Sixteenth Edition

LOVEJOY'S College Guide

A COMPLETE REFERENCE BOOK TO SOME 3,000 AMERICAN COLLEGES AND UNIVERSITIES FOR USE BY STUDENTS, PARENTS, TEACHERS, REFERENCE LIBRARIES, YOUTH AGENCIES, GUIDANCE COUNSELORS, INDUSTRIAL CORPORATIONS, FOUNDATIONS, ARMY, NAVY, AIR FORCE STATIONS, OTHER FEDERAL SERVICES, AND BY FOREIGN GOVERNMENTS AND AGENCIES.

Edited by Charles T. Straughn and Barbarasue Lovejoy Straughn

Authors of the companion books, *Lovejoy's Career and Vocational School Guide* and *Lovejoy's Prep and Private School Guide;* editors and publishers of the monthly *Lovejoy's Guidance Digest.*

LOVEJOY'S EDUCATIONAL GUIDES

MONARCH PRESS NEW YORK

This book is dedicated to the memory of Dr. Clarence E. Lovejoy whose interest in the education of young people led him to write his first book, "So You're Going to College" published in 1940, the forerunner of *Lovejoy's College Guide;* to his wife, Madelyn, who was devoted to his work and was his aid and able assistant during the first book and the many succeeding revisions of Lovejoy's College Guide; to our own two children, Amy-Beth and Jeffrey Lovejoy Straughn, who are using it for their college preparation.
Charles T. Straughn II
Barbarasue Lovejoy Straughn
Editors

ACKNOWLEDGED WITH THANKS
We wish to thank our editorial assistants, Mrs. Gayle Thompson August and Mrs. Nancy Hemmes Boylan, for their intelligent and painstaking efforts and professionalism in helping with the preparation of this book.

Published by MONARCH PRESS
A Simon & Schuster Division of Gulf & Western Corporation
Simon & Schuster Building
1230 Avenue of the Americas
New York, New York 10020

MONARCH PRESS and colophon are trademarks of Simon & Schuster registered in the U.S Patent and Trademark Office.
Manufactured in the United States of America

10 9 8 7 6 5 4 3 2 1

ISBN 0-671-47201-1 cloth
ISBN 0-671-47170-8 paperback

CONTENTS

NOTE TO COLLEGES AND UNIVERSITIES

Colleges listed in the *Guide* are urged to keep their entries up to date by sending all significant changes to *Lovejoy's College Guide* as soon as they are determined. Colleges not listed are invited to submit basic information to:

Lovejoy's College Guide
2 Drummond Place
P.O. Drawer Q
Red Bank, New Jersey 07701

NOTE TO USERS OF *LOVEJOY'S COLLEGE GUIDE*

With the increase in demands being made on our educational institutions, colleges are constantly changing tuition and other fees, adding component schools, acquiring or losing ROTC units of the Army, Navy, and Air Force, and otherwise changing their characteristics. The authors and publishers plan to keep this *Lovejoy's College Guide* up to date by bringing out recurrent revisions. The monthly *Lovejoy's Guidance Digest* is published from offices at 2 Drummond Place, Red Bank, New Jersey 07701, to bridge the gaps between revisions of the *Guide,* with up-to-date developments in college admissions, accreditations, degree programs, costs, scholarships, etc.

While developing and organizing the revisions of *Lovejoy's College Guide* we are in constant communication with each of the institutions listed in our book requesting updated information for each entry. Most will exercise this option and supply us with complete data.

We also give each institution the opportunity to respond to a questionnaire for inclusion in our special Section Two: Career Curricula and Special Programs–Guidance and Tips. Only those institutions that respond are listed in this section.

Lovejoy's College Guide is composed of four main sections. The first section consists of general information on colleges and the selection process. Section Two is the Career Curricula Section. In this part of the book a student may find various majors and the colleges and universities which offer them. After selecting the major and the institutions which offer it, the student then turns to Section Three of the book and proceeds to study the colleges which are of interest.

In many cases community colleges are only listed by name and address. This is because community colleges are basically for the commuter students who reside in that particular area. However, those community colleges which offer dormitory facilities are given a more complete profile. Institutions which are specific in nature (religious, fine arts, professional, career, etc.) are also only listed by name and address.

A new fourth section of the book contains information on college and university varsity intercollegiate sports for men and women and those which offer athletic scholarships in these various sports.

ABOUT THE FOUNDING AUTHOR

(adapted from *"Who's Who in America"*) 1884-1974

CLARENCE E. LOVEJOY spent most of his life in or near colleges and universities, visiting campuses repeatedly, analyzing the ever-changing college scene, addressing college audiences, writing about colleges, getting acquainted with college presidents, deans, and directors. Born in a college town in Maine, he grew up in the Berkshires near other colleges, studied at Columbia and the Sorbonne, was a professor at Rutgers and held honorary degrees from Colby College and Parsons College. As an editor, faculty member, university official, newspaperman and Army officer he knew students, their ambitions, their worries, their successes. He was a friend and counselor to thousands of their parents. The educational consulting office he established continues to offer personalized, individualized, professional college counseling at 2 Drummond Place, Red Bank, New Jersey 07701, and to publish the monthly *Lovejoy's Guidance Digest*.

For more than twenty years of his life Dr. Lovejoy was a soldier, including participation in two World Wars. He spent eight years during and following World War I as a combat infantry lieutenant and captain of the Regular Army, including service in France and Germany, before resigning his Regular commission in 1925 to return to civilian life as a Reserve officer.

Called back into uniform following Pearl Harbor, he served for five years as a major, lieutenant colonel, and colonel, first as Director of Security and Intelligence for New York City and vicinity, and then overseas as a General Staff corps officer at SHAEF and USFET as Chief of the Public Relations Branch of G-5 (Military Government). He was later elevated by General Eisenhower to become Director of the Public Relations Division at Frankfurt for the entire European theatre, frequently accompanying General Eisenhower and later Generals McNarney and Clay to meetings of the Allied Control Council at Berlin.

Dr. Lovejoy was a professional member of the National Vocational Guidance Association and of other educational bodies, including the New York State Association of Deans and Guidance Personnel, the New York State Counselors Association, New Jersey Personnel and Guidance Association, National Association of Secondary School Principals, and American Personnel and Guidance Association. He was also for many years a department editor on the staff of *The New York Times*. His wife, Madelyn Dunphy Lovejoy (a former student at Skidmore and Columbia), collaborated in his college research work. His two daughters, Barbarasue and Joan who were graduated from college with B.A. degrees, helped in the preparation of the books as did his son-in-law, Charles T. Straughn II.

SECTION ONE

SO YOU'RE GOING TO COLLEGE!

Before selecting a particular institution, many factors must be considered. This section contains general, essential information on:

1. Educational Financial Aid
2. U.S.A. Federal Aids
3. Admissions
4. Which College for You?

EDUCATIONAL FINANCIAL AID

National Merit Scholarship Program

America's largest private scholarship program in history is the National Merit Scholarship. Formerly students applying for these scholarships were required to take the National Merit Scholarship Qualifying Test (NMSQT). However, both the National Merit Scholarship Corporation and the College Board agreed that the number and variety of tests put too much strain on schools and students and a multipurpose test, the PSAT/NMSQT, was substituted.

College Scholarship Service (CSS)

The College Scholarship Service is an agency of the College Board which analyzes a student's need for financial aid.

CSS Financial Aid Form

Colleges and Universities which are participating institutions of the College Scholarship Service require parents of applicants for financial aid to file a Financial Aid Form. This contains data about income and expenses of both father and mother; number and ages of children, whether they are dependent, in school or college; data about other dependents and their relationship; data about parents' federal income tax; home and other real estate, including present sale value and unpaid mortgage; and data about any unusual family circumstance, such as divorce, illnesses, special housing problems, etc.

The CSS emphasizes that the amounts of aid awarded should be determined according to financial need. Some colleges offer special prizes and certain scholarships whose terms stipulate that they are awarded for reasons which do not include financial need. The CSS colleges believe, however, that by and large their unrestricted financial aid funds should be administered according to need. It is an honor to win a scholarship whether or not a stipend is attached to it. If there is a stipend, its size should be a reflection of the financial need of the student and not a measure of the honor awarded.

Parents of students who are entering or continuing college and who are applying for financial aid should complete the Financial Aid Form. The FAF helps colleges, universities, and scholarship-granting agencies determine the amount of financial assistance a student may need to pursue his college education. Copies are submitted to the colleges and agencies named to receive them.

The CSS Form is *confidential*. The student's secondary school is not informed of the statement's contents unless it is informed by the parents themselves.

Recommended Financial Aid Literature

Many posts of the American Legion have appointed Education and Scholarship Committees to assemble information about scholarships. The Legion's headquarters, at Indianapolis, Indiana, compiles a booklet entitled "Need a Lift?" It describes scholarships for children of deceased or disabled war veterans.

Robert Leider, an expert in the many financial avenues available through both federal and state governments, has developed booklets used by families and guidance counselors throughout the country. They include: "The A's & B's of Academic Scholarships," "Don't Miss Out," "College Grants From Uncle Sam," "Cooperative Education Opportunities Offered By The Federal Government" and "College Loans From Uncle Sam." They can be purchased at a nominal fee from Octameron Associates, Inc. P.O.Box 3437, Alexandria, Virginia 22302.

Federally Supported Financial Aid Programs

There have been changes in the federally supported programs of financial aid administered by the U.S. Office of Education under the Education Amendments of 1972. The financial aid officer of the school, college or university selects those students who will receive grants and the amount needed, those eligible for and the amount of loans, and determines students to be employed and suitable jobs for them in the Educational Opportunity Grants Program (EOG), National Direct Student Loan Program (NDSLP) and the College Work-Study Program (CWSP). The Guaranteed Student Loan Program eligibility information may be obtained from the regional office of the U.S. Office of Education, state guarantee agency, lender, or student financial aid officer of approved institutions.

Educational Opportunity Grants Program (Pell Grant and SEOG)

The Pell Grant and the SEOG are a great boon to students who might not otherwise be able to continue their education. Grants of up to $2,000 for the SEOG and $1,750 for the Pell Grant per year for four years of undergraduate study are available.

National Direct Student Loan Program (NDSLP)

Under the NDSLP undergraduate students who have completed two years of a 4-year program in an approved post-secondary institution may borrow each year, for college expenses, a sum not exceeding a total of $6,000 for the undergraduate college program. The graduate or professional student will be able to borrow up to a total of $12,000 for both undergraduate and graduate study. Repayment extends over a ten-year period beginning six months after the borrower graduates or leaves school. Interest at 4% starts to accrue at the beginning of the repayment period. Students who enter certain fields of teaching in a poverty or Headstart Program or in a public or other non-profit elementary or secondary school for disabled children, or specified military duty are provided with partial or total loan cancellation under the NDSLP.

College Work-Study Program (CWSP)

The College Work-Study Program gives a student who is enrolled at least half-time the opportunity to pay off part or all of his educational expenses by working at a part-time job at the college itself or with a public or private nonprofit agency working in cooperation with the college. Students may work up to 40 hours per week depending on the determination of the college financial aid officer. Generally the salary paid is at least equal to the current minimum wage but frequently it is higher.

Guaranteed Student Loan Program(GSLP)

Under the Guaranteed Student Loan Program a student who is enrolled or has been accepted for enrollment as an undergraduate or graduate student, on at least a half-time basis, at an eligible college or university or hospital school of nursing or an approved vocational, technical, trade, business, or home study school may borrow money directly from a bank, credit union, savings and loan association, or other participating lender. This loan is guaranteed by a State or private nonprofit guarantee agency or insured by the federal government. A student may borrow up to a maximum of $2,500 per academic year; however, in some states the maximum per academic year is less and lenders must adhere to state regulations. The total amount for undergraduate or vocational study which may be borrowed is $12,500. Independent undergraduates may borrow up to $3,000 to a total of $15,000. Students are eligible for federal payment of interest charges of 9% on their loans during school years during a 9- to 12-month grace period prior to repayment period and during authorized periods of deferrment. The maximum repayment period takes 5 to 10 years; however, the minimum monthly payment of $30 plus interest may reduce this period, depending upon the size of the loan. If a student serves in the military, Peace Corps, or VISTA, or for any period returns to full-time study, repayment may be deferred for up to 3 years.

Sources of Information on the Guaranteed Student Loan Programs

ALABAMA
Office of Education, Region IV, 101 Marietta Tower, Suite 423, Atlanta, Georgia 30323

ALASKA
Student Aid Office, State Education Department, Pouch F, AOB, Juneau, Alaska 99801

ARIZONA
Office of Education, Region IX, 50 United Nations Plaza, Room 250, San Francisco, California 94102

ARKANSAS
Student Loan Guarantee Foundation of Arkansas, Suite 515, 1515 West 7th Street, Little Rock, Arkansas 72202

CALIFORNIA
California Student Aid Commission, 1410 Fifth Street, Sacramento, California 95814

COLORADO
Guaranteed Student Loan Program, ABS Building, 7000 North Broadway, Suite 100, Denver, Colorado 80221

CONNECTICUT
Connecticut Student Loan Foundation, 25 Pratt Street, Hartford, Connecticut 06103

DELAWARE
Delaware Higher Education Loan Program, Brandywine College, Box 7139, Wilmington, Delaware 19803

DISTRICT OF COLUMBIA
Higher Education Loan Program of D.C. Inc., 1001 Connecticut Ave., N.W., Suite 825, Washington, D.C. 20036

FLORIDA
Florida Student Financial Assistance Commission, Room 563, Knott Building, Tallahassee, Florida 32301

GEORGIA
Georgia Higher Education Assistance Corporation, 9 LaVista Perimeter Park, 2187 Northlake Parkway, Tucker, Georgia 30084

HAWAII
Education Loan Program, 1314 King Street, Suite 613, Honolulu, Hawaii 96814

IDAHO
Student Loan Fund of Idaho, Route 5, Caldwell, Idaho 83605

ILLINOIS
Illinois Guaranteed Loan Program, 102 Wilmot Road, Deerfield, Illinois 60015

INDIANA
State Student Assistance Commission, 219 North Senate Avenue, First Floor, Indianapolis, Indiana 46202

IOWA
Iowa College Aid Commission, 904 Grand Avenue, Des Moines, Iowa 50309

KANSAS
Higher Education Assistance Foundation, 34 Corporate Woods, 10950 Grand View Drive, Overland Park, Kansas 66210

KENTUCKY
Kentucky Higher Education Assistance Authority, 691 Teton Trail, Frankfort, Kentucky 40601

LOUISIANA
Governor's Special Commission on Educational Services, 4637 Jamestown Street, Post Office Box 44127, Baton Rouge, Louisiana 70804

MAINE
Maine State Department of Education, State House Complex, State House Station 23, Augusta, Maine 04333

MARYLAND
Maryland Higher Education Loan Corporation, 2100 Guilford Avenue, Baltimore, Maryland 21218

MASSACHUSETTS
Massachusetts Higher Education Assistance Corporation, 1010 Park Square Building, Boston, Massachusetts 02116

MICHIGAN
Michigan Department of Education, Guaranteed Student Loan Program, Box 30047, Lansing, Michigan 48909

MINNESOTA
Higher Education Assistance Foundation, 1100 Northwestern Bank Building, 55 East 5th Street, St. Paul, Minnesota 55101

MISSISSIPPI (see ALABAMA)

MISSOURI
Department of Higher Education, P.O. Box 1438, Jefferson City, Missouri 65102

MONTANA
Regional Administrator, Guaranteed Student Loan Program, Region VIII, 33 South Last Chance Gulch, Helena, Montana 59601

NEBRASKA
Higher Education Asst. Foundation, 3600 South 48th Street, Lincoln, Nebraska 68506

NEVADA
State Department of Education, 400 West King Street, Carson City, Nevada 89701

NEW HAMPSHIRE
New Hampshire Higher Education Assistance Foundation, 143 North Main Street, P.O. Box 877, Concord, New Hampshire 03301

NEW JERSEY
New Jersey Higher Education Assistance Authority, C.N. 00538, Trenton, New Jersey 08638

NEW MEXICO
Student Loan Program, Student Loan Services, Bandelier West, U. of New Mexico, Albuquerque, New Mexico 87131

NEW YORK
New York State Higher Education Services, 99 Washington Ave., Albany, New York 12255

NORTH CAROLINA
State Education Assistance Authority, Post Office Box 2688, Chapel Hill, North Carolina 27514

NORTH DAKOTA
Student Financial Assistance, Department of Education, Region VIII, 11037 Federal Office Building, 19th and Stout Streets, Denver, Colorado 80294

OHIO
Ohio Student Loan Commission, P.O. Box 16610, Columbus, Ohio 43216

OKLAHOMA
Oklahoma State Regents for Higher Education, 500 Education Building, State Capital Complex, Oklahoma City, Oklahoma 73105

OREGON
State of Oregon Scholarship Commission, 1445 Willamette Street, Eugene, Oregon 97401

PENNSYLVANIA
Pennsylvania Higher Education Assistance Agency, 660 Boas Street, Harrisburg, Pennsylvania 17102

PUERTO RICO
Director of Higher Education, Office of Education, Region II, 26 Federal Plaza, New York, New York 10007

RHODE ISLAND
Rhode Island Higher Education Assistance Authority, 274 Weybosset Street, Providence, Rhode Island 02903

SOUTH CAROLINA
South Carolina Student Loan Corporation, Interstate Center, Suite 210, Post Office Box 21337, Columbia, South Carolina 29221

SOUTH DAKOTA
South Dakota Education Assistance Corporation, 105 First Avenue, S.W., Aberdeen, South Dakota 57401

TENNESSEE
Tennessee Student Assistance Corporation, B-3 Capitol Tower, Suite 9, Nashville, Tennessee 37219

TEXAS
Regional Administrator, Office of Education, Region VI, 1200 Main Tower Building, 15th Floor, Dallas, Texas 75202

UTAH
Utah Education Loan Service, 1800 South West Temple, Salt Lake City, Utah 84108

VERMONT
Vermont Student Assistance Corporation, 5 Burlington Square, Burlington, Vermont 05401

VIRGINIA
Virginia State Education Assistance Authority, 6 North 6th Street, Suite 400, Richmond, Virginia 23219

WASHINGTON
Student Loan Guaranty Assn., 100 South King Street, Suite 560, Westland Building, Seattle, Washington 98104

WEST VIRGINIA
Higher Education Assistance Foundation, Loan Program of West Virginia Inc., P.O. Box 591, Union Bldg. Suite 900, 723 Kanawha Blvd. East, Charleston, West Virginia 25322

WISCONSIN
Wisconsin Higher Education Corporation, 137 East Wilson Street, Madison, Wisconsin 53702

WYOMING
Higher Education Asst. Foundation, American National Bank Building, 20th Street at Capitol, Suite 320, Cheyenne, Wyoming 82001

U.S.A. FEDERAL AIDS

ROTC

Federal government money has helped thousands get their college education. The Reserve Officers Training Corps in many colleges and universities and some of its adaptations in private and public secondary schools have been a boon to men and women students.

Institutions offering ROTC programs are listed in Section Two, Special Programs, of this book. Pertinent information may be obtained by writing to the individual institutions or ROTC headquarters at:

Army ROTC
Headquarters U.S. Training and Doctrine Command
Fort Monroe, Virginia 23651

Navy Recruiting Command (Code 314)
4015 Wilson Boulevard
Arlington, Virginia 22203

Air Force ROTC
Advisory Service
Maxwell Air Force Base, Alabama 36112

SERVICE ACADEMIES

Admission to the United States Military Academy at West Point, the United States Naval Academy at Annapolis, and the United States Air Force Academy at Colorado Springs is by appointment and involves, of course, exams that are sometimes competitive for the appointment and exams for admission. There are also appointments made by the President and members of Congress for certain numbers of enlisted regulars and reservists and a few others. Admission to the United States Coast Guard Academy at New London is on the basis of competitive examination and to the United States Merchant Marine Academy at Kings Point on the basis of competitive examination after allocations of authority to take the exams.

FEDERAL AVIATION AGENCY

The following institutions are included among the FAA pilot, flight, and ground schools, including those operated by or in conjunction with an accredited college or university:

ABBREVIATIONS
Certificated Pilot School Ratings

Private Pilot Certification Course

- PC(A)—Airplane
- PC(R)—Rotorcraft
- PC(G)—Glider
- PC(L)—Lighter-Than-Glider

Private Test Course

- PT(A)—Airplane
- PT(R)—Rotorcraft
- PT(G)—Glider
- PT(L)—Lighter-Than-Air

Commercial Pilot Certification Course

- CC(A)—Airplane
- CC(R)—Rotorcraft
- CC(G)—Glider
- CC(L)—Lighter-Than-Air

Commercial Test Course

- CT(A)—Airplane
- CT(R)—Rotorcraft
- CT(G)—Glider
- CT(L)—Lighter-Than-Air

Instrument Rating

- IR(A)—Airplane
- IR(H)—Helicopter

Pilot Ground School Courses

- PG(P)—Private Pilot
- PG(I)—Instrumental Rating
- PG(C)—Commercial Pilot
- PG(F)—Flight Instructor
- PG(T)—Airline Transport Pilot
- PG(R)—Additional Flight Instructor
- PG(A)—Additional Instrument

Additional Aircraft Rating

- AR(A)—Airplane
- AR(R)—Rotorcraft
- AR(G)—Glider
- AR(L)—Lighter-Than-Air

Test Preparation Courses

- FI—Flight Instructor Certification
- AF—Additional Flight Instructor Rating
- AI—Additional Instrument Rating
- AT—Airline Transport Pilot Certification
- PR—Pilot Refresher Course
- AG—Agricultural Aircraft Operations Course
- XL—Rotorcraft External Load Operations Course

ALABAMA

Auburn U .... PC(A)—CC(A)—IR(A)—PT(A)—AR(A)
Gadsden State Jr. Coll .... PC(A)—CC(A)—IR(A)—PG(P-I-C)—PT(A)
Jacksonville State U .... PG(P)
South Alabama, U. of .... PC(A)—PG(P)
Wallace State Comm. Coll .... PC(A)—CC(A)—IR(A)—AR(A)

ALASKA

Anchorage Comm. Coll .... PG(P-I-C-F-T)
Tanana Valley Comm. Coll .... PG(P)

ARIZONA

Cochise Coll .... PC(A)—CC(A)—AR(A)
Cochise Coll. Flight Sch .... AC(A)—PT(A)—CC(A)—CT(A)—IR(A)—AR(A)
Embry-Riddle Aeronautical U .... PC(A)—CC(A)—IR(A)—AR(A)

CALIFORNIA

Alameda, Coll. of .... PG(P)
Glendale Comm. Coll .... PG(P)
Grossmont Comm. Coll .... PG(P-I-C)
Merced Coll .... PG(P-I-C)
Mt. San Antonio Coll .... PG(P-I-C)
Harvey Mudd Coll .... PC(A)—CC(A)—IR(A)
Ohlone Coll .... PG(P-I-C)
Pasadena City Coll .... PG(P-I-C)
San Diego Mesa Coll .... PC(A)—CC(A)—IR(A)

San Mateo, Coll. of .... PG(P-I-C)
Santa Ana Coll .... PG(P-I-C)
Santa Rosa Jr. Coll .... PG(P)
Sierra Coll .... PG(P-I)
Sweetwater Comm. Coll .... PG(P-I-C)

COLORADO
Aims Comm. Coll .... PG(P-I-C)
Colorado Northwestern Comm. Coll .... PC(A)—CC(A)—IR(A)
Metropolitan State Coll .... PG(P-I-C)
U.S. Air Force Acad .... PC(A)—CC(A)—IR(A)

FLORIDA
Broward Comm. Coll .... PG(P-I-C-F-R)
Embry Riddle Aeronautical U .... PC(A)—CC(A)—IR(A)—AR(A)—PG(P-I-C-A)
Florida Instit. of Tech .... PC(A)—CC(A)—IR(A)—AR(A)
Manatee Jr. Coll .... PG(P-I-C-A)
Miami-Dade Comm. Coll. (North) .... PG(P)
Miami-Dade Comm. Coll. (South) .... PG(P-I-C)
St. Petersburg Jr. Coll .... PG(P-I-C)

IDAHO
Boise State U .... PG(P-I-C)

ILLINOIS
Belleville Area Coll .... PC(A)—CC(A)—IR(A)—AR(A)
Illinois Central Coll .... PG(P)
Illinois, U. of .... PC(A)—CC(A)—IR(A)
Prairie State Coll .... PG(P)
Rock Valley Coll .... PG(P-C)
St. Louis U., Parks Coll .... PC(A)—CC(A)—IR(A)—AR(A)

INDIANA
Indiana State U .... PG(P-I-C-F)
Purdue U .... AR(A)

IOWA
Dubuque, U. of .... PC(A)—CC(A)—IR(A)—AR(A)
Iowa Lakes Comm. Coll .... PC(A)—CC(A)—IR(A)
Iowa State U .... PC(A)—PG(P)
Iowa Western Comm. Coll .... PC(R)—PT(A)—CC(R)—CT(A)—IR(A)—AR(A)

KANSAS
Hesston Coll .... PC(A)—CC(A)—IR(A)—PG(P)

LOUISIANA
Louisiana Tech. U .... PC(A)—CC(A)—IR(A)—AR(A)—PG(P-I-C-F-T-R-A)
Northwestern State U .... PC(A)—CC(A)—IR(A)—AR(A)

MASSACHUSETTS
North Shore Comm. Coll .... PG(P-I-C)
Northeastern U .... PG(P-I-C)

MICHIGAN
Andrews U .... PC(A)—CC(A)—IR(A)—AR(A)
Grand Rapids Sch. of Bible and Music .... PC(A)—CC(A)—IR(A)
Henry Ford Comm. Coll .... PG(P-I-C)
Jackson Comm. Coll .... PC(A)—CC(A)—IR(A)
Lansing Comm. Coll .... PC(A)—CC(A)—IR(A)—PG(P-I-C)
Northern Michigan U .... PC(A)—CC(A)—PT(A)—CT(A)—IR(A)—AR(A)
Northwestern Michigan Coll .... PC(A)—CC(A)—IR(A)—AR(A)
Schoolcraft Coll .... PG(P-I-C)
Western Michigan U .... PC(A)—CC(A)

MINNESOTA
Minnesota, U. of, Technical Coll .... PC(A)—CC(A)
Minnesota, U. of (Minneapolis) .... PC(A)—CC(A)—IR(A)—AR(A)—PG(P)
St. Cloud State U .... PG(P-I-C)
Winona State U .... PG(P)

MISSISSIPPI
Mississippi State U .... PG(P)

MISSOURI
Meramec Comm. Coll .... PG(P-I-C)
Ozarks, Sch. of the .... PC(A)—CC(A)—IR(A)—AR(A)—PG(P-I-C-F-T)
Penn Valley Comm. Coll .... PG(P-I-C)

NEW HAMPSHIRE
Hawthorne Coll .... PC(A)—CC(A)—IR(A)
Daniel Webster Coll .... PG(P-I-C)

NEW JERSEY
Mercer Cty. Comm. Coll .... PC(A)—CC(A)—IR(A)—PG(P-I-C)
Stockton State Coll .... PG(P-I)

NEW MEXICO
New Mexico Jr. Coll .... PG(P)

NEW YORK
Dowling Coll .... PG(P-I-C-F)
Queensborough Comm. Coll .... PG(P-I)

NORTH CAROLINA
Guilford Tech. Inst .... PG(P-C)
Lenoir Comm. Coll .... PG(P-I-C)
Wayne Comm. Coll .... PG(P)

NORTH DAKOTA
North Dakota, U. of .... PC(A)—CC(A)—IR(A)—AR(A-R)—PT(A)—CT(A)

OHIO
Cuyahoga Comm. Coll .... PG(P-I-C-F)
Kent State U .... PC(A)—CC(A)—IR(A)—PG(P-I-C)
Lorain Cty. Comm. Coll .... PG(P)
Miami U .... PC(A)—CC(A)—IR(A)
Ohio State U .... PC(A-R)—CC(A-R)—IR(A)—PG(P)—AR(A-R)
Ohio U .... PC(A)—CC(A)—IR(A)—AR(A)—PG(P)

OKLAHOMA
Oklahoma, U. of .... PC(A)—CC(A)—IR(A)—PG(P-I-C-F)
Oklahoma State U .... PC(A)—PG(P-C)
Southeastern Oklahoma State U .... PC(A)—CC(A)—IR(A)—AR(A)
Western Oklahoma State Coll .... PG(P-I-C-F-T)—PC(A)

OREGON
Lane Comm. Coll .... PC(A)—CC(A)—IR(A)—AR(A)—PG(P-I-C-F)
Southern Oregon State College .... PG(P)
Treasure Valley Comm. Coll .... PG(P-I-C-F)

PENNSYLVANIA
Beaver Cty., Comm. Coll. of .... PG(P-I-C)
Harrisburg Area Comm. Coll .... PG(P)
Pennsylvania State U. (University Park) .... PC(A)—CC(A)—PG(P)
Swarthmore Coll .... PG(P)

SOUTH DAKOTA
Augustana Coll .... PG(P-I-C)

TENNESSEE
Steed Coll .... PC(A)—CC(A)—IR(A)—AR(A)

TEXAS
Central Texas Coll .... PC(A)—IR(A)—CC(A)—AR(A)—PG(P)
LeTourneau Coll .... PC(A)
Mountain View Coll .... PG(P-I-C)
Navarro Coll .... PC(A)—CC(A)—IR(A)—AR(A)—PG(P-I-C)
North Lake Coll .... PG(P-I-C)
Southwest Texas Jr. Coll .... PC(A)—CC(A)—PT(A)—CT(A)—IR(A)
Texarkana Comm. Coll .... PC(A)—CC(A)—IR(A)—PG(P-I-C)
Texas State Tech. Inst .... PC(A)—IR(A)—PG(P-I-C-F)—CC(A)

UTAH
Westminster Coll .... PG(P-C-F)

VIRGINIA
Central Virginia Comm. Coll ....PG(I)
Tidewater Comm. Coll ....PG(P-I-C)
Virginia Poly. Inst ....PC(A)—PT(A)—CC(A)—CT(A)—IR(A)

WASHINGTON
Big Bend Comm. Coll ....PC(A)—CC(A)
Central Washington U ....PG(P-I-C)
Green River Comm. Coll ....PG(P-I-C)
South Seattle Comm. Coll ....PG(P-I-C)

WISCONSIN
Gateway Tech. Inst ....PC(A)—CC(A)—IR(A)

ADMISSIONS

Multiple Applications Are a Necessity

Let's examine this business of being admitted to college. The truth of the matter is that it frightens a good many students and their parents. Admissions procedures are important and necessary.

Educators have been disagreeing for generations about which students are suited for college. They have argued about aptitudes, validity studies, and pre-college tests. They have been tabulating, figuring, and graphing for decades. They rarely talk about averages. Instead, they use such terms as *median, norm, percentile, converted rank*. Sometimes they sound like an algebraic formula.

We must give credit to these admissions directors and other educators for trying to determine, with their scientific studies, which applicants are likely to have the ability to stay in college, do creditable work, and ultimately earn a degree. They size up applicants, as a life insurance examiner would, as good or bad "risks."

Many colleges have selective, or competitive, admissions with four or five, perhaps as many as ten, applicants for every opening. Standards are getting higher.

Moreover, the widespread practice of "multiple applications" presents an admissions problem. Today most college applicants apply concurrently to at least six institutions or more. Even valedictorians dare not put their eggs in fewer baskets.

Before the unreasonable, artificial first-second-third-choice rule was voted out of practice about 1951, some secondary school counselors assumed erroneously that only three concurrent applications should be permitted. Even now they sometimes take the position that their school has insufficient clerical help to supply a fourth, fifth, or sixth transcript. Nevertheless, it is unfair to limit a student to three if he feels he needs six transcripts, as many do. Some public high schools, which arbitrarily allow only three, charge fees for the fourth, fifth, and sixth.

The multiple application practice is not necessarily a happy one as far as some admissions offices are concerned. When a college wants to enroll, say, 300 freshmen for the ensuing September, it may be obliged actually to accept 600 or perhaps 700. Each accepted applicant probably was also accepted by several other colleges and sometimes takes advantage of the Candidates Reply Date Agreement on May 1 to determine which to choose.

Early Decision Plan and Early Admissions Plan

The Early Decision Plan is not to be confused with the Early Admissions Plan which the University of Chicago and other institutions have used to enroll exceptionally bright students who have finished the tenth or eleventh grade and are regarded as ready for college without the formality of a secondary school graduation diploma at the end of twelve grades.

In the Early Decision Plan these students of unusual promise who make outstandingly good scores on eleventh grade CEEB SATs and have high rank in class and high academic marks are assured college admissions as early as December in the twelfth grade if they apply by October 1 to only the one institution.

Rolling Admissions

Rolling Admissions is part of the admissions procedure at many colleges. Students can apply any time after six semesters of secondary school work. Candidates are notified as soon as their files with the college admissions department have been completed and they have fulfilled all the college's entrance requirements. The Admissions Committee then either accepts or rejects the candidate.

Quarter, Trimester, and 4-1-4 Systems

Because there has been a growing feeling that colleges should utilize more of the 52 weeks each year, there has been a disposition to change over from the two 16-week or two 17-week semesters into trimesters or quarters. This would permit more applicants to be accepted and would permit colleges to utilize more of the calendar year instead of leaving classrooms, laboratories, and libraries idle and unused.

Colleges on the quarter system usually have 12-week quarters, utilizing 48 weeks of the 52 in the year. Trimester colleges have worked out schedules to have trimesters of 17 weeks each for a total of 51 weeks out of 52. Both types of institutions permit students to earn degrees in three years or even less. Quarter-system colleges and trimester-system colleges sometimes permit freshmen to enter at the start of any quarter or trimester term.

Another calendar system incorporated within the past few years is the 4-1-4 plan. This is comprised of three terms: a four-month term, a one-month or interim term, and a four-month term. The one-month term is generally used for independent study.

Institutions offering the various types of calendar systems are listed in Section Two, Special Programs.

The Admissions Procedure: From Application Form to Carnegie Units

Colleges are not alike. Part of the application may require a brief essay by the applicant and in his or her own handwriting. In general, college application forms have several parts which vary from college to college. All institutions want biological facts about the applicant; in addition, they will need information about his or her academic preparation and career objectives.

The academic record or transcript of grades, marks, and rank in class in the secondary school is also one of the parts of completed application forms. This is usually forwarded direct from the secondary schools to the college along with the endorsement and recommendation of the principal, guidance counselor, headmaster or headmistress. Similarly, some of the colleges requiring medical and physical examinations by physicians ask that these be sent directly to the college instead of through the student.

How do colleges select their students? There is no single yardstick, no infallible and revealing slide rule. Admissions procedures have come a long way from the early rigidity of stated examinations when an applicant had to pass tests in various subjects for each college. Colleges have become increasingly flexible. Several criteria are now evaluated, instead of, as in the past, merely examination scores.

Most colleges use several yardsticks. The secondary school record is, of course, highly important. Many admissions directors first look at an applicant's rank in class.

This relative appraisal reveals an important fact. Is he or she in the upper tenth of the class, upper fifth, fourth, third? Most selective, or competitive, colleges insist at the very minimum that an applicant's ranking be in the upper half of his or her class. It is next to impossible to be accepted by any selective college if you are in the lower half. Those willing to give you consideration will usually require additional data of one kind or another.

Most colleges adhere to the traditional 16 Carnegie units as a requirement (12 for the tenth, eleventh and twelfth grades). Customarily 16 units include four years of secondary school English, one year of algebra, one year of geometry and, depending upon college curriculum or program sought, units in social studies, sciences, foreign languages and, in the case of those headed for engineering careers, courses in advanced math.

The required 16 units (or in some special cases 14) may be built up from various academic subjects. Some colleges, accepting for only half credits courses in music and art, do not accept for admissions credits such vocational or industrial subjects as carpentry, shop practice, bookkeeping, etc.

High school pupils and their parents should assure themselves by the tenth grade that they are pursuing and passing the number and variety of courses required.

An important criterion is the recommendation of the secondary school principal, headmaster or headmistress. Obviously in large schools, they cannot know every pupil personally but must have department chairmen, guidance counselors, or perhaps home room teachers prepare the recommendations for their signatures on the transcripts sent to colleges.

College Board: SAT and TOEFL

Other criteria used by colleges are the tests of the College Board's Admissions Testing Program (ATP). The ATP includes the Scholastic Aptitude Test (SAT) which is comprised of a verbal section to measure reading comprehension and vocabulary, and a mathematical section to measure aptitude for handling quantitative abilities closely related to college work. The SAT provides colleges with a common national standard for evaluating students from different schools. SAT scores, combined with the high school record, are used for predicting students' academic performance in college.

The Test of Standard Written English (TSWE) is a half-hour objective test of writing abilities used for placement in college English courses. It is administered at the same time as the SAT and at no additional charge.

Fourteen one-hour subject matter Achievement Tests, offered on most of the same test dates as the SAT and Test of Standard Written English, measure skills and knowledge students have developed in a particular subject. A student can take either the SAT or as many as three one-hour Achievement Tests, but not both, on a given morning.

Also, the Student Descriptive Questionnaire, another component of the Admissions Testing Program, provides students with the opportunity to describe themselves in greater detail so that colleges can get an idea of their background, skills, plans, and interests. The Questionnaire, an optional feature, is filled out at home when the student registers for the test.

Students can review for Achievement Tests and select preferred subjects. Achievement Tests cover American History and Social Studies, Biology, Chemistry, English Composition, European History and World Cultures, French, German, Spanish, Hebrew, Latin, Literature, Mathematics—Level I, Mathematics—Level II, and Physics. Language proficiency tests measure reading ability only.

For specific information on test dates and which Achievement Tests are given on each date, a student should contact his or her guidance counselor for copies of the *Student Bulletin* for the Admissions Testing Program. Students planning to take the SAT should also ask for a copy of *Taking the SAT* which contains a description of each type of question appearing on an SAT and a full length SAT and TSWE for practice and self-scoring. Students who register for Achievement Tests will be mailed a descriptive booklet with their admissions tickets.

The College Board jointly sponsors the Test of English as a Foreign Language (TOEFL) with the Graduate Record Examinations Board; the test is administered by Educational Testing Service. The major purpose of the TOEFL is to evaluate the English proficiency of people whose native language is not English. It is designed for students in grades 11 or above who are applying for undergraduate or graduate admission to academic institutions in the United States or Canada. The test uses a multiple-choice format and consists of three sections. The Listening Comprehensive Section measures ability to understand spoken English; the Structure and Written Expression Section measures ability to recognize language that is appropriate for standard written English; the Reading Comprehension and Vocabulary Section measures ability to understand nontechnical reading matter. More than 2,000 colleges and universities in the United States and Canada, as well as in other countries where English is the language of instruction, require applicants who are not native speakers of English to take the TOEFL.

The TOEFL is administered twelve times each year under two testing programs: the International Testing Program on regularly scheduled Saturday test dates and the Special Center Testing Program on regularly scheduled Friday test dates. In the United States and Canada, the test fee is $21 for the International Testing Program and $29 for the Special Center Testing Program. In all other countries and areas, the fee is $23 for the International Testing Program and $31 for the Special Center Testing Program.

The test is given at 850 test centers in 135 countries and areas. Persons wishing to take TOEFL must obtain the appropriate Bulletin of Information and Application Form for the country or area in which they plan to take the test. For further information, write to Educational Testing Service, TOEFL, Box 899, Princeton, NJ 08541, USA.

The College Board maintains headquarters offices in New

York City at 888 Seventh Ave., New York, NY 10019, and has the following regional offices: Midwest, 500 Davis St., Evanston, IL 60201; Middle States, Suite 1418, 1700 Market St., Philadelphia, PA 19103; New England, 470 Totten Pond Rd., Waltham, MA 02154; South, Suite 200, 17 Executive Park Dr. N.E., Atlanta, GA 30329; Southwest, Suite 922, 211 East Seventh St., Austin, TX 78701; West, Suite 228, 2700 Augustine Drive, Santa Clara, CA 95051; and Suite 705, 4155 East Jewell Avenue, Denver, CO 80222. The tests are prepared and administered for the College Board by the Educational Testing Service whose addresses are CBATP, Box 592, Princeton, NJ 08541.

CEEB test charges are $10.50 for the SAT and $16.75 for the Achievement Tests. Scores are forwarded to three colleges as part of CEEB's service for these fees. It charges $4.00 for each report needed for fourth, fifth, and sixth college, etc.

College-bound students should realize that, in addition to member colleges, there are many more that require CEEB test scores for their applicants.

The SATs and Achievement Tests are held seven times in an academic year: a Saturday in October (in Texas, Florida, Georgia, North Carolina, California, Illinois only), November, December, January, March, May, and June. The New SAT Question-and-Answer Service is available for these test dates: Saturday, May 7, 1983; Saturday, June 4, 1983 and Sunday, June 5, 1983. The tests are given in more than 3,000 test centers in American and foreign cities.

Students who are unable to take the tests on Saturdays because of religious convictions can make arrangements to have them given on Sundays.

The College Board will make special arrangements for administering the Admissions Tests to disabled students.

Scoring is not on the numerical range from 0 to 100 but on a relative range from a minimum of 200 to a maximum of 800.

The College Board has pointed out that a good school record is the single most important part of a student's application for college. The SAT measures verbal and mathematical abilities developed over a long period of time both in and out of school. These abilities are closely related to both school and college success.

The number of eleventh and twelfth grade students at public and private secondary schools throughout the nation taking the Preliminary Scholastic Aptitude Test/National Merit Scholarship Qualifying Test and the Scholastic Aptitude Test has grown into the hundreds of thousands. The PSAT/NMSQT, costing a fee of $4.25 per student, is a two-hour version of the three-hour SAT and uses the scoring range of 20 to 80 instead of the SAT's three digit scoring range of 200 to 800.

The PSAT/NMSQT may be given by any one school on either the Tuesday or the Saturday of a specified week in October, whichever day is more convenient for the school.

American College Testing Program (ACT)

The American College Testing Program (ACT) is an independent, nonprofit organization that provides a variety of educational programs and services.

The ACT Assessment Program is a comprehensive system of information gathering, processing, and reporting designed to help students planning to enter a postsecondary institution. The ACT Assessment instrument consists of a battery of four academic tests, taken under timed conditions, and a Student Profile Section and Interest Inventory, completed when students register for the Assessment.

The academic tests cover about four subject matter areas: English, mathematics, social studies, and natural sciences. These tests are designed to assess each student's general educational development and ability to complete college-level work. The test items require that the student demonstrate knowledge and both problem-solving and reasoning ability.

The Student Profile Section requests information about each student's admissions and enrollment plans, academic and out-of-class high school achievements and aspirations, and high school coursework. The student is also asked to supply biographical data and self-reported high school grades in the four subject matter areas covered by the academic tests.

The ACT Interest Inventory is designed to measure six major interest dimensions. Results are used to compare the student's interests with those of college-bound students who later majored in each of a wide variety of areas. Inventory results are also used to help students compare their work activity preferences with work activities that characterize specific families of jobs.

The ACT Assessment is administered on five national test dates each academic year throughout the United States, and four times a year in Canada and about 70 other countries. Each year, approximately one million students participate in the ACT Assessment program.

ACT's Student Need Analysis Service helps students applying for financial aid demonstrate their eligibility for assistance. This service collects, analyzes, and disseminates demographic and financial information on which more than 3,000 institutions and agencies base the awarding of scholarships, loans, and other financial assistance.

To apply for financial assistance at a postsecondary institution or scholarship agency using the ACT Student Need Analysis Service, a student obtains an ACT Family Financial Statement (FFS) packet from a high school counselor, from a college aid administrator, or directly from ACT. FFS packets—each containing an FFS with instructions, a list of institutions and agencies accepting ACT need analysis reports, and, in most states, a Student Data Form—are mailed to all high schools each year in late fall. The FFS, a mark-sense form designed for rapid processing and reporting, collects financial information from the student and family. This information, treated confidentially, is based on federal income data and thus is accurate and easy to report.

ACT's *College Planning/Search Book* has helped hundreds of thousands of students make college plans and decisions. The book is divided into two sections that encourage students to organize their thinking and their activities at each step in the process of making plans and choosing a college. The Planning Section helps students decide what they want from college. Worksheets, logs, questions, and illustrations help students define their needs and preferences. The Search Section displays information about colleges in a compact and accessible format. Students can compare cost, size, location, availability of majors, facts about the student body, admission selectivity, religious affiliation, and other significant college characteristics.

The facts about colleges provided by the *College Planning/Search Book* are drawn from ACT's comprehensive bank of information about more than 3,000 two-year and four-year institutions. Each year, this information bank is completely updated.

The Educational Opportunity Service (EOS) helps inform

students who have particular educational needs and goals about schools that have pertinent programs. EOS-participating institutions send ACT descriptions of their programs and specify the characteristics of appropriate students. When students register for the ACT Assessment, they indicate whether they want information about colleges or educational programs available through the EOS. Several times each year, ACT searches its Assessment files and matches students and programs.

Each year, about a million students receive EOS letters containing brief program descriptions along with preaddressed cards to be returned directly to the institutions for more information about programs that interest them.

More information about these programs can be obtained from the ACT National Office:

P.O.Box 168
2201 North Dodge Street
Iowa City, Iowa 52243
(319) 337-1000

Advanced Placement Program (AP)

A development over the past thirty years that has been gaining in strength, popularity, and usefulness is the Advanced Placement Program of the College Board whereby abler students may "leapfrog" some of the early work in college by taking freshman-level courses in the latter days of their secondary schooling and receive advanced placement and/or credit for them in college.

Planning, originated largely by the faculty of Kenyon College, began about 1951. The Advanced Placement Program exists primarily to serve the interests of three groups: able and ambitious secondary-school students capable of doing college-level work in school; secondary schools interested in providing such students with an opportunity to work up to capacity; and colleges prepared to recognize and reward their achievements. In serving these ends, the program encourages schools and colleges to work together to eliminate wasted time and duplicated studies and to stimulate students and teachers to higher achievements.

The program includes American History, Art (Studio, History), Biology, Chemistry, English (Language, Literature), European History, French (Language, Literature), German Language, Latin (Virgil, Catullus-Horace), Mathematics (Calculus AB, Calculus BC), Music (Listening and Literature, Theory), Physics (Physics B, Physics C), and Spanish (Language, Literature). Computer Science will be added in 1983-84.

Each college makes its own decision regarding credit and advanced placement. Although few students plan to complete their formal education in less than four years, many can finish college in three years, and enter graduate schools earlier, with a saving of both time and money.

College-Level Examination Program (CLEP)

Another activity of the College Board is the College-Level Examination Program (CLEP). This is designed to increase access to higher education and to facilitate the proper placement of students regardless of how or where they gained their knowledge.

The program has four major objectives: a national program of general and subject examinations that can be used to evaluate non-traditional college level education, including independent study, correspondence work, on-the-job and military training; to stimulate colleges and universities to develop appropriate procedures for the placement, accreditation, and admission of nontraditional, traditional, and transfer students; to provide colleges and universities with a means by which to evaluate their programs and their students' achievement; and to assist adults who wish to meet licensing requirements or qualify for higher positions.

Students are smarter about colleges than they were a generation ago. Their parents are smarter. With the country's vast array of colleges and universities, including two-year terminal and sometimes semi-professional programs, young people today need not confine their thoughts only to the traditional or conventional institutions.

Law School Admission Test (LSAT)

A Law School Admission Test is administered by the Law School Admission Services, Box 2000, New Town, PA 18940. Law schools require that all of their applicants submit scores on this test. It is given four times a year, on Saturdays, in October, December, February, and on Wednesday in June. Students whose religious convictions prevent their taking tests on Saturdays may apply to take them on the Monday following some of the Saturday test dates.

The test fee is $20.

The Law School Admission Test is held on many college campuses, in many cities of the United States and in a number of foreign large cities.

Medical College Admission Test (MCAT)

The Medical College Admission Test is administered by the American College Testing Program, P.O. Box 414, Iowa City, IA 52243, under the direction of the Association of American Medical Colleges. It is given twice a year, in the fall and spring at established testing centers, and is designed to be a measure of specified science knowledge in biology, chemistry, and physics; the application of this knowledge to solving related problems in the sciences; a measure of basic reasoning skills through the ability to comprehend, evaluate, and utilize information presented in narrative, tabular, and graphic formats.

The examination fee is $45. Tests will be arranged for Sundays, with an extra fee of $5, for registrants presenting satisfactory evidence that their religious convictions prevent them from taking tests on Saturday.

The extent to which test results are used in deciding about applicants varies from one school of medicine to another.

Graduate Record Examinations (GRE)

Many graduate and professional schools require that admission applicants take the Graduate Record Examinations. These are prepared annually by the Educational Testing Service and consist of several tests.

The General Aptitude Test, a three-hour-and-thirty-minute examination given in the morning, provides a measure of general scholastic ability at the graduate level. It yields separate scores for verbal, quantitative, and analytical ability. Included are verbal reasoning questions, reading comprehension questions from several fields, arithmetic reasoning, algebraic problems, and interpretation of graphs, diagrams, and descriptive data.

The Subject (Advanced) Tests, two hours and fifty minutes long, are given in the afternoon to measure one's mastery and comprehension of materials basic to success in the field of a specific graduate major. Subject (Advanced) Tests are offered in the following subjects: Biology, Chemistry, Computer Science, Economics, Education, Engineering, French, Geography, Geology, German, History, Literature in English, Mathematics, Music, Philosophy, Physics, Political Science, Psychology, Sociology, Spanish.

The Graduate Record Examinations are offered in many cities in this country and in 106 foreign nations and United States territories in February, April, October, and December. In June, only the General (Aptitude) Test is offered. A few of the Subject (Advanced) Tests are available less frequently.

A fee of $24 is charged for each test in the United States and Puerto Rico. In other locations the fee is $31 for a single test, or $55 for both the General (Aptitude) Test and a Subject (Advanced) Test on the same day. Fees are partially refundable if the registrant is absent from the test.

Graduate Management Admission Test (GMAT)

The Graduate Management Admission Test is a four-hour test measuring general verbal abilities that are developed over a long period of time and that are associated with success in the first year of study at graduate schools of management. The Graduate Management Admission Council, representing 64 graduate management schools, directs Educational Testing Service in the conduct of the GMAT program. The test is offered on a Saturday in October, January, March, and June. The test fee is $30 for test centers in the United States, Guam, Puerto Rico, the U.S. Virgin Islands, and U.S. territories and $36 for test centers elsewhere.

Students from Abroad: Special Procedures

Students in foreign countries in increasing numbers have ambitions to study at colleges and universities in the United States. They find, however, that American institutions differ from their native colleges.

A great deal is strange. The matter of pre-college tests, including the College Board exams, is unknown to the overseas student. There are various other unfamiliar items about passports, visas, alien registration cards, port-of-entry procedures.

The Institute of International Education, 809 United Nations Plaza, New York, NY 10017, publishes the *Handbook on International Study for Foreign Nationals* which describes study opportunities in the United States for foreign students.

WHICH COLLEGE FOR YOU?

The Importance of Choosing Carefully

Now comes the problem of choosing your college. You have made up your mind to go. You and your family have been calculating the costs, adding up the savings bank books, eying scholarship possiblities, loans, and part-time jobs.

Picking the right college has lasting effects. It must be done carefully and earnestly. If the high school senior knows his or her choice of a life's career, it may be easier. A wise and discerning principal once said, "A first-class student doesn't select a third-class college."

Don't flip a coin. Don't pick because of a whim. Some have not chosen a college at all but a college atmosphere. They thought they wanted to attend a country club.

Sooner or later parents must be willing to allow their child to make the final selection of a college. They can help in the examination of guide books and catalogs and in visits to campuses. But in the end the student should make the decision. The student is going to college, not the parents. The student is going to do the best work on the campus where he or she is most contented.

Perhaps as the student analyzes colleges he or she finds two almost exactly even in size, excellence, endowments, curricula, pride, reputation, and in the "creature comforts" for its students. Yet he or she will pick one over the other because of some subconscious, intangible reason.

As a matter of fact, and because of the competitive selective admissions policies, many students go where they can get in and not always to the college that was their initial choice. College will continue to be a seller's market and you, the student, are the buyer of education!

This great nation of ours has all kinds of institutions: great universities famed the world over; state and municipal institutions supported largely by taxes; private, independent, and endowed colleges that are for men or women or co-ed; denominational colleges affiliated with or actually operated by religious bodies; colleges for teachers; independent professional and technological institutes offering specialized training such as for engineering, medicine, dentistry, perhaps optometry, osteopathy, chiropractic, chiropody; independent theological and Bible institutions; and the post-high-school junior, terminal, and community colleges and technical institutes.

By and large, any good student in sound health with a rank in the top third of the class and with an average of B or better can look with confidence toward being accepted by any college. Rejections are not likely to be made because of academic deficiencies. They might stem from the accident of residence, however.

Colleges like to have geographical dispersion. They like to brag in their literature that their students come from every state in the Union and from twenty-odd foreign nations. Some are likely to accept students from North Dakota or Wyoming and reject additional applicants from metropolitan areas of New York, Boston, Chicago, or Philadelphia.

This edition of *Lovejoy's College Guide* includes about 3,000 institutions of higher education in the United States plus some selected foreign institutions, counting every kind and gradation. Many confer baccalaureate or higher degrees; the others have programs shorter than four years, some of which are empowered to confer the A.A., A.S. degrees, etc.

Every college-bound student and family won't be interested in all of the aforementioned institutions. They will narrow their horizons to a workable number and then will examine several college catalogs, fine print and all. They will analyze the college bulletins from cover to cover, sizing up the faculty and their backgrounds, examining the financial structure, endowment, expenditures, value and size of plant.

College Fairs/College Nights

The National Association of College Admissions Counselors holds large college fairs throughout the country. There are hundreds of colleges represented at these fairs. It would be very unlikely if your selected group of colleges were not at these. Since these gatherings are large it is to your advantage to have researched your five to seven colleges so when you attend one of these fairs or a College Night you will not waste time wandering around not knowing what colleges to visit.

Visiting Colleges

Prospective students should try to visit colleges after they have narrowed their list of considerations to perhaps ten or twelve. They can drive around the campuses, look into some of the buildings and while on the campuses, call the Admissions Office for a brief chat with the director, committee member, or one of the assistants if possible.

Colleges encourage visits by prospective students and their parents. They prefer them to visit on weekdays between the hours of, say, 8:30 and 4:30. But, more and more, they are beginning to understand that some visitors can only come on a Saturday, Sunday, or holiday; and they are providing for their welcome by having specially assigned officers—one college uses some emeritus professors—to be on hand to greet guests.

It is advisable to notify the institution in advance of intended visits. But college officers realize this is not always possible because of the vagaries and delays of auto, air, and train travel. Even if directors of admission are away on speaking trips or attending educational conventions, they invariably leave behind one or two deputies and assistants.

In visiting a college, prospective students should wander around the campus by car or afoot, looking into laboratories, libraries, residence halls, dining halls, student union buildings, gymnasiums, field houses, and even conceivably fraternity and sorority houses or the equivalent in clubs if opportunities present themselves. It is valuable, when possible, to spend a night with students in a freshman dormitory, eat dinner or breakfast in the campus commons, and talk with some students.

It is important to visit colleges. The selection should not be left to whim or to a teacher's sometimes biased advice or to an uncle's casual suggestion, or because an acquaintance or friend is planning to attend or because of the influence of fraternity rushers. Parents should be concerned with where their sons and daughters are going to study for the next four or more years. And so should students.

Accreditation

Sooner or later someone will point out that this college is accredited but that one is not. What about this business of accrediting?

Two kinds of accreditation are attainable: regional and professional.

There are six regional associations, covering the United States and territories, which either do formal accrediting and approving or have a membership list that is practically the equivalent. These are the New England Association of Schools and Colleges, Inc., Middle States Association of Colleges and Secondary Schools, Southern Association of Colleges and Secondary Schools, North Central Association of Colleges and Secondary Schools, Northwest Association of Secondary and Higher Schools, Western Association of Schools and Colleges. The addresses and states each encompasses can be found on page 16 .

There are many national professional associations which accredit or approve college programs in a specific area of study such as music, business schools, Bible schools, law, etc.

Intangible Factors to Consider

It is utterly impossible to measure with a yardstick some of the intangibles and imponderables about colleges. One of the arguments against early practices of some of the accrediting bodies with their quantitative requirements calling for, say, ten departments, 10,000 library volumes, and 1,000 students, was that it was sheer nonsense to aver such a college was superior to one with nine departments, 9,999 volumes, and 999 students.

One of the difficult problems in selecting a college is whether to choose a small one or a large one. The small one will make you, some say, a bigger frog in a little puddle because you will be closer to your professors and know the student body more intimately. On the other hand, you will be told that the larger institutions with larger resources can command and pay for better faculty brains for your instruction and that the laboratories, libraries, and other facilities will be more ample.

Proximity to home is often an influential factor. Attractive regional scholarships, if available, must be weighed. Families should be sensible. To go to college 3,000 miles away from home may mean using up, in railroad and plane fares at vacation times, too much of a liberal grant.

Professional Counseling

High school pupils need guidance and counseling, advice and information about selecting their colleges. Too few high schools, regrettably, have adequate guidance service. Or, at best, they do it poorly by using overburdened teachers to give a smattering of counseling in addition to their normal teaching duties.

A few college counselors have begun to appear who decline payments from institutions, but, instead, charge the parents or pupil clients a professional fee for advice and consultation in the manner a lawyer or doctor or dentist or C.P.A. would charge a professional consulting fee. This sound practice is followed by the Lovejoy Counseling Service.

If a family is about ready to spend $32,000 or more for a child's higher education (four years at $8,000), it is a good, sound investment to pay a fee for professional advice, just as a family would go to another professional called an architect if it were ready to invest thousands of dollars in building a home.

A monthly LOVEJOY'S GUIDANCE DIGEST is published from offices at 2 Drummond Place, Red Bank, New Jersey 07701, to bridge the gaps between revisions of the Guide, with up-to-date developments in college admissions, accreditations, degree programs, expenses, scholarships, free research service, etc. and is available by subscription to parents, students, and guidance counselors.

LOVEJOY'S COUNSELING SERVICE is available at this office counseling families on a personalized, effective, and understanding professional basis.

A Note on "Degree Mills"

The lax chartering laws in some states permit the existence of correspondence schools whose practices amount virtually to the sale of degrees. Such organizations are commonly referred to as "degree mills."

The Office of Education defines a degree mill as "an organization that awards degrees without requiring courses of instruction that all reputable educational institutions require before conferring degrees." Most of these degree mills operate solely by mail. In many cases staffs and plants do not even exist.

Degree mills seriously threaten American educational standards in several ways. First, by misleading the public, they damage the legitimate and reputable correspondence schools which are filling an important and necessary role by providing correspondence study in the areas of vocational and adult education. Second, degree mills defraud those who honestly believe that they have received recognition from a legitimate institution of higher education. Third, they lower American prestige abroad by deceiving foreign students. They cause legitimate American educational degrees to be undervalued because of the confusion they create overseas.

In view of the inadequacy and utter worthlessness of degree mills and their disservice to American higher education, the U.S. Office of Education strongly urges the public to be on guard against organizations advertising degrees based solely on correspondence study. Caution should be exercised in evaluating degrees and other credentials, to determine whether or not they have been obtained from degree mills.

The following is the Statement of Student's Rights from the National Association of College Counselors Admissions Process booklet.

The Student's Rights:

1. To full information from colleges and universities concerning their admission, financial aid, and scholarship policies. Prior to applying you should be fully informed of policies and procedures concerning application fees, deposits, refunds, housing, financial aid, and scholarships.

2. To defer responding to an offer of admission and/or financial aid and scholarships until you have heard from all colleges and universities to which you have applied, or until May 1 (whichever is earlier).

Should you be denied this right: (1) immediately request the college/university to extend the reply date; (2) notify your counselor and ask him/her to notify the President of the State or Regional ACAC. For additional assistance send a copy of your admission notification letter and all correspondence to: Executive Director, NACAC, 9933 Lawler Avenue, Suite 500, Skokie, Illinois 60077.

The Student's Responsibility:

1. To be aware of the policies (deadlines, restrictions, etc.) regarding admissions, financial aid, and scholarships of the colleges and universities of your choice.

2. To complete and submit required material to colleges and universities.

3. To meet all application deadlines.

4. To follow college application procedures of your high school.

5. To notify the colleges and universities which have offered you admission of your acceptance or rejection of their offer as soon as you have heard from all to which you have applied or before May 1 (whichever is earlier).

6. To confirm your intention to enroll at—and submit a deposit to—*only one institution* by the required notification date, usually May 1. If you have been put on a waiting list and later accepted by another college you decide to attend, it is of course permissable to send your acknowledgement and deposit to this second college; it is also your obligation to notify the former college immediately of your change in circumstances and your plan to go elsewhere.

SECTION TWO

CAREER CURRICULA AND SPECIAL PROGRAMS—GUIDANCE AND TIPS

This section is designed to facilitate the selection of a college according to your career objectives. You will find a list of the Professional Accrediting Bodies and Recognized Member Associations to which references are made in the material that follows.

The material is divided into two main parts:

I: PROFESSIONAL CURRICULA—consists of the list of nearly 500 career fields, from Accounting through Zoology, and institutions where they are taught.

II: SPECIAL PROGRAMS—consists of 18 Special Programs and institutions where they are offered.

NOTE: Certain curricula and special programs listed in the previous edition of this book have now become so widely available that we have dropped them in order to provide space for new categories that can be found at a limited number of colleges only.

The new listings in this edition are: Arts Management, 5-Year MBA, Commercial Music, Computer Repair, Culinary Arts, Electronic Music, Future Studies, Geriatrics/Gerontology, Golf Management, Humanities, Journalism, Music Media, Musical Theatre, Medical Secretarial, Legal Secretarial, Sports Medicine, Store/Shop Management, Special Education, Ultra Sound Studies, Basic Studies.

PROFESSIONAL ACCREDITING BODIES AND RECOGNIZED MEMBER ASSOCIATIONS

Most of the traditional fields now have well-defined professional accrediting procedures by recognized bodies. Not all professional schools have professional accreditation. Some of the accrediting bodies have gradations of approval, for example, "provisional," "probationary," or "associate."

The following list of names and addresses of professional accrediting bodies and recognized member associations is included for your convenience. You may contact these organizations directly for information on criteria for accreditation, or for clarification of the professional standing of a particular institution.

Accreditation Board for Engineering and Technology, Inc., 345 East 47th St., New York, NY 10017

Advertising Education Publications, 3429 Fifty-Fifth St., Lubbock, TX 79413

American Assembly of Collegiate Schools of Business, 11500 Olive Blvd., Suite 142, St. Louis, MO 63141

American Association of Bible Colleges, Box 1523, Fayetteville, AR 72701

American Association of Colleges of Podiatric Medicine, 20 Chevy Chase Circle, N.W., Washington, DC 20015

American Bar Association (Law), II55 E. 60th St., Chicago, IL 60637

American Board of Funeral Service Education, P.O. Box 2098, Fairmont, WV 26554

American Chemical Society, 1155 Sixteenth St., N.W., Washington, DC 20036

American College of Nurse Midwives, 1552 K St., N.W., Suite 1120, Washington, DC 20005

American Collegiate Retailing Association, Rochester Institute of Technology, College of Business, 1 Lomb Memorial Drive, Rochester, NY 14623

American Council on Education in Journalism and Mass Communications, School of Journalism, U. of Missouri, Box 838, Columbia, MO 65205

American Council on Pharmaceutical Education, 1 E. Wacker Dr., Suite 2210, Chicago, IL 60601

American Dance Therapy Assn., 2000 Century Plaza, Columbia, MD 21044

American Dental Association, 211 E. Chicago Ave., Chicago, IL 60611

American Dietetic Association, 430 N. Michigan Ave., Chicago, IL 60611

American Institute of Physics, 335 East 45th Street, New York, NY 10017

American Library Association, 50 E. Huron St., Chicago, IL 60611

American Medical Association, 535 N. Dearborn St., Chicago, IL 60610

American Meterological Society, 45 Beacon St., Boston, MA 02108

American Montessori Society, 150 Fifth Ave., New York, NY 10011

American Optometric Association, 243 N. Lindbergh Blvd., St. Louis, MO 63141

American Osteopathic Association, 212 E. Ohio St., Chicago, IL 60611

American Physical Therapy Association, 1156 Fifteenth St., N.W., Washington, DC 20005

American Physiological Society, 9650 Rockville Pike, Bethesda, MD 20814

American Planning Association, 1776 Massachusetts Ave., N.W., Washington, DC 20036

American Psychological Association, 1200 Seventeenth St., N.W., Washington, DC 20036

American Society of Agricultural Engineers, P.O. Box 410, St. Joseph, MI 49085

American Society of Landscape Architects, 1900 M St., N.W., Suite 750, Washington, DC 20036

American Speech-Language-Hearing Association, 10801 Rockville Pike, Rockville, MD 20852

American Theatre Association, 1029 Vermont Ave., N.W., Washington, DC 20005

American Veterinary Medical Association, 930 N. Meacham Rd., Schaumburg, IL 60196

Association of Physician Assistant Programs, 2341 Jefferson Davis Highway, Suite 700, Arlington, VA 22202

Association of Theological Schools, P.O. Box 130, Vandalia, OH 45377

Association of University Programs in Health Administration, 1911 North Fort Meyer Drive, Suite 503, Arlington, VA 22209

Council on Accreditation of Nurse Anesthesia, 216 W. Higgins Rd., Park Ridge, IL 60068

Council on Chiropractic Education, 3209 Ingersoll Ave., Des Moines, IA 50312

Council on Education for Public Health, 1015 Fifteenth St., N.W., Washington, DC 20036

Council on Hotel, Restaurant and Institutional Education, Inc., Human Development Bldg., Room 21, University Park, PA 16802

Council on Social Work Education, 111 Eighth Ave., New York, NY 10011

Federal Aviation Administration, Distribution Unit, Publications Section, TAD-443.1, Washington, DC 20590

Foundation for Interior Design Education, 242 West 27th St., New York, NY 10001

National Aeronautics and Space Administration, Employees Relations Div., Office of Personnel, Washington, DC 20546

National Architectural Accrediting Board, 1735 New York Ave., N.W., Washington, DC 20006

National Association of Broadcasters, 1771 N Street, N.W., Washington, DC 20036

National Association for Musical Therapy, 901 Kentucky St., Suite 206, P.O. Box 610, Lawrence, KS 66044

National Association of Schools of Art, 11250 Roger Bacon Dr. #5, Reston, VA 22090

National Association of Schools of Music, 11250 Roger Bacon Dr. #5, Reston, VA 22090

National Commission for Cooperative Education, 360 Huntington Ave., Boston, MA 02115

National Council for Accreditation of Teacher Education, 1919 Pennsylvania Ave., N.W., Suite 202, Washington, DC 20006

National Dance Association, 1900 Association Drive, Reston, VA 22091

National League for Nursing, 10 Columbus Circle, New York, NY 10019

National University Extension Assn., One Dupont Circle, Suite 360, Washington, DC 20036 (Correspondence study)

National Women's Studies Association, University of Maryland, College Park, MD 20742

Plastics Education Foundation, 1913 Central Ave., Albany, NY 12205

Society of Actuaries, 208 S. LaSalle St., Chicago, IL 60604

Society of American Foresters, 5400 Grosvenor Lane, Bethesda MD 20814

Sports Fishing Institute, 608-13th St. N.W., Washington, DC 20005

United Nations Semester Program, Drew University, Madison, NJ 07940

Washington Semester Program, American University, Massachusetts and Nebraska Aves., Washington, DC 20016

I-PROFESSIONAL CURRICULA: SPECIAL PROGRAMS AND WHERE TO FIND THEM

Accounting

Institutions awarding 20 or more undergraduate degrees as major field in single year according to U.S. Office of Education statistics

Abilene Christian U	TX
Adelphi	NY
Akron, U. of	OH
Alabama, U. of	AL
Alabama A&M	AL
Alabama State U	AL
Albright	PA
Albuquerque, U. of	NM
American International	MA
American U	DC
Angelo State	TX
Appalachian State	NC
Aquinas	MI
Arizona, U. of	AZ
Arizona State U	AZ
Arkansas, U. of	AR
Arkansas State	AR
Arkansas Tech. U	AR
Armstrong	GA
Athens State	AL
Auburn	AL
Augsburg Coll	MN
Augusta	GA
Augustana Coll	IL
Austin Peay	TN
Baldwin-Wallace Coll	OH
Ball State U	IN
Baruch Coll	NY
Bayamon Central U	PR
Baylor	TX
Bellarmine	KY
Belmont Abbey	NC
Benedictine Coll	KS
Bentley	MA
Biscayne	FL
Bloomsburg State	PA
Bloomfield Coll	NJ
Bob Jones U	SC
Boise State	ID
Boston Coll	MA
Bowling Green State U	OH
Bradley	IL
Bridgeport, U. of	CT
Brigham Young	UT
Brooklyn Coll	NY
Bryant Coll	RI
Bucknell	PA
Buena Vista Coll	IA
Butler U	IN
Calumet Coll	IN
Canisius	NY
Carson-Newman	TN
Carthage Coll	WI
Catholic U	PR
Central Arkansas, U. of	AR
Central Connecticut	CT
Central Michigan U	MI
Central Missouri State	MO
Central State	OK
Central Washington	WA
Chaminade U	HI
Christian Bros	TN
Cincinnati, U. of	OH
Clarion State	PA
Clark Coll	GA
Clarkson Coll. of Tech	NY
Clemson	SC
Cleveland State U	OH
Colorado, U. of	CO
Columbus Coll	GA
Concord Coll	WV
Concordia	MN
Connecticut, U. of	CT
Corpus Christi State U	TX
Creighton	NE
David Lipscomb	TN
Dayton, U. of	OH
Delaware, U. of	DE
Delaware State	DE
Delta State	MS
Denver, U. of	CO
DePaul	IL
Detroit, U. of	MI
Detroit Coll. of Business	MI
Dillard U	LA
District of Columbia, U. of (Van Ness)	DC
Dominican Coll	NY
Dowling	NY
Drake	IA
Duke U	NC
Dyke	OH
East Central	OK
East Tennessee State U	TN
East Texas State U	TX
Eastern Illinois	IL
Eastern Kentucky	KY
Eastern Michigan U	MI
Eastern New Mexico	NM
Eastern Washington State	WA
Edinboro State	PA
Elizabethtown	PA
Elmhurst Coll	IL
Emporia Kansas State	KS
Elon Coll	NC
Evansville, U. of	IN
Fairfield U	CT
Fairleigh Dickinson	NJ
Ferris State	MI
Florida, U. of	FL
Florida A&M	FL
Florida Atlantic	FL
Florida International	FL
Florida Southern	FL
Florida State U	FL
Florida Tech	FL
Fordham	NY
Fort Hays	KS
Fort Lewis Coll	CO
Franklin	OH
Franklin and Marshall	PA
Freed-Hardeman	TN
Furman U	SC
Gannon	PA
Geneva	PA
George Washington	DC
Georgetown	DC
Georgia, U. of	GA
Georgia Coll	GA
Georgia Southern	GA
Georgia State U	GA
Golden Gate	CA
Gonzaga	WA
Grambling	LA
Grove City Coll	PA
Guilford	NC
Harding	AR
Hartford, U. of	CT
Hawaii, U. of	HI
Henderson State	AR
Hofstra	NY
Houston, U. of	TX
Howard	DC
Hunter Coll	NY
Husson	ME
Idaho, U. of	ID
Idaho State U	ID
Illinois, U. of	IL
Illinois State U	IL
Illinois Wesleyan U	IL
Indiana State U	IN
Indiana U	IN
Indiana-Purdue U	IN
Inter-America U	PR
Iona	NY
Iowa, U. of	IA
Ithaca Coll	NY
Jackson State	MS
Jacksonville State	AL
James Madison U	VA
John Carroll U	OH
Johnson and Wales	RI
Jones	FL
Kansas, U. of	KS
Kansas State U	KS
Kent State U	OH
Kentucky, U. of	KY
King's	PA
La Salle	PA
Lake Erie Coll	OH
Lake Superior State	MI
Lamar U	TX
Le Moyne	NY
Lehigh	PA
Lehman	NY
Lewis U	IL
Long Island U	NY
Loras	IA
Louisiana State U	LA
Louisiana Tech	LA
Louisville, U. of	KY
Lowell, U. of	MA
Loyola	IL
Loyola	LA
Loyola	MD
Loyola Marymount U	CA
Luther	IA
Lycoming	PA
Manchester Coll	IN
Manhattan	NY
Mankato State	MN
Marietta	OH
Marist Coll	NY
Marquette	WI
Marshall	WV
Maryland, U. of	MD
Massachusetts, U. of (Amherst)	MA
McNeese State	LA
Medgar Evers	NY
Memphis State	TN
Merrimack	MA
Metropolitan State	CO
Miami, U. of	FL
Miami U	OH
Michigan, U. of (Flint)	MI
Michigan State U	MI
Middle Tennessee State U	TN
Midwestern	TX
Millikin	IL
Minnesota, U. of	MN
Mississippi, U. of	MS
Mississippi Coll	MS
Mississippi State U	MS
Missouri Southern	MO
Missouri Western	MO
Monmouth Coll	NJ
Montana, U. of	MT
Moorhead State	MN
Moravian Coll	PA
Morgan State U	MD
Mount Union	OH
Mt. St. Mary's Coll	MD
Muhlenberg Coll	PA
Murray State	KY
National Coll. of Bus	SD
Nebraska, U. of (Omaha)	NE
Nevada, U. of	NV
New Hampshire, U. of	NH
New Hampshire Coll	NH
New Haven, U. of	CT
New Mexico State	NM
New Orleans, U. of	LA
New York Inst. of Tech	NY
New York U	NY
Niagara	NY
Nicholls State U	LA
Nichols	MA
Norfolk State	VA
North Alabama, U. of	AL
North Carolina, U. of (Charlotte, Greensboro, Wilmington)	NC
North Carolina A&T State U	NC
North Carolina Central	NC
North Carolina State U	NC
North Dakota, U. of	ND
North Florida, U. of	FL
North Georgia Coll	GA
North Texas State U	TX
Northeast Louisiana State	LA
Northeast Missouri	MO
Northeastern	MA
Northeastern State Coll	OK
Northern Arizona	AZ
Northern Colorado, U. of	CO
Northern Illinois U	IL
Northern Iowa, U. of	IA
Northern Kentucky U	KY
Northern Michigan	MI
Northern State	SD
Northwest Missouri	MO
Notre Dame, U. of	IN
Ohio Northern U	OH
Ohio State U	OH
Ohio U	OH
Oklahoma, U. of	OK
Oklahoma State U	OK
Old Dominion Coll	VA
Oral Roberts	OK
Oregon, U. of	OR
Ouachita Baptist	AR
Pace	NY
Pan American U	TX
Pennsylvania, U. of	PA
Pennsylvania State U	PA
Philadelphia Coll. Textiles and Sci	PA
Pittsburg State U	KS
Portland, U. of	OR
Providence	RI
Puerto Rico, U. of	PR
Queens	NY
Quincy	IL
Quinnipiac	CT
Regis Coll	CO
Rhode Island, U. of	RI
Richmond, U. of	VA
Rider	NJ
Robert Morris	PA
Rochester Inst. of Tech	NY
Rockhurst	MO
Rollins Coll	FL
Roosevelt	IL
Rutgers	NJ
Sacred Heart	CT
Sacred Heart U	PR
Saginaw Valley State	MI
Salem State	MA
Sam Houston State	TX
San Diego, U. of	CA
San Francisco, U. of	CA
Scranton, U. of	PA
Seattle U	WA
Seton Hall	NJ
Shippensburg State Coll	PA
Siena Coll	NY
South Alabama, U. of	AL
South Carolina, U. of	SC
South Dakota, U. of	SD
South Florida, U. of	FL
Southeast Missouri State U	MO
Southeastern Louisiana	LA
Southeastern Massachusetts U	MA
Southeastern Oklahoma	OK
Southeastern U	DC
Southern Arkansas	AR
Southern Colorado, U. of	CO
Southern Illinois U	IL
Southern Maine, U. of	ME
Southern Mississippi, U. of	MS
Southern U. (Baton Rouge, New Orleans)	LA
Southwest Missouri	MO

Southwestern Louisiana, U. of .. LA
Southwestern State .... OK
St. Ambrose .... IA
St. Bonaventure .... NY
St. Cloud State Coll .... MN
St. Francis .... NY
St. Francis .... PA
St. John Fisher .... NY
St. John's .... MN
St. John's .... NY
St. Joseph's .... PA
St. Joseph's Coll .... IN
St. Louis U .... MO
St. Mary's .... TX
St. Norbert Coll .... WI
St. Peter's .... NJ
St. Thomas, Coll. of .... MN
St. Vincent .... PA
State U. of New York (Albany, Binghamton, Oswego, Plattsburgh) .... NY
Stephen F. Austin State .... TX
Stetson U .... FL
Steubenville, Coll. of .... OH
Stonehill .... MA
Strayer .... DC
Suffolk .... MA
Susquehanna .... PA
Syracuse .... NY
Tampa, U. of .... FL
Temple .... PA
Tennessee, U. of .... TN
Tennessee Tech. U .... TN
Texas, U. of (Arlington, Austin, El Paso, Permian Basin, San Antonio) .... TX
Texas A&I .... TX
Texas A&M .... TX
Texas Christian U .... TX
Texas Eastern U .... TX
Texas Lutheran U .... TX
Texas Southern .... TX
Texas Tech. U .... TX
Texas Wesleyan .... TX
Thiel Coll .... PA
Thomas Coll .... ME
Thomas More .... KY
Tiffin U .... OH
Toledo, U. of .... OH
Tri-State .... IN
Troy State .... AL
Tulsa, U. of .... OK
Tuskegee Inst .... AL
Upsala Coll .... NJ
Utah, U. of .... UT
Utah State .... UT
Utica Coll .... NY
Valdosta State .... GA
Valparaiso U .... IN
Villanova .... PA
Virginia, U. of .... VA
Virginia Commonwealth U ...... VA
Virginia Poly. Inst .... VA
Virginia State .... VA
Wake Forest U .... NC
Walsh .... MI
Washburn .... KS
Washington, U. of .... WA
Wayne State U .... MI
Waynesburg .... PA
Weber State .... UT
West Chester State Coll .... PA
West Florida, U. of .... FL
West Georgia .... GA
West Texas State .... TX
West Virginia State .... WV
West Virginia U .... WV
Western Carolina .... NC
Western Illinois IL
Western Kentucky U .... KY
Western Michigan U .... MI
Western New England .... MA
Western State Coll .... CO
Western Washington State ..... WA
Wheeling Coll .... WV
Wichita State U .... KS
Widener .... PA
Wilkes .... PA
William Paterson .... NJ
Winona State .... MN
Wisconsin, U. of (Eau Claire, Madison, Oshkosh, Platteville, Whitewater) .... WI
Woodbury .... CA
World U .... PR
Wright State .... OH
Wyoming, U. of .... WY
Xavier .... OH
Xavier U .... LA
York .... PA
Youngstown State U .... OH

Actuarial Science

According to the Society of Actuaries the following institutions offer bachelor's and master's degrees

⋆Indicates bachelor's degree only
•Indicates master's degree only

Ball State U .... IN
⋆Butler U .... IN
⋆Cincinnati, U. of .... OH
Connecticut, U. of .... CT
⋆Drake U .... IA
Georgia State U .... GA
Illinois, U. of IL
⋆Indiana U. Northwest .... IN
⋆Insurance, Coll. of .... NY
Iowa, U. of .... IA
⋆Lebanon Valley Coll .... PA
•Loyola Coll .... MD
⋆Maryville Coll .... MO
Michigan, U. of .... MI
Minnesota, U. of .... MN
Nebraska, U. of .... NE
New York U .... NY
North Carolina, U. of .... NC
•Northeastern U .... MA
Ohio State U .... OH
Pennsylvania, U. of .... PA
⋆Pennsylvania State U .... PA
Roosevelt U IL
SUNY (Albany) .... NY
Temple U .... PA
Texas, U. of (Austin) .... TX
Wisconsin, U. of (Madison) ..... WI

Acupuncture

Alabama A&M .... AL

Advertising

Curricula approved by American Council on Education in Journalism and Mass Communications

California State U. (Fullerton) ... CA
Colorado, U. of .... CO
Drake .... IA
Florida, U. of .... FL
Georgia, U. of .... GA
Illinois, U. of IL
Iowa State U .... IA
Kansas, U. of .... KS
Louisiana State U .... LA
Michigan State U .... MI
Minnesota, U. of .... MN
Missouri, U. of .... MO
Nebraska, U. of .... NE
North Carolina, U. of .... NC
Northern Illinois U IL
Northwestern IL
Ohio U .... OH
Oklahoma, U. of .... OK
Oklahoma State U .... OK
Oregon, U. of .... OR
Pennsylvania State .... PA
San Jose State U .... CA
South Carolina, U. of .... SC
Syracuse .... NY
Tennessee, U. of .... TN
Texas, U. of (Austin) .... TX
Texas Tech. U .... TX
Washington, U. of .... WA
West Virginia U .... WV
Wisconsin, U. of (Madison) ..... WI

Aeronautical Engineering,

See
ENGINEERING, AERONAUTICAL

Agricultural Business

Abilene Christian .... TX
Alfred U .... NY
Andrews U .... MI
Arizona State U .... AZ
Arizona Western .... AZ
Arkansas, U. of (Fayetteville) ... AR
Arkansas State U .... AR
Arkansas Tech .... AR
Austin Peay State .... TN
Auburn U .... AL
Barton Co. Comm .... KS
Bismark Jr .... ND
Blinn Coll .... TX
Butte Coll .... CA
Brigham Young U .... UT
California, U. of (Davis) .... CA
California State Poly. (Pomona) .... CA
California State U. (Fresno) ..... CA
Casper .... WY
Central Arizona .... AZ
Central Coll .... KS
Chadron State .... NE
Coffeyville .... KS
Cowley Co. Comm. Jr .... KS
Dakota State Coll .... SD
Dakota Wesleyan .... SD
Dawson Comm .... MT
Delaware, U. of .... DE
Dickinson State .... SD
Dordt .... IA
Eastern Arizona .... AZ
Eastern Kentucky U .... KY
Eastern Oregon State .... OR
Eastern Wyoming .... WY
Ferrum .... VA
Florida A&M .... FL
Fort Hays State .... KS
Fort Lewis .... CO
Fort Scott Comm .... KS
Freed-Hardeman .... TN
Freeman Jr .... SD
Georgia Southwestern .... GA
Goddard College .... VT
Hannibal-Lagrange .... MO
Hesston .... KS
Highland Comm .... KS
Huron .... SD
Hutchinson Comm .... KS
Idaho, U. of .... ID
Illinois, U. of IL
Illinois Central IL
Illinois State U IL
Iowa State U .... IA
James Madison .... VA
Kaskaskia IL
Kearney State .... NE
Lincoln IL
McPherson .... KS
Maine, U. of (Orono) .... ME
Middle Tennessee State .... TN
Missouri Valley .... MO
Murray State U .... KY
Morehead State .... KY
Morningside Coll .... IA
National .... SD
Nebraska Western .... NE
New Mexico Military Inst ...... NM
Nicholls State .... LA
North Carolina Agric. Tech .... NC
North Dakota State U. (Fargo, Bottineau) .... ND
Northeast Louisiana U .... LA
Northeast Mississippi Jr .... MS
Northeast Missouri State ...... MO
Northeastern Jr .... CO
Northern Montana .... MT
Northern Oklahoma .... OK
Northwest Missouri State ...... MO
Northwestern Oklahoma State . OK
Northwestern State U .... LA
Ohio State U .... OH
Oklahoma Panhandle State .... OK
Oklahoma State U .... OK
Otero Jr .... CO
Ozarks, Sch. of the .... MO
Pennsylvania State U .... PA
Purdue U .... IN
Puerto Rico, U. of .... PR
Sheridan Coll .... WY
Simpson Coll .... IA
Snow Coll .... UT
South Dakota State .... SD
South Georgia .... GA
Southeast Missouri .... MO
Southern Arkansas U .... AR
Southern Idaho, Coll. of .... ID
Southern Illinois U IL
Southwest Missouri State ...... MO
Southwest State U .... MN
St. Mary's of the Plains .... KS
State U. of New York (Cobleskill, Delhi, Farmingdale, Morrisville) .... NY
State U. of New York Coll. of Agri. & Life Sci .... NY
Stephen F. Austin .... TX
Tennessee, U. of .... TN
Tennessee Tech. U .... TN
Texas A&I U .... TX
Truett McConnell .... GA
Tuskegee Inst .... AL
Upper Iowa U .... IA
Virginia State .... VA
West Texas State .... TX
Western Kentucky U .... KY
Western Michigan U .... MI
Wharton Co. Jr .... TX
Wilmington Coll .... OH
Wisconsin, U. of (River Falls) ... WI
Worthington Comm .... MN
Wyoming, U. of .... WY
Yakima Valley Comm .... WA

Agricultural Economics

Alabama A&M .... AL
Arizona, U. of .... AZ
Arkansas, U. of .... AR
Blinn Coll .... TX
Brigham Young .... UT
California, U. of (Davis) .... CA
California State U. (Fresno) ..... CA
Central Missouri .... MO
Clemson U .... SC
Colorado State .... CO
Cowley Co. Comm. Coll .... KS
Delaware, U. of .... DE
Eastern Kentucky U .... KY
Eastern Oklahoma State .... OK
Florida, U. of .... FL
Fort Scott Comm .... KS
Georgia, U. of .... GA
Goddard .... VT
Hawaii, U. of .... HI
Highland Comm .... KS
Idaho, U. of .... ID
Illinois, U. of (Urbana) IL

Kansas State U . . . . . KS
Kentucky, U. of . . . . . KY
Langston U . . . . . OK
Lincoln Coll IL
Macalester Coll . . . . . MN
McPherson Coll . . . . . KS
Maine, U. of (Orono) . . . . . ME
Massachusetts, U. of (Amherst) . . . . . MA
Michigan State U . . . . . MI
Minnesota, U. of . . . . . MN
Missouri, U. of . . . . . MO
Missouri Western State . . . . . MO
Morehead State . . . . . KY
Nebraska, U. of . . . . . NE
Nevada, U. of . . . . . NV
New Mexico State U . . . . . NM
North Carolina A&T State U . . . NC
North Dakota State U. (Fargo) . ND
Northeast Mississippi Jr . . . . . MS
Northeast Missouri State . . . . . MO
Northeastern Jr . . . . . CO
Northwest Missouri State . . . . . MO
Ohio State U . . . . . OH
Oklahoma State U . . . . . OK
Oregon State U . . . . . OR
Pennsylvania State U . . . . . PA
Purdue U . . . . . IN
Puerto Rico, U. of . . . . . PR
Sheridan Coll . . . . . WY
Snow Coll . . . . . UT
South Dakota State U . . . . . SD
South Georgia Coll . . . . . GA
Southeast Missouri State . . . . . MO
Southern Illinois U IL
Southwest Missouri State . . . . . MO
State U. of New York (Coll. of Agri. & Life Sci.) . . . . . NY
Stephen F. Austin . . . . . TX
Tennessee, U. of . . . . . TN
Texas A&M . . . . . TX
Utah State U . . . . . UT
Vermont, U. of . . . . . VT
Virginia Poly. Inst . . . . . VA
Virginia State U . . . . . VA
Washington State U . . . . . WA
West Texas State . . . . . TX
West Virginia U . . . . . WV
Wisconsin, U. of (Madison, River Falls) . . . . . WI
Wyoming, U. of . . . . . WY

Agricultural Education

Institutions awarding undergraduate degrees as major field according to U.S. Office of Education latest statistics

Alcorn State U . . . . . MS
Arizona, U. of . . . . . AZ
Arkansas, U. of . . . . . AR
Arkansas State U . . . . . AR
Auburn U . . . . . AL
Brigham Young U . . . . . UT
Central Missouri State . . . . . MO
Clemson U . . . . . SC
Colorado State U . . . . . CO
Connecticut, U. of . . . . . CT
Cornell U . . . . . NY
Delaware, U. of . . . . . DE
East Texas State U . . . . . TX
Florida, U. of . . . . . FL
Florida A&M U . . . . . FL
Fort Valley State Coll . . . . . GA
Georgia, U. of . . . . . GA
Idaho, U. of . . . . . ID
Illinois, U. of IL
Iowa State U . . . . . IA
Kansas State U . . . . . KS
Kentucky, U. of . . . . . KY
Louisiana State U . . . . . LA
Louisiana Tech . . . . . LA
Michigan State U . . . . . MI
Minnesota, U. of . . . . . MN
Mississippi State U . . . . . MS
Missouri, U. of . . . . . MO
Montana State U . . . . . MT
Murray State U . . . . . KY
Nebraska, U. of . . . . . NE
North Carolina State U. (Raleigh) . . . . . NC
North Dakota State U . . . . . ND
Northeast Missouri State U . . . . MO
Northwest Missouri State . . . . . MO
Oregon State U . . . . . OR
Pennsylvania State U . . . . . PA
Prairie View A&M . . . . . TX
Puerto Rico, U. of . . . . . PR
Purdue U . . . . . IN
South Dakota State U . . . . . SD
Southern Illinois IL
Southern U. and A&M Coll . . . . . LA
Southwest Texas State U . . . . . TX
Southwestern Louisiana, U. of . . LA
Stephen F. Austin State U . . . . . TX
Tabor Coll . . . . . KS
Tarleton State U . . . . . TX
Tennessee, U. of (Knoxville, Martin) . . . . . TN
Texas A&I U . . . . . TX
Texas A&M . . . . . TX
Texas Tech. U . . . . . TX
Tuskegee Inst . . . . . AL
Utah State U . . . . . UT
Washington State U . . . . . WA
West Texas State U . . . . . TX
West Virginia U . . . . . WV
Wisconsin, U. of (Madison, Platteville, River Falls) . . . . . WI

Agricultural Engineering

According to American Society of Agricultural Engineers
•Accredited ASAE program

California State Poly. U. (Pomona) . . . . . CA
California State U. (Chico, •Fresno) . . . . . CA
Connecticut, U. of . . . . . CT
Delaware, U. of . . . . . DE
Hawaii, U. of . . . . . HI
Massachusetts, U. of . . . . . MA
North Carolina, Ag. & Tech. State U . . . . . NC
•Puerto Rico, U. of . . . . . PR
Prairie View Ag. & Mech. Coll . . . TX
Southern Illinois U IL
Southwestern Louisiana, U. of . . LA
State U. of New York, Coll. of Environ. Sci. & Forestry . . . . . NY
Vermont, U. of . . . . . VT
West Virginia U . . . . . WV
Wisconsin, U. of (Platteville, •River Falls) . . . . . WI

Agricultural Engineering,

See also
ENGINEERING, AGRICULTURAL

AGRICULTURAL-Liberal Arts 3-2 Binary Plan

Student is awarded a Bachelor's degree from the Liberal Arts college and the appropriate Agricultural degree both within a five-year period

Cornell U., 3-2 Plan with

State U. of New York (Fredonia) . . . . . NY

Ohio State, Binary Plan with

Heidelberg . . . . . OH
Hiram . . . . . OH

Purdue U., 3-2 Plan with

St. Joseph's . . . . . IN

Agriculture

Institutions awarding 10 or more undergraduate degrees as major field in single year according to latest statistics from U.S. Office of Education

Arkansas, U. of . . . . . AR
Auburn U . . . . . AL
Austin Peay State . . . . . TN
Berea . . . . . KY
Berry Coll . . . . . GA
California, U. of (Riverside) . . . . . CA
California Poly. State U . . . . . CA
California State Poly. U . . . . . CA
California State U. (Chico, Fresno) . . . . . CA
Cameron U . . . . . OK
Delaware, U. of . . . . . DE
Delaware State U . . . . . DE
East Texas State U . . . . . TX
Fort Hays Kansas State Coll . . . . KS
Georgia, U. of . . . . . GA
Hawaii, U. of . . . . . HI
Illinois, U. of (Urbana) IL
Illinois State U IL
Maryland, U. of . . . . . MD
Mississippi State U . . . . . MS
Missouri, U. of . . . . . MO
Montana State U . . . . . MT
Morehead State U . . . . . KY
Murray State . . . . . KY
Nebraska, U. of . . . . . NE
New Hampshire, U. of . . . . . NH
North Carolina A&T State U . . . NC
Northeast Missouri . . . . . MO
Northwestern State U . . . . . LA
Ohio State U . . . . . OH
Oregon State . . . . . OR
Ozarks, School of the . . . . . MO
Pennsylvania State . . . . . PA
Puerto Rico, U. of . . . . . PR
Purdue . . . . . IN
Rutgers U . . . . . NJ
Sam Houston State . . . . . TX
South Dakota State U . . . . . SD
Southern Illinois U. (Carbondale) IL
Southwest Texas State Coll . . . . . TX
Stephen F. Austin State U . . . . . TX
Tarleton State . . . . . TX
Vermont, U. of, State Agric . . . . . VT
Virginia State Coll . . . . . VA
Washington State U . . . . . WA
Western Illinois U IL
Western Kentucky . . . . . KY
Western Michigan U . . . . . MI
Wisconsin, U. of (Madison, River Falls) . . . . . WI

Agri-Equine

Averett Coll . . . . . VA
Eastern Wyoming . . . . . WY
Johnson & Wales . . . . . RI
Louisiana Tech . . . . . LA
Northwestern State U . . . . . LA
State U. of New York (Cobleskill, Morrisville) . . . . . NY
Wisconsin, U. of (River Falls) . . . WI

Agronomy

Institutions awarding 20 or more undergraduate degrees as major field in single year according to latest statistics from U.S. Office of Education

Arizona, U. of . . . . . AZ
Auburn . . . . . AL
Brigham Young U . . . . . UT
California Poly. State . . . . . CA
California State Poly . . . . . CA
California, U. of . . . . . CA
Clemson U . . . . . SC
Colorado State U . . . . . CO
Delaware Valley Coll . . . . . PA
Florida, U. of . . . . . FL
Florida Southern . . . . . FL
Georgia, U. of . . . . . GA
Idaho, U. of . . . . . ID
Illinois, U. of IL
Iowa State . . . . . IA
Kansas State U . . . . . KS
Kentucky, U. of . . . . . KY
Maryland, U. of . . . . . MD
Michigan State . . . . . MI
Minnesota, U. of . . . . . MN
Mississippi State U . . . . . MS
Missouri, U. of . . . . . MO
Nebraska, U. of . . . . . NE
New Mexico State U . . . . . NM
North Carolina State . . . . . NC
North Dakota State U . . . . . ND
Ohio State U . . . . . OH
Oklahoma State U . . . . . OK
Oregon State U . . . . . OR
Pennsylvania State U . . . . . PA
Puerto Rico, U. of . . . . . PR
Purdue U . . . . . IN
Rutgers U . . . . . NJ
Texas A&M . . . . . TX
Texas Tech. U . . . . . TX
Utah State U . . . . . UT
Virginia Poly. Inst . . . . . VA
Washington State U . . . . . WA
Wisconsin, U. of (Madison) . . . . . WI

Air Conditioning, Heating and Refrigeration

Alfred State . . . . . NY
Arizona Western Coll . . . . . AZ
Barton County Comm. Coll . . . . . KS
Central Missouri . . . . . MO
Cincinnati, U. of . . . . . OH
DuPage, Coll. of IL
Eastern Wyoming Coll . . . . . WY
Eastfield Coll . . . . . TX
Ferris State . . . . . MI
Harper Coll IL
Kaskaskia Coll IL
Lake Superior State Coll . . . . . MI
Lamar U . . . . . TX
McNeese . . . . . LA
Miami U . . . . . OH
Mississippi Delta Jr. Coll . . . . . MS
Navarro Coll . . . . . TX
New England Inst. of Tech . . . . . RI
Northeast Mississippi Jr. Coll . . MS
Pearl River Jr . . . . . MS
Pittsburg State . . . . . KS
South Dakota, U. at (Springfield) . . . . . SD
Southern Idaho, Coll. of . . . . . ID
Southwest Mississippi Jr. Coll . MS
St. Catherine Coll . . . . . KY
State U. of New York A&T Coll. (Canton, Delhi, Farmingdale) . NY
Texas State Tech. Inst. (Rio Grande) . . . . . TX
Toledo, U. of . . . . . OH

Air Traffic Control

Alaska, U. of .... AK
Albuquerque, U. of .... NM
Antelope Valley .... CA
Daniel Webster .... NH
Mt. San Antonio .... CA
North Dakota, U. of .... ND
Oscar Rose Jr .... OK
Palomar .... CA
San Diego Mesa .... CA
Troy State U .... AL

Air Transportation

Biscayne Coll .... FL
Central Missouri .... MO
Daniel Webster Coll .... NH
Delta State U .... MS
Florida Inst. of Tech .... FL
New Haven, U. of .... CT
Niagara U .... NY
Purdue U .... IN

Airline Flight Attendant

Bay State Jr. Coll .... MA
Brevard Coll .... NC
Citrus Coll .... CA
Compton .... CA
Cypress .... CA
Daniel Webster Coll .... NH
Dubuque, U. of .... IA
El Camino .... CA
Fisher Jr. Coll .... MA
Foothill .... CA
John Logan IL
Long Beach City .... CA
Los Angeles City .... CA
Mac Cormac Jr. Coll IL
Manatee Jr .... FL
Mt. San Antonio .... CA
National Coll .... SD
Niagara U .... NY
North Dakota, U. of .... ND
Northeast Louisiana U .... LA
Orange Coast Coll .... CA
Rio Hondo Coll .... CA
San Bernardino Valley .... CA
San Diego Mesa .... CA
San Jacinto Coll .... CA
Southern Vermont Coll .... VT
Southwestern Coll .... CA
Suomi Coll .... MI
Webber Coll .... FL

Airline Pilot, *See*

FAA, SECTION ONE

Animal Science

Abilene Christian .... TX
Alabama A&M .... AL
Alcorn State .... MS
Alfred State .... NY
Angelo State .... TX
Arizona, U. of .... AZ
Arizona Western Coll .... AZ
Arkansas State U .... AR
Auburn U .... AL
Bennet Coll .... NC
Blinn Coll .... TX
Bucknell U .... PA
Butte Coll .... CA
California, U. of (Davis) .... CA
California Poly. State .... CA
California State U. (Chico, Fresno) .... CA
Casper Coll .... WY
Central Missouri .... MO
Clemson .... SC
Colorado Mountain .... CO
Colorado State U .... CO
Connecticut, U. of .... CT
Cornell U .... NY
Cowley Co. Comm. Coll .... KS
Dawson Comm. Coll .... MT
Delaware, U. of .... DE
Delaware Valley Coll .... PA
Denver, U. of .... CO
District of Columbia .... DC
Eastern Kentucky .... KY
Eastern Oklahoma State .... OK
Florida, U. of .... FL
Florida A&M U .... FL
Fort Hays State Coll .... KS
Fort Scott Comm. Coll .... KS
Fort Valley State .... GA
Freeman Jr. Coll .... SD
Hampshire College .... MA
Harcum Jr. Coll .... PA
Hawaii, U. of .... HI
Idaho, U. of .... ID
Illinois, U. of (Urbana) IL
Iowa, U. of .... IA
Iowa State Agri. & App. Sci .... IA
Kansas State U .... KS
Kentucky, U. of .... KY
Lincoln Coll IL
Lincoln U .... MO
Louisiana Tech .... LA
Luther Coll .... IA
McNeese State .... LA
McPherson Coll .... KS
Maine, U. of (Orono) .... ME
Marlboro Coll .... VT
Maryland, U. of .... MD
Massachusetts, U. of (Amherst) MA
Mesa Coll .... CO
Michigan State U .... MI
Minnesota, U. of (Crookston, Minneapolis) .... MN
Mississippi Delta Jr. Coll .... MS
Missouri, U. of .... MO
Missouri Western .... MO
Montana State U .... MT
Morehead State .... KY
Nebraska, U. of (Lincoln, Sch. of Tech. Agric.) .... NE
Nevada, U. of .... NV
New Hampshire, U. of .... NH
New Mexico State .... NM
Newbury Jr. Coll .... MA
Nicholls State .... LA
North Carolina A&T State U .... NC
North Carolina State .... NC
North Dakota State .... ND
Northeast Louisiana U .... LA
Northeast Mississippi Jr. Coll .... MS
Northeast Missouri State Coll .... MO
Northeastern Jr. Coll .... CO
Northern Oklahoma Coll .... OK
Northwest Missouri .... MO
Northwestern State U .... LA
Ohio State U .... OH
Oklahoma Panhandle .... OK
Oklahoma State U .... OK
Oregon State U .... OR
Park Coll .... MO
Pennsylvania State U. (Allentown, Behrend, Schuylkill, Shenango, University Park) .... PA
Prairie View .... TX
Pratt Comm. Coll .... KS
Puerto Rico, U. of .... PR
Purdue U. (Lafayette) .... IN
Rhode Island, U. of .... RI
Rutgers U .... NJ
Snow Coll .... UT
South Georgia Coll .... GA
Southeastern .... LA
Southern Idaho, Coll. of .... ID
Southern Illinois U. (Carbondale) IL
Southern Sem .... VA
Southern U. A&M .... LA
Southwest Missouri .... MO
Southwest Texas State .... TX
State U. of New York (Coll. of Environmental Sci. and Forestry, Cobleskill, Farmingdale, Geneseo, Morrisville) .... NY
Stephen F. Austin .... TX
Sul Ross State .... TX
Tennessee, U. of (Martin) .... TN
Tennessee State .... TN
Texas A&I .... TX
Texas A&M .... TX
Texas Tech .... TX
Tuskegee Inst .... AL
Utah State U .... UT
Vermont, U. of .... VT
Virginia Poly. Inst. and State U .... VA
Virginia State U .... VA
Washington State U .... WA
West Texas State U .... TX
West Virginia U .... WV
Western Kentucky U .... KY
Western Texas Coll .... TX
William Woods Coll .... MO
Wisconsin, U. of (Madison, Platteville, River Falls) .... WI
Yakima Valley Comm. Coll .... WA

Animal Technology

Accredited by American Veterinary Medical Assn.
•Indicates probational accreditation
⋆Indicates not accredited

Abraham Baldwin Ag. Coll .... GA
•Becker Jr. Coll .... MA
Bel-Rea Inst. of Animal Tech .... CO
Blue Ridge Comm. Coll .... VA
Camden County Coll .... NJ
•Cedar Valley Coll .... TX
Central Carolina Tech .... NC
Cincinnati, U. of .... OH
Colby Comm. Jr. Coll .... KS
Colorado Mountain Coll .... CO
Columbia State Comm. Coll .... TN
Columbus Tech. Inst .... OH
•Consumnes River Coll .... CA
Eastern Wyoming Coll .... WY
Essex Comm. Coll .... MD
•Fairmont State .... WV
•Foothill de Anza Comm .... CA
Fort Steilacoom Comm. Coll .... WA
•Fort Valley State Coll .... GA
•Garret Community Coll .... MD
•Harcum Jr. Coll .... PA
Hartnell Coll .... CA
⋆Hinds Jr. Coll .... MS
⋆Holyoke Comm. Coll .... MA
Jefferson Coll .... MO
Los Angeles Pierce Coll .... CA
•Macomb County Community Coll .... MI
•Madison Area Tech .... WI
Maine, U. of .... ME
Maple Woods Comm .... MO
•Median School of Allied Health Careers .... PA
Minnesota, U. of .... MN
Morehead State .... KY
•Mount San Antonio Coll .... CA
Murray State Coll .... OK
National Coll. (provisional) .... SD
⋆Navajo Comm. Coll .... AZ
Nebraska, U. of .... NE
•Newbury Jr. Coll .... MA
North Dakota State U .... ND
Northern Virginia Comm .... VA
•Northwestern State U .... LA
•Orange Coast Coll .... CA
Parkland Coll IL
⋆Portland Comm. Coll .... OR
Purdue U .... IN
•Quinnipiac Coll .... CT
St. Petersburg Jr. Coll .... FL
San Diego Mesa .... CA
Snead State Junior Coll .... AL
State U. of New York A&T Coll. (•Delhi, Canton, ⋆Farmingdale) .... NY
•Texas State Tech. (James Connally Campus) .... TX
Tri-County Tech. Coll .... SC
Wayne Co. Comm. Coll .... MI
•Yuba .... CA

Anthropology

Institutions awarding 20 or more undergraduate degrees as major field in single year according to U.S. Office of Education latest statistics

Arizona, U. of .... AZ
Arizona State U .... AZ
Beloit .... WI
California, U. of (Berkeley, Davis, Los Angeles, San Diego, Santa Barbara, Santa Cruz) .... CA
California State U. (Fullerton, Long Beach, Northridge, Sacramento) .... CA
Colorado, U. of .... CO
Columbia .... NY
Duke .... NC
Florida, U. of .... FL
Florida State U .... FL
Harvard U .... MA
Hawaii, U. of .... HI
Hunter Coll .... NY
Illinois, U. of (Chicago Circle, Urbana) IL
Indiana U .... IN
Massachusetts, U. of .... MA
Michigan, U. of .... MI
Michigan State U .... MI
Minnesota, U. of .... MN
New Mexico, U. of .... NM
Northwestern U IL
Ohio State U .... OH
Oregon, U. of .... OR
Pennsylvania, U. of .... PA
Pennsylvania State .... PA
Pittsburgh, U. of .... PA
Queens .... NY
Radcliffe Coll .... MA
Rutgers U .... NJ
San Diego State U .... CA
San Francisco State .... CA
South Florida, U. of .... FL
Southern Methodist .... TX
Southwestern at Memphis .... TN
Stanford U .... CA
State U. of New York (Albany, Buffalo, Oswego, Stony Brook) .... NY
Tennessee, U. of .... TN
Texas, U. of (Austin) .... TX
Utah, U. of .... UT
Vassar Coll .... NY
Virginia, U. of .... VA
Washington, U. of .... WA
William and Mary, Coll. of .... VA
Wisconsin, U. of (Madison) .... WI

Apiculture

Barton County Comm. Coll .... KS
Pratt Comm. Coll .... KS
Sam Houston State .... TX
Southeast Missouri .... MO
SUNY Coll. of Agri. & Life Sci .... NY

Archaeology

Baylor U .... TX
Beloit Coll .... WI
Boston U .... MA
Bowdoin .... ME
Bridgewater State .... MA
Brooklyn Coll .... NY
Brown U .... RI
Bryn Mawr .... PA
Catholic U .... DC
Cleveland State .... OH
Colorado State .... CO
Cornell U .... NY
Dropsie Coll .... PA
Eastern Kentucky U .... KY
Florida State U .... FL
Franklin Pierce .... NH
Gannon U .... PA
George Washington U .... DC
Goddard Coll .... VT
Harvard U .... MA
Haverford Coll .... PA
Holy Cross .... MA
Hunter Coll .... NY
Indiana U. (Bloomington) .... IN
Lycoming Coll .... PA
Missouri, U. of .... MO
Muskingum Coll .... OH
New York U .... NY
Radcliffe Coll .... MA
Sonoma State U .... CA
South Dakota, U. of .... SD
South Georgia Coll .... GA
Tennessee, U. of .... TN
Texas, U. of (Austin) .... TX
Washington U .... MO
Wellesley Coll .... MA
Wesleyan U .... CT
Wheaton Coll IL
West Georgia Coll .... GA
William & Mary, Coll. of .... VA
Yale U .... CT

Architectural Engineering, *See* ENGINEERING, ARCHITECTURAL

Architecture

Institutions accredited by National Architectural Accrediting Board

Arizona, U. of .... AZ
Arizona State U .... AZ
Arkansas, U. of .... AR
Auburn U .... AL
Ball State U .... IN
Boston Architectural Ctr .... MA
California, U. of (Berkeley, Los Angeles) .... CA
California Poly. State U. (San Luis Obispo) .... CA
California State Poly. U. (Pomona) .... CA
Carnegie-Mellon U .... PA
Catholic U .... DC
Cincinnati, U. of .... OH
City Coll .... NY
Clemson .... SC
Colorado, U. of .... CO
Columbia .... NY
Cooper Union .... NY
Cornell .... NY
Detroit, U. of .... MI
Drexel U .... PA
Florida, U. of .... FL
Florida A&M U .... FL
Georgia Inst. of Tech .... GA
Hampton Inst .... VA
Harvard .... MA
Hawaii, U. of .... HI
Houston, U. of .... TX
Idaho, U. of .... ID
Illinois, U. of (Champaign, Chicago Circle) IL
Illinois Inst. of Tech IL
Iowa State U .... IA
Kansas, U. of .... KS
Kansas State U .... KS
Kent State U .... OH
Kentucky, U. of .... KY
Lawrence Inst. of Tech .... MI
Louisiana State U .... LA
Louisiana Tech. U .... LA
Maryland, U. of .... MD
Massachusetts Inst. of Tech .... MA
Miami, U. of .... FL
Miami U .... OH
Michigan, U. of .... MI
Minnesota, U. of .... MN
Mississippi State U .... MS
Montana State U .... MT
Nebraska, U. of .... NE
New Jersey Inst. of Tech .... NJ
New Mexico, U. of .... NM
New York Inst. of Tech .... NY
North Carolina, U. of (Charlotte) .... NC
North Carolina State U .... NC
North Dakota State U .... ND
Notre Dame, U. of .... IN
Ohio State U .... OH
Oklahoma, U. of .... OK
Oklahoma State U .... OK
Oregon, U. of .... OR
Pennsylvania, U. of .... PA
Pennsylvania State U .... PA
Pratt Inst .... NY
Princeton .... NJ
Puerto Rico, U. of .... PR
Rensselaer Poly. Inst .... NY
Rhode Island Sch.of Design .... RI
Rice U .... TX
Southern California, U. of .... CA
Southern California Inst. of Architecture .... CA
Southern U .... LA
Southwestern Louisiana, U. of .... LA
State U. of New York (Buffalo) .... NY
Syracuse .... NY
Temple U .... PA
Tennessee, U. of .... TN
Texas, U. of (Arlington, Austin) .... TX
Texas A&M .... TX
Texas Tech. U .... TX
Tulane .... LA
Tuskegee Inst .... AL
Utah, U. of .... UT
Virginia, U. of .... VA
Virginia Poly. Inst .... VA
Washington, U. of .... WA
Washington State U .... WA
Washington U .... MO
Wisconsin, U. of (Milwaukee) .... WI
Yale .... CT

AREA STUDIES

African

Austin Coll .... TX
Boston U .... MA
Brandeis U .... MA
Chicago, U. of IL
Cincinnati, U. of .... OH
Colorado, U. of .... CO
Dartmouth Coll .... NH
DePauw U .... IN
Duke U .... NC
East Carolina U .... NC
Florida, U. of .... FL
George Washington U .... DC
Governors State U IL
Harvard U .... MA
Hofstra U .... NY
Johns Hopkins U .... MD
Kansas, U. of .... KS
Michigan, U. of (Flint) .... MI
New Coll .... FL
North Carolina, U. of (Chapel Hill) .... NC
Northwestern U IL
Oakland U .... MI
Occidental .... CA
Pennsylvania, U. of .... PA
Pitzer Coll .... CA
Princeton U .... NJ
Radcliffe Coll .... MA
State U. of New York (Albany) .... NY
Temple U .... PA
Tennessee, U. of .... TN
Towson State .... MD
Vassar Coll .... NY
Wellesley Coll .... MA
Wesleyan U .... CT
William Paterson .... NJ
Williams Coll .... MA
Wooster, Coll. of .... OH

Afro-American

Amherst Coll .... MA
Baruch Coll .... NY
Boston U .... MA
Bowdoin .... ME
Bowling Green .... OH
Brandeis U .... MA
Brooklyn Coll .... NY
Brown U .... RI
California, U. of (Berkeley, Davis, Los Angeles, Riverside) .... CA
California State U. (Chico, Dominguez Hills, Hayward, Los Angeles, Northridge, Sacramento) .... CA
Carleton Coll .... MN
Central Washington U .... WA
Cheyney State Coll .... PA
Chicago State U IL
Cincinnati, U. of .... OH
Coe Coll .... IA
Cornell U .... NY
Dartmouth Coll .... NH
Duke U .... NC
Earlham .... IN
Eastern Illinois U IL
Eastern Washington U .... WA
Emory .... GA
Fayetteville State U .... NC
Florida A&M U .... FL
Fordham U .... NY
Goddard Coll .... VT
Grinnell Coll .... IA
Hampton Institute .... VA
Hartford, U. of .... CT
Harvard U .... MA
Indiana State .... IN
Indiana U. (Bloomington) .... IN
Iowa, U. of .... IA
Kansas, U. of .... KS
Kent State .... OH
Lehman Coll .... NY
Louisville, U. of .... KY
Loyola Marymount U .... CA
Luther Coll .... IA
Maryland, U. of (Baltimore) .... MD
Massachusetts, U. of (Amherst, Boston) .... MA
Metropolitan State Coll .... CO
Michigan, U. of (Flint) .... MI
Mills Coll .... CA
Minnesota, U. of (Minneapolis) .... MN
New Coll. of U.S.F .... FL
New York U .... NY
North Carolina, U. of (Chapel Hill, Charlotte) .... NC
North Carolina Cent. U .... NC
Northeastern U .... MA
Northwestern U IL
Notre Dame, U. of .... IN
Occidental .... CA
Pennsylvania, U. of .... PA
Pittsburgh, U. of .... PA
Princeton U .... NJ
Purdue U .... IN
Radcliffe Coll .... MA
Rhode Island Coll .... RI
Rutgers U .... NJ
San Diego State U .... CA
San Francisco State .... CA
San Jose State .... CA
Seattle Pacific U .... WA
Seton Hall .... NJ
Smith .... MA
Sonoma State U .... CA
South Carolina, U. of (Columbia) .... SC
South Florida, U. of .... FL
Southern Illinois U. (Carbondale) IL
Southern Methodist .... TX
State U. of New York (Albany, Binghamton, Brockport, Buffalo, Oneonta, Stony Brook) .... NY
Staten Island, Coll. of .... NY
Syracuse U .... NY
Tennessee, U. of .... TN
Tougaloo Coll .... MS
Texas, U. of (Austin) .... TX
Towson State .... MD
Trenton State .... NJ
Tufts U .... MA
Tuskegee Inst .... AL
Upsala Coll .... NJ
Vanderbilt U .... TN
Virginia, U. of .... VA
Virginia Commonwealth .... VA
Washington, U. of .... WA
Washington U .... MO
Wellesley Coll .... MA
Wesleyan U .... CT
Western Illinois U IL
William Paterson Coll .... NJ
Williams Coll .... MA
Wisconsin, U. of (Madison, Milwaukee) .... WI
Wooster, Coll. of .... OH
Yale U .... CT
York Coll. (CUNY) .... NY
Youngstown State .... OH

American

Adelphi U .... NY
Alabama, U. of .... AL
Albion .... MI
Albright Coll .... PA
Alma Coll .... MI
American International .... MA
American U .... DC
Amherst .... MA
Ashland .... OH
Babson .... MA
Bard .... NY
Barrington .... RI
Baylor U .... TX
Bennington .... VT
Black Hills State .... SD
Boston U .... MA
Bowling Green .... OH
Brandeis .... MA
Bridgeport, U. of .... CT
Bridgewater State .... MA
Brown U .... RI
Butler U .... IN
Cabrini Coll .... PA
California, U. of (Davis, Santa Cruz) .... CA

- California State Coll ... CA
- California Baptist ... CA
- California State Poly ... CA
- California State U. (Chico, Fullerton, Los Angeles, San Bernardino) ... CA
- Calvin ... MI
- Carleton ... MN
- Case Western ... OH
- Chaminade U ... HI
- Cincinnati, U. of ... OH
- Claremont-McKenna ... CA
- Coe Coll ... IA
- Colby ... ME
- Colby-Sawyer ... NH
- Colgate U ... NY
- Colorado, U. of ... CO
- Connecticut Coll ... CT
- Cornell U ... NY
- C.W. Post ... NY
- David Lipscomb ... TN
- Davidson ... NC
- Dayton, U. of ... OH
- Delaware, U. of ... DE
- DePauw U ... IN
- Denver, U. of ... CO
- Dickinson Coll ... PA
- East Tennessee State ... TN
- Eastern New Mexico ... NM
- Eckerd Coll ... FL
- Elms Coll ... MA
- Evergreen State ... WA
- Fairfield U ... CT
- Felician Coll ... IL
- Florida, U. of ... FL
- Florida State U ... FL
- Fordham U ... NY
- Fort Lewis Coll ... CO
- Franklin and Marshall ... PA
- Gallaudet ... DC
- George Washington U ... DC
- Georgetown Coll ... KY
- Georgetown U ... DC
- Goddard Coll ... VT
- Goucher Coll ... MD
- Grinnell ... IA
- Gustavus Adolphus ... MN
- Hamilton ... NY
- Hampshire ... MA
- Harvard U ... MA
- Haverford Coll ... PA
- Hawaii, U. of ... HI
- Hawaii Loa Coll ... HI
- Hillsdale Coll ... MI
- Hobart-William Smith ... NY
- Hofstra ... NY
- Hollins ... VA
- Hunter ... NY
- Illinois, U. of (Urbana) ... IL
- Illinois Wesleyan U ... IL
- Indiana State U ... IN
- Iowa, U. of ... IA
- Kansas,, U. of ... KS
- Kansas Newman ... KS
- Keene State ... NH
- Kendall ... IL
- Kent State ... OH
- Kentucky Wesleyan ... KY
- Knox ... IL
- Lake Erie ... OH
- Lake Forest ... IL
- La Salle ... PA
- Lenoir-Rhyne ... NC
- Lincoln Coll ... IL
- Lowell, U. of ... MA
- Lynchburg ... VA
- Manhattan Coll ... NY
- Manhattanville Coll ... NY
- Mankato State ... MN
- Marist ... NY
- Marlboro Coll ... VT
- Maryland, U. of (Baltimore Co.) ... MD
- Meredith Coll ... NC
- Miami, U. of ... FL
- Miami U ... OH
- Michigan, U. of (Dearborn) ... MI
- Michigan State U ... MI
- Millikin ... IL
- Minnesota, U. of (Minneapolis) . MN
- Moorhead State U ... MN
- Mount St. Mary ... NY
- Mount St. Mary's ... CA
- Mount Holyoke ... MA
- Muhlenberg ... PA
- Muskingum ... OH
- Nazareth ... MI
- Nazareth ... NY
- Nebraska, U. of (Lincoln) ... NE
- New Coll ... FL
- New Rochelle, Coll. of ... NY
- Newcomb Coll ... LA
- North Carolina, U. of (Chapel Hill) ... NC
- North Carolina Central U ... NC
- Northeast Mississippi Jr ... MS
- Northern Iowa, U. of ... IA
- Northwestern ... IL
- Notre Dame ... IN
- Occidental ... CA
- Oglethorpe ... GA
- Pacific, U. of the ... CA
- Pennsylvania, U. of ... PA
- Pennsylvania State U ... PA
- Pepperdine U ... CA
- Pfeiffer Coll ... NC
- Pine Manor ... MA
- Pittsburgh, U. of (Johnstown) ... PA
- Pitzer Coll ... CA
- Pomona Coll ... CA
- Princeton U ... NJ
- Providence Coll ... RI
- Puerto Rico, U. of ... PR
- Purdue U ... IN
- Queens Coll ... NC
- Radcliffe Coll ... MA
- Ramapo ... NJ
- Randolph-Macon ... VA
- Reed Coll ... OR
- Richmond, U. of ... VA
- Rider Coll ... NJ
- Rio Grande Coll ... OH
- Roger Williams Coll ... RI
- Rosary Coll ... IL
- Rosemont Coll ... PA
- Salem Coll ... NC
- San Diego, U. of ... CA
- San Diego State U ... CA
- San Jose State ... CA
- Sarah Lawrence ... NY
- Scripps Coll ... CA
- Seton Hall ... NJ
- Seton Hill ... PA
- Shepherd Coll ... WV
- Siena Coll ... NY
- Simmons Coll ... MA
- Skidmore ... NY
- Smith ... MA
- South, U. of the ... TN
- South Florida, U. of ... FL
- Southeast Missouri State ... MO
- Southern Mississippi ... MS
- Southwestern U ... TX
- St. Cloud State ... MN
- St. Francis ... PA
- St. Joseph ... CT
- St. Mary's Coll ... MN
- St. Michael's ... VT
- St. Olaf ... MN
- St. Rose ... NY
- State U. of New York (Binghamton, Brockport, Buffalo, Geneseo, Oswego) ... NY
- Stetson ... FL
- Stonehill Coll ... MA
- Syracuse U ... NY
- Temple U ... PA
- Tennessee, U. of ... TN
- Texas, U. of (Dallas, San Antonio) ... TX
- Toledo, U. of ... OH
- Towson State U ... MD
- Trinity ... CT
- Trinity Coll ... VT
- Tufts U ... MA
- Tulane ... LA
- U.S. Military Acad ... NY
- Union ... NY
- Upsala Coll ... NJ
- Utah State U ... UT
- Valparaiso U ... IN
- Vassar Coll ... NY
- Virginia, U. of ... VA
- Virginia Wesleyan ... VA
- Washington Coll ... MD
- Wayne State U ... MI
- Wellesley Coll ... MA
- Wells Coll ... NY
- Wesleyan Coll ... GA
- Wesleyan U ... CT
- West Chester State ... PA
- Western Maryland Coll ... MD
- Western Michigan U ... MI
- Western Washington U ... WA
- Wheaton ... MA
- Wichita State ... KS
- Willamette ... OR
- William Smith Coll ... NY
- William Woods Coll ... MO
- Williams Coll ... MA
- Wilson ... PA
- Wisconsin, U. of (River Falls) ... WI
- Wittenberg ... OH
- Yale ... CT
- Youngstown State U ... OH

Asian

- Austin ... TX
- Barnard Coll ... NY
- Bowling Green State U ... OH
- Brigham Young ... UT
- Brown U ... RI
- Bucknell U ... PA
- California, U. of (Berkeley, Davis, Los Angeles, San Diego, Santa Barbara) ... CA
- California State U ... CA
- Carleton Coll ... MN
- Case Western ... OH
- Chaminade U ... HI
- Chicago, U. of ... IL
- Cincinnati, U. of ... OH
- City Coll ... NY
- Claremont-McKenna ... CA
- Cleveland State ... OH
- Colorado, U. of ... CO
- Connecticut Coll ... CT
- Cornell U ... NY
- Dartmouth Coll ... NH
- DePauw U ... IN
- Detroit, U. of ... MI
- Drake U ... IA
- Duke ... NC
- East Carolina ... NC
- Eastern Washington ... WA
- Florida, U. of ... FL
- Florida State U ... FL
- Fort Lewis Coll ... CO
- George Washington U ... DC
- Hamilton Coll ... NY
- Harvard U ... MA
- Hawaii, U. of (Honolulu) ... HI
- Hawaii Loa Coll ... HI
- Hofstra U ... NY
- Illinois, U. of (Urbana) ... IL
- Iowa, U. of ... IA
- Kansas, U. of ... KS
- Knox Coll ... IL
- La Salle ... PA
- Manhattanville Coll ... NY
- Michigan, U. of (Ann Arbor) ... MI
- Mills Coll ... CA
- Mount Holyoke ... MA
- Mundelein Coll ... IL
- New Coll. of U.S.F ... FL
- New York U ... NY
- Northern Iowa, U. of ... IA
- Northern Kentucky U ... KY
- Northwestern U ... IL
- Notre Dame, U. of ... IN
- Oakland U ... MI
- Occidental ... CA
- Oklahoma, U. of ... OK
- Oregon, U. of ... OR
- Pacific, U. of ... CA
- Pitzer Coll ... CA
- Pomona Coll ... CA
- Princeton U ... NJ
- Principia Coll ... IL
- Puget Sound, U. of ... WA
- Queens Coll ... NY
- Radcliffe Coll ... MA
- Randolph-Macon Woman's ... VA
- Rutgers ... NJ
- San Diego, U. of ... CA
- San Diego State ... CA
- Sarah Lawrence ... NY
- Scripps Coll ... CA
- Seton Hall ... NJ
- South, U. of the ... TN
- Southern Illinois U ... IL
- St. John's U ... NY
- St. Olaf Coll ... MN
- St. Thomas Coll ... MN
- State U. of New York (Albany) .. NY
- Stonehill Coll ... MA
- Swarthore Coll ... PA
- Temple U ... PA
- Tennessee, U. of ... TN
- Toledo, U. of ... OH
- Towson State U ... MD
- Trinity U ... TX
- Valparaiso U ... IN
- Virginia, U. of ... VA
- Washington U ... MO
- Wayne State ... MI
- Weber State Coll ... UT
- Wellesley Coll ... MA
- Wesleyan U ... CT
- Western Kentucky ... KY
- Wheaton Coll ... MA
- Williams College ... MA
- Wisconsin, U. of (Madison) ... WI
- Wittenberg U ... OH

Brazilian

- Brown U ... RI
- Kansas, U. of ... KS

British

- Barnard Coll ... NY
- La Salle ... PA
- Marlboro Coll ... VT
- Pfeiffer Coll ... NC
- Rosary Coll ... IL
- Valparaiso U ... IN
- Willamette U ... OR
- Yale U ... CT

Canadian

- Bridgewater State Coll ... MA
- Duke U ... NC
- Maine, U. of ... ME
- Smith Coll ... MA
- St. Lawrence U ... NY
- State U. of New York at Plattsburgh ... NY

Trinity Coll ... VT
Vermont, U. of ... VT

Caribbean

International Coll. of Cayman Islands ... FL
Puerto Rico, U. of ... PR
State U. of New York (Binghamton) ... NY
Temple U ... PA

Central European

Colorado, U. of ... CO
Cornell U ... NY
George Washington U ... DC
Marlboro Coll ... VT
Minnesota, U. of ... MN
New Coll. of U.S.F ... FL
Princeton U ... NJ
Temple U ... PA

Chicano

Arizona, U. of ... AZ
California, U. of (Berkeley, Davis, San Diego) ... CA
California State U. (Los Angeles, Northridge, Sacramento) ... CA
Central Washington U ... WA
Colorado, U. of ... CO
Eastern Washington U ... WA
Goddard Coll ... VT
Loyola Marymount U ... CA
Metropolitan State Coll ... CO
Minnesota, U. of (Minneapolis) .. MN
New Mexico Highlands ... NM
Pitzer Coll ... CA
Pomona Coll ... CA
Randolph-Macon Woman's ... VA
Roosevelt U ... IL
San Francisco State ... CA
Sonoma State U ... CA
Southern Methodist ... TX
Texas, U. of (Austin, El Paso) ... TX
Washington, U. of ... WA

East Asian

Auburn U ... AL
Augsburg Coll ... MN
California, U. of (Davis, Los Angeles, Santa Cruz) ... CA
Chicago, U. of ... IL
Colby ... ME
Colgate U ... NY
Columbia U. (College, Sch. of General Studies) ... NY
Cornell U ... NY
Earlham Coll ... IN
George Washington ... DC
Hamline U ... MN
Harvard U ... MA
Hobart Coll ... NY
Humboldt State ... CA
Indiana U ... IN
Kansas, U. of ... KS
Linfield Coll ... OR
Macalester ... MN
Massachusetts, U. of (Boston) . MA
Minnesota, U. of ... MN
Monmouth Coll ... IL
New York U ... NY
North Carolina, U. of ... NC
Oberlin ... OH
Occidental ... CA
Ohio State U ... OH
Pacific, U. of the ... CA
Pennsylvania, U. of ... PA
Pennsylvania State U. (Allentown, Shenango) ... PA
Princeton ... NJ
Queens ... NY
Radcliffe Coll ... MA
St. Olaf Coll ... MN
Tennessee, U. of ... TN
U.S. Military Acad ... NY
Vanderbilt U ... TN
Vassar Coll ... NY
Vermont, U. of ... VT
Washington & Lee U ... VA
Washington, U. of ... WA
Wayne State U ... MI
Wellesley Coll ... MA
Wesleyan U ... CT
Western Washington U ... WA
Williams Coll ... MA
Wooster, Coll. of ... OH
Yale U ... CT

East European

American U ... DC
Auburn U ... AL
Boston U ... MA
California State Coll ... PA
California State U. (Fullerton) ... CA
Colorado, U. of ... CO
Connecticut, U. of ... CT
Cornell U ... NY
Denison ... OH
Duke U ... NC
Fort Lewis Coll ... CO
George Washington U ... DC
Grinnell Coll ... IA
Harvard U ... MA
Illinois, U of (Urbana) ... IL
Kansas, U. of ... KS
Kent State ... OH
Marlboro Coll ... VT
Massachusetts, U. of (Amherst) .. MA
Minnesota, U. of ... MN
New Coll. of U.S.F ... FL
Notre Dame, U. of ... IN
Oakland U ... MI
Ohio State ... OH
Radcliffe Coll ... MA
San Diego State U ... CA
Tennessee, U. of ... TN
Vermont, U. of ... VT
Williams Coll ... MA
Wittenberg U ... OH
Yale U ... CT

European

Barnard Coll ... NY
Boston U ... MA
Calvin Coll ... MI
Connecticut, U. of ... CT
Connecticut Coll ... CT
David Lipscomb ... TN
Drake U ... IA
Eastern Washington ... WA
Evergreen State ... WA
Franklin Coll ... Switzerland
Franklin and Marshall ... PA
George Mason U ... VA
George Washington U ... DC
Georgetown Coll ... KY
Goucher Coll ... MD
Harvard U ... MA
Hillsdale Coll ... MI
Marlboro Coll ... VT
New Coll of U.S.F ... FL
North Carolina, U. of (Greensboro) ... NC
Northern Kentucky U ... KY
Notre Dame, U. of ... IN
Occidental ... CA
Oklahoma, U. of ... OK
Princeton U ... NJ
Queens Coll ... NC
Radcliffe Coll ... MA
Redlands, U. of the ... CA
Rosary Coll ... IL
San Diego State U ... CA
Sarah Lawrence ... NY
Scripps Coll ... CA
Shepherd Coll ... WV
St. Joseph Coll ... CT
State U. of New York (Albany) .. NY
Susquehanna U ... PA
Tennessee, U. of ... TN
Toledo, U. of ... OH
Vermont, U. of ... VT

Far East

Chicago, U. of ... IL
Cornell U ... NY
Duke U ... NC
Felician Coll ... IL
George Washington U ... DC
Harvard U ... MA
International U ... MO
Minnesota, U. of ... MN
Montana, U. of ... MT
New College of U.S.F ... FL
Princeton U ... NJ
Radcliffe Coll ... MA
Williams Coll ... MA

Finnish

Harvard U ... MA
Minnesota, U. of ... MN
Radcliffe Coll ... MA

French

Alabama A&M ... AL
Alvernia Coll ... PA
American U. (with West European) ... DC
Anna Maria Coll ... MA
Brown U ... RI
Bryn Mawr ... PA
Butler U ... IN
California, U. of (Santa Cruz) ... CA
Carleton Coll ... MN
Chatham Coll ... PA
Cincinnati, U. of ... OH
Clinch Valley ... VA
Colgate ... NY
Cornell U ... NY
Denison ... OH
Dominican Coll ... CA
Drew ... NJ
Eastern Montana ... MT
Eckerd Coll ... FL
Emory ... GA
Franklin and Marshall ... PA
Franklin Pierce ... NH
Hartford, U. of ... CT
Harvard U ... MA
Hood Coll ... MD
Hope Coll ... MI
Idaho, U. of ... ID
Indiana U. (Bloomington) ... IN
Johns Hopkins U ... MD
Kansas, U. of ... KS
Lander Coll ... SC
La Salle ... PA
Lincoln U ... MO
Lincoln U ... PA
Lock Haven State ... PA
Maine, U. of (Fort Kent, Orono) ... ME
Marlboro Coll ... VT
Mars Hill ... NC
Mary Washington ... VA
Minnesota, U. of ... MN
Mount St. Clare ... IA
New Coll. of U.S.F ... FL
New Hampshire, U. of ... NH
North Carolina Cent. U ... NC
Northeast Mississippi Jr. Coll .. MS
Northeast Missouri ... MO
Old Dominion ... VA
Pennsylvania, U. of ... PA
Puerto Rico, U. of ... PR
Radcliffe Coll ... MA
Randolph-Macon Woman's ... VA
St. Bonaventure ... NY
St. Mary's Coll ... IN
Taylor U ... IN
Tennessee, U. of ... TN
Texas Women's ... TX
Toledo, U. of ... OH
Trenton State ... NJ
Upsala Coll ... NJ
Virginia Commonwealth ... VA
Virginia State U ... VA
Wellesley Coll ... MA
Wesleyan U ... CT
Western Carolina ... NC
Western State Coll ... CO
Willamette U ... OR

German

Alabama A&M ... AL
Alvernia Coll ... PA
American U ... DC
Butler U ... IN
Chatham Coll ... PA
Cincinnati, U. of ... OH
Colgate U ... NY
Cornell Coll ... IA
Cornell U ... NY
Drew ... NJ
Eastern Montana ... MT
Eckerd ... FL
Emory ... GA
Hartford, U. of ... CT
Harvard U ... MA
Hood Coll ... MD
Hope Coll ... MI
Idaho, U. of ... ID
Indiana U. (Bloomington) ... IN
Johns Hopkins U ... MD
Kansas, U. of ... KS
La Salle ... PA
Lincoln U ... PA
Lock Haven State ... PA
Maine, U. of (Orono) ... ME
Manhattanville Coll ... NY
Marlboro Coll ... VT
Mars Hill ... NC
Mary Washington ... VA
New Coll. of U.S.F ... FL
New Hampshire, U. of ... NH
North Carolina Cent. U ... NC
Northeast Mississippi Jr. Coll .. MS
Old Dominion ... VA
Pennsylvania, U. of ... PA
Principia Coll ... IL
Radcliffe Coll ... MA
Randolph-Macon Woman's ... VA
St. Bonaventure ... NY
Tennessee, U. of ... TN
Toledo, U. of ... OH
Trenton State ... NJ
Virginia Commonwealth ... VA
Washington U ... MO
Western Carolina U ... NC
Willamette U ... OR

Indian, American

Black Hills State Coll ... SD
California, U. of (Berkeley, Davis) ... CA
Central Washington U ... WA
Dakota Wesleyan ... SD

Darmouth Coll ... NH
Eastern Washington U ... WA
Fort Lewis Coll ... CO
Gettysburg Coll ... PA
Goddard Coll ... VT
Hamline U ... MN
Harvard U ... MA
Minnesota, U. of (Minneapolis) . MN
Morningside Coll ... IA
Northeastern Oklahoma State .. OK
Northland Coll ... WI
Oklahoma, U. of Science & Arts of ... OK
Pembroke State U ... NC
Radcliffe Coll ... MA
South Dakota U ... SD
Southeastern Oklahoma State U ... OK
St. Scholastica ... MN
Union for Experimenting Colls . OH
Washington, U. of ... WA

Indian, Asian

Chicago, U. of ... IL
Duke U ... NC
Kansas, U. of ... KS
Oakland U ... MI
Sonoma State U ... CA
Tennessee, U. of ... TN

Jewish

Brandeis U ... MA
City Coll ... NY
Clark U ... MA
Dickinson ... PA
Dropsie U ... PA
Emory ... GA
George Washington U ... DC
Harvard U ... MA
Illinois, U. of (Chicago) ... IL
Massachusetts, U. of (Amherst) .. MA
Miami, U. of ... FL
Minnesota, U. of (Minneapolis) . MN
Missouri, U. of ... MO
Newcomb ... LA
Ohio State U ... OH
Pennsylvania, U. of ... PA
Radcliffe Coll ... MA
State U. of New York (Binghamton) ... NY
Syracuse U ... NY
Temple U ... PA
Tulane U ... LA
Upsala Coll ... NJ
Washington U ... MO
Wesleyan U ... CT
Wisconsin, U. of (Milwaukee) ... WI
Yale U ... CT
Yeshiva U ... NY

Latin American

Adelphi ... NY
Alabama, U. of ... AL
Arizona, U. of ... AZ
Auburn U ... AL
Austin ... TX
Ball State ... IN
Barnard Coll ... NY
Baylor U ... TX
Boston U ... MA
Bowling Green State U ... OH
Brandeis ... MA
Brooklyn ... NY
Brown U ... RI
California, U. of (Riverside, Santa Cruz) ... CA
California State U. (Chico, Fullerton, Hayward, Los Angeles) ... CA
Carthage Coll ... WI
Chicago, U. of ... IL
City Coll ... NY
Colorado, U. of ... CO
Connecticut, U. of ... CT
C.W. Post ... NY
Denison U ... OH
Denver, U. of ... CO
DePauw U ... IN
Dominican Coll ... CA
Drake U ... IA
Duke U ... NC
Eastern New Mexico ... NM
Eastern Washington ... WA
Eckerd Coll ... FL
Elmhurst Coll ... IL
Emory U ... GA
Flagler Coll ... FL
Florida, U. of ... FL
Florida Int. U ... FL
Fordham U ... NY
George Mason U ... VA
George Washington ... DC
Grinnell Coll ... IA
Gustavus Adolphus ... MN
Harvard U ... MA
Hood ... MD
Illinois, U. of (Chicago Circle, Urbana) ... IL
International U ... MO
Iowa, U. of ... IA
Kansas, U. of ... KS
Kent State U ... OH
Kentucky, U. of ... KY
La Salle ... PA
Lehman ... NY
Lock Haven State ... PA
Loma Linda U ... CA
Luther ... IA
Macalester ... MN
Mars Hill Coll ... NC
Minnesota, U. of (Minneapolis) . MN
Mount Holyoke ... MA
Nebraska, U. of (Lincoln) ... NE
New Coll. of U.S.F ... FL
New Mexico, U. of ... NM
New York U ... NY
Newcomb Coll ... LA
North Carolina, U. of (Chapel Hill, Greensboro) ... NC
Northeast Missouri State ... MO
Northern Iowa, U. of ... IA
Northern Kentucky U ... KY
Notre Dame, U. of ... IN
Oakland U ... MI
Occidental ... CA
Oklahoma, U. of ... OK
Pacific, U. of the ... CA
Pennsylvania State U. (McKeesport, Shenango) ... PA
Pitzer Coll ... CA
Princeton U ... NJ
Providence Coll ... RI
Puerto Rico, U. of ... PR
Queens Coll ... NC
Radcliffe Coll ... MA
Randolph-Macon Woman's ... VA
Rhode Island Coll ... RI
Rosary Coll ... IL
San Diego State U ... CA
South Carolina, U. of ... SC
Southeastern Missouri State ... MO
Southeastern Oklahoma U ... OK
Southern Illinois ... IL
Southwest Missouri State ... MO
St. Cloud State ... MN
St. Mary's ... TX
State U. of New York (Albany, Binghamton, Plattsburgh) ... NY
Syracuse U ... NY
Temple U ... PA
Tennessee, U. of ... TN
Texas, U. of (El Paso, Austin) ... TX
Texas Christian U ... TX
Texas Tech ... TX
Toldeo, U. of ... OH
Towson State ... MD
Tulane ... LA
U.S. Military Acad ... NY
U.S. Naval Academy ... MD
Vanderbilt U ... TN
Vassar ... NY
Vermont, U. of ... VT
Virginia, U. of ... VA
Washington U ... MO
Weber State Coll ... UT
Wesleyan U ... CT
West Chester State ... PA
Western Kentucky ... KY
Wichita State U ... KS
Williams Coll ... MA
Wisconsin, U. of (Madison, Stevens Point) ... WI
Wooster, Coll. of ... OH
Yale ... CT

Mediterranean

Chicago, U. of ... IL
Franklin Coll ... Switzerland
Hollins Coll ... VA
International U ... MO
Tennessee, U. of ... TN

Native American

Black Hills State Coll ... SD
Cornell U ... NY
Dartmouth Coll ... NH
Eastern Montana ... MT
Eastern Washington U ... WA
Fort Lewis Coll ... CO
Goddard Coll ... VT
Great Falls, Coll. of ... MT
Northeastern Oklahoma State .. OK
Pembroke State U ... NC

Near and Middle East

Brandeis U ... MA
Brooklyn Coll ... NY
California, U. of (Berkeley, Santa Barbara) ... CA
Chicago, U. of ... IL
City Coll ... NY
Colorado, U. of ... CO
Cornell U ... NY
Dartmouth Coll ... NH
Dropsie U ... PA
Duke U ... NC
Fort Lewis Coll ... CO
George Washington U ... DC
Harvard U ... MA
Hunter Coll ... NY
Incarnate Word Coll ... TX
Johns Hopkins U ... MD
Kansas, U. of ... KS
Kentucky, U. of ... KY
Kenyon Coll ... OH
La Salle ... PA
La Verne, U. of ... CA
Lycoming Coll. (Near East only) . PA
Michigan, U. of (Ann Arbor) ... MI
Minnesota, U. of (Minneapolis) . MN
New Coll. of U.S.F ... FL
Occidental ... CA
Pennsylvania, U. of ... PA
Princeton U ... NJ
Radcliffe Coll ... MA
Tennessee, U. of ... TN
Upsala Coll ... NJ
Utah, U. of ... UT
Williams Coll ... MA
Wisconsin, U. of (Milwaukee) ... WI
Yale U ... CT

Non-Western

Felician Coll ... IL
Fort Lewis Coll ... CO
Meredith Coll ... NC
Pacific, U. of the ... CA
Tennessee, U. of ... TN

Northern Studies—Arctic

Alaska, U. of ... AK

Oriental

Arizona, U. of ... AZ
Brandeis U ... MA
Harvard U ... MA
Indiana U ... IN
Pennsylvania, U. of ... PA
Princeton U ... NJ
Radcliffe Coll ... MA
Tennessee, U. of ... TN

Portuguese

Brown U ... RI
California, U. of (Santa Barbara) ... CA
Cornell U ... NY
Harvard U ... MA
Kansas, U. of ... KS
La Salle ... PA
Minnesota, U. of ... MN
Pennsylvania, U. of ... PA
Providence ... RI
Radcliffe Coll ... MA
Tennessee, U. of ... TN
Vanderbilt U ... TN

Russian

Alaska, U. of ... AK
American U ... DC
Auburn U ... AL
Augsburg Coll ... MN
Barnard Coll ... NY
Boston Coll ... MA
Boston U ... MA
Bowling Green ... OH
Brandeis U ... MA
Brown U ... RI
Bryn Mawr ... PA
California, U. of (Riverside, Santa Cruz) ... CA
California State U. (Fullerton) ... CA
Chicago, U. of ... IL
Cincinnati, U. of ... OH
City Coll ... NY
Colgate ... NY
Colorado Coll ... CO
Connecticut, U. of ... CT
Connecticut Coll ... CT
Cornell Coll ... IA
Cornell U ... NY
C.W. Post ... NY
Denison U ... OH
Denver, U. of ... CO
DePauw U ... IN
Dickinson ... PA
Duke U ... NC
Eastern Washington ... WA
Fordham ... NY
Fort Lewis Coll ... CO
George Mason U ... VA
George Washington U ... DC
Grand Valley State ... MI
Grinnell Coll ... IA
Gustavus Adolphus ... MN
Harvard U ... MA
Haverford Coll ... PA

Illinois, U. of (Urbana) IL
Illinois State U IL
Indiana U. (Bloomington) .... IN
Johns Hopkins U.............. MD
Kansas, U. of .... KS
Kent State U .... OH
Kentucky, U. of .... KY
Knox Coll IL
Kutztown State................. PA
La Salle .... PA
Macalester Coll .... MN
Manhattan Coll .... NY
Manhattanville .... NY
Marlboro Coll .... VT
Maryland, U. of .... MD
Michigan, U. of (Ann Arbor) .... MI
Minnesota, U. of .... MN
Missouri, U. of .... MO
Montana, U. of .... MT
Muhlenberg .... PA
New Hampshire, U. of .... NH
New Mexico, U. of............. NM
North Carolina, U. of (Greensboro) .... NC
Northern Iowa, U. of .... IA
Northwestern U IL
Oakland U .... MI
Oklahoma, U. of .... OK
Old Dominion .... VA
Pennsylvania, U. of............ PA
Princeton U .... NJ
Principia Coll IL
Radcliffe Coll .... MA
Randolph-Macon Woman's ..... VA
Rutgers .... NJ
San Diego State U .... CA
Seton Hall U .... NJ
South, U. of the .... TN
Southern Methodist U .... TX
St. Catherine, Coll. of .... MN
St. Olaf Coll .... MN
Stanford .... CA
Syracuse .... NY
Tennessee, U. of .... TN
U.S. Military Acad .... NY
U.S. Naval Academy........... MD
Vanderbilt U .... TN
Vermont, U. of .... VT
Virginia, U. of .... VA
Washington, U. of .... WA
Wells Coll..................... NY
Wesleyan U .... CT
West Chester State .... PA
Wheaton Coll .... MA
Willamette U .... OR
Williams Coll.................. MA
Wisconsin, U. of (Stevens Point) .... WI
Wooster, Coll. of .... OH
Yale U .... CT

Scandinavian

Augsburg .... MN
Cornell U .... NY
Eastern Montana .... MT
Goddard Coll .... VT
Gustavus Adolphus Coll .... MN
Harvard U .... MA
Kansas, U. of .... KS
Luther .... IA
Mankato State .... MN
Michigan, U. of................ MI
Minnesota, U. of .... MN
Pennsylvania, U. of............ PA
Radcliffe Coll .... MA
Upsala Coll .... NJ
Washington U.................. MO
Wisconsin, U. of (Madison) ..... WI

Slavic

Boston U .... MA
Brown U....................... RI
California State Coll .... PA
Chicago, U. of IL
Connecticut, U. of............. CT
Connecticut Coll .... CT
Cornell U .... NY
DePauw U .... IN
Goddard .... VT
Harvard U .... MA
Indiana U. (Bloomington) .... IN
Kansas, U. of .... KS
Kent State .... OH
Kutztown .... PA
La Salle .... PA
Macalester .... MN
Maryland, U. of .... MD
Michigan, U. of (Ann Arbor) .... MI
Minnesota, U. of .... MN
Northwestern U IL
Ohio State U .... OH
Pennsylvania, U. of............ PA
Radcliffe Coll .... MA
San Diego State............... CA
Stanford .... CA
Syracuse .... NY
U.S. Naval Academy........... MD
Vanderbilt U .... TN
Vermont, U. of .... VT
Virginia, U. of .... VA
Washington, U. of .... WA
Wisconsin, U. of (Stevens Point) .... WI
Yale U .... CT

Southeast Asia

California, U. of (Santa Cruz) ... CA
Duke U .... NC
Eastern Washington .... WA
Kansas State U................ KS
Missouri, U. of .... MO
Pennsylvania, U. of............ PA
Princeton U .... NJ
Williams Coll.................. MA
Wooster, Coll. of .... OH

Southwest Asia

Pennsylvania, U. of............ PA
Princeton U .... NJ
Tennessee, U. of .... TN

Spanish

Alabama A&M.................. AL
Alvernia Coll .... PA
American U .... DC
Anna Maria Coll............... MA
Azusa Pacific Coll .... CA
Biscayne Coll .... FL
Brown U...................... RI
Butler U .... IN
California State U. (Northridge) . CA
Chatham Coll .... PA
Cincinnati, U. of .... OH
Colgate U..................... NY
Cornell U .... NY
Dominican .... CA
Drew .... NJ
Eastern Montana .... MT
Eckerd Coll .... FL
Franklin Pierce .... NH
Hartford, U. of .... CT
Harvard U .... MA
Hood Coll .... MD
Hope Coll..................... MI
Idaho, U. of .... ID
Indiana U. (Bloomington) .... IN
Johns Hopkins .... MD
Kansas, U. of .... KS
Kansas Newman Coll .... KS
La Salle .... PA
Lincoln U .... PA
Lock Haven State .... PA
Loyola U .... LA
Maine, U. of (Orono) .... ME
Marlboro Coll .... VT
Mars Hill...................... NC
Mary Washington .... VA
Massachusetts, U. of (Boston) . MA
Minnesota, U. of .... MN
Mount St. Clare .... IA
New Coll. of U.S.F .... FL
New Hampshire, U. of .... NH
North Carolina Cent. U .... NC
Northeast Mississippi Jr. Coll .. MS
Northeast Missouri .... MO
Old Dominion .... VA
Pennsylvania, U. of............ PA
Puerto Rico, U. of .... PR
Radcliffe Coll .... MA
Randolph-Macon Woman's ..... VA
St. Bonaventure .... NY
St. Mary's Coll .... IN
Sul Ross State .... TX
Taylor U .... IN
Tennessee, U. of .... TN
Texas Woman's .... TX
Trenton State .... NJ
Vanderbilt U .... TN
Vassar Coll .... NY
Virginia Commonwealth .... VA
Virginia State U .... VA
Wesleyan U .... CT
Western Carolina U .... NC
Western State Coll .... CO
Wharton County Jr. Coll........ TX
Willamette U .... OR

Third World

California, U. of (San Diego).... CA
Fort Lewis Coll............... CO
Hampshire Coll .... MA
Notre Dame, U. of............. IN
World Coll. West .... CA

Western European

Austin Coll .... TX
Boston U .... MA
Barnard Coll .... NY
Cornell U .... NY
Felician Coll IL
Fort Lewis Coll................ CO
George Washington U .... DC
Goddard .... VT
Grinnell Coll .... IA
Harvard U .... MA
Illinois State U IL
Kansas, U. of .... KS
Kentucky Wesleyan .... KY
La Salle .... PA
Marietta Coll .... OH
Marlboro Coll .... VT
New Coll of U.S.F .... FL
Northeast Mississippi Jr. Coll .. MS
Notre Dame, U. of............. IN
Princeton U .... NJ
Rutgers U..................... NJ
St. Olaf .... MN
Tennessee, U. of .... TN
U.S. Naval Academy........... MD
Vermont, U. of .... VT
Washington, U. of .... WA
West Virginia Wesleyan........ WV
William Smith Coll .... NY
Yale .... CT

World

California Baptist .... CA
Calvin Coll.................... MI
Northeast Mississippi Jr. Coll .. MS
Ramapo Coll.................. NJ
Reed Coll..................... OR
World Coll. West .... CA

Art

Members of National Assn. of Schools of Art

Akron, U. of .... OH
Albany, Jr. Coll. of .... NY
Art Center Coll. of Design ...... CA
Art Inst. of Chicago, Sch. of the.. IL
Atlanta Coll. of Art .... GA
Auburn U .... AL
Beaver Coll .... PA
California Coll. of Arts and Crafts .... CA
California Inst. of the Arts ...... CA
California State U. (Chico, Dominguez Hills, Fullerton, Hayward, Long Beach, Los Angeles, Sacramento) .... CA
Carleton Coll .... MN
Carnegie-Mellon U .... PA
Center for Creative Studies— Coll. of Art and Design .... MI
Cincinnati, Art Acad. of........ OH
Cincinnati, U. of .... OH
Cleveland Inst. of Art.......... OH
Columbus Coll. of Art and Design .... OH
Cooper Union Sch .... NY
Corcoran Sch. of Art .... DC
Cranbrook Acad. of Art (Bloomfield) .... MI
Drake U .... IA
East Carolina U .... NC
Eastern Montana Coll .... MT
Georgia, U. of................. GA
Georgia State U............... GA
Grand Valley State Colleges .... MI
Hartford, U. of .... CT
Herron Sch. of Art............. IN
Hope Coll..................... MI
Howard U..................... DC
Humboldt State U .... CA
Illinois, U. of IL
Illinois Inst. Tech............... IL
Illinois State U IL
Inst. of American Indian Arts .. NM
Jackson State U .... MS
Jersey City State .... NJ
Kansas, U. of .... KS
Kansas City Art Inst .... MO
Kendall Sch. of Design .... MI
Kent State U .... OH
Louisiana Tech U .... LA
Louisville Sch. of Art .... KY
Maine, U. of (Orono) .... ME
Mankato State U .... MN
Maryland Coll. of Art and Design .... MD
Maryland Inst .... MD
Massachusetts Coll. of Art ..... MA
Memphis Acad. of Arts .... TN
Michigan, U. of................ MI
Milwaukee Inst. of Art and Design .... WI
Minneapolis Coll. of Art and Design .... MN
Mississippi Valley State U ..... MS
Montana State U .... MT
Moore Coll. of Art .... PA
Moorhead State U .... MN
Morgan State U .... MD
Museum Art School .... OR

Museum of Fine Arts, School of the ... MA
North Dakota, U. of ... ND
N.Y. State Coll. of Ceramics at Alfred ... NY
Northern Illinois U ... IL
Northern Iowa, U. of ... IA
Oberlin Coll ... OH
Otis Art Inst ... CA
Pacific, U. of the ... CA
Parsons School of Design ... NY
Pennsylvania Acad. of Fine Arts ... PA
Philadelphia Coll. of Art ... PA
Portland Sch. of Art ... ME
Pratt Inst ... NY
Rhode Island Coll ... RI
Rochester Inst. of Tech ... NY
San Diego State U ... CA
San Francisco Art Inst ... CA
San Jose State U ... CA
Skidmore Coll ... NY
South Dakota, U. of ... SD
Southeastern Massachusetts ... MA
Southern Illinois U. (Carbondale) ... IL
Southern Maine, U. of ... ME
St. Cloud State U ... MN
St. Louis Comm. Coll. (Florissant Valley) ... MO
St. Mary's Coll ... IN
State U. of New York (Alfred, Buffalo) ... NY
Swain Sch. of Design ... MA
Syracuse U ... NY
Temple U. (Tyler Sch. of Art) ... PA
Texas, U. of ... TX
Texas Tech. U ... TX
Tulane U. (Newcomb Coll.) ... LA
Virginia Commonwealth U ... VA
Washington, U. of ... WA
Washington U ... MO
West Virginia U ... WV
Western Michigan U ... MI
Wooster, Coll. of ... OH
Worcester Art Museum, School of the ... MA

Art Education

Institutions awarding 10 or more undergraduate degrees as major field in single year according to U.S. Office of Education latest statistics

Akron, U. of ... OH
Appalachian State ... NC
Arizona, U. of ... AZ
Auburn U ... AL
Bemidji State ... MN
Bowling Green ... OH
Brigham Young U ... UT
Calvin Coll ... MI
Central Connecticut ... CT
Central Michigan U ... MI
Central State U ... OH
Central State U ... OK
Cincinnati, U. of ... OH
Colorado, U. of ... CO
Daemen Coll ... NY
Delaware, U. of ... DE
Drake ... IA
Eastern Illinois ... IL
Eastern Michigan U ... MI
Edinboro State ... PA
Florida, U. of ... FL
Florida International U ... FL
Florida State U ... FL
Florida Tech ... FL
Georgia, U. of ... GA
Hartford, U. of ... CT
Houston, U. of ... TX
Illinois, U. of ... IL
Indiana State ... IN
Indiana U. of Pennsylvania ... PA
International American ... PR
Iowa State ... IA
Kansas, U. of ... KS
Kansas State U ... KS
Kearney State ... NE
Kent State ... OH
Kentucky, U. of ... KY
Kutztown State ... PA
Long Island U ... NY
Longwood Coll ... VA
Louisiana State U. (Baton Rouge) ... LA
Louisiana Tech U ... LA
Maine, U. of ... ME
Mansfield State ... PA
Maryland, U. of ... MD
Maryland Inst. Coll. of Art ... MD
Massachusetts, U. of ... MA
Massachusetts Coll. of Art ... MA
Miami U ... OH
Middle Tennessee ... TN
Millersville State ... PA
Minnesota, U. of ... MN
Missouri, U. of ... MO
Moore Coll. of Art ... PA
Moorhead ... MN
New Mexico, U of ... NM
New York U ... NY
North Carolina, U. of (Greensboro) ... NC
Northern Arizona U ... AZ
Northern Illinois U ... IL
Ohio State U ... OH
Old Dominion U ... VA
Oregon, U. of ... OR
Oregon Coll. of Educ ... OR
Pennsylvania State U ... PA
Puerto Rico, U. of ... PR
Rhode Island Coll ... RI
Skidmore Coll ... NY
South Carolina, U. of ... SC
South Carolina State ... SC
South Florida, U. of ... FL
Southeast Missouri ... MO
Southeastern Louisiana U ... LA
Southeastern Massachusetts U ... MA
Southern Illinois U. (Edwardsville) ... IL
Southern Methodist U ... TX
Southern Mississippi, U. of ... MS
Southwest Missouri ... MO
Southwest Texas State U ... TX
St. Rose, College of ... NY
State U. of New York (Buffalo, New Paltz) ... NY
Syracuse ... NY
Temple U ... PA
Tennessee, U. of (Knoxville) ... TN
Texas, U. of (Austin) ... TX
Texas Tech ... TX
Towson State ... MD
Trenton State ... NJ
Virginia Commonwealth U ... VA
Washington, U. of ... WA
Wayne State U ... MI
West Florida, U. of ... FL
Western Michigan U ... MI
Western Washington State ... WA
Wichita State U ... KS
William Paterson ... NJ
Winona State ... MN
Wisconsin, U. of (Madison, Milwaukee, Stevens Point, Stout, Whitewater) ... WI
Wright State ... OH

Art Therapy

Albertus Magnus Coll ... CT
Alverno Coll ... WI
Anna Maria Coll ... MA
Avila ... MO
Barat Coll ... IL
Baylor U ... TX
Bennett Coll ... NC
Bowling Green State U ... OH
Brevard Coll ... NC
Bridgewater State ... MA
California State Coll ... PA
California State U. (Sacramento) ... CA
Capital U ... OH
Cheyney State ... PA
C.W. Post ... NY
Drake U ... IA
Eastern Montana ... MT
Elizabeth Seton ... NY
Emmanuel Coll ... MA
Emporia State U ... KS
Eureka Coll ... IL
Evansville, U. of ... IN
Florida Southern ... FL
Fort Hays State U ... KS
Goddard Coll ... VT
Grand Valley ... MI
Hampshire Coll ... MA
Hawaii Loa Coll ... HI
Indiana Central U ... IN
Jersey City State ... NJ
Kansas Newman Coll ... KS
Lake Erie Coll ... OH
Marian Coll ... IN
Maryville ... MO
Marywood ... PA
Mercyhurst Coll ... PA
Milliken U ... IL
Mt. Aloysius Jr ... PA
Mount Mary Coll ... WI
National Coll. of Education ... IL
Nebraska Wesleyan ... NE
New Rochelle, Coll. of ... NY
New York U ... NY
North Carolina Cent ... NC
Northeast Mississippi Jr. Coll ... MS
Norwich U ... VT
Notre Dame, Coll. of ... CA
Ohio U ... OH
Philadelphia Coll. of Art ... PA
Pittsburg State U ... KS
Pratt Inst ... NY
Puerto Rico, U. of ... PR
Regis Coll ... MA
Rivier Coll ... NH
Russell Sage Coll ... NY
Seton Hill ... PA
Shepherd Coll ... WV
St. Teresa, Coll. of ... MN
St. Thomas Aquinas Coll ... NY
Thiel Coll ... PA
Trenton State ... NJ
West Texas State ... TX
Wisconsin, U. of (Superior) ... WI
Wright State U ... OH
Xavier U ... OH

Arts and Crafts

Akron, U. of ... OH
Allen U ... SC
Alma Coll ... MI
Alvernia Coll ... PA
Alverno Coll ... WI
Andrews U ... MI
Artesia Christian Coll ... NM
Austin Peay State U ... TN
Averett Coll ... VA
Bennington Coll ... VT
Bethel Coll ... IN
Blake Coll ... OR
Blue Mountain Coll ... MS
Brenau ... GA
Brevard Coll ... NC
California Coll. of Arts and Crafts ... CA
California State Coll ... PA
Casper Coll ... WY
Center for Creative Studies ... MI
Colorado Mountain Coll ... CO
Columbia Coll ... IL
Columbia Coll ... MO
Cowley County Comm. Coll ... KS
C.W. Post ... NY
Delta State U ... MS
DuPage, Coll. of ... IL
Eastern Kentucky ... KY
Eastern Washington ... WA
Elizabeth Seton Coll ... NY
Felician Coll ... IL
Ferrum Coll ... VA
Fisk U ... TN
Florida Southern Coll ... FL
Fort Hays State ... KS
Franklin Coll ... IN
Glassboro ... NJ
Goddard Coll ... VT
Green Mountain Coll ... VT
Hastings Coll ... NE
Highland Comm. Coll ... KS
Illinois, U. of (Urbana) ... IL
Independence Comm. Coll ... KS
Indiana State U ... IN
Indiana U ... PA
Kansas, U. of ... KS
Kansas City Art Inst ... MO
Kent State ... OH
Kutztown State ... PA
Lasell Jr. Coll ... MA
Lincoln Coll ... IL
McKendree Coll ... IL
Mary Washington ... VA
Marygrove Coll ... MI
Maryland, U. of (Eastern Shore) ... MD
Marylhurst Educ. Ctr ... OR
Maryville Coll ... TN
Midway Coll ... KY
Minnesota, U. of ... MN
Mississippi Delta Jr. Coll ... MS
Montana State U ... MT
Mt. St. Joseph, Coll. of ... OH
Nebraska Western ... NE
Northeast Louisiana U ... LA
Northeast Mississippi Jr. Coll ... MS
Northern Michigan ... MI
Notre Dame, Coll. of ... OH
Old Dominion ... VA
Pembroke State U ... NC
Philadelphia Coll. of Art ... PA
Pittsburg State U ... KS
Pratt Inst ... NY
Puerto Rico, U. of ... PR
Purdue (Lafayette) ... IN
St. Mary Coll ... KS
Schreiner Coll ... TX
Shepherd ... WV
South Dakota, U. of ... SD
South Georgia Coll ... GA
Southeast Missouri State ... MO
Southeastern Oklahoma State U ... OK
Southern Arkansas U ... AR
Southern Idaho, Coll. of ... ID
Tennessee, U. of ... TN
Texas A&I ... TX
Texas Woman's U ... TX
Towson State U ... MD
Trinity Christian ... IL
Truett McConnell ... GA
Union Coll ... NE
Union U ... TN
U.S. International U ... CA
Upper Iowa U ... IA
Virginia Commonwealth ... VA
Waldorf Coll ... IA
Weber State Coll ... UT
Webster Coll ... MO
Western Montana ... MT
Western Texas Coll ... TX

Wharton County Jr. Coll .... TX
Whitworth Coll .... WA
William Woods Coll .... MO
Wittenberg U .... OH
Xavier U .... OH

Arts Management

American U .... DC
Baldwin-Wallace .... OH
Baruch Coll .... NY
Brenau Coll .... GA
Brevard .... NC
Butler U .... IN
Columbia Coll IL
C.W. Post .... NY
Eastern Washington U .... WA
Evansville, U. of .... IN
Goddard Coll .... VT
Hastings .... NE
Indiana U. (Bloomington) .... IN
Iowa, U. of .... IA
Lake Erie Coll .... OH
Mary Baldwin Coll .... VA
Marywood Coll .... PA
Medaille Coll .... NY
Miami U .... OH
Milliken U IL
Mount Vernon .... DC
Nebraska, U. of .... NE
New Mexico State U .... NM
Northern Arizona .... AZ
Ottawa U .... KS
Russell Sage Coll .... NY
Saint Leo Coll .... FL
Saint Teresa, Coll. of .... MN
Salem Coll .... NC
Santa Fe Coll .... NM
Seton Hill .... PA
Shenandoah Coll .... VA
St. Andrew's Presbyterian ..... NC
St. Catherine .... KY
St. Mary .... KS
State U. of New York (Fredonia, Potsdam) .... NY
U.S. International U .... CA
Viterbo .... WI
Webster Coll .... MO
Wesleyan Coll .... GA
Wheeling Coll .... WV
Whitworth Coll .... WA
Yankton Coll .... SD

Astronautical Engineering, *See* ENGINEERING, ASTRONAUTICAL

Astronomy

Arizona, U. of .... AZ
Boston U .... MA
Brigham Young U .... UT
Brown U .... RI
Bryn Mawr .... PA
California, U. of (Berkeley, Los Angeles, Santa Cruz) .... CA
California Inst. of Tech .... CA
Case Western Reserve .... OH
Central Methodist U .... MO
Chicago, U. of IL
Clarion State Coll .... PA
Clark Coll .... GA
Clemson U .... SC
Colgate .... NY
Colorado, U. of .... CO
Colorado Mountain Coll .... CO
Columbia U .... NY
Cornell U .... NY
C.U.N.Y .... NY
Delaware, U. of .... DE
Drury Coll .... MO
Earlham .... IN
Eastern Kentucky .... KY
Florida, U. of .... FL
Goddard Coll .... VT
Hampshire .... MA
Harvard U .... MA
Hawaii, U. of .... HI
Indiana U. (Bloomington) .... IN
Iowa, U. of .... IA
Iowa State U .... IA
Kansas, U. of .... KS
Kentucky, U. of .... KY
Louisiana State U .... LA
Lycoming Coll .... PA
Macalester .... MN
Mankato State U .... MN
Marlboro Coll .... VT
Maryland, U. of .... MD
Michigan State U .... MI
Minnesota, U. of .... MN
Missouri, U. of .... MO
Montana, U. of .... MT
Mount Holyoke .... MA
Nebraska, U. of (Lincoln) .... NE
New Mexico Inst. of Mining & Tech .... NM
New Mexico State U .... NM
North Carolina, U. of .... NC
Northeast Mississippi Jr. Coll .. MS
Northern Arizona U .... AZ
Northwestern U IL
Ohio State U .... OH
Ohio Wesleyan .... OH
Oklahoma, U. of .... OK
Old Dominion .... VA
Pacific Union Coll .... CA
Pennsylvania, U. of .... PA
Pennsylvania State U .... PA
Pittsburgh, U. of .... PA
Pomona Coll .... CA
Princeton U .... NJ
Radcliffe Coll .... MA
Rice U .... TX
Rio Piedras .... PR
Rochester, U. of .... NY
Sam Houston State U .... TX
San Diego State .... CA
San Francisco State U .... CA
Sangamon State IL
Smith Coll .... MA
Sonoma State U .... CA
Southern Mississippi, U. of .... MS
St. John's Coll .... MD
State U. of New York (Maritime Coll., Stony Brook) .... NY
Swarthmore Coll .... PA
Tennessee, U. of (Martin) .... TN
Texas, U. of .... TX
Texas Christian U .... TX
Toledo .... OH
Utah, U. of .... UT
Vanderbilt U .... TN
Vassar Coll .... NY
Villanova U .... PA
Virginia, U. of .... VA
Washington, U. of .... WA
Wellesley Coll .... MA
Wesleyan U .... CT
Western Kentucky .... KY
Western Washington U .... WA
Williams Coll .... MA
Wisconsin, U. of .... WI
Wyoming, U. of .... WY
Yale U .... CT
Youngstown State U .... OH

Astrophysics

Boston U .... MA
California Institute of Tech ..... CA
Chicago, U. of IL
Colgate .... NY
Cornell U .... NY
Dordt .... IA
Harvard U .... MA
Indiana U. (Bloomington) .... IN
Iowa, U. of .... IA
Michigan State U .... MI
New Mexico, U. of .... NM
Oklahoma, U. of .... OK
Pennsylvania, U. of .... PA
Princeton U .... NJ
Radcliffe Coll .... MA
Virginia, U. of .... VA
Wesleyan U .... CT
Williams Coll .... MA
Worcester Poly. Inst .... MA

Athletic or Sports Administration

Alabama A&M .... AL
Averett Coll .... VA
Becker Jr. Coll .... MA
Biscayne Coll .... FL
Blue Mountain Coll .... MS
Brevard Coll .... NC
Briar Cliff Coll .... IA
Bridgewater State .... MA
Central Missouri .... MO
Connecticut, U. of .... CT
Eastern Kentucky U .... KY
Eastern Washington U .... WA
Elon Coll .... NC
Ferrum Coll .... VA
Florida Southern Coll .... FL
Franklin Coll .... IN
George Fox Coll .... OR
George Williams Coll IL
Gonzaga U .... WA
Harcum Jr. Coll .... PA
Huron Coll .... SD
Kansas, U. of .... KS
Lamar U .... TX
Lenoir-Rhyne Coll .... NC
Lincoln Coll IL
Marietta Coll .... OH
Marlboro Coll .... VT
Marywood Coll .... PA
Midway Coll .... KY
Minnesota, U. of .... MN
Mississippi Delta Jr. Coll ...... MS
New Mexico Military Inst ...... NM
New Mexico State U .... NM
North Dakota State U. (Fargo) . ND
Northeast Mississippi Jr. Coll .. MS
Norwich U .... VT
Ohio U. (Graduate) .... OH
Old Dominion U .... VA
Puerto Rico, U. of .... PR
Purdue U .... IN
Robert Morris Coll .... PA
Seattle Pacific .... WA
St. Leo Coll .... FL
South Georgia Coll .... GA
Springfield Coll .... MA
Suomi Coll .... MI
Temple U .... PA
Texas, U. of (Austin) .... TX
Towson State .... MD
Trinity Christian IL
Truett McConnell .... GA
Union U .... TN
Wayne State U .... MI
Weber State .... UT
Wesley Coll .... DE
West Florida, U. of .... FL
Western Carolina U .... NC
William Woods .... MO
Winona State .... MN
Yankton Coll .... SD

Athletic Trainer

Akron, U. of .... OH
Anderson Coll .... IN
Arizona State U. (Tempe) .... AZ
Arkansas, U. of (Fayetteville) ... AR
Baldwin-Wallace Coll .... OH
Ball State U .... IN
California State U. (Sacramento) .... CA
California State Coll .... PA
Central Michigan U .... MI
Central Missouri .... MO
Chapman Coll .... CA
Cincinnati, U. of .... OH
Clarion State .... PA
Colgate U .... NY
Denver, U. of .... CO
Drake U .... IA
Eastern Kentucky U .... KY
Eastern Washington U .... WA
Eureka Coll IL
Evansville, U. of .... IN
Fort Hays State .... KS
George Williams Coll IL
Gustavus Adolphus .... MN
Hutchinson Comm. Coll .... KS
Indiana U. (Bloomington) .... IN
Indiana U .... PA
Iowa, U. of .... IA
John Carroll U .... OH
Kean Coll .... NJ
Kearney State .... NE
Keene State Coll .... NH
Lenoir-Rhyne .... NC
Lock Haven State .... PA
McMurray Coll .... TX
Mankato State .... MN
Mansfield State .... PA
Marietta .... OH
Mars Hill .... NC
Marywood Coll .... PA
Miami, U. of .... FL
Midwestern State .... TX
Mitchell Coll .... CT
Nebraska, U. of (Lincoln) .... NE
Nebraska Wesleyan U .... NE
Nevada, U. of (Las Vegas) ...... NV
North Dakota State U .... ND
Northern Colorado, U. of ..... CO
Northwest Missouri State ...... MO
Northwest Nazarene Coll .... ID
Norwich U .... VT
Old Dominion .... VA
Pacific U .... OR
Pittsburg State .... KS
Plymouth State .... NH
Point Loma Coll .... CA
Purdue .... IN
Slippery Rock State .... PA
South Dakota State U .... SD
Southwest Missouri State ...... MO
Springfield Coll .... MA
Temple U .... PA
Texas A&I .... TX
Texas Christian U .... TX
Toledo, U. of .... OH
Towson State .... MD
Valparaiso U .... IN
Washington State U .... WA
Wayne State U .... MI
West Chester State .... PA
West Virginia Wesleyan .... WV
Western Montana .... MT
Whittier Coll .... CA
Whitworth Coll .... WA
William Paterson Coll .... NJ
Wilmington Coll .... OH
Wisconsin, U. of (LaCrosse, Superior) .... WI

Atmospheric Science

Arizona, U. of .... AZ
California, U. of (Davis) .... CA
Colorado State .... CO
Cornell U .... NY
Drexel U .... PA

Lincoln Coll IL
Missouri, U. of .... MO
Northeast Louisiana U .... LA
Northland Coll .... WI
Ohio State U .... OH
Old Dominion .... VA
Plymouth State Coll .... NH
Purdue U .... IN
Southwest Missouri State ...... MO
SUNY Coll. of Agric. & Life Sci . NY
Washington, U. of .... WA

Audio or Recording Technology

American U .... DC
Artesia Christian Coll .... NM
Belmont Coll .... TN
Berklee Coll. of Music .... MA
California State Coll .... PA
Case Western .... OH
Central Missouri .... MO
Columbia Coll IL
Ferris State .... MI
Florida Southern .... FL
Goddard Coll .... VT
Indiana U. (Bloomington) .... IN
New York U .... NY
Northern Iowa, U. of .... IA
Ohio State U .... OH
South Dakota, U. of .... SD
State U. of New York (Fredonia) .... NY
Washington, U of .... WA
William Woods .... MO

Audiology

Accredited by the American Speech-Language-Hearing Association

Akron, U. of .... OH
Alabama, U. of .... AL
Arizona, U. of .... AZ
Arizona State U .... AZ
Auburn U .... AL
Ball State .... IN
Boston U .... MA
Bowling Green State U .... OH
Brigham Young .... UT
Brooklyn Coll .... NY
California State U. (Sacramento) .... CA
Case Western Reserve U .... OH
Central Michigan U .... MI
Cincinnati, U. of .... OH
Cleveland State U .... OH
Colorado, U. of .... CO
Colorado State U .... CO
Columbia U. (Teachers Coll.) ... NY
Connecticut, U. of .... CT
Denver, U. of .... CO
Emory U .... GA
Florida, U. of .... FL
Florida State U .... FL
Gallaudet Coll .... DC
George Washington U .... DC
Hofstra U .... NY
Hunter Coll .... NY
Idaho State .... ID
Illinois, U. of IL
Illinois State U IL
Indiana U .... IN
Iowa, U. of .... IA
Ithaca U .... NY
James Madison U .... VA
Kansas, U. of .... KS
Kent State U .... OH
Louisiana State .... LA
Maryland, U. of .... MD
Massachusetts, U. of .... MA
Memphis State U .... TN
Michigan, U. of .... MI
Michigan State U .... MI
Mississippi, U. of .... MS
Montana, U. of .... MT
Nebraska, U. of .... NE
New Mexico, U. of .... NM
New York U .... NY
North Texas State .... TX
Northeastern U .... MA
Northern Colorado, U. of .... CO
Northern Illinois IL
Northwestern U IL
Ohio State U .... OH
Ohio U .... OH
Oklahoma, U. of .... OK
Pennsylvania State U .... PA
Pittsburgh, U. of .... PA
Portland State U .... OR
Purdue U .... IN
Queens Coll .... NY
San Diego State U .... CA
San Francisco State U .... CA
South Carolina, U. of .... SC
South Florida, U. of .... FL
Southern Methodist U .... TX
Southern Mississippi, U. of .... MS
State U. of New York (Buffalo) .. NY
Syracuse U .... NY
Temple U .... PA
Tennessee, U. of .... TN
Texas, U. of (Austin) .... TX
Utah, U. of .... UT
Vanderbilt U .... TN
Virginia, U. of .... VA
Washington, U. of .... WA
Washington U .... MO
Wayne State U. Sch. of Medicine .... MI
West Virginia U .... WV
Western Illinois IL
Western Michigan U .... MI
Wichita State .... KS
Wisconsin, U. of (Madison, Stevens Point) .... WI
Wyoming, U. of .... WY

Audiovisual Aids

Bridgewater State .... MA
Central Missouri .... MO
Columbia Coll IL
Cowley County Comm. Coll .... KS
Ferris State .... MI
Goddard Coll .... VT
Kansas, U. of .... KS
Kearney State .... NE
Marywood Coll .... PA
Northeastern Oklahoma State .. OK
South Dakota, U. of .... SD
Texas State Tech .... TX
Utah State U .... UT
William Woods .... MO

Automotive Design

Center for Creative Studies ..... MI
Navajo Comm. Coll .... AZ
Northeast Mississippi Jr. Coll .. MS

Automotive Technology

Andrews U .... MI
Angelina Coll .... TX
Arizona Western Coll .... AZ
Artesia Christian .... NM
Barton Co. Comm. Coll .... KS
Bismarck Jr. Coll .... ND
Butte Coll .... CA
California State (Fresno) ...... CA
Casper Coll .... WY
Central Arizona .... AZ
Central Coll .... KS
Central Missouri .... MO
Coffeyville .... KS
Cooke Co .... TX
Cowley Co .... KS
Dawson Comm. Coll .... MT
DuPage, Coll. of IL
Eastern Arizona Coll .... AZ
Eastern Oklahoma State .... OK
Eastfield Coll .... TX
Evergreen Valley Coll .... CA
Fairmont State Coll .... WV
Hesston Coll .... KS
Highland Comm. Coll IL
Hocking Tech. Coll .... OH
Howard Co. Jr. Coll .... TX
Illinois Central Coll IL
Independence Comm. Coll .... KS
Indiana Voc. Tech. (North Central, Northwest, South Central, Terre Haute) .... IN
Kaskaskia Coll IL
Lamar U .... TX
LeTourneau Coll .... TX
McNeese State U .... LA
Miami U. (Hamilton) .... OH
Mississippi Delta Jr. Coll ..... MS
Missouri Western .... MO
Navajo Comm. Coll .... AZ
Nebraska Western Coll .... NE
North Carolina A&T State U ... NC
Northeast Louisiana U .... LA
Northeast Mississippi Jr. Coll .. MS
Northeastern Jr. Coll .... CO
Northern Iowa, U. of .... IA
Northern Montana Coll .... MT
Northwestern State U .... LA
Northwood Inst .... MI
Ohio State U .... OH
Ohio U .... OH
Pacific Union Coll .... CA
Pearl River Jr. Coll .... MS
Peninsula Coll .... WA
Pittsburg State U .... KS
Pratt Comm. Coll .... KS
Puerto Rico, U. of .... PR
Rio Grande Coll .... OH
Snow Coll .... UT
South Dakota, U. of (Springfield) .... SD
Southeastern Louisiana U .... LA
Southeastern Oklahoma State U .... OK
Southern Idaho, Coll. of .... ID
Southern Illinois U IL
Southwestern Adventist Coll .... TX
State U. of New York (Canton, Farmingdale, Morrisville) ..... NY
Texas State Tech .... TX
Trinidad State Jr. Coll .... CO
Utah State U .... UT
Vernon Regional Jr. Coll .... TX
Walla Walla Coll .... WA
Weber State Coll .... UT
Western Texas Coll .... TX
Wharton Co. Jr. Coll .... TX
Winona State U .... MN
Wright State U .... OH
Yakima Valley Comm. Coll .... WA

Aviation Administration

Aero Space Inst IL
Akron, U. of .... OH
Alameda, Coll. of .... CA
Albuquerque, U. of .... NM
Amarillo Coll .... TX
American Tech. U .... TX
Arizona State U .... AZ
Auburn U .... AL
Augustana Coll .... SD
Averett Coll .... VA
Bay State Jr. Coll .... MA
Biscayne Coll .... FL
Boise State U .... UT
Bridgewater State .... MA
Broward County Comm. Coll ... FL
California, U. of (Berkeley) ..... CA
California State U. (Long Beach, Los Angeles) .... CA
Central Missouri State U .... MO
Central New England Coll. of Tech .... MA
Central Pennsylvania Business School .... PA
Clayton Jr. Coll .... GA
Cochise Coll .... AZ
Cypress .... CA
Daniel Webster .... NH
DeAnza Coll .... CA
Delta State U .... MS
District of Columbia, U. of ..... DC
Dowling Coll .... NY
Dubuque, U. of .... IA
Embry-Riddle Aeronautical U ... FL
Florida Inst. of Tech .... FL
Florida International U .... FL
Fort Lauderdale U .... FL
Gateway Tech. Inst .... WI
Geneva Coll .... PA
Georgia State U .... GA
Glendale Coll .... CA
Grossmont Coll .... CA
Guilford Tech. Inst .... NC
Hiwassee Coll .... TN
Houston, U. of .... TX
Indiana State U .... IN
Kansas Newman .... KS
Kent State U .... OH
Lewis U IL
Long Beach City .... CA
Los Angeles City .... CA
Louisiana Tech. U .... LA
Mankato State U .... MN
Metropolitan State .... CO
Middle Tennessee U .... TN
Mountain View .... TX
Nathaniel Hawthorne .... NH
National Coll .... SD
New Haven, U. of .... CT
New York, State U. of (Farmingdale) .... NY
Newbury Jr .... MA
North Dakota, U. of .... ND
Northeast Louisiana U .... LA
Ohio State U .... OH
Oklahoma City U .... OK
Oklahoma State U .... OK
Orange Coast Coll .... CA
Our Lady of the Lake U .... TX
Palomar Coll .... CA
Parks Coll IL
Purdue U .... IN
Saint Martins Coll .... WA
Salem Coll .... WV
San Diego Mesa Coll .... CA
San Francisco City Coll .... CA
San Jacinto Coll .... TX
San Jose State U .... CA
Santa Ana Coll .... CA
Shepherd Coll .... WV
Southwestern Coll .... CA
Southwestern Coll .... KS
St. Petersburg Jr .... FL
Steed Coll .... TN
Tennessee, U. of, Space Inst ... TN
Texas, U. of, Permian Basin ..... TX
Troy State U .... AL
Western Michigan U .... MI
Western Oklahoma State .... OK
Wichita State U .... KS
Wilmington Coll .... DE
Worcester Jr .... MA

Aviation Maintenance Technician

FAA certificated schools

Aeronautics, Acad. of .... NY
Alameda, Coll. of .... CA
Anchorage Comm. Coll .... AK
Andrews U. Coll. of Tech .... MI
Belleville Area Coll IL
Big Bend Comm. Coll .... WA
Blackhawk Tech. Inst .... WI
Chaffey Coll .... CA
Cochise Coll .... AZ
Columbus Tech. Inst .... OH
Delgado Coll .... LA
District of Columbia, U. of ..... DC
Dixie Coll .... UT
Eastern New Mexico U. (Roswell) .... NM
Embry-Riddle Aeronautical U ... FL
Everett Comm. Coll .... WA
Florence Darlington Tech. Coll .. SC
Gateway Tech. Inst .... WI
Gavilan Coll .... CA
Hawkeye Inst. of Tech .... IA
Hinds Junior Coll .... MS
Honolulu Comm. Coll .... HI
Idaho State U .... ID
Illinois, U. of, Inst. of Aviation IL
Indian Hills Comm. Coll .... IA
Iowa Western Comm. Coll ...... IA
Kansas Tech. Inst .... KS
Kings River Comm. Coll .... CA
Kirtland Comm. Coll .... MI
Lake Area Voc. Tech. Sch ...... SD
Lane Comm. Coll .... OR
Lansing Comm. Coll .... MI
LeTourneau Coll .... TX
Lewis U IL
Linn Tech. Coll .... MO
Long Beach City Coll .... CA
Maple Wood Comm. Coll ...... MO
Memphis Area Voc. Tech. Sch .. TN
Milwaukee Area Tech. Coll ..... WI
Minneapolis Area Voc. Tech. Inst .... MN
Montcalm Comm. Coll .... MI
Mt. San Antonio Coll .... CA
Oklahoma State U. Tech. Inst .. OK
Orange Coast Coll .... CA
Ozarks, School of the .... MO
Parks Coll IL
Pittsburgh Inst. of Aeronautics .. PA
Portland Comm. Coll .... OR
Purdue U. Dept. of Aviation Tech .... IN
Rock Valley Coll IL
Sacramento City Coll .... CA
San Bernardino Valley Coll ..... CA
San Francisco, City Coll. of ..... CA
San Jose State U .... CA
San Mateo, Coll. of .... CA
Shasta Coll .... CA
Solano Comm. Coll .... CA
South Seattle Comm. Coll ..... WA
Southern Arkansas U. Tech. Branch .... AR
Southern Illinois U. Avn. Tech ... IL
Southwestern Michigan Coll .... MI
Sowela Tech. Inst .... LA
Spokane Comm. Coll .... WA
Tarrant County Jr. Coll .... TX
Texas State Tech. Inst .... TX
Trident Tech. Coll .... SC
Utah State U .... UT
Victor Valley Coll .... CA
Vincennes U .... IN
Wayne Comm. Coll .... NC
Wentworth Inst .... MA
Western Michigan U .... MI
Williamsport Area Comm. Coll .. PA

Aviation Systems

Central Missouri .... MO
Kansas, U. of .... KS

Aviation Technology

Alameda, Coll. of .... CA
Alaska, U. of .... AK
Albuquerque, U. of .... NM
American Technological U ...... TX
Andrews U .... MI
Arizona State .... AZ
Blue Mt. Jr. Coll .... OR
Bowling Green State U .... OH
Catholic Coll .... DC
Central Arkansas, U. of .... AR
Central Missouri State Coll .... MO
Central Washington, U. of ..... WA
Chaffey Coll .... CA
Cypress Jr. Coll .... CA
Daniel Webster Coll .... NH
District of Columbia, U. of ..... DC
Dixie Coll .... UT
Dowling Coll .... NY
Embry-Riddle .... FL
Everett Comm. Coll .... WA
Ferris State .... MI
Florence-Darlington Tech. Coll . SC
Florida Inst. of Tech .... FL
Fort Scott Comm. Coll .... KS
Hesston Coll .... KS
Hiwassee Coll .... TN
Houston, U of .... TX
Indiana State U .... IN
Kansas, U. of .... KS
Kent State U .... OH
Lewis U IL
LeTourneau .... TX
Los Angeles Trade Tech. Coll ... CA
Louisiana Tech .... LA
Mitchell Coll .... CT
Mountain View Coll .... TX
Mt. San Antonio .... CA
Navajo Comm. Coll .... AZ
New Haven, U. of .... CT
North Dakota, U. of .... ND
Northeast Louisiana U .... LA
Northeastern U .... MA
Northern Michigan U .... MI
Northrop U .... CA
Northwestern State U .... LA
Oklahoma State U .... OK
Oscar Rose Jr. Coll .... OK
Ozarks, School of the .... MO
Palm Beach Jr. Coll .... FL
Palomar Coll .... CA
Parks Coll IL
Piedmont Aero. Inst .... NC
Purdue U .... IN
Rock Valley Coll IL
San Bernardino .... CA
San Francisco, City Coll. of ..... CA
San Francisco, City Coll. of ..... CA
San Jacinto Jr. Coll .... TX
San Jose State U .... CA
San Mateo Coll .... CA
Skyline Coll .... CA
Southeastern Oklahoma State U .... OK
Southern Arkansas U .... AR
Southern Illinois U. (Carbondale) IL
Southwestern Jr. Coll .... CA
Southwest Texas Jr .... TX
St. Cloud State U .... MN
St. Phillips .... TX
State U. of New York (Farmingdale) .... NY
Tennessee State U .... TN
Troy State .... AL
Utah State U .... UT
Vernon Regional Jr. Coll .... TX
Victor Valley .... CA
Walla Walla Coll .... WA
Webster Coll .... NH
Western Oklahoma State ...... OK
Westminster Coll .... UT

Bacteriology

Institutions awarding undergraduate degrees as major field in single year according to U.S. Office of Education latest statistics

Arkansas, U. of .... AR
California, U. of (Berkeley, Davis, Los Angeles) .... CA
Idaho, U. of .... ID
Iowa State U .... IA
North Dakota State .... ND
Wagner .... NY
Washington State U .... WA
Wisconsin, U. of (Madison) ..... WI

Baking

Indiana State U .... IN
Johnson & Wales Coll .... RI
Mars Hill Coll .... NC
Thomas More Coll .... KY

Beef Cattle Raising

Angelina Coll .... TX
Barton County Comm. Coll ..... KS
California State U. (Fresno) ..... CA
Eastern Kentucky U .... KY
Eastern Oklahoma State .... OK
Eastern Washington U .... WA
Freeman Jr. Coll .... SD
North Dakota State U .... ND
Purdue U .... IN
Southern Arkansas U .... AR
State U. of New York (Cobleskill) .... NY
SUNY Coll. of Agri. & Life Sci .. NY
Texas A&I .... TX
Texas State Tech. Inst .... TX
Utah State U .... UT
Western Texas Coll .... TX

Bible

Institutions accredited by American Association of Bible Colleges

American Baptist Coll .... TN
Appalachian Bible Coll .... WV
Arizona Coll. of the Bible .... AZ
Arlington Baptist Coll .... TX
Atlanta Christian Coll .... GA
Baptist Bible Coll .... MO
Baptist Bible Coll of Pennsylvania .... PA
Berkshire Christian Coll .... MA
Bethany Bible Coll .... CA
Biola Coll .... CA
Calvary Bible Coll .... MO
Central Baptist Coll .... AR
Central Bible Coll .... MO
Cincinnati Bible Coll .... OH
Circleville Bible Coll .... OH
Columbia Bible Coll .... SC
Criswell Bible Coll .... TX
Dallas Bible Coll .... TX
Dallas Christian Coll .... TX
Emmanuel Coll .... GA
Faith Baptist Bible Coll .... IA
Fort Wayne Bible Coll .... IN
Free Will Baptist Bible Coll ..... TN
Friends Bible Coll .... KS
Grace Bible Coll .... MI
Grace Coll. of the Bible .... NE
Great Lakes Bible Coll .... MI
Gulf-Coast Bible Coll .... TX
Johnson Bible Coll .... TN
Kentucky Christian Coll .... KY
L.I.F.E. Bible Coll .... CA
Lancaster Bible Coll .... PA
Lincoln Christian Coll IL
Lutheran Bible Inst .... WA
Manhattan Christian Coll .... KS
Miami Christian Coll .... FL
Mid-South Bible Coll .... TN
Midwest Christian Coll .... OK
Minnesota Bible Coll .... MN
Moody Bible Inst IL
Multnomah Sch. of the Bible ... OR
Nazarene Bible Coll .... CO
North Central Bible Coll .... MN
Northeastern Bible Coll .... NJ
Northwest Bible Coll .... ND
Northwest Coll. of the Assemblies of God .... WA
Open Bible Coll .... IA
Pacific Christian Coll .... CA
Philadelphia Coll. of Bible ...... PA
Piedmont Bible Coll .... NC
Puget Sound Coll. of the Bible . WA
Reformed Bible Coll .... MI
Roanoke Bible Coll .... NC
San Jose Bible Coll .... CA
Simpson Bible Coll .... CA
Southeastern Coll. of the Assemblies of God .... FL
Southeastern Bible Coll .... AL
Southern Bible Coll .... TX
Southwestern Assemblies of God Coll .... TX
Southwestern Cons. Bapt. Coll .. AZ
St. Louis Christian Coll .... MO
St. Paul Bible Coll .... MN
Toccoa Falls Coll .... GA
Trinity Bible Inst .... ND
United Wesleyan Coll .... PA
Valley Forge Christian Coll ..... PA
Vennard Coll .... IA
Washington Bible Coll .... MD
Wesley Coll .... MS
West Coast Bible Coll .... CA
Western Baptist Bible Coll ..... OR
Western Bible Coll .... CO
William Tyndale Coll .... MI

Biochemistry

Institutions awarding undergraduate degrees as a major field according to U.S. Office of Education latest statistics

Albright .... PA
Alvernia Coll .... PA
Andrews U .... MI
Ashland Coll .... OH
Barnard .... NY
Bethel Coll .... MN
Bloomfield Coll .... NJ
Bowdoin .... ME
Brandeis .... MA
Brown U .... RI
California, U. of (Berkeley, Davis, Los Angeles, Riverside) .... CA
California Poly. State Coll. (San Luis Obispo) .... CA
California State U. (Los Angeles) .... CA
Canisius Coll .... NY
Carnegie-Mellon .... PA
Carleton Coll .... MN
Catholic U .... DC
Clemson U .... SC
Columbia .... NY

Columbia Union .... MD
Connecticut Coll .... CT
Cornell U .... NY
CUNY .... NY
Dallas, U. of .... TX
Dartmouth Coll .... NH
David Lipscomb .... TN
East Carolina U .... NC
Eastern Michigan U .... MI
Elmira .... NY
Fairleigh Dickinson .... NJ
Georgia, U. of .... GA
Georgian Court .... NJ
Harvard U .... MA
Holy Family Coll .... PA
Idaho State U .... ID
Illinois, U. of IL
Illinois Benedictine IL
Iowa, U. of .... IA
Iowa State U .... IA
Juniata Coll .... PA
Kansas, U. of .... KS
Kansas State U .... KS
Lehigh U .... PA
Loma Linda .... CA
Louisiana State U .... LA
Maine, U. of .... ME
Manhattan .... NY
Maryland, U. of .... MD
Massachusetts, U. of .... MA
Miami, U. of .... FL
Michigan, U. of .... MI
Michigan State U .... MI
Middlebury Coll .... VT
Minnesota, U. of .... MN
Mississippi State .... MS
Missouri, U. of .... MO
Mt. Holyoke .... MA
Mt. St. Mary's .... CA
Mt. St. Vincent .... NY
New Hampshire, U. of .... NH
New York U .... NY
North Carolina State U .... NC
North Texas State U .... TX
Northeastern U .... MA
Northern Michigan U .... MI
Northwest Missouri State .... MO
Northwestern U IL
Notre Dame, U. of .... IN
Occidental Coll .... CA
Ohio State U .... OH
Oklahoma State U .... OK
Oregon, U. of .... OR
Oregon State U .... OR
Ottawa U .... KS
Pacific Union Coll .... CA
Pennsylvania, U. of .... PA
Pennsylvania State U .... PA
Pittsburgh, U. of .... PA
Point Loma Coll .... CA
Princeton U .... NJ
Purdue U .... IN
Radcliffe Coll .... MA
Rice U .... TX
Ripon Coll .... WI
Rutgers .... NJ
San Francisco State U .... CA
Scranton, U. of .... PA
Skidmore Coll .... NY
Smith Coll .... MA
Southern Connecticut State Coll .... CT
Southwestern at Memphis .... TN
St. Mary's Coll .... CA
Suffolk U .... MA
SUNY (Binghamton, Buffalo, Stony Brook) .... NY
Temple U .... PA
Tennessee State U .... TN
Texas, U. of (Austin, Arlington) . TX
Texas A&M .... TX
Texas Christian U .... TX
Trinity Coll .... CT
Trinity Coll .... DC
Tulane .... LA
Vassar Coll .... NY
Vermont, U. of .... VT
Virginia Poly. Tech. Inst .... VA
Washington State U .... WA
Wellesley Coll .... MA
Wells Coll .... NY
West Chester State .... PA
West Texas State .... TX
Western Connecticut State .... CT
Wheaton Coll .... MA
Whitworth Coll .... WA
Wilson Coll .... PA
Wisconsin, U. of (Madison) .... WI
Wyoming, U. of .... WY

Bioengineering

Arizona State U. (Tempe) .... AZ
Boston U .... MA
Bridgeport, U. of .... CT
Brigham Young U .... UT
Brown U .... RI
Bucknell U .... PA
California, U. of (Berkeley, Davis, San Diego) .... CA
Carnegie-Mellon U .... PA
Case Western .... OH
Catholic U .... DC
Cincinnati, U. of .... OH
Cleveland State U .... OH
Columbia U .... NY
Cornell U .... NY
Duke .... NC
Harvard U .... MA
Illinois, U. of (Chicago Circle, Urbana) IL
Illinois Inst. of Tech IL
International U .... MO
Johns Hopkins .... MD
Louisiana Tech .... LA
Marquette U .... WI
Michigan Tech. U .... MI
Minnesota, U. of .... MN
Mississippi State U .... MS
Missouri, U. of .... MO
North Dakota State U .... ND
Northwestern U IL
Ohio State U .... OH
Oral Roberts .... OK
Pennsylvania, U. of .... PA
Pennsylvania State U. (Behrend, University Park, Wilkes-Barre) PA
Purdue .... IN
Radcliffe Coll .... MA
Rhode Island, U. of .... RI
Southern Methodist .... TX
Syracuse U .... NY
Temple .... PA
Texas A&M .... TX
Utah, U. of .... UT
Vanderbilt U .... TN
Vermont, U. of .... VT
Washington U .... MO
Western New England Coll .... MA
Worcester Poly Inst .... MA
Wright State U .... OH
Wyoming, U. of .... WY

Biological Illustration

Beaver Coll .... PA
Felician Coll IL
Minnesota, U. of .... MN
New Haven, U. of .... CT
Newcomb Coll .... LA
Purdue U .... IN
Salem Coll .... WV
St. Mary Coll .... KS

Biology

Institutions awarding 20 or more undergraduate degrees as major field in single year according to U.S. Office of Education latest statistics

Abilene Christian .... TX
Adelphi U .... NY
Akron, U. of .... OH
Alabama, U. of .... AL
Alaska, U. of .... AK
Albion .... MI
Albright .... PA
Alcorn State .... MS
Allegheny .... PA
Alma .... MI
Amherst Coll .... MA
Andrews U .... MI
Angelo State .... TX
Appalachian State U .... NC
Aquinas Coll .... MI
Arizona, U. of .... AZ
Arizona State .... AZ
Arkansas, U. of (Little Rock) .... AR
Assumption Coll .... MA
Auburn U .... AL
Augusta Coll .... GA
Augustana IL
Augustana .... SD
Austin Coll .... TX
Austin Peay State U .... TN
Baker U .... KS
Baldwin-Wallace .... OH
Ball State U .... IN
Barnard .... NY
Bates Coll .... ME
Baylor U .... TX
Bemidji State .... MN
Benedict Coll .... SC
Berry Coll .... GA
Bloomsburg State .... PA
Boise State .... ID
Boston Coll .... MA
Boston U .... MA
Bowdoin Coll .... ME
Bowling Green State U .... OH
Bradley U IL
Brandeis U .... MA
Bridgewater Coll .... VA
Bridgewater State .... MA
Brooklyn .... NY
Brown U .... RI
Bryn Mawr .... PA
Bucknell U .... PA
California, U. of (Berkeley, Davis, Irvine, Los Angeles, Riverside, San Diego, Santa Barbara, Santa Cruz) .... CA
California Poly. State .... CA
California State Coll. (Dominguez Hills, San Bernardino, Stanislaus) CA
California State Poly. (Pomona) . CA
California State U. (Chico, Fresno, Fullerton, Hayward, Long Beach, Los Angeles, Northridge, Sacramento) CA
Calvin .... MI
Cameron U .... OK
Canisius .... NY
Carleton .... MN
Carroll .... WI
Carroll Coll .... MT
Carson-Newman .... TN
Case Western Reserve U .... OH
Catholic U .... PR
Central Arkansas, U. of .... AR
Central Connecticut .... CT
Central Michigan U .... MI
Central Missouri State .... MO
Central State .... OK
Central Washington State .... WA
Centre Coll .... KY
Charleston, Coll. of .... SC
Chicago, U. of IL
Chicago State IL
Cincinnati, U. of .... OH
Citadel Military .... SC
City Coll .... NY
Clarion State .... PA
Clark U .... MA
Clemson U .... SC
Cleveland State U .... OH
Colby .... ME
Colgate U .... NY
Colorado, U. of .... CO
Colorado Coll .... CO
Colorado State U .... CO
Columbia U .... NY
Columbus Coll .... GA
Concordia (Moorhead) .... MN
Connecticut, U. of .... CT
Cornell U .... NY
Creighton U .... NE
Cumberland Coll .... KY
Dartmouth .... NH
David Lipscomb Coll .... TN
Davidson Coll .... NC
Dayton, U. of .... OH
Delaware, U. of .... DE
Delaware Valley .... PA
Delta State .... MS
Denison U .... OH
DePaul IL
Detroit, U. of .... MI
Dickinson .... PA
Dillard U .... LA
District of Columbia, U. of .... DC
Drake U .... IA
Drexel .... PA
Drury Coll .... MO
Earlham .... IN
East Carolina U .... NC
East Stroudsburg Coll .... PA
East Tennessee State U .... TN
East Texas State U .... TX
Eastern Connecticut State .... CT
Eastern Illinois U IL
Eastern Kentucky U .... KY
Eastern Mennonite .... VA
Eastern Michigan U .... MI
Eastern Washington State .... WA
Edinboro State .... PA
Elmhurst Coll IL
Elon Coll .... NC
Emory .... GA
Emporia State U .... KS
Fairfield U .... CT
Fairleigh Dickinson U. (Madison, Rutherford, Teaneck) .... NJ
Ferris State .... MI
Fisk U .... TN
Fitchburg State .... MA
Florida Atlantic .... FL
Florida International U .... FL
Florida Southern .... FL
Florida State .... FL
Florida Tech .... FL
Fordham U .... NY
Fort Lewis Coll .... CO
Franklin and Marshall .... PA
Frostburg State Coll .... MD
Furman U .... SC
Gannon .... PA
Geneva .... PA
George Mason U .... VA
George Washington U .... DC
Georgetown U .... DC
Georgia, U. of .... GA
Georgia Coll .... GA
Georgia Southern .... GA
Georgia State U .... GA
Gettysburg .... PA
Glassboro State .... NJ
Goucher Coll .... MD
Grand Valley State .... MI
Grinnell .... IA
Grove City .... PA

Guilford Coll ... NC
Gustavus Adolphus ... MN
Hamilton Coll ... NY
Hamline U ... MN
Hampden-Sydney Coll ... VA
Hampton Inst ... VA
Harding Coll ... AR
Hartford, U. of ... CT
Hartwick ... NY
Harvard U ... MA
Haverford ... PA
Hawaii, U. of ... HI
Heidelberg Coll ... OH
Hendrix ... AR
Hiram Coll ... OH
Hofstra U ... NY
Holy Cross, Coll. of the ... MA
Hood ... MD
Hope ... MI
Houston, U. of ... TX
Houston Baptist U ... TX
Humboldt State U ... CA
Hunter ... NY
Illinois, U. of (Chicago Circle, Urbana) ... IL
Illinois Benedictine Coll ... IL
Illinois Coll. of Podiatric Med ... IL
Illinois State ... IL
Illinois Wesleyan U ... IL
Indiana State U ... IN
Indiana U ... IN
Indiana U. of Pennsylvania ... PA
Inter-American U ... PR
Iona Coll ... NY
Iowa State ... IA
Jackson State U ... MS
Jacksonville State ... AL
Jacksonville U ... FL
James Madison U ... VA
Jersey City State ... NJ
John Carroll U ... OH
Johns Hopkins ... MD
Juniata Coll ... PA
Kalamazoo ... MI
Kansas, U. of ... KS
Kansas Newman Coll ... KS
Kansas State U. (Agri. & Applied Sci.) ... KS
Kean Coll ... NJ
Kearney State ... NE
Kent State U ... OH
Kentucky, U. of ... KY
Kenyon Coll ... OH
King's Coll ... PA
Knox Coll ... IL
Kutztown State ... PA
La Salle ... PA
Lafayette ... PA
Lake Forest ... IL
Lake Superior ... MI
Lamar U ... TX
Le Moyne ... NY
Lehigh U ... PA
Lehman ... NY
Lewis and Clark ... OR
Lincoln U ... PA
Loma Linda ... CA
Long Island U ... NY
Loras Coll ... IA
Los Angeles Coll. of Chiropractic ... CA
Louisville, U. of ... KY
Lowell, U. of ... MA
Loyola ... MD
Loyola Marymount U ... CA
Loyola U ... IL
Luther ... IA
Lycoming Coll ... PA
Macalester ... MN
Maine, U. of (Orono) ... ME
Manchester ... IN
Manhattan ... NY
Mankato State ... MN
Marietta Coll ... OH

Marquette ... WI
Mary Washington Coll ... VA
Maryland, U. of ... MD
Massachusetts, U. of (Boston) . MA
Massachusetts Inst. of Tech ... MA
Memphis State U ... TN
Mercer U ... GA
Mercy Coll ... NY
Merrimack ... MA
Metropolitan State ... CO
Miami, U. of ... FL
Michigan, U. of ... MI
Michigan State U ... MI
Michigan Tech ... MI
Middle Tennessee State U ... TN
Middlebury ... VT
Millersville State ... PA
Millikin ... IL
Millsaps ... MS
Minnesota, U. of (Duluth, Morris, St. Paul) ... MN
Mississippi, U. of ... MS
Missouri, U. of (Columbia, Kansas City, St. Louis) ... MO
Missouri Southern ... MO
Monmouth Coll ... NJ
Montclair State ... NJ
Moorhead State ... MN
Moravian Coll ... PA
Morehouse Coll ... GA
Morgan State U ... MD
Mount Holyoke ... MA
Mount St. Mary's ... MD
Muhlenberg ... PA
Murray State U ... KY
National Coll. of Chiropractic ... IL
Nebraska, U. of ... NE
Nebraska Wesleyan ... NE
Nevada, U. of (Reno) ... NV
New Mexico, U. of ... NM
New Mexico State U ... NM
New Orleans, U. of ... LA
New York Inst. Tech ... NY
New York U ... NY
Niagara ... NY
North Alabama, U. of ... AL
North Adams State ... MA
North Carolina, U. of (all campuses) ... NC
North Carolina Central U ... NC
North Carolina State ... NC
North Dakota, U. of ... ND
North Texas State U ... TX
Northeast Missouri State ... MO
Northeastern Illinois ... IL
Northeastern U ... MA
Northern Arizona U ... AZ
Northern Illinois U ... IL
Northern Iowa, U. of ... IA
Northern Kentucky U ... KY
Northern Michigan U ... MI
Northland Coll ... WI
Northwest Missouri ... MO
Northwestern U ... IL
Notre Dame ... IN
Oakland U ... MI
Oberlin ... OH
Occidental ... CA
Oklahoma Christian ... OK
Oklahoma State U ... OK
Old Dominion U ... VA
Oral Roberts U ... OK
Oregon, U. of ... OR
Pace U ... NY
Pacific, U. of the ... CA
Pacific Lutheran U ... WA
Pacific Union Coll ... CA
Pan American U ... TX
Pembroke State ... NC
Pennsylvania, U. of ... PA
Pennsylvania State U ... PA
Pittsburg State U ... KS
Pittsburgh, U. of ... PA
Plymouth State ... NH

Pomona Coll ... CA
Portland State ... OR
Prairie View A&M ... TX
Presbyterian Coll ... SC
Princeton U ... NJ
Providence ... RI
Puerto Rico, U. of ... PR
Puget Sound, U. of ... WA
Purdue U ... IN
Queens ... NY
Radcliffe Coll ... MA
Radford ... VA
Randolph-Macon ... VA
Reed Coll ... OR
Rensselaer Poly. Inst ... NY
Rice U ... TX
Richmond, U. of ... VA
Roanoke Coll ... VA
Rochester, U. of ... NY
Rockhurst Coll ... MO
Roosevelt U ... IL
Rutgers U ... NJ
Sacred Heart U ... PR
Salisbury State ... MD
Sam Houston State U ... TX
San Diego, U. of ... CA
San Diego State ... CA
San Francisco, U. of ... CA
San Francisco State ... CA
San Jose State ... CA
Santa Clara, U. of ... CA
Scranton, U. of ... PA
Seton Hall U ... NJ
Shippensburg State ... PA
Siena Coll ... NY
Slippery Rock State ... PA
Smith ... MA
Sonoma State U ... CA
South Alabama, U. of ... AL
South Carolina, U. of ... SC
South Dakota State ... SD
South Florida, U. of ... FL
Southeast Missouri State ... MO
Southeastern Massachusetts U .. MA
Southern California, U. of ... CA
Southern Coll. of Optometry ... TN
Southern Colorado, U. of ... CO
Southern Connecticut ... CT
Southern Illinois U ... IL
Southern Methodist U ... TX
Southern Missionary ... TN
Southern Mississippi, U. of ... MS
Southwest Missouri State ... MO
Southwest Texas State ... TX
Southwestern Oklahoma ... OK
Southwestern at Memphis ... TN
Spelman Coll ... GA
Springfield Coll ... MA
St. Anselm ... NH
St. Bonaventure ... NY
St. Catherine ... MN
St. Cloud State ... MN
St. Francis Coll ... PA
St. John Fisher Coll ... NY
St. John's ... NY
St. John's U ... MN
St. Joseph's ... PA
St. Lawrence ... NY
St. Louis U ... MO
St. Mary's Coll ... IN
St. Mary's Coll ... MD
St. Mary's U ... TX
St. Michael's Coll ... VT
St. Olaf ... MN
St. Peter's ... NJ
St. Thomas, Coll. of ... MN
Stanford ... CA
State U. of New York (Albany, Binghamton, Brockport, Buffalo, Cortland, Fredonia, Geneseo, New Paltz, Old Westbury, Oneonta, Oswego, Plattsburgh, Potsdam, Stony Brook) ... NY
Stephen F. Austin State U ... TX

Stetson U ... FL
Stockton State ... NJ
Stonehill ... MA
Suffolk U ... MA
Swarthmore ... PA
Syracuse ... NY
Tampa, U. of ... FL
Tarleton State ... TX
Temple U ... PA
Tennessee, U. of (Chattanooga, Knoxville, Martin) ... TN
Tennessee State ... TN
Tennessee Tech U ... TN
Texas, U. of (Arlington, Austin, El Paso, Plano, San Antonio) . TX
Texas A&I U ... TX
Texas A&M U ... TX
Texas Christian U ... TX
Texas Lutheran ... TX
Texas Southern U ... TX
Texas Woman's U ... TX
Toledo, U. of ... OH
Tougaloo Coll ... MS
Towson State U ... MD
Trenton State Coll ... NJ
Trinity ... CT
Trinity U ... TX
Troy State U ... AL
Tufts ... MA
Tulane U ... LA
Tulsa, U. of ... OK
Tuskegee Inst ... AL
Union ... NY
Upsala Coll ... NJ
Ursinus ... PA
U.S. Air Force Acad ... CO
Utah, U. of ... UT
Utah State U ... UT
Valdosta State ... GA
Valparaiso U ... IN
Vanderbilt U ... TN
Vassar Coll ... NY
Vermont, U. of ... VT
Villanova ... PA
Virginia, U. of ... VA
Virginia Commonwealth ... VA
Virginia Poly. Inst ... VA
Virginia Union ... VA
Wabash ... IN
Wagner ... NY
Wake Forest U ... NC
Walla Walla ... WA
Wartburg Coll ... IA
Washington, U. of ... WA
Washington and Jefferson ... PA
Washington and Lee ... VA
Washington State U ... WA
Washington U ... MO
Wayne State U ... MI
Wellesley ... MA
Wesleyan U ... CT
West Florida, U. of ... FL
West Texas State U ... TX
West Virginia U ... WV
West Virginia Wesleyan ... WV
Western Connecticut State ... CT
Western Illinois U ... IL
Western Kentucky U ... KY
Western Maryland Coll ... MD
Western Michigan U ... MI
Western State Coll ... CO
Western Washington State ... WA
Westfield State ... MA
Westminster ... PA
Wheaton ... IL
Wheaton Coll ... MA
Whitman ... WA
Whittier ... CA
Wichita State U ... KS
Wilkes Coll ... PA
William and Mary ... VA
William Paterson Coll ... NJ
Williams ... MA
Winston-Salem ... NC

Winthrop Coll .... SC
Wisconsin, U. of (Eau Claire, La Crosse, Oshkosh, River Falls, Stevens Point, Superior, Whitewater) .... WI
Wittenberg U .... OH
Wofford .... SC
Wooster, Coll. of .... OH
Wright State .... OH
Yale .... CT
Yeshiva U .... NY
York Coll. (CUNY) .... NY
Youngstown State U .... OH

Biomedical Engineering, *See* ENGINEERING, BIOMEDICAL

Biomedical Science

Alvernia Coll .... PA
Bennett Coll .... NC
Bennington Coll .... VT
Blake Coll .... OR
Brown U .... RI
California, U. of (Davis, Riverside) .... CA
Carnegie-Mellon U .... PA
Carthage Coll .... WI
Catholic U .... DC
Cincinnati, U. of .... OH
Clinch Valley .... VA
Dartmouth Coll .... NH
Drew U .... NJ
Florida Southern .... FL
Franklin Coll .... IN
Grand Valley State .... MI
Hampshire Coll .... MA
Harvard U .... MA
Hawaii, U. of (Honolulu) .... HI
Hofstra U .... NY
Illinois Inst. of Tech IL
Immaculata Coll .... PA
Iowa, U. of .... IA
John Carroll U .... OH
Kansas, U. of .... KS
La Salle .... PA
LeTourneau .... TX
Lincoln Coll IL
Louisiana Tech .... LA
Maine, U. of (Fort Kent) .... ME
Marian Coll .... IN
Maryland, U. of (Eastern Shore) .... MD
Mary Washington Coll .... VA
Michigan State .... MI
Montana State U .... MT
Nebraska, U. of .... NE
New Coll. of U.S.F .... FL
New England, U. of .... ME
New Mexico Military Inst .... NM
New York Inst. of Tech .... NY
Oral Roberts .... OK
Puerto Rico, U. of .... PR
Purdue .... IN
Radcliffe Coll .... MA
Saint Theresa, Coll. of .... MN
Schreiner Coll .... TX
South Carolina, U. of .... SC
South Dakota, U. of (Springfield) .... SD
St. Andrew's Presbyterian .... NC
Stevens Inst. of Tech .... NJ
Stockton State .... NJ
Tennessee, U. of .... TN
Texas A&M .... TX
Texas State Tech .... TX
Trinity Christian IL
Walsh Coll .... OH
Washington U .... MO
Wright State U .... OH

Biophysics

Andrews .... MI
Augustana Coll .... SD
Bennett Coll .... NC
Brown U .... RI
California, U. of (Berkeley, Davis, San Diego) .... CA
California State U (Los Angeles) .... CA
Columbia U .... NY
Connecticut, U. of .... CT
Eastern New Mexico .... NM
Franklin Coll .... IN
Hampden-Sydney Coll .... VA
Hampshire Coll .... MA
Harvard U .... MA
Hawaii, U. of .... HI
Houston, U. of .... TX
Illinois, U. of IL
Indiana State .... IN
Iowa, U. of .... IA
Iowa State U .... IA
Johns Hopkins .... MD
Kansas, U. of .... KS
Keene State Coll .... NH
Loma Linda U .... CA
Marlboro Coll .... VT
Michigan, U. of .... MI
Michigan State .... MI
Midwestern State .... TX
Nebraska Wesleyan U .... NE
New Coll. of U.S.F .... FL
Northwestern U IL
Ohio State U .... OH
Oregon State U .... OR
Pacific Union Coll .... CA
Pennsylvania, U. of .... PA
Pennsylvania State U. (Allentown, McKeesport, Schuykill, Shenango, University Park) .... PA
Pittsburgh, U. of .... PA
Puerto Rico, U. of .... PR
Purdue U .... IN
Radcliffe Coll .... MA
Reed Coll .... OR
St. Lawrence U .... NY
Scranton, U. of .... PA
Southwestern Oklahoma State U .... OK
State U. of New York (New Paltz, Plattsburgh) .... NY
Texas, U. of (Austin) .... TX
Texas A&M U .... TX
Trinity U .... TX
Walla Walla Coll .... WA
Washington State U .... WA
Wayne State .... MI
Yale U .... CT

Biostatistics

Hawaii, U. of (Honolulu) .... HI
Kansas, U. of .... KS
Ohio State U .... OH
Purdue U .... IN
Southwestern Adventist Coll .... TX

Blacksmithing

Bernadean U .... CA

Blind, Preparation for Teaching the

D'Youville Coll .... NY
Kansas, U. of .... KS
Northern Illinois U IL
Mt. St. Joseph, Coll. of .... OH
Puerto Rico U .... PR
Shepherd .... WV

South Dakota, U. of .... SD
State U. of New York (Geneseo) .... NY
Stephen F. Austin .... TX
Toledo, U. of .... OH
Wayne State .... MI

Botany

Institutions awarding 5 or more undergraduate degrees as major field in single year according to U.S. Office of Education latest statistics

Arizona State U .... AZ
Auburn U .... AL
Brigham Young U .... UT
Butler U .... IN
California, U. of (Berkeley, Davis, Santa Barbara) .... CA
California State U. (Long Beach) .... CA
Colorado State .... CO
Connecticut Coll .... CT
DePauw .... IN
Drew U .... NJ
Duke U .... NC
Eastern Illinois U IL
Florida, U. of .... FL
Georgia, U. of .... GA
Humboldt State .... CA
Illinois, U. of (Urbana) IL
Iowa State U .... IA
Lee Coll .... TN
Marshall U .... WV
Maryland, U. of .... MD
Marymount Coll .... KS
Massachusetts, U. of .... MA
Miami U .... OH
Michigan, U. of .... MI
Michigan State .... MI
Minnesota, U. of .... MN
Montana, U. of .... MT
Montana State U .... MT
New Hampshire, U.of .... NH
North Carolina, U. of (Chapel Hill) .... NC
North Carolina State .... NC
North Dakota State .... ND
Ohio State U .... OH
Ohio U .... OH
Ohio Wesleyan U .... OH
Oklahoma, U. of .... OK
Oregon State U .... OR
Pennsylvania State U .... PA
Pomona .... CA
Purdue U .... IN
Rhode Island, U. of .... RI
Rutgers U .... NJ
San Diego State U .... CA
San Jose State U .... CA
South Florida, U. of .... FL
Southern Illinois IL
Tennessee, U. of .... TN
Texas Tech .... TX
Vermont, U. of .... VT
Washington, U. of .... WA
Weber State .... UT
Wisconsin, U. of (Madison, Milwaukee) .... WI
Wyoming, U. of .... WY

Broadcasting

Undergraduate degree programs according to the National Assn. of Broadcasters

Akron, U. of .... OH
Alabama, U. of .... AL
Alabama A&M U .... AL
Alaska, U. of .... AK
American U .... DC
Appalachian State U .... NC
Arizona, U. of .... AZ
Arizona State U .... AZ
Arkansas, U. of .... AR
Arkansas State U .... AR
Ashland Coll .... OH
Auburn U .... AL
Ball State U .... IN
Baylor U .... TX
Bemidji State U .... MN
Boston Coll .... MA
Boston U .... MA
Bowling Green State U .... OH
Bridgeport, U. of .... CT
Brigham Young U .... UT
Brooklyn Coll .... NY
Butler U .... IN
California Inst. of the Arts .... CA
California State U. (Chico, Fresno, Fullerton, Long Beach, Los Angeles, Northridge, Sacramento) .... CA
Canisius Coll .... NY
Capital U .... OH
Central Florida, U. of .... FL
Central Michigan U .... MI
Central Missouri State U .... MO
Central State U .... OK
Central Washington U .... WA
Cincinnati, U. of .... OH
Clarion State Coll .... PA
Clark Coll .... GA
Colorado, U. of .... CO
Colorado State U .... CO
Columbia U .... NY
Creighton U .... NE
Dayton, U. of .... OH
Delaware, U. of .... DE
Denison U .... OH
Denver, U. of .... CO
DePauw U .... IN
Detroit, U. of .... MI
Drake U .... IA
Duquesne U .... PA
East Texas State U .... TX
Eastern Illinois U IL
Eastern Kentucky U .... KY
Eastern Michigan U .... MI
Eastern Montana Coll .... MT
Eastern Washington U .... WA
Elizabethtown Coll .... PA
Emerson Coll .... MA
Evangel Coll .... MO
Fairmont State Coll .... WV
Florida, U. of .... FL
Florida A&M U .... FL
Florida Atlantic U .... FL
Florida Southern Coll .... FL
Florida State U .... FL
Fordham U .... NY
Fort Hays State U .... KS
Geneva Coll .... PA
George Washington U .... DC
Georgia, U. of .... GA
Georgia State U .... GA
Governors State U IL
Grambling State U .... LA
Grand View Coll .... IA
Hampton Inst .... VA
Henderson State U .... AR
Herbert Lehman Coll. of CUNY .... NY
Hofstra U .... NY
Houston, U. of .... TX
Howard U .... DC
Idaho, U. of .... ID
Idaho State U .... ID
Illinois, U. of IL
Illinois State U IL
Indiana State U .... IN
Indiana U .... IN
Iona Coll .... NY
Iowa, U. of .... IA
Iowa State U .... IA

Ithaca Coll .... NY
James Madison U .... VA
John Brown U .... AR
Kansas, U. of .... KS
Kansas State U .... KS
Kearney State Coll .... NE
Kent State U .... OH
Kentucky, U. of .... KY
King's Coll .... PA
Kutztown State Coll .... PA
Lamar U .... TX
Langston U .... OK
Liberty Baptist Coll .... VA
Lindenwood Coll .... MO
Louisiana State U .... LA
Louisville, U. of .... KY
Loyola U IL
Loyola U .... LA
Maine, U. of .... ME
Marietta Coll .... OH
Marist Coll .... NY
Marquette U .... WI
Marshall U .... WV
Maryland, U. of .... MD
Massachusetts, U. of .... MA
McNeese State U .... LA
Memphis State U .... TN
Miami, U. of .... FL
Miami U .... OH
Michigan, U. of .... MI
Michigan State U .... MI
Minnesota, U. of .... MN
Minot State Coll .... ND
Mississippi, U. of .... MS
Mississippi State U .... MS
Mississippi U. for Women .... MS
Missouri, U. of (Columbia, Kansas City) .... MO
Montana, U. of .... MT
Montana State U .... MT
Morehead State U .... KY
Morgan State U .... MD
Mount Vernon Coll .... DC
Murray State U .... KY
Nebraska, U. of .... NE
Nevada, U. of .... NV
New Hampshire, U. of .... NH
New Mexico State U .... NM
New Rochelle, Coll. of .... NY
New York Inst. of Tech .... NY
New York U .... NY
Norfolk State U .... VA
North Carolina, U. of (Chapel Hill) .... NC
North Carolina State U .... NC
North Central Coll IL
North Dakota, U. of .... ND
North Texas State U .... TX
Northeast Louisiana U .... LA
Northern Arizona U .... AZ
Northern Illinois U IL
Northern Iowa, U. of .... IA
Northern Michigan U .... MI
Northwest Missouri State U .... MO
Northwestern U IL
Notre Dame of Maryland, Coll of .... MD
Ohio State U .... OH
Ohio U .... OH
Oklahoma, U. of .... OK
Oklahoma State U .... OK
Oregon, U. of .... OR
Oregon State U .... OR
Otterbein Coll .... OH
Pacific U .... OR
Park Coll .... MO
Pennsylvania State U .... PA
Pittsburg State U .... KS
Point Park Coll .... PA
Purdue U .... IN
Queens Coll .... NY
Rutgers U .... NJ
Saint Louis U .... MO
Saint Mary's Coll .... MN
Saint Xavier Coll IL
Sam Houston State U .... TX
San Diego State U .... CA
San Francisco State U .... CA
San Jose State U .... CA
Seton Hall U .... NJ
Shaw U .... NC
Shippensburg State Coll .... PA
South Carolina, U. of .... SC
South Dakota, U. of .... SD
South Dakota State U .... SD
South Florida, U. of .... FL
Southern Arkansas U .... AR
Southern California, U. of ..... CA
Southern Colorado, U. of .... CO
Southern Illinois U IL
Southern Methodist U .... TX
Southern Missionary Coll .... TN
Southern Mississippi, U. of .... MS
Southern Oregon State Coll ..... OR
Southwest Missouri State U .... MO
Southwest Texas State U .... TX
Southwestern Louisiana, U. of .. LA
St. John Fisher Coll .... NY
Stanford U .... CA
State U. of New York (Brockport, Buffalo, Fredonia, Geneseo, Oswego, Plattsburgh) .... NY
Stephen F. Austin State U ...... TX
Stephens Coll .... MO
Syracuse U .... NY
Temple U .... PA
Tennessee, U. of .... TN
Texas, U. of (Arlington, Austin, El Paso) .... TX
Texas Christian U .... TX
Texas Tech U .... TX
Texas Woman's U .... TX
Toledo, U. of .... OH
Towson State U .... MD
Tulsa, U. of .... OK
Utah, U. of .... UT
Utah State U .... UT
Vermont, U. of .... VT
Villanova U .... PA
Virginia Poly. Inst .... VA
Wake Forest U .... NC
Washburn U. of Topeka .... KS
Washington, U. of .... WA
Washington & Lee U .... VA
Washington State U .... WA
Wayne State U .... MI
Weber State Coll .... UT
West Florida, U. of .... FL
West Texas State U .... TX
West Virginia U .... WV
Western Connecticut State Coll . CT
Western Illinois U IL
Western Michigan U .... MI
Western Washington U .... WA
Wheaton Coll .... MA
Wichita State U .... KS
William Paterson Coll .... NJ
Wisconsin, U. of (Eau Claire, La Crosse, Madison, Oshkosh, Parkside, Platteville, Stevens Point, Whitewater) .... WI
Wooster, Coll. of .... OH
Wright State U .... OH
Wyoming, U. of .... WY
Xavier U .... OH
Xavier U. of Louisiana .... LA
York Coll .... PA
Youngstown State U .... OH

Building Industry

Central Coll .... KS
Central Missouri .... MO
Cowley County Comm. Jr .... KS
Eastern Oklahoma .... OK
John Brown U .... AR
Lake Superior State Coll .... MI
Mississippi Delta Jr. Coll ..... MS
Northwest Missouri State U .... MO
Pratt Comm. Coll .... KS
South Dakota, U. of (Springfield) .... SD
Southwestern Adventist .... TX
Waldorf Coll .... IA
Western Texas Coll .... TX

Business Administration

Members of Accreditation Council of American Assembly of Collegiate Schools of Business

Akron, U. of .... OH
Alabama, U. of (Birmingham, University) .... AL
Appalachian State U .... NC
Arizona, U. of .... AZ
Arizona State U. (Tempe) .... AZ
Arkansas, U. of (Fayetteville, Little Rock) .... AR
Arkansas State U .... AR
Atlanta U .... GA
Auburn .... AL
Babson Coll .... MA
Ball State U .... IN
Baylor .... TX
Bernard Baruch Sch. of Bus., City U .... NY
Boise State U .... ID
Boston Coll .... MA
Boston U .... MA
Bowling Green State U .... OH
Bradley U IL
Bridgeport, U. of .... CT
Brigham Young U .... UT
California, U. of (Berkeley, Los Angeles) .... CA
California Polytechnic .... CA
California State Coll. (Bakersfield) .... CA
California State U. (Chico, Fresno, Fullerton, Hayward, Long Beach, Los Angeles, Northridge, Sacramento) ..... CA
Canisius .... NY
Carnegie-Mellon U .... PA
Case Western Reserve .... OH
Central Florida, U. of .... FL
Chicago, U. of IL
Cincinnati, U. of .... OH
Clarkson Coll .... NY
Clemson U .... SC
Cleveland State U .... OH
Colorado, U. of .... CO
Colorado State U .... CO
Columbia .... NY
Connecticut, U. of .... CT
Cornell U .... NY
Creighton .... NE
Dartmouth .... NH
Delaware, U. of .... DE
Denver, U. of .... CO
DePaul IL
Detroit, U. of .... MI
Drake .... IA
Drexel U .... PA
Duke U .... NC
Duquesne U .... PA
East Carolina U .... NC
East Texas State U .... TX
Eastern Michigan U .... MI
Eastern Washington U .... WA
Emory .... GA
Florida, U. of .... FL
Florida Atlantic .... FL
Florida State U .... FL
Fordham .... NY
Fort Lewis Coll .... CO
George Washington .... DC
Georgia, U. of .... GA
Georgia Inst. of Tech .... GA
Georgia Southern .... GA
Georgia State U .... GA
Harvard U .... MA
Hawaii, U. of .... HI
Hofstra .... NY
Houston, U. of .... TX
Howard U .... DC
Idaho State U .... ID
Illinois, U. of (Chicago Circle, Urbana) IL
Illinois State U IL
Indiana State U .... IN
Indiana U .... IN
Iowa, U. of .... IA
John Carroll U .... OH
Kansas, U. of .... KS
Kansas State U .... KS
Kent State .... OH
Kentucky, U. of .... KY
Lamar U .... TX
Lehigh .... PA
Louisiana State U. (Baton Rouge) .... LA
Louisiana Tech. U .... LA
Loyola IL
Loyola Marymount U .... CA
Loyola U .... LA
Maine, U. of (Orono) .... ME
Marquette .... WI
Maryland, U. of .... MD
Massachusetts, U. of .... MA
Massachusetts Inst. of Tech ... MA
Memphis State U .... TN
Miami, U. of .... FL
Miami U .... OH
Michigan, U. of .... MI
Michigan State U .... MI
Middle Tennessee State .... TN
Minnesota, U. of .... MN
Mississippi, U. of .... MS
Mississippi State U .... MS
Missouri, U. of (Columbia, Kansas City, St. Louis) ...... MO
Montana, U. of .... MT
Murray State U .... KY
Nebraska, U. of (Lincoln, Omaha) .... NE
Nevada, U. of (Reno) .... NV
New Mexico, U. of .... NM
New Mexico State U .... NM
New Orleans, U. of .... LA
New York U .... NY
North Carolina, U. of .... NC
North Carolina A&T State U ... NC
North Florida, U. of .... FL
North Texas State U .... TX
Northeast Louisiana U .... LA
Northeastern U .... MA
Northern Arizona U .... AZ
Northern Illinois U IL
Northwestern IL
Notre Dame, U. of .... IN
Ohio State U .... OH
Ohio U .... OH
Oklahoma, U. of .... OK
Oklahoma State U .... OK
Old Dominion U .... VA
Oregon, U. of .... OR
Oregon State U .... OR
Pacific Lutheran U .... WA
Pan American U .... TX
Pennsylvania, U. of .... PA
Pennsylvania State U .... PA
Pittsburgh, U. of .... PA
Portland, U. of .... OR
Portland State U .... OR
Purdue .... IN
Rensselaer Poly. Inst .... NY
Rhode Island, U. of .... RI
Richmond, U. of .... VA
Rochester, U. of .... NY
Roosevelt U IL
Rutgers U .... NJ

San Diego, U. of .... CA
San Diego State U .... CA
San Francisco, U. of .... CA
San Francisco State U .... CA
San Jose State U .... CA
Santa Clara, U. of .... CA
Seattle U .... WA
Seton Hall U .... NJ
Shippensburg State Coll .... PA
South Alabama, U. of .... AL
South Carolina, U. of .... SC
South Dakota, U. of .... SD
South Florida, U. of .... FL
Southern California, U. of ...... CA
Southern Illinois U. (Carbondale, Edwardsville) IL
Southern Methodist .... TX
Southern Mississippi, U. of .... MS
St. Cloud State U .... MN
St. John's U .... NY
St. Louis U .... MO
Stanford .... CA
State U. of New York (Albany, Buffalo) .... NY
Stephen F. Austin State .... TX
Syracuse .... NY
Temple .... PA
Tennessee, U. of .... TN
Tennessee Tech. U .... TN
Texas, U. of (Arlington, Austin) . TX
Texas A&M U .... TX
Texas Christian U .... TX
Texas Southern .... TX
Texas Tech U .... TX
Toledo, U. of .... OH
Tulane .... LA
Tulsa, U. of .... OK
Utah, U. of .... UT
Utah State U .... UT
Valdosta State Coll .... GA
Vanderbilt U .... TN
Villanova .... PA
Virginia, U. of .... VA
Virginia Commonwealth .... VA
Virginia Polytechnic Inst .... VA
Washington, U. of .... WA
Washington and Lee .... VA
Washington State U .... WA
Washington U .... MO
Wayne State U .... MI
West Virginia U .... WV
Western Illinois U IL
Western Michigan U .... MI
Wichita State .... KS
William and Mary, Coll. of ...... VA
Winthrop Coll .... SC
Wisconsin, U. of (Eau Claire, Madison, Milwaukee, Oshkosh, Whitewater) .... WI
Wright State U .... OH
Wyoming, U. of .... WY

Business Administration

5 year master's program

Adelphi U .... NY
Akron, U. of .... OH
Alabama, U. of .... AL
Alfred U. (with Clarkson) .... NY
Andrews U .... MI
Angelina Coll .... TX
Anna Maria Coll .... MA
Appalachian State .... NC
Arizona, U. of .... AZ
Arkansas, U. of (Little Rock) .... AR
Ashland Coll .... OH
Babson Coll .... MA
Baylor U .... TX
Bernadean U .... CA
Baruch Coll .... NY
Bradley U IL
Brevard Coll .... NC
California, U. of (Irvine) .... CA
California State Coll .... PA
California State U. (Hayward, Sacramento) .... CA
Case Western .... OH
Central Missouri .... MO
Central State U .... OK
Chicago, U. of IL
Clarion State .... PA
Clark U .... MA
Colorado, U. of .... CO
Columbus Coll .... GA
Cornell U .... NY
Dallas, U. of .... TX
Delta State U .... MS
Denver, U. of .... CO
Drake U .... IA
East Carolina .... NC
Eastern Kentucky .... KY
Eastern New Mexico .... NM
Eastern Washington .... WA
Fisk U .... TN
Florida A&M .... FL
Fort Hays State .... KS
Gannon U .... PA
Georgia Coll .... GA
Gonzaga U .... WA
Grand Valley .... MI
Hartford, U. of .... CT
Henderson State U .... AR
Hofstra U .... NY
Illinois Inst. of Tech IL
Indiana U. (Bloomington) .... IN
Indiana U.—Purdue U .... IN
International Coll .... FL
Iona Coll .... NY
Iowa, U. of .... IA
Kansas, U. of .... KS
Kansas State U .... KS
La Salle Coll .... PA
Louisville, U. of .... KY
Loyola Coll .... MD
Loyola U .... LA
Manhattanville Coll .... NY
Mankato State .... MN
Mary Washington .... VA
Marymount Coll. of Virginia ..... VA
Marywood .... PA
Mercy Coll .... NY
Michigan, U. of .... MI
Minnesota, U. of .... MN
Montana, U. of .... MT
Mount St. Mary's .... MD
Murray State U .... KY
Nevada, U. of .... NV
Newcomb Coll .... LA
New Hampshire, U. of .... NH
New York U .... NY
Nicholls State U .... LA
North Carolina Cent. U .... NC
North Texas State .... TX
Northern Kentucky U .... KY
Notre Dame, Coll of .... CA
Oakland U .... MI
Oral Roberts U .... OK
Oregon, U. of .... OR
Pace U .... NY
Pittsburg State .... KS
Plymouth State .... NH
Puerto Rico, U. of .... PR
Puget Sound, U. of .... WA
Queens Coll .... NC
Richmond, U. of .... VA
Rosary Coll IL
Scranton, U. of .... PA
Shenandoah Coll .... VA
Shippensburg State .... PA
Skidmore Coll .... NY
South Dakota, U. of .... SD
Southeastern Oklahoma State . OK
Southwest Missouri State ...... MO
St. Bonaventure U .... NY
State U. of New York (Binghamton, Buffalo, Geneseo, Oneonta) .... NY
State U. of New York Coll. of Ag. & Life Sci .... NY
Stephen F. Austin .... TX
Steubenville, U. of .... OH
Sweet Briar Coll .... VA
Tennessee, U. of .... TN
Tennessee State .... TN
Texas, U. of (Austin, San Antonio) .... TX
Texas A&I U .... TX
Texas Woman's .... TX
Tulane U .... LA
U.S. International U .... CA
Utah State U .... UT
Vanderbilt U .... TN
Washington U .... MO
Webber Coll .... FL
West Georgia Coll .... GA
Western Connecticut State ...... CT
Western Kentucky U .... KY
Wheaton Coll .... MA
White Plains, Coll. of .... NY
Whittier Coll .... CA
Willamette U .... OR
William Smith .... NY
Wilmington Coll .... DE
Winona State U .... MN
Wisconsin, U. of (Whitewater) ... WI
Worcester Poly. Inst .... MA
Xavier U .... LA
Youngstown State U .... OH

Cabinetmaking

Marlboro Coll .... VT
New England Inst. of Tech ...... RI
Northeast Mississippi Jr. Coll .. MS
Pearl River .... MS
Pittsburg State .... KS

Cartography

Akron, U. of .... OH
Bridgewater State Coll .... MA
Colorado Mountain Coll .... CO
East Central Oklahoma State .. OK
George Washington U .... DC
Macalester Coll .... KS
Mary Washington .... VA
Plymouth State .... NH
Southwest Missouri State ...... MO
Temple U .... PA
Valparaiso U .... IN
Wittenberg U .... OH

Cartooning

Columbia Coll IL
Columbia Coll .... MO

Ceramic Art

Akron, U. of .... OH
Alabama A&M .... AL
Alabama State U .... AL
Atlantic Christian Coll .... NC
Baldwin-Wallace Coll .... OH
Barat IL
Baylor U .... TX
Beaver Coll .... PA
Bennington Coll .... VT
Boston U .... MA
Bowling Green State U .... OH
Brevard Coll .... NC
California, U. of (Santa Cruz) ... CA
California Coll. of Arts and Crafts .... CA
California State U. (Sacramento) .... CA
Carnegie-Mellon U .... PA
Center for Creative Studies ..... MI
Clark U .... MA
Columbia Coll .... MO
Drake U .... IA
East Carolina .... NC
Eastern Kentucky U .... KY
Eastern New Mexico U .... NM
Eastern Washington U .... WA
Endicott .... MA
George Washington U .... DC
Goddard Coll .... VT
Hampton Institute .... VA
Hartford, U. of .... CT
Hastings Coll .... NE
Hope Coll .... MI
Iowa, U. of .... IA
Kansas, U. of .... KS
Kansas City Art Inst .... MO
LaGrange Coll .... GA
Lincoln Coll IL
Marlboro Coll .... VT
Marywood .... PA
Midwestern State .... TX
Mills Coll .... CA
Minnesota, U. of .... MN
Mississippi Delta Jr. Coll ...... MS
Montana, U. of .... MT
Mount Aloysius Jr. Coll .... PA
Mount Senario .... WI
Mount St. Joseph, Coll. of ..... OH
Nebraska Wesleyan .... NE
New Rochelle, Coll of .... NY
North Texas State U .... TX
Northeast Mississippi Jr. Coll .. MS
Northeastern Louisiana U .... LA
Northern Michigan .... MI
Northwest Missouri State ...... MO
Ohio State U .... OH
Old Dominion .... VA
Otis Art Inst .... CA
Philadelphia Coll. of Art .... PA
Pittsburg State .... KS
Pratt Inst .... NY
Rhode Island Sch. of Design .... RI
Rochester Inst. of Tech .... NY
Rockford Coll IL
Savannah Coll. of Art and Design .... GA
Seton Hill .... PA
Shepherd .... WV
Shorter Coll .... GA
South Dakota, U. of .... SD
South Georgia Coll .... GA
Southern Idaho, Coll. of .... ID
Southern Methodist .... TX
St. Benedict .... MN
St. Gregory's Coll .... OK
St. Mary Coll .... KS
Syracuse U .... NY
Temple U .... PA
Tennessee, U. of .... TN
Texas, U. of (El Paso) .... TX
Texas Woman's U .... TX
Thiel Coll .... PA
Trinity Christian IL
Tulsa, U. of .... OK
Waldorf Coll .... IA
Washington U .... MO
Wayne State U .... MI
Webster Coll .... MO
Wesleyan Coll .... GA
Wesleyan U .... CT
Wichita State U .... KS
William Woods .... MO
Wisconsin, U. of (Milwaukee, Oshkosh, Superior) .... WI

Ceramic Engineering, *See* ENGINEERING, CERAMIC

Ceramic Science

Carnegie-Mellon U .... PA
Marlboro Coll .... VT
Ohio State .... OH
Pennsylvania State U. (Allentown, McKeesport, Shenango, University Park) .... PA

Chefs, Training for

El Centro Coll .... TX
Hocking Tech. Coll .... OH
Johnson and Wales Coll .... RI
Paul Smith's Coll .... NY
Southern Idaho, Coll. of .... ID
State U. of New York (Cobleskill) .... NY

Chemical Engineering, *See* ENGINEERING, CHEMICAL

Chemistry

Approved by American Chemical Society. The Society recognizes, however, that there are many institutions having adequate instruction in chemistry which are not on its list of approved schools

Abilene Christian .... TX
Adelphi .... NY
Agnes Scott .... GA
Akron, U. of .... OH
Alabama, U. of (Birmingham, Huntsville, University) .... AL
Alaska, U. of .... AK
Albion .... MI
Albright .... PA
Alfred U .... NY
Allegheny .... PA
Alma .... MI
American U .... DC
Amherst .... MA
Andrews U .... MI
Appalachian State U .... NC
Arizona, U. of .... AZ
Arizona State U. (Tempe) .... AZ
Arkansas, U. of (Fayetteville, Little Rock) .... AR
Ashland Coll .... OH
Auburn U .... AL
Augsburg .... MN
Augustana IL
Augustana Coll .... SD
Austin .... TX
Baldwin-Wallace .... OH
Ball State .... IN
Barnard .... NY
Bates .... ME
Baylor .... TX
Beloit .... WI
Bemidji State U .... MN
Birmingham-Southern Coll ..... AL
Bloomsburg State Coll .... PA
Boston Coll .... MA
Boston U .... MA
Bowdoin .... ME
Bowling Green State U .... OH
Bradley IL
Brandeis .... MA
Bridgeport, U. of .... CT
Bridgewater State .... MA
Brigham Young .... UT
Brooklyn Coll .... NY
Brown .... RI
Bryn Mawr .... PA
Bucknell .... PA
Butler U .... IN
California, U. of (Berkeley, Davis, Irvine, Los Angeles, Riverside, San Diego, Santa Barbara, Santa Cruz) .... CA
California Inst. of Tech .... CA
California Poly. State U .... CA
California State Coll. (Bakersfield, San Bernardino, Stanislaus) .. CA
California State Poly .... CA
California State U. (Chico, Dominguez Hills, Fresno, Fullerton, Hayward, Long Beach, Los Angeles, Northridge, Sacramento) ..... CA
Calvin .... MI
Canisius .... NY
Capital U .... OH
Carleton .... MN
Carnegie-Mellon .... PA
Carroll Coll .... WI
Carthage Coll .... WI
Case Western Reserve U ...... OH
Catholic U .... DC
Centenary .... LA
Central Coll .... IA
Central Connecticut State Coll .. CT
Central Florida, U. of .... FL
Central Michigan U .... MI
Central State U .... OH
Central State U .... OK
Charleston, Coll of .... SC
Chatham .... PA
Chestnut Hill Coll .... PA
Chicago, U. of IL
Cincinnati, U. of .... OH
Citadel .... SC
City Univ. of N.Y .... NY
Clarion State Coll .... PA
Clark .... MA
Clarkson Coll. of Tech .... NY
Clemson .... SC
Cleveland State U .... OH
Coe Coll .... IA
Colby .... ME
Colgate .... NY
Colorado, U. of (Boulder, Denver) .... CO
Colorado Coll .... CO
Colorado Sch. of Mines .... CO
Colorado State U .... CO
Columbia .... NY
Concordia .... MN
Connecticut, U. of .... CT
Cornell .... IA
Cornell U .... NY
Creighton U .... NE
Dartmouth .... NH
David Lipscomb Coll .... TN
Davidson .... NC
Dayton, U. of .... OH
Delaware, U. of .... DE
Delaware State .... DE
Delware Valley State Coll .... PA
Delta State U .... MS
Denison .... OH
Denver, U. of .... CO
DePaul IL
DePauw .... IN
Detroit, U. of .... MI
Dickinson .... PA
Douglass .... NJ
Drake U .... IA
Drew .... NJ
Drexel U .... PA
Duke U .... NC
Duquesne .... PA
Earlham .... IN
East Carolina U .... NC
East Stroudsburg State Coll .... PA
East Tennessee State U .... TN
East Texas State U .... TX
Eastern Illinois U IL
Eastern Kentucky, U. of .... KY
Eastern Michigan U .... MI
Elizabethtown .... PA
Elmhurst Coll IL
Emory .... GA
Emporia Kansas State U .... KS
Evansville, U. of .... IN
Fairfield U .... CT
Fairleigh Dickinson U. (Rutherford, Teaneck) .... NJ
Fisk U .... TN
Florida, U. of .... FL
Florida Atlantic U .... FL
Florida State U .... FL
Fordham .... NY
Fort Lewis Coll .... CO
Franklin and Marshall .... PA
Furman .... SC
Geneva .... PA
George Mason U .... VA
George Washington .... DC
Georgetown .... DC
Georgia, U. of .... GA
Georgia Inst. of Tech .... GA
Georgia State U .... GA
Gettysburg .... PA
Gonzaga .... WA
Glassboro State Coll .... NJ
Goucher .... MD
Grand Valley State Coll .... MI
Grinnell .... IA
Gustavus Adolphus .... MN
Hamilton .... NY
Hamline .... MN
Hampden-Sydney .... VA
Hampton Inst .... VA
Hartford, U. of .... CT
Hartwick Coll .... NY
Harvard U .... MA
Harvey Mudd .... CA
Haverford .... PA
Hawaii, U. of .... HI
Hiram .... OH
Hobart and William Smith Coll .. NY
Hofstra .... NY
Hollins Coll .... VA
Holy Cross .... MA
Hope .... MI
Houston, U. of .... TX
Howard .... DC
Humboldt State U .... CA
Hunter .... NY
Idaho, U. of .... ID
Idaho State U .... ID
Illinois, U. of (Chicago, Urbana) .. IL
Illinois Benedictine Coll IL
Illinois Inst. of Tech IL
Illinois State U IL
Illinois Wesleyan U IL
Indiana State .... IN
Indiana U .... IN
Indiana U. of Pennsylvania ...... PA
Indiana U.—Purdue U .... IN
Iowa, U. of .... IA
Iowa State U. of Science and Tech .... IA
Ithaca .... NY
Jackson State U .... MS
James Madison U .... VA
John Carroll U .... OH
Johns Hopkins .... MD
Juniata .... PA
Kalamazoo .... MI
Kansas, U. of .... KS
Kansas State U .... KS
Kearney State Coll .... NE
Kent State U .... OH
Kentucky, U. of .... KY
Kenyon .... OH
King's .... PA
Knox IL
La Salle .... PA
Lafayette .... PA
Lake Forest Coll IL
Lamar .... TX
Lawrence .... WI
Le Moyne .... NY
Lebanon Valley .... PA
Lehigh .... PA
Lehman Coll .... NY
Lincoln U .... PA
Long Island U .... NY
Loras Coll .... IA
Louisiana State U. (Baton Rouge, Shreveport) .... LA
Louisiana Tech. U .... LA
Louisville, U. of .... KY
Lowell, U. of .... MA
Loyola IL
Loyola .... LA
Loyola Coll .... MD
Loyola Marymount .... CA
Luther .... IA
Macalester .... MN
MacMurray IL
Maine, U. of .... ME
Manhattan .... NY
Manhattanville Coll .... NY
Mankato State .... MN
Marietta .... OH
Marist Coll .... NY
Marquette .... WI
Marshall .... WV
Maryland, U. of .... MD
Massachusetts, U. of .... MA
Massachusetts Inst. of Tech ... MA
McMurry .... TX
McNeese State U .... LA
Memphis State U .... TN
Merrimack .... MA
Metropolitan State .... CO
Miami, U. of .... FL
Miami U .... OH
Michigan, U. of (Ann Arbor, Dearborn, Flint) .... MI
Michigan State U .... MI
Michigan Tech. U .... MI
Middle Tennessee State U ...... TN
Middlebury .... VT
Midwestern .... TX
Millersville State .... PA
Milsaps Coll .... MS
Minnesota, U. of (Duluth, Minneapolis) .... MN
Mississippi, U. of .... MS
Mississippi Coll .... MS
Mississippi State U .... MS
Missouri, U. of (Columbia, Kansas City, Rolla, St. Louis) .... MO
Monmouth IL
Montana, U. of .... MT
Montana Coll. of Min. Sci. and Tech .... MT
Montana State U .... MT
Montclair State Coll .... NJ
Moorhead State .... MN
Moravian .... PA
Morehouse Coll .... GA
Morgan State .... MD
Mount Holyoke Coll .... MA
Mount St. Vincent .... NY
Muhlenberg .... PA
Murray State .... KY
Muskingum .... OH
Nebraska, U. of (Lincoln, Omaha) .... NE
Nebraska Wesleyan U .... NE
Nevada, U. of (Las Vegas, Reno) .... NV
New Hampshire, U. of .... NH
New Mexico, U. of .... NM
New Mexico Highlands .... NM
New Mexico Inst. of Min. and Tech .... NM
New Mexico State U .... NM
New Orleans, U. of .... LA
New York Poly. Inst. of .... NY
New York U .... NY
North Alabama, U. of .... AL

North Carolina, U. of (Asheville, Chapel Hill, Charlotte, Greensboro, Wilmington) .... NC
North Carolina A&T U .... NC
North Carolina Central U ...... NC
North Carolina State U .... NC
North Dakota, U. of .... ND
North Dakota State .... ND
North Texas State .... TX
Northeast Louisiana U .... LA
Northeastern .... MA
Northern Arizona U .... AZ
Northern Colorado, U. of ...... CO
Northern Illinois IL
Northern Iowa, U. of .... IA
Northern Michigan U .... MI
Northwest Missouri State ...... MO
Northwestern IL
Northwestern State U .... LA
Norwich .... VT
Notre Dame .... IN
Oakland U .... MI
Oberlin .... OH
Occidental .... CA
Ohio Northern U .... OH
Ohio State U .... OH
Ohio U .... OH
Ohio Wesleyan .... OH
Oklahoma, U. of .... OK
Oklahoma State U .... OK
Old Dominion U .... VA
Oregon, U. of .... OR
Oregon State U .... OR
Pace U .... NY
Pacific, U. of the .... CA
Pacific Lutheran .... WA
Pennsylvania, U. of .... PA
Pennsylvania State U .... PA
Philadelphia Coll. of Phar. and Science .... PA
Philadelphia Coll. of Textiles and Science .... PA
Pittsburg State U .... KS
Pittsburgh, U. of .... PA
Pomona .... CA
Portland State U .... OR
Princeton .... NJ
Providence Coll .... RI
Puerto Rico, U. of (Mayaguez, Rio Piedras) .... PR
Puget Sound, U. of .... WA
Purdue .... IN
Queens .... NY
Randolph-Macon Woman's ..... VA
Redlands, U. of .... CA
Reed .... OR
Regis Coll .... CO
Rensselaer Poly Inst .... NY
Rhode Island, U. of .... RI
Rice .... TX
Richmond, U. of .... VA
Rider .... NJ
Ripon .... WI
Roanoke Coll .... VA
Rochester, U. of .... NY
Rochester Inst. of Tech .... NY
Rollins Coll .... FL
Roosevelt U IL
Rose-Hulman Inst. of Tech ..... IN
Russell Sage Coll .... NY
Rutgers .... NJ
Saginaw Valley Coll .... MI
Sam Houston State .... TX
San Diego State U .... CA
San Francisco, U. of .... CA
San Francisco State U .... CA
San Jose State U .... CA
Santa Clara, U. of .... CA
Scranton, U. of .... PA
Seattle U .... WA
Seton Hall .... NJ
Shippensburg State .... PA
Siena Coll .... NY
Simmons .... MA
Skidmore Coll .... NY
Slippery Rock State Coll .... PA
Smith .... MA
Sonoma State U .... CA
South Carolina, U. of .... SC
South Dakota, U. of .... SD
South Dakota Sch. of Mines and Tech .... SD
South Dakota State U .... SD
South Florida, U. of .... FL
Southeast Missouri .... MO
Southeastern Massachusetts U . MA
Southern California, U. of ...... CA
Southern Illinois U. (Carbondale, Edwardsville) IL
Southern Methodist .... TX
Southern Mississippi, U. of .... MS
Southern Oregon State Coll ... OR
Southern U .... LA
Southwest Minnesota State U .. MN
Southwest Missouri State U .... MO
Southwest Texas State U .... TX
Southwestern at Memphis ...... TN
Southwestern Louisiana, U. of .. LA
Southwestern State .... OK
St. Anselm Coll .... NH
St. Cloud State U .... MN
St. John Fisher .... NY
St. John's .... NY
St. Joseph Coll .... CT
St. Joseph's .... PA
St. Lawrence U .... NY
St. Louis U .... MO
St. Mary's Coll .... IN
St. Olaf .... MN
St. Peters .... NJ
St. Thomas, Coll. of .... MN
Stanford .... CA
State U. of New York (Albany, Binghamton, Buffalo, Stony Brook) .... NY
State U. of New York Colleges (Brockport, Buffalo, Cortland, Fredonia, Geneseo, New Paltz, Oneonta, Oswego, Plattsburgh, Potsdam) .... NY
Stephen F. Austin State U ...... TX
Stetson U .... FL
Stevens Inst. of Tech .... NJ
Suffolk U .... MA
Susquehanna U .... PA
Swarthmore .... PA
Syracuse .... NY
Temple .... PA
Tennessee, U. of (Chattanooga, Knoxville, Martin) .... TN
Tennessee Tech .... TN
Texas, U. of (Arlington, Austin, Dallas, El Paso) .... TX
Texas A&I .... TX
Texas A&M .... TX
Texas Christian .... TX
Texas Southern U .... TX
Texas Tech .... TX
Texas Woman's U .... TX
Thiel .... PA
Thomas More Coll .... KY
Toledo, U. of .... OH
Towson State .... MD
Trenton State .... NJ
Trinity .... CT
Trinity U .... TX
Tufts .... MA
Tulane .... LA
Tulsa, U. of .... OK
Tuskegee Inst .... AL
Union .... NY
Ursinus .... PA
U.S. Air Force Acad .... CO
U.S. Naval Acad .... MD
Utah, U. of .... UT
Utah State U .... UT
Valparaiso .... IN
Vanderbilt .... TN
Vassar .... NY
Vermont, U. of .... VT
Villanova .... PA
Virginia, U. of .... VA
Virginia Commonwealth U ...... VA
Virginia Military Inst .... VA
Virginia Poly. Inst .... VA
Wabash .... IN
Wagner .... NY
Wake Forest .... NC
Washburn, U. of .... KS
Washington, U. of .... WA
Washington and Jefferson ...... PA
Washington and Lee .... VA
Washington Coll .... MD
Washington State U .... WA
Washington U .... MO
Wayne State U .... MI
Waynesburg .... PA
Weber State .... UT
Wellesley .... MA
Wesleyan .... CT
West Chester State Coll .... PA
West Florida, U. of .... FL
West Texas State U .... TX
West Virginia Inst. of Tech ..... WV
West Virginia State Coll .... WV
West Virginia U .... WV
Western Illinois U IL
Western Kentucky .... KY
Western Maryland Coll .... MD
Western Michigan U .... MI
Western New England Coll .... MA
Western Washington .... WA
Westminster .... PA
Wheaton IL
Wheaton .... MA
Wheeling Coll .... WV
Whitman Coll .... WA
Whittier .... CA
Wichita State .... KS
Widener .... PA
Wilkes .... PA
Willamette U .... OR
William and Mary .... VA
William Paterson Coll .... NJ
Williams .... MA
Wisconsin, U. of (Eau Claire, Green Bay, La Crosse, Madison, Milwaukee, Oshkosh, Parkside, Platteville, River Falls, Stevens Point, Superior) ...... WI
Wittenberg .... OH
Wooster, Coll. of .... OH
Worcester Poly. Inst .... MA
Wright State U .... OH
Wyoming, U. of .... WY
Xavier .... LA
Xavier .... OH
Yale .... CT
Youngstown State .... OH

Children's Literature

Central Missouri .... MO
Colorado Mountain Coll .... CO
Columbia Coll .... MO
Eastern Kentucky U .... KY
Eastern Washington U .... WA
Felician Coll IL
Goddard Coll .... VT
Hope Coll .... MI
Kansas, U. of .... KS
William Woods .... MO

Chiropody, *See*

PODIATRY

Chiropractic

Institutions accredited by Council on Chiropractic Education

Logan Coll. of Chiropractic .... MO
Los Angeles Coll. of Chiropractic .... CA
National Coll. of Chiropractic (Lombard) IL
New York Chiropractic Coll ..... NY
Northwestern Coll. of Chiropractic (St. Paul) .... MN
Palmer Coll. of Chiropractic .... IA
Texas Chiropractic Coll. (Pasadena) .... TX
Western States Chiropractic Coll .... OR

Church Vocations

Alderson-Broaddus .... WV
Anderson Coll .... IN
Anderson Coll .... SC
Artesia Christian Coll .... NM
Atlanta Christian Coll .... GA
Aurora Coll IL
Averett Coll .... VA
Baptist Christian Coll .... LA
Baylor U .... TX
Belhaven Coll .... MS
Bernadean U .... CA
Bethany Nazarene Coll .... OK
Bethel Coll .... IN
Blue Mountain Coll .... MS
Bluffton Coll .... OH
Bob Jones U .... SC
Carson-Newman .... TN
Central Coll .... KS
Christian Heritage .... CA
Concordia Coll IL
Concordia Coll .... OR
Dallas Christian Coll .... TX
David Lipscomb Coll .... TN
Drake U .... IA
Florida Southern .... FL
Franklin Coll .... IN
Freed-Hardeman Coll .... TN
Freeman Jr. Coll .... SD
Friends U .... KS
Goshen Coll .... IN
Gustavus Adolphus Coll .... MN
Hardin-Simmons U .... TX
Harding U .... AR
Hope Coll .... MI
Huntingdon Coll .... AL
John Brown U .... AR
John Wesley Coll .... NC
Judson Baptist Coll .... OR
Judson Coll .... AL
Judson Coll IL
Lincoln Christian IL
Lindsey Wilson .... KY
McMurray Coll .... TX
Manchester Coll .... IN
Marian Coll. of Fond du Lac .... WI
Mars Hill .... NC
Messiah Coll .... PA
Mississippi Coll .... MS
Mobile Coll .... AL
Mount St. Joseph, Coll. of ..... OH
New Rochelle, Coll. of .... NY
Nyack Coll .... NY
Pacific Christian Coll .... CA
Pfeiffer Coll .... NC
Point Loma .... CA
Rockmount .... CO
Shenandoah Coll. & Cons. of Music .... VA
Shorter Coll .... GA
Southwestern .... TX
St. Paul's Coll .... MO
St. Scholastica, Coll. of .... MN

Stetson U ..... FL
Tift Coll ..... GA
Toccoa Falls ..... GA
Trevecca Nazarene ..... TN
Trinity Christian IL
United Wesleyan Coll ..... PA
Valparaiso U ..... IN
West Virginia Wesleyan ..... WV
Westminster Choir Coll ..... NJ
Western Baptist ..... OR
Wheaton Coll IL
Whitworth Coll ..... WA

Cinema, *See*
MOTION PICTURES/FILM/CINEMA

Citrus Fruit Farming and Processing

Florida, U. of ..... FL
Florida Southern ..... FL
Texas A&I ..... TX

City and/or Urban Planning

•*Indicates that the program is recognized by the American Planning Association for membership credit*

Akron, U. of ..... OH
Alabama, U. of ..... AL
•Alabama A&M U ..... AL
•Arizona, U. of ..... AZ
Arizona State U ..... AZ
Auburn U ..... AL
Boston Coll ..... MA
Boston U ..... MA
•California, U. of (Berkeley, Los Angeles) ..... CA
•California Poly. State U. (San Luis Obispo) ..... CA
•California State Poly. (Pomona) . CA
•California State U. (Fresno) ..... CA
California State Coll ..... PA
Carnegie-Mellon ..... PA
Catholic U ..... DC
•Cincinnati, U. of ..... OH
•Clemson U ..... SC
Cleveland State ..... OH
•Colorado, U. of ..... CO
•Columbia ..... NY
Connecticut Coll ..... CT
•Cornell U ..... NY
•District of Columbia, U. of ..... DC
East Carolina U ..... NC
East Tennessee State ..... TN
Eastern Kentucky U ..... KY
Eastern Washington U ..... WA
Elmhurst IL
Evansville, U. of ..... IN
•Florida, U. of ..... FL
Florida Atlantic U ..... FL
•Florida State ..... FL
•George Washington U ..... DC
•Goddard Coll ..... VT
Governors State U IL
Hampton Institute ..... VA
Hampshire Coll ..... MA
•Harvard U ..... MA
•Hawaii, U. of ..... HI
•Howard U ..... DC
•Illinois, U. of (Urbana) IL
Illinois Inst. of Tech IL
Indiana U. (Bloomington) ..... IN
Indiana U ..... PA
Indiana State U ..... IN
•Iowa, U. of ..... IA
•Iowa State ..... IA
Kansas, U. of ..... KS
Kansas State U ..... KS
Lake Forest Coll IL
Louisville, U. of ..... KY
Mankato State ..... MN
Mansfield State ..... PA
•Maryland, U. of (Baltimore, College Park) ..... MD
Massachusetts, U. of ..... MA
•Massachusetts Inst. of Tech ..... MA
•Memphis State U ..... TN
Miami U ..... OH
•Michigan, U. of ..... MI
•Michigan State U ..... MI
Minnesota, U. of ..... MN
•Mississippi, U. of ..... MS
Missouri, U. of (Rolla) ..... MO
•Morgan State ..... MD
•Nebraska, U. of ..... NE
New Hampshire, U. of ..... NH
New Mexico, U. of ..... NM
New Mexico State U ..... NM
•New Orleans, U. of ..... LA
New School for Social Research ..... NY
•New York U ..... NY
•North Carolina, U. of (Chapel Hill) ..... NC
North Carolina, U. of (Greensboro) ..... NC
•North Dakota State U. (Fargo) ..... ND
•Ohio State U ..... OH
•Oklahoma, U. of ..... OK
•Oregon, U. of ..... OR
Pacific, U. of the ..... CA
•Pennsylvania, U. of ..... PA
•Pennsylvania State U. (Middleton) ..... PA
Pennsylvania State U. (University Park) ..... PA
•Pittsburgh, U. of ..... PA
•Portland State U ..... OR
•Pratt Inst ..... NY
Princeton U ..... NJ
•Puerto Rico, U. of ..... PR
Rhode Island Coll ..... RI
•Rutgers ..... NJ
•San Jose State ..... CA
Southern Arkansas U ..... AR
•Southern California, U. of ..... CA
•Southern Illinois IL
Southwest Missouri State ..... MO
Southwest Texas State U ..... TX
State U. of New York Coll. (Buffalo) ..... NY
Syracuse U ..... NY
Temple U ..... PA
•Tennessee, U. of ..... TN
•Texas, U. of (Arlington, Austin) . TX
•Texas A&M ..... TX
Texas Southern U ..... TX
Toledo, U. of ..... OH
Upsala Coll ..... NJ
Valparaiso U ..... IN
•Virginia, U. of ..... VA
•Virginia Commonwealth U ..... VA
•Virginia Poly. Inst ..... VA
•Washington, U. of ..... WA
Washington U ..... MO
•Wayne State ..... MI
West Florida, U. of ..... FL
Western Kentucky ..... KY
Western Maryland Coll ..... MD
•Wisconsin, U. of (Green Bay, Platteville) ..... WI
Wyoming, U. of ..... WY
Wright State ..... OH

Civil Engineering, *See*
ENGINEERING, CIVIL

Climatology

Purdue U ..... IN
Valparaiso U ..... IN

Clinical Dental Sciences

Boston U ..... MA
Case Western ..... OH
Columbus ..... GA
Creighton ..... NE
Harcum Jr. Coll ..... PA
Harper Coll IL
Iowa, U. of ..... IA
John Carroll U ..... OH
McKendree Coll IL
Maine, U. of ..... ME
Marian Coll ..... IN
Minnesota, U. of (Minneapolis) .. MN
Northwestern U IL
Pittsburgh, U. of ..... PA
Puerto Rico, U. of ..... PR
South Dakota, U. of ..... SD
Temple U ..... PA
Tennessee, U. of ..... TN
Trinity Christian IL
Walsh Coll ..... OH

Clinical Medical Sciences

Alderson-Broaddus ..... WV
Anna Maria Coll ..... MA
Boston U ..... MA
California State U. (Sacramento) ..... CA
Case Western ..... OH
Catholic U ..... DC
Creighton ..... NE
Davenport Coll. of Bus ..... MI
DuPage, Coll. of IL
Harcum Jr. Coll ..... PA
Harper Coll IL
Hawaii, U. of ..... HI
Iowa, U. of ..... IA
John Carroll U ..... OH
Kansas, U. of ..... KS
Maine, U. of ..... ME
Marian Coll ..... IN
McKendree Coll IL
Minnesota, U. of (Minneapolis) .. MN
Navajo Comm. Coll ..... AZ
Nebraska Wesleyan ..... NE
Northern Michigan ..... MI
Northwestern U IL
Ohio State ..... OH
Puerto Rico, U. of ..... PR
Rochester Inst. of Tech ..... NY
Southwest Texas State ..... TX
Tennessee, U. of ..... TN
Trinity Christian IL
Walsh Coll ..... OH
Washington U ..... MO
Wheeling Coll ..... WV

Clinical Veterinary Medical Sciences

Bennett Coll ..... NC
Colorado State U ..... CO
Colorado Mountain Coll ..... CO
Cornell U ..... NY
Eastern Kentucky ..... KY
Eastern Wyoming ..... WY
Franklin Coll ..... IN
Harcum Jr. Coll ..... PA
John Carroll U ..... OH
Kansas State U ..... KS
La Salle ..... PA
Maine, U. of, at Orono ..... ME
McKendree Coll IL
Michigan State ..... MI
Minnesota, U. of (Minneapolis) .. MN
Missouri, U. of ..... MO
Ohio State ..... OH
Puerto Rico, U. of ..... PR
Purdue U ..... IN
State U. of New York (Delhi) ..... NY
Tennessee, U. of ..... TN
Walsh Coll ..... OH
Wesleyan Coll ..... GA

Commercial Fishing

Rhode Island, U. of ..... RI

Commercial Music

Belmont Coll ..... TN
Berklee Coll. of Music ..... MA
Brevard Coll ..... NC
California State U. (Los Angeles) ..... CA
Eastern Kentucky U ..... KY
Eastern Montana Coll ..... MT
Fontbonne Coll ..... MO
Georgia State U ..... GA
Kansas, U. of ..... KS
Kearney State ..... NE
Milliken U IL
Minnesota, U. of ..... MN
North Alabama, U. of ..... AL
Northeast Mississippi Jr ..... MS
Northeast Missouri State ..... MO
Oakland U ..... MI
St. Rose, Coll. of ..... NY
Shenandoah Coll ..... VA
State U. of New York (Potsdam) . NY
Temple U ..... PA
Valparaiso U ..... IN

Communications Engineering,
See ENGINEERING, COMMUNICATIONS

Community Work

Akron, U. of ..... OH
Alabama State U ..... AL
Bemidji State U ..... MN
Bennett Coll ..... NC
California State Coll ..... PA
Cincinnati, U. of ..... OH
Drake U ..... IA
DuPage, Coll. of IL
Eastern Kentucky ..... KY
Eastern Montana Coll ..... MT
Fort Lewis Coll ..... CO
Franklin Coll ..... IN
Freed-Hardeman ..... TN
George Williams IL
Goddard Coll ..... VT
International Coll ..... FL
Lincoln Coll IL
Maria Regina ..... NY
Mars Hill Coll ..... NC
Marlboro Coll ..... VT
Missouri, U. of ..... MO
National Coll. of Educ IL
Sangamon State IL
Springfield ..... MA
Syracuse U ..... NY
Temple U ..... PA
Tennessee, U. of ..... TN
Trinity Christian IL
Upsala Coll ..... NJ
Waldorf Coll ..... IA
World Coll. West ..... CA

Comparative Literature

Alderson-Broaddus .... WV
American Coll. in Paris ..... France
Augustana .... SD
Beloit Coll .... WI
Brandeis .... MA
Brevard .... NC
Brown U .... RI
California, U. of (Davis, Irvine Riverside, San Diego, Santa Barbara) .... CA
California State U. (Fullerton, Sacramento) .... CA
Carnegie-Mellon .... PA
Carthage .... WI
Case Western Reserve .... OH
Catholic U .... DC
Cedar Crest .... PA
Central Missouri .... MO
Coe Coll .... IA
Creighton .... NE
Darmouth Coll .... NH
Delaware, U. of .... DE
Denver, U. of .... CO
DePauw U .... IN
Duke U .... NC
Eastern Washington U .... WA
Eckerd Coll .... FL
Fordham U .... NY
Franklin Coll .... IN
George Washington U .... DC
Goddard Coll .... VT
Gonzaga U .... WA
Governors State U IL
Hampshire Coll .... PA
Hillsdale Coll .... MI
Hiram Coll .... OH
Hobart Coll .... NY
Hofstra U .... NY
Illinois, U. of IL
Immaculata Coll .... PA
Indiana U. (Bloomington) .... IN
International U .... MO
Iowa, U. of .... IA
John Carroll U .... OH
Johns Hopkins .... MD
Judson Coll IL
Kansas, U. of .... KS
Knox Coll IL
Lake Forest IL
La Salle .... PA
Marlboro Coll .... VT
Massachusetts, U. of (Amherst) .... MA
Mills Coll .... CA
New Coll .... FL
New Mexico, U. of .... NM
North Carolina, U. of (Chapel Hill) .... NC
Northwestern U IL
Oglethorpe .... GA
Pennsylvania State (Allentown, Behrend, Shenango, University Park) .... PA
Princeton U .... NJ
Reed Coll .... OR
Rhode Island, U. of .... RI
Rio Piedras .... PR
San Diego State .... CA
Seattle U .... WA
Smith .... MA
South, U. of the .... TN
South Carolina, U. of .... SC
South Georgia Coll .... GA
State U. of New York (Binghamton, Geneseo, Stony Brook) .... NY
Syracuse U .... NY
Tennessee, U. of .... TN
Trinity Coll .... CT
Trinity Christian IL
Virginia Commonwealth .... VA
Washington, U. of .... WA
Washington U .... MO
Wesleyan U .... CT
Western Maryland .... MD
William Smith .... NY
William Woods .... MO
Williams Coll .... MA
Wisconsin, U. of (Milwaukee) ... WI
Wright State U .... OH

Computer Engineering, *See* ENGINEERING, COMPUTER

Computer Information Sciences

Institutions awarding 20 or more undergraduate degrees as major field in single year according to U.S. Office of Education

Alabama A&M .... AL
American Tech. U .... TX
American U .... DC
Arizona, U. of .... AZ
Arizona State U .... AZ
Arkansas State U .... AR
Bentley Coll .... MA
Bernard Baruch .... NY
Boston Coll .... MA
Bowling Green .... OH
Bradley U IL
Brigham Young U .... UT
Brooklyn Coll .... NY
Brown U .... RI
California, U. of (Berkeley, Irvine, San Diego, Santa Barbara, Santa Cruz .... CA
California State Poly. (San Luis Obispo) .... CA
California State U. (Chico, Fullerton, Northridge, Sacramento) .... CA
Central Michigan U .... MI
Central Missouri State .... MO
Central State .... OK
Cincinnati, U. of .... OH
City Coll .... NY
Cleveland State U .... OH
Coleman Coll .... CA
Colorado State U .... CO
Connecticut, U. of .... CT
Dayton, U. of .... OH
Delaware, U. of .... DE
District of Columbia, U. of ..... DC
Duke U .... NC
East Tennessee State .... TN
East Texas State .... TX
Eastern Illinois U IL
Fairleigh Dickinson .... NJ
Ferris State U .... MI
Florida, U. of .... FL
Florida Atlantic .... FL
Florida International U .... FL
Florida Tech. U .... FL
Georgia, U. of .... GA
Georgia Inst. of Tech .... GA
Georgia State U .... GA
Grambling State U .... LA
Hawaii, U. of .... HI
Hofstra U .... NY
Houston, U. of .... TX
Hunter Coll .... NY
Illinois, U. of IL
Illinois Inst. of Tech IL
Indiana U .... IN
Indiana U .... PA
Iowa, U. of .... IA
Iowa State U .... IA
Jackson State U .... MS
Johnson & Wales Coll .... RI
Kansas, U. of .... KS
Kansas State U .... KS
Kean Coll .... NJ
Kent State U .... OH
Kentucky, U. of .... KY
Lock Haven State .... PA
Louisiana Tech. U .... LA
Mankato State .... MN
Maryland, U. of .... MD
Massachusetts, U. of .... MA
Massachusetts Inst. of Tech ... MA
Metropolitan State U .... CO
Miama, U. of .... FL
Miami U .... OH
Michigan, U. of (Ann Arbor) .... MI
Michigan State U .... MI
Middle Tennessee State .... TN
Millersville State Coll .... PA
Minnesota, U. of (Minneapolis) .... MN
Mississippi State U .... MS
Missouri, U. of (Rolla) .... MO
Monmouth Coll .... NJ
Nebraska, U. of (Lincoln) .... NE
New Hampshire Coll .... NH
New York Inst. of Tech .... NY
New York U .... NY
Nicholls State U .... LA
North Carolina State .... NC
North Dakota, U. of .... ND
North Texas State .... TX
Northeastern Illinois U IL
Northeastern U .... MA
Northern Illinois U IL
Northwestern Illinois U IL
Oakland U .... MI
Ohio State .... OH
Oregon, U. of .... OR
Oregon State .... OR
Pennsylvania State U. (University Park) .... PA
Pittsburg State U .... KS
Pittsburgh, U. of .... PA
Point Park Coll .... PA
Puerto Rico, U. of .... PR
Purdue .... IN
Queens Coll .... NY
Rensselaer Poly. Inst .... NY
Robert Morris Coll .... PA
Rochester Inst. of Tech .... NY
Roosevelt U IL
Rutgers U .... NJ
San Diego State U .... CA
South Alabama, U. of .... AL
South Carolina, U. of .... SC
Southeast Missouri State ...... MO
Southern California, U. of ...... CA
Southern Illinois U IL
Southern Mississippi, U. of .... MS
Southern U .... LA
Southwest Missouri .... MO
Southwest Texas State .... TX
Southwestern Louisiana, U. of .. LA
St. John's U .... NY
State U. of New York (Brockport, Buffalo, Oswego, Potsdam, Stony Brook) .... NY
Stephen F. Austin .... TX
Stockton State .... NJ
Temple U .... PA
Tennessee, U. of .... TN
Texas, U. of (Austin) .... TX
Texas A&M .... TX
Troy State U .... AL
U.S. Air Force Acad .... CO
Union Coll .... NY
Utah, U. of .... UT
Vanderbilt U .... TN
Virginia Poly. Inst .... VA
Washington, U. of .... WA
Washington State U .... WA
Washington U .... MO
Wayne State U .... MI
West Florida, U. of .... FL
Western Illinois U IL
Wisconsin, U. of (La Crosse, Madison) .... WI
Wichita State U .... KS
Wright State U .... OH
Youngstown State U .... OH

Computer Repair and Maintenance

Colorado Tech .... CO
Eastern Kentucky U .... KY
Hartford, U. of .... CT
Indiana State U .... IN
Lake Superior State .... MI
Miami U .... OH
Missouri, U. of .... MO
Trinidad State Jr .... CO

Conservation and/or Wildlife Management

Alaska, U. of .... AK
Arkansas State U .... AR
Auburn U .... AL
Becker Jr. Coll .... MA
Brevard Coll .... NC
California, U. of (Davis) .... CA
California State Coll .... PA
California State U. (Sacramento) .... CA
Carthage Coll .... WI
Central Missouri .... MO
Clinch Valley .... VA
Colorado Mountain Coll .... CO
Colorado State U .... CO
Cornell U .... NY
Eastern Kentucky U .... KY
Eastern Oklahoma State .... OK
Ferrum Coll .... VA
Florida, U. of .... FL
Franklin Coll .... IN
Goddard Coll .... VT
Hampshire Coll .... MA
Hocking Tech .... OH
Humboldt State .... CA
Kansas State U .... KS
Kent State U .... OH
Lake Superior State .... MI
Lincoln Coll IL
Louisiana Tech .... LA
Maine, U. of (Fort Kent, Orono, Presque Isle) .... ME
Maryland, U. of .... MD
Michigan State .... MI
Missouri, U. of .... MO
Montana, U. of .... MT
Murray State Coll .... OK
Nebraska, U. of .... NE
New Hampshire, U. of .... NH
New Mexico State U .... NM
North Dakota State U. (Bottineau, Fargo) .... ND
Northeast Louisiana U .... LA
Northeast Mississippi Jr. Coll .. MS
Northeast Missouri .... MO
Northern Michigan U .... MI
Northland Coll .... WI
Northwest Missouri State ...... MO
Northwestern Oklahoma State . OK
Northwestern State U .... LA
Ohio State U .... OH
Oklahoma State U .... OK
Pennsylvania State U. (Allentown, Behrend, Shenango, University Park, Wilkes-Barre) .... PA
Purdue U .... IN
Rhode Island, U. of .... RI
Southeastern Oklahoma State . OK
Southwest Missouri State ...... MO
Springfield Coll .... MA
State U. of New York A&T (Cobleskill, Morrisville) .... NY

State U. of New York Coll. of Agri. and Life Sci .... NY
Stephen F. Austin .... TX
Tennessee, U. of .... TN
Texas A&I .... TX
Thiel Coll .... PA
Unity Coll .... ME
Upper Iowa U .... IA
Utah State U .... UT
Vermont, U. of .... VT
Virginia Poly. Inst .... VA
Walsh Coll .... OH
Western Montana .... MT
Winona State U .... MN
Wisconsin, U. of (Milwaukee, River Falls, Stevens Point) .... WI

Construction Engineering,
See ENGINEERING, CONSTRUCTION

Construction Technology

Akron, U. of .... OH
Alfred State .... NY
Andrews U .... MI
Bismarck Jr. Coll .... ND
Bob Jones U .... SC
Bowling Green .... OH
Brigham Young .... HI
California Poly. State .... CA
California State U. (Chico, Fresno, Sacramento) .... CA
Casper Coll .... WY
Central Arizona .... AZ
Central Coll .... KS
Central Missouri .... MO
Cincinnati, U. of .... OH
Eastern Kentucky U .... KY
Eastern Oklahoma State .... OK
Eastern Washington U .... WA
Fairmont State Coll .... WV
Ferris State .... MI
Florida A&M .... FL
Harper Coll IL
Hutchinson Comm. Coll .... KS
Illinois Central Coll IL
Indiana U.-Purdue (Fort Wayne) .... IN
Kansas State U .... KS
Kaskaskia Coll IL
Lake Superior State .... MI
Lawrence Inst. of Tech .... MI
Louisiana Tech .... LA
Maryland, U. of, Eastern Shore .... MD
Minnesota, U. of .... MN
Mississippi Delta Jr. Coll ...... MS
Missouri, U. of .... MO
Missouri Western .... MO
Moorhead State .... MN
Morehead State U .... KY
Morrison Inst. of Tech IL
Nebraska, U. of (Lincoln, Omaha) .... NE
New England Inst. of Tech ...... RI
North Dakota State U .... ND
North Florida, U. of .... FL
Northeast Louisiana U .... LA
Northeast Mississippi Jr. Coll .. MS
Northeastern Okla. State ...... OK
Northern Iowa, U. of .... IA
Northern Kentucky U .... KY
Northern Montana .... MT
Northern Oklahoma Coll .... OK
Northwest Missouri State ...... MO
Oklahoma State U .... OK
Oregon Inst. of Tech .... OR
Pacific Union Coll .... CA
Pennsylvania State U. (Shenango, University Park) .. PA
Pittsburg State U .... KS

Puerto Rico, U. of .... PR
Purdue U .... IN
Saginaw Valley .... MI
Snow Coll .... UT
South Dakota, U. of .... SD
Southeastern Louisiana U ...... LA
Southern Arkansas U. (Tech.) ... AR
Southern Coll .... FL
Southern Illinois U IL
Southern Mississippi, U. of .... MS
Southwest Missouri State ...... MO
Southwestern Adventist Coll .... TX
State U. of New York A&T (Canton, Delhi, Farmingdale) .... NY
Temple U .... PA
Texas State Tech. Inst .... TX
Toledo, U. of .... OH
Trinidad State Jr. Coll .... CO
Tuskegee Inst .... AL
Vernon Regional Jr. Coll .... TX
Virgin Islands, Coll. of the VI
Weber State .... UT
West Virginia State Coll .... WV
Western Wyoming Comm ...... WY

Controls Systems Engineering

Case Western Reserve .... OH
Cincinnati, U. of .... OH
Kansas, U. of .... KS
Missouri, U. of .... MO
Purdue U .... IN
State U. of New York (Coll. of Technology) .... NY

Cosmetology

Barton Co. Comm. Coll .... KS
Butte Coll .... CA
Cowley Co .... KS
Eastern Wyoming Coll .... WY
Ferris State .... MI
Fort Scott Comm. Coll .... KS
Kaskaskia Coll IL
Lamar U .... TX
Northeast Mississippi Jr .... MS
Northeastern Jr .... CO
Pearl River Jr .... MS
Pittsburg State .... KS
Trinidad State Jr. Coll .... CO
Virginia State .... VA
Weber State .... UT
Western Texas .... TX

Costume Design and/or Illustration

Carnegie-Mellon .... PA
Chamberlayne Jr. Coll .... MA
Columbia Coll .... MO
El Centro Coll .... TX
Endicott .... MA
Indiana U .... PA
Kansas, U. of .... KS
Kansas State U .... KS
Marlboro Coll .... VT
Marymount Coll .... NY
Rockford Coll IL
St. Benedict .... MN
St. Mary Coll .... KS
Syracuse U .... NY
U.S. International U .... CA
Webster Coll .... MO
William Woods Coll .... MO

Cotton Growing

California State U. (Fresno) ..... CA
Mississippi Delta Jr. Coll ...... MS

Counseling and Guidance,
See GUIDANCE AND STUDENT PERSONNEL WORK

Court Reporting

Alfred State .... NY
Bliss Coll .... OH
Central Michigan U .... MI
Central Pennsylvania Bus. Sch .. PA
Champlain Coll .... VT
Cincinnati, U. of .... OH
Concordia Coll .... OR
Eastern Wyoming Coll .... WY
Ferris State .... MI
Humphreys Coll .... CA
Illinois Central Coll IL
Johnson and Wales .... RI
MacCormac IL
Manor Jr. Coll .... PA
Norwich U .... VT
Southern Coll .... FL
Southern Illinois U IL
Temple U .... PA
Youngstown State .... OH

Crafts, *See* ARTS AND CRAFTS

Creative Writing

Institutions awarding undergraduate degrees as major field according to U.S. Office of Education latest statistics

Alabama, U. of .... AL
Alderson-Broaddus Coll .... WV
Arizona, U. of .... AZ
Arkansas Tech. U .... AR
Bowling Green .... OH
Carnegie-Mellon .... PA
Carroll Coll .... WI
Columbia Coll IL
Columbia U .... NY
Davis and Elkins Coll .... WV
Denison U .... OH
Eastern Coll .... PA
Eckerd Coll .... FL
Emerson Coll .... MA
Goddard Coll .... VT
Houghton Coll .... NY
International Coll .... CA
Johns Hopkins .... MD
Knox Coll IL
Loma Linda Coll .... CA
Madonna Coll .... MI
Marlboro Coll .... VT
Miami, U. of .... FL
Michigan, U. of (Ann Arbor) .... MI
Nebraska, U. of .... NE
New Mexico, U. of .... NM
North Carolina, U. of (Charlotte) .... NC
Pittsburgh, U. of .... PA
Prescott Ctr. Coll .... AZ
Roger Williams .... RI
South Alabama, U. of .... AL
Southern Methodist U .... TX
Southwest Missouri .... MO
St. Mary's Coll .... IN
Stephens Coll .... MO
Sweet Briar .... VA
Syracuse U .... NY
Tampa, U. of .... FL
Wheaton Coll .... MA

Credit Management

Gonzaga U .... WA
Huron Coll .... SD

Indiana Central U .... IN
La Salle .... PA
Minnesota, U. of (Duluth) ...... MN
Northwood Inst .... MI
Trinity Christian IL
William Woods .... MO

Criminology

Institutions awarding 10 or more undergraduate degrees according to the latest statistics of the U.S. Office of Education

Albuquerque, U. of .... NM
Arizona State U .... AZ
Arkansas State U .... AR
Athens State Coll .... AL
Brenau Coll .... GA
California, U. of (Fresno) ...... CA
Central State .... OK
Chadron State .... NE
Chaminade Coll .... HI
Chapman Coll .... CA
Delaware, U. of .... DE
Detroit, U. of .... MI
Eastern Washington U .... WA
Florida Memorial .... FL
Fort Valley State .... GA
Gustavus Adolphus .... MN
Illinois, U. of (Chicago Circle) ... IL
Indiana State U .... IN
Indiana U. of Pennsylvania ...... PA
Louisiana State .... LA
Lowell, U. of .... MA
Maryland, U. of .... MD
Mercy Coll .... MI
Nevada, U. of .... NV
North Georgia Coll .... GA
Northeastern Illinois U IL
Northeastern Oklahoma .... OK
Ohio U .... OH
Old Dominion .... VA
Sam Houston .... TX
Savannah State .... GA
Southern Alabama .... AL
Southern Oregon .... OR
St. Ambrose .... IA
St. Edward's .... TX
St. Leo Coll .... FL
St. Xavier IL
Stephen F. Austin .... TX
Stockton State .... NJ
Tampa, U. of .... FL
Valdosta State .... GA
Westfield State .... MA
Wilmington Coll .... DE

Culinary Arts

Baylor U .... TX
Culinary Inst. of America ...... NY
DuPage, Coll. of IL
El Centro Coll .... TX
Hocking Tech. Coll .... OH
Newbury Jr .... MA
Southern Idaho, Coll. of .... ID
St. Mary Coll .... KS
State U. of New York (Cobleskill) .... NY
William Woods .... MO

Cytology, Exfoliative

Notre Dame Coll .... NH

Cytotechnology

Degree or certificate programs approved by Council on Medical Education of the American Medical Assn. in collaboration with American Society of Cytology

Alabama, U. of (Birmingham) ... AL
Bowman Gray Sch. of Med. of Wake Forest U ... NC
California, U. of (San Francisco) ... CA
Duke U ... NC
Elon College ... NC
Indiana U. Sch. of Medicine ... IN
Johns Hopkins U ... MD
Kansas, U. of, Med. Ctr ... KS
Louisiana State U. Med. Ctr ... LA
Louisville, U. of ... KY
Miami, U. of ... FL
Michigan, U. of ... MI
Mississippi, U. of ... MS
Missouri, U. of ... MO
New Jersey Coll. of Medicine and Dentistry (Newark) ... NJ
North Carolina, U. of ... NC
North Dakota, U. of, Sch. of Med ... ND
Oklahoma, U. of ... OK
Pennsylvania, U. of ... PA
Puerto Rico, U. of ... PR
South Alabama, U. of ... AL
South Carolina, Med. U. of ... SC
Southern California, U. of ... CA
State U. of New York (Upstate Med. Ctr.) ... NY
Tennessee, U. of ... TN
Texas, U. of (Houston) ... TX
Thomas Jefferson U ... PA
Vermont, U. of ... VT
Virginia, U. of, Med. Ctr ... VA
Virginia Commonwealth U ... VA
Washington, U. of ... WA
Wayne State U ... MI
Wisconsin, U. of (Madison) ... WI

Dairy Science

Institutions awarding 4 or more undergraduate degrees as major field in single year according to U.S. Office of Education latest statistics

California Poly. State Coll. (San Luis Obispo) ... CA
Delaware Valley Coll ... PA
Florida, U. of ... FL
Georgia, U. of ... GA
Illinois, U. of ... IL
Iowa State U ... IA
Kansas State U ... KS
Louisiana State U. (Baton Rouge) ... LA
Michigan State U ... MI
Mississippi State U ... MS
Missouri, U. of ... MO
Ohio State U ... OH
Pennsylvania State U ... PA
South Dakota State ... SD
Texas A&M U ... TX
Vermont, U. of ... VT
Virginia Poly. Inst ... VA
Wisconsin, U. of (Madison) ... WI

Dance

Undergraduate degree programs according to National Dance Assn.

Adelphi U ... NY
Akron, U. of ... OH
Alabama, U. of (Birmingham) ... AL
American U ... DC
Amherst Coll ... MA
Arizona, U. of ... AZ
Arizona State U ... AZ
Arkansas, U. of ... AR
Auburn U ... AL
Baldwin-Wallace Coll ... OH
Barat Coll ... IL
Bard Coll ... NY
Barnard Coll ... NY
Bennett Coll ... NC
Bennington Coll ... VT
Boston Cons. of Music ... MA
Bowling Green State U ... OH
Brenau Coll ... GA
Bridgeport, U. of ... CT
Brigham Young U ... UT
Brooklyn Coll ... NY
Butler U ... IN
California, U. of (Irvine, Los Angeles, Riverside, Santa Barbara, Santa Cruz) ... CA
California State U. (Chico, Fresno, Hayward, Long Beach, Los Angeles, Sacramento) ... CA
Castleton State Coll ... VT
Centenary Coll ... NJ
Central Washington U ... WA
Chapman Coll ... CA
Cincinnati, U. of ... OH
City Coll. of CUNY ... NY
Cleveland State U ... OH
Coker Coll ... SC
Colby-Sawyer ... NH
Colorado, U. of ... CO
Colorado Coll ... CO
Colorado Mountain Coll ... CO
Colorado State U ... CO
Columbia Coll ... IL
Columbia Coll ... SC
Connecticut Coll ... CT
Cornell U ... NY
Cornish Inst. of Allied Art ... WA
Creighton U ... NE
Dean Jr. Coll ... MA
Denison U ... OH
Dominican Coll. of San Rafael ... CA
Douglass Coll ... NJ
East Carolina U ... NC
East Stroudsburg State Coll ... PA
Eastern Kentucky U ... KY
Eastern Michigan U ... MI
Eastern Washington U ... WA
El Centro Coll ... TX
Florida, U. of ... FL
Florida State U ... FL
Furman U ... SC
George Mason U ... VA
George Washington U ... DC
Georgia, U. of ... GA
Georgia State U ... GA
Glassboro State Coll ... NJ
Goucher Coll ... MD
Hamilton Coll ... NY
Hampshire Coll ... MA
Harcum Jr. Coll ... PA
Hawaii, U. of ... HI
Herbert H. Lehman of CUNY ... NY
Hofstra U ... NY
Hollins Coll ... VA
Hope Coll ... MI
Hunter Coll. of CUNY ... NY
Idaho, U. of ... ID
Illinois, U. of ... IL
Illinois Central Coll ... IL
Illinois State U ... IL
Indiana State U ... IN
Indiana U ... IN
Iowa, U. of ... IA
Iowa State ... IA
Jacksonville U ... FL
James Madison U ... VA
Johnson State Coll ... VT
Juilliard School ... NY
Kansas, U. of ... KS
Kansas State U ... KS
Kearney State ... NE
Kent State U ... OH
Kentucky, U. of ... KY
Lake Erie Coll ... OH
Lamar U ... TX
Lincoln Coll ... IL
Lindenwood Colleges ... MO
Loretto Heights Coll ... CO
Loyola Marymount U ... CA
Mankato State U ... MN
Marlboro Coll ... VT
Mars Hill Coll ... NC
Mary Washington Coll ... VA
Marygrove Coll ... MI
Maryland, U. of ... MD
Marymount Manhattan Coll ... NY
Massachusetts, U. of ... MA
Mercyhurst Coll ... PA
Mesa Coll ... CO
Miami, U. of ... FL
Miami U ... OH
Michigan, U. of ... MI
Michigan State U ... MI
Middle Tennessee State U ... TN
Mills Coll ... CA
Minnesota, U. of ... MN
Missouri, U. of (Columbia, Kansas City) ... MO
Montana, U. of ... MT
Montclair State ... NJ
Mount Holyoke Coll ... MA
Nebraska, U. of ... NE
Nevada, U. of ... NV
New Hampshire, U. of ... NH
New Mexico, U. of ... NM
New York U ... NY
North Carolina, U. of (Charlotte, Greensboro) ... NC
North Carolina Sch. of the Arts ... NC
North Texas State U ... TX
Northeastern U ... MA
Northern Arizona U ... AZ
Northern Colorado, U. of ... CO
Northern Illinois U ... IL
Northwest Missouri State U ... MO
Northwestern State U. of Louisiana ... LA
Northwestern U ... IL
Oakland U ... MI
Oberlin Coll ... OH
Ohio State U ... OH
Ohio U ... OH
Oklahoma, U. of ... OK
Old Dominion ... VA
Oregon, U. of ... OR
Oregon State U ... OR
Pacific, U. of the ... CA
Pennsylvania State U ... PA
Pittsburgh, U. of ... PA
Point Park Coll ... PA
Purdue U ... IN
Radford Coll ... VA
Randolph-Macon Woman's ... VA
Reed Coll ... OR
Rockford Coll ... IL
Russell Sage Coll ... NY
Saint Leo Coll ... FL
Saint Teresa, Coll. of ... MN
Sam Houston State U ... TX
San Diego State U ... CA
San Francisco State U ... CA
San Jose State U ... CA
Santa Clara, U. of ... CA
Santa Fe, Coll. of ... NM
Sarah Lawrence Coll ... NY
Scripps Coll ... CA
Shenandoah Coll. & Cons. of Mus ... VA
Skidmore Coll ... NY
Snow Coll ... UT
South Dakota, U. of ... SD
South Florida, U. of ... FL
Southeastern Louisiana U ... LA
Southern Connecticut State Coll ... CT
Southern Methodist U ... TX
Southwest Missouri State U ... MO
Southwest State U ... MN
Southwest Texas State U ... TX
Spelman Coll ... GA
St. Gregory's ... OK
St. Joseph Coll ... CT
St. Mary Coll ... KS
St. Olaf Coll ... MN
State U. of New York (Brockport, Geneseo, Potsdam) ... NY
Stephens Coll ... MO
Temple U ... PA
Tennessee, U. of ... TN
Texas, U. of ... TX
Texas Christian U ... TX
Texas Tech. U ... TX
Texas Woman's U ... TX
Toledo, U. of ... OH
Towson State U ... MD
Tufts U ... MA
U.S. International U ... CA
Utah, U. of ... UT
Utah State U ... UT
Vanderbilt U ... TN
Virginia Intermont Coll ... VA
Washington, U. of ... WA
Washington Coll ... MD
Washington State U ... WA
Washington U ... MO
Wayne State U ... MI
Webster Coll ... MO
Wesleyan U ... CT
West Chester State Coll ... PA
Western Michigan U ... MI
Western Washington U ... WA
Wichita State U ... KS
William Paterson Coll. of New Jersey ... NJ
William Woods Coll ... MO
Winthrop Coll ... SC
Wisconsin, U. of (Green Bay, Madison, Milwaukee, Stevens Point) ... WI
Wittenberg U ... OH
Wright State U ... OH
Wyoming, U. of ... WY

Dance Therapy

★Approved grad. program
•Graduate program according to American Dance Therapy Assn.

★Antioch U ... NH
Barat ... IL
★California, U. of (Los Angeles) ... CA
Columbia Coll ... IL
•Goucher Coll ... MD
★Hahnemann Medical Coll ... PA
★Hunter Coll ... NY
•John F. Kennedy U ... CA
★Loyola Marymount U ... CA
Marygrove Coll ... MI
Marywood ... PA
★New York U ... NY
Pacific, U. of the ... CA
•Pratt Institute ... NY
Russell Sage Coll ... NY
St. Teresa, Coll. of ... MN
Wisconsin, U of (Madison) ... WI

Deaf and Hard of Hearing, Preparation for Teaching of

Akron, U. of ... OH
Atlantic Christian ... NC
Augustana Coll ... SD
Baruch Coll ... NY

Baylor U .... TX
Bowling Green .... OH
Bridgewater State .... MA
California, U. of (Santa Barbara) .... CA
California State Coll .... PA
California State U. (Los Angeles) .... CA
Calvin Coll .... MI
Central Missouri .... MO
Central State U .... OK
Converse Coll .... SC
C.W. Post Ctr. (Long Island U.) . NY
Eastern Kentucky U .... KY
Eastern Montana .... MT
Emerson Coll .... MA
Flagler Coll .... FL
Florida State U .... FL
Fontbonne Coll .... MO
Georgia State U .... GA
Goddard Coll .... VT
Huntingdon Coll .... AL
Iowa, U. of .... IA
James Madison U .... VA
John Carroll U .... OH
Kansas, U. of .... KS
Kent State .... OH
Lamar U .... TX
Lenoir-Rhyne Coll .... NC
Louisiana Tech .... LA
Marymount Manhattan Coll ..... NY
Marywood .... PA
Mercy Coll .... NY
Michigan State U .... MI
Mississippi Coll .... MS
Missouri, U. of .... MO
Mount St. Joseph, Coll. of ..... OH
New York U .... NY
North Carolina, U. of (Greensboro) .... NC
North Florida, U. of .... FL
Northern Arizona .... AZ
Northwestern State U .... LA
Ohio U .... OH
Old Dominion U .... VA
Pennsylvania State U. (Allentown, Behrend, Shenango) .... PA
Purdue U .... IN
Saint Rose, Coll. of .... NY
Shepherd Coll .... WV
South Dakota, U. of .... SD
South Florida, U. of .... FL
Southwestern Jr. Coll .... TX
State U. of New York Coll. (New Paltz) .... NY
Stephen F. Austin .... TX
Syracuse U .... NY
Tennessee, U. of .... TN
Texas, U. of (El Paso) .... TX
Texas Woman's U .... TX
Toledo .... OH
Trenton State .... NJ
Trevecca Nazarene .... TN
Tulsa, U. of .... OK
Utah State .... UT
Western Maryland .... MD
William Woods .... MO
Wisconsin, U. of (Milwaukee) ... WI

Dental Assistant

Accredited by Commission on Dental Accreditation of the American Dental Association

Alabama, U. of .... AL
Alamance, Tech. Coll. of ...... NC
Alameda, Coll. of .... CA
Albert I. Prince .... CT
Allan Hancock Coll .... CA
Allegany Comm .... MD
Amarillo Coll .... TX
Anchorage Comm. Coll .... AK
Andon Coll .... CA
Asheville-Buncombe Tech. Inst NC
Assabet Valley .... MA
Atlanta Area Tech. Sch .... GA
Augusta Area Voc.-Tech. Sch .. GA
Aurora P.S. Tech. Cent .... CO
Bakersfield Coll .... CA
Baltimore, Comm. Coll. of ..... MD
Bangor Comm. Coll .... ME
Bemidji Voc.-Tech .... MN
Bessemer State Tech. Coll ...... AL
Bellingham Voc.-Tech .... WA
Black Hawk IL
Blackhawk Tech .... WI
Blue Hills Reg. Tech. Inst ...... MA
Blue Mountain .... OR
Boise State .... ID
Boston U .... MA
Bowling Green Voc.-Tech ...... KY
Brainerd Area .... MN
Bervard Comm. Coll .... FL
Briarwood Coll .... CT
Broward Comm .... FL
Cabrillo Coll .... CA
California, U. of .... CA
Camden Co .... NJ
Canby Area Voc.-Tech .... MN
Central City Occ. Center .... CA
Central Piedmont Comm ...... NC
Central Tech. Comm. Coll ...... NE
Cerritos .... CA
Chabot .... CA
Chaffey Comm. Coll .... CA
Champlain Coll .... VT
Charles H. McCann Tech. Sch . MA
Chattanooga State .... TN
Chemeketa Comm .... OR
Citrus Coll .... CA
Clover Park Voc .... WA
Coastal Carolina Comm. Coll .. NC
Contra Costa Coll .... CA
Cotton Boll Voc .... AR
Council Trenholm State Tech. Coll .... AL
Cypress Coll .... CA
Daytona Beach .... FL
Del Mar Coll .... TX
Delaware Tech. and Comm. Coll .... DE
Delta .... MI
Denver Comm. Coll .... CO
Des Moines Area Comm. Coll ... IA
Diablo Valley .... CA
Diman Reg. Tech. Inst .... MA
Dutchess Comm. Coll .... NY
East Central Missouri Coll ..... MO
East Los Angeles Occ. Cent .... CA
East Tennessee State .... TN
Eastern Idaho .... ID
Edmonds Comm. Coll .... WA
El Centro Coll .... TX
El Paso Comm. Coll .... CO
Elgin Comm. Coll IL
Eli Whitney .... CT
Emily Griffith Sch .... CO
Essex Comm. Coll .... MD
Fayetteville Tech .... NC
Ferris State .... MI
Flint Hills Area Voc. Tech. Sch .. KS
Florence-Darlington .... SC
Florida Jr. Coll .... FL
Foothill Coll .... CA
Fox Valley Tech .... WI
Frederick Comm. Coll .... MD
Gateway Tech. Inst .... WI
Graff Area Voc. Tech. Ctr ...... MO
Grand Rapids Jr .... MI
Grayson Co .... TX
Great Falls Voc.-Tech .... MT
Greater Lawrence Reg .... MA
Green Mountain Coll .... VT
Greenville Tech. Comm .... SC
Guilford Tech. Inst .... NC
Gulf Coast Comm .... FL
Harcum Jr. Coll .... PA
Haskell Indian Jr .... KS
Hawkeye Inst. of Tech .... IA
Hennepin Tech. Center .... MN
Hibbing Area Tech. Inst .... MN
Highline Comm. Coll .... WA
Hinds Jr. Coll .... MS
Hudson Valley .... NY
Huston Comm. Coll .... TX
Illinois Central IL
Illinois Valley IL
Indian River Comm. Coll .... FL
Indiana State U .... IN
Indiana U .... IN
Indiana Voc.-Tech. (Lafayette) .. IN
Iowa Central .... IA
Iowa Western Comm .... IA
J. M. Wright Voc. Tech. Inst .... CT
J. Sargeant Reynolds Comm .... VA
James Faulkner Jr. Coll .... AL
Jane Adams School .... OH
Jefferson State Voc.-Tech ...... KY
Jefferson Tech. Coll .... OH
John A. Logan IL
John C. Calhoun Comm .... AL
Kapiolani Comm. Coll .... HI
Kaskaskia Comm. Coll IL
Kellogg Comm .... MI
Kings River Coll .... CA
Kinman Business U .... WA
Kirkwood Comm .... IA
Lake Area Voc. Tech .... SD
Lake County, Coll. of IL
Lake Land Coll IL
Lakeland Medical-Dental ...... MN
Lake Michigan Coll .... MI
Lakeshore Tech. Inst .... WI
Lane Comm .... OR
Lansing Comm. Coll .... MI
La Puente Valley .... CA
Larimer Co .... CO
Lehigh Co. Comm. Coll .... PA
Lewis and Clark IL
Lincoln Land IL
Lindsey Hopkins Tech .... FL
Linn Benton Comm. Coll ...... OR
Loma Linda U .... CA
Loop Coll IL
Los Angeles City Coll .... CA
Louisiana State U .... LA
Louisville, U. of .... KY
Luzerne County Coll .... PA
Macomb Co. Comm .... MI
Madison Area Tech. Coll .... WI
Manatee Area Voc.-Tech .... FL
Mankato State U .... MN
Manor Jr. Coll .... PA
Margaret Murray Washington .. DC
Maricopa Tech. Coll .... AZ
Marin, Coll. of .... CA
Marshalltown Comm .... IA
McDuffie Voc. Sch .... PA
Median Sch. of Allied H .... PA
Memphis Area Voc. Tech. Sch .. TN
Merced Comm. Coll .... CA
Mercer Co .... NJ
Mercyhurst Coll .... PA
Mesa Coll .... CO
Metropolitan Tech .... NE
Middlesex Comm .... MA
Middlesex Comm .... NJ
Midlands Tech. Coll .... SC
Mid-Plains Comm. Coll .... NE
Milwaukee Area Tech .... WI
Mineral Area Coll .... MO
Minneapolis Tech. Inst .... MN
Minnesota Institute of Medical & Dental Assts .... MN
Missouri Southern .... MO
Modesto Jr. Coll .... CA
Monterey Peninsula .... CA
Montgomery Comm .... MD
Moorhead Area Voc.-Tech ..... MN
Morris, County Coll. of .... NJ
Morton IL
Mott Comm. Coll .... MI
Mt. Ida Jr. Coll .... MA
Muskegon Comm .... MI
Muskingum Area Tech .... OH
Murrell Dobbins Area Voc.-Tech .... PA
National School of Health Tech .... PA
New Hampshire Tech. Inst ..... NH
New Jersey Coll. of Medicine and Dentistry (Newark) .... NJ
New Mexico, U. of .... NM
New York U .... NY
Niagara County Comm .... NY
Nichols Career Center .... MO
916 Area Voc. Tech. Inst .... MN
Normandale Comm. Coll ...... MN
North Carolina, U. of .... NC
North Dakota State Sch. of Science .... ND
North Valley Occ. Center .... CA
Northampton Co. Area Comm. Coll .... PA
Northeast Iowa Tech .... IA
Northeast Metropolitan Regional .... MA
Northeast Wisconsin Tech. Inst . WI
Northeastern-Tufts U .... MA
Northern Virginia Comm. Coll .. VA
Northwestern Michigan Coll .... MI
Oakland Comm .... MI
Old Dominion U .... VA
Olney Central Coll IL
Olympia Comm. Coll .... WA
Omaha Coll. of Health Careers .. NE
Orange Coast Coll .... CA
Orlando Voc .... FL
Oscar Rose Jr. Coll .... OK
Oregon Inst. of Tech .... OR
Palm Beach Jr. Coll .... FL
Palomar Coll .... CA
Parkland Coll IL
Pasadena City College .... CA
Penn Valley Comm. Coll .... MO
Pensacola Jr. Coll .... FL
Philadelphia, C. Coll. of .... PA
Pikes Peak Comm. Coll .... CO
Pima Comm .... AZ
Pittsburgh, U. of .... PA
Portland Comm. Coll .... OR
Prairie State IL
Prince George's Comm. Coll ... MD
Professional Careers Inst IL
Puerto Rico, U. of .... PR
Pulaski Voc .... AR
Quincy Jr. Coll .... MA
Redwoods, Coll. of the .... CA
Rhode Island Comm. Coll ...... RI
Rio Hondo Coll .... CA
Robert Morris IL
Rochester Area Voc.-Tech. Inst .... MN
Rock Valley Coll IL
Rockland Comm. Coll .... NY
Rowan Tech .... NC
Sacramento City Coll .... CA
San Antonio Coll .... TX
San Diego Mesa .... CA
San Francisco, City Coll. of ..... CA
San Jose City Coll .... CA
San Mateo, Coll. of .... CA
Santa Barbara Coll .... CA
Santa Fe Comm .... FL
Santa Rosa Jr. Coll .... CA
Seattle Central C. Coll .... WA
Shaw .... MI
Sheridan Coll .... WY
Simi Valley Sch .... CA
South Carolina, Med. U. of ...... SC
Southeast Comm. Coll .... NE
Southeastern Tech .... MA
Southern Arkansas U .... AR
Southern Coll .... FL

Spartanburg Tech. Coll . . . . SC
Spokane Comm . . . . WA
Springfield Tech. Comm. Coll . . MA
St. Cloud Area Voc. Tech. Inst . MN
St. Louis Comm. Coll. (Forest Park, Meramec) . . . . MO
St. Petersburg . . . . FL
State U. of NY . . . . NY
Suffolk County C. Coll . . . . NY
Tarrant Co. Jr. Coll . . . . TX
Texas, U. of (Houston, San Antonio) . . . . TX
Texas State Tech. Inst . . . . TX
Three Rivers Comm. Coll . . . . . . MO
Triton Coll IL
Truckee Meadows . . . . NV
Tunxis Comm. Coll . . . . CT
Union County Tech . . . . NJ
Utah Tech . . . . UT
Virginia Western Comm. Coll . . . VA
Volunteer State Comm. Coll . . . . TN
Wallace State Comm. Coll . . . . . . AL
Washtenaw Comm . . . . MI
Watterson Coll . . . . KY
Wayne Comm. Coll . . . . NC
West Kentucky State . . . . KY
Western Iowa Tech . . . . IA
Western Piedmont . . . . NC
Western Wisconsin Tech. Inst . . . WI
Wichita Area Voc.-Tech . . . . KS
Windham Sch . . . . CT
Wytheville Comm. Coll . . . . VA
York Tech. Coll . . . . SC

Dental Hygienist

Accredited by Commission on Dental Accreditation of the American Dental Association

Alabama, U. of . . . . AL
Albany Jr. Coll . . . . GA
Allegany Comm. Coll . . . . MD
Amarillo Coll . . . . TX
Anchorage Comm. Coll . . . . AK
Arkansas, U. of . . . . AR
Armstrong State Coll . . . . GA
Asheville-Buncombe . . . . NC
Baltimore, Comm. Coll. of . . . . . MD
Baylor . . . . TX
Bee Co . . . . TX
Bergen Comm . . . . NJ
Bridgeport, U. of . . . . CT
Bristol Comm. Coll . . . . MA
Broome Comm . . . . NY
Cabrillo Coll . . . . CA
California, U. of (San Francisco) . . . . CA
Camden City Coll . . . . NJ
Cape Cod Comm. Coll . . . . MA
Carroll Coll . . . . MT
Central Piedmont Comm. Coll . NC
Central Tech. C. Coll . . . . NE
Cerritos Coll . . . . CA
Chabot Coll . . . . CA
Charles S. Mott Comm. Coll . . . . MI
Chattanooga State Tech . . . . TN
Cincinnati, U. of . . . . OH
Clark Coll . . . . WA
Clark Co. Comm. Coll . . . . NV
Clayton Jr. Coll . . . . GA
Coastal Carolina . . . . NC
Colorado, U. of . . . . CO
Colorado Northwestern Comm. Coll . . . . CO
Columbia . . . . NY
Columbus Coll . . . . GA
Cuyahoga Comm. Coll . . . . OH
Cypress Coll . . . . CA
DeKalb Comm. Coll . . . . GA
Del Mar Coll . . . . TX
Delaware Tech. and Comm. Coll . . . . DE
Delta Coll . . . . MI
Des Moines Area (Ankeny) . . . . . IA
Detroit, U. of . . . . MI
Diablo Valley . . . . CA
East Tennessee State U . . . . TN
Eastern Washington U . . . . WA
El Paso Comm . . . . TX
Erie Comm . . . . NY
Eugenio Maria de Hostos . . . . NY
Fairleigh Dickinson . . . . NJ
Fayetteville Tech. Inst . . . . NC
Ferris State . . . . MI
Florence-Darlington Tech. Coll . . . . SC
Florida Jr. Coll . . . . FL
Foothill Coll . . . . CA
Forsyth School . . . . MA
Fort Steilacoom Comm. Coll . . . WA
Fresno City . . . . CA
Georgia, Medical Coll. of . . . . . . GA
Grand Rapids Jr. Coll . . . . MI
Greenville Tech. Coll . . . . SC
Guilford Tech. Inst . . . . NC
Harper Coll IL
Hawaii, U. of . . . . HI
Hawkeye Inst. of Tech . . . . IA
Howard . . . . DC
Hudson Valley Comm . . . . NY
Idaho State . . . . ID
Illinois Central Coll IL
Indiana State U . . . . IN
Indiana U. (Fort Wayne, Indianapolis, Northwest, South Bend) . . . . IN
Iowa, U. of . . . . IA
Johnson Co. Comm . . . . KS
Kalamazoo Valley . . . . MI
Kellogg Comm. Coll . . . . MI
Kentucky, U. of (Comm. Coll. Sys.) . . . . KY
Lake Land Coll IL
Lakeland Comm . . . . OH
Lamar U . . . . TX
Lane Comm. Coll . . . . OR
Lansing Comm. Coll . . . . MI
Lima Tech. Coll . . . . OH
Loma Linda U . . . . CA
Louisiana State U . . . . LA
Louisville, U. of . . . . KY
Loyola U IL
Loyola U . . . . LA
Luzerne County C. Coll . . . . PA
Macon Jr. Coll . . . . GA
Madison Area Tech. Coll . . . . WI
Maine, U. of (Orono) . . . . ME
Mankato State U . . . . MN
Marquette . . . . WI
Maryland, U. of . . . . MD
Meridian Jr. Coll . . . . MS
Miami-Dade Comm. Coll . . . . FL
Michael J. Owens Tech . . . . OH
Michigan, U. of . . . . MI
Middlesex Comm. Coll . . . . MA
Middlesex Co. Coll . . . . NJ
Midlands Tech. Coll . . . . SC
Midwestern U . . . . TX
Milwaukee Area Tech . . . . WI
Minnesota, U. of . . . . MN
Mississippi, U. of . . . . MS
Missouri, U. of (Kansas City) . . MO
Missouri Southern State . . . . MO
Monroe Comm . . . . NY
Montgomery Co. Comm . . . . PA
Mt. Hood Comm. Coll . . . . OR
Nebraska, U. of . . . . NE
New Hampshire Tech. (Concord) . . . . NH
New Jersey Coll. of Medicine and Dentistry (Newark) . . . . NJ
New Mexico, U. of . . . . NM
New York City Comm . . . . NY
Normandale Comm. Coll . . . . . . MN
North Carolina, U. of . . . . NC
North Central Tech. Inst . . . . WI
North Dakota State Sch. of Science . . . . ND
Northampton County Area Comm . . . . PA
Northeast Louisiana U . . . . LA
Northeast Mississippi Jr. Coll . . . . MS
Northeast Wisconsin Tech. Inst . . . . WI
Northern Arizona U . . . . AZ
Northern Virginia C. Coll . . . . . . VA
Northwestern IL
Oakland Comm. Coll . . . . MI
Ohio State U . . . . OH
Oklahoma, U. of . . . . OK
Old Dominion U . . . . VA
Onondaga Comm. Coll . . . . NY
Orange Co. Comm . . . . NY
Oregon, U. of . . . . OR
Oregon Inst. of Tech . . . . OR
Oscar Rose Jr . . . . OK
Palm Beach Jr. Coll . . . . FL
Parkland Coll IL
Pasadena City Coll . . . . CA
Pennsylvania, U. of . . . . PA
Pensacola Jr. Coll . . . . FL
Philadelphia, C. Coll. of . . . . PA
Phoenix Coll . . . . AZ
Pittsburgh, U. of . . . . PA
Portland Comm. Coll . . . . OR
Prairie State IL
Pueblo Voc. C. Coll . . . . CO
Puerto Rico, U. of . . . . PR
Quinsigamond Comm. Coll . . . . MA
Rhode Island, U. of . . . . RI
Sacramento City Coll . . . . CA
Santa Fe Comm. Coll . . . . FL
Shawnee State . . . . OH
Sheridan Coll . . . . WY
Shoreline Comm. Coll . . . . WA
Sinclair Comm . . . . OH
South Carolina, Med. U. of . . . . . SC
South Dakota, U. of . . . . SD
Southern California, U. of . . . . . CA
Southern Illinois IL
Springfield Tech. Comm. Coll . . . . MA
St. Louis Comm. Coll . . . . MO
St. Petersburg Jr . . . . FL
State U. of New York (Farmingdale) . . . . NY
Tallahassee C. Coll . . . . FL
Tarrant Co. Jr. Coll . . . . TX
Temple . . . . PA
Tennessee, U. of . . . . TN
Tennessee State . . . . TN
Texas, U. of (Houston, San Antonio) . . . . TX
Texas Woman's U . . . . TX
Thomas Jefferson U . . . . PA
Tunxis Comm. Coll . . . . CT
Tyler Jr. Coll . . . . TX
Union County Tech . . . . NJ
Valencia C. Coll . . . . FL
Vermont, U. of . . . . VT
Virginia Commonwealth U . . . . . . VA
Virginia Western Comm. Coll . . . . VA
Washington, U. of . . . . WA
Wayne Comm . . . . NC
Weber State . . . . UT
West Liberty State . . . . WV
West Los Angeles Coll . . . . CA
West Virginia Inst. of Tech . . . . . WV
West Virginia U . . . . WV
Westbrook Coll . . . . ME
Western Kentucky U . . . . KY
Wharton Co. Jr. Coll . . . . TX
Wichita State U . . . . KS
Williamsport Area C. Coll . . . . . . PA
Yakima Valley Coll . . . . WA
Youngstown State U . . . . OH

Dental Laboratory Technician

Accredited by Commission on Dental Accreditation of the American Dental Association

Alabama, U. of . . . . AL
Atlanta Area Tech. Sch . . . . GA
Atlanta Coll. of Med. and Dental Car . . . . GA
Augusta Area Tech . . . . GA
Baltimore, Comm. Coll. of . . . . . MD
Bates Voc. Tech. Inst . . . . WA
Central Tech. Comm. Coll . . . . . . NE
Cleveland State C. Coll . . . . TN
Columbus Tech. Inst . . . . OH
Diablo Valley Coll . . . . CA
Dutchess Comm. Coll . . . . NY
Durham Tech. Inst . . . . NC
East Tennessee State U . . . . TN
Edinboro St. Coll . . . . PA
Ferris State . . . . MI
Grand Rapids Jr. Coll . . . . MI
Greenville Tech. Coll . . . . SC
Indian River Comm. C . . . . FL
Indiana U. (Evansville, Fort Wayne) . . . . IN
J. Sargeant Reynolds Comm . . . . VA
Kirkwood Comm. Coll . . . . IA
Lake Area Voc.-Tech. Sch . . . . . . SD
Lewis and Clark IL
Lexington Tech. Inst . . . . KY
Louisiana State U . . . . LA
Los Angeles City C . . . . CA
Merced Coll . . . . CA
Mastbaum Area Voc. Tech . . . . . . PA
Middlesex Comm. Coll . . . . MA
Milwaukee Area Tech. Coll . . . . . WI
Montgomery Coll . . . . MD
New York City Tech. Coll . . . . NY
916 Area Voc.-Tech. Inst . . . . . . MN
Northern Virginia Comm . . . . VA
Oscar Rose Jr. Coll . . . . OK
Orange Coast Coll . . . . CA
Palm Beach Jr. Coll . . . . FL
Pasadena City C . . . . CA
Pensacola Jr. Coll . . . . FL
Pima Comm. Coll . . . . AZ
Quincy Voc.-Tech. Sch . . . . MA
Riverside City C . . . . CA
San Francisco, City C. of . . . . CA
Seattle Central Comm. C . . . . . . WA
Southern Coll . . . . FL
Southern Illinois U IL
St. Lewis Comm . . . . MO
Suburban Hennepin Area Voc. Tech. Inst . . . . MN
Texas, U. of (San Antonio) . . . . . . TX
Texas State Tech. Inst . . . . TX
Trident Tech. Coll . . . . SC
Triton Coll IL
Union Co. Tech. Inst . . . . NJ

Dental Schools

Accredited by Commission on Dental Accreditation of the American Dental Association
•Conditional Approval
★Provisional Approval

Alabama, U. of . . . . AL
Baylor . . . . TX
Boston U . . . . MA
California, U. of (Los Angeles, San Francisco) . . . . CA
Case Western Reserve . . . . OH
Colorado, U. of . . . . CO
Columbia . . . . NY
Connecticut, U. of . . . . CT
Creighton . . . . NE
★Detroit, U. of . . . . MI

Emory .... GA
Fairleigh Dickinson U .... NJ
Florida, U. of .... FL
Georgetown .... DC
Georgia, Med. Coll. of .... GA
Harvard .... MA
Howard .... DC
Illinois, U. of IL
Indiana U .... IN
Iowa, U. of .... IA
Kentucky, U. of .... KY
Loma Linda U .... CA
Louisiana State U .... LA
Louisville, U. of .... KY
Loyola IL
Marquette .... WI
Maryland, U. of .... MD
★Meharry Med. Coll .... TN
Michigan, U. of .... MI
Minnesota, U. of .... MN
Mississippi, U. of .... MS
Missouri, U. of (Kansas City) .. MO
Nebraska, U. of .... NE
New Jersey Coll. of Medicine & Dentistry (Newark) .... NJ
New York U .... NY
North Carolina, U. of .... NC
Northwestern IL
Ohio State U .... OH
Oklahoma, U. of .... OK
Oregon, U. of .... OR
Pacific, U. of the .... CA
Pennsylvania, U. of the .... PA
Pittsburgh, U. of .... PA
Puerto Rico, U. of .... PR
South Carolina, U. of .... SC
•Southern California, U. of .... CA
Southern Illinois IL
•State U. of New York (Buffalo) .. NY
State U. of New York (Stony Brook) .... NY
•Temple .... PA
Tennessee, U. of .... TN
Texas, U. of (Houston, San Antonio) .... TX
Tufts .... MA
Virginia Commonwealth U ...... VA
•Washington, U. of .... WA
Washington U .... MO
West Virginia U .... WV

Dental Schools—Accelerated Programs

•Indicates program available only to the University's undergraduates

•Case Western Reserve .... OH
Florida, U. of .... FL
•Howard .... DC
Lehigh U .... PA
Pacific, U. of the .... CA
Pennsylvania, U. of .... PA
Pittsburgh, U. of .... PA
Rensselaer Inst .... NY
•South Carolina, U. of .... SC

Diesel Mechanics and/or Technology

Alfred State .... NY
Barton Co. Comm. Coll .... KS
Bob Jones U .... SC
Casper Coll .... WY
Central Arizona Coll .... AZ
Central Missouri .... MO
Eastern Arizona .... AZ
Florida Inst. of Tech.—Sch. of App. Tech .... FL
Fort Scott Comm. C .... KS
Hawaii, U. of (Hilo) .... HI
Howard Co. Jr. Coll .... TX
Hutchinson Comm. C .... KS
Illinois Central Coll IL
Kansas, U. of .... KS
Kirkwood Comm .... IA
Lamar U .... TX
Mississippi Delta Jr. Coll ...... MS
Missouri, U. of .... MO
North Idaho Coll .... ID
Northeast Mississippi Jr .... MS
Northern Iowa, U. of .... IA
Northern Montana .... MT
Oregon Inst. of Tech .... OR
Pearl River Jr .... MS
Pittsburg State .... KS
Pratt Comm. Coll .... KS
Sheridan Coll .... WY
South Dakota, U. of (Springfield) .... SD
Trinidad State Jr .... CO
Yakima Valley Comm. Coll ..... WA

Dietetics

Baccalaureate degree programs approved by the American Dietetic Association

Abilene Christian U .... TX
Akron, U. of .... OH
Alabama, U. of .... AL
Alabama A&M .... AL
Albertus Magnus Coll .... CT
Albright Coll .... PA
Andrews U .... MI
Appalachian State U .... NC
Arizona, U. of .... AZ
Arizona State U .... AZ
Arkansas, U. of .... AR
Atlantic Union Coll .... MA
Auburn U .... AL
Ball State U .... IN
Benedictine Coll .... KS
Berea .... KY
Bowling Green .... OH
Bradley U IL
Brigham Young .... UT
Brooklyn Coll .... NY
California, U. of (Berkeley, Davis) .... CA
California Poly. State U .... CA
California State Poly. U .... CA
California State U. (Chico, Fresno, Long Beach, Los Angeles, Northridge) .... CA
Cardinal Stritch Coll .... WI
Carson-Newman .... TN
Case Western Reserve U ...... OH
Central Michigan U .... MI
Central Missouri .... MO
Central Washington U .... WA
Cheyney State Coll .... PA
Chicago State U IL
Cincinnati, U. of .... OH
Clark Coll .... GA
Colorado State U .... CO
Concordia Coll .... MN
Connecticut, U. of .... CT
Cornell .... NY
David Lipscomb Coll .... TN
Dayton, U. of .... OH
Delaware, U. of .... DE
Douglass .... NJ
Drexel U .... PA
Drury Coll .... MO
East Carolina U .... NC
East Tennessee State U .... TN
East Texas State U .... TX
Eastern Illinois U IL
Eastern Kentucky U .... KY
Eastern Mennonite Coll .... PA
Eastern Michigan U .... MI
Edinboro State Coll .... PA
Florida, U. of .... FL
Florida A&M .... FL
Florida International U .... FL
Florida State U .... FL
Fontbonne Coll .... MO
Fort Hays Kansas State U ...... KS
Fort Valley St. Coll .... GA
Framingham State Coll .... MA
Georgia, U. of .... GA
Georgia Coll .... GA
Georgia Southern .... GA
Georgia State U .... GA
Grambling Coll .... LA
Hampton U .... VA
Harding U .... AR
Hawaii, U. of (Manoa) .... HI
Hood .... MD
Houston, U. of .... TX
Howard U .... DC
Hunter Coll .... NY
Idaho, U. of .... ID
Idaho State U .... ID
Illinois, U. of IL
Illinois Benedictine Coll IL
Illinois State U IL
Immaculata .... PA
Incarnate Word .... TX
Indiana State U .... IN
Indiana U. of Pennsylvania ...... PA
Iowa, U. of .... IA
Iowa State U .... IA
Iowa Wesleyan Coll .... IA
Jacksonville State U .... AL
James Madison U .... VA
Kansas State U .... KS
Kearney State .... NE
Keene State .... NH
Kent State U .... OH
Kentucky, U. of .... KY
Kentucky State U .... KY
Lamar U .... TX
Lehman Coll .... NY
Lincoln U .... MO
Louisiana State U .... LA
Louisiana Tech. U .... LA
Louisville, U. of .... KY
Loma Linda U .... CA
Madonna Coll .... MI
Maine, U. of .... ME
Mankato State U .... MN
Mansfield State Coll .... PA
Marian .... IN
Marshall U .... WV
Mary Hardin-Baylor Coll .... TX
Marycrest .... IA
Marygrove Coll .... MI
Maryland, U. of (College Park and Eastern Shore) .... MD
Marymount .... NY
Marywood Coll .... PA
Massachusetts, U. of .... MA
Mercy Coll. of Detroit .... MI
Mercyhurst Coll .... PA
Memphis St. U .... TN
Messiah Coll .... PA
Miami U .... OH
Michigan, U. of .... MI
Michigan State U .... MI
Middle Tennessee State .... TN
Minnesota, U. of .... MN
Misericordia .... PA
Mississippi, U. of .... MS
Mississippi Coll .... MS
Mississippi State .... MS
Mississippi U. for Women ...... MS
Missouri, U. of (Columbia) ..... MO
Montana, U of .... MT
Montana State U .... MT
Montclair State Coll .... NJ
Morehead State U .... KY
Mount Mary .... WI
Mount Marty .... SD
Mount St. Joseph, Coll. of ..... OH
Mount St. Mary Coll .... NH
Mundelein Coll IL
Murray State U .... KY
Nebraska, U. of .... NE
Nevada, U. of .... NV
New Hampshire, U. of .... NH
New Mexico, U. of .... NM
New Mexico State U .... NM
New York U .... NY
Nicholls State .... LA
North Carolina, U. of (Greensboro) .... NC
North Carolina A&T State U ... NC
North Carolina Central .... NC
North Dakota, U. of .... ND
North Dakota State U (Fargo) .. ND
North Texas State U .... TX
Northeast Louisiana U .... LA
Northern Arizona U .... AZ
Northern Colorado, U. of ...... CO
Northern Illinois U IL
Northern Michigan .... MI
Northwest State U .... LA
Notre Dame, Coll. of .... CA
Notre Dame Coll. of Ohio ...... OH
Oakwood Coll .... AL
Ohio State U .... OH
Ohio U .... OH
Oklahoma, U. of .... OK
Oklahoma State U .... OK
Olivet Nazarene Coll IL
Oregon State U .... OR
Otterbein Coll .... OH
Ouachita Baptist U .... AR
Ozarks, Sch. of the .... MO
Pacific Union Coll .... CA
Pennsylvania State U .... PA
Pepperdine .... CA
Pittsburgh, U. of .... PA
Prairie View A&M .... TX
Pratt Inst .... NY
Puerto Rico, U. of .... PR
Purdue .... IN
Queens Coll .... NY
Radford Coll .... VA
Rhode Island, U. of .... RI
Rivier .... NH
Rochester Inst. of Tech .... NY
Rosary IL
Russell Sage Coll .... NY
Salem Coll .... NC
Sam Houston State .... TX
Samford U .... AL
San Diego State U .... CA
San Francisco State U .... CA
San Jose State U .... CA
Savannah State Coll .... GA
Seton Hill Coll .... PA
Simmons Coll .... MA
South Carolina State .... SC
South Dakota State U .... SD
Southeast Missouri .... MO
Southeastern Louisiana .... LA
Southern Idaho, Coll. of .... ID
Southern Illinois U. (Carbondale) IL
Southern Mississippi, U. of .... MS
Southern U .... LA
Southwest Missouri State ...... MO
Southwest Texas State U .... TX
Southwestern Adventist Coll .... TX
Southwestern Louisiana, U. of .. LA
Spalding .... KY
St. Benedict, Coll of .... MN
St. Catherine, Coll. of .... MN
St. Elizabeth, Coll. of .... NJ
St. Joseph .... CT
St. Mary .... KS
St. Mary's Dominican Coll ...... LA
St. Mary's-of-the-Woods .... IN
St. Scholastica, Coll. of .... MN
St. Teresa, Coll. of .... MN
State U. of New York (Buffalo, Oneonta, Plattsburgh) .... NY
Stephen F. Austin State U ...... TX
Syracuse U .... NY
Tennessee, U. of .... TN
Tennessee State U .... TN
Tennessee Tech. U .... TN
Texas A&I .... TX

Texas A&M .... TX
Texas Christian U .... TX
Texas Southern U .... TX
Texas Tech. U .... TX
Texas Woman's U .... TX
Tuskegee Inst .... AL
Union Coll .... NE
Utah, U. of .... UT
Utah State U .... UT
Valparaiso U .... IN
Vermont, U. of .... VT
Virginia Poly. Inst .... VA
Virginia State Coll .... VA
Viterbo Coll .... WI
Washington, U. of .... WA
Washington State U .... WA
Walla Walla Coll .... WA
Wayne State U .... MI
West Florida, U. of .... FL
West Virginia Wesleyan .... WV
Western Carolina U .... NC
Western Illinois U IL
Western Kentucky U .... KY
Western Michigan U .... MI
Western Texas Coll .... TX
Whittier Coll .... CA
William Woods Coll .... MO
Winthrop .... SC
Wisconsin, U. of (Green Bay, Madison, Stevens Point, Stout) .... WI
Wyoming, U. of .... WY
Youngstown State U .... OH

Distributive Education

Institutions awarding 20 or more undergraduate degrees as major field in single year according to U.S. Office of Education latest statistics

Alabama A&M .... AL
Alabama State U .... AL
Akron, U. of .... OH
Appalachian State U .... NC
Arkansas State U .... AR
Auburn U .... AL
Bloomsburg State .... PA
Bowling Green State .... OH
Brigham Young U .... UT
Central Connecticut State .... CT
Central Michigan U .... MI
Central Missouri .... MO
Central State U .... OK
Central Washington .... WA
Chicago State U IL
Cincinnati, U. of .... OH
District of Columbia, U. of .... DC
Delaware, U. of .... DE
East Carolina U .... NC
East Texas State U .... TX
Eastern Illinois U IL
Emporia State .... KS
Fayetteville State .... NC
Florida, U. of .... FL
Georgia, U. of .... GA
Georgia State U .... GA
Illinois State U IL
Indiana U .... PA
Jackson State .... MS
James Madison U .... VA
Kearney State .... NE
Kent State U .... OH
Kentucky, U. of .... KY
Mississippi State .... MS
Montclair State Coll .... NJ
New Mexico, U. of .... NM
North Carolina Central U .... NC
North Dakota, U. of .... ND
Northeast Missouri State .... MO
Northeastern Oklahoma State .... OK
Northern Iowa .... IA
Ohio State .... OH
Oklahoma, U. of .... OK
Oklahoma State U .... OK
Old Dominion U .... VA
Oregon State U .... OR
Pittsburgh, U. of .... PA
Puerto Rico, U. of .... PR
Rider Coll .... NJ
Salem State .... MA
Sam Houston .... TX
Shippensburg State .... PA
South Carolina, U. of .... SC
South Florida, U. of .... FL
Southeast Missouri .... MO
Southern U. A&M .... LA
Southwest Texas .... TX
Southwestern Oklahoma .... OK
State U. of New York (Albany, Buffalo) .... NY
Temple U .... PA
Trenton State .... NJ
Utah State U .... UT
Virginia Commonwealth U .... VA
Virginia State .... VA
West Texas State .... TX
Western Illinois U IL
Western Kentucky U .... KY
Western Michigan U .... MI
Western Texas .... TX
Wisconsin, U. of (Eau Claire, Whitewater) .... WI

Drafting

Akron, U. of .... OH
Alabama A&M .... AL
Alfred State .... NY
Alliance Coll .... PA
Angelina Coll .... TX
Barton County Comm .... KS
Black Hills State .... SD
Butte Coll .... CA
California State Coll .... PA
Casper Coll .... WY
Central Missouri .... MO
Cheyney State Coll .... PA
Coffeyville .... KS
Cooke County Coll .... TX
Cowley County Comm .... KS
Dean Jr. Coll .... MA
DuPage, Coll. of IL
East Central Jr. Coll .... MS
Eastern Arizona Coll .... AZ
Eastern Kentucky U .... KY
Eastern Oklahoma State .... OK
El Centro Coll .... TX
Evergreen Valley Coll .... CA
Fairmont State .... WV
Ferris State .... MI
Harper Coll IL
Hawaii, U. of (Hilo) .... HI
Hocking Tech. Coll .... OH
Howard Co. Jr. Coll .... TX
Hutchinson Comm. Coll .... KS
Indiana State U .... IN
Kaskaskia IL
Kearney State .... NE
Keene State Coll .... NH
Lake Superior State .... MI
Mississippi Delta Junior Coll .... MS
Morehead State U .... KY
Morrison Inst. of Tech IL
Navarro Coll .... TX
New England Inst. of Tech .... RI
Northeast Mississippi Jr .... MS
Northern Arizona .... AZ
Northern Michigan .... MI
Northern Montana Coll .... MT
Northern Oklahoma Coll .... OK
Northwest Missouri State Coll .... MO
Northwestern Oklahoma State U .... OK
Northwestern State U .... LA
Oregon Inst. of Tech .... OR
Otero Jr. Coll .... CO
Pearl River Jr. Coll .... MS
Purdue U .... IN
Rio Grande Coll .... OH
Savannah Coll. of Art and Design .... GA
Sheridan Coll .... WY
Snow Coll .... UT
South Dakota, U. of .... SD
South Dakota State .... SD
South Georgia Coll .... GA
Southeastern Oklahoma State U .... OK
Southern Idaho, Coll. of .... ID
Southwest Missouri State U .... MO
Southwestern Adventist .... TX
State U. of New York (Delhi, Morrisville) .... NY
Texas State Tech. Inst. (Harlingen) .... TX
Toledo, U. of .... OH
Trinidad State Jr. Coll .... CO
Utah State U .... UT
Vernon Reg. Jr. Coll .... TX
Waldorf Coll .... IA
West Virginia State Coll .... WV
Wharton Co. Jr. Coll .... TX
Wisconsin, U. of (Platteville) .... WI
Wright State U .... OH
Wytheville Comm. Coll .... VA
Youngstown State U .... OH
Yuba Coll .... CA

Drama and/or Theater

Abilene Christian .... TX
Alabama, U. of .... AL
Alabama State U .... AL
Alaska, U. of .... AK
Albion Coll .... MI
Albuquerque, U. of .... NM
Alderson-Broaddus .... WV
American U .... DC
Anderson Coll .... SC
Angelo .... TX
Antioch Coll .... OH
Ashland .... OH
Atlantic Christian .... NC
Auburn U .... AL
Augustana .... SD
Baldwin-Wallace .... OH
Barry U .... FL
Baruch Coll .... NY
Bay Path Jr .... MA
Baylor U .... TX
Beaver Coll .... PA
Bee County Coll .... TX
Belmont Coll .... TN
Bemidji State .... MN
Benedictine Coll .... IA
Bennett Coll .... NC
Bennington Coll .... VT
Bethany Coll .... WV
Birmingham Southern .... AL
Black Hawk Comm IL
Black Hills .... SD
Blackburn Coll IL
Blinn Coll .... TX
Blue Mountain .... MS
Bluffton Coll .... OH
Boston U .... MA
Bowie State .... MD
Bowling Green .... OH
Bradley U IL
Brandeis U .... MA
Brenau Coll .... GA
Brevard .... NC
Bridgeport, U. of .... CT
Bridgewater State .... MA
Broward Comm .... FL
Brown U .... RI
Bucknell U .... PA
Butler U .... IN
California, U. of (Irvine, San Diego, Santa Cruz) .... CA
California Baptist Coll .... CA
California Inst. of the Arts .... CA
California Lutheran .... CA
California State Coll. (Dominguez Hills, San Bernardino, Stanislaus) .... CA
California State Coll .... PA
California State Poly. (Pomona) .... CA
California State U. (Chico, Hayward, Los Angeles, San Bernardino) .... CA
Carnegie-Mellon U .... PA
Carson Newman .... TN
Carthage .... WI
Case Western Reserve .... OH
Casper Coll .... WY
Catholic U .... DC
Centenary Coll .... NJ
Central Arkansas, U. of .... AR
Central Coll .... IA
Central Connecticut State .... CT
Central Florida, U. of .... FL
Central Michigan U .... MI
Central Missouri .... MO
Central Washington State .... WA
Centre Coll .... KY
Chadron State .... NE
Chapman Coll .... CA
Chatham .... PA
Cheyney State .... PA
Clark U .... MA
Clarke Coll .... IA
Cleveland State .... OH
Coe Coll .... IA
Coker Coll .... SC
Colby-Sawyer .... NH
Columbia IL
Columbus .... GA
Colorado, U. of .... CO
Compton Coll .... CA
Connecticut, U. of .... CT
Connecticut Coll .... CT
Converse Coll .... SC
Creighton U .... NE
C.W. Post Coll .... NY
Daemen .... NY
Dakota State .... SD
Dallas, U. of .... TX
Dana .... NE
Davis & Elkins Coll .... WV
Dayton, U. of .... OH
Dean Jr. Coll .... MA
De Anza Coll .... CA
Delaware, U. of .... DE
Delta State U .... MS
Denison .... OH
Denver, U. of .... CO
DePauw U .... IN
Detroit, U. of .... MI
Dickinson .... PA
Dillard U .... LA
Dominican Coll .... CA
Dordt Coll .... IA
Drake U .... IA
Drew U .... NJ
Drury .... MO
DuPage, Coll. of IL
Duquesne U .... PA
East Carolina .... NC
East Central Oklahoma State .... OK
East Los Angeles .... CA
East Tennessee State .... TN
East Texas State U .... TX
Eastern Arizona .... AZ
Eastern Kentucky U .... KY
Eastern New Mexico .... NM
Eastern Oklahoma State .... OK
Eastern Washington .... WA
Eckerd Coll .... FL
Edgewood .... WI
Edinboro State .... PA

El Camino Coll . . . CA
Elmhurst Coll . . . IL
Elmira . . . NY
Emerson . . . MA
Emporia State U . . . KS
Eureka Coll . . . IL
Evangel Coll . . . MO
Evansville, U. of . . . IN
Fayetteville State U . . . NC
Ferris State . . . MI
Ferrum . . . VA
Findlay Coll . . . OH
Fisk U . . . TN
Flagler Coll . . . FL
Florida, U. of . . . FL
Florida A&M . . . FL
Florida Atlantic . . . FL
Florida International . . . FL
Florida Southern Coll . . . FL
Florida State U . . . FL
Fontbonne Coll . . . MO
Fordham . . . NY
Fort Lewis Coll . . . CO
Fort Scott Comm. C . . . KS
Franklin and Marshall . . . PA
Freed-Hardeman Coll . . . TN
Gallaudet Coll . . . DC
Gaston Coll . . . NC
George Mason U . . . VA
George Peabody Coll . . . TN
George Washington U . . . DC
Georgia State . . . GA
Gettysburg Coll . . . PA
Glassboro . . . NJ
Goddard Coll . . . VT
Gonzaga . . . WA
Goucher Coll . . . MD
Grinnell Coll . . . IA
Gustavus Adolphus . . . MN
Hamilton Coll . . . NY
Hamline U . . . MN
Hampshire . . . MA
Hampton Institute . . . VA
Hanover Coll . . . IN
Harcum Jr . . . PA
Hardin-Simmons . . . TX
Harding U . . . AR
Hartford, U. of . . . CT
Hastings Coll . . . NE
Hawaii, U. of . . . HI
Hendrix Coll . . . AR
Hillsdale Coll . . . MI
Hiram . . . OH
Holy Cross Coll . . . MA
Howard U . . . DC
Huntingdon Coll . . . AL
Huron Coll . . . SD
Hutchinson Comm. Coll . . . KS
Idaho, U. of . . . ID
Illinois, U. of . . . IL
Illinois Coll . . . IL
Illinois State U . . . IL
Illinois Wesleyan U . . . IL
Incarnate Word . . . TX
Indiana State U . . . IN
Indiana U . . . PA
Indiana U. (Bloomington) . . . IN
Iowa, U. of . . . IA
Iowa State U . . . IA
Iowa Wesleyan . . . IA
Ithaca . . . NY
Jacksonville State U . . . AL
Jacksonville U . . . FL
James Madison . . . VA
Jersey City State . . . NJ
John A. Logan Coll . . . IL
Johnson State Coll . . . VT
Judson Baptist . . . OR
Judson Coll . . . IL
Juilliard Sch . . . NY
Kalamazoo Coll . . . MI
Kansas, U. of . . . KS
Kansas State U . . . KS
Kansas Wesleyan . . . KS
Kearney State . . . NE
Keene State . . . NH
Kent State . . . OH
Kentucky Wesleyan . . . KY
Kenyon Coll . . . OH
Keuka Coll . . . NY
Kings Coll . . . PA
Kirkland Coll . . . NY
Knox Coll . . . IL
Kutztown State . . . PA
La Grange Coll . . . GA
Lake Erie . . . OH
Lamar U . . . TX
Lander Coll . . . SC
Langston U . . . OK
Lawrence . . . WI
Lehigh U . . . PA
Lewis and Clark Coll . . . OR
Lewis U . . . IL
Limestone Coll . . . SC
Lincoln Coll . . . IL
Lindsey Wilson Coll . . . KY
Linfield Coll . . . OR
Lock Haven State . . . PA
Lon Morris Coll . . . TX
Longwood Coll . . . VA
Los Medanos Coll . . . CA
Louisville, U. of . . . KY
Lower Columbia Coll . . . WA
Loyola . . . IL
Loyola U . . . LA
Lynchburg Coll . . . VA
McMurray Coll . . . TX
McPherson Coll . . . KS
Maine, U. of (Orono) . . . ME
Mankato State . . . MN
Marian Coll . . . IN
Marist Coll . . . NY
Marlboro Coll . . . VT
Mary Washington . . . VA
Marygrove Coll . . . MI
Marymount Manhattan . . . NY
Marymount Palos Verdes . . . CA
Marywood . . . PA
Massachusetts, U. of (Amherst) MA
Memphis State U . . . TN
Messiah Coll . . . PA
Miami, U. of . . . FL
Miami U . . . OH
Michigan State U . . . MI
Midland Lutheran Coll . . . NE
Midway Coll . . . KY
Midwestern . . . TX
Millikin U . . . IL
Mills Coll . . . CA
Millsaps Coll . . . MS
Minnesota, U. of (Minneapolis) . MN
Mississippi Delta Jr. Coll . . . MS
Missouri, U. of . . . MO
Modesto Jr. Coll . . . CA
Montana, U. of . . . MT
Montclair State . . . NJ
Monterey Peninsula Coll . . . CA
Montevallo, U. of . . . AL
Moorhead State . . . MN
Moorpark Coll . . . CA
Morehead State U . . . KY
Morningside Coll . . . IA
Mount Holyoke . . . MA
Mount Mercy Coll . . . IA
Mount St. Mary Coll . . . NY
Mount Union Coll . . . OH
Muskingum Coll . . . OH
Navajo Comm. Coll . . . AZ
Nazareth Coll. of Rochester . . . NY
Nebraska, U. of (Lincoln) . . . NE
Nevada, U. of (Las Vegas) . . . NV
New Hampshire, U. of . . . NH
New Mexico, U. of . . . NM
New Mexico State U . . . NM
New York U . . . NY
Niagara U . . . NY
Nicholls State . . . LA
North Carolina, U. of (Asheville, Chapel Hill, Charlotte, Greensboro, Wilmington) . . . NC
North Carolina A&T . . . NC
North Carolina Cent. U . . . NC
North Carolina Sch. of the Arts . NC
North Carolina Wesleyan . . . NC
North Central Coll . . . IL
North Dakota State U . . . ND
North Idaho Coll . . . ID
North Park Coll . . . IL
North Texas State . . . TX
Northeast Mississippi Jr . . . MS
Northeast Missouri State . . . MO
Northeastern Illinois U . . . IL
Northeastern Jr . . . CO
Northern Arizona . . . AZ
Northern Colorado, U. of . . . CO
Northern Illinois U . . . IL
Northern Michigan . . . MI
Northwest Missouri State . . . MO
Northwestern State U . . . LA
Northwestern U . . . IL
Notre Dame, Coll. of . . . CA
Oakland U . . . MI
Ohio State . . . OH
Ohio U. (Athens) . . . OH
Ohio Valley Coll . . . WV
Ohio Wesleyan . . . OH
Oklahoma, U. of . . . OK
Oklahoma State U . . . OK
Old Dominion U . . . VA
Olivet Coll . . . MI
Oral Roberts . . . OK
Oregon, U. of . . . OR
Oregon State U . . . OR
Otterbein Coll . . . OH
Pacific, U. of . . . CA
Palomar Coll . . . CA
Park Coll . . . MO
Patrick Henry St. Jr. Coll . . . AL
Pennsylvania, U. of . . . PA
Pennsylvnia State U. (Allentown, Behrend, Schuylkill, Shenango, University Park) . . . PA
Pepperdine U . . . CA
Peru State . . . NE
Pittsburg State . . . KS
Pittsburgh, U. of (Johnstown) . . . PA
Pitzer Coll . . . CA
Point Loma . . . CA
Point Park Coll . . . PA
Pomona Coll . . . CA
Prairie State Coll . . . IL
Pratt Inst . . . NY
Princeton U . . . NJ
Puerto Rico, U. of . . . PR
Puget Sound, U. of . . . WA
Purdue U . . . IN
Quinnipiac Coll . . . CT
Radford Coll . . . VA
Randolph-Macon Woman's Coll . VA
Redlands, U. of . . . CA
Reed Coll . . . OR
Rhode Island Coll . . . RI
Richmond, U. of . . . VA
Rio Piedras . . . PR
Riverside City . . . CA
Rochester, U. of . . . NY
Rockford Coll . . . IL
Rockmont Coll . . . CO
Roger Williams . . . RI
Rosary Hill Coll . . . NY
Rosemont Coll . . . PA
Russell Sage Coll . . . NY
Rutgers U . . . NJ
Saint Teresa, Coll. of . . . MN
Sacramento City Coll . . . CA
Saginaw Valley . . . MI
Salisbury State . . . MD
Sam Houston State . . . TX
San Antonio Coll . . . TX
San Diego City Coll . . . CA
San Diego State U . . . CA
San Francisco State Coll . . . CA
San Jose State . . . CA
Santa Fe, Coll. of . . . NM
Sarah Lawrence . . . NY
School of the Arts . . . NC
Schreiner Coll . . . TX
Science & Arts of Okla., U. of . . OK
Scripps Coll . . . CA
Seattle Pacific . . . WA
Seattle U . . . WA
Shasta Coll . . . CA
Shenandoah Coll . . . VA
Shepherd Coll . . . WV
Shippensburg State Coll . . . PA
Simpson Coll . . . IA
Siskiyous, Coll. of the . . . CA
Skidmore Coll . . . NY
Slippery Rock . . . PA
Snow Coll . . . UT
Sonoma State U . . . CA
South Alabama, U. of . . . AL
South Carolina, U. of (Columbia) . . . SC
South Carolina State . . . SC
South Dakota, U. of . . . SD
South Florida, U. of . . . FL
South Georgia Coll . . . GA
Southeast Missouri State . . . MO
Southern Arkansas U . . . AR
Southern California, U. of . . . CA
Southern California Coll . . . CA
Southern Connecticut State . . . CT
Southern Idaho, Coll. of . . . ID
Southern Methodist . . . TX
Southern Mississippi, U. of . . . MS
Southwest Minnesota . . . MN
Southwest Missouri St . . . MO
Southwest Texas State . . . TX
Southwestern at Memphis . . . TN
Southwestern Coll . . . KS
Southwestern Louisiana . . . LA
Southwestern U . . . TX
Spelman Coll . . . GA
St. Andrews Presbyterian . . . NC
St. Benedict, Coll. of . . . MN
St. Catherine, Coll. of . . . MN
St. Cloud State U . . . MN
St. Francis Coll . . . PA
St. Gregory's . . . OK
St. Leo Coll . . . FL
St. Louis U . . . MO
St. Mary Coll . . . KS
St. Mary of the Plains . . . KS
St. Mary's . . . MN
St. Mary's U . . . TX
St. Michael's . . . VT
St. Thomas, Coll. of . . . MN
State U. of New York (Albany, Brockport, Buffalo, Geneseo, Oswego, Pittsburgh, Potsdam, Purchase) . . . NY
Stephen F. Austin . . . TX
Stephens Coll . . . MO
Stetson . . . FL
Sul Ross State U . . . TX
Sullins Coll . . . VA
Suomi Coll . . . MI
Susquehanna U . . . PA
Sweet Briar Coll . . . VA
Syracuse U . . . NY
Taylor U . . . IN
Temple . . . PA
Tennessee, U. of (Chattanooga, Martin) . . . TN
Tennessee State U . . . TN
Texas, U. of (Austin, Dallas, El Paso) . . . TX
Texas A&M U . . . TX
Texas Woman's U . . . TX
Thomas More Coll . . . KY
Tift Coll . . . GA
Towson State . . . MD
Trinidad State Jr . . . CO
Trinity Coll . . . CT

Troy State U ... AL
Truett McConnell ... GA
Tulsa, U. of ... OK
Tusculum ... TN
U.S. International U ... CA
Union Coll ... KY
Upper Iowa ... IA
Upsala Coll ... NJ
Utah, U. of ... UT
Utah State U ... UT
Valparaiso U ... IN
Vanderbilt U ... TN
Vassar Coll ... NY
Virginia Commonwealth ... VA
Virginia Poly. Inst ... VA
Viterbo ... WI
Wagner Coll ... NY
Wake Forest U ... NC
Waldorf Coll ... IA
Washburn U ... KS
Washington, U. of ... WA
Washington and Lee ... VA
Washington International ... DC
Washington U ... MO
Wayne State ... NE
Wayne State U ... MI
Weber ... UT
Webster Coll ... MO
Wellesley Coll ... MA
Wesleyan ... GA
West Chester State Coll ... PA
West Florida, U. of ... FL
West Liberty State ... WV
West Virginia Wesleyan ... WV
Western Carolina U ... NC
Western Illinois U ... IL
Western Kentucky ... KY
Western Maryland ... MD
Western State ... CO
Westminster Coll ... UT
Wharton Count. Jr. Coll ... TX
Whitman Coll ... WA
Whittier Coll ... CA
Wichita ... KS
Wilbur Wright Coll ... IL
Wilkes Coll ... PA
Willamette ... OR
William Woods Coll ... MO
Williams Coll ... MA
Wilmington Coll ... OH
Windham Coll ... VT
Winona State ... MN
Wisconsin, U. of (Green Bay, Madison, Milwaukee, Oshkosh, River Falls, Stevens Point, Superior, Whitewater) ... WI
Wood Jr. Coll ... MS
Wooster, Coll. of ... OH
Wright State ... OH
Xavier U ... OH
Yale U ... CT
Yankton Coll ... SD
Youngstown State U ... OH

Early Childhood Education,

See TEACHER EDUCATION

Earth Sciences

Adelphi ... NY
Adrian Coll ... MI
Alabama A&M ... AL
Alaska, U. of ... AK
Antioch Coll ... OH
Appalachian State U ... NC
Arizona, U. of ... AZ
Arizona Western Coll ... AZ
Arkansas, U. of ... AR
Ashland ... OH
Auburn U ... AL
Ball State ... IN
Barton Co. Comm. Coll ... KS
Baylor U ... TX
Bennett Coll ... NC
Bennington Coll ... VT
Berea Coll ... KY
Black Hills State ... SD
Bloomsburg State ... PA
Boston U ... MA
Bowling Green ... OH
Brevard ... NC
Bridgewater State ... MA
California, U. of (Davis, Los Angeles, Riverside, San Diego, Santa Cruz) ... CA
California State Coll. (Bakersfield, Long Beach, Stanislaus) ... CA
California State Coll ... PA
California State Poly. (Pomona) ... CA
California State U. (Chico, Los Angeles, Northridge) ... CA
Case Western Reserve ... OH
Casper ... WY
Central Connecticut State ... CT
Central Michigan ... MI
Central Missouri State ... MO
Central State ... OH
Chadron ... NE
Cheyney State ... PA
Cincinnati, U. of ... OH
City Coll ... NY
Clarion State ... PA
Colorado, U. of ... CO
Colorado Mountain State ... CO
Colorado Sch. of Mines ... CO
Colorado State U ... CO
Columbus Coll ... GA
Concordia Tech. Coll ... IL
Cornell U ... NY
C.W. Post Ctr ... NY
Dartmouth ... NH
Davis & Elkins Coll ... WV
Denison U ... OH
DePauw U ... IN
District of Columbia, U. of ... DC
Drake U ... IA
Drew U ... NJ
DuPage Coll ... IA
East Texas State ... TX
Eastern Connecticut State ... CT
Eastern Kentucky U ... KY
Eastern Montana ... MT
Eastern New Mexico ... NM
Eastern Washington U ... WA
Edinboro State ... PA
Elizabeth Seton Coll ... NY
Emporia State ... KS
Fairleigh Dickinson ... NJ
Fitchburg State ... MA
Florida, U. of ... FL
Florida International U ... FL
Florida Southern ... FL
Fort Hays State ... KS
Franklin Coll ... IN
George Washington U ... DC
Georgia Southwestern Coll ... GA
Goddard Coll ... VT
Grand Valley State ... MI
Guilford Coll ... NC
Gustavus Adolphus ... MN
Hampshire Coll ... MA
Hastings Coll ... NE
Hawaii, U. of (Honolulu) ... HI
Hope Coll ... MI
Illinois, U. of (Urbana) ... IL
Illinois Central Coll ... IL
Indiana Central ... IN
Indiana State U ... IN
Indiana U. (Bloomington) ... IN
Iowa State U ... IA
Iowa Wesleyan ... IA
Jacksonville State U ... AL
John Brown U ... AR
Johns Hopkins U ... MD
Juniata Coll ... PA
Kansas State U ... KS
Kean State ... NJ
Kearney State ... NE
Keene State ... NH
Kent State ... OH
Knox Coll ... IL
Kutztown ... PA
La Salle Coll ... PA
Lewis-Clark State Coll ... ID
Lincoln Coll ... IL
Linfield Coll ... OR
Lock Haven State Coll ... PA
Loma Linda U ... CA
Longwood ... VA
Lowell, U. of ... MA
Mankato State Coll ... MN
Marlboro Coll ... VT
Mars Hill ... NC
Massachusetts, U. of (Boston) . MA
Massachusetts Inst. of Tech ... MA
McMurray Coll ... TX
Miami U ... OH
Michigan State U ... MI
Millersville State ... PA
Minnesota, U. of (Duluth, Minneapolis) ... MN
Minot State Coll ... ND
Missouri, U. of (Kansas City, Rolla) ... MO
Montana, U. of ... MT
Montana State U ... MT
Montclair State Coll ... NJ
Moorhead State ... MN
Moravian Coll ... PA
Morehead State U ... KY
Nebraska Wesleyan Coll ... NE
New Hampshire, U. of (Durham) ... NH
New Mexico, U. of ... NM
New Mexico Highlands ... NM
New Mexico State U ... NM
New Orleans, U. of ... LA
Nicholls State U ... LA
North Carolina, U. of (Charlotte, Wilmington) ... NC
North Texas State ... TX
Northeast Louisiana ... LA
Northeast Mississippi Jr ... MS
Northeast Missouri State Coll .. MO
Northeastern Illinois ... IL
Northeastern U ... MA
Northern Arizona ... AZ
Northern Colorado, U. of ... CO
Northern Iowa, U. of ... IA
Northland ... WI
Northwest Missouri State U ... MO
Northwestern State U ... LA
Norwich U ... VT
Notre Dame, U. of ... IN
Old Dominion U ... VA
Olivet Nazarene ... IL
Pacific Lutheran ... WA
Pacific Union Coll ... CA
Pennsylvania State U. (Allentown, Behrend, McKeesport, Schuylkill, Shenango) ... PA
Pittsburgh, U. of ... PA
Plymouth State ... NH
Portland State ... OR
Principia Coll ... IL
Purdue ... IN
Rider Coll ... NJ
Salem State ... MA
Sam Houston State ... TX
Santa Barbara City Coll ... CA
Shippensburg State ... PA
Shorter Coll ... GA
Slippery Rock State ... PA
Snow Coll ... UT
South Alabama, U. of ... AL
South Carolina, U. of ... SC
South Dakota, U. of ... SD
Southeast Missouri State U ... MO
Southern Connecticut State ... CT
Southern Idaho, Coll. of ... ID
Southern Illinois (Edwardsville) ... IL
Southern Methodist ... TX
Southwest Missouri State ... MO
St. Andrews Presbyterian ... NC
St. Cloud State ... MN
St. Louis U ... MO
St. Mary Coll ... KS
St. Mary's U ... TX
Stanford U ... CA
State U. of New York (Albany, Brockport, Buffalo, Geneseo, Oneonta, Oswego, Plattsburgh, Potsdam, Stony Brook) ... NY
Suomi Coll ... MI
Tennessee ... TN
Tennessee Tech. U ... TN
Texas, U. of (Permian Basin, San Antonio) ... TX
Toledo, U. of ... OH
Trinity Christian ... IL
Truett McConnell ... GA
Tulane ... LA
Vanderbilt U ... TN
Virginia State U ... VA
Walsh Coll ... OH
Washington U ... MO
Weber State ... UT
Wesleyan U ... CT
West Chester State ... PA
West Georgia ... GA
Western Carolina U ... NC
Western Connecticut State Coll. CT
Western Kentucky U ... KY
Whittier Coll ... CA
Whitworth ... WA
Wilkes Coll ... PA
William Woods ... MO
Winona State ... MN
Wisconsin, U. of (Green Bay, Madison, Oshkosh, Platteville, River Falls, Superior, Whitewater) ... WI
Wittenberg ... OH
World College West ... CA
Wright State U ... OH
Youngstown ... OH

Ecology and/or Environmental Science

Akron, U. of ... OH
Alfred U ... NY
Allegheny Coll ... PA
American U ... DC
Antioch Coll ... OH
Aquinas ... MI
Arizona, U. of ... AZ
Atlantic, Coll. of the ... ME
Augustana Coll ... SD
Aurora Coll ... IL
Baruch Coll ... NY
Baylor U ... TX
Belmont Abbey ... NC
Beloit Coll ... WI
Bemidji State U ... MN
Bennington Coll ... VT
Bethel Coll ... KS
Bowdoin Coll ... ME
Bowling Green State ... OH
Brevard Coll ... NC
Brown U ... RI
Butler U ... IN
California, U. of (Davis, Irvine, Riverside, Santa Cruz) ... CA
California Poly. State ... CA
California State Coll ... PA
California State U (Hayward, Sacramento, San Bernardino) . CA
Carleton Coll ... MN
Catholic U ... DC
City Coll ... NY

Cleveland State .... OH
Coe Coll .... IA
Colorado, U. of .... CO
Colorado Mountain .... CO
Colorado State U .... CO
Concordia Coll .... NY
Connecticut Coll .... CT
Cornell Coll .... IA
Cornell U .... NY
C.W. Post .... NY
Dartmouth Coll .... NH
Davis & Elkins .... WV
Delta State U .... MS
Denver, U. of .... CO
Drexel U .... PA
Dubuque, U. of .... IA
Earlham Coll .... IN
East Central Oklahoma State U OK
East Stroudsburg Coll .... PA
Eastern Kentucky U .... KY
Eastern Montana .... MT
Eastern Washington U .... WA
Eckerd Coll .... FL
Edgewood Coll .... WI
Elmira Coll .... NY
Evansville, U. of .... IN
Evergreen State .... WA
Fairleigh Dickinson U .... NJ
Ferrum Coll .... VA
Findlay Coll .... OH
Florida Inst. of Tech .... FL
Florida International .... FL
Florida Tech .... FL
Fort Lewis Coll .... CO
Franklin Coll .... IN
Franklin Pierce .... NH
Friends U .... KS
George Washington U .... DC
George Williams IL
Georgetown Coll .... KY
Georgia, U. of .... GA
Georgia Coll .... GA
Goddard Coll .... VT
Governors State IL
Grand Canyon Coll .... AZ
Grand Valley State .... MI
Hampshire Coll .... MA
Harvard .... MA
Hillsdale Coll .... MI
Hood Coll .... MD
Houston, U. of .... TX
Humboldt State .... CA
Hunter Coll .... NY
Illinois, U. of IL
Indiana State U .... IN
Indiana U. (Bloomington) .... IN
Iona Coll .... NY
Iowa State U .... IA
Iowa Wesleyan .... IA
John Carroll U .... OH
Johnson State .... VT
Juniata .... PA
Kansas, U. of .... KS
Keene State .... NH
Keystone Jr .... PA
Lake Forest Coll IL
Lamar U .... TX
La Salle .... PA
Lenoir-Rhyne .... NC
Lincoln Coll IL
Linfield Coll .... OR
Livingston U .... AL
Lowell, U. of .... MA
Maine, U. of (Fort Kent, Machias, Presque Isle) ...... ME
Manchester Coll .... IN
Manhattanville Coll .... NY
Mankato State U .... MN
Marlboro Coll .... VT
Mars Hill .... NC
Mary Washington .... VA
Maryland, U. of .... MD
Massachusetts, U. of .... MA
McNeese State U .... LA
Michigan, U. of (Dearborn) ..... MI
Michigan State .... MI
Middlebury Coll .... VT
Midwestern State .... TX
Millersville State .... PA
Minnesota, U. of (Minneapolis)..MN
Mitchell Coll .... CT
Monmouth Coll .... NJ
Montana, U. of .... MT
Montclair State .... NJ
Morehead State U .... KY
Mt. St. Vincent .... NY
Muhlenberg Coll .... PA
Nasson Coll .... ME
New England U .... ME
New Hampshire, U. of .... NH
New Haven, U. of .... CT
New York Inst. of Tech .... NY
North Carolina, U. of (Wilmington) .... NC
North Carolina Wesleyan ...... NC
North Dakota State U. (Bottineau, Fargo) .... ND
Northeast Missouri .... MO
Northeastern Illinois IL
Northern Arizona U .... AZ
Northern Iowa, U. of .... IA
Northern Michigan U .... MI
Northland Coll .... WI
Northwest Missouri State ...... MO
Northwestern Oklahoma State . OK
Northwestern U IL
Ohio State U .... OH
Oklahoma State U .... OK
Ottawa .... KS
Pacific, U. of the .... CA
Paul Smith's Coll .... NY
Pennsylvania, U. of .... PA
Pennsylvania State U. (Behrend, University) .... PA
Pittsburgh, U. of .... PA
Prescott Ctr. Coll .... AZ
Purdue U .... IN
Quinnipiac Coll .... CT
Radcliffe Coll .... MA
Ramapo .... NJ
Rio Piedras .... PR
Rutgers U .... NJ
Sam Houston U .... TX
San Diego State .... CA
San Jose State .... CA
Seattle Pacific .... WA
Shorter Coll .... GA
Slippery Rock State .... PA
South Dakota State .... SD
Southampton Coll .... NY
Southern Idaho, Coll. of .... ID
Southern Illinois U IL
Southern Vermont Coll .... VT
Springfield Coll .... MA
St. Andrews Presbyterian ...... NC
St. Cloud State .... MN
St. Francis Coll .... PA
St. John's U .... NY
St. Joseph Coll .... ME
St. Mary Coll .... KS
St. Mary's Coll .... MN
State U. of New York (Geneseo, Plattsburgh, Coll. of Environmental Science & Forestry) .... NY
State U. of New York Coll. of Ag. & Life Sci .... NY
Stephen F. Austin .... TX
Stockton State .... NJ
Syracuse U .... NY
Temple U .... PA
Tennessee, U. of .... TN
Texas, U. of .... TX
Thiel Coll .... PA
Toledo, U. of .... OH
Towson State .... MD
Trinity Christian IL
Trinity Coll .... CT
Troy State U .... AL
Unity Coll .... ME
Upsala Coll .... NJ
Utah State .... UT
Vassar Coll .... NY
Virginia, U. of .... VA
Warren Wilson .... NC
Washington State U .... WA
Wellesley Coll .... MA
Wesley Coll .... DE
Wesleyan U .... CT
West Virginia State .... WV
Western Kentucky .... KY
Whitworth Coll .... WA
Wilkes Coll .... PA
Willamette U .... OR
Williams Coll .... MA
Winona State .... MN
Wisconsin, U. of (Green Bay, Madison) .... WI
Wright State .... OH

Economics

Institutions awarding 20 or more undergraduate degrees as major field in a single year according to U.S. Office of Education latest statistics

Alabama A&M U .... AL
Albion .... MI
Allegheny Coll .... PA
American U .... DC
Amherst .... MA
Arizona, U. of .... AZ
Barnard Coll .... NY
Bates .... ME
Bethany .... WV
Boston Coll .... MA
Boston U .... MA
Bowdoin Coll .... ME
Brandeis U .... MA
Brigham Young .... UT
Brooklyn Coll .... NY
Brown U .... RI
Bucknell .... PA
California State Coll. (San Bernardino) .... CA
California, U. of (Berkeley, Davis, Irvine, Los Angeles, Riverside, San Diego, Santa Barbara, Santa Cruz) .... CA
California Poly. State U .... CA
California State U. (Chico, Fullerton, Long Beach, Sacramento) .... CA
Carleton Coll .... MN
Catholic U .... DC
Centre Coll .... KY
Chicago, U. of IL
Cincinnati, U. of .... OH
City Coll .... NY
Claremont Coll .... CA
Clark U .... MA
Clemson .... SC
Colby Coll .... ME
Colgate .... NY
Colorado, U. of .... CO
Colorado Coll .... CO
Colorado State U .... CO
Columbia .... NY
Connecticut, U. of .... CT
Connecticut Coll .... CT
Cornell .... NY
Dallas, U. of .... TX
Dartmouth .... NH
Davidson .... NC
Delaware, U. of .... DE
Denver, U. of .... CO
Denison .... OH
DePauw .... IN
Dickinson .... PA
Drake U .... IA
Drew U .... NJ
Duke .... NC
East Stroudsburg State .... PA
Eastern Connecticut State ...... CT
Eastern Illinois U IL
Fairfield .... CT
Florida, U. of .... FL
Florida State U .... FL
Fordham .... NY
Framingham State Coll .... MA
Franklin and Marshall .... PA
George Mason U .... VA
George Washington U .... DC
Georgetown .... DC
Georgia, U. of .... GA
Hamilton Coll .... NY
Hampden-Sydney Coll .... VA
Hartwick Coll .... NY
Harvard .... MA
Haverford Coll .... PA
Hawaii, U. of .... HI
Hobart and William Smith ...... NY
Holy Cross, Coll. of the .... MA
Houston, U. of .... TX
Howard .... DC
Hunter .... NY
Illinois, U. of IL
Illinois State IL
Indiana U. at Bloomington ...... IN
Iowa, U. of .... IA
Iowa State U .... IA
Jersey City State .... NJ
Johns Hopkins U .... MD
Kalamazoo Coll .... MI
Kansas, U. of .... KS
Kean Coll .... NJ
Kenyon Coll .... OH
Knox IL
Lafayette .... PA
Lake Forest Coll IL
Lawrence U .... WI
Lehman Coll .... NY
Long Island U .... NY
Loyola U IL
Macalester .... MN
Maryland, U. of .... MD
Marymount Coll .... NY
Mary Washington Coll .... VA
Massachusetts, U. of .... MA
Massachusetts Inst. of Tech ... MA
Miami U .... OH
Michigan, U. of .... MI
Michigan State U .... MI
Middlebury .... VT
Millersville State .... PA
Minnesota, U. of .... MN
Missouri, U. of .... MO
Mt. Holyoke .... MA
New Hampshire, U. of .... NH
New Mexico, U. of .... NM
New York U .... NY
North Carolina, U. of (Chapel Hill, Charlotte) .... NC
North Carolina State U. (Raleigh) .... NC
Northern Illinois U IL
Northwestern U IL
Note Dame, U. of .... IN
Occidental .... CA
Ohio State U .... OH
Ohio U .... OH
Ohio Wesleyan .... OH
Oregon, U. of .... OR
Pennsylvania, U. of .... PA
Pennsylvania State U .... PA
Pittsburgh, U. of .... PA
Pomona Coll .... CA
Portland State .... OR
Princeton .... NJ
Puerto Rico, U. of .... PR
Puget Sound, U. of .... WA
Queens Coll .... NY
Radcliffe Coll .... MA

Randolph-Macon Woman's Coll . VA
Rhode Island, U. of . . . . RI
Rhode Island Coll . . . . RI
Rice . . . . TX
Richmond, U. of . . . . VA
Ripon . . . . WI
Rochester, U. of . . . . NY
Rutgers . . . . NJ
San Diego State . . . . CA
San Francisco, U. of . . . . CA
San Francisco State U . . . . CA
San Jose State . . . . CA
Santa Clara, U. of . . . . CA
Slippery Rock . . . . PA
Smith Coll . . . . MA
South, U. of the . . . . TN
South Dakota State . . . . SD
Southern California, U. of . . . . CA
Southern Connecticut . . . . CT
Southern Methodist U . . . . TX
Southwestern at Memphis . . . . TN
Spelman Coll . . . . GA
St. Anselm . . . . NH
St. Lawrence U . . . . NY
St. Olaf . . . . MN
Stanford . . . . CA
State U. of New York (Albany, Binghamton, Buffalo, Cortland, New Paltz, Oneonta, Oswego, Potsdam, Stony Brook) . . . . NY
Staten Island, Coll. of . . . . NY
Swarthmore Coll . . . . PA
Syracuse . . . . NY
Temple U . . . . PA
Texas, U. of (Arlington, Austin) . TX
Texas A&M . . . . TX
Trinity . . . . CT
Tufts . . . . MA
Tulane . . . . LA
Union . . . . NY
Ursinus . . . . PA
Utah, U. of . . . . UT
Vanderbilt . . . . TN
Vassar Coll . . . . NY
Vermont, U. of . . . . VT
Villanova U . . . . PA
Virginia, U. of . . . . VA
Virginia Military Inst . . . . VA
Virginia Poly. Inst . . . . VA
Wabash Coll . . . . IN
Wake Forest . . . . NC
Washington, U. of . . . . WA
Washington and Jefferson . . . . PA
Washington and Lee . . . . VA
Washington State U . . . . WA
Washington U . . . . MO
Wellesley . . . . MA
Wesleyan U . . . . CT
Westfield State . . . . MA
Westminster Coll . . . . MO
Westmont Coll . . . . CA
Wheaton IL
Wheaton . . . . MA
Whitman Coll . . . . WA
Willamette . . . . OR
William and Mary . . . . VA
Williams . . . . MA
Wisconsin, U. of (Madison, Milwaukee, Stevens Point) . . . . WI
Wofford Coll . . . . SC
Wooster, Coll. of . . . . OH
Worcester State Coll . . . . MA
Yale . . . . CT
York Coll . . . . NY

Education, Montessori Plan

•*Accredited teacher preparation programs according to American Montessori Society*

Bennett Coll . . . . NC
•Chaminade U . . . . HI
•Chestnut Hill . . . . PA
•Concordia T.C . . . . NE
Eastern Washington U . . . . WA
El Centro Coll . . . . TX
La Salle Coll . . . . PA
Mills Coll . . . . CA
•Notre Dame, Coll. of . . . . CA
•Oklahoma City U . . . . OK
•Palm Beach Jr. Coll . . . . FL
Russell Sage . . . . NY
St. Leo Coll . . . . FL
•St. Mary, Coll. of . . . . NE
•St. Mary-of-the-Woods Coll . . . . IN
•St. Mary's Coll . . . . CA
•Seattle U . . . . WA
Southwest Texas State . . . . TX
Tennessee U. of . . . . TN
•Xavier U . . . . OH

Educational Administration

Institutions offering 25 or more graduate degrees according to U.S. Office of Education latest statistics

Akron, U. of . . . . OH
Alabama, U. of . . . . AL
Alabama A&M . . . . AL
Antioch Coll . . . . OH
Appalachian State U . . . . NC
Arizona, U. of . . . . AZ
Arkansas, U. of . . . . AR
Arkansas State U . . . . AR
Austin Peay State . . . . TN
Ball State . . . . IN
Bob Jones U . . . . SC
Bowling Green . . . . OH
Bridgeport, U. of . . . . CT
Bridgewater State . . . . MA
Brigham Young U . . . . UT
California Lutheran Coll . . . . CA
Central Connecticut . . . . CT
Central Michigan U . . . . MI
Central Missouri State . . . . MO
Citadel, The . . . . SC
Clemson . . . . SC
Colorado, U. of . . . . CO
Columbia . . . . NY
Corpus Christi State U . . . . TX
Dayton, U. of . . . . OH
East Carolina . . . . NC
East Texas State . . . . TX
Eastern Illinois U IL
Eastern Michigan U . . . . MI
Fairfield U . . . . CT
Florida Atlantic U . . . . FL
Florida International . . . . FL
Florida Tech. U . . . . FL
Fordham . . . . NY
George Mason U . . . . VA
George Peabody . . . . TN
Georgia, U. of . . . . GA
Georgia State . . . . GA
Glassboro State . . . . NJ
Gonzaga U . . . . WA
Hawaii, U. of . . . . HI
Houston, U. of . . . . TX
Illinois, U. of IL
Indiana State . . . . IN
Indiana U . . . . IN
International American . . . . PR
Iowa, U. of . . . . IA
Kean Coll . . . . NJ
Kearney State . . . . NE
Kent State . . . . OH
Lehigh U . . . . PA
Louisiana State U . . . . LA
Lowell, U. of . . . . MA
Loyola IL
Loyola Coll . . . . MD
Mankato State . . . . MN
Marshall U . . . . WV
Maryland, U. of . . . . MD
McNeese State . . . . LA
Memphis State U . . . . TN
Michigan State U . . . . MI
Middle Tennessee . . . . TN
Missouri, U. of . . . . MO
Monmouth Coll . . . . NJ
Montana, U. of . . . . MT
Montclair State . . . . NJ
Nebraska, U. of . . . . NE
Nevada, U. of . . . . NV
New Mexico, U. of . . . . NM
New Mexico State . . . . NM
New Orleans, U. of . . . . LA
Niagara U . . . . NY
North Carolina Agr. & Tech . . . . NC
North Florida, U. of . . . . FL
North Texas State U . . . . TX
Northeast Louisiana State . . . . LA
Northeast Missouri State . . . . MO
Northern Colorado, U. of . . . . CO
Northern Illinois IL
Northern Iowa, U. of . . . . IA
Northern Michigan . . . . MI
Nova U . . . . FL
Ohio U . . . . OH
Oklahoma, U. of . . . . OK
Old Dominion . . . . VA
Our Lady of the Lake . . . . TX
Pan American U . . . . TX
Pennsylvania State . . . . PA
Pepperdine . . . . CA
Pittsburg State U . . . . KS
Prairie View A&M . . . . TX
Providence Coll . . . . RI
Puerto Rico, U. of . . . . PR
Purdue U . . . . IN
Radford . . . . VA
Roosevelt U IL
Salem State . . . . MA
Scranton, U. of . . . . PA
Seton Hall . . . . NJ
South Carolina, U. of . . . . SC
South Dakota, U. of . . . . SD
South Dakota State . . . . SD
South Florida, U. of . . . . FL
Southeast Missouri State . . . . MO
Southeastern Louisiana . . . . LA
Southern Connecticut . . . . CT
Southern Illinois IL
Southern Maine, U. of . . . . ME
Southern Mississippi, U. of . . . . MS
Southern U . . . . LA
Southwest Missouri State . . . . MO
St. Cloud State U . . . . MN
St. Thomas, Coll. of . . . . MN
State U. of New York (Albany) . . NY
Tarleton State . . . . TX
Tennessee, U. of . . . . TN
Tennessee State U . . . . TN
Tennessee Tech . . . . TN
Texas, U. of (El Paso, San Antonio) . . . . TX
Texas A&I U . . . . TX
Texas Southern U . . . . TX
Toledo, U. of . . . . OH
Troy State U . . . . AL
Villanova U . . . . PA
Virginia, U. of . . . . VA
Virginia Commonwealth . . . . VA
Virginia State Coll . . . . VA
Wayne State . . . . MI
West Florida, U. of . . . . FL
West Georgia . . . . GA
West Virginia Coll. of Grad. Studies . . . . WV
West Virginia U . . . . WV
Western Carolina U . . . . NC
Western Illinois U IL
Western Michigan . . . . MI
Western Washington State . . . . WA
Westfield State Coll . . . . MA
Wichita State . . . . KS
William Paterson Coll . . . . NJ
Wisconsin, U. of (Madison, Milwaukee, Superior) . . . . WI
Wright State . . . . OH
Xavier U . . . . OH
Youngstown State . . . . OH

Electrical Engineering, *See* ENGINEERING, ELECTRICAL

Electroencephalographic Technology

Degree programs approved by Council on Medical Education of American Medical Assn. in collaboration with American Society of Electroencephalographic Technologists, American Electroencephalographic Society, American Medical Electroencephalographic Assn.

Galveston Coll . . . . TX
Laboure Jr. Coll . . . . MA
Phoenix Jr. Coll . . . . AZ
Western Wisconsin Tech. Inst . . . WI

Electronics Engineering, *See* ENGINEERING, ELECTRONICS

Electronic Music

Akron, U. of . . . . OH
Berklee Coll. of Music . . . . MA
Brevard Coll . . . . NC
Indiana U. (Bloomington) . . . . IN
Jacksonville U . . . . FL
Marlboro Coll . . . . VT
Mills Coll . . . . CA
State U. of New York (Potsdam) NY

Elementary Education, *See* TEACHER EDUCATION

Endocrinology

California, U. of (Davis) . . . . CA
Purdue U . . . . IN
Puerto Rico, U. of . . . . PR
Western Kentucky . . . . KY

ENGINEERING

All of the following Engineering programs have been accredited by the Accreditation Board for Engineering and Technology, Inc.
•Master's Degree

Engineering, Aeronautical and/or Astronautical

•Air Force Inst. of Tech . . . . OH
California Poly. State U. (San Luis Obispo) . . . . CA
Embry-Riddle . . . . FL
Illinois, U. of (Urbana) IL
Massachusetts Inst. of Tech . . . MA
Ohio State U . . . . OH
Purdue U . . . . IN
Rensselaer Poly. Inst . . . . NY
•Stanford U . . . . CA
U.S. Air Force Acad . . . . CO
•U.S. Naval Postgraduate Sch . . . . CA
Washington, U. of . . . . WA
Wichita State U . . . . KS

Engineering, Aeronautics and Astronautics

•California Inst. of Tech .... CA
Massachusetts Inst. of Tech ... MA
Washington, U of .... WA

Engineering, Aerospace

Alabama, U. of (University) ..... AL
Arizona, U. of .... AZ
Auburn U .... AL
Boston U .... MA
California State Poly. U. (Pomona) .... CA
Cincinnati, U. of .... OH
Colorado, U. of .... CO
•Cornell .... NY
Florida, U. of .... FL
Georgia Inst. of Tech .... GA
Illinois Inst. of Tech IL
Iowa State U .... IA
Kansas, U. of .... KS
Maryland, U. of .... MD
Michigan, U. of (Ann Arbor) .... MI
Minnesota, U. of .... MN
Mississippi State .... MS
Missouri, U. of (Rolla) .... MO
New York, Poly. Inst. of .... NY
North Carolina State U. (Raleigh) .... NC
Northrop U .... CA
Notre Dame, U. of .... IN
Oklahoma, U. of .... OK
Oklahoma State U .... OK
Pennsylvania State U .... PA
Princeton .... NJ
San Diego State U .... CA
Southern California, U. of ...... CA
St. Louis U (Parks Coll.) .... MO
State U. of New York (Buffalo) .... NY
Syracuse U .... NY
Tennessee, U. of (Knoxville) .... TN
Texas, U. of (Arlington, Austin) . TX
Texas A&M .... TX
Tri-State U .... IN
U.S. Naval Acad .... MD
Virginia, U. of .... VA
Virginia Poly. Inst .... VA
West Virginia U .... WV

Engineering, Aerospace and Ocean

Virginia Poly. Inst .... VA

Engineering, Agricultural

Arizona, U. of .... AZ
Arkansas, U. of .... AR
Arkansas State U .... AR
Auburn U .... AL
California, U. of (Davis) .... CA
California Poly. State U. (San Luis Obispo) .... CA
Clemson .... SC
Colorado State U .... CO
Cornell U .... NY
Florida, U. of .... FL
Georgia, U. of .... GA
Idaho, U of .... ID
Illinois, U. of (Urbana) IL
Iowa State U .... IA
Kansas State U .... KS
Kentucky, U. of .... KY
Louisiana State U. (Baton Rouge) .... LA
Louisiana Tech. Inst .... LA
Maine, U. of (Orono) .... ME
Maryland, U. of .... MD
Michigan State U .... MI
Minnesota, U. of .... MN
Mississippi State U .... MS
Missouri, U. of (Columbia) ..... MO
Montana State U .... MT
Nebraska, U. of (Lincoln) .... NE
New Mexico State U .... NM
North Carolina State .... NC
North Dakota State .... ND
Ohio State U .... OH
Oklahoma State U .... OK
Oregon State U .... OR
Pennsylvania State U .... PA
Purdue .... IN
Rutgers .... NJ
South Dakota State U .... SD
Tennessee, U. of (Knoxville) .... TN
Texas A&M .... TX
Texas Tech. U .... TX
Utah State .... UT
Virginia Poly. Inst .... VA
Washington State U .... WA
Wisconsin, U. of (Madison) ..... WI
Wyoming, U. of .... WY

Engineering, Agricultural and Irrigation

Utah State U .... UT

Engineering, Applied Mechanics

Illinois, U. of (Chicago Circle) ... IL
Pennsylvania, U. of .... PA

Engineering, Applied and Engineering Physics

Cornell U .... NY

Engineering, Architectural

California Poly. State U. (San Luis Obispo) .... CA
Colorado, U. of .... CO
Kansas, U. of .... KS
Kansas State U .... KS
Miami, U. of .... FL
North Carolina A&T State U ... NC
•Oklahoma State U .... OK
Pennsylvania State U .... PA
Tennessee State U .... TN
Texas, U. of (Austin) .... TX

Engineering, Bioengineering

Illinois, U. of (Chicago) IL
Texas A&M U .... TX

Engineering, Biological

Mississippi State U .... MS
North Carolina State U. (Raleigh) .... NC

Engineering, Biological and Agricultural

North Carolina State U. (Raleigh) .... NC

Engineering, Biomedical

Brown U .... RI
Case Western Reserve U ...... OH
Duke U .... NC
Louisiana Tech. U .... LA
Rensselaer Poly. Inst .... NY
Tulane U .... LA

Engineering, Ceramic

Alfred U .... NY
Clemson .... SC
Florida, U. of .... FL
Georgia Inst. of Tech .... GA
Illinois, U. of (Urbana) IL
Iowa State U .... IA
Missouri, U. of (Rolla) .... MO
Ohio State U .... OH
Pennsylvania State U .... PA
Rutgers .... NJ
Washington, U. of .... WA

Engineering, Chemical

Akron, U. of .... OH
Alabama, U. of (University) ..... AL
Arizona, U. of .... AZ
Arizona State U .... AZ
Arkansas, U. of .... AR
Auburn U .... AL
Brigham Young .... UT
Bucknell .... PA
California, U. of (Berkeley, Davis, Santa Barbara) .... CA
California Inst. of Tech .... CA
California State Poly. U. (Pomona) .... CA
California State U. (Long Beach) .... CA
Carnegie-Mellon U .... PA
Case Western Reserve U ...... OH
Catholic U .... DC
Cincinnati, U. of .... OH
City Coll. of the City U. of New York .... NY
Clarkson Coll. of Tech .... NY
Clemson .... SC
Cleveland State U .... OH
Colorado, U. of .... CO
Colorado School of Mines ..... CO
Colorado State U .... CO
Columbia .... NY
Connecticut, U. of .... CT
Cooper Union .... NY
Cornell .... NY
Dayton, U. of .... OH
Delaware, U. of .... DE
Detroit, U. of .... MI
Drexel U .... PA
Florida, U. of .... FL
Georgia Inst. of Tech .... GA
Houston, U. of .... TX
Howard U .... DC
Idaho, U. of .... ID
Illinois, U. of (Chicago Circle, Urbana) IL
Illinois Inst. of Tech IL
Iowa, U. of .... IA
Iowa State U .... IA
Kansas, U. of .... KS
Kansas State U .... KS
Kentucky, U. of .... KY
Lafayette .... PA
Lamar U .... TX
Lehigh .... PA
Louisiana State U. (Baton Rouge) .... LA
Louisiana Tech. U .... LA
•Louisville, U. of .... KY
Lowell, U. of .... MA
Maine, U. of (Orono) .... ME
Manhattan .... NY
Maryland, U. of .... MD
Massachusetts, U. of (Amherst) .... MA
Massachusetts Inst. of Tech ... MA
Michigan, U. of (Ann Arbor) .... MI
Michigan State U .... MI
Michigan Tech. U .... MI
Minnesota, U. of .... MN
Mississippi, U. of .... MS
Mississippi State U .... MS
Missouri, U. of (Columbia, Rolla) .... MO
Montana State U .... MT
Nebraska, U. of (Lincoln) .... NE
New Hampshire, U. of .... NH
New Jersey Inst. of Tech .... NJ
New Mexico, U. of .... NM
New Mexico State U .... NM
New York, Poly. Inst. of .... NY
North Carolina State U. (Raleigh) .... NC
North Dakota, U. of .... ND
Northeastern .... MA
Northwestern IL
Notre Dame, U. of .... IN
Ohio State U .... OH
Ohio U .... OH
Oklahoma, U. of .... OK
•Oklahoma State U .... OK
Oregon State U .... OR
Pennsylvania, U. of .... PA
Pennsylvania State U .... PA
Pittsburgh, U. of .... PA
Pratt Inst .... NY
Princeton .... NJ
Puerto Rico, U. of .... PR
Purdue .... IN
Rensselaer Poly. Inst .... NY
Rhode Island, U. of .... RI
Rice U .... TX
Rochester, U. of .... NY
Rose-Hulman Inst. of Tech ..... IN
Rutgers U .... NJ
San Jose State U .... CA
South Carolina, U. of .... SC
South Dakota Sch. of Mines and Tech .... SD
South Florida, U. of .... FL
Southern California, U. of ...... CA
Southwestern Louisiana, U. of .. LA
Stanford .... CA
State U. of New York (Buffalo) .. NY
Syracuse U .... NY
Tennessee, U. of (Knoxville) .... TN
Tennessee Tech. U .... TN
Texas, U. of (Austin) .... TX
Texas A&I .... TX
Texas A&M .... TX
Texas Tech. U .... TX
Toledo, U. of .... OH
Tri-State U .... IN
Tufts .... MA
Tulane .... LA
Tulsa, U. of .... OK
Utah, U. of .... UT
Vanderbilt .... TN
Villanova .... PA
Virginia, U. of .... VA
Virginia Poly. Inst .... VA
Washington, U. of .... WA
Washington State U .... WA
Washington U .... MO
Wayne State U .... MI
West Virginia Inst. of Tech ..... WV
West Virginia U .... WV
Wisconsin, U. of (Madison) ..... WI
Worcester Poly. Inst .... MA
Wyoming, U. of .... WY
Youngstown State U .... OH

Engineering, Chemical and Petroleum-Refining

Colorado Sch. of Mines .... CO

Engineering, Civil

Akron, U. of .... OH
Alabama, U. of (University) ..... AL
Alaska, U. of .... AK
Arizona, U. of .... AZ
Arizona State U .... AZ
Arkansas, U. of................. AR
Auburn U .... AL
Bradley IL
Brigham Young U .... UT
Brown .... RI
Bucknell .... PA
California, U. of (Berkeley, Davis, Irvine) .... CA
California Poly. State U. (San Luis Obispo) .... CA
California State Poly. Coll. (Pomona) .... CA
California State U. (Chico, Fresno, Long Beach, Los Angeles, Sacramento) .... CA
Carnegie-Mellon U .... PA
Case Western Reserve U ...... OH
Catholic U .... DC
Cincinnati, U. of .... OH
Citadel .... SC
City Coll. of the City U. of New York .... NY
Clarkson Coll. of Tech.......... NY
Clemson .... SC
Cleveland State U .... OH
Colorado, U. of (Boulder, Denver) .... CO
Colorado State U .... CO
Columbia .... NY
Connecticut, U. of.............. CT
Cooper Union .... NY
Cornell .... NY
Dayton, U. of .... OH
Delaware, U. of .... DE
Detroit, U. of .... MI
District of Columbia, U. of ..... DC
Drexel U .... PA
Duke .... NC
Florida, U. of.................. FL
George Washington U .... DC
Georgia Inst. of Tech.......... GA
Hartford, U. of .... CT
Hawaii, U. of .... HI
Houston, U. of .... TX
Howard U...................... DC
Idaho, U. of .... ID
Illinois, U. of (Urbana) IL
Illinois Inst. of Tech IL
Iowa, U. of .... IA
Iowa State U .... IA
Kansas, U. of .... KS
Kansas State U................. KS
Kentucky, U. of .... KY
Lafayette .... PA
Lamar U .... TX
Lehigh .... PA
Louisiana State U. (Baton Rouge) .... LA
Louisiana Tech. U .... LA
•Louisville, U. of .... KY
Lowell, U. of .... MA
Loyola Marymount U .... CA
Maine, U. of (Orono) .... ME
Manhattan .... NY
Marquette...................... WI
Maryland, U. of .... MD
Massachusetts, U. of (Amherst) .... MA
Massachusetts Inst. of Tech ... MA
Memphis State U .... TN
Merrimack Coll .... MA
Miami, U. of .... FL
Michigan State U............... MI
Michigan Tech U .... MI
Minnesota, U. of .... MN
Mississippi, U. of .... MS
Mississippi State U .... MS
Missouri, U. of (Columbia, Kansas City, Rolla) .... MO
Montana State U .... MT
Nebraska, U. of (Lincoln, Omaha)..................... NE
Nevada, U. of (Reno) .... NV
New England Coll .... NH
New Hampshire, U. of .... NH
New Haven, U. of .... CT
New Jersey Inst. of Tech .... NJ
New Mexico, U. of............. NM
New Mexico State U........... NM
New Orleans, U. of .... LA
New York, Poly. Inst. of......... NY
North Carolina State U. (Raleigh) .... NC
North Dakota, U. of .... ND
North Dakota State U .... ND
Northeastern .... MA
Northern Arizona U .... AZ
Northwestern IL
Norwich .... VT
Notre Dame, U. of.............. IN
Ohio Northern .... OH
Ohio State U .... OH
Ohio U .... OH
Oklahoma, U. of .... OK
Oklahoma State U............. OK
Old Dominion U .... VA
Oregon State U .... OR
Pacific, U. of the .... CA
Pennsylvania, U. of............. PA
Pennsylvania State U .... PA
Pittsburgh, U. of .... PA
Portland, U. of .... OR
Prairie View A&M U .... TX
Princeton .... NJ
Puerto Rico, U. of (Mayaguez) .. PR
Purdue .... IN
Rensselaer Poly. Inst .... NY
Rhode Island, U. of............. RI
Rice U .... TX
Rose-Hulman Inst. of Tech ..... IN
Rutgers U...................... NJ
San Diego State U .... CA
San Jose State U............... CA
Santa Clara, U. of .... CA
South Carolina, U. of .... SC
South Dakota Sch. of Mines .... SD
South Dakota State U .... SD
Southeastern Massachusetts ... MA
Southern California, U. of ...... CA
Southern Illinois U. (Edwardsville)................. IL
Southern Methodist .... TX
Southern U .... LA
Southwestern Louisiana, U. of .. LA
St. Martin's Coll .... WA
Stanford .... CA
State U. of New York (Buffalo)...................... NY
Syracuse .... NY
Tennessee, U. of (Knoxville) .... TN
Tennessee State U .... TN
Tennessee Tech. U .... TN
Texas, U. of (Arlington, Austin, El Paso) .... TX
Texas A&I .... TX
Texas A&M .... TX
Texas Tech. U .... TX
Toledo, U. of................... OH
Tri-State U .... IN
Tufts .... MA
Tulane......................... LA
U.S. Air Force Acad .... CO
U.S. Coast Guard Acad .... CT
Union .... NY
Utah, U. of..................... UT
Utah State U .... UT
Valparaiso U .... IN
Vanderbilt .... TN
Vermont, U. of .... VT
Villanova .... PA
Virginia, U. of .... VA
Virginia Military Inst .... VA
Virginia Poly. Inst .... VA
Washington, U. of .... WA
Washington State U .... WA
Washington U .... MO
Wayne State U .... MI
West Virginia Inst. of Tech ..... WV
West Virginia U .... WV
Wisconsin, U. of (Madison, Milwaukee, Platteville) .... WI
Worcester Poly. Inst .... MA
Wyoming, U. of .... WY
Youngstown State U .... OH

Engineering, Civil/Building Sciences

Southern California, U. of ...... CA

Engineering, Civil and Environmental

Cornell U .... NY
Vanderbilt U .... TN
Wisconsin, U. of (Madison) ..... WI

Engineering, Civil and Urban

Pennsylvania, U. of............. PA

Engineering, Coastal and Oceanographic

Florida, U. of................... FL

Engineering, Communication

Illinois, U. of (Chicago) IL

Engineering, Computer

California State U. (Long Beach) .... CA
Case Western Reserve......... OH
Illinois, U. of (Chicago Circle, Urbana) IL
Iowa State U .... IA
Massachusetts Inst. of Tech ... MA
Michigan, U. of (Ann Arbor) .... MI
New Mexico, U. of............. NM
Oakland U .... MI
Syracuse U .... NY

Engineering, Computer and Information Systems

Illinois, U. of (Chicago Circle) ... IL

Engineering, Computer Science

Connecticut, U. of............. CT
Washington U................. MO

Engineering, Computer Systems

Arizona State U .... AZ
Massachusetts, U. of (Amherst).................. MA
Rensselaer Poly. Inst .... NY

Engineering, Construction

Iowa State U .... IA
Lawrence Inst .... MI
North Carolina State U. (Raleigh) .... NC

Engineering, Design

Colorado, U. of .... CO
North Carolina, U. of (Charlotte) .... NC

Engineering, Electric Power

Rennsselaer Poly. Inst .... NY

Engineering, Electrical

Air Force Inst. of Tech......... OH
Akron, U. of .... OH
Alabama, U. of (Huntsville, University) .... AL
Alaska, U. of .... AK
Arizona, U. of .... AZ
Arizona State U .... AZ
Arkansas, U. of................. AR
Auburn U .... AL
Bradley IL
Bridgeport, U. of .... CT
Brigham Young U .... UT
Brown .... RI
Bucknell .... PA
California, U. of (Berkeley, Davis, Irvine, Santa Barbara) .... CA
California Poly. State U. (San Luis Obispo) .... CA
California State Poly. U. (Pomona) .... CA
California State U. (Chico, Fresno, Long Beach, Los Angeles)................. CA
Carnegie-Mellon U .... PA
Case Western Reserve U ...... OH
Catholic U .... DC
Central Florida, U. of .... FL
Christian Brothers Coll .... TN
Cincinnati, U. of .... OH
Citadel, The .... SC
City Coll. of the City U. of NY .. NY
Clarkson Coll. of Tech.......... NY
Clemson .... SC
Cleveland State U .... OH
Colorado, U. of (Boulder, Colorado Springs, Denver) .. CO
Colorado State U .... CO
Columbia .... NY
Connecticut, U. of.............. CT
Cooper Union .... NY
Cornell .... NY
Dayton, U. of .... OH
Delaware, U. of .... DE
Detroit, U. of .... MI
District of Columbia, U. of ..... DC
Drexel U .... PA
Duke .... NC
Evansville, U. of .... IN
Fairleigh Dickinson............. NJ
Florida, U. of................... FL
Florida Atlantic U .... FL
Florida Inst. of Tech .... FL
Gannon .... PA
General Motors Inst .... MI
George Washington U .... DC
Georgia Inst. of Tech.......... GA
Hartford, U. of .... CT
Hawaii, U. of .... HI
Houston, U. of .... TX
Howard U..................... DC
Idaho, U. of .... ID
Illinois, U. of (Urbana) IL
Illinois Inst. of Tech IL
Indiana U.-Purdue U .... IN

Iowa, U. of ... IA
Iowa State U ... IA
Johns Hopkins ... MD
Kansas, U. of ... KS
Kansas State U ... KS
Kentucky, U. of ... KY
Lafayette ... PA
Lamar U ... TX
Lawrence Inst ... MI
Lehigh ... PA
LeTourneau Coll ... TX
Louisiana State U ... LA
Louisiana Tech. U ... LA
•Louisville, U. of ... KY
Lowell, U. of ... MA
Loyola Marymount U ... CA
Maine, U. of (Orono) ... ME
Manhattan ... NY
Marquette ... WI
Maryland, U. of ... MD
Massachusetts, U. of (Amherst) ... MA
Massachusetts Inst. of Tech ... MA
Memphis State U ... TN
Merrimack Coll ... MA
Miami, U. of ... FL
Michigan, U. of (Ann Arbor, Dearborn) ... MI
Michigan State U ... MI
Michigan Tech. U ... MI
Milwaukee School of Engineering ... WI
Minnesota, U. of ... MN
Mississippi, U. of ... MS
Mississippi State U ... MS
Missouri, U. of (Columbia, Kansas City, Rolla) ... MO
Montana State U ... MT
Naval Postgraduate School ... CA
Nebraska, U. of (Lincoln) ... NE
Nevada, U. of (Reno) ... NV
New Hampshire, U. of ... NH
New Haven, U. of ... CT
New Jersey Inst. of Tech ... NJ
New Mexico, U. of ... NM
New Mexico State U ... NM
New Orleans, U. of ... LA
New York, Poly. Inst. of ... NY
North Carolina A&T State U ... NC
North Carolina State U. (Raleigh) ... NC
North Dakota, U. of ... ND
North Dakota State ... ND
Northeastern ... MA
Northern Arizona U ... AZ
Northwestern U ... IL
Norwich ... VT
Notre Dame, U. of ... IN
Oakland U ... MI
Ohio Northern ... OH
Ohio State U ... OH
Ohio U ... OH
Oklahoma, U. of ... OK
Oklahoma State U ... OK
Old Dominion U ... VA
Oregon State U ... OR
Pacific, U. of the ... CA
Pennsylvania, U. of ... PA
Pennsylvania State U ... PA
Pittsburgh, U. of ... PA
Portland, U. of ... OR
Prairie View A&M ... TX
Pratt ... NY
Princeton ... NJ
Puerto Rico, U. of (Mayaguez) ... PR
Purdue ... IN
Rensselaer Poly. Inst ... NY
Rhode Island, U. of ... RI
Rice U ... TX
Rochester, U. of ... NY
Rochester Inst. of Tech ... NY
Rose-Hulman Inst. of Tech ... IN
Rutgers ... NJ
San Diego State U ... CA
San Jose State U ... CA
Santa Clara, U. of ... CA
Seattle U ... WA
South Alabama, U. of ... AL
South Carolina, U. of ... SC
South Dakota Sch. of Mines ... SD
South Dakota State U ... SD
South Florida, U. of ... FL
Southeastern Massachusetts U ... MA
Southern California, U. of ... CA
Southern Illinois U. (Carbondale, Edwardsville) ... IL
Southern Methodist ... TX
Southern U ... LA
Southwestern Louisiana, U. of ... LA
Stanford ... CA
State U. of New York (Buffalo, Maritime Coll., Stony Brook) ... NY
Syracuse U ... NY
Tennessee, U. of (Knoxville) ... TN
Tennessee State U ... TN
Tennessee Tech. U ... TN
Texas, U. of (Arlington, Austin, El Paso) ... TX
Texas A&I U ... TX
Texas A&M ... TX
Texas Tech. U ... TX
Toledo, U. of ... OH
Tri-State U ... IN
Tufts ... MA
Tulane ... LA
Tulsa, U. of ... OK
Tuskegee Inst ... AL
U.S. Air Force Acad ... CO
U.S. Coast Guard Acad ... CT
•U.S. Naval Postgraduate School ... CA
Union ... NY
Utah, U. of ... UT
Utah State U ... UT
Valparaiso U ... IN
Vanderbilt ... TN
Vermont, U. of ... VT
Villanova ... PA
Virginia, U. of ... VA
Virginia Military Inst ... VA
Virginia Poly. Inst ... VA
Washington, U. of ... WA
Washington State U ... WA
Washington U ... MO
Wayne State U ... MI
West Virginia Inst. of Tech ... WV
West Virginia U ... WV
Western New England Coll ... MA
Wichita State U ... KS
Wilkes Coll ... PA
Wisconsin U. of (Madison, Milwaukee) ... WI
Worcester Poly. Inst ... MA
Wright State U ... OH
Wyoming, U. of ... WY
Youngstown State U ... OH

Engineering, Electrical and Computer and/or Science

California, U. of (Berkeley) ... CA
Oregon State U ... OR
Santa Clara, U. of ... CA
Wisconsin, U. of (Madison) ... WI

Engineering, Electrical and Electronic

California State Poly. U. (Pomona) ... CA
California State U. (Chico, Sacramento) ... CA

Engineering, Electrical Sciences and Systems

Southern Illinois U. (Carbondale) ... IL

Engineering, Electronic

California Poly. State U. (San Luis Obispo) ... CA
California State Poly. U. (Pomona) ... CA
California State U. (Chico) ... CA
Illinois, U. of (Chicago) ... IL
Monmouth Coll ... NJ
Northrop U ... CA
Yale ... CT

Engineering, Energy Conversion

Illinois, U. of (Chicago) ... IL

Engineering, Environmental

California Poly. State U. (San Luis Obispo) ... CA
Central Florida, U. of ... FL
•Cincinnati, U. of ... OH
•Clemson U ... SC
•Colorado State U ... CO
Cornell ... NY
Florida, U. of ... FL
Harvard ... MA
Humboldt State U ... CA
•Manhattan Coll ... NY
•Massachusetts, U. of (Amherst) ... MA
Montana Coll. of Tech ... MT
North Carolina, U. of (•Chapel Hill, Charlotte) ... NC
Northwestern ... IL
Pennsylvania State U ... PA
Rensselaer Poly. Inst ... NY
Southern Illinois U. (Carbondale) ... IL
•Tennessee, U. of (Knoxville) ... TN
Vanderbilt U ... TN
Wisconsin, U. of (Madison) ... WI

Engineering, Environmental Health and/or Sciences

•California Inst. of Tech ... CA
Michigan, U. of (Ann Arbor) ... MI
•Texas, U. of (Austin) ... TX

Engineering, Fire Protection

Maryland, U. of ... MD

Engineering, Fluid and/or Thermal Science

Case Western Reserve U ... OH
Illinois, U. of (Chicago) ... IL
South Florida, U. of ... FL

Engineering, Forest

Maine, U. of (Orono) ... ME

Engineering, General

Alabama, U. of (Birmingham, Huntsville) ... AL
Arizona State U ... AZ
California, U. of (Irvine, Los Angeles) ... CA
California Inst. of Tech ... CA
California State U. (Fullerton, •Long Beach, Northridge) ... CA
Carnegie-Mellon U ... PA
Case Western Reserve U ... OH
Central Florida, U. of ... FL
Dartmouth ... NH
Harvey Mudd ... CA
Illinois, U. of (Chicago, Urbana) ... IL
LeTourneau Coll ... TX
Maryland, U. of ... MD
McNeese State U ... LA
Michigan Tech. U ... MI
Oakland U ... MI
Oklahoma, U. of ... OK
•Oklahoma State U ... OK
Portland State U ... OR
Purdue U. (Calumet) ... IN
San Francisco State U ... CA
Southern Illinois U. (Carbondale) ... IL
Stevens Inst. of Tech ... NJ
Swarthmore ... PA
Tennessee, U. of (Chattanooga, Nashville) ... TN
Walla Walla Coll ... WA
Widener Coll ... PA

Engineering, Geological

Alaska, U. of ... AK
Arizona, U. of ... AZ
Colorado Sch. of Mines ... CO
Idaho, U. of ... ID
Michigan Tech. U ... MI
Minnesota, U. of ... MN
Mississippi, U. of ... MS
Missouri, U. of (Rolla) ... MO
Montana Coll. of Mineral Science ... MT
Nevada, U. of (Reno) ... NV
New Mexico Inst. of Mining and Tech ... NM
Princeton ... NJ
South Dakota Sch. of Mines ... SD
Utah, U. of ... UT

Engineering, Geophysical

Colorado School of Mines ... CO
Montana Coll. of Mineral Science ... MT

Engineering, Glass Science

Alfred U ... NY

Engineering, Industrial

•Alabama, U. of (Huntsville, University) ... AL
Arizona, U. of ... AZ
•Arizona State U ... AZ
•Arkansas, U. of ... AR
•Auburn U ... AL
•Bradley ... IL
California, U. of (Berkeley) ... CA
•California Poly. State U. (San Luis Obispo) ... CA
•California State Poly. U. (Pomona) ... CA
•Central Florida, U. of ... FL
•Cleveland State U ... OH
•Columbia U ... NY
Cornell ... NY
•Fairleigh Dickinson U ... NJ
•Florida, U. of ... FL
•General Motors Inst ... MI
•Georgia Inst. of Tech ... GA

•Houston, U. of .... TX
•Illinois, U. of (Chicago Circle, Urbana) IL
•Illinois Inst. of Tech IL
•Iowa, U. of .... IA
•Iowa State U .... IA
•Kansas State U .... KS
•Lamar U .... TX
•Lehigh .... PA
•Louisiana State U .... LA
•Louisiana Tech. U .... LA
Massachusetts, U. of (Amherst) .... MA
•Miami, U. of .... FL
•Michigan, U. of (Ann Arbor, Dearborn) .... MI
•Mississippi State U .... MS
•Missouri, U. of (Columbia) .... MO
•Montana State U .... MT
•Nebraska, U. of (Lincoln) .... NE
•New Haven, U. of .... CT
•New Jersey Inst. of Tech .... NJ
•New Mexico State U .... NM
•New York, Poly. Inst. of .... NY
North Carolina Ag. and Tech .. NC
•North Carolina State U. (Raleigh) .... NC
•North Dakota State U .... ND
•Northeastern .... MA
•Northwestern IL
•Ohio State U .... OH
•Ohio U .... OH
•Oklahoma, U. of .... OK
•Oklahoma State U .... OK
•Oregon State U .... OR
•Pennsylvania State U .... PA
•Pittsburgh, U. of .... PA
•Puerto Rico, U. of (Mayaguez) .. PR
•Purdue .... IN
•Rhode Island, U. of .... RI
•Rochester Inst. of Tech .... NY
•Rutgers .... NJ
•San Jose State U .... CA
•South Florida, U. of .... FL
•Southern California, U. of .... CA
•Stanford .... CA
•State U. of New York (Buffalo) .. NY
Syracuse U .... NY
•Tennessee, U. of (Knoxville) .... TN
•Tennessee Tech. U .... TN
•Texas, U. of (Arlington) .... TX
•Texas A&M .... TX
•Texas Tech. U .... TX
•Toledo, U. of .... OH
•Utah, U. of .... UT
Virginia Poly. Inst .... VA
•Wayne State U .... MI
•West Virginia U .... WV
•Western Michigan U .... MI
•Wichita State U .... KS
•Wisconsin, U. of (Madison, Milwaukee) .... WI

Engineering, Industrial and Operations Research

California, U. of (Berkeley) .... CA
Cornell U .... NY
Massachusetts, U. of .... MA
Michigan, U. of (Ann Arbor) .... MI
Syracuse U .... NY
Virginia Poly. Inst .... VA

Engineering, Management

Columbia U .... NY
Missouri, U. of (Rolla) .... MO
•Rensselaer Poly. Inst .... NY
Southern Methodist U .... TX

Engineering, Manufacturing

Boston U .... MA
•Massachusetts, U. of (Amherst) .... MA
Utah State U .... UT

Engineering, Marine

Massachusetts Inst. of Tech ... MA
Michigan, U. of (Ann Arbor) .... MI
State U. of New York (Maritime Coll.) .... NY
Texas A&M U. (Galveston) .... TX
U.S. Coast Guard Acad .... CT
U.S. Naval Acad .... MD
Webb Inst .... NY

Engineering, Materials

Auburn .... AL
Brown .... RI
California, U. of (Berkeley) .... CA
California State U. (Long Beach) .... CA
Carnegie-Mellon U .... PA
Case Western Reserve .... OH
Cornell .... NY
Drexel U .... PA
General Motors Inst .... MI
Lehigh U .... PA
Massachusetts Inst. of Tech ... MA
Michigan Tech. U .... MI
North Carolina, U. of (Charlotte) .... NC
North Carolina State .... NC
Northwestern U IL
Pennsylvania, U. of .... PA
Rensselaer Poly. Inst .... NY
Rice .... TX
San Jose State U .... CA
South Florida, U. of .... FL
Utah, U. of .... UT
Virginia Poly. Inst .... VA
Wisconsin, U. of (Milwaukee) ... WI
Wright State U .... OH

Engineering, Mathematics

Central Florida, U. of .... FL
Washington U .... MO

Engineering, Mechanical

Akron, U. of .... OH
Alabama, U. of (Huntsville, University) .... AL
Alaska, U. of .... AK
Arizona, U. of .... AZ
Arizona State U .... AZ
Arkansas, U. of .... AR
Auburn U .... AL
Bradley IL
Bridgeport, U. of .... CT
Brigham Young U .... UT
Brown .... RI
Bucknell .... PA
California, U. of (Berkeley, Davis, Irvine, Santa Barbara) .... CA
California Poly. State U. (San Luis Obispo) .... CA
California State Poly. U. (Pomona) .... CA
California State U. (Chico, Fresno, Long Beach, Los Angeles, Sacramento) .... CA
Carnegie-Mellon U .... PA
Case Western Reserve U .... OH
Catholic U .... DC
Central Florida, U. of .... FL
Christian Brothers Coll .... TN
Cincinnati, U. of .... OH
City Coll. of the City U. of New York .... NY
Clarkson Coll. of Tech .... NY
Clemson .... SC
Cleveland State U .... OH
Colorado, U. of .... CO
Colorado State U .... CO
Columbia .... NY
Connecticut, U. of .... CT
Cooper Union .... NY
Cornell .... NY
Dayton, U. of .... OH
Delaware, U. of .... DE
Detroit, U. of .... MI
Drexel U .... PA
Duke .... NC
Evansville, U. of .... IN
Fairleigh Dickinson .... NJ
Florida, U. of .... FL
Florida Atlantic U .... FL
Florida Inst. of Tech .... FL
Gannon .... PA
General Motors Inst .... MI
George Washington U .... DC
Georgia Inst. of Tech .... GA
Hartford, U. of .... CT
Hawaii, U. of .... HI
Houston, U. of .... TX
Howard U .... DC
Idaho, U. of .... ID
Illinois, U. of (Urbana) IL
Illinois Inst. of Tech IL
Indiana U.-Purdue U .... IN
Iowa, U. of .... IA
Iowa State U .... IA
Kansas, U. of .... KS
Kansas State U .... KS
Kentucky, U. of .... KY
Lafayette .... PA
Lamar U .... TX
Lawrence Inst .... MI
Lehigh .... PA
LeTourneau Coll .... TX
Louisiana State U .... LA
Louisiana Tech. U .... LA
•Louisville, U. of .... KY
Lowell, U. of .... MA
Loyola Marymount U .... CA
Maine, U. of (Orono) .... ME
Manhattan Coll .... NY
Marquette .... WI
Maryland, U. of .... MD
Massachusetts, U. of .... MA
Massachusetts Inst. of Tech ... MA
Memphis State U .... TN
Miami, U. of .... FL
Michigan, U. of (Ann Arbor, Dearborn) .... MI
Michigan State U .... MI
Michigan Tech. U .... MI
Milwaukee Sch. of Engr .... WI
Minnesota, U. of .... MN
Mississippi, U. of .... MS
Mississippi State U .... MS
Missouri, U. of (Columbia, Kansas City, Rolla) .... MO
Montana State U .... MT
Nebraska, U. of (Lincoln) .... NE
Nevada, U. of (Reno) .... NV
New Hampshire, U. of .... NH
New Haven, U. of .... CT
New Jersey Inst. of Tech .... NJ
New Mexico, U. of .... NM
New Mexico State U .... NM
New Orleans, U. of .... LA
New York, Poly. Inst. of .... NY
North Carolina A&T State U ... NC
North Carolina State U. (Raleigh) .... NC
North Dakota, U. of .... ND
North Dakota State U .... ND
Northeastern .... MA
Northern Arizona U .... AZ
Northrop U .... CA
Northwestern IL
Norwich .... VT
Notre Dame, U. of .... IN
Oakland U .... MI
Ohio Northern .... OH
Ohio State U .... OH
Ohio U .... OH
Oklahoma, U. of .... OK
Oklahoma State U .... OK
Old Dominion .... VA
Oregon State U .... OR
Pennsylvania, U. of .... PA
Pennsylvania State U .... PA
Pittsburgh, U. of .... PA
Portland, U. of .... OR
Prairie View A&M .... TX
Pratt .... NY
Princeton .... NJ
Puerto Rico, U. of (Mayaguez) .. PR
Purdue .... IN
Rensselaer Poly. Inst .... NY
Rhode Island, U. of .... RI
Rice U .... TX
Rochester, U. of .... NY
Rochester Inst. of Tech .... NY
Rose-Hulman Inst. of Tech ..... IN
Rutgers .... NJ
San Diego State U .... CA
San Jose State U .... CA
Santa Clara, U. of .... CA
Seattle U .... WA
South Carolina, U. of .... SC
South Dakota Sch. of Mines .... SD
South Dakota State U .... SD
South Florida, U. of .... FL
Southeastern Massachusetts U . MA
Southern California, U. of .... CA
Southern Methodist .... TX
Southern U .... LA
Southwestern Louisiana, U. of .. LA
Stanford .... CA
State U. of New York (Buffalo, Stony Brook) .... NY
Syracuse U .... NY
Tennessee, U. of (Knoxville) .... TN
Tennessee State U .... TN
Tennessee Tech. U .... TN
Texas, U. of (Arlington, Austin, El Paso) .... TX
Texas A&I U .... TX
Texas A&M .... TX
Texas Tech. U .... TX
Toledo, U. of .... OH
Tri-State U .... IN
Tufts .... MA
Tulane .... LA
Tulsa, U. of .... OK
Tuskegee Inst .... AL
U.S. Naval Acad .... MD
U.S. Naval Postgraduate Sch ... CA
Union .... NY
Utah, U. of .... UT
Utah State U .... UT
Valparaiso U .... IN
Vanderbilt .... TN
Vermont, U. of .... VT
Villanova .... PA
Virginia, U. of .... VA
Virginia Poly. Inst .... VA
Washington, U. of .... WA
Washington State U .... WA
Washington U .... MO
Wayne State U .... MI
West Virginia Inst. of Tech ..... WV
West Virginia U .... WV
Western New England Coll .... MA
Wichita State U .... KS
Wisconsin, U. of (Madison, Milwaukee) .... WI
Worcester Poly. Inst .... MA
Wright State U .... OH

Wyoming, U. of .... WY
Youngstown State U .... OH

Engineering, Mechanical Design

Illinois, U. of (Chicago Circle) ... IL

Engineering, Mechanics

Columbia U .... NY
Illinois, U. of (Urbana) IL
Lehigh .... PA
Missouri, U. of (Rolla) .... MO
North Carolina, U. of (Charlotte) .... NC
Southern Illinois U. (Carbondale) IL
Tennesee Tech. U .... TN
U.S. Air Force Acad .... CO
Virginia Poly. Inst .... VA
Wisconsin, U. of (Madison) ..... WI
Yale .... CT

Engineering, Metallurgical

Alabama, U. of (University) ..... AL
Arizona, U. of .... AZ
California Poly. State U. (San Luis Obispo) .... CA
Cincinnati, U. of .... OH
Colorado Sch. of Mines .... CO
Columbia U .... NY
Florida, U. of .... FL
Idaho, U. of .... ID
Illinois, U. of (Urbana) IL
Illinois Inst. of Tech IL
Iowa State U .... IA
Kentucky, U. of .... KY
Lafayette .... PA
Michigan Tech. U .... MI
Minnesota, U. of .... MN
Missouri, U. of (Rolla) .... MO
Montana Coll. of Mineral Sci. and Tech .... MT
Nevada, U. of (Reno) .... NV
New Mexico Inst. of Mining and Tech .... NM
New York, Poly. Inst. of .... NY
Notre Dame, U. of .... IN
Ohio State U .... OH
Oklahoma, U. of .... OK
Pittsburgh, U. of .... PA
Purdue .... IN
South Dakota Sch. of Mines .... SD
Tennessee, U. of (Knoxville) .... TN
Texas, U. of (El Paso) .... TX
Utah, U. of .... UT
Washington, U. of .... WA
Wayne State U .... MI
Wisconsin, U. of (Madison) ..... WI

Engineering, Metallurgy

Carnegie-Mellon U .... PA
Case Western Reserve .... OH
•Georgia Inst. of Tech .... GA
Illinois, U. of (Chicago) IL
Lehigh .... PA
Pennsylvania, U. of .... PA
Pennsylvania State U .... PA
Washington State U .... WA

Engineering, Metals

Florida, U. of .... FL

Engineering, Mineral

Alabama, U. of (University) ..... AL
Colorado Sch. of Mines .... CO
Minnesota, U. of .... MN

Engineering, Mineral Process

Michigan Tech. U .... MI
Montana Coll. of Mineral Sci ... MT

Engineering, Mining

Alaska, U. of .... AK
Arizona, U. of .... AZ
Colorado Sch. of Mines .... CO
Columbia U .... NY
Idaho, U. of .... ID
Michigan Tech. U .... MI
Missouri, U. of (Rolla) .... MO
Montana Coll. of Mineral Sci. and Tech .... MT
Nevada, U. of (Reno) .... NV
New Mexico Inst. of Mining and Tech .... NM
Pennsylvania State U .... PA
South Dakota School of Mines and Tech .... SD
Utah, U. of .... UT
Virginia Poly. Inst .... VA
West Virginia U .... WV
Wisconsin, U. of (Madison, Platteville) .... WI

Engineering, Natural Gas

Pennsylvania State U .... PA
Texas A&I U .... TX

Engineering, Naval Architecture

•California, U. of (Berkeley) ..... CA
Massachusetts Inst. of Tech ... MA
Michigan, U. of (Ann Arbor) .... MI
State U. of New York (Maritime Coll.) .... NY
U.S. Naval Acad .... MD
Webb Inst. of Naval Arch .... NY

Engineering, Nuclear

•Air Force Inst. of Tech .... OH
Arizona, U. of .... AZ
California, U. of (Berkeley, Santa Barbara) .... CA
Cincinnati, U. of .... OH
Columbia U .... NY
Florida, U. of .... FL
Georgia Inst. of Tech .... GA
Illinois, U. of (Urbana) IL
Iowa State U .... IA
Kansas State U .... KS
Lowell, U. of .... MA
Maryland, U. of .... MD
Massachusetts Inst. of Tech ... MA
Michigan, U. of (Ann Arbor) .... MI
Mississippi State U .... MS
Missouri, U. of (Rolla) .... MO
New York, Poly. Inst. of .... NY
North Carolina State (Raleigh) . NC
Oklahoma, U. of .... OK
Oregon State .... OR
Pennsylvania State U .... PA
Purdue U .... IN
Rensselaer Poly. Inst .... NY
State U. of New York (Buffalo) .. NY
Tennessee, U. of (Knoxville) .... TN
Texas A&M .... TX
Virginia, U. of .... VA
Wisconsin, U. of (Madison) ..... WI

Engineering, Ocean

California State U. (Long Beach) .... CA
Florida Atlantic U .... FL
Florida Inst. of Tech .... FL
•Hawaii, U. of .... HI
Massachusetts Inst. of Tech ... MA
Texas A&M U .... TX
U.S. Coast Guard Acad .... CT
U.S. Naval Acad .... MD
Virginia Poly. Inst .... VA

Engineering, Petroleum

Colorado Sch. of Mines .... CO
Kansas, U. of .... KS
Louisiana State U .... LA
Louisiana Tech. U .... LA
Mississippi State U .... MS
Missouri, U. of (Rolla) .... MO
Montana Coll. of Mineral Science .... MT
New Mexico Inst. of Mining and Tech .... NM
Oklahoma, U. of .... OK
Pennsylvania State U .... PA
Southern California, U. of ...... CA
Southwestern Louisiana, U. of .. LA
Stanford .... CA
Texas, U. of (Austin) .... TX
Texas A&M .... TX
Texas Tech. U .... TX
Tulsa, U. of .... OK
West Virginia U .... WV
Wyoming, U. of .... WY

Engineering, Physics

Cornell .... NY
Kansas, U. of .... KS
Maine, U. of (Orono) .... ME
Oklahoma, U. of .... OK
Princeton .... NJ
Texas Tech. U .... TX
Toledo, U. of .... OH
Tulsa, U. of .... OK

Engineering, Plant

General Motors Inst .... MI

Engineering, Plastics

Lowell, U. of .... MA

Engineering, Polymer Science

Case Western Reserve U ...... OH

Engineering, Power and Nuclear

Cincinnati, U. of .... OH

Engineering, Process

General Motors Inst .... MI

Engineering, Sanitary

•California, U. of (Berkeley) ..... CA
•Georgia Inst. of Tech .... GA

Engineering Science

Arizona State U .... AZ
Arkansas, U. of .... AR
Colorado State U .... CO
Florida, U. of .... FL
Georgia Inst. of Tech .... GA
Harvard .... MA
Hofstra U .... NY
Illinois, U. of (Chicago) IL
Iowa State U .... IA
Michigan, U. of (Ann Arbor) .... MI
Montana Coll. of Tech .... MT
North Carolina, U. of (Charlotte) .... NC
Notre Dame, U. of .... IN
Pennsylvania State U .... PA
State U. of New York (Buffalo, Stony Brook) .... NY
Tennessee, U. of (Knoxville) .... TN
Tennessee Tech. U .... TN
Texas, U. of (Austin) .... TX
Trinity U .... TX
U.S. Air Force Acad .... CO
Virginia Poly. Inst .... VA

Engineering, Structural or Structures

Illinois, U. of (Chicago) IL
Portland State U .... OR
South Florida, U. of .... FL

Engineering, Surveying and/or Photogrammetry

California State U. (Fresno) ..... CA
Maine, U. of (Orono) .... ME

Engineering, Systems

•Air Force Inst. of Tech .... OH
Arizona, U. of .... AZ
Boston U .... MA
Case Western Reserve U ...... OH
Florida, U. of .... FL
Oakland U .... MI
U.S. Naval Acad .... MD
Virginia, U. of .... VA
Washington U .... MO
Wright State U .... OH

Engineering, Technology

Accredited by the Accreditation Board for Engineering and Technology for degree programs in Engineering Technology and offering variety of programs as described in the individual college entries

Aeronautics, Acad. of .... NY
Akron, U. of (Community and Tech. Coll.) .... OH
Alabama A&M .... AL
Alamance, Tech. Inst. of .... NC
Anoka-Ramsey Comm .... MN
Arizona State U .... AZ
Atlantic Comm. Coll .... NJ
Belleville Area Coll IL
Blue Mountain Comm. Coll .... OR
Bluefield State Coll .... WV
Bradley IL
Brigham Young U .... UT
Bronx Comm. Coll .... NY
Broome Comm. Coll .... NY
California Maritime Acad .... CA
California Poly. State U. (San Luis Obispo) .... CA
California State Poly. (Pomona) . CA
California State U. (Sacramento) .... CA

Capitol Inst. of Tech ... MD
Central Florida, U. of ... FL
Chattanooga State Tech. Comm. Coll ... TN
Cincinnati, U. of ... OH
Cincinnati Tech. Coll ... OH
City Coll. of CUNY ... NY
Clemson U ... SC
Cogswell Coll ... CA
Colorado Tech. Coll ... CO
Columbus Tech. Inst ... OH
Connecticut, U. of ... CT
Dayton, U. of ... OH
Del Mar Coll ... TX
Delta Coll ... MI
DeVry Inst. of Tech ... AZ
DeVry Inst. of Tech ... GA
DeVry Inst. of Tech ... IL
DeVry Inst. of Tech ... TX
District of Columbia, U. of (Van Ness Campus) ... DC
East Tennessee State U ... TN
Eastern Maine Voc.-Tech. Inst ... ME
Embry-Riddle Aeronautical Inst ... FL
Erie Comm. Coll ... NY
Fayetteville Tech. Inst ... NC
Florence Darlington Tech. Coll ... SC
Florida A&M U ... FL
Florida International U ... FL
Fort Valley State Coll ... GA
Franklin Inst. of Boston ... MA
Franklin U ... OH
Gaston Coll ... NC
Georgia Southern Coll ... GA
Glendale Comm. Coll ... AZ
Greenville Tech. Coll ... SC
Guilford Tech. Inst ... NC
Hartford, U. of ... CT
Hartford State Tech. Coll ... CT
Hawkeye Inst. of Tech ... IA
Houston, U. of (Coll. of Tech.) ... TX
Hudson Valley Comm. Coll ... NY
Indiana State U ... IN
Indiana U.-Purdue U. (Fort Wayne, Indianapolis) ... IN
Kansas State U ... KS
Kansas Tech. Inst ... KS
Kent State U ... OH
Knoxville State Tech. Inst ... TN
Lake Superior State Coll ... MI
Lawrence Inst. of Tech ... MI
Longview Comm. Coll ... MO
Louisiana Tech. U ... LA
Lowell, U. of ... MA
Maine, U. of, at Orono ... ME
Memphis, State Tech. Inst. at ... TN
Memphis State U ... TN
Mercer County Comm. Coll ... NJ
Metropolitan State Coll ... CO
Michael J. Owens Tech. Coll ... OH
Michigan Tech. U ... MI
Middlesex County Coll ... NJ
Midlands Tech. Coll ... SC
Milwaukee Sch. of Engineering ... WI
Missouri Inst. of Tech ... MO
Mohawk Valley Comm. Coll ... MY
Monroe Comm. Coll ... NY
Montana State U ... MT
Montgomery Coll ... MD
Morrison Inst. of Tech ... IL
Murray State U ... KY
Nashville State Tech. Inst ... TN
Nassau Comm. Coll ... NY
Nebraska, U. of (Omaha) ... NE
Nevada, U. of ... NV
New Hampshire, U. of ... NH
New Hampshire Tech. Inst ... NH
New Jersey Inst. of Tech ... NJ
New Mexico State U ... NM
New York City Tech. Coll ... NY
New York Inst. of Tech. (Metropolitan, Old Westbury) ... NY
North Carolina, U. of (Charlotte) ... NC
Northeastern U. (Lincoln Coll.) ... MA
Northern Arizona U ... AZ
Northrop U ... CA
Norwalk State Tech. Coll ... CT
Norwich U ... VT
Ocean County Coll ... NJ
Ohio Inst. of Tech ... OH
Oklahoma State U. (Sch. of Tech.) ... OK
Old Dominion U ... VA
Orange Co. Comm. Coll ... NY
Oregon Inst. of Tech ... OR
Oregon State U ... OR
Parkland Coll ... IL
Pennsylvania State U. (Altoona, Beaver, Behrend [Erie], Berks Ctr., Capitol, Delaware County, Dubois, Fayette, Hazleton, McKeesport, Mont Alto, New Kensington, Ogontz, Schuylkill, Shenango Valley [Sharon], Wilkes-Barre, Worthington-Scranton, York) ... PA
Phoenix Coll ... AZ
Piedmont Tech ... SC
Pittsburg State U ... KS
Pittsburgh, U. of (Johnstown) ... PA
Prince George's Comm. Coll ... MD
Purdue (Calumet, Lafayette, West Lafayette) ... IN
Queensborough Comm. Coll ... NY
Ricks ... ID
Roane Stat. Comm. Coll ... TN
Rochester Comm. Coll ... MN
Rochester Inst. of Tech ... NY
Roger Williams Coll ... RI
San Francisco, City Coll. of ... CA
Sandhills Comm. Coll ... NC
Savannah State Coll ... GA
Sinclair Comm. Coll ... OH
Southeastern Massachusetts U ... MA
Southern Colorado, U. of ... CO
Southern Illinois, U. of (Carbondale) ... IL
Southern Mississippi, U. of ... MS
Southern Tech. Inst. (Div. of Ga. Inst. of Tech.) ... GA
Spartanburg Tech. Coll ... SC
Spring Garden Coll ... PA
St. Louis Comm. Coll ... MO
Stark Tech. Coll ... OH
State U. of New York A&T (Alfred, Binghamton, Canton, Farmingdale) ... NY
Sumter Area Tech. Coll ... SC
Temple U ... PA
Tennessee, U. of (Martin) ... TN
Texas A&M U ... TX
Texas Tech. U ... TX
Thames Valley State Tech ... CT
Toledo, U. of, Comm. and Tech. Coll ... OH
Trenton State Coll ... NJ
Trident Tech. Coll ... SC
Vermont Tech. Coll ... VT
Wake Tech. Inst ... NC
Walters State Comm. Coll ... TN
Waterbury State Tech. Coll ... CT
Weber State Coll ... UT
Wentworth Inst ... MA
West Virginia Inst. of Tech ... WV
Western Kentucky U ... KY
Wichita State U ... KS
York Tech. Coll ... SC
Youngstown State U ... OH

Engineering, Textile

Boston U ... MA
Georgia Inst. of Tech ... GA

Engineering, Thermal

Southern Illinois U. (Carbondale) ... IL

Engineering, Thermomechanical

Illinois, U. of (Chicago) ... IL

Engineering, Transportation

•California, U. of (Berkeley) ... CA

Engineering, Urban and Environmental

North Carolina, U. of (Charlotte) ... NC
Pennsylvania, U. of ... PA

Engineering, Welding

Ohio State U ... OH

ENGINEERING—Liberal Arts 3-2 Binary or Dual Degree Plan

Student is awarded a Bachelor's degree from the Liberal Arts College and a Bachelor of Science degree in Engineering from the Engineering College, both within a five-year period.

Arkansas, U. of, Binary Plan with

Centenary Coll ... LA
Harding U ... AR
Ouachita Baptist U ... AR
Ozarks, Coll. of the ... AR
Ozarks, School of the ... MO

Auburn U., 3-2 Plan with

Huntingdon ... AL
Rollins ... FL

California Inst. of Tech., Dual Degree with

Arkansas, U. of ... AR
Bowdoin Coll ... ME
Bryn Mawr Coll ... PA
Grinnell ... IA
Occidental ... CA
Ohio Wesleyan ... OH
Pomona ... CA
Reed ... OR
Wesleyan U ... CT

Case Western Reserve U., 3-2 Plan with

Monmouth Coll ... IL
Wittenberg U ... OH

Clarkson Coll., 3-2 Plan with

Houghton ... NY
Siena Coll ... NY
St. John Fisher ... NY

Clemson U., Dual Degree with

Baptist Coll ... SC
Charleston, Coll. of ... SC
Francis Marion Coll ... SC
Furman U ... SC
Georgia State U ... GA
Lander Coll ... SC
Livingstone Coll ... NC
Newberry Coll ... SC
Presbyterian Coll ... SC

Columbia U., Binary Plan with

Adelphi U ... NY
Albion ... MI
Alfred ... NY
Allegheny ... PA
Augustana ... SD
Baldwin-Wallace ... OH
Bard ... NY
Barnard ... NY
Bates ... ME
Baylor ... TX
Beaver ... PA
Beloit ... WI
Bethany ... WV
Bowdoin ... ME
Carleton ... MN
Carroll ... MT
Centenary Coll. of Louisiana ... LA
Centre Coll ... KY
Colgate ... NY
Colorado, U. of ... CO
Colorado Coll ... CO
Columbia U. (College and Sch. of General Studies) ... NY
Davidson ... NC
Denison U ... OH
DePauw ... IN
Dillard U ... LA
Doane ... NE
Earlham Coll ... IN
Eckerd Coll ... FL
Emmanuel Coll ... MA
Fordham ... NY
Grinnell ... IA
Hamilton ... NY
Hartwick Coll ... NY
Hastings ... NE
Hendrix ... AR
Hobart & William Smith ... NY
Hofstra ... NY
Hope ... MI
Idaho, Coll. of ... ID
Inter-American U. of Puerto Rico (Hato Rey, San German) ... PR
Jacksonville U ... FL
Juniata ... PA
Kansas Wesleyan U ... KS
Knox ... IL
Lawrence U ... WI
Lewis and Clark ... OR
MacMurray ... IL
Marietta ... OH
Miami ... OH
Middlebury ... VT
Millsaps ... MS
Muhlenberg ... PA
Nebraska Wesleyan ... NE
Occidental ... CA
Pacific Lutheran U ... WA
Pan American Coll ... TX
Providence ... RI
Puget Sound, U. of ... WA
Queens ... NY
Randolph-Macon Coll ... VA
Reed ... OR
Rollins ... FL
Seattle Pacific U ... WA
South, U. of the ... TN
St. John Fisher Coll ... NY
St. Lawrence ... NY

State U. of New York (Binghamton, Brockport, Fredonia, New Paltz, Oneonta, Oswego, Plattsburgh, Potsdam) .... NY
Sweet Briar .... VA
Wabash .... IN
Washington & Lee .... VA
Wells .... NY
Wesleyan U .... CT
Whitman .... WA
Willamette .... OR
William and Mary .... VA
William Jewell .... MO
William Smith .... NY
Williams Coll .... MA
Wittenberg .... OH
Wofford .... SC
Yeshiva U .... NY
York Coll .... PA

Detroit, U. of, 3-2 Plan with

St. John Fisher .... NY

George Washington U., 3-2 Plan with

Hampton Inst .... VA

Georgia Inst. of Tech., Dual Degree with

Agnes Scott Coll .... GA
Alabama A&M .... AL
Alabama State U .... AL
Albany State Coll .... GA
Antioch Coll .... OH
Armstrong State Coll .... GA
Belmont .... TN
Benedict Coll .... SC
Berry Coll .... GA
Bethany Coll .... WV
Bridgewater Coll .... VA
Campbellsville Coll .... KY
Carson-Newman .... TN
Cedar Crest Coll .... PA
Charleston, Coll. of .... SC
Clark Coll .... GA
Columbus .... GA
Covenant .... GA
David Lipscomb .... TN
Davidson .... NC
DePauw U .... IN
Dillard U .... LA
Drew U .... NJ
Eastern Kentucky U .... KY
Eckerd Coll .... FL
Edgecliff .... OH
Elmira Coll .... NY
Emory and Henry Coll .... VA
Erskine .... SC
Franklin and Marshall Coll ...... PA
Furman U .... SC
Georgetown Coll .... KY
Georgia, U. of .... GA
Georgia Coll .... GA
Georgia Southern .... GA
Georgia Southwestern .... GA
Guilford Coll .... NC
Hampden-Sydney Coll .... VA
Hartwick Coll .... NY
Hastings .... NE
Jacksonville U .... FL
Juniata Coll .... PA
Kalamazoo Coll .... MI
King Coll .... TN
La Grange .... GA
Lenoir-Rhyne Coll .... NC
Livingstone Coll .... NC
Maine, U. of (Presque Isle) ..... ME
Marymount Coll .... NY
Maryville Coll .... TN
Methodist Coll .... NC
Middle Tennessee State U ...... TN
Middlebury Coll .... VT
Milligan .... TN
Millsaps Coll .... MS
Morehouse Coll .... GA
Morris Brown U .... GA
Mount Marty .... SD
Mundelein Coll IL
Newberry Coll .... SC
North Carolina Central .... NC
North Georgia .... GA
Oglethorpe .... GA
Ohio Wesleyan U .... OH
Pacific U .... OR
Paine Coll .... GA
Pfeiffer Coll .... NC
Rollins Coll .... FL
Rust Coll .... MS
Samford .... AL
Savannah State Coll .... GA
South, U. of the .... TN
Spelman .... GA
Spring Hill Coll .... AL
St. Teresa, Coll. of .... MN
State U. of New York (Oneonta) . NY
Stephens Coll .... MO
Sweet Briar .... VA
Tampa, U. of .... FL
Tennessee, U. of (Chattanooga) . TN
Tougaloo Coll .... MS
Ursinus .... PA
Valdosta State Coll .... GA
Wesleyan Coll .... GA
West Georgia .... GA
Wheaton Coll .... MA
William Woods Coll .... MO
Wittenberg U .... OH
Wofford Coll .... SC

Illinois, U. of, Binary Plan with

Adrian Coll .... MI
Anderson Coll .... IN
Augustana IL
Beloit Coll .... WI
Butler U .... IN
Carthage .... WI
DePaul U IL
Eastern Illinois U IL
Elmhurst IL
Greenville IL
Illinois Benedictine Coll IL
Illinois Coll IL
Illinois State U IL
Illinois Wesleyan IL
Knox Coll IL
Lewis U IL
Loras .... IA
Loyola U IL
MacMurray IL
McKendree IL
Millikin U IL
Monmouth IL
Northern Illinois U IL
Olivet Nazarene IL
Rockford IL
St. Ambrose Coll .... IA
St. Joseph's .... IN
Wartburg .... IA
Western Illinois U IL
Wheaton IL
Yankton .... SD

Manhattan Coll., 3-2 Plan with

Siena Coll .... NY
St. John Fisher .... NY

Marquette U., Binary Plan with

Concordia Coll .... WI
St. Norbert's .... WI

Michigan, U. of, Binary Plan with

Adrian Coll .... MI
Albion .... MI
Alma .... MI
Andrews U .... MI
Beloit Coll .... WI
Bowling Green State U .... OH
Calvin .... MI
Central Michigan .... MI
Eastern Michigan .... MI
Grand Valley State .... MI
Hope .... MI
Kalamazoo .... MI
Michigan, U. of (Flint) .... MI
Shaw Coll .... MI
South, U. of the .... TN
Spring Arbor Coll .... MI
Virginia Union .... VA

Old Dominion U., 3-2 Plan with

Hampton Inst .... VA

Pennsylvania, U. of, Binary Plan with

Albright Coll .... PA
Dickinson Coll .... PA
Franklin and Marshall Coll ...... PA
Lebanon Valley Coll .... PA
Marietta Coll .... OH
Millersville State Coll .... PA
Moravian Coll .... PA
Morgan State U .... MD
Muhlenberg Coll .... PA
Oberlin Coll .... OH
Susquehanna U .... PA
Ursinus Coll .... PA
West Virginia Wesleyan Coll ... WV

Pennsylvania State U., Binary Plan with

Albright .... PA
Bloomsburg State Coll .... PA
California State Coll .... PA
East Stroudsburg State .... PA
Edinboro State Coll .... PA
Elizabethtown .... PA
Gettysburg Coll .... PA
Juniata .... PA
Kutztown State Coll .... PA
Lincoln U .... PA
Lock Haven Coll .... PA
Lycoming .... PA
Mansfield State .... PA
Millersville State Coll .... PA
Seton Hill Coll .... PA
Shippensburg State .... PA
Slippery Rock State .... PA
St. Francis Coll .... PA
St. Vincent .... PA
West Chester State .... PA
Westminster .... PA
Wilson Coll .... PA

Purdue U., 3-2 Plan with

St. Joseph's .... IN

Rensselaer Poly. Inst., Binary Plan with

Amherst Coll .... MA
Bates .... ME
Beloit .... WI
Colgate .... NY
Colorado Coll .... CO
Denison .... OH
Dickinson .... PA
Earlham .... IN
Franklin and Marshall .... PA
Gettysburg .... PA
Grinnell .... IA
Hamilton .... NY
Hobart and William Smith ...... NY
Hope .... MI
Kenyon .... OH
Knox IL
Lawrence U .... WI
Ohio Wesleyan .... OH
Reed .... OR
Ripon .... WI
South, U. of the .... TN
St. Lawrence .... NY
State U. of N.Y. Coll. (Fredonia) .... NY
Washington and Lee .... VA
William and Mary, Coll. of ...... VA

Rochester, U. of, 3-2 Plan with

William Smith Coll .... NY

Southern California, U. of, 3-2 Plan with

Ripon Coll .... WI
Ursinus Coll .... PA

Stanford U., Dual Degree with

Centenary Coll. of Louisiana .... LA
Central Methodist Coll .... MO
Claremont McKenna Coll .... CA
Colorado Coll .... CO
Hastings Coll .... NE
Idaho, Coll. of .... ID
Knox Coll IL
Mills Coll .... CA
Pacific Lutheran U .... WA
Pepperdine U .... CA
Redlands, U. of .... CA
Scripps Coll .... CA
Westmont Coll .... CA
Whittier Coll .... CA
Willamette U .... OR

Tennessee, U. of, Binary Plan with

Belmont .... TN
Bethel Coll .... TN
Carson-Newman .... TN
David Lipscomb .... TN
East Tennessee .... TN
King .... TN
Knoxville Coll .... TN
Maryville Coll .... TN
Middle Tennessee State .... TN
Southwestern U .... TN
Tennessee Wesleyan .... TN
Union U .... TN

Washington U., 3-2 Plan with

Lake Forest Coll IL

Monmouth Coll IL
Pomona Coll .... CA
Ripon Coll .... WI
Rollins .... FL
Wabash .... IN
Wittenberg U .... OH

West Virginia U., 3-2 Plan with

Davis and Elkins .... WV

English

Institutions awarding 40 or more undergraduate degrees in single year according to U.S. Office of Education latest statistics

Alabama. U. of .... AL
Arizona, U. of .... AZ
Arizona State U .... AZ
Auburn U .... AL
Barnard Coll .... NY
Boston Coll .... MA
Boston U .... MA
Brigham Young U .... UT
Bucknell U .... PA
California, U. of (Berkeley, Davis, Irvine, Los Angeles, Santa Barbara) .... CA
California State U. (Chico, Fullerton, Long Beach, Los Angeles, Northridge, Sacramento) .... CA
Calvin .... MI
Carleton Coll .... MN
Central Connecticut State ...... CT
Central Michigan U .... MI
City U (Brooklyn, City Coll., Lehman, Queens Coll.) .... NY
Clemson U .... SC
Cleveland State U .... OH
Colgate U .... NY
Colorado, U. of .... CO
Colorado Coll .... CO
Colorado State U .... CO
Connecticut, U. of .... CT
Cornell U .... NY
Delaware, U of .... DE
Dickinson Coll .... PA
Duke U .... NC
East Carolina U .... NC
Eastern Connecticut State ...... CT
Eastern Michigan U .... MI
Fairfield U .... CT
Florida, U. of .... FL
Florida Atlantic U .... FL
Florida State U .... FL
Fordham U .... NY
Harvard U .... MA
Hawaii, U. of (Manoa) .... HI
Hofstra U .... NY
Holy Cross, Coll. of the .... MA
Houston, U. of .... TX
Illinois, U. of (Circle, Urbana) IL
Illinois State U IL
Indiana U. (Bloomington) .... IN
Iowa, U. of .... IA
Iowa State U .... IA
Kansas, U. of .... KS
Kean Coll .... NJ
Kent State U .... OH
Kentucky, U of .... KY
Kenyon Coll .... OH
Louisiana State U. and A&M .... LA
Maryland, U. of .... MD
Massachusetts, U. of (Amherst, Boston) .... MA
Miami U .... OH
Michigan, U. of .... MI
Michigan State U .... MI
Middlebury Coll .... VT
Minnesota, U. of .... MN
Mississippi, U. of .... MS
Missouri, U. of .... MO
Montclair State .... NJ
Mount Holyoke .... MA
Nebraska, U. of .... NE
New Hampshire, U. of .... NH
New Orleans, U. of .... LA
New York U .... NY
North Carolina, U. of (Chapel Hill, Charlotte, Greensville) .. NC
Northern Illinois U IL
Northern Iowa, U of .... IA
Northwestern U IL
Notre Dame, U. of .... IN
Oakland U .... MI
Oberlin Coll .... OH
Ohio State U .... OH
Old Dominion U .... VA
Oregon, U. of .... OR
Pennsylvania, U. of .... PA
Pennsylvania State U .... PA
Pittsburgh, U. of .... PA
Portland State U .... OR
Princeton U .... NJ
Providence Coll .... RI
Puerto Rico, U. of .... PR
Radcliffe Coll .... MA
Rhode Island, U. of .... RI
Rutgers U .... NJ
San Diego State .... CA
San Francisco State .... CA
San Jose State .... CA
Santa Clara, U. of .... CA
Smith Coll .... MA
Sonoma State U .... CA
South Carolina, U. of .... SC
South Florida, U. of .... FL
Southern Illinois U IL
St. Olaf Coll .... MN
Stanford U .... CA
State U. of New York (Albany, Binghamton, Brockport, Buffalo, Coll. at Buffalo, Fredonia, Geneseo, New Paltz, Oneonta, Oswego, Potsdam, Stony Brook) .... NY
Temple U .... PA
Tennessee, U. of .... TN
Texas, U. of (Arlington, Austin) . TX
Towson State U .... MD
Tulane U .... LA
Utah, U. of .... UT
Vanderbilt U .... TN
Vassar Coll .... NY
Villanova U .... PA
Virginia, U. of .... VA
Washington, U. of .... WA
Wayne State U .... MI
Wellesley Coll .... MA
Wesleyan U .... CT
Western Michigan U .... MI
Western Washington U .... WA
William & Mary, Coll. of .... VA
Williams Coll .... MA
Wisconsin, U. of (Eau Claire, Madison, Milwaukee) .... WI

English for Foreign Students

Adrian Coll .... MI
Akron, U. of .... OH
Amarillo Coll .... TX
American Coll. of Switzerland .... Switzerland
American U .... DC
Andrews .... MI
Arizona State U .... AZ
Arizona Western Coll .... AZ
Armstrong Coll .... CA
Ashland Coll .... OH
Azusa Pacific Coll .... CA
Ball State .... IN
Bee Co. Coll .... TX
Bennett Coll .... NC
Biscayne Coll .... FL
Blake Coll .... OR
Boston U .... MA
Bradford Coll .... MA
Brevard Coll .... NC
Brevard Comm. Coll .... FL
Brigham Young .... UT
Broome Comm. Coll .... NY
California, U. of (Davis) .... CA
California State Coll .... PA
Calvin Coll .... MI
Campbellsville Coll .... KY
Case Western .... OH
Central Missouri .... MO
Central New England .... MA
Central Texas Coll .... TX
Chamberlayne Jr. Coll .... MA
City U .... NY
Cochise .... AZ
Cornell Coll .... IA
Curry Coll .... MA
C.W. Post Ctr. (Long Island U.) . NY
Danville Area Comm. Coll IL
Delaware Tech. and Comm. Coll .... DE
Detroit, U. of .... MI
DuPage, Coll. of IL
Eastern Washington U .... WA
El Centro Coll .... TX
Findlay Coll .... OH
Florida Inst. of Tech .... FL
Florida Int. U .... FL
Fontbonne Coll .... MO
Freeman Jr. Coll .... SD
Friends World Coll .... NY
Fulton-Montgomery Comm. Coll .... NY
Gadsden State .... AL
George Mason U .... VA
Gonzaga U .... WA
Gwynedd-Mercy .... PA
Hocking Tech. Coll .... OH
Illinois Central Coll IL
Immaculata Coll .... PA
Incarnate Word .... TX
International Coll .... FL
International Fine Arts .... FL
Jacksonville U .... FL
Kansas, U. of .... KS
Kean Coll .... NJ
King's Coll .... PA
Kirkwood Comm. Coll .... IA
La Salle Coll .... PA
Lake Co., Coll. of IL
Lansing Comm. Coll .... MI
Lincoln Coll IL
Lincoln Trail Coll IL
Lindenwood Colleges .... MO
Linfield Coll .... OR
Loma Linda U .... CA
Long Beach City Coll .... CA
Los Angeles City Coll .... CA
Los Angeles Southwest Coll .... CA
Louisiana Tech .... LA
Louisville, U. of .... KY
Loyola U .... LA
MacCormac Jr. Coll IL
Macalaster Coll .... MN
Mallinckrodt Coll IL
Malone Coll .... OH
Manhattanville Coll .... NY
Maryland, U. of .... MD
Marywood .... PA
Memphis State U .... TN
Miami, U. of .... FL
Michigan, U. of (Ann Arbor) .... MI
Michigan State U .... MI
Midland Coll .... TX
Minnesota, U. of (Minneapolis) . MN
Miracosta Comm. Coll .... CA
Missouri, U. of (Rolla) .... MO
Mitchell Coll .... CT
Monterey Inst .... CA
Mount Hood Comm. Coll ...... OR
Mount St. Joseph, Coll. of ..... OH
Mount Wachusett Comm. Coll . MA
Nebraska, U. of .... NE
Nevada, U. of .... NV
New Hampshire Coll .... NH
New Mexico, U. of .... NM
New Mexico Military Inst ...... NM
New York U .... NY
North Carolina, U. of (Charlotte) .... NC
Northampton Co. Area Comm. Coll .... PA
Northeast State Jr. Coll .... AL
Northeastern U .... MA
Northern Essex Comm. Coll ... MA
Northern Iowa, U. of .... IA
Northrop U .... CA
Northwest Missouri State ...... MO
Northwestern State U .... LA
Notre Dame, Coll. of .... CA
Old Dominion .... VA
Olympia Tech. Comm. Coll .... WA
Oregon, U. of .... OR
Oregon State U .... OR
Ottawa .... KS
Otterbein Coll .... OH
Pacific, U. of the .... CA
Pacific Lutheran U .... WA
Pennsylvania State U. (McKeesport) .... PA
Pensacola Jr. Coll .... FL
Pikes Peak Comm. Coll .... CO
Pittsburg State U .... KS
Rio Piedras .... PR
Sacred Heart .... CT
San Francisco, City Coll. of ..... CA
Schreiner Coll .... TX
Snow Coll .... UT
Sonoma State U .... CA
Southeastern Oklahoma State U .... OK
Southern Idaho, Coll. of .... ID
Southwestern Adventist .... TX
Springfield Tech. Comm. Coll .. MA
St. Gregory's Coll .... OK
St. Mary Coll .... KS
St. Mary-of-the-Woods .... IN
St. Mary's Coll .... CA
St. Mary's Dominican Coll ...... LA
St. Michael's .... VT
Strayer .... DC
Suomi Coll .... MI
Syracuse U .... NY
Temple U .... PA
Tennessee, U. of .... TN
Tennessee Tech. U .... TN
Texas, U. of (San Antonio) ...... TX
Thomas More Coll .... KY
Trinidad State Jr .... CO
Trinity Coll .... DC
Tri-State U .... IN
Tulane .... LA
Tulsa, U. of .... OK
U.S. International U .... CA
Utah State U .... UT
Valley Forge Military .... PA
Washington U .... MO
Wayne State U .... MI
Webster Coll .... MO
West Hills Coll .... CA
Whittier Coll .... CA
Whitworth Coll .... WA
Wilbur Wright Coll IL
Wisconsin, U. of (Green Bay, Superior) .... WI
Wittenberg U .... OH

Yakima Valley Comm. Coll ..... WA

Enology (Winemaking)

California, U. of (Davis) .... CA
California State U. (Fresno) ..... CA

Entomology

Institutions awarding 5 or more undergraduate degrees as major field in single year according to U.S. Office of Education latest statistics

Arizona, U. of .... AZ
Auburn U .... AL
California, U. of (Davis, Riverside) .... CA
California State U. (Long Beach) .... CA
Colorado State U .... CO
Cornell .... NY
Delaware, U. of .... DE
Florida, U. of .... FL
Georgia, U. of .... GA
Iowa State U .... IA
Louisiana State U .... LA
Maryland, U. of .... MD
Massachusetts, U. of .... MA
Michigan State U .... MI
Mississippi State .... MS
Missouri, U. of .... MO
New Hampshire, U. of .... NH
Ohio State .... OH
Oklahoma State U .... OK
Oregon State U .... OR
Pennsylvania State U .... PA
Purdue U .... IN
San Jose State .... CA
Texas A&M U .... TX
Texas Tech. U .... TX

Environmental Health Engineering, *See* ENGINEERING, ENVIRONMENTAL HEALTH

Ethnomusicology

Goddard Coll .... VT
Jersey City State .... NJ
New Coll .... FL
New Haven, U. of .... CT

Exceptional Children, Preparation for Teaching of

Institutions offering specialization in one or more areas of the education of exceptional children, including blind, deaf, crippled, disadvantaged, gifted, etc.

Akron, U. of .... OH
Alabama A&M .... AL
Alderson-Broaddus .... WV
American U .... DC
Averett Coll .... VA
Barat IL
Barry U .... FL
Baruch Coll .... NY
Bennett Coll .... NC
Blue Mountain Coll .... MS
Bradley U IL
Brevard Coll .... NC
Bridgewater State .... MA
California Poly. U .... CA
California State Coll .... PA
California State U. (Chico, Los Angeles, Sacramento) .... CA
Calvin Coll .... MI
Central Arkansas, U. of .... AR
Central Missouri .... MO
Cheyney State .... PA
Colorado Mountain Coll .... CO
Columbia Coll .... MO
Columbus Coll .... GA
Converse Coll .... SC
Coppin State Coll .... MD
Daemen Coll .... NY
Delaware, U. of .... DE
Denver, U. of .... CO
Drake U .... IA
East Carolina .... NC
East Texas State .... TX
Eastern Kentucky U .... KY
Eastern Montana .... MT
Eastern New Mexico .... NM
Eastern Washington .... WA
Edgewood Coll .... WI
Emporia State U .... KS
Felician Coll .... NJ
Findlay Coll .... OH
Flagler Coll .... FL
Florida Atlantic .... FL
Florida Southern Coll .... FL
Fontbonne Coll .... MO
Fort Hays State U .... KS
Georgia Coll .... GA
Goddard Coll .... VT
Guilford Coll .... NC
Gwynedd-Mercy .... PA
Harcum Jr. Coll .... PA
Hardin-Simmons U .... TX
Hartford, U. of .... CT
Huntingdon Coll .... AL
Incarnate Word Coll .... TX
Iowa, U. of .... IA
Iowa Wesleyan .... IA
Jacksonville U .... FL
Johnson State Coll .... VT
Kansas, U. of .... KS
Kansas State U .... KS
Keene State Coll .... NH
Kent State .... OH
Keystone Jr. Coll .... PA
King's Coll .... PA
La Salle .... PA
Lesley .... MA
Lindenwood Coll .... MO
Lincoln Coll IL
Maine, U. of (Farmington) ..... ME
Marian Coll .... IN
Maryland, U. of .... MD
Marywood .... PA
Missouri, U. of .... MO
Moorhead State .... MN
Mount St. Mary's .... CA
National Coll. of Educ IL
Nazareth Coll .... MI
Nazareth Coll. of Rochester ..... NY
North Carolina Cent. U .... NC
North Carolina Wesleyan ...... NC
North Florida, U. of .... FL
Northeast Louisiana .... LA
Northeast Missouri .... MO
Northeastern Oklahoma State .. OK
Northern Arizona .... AZ
Northern Iowa, U. of .... IA
Northwest Missouri State ...... MO
Northwestern Oklahoma State . OK
Northwestern State .... LA
Ohio State U .... OH
Oklahoma, U. of .... OK
Old Dominion U .... VA
Pacific, U. of the .... CA
Pennsylvania State U .... PA
Providence Coll .... RI
Purdue U .... IN
Rhode Island Coll .... RI
Rio Piedras .... PR
Rivier .... NH
Seattle U .... WA
Slippery Rock State .... PA
South Carolina, U. of .... SC
South Dakota, U. of .... SD
South Florida .... FL
Southeast Missouri State U .... MO
Southwest Missouri State ...... MO
St. Andrews Presbyterian ...... NC
St. Gregory's .... OK
St. Joseph .... CT
St. Leo Coll .... FL
St. Mary Coll .... KS
St. Rose, Coll. of .... NY
State U. of New York (Buffalo, Cobleskill, Geneseo) .... NY
Stephen F. Austin .... TX
Stetson U .... TX
Steubenville, U. of .... OH
Tennessee, U. of .... TN
Tennessee Temple U .... TN
Texas, U. of (Dallas, El Paso) ... TX
Texas Woman's U .... TX
Tift Coll .... GA
Trenton State .... NJ
Trinity Christian IL
Trinity Coll .... VT
Union Coll .... KY
Utah State U .... UT
Vanderbilt U .... TN
Vermont, U. of .... VT
Walsh Coll .... OH
Wayne State .... MI
West Florida, U. of .... FL
West Virginia State Coll .... WV
Western Carolina U .... NC
William Woods .... MO
Wisconsin, U. of (Milwaukee, Whitewater) .... WI
Wright State U .... OH

Executive Management

Alderson-Broaddus .... WV
Armstrong Coll .... CA
Baruch Coll .... NY
Bennett Coll .... NC
Bliss Coll .... OH
Boca Raton, Coll. of .... FL
Central Missouri .... MO
Columbia Union Coll .... MD
Coppin State Coll .... MD
Eastfield Coll .... TX
Fisher Jr. Coll .... MA
Franklin Coll .... IN
Franklin Pierce .... NH
Freed-Hardeman Coll .... TN
George Washington U .... DC
Golden Gate U .... CA
Gwynedd-Mercy .... PA
Hawaii, U. of (Honolulu) .... HI
Indiana U. (Bloomington) .... IN
International U .... MO
Jacksonville State U .... AL
La Salle .... PA
Lasell Jr. Coll .... MA
Lincoln IL
Marymount Manhattan .... NY
Michigan, U. of .... MI
Minnesota, U. of .... MN
Mount Vernon .... DC
New Mexico State U .... NM
Newbury Jr. Coll .... MA
Northeast Missouri .... MO
Northeastern Oklahoma State .. OK
Northern Arizona .... AZ
Northern Iowa, U. of .... IA
Northwood Inst .... MI
Oklahoma State U .... OK
Quinnipiac Coll .... CT
Rivier Coll .... NH
Robert Morris Coll .... PA
Shenandoah Coll .... VA
South Dakota, U. of .... SD
Southwest Texas State .... TX
Syracuse U .... NY
Tennessee Temple U .... TN
Trinity Christian IL
Valparaiso U .... IN
Wesleyan Coll .... GA
William Woods .... MO
York Coll .... PA

Farm and Agricultural Management

Institutions awarding undergraduate degrees as major field in single year according to U.S. Office of Education latest statistics

California, U. of (Davis) .... CA
California Poly. State (San Luis Obispo) .... CA
Colorado State U .... CO
Cornell .... NY
Delaware, U. of .... DE
Iowa State U .... IA
Kansas State U .... KS
Kentucky, U. of .... KY
Louisiana State U .... LA
Montana State U .... MT
New Mexico State .... NM
Southwestern Louisiana, U. of .. LA
Wisconsin State U. (River Falls) .... WI
Wyoming, U. of .... WY

Farriery, *See* BLACKSMITHING

Fashion Design and Related Fields

Barton County Comm. Coll ..... KS
Baylor U .... TX
Becker Jr .... MA
Bennett Coll .... NC
Bliss Coll .... OH
Boca Raton, Coll. of .... FL
Bowling Green State U .... OH
Brooks Coll .... CA
Butte Coll .... CA
California State U. (Los Angeles) .... CA
Cazenovia .... NY
Centenary Coll .... NJ
Central Arkansas, U. of .... AR
Central Coll .... KS
Central Michigan U .... MI
Central Missouri .... MO
Chamberlayne Jr .... MA
Cheyney State .... PA
Cincinnati, U. of .... OH
Columbia Coll .... MO
Delaware, U. of .... DE
Delta State U .... MS
Drexel .... PA
DuPage, Coll. of IL
Eastern Oklahoma State .... OK
El Centro Coll .... TX
Endicott Coll .... MA
Fashion Inst. of Tech .... NY
Fisher Jr. Coll .... MA
Flagler Coll .... FL
Florida State U .... FL
Hampton Institute .... VA
Harcum Jr .... PA
Harper Coll IL
Hawaii, U. of (Honolulu) .... HI
Illinois Central Coll IL
Immaculata Coll .... PA
Incarnate Word .... TX
Indiana U. (Bloomington) .... IN
Indiana U .... PA

James Madison U .... VA
Judson Coll .... AL
Kansas State U .... KS
Kearney State .... NE
Kent State .... OH
Lamar U .... TX
Lasell Jr. Coll .... MA
Lincoln Coll IL
Marian Coll .... IN
Marist Coll .... NY
Mars Hill .... NC
Marymount .... NY
Marymount .... VA
Marymount Palos Verdes .... CA
Michigan State .... MI
Midway Coll .... KY
Mt. Mary .... WI
Mundelein Coll IL
Nebraska, U. of (Lincoln) .... NE
New Haven, U. of .... CT
Newbury Jr. Coll .... MA
North Carolina Central U .... NC
North Dakota State U .... ND
North Texas State U .... TX
Northeast Mississippi Jr. Coll .... MS
Northeastern Oklahoma State .... OK
Northern Arizona .... AZ
Northwest Missouri State .... MO
Northwestern State .... LA
Northwood Inst .... MI
Oklahoma Panhandle State U .... OK
Otis Art Inst .... CA
Pittsburg State .... KS
Pratt Inst .... NY
Purdue (Lafayette) .... IN
Rockmont Coll .... CO
Rosary Coll IL
Seattle Pacific Coll .... WA
Seton Hill .... PA
Southeast Missouri State .... MO
Southern Coll .... FL
Southern Idaho, Coll. of .... ID
Southern Illinois IL
St. Benedict, Coll. of .... MN
St. Mary Coll .... KS
Stephens Coll .... MO
Syracuse U .... NY
Tennessee, U. of .... TN
Texas Woman's U .... TX
Thiel Coll .... PA
U.S. International U .... CA
Ursuline Coll .... OH
Valparaiso U .... IN
Vermont, U. of .... VT
Virginia Commonwealth .... VA
Virginia Polytech .... VA
Viterbo Coll .... WI
Washington U .... MO
Wayne State U .... MI
Weber State Coll .... UT
Western Carolina U .... NC
William Woods Coll .... MO
Wisconsin, U. of (Madison) .... WI

Fashion Merchandising

Abilene Christian .... TX
Adrian Coll .... MI
Akron, U. of .... OH
Alabama A&M .... AL
Albright Coll .... PA
Anderson Coll .... SC
Arizona, U. of .... AZ
Art Institute of Pittsburgh .... PA
Ashland Coll .... OH
Auburn U .... AL
Barton County Comm. Coll .... KS
Bay Path Jr. Coll .... MA
Bay State Jr. Coll .... MA
Baylor U .... TX
Becker Jr .... MA
Bee Co. Coll .... TX
Belmont Coll .... TN
Bethany Nazarene .... OK
Blinn .... TX
Bliss Coll .... OH
Boca Raton .... FL
Bowling Green .... OH
Brandywine Coll .... DE
Brenau Coll .... GA
Briarwood Coll .... CT
Bridgeport, U. of .... CT
Brooks Coll .... CA
Butler U .... IN
California State U. (Fresno, Los Angeles) .... CA
Carson-Newman .... TN
Cazenovia Coll .... NY
Centenary .... NJ
Central Arkansas, U. of .... AR
Central Coll .... KS
Central Michigan U .... MI
Central Missouri .... MO
Central Washington U .... WA
Champlain Coll .... VT
Cheyney State .... PA
College Misericordia .... PA
Colorado State U .... CO
Columbia Coll .... MO
Columbia Jr. Coll .... SC
Davenport Coll. of Bus .... MI
David Lipscomb Coll .... TN
Davis and Elkins .... WV
Dean Jr. Coll .... MA
Delta State U .... MS
Drexel U .... PA
DuPage, Coll. of IL
Eastern Arizona Coll .... AZ
Eastern Kentucky U .... KY
Eastern Oklahoma State .... OK
Eastern Washington U .... WA
Endicott Coll .... MA
Evergreen Valley Coll .... CA
Fashion Inst. of Tech .... NY
Ferris State .... MI
Fisher Jr. Coll .... MA
Flagler Coll .... FL
Florida International U .... FL
Florida State U .... FL
Fontbonne Coll .... MO
Francis Marion Coll .... SC
Franklin Coll .... IN
Freed-Hardeman Coll .... IN
Georgia Coll .... GA
Hampton Institute .... VA
Harcum Jr .... PA
Harding U .... AR
Harper Coll IL
Hawaii, U, of (Honolulu) .... HI
Hesser Coll .... NH
Hood Coll .... MD
Hutchinson Comm. Coll .... KS
Immaculata Coll .... PA
Incarnate Word .... TX
Indiana U. (Bloomington) .... IN
Indiana U .... PA
International Fine Arts Coll. of Fashion .... FL
Iowa State U .... IA
James Madison U .... VA
Johnson and Wales Coll .... RI
Judson Coll .... AL
Kansas State U .... KS
Kearney State .... NE
Kent State U .... OH
Kentucky, U. of .... KY
Laboratory Inst. of Merchandising .... NY
Lamar U .... TX
Lasell Jr. Coll .... MA
Limestone Coll .... SC
Lincoln Coll IL
Lincoln U .... MO
Lindenwood .... MO
Louisiana Tech .... LA
Maine, U. of .... ME
Marian Coll .... IN
Mars Hill Coll .... NC
Mary Hardin-Baylor .... TX
Marycrest Coll .... IA
Marymount .... NY
Marymount Coll. of Virginia .... VA
Marymount Palos Verdes .... CA
Marywood .... PA
Mercy Coll. of Detorit .... MI
Mercyhurst Coll .... PA
Miami U .... OH
Michigan State U .... MI
Midway Coll .... KY
Morehead State .... KY
Mt. Aloysius Jr .... PA
Mt. Mary .... WI
Mundelein Coll IL
Nebraska, U. of .... NE
Nevada, U. of .... NV
New York U .... NY
Newbury Jr .... MA
New Hampshire Coll .... NH
Nicholls State U .... LA
North Alabama, U. of .... AL
North Carolina, U. of (Greensboro) .... NC
North Dakota State U .... ND
North Idaho Coll .... ID
North Texas State U .... TX
Northeast Louisiana U .... LA
Northeast Mississippi Jr .... MS
Northeast Missouri State Coll .... MO
Northeastern Jr. Coll .... CO
Northeastern Oklahoma State .... OK
Northern Arizona .... AZ
Northern Iowa, U. of .... IA
Northern Michigan U .... MI
Northwest Missouri State .... MO
Northwestern State U .... LA
Northwood Inst .... IN
Ohio U .... OH
Oklahoma Panhandle State U .... OK
Oklahoma State U .... OK
Otterbein Coll .... OH
Our Lady of the Lake .... TX
Pittsburg State U .... KS
Post College .... CT
Pratt Inst .... NY
Purdue U. (Lafayette) .... IN
Rochester Inst. of Tech .... NY
Rosary Coll IL
Samford U .... AL
Seton Hill .... PA
Seward County C. Coll .... KS
Shepherd Coll .... WV
Snow Coll .... UT
South Dakota State U .... SD
South Georgia Coll .... GA
Southeast Missouri State U .... MO
Southern Coll .... FL
Southern Idaho, Coll. of .... ID
Southern Illinois U IL
Southern Sem. Jr .... VA
Southwest Texas State .... TX
St. Benedict, Coll. of .... MN
St. Catherine, Coll. of .... MN
Stephen F. Austin State U .... TX
Stephens Coll .... MO
Syracuse U .... NY
Tennessee, U. of .... TN
Texas Woman's U .... TX
Thiel Coll .... PA
Union Coll .... NE
Ursuline Coll .... OH
Valparaiso U .... IN
Virginia Commonwealth .... VA
Virginia Intermont Coll .... VA
Washington State U .... WA
Wayne State .... NE
Wayne State .... MI
Webber Coll .... FL
Weber State .... UT
West Virginia State Coll .... WV
Western Michigan U .... MI
William Woods Coll .... MO
Winthrop Coll .... SC
Wisconsin, U. of (Madison, Stevens Point, Stout) .... WI
Xavier U .... OH
Youngstown U .... OH

Film, *See*

MOTION PICTURES/FILM/CINEMA

Fire Science and/or Prevention

Akron, U. of .... OH
Arizona Western Coll .... AZ
Bee Co. Coll .... TX
Blinn Coll .... TX
Butte Coll .... CA
California State U. (Los Angeles) .... CA
Central Missouri .... MO
Cincinnati, U. of .... OH
DuPage, Coll of IL
Eastern Kentucky U .... KY
El Centro Coll .... TX
Fairmont State Coll .... WV
Florida International .... FL
George Mason U .... VA
Goddard Coll .... VT
Harper Coll IL
Hawaii, U. of, at Hilo .... HI
Holy Family Coll .... PA
Hutchinson Comm. Coll .... KS
Illinois Central Coll IL
Illinois Inst. of Tech IL
Lamar U .... TX
Lewis U IL
Mercy Coll .... NY
Minnesota, U. of .... MN
Navarro Coll .... TX
New Haven, U. of .... CT
North Florida, U. of .... FL
North Idaho Coll .... ID
Northern Kentucky .... KY
Oklahoma State U .... OK
Shepherd Coll .... WV
Southern Arkansas U. Tech .... AR
Southern Idaho, Coll. of .... ID
West Virginia State Coll .... WV
Wichita State U .... KS
Wright State .... OH
Yakima Valley Comm. Coll .... WA

Fisheries

Undergraduate degree programs according to Sports Fishing Institute

Alabama, U. of .... AL
Alaska, U. of .... AK
Arizona, U. of .... AZ
Arkansas Tech .... AR
Auburn U .... AL
Ball State U .... IN
Bemidji State U .... MN
Brigham Young U .... UT
California, U. of (Davis) .... CA
California Poly. State U. (San Luis Obispo) .... CA
California State U. (Sacramento) .... CA
Central Michigan U .... MI
City U. of New York .... NY
Colorado State U .... CO
Connecticut, U. of .... CT
Cornell .... NY
Delaware State Coll .... DE
Eastern Illinois U IL
Eastern Kentucky U .... KY
Emporia State U .... KS
Florida Inst. of Tech .... FL

Idaho, U. of .... ID
Illinois, U. of (Urbana) IL
Iowa State U .... IA
Kansas State U .... KS
Lehigh U .... PA
Louisiana Tech. U .... LA
Louisville, U. of .... KY
Maine, U. of (Orono) .... ME
Maryland, U. of .... MD
Massachusetts, U. of .... MA
Miami, U. of .... FL
Michigan, U. of .... MI
Michigan State U .... MI
Minnesota, U. of .... MN
Mississippi State U .... MS
Missouri, U. of (Columbia) ..... MO
Montana State U .... MT
Morehead State U .... KY
Murray State U .... KY
Nevada, U. of .... NV
New Hampshire, U. of .... NH
New Mexico State U .... NM
New York, State U. of, Coll. at Oneonta .... NY
Nicholls State U .... LA
North Carolina, U. of .... NC
North Carolina State U .... NC
North Dakota State U .... ND
Northeast Louisiana U .... LA
Northeastern U .... MA
Northern Illinois U IL
Northwestern State U .... LA
Oklahoma, U. of .... OK
Old Dominion U .... VA
Oregon State U .... OR
Pennsylvania State U .... PA
Purdue U .... IN
Richmond, U. of .... VA
Saint Mary's Coll .... MN
San Diego State U .... CA
San Francisco State U .... CA
San Jose State U .... CA
South Alabama, U. of .... AL
Southampton Coll. of L.I.U ..... NY
South Dakota, U. of .... SD
South Dakota State U .... SD
South Florida, U. of .... FL
Southeastern Louisiana U ...... LA
Southeastern Massachusetts U ... MA
Southern Mississippi, U. of .... MS
Southwest Missouri State U .... MO
Southwest Texas State U .... TX
Tennessee, U. of .... TN
Tennessee Tech. U .... TN
Texas, U. of .... TX
Texas A&M U .... TX
Texas Christian U .... TX
Utah State U .... UT
Vermont, U. of .... VT
Virginia, U. of .... VA
Virginia Poly. Inst. and State U .. VA
Washington, U. of .... WA
West Florida, U. of .... FL
West Virginia U .... WV
Western Kentucky U .... KY
Wisconsin, U. of (LaCrosse, Stevens Point) .... WI
Wyoming, U. of .... WY

Fisheries, *See also* MARINE BIOLOGY AND/OR FISHERIES

Floriculture

Alfred State .... NY
Becker Jr .... MA
Cornell U .... NY
Eastern Kentucky .... KY
Kansas State U .... KS
Michigan State U .... MI
Nicholls State .... LA
North Dakota State .... ND
Purdue U .... IN
Southwest Texas State .... TX
State U. of New York (Cobleskill, Farmingdale, Morrisville) .... NY
SUNY Coll. of Agri. & Life Sci .... NY
Texas A&M .... TX
Texas State Tech .... TX
Washington State U .... WA

Folklore

Goddard Coll .... VT
Harvard U .... MA
Indiana U. (Bloomington) .... IN
Marlboro Coll .... VT
Pennsylvania, U. of .... PA
Radcliffe Coll .... MA
Tennessee, U. of .... TN

Food Marketing and Related Fields

Alabama A&M .... AL
Alfred State .... NY
Bennett Coll .... NC
DuPage, Coll. of IL
Fontbonne Coll .... MO
Harper Coll IL
Illinois, U. of (Urbana) IL
Indiana State U .... IN
Johnson and Wales Coll .... RI
Kansas State U .... KS
Kent State .... OH
Marywood .... PA
Michigan State .... MI
Missouri, U. of .... MO
Niagara U .... NY
North Dakota State U .... ND
Northern Arizona .... AZ
Northern Iowa, U. of .... IA
Purdue U .... IN
Rochester Institute of Technology .... NY
Rosary Coll IL
Seattle Pacific .... WA
Shepherd Coll .... WV
State U. of New York Coll. (Buffalo) .... NY
SUNY Coll. of Agri. & Life Sci .... NY
Syracuse U .... NY
Texas State Tech .... TX
Toledo .... OH
Valparaiso U .... IN
Viterbo Coll .... WI
William Woods .... MO

Food Processing Technology

Akron, U. of .... OH
Austin Peay State U .... TN
Bennett Coll .... NC
Central Missouri .... MO
Chapman Coll .... CA
Cincinnati, U. of .... OH
Fairmont State .... WV
Harper Coll IL
Kansas State U .... KS
Louisiana Tech .... LA
Northeast Missouri .... MD
Rosary Coll IL
State U. of New York (Farmingdale, Morrisville) ..... NY
SUNY Coll. of Agri. & Life Sci .... NY
Tennessee, U. of .... TN
Wisconsin, U. of (Madison, River Falls) .... WI

Food Technology

Alabama A&M U .... AL
Arizona, U. of .... AZ
Arkansas, U. of .... AK
Auburn U .... AL
Bennett Coll .... NC
California, U. of (Berkeley, Davis) .... CA
California Poly U. (Pomona) .... CA
California State Poly. (San Luis Obispo) .... CA
Central Coll .... KS
Central Missouri .... MO
Clemson U .... SC
Colorado State U .... CO
Connecticut, U. of .... CT
Cornell U .... NY
Delaware Valley .... DE
District of Columbia, U. of ..... DC
El Centro Coll .... TX
Florida, U. of .... FL
Harper Coll IL
Hawaii, U. of (Honolulu) .... HI
Hawaii Pacific Coll .... HI
Illinois, U. of IL
Illinois Inst. of Tech IL
Iowa State .... IA
John Brown U .... AR
Kansas State U .... KS
Kentucky, U. of .... KY
Keystone Jr .... PA
Loma Linda U .... CA
Louisiana State U .... LA
Maine, U. of (Farmington) ..... ME
Marian Coll .... IN
Maryland, U. of .... MD
Massachusetts, U. of .... MA
Michigan State U .... MI
Minnesota, U. of (Minneapolis) .... MN
Mississippi State .... MS
Missouri, U. of .... MO
Morehead State .... KY
Nebraska, U. of (Lincoln) .... NE
Nevada, U. of .... NV
New Hampshire, U. of .... NH
Nicholls State U .... LA
North Carolina, U. of (Raleigh) .... NC
North Carolina Central U ...... NC
North Dakota State U .... ND
Northeast Mississippi Jr .... MS
Northwest Missouri State ...... MO
Ohio State .... OH
Oregon State U .... OR
Pennsylvania State U. (McKeesport) .... PA
Puerto Rico, U. of .... PR
Purdue (Calumet, West Lafayette) .... IN
Rhode Island, U. of .... RI
Rosary Coll IL
Rutgers, U. of .... NJ
Saint Paul's College .... MO
Seattle Pacific .... WA
South Dakota State .... SD
State U. of New York (Cobleskill) .... NY
SUNY Coll. of Agri. & Life Sci .. NY
Tennessee, U. of (Knoxville) .... TN
Texas A&M .... TX
Texas Tech .... TX
Texas Woman's U .... TX
Toledo, U. of .... OH
Utah State .... UT
Vermont, U. of .... VT
Virginia Poly. Inst .... VA
Washington State U .... WA
Washington, U. of .... WA
Western Carolina U .... NC
Wisconsin, U. of .... WI
Wyoming, U. of .... WY

Foreign Service and Diplomacy

Colorado, U. of .... CO
Eckerd Coll .... FL
George Washington U .... DC
Johns Hopkins U .... MD
Mary Washington .... VA
Pepperdine U .... CA
Southwestern at Memphis ...... TN
Valparaiso U .... IN

Foreign Trade

Auburn U .... AL
Baruch Coll .... NY
Bernadean U .... CA
Biscayne Coll .... FL
George Washington U .... DC
Hawaii, U. of (Honolulu) .... HI

Forensic Medicine

Eastern Kentucky U .... KY
Jacksonville State U .... AL
Mercy Coll. of Detroit .... MI

Forestry

Accredited by the Society of American Foresters

Arizona, U. of .... AZ
Auburn U .... AL
California, U. of (Berkeley) ..... CA
Clemson .... SC
Colorado State U .... CO
Duke (Grad. only) .... NC
Florida, U. of .... FL
Georgia, U. of .... GA
Humboldt State U .... CA
Idaho, U. of .... ID
Illinois, U. of IL
Iowa State U .... IA
Kentucky, U. of .... KY
Louisiana State U .... LA
Maine, U. of .... ME
Massachusetts, U. of .... MA
Michigan, U. of .... MI
Michigan State U .... MI
Michigan Tech. U .... MI
Minnesota, U. of .... MN
Mississippi State U .... MS
Missouri, U. of, at Columbia ... MO
Montana, U. of .... MT
New Hampshire, U. of .... NH
North Carolina State U .... NC
Northern Arizona U .... AZ
Oklahoma State U .... OK
Oregon State U .... OR
Pennsylvania State U .... PA
Purdue .... IN
Southern Illinois IL
State U. of New York Sch. of Environmental and Resource Mgt. (Syracuse) .... NY
Stephen F. Austin State Coll .... TX
Tennessee, U. of .... TN
Texas A&M .... TX
Utah State U .... UT
Vermont, U. of .... VT
Virginia Poly. Inst .... VA
Washington, U. of .... WA
Washington State U .... WA
West Virginia U .... WV
Wisconsin, U. of (Madison, Stevens Point) .... WI
Yale (Grad. only) .... CT

Forestry Technician

•Recognized by Society of American Foresters

•Abraham Baldwin .... GA
•Allegany Comm .... MD
•Alpena Comm .... MI
•American River .... CA
•Brainerd Area Voc. Tech .... MN
Brevard .... NC
•Central Oregon Comm .... OR
•Centralia Coll .... WA
•Chemeketa Comm .... OR
•Clatsop Comm .... OR
•Dabney S. Lancaster Comm .... VA
•Eastern Oklahoma State .... OK
•Everett Comm .... WA
•Flathead Valley Comm .... MT
•Glenville State .... WV
•Green River Comm .... WA
•Haywood Tech. Inst .... NC
•Hocking Tech .... OH
•Horry-Georgetown Tech .... SC
•Itasca Comm .... MN
•Kentucky, U. of .... KY
Keystone Jr .... PA
•Kings River .... CA
•Lake City Comm .... FL
•Lane Comm .... OR
•Lassen Comm .... CA
•Maine, U. of (Orono) .... ME
•Martin Comm .... NC
Michigan State U .... MI
•Michigan Tech .... MI
Mississippi Delta Jr .... MS
•Missoula Vo-Tech. Ctr .... MT
•Mt. Hood Comm .... OR
•Mt. San Antonio .... CA
•New Hampshire, U. of .... NH
North Dakota State (Bottineau) .... ND
•North Idaho .... ID
Northeast Mississippi Jr .... MS
Northern Arizona .... AZ
•Paul Smith's .... NY
•Peninsula Coll .... WA
•Pennsylvania State U. (Mont Alto) .... PA
•Redwoods, Coll. of the .... CA
•Santa Rosa Jr .... CA
•Savannah Area Voc. Tech .... GA
•Shoreline Comm .... WA
•Sierra Coll .... CA
•Southeastern Illinois IL
•Southwestern Oregon Comm .... OR
•Spokane Comm .... WA
State U. of New York (•Coll. of Env. Sci., Canton, Cobleskill, •Morrisville) .... NY
Stephen F. Austin .... TX
Tennessee, U. of .... TN
Tennessee Temple U .... TN
•Treasure Valley Comm .... OR
•Umpqua Comm .... OR
•Unity .... ME
•Vermilion Comm .... MN
•Wayne Comm .... NC
•Wenatchee Valley .... WA
Western Montana .... MT
•Williamsport Area Comm .... PA

Foundry Industry, *See* METAL AND FOUNDRY WORK

Furniture Industry

Catawba Valley Tech. Inst .... NC
High Point Coll .... NC

Future Studies

Akron, U. of .... OH
Goddard Coll .... VT
Hampshire Coll .... MA
Northern Iowa, U. of .... IA
Southeastern U .... LA

Genealogical Research

California, U. of (Irvine) .... CA

General Studies

Associate or Baccalaureate Degree

Alabama State U .... AL
Albertus Magnus .... CT
Alderson-Broaddus .... WV
Alverno Coll .... WI
American Coll. of Switzerland .... Switzerland
American Tech. U .... TX
American U .... DC
Andrews U .... MI
Antioch Coll .... OH
Aquinas Coll .... MI
Arizona, U. of .... AZ
Arkansas State .... AR
Arkansas Tech. U .... AR
Armstrong Coll .... CA
Armstrong State .... GA
Athens State .... AL
Auburn U .... AL
Austin Peay State U .... TN
Averett Coll .... VA
Barat Coll IL
Barrington Coll .... RI
Bee County Coll .... TX
Bernadean U .... CA
Bethany Lutheran Coll .... MN
Bethel Coll .... KS
Bismarck Jr .... ND
Black Hills State .... SD
Blinn Coll .... TX
Bowling Green State .... OH
Brandywine Coll .... DE
Brevard Coll .... NC
Bridgeport, U. of .... CT
Butte Coll .... CA
California, U. of (Riverside) .... CA
California State Coll .... PA
California State U. (Sacramento) .... CA
Carroll Coll .... MT
Carson-Newman .... TN
Carthage Coll .... WI
Central Coll .... KS
Central Florida, U. of .... FL
Central State .... OK
Central Texas .... TX
Chadron State .... NE
Chamberlayne Jr .... MA
Charleston, U. of .... WV
Chicago, U. of IL
Cincinnati, U. of .... OH
Coffeyville .... KS
College Misericordia .... PA
Colorado Mountain Coll .... CO
Columbia Coll .... MO
Columbia Union .... MD
Columbus Coll .... GA
Connecticut, U. of .... CT
Davis & Elkins Coll .... WV
Dawson Comm .... MT
Dayton, U. of .... OH
Dean Jr. Coll .... MA
Delaware, U. of .... DE
Delta State U .... MS
Drake U .... IA
Drew U .... NJ
D'Youville Coll .... NY
Eastern Arizona Coll .... AZ
Eastern Kentucky .... KY
Eastern Montana .... MT
Eastern New Mexico .... NM
Eastern Oregon State .... OR
Eastern Washington U .... WA
Eastfield Coll .... TX
El Centro Coll .... TX
Elmira Coll .... NY
Emmanuel Coll .... GA
Emporia State U .... KS
Evangel Coll .... MO
Evergreen State .... WA
Evergreen Valley .... CA
Felician Coll .... NJ
Flagler Coll .... FL
Florida A&M .... FL
Florida Southern .... FL
Fordham U .... NY
Fort Hays State U .... KS
Franklin Coll .... Switzerland
Freed-Hardeman Coll .... TN
Freeman Jr .... SD
George Fox Coll .... OR
George Washington U .... DC
Georgia State U .... GA
Goddard Coll .... VT
Goshen Coll .... IN
Governors State U IL
Grand Canyon Coll .... AZ
Grandview .... IA
Harcum Jr .... PA
Harper Coll IL
Hendrix Coll .... AR
Huntingdon Coll .... AL
Hutchinson Comm .... KS
Idaho, U. of .... ID
Illinois Central IL
Indiana Central U .... IN
Indiana U. (Bloomington) .... IN
Indiana U.-Purdue U .... IN
International .... MO
Iowa, U. of .... IA
Jacksonville State U .... AL
James Madison U .... VA
John Brown U .... AR
John F. Kennedy U .... CA
Johnson State .... VT
Judson Baptist Coll .... OR
Kansas, U. of .... KS
Kansas State U .... KS
Kearney State .... NE
Keene State .... NH
Kendall Coll IL
Kent State U. (Ashtabula Regional) .... OH
Kentucky, U. of .... KY
Keystone Jr. Coll .... PA
Kutztown State .... PA
Lamar U .... TX
Lander Coll .... SC
Lasell Jr .... MA
Lenoir-Rhyne .... NC
Lewis-Clark State .... ID
Lincoln Coll IL
Lincoln U .... PA
Lock Haven State .... PA
Louisburg Coll .... NC
Louisville, U. of .... KY
Maine, U. of (Farmington, Fort Kent, Machias) .... ME
Mallinckrodt Coll IL
Mankato State .... MN
Manor Jr. Coll .... PA
Mansfield State .... PA
Marian Coll. of Fond du Lac .... WI
Maria Regina .... NY
Marlboro Coll .... VT
Mary Hardin-Baylor .... TX
Mary Washington .... VA
Maryland, U. of .... MD
Marymount Coll. of Va .... VA
Maryville State .... ND
Marywood Coll .... PA
McNeese State .... LA
Miami, U. of .... FL
Miami U. (Hamilton, Middletown) .... OH
Michigan, U. of (Dearborn) .... MI
Michigan Tech. U .... MI
Minnesota, U. of (Minneapolis) .... MN
Mississippi Coll .... MS
Missouri, U. of .... MO
Missouri Western .... MO
Mitchell Coll .... CT
Morehead State .... KY
Morrison Inst. of Tech IL
Mount Mary Coll .... WI
Mount Mercy Coll .... IA
Mount St. Mary Coll .... NY
Natchez Jr. Coll .... MS
Navajo Comm. Coll .... AZ
Navarro Coll .... TX
Nebraska Western .... NE
New Coll .... FL
New Hampshire, U. of .... NH
New Hampshire Coll .... NH
New Haven, U. of .... CT
New Mexico Inst. of Mining & Tech .... NM
New Mexico Military Inst .... NM
New York Inst. of Tech .... NY
New York U .... NY
Nicholls State U .... LA
North Carolina Wesleyan .... NC
North Dakota State U .... ND
North Florida, U. of .... FL
North Idaho, U. of .... ID
Northeast Louisiana U .... LA
Northeast Mississippi Jr .... MS
Northeastern Jr .... CO
Northern Arizona U .... AZ
Northern Colorado, U. of .... CO
Northern Iowa, U. of .... IA
Northwest Nazarene Coll .... ID
Northwestern State .... LA
Oakland U .... MI
Oakwood Coll .... AL
Oglethorpe U .... GA
Ohio State U .... OH
Ohio U .... OH
Ohio Valley Coll .... WV
Oklahoma State U .... OK
Old Dominion U .... VA
Otero Jr. Coll .... CO
Ottawa U .... KS
Pace U .... NY
Pacific Christian Coll .... CA
Pennsylvania State U. (Allentown) .... PA
Pine Manor Coll .... MA
Pittsburg State U .... KS
Pittsburgh, U. of .... PA
Plymouth State Coll .... NH
Post Coll .... CT
Queens Coll .... NC
Rhode Island Coll .... RI
Rider Coll .... NJ
Rio Piedras .... PR
Rivier Coll .... NH
Robert Morris Coll .... PA
Rockmont Coll .... CO
Rollins .... FL
San Diego State .... CA
Sacred Heart .... CT
Salisbury State .... MD
Sarah Lawrence .... NY
Schreiner Coll .... TX
Seattle Pacific U .... WA
Seattle U .... WA
Seward Co. Comm .... KS
Shenandoah Coll .... VA
Shepherd Coll .... WV
Sheridan Coll .... WY
Shorter Coll .... GA
South Carolina, U. of .... SC
South Dakota State U .... SD
South Georgia Coll .... GA

Southeast Missouri State ...... MO
Southern Arkansas U .... AR
Southern Idaho, Coll. of .... ID
Southern Vermont Coll .... VT
Spring Arbor Coll .... MI
Spring Hill .... AL
Springfield Coll .... MA
St. Benedict, Coll. of .... MN
St. Cloud State U .... MN
St. Gregory's Coll .... OK
St. John's Coll .... MD
St. Mary-of-the-Woods .... IN
St. Mary's Coll .... KS
St. Scholastica .... MN
State U. of New York (Brockport, Oneonta, Plattsburgh) .... NY
State U. of New York Coll. of Tech .... NY
Stephens Coll .... MO
Sue Bennett .... KY
Talladega Coll .... AL
Texas, U. of (Dallas, Tyler) ..... TX
Toccoa Falls Coll .... GA
Toledo, U. of .... OH
Towson State .... MD
Trevecca Nazarene Coll .... TN
Trinity Christian IL
Trinity Coll IL
Truett McConnell .... GA
Urbana Coll .... OH
Utah, U. of .... UT
Utah State U .... UT
Valley Forge Military .... PA
Valparaiso U .... IN
Virgin Islands, Coll. of VI
Virginia Commonwealth U ...... VA
Walsh Coll .... OH
Warren Wilson .... NC
Washington, U. of .... WA
Washington U .... MO
Wayne State U .... MI
Webster Coll .... MO
West Chester State .... PA
West Coast Christian .... CA
Wharton Co. Jr .... TX
Wheeling Coll .... WV
White Plains, Coll. of .... NY
Whittier Coll .... CA
Wichita State U .... KS
Worthington Comm .... MN
Wright State U .... OH
Yakima Valley Comm .... WA
Yankton Coll .... SD
York Coll .... PA

Genetics

Arizona, U. of .... AZ
California, U. of (Berkeley, Davis, Irvine, Riverside, San Diego) .... CA
California Inst. of Tech .... CA
Carnegie-Mellon .... PA
Chicago, U. of IL
Connecticut, U. of .... CT
Cornell U .... NY
George Washington U .... DC
Hampshire .... MA
Hawaii, U. of .... HI
Illinois, U. of (Urbana) IL
Indiana U .... IN
Iowa, U. of .... IA
Michigan, U. of .... MI
Michigan State .... MI
Minnesota, U. of (Minneapolis) . MN
Missouri, U. of .... MO
New Coll .... FL
North Carolina, U. of .... NC
North Carolina State .... NC
North Dakota State U .... ND
Ohio State U .... OH
Pennsylvania State U. (Shenango, University Park) .. PA

Purdue U .... IN
Rutgers U .... NJ
Sarah Lawrence Coll .... NY
State U. of New York (Coll. of Agr. & Life Sci.) ..... NY
Tennessee, U. of .... TN
Texas A&M U .... TX
Virginia Commonwealth .... VA
Wesleyan U .... CT
West Texas State .... TX
Western Baptist .... OR
William Woods .... MO
Winona State .... MN
Wisconsin, U. of (Green Bay, Madison, Milwaukee, Stevens Point, Superior, Whitewater) .... WI
Worcester Poly. Inst .... MA
Yeshiva .... NY

Geography

Institutions awarding 15 or more undergraduate degrees as major field in single year according to U.S. Office of Education latest statistics

Arizona State U .... AZ
Boston U .... MA
Bowling Green State .... OH
Brigham Young U .... UT
California, U. of (Berkeley, Davis, Los Angeles, Santa Barbara) .... CA
California State Coll. (Dominguez Hills, Sonoma) ... CA
California State U. (Chico, Fresno, Fullerton, Hayward, Long Beach, Los Angeles, Northridge, Sacramento) ..... CA
Central Michigan U .... MI
Clark U .... MA
Colorado, U. of .... CO
Dartmouth .... NH
Delaware, U. of .... DE
Denver, U. of .... CO
East Carolina U .... NC
Florida State U .... FL
Framingham State .... MA
Frostburg State Coll .... MD
Georgia, U. of .... GA
Georgia Southern .... GA
Gustavus Adolphus .... MN
Howard U .... DC
Humboldt State .... CA
Illinois, U. of IL
Kansas, U. of .... KS
Kansas State U .... KS
Mankato State U .... MN
Maryland, U. of .... MD
Massachusetts, U. of .... MA
Michigan State U .... MI
Middlebury .... VT
Minnesota, U. of .... MN
Montana, U. of .... MT
North Alabama U .... AL
North Carolina, U. of .... NC
Northern Colorado, U. of ...... CO
Northern Illinois U IL
Northern Michigan U .... MI
Oklahoma, U. of .... OK
Oregon, U. of .... OR
Pacific, U. of the .... CA
Pennsylvania State .... PA
Pittsburgh, U. of .... PA
Portland State Coll .... OR
Salem State .... MA
Salisbury State .... MD
San Diego State .... CA
San Francisco State .... CA
San Jose State .... CA
Slippery Rock State .... PA

South Alabama, U. of .... AL
South Carolina, U. of .... SC
South Dakota State .... SD
South Florida, U. of .... FL
Southern Connecticut State .... CT
Southern Illinois U IL
Southern Oregon State U ...... OR
Southwest Missouri State U .... MO
Southwest Texas State .... TX
St. Cloud State .... MN
State U. of New York (Albany, Buffalo, Geneseo, Oswego, Plattsburgh, Potsdam) .... NY
Stetson U .... FL
Syracuse .... NY
Tennessee, U. of (Knoxville) .... TN
Texas, U. of (Austin) .... TX
Towson State U .... MD
U.S. Air Force Acad .... CO
Utah, U. of .... UT
Virginia Poly. Inst .... VA
Washington, U. of .... WA
West Georgia Coll .... GA
Western Illinois U IL
Western Michigan U .... MI
Western Washington State ..... WA
Wisconsin, U. of (Eau Claire, Madison, Milwaukee, Oshkosh, Whitewater) .... WI
Worcester State .... MA

Geological Engineering, *See* ENGINEERING, GEOLOGICAL

Geology

Institutions awarding 10 or more undergraduate degrees as major field in single year according to U.S. Office of Education latest statistics

Alabama, U. of .... AL
Allegheny .... PA
Appalachian State U .... NC
Arizona State U .... AZ
Arkansas, U. of .... AR
Auburn .... AL
Ball State U .... IN
Baylor U .... TX
Bemidji State U .... MN
Boise State .... ID
Boston Coll .... MA
Boston U .... MA
Bowling Green State .... OH
Brigham Young .... UT
California, U. of (Berkeley, Davis, Los Angeles, Santa Barbara) .... CA
California State U. (Chico, Los Angeles, Northridge) .... CA
Campbell .... NC
Carleton Coll .... MN
Central Washington .... WA
Charleston, U. of .... SC
Cincinnati, U. of .... OH
Colgate .... NY
Colorado, U. of .... CO
Colorado Coll .... CO
Connecticut, U. of .... CT
Cornell .... NY
Delaware, U. of .... DE
Dickinson .... PA
Duke U .... NC
Earlham Coll .... IN
Eastern Illinois U IL
Eastern Michigan U .... MI
Eastern New Mexico .... NM
Eastern Washington .... WA
Emory U .... GA
Florida, U. of .... FL
Florida Atlantic U .... FL

Florida State U .... FL
Fort Lewis .... CO
Franklin and Marshall .... PA
Georgia, U. of .... GA
Georgia Southwestern .... GA
Georgia State .... GA
Hardin-Simmons U .... TX
Hartwick Coll .... NY
Harvard U .... MA
Hope Coll .... MI
Houston, U. of .... TX
Humboldt State U .... CA
Hunter Coll .... NY
Idaho, U. of .... ID
Illinois, U. of IL
Illinois State IL
Indiana U .... IN
Iowa, U. of .... IA
James Madison U .... VA
Kansas, U. of .... KS
Kent State U .... OH
Lawrence U .... WI
Louisiana State U .... LA
Macalester Coll .... MN
Maine, U. of .... ME
Maryland, U. of .... MD
Massachusetts, U. of .... MA
Mesa Coll .... CO
Miami, U. of .... FL
Miami U .... OH
Michigan, U of .... MI
Middlebury .... VT
Minnesota, U. of .... MN
Missouri, U. of .... MO
Montana, U. of .... MT
Nebraska, U. of .... NE
Nevada, U. of .... NV
New Mexico, U. of .... NM
North Carolina, U. of .... NC
Northern Arizona U .... AZ
Northern Illinois U IL
Ohio State U .... OH
Ohio U .... OH
Oklahoma State U .... OK
Oregon, U. of .... OR
Oregon State .... OR
Pomoma Coll .... CA
Princeton U .... NJ
Radford Coll .... VA
Rhode Island, U. of .... RI
Rochester, U. of .... NY
Rutgers .... NJ
San Diego State .... CA
San Jose State .... CA
Skidmore Coll .... NY
Smith Coll .... MA
South Alabama, U. of .... AL
South Florida, U. of .... FL
Southern California, U. of ...... CA
Southern Illinois U IL
Southern Methodist U .... TX
Southwest Missouri State U .... MO
Southwestern Louisiana .... LA
Stanford .... CA
State U. of New York (Binghamton, Brockport, Buffalo, Cortland, New Paltz, Oneonta) .... NY
Stephen Austin .... TX
Sul Ross .... TX
Syracuse U .... NY
Tennessee, U. of .... TN
Texas, U. of (Arlington, Austin) . TX
Texas A&M U .... TX
Trinity U .... TX
Tufts U .... MA
Utah, U. of .... UT
Utah State U .... UT
Vermont, U. of .... VT
Virginia Poly. Inst .... VA
Washington, U. of .... WA
Washington State U .... WA
Weber State .... UT
West Virginia U .... WV

Western Illinois IL
Western Michigan MI
Western Washington State WA
Wheaton Coll IL
William and Mary, Coll. of VA
Williams MA
Wisconsin, U. of (Oshkosh) WI
Wittenberg U OH
Wooster, Coll. of OH
Wright State OH
Yale CT

Geophysical Engineering, *See* ENGINEERING, GEOPHYSICAL

Geophysics

Alaska, U. of AK
Boise State U ID
Brown U RI
California, U. of (Riverside, San Diego, Santa Cruz) CA
California Inst. of Tech CA
Chicago, U. of IL
Colorado School of Mines CO
Connecticut, U. of CT
Cornell U NY
Delaware, U. of DE
Harvard U MA
Hawaii, U. of (Honolulu) HI
Indiana U. (Bloomington) IN
Iowa, U. of IA
Kansas, U. of KS
Keene State Coll NH
Lehigh PA
Michigan Tech. U MI
Minnesota, U. of (Minneapolis) MN
Northeast Louisiana U LA
Occidental CA
Oklahoma, U. of OK
Oregon State U OR
Pacific, U. of the CA
Pennsylvania State U. (Allentown, McKeesport, Schuylkill Campus, Shenango, University Park) PA
Purdue IN
Radcliffe MA
St. Joseph's IN
State U. of New York (Binghamton, Fredonia, Geneseo) NY
Texas, U. of (Austin, Dallas, El Paso) TX
Texas A&M TX
Tulsa, U. of OK
Utah, U. of UT
Virginia Poly. Inst. VA
Washington and Lee VA
Western Kentucky KY
Wisconsin, U. of WI
Wright State U OH
Yale U CT

Geosciences

Arizona, U. of AZ
California, U. of (Santa Barbara) CA
California Inst. of Tech CA
California State U. (Hayward, Long Beach) CA
District of Columbia, U. of DC
Elizabeth City State NC
Emporia State U KS
Hobart-William Smith NY
Indiana U. of Pennsylvania PA
Jersey City State NJ
Lock Haven State PA
Louisiana Tech. U LA
Missouri, U. of (Kansas City) MO
Murray State U KY

Nevada, U. of NV
New Mexico Inst. of Mining & Tech NM
Northeast Louisiana U LA
Pennsylvania State U PA
Purdue U IN
Rider Coll NJ
San Francisco State U CA
Southern Colorado, U. of CO
Tennessee, U. of TN
Texas, U. of TX
Texas Tech. U TX
Tulsa, U. of OK
West Texas State TX
Wisconsin, U. of (Platteville, Superior) WI

Geriatrics/Gerontology

Albertus Magnus CT
Alfred U NY
Baylor U TX
California State Coll PA
Case Western Reserve OH
Duquesne U PA
Eastern Montana MT
Emmanuel Coll MA
Endicott MA
Fontbonne Coll MO
Fordham U NY
Gwynedd-Mercy PA
High Point Coll NC
Kent State OH
King's Coll PA
Langston U OK
Livingstone Coll NC
McKendree Coll IL
Manchester IN
Marywood PA
Mississippi Valley State MS
Missouri Baptist MO
Mount Aloysius PA
National Coll. of Education IL
Nazareth Coll MI
Northeast Missouri State MO
Northern Colorado, U. of CO
Oakland U MI
Scranton, U. of PA
South Carolina, U. of SC
South Dakota, U. of (Springfield) SD
Southwest Missouri State MO
State U. of New York (Cobleskill) NY
Syracuse U NY
Temple U PA
Towson State MD
Tusculum Coll TN
Virginia Commonwealth U VA
White Pines Coll NH
Wichita State U KS
William Woods MO

Glass Technology

California Coll. of Arts and Crafts CA
Ohio State U OH
Rhode Island Sch. of Design RI

Golf Management

Ferris State U MI
Purdue U IN
Western Texas Coll TX

Graphic Arts and/or Printing

Akron, U. of OH
Anderson Coll IN
Andrews U MI
Arizona, U. of AZ
Arkansas State U AR
Artesia Christian Coll NM
Austin Peay State U TN
Ball State U IN
Baruch Coll NY
Baylor U TX
Boca Raton, Coll. of FL
Brevard Coll NC
Bridgeport, U. of CT
California Coll. of Arts and Crafts CA
California State Coll PA
California State U. (Fresno, Los Angeles) CA
Carnegie-Mellon PA
Cazenovia Coll NY
Center for Creative Studies MI
Central Washington U WA
Chamberlayne Jr. Coll MA
Cheyney State PA
Chowan Coll NC
Cincinnati, U. of OH
Coker Coll SC
Columbia MO
Columbia Coll IL
Daemen Coll NY
Drake U IA
DuPage, Coll. of IL
Eastern Kentucky KY
Eastern New Mexico NM
Fairmont State Coll WV
Ferris State MI
Florida A&M FL
Franklin Pierce Coll NH
George Washington U DC
Goddard Coll VT
Hampshire Coll MA
Harcum Jr. Coll PA
Illinois Central Coll IL
Kansas, U. of KS
Kansas City Art Inst MO
Kent State U OH
La Grange Coll GA
LaRoche Coll PA
Lincoln Coll IL
Loma Linda U CA
Maine, U. of (Augusta) ME
Marywood Coll PA
Midwestern State TX
Minnesota, U. of MN
Mississippi Valley State MS
Moorhead State U MN
Morehead State KY
Morrison Inst. of Tech IL
Mount Aloysius PA
Mt. St. Joseph, Coll. of OH
New York Inst. of Tech NY
North Florida, U. of FL
Northeast Missouri State Coll MO
Northeastern Oklahoma State U OK
Northern Arizona U AZ
Northern Colorado, U. of CO
Northern Iowa, U. of IA
Northern Michigan U MI
Northern Oklahoma Coll OK
Northwestern State U LA
Ohio State U OH
Otis Art Inst CA
Ozarks, Sch. of the MO
Pennsylvania Acad. of the Fine Arts PA
Philadelphia Coll. of Arts PA
Purdue U IN
Rhode Island Sch. of Design RI
Rivier Coll NH
Rochester Inst. of Tech NY
Rockford Coll IL
Saint Rose, Coll. of NY
Savannah Coll. of Art and Design GA
Seton Hill PA
South Dakota, U. of SD
Southern Illinois U IL
State U. of New York (Farmingdale) NY
State U. of N.Y. Coll. (Buffalo) NY
Stephens Coll MO
Temple U PA
Tennessee, U. of TN
Thiel Coll PA
Trenton State NJ
Trinity Christian IL
U.S. International U CA
Virginia Commonwealth VA
Washington U MO
Wesleyan Coll GA
William Woods MO
Wisconsin, U. of (Superior) WI
Wittenberg U OH
Xavier U LA

Guidance and Student Personnel Work

Akron, U. of OH
Alabama, U. of AL
Alabama A&M AL
Alfred U NY
American Tech. U TX
Antioch U OH
Appalachian State U NC
Arizona, U. of AZ
Arizona State U AZ
Arkansas, U. of AR
Auburn U AL
Ball State U IN
Bank Street Coll NY
Boston U MA
Bowie State MD
Bowling Green State U OH
Bradley U IL
Brevard Coll NC
Bridgeport, U. of CT
Bridgewater State MA
Brigham Young U UT
California Lutheran CA
California State Coll PA
California State U. (Los Angeles, Sacramento) CA
Central Arkansas, U. of AR
Central Connecticut State CT
Central Florida, U. of FL
Central Michigan U MI
Central Missouri State MO
Central State OK
Chicago State U IL
Chadron State Coll NE
Citadel SC
City U. of New York NY
Clemson SC
Colorado, U. of CO
Columbia U NY
Concordia Coll IL
Connecticut, U. of CT
Corpus Christi State U TX
Dayton, U. of OH
Delaware, U. of DE
Delta State U MS
Denver, U. of CO
Detroit, U. of MI
Drake U IA
Duquesne PA
East Carolina U NC
East Texas State U TX
Eastern Illinois U IL
Eastern Kentucky U KY
Eastern Michigan U MI
Eastern Montana MT
Eastern New Mexico NM
Emporia State KS
Fairfield U CT
Florida, U. of FL

Florida A&M .... FL
Florida Atlantic U .... FL
Florida International .... FL
Florida State U .... FL
Florida Tech. U .... FL
Fordham U .... NY
Fort Hays State .... KS
Framingham State .... MA
George Mason U .... VA
George Washington U .... DC
Georgia, U. of .... GA
Georgia State U .... GA
Glassboro State .... NJ
Goddard Coll .... VT
Gonzaga U .... WA
Governors State U IL
Hampton Institute .... VA
Hardin-Simmons U .... TX
Harvard U .... MA
Hawaii, U. of .... HI
Henderson State .... AR
Houston, U. of .... TX
Houston Baptist U .... TX
Idaho, U. of .... ID
Illinois State U IL
Indiana U .... IN
Indiana-Purdue U .... IN
Indiana U. of Pa. .... PA
Iowa, U. of .... IA
Jackson State U .... MS
Jacksonville State .... AL
James Madison U .... VA
Jersey City State .... NJ
John Carroll .... OH
Kansas, U. of .... KS
Kansas State U .... KS
Kean Coll .... NJ
Kearney State .... NE
Kent State U .... OH
La Verne, U. of .... CA
Lesley Coll .... MA
Lewis & Clark .... OR
Long Island U .... NY
Louisiana Tech .... LA
Louisville, U. of .... KY
Loyola U IL
Lynchburg Coll .... VA
Mankato State .... MN
Marshall U .... WV
Maryland, U. of .... MD
Marywood .... PA
Memphis State U .... TN
Miami U .... OH
Michigan State U .... MI
Midwestern State .... TX
Millersville State .... PA
Minnesota, U. of .... MN
Mississippi State U .... MS
Missouri, U. of .... MO
Montana, U. of .... MT
Montclair State .... NJ
Montevallo, U. of .... AL
Moorhead State .... MN
Mount St. Mary's .... CA
Murray State U .... KY
Nebraska, U. of .... NE
Nevada, U. of .... NV
New Hampshire, U. of .... NH
New Mexico, U. of .... NM
New Mexico State U .... NM
New York U .... NY
North Alabama, U. of .... AL
North Carolina Ag. & Tech ..... NC
North Carolina, U. of (Charlotte, Greensboro) .... NC
North Carolina Central U ...... NC
North Dakota, U. of .... ND
North Dakota State U .... ND
North Florida, U. of .... FL
North Texas State U .... TX
Northeast Louisiana U .... LA
Northeast Missouri State ...... MO
Northeastern Illinois U IL
Northeastern Oklahoma State .. OK
Northeastern U .... MA
Northern Arizona U .... AZ
Northern Illinois U IL
Northern Iowa, U. of .... IA
Northern Michigan U .... MI
Northern Montana .... MT
Northwest Missouri State ...... MO
Northwestern Oklahoma State . OK
Northwestern State U .... LA
Nova U .... FL
Oakland U .... MI
Ohio State U .... OH
Ohio U .... OH
Oklahoma, U. of .... OK
Oklahoma State U .... OK
Old Dominion U .... VA
Oregon, U. of .... OR
Pacific Lutheran .... WA
Pan American U .... TX
Pennsylvania State U .... PA
Pittsburg State U .... KS
Pittsburgh, U. of .... PA
Plymouth State .... NH
Prairie View A&M .... TX
Providence Coll .... RI
Puerto Rico, U. of .... PR
Purdue U .... IN
Rhode Island Coll .... RI
Rider Coll .... NJ
Rio Piedras .... PR
Rollins .... FL
Roosevelt U IL
Salem State .... MA
San Diego State .... CA
Seattle U .... WA
Seton Hall .... NJ
Shippensburg State .... PA
Siena Heights Coll .... MI
Slippery Rock State .... PA
Sonoma State U .... CA
South Alabama, U. of .... AL
South Carolina, U. of .... SC
South Carolina State .... SC
South Dakota, U. of .... SD
South Dakota State .... SD
South Florida, U. of .... FL
South Georgia Coll .... GA
Southern Arkansas U .... AR
Southern California, U. of ...... CA
Southern Connecticut .... CT
Southern Illinois U IL
Southern Maine, U. of .... ME
Southern Mississippi, U. of .... MS
Southern U. A&M .... LA
Southwest Missouri State ...... MO
Southwest Texas State .... TX
Southwestern Oklahoma State U .... OK
Springfield Coll .... MA
St. Bonaventure U .... NY
St. Cloud State .... MN
St. John's U .... NY
St. Lawrence U .... NY
St. Thomas, Coll. of .... MN
State U. of New York (Brockport, Plattsburgh) ...... NY
Stetson U .... FL
Suffolk U .... MA
Syracuse U .... NY
Tennessee, U. of .... TN
Tennessee State U .... TN
Texas, U. of .... TX
Texas A&I .... TX
Texas A&M .... TX
Texas Southern U .... TX
Texas Woman's U .... TX
Toledo, U. of .... OH
Trenton State .... NJ
Trinity Christian IL
Trinity Coll .... DC
Troy State .... AL
Upsala Coll .... NJ
Vermont, U. of .... VT
Villanova U .... PA
Virginia, U. of .... VA
Virginia Commonwealth U ...... VA
Wayne State U .... MI
West Chester State .... PA
West Georgia .... GA
West Virginia U .... WV
Western Kentucky U .... KY
Western Michigan U .... MI
Western New Mexico U .... NM
Wichita State U .... KS
William Woods .... MO
Winona State U .... MN
Winthrop Coll .... SC
Wisconsin, U. of (Oshkosh, Whitewater) .... WI
Wright State U .... OH
Wyoming, U. of .... WY
Xavier U .... OH
Youngstown State U .... OH

Gunsmithing

Barton County Comm. Coll ..... KS
Murray State Coll .... OK
Trinidad State Jr. Coll .... CO

Health Administration

(According to the Assn. of University Programs in Health Administration)
•program satisfies AUPHA's criteria for full membership

Appalachian State U .... NC
California State U. (Northridge) .... CA
California State Coll. (San Bernardino) .... CA
•Cincinnati, U. of .... OH
•City U. of New York (Lehman Coll.) .... NY
•Concordia Coll .... MN
Eastern Michigan U .... MI
•Fisk U .... TN
Florida Atlantic U .... FL
Golden Gate U .... CA
Governors State U IL
•Ithaca Coll .... NY
Kansas, U. of (Kansas City) ..... KS
Kentucky, U. of .... KY
La Salle Coll .... PA
La Verne, U. of .... CA
•Lowell, U. of .... MA
•Meharry Medical Coll .... TN
•Metropolitan State Coll .... CO
Missouri, U. of (Columbia) ..... MO
•New Hampshire, U. of .... NH
Park Coll .... MO
•Pennsylvania State U .... PA
•Providence Coll .... RI
•Quinnipiac Coll .... CT
Saint Mary's Coll. of California .. CA
•Sangamon State U IL
South Dakota, U. of .... SD
Southern Illinois U IL
Southwest Texas State U .... TX
•Tennessee State U .... TN
Texas, U. of (Galveston) .... TX
•Virginia, Medical Coll. of .... VA
•Virginia Commonwealth U ...... VA
•Wichita State U .... KS

Health Education

Institutions awarding 10 or more undergraduate degrees according to latest statistics of U.S. Office of Education

Alabama, U. of .... AL
Alcorn State U .... MS
Appalachian State .... NC
Arizona State U .... AZ
Ball State U .... IN
Bemidji State .... MN
Bowling Green .... OH
Brigham Young .... UT
California, U. of (Santa Barbara) .... CA
California State U. (Los Angeles, Sacramento) .... CA
Central Arkansas, U. of .... AR
Central Michigan U .... MI
Central State U .... OH
Central Washington .... WA
Columbus Coll .... GA
Cumberland .... KY
District of Columbia, U. of ..... DC
East Carolina U .... NC
East Tennessee State U .... TN
Eastern Illinois IL
Ferris .... MI
Florida, U. of .... FL
Florida State U .... FL
George Williams Coll IL
Georgia, U. of .... GA
Hunter Coll .... NY
Illinois, U. of IL
James Madison Coll .... VA
Kent State U .... OH
Lehman Coll .... NY
Long Island U .... NY
Mankato State .... MN
Maryland, U. of .... MD
Minnesota, U. of .... MN
Montclair State .... NJ
Moorhead State U .... MN
Nebraska, U. of .... NE
Nevada, U. of .... NV
New Mexico, U. of .... NM
Nicholls State U .... LA
North Carolina, U. of (Chapel Hill, Greensboro) .... NC
North Carolina Central U ...... NC
Northeastern U .... MA
Northern Colorado, U. of ...... CO
Northern Michigan U .... MI
Ohio Northern U .... OH
Ohio State U .... OH
Oregon, U. of .... OR
Portland State .... OR
Purdue U .... IN
Queens Coll .... NY
Russell Sage Coll .... NY
Slippery Rock .... PA
South Carolina, U. of .... SC
South Florida, U. of .... FL
Southeastern Oklahoma State . OK
Southern Connecticut .... CT
Southern Illinois IL
Southwest Texas .... TX
Springfield Coll .... MA
St. Cloud State .... MN
State U. of New York (Cortland, Plattsburgh) .... NY
Temple U .... PA
Tennessee, U. of .... TN
Tennessee Tech. U .... TN
Texas, U. of (Austin) .... TX
Texas A&M .... TX
Toledo, U. of .... OH
Utah, U. of .... UT
Washington, U. of .... WA
West Chester State .... PA
West Liberty State .... WV
Western Connecticut U .... CT
Western Michigan U .... MI
William Paterson Coll .... NJ
Winona State U .... MN
Wisconsin, U. of (La Crosse) .... WI

Health Physics

California State U. (Los Angeles) .... CA

Carson-Newman .... TN
David Lipscomb Coll .... IN
Francis Marion Coll .... SC
Goddard Coll .... VT
Hawaii, U. of (Honolulu) .... HI
Purdue U .... IN
Trenton State Coll............. NJ
Truett McConnell .... GA
West Virginia State .... WV
West Virginia Wesleyan .... WV

Heating and Plumbing

Alfred State .... NY
New England Inst. Tech......... RI
State U. of New York (Delhi) .... NY

Heavy Construction Equipment

Casper Coll .... WY
Central Arizona .... AZ
Colorado Mountain Coll .... CO
Ferris State .... MI
Northeast Mississippi Jr .... MS
Oklahoma State U............. OK

Histologic Technology

Approved by Council on Medical Education of the American Medical Assn. in collaboration with American Society of Clinical Pathologists and American Society of Medical Technologists and National Society for Histotechnology

Chicago, U. of IL
Fergus Falls Comm. Coll ...... MN
Harford Comm. Coll .... MD
Miami, U. of .... FL
North Dakota, U. of .... ND
Oscar Rose Jr. Coll .... OK
Pennsylvania, U. of............. PA
Shoreline Comm. Coll .... WA
South Carolina, Medical U. of ... SC
State U. of New York A&T Coll. (Cobleskill) .... NY
Tennessee, U. of .... TN
Texas, U. of (Houston) .... TX

Holistic Medicine

Bernadean U.................. CA
Goddard Coll .... VT

Home Economics, Child Development and Family Relations

Institutions awarding undergraduate degrees as major field in a single year according to U.S. Office of Education latest statistics

Akron, U. of .... OH
Alabama, U. of .... AL
Arizona, U. of .... AZ
Arkansas, U. of................ AR
Auburn U .... AL
Berea .... KY
Bowling Green .... OH
Brigham Young U .... UT
California, U. of (Davis)........ CA
Carson-Newman Coll........... TN
Central Michigan U............. MI
Central Missouri .... MO
Central Washington .... WA
Cincinnati, U. of .... OH
Clark College .... GA
Colorado State U .... CO
Connecticut, U. of............. CT
Connecticut Coll .... CT
Cornell .... NY
Delaware, U. of .... DE
Delaware State Coll .... DE
Drexel U .... PA
Eastern Illinois IL
Eastern Kentucky U .... KY
Eastern Michigan .... MI
Florida A&M .... FL
Florida State U................. FL
Fontbonne Coll .... MO
Freed-Hardeman Coll .... TN
Georgia, U. of................. GA
Hawaii, U. of .... HI
Idaho, U. of .... ID
Indiana State U .... IN
Iowa State U .... IA
Kansas State U................ KS
Kent State U .... OH
Kentucky, U. of .... KY
Kentucky State U .... KY
Loma Linda .... CA
Louisiana State U .... LA
Luther Coll .... IA
Madonna Coll.................. MI
Maine, U. of .... ME
Mankato State .... MN
Mansfield State .... PA
Massachusetts, U. of .... MA
Memphis State .... TN
Mercy Coll .... MI
Middle Tennessee State .... TN
Mills Coll .... CA
Minnesota, U. of .... MN
Mississippi U. for Women ...... MS
Missouri, U. of .... MO
Morehouse Coll .... GA
Mundelein Coll.................. IL
Murray State .... KY
Nebraska, U. of .... NE
Nevada, U. of .... NV
New Mexico State U........... NM
North Carolina, U. of (Greensboro) .... NC
North Carolina Agri. & Tech. State U .... NC
North Dakota State U .... ND
Northeast Louisiana .... LA
Northeast Missouri .... MO
Northern Illinois................. IL
Northwest Missouri............ MO
Northwestern State U .... LA
Ohio State U.................. OH
Ohio U .... OH
Ohio Wesleyan................ OH
Oklahoma State U............ OK
Oregon State U .... OR
Pacific Union Coll.............. CA
Pennsylvania State U .... PA
Point Loma .... CA
Prairie View A&M .... TX
Puerto Rico, U. of .... PR
Purdue .... IN
Rhode Island, U. of............ RI
San Jose State .... CA
Seton Hill Coll .... PA
South Carolina State Coll....... SC
South Dakota State U .... SD
Southern Illinois IL
Southern Mississippi, U. of .... MS
Southern U. A&M Coll.......... LA
Southwest Missouri .... MO
St. Benedict, Coll. of .... MN
St. Olaf Coll .... MN
State U. of New York (Plattsburgh)................ NY
Stephen F. Austin State .... TX
Stephens Coll .... MO
Syracuse U .... NY
Tennessee, U. of .... TN
Texas, U. of (Austin) .... TX
Texas Tech. U .... TX
Texas Woman's U .... TX
Utah, U. of.................... UT
Utah State U .... UT
Vermont U. & State Agri. Coll ... VT
Virginia Poly. Inst .... VA
Washington State .... WA
Weber State Coll .... UT
Western Washington State ..... WA
Whittier .... CA
Winthrop .... SC
Wisconsin, U. of (Madison, Stout) .... WI

Home Economics, Clothing and Textiles

Institutions awarding 10 or more undergraduate degrees as major field in single year according to U.S. Office of Education latest statistics

Akron, U. of .... OH
Alabama, U. of .... AL
Appalachian State U .... NC
Arkansas, U. of................ AR
Bowling Green State U .... OH
Brigham Young U .... UT
California, U. of (Davis)......... CA
Campbell Coll................. NC
Central Missouri .... MO
Colorado State U .... CO
Columbia Coll .... MO
Connecticut, U. of............. CT
Delaware, U. of .... DE
Drexel .... PA
Eastern Washington .... WA
Florida A&M .... FL
Florida State U................ FL
Framingham State............. MA
Georgia, U. of................ GA
Hawaii, U. of .... HI
Idaho, U. of .... ID
Indiana State .... IN
Iowa State U .... IA
Kansas State U................. KS
Kent State .... OH
Kentucky, U. of .... KY
Louisiana State .... LA
Louisiana Tech. U .... LA
Maryland, U. of .... MD
Memphis State .... TN
Michigan State U............... MI
Minnesota, U. of .... MN
Missouri, U. of .... MO
Montevallo, U. of .... AL
Mundelein Coll................. IL
North Carolina, U. of (Greensboro) .... NC
North Carolina A&T .... NC
North Carolina Central U ...... NC
North Dakota State............ ND
North Texas State U........... TX
Northeast Louisiana .... LA
Northern Illinois................ IL
Northern Iowa .... IA
Northwest Missouri............ MO
Ohio State U.................. OH
Oklahoma, U. of .... OK
Oklahoma State U............ OK
Oregon State U .... OR
Prairie View A&M .... TX
Purdue U .... IN
Rhode Island, U. of............ RI
Seton Hill Coll .... PA
Southern Illinois IL
Southern Mississippi .... MS
Southern U .... LA
Tennessee, U. of .... TN
Texas, U. of (Austin) .... TX
Texas Tech. U .... TX
Tuskegee Inst.................. AL
Ursuline Coll.................. OH
Vermont, U. of .... VT
Virginia Poly. Inst .... VA
Washington, U. of .... WA
Washington State .... WA
Western Kentucky............. KY
Western Michigan U........... MI
Wisconsin, U. of (Madison, Stout) .... WI

Home Economics, Foods and Nutrition

Institutions awarding 5 or more undergraduate degrees as major field in single year according to U.S. Office of Education latest statistics

Akron, U. of .... OH
Albright Coll .... PA
Andrews U .... MI
Appalachian State............ NC
Arizona, U. of .... AZ
Arkansas, U. of................. AR
Auburn U .... AL
Ball State U .... IN
Berea Coll .... KY
Bowling Green .... OH
Brigham Young .... UT
California, U. of (Berkeley, Davis) .... CA
California Poly. State .... CA
California State Poly .... CA
California State U. (Long Beach) .... CA
Central Missouri .... MO
Central Washington U .... WA
Cincinnati, U. of .... OH
College Misericordia .... PA
Colorado State U .... CO
Concordia Coll. (Moorhead) ... MN
Cornell U .... NY
Dayton, U. of .... OH
Delaware, U of .... DE
Drexel U .... PA
Eastern Illinois IL
Eastern Kentucky U .... KY
Eastern Michigan U .... MI
Eastern Washington .... WA
Florida, U. of.................. FL
Florida A&M .... FL
Florida International............ FL
Florida State U................. FL
Fontbonne .... MO
Framingham State............ MA
Georgia, U. of................ GA
Georgia State U .... GA
Hawaii, U. of .... HI
Immaculata Coll .... PA
Incarnate Word .... TX
Indiana State .... IN
Indiana U .... PA
Iowa State U .... IA
Jacksonville State U .... AL
James Madison U .... VA
Kansas State U................ KS
Kent State .... OH
Kentucky, U. of .... KY
Loma Linda U................. CA
Louisiana State U .... LA
Louisiana Tech U .... LA
Maine, U. of (Orono) .... ME
Mankato State .... MN
Mansfield State .... PA
Maryland, U. of .... MD
Marywood .... PA
Miami U .... OH

Michigan State U . . . . . MI
Middle Tennessee . . . . . TN
Minnesota, U. of . . . . . MN
Missouri, U. of . . . . . MO
Morehead State U . . . . . KY
Mt. Mary Coll . . . . . WI
Mt. St. Joseph . . . . . OH
Mundelein IL
Nebraska, U. of . . . . . NE
Nevada, U. of . . . . . NV
New Mexico State . . . . . NM
New York U . . . . . NY
Norfolk State . . . . . VA
North Carolina, U. of (Greensboro) . . . . . NC
North Carolina A&T . . . . . NC
North Carolina Central U . . . . . NC
North Dakota, U. of . . . . . ND
North Dakota State U . . . . . ND
Northern Colorado . . . . . CO
Northern Illinois IL
Northern Iowa . . . . . IA
Northern Michigan . . . . . MI
Ohio State U . . . . . OH
Ohio U . . . . . OH
Oklahoma, U. of . . . . . OK
Oklahoma State U . . . . . OK
Oregon State U . . . . . OR
Pennsylvania State U . . . . . PA
Prairie View A&M . . . . . TX
Pratt U . . . . . NY
Puerto Rico, U. of . . . . . PR
Purdue U . . . . . IN
Rhode Island, U. of . . . . . RI
Rivier Coll . . . . . NH
Rochester Inst. of Tech . . . . . NY
Rosary Coll IL
San Jose State . . . . . CA
Seattle Pacific . . . . . WA
Seton Hill Coll . . . . . PA
Simmons . . . . . MA
South Dakota State U . . . . . SD
Southern Illinois IL
Southern Mississippi, U. of . . . . . MS
Southern U . . . . . LA
Southwest Missouri State U . . . . . MO
Southwestern Louisiana, U. of . . . . . LA
St. Elizabeth, Coll. of . . . . . NJ
St. Joseph Coll . . . . . CT
St. Mary's Dominican . . . . . LA
St. Scholastica, Coll. of . . . . . MN
State U. of New York (Buffalo, Plattsburgh) . . . . . NY
Syracuse U . . . . . NY
Tennessee, U. of . . . . . TN
Texas, U. of (Austin) . . . . . TX
Texas A&I . . . . . TX
Texas Tech. U . . . . . TX
Tuskegee Inst . . . . . AL
Ursuline Coll . . . . . OH
Utah, U of . . . . . UT
Vermont, U. of . . . . . VT
Virginia Poly. Inst . . . . . VA
Washington, U. of . . . . . WA
Washington State . . . . . WA
Western Michigan . . . . . MI
Wisconsin, U. of (Madison, Stevens Point, Stout) . . . . . WI
Youngstown . . . . . OH

Home Economics, General

Institutions awarding 10 or more undergraduate degrees as major field in single year according to U.S. Office of Education latest statistics

Akron, U. of . . . . . OH
Albion . . . . . MI
Arizona, U. of . . . . . AZ
Arizona State U . . . . . AZ
Arkansas, U. of . . . . . AR
Ball State . . . . . IN
Baylor U . . . . . TX
Bob Jones U . . . . . SC
Bradley U IL
Brooklyn Coll . . . . . NY
Butler U . . . . . IN
California, U. of (Davis) . . . . . CA
California Poly. State (San Luis Obispo) . . . . . CA
California State Poly. U. (Pomona) . . . . . CA
California State U. (Chico, Fresno, Long Beach, Los Angeles, Northridge, Sacramento) . . . . . CA
Cameron U . . . . . OK
Carson-Newman . . . . . TN
Catholic U. of Puerto Rico . . . . . PR
Central Arkansas, U. of . . . . . AR
Central Michigan . . . . . MI
Central State . . . . . OK
Christian Heritage . . . . . CA
David Lipscomb Coll . . . . . TN
Dayton, U. of . . . . . OH
Delaware, U. of . . . . . DE
East Carolina U . . . . . NC
East Texas State . . . . . TX
Emporia State U . . . . . KS
Florida International . . . . . FL
Fort Hays Kansas State . . . . . KS
Framingham State . . . . . MA
Gallaudet Coll . . . . . DC
Georgia, U. of . . . . . GA
Georgia Coll . . . . . GA
Hawaii, U. of . . . . . HI
Hood . . . . . MD
Houston, U. of . . . . . TX
Howard U . . . . . DC
Humboldt State U . . . . . CA
Hunter . . . . . NY
Illinois, U. of IL
Illinois State IL
Indiana U . . . . . IN
Iowa, U. of . . . . . IA
James Madison U . . . . . VA
Kansas State U . . . . . KS
Lamar U . . . . . TX
Lander Coll . . . . . SC
Lehman Coll . . . . . NY
Longwood Coll . . . . . VA
Louisville, U. of . . . . . KY
Marymount . . . . . NY
Marywood . . . . . PA
Massachusetts, U. of . . . . . MA
McNeese State . . . . . LA
Mercy Coll. of Detroit . . . . . MI
Meredith Coll . . . . . NC
Messiah Coll . . . . . PA
Middle Tennessee . . . . . TN
Minnesota, U. of . . . . . MN
Mississippi, U. of . . . . . MS
Mississippi State . . . . . MS
Montana, U. of . . . . . MT
Montana State . . . . . MT
Montclair State . . . . . NJ
Morehead State . . . . . KY
Morgan State . . . . . MD
New Hampshire, U. of . . . . . NH
Nicholls State U . . . . . LA
Norfolk State . . . . . VA
North Carolina, U. of . . . . . NC
North Carolina Central . . . . . NC
Northeastern State U . . . . . OK
Northern Arizona . . . . . AZ
Northern Colorado, U. of . . . . . CO
Northern Iowa . . . . . IA
Ohio State U . . . . . OH
Oklahoma Christian . . . . . OK
Oregon State U . . . . . OR
Pembroke State . . . . . NC
Pepperdine U . . . . . CA
Puerto Rico, U. of . . . . . PR
Puget Sound, U. of . . . . . WA
Purdue U . . . . . IN
Queens Coll . . . . . NY
Radford . . . . . VA
Rutgers . . . . . NJ
Sam Houston State . . . . . TX
San Diego State . . . . . CA
San Francisco State . . . . . CA
San Jose State . . . . . CA
Seattle Pacific U . . . . . WA
Southeast Missouri State . . . . . MO
Southwest Texas State . . . . . TX
Southwestern Louisiana . . . . . LA
Spalding Coll . . . . . KY
State U. of New York (Oneonta) . . . . . NY
Stephen F. Austin . . . . . TX
Sterling Coll . . . . . KS
Syracuse . . . . . NY
Tarleton . . . . . TX
Tennessee, U. of . . . . . TN
Tennessee State U . . . . . TN
Tennessee Tech . . . . . TN
Texas, U. of (Austin) . . . . . TX
Texas Christian U . . . . . TX
Texas Coll . . . . . TX
Texas Southern . . . . . TX
Utah State . . . . . UT
Valparaiso U . . . . . IN
Wayne State U . . . . . MI
West Virginia U . . . . . WV
West Virginia Wesleyan . . . . . WV
Western Carolina U . . . . . NC
Western Illinois IL
Western Washington . . . . . WA
William Woods . . . . . MO
Wisconsin, U. of (Madison, Stevens Point, Stout) . . . . . WI

Home Economics, Institutional and Cafeteria Management

Institutions awarding 5 or more undergraduate degrees as major field in single year according to U.S. Office of Education latest statistics

Alabama, U. of . . . . . AL
Grambling . . . . . LA
Illinois, U. of IL
Iowa State . . . . . IA
Johnson & Wales Coll . . . . . RI
Kansas State . . . . . KS
Minnesota, U. of . . . . . MN
Morehead State . . . . . KY
Northeast Louisiana U . . . . . LA
Northern Michigan U . . . . . MI
Oregon State U . . . . . OR
Pennsylvania State U . . . . . PA
Purdue . . . . . IN
Rochester Inst. of Tech . . . . . NY
Tennessee, U. of . . . . . TN
Wisconsin, U. of (Stout) . . . . . WI

Home Economics Education

Institutions awarding 15 or more undergraduate degrees as major field in a single year according to U.S. Office of Education latest statistics

Abilene Christian . . . . . TX
Arizona, U. of . . . . . AZ
Auburn U . . . . . AL
Bowling Green State . . . . . OH
Central Washington U . . . . . WA
Cincinnati, U. of . . . . . OH
East Texas State . . . . . TX
Eastern Illinois U IL
Florida State U . . . . . FL
Georgia, U. of . . . . . GA
Glassboro State . . . . . NJ
Hampton Institute . . . . . VA
Indiana State . . . . . IN
Indiana U. of Pennsylvania . . . . . PA
Inter-American U . . . . . PR
Iowa State U . . . . . IA
Kearney State . . . . . NE
Kentucky, U. of . . . . . KY
Louisiana Tech . . . . . LA
Mankato State . . . . . MN
Mansfield State . . . . . PA
Miami U . . . . . OH
Michigan State U . . . . . MI
Middle Tennessee . . . . . TN
Minnesota, U. of . . . . . MN
Mississippi U. for Women . . . . . MS
Montevallo, U. of . . . . . AL
Nebraska, U. of . . . . . NE
North Dakota, U. of . . . . . ND
North Dakota State U . . . . . ND
North Texas State . . . . . TX
Northeast Missouri State U . . . . . MO
Northwest Missouri State . . . . . MO
Oregon State U . . . . . OR
Pennsylvania State U . . . . . PA
Prairie View A&M . . . . . TX
Puerto Rico, U. of . . . . . PR
South Carolina State . . . . . SC
South Dakota State . . . . . SD
Southeast Missouri . . . . . MO
Southwest Missouri State . . . . . MO
Southwest Texas . . . . . TX
State U. of New York (Buffalo, Oneonta, Plattsburgh) . . . . . NY
Stephen F. Austin State U . . . . . TX
Tennessee, U. of . . . . . TN
Texas, U. of (Austin) . . . . . TX
Texas Tech. U . . . . . TX
Texas Woman's U . . . . . TX
Vermont, U. of . . . . . VT
Virginia State Coll . . . . . VA
Washington State . . . . . WA
Western Kentucky U . . . . . KY
Western Michigan U . . . . . MI
Wisconsin, U. of (Madison, Stevens Point, Stout) . . . . . WI

Horsemanship

Averett . . . . . VA
Becker Jr. Coll (Leicester) . . . . . MA
Cazenovia . . . . . NY
Centenary Coll . . . . . NJ
Colorado Mountain Coll . . . . . CO
Dawson Comm. Coll . . . . . MT
Findlay Coll . . . . . OH
Johnson and Wales . . . . . RI
Lake Erie . . . . . OH
Loma Linda U . . . . . CA
Louisiana Tech . . . . . LA
Midway Coll . . . . . KY
Mount Senario . . . . . WI
Newberry Jr. Coll . . . . . SC
Northwestern State U . . . . . LA
Otterbein Coll . . . . . OH
Pepperdine U . . . . . CA
Post Coll . . . . . CT
Purdue U . . . . . IN
Salem Coll . . . . . WV
Shenandoah Coll . . . . . VA
Southeastern Oklahoma State U . . . . . OK
Southern Idaho, Coll. of . . . . . ID
Southern Seminary . . . . . VA
State U. of New York (Delhi) . . . . . NY
Virginia Intermont . . . . . VA
Wesleyan Coll . . . . . GA
Western Wyoming Comm. Coll . . . . . WY
William Woods Coll . . . . . MO
Wood Jr. Coll . . . . . MS

Horticulture

Institutions offering 5 or more undergraduate degrees as major field in single year according to U.S. Office of Education latest statistics

Arizona, U. of .... AZ
Arkansas, U. of.................. AR
Brigham Young .... UT
California State Poly. Coll. (Pomona).................. CA
Colorado State U .... CO
Connecticut, U. of.............. CT
Cornell .... NY
Delaware Valley Coll .... PA
Florida, U. of.................... FL
Georgia, U. of.................... GA
Hawaii, U. of .... HI
Illinois, U. of IL
Iowa State U .... IA
Kansas State U.................. KS
Kentucky, U. of .... KY
Louisiana State .... LA
Louisiana Tech.................. LA
Maryland, U. of .... MD
Michigan State.................. MI
Minnesota, U. of .... MN
Mississippi State .... MS
Missouri, U. of .... MO
Nebraska, U. of .... NE
New Mexico State U........... NM
North Carolina State U .... NC
North Dakota State............ ND
Ohio State U .... OH
Oklahoma State .... OK
Oregon State U .... OR
Pennsylvania State U .... PA
Puerto Rico, U. of .... PR
Purdue .... IN
South Dakota State U .... SD
Southwestern Louisiana, U. of .. LA
Texas A&M .... TX
Texas Tech .... TX
Virginia Poly. Inst .... VA
Washington State U .... WA
Wisconsin, U. of (Madison) ..... WI

Horticulture, Ornamental

Institutions offering 5 or more undergraduate degrees as major field in single year according to U.S. Office of Education latest statistics

Arkansas, U. of.................. AR
Auburn U .... AL
California Poly. State U......... CA
California State Poly. (Pomona) . CA
Colorado State U .... CO
Cornell .... NY
Delaware Valley Coll .... PA
Eastern Kentucky U .... KY
Florida, U. of.................... FL
Illinois, U. of IL
Iowa State U .... IA
Tennessee, U. of .... TN
Texas A&M .... TX

Hospital Administration

Arizona, U. of .... AZ
Ashland Coll .... OH
Auburn U .... AL
Augustana Coll .... SD
Avila Coll .... MO
Barton Comm. Coll.............. KS
Bowling Green .... OH
Cincinnati, U. of .... OH
Chatham Coll .... PA
Concordia Coll................ MN
Davis & Elkins .... WV
East Central Oklahoma State U .... OK
East Texas State U .... TX
Eastern Kentucky U .... KY
Eastern Washington U .... WA
Ferris State U .... MI
Florida, U. of.................... FL
Florida Atlantic U .... FL
George Washington U .... DC
Georgia State U .... GA
Goddard Coll .... VT
Governors State U IL
Houston, U. of .... TX
Idaho State U .... ID
Indiana U. (Bloomington)....... IN
Indiana U .... PA
International U .... MO
Iona Coll .... NY
Iowa, U. of .... IA
Ithaca Coll .... NY
Kean Coll .... NJ
La Salle .... PA
La Verne, U. of................. CA
Lake Superior State .... MI
Langston U .... OK
Lehman Coll .... NY
Lindenwood Colleges .... MO
Loma Linda .... CA
Louisiana State U .... LA
Lowell, U. of .... MA
Marymount Coll .... VA
Mercy Coll. of Detroit .... MI
Metropolitan State............. CO
Miami, U. of .... FL
Michigan, U. of (Dearborn) ..... MI
Minnesota, U. of .... MN
Missouri, U. of .... MO
Morehead State U .... KY
National U .... CA
Nazareth Coll .... MI
Nebraska, U. of .... NE
New Hampshire, U. of .... NH
Northeastern Oklahoma State .. OK
Northeastern U................. MA
Northern Iowa, U. of .... IA
Ohio State U .... OH
Oklahoma Baptist .... OK
Oregon State U .... OR
Ottawa U .... KS
Park Coll .... MO
Pennsylvania, U. of............ PA
Pennsylvania State U .... PA
Pittsburgh, U. of .... PA
Quinnipiac Coll .... CT
Sangamon State IL
Shepherd Coll .... WV
South Carolina, U. of .... SC
South Dakota, U. of .... SD
Southern Vermont Coll .... VT
Southwest Texas State .... TX
Southwestern Oklahoma State . OK
St. Andrews Presbyterian .... SC
St. Mary's .... CA
St. Norbert..................... WI
State U. of New York (Coll. of Tech.) .... NY
Stephen F. Austin .... TX
Stonehill .... MA
Stockton State .... NJ
Tarkio Coll .... MO
Temple U .... PA
Tennessee State U .... TN
Texas Woman's U .... TX
Trinity Christian................ IL
Union Experimenting .... OH
Ursuline Coll................... OH
Virginia Commonwealth .... VA
Washburn U .... KS
Washington U.................. MO
Western Kentucky U .... KY
Wichita State .... KS
Wisconsin, U. of .... WI

Hospital Housekeeping

North Dakota State U .... ND
State U. of New York Cobleskill) .... NY

Hotel, Institutional, Motel and/or Restaurant Administration

Alaska, U. of .... AK
Appalachian State U .... NC
Arkansas Tech. U .... AR
Ashland Coll .... OH
Auburn U .... AL
Belmont Coll................... TN
Biscayne Coll .... FL
Bismarck Jr. Coll.............. ND
Black Hills State Coll .... SD
Boca Raton .... FL
Boston U .... MA
Bowling Green State U .... OH
Bradley U IL
Brandywine Coll .... DE
Brigham Young U .... UT
California, U. of .... CA
California State Poly. U......... CA
California State U .... CA
Central Missouri State U....... MO
Central Pa. Business Sch .... PA
Chamberlayne Jr. Coll......... MA
Champlain Coll .... VT
Cheyney State .... PA
Cincinnati, U. of .... OH
Colorado Mountain Coll .... CO
Colorado State U .... CO
Cornell U .... NY
Culinary Inst .... NY
Davenport Coll. of Bus .... MI
Davis & Elkins .... WV
Denver, U. of .... CO
Drexel U .... PA
DuPage, Coll. of IL
East Carolina U .... NC
Eastern Illinois U IL
Eastern Kentucky U .... KY
Eastern Michigan U .... MI
El Centro Coll.................. TX
Endicott Coll................... MA
Fairleigh Dickinson U .... NJ
Ferris State Coll............... MD
Florida International U.......... FL
Florida State U .... FL
Georgia, U. of.................. GA
Georgia State U .... GA
Golden Gate U .... CA
Grand Valley State Colls........ MI
Hawaii, U. of (Honolulu) .... HI
Hawaii Pacific Coll .... HI
Hocking Tech .... OH
Houston, U. of .... TX
Howard U...................... DC
Huron Coll..................... SD
Illinois, U. of (Urbana) IL
Indiana State U .... IN
Indiana U .... IN
Indiana U. of Pennsylvania...... PA
International .... FL
Iowa State U .... IA
James Madison .... VA
Johnson and Wales Coll .... RI
Kansas State U................. KS
Kentucky, U. of .... KY
Keystone Jr.................... PA
Kirkoff Coll .... MI
Laboure Jr..................... MA
Loma Linda U.................. CA
Mankato State U .... MN
Maryland, U. of (Eastern Shore)...................... MD
Massachusetts, U. of (Amherst)................... MA
Mercy Coll..................... MI
Mercyhurst Coll .... PA
Messiah Coll .... PA
Metropolitan State............. CO
Miami U .... OH
Michigan State U.............. MI
Minnesota, U. of (Crookston, Minneapolis) .... MN
Missouri, U. of .... MO
Montana, U. of .... MT
Montclair State Coll .... NJ
Moorhead State .... MN
Morehead State U .... KY
Morris Brown Coll.............. GA
Nevada, U. of (Las Vegas) ...... NV
New Hampshire Coll .... NH
New Hampshire, U. of (Durham) .... NH
New Haven, U. of .... CT
New Orleans, U. of .... LA
New York Inst. of Tech .... NY
New York U..................... NY
Newbury Jr .... MA
Niagara U...................... NY
North Carolina, U. of .... NC
North Carolina Wesleyan ...... NC
North Dakota State U .... ND
Northeast Mississippi Jr .... MS
Northern Arizona U .... AZ
Northern Illinois U IL
Northwood Inst .... IN
Northwood Inst .... MI
Ohio State U .... OH
Oklahoma State U............. OK
Paul Smith..................... NY
Pennsylvania State U. (Allentown, McKeesport, Schuylkill, University Park) .... PA
Pratt Institute .... NY
Purdue U .... IN
Radford U .... VA
Rhode Island, U. of............. RI
Rochester Inst. of Tech......... NY
Rosary Coll IL
Shepherd Coll .... WV
South Carolina, U. of .... SC
South Dakota State U .... SD
Southern Arkansas U. (Tech. Branch)....................... AR
Southern Illinois U IL
Southern Maine, U. of .... ME
Southern Mississippi, U. of .... MS
Southwest Missouri State ...... MO
Southwest State U .... MN
State U. of New York (Canton, Cobleskill, Delhi, Morrisville) .... NY
Syracuse U .... NY
Tennessee, U. of .... TN
Texas Woman's U .... TX
Transylvania U .... KY
Trinity Christian................ IL
Tuskegee Institute.............. AL
U.S. International U .... CA
Vermont, U. of .... VT
Virginia State U .... VA
Webber Coll .... FL
West Virginia State Coll .... WV
Western Illinois U IL
Western Kentucky.............. KY
Wiley Coll .... TX
Wisconsin, U. of (Stout) .... WI

Humanities

Alabama, U. of .... AL
Alabama State U .... AL
Albertus Magnus .... CT
Alderson-Broaddus............ WV
Alfred U .... NY
Angelina....................... TX
Antioch .... OH
Augustana IL
Aurora.......................... IL

Averett VA
Baldwin-Wallace OH
Barat IL
Baylor U TX
Bennett Coll NC
Bernadean U CA
Blinn Coll TX
Bob Jones U SC
Boston U MA
Bradford MA
Brevard Coll NC
Bridgewater State MA
California, U. of (Irvine, Riverside) CA
California Poly. U. (Pomona) CA
California State Coll PA
California State U. (Northridge, Sacramento, San Bernardino) CA
Carnegie-Mellon PA
Case Western OH
Cedar Crest PA
Central Florida, U. of FL
Chapman Coll CA
Cheyney State PA
Chicago, U. of IL
Christian Brothers TN
Clearwater Christian FL
Colgate U NY
College Misericordia PA
Colorado Coll CO
Colorado Mountain CO
Columbia Coll IL
Columbia Coll MO
Connecticut, U. of CT
Converse Coll SC
Daemen Coll NY
Dana Coll NE
Dayton, U. of OH
Dean Jr MA
DePauw U IN
Drake U IA
Drew U NJ
DuPage, Coll. of IL
D'Youville Coll NY
Eastern Kentucky U KY
Eastern Washington U WA
Eckerd Coll FL
Elizabethtown Coll PA
Elmira Coll NY
Emporia State KS
Evergreen State WA
Felician Coll IL
Ferris State MI
Ferrum Coll VA
Findlay Coll OH
Florida, U. of FL
Florida Beacon Coll FL
Florida Inst. of Tech FL
Florida International FL
Gannon U PA
George Washington U DC
Goddard Coll VT
Gonzaga U WA
Grand Valley State MI
Green Mountain VT
Grinnell Coll IA
Hampden-Sydney Coll VA
Hampshire Coll MA
Harcum Jr PA
Harvard U MA
Hastings Coll NE
Hawaii Loa HI
Hawaii Pacific Coll HI
Hendrix Coll AR
High Point Coll NC
Hillsdale Coll MI
Holy Family PA
Houghton Coll NY
Illinois, U. of (Urbana) IL
Illinois Inst. of Tech IL
Indiana State U IN
Iowa State U IA
Jacksonville State U AL
Jacksonville U FL
John Carroll U OH
John F. Kennedy CA
John Wesley Coll NC
Johns Hopkins U MD
Judson Baptist Coll OR
Judson Coll AL
Juniata Coll PA
Kansas, U. of KS
Kearney State NE
Kent State U OH
Knox Coll IL
La Salle Coll PA
Lasell Jr MA
Lawrence Inst. of Tech MI
Lawrence U WI
Lees Jr KY
Lincoln Coll IL
Lincoln U IL
Loretto Heights CO
Louisiana Tech LA
Louisville, U. of KY
Maine, U. of (Fort Kent) ME
Mankato State MN
Marlboro Coll VT
Mars Hill NC
Marylhurst Coll OR
Marymount Manhattan NY
Maryville MO
Massachusetts Inst. of Tech MA
Michigan, U. of (Dearborn) MI
Michigan State U MI
Mid-America Nazarene KS
Milligan Coll TN
Millikin U IL
Minnesota, U. of MN
Mobile Coll AL
Montana, U. of MT
Moorhead State MN
Muhlenberg PA
Muskingum Coll OH
New Coll. of U.S.F FL
North Central Coll IL
North Dakota State U ND
Northeastern Jr CO
Northern Iowa, U. of IA
Northern Michigan, U. of MI
Northwest Missouri State MO
Notre Dame, U. of IN
Norwich U VT
Occidental Coll CA
Ohio State U OH
Oklahoma State U OK
Pacific, U. of the CA
Pacific Union Coll CA
Pennsylvania State U PA
Pepperdine U CA
Peru State NE
Pittsburgh, U. of PA
Plymouth State NH
Providence Coll RI
Puerto Rico, U. of PR
Purdue U IN
Radcliffe MA
Richmond Coll England
Rio Grande Coll OH
Rio Piedras PR
Rockford Coll IL
Rockmont Coll CO
Roger Williams RI
Rosemont PA
Saint Joseph Coll CT
Saint Joseph's Coll IN
Saint Leo FL
Saint Mary's MN
Saint Michael's VT
Saint Paul's MO
Saint Rose, Coll. of NY
Sam Houston TX
Santa Fe, Coll. of NM
Sarah Lawrence NY
Seattle Pacific WA
Seattle U WA
Simpson Coll CA
Sioux Falls SD
South Carolina, U. of SC
South Dakota, U. of SD
South Georgia Coll GA
Southeastern U LA
Southern Idaho, Coll. of ID
Southern Maine, U. of ME
Southern Vermont Coll VT
Southwestern Coll KS
Southwestern U TX
Spring Hill AL
Springfield MA
St. Benedict, Coll. of MN
St. Catherine, Coll. of MN
St. Gregory's Coll OK
St. John's U MN
St. Mary Coll KS
St. Mary's Coll IN
St. Scholastica, Coll. of MN
State U. of New York (Buffalo, Morrisville, Stony Brook) NY
Stephens Coll MO
Stetson U FL
Steubenville, U. of OH
Tennessee State U TN
Texas, U. of (Austin, Dallas, San Antonio) TX
Thiel Coll PA
Toledo, U. of OH
Trevecca Nazarene TN
Trinity Christian IL
Trinity Coll IL
U.S. Military Acad NY
Union Coll NY
Urbana Coll OH
Utah State U UT
Valley Forge Military PA
Valparaiso U IN
Voorhees Coll SC
Washington U MO
Wayne State MI
Weber State UT
Webster Coll MO
Wellesley Coll MA
West Florida, U. of FL
Western Oregon State OR
Westminster Coll UT
White Plains, Coll. of NY
Wichita State U KS
Wiley Coll TX
Willamette U OR
William Woods MO
Wisconsin, U. of (Green Bay, Madison, Superior) WI
Wofford Coll SC
Worcester Poly. Inst MA
Youngstown State OH

Industrial Arts

Abilene Christian TX
Adams State Coll CO
Alabama A&M AL
Angelina Coll TX
Appalachian State U NC
Ball State IN
Barton County Comm. Coll KS
Bemidji State U MN
Berea Coll KY
Bethel Coll KS
Blinn Coll TX
California State Coll PA
California State U. (Chico, Fresno, Los Angeles) CA
Casper Coll WY
Central Arkansas, U. of AR
Central Coll KS
Central Michigan U MI
Chadron State Coll NE
Cheyney State Coll PA
Cincinnati, U. of OH
Colorado State U CO
Coppin State Coll MD
Cowley County Comm. Coll KS
Dakota State Coll SD
East Central Oklahoma State U OK
East Tennessee State TN
Eastern Arizona AZ
Eastern Kentucky U KY
Eastern New Mexico NM
Eastern Oklahoma State OK
Eastern Washington U WA
Emporia State KS
Florida A&M FL
Florida International U FL
Fort Hays State U KS
Fort Scott Comm. Coll KS
Freeman Jr. Coll SD
George Mason U VA
Humboldt State CA
Hutchinson Comm. Coll KS
Idaho, U. of ID
Jackson State U MS
Kean Coll NJ
Kearney State NE
Kent State OH
Langston U OK
Lincoln U MO
Loma Linda CA
Mankato State U MN
Maryland, U. of MD
Marywood PA
McPherson Coll KS
Miami U OH
Michigan State U MI
Millersville State PA
Minnesota, U. of (Duluth) MN
Mississippi Delta Jr. Coll MS
Montana State U MT
Montclair State Coll NJ
Moorhead State Coll MN
Morehead State KY
New Mexico, U. of NM
New Mexico State U NM
Norfolk State U VA
North Carolina A&T State U NC
North Texas State U TX
Northeast Missouri State Coll MO
Northeastern Oklahoma State U OK
Northern Arizona U AZ
Northern Colorado CO
Northern Iowa, U. of IA
Northern Michigan U MI
Northern Montana Coll MT
Northern Oklahoma Coll OK
Northwest Missouri State MO
Northwestern Oklahoma State OK
Northwestern State U LA
Ohio State OH
Oklahoma Panhandle OK
Oklahoma State U OK
Ozarks, Sch. of the MO
Pacific Union Coll CA
Peru State Coll NE
Pittsburg State KS
Puerto Rico, U. of PR
Purdue (Calumet) IN
Rhode Island Coll RI
Rio Piedras PR
Rochester Inst. of Tech NY
Salem Coll WV
San Diego State CA
San Jose State U CA
South Carolina State SC
South Dakota, U. of (Springfield) SD
South Georgia Coll GA
Southeastern Louisiana U LA
Southwest Missouri State MO
Southwest Texas State U TX
State U. of New York (Oswego) NY
State U. of N.Y. Coll. (Buffalo) NY
Sul Ross State U TX
Temple U PA
Tennessee State U TN
Texas A&I TX
Trenton State Coll NJ
Trinity Christian IL

Virginia Poly. Inst .... VA
Virginia State U .... VA
Waldorf .... IA
Wayne State U .... MI
West Florida, U. of .... FL
West Virginia Inst. of Tech ..... WV
Western Carolina U .... NC
Western Kentucky U .... KY
Western State Coll .... CO
Westmar .... IA
William Penn Coll .... IA
Winona State U .... MN
Wisconsin, U. of (Platteville) .... WI

Industrial Arts, Vocational and Technical Education

Institutions awarding 30 or more undergraduate degrees as major field in single year according to the U.S. Office of Education latest statistics

Akron, U. of .... OH
American Tech. U .... TX
Appalachian State .... NC
Athens State .... AL
Ball State U .... IN
Bemidji State .... MN
Bowling Green State U .... OH
Brigham Young U .... UT
California Poly. State .... CA
California State Coll .... PA
California State U. (Chico, Fresno, Long Beach, Los Angeles) .... CA
Central Connecticut State ...... CT
Central Michigan U .... MI
Central State U .... OK
Central Washington .... WA
City Coll .... NY
Clemson U .... SC
Colorado State .... CO
East Carolina .... NC
East Texas State U .... TX
Eastern Illinois IL
Ferris State .... MI
Fitchburg State Coll .... MA
Fort Hays Kansas State .... KS
Glassboro State .... NJ
Humboldt State U .... CA
Indiana State U .... IN
Iowa State .... IA
Kean Coll .... NJ
Kearney State .... NE
Kent State U .... OH
Miami U .... OH
Millersville State .... PA
Minnesota, U. of .... MN
Mississippi State .... MS
Mississippi Valley .... MS
Montclair State .... NJ
Morehead State U .... KY
Nebraska, U. of .... NE
New Hampshire, U. of .... NH
North Carolina State .... NC
North Texas State U .... TX
Northeastern State .... OK
Northern Arizona U .... AZ
Northern Illinois IL
Northern Iowa .... IA
Northern Michigan .... MI
Ohio State .... OH
Oklahoma State .... OK
Oregon State .... OR
Pennsylvania State .... PA
Prairie View A&M .... TX
Puerto Rico, U. of .... PR
Purdue .... IN
Rhode Island Coll .... RI
Sam Houston State .... TX
San Diego State .... CA
San Francisco State .... CA
San Jose State .... CA
South Dakota, U. of .... SD
Southern Illinois IL
Southern Maine, U. of .... ME
Southern Mississippi .... MS
Southwest Texas State .... TX
St. Cloud State U .... MN
State U. of New York (Buffalo, Oswego, Utica) .... NY
Tarleton State .... TX
Temple .... PA
Texas A&M .... TX
Trenton State .... NJ
Virginia State .... VA
West Florida, U. of .... FL
Western Carolina U .... NC
Western Illinois U IL
Western Michigan U .... MI
Wisconsin, U. of (Stout) .... WI
Wyoming, U. of .... WY

Industrial Design

Art Center Coll. of Design ...... CA
Auburn U .... AL
Bowling Green State U .... OH
Bridgeport, U. of .... CT
California State Coll .... PA
Carnegie-Mellon .... PA
Center For Creative Studies ..... MI
Cincinnati, U. of .... OH
Eastern Washington U .... WA
Illinois, U. of (Chicago, Urbana) .. IL
Illinois Inst. of Tech IL
Kansas, U. of .... KS
Kansas City Art Inst .... MO
Kent State .... OH
Missouri, U. of .... MO
Moorhead State .... MN
Morrison Inst. of Tech IL
Northern Michigan U .... MI
Ohio State U .... OH
Philadelphia Coll. of Art .... PA
Pittsburg State .... KS
Pratt Inst .... NY
Purdue .... IN
Rhode Island Sch. of Design .... RI
San Jose State .... CA
South Dakota, U. of .... SD
Syracuse U .... NY

Industrial Distribution

California State Coll .... PA
Central Washington U .... WA
Eastern Washington .... WA
Hawaii Pacific Coll .... HI
Kansas, U. of .... KS
Texas A&M .... TX
West Texas State .... TX

Industrial Electronics

Alfred State .... NY
Angelina Coll .... TX
California State Coll .... PA
Central Washington U .... WA
Eastern Arizona .... AZ
Eastern Kentucky U .... KY
Eastern Oklahoma State .... OK
Ferris State .... MI
Indiana State U .... IN
Kansas, U. of .... KS
Marywood Coll .... PA
Missouri, U. of .... MO
Moorhead State .... MN
Morehead State .... KY
Murray State U .... KY
North Idaho .... ID
Northeastern Oklahoma State .. OK
Northwestern State U .... LA
Pearl River Jr. Coll .... MS
South Dakota, U. of .... SD
Southeast Missouri State ...... MO
Southeastern Oklahoma State U .... OK
Southwest Missouri State ...... MO
State U. of New York (Morrisville) .... NY
SUNY Coll. of Tech .... NY
Texas State Tech. Inst. (Harlingen) .... TX
Valparaiso Tech. Inst .... IN

Industrial Engineering, *See* ENGINEERING, INDUSTRIAL

Industrial Hygiene

Clarkson Coll .... NY
Minnesota, U. of .... MN
New York Inst. of Tech .... NY
North Alabama, U. of .... AL
Ohio U .... OH
Purdue U .... IN
Quinnipiac .... CT
Texas A&M .... TX
Toledo, U. of .... OH
West Virginia U .... WV

Industrial Instrumentation

California State Coll .... PA
Texas State Tech .... TX

Industrial Management

Abilene Christian .... TX
Akron, U. of .... OH
Arkansas, U. of .... AR
Aurora Coll IL
Averett Coll .... VA
Boston U .... MA
California State Coll .... CA
California State U. (Hayward, Sacramento) .... CA
Carnegie-Mellon .... PA
Case Western .... OH
Central Washington U .... WA
Chadron State Coll .... NE
Cheyney State .... PA
Cincinnati, U. of .... OH
Clarion State .... PA
Clarkson Coll .... NY
Colorado State U .... CO
Coloardo Tech. Coll .... CO
Columbia Coll .... MO
Ferrum Coll .... VA
Franklin U .... OH
Gannon U .... PA
GMI .... MI
George Washington U .... DC
Georgia Inst. of Tech .... GA
Illinois Inst. of Tech IL
International U .... MO
Iowa, U. of .... IA
Kansas, U. of .... KS
Kansas Newman .... KS
Kearney State .... NE
Kent State U .... OH
La Salle .... PA
Lambuth Coll .... TN
Lawrence Inst. of Tech .... MI
LeTourneau Coll .... TX
Lincoln Coll IL
Lowell, U. of .... MA
Marietta Coll .... OH
Miami U .... OH
Michigan, U. of (Dearborn) ..... MI
Millikin U IL
Minnesota, U. of .... MN
Moorhead State .... MN
Navarro Coll .... TX
Northeast Missouri .... MO
Northern Iowa, U. of .... IA
Northwestern State U .... LA
Ohio State .... OH
Oklahoma State U .... OK
Oregon Instit. of Tech .... OR
Peru State .... NE
Pratt Inst .... NY
Purdue .... IN
Saginaw Valley .... MI
San Jose State .... CA
South Georgia .... GA
Southeastern Louisiana U ...... LA
Southern Arkansas U .... AR
Southwest Missouri .... MO
St. Andrews Presbyterian ...... NC
St. Scholastica .... MN
State U. of New York Coll. (Buffalo, Coll. of Tech) .... NY
Stevens Inst. of Tech .... NJ
Temple U .... PA
Tennessee, U. of .... TN
Trinity Christian IL
Wayne State U .... MI
Wesleyan Coll .... GA
West Virginia Inst. of Tech ..... WV
Youngstown State .... OH

Industrial Psychology

Akron, U. of .... OH
Albertus Magnus .... CT
Averett Coll .... VA
Baruch Coll .... NY
Bridgewater State .... MA
Carnegie-Mellon .... PA
Central Florida, U. of .... FL
Clarkson Coll .... NY
Columbia Coll .... MO
Emporia State U .... KS
George Washington U .... DC
Hawaii Pacific Coll .... HI
Illinois Inst. of Tech IL
International U .... MO
Iowa Wesleyan .... IA
La Salle Coll .... PA
Lamar U .... TX
Marietta Coll .... OH
Morningside Coll .... IA
Nebraska, U. of .... NE
Pepperdine U .... CA
Purdue U .... IN
Springfield .... MA
Trinity Christian IL
Wayne State U .... MI

Industrial Relations and Labor

Institutions awarding 10 or more undergraduate degrees as major field in single year according to U.S. Office of Education latest statistics

Alabama, U. of .... AL
Auburn .... AL
Bridgeport, U. of .... CT
Cincinnati, U. of .... OH
Cleveland State U .... OH
Colorado, U. of .... CO
Connecticut, U. of .... CT
Cornell .... NY
Hawaii, U. of .... HI
Iowa, U. of .... IA
Kent State U .... OH
La Salle Coll .... PA
Le Moyne Coll .... NY
Louisiana State .... LA
Mankato State .... MN
North Carolina, U. of .... NC

North Texas State .... TX
Northeastern U .... MA
Ohio State .... OH
Pace U .... NY
Pennsylvania State U .... PA
Puerto Rico, U. of .... PR
Rider .... NJ
Rockhurst Coll .... MO
Rutgers U .... NJ
Seton Hall U .... NJ
South Alabama .... AL
Southeastern Massachusetts U . MA
Southern Illinois, U. of IL
St. Louis U .... MO
St. Vincent Coll .... PA
State U. of New York (Empire State) .... NY
Syracuse .... NY
Temple U .... PA
West Virginia Inst. of Tech ... WV
Wisconsin, U. of .... WI

Inhalation Therapy, *See* RESPIRATORY THERAPY

Insurance

American Coll. of Life Underwriters .... PA
Appalachian State U .... NC
Arizona State U .... AZ
Arkansas, U. of (Fayetteville, Little Rock) .... AR
Arkansas State U .... AR
Baylor U .... TX
Bennett Coll .... NC
Bowling Green .... OH
California State Poly. Coll. (Pomona) .... CA
California State U. (Fresno, Sacramento) .... CA
Cincinnati, U. of .... OH
Clarion State .... PA
Connecticut, U. of .... CT
Delta State U .... MS
Drake U .... IA
Eastern Kentucky U .... KY
Eastern New Mexico U .... NM
Evansville, U. of .... IN
Fairmont State .... WV
Ferris State .... MI
Florida, U. of .... FL
Florida International U .... FL
Florida State U .... FL
Georgia, U. of .... GA
Georgia State .... GA
Golden Gate U .... CA
Hartford, U. of .... CT
Husson Coll .... ME
Hutchinson Comm. Coll .... KS
Illinois Wesleyan U IL
Indiana U .... IN
Insurance, Coll. of .... NY
International Coll .... FL
International U .... MO
Iowa, U. of .... IA
Jacksonville State U .... AL
Johnson and Wales .... RI
La Salle Coll .... PA
Lake Erie Coll .... OH
Louisiana State U .... LA
Memphis State U .... TN
Miami, U. of .... FL
Miami U .... OH
Michigan State U .... MI
Mississippi, U. of .... MS
Mississippi State .... MS
Nebraska, U. of (Omaha) .... NE
New Hampshire, U. of .... NH
North Florida, U. of .... FL
North Texas State U .... TX
Northeastern U .... MA
Northern Colorado, U. of ...... CO
Northwestern Oklahoma State . OK
Ohio State .... OH
Pennsylvania, U. of .... PA
Pennsylvania State U. (Allentown, McKeesport, University Park) .... PA
Puerto Rico, U. of .... PR
Purdue U .... IN
Rhode Island, U. of .... RI
Rider Coll .... NJ
Rio Piedras .... PR
San Diego State .... CA
South Carolina, U. of .... SC
St. Mary's U .... TX
State U. of New York (Canton) .. NY
Syracuse U .... NY
Temple U .... PA
Tennessee, U. of .... TN
Texas, U. of (Austin) .... TX
Thiel Coll .... PA
Thomas Edison .... NJ
Thomas More Coll .... KY
West Virginia State Coll ...... WV
Western Michigan U .... MI
Wisconsin, U. of .... WI

Interior Decoration

Artesia Christian Coll .... NM
Ball State U .... IN
Brooks Coll .... CA
Central Coll .... KS
Columbia Coll .... MO
Delta State U .... MS
Eastern Kentucky U .... KY
Fisher Jr. Coll .... MA
Harper Coll IL
Lasell Jr. Coll .... MA
Marian Coll .... IN
Marywood .... PA
Mississippi Coll .... MS
Morehead State .... KY
Nebraska, U. of .... NE
Northern Arizona, U. of .... AZ
Northern Iowa, U. of .... IA
Puerto Rico, U. of .... PR
Savannah Coll. of Art and Design .... GA
Seton Hill .... PA
South Georgia Coll .... GA
Southeast Missouri State ...... MO
Southern Coll .... FL
Southwest Missouri State ...... MO
Southwest Texas State .... TX
Texas Woman's U .... TX
U.S. International U .... CA
Western Carolina U .... NC
William Woods .... MO

Interior Design

According to survey by the Foundation for Interior Design Education Research
•Indicates accredited program

Adelphi .... NY
Adrian .... MI
•Alabama, U. of .... AL
Albion .... MI
•Alexandria Tech. Inst .... MN
Alfred U .... NY
Andrews U .... MI
Appalachian State .... NC
Arizona, U. of .... AZ
Arizona State U .... AZ
Arkansas, U. of .... AR
Art Inst. of Atlanta .... GA
Art Inst. of Chicago IL
Art Inst. of Fort Lauderdale .. FL
Art Inst. of Philadelphia ..... PA
Art Inst. of Pittsburgh .... PA
•Auburn U .... AL
Bakersfield Coll .... CA
Ball State U .... IN
•Bauder Fashion Coll .... FL
Bauder Fashion Coll .... TX
Beaver Coll .... PA
Bellevue Comm. Coll .... WA
Bowling Green State U .... OH
Bradley U IL
Brenau Coll .... GA
Bridgeport, U. of .... CT
Brigham Young U .... UT
•California Coll. of Arts & Crafts . CA
California State U. (Fresno, •Long Beach, Los Angeles, Northridge) .... CA
Centenary Coll .... NJ
Central Michigan U .... MI
Central Missouri State U ...... MO
Central Piedmont Comm. Coll . NC
Central State U .... OH
•Chamberlayne Jr. Coll .... MA
Chicago State U IL
•Cincinnati, U. of .... OH
Clemson U .... SC
Colorado State U .... CO
Columbus Coll. of Art & Design .... OH
Connecticut, U. of .... CT
Contra Costa Coll .... CA
Converse Coll .... SC
Cornell U .... NY
Cornish Inst. of Allied Art ... WA
Cuyahoga Comm. Coll .... OH
•Dakota Co. Area Voc. Tech. Inst .... MN
DeAnza Coll .... CA
Delaware, U. of .... DE
Delgado Coll .... LA
Delta Coll .... MI
Desert, Coll. of the .... CA
•Drexel U .... PA
Drury Coll .... MO
DuPage, Coll. of IL
East Carolina U .... NC
East Texas State U .... TX
Eastern Kentucky U .... KY
Eastern Michigan U .... MI
El Camino .... CA
Endicott Coll .... MA
Everett Comm. Coll .... WA
•Fashion Inst. of Merchandising .. CA
•Fashion Inst. of Tech .... NY
•Florida, U. of .... FL
•Florida State U .... FL
Fort Hays State .... KS
Fullerton Coll .... CA
•Georgia, U. of .... GA
Georgia Southern Coll .... GA
Georgia State U .... GA
Halifax Comm. Coll .... NC
Harcum Jr. Coll .... PA
•Harrington Inst. of Interior Design IL
Hawkeye Inst. of Tech .... IA
Henry Ford Comm. Coll .... MI
Highline Comm. Coll .... WA
Hood Coll .... MD
Houston, U. of .... TX
Howard U .... DC
Idaho, U. of .... ID
Illinois, U. of IL
Illinois Central IL
Illinois State U IL
Incarnate Word .... TX
•Indiana State U .... IN
Indiana U .... IN
Indiana U. of Pennsylvania ..... PA
Indiana Voc. Tech. Coll. (Columbus, Kokomo) .... IN
International Fine Arts Coll .. FL
Iowa, U. of .... IA
Iowa State U .... IA
Iowa Wesleyan .... IA
James Madison U .... VA
Jefferson State Jr .... AL
Joliet Jr IL
Judson Coll .... AL
Kansas, U. of .... KS
•Kansas State U .... KS
Kean Coll .... NJ
•Kendall Sch. of Design .... MI
Kent State U .... OH
•Kentucky, U. of .... KY
La Roche Coll .... PA
Lake Land Coll IL
Lambuth Coll .... TN
Lansing Comm. Coll .... MI
Lawrence Inst. of Tech .... MI
Long Beach City .... CA
Los Angeles Valley .... CA
•Louisiana State U. & Ag. & Mech .... LA
Louisiana Tech. U .... LA
Louisville, U. of .... KY
Madison Area Tech. Coll .... WI
Maine, U. of .... ME
Mankato State U .... MN
Marygrove Coll .... MI
Maryland, U. of .... MD
Maryland Inst. of Art .... MD
Marymount Coll .... NY
•Maryville Coll .... MO
Marywood Coll .... PA
•Massachusetts, U. of .... MA
Memphis State U .... TN
Meredith Coll .... NC
Miami Dade Coll .... FL
Miami U .... OH
Michigan, U. of .... MI
•Michigan State U .... MI
Middle Tennessee State U ...... TN
Midway Coll .... KY
•Minnesota, U. of .... MN
Mississippi, U. of .... MS
Mississippi Coll .... MS
Mississippi State U .... MS
Mississippi U. for Women ...... MS
•Missouri, U. of .... MO
Modesto Jr. Coll .... CA
Montana State U .... MT
Moore Coll. of Art .... PA
Morehead State U .... KY
Mount Mary Coll .... WI
Mount St. Joseph-on-the-Ohio . OH
•Mount Vernon .... DC
Mt. San Antonio .... CA
•Nebraska, U. of .... NE
Nevada, U. of .... NV
New Haven, U. of .... CT
New York Inst. of Tech .... NY
•New York Sch. of Interior Design .... NY
New York U .... NY
North Alabama, U. of .... AL
North Carolina, U. of (Greensboro) .... NC
North Dakota State U .... ND
•North Texas State U .... TX
Northampton County Area Comm .... PA
Northeast Louisiana U .... LA
Northeastern Oklahoma State U .... OK
Northern Arizona U .... AZ
Northern Illinois U IL
Northern Iowa, U. of .... IA
Northern Michigan U .... MI
Northern Virginia Comm .... VA
Northwest Missouri State U .... MO
Northwestern State U of Louisiana .... LA
Northwood Inst .... MI
Ohio U .... OH
Ohlone Coll .... CA
Oklahoma, U. of .... OK
Oklahoma State U .... OK
•O'More Sch. of Interior Arch. & Design .... TN

Orange Coast .... CA
•Oregon, U. of .... OR
Pace U .... NY
Palomar Coll .... CA
Parsons Sch. of Design .... NY
Peace Coll .... NC
Phoenix Coll .... AZ
Piedmont Virginia Comm .... VA
Pittsburg State U .... KS
Post Coll .... CT
Prairie State IL
Pratt Inst .... NY
•Purdue U .... IN
Radford U .... VA
Randolph Tech. Inst .... NC
•Rhode Island Sch. of Design .. RI
Ricks Coll .... ID
Ringling Sch. of Art .... FL
Rochester Institute of Technology ... NY
Roosevelt U IL
Saint Benedict, Coll. of ...... MN
Samford U .... AL
San Bernardino Valley .... CA
San Diego Mesa .... CA
San Diego State U .... CA
San Jacinto .... TX
Santa Ana .... CA
Santa Monica City .... CA
Scottsdale Comm. Coll .... AZ
Seattle Pacific U .... WA
Seton Hill .... PA
Shelby State Comm .... TN
Shoreline Comm. Coll .... WA
South Dakota State U .... SD
South Georgia Coll .... GA
•Southern Illinois U IL
Southern Inst .... AL
Southern Mississippi, U. of ... MS
Southern U .... LA
Southwest Missouri State U .... MO
Southwest Texas State U .... TX
Southwestern Louisiana U. of .. LA
•Spokane Falls Comm .... WA
Spring Garden .... PA
St. Louis Comm .... MO
St. Petersburg Jr .... FL
State U. of New York (Coll. at Buffalo) ... NY
Stephen F. Austin State U ..... TX
•Syracuse U .... NY
•Tennessee, U. of .... TN
•Texas, U. of (Arlington, Austin) ... TX
•Texas Christian U .... TX
Texas Southern U .... TX
•Texas Tech U .... TX
•Texas Woman's U .... TX
Trenton State U .... NJ
Triton Coll IL
Vermont, U. of .... VT
•Virginia Commonwealth U ...... VA
Virginia Poly. Institute & State U ... VA
Virginia State U .... VA
Walla Walla Comm. Coll .... WA
Washington, U. of .... WA
•Washington State U .... WA
Wayne State U .... MI
Weber State Coll .... UT
West Virginia U .... WV
Western Carolina U .... NC
Western Illinois U IL
Western Kentucky U .... KY
Western Michigan U .... MI
Western Washington U .... WA
William Rainey Harper IL
Winthrop Coll .... SC
Wisconsin, U. of (Madison, Stevens Point) ... WI
Woodbury U .... CA

International Relations

According to latest statistics of U.S. Office of Education

Alabama, U. of .... AL
American .... DC
Aquinas .... MI
Arkansas, U. of .... AR
Assumption .... MA
Aurora Coll IL
Barat IL
Baylor .... TX
Beloit .... WI
Bethel Coll .... MN
Boston U .... MA
Bowie State .... MD
Bowling Green State U .... OH
Bradley IL
Brigham Young U .... UT
Brown .... RI
California, U. of (Davis) ..... CA
California State (Chico) ...... CA
Canisius Coll .... NY
Carleton .... MN
Chaminade U .... HI
Cincinnati, U. of .... OH
City Coll .... NY
Claremont Men's Coll .... CA
Colgate U .... NY
Colorado, U. of .... CO
Concordia Coll .... MN
Delaware, U. of .... DE
Drake .... IA
Eastern Coll .... PA
Eastern Washington .... WA
Eckerd .... FL
Eisenhower .... NY
Elmira .... NY
Florida International .... FL
Florida State U .... FL
George Mason U .... VA
George Washington U .... DC
Georgetown .... DC
Goucher .... MD
Hamline .... MN
Haverford .... PA
Hunter Coll .... NY
Indiana U. of Pennsylvania .... PA
Jacksonville U .... FL
Johns Hopkins .... MD
Knox IL
Lafayette .... PA
Lake Erie .... OH
Lake Forest IL
Lehigh .... PA
Lewis and Clark .... OR
Loretto Heights Coll .... CO
Louisville, U. of .... KY
Macalester Coll .... MN
Manhattan Coll .... NY
Mankato State .... MN
Marshall U .... WV
Mary Washington .... VA
Maryville .... MO
Memphis State .... TN
Miami U .... OH
Middle Tennessee .... TN
Midwestern State .... TX
Minnesota, U. of .... MN
Monterey Inst .... CA
Montevallo, U. of .... AL
Morgan State .... MD
Mount Holyoke .... MA
Muhlenberg .... PA
Nebraska, U. of .... NE
North Park IL
Occidental Coll .... CA
Ohio State .... OH
Pacific, U. of the .... CA
Pennsylvania, U. of .... PA
Pomona Coll .... CA
Redlands, U. of .... CA
Rio Grande .... OH
Roanoke, Coll. of .... VA
Rosemont .... PA
San Diego, U. of .... CA
San Francisco State .... CA
Scripps .... CA
Shaw U .... NC
South Alabama, U. of .... AL
South Carolina, U. of .... SC
South Florida, U. of .... FL
Southern California, U. of .... CA
Southwest Texas .... TX
Southwestern at Memphis .... TN
St. Catherine, Coll. of .... MN
St. Joseph .... PA
St. Mary's U .... TX
St. Thomas, U. of .... TX
Stanford U .... CA
Stonehill .... MA
Swarthmore .... PA
Sweet Briar .... VA
Syracuse .... NY
Texas Christian .... TX
Toledo, U. of .... OH
Towson State .... MD
Tufts .... MA
U.S. Air Force Acad .... CO
U.S. International U .... CA
U.S. Naval Acad .... MD
Utica Coll .... NY
Virginia, U. of .... VA
Washington Coll .... MD
Wellesley .... MA
Wheaton .... MA
Widener .... PA
Wisconsin, U. of (Madison, Milwaukee, Oshkosh, Platteville, Superior, Whitewater) ... WI
York Coll .... PA

Interpreter

Drake U .... IA
Howard Co. Jr. Coll .... TX
Mount Aloysius Jr. Coll .... PA
Puerto Rico, U. of .... PR
Rochester Inst. of Tech .... NY
Sacred Heart .... CT
Southern Idaho, Coll. of ...... ID

Irrigation

California, U. of (Davis, Fresno) ... CA

Jazz

Akron, U. of .... OH
Aquinas Coll .... MI
Arizona, U. of .... AZ
Arizona State U .... AZ
Bellarmine Coll .... KY
Bennington Coll .... VT
Berklee Coll. of Music .... MA
Bethel Coll .... KS
Brevard Coll .... NC
Bridgeport, U. of .... CT
California State U. (Los Angeles) ... CA
Capital U .... OH
Cincinnati, U. of .... OH
City Coll .... NY
Coe Coll .... IA
Columbia Coll IL
Georgia State U .... GA
Gonzaga U .... WA
Hampshire Coll .... MA
Hampton Institute .... VA
Hartford, U. of .... CT
Hutchinson Comm. Coll .... KS
Indiana U. (Bloomington) ...... IN
International U .... MO
Ithaca .... NY
Jersey City State .... NJ
Kansas, U. of .... KS
Lincoln Coll IL
Loyola U .... LA
Mansfield State .... PA
Marlboro Coll .... VT
Miami, U. of .... FL
Minnesota, U. of (Duluth) ..... MN
Mount Senario Coll .... WI
Nevada, U. of .... NV
North Carolina Cent. U .... NC
North Texas State U .... TX
Oakwood U .... MI
Ohio State U .... OH
Sangamon State IL
Shepherd Coll .... WV
Southern, Mississippi U. of ... MS
Temple U .... PA
U.S. International U .... CA
Webster Coll .... MO
Wesleyan U .... CT
Western Washington U .... WA
William Paterson Coll .... NJ
Wisconsin, U. of (Milwaukee) .. WI

Journalism and Mass Communications

Accredited by American Council on Education for Journalism and Mass Communications

Alabama, U. of .... AL
American U .... DC
Arizona, U. of .... AZ
Arizona State U .... AZ
Arkansas, U. of (Fayetteville, Little Rock) ... AR
Arkansas State U .... AR
Ball State U .... IN
Boston U .... MA
Bowling Green State U .... OH
California, U. of (Berkeley) .. CA
California State U. (Fresno, Fullerton, Long Beach, Northridge) ... CA
Colorado, U. of .... CO
Colorado State U .... CO
Columbia .... NY
Drake U .... IA
Florida, U. of .... FL
Georgia, U. of .... GA
Hawaii, U. of, at Manoa .... HI
Illinois, U. of IL
Indiana U .... IN
Iowa, U. of .... IA
Iowa State U .... IA
Kansas, U. of .... KS
Kansas State U .... KS
La Salle Coll .... PA
Louisiana State U .... LA
Marshall U .... WV
Maryland, U. of .... MD
Memphis State U .... TN
Michigan, U. of .... MI
Michigan State U .... MI
Minnesota, U. of .... MN
Mississippi, U. of .... MS
Missouri, U. of .... MO
Montana, U. of .... MT
Nebraska, U. of (Lincoln) ..... NE
Nevada, U. of .... NV
New Mexico, U. of .... NM
New York U .... NY
North Carolina, U. of .... NC
North Dakota, U. of .... ND
North Texas State U .... TX
Northern Illinois U IL
Northwestern IL
Ohio State U .... OH

Ohio U .... OH
Oklahoma, U. of .... OK
Oklahoma State U .... OK
Oregon, U. of .... OR
Oregon State U .... OR
Pennsylvania State U .... PA
San Jose State .... CA
South Carolina, U. of .... SC
South Dakota State U .... SD
South Florida, U. of .... FL
Southern California, U. of ...... CA
Southern Illinois U IL
Syracuse .... NY
Temple U .... PA
Tennessee, U. of .... TN
Texas, U. of (Austin, El Paso) ... TX
Texas A&M .... TX
Texas Christian U .... TX
Texas Tech. U .... TX
Utah, U. of .... UT
Virginia Commonwealth U ...... VA
Washington, U. of .... WA
Washington and Lee .... VA
West Virginia U .... WV
Western Kentucky U .... KY
Wisconsin, U. of (Eau Claire, Madison, Milwaukee, Oshkosh) .... WI

Journalism

Abilene Christian .... TX
Adams State .... CO
Alabama State U .... AL
Alaska, U. of .... AK
Albertus Magnus .... CT
Andrews U .... MI
Angelo State .... TX
Ashland Coll .... OH
Auburn U .... AL
Augustana Coll .... SD
Averett Coll .... VA
Azusa Pacific .... CA
Baldwin-Wallace .... OH
Baruch Coll .... NY
Baylor U .... TX
Belmont Coll .... TN
Bennett Coll .... NC
Black Hills State .... SD
Blinn .... TX
Bluffton Coll .... OH
Bob Jones U .... SC
Bowie State .... MD
Brevard Coll .... NC
Bridgeport, U. of .... CT
Butler U .... IN
C.W. Post .... NY
California State Coll .... PA
Cardinal Newman Coll .... MO
Carnegie-Mellon U .... PA
Central Arkansas, U. of .... AR
Central Florida, U. of .... FL
Central Michigan U .... MI
Central Missouri .... MO
Central State U .... OK
Cincinnati, U. of .... OH
Clarion State .... PA
Clark U .... MA
Colorado Mountain Coll .... CO
Connecticut, U. of .... CT
Davis & Elkins .... WV
Dayton, U. of .... OH
Delaware, U. of .... DE
DePauw U .... IN
Dordt .... IA
Duquesne U .... PA
East Carolina .... NC
East Central Oklahoma State .. OK
East Tennessee State U .... TN
Eastern Arizona Coll .... AZ
Eastern Kentucky U .... KY
Eastern New Mexico .... NM
Eastern Washington U .... WA
Emerson Coll .... MA
Evangel Coll .... MO
Evansville, U. of .... IN
Findlay Coll .... OH
Florida A&M .... FL
Florida Atlantic U .... FL
Florida Southern Coll .... FL
Fordham U .... NY
Fort Lewis Coll .... CO
Gannon U .... PA
George Washington U .... DC
Georgia State U .... GA
Glassboro State .... NJ
Goddard Coll .... VT
Gonzaga U .... WA
Grand View Coll .... IA
Hampshire Coll .... MA
Hampton Inst .... VA
Henderson State U .... AR
High Point Coll .... NC
Hofstra U .... NY
Howard Payne U .... TX
Huron Coll .... SD
Idaho, U. of .... ID
Immaculata Coll .... PA
Indiana State U .... IN
Indiana U .... PA
International U .... MO
Jackson State U .... MS
Jacksonville U .... FL
James Madison U .... VA
Judson Coll IL
Kansas Newman Coll .... KS
Kearney State .... NE
Keene State .... NH
King's Coll .... PA
Lamar U .... TX
Lewis U IL
Lincoln U .... MO
Lincoln U .... PA
Loma Linda .... CA
Louisiana Tech .... LA
Louisville, U. of .... KY
Loyola U .... LA
Lynchburg Coll .... VA
Macalester Coll .... MN
Maine, U. of (Orono) .... ME
Mankato State U .... MN
Marietta Coll .... OH
Marquette U .... WI
Mars Hill .... NC
Marywood Coll .... PA
Medaille Coll .... NY
Mercy Coll .... NY
Messiah Coll .... PA
Midland Coll .... NE
Midway Coll .... KY
Midwestern State U .... TX
Mills Coll .... CA
Moorhead State U .... MN
Moravian Coll .... PA
Morehead State U .... KY
Mount Vernon .... DC
Nasson .... ME
Nazareth Coll .... MI
New Haven, U. of .... CT
New Mexico State U .... NM
New Rochelle, Coll. of .... NY
Norfolk State U .... VA
North Alabama, U. of .... AL
Northeast Louisiana U .... LA
Northeast Missouri State ...... MO
Northeastern U .... MA
Northern Arizona U .... AZ
Northern Colorado, U. of ...... CO
Northern Kentucky .... KY
Northwest Missouri State ...... MO
Northwestern State U .... LA
Notre Dame of Ohio, Coll. of .. OH
Oakland U .... MI
Ohio Valley Coll .... WV
Otterbein Coll .... OH
Pacific Lutheran U .... WA
Pembroke State U .... NC
Pepperdine U .... CA
Peru State .... NE
Pittsburgh, U. of .... PA
Point Park Coll .... PA
Purdue U .... IN
Radford U .... VA
Randolph-Macon Woman's ..... VA
Rhode Island, U. of .... RI
Richmond, U. of .... VA
Rider Coll .... NJ
Rio Piedras .... PR
Rockford Coll IL
Rockmont Coll .... CO
Roger Williams .... RI
Sacred Heart .... CT
Saint Francis Coll .... PA
Saint Mary of the Plains Coll .... KS
Saint Mary-of-the-Woods .... IN
Saint Mary's .... MN
Saint Michael's Coll .... VT
Saint Rose, Coll. of .... NY
Salem Coll .... WV
Sam Houston State U .... TX
San Diego State .... CA
Schreiner Coll .... TX
Scranton, U. of .... PA
Seattle Pacific U .... WA
Seattle U .... WA
Seton Hill .... PA
Shepherd Coll .... WV
Shippensburg State .... PA
South Alabama, U. of .... AL
South Dakota, U. of .... SD
South Georgia Coll .... GA
Southern Methodist U .... TX
Southern Mississippi, U. of .... MS
Southwest Texas State .... TX
St. Bonaventure U .... NY
St. Catherine, Coll. of .... MN
St. Francis, Coll. of IL
St. John Fisher Coll .... NY
St. Thomas Aquinas .... NY
State U. of New York (Buffalo, New Paltz) .... NY
Stephen F. Austin .... TX
Steubenville, U. of .... OH
Tarkio Coll .... MO
Tennessee, U. of .... TN
Texas Woman's .... TX
Union Coll .... NE
Union U .... TN
Utica Coll .... NY
Valparaiso U .... IN
Washington State U .... WA
Wayne State .... MI
Wayne State .... NE
Weber State .... UT
Webster Coll .... MO
Wesleyan Coll .... GA
West Texas State U .... TX
Western Texas Coll .... TX
Westminster Coll .... UT
White Plains, Coll. of .... NY
Wichita State U .... KS
William Paterson .... NJ
William Woods .... MO
Winona State .... MN
Wisconsin, U. of (River Falls, Whitewater) .... WI
Wright State U .... OH

Journalism—Two Year

Anderson Coll .... SC
Angelina Coll .... TX
Arizona Western Coll .... AZ
Artesia Christian Coll .... NM
Ball State U .... IN
Bee Co. Coll .... TX
Bethel Coll .... IN
Bismarck Jr .... ND
Brevard Coll .... NC
Casper Coll .... WY
Centenary Coll .... NJ
Central Arizona .... AZ
Cowley Co. Comm. Coll .... KS
DuPage, Coll. of IL
Eastern Oklahoma State .... OK
Evangel Coll .... MO
Evansville, U. of .... IN
Ferris State .... MI
Flagler Coll .... FL
Fort Hays State Coll .... KS
Fort Scott Comm. Coll .... KS
Hastings Coll .... NE
Highland Comm .... KS
Hutchinson Comm. Coll .... KS
Illinois, U. of IL
Illinois Central Coll .... KS
Kansas, U. of .... KS
Lincoln Coll IL
Manchester Coll .... IN
Minnesota, U. of (Duluth) ...... MN
Mississippi Delta Jr .... MS
Morehead State .... KY
North Idaho Coll .... ID
Northeast Mississippi Jr .... MS
Northeastern Jr. Coll .... CO
Northwestern Oklahoma State . OK
Pennsylvania State (McKeesport, University Park) .... PA
Point Park .... PA
Rockhurst Coll .... MO
Seward County Comm. Coll .... KS
Sheridan Coll .... NY
South Georgia Coll .... GA
Southern Arkansas U .... AR
Southern Idaho, Coll. of .... ID
Southwestern Jr. Coll .... TX
St. Gregory's Coll .... OK
State U. of New York (Morrisville) .... NY
Trinidad State Jr. Coll .... CO
Truett McConnell .... GA
Weber State .... UT
White Pines .... NH

Landscape Architecture

Approved by Amer. Soc. of Landscape Architects
•"Provisional" accreditation

Arizona, U. of .... AZ
Ball State U .... IN
California, U. of (Berkeley, Davis) .... CA
California Poly. State (San Luis Obispo) .... CA
California State Poly. Coll. (Pomona) .... CA
City Coll .... NY
Colorado, U. of .... CO
Cornell U .... NY
Florida, U. of .... FL
Georgia, U. of .... GA
Harvard .... MA
Idaho, U. of .... ID
Illinois, U. of IL
Iowa State U .... IA
Kansas State U .... KS
Kentucky, U. of .... KY
Louisiana State U .... LA
Massachusetts, U. of .... MA
Michigan, U. of .... MI
Michigan State U .... MI
Minnesota, U. of .... MN
Mississippi State U .... MS
North Carolina State U .... NC
Ohio State U .... OH
Oregon, U. of .... OR
Pennsylvania, U. of .... PA
Pennsylvania State U .... PA
Purdue U .... IN
Rhode Island Sch. of Design .... RI
Rutgers U .... NJ

State U. of New York Coll. of Environmental Science and Forestry at Syracuse .... NY
Texas A&M U .... TX
Texas Tech. U .... TX
Utah State U .... UT
Virginia, U. of .... VA
•Virginia Poly. Inst .... VA
Washington, U. of .... WA
Washington State U .... WA
•West Virginia, U. of........... WV
Wisconsin, U. of (Madison) ..... WI

Landscape Management

Alabama A&M.................. AL
Alfred State .... NY
Auburn U .... AL
Becker Jr. Coll .... MA
Butte Coll...................... CA
California, U. of (Davis)......... CA
Central Coll.................... KS
Central Missouri .... MO
Colorado State U .... CO
Connecticut, U. of............. CT
Eastern Kentucky .... KY
Eastern Oklahoma State .... OK
Florida Southern .... FL
Goddard Coll .... VT
Illinois, U. of (Urbana) IL
Illinois Central Coll............. IL
Maine, U. of (Orono) .... ME
Massachusetts, U. of (Amherst) MA
Nebraska, U. of .... NE
North Dakota State U. (Fargo) . ND
Northeastern Jr. Coll .... CO
Ohio State U.................. OH
Oklahoma State U............ OK
Purdue U .... IN
South Dakota State U .... SD
State U. of New York (Cobleskill, Geneseo, Morrisville) .... NY
Stephen F. Austin .... TX
Temple U .... PA
Texas A&M U .... TX
Wisconsin, U. of (Madison) ..... WI

Languages, Arabic

Chicago, U. of IL
Cornell U .... NY
Dropsie U...................... PA
Georgetown U .... DC
Harvard U .... MA
Johns Hopkins U.............. MD
Kansas, U. of .... KS
Middlebury Coll .... VT
Minnesota, U. of .... MN
New York U.................... NY
Ohio State .... OH
Pennsylvania, U. of............ PA
Princeton U.................... NJ
Radcliffe Coll .... MA
State U. of New York (Binghamton) .... NY
Temple U .... PA
Tennessee, U. of .... TN
Texas, U. of (Austin) .... TX
Wayne State U .... MI
Wisconsin, U. of (Madison) ..... WI

Languages, Chinese

Arizona State U .... AZ
Brown U....................... RI
California, U. of (Berkeley, Los Angeles, Riverside, San Diego, Santa Barbara) .... CA
Chicago, U. of IL
Colorado, U. of .... CO
Connecticut, U. of............. CT
Connecticut Coll .... CT
Cornell U .... NY
Dartmouth Coll .... NH
Dominican Coll .... CA
Eastern Washington .... WA
George Washington U .... DC
Harvard U .... MA
Hawaii, U. of (Honolulu) .... HI
Hawaii Loa Coll .... HI
Hofstra U .... NY
Indiana U .... IN
International U .... MO
Iowa, U. of.................... IA
Kansas, U. of .... KS
Lewis and Clark Coll .... OR
Macalester Coll .... MN
Massachusetts, U. of (Amherst) MA
Michigan State U.............. MI
Middlebury Coll............... VT
Minnesota, U. of .... MN
Mundelein Coll................. IL
New York U................... NY
Northwestern U IL
Notre Dame, U. of............ IN
Oakland U .... MI
Occidental Coll .... CA
Ohio State U.................. OH
Pennsylvania, U. of............ PA
Pittsburgh, U. of .... PA
Pomona Coll.................. CA
Princeton U................... NJ
Principia Coll IL
Radcliffe Coll .... MA
Rochester, U. of............... NY
Rockford Coll.................. IL
Rutgers .... NJ
Seton Hall .... NJ
Smith .... MA
South Florida, U. of .... FL
Temple U .... PA
Tennessee, U. of .... TN
Texas, U. of, at Austin .... TX
Tufts .... MA
Washington U................. MO
Wellesley Coll................. MA
Wesleyan U .... CT
Whittier Coll .... CA
William and Mary .... VA
Wisconsin, U. of (Madison) ..... WI
Wittenberg U .... OH
Wooster, Coll. of .... OH
Yale U .... CT

Languages, Classical

Bard Coll .... NY
Barnard Coll .... NY
Baylor U .... TX
Beloit .... WI
Brandeis .... MA
Brigham Young U .... UT
Brown U .... RI
Bryn Mawr .... PA
Butler U .... IN
California, U. of (Davis, San Diego) .... CA
Carleton Coll .... MN
Case Western Reserve......... OH
Catholic U .... DC
Chicago, U. of IL
Cincinnati, U. of .... OH
City U .... NY
Colorado, U. of .... CO
Colorado Coll .... CO
Columbia .... NY
Connecticut, U. of............. CT
Connecticut Coll .... CT
Cornell Coll.................... IA
Cornell U .... NY
Creighton U .... NE
Dartmouth Coll .... NH
Dayton, U. of .... OH
Delaware, U. of .... DE
Dickinson..................... PA
Drew U .... NJ
Duke U .... NC
Fordham U .... NY
George Washington U .... DC
Gettysburg Coll .... PA
Grinnell Coll .... IA
Gustavus Adolphus........... MN
Hamilton Coll .... NY
Harvard U .... MA
Hawaii, U. of .... HI
Hobart Coll .... NY
Hofstra .... NY
Illinois, U. of (Chicago) IL
Indiana U .... IN
Iowa, U. of.................... IA
Johns Hopkins .... MD
Kansas, U. of .... KS
Kent State .... OH
Knox Coll...................... IL
Kutztown State................ PA
La Salle .... PA
Lehigh U .... PA
Lehman Coll .... NY
Lenoir-Rhyne Coll............ NC
Luther .... IA
Manhattan Coll .... NY
Marlboro Coll .... VT
Massachusetts, U. of (Amherst).................. MA
Minnesota, U. of .... MN
Missouri, U. of .... MO
Montana, U. of .... MT
Mount St. Vincent .... NY
New Coll. of U.S.F .... FL
New Hampshire, U. of .... NH
Newcomb..................... LA
Northwestern U IL
Notre Dame, U. of............. IN
Ohio State U.................. OH
Pacific, U. of the .... CA
Pacific Lutheran U .... WA
Pennsylvania, U. of............ PA
Pittsburgh, U. of .... PA
Pomona Coll.................. CA
Princeton U................... NJ
Radcliffe...................... MA
Regis Coll .... MA
Rhode Island, U. of............ RI
Rice .... TX
Rutgers .... NJ
San Diego State............... CA
Scranton, U. of................ PA
Smith .... MA
South, U. of the .... TN
Southwestern at Memphis ...... TN
St. Mary Coll.................. KS
St. Norbert Coll .... WI
St. Olaf Coll .... MN
State U. of New York (Binghamton) .... NY
Susquehanna .... PA
Swarthmore Coll .... PA
Temple U .... PA
Tennessee, U. of .... TN
Tufts .... MA
Upsala Coll .... NJ
Utah, U. of.................... UT
Vassar Coll .... NY
Vermont, U. of .... VT
Virginia, U. of .... VA
Wabash....................... IN
Washington & Lee............. VA
Washington U................. MO
Wellesley Coll................. MA
Wesleyan U .... CT
Wheaton Coll .... MA
William Woods .... MO
Williams Coll.................. MA
Wisconsin, U. of (Madison) .... WI
Wright State .... OH
Xavier U .... OH
Yale U .... CT

Languages, Czech

Kansas, U. of .... KS
Minnesota, U. of .... MN

Languages, Danish

Dana .... NE
Harvard....................... MA
Macalester .... MN
Minnesota, U. of .... MN
Radcliffe .... MA

Languages, Dutch

Cornell U .... NY
Macalester .... MN
Minnesota, U. of .... MN
Pennsylvania, U. of............ PA
Temple U .... PA

Languages, English, *See*

ENGLISH FOR FOREIGN STUDENTS

Languages, Finnish

Harvard....................... MA
Minnesota, U. of .... MN
Radcliffe .... MA

Languages, French

Institutions awarding 10 or more undergraduate degrees as major field in single year according to U.S. Office of Education latest statistics

Akron, U. of .... OH
Arizona, U. of .... AZ
Arizona State U .... AZ
Assumption Coll .... MA
Auburn U .... AL
Barnard Coll .... NY
Boston Coll .... MA
Boston U .... MA
Brigham Young .... UT
Brooklyn Coll .... NY
Brown U .... RI
California, U. of (Berkeley, Davis, Irvine, Los Angeles, Santa Barbara) .... CA
California State U. (Long Beach, Northridge) .... CA
Central Michigan U............ MI
Central U. of Iowa............ IA
Colby......................... ME
Colorado, U. of .... CO
Colorado Coll .... CO
Concordia Coll................ MN
Connecticut, U. of............. CT
Connecticut Coll .... CT
Dartmouth .... NH
Duke .... NC
Emmanuel Coll .... MA
Fordham U .... NY
George Washington U .... DC
Georgetown U .... DC
Georgia State .... GA
Hollins Coll .... VA
Holy Cross, Coll. of .... MA
Houston, U. of .... TX
Hunter Coll .... NY
Illinois, U. of IL
Illinois State U IL
Indiana U .... IN
Iowa, U. of.................... IA
Kansas, U. of .... KS
Louisiana State U. and A&M Coll .... LA

Maryland, U. of .... MD
Massachusetts, U. of .... MA
Miami U .... OH
Michigan, U. of................ MI
Michigan State .... MI
Middlebury .... VT
Minnesota, U. of .... MN
Montclair State................. NJ
Mount Holyoke .... MA
New York U.................... NY
North Carolina, U. of (Chapel Hill) .... NC
Northeastern Illinois IL
Northern Illinois................ IL
Northwestern U IL
Ohio State .... OH
Oregon, U. of .... OR
Pennsylvania, U. of............ PA
Pennsylvania State .... PA
Pittsburgh, U. of .... PA
Portland State U .... OR
Puerto Rico, U. of .... PR
Queens .... NY
Rutgers .... NJ
San Diego State............... CA
San Francisco State .... CA
San Jose State .... CA
South Carolina, U. of .... SC
Southern California, U. of ...... CA
State U. of New York (Albany, Binghamton, Buffalo, New Paltz, Oswego, Potsdam, Stony Brook) .... NY
Tennessee, U. of .... TN
Texas, U. of (Arlington, Austin) . TX
Tufts .... MA
Utah, U. of.................... UT
Vanderbilt .... TN
Vassar .... NY
Vermont, U. of .... VT
Virginia, U. of .... VA
Wake Forest .... NC
Washington, U. of .... WA
Wellesley .... MA
West Chester State .... PA
Western Michigan U .... MI
Western Washington .... WA
Wheaton Coll IL
William and Mary .... VA
Wisconsin, U. of (Madison) ..... WI

Languages, German

Institutions awarding 5 or more undergraduate degrees as major field in single year according to U.S. Office of Education latest statistics

Akron, U. of .... OH
Albion .... MI
Arizona, U. of .... AZ
Arizona State U .... AZ
Auburn U .... AL
Ball State U.................... IN
Barnard Coll .... NY
Baylor U .... TX
Bowdoin Coll .... ME
Brigham Young .... UT
California, U. of (Berkeley, Irvine, Los Angeles) .... CA
California State U. (Fullerton, Sacramento) .... CA
Calvin .... MI
Carleton Coll .... MN
Central U. of Iowa............. IA
Clarion State.................. PA
Colorado, U. of .... CO
Columbia U .... NY
Concordia Coll .... MN
Connecticut, U. of............. CT
Cornell U .... NY
Dallas, U. of .... TX
Dartmouth .... NH
Delaware, U. of .... DE
Duke .... NC
Florida, U. of.................. FL
Florida State .... FL
George Washington U .... DC
Georgetown U .... DC
Georgia, U. of................. GA
Hamilton Coll .... NY
Hope Coll..................... MI
Hunter Coll .... NY
Illinois, U. of IL
Indiana U. at Bloomington ...... IN
Iowa, U. of.................... IA
Kansas, U. of .... KS
Kent State .... OH
Lewis and Clark .... OR
Macalester Coll .... MN
Marquette..................... WI
Maryland, U. of .... MD
Massachusetts, U. of .... MA
Miami U .... OH
Michigan, U. of................ MI
Michigan State U.............. MI
Middlebury .... VT
Millersville State .... PA
Minnesota, U. of .... MN
Missouri, U. of .... MO
Montana, U. of .... MT
Montclair State................ NJ
Mount Holyoke .... MA
Nebraska, U. of .... NE
New Hampshire, U. of .... NH
New Mexico State U........... NM
Northern Colorado .... CO
Northern Illinois U IL
Northwestern U IL
Notre Dame, U. of............. IN
Ohio State .... OH
Oklahoma, U. of .... OK
Old Dominion .... VA
Oregon, U. of .... OR
Oregon State .... OR
Pennsylvania, U. of............ PA
Pennsylvania State U .... PA
Pittsburgh, U. of .... PA
Portland State................ OR
Queens .... NY
Rutgers .... NJ
Saint Cloud .... MN
Saint Olaf.................... MN
San Diego State............... CA
San Francisco State .... CA
San Jose State .... CA
Smith Coll .... MA
Southern Illinois U. (Carbondale)................. IL
Southern Methodist .... TX
Southwest Texas .... TX
Stanford .... CA
State U. of New York (Albany, Binghamton, Buffalo, Oneonta, Oswego, Stony Brook) .... NY
Stetson U .... FL
Texas, U. of (Arlington, Austin) . TX
Texas Tech., U. of............. TX
Tufts .... MA
Valdosta State .... GA
Valparaiso U .... IN
Vanderbilt .... TN
Virginia, U. of .... VA
Wake Forest .... NC
Washington, U. of .... WA
Washington and Lee .... VA
Washington U................ MO
Wayne State U .... MI
Western Washington U .... WA
William and Mary, Coll. of ...... VA
Wisconsin, U. of (Eau Claire, Madison, Milwaukee, Stevens Point) .... WI

Languages, Greek

Anderson Coll .... IN
Arizona, U. of .... AZ
Azusa Pacific Coll .... CA
Bard.......................... NY
Barnard Coll .... NY
Baylor U .... TX
Belhaven Coll .... MS
Beloit Coll .... WI
Bethany Lutheran .... MN
Boston U .... MA
Brown U...................... RI
Bryn Mawr.................... PA
Bucknell .... PA
California, U. of (Berkeley, Davis, Los Angeles, Riverside, Santa Barbara) .... CA
Capital U .... OH
Cardinal Newman Coll......... MO
Carleton Coll .... MN
Case Western Reserve......... OH
Charleston, Coll. of............ SC
Chicago, U. of IL
Cincinnati, U. of .... OH
Colgate .... NY
Colorado, U. of .... CO
Columbia U. (Sch. of General Studies) .... NY
Concordia Coll................ MI
Concordia Coll................ MN
Connecticut, U. of............. CT
Connecticut Coll .... CT
Cornell Coll................... IA
Cornell U .... NY
Creighton U .... NE
Dallas Christian Coll .... TX
David Lipscomb Coll .... TN
Davidson Coll .... NC
DePauw U .... IN
Dickinson..................... PA
Drake U .... IA
Dropsie U..................... PA
Duke U .... NC
Elmira Coll .... NY
Emory U .... GA
Florida State U .... FL
Fordham...................... NY
Franklin and Marshall .... PA
Furman U..................... SC
Gannon U .... PA
George Washington U .... DC
Gettysburg Coll .... PA
Hamilton Coll .... NY
Hampden-Sydney .... VA
Harvard .... MA
Haverford..................... PA
Hawaii, U. of (Honolulu) .... HI
Hellenic Coll .... MA
Hobart Coll .... NY
Hofstra U .... NY
Hollins Coll .... VA
Hope .... MI
Houghton .... NY
Illinois, U. of (Urbana) IL
Indiana U. (Bloomington) .... IN
Iowa, U. of.................... IA
Kansas, U. of .... KS
Kentucky, U. of .... KY
Knox Coll IL
La Salle .... PA
Lehigh........................ PA
Lewis and Clark Coll .... OR
Loras Coll .... IA
Louisiana State .... LA
Louisville, U. of .... KY
Loyola U .... LA
Manhattan Coll .... NY
Michigan, U. of................ MI
Millersville State .... PA
Millsaps Coll .... MS
Minnesota, U. of .... MN
Missouri Baptist .... MO
Mount Holyoke .... MA
Mount St. Vincent .... NY
Muhlenberg .... PA
New Hampshire, U. of (Durham) .... NH
New Rochelle, Coll. of.......... NY
New York U.................... NY
North Carolina, U. of (Asheville, Chapel Hill, Greensboro) .... NC
North Central Coll.............. IL
North Dakota State........... ND
Northwest Nazarene Coll .... ID
Northwestern U IL
Notre Dame, U. of............. IN
Oberlin Coll .... OH
Ohio Valley Coll .... OH
Oklahoma, U. of .... OK
Pacific, U. of the .... CA
Pennsylvania, U. of............ PA
Pomona Coll .... CA
Princeton U .... NJ
Queens Coll .... NY
Radcliffe Coll .... MA
Randolph-Macon Woman's ..... VA
Rockford IL
Rockmont Coll .... CO
Sarah Lawrence............... NY
Scranton, U. of................ PA
Seattle Pacific................ WA
Smith .... MA
South, U. of the .... TN
South Carolina, U. of (Columbia) .... SC
South Dakota, U. of .... SD
Southwestern U .... TX
St. Bonaventure .... NY
St. John's Coll .... MD
St. Mary's .... MN
St. Olaf .... MN
St. Paul's .... MO
St. Thomas, Coll. of .... MN
State U. of New York (Albany) .. NY
Swarthmore Coll .... PA
Sweet Briar Coll .... VA
Temple U .... PA
Tennessee, U. of .... TN
Texas, U. of.................... TX
Tufts .... MA
Union U .... TN
Utah, U. of.................... UT
Valparaiso U .... IN
Vassar Coll .... NY
Vermont, U. of .... VT
Villanova U .... PA
Virginia, U. of .... VA
Washington & Lee............. VA
Washington U................ MO
Wayne State U .... MI
Wellesley Coll................. MA
Wesleyan U .... CT
William Smith .... NY
Wisconsin, U. of (Madison, Milwaukee) .... WI
Wooster, Coll. of .... OH
Yale U .... CT

Languages, Hebrew

Baltimore Hebrew Coll .... MD
Bard.......................... NY
Baruch Coll................... NY
Baylor U .... TX
Bethany Lutheran Coll......... MN
Brooklyn Coll .... NY
Brown U .... RI
Bryn Mawr .... PA
C.W. Post Ctr .... NY
California, U. of .... CA
California State U. (Northridge) .... CA
Chicago, U. of IL
Cincinnati, U. of .... OH
City Coll .... NY
Connecticut, U. of............. CT

Cornell U ..... NY
Dallas Christian Coll ..... TX
David Lipscomb Coll ..... TN
Drake U ..... IA
Dropsie U ..... PA
George Washington U ..... DC
Harvard ..... MA
Haverford Coll ..... PA
Hebrew Coll ..... MA
Hebrew Theo. Coll IL
Hobart Coll ..... NY
Hofstra ..... NY
Houghton Coll ..... NY
Hunter Coll ..... NY
Johns Hopkins U ..... MD
Lehigh U ..... PA
Long Island U ..... NY
Minnesota, U. of ..... MN
Mundelein Coll IL
New York U ..... NY
Ohio State ..... OH
Ohio Valley Coll ..... WV
Pennsylvania, U. of ..... PA
Pomona Coll ..... CA
Princeton U ..... NJ
Queens Coll ..... NY
Radcliffe Coll ..... MA
Rockmont Coll ..... CO
State U. of New York (Binghamton) ..... NY
Temple U ..... PA
Texas, U. of ..... TX
Valparaiso U ..... IN
Washington U ..... MO
Wayne State U ..... MI
Wellesley Coll ..... MA
Wesleyan U ..... CT
Wisconsin, U. of (Madison) ..... WI
Yeshiva U ..... NY

Languages, Hindi

Cornell U ..... NY
Harvard ..... MA
Minnesota, U. of ..... MN
Pennsylvania, U. of ..... PA
Radcliffe Coll ..... MA
Temple U ..... PA

Languages, Indonesian

Cornell U ..... NY
Harvard ..... MA
Radcliffe ..... MA
Temple U ..... PA

Languages, Italian

Albertus Magnus Coll ..... CT
Alvernia ..... PA
Arizona, U. of ..... AZ
Biscayne Coll ..... FL
Boston U ..... MA
Bridgewater State ..... MA
Brooklyn Coll ..... NY
Brown U ..... RI
Bryn Mawr ..... PA
California, U. of (Berkeley, Davis, Los Angeles, Riverside, Santa Barbara) ..... CA
California State U ..... CA
Catholic U ..... DC
Central Connecticut ..... CT
Chicago, U. of IL
City Coll ..... NY
Colby ..... ME
Colorado, U. of ..... CO
Columbia U. (Sch. of General Studies) ..... NY
Connecticut, U. of ..... CT
Connecticut Coll ..... CT
Cornell U ..... NY
Dartmouth Coll ..... NH
Drake U ..... IA
DuPage, Coll. of ..... IA
Emmanuel ..... MA
Florida International ..... FL
Florida State U ..... FL
Fordham ..... NY
Franklin Coll ..... Switzerland
Gannon U ..... PA
George Washington U ..... DC
Georgetown U ..... DC
Gonzaga U ..... WA
Hartford, U. of ..... CT
Harvard ..... MA
Haverford ..... PA
Hofstra ..... NY
Illinois, U. of (Chicago Circle, Urbana) IL
Immaculata Coll ..... PA
Indiana U. (Bloomington) ..... IN
Iona Coll ..... NY
Iowa, U. of ..... IA
Johns Hopkins U ..... MD
Kansas, U. of ..... KS
Kentucky, U. of ..... KY
La Salle Coll ..... PA
Lake Erie ..... OH
Lehigh U ..... PA
Lewis and Clark Coll ..... OR
Long Island U ..... NY
Loyola IL
Loyola U ..... LA
Manhattan Coll ..... NY
Manhattanville ..... NY
Marlboro Coll ..... VT
Marymount Manhattan Coll ..... NY
Marywood ..... PA
Massachusetts, U. of (Amherst, Boston) ..... MA
Mercy Coll ..... NY
Middlebury ..... VT
Minnesota, U. of ..... MN
Missouri, U. of ..... MO
Mount Holyoke ..... MA
Mount St. Vincent, Coll. of ..... NY
Nazareth Coll ..... NY
New Rochelle, Coll. of ..... NY
New York U ..... NY
Newcomb Coll ..... LA
North Carolina, U. of (Chapel Hill) ..... NC
Northwestern U IL
Notre Dame, U. of ..... IN
Occidental ..... CA
Ohio State U ..... OH
Ohio Valley Coll ..... OH
Pennsylvania, U. of ..... PA
Pittsburgh, U. of ..... PA
Princeton U ..... NJ
Providence Coll ..... RI
Puerto Rico, U. of ..... PR
Queens Coll ..... NY
Radcliffe Coll ..... MA
Rhode Island, U. of ..... RI
Rio Piedras ..... PR
Rosary Coll IL
Rosemont Coll ..... PA
San Francisco State ..... CA
Sarah Lawrence ..... NY
Smith ..... MA
South Carolina, U. of ..... SC
Southern Connecticut ..... CT
Spring Arbor ..... MI
St. John Fisher Coll ..... NY
Stanford U ..... CA
State U. of New York (Albany, Binghamton, Stony Brook) ..... NY
Sweet Briar Coll ..... VA
Syracuse U ..... NY
Temple ..... PA
Tennessee, U. of ..... TN
Texas, U. of ..... TX
Trinity Coll ..... CT
Tulane ..... LA
Vassar Coll ..... NY
Villanova U ..... PA
Washington, U. of ..... WA
Washington U ..... MO
Wayne State ..... MI
Wellesley Coll ..... MA
Wesleyan U ..... CT
Wisconsin, U. of (Madison, Milwaukee) ..... WI
Wooster ..... OH
Yale ..... CT
Youngstown State ..... OH

Languages, Japanese

Alaska, U. of ..... AK
Arizona State ..... AZ
Baylor U ..... TX
Brigham Young ..... UT
Brown U ..... RI
Bucknell U ..... PA
California, U. of ..... CA
California State U. (Los Angeles, Northridge) ..... CA
Chicago, U. of IL
Colorado, U. of ..... CO
Connecticut, U. of ..... CT
Cornell U ..... NY
Earlham Coll ..... IN
Eastern Washington U ..... WA
George Washington U ..... DC
Georgetown U ..... DC
Harvard ..... MA
Hawaii, U. of (Honolulu) ..... HI
Hawaii Loa Coll ..... HI
Indiana U ..... IN
International U ..... MO
Iowa, U. of ..... IA
Kansas, U. of ..... KS
Knox Coll IL
Lewis and Clark ..... OR
Manhattanville Coll ..... NY
Massachusetts, U. of (Amherst) ..... MA
Michigan, U. of ..... MI
Middlebury Coll ..... VT
Minnesota, U. of ..... MN
Mundelein Coll IL
Northwestern U IL
Notre Dame ..... IN
Occidental ..... CA
Ohio State U ..... OH
Oregon, U. of ..... OR
Pacific, U. of the ..... CA
Pennsylvania, U. of ..... PA
Pittsburgh, U. of ..... PA
Princeton U ..... NJ
Radcliffe Coll ..... MA
Randolph-Macon Woman's ..... VA
San Francisco State ..... CA
Seton Hall ..... NJ
Temple U ..... PA
Tennessee, U. of ..... TN
Texas, U. of ..... TX
Washington, U. of ..... WA
Washington U ..... MO
Wesleyan U ..... CT
Whitman Coll ..... WA
William Jewell Coll ..... MO
Wisconsin, U. of ..... WI
Wittenberg ..... OH
Yale U ..... CT

Languages, Korean

Cornell U ..... NY
Temple U ..... PA
Texas, U. of (Austin) ..... TX

Languages, Latvian

Minnesota, U. of ..... MN

Languages, Nahuatl

Temple U ..... PA

Languages, Norwegian

Cornell U ..... NY
Eastern Montana Coll ..... MT
Harvard ..... MA
Luther ..... IA
Macalester ..... MN
Minnesota, U. of ..... MN
Pacific Lutheran ..... WA
Radcliffe ..... MA
St. Olaf ..... MN

Languages, Persian

Cornell U ..... NY
Dropsie U ..... PA
New York U ..... NY
Princeton U ..... NJ
Temple U ..... PA
Tennessee, U. of ..... TN
Texas, U. of (Austin) ..... TX

Languages, Polish

Alvernia Coll ..... PA
Cornell U ..... NY
Felician Coll IL
Harvard ..... MA
Illinois, U. of (Chicago Circle) IL
Kansas, U. of ..... KS
Pennsylvania, U. of ..... PA
Pittsburgh, U. of ..... PA
Radcliffe Coll ..... MA
St. Mary's Coll ..... MI
Temple U ..... PA
Wayne State U ..... MI
Wisconsin, U. of (Madison) ..... WI

Languages, Portuguese

Arizona, U. of ..... AZ
Baylor U ..... TX
Bridgewater State ..... MA
Brown U ..... RI
California, U. of (Riverside, Santa Barbara) ..... CA
Colorado, U. of ..... CO
Connecticut, U. of ..... CT
Cornell U ..... NY
Dartmouth Coll ..... NH
Florida International ..... FL
Harvard ..... MA
Illinois, U. of (Urbana) IL
Iowa, U. of ..... IA
Kansas, U. of ..... KS
La Salle Coll ..... PA
Massachusetts, U. of (Amherst, Boston) ..... MA
Miami U ..... OH
Minnesota, U. of ..... MN
New Mexico, U. of ..... NM
New York U ..... NY
North Carolina, U. of (Chapel Hill) ..... NC
Northwestern U IL
Pennsylvania, U. of ..... PA
Providence ..... RI
Radcliffe Coll ..... MA
Smith ..... MA
Temple U ..... PA
Texas, U. of (Austin) ..... TX
Tulane ..... LA
Vanderbilt U ..... TN
Wisconsin, U. of (Madison) ..... WI
Wittenberg U ..... OH

Languages, Russian

Akron, U. of ... OH
Alaska, U. of ... AK
Arizona, U. of ... AZ
Barnard ... NY
Baylor U ... TX
Bennington Coll ... VT
Boston Coll ... MA
Boston U ... MA
Bowling Green ... OH
Brandeis ... MA
Bridgewater State ... MA
Brigham Young ... UT
Brooklyn Coll ... NY
Brown U ... RI
Bryn Mawr ... PA
Bucknell U ... PA
California, U. of (Davis, Irvine, Riverside, San Diego) ... CA
California State U. (Fresno, Long Beach, Northridge) ... CA
Canada Coll ... CA
Carleton Coll ... MN
Case Western Reserve ... OH
Chatham Coll ... PA
Chicago, U. of ... IL
Cincinnati, U. of ... OH
City Coll ... NY
Clarion State ... PA
Colgate ... NY
Colorado, U. of ... CO
Columbia ... NY
Connecticut, U. of ... CT
Connecticut Coll ... CT
Cornell ... NY
Cornell Coll ... IA
Dartmouth Coll ... NH
Delaware, U. of ... DE
Denison ... OH
Denver, U. of ... CO
DePauw U ... IN
Drake U ... IA
Drew ... NJ
Duke U ... NC
DuPage, Coll. of ... IL
Eastern Kentucky U ... KY
Eastern Washington U ... WA
Eckerd Coll ... FL
Edinboro State ... PA
Emmanuel Coll ... MA
Emory U ... GA
Fairleigh Dickinson U ... NJ
Ferrum Coll ... VA
Florida, U. of ... FL
Florida State U ... FL
Fordham ... NY
Franklin and Marshall ... PA
George Washington U ... DC
Georgetown U ... DC
Goucher Coll ... MD
Grinnell Coll ... IA
Gustavus Adolphus ... MN
Hamilton Coll ... NY
Hartwick Coll ... NY
Harvard ... MA
Haverford Coll ... PA
Hawaii, U. of (Honolulu) ... HI
Holy Cross ... MA
Howard U ... DC
Hunter Coll ... NY
Illinois, U. of (Chicago Circle, Urbana) ... IL
Immaculata Coll ... PA
Indiana State U ... IN
Indiana U ... IN
Iowa, U. of ... IA
Iowa State U ... IA
James Madison ... VA
Johns Hopkins U ... MD
Juniata ... PA
Kansas, U. of ... KS
Kent State ... OH
Kentucky, U. of ... KY
Kutztown State ... PA
La Salle Coll ... PA
Lafayette Coll ... PA
Lawrence U ... WI
Lehigh U ... PA
Lehman Coll ... NY
Lewis and Clark Coll ... OR
Louisiana State ... LA
Louisville, U. of ... KY
Loyola U ... LA
Lycoming Coll ... PA
Macalester Coll ... MN
Manhattan Coll ... NY
Manhattanville Coll ... NY
Marist Coll ... NY
Marlboro Coll ... VT
Maryland, U.of (Baltimore Co.) ... MD
Massachusetts, U. of (Amherst, Boston) ... MA
Miami, U. of ... FL
Miami U ... OH
Michigan, U. of ... MI
Michigan State U ... MI
Middlebury ... VT
Millersville State ... PA
Minnesota, U. of ... MN
Missouri, U. of (Columbia, Rolla) ... MO
Montana, U. of ... MT
Monterey Inst ... CA
Mount Holyoke ... MA
Muhlenberg ... PA
Muskingum ... OH
Nebraska, U. of (Lincoln) ... NE
New Coll ... FL
New Hampshire, U. of ... NH
New Mexico State ... NM
New York U ... NY
North Carolina, U. of (Chapel Hill) ... NC
North Dakota, U. of ... ND
Northern Iowa, U. of ... IA
Northwestern U ... IL
Norwich U ... VT
Notre Dame ... IN
Oakland U ... MI
Oberlin Coll ... OH
Occidental ... CA
Ohio State U ... OH
Ohio U ... OH
Oklahoma, U. of ... OK
Old Dominion U ... VA
Oregon, U. of ... OR
Pennsylvania, U. of ... PA
Pennsylvania, U. of (Allentown, University Park) ... PA
Pittsburgh, U. of ... PA
Pomona Coll ... CA
Portland State ... OR
Princeton U ... NJ
Principia Coll ... IL
Queens Coll ... NY
Randolph-Macon ... VA
Reed ... OR
Rhode Island, U. of ... RI
Rice U ... TX
Richmond, U. of ... VA
Rochester, U. of ... NY
Rutgers ... NJ
Saint Mary's Coll ... MN
San Diego State ... CA
San Francisco State ... CA
Sarah Lawrence ... NY
Smith ... MA
South, U. of the ... TN
South Alabama, U. of ... AL
South Florida, U. of ... FL
Southern Illinois (Carbondale) ... IL
Southern Methodist ... TX
St. Catherine, Coll. of ... MN
St. Louis U ... MO
St. Olaf ... MN
State U. of New York (Albany, Oswego, Stony Brook) ... NY
Swarthmore Coll ... PA
Syracuse U ... NY
Temple ... PA
Tennessee, U. of ... TN
Texas, U. of (Arlington, Austin) . TX
Tufts ... MA
Tulane ... LA
Utah, U. of ... UT
Vanderbilt U ... TN
Vassar Coll ... NY
Vermont, U. of ... VT
Villanova U ... PA
Virginia, U. of ... VA
Wabash Coll ... IN
Washington, U. of ... WA
Washington State U ... WA
Washington U ... MO
Wayne State U ... MI
Wellesley Coll ... MA
Wesleyan U ... CT
West Chester State ... PA
Western Illinois ... IL
Western Michigan U ... MI
Westminster Coll ... MO
Wheaton Coll ... MA
Williams Coll ... MA
Wisconsin, U. of (Madison, Milwaukee) ... WI
Wittenberg ... OH
Wooster ... OH
Yale U ... CT
Youngstown State U ... OH

Languages, Serbo-Croatian

Cornell U ... NY
George Washington U ... DC
Kansas, U. of ... KS
Minnesota, U. of ... MN
Princeton U ... NJ

Languages, Slavic

California, U. of (Santa Barbara) ... CA
Chicago, U. of ... IL
Cornell U ... NY
Florida State U ... FL
Harvard ... MA
Illinois, U. of (Chicago) ... IL
Kansas, U. of ... KS
Knox Coll ... IL
Kutztown State ... PA
La Salle Coll ... PA
Minnesota, U. of ... MN
Northwestern U ... IL
Pennsylvania, U. of ... PA
Princeton U ... NJ
Radcliffe Coll ... MA
Texas, U. of (Austin) ... TX
Virginia, U. of ... VA
Wisconsin, U. of (Madison) ... WI

Languages, Spanish

Institutions awarding 15 or more undergraduate degrees as major field in single year according to U.S. Office of Education latest statistics

Akron, U. of ... OH
Arizona, U. of ... AZ
Arizona State U ... AZ
Auburn U ... AL
Biscayne ... FL
Bowling Green State U ... OH
Brigham Young ... UT
Brooklyn Coll ... NY
California, U. of (Berkeley, Irvine, Los Angeles, Santa Barbara) ... CA
California State U. (Chico, Fresno, Fullerton, Long Beach, Los Angeles, Northridge, Sacramento) ... CA
Catholic U. of Puerto Rico ... PR
Colorado, U. of ... CO
Connecticut, U. of ... CT
Florida International ... FL
Florida State ... FL
Fordham U ... NY
Georgetown U ... DC
Georgia State U ... GA
Glassboro State ... NJ
Hunter ... NY
Illinois, U. of ... IL
Illinois State U ... IL
Indiana U. at Bloomington ... IN
Indiana U. of Pennsylvania ... PA
Iowa, U. of ... IA
Kean Coll ... NJ
Laredo State U ... TX
Lehman Coll ... NY
Marquette U ... WI
Maryland, U. of ... MD
Massachusetts, U. of ... MA
Mercy Coll ... NY
Miami U ... OH
Middlebury Coll ... VT
Minnesota, U. of ... MN
Montclair State ... NJ
New Hampshire, U. of ... NH
New Mexico, U. of ... NM
New York U ... NY
Northeastern Illinois State ... IL
Northern Arizona ... AZ
Northern Illinois U ... IL
Northern Iowa, U. of ... IA
Ohio State U ... OH
Our Lady of the Lake ... TX
Pennsylvania State U ... PA
Puerto Rico, U. of ... PR
Queens ... NY
Rutgers ... NJ
Saint Thomas Aquinas ... NY
San Diego State ... CA
San Francisco State ... CA
San Jose State ... CA
Santa Clara, U. of ... CA
Southwest Texas State ... TX
State U. of New York (Albany, Binghamton, Brockport, Buffalo, New Paltz, Oneonta, Oswego, Stony Brook) ... NY
Texas, U. of (Arlington, Austin) ... TX
Texas Tech. U ... TX
Utah, U. of ... UT
Washington, U. of ... WA
Wisconsin, U. of (Eau Claire, Madison) ... WI

Languages, Swahili

Cornell U ... NY
Texas, U. of (Austin) ... TX
Wayne State U ... MI

Languages, Swedish

Augustana ... IL
Chicago, U. of ... IL
Cornell U ... NY
Gustavus Adolphus ... MN
Harvard ... MA
Minnesota, U. of ... MN
North Park Coll ... IL
Pennsylvania, U. of ... PA
Radcliffe Coll ... MA
Upsala Coll ... NJ

Languages, Thai

Cornell U .... NY

Languages, Turkish

Cornell U .... NY
Harvard .... MA
New York U .... NY
Pennsylvania, U. of .... PA
Radcliffe .... MA

Languages, Ukrainian

Cornell U .... NY
Harvard U .... MA
Manor Jr .... PA
Radcliffe .... MA

Languages, Vietnamese

Cornell U .... NY

Languages, Welsh

Cornell U .... NY

Languages, Elementary School Teaching of

Adrian Coll .... MI
Allentown Coll. of St. Francis de Sales .... PA
Anderson Coll .... IN
Bluffton Coll .... OH
California State Coll .... PA
Calvin Coll .... MI
Central Washington U .... WA
Cheyney State Coll .... PA
Connecticut, U. of .... CT
Drake U .... IA
Eastern Washington U .... WA
Elon Coll .... NC
Evansville, U. of .... IN
Fairleigh Dickinson .... NJ
Findlay Coll .... OH
Fort Hays State .... KS
Fort Lewis Coll .... CO
Gannon U .... PA
Goshen Coll .... IN
Hastings Coll .... NE
Hawaii, U. of (Honolulu) .... HI
Hope Coll .... MI
Iowa, U. of .... IA
Kansas, U. of .... KS
Kean Coll .... NJ
Kutztown State .... PA
Lindenwood Colleges .... MO
Linfield Coll .... OR
Manhattan Coll .... NY
Marywood .... PA
Michigan, U. of .... MI
Miles Coll .... AL
Millersville State .... PA
Minnesota, U. of .... MN
Missouri, U. of .... MO
Nazareth Coll .... NY
Nebraska Wesleyan U .... NE
North Carolina Central U .... NC
North Central Coll IL
Northwest Missouri State Coll .... MO
Notre Dame Coll. of Ohio .... OH
Plymouth State .... NH
Rhode Island Coll .... RI
Rio Piedras .... PR
Rivier Coll .... NH
Saint Rose, Coll. of .... NY
Schreiner Coll .... TX
Southern Illinois U IL
Southwest Missouri .... MO
State U. of New York (Geneseo) NY
Tennessee, U. of (Chattanooga) .... TN
Texas A&I U .... TX
Trinity Christian IL
William Woods Coll .... MO

Law

Approved by American Bar Association

Akron, U. of .... OH
Alabama, U. of .... AL
American .... DC
Antioch Sch. of Law .... DC
Arizona, U. of .... AZ
Arizona State U .... AZ
Arkansas, U. of (Fayetteville, Little Rock) .... AR
Baltimore, U. of .... MD
Baylor .... TX
Boston Coll .... MA
Boston U .... MA
Bridgeport, U. of .... CT
Brigham Young U .... UT
Brooklyn Law Sch .... NY
California, U. of (Berkeley, Davis, Los Angeles) .... CA
California Western Sch. of Law .... CA
Campbell U .... NC
Capital U .... OH
Case Western Reserve U .... OH
Catholic U .... DC
Catholic U. of Puerto Rico .... PR
Chicago, U. of IL
Chicago-Kent Coll. of Law, see Illinois Inst. of Tech IL
Cincinnati, U. of .... OH
Cleveland-Marshall Coll. of Law .... OH
Colorado, U. of .... CO
Columbia .... NY
Connecticut, U. of .... CT
Cornell .... NY
Creighton .... NE
Dayton, U. of .... OH
Delaware Law Sch .... DE
Denver, U. of .... CO
DePaul IL
Detroit, U. of .... MI
Detroit Coll. of Law .... MI
Dickinson Sch. of Law .... PA
Drake .... IA
Duke .... NC
Duquesne U .... PA
Emory .... GA
Florida, U. of .... FL
Florida State U .... FL
Fordham .... NY
Franklin Pierce Law Ctr .... NH
George Washington .... DC
Georgetown .... DC
Georgia, U. of .... GA
Golden Gate .... CA
Gonzaga .... WA
Hamline .... MN
Harvard .... MA
Hastings Coll. of the Law (San Francisco) .... CA
Hawaii, U. of .... HI
Hofstra U .... NY
Houston, U. of .... TX
Howard .... DC
Idaho, U. of .... ID
Illinois, U. of IL
Illinois Inst. of Tech IL
Indiana U .... IN
Inter-American U. of Puerto Rico .... PR
Iowa, U. of .... IA
John Marshall Law School IL
Judge Advocate General's Sch .... VA
Kansas, U. of .... KS
Kentucky, U. of .... KY
Lewis and Clark Coll .... OR
Louisiana State U .... LA
Louisville, U. of .... KY
Loyola .... CA
Loyola IL
Loyola .... LA
Maine, U. of .... ME
Marquette .... WI
Maryland, U. of .... MD
Memphis State U .... TN
Mercer .... GA
Miami, U. of .... FL
Michigan, U. of .... MI
Minnesota, U. of .... MN
Mississippi, U. of .... MS
Missouri, U. of (Columbia, Kansas City) .... MO
Montana, U. of .... MT
Nebraska, U. of .... NE
New England Sch. of Law .... MA
New Mexico, U. of .... NM
New York Law Sch .... NY
New York U .... NY
North Carolina, U. of .... NC
North Carolina Central U .... NC
North Dakota, U. of .... ND
Northeastern U .... MA
Northern Illinois U IL
Northern Kentucky U .... KY
Northwestern IL
Notre Dame, U. of .... IN
Nova U .... FL
Ohio Northern U .... OH
Ohio State U .... OH
Oklahoma, U. of .... OK
Oklahoma City U .... OK
Oregon, U. of .... OR
Pace U .... NY
Pacific, U. of the .... CA
Pennsylvania, U. of .... PA
Pepperdine U .... CA
Pittsburgh, U. of .... PA
Puerto Rico, U. of .... PR
Puget Sound, U. of .... WA
Richmond, U. of .... VA
Rutgers, State U. (Camden, Newark) .... NJ
Saint Mary's .... TX
Samford U .... AL
San Diego, U. of .... CA
San Francisco, U. of .... CA
Santa Clara, U. of .... CA
Seton Hall .... NJ
South Carolina, U. of .... SC
South Dakota, U. of .... SD
South Texas Coll. Law School .... TX
Southern California, U. of .... CA
Southern Illinois U IL
Southern Methodist .... TX
Southern U .... LA
Southwestern U .... CA
St. John's .... NY
St. Louis U .... MO
Stanford .... CA
State U. of New York (Buffalo) .... NY
Stetson .... FL
Suffolk .... MA
Syracuse .... NY
Temple .... PA
Tennessee, U. of .... TN
Texas, U. of (Austin) .... TX
Texas Southern U .... TX
Texas Tech. U .... TX
Thomas M. Cooley Law Sch .... MI
Toledo, U. of .... OH
Tulane .... LA
Tulsa, U. of .... OK
Union (Albany Law Sch.) .... NY
Utah, U. of .... UT
Valparaiso .... IN
Vanderbilt .... TN
Vermont Law Sch .... VT
Villanova .... PA
Virginia, U. of .... VA
Wake Forest .... NC
Washburn .... KS
Washington, U. of .... WA
Washington and Lee .... VA
Washington U .... MO
Wayne State U .... MI
West Virginia U .... WV
Western New England Coll .... MA
Whittier Coll .... CA
Willamette .... OR
William and Mary .... VA
William Mitchell Coll. of Law .... MN
Wisconsin, U. of (Madison) .... WI
Wyoming, U. of .... WY
Yale .... CT
Yeshiva U .... NY

Law, Patent

Bernadean U .... CA
Case Western .... OH
Eastern Kentucky .... KY
Findlay Coll .... OH
Illinois Inst. of Tech IL
Iowa, U. of .... IA
La Salle Coll .... PA
Marywood Coll .... PA
Missouri, U. of .... MO
North Carolina Cent. U .... NC
Rio Piedras .... PR
Tennessee, U. of .... TN

Law and Liberal Arts

6-year combination programs

•Indicates program available only to that particular institution's undergraduates

Baylor U .... TX
Boston U .... MA
Campbell U .... NC
•Catholic U .... DC
Chicago, U. of IL
Columbia U .... NY
•Cornell U .... NY
•Fordham Coll .... NY
Hamline U .... MN
Howard U .... DC
Idaho, U. of .... ID
•Illinois Inst. of Tech IL
Missouri, U. of (Columbia, Kansas City .... MO
Nebraska, U. of .... NE
•North Carolina, U. of .... NC
North Carolina Central U .... NC
Richmond, U. of .... VA
•Suffolk U .... MA
Syracuse .... NY
Tulane .... LA
Union (also Rensselaer Poly. Inst.) .... NY
Utah, U. of .... UT
Vanderbilt U .... TN
Vermont Law Sch .... VT
Wabash Coll. (with Columbia U.) .... IN
•Wake Forest .... NC
•Washington & Lee U .... VA
Wisconsin, U. of (Madison) .... WI

Legal Assistant/Paralegal Studies

•Program has received final approval from the American Bar Assn.

•Adelphi U .... NY
•Arapahoe Comm .... CO
•Avila Coll .... MO
•Bentley Coll .... MA
•Burlington Co. Coll .... NJ
•California, U. of (Los Angeles) .. CA
•California State U. (Los Angeles) CA
•Cedar Crest Coll .... PA
•Central Pennsylvania Bus. Sch .. PA
•Cleveland State Comm .... OH
•Cumberland County Coll .... NJ
•Denver Paralegal Inst .... CO
•Dyke Coll .... OH
•Eastern Kentucky U .... KY
•Edmonds Comm .... WA
•Elizabeth Seton Coll .... NY
•Evansville, U. of .... IN
•Fayetteville Tech. Inst .... NC
•Ferris State U .... MI
Gannon U .... PA
•George Washington U .... DC
•Georgetown U .... DC
Greensboro Coll .... NC
•Harper Coll IL
•Highline Comm .... WA
•Hilbert Coll .... NY
Huntingdon Coll .... AL
Husson Coll .... MN
Hutchinson Comm .... KS
•Inver Hills Comm .... MN
Indiana Central U .... IN
•Inst. for Paralegal Training .... PA
•Johnson Co. Comm .... KS
•Kapiolani Comm. Coll .... HI
King's Coll .... PA
•Kirkwood Comm. Coll .... IA
•Lakeshore Tech. Inst .... WI
•Lincoln Sch. of Commerce .... NE
•Long Island U .... NY
•Mallinckrodt Coll IL
Manhattanville Coll .... NY
Marymount Coll .... VA
Marywood Coll .... PA
•Mercer Co. Comm .... NJ
Mercy Coll .... MI
•Mercy Coll .... NY
Michigan Christian IL
•Midlands Tech .... SC
Midway Coll .... KY
•Minnesota, U. of .... MN
Missouri Western State .... MO
Moorhead State U .... MN
•National Center for Paralegal Training .... GA
Nicholls State U .... LA
•North Hennepin Comm .... MN
Northeast Mississippi Jr .... MS
•Northern Arizona U .... AZ
•Norwalk Comm .... CT
•Oakland U .... MI
•Oklahoma, U. of .... OK
•Oscar Rose Jr .... OK
Pittsburg State .... KS
Pittsburgh, U. of .... PA
•Portland Comm .... OR
Post Coll .... CT
•Quinnipiac Coll .... CT
•Rivier Coll .... NH
Rocky Mountain Coll .... MT
Roger Williams Coll .... RI
•Roosevelt U IL
•Sacred Heart .... CT
•Samford U .... AL
•San Diego, U. of .... CA
•San Francisco, City Coll. of .... CA
•Sangamon State U IL
•Santa Fe Comm Coll .... FL
•Southern California, U. of .... CA
•Southwestern Paralegal Inst .... TX
•St. Mary's Coll .... CA
•Toledo, U. of .... OH
•Tulane U .... LA
•Villa Julie Coll .... MD
Virgin Islands, Coll. of VI
Webster Coll .... MO
Wesley Coll .... DE
West Florida, U. of .... FL
•West Los Angeles, U. of .... CA
•Wichita State U .... KS
•Widener U .... PA
•William Woods .... MO
•Winona State U .... MN

Librarianship

Alabama A&M .... AL
Alverno Coll .... WI
Andrews U .... MI
Appalachian State U .... NC
Arizona, U. of .... AZ
Arizona State U .... AZ
Arkansas, U. of .... AR
Ball State U .... IN
Baylor U .... TX
Bethany Lutheran Coll .... MN
Bob Jones U .... SC
Boston U .... MA
Bowling Green State U .... OH
Brevard Coll .... NC
Brevard Comm. Coll .... FL
Bridgewater State .... MA
Brigham Young .... UT
California State U. (Sacramento) .... CA
Calvin Coll .... MI
Case Western .... OH
Central Coll .... KS
Central Michigan .... MI
Central Missouri .... MO
Chadron .... NE
Clarion State .... PA
Clinch Valley Coll .... VA
Columbia Coll .... NY
Creighton U .... NE
Delta State U .... MS
Denver, U. of .... CO
Desert, Coll. of the .... CA
DuPage, Coll. of IL
Eastern Kentucky U .... KY
Emporia State .... KS
Georgia Coll .... GA
Grossmont Coll .... CA
Hartnell Comm. Coll .... CA
Henry Ford Comm. Coll .... MI
International U .... MO
Iowa, U. of .... IA
Kentucky Wesleyan Coll .... KY
Kutztown State .... PA
Lansing Comm. Coll .... MI
Lock Haven State .... PA
Maria Regina .... NY
Mars Hill Coll .... NC
Marshall U .... WV
Marywood .... PA
Mercer Co. Comm. Coll .... NJ
Michigan, U. of .... MI
Middle Georgia Coll .... GA
Minnesota, U. of .... MN
Missouri, U. of .... MO
Mississippi U. for Women .... MS
Moraine Valley Comm. Coll IL
North Carolina Cent. U .... NC
Northeastern Oklahoma State U .... OK
Northern Iowa, U. of .... IA
Northwest Missouri State U .... MO
Northwestern State U .... LA
Ohio Dominican Coll .... OH
Oklahoma Panhandle State .... OK
Pittsburg State U .... KS
Pratt Inst .... NY
Puerto Rico, U. of .... PR
Purdue U .... IN
Radford U .... VA
Rio Piedras .... PR
Sacramento City Coll .... CA
San Francisco, City Coll. of .... CA
Santa Ana Coll .... CA
S.D. Bishop State Jr. Coll .... AL
Shepherd .... WV
Shippensburg State .... PA
Sierra Coll .... CA
Simmons .... MA
Siskiyous, Coll. of the .... CA
Slippery Rock State .... PA
South Carolina, U. of .... SC
South Dakota, U. of .... SD
South Florida, U. of .... FL
South Georgia Coll .... GA
Southern California, U. of .... CA
Southern Idaho, Coll. of .... ID
Southwestern Michigan Coll .... MI
St. Catherine, Coll. of .... MN
State U. of New York (Geneseo) NY
Tennessee, U. of .... TN
Texas Woman's Coll .... TX
Umpqua Comm. Coll .... OR
Union U .... TN
Urbana Coll .... OH
Wayne State .... MI
Weber State Coll .... UT
West Virginia Wesleyan .... WV
Western Michigan .... MI
Wilbur Wright Coll IL
William Woods Coll .... MO
Wisconsin, U. of (Milwaukee) .... WI

Library Education—Graduate Programs

Accredited by the American Library Association

Alabama, U. of .... AL
Arizona, U. of .... AZ
Atlanta .... GA
Ball State U .... IN
Brigham Young U .... UT
California, U. of (Berkeley, Los Angeles) .... CA
Case Western Reserve .... OH
Catholic U .... DC
Chicago, U. of IL
Clarion State .... PA
Columbia .... NY
Denver, U. of .... CO
Drexel U .... PA
Emory .... GA
Emporia State .... KS
Florida State U .... FL
Hawaii, U. of .... HI
Illinois, U. of IL
Indiana U .... IN
Iowa, U. of .... IA
Kent State .... OH
Kentucky, U. of .... KY
Long Island U .... NY
Louisiana State U .... LA
Maryland, U. of .... MD
Michigan, U. of .... MI
Minnesota, U. of .... MN
Mississippi, U. of .... MS
Missouri, U. of (Columbia) .... MO
North Carolina, U. of (Chapel Hill, Greensboro) .... NC
North Carolina Central .... NC
North Texas State U .... TX
Northern Illinois U IL
Oklahoma, U. of .... OK
Pittsburgh, U. of .... PA
Pratt Inst .... NY
Queens Coll .... NY
Rhode Island, U. of .... RI
Rosary Coll IL
Rutgers .... NJ
San Jose State U .... CA
Simmons .... MA
South Carolina, U. of .... SC
South Florida, U. of .... FL
Southern California, U. of .... CA
Southern Connecticut State .... CT
Southern Mississippi, U. of .... MS
St. John's U .... NY
State U. of New York (Albany, Buffalo, Geneseo) .... NY
Syracuse .... NY
Tennessee, U. of .... TN
Texas, U. of (Austin) .... TX
Texas Woman's .... TX
Vanderbilt U .... TN
Washington, U. of .... WA
Wayne State U .... MI
Western Michigan U .... MI
Wisconsin, U. of (Madison, Milwaukee) .... WI

Linguistics

Alaska, U. of .... AK
Arizona, U. of .... AZ
Barnard Coll .... NY
Bethel Coll .... MN
Blake Coll .... OR
Boston Coll .... MA
Boston U .... MA
Bowie State .... MD
Brandeis U .... MA
Bridgewater State .... MA
Brigham Young U .... UT
Brown U .... RI
California, U. of (Berkeley, Irvine, Los Angeles, Riverside, San Diego, Santa Cruz) .... CA
California State U. (Fresno, Fullerton) .... CA
Carnegie-Mellon U .... PA
Central Coll .... IA
Central Michigan U .... MI
Central Missouri .... MO
Chicago, U. of IL
Cincinnati, U. of .... OH
City U .... NY
Cleveland State .... OH
Colorado, U. of .... CO
Columbia U .... NY
Cornell U .... NY
DePauw U .... IN
Eastern Washington U .... WA
Florida, U. of .... FL
Florida Atlantic U .... FL
Gannon .... PA
Georgetown U .... DC
Gordon Coll .... MA
Hampshire Coll .... MA
Hartford, U. of .... CT
Harvard U .... MA
Hawaii, U. of (Honolulu) .... HI
Illinois, U. of IL
Indiana U .... IN
Iowa, U. of .... IA
Kansas, U. of .... KS
Kansas State U .... KS
Kentucky, U. of .... KY
La Salle .... PA
Loyola U IL
Macalester Coll .... MN
Massachusetts, U. of (Amherst) MA
Michigan, U. of .... MI
Michigan State U .... MI
Minnesota, U. of (Minneapolis) . MN
Montclair State .... NJ
New Hampshire, U. of .... NH
New Mexico, U. of .... NM
New York U .... NY
North Carolina, U. of (Chapel Hill, Greensboro) .... NC

Northeastern U .... MA
Northeastern Illinois U IL
Northern Iowa, U. of .... IA
Northwestern U IL
Oakland U .... MI
Ohio State U .... OH
Oklahoma, U. of .... OK
Oregon, U. of .... OR
Pacific, U. of the .... CA
Pennsylvania, U. of .... PA
Pennsylvania State U .... PA
Pittsburgh, U. of .... PA
Pomona Coll .... CA
Radcliffe Coll .... MA
Rhode Island, U. of .... RI
Rio Piedras .... PR
Rochester, U. of .... NY
San Diego State U .... CA
South Carolina, U. of .... SC
South Florida, U. of .... FL
Southern Illinois U IL
Stanford U .... CA
State U. of New York (Buffalo, Binghamton, Geneseo, Stony Brook) .... NY
Syracuse U .... NY
Temple U .... PA
Tennessee, U. of .... TN
Texas, U. of (Austin) .... TX
Texas A&M U .... TX
Utah, U. of .... UT
Washington, U. of .... WA
Washington U .... MO
Wellesley .... MA
Wesleyan .... CT
Western Michigan .... MI
Wichita State .... KS
William Woods .... MO
Wisconsin, U. of (Milwaukee) ... WI
Wright State U .... OH
Yale U .... CT

Mammalogy

Cornell U .... NY

Marine Biology and/or Fisheries

Alabama State U .... AL
Alaska, U. of .... AK
American U .... DC
Atlantic, Coll. of the .... ME
Auburn U .... AL
Barrington Coll .... RI
Beaver Coll .... PA
Bemidji State U .... MN
Bridgewater State .... MA
Brown U .... RI
California, U. of (Davis, San Diego, Santa Cruz) .... CA
California State U .... CA
Charleston, Coll. of .... SC
Cheyney State .... PA
Cornell U .... NY
Corpus Christi State U .... TX
Eckerd Coll .... FL
Evergreen State Coll .... WA
Fairleigh Dickinson .... NJ
Florida Atlantic .... FL
Florida Inst. of Tech .... FL
Florida Inst. of Tech—Sch. of App. Tech .... FL
Goddard Coll .... VT
Hampshire Coll .... MA
Hampton Institute .... VA
Hawaii, U. of .... HI
Hawaii Loa Coll .... HI
Illinois Central Coll IL
Jackson State U .... MS
Jacksonville U .... FL
Kutztown State .... PA
Lebanon Valley Coll .... PA
Lincoln Coll IL
Michigan State U .... MI
Mitchell Coll .... CT
Montevallo, U. of .... AL
New Coll .... FL
New England, U. of .... ME
Nicholls State U .... LA
North Alabama, U. of .... AL
North Carolina, U. of (Wilmington) .... NC
Northeast Missouri .... MO
Northeastern Oklahoma .... OK
Northern Michigan U .... MI
Northland Coll .... WI
Occidental .... CA
Ohio State U .... OH
Oklahoma State U .... OK
Old Dominion U .... VA
Palm Beach Atlantic .... FL
Pomona Coll .... CA
Puerto Rico, U. of .... PR
Roger Williams Coll .... RI
Samford U .... AL
South Alabama, U. of .... AL
South Carolina, U. of .... SC
Southampton Coll .... NY
Southwest Texas State U .... TX
Southwestern Oklahoma State U OK
Spring Hill Coll .... AL
St. Francis Coll .... PA
State U. of New York (Coll. of Environmental Science and Forestry) .... NY
Stephen F. Austin .... TX
Tennessee, U. of .... TN
Texas A&M .... TX
Unity Coll .... ME
Washington, U. of .... WA
West Florida, U. of .... FL
Wisconsin, U. of (Stevens Point) .... WI
Wittenberg .... OH

Marine Engineering, *See* ENGINEERING, MARINE

Marine Geology

Brown U .... RI
Cornell U .... NY
Corpus Christi State .... TX
Goddard Coll .... VT
Lamar U .... TX
Massachusetts, U. of .... MA
Miami, U. of .... FL
Southampton Coll .... NY
Wittenberg U .... OH

Marine Science

Alabama, U. of .... AL
Alaska, U. of .... AK
American U .... DC
Brevard Coll .... NC
California, U. of (San Diego) .... CA
California Maritime Acad .... CA
California State U. (Fresno, Hayward) .... CA
Drake U .... IA
Eckerd Coll .... FL
Evergreen State Coll .... WA
Florida, U. of .... FL
Goddard Coll .... VT
Hampshire Coll .... MA
Hampton Institute .... VA
Jacksonville State .... AL
Jacksonville U .... FL
Kutztown State Coll .... PA
Lincoln Coll IL
Maryland, U. of (Eastern Shore) .... MD
Masschusetts, U. of .... MA
Miami, U. of .... FL
Millersville State Coll .... PA
Mitchell Coll .... CT
Nasson Coll .... ME
North Carolina State .... NC
Northeastern Illinois U IL
Occidental .... CA
Old Dominion .... VA
Puerto Rico, U. of .... PR
Purdue U .... IN
Roger Williams .... RI
South Carolina, U. of .... SC
Southampton Coll .... NY
St. Andrew's Presbyterian ..... NC
Stockton State .... NJ
Tampa, U. of .... FL
Temple U .... PA
Texas A&M .... TX
U.S. Coast Guard Acad .... CT
Virgin Islands, Coll. of VI
William and Mary, Coll. of ...... VA
Wittenberg U .... OH

Marine Technology

According to U.S. Dept. of Commerce, National Oceanic and Atmospheric Administration

Brazosport Coll .... TX
California Maritime Acad .... CA
Cape Fear Tech. Inst .... NC
Florida Inst. of Tech .... FL
Mississippi State U .... MS

Marine Transportation, *See* TRANSPORTATION, MARINE

Marketing

Institutions awarding 25 or more undergraduate degrees as major field in single year according to U.S. Office of Education latest statistics

Abilene Christian U .... TX
Akron, U. of .... OH
Alabama, U. of .... AL
American U .... DC
Appalachian State U .... NC
Arizona, U. of .... AZ
Arizona State U .... AZ
Arkansas, U. of .... AR
Arkansas State U .... AR
Ashland Coll .... OH
Auburn U .... AL
Babson Coll .... MA
Baldwin-Wallace .... OH
Ball State U .... IN
Baylor U .... TX
Benedict Coll .... SC
Bentley Coll .... MA
Bernard Baruch Coll .... NY
Boise State U .... ID
Boston Coll .... MA
Bowling Green State U .... OH
Bradley U IL
Bridgeport, U. of .... CT
Brigham Young U .... UT
Bryant Coll .... RI
Canisius Coll .... NY
Central Arizona, U. of .... AZ
Central Connecticut State ...... CT
Central Missouri State U .... MO
Central Pennsylvania Business Sch .... PA
Central State U .... OK
Central Washington U .... WA
Cincinnati, U. of .... OH
Clarion State .... PA
Cleveland State U .... OH
Colorado, U. of .... CO
Connecticut, U. of .... CT
Creighton U .... NE
Dayton, U. of .... OH
Delaware, U. of .... DE
Denver, U. of .... CO
DePaul U IL
Drake U .... IA
East Tennessee State U .... TN
East Texas State U .... TX
Eastern Illinois U IL
Eastern Kentucky U .... KY
Eastern Michigan U .... MI
Eastern Washington U .... WA
Fairfield U .... CT
Fairleigh Dickinson U .... NJ
Ferris State U .... MI
Florida, U. of .... FL
Florida Atlantic U .... FL
Florida International U .... FL
Florida State U .... FL
Florida Tech. U .... FL
Fort Hays State U .... KS
Georgetown U .... DC
Georgia, U. of .... GA
Georgia Southern U .... GA
Georgia State U .... GA
Hampton Inst .... VA
Hartford, U. of .... CT
Hawaii, U. of (Manoa) .... HI
Hofstra U .... NY
Houston, U. of .... TX
Illinois, U. of IL
Illinois State U IL
Indiana State U .... IN
Indiana U .... IN
Indianapolis U.-Purdue U .... IN
Iona Coll .... NY
Iowa, U. of .... IA
Jacksonville State U .... AL
Jacksonville U .... FL
James Madison U .... VA
John Carroll U .... OH
Kansas State U .... KS
Kent State U .... OH
La Salle Coll .... PA
Lamar U .... TX
Lehigh U .... PA
Long Island U. (C.W. Post) ..... NY
Louisiana State U. and A&M Coll .... LA
Louisville, U. of .... KY
Loyola U IL
Manhattan Coll .... NY
Mankato State U .... MN
Marquette U .... WI
Marshall U .... WV
Maryland, U. of .... MD
Massachusetts, U. of .... MA
Merrimack Coll .... MA
Miami U .... OH
Michigan State U .... MI
Middle Tennessee State U ...... TN
Millikin U IL
Mississippi, U. of .... MS
Mississippi State U .... MS
Missouri Western State .... MO
Moorhead State U .... MN
Murray State U .... KY
Nebraska, U. of .... NE
New Hampshire Coll .... NH
New Haven, U. of .... CT
New Mexico State U .... NM
New Orleans, U. of .... LA
New York Inst. of Tech .... NY
New York U .... NY
North Alabama, U. of .... AL
North Dakota, U. of .... ND
North Texas State U .... TX
Northeastern U .... MA
Northern Arizona U .... AZ

Northern Colorado, U. of ...... CO
Northern Illinois U IL
Northern Iowa, U. of .... IA
Northern Kentucky U .... KY
Northwest Missouri State U .... MO
Notre Dame, U. of .... IN
Ohio State U .... OH
Ohio U .... OH
Oklahoma, U. of .... OK
Oklahoma State U .... OK
Old Dominion U .... VA
Oregon, U. of .... OR
Pace U .... NY
Pennsylvania, U. of .... PA
Pennsylvania State U .... PA
Philadelphia Coll. of Textiles & Sci .... PA
Plymouth State Coll .... NH
Quinnipiac Coll .... CT
Rhode Island, U. of .... RI
Rider Coll .... NJ
Robert Morris .... PA
Rochester Inst. of Tech .... NY
Roosevelt U IL
Rutgers U .... NJ
Saint Joseph's U .... PA
Saint Louis U .... MO
Saint Peter's Coll .... NJ
Sam Houston State U .... TX
Seton Hall U .... NJ
Shippensburg State .... PA
Siena Coll .... NY
South Alabama, U. of .... AL
South Carolina, U. of .... SC
South Florida, U. of .... FL
Southeast Missouri State U .... MO
Southeastern Louisiana U ...... LA
Southeastern Massachusetts U . MA
Southern California, U. of ...... CA
Southern Illinois U IL
Southern Mississippi, U. of .... MS
Southern U .... LA
Southwest Missouri State U .... MO
Southwestern Louisiana, U. of .. LA
St. Bonaventure U .... NY
St. Cloud State U .... MN
St. John's U .... NY
St. Thomas, U. of .... MN
St. Thomas Aquinas Coll .... NY
Stephen F. Austin State U ...... TX
Stonehill Coll .... MA
Suffolk U .... MA
Susquehanna U .... PA
Syracuse U .... NY
Temple U .... PA
Tennessee, U. of .... TN
Tennessee Tech U .... TN
Texas, U. of (Austin, El Paso, San Antonio) .... TX
Texas A&M U .... TX
Texas Christian U .... TX
Texas Tech. U .... TX
Toledo, U. of .... OH
Troy State U .... AL
Tulsa, U. of .... OK
Utah, U. of .... UT
Utah State U .... UT
Villanova U .... PA
Virginia, U. of .... VA
Virginia Commonwealth U ...... VA
Virginia Poly. Inst .... VA
Wayne State U .... MI
West Florida, U. of .... FL
West Virginia U .... WV
Western Colorado U .... CO
Western Illinois U IL
Western Michigan U .... MI
Western New England Coll .... MA
Wisconsin, U. of (Eau Claire, La Crosse, Madison, Oshkosh Whitewater) .... WI
Wright State U .... OH
Xavier U .... OH
Youngstown State U .... OH

Mass Communications, *See* JOURNALISM AND MASS COMMUNICATIONS

Materials Engineering, *See* ENGINEERING, MATERIALS

Mathematics

Institutions awarding 15 or more undergraduate degrees as major field in single year according to U.S. Office of Education latest statistics

Akron, U. of .... OH
Alabama, U. of .... AL
American U .... DC
Appalachian State .... NC
Arizona, U. of .... AZ
Arizona State U .... AZ
Armstrong State .... GA
Auburn U .... AL
Ball State U .... IN
Bates Coll .... ME
Boston Coll .... MA
Boston U .... MA
Bowdoin Coll .... ME
Bridgewater State Coll .... MA
Brigham Young .... UT
Brooklyn Coll .... NY
Brown .... RI
Bucknell .... PA
California, U. of (Berkeley, Davis, Irvine, Los Angeles, Riverside, San Diego, Santa Barbara, Santa Cruz) .... CA
California Poly. State (San Luis Obispo) .... CA
California State Coll .... PA
California State U. (Chico, Fresno, Fullerton, Hayward, Long Beach, Los Angeles, Northridge) .... CA
Carnegie-Mellon .... PA
Case Western .... OH
Catholic U. of Puerto Rico ...... PR
Central Connecticut State Coll .. CT
Chicago, U. of IL
Cincinnati, U. of .... OH
Citadel, The .... SC
City Coll .... NY
Clafin Coll .... SC
Clarion State .... PA
Clark Coll .... MA
Clemson U .... SC
Cleveland State U .... OH
Colgate U .... NY
Colorado, U. of .... CO
Colorado State .... CO
Columbia U .... NY
Connecticut, U. of .... CT
Cornell .... NY
Dartmouth .... NH
Delaware, U. of .... DE
Denver, U. of .... CO
Drexel U .... PA
Duke .... NC
East Carolina .... NC
East Texas .... TX
Emporia Kansas State .... KS
Fairleigh Dickinson .... NJ
Florida, U. of .... FL
Florida State U .... FL
Fordham .... NY
Francis Marion Coll .... SC
George Mason .... VA
George Washington .... DC
Georgia, U. of .... GA
Georgia Southern .... GA
Gettysburg .... PA
Glassboro State Coll .... NJ
Grand Valley .... MI
Grove City .... PA
Gustavus Adolphus .... MN
Harvard .... MA
Harvey Mudd Coll .... CA
Hawaii, U. of .... HI
Holy Cross .... MA
Houston, U. of .... TX
Hunter .... NY
Illinois, U. of IL
Illinois State U IL
Indiana State .... IN
Indiana U .... IN
Indiana U. of Pa .... PA
Iowa, U. of .... IA
Iowa State .... IA
James Madison Coll .... VA
Jersey City State .... NJ
John Carroll .... OH
Johns Hopkins .... MD
Kean Coll .... NJ
Kearney State Coll .... NE
Kent State .... OH
La Salle .... PA
Lamar U .... TX
Lawrence Inst. of Tech .... MI
Lebanon Valley .... PA
Lehman Coll .... NY
Long Island U .... NY
Lowell, U. of .... MA
Maine, U. of .... ME
Mary Washington .... VA
Maryland, U. of .... MD
Massachusetts, U. of .... MA
Massachusetts Inst. of Tech ... MA
Meredith Coll .... NC
Metropolitan State .... CO
Miami U .... OH
Michigan, U. of .... MI
Michigan State U .... MI
Middle Tennessee State .... TN
Millersville State Coll .... PA
Minnesota, U. of .... MN
Missouri, U. of .... MO
Montana State .... MT
Montclair State .... NJ
Mount Holyoke .... MA
Muskingum .... OH
Nebraska, U. of .... NE
New Hampshire, U. of .... NH
New Mexico, U. of .... NM
New Mexico State .... NM
New York U .... NY
North Carolina, U. of .... NC
North Carolina State U .... NC
Northeastern .... MA
Northeastern Illinois U IL
Northeastern Oklahoma .... OK
Northern Illinois IL
Northern Iowa, U. of .... IA
Northwestern IL
Notre Dame, U. of .... IN
Oakland U .... MI
Oberlin .... OH
Occidental .... CA
Ohio State .... OH
Ohio U .... OH
Ohio Wesleyan U .... OH
Oklahoma, U. of .... OK
Old Dominion U .... VA
Oregon, U. of .... OR
Pan American .... TX
Pennsylvania State U .... PA
Pittsburgh, U. of .... PA
Pomona Coll .... CA
Portland State .... OR
Princeton .... NJ
Puerto Rico, U. of .... PR
Purdue .... IN
Queens .... NY
Radford .... VA
Reed Coll .... OR
Rensselaer Poly. Inst .... NY
Rice U .... TX
Richmond, U. of .... VA
Rochester, U. of .... NY
Rutgers .... NJ
Sam Houston .... TX
San Diego State .... CA
San Francisco State .... CA
San Jose State .... CA
Seton Hall .... NJ
Shippensburg State Coll .... PA
Smith Coll .... MA
South Carolina, U. of .... SC
South Florida, U. of .... FL
Southeastern Massachusetts ... MA
Southern Illinois U IL
Southern Methodist .... TX
Southern Mississippi, U. of .... MS
St. Cloud .... MN
St. John's U .... NY
St. Olaf .... MN
Stanford .... CA
State U. of New York (Albany, Binghamton, Brockport, Buffalo, Cortland, Geneseo, Oneonta, Oswego, Potsdam, Stony Brook) .... NY
Stephen F. Austin State Coll .... TX
Tennessee, U. of .... TN
Texas, U. of (Arlington, Austin, Dallas, San Antonio) .... TX
Texas A&M .... TX
Toledo, U. of .... OH
Towson State U .... MD
Trenton State Coll .... NJ
Tulane U .... LA
U.S. Coast Guard .... CT
U.S. Naval Academy .... MD
Utah, U. of .... UT
Vanderbilt .... TN
Vermont U. & State Agric. Coll .. VT
Villanova U .... PA
Virginia, U. of .... VA
Virginia Poly. Inst .... VA
Wabash Coll .... IN
Wake Forest .... NC
Washington, U. of .... WA
Washington U .... MO
West Texas .... TX
Western Illinois IL
Western Michigan U .... MI
Westfield State .... MA
Westminster Coll .... PA
Wheaton Coll IL
William and Mary .... VA
William Paterson .... NJ
Winthrop .... SC
Wisconsin, U. of (Eau Claire, La Crosse, Madison, Milwaukee, Oshkosh, Stevens Point, Stout, Whitewater) .... WI
Worcester State Coll .... MA
Yale U .... CT
York .... NY
Youngstown State U .... OH

Mechanical Engineering, *See* ENGINEERING, MECHANICAL

Medical Assistants

Degree programs approved by Council on Medical Education of American Medical Assn. in collaboration with American Assn. of Medical Assistants

Alameda, Coll. of .... CA
Allan Hancock Coll .... CA
Allegheny Co., Comm. Coll. of .. PA
Aquinas Jr. Coll .... MA
Arapahoe Comm. Coll .... CO
Arkansas Tech. U .... AR
Baker Jr. Coll .... MI

Bay Path Jr. Coll . . . . MA
Becker Jr. Coll . . . . MA
Belleville Area IL
Bergen Comm. Coll . . . . NJ
Broome Comm. Coll . . . . NY
Broward Comm . . . . FL
Central Pennsylvania Bus. Sch . . PA
Central Tech. C. Coll . . . . NE
Charles Stewart Mott Comm. Coll . . . . MI
Cincinnati Tech. Coll . . . . OH
Consumnes Coll . . . . CA
Cuyahoga Comm. Coll . . . . OH
Cypress . . . . CA
DeAnza Coll . . . . CA
Dutchess Comm . . . . NY
Eastern Kentucky . . . . KY
Edmonson Coll . . . . TN
El Camino Coll . . . . CA
El Centro . . . . TX
Ferris State . . . . MI
Fisher Jr . . . . MA
Gannon U . . . . PA
Georgia State U . . . . GA
Greater Hartford Comm. Coll . . . CT
Green Mountain Coll . . . . VT
Harper Coll IL
Highline Comm. C . . . . WA
Hocking Tech. Coll . . . . OH
Indiana Voc. Tech. Coll. (Evansville, Fort Wayne, Indianapolis, Terre Haute) . . . . IN
Iowa Western . . . . IA
Jefferson Tech . . . . OH
Kalamazoo Valley . . . . MI
Kapiolani Comm. Coll . . . . HI
Lasell Jr. Coll . . . . MA
Long Beach City Coll . . . . CA
Middlesex Comm. Coll . . . . MA
Millersville State . . . . PA
Minnesota, Med. Inst. of . . . . MN
Modesto Junior Coll . . . . CA
Montgomery Coll . . . . MD
Morehead State U . . . . KY
Mt. Ida Jr. Coll . . . . MA
Muskingum Area Tech . . . . OH
Normandale Comm. Coll . . . . . . MN
North Seattle Comm. Coll . . . . . WA
Northeast Mississippi Jr. Coll . . MS
Ohlone Coll . . . . CA
Orange Coast . . . . CA
Parks Coll . . . . CO
Pasadena City Coll . . . . CA
Philadelphia, C. Coll. of . . . . PA
Portland Comm . . . . OR
Robert Morris Coll IL
San Diego Mesa . . . . CA
San Francisco, City Coll. of . . . . . CA
Shasta Coll . . . . CA
South Carolina, Medical U. of . . . SC
Southeastern Comm . . . . IA
Southern Ohio Coll . . . . OH
Springfield Tech . . . . MA
Stark Tech . . . . OH
Toledo, U. of . . . . OH
Tri-County Tech. Coll . . . . SC
Triton Coll IL
Tulsa Jr. Coll . . . . OK
West Valley Coll . . . . CA
Westbrook . . . . ME
Western Piedmont . . . . NC
Wingate Coll . . . . NC

Medical Illustration

Beaver Coll . . . . PA
Bridgewater State . . . . MA
Illinois, U. of IL
Michigan, U. of . . . . MI
Ohio State . . . . OH
Purdue U . . . . IN
Salem Coll . . . . WV
Springfield Coll . . . . MA
Thiel . . . . PA

Medical Laboratory Technician

Associate degree programs approved by the National Accrediting Agency for Clinical Laboratory Sciences and the American Medical Association in collaboration with the American Society of Clinical Pathologists and American Society for Medical Technology

Albany Jr. Coll . . . . GA
Allegheny C. Coll . . . . MD
Allegheny Co., Comm. Coll. of . . PA
Arapahoe Comm. Coll . . . . CO
Asheville-Buncombe Tech. Inst NC
Atlantic Comm. Coll . . . . NJ
Belleville Area Coll IL
Bergen Comm. Coll . . . . NJ
Bismarck Jr . . . . ND
Brevard Comm. Coll . . . . FL
Brookdale Comm. Coll . . . . NJ
Broward Comm. Coll . . . . FL
Brunswick Jr . . . . GA
Central Methodist Coll . . . . MO
Chesapeake Coll . . . . MD
Cleveland State Comm. Coll . . . . TN
Coastal Carolina C. Coll . . . . NC
Columbia Union Coll . . . . MD
Columbus Tech. Inst . . . . OH
CUNY (Coll. of Staten Island) . . . NY
Cuyahoga Comm. Coll . . . . OH
Dakota Wesleyan U . . . . SD
Dalton Jr. Coll . . . . GA
DeKalb Comm. Coll . . . . GA
Delaware Tech. and Comm. Coll . . . . DE
Des Moines Area Comm. Coll . . . IA
District One Tech. Inst . . . . WI
Eastern Maine Voc-Tech . . . . ME
Erie Comm. Coll . . . . NY
Essex C. Coll . . . . MD
Ferris State Coll . . . . MI
Florida Inst. of Tech . . . . FL
Forest Park Comm. Coll . . . . MO
Grayson C. Comm. Coll . . . . TX
Greenville Tech. Coll . . . . SC
Gwynedd-Mercy Coll . . . . PA
Hahnemann Med. Coll . . . . PA
Hinds Jr. Coll . . . . MS
Housatonic Comm. Coll . . . . CT
Houston Comm. Coll . . . . TX
Illinois Central IL
Indiana U . . . . IN
Indiana Voc.-Tech. Coll. (Indianapolis) . . . . IN
Jackson State Comm. Coll . . . . . . TN
Jefferson State Jr . . . . AL
Jefferson Tech. Coll . . . . OH
Kettering Coll. of Med. Arts . . . . OH
Lake Co., Coll. of IL
Lake Michigan Coll . . . . MI
Lakeland Comm. Coll . . . . OH
Laredo Jr. Coll . . . . TX
Lewis and Clark Comm. Coll IL
Macomb Co. Comm. Coll . . . . MI
Maine, U. of . . . . ME
Mankato State U . . . . MN
Mercer C. Comm. Coll . . . . NJ
Mercy Coll . . . . MI
Miami-Dade Jr. Coll . . . . FL
Midland Tech. Coll . . . . SC
Midway Coll . . . . KY
Midwestern U . . . . TX
Milwaukee Area Tech. Coll . . . . . WI
Mississippi Gulf Coast Jr. Coll . MS
Montgomery Coll . . . . MD
Moraine Valley Comm. Coll IL
New Hampshire Voc-Tech . . . . . NH
New Mexico State U . . . . NM
North Shore Comm. Coll . . . . . . MA
Northampton Co. Area Comm. Coll . . . . PA
Northern Michigan U . . . . MI
Northern Virginia Comm. Coll . . . . VA
Oakton Comm. Coll IL
Orange County C. Coll . . . . NY
Orangeburg-Calhoun Tech. Coll . . . . SC
Oscar Rose Jr. Coll . . . . OK
Parkersburg Comm. Coll . . . . . . WV
Philadelphia, Comm. Coll. of . . . . PA
Phoenix Coll . . . . AZ
Presentation Coll . . . . SD
Reading Area C. Coll . . . . PA
Rio Grande Coll . . . . OH
Rivier Coll . . . . NH
Rockland C. Coll . . . . NY
Sandhills Comm. Coll . . . . NC
Sauk Valley Coll IL
Schoolcraft Coll . . . . MI
Shawnee State Coll . . . . OH
Shoreline C. Coll . . . . WA
South Carolina, Med. U. of . . . . . SC
Southeastern C. Coll . . . . KY
Spartanburg Tech. Coll . . . . SC
Springfield Tech. C. Coll . . . . . . MA
St. Mary's Jr. Coll . . . . MN
St. Petersburg Jr . . . . FL
State U. of New York (A&T Coll. at Alfred) . . . . NY
Tarrant Co. Jr. Coll . . . . TX
Tri-County Tech. Coll . . . . SC
Tulsa Jr. Coll . . . . OK
Union Co. Tech. Inst . . . . NJ
Vermont, U. of . . . . VT
Vermont Coll . . . . VT
Villa Julie . . . . MD
Wallace State Comm. Coll . . . . . . AL
Weber State . . . . UT
West Virginia Northern C. Coll . . . . WV
Western Piedmont Comm. Coll. NC
Western Wisconsin Tech. Inst . . . WI
Wytheville Comm. Coll . . . . VA
York Tech. Coll . . . . SC

Medical Physicist

Bennett Coll . . . . NC
Chipola Jr. Coll . . . . FL
Cornell U . . . . NY
Illinois Inst. of Tech IL
Wilkes Coll . . . . PA

Medical Record Administrator

College programs approved by the Council on Medical Education of the American Medical Association and the American Medical Record Association

Alabama, U. of (Birmingham) . . . AL
Alderson-Broaddus . . . . WV
Arkansas Tech. U . . . . AR
Avila Coll . . . . MO
Bridgeport, U. of . . . . CT
California, U. of (Los Angeles) . . CA
Carroll Coll . . . . MT
Central Florida, U. of . . . . FL
Chicago State U IL
Daemen Coll . . . . NY
East Carolina U . . . . NC
East Central Oklahoma State . . OK
Eastern Kentucky U . . . . KY
Emory U . . . . GA
Ferris State Coll . . . . MI
Florida International U . . . . FL
Georgia, Med. Coll. of . . . . GA
Golden Gate U . . . . CA
Illinois, U. of IL
Illinois State U IL
Incarnate Word Coll . . . . TX
Indiana U . . . . IN
Ithaca Coll . . . . NY
Kansas, U. of . . . . KS
Loma Linda U . . . . CA
Louisiana Tech . . . . LA
Mercy Coll . . . . MI
Mississippi, U. of . . . . MS
Northeastern U . . . . MA
Ohio State . . . . OH
Pittsburgh, U. of . . . . PA
Puerto Rico, U. of . . . . PR
Regis Coll . . . . CO
Seattle U . . . . WA
South Carolina, Med. Coll. of . . . SC
Southwest Texas State . . . . TX
Southwestern Louisiana, U. of . . LA
Southwestern Oklahoma State . OK
St. Louis U . . . . MO
St. Mary, Coll. of . . . . NE
St. Scholastica, Coll. of . . . . MN
State U. of New York (Downstate Med. Ctr.) . . . . NY
Stephens Coll . . . . MO
Temple U . . . . PA
Tennessee, U. of (Memphis) . . . . TN
Tennessee State . . . . TN
Texas, U. of, Med. Branch (Galveston) . . . . TX
Texas Woman's U . . . . TX
Tulsa, U. of . . . . OK
Virginia Commonwealth . . . . VA
Viterbo Coll . . . . WI
Western Carolina U . . . . NC
Wisconsin, U. of (Milwaukee) . . . WI

Medical Record Librarian

Alabama, U. of . . . . AL
Alfred State . . . . NY
Arkansas Tech . . . . AR
Avila . . . . MO
Bowling Green State . . . . OH
Carroll Coll . . . . MT
Carson-Newman Coll . . . . TN
Case Western . . . . OH
Central Missouri . . . . MO
Christian Brothers . . . . TN
Clark Coll . . . . GA
Colby-Sawyer Coll . . . . NH
Colorado Women's Coll . . . . CO
Daemen . . . . NY
East Carolina U . . . . NC
East Central Oklahoma . . . . OK
Eastern Kentucky U . . . . KY
Emory U . . . . GA
Ferris State . . . . MI
Florida Tech. U . . . . FL
Georgia, Med. Coll. of . . . . GA
Gwynedd-Mercy . . . . PA
Howard Co. Jr . . . . TX
Hutchinson Comm. Coll . . . . KS
Illinois, U. of IL
Illinois Central Coll IL
Illinois State U IL
Incarnate Word . . . . TX
Ithaca Coll . . . . NY
Kansas, U. of . . . . KS
Kean Coll . . . . NJ
Loma Linda U . . . . CA
Louisiana Tech . . . . LA
Marymount Coll . . . . KS
Mercy Coll . . . . MI
Miami U . . . . OH
Mississippi, U. of . . . . MS
Mississippi Delta Jr. Coll . . . . . . MS
Mount St. Joseph . . . . OH
Northeast Mississippi Jr . . . . MS

Northeastern U . . . . MA
Ohio State U . . . . OH
Pittsburgh, U. of (Bradford) . . . . PA
Purdue U . . . . IN
Seattle U . . . . WA
South Carolina, Med. Coll. of . . . SC
South Georgia Coll . . . . GA
Southwest Texas State U . . . . TX
Southwestern Louisiana, U. of . . LA
Southwestern Oklahoma State . OK
St. Louis U . . . . MO
St. Mary . . . . NE
St. Mary's Jr . . . . MN
St. Scholastica . . . . MN
State U. of New York (Coll. of Tech., Downstate Med. Ctr.) . . NY
Temple U . . . . PA
Tennessee, U. of . . . . TN
Texas, U. of . . . . TX
Toledo, U. of . . . . OH
Tulsa, U. of . . . . OK
Viterbo Coll . . . . WI
Wayne State . . . . MI
Western Carolina U . . . . NC
Wichita State U . . . . KS
Wisconsin, U. of (Milwaukee) . . . WI
York Coll . . . . PA

Medical Record Technician

College programs accredited by Council on Medical Education of the American Medical Association and American Medical Record Association

Alabama, U. of (Birmingham) . . . AL
Allegheny Co., Comm. Coll. of . . PA
Amarillo Coll . . . . TX
Arapahoe Comm. Coll . . . . CO
Armstrong State Coll . . . . GA
Avila Coll . . . . MO
Baltimore, Comm. Coll of . . . . MD
Belleville Area Coll IL
Boise State U . . . . ID
Bowling Green State U . . . . OH
Broome Comm. Coll . . . . NY
Central Oregon . . . . OR
Central Piedmont Comm. Coll . NC
Central Virginia . . . . VA
Central YMCA Comm IL
Chabot Coll . . . . CA
Chattanooga State Tech. Comm. Coll . . . . TN
Cincinnati Tech . . . . OH
Colegio Universitario Metropolitano . . . . PR
Cuyahoga Comm . . . . OH
Cypress Coll . . . . CA
Dakota State Coll . . . . SD
District One Tech . . . . WI
East Los Angeles Coll . . . . CA
Eastern Kentucky U . . . . KY
Fairmont State Coll . . . . WV
Ferris State . . . . MI
Gwynedd-Mercy Coll . . . . PA
Hinds Jr. Coll . . . . MS
Hocking Tech. Coll . . . . OH
Holyoke Comm. Coll . . . . MA
Hutchinson Comm. Jr. Coll . . . . KS
Indiana U. (Northwest) . . . . IN
Indiana U. (Sch. of Med.) . . . . IN
Lake County, Coll. of IL
Manhattan Comm. Coll . . . . NY
Massachusetts Bay Comm . . . . MA
Mercy Coll . . . . MI
Meridian Jr. Coll . . . . MS
Miami-Dade Jr. Coll . . . . FL
Monroe Comm. Coll . . . . NY
Moraine Park Tech. Inst . . . . WI
Moraine Valley Comm. Coll IL
New Hampshire Voc-Tech. Coll . . . . NH
Northern Essex Comm. Coll . . . MA
Northern Virginia Comm . . . . VA
Oakton Comm IL
Philadelphia, Comm. Coll. of . . . . PA
Phoenix Coll . . . . AZ
Portland Comm. Coll . . . . OR
Prince George's Comm. Coll . . . MD
Roane State Comm . . . . TN
Rochester Inst. of Tech . . . . NY
Rockland Comm. Coll . . . . NY
San Diego Mesa Coll . . . . CA
San Francisco, City Coll. of . . . . CA
Schoolcraft Coll . . . . MI
Shoreline Comm. Coll . . . . WA
Sinclair Comm. Coll . . . . OH
Spokane Comm. Coll . . . . WA
St. Mary's Jr. Coll . . . . MN
St. Philips Coll . . . . TX
Stark Tech. Coll . . . . OH
State U. of New York (Alfred) . . . NY
Tacoma Comm. Coll . . . . WA
Tarrant Co. Jr. Coll . . . . TX
Temple Jr . . . . TX
Union Co. Tech. Inst . . . . NJ
Volunteer State Comm. Coll . . . . TN
Wallace State Comm. Coll . . . . AL
Wayne Co. Comm. Coll . . . . MI
West Valley Coll . . . . CA
Western Kentucky U . . . . KY
Western Wisconsin Tech . . . . WI
Wharton Co. Jr . . . . TX

Medical Schools

Schools accredited by the Liaison Committee on Medical Education sponsored jointly by the American Medical Association and the Association of American Medical Colleges

Alabama, U. of (Birmingham) . . . AL
Albany Medical Coll. of Union U . . . . NY
Arizona, U. of . . . . AZ
Arkansas, U. of . . . . AR
Baylor . . . . TX
Boston U . . . . MA
Brown U . . . . RI
California, U. of (Davis, Irvine, Los Angeles, San Diego, San Francisco) . . . . CA
Case Western Reserve U . . . . OH
Central del Caribe Escuela de Medicina de Cayey . . . . PR
Chicago, U. of IL
Chicago Medical Sch IL
Cincinnati, U. of . . . . OH
Colorado, U. of . . . . CO
Columbia . . . . NY
Connecticut, U. of . . . . CT
Cornell . . . . NY
Creighton . . . . NE
CUNY (Mt. Sinai Sch. of Med.) . . NY
Dartmouth Medical Sch . . . . NH
Duke . . . . NC
East Carolina U . . . . NC
East Tennessee State U . . . . TN
Eastern Virginia Medical Sch . . . VA
Emory . . . . GA
Florida, U. of . . . . FL
George Washington . . . . DC
Georgetown . . . . DC
Georgia, Medical Coll. of . . . . GA
Hahnemann Medical Coll . . . . PA
Harvard . . . . MA
Hawaii, U. of . . . . HI
Howard . . . . DC
Illinois, U. of IL
Indiana U . . . . IN
Iowa, U. of . . . . IA
Johns Hopkins . . . . MD
Kansas, U. of . . . . KS
Kentucky, U. of . . . . KY
Loma Linda U . . . . CA
Louisiana State U. (New Orleans, Shreveport) . . . . LA
Louisville, U. of . . . . KY
Loyola IL
Marshall U . . . . WV
Maryland, U. of . . . . MD
Massachusetts, U. of . . . . MA
Mayo Medical Sch . . . . MN
Medical Coll. of Pennsylvania . . . PA
Medical U. of South Carolina . . . SC
Meharry Medical Coll . . . . TN
Miami, U. of . . . . FL
Michigan, U. of . . . . MI
Michigan State U . . . . MI
Minnesota, U. of (Duluth) . . . . MN
Minnesota, U. of (Minneapolis) . MN
Mississippi, U. of . . . . MS
Missouri, U. of (Columbia, Kansas City) . . . . MO
Morehouse Coll . . . . GA
Nebraska, U. of . . . . NE
Nevada, U. of . . . . NV
New Jersey Medical School . . . . NJ
New Mexico U. of . . . . NM
New York Medical Coll . . . . NY
New York U . . . . NY
North Carolina, U. of . . . . NC
North Dakota, U. of . . . . ND
Northeastern Ohio U . . . . OH
Northwestern IL
Ohio, Medical Coll. of . . . . OH
Ohio State U . . . . OH
Oklahoma, U. of . . . . OK
Oral Roberts U . . . . OK
Oregon, U. of . . . . OR
Pennsylvania, U. of . . . . PA
Pennsylvania State U . . . . PA
Pittsburgh, U. of . . . . PA
Ponce School of Medicine . . . . PR
Puerto Rico, U. of . . . . PR
Rochester, U. of . . . . NY
Rush Medical Coll IL
Rutgers Medical School . . . . NJ
South Alabama, U. of . . . . AL
South Carolina, U. of . . . . SC
South Dakota, U. of . . . . SD
South Florida, U. of . . . . FL
Southern California, U. of . . . . CA
Southern Illinois IL
St. Louis U . . . . MO
Stanford . . . . CA
State U. of New York (Buffalo, Downstate Med. Ctr., Stony Brook, Upstate Med. Ctr.) . . . . NY
Temple . . . . PA
Tennessee, U. of . . . . TN
Texas, U. of (Dallas, Galveston, Houston, San Antonio) . . . . TX
Texas A&M U . . . . TX
Texas Tech. U . . . . TX
Thomas Jefferson U . . . . PA
Tufts . . . . MA
Tulane . . . . LA
Uniformed Services U . . . . MD
Utah, U. of . . . . UT
Vanderbilt . . . . TN
Vermont, U. of . . . . VT
Virginia, U. of . . . . VA
Virginia Commonwealth U . . . . VA
Wake Forest (Bowman Gray) . . NC
Washington, U. of . . . . WA
Washington U . . . . MO
Wayne State U . . . . MI
West Virginia U . . . . WV
Wisconsin, Med. Coll. of . . . . WI
Wisconsin, U. of (Madison) . . . . WI
Wright State U . . . . OH
Yale . . . . CT
Yeshiva (Albert Einstein) . . . . NY

Medical Schools—Accelerated Programs

•Indicates program is limited to students entering from high school

•Albany Med. Coll . . . . NY
Baylor Coll. of Medicine . . . . TX
•Boston U . . . . MA
Brown U. (for its undergraduates only) . . . . RI
California, U. of (at Irvine) . . . . CA
Howard U. (for its undergraduates only) . . . . DC
Johns Hopkins U . . . . MD
•Louisiana State U. (Shreveport) (Louisiana residents only) . . . . LA
Medical Coll. of Pennsylvania (programs with Lehigh U. and Bryn Mawr Coll.) . . . . PA
Miami, U. of . . . . FL
•Michigan, U. of (for its undergraduates only) . . . . MI
•Missouri, U. of (Kansas City) (available primarily to residents of Missouri) . . . . MO
New York, State U. of at Stonybrook (only students from Sophie-Davis BW-Med. Science program) . . . . NY
Northeastern Ohio U . . . . OH
Ohio State U . . . . OH
Texas A&M U . . . . TX
Wisconsin, Medical Coll. of . . . . WI
•Wisconsin, U. of, at Madison . . . . WI

Medical Technology

Affiliated in a degree program in medical technology with Schools of Medical Technology that are approved by the American Medical Association's Council on Medical Education in cooperation with the American Society of Clinical Pathologists and American Society for Medical Technology

Abilene Christian . . . . TX
Adams State Coll . . . . CO
Adelphi . . . . NY
Akron, U. of . . . . OH
Alabama, U. of (Birmingham) . . . AL
Albany Coll. of Pharmacy . . . . NY
Albion . . . . MI
Albright . . . . PA
Alderson-Broaddus . . . . WV
Alma . . . . MI
American International . . . . MA
American U . . . . DC
Anderson . . . . IN
Andrews U . . . . MI
Angelo State . . . . TX
Anna Maria Coll . . . . MA
Appalachian State . . . . NC
Aquinas . . . . MA
Arizona, U. of . . . . AZ
Arizona State U . . . . AZ
Arkansas, U. of (Little Rock) . . . . AR
Arkansas, State Coll. of . . . . AR
Arkansas Poly. Coll . . . . AR
Arkansas State U . . . . AR
Arkansas Tech U . . . . AR
Armstrong State . . . . GA
Asbury Coll . . . . KY
Ashland . . . . OH
Atlantic Christian Coll . . . . NC
Auburn U . . . . AL
Augsburg . . . . MN
Augusta . . . . GA
Augustana IL
Augustana . . . . SD

Northern Missouri State .... MO
Northern State Coll .... SD
Northwest Nazarene .... ID
Northwestern Coll .... IA
Northwestern State U .... LA
Northwestern U IL
Notre Dame .... MO
Oakland U .... MI
Oakwood .... AL
Ohio Northern U .... OH
Ohio State U .... OH
Ohio U .... OH
Oklahoma, U. of .... OK
Oklahoma, U. of, Sci. and Arts . OK
Oklahoma Baptist .... OK
Oklahoma Christian .... OK
Oklahoma City U .... OK
Oklahoma Panhandle State Coll OK
Oklahoma State U .... OK
Old Dominion U .... VA
Oregon, U. of .... OR
Oregon Tech. Inst .... OR
Otterbein .... OH
Ouachita Baptist U .... AR
Our Lady of the Elms .... MA
Ozarks, Coll. of the .... AR
Ozarks, Sch. of the .... MO
Pace .... NY
Pan American U .... TX
Panama Canal Coll .... Balboa
Panhandle State U .... OK
Pembroke State U .... NC
Pennsylvania Medical Coll ...... PA
Pennsylvania State U .... PA
Philadelphia Coll .... PA
Philander Smith .... AR
Phillips .... OK
Pikeville Coll .... KY
Pittsburg State U .... KS
Pittsburgh, U. of .... PA
Point Park Coll .... PA
Prairie View .... TX
Presbyterian Coll .... SC
Princeton U .... NJ
Puerto Rico, Catholic U. of ..... PR
Puerto Rico, U. of .... PR
Purdue .... IN
Quincy IL
Quinnipiac .... CT
Radford U .... VA
Randolph Macon .... VA
Regis .... CO
Regis Coll .... MA
Rhode Island, U. of .... RI
Rhode Island Coll .... RI
Rochester Inst. of Tech .... NY
Rockford Coll IL
Rockhurst .... MO
Roosevelt IL
Russell Sage .... NY
Rust Coll .... MS
Rutgers .... NJ
Saginaw Valley .... MI
Salem .... NC
Salisbury State .... MD
Salve Regina Coll .... RI
Sam Houston State .... TX
San Francisco State U .... CA
Sangamon State U IL
Savannah State .... GA
Scranton, U. of .... PA
Seattle U .... WA
Seton Hall .... NJ
Seton Hill .... PA
Shippensburg State Coll .... PA
Siena Heights .... MI
Simpson Coll .... IA
Slippery Rock .... PA
South Alabama, U. of .... AL
South Carolina, Med. U. of ...... SC
South Dakota, U. of .... SD
South Dakota State .... SD
Southeastern Louisiana .... LA
Southeastern Massachusetts U . MA
Southeastern Missouri State ... MO
Southeastern Oklahoma .... OK
Southern Colorado, U. of ...... CO
Southern Florida, U. of .... FL
Southern Illinois U IL
Southern Missionary Coll .... TN
Southern Mississippi, U. of .... MS
Southern U .... LA
Southwest Adventist Coll ...... TX
Southwest Baptist Coll .... MO
Southwest Texas State .... TX
Southwestern .... KS
Southwestern Louisiana, U. of .. LA
Southwestern Oklahoma State U .... OK
Southwestern State U .... MN
Southwestern State U .... OK
Spring Garden .... PA
Springfield .... MA
St. Andrews Presbyterian Coll . NC
St. Augustines Coll .... NC
St. Benedict, Coll. of .... MN
St. Cloud State Coll .... MN
St. Edward's U .... TX
St. Francis .... IN
St. Francis, Coll. of IL
St. John's U .... NY
St. Joseph .... CT
St. Joseph's Coll .... IN
St. Leo Coll .... FL
St. Louis U .... MO
St. Mary .... MN
St. Mary, Coll. of .... NE
St. Mary of the Plains .... KS
St. Mary-of-the-Woods .... IN
St. Mary's .... IN
St. Mary's Dominican Coll ...... LA
St. Norbert .... WI
St. Scholastica, Coll. of .... MN
St. Thomas Aquinas .... NY
St. Vincent Coll .... PA
State U. of New York (Albany, Buffalo, Fredonia, Plattsburgh, Stony Brook, Syracuse, Upstate Med. Ctr.) .... NY
Staten Island, Coll. of .... NY
Stephen F. Austin State Coll .... TX
Sterling .... KS
Stetson U .... FL
Steubenville, Coll. of .... OH
Stonehill Coll .... MA
Suffolk U .... MA
Tabor Coll .... KS
Tarleton State U .... TX
Taylor U .... IN
Temple .... PA
Tennessee, U. of .... TN
Tennessee A&I .... TN
Tennessee State U .... TN
Tennessee Tech. U .... TN
Tennessee Wesleyan .... TN
Texas, U. of (Arlington, Austin, Dallas, El Paso, Galveston, Houston, San Antonio, Tyler) .... TX
Texas A&I .... TX
Texas Christian .... TX
Texas Lutheran Coll .... TX
Texas Southern U .... TX
Texas Tech. U .... TX
Texas Wesleyan Coll .... TX
Texas Woman's .... TX
Thiel .... PA
Thomas Jefferson .... PA
Thomas More Coll .... KY
Toledo, U. of .... OH
Tougaloo Coll .... MS
Towson State Coll .... MD
Trevecca Nazarene .... TN
Trinity .... DC
Trinity IL
Trinity .... VT
Trinity Christian IL
Troy State U .... AL
Tulsa, U. of .... OK
Tusculum .... TN
Tuskegee Inst .... AL
Union Coll .... KY
Union U .... TN
Utah, U. of .... UT
Utah State U .... UT
Utica Coll .... NY
Valparaiso U .... IN
Vanderbilt .... TN
Vermont, U. of .... VT
Vermont Coll .... VT
Villa Maria .... PA
Virgin Islands, Coll. of VI
Virginia, Medical Coll. of .... VA
Virginia, U. of .... VA
Virginia Intermont .... VA
Viterbo .... WI
Wagner .... NY
Wake Forest .... NC
Wartburg .... IA
Washburn .... KS
Washington, U. of .... WA
Washington and Jefferson ...... PA
Washington State U .... WA
Wayne State U .... MI
Waynesburg Coll .... PA
Weber State Coll .... UT
Wesley Coll .... DE
West Florida, U. of .... FL
West Liberty State .... WV
West Texas State U .... TX
West Virginia U .... WV
Westbrook Coll .... ME
Western Carolina U .... NC
Western Connecticut State ...... CT
Western Illinois U IL
Western Kentucky U .... KY
Western Michigan U .... MI
Westmar .... IA
Wheeling Coll .... WV
Wichita State U .... KS
Wilkes .... PA
William Jewell .... MO
William Woods .... MO
Wilson .... PA
Winona State Coll .... MN
Winston-Salem .... NC
Winthrop Coll .... SC
Wisconsin, U. of (Eau Claire, La Crosse, Madison, Milwaukee, Oshkosh, Parkside, Platteville, River Falls, Stevens Point, Superior, Whitewater) .... WI
Wright State U .... OH
Wyoming, U. of .... WY
Xavier U .... OH
York Coll. (CUNY) .... NY
Youngstown State U .... OH

Mentally Handicapped, Preparation for Teaching of

Abilene Christian .... TX
Akron, U. of .... OH
Alabama A&M .... AL
Alderson-Broaddus Coll .... WV
Arizona State .... AZ
Auburn U .... AL
Augustana Coll .... SD
Averett Coll .... VA
Ball State U .... IN
Baruch Coll .... NY
Beaver Coll .... PA
Belmont Abbey Coll .... NC
Bennett Coll .... NC
Bluffton Coll .... OH
Bowling Green State .... OH
Brenau Coll .... GA
Brevard Coll .... NC
Bridgewater State .... MA
Butler .... IN
California State Coll .... PA
California State U. (Los Angeles) CA
Calvin Coll .... MI
Cardinal Stritch .... WI
Carthage Coll .... WI
Central Arkansas, U. of .... AR
Central Michigan U .... MI
Central Missouri .... MO
Central Wesleyan .... SC
Chadron .... NE
Charleston, U. of .... WV
Cincinnati, U. of .... OH
Clarion State .... PA
Cleveland State .... OH
Coker Coll .... SC
Colorado Mountain Coll. (West) .... CO
Columbus Coll .... GA
Coppin State Coll .... MD
Daemen Coll .... NY
Delta State U .... MS
Denver, U. of .... CO
Drake U .... IA
East Carolina .... NC
East Texas State U .... TX
Eastern Kentucky U .... KY
Eastern Montana Coll .... MT
Eastern New Mexico .... NM
Eastern Washington U .... WA
Emporia State U .... KS
Evansville, U. of .... IN
Felician .... NJ
Findlay Coll .... OH
Flagler Coll .... FL
Florida Atlantic .... FL
Florida International U .... FL
Florida State U .... FL
Fontbonne Coll .... MO
Fort Hays State .... KS
Georgia Coll .... GA
Georgia State .... GA
Goddard Coll .... VT
Hampton Inst .... VA
Harding U .... AR
Hartford, U. of .... CT
Hastings Coll .... NE
Hawaii, U. of (Honolulu) .... HI
Henderson State U .... AR
Huntingdon Coll .... AL
Huron Coll .... SD
Indiana U .... PA
Iowa, U. of .... IA
Jacksonville State .... AL
James Madison U .... VA
John Carroll U .... OH
Kansas, U. of .... KS
Kansas State U .... KS
Kearney State .... NE
Keene State .... NH
Kent State .... OH
Kutztown State .... PA
La Salle Coll .... PA
Lincoln Coll IL
Lindenwood Colleges .... MO
Lock Haven State .... PA
Lynchburg Coll .... VA
Maine, U. of (Farmington) ..... ME
Manchester Coll .... IN
Mansfield State .... PA
Marian .... IN
Mary Hardin-Baylor, U. of ...... TX
Marymount Coll .... NY
Marymount Coll of Virginia ..... VA
Maryville State .... ND
Marywood .... PA
Michigan State U .... MI
Midland Coll .... NE
Mississippi Coll .... MS
Missouri, U. of .... MO
Monmouth Coll .... NJ
Moorhead State .... MN
Morehead State .... KY
Mt. St. Joseph, Coll. of .... OH
Nazareth Coll .... NY
Nebraska Wesleyan .... NE

Nevada, U. of .... NV
Nicholls State .... LA
North Carolina, U. of (Wilmington) .... NC
North Carolina Cent. U .... NC
North Florida, U. of............. FL
Northeast Missouri State College .... MO
Northeastern Illinois IL
Northeastern Oklahoma .... OK
Northern Colorado .... CO
Northern Iowa, U. of .... IA
Northwestern Oklahoma State .... OK
Northwestern State U .... LA
Notre Dame................... OH
Ohio State .... OH
Ohio U. (Athens) .... OH
Oklahoma State U............. OK
Old Dominion U .... VA
Ozarks, Sch.of the............. MO
Pacific, U. of the .... CA
Pennsylvania State U. (Allentown, University Park) .... PA
Plymouth State .... NH
Puerto Rico, U. of .... PR
Radford U .... VA
Rhode Island Coll .... RI
Rivier Coll .... NH
Saint Mary-of-the-Woods .... IN
Slippery Rock State .... PA
South Carolina, U. of .... SC
South Dakota, U. of .... SD
South Florida, U. of .... FL
Southeast Missouri .... MO
Southern Illinois U IL
Southwest Missouri .... MO
Southwest Texas State .... TX
St. Francis Coll .... IN
St. Leo Coll .... FL
St. Rose, The Coll. of........... NY
State U. of New York (Plattsburgh)................ NY
State U. of N.Y. Coll. (Buffalo).................... NY
Steubenville, U. of............. OH
Syracuse U .... NY
Tennessee, U. of (Martin) .... TN
Texas, U. of (Dallas, El Paso) ... TX
Texas A&I .... TX
Texas Woman's U .... TX
Tift Coll .... GA
Toledo, U. of................... OH
Trenton State Coll............. NJ
Trevecca Nazarene .... TN
Trinity .... VT
Trinity Christian................ IL
Tulsa, U. of .... OK
Tusculum Coll .... TN
Valparaiso U .... IN
Walsh Coll .... OH
Wayne State .... MI
Webster Coll .... MO
West Florida, U. of .... FL
West Texas State.............. TX
West Virginia State .... WV
West Virginia Wesleyan .... WV
William Woods Coll .... MO
Winona State U .... MN
Wisconsin, U. of (Milwaukee, Whitewater) .... WI
Wittenberg U .... OH
Xavier U .... OH
Youngstown State .... OH

Merchandising, *See* RETAILING

Merchant Marine and Maritime

California Maritime Acad .... CA
Massachusetts Maritime Acad .. MA
State U. Maritime Coll .... NY

Metal and Foundry Work

Angelina Coll .... TX
California State Coll .... PA
Kansas City Art Inst .... MO
Mississippi Delta Jr. Coll ...... MS
Northeastern Oklahoma State .. OK
Northern Montana Coll .... MT
Southwest Missouri .... MO
Wisconsin, U. of (Superior) ..... WI

Metal Smithing

Beaver Coll .... PA
Boston U .... MA
Philadelphia Coll. of Art .... PA
Seton Hill Coll .... PA
State U. of New York (New Paltz) .... NY
Temple U .... PA
Washington U................. MO

Metallurgical Engineering, *See* ENGINEERING, METALLURGICAL

Metallurgy

Carnegie-Mellon .... PA
Case Western .... OH
Colorado Sch. of Mines........ CO
Cornell U .... NY
Drexel U .... PA
Florida, U. of................... FL
Idaho, U. of .... ID
Illinois, U. of (Chicago) IL
Miami U .... OH
Michigan State U.............. MI
Michigan Tech U .... MI
Nebraska, U. of .... NE
Ohio State U.................. OH
Pennsylvania, U. of............ PA
Pennsylvania State U .... PA
Texas, U. of (Austin) .... TX
Wayne State U .... MI
Wisconsin, U. of (Madison) ..... WI
Youngstown State............ OH

Metallurgy Engineering, *See* ENGINEERING, METALLURGY

Metals Engineering, *See* ENGINEERING, METALS

Meteorology

Undergraduate degree programs according to the American Meteorological Society

Alaska, U. of .... AK
California, U. of (Davis, Los Angeles) .... CA
California State U. (Northridge) .... CA
Chicago, U. of IL
City Coll. of City U. of New York .... NY
Columbia U .... NY
Cornell U .... NY
Delaware, U. of .... DE
Denver, U. of .... CO
Florida Inst. of Tech .... FL
Florida State U .... FL
Hawaii, U. of .... HI
Iowa State U .... IA
Jackson State U .... MS
Johns Hopkins U.............. MD
Kansas, U. of .... KS
Kean Coll .... NJ
Lincoln Coll IL
Lowell, U. of .... MA
Lyndon State Coll .... VT
Metropolitan State Coll .... CO
Michigan, U. of................ MI
Minnesota, U.of .... MN
Missouri, U. of (Columbia) ..... MO
Montana State U .... MT
Nebraska, U. of .... NE
New Mexico Inst. of Mining and Tech .... NM
North Carolina, U. of (Chapel Hill, Charlotte) .... NC
North Carolina State U .... NC
Northeast Louisiana U .... LA
Northern Arizona U .... AZ
Northern Illinois U IL
Oklahoma, U. of .... OK
Oregon State U .... OR
Park Coll .... MO
Pennsylvania State U .... PA
Plymouth State Coll .... NH
Purdue U .... IN
Rhode Island, U. of............ RI
Rutgers U..................... NJ
Saint Louis U .... MO
Saint Thomas, U. of .... TX
San Jose State U.............. CA
South Dakota School of Mines and Technology............. SD
Southern Illinois U IL
State U. of New York (Albany, Brockport, Maritime Coll., Oneonta, Oswego) .... NY
Texas, U. of (Austin) .... TX
Texas A&M U .... TX
U.S. Air Force Acad .... CO
U.S. Naval Acad.............. MD
U.S. Coast Guard Acad .... CT
Utah, U. of.................... UT
Virginia, U. of .... VA
Washington, U. of .... WA
Wisconsin, U. of (Milwaukee) ... WI
Yale U .... CT

Microbiology

Akron, U. of .... OH
Alabama, U. of .... AL
Alderson-Broaddus............ WV
American U .... DC
Arizona, U. of .... AZ
Arizona State U .... AZ
Auburn U .... AL
Boston U .... MA
Bowling Green .... OH
Brigham Young .... UT
Butler U .... IN
California, U. of (Davis, Irvine, Los Angeles, San Diego, Santa Barbara) .... CA
California Poly. State .... CA
California State Poly. (Pomona) .... CA
California State U. (Chico, Fresno, Long Beach, Los Angeles) .... CA
Central Florida, U. of .... FL
Cincinnati, U. of .... OH
Colorado, U. of .... CO
Colorado State U .... CO
Connecticut, U. of............. CT
Cornell U .... NY
East Tennessee State........... TN
Eastern Kentucky U .... KY
Eastern Michigan U .... MI
Eastern Washington U .... WA
Florida, U. of.................. FL
Florida Atlantic U .... FL
Florida Tech. U .... FL
Georgia, U. of................. GA
Goddard Coll .... VT
Hawaii, U. of .... HI
Howard U.................... DC
Idaho State U .... ID
Illinois, U. of IL
Illinois Central Coll............. IL
Illinois Inst. of Tech IL
Indiana State U .... IN
Indiana U. (Bloomington) .... IN
Iowa, U. of .... IA
Iowa State U .... IA
Kansas, U. of .... KS
Kansas State U................ KS
Kentucky, U. of .... KY
Knox Coll IL
La Salle Coll .... PA
Lincoln Coll IL
Louisiana State U .... LA
Louisiana Tech................ LA
Maine, U. of .... ME
Marlboro Coll .... VT
Maryland, U. of .... MD
Massachusetts, U. of (Amherst) MA
McNeese State .... LA
Mercy Coll .... MI
Miami, U. of .... FL
Miami U .... OH
Michigan, U. of................ MI
Michigan State U.............. MI
Minnesota, U. of .... MN
Mississippi, U. of .... MS
Mississippi State .... MS
Mississippi U. for Women...... MS
Missouri, U. of .... MO
Montana, U. of .... MT
Montana State .... MT
Nebraska, U. of .... NE
New Coll. of U.S.F .... FL
New Hampshire, U. of .... NH
New Haven, U. of .... CT
North Carolina State .... NC
Northeast Mississippi Jr .... MS
Northern Arizona U .... AZ
Northwestern .... LA
Northwestern U IL
Notre Dame................... IN
Ohio State .... OH
Ohio U. (Athens) .... OH
Oklahoma, U. of .... OK
Oklahoma State .... OK
Oregon State U .... OR
Ottawa U .... KS
Pennsylvania, U. of............ PA
Pennsylvania State U. (Allentown, McKeesport, University Park) .... PA
Pittsburgh, U. of .... PA
Puerto Rico, U. of .... PR
Purdue U. (Lafayette, North Central) .... IN
Quinnipiac Coll .... CT
Rhode Island, U. of............ RI
Rochester, U. of............... NY
Rutgers .... NJ
San Diego State U .... CA
San Jose State .... CA
Schreiner Coll .... TX
South Carolina, U. of .... SC
South Dakota State U .... SD
South Florida .... FL
Southeastern Louisiana U ...... LA
Southern Illinois U IL
Southern Mississippi .... MS
Southern U .... LA
Southwestern Louisiana U ...... LA

St. Bonaventure . . . . NY
Stanford U . . . . CA
State U. of New York Coll. of Agr. and Life Sci. (Canton) . . . NY
Tennessee, U. of . . . . TN
Texas, U. of (Austin, El Paso) . . . TX
Texas A&M . . . . TX
Texas Tech . . . . TX
Texas Woman's U . . . . TX
Trinity Christian IL
Tulsa, U. of . . . . OK
Tuskegee . . . . AL
Virginia Commonwealth . . . . VA
Washington, U. of . . . . WA
Washington U . . . . MO
Wayne State U . . . . MI
Weber State . . . . UT
Western Kentucky U . . . . KY
William Woods . . . . MO
Wisconsin, U. of (La Crosse) . . . . WI
Wittenberg U . . . . OH
Wright State U . . . . OH
Xavier U . . . . LA

Military, Naval, or Air Force Science

Ball State U . . . . IN
Baylor U . . . . TX
California State Coll . . . . PA
California State U. (Sacramento) . . . . CA
Carnegie-Mellon U . . . . PA
Chaminade U . . . . HI
Cincinnati, U. of . . . . OH
Connecticut, U. of . . . . CT
Cornell U . . . . NY
Eastern Kentucky U . . . . KY
Florida, U. of . . . . FL
Henderson State . . . . AR
Illinois Inst. of Tech IL
Jacksonville State . . . . AL
Jacksonville U . . . . FL
Kansas, U. of . . . . KS
Kutztown State . . . . PA
Miami U . . . . OH
Minnesota, U. of . . . . MN
New Mexico Military Inst . . . . . . NM
North Carolina A&T State U . . . NC
Northeast Mississippi Jr . . . . MS
Northern Arizona . . . . AZ
Northern Colorado, U. of . . . . . . CO
Northern Michigan . . . . MI
Northwestern State . . . . LA
Norwich U . . . . VT
Oklahoma State U . . . . OK
Seton Hall U . . . . NJ
Shepherd Coll . . . . WV
South Dakota, U. of . . . . SD
State U. of New York Maritime Coll . . . . NY
Syracuse U . . . . NY
Temple U . . . . PA
Tennessee, U. of . . . . TN
Texas A&I . . . . TX
Tuskegee Inst . . . . AL
U.S. Military Acad . . . . NY
Utah State U . . . . UT
Valley Forge Military . . . . PA
Virginia Poly . . . . VA
Washington, U. of . . . . WA
Washington U . . . . MO
West Florida, U. of . . . . FL
Westminster Coll . . . . UT
William & Mary . . . . VA
Wisconsin, U. of (Madison) . . . . . WI
York Coll . . . . PA

Mineral Engineering, *See* ENGINEERING, MINERAL

Mining Engineering, *See* ENGINEERING, MINING

Montessori Plan, *See* EDUCATION, MONTESSORI PLAN

Mortuary Science

Accredited by the American Board of Funeral Service Education

Catonsville Comm . . . . MD
Central State U . . . . OK
Cincinnati Coll. of Mortuary Sci . . . . OH
Cypress Coll . . . . CA
Delgado Comm. Coll . . . . LA
District of Columbia, U. of . . . . . DC
East Mississippi Jr. Coll . . . . MS
Fayetteville Tech . . . . NC
Hudson Valley Comm . . . . NY
Jefferson State Jr. Coll . . . . AL
John A. Gupton Coll . . . . TN
John Tyler Comm. Coll . . . . VA
Kansas City Comm. Coll . . . . KS
McNeese State . . . . LA
Mercer Co. Comm . . . . NJ
Miami-Dade Comm. Coll . . . . FL
Milwaukee Area Tech. Coll . . . . . WI
Minnesota, U. of . . . . MN
Mt. Hood Comm. Coll . . . . OR
New England Inst. of Applied Arts & Sciences . . . . MA
Northampton Co. Area Comm. Coll . . . . PA
Northwest Mississippi Jr. Coll . . MS
San Antonio Coll . . . . TX
San Francisco Coll. of Mortuary Sci . . . . CA
Southern Illinois U IL
St. Louis Comm. Coll . . . . MO
State U. of New York (Canton, Farmingdale) . . . . NY
Vincennes U . . . . IN
Wayne State U . . . . MI
Worsham Coll IL

Motel Management, *See* HOTEL, MOTEL AND/OR RESTAURANT ADMINISTRATION

Motion Pictures/Film/Cinema

Alabama, U. of . . . . AL
Arkansas, U. of . . . . AR
Ball State . . . . IN
Bard Coll . . . . NY
Bob Jones U . . . . SC
Bridgeport, U. of . . . . CT
C.W. Post Coll . . . . NY
California, U. of (Santa Cruz) . . . CA
California Inst. of the Arts . . . . . . CA
Chapman Coll . . . . CA
Columbia Coll . . . . CA
Columbia Coll IL
Denison . . . . OH
Eastern Kentucky . . . . KY
Emerson Coll . . . . MA
Florida, U. of . . . . FL
Georgia, U. of . . . . GA
Governors State IL
Hampshire Coll . . . . MA
Howard U . . . . DC
International . . . . MO
Iowa, U. of . . . . IA
Ithaca Coll . . . . NY
Kansas, U. of . . . . KS
Kent State U . . . . OH
Loyola Marymount . . . . CA
Montana State U . . . . MT
New York U . . . . NY
North Carolina, U. of . . . . NC
North Texas State . . . . TX
Northwestern U IL
Ohio State . . . . OH
Oklahoma, U. of . . . . OK
Oklahoma State U . . . . OK
Oregon, U. of . . . . OR
Pennsylvania State U . . . . PA
Point Park Coll . . . . PA
Rhode Island Sch. of Design . . . . RI
San Diego State . . . . CA
Shaw U . . . . NC
Southern California, U. of . . . . . . CA
Southern Methodist U . . . . TX
Southern Mississippi, U. of . . . . MS
Spring Hill . . . . AL
Syracuse U . . . . NY
Temple U . . . . PA
Wayne State U . . . . MI
Wisconsin, U. of (Milwaukee) . . . WI
Wright State U . . . . OH

Museum Curators

Baylor U . . . . TX
Butler U . . . . IN
Iowa, U of . . . . IA
John F. Kennedy U . . . . CA
Luther Coll . . . . IA
Pennsylvania, U. of . . . . PA
South Carolina, U. of . . . . SC
Wayne State . . . . MI
Wesleyan Coll . . . . GA
Wright State U . . . . OH

Museum Studies

Degree programs listed by the Office of Museum Programs, Smithsonian Institution
•Bachelor's level programs. All others are Master's level.

•Anderson Coll . . . . IN
Arizona, U. of . . . . AZ
Arizona State U . . . . AZ
Bank Street Coll. of Ed . . . . NY
•Baylor U . . . . TX
Boston U . . . . MA
California, U. of (Davis) . . . . CA
California State U. (Fullerton, Long Beach) . . . . CA
Case Western Reserve U . . . . . . OH
Central Michigan U . . . . MI
City U. of New York . . . . NY
Colorado, U. of . . . . CO
•Corpus Christi State U . . . . TX
Delaware, U. of . . . . DE
Duquesne U . . . . PA
•East Carolina U . . . . NC
Eastern Illinois U IL
Eastern New Mexico U . . . . NM
George Washington U . . . . DC
•Hartwick Coll . . . . NY
•Idaho, U. of . . . . ID
Illinois, U. of IL
•Indiana U . . . . IN
John Kennedy U . . . . CA
Leslie Coll . . . . MA
•Mary Baldwin Coll . . . . VA
•Mary Washington Coll . . . . VA
Minnesota, U. of . . . . MN
New York, State U. of (Oneonta, •Oswego) . . . . NY
New York U . . . . NY
Oklahoma, U. of . . . . OK
Pennsylvania State U . . . . PA
Portland State U . . . . OR
Rensselaer Poly. Inst . . . . NY
Rochester Inst. of Tech . . . . NY
•Roger Williams Coll . . . . RI
San Diego, U. of . . . . CA
San Francisco State U . . . . CA
South Carolina, U. of . . . . SC
South Dakota Sch. of Mines . . . . SD
Southern California, U. of . . . . . . CA
•Southern Illinois U IL
•Southwestern at Memphis . . . . . . TN
Syracuse U . . . . NY
Temple U . . . . PA
Texas, U. of . . . . TX
•Texas A&M U . . . . TX
Texas Tech U . . . . TX
Trinity Coll . . . . CT
Vincennes U. (associate) . . . . IN
•Virginia Commonwealth U . . . . . . VA
Wake Forest U . . . . NC
•Washington, U. of . . . . WA
Wayne State U . . . . MI
William & Mary, Coll. of . . . . VA
Williams Coll . . . . MA
Wright State U . . . . OH

Music

Members of National Association of Schools of Music, the Accrediting body
•Indicates associate member

Abilene Christian Coll . . . . TX
Akron, U. of . . . . OH
Alabama, U. of . . . . AL
Alabama State U . . . . AL
Alaska, U. of . . . . AK
Albion . . . . MI
•Allegheny Coll . . . . PA
Alma . . . . MI
Alverno . . . . WI
Amarillo Coll . . . . TX
American Conservatory of Music IL
American U . . . . DC
Anderson Coll . . . . IN
Anderson Coll . . . . SC
Andrews U . . . . MI
Angelo State U . . . . TX
Anna Maria Coll . . . . MA
Appalachian State . . . . NC
Arizona, U. of . . . . AZ
Arizona State U . . . . AZ
Arkansas, U. of (Fayetteville) . . . AR
•Arkansas, U. of (Little Rock) . . . . AR
Arkansas State U . . . . AR
Arkansas Tech U . . . . AR
•Asbury Coll . . . . KY
Ashland Coll . . . . OH
•Atlantic Christian . . . . NC
Auburn U . . . . AL
Augusta Coll . . . . GA
Augustana IL
Augustana Coll . . . . SD
Austin Peay . . . . TN
Baldwin-Wallace . . . . OH
Ball State U . . . . IN
•Baptist Coll. at Charleston . . . . . . SC
Barrington Coll . . . . RI
Baylor . . . . TX
Belhaven . . . . MS
Belmont Coll . . . . TN
Benedictine Coll . . . . KS
Berry Coll . . . . GA
Bethany . . . . KS
Biola Coll . . . . CA
Birmingham Southern . . . . AL
Black Hills State Coll . . . . SD
Bluffton Coll . . . . OH
Boise State U . . . . ID
Boston Conservatory . . . . MA
Boston U . . . . MA
Bowling Green State U . . . . OH
Bradley IL
Brevard . . . . NC

Bridgeport, U. of	CT
Brigham Young	UT
Bucknell	PA
Butler (Jordan Coll)	IN
California Inst. of the Arts	CA
California State U. (Chico, Fresno, Fullerton, Hayward, Long Beach, Los Angeles, Northridge, Sacramento)	CA
•California State U. (Dominguez Hills)	CA
Cameron U	OK
Capital	OH
Carnegie-Mellon U	PA
Carson-Newman	TN
•Carthage Coll	WI
Case Western Reserve	OH
Catholic U	DC
Centenary	LA
Central Arkansas	AR
Central Methodist Coll	MO
Central Michigan U	MI
Central Missouri State Coll	MO
Central State	OH
Central Washington U	WA
Chicago Conservatory Coll	IL
Cincinnati, U. of	OH
•Clarke	IA
Cleveland Inst. of Music	OH
•Cleveland State	OH
Coe Coll	IA
Coker	SC
College Misericordia	PA
Colorado, U. of	CO
•Colorado, U. of, at Denver	CO
Colorado Coll	CO
Colorado State U	CO
Columbia Coll	SC
•Columbia Union Coll	MD
•Columbus	GA
Concordia Coll	MN
Connecticut, U. of	CT
Converse	SC
Cornell	IA
•Corpus Christi	TX
Cottey Coll	MO
Cumberland Coll	KY
•Curtis Inst. of Music	PA
Dayton, U. of	OH
Del Mar Coll	TX
Delaware, U. of	DE
Delta State	MS
Denison	OH
Denver, U. of (Lamont Sch.)	CO
DePaul	IL
DePauw	IN
•Dillard U	LA
Douglass	NJ
Drake	IA
Duquesne	PA
East Carolina U	NC
•East Tennessee State U	TN
•East Texas Baptist Coll	TX
East Texas State U	TX
Eastern Illinois U	IL
Eastern Kentucky U	KY
Eastern Michigan U	MI
•Eastern Montana	MT
Eastern New Mexico U	NM
Eastern Washington U	WA
•Edinboro State	PA
Elizabethtown Coll	PA
Emporia State U	KS
Essex Comm	MD
Evangel Coll	MO
Evansville, U. of	IN
Fisk	TN
Florida, U. of	FL
Florida Atlantic Coll	FL
Florida State U	FL
Fontbonne Coll	MO
Fort Hays Kansas State U	KS
Friends	KS
Furman	SC
•Gardner-Webb Coll	NC
George Peabody Coll. for Teachers	TN
•George Washington U	DC
Georgia, U. of	GA
Georgia Coll	GA
Georgia Southern Coll	GA
Georgia State U	GA
Glassboro State Coll	NJ
Gordon	MA
•Grambling State U	LA
Grand Rapids Jr	MI
•Grand Valley State Colls	MI
Greensboro	NC
Gustavus Adolphus	MN
Hamline U	MN
Hampton Inst	VA
Hardin-Simmons	TX
Hartt	CT
Hastings	NE
Hawaii, U. of	HI
Heidelberg	OH
Henderson State Coll	AR
Hendrix	AR
Hiram Coll	OH
Hollins	VA
Holy Names, Coll. of the	CA
Hope	MI
Houghton	NY
Houston, U. of	TX
Howard	DC
•Humboldt State U	CA
Idaho, U. of	ID
•Idaho State	ID
Illinois, U. of (Urbana)	IL
Illinois Central	IL
Illinois State U at Normal	IL
Illinois Wesleyan	IL
Immaculata Coll	PA
•Indiana Central U	IN
Indiana State U	IN
Indiana U	IN
Indiana U. of Pennsylvania	PA
•Indiana U.—Purdue U. at Fort Wayne	IN
Iowa, U. of	IA
Iowa State U	IA
Ithaca	NY
•Jackson State	MS
Jacksonville U	FL
James Madison	VA
Jersey City State Coll	NJ
Judson	AL
Kansas, U. of	KS
Kansas State U	KS
•Kean Coll	NJ
•Kearney State	NE
Kent State	OH
Kentucky, U. of	KY
Kentucky State U	KY
Lamar U	TX
Lawrence	WI
Lebanon Valley	PA
Lewis and Clark	OR
Limestone	SC
Lincoln	MO
Linfield	OR
•Louisiana Coll	LA
Louisiana State U. (Baton Rouge)	LA
Louisiana Tech U	LA
Louisville, U. of	KY
Lowell, U. of	MA
Loyola	LA
Luther Coll	IA
Macalester Coll	MN
MacMurray Coll	IL
Maine, U. of (Orono)	ME
•Malone Coll	OH
Manchester	IN
Manhattan Sch. of Music	NY
Manhattanville	NY
Mankato State	MN
Mansfield State Coll	PA
Mars Hills Coll	NC
•Marshall U	WV
Mary Washington Coll	VA
Maryland, U. of	MD
Marylhurst Ed. Ctr	OR
Marymount	KS
Maryville	TN
Marywood	PA
Massachusetts, U. of	MA
McNeese State U	LA
Memphis State U	TN
•Mercer U	GA
Meredith	NC
•Metropolitan State	CO
Miami, U. of	FL
Miami U	OH
Michigan, U. of	MI
•Michigan-Flint, U. of	MI
Michigan State U	MI
Middle Tennessee State U	TN
Midwestern	TX
•Millersville State	PA
Millikin	IL
Minnesota, U. of (Duluth, Minneapolis)	MN
Minot State Coll	ND
Mississippi, U. of	MS
Mississippi Coll	MS
Mississippi U. for Women	MS
Missouri, U. of (Columbia and Kansas City)	MO
Montana, U. of	MT
•Montana State U	MT
Montclair	NJ
Montevallo, U. of	AL
Montgomery Coll	MD
Moorhead State U	MN
Morehead State U	KY
•Morgan State U	MD
Morningside	IA
Mount St. Mary's	CA
Mt. Union	OH
Murray State U	KY
Muskingum	OH
Nassau Comm. Coll	NY
Nazareth Coll	NY
Nebraska, U. of	NE
Nebraska Wesleyan U	NE
New England Conservatory	MA
New Hampshire, U. of	NH
New Mexico, U. of	NM
New Mexico State U	NM
•New Orleans, U. of	LA
New Orleans Baptist Theol. Sem	LA
New York U	NY
•Newberry Coll	SC
Norfolk State	VA
North Carolina, U. of	NC
•North Dakota, U. of	ND
North Dakota State U	ND
North Park	IL
North Texas State	TX
Northeast Louisiana U	LA
Northeast Missouri	MO
Northern Arizona U	AZ
Northern Colorado, U. of	CO
•Northern Illinois U	IL
Northern Iowa, U. of	IA
Northern Michigan U	MI
Northern State Coll	SD
Northwest Missouri	MO
Northwestern	IL
Northwestern State U	LA
Notre Dame, Coll. of	CA
•Notre Dame, U. of	IN
Nyack Coll	NY
Oberlin	OH
Odessa Coll	TX
Ohio Northern U	OH
Ohio State U	OH
Ohio U	OH
Ohio Wesleyan	OH
Oklahoma, U. of	OK
Oklahoma, U. of Science & Arts of	OK
Oklahoma Baptist U	OK
Oklahoma City U	OK
Oklahoma State U	OK
•Old Dominion U	VA
Oregon, U. of	OR
Oregon Coll. of Education	OR
•Oregon State U	OR
Otterbein	OH
Ouachita Baptist	AR
Ozarks, Sch. of the	MO
Pacific, U. of the	CA
•Pacific Lutheran U	WA
Pacific Union Coll	CA
Pacific U	OR
•Park Coll	MO
Peabody Inst	MD
Pembroke State	NC
•Pennsylvania State U	PA
Pepperdine U	CA
Pfeiffer Coll	NC
Philadelphia Coll. of Bible	PA
Philadelphia Coll. of Performing Arts	PA
Phillips	OK
Pittsburg State	KS
•Portland State U	OR
Puget Sound, U. of	WA
Queens	NC
Quincy	IL
•Radford	VA
Redlands, U. of	CA
Rhode Island, U. of	RI
Rhode Island Coll	RI
Richmond, U. of	VA
Ricks Coll	ID
•Roberts Wesleyan	NY
Rochester, U. of (Eastman Sch. of Music)	NY
Rollings	FL
Roosevelt (Chicago Musical Coll.)	IL
Rosary	IL
Salem	NC
Sam Houston State	TX
Samford U	AL
San Diego State U	CA
San Francisco Conservatory of Music	CA
San Francisco State U	CA
San Jose State U	CA
•Santa Clara, U. of	CA
Seattle Pacific Coll	WA
Seton Hill	PA
Shenandoah Conserv	VA
Sherwood Music Sch	IL
Shorter	GA
Simpson	IA
•Slippery Rock	PA
Sonoma State	CA
South Alabama, U. of	AL
South Carolina, U. of	SC
South Dakota, U. of	SD
South Dakota State U	SD
Southeast Missouri	MO
Southeastern Louisiana U	LA
•Southeastern Oklahoma State U	OK
Southern Arkansas	AR
Southern Baptist Theol. Sem	KY
Southern California, U. of	CA
Southern Colorado, U. of	CO
Southern Illinois U. (Carbondale, Edwardsville)	IL
•Southern Maine, U. of	ME
Southern Methodist	TX
Southern Missionary	TN
Southern Mississippi, U. of	MS
Southern Oregon State	OR
Southern U	LA
•Southwest Baptist Coll	MO
Southwest Missouri	MO
•Southwest Texas	TX

Southwestern .... KS
Southwestern .... TX
Southwestern at Memphis ...... TN
Southwestern Baptist Theol. Sem .... TX
Southwestern Louisiana, U. of .. LA
Southwestern Oklahoma State U .... OK
Spelman Coll .... GA
Springfield Coll IL
St. Catherine, Coll. of .... MN
St. Cloud State .... MN
St. Louis Conservatory of Music .... MO
St. Mary .... KS
•St. Mary of the Plains .... KS
St. Mary-of-the-Woods .... IN
•St. Mary's Coll .... IN
•St. Mary's Coll. of Maryland .... MD
St. Olaf .... MN
•St. Teresa, Coll. of .... MN
State U. of New York (Fredonia, Potsdam) .... NY
•State U. of New York (Buffalo, New Paltz, Oswego) .... NY
Stephen F. Austin State U ...... TX
•Stephens Coll .... MO
Stetson .... FL
Susquehanna U .... PA
Syracuse .... NY
Tabor Coll .... KS
Tampa, U. of .... FL
Taylor U .... IN
Temple U .... PA
Tennessee, U. of (Chattanooga, Knoxville, Martin) .... TN
Tennessee State U .... TN
Tennessee Tech U .... TN
Texarkana Coll .... TX
Texas, U. of (Arlington, Austin, El Paso) .... TX
•Texas, U. of (San Antonio) ...... TX
Texas A&I .... TX
Texas Christian .... TX
Texas Tech U .... TX
Texas Wesleyan .... TX
Texas Woman's U .... TX
Thornton Comm. Coll IL
Toledo, U. of .... OH
Towson State U .... MD
Trenton State Coll .... NJ
•Trevecca Nazarene .... TN
Truett McConnell Coll .... GA
Tulane .... LA
Tulsa, U. of .... OK
Union Coll .... NE
Union U .... TN
Utah, U. of .... UT
•Utah State U .... UT
Valparaiso U .... IN
Vander Cook Coll. of Music IL
Vermont U. of .... VT
Virginia Commonwealth .... VA
Virginia State U .... VA
Viterbo .... WI
Walla Walla Coll .... WA
Wartburg .... IA
Washburn U .... KS
Washington, U. of .... WA
Washington State U .... WA
Washington U .... MO
Wayne State U .... MI
•Weber State Coll .... UT
Webster .... MO
Wesleyan .... GA
West Chester State Coll .... PA
West Florida, U. of .... FL
West Georgia Coll .... GA
West Liberty State Coll .... WV
West Texas State U .... TX
West Virginia U .... WV
West Virginia Wesleyan .... WV
Western Illinois U IL
Western Kentucky U .... KY
Western Maryland .... MD
Western Michigan U .... MI
Western State Coll .... CO
•Western Washington U .... WA
Westminster Choir Coll .... NJ
Westminster Coll .... PA
Wheaton IL
Whitman .... WA
•Whitworth Coll .... WA
Wichita State U .... KS
Willamette .... OR
William Carey Coll .... MS
•William Jewell Coll .... MO
•William Paterson Coll .... NJ
William Rainey Harper Coll IL
Wingate Coll .... NC
Winona State .... MN
Winston-Salem State U .... NC
Winthrop .... SC
Wisconsin, U. of (Eau Claire, Madison, Milwaukee, Oshkosh, Stevens Point) ...... WI
•Wisconsin, U. of (Green Bay, Whitewater) .... WI
Wisconsin Conservatory .... WI
Wittenberg .... OH
Wooster .... OH
Wright State U .... OH
Wyoming, U. of .... WY
Xavier U .... LA
Yale .... CT
Yankton Coll .... SD
Youngstown .... OH

Music Business

Barrington Coll .... RI
Baruch Coll .... NY
Belmont Coll .... TN
Blue Mountain Coll .... MS
Bradley U IL
Central Missouri U .... MO
Columbia Coll IL
Cumberland Coll .... KY
DePauw U .... IN
Drake U .... IA
Elmhurst Coll IL
Florida Southern Coll .... FL
Fontbonne Coll .... MO
Franklin Pierce .... NH
Goddard Coll .... VT
Hartford, U. of .... CT
Hastings Coll .... NE
Jacksonville U .... FL
James Madison U .... VA
Jersey City State .... NJ
Kearney State .... NE
Mars Hill Coll .... NC
Millikin U IL
Mount Senario .... WI
Mount St. Joseph .... OH
New York U .... NY
North Park Coll IL
Northeast Missouri State ...... MO
Northland Coll .... WI
Otterbein Coll .... OH
Pacific, U. of the .... CA
Peru State .... NE
Plymouth State .... NH
Shenandoah Coll .... VA
Southern Illinois U IL
St. Catherine, Coll. of .... MN
St. Leo Coll .... FL
St. Rose, Coll. of .... NY
St. Scholastica .... MN
St. Thomas .... MN
State U. of New York (Fredonia, Potsdam) .... NY
Syracuse U .... NY
Union Coll .... KY
Ursuline Coll .... OH
Valparaiso U .... IN
Wayne State .... MI
Wesleyan Coll .... GA
William Woods .... MO
Wingate Coll .... NC
Wisconsin, U. of (Green Bay) ... WI
Wittenberg U .... OH
Yankton Coll .... SD

Music Education

Institutions awarding 20 or more undergraduate degrees as a major field in a single year according to U.S. Office of Education latest statistics

Alabama State U .... AL
Appalachian State U .... NC
Arizona, U. of .... AZ
Arkansas State U .... AR
Auburn U .... AL
Baylor U .... TX
Berklee Coll .... MA
Bob Jones U .... SC
Boston U .... MA
Bowling Green .... OH
Brigham Young U .... HI
Brigham Young U .... UT
Capital U .... OH
Central Michigan U .... MI
Central State .... OK
Clarion State .... PA
Colorado, U. of .... CO
Concordia Coll. (Moorhead) ... MN
DePaul IL
Duquesne .... PA
East Texas .... TX
Eastern Illinois IL
Eastern Kentucky U .... KY
Eastern Michigan .... MI
Edinboro State .... PA
Florida, U. of .... FL
Florida State U .... FL
Georgia, U. of .... GA
Hartford, U. of .... CT
Houston, U. of .... TX
Illinois, U. of IL
Illinois State U IL
Illinois Wesleyan IL
Indiana U .... IN
Indiana U. of Pennsylvania ...... PA
Ithaca Coll .... NY
Jacksonville .... AL
James Madison Coll .... VA
Kansas, U. of .... KS
Kansas State U .... KS
Kent State .... OH
Kentucky, U. of .... KY
Lebanon Valley .... PA
Long Island U .... NY
Louisiana Tech U .... LA
Lowell, U. of .... MA
Mankato State .... MN
Mansfield State .... PA
Maryland, U. of .... MD
Metropolitan State .... CO
Miami, U. of .... FL
Miami U .... OH
Michigan, U. of .... MI
Michigan State U .... MI
Millersville State .... PA
Minnesota, U. of .... MN
Mississippi, U. of .... MS
Mississippi State .... MS
Missouri, U. of (Columbia) ..... MO
Montevallo, U. of .... AL
Morehead State .... KY
Murray State .... KY
Nebraska, U. of .... NE
North Carolina, U. of (Greensboro) .... NC
North Texas State .... TX
Northern Colorado, U. of ...... CO
Northern Illinois U IL
Ohio State .... OH
Oklahoma, U. of .... OK
Pennsylvania State U .... PA
Rochester, U. of .... NY
Sam Houston .... TX
Samford .... AL
Shenandoah Coll .... VA
South Carolina, U. of .... SC
Southeast Missouri State ...... MO
Southern Mississippi, U. of .... MS
Southwest Missouri State ...... MO
Southwest Texas U .... TX
St. Olaf .... MN
State U. of New York (Fredonia, Potsdam) .... NY
Syracuse U .... NY
Temple U .... PA
Tennessee Tech U .... TN
Texas, U. of (Austin) .... TX
Texas Tech .... TX
Towson State .... MD
Troy State U .... AL
West Chester State .... PA
West Texas .... TX
Western Connecticut .... CT
Western Michigan U .... MI
Western Washington U .... WA
Westminster Choir Coll .... NJ
William Paterson Coll .... NJ
Wisconsin, U. of (Eau Claire, Madison, Milwaukee, Stevens Point) .... WI
Youngstown State U .... OH

Music Media

Bennett Coll .... NC
Lincoln Coll IL
Norfolk State U .... VA
Shenandoah Coll .... VA
Southern Idaho, Coll. of .... ID
Trevecca Nazarene .... TN
Wayne State .... MI

Music Merchandising

Appalachian State U .... NC
Ashland Coll .... OH
Augustana Coll .... SD
Cheyney State .... PA
Clarion State .... PA
Eastern Kentucky U .... KY
Eastern Montana .... MT
Emporia State U .... KS
Evangel Coll .... MO
Fairmont State Coll .... WV
Heidelberg Coll .... OH
Hofstra U .... NY
Jacksonville U .... FL
James Madison U .... VA
Kearney State .... NE
Lewis U IL
Mansfield State .... PA
Miami, U. of .... FL
Millersville State .... PA
Mt. St. Joseph, Coll. of .... OH
North Idaho .... ID
Saint Mary's Coll .... MN
Shenandoah Coll .... VA
Southwestern Oklahoma State U .... OK
State U. of New York (Potsdam) NY
Valparaiso U .... IN
William Woods .... MO
Wisconsin, U. of (Oshkosh) ..... WI

Music Therapy

Approved by the Assn. for Music Therapy Inc.

Alverno Coll .... WI

Anna Maria .... MA
Arizona State U .... AZ
Augsburg .... MN
Baldwin-Wallace .... OH
Baptist Coll. at Charleston ...... SC
Brevard .... NC
California State U .... CA
Case Western Reserve .... OH
Catholic U .... DC
Cleveland State U .... OH
Colorado State U .... CO
Columbia U. Teachers Coll ..... NY
Dayton, U. of .... OH
DePaul U IL
Duquesne U .... PA
East Carolina .... NC
Eastern Michigan .... MI
Eastern Montana Coll .... MT
Eastern New Mexico .... NM
Elizabethtown Coll .... PA
Evansville, U. of .... IN
Florida State U .... FL
Georgia, U. of .... GA
Georgia Coll .... GA
Hahnemann Med. Cent .... PA
Henderson State U .... AR
Howard U .... DC
Illinois State U IL
Indiana U.-Purdue U. (Fort Wayne) .... IN
Iowa, U. of .... IA
Kansas, U. of .... KS
Loyola .... LA
Mansfield State .... PA
Maryville Coll .... MO
Marywood Coll .... PA
Miami, U. of .... FL
Michigan State U .... MI
Minnesota, U. of .... MN
Misericordia Coll .... PA
Missouri, U. of (Kansas City) .. MO
Montclair State Coll .... NJ
Mt. St. Joseph .... OH
Nazareth Coll .... NY
Oberlin Coll .... OH
Ohio U .... OH
Pacific, U. of the .... CA
Phillips U .... OK
Queens Coll .... NC
Shenandoah .... VA
Slippery Rock State .... PA
Southern Methodist U .... TX
St. Teresa, Coll. of .... MN
State Univ. Coll. (Fredonia, New Paltz) .... NY
Temple U .... PA
Tennessee Tech U .... TN
Texas Woman's U .... TX
Utah State U .... UT
Wartburg Coll .... IA
Wayne State .... MI
West Texas State .... TX
Western Illinois U IL
Western Michigan U .... MI
Willamette U .... OR
William Carey Coll .... MS
Wisconsin, U. of (Eau Claire, Milwaukee, Oshkosh) .... WI
Wooster, Coll. of .... OH
Xavier U. of Louisiana .... LA

Musical Theatre

Baldwin-Wallace Coll .... OH
Baylor U .... TX
Boston U .... MA
Brevard .... NC
California, U. of (Irvine) .... CA
Carnegie-Mellon U .... PA
Cincinnati, U. of .... OH
Columbia Coll IL
Connecticut, U. of .... CT
Cornell U .... NY
Creighton U .... NE
Eastern Kentucky U .... KY
Emerson Coll .... MA
Florida State U .... Fl
Fontbonne Coll .... MO
Goddard Coll .... VT
Gonzaga U .... WA
Hartford, U. of .... CT
Hope Coll .... MI
Indiana State U .... IN
Indiana U. (Bloomington) .... IN
Ithaca Coll .... NY
Jacksonville U .... FL
Kent State U .... OH
Lincoln Coll IL
Loretto Heights .... CO
Loyola U .... LA
Marlboro Coll .... VT
Mars Hill .... NC
Marywood Coll .... PA
Miami, U. of .... FL
Milliken U IL
Minnesota, U. of .... MN
Nebraska Wesleyan .... NE
New York U .... NY
Northeast Mississippi Jr .... MS
Northern Colorado, U. of ...... CO
Northern Iowa, U. of .... IA
Ohio State U .... OH
Otterbein .... OH
Pfeiffer Coll .... NC
Plymouth State .... NH
Redlands, U. of .... CA
Santa Fe, Coll. of .... NM
Shenandoah Coll .... VA
South Georgia Coll .... GA
State U. of New York (Fredonia, Geneseo) .... NY
Stephens Coll .... MO
Syracuse U .... NY
Tennessee, U. of .... TN
Viterbo Coll .... WI
Webster Coll .... MO
William Woods .... MO

Naval Architecture Engineering,

See ENGINEERING, NAVAL ARCHITECTURE

Nuclear Medicine Technology

Approved by Council on Medical Education of American Medical Assn. in collaboration with American College of Radiology, American Society of Clinical Pathologists, American Society for Medical Technology, American Society of Radiologic Technologists, and Society of Nuclear Medicine

Alabama, U. of .... AL
Allegheny County, C. Coll. of ... PA
Arizona, U. of .... AZ
Baylor Coll .... TX
Bunker Hill Comm. Coll .... MA
Butler U .... IN
Caldwell Comm. Coll .... NC
California, U. of (Davis, San Francisco) .... CA
Cedar Crest Coll .... PA
Cincinnati, U. of .... OH
Delaware Tech. Comm. Coll .... DE
Denver, Comm. Coll. of .... CO
Detroit, U. of .... MI
Duke U .... NC
Emory U .... GA
Essex Comm. Coll .... MD
Ferris State Coll .... MI
Forsyth Tech. Inst .... NC
Georgia, Med. Coll. of .... GA
Gwynedd-Mercy Coll .... PA
Hillsborough Comm .... FL
Houston Comm. Coll .... TX
Incarnate Word Coll .... TX
Indiana U .... IN
Iowa, U. of .... IA
Kansas, U. of .... KS
Loma Linda .... CA
Los Angeles City .... CA
Louisville, U. of .... KY
Manhattan Coll .... NY
Miami, U. of .... FL
Midlands Tech. Coll .... SC
Mississippi, U. of .... MS
Missouri, U. of .... MO
Nebraska, U. of .... NE
Nevada, U. of .... NV
North Carolina, U. of .... NC
Ohio State .... OH
Oklahoma, U. of .... OK
Prince George's Comm. Coll ... MD
Puerto Rico, U. of .... PR
Quinnipiac Coll .... CT
Queen's Coll .... NC
Rochester Inst. of Tech .... NY
Santa Fe Comm .... NM
Seattle U .... WA
South Carolina, Med. U. of ...... SC
South Central Comm. Coll ...... CT
Springfield Tech. Comm. Coll .. MA
St. Mary's Coll .... MN
State U. of New York (Buffalo) .. NY
Triton IL
Utah, U. of .... UT
Vanderbilt U .... SC
Vermont, U. of .... VT
Virginia, U. of .... VA
Wagner Coll .... NY
Washington U .... MO
West Virginia State Coll .... WV
West Virginia U .... WV
Wheeling Coll .... WV
Worcester State Coll .... MA

Nuclear Metallurgy

Missouri, U. of (Rolla) .... MO

Nuclear Physics

California Inst. of Tech .... CA
Carnegie-Mellon .... PA
Cincinnati, U. of .... OH
Colorado State U .... CO
Cornell U .... NY
Kansas, U. of .... KS
Lynchburg Coll .... VA
Missouri, U. of (Rolla) .... MO
Purdue U .... IN
Syracuse U .... NY
Valparaiso U .... IN
Worcester Poly. Inst .... MA

Nuclear Technology Training

Anna Maria Coll .... MA
Barry U .... FL
C.W. Post .... NY
Ferris State .... MI
Findlay Coll .... OH
Iowa, U. of .... IA
Kansas Newman Coll .... KS
Lycoming Coll .... PA
Manhattan Coll .... NY
Missouri, U. of .... MO
Notre Dame, U. of .... IN
Seattle U .... WA
Texas State Tech .... TX
Wisconsin, U. of (La Crosse) .... WI

Nurse Anesthesia

Approved by Council on Accreditation of Nurse Anesthesia educational degree programs

Alabama, U. of (Birmingham) .... AL
Bowman Gray School of Medicine .... NC
Brooklyn Coll .... NY
Columbia U .... NY
Creighton U .... NE
Detroit, U. of .... MI
Duke U .... NC
Edinboro State Coll .... PA
Friends U .... KS
George Washington U .... DC
Gonzaga U .... WA
Kansas, U. of .... KS
Kansas Newman Coll .... KS
La Roche Coll .... PA
Loma Linda U .... CA
Medical Coll. of Pennsylvania .... PA
Mercy Coll. of Detroit .... MI
Michigan, U. of .... MI
Mississippi, U. of .... MS
Missouri, U. of (Kansas City) .... MO
Mount Marty Coll .... SD
Nebraska, U. of .... NE
Nebraska Wesleyan U .... NE
New York Medical Coll .... NY
Ohio State U .... OH
Old Dominion U .... VA
Pittsburgh, U. of (Johnstown) .... PA
Rush U IL
Samford U .... AL
Sangamon State U IL
South Carolina, U. of .... SC
South Dakota, U. of .... SD
Southwest Missouri State U .... MO
State U. of New York at Buffalo .... NY
Susquehanna U .... PA
Virginia Commonwealth U ...... VA
Warren Wilson Coll .... NC
Wayne State U .... MI
Wesley Coll .... DE
Wheeling Coll .... WV

Nurse-Midwife

Accredited by The American College of Nurse-Midwives

Arizona, U. of .... AZ
California, U. of (San Diego, San Francisco) .... CA
Colorado, U. of (Denver) ...... CO
Columbia U .... NY
Emory .... GA
Georgetown .... DC
Illinois, U. of IL
Kentucky, U. of .... KY
Meharry Medical Coll .... TN
Miami, U. of .... FL
Minnesota, U. of .... MN
Mississippi, U. of .... MS
New Jersey Coll. of Medicine and Dentistry (Newark) .... NJ
Pennsylvania, U. of .... PA
South Carolina, Medical Coll. of .... SC
Southern California, U. of ...... CA
St. Louis U .... MO
State U. of New York (Downstate Medical Ctr.) ..... NY
Utah, U. of .... UT
Yale U .... CT

Nursing, Associate Degree

Accredited by National League for Nursing

Abraham Baldwin Agric. Coll .. GA
Albany, Jr. Coll. of ....NY
Albany Jr. Coll .... GA
Albuquerque, U. of .... NM
Allegheny County, Comm. Coll of ....PA
Amarillo Coll ....TX
Anchorage Comm. Coll ....AK
Anderson Coll .... IN
Angelina Coll ....TX
Angelo State U ....TX
Anne Arundel Comm. Coll ..... MD
Anoka-Ramsey Comm. Coll .... MN
Arizona Western Coll ....AZ
Arkansas, U. of (Fayetteville, Little Rock) ....AR
Arkansas State U ....AR
Armstrong State Coll .... GA
Atlantic Comm ....NJ
Atlantic Union .... MA
Augusta .... GA
Austin Comm .... MN
Austin Peay State U ....TN
Bacone Coll .... OK
Baltimore, Comm. Coll. of ..... MD
Barton County Comm. Coll .....KS
Belleville Area Coll IL
Bellevue Comm. Coll .... WA
Belmont Coll ....TN
Bergen Comm ....NJ
Berkshire Comm. Coll .... MA
Black Hawk Coll IL
Blackhawk Tech. Inst .... WI
Bluefield State Coll .... WV
Boise State U .... ID
Brazosport-Galveston Colls ..... TX
Bridgeport, U. of ....CT
Brigham Young U ....UT
Bristol Comm. Coll .... MA
Bronx Comm. Coll ....NY
Brookdale Comm. Coll .... NJ
Broome Comm. Coll ....NY
Broward Comm .... FL
Brunswick Jr. Coll .... GA
Bucks County Comm. Coll ......PA
Bunker Hill Comm. Coll .... MA
Cameron U .... OK
Cape Cod Comm. Coll .... MA
Casper Coll .... WY
Castleton State Coll .... VT
Central Arizona Coll ....AZ
Central Ohio Tech. Coll .... OH
Central Texas Coll .... TX
Chaffey Comm. Coll ....CA
Charles Stewart Mott Comm. Coll .... MI
Charleston, U. of .... WV
Chattahoochee Valley Comm. Coll ....AL
Chemetka Comm. Coll .... OR
Cincinnati, U. of (Raymond Walters Branch) .... OH
Clark Coll ....WA
Clark Tech. Coll .... OH
Clayton Jr. Coll .... GA
Cleveland State Comm. Coll ....TN
Cloud County Comm. Coll ......KS
Columbia State Comm. Coll ....TN
Columbus Coll .... GA
Cooke County ....TX
Corning Comm ....NY
Cumberland Coll ....KY
Cumberland County .... NJ
Cuyahoga Comm. Coll. (Western Campus, Metropolitan Campus) .... OH
Dakota Wesleyan U ....SD
Dalton Jr. Coll .... GA
DeKalb Comm. Coll .... GA
Del Mar Coll ....TX
Delaware County Comm. Coll .. PA
Delaware Tech. and Comm. Coll ....DE
Delta Coll .... MI
Desert, Coll. of the ....CA
Dickinson State Coll .... ND
District of Columbia, U. of ..... DC
DuPage, Coll. of IL
Dutchess Comm ....NY
East Tennessee State U ....TN
Eastern Kentucky U ....KY
Eastern New Mexico U at Roswell .... NM
Eastern Oklahoma State Coll .. OK
El Centro Coll ....TX
El Paso Comm .... TX
Elgin Comm. Coll IL
Essex Comm. Coll .... MD
Essex County Coll .... NJ
Evansville, U. of .... IN
Everett Comm. Coll .... WA
Evergreen Valley ....CA
Fairmont State .... WV
Fayetteville Tech. Inst .... NC
Felician Coll ....NJ
Finger Lakes, Comm. Coll. of ...NY
Florence-Darlington Tech. Ed. Ctr ....SC
Florida Jr. Coll. at Jacksonville .... FL
Floyd Jr .... GA
Fox Valley Tech. Inst .... WI
Gardner-Webb Coll .... NC
Gateway Tech. Inst .... WI
Genesee Comm ....NY
George C. Wallace State Comm. Coll .... AL
Georgia Southwestern Coll .... GA
Germanna Comm. Coll ....VA
Glendale Comm. Coll .... AZ
Gloucester County .... NJ
Golden West ....CA
Gordon Jr. Coll .... GA
Grand Rapids Jr. Coll .... MI
Grayson County Coll .... TX
Greater Hartford Comm. Coll ...CT
Gwynedd-Mercy .... PA
Hahnemann Med. Coll .... PA
Harford Comm .... MD
Hawaii, U. of .... HI
Helene Fuld Sch. of Nursing ....NY
Henry Ford Comm. Coll .... MI
Hesston Coll ....KS
Highline Comm. Coll .... WA
Hinds Jr. Coll .... MS
Holyoke Comm. Coll .... MA
Howard Comm .... MD
Howard Co. Jr. Coll .... TX
Hudson Valley Comm ....NY
Illinois Central Coll IL
Illinois Valley Comm. Coll IL
Imperial Valley ....CA
Indian River Comm. Coll .... FL
Indiana Central U .... IN
Indiana State U .... IN
Indiana U. (Indianapolis, Kokomo, Northwest Campus) .... IN
Indiana U.-Purdue U. (Fort Wayne) .... IN
Inver Hills Comm. Coll .... MN
J. Sargeant Reynolds Comm. Coll ....VA
Jamestown Comm ....NY
Jefferson Comm ....NY
Jefferson Comm. Coll ....KY
Jefferson State Jr. Coll .... AL
John C. Calhoun State Comm .. AL
Johnson County Comm. Coll ... KS
Joliet Jr. Coll IL
Kansas City Comm ....KS
Kansas Newman ....KS
Kaskaskia Coll IL
Kennesaw Coll .... GA
Kent State U. (Ashtabula, East Liverpool, Tuscarawas Branch) .... OH
Kentucky State U ....KY
Kilgore Coll .... TX
Kingsborough Comm ....NY
La Grange Coll .... GA
Labette Comm. Jr. Coll ....KS
Laboure Jr .... MA
Lake Co., Coll. of IL
Lake Michigan Coll .... MI
Lakeshore Tech. Inst .... WI
Lander Coll ....SC
Lane Comm. Coll .... OR
Lansing Comm. Coll .... MI
Laredo Jr .... TX
Lewis and Clark Comm IL
Lewis-Clark State Coll .... ID
Lexington Tech. Inst ....KY
Lima Tech. Coll .... OH
Lincoln Land Comm. Coll IL
Linn-Benton Comm .... OR
Livingston U ....AL
Loma Linda U ....CA
Long Beach City ....CA
Lorain County Comm. Coll .... OH
Los Angeles City ....CA
Los Angeles Pierce ....CA
Los Angeles Valley ....CA
Louisiana State U. (Alexandria, New Orleans) .... LA
Louisiana Tech ....LA
Louisville, U. of ....KY
Lower Columbia Comm. Coll .. WA
Luzerne Co. Comm. Coll .... PA
Macomb County Comm. Coll ... MI
Macon Jr. Coll .... GA
Madison Area Tech. Coll .... WI
Maine, U. of (Augusta) .... ME
Mainland, Coll. of the .... TX
Manatee Jr .... FL
Manhattan, Borough of, Comm. Coll ....NY
Maria Coll ....NY
Maricopa Tech .... AZ
Marin, Coll. of ....CA
Marion Tech. Coll .... OH
Marshall U .... WV
Marymount Coll. of Virginia .....VA
Maryville Coll .... MO
Massasoit Comm. Coll .... MA
Mattatuck Comm ....CT
McLennan Comm. Coll .... TX
Mercer County Comm ....NJ
Meridian Jr. Coll .... MS
Mesa .... CO
Mesa Comm. Coll .... AZ
Miami U. (Hamilton, Middletown Branch) .... OH
Miami-Dade Comm. Coll .... FL
Michael J. Owens Tech .... OH
Middle Tennessee State U ......TN
Middlesex County ....NJ
Midway Coll ....KY
Midwestern U .... TX
Milwaukee Area Tech. Coll ..... WI
Minneapolis Comm. Coll ...... MN
Mississippi Delta .... MS
Mississippi U. for Women ...... MS
Missouri Southern .... MO
Mobile Coll .... AL
Mohawk Valley Comm ....NY
Mohegan Comm. Coll ....CT
Monroe Comm ....NY
Montgomery Comm .... MD
Moraine Valley Comm. Coll IL
Morris, County Coll. of .... NJ
Motlow State Comm. Coll ......TN
Mountain Empire Comm. Coll ... VA
Mount Aloysius Jr. Coll ....PA
Mount Hood Comm. Coll ...... OR
Mount St. Mary's Coll ....CA
Mount Wachusett Comm. Coll . MA
Murray State Coll .... OK
Nassau Comm. Coll ....NY
Nebraska, U. of ....NE
Nevada, U. of—Coll. of Allied Health Professions ....NV
New Hampshire Tech. Inst. (Concord) .... NH
New Mexico Jr .... NM
New York Technical Coll ....NY
Niagara Co. Comm. Coll ....NY
Nicholls State U ....LA
Norfolk State U ....VA
Normandale Comm .... MN
North Central Tech. Coll ...... OH
North Dakota State U .... ND
North Georgia Coll .... GA
North Harris County Coll .... TX
North Hennepin Comm. Coll ... MN
North Idaho Coll .... ID
North Shore Comm. Coll ...... MA
Northampton County Area Comm. Coll ....PA
Northeastern Oklahoma .... OK
Northern Arizona U ....AZ
Northern Essex Comm. Coll ... MA
Northern Kentucky U ....KY
Northern Oklahoma Coll .... OK
Northern Virginia Comm. Coll .. VA
Northwest Alabama State Jr .... AL
Northwest Mississippi Jr. Coll .. MS
Northwestern State U ....LA
Norwalk Comm ....CT
Ocean County Coll .... NJ
Odessa Coll .... TX
Ohio U. (Zanesville) .... OH
Ohlone Coll ....CA
Oklahoma State U. Tech. Inst .. OK
Onondaga Comm. Coll ....NY
Orange County Comm. Coll ....NY
Oregon Inst. of Tech .... OR
Pace U. (Pleasantville) ....NY
Pacific Union ....CA
Paducah Comm ....KY
Palomar ....CA
Pan American U .... TX
Paris Jr. Coll .... TX
Parkersburg Comm. Coll ...... WV
Parkland Coll IL
Pasadena City ....CA
Passaic County Comm. Coll .... NJ
Penn Valley Comm. Coll ...... MO
Philadelphia, Comm. Coll. of .... PA
Phoenix Coll ....AZ
Pikes Peak Comm. Coll .... CO
Pima Comm. Coll .... AZ
Portland Comm. Coll .... OR
Prairie State Coll IL
Presentation Coll ....SD
Prince George's Comm. Coll ... MD
Puerto Rico, U. of (Arecibo, Humacao) .... PR
Puerto Rico Jr. Coll .... PR
Purdue U. (Calumet, North Central) .... IN
Queensborough Comm. Coll ....NY
Quinnipiac Coll ....CT
Rhode Island Jr. Coll. (Flanagan, Knight) .... RI
Ricks Coll .... ID
Rochester Comm ....NY
Rockingham Comm. Coll ...... NC
Rockland Comm. Coll ....NY
S.D. Bishop State Jr. Coll .... AL
Sacramento City ....CA
Samford U ....AL
San Antonio Coll .... TX
San Joaquin Delta ....CA
San Mateo, Coll. of ....CA
Sandhills Comm. Coll .... NC
Santa Barbara City ....CA
Santa Fe, Coll. of .... NM
Scottsdale Comm .... AZ
Seminole Jr. Coll .... OK
Shenandoah Coll ....VA

Shepherd Coll ... WV
Shoreline Community Coll ... WA
Sinclair Community College ... OH
Somerset County Coll ... NJ
South Carolina, U. of (Aiken, Columbia, Spartanburg) ... SC
South Dakota, U. of ... SD
South Georgia Coll ... GA
South Oklahoma City Junior Coll ... OK
Southern Arkansas U ... AR
Southern Colorado, U. of ... CO
Southern Idaho, Coll. of ... ID
Southern Illinois ... IL
Southern Missionary Coll ... TN
Southern Oregon Coll ... OR
Southwest Virginia Comm. Coll ... VA
Southwestern Adventist Coll ... TX
Springfield Tech. Comm. Coll ... MA
St. Louis Community Coll ... MO
St. Mary, Coll. of ... NE
St. Mary's Coll. of O'Fallon ... MO
St. Mary's Jr. Coll ... MN
St. Petersburg Jr. Coll ... FL
State U. of New York (Alfred, Canton, Farmingdale, Morrisville) ... NY
State U. of New York (Regents External Degree) ... NY
Staten Island Community Coll ... NY
Suffolk County Community Coll ... NY
Tacoma Community Coll ... WA
Tarrant County Jr. Coll ... TX
Tennessee, U. of (Martin) ... TN
Tennessee State U ... TN
Texarkana Coll ... TX
Thornton Comm. Coll ... IL
Tidewater Comm. Coll ... VA
Toledo, U. of ... OH
Tompkins-Cortland Comm. Coll ... NY
Triton Coll ... IL
Trocaire Coll ... NY
Troy State U ... AL
Tulsa Jr. Coll ... OK
Union U ... TN
Valencia Comm. Coll ... FL
Vermont, U. of—Division of Health Sciences ... VT
Vermont Coll. (Norwich U.) ... VT
Victor Valley Coll ... CA
Vincennes U ... IN
Virgin Islands, Coll. of the ... VI
Virginia Highlands Comm. Coll ... VA
Virginia Western Community Coll ... VA
Walla Walla Community Coll ... WA
Walters State Comm. Coll ... TN
Waukesha County Tech ... WI
Weber State Coll ... UT
Wesley ... DE
West Georgia Coll ... GA
West Virginia Northern Comm. Coll ... WV
Westark Comm. Coll ... AR
Westbrook Coll ... ME
Western Kentucky U ... KY
Western Piedmont ... NC
Western Wisconsin Tech ... WI
William Rainey Harper Coll ... IL
Wytheville Comm. Coll ... VA
Yakima Valley Coll ... WA
Yavapai Coll ... AZ
Youngstown State U ... OH

Nursing, Baccalaureate Degree

Baccalaureate degree programs accredited by the Council of Baccalaureate and Higher Degree Programs of the National League for Nursing; all programs include preparation in community health nursing

Adelphi ... NY
Akron, U. of ... OH
Alabama, U. of (Birmingham, Huntsville, Tuscaloosa) ... AL
Alaska, U. of ... AK
Albright Coll ... PA
Alderson-Broaddus ... WV
Alfred U ... NY
Allentown Coll. of St. Francis de Sales ... PA
Alverno ... WI
American U ... DC
Andrews U ... MI
Arizona, U. of ... AZ
Arizona State U ... AZ
Arkansas, U. of (Little Rock, Pine Bluff) ... AR
Arkansas State U ... AR
Atlantic Christian Coll ... NC
Augsburg Coll ... MN
Augustana Coll ... SD
Avila Coll ... MO
Azusa Pacific Coll ... MT
Ball State U ... IN
Barry Coll ... FL
Baylor U ... TX
Berea Coll ... KY
Biola Coll ... CA
Bloomfield Coll ... NJ
Boise State U ... ID
Boston Coll ... MA
Boston U ... MA
Bowling Green State ... OH
Bradley U ... IL
Bridgeport, U. of ... CT
Brigham Young ... UT
California, U. of (Los Angeles, San Francisco) ... CA
California State Coll. (Bakersfield) ... CA
California State U. (Chico, Fresno, Hayward, Long Beach, Los Angeles, Sacramento, San Bernardino) ... CA
Capital U ... OH
Carlow Coll ... PA
Carroll Coll ... MT
Case Western Reserve U ... OH
Catholic U. of America ... DC
Catholic U. of Puerto Rico ... PR
Cedar Crest Coll ... PA
Central Arkansas, U. of ... AR
Central Missouri State ... MO
Central State U ... OK
Chicago State U ... IL
Cincinnati, U. of ... OH
City Coll. of City U ... NY
Clemson U ... SC
Coll. Misericordia ... PA
Colorado, U. of ... CO
Columbia ... NY
Columbia Union Coll ... MD
Connecticut, U. of ... CT
Coppin State Coll ... MD
Corpus Christi State ... TX
Creighton ... NE
Dallas Baptist Coll ... TX
Delaware, U. of ... DE
DePaul U ... IL
DePauw ... IN
Dillard ... LA
District of Columbia, U. of ... DC
Dominican Coll ... NY
Duke ... NC
Duquesne ... PA
D'Youville Coll ... NY
East Carolina U ... NC
East Central Oklahoma State ... OK
East Tennessee State U ... TN
Eastern Kentucky U ... KY
Eastern Mennonite Coll ... VA
Eastern Michigan U ... MI
Elmhurst Coll ... IL
Emory ... GA
Evansville, U. of ... IN
Fairfield U ... CT
Fairleigh Dickinson U ... NJ
Fitchburg State Coll ... MA
Florida, U. of ... FL
Florida A&M U ... FL
Florida State U ... FL
Fort Hays State ... KS
George Mason U ... VA
Georgetown ... DC
Georgia, Medical Coll. of ... GA
Georgia State U ... GA
Goshen Coll ... IN
Graceland Coll ... IA
Grand Valley State ... MI
Grand View Coll ... IA
Gustavus Adolphus ... MN
Gwynedd-Mercy Coll ... PA
Hahnemann Med. Coll. and Hosp ... PA
Hampton Inst ... VA
Harding U ... AR
Hartwick Coll ... NY
Hawaii, U. of ... HI
Herbert H. Lehmann Coll ... NY
Holy Family Coll ... PA
Holy Names Coll ... CA
Houston Baptist U ... TX
Howard U ... DC
Humboldt State U ... CA
Hunter ... NY
Idaho State U ... ID
Illinois, U. of ... IL
Illinois Wesleyan ... IL
Incarnate Word ... TX
Indiana State U ... IN
Indiana U ... IN
Indiana U. of Pennsylvania ... PA
Intercollegiate Ctr. for Nursing Educ ... WA
Iowa, U. of ... IA
Iowa Wesleyan ... IA
Jacksonville State U ... AL
Jamestown Coll ... ND
Jersey City State ... NJ
Kansas, U. of ... KS
Kent State U ... OH
Kentucky, U. of ... KY
Keuka Coll ... NY
LaRoche Coll ... PA
Lenoir-Rhyne Coll ... NC
Lewis U ... IL
Loma Linda U ... CA
Long Island U. (Richard L. Conolly Coll.) ... NY
Loretto Heights ... CO
Louisiana State U ... LA
Lowell, U. of ... MA
Loyola ... IL
Luther Coll ... IA
Madonna Coll ... MI
Mankato State ... MN
Marian Coll. of Fond du Lac ... WI
Marion Coll ... IN
Marquette U ... WI
Marshall Coll ... WV
Mary Coll ... ND
Mary Hardin-Baylor ... TX
Marycrest Coll ... IA
Maryland, U. of ... MD
Marymount Coll ... KS
Marymount Coll ... VA
Maryville Coll ... MO
Massachusetts, U. of ... MA
Medgar Evars Coll ... NY
Memphis State ... TN
Mercy ... MI
Mercy Coll ... NY
Metropolitan State Coll ... CO
McKendree Coll ... IL
Miami, U. of ... FL
Michigan, U. of ... MI
Michigan State U ... MI
Mid-America Nazarene ... KS
Millikin U ... IL
Midland Lutheran ... NE
Minnesota, U. of ... MN
Mississippi, U. of ... MS
Mississippi, U. of for Women ... MS
Mississippi Coll ... MS
Missouri, U. of ... MO
Mobile Coll ... AL
Molloy ... NY
Montana State U ... MT
Moorhead State U ... MN
Mt. Marty Coll ... SD
Mt. Mercy Coll ... IA
Mt. St. Joseph-on-the-Ohio ... OH
Mt. St. Mary Coll ... NY
Mt. St. Mary's ... CA
Mt. St. Vincent, Coll. of ... NY
Murray State U ... KY
Nazareth Coll ... MI
Nebraska, U. of ... NE
Neumann Coll ... PA
Nevada, U. of (Reno, Las Vegas) NV
New Hampshire, U. of ... NH
New Mexico, U. of ... NM
New Rochelle, Coll. of ... NY
New York U ... NY
Niagara U ... NY
North Carolina, U. of (Chapel Hill, Charlotte, Greensboro) . NC
North Carolina A&T ... NC
North Carolina Central U ... NC
North Dakota, U. of ... ND
North Park Coll ... IL
Northeast Louisiana State U ... LA
Northeast Missouri State ... MO
Northeastern U ... MA
Northern Colorado, U. of ... CO
Northern Illinois U ... IL
Northern Michigan U ... MI
Northwestern U ... IL
Northwestern State U. of Louisiana ... LA
Oakland U ... MI
Ohio State U ... OH
Ohio Wesleyan U ... OH
Oklahoma, U. of ... OK
Oklahoma Baptist U ... OK
Old Dominion U ... VA
Olivet Nazarene Coll ... IL
Oral Roberts U ... OK
Oregon, U. of ... OR
Pace U ... NY
Pacific Lutheran U ... WA
Pennsylvania, U. of ... PA
Pennsylvania State U ... PA
Pittsburg State ... KS
Pittsburgh, U. of ... PA
Point Loma Coll ... CA
Portland, U. of ... OR
Prairie View A&M ... TX
Puerto Rico, U. of ... PR
Purdue U. (Calumet Campus, Lafayette) ... IN
Radford Coll ... VA
Rhode Island, U. of ... RI
Rhode Island Coll ... RI
Roberts Wesleyan Coll ... NY
Rochester, U. of ... NY
Rush U ... IL
Russell Sage ... NY
Rutgers ... NJ
Salem State ... MA
Salisbury State Coll ... MD

Salve Regina .... RI
Samford U .... AL
San Diego, U. of ....CA
San Diego State U ....CA
San Francisco, U. of...........CA
San Francisco State ....CA
San Jose State ....CA
Sangamon State IL
Seattle Pacific Coll .... WA
Seattle U .... WA
Seton Hall ....NJ
Simmons .... MA
Skidmore ....NY
Slippery Rock..................PA
Sonoma State U ....CA
South Alabama, U. of........... AL
South Carolina, Med. U. of......SC
South Carolina, U. of (Columbia, Spartanburg)..................SC
South Dakota State U ....SD
South Florida, U. of .... FL
Southeastern Louisiana U ...... LA
Southeastern Massachusetts U . MA
Southern Colorado, U. of...... CO
Southern Connecticut State ....CT
Southern Illinois U IL
Southern Maine, U. of .... ME
Southern Missionary Coll.......TN
Southern Mississippi, U. of .... MS
Southern Oregon State .... OR
Southwestern Oklahoma State . OK
Spalding Coll ....KY
St. Anselm .... NH
St. Benedict, Coll. of .... MN
St. Catherine, Coll. of .... MN
St. Joseph's................... ME
St. Louis U.................... MO
St. Mary of the Plains ....KS
St. Mary's Coll .... IN
St. Olaf Coll .... MN
St. Scholastica, Coll. of........ MN
St. Teresa..................... MN
St. Thomas, U. of ....TX
St. Xavier IL
State U. of New York (Binghamton, Brockport, Buffalo, Downstate Med. Ctr., Plattsburgh, Stony Brook).......................NY
Stephen F. Austin State ....TX
Stockton State Coll ....NJ
Syracuse ....NY
Temple U......................PA
Tennessee, U. of (Chattanooga, Knoxville, Memphis)..........TN
Texas, U. of (Arlington, Austin, El Paso, Galveston, Houston, San Antonio).................TX
Texas Christian U ....TX
Texas Woman's U ....TX
Thomas Jefferson U............PA
Toledo, U. of.................. OH
Towson State U .... MD
Trenton State Coll.............NJ
Troy State U ....AL
Tulsa, U. of .... OK
Tuskegee Inst..................AL
Union Coll.....................NE
Ursuline Coll.................. OH
Utah, U. of.....................UT
Valdosta State .... GA
Valparaiso U .... IN
Vanderbilt ....TN
Vermont, U. of ....VT
Villa Maria ....PA
Villanova ....PA
Virginia, U. of ....VA
Virginia Commonwealth U ......VA
Viterbo Coll.................... WI
Wagner........................NY
Walla Walla Coll .... WA
Washburn U ....KS
Washington, U. of .... WA
Wayne State U .... MI
West Chester State ....PA
West Texas State...............TX
West Virginia U .... WV
West Virginia Wesleyan........ WV
Western Carolina U .... NC
Western Connecticut ....CT
Western Kentucky U ....KY
Wheeling Coll................. WV
Wichita State ....KS
Widener ....PA
Wilkes Coll ....PA
William Carey Coll .... MS
William Jewell................. MO
William Paterson ....NJ
Winona State .... MN
Winston-Salem State .... NC
Wisconsin, U. of (Eau Claire, Madison, Milwaukee, Oshkosh)WI
Worcester State Coll .... MA
Wright State U .... OH
Wyoming, U. of .... WY
Yale ....CT

Nursing, Missionary

Becker Jr. Coll .... MA
Bennett Coll .... NC
Bob Jones U...................SC
Eastern Kentucky ....KY
Fort Scott Comm C ....KS
Freeman Jr. Coll ....SD
Hesston Coll...................KS
Hope Coll...................... MI
Lamar U ....TX
Marywood Coll.................PA
Messiah Coll ....PA
Miami U .... FL
Mississippi Delta Jr............ MS
North Carolina Cent. U .... NC
Tennessee, U. of ....TN
Tennessee Temple U ....TN
Trinity Christian.................IL

Occupational Therapy

College programs accredited by the Council on Medical Education of the American Medical Association and the American Occupational Therapy Association

Alabama, U. of ....AL
Boston U .... MA
Central Arkansas U.............AR
Cleveland State U .... OH
Colorado State U .... CO
Columbia U....................NY
East Carolina .... NC
Eastern Kentucky U ....KY
Eastern Michigan U .... MI
Elizabethtown Coll ....PA
Florida, U. of.................. FL
Florida International .... FL
Georgia, Medical Coll. of ...... GA
Howard U..................... DC
Illinois, U. of IL
Indiana U .... IN
Kansas, U. of ....KS
Kean Coll......................NJ
Loma Linda U..................CA
Louisiana State U .... LA
Minnesota, U. of .... MN
Missouri, U. of .... MO
Mount Mary.................... WI
New Hampshire, U. of .... NH
New York U.....................NY
North Carolina, U. of .... NC
North Dakota, U. of .... ND
Northeast Louisiana ....LA
Ohio State U.................. OH
Oklahoma, U. of .... OK
Pennsylvania, U. of.............PA
Puerto Rico, U. of ....PR
Puget Sound, U. of............ WA
Quinnipiac.....................CT
San Jose State ....CA
South Carolina, Med. U. of......SC
Southern California, U. of ......CA
St. Catherine, Coll. of .... MN
State U. of New York (Buffalo, Downstate Med. Center) ......NY
Temple U......................PA
Texas, U. of (San Antonio)......TX
Texas, U. of, Medical Branch (Galveston) ....TX
Texas Woman's U ....TX
Towson State U .... MD
Tufts .... MA
Tuskegee Inst..................AL
Utica Coll. of Syracuse U ....NY
Virginia Commonwealth U ......VA
Washington, U. of .... WA
Washington U................. MO
Wayne State U .... MI
Western Michigan U........... MI
Wisconsin, U. of (Madison, Milwaukee) .... WI
York Coll. (CUNY) ....NY

Ocean Engineering *See*
ENGINEERING, OCEAN

Oceanography

Undergraduate and/or graduate levels

Alaska, U. of ....AK
Arizona Western Coll ....AZ
Boston U .... MA
Bridgewater State .... MA
California State U. (San Diego) .CA
Catholic U .... DC
City Coll.......................NY
Delaware, U. of ....DE
Florida Inst. of Tech .... FL
Hawaii, U. of (Honolulu) .... HI
Hawaii Loa Coll .... HI
High Point Coll .... NC
Humboldt State U ....CA
Kansas, U. of ....KS
Massachusetts Inst. of Tech ... MA
Millersville State ....PA
Occidental ....CA
Old Dominion U ....VA
Oregon State U .... OR
Southampton Coll.............NY
State U. of New York (Maritime Coll., Farmingdale)..........NY
Texas A&M ....TX
U.S. Naval Acad............... MD
Virginia Polytech ....VA
Virginia Wesleyan Coll..........VA
Washington, U. of .... WA
Washington & Lee.............VA

Operations Research

Baruch Coll....................NY
Bloomfield Coll ....NJ
Boston U .... MA
Bowling Green .... OH
California State U. (Fresno, Northridge) ....CA
Carnegie-Mellon ....PA
Case Western Reserve U ...... OH
Cincinnati, U. of .... OH
Colorado, U. of .... CO
Colorado State U .... CO
Cornell U ....NY
Denver, U. of .... CO
Eastern Washington U......... WA
Florida Atlantic U .... FL
Florida Inst. of Tech .... FL
George Washington U .... DC
Illinois Inst. of Tech IL
Indiana U .... IN
Jones Coll .... FL
Lebanon Valley Coll ....PA
Long Island U..................NY
Louisiana Tech. U ....LA
Massachusetts Inst. of Tech ... MA
Miami, U. of .... FL
Michigan State U............... MI
Minnesota, U. of .... MN
New Haven, U. of ....CT
Nicholls State U................LA
Ohio State U.................. OH
Oklahoma, U. of .... OK
Pennsylvania, U. of............PA
Pennsylvania State U ....PA
Rensselaer Poly. Inst ....NY
Sacred Heart...................CT
South Alabama, U. of........... AL
Southern California, U. of ......CA
Southern Illinois U IL
Southern Methodist U ....TX
St. Ambrose Coll .... IA
St. Cloud State U .... MN
St. John's U ....NY
Syracuse U ....NY
Texas, U. of (Austin) ....TX
Thomas Edison Coll............NJ
Toledo, U. of.................. OH
Trinity Christian.................IL
U.S. Air Force Acad .... CO
U.S. Military Acad ....NY
Villanova U ....PA

Ophthalmology, Ophthalmic Dispensing, Opticianry

Ferris State .... MI
Mater Dei Coll ....NY
Newbury Jr. Coll .... MA

Optometry

Accredited by American Optometric Assn.

Alabama, U. of (Birmingham) ... AL
California, U. of (Berkeley) .....CA
Ferris State .... MI
Houston, U. of ....TX
Illinois Coll. of Opt IL
Indiana U .... IN
Inter-American U...............PR
Missouri, U. of (St. Louis) ..... MO
New England Coll. of Optometry .... MA
Northeastern State U .... OK
Ohio State U.................. OH
Pacific U .... OR
Pennsylvania Coll. of Opt.......PA
Southern California Coll. of Optometry ....CA
Southern Coll. of Opt ....TN
State U. of New York Coll. of Optometry ....NY

Ornamental Horticulture

Alabama A&M...................AL
Auburn U ....AL
California, U. of (Davis).........CA
California State Poly. U ....CA
California State U. (Chico, Fresno) ....CA
Cornell U ....NY
Delaware Valley Coll ....PA
Eastern Kentucky ....KY
Ferris State .... MI
Florida, U. of.................. FL
Florida A&M U .... FL
Florida Southern .... FL
Harper Coll IL
Illinois, U. of (Urbana)...........IL

Morehead State .... KY
Northeast Louisiana U .... LA
Northeast Mississippi Jr .... MS
Purdue U .... IN
State U. of New York (Cobleskill, Farmingdale, Morrisville) ..... NY
SUNY Coll. of Agr. & Life Sci ... NY
Temple U .... PA
Tennessee, U. of .... TN

Ornithology

Cornell U .... NY
Goddard Coll .... VT
Purdue U .... IN
SUNY Coll. of Agr. & Life Sci ... NY

Orthoptics

Colby-Sawyer .... NH

Osteopathy

Accredited by American Osteopathic Association

Chicago Coll. of Osteopathic Medicine IL
College of Medicine and Dentistry .... NJ
Coll. of Osteopathic Medicine and Surgery .... IA
Coll. of Osteopathic Medicine of the Pacific .... CA
Kirksville Coll. of Osteopathic Medicine .... MO
Michigan State U. Coll of Osteopathic Medicine .... MI
New England Coll. of Osteopathic Medicine .... ME
New York Coll. of Osteopathic Medicine .... NY
Oklahoma Coll. of Osteopathic Medicine and Surgery .... OK
Ohio U. Coll. of Osteopathic Medicine .... OH
Philadelphia Coll. of Osteopathic Medicine .... PA
Southeastern Coll. of Osteopathic Medicine .... FL
Texas Coll. of Osteopathic Medicine .... TX
U. of Health Sciences Coll. of Osteopathic Medicine ..... MO
West Virginia School of Osteopathic Medicine .... WV

Outdoor Entertainment Industries

Colorado Mountain Coll .... CO
Minnesota, U. of .... MN

Packaging

Center for Creative Studies ..... MI
Indiana State U .... IN
Kansas City Art Inst .... MO
Michigan State U............... MI
Northern Michigan U .... MI
Philadelphia Coll. of Art .... PA
Rochester Inst. of Tech .... NY

Paleontology

California, U. of (Berkeley, Davis) .... CA
Cornell U .... NY
Kansas, U. of .... KS
South Dakota School of Mines and Technology .... SD
Washington U .... MO

Paper and Pulp Industry

Brevard Coll .... NC
Miami U .... OH
Minnesota, U. of .... MN
North Carolina State U .... NC
Paper Chemistry, Inst. of .... WI
State U. of New York Coll. of Environmental Sci. and Forestry .... NY
Syracuse U .... NY
Washington, U. of .... WA
Wisconsin, U. of (Stevens Point) .... WI

Paralegal Studies, *See* LEGAL ASSISTANT

Paramedical Studies

Central Washington U .... WA
Davenport Coll. of Bus .... MI
El Centro Coll................. TX
Evansville, U. of .... IN
Huntingdon Coll .... AL
Jacksonville State .... AL
Kansas, U. of .... KS
Marywood Coll................. PA
Montana, U. of .... MT
South Alabama, U. of.......... AL

Parapsychology

Goddard Coll .... VT
John F. Kennedy .... CA

Parasitology

Cornell U .... NY
Tuskegee Inst .... AL

Parks and Recreation Management

Institutions awarding more than 25 undergraduate degrees according to statistics of the U.S. Office of Education

Appalachian State U .... NC
Arizona State U .... AZ
Arkansas Tech. U .... AR
Auburn U .... AL
Bowling Green .... OH
California State Poly. (Pomona) .... CA
California State U. (Chico, Fresno, Hayward, Long Beach, Los Angeles, Northridge, Sacramento) .... CA
Central Michigan U............ MI
Central Missouri .... MO
Central Washington State...... WA
Clemson...................... SC
Colorado, U. of .... CO
Colorado State .... CO
East Carolina .... NC
Eastern Illinois IL
Eastern Kentucky .... KY
Eastern Michigan U .... MI
Eastern Washington .... WA
Ferris State .... MI
Florida State U............... FL
George Williams Coll IL
Georgia Southern .... GA
Hawaii, U. of .... HI
Idaho, U. of .... ID
Illinois, U. of IL
Illinois State U IL
Indiana U .... IN
Iowa State U .... IA
Ithaca Coll.................... NY
Kansas State .... KS
Kean Coll .... NJ
Kent State U .... OH
Lyndon State Coll .... VT
Mankato State .... MN
Marshall U .... WV
Maryland, U. of .... MD
Massachusetts, U. of (Amherst) MA
Minnesota, U. of .... MN
Missouri, U. of (Columbia) ..... MO
Morehead State .... KY
Nebraska, U. of .... NE
North Carolina, U. of .... NC
North Carolina State .... NC
Northeastern U .... MA
Northern Arizona U .... AZ
Northern Colorado .... CO
Northern Michigan U .... MI
Oklahoma, U. of .... OK
Oregon, U. of .... OR
Oregon State U .... OR
Pennsylvania State U .... PA
Purdue .... IN
Radford College .... VA
San Diego State U .... CA
San Francisco State U .... CA
San Jose State U.............. CA
Slippery Rock State .... PA
Southern Connecticut State .... CT
Southern Illinois IL
Southwest Missouri State ...... MO
Springfield U .... MA
State U. of New York (Brockport, Cortland) .... NY
Texas A&M .... TX
Texas Tech .... TX
Utah, U. of.................... UT
Virginia Commonwealth .... VA
Washington, U. of .... WA
Washington State U .... WA
West Virginia U .... WV
Western Carolina U .... NC
Western Illinois IL
Western Washington .... WA
Wisconsin, U. of (La Crosse, Madison) .... WI
Wyoming, U. of .... WY

Pathology

Alabama, U. of .... AL
Albany Med. Coll.............. NY
Albert Einstein Coll of Medicine .... NY
Arkansas, U. of................ AR
Baylor U .... TX
Boston U .... MA
Brown U .... RI
California, U. of (Davis, Irvine, Los Angeles, San Diego, San Francisco) .... CA
Case Western Reserve U ...... OH
Chicago, U. of IL
Cincinnati, U. of .... OH
Colorado, U. of .... CO
Colorado State U .... CO
Connecticut, U. of............. CT
Cornell U .... NY
Creighton U .... NE
Duke U .... NC
Eastern Virginia Medical School .... VA
Emory U .... GA
Florida, U. of.................. FL
George Washington U .... DC
Georgia, Medical Coll. of ...... GA
Hahnemann Medical Coll .... PA
Hawaii, U. of .... HI
Howard U.................... DC
Illinois, U. of IL
Indiana U .... IN
Iowa, U. of .... IA
Johns Hopkins U............. MD
Kansas, U. of .... KS
Kentucky, U. of .... KY
Louisiana State U .... LA
Loyola U IL
Marshall U................... WV
Maryland, U. of .... MD
Massachusetts, U. of .... MA
Mayo Medical School .... MN
Miami, U. of .... FL
Michigan, U. of................ MI
Michigan State U.............. MI
Minnesota, U. of .... MN
Missouri, U. of .... MO
Mount Sinai School of Medicine of CUNY..................... NY
Nebraska, U. of .... NE
New Jersey Medical Sch........ NJ
New Mexico, U. of............. NM
New York Medical Coll .... NY
New York State U. of (U. at Buffalo, Downstate Med. Ctr., Upstate Med. Ctr.) .... NY
New York U................... NY
North Carolina, U. of .... NC
Northwestern U IL
Ohio, Med. Coll. of .... OH
Ohio State U .... OH
Oregon, U. of .... OR
Pennsylvania, Med. Coll. of ..... PA
Pennsylvania, U. of............ PA
Pennsylvania State U .... PA
Pittsburgh, U. of .... PA
Rochester, U. of............... NY
Rush U IL
Rutgers U. Medical Sch......... NJ
Saint Louis U .... MO
South Alabama, U. of.......... AL
South Carolina, Medical U. of... SC
South Florida, U. of .... FL
Southern California, U. of ...... CA
Stanford U.................... CA
Temple U .... PA
Tennessee, U. of .... TN
Texas, U. of................... TX
Thomas Jefferson U .... PA
Tufts U .... MA
Tulane U .... LA
Tuskegee Inst .... AL
Utah, U. of.................... UT
Vanderbilt U .... TN
Vermont, U. of .... VT
Virginia, Medical Coll. of .... VA
Wake Forest U .... NC
Washington, U. of .... WA
Washington U................ MO
Wayne State U .... MI
West Virginia U .... WV
Wisconsin, U. of .... WI
Wisconsin, Medical Coll. of ..... WI
Wright State U .... OH
Yale U .... CT

Petroleum Engineering, *See* ENGINEERING, PETROLEUM

Pharmacology

Bee County Coll .... TX
Boston U .... MA
Butler U .... IN
California, U. of (Davis, San Diego, Santa Barbara) .... CA
Cincinnati, U. of .... OH
Clatsop Comm. Coll........... OR
Creighton .... NE

Drake U .... IA
Duquesne U .... PA
Florida, U. of .... FL
Florida A&M .... FL
Gannon U .... PA
Hawaii, U. of .... HI
Iowa, U. of .... IA
Kansas, U. of .... KS
Mercer U .... GA
Michigan State U .... MI
Missouri, U. of (Kansas City) .... MO
Ohio State .... OH
Old Dominion .... VA
Pennsylvania State U. (University Park) .... PA
Purdue .... IN
South Carolina, U. of .... SC
Texas, U. of (Austin) .... TX
Tuskegee Inst .... AL
Utah, U. of .... UT
Virginia Commonwealth U .... VA
Wayne State U .... MI
West Virginia U .... WV

Pharmacy

Accredited by American Council on Pharmaceutical Education

Arizona, U. of .... AZ
Arkansas, U. of (Little Rock) .... AR
Auburn U .... AL
Butler U .... IN
California, U. of (San Francisco) .... CA
Cincinnati, U. of .... OH
Colorado, U. of .... CO
Connecticut, U. of .... CT
Creighton U .... NE
Drake U .... IA
Duquesne U .... PA
Ferris State Coll .... MI
Florida, U. of .... FL
Florida A&M U .... FL
Georgia, U. of .... GA
Houston, U. of .... TX
Howard U .... DC
Idaho State U .... ID
Illinois, U. of IL
Iowa, U. of .... IA
Kansas, U. of .... KS
Kentucky, U. of .... KY
Long Island U. (Schwartz Coll. of Pharmacy) .... NY
Maryland, U. of .... MD
Massachusetts Coll. of Pharmacy .... MA
Mercer U .... GA
Michigan, U. of .... MI
Minnesota, U. of .... MN
Mississippi, U. of .... MS
Missouri, U. of (Kansas City) .... MO
Montana, U. of .... MT
Nebraska, U. of .... NE
New Mexico, U. of .... NM
North Carolina, U. of .... NC
North Dakota State U .... ND
Northeast Louisiana U .... LA
Northeastern U .... MA
Ohio Northern U .... OH
Ohio State U .... OH
Oklahoma, U. of .... OK
Oregon State U .... OR
Pacific, U. of the .... CA
Philadelphia Coll. of Pharmacy and Science .... PA
Pittsburgh, U. of .... PA
Puerto Rico, U. of .... PR
Purdue U .... IN
Rhode Island, U. of .... RI
Rutgers U .... NJ
Samford U .... AL
South Carolina, Medical U. of .... SC
South Carolina, U. of .... SC
South Dakota State U .... SD
Southern California, U. of .... CA
Southwestern Oklahoma State U .... OK
St. John's U .... NY
St. Louis Coll. of Pharmacy .... MO
State U. of New York (Buffalo) .... NY
Temple U .... PA
Tennessee, U. of .... TN
Texas, U. of (Austin) .... TX
Texas Southern U .... TX
Toledo, U. of .... OH
Union (Albany Coll. of Pharmacy) .... NY
Utah, U. of .... UT
Virginia Commonwealth U .... VA
Washington, U. of .... WA
Washington State U .... WA
Wayne State U .... MI
West Virginia U .... WV
Wisconsin, U. of (Madison) .... WI
Wyoming, U. of .... WY
Xavier U .... LA

Philology

Beloit Coll .... WI
Brevard Coll .... NC
Charleston, U. of .... WV
Cincinnati, U. of .... OH
D'Youville Coll .... NY
Hampshire Coll .... MA
Jacksonville U .... FL
Lincoln U .... MO
Northern Iowa, U. of .... IA
Schreiner Coll .... TX
St. Bonaventure U .... NY
Stockton State .... NJ

Philosophy

Institutions awarding 10 or more undergraduate degrees as major field in single year according to U.S. Office of Education latest statistics

Amherst .... MA
Arizona, U. of .... AZ
Arizona State .... AZ
Beloit .... WI
Boston Coll .... MA
Boston U .... MA
Brandeis .... MA
Brown .... RI
California, U. of (Berkeley, Irvine, Los Angeles, San Diego, Santa Barbara, Santa Cruz) .... CA
California State U. (Dominguez Hills, Fullerton, Long Beach, Los Angeles, Northridge) .... CA
Calvin Coll .... MI
Cardinal Glennon Coll .... MO
Catholic U .... DC
Clark U .... MA
Colgate .... NY
Colorado, U. of .... CO
Colorado State .... CO
Columbia .... NY
Connecticut, U. of .... CT
Denver, U. of .... CO
Dominican School .... CA
Don Bosco .... NJ
Duke U .... NC
Duquesne U .... PA
Emory U .... GA
Florida, U. of .... FL
Fordham .... NY
George Washington U .... DC
Georgetown .... DC
Georgia, U. of .... GA
Greenville Coll IL
Harvard .... MA
Haverford .... PA
Holy Cross, Coll. of the .... MA
Hunter Coll .... NY
Illinois, U. of IL
Illinois State IL
Indiana U .... IN
Iona Coll .... NY
Kansas, U. of .... KS
Lehman Coll .... NY
Loyola U IL
Maharishi International .... IA
Marquette U .... WI
Maryland, U. of .... MD
Massachusetts, U. of .... MA
Michigan, U. of .... MI
Michigan State U .... MI
Minnesota, U. of .... MN
New Hampshire, U. of .... NH
New York U .... NY
North Texas State .... TX
Northwestern U IL
Notre Dame .... IN
Oregon, U. of .... OR
Pennsylvania State U .... PA
Pittsburgh, U. of .... PA
Pomona .... CA
Portland State .... OR
Princeton .... NJ
Queens .... NY
Reed Coll .... OR
Rhode Island, U. of .... RI
Ripon Coll .... WI
Roberts Wesleyan .... NY
Rutgers .... NJ
San Diego State .... CA
San Francisco State .... CA
San Jose State .... CA
Scranton, U. of .... PA
South Carolina, U. of .... SC
South Florida, U. of .... FL
St. Charles Borromeo Sem .... PA
St. John's Coll .... CA
St. Louis U .... MO
St. Pius .... KY
Stanford .... CA
State U. of New York (Albany, Binghamton, Buffalo, New Paltz, Purchase, Stony Brook) .... NY
Swarthmore .... PA
Syracuse .... NY
Tennessee, U. of .... TN
Texas, U. of (Austin) .... TX
Trinity Coll .... CT
Tulane U .... LA
Utah, U. of .... UT
Vanderbilt .... TN
Vassar Coll .... NY
Wadhams Hall .... NY
Washington, U. of .... WA
Wellesley .... MA
Wheaton IL
William and Mary .... VA
Wisconsin, U. of (Madison, Milwaukee) .... WI
Yale .... CT

Photogrammetry

California State U. (Fresno) .... CA
Purdue U .... IN
South Dakota, U. of (Springfield) .... SD

Photographic Equipment Technology

California State Coll .... PA
Emporia State .... KS
Southern Illinois U IL

Photographic Science and Instrumentation

California State Coll .... PA
Central Missouri .... MO
Rochester Inst. of Tech .... NY
St. Cloud State U .... MN

Photography

Akron, U. of .... OH
American Coll. in Paris .... France
Arizona State U .... AZ
Art Inst. of Pittsburgh .... PA
Artesia Christian Coll .... NM
Ball State U .... IN
Barat IL
Bard .... NY
Bennett Coll .... NC
Bradley IL
Brevard .... NC
Bridgeport, U. of .... CT
Brooks Inst .... CA
C.W. Post .... NY
California, U. of (Santa Cruz) .... CA
California Coll. of Arts and Crafts .... CA
California Institute of the Arts .... CA
California State U. (Los Angeles) .... CA
Carson-Newman .... TN
Center for Creative Studies .... MI
Central Missouri .... MO
Coker Coll .... SC
Coll. of Design .... CA
Colorado Inst. of Art .... CO
Colorado Mountain .... CO
Columbia Coll IL
Columbia .... MO
Connecticut, U. of .... CT
Creighton U .... NE
Dayton, U. of .... OH
DuPage, Coll. of IL
East Texas State .... TX
Eastern Kentucky .... KY
Eastern Washington U .... WA
Endicott Coll .... MA
Ferris State .... MI
Florida, U. of .... FL
Florida Inst. of Tech .... FL
Florida Inst. of Tech.-Sch. of App. Tech .... FL
George Washington U .... DC
Georgia State U .... GA
Goddard Coll .... VT
Grand Valley .... MI
Hampton Institute .... VA
Hampshire Coll .... MA
Hartford, U. of .... CT
High Point Coll .... NC
Hofstra U .... NY
Illinois Central Coll IL
Illinois Inst. of Tech IL
Indiana State U .... IN
Iowa, U. of .... IA
Ithaca .... NY
Jersey City State .... NJ
Kansas, U. of .... KS
Kansas City Art Inst .... MO
Kendall IL
Kent State U .... OH
Lincoln IL
Loma Linda .... CA
Louisiana Tech .... LA

Louisville, U. of .... KY
Massachusetts Coll. of Art ..... MA
Minnesota, U. of .... MN
Montana State U .... MT
New Haven, U. of .... CT
New Rochelle, Coll. of .... NY
New York U .... NY
North Alabama, U. of .... AL
North Florida, U. of .... FL
North Texas State U .... TX
Northeast Louisiana .... LA
Northeast Mississippi Jr. Coll .. MS
Northeast Missouri State Coll .. MO
Northern Arizona U .... AZ
Northern Kentucky .... KY
Northern Michigan .... MI
Northwestern State U .... LA
Ohio State U .... OH
Ohio U .... OH
Oklahoma Christian Coll .... OK
Otis Art Inst .... CA
Pepperdine U .... CA
Philadelphia Coll. of Art .... PA
Pratt Inst .... NY
Providence .... RI
Purdue U .... IN
Rhode Island Sch. of Design .... RI
Rochester Inst. of Tech .... NY
Rockmont Coll .... CO
Saint Edward's U .... TX
Sam Houston State .... TX
San Francisco Art Inst .... CA
Savannah Coll. of Art and Design .... GA
Seton Hill Coll .... PA
Shepherd Coll .... WV
South Alabama, U. of .... AL
South Dakota, U. of .... SD
Southern Idaho, Coll. of .... ID
Southern Illinois U IL
Southwest Missouri .... MO
St. Gregory's Coll .... OK
State U. of New York (Buffalo) .. NY
State U. of N.Y. Coll. (Buffalo, Potsdam) .... NY
Stephen F. Austin .... TX
Syracuse U .... NY
Temple U .... PA
Tennessee Temple U .... TN
Texas Woman's U .... TX
Unity Coll .... ME
Valparaiso U .... IN
Virginia Commonwealth .... VA
Virginia Intermont .... VA
Visual Arts, School of .... NY
Washington U .... MO
Wayne State U .... MI
Webster Coll .... MO
Western Kentucky U .... KY
White Pines Coll .... NH
William Woods .... MO
Winona State .... MN
Wisconsin, U. of (Milwaukee, Superior) .... WI
Wright State U .... OH

Physical Education

Institutions awarding 30 or more undergraduate degrees as major field in single year according to U.S. Office of Education latest statistics

Adelphi U .... NY
Akron, U. of .... OH
Alabama State .... AL
Angelo State .... TX
Appalachian State U .... NC
Arizona, U. of .... AZ
Arkansas, U. of .... AR
Arkansas State U .... AR
Auburn U .... AL
Ball State U .... IN
Boise State .... ID
Bowling Green State .... OH
Bridgewater State Coll .... MA
Brigham Young .... UT
Brooklyn Coll .... NY
California, U. of (Berkeley, Santa Barbara) .... CA
California Poly. State U .... CA
California State Poly. U .... CA
California State U. (Chico, Fresno, Fullerton, Hayward, Long Beach, Los Angeles, Northridge, Sacramento) ..... CA
Cameron U .... OK
Carson-Newman .... TN
Central Arkansas, U. of .... AR
Central Connecticut .... CT
Central Michigan .... MI
Central Missouri State .... MO
Central State U .... OK
Central Washington .... WA
Cincinnati, U. of .... OH
Colorado, U. of .... CO
Colorado State U .... CO
Connecticut, U. of .... CT
Dayton, U. of .... OH
Delaware, U. of .... DE
Delta State Coll .... MS
East Carolina U .... NC
East Stroudsburg State Coll .... PA
East Tennessee State .... TN
East Texas State U .... TX
Eastern Illinois U IL
Eastern Kentucky U .... KY
Eastern Michigan .... MI
Eastern New Mexico .... NM
Eastern Washington .... WA
Elon .... NC
Emporia Kansas State .... KS
Florida, U. of .... FL
Florida A&M .... FL
Florida Atlantic U .... FL
Florida International .... FL
Florida Southern .... FL
Florida State U .... FL
Florida Tech .... FL
Fort Hays Kansas State .... KS
Frostburg State Coll .... MD
Georgia, U. of .... GA
Georgia Southern .... GA
Glassboro .... NJ
Grand Valley .... MI
Hawaii, U. of .... HI
Henderson State Coll .... AR
Houston, U. of .... TX
Humboldt State .... CA
Illinois, U. of IL
Illinois State U IL
Indiana State U .... IN
Indiana U .... IN
Indiana U. of Pennsylvania .... PA
Iowa, U. of .... IA
Iowa State U .... IA
Ithaca .... NY
Jackson State U .... MS
Jacksonville State U .... AL
James Madison U .... VA
Kansas, U. of .... KS
Kansas State U .... KS
Kean Coll .... NJ
Kearney State Coll .... NE
Keene State .... NH
Kent State U .... OH
Lamar U .... TX
Lehman .... NY
Lock Haven State .... PA
Louisiana State .... LA
Maine, U. of (Orono) .... ME
Manhattan Coll .... NY
Mankato State .... MN
Maryland, U. of .... MD
Massachusetts, U. of .... MA
Memphis State .... TN
Miami U .... OH
Michigan State U .... MI
Middle Tennessee State .... TN
Minnesota, U. of .... MN
Mississippi, U. of .... MS
Mississippi State U .... MS
Mississippi Valley State .... MS
Missouri, U. of .... MO
Missouri Southern .... MO
Montana, U. of .... MT
Montana State .... MT
Montclair State .... NJ
Montevallo, U. of .... AL
Moorhead State U .... MN
Morehead State U .... KY
Nebraska, U. of .... NE
Nevada, U. of .... NV
New Mexico, U. of .... NM
New Orleans, U. of .... LA
Norfolk State .... VA
North Alabama, U. of .... AL
North Carolina, U. of .... NC
North Dakota, U. of .... ND
North Texas .... TX
Northeast Missouri State U .... MO
Northeastern Illinois U IL
Northeastern State .... OK
Northeastern U .... MA
Northern Arizona .... AZ
Northern Colorado .... CO
Northern Illinois U IL
Northern Iowa, U. of .... IA
Northern Michigan .... MI
Northwest Missouri .... MO
Ohio State U .... OH
Ohio U .... OH
Oklahoma State U .... OK
Old Dominion .... VA
Oregon, U. of .... OR
Oregon Coll. of Educ .... OR
Oregon State U .... OR
Pan American U .... TX
Pembroke .... NC
Pennsylvania State U .... PA
Pittsburg State U .... KS
Pittsburgh, U. of .... PA
Plymouth State Coll .... NH
Portland State U .... OR
Puerto Rico, U. of .... PR
Purdue .... IN
Queens Coll .... NY
Rhode Island, U. of .... RI
Rutgers U .... NJ
Sam Houston State U .... TX
San Diego State .... CA
San Francisco State .... CA
San Jose State .... CA
Slippery Rock State .... PA
South Carolina, U. of .... SC
South Carolina State .... SC
South Dakota State U .... SD
South Florida, U. of .... FL
Southeast Missouri State .... MO
Southern California, U. of .... CA
Southern Connecticut State Coll .... CT
Southern Illinois U IL
Southern Mississippi, U. of .... MS
Southwest Missouri State .... MO
Southwest Texas State U .... TX
Southwestern Louisiana .... LA
Southwestern State .... OK
Springfield .... MA
St. Cloud State U .... MN
State U. of New York (Brockport, Buffalo, Cortland) .... NY
Stephen F. Austin State U .... TX
Tarleton .... TX
Temple U .... PA
Tennessee, U. of .... TN
Tennessee State .... TN
Tennessee Tech. U .... TN
Texas, U. of (Arlington, Austin, El Paso) .... TX
Texas A&M .... TX
Texas Tech .... TX
Towson State U .... MD
Trenton State .... NJ
Utah, U. of .... UT
Utah State U .... UT
Vermont, U. of .... VT
Virginia State .... VA
Washingtin, U. of .... WA
Washington State U .... WA
Wayne State U .... MI
West Chester State .... PA
West Florida, U. of .... FL
West Texas State U .... TX
West Virginia U .... WV
Western Carolina U .... NC
Western Illinois IL
Western Kentucky .... KY
Western Michigan .... MI
Western State .... CO
Western Washington .... WA
Westfield State Coll .... MA
William Paterson State .... NJ
Winthrop .... NC
Wisconsin, U. of (La Crosse, Madison, Milwaukee, Oshkosh, River Falls, Stevens Point, Whitewater) .... WI

Physical Therapist Assistant

Program accredited by the American Physical Therapy Association

Alabama, U. of (Birmingham) ... AL
Atlantic Comm. Coll .... NJ
Baltimore, Comm. Coll. of ..... MD
Becker Jr .... MA
Belleville Area Coll IL
Broward Comm. Coll .... FL
Central Piedmont Comm. Coll . NC
Cerritos Coll .... CA
Chattanooga State Comm. Coll .... TN
Colby Comm. Coll .... KS
Cuyahoga Comm. Coll .... OH
DeAnza Comm. Coll .... CA
Delta Coll .... MI
Essex County Coll .... NJ
Evansville, U. of .... IN
Fairleigh Dickinson U .... NJ
Fayetteville Tech. Inst .... NC
Georgia, Medical Coll. of .... GA
Green River Comm. Coll .... WA
Greenville Tech. Comm. Coll ... SC
Houston Comm. Coll .... TX
Humacao Regional Coll .... PR
Illinois Central Coll IL
Jefferson Comm .... KY
Kellogg Comm. Coll .... MI
Lasell Jr. Coll .... MA
Lehigh County Comm. Coll ..... PA
Los Angeles Pierce .... CA
Maria Coll .... NY
Miami-Dade Comm. Coll .... FL
Milwaukee Area Tech. Coll ..... WI
Morton Coll IL
Mount Hood Comm. Coll .... OR
Mount St. Mary's .... CA
Nassau Comm. Coll .... NY
New Hampshire Voc.-Tech. Coll. (Claremont) .... NH
New York U. (Rehabilitation Medicine, Inst. of) .... NY
Newbury Jr. Coll .... MA
North Shore Comm. Coll .... MA
Northern Virginia Comm .... VA
Oakton Comm IL
Orange County Comm. Coll .... NY
Penn Valley Comm .... MO

Puerto Rico, U. of .... PR
San Diego Mesa Coll .... CA
Shelby State Comm. Coll .... TN
Sinclair Comm. C .... OH
Southern Illinois U IL
Springfield Tech. Comm. Coll .. MA
St. Mary's Jr. Coll .... MN
St. Petersburg Jr. Coll .... FL
St. Philip's Coll .... TX
Suffolk County Comm. Coll .... NY
Tarrant County Jr. Coll .... TX
Union County Tech. Inst .... NJ
Vincennes U .... IN
Volunteer State Comm .... TN

Physical Therapy

College programs accredited by the American Physical Therapy Association

Alabama, U. of (Birmingham) ... AL
Baylor .... TX
Boston U .... MA
California, U. of (San Francisco) .... CA
California State U. (Fresno, Long Beach, Northridge) .... CA
Central Arkansas, U. of .... AR
Chicago Medical Sch IL
Cleveland State U .... OH
Colorado, U. of .... CO
Columbia U .... NY
Connecticut, U. of .... CT
Daemen Coll .... NY
Delaware, U. of .... DE
Duke U .... NC
East Carolina U .... NC
Emory .... GA
Evansville, U. of .... IN
Florida, U. of .... FL
Florida International .... FL
Georgia, Medical Coll. of .... GA
Georgia State U .... GA
Hahnemann Med. Coll .... PA
Howard U .... DC
Hunter Coll .... NY
Illinois, U. of., Med. Ctr IL
Indiana U .... IN
Iowa, U. of .... IA
Ithaca Coll .... NY
Kansas, U. of .... KS
Kentucky, U. of .... KY
Loma Linda U .... CA
Louisiana State U .... LA
Lowell, U. of .... MA
Marquette U .... WI
Maryland, U. of .... MD
Michigan, U. of .... MI
Minnesota, U. of .... MN
Mississippi, U. of .... MS
Missouri, U. of .... MO
Montana, U. of .... MT
Mt. St. Mary's .... CA
Nebraska, U. of .... NE
New Jersey Coll. of Medicine and Dentistry .... NJ
New Mexico, U. of .... NM
New York U .... NY
North Carolina, U. of .... NC
North Dakota, U. of .... ND
Northeastern U .... MA
Northern Arizona U .... AZ
Northwestern U IL
Oakland U .... MI
Ohio State U .... OH
Oklahoma, U. of .... OK
Old Dominion U .... VA
Pacific U .... OR
Pittsburgh, U. of .... PA
Puerto Rico, U. of .... PR
Puget Sound, U. of .... WA
Quinnipiac Coll .... CT
Russell Sage Coll .... NY
Simmons Coll .... MA
South Alabama, U. of .... AL
South Carolina, Med. U. of .... SC
Southern California, U. of .... CA
St. Louis U .... MO
St. Scholastica, Coll. of .... MN
Stanford U .... CA
State U. of New York (Buffalo, Downstate Med. Ctr., Stony Brook, Upstate Med. Ctr.) .... NY
Temple U .... PA
Tennessee, U. of .... TN
Texas, U. of (Medical Branch-Galveston, Health Science Ctr. at Dallas, San Antonio) .... TX
Texas Woman's U .... TX
Tuskegee Inst .... AL
Utah, U. of .... UT
Vermont, U. of .... VT
Virginia Commonwealth U .... VA
Washington, U. of .... WA
Washington U .... MO
Wayne State U .... MI
West Virginia U .... WV
Wichita State U .... KS
Wisconsin, U. of (La Crosse, Madison) .... WI

Physician's Assistant, *See*

PRIMARY CARE PHYSICIANS, ASSISTANT TO

Physics

Institutions awarding 10 or more undergraduate degrees as major field in single year according to U.S. Office of Education latest statistics

Alabama A&M .... AL
Amherst Coll .... MA
Appalachian State .... NC
Arizona, U. of .... AZ
Arkansas, U. of .... AR
Auburn U .... AL
Brigham Young U .... UT
Brown U .... RI
California, U. of (Berkeley, Irvine, Los Angeles, San Diego, Santa Barbara, Santa Cruz) .... CA
California Inst. of Tech .... CA
California Poly St. U .... CA
California State Poly. U .... CA
California State U. (Sonoma) ... CA
California State U. (Bakersfield, Fullerton, Northridge) .... CA
Calvin Coll .... MI
Carnegie-Mellon U .... PA
Case Western .... OH
Central Connecticut .... CT
Central State .... OK
Chicago, U. of IL
Clarkson .... NY
Colorado, U. of .... CO
Colorado School of Mines .... CO
Colorado State U .... CO
Cornell .... NY
Dartmouth .... NH
Drexel U .... PA
Eastern Illinois U IL
Emory U .... GA
Florida State .... FL
Franklin and Marshall .... PA
Georgia Inst. of Tech .... GA
Gettysburg .... PA
Harvard .... MA
Harvey Mudd Coll .... CA
Holy Cross, Coll. of .... MA
Humboldt State U .... CA
Illinois, U. of IL
Illinois Inst. of Tech IL
Illinois State U IL
Indiana U .... IN
Iowa State U .... IA
John Carroll .... OH
La Salle .... PA
Lowell, U. of .... MA
Manhattan Coll .... NY
Maryland, U. of .... MD
Massachusetts, U. of .... MA
Massachusetts Inst. of Tech ... MA
Miami U .... OH
Michigan, U. of .... MI
Michigan State U .... MI
Minnesota, U. of .... MN
Missouri, U. of (Rolla, St. Louis) .... MO
Nebraska, U. of .... NE
North Carolina, U. of .... NC
Northeastern U .... MA
Northern Arizona .... AZ
Northern Illinois U IL
Oakland U .... MI
Oberlin Coll .... OH
Pennsylvania, U. of .... PA
Pennsylvania State U .... PA
Princeton .... NJ
Purdue .... IN
Reed Coll .... OR
Rensselaer Poly. Inst .... NY
Rice .... TX
Rutgers .... NJ
San Jose State .... CA
South Dakota, U. of .... SD
Southwest Missouri State .... MO
Southwestern Oklahoma State . OK
Stanford .... CA
State U. of New York (Albany, Buffalo, Oneonta, Stony Brook) .... NY
Stockton State Coll .... NJ
Tennessee, U. of .... TN
Texas, U. of (Arlington, Austin, El Paso) .... TX
Texas A&M .... TX
Towson State .... MD
U.S. Air Force Acad .... CO
U.S. Naval Acad .... MD
Utah, U. of .... UT
Virginia, U. of .... VA
Virginia Poly. Inst .... VA
Washington, U. of .... WA
Washington State U .... WA
William and Mary, Coll. of .... VA
Williams .... MA
Wisconsin, U. of (Eau Claire, Madison, Whitewater) .... WI
Worcester Poly .... MA
Yale .... CT

Physiology

Institutions awarding undergraduate degrees as major field according to American Physiological Society

Akron, U. of .... OH
Alaska, U. of .... AK
Albany Medical Coll .... NY
Arkansas, U. of .... AR
Aurora Coll IL
Bowling Green State U .... OH
California, U. of (Berkeley, Davis, San Diego, Santa Barbara) ... CA
California State U. (Hayward, Los Angeles) .... CA
Case Western Reserve U .... OH
Clark U .... MA
Clemson U .... SC
Connecticut, U. of .... CT
Cornell U .... NY
Dayton, U. of .... OH
Delaware, U. of .... DE
Detroit, U. of .... MI
Drake U .... IA
Duke U .... NC
East Tennessee State Coll .... TN
East Texas State U .... TX
Eastern Illinois U IL
Eastern Michigan U .... MI
Fairleigh Dickinson U .... NJ
Florida State U .... FL
Fort Hays State U .... KS
Georgetown U .... DC
Glenville State Coll .... WV
Hawaii, U. of .... HI
Idaho, U. of .... ID
Idaho State U .... ID
Illinois, U. of (Urbana) IL
Indiana State U .... IN
Indiana U. School of Medicine .. IN
Iowa, U. of .... IA
Kansas, U. of .... KS
Kentucky, U. of .... KY
Kenyon Coll .... OH
Louisiana Tech. U .... LA
Mankato State U .... MN
Massachusetts, U. of .... MA
Massachusetts Inst. of Tech ... MA
Miami U .... OH
Michigan, U. of .... MI
Michigan State U .... MI
Michigan Tech. U .... MI
Minnesota, U. of .... MN
Missouri, U. of (Kansas City) .. MO
New Hampshire, U. of .... NH
North Dakota State U .... ND
Northern Colorado, U. of .... CO
Notre Dame, U. of .... IN
Oberlin Coll .... OH
Ohio Wesleyan .... OH
Oklahoma, U. of .... OK
Oklahoma State U .... OK
Oregon State U .... OR
Pacific, U. of the .... CA
Pomona Coll .... CA
Princeton U .... NJ
Purdue U .... IN
Rhode Island, U. of .... RI
Rice U .... TX
Rutgers State U .... NJ
St. Scholastica, Coll. of .... MN
San Diego State U .... CA
San Francisco State U .... CA
South Dakota State .... SD
Southeast Missouri State U .... MO
Southern California, U. of .... CA
Southern Illinois U IL
Stockton State Coll .... NJ
Syracuse U .... NY
Tennessee, U. of (Knoxville) .... TN
Texas, U. of (Austin, El Paso) ... TX
Toledo, U. of .... OH
Utah State U .... UT
Virginia Poly. Inst .... VA
Washington, U. of .... WA
Wayne State U .... MI
Weber State Coll .... UT
Wellesley Coll .... MA
Western Michigan U .... MI
Wisconsin, U. of (Platteville) .... WI
Wittenberg U .... OH
Wyoming, U. of .... WY

Piano Tuning Technology

Evangel Coll .... MO
Mount Aloysius Jr. Coll .... PA
Pittsburg State .... KS
Shenandoah Coll. and Conservatory of Music .... VA

Plant Pathology

Arizona, U. of .... AZ
California, U. of (Davis, Riverside) .... CA
Colorado State U .... CO
Cornell U .... NY
Delaware, U. of .... DE
Florida, U. of.................. FL
Goddard Coll .... VT
Illinois, U. of (Urbana) IL
Kentucky, U. of .... KY
Marlboro Coll .... VT
Massachusetts, U. of .... MA
Missouri, U. of .... MO
North Dakota State U .... ND
Ohio State U .... OH
Oklahoma State U.............. OK
Pennsylvania State U .... PA
Purdue .... IN
SUNY Coll. of Agri. & Life Sci .. NY
Tennessee, U. of .... TN
Texas A&M .... TX
West Virginia U .... WV
Wisconsin, U. of (Madison) ..... WI

Plant Physiology

California, U. of (Davis, Riverside) .... CA
Cornell U .... NY
Goddard Coll .... VT
Maine, U. of .... ME
Marlboro Coll .... VT
Mars Hill...................... NC
North Dakota State U .... ND
Purdue U .... IN
St. Andrew's Presbyterian ..... NC
SUNY Coll. of Agri. & Life Sci .. NY
Tennessee, U. of .... TN
Texas A&M .... TX
Trinity Christian................ IL
Western Kentucky U .... KY

Plastics Technology

Institutions according to statistics of the Plastics Technology Education Foundation

Berkshire Comm. Coll .... MA
California Poly State U. (San Luis Obispo) .... CA
California State U. (Chico) ...... CA
Carnegie-Mellon U .... PA
Case Western Reserve .... OH
Central Connecticut State U .... CT
Cincinnati Tech. Inst .... OH
Dayton, U. of .... OH
Detroit, U. of.................. MI
DuPage, Coll. of IL
Elgin Comm. Coll IL
Ferris State Coll................ MI
Illinois State U IL
Lakeshore Tech. Inst .... WI
Los Angeles Trade & Tech. Coll .... CA
Ohio U .... OH
Pennsylvania State U .... PA
Pittsburg State U .... KS
Ricks Coll .... ID
Shawnee State Comm. Coll .... OH
Southern California, U. of ...... CA
Southern Mississippi, U. of .... MS
State U. of New York A&T Coll. (Morrisville) .... NY
Utah, U. of.................... UT
Virginia Poly. Inst .... VA
Western Washington State Coll WA

Podiatry

Accredited by the American Association of Colleges of Podiatric Medicine

California Coll. of Podiatric Medicine .... CA
Coll. of Podiatric Medicine and Surgery .... IA
Dr. William Scholl Coll. of Podiatric Medicine IL
New York Coll. of Podiatric Medicine .... NY
Ohio Coll. of Podiatric Medicine .... OH
Pennsylvania Coll. of Podiatric Medicine .... PA

Police Science, *See* CRIMINOLOGY

Political Science and Government

Institutions awarding 30 or more undergraduate degrees as major field in single year according to U.S. Office of Education latest statistics

Akron, U. of .... OH
Alabama, U. of .... AL
Allegheny Coll .... PA
American U .... DC
Amherst .... MA
Arizona, U. of .... AZ
Arizona State U .... AZ
Arkansas, U. of................ AR
Auburn .... AL
Ball State U .... IN
Baltimore, U. of .... MD
Barnard .... NY
Biscayne Coll .... FL
Boston Coll .... MA
Boston U .... MA
Bowdoin...................... ME
Brandeis...................... MA
Brigham Young .... UT
Brooklyn Coll .... NY
Brown .... RI
California, U. of (Berkeley, Davis, Irvine, Los Angeles, Riverside, San Diego, Santa Barbara, Santa Cruz) .... CA
California Poly. State .... CA
California State Poly. (Pomona) .... CA
California State U. (Chico, Fullerton, Hayward, Long Beach, Los Angeles, Northridge, Sacramento) .... CA
Central Connecticut .... CT
Central Michigan U............ MI
Charleston, Coll. of............ SC
Chicago, U. of IL
Cincinnati, U. of .... OH
Citadel .... SC
City Coll .... NY
Claremont McKenna Coll .... CA
Clark Coll..................... MA
Clemson .... SC
Cleveland State .... OH
Colby Coll .... ME
Colgate .... NY
Colorado, U. of .... CO
Colorado Coll .... CO
Colorado State U .... CO
Columbia .... NY
Connecticut, U. of .... CT
Connecticut Coll .... CT
Cornell .... NY
Dartmouth .... NH
Delaware, U. of .... DE
Denison U .... OH
Denver, U. of .... CO
DePaul U IL
Dickinson Coll .... PA
Drake.......................... IA
Drew U .... NJ
Duke .... NC
Duquesne...................... PA
East Carolina .... NC
East Tennessee State U .... TN
Eastern Illinois IL
Emory .... GA
Fairfield U .... CT
Fayetteville State .... NC
Florida, U. of.................. FL
Florida A&M .... FL
Florida International............ FL
Florida State .... FL
Florida Tech .... FL
Fordham...................... NY
Franklin and Marshall Coll ...... PA
Frostburg State Coll .... MD
Furman .... SC
George Mason U .... VA
George Washington .... DC
Georgetown .... DC
Georgia, U. of................ GA
Georgia State U .... GA
Gettysburg.................... PA
Hamilton Coll .... NY
Harvard........................ MA
Hawaii, U. of.................. HI
Hofstra .... NY
Holy Cross, Coll. of the........ MA
Houston, U. of .... TX
Howard U...................... DC
Hunter Coll .... NY
Illinois, U. of IL
Illinois State U IL
Indiana State U .... IN
Indiana U .... IN
Indiana U. of Pennsylvania...... PA
Iowa, U. of.................... IA
Iowa State U .... IA
Jacksonville .... AL
James Madison Coll............ VA
John Carroll U .... OH
John Jay Coll.................. NY
Johns Hopkins U.............. MD
Kansas, U. of .... KS
Kansas State U................ KS
Kean Coll...................... NJ
Kent State .... OH
Kentucky, U. of .... KY
Kenyon Coll .... OH
Lafayette Coll .... PA
Lehigh U .... PA
Lehman .... NY
Long Island U.................. NY
Louisiana State U. (Baton Rouge) .... LA
Louisville, U. of .... KY
Loyola........................ IL
Loyola Marymount U .... CA
Maine, U. of .... ME
Marquette...................... WI
Maryland, U. of .... MD
Massachusetts, U. of .... MA
Memphis State U.............. TN
Mercer U .... GA
Merrimack Coll .... MA
Miami, U. of .... FL
Miami U .... OH
Michigan, U. of................ MI
Michigan State .... MI
Middle Tennessee.............. TN
Middlebury Coll .... VT
Minnesota, U. of .... MN
Mississippi, U. of .... MS
Mississippi State U .... MS
Missouri, U. of .... MO
Montana State .... MT
Montclair State................ NJ
Mount Holyoke .... MA
Mount St. Mary''s .... MD
Nebraska, U. of .... NE
New Hampshire, U. of .... NH
New Mexico, U. of............ NM
New Orleans, U. of .... LA
New York U.................... NY
North Carolina, U. of .... NC
North Carolina Central U ...... NC
North Carolina State .... NC
North Texas State .... TX
Northeastern Illinois............ IL
Northeastern U................ MA
Northern Illinois U IL
Northwestern IL
Notre Dame, U. of............ IN
Oakland U .... MI
Oberlin .... OH
Occidental .... CA
Ohio State U.................. OH
Ohio U .... OH
Ohio Wesleyan................ OH
Oklahoma, U. of .... OK
Oklahoma State U............ OK
Old Dominion U .... VA
Oregon, U. of .... OR
Oregon State U .... OR
Pan American.................. TX
Pennsylvania, U. of............ PA
Pennsylvania State U .... PA
Pittsburgh, U. of .... PA
Princeton .... NJ
Puerto Rico, U. of .... PR
Purdue U .... IN
Queens .... NY
Radcliffe...................... MA
Rhode Island, U. of............ RI
Rice U........................ TX
Richmond, U. of .... VA
Rochester, U. of.............. NY
Rutgers........................ NJ
San Diego State................ CA
San Francisco, U. of............ CA
San Francisco State .... CA
San Jose State................ CA
Santa Clara, U. of .... CA
Scranton, U. of................ PA
Seton Hall U .... NJ
Smith .... MA
South Alabama, U. of.......... AL
South Carolina, U. of .... SC
South Dakota, U. of .... SD
South Florida, U. of .... FL
Southern California, U. of ...... CA
Southern Illinois IL
Southern Methodist U .... TX
Southwest Texas State .... TX
St. Johns U .... NY
St. Lawrence.................. NY
St. Louis U.................... MO
St. Mary's U .... TX
St. Olaf Coll .... MN
Stanford .... CA
State U. of New York (Albany, Binghamton, Brockport, Buffalo, Cortland, Fredonia, New Paltz, Oneonta, Oswego, Stony Brook) .... NY
Stonehill Coll .... MA
Syracuse .... NY
Temple U .... PA
Tennessee, U. of .... TN
Texas, U. of (Arlington, Austin, San Antonio).................. TX
Texas A&M U .... TX
Texas Tech. U .... TX
Toledo, U. of.................. OH
Trenton State .... NJ
Tufts .... MA
Tulane........................ LA
Tuskegee Inst.................. AL
Union Coll .... NY
Utah, U. of.................... UT

Utah State U ... UT
Valparaiso ... IN
Vanderbilt ... TN
Vassar Coll ... NY
Vermont, U. of, & State Agric. Coll ... VT
Villanova ... PA
Virginia, U. of ... VA
Virginia Poly. Inst ... VA
Wake Forest ... NC
Washington, U. of ... WA
Washington State ... WA
Washington U ... MO
Wayne State U ... MI
Wellesley Coll ... MA
Wesleyan U ... CT
West Virginia U ... WV
Western Illinois U ... IL
Western Michigan U ... MI
Western Washington State ... WA
Whittier Coll ... CA
Willamette U ... OR
William and Mary ... VA
William Paterson ... NJ
Williams Coll ... MA
Wisconsin, U. of (Madison, Milwaukee) ... WI
Wittenberg ... OH
Wright State ... OH
Wyoming, U. of ... WY
Yale ... CT

Poultry Husbandry

Alabama A&M ... AL
Auburn U ... AL
California, U. of (Davis) ... CA
California State U. (Fresno) ... CA
Cornell U ... NY
Florida, U. of ... FL
Michigan State U ... MI
Minnesota, U. of ... MN
Missouri, U. of ... MO
North Dakota State U ... ND
Ohio State U ... OH
Pennsylvania State U ... PA
Purdue ... IN
Southern Illinois U ... IL
State U. of New York Coll. of Agri. (Farmingdale), Coll. of Agri. & Life Sci ... NY
Tennessee, U. of ... TN
Wisconsin, U. of (Madison) ... WI

Primary Care Physicians, Assistant to

Institutions approved by the American Medical Association in collaboration with the merican Academy of Family Physicians, the American Academy of Pediatrics, American Academy of Physician Assistants, American College of Physicians, American College of Surgeons, American Society of Internal Medicine, Association of Physician Assistant Programs.

Alderson-Broaddus Coll ... WV
Baylor U ... TX
Bowman Gray Sch. of Medicine ... NC
City Coll ... NY
Colorado, U. of ... CO
Cuyahoga Comm. Coll ... OH
Duke U ... NC
Emory U ... GA
Essex Comm. Coll ... MD
Gannon Coll ... PA
George Washington U ... DC
Georgia, Medical Coll. of ... GA
Hahnemann Medical Coll ... PA
Howard U ... DC
Hudson Valley Comm. Coll ... NY
Iowa, U. of ... IA
Kettering Coll. of Medical Arts . OH
King's Coll ... PA
Lake Erie Coll ... OH
Loma Linda U ... CA
Long Island U ... NY
Mercy Coll ... MI
Nebraska, U. of ... NE
New Mexico, U. of ... NM
Northeastern U ... MA
Oklahoma, U. of ... OK
Pennsylvania State U ... PA
Rutgers U ... NJ
Southern California, U. of ... CA
St. Francis Coll ... PA
St. Louis U ... MO
Stanford U ... CA
State U. of New York (Stony Brook) ... NY
Texas, U. of (Dallas, Galveston) . TX
Touro Coll ... NY
Trevecca Nazarene Coll ... TN
Western Michigan U ... MI
Wichita State U ... KS
Wisconsin, U. of (Madison) ... WI

Primatology

Hampshire Coll ... MA

Printing, *See* GRAPHIC ARTS AND/OR PRINTING

Prosthetics

Iowa, U. of ... IA
New York U ... NY
Washington, U. of ... WA

Psychology

Institutions having doctoral programs in clinical and/or counseling and school psychology approved by the American Psychological Association

Adelphi U ... NY
Alabama, U. of ... AL
American U ... DC
Arizona, U. of ... AZ
Arizona State U ... AZ
Arkansas, U. of ... AR
Auburn U ... AL
Baylor U ... TX
Boston U ... MA
Bowling Green State U ... OH
Brigham Young U ... UT
California, U. of (Berkeley, Los Angeles, Santa Barbara) ... CA
Case Western Reserve ... OH
Catholic U ... DC
Cincinnati, U. of ... OH
City Coll. (CUNY) ... NY
Clark ... MA
Colorado, U. of ... CO
Colorado State U ... CO
Columbia U. T.C ... NY
Connecticut, U. of ... CT
Delaware, U. of ... DE
Denver, U. of ... CO
DePaul U ... IL
Duke ... NC
East Texas State U ... TX
Emory U ... GA
Florida, U. of ... FL
Florida State U ... FL
Fordham U ... NY
Fuller Theo. Sem ... CA
George Washington U ... DC
Georgia, U. of ... GA
Georgia State U ... GA
Hahnemann Medical Coll ... PA
Hawaii, U. of ... HI
Houston, U. of ... TX
Illinois, U. of (Chicago Circle, Urbana) ... IL
Indiana U ... IN
Iowa, U.of ... IA
Iowa State U ... IA
Kansas, U. of ... KS
Kent State U ... OH
Kentucky, U. of ... KY
Long Island U ... NY
Louisiana State U ... LA
Louisville, U. of ... KY
Loyola U ... IL
Maine, U. of ... ME
Maryland, U. of ... MD
Massachusetts, U. of ... MA
Memphis State U ... TN
Miami, U. of ... FL
Miami U ... OH
Michigan, U. of ... MI
Michigan State U ... MI
Minnesota, U. of ... MN
Mississippi, U. of ... MS
Missouri, U. of (Columbia, St. Louis) ... MO
Montana, U. of ... MT
Nebraska, U. of ... NE
Nevada, U. of ... NV
New Mexico, U. of ... NM
New York U ... NY
North Carolina, U. of ... NC
North Dakota, U. of ... ND
North Texas State U ... TX
Northern Illinois U ... IL
Notre Dame, U. of ... IN
Ohio State U ... OH
Ohio U ... OH
Oklahoma State U ... OK
Oregon, U. of ... OR
Pennsylvania, U. of ... PA
Pennsylvania State U ... PA
Pittsburgh, U. of ... PA
Purdue ... IN
Rhode Island, U. of ... RI
Rochester, U. of ... NY
Rutgers (New Brunswick, Piscataway) ... NJ
South Carolina, U. of ... SC
South Dakota, U. of ... SD
South Florida, U. of ... FL
Southern California, U. of ... CA
Southern Illinois U ... IL
Southern Mississippi, U. of ... MS
St. Louis U ... MO
Stanford U ... CA
State U. of New York (Albany, Buffalo, Stony Brook) ... NY
Syracuse ... NY
Temple U ... PA
Tennessee, U. of ... TN
Texas, U. of (Austin) ... TX
Texas Tech. U ... TX
Toledo, U. of ... OH
Utah, U. of ... UT
Vanderbilt ... TN
Virginia Commonwealth ... VA
Virginia Polytechnic Inst ... VA
Washington, U. of ... WA
Washington State U ... WA
Washington U ... MO
Wayne State U ... MI
West Virginia U ... WV
Wisconsin, U. of (Madison) ... WI
Wyoming, U. of ... WY
Yale ... CT
Yeshiva ... NY

Psychotherapy

Goddard Coll ... VT
Hampshire Coll ... MA
Indiana State U ... IN
Kansas, U. of ... KS
Trinity Christian ... IL

Public Administration

Institutions awarding 10 or more undergraduate degrees as a major field in single year according to U.S. Office of Education latest statistics

Antioch ... OH
Arizona, U. of ... AZ
Arkansas, U. of ... AR
Auburn ... AL
Bernard Baruch ... NY
Bowling Green ... OH
California State U. (Chico, Dominguez Hills, Fresno, Sacramento) ... CA
Carthage Coll ... WI
Christopher Newport Coll ... VA
City Coll ... WA
District of Columbia, U. of ... DC
Drake ... IA
Eastern Michigan U ... MI
Evansville, U. of ... IN
Ferris State ... MI
Florida International U ... FL
Florida Tech ... FL
Franklin U ... OH
George Mason U ... VA
George Washington U ... DC
Golden Gate U ... CA
Governors State U ... IL
Grand Valley State ... MI
Green Mountain Coll ... VT
Houston Clear Lake City ... TX
Indiana U ... IN
International Am. U ... PR
Iowa State ... IA
Kean Coll ... NJ
LaVerne Coll ... CA
Maine, U. of ... ME
Miami U ... OH
Michigan State U ... MI
Mississippi, U. of ... MS
Missouri, U. of ... MO
National U ... CA
Oregon, U. of ... OR
Park Coll ... MO
Pepperdine ... CA
Pittsburgh, U. of ... PA
Puget Sound, U. of ... WA
Roosevelt U ... IL
San Diego State ... CA
Shaw U ... NC
Southern California, U. of ... CA
Southwest Missouri State ... MO
St. Cloud State U ... MN
St. Edward's U ... TX
Syracuse U ... NY
Tariko Coll ... MO
Tennessee, U. of ... TN
Upper Iowa ... IA
Virginia Poly. Inst ... VA
William Paterson Coll ... NJ

Public Health

Accredited by Council on Education for Public Health

Alabama, U. of ... AL
Boston U ... MA
California, U. of (Berkeley, Los Angeles) ... CA

California State U. (Northridge) (Grad) ..... CA
Columbia ..... NY
Emory U ..... GA
Harvard ..... MA
Hawaii, U. of ..... HI
Hunter Coll. (Grad) ..... NY
Illinois, U. of IL
Johns Hopkins ..... MD
Loma Linda U ..... CA
Massachusetts, U. of ..... MA
Michigan, U. of ..... MI
Minnesota, U. of ..... MN
Missouri, U. of (Grad) ..... MO
New York U. (Grad) ..... NY
North Carolina, U. of ..... NC
Oklahoma, U. of ..... OK
Pittsburgh, U. of ..... PA
Puerto Rico, U. of ..... PR
Rochester, U. of ..... NY
San Jose State U. (Grad) ..... CA
South Carolina, U. of ..... SC
Tennessee, U. of (Grad) ..... TN
Texas, U. of (Houston) ..... TX
Tulane ..... LA
Utah, U. of ..... UT
Washington, U. of ..... WA
Yale ..... CT

Public Relations

Abilene Christian ..... TX
Akron, U. of ..... OH
Alabama, U. of ..... AL
Alverno Coll ..... WI
Anderson Coll ..... IN
Arkansas State U ..... AR
Auburn U ..... AL
Averett Coll ..... VA
Ball State U ..... IN
Baltimore, U. of ..... MD
Baylor U ..... TX
Bennett Coll ..... NC
Bliss Coll ..... OH
Bob Jones U ..... SC
Boston U ..... MA
Bowling Green State U ..... OH
Bradley U IL
Brenau Coll ..... GA
Bridgewater State ..... MA
Butler U ..... IN
California State Poly. (Pomona) ..... CA
California State U. (Fresno) ..... CA
Cardinal Newman ..... MO
Central Michigan U ..... MO
Central Missouri ..... MO
Central Washington U ..... WA
Chapman Coll ..... CA
Cincinnati, U. of ..... OH
Clarion State ..... PA
Colorado State U ..... CO
Columbia Coll IL
Columbia Coll ..... MO
Creighton U ..... NE
Dayton, U. of ..... OH
Drake U ..... IA
Eastern Kentucky U ..... KY
Eastern Montana ..... MT
Eastern Washington U ..... WA
Emerson Coll ..... MA
Evansville, U. of ..... IN
Findlay Coll ..... OH
Florida, U. of ..... FL
Florida Southern ..... FL
Florida State U ..... FL
Fontbonne Coll ..... MO
Franklin Coll ..... IN
Franklin Pierce ..... NH
Grand Valley ..... MI
Gustavus Adolphus ..... MN
Hampton Inst ..... VA
Harcum Jr ..... PA
Harding U ..... AR
Huron Coll ..... SD
Indiana U. (Bloomington) ..... IN
Johnson & Wales Coll ..... RI
Kansas, U. of ..... KS
Kansas State U ..... KS
Kearney State ..... NE
Kent State U ..... OH
Kentucky Wesleyan ..... KY
La Salle Coll ..... PA
Louisville, U. of ..... KY
Mansfield State ..... PA
Maryland, U. of ..... MD
Marywood ..... PA
Medaille Coll ..... NY
Michigan State U ..... MI
Montana State U ..... MT
Morehead State ..... KY
Mount Mary ..... WI
Mount St. Mary ..... NY
Nebraska, U. of ..... NE
New York U ..... NY
North Dakota State U ..... ND
Northeast Missouri State ..... MO
Northern Illinois U IL
Northern Iowa, U. of ..... IA
Northern Kentucky ..... KY
Northwest Missouri State U ..... MO
Northwestern State U ..... LA
Ohio U ..... OH
Oklahoma Christian Coll ..... OK
Ottawa U ..... KS
Otterbein Coll ..... OH
Pacific Union Coll ..... CA
Pittsburg State ..... KS
Purdue U ..... IN
Rio Piedras ..... PR
Saint Mary's Coll ..... MN
San Jose State ..... CA
Scranton, U. of ..... PA
Shippensburg State ..... PA
South Carolina, U. of ..... SC
South Dakota, U. of ..... SD
South Florida, U. of ..... FL
South Georgia Coll ..... GA
Southern Illinois U IL
Southern Methodist U ..... TX
St. Andrew's Presbyterian ..... NC
St. Scholastica ..... MN
State U. of New York (Geneseo) ..... NY
State U. of New York Coll. of Agri. & Life Sci ..... NY
Syracuse U ..... NY
Tennessee, U. of ..... TN
Temple U ..... PA
Texas, U. of (Austin) ..... TX
Texas Christian U ..... TX
Texas Tech ..... TX
Toledo, U. of ..... OK
Tulsa, U. of ..... OK
Utica Coll. of Syracuse U ..... NY
Valparaiso U ..... IN
Wayne State U ..... MI
Weber State Coll ..... UT
West Virginia U ..... WV
Wesleyan Coll ..... GA
Western Kentucky U ..... KY
Whitworth Coll ..... WA
William Woods ..... MO
Wisconsin, U. of (Superior) ..... WI
Youngstown ..... OH

Publishing

Baltimore, U. of ..... MD
Eastern Montana ..... MT
Emerson Coll ..... MA
Goddard Coll ..... VT
La Salle ..... PA
Puerto Rico, U. of ..... PR

Purchasing, *See* BUSINESS ADMINISTRATION

Quantum Mechanics

Hampshire Coll ..... MA
Missouri, U. of (Rolla) ..... MO

Radiation Therapy Technologist

Approved by Council on Medical Education of the American Medical Assn. in collaboration with the American College of Radiology and the American Society of Radiologic Technologists

Allegheny, Comm. Coll. of ..... PA
Arizona, U. of ..... AZ
Baylor U ..... TX
Broward Comm ..... FL
California, U. of (Los Angeles, San Francisco) ..... CA
Chicago State U IL
City Wide Coll IL
Denver, Comm. Coll. of ..... CO
Erie Comm. Coll ..... NY
Essex Comm. Coll ..... MD
Foothill Comm. Coll ..... CA
George Washington U ..... DC
Georgia, Medical Coll. of ..... GA
Gwynedd-Mercy ..... PA
Howard U ..... DC
Indiana U ..... IN
Iowa, U. of ..... IA
Kansas, U. of ..... KS
Kentucky, U. of ..... KY
Loma Linda ..... CA
Manhattan Coll ..... NY
Michael J. Owens Tech ..... OH
Minnesota, U. of ..... MN
Missouri, U. of ..... MO
Nebraska, U. of ..... NE
Oklahoma, U. of ..... OK
Oregon, U. of ..... OR
South Carolina, Medical U. of ..... SC
South Central Comm ..... CT
Springfield Tech ..... MA
State U. of New York (Upstate Medical Center) ..... NY
Utah, U. of ..... UT
Vanderbilt ..... TN
Vermont, U. of ..... VT
Virginia, U. of ..... VA
Virginia Commonwealth U ..... VA
Washington U ..... MO
Wayne State U ..... MI
West Virginia U ..... WV
Wisconsin, Medical Coll. of ..... WI
Wisconsin, U. of (Madison) ..... WI

Radio and/or TV

Abilene Christian ..... TX
Akron, U. of ..... OH
Alabama A&M ..... AL
Alabama State U ..... AL
Alderson-Broaddus ..... WV
Andrews U ..... MI
Arizona, U. of ..... AZ
Arizona Western Coll ..... AZ
Arkansas, U. of ..... AR
Arkansas State U ..... AR
Artesia Christian Coll ..... NM
Ashland ..... OH
Augustana Coll ..... SD
Baldwin-Wallace Coll ..... OH
Ball State U ..... IN
Baylor U ..... TX
Belmont Coll ..... TN
Bennett Coll ..... NC
Biscayne Coll ..... FL
Bismarck Jr. Coll ..... ND
Black Hills State ..... SD
Bob Jones U ..... SC
Boston U ..... MA
Bradley IL
Brenau Coll ..... GA
Bridgewater State ..... MA
Brooklyn Coll ..... NY
Butler U ..... IN
C.W. Post Ctr ..... NY
California Poly. U ..... CA
California State Coll ..... PA
California State U. (Fresno, Los Angeles, Northridge) ..... CA
Cardinal Newman ..... MO
Centenary ..... NJ
Central Arkansas, U. of ..... AR
Central Florida, U. of ..... FL
Central Michigan ..... MI
Central Missouri ..... MO
Central Wyoming Coll ..... WY
Chapman Coll ..... CA
Cincinnati, U. of ..... OH
Clarion State ..... PA
Colby Comm. Coll ..... KS
Columbia Coll ..... CA
Columbia Coll IL
Columbia Union Coll ..... MD
David Lipscomb Coll ..... IN
Dayton, U. of ..... OH
Dean Jr ..... MA
Defense Info. Sch ..... IN
DePauw U ..... IN
Detroit, U. of ..... MI
Drake U ..... IA
East Texas State U ..... TX
Eastern Kentucky, U. of ..... KY
Eastern Montana Coll ..... MT
Eastern New Mexico ..... NM
Eastern Washington U ..... WA
Elizabeth Seton Coll ..... NY
Elizabethtown Coll ..... PA
Emerson Coll ..... MA
Endicott Coll ..... MA
Evansville, U. of ..... IN
Ferris State ..... MI
Florida, U. of ..... FL
Florida Atlantic U ..... FL
Florida Southern ..... FL
Fontbonne Coll ..... MO
Fordham U ..... NY
Franklin Coll ..... IN
Gannon U ..... PA
George Fox Coll ..... OR
George Washington ..... DC
Georgia, U. of ..... GA
Gonzaga U ..... WA
Grand View ..... IA
Gulf Coast Comm. Coll ..... FL
Hampton Institute ..... VA
Harding U ..... AR
Herkimer County ..... NY
High Point Coll ..... NC
Howard U ..... DC
Hutchinson Comm. Coll ..... KS
Illinois, U. of IL
Illinois Central Coll IL
Illinois Coll IL
Indiana State U ..... IN
Indiana U ..... IN
International Coll ..... FL
Iowa, U. of ..... IA
Ithaca Coll ..... NY
James Madison ..... VA
Jersey City State ..... NJ
John Brown U ..... AR
John Carroll U ..... OH
Kansas, U. of ..... KS
Kansas State U ..... KS
Kent State U ..... OH
Kentucky Wesleyan ..... KY
Kutztown State ..... PA

Lake Land ... IL
Lees Jr. Coll ... KY
Lenoir Comm ... NC
Liberty Baptist Coll ... VA
Lincoln Coll ... IL
Lock Haven State ... PA
Los Angeles City Coll ... CA
Louisville, U. of ... KY
Loyola U ... LA
Loyola Marymount ... CA
Maine, U. of ... ME
Marietta Coll ... OH
Marquette U ... WI
Maryland, U. of ... MD
Marywood ... PA
Medaille Coll ... NY
Messiah Coll ... PA
Miami U ... OH
Minnesota, U. of ... MN
Mississippi Delta Jr. Coll ... MS
Missouri, U. of ... MO
Montana, U. of ... MT
Moorhead State ... MN
Morehead State ... KY
Mount Vernon ... DC
Murray State U ... KY
Navarro ... TX
New England Inst. Tech ... RI
New Mexico State ... NM
New Rochelle, Coll. of ... NY
New York Inst. of Tech ... NY
New York U ... NY
Niagara U ... NY
North Alabama, U. of ... AL
North Carolina, U. of (Chapel Hill, Greensboro) ... NC
North Central Coll ... IL
North Texas State U ... TX
Northeast Louisiana U ... LA
Northeast Mississippi Jr ... MS
Northeast Missouri State ... MO
Northern Iowa, U. of ... IA
Northern Kentucky U ... KY
Northern Michigan ... MI
Northwestern U ... IL
Ohio State U ... OH
Ohio U ... OH
Oklahoma, U. of ... OK
Oklahoma Christian Coll ... OK
Oklahoma State U ... OK
Oral Roberts ... OK
Ottawa ... KS
Otterbein Coll ... OH
Pacific U ... OR
Pembroke State ... NC
Pennsylvania State U. (Allentown, Schuylkill, Wilkes-Barre) ... PA
Point Park Coll ... PA
Purdue U ... IN
Saint Mary's Coll ... MN
Salem Coll ... WV
Sam Houston State ... TX
San Diego State ... CA
Scranton, U. of ... PA
Shaw U ... NC
Shepard Coll ... WV
Shippensburg State ... PA
Slippery Rock State ... PA
South Carolina, U. of ... SC
South Dakota, U. of ... SD
Southeast Missouri State ... MO
Southern California, U. of ... CA
Southern Idaho, Coll. of ... ID
Southern Illinois U ... IL
Southern Mississippi, U. of ... MS
Spring Hill Coll ... AL
St. Thomas Aquinas ... NY
State U. of New York (Geneseo, New Paltz) ... NY
State U. of N.Y. Coll. (Buffalo) ... NY
Stephen F. Austin ... TX
Stephens ... MO
Susquehanna U ... PA
Syracuse U ... NY
Temple U ... PA
Tennessee, U. of (Martin) ... TN
Tennessee Temple U ... TN
Texas, U. of ... TX
Texas Christian ... TX
Texas Tech ... TX
Texas Woman's ... TX
Toledo, U. of ... OH
Union U ... TN
Wayne State Coll ... NE
Wayne State U ... MI
Webster Coll ... MO
Western Carolina U ... NC
Western Kentucky U ... KY
Wilkes Comm. Coll ... NC
William Woods ... MO
Winona State U ... MN
Wisconsin, U. of (La Crosse, Platteville, Superior) ... WI
Wright State U ... OH
Xavier ... OH
Xavier U ... LA
York ... PA

Radiobiology

California, U. of (Davis) ... CA
Cincinnati, U. of ... OH
Cornell U ... NY
Iowa, U. of ... IA
Kansas, U. of ... KS
Purdue U ... IN

Radiochemistry

Kansas, U. of ... KS

Radiographer

College programs approved by the Council on Medical Education of the American Medical Association in collaboration with the American College of Radiology and the American Society of Radiologic Technologists

Aims Comm. Coll ... CO
Alabama, U. of (Birmingham) ... AL
Albuquerque, U. of ... NM
Amarillo Coll ... TX
Angelina Coll ... TX
Antelope Valley ... CA
Aquinas Jr. Coll ... TN
Arkansas, U. of (Little Rock) ... AR
Asheville-Buncombe Tech ... NC
Austin Comm. Coll ... TX
Avila Coll ... MO
Bakersfield Coll ... CA
Baylor U ... TX
Belleville Area Coll ... IL
Bellvue Comm. Coll ... WA
Bergen Comm. Coll ... NJ
Bluefield State Coll ... WV
Boise State U ... ID
Brevard Comm. Coll ... FL
Broome Comm. Coll ... NY
Broward Comm. Coll ... FL
Brunswick Jr. Coll ... GA
Bunker Hill Comm. Coll ... MA
Butler U ... IN
Cabrillo Coll ... CA
Caldwell Comm ... NC
California State U ... CA
California, U. of (Los Angeles, Torrance) ... CA
Canada Coll ... CA
Carl Sandburg Coll ... IL
Carteret Tech. Inst ... NC
Casper Coll ... WY
Central Florida, U. of ... FL
Central Ohio Tech ... OH
Central Virginia Comm. Coll ... VA
Central Y.M.C.A. Jr. Coll ... IL
Chaffey Comm. Coll ... CA
Charleston, U. of ... WV
Chattanooga State Tech ... TN
Cincinnati, U. of ... OH
Cleveland Co. Tech ... NC
College Misericordia ... PA
Columbia State Comm ... TN
Copiah-Lincoln Jr. Coll ... MS
Cuyahoga Comm. Coll ... OH
Cypress Coll ... CA
Dakota Wesleyan U ... SD
Del Mar Coll ... TX
Delgado Coll ... LA
Delta Coll ... MI
Denver, Comm. Coll of ... CO
DePaul ... IL
District of Columbia, U. of ... DC
Districk One Tech. Inst ... WI
DuPage, Coll. of ... IL
East Tennessee State U ... TN
Edgecombe Tech ... NC
El Camino Coll ... CA
El Centro Coll ... TX
El Paso Comm. Coll ... TX
Emory ... GA
Essex Comm ... MD
Essex Co. Coll ... NJ
Evansville, U. of ... IN
Fairleigh Dickinson ... NJ
Fayetteville Tech. Inst ... NC
Ferris State Coll ... MI
Foothill Coll ... CA
Forsyth Tech ... NC
Fort Hays State U ... KS
Fresno City Coll ... CA
Gadsden State Jr ... AL
Gannon Coll ... PA
Georgia, Medical Coll. of ... GA
Grand Rapids Jr ... MI
Greenville Tech. Coll ... SC
Gwynedd-Mercy ... PA
Hagerstown Jr. Coll ... PA
Hahnemann Med. Coll ... PA
Hillsborough Comm ... FL
Holyoke Comm. Coll ... MA
Hood Coll ... MD
Hostos Comm. Coll ... NY
Houston Comm ... TX
Howard U ... DC
Hudson Valley Comm. Coll ... NY
Hutchison Comm. Jr. Coll ... KS
Idaho State U ... ID
Illinois Central ... IL
Indian Hills Comm. C ... IA
Indian River Comm ... FL
Indiana State U. (Evansville) ... IN
Indiana U ... IN
Indiana Voc. Tech. Coll. (Indianapolis) ... IN
Iowa, U. of ... IA
Itawamba Jr. Coll ... MS
Jackson Comm. Coll ... MI
Jackson State Comm. Coll ... TN
Jefferson State Jr. Coll ... AL
Jefferson Tech ... OH
Johnston Tech. Inst ... NC
Kankakee Comm ... IL
Kansas, U. of ... KS
Kapiolani Comm ... HI
Kaskaskia Coll ... IL
Kellogg Comm. Coll ... MI
Kentucky, U. of ... KY
Kettering Coll. of Medical Arts ... OH
Kishwaukee Coll ... IL
Labette Comm. Coll ... KS
Lake County, Coll. of ... IL
Lake Michigan Coll ... MI
Lamar U ... TX
Lansing Comm ... MI
Laramie County Comm ... WY
Laredo Jr. Coll ... TX
Lima Tech. Coll ... OH
Lincoln Land Comm. Coll ... IL
Loma Linda U ... CA
Long Beach City ... CA
Long Island U ... NY
Lorain County Comm. Coll ... OH
Los Angeles City Coll ... CA
Louisiana State U ... LA
Louisville, U. of ... KY
Lyons Tech. Inst ... PA
Malcolm X Coll ... IL
Manatee ... FL
Mansfield State Coll ... PA
Maricopa Tech. Comm. Coll ... AZ
Maryland, U. of ... MD
Massachusetts Bay Comm ... MA
Mattatuck Comm. Coll ... CT
McLennan Comm ... TX
McNeese State U ... LA
Merced Coll ... CA
Mercer County Comm. Coll ... NJ
Meridian Jr. Coll ... MS
Merritt Coll ... CA
Mesa Coll ... CA
Miami, U. of ... FL
Miami-Dade Comm ... FL
Michael Owens Tech ... OH
Mid-Michigan Comm. Coll ... MI
Middlesex Comm. Coll ... CT
Middlesex Comm. Coll ... MA
Middlesex County Coll ... NJ
Midlands Tech ... SC
Midwestern U ... TX
Milwaukee Area Tech. Coll ... WI
Minnesota, U. of ... MN
Mississippi, U. of ... MS
Mississippi Gulf Coast ... MS
Missouri, U. of ... MO
Missouri Southern ... MO
Monroe Comm. Coll ... NY
Montgomery Coll ... MD
Moraine Valley Comm. Coll ... IL
Morehead State U ... KY
Mt. San Antonio Coll ... CA
Muskingum Area Tech ... OH
Nassau Comm ... NY
Nebraska, U. of (Omaha) ... NE
Nebraska Western Coll ... NE
Nevada, U. of (Las Vegas) ... NV
New Jersey Coll. of Medicine and Dentistry (Newark) ... NJ
New Mexico, U. of ... NM
New Mexico State U ... NM
New York City Tech ... NY
North Carolina, U. of ... NC
North Central Tech ... WI
North Country Comm. Coll ... NY
North Shore Comm. Coll ... MA
Northampton Co. Area Comm. Coll ... PA
Northeast Louisiana U ... LA
Northeastern ... MA
Northern Arizona U ... AZ
Northern Essex Comm ... MA
Northern Kentucky U ... KY
Northern New Mexico Comm. Coll ... NM
Northern Virginia Comm. Coll ... VA
Northwestern State U ... LA
Oakton Comm ... IL
Odessa Coll ... TX
Ohio State U ... OH
Oklahoma, U. of ... OK
Orange Coast Coll ... CA
Orangeburg-Calhoun Tech. Educ. Ctr ... SC
Oregon Inst. of Tech ... OR
Oscar Rose ... OK
Parkersburg Comm. Coll ... WV
Parkland Coll ... IL
Pasadena City Coll ... CA
Passaic Co. Comm ... NJ
Penn Valley Comm ... MO

Pennsylvania, Med. Coll. of ..... PA
Pennsylvania State U .... PA
Philadelphia, Comm. Coll. of.... PA
Piedmont Tech. Coll .... SC
Pima Coll .... AZ
Pitt Comm. Coll .... NC
Portland Comm. Coll .... OR
Prince George's Comm. Coll ... MD
Pueblo Voc. Comm. Coll ...... CO
Quinsigamond Comm. Coll .... MA
Rhode Island, Comm. Coll. of ... RI
Roane State Comm. Coll .... TN
Rowan Tech. Inst .... NC
San Diego Mesa Coll .... CA
San Francisco, City Coll. of..... CA
San Jacinto Coll .... TX
Sandhills Comm. Coll .... NC
Santa Barbara City Coll .... CA
Santa Fe Comm. Coll........... FL
Santa Rosa .... CA
Sauk Valley IL
Scott Comm. Coll .... IA
Shawnee State .... OH
Shelby State Comm. Coll .... TN
Sinclair Comm .... OH
South Alabama, U. of........... AL
South Carolina, Med. U. of...... SC
South Central Comm .... CT
South Plains Coll .... TX
Southeast Comm. Coll.......... NE
Southern Arkansas U .... AR
Southern California, U. of ...... CA
Southern Illinois U IL
Southwest State............... MN
Southwest Virginia Comm. Coll . VA
Spartanburg Tech. Coll .... SC
Springfield Tech. Comm. Coll.. MA
St. Louis Comm. Coll.......... MO
St. Philip's .... TX
State U. of New York (Upstate Med. Ctr.) .... NY
Tacoma Comm. Coll .... WA
Tallahassee Comm .... FL
Tarrant County Jr. Coll .... TX
Temple U .... PA
Tennessee, U. of .... TN
Texas, U. of (Med. Branch at Galveston, Houston).......... TX
Texas Southmost .... TX
Thomas Jefferson U .... PA
Thornton Comm. Coll IL
Triton IL
Trocaire Coll.................. NY
Truckee Meadows .... NV
Tulsa Jr. Coll .... OK
Tyler Jr........................ TX
Union Coll .... KY
Universidad Central del Caribe .. PR
Utah, U. of..................... UT
Vermont, U. of .... VT
Virginia, U. of .... VA
Virginia Commonwealth U ...... VA
Virginia Western Comm .... VA
Wake County Tech .... NC
Wallace State Comm. Coll ...... AL
Washtenaw Comm. Coll .... MI
Weber State Coll .... UT
Wenatchee Valley Coll......... WA
Westchester Comm. Coll .... NY
Western Wisconsin Tech .... WI
Western Wyoming Comm...... WY
Williamsport Area Comm .... PA
Wisconsin, U. of (Madison) ..... WI
Wittenberg.................... OH
Wright Coll IL
Xavier .... OH
Yakima Valley Coll .... WA
Yuba Coll...................... CA

Radioisotope Technology

Butler U .... IN
Seattle U .... WA

Range and/or Ranch Management

Abilene Christian.............. TX
Arizona, U. of .... AZ
California, U. of (Davis)......... CA
California State U. (Chico, Fresno) .... CA
Colorado State U .... CO
Humboldt State .... CA
Kansas State U................ KS
Navarro Coll .... TX
Nebraska, U. of (Lincoln) .... NE
New Mexico State U........... NM
North Dakota State U. (Bottineau, Fargo).......... ND
Northeastern Jr. Coll .... CO
Northern Montana Coll .... MT
Oklahoma State U............ OK
South Dakota State .... SD
Southeastern Oklahoma State U .... OK
Stephen F. Austin .... TX

Ranger Studies

North Dakota State U. (Bottineau) .... ND

Real Estate

Akron, U. of .... OH
Albuquerque, U. of .... NM
Alfred State .... NY
American U .... DC
Angelina .... TX
Appalachian State U .... NC
Arizona, U. of .... AZ
Arizona State U. (Tempe)....... AZ
Arizona Western Coll .... AZ
Arkansas, U. of (Fayetteville) ... AR
Arkansas State U............... AR
Baylor U...................... TX
Bee Co. Coll .... TX
Blinn Coll...................... TX
Bliss Coll .... OH
Boise State U .... ID
California State Poly. (Pomona)................... CA
California State U. (Fresno, Hayward, Los Angeles, Northridge, Sacramento) ..... CA
Central Pennsylvania Bus. Sch .. PA
Central State U .... OK
Chadron .... NE
Charleston, U. of .... WV
Cincinnati, U. of .... OH
City Coll .... WA
Clarion State Coll .... PA
Colorado, U. of .... CO
Columbia Coll .... MO
Columbus .... GA
Connecticut, U. of............. CT
Cooke County Coll............. TX
Dakota State .... SD
Delta State U .... MS
Denver, U. of .... CO
DuPage, Coll. of IL
Dyke .... OH
East Tennessee State........... TN
Eastern Kentucky U .... KY
Eastern New Mexico U .... NM
Evansville, U. of .... IN
Felician Coll IL
Ferris State .... MI
Florida .... FL
Florida, U. of.................. FL
Florida Atlantic .... FL
Florida International .... FL
Florida State U................ FL
Fort Lauderdale Coll .... FL
Franklin U .... OH
Georgia, U. of .... GA
Georgia State U .... GA
Golden Gate U .... CA
Harper Coll IL
Hawaii, U. of .... HI
Howard Co. Jr. Coll .... TX
Illinois Central IL
Immaculata Coll .... PA
Indiana U. (Bloomington) ...... IN
Jacksonville State U .... AL
Johnson and Wales Coll .... RI
Kearney State .... NE
Kent State .... OH
La Salle Coll .... PA
Lamar U .... TX
Louisiana State U. (Eunice) ..... LA
Manor Jr. Coll .... PA
Memphis State U.............. TN
Miami, U. of .... FL
Mississippi State U .... MS
Morehead State .... KY
Murray State U................ KY
National U .... CA
Navarro....................... TX
Nebraska Western Coll .... NE
Nevada, U. of .... NV
New Hampshire, U. of .... NH
New Mexico State .... NM
North Florida, U. of............ FL
North Texas State U........... TX
Northeast Louisiana U .... LA
Northeast Mississippi Jr .... MS
Northeastern Oklahoma State .... OK
Northern Kentucky .... KY
Northwestern Oklahoma State .... OK
Ohio State U .... OH
Oklahoma, U. of .... OK
Oregon, U. of .... OR
Pace Coll .... NY
Pennsylvania State U. (Allentown, Behrend, McKeesport, Schuylkill campus, University Park) ..... PA
Pfeiffer Coll .... NC
Plymouth State Coll .... NH
Purdue U .... IN
Richmond, U. of .... TX
Samford U .... AL
San Diego State............... CA
Shippensburg State Coll .... PA
Southern Idaho, Coll. of .... ID
Southern Mississippi, U. of .... MS
Southern Methodist U .... TX
St. Cloud State U .... MN
St. Leo Coll .... FL
State U. of New York (Canton).................... NY
Syracuse U .... NY
Temple .... PA
Tennessee, U. of .... TN
Texas, U. of................... TX
Texas A&I U .... TX
Texas Christian .... TX
Thiel Coll .... PA
Thomas Coll .... ME
Toledo........................ OH
Vernon Reg. Jr................ TX
Virginia Commonwealth .... VA
Walsh Coll .... OH
Webber Coll .... FL
Weber State U .... UT
West Virginia State .... WV
Western Carolina U .... NC
Western Texas .... TX
Wharton County Jr .... TX
Wichita State U .... KS
William Woods .... MO
Wisconsin, U. of (Milwaukee) ... WI
Wittenberg U .... OH
Xavier U .... OH
York Coll .... PA

Recreation, *See* PARKS AND RECREATION MANAGEMENT

Rehabilitation Counseling

Akron, U. of .... OH
Arizona, U. of .... AZ
California State U. (Fresno, Los Angeles) .... CA
Central Arkansas, U. of .... AR
Central Missouri .... MO
Cincinnati, U. of .... OH
Drake U .... IA
East Central Oklahoma State .. OK
Eastern Kentucky U .... KY
Eastern Montana .... MT
Emmanuel .... MA
Emporia State U .... KS
Florida, U. of.................. FL
Georgia State U .... GA
Illinois Inst. of Tech IL
Indiana U. (Purdue) .... IN
Iowa, U. of .... IA
Kansas, U. of .... KS
La Salle Coll .... PA
Maine, U. of (Farmington) ..... ME
Mankato State .... MN
Nebraska Wesleyan .... NE
Northeastern U................ MA
Northeastern Oklahoma .... OK
North Texas State .... TX
Northwestern State U .... LA
Puerto Rico, U. of .... PR
Rhode Island Coll .... RI
Rio Piedras .... PR
Seattle U .... WA
Seton Hall .... NJ
South Carolina, U. of .... SC
South Carolina State .... SC
Southern Illinois U IL
Springfield.................... MA
St. Cloud State................ MN
Trinity Christian................. IL
Virginia Commonwealth U ...... VA
West Virginia U .... WV
West Virginia Wesleyan........ WV
Wright State .... OH

Respiratory Therapy

Approved by the Council on Medical Education of the American Medical Association in collaboration with the American Association for Respiratory Therapy, the American College of Chest Physicians, American Thoracic Society, and the American Society of Anesthesiologists

Akron, U. of .... OH
Alabama, U. of .... AL
Albuquerque, U. of .... NM
Allegheny, Comm. Coll. of ...... PA
Amarillo .... TX
American River................. CA
Arkansas, U. of................ AR
Atlantic Comm. Coll .... NJ
Baltimore, Comm. Coll. of ..... MD
Bergen Comm .... NJ
Black Hawk Coll IL
Boise State Coll .... ID
Bridgeport, U. of .... CT
Brookdale Comm .... NJ
Broward Comm. Coll .... FL
Butte Coll..................... CA
California, U. of (Davis, Los Angeles) .... CA
Central Florida, U. of .... FL
Central Piedmont .... NC
Central YMCA Comm IL
Cleveland State Comm. Coll .... TN

Colegio Universitario .... PR
Columbia State Comm .... TN
Columbia Union .... MD
Columbus Coll .... GA
Columbus Tech. Inst .... OH
Crafton Hills Coll .... CA
Cuyahoga Comm. Coll .... OH
Del Mar .... TX
Delaware County Comm .... PA
Delaware Tech. Comm. Coll .... DE
Delgado .... LA
Denver, Comm. Coll. of .... CO
Des Moines Area Comm. Coll ... IA
Desert, Coll. of the .... CA
District of Columbia, U. of ..... DC
Durham Tech. Inst .... NC
East Los Angeles Coll .... CA
El Camino Coll .... CA
El Centro Coll .... TX
El Paso Comm .... TX
Emory .... GA
Erie Comm. Coll .... NY
Fairleigh Dickinson .... NJ
Ferris State .... MI
Florida Jr. Coll .... FL
Foothill Coll .... CA
Forsyth Tech .... NC
Fresno City Coll .... CA
George C. Wallace Comm. Coll . AL
Georgia, Medical Coll. of ...... GA
Georgia State U .... GA
Grossmont Coll .... CA
Hahnemann Medical Coll .... PA
Highland Park Coll .... MI
Highline Coll .... WA
Hinds Jr. Coll .... MS
Houston Comm .... TX
Hudson Valley Comm. Coll ..... NY
Indiana State U .... IN
Indiana U .... IN
Indiana U. of Pennsylvania ...... PA
Jackson State Comm. Coll ...... TN
Johnson County Comm. Jr. Coll .... KS
Kalamazoo Valley .... MI
Kansas, U. of .... KS
Kapiolani Comm .... HI
Kentucky, U. of .... KY
Kettering Coll. of Medical Arts . OH
Kirkwood Comm .... IA
Laboure Jr. Coll .... MA
Lakeland Comm. Coll .... OH
Lane Comm. Coll .... OR
Lansing Comm. Coll .... MI
Lexington Tech. Inst .... KY
Lincoln Land Comm IL
Loma Linda .... CA
Long Beach City Coll .... CA
Long Island U .... NY
Louisiana State U .... LA
Madison Area .... WI
Malcolm X Coll IL
Manchester Comm. Coll .... CT
Manhattan Comm .... NY
Mansfield State .... PA
Maricopa Tech. Comm. Coll .... AZ
Maryville .... MO
Massasoit Comm. Coll .... MA
Mercy Coll .... MI
Miami-Dade Jr. Coll .... FL
Midlands Tech .... SC
Milwaukee Area Tech. Coll ..... WI
Minnesota, U. of .... MN
Missouri, U. of .... MO
Moraine Valley IL
Mt. Hood Comm. Coll .... OR
Mt. Marty .... SD
Mt. San Antonio Coll .... CA
Mt. St. Joseph .... OH
Napa Coll .... CA
Nassau Comm. Coll .... NY
Nebraska, U. of .... NE
Newbury Jr. Coll .... MA
North Dakota School .... ND
North Hennepin Comm. Coll ... MN
North Shore Comm. Coll ...... MA
Northeastern U .... MA
Northern Essex Comm. Coll ... MA
Northern Virginia Comm .... VA
Northwest Mississippi Jr. Coll .. MS
Norwalk Comm. Coll .... CT
Oakland Comm .... MI
Odessa Coll .... TX
Ohio State U .... OH
Oklahoma, U. of .... OK
Onondaga Comm. Coll .... NY
Orange Coast Coll .... CA
Oscar Rose Jr. Coll .... OK
Parkland IL
Philadelphia, Comm. Coll. of .... PA
Piedmont Virginia Comm ...... VA
Pima Comm .... AZ
Prince George's Comm .... MD
Pueblo Voc .... CO
Quinnipiac Coll .... CT
Quinsigamond Comm. Coll .... MA
Rio Hondo Coll .... CA
Rochester State .... MN
Rock Valley Coll IL
Santa Fe Comm. Coll .... FL
Shenandoah Coll .... VA
Sinclair Comm .... OH
Skyline .... CA
South Carolina, Medical Coll. of .... SC
Southwest Missouri .... MO
Southwest Texas .... TX
Spokane Comm. Coll .... WA
Springfield Tech. Comm. Coll .. MA
St. Louis Comm. Coll .... MO
St. Mary, Coll. of .... NE
St. Mary's Dominican .... LA
St. Mary's Jr. Coll .... MN
St. Paul Tech .... MN
St. Petersburg Jr. Coll .... FL
State U. of New York (Stony Brook, Syracuse, Upstate Med. Ctr.) .... NY
Tarrant Co. Jr .... TX
Temple Jr. Coll .... TX
Texas, U. of (Galveston) .... TX
Texas Southern U .... TX
Toledo, U. of .... OH
Triton Coll IL
Tulsa Jr .... OK
Tyler Jr .... TX
Union Co. Tech. Inst .... NJ
Valencia Comm .... FL
Vanderbilt .... TN
Ventura Coll .... CA
Victor Valley Comm. Coll ...... CA
Vincennes U .... IN
Washtenaw Comm. Coll .... MI
Weber State Coll .... UT
Westchester Comm. Coll .... NY
Wichita State U .... KS
York Coll .... PA
Youngstown State U .... OH

Restaurant Management, *See*

HOTEL, MOTEL AND/OR RESTAURANT ADMINISTRATION

Retailing

Members American Collegiate Retailing Association

Alabama, U. of .... AL
Appalachian State U .... NC
Arkansas, U. of .... AR
Ball State .... IN
Baruch Coll. (CUNY) .... NY
Bloomfield Coll .... NJ
Boston U .... MA
Bowling Green State U .... OH
Brigham Young U .... UT
Bryant Coll .... NY
California State Coll. (Los Angeles) .... CA
California State U. (Long Beach) .... CA
Central Arkansas, U. of .... AR
Central Connecticut .... CT
Central Michigan U .... MI
Christopher Newport Coll ...... VA
Cincinnati, U. of .... OH
Colorado State U .... CO
Dayton, U. of .... OH
Drake U .... IA
Delta State U .... MS
Drexel U .... PA
Eastern Michigan U .... MI
Eastern Tennessee State U ..... TN
Eastern Washington U .... WA
Florida, U. of .... FL
Florida Atlantic U .... FL
Florida State U .... FL
Georgia Southern .... GA
Hawaii, U. of .... HI
Henderson State .... AR
Hofstra U .... NY
Houston, U. of .... TX
Iowa State U .... IA
Kent State U .... OH
Lamar U .... TX
Louisiana Tech. U .... LA
Lowell, U. of .... MA
Marquette U .... WI
Maryland, U. of .... MD
Massachusetts, U. of .... MA
Memphis State U .... TN
Miami U .... OH
Michigan, U. of .... MI
Michigan State U .... MI
Mississippi, U. of .... MS
Montana State U .... MT
Nebraska, U. of (Omaha) .... NE
New Hampshire Coll .... NH
New York U .... NY
North Texas State .... TX
Northern Iowa, U. of .... IA
Providence Coll .... RI
Rochester Inst. of Tech .... NY
Rutgers U .... NJ
Sam Houston State U .... TX
Shippensburg State Coll .... PA
Simmons Coll .... MA
Skidmore Coll .... NY
South Carolina, U. of .... SC
South Dakota State U .... SD
Stephen F. Austin .... TX
Syracuse U .... NY
Temple U .... PA
Tennessee, U. of .... TN
Texas, U. of, at Arlington .... TX
Texas A&M U .... TX
Texas Tech. U .... TX
Troy State U .... AL
Valpariso U .... IN
Virginia, U. of .... VA
Virginia Intermont Coll .... VA
Wayne State U .... NE
West Liberty State Coll .... WV
Western Illinois U IL
Western Michigan U .... MI
Winthrop Coll .... SC
Wisconsin, U. of (Whitewater) ... WI
Wisconsin State U .... WI
Wittenberg U .... OH
Wyoming, U. of .... WY
Youngstown State U .... OH

Retailing, Teaching of, *See*

DISTRIBUTIVE EDUCATION

Rubber Chemistry and Technology

Akron, U. of .... OH

Safety and Driver Education, Preparation for Teaching of

Appalachian State .... NC
California State U. (Los Angeles) .... CA
Central Missouri .... MO
Central State .... OK
Chadron State Coll .... NE
Delta State U .... MS
East Carolina U .... NC
Eastern Kentucky U .... KY
Emporia State U .... KS
Evansville, U. of .... IN
Glenville State .... WV
Jacksonville State U .... AL
James Madison U .... VA
Kearney State .... NE
Keene State Coll .... NH
Lamar U .... TX
Lock Haven State Coll .... PA
Michigan State U .... MI
Millersville State .... PA
Minnesota, U. of .... MN
Missouri Western .... MO
Montevallo, U. of .... AL
North Carolina A&T .... NC
North Dakota State .... ND
Northeast Missouri State Coll .. MO
Northeastern Illinois U IL
Northern Iowa, U. of .... IA
Northwestern State U .... LA
Ozarks, Sch. of the .... MO
Pittsburg State U .... KS
Purdue U .... IN
Shepherd Coll .... WV
Southeastern Oklahoma State U .... OK
Southern Illinois U IL
Southwestern Oklahoma State . OK
Stephen F. Austin .... TX
Wayne State U .... MI
West Liberty State .... WV
West Virginia U .... WV
Western Kentucky U .... KY
Winona State U .... MN
Wisconsin, U. of (Platteville) .... WI

Sanitary Engineering, *See*

ENGINEERING, SANITARY

Scientific and Technical Editing

Alderson-Broaddus .... WV
California State Coll .... PA
Carnegie-Mellon .... PA
Drexel U .... PA
Michigan Tech U .... MI
Nazareth Coll .... MI
SUNY Coll. of Agri. & Life Sci .. NY
Washington, U. of .... WA

Secondary Education, *See*

TEACHER EDUCATION

SECRETARIAL STUDIES

Secretarial Studies, General

Institutions offering 5 or more undergraduate degrees as major field in single year according to the U.S. Office of Education latest statistics

Abilene Christian U .... TX

Alabama, U. of .... AL
Alcorn State .... MS
Andrews U .... MI
Arkansas, U. of .... AR
Arkansas State .... AR
Athens State .... AL
Auburn U .... AL
Austin-Peay .... TN
Ball State .... IN
Baylor U .... TX
Benedict .... SC
Bernard Baruch .... NY
Berry .... GA
Bob Jones U .... SC
Boise State .... ID
Bowling Green State U .... OH
Brigham Young .... UT
Bryant Coll .... RI
Catholic U .... PR
Central Connecticut .... CT
Central Michigan .... MI
Central Missouri .... MO
Central State .... OK
Central Washington U .... WA
David Lipscomb .... TN
Delta State .... MS
Detroit Coll. of Bus .... MI
East Carolina .... NC
East Central State .... OK
East Tennessee .... TN
Eastern Illinois U IL
Eastern Michigan .... MI
Emporia State U .... KS
Evansville, U. of IL
Ferris State .... MI
Freed-Hardeman .... TN
Georgia Southern .... GA
Harding .... AR
Houston, U. of .... TX
Idaho, U. of .... ID
Illinois State U IL
Indiana State .... IN
Jacksonville .... AL
James Madison U .... VA
Kansas State .... KS
Lamar State .... TX
Loma Linda U .... CA
Louisiana State U .... LA
Louisiana Tech .... LA
Mankato State U .... MN
Mars Hill Coll .... NC
McNeese .... LA
Memphis State .... TN
Miami U .... OH
Michigan State U .... MI
Middle Tennessee .... TN
Midwestern U .... TX
Miles .... AL
Mississippi, U. of .... MS
Mississippi Coll .... MS
Mississippi State U .... MS
Mississippi Valley State ...... MS
Montevallo, U. of .... AL
Morehead State U .... KY
Morgan State .... MD
Morris Brown .... GA
Nebraska, U. of .... NE
New Hampshire, U. of .... NH
New Orleans, U. of .... LA
Norfolk State .... VA
North Alabama, U. of .... AL
North Carolina, U. of .... NC
North Carolina A&T .... NC
North Dakota, U. of .... ND
North Texas State U .... TX
Northeast Louisiana State ..... LA
Northeastern State .... OK
Northern Illinois U IL
Northern Iowa .... IA
Northwest Missouri State ...... MO
Northwestern State U .... LA
Oklahoma Bapt. U .... OK
Oklahoma Christian Coll ...... OK
Oklahoma State U .... OK
Old Dominion U .... VA
Prairie View A&M .... TX
Puerto Rico, U. of .... PR
Robert Morris .... PA
Sacred Heart .... PR
Sam Houston .... TX
Samford .... AL
Shippensburg .... PA
South Carolina, U. of .... SC
Southeastern Louisiana .... LA
Southern Missionary .... TN
Southwest Missouri State ...... MO
Southwestern Louisiana, U. of .. LA
Southwestern Oklahoma State . OK
Stephen F. Austin .... TX
Tennessee, U. of (Knoxville) .... TN
Tennessee State .... TN
Tennessee Tech. U .... TN
Texas, U. of (Austin, San Antonio) .... TX
Texas Christian .... TX
Texas Southern .... TX
Troy State .... AL
Valdosta .... GA
Washington State U .... WA
West Georgia .... GA
West Texas .... TX
Western Carolina .... NC
Western Illinois U IL
Western Michigan .... MI
William Carey .... MS
Winona State .... MN
Winston-Salem State U .... NC
Wisconsin, U. of (Whitewater) ... WI
World U .... PR
Xavier U .... LA
Youngstown State .... OH

Secretarial, Legal

Akron, U. of .... OH
Ancilla Coll .... IN
Aquinas Jr .... MA
Bay Path Jr .... MA
Bay State Jr .... MA
Becker Jr .... MA
Beckley Coll .... WV
Bismarck Jr .... ND
Black Hills State .... SD
Blinn Coll .... TX
Bliss Coll .... OH
Brandywine Coll .... DE
Brevard .... NC
Briarwood Coll .... CT
Bristol Coll .... TN
Campbell U .... NC
Campbellsville Coll .... KY
Castleton State .... VT
Central Coll .... KS
Central Missouri .... MO
Central Pennsylvania Bus. Sch .. PA
Champlain Coll .... VT
Cincinnati, U. of .... OH
Coffeyville .... KS
Colby-Sawyer .... NH
Dakota State Coll .... SD
Davenport Coll. of Bus .... MI
David Lipscomb Coll .... TN
Davis & Elkins Coll .... WV
Dean Jr .... MA
Dickinson State .... ND
Eastern Arizona Coll .... AZ
Eastern Kentucky U .... KY
Eastern New Mexico U .... NM
Eastern Wyoming Coll .... WY
Emporia State .... KS
Endicott .... MA
Fairmont State .... WV
Ferris State .... MI
Ferrum Coll .... VA
Fisher Jr. Coll .... MA
Gannon U .... PA
Goldey Beacom Coll .... DE
Gwynedd-Mercy .... PA
Harcum Jr .... PA
Harper Coll IL
Hesser Coll .... NH
Hilbert Coll .... NY
Hocking Technical Coll .... OH
Humphreys Coll .... CA
Husson Coll .... MN
Hutchinson Community Coll .... KS
Indiana Central U .... IN
Indiana State U .... IN
Johnson & Wales .... RI
Kaskaskia Coll IL
Keystone Jr .... PA
Lamar U .... TX
Lasell Jr .... MA
Lewis & Clark State .... ID
Loma Linda U .... CA
Louisburg Coll .... NC
MacCormac Jr IL
Maine, U. of (Machias) .... ME
Mallinckrodt Coll IL
Mankato State .... MN
Manor Jr .... PA
Maria Regina .... NY
Maryville State Coll .... ND
Mount St. Mary's .... CA
Navarro Coll .... TX
New Hampshire Coll .... NH
Newbury Jr .... MA
North Carolina Central U ...... NC
North Dakota State U .... ND
North Idaho Coll .... ID
Northeast Mississippi Jr ...... MS
Northern Kentucky U .... KY
Norwich U .... VT
Notre Dame Coll .... NH
Oregon Institute of Technology .... OR
Otero Jr. Coll .... CO
Pacific Union Coll .... CA
Pittsburg State .... KS
Post Coll .... CT
Quinnipiac Coll .... CT
Rider Coll .... NJ
Rio Grande Coll .... OH
Rivier Coll .... NH
Robert Morris .... PA
Sacred Heart U .... CT
Schreiner Coll .... TX
Sheridan Coll .... WY
South Dakota, U. of .... SD
South Georgia Coll .... GA
Southern Coll .... FL
Southern Idaho, Coll. of .... ID
Southern Illinois U IL
Southern Vermont Coll .... VT
Southwestern Adventist .... TX
Southwestern Oklahoma State U .... OK
St. Catherine Coll .... KY
State U. of New York (Cobleskill, Delhi, Farmingdale, Morrisville) .... NY
Sue Bennett .... KY
Suomi Coll .... MI
Tennessee, U. of .... TN
Thomas Coll .... ME
Toledo, U. of .... OH
Waldorf Coll .... IA
Walla Walla Coll .... WA
Wesley Coll .... DE
West Virginia State .... WV
Western Kentucky U .... KY
Western Texas Coll .... TX
Wichita State U .... KS
Yakima Valley Community Coll .... WA
York Coll .... PA

Secretarial, Medical

Ancilla .... IN
Andrews U .... MI
Aquinas Jr .... MA
Bay State Jr .... MA
Becker Jr .... MA
Beckley .... WV
Bismarck Jr .... ND
Black Hills State .... SD
Blinn .... TX
Bliss .... OH
Brandywine .... DE
Briarwood .... CT
Bristol Coll .... TN
Campbellsville Coll .... KY
Castleton State .... VT
Cazenovia Coll .... NY
Central Coll .... KS
Central Missouri .... MO
Central Pennsylvania Bus. Sch .. PA
Champlain Coll .... VT
Chowan Coll .... NC
Cincinnati, U. of .... OH
Coffeyville .... KS
Colby-Sawyer Coll .... NH
Columbia Union .... MD
Dakota State .... SD
Davenport Coll. of Bus .... MI
David Lipscomb Coll .... TN
Davis & Elkins .... WV
Dean Jr .... MA
Dickinson State .... ND
East Central Oklahoma State .. OK
Eastern Arizona .... AZ
Eastern Kentucky U .... KY
Eastern New Mexico U .... NM
Eastern Wyoming Coll .... WY
Elizabethtown Coll .... PA
Endicott .... MA
Fairmont State .... WV
Ferris State .... MI
Ferrum Coll .... VA
Fisher Jr .... MA
Gannon U .... PA
Georgia State U .... GA
Goldey Beacom Coll .... DE
Gwynedd-Mercy .... PA
Harcum Jr .... PA
Harper Coll IL
Hesser Coll .... NH
Hesston Coll .... KS
Hilbert .... NY
Hocking Tech. Coll .... OH
Howard Comm. Jr .... TX
Humphreys Coll .... CA
Husson Coll .... MN
Hutchinson Comm .... KS
Indiana State U .... IN
Johnson & Wales .... RI
Keystone Jr .... PA
Lamar U .... TX
Lasell Jr .... MA
Lewis & Clark State .... ID
Loma Linda U .... CA
Louisburg Coll .... NC
Maine, U. of (Machias) .... ME
Mallinckrodt IL
Mankato State .... MN
Manor Jr .... PA
Maria Regina Coll .... NY
Maryville State .... ND
Miami, U. of .... OH
Missouri, U. of (Kansas City) .. MO
Morehead State .... KY
Mount Alousius Jr .... PA
Navarro Coll .... TX
Newbury Jr .... MA
North Carolina Central U ...... NC
North Dakota State U .... ND
North Idaho .... ID
Northeast Mississippi Jr ...... MS
Northern Kentucky U .... KY

Northern Michigan U .... MI
Norwich U .... VT
Notre Dame Coll .... NH
Oregon Inst. of Tech .... OR
Otero Jr .... CO
Pacific Union .... CA
Pearl River Coll .... MS
Pittsburg State .... KS
Post Coll .... CT
Quinnipiac Coll .... CT
Rio Grande Coll................ OH
Rivier Coll .... NH
Robert Morris .... PA
Sacred Heart U .... CT
Schreiner Coll .... TX
Sheridan Coll .... WY
South Dakota, U. of .... SD
South Georgia Coll............ GA
Southern Coll .... FL
Southern Illinois U IL
Southern Vermont Coll .... VT
Southwest Missouri .... MO
Southwestern Adventist......... TX
Southwestern Oklahoma State U .... OK
St. Catherine Coll .... KY
State U. of New York (Cobleskill, Farmingdale, Morrisville) .... NY
Sue Bennett .... KY
Suomi Coll .... MI
Tennessee, U. of .... TN
Thomas Coll .... ME
Toledo, U. of.................. OH
Trevecca Nazarene............. TN
Waldorf Coll .... IA
Walla Walla Coll .... WA
West Virginia State .... WV
Western Kentucky U .... KY
Western Montana Coll......... MT
Western Texas Coll .... TX
Wichita State U .... KS
Yakima Valley Comm.......... WA
York Coll .... PA

Secretarial Science

Bluefield Coll .... VA
Crandall Coll .... GA
Eastern Oregon State .... OR
Geneva Coll .... PA
Hawaii, U. of (Hilo)............ HI
Indiana Inst. of Tech .... IN
Sioux Empire .... IA
Southwest Mississippi Jr ...... MS

Secretarial Studies, Overseas

Alabama A&M.................. AL
International Coll .... FL
Marywood Coll................. PA
Rio Piedras .... PR

Secretary, Bilingual

Baruch Coll.................... NY
Bay State Jr. Coll .... MA
Bennett Coll .... NC
Chamberlayne Jr. Coll......... MA
Coffeyville .... KS
David Lipscomb Coll .... TN
Eastern Kentucky U .... KY
Endicott Coll.................. MA
Findlay Coll.................... OH
Hutchinson .... KS
Marywood Coll................. PA
Newbury Jr. Coll .... MA
Pacific Union Coll.............. CA
Puerto Rico, U. of .... PR
Rider Coll...................... NJ
Tennessee, U. of .... TN

Silk Screening

California Coll. of Arts and Crafts .... CA
Carnegie-Mellon .... PA
Columbia Coll .... MO
George Washington U .... DC
Goddard Coll .... VT
Hampshire Coll .... MA
Kansas City Art Inst .... MO
Savannah Coll. of Art and Design .... GA
Skidmore Coll.................. NY
William Woods .... MO
Wittenberg U .... OH

Social Psychology

Alabama Agricultural & Mechanical U .... AL
Belmont Coll................... TN
Bennett Coll .... NC
Bernadean U................... CA
Brevard .... NC
Bridgewater State .... MA
California, U. of (Davis, Irvine, San Diego) .... CA
Carnegie-Mellon .... PA
Charleston, U. of .... WV
Cheyney State .... PA
Clarion State................... PA
Columbia Coll .... MO
Connecticut, U. of.............. CT
Davis & Elkins .... WV
Eastern Kentucky U .... KY
Eastern Washington .... WA
Eckerd Coll .... FL
Franklin Coll .... IN
Franklin Pierce Coll .... NH
George Washington U .... DC
Goddard Coll .... VT
Illinois Central Coll............. IL
Indiana State U .... IN
Indiana U. (Bloomington) .... IN
International .... MO
Iowa, U. of..................... IA
John F. Kennedy U............. CA
Johns Hopkins U.............. MD
Kansas, U. of .... KS
Knox Coll....................... IL
La Salle Coll .... PA
Lincoln Coll IL
Marlboro Coll .... VT
Michigan, U. of................. MI
Minnesota, U.of .... MN
Montevallo, U. of .... AL
Nebraska Wesleyan .... NE
New York Institute of Technology.................. NY
North Carolina Central U.......................... NC
Northwest Missouri State Coll .... MO
Puerto Rico, U. of .... PR
Rio Piedras .... PR
Shorter Coll .... GA
South Georgia Coll............ GA
Southeastern U .... LA
St. Andrew's Presbyterian ..... NC
St. Leo Coll .... FL
Tennessee, U. of .... TN
Texas A&I .... TX
Trinity Christian................. IL
Truett McConnell .... GA
Washington U................. MO
Wesleyan U .... CT
West Florida, U. of .... FL
Westminster Coll............... UT
White Pines Coll .... NH
William Woods .... MO
Wisconsin, U. of (Superior) ..... WI

Social Work

Undergraduate and graduate programs with social welfare content; members of Council on Social Work Education
•Undergraduate only
★Graduate only

Adelphi .... NY
•Alabama, U. of (Birmingham) ... AL
Alabama, U. of (University) ..... AL
•Alabama A&M.................. AL
•Alaska, U. of .... AK
•Alma Coll...................... MI
•Anderson Coll .... IN
•Andrews U..................... MI
•Anna Maria Coll............... MA
Arizona State U (Tempe) .... AZ
★Arkansas, U. of .... AR
•Arkansas State U............... AR
★Atlanta U .... GA
•Auburn U .... AL
•Augsburg Coll .... MN
•Augustana .... SD
•Averett Coll .... VA
•Avila Coll .... MO
•Ball State U................... IN
Barry Coll .... FL
•Baylor U...................... TX
•Bemidji State U .... MN
•Benedict Coll .... SC
•Bethany Coll .... KS
•Bethel Coll..................... KS
•Boise State U .... ID
★Boston Coll................... MA
Boston U .... MA
•Bowie State Coll .... MD
•Bowling Green State U .... OH
•Briar Cliff Coll .... IA
•Brigham Young .... UT
•Brigham Young U .... HI
★Bryn Mawr Coll .... PA
★California, U. of (Berkeley, Los Angeles)................ CA
•California State Coll .... PA
•California State Poly U. (Pomona) .... CA
•California State U. (Chico, Long Beach, Los Angeles) .... CA
California State U. (Fresno) ..... CA
★California State U. (Sacramento) .... CA
•Capital U .... OH
•Carroll Coll .... MT
•Carroll Coll .... WI
★Case Western Reserve......... OH
Catholic U .... DC
•Catholic U of Puerto Rico ...... PR
•Cedar Crest Coll .... PA
•Central Florida, U. of .... FL
•Chapman Coll .... CA
★Chicago, U. of IL
Cincinnati, U. of .... OH
•Clarke Coll .... IA
•Cleveland State U .... OH
•College Misericordia .... PA
•Colorado State U............. CO
•Columbia Coll .... SC
★Columbia U................... NY
•Concord Coll .... WV
•Concordia Coll................. NY
★Connecticut, U. of .... CT
•Coppin State Coll .... MD
•Cornell U .... NY
•Daemen Coll................... NY
•Dakota Wesleyan.............. SD
•Dayton, U. of .... OH
•Defiance Coll .... OH
★Denver, U. of .... CO
•Detroit, U. of .... MI
•District of Columbia, U. of ..... DC
•Dominican Coll .... NY
•Dubuque, U. of................. IA
•East Carolina U .... NC
•East Tennessee State U .... TN
•East Texas State U .... TX
•Eastern Coll .... PA
•Eastern Kentucky U .... KY
•Eastern Mennonite .... VA
•Eastern Michigan U .... MI
•Eastern Nazarene Coll......... MA
Eastern Washington .... WA
•Elizabethtown Coll .... PA
•Evansville, U. of................ IN
•Fairleigh Dickinson............. NJ
•Fairmont State Coll............ WV
•Ferrum Coll.................... VA
•Florida A&M Coll.............. FL
•Florida International .... FL
Florida State U................. FL
Fordham U .... NY
•Freed-Hardeman Coll........... TN
•Gallaudet Coll .... DC
•Gannon Coll .... PA
•George Mason U .... VA
George Williams IL
Georgia, U. of................. GA
•Glenville State Coll .... WV
•Goshen Coll .... IN
•Graceland Coll.................. IA
•Harding Coll .... AR
Hawaii, U. of .... HI
•Hood Coll .... MD
★Houston, U. of .... TX
•Houston Baptist................ TX
★Howard U .... DC
★Hunter .... NY
★Idaho State U.................. ID
Illinois, U. of (Chicago, Urbana) IL
•Illinois State U IL
•Indiana State U .... IN
★Indiana U. (Indianapolis) .... IN
•Inter-American U............... PR
•Iona Coll .... NY
Iowa, U. of..................... IA
•Iowa State U .... IA
•Jackson State U............... MS
•James Madison U .... VA
Kansas, U. of .... KS
•Kansas State U................. KS
•Kean Coll. of New Jersey .... NJ
Kentucky, U. of .... KY
•Kentucky State U .... KY
•Lamar U .... TX
•Lambuth Coll .... TN
•Livingston Coll................. NJ
•Livingstone Coll............... NC
•Lock Haven State Coll.......... PA
•Loma Linda U.................. CA
•Longwood Coll................. VA
•Loras Coll .... IA
★Louisiana State U .... LA
Louisville, U. of .... KY
Loyola U IL
•Loyola U....................... LA
•Luther Coll .... IA
•Maine, U. of (Orono) .... ME
•Manchester Coll................. IN
•Mankato State Coll .... MN
•Marquette U .... WI
•Mars Hill...................... NC
•Marycrest Coll .... IA
•Marygrove Coll................. MI
Maryland, U. of (Baltimore) .... MD
Marywood Coll................ PA
•Memphis State U .... TN
•Mercy Coll..................... NY
•Mercyhurst Coll .... PA
•Meredith Coll .... NC
★Michigan, U. of .... MI
Michigan State U............... MI
•Middle Tennessee State U ...... TN
★Minnesota, U. of (Duluth, Minneapolis) .... MN
•Minot State Coll............... ND
•Mississippi, U. of .... MS

•Mississippi U. for Women ... MS
•Mississippi Valley State U ... MS
Missouri, U. of (Columbia) ... MO
•Missouri Western State Coll ... MO
•Molloy Coll ... NY
•Monmouth Coll ... NJ
•Montana, U. of ... MT
•Montevallo, U. of ... AL
•Moorhead State Coll ... MN
•Moravian Coll ... PA
•Morehead State U ... KY
•Morgan State Coll ... MD
•Morningside Coll ... IA
•Mount Marty Coll ... SD
•Mount Mary Coll ... WI
•Mount Mercy Coll ... IA
•Muhlenberg ... PA
•Murray State U ... KY
•Nazareth Coll ... MI
•Nazareth Coll ... NY
Nebraska, U. of (Omaha) ... NE
•Nevada, U. of (Las Vegas, Reno) ... NV
•New Hampshire, U. of ... NH
New Mexico Highlands ... NM
•New Mexico State U ... NM
•New Orleans, U. of ... LA
•New Rochelle, Coll. of ... NY
New York U ... NY
Norfolk State U ... VA
•North Alabama, U. of ... AL
★North Carolina, U. of (Chapel Hill) ... NC
•North Carolina, U. of (Greensboro) ... NC
•North Carolina A&T State U ... NC
•North Carolina State U ... NC
•North Dakota, U. of ... ND
•North Texas State U ... TX
•Northeast Louisiana U ... LA
•Northern Iowa, U. of ... IA
•Northern Kentucky U ... KY
•Northern Michigan U ... MI
•Northwest Nazarene Coll ... ID
•Northwestern State U ... LA
Ohio State U ... OH
•Ohio U ... OH
Oklahoma, U. of ... OK
Our Lady of the Lake U ... TX
•Pacific Lutheran ... WA
•Pan American U ... TX
•Paul Quinn Coll ... TX
★Pennsylvania, U. of ... PA
•Pennsylvania State U ... PA
•Pfeiffer Coll ... NC
•Philadelphia Coll. of the Bible ... PA
•Pittsburg State ... KS
Pittsburgh, U. of ... PA
Portland State U ... OR
•Prarie View A&M U ... TX
•Providence Coll ... RI
Puerto Rico, U. of ... PR
•Radford Coll ... VA
•Ramapo Coll ... NJ
•Regis Coll ... MA
Rhode Island Coll ... RI
•Roberts Wesleyan Coll ... NY
•Rochester Inst. of Tech ... NY
•Roosevelt U ... IL
•Rutgers (Camden Coll. of Arts and Sciences) ... NJ
Rutgers (New Brunswick) ... NJ
•Salem State Coll ... MA
•Salisbury State Coll ... MD
San Diego State U ... CA
San Francisco State U ... CA
San Jose State U ... CA
•Santa Fe, Coll. of ... NM
•Seton Hall U ... NJ
•Shepherd Coll ... WV
•Shippensburg State Coll ... PA
★Simmons Coll ... MA
•Sioux Falls Coll ... SD
★Smith Coll ... MA
★South Carolina, U. of ... SC
•South Dakota, U. of ... SD
•South Florida, U. of ... FL
★Southern California, U. of ... CA
•Southern Connecticut State Coll ... CT
•Southern Illinois U ... IL
•Southern Maine, U. of ... ME
★Southern Mississippi, U. of ... MS
•Southern U. and A&M Coll ... LA
•Southern U. in New Orleans ... LA
•Southern Utah State Coll ... UT
•Southwest Missouri State U ... MO
•Southwest Texas State U ... TX
•Spalding Coll ... KY
•St. Catherine, Coll. of ... MN
•St. Cloud U ... MN
•St. Edwards U ... TX
•St. Francis Coll ... IN
•St. Francis Coll ... PA
•St. Joseph Coll ... CT
St. Louis U ... MO
•St. Mary's Dominican Coll ... LA
•St. Mary of the Plains Coll ... KS
•St. Scholastica, Coll. of ... MN
•St. Teresa, Coll. of ... MN
•St. Thomas, Coll. of ... MN
State U. of New York (Albany, Stony Brook) ... NY
★State U. of New York (Buffalo) ... NY
•State U. of New York Coll. (Brockport, Buffalo) ... NY
•Stockton State Coll ... NJ
Syracuse ... NY
•Tabor Coll ... KS
•Talladega Coll ... AL
•Tarleton State U ... TX
•Taylor U ... IN
Temple ... PA
•Tennessee, U. of (Chattanooga, Martin) ... TN
★Tennessee, U. of (Memphis, Knoxville, Nashville) ... TN
•Tennessee State U ... TN
★Texas, U. of (Arlington) ... TX
Texas, U. of (Austin) ... TX
•Texas Christian U ... TX
•Texas Lutheran Coll ... TX
•Texas Southern U ... TX
•Texas Tech. U ... TX
•Texas Woman's U ... TX
•Thomas More Coll ... KY
•Trinity Coll ... VT
★Tulane U ... LA
•Tuskegee Inst ... AL
★Utah, U. of ... UT
•Utah State U ... UT
•Valparaiso U ... IN
•Vermont, U. of ... VT
•Villa Maria Coll ... PA
Virginia Commonwealth U ... VA
•Virginia Intermont Coll ... VA
•Virginia State Coll ... VA
•Virginia Union ... VA
•Walla Walla Coll ... WA
•Warren Wilson Coll ... NC
•Wartburg Coll ... IA
•Washburn U. of Topeka ... KS
Washington, U. of ... WA
•Washington U ... MO
Wayne State U ... MI
•Weber State Coll ... UT
•West Chester State Coll ... PA
•West Florida, U. of ... FL
•West Texas State ... TX
•West Virginia State ... WV
West Virginia U ... WV
•Western Carolina U ... NC
•Western Kentucky U ... KY
•Western Maryland Coll ... MD
Western Michigan U ... MI
•Whittier Coll ... CA
•Wichita State U ... KS
•Widener Coll ... PA
•Winthrop ... SC
•Wisconsin, U. of (Eau Claire, La Crosse, Oshkosh, Superior, Whitewater) ... WI
Wisconsin, U. of (Madison, Milwaukee) ... WI
•Wright State U ... OH
•Wyoming, U. of ... WY
•Xavier U ... LA
•Xavier U ... OH
★Yeshiva U ... NY

Sociology

Institutions awarding 20 or more undergraduate degrees as major field in single year according to U.S. Office of Education latest statistics

Adams State Coll ... CO
Albany State Coll ... GA
Alcorn State U ... MS
American U ... DC
Appalachian State ... NC
Arizona, U. of ... AZ
Arizona State U ... AZ
Atlantic Christian ... NC
Austin Peay ... TN
Baruch Coll ... NY
Bethune-Cookman Coll ... FL
Biscayne Coll ... FL
Black Hills State ... SD
Bloomsburg State ... PA
Boston Coll ... MA
Boston U ... MA
Bowling Green ... OH
Brandeis ... MA
Bridgewater State ... MA
Brigham Young ... UT
Brooklyn ... NY
California, U. of (Berkeley, Davis, Los Angeles, Riverside, San Diego, Santa Barbara, Santa Cruz) ... CA
California State Coll. (San Bernardino, Stanislaus) ... CA
California State U. (Chico, Dominguez Hills, Fresno, Fullerton, Hayward, Long Beach, Los Angeles, Northridge, Sacramento) ... CA
Calvin Coll ... MI
Cameron U ... OK
Canisius ... NY
Catholic U ... PR
Centenary Coll ... LA
Central Connecticut ... CT
Central Michigan U ... MI
Central State U ... OK
Charleston, Coll. of ... SC
City Coll ... NY
Clark U ... MA
Clemson ... SC
Cleveland State U ... OH
Colgate U ... NY
Colorado, U. of ... CO
Connecticut, U. of ... CT
Corpus Christi State ... TX
David Lipscomb ... TN
Delaware, U. of ... DE
DePaul U ... IL
Drake ... IA
Duquesne U ... PA
Earlham Coll ... IN
East Stroudsburg ... PA
East Texas State U ... TX
Eastern Connecticut ... CT
Eastern Illinois U ... IL
Eastern New Mexico ... NM
Eastern Washington U ... WA
Elizabeth City State ... NC
Fairfield U ... CT
Fairleigh Dickinson ... NJ
Fayetteville State U ... NC
Florida, U. of ... FL
Florida A&M ... FL
Florida International U ... FL
Florida Southern ... FL
Florida State U ... FL
Florida Tech ... FL
Fordham U ... NY
Framingham State Coll ... MA
Francis Marion Coll ... SC
Frostburg State ... MD
Furman U ... SC
George Mason ... VA
George Washington ... DC
Georgetown ... DC
Georgia Southern ... GA
Georgia State ... GA
Gettysburg ... PA
Glassboro ... NJ
Hamline ... MN
Hampton ... VA
Hartford, U. of ... CT
Hartwick Coll ... NY
Harvard U ... MA
Hawaii, U. of ... HI
Hobart & William Smith Coll ... NY
Hofstra ... NY
Holy Cross, Coll. of the ... MA
Houston, U. of ... TX
Howard U ... DC
Hunter ... NY
Idaho State U ... ID
Illinois, U. of ... IL
Illinois State U ... IL
Indiana State U ... IN
Indiana U ... IN
Inter-American U ... PR
Iowa, U. of ... IA
Iowa State U ... IA
Ithaca ... NY
Jacksonville ... AL
Jersey City State Coll ... NJ
John Carroll ... OH
John Jay ... NY
Kansas, U. of ... KS
Kansas State U ... KS
Kean Coll ... NJ
Kent State U ... OH
La Salle Coll ... PA
Lamar U ... TX
Lehman Coll ... NY
Lincoln ... PA
Long Island U ... NY
Louisiana State U ... LA
Louisville, U. of ... KY
Lowell, U. of ... MA
Loyola ... IL
Loyola Coll ... MD
Loyola Marymount ... CA
Lycoming Coll ... PA
Lynchburg ... VA
Maine, U. of ... ME
Mankato State ... MN
Mary Washington Coll ... VA
Maryland, U. of ... MD
Marymount Manhattan Coll ... NY
Massachusetts, U. of ... MA
Memphis State ... TN
Mercer ... GA
Mercy ... NY
Meredith ... NC
Metropolitan ... CO
Miami, U. of ... FL
Miami U ... OH
Michigan, U. of ... MI
Middle Tennessee State U ... TN
Minnesota, U. of ... MN
Mississippi Valley ... MS
Missouri, U. of ... MO
Missouri Southern ... MO
Montana, U. of ... MT
Montana State U ... MT

Montclair State NJ
Morgan State MD
Mount St. Mary's MD
Nebraska, U. of NE
New Mexico, U. of NM
New Mexico State NM
New Orleans, U. of LA
New York U NY
Norfolk State Coll VA
North Adams State MA
North Alabama AL
North Carolina, U. of (Chapel Hill, Charlotte, Greensboro, Wilmington) NC
North Carolina Central U NC
North Carolina State U NC
North Dakota State U ND
North Florida FL
Northeast Missouri State U MO
Northeastern Illinois IL
Northeastern State Coll OK
Northeastern U MA
Northern Arizona U AZ
Northern Colorado, U. of CO
Northern Illinois U IL
Northwestern IL
Notre Dame, U. of IN
Oakland U MI
Ohio State OH
Oklahoma, U. of OK
Oklahoma State U OK
Old Dominion U VA
Oregon, U. of OR
Oregon State U OR
Pan American U TX
Pembroke State U NC
Pennsylvania, U. of PA
Pennsylvania State U PA
Pittsburgh, U. of PA
Pitzer Coll CA
Portland State U OR
Princeton U NJ
Providence Coll RI
Puerto Rico, U. of PR
Puget Sound, U. of WA
Purdue IN
Queens NY
Ramapo NJ
Regis Coll MA
Rhode Island, U. of RI
Rhode Island Coll RI
Richmond, U. of VA
Rider Coll NJ
Roosevelt IL
Rutgers NJ
Saginaw Valley MI
San Diego State CA
San Francisco, U. of CA
San Francisco State CA
San Jose State CA
Santa Clara, U. of CA
Seton Hall U NJ
Shippensburg State Coll PA
Siena Coll NY
Sonoma CA
South Carolina, U. of SC
South Carolina State SC
South Dakota State SD
South Florida, U. of FL
Southeastern Massachusetts U MA
Southern California, U. of CA
Southern Colorado, U. of CO
Southern Connecticut State Coll CT
Southern Illinois IL
Southern Mississippi, U. of MS
Southwest Missouri MO
Southwest Texas TX
Southwestern Louisiana LA
Spelman Coll GA
St. Augustine's NC
St. John's U NY
St. Joseph's PA
St. Lawrence U NY
St. Martin's WA
St. Mary's IN
St. Olaf MN
St. Rose, Coll. of NY
State U. of New York (all campuses) NY
Stanford CA
Stephen F. Austin TX
Stillman Coll AL
Stockton State NJ
Suffolk U MA
Syracuse NY
Tampa, U. of FL
Tarleton State U TX
Temple PA
Tennessee, U. of TN
Texas, U. of TX
Texas A&I TX
Texas A&M TX
Texas Eastern TX
Texas Tech. U TX
Toledo, U. of OH
Trenton State U NJ
Trinity U TX
Tulane U LA
Upsala Coll NJ
Utah, U. of UT
Valdosta State Coll GA
Vanderbilt U TN
Vermont, U. of VT
Villanova U PA
Virginia, U. of VA
Virginia Commonwealth U VA
Virginia Poly. Inst VA
Virginia State Coll VA
Wake Forest NC
Washington, U. of WA
Washington State U WA
Washington U MO
Wayne State U MI
Weber State UT
West Georgia Coll GA
West Virginia U WV
Western Illinois U IL
Western Kentucky U KY
Western Maryland Coll MD
Western Michigan U MI
Western Washington WA
William and Mary VA
William Paterson NJ
Winona State MN
Winston-Salem NC
Winthrop Coll SC
Wisconsin, U. of WI
Wofford Coll SC
Wright State OH
York NY

Soil Science Management, Conservation

Abilene Christian TX
Arizona, U. of AZ
Ball State U IN
California, U. of (Davis) CA
California Poly. State U CA
California State Coll PA
Central Missouri MO
Colorado Mountain CO
Cornell U NY
Cowley County Comm KS
Dickinson State Coll ND
Eastern Washington WA
Florida, U. of FL
Goddard Coll VT
Hawaii, U. of (Honolulu) HI
Kansas State U KS
Lincoln Coll IL
Maine, U. of (Farmington) ME
Michigan State MI
Minnesota, U. of (Crookston, Minneapolis) MN
Mississippi Delta Jr MS
New Hampshire, U. of NH
New Mexico State U NM
North Dakota State U ND
Northeast Louisiana U LA
Northeast Missouri MO
Purdue IN
South Dakota State U SD
Southern Idaho, Coll. of ID
Southern Illinois U IL
State U. of New York (Morrisville) NY
SUNY Coll. of Agri. & Life Sci NY
Western Kentucky U KY
Wisconsin, U. of (River Falls, Stevens Point, Superior) WI
World Coll. West CA

Solar Energy

According, in part, to information obtained from the Solar Energy Information Data Bank

Alabama, U. of (Huntsville) AL
Arizona, U. of AZ
Arizona State U AZ
Arkansas, U. of AR
Atlantic, Coll. of the ME
Ball State U IN
Beacon Coll DC
Bemidji State U MN
Bridgewater State Coll MA
California Poly. State U. (San Luis Obispo) CA
California State U. (Hayward, Long Beach) CA
Cincinnati, U. of OH
Colorado, U. of (Boulder) CO
Colorado Mountain Coll CO
Colorado Sch. of Mines CO
Colorado State U CO
Colorado Tech. Coll CO
Dayton, U. of OH
Dordt Coll IA
East Tennessee State U TN
Florida, U. of FL
Georgia Inst. of Tech GA
Goddard Coll VT
Governors State U IL
Grand Valley State U MI
Hampshire Coll MA
Idaho, U. of ID
Idaho State U ID
Illinois Inst. of Tech IL
Illinois State U IL
Jordan Coll MI
Kansas, U. of KS
Kansas State U KS
Kentucky, U. of KY
Lake Superior State Coll MI
Lowell, U. of MA
Louisiana State U LA
Marlboro Coll VT
Marquette U WI
Maryland, U. of MD
Massachusetts, U. of (Amherst) MA
Metropolitan State Coll CO
Michigan State U MI
Middlebury Coll VT
Minnesota, U. of (Minneapolis-St. Paul) MN
Mississippi, U. of MS
Montana Coll. of Mineral Sci. & Tech MT
Navarro Coll TX
New England Inst. of Tech RI
New Jersey Inst. of Tech NJ
New Mexico, U. of NM
New York, State U. of (Binghamton, Buffalo, Plattsburgh) NY
New York, State U. of, Coll. of Tech NY
North Adams State MA
Northeastern U MA
Northern Arizona U AZ
Northern Colorado, U. of CO
Northern Illinois U IL
Northrop U CA
Old Dominion U VA
Oregon State U OR
Pennsylvania State U PA
Portland State U OR
Princeton U NJ
Purdue U IN
Ramapo Coll NJ
Rose-Hulman Inst. of Tech IN
Saint Louis U MO
Sangamon State U IL
Sheridan Coll WY
Sonoma State U CA
Southern Idaho, Coll. of ID
Southwest Missouri State U MO
Texas A&M U TX
Union Coll OH
Washington, U. of WA
Wesley Coll DE
Wisconsin, U. of (Stout) WI
Worcester Poly. Inst MA
Worcester State Coll MA
World Coll. West CA
Wyoming, U. of WY
Youngstown State U OH

Space Technology

Florida Inst. of Tech FL
Kansas, U. of KS

Special Education, *See* EXCEPTIONAL CHILDREN, PREPARATION FOR TEACHING OF

Speech and Hearing Therapy

Abilene Christian TX
Adelphi NY
Akron, U. of OH
Alabama A&M AL
Andrews U MI
Arizona, U. of AZ
Arizona State U AZ
Arkansas State U AR
Ashland Coll OH
Augustana Coll IL
Baldwin-Wallace Coll OH
Baylor U TX
Bennett Coll NC
Boston U MA
Bradley IL
Bridgewater State MA
Butler U IN
C.W. Post NY
California State Coll PA
California State U. (Fresno, Los Angeles, Northridge, Sacramento) CA
Calvin Coll MI
Case Western OH
Central Michigan U MI
Central Missouri MO
Chapman Coll CA
City Coll NY
Clarion State PA
Cleveland State OH
Colorado, U. of CO
Colorado State U CO
Columbus Coll GA
Connecticut, U. of CT
Delta State U MS
Denver, U. of CO
Duquesne U PA

Eastern New Mexico .... NM
Elmhurst IL
Elmira .... NY
Elms Coll .... MA
Emerson .... MA
Evangel Coll .... MO
Florida State U .... FL
Fontbonne Coll .... MO
George Washington U .... DC
Governors State U IL
Hardin-Simmons .... TX
Harding U .... AR
Hawaii, U. of (Honolulu) .... HI
Illinois, U. of IL
Illinois State U IL
Indiana State U .... IN
Indiana U. (Bloomington) .... IN
Indiana U .... PA
Iowa, U. of .... IA
Ithaca .... NY
James Madison .... VA
Kansas, U. of .... KS
Kearney State .... NE
Kent State U .... OH
Kentucky, U. of .... KY
Lamar U .... TX
Loma Linda .... CA
Louisiana Tech .... LA
Maine, U. of (Farmington, Orono) .... ME
Mankato State .... MN
Marquette U .... WI
Mary Washington Coll .... VA
Marymount Manhattan .... NY
Marywood .... PA
Miami U .... OH
Michigan State U .... MI
Midwestern State U .... TX
Minnesota, U. of (Duluth, Minneapolis) .... MN
Missouri, U. of .... MO
Montana, U. of .... MT
Montclair State .... NJ
Montevallo, U. of .... AL
Moorhead State .... MN
Mount St. Joseph .... OH
Nazareth .... NY
New Mexico State U .... NM
Nicholls State U .... LA
North Carolina, U. of (Greensboro) .... NC
North Dakota State U .... ND
North Texas State .... TX
Northeast Louisiana State ...... LA
Northeast Mississippi Jr. Coll .. MS
Northeast Missouri .... MO
Northern Arizona U .... AZ
Northern Iowa, U. of .... IA
Northern Michigan U .... MI
Northwest Missouri State ...... MO
Northwest Nazarene Coll .... ID
Northwestern Oklahoma State . OK
Northwestern State .... LA
Northwestern U IL
Ohio State U .... OH
Ohio U .... OH
Oklahoma Christian Coll .... OK
Oklahoma State U .... OK
Pacific, U. of the .... CA
Pennsylvania State U .... PA
Purdue .... IN
Radford U .... VA
St. Rose, Coll. of .... NY
Seton Hall .... NJ
South Georgia Coll .... GA
Southern Illinois U IL
Southern Mississippi, U. of .... MS
Southwest Missouri .... MO
Southwest Texas State .... TX
State U. of New York (Geneseo, Fredonia) .... NY
State U. of N.Y. Coll. (Buffalo) .. NY
Stephen F. Austin .... TX
Syracuse U .... NY
Temple U .... PA
Tennessee, U. of .... TN
Tennessee Temple U .... TN
Texas, U. of (El Paso) .... TX
Texas Christian .... TX
Texas Woman's U .... TX
Thiel Coll .... PA
Toledo, U. of .... OH
Towson State .... MD
Trenton State .... NJ
Utah, U. of .... UT
Valparaiso U .... IN
Vermont, U. of .... VT
Walla Walla Coll .... WA
Washington, U. of .... WA
Washington U .... MO
West Chester State .... PA
West Texas State .... TX
Western Carolina U .... NC
Wichita State U .... KS
Wisconsin, U. of (Milwaukee, River Falls, Stevens Point) .... WI
Worcester State Coll .... MA
Xavier U .... LA

Speech-Language Pathology

Accredited by the American Speech-Language-Hearing Association

Adelphi U .... NY
Akron, U. of .... OH
Alabama, U. of .... AL
Arizona, U. of .... AZ
Arizona State U .... AZ
Arkansas, U. of .... AR
Auburn U .... AL
Ball State U .... IN
Boston U .... MA
Bradley U IL
Brigham Young .... UT
Brooklyn Coll .... NY
California, U. of (Santa Barbara) .... CA
California State U. (Fullerton, Long Beach, Northridge, Sacramento) .... CA
Case Western Reserve U ...... OH
Central Michigan U .... MI
Central Missouri State .... MO
Cincinnati, U. of .... OH
Cleveland State U .... OH
Colorado, U. of .... CO
Colorado State U .... CO
Columbia U. (Teachers Coll.) ... NY
Connecticut, U. of .... CT
Denver, U. of .... CO
Eastern Illinois U IL
Eastern Michigan U .... MI
Emory U .... GA
Florida, U. of .... FL
Florida State U .... FL
George Washington U .... DC
Georgia, U. of .... GA
Hofstra U .... NY
Houston, U. of .... TX
Hunter Coll .... NY
Idaho State U .... ID
Illinois, U. of IL
Illinois State U IL
Indiana State U .... IN
Indiana U .... IN
Iowa, U. of .... IA
Ithaca Coll .... NY
Kansas, U. of .... KS
Kansas State U .... KS
Kent State .... OH
Louisiana State U .... LA
Marquette U .... WI
Maryland, U. of .... MD
Massachusetts, U. of .... MA
Memphis State U .... TN
Michigan, U. of .... MI
Michigan State U .... MI
Minnesota, U. of (Duluth, Minneapolis) .... MN
Minot State Coll .... ND
Missouri, U. of (Columbia) ..... MO
Montana, U. of .... MT
Nebraska, U. of .... NE
New Mexico, U. of .... NM
New York U .... NY
North Dakota, U. of .... ND
North Texas State .... TX
Northeast Missouri State ...... MO
Northern Colorado, U. of ...... CO
Northern Illinois U IL
Northern Iowa, U. of .... IA
Northern Michigan U .... MI
Northwestern U IL
Ohio State U .... OH
Ohio U .... OH
Oklahoma, U. of .... OK
Oklahoma State U .... OK
Our Lady of the Lake Coll ...... TX
Pacific, U. of the .... CA
Pennsylvania State U .... PA
Phillips U .... OK
Pittsburgh, U. of .... PA
Portland State U .... OR
Purdue U .... IN
Queens Coll .... NY
San Diego State U .... CA
San Francisco State .... CA
San Jose State .... CA
South Carolina, U. of .... SC
South Dakota, U. of .... SD
Southern Connecticut State Coll .... CT
Southern Illinois U IL
Southern Methodist U .... TX
Southern Mississippi, U. of .... MS
Southwest Texas State .... TX
State U. of New York (Buffalo) .... NY
State U. of New York Coll. (Geneseo) .... NY
Syracuse U .... NY
Temple U .... PA
Tennessee, U. of .... TN
Texas, U. of (Austin) .... TX
Tulane .... LA
Utah, U. of .... UT
Vanderbilt U .... TN
Vermont, U. of .... VT
Virginia, U. of .... VA
Washington, U. of .... WA
Washington State U .... WA
Wayne State U .... MI
West Virginia U .... WV
Western Illinois IL
Western Michigan U .... MI
Wichita State U .... KS
Wisconsin, U. of (Eau Claire, Madison, Milwaukee, Stevens Point) .... WI
Wyoming, U. of .... WY

Sports Administration, *See* ATHLETIC OR SPORTS ADMINISTRATION

Sports Medicine

Akron,U. of .... OH
Alabama, U. of .... AL
Ashland Coll .... OH
Baylor U .... TX
California State U. (Sacramento) .... CA
Central Michigan U .... MI
Central Missouri .... MO
Chapman Coll .... CA
Cincinnati, U. of .... OH
Denver, U. of .... CO
George Williams IL
Guilford .... NC
Hope Coll .... MI
Hutchinson Comm. Coll .... KS
John Carroll U .... OH
Marietta Coll .... OH
Mars Hill .... NC
Marywood .... PA
New Mexico State U .... NM
North Dakota State U .... ND
Northern Kentucky U .... KY
Northern Michigan U .... MI
Northwest Nazarene Coll .... ID
Pacific, U. of the .... CA
Pepperdine U .... CA
Purdue U .... IN
Springfield Coll .... MA
Valparaiso U .... IN
William Woods .... MO
Wisconsin, U. of (La Crosse) .... WI

Statistics

Akron, U. of .... OH
Appalachian State .... NC
Ball State U .... IN
Baruch Coll .... NY
Baylor U .... TX
Belmont Coll .... TN
Boston U .... MA
Bowling Green .... OH
California, U. of (Davis, Riverside) .... CA
California State U. (Chico, Hayward) .... CA
Carnegie-Mellon .... PA
Case Western Reserve .... OH
Central Florida, U. of .... FL
Central Missouri .... MO
Chicago, U. of IL
City Coll .... NY
Colorado State U .... CO
Connecticut, U. of .... CT
Denver, U. of .... CO
Drake U .... IA
Eastern Kentucky U .... KY
Eastern New Mexico .... NM
Florida, U. of .... FL
Florida State U .... FL
Franklin Coll .... IN
George Washington U .... DC
Harvard U .... MA
Hollins Coll .... VA
Hope Coll .... MI
Illinois, U. of IL
Indiana U. (Bloomington) .... IN
Iowa, U. of .... IA
Iowa State U .... IA
Jacksonville State U .... AL
Johns Hopkins .... MD
Kansas, U. of .... KS
Kansas State U .... KS
Kearney State .... NE
La Salle Coll .... PA
Lehigh U .... PA
Marquette U .... WI
Miami U .... OH
Michigan State U .... MI
Minnesota, U. of (Duluth, Minneapolis) .... MN
Missouri, U. of (Columbia, Rolla) .... MO
Montevallo, U. of .... AL
Nebraska, U. of .... NE
New Coll. of U.S.F .... FL
North Florida, U. of .... FL
Northeast Missouri .... MO
Northern Michigan U .... MI
Northwest Missouri State ...... MO
Oakland U .... MI
Ohio State .... OH

Oklahoma State U . . . . OK
Oregon State U . . . . OR
Pennsylvania State U. (University Park) . . . . PA
Pittsburgh, U. of . . . . PA
Princeton U . . . . NJ
Puerto Rico, U. of . . . . PR
Purdue . . . . IN
Radcliffe . . . . MA
Radford U . . . . VA
Rider Coll . . . . NJ
Rio Piedras . . . . PR
Rochester, U. of . . . . NY
Saint Mary's Coll . . . . MN
San Diego State . . . . CA
South Carolina, U. of . . . . SC
State U. of New York (Oneonta, Stony Brook, Coll. of Agri. & Life Sci.) . . . . NY
Stevens Inst. of Tech . . . . NJ
Syracuse U . . . . NY
Temple U . . . . PA
Tennessee, U. of . . . . TN
Texas A&M . . . . TX
Trinity Christian IL
Truett McConnell . . . . GA
Utah, U. of . . . . UT
Utah State . . . . UT
Virginia Polytech . . . . VA
Washington, U. of . . . . WA
Washington U . . . . MO
Wayne State U . . . . MI
West Florida, U. of . . . . FL
William Woods . . . . MO
Winona State U . . . . MN
Wisconsin, U. of (Madison, Milwaukee) . . . . WI
Wright State U . . . . OH
Wyoming, U. of . . . . WY

Store/Shop Management

Alabama A&M . . . . AL
Averett Coll . . . . VA
Central Missouri . . . . MO
Columbia Coll . . . . MO
Davenport Coll. of Business . . . . MI
Drexel U . . . . PA
Eastern Montana Coll . . . . MT
Huron Coll . . . . SD
Indiana U. (Bloomington) . . . . IN
Johnson & Wales Coll . . . . RI
Lincoln Coll IL
Maria Regina Coll . . . . NY
Medaille Coll . . . . NY
Minnesota, U. of . . . . MN
Morehead State . . . . KY
Navarro Coll . . . . TX
North Dakota State U. (Bottineau) . . . . ND
Plymouth State . . . . NH
Schreiner Coll . . . . TX
South Dakota, U. of (Springfield) . . . . SD
South Georgia Coll . . . . GA
State U. of New York (Canton) . . NY
Trinity Christian IL
Webber Coll . . . . FL
Western Texas Coll . . . . TX
William Woods . . . . MO

Surgical Assistant

⋆Accredited by the American Medical Assn. in collaboration with the Assn. of Physician Assistant Programs.
•Accredited by the American Medical Assn., American Coll. of Surgeons, American Hospital Assn., Association of Surgical Technologists.

⋆Alabama, U. of . . . . AL
•Cincinnati Tech . . . . OH
⋆Cuyahoga Comm . . . . OH
East Tennessee State . . . . TN
El Centro Coll . . . . TX
Harper Coll IL
Illinois Central Coll IL
Kaskaskia Coll IL
•Manchester Comm. Coll . . . . CT
•Michael J. Owens Tech. Coll . . . OH
Mount Aloysius Jr. Coll . . . . PA
•Mt. Hood Comm. Coll . . . . OR
•Nassau Comm. Coll . . . . NY
•Spokane Comm. Coll . . . . WA
Trinity Christian IL
•Utica Coll . . . . NY
Wichita State U . . . . KS

Surgical Technologist

College Programs accredited by the American Medical Assn. in collaboration with the American College of Surgeons, American Hospital Assn., and Assn. of Surgical Technologists.

Cincinnati Tech. Coll . . . . OH
Manchester Comm. Coll . . . . CT
Michael J. Owens Tech. Coll . . . OH
Mt. Hood Comm. Coll . . . . OR
Nassau Comm. Coll . . . . NY
Spokane Comm. Coll . . . . WA
Utica Coll. of Syracuse U . . . . . . NY

Teacher Education, Elementary and Secondary

Accredited by National Council for Accreditation of Teacher Education; many other institutions also have graduates entering the teaching profession
•Elementary only
⋆Secondary only

Abilene Christian Coll . . . . TX
Adams State Coll . . . . CO
Adrian Coll . . . . MI
Akron, U. of . . . . OH
Alabama, U. of (Birmingham, University) . . . . AL
Alabama A&M U . . . . AL
Alabama State U . . . . AL
Albany State Coll . . . . GA
Alcorn State U . . . . MS
Alma Coll . . . . MI
Alverno Coll . . . . WI
American International Coll . . . . MA
American U . . . . DC
Anderson Coll . . . . IN
Andrews U . . . . MI
Appalachian State U . . . . NC
Arizona, U. of . . . . AZ
Arizona State U . . . . AZ
Arkansas, U. of (Fayetteville, Little Rock, Monticello) . . . . AR
⋆Arkansas, U. of (Pine Bluff) . . . . . AR
Arkansas Coll . . . . AR
Arkansas State U . . . . AR
Arkansas Tech . . . . AR
Ashland Coll . . . . OH
Atlanta U. (Grad) . . . . GA
Atlantic Christian Coll . . . . NC
Atlantic Union Coll . . . . MA
Auburn U . . . . AL
Augsburg Coll . . . . MN
Augusta Coll . . . . GA
Augustana Coll IL
Augustana Coll . . . . SD
Austin Peay State U . . . . TN
Baker U . . . . KS
Baldwin-Wallace Coll . . . . OH
Ball State U . . . . IN
Bemidji State U . . . . MN
Benedictine Coll . . . . KS
Berea Coll . . . . KY
Berry Coll . . . . GA
Bethany Coll . . . . KS
Bethany Coll . . . . WV
Bethel Coll . . . . MN
Birmingham-Southern . . . . AL
Black Hills State Coll . . . . SD
Bloomsburg State Coll . . . . PA
Boise State U . . . . ID
Boston Coll . . . . MA
Boston U . . . . MA
Bowie State Coll . . . . MD
Bowling Green State U . . . . OH
Bradley U IL
Bridgeport, U. of . . . . CT
Bridgewater State Coll . . . . MA
Brigham Young U . . . . UT
Brooklyn Coll . . . . NY
Buena Vista Coll . . . . IA
Butler U . . . . IN
California State Coll . . . . PA
California State U. (Chico, Dominguez Hills, Fresno, Fullerton, Hayward, Los Angeles, Sacramento) . . . . CA
Calvin Coll . . . . MI
Campbell Coll . . . . NC
⋆Canisius Coll . . . . NY
Capital U . . . . OH
Cardinal Stritch Coll . . . . WI
⋆Carleton Coll . . . . MN
Carson-Newman Coll . . . . TN
•Catholic U . . . . DC
Central Arkansas . . . . AR
Central Connecticut State Coll . . . . CT
Central Methodist Coll . . . . MO
Central Michigan U . . . . MI
Central Missouri State U . . . . MO
Central State U . . . . OH
Central State U . . . . OK
Central U . . . . IA
Central Washington State Coll . WA
Chadron State Coll . . . . NE
Cheyney State Coll . . . . PA
Chicago State U IL
Cincinnati, U. of . . . . OH
⋆Citadel, The . . . . SC
City Coll . . . . NY
Clarion State Coll . . . . PA
Clark Coll . . . . GA
Clarke Coll . . . . IA
Clemson U . . . . SC
Cleveland State U . . . . OH
Colorado, U. of . . . . CO
⋆Colorado State U . . . . CO
Columbia Coll . . . . SC
Columbia U. Teachers Coll. (Grad) . . . . NY
Columbus Coll . . . . GA
Concord Coll . . . . WV
Concordia Coll. (Moorhead) . . . . MN
•Concordia Coll. (St. Paul) . . . . . MN
Concordia T.C IL
Concordia T.C . . . . NE
Connecticut, U. of . . . . CT
Coppin State Coll . . . . MD
Creighton U . . . . NE
Dakota State Coll . . . . SD
Dana Coll . . . . NE
David Lipscomb Coll . . . . TN
Dayton, U. of . . . . OH
Delta State U . . . . MS
Denver, U. of . . . . CO
DePaul U IL
DePauw U . . . . IN
Dickinson State Coll . . . . ND
Doane Coll . . . . NE
Drake U . . . . IA
Drury Coll . . . . MO
Dubuque, U. of . . . . IA
Duke U . . . . NC
East Carolina U . . . . NC
East Central State U . . . . OK
East Stroudsburg State Coll . . . . PA
East Tennessee State U . . . . TN
East Texas State U . . . . TX
Eastern Illinois U IL
Eastern Kentucky U . . . . KY
Eastern Mennonite Coll . . . . VA
Eastern Michigan U . . . . MI
Eastern Montana Coll . . . . MT
Eastern New Mexico U . . . . NM
Eastern Oregon Coll . . . . OR
Eastern Washington State Coll . . . . WA
Edgewood Coll . . . . WI
Edinboro State Coll . . . . PA
Elmhurst Coll IL
Emporia Kansas State Coll . . . . . . KS
Evangel Coll . . . . MO
Evansville, U. of . . . . IN
Fairmont State Coll . . . . WV
Fayetteville State U . . . . NC
Fitchburg State Coll . . . . MA
Florida, U. of . . . . FL
Florida A&M . . . . FL
Florida Atlantic U . . . . FL
Florida State U . . . . FL
Fontbonne Coll . . . . MO
Fordham U . . . . NY
Fort Hays Kansas State Coll . . . . KS
Fort Lewis Coll . . . . CO
Fort Valley State Coll . . . . GA
Framingham State Coll . . . . MA
Friends U . . . . KS
Frostburg State Coll . . . . MD
Gallaudet Coll. (Grad) . . . . DC
⋆Gannon Coll . . . . PA
George Mason U . . . . VA
George Washington U . . . . DC
Georgia, U. of . . . . GA
Georgia Coll . . . . GA
Georgia Southern Coll . . . . GA
Georgia Southwestern Coll . . . . GA
Georgia State U . . . . GA
Glassboro State Coll . . . . NJ
Glenville State Coll . . . . WV
Gonzaga U . . . . WA
Goshen Coll . . . . IN
Graceland Coll . . . . IA
Grambling State U . . . . LA
Greenville Coll IL
Gustavus Adolphus Coll . . . . MN
Hamline U . . . . MN
Hampton Institute . . . . VA
Harding Coll . . . . AR
Hardin-Simmons U . . . . TX
•Harris-Stowe State Coll . . . . MO
Hartford, U. of . . . . CT
Hastings Coll . . . . NE
Henderson State U . . . . AR
Hendrix Coll . . . . AR
High Point Coll . . . . NC
•Hiram Coll . . . . OH
Hofstra U . . . . NY
Hope Coll . . . . MI
Houston, U. of . . . . TX
Hunter Coll . . . . NY
Idaho, U. of . . . . ID
Idaho State U . . . . ID
Illinois, U. of (Urbana) IL
Illinois State U IL
•Illinois Wesleyan U IL
Incarnate Word Coll . . . . TX
Indiana Central Coll . . . . IN
Indiana State U. (Evansville, Terre Haute) . . . . IN
Indiana U . . . . IN
Indiana U. of Pennsylvania . . . . . . PA
Iowa, U. of . . . . IA
Iowa State U. of Science and Tech . . . . IA
⋆Ithaca Coll . . . . NY
Jackson State U . . . . MS

Jacksonville State U .... AL
James Madison U .... VA
Jersey City State Coll .... NJ
John Brown U .... AR
John Carroll U .... OH
Kansas, U .of .... KS
Kansas State U .... KS
Kean Coll. of New Jersey .... NJ
Kearney State Coll .... NE
Keene State Coll .... NH
Kent State U .... OH
Kentucky, U. of .... KY
Kentucky State U .... KY
★King's Coll .... PA
Knox Coll IL
Kutztown State Coll .... PA
Lamar U .... TX
Langston U .... OK
Lehigh U. (Grad) .... PA
Lehman Coll .... NY
Lenoir-Rhyne Coll .... NC
Lewis & Clark Coll .... OR
Lewis-Clark State Coll .... ID
Lincoln U .... MO
Lindenwood Colleges .... MO
Livingston U .... AL
Lock Haven State Coll .... PA
Longwood Coll .... VA
Loras Coll .... IA
Loretto Heights Coll .... CO
Louisiana State U. (Baton Rouge, Shreveport) .... LA
Louisiana Tech. U .... LA
Louisville, U. of .... KY
Lowell, U. of .... MA
Loyola U IL
Lubbock Christian Coll .... TX
Luther Coll .... IA
Macalester Coll .... MN
Madonna Coll .... MI
Maine, U. of (Farmington, Orono) .... ME
Manchester Coll .... IN
Mankato State U .... MN
Mansfield State Coll .... PA
Marian Coll .... IN
Marian Coll. of Fond du Lac .... WI
Marquette U .... WI
Marshall U .... WV
Marycrest Coll .... IA
Marygrove Coll .... MI
Maryland, U. of .... MD
Marymount Coll .... KS
•Maryville Coll .... MO
Marywood Coll .... PA
Massachusetts, U. of .... MA
Mayville State Coll .... ND
McMurry Coll .... TX
McNeese State U .... LA
Memphis State U .... TN
Mercer U .... GA
Metropolitan State Coll .... CO
Miami, U. of .... FL
Miami U .... OH
Michigan, U. of .... MI
Michigan State U .... MI
Middle Tennessee State U ...... TN
Midwestern U .... TX
Milligan Coll .... TN
Minnesota, U. of (Duluth, Minneapolis, Morris) .... MN
Minot State Coll .... ND
Mississippi, U. of .... MS
Mississippi Coll .... MS
Mississippi State U .... MS
Mississippi U. for Women ...... MS
Mississippi Valley State U ..... MS
Missouri, U. of (Columbia, Kansas City, St. Louis) ...... MO
Missouri Southern State Coll .. MO
Missouri Western State Coll ... MO
Montana, U. of .... MT
Montana State U .... MT
Montclair State Coll .... NJ
Montevallo, U. of .... AL
Moorhead State U .... MN
Morehead State U .... KY
Morgan State U .... MD
Morningside Coll .... IA
Mount Marty Coll .... SD
Mt. Mary Coll .... WI
Muhlenberg Coll .... PA
Mundelein Coll IL
Murray State U .... KY
•National Coll. of Educ IL
•Nazareth Coll .... MI
Nebraska, U. of (Lincoln, Omaha) .... NE
Nebraska Wesleyan U .... NE
Nevada, U. of .... NV
New Hampshire, U. of (Grad. in both) .... NH
New Mexico, U. of .... NM
New Mexico State U .... NM
New Orleans, U. of .... LA
New York U .... NY
•Newberry Coll .... SC
Nicholls State U .... LA
Norfolk State Coll .... VA
•North Adams State Coll ...... MA
North Alabama, U. of .... AL
North Carolina, U. of (Chapel Hill, Greensboro) .... NC
North Carolina A&T .... NC
North Carolina Central U ...... NC
★North Carolina State U .... NC
North Dakota, U. of .... ND
★North Dakota State U .... ND
North Georgia Coll .... GA
North Texas State U .... TX
Northeast Louisiana U .... LA
Northeast Missouri State U .... MO
Northeastern Illinois U IL
Northeastern Oklahoma State U .... OK
Northeastern U .... MA
Northern Arizona U .... AZ
Northern Colorado, U. of ...... CO
Northern Illinois U IL
Northern Iowa, U. of .... IA
Northern Michigan U .... MI
Northern State Coll .... SD
Northwest Missouri State U .... MO
Northwest Nazarene Coll .... ID
Northwestern Coll .... IA
Northwestern Oklahoma State U .... OK
Northwestern State U .... LA
Notre Dame, Coll. of .... CA
Oakland U .... MI
Ohio State U .... OH
Ohio U .... OH
Oklahoma, U. of .... OK
Oklahoma Baptist Coll .... OK
Oklahoma Christian Coll ...... OK
Oklahoma State U .... OK
Old Dominion Coll .... VA
Olivet Nazarene Coll IL
Oregon, U. of .... OR
Oregon State U .... OR
Otterbein Coll .... OH
Ouachita Baptist .... AR
Ozarks, Sch. of the .... MO
Pacific, U. of the .... CA
Pacific Lutheran U .... WA
Pan American U .... TX
Panhandle State U .... OK
Pembroke State Coll .... NC
Pennsylvania State U .... PA
Peru State Coll .... NE
Pittsburg State U .... KS
Pittsburgh, U. of .... PA
Plymouth State Coll .... NH
Portland State U .... OR
Prairie View A&M .... TX
★Puerto Rico, U. of .... PR
Puget Sound, U. of .... WA
Purdue U. (Calumet, Lafayette) . IN
Radford Coll .... VA
Rhode Island Coll .... RI
Rider Coll .... NJ
Roosevelt U IL
Rutgers (including Douglass; also Grad) .... NJ
Salem Coll .... NC
Salem State Coll .... MA
Salisbury State Coll .... MD
Sam Houston State Coll .... TX
Samford U .... AL
San Diego State U .... CA
San Francisco State U .... CA
San Jose State .... CA
★Scranton, U. of .... PA
Sciences and Arts of Oklahoma, U. of .... OK
Seattle Pacific Coll .... WA
Seattle U .... WA
Seton Hall .... NJ
Shepherd Coll .... WV
Shippensburg State Coll .... PA
Silver Lake Coll. of the Holy Family .... WI
Simpson Coll .... IA
Sioux Falls Coll .... SD
Slippery Rock State Coll .... PA
South Alabama, U. of .... AL
South Carolina, U. of .... SC
South Carolina State Coll .... SC
South Dakota, U. of .... SD
★South Dakota State U .... SD
Southeast Missouri State U .... MO
Southeastern Louisiana U ...... LA
Southeastern Oklahoma State U .... OK
Southern Arkansas U .... AR
Southern California, U. of ...... CA
Southern Colorado, U. of ...... CO
Southern Illinois U. (Carbondale, Edwardsville) IL
Southern Maine, U. of .... ME
Southern Methodist U .... TX
Southern Missionary Coll .... TN
Southern Mississippi, U. of .... MS
Southern Oregon State Coll ... OR
Southern U .... LA
Southern Utah State Coll .... UT
Southwest Missouri State U .... MO
Southwest Texas State U .... TX
Southwestern Louisiana, U. of .. LA
Southwestern Oklahoma State U .... OK
St. Benedict and St. John's, Coll. of .... MN
St. Catherine, Coll. of .... MN
St. Cloud State U .... MN
St. Francis Coll .... IN
St. Joseph's Coll .... IN
St. Louis U .... MO
St. Mary Coll .... KS
St. Mary of the Plains .... KS
St. Mary's Coll .... IN
St. Norbert Coll .... WI
★St. Olaf Coll .... MN
St. Teresa, Coll. of .... MN
★St. Thomas, Coll. of .... MN
State U. of New York Coll. (Buffalo, Cortland, Oswego) .. NY
Stephen F. Austin State U ...... TX
Sterling Coll .... KS
Stonehill Coll .... MA
Syracuse U .... NY
Tarleton State U .... TX
Taylor U .... IN
Temple U .... PA
Tennessee, U. of (Chattanooga, Knoxville, Martin) .... TN
Tennessee State U .... TN
Tennessee Tech. U .... TN
Texas, U. of (Austin, El Paso) ... TX
Texas A&I U .... TX
Texas A&M U .... TX
Texas Christian U .... TX
Texas Southern U .... TX
Texas Tech. U .... TX
Texas Wesleyan Coll .... TX
Texas Woman's U .... TX
Toledo, U. of .... OH
Towson State U .... MD
Trenton State Coll .... NJ
Trinity U .... TX
Tulsa, U. of .... OK
Union Coll .... NE
Utah, U. of .... UT
Utah State U .... UT
Valdosta State Coll .... GA
Valley City State Coll .... ND
Valparaiso U .... IN
Vanderbilt U .... TN
Vermont, U. of .... VT
Virginia, U. of .... VA
Virginia Poly. Inst .... VA
Virginia State Coll .... VA
Viterbo Coll .... WI
★Wake Forest U .... NC
Washburn U .... KS
Washington, U. of .... WA
Washington State U .... WA
Washington U .... MO
Wayne State Coll .... NE
Wayne State U .... MI
Weber State Coll .... UT
West Chester State Coll .... PA
West Georgia Coll .... GA
West Liberty State Coll .... WV
West Texas State U .... TX
West Virginia Coll. of Grad. Studies .... WV
★West Virginia Inst. of Tech ..... WV
West Virginia State Coll .... WV
West Virginia U .... WV
Western Carolina U .... NC
Western Connecticut State ...... CT
Western Illinois U IL
Western Kentucky U .... KY
Western Michigan U .... MI
Western Oregon State .... OR
Western State Coll .... CO
Western Washington U .... WA
Westfield State Coll .... MA
Wheaton Coll IL
•Wheelock Coll .... MA
Whitworth Coll .... WA
Wichita State U .... KS
William and Mary, Coll. of ...... VA
William Paterson Coll .... NJ
William Penn Coll .... IA
William Woods Coll .... MO
Winona State U .... MN
Winston-Salem State U .... NC
Winthrop Coll .... SC
Wisconsin, U. of (Eau Claire, La Crosse, Madison, Milwaukee, Oshkosh, Platteville, River Falls, Stevens Point, Stout, Superior, Whitewater) .... WI
Wittenberg U .... OH
Worcester State Coll .... MA
Wright State Coll .... OH
Wyoming, U. of .... WY
Youngstown State U .... OH

Teaching, College Level

Alabama A&M .... AL
Blue Mountain Coll .... MS
Boston U .... MA
California State U. (Sacramento) .... CA
Central Missouri .... MO
Chapman Coll .... CA
Colgate U .... NY
Colorado, U. of .... CO
Connecticut, U. of .... CT
Creighton U .... NE
Denver, U. of .... CO

Drake U .... IA
Eastern Kentucky U .... KY
Eastern Washington .... WA
Eckerd Coll .... FL
Evansville, U. of .... IN
George Mason U .... VA
Goddard Coll .... VT
Gonzaga U .... WA
Hampshire Coll .... MA
Iowa, U. of .... IA
La Salle Coll .... PA
Marywood Coll .... PA
Mills Coll .... CA
Missouri, U. of (Kansas City, St. Louis) .... MO
Montana, U. of .... MT
Montevallo, U. of .... AL
Moorhead State .... MN
Niagara U .... NY
North Dakota State U .... ND
Northeastern U .... MA
Northern Arizona U .... AZ
Northern Iowa, U. of .... IA
Northwest Missouri .... MO
Northwestern State .... LA
Pepperdine U .... CA
Plymouth State .... NH
South Dakota, U. of (Springfield) .... SD
Southwestern Oklahoma State U .... OK
Springfield Coll .... MA
Syracuse U .... NY
Tennessee, U. of .... TN
Texas A&M .... TX
Texas Woman's U .... TX
Truett McConnell .... GA
Valparaiso U .... IN
Wisconsin, U. of (Superior) .... WI

Teacher Education, Early Childhood/Pre-Elementary

Institutions awarding 25 or more undergraduate degrees as major field in single year according to latest statistics from U.S. Office of Education

Alabama, U. of .... AL
Alabama State U .... AL
Arkansas State U .... AR
Auburn U .... AL
Bemidji State U .... MN
Bradley U IL
Bridgewater State Coll .... MA
California Poly. State U .... CA
California State U. (Chico, Fresno, Fullerton, Los Angeles, Northridge, Sacramento) .... CA
Central Arkansas, U. of .... AR
Central Connecticut State .... CT
Chicago State U IL
Clemson U .... SC
Concord Coll .... WV
Concordia Teachers .... NE
Delaware, U. of .... DE
Eastern Connecticut State .... CT
Eastern Michigan U .... MI
Fitchburg State .... MA
Florida State U .... FL
Framingham State .... MA
Frostburg State .... MD
George Mason U .... VA
Georgia Southern .... GA
Georgia State U .... GA
Hawaii, U. of (Manoa) .... HI
Jacksonville State U .... AL
James Madison U .... VA
Jersey City State .... NJ
Kean Coll .... NJ
Kent State U .... OH
Lander Coll .... SC
Lesley Coll .... MA
Lock Haven State .... PA
Louisiana Tech. U .... LA
Maryland, U. of .... MD
Metropolitan State .... CO
Middle Tennessee State U .... TN
Northeastern Illinois U IL
Northern Colorado, U. of .... CO
Northern Iowa, U. of .... IA
Ohio State U .... OH
Old Dominion U .... VA
Puerto Rico, Catholic U. of .... PR
Purdue U .... IN
Radford U .... VA
Rhode Island Coll .... RI
San Diego State U .... CA
South Carolina, U. of (Columbia, Spartanburg) .... SC
Southern Connecticut State .... CT
Southern U. A&M Coll .... LA
Temple U .... PA
Tennessee, U. of (Martin) .... TN
Towson State .... MD
Trenton State .... NJ
Troy State .... AL
Tufts U .... MA
Valdosta State .... GA
West Florida, U. of .... FL
West Georgia Coll .... GA
Wisconsin, U. of (Madison, Milwaukee, Stevens Point, Stout) .... WI
Worcester State .... MA
Wright State .... OH

Teaching of English as a Foreign Language, *See* ENGLISH FOR FOREIGN STUDENTS

Teaching, Special Education

Undergraduate programs accredited by the National Council for Accreditation of Teacher Education

Abilene Christian U .... TX
Adams State .... CO
Akron, U. of .... OH
Alabama, U. of .... AL
Alabama Agric. & Mech. U .... AL
Alabama State U .... AL
Albany State .... GA
Alcorn State U .... MS
American International .... MA
American U .... DC
Appalachian State U .... NC
Arizona, U. of .... AZ
Arizona State U .... AZ
Arkansas, U. of .... AR
Arkansas State U .... AR
Ashland Coll .... OH
Atlanta Christian .... GA
Auburn U .... AL
Augusta Coll .... GA
Augustana Coll .... SD
Austin Peay State U .... TN
Ball State U .... IN
Benedictine Coll .... KS
Bethany Coll .... KS
Black Hills State Coll .... SD
Bloomsburg State .... PA
Boston Coll .... MA
Boston U .... MA
Bowling Green State U .... OH
Bradley U IL
Bridgewater State .... MA
Brigham Young U .... UT
Buena Vista Coll .... IA
California State Coll .... PA
California State U. (Fresno, Hayward, Los Angeles) .... CA
Cardinal Stritch .... WI
Carson-Newman .... TN
Central Arkansas, U. of .... AR
Central Connecticut State .... CT
Central Michigan U .... MI
Central Missouri State U .... MO
Central State U .... OH
Central State U .... OK
Central Washington U .... WA
Cheyney State .... PA
Chicago State U IL
Cincinnati, U. of .... OH
City U. of New York .... NY
Clarion State .... PA
Cleveland State U .... OH
Columbia Coll .... SC
Columbus Coll .... GA
Concord Coll .... WV
Concordia Teachers .... NE
Connecticut, U. of .... CT
Coppin State .... MD
Creighton U .... NE
Dana Coll .... NE
Dayton, U. of .... OH
De Paul U IL
Delta State .... MS
Drake U .... IA
Drury Coll .... MO
Dubuque, U. of .... IA
East Carolina U .... NC
East Central Oklahoma State U .... OK
East Stroudsburg State .... PA
East Tennessee State U .... TN
East Texas State U .... TX
Eastern Illinois U IL
Eastern Kentucky U .... KY
Eastern Michigan U .... MI
Eastern Montana .... MT
Eastern Washington U .... WA
Edgewood Coll .... WI
Edinboro State .... PA
Emporia State U .... KS
Evangel Coll .... MO
Evansville, U. of .... IN
Fairmont State .... WV
Fitchburg State .... MA
Florida, U. of .... FL
Florida Atlantic U .... FL
Florida State U .... FL
Fontbonne Coll .... MO
Fort Hays State U .... KS
George Washington U .... DC
Georgia, U. of .... GA
Georgia Coll .... GA
Georgia State U .... GA
Glassboro State .... NJ
Glenville State .... WV
Graceland .... IA
Grambling State U .... LA
Hampton Inst .... VA
Harding U .... AR
Hartford, U. of .... CT
Hastings Coll .... NE
Hiram Coll .... OH
Hope Coll .... MI
Idaho, U. of .... ID
Idaho State U .... ID
Illinois, U. of IL
Illinois State U IL
Incarnate Word .... TX
Indiana Central U .... IN
Indiana State U .... IN
Indiana U. of Pa .... PA
Iowa, U. of .... IA
Jackson State .... MS
Jacksonville State U .... AL
James Madison U .... VA
Jersey City State U .... NJ
Kean Coll .... NJ
Kearney State .... NE
Keene State .... NH
Kent State U .... OH
Kentucky, U. of .... KY
Kutztown State .... PA
Lamar U .... TX
Lenoir-Rhyne .... NC
Lewis-Clark State .... ID
Lincoln U .... MO
Lindenwood Colleges .... MO
Lock Haven State .... PA
Loretto Heights .... CO
Louisiana State U. and A&M U .... LA
Louisiana State U. (Shreveport) .... LA
Louisiana Tech. U .... LA
Louisville, U. of .... KY
Loyola U IL
Madonna Coll .... MI
Maine, U. of (Farmington) .... ME
Mansfield State .... PA
Marian Coll .... IN
Marshall U .... WV
Marygrove Coll .... MI
Maryland, U. of .... MD
Maryville Coll .... MO
Marywood Coll .... PA
McNeese State U .... LA
Memphis State U .... TN
Mercer U .... GA
Metropolitan State Coll .... CO
Miami, U. of .... FL
Miami U .... OH
Michigan, U. of .... MI
Michigan State U .... MI
Middle Tennessee State U .... TN
Midwestern State U .... TX
Milligan Coll .... TN
Minnesota, U. of .... MN
Minot State .... ND
Mississippi, U. of .... MS
Mississippi State U .... MS
Mississippi U. for Women .... MS
Mississippi Valley State .... MS
Missouri, U. of (Columbia, St. Louis) .... MO
Missouri Southern State .... MO
Moorhead State U .... MN
Morehead State U .... KY
Morningside .... IA
Mundelein Coll IL
Murray State .... KY
National Coll. of Ed IL
Nebraska, U. of .... NE
Nebraska Wesleyan .... NE
Nevada, U. of .... NV
New Mexico State U .... NM
New York U .... NY
Nicholls State U .... LA
Norfolk State U .... VA
North Alabama, U. of .... AL
North Dakota, U. of .... ND
North Georgia Coll .... GA
Northeast Louisiana U .... LA
Northeast Missouri State U .... MO
Northeastern Illinois U IL
Northeastern Oklahoma State U .... OK
Northern Arizona U .... AZ
Northern Colorado, U. of .... CO
Northern Illinois U IL
Northern Iowa, U. of .... IA
Northern Michigan U .... MI
Northern State Coll .... SD
Northwest Missouri State U .... MO
Northwest Nazarene .... ID
Northwestern Coll .... IA
Northwestern State U. of Louisiana .... LA
Ohio State U .... OH
Ohio U .... OH
Oklahoma, U. of .... OK
Oklahoma, U. of Science and Arts .... OK
Oklahoma Christian U .... OK
Oklahoma State U .... OK
Old Dominion U .... VA

Oregon, U. of .... OR
Ouachita Baptist U .... AR
Pacific Lutheran U .... WA
Pembroke State U .... NC
Pennsylvania State U .... PA
Peru State .... NE
Pittsburg State U .... KS
Prairie View A&M .... TX
Radford U .... VA
Rhode Island Coll .... RI
Roosevelt U IL
Rutgers U .... NJ
Saint Louis U .... MO
Saint Teresa, Coll. of .... MN
Salem Coll .... NC
Sam Houston State .... TX
San Jose State U .... CA
Seattle Pacific U .... WA
Seattle U .... WA
Seton Hall U .... NJ
Silver Lake Coll .... WI
Simpson Coll .... IA
Slippery Rock State .... PA
South Alabama, U. of .... AL
South Carolina State Coll .... SC
South Dakota, U. of .... SD
Southeast Missouri State U .... MO
Southeastern Louisiana U .... LA
Southern California, U. of .... CA
Southern Illinois U IL
Southern Methodist U .... TX
Southern Mississippi, U. of .... MS
Southwest Missouri State U .... MO
Southwest Texas State U .... TX
Southwestern Louisiana, U. of .... LA
Southwestern Oklahoma State U .... OK
St. Cloud State U .... MN
St. Francis Coll .... IN
State U. of New York (Buffalo, Cortland) .... NY
Stephen F. Austin State U .... TX
Syracuse U .... NY
Temple U .... PA
Tennessee, U. of (Chattanooga, Knoxville, Martin) .... TN
Tennessee Tech. U .... TN
Texas, U. of (Austin, El Paso) .... TX
Texas A&I U .... TX
Texas Christian U .... TX
Texas Southern U .... TX
Texas Wesleyan .... TX
Texas Woman's U .... TX
Toledo, U. of .... OH
Trenton State .... NJ
Trinity U .... TX
Tulsa, U. of .... OK
Utah, U. of .... UT
Utah State U. of Ag. & App. Sci .... UT
Valdosta State .... GA
Vanderbilt U .... TN
Vermont, U. of .... VT
Virginia, U. of .... VA
Virginia State Coll .... VA
Washington U .... MO
Wayne State Coll .... NE
Wayne State U .... MI
West Chester State .... PA
West Georgia Coll .... GA
West Liberty State .... WV
West Texas State U .... TX
West Virginia State Coll .... WV
Western Carolina U .... NC
Western Illinois U IL
Western Kentucky U .... KY
Western Michigan U .... MI
Western State Coll. of Colorado .... CO
Western Washington U .... WA
Westfield State .... MA
Wheelock Coll .... MA
William Paterson Coll .... NJ
William Woods .... MO
Winona State U .... MN
Winston-Salem State U .... NC
Winthrop Coll .... SC
Wisconsin, U. of (Madison, Milwaukee, Oshkosh, Stevens Point, Stout, Whitewater) .... WI
Wittenberg U .... OH
Wright State U .... OH
Wyoming, U. of .... WY
Youngstown State U .... OH

Television, *See*

RADIO AND/OR T.V.

Textile Design

Akron, U. of .... OH
Arkansas, U. of .... AR
Bennett Coll .... NC
Bowling Green .... OH
California, U. of (Davis) .... CA
California Coll. of Arts and Crafts .... CA
California State U .... CA
Center for Creative Studies .... MI
Central Missouri .... MO
Cleveland Inst. of Art .... OH
Colorado State U .... CO
Cornell U .... NY
East Carolina U .... NC
Eastern Kentucky .... KY
Fashion Inst. of Tech .... NY
Hawaii, U. of (Honolulu) .... HI
Illinois, U. of (Urbana) IL
Indiana State U .... IN
Kansas, U. of .... KS
Kansas City Art Inst .... MO
Lincoln Coll IL
Loma Linda U .... CA
Louisville Sch. of Art .... KY
Michigan State U .... MI
Minnesota, U. of (Minneapolis) .... MN
Nebraska, U. of .... NE
North Dakota State U .... ND
Northern Michigan U .... MI
Ohio State U .... OH
Philadelphia Coll. of Art .... PA
Pratt Institute .... NY
Purdue U .... IN
Rhode Island School of Design .... RI
Rochester Inst. of Tech .... NY
Savannah Coll. of Art and Design .... GA
Skidmore Coll .... NY
Southeastern Massachusetts U .... MA
Syracuse U .... NY
Tennessee, U. of .... TN
Texas Woman's U .... TX
Utah State .... UT
Washington, U. of .... WA
Western Michigan U .... MI
Wisconsin, U. of (Madison) .... WI

Textile Engineering, *See*

ENGINEERING, TEXTILE

Textile Management

Auburn U .... AL
Bennett Coll .... NC
California, U. of (Davis) .... CA
La Grange Coll .... GA
North Dakota State U .... ND
Ohio State U .... OH
Purdue U .... IN
South Dakota State U .... SD
Southern Tech .... GA
Tennessee, U. of .... TN
Texas Woman's .... TX
Trinity Christian IL

Textile Merchandising

Alabama A&M .... AL
Arkansas, U. of .... AR
Bennett Coll .... NC
California, U. of (Davis) .... CA
Central Missouri .... MO
Columbia Coll .... MO
Cheyney State .... PA
Delaware, U. of .... DE
Hawaii, U. of (Honolulu) .... HI
Kentucky, U. of .... KY
Maryland, U. of .... MD
Morehead State .... KY
North Dakota State U .... ND
Northeast Missouri .... MO
Northern Illinois U IL
Ohio State U .... OH
Oklahoma State U .... OK
Purdue U .... IN
Rhode Island, U. of .... RI
South Dakota State .... SD
Tennessee, U. of .... TN
Texas Woman's U .... TX
William Woods .... MO

Textiles and Textile Engineering, *See also*

ENGINEERING, TEXTILE

Auburn U .... AL
Baylor U .... TX

Theatre, *See*

DRAMA/THEATRE

Theological Schools

Members of Association of Theological Schools

American Baptist Sem. of the West (Berkeley) .... CA
Anderson Coll. Sch. of Theol .... IN
Andover Newton Theol. Sch .... MA
Aquinas Inst. of Theol .... IA
Asbury Theol. Sem .... KY
Ashland Theol. Sem .... OH
Austin Presbyterian Theol. Sem .... TX
Bangor Theol. Sem .... ME
Berkeley Divinity School .... CT
Bethany Theological Sem IL
Bethel Theol. Sem .... MN
Bexley Hall .... NY
Boston U. Sch. of Theol .... MA
Brite Divinity Sch., T.C.U .... TX
Calvin Theol. Sem .... MI
Catholic Theological Union IL
Catholic U .... DC
Central Baptist Theol. Sem .... KS
Chicago, U. of, Divinity School IL
Chicago Theol. Sem IL
Christ Sem .... MO
Christ the King Sem .... NY
Christian Theol. Sem .... IN
Church Div. Sch. of the Pacific .... CA
Claremont, School of Theology .... CA
Colgate Rochester/Bexley Hall/Crozer Divinity Sch .... NY
Columbia Theol. Sem .... GA
Concordia Sem .... MO
Concordia Theol. Sem .... IN
De Sales Hall Sch. of Theol .... MD
Denver Conservative Baptist Sem .... CO
Dominican House of Studies .... DC
Dominican Sch. of Philosophy and Theol .... CA
Drew U. Theol. Sch .... NJ
Dubuque, Theol. Sem. of U. of .... IA
Duke U. Divinity Sch .... NC
Earlham Sch. of Religion .... IN
Eastern Baptist Theol. Sem .... PA
Eden Theol. Sem .... MO
Emmanuel School of Religion .... TN
Emory (Candler School) .... GA
Episcopal Divinity Sch .... MA
Episcopal Theol. Sem. of the Southwest .... TX
Erskine Theol. Sem .... SC
Franciscan Sch. of Theol .... CA
Fuller Theol. Sem .... CA
Garrett Evangelical Theol. Sem IL
General Theol. Sem .... NY
Golden Gate Baptist Theol. Sem .... CA
Gordon-Conwell Theol. Sem .... MA
Goshen Biblical Sem .... IN
Graduate Theol. Union .... CA
Hartford Sem. Foundation .... CT
Harvard Divinity Sch .... MA
Holy Cross Greek Orthodox Sch. of Theol .... MA
Howard U. Sch. of Religion .... DC
Iliff School of Theol .... CO
Immaculate Conception, Sem. of the .... NY
Immaculate Conception Sem .... NJ
Interdenominational Theol. Center .... GA
Jesuit Sch. of Theol .... CA
Kenrick Sem .... MO
Lancaster Theol. Sem .... PA
Lexington Theol. Sem .... KY
Louisville Presbyterian Theol. Sem .... KY
Luther Theol. Sem .... MN
Lutheran Sch. of Theol. at Chicago IL
Lutheran Theol. Sem. at Gettysburg .... PA
Lutheran Theol. Sem. (Philadelphia) .... PA
Lutheran Theol. Southern Sem .... SC
Mary Immaculate Sem .... PA
Maryknoll Sem .... NY
McCormick Theol. Sem IL
Meadville Lombard Theol. School IL
Memphis Theol. Sem .... TN
Mennonite Biblical Sem .... IN
Mennonite Brethren Biblical Sem .... CA
Methodist Theol. Sch .... OH
Midwestern Baptist Theol. Sem .... MO
Moravian Theol. Sem .... PA
Mt. Angel Sem .... OR
Mt. St. Alphonsus Sem .... NY
Mt. St. Mary's Sem. of the West .... OH
Nashotah House .... WI
Nazarene Theol. Sem .... MO
New Brunswick Theol. Sem .... NJ
New Orleans Baptist Theol. Sem .... LA
New York Theol. Sem .... NY
North American Baptist Sem .... SD
North Park Theol. Sem IL
Northern Baptist Theol. Sem IL
Northwestern Lutheran Theol. Sem .... MN
Notre Dame, U. of, Theol. Dept .... IN
Oblate Coll .... DC
Oral Roberts U. Sch. of Theol .... OK
Pacific Lutheran Theol. Sem .... CA
Pacific School of Religion .... CA
Perkins Sch. of Theol .... TX
Phillips U. Graduate Sem .... OK
Pittsburgh Theol. Sem .... PA

Pontifical Coll. Josephinum .... OH
Presbyterian Sch. of Christian Educ .... VA
Princeton Theol. Sem .... NJ
Protestant Episcopal Theol. Sem .... VA
Reformed Theol. Sem .... MS
San Francisco Theol. Sem ...... CA
Seabury-Western Theol. Sem IL
Seventh-Day Adventist Theol. Sem. of Andrews U .... MI
South, U. of the, Sch. of Theol .. TN
Southeastern Baptist Theol. Sem .... NC
Southern Baptist Theol. Sem ... KY
Southwestern Baptist Theol. Sem .... TX
St. Bernard's Sem .... NY
St. Charles Borromeo Sem ...... PA
St. Francis Sem .... WI
St. John's Provincial Sem .... MI
St. John's Sem .... CA
St. John's Sem .... MA
St. John's U. Sch. of Theol .... MN
St. Joseph's Sem .... NY
St. Mary of the Lake Sem IL
St. Mary Sem .... OH
St. Mary's Sem. and U .... MD
St. Meinrad Sch. of Theol .... IN
St. Patrick's Sem .... CA
St. Paul Sch. of Theol. Methodist .... MO
St. Paul Sem .... MN
St. Thomas Sem .... CO
St. Vladimir's Orthodox Theol. Sem .... NY
Starr King Sch. for the Ministry .... CA
Talbot Theol. Sem .... CA
Trinity Evangelical Divinity Sch IL
Trinity Lutheran Sem .... OH
Union Theol. Sem .... NY
Union Theol. Sem .... VA
United Theol. Sem .... OH
United Theol. Sem. of the Twin Cities .... MN
Vanderbilt U. Divinity Sch ...... TN
Virginia Union U. Sch. of Theol .... VA
Wartburg Theol. Sem .... IA
Washington Theol. Sem .... MD
Wesley Theol. Sem .... DC
Western Evangelical Sem ...... OR
Western Theol. Sem .... MI
Weston Sch. of Theol .... MA
Yale U. Divinity Sch .... CT

Tourism and Travel

Bay Path Jr. Coll .... MA
Bay State Jr. Coll .... MA
Becker Jr .... MA
Belmont Coll .... TN
Biscayne Coll .... FL
Black Hills State Coll .... SD
Bliss Coll .... OH
Brandywine Coll .... DE
Briarwood Coll .... CT
Central Pennsylvania Bus. Sch .. PA
Columbia Coll .... MO
Concord Coll .... WV
Daeman Coll .... NY
Dakota State Coll .... SD
Daniel Webster Coll .... NH
Davenport Coll. of Bus .... MI
DuPage, Coll. of IL
Endicott Coll .... MA
Fisher Jr. Coll .... MA
Florida International U .... FL
George Washington U .... DC
Georgia State U .... GA
Harcum Jr .... PA
Hawaii, U. of .... HI
Henderson State U .... AR
Hesser Coll .... NH
Hocking Tech. Coll .... OH
Johnson and Wales Coll .... RI
MacCormac Jr IL
Mansfield State .... PA
Massachusetts, U. of (Amherst) MA
Michigan State U .... MI
New Haven, U. of .... CT
New Orleans, U. of .... LA
Newbury Jr. Coll .... MA
Northeastern Oklahoma State .. OK
Parks Coll IL
Paul Smith's .... NY
Purdue U .... IN
Rochester Inst. of Tech .... NY
Southern Coll .... FL
Suomi Coll .... MI
Tennessee, U. of .... TN
Valparaiso U .... IN
Webber Coll .... FL
Wisconsin, U. of (Stout) .... WI

Trade and Industrial Training

Central Missouri .... MO
Georgia State U .... GA
Morehead State U .... KY
Oklahoma State U .... OK
South Dakota, U. of (Springfield) .... SD
Southern Idaho, Coll. of .... ID
Wayne State .... NE

Traffic, *See* TRANSPORTATION AND TRAFFIC

Transportation, Marine

Davenport Coll. of Bus .... MI
Florida Inst. of Tech.-Sch. of App. Tech .... FL
Massachusetts Maritime Acad .. MA
State U. of New York Maritime Coll .... NY
Texas A&M .... TX

Transportation and Traffic

Akron, U. of .... OH
Auburn U .... AL
Baltimore, U. of .... MD
Biscayne Coll .... FL
California, U. of (Irvine) .... CA
California State U. (Los Angeles) .... CA
Colorado, U. of .... CO
Daemen Coll .... NY
Davenport Coll. of Bus .... MI
East Tennessee State .... TN
Eastern Kentucky .... KY
Eastern Montana .... MT
Eastfield Coll .... TX
Elmhurst IL
Evansville, U. of .... IN
Fort Scott Comm. Coll .... KS
Golden Gate U .... CA
Hawaii Pacific Coll .... HI
Hilbert Coll .... NY
John Carroll U .... OH
Kent State .... OH
Maryland, U. of .... MD
Missouri, U. of (Kansas City) .. MO
Niagara U .... NY
Ohio State .... OH
Parks Coll IL
Purdue U .... IN
Robert Morris .... PA
Shippensburg State .... PA
South Alabama, U. of .... AL
Syracuse U .... NY
Tennessee, U. of .... TN
Tennessee State .... TN
Worcester Poly. Inst .... MA

Transportation Engineering, *See* ENGINEERING, TRANSPORTATION

Travel and Tourism, *See* TOURISM AND TRAVEL

Turf Management

Becker Jr. Coll. (Leicester Campus) .... MA
Eastern Kentucky U .... KY
Illinois Central Coll IL
Massachusetts, U. of (Amherst) MA
Nevada, U. of .... NV
Northeast Louisiana State ...... LA
Northeastern Jr. Coll .... CO
Purdue (Lafayette) .... IN
State U. of New York (Cobleskill, Delhi, Farmingdale) .... NY
Western Texas Coll .... TX

Typography

California Coll. of Arts and Crafts .... CA
Kansas City Art Inst .... MO

Ultra-Sound Technology

Barry U .... FL
Butler U .... IN
Puerto Rico, U. of .... PR
Quinnipiac Coll .... CT
Rochester Inst. of Tech .... NY
Seattle U .... WA
Weber State .... UT

Urban Planning Education *See* CITY AND/OR URBAN PLANNING

Veterinary Assistant, *See* ANIMAL TECHNOLOGY

Veterinary Medicine

Accredited by American Veterinary Medical Association

Auburn U .... AL
California, U. of (Davis) .... CA
Colorado State U .... CO
Florida, U. of .... FL
Georgia, U. of .... GA
Illinois, U. of IL
Iowa State U .... IA
Kansas State U .... KS
Louisiana State U. at Baton Rouge .... LA
Michigan State U .... MI
Minnesota, U. of .... MN
Mississippi State U .... MS
Missouri, U. of .... MO
North Carolina State U .... NC
Ohio State U .... OH
Oklahoma State U .... OK
Oregon State U .... OR
Pennsylvania, U. of .... PA
Purdue .... IN
State U. of New York Vet. Coll. (Cornell) .... NY
Tennessee, U. of .... TN
Texas A&M .... TX
Tufts U .... MA
Tuskegee Inst .... AL
Virginia Polytechnic Inst .... VA
Washington State U .... WA

Visual Art

Albion Coll .... MI
Antioch Coll .... OH
Art Inst. of Pittsburgh .... PA
Auburn U .... AL
Averett Coll .... VA
Baldwin-Wallace Coll .... OH
Barnard Coll .... NY
Baylor U .... TX
Bennett Coll .... NC
Bowdoin Coll .... ME
California, U. of (San Diego) .... CA
California Coll. of Arts and Crafts .... CA
California Institute of the Arts ... CA
California State Coll .... PA
Carnegie-Mellon .... PA
Carthage Coll .... WI
Chicago, U. of IL
City Coll .... NY
Columbia Coll .... MO
Curry Coll .... MA
Dartmouth Coll .... NH
Dean Jr. Coll .... MA
Delta State U .... MS
Denison U .... OH
Eckerd .... FL
Evergreen State .... WA
Flagler Coll .... FL
Florida International .... FL
George Washington U .... DC
Georgia State U .... GA
Goddard Coll .... VT
Goucher Coll .... MD
Governors State IL
Harcum Jr. Coll .... PA
Harvard U .... MA
Hawaii, U. of .... HI
Jackson State U .... MS
Kansas, U. of .... KS
Kansas City Art Inst .... MO
Kutztown State .... PA
La Grange Coll .... GA
Lake Erie Coll .... OH
Lamar U .... TX
Lincoln Coll IL
Loyola U .... LA
Marlboro Coll .... VT
Mount Senario .... WI
North Carolina Cent. U .... NC
Northeastern Illinois IL
Northern Illinois State IL
Northern Iowa, U. of .... IA
Ohio State U .... OH
Old Dominion .... VA
Otis Art Inst .... CA
Otterbein Coll .... OH
Philadelphia Coll. of Art .... PA
Pine Manor Coll .... MA
Plymouth State .... NH
Pratt Inst .... NY
Princeton U .... NJ
Purdue .... IN
Radcliffe .... MA
Saint Rose, Coll. of .... NY
Santa Fe, Coll. of .... NM
Savannah Coll. of Art and Design .... GA
Seton Hill Coll .... PA
Shepherd Coll .... WV
State U. of New York (New Paltz) .... NY
Syracuse U .... NY

Tennessee, U. of .... TN
Texas, U. of (Dallas) .... TX
Texas Lutheran .... TX
Trinity Christian................. IL
Unity Coll..................... ME
U.S. International U ....CA
West Virginia U .... WV
Winthrop Coll ....SC
Wisconsin, U. of (Green Bay, Superior) .... WI
Xavier U .... LA

Viticulture

Grape Growing

California, U. of (Davis).........CA
California State U. (Fresno).....CA
SUNY Coll. of Agri. & Life Sci ..NY

Volcanology

Hampshire Coll .... MA

Weather Technology

Kansas, U. of ....KS
Lincoln Coll IL

Welding Engineering, *See* ENGINEERING, WELDING

Wildlife Training and Management, *See* CONSERVATION AND/OR WILDLIFE MANAGEMENT

Women's Studies

Institutions awarding a bachelor's degree according to the National Women's Studies Association and the Women's Studies Quarterly

Alabama, U. of .... AL
Antioch U. West................CA
Appalachian State U .... NC
Barnard Coll ....NY
Beacon Coll .... MA
Bowling Green State U .... OH
California, U. of (Berkeley, Davis, Santa Cruz) ....CA
California State U. (Long Beach, Sacramento)..........CA
Case Western Reserve U ...... OH
Cincinnati, U. of .... OH
City Coll.......................NY
Colorado, U. of (Boulder, Denver).................... CO
Connecticut, U. of.............CT
Dartmouth Coll .... NH
Denison U .... OH
Douglass Coll..................NJ
Eastern Washington U......... WA
Florida Atlantic U .... FL
Goddard Coll ....VT
Goucher Coll .... MD
Governors State U IL
Hawaii, U. of .... HI
Henderson State U ....AR
Hobart and William Smith Coll ..NY
Hofstra U ....NY
Hood Coll .... MD
Humboldt State U ....CA
Hunter Coll ....NY
Illinois, U. of (Chicago) IL
Illinois State U IL
Indiana U .... IN
Indiana U.-Purdue U .... IN
Jersey City State Coll .... NJ
Kansas, U. of .... KS
Kansas State U.................KS
Livingston Coll.................NJ
Mankato State U .... MN
Maryland, U. of .... MD
Massachusetts, U. of (Amherst, Boston)..................... MA
Memphis State U...............TN
Michigan, U. of................. MI
Mills Coll ....CA
Minnesota, U. of (Minneapolis) . MN
Missouri, U. of .... MO
Mundelein Coll..................IL
Nebraska, U. of ....NE
New England Coll .... NH
New Mexico, U. of............ NM
New Rochelle, Coll. of..........NY
North Carolina, U. of .... NC
Northeastern Illinois U...........IL
Northern Colorado, U. of ...... CO
Oberlin Coll .... OH
Ohio State .... OH
Ohio Wesleyan U .... OH
Oklahoma,U. of .... OK
Old Dominion U ....VA
Pennsylvania, U. of............PA
Pittsburgh, U. of ....PA
Pitzer Coll ....CA
Quinnipiac Coll ....CT
Rhode Island Coll .... RI
Roosevelt U.....................IL
San Diego State U ....CA
San Francisco State U..........CA
Sangamon State U IL
Simmons Coll................ MA
Sonoma State U ....CA
South Carolina, U. of ....SC
South Florida, U. of .... FL
Southeastern Massachusetts U.......................... MA
Southern California, U. of ......CA
St. Benedict, Coll. of .... MN
St. Catherine, Coll. of .... MN
Stanford U......................CA
State U. of New York (Albany, Binghamton, Brockport, Buffalo, Fredonia, New Paltz, Old Westbury, Plattsburgh, Stony Brook) ....NY
Staten Island, Coll. of ....NY
Stephens Coll................. MO
Temple U ....PA
Texas, U. of (Dallas) .... TX
Towson State U .... MD
Utah, U. of.....................UT
Vassar Coll ....NY
Washington, U. of .... WA
Washington U................. MO
Wayne State U .... MI
Wellesley Coll................ MA
Wichita State U .... KS
Wisconsin, U. of (Green Bay, Madison, Milwaukee) .... WI

Wood Utilization and Technology

Idaho, U. of .... ID
Marlboro Coll .... VT
Michigan Tech. U .... MI
Missouri, U. of .... MO
Northeast Missouri State Coll .. MO
Northwestern State U .... LA
Pittsburg State .... KS
State U. of New York (Morrisville)..................NY

Woodworking

Blinn Coll...................... TX
Boston U .... MA
California Coll. of Arts and Crafts ....CA
Marlboro Coll .... VT
Morehead State U ....KY
Northern Michigan U .... MI
Northwestern Oklahoma State Coll .... OK
Philadelphia Coll. of Art ....PA
Pittsburg State ....KS
Rochester Inst. of Tech ....NY
Southeastern Oklahoma State U .... OK
Southwest Mississippi Jr. Coll . MS
Southwest Missouri .... MO
Southwestern Oklahoma State U .... OK
State U. of New York (New Paltz)........................NY

X-Ray Technology, *See* RADIOLOGIC TECHNOLOGY

Youth Leadership, Professional Careers in

Anderson Coll .... IN
Barrington Coll .... RI
Bethel Coll .... IN
Central Coll....................KS
Franklin Pierce Coll .... NH
George Williams Coll IL
Hastings Coll ....NE
High Point Coll .... NC
Indiana Central U .... IN
Michigan State U.............. MI
Milligan Coll ....TN
Pepperdine U ....CA
Rockhurst Coll................ MO
Rockmont Coll................ CO
Springfield.................... MA
St. Paul's Coll .... MO
Trinity Christian.................IL
Whitworth Coll................ WA

Zoology

Institutions awarding 15 or more undergraduate degrees as major field in single year according to U.S. Office of Education latest statistics

Arizona State U .... AZ
Arkansas, U. of.................AR
Arkansas State U...............AR
Auburn U .... AL
Brigham Young ....UT
California, U. of (Berkeley, Davis, Santa Barbara) ....CA
California State Poly. U.........CA
California State U. (Long Beach) ....CA
Clemson.......................SC
Colorado State U .... CO
Connecticut Coll ....CT
DePauw .... IN
Drew ....NJ
Duke .... NC
Eastern Illinois U................IL
East Texas.....................TX
Florida, U. of.................. FL
George Washington .... DC
Georgia, U. of................. GA
Hawaii, U. of .... HI
Howard .... DC
Humboldt State U ....CA
Idaho, Coll. of.................. ID
Iowa, U. of .... IA
Iowa State U .... IA
Kent State .... OH
Kentucky, U. of ....KY
Louisiana State .... LA
Louisiana Tech. U .... LA
Maine, U. of .... ME
Marshall U .... WV
Maryland, U. of .... MD
Massachusetts, U. of .... MA
Miami U .... OH
Michigan, U. of................. MI
Michigan State U............... MI
Mississippi, U. of .... MS
Montana, U. of................ MT
Montana State U .... MT
Nebraska, U. of ....NE
New Hampshire, U. of .... NH
North Carolina, U. of .... NC
North Carolina State U .... NC
North Dakota State............ ND
Northern Arizona...............AZ
Northern Colorado .... CO
Ohio State U .... OH
Ohio U .... OH
Ohio Weslayan................ OH
Oklahoma, U. of .... OK
Oklahoma State U............. OK
Oregon State U .... OR
Rhode Island, U. of............. RI
Rutgers State U ....NJ
San Diego State................CA
San Jose State ....CA
South Florida, U. of .... FL
Southeastern Louisiana U...........................LA
Southern Illinois U IL
State U. of New York (Oswego) ....NY
Tennessee, U. of ....TN
Texas, U. of (Austin) .... TX
Texas A&M ....TX
Texas Tech ....TX
Vermont, U. of ....VT
Washington, U. of .... WA
Washington State U .... WA
Weber State ....UT
Wisconsin, U. of (Madison, Milwaukee) .... WI
Wyoming, U. of .... WY

II-SPECIAL PROGRAMS: WHERE TO FIND 18 SPECIAL PROGRAMS

Basic Studies

Bernadean U .... CA
Biscayne .... FL
Black Hills State .... SD
Boston U .... MA
Brevard Coll .... NC
Bridgeport, U. of .... CT
California, U. of (Riverside) ..... CA
Campbell U .... NC
Carson-Newman .... TN
Columbus Coll .... GA
Cottey Coll .... MO
Evergreen State .... WA
Ferris State .... MI
Florida A&M .... FL
Fort Hays State .... KS
Goddard Coll .... VT
Goshen Coll .... IN
Hartford, U. of .... CT
James Madison U .... VA
Kansas, U. of .... KS
Lakeland Coll .... WI
Lincoln Coll IL
Louisburg Coll .... NC
Louisville, U. of .... KY
Maine, U. of (Fort Kent) .... ME
Montana, U. of .... MT
New Mexico Inst. of Mining and Tech .... NM
Northwestern State U .... LA
Otero Jr. Coll .... CO
Plymouth State .... NH
Puerto Rico, U. of .... PR
Rider Coll .... NJ
Rio Piedras .... PR
Saint Peter's Coll .... NJ
Salem Coll .... WV
Slippery Rock State .... PA
South Carolina, U. of .... SC
Southwestern Coll .... KS
St. Leo Coll .... FL
Trenton State .... NJ
Trinity Christian IL
Truett McConnell .... GA
Union Coll .... NJ
West Chester State .... PA
Western Baptist Coll .... OR
Western Connecticut State ...... CT
Winona State .... MN
Wisconsin, U. of (Whitewater) ... WI

Cooperative Education

Integration of classroom study and practical work experience in the community. About 1,000 colleges and universities now offer this program. It is suggested that interested parties contact the National Commission for Cooperative Education, 360 Huntington Ave., Boston, MA 02115, for its publication listing the names of the institutions as well as the specific cooperative education program offered.

Correspondence Studies

Interested parties wishing information on study through correspondence should contact the National University Extension Assn., One Dupont Circle, Suite 360, Washington, D.C. 20036, for further information.

External Curriculum

Institutions offering extensive off-campus programs

Albertus Magnus .... CT
California State U. (Sacramento) CA
Central Michigan .... MI
Central Missouri .... MO
Chadron .... NE
Cleveland State .... OH
Colgate U .... NY
College Miseracordia .... PA
Columbia Union Coll .... MD
D.C., U. of .... DC
DePauw U .... IN
Goddard Coll .... VT
Hastings Coll .... NE
Hawaii Pacific Coll .... HI
Houghton Coll .... NY
Hutchinson Comm. Coll .... KS
Illinois, U. of IL
Illinois State U IL
International U .... MO
International Coll .... FL
Iowa, U. of .... IA
Kearney State .... NE
Lawrence U .... WI
Lewis and Clark Coll .... OR
Linfield Coll .... OR
Luther Coll .... IA
Marlboro Coll .... VT
Marywood .... PA
Michigan State U .... MI
Moorhead State U .... MN
Morehead State U .... KY
New Hampshire, U. of .... NH
New York Instit. of Tech .... NY
Niagara U .... NY
Northern Iowa, U. of .... IA
Northern Kentucky U .... KY
Northwestern State U .... LA
Northwood Inst .... MI
Oklahoma, U. of .... OK
South Georgia Coll .... GA
Spring Arbor Coll .... MI
St. Benedict .... MN
St. Cloud .... MN
St. Mary's of California .... CA
State U. of New York (Binghamton, Morrisville) ..... NY
Stephens Coll .... MO
Temple U .... PA
Tennessee, U. of (Chattanooga) . TN
Trenton State .... NJ
Wayne State .... MI
Webster Coll .... MO
West Florida, U. of .... FL
Western Kentucky U .... KY
Winona State .... MN
Wisconsin, U. of (Green Bay, Stevens Point) .... WI
Worcester Poly. Inst .... MA
Wright State U .... OH

Four-One-Four System

Schools offering a three-term calendar system: a four-month term, a one-month or interim term, and a four-month term. The one-month term is generally used for independent study.

Adelphi U .... NY
Albion Coll .... PA
Anna Maria .... MA
Averett .... VA
Bates Coll .... ME
Beaver Coll .... PA
Bethany Coll .... WV
Bethel Coll .... MN
Buena Vista Coll .... IA
California Lutheran .... CA
Calvin Coll .... MI
Carthage Coll .... WI
Chapman Coll .... CA
Chatham Coll .... PA
Colby Coll .... ME
Colby-Sawyer Coll .... NH
Colgate .... NY
Dakota Wesleyan U .... SD
Davis and Elkins Coll .... WV
DePauw U .... IN
Delaware, U. of .... DE
Denison U .... OH
Drew .... NJ
Eckerd Coll .... FL
Elmhurst Coll IL
Florida Southern Coll .... FL
Franklin Pierce Coll .... NH
Freeman Jr. Coll .... SD
Gettysburg Coll .... PA
Gustavus Adolphus Coll .... MN
Hamilton Coll .... NY
Hampshire Coll .... MA
Hastings Coll .... NE
Hofstra U .... NY
Hollins Coll .... VA
Huntingdon Coll .... AL
Illinois Wesleyan U IL
Iona Coll .... NY
Iowa Wesleyan Coll .... IA
Johns Hopkins U .... MD
Judson Coll IL
Lakeland Coll .... WI
Linfield Coll .... OR
Loyola Coll .... MD
Luther .... IA
Manchester Coll .... IN
Marymount Palos Verdes Coll ... CA
McPherson Coll .... KS
Midland Coll .... NE
Mount St. Mary .... MD
Mount St. Mary Coll .... NY
Nevada, U. of .... NV
New England, U. of .... ME
New Haven, U. of .... CT
Northland Coll .... WI
Oklahoma Baptist U .... OK
Pace U .... NY
Pacific Christian Coll .... CA
Pacific Lutheran U .... WA
Pratt Instit .... NY
Puget Sound, U. of .... WA
Queens Coll .... NC
Redlands, U. of the .... CA
Regis Coll .... MA
Rider .... NJ
Rockford Coll IL
Roger Williams .... RI
Salem Coll .... NC
Simpson Coll .... IA
Skidmore Coll .... NY
Southampton Coll .... NY
Spring Arbor .... MI
St. Andrews Presbyterian Coll . NC
St. Benedict, Coll of .... MN
St. Catherine, Coll. of .... MN
St. John's U .... MN
St. Mary's Coll. of California .... CA
St. Olaf Coll .... MN
St. Paul's .... MO
St. Thomas Aquinas .... NY
Stetson U .... FL
Sweet Briar Coll .... VA
Texas Lutheran Coll .... TX
Thiel Coll .... PA
Towson State Coll .... MD
Trinity Christian Coll IL
United Wesleyan Coll .... PA
Upsala Coll .... NJ
Valley Forge Military .... PA
Washington and Jefferson Coll .. PA
Wellesley Coll .... MA
Wells Coll .... NY
West Virginia Wesleyan .... WV
Western Maryland Coll .... MD
Westminster Coll .... PA
White Pines Coll .... NH
White Plains, Coll. of .... NY
Whittier Coll .... CA
Whitworth Coll .... WA
William Jewell Coll .... MO
Williams Coll .... MA
Wisconsin, U. of (Green Bay) ... WI
Yankton Coll .... SD

Handicapped, Colleges Having Facilities for

(According to Public Law 504 of the Federal Government, all colleges as of June 1, 1980, must provide accessibility to all facilities for handicapped students)

Handicapped, Education by Telephone for

Ramapo .... NJ
Southwest State .... MN

Kosher Meals, Colleges Serving

Adelphi U .... NY
Barnard .... NY
Bridgeport, U. of .... CT
Case Western Reserve .... OH
Central Missouri .... MO
Clark U .... MA
Colgate .... NY
Cornell U .... NY
Drexel U .... PA
Eckerd Coll .... FL
George Washington U .... DC
Grinnell Coll .... IA
Johns Hopkins U .... MD
Macalester Coll .... MN
Maryland, U. of .... MD
New York U .... NY
Oglethorpe .... GA
Princeton U .... NJ
State U. of New York (Brockport, Binghamton) ..... NY
Temple U .... PA
Trenton State .... NJ
Washington U .... MO
Wellesley Coll .... MA
Wells Coll .... NY
Willamette U .... OR
Yeshiva U .... NY

Language Houses

Ball State U .... IN
Beloit Coll .... WI
Brown U .... RI
Bryn Mawr Coll .... PA
California, U. of (Davis, Riverside) .... CA
Calvin Coll .... MI
Capital U .... OH
Central Coll .... IA
Colgate U .... NY
Colorado, U. of .... CO
Colorado Coll .... CO
Cornell U .... NY
Davis & Elkins .... WV
Delaware, U. of .... DE
Dickinson .... PA
Earlham .... IN

Gordon Coll .... MA
Grinnell Coll .... IA
Gustavus Adolphus........... MN
Hollins Coll .... VA
Hood Coll .... MD
Illinois, U. of IL
Indiana U .... IN
Iowa, U. of .... IA
James Madison U .... VA
Macalester .... MN
Mary Washington Coll .... VA
Middlebury Coll .... VT
Muhlenberg Coll .... PA
Nebraska, U. of .... NE
New Hampshire, U. of .... NH
New York U .... NY
Newcomb Coll .... LA
Northwestern U IL
Occidental .... CA
Ohio Wesleyan U .... OH
Plymouth State Coll .... NH
Princeton U .... NJ
Puget Sound, U. of .... WA
Southern Methodist .... TX
Southwestern at Memphis ...... TN
St. Olaf .... MN
Stephens Coll .... MO
Texas, U. of (Austin) .... TX
Tufts .... MA
Washington, U. of .... WA
Wells Coll .... NY
Whitman Coll .... WA
Willamette U .... OR
William and Mary .... VA

Learning Disabilities, Colleges which accept Students with

Adelphi U .... NY
Alderson-Broaddus........... WV
Appalachian State .... NC
Arizona State U .... AZ
Arkansas, U. of .... AR
Barat Coll IL
Bennett Coll .... NC
Bradford Coll .... MA
California, U. of (San Diego) .... CA
California State U. (Northridge) . CA
Calvin Coll .... MI
Central Missouri .... MO
College Miseracordia .... PA
Colorado, U. of .... CO
Curry Coll .... MA
Delaware, U. of .... DE
Findlay Coll .... OH
Fort Hays State .... KS
George Mason U .... VA
Georgia State U .... GA
Harding U .... AR
Hastings Coll .... NE
Hofstra U .... NY
Husson Coll .... ME
Iowa, U. of .... IA
Kansas, U. of .... KS
Kansas State U .... KS
Kent State U .... OH
Kutztown State .... PA
Lamar U .... TX
Lock Haven State .... PA
Maine, U. of (Farmington) ..... ME
Minnesota, U. of (Duluth, Minneapolis) .... MN
Moorhead State U .... MN
Nevada, U. of .... NV
North Florida, U. of............ FL
Northeastern Oklahoma State .. OK
Northwest Nazarene Coll .... ID
Notre Dame Coll .... NH
Notre Dame Coll .... OH
Oral Roberts U .... OK
Pine Manor Coll............... MA
Salem Coll .... WV
Schreiner Coll .... TX
Southwest State .... MN
Southwestern Oklahoma State U .... OK
St. Mary's Jr. Coll .... MN
State U. of New York (Binghamton, Plattsburgh) .... NY
Syracuse U .... NY
Temple U .... PA
Tennessee, U. of .... TN
Texas Woman's U .... TX
Towson State .... MD
Unity Coll .... ME
Utah State U .... UT
Wayne State .... MI
West Virginia Wesleyan .... WV
Western Carolina U .... NC
Westminster .... MO
Wisconsin, U. of (Stevens Point, Whitewater) .... WI
Wright State U .... OH

NASA Work-Study Program

Institutions having an active cooperative work-study agreement with the National Aeronautics and Space Administration

Akron, U. of .... OH
Alabama, U. of .... AL
Alabama A&M.................. AL
Albany State .... GA
American U .... DC
Arizona, U. of .... AZ
Arizona State U .... AZ
Arkansas, U. of................ AR
Auburn .... AL
Bethune-Cookman .... FL
Bowie State .... MD
California, U. of (Berkeley, Davis, Santa Barbara, Santa Cruz) ... CA
California Poly. State .... CA
California State U. (San Jose) .. CA
Case Western .... OH
Central Florida, U. of .... FL
Cincinnati, U. of .... OH
Clemson U .... SC
Cleveland State U .... OH
Columbia Union Coll .... MD
Coppin State .... MD
Davidson Coll .... NC
Dayton, U. of .... OH
Detroit, U. of.................. MI
District of Columbia, U. of ..... DC
Drexel U .... PA
Duke .... NC
Dyke Coll .... OH
East Carolina .... NC
Elizabeth City State U .... NC
Embry-Riddle .... FL
Evansville, U. of .... IN
Florida, U. of.................. FL
Florida Inst. of Tech .... FL
Florida State U .... FL
George Washington U .... DC
George Mason U .... VA
Georgia Tech .... GA
Hampton Inst .... VA
Houston, U. of .... TX
Howard U .... DC
Jacksonville State U .... AL
John Carroll U .... OH
Kansas, U. of .... KS
Lamar U .... TX
Louisville, U. of .... KY
Marquette U .... WI
Maryland, U. of .... MD
Massachusetts Instit. of Tech .. MA
Miami, U. of .... FL
Michigan, U. of................ MI
Minnesota, U. of .... MN
Mississippi Coll .... MS
Mississippi State U .... MS
Mississippi Valley State .... MS
Missouri, U. of .... MO
Morgan State .... MD
Mt. Union .... OH
Murray State U .... KY
New Mexico, U. of............ NM
New Mexico Highlands .... NM
New Mexico State U........... NM
New Orleans, U. of .... LA
Norfolk State Coll .... VA
North Carolina A&T State U ... NC
North Carolina State U .... NC
Northeastern .... MA
Northwestern U IL
Oakwood Coll.................. AL
Ohio State .... OH
Oklahoma, U. of .... OK
Old Dominion .... VA
Oregon State .... OR
Pacific, U. of the .... CA
Pennsylvania, U. of............ PA
Prairie View A&M .... TX
Puerto Rico, U. of .... PR
Purdue U .... IN
Rensselaer Poly. Inst .... NY
Rochester Inst. of Tech .... NY
South Florida, U. of .... FL
Southern California, U. of ..... CA
Southern Oregon State U ...... OR
Southern U .... LA
Southwestern U .... TX
Strayer Coll .... DC
Tennessee, U. of .... TN
Tennessee State U .... TN
Tennessee Tech. U .... TN
Texas, U. of (Austin, El Paso) ... TX
Texas A&I .... TX
Texas A&M .... TX
Texas Southern .... TX
Texas Woman's U .... TX
Towson State .... MD
Tri-State .... IN
Tulane U .... LA
Tuskegee Inst .... AL
Vanderbilt .... TN
Virginia Poly. Inst .... VA
Washington, U. of .... WA
West Florida, U. of .... FL
West Virginia Inst. of Tech ..... WV
Western Carolina State .... NC
Western Kentucky U .... KY
Wilberforce .... OH
Williams Coll.................. MA
Wisconsin, U. of (Madison, Platteville) .... WI
Wright State .... OH
Xavier .... LA

Quarter System

Andrews U .... MI
Antioch Coll .... OH
Armstrong Coll .... CA
Art Inst. of Pittsburgh .... PA
Augustana Coll IL
Ball State U .... IN
Bliss Coll .... OH
Bristol Coll .... TN
California, U. of (Davis, Irvine, Riverside, San Diego, Santa Barbara, Santa Cruz) .... CA
California Inst. of Tech .... CA
California Poly. State U .... CA
California State U. (Hayward, Los Angeles) .... CA
Central Coll .... IA
Central Missouri .... MO
Chicago, U. of IL
Cincinnati, U. of .... OH
Cleveland State U .... OH
Colorado Mountain............ CO
Colorado Tech Coll .... CO
Columbia Coll .... CA
Columbus Coll .... GA
Concordia Coll .... OR
Crandall Coll .... GA
David Lipscomb Coll .... TN
Denver, U. of .... CO
DuPage, Coll. of IL
Eastern Montana Coll .... MT
Emmanuel Coll .... GA
Evansville, U. of .... IN
Evergreen State Coll .... WA
Florida Inst. of Tech .... FL
Florida Inst. of Tech-Sch. of App. Tech .... FL
George Williams Coll IL
Georgia, U. of .... GA
Hiram Coll .... OH
Illinois, U. of IL
International Coll .... FL
International U .... MO
John F. Kennedy U .... CA
Kalamazoo Coll .... MI
La Grange Coll .... GA
Lake Superior State Coll........ MI
Lawrence Inst. Tech .... MI
Lewis and Clark Coll .... OR
Louisiana Tech .... LA
MacCormac Jr. Coll IL
Mankato State .... MN
Marylhurst Coll .... OR
Michigan Tech. U. (Houghton) .. MI
Minnesota, U. of (Crookston, Duluth, Minneapolis) .... MN
Montana, U. of .... MT
Moorhead State U .... MN
National Coll. of Educ IL
Northeastern Jr. Coll .... CO
Northern Colorado, U. of ...... CO
Northern Montana Coll .... MT
Northwest Nazarene Coll .... ID
Northwestern U IL
Oakwood Coll.................. AL
Ohio State .... OH
Ohio U .... OH
Oregon, U. of .... OR
Oregon State U .... OR
Otero Jr. Coll .... CO
Otterbein Coll................. OH
Pacific Union Coll .... CA
Point Loma .... CA
Rochester Inst. of Tech .... NY
Rockmont Coll .... CO
Seattle U .... WA
South Georgia Coll............ GA
Southern Illinois U. (Edwardsville) IL
Southwest State U .... MN
St. Cloud State................ MN
Tennessee, U. of .... TN
Texas State Tech. Inst.......... TX
Toledo, U. of................. OH
Trinidad State Jr. Coll .... CO
U.S. International U .... CA
Utah, U. of .... UT
Virginia Poly. Inst .... VA
Walla Walla Coll .... WA
Washington, U. of .... WA
West Georgia Coll............. GA
Western Baptist Coll .... OR
Winona State U .... MN
Wisconsin, U. of (River Falls, Superior) .... WI
Wooster, Coll. of .... OH
Worcester Poly. Inst .... MA
Worthington Comm. Coll ...... MN
Youngstown U .... OH

ROTC

Air Force ROTC

Those with the bullet host cross-enrollment with nearby institutions

Akron, U. of .... OH

Alabama, U. of ... AL
•Alabama State U ... AL
Angelo State U ... TX
•Arizona, U. of ... AZ
•Arizona State U ... AZ
Arkansas, U. of ... AR
Auburn ... AL
•Baptist Coll. at Charleston ... SC
•Baylor U ... TX
Boston U ... MA
•Bowling Green State U ... OH
•Brigham Young U ... UT
•California, U. of (Berkeley, Los Angeles) ... CA
California State U. (Fresno, Long Beach, Sacramento) ... CA
Carnegie-Mellon U ... PA
•Central Florida, U. of ... FL
Central Washington U ... WA
•Cincinnati, U. of ... OH
Citadel, The ... SC
Clarkson Coll. of Tech ... NY
•Clemson U ... SC
•Colorado, U. of ... CO
Colorado State U ... CO
•Connecticut, U. of (Storrs) ... CT
•Cornell U ... NY
•Duke U ... NC
•East Carolina U ... NC
•East Texas State U ... TX
Embry-Riddle ... AR
•Embry-Riddle ... FL
•Fayetteville State U ... NC
Florida, U. of ... FL
•Florida State U ... FL
Georgia, U. of ... GA
•Georgia Inst. of Tech ... GA
Grambling Coll ... LA
•Grove City Coll ... PA
•Hawaii, U. of ... HI
•Holy Cross, Coll. of ... MA
•Howard U ... DC
•Illinois, U. of (Urbana) ... IL
•Illinois Inst. of Tech ... IL
•Indiana U ... IN
Iowa, U. of ... IA
•Iowa State U ... IA
Kansas, U. of ... KS
Kansas State U ... KS
Kent State U ... OH
•Kentucky, U. of ... KY
•Lehigh U ... PA
•Louisiana State U. and A&M Coll ... LA
Louisiana Tech. U ... LA
•Louisville, U. of ... KY
•Lowell, U. of ... MA
•Loyola Marymount U ... CA
Maine, U. of ... ME
•Manhattan Coll ... NY
Maryland, U. of (College Park) . MD
•Massachusetts, U. of (Amherst) MA
•Massachusetts Inst. of Tech ... MA
•Memphis State U ... TN
•Miami, U. of ... FL
Miami U ... OH
•Michigan, U. of ... MI
•Michigan State U ... MI
•Michigan Tech U ... MI
•Minnesota, U. of (Duluth) ... MN
Minnesota, U. of (Minneapolis) . MN
Mississippi, U. of ... MS
•Mississippi State U ... MS
•Mississippi Valley State Coll ... MS
•Missouri, U. of (Columbia) ... MO
Missouri-Rolla, U. of ... MO
Montana State U ... MT
•Nebraska, U. of (Lincoln, Omaha) ... NE
•New Hampshire, U. of ... NH
•New Jersey Inst. of Tech ... NJ
•New Mexico, U. of ... NM
•New Mexico State U ... NM
•New Orleans, U. of ... LA
North Carolina, U. of (Chapel Hill) ... NC
•North Carolina, U. of (Charlotte) NC
•North Carolina A&T State U ... NC
•North Carolina State U ... NC
•North Dakota State U. of A&AS ND
•North Texas State U ... TX
Northern Arizona U ... AZ
•Northern Colorado, U. of ... CO
Norwich U ... VT
•Notre Dame, U. of ... IN
•Ohio State U ... OH
Ohio U ... OH
•Oklahoma, U. of ... OK
Oklahoma State U ... OK
•Oregon State U ... OR
•Parks Coll ... IL
Pennsylvania State U. (University Park) ... PA
•Pittsburgh, U. of ... PA
•Portland, U. of ... OR
•Puerto Rico, U. of (Mayaguez, San Juan) ... PR
•Puget Sound, U. of ... WA
Purdue U ... IN
•Rensselaer Poly. Inst ... NY
•Rutgers U ... NJ
•Samford ... AL
•San Diego State U ... CA
•San Francisco State U ... CA
San Jose State U ... CA
•South Carolina, U. of ... SC
South Dakota State U ... SD
South Florida, U. of ... FL
Southeast Missouri ... MO
•Southern California, U. of ... CA
Southern Illinois U. (Carbondale) ... IL
•Southern Illinois U. (Edwardsville) ... IL
•Southern Mississippi, U. of ... MS
•Southwest Texas State ... TX
Southwestern Louisiana, U. of .. LA
•St. Joseph's U ... PA
•St. Michael's Coll ... VT
•St. Thomas, Coll. of ... MN
•Syracuse U ... NY
•Tennessee, U. of (Knoxville) ... TN
•Tennessee State U ... TN
•Texas, U. of (Austin) ... TX
Texas A&M U ... TX
•Texas Christian U ... TX
•Texas Tech U ... TX
Troy State ... AL
Tuskegee ... AL
•Utah, U. of ... UT
Utah State U ... UT
Valdosta State Coll ... GA
•Virginia, U. of ... VA
Virginia Military Inst ... VA
Virginia Poly. Inst ... VA
Washburn U ... KS
•Washington, U. of ... WA
•Washington State U ... WA
•West Virginia U ... WV
•Wilkes Coll ... PA
Wisconsin, U. of (Madison, Superior) ... WI
Wright State U ... OH
Wyoming, U. of ... WY

Army ROTC

Akron, U. of ... OH
Alabama, U. of ... AL
Alabama A&M ... AL
Alaska, U. of ... AK
Alcorn State U ... MS
Appalachian State U ... NC
Arizona, U. of ... AZ
Arizona State U ... AZ
Arkansas, U. of (Fayetteville, Pine Bluff) ... AR
Arkansas State U ... AR
Arkansas Tech ... AR
Auburn ... AL
Austin Peay State U ... TN
Bishop Coll ... TX
Bowling Green State U ... OH
Brigham Young U ... UT
Bucknell U ... PA
California, U. of (Berkeley, Davis, Los Angeles, Santa Barbara) ... CA
California Poly. State (San Luis Obispo) ... CA
Cameron U ... OK
Campbell Coll ... NC
Canisius Coll ... NY
Carnegie-Mellon U ... PA
Carson-Newman Coll ... TN
Central Arkansas, U. of ... AR
Central Michigan U ... MI
Central Missouri State Coll ... MO
Central State U ... OH
Central State U ... OK
Cincinnati, U. of ... OH
Citadel, The ... SC
Claremont Colleges ... CA
Clarkson Coll. of Tech ... NY
Clemson U ... SC
Colorado, U. of ... CO
Colorado School of Mines ... CO
Colorado State U ... CO
Columbus Coll ... GA
Connecticut, U. of (Storrs) ... CT
Cornell U ... NY
Creighton U ... NE
Davidson Coll ... NC
Dayton, U. of ... OH
Delaware, U. of ... DE
Detroit, U. of ... MI
Dickinson Coll ... PA
Drexel U ... PA
Duquesne U ... PA
East Central State Coll ... OK
East Tennessee State U ... TN
Eastern Kentucky U ... KY
Eastern Michigan U ... MI
Eastern New Mexico U ... NM
Eastern Washington U ... WA
Florida, U. of ... FL
Florida A&M ... FL
Florida Inst. of Tech ... FL
Florida Southern Coll ... FL
Florida State U ... FL
Fordham U ... NY
Fort Valley State Coll ... GA
Furman U ... SC
Gannon Coll ... PA
Georgetown U ... DC
Georgia, U. of ... GA
Georgia Inst. of Tech ... GA
Georgia Military Coll ... GA
Georgia State U ... GA
Gettysburg Coll ... PA
Gonzaga U ... WA
Guam, U. of ... GU
Hampton Inst ... VA
Hardin-Simmons U ... TX
Hawaii, U. of ... HI
Henderson State ... AR
Hofstra U ... NY
Houston, U. of ... TX
Howard U ... DC
Idaho, U. of ... ID
Idaho State U ... ID
Illinois, U. of (Chicago Circle, Urbana) ... IL
Indiana Inst. of Tech ... IN
Indiana U ... IN
Indiana U. of Pennsylvania ... PA
Iowa, U. of ... IA
Iowa State U ... IA
Jackson State Coll ... MS
Jacksonville State ... AL
James Madison U ... VA
John Carroll U ... OH
Johns Hopkins U ... MD
Kansas, U. of ... KS
Kansas State U ... KS
Kearney State Coll ... NE
Kemper Military School and Coll ... MO
Kent State U ... OH
Kentucky, U. of ... KY
Knox Coll ... IL
La Salle ... PA
Lafayette Coll ... PA
Lehigh U ... PA
Lincoln U ... MO
Louisiana State U. and A&M Coll ... LA
Loyola Coll ... MD
Loyola U ... LA
Loyola U. of Chicago ... IL
Maine, U. of ... ME
Marion Military Inst ... AL
Marquette U ... WI
Marshall U ... WV
Massachusetts, U. of (Amherst) MA
Massachusetts Inst. of Tech ... MA
McNeese State U ... LA
Mercer U ... GA
Miami, U. of ... FL
Michigan, U. of ... MI
Michigan State U ... MI
Michigan Tech. U ... MI
Middle Tennessee State U ... TN
Midwestern U ... TX
Minnesota, U. of (Minneapolis) . MN
Mississippi, U. of ... MS
Mississippi State U ... MS
Missouri, U. of (Columbia, Rolla) ... MO
Missouri Western Coll ... MO
Montana, U. of ... MT
Montana State U ... MT
Morehead State U ... KY
Morgan State Coll ... MD
Murray State U ... KY
Nebraska, U. of (Lincoln) ... NE
Nevada, U. of ... NV
New Hampshire, U. of ... NH
New Mexico Military Inst ... NM
New Mexico State U ... NM
New York, Poly. Inst. of ... NY
Niagara U ... NY
Nicholls State U ... LA
Norfolk State Coll ... VA
North Alabama, U. of ... AL
North Carolina A&T State U ... NC
North Carolina State U ... NC
North Dakota, U. of ... ND
North Dakota State U. of A&AS ND
North Georgia Coll ... GA
Northeast Louisiana U ... LA
Northeast Missouri State Coll . MO
Northeastern U ... MA
Northern Illinois U ... IL
Northern Michigan U ... MI
Northwestern Oklahoma State U ... OK
Northwestern State U. of Louisiana ... LA
Norwich U ... VT
Notre Dame, U. of ... IN
Ohio State U ... OH
Ohio U ... OH
Oklahoma, U. of ... OK
Oklahoma State U ... OK
Old Dominion U ... VA
Oregon, U. of ... OR
Oregon State U ... OR
Ouachita Baptist ... AR
Pennsylvania, U. of ... PA
Pennsylvania State U. (University Park) ... PA
Pittsburg State U ... KS
Pittsburgh, U. of ... PA
Prairie View A&M Coll ... TX

Presbyterian Coll .... SC
Princeton .... NJ
Providence Coll .... RI
Puerto Rico, U. of (Mayaguez, Rio Piedras) .... PR
Purdue U .... IN
Rensselaer Poly. Inst .... NY
Rhode Island, U. of .... RI
Rice U .... TX
Richmond, U. of .... VA
Rider Coll .... NJ
Ripon Coll .... WI
Rochester Inst. of Tech .... NY
Rose-Hulman Inst. of Tech .... IN
Rutgers .... NJ
Sam Houston State U .... TX
San Francisco, U. of .... CA
San Jose State U .... CA
Santa Clara, U. of .... CA
Scranton, U. of .... PA
Seattle U .... WA
Seton Hall U .... NJ
Siena Coll .... NY
South Alabama, U. of .... AL
South Carolina State Coll .... SC
South Dakota, U. of .... SD
South Dakota School of Mines and Tech .... SD
South Dakota State U .... SD
South Florida, U. of .... FL
Southeastern Louisiana U .... LA
Southern Arkansas U .... AR
Southern Colorado, U. of .... CO
Southern Mississippi, U. of .... MS
Southern U. and A&M Coll .... LA
Southwest Missouri State Coll .... MO
Southwestern Oklahoma State U .... OK
St. Augustine's Coll .... NC
St. Bonaventure .... NY
St. John's U .... MN
St. John's U .... NY
St. Lawrence U .... NY
St. Mary's U. of San Antonio .... TX
St. Norbert Coll .... WI
St. Peter's Coll .... NJ
Stephen F. Austin State Coll .... TX
Stetson U .... FL
Syracuse U .... NY
Tampa, U. of .... FL
Temple U .... PA
Tennessee, U. of (Chattanooga, Knoxville, Martin) .... TN
Tennessee Tech. U .... TN
Texas, U. of (Arlington, Austin, El Paso) .... TX
Texas A&I U .... TX
Texas A&M U .... TX
Texas Christian U .... TX
Texas Tech. U .... TX
Toledo, U. of .... OH
Trinity U .... TX
Tulane U .... LA
Tuskegee .... AL
Utah, U. of .... UT
Utah State U .... UT
Valley Forge Military Acad .... PA
Vanderbilt .... TN
Vermont, U. of .... VT
Virginia, U. of .... VA
Virginia Military Inst .... VA
Virginia Poly. Inst .... VA
Virginia State Coll .... VA
Wake Forest U .... NC
Washington, U. of .... WA
Washington and Jefferson Coll .... PA
Washington and Lee U .... VA
Washington State U .... WA
Washington U .... MO
Weber State Coll .... UT
Wentworth Military Acad. and Jr. Coll .... MO
West Texas State U .... TX
West Virginia State Coll .... WV
West Virginia U .... WV
Western Carolina U .... NC
Western Illinois U IL
Western Kentucky U .... KY
Western Maryland Coll .... MD
Western Michigan U .... MI
Westminster Coll .... MO
Wheaton Coll IL
Wichita State U .... KS
Widener Coll .... PA
William and Mary, Coll. of .... VA
Wisconsin, U. of (La Crosse, Madison, Milwaukee, Oshkosh, Platteville, Stevens Point, Whitewater) .... WI
Wofford Coll .... SC
Worcester Poly. Inst .... MA
Wyoming, U. of .... WY
Xavier U .... OH
Youngstown State U .... OH

Navy ROTC

•Crosstown enrollment agreements with other area schools.

Auburn .... AL
•California, U. of (Berkeley, Los Angeles) .... CA
Citadel, The .... SC
Colorado, U. of .... CO
•Cornell U .... NY
Duke U .... NC
Florida, U. of .... FL
•Florida A&M .... FL
Georgia Inst. of Tech .... GA
•Holy Cross, Coll. of .... MA
Idaho, U. of .... ID
Illinois, U. of (Champaign) IL
•Illinois Inst. of Tech IL
Iowa State U. of S&T .... IA
•Jacksonville U .... FL
Kansas, U. of .... KS
Maine Maritime Acad .... ME
•Marquette U .... WI
•Massachusetts Inst. of Tech .... MA
Miami U .... OH
•Michigan, U. of .... MI
•Minnesota, U. of (Minneapolis) .... MN
Mississippi, U. of .... MS
Missouri, U. of (Columbia) .... MO
•Nebraska, U. of (Lincoln) .... NE
•New Mexico, U. of .... NM
Norfolk State U .... VA
•North Carolina, U. of .... NC
•Northwestern U IL
•Notre Dame, U. of .... IN
Ohio State U .... OH
•Oklahoma, U. of .... OK
Old Dominion U .... VA
•Oregon State U .... OR
Pennsylvania, U. of .... PA
Pennsylvania State U. (University Park) .... PA
Prairie View A&M Coll .... TX
Purdue U .... IN
•Rensselaer Poly. Inst .... NY
Rice U .... TX
Rochester, U. of .... NY
San Diego, U. of .... CA
San Diego State U .... CA
•Savannah State Coll .... GA
South Carolina, U. of .... SD
•Southern California, U. of .... CA
•Southern U. and A&M Coll .... LA
State of New York (Maritime Coll.) .... NY
Texas, U. of (Austin) .... TX
Texas A&M .... TX
•Tulane U .... LA
Utah, U. of .... UT
Vanderbilt .... TN
Villanova U .... PA
Virginia, U. of .... VA
Virginia Military Inst .... VA
Virginia Poly. Inst .... VA
•Washington, U. of .... WA
Wisconsin, U. of (Madison) .... WI

Senior Colleges

Only junior and senior years of undergraduate work

Baltimore, U. of .... MD
Chowan Coll .... NC
Corpus Christi State .... TX
Evergreen State Coll .... WA
Governors State U IL
Illinois, U. of IL
John F. Kennedy .... CA
North Florida, U. of .... FL
Northwestern Oklahoma State .... OK
Sangamon State U IL
State U. of New York (Coll. of Env. Sci. and Tech.) .... NY
Stephens Coll .... MO
Texas, U. of (Dallas) .... TX
West Florida, U. of .... FL

Trimester System

Alderson-Broaddus .... WV
Allegheny Coll .... PA
Art Center Coll. of Design .... CA
Brooks Coll .... CA
California Coll. of Arts and Crafts .... CA
Central New England Coll .... MA
Central Pennsylvania Bus. Sch .... PA
Dayton, U. of .... OH
Detroit, U. of .... MI
Drexel U .... PA
Earlham Coll .... IN
Elmira Coll .... NY
Embry-Riddle Aero. U .... FL
Emory and Henry Coll .... VA
Florida Atlantic U .... FL
Fort Lewis Coll .... CO
Golden Gate U .... CA
Gordon Coll .... MA
Governors State U IL
Hobart Coll .... NY
Insurance, Coll. of .... NY
Johnson and Wales Coll .... RI
Judson Coll .... AL
Knox Coll IL
Lincoln U .... PA
Michigan, U. of (Dearborn) .... MI
Morrison Inst. of Tech IL
North Central Coll IL
Northeastern Illinois IL
Occidental .... CA
Oklahoma Christian Coll .... OK
Parks Coll IL
Pepperdine U .... CA
Union .... NY
William Smith Coll .... NY
Wilmington Coll .... DE

Two-Year Terminal Programs at Four-Year Colleges

Andrews U IL
Arkansas, U. of .... AR
Ball State U .... IN
Baltimore, U. of .... MO
Bemidji State U .... MN
Black Hills State Coll .... SD
Bridgeport, U. of .... CT
Butler U .... IN
California State U .... PA
Campbell U .... NC
Castleton State .... VT
Central Missouri .... MO
Chadron .... NE
Cincinnati, U. of .... OH
Clarion State .... PA
Clearwater Christian .... FL
Colby-Sawyer .... NH
Colorado State U .... CO
Columbus Coll .... GA
District of Columbia, U. of .... DC
East Tennessee State .... TN
Eastern Kentucky .... KY
Edinboro State Coll .... PA
Elizabethtown Coll .... PA
Embry-Riddle Aero. U .... FL
Ferris State .... MI
Florida Inst. of Tech.-Sch. of App. Tech .... FL
Fort Hays State .... KS
Hannibal-LaGrange .... MO
Hartford, U. of .... CT
Hawaii, U. of (Honolulu) .... HI
Houghton Coll .... NY
Immaculata Coll .... PA
Indiana State U .... IN
Indiana U. (Bloomington) .... IN
International Coll .... FL
John Brown U .... AR
Johnson & Wales .... RI
Lamar U .... TX
Louisiana Tech .... LA
Louisville, U. of .... KY
Maine, U. of (Fort Kent, Orono) .... ME
Manchester Coll .... IN
Marymount Coll .... VA
Medgar Evers Coll .... NY
Midland Coll .... TX
Midwestern State U .... TX
Milligan Coll .... TN
Missouri Western State .... MO
Morehead State .... KY
Mount St. Claire Coll .... IA
Mount St. Mary's .... CA
Murray State U .... KY
Nevada, U. of .... NV
Nicholls State .... LA
Northeast Louisiana .... LA
Northwestern State U .... LA
Norwich U .... VT
Notre Dame Coll .... NH
Ohio U .... OH
Oklahoma Christian Coll .... OK
Otterbein Coll .... OH
Pikeville Coll .... KY
Plymouth State .... NH
Post Coll .... CT
Rider Coll .... NJ
Robert Morris .... PA
Salem Coll .... WV
Shenandoah Coll .... VA
Shepherd Coll .... WV
South Dakota State .... SD
Southeastern Oklahoma State U .... OK
Southern Maine, U. of .... ME
Southern Methodist Coll .... SC
Southwest Missouri .... MO
Southwest State .... MN
Temple U .... PA
Thiel Coll .... PA
Trinity Coll .... VT
Union Coll .... NE
Valparaiso U .... IN
Virgin Islands, Coll. of the VI
Walsh Coll .... OH
West Coast Christian .... CA
West Virginia State .... WV
West Virginia Wesleyan .... WV
Western Baptist Coll .... OR
Wisconsin, U. of (Stevens Point) .... WI

United Nations Semester

The UN Semester Program is sponsored by Drew University and offered each semester, with some students studying for a single semester and others for a longer period of time.

Participating students live on the Drew campus at Madison, NJ, and go into New York City twice weekly. Drew also maintains a facility across the street from the United Nations.

Students engage in individual research projects on the functions and operations of the working units of the United Nations or related agencies. Expenses are based on Drew University's regular charges, plus small additional fees.

Adelphi U ..... NY
Akron, U. of ..... OH
Albion ..... MI
American U ..... DC
Ashland ..... OH
Augustana IL
Baker U ..... KS
Baldwin-Wallace ..... OH
Barat Coll IL
Bates ..... ME
Bethany Coll ..... WV
Bowdoin Coll ..... ME
Bradley U IL
Brooklyn Coll ..... NY
Bucknell U ..... PA
Caldwell Coll. for Women ..... NJ
California, U. of (Irvine, Riverside) ..... CA
California State U ..... CA
Carroll Coll ..... WI
Central Methodist ..... MO
Colorado Coll ..... CO
Colorado State U ..... CO
Dayton, U. of ..... OH
Delaware, U. of ..... DE
Denison ..... OH
DePauw U ..... IN
Dickinson ..... PA
Drake ..... IA
Drew ..... NJ
Duke U ..... NC
Elmira ..... NY
Florida Southern ..... FL
Franklin Coll ..... IN
George Washington U ..... DC
Gettysburg ..... PA
Hamilton ..... NY
Hamline U ..... MN
Hartwick ..... NY
Heidelberg ..... OH
Hiram Coll ..... OH
Hollins ..... VA
Illinois Wesleyan U IL
Ithaca Coll ..... NY
Juniata ..... PA
Kansas, U. of ..... KS
Kansas Wesleyan U ..... KS
Kirkland ..... NY
Lake Forest Coll IL
Linfield Coll ..... OR
Lycoming ..... PA
MacMurray IL
Maine, U. of ..... ME
Massachusetts, U. of ..... MA
Meredith Coll ..... NC
Miami U ..... OH
Millikin IL
Morningside ..... IA
Muskingum Coll ..... OH
Nebraska Wesleyan ..... NE
New Hampshire, U. of ..... NH
New Rochelle, Coll. of ..... NY
North Central IL
Ohio Wesleyan U ..... OH
Oklahoma City U ..... OK
Otterbein ..... OH
Pacific, U. of the ..... CA
Pennsylvania, U. of ..... PA
Puget Sound, U. of ..... WA
Randolph-Macon Woman's Coll ..... VA
Redlands, U. of ..... CA
Rockford IL
Russell Sage ..... NY
Rutgers U ..... NJ
Salem Coll ..... NC
Santa Clara, U. of ..... CA
Scripps ..... CA
Seton Hall ..... NJ
Seton Hill ..... PA
Simpson Coll ..... IA
Southern Methodist U ..... TX
Southwestern U ..... KS
St. Andrews Presbyterian ..... NC
Stephens Coll ..... MO
Susquehanna U ..... PA
Thiel ..... PA
Trinity Coll ..... DC
Tufts ..... MA
Union Coll ..... NY
Upsala ..... NJ
Valparaiso U ..... IN
Wabash Coll ..... IN
Wartburg Coll ..... IA
Washington State U ..... WA
Wells Coll ..... NY
Western Maryland U ..... MD
Westminster ..... MO
Wheaton Coll ..... MA
Willamette U ..... OR
William Jewell Coll ..... MO
William Woods ..... MO
Williams Coll ..... MA
Wisconsin, U. of (Milwaukee) ..... WI
Wittenberg U ..... OH
Wooster, Coll. of ..... OH

Washington, DC, Semester

Cooperative programs arranged between the American University College of Public Affairs, in Washington, DC, and many other schools throughout the country. Honors-level undergraduates are nominated by their colleges to attend a semester of field study and research in one of the six programs offered: the Washington Semester (the original program, established in 1947), the Washington Urban Semester, the Foreign Policy Semester, the Economic Policy Semester, the Semester in Arts & Humanities, and the Criminal Justice Semester. Emphasis is on direct contact with public officials and others active in the area being studied. Tuition is paid through the student's home college.

Agnes Scott Coll ..... GA
Albion Coll ..... MI
Alfred U ..... NY
Allegheny Coll ..... PA
Alma Coll ..... MI
American U., The ..... DC
Arizona State U ..... AZ
Ashland Coll ..... OH
Augustana Coll IL
Augustana Coll ..... SD
Austin Coll ..... TX
Baldwin-Wallace Coll ..... OH
Bard Coll ..... NY
Bates Coll ..... ME
Beaver Coll ..... PA
Beloit Coll ..... WI
Bethany Coll ..... WV
Blackburn Coll IL
Boston Coll ..... MA
Bowdoin Coll ..... ME
Bowling Green State U ..... OH
Bradley U IL
Bucknell U ..... PA
Buena Vista Coll ..... IA
Calvin Coll ..... MI
Canisius Coll ..... NY
Carleton Coll ..... MN
Carnegie-Mellon U ..... PA
Carroll Coll ..... WI
Case Western Reserve U ..... OH
Cedar Crest Coll ..... PA
Centenary Coll. of Louisiana ..... LA
Chapman Coll ..... CA
Chatham Coll ..... PA
Cincinnati, U. of ..... OH
City U. of New York, Lehman Coll ..... NY
Clark U ..... MA
Colby Coll ..... ME
Colby-Sawyer ..... NH
Colorado Coll ..... CO
Colorado Women's Coll ..... CO
Concordia Coll. (Moorhead) ..... MN
Connecticut Coll ..... CT
Cornell Coll ..... IA
Davidson Coll ..... NC
Davis and Elkins Coll ..... WV
Defiance Coll ..... OH
Denison U ..... OH
DePauw U ..... IN
Dickinson Coll ..... PA
Doane Coll ..... NE
Drake U ..... IA
Drury Coll ..... MO
Duke U ..... NC
Duquesne U ..... PA
Eastern Michigan U ..... MI
Eisenhower Coll ..... NY
Elmhurst Coll IL
Elmira Coll ..... NY
Emory U ..... GA
Fairfield U ..... CT
Florida Southern ..... FL
Franklin and Marshall ..... PA
Franklin Coll. of Indiana ..... IN
Gettysburg Coll ..... PA
Grinnell Coll ..... IA
Gustavus Adolphus Coll ..... MN
Hamline U ..... MN
Hampden-Sydney Coll ..... VA
Hanover Coll ..... IN
Hartwick Coll ..... NY
Hawaii, U. of (Manoa) ..... HI
Heidelberg Coll ..... OH
Hendrix Coll ..... AR
Hiram Coll ..... OH
Hobart and William Smith ..... NY
Hollins Coll ..... VA
Hood Coll ..... MD
Houston, U. of ..... TX
Idaho, The Coll. of ..... ID
Illinois Wesleyan U IL
Indiana State U ..... IN
Kansas Wesleyan U ..... KS
Kenyon Coll ..... OH
Knox Coll IL
Lawrence U ..... WI
Le Moyne-Owen Coll ..... TN
Lebanon Valley Coll ..... PA
Lehigh U ..... PA
Lenoir-Rhyne Coll ..... NC
Lindenwood Colleges ..... MO
Luther Coll ..... IA
Lycoming Coll ..... PA
Manhattanville Coll ..... NY
Marietta Coll ..... OH
Marist Coll ..... NY
Meredith Coll ..... NC
Middlebury Coll ..... VT
Millikin U IL
Mills ..... CA
Millsaps Coll ..... MS
Monmouth Coll IL
Montana, U. of ..... MT
Montana State U ..... MT
Moravian Coll ..... PA
Morningside Coll ..... IA
Mount St. Mary's ..... CA
Muskingum ..... OH
Nebraska Wesleyan U ..... NE
North Central Coll IL
Occidental Coll ..... CA
Ohio Northern U ..... OH
Ohio Wesleyan U ..... OH
Oklahoma City U ..... OK
Otterbein Coll ..... OH
Pacific, U. of the ..... CA
Park Coll ..... MO
Phillips U ..... OK
Queens Coll ..... NC
Randolph-Macon Woman's Coll ..... VA
Regis Coll ..... MA
Ripon ..... WI
Rockford Coll IL
Rollins Coll ..... FL
Salem Coll ..... NC
San Diego State U ..... CA
Santa Clara, U. of ..... CA
Scripps Coll ..... CA
Seton Hill Coll ..... PA
Simmons Coll ..... MA
Simpson Coll ..... IA
Skidmore Coll ..... NY
South Dakota, U. of ..... SD
Southern U ..... LA
Southwestern at Memphis ..... TN
Spring Hill Coll ..... AL
St. Francis Coll ..... PA
St. Lawrence U ..... NY
St. Mary's Coll ..... IN
St. Olaf Coll ..... MN
State U. of New York (Buffalo, Oswego, Potsdam) ..... NY
Stetson U ..... FL
Susquehanna U ..... PA
Sweet Briar Coll ..... VA
Syracuse U ..... NY
Tarkio Coll ..... MO
Texas Lutheran Coll ..... TX
Thiel ..... PA
Tougaloo Coll ..... MA
Transylvania Coll ..... KY
Trinity Coll ..... CT
Tufts ..... MA
Tulane ..... LA
Union Coll ..... KY
Union Coll ..... NY
Valparaiso U ..... IN
Vassar Coll ..... NY
Vermont, U. of ..... VT
Wabash Coll ..... IN
Washington and Jefferson ..... PA
Washington Coll ..... MD
Wells ..... NY
Wesleyan U ..... CT
Western Maryland Coll ..... MD
Western New England Coll ..... MA
Westmar ..... IA
Westminster Coll ..... MO
Westminster Coll ..... PA
Westminster Coll ..... UT
Westmont Coll ..... CA
Wheaton Coll IL
Wheaton Coll ..... MA
Wheeling Coll ..... WV
Whitman Coll ..... WA
Widener Coll ..... PA
Willamette U ..... OR
Wilmington Coll ..... OH
Wisconsin, U. of (Stevens Point) ..... WI
Wittenberg U ..... OH
Wooster, Coll. of ..... OH
York Coll ..... PA

SECTION THREE

THE SCHOOLS

With the help of Sections One and Two, you are ready to select a particular institution. The third section offers *Capsule Descriptions of the Schools* themselves—individual description and rating of some 3,000 colleges and universities, listed alphabetically within each state.

Before the actual listings, you will find the symbols and abbreviations used in the section for instant reference.

SYMBOLS AND ABBREVIATIONS USED IN SECTION THREE

Although abbreviations in *Lovejoy's College Guide* have been kept to the minimum, some symbols and abbreviations are necessary. Most are obvious; all others are clarified in this introductory text.

Section Three of *Lovejoy's College Guide* provides a profile on each institution. There are briefer entries for the junior, terminal, technical, transfer, and community colleges and for some of the institutions of special appeal.

Definition Of Symbols

[1] Four-year institution, having regional accreditation, the highest attainable.

[2] Other institutions which do not have accreditation by one of the six regional bodies but which may have approval or recognition by their state universities, state boards or departments of education. Some of these [2] colleges may have had regional accreditation in past years but lost it because of one weakness or another. Some, conceivably, might have obtained regional accreditation but elected not to seek it. Some are among the nation's oldest colleges, some are commendable new institutions, while others are not impressive because of their limited facilities.

[J1] Institutions with regional accreditation that do not confer baccalaureate degrees and are in various categories of junior, terminal, transfer, or community colleges or technical institutes. They have a two-year program and offer the degree of Associate in Arts, Associate in Science, etc.

[J2] Institutions below baccalaureate-degree level which are not regionally accredited but may have recognition and approval by their state universities, state boards or departments of education.

[G] Graduate institutions. Students need a baccalaureate degree or its equivalent for admission and usually must take entrance examinations.

[P] Instead of giving these institutions what might be the lesser prefix of [2] or [J2], since they are not regionally accredited, the prefix [P] has been substituted because of their professional accreditation by one or more of the professional accrediting bodies.

[R] Institutions whose student body almost entirely comprises students studying for the Roman Catholic priesthood or as clergy or missionaries in other faiths.

[S] Special institutions which are in the realm of higher education but whose programs are unusual. Some do not give formal degrees.

Regional Accrediting Bodies

MIDDLE STATES ASSN. 3624 Market Street, Philadelphia, PA 19104.
Middle States Association of Colleges and Secondary Schools, embracing states of New York, New Jersey, Pennsylvania, Delaware, Maryland, District of Columbia, Puerto Rico, Republic of Panama, and the Virgin Islands.

NEW ENGLAND ASSN. 131 Middlesex Turnpike, Burlington, MA 01803.
New England Association of Schools and Colleges, Inc., membership in which is regarded as tantamount to accreditation, embracing states of Maine, New Hampshire, Vermont, Massachusetts, Rhode Island, Connecticut.

NORTH CENTRAL ASSN. 1540 Thirtieth St., P.O. Box 18, Boulder, CO 80306
North Central Association of Colleges and Secondary Schools, embracing states of Arizona, Arkansas, Colorado, Illinois, Indiana, Iowa, Kansas, Michigan, Minnesota, Missouri, Nebraska, New Mexico, North Dakota, Ohio, Oklahoma, South Dakota, West Virginia, Wisconsin, Wyoming.

NORTHWEST ASSN. 3700B University Way N.E., Seattle, WA 98105.
Northwest Association of Secondary and Higher Schools, embracing states of Alaska, Idaho, Montana, Nevada, Oregon, Utah, Washington.

SOUTHERN ASSN. 795 Peachtree St., N.E., Atlanta, GA 30308.
Southern Association of Colleges and Secondary Schools, which has a membership list as well as an approved list and embraces states of Alabama, Florida, Georgia, Kentucky, Louisiana, Mississippi, North Carolina, South Carolina, Tennessee, Texas, Virginia.

WESTERN ASSN. 1614 Rollins Road, Burlingame, CA 94010.
Western Association of Schools and Colleges embraces states of California, Hawaii, American Samoa, Trust Territory of the Pacific, and Territory of Guam.

Miscellaneous Abbreviations

ACH—Achievement (CEEB)
ACT—American College Testing Program (E-English, M-Math)
AP—Advanced Placement
CEEB—College Entrance Examination Board
CGP—Comparative Guidance and Placement Test
CSS—Signifies participating institution in College Scholarship Service in which parents of candidates for scholarships and financial aid agree to file confidential statements before specified winter and early spring dates. Some of the CSS participants are not members of the College Entrance Examination Board (CEEB) which organized it.
CUNY—City University of New York
CWS or CWSP—College Work-Study Program
FAF—Financial Aid Form
FFS—Family Financial Statement of the American College Testing Program
FISL—Federally Insured Student Loan
GED—General Equivalency Diploma
GSL—Guarenteed Student Loan
GRE—Graduate Record Examinations
NDEA—National Defense Education Act
NDSL—National Direct Student Loan
NMSQT—National Merit Scholarship Qualifying Test
PELL—Basic Educational Opportunity Grant
PSAT—Preliminary Scholastic Aptitude Test
SACS—Southern Assn. of Colleges and Schools
SAT—Scholastic Aptitude Test (M-Math, V-Verbal)
SCAT—School and College Ability Test
SEEK—Search for Education, Elevation and Knowledge
SEOG—Supplemental Educational Opportunity Grant
SUNY—State University of New York
TAP—Tuition Assistance Plan

Some Degree Abbreviations

AA—Associate in Arts
AAA—Associate in Applied Arts
AAAS—Associate in Applied Arts and Sciences
AAS—Associate in Applied Science
AB—Bachelor of Arts
ABA—Associate in Business Administration

ABEd—Bachelor of Arts in Education
AE—Agricultural Engineer or Aeronautical Engineer
AFA—Associate in Fine Arts
AGE—Associate in General Education
AGS—Associate in General Studies
ALA—Associate in Liberal Arts
AM—Master of Arts
AME—Advanced Master of Education
AMT—Master of Arts in Teaching
AgE—Agricultural Engineer
AOS—Associate in Occupational Studies
AS—Associate in Science
ASB—Associate in Specialized Business
ASN—Associate of Science in Nursing
AST—Associate in Specialized Technology
ATE—Associate in Technical Education
AVE—Associate in Vocational Education
BA—Bachelor of Arts
BAEd—Bachelor of Arts in Education
BAGE—Bachelor of Arts in General Education
BAMus—Bachelor of Arts in Music
BArch—Bachelor of Arts in Architecture
BBA—Bachelor of Business Administration
BBS—Bachelor of Business Science
BCS—Bachelor of Continuing Studies
BD—Bachelor of Divinity
BES—Bachelor of Elective Studies
BFA—Bachelor of Fine Arts
BGS—Bachelor of General Studies
BHL—Bachelor of Hebrew Literature (or Letters)
BID—Bachelor of Industrial Design
BIM—Bachelor of Industrial Management
BIS—Bachelor of Independent Studies
BLS—Bachelor of Library Science or Liberal Studies
BMus—Bachelor of Music
BMus Ed—Bachelor of Music Education
BPA—Bachelor of Professional Arts
BRE—Bachelor of Religious Education
BS—Bachelor of Science
BSAA—Bachelor of Science in Applied Arts
BSBA—Bachelor of Science in Business Administration
BSCE—Bachelor of Science in Civil Engineering
BSE—Bachelor of Science in Engineering
BSEd—Bachelor of Science in Education
BSEE—Bachelor of Science in Electrical Engineering
BSM—Bachelor in Sacred Music
BSME—Bachelor of Science in Mechanical Engineering
BSN—Bachelor of Science in Nursing
BSPA—Bachelor of Science in Public Administration
BSPh—Bachelor of Science in Pharmacy
BSS—Bachelor of Secretarial Science
BSW—Bachelor of Social Work
BT—Bachelor of Technology
BTh—Bachelor of Theology
CAS—Certificate Administrative Specialist, or Certificate in Advanced Studies
CE—Civil Engineer
ChE—Chemical Engineer
DB—Bachelor of Divinity
DC—Doctor of Chiropractic
DCL—Doctor of Civil Law
DD—Doctor of Divinity
DDS—Doctor of Dental Surgery
DHL—Doctor of Hebrew Literature
DLS—Doctor of Library Science
DML—Doctor of Modern Languages
DPH—Doctor of Public Health
DSW—Doctor of Social Work
DVM—Doctor of Veterinary Medicine
EE—Electrical Engineer
EM—Mining Engineer
EdB—Bachelor of Education
EdD—Doctor of Education
EdM—Master of Education
ExM—Master of Extension (Agriculture)
JD—Doctor of Jurisprudence
JSD—Doctor of Juridical Science
MA—Master of Arts
MAEd—Master of Arts in Education
MALL—Master of Arts in Liberal Learning
MALS—Master of Arts in Liberal Studies
MAR—Master of Arts in Religion
MAT—Master of Arts in Teaching
MBA—Master of Business Administration
MC—Master in Counseling
MCL—Master of Comparative Law, or Master of Civil Law
MCP—Master in Civic Planning
MDS—Master in Dental Surgery
MDiv—Master of Divinity
MFA—Master in Fine Arts
MI—Master in Instruction
MLS—Master in Library Science
MMEd—Master in Music Education
MMP—Master in Marine Policy
MPA—Master of Public Administration, or Master of Public Affairs
MPH—Master of Public Health
MPL—Master in Parliamentary Law
MRE—Master in Religious Education
MS—Master of Science
MSHE—Master of Science in Home Economics
MST—Master of Science in Teaching
MSW—Master of Social Work
MTh—Master of Theology
MURP—Master in Urban and Regional Planning
NE—Nuclear Engineer
OD—Doctor of Optometry
PhB—Bachelor of Philosophy
PhC—Pharmaceutical Chemistry, or Philosopher of Chiropractic
PhD—Doctor of Philosophy
PhM—Master of Philosophy
SJD—Doctor of Juridical Science
ScD—Doctor of Science
SEd—Specialist in Education
STD—Doctor of Sacred Theology
STL—Licentiate in Sacred Theology
STM—Master of Sacred Theology
ThB—Bachelor of Theology
ThM—Master of Theology

CAPSULE DESCRIPTIONS OF THE SCHOOLS

ALABAMA (AL)

[J1] AIR FORCE, COMMUNITY COLLEGE OF THE
Maxwell Air Force Base 36112

[1] ALABAMA, UNIVERSITY OF
University 35486, (205) 348-5666
Dean of Admissions: Dr. Lawrence Durham

- **Undergraduates: 6,490m, 6,267w; 16,385 total (including graduates)**
- **Tuition & Fees (1982/83): $1,075 (in-state), $2,290 (out-of-state)**
- **Room & Board: $2,175**
- **Degrees offered: BA, BS, BFA, BMus, BSN, BSW, BSEd, BSBA, BSE's**
- **Mean ACT 21; mean SAT 450v, 470m**
- **Student-faculty ratio: 18 to 1**

A public university established in 1831. 520-acre small city main campus 56 miles southwest of Birmingham. Served by air, rail, and bus.
Academic Character SACS and professional accreditation. Semester system, 3-week May interim, 2 5-week summer terms. 48 majors offered by the College of Arts & Sciences, 16 by the College of Commerce & Business Administration, 15 by the College of Education, 11 by the College of Engineering, 8 by the School of Communication, 13 by the School of Home Economics, 1 by the School of Nursing, and 3 by the School of Social Work. New College offers flexible, independent programs for highly motivated students leading to a BA or BS. Special and double majors. Minor sometimes required. Minors offered in most major fields and many additional areas. Distributive requirements. Graduate and professional degrees granted. Independent study, honors program, Phi Beta Kappa, cooperative work/study, pass/fail, internships. Preprofessional programs in dentistry, law, medicine, optometry, physical therapy, social work, and speech-language pathology. 2-year preprofessional transfer programs in dental hygiene, medical record administration, occupational therapy, pharmacy, physical therapy. 3-1 programs in dentistry and medicine. 5-year BA/MBA or BS/MBA program. Study abroad. Early childhood, elementary, secondary, and special education certification. AFROTC, ROTC. Computer center, observatory. 1,300,000-volume library.
Financial ACT FAS. University scholarships, grants, loans; PELL, SEOG, NDSL, GSL, NSL, CWS. Priority application deadline March 15.
Admissions High school graduation with 12 units required. GED accepted. ACT or SAT required. $15 application fee. Rolling admissions; deadline August 1. *Early Admission* Program. SEARCH program for concurrent enrollment. Transfers accepted. Credit possible for CEEB AP and CLEP exams. Summer Trial Admission Program.
Student Life Student government. Newspaper, magazines, yearbook, radio & TV stations. Music, debate, and drama groups. Afro-American Association. Numerous academic, honorary, political, professional, recreational, religious, service, and special interest organizations. 29 fraternities and 20 sororities, all with houses. 35% of men and 22% of women join. No coed dorms. Married-student housing. 33% of students live on campus. Liquor prohibited on campus. 9 intercollegiate sports for men, 8 for women; several intramurals. NCAA, Southeastern Conference. Student body composition: 10% Black, 89% White, 1% Other. 25% from out of state.

■[1] ALABAMA, UNIVERSITY OF
University Station, Birmingham 35294, (205) 934-4011, 5268
Director of Admissions: Don Belcher

- **Undergraduates: 2,608m, 3,628w; 14,867 total (including graduates)**
- **Tuition (1982/83): $1,026 (in-state), $2,052 (out-of-state)**
- **Fees: $5-$40**
- **Degrees offered: BA, BS, BSE, BSN, BSSW**
- **Mean ACT 18**
- **Student-faculty ratio: 9 to 1**

A public university established in 1966. 241-acre urban campus in Birmingham. Served by air, rail, and bus.
Academic Character SACS and professional accreditation. Trimester system with miniterms, 10-week summer term. 6 majors offered by the School of Business, 8 by the School of Education, 4 by the School of Engineering, 11 by the School of Humanities, 7 by the School of Natural Sciences & Mathematics, and 9 by the School of Social & Behavioral Sciences. Graduate schools of medicine, dentistry, optometry, nursing, and community & allied health also on campus. Minor required. Interdepartmental and self-designed majors and minors possible. Minors offered in most major fields. Distributive requirements. Graduate and professional degrees granted. Honors program, cooperative work/study, limited pass/fail, credit by exam. Preprofessional transfer programs in community & allied health and nursing. Member Marine Environmental Sciences Consortium. Cross-registration with Birmingham Southern, Jefferson State Junior College, Miles, and Samford. Elementary, secondary, and special education certification. ROTC; AFROTC at Samford. 650,000-volume combined libraries.
Financial CEEB CSS. University scholarships, grants, loans; PELL, SEOG, AL state grants, FISL, NDSL, GSL, CWS. Apply for federal programs by April 1.
Admissions High school graduation with 16 units required. GED accepted in special cases. ACT or SAT required (ACT preferred). $15 application fee. Rolling admissions; suggest applying by 4 weeks before beginning of fall term. *Early Entrance* and *Early Decision* programs. Transfers accepted. Credit possible for CEEB AP and CLEP exams; university has own advanced placement program.
Student Life Student government, newspaper, literary magazine. Dance, drama, film, and music groups. Athletic, honorary, and special interest organizations. 10 fraternities and 6 sororities. 4% join. Limited housing on first-come basis. 20% of students live on campus. Liquor prohibited. 6 intercollegiate sports for men, 5 for women; intramurals. NCAA and Sun Belt Conference. Student body composition: 1% Asian, 19% Black, 79% White, 1% Other. 4% from out of state.

■[1] ALABAMA, UNIVERSITY OF
Huntsville 35899, (205) 895-6210
Registrar and Director of Admissions: Nan G. Hall

- **Enrollment: 2,829m, 2,630w**
- **Tuition (1982/83): $966 (in-state), $1,932 (out-of-state)**
- **Room: $1,000 (apartments)**
- **Degrees offered: BA, BS, BSBA, BSE, BSN**
- **Mean ACT 22.7**
- **Student-faculty ratio: 25 to 1**

A public university established in 1950. 332-acre urban campus in research park area of Huntsville, 100 miles north of Birmingham and 100 miles south of Nashville. Air, bus, and rail service.
Academic Character SACS and professional accreditation. Trimester system, summer term. 38 majors offered by the schools of Administrative Sciences, Humanities & Behavioral Sciences, Nursing, and Science & Engineering. Environmental science certificate program. MSN, MAS, MA, MS, MSE, MSOR, PhD granted. Independent study, cooperative work/study. Pass/fail for juniors and seniors. Preprofessional programs in dentistry, law, medical technology, and medicine. Limited cross-registration with Alabama A&M, Athens, John C. Calhoun Junior, and Oakwood colleges. Close cooperation with NASA's Marshall Space Center and the US Army Missile Command, and with numerous private businesses. Elementary and secondary education certification. ROTC at Alabama A&M. 180,000-volume library.
Financial ACT FAS. University scholarships, grants, loans, nursing scholarships; PELL, SEOG, NDSL, NSL, CWS. Apply for federal programs by April 1.
Admissions High school graduation with 16 units required. GED accepted. ACT required; SAT accepted. $15 application fee. Rolling admissions; suggest applying in fall of 12th year. Deadline 2 weeks before beginning of term. *Early Decision* Program. Admission deferral possible. Transfers accepted. Credit possible for CLEP exams. University has own advanced placement program.
Student Life Student government. Newspaper, music and drama groups. Athletic, academic, honorary, service, religious, and special interest organizations. 4 fraternities and 4 sororities. No dorms, only university apartments. 5% of students live on campus. Liquor restricted; unauthorized drugs, fireworks, gambling prohibited. 2 intercollegiate sports for men, 2 for women; several intramural and club sports. NAIA, Southern States Conference. Student body composition: 4% Black, 93% White, 3% Other. 1% from out of state.

[1] ALABAMA AGRICULTURAL AND MECHANICAL UNIVERSITY
PO Box 285, Normal 35762, (205) 859-7468
Director of Admissions: A. G. Adams

- **Undergraduates: 1,853m, 1,612w**
- **Tuition (1982/83): $620 (in-state), $1,180 (out-of-state)**
- **Room & Board: $1,380**
- **Degrees offered: BA, BS, AS**
- **Student-faculty ratio: 15 to 1**

A public land-grant university established in 1875. Suburban 800-acre campus 2 miles from downtown Huntsville. Bus service; air, rail, and bus in Huntsville.
Academic Character SACS and professional accreditation. Semester system, summer term. 58 majors offered in the areas of accounting, agriculture, business, clothing & merchandising, communications, education, engineering, home economics, humanities, office administration, printing, sciences, social sciences, social work, and timber harvesting management. Distributive requirements. Graduate degrees granted. Independent study, honors program, cooperative work/study, internships. Preprofessional programs in dentistry and medicine. 3-1 program in medical technology. Dual degree programs in engineering, industrial management, and other areas with Georgia Institute of Technology. 2-2 nursing programs with Emory. 6-year dual degree program with Tuskegee Institute for Veterinary Medicine. Other programs with 7 area colleges. Exchange program with Calhoun Community College. Elementary, secondary, and special education certification. ROTC. 400,000-volume library.
Financial CEEB CSS and ACT FAS. University scholarships, grants, loans, athletic grants-in-aid; PELL, SEOG, Alabama Student Assistance Program, NDSL, FISL, GSL, CWS, Project Biweekly Program. Aid application deadline April 1.
Admissions High school graduation with a GPA of 'C' in major courses required. GED accepted. SAT or ACT required. $10 application fee. Rolling admissions; suggest applying early in 12th year. *Early Admission* and *Early Decision* programs. Admission deferral possible. Transfers accepted. Credit possible for CEEB AP and CLEP exams. Conditional admission possible.

Student Life Student, class, and residence hall governments. Angelic Voice of Faith. Music, dance, and drama groups. Honorary, service, religious, academic, and special interest organizations. 4 fraternities and 3 sororities. 40% of students live on campus. No coed dorms. Resident freshmen may not have cars on campus. Class attendance required. 8 intercollegiate sports for men; several intramural sports. NAIA, NCAA, SIAC. Student body composition: 1% Asian, 88% Black, 2% Hispanic, 3% Native American, 6% White. 10% from out of state.

[J1] ALABAMA CHRISTIAN COLLEGE
5345 Atlanta Hwy., Montgomery 36193, (205) 272-5820
- **Undergraduates: 744m, 622w; 1,512 total (including part-time)**
- **Degrees offered: AA**
- **Mean ACT 17**

A private coeducational college affiliated with the Church of Christ. Located in the capital of Alabama. Air and bus service.
Academic Character SACS accreditation. Trimester system, summer term. Montgomery traditional program awards associate degrees.
Admissions Rolling admissions. ACT of 17 for standard-admittance students. *Early Admissions* and *Early Decision* programs.
Student Life Student body composition: 18% minority.

[J2] ALABAMA LUTHERAN ACADEMY AND COLLEGE
Selma — see Concordia College of Selma

[1] ALABAMA STATE UNIVERSITY
Montgomery 36195, (205) 832-6072
Acting Director of Admissions: Gregory Singleton
- **Undergraduates: 1,450m, 1,969w; 4,034 total (including graduates)**
- **Tuition (1982/83): $600 (in-state), $1,200 (out-of-state)**
- **Room & Board: $1,320**
- **Degrees offered: BA, BS, BFA, AA**
- **Student-faculty ratio: 20 to 1**

A public university established in 1874. 81-acre urban campus located in the capital of Alabama. Air and bus service.
Academic Character SACS and professional accreditation. Trimester system, 11-week summer term. 15 majors offered by the College of Arts & Sciences, 6 by the College of Business Administration, 7 by the College of Education, 1 by the School of Music, and 2 by the Division of Health, Physical Education, Safety, & Recreation. Minors in most major fields and in additional areas. Masters degrees offered. Associate degrees in business administration, child development, community services, general studies, recreation leadership, secretarial science. Independent study, honors program, cooperative work/study, pass/fail, internships. Pre-law major. Dual degree program in engineering with Auburn. Early childhood, elementary, secondary, special, music, and teacher-librarian education certification. AFROTC; NROTC & ROTC available nearby. 145,300-volume library.
Financial University scholarships, loans; PELL, SEOG, NDSL, CWS. Application deadline June 1.
Admissions High school graduation or equivalency exam required. SAT or ACT required. No application fee. Rolling admissions; deadline late August. $50 room deposit required on acceptance of admissions offer. Transfers accepted. Credit possible for CEEB AP and CLEP exams.
Student Life Student government. Newspaper, yearbook. Marching band, choir, other music and drama groups. Religious, service, honorary, athletic, academic, and special interest groups. 4 fraternities and 3 sororities; none with houses. No coed dorms. Some married-student housing. 40% of students live on campus. Liquor prohibited. Class attendance expected. 5 hour phys ed requirement. 6 intercollegiate sports for men, 5 for women; intramurals. NAIA, NCAA. Student body composition: 99.5% Black, 0.2% White, 0.3% Other. 15% from out of state.

[J1] ALEXANDER CITY STATE JUNIOR COLLEGE
PO Box 699, Alexander City 35010

[1] ATHENS STATE COLLEGE
Athens 35611, (205) 232-1802
Director of Admissions & Registrar: John W. King
- **Undergraduates: 479m, 484w**
- **Tuition (1982/83): $900-$1,080 (in-state), $1,800-2,160 (out-of-state)**
- **Room: $450-$585**
- **Degrees offered: BA, BS, BSEd**
- **Student-faculty ratio: 16 to 1**

A public upper-division university founded in 1822. Small-town environment located 20 miles west of Huntsville, 90 miles north of Birmingham, and 90 miles south of Nashville.
Academic Character SACS accreditation. Trimester system, summer terms. Majors offered in accounting, art, behavioral science, biology, business administration, chemistry, comprehensive science, criminal justice, education (8), English, health science, history, instrumentation science, instrumentation technology, language arts, mathematics, nondestructive testing science, nondestructive testing technology, office administration, personnel psychology, physics, political science, psychology, religion, religion & philosophy, social science, sociology, technical-general business, and technical management. Minors in some major fields and in computer science, music, philosophy. Courses in anthropology, geography. Distributive requirements. Cooperative work/study. Preprofessional programs in dentistry, law, medicine, theology. Early childhood, elementary, middle school, secondary, trade & industrial, vocational, and special education certification. 63,000-volume library plus access to area libraries.
Financial ACT FAS. PELL, SEOG, AL state grants, FISL, NDSL, CWS. Application deadline March 15 (federal aid).
Admissions 2-year college degree, or 96 quarter-hours of college credit with a 2.0 avg, or 86 quarter-hours of credit with a 2.0 avg and prior college's Deans's permission, or technical school diploma required. Transcript from previously attended college required. $15 application fee. Rolling admissions. Dual enrollment with a junior/community college possible. Non-degree seeking students accepted. Credit possible for CLEP exams and for non-traditional learning.
Student Life Student government. Newspaper, yearbook, literary magazine. Baptist Student Union, Ministerial Association. Academic, honorary, and professional groups. 1 fraternity and 2 sororities. Dorms for men and women. Intercollegiate basketball; intramural & recreational sports. NAIA, Southern States Conference. Student body composition: 19% minority.

[1] AUBURN UNIVERSITY
Auburn 36849, (205) 826-4000
Director of Admissions: Charles E. Reeder
- **Undergraduates: 9,116m, 6,681w; 18,677 total (including graduates)**
- **Tuition (1982/83): $990 (in-state), $2,280 (out-of-state)**
- **Room: $555-$1,125**
- **Degrees offered: BA, BS, BArch, BAv Mgt, BFA, BInd Des, BInt Des, BLArch, BMus, BSBA, BSEd, BSN, BSPharm, BText's and BE's**
- **Mean ACT 23; mean SAT 490v, 550m**
- **Student-faculty ratio: 17 to 1**

A public land-grant university founded in 1856. 1,871-acre small town campus 59 miles east of Montgomery and 116 miles southwest of Atlanta. Air and bus service.
Academic Character SACS and professional accreditation. Trimester system, 11-week summer term. 147 majors offered by the schools of Arts & Sciences, Education, Agriculture, Architecture & Fine Arts, Engineering, Home Economics, Business, Nursing, Pharmacy, and Veterinary Medicine. Distributive requirements. Graduate and professional degrees granted. Independent study, honors program, cooperative work/study, pass/fail, internships. Program in environmental health. Preprofessional program in hospital administration. Preprofessional and 3-1 programs in law, medicine, dentistry, optometry, and veterinary medicine. 3-2 programs in many areas including agriculture, business, engineering. Study abroad. Elementary, secondary, and special education certification. AFROTC, NROTC, ROTC. Computer center. 1,100,000-volume library with microform resources.
Financial ACT FAS. University scholarships, loans; PELL, SEOG, NDSL, GSL, CWS. Priority application deadline for scholarships & loans March 15. Loan deadline 8 weeks before beginning of quarter.
Admissions High school graduation with 16 units required. Equivalency exams may be accepted. ACT or SAT required (must be ACT for AL residents). 'C' average and 18 composite ACT or similar SAT required for admission. $15 application fee. Rolling admissions; suggest applying by January of 12th year. Deadline 3 weeks before beginning of term. *Early Entrance* and *Concurrent Enrollment* programs. Admission deferral possible. Transfers accepted. Credit possible for CEEB AP and CLEP exams; departments have own placement exams.
Student Life Student government. Debate, community service. Radio and TV stations, several music, dance, and drama groups. Many athletic, academic, political, religious, honorary, and special interest organizations. 30 fraternities and 17 sororities. No coed dorms. Married-student apartments. 30% of students live on campus. Liquor prohibited. Numerous intercollegiate and intramural sports for men and women. Southeastern Conference. Student body composition: 0.5% Asian, 2.3% Black, 0.3% Hispanic, 0.1% Native American, 95.6% White, 1.2% Other. 35% from out of state.

■[1] AUBURN UNIVERSITY
Montgomery 36193, (205) 279-9110
Director of Admissions: Lee Davis
- **Undergraduates: 1,616m, 1,515w**
- **Tuition (1982/83): $795 (in-state), $1,590 (out-of-state)**
- **Room: $810-$900**
- **Degrees offered: BA, BS, BSBA, BSN, BSElem Ed**

A public university established in 1967. 500-acre campus 7 miles east of downtown Montgomery, the capital of Alabama. Air and bus service.
Academic Character SACS accreditation. Trimester system, summer term. 21 majors offered by the School of Science, 10 by the School of Business, 8 by the School of Education, 13 by the School of Liberal Arts, and 1 by the School of Nursing. Double majors. Distributive requirements. MBA, MEd, MPA, MPS, MSCJ, MSPg granted. Cooperative work/study, internships. Preprofessional programs in law, engineering, medicine, dentistry, optometry, pharmacy, and veterinary medicine. Cross-registration with Auburn (at Auburn) and Huntington College. Member Marine Environmental Sciences Consortium. Study abroad. Elementary and secondary education certification. AFROTC, ROTC. Computer center. Library.
Financial University scholarships, loans; PELL, SEOG, NSL, NDSL, GSL, CWS. Application deadline March 15.
Admissions High school graduation or equivalent required. GED accepted. ACT or SAT required (must be ACT for AL residents). $10 application fee. Rolling admissions; suggest applying early in 12th year. Application deadline September 2. Credit possible for CLEP exams.
Student Life University chorus, drama groups. Fraternities and sororities. Limited housing available in university-owned apartments. Regular class attendance expected. 2 intercollegiate and 14 intramural sports. Student body composition: 0.9% Asian, 15% Black, 84.1% White.

[1] BIRMINGHAM—SOUTHERN COLLEGE
800 Eighth Ave. W., Birmingham 35254, (205) 328-5250
Vice President for Admissions: Robert Dortch

- **Undergraduates: 763m, 771w**
- **Tuition (1982/83): $3,990**
- **Room & Board: $1,835; Fees: $75**
- **Degrees offered: BA, BS, BFA, BMus, BMus Ed, BSN**
- **Mean ACT 25; mean SAT 510v, 525m**
- **Student-faculty ratio: 16 to 1**

A private college founded in 1856, associated with the United Methodist Church. 200-acre wooded campus 3 miles west of Birmingham business district. Air, rail, and bus service.

Academic Character SACS and professional accreditation. 4-1-4 calendar, 9-week summer term. Majors offered in the areas of accounting, art, business administration, computer science, dance, drama & speech, education, health/phys ed/athletics, mathematics, languages & literatures, music (8), music education, music merchandising, nursing, philosophy, psychology, religion, sciences, and social sciences. Interdisciplinary and self-designed majors. Distributive requirements. Honors program, Phi Beta Kappa, pass/fail, internships. Preprofessional programs in business, law, dentistry, medicine, medical technology, optometry, and pharmacy. 3-2 engineering program with Auburn. Exchange program with U Alabama (Birmingham). Member Marine Environmental Sciences Consortium, Southern College and University Union. Washington Semester. Study abroad. Early childhood, elementary, and secondary education certification. AFROTC at Samford; ROTC at UAB. Planetarium, computer center, language lab. 132,000-volume library.

Financial CEEB CSS. College scholarships, grants, loans, tuition reduction for children of ministers and for those preparing for Christian service, deferred payment; PELL, SEOG, AL state grants, NDSL, FISL, CWS. Application deadlines March 15 (scholarships), April 15 (loans).

Admissions High school graduation with 15 units required. GED accepted. Music majors must audition. ACT or SAT required. $10 application fee. Rolling admissions; suggest applying before February 15 of 12th year. $25 deposit required on acceptance of admissions offer. *Early Admission* and *Concurrent Enrollment* programs. Admission deferral possible. Transfers accepted. Credit possible for CEEB AP and CLEP exams.

Student Life Student government. Newspaper, literary magazine, yearbook. Many music, dance, and drama groups. Black Student Union. Academic, honorary, and special interest organizations. 5 fraternities and 6 sororities, some with houses. 41% of men and women join. Unmarried students under 21 must live at home or on campus. No coed dorms. Married-student apartments. 80% of students live on campus. Liquor prohibited. Honor Code. 4 intercollegiate sports for men, 1 for women; several intramurals. NAIA, Southern States Conference. Student body composition: 0.5% Asian, 12% Black, 0.2% Hispanic, 87.3% White. 20% from out of state.

[J1] BREWER STATE JUNIOR COLLEGE
Fayette 35555

[J1] CHATTAHOOCHEE VALLEY COMMUNITY COLLEGE
2602 Savage Drive, Phenix City 36867

[J2] CONCORDIA COLLEGE OF SELMA
1804 Green Street, Selma 36701

[J1] ENTERPRISE STATE JUNIOR COLLEGE
Enterprise 36361

[J1] GADSDEN STATE JUNIOR COLLEGE
George Wallace Drive, Gadsden 35999, (205) 546-0484, ext. 250
Director of Admissions & Registrar: Jack N. Little

- **Enrollment: 3,538 (for credit); 4,873 total**
- **Tuition (1982/83): $375 (in-state), $750 (out-of-state)**
- **Room & Board: $1,395**
- **Degrees offered: AA, AS, AAS**

A public junior college established in 1963. 246-acre campus with 4 off-campus centers.

Academic Character SACS and professional accreditation. Trimester system, 10-week summer term. AA offered with a major in liberal arts; AS with 20 majors in the areas of agriculture, business administration, computer science, education, engineering, home economics, mathematics, music, office administration, religion, sciences, and health, physical education, & recreation; AAS with 25 majors in the areas of agribusiness, allied health fields, aviation, banking & finance, broadcasting, business, computer science, court reporting, early childhood, electronic engineering, fire science, food marketing, human services, insurance, law enforcement, management, merchandising, nursing, office administration, and religion. Preprofessional degrees in forestry, law, medical technology, medicine, dentistry, pharmacy, veterinary medicine. Distributive requirements. Independent study. Cooperative work/study in engineering. Linkage programs for degrees in many allied health and technological fields. Continuing education & certificate programs. Summer study abroad. Computer. A-V materials, over 70,000-volume library.

Financial CEEB CSS. College & nursing scholarships, state grants; PELL, SEOG, NDSL, GSL, NSL, CWS, college work program. Priority application deadline May 1.

Admissions High school graduation required. GED or equivalent accepted. Special requirements for some programs. $5 application fee. Rolling admissions. *Early Admission* and *Early Decision* programs. Dual Enrollment & summer programs for high school students. Admission deferral possible. Transfers accepted. Credit possible for CEEB CLEP exams, other tests, & experience. Provisional acceptance possible. Special Services Program, Upward Bound.

Student Life Student government, newspaper. Circle K, Jaycees. Academic, honorary, musical, professional, religious, and special interest clubs. 1 dorm with separate facilities for 112 women & 112 men. Class attendance expected. Gambling & firearms prohibited. 3 quarters of phys ed required except for over 26 & veterans. 4 intercollegiate sports; intramurals. Student body composition: 14% minority.

[J1] GEORGE C. WALLACE STATE COMMUNITY COLLEGE
Dothan 36303

[J1] GEORGE C. WALLACE STATE COMMUNITY COLLEGE
PO Box 1049, Selma 36701

[J1] GEORGE C. WALLACE STATE TECHNICAL COMMUNITY COLLEGE
Hanceville 35077

[1] HUNTINGDON COLLEGE
Montgomery 36106, (205) 834-3300
Director of Admissions: Jerald T. Lipscomb

- **Enrollment: 243m, 296w; total 737 (including part-time)**
- **Tuition (1982/83): $2,650**
- **Room & Board: $2,100; Fees: $50**
- **Degrees offered: BA**
- **Mean ACT 20; mean SAT 884**
- **Student-faculty ratio: 13 to 1**

A private college affiliated with the United Methodist Church. Established in 1854 as Alabama Conference Female College, became coed in 1946. 58-acre campus in city of Montgomery. Air, rail, and bus service nearby.

Academic Character SACS accreditation. Semester system, January term, 2 summer terms. Majors offered in accounting, art, biology, business administration, chemistry, Christian education, economics, elementary education, English, history, management science, mathematics, medical administration, music, physical education, psychology, religion & philosophy, social work, and speech & drama. Self-designed majors. Courses in 8 additional areas. Distributive requirements; 12 hours in Bible and Bible-related courses required. Evening program offers BA and AA in general studies. Independent study, honors program, cooperative work/study, pass/fail, internships. Preprofessional programs in dentistry, law, medical technology, medicine, theology. 3-2 engineering program with Auburn. Allied health program with U Alabama (Birmingham). Cross-registration with Auburn. Member of Alabama Consortium for the Development of Higher Education and Marine Environmental Sciences Consortium at Dauphin Island. Study abroad. Elementary, secondary, and special education certification. ROTC at Auburn; AFROTC at Alabama State U. Computer center, art gallery. 95,000-volume library.

Financial CEEB CSS and ACT FAS. College scholarships, loans, deferred payment; PELL, SEOG, NDSL, FISL, CWS. File FAF by June 1; aid application deadline August 1.

Admissions High school graduation with at least 9 units required. GED accepted. Interview encouraged. SAT or ACT required. $10 application fee. Rolling admissions; suggest applying early. $50 tuition and $50 room deposits required with acceptance of admissions offer. *Early Entrance* and *Concurrent Enrollment* programs. Transfers accepted. Credit possible for CEEB AP and CLEP exams.

Student Life Student government. Newspaper, literary magazine, yearbook. Huntingdon Players, summer rep theater. International Relations Club, Campus Ministries, academic, honorary, other special interest organizations. 2 fraternities and 2 sororities. Students must live at home or on campus. No coed dorms. 52% of students live on campus. Class attendance expected; attendance at specified convocations required. 3 intercollegiate sports for men, 3 for women; intramurals. NAIA, Southern States Conference. Student body composition: 1% Asian, 11% Black, 88% White. 25% from out of state.

[1] JACKSONVILLE STATE UNIVERSITY
Jacksonville 36265, (205) 435-9820
University Registrar: Jerry D. Smith

- **Undergraduates: 2,164m, 2,356w; 6,328 total (including graduates)**
- **Tuition (1982/83): $700 (in-state), $1,050 (out-of-state)**
- **Room & Board: $1,388-$1,488**
- **Degrees offered: BA, BS, BSEd**
- **Student-faculty ratio: 24 to 1**

A public university located in the foothills of the Appalachians, established in 1883. 175-acre small town campus 60 miles east of Birmingham and 80 miles west of Atlanta. Airport 15 miles away.

Academic Character SACS and professional accreditation. 4-1-4 calendar, split summer term with minimester in May. Majors offered in art, biology, business (6), chemistry, clothing, computer science, corrections, dietetics, drama, economics, education (11), English, food services, forensic science, general studies, geography, history, home economics, law enforcement, mathematics, military science, music (5), nursing, physics, political science, production management, psychology, recreation, sociology. Minor required. Minors offered in major fields and in basic engineering. MSEd, MA, MS, MBA, MPA granted. Independent study, cooperative work/study, internships. Preprofessional programs in agriculture, dentistry, engineering, law, medicine, pharmacy, and veterinary medicine. 3-1 programs in medical technology and law. Courses at Marine Environmental

Sciences Consortium Sea Lab, Dauphin Island. Elementary, secondary, and special education certification. ROTC. 345,000-volume library with microform resources.
Financial University scholarships, loans, nursing scholarships; PELL, SEOG, SSIG, NDSL, FISL, NSL, HELP, CWS, University Aid Program. Preferred application deadline April 15.
Admissions High school graduation with 15 units required. GED accepted. ACT or SAT (ACT preferred) by end of first year. Nursing & education programs have GPA requirements. $10 application fee. Rolling admissions; suggest applying at least 3 months prior to registration. $20 room deposit required as early as possible. *Concurrent Enrollment* Program. Transfers accepted. Credit possible for CEEB AP and CLEP exams. University has own advanced placement exams.
Student Life Student government. Newspaper, yearbook, music, dance, and drama groups. Honorary societies. 3rd and 4th year students may live off campus. 1 coed and several single-sex dorms. International House, married-student housing. 35% of students live on campus. Liquor prohibited. Attendance at 75% of classes necessary for credit. 9 intercollegiate sports for men, 5 for women; several intramural sports. AIAW, Alabama Collegiate and Gulf South Conferences. Student body composition: 14% Black, 84% White, 2% Other. 10% from out of state.

[J1] JAMES C. FAULKNER STATE COMMUNITY COLLEGE
Bay Minette 36507

[J1] JEFFERSON DAVIS STATE JUNIOR COLLEGE
Brewton 36427

[J1] JEFFERSON STATE JUNIOR COLLEGE
Birmingham 35215

[J1] JOHN C. CALHOUN STATE COMMUNITY COLLEGE
Decatur 35602

[1] JUDSON COLLEGE
Marion 36756, (205) 683-6161
Dean of Admissions: Helen Patricia Turnipseed

- **Undergraduates: 400w • Tuition & Fees(1981/82): $2,190**
- **Room & Board: $1,460-$1,580 (2-terms), $1,960-$2,080 (3-terms)**
- **Degrees offered: BA, BS**
- **Student-faculty ratio: 12 to 1**

A private women's college founded in 1838, owned and operated by the Alabama Baptist State Convention. Small town campus 80 miles southwest of Birmingham.
Academic Character SACS and professional accreditation. Semester system, optional May/June term allows degree in 3 or 4 years. Majors in applied music (3), art, biology, business (4), chemistry, clothing & textiles, computer technology & management, education areas, English, history & political science, home economics education, interior design, mathematics, modern foreign languages, psychology, religious studies, retail fashion merchandising, social work, and sociology. Major & minor, double major, or area of concentration & related courses required. Minors in major fields and in drama & speech, equitation, French, journalism, organ, physics, piano, Spanish, and voice. Distributive requirements. Certificate programs in church office management, office administration. Honors program, cooperative work/study, internships. Preprofessional programs in dentistry, law, medicine, nursing, pharmacy, physical therapy. Some shared classes with Marion Military Institute. Combined BS/Medical Technology degree with Birmingham Baptist hospitals. 2-2 BSN and BS/BSN programs with Samford U. Cooperative program with Birmingham airport in air traffic control. Study abroad. Early childhood, elementary, health & physical education, music, and secondary education certification. ROTC at Marion Military Institute. 50,000-volume library.
Financial ACT FAS. College scholarships, grants, loans, state grants, Baptist Women's Missionary Union work scholarships, discounts for Baptist ministers' dependents, deferred payment. PELL, SEOG, NDSL, GSL, CWS.
Admissions High school graduation with 15 units required. ACT or SAT required. $10 application fee. Rolling admissions. $45 room deposit required on acceptance of admissions offer. *Early Admission* and *Early Decision* programs. Admission deferral possible. Transfers accepted. Credit possible for CEEB AP, CLEP, ACT, and college exams. College Opportunity Program, special admission for adult students.
Student Life Student government. Journals, yearbook. Campus Ministries. Academic, honorary, musical, professional, and special interest groups. Women's dorms. Honor code. No liquor on campus. Class attendance required except for Dean's list students. Intercollegiate tennis, basketball, riding, volleyball; intramurals.

[J1] LAWSON STATE COMMUNITY COLLEGE
3060 Wilson Road, Birmingham 35221

[1] LIVINGSTON UNIVERSITY
Livingston 35470, (205) 652-9661
Director of Admissions: Ervin L. Wood

- **Undergraduates: 466m, 472w; 1,280 total (including graduates)**
- **Tuition (1982/83): $750**
- **Room & Board: $1,485; Fees: $138**
- **Degrees offered: BA, BS, BMus Ed, AS**
- **Mean ACT 14.5**
- **Student-faculty ratio: 18 to 1**

A public university established in 1840. 272-acre rural campus 116 miles from Birmingham and 60 miles from Tuscaloosa. Served by bus and rail.
Academic Character SACS and professional accreditation. Trimester system, summer term. Majors offered in accounting, biology, business administration, chemistry, computer information processing, English, environmental science, general business, history, management, marine biology, mathematics, music, physical science, sociology, and in education (early childhood, elementary, secondary (4), industrial arts, physical, music, natural science, secretarial, & social science). Minors and courses offered in 16 additional fields. Distributive requirements. Freshman Studies Program. MEd, MSCE, MS granted. Independent study, honors program. Preprofessional programs in allied health, dentistry, law, medicine, and pharmacy. 2-year transfer programs in fisheries & wildlife management and forestry. 3-1 program in medical technology. Associate degrees in 14 allied health fields with U Alabama (Birmingham). 3-2 engineering program with Auburn. Member Alabama Marine Environmental Consortium. Elementary, secondary, industrial, library science, and special education certification. Computer center. 111,000-volume library.
Financial ACT FAS. University scholarships, grants, loans, nursing scholarship, deferred payment; PELL, SEOG, NDSL, FISL, NSL, CWS. Application deadline April 20.
Admissions High school graduation with 15 units required. GED accepted. ACT or SAT required; ACT preferred. $10 application fee. Rolling admissions; suggest applying between January 1 and September 1. *Early Entrance* and *Early Decision* programs. Admission deferral possible. Transfers accepted. Credit possible for CLEP exams; university has own advanced placement program.
Student Life Student government, newspaper, yearbook. Association for Women Students, Afro American Society. Music, athletic, academic, honorary, religious, and special interest groups. 5 fraternities with houses, 3 sororities without houses. 15% of men and 12% of women join. All unmarried 1st and 2nd year students under 20 must live at home or on campus. No coed dorms. Married-student apartments. 50% of students live on campus. Liquor, drugs, gambling, firearms, and fireworks prohibited. Class attendance required. 6 intercollegiate sports for men, 4 for women; several intramurals. AIAW, NCAA, Gulf South Conference. Student body composition: 1% Asian, 32% Black, 67% White. 20% from out of state.

[J1] LURLEEN B. WALLACE STATE JUNIOR COLLEGE
PO Box 1418, Andalusia 36420

[J1] MARION MILITARY INSTITUTE
Marion 36756, (205) 683-6173
Director of Admissions: Lieut. Colonel James Alfred Jackson, Jr.

- **Undergraduates: 400m**
- **Tuition & Fees (1982/83): $3,817**
- **Room & Board: $2,250**
- **Degrees offered: AA, AS**

A private military men's junior college and coed preparatory school founded in 1842. 120-acre small town campus in the hills of west central Alabama.
Academic Character SACS accreditation. Semester system, summer school. 2-year transfer degrees in the fields of liberal arts, science, business administration, pre-medicine, pre-dentistry, pre-law, and pre-engineering. Distributive requirements. ROTC required. Cross-registration with Judson College. ROTC basic and advanced courses offered. A-V center. 75,000-volume library plus access to Judson library.
Financial ACT FAS. College scholarships, ROTC pay (for advanced course), tuition discount for 2nd family member; PELL, SEOG, NDSL, GSL, CWS.
Admissions High school graduation with 16 units required. Entrance exam, SAT, ACT, or Armed Forces Qualifications Test required. Interview encouraged. "Students seeking admission must be of good moral character." Rolling admissions. $50 room deposit required on acceptance of admissions offer, refundable to August 15. *Early Admission* and *Early Decision* programs. Admissions deferral possible. Transfers accepted.
Student Life Newspaper, yearbook. Drama and several music groups. Academic, athletic, honorary, religious, social, and special interest groups. Students must live on campus. 4 men's dorms. Honor system. Class attendance required. 6 intercollegiate sports; extensive intramural & recreational sports.

[1] MILES COLLEGE
PO Box 3800, Birmingham 35208, (205) 923-2771
Director of Admissions: Ethel Van Buren

- **Undergraduates: 438m, 521w**
- **Tuition (1982/83): $2,400**
- **Room & Board: $2,100**
- **Degrees offered: BA, BS**
- **Student-faculty ratio: 13 to 1**

A private college controlled by the Christian Methodist Episcopal Church, established in 1908. 25-acre urban campus located in Fairfield, 6 miles west of downtown Birmingham. Air, rail, and bus in Birmingham.
Academic Character SACS accreditation. Semester system, 8-week summer term. Majors offered in biology, business administration (accounting, finance, management, marketing), business education, chemistry, early childhood education, elementary education, English, mathematics, music, political science, science education, social science, social work, and sociology. Minors. Courses in 6 additional areas. Distributive requirements. Senior comprehensive exams. Independent study, honors program,

cooperative work/study, internships. Member of 4 consortia. Cooperative programs in engineering, physics, veterinary medicine with Tuskegee Inst., Alabama A&M. Cross-registration with U of Alabama (Birmingham). Elementary and secondary education certification. ROTC, AFROTC at Samford and UAB. Afro-American Materials Center. 80,000-volume library.
Financial College scholarships, grants, loans; PELL, SEOG, AL state grants, NDSL, GSL, CWS. United Negro College Fund.
Admissions High school graduation with 20 units required. GED accepted. ACT required. $15 application fee. Rolling admissions; application deadline July 31. *Concurrent Enrollment* Program. Transfers accepted. College has own advanced placement program; exams administered to all entering students. Special Services and Upward Bound programs.
Student Life Student government. Newspaper, yearbook. Music and drama groups, YMCA, YWCA. Academic, professional, and special interest groups. No coed dorms. On-campus apartments. 36% of students live on campus. Class attendance and attendance at 13 College Forum assemblies each semester required. Intercollegiate and intramural sports for men and women. Student body composition: 98% Black, 2% Other. 10% from out of state.

[1] MOBILE COLLEGE
PO Box 13220, Mobile 36613, (205) 675-5990
Director of Admissions: Dr. Leon Pirkle

- **Undergraduates: 230m, 434w; total 1,002 (including part-time)**
- **Tuition (1982/83): $2,250**
- **Room & Board: $1,940; Fees: $55**
- **Degrees offered: BA, BS, BSN**
- **Mean ACT 16**
- **Student-faculty ratio: 20 to 1**

A private college affiliated with the Alabama Baptist Convention, established in 1961. 700-acre urban campus served by air and bus.
Academic Character SACS and professional accreditation. Semester system, 2 5-week summer terms. Majors offered in art, biology, business administration, early childhood education, elementary education, English, health, history, mathematics, music, music education, physical education/recreation, psychology, religion, sociology. Minor required. Minors offered in major fields and in computer science, chemistry, French, German, and speech. Distributives and 5 semesters of religious education required. Independent study, cooperative work/study. Preprofessional programs in medicine, dentistry, engineering, nursing, law, and the ministry. 2-2 program in engineering. Elementary and secondary education certification. ROTC at U of South Alabama. Language lab. 74,000-volume library with microform resources.
Financial CEEB CSS and ACT FAS. University scholarships, grants, loans, nursing scholarships, ministerial grant & ministers' dependents scholarships, deferred payment; PELL, SEOG, NDSL, FISL, NSL, college work program.
Admissions High school graduation required. GED accepted. ACT required. $10 application fee. Suggest applying by July; no deadline. Tuition and room deposits required on acceptance of offer of admission. *Early Entrance* Program. Admission deferral possible. Transfers accepted. Credit possible for CLEP exams.
Student Life Student government. Literary magazine, yearbook, music and drama groups. Ethnic, religious, service, and special interest clubs. Students must live at home or on campus. No coed dorms. Married-student housing. 35% of students live on campus. No liquor or drugs on campus. Class attendance expected; weekly chapel attendance required. 4 semesters of phys ed required. Dress code. 1 intercollegiate sport for men, 1 for women; several intramurals. Student body composition: 13.7% Black, 0.3% Hispanic, 0.1% Native American, 85.7% White, 0.2% Other.

[1] MONTEVALLO, UNIVERSITY OF
Montevallo 35115, (205) 665-2521
Director of Admissions: Robert A. Doyle

- **Undergraduates: 880m, 1,469w**
- **Tuition (1982/83): $868 (in-state), $1,468 (out-of-state)**
- **Room & Board: $1,404-$1,752; Fees: $100**
- **Degrees offered: BA, BS, BFA, BBA, BMus Ed, BMus**
- **Mean ACT 19**
- **Student-faculty ratio: 19 to 1**

A public university established in 1896, became coed in 1956. 500-acre suburban campus 30 miles from Birmingham. Air, bus, and rail in Birmingham.
Academic Character SACS and professional accreditation. Semester system, 2 5-week summer terms. 42 majors offered in the areas of business, home economics, sciences, humanities, social sciences, music, health, communications, and education. Minors in some major fields and in 12 additional areas. Distributives and 3 hours of religion, philosophy, or psychology required. MA, MS, MM, MEd granted. Secretarial science certificate. Independent study, honors program, pass/fail, credit by exam, internships. Preprofessional programs in dentistry, law, medicine, nursing, optometry, pharmacy. 3-2 engineering program with Auburn. Member 2 consortia. Study abroad at several locations. Elementary, secondary, and special education certification. ROTC, AFROTC. Media Center. 162,000-volume library.
Financial CEEB CSS and ACT FAS. University scholarships, loans, departmental scholarships; PELL, SEOG, NDSL, FISL, CWS, University Jobship Program. Priority application deadlines March 1 (scholarships), April 15 (loans).
Admissions High school graduation with 15 units required. GED accepted. ACT or SAT required. $10 application fee. Rolling admissions; suggest applying soon after September 15 of 12th year. Tuition and room deposits required on acceptance of admissions offer. *Early Entrance* and *Concurrent Enrollment* programs. Transfers accepted. Credit possible for CEEB AP and CLEP exams. Conditional admission possible.
Student Life Student government. Newspaper, literary magazine, yearbook. Several music groups. University Theatre, Communications Center, debate. Academic, athletic, honorary, professional, and special interest organizations. 6 fraternities, 2 with houses, and 6 sororities without houses. Unmarried students under 19 must live at home or on campus. No coed dorms. Married-student housing. Students must attend 5/6 of classes. 4 hours of phys ed required. Honor code. 4 intercollegiate sports for men, 3 for women; intramurals. AIAW, NAIA, Southern State Conference. Student body composition: 7% Black, 1% Native American, 91% White, 1% Other. 7% from out of state.

[1] NORTH ALABAMA, UNIVERSITY OF
Florence 35632, (205) 766-4100
Director of Admissions: J. Hollie Allen

- **Undergraduates: 2,144m, 2,607w; 5,272 total (including graduates)**
- **Tuition & Fees (1982/83): $870 (in-state), $1,740 (out-of-state)**
- **Room & Board: $1,790**
- **Degrees offered: BA, BS, BSEd, BSN, BSW**
- **Mean ACT 16.7**
- **Student-faculty ratio: 23 to 1**

A public university established in 1872. 92-acre urban campus, 125 miles from Birmingham. Bus service; airport in Muscle Shoals.
Academic Character SACS and professional accreditation. Semester system, 8-week summer term. 42 majors offered in the areas of art, music, humanities, sciences, social sciences, social work, business, education, nursing, home economics, and communications. Minors in most major fields and in 8 additional areas. Distributive requirements. 2-year secretarial training. MA, MBA, EdS granted. Independent study, honors program. Cooperative work/study in chemistry. Preprofessional programs in agriculture, dentistry, engineering, forestry, health sciences, law, medicine, medical technology, pharmacy, veterinary medicine. Dual degree program in engineering with Auburn. Member 2 consortia; associated with 16 other schools. Early childhood, elementary, secondary, and special education certification. ROTC. Planetarium-observatory. 203,147-volume library.
Financial ACT FAS. University scholarships, grants, loans, nursing scholarships, deferred payment; PELL, SEOG, GSL, NDSL, NSL, CWS, institutional work program. Application deadlines February 15 (academic scholarships), April 1 (other aid).
Admissions High school graduation required. GED or high school equivalency certificate accepted. ACT required. $15 application fee. Rolling admissions; suggest applying as early as possible. Deadline 2 weeks before beginning of term. Transfers accepted. Credit possible for CEEB AP and CLEP exams.
Student Life Student government. Newspaper, literary magazine, yearbook. Several music and drama groups. Many academic, professional, religious, service, and special interest organizations. 8 fraternities, 4 with houses, and 7 sororities without houses. 7% of men and 6% of women join. No coed dorms. Married-student housing. 20% of students live on campus. Regular class attendance expected. 2 semesters of phys ed required. Use of liquor limited. 8 intercollegiate, several club and intramural sports. AIAW, NCAA, Gulf South Conference. Student body composition: 7.6% Black, 0.05% Hispanic, 92.3% White, 0.05% Other. 10% from out of state.

[J1] NORTHEAST ALABAMA STATE JUNIOR COLLEGE
Rainsville 35986

[J1] NORTHWEST ALABAMA STATE JUNIOR COLLEGE
Phil Campbell 35581

[1] OAKWOOD COLLEGE
Huntsville 35896, (205) 837-1630
Assistant Dean for Admissions and Records: Roy Malcolm

- **Undergraduates: 654m, 805w**
- **Tuition (1982/83): $3,663**
- **Room & Board: $1,920**
- **Degrees offered: BA, BS, BGS, AA, AS**
- **Student-faculty ratio: 20 to 1**

A private college affiliated with the General Conference of Seventh-Day Adventists, established in 1896. 1,185-acre small city campus. Air and bus service.
Academic Character SACS accreditation. Trimester system, 6-week summer term. Majors offered in accounting, biology, business administration, chemistry, education (business, early childhood, elementary, secondary, special), English, foods & nutrition, history, home economics, mathematics, medical technology, music, office administration, psychology, religion, social work, theology. Double major or minor required. Minors in most major fields and 8 other areas. Distributives and GRE required for graduation. Freshman Studies Program. AA/AS granted in 7 areas. Independent study, honors program, cooperative work/study, pass/fail, credit by exam. Preprofessional programs in allied health sciences, dentistry, engineering, law, medicine, veterinary medicine, pharmacy. 2-year transfer programs with Loma Linda U in anesthesia, dental hygiene, occupational therapy, physical therapy, public health; in engineering with Walla Walla College. 3-2 cooperative programs in architecture and engineering with Tuskegee Institute. 2-4 program in veterinary medicine, 3-1 programs in natural science and medical technology. Cross-registration with 3 area schools. Member Alabama Center for Higher Education. Elementary and secondary education certification. 82,000-volume library.
Financial CEEB CSS. College scholarships, grants, loans, Denominational Educational Grants, nursing scholarships, 2nd-family-member discount,

deferred payment; PELL, SEOG, NDSL, GSL, NSL, CWS. United Negro College Fund. Apply for federal programs by April 1.

Admissions High school graduation or 18 units required. ACT required. $5 application fee ($10 after July 1). Rolling admissions; no deadline. $50 room deposit required on acceptance of admissions offer. *Early Admission, Early Decision* programs. Admission deferral possible. Transfers accepted. Credit possible for CEEB AP and CLEP exams, college advanced placement program.

Student Life Student government. Newspaper, yearbook, radio station. Academic, music, social, and special interest groups. Unmarried students under 23 must live at home or on campus. No coed dorms. Married-student housing. Cars discouraged; freshmen may not drive on campus. Class and evening worship, chapel, Friday evening vespers, Sabbath school, & Sabbath morning church service attendance required. 4-hours of phys ed required. No intercollegiate sports; some intramurals. Student body composition: 99.1% Black, 0.9% White.

[J1] PATRICK HENRY STATE JUNIOR COLLEGE

Monroeville 36460

[1] SAMFORD UNIVERSITY

800 Lakeshore Drive, Birmingham 35229, (205) 870-2901
Dean of Admissions & Financial Aid: E. Thomas Cleveland

- **Undergraduates: 957m, 1,180w; 3,955 total (including graduates)**
- **Tuition (1982/83): $3,104 (in-state), $3,200 (out-of-state)**
- **Room & Board: $1,750; Fees: $50**
- **Degrees offered: AB, BS, BGS, BMus, BSBA, BSEd, BSPharm, BSN, BS in Anesthesia, AGS, ASN**
- **Mean ACT 21; mean SAT 500**
- **Student-faculty ratio: 20 to 1**

A private university affiliated with the Alabama Baptist State Convention, established in 1841. 500-acre suburban campus in Shades Valley, 6 miles from center of Birmingham. Air, rail, and bus service.

Academic Character SACS and professional accreditation. 4-1-4 calendar, 2 5½-week summer terms. 20 majors offered by the Howard College of Arts & Sciences, 5 by the School of Business, 2 by the School of Education, 5 by the School of Music, 1 by the School of Nursing, and 1 by the School of Pharmacy. Minors in most major fields and 4 additional areas. Distributives and 2 religion survey courses required. GRE required for graduation. Graduate and professional degrees granted. Independent study, honors program, pass/fail. Preprofessional programs in dentistry, law, medicine, seminary studies. Paralegal program. 3-2 forestry program with Duke. 3-2 engineering programs. 3-1 medical technology program with Alabama hospitals. Exchange with U of Alabama (Birmingham). Marine biology program at Dauphin Island Sea Lab. Study abroad. Elementary and secondary teacher training. AFROTC; ROTC at UAB. Language lab. 361,458-volume library with microform resources.

Financial CEEB CSS and ACT FAS. University scholarships, grants, loans, ministerial & health professions scholarships, loans; PELL, SEOG, NDSL, FISL, GSL, CWS. Priority application deadline April 1.

Admissions High school graduation with 16 units required. GED or equivalent accepted for students over 20. Interview encouraged. ACT or SAT required. $25 application fee; $25 room reservation fee (refunded if applicant not admitted). Rolling admissions; suggest applying as soon as possible in 12th year. Deadline in early August. *Early Entrance* Program. Transfers accepted. Credit possible for CEEB AP and CLEP exams.

Student Life Student government. Newspaper, literary magazine, yearbook. Debate, music, & drama groups. Campus Ministries. Academic, honorary, professional, religious, and service organizations. 4 fraternities and 6 sororities, some with houses. 19% of men and 27% of women join. Unmarried 1st and 2nd year students must live at home or on campus. No coed dorms. Married-student apartments. 34% of students live on campus. 4 semester hours of phys ed required. Attendance required at 9 convocations per semester. 5 intercollegiate sports for men; intramurals for men and women. Student body composition: 5% Black, 94% White, 1% Other. 32% from out of state.

■[P] CUMBERLAND SCHOOL OF LAW OF SAMFORD UNIVERSITY

Birmingham 35229

[J1] S. D. BISHOP STATE JUNIOR COLLEGE

351 North Broad St., Mobile 36603

[J1] SHELTON STATE COMMUNITY COLLEGE

Drawer J, Tuscaloosa 35404

[J1] SNEAD STATE JUNIOR COLLEGE

PO Drawer D, Boaz 35957, (205) 593-5120
Director of Admissions: Joan Ables

- **Enrollment: 1,200 men & women**
- **Tuition (1982/83): $375 (in-state), $750 (out-of-state)**
- **Room & Board: $1,404-$1,554**
- **Degrees offered: AA, AS, AAS**
- **Student-faculty ratio: 33 to 1**

A public junior college established in 1935. 35-acre campus 2 blocks west of downtown Boaz.

Academic Character SACS accreditation. Trimester system, 11-week summer term. Terminal majors offered in animal health technology, library technology, management & supervision, retail merchandising, data processing, and secretarial science. Transfer majors offered in agricultural business & economics, agricultural science, biological science, business administration, chemistry/chemical engineering, computer science, criminal justice, general education, liberal arts, mathematics/physics, medical technology, music, secretarial administration, and agricultural, early childhood, elementary, health & physical, music, secondary, & special education. Preprofessional transfer majors in dentistry, engineering, forestry, law, medicine, nursing, pharmacy, and veterinary medicine. Allied Health Linkage Program with Regional Technical Institute in Birmingham offers 2-2 programs in biomedical equipment technician, multiple competency clinical technician, occupational therapy assistant, medical assistant, medical laboratory technician, medical record technician, respiratory therapy, physical therapist assistant, radiographer, and emergency medical technician. Distributive requirements. A-V center, TV studio, language lab, computer. 35,043-volume library.

Financial ACT FAS. College scholarships, loans, state grants; PELL, SEOG, NDSL, CWS. Priority application deadline April 15.

Admissions High school graduation required. GED or equivalent accepted. $5 application fee. Application deadline 2 weeks prior to registration. *Concurrent Enrollment* Program. Summer Accelerated High School Program. Transfers accepted. Credit possible for CLEP exams. Provisional admission possible.

Student Life Student government. Drama & music groups. Baptist Student Union. College Bowl. EARTH. Academic, honorary, professional, service, and special interest clubs. Class attendance expected. 3 quarter hours of health & phys ed required. 2 intercollegiate sports for men, 1 for women; intramurals. AJCC, NJCAA.

[1] SOUTH ALABAMA, UNIVERSITY OF

Mobile 36688, (205) 460-6101
Director of Admissions: J. David Stearns

- **Undergraduates: 3,010m, 3,075w; 9,549 total (including graduates)**
- **Tuition (1982/83): $1,248 (in-state), $1,848 (out-of-state)**
- **Room & Board: $1,683-$2,328; Fees: $141**
- **Degrees offered: BA, BS, BFA, BMus, BSN, BS in 5 medical fields, AA**
- **Mean ACT 21**
- **Student-faculty ratio: 30 to 1**

A public university founded in 1963. 1,200-acre suburban campus. Air, rail, and bus service.

Academic Character SACS and professional accreditation. Trimester system, 11-week summer term. 22 majors offered by the College of Arts & Sciences, 5 by the College of Business & Management Studies, 9 by the College of Education, 4 by the College of Engineering, 6 by the Division of Allied Health Professions, 1 by the School of Nursing, and 1 in computer science. Self-designed majors. Distributive requirements. Graduate and professional degrees granted. Independent study, honors program, cooperative work/study, internships. Preprofessional programs in dentistry, medicine, optometry, pharmacy, and veterinary medicine. Dual degree programs. Elementary, secondary, and special education certification. ROTC. Medical Center, computer center, engineering labs, museum/gallery complex. 267,995-volume library with microform resources.

Financial ACT FAS. University scholarships, grants, loans, nursing scholarships, AL state grants; PELL, SEOG, NDSL, FISL, NSL, CWS, university work program. Application deadline April 1.

Admissions High school graduation with college prep program recommended. GED accepted. SAT or ACT required. Special requirements for engineering and nursing programs. $10 application fee. Rolling admissions; suggest applying by February of 12th year. Deadline September 10. *Early Entrance* Program. Transfers accepted. Credit possible for CEEB AP and CLEP exams. University has own advanced placement program. Academic Opportunity Program.

Student Life Student government. Newspaper, literary magazine, music and drama groups. Social, professional, religious, and special interest groups. 12 fraternities and 6 sororities. Coed and single-sex dorms, international students house, married-student apartments. 20% of students live on campus. 6 activity (phys ed) courses required. 9 intercollegiate and several intramural sports. AIAW, NCAA. Student body composition: 0.3% Asian, 9.7% Black, 0.5% Hispanic, 0.4% Native American, 84.8% White, 4.3% Other. 16% from out of state.

[P] SOUTHEASTERN BIBLE COLLEGE

2901 Pawnee Avenue, Birmingham 35205

[J1] SOUTHERN INSTITUTE

2015-19 Highland Avenue South, Birmingham 35205

[J1] SOUTHERN JUNIOR COLLEGE OF BUSINESS

1724 First Avenue North, Birmingham 35203

[J1] SOUTHERN UNION STATE JUNIOR COLLEGE

Wadley 36276, (205) 395-2211
Registrar: Larry East

- **Enrollment: 458m, 514w; 1,500 total (including part-time)**
- **Tuition (1982/83): $375 (in-state), $750 (out-of-state)**
- **Room & Board: $1,238-$1,403**
- **Degrees offered: AA, AS, AAS**

A public junior college established in 1922. Main campus in the small town of Wadley, 90 miles SW of Atlanta & 90 miles SE of Birmingham, with centers in Opelika, Heflin, and the Valley. Bus service.

Academic Character SACS accreditation. Trimester system, 10-week summer term. Transfer majors in art, biology, chemistry, English, foreign

languages, journalism, mathematics, physics, psychology, sociology, and speech communication; preprofessional transfer majors in business, elementary education, home economics education, law, law enforcement, secondary education, vocational & adult education, and health, physical education, & recreation. Terminal majors in aquatic technology, business management & supervision technology, police science, secretarial science, and nursing. Distributive requirements. Numerous other occupational degrees offered in conjuction with various state institutions. Linkage program with Regional Technical Institute in Birmingham offers 9 degrees in allied health fields.
Financial ACT FAS. College scholarships, loans; PELL, SEOG, NDSL, FISL, CWS, college work program.
Admissions High school graduation required. GED or equivalent accepted. $5 application fee. Transfers accepted. *Concurrent Enrollment* Program. Summer Accelerated High School Program. Credit possible for CLEP exams. Provisional admission possible.
Student Life Student government. Newspaper, yearbook. Music and drama groups. Environmental Study Club. Circle K. Academic, religious, and special interest clubs. Single-sex housing for 100 men and 64 women. Liquor prohibited on campus. 3 quarter hours of phys ed required. Intercollegiate basketball & baseball. NJCAA, National Little College Athletic Association.

[1] SPRING HILL COLLEGE

4307 Old Shell Road, Mobile 36608, (205) 460-2130
Vice President for Enrollment Planning: Anne M. Kennedy

- **Undergraduates: 430m, 407w; 1,020 total (including part-time)**
- **Tuition & Fees (1982/83): $4,500**
- **Room & Board: $2,426**
- **Degrees offered: BA, BS, BGS**
- **Mean ACT 23; mean SAT 1000**
- **Student-faculty ratio: 14 to 1**

A private Jesuit college founded in 1830, became coed in 1952. 500-acre suburban campus. Air, rail, and bus service.
Academic Character SACS accreditation. Semester system, May term, 6- and 10-week summer terms. Majors offered in art therapy, biology, business & management (4), chemistry, communications (4), economics, education (2), English, fine arts, history, legal studies, marine biology, mathematics, medical technology, philosophy, political science, psychology, sociology, theology. Self-designed and double majors. Courses in 7 additional areas. Core curriculum and 12 hours of theology required. GRE, departmental exam, paper, project, or seminar required of seniors. Independent study, pass/fail, internships. Preprofessional programs in engineering, dentistry, law, medicine. Legal assistant and real estate certification. 3-1 & 4-1 medical technology, and 3-1 respiratory therapy programs. 3-2 engineering programs with Auburn and Georgia Tech. Member Marine Environmental Sciences Consortium. Washington Semester. Study abroad. Early childhood and elementary education certification. ROTC. Human Relations Center, US Siesmograph Station, language lab, computer. 160,000-volume library.
Financial CEEB CSS. College scholarships, grants, loans, 2nd-family-member tuition rebates, deferred payment; PELL, SEOG, NDSL, GSL, FISL, CWS, College Employment Program. Application deadline March 1.
Admissions High school graduation with 12 units required. SAT or ACT required. $20 application fee. Rolling admissions; suggest applying by February 1 of 12th year. Deadline August 15. $50 tuition and $100 room deposits required on acceptance of admissions offer. *Early Entrance* Program. Admission deferral possible. Transfers accepted. Credit possible for CEEB AP and CLEP exams, and high SAT or ACT scores. College has own advanced placement exams. Summer Development and Upward Bound programs.
Student Life Student government. Newspaper, literary magazine, yearbook, radio station. Music & drama groups. Academic, honorary, religious, military, service, and social clubs. 4 fraternities and 3 sororities, some with houses. 25% of men and women join. Unmarried students must live at home or on campus. No coed dorms. 75% live on campus. Class attendance required except for Dean's List students. 4 intercollegiate sports for men, 3 for women; club and intramural sports. AIAW, NAIA, Gulf Coast Athletic Conference. Student body composition: 1% Asian, 8% Black, 3% Hispanic, 88% White. 65% from out of state.

[1] STILLMAN COLLEGE

PO Box 1430, Tuscaloosa 35403, (205) 349-4240 ext 35-36
Director of Admissions & Recruitment: Eddie R. Johnson

- **Undergraduates: 276m, 384w**
- **Tuition (1982/83): $2,180**
- **Room & Board: $2,003**
- **Degrees offered: BA, BS**
- **Student-faculty ratio: 18 to 1**

A private Presbyterian college establised in 1876. 100-acre tree-lined campus within walking distance of downtown Tuscaloosa, 52 miles southwest of Birmingham. Air, rail, and bus service.
Academic Character SACS accreditation. Semester system, 8-week summer term. Majors offered in biology, business, chemistry, elementary education, English, French, health & physical education, history, ,mathematics, music, physics, sociology, and Spanish. Minor required. Minors offered in major fields (except elem ed) and in art, computer science, foreign languages, political science, psychology, and religion & philosophy. Courses in geography, speech. Distributives and 12 credit hours of Bible required. Cooperative work/study. 3-2 bachelor's degree programs in engineering and architecture, and 2-4 BS/DVM program with Tuskegee Institute. BS/MD program possible. Exchanges with U Alabama. ROTC at UAL. Language labs, Afro-American research center. 80,000-volume library with microform resources; access to UAL library.
Financial College & ROTC scholarships, private loans; PELL, SEOG, NDSL, FISL, CWS, college work/credit program. Member United Negro College Fund. Priority application deadline May 1.
Admissions High school graduation with 15 units recommended. SAT or ACT required. $10 application fee. $25 deposit required on acceptance of admissions offer. Transfers accepted. Developmental Studies Program. Upward Bound.
Student Life Student government. Newspaper, yearbook. College band, choir, several religious activities. Academic, honorary, social, and special interest groups. 8 fraternities & sororities. Married students must live off campus. No coed dorms. Most students live on campus. Class attendance required. Attendance at 11 assemblies & chapels and at 2 cultural events per semester required. 2 credit hours of phys ed or military science required. 5 intercollegiate sports; intramurals. NCAA, SIAC. 30% of students from out of state.

[1] TALLADEGA COLLEGE

Talladega 35160, (205) 362-0206
Director of Admissions: Robert L. Clayton

- **Undergraduates: 171m, 321w; 532 total (including part-time)**
- **Tuition & Fees (1982/83): $2,909**
- **Room & Board: $1,891**
- **Degree offered: BA**
- **Mean ACT 13; mean SAT 337**
- **Student-faculty ratio: 10 to 1**

A private college established in 1867, affiliated with the American Missionary Association of the United Church of Christ. 130-acre small town campus in the foothills of the Blue Ridge Mountains, 55 miles east of Birmingham. Served by bus; air, rail, and bus in Birmingham.
Academic Character SACS accreditation. Semester system, 8-week summer term. Majors offered in biology, business administration, chemistry, early education for the handicapped, economics, English, history, mathematics, modern languages, music, physical education/recreation, physics, psychology, public administration, rehabilitation education services, social work, sociology. Courses in 13 other areas. Distributive requirements. Honors program, pass/fail, internships. Preprofessional programs in allied health fields, dentistry, law, medicine, and nursing. Dual degree programs. Transfer programs in engineering, physics, and veterinary medicine with 7-member Alabama Center for Higher Education. 3-2 engineering and 2-2 veterinary medicine programs with Tuskegee Institute and Auburn. Secondary and special education certification. Computer. 74,423-volume library.
Financial CEEB CSS and ACT FAS. College scholarships, loans, AL state grants, UNCF loans; PELL, SEOG, USAF, GSL, CWS, college work program. United Negro College Fund. Application deadline May 15.
Admissions High school graduation with 16 units required. Admission by exam possible. Applicants for a BA in Music must take a college music aptitude test and should be familiar with the piano. SAT or ACT required. $10 application fee. Rolling admissions; suggest applying by February 1 of 12th year. Deadline August 1. $25 deposit required on acceptance of admissions offer. *Early Entrance* and *Early Decision* programs. Admission deferral possible. Transfers accepted. Advanced placement program.
Student Life Student government. Newspaper, yearbook, literary magazine, arts festival. Music, drama, and dance groups. Debate, academic, religious, and special interest clubs. 4 fraternities and 4 sororities, none with houses. 40% of men and 45% of women join. No coed dorms. 81% live on campus. No weapons permitted on campus. 1 year phys ed required. Regular class attendance expected. 2 intercollegiate and several intramural sports for men and women. AIAW, NAIA. Student body composition: 98% Black, 2% White. 44% from out of state.

[1] TROY STATE UNIVERSITY

Troy 36082, (205) 566-3000
Director of Admissions: Rick Sandretto

- **Undergraduates: 2,311m, 2,309w; 5,341 total (including graduates)**
- **Tuition (1982/83): $840 (in-state), $1,260 (out-of-state)**
- **Room & Board: $1,245-$1,500**
- **Degrees offered: BA, BS, BAEd, BSEd, BMus Ed, BSN, BApplied Science, AS**
- **Mean ACT 17; mean SAT 400v, 440m**
- **Student-faculty ratio: 22 to 1**

A public university established in 1887. 433-acre suburban campus 50 miles from Montgomery. Branch campuses in Dothan and Montgomery. Served by bus; air and rail in Montgomery.
Academic Character SACS and professional accreditation. Trimester system, 8-week summer term. 8 majors offered in Applied Science Programs, 18 by the College of Arts & Sciences, 9 by the School of Business & Commerce, 8 by the School of Education, 7 by the School of Fine Arts, 2 by the School of Journalism, and 1 by the School of Nursing. Self-designed majors. Minors in most major fields and in 8 additional areas. General studies program required. MS and MBA granted. AS granted in business, nursing, criminal justice, general education. Independent study, honors program. Preprofessional programs in dentistry, law, medicine. Elementary, secondary, and special education certification. AFROTC. 285,000-volume library.
Financial CEEB CSS. University scholarships, grants, loans, nursing scholarships, deferred payment; PELL, SEOG, NDSL, FISL, NSL, CWS, workship program. Priority application deadline for scholarships May 1.
Admissions High school graduation with 15 units required. GED accepted. Interview recommended. SAT or ACT required. $10 application fee. Rolling admissions; suggest applying as early as possible. $35 room deposit required on acceptance of admissions offer. *Early Entrance, Concurrent Enrollment, Early Decision* programs. Admission deferral possible. Transfers accepted. Credit possible for CLEP exams. University has own placement exams.

Student Life Student government. Newspaper, literary magazine, yearbook, radio and TV stations. Music, dance, and drama groups. Debate, Afro Club. Academic, professional, religious, political, honorary, and service organizations. 11 fraternities, 8 with houses, and 7 sororities with rooms in dorms. 20% of men and 10% of women join. Unmarried students under 19 must live at home or on campus. Coed, single-sex, special interest, and married-student housing. University apartments. 50% of students live on campus. Liquor prohibited on campus. Class attendance expected. 3 quarters of phys ed required. 7 intercollegiate sports; intramurals. Gulf South Conference. Student body composition: 1% Asian, 19% Black, 1% Hispanic, 1% Native American, 78% White. 40% from out of state.

[1] TUSKEGEE INSTITUTE
Tuskegee 36088, (205) 727-8500
Director of Admissions: Herbert Carter

- **Enrollment: 1,713m, 1,684w**
- **Tuition (1982/83): $2,750**
- **Room & Board: $1,375**
- **Degrees offered: BA, BS, BArch, BSB, BSIT, BSEE, BSME**
- **Mean SAT 340v, 375m**
- **Student-faculty ratio: 14 to 1**

A private institute founded in 1881 by Booker T. Washington. 5,000-acre rural campus 40 miles east of Montgomery. Air, rail, and bus in Montgomery.
Academic Character SACS accreditation. Semester system, 8-week summer term. 12 majors offered by the College of Arts & Sciences, 16 by the School of Applied Sciences, 13 by the School of Education, 3 by the School of Engineering, and 1 by the School of Nursing. Courses offered in 7 additional areas. Distributive requirements. GRE required for graduation. Graduate and professional degrees granted. Independent study, honors program, pass/fail, cooperative work/study. 3-2 programs in dentistry and medicine. 2-year pre-forestry and veterinary medicine programs. Elementary, secondary, and special education certification. AFROTC, ROTC. 155,000-volume library.
Financial CEEB CSS. Institute scholarships, loans, nursing scholarships; PELL, SEOG,, NDSL, CWS. Application deadlines March 1 (scholarships), April 15 (loans).
Admissions High school graduation with 15 units required. SAT or ACT required. No application fee. Rolling admissions; suggest applying in January or February of 12th year. Deadline April 15. $15 acceptance fee and $100 room deposit required on acceptance of offer of admission. *Early Entrance* and *Early Decision* programs. Transfers accepted. Credit possible for CEEB AP and CLEP exams.
Student Life Student government, newspaper, yearbook, several music groups. Theater group, professional, honorary, and special interest organizations. 6 fraternities and 3 sororities, none with houses. 20% of men and 15% of women join. Students not living at home must live on campus. Men's and women's dorms. Married-student apartments. 75% of students live on campus. Liquor and firearms prohibited on campus. Class attendance expected. 2 semesters of phys ed required in first year. 6 intercollegiate sports; intramurals. Southern Intercollegiate Athletic Conference. Student body composition: 95% Black, 1% Hispanic, 0.7% Native American, 3% White, 0.3% Other. 65% from out of state.

[J1] WALKER COLLEGE
Jasper 35501

ALASKA (AK)

[1] ALASKA, UNIVERSITY OF
Fairbanks 99701, (907) 479-7821
Director of Admissions: Ann Tremarello

- **Undergraduates: 2,083m, 2,032w**
- **Tuition (1982/83): $410 (in-state), $1,190 (out-of-state)**
- **Room & Board: $2,080; Fees: $174**
- **Degrees offered: BA, BS, BBA, BEd, BMus, BTech, AA, AAS**
- **Student-faculty ratio: 12 to 1**

A public university established in 1915. 2,400-acre suburban campus 5 miles from Fairbanks, which has air, rail, bus service.
Academic Character NASC and professional accreditation. Semester system, 3 3-week summer terms, 1 to 6-week summer workshops. 54 majors offered by the colleges of Arts & Sciences, Environmental Sciences, and the schools of Agriculture & Land Resources Management, Education, Engineering, Management, and Mineral Industry. Minors offered in most major fields. Courses in natural and social sciences, humanities. Distributive requirements. Graduate and professional degrees granted. Preprofessional programs in dentistry, medicine, nursing, veterinary medicine. Exchange program in Japan. Elementary and secondary education certification. ROTC. Language labs. 750,000-volume library.
Financial CEEB CSS. University scholarships, grants, loans. 1st-semester non-state residents not eligible for scholarships or grants. PELL, SEOG, NDSL, CWS. Application deadlines March 1 (scholarships, grants) and August 1 (loans).
Admissions High school graduation with 16 units required. ACT required. $10 application fee. Rolling admissions; deadline August 1. $50 housing deposit required on acceptance of offer of admission. Transfers accepted. Credit possible for CEEB AP and CLEP exams; university administers departmental exams. Older residents with no formal high school education but with acceptable test scores may be accepted provisionally.
Student Life Student government, campus union. Newspaper, yearbook, radio station. Musical, athletic, honorary, religious, service, and special interest groups. Single freshmen under 21 must live at home or on campus. Coed and single-sex dorms; some married-student housing. 41% of students live on campus. Class attendance expected. 5 intercollegiate sports for men, 5 for women; intramurals. Student body composition: 1.8% Asian, 2.3% Black, 0.5% Hispanic, 12.2% Native American, 82.6% White, 0.6% Other. 19% from out of state.

■[1] ALASKA, UNIVERSITY OF
3211 Providence Ave., Anchorage 99504, (907) 263-1481
Director of Admissions & Records: Kay Wilson

- **Enrollment: 1,350m, 2,275w**
- **Tuition (1982/83): $615 (AL, HI, Yukon & North Territories residents), $1,785 (others)**
- **Est. living expenses: $4,000 (no university housing)**
- **Degrees offered: BA, BS, BBA, BEd, BFA, BMus, BSW, BTech**
- **Student-faculty ratio: 28 to 1**

A public university established in 1954. 424-acre campus in Anchorage, which has air, rail, and bus service.
Academic Character NASC and professional accreditation. Semester system, summer term. 40 majors offered by the College of Arts & Sciences, schools of Business & Public Administration, Education, Engineering, Nursing, and the Justice Center. Minors offered in most major areas. Distributive requirements. Master's and associate's degrees granted. Independent study. Some pass/fail courses, credit/no credit options. Professional certificate programs in labor/management relations, planning, real estate. Elementary, secondary, physical education, counseling & guidance, reading specialist, school administration, and special education certification. Media services. Anchorage Urban Research Observatory. 300,000-volume library.
Financial CEEB CSS. University scholarships, grants, loans; PELL, SEOG, BIA, NSS, GSL, NDSL, NSL, CWS. Priority application deadline June 1.
Admissions High school graduation with GPA of 2.5 required. ACT or SAT required. $10 application fee. Rolling admissions; application deadline May 1. Transfers accepted. Credit possible for CEEB AP, CLEP, and DANTES exams. University also administers own challenge exams. Probationary admission possible.
Student Life United Students of U of Alaska. Newspaper. Athletic, academic, religious, service, and special interest groups. No university housing. Class attendance required. 6 intercollegiate sports for men, 6 for women; intramurals. NCAA, AIAW, NCWSA, NAIA, NCSA. 6% of students from out of state.

■[2] ALASKA, UNIVERSITY OF
11120 Glacier Highway, Juneau 99803, (907) 789-2101
Director of Admissions & Records: Meribeth Dahlberg

- **Enrollment: 846m, 1,512w**
- **Tuition (1982/83): $600 (AL, HI, Yukon & Northwest Territories residents), $1,560 (others)**
- **Room & Board: $2,800-$4,100**
- **Degrees offered: BA, BS, BEd, BBA, BLS, AA, AAS**
- **Student-faculty ratio: 10 to 1**

A public university founded in 1972. Campus 9 miles north of Juneau, located in the Tongass National Forest. Airport in Juneau.
Academic Character NASC accreditation candidate. Semester system. Majors in accounting, biology, computer information systems, construction technology, early childhood education, elementary education, fisheries, government, legal administration, management, marine technology, music, office administration, paralegal studies, power technology, secondary education. Interdisciplinary Certificates. Distributive requirements for bachelor's degree candidates. Master's degrees and post-graduate certificates granted. Credit/no credit option. Early childhood, elementary, and secondary education certification. 40,000-volume library with microform resources.
Financial CEEB CSS. University talent scholarships and loans, state incentive grants, loans, deferred payment; PELL, SEOG, BIA, NDSL, CWS, university part-time employment. Apply at least 1 month before registration.
Admissions High school graduation, GED, or minimum age of 18 required. No tests or minimum GPA required. $10 application fee. Rolling admissions. *Concurrent Enrollment* Program. Transfers accepted.
Student Life Student government. Newspaper. Student study center. Limited on-campus housing; preference given to full-time single students.

■[J1] ANCHORAGE COMMUNITY COLLEGE
2533 Providence Avenue, Anchorage 99508

■[J1] KENAI PENINSULA COMMUNITY COLLEGE
Soldotna 99669

■[J1] KETCHIKAN COMMUNITY COLLEGE
Ketchikan 99901

■[J1] KODIAK COMMUNITY COLLEGE
Kodiak 99615

■[J1] KUSKOKWIM COMMUNITY COLLEGE
PO Box 368, Bethel 99559

■[J1] MATANUSKA-SUSITNA COMMUNITY COLLEGE
Palmer 99645

■[J2] SITKA COMMUNITY COLLEGE
Sitka 99835

■[J2] TANANA VALLEY COMMUNITY COLLEGE
Fairbanks 99701

[2] ALASKA BIBLE COLLEGE
Box 289, Glennallen 99588

[1] ALASKA PACIFIC UNIVERSITY
3500 University Drive, Anchorage 99508, (907) 276-8181
Director of Admissions: Frank Schlehofer

- **Enrollment: 800 men and women**
- **Tuition (1982/83): $3,000**
- **Room & Board: $2,800-$3,050; Fees: $215**
- **Degrees offered: BA, AA**
- **Student-faculty ratio: 15 to 1**

A private university founded by the Methodists. Wooded 270-acre campus in Anchorage, with a view of the Arugach Mountains. Bus station, airport.
Academic Character NASC accreditation. Semester system, 3-week spring Intensive in May; a 6-week, a 9-week, and 3 3-week summer terms. Areas of concentration offered are communications, education, human resources development, management sciences, natural resources, Pacific Rim studies, and value & religious service. Courses in behavioral sciences, economics, graphic arts, math, music, physical & outdoor education, public administration, languages, literature, fine & performing arts, travel industry management. Distributive requirements. MAT, MLA, MSM granted. Internships, cooperative work/study. PLATO (computer-assisted instruction system) offers self-paced courses. Hawaii semester, Washington D.C. semester. Exchange program with Duke, Southern Methodist, Tufts universities, and others. Study abroad. Alaskana Library: extensive collection of documents on the discovery, exploration, and growth of Alaska.
Financial ACT FAS. University scholarships and grants. Alaska State Student Loan Program. CWS. Apply as early as possible; deadline is 10 weeks prior to registration.
Admissions High school graduation required, with at least a 2.5 GPA, 800 SAT composite, and/or 20 ACT composite. GED accepted. SAT, ACT, or Washington Pre-College Test (WPCT) required. $20 application fee. Rolling admissions; no deadline. Transfers accepted. Provisional acceptance possible for academically disadvantaged applicants.
Student Life Drama, dance, music, and art-related activities. Sports clubs. Annual International Student Potluck, Native Awareness Week, Model UN Security Council. Coed dorms. Student body composition: 8% Foreign, 7% Native American, 85% from Alaska and the lower 48 states.

[1 & J1] SHELDON JACKSON COLLEGE
Sitka 99835, (907) 479-7211

- **Enrollment: 76m, 78w; 199 total**
- **Tuition (1982/83): $3,000**
- **Room & Board: $3,000**
- **Degrees offered: BA, AA, AS**

A private, coeducational college affiliated with the United Presbyterian Church.
Academic Character NASC accreditation. 4-1-4 system. Majors offered in liberal arts, forestry, fisheries, Christian service, native studies, business administration, teacher education. BA degree is in teacher education only. Remedial mathematics and English programs. Functioning salmon hatchery on campus.
Financial CEEB CSS. Scholarships, grants, and loans for eligible students. Work program.
Admissions High school graduation or GED required. Admissions notification done on a rolling basis. *Early Admission* Program for qualified high school students.
Student Life Five dormitories on campus house up to 200 students. 54% of students are from minority groups.

ARIZONA *(AZ)*

[G1] AMERICAN GRADUATE SCHOOL OF INTERNATIONAL MANAGEMENT
Glendale 85306

[1] ARIZONA, UNIVERSITY OF
Tucson 85721, (602) 626-0111
Dean of Admissions: David L. Windsor

- **Undergraduates: 10,161m, 8,975w; 33,914 total (including graduates)**
- **Tuition (1982/83): $710 (in-state), $3,250 (out-of-state)**
- **Room & Board: $2,002-$2,603**
- **Degrees offered: BA, BS, BArch, BFA, BMus, BSPharm, BLA, BSN**
- **Mean ACT 21**
- **Student-faculty ratio: 18 to 1**

A public land-grant university established in 1885. 319-acre urban campus located in residential Tucson, which is served by air, rail, and bus.
Academic Character NCACS and professional accreditation. Semester system, 2 summer terms. 127 majors offered by the Colleges of Agriculture, Architecture, Business & Public Administration, Earth Sciences, Education, Engineering, Fine Arts, Liberal Arts, Mines, Nursing, Pharmacy, and the Schools of Health Related Professions and Home Economics. Minors in most major areas and in American Indian, Black, and women's studies. Graduate and professional degrees granted. Independent study, honors program. Phi Beta Kappa. Cooperative work/study, pass/fail, internships. Preprofessional preparation in dental hygiene, dentistry, foreign service, law, medicine, occupational therapy, optometry, osteopathy, pharmacy, physical therapy, podiatry. Study abroad in Mexico, Europe, Brazil, Egypt, Far East. Elementary, secondary, and special education certification. AFROTC, ROTC. 4,574,445-volume library.
Financial University scholarships, grants, loans. PELL, SEOG, NSS, NDSL, GSL, NSL, CWS. Priority application deadline is May 1.
Admissions High school graduation with 16 units required. ACT or SAT required. $10 application fee for out-of-state students, none for in-state. Rolling admissions; deadline July 1. $50 room deposit required on acceptance of offer of admission. Credit possible for CEEB AP and CLEP exams; university has own placement exams.
Student Life Student government, newspaper, magazines. About 200 campus organizations. 18 fraternities and 12 sororities with houses. Coed and single-sex dorms, women's cooperative dorm. Some married-student housing. 34% of students live on campus. 9 intercollegiate sports for men, 11 for women; intramurals. NCAA, Pacific-10, Western Collegiate Athletic Association. Student body composition: 1.2% Asian, 1.2% Black, 5.1% Hispanic, 0.8% Native American, 51.4% White, 40.3% Other. 21% from out of state.

[P] ARIZONA COLLEGE OF THE BIBLE
2045 W. Northern, Phoenix 85021

[1] ARIZONA STATE UNIVERSITY
Tempe 85287, (602) 965-7788
Director of Admissions: Christine A. Wilkinson

- **Undergraduates: 11,728m, 10,132w; 37,828 total (including graduates)**
- **Tuition (1982/83): $710 (in-state), $3,250 (out-of-state)**
- **Room & Board: $2,320**
- **Degrees offered: BA, BS, BArch, BEd, BFA, BMus, BSE, BSN, BSW, BSCS**
- **Mean ACT 21**
- **Student-faculty ratio: 25 to 1**

A public university established in 1885. 566-acre suburban campus just east of Phoenix, plus 320-acre University farm. Air, bus, and rail service.
Academic Character NCACS and professional accreditation. Semester system, 2 5-week and 1 8-week summer terms. 88 majors offered by the Colleges of Architecture, Business Administration, Education, Engineering & Applied Sciences, Fine Arts, Law, Liberal Arts, Nursing, Public Programs, and by the School of Social Work. Interdisciplinary majors possible in American, Asian, energy & environmental, film, liberal arts, Latin American, religious, and women's studies, and in gerontology. Distributive requirements. Graduate degrees granted. Independent study. Honors program. Phi Beta Kappa. Cooperative work/study, internships. Pass/fail, credit by exam. Preprofessional programs in bilingual secretarial, dentistry, foreign service, law, medicine, ministry, occupational therapy, optometry, osteopathy, pharmacy, physical therapy, podiatry. 5-year BS/MS in engineering. Study abroad. Elementary, secondary, and special education certification. AFROTC, ROTC. Language lab. 1,650,000-volume library with microform resources.
Financial CEEB CSS and ACT FAS. University scholarships, grants, and loans; PELL, SEOG, NDSL, FISL, CWS. Apply by April 15.
Admissions High school graduation required with 16 units recommended. GED accepted. Audition required for music majors. ACT or SAT required. $10 application fee for out-of-state students, none for in-state. Apply by July 31. $50 room reservation deposit suggested for boarders. *Concurrent Enrollment* Program. Transfers accepted. Credit possible for CEEB AP, CLEP, and university proficiency exams.
Student Life Student government. Newspaper, TV station. Music, drama, political, environmental, athletic, academic, religious, service, and special interest groups. 21 fraternities, 13 sororities. No coed dorms. 15% of undergraduates live on campus. 12 intercollegiate sports for men, 9 for women; intramurals. AIAW, NCAA, PAC-10, Western Collegiate Athletic Association. Student body composition: 2% Asian, 3% Black, 4% Hispanic, 2% Native American, 89% White. 25% from out of state.

[J1] ARIZONA WESTERN COLLEGE
Yuma 85364, (602) 344-0264

- **Enrollment: 1,144 men & women; 4,064 total (including part-time)**
- **Tuition (1982/83): $5 per credit hour (in-state), $2,424 (out-of-state)**
- **Fees: $240**
- **Degrees offered: AA, AAS**

A public coeducational county-operated college 7 miles east of Yuma.
Academic Character NCACS and professional accreditation. Semester system. College offers first two years of general education for students planning to transfer to baccalaureate colleges, and offers terminal programs

in secretarial science, office, general business, banking & finance, marketing & management, data processing, education, welding technology, broadcasting, agricultural technology, home economics, nursing (PN, RN). Remedial math and reading programs.
Admissions High school graduation or GED required in order to be considered for admission. No application deadline. Notification of admission is on a rolling basis. *Early Decision* Program for applicants who know that Arizona Western is their first choice. Admission may be deferred. Credit possible for CEEB's Advanced Placement exams.
Student Life Three coeducational dormitories. Cafeteria service available on campus.

[J1] CENTRAL ARIZONA COLLEGE
Woodruff at Overfield Rd., Coolidge 85228, (602) 836-8243
Director of Admissions: Cherie McGlynn

- **Enrollment: 2,027m, 3,148w (including full and part-time)**
- **Tuition & Fees (1982/83): $216 (in-state), $2,304 (out-of-state)**
- **Room & Board: $1,400**
- **Degrees offered: AA, AS, AAS, AGS**

A public community college established in 1961. 2 campuses serving Pinal County between Tucson and Phoenix. Second campus in Winkelman.
Academic Character NCACS accreditation. Semester system. Terminal and transfer programs with majors in accounting, advanced emergency medical technology, administration of justice, agriculture mechanics, agriculture sciences, general agriculture, automotive technology business & sales, automotive mechanics technology, banking & finance, building trades, civil engineering technology, computer science, diesel technology, diesel & heavy equipment mechanic, dietetic education, general technology, heavy equipment operator, industrial electricity technology, legal assistant, legal secretary, machine trades technology, medical technology, mid-management, mining technology, mining process technology, nursing, office administration, piano teaching, pre-construction, pre-engineering, special education, and welding technology. Certificates. Distributive requirements. Special career awareness, work experience, career preparation, and career advancement courses. Credit by exam. Vocational education programs at Arizona State Prison. Career Center. Child Development Center. 75,000-volume library.
Financial College scholarships, federal grants, long & short-term loans, and employment. Contact financial aid director for more information.
Admissions High school graduation, GED, or minimum age of 18 required. Some programs may require entrance exams and prerequisites. *Concurrent Enrollment* Program. Transfers accepted.
Student Life Large number of clubs and organizations. Special activities. Lounge and recreation area. No housing on Winkelman campus. Intercollegiate and intramural sports.

[J1] COCHISE COLLEGE
Douglas 85607, (602) 364-7943

- **Enrollment: 558m, 604w; 4,085 total (including part-time)**
- **Tuition (1982/83): $160 (in-state), $1,030 (out-of-state)**
- **Room & Board: $1,460; Fees: $200**
- **Degrees offered: AA, AS, AAS**

A public community college established in 1964 on a 500-acre campus 8 miles west of Douglas. 40-acre branch campus in Sierra Vista.
Academic Character NCACS and professional accreditation. Semester system. University parallel and occupational programs offered in administration of justice, agriculture, anthropology, aviation technology, business, chemistry, dental assisting technology, drafting technology, electronics technology, English, environmental studies, fire science technology, health education, history, journalism, liberal arts, medical technology, nursing, ophthalmic dispensing technology, phys ed, political science, pre-dentistry, pre-engineering, pre-forestry, pre-law, pre-medicine, pre-pharmacy, pre-physical therapy, pre-veterinary, psychology, social work, Spanish, and welding. Radiologic technology and respiratory technology offered in cooperation with Pima Community College. Certificates of Completion and Life-Long Learning Certificates. Distributive requirements. Independent study. Cooperative work/study. Credit by exam. Spanish and English Immersion Programs offer intensive instruction to non-native speakers. On-campus airport. Library.
Financial ACT FAS. College scholarships, grants, and loans, Migrant Opportunity Program and BIA grants, Dougherty Foundation loans and grants; PELL, SEOG, SSIG, NSP, NSL, FISL, NDSL, CWS, college part-time employment.
Admissions High school graduation, GED, or minimum age of 19 required. Nursing and aviation programs have more specific admission requirements. $5 application fee. Rolling admissions. $50 housing deposit required. *Concurrent Enrollment* Program. Transfers accepted. Credit possible for CEEB CLEP exams.
Student Life Student government. Newspaper, literary magazine. International club, honor societies, Rodeo Club, Running Club, Newman Club. Several other student organizations. Non-commuting single students advised to live on campus. Single-sex dormitories. 4 intercollegiate sports for men and women.

[1] DEVRY INSTITUTE OF TECHNOLOGY
4702 North 24th Street, Phoenix 85016, (602) 956-8806
Director of Admissions: Arthur L. Geiger

- **Undergraduates: 2,386m, 181w**
- **Tuition & Fees (1982/83): $3,025**
- **Degrees offered: BS, AAS**

Private institute, part of the Bell and Howell Education Group, established in 1967. Air and bus service in Phoenix.
Academic Character NCACS, NATTS, and professional accreditation. Semester system, 15-week summer term. Major offered in Electronics Engineering Technology. Electronic technician diplomas offered. Electronics and audio-visual labs. Library.
Financial CEEB CSS. Institute scholarships, grants, and loans. PELL, SEOG, NDSL, FISL. Educard installment plan. Scholarship and grant application deadline is March 31; loan application deadline 2 weeks after receipt of aid forms.
Admissions High school diploma or GED certificate required. Institute entrance exam and interview required. $25 application fee. Rolling admissions; suggest applying at least 2 weeks before classes begin. $50 tuition deposit required with acceptance of offer of admission. *Concurrent Enrollment* Program. Transfers accepted. Institute offers challenge exams for advanced placement.
Student Life Student government. Newspaper. Radio, audio-recording, ski, computer clubs. Music groups. Professional organizations. No institute housing. Liquor prohibited on campus. Class attendance expected. 4 intramural sports. Student body composition: 1.3% Asian, 2.9% Black, 4.3% Hispanic, 1.1% Native American, 90.4% White. 75% from out of state.

[J1] EASTERN ARIZONA COLLEGE
Thatcher 85552, (602) 428-1133
Associate Dean of Admissions, Research, & Development: Jesse U. DeVaney

- **Undergraduates: 620m, 386w; 3,633 total (including part-time)**
- **Tuition & Fees (1982/83): $312 (in-state), $2,612 (out-of-state)**
- **Room & Board: $1,990**
- **Degrees offered: AA, AAS**

A public 2-year community college founded in 1888. Campus in the Upper Gila Valley of Arizona.
Academic Character NCACS accreditation. Semester system. Transfer and terminal programs with majors in agriculture, anthropology, art, business, education, biology, forestry, geology, home economics, justice administration, mass communications, political science, pre-engineering, pre-law, pre-medical science, pre-nursing, pre-optometry, pre-pharmacy, psychology, sociology, and technologies. Distributive requirements. Credit by exam. Courses may be repeated for credit. Evening school. Continuing education program.
Financial ACT FAS. College scholarships and loans; PELL, SEOG, NSS, NDSL, GSL, NSL, CWS. Priority application deadline March 15th.
Admissions High school graduation, GED, or minimum age of 18 required. ACT, SAT, and/or ACH recommended. $5 application fee for out-of-state students. If housing desired, include $50 deposit with application. Rolling admissions. *Early Admission, Early Decision, Concurrent Enrollment* programs. Transfers accepted. Credit possible for CLEP exams and departmental exams.
Student Life Student publications. Drama, music, religious, and political organizations. Social and scholastic clubs. All students under 18 must live at home or on campus. Dormitories and dining hall. Use or possession of liquor and/or illegal drugs prohibited. Organized sports. Student body composition: 25% minority.

[S] FRANK LLOYD WRIGHT SCHOOL OF ARCHITECTURE
Taliesin West, Scottsdale 85258

[J1] GANADO, COLLEGE OF
Ganado 86505

[J1] GLENDALE COMMUNITY COLLEGE
Glendale 85302

[1] GRAND CANYON COLLEGE
3300 West Camelback Road, Phoenix 85017, (602) 249-3300
Director of Admissions: Dori Wilson

- **Enrollment: 585m, 629w**
- **Tuition (1982/83): $2,272**
- **Room & Board: $2,190; Fees: $165**
- **Degrees offered: BA, BS, BGS, BSN**
- **Mean ACT 20; mean SAT 424v, 448m**
- **Student-faculty ratio: 25 to 1**

A private college established in 1949, affiliated with the Arizona Southern Baptist Convention. 70-acre urban campus in Phoenix, which is served by air and bus.
Academic Character NCACS accreditation. 4-1-4 system, 2 5-week summer terms. Majors offered in art, art education, behavioral sciences, Bible, biology, business, chemistry, church music, computer science, criminal justice, elementary education, English, environmental science, general studies, history, mathematics, music, music education, nursing, performing arts, physical education, psychology, religion, secondary education, social studies, sociology, special education, studio art, theatre & speech, and training & development. Minor required; offered in some major areas and in 7 additional areas. 6 hours of religion and Bible required. Independent study, honors program. Internships. Pass/fail. Preprofessional programs in 7 health fields and in law. Cooperative programs with other Baptist colleges. Study abroad. Elementary, secondary, and special education certification. ROTC, AFROTC. 131,256-volume library.
Financial ACT FAS. College scholarships, grants, loans, tuition reduction for children of Southern Baptist ministers, minority grants, deferred payment;

PELL, SEOG, NDSL, FISL, CWS. Application deadlines March 15 (scholarships & grants), August 1 (loans).
Admissions High school graduation with 16 units required. GED accepted. ACT or SAT required. $15 application fee. Rolling admissions; deadline August 1. $40 room deposit (for boarders) required on acceptance of offer of admission. *Early Decision, Early Admission* programs. Transfers accepted. Credit possible for CEEB AP and CLEP subject exams. Probational admission possible.
Student Life Student Association. Newspaper, literary journal, yearbook. Music and drama groups. Intercollegiate debate. Academic, professional, service, honorary, religious groups. Single students under 20 must live at home or on campus. No coed dorms. 25% live on campus. Drugs, liquor, gambling, dancing, profane language, firearms prohibited; smoking discouraged. Class attendance mandatory. 4 semesters of physical education and twice-weekly attendance at assembly required. 4 intercollegiate sports for men, 2 for women; intramurals. NAIA, AIAW. Student body composition: 1% Asian, 4% Black, 6% Hispanic, 4% Native American, 82% White, 3% Other. 20% from out of state.

[J1] MARICOPA TECHNICAL COMMUNITY COLLEGE
Phoenix 85034

[J1] MESA COMMUNITY COLLEGE
Mesa 85202

[J1] MOHAVE COMMUNITY COLLEGE
1971 Jagerson Avenue, Kingman 86401

[J1] NAVAJO COMMUNITY COLLEGE
Tsaile 86556, (602) 724-3311
Student Admissions & Recruitment: Lillie Peterman

- **Enrollment: 147m, 256w; 1,707 total (including part-time)**
- **Tuition (1982/83): $2,400**
- **Room & Board: $2,154-$2,370**
- **Degrees offered: AA, AS, AAS**

A private college controlled by the Navajo Tribe, established in 1968. Campuses in Tsaile and Shiprock, New Mexico. Community campuses in Window Rock and Tuba City, and in Crownpoint, NM. Tsaile campus is 24 miles from Chinle; Shiprock campus is 90 miles from Tsaile.
Academic Character NCACS accreditation. Semester system, summer term. AA offered in bilingual/bicultural education, business administration, communicative disorders, computer science, elementary education, fine arts, liberal arts, mass communications, Navajo bilingual/bicultural education, Navajo culture/history/language, sociology/human services, and special education rehabilitation. AS offered in advocates training program, automotive mechanics, computer science, nursing, phys ed, preprofessional, social work, welding. AAS offered in administration of justice, agriculture, automotive mechanics, business management, environmental health, human services & community education, secretarial science, welding. Certificates of Proficiency in several areas. Not all programs are offered at all campuses. Distributive requirements. Credit by exam possible. Cooperative work/study. Conferences, workshops. Preprofessional programs in biomedical sciences, math, engineering, forestry, resource science. Native American Health Career Opportunity Program. Minority Biomedical Research Support Program. The Support System for Science Teachers. Navajo Community College Press. Computer services, museum. Library with extensive collections on American Indians.
Financial ACT FAS. College scholarships & tuition waivers, Navajo and other tribal scholarships, BIA grants, deferred payment; PELL, SEOG, NSS, NDSL, SSIG, NSL, CWS. Application deadline March 15; applicants for tuition waiver must submit a Certification of Indian Blood.
Admissions High school graduation with a 2.0 GPA. GED accepted. Candidates without high school diploma must be 18 or over. ACT recommended. Rolling admissions; deadline August 1. $50 room deposit required on acceptance of offer of admission. *Early Admission, Concurrent Enrollment* programs. Admission deferral possible. Transfers accepted. Credit possible for CEEB AP and CLEP exams. Provisional admissions.
Student Life Student government. Radio station. Native American Folk Festival. 10 hogan-shaped residence halls. Married-student housing at Tsaile. 2 phys ed courses required. 4 intercollegiate sports for men, 4 for women; intramurals.

[1] NORTHERN ARIZONA UNIVERSITY
Flagstaff 86011, (602) 523-5511
Director of Admissions: Dr. Margaret Cibik

- **Enrollment: 4,271m, 4,068w; 11,000 total (including part-time)**
- **Tuition (1982/83): $710 (in-state), $2,750 (out-of-state)**
- **Room & Board: $1,700; Fees: $104**
- **Degrees offered: BA, BS, BFA, BMus, BMus Ed, BSEd, AA, AS**
- **Mean ACT 19**
- **Student-faculty ratio: 26 to 1**

A public university established in 1899. 689-acre small city campus in the Coconino National Forest, 2½ hour's drive from Phoenix. Air, rail, and bus service.
Academic Character NCACS and professional accreditation. Semester system, 2 5-week summer terms. 24 majors offered by the College of Arts & Sciences, 9 by Business Administration, 15 by Creative Arts, 4 by Education, 7 by Engineering & Technology, 6 by Social & Behavioral Sciences, and 7 by the Schools of Applied Sciences, 1 by Forestry, and 5 by Health Professions. Interdisciplinary and self-designed majors, area studies. Minors in some major areas and in 5 others, including Navajo. Distributive requirements. Graduate and professional degrees granted. Independent study. Honors program. Phi Beta Kappa. Cooperative work/study internships, pass/fail, credit by examination. Preprofessional programs. 3-1 medical technology and park service programs. Intensive Spanish, Traveling Scholars programs. Study abroad. Elementary, secondary, and special education certification. AFROTC, ROTC. Language lab, art gallery, observatory, 4,000-acre School Forest. 647,722-item library.
Financial ACT FAS. University scholarships, grants, loans; minority & athletic scholarships, activity grants. PELL, SEOG, NDSL, FISL, CWS, institutional work-study. Priority application deadline April 15.
Admissions High school graduation with 16 units recommended. GED accepted. Special requirements for some programs. ACT or SAT required. $10 fee for out-of-state applicants. Rolling admissions; suggest applying in November of 12th year. Deadline July 1. $75 room deposit required with acceptance of offer of admission. *Early Admission, Early Decision, Concurrent Enrollment* programs. Admission deferral possible. Transfers accepted. Credit possible for CEEB AP and CLEP exams. Probational acceptance possible.
Student Life Student-faculty government, Associated Students. Newspaper, literary magazine, radio & TV stations. Music, drama, athletic, academic, political, special interest groups. Debate team. 8 fraternities and 4 sororities, some with houses. 6% of men and women join. Coed and single-sex dorms, honors dorm, married-student apartments. 46% of students live on campus. 7 intercollegiate sports for men, 6 for women; intramurals. AIAW, NCAA, Big Sky Conference. Student body composition: 1% Asian, 1% Black, 6% Hispanic, 5% Native American, 85% White, 2% Other. 14% from out of state.

[J1] NORTHLAND PIONEER COLLEGE
1200 East Hermosa Drive, Holbrook 86025

[1] PHOENIX, UNIVERSITY OF
2525 North Third Street, Phoenix 85004, (602) 258-3666

- **Enrollment: 140m, 83w; 2,000 total (including part-time & branches)**
- **Tuition (1982/83): $X,XXX**
- **Degrees offered: BA, BS**

A private, coeducational, non-sectarian, upper-division university. Branch campuses in California, Colorado, Mexico, Puerto Rico, and the Virgin Islands.
Academic Character NCACS accreditation. Semester system with additional 8-week terms year-round. Majors offered in business administration, health services administration, management, management/quality control, and nursing. Master's degrees granted in education, management, management/quality control, and management in human relations & organizational behavior. MBA also granted. University programs are designed to meet the needs of adult professionals. Degree programs can commence at any time during the year. Not all programs are available in all geographical areas.
Admissions Applicants must have a minimum of thirty transferable semester units and two years of degree-related work exprience in order to apply. Rolling admissions policy. Advanced placement credit possible for CEEB Advanced Placement examinations.

[J1] PHOENIX COLLEGE
Phoenix 85013

[J1] PIMA COMMUNITY COLLEGE
Tucson 85709

[2] PRESCOTT COLLEGE
220 Grove Avenue, Prescott 86301

[J1] RIO SALADO COLLEGE
PO Box 13349, Phoenix 85002

[J1] SCOTTSDALE COMMUNITY COLLEGE
Scottsdale 85253

[P] SOUTHWESTERN BAPTIST BIBLE COLLEGE
2625 East Cactus Road, Phoenix 85032

[2] SOUTHWESTERN UNIVERSITY
4621 N. First Avenue, Dept.5, Tucson 85718

[J1] YAVAPAI COLLEGE
Prescott 86301

ARKANSAS (AR)

[1] ARKANSAS, UNIVERSITY OF
Fayetteville 72701, (501) 575-5346
Director of Admissions: Larry F. Matthews

- **Enrollment: 8,792m, 6,383w**
- **Tuition & Fees (1982/83): $780 (in-state), $1,920 (out-of-state)**
- **Room & Board: $1,750**
- **Degrees offered: BA, BS, BArch, BLArch, BMus, BSEngs, AA, AS**
- **Mean ACT 19**
- **Student-faculty ratio: 18 to 1**

A public university established in 1871. 329-acre urban campus located in small city of Fayetteville, 2½ hours from Tulsa, 4 hours from Little Rock. Served by air and bus.

Academic Character NCACS and professional accreditation. Semester system, 9 summer terms of 3 to 12 weeks. 32 majors offered by the College of Agriculture & Home Economics, 35 by the College of Arts & Sciences, 15 by the College of Business Administration, 17 by the College of Education, 8 by the College of Engineering, and 2 by the School of Architecture. Self-designed majors. Associate degrees offered by Business Administration, Engineering, and the School of Nursing. Distributive requirements. Graduate and professional degrees granted. Independent study. Honors program. Phi Beta Kappa. Pass/fail. Preprofessional programs in chiropractic medicine, dental hygiene, dentistry, medical technology, medicine, nursing, optometry, pharmacy, physical therapy, theology. Study abroad in Japan. Elementary, secondary, and special education certification. ROTC, AFROTC. 981,000-volume library.

Financial CEEB CSS and ACT FAS. University scholarships, grants, athletic scholarships, loans; state residents receive priority consideration. PELL, NSS, NDSL, CWS. Application deadline April 1.

Admissions High school graduation with 15 units required. GED accepted. ACT with composite score of 18 required; lower scores may be accepted conditionally. $15 application fee. Rolling admissions. $60 room deposit required on acceptance of offer of admission. *Early Admission* Program. Transfers accepted. Credit possible for CEEB AP and CLEP exams.

Student Life Student government. Publications. Music and drama groups. Debate team. Religious, service, political, honorary, and special interest groups. 19 fraternities and 12 sororities. Single freshmen under 21 must live at home or on campus. Dorms for men and women. Married-student housing. 55% of students live on campus. 8 intercollegiate sports for men, 5 for women; over 100 intramural and club sports. AIAW, Southwest Conference. Student body composition: 2% Asian, 5% Black, 1% Hispanic, 1% Native American, 91% White. 18% from out of state.

■[1] ARKANSAS, UNIVERSITY OF, AT LITTLE ROCK
33rd and University, Little Rock 72204, (501) 569-3127
Director of Admissions: D. Sue Pine

- **Undergraduates: 2,090m, 2,311w; 9,729 total (including graduates)**
- **Tuition & Fees (1982/83): $730 (in-state), $1,760 (out-of-state)**
- **Degrees offered: BA, BS, BBA, BMus, BMus Ed, BSEd, AA, AS**
- **Mean ACT 16.9**
- **Student-faculty ratio: 17 to 1**

A public university established in 1927. 150-acre urban campus. Served by air and bus.

Academic Character NCACS and professional accreditation. Semester system, 2 6-week summer terms. 65 majors offered by the colleges of Business Administration, Communication, Education, Fine Arts, Liberal Arts, Sciences, and by the School of Engineering. Minors offered in most major fields and in several additional areas. Courses in 6 additional areas. Distributive requirements. Graduate and professional degrees granted. Independent study. Honors program. Cooperative work/study, pass/fail, credit by exam, internships. Preprofessional programs in 12 areas. 2-year transfer programs in pharmacy and engineering. Elementary and secondary education certification. ROTC. Language lab. 320,500-volume library.

Financial CEEB CSS and ACT FAS. University scholarships, grants, loans, deferred payment; PELL, SEOG, NSS, NDSL, GSL, NSL, CWS. Application deadlines March 15 (scholarships), May 1 (grants and loans).

Admissions High school graduation with 15 units required. GED accepted. SAT or ACT required. $5 application fee. Rolling admissions; suggest applying at least 30 days before registration. *Early Admission, Early Decision, Concurrent Enrollment* programs. Admission deferral possible. Transfers accepted. Credit possible for CLEP exams; placement possible for CEEB AP.

Student Life Student government. Newspaper, magazine, yearbook. Music and drama guilds. Political, religious, service, honorary, academic, and special interest groups. 8 fraternities and 7 sororities, all with houses. No university housing. Cafeteria. 1 hour of phys ed required. 6 intercollegiate sports for men, 5 for women; 14 intramurals. AIAW, NCAA. Student body composition: 12.5% Black, 0.3% Hispanic, 1.5% Native American, 85.7% White. 3% from out of state.

■[1] ARKANSAS, UNIVERSITY OF, AT MONTICELLO
Monticello 71655, (501) 367-6811
Registrar: Robert L. Kirchman

- **Undergraduates: 779m, 769w; 1,824 total (including part-time)**
- **Tuition & Fees (1982/83): $768 (in-state), $1,678 (out-of-state)**
- **Room & Board: $1,400-$1,510**
- **Degrees offered: BA, BS**
- **Mean ACT 15**
- **Student-faculty ratio: 20 to 1**

A public university established in 1909. 1,600-acre wooded, rural campus in Southeast Arkansas, 85 miles from Little Rock. Served by bus; air in Little Rock.

Academic Character NCACS and professional accreditation. Semester system, 2 5½-week summer terms. Majors offered in accounting, agriculture, art, biology, business administration, business education, chemistry, computer science, elementary education, English, forestry, French, general science, geology, history, history & social studies, management, marketing, mathematics, music, office administration, physical science, physics, political science, psychology, speech & dramatic arts, wildlife & fisheries management, and health, physical education, & recreation. Minors offered. Courses in 4 additional fields. Distributive requirements. Independent study. Preprofessional programs in agriculture, engineering, law, medicine, nursing, and pharmacy. 3-1 programs in medical science and medical technology. Elementary, secondary, early childhood, and special education certification. ROTC. Language lab. 92,669-volume library with microform resources.

Financial ACT FAS. University scholarships (for AR residents only), grants, loans; PELL, SEOG, NSS, NDSL, NSL, CWS, university work program. Application deadlines April 15 (scholarships), July 15 (loans).

Admissions High school graduation with 15 units required. GED accepted. Exam required for applicants without diploma/GED. ACT required. Rolling admissions; application deadline 2 weeks before registration. $20 room deposit required on acceptance of offer of admission. *Early Admission, Early Decision, Concurrent Enrollment* programs. Admission deferral possible. Transfers accepted. Credit possible for CLEP exams; university has own advanced placement program.

Student Life Student government. Newspaper, yearbook. Debate, music, religious, political, honorary, academic, service, and special interest groups. 5 fraternities and 3 sororities. 15% of men and 10% of women join. No coed dorms. Married-student housing. 34% of students live on campus. Liquor prohibited on campus. Class attendance required. 7 intercollegiate sports for men, 3 for women; intramurals. AIAW, AWISA, NAIA, Arkansas Intercollegiate Conference. Student body composition: 0.2% Asian, 20% Black, 0.4% Hispanic, 0.4% Native American, 79% White. 6% from out of state.

■[1] ARKANSAS, UNIVERSITY OF, AT PINE BLUFF
Box 31, University Drive, Pine Bluff 71601, (501) 541-6500
Director of Admissions: C. N. Toney

- **Undergraduates: 1,125m, 1,429w**
- **Tuition (1982/83): $710 (in-state), $1,842 (out-of-state)**
- **Room & Board: $1,750; Fees: $74**
- **Degrees offered: BA, BS, AA, AAS**
- **Student-faculty ratio: 12 to 1**

A public university established in 1873. 295-acre urban campus, 40 miles southeast of Little Rock. Served by air and bus.

Academic Character NCACS and professional accreditation. Semester system, 2 5-week summer terms. 56 majors offered in the areas of arts, sciences, agriculture, business, communications, education, home economics, social sciences, physical education. Distributive requirements. Cooperative work/study. Preprofessional programs in law, medical technology, medicine, nursing. Elementary and secondary education certification. ROTC. University farm. 140,000-volume library.

Financial University scholarships, grants, loans; PELL, NDSL, GSL, CWS. Preferred application deadline 6 weeks before semester begins.

Admissions High school graduation with 15 units required. GED accepted. Interview recommended. ACT required. Rolling admissions; suggest applying by fall of senior year. $10 room deposit required on acceptance of offer of admission. *Early Admission* Program. Transfers accepted. Credit possible for CLEP exams.

Student Life Student government. Newspaper, yearbook. Music, speech, and drama groups. Religious, academic, and special interest organizations. 4 fraternities, 1 with house, and 4 sororities without houses. 5% of men and 2% of women join. All students must live at home, on campus, or in approved housing. 32% live on campus. Liquor prohibited on campus. 2 semesters of phys ed required. ROTC required for 1st-year men. 5 intercollegiate sports for men, 2 for women; intramurals. NAIA, NCAA. Student body composition: 0.2% Asian, 85.5% Black, 1.6% Hispanic, 0.2% Native American, 11.1% White. 10% from out of state.

[2] ARKANSAS BAPTIST COLLEGE
Little Rock 72200

[1] ARKANSAS COLLEGE
Batesville 72501, (501) 793-9813
Director of Admissions: John A. Thompson

- **Undergraduates: 170m, 225w; 514 total (including part-time)**
- **Tuition (1982/83): $3,300**
- **Room & Board: $1,596-$1,696**
- **Degree offered: BA**
- **Mean ACT 18**
- **Student-faculty ratio: 13 to 1**

A private college affiliated with the Presbyterian Church, US, founded in 1872. 122-acre campus in small town of Batesville, 90 miles from Little Rock. Served by air and bus.
Academic Character NCACS and professional accreditation. 4-1-4 system, 6-week summer term. Majors offered in accounting, business administration, data processing, management, elementary education, physical education, psychology, social work, biology, chemistry, health care administration, mathematics, medical technology, history, English, media arts, music, and theatre. Distributive requirements. Independent study. Cooperative work/study. Credit by exam. Preprofessional programs in several health and science fields, law, and ministry. Computer centers, media center. 69,000-volume library with microform resources.
Financial ACT FAS. College scholarships, grants, Presbyterian grants, state scholarships and loans; PELL, SEOG, NDSL, GSL, CWS, college work program. Application deadlines April 1 (PELL, FFS), June 24 (state scholarships).
Admissions High school graduation with 16 units required. GED accepted. ACT or SAT required. $15 application fee. Rolling admissions; application deadline July 15. $100 deposit required on acceptance of offer of admission. Transfers accepted. Credit possible for CEEB AP and CLEP exams; college has own advanced placement program.
Student Life Student government. Newspaper, yearbook, radio station. Music and drama groups. Over 20 academic, religious, and special interest groups. Single students must live at home or on campus. Married-student housing. 2 credits in physical fitness/activity required. 5 intercollegiate sports for men, 2 for women; intramurals. NAIA, AWISA, AIC.

[1] ARKANSAS STATE UNIVERSITY
State University, Jonesboro 72467, (501) 972-3024
Dean of Admissions & Records: Greta Mack

- **Undergraduates: 3,164m, 3,639w; 7,448 total (including graduates)**
- **Tuition & Fees (1982/83): $730 (in-state), $1,280 (out-of-state)**
- **Room & Board: $1,520-$1,750**
- **Degrees offered: BA, BS, BFA, BGS, BMus, BMus Ed, BSAgr, BSAgr Eng, BSEd, BSE, BSN, AAS, ASN, AGS, AS**
- **Student-faculty ratio: 21 to 1**

A public university established in 1909. 800-acre campus on Crowley's Ridge in Jonesboro, bordering Mississippi Delta. 65 miles from Memphis and 133 miles from Little Rock. Branch junior college campus in Beebe. Served by air, rail, and bus.
Academic Character NCACS and professional accreditation. Semester system, 2 5-week summer terms. 64 majors offered by the colleges of Business, Communications, Engineering & Agriculture, Fine Arts, Liberal Arts, Science, and Nursing. Self-designed majors. Distributive requirements for some students. English proficiency requirement. Masters degrees granted. Independent study. Honors program. Cooperative work/study, internships. Combined degree programs with dentistry, law, medicine, and pharmacy schools. Double degrees. Elementary, secondary, and special education certification. ROTC. Museum. Language lab. 377,441-volume library with microform resources.
Financial Guaranteed tuition. CEEB CSS. University scholarships, loans, grants; PELL, SEOG, NDSL, NSL, CWS. Application deadline May 1.
Admissions High school graduation with 15 units required. All Arkansas high school graduates admitted; 'C' average required for out-of-state students. GED accepted. ACT required. Rolling admissions; suggest applying by July 31. *Early Admission* and *Concurrent Enrollment* programs. Transfers accepted. Credit possible for CLEP exams; university has own advanced placement program.
Student Life Student government. Newspaper, magazine, yearbook, folklore journal, radio and TV stations. Music and drama groups. Debate. Religious, political, academic, service, and special interest organizations. 11 fraternities, 1 with house, 8 sororities without houses, and one local social club. 16% of students join. No coed dorms. Married-student housing. 32% of students live on campus. Liquor prohibited on campus. 2 semesters of phys ed required. 10 intercollegiate sports for men, 6 for women; extensive intramural program. AIAW, NCAA, Southland Conference. Student body composition: 0.5% Asian, 10.4% Black, 0.4% Hispanic, 0.7% Native American, 87.2% White, 0.8% Other. 12% from out of state.

[1] ARKANSAS TECH UNIVERSITY
Russellville 72801, (501) 968-0272
Registrar: Charles M. Shelton

- **Undergraduates: 1,446m, 1,219w**
- **Tuition & Fees (1982/83): $750 (in-state), $1,450 (out-of-state)**
- **Room & Board: $1,440-$1,480**
- **Degrees offered: BA, BS, BFA, BSN, AS, AA**
- **Mean ACT 18**
- **Student-faculty ratio: 20 to 1**

A public university established in 1909. 487-acre campus on Lake Dardanelle in small city of Russellville, 75 miles from Little Rock. Served by rail.
Academic Character NCACS and professional accreditation. Semester system, 2 5-week summer terms. 3 majors offered by the School of Education, 12 by the School of Liberal & Fine Arts, 9 by the School of Physical & Life Sciences, and 13 by the School of Systems Science. Courses in 10 additional areas. Distributive requirements. MEd granted. AS offered in medical assistance, mining & minerals technology, secretarial science; AA in general studies. Independent study. Preprofessional programs in dentistry, forestry, law, medicine, pharmacy, veterinary medicine. Exchange program with Westfield State College, Westfield, Mass. Elementary, secondary, and library media education certification. ROTC. 166,034-volume library with microform resources.
Financial University scholarships, grants, loans; state, music, and ROTC scholarships; PELL, SEOG, NDSL, FISL, GSL, CWS. Loan application deadline May 1.
Admissions High school graduation or 15 units and principal's recommendation required. GED or University tests accepted for veterans and applicants over 21. Rolling admissions. $50 room deposit required on acceptance of offer of admission. *Early Admission* Program. Admission deferral possible. Transfers accepted. Credit possible for CLEP exams.
Student Life Student government. Newspaper, yearbook. Music and drama groups. Women's and Black Student Associations. Religious, political, academic, service, and special interest groups. 7 fraternities and 5 sororities. Single students under 21 must live at home or on campus. No coed dorms. Married-student housing. 40% of students live on campus. 2 semesters of phys ed required. 9 intercollegiate sports for men, 5 for women; several intramural and club sports. NAIA, Arkansas Intercollegiate and Arkansas Women's Intercollegiate Sports Conferences. Student body composition: 0.2% Asian, 4.1% Black, 0.2% Hispanic, 0.5% Native American, 95% White. 3.8% from out of state.

[1] CENTRAL ARKANSAS, UNIVERSITY OF
Conway 72032, (501) 450-3128 *OR* 327-1837
Director of Admissions: Tommy G. Smith

- **Undergraduates: 1,964m, 2,945w; 6,007 total (including graduates)**
- **Tuition & Fees (1982/83): $710 (in-state), $1,420 (out-of-state)**
- **Room & Board: $1,680**
- **Degrees offered: BA, BS, BBA, BMus, BMus Ed, BSEd**
- **Student-faculty ratio: 20 to 1**

A public university established in 1907. 200-acre campus 27 miles north of Little Rock. Air and rail in Little Rock.
Academic Character NCACS and professional accreditation. Semester system, 2 5-week summer terms. 63 majors offered in the areas of arts, sciences, business/management, communications, education, languages, health, home economics, library science, computer science, and social sciences. Distributive requirements. MA, MBA, MME, MS, MSE, MSN granted. Independent study. Honors program. Pass/fail. Elementary, secondary, and special education certification. ROTC. 310,000-volume library.
Financial ACT FAS. University scholarships, grants, loans, ROTC scholarships; PELL, SEOG, NSL, NDSL, CWS. Application deadline May 1.
Admissions High school graduation with 15 units required. GED accepted. ACT required. Rolling admissions; suggest applying by April. $50 room deposit required on acceptance of offer of admission. *Early Admission* and *Early Decision* programs. Admission deferral possible. Transfers accepted. Credit possible for CLEP exams. University has own advanced placement program.
Student Life Student government. Newspaper, magazine, yearbook. Music and drama groups. Debate. Religious, service, honorary, professional, and special interest organizations. 10 fraternities and 8 sororities; none have houses. 30% of men and 25% of women join. No coed dorms. Married-student housing. 30% of students live on campus. Liquor prohibited on campus. 4 semesters of phys ed required. 10 intercollegiate sports; several intramurals. Student body composition: 12% Black, 87% White, 1% Other. 5% from out of state.

[2] CENTRAL BAPTIST COLLEGE
College Ave., Conway 72032, (501) 329-6872
Registar & Admissions Officer: Norma Jean Tio

- **Enrollment: 118m, 79w; 271 total (including part-time)**
- **Tuition (1982/83): $720**
- **Room & Board: $1,200**
- **Degrees offered: BA, BS, AA**

A private college established in 1950, controlled by the Arkansas Missionary Baptist Association. 11-acre campus in the small city of Conway in central Arkansas, 30 miles from Little Rock. Served by rail.
Academic Character AABC accreditation. Semester system. Majors offered in Bible, church music, nursing, missions, and religious education. Minor may be required. Minors offered in English, history, music, religious education, pastoral studies. Courses offered in 10 additional areas. Distributive requirements. MA offered. Pre-seminary studies program. 1-year business course. BS/RN program with the University of Central Arkansas. ROTC. Correspondence school.
Financial College scholarships, ministerial and religious education discounts, music and athletic scholarships, state grants; PELL, CWS.
Admissions High school graduation or 15 units required. GED accepted for veterans. ACT required. $10 room deposit (for boarders) required with application. Rolling admissions; application deadline August 15. Transfers accepted.
Student Life Student government. Association of Baptist Students. Ministers' Association. Students under 21 must live at home or on campus. No coed dorms. Married-student housing. Liquor, gambling, drugs prohibited on campus. Attendance at chapel services required. 4 hours of phys ed required. Intercollegiate basketball.

[J2] CROWLEY'S RIDGE COLLEGE
Paragould 72450

[J1] EAST ARKANSAS COMMUNITY COLLEGE
Forrest City 72335

[J1] GARLAND COUNTY COMMUNITY COLLEGE
Hot Springs 71913

[1] HARDING UNIVERSITY
Searcy 72143, (501) 268-6161
Director of Admissions: Durward McGaha

- **Enrollment: 1,303m, 1,448w**
- **Tuition (1982/83): $2,460**
- **Room & Board: $1,950; Fees: $177**
- **Degrees offered: BA, BS, BBA, BSMedTech, BSN, AA**
- **Student-faculty ratio: 21 to 1**

A private university affiliated with the Church of Christ, established in 1919. 200-acre rural campus located in the small city of Searcy, 45 miles from Little Rock. Served by bus; air in Little Rock.
Academic Character NCACS and professional accreditation. Semester system, 2 5-week summer terms, May intersession. 51 majors offered by the College of Arts & Sciences and the schools of Business, Education, and Nursing. Self-designed majors. American Studies program. Minor required. Minors offered in all major fields and in Greek. Courses in geography, German, Hebrew. Distributive requirements may be waived by exam. 4 Bible courses required. Masters degrees granted. Independent study. Honors program. Cooperative work/study, pass/fail, internships. Preprofessional programs in agriculture, architecture, optometry, pharmacy. 3-2 programs in engineering, dentistry, law, medical technology, medicine, nursing. 4-2 program in engineering. Study abroad. Elementary, secondary, and special education certification. Computer center. Over 200,000-volume library with microfilm resources.
Financial ACT FAS. University scholarships, loans, deferred payment; PELL, SEOG, NDSL, FISL, CWS. Application deadlines May 1 (scholarships), April 1 (loans).
Admissions High school graduation with 15 units required. ACT required. $15 application fee, $25 housing reservation due with application. Rolling admissions; suggest applying between November and February. *Early Admission* Program. Transfers accepted. Credit possible for CEEB AP and CLEP exams.
Student Life Student government. Newspaper, yearbook, radio station. Music, drama, debate groups. Intercollegiate business games. Religious, political, honorary, academic, and special interest organizations. 20 men's and 23 women's social clubs; none have houses. Single students under 23 must live on campus. No coed dorms. Married-student apartments. 80% of students live on campus. Liquor, gambling, hazing, smoking, obscene literature, profanity prohibited on campus. Students who falsify marital status dismissed. Class attendance and daily chapel required. 4 semester hours of phys ed required, except for veterans. 8 intercollegiate sports for men, 3 for women; intramurals. NAIA and Arkansas Intercollegiate Conference. Student body composition: 3% Black, 96% White, 1% Other. 72% from out of state.

[1] HENDERSON STATE UNIVERSITY
1100 Henderson St., Arkadelphia 71923, (501) 246-5511
Director of Admissions: Hershel F. Lucht

- **Enrollment: 1,204m, 1,432w**
- **Tuition (1982/83): $720 (in-state), $1,440 (out-of-state)**
- **Room & Board: $1,456; Fees: $40**
- **Degrees offered: BA, BS, BMus, BMus Ed, BFA, BSN, BSBA, BSEd, AA**
- **Mean ACT 17**
- **Student-faculty ratio: 15 to 1**

A public university established in 1929. 132-acre campus in the small city of Arkadelphia, 70 miles from Little Rock. Served by bus and rail; air in Little Rock.
Academic Character NCACS and professional accreditation. Semester system, 2 5-week summer terms. 36 majors offered by the schools of Business, Education, Fine Arts, Liberal Arts, and Natural Sciences & Mathematics. Courses in 8 additional areas. Distributive requirements. Masters degrees granted. Honors program. Pass/fail. Preprofessional programs in dentistry, engineering, law, medicine, pharmacy. Elementary, secondary, and special education certification. ROTC. Computer center, closed-circuit TV studio. 200,000-volume library.
Financial ACT FAS. University scholarships, loans, music, ROTC, and athletic scholarships, deferred payment; PELL, SEOG, NDSL, FISL, GSL, CWS, university work program. Scholarship application deadline March 1.
Admissions High school graduation with 15 units required. GED accepted. ACT required. Rolling admissions; deadline is August 26. *Early Admission, Early Decision, Concurrent Enrollment* programs. Admission deferral possible. Transfers accepted. Credit possible for CEEB AP and CLEP exams.
Student Life Student government. Newspaper, magazine, yearbook, radio station. Debate, music, and drama groups. Religious, political, honorary, academic, service, and special interest organizations. 7 fraternities without houses, and 6 sororities with houses. 15% of men and 10% of women join. Single students under 21 must live at home or on campus. No coed dorms. Married-student housing. 50% of students live on campus. Liquor prohibited on campus. 2 hours phys ed or military science required. 8 intercollegiate sports for men, 4 for women. AIC, AWISA, NAIA. Student body composition: 19% minority. 4% of students from out of state.

[1] HENDRIX COLLEGE
Conway 72032, (501) 329-6811
Dean of Admissions: Rudy Pollan

- **Undergraduates: 488m, 475w**
- **Tuition (1982/83): $3,200**
- **Room & Board: $1,500-$1,560; Fees: $75**
- **Degree offered: BA**
- **Mean ACT 23.5; mean SAT 509v, 535m**
- **Student-faculty ratio: 15 to 1**

A private college established in 1884, affiliated with United Methodist Church. 120-acre suburban campus, 30 miles from Little Rock. Served by air and bus.
Academic Character NCACS and professional accreditation. Trimester system. Majors offered in art, biology, chemistry, economics/business, elementary education, English, French, German, history, humanities, mathematics, music, philosophy, physical education, physics, political science, psychology, religion, sociology, Spanish, and theatre arts. Special majors. Courses in Latin, Greek. Distributive requirements. Independent study. Honors program. Pass/fail. Preprofessional programs in dentistry, law, medical technology, medicine, pharmacy, theology. 3-2 program, in engineering with Columbia U. Summer courses at Gulf Coast Research Lab. Exchange program with Southern College University Union. Washington Semester. Study abroad. Elementary and secondary education certification. ROTC at U. of Central Arkansas. Language lab. 130,000-volume library.
Financial ACT FAS. University scholarships, grants, loans, state scholarships, ½-tuition scholarships to ministerial students and children of ministers, deferred payment; PELL, SEOG, NDSL, FISL, CWS, college has own work program. Scholarship application deadline April 1.
Admissions High school graduation with 16 units required. SAT or ACT required. $10 application fee. Rolling admissions. $100 deposit required on acceptance of offer of admission. *Early Decision* and *Early Admission* programs. Transfers accepted. Credit possible for CEEB AP and CLEP exams.
Student Life Student government. Newspaper, magazine, yearbook. Music and drama groups. Outdoor activities program. Religious, honorary, academic, and special interest organizations. All 1st-year students must live at home or on campus. No coed dorms. No married-student housing. 77% live on campus. Liquor and nonprescription drugs prohibited on campus. 7 intercollegiate sports for men, 3 for women; several intramural and club sports. NAIA, Arkansas Intercollegiate Conference, Arkansas Women's Intercollegiate Sports Association. Student body composition: 4.5% Black, 89.4% White, 6.1% Other. 8% from out of state.

[1] JOHN BROWN UNIVERSITY
Siloam Springs 72761, (501) 524-3131
Acting Director of Admissions: Roger Kline

- **Undergraduates: 383m, 320w**
- **Tuition (1982/83): $2,500**
- **Room & Board: $1,900**
- **Degrees offered: BA, BS, BSEd, BMus, BMus Ed, AS, AA**
- **Student-faculty ratio: 15 to 1**

A private, Christian university established in 1919. 300-acre small-city campus in northwest Arkansas, 90 miles from Tulsa, Oklahoma. Served by bus. Air in Fayetteville.
Academic Character NCACS and professional accreditation. Semester system. 34 majors offered in the areas of arts & literature, Biblical studies, engineering, natural science, social studies, and teacher education. Minor required. Minors offered in most major fields and 3 additional areas. Courses in 6 additional areas. Distributive requirements. 12 semester hours of religion required. Cooperative work/study. Credit by exam. Preprofessional programs in dentistry, engineering, law, medicine, ministry, nursing, pharmacy. Member Small-College Consortium. Elementary and secondary education certification. 76, 631-volume library.
Financial ACT FAS. University scholarships, loans, grants; PELL, SEOG, NDSL, FISL, CWS. Scholarship application deadline April 1.
Admissions High school graduation with 15 units required. ACT, SAT, PSAT, or CQT required; ACT preferred. $25 application fee; $50 room deposit due with application (refunded if not admitted). Rolling admissions; suggest applying by March 1. *Early Admission* Program. Transfers accepted. Credit possible for CEEB AP and CLEP exams; university has own advanced placement program.
Student Life Student government. Newspaper, yearbook, radio & TV stations. Music and drama groups. Religious, service, academic, and special interest groups. Seniors over 21 may live off campus. No coed dorms. Married-student housing. 80% of students live on campus. Liquor prohibited on campus. Attendance in class and at 2 convocations per week required. 2 semesters of phys ed required. 4 intercollegiate sports for men, 5 for women; several intramural and club sports. Student body composition: 5% Black, 90% White, 5% Other. 75% from out of state.

[J1] MISSISSIPPI COUNTY COMMUNITY COLLEGE
PO Box 1309, Blytheville 72315

[J1] NORTH ARKANSAS COMMUNITY COLLEGE
Harrison 72601

[1] OUACHITA BAPTIST UNIVERSITY
Arkadelphia 71923, (501) 246-4531
Director of Admissions Counseling: Harold Johnson

- **Enrollment: 736m, 734w; 1,704 total (including part-time)**
- **Tuition (1982/83): $2,460**
- **Room & Board: $1,620; Fees: $40**
- **Degrees offered: BA, BS, BSEd, BMus, BMus Ed**
- **Mean ACT 20**
- **Student-faculty ratio: 16 to 1**

A private university established in 1886, affiliated with the Southern Baptist Church. 200-acre small-city campus, 70 miles from Little Rock. Served by bus and rail. Air 35 miles away in Hot Springs, and in Little Rock.

Academic Character NCACS and professional accreditation. Semester system, 2 5-week summer terms. 32 majors offered in the areas of business & economics, education, humanities, natural science, religion & philosophy, social science, and music. Distributive requirements. 2 semesters of religion required. Masters degrees granted. Independent study. Honors program. Pass/fail. Internships. Preprofessional programs in architecture, dental hygiene, dentistry, dietetics, engineering, landscape architecture, medical technology, medicine, nursing, pharmacy, physical therapy. 3-2 programs in dentistry, engineering, medicine, pharmacy. Cross-registration with Henderson State. Exchange programs with schools in Japan and Nigeria. Elementary, secondary, and special education certification. ROTC. Computer center, language lab, museum, TV studio. 104,000-volume library with microform resources.
Financial ACT FAS. University scholarships, grants, loans, ministerial scholarships; PELL, SEOG, NDSL, GSL, CWS, university has own work program. Application deadline May 1.
Admissions High school graduation with 15 units required. GED accepted. ACT required. $25 application fee. Rolling admissions; suggest applying by May 1. $100 deposit required on acceptance of offer of admission. *Early Admission* and *Concurrent Enrollment* programs. Transfers accepted. Credit possible for CEEB AP, CLEP, and ACT PEP exams; university has own advanced placement program. Academic Skills Development Program.
Student Life Student government. Newspaper, yearbook, magazine. Music and drama groups. Ethnic and women's organizations. Religious, political, academic, service, and special interest groups. 4 fraternities and 4 sororities. 10% of men and women join. All students must live at home or on campus. No coed dorms. Married-student housing. 82% of students live on campus. Liquor, drugs, gambling prohibited on campus. Class attendance required for freshmen and sophomores. Weekly chapel attendance required. 4 semesters of phys ed required. 9 intercollegiate sports for men, 3 for women; several intramural and club sports. AWISA, NAIA. Student body composition: 6% Black, 1% Hispanic, 92% White, 1% Other. 25% from out of state.

[1] OZARKS, COLLEGE OF THE
Clarksville 72830, (501) 754-2788
Director of Admissions & Coordinator of Student Life: Greg Blackburn

- **Undergraduates: 335m, 292w; 684 total (including part-time)**
- **Tuition (1982/83): $1,425**
- **Room & Board: $1,300-$1,350**
- **Degrees offered: BA, BS, BGS, BApp Sc, AAS**
- **Student-faculty ratio: 15 to 1**

A private college founded in 1834, affiliated with the Presbyterian Synod of Red River and Synod of the Sun. 30-acre small-town campus located east of Fort Smith and 105 miles from Little Rock. Served by bus.
Academic Character NCACS accreditation. 4-1-4 system. 9 majors offered by the Division of Business Administration, 6 by the Division of Education, 8 in secondary education, 5 by the Division of Fine Arts & Humanities, 8 by the Division of Natural Sciences & Mathematics, and 5 by the Division of Social Sciences. Minor required for some majors. Minors offered in some major fields and in 3 additional areas. Distributive requirements. 1 religion course required. Honors program. Pass/fail. Elementary, secondary, physical, special, middle school, and kindergarten education certification. ROTC. 70,000-volume library with microform resources.
Financial ACT FAS. College scholarships and loans, state scholarships, ROTC scholarships; PELL, SEOG, NDSL, GSL, CWS.
Admissions High school graduation with 15 units required. GED accepted. ACT or SAT required. $20 application fee. Rolling admissions. Transfers accepted. Credit possible for CLEP exams. SSDS program.
Student Life Student government. Music and drama groups. Honorary, religious, academic, service, and special interest groups. Coed and single-sex dorms. Married-student housing. Attendance in class and at 4-8 convocations per year required. 4 hours of phys ed or ROTC required. 5 intercollegiate sports for men, 1 for women. AIC.

[1] PHILANDER SMITH COLLEGE
812 West 13th Street, Little Rock 72202, (501) 375-9845

- **Enrollment: 302m, 238w; 596 total (including part-time)**
- **Tuition & Fees (1982/83): $1,600**
- **Room & Board: $2,000**
- **Degrees offered: BA, BS, BS in Home Economics**

A private, coeducational, liberal arts college affiliated with the United Methodist Church. Founded as a seminary in 1877, merged wih George R. Smith College in 1933. Campus in urban Little Rock, which is served by air and bus.
Academic Character NCACS accreditation. Semester system. College offers liberal arts and preprofessional curricula leading to the degrees of Bachelor of Arts, Bachelor of Science, and Bachelor of Science in home economics. Remedial mathematics and English programs available.
Financial Financial aid available includes scholarships, grants-in-aid, loans, and work/study. PELL, SEOG, NDSL, CWS. United Student Aid Fund.
Admissions Admissions notification is done on a rolling basis. *Early Admission* Program for high school juniors. *Early Decision* Program for applicants whose first choice is Philander Smith College. Advanced placement credit possible.

[J1] PHILLIPS COUNTY COMMUNITY COLLEGE
Helena 72342

[J1] SHORTER COLLEGE
North Little Rock 72114, (501) 374-6305

- **Enrollment: 95m, 44w; 161 total (including part-time)**
- **Tuition & Fees (1982/83): $2,950**
- **Degrees offered: AA**

A private, coeducational junior college related to the A.M.E. Church. Founded in 1886 as the Bethel Institute, adopted present name in 1903. Campus in urban Little Rock, which is served by air and bus.
Academic Character NCACS accreditation. Semester system. Transfer and preprofessional programs in the areas of liberal arts, secretarial science, teacher training, business education, religious education, and home economics. The College is affiliated with Jackson Theological Seminary which confers the B.D. degree.
Student Life Dormitories and dining hall available.

[1] SOUTHERN ARKANSAS UNIVERSITY
Magnolia 71753, (501) 234-5120

- **Undergraduates: 705m, 843w; 2,037 total**
- **Tuition (1982/83): $720 (in-state), $1,150 (out-of-state)**
- **Room & Board: $1,430; Fees: $30**
- **Degrees offered: BA, BS, BBA, BMus Ed, BSEd, BApp Studies, AA, AS**
- **Student-faculty ratio: 12 to 1**

A public university established in 1909. 120-acre campus in southwestern Arkansas. Served by bus.
Academic Character NCACS and professional accreditation. Semester system, 2 5-week summer terms. 54 majors offered by the schools of Business Administration, Education, Liberal & Performing Arts, Science & Technology, and by the Division of Applied Studies. Minors offered in most major fields and in 11 additional areas. Distributive requirements. Exams required for graduation. MEd granted. Independent study. Honors program. Credit by exam. Preprofessional programs in agricultural engineering, dentistry, engineering, forestry, law, medicine, nursing, optometry, pharmacy, veterinary science. Elementary and secondary education certification. ROTC. 150,000-volume library.
Financial ACT FAS. University scholarships, grants; PELL, SEOG, NSS, NDSL, GSL, NSL, CWS. Application deadline March 15.
Admissions High school graduation with 15 units required. GED accepted; university has own entrance exam. Out of state students must rank in upper half of class. ACT required. Rolling admissions. $40 room deposit required on acceptance of offer of admission. *Early Admission* and *Concurrent Enrollment* programs. Transfers accepted. Credit possible for CLEP exams. Academic Opportunity Program.
Student Life Student government. Newspaper, yearbook. Music and drama groups. Rodeo club. Men's and women's associations. Religious, political, honorary, academic, professional, and special interest groups. Social fraternities and sororities. Married students, veterans, and those over 21 may live off campus. No coed dorms. Married-student housing. 7 semesters of phys ed required. 8 intercollegiate sports for men, 4 for women; intramurals. AIAW, NAIA. Student body composition: 0.3% Asian, 22.1% Black, 0.2% Hispanic, 0.1% Native American, 76.7% White.

■[J2] SOUTHERN ARKANSAS UNIVERSITY
300 Southwest Avenue, El Dorado 71730

■[J1] SOUTHERN ARKANSAS UNIVERSITY — TECHNICAL BRANCH
PO Box 3048, East Camden 71701

[J1] SOUTHERN BAPTIST COLLEGE
College City Branch PO, Walnut Ridge 72476, (501) 886-6741, ext.121
Director of Admissions: Harry Black

- **Undergraduates: 135m, 164w; 344 total (including part-time)**
- **Tuition (1982/83): $1,998**
- **Room & Board: $1,490; Fees: $32**
- **Degrees offered: AA, AMus, AS, AAS**
- **Student-faculty ratio: 15 to 1**

A private college established in 1941, affiliated with the Arkansas Baptist Convention. 180-acre campus in small town of Walnut Ridge in Northeast Arkansas.
Academic Character NCACS and professional accreditation. Semester system, 5-week summer term. Majors offered in business administration, business education, education, health & physical education, recreation/church recreation, art, English, journalism, language, speech/drama, music, biology, chemistry, general science, mathematics, physical science, religion & philosophy, Greek, and social sciences. Courses in data processing. Distributive requirements. 2 courses in Bible required. Independent study. Credit by exam. Certificate programs in recreation, secretarial science. Diploma in theology. Media center. 50,000-volume library with microform resources.
Financial ACT FAS. College scholarships, music, athletic, ministerial, state scholarships and loans; PELL, SEOG, NDSL, GSL, CWS. United Student Aid Fund. Priority application deadline June 1.
Admissions 5 units required. $15 application fee. Rolling admissions. $25 deposit required on acceptance of offer of admission. Transfers accepted. Credit possible for CEEB CLEP exams.
Student Life Student government. Yearbook. Music and hostess groups. Black Renaissance Organization. International Students. Religious, academic, professional, service, political, and special interest groups. Single students must live at home or on campus. No coed dorms. Married-student housing. Liquor, drugs prohibited on campus. Class and chapel attendance required. Phys ed requirements vary with major. Intercollegiate basketball. Ozark Junior College Conference. 21% of students from out of state.

[2] THOMAS A. EDISON COLLEGE
Corner 1st & 2nd Sts. and Edison Ave., Benton 72015

[J1] WESTARK COMMUNITY COLLEGE
PO Box 3649, Fort Smith 72913

CALIFORNIA (CA)

[J1] ALAMEDA, COLLEGE OF
555 Atlantic Avenue, Alameda 94501

[J1] ALLAN HANCOCK COLLEGE
800 S. College Drive, Santa Maria 93454

[J1] AMERICAN ACADEMY OF DRAMATIC ARTS WEST
2550 Paloma Street, Pasadena 91107

[P] AMERICAN BAPTIST SEMINARY OF THE WEST
2515 Hillegass Avenue, Berkeley 94704

[G2] AMERICAN CONSERVATORY THEATRE
450 Geary Street, San Francisco 94102

[J1] AMERICAN RIVER COLLEGE
4700 College Oak Drive, Sacramento 95841

[J1] ANTELOPE VALLEY COLLEGE
3041 West Avenue K, Lancaster 93534

[1] ARMSTRONG COLLEGE
2222 Harold Way, Berkeley 94704, (415) 848-2500

- **Enrollment: 187m, 120w; 410 total (including part-time)**
- **Tuition (1982/83): $720 per term**
- **Room & Board: $300 per month**
- **Degrees offered: BS, BBA, AA**
- **Student-faculty ratio: 14 to 1**

A private college of business administration founded in 1918. Small city campus. Air, rail, and bus service.
Academic Character WASC accreditation. System of 4 11-week terms. Majors offered include accounting, business administration, business management, finance, international business, marketing, and secretarial administration. Graduate programs in business administration, accounting, law, and CPA review. MS, MBA, JD granted. 18,000-volume library.
Financial Financial aid available, including part-time work/study. Over 50% of students earn part or all of their expenses.
Admissions High school graduation required. Rolling admissions. *Early Decision* Program. Admission deferral possible. Transfers accepted. Advanced placement credit possible.
Student Life Intramural sports program including baseball, basketball, bowling, soccer, and volleyball.

[1] ART CENTER COLLEGE OF DESIGN
1700 Lida St., Pasadena 91103, (213) 577-1700
Director of Admissions: Rosa Maria Zaldivar

- **Enrollment: 699m, 500w; 1,596 total (including evening)**
- **Tuition (1982/83): $3,920**
- **Supplies: $1,000-$1,500**
- **Degrees offered: BFA, BS**
- **Mean ACT 23; mean SAT 550v, 480m**
- **Student-faculty ratio: 6 to 1**

A private college founded in 1930. 175-acre campus in the city of Pasadena, located in the Linda Vista Hills.
Academic Character WASC and professional accreditation. Year-round trimester system. Majors offered in communications design, advertising design, advertising illustration, graphic design/packaging, film, fine arts, painting, illustration, fashion illustration, industrial design, environmental design, product design, transportation design, photography. Courses in American studies, communication, history of art, humanities, behavioral sciences, natural sciences. Distributive requirements in academic studies. MFA and MS granted. Industrial design workshops, photography labs, shooting studios, film editing & animation facilities, galleries for student work. Library.
Financial CEEB CSS. College scholarships, grants, short-term loans, deferred payment; PELL, NDSL, FISL, limited part-time work.
Admissions High school graduation required. Some prior college work recommended. Portfolio with at least 12 samples of original work required. Super 8mm film required for film majors. SAT or ACT required unless applicant has attended college for 1 year. $25 application fee. Rolling admissions; suggest applying 10 months before desired entry (especially photography majors). Deadline 5 months before beginning of term. $100 deposit required on acceptance of offer of admission. Admission deferral possible. Transfers accepted. Credit possible for CEEB AP, CLEP, and ACT PEP exams.
Student Life Informal special interest activities. No college housing. Class attendance required. No athletics. 25% of entering students have college degrees; 77% of undergraduates are over 21. Student body composition: 1% Black, 3% Hispanic, 1% Native American, 78% White, 17% Other. 40% from out of state.

[1] AZUSA PACIFIC UNIVERSITY
Citrus Ave. & Alosta, Azusa 91702, (213) 969-3434
Director of Admissions: David Bixby

- **Undergraduates: 650m, 680w; 1,550 (including graduates)**
- **Tuition (1982/83): $4,312**
- **Room & Board: $2,210; Fees: $60**
- **Degrees offered: BA, BS**
- **Mean ACT 20 composite; mean SAT 920**
- **Student-faculty ratio: 17 to 1**

A private interdenominational university established in 1899. 77-acre suburban campus in the San Gabriel Valley, 25 miles northeast of Los Angeles. Air, rail, and bus in Los Angeles.
Academic Character WASC and professional accreditation. 4-4-1 calendar, 2 summer terms. Majors offered in accounting, art, Biblical literature, biology, business administration, chemistry, communication arts, English, history, liberal studies, mathematics, music, nursing, philosophy, physical education, political science, psychology, recreation, religion, social science, social work, sociology, Spanish. Self-designed majors, interdisciplinary programs. Minors. Distributive requirements. 24 credits in philosophy/religion and 4 semesters of student ministry assignments required. MA granted. Associate degrees offered on video cassettes for those unable to attend classes. Independent study, honors program, pass/fail, business internships. Preprofessional programs in dentistry, law, medicine, and the ministry. Elementary, secondary, and special education certification. 310,000-volume library.
Financial CEEB CSS. University scholarships, grants, tuition discounts for students in full-time Christian service and for dependents of ministers and missionaries, deferred payment; PELL, SEOG, NSS, Cal grants, NDSL, GSL, NSL, CWS. Priority application deadline for scholarships is March 1.
Admissions High school graduation with 15 units and minimum GPA of 2.5 required. GED accepted. Interview may be required. SAT or ACT required. $30 application fee. Rolling admissions. $50 room deposit required on acceptance of offer of admission. Transfers accepted with minimum GPA of 2.0. Credit possible for CEEB AP exams. Provisional admission with study skills classwork possible.
Student Life Associated Student Body, Koinonia. Music, honorary, religious, service organizations. Business, ski, and other special interest clubs initiated by students. No coed dorms. 80% of students live on campus. Smoking, liquor, illegal drugs, and dancing not allowed on campus. Attendance at chapel 3 times each week required. 1 health education and 2 activity courses required. 8 intercollegiate and several intramural sports for men and women. Outdoor Adventure Program. AIAW, NAIA. Student body composition: 25% minority. 20% of students from out of state.

[J1] BAKERSFIELD COLLEGE
1801 Panorama Drive, Bakersfield 93305, (805) 395-4011
Director of Admissions & Records: Sue Scoggins

- **Undergraduates: 1,523m, 1,622w; 11,940 total (including part-time)**
- **Tuition & Fees (1982/83): $30 (in-state), $1,830-$2,280 (out-of-state)**
- **Degrees offered: AA, AS**

A public community college established in 1913. Additional campuses downtown and in Delano.
Academic Character WASC and professional accreditation. Semester system, 6-week summer term. Career and transfer degrees in the areas of agriculture, art, behavioral science, business, communications, English, family & consumer education, French, German, health & physical education, health careers, industrial education, computer, life science, mathematics, music, philosophy, physical science, public service, social science, and theatre arts. Women's studies program. Distributive requirements. Numerous certificate programs. Pass/fail, credit by exam, cooperative work/study. Preprofessional programs in dentistry, law, medicine, optometry, pharmacy, and veterinary medicine. Member of League for Innovation in the Community College and of Southern California Consortium for Community College Television. Learning Center for remedial work. Planetarium, computer center. Over 55,000-volume library.
Financial College scholarships, loans; PELL, SEOG, EOPS, NDSL, GSL, NSL, CWS, college work program.
Admissions High school graduation, GED, or equivalent required. Non-high school graduates over 18 may be admitted with approval of Director of Admissions. California residents outside the Kern Community College District may need permit to attend. Application deadline August 1. *Concurrent Enrollment* Program. SAT, ACT, or college exam used for placement. Extended Opportunity Program & Services provides financial and/or academic support for low-income students.
Student Life Associated students. Athletic, professional, religious, service, and special interest groups. 2 dorms house 120 students. Dining hall. 2 units of phys ed required.

[J1] BARSTOW COLLEGE
2700 Barstow Road, Barstow 92311

[J2] BAUDER FASHION COLLEGE
1321 Howe Avenue, Sacramento 95825

[R] BEREAN CHRISTIAN COLLEGE
2132 East Broadway, Long Beach 90803

[2] BERNADEAN UNIVERSITY
13615 Victory Blvd., Van Nuys 91401

[1] BETHANY BIBLE COLLEGE
800 Bethany Drive, Santa Cruz 95066, (408) 438-3800
Director of Admissions & Records: Carmine Wilson

- **Undergraduates: 275m, 254w; 600 total (including part-time)**
- **Tuition (1982/83): $2,410**
- **Room & Board: $1,990; Fees: $300**
- **Degrees offered: BA, BS**
- **Student-faculty ratio: 17 to 1**

A private Christian college founded in 1919, owned and operated by the Northern California and Nevada District of the Assemblies of God. 40-acre rural campus 7 miles from Santa Cruz and the Pacific.
Academic Character WASC and AABC accreditation. 4-1-4 system, 2 3-week summer terms. Majors offered in communication arts, early childhood education, English, history, ministerial studies, multiple subjects, music (5), psychology, religious education, and social science. Missions program. Courses in Biblical languages, business administration, geography, mathematics, natural science, political science. Distributive requirements. 7 Bible and 4 theology courses required. 3-year diplomas in religious education, ministerial studies, and music. 2-year programs in ministerial studies, religious education. Pass/fail, internships. Preprofessional program in theology. Evangelical Teacher Training Certificate. 5-year elementary and secondary education certification. Recording & broadcasting studio. 50,000-volume library.
Financial CEEB CSS. College scholarships, loans, missionaries' and ministers' dependents tuition grants, 2nd-family-member discount, Cal grants, deferred payment; PELL, SEOG, NDSL, GSL, CWS. Application deadline June 1.
Admissions High school graduation required. GED accepted. "A definite experience of Christian conversion is essential for admission." ACT required. $20 application fee. Transfers accepted. Rolling admissions. Deadline August 1. Credit possible for CEEB CLEP exams. Probationary admission possible.
Student Life Student Council. Newspaper, yearbook. Student Ministries. Several music, missions, and prayer groups. Single students under 21 must live on campus. Men's and women's dorms. Married-student housing. Daily chapel attendance required. 4 semesters of phys ed required. Dress code. Premarital counseling required for those who plan to marry while in college. Intercollegiate and intramural sports. Northern California Christian College Conference. Student body composition: 15% minority.

[1] BIOLA UNIVERSITY
13800 Biola Ave., La Mirada 90639, (213) 944-0351
Dean of Admissions & Records: Wayne Chute

- **Enrollment: 1,380m, 1,351w**
- **Tuition & Fees (1982/83): $4,082**
- **Room & Board: $2,390**
- **Degrees offered: BA, BS, BMus, BSN**
- **Mean SAT 460v, 470m**
- **Student-faculty ratio: 18 to 1**

A private non-denominational Christian university founded in 1908. 100-acre suburban campus, 22 miles from Los Angeles. Air, rail, and bus in Los Angeles.
Academic Character WASC, AABC, and professional accreditation. 4-1-4 calendar, 3- and 5-week summer terms. Majors offered in American studies, art, Biblical studies & theology, biological science, business administration & economics, Christian education, communication, education, English, history & geography, humanities (6), intercultural studies, liberal studies/education, mathematical sciences, music (3), nursing, physical education, physical science, public administration, psychology, recreation & camp administration, social science, and sociology. Double, self-designed, and interdisciplinary majors. Minors offered in most major areas. Courses in 6 additional areas. Distributives and 30 credit hours of Biblical studies required. Graduate and professional degrees granted. Internships. Preprofessional programs in law, medicine, seminary. Member Christian College Consortium. Study abroad in France and Germany. Elementary and secondary education certification. AFROTC at USC; ROTC at UCLA. Talbot Theological Seminary, Rosemead Graduate School of Psychology. 180,000-volume library.
Financial CEEB CSS. University scholarships, grants, loans, art, athletic, and music scholarships, deferred payment; PELL, SEOG, NSS, GSL, NDSL, NSL, FISL, CWS. FAF and application deadlines March 1.
Admissions High school graduation with 16 units required. Interview recommended. SAT or ACT required. $25 application fee. Rolling admissions; suggest applying before February 28. *Early Decision* Program. $50 tuition and $50 room deposits required on acceptance of admissions offer. Admission deferral possible. Transfers accepted. Credit possible for CEEB AP and CLEP exams. University has own advanced placement program.
Student Life Associated Students, Student Missionary Union. Newspaper, yearbook, literary magazine. Several music and drama groups. Debate. Academic, religious, service, and special interest clubs. Underclass students under 21 must live at home or on campus. No married-student housing. 60% of students live on campus. Smoking, alcohol, gambling, and dancing prohibited. Dress and hair code. Permission required for marriage during school year. Class, daily chapel, and graduation attendance required. Weekly student ministry required. 4 semesters of phys ed required. 8 intercollegiate and several intramural sports for men and women. NCAA, NAIA. Student body composition: 4.8% Asian, 2.9% Black, 3.1% Hispanic, 0.5% Native American, 85.3% White, 3.4% Other. 30% from out of state.

[J1] BROOKS COLLEGE
4825 E. Pacific Coast Hwy., Long Beach 90804
In-state: (213) 597-6611, Out-of-state: (800) 421-3775
Director of Admissions: Dr. Charles A. Folcke

- **Undergraduates: 900 men & women**
- **Tuition & Fees (1982/83): $3,730**
- **Room & Board: $2,780**
- **Degree offered: AA**

A private college of fashion and interior design founded in 1969. 6½-acre campus south of Los Angeles, 1½ miles from the Pacific Ocean. Bus service.
Academic Character WASC accreditation. Trimester system. 1-year diploma or 2-year AA degree with majors in fashion merchandising, fashion design, and interior design. Minor/certificate in professional modeling. Courses offered in advertising, art, business law, English, math, sociology. Internships & apprenticeships. 2-week fashion study in Europe. Library.
Financial College & industry scholarships, Cal grants; PELL, SEOG, NDSL, GSL, PLUS.
Admissions High school graduation or equivalent required. Personal or telephone interview required. $20 application fee. $30 fee required on acceptance of admissions offer. Rolling admissions. *Early Admission* and *Early Decision* programs. Admission deferral possible. Advanced placement credit possible.
Student Life Newspaper, yearbook. Dorm housing. Regular class attendance expected. Dress code. Student body composition: 17% minority.

[1] BROOKS INSTITUTE OF PHOTOGRAPHY
2190 Alston Road, Santa Barbara 93108

[J1] BUTTE COLLEGE
3536 Butte Campus Drive, Oroville 95965

[J1] CABRILLO COLLEGE
6500 Soquel Drive, Aptos 95003

[1] CALIFORNIA, UNIVERSITY OF
131 University Hall, Berkeley 94720, (415) 642-0505
President: David S. Saxon

Central administration for a public university with campuses at Berkeley, Davis, Irvine, Los Angeles, Riverside, San Diego, San Francisco, Santa Barbara, and Santa Cruz. San Francisco campus is devoted to medical & health sciences; medical schools are also located at Davis, Irvine, Los Angeles, and San Diego. Hastings College of Law located in San Francisco. Total enrollment of approximately 138,700 men and women (98,508 undergraduate, 27,544 graduate, and 12,648 health science students). Phi Beta Kappa. Extensive study abroad opportunities through Education Abroad Program. Total library of over 18,150,000 volumes. University campuses have identical admissions requirements and accept freshmen, transfer, and graduate students.

■[1] CALIFORNIA, UNIVERSITY OF
Berkeley 94720, (415) 642-0200
Director of Admissions & Records: Robert L. Bailey

- **Undergraduates: 12,358m, 9,268w; 30,882 total (including graduates)**
- **Tuition & Fees (1982/83): $1,172 (in-state), $4,322 (out-of-state)**
- **Room & Board: $3,252**
- **Degrees offered: AB, BS**
- **Mean SAT 553v, 585m**
- **Student-faculty ratio: 15 to 1**

A public university established in 1868. 1,200-acre urban campus on eastern shore of San Francisco Bay. Bus and rapid transit to San Francisco; air, rail, and bus in San Francisco.
Academic Character WASC and professional accreditation. Trimester system, 8-week summer term. Over 100 majors offered in the areas of area studies, anthropolgy, architecture, arts, astronomy, biological sciences, business administration, chemistry, computer science, economics, engineering, environmental studies, film, forestry, geology, health, humanities, classical & modern languages & literatures, mass communications, mathematics, music, nutrition, philosophy & religion, physical education, physics, psychology, rhetoric, social sciences, social welfare, and zoology. Graduate and professional degrees granted. Honors program, Phi Beta Kappa. Cooperative work/study. Preprofessional programs in city & regional planning, education, law, library science, medicine, social welfare. Exchanges and transfers with other universities in the California system, and with professional schools in business administration, forestry, journalism, optometry, and veterinary science. Numerous study abroad programs. AFROTC, NROTC, ROTC. Space Sciences Lab, computer facilities, several research institutes, labs, museums. Law School. 6,000,000-volume library.
Financial CEEB CSS. University scholarships, grants, loans; PELL, SEOG, NDSL, CWS, university work program. Application deadlines November 30 (scholarships), January 15 (loans).
Admissions High school graduation with 15 units required. SAT or ACT, and 3 ACH required. Minimum GPAs and test scores. $25 application fee. Rolling admissions; deadline November 30. $50 deposit required on

acceptance of offer of admission. *Early Decision* and informal *Early Entrance* programs. Transfers accepted. Credit possible for CEEB AP exams. Educational Opportunity Program.
Student Life Student government. Men's and Women's Boards. Several student publications. Debate, Radio-TV Theatre, music, dance, and drama groups. Community Project Committee, CalPIRG, Cal Camp. Many other academic, honorary, professional, and special interest organizations. 36 fraternities and 14 sororities, most with houses. 11% of students join. Coed, single-sex, special interest, cooperative, and married-student housing. 28% of students live on campus (including fraternities and sororities). 19 intercollegiate sports for men, 9 for women; intramurals. 5% of students from out of state.

■[1] CALIFORNIA, UNIVERSITY OF

Davis 95616, (916) 752-2971
Registrar & Admissions Officer: Maynard C. Skinner

- **Undergraduates: 6,562m, 7,133w; 19,321 total (including graduates)**
- **Tuition & Fees (1982/83): $1,186 (in-state), $4,336 (out-of-state)**
- **Room & Board: $2,440**
- **Degrees offered: AB, BS, BSAgr, BSEng**
- **Mean SAT 494v, 555m**
- **Student-faculty ratio: 19 to 1**

A public university established in 1922. 3,700-acre rural campus 13 miles west of Sacramento. Served by air, rail, and bus.
Academic Character WASC and professional accreditation. Trimester system, 2 6-week summer terms. 49 majors offered by the College of Letters & Science, 40 by the College of Agricultural & Environmental Sciences, and 7 by the College of Engineering. Self-designed, dual, and multiple majors. Minors. Distributive requirements. Graduate and professional degrees granted. Independent study, honors program, Phi Beta Kappa, pass/fail, credit by exam, internships. Planned Education Leave and Work-Learn programs. Preprofessional programs in forestry and veterinary science. 2- and 3-year transfer programs with professional schools and other universities in California system. Study abroad in 19 centers. Elementary, secondary, and special education certification. ROTC. Language lab, computer center, art galleries, several research institutes. Law and medical schools. 1,755,000-volume library.
Financial CEEB CSS. University scholarships, grants, loans, Cal grants, deferred payment; PELL, SEOG, NDSL, GSL, CWS. Application deadlines January 15 (institutional scholarships), February 12 (priority: grants, loans, California Student Aid Commission).
Admissions High school graduation with 15 units required. SAT or ACT, and 3 ACH required. Minimum GPAs and test scores. $30 application fee. Rolling admissions; suggest applying after November 1 of 12th year. Deadline November 30. $50 deposit required on acceptance of admissions offer. Admission deferral possible. Transfers accepted. Credit possible for CEEB AP exams. Educational Opportunity Program.
Student Life Associated Students. Newspaper, yearbook, radio station. Several music, dance, film, and drama groups. Many athletic, academic, ethnic, honorary, political, religious, service, and special interest organizations. 19 fraternities and 12 sororities. Coed, special interest, and married-student housing. 35% of students live on campus. 10 intercollegiate sports for men, 7 for women; numerous intramural sports. Student body composition: 9% Asian, 3% Black, 3% Hispanic, 1% Native American, 71% White, 13% Other. 10% from out of state.

■[1] CALIFORNIA, UNIVERSITY OF

Irvine 92717, (714) 833-6703
Director of Admissions: James E. Dunning

- **Undergraduates: 4,286m, 4,199w; 11,057 total (including graduates)**
- **Tuition & Fees (1982/83): $1,215 (in-state), $4,365 (out-of-state)**
- **Room & Board: $3,100**
- **Degrees offered: BA, BS**
- **Mean SAT 460v, 570m**
- **Student-faculty ratio: 17 to 1**

A public university established in 1965. 1,510-acre suburban campus with 200-acre San Joaquin Marsh Preserve. Located 5 miles from the Pacific and 40 miles south of Los Angeles. Air and bus service.
Academic Character WASC and professional accreditation. Trimester system, 2 6-week summer terms. 37 majors offered in the areas of arts, humanities, social sciences, sciences, ecology, engineering, geography, languages,and information & computer science. Double and interdisciplinary majors. Courses in Hebrew, Italian, Portuguese. Distributive requirements. Graduate and professional degrees granted. Independent study and seminars stressed. Honors program, Phi Beta Kappa, challenge exams, internships. Preprofessional programs in medicine and other areas. 3-2 program with Graduate School of Management. Study abroad in many locations. Elementary, secondary, and special education certification. AFROTC with USC, Loyola Marymount, and UCLA. Public Policy Research Organization, laser microbeam program, computer facilities. 1,000,000-volume library with microform resources.
Financial CEEB CSS. University scholarships, loans, handicapped student aid, Regents' scholarships; PELL, SEOG, GSL, NDSL, FISL, CWS. Application deadline April 18.
Admissions High school graduation with 15 units required. SAT or ACT, and 3 ACH required. Minimum GPAs and test scores. $30 application fee. Rolling admissions. Suggest applying in November; applications accepted after November 30 for available spaces. Experimental *Early Admission* Program. Admission deferral possible. Transfers accepted. Credit possible for CEEB AP exams; university has own placement program. Educational Opportunity Program.
Student Life Associated Students. Newspaper, radio station. Music, dance, and drama groups. Chicano Pride. Athletic, academic, honorary, political, religious, service, and special interest clubs. 5 fraternities and 6 sororities. Coed, single-sex, cooperative, apartment, and married-student housing. 31% of students live on campus. 11 intercollegiate sports for men, 5 for women; intramurals, cooperative outdoor program. AIAW, NCAA, PCAA. Student body composition: 11.5% Asian, 3.6% Black, 6.8% Hispanic, 0.5% Native American, 56.1% White, 21.5% Other. 6% from out of state.

■[1] CALIFORNIA, UNIVERSITY OF

405 Hilgard Ave., Los Angeles 90024, (213) 825-3101
Director, Undergraduate Admissions: Rae Lee Siporin

- **Undergraduates: 10,812m, 10,997w; 33,435 total (including graduates)**
- **Tuition & Fees (1982/83): $1,452 (in-state), $4,080 (out-of-state)**
- **Room & Board: $3,000**
- **Degrees offered: BA, BS**
- **Student-faculty ratio: 17 to 1**

A public university established in Los Angeles in 1919. 411-acre urban campus in the Westwood section of L.A. Air, rail, and bus service.
Academic Character WASC and professional accreditation. Trimester system, 2 6-week summer terms. 14 majors offered by the College of Fine Arts, 66 by the College of Letters & Science, 19 by the School of Engineering & Applied Science, and 1 each by the schools of Nursing and Public Health. Self-designed majors. Numerous special programs. Distributive requirements. Graduate and professional degrees granted. Independent study, honors program, Phi Beta Kappa, cooperative work/study. Preprofessional programs in architecture, dentistry, journalism, medicine. 2-2 programs with various schools in criminology, dental hygiene, nursing, optometry, pharmacy, physical therapy, public health. Study abroad. AFROTC, NROTC, ROTC. Computer. 4,346,526-volume library.
Financial University scholarships, grants, loans; PELL, SEOG, NDSL, NSL, FISL, CWS. Application deadline February 1.
Admissions High school graduation with 15 units required. SAT or ACT, and 3 ACH required. Minimum GPAs and test scores. $30 application fee. Rolling admissions. Apply as soon as possible beginning November 1. *Early Entrance* Program. Transfers accepted. Credit possible for CEEB AP exams.
Student Life Associated Students. Newspaper, yearbook. Several music, drama, film, TV, and radio groups. Debate. Many other student organizations. 27 fraternities and 18 sororities, most with houses. 22% of students join. Coed and cooperative dorms. Married-student apartments. 20% of students live on campus. 15 intercollegiate sports for men, 11 for women; several intramurals. AIAW, Pacific-10. Student body composition: 14.4% Asian, 5.3% Black, 1.5% Filipino, 6.7% Hispanic, 0.4% Native American, 70.2% White, 1.5% Other. 14% from out of state.

■[1] CALIFORNIA, UNIVERSITY OF

Riverside 92521, (714) 787-3411
Admissions Officer: Robert B. Herschler

- **Undergraduates: 1,527m, 1,597w; 4,787 total (including graduates)**
- **Tuition & Fees (1983/84): $1,225 (in-state), $4,585 (out-of-state)**
- **Room & Board: $2,600**
- **Degrees offered: AB, BS**
- **Mean SAT 500v, 563m**
- **Student-faculty ratio: 14 to 1**

A public university established in 1954. 1,200-acre suburban campus 60 miles east of Los Angeles. Air, rail, and bus service.
Academic Character WASC and professional accreditation. Trimester system, 6-week summer term. Over 50 majors offered in the areas of administrative studies, area studies, biology, chemistry, computer, English, environmental sciences, fine & performing arts, geography, geology, languages & literatures, mathematics, philosophy & religion, physical sciences, physics, psychology, and social sciences. Interdisciplinary, individual, and cooperative majors. Minors in Chicano, Marxist, urban, Western American, and women's studies, and in international relations. Courses in 6 other areas. Distributive requirements. MA, MS, PhD granted. Independent study, honors programs, Phi Beta Kappa. Credit/no credit, credit by exam, cooperative work/study, internships. Preprofessional programs in business administration, dentistry, education, engineering, forestry, law, library science, medicine, medical technology, public administration, public health, social welfare, veterinary medicine, and museums/preservation. Several dual degree programs including: 3-1 medical technology; 5-yr master's in administration; 7-yr BS/MD biomedical sciences; 2-2 engineering with UCLA. Many study abroad programs. Administration, elementary, secondary, and special education certification. AFROTC at Loyola-Marymount, UCLA, USC; ROTC at Claremont Colleges. Numerous research institutes, A-V, center, language lab, computer, galleries & museums. 1,085,000-volume library.
Financial CEEB CSS. University scholarships, grants, loans, regents' scholarships, Cal grants; PELL, SEOG, NDSL, GSL, CWS. Application deadlines February 9 (Cal grants), February 18 (scholarships). Suggest applying for other aid as soon as possible.
Admissions High school graduation with 15 units required. California High School Proficiency Exam accepted. SAT or ACT, and 3 ACH required. Minimum GPAs and test scores. $30 application fee. Rolling admissions; suggest applying in November of 12th year. $50 deposit required on acceptance of admissions offer. *Concurrent Enrollment* Program. Transfers accepted. Credit possible for CEEB AP exams. Educational Opportunity Program.
Student Life Newspaper, literary magazine, radio & TV stations. Several music groups. Coffeehouse, Black Student Theatre, film society, folk dancing. Athletic, academic, service, honorary, religious, and special interest clubs. 10 fraternities and sororities. Coed and single-sex dorms. Married-student housing. 45% of students live on campus. 9 intercollegiate sports for men, 7 for women; many intramurals. NCAA, CCAA. Student body composition: 8.3% Asian, 5.7% Black, 10.8% Hispanic, 0.7% Native American, 72.8% White, 1.7% Other. 10% from out of state.

■[1] CALIFORNIA, UNIVERSITY OF

3rd Ave. & Parnassus, San Francisco 94143, (415) 666-9000

- **Enrollment: 2,205m, 1,606w**
- **Tuition & Fees (1982/83): $1,221 (in-state), $4,371 (out-of-state)**
- **Degree offered: BS**

A public university founded in 1864. Urban campus. Air, rail, and bus service.
Academic Character WASC and professional accreditation. Trimester system, summer term. Majors offered by the Schools of Dentistry, Medicine, Nursing, and Pharmacy, and in dental hygiene, exfoliative cytology, physical therapy. University also has Graduate Division, Continuing Education in Medical & Health Sciences, Postgraduate Dentistry. MA, MS, MCLS, DNS, PhD, MD, DDS, PharmD granted. University contains several research facilities including Cancer Research Institute, Hormone Research Laboratory, Cardiovascular Research Institute, Metabolic Research Unit, Radiological Research Laboratory, Biomechanics Laboratory, George Williams Hooper Foundation, Francis I. Proctor Foundation, International Center for Medical Research & Training, International Reference Center of Trachoma, World Health Organization, Surgical Research Laboratories, and Laboratory of Radiobiology. 468,620-volume library.
Financial CEEB CSS. University scholarships, grants, loans, Cal grants; PELL, SEOG, NDSL, GSL, CWS. File SAAC by February 12.
Admissions High school graduation with 15 units required. SAT or ACT required. Minimum grades and test scores. $30 application fee. Rolling admissions; suggest applying soon after November 1. Admission deferral possible. Transfers accepted. Credit possible for CEEB AP exams. Educational Opportunity Program.

■[1] CALIFORNIA, UNIVERSITY OF

Santa Barbara 93106, (805) 961-2881
Registrar & Dean of Admissions: Dr. Charles W. McKinney

- **Undergraduates: 6,483m, 6,880w**
- **Tuition & Fees (1982/83): $1,194 (in-state), $4,344 (out-of-state)**
- **Room & Board: $3,200**
- **Degrees offered: BA, BS, BMus**
- **Mean SAT 525v, 543m**
- **Student-faculty ratio: 18 to 1**

A public university founded in 1891, joined University in 1944. 850-acre suburban campus on Pacific coast, 100 miles northwest of Los Angeles. Air, rail, and bus service.
Academic Character WASC and professional accreditation. Trimester system, 6-week summer term. 50 majors in the areas of fine & performing arts (7), anthropology, archaeology, biology (6), Black studies, botany, chemistry, classics, economics (2), engineering (5), English, geography, geology, history, languages (9), linguistics, mathematics, pharmacology, philosophy, physics, political science, psychology, religion, sociology, speech & hearing sciences, zoology. Interdepartmental majors in Asian-American studies, classical civilization, comparative literature, computer science, economics/mathematics, environmental studies, Hispanic civilization, law & society, liberal studies, medieval studies, public/social affairs, renaissance studies. College of Creative Studies for individually talented students offers majors in art (painting, sculpture), biology, chemistry, literature, mathematics, music (theory, history, composition, performance), and physics. Individual majors. MA, MS, PhD granted. Independent study, Phi Beta Kappa, pass/fail, credit by exam. Preprofessional programs in dentistry, medical technology, medicine, nursing, physical therapy, speech therapy. Extensive foreign study program. Early childhood, elementary, secondary, bilingual/crosscultural, and reading education certification. ROTC. Several research institutes. 1,325,000-volume library.
Financial CEEB CSS. University scholarships, grants, loans, Cal grants; PELL, SEOG, NDSL, GSL, CWS. File SAAC by February 12.
Admissions High school graduation with 15 units required. Dance majors must audition. SAT or ACT, and 3 ACH required. Minimum grades and test scores. $30 application fee. Rolling admissions; suggest applying soon after November 1. $50 deposit required on acceptance of admissions offer. Admission deferral possible. Transfers accepted. Credit possible for CEEB AP exams. Educational Opportunity Program.
Student Life Associated Students. Newspaper, literary magazine, yearbook. Many music, dance, drama groups. Academic, honorary, religious, service, and special interest organizations. 9 fraternities and 13 sororities, all with houses. 5% of students join. Coed dorms, single and married-student apartments. 17% of students live on campus. 11 intercollegiate sports for men, 8 for women; many intramurals. NCAA, SCAA, AIAW. Student body composition: 2.3% Black, 6.2% Hispanic, 0.7% Native American, 83.6% White, 7.2% Other. 10% from out of state.

■[1] CALIFORNIA, UNIVERSITY OF

Santa Cruz 95064, (408) 429-4008
Dean of Admissions: Richard Moll

- **Enrollment: 3,170m, 3,164w**
- **Tuition & Fees (1982/83): $1,261 (in-state), $4,411 (out-of-state)**
- **Room & Board: $2,800**
- **Degrees offered: BA, BS Earth Sciences**
- **Mean SAT 545v, 560m**
- **Student-faculty ratio: 18 to 1**

A public university established in 1965. 2,000-acre campus composed of 8 residential colleges overlooking Monterey Bay and the small city of Santa Cruz, 75 miles south of San Francisco. Bus service; air and rail 35 miles away in San Jose.
Academic Character WASC accreditation. Trimester system, 2 summer terms, special summer programs. Majors offered in American studies, anthropology, art, art history, biology, chemistry, community studies, computer & information sciences, earth sciences, economics, environmental studies, history, Latin American studies, linguistics, literature and languages (9), mathematics, modern society & social thought, music, philosophy, physics, politics, psychobiology, psychology, sociology, theater arts, women's studies. 8 individualized majors. Double majors. Minors in 17 areas. Courses in education. Distributive requirements. Comprehensive exam and/or thesis required in major field. MA, MS, PhD granted. Independent study, field study, pass/no record, internships, cooperative work/study. Preprofessional programs in law, forestry, health sciences, medicine. 3-2 engineering program with UC Berkeley. Many study abroad programs. Elementary and secondary education certification. Research institutes, observatory, computer center, media center. 661,500-volume library.
Financial CEEB CSS. University scholarships, grants, loans, Cal grants; PELL, SEOG, GSL, NDSL, CWS, university work program. File SAAC by February 10.
Admissions High school graduation with 15 units required. GED accepted. SAT or ACT, and 3 ACH required. Minimum grades and test scores. $30 application fee. Rolling admissions; suggest applying soon after November 1. Admission deferral possible. Transfers accepted. Credit possible for CEEB AP exams.
Student Life Newspaper, radio station. Drama, music, photography, and literary groups. Many political, ethnic, religious, academic, service, social, and special interest organizations. Coed, single-sex, special interest, and married-student housing. Dorms and apartments clustered by college. 50% of students live on campus. Many intramural sports for men and women. Student body composition: 4.6% Asian, 2% Black, 5.6% Hispanic, 0.5% Native American, 85.6% White, 1.6% Other. 9% from out of state.

■[1] CALIFORNIA, UNIVERSITY OF, SAN DIEGO

La Jolla 92093, (714) 452-3160
Registrar and Admissions Officer: Ronald J. Bowker

- **Undergraduates: 5,775m, 4,800w; 13,108 total(including graduates)**
- **Tuition & Fees (1982/83): $1,199 (in-state), $4,349 (out-of-state)**
- **Room & Board: $3,300**
- **Degrees offered: BA, BS**
- **Mean SAT 510v, 580m**
- **Student-faculty ratio: 18 to 1**

A public university established in 1912 from Scripps Institution of Oceanography. 1,200-acre campus on Pacific coast, 12 miles from San Diego. University composed of 4 undergraduate colleges, each with a distinct educational philosophy, graduate schools, and the School of Medicine. Air, bus, and rail service.
Academic Character WASC accreditation. Trimester system, 6-week summer term, 2- to 11-week summer programs. Over 50 majors offered in the areas of anthropology, applied mechanics/engineering science, biology, chemistry, Chicano studies, Chinese studies, classical studies, communications,, drama, economics, electrical engineering/computer science, history, linguistics, literature, mathematics, music, philosophy, physics, political science, psychology, sociology, third world studies, urban studies & planning, and visual arts. Special and self-designed majors. Other programs in Judaic studies, science & technology, and science, technology, & public affairs. Distributive requirements. MA, MS, MFA, PhD, MD granted. Independent study, honors program, Phi Beta Kappa. Pass/fail, internships. Preprofessional programs in law, medicine, and education. Exchange programs with Dartmouth College and other U of C campuses. Many study abroad programs. Partial elementary education certification. AFROTC, NROTC, ROTC at San Diego State U. Research institutes, Scripps Institution of Oceanography, medical school. Computer. 1,400,000-volume library.
Financial CEEB CSS. University scholarships, loans, regents' scholarships, Cal grants; PELL, SEOG, GSL, NDSL, PLUS, CWS. Priority application deadline February 9.
Admissions High school graduation with 15 units required. SAT or ACT, and 3 ACH required. Minimum GPAs and test scores. $30 application fee. Rolling admissions; suggest applying in November of 12th year. Priority application deadline November 30. $50 deposit required on acceptance of admissions offer. *Early Admission* and *Concurrent Enrollment* programs. Admission deferral possible. Transfers accepted. Credit possible for CEEB AP exams. Educational Opportunity Program.
Student Life Newspapers, literary magazine, radio station. Several music groups. Athletic, academic, honorary, service, and special interest groups. 2 fraternities and sororities. Dorms and apartments for single students. Married-student apartments. 30% of students live on campus. 30 intercollegiate sports; many intramural and club sports. AIAW. Student body composition: 11.7% Asian, 3% Black, 5.1% Hispanic, 66.6% White, 2.2% Other, 11.4% Unknown. 9% from out of state.

[1] CALIFORNIA BAPTIST COLLEGE

8432 Magnolia Ave., Riverside 92504, (714) 689-5771
Director of Admissions: John E. Potter

- **Undergraduates: 275m, 265w**
- **Tuition (1982/83): $2,730**
- **Room & Board: $1,890; Fees: $292**
- **Degrees offered: BA, BS, BMus**
- **Mean ACT 17e, 14m; mean SAT 432v, 430m**
- **Student-faculty ratio: 17 to 1**

A private college founded in 1950, affiliated with the Southern Baptist Convention. 75-acre campus 50 miles east of Los Angeles. Served by air, rail, and bus.
Academic Character WASC accreditation. 4-1-4 system, 5-week summer term. Majors offered in art, behavioral science, business administration, communication arts, education, English, history, liberal arts, life science, music, physical education, physical science, political science/public administration, psychology, recreation, religion, social science, sociology,

Spanish, and teacher education. Interdepartmental majors. Minors in most major fields and in Bible, chemistry, math, and religious education. Courses in 5 other areas. Distributives and 3 semesters of religion required. Honors program, independent study. Pass/fail, internships. Preprofessional programs in nursing and physical therapy. Elementary, secondary, and special education certification. Language lab. 105,000-volume library.
Financial CEEB CSS and ACT FAS. College scholarships, academic, church/vocational, performance, athletic scholarships, Cal grants, deferred payment; PELL, SEOG, NDSL, FISL, GSL, CWS. Priority application deadline April 1.
Admissions High school graduation with 12 units recommended. SAT or ACT required. $15 application fee. Rolling admissions; suggest applying after October 5 of 12th year. *Early Decision* and *Early Entrance* programs. Transfers accepted. Credit possible for CEEB AP and CLEP exams. College has own advanced placement program. Conditional acceptance possible.
Student Life Student council. Newspaper, yearbook. Campus Ministry, Circle K. Drama, debate, and several music groups. Athletic, academic, political, honorary, religious, service, and special interest clubs. Students under 21 and those with college scholarships must live at home or on campus. Single-sex dorms, apartments, married-student housing. 65% of students live on campus. Liquor, drugs, gambling, hazing, tobacco prohibited. 2 semesters of phys ed required. 2 intercollegiate sports for men, 2 for women; intramurals. NAIA. Student body composition: 0.8% Asian, 7.1% Black, 2.8% Hispanic, 1.1% Native American, 83.7% White, 4.5% Other. 19% from out of state.

[P] CALIFORNIA CHRISTIAN COLLEGE
4881 East University, Fresno 93703

[1] CALIFORNIA COLLEGE OF ARTS AND CRAFTS
5212 Broadway, Oakland 94618, (415) 653-8118
Director of Admissions: Jean T. Thomma

- **Enrollment: 284m, 563w; 1,025 total (including part-time)**
- **Tuition (1982/83): $4,810**
- **Room: $1,000**
- **Degree offered: BFA**
- **Student-faculty ratio: 12 to 1**

A private college established in 1907. 4-acre urban campus overlooking San Francisco Bay, 12 miles from San Francisco. Served by air, rail, bus, and metro.
Academic Character WASC and professional accreditation. Semester system, 3 5-week summer terms. Majors offered in drawing, painting, printmaking, sculpture, photography, film/video, general fine arts, ceramics, glass, metal arts, textiles, wood design, general crafts, interior architectural design, graphic design & illustration, general design, and ethnic art studies. Self-designed majors. Major not required. Courses in art history, English, general studies, environmental studies, art therapy. Distributive requirements. MFA, MAEd granted. 3-year Certificate in Art program. Independent study, pass/fail, cooperative work/study, internships. Courses available at Mills and Holy Names Colleges and through the Union of Independent Colleges of Art. Member Regional Association of East Bay Colleges & Universities. Semester and year exchanges with several colleges in Student Mobility Program. Study abroad in Japan. Elementary and secondary education certification. Art galleries, media center. 27,000-volume and 300-film libraries.
Financial CEEB CSS. College grants, scholarships, Cal grants, deferred payment; PELL, SEOG, FISL, NDSL, CWS. Application deadline February 1.
Admissions High school graduation with C average required. 9 units recommended. GED accepted. SAT or ACT recommended. $20 application fee. Rolling admissions; suggest applying by February 1. $150 deposit required on acceptance of admissions offer. Admission deferral possible. Transfers accepted. Credit possible for CEEB AP and CLEP exams.
Student Life Student Association. Newspaper. Special interest groups. 1 dorm for women (co-ed in summer term). No married-student housing. 6% of students live on campus. Student body composition: 8% Asian, 5% Black, 6% Hispanic, 2% Native American, 67% White, 12% Other. 35% from out of state.

[1] CALIFORNIA COLLEGE OF PODIATRIC MEDICINE
1210 Scott Street, San Francisco 94115

[1] CALIFORNIA INSTITUTE OF THE ARTS
24700 McBean Pkwy., Valencia 91355, (805) 255-1050
Director of Admissions: Renee Levine

- **Enrollment: 446m, 320w; 798 total (including part-time)**
- **Tuition (1982/83): $5,600**
- **Room & Board: $2,950-$3,450**
- **Degree offered: BFA**
- **Student-faculty ratio: 8 to 1**

A private institute established in 1961. 60-acre suburban campus 35 miles from Los Angeles. Air, rail, and bus nearby.
Academic Character WASC and professional accreditation. Semester system. Majors offered in acting, character animation, dance, directing, film graphics animation, fine art, general music, graphic design, live action film & video, music composition, music performance, photography, and technical theatre. Distributive requirements. MFA granted. Certificate of Fine Arts program. Independent and accelerated study. TV studio, museum, gallery. 46,000-volume library with microform resources.
Financial CEEB CSS. Institute scholarships, grants, loans, Cal grants; PELL, SEOG, NDSL, FISL, CWS.
Admissions High school graduation required. GED accepted. Portfolio required. Audition may be required. Interview encouraged. $25 application fee. Rolling admissions; suggest applying by January 1. Deadline April 1 (February 1 for film majors). $200 tuition and $150 room deposits (for boarders) required on acceptance of admissions offer. *Early Entrance* and *Concurrent Enrollment* programs. Admission deferral possible. Transfers accepted. Advanced placement credit possible.
Student Life Special interest groups. Coed dorms. No married-student housing. 42% of students live on campus. Student body composition: 1.9% Asian, 5.8% Black, 3.5% Hispanic, 0.2% Native American, 83.6% White, 5% Other. 42% from out of state.

[G1] CALIFORNIA INSTITUTE OF INTEGRAL STUDIES
3494 21st Street, San Francisco 94110

[1] CALIFORNIA INSTITUTE OF TECHNOLOGY
1201 E. California Blvd., Pasadena 91125, (213) 356-6341
Director of Admissions: Stirling L. Huntley

- **Undergraduates: 730m, 144w; 1,810 total (including graduates)**
- **Tuition (1982/83): $7,500**
- **Room & Board: $3,150; Fees: $60**
- **Degree offered: BS**
- **Mean SAT 650v, 760m**
- **Student-faculty ratio: 3 to 1**

A private institute known as Caltech, established in 1891, became coed in 1970. 82-acre central campus in residential area of Pasadena, ½ mile from downtown. Located 25 miles from Pacific Ocean, ½ hour from Los Angeles.
Academic Character WASC and professional accreditation. Trimester system. Majors offered in applied mathematics, applied physics, astronomy, biology, chemical engineering, chemistry, economics, electrical engineering, engineering & applied science, geochemistry, geology, geophysics, history, independent studies, literature, mathematics, physics, planetary science, and social science. Self-designed majors. Courses in 5 areas of engineering and 13 additional areas. Distributive requirements in 1st year; all graded pass/fail. Graduate and professional degrees granted. Independent study & research encouraged in all majors. Honors programs. Humanities/Social Science Tutorial program. 5-year BA/BSEng program with 9 colleges including Bryn Mawr. Exchanges with Occidental, Scripps Colleges, and Art Center College of Design. AFROTC & NROTC at USC. Aeronautical, seismological, jet propulsion, marine, and environmental quality labs. Industrial Relations Center. 4 observatories. Computer center. 388,000-volume library.
Financial CEEB CSS. Institute scholarships, grants, loans, Cal grants; PELL, SEOG, NDSL, CWS. Application deadline February 1.
Admissions High school graduation with 15 units required. SAT and 3 ACH required. $25 application fee. Application deadline January 15. $10 fee required on acceptance of offer of admission. *Early Decision* and *Early Entrance* programs. Admission deferral possible. Transfers accepted. Institute has own advanced placement program.
Student Life Student government. Newspaper, literary magazine, yearbook. Drama, art, radio, photography, and several music groups. Elementary & secondary school tutoring. YMCA. Society of Women Engineers. Athletic, academic, political, professional, religious, honorary, and special interest groups. Freshmen urged to live in dorms. Coed, women's, and coop dorms. No married-student housing. 65% of students live on campus. 3 terms of phys ed required. 12 intercollegiate sports for men, 6 for women; men's teams (except for football & wrestling) open to women. Intramurals. SCIAC. Student body composition: 15% Asian, 2% Black, 4% Hispanic, 71% White, 8% Other (Foreign). 63% from out of state.

[1] CALIFORNIA LUTHERAN COLLEGE
Thousand Oaks 91360, (805) 492-2411
Director of Admissions: Ronald Timmons

- **Undergraduates: 550m, 637w; 1,367 total (including graduates)**
- **Tuition (1982/83): $4,500**
- **Room & Board: $2,450**
- **Degrees offered: BA, BS**
- **Mean SAT 500v, 525m**
- **Student-faculty ratio: 15 to 1**

A private college established in 1959, affiliated with the Lutheran Church. 285-acre suburban campus, 50 miles northwest of Los Angeles.
Academic Character WASC accreditation. 4-1-4 system, 2 5-week summer terms. Majors offered in accounting, administration of justice, art, biological sciences, business administration, chemistry, communications, drama, economics, education/liberal arts, English, French, geology, German, history, mathematics, medical technology, music, philosophy, physical education, physics/computer science, political science, psychology, religion, sociology, Spanish, and speech. Interdisciplinary majors. Courses in anthropology, Greek, international studies. Distributive requirements. Minimum of 2 religion courses required. MBA, MAEd, MPA granted. Independent study, honors program, pass/no credit, tutorial programs, internships. Preprofessioal programs in dentistry, engineering, law, church work, medicine, nursing, theology. 3-1 mental health specialist program. 3-2 engineering program with Washington U. Exchange program with Wagner College. Interim exchange program with about 400 colleges. Study abroad, including 5th year advanced pottery in the Netherlands, summer Holy Land tours. Elementary, secondary, and special education certification. ROTC, AFROTC. Language lab. 100,000-volume library.
Financial CEEB CSS. College and ROTC scholarships, Lutheran student awards, 2nd-family-member and Lutheran pastors' family discounts, Cal grants, deferred payment; PELL, NDSL, FISL, GSL, CWS. Application deadline February 1.
Admissions High school graduation required. 12 units recommended. GED or equivalent accepted. Interview encouraged. ACT or SAT required. $20 application fee. Rolling admissions; suggest applying in fall or winter of 12th year. Deadline June 1. $100 tuition deposit required on acceptance of

admissions offer; refundable to May 1. *Early Entrance* and *Early Decision* programs. Admission deferral possible. Transfers accepted. Credit possible for CEEB AP and CLEP exams; college has own advanced placement exams. College Achievement Program.
Student Life Associated Student Body. Newspaper, literary magazine, yearbook. Several music groups, coffeehouse, Little Theatre. Debate. Academic, political, honorary, religious, and special interest groups. 1st and 2nd year students must live at home, on campus, or in approved housing. Coed dorms. No married-student housing. 80% of students live on campus. Liquor, drugs, gambling, profanity, hazing prohibited. 3 phys ed courses required. Attendance at monthly convocations urged. 9 intercollegiate sports for men, 6 for women; equestrian team, intramurals. AIAW, NAIA. Student body composition: 4% Asian, 5% Black, 6% Hispanic, 1% Native American, 84% White. 15% from out of state.

[1] CALIFORNIA MARITIME ACADEMY

PO Box 1392, Vallejo 94590, (707) 644-5601
Director of Admissions: David Buchanan

- **Undergraduates: 460m, 40w**
- **Tuition & Fees (1982/83): $1,192 (in-state), $2,944 (out-of-state)**
- **Room & Board: $3,015**
- **Degree offered: BS**
- **Mean SAT 480v, 530m**
- **Student-faculty ratio: 15 to 1**

A public academy established in 1929, became coed in 1973. 67-acre small city campus on the north shore of the Carquinez Strait, 30 miles from San Francisco. Bus and rail nearby.
Academic Character WASC and professional accreditation. Trimester system, summer term. Majors offered in marine engineering technology and nautical industrial technology. Options in computer science, instrumentation & automation, marine business management, marine engineering, maritime specialties, naval architectural technology, nuclear technology, and ocean technology. Liberal arts courses available. Required 1st year curriculum. 3 12-week training programs at sea required. Merchant Marine Licensing Program stresses practical training, officer development, and academics, and qualifies students for Merchant Marine Officer's License and a reserve commission as Ensign in U.S. Naval or Coast Guard Reserves. Credit by exam, internships. Cadet Shipping Training Program after 2nd year. NROTC. Tanker loading-simulator. Several labs. Yachts, sloops, dinghies, motor cruiser. 20,600-volume library plus 1,000-volume shipboard library.
Financial CEEB CSS. Academy scholarships, grants, loans, Cal grants; PELL, SEOG, NDSL, FISL, CWS. Application deadlines February 1 (Cal state aid), March 1 (priority: other aid).
Admissions High school graduation with strong math or science preparation required. GED accepted. Applicant must be over 16, a U.S. citizen, and healthy. Interview urged. SAT or ACT required. $25 application fee. Rolling admissions; suggest applying between October 1 and January 30. Deadline March 15. $50 refundable deposit due on acceptance of admissions offer. Transfers accepted (must attend min. 3 years). Credit possible for CEEB AP and CLEP exams, Academy placement exams.
Student Life Midshipmen Council. Yearbook, camera & radio clubs. Color Guard, Drill team. Propeller, sailing, scuba, service, and special interest clubs. All students must live on campus. No coed dorms. No married-student housing. Parking space limited. Liquor prohiited on campus. Class attendance and 2 semsters of phys ed required. Uniforms, adherence to military rules required. 6 intercollegiate and several intramural sports. Student body composition: 6% Asian, 2% Black, 3% Hispanic, 1% Native American, 87% White, 1% Other. 20% from out of state.

[G1] CALIFORNIA SCHOOL OF PROFESSIONAL PSYCHOLOGY

2152 Union Street, San Francisco 94123

CALIFORNIA STATE UNIVERSITY SYSTEM

■[1] CALIFORNIA POLYTECHNIC STATE UNIVERSITY

San Luis Obispo 93407, (805) 546-0111
Director of Admissions: F. Jerald Holley

- **Enrollment: 9,332m, 7,060w**
- **Tuition (1982/83): $0 (in-state), $70 per unit (out-of-state)**
- **Room & Board: $2,721; Fees: $465**
- **Degrees offered: BA, BS, BArch**
- **Mean SAT 995**
- **Student-faculty ratio: 18 to 1**

A public university founded in 1901, became coed in 1956. 5,000-acre rural campus 12 miles from Pacific between Los Angeles and San Francisco. Air, rail, and bus service.
Academic Character WASC and professional accreditation. Trimester system, summer terms. 13 majors offered by the School of Agriculture & Natural Resources, 5 by Architecture & Environmental Design, 2 by Business, 8 by Communicative Arts & Humanities, 12 by Engineering & Technology, 6 by Human Development & Education, and 10 by Science & Mathematics. Double majors. Courses in 6 additional areas. Distributive requirements. Educational program puts emphasis on occupational and career training. Masters degrees granted. 2-year technical certificate program in agriculture. Credit/no credit, credit by exam, cooperative work/study. Extensive study abroad program. Elementary, secondary, administrative, pupil personnel, reading specialist, and special education training. ROTC. 580,000-volume library with microform resources.
Financial CEEB CSS. University scholarships, loans; PELL, SEOG, NDSL, GSL, CWS. Application deadline March 1.
Admissions At present only in-state applicants accepted. High school graduation with minimum 2.0 GPA required. SAT or ACT required. $30 application fee. Apply during November of 12th year; notification after February 1. Students apply for specific major program(s). Transfers accepted. Credit possible for CEEB AP and CLEP exams. University has own advanced placement program. Educational Opportunity Program.
Student Life Student government. Newspaper, radio station. Debate, drama, and several music groups. Athletic, academic, service, honorary, and special interest groups. 11 fraternities and 7 sororities. Coed and single-sex dorms. No married-student housing. 20% of students live on campus. Liquor prohibited on campus. Class attendance required. 3-5 units of physical or health education required. 11 intercollegiate sports for men, 6 for women; many intramurals. NCAA, CCAA. Student body composition: 1% Black, 3% Hispanic, 1% Native American, 76% White, 19% Other. 1% from out of state.

■[1] CALIFORNIA STATE COLLEGE, BAKERSFIELD

9001 Stockdale Highway, Bakersfield 93309, (805) 833-2011
Associate Dean of Admissions & Records: Homer S. Montalvo

- **Undergraduates: 1,060m, 1,524w; 3,400 total (including part-time)**
- **Tuition (1982/83): $0 (in-state), $2,428 (out-of-state)**
- **Room & Board: $2,200; Fees: $360**
- **Degrees offered: BA, BS**
- **Student-faculty ratio: 18 to 1**

A public college established in 1970. 375-acre small city campus 110 miles from Los Angeles. Air, rail, and bus service.
Academic Character WASC and professional accreditation. Trimester system, 3- and 6-week summer terms. Majors offered in anthropology, biology, business administration, chemistry, child development, criminal justice, economics, English, fine arts, French, geology, health science, history, liberal studies, mathematics, nursing, philosophy, physical education, physical science, political science, psychology, public administration, sociology, Spanish, special studies. Self-designed majors. Minors in 20 additional areas. Distributive requirements. MA, MS, MBA, MPA granted. Independent study, honors program, cooperative work/study. Pass/fail, credit by exam, internships. Preprofessional programs in business administration, teaching, engineering, forestry, law, medicine, and theology. National Student Exchange. Study abroad. Elementary, secondary, and special education certification. 238,000-volume library.
Financial CEEB CSS and ACT FAS. College scholarships, loans, Cal grants; PELL, SEOG, NSS, NDSL, FISL, NSL, CWS. Priority application deadline March 1.
Admissions High school graduation required. College prep program suggested. SAT or ACT required. Minimum grades and test scores. $30 application fee. Rolling admissions with notification beginning in February; suggest applying in November. *Early Decision* and *Early Admission* programs. Transfers accepted. Credit possible for CEEB AP and CLEP exams. Educational Opportunity Program.
Student Life Newspaper, yearbook. Academic, athletic, honorary, service, and special interest organizations. Coed and women's dormitories. 9% of students live on campus. Liquor on campus only in restricted areas for students over 21. 6 intercollegiate sports for men, 4 for women; intramurals. NCAA. Student body composition: 3% Asian, 6% Black, 4% Filipino, 9% Hispanic, 5% Native American, 57% White, 16% Unknown. 1% from out of state.

■[1] CALIFORNIA STATE COLLEGE, SAN BERNARDINO

5550 State College Pkwy., San Bernardino 92407, (714) 887-7301
Dean of Admissions & Records: H. Stephen Prouty

- **Undergraduates: 1,475m, 1,980w; 5,100 total (including graduates)**
- **Tuition (1982/83): $0 (in-state), $3,150 (out-of-state)**
- **Room & Board: $2,330; Fees: $450**
- **Degrees offered: BA, BS, BVEd**
- **Mean ACT 20; mean SAT 454v, 460m**
- **Student-faculty ratio: 17 to 1**

A public college established in 1962. 450-acre campus 50 miles east of Los Angeles and 100 miles north of San Diego. Air, rail, and bus service.
Academic Character WASC accreditation. Trimester system. Majors offered in administration, American studies, anthropology, art, biology, chemistry, child development, computer science, criminal justice, economics, English, environmental studies, French, geography, health science, history, human services, humanities, liberal studies, mathematics, music, nursing, philosophy, physical education, political science, psychology, social science, sociology, Spanish, theatre arts, and vocational education. Special and self-designed majors. Distributive requirements. MA, MS, MBA, MPA granted. Independent study encouraged. Credit by exam. Preprofessional programs in dentistry, engineering, law, medicine, pharmacy, veterinary medicine. Several study abroad programs. 5-year elementary, secondary, and special education certification. ROTC; AFROTC at Claremont, UCLA, USC. Language lab, simulation labs, computer. Desert studies center. Electronic music. 315,000-volume library.
Financial CEEB CSS. College scholarships (in-state only), loans; PELL, SEOG, NDSL, FISL, NSL, CWS. Application deadline March 1.
Admissions High school graduation required. ACT or SAT required. Minimum grades and test scores. $30 application fee. Rolling admissions; suggest applying November 1. Deadline July 1. *Early Admission* and *Concurrent Enrollment* programs. Transfers accepted. Credit possible for CEEB AP exams. Educational Opportunity Program.
Student Life Associated Students, Student Union. Newspaper. Music and drama groups. Outdoors club. Academic, political, religious, service, and special interest groups. Coed and single-sex dorms. Apartments. No married-student housing. 7% of students live on campus. 1 year of phys ed required for students under 25. Intramural sports. Student body composition: 2% Asian, 12% Black, 15% Hispanic, 2% Native American, 67% White, 2% Other. 6% from out of state.

■[1] CALIFORNIA STATE COLLEGE, STANISLAUS

800 Monte Vista Ave., Turlock 95380, (209) 667-3122
Director of Admissions & Articulation: Edward J. Aubert

- **Enrollment: 1,757m, 2,169w**
- **Tuition (1982/83): $284 (in-state), $3,119 (out-of-state)**
- **Room & Board: $2,100**
- **Degrees offered: BA, BS, BVEd**
- **Mean SAT 440v, 469m**
- **Student-faculty ratio: 17 to 1**

A public college established in 1957. 230-acre semi-rural campus in San Joaquin Valley. Air, rail, and bus 13 miles away in Modesto.

Academic Character WASC and professional accreditation. 4-1-4 system, 3- and 6-week summer terms. Majors offered in the areas of anthropology, art, biological sciences, business administration, chemistry, child development, drama, economics, English, French, geography, history, liberal studies, mathematics, music, physical education, physical sciences, physics, political science, psychology, social sciences, sociology, Spanish, speech, and vocational education. Special and self-designed majors. Minors in 11 additional areas. Distributive requirements. MA, MS, MBA, MPA granted. Nursing program for students who have an RN. Certificate program in printmaking. Independent study, honors program, pass/fail. Credit by exam, internships. Preprofessional programs in dentistry, lab technology, law, medical lab technology, medicine, nursing, optometry, pharmacy, school supervision, counseling & psychology, and veterinary medicine. Many study abroad programs. Other special programs during January term. Elementary, secondary, speech & hearing, and special education certification. Marine sciences station. Over 200,000-volume library with microform resources.

Financial CEEB CSS. College scholarships, grants, loans; PELL, SEOG, NDSL, FISL, CWS. Priority application deadline March 1.

Admissions High school graduation required. College prep program recommended. SAT or ACT required. Minimum grades and test scores. $25 application fee. Rolling admissions; suggest applying early in November. *Early Entrance* Program. Informal early decision and concurrent enrollment. Admission deferral possible. Transfers accepted. Credit possible for CEEB AP and CLEP exams. College has own advanced placement program. Educational Opportunity Program. Special admissions for veterans and mature students.

Student Life Associated Students. Newspaper, yearbook, debate. Several music groups. Asian Student Alliance. Black Student Union. Chicano group. Native American Indian Council. World Students Alliance. Young Americans for Freedom. Athletic, academic, drama, ecology, honorary, religious, service, and special interest groups. 1 fraternity and 1 sorority. Coed dorms. 5% of students live on campus. One semester of phys ed required. Class attendance expected. 8 intercollegiate sports for men, 4 for women; several intramurals. Student body composition: 6% Asian, 6% Black, 9% Hispanic, 2% Native American, 77% White. 5% from out of state.

■[1] CALIFORNIA STATE POLYTECHNIC UNIVERSITY

3801 W. Temple Ave., Pomona 91768, (714) 598-4592
Director of Admissions: Richard G. York

- **Enrollment: 6,856m, 4,463w; 16,170 total (including part-time)**
- **Tuition (1982/83): $0 (in-state), $63 per unit (out-of-state)**
- **Room & Board: $2,500; Fees: $345**
- **Degrees offered: BA, BS**
- **Mean ACT 19 • Student-faculty ratio: 18 to 1**

A public university established in 1938, became coed in 1961. 813-acre suburban campus 30 miles from Los Angeles. Air, rail, and bus service.

Academic Character WASC and professional accreditation. Trimester system, summer term. 13 majors offered by the School of Agriculture, 18 by the School of Arts, 6 by the School of Business Administration, 7 by the School of Engineering, 3 by the School of Environmental Design, and 10 by the School of Science. Distributive requirements. GRE required for graduation. Masters degrees granted. Internships, cooperative work/study. Preprofessional programs in dentistry, medicine, veterinary medicine. Southern California Ocean & Desert Studies Consortium. Numerous study abroad programs. Elementary, secondary, and special education certification. ROTC on campus & at Claremont Colleges; AFROTC at UCLA & USC. Extensive agricultural facilities. Computer. 342,000-volume library with microform resources.

Financial CEEB CSS. University scholarships, grants, loans, Cal grants; PELL, SEOG, NDSL, CWS. Application deadline April 15.

Admissions High school graduation with college prep program required. Interview & portfolio required for architecture applicants. SAT or ACT required. Minimum grades and test scores. $30 application fee. Rolling admissions; suggest applying in November. *Early Entrance* Program. Transfers accepted. Credit possible for CEEB AP exams, and for previous military experience. Educational Opportunity Program.

Student Life Student government. Newspaper, literary magazine, yearbook. Several music groups. Arabian horse shows. Drama, debate, religious, and special interest clubs. Fraternities and sororities. Coed and single-sex dorms. No married-student housing. 7% of students live on campus. 8 intercollegiate sports for men, 5 for women; numerous intramurals. AIAW, NCAA, CCAA. Student body composition: 8.1% Asian, 2.7% Black, 8.5% Hispanic, 0.9% Native American, 76.8% White, 3% Other. 1.3% from out of state.

■[1] CALIFORNIA STATE UNIVERSITY, CHICO

1st & Normal Streets, Chico 95929, (916) 895-6116
Director of Admissions: Ken Edson

- **Enrollment: 6,185m, 6,366w; 14,238 total (including graduates)**
- **Tuition (1982/83): $0 (in-state), $105 per unit (out-of-state)**
- **Room & Board: $2,550; Fees: $580**
- **Degrees offered: BA, BS**
- **Mean ACT 19; mean SAT 435v, 475m**
- **Student-faculty ratio: 18 to 1**

A public university founded in 1887. Small city campus and farm located in the Sierra foothills 90 miles north of Sacramento. Air and bus nearby.

Academic Character WASC and professional accreditation. Semester system, winter intersession, 2 5½- and 1 11-week summer terms. Over 70 majors offered in the areas of agriculture, area studies, arts & humanities, biological sciences, business administration, child development, community services, computer science, engineering, home economics, industrial arts & technologies, languages & literatures, mathematics, nursing, physical education, physical sciences, psychology, public administration, social sciences, speech, and vocational education. Self-designed and special majors. Distributive requirements. MA, MS, MBA, MPA granted. Independent study, honors program, cooperative work/study, pass/fail, credit by exam, internships. Preprofessional programs in dentistry, forestry, law, library science, medicine, optometry, pharmacy, physical therapy, theology, veterinary medicine. Exchanges with U of New Hampshire, Center for Intercultural Studies, Eagle Lake Field Station. Study abroad. Elementary, secondary, and special education certification with graduate work. ROTC at UCal, Davis. Computer. Language lab. Media center. 556,277-volume library.

Financial CEEB CSS and ACT FAS. University scholarships, loans, Cal grants; PELL, SEOG, NSS, GSL, NDSL, NSL, CWS. Application deadline March 1.

Admissions High school graduation with college prep program recommended. Furthur requirements for nursing applicants. SAT or ACT required. Minimum grades and test scores. $30 application fee. Rolling admissions; suggest applying soon after November 1. *Early Entrance* Program. Admission deferral possible. Transfers accepted. Credit possible for CEEB AP and CLEP exams. Educational Opportunity Program. Alternative admissions for creative arts applicants.

Student Life Student Association. Newspapers, magazines, radio & TV stations. Drama, debate, several music groups. Community service projects. Athletic, academic, honorary, religious, and special interest clubs. 12 fraternities, 9 with houses, and 7 sororities, 5 with houses. 5% join. Coed & single-sex dorms, foreign-language houses. No married-student housing. 8% of students live on campus. 11 intercollegiate sports for men, 12 for women; several intramurals. AIAW, NCAA, Far Western Athletic Conference. Student body composition: 2.1% Asian, 2.3% Black, 4% Hispanic, 0.7% Native American, 88.4% White, 2.5% Other. 1% from out of state.

■[1] CALIFORNIA STATE UNIVERSITY, DOMINGUEZ HILLS

1000 E. Victoria St., Carson 90747, (213) 516-3696
Director of Admissions: Dr. Kenneth Finlay

- **Undergraduates: 1,635m, 2,204w; 8,279 total (including part-time)**
- **Tuition & Fees (1982/83): $345 (in-state), $3,495 (out-of-state)**
- **Room: $1,120-$1,580**
- **Degrees offered: BA, BS**
- **Student-faculty ratio: 18 to 1**

A public university established in 1965. 346-acre campus near Los Angeles and Pacific beaches.

Academic Character WASC and professional accreditation. Trimester system, 4- and 6-week summer terms. 21 majors offered by the School of Humanities & Fine Arts, 19 by Management, 17 by Social & Behavioral Sciences, 11 by Natural Sciences & Mathematics, and 2 by Education. University College offers 7 majors in interdisciplinary and experimental academics. Special and self-designed majors. Minors in most major fields and in 14 additional areas. Courses in Japanese. Distributive requirements. MA, MS, MBA, MPA granted. Several certificate and evening programs. Independent study, pass/fail, credit by exam, cooperative work/study, internships. Preprofessional programs in dentistry, law, medicine, optometry, osteopathy, pharmacy, podiatry, veterinary medicine. Many study abroad programs. Elementary, secondary, bilingual/cross-cultural, and special education certification. AFROTC & ROTC nearby. A-V and computer centers. 230,000-volume library.

Financial University scholarships, loans; PELL, SEOG, NDSL, FISL, CWS. Priority application deadline March 1.

Admissions High school graduation with college prep program recommended. ACT or SAT required. Minimum grades and test scores. $30 application fee. Rolling admissions; suggest applying soon after November 1. Transfers accepted. Credit possible for CEEB AP exams. Educational Opportunity Program.

Student Life Student government. Newspaper, magazine. Black Students Association, Women's Center. Music, drama, academic, professional, religious, social, and special interest groups. 1- and 2-bedroom apartments for 346 students. 1% of students live on campus. Cafeteria. 5 intercollegiate sports for men, 4 for women, and 2 coed (badminton & golf). Club sports. AIAW, NAIA. Student body composition: 9% Asian, 36% Black, 7% Hispanic, 2.5% Native American, 39% White, 6.5% Other. 4% from out of state.

■[1] CALIFORNIA STATE UNIVERSITY, FRESNO

Shaw & Cedar Avenues, Fresno 93740, (209) 294-4240
Director of Admissions: Kent Davies

- **Undergraduates: 6,487m, 6,693w; 16,243 total (including graduates)**
- **Tuition & Fees (1982/83): $312 (in-state), $3,462 (out-of-state)**
- **Room & Board: $2,334-$2,764**
- **Degrees offered: BA, BS, BVEd**
- **Mean ACT 19.4; mean SAT 424v, 464m**
- **Student-faculty ratio: 18 to 1**

A public university established in 1911. 1,410-acre suburban campus 7 miles from downtown Fresno. Air, rail, and bus service.

Academic Character WASC and professional accreditation. Semester system, 2 3- and 1 6-week summer terms. 10 majors offered by the School of

Agriculture & Home Economics, 19 by the School of Arts & Humanities, 15 by the School of Business & Administrative Sciences, 2 by the School of Education & Human Development, 6 by the School of Engineering, 11 by the School of Health & Social Work, 13 by the School of Natural Sciences, and 10 by the School of Social Sciences. Special, interdisciplinary, and self-designed majors. Minors in most major fields and in aerospace studies, Armenian, Asian studies, business, classics, ethnic studies, gerontology, La Raza studies, Latin, Latin American studies, office administration, performing arts administration, physical science, and women's studies. Distributive requirements. Masters degrees granted. Independent study, honors program, pass/fail, credit by exam. Preprofessional programs in dentistry, forestry, law, library science, medicine, optometry, pharmacy, theology, and veterinary medicine. Numerous study abroad programs. Elementary, secondary, and special education certification. AFROTC, ROTC. Marine lab, computer center. 620,000-volume library.

Financial CEEB CSS. University scholarships, grants, loans, Cal grants, deferred payment; PELL, SEOG, SEOPG, NSS, NDSL, GSL, NSL, CWS. Application deadline March 1.

Admissions High school graduation with college prep program recommended. Special requirements for some programs. SAT or ACT required. Minimum grades and test scores. $30 application fee. Rolling admissions; suggest applying soon after November 1, and before November 30. *Early Decision* and *Concurrent Enrollment* programs. Transfers accepted. Credit possible for CEEB AP and CLEP exams. University has own advanced placement exams. Educational Opportunity Program. Special admission possible.

Student Life Student government. Newspaper, magazine. Academic, honorary, religious, service, and special interest groups. 10 fraternities and 6 sororities, most with houses. Coed and single-sex dorms. No married-student housing. 8% of students live on campus. 11 intercollegiate sports for men, 6 for women, and coed badminton; many intramurals. AIAW, NCAA, NCAC, NCBA, PCAA, PSCN. Student body composition: 4.3% Asian, 3.5% Black, 12.3% Hispanic, 1.2% Native American, 69.1% White, 9.6% Other. 10% from out of state.

■[1] CALIFORNIA STATE UNIVERSITY, FULLERTON

800 N. State College Blvd., Fullerton 92634, (714) 773-2011
Director of Admissions: Mildred Scott

- **Enrollment: 10,605m, 11,609w**
- **Tuition (1982/83): $196 (in-state), $2,835 (out-of-state)**
- **Estimated expenses: $3,500**
- **Degrees offered: BA, BS, BMus**
- **Mean ACT 18.7; mean SAT 435v, 485m**
- **Student-faculty ratio: 14 to 1**

A public university founded in 1957. 225-acre high-rise campus in suburban Fullerton, 30 miles from Los Angeles. Rail and bus service; airport nearby.

Academic Character WASC and professional accreditation. Semester system, 2 6-week summer terms. 45 majors offered in the areas of area studies, arts, biological & physical sciences, business administration, child development, communications, communicative disorders, computer science, criminal justice, engineering, human services, languages & literatures, mathematics, medical technology, philosophy & religion, physical education, psychology, and social sciences. Nursing program for students with an RN. Distributive requirements. MA, MS, MBA, MFA, MPA granted. Independent study, cooperative work/study, pass/fail, internships, tutorials. Preprofessional programs in dentistry, law, medicine, nursing, optometry, podiatry, social welfare, and theology. Many study abroad programs. Elementary, secondary, and special education certification. AFROTC at Loyola, UCLA, USC; ROTC at Claremont Colleges, CSU (Long Beach), UCLA. Several research centers. Wildlife sanctuary. A-V, media, and computer centers. 500,000-volume library with microform resources.

Financial CEEB CSS and ACT FAS. University scholarships, grants, loans; PELL, SEOG, EOPG, NDSL, FISL, CWS. Application deadline March 1.

Admissions High school graduation with college prep program recommended. SAT or ACT required. Minimum grades and test scores. $30 application fee. Rolling admissions; suggest applying soon after November 1, and before November 30. *Early Commitment* and *Early Entrance* programs. Transfers accepted. Credit possible for CEEB AP; placement for CLEP exams. Educational Opportunity Program.

Student Life Student government. Newspaper, literary magazine. Music, drama, debate, public speaking groups. Academic, honorary, political, religious, service, and special interest clubs. 7 fraternities and 4 sororities. No university housing. Liquor only in approved areas on campus. 10 intercollegiate sports for men, 8 for women; intramurals. AIAW, NCAA, Pacific Coast Athletic Conference, Western Collegiate Athletic Association. Student body composition: 3% Asian, 2.3% Black, 6.7% Foreign, 5.8% Hispanic, 0.5% Native American, 56.9% White, 24.8% Other. 3% from out of state.

■[1] CALIFORNIA STATE UNIVERSITY, HAYWARD

Hayward 94542, (415) 881-3811
Asst. Vice-President, Admissions & Records: Judith L. Hirsch

- **Undergraduates: 3,788m, 4,629w; 11,483 total (including graduates)**
- **Tuition & Fees (1982/83): $426 (in-state), $3,576 (out-of-state)**
- **Degrees offered: BA, BS**
- **Mean ACT 25; mean SAT 584v, 585m**
- **Student-faculty ratio: 18 to 1**

A public university founded in 1957. 354-acre suburban campus overlooking San Francisco Bay, 25 miles from San Francisco. Served by rapid transit; air and rail in Oakland.

Academic Character WASC and professional accreditation. Trimester system, 6-week summer term. 39 majors offered in the areas of Afro-American studies, arts, business administration, communications, computer science, criminal justice, English, environmental studies, French, German, health sciences, human development, Latin American studies, liberal studies, math, Mexican-American studies, nursing, philosophy, physical education, psychology, recreation, social sciences, Spanish, speech, and statistics. Self-designed and special majors. Minors. Several interdisciplinary programs. Distributive requirements. MA, MS, MSEd, MBA, MPA granted. Independent study, honors program, Phi Beta Kappa. Cooperative work/study, pass/fail, credit by exam, internships. Preprofessional programs in dentistry, engineering, law, medicine, theology, and veterinary medicine. 3-2 MS program in accountancy. Cross-registration with East Bay Area schools. Many study abroad programs. Elementary, secondary, community college, and special education certification. AFROTC, NROTC at UCal, Berkeley. Asian-American and Intercultural Education centers. Marine lab. A-V, computer centers. Art gallery. 640,888-volume library.

Financial CEEB CSS. PELL, SEOG, NSS, NDSL, FISL, GSL, CWS. Priority application deadline April 15.

Admissions High school graduation with college prep program recommended. SAT or ACT required. Minimum grades and test scores. $30 application fee. Rolling admissions; suggest applying soon after November 1, and before November 30. *Early Decision* Program for military personnel. *Concurrent Enrollment* through continuing education. Transfers accepted. Credit possible for CEEB AP and CLEP exams. University has own advanced placement exams. Educational Opportunity Program. Non-high school graduates with 2 full years at a community college may be accepted.

Student Life Student governments. Newspaper, literary magazine. Athletic, academic, religious, service, honorary, and special interest clubs. 3 fraternities and 1 sorority. No university housing, but private dorm near campus. Liquor on campus only in approved areas. Class attendance expected. 10 intercollegiate sports for men, 7 for women; intramurals. NCAC. Student body composition: 10.9% Asian, 11.5% Black, 6% Hispanic, 2.4% Native American, 64.3% White, 4.9% Other. 3% from out of state.

■[1] CALIFORNIA STATE UNIVERSITY, LONG BEACH

1250 Bellflower Blvd., Long Beach 90840, (213) 498-4111
Dean of Admissions & Records: Leonard Kreutner

- **Undergraduates: 7,622m, 8,836w; 31,928 total (including graduates)**
- **Tuition & Fees (1982/83): $400 (in-state), $3,550 (out-of-state)**
- **Room & Board: $2,200-$2,500**
- **Degrees offered: BA, BS, BMus, BFA, BVEd**
- **Student-faculty ratio: 18 to 1**

A public university established in 1949. 322-acre suburban campus south of Los Angeles. Air, rail, and bus in LA.

Academic Character WASC and professional accreditation. Semester system, 3 summer terms. 68 majors offered in the areas of arts, business & management, communications, education, engineering, health sciences, home economics, humanities, industrial arts, modern languages & literatures, music, recreation, sciences, and social sciences. Minors in religious studies, women's studies. Certificates in over 15 interdisciplinary areas. Distributive requirements. Masters degrees granted. Independent study, honors program, Phi Beta Kappa, pass/fail, cooperative work/study, credit by exam. Preprofessional programs in dentistry, education, law, medicine. Educational Participation in the Community program. Several study abroad programs. AFROTC. ROTC. Over 773,610-volume library.

Financial PELL, SEOG, NDSL, FISL, NSL, CWS. Application deadline March 15.

Admissions High school graduation with college prep program recommended. SAT or ACT required. Minimum grades and test scores. $30 application fee. Rolling admissions; suggest applying soon after November 1, and before November 30. *Concurrent Enrollment* Program. Transfers accepted. Credit possible for CEEB AP exams. Educational Opportunity Program.

Student Life Student government. Newspaper, literary magazine, yearbook, radio station. Music, dance, & drama groups. Academic, athletic, service, honorary, political, religious, and special interest clubs. 12 fraternities and 7 sororities. Single students under 18 urged to live on campus. Coed and single-sex dorms. 3% of students live on campus. 12 intercollegiate sports for men, 8 for women, and coed archery, badminton, fencing; several intramurals. AIAW, NCAA, Pacific Coast Athletic Conference. Student body composition: 12% Asian, 8% Black, 7% Hispanic, 1% Native American, 56% White, 16% Other. 3% from out of state.

■[1] CALIFORNIA STATE UNIVERSITY, LOS ANGELES

5151 State University Drive, Los Angeles 90032, (213) 224-0111
Director of Admissions: Ronald L. Gibson

- **Undergraduates: 3,940m, 4,637w; 22,250 total (including graduates)**
- **Tuition & Fees (1982/83): $330 (in-state), $3,500 (out-of-state) • Degrees offered: BA, BS, BMus, BVEd**
- **Mean ACT 19**
- **Student-faculty ratio: 18 to 1**

A public university established in 1947. 100-acre urban campus. Air, rail, and bus service.

Academic Character WASC and professional accreditation. Trimester system, summer term. 84 majors offered in the areas of arts, business administration, communications, computer science, education, engineering, fire protection, home economics, industrial arts, languages & literatures, music, nursing, sciences, social sciences, and social welfare. Self-designed and special majors. Distributive requirements. Graduate and professional degrees granted. Honors program, cooperative work/study, credit by exam, internships. Preprofessional programs in dentistry, law, libarianship, medicine, optometry, pharmacy, and veterinary medicine. Many study abroad programs. Elementary, secondary, and special education certification. AFROTC at Loyola-Marymount, USC, UCLA; NROTC, ROTC at UCLA. Research centers. Computer, A-V center. Over 800,000-volume library.

Key to ratings **[1, 2, J1, J2, G, P, R, S]** *and list of abbreviations start on page 120*

Financial CEEB CSS. PELL, SEOG, NDSL, NSL, CWS.
Admissions High school graduation with college prep program recommended. SAT or ACT required. Minimum grades and test scores. $30 application fee. Rolling admissions; suggest applying soon after November 1, and before November 30. *Early Entrance* and *Concurrent Enrollment* programs. Transfers accepted. Credit possible for CEEB AP, CLEP, and university exams, and for military and Peace Corps experience. Educational Opportunity Program.
Student Life Student government. Newspaper, magazines. Several music groups. Intercollegiate debate. Drama clubs. Academic, athletic, honorary, service, religious, and special interest organizations. 8 fraternities and 4 sororities. 3% of men and women join. No university housing. 4 cafeterias on campus. 8 intercollegiate sports for men, 5 for women, and coed archery & badminton; intramurals. AIAW, NCAA, California Women's Intercollegiate Athletic Association. Student body composition: 19% Asian, 13% Black, 23% Hispanic, 1% Native American, 42% White, 2% Other. 3% from out of state.

■[1] CALIFORNIA STATE UNIVERSITY, NORTHRIDGE

18111 Nordhoff St., Northridge 91330, (213) 885-1200
Director of Admissions & Records: Ned Reynolds

- **Enrollment: 10,683m, 11,768w; 25,438 total (including part-time)**
- **Tuition & Fees (1982/83): $374 (in-state), $2,920 (out-of-state)**
- **Degrees offered: BA, BS, BMus**
- **Mean SAT 877**
- **Student-faculty ratio: 19 to 1**

A public university established in 1958. 350-acre suburban campus in the San Fernando Valley, 30 miles from downtown Los Angeles. Air, rail, and bus in LA.
Academic Character WASC and professional accreditation. Semester system, 2 6-week summer terms. 43 majors offered in the fields of arts, business administration, child development, communications, communicative disorders, computer science, engineering, health science, home economics, humanities, languages & literatures, music, psychology, recreation, sciences, social sciences. Interdisciplinary majors and minors. Distributive requirements. MA, MS, MBA, MPA, MPH granted. Independent study, pass/fail, credit by exam, internships. Preprofessional programs in dentistry, law, medicine, optometry, physical therapy. Concurrent enrollment with other state schools. Study abroad in Brazil, Canada, China, Europe, Israel, Mexico, New Zealand, Peru. Elementary, secondary, and special education certification. AFROTC at Loyola-Marymount, USC, UCLA; NROTC, ROTC at UCLA. Art gallery. Computer center. Over 800,000-volume library.
Financial CEEB CSS. University scholarships, loans, Cal grants; PELL, SEOG, NDSL, FISL, GSL, CWS. Priority application deadline March 1.
Admissions High school graduation with college prep program recommended. SAT or ACT required. Minimum grades and test scores. Some programs closed to non-residents. $30 application fee. Rolling admissions; suggest applying soon after November 1, and before November 30. *Early Decision, Early Admission, Concurrent Enrollment* programs. Transfers accepted. Credit possible for CEEB AP and CLEP exams. University has own advanced placement exams. Educational Opportunity Program.
Student Life Student government. Newspaper, literary magazine, radio station. Music groups. Intercollegiate debate. Academic, athletic, service, outing, honorary, religious, and special interest clubs. 11 fraternities and 7 sororities, all with houses. 1% of men and women join. Campus apartments. 1% of students live on campus. Liquor prohibited on campus. 10 intercollegiate sports for men, 9 for women; intramural and club sports. AIAW, NCAA, California Collegiate Athletic Association. Student body composition: 7.2% Asian, 5.1% Black, 7.2% Hispanic, 0.7% Native American, 61.4% White, 18.4% Other. 3% from out of state.

■[1] CALIFORNIA STATE UNIVERSITY, SACRAMENTO

6000 J St., Sacramento 95819, (916) 454-6011
Director of Admissions & Records: Duane Anderson

- **Enrollment: 7,100m, 7,600w; 22,700 total (including part-time)**
- **Tuition & Fees (1982/83): $313 (in-state), $3,150 (out-of-state)**
- **Room & Board: $2,350**
- **Degrees offered: BA, BS, BMus**
- **Mean ACT 19.5; mean SAT 420v, 470m**
- **Student-faculty ratio: 19 to 1**

A public university established in 1947. 288-acre urban campus bordering the American River. Air, rail, and bus service.
Academic Character WASC and professional accreditation. Semester system, 4- and 6-week summer terms. Over 80 majors offered in the areas of arts, biological sciences, business administration, child development, communications, computer science, criminal justice, engineering, environmental studies, ethnic studies, forensic science, health & safety studies, home economics, humanities, languages & literatures, mathematics, music, nursing, physical education, physical sciences, psychology, recreation administration, social sciences, social work, and speech pathology & audiology. Self-designed majors. Minors in major fields and additional areas. Distributive requirements. MA, MS, MBA, MPA, MSW granted. Independent study, honors program, pass/fail, credit by exam, internships. Preprofessional programs in dentistry, law, medicine, optometry, pharmacy, and veterinary medicine. Several study abroad programs. 5-year programs for elementary, secondary, service, and special education certification. ROTC, AFROTC. Computer center, language lab. 740,000-volume library with microform resources.
Financial CEEB CSS. University scholarships, grants, loans, Cal grants; PELL, SEOG, NDSL, NSS, GSL, NSL, CWS. Priority application deadline March 1.
Admissions High school graduation with college prep program recommended. SAT or ACT required. Minimum grades and test scores. $30 application fee. Rolling admissions; suggest applying soon after November 1, and before November 30. *Early Admission, Early Decision, Concurrent Enrollment* programs. Transfers accepted. Credit possible for CEEB AP and CLEP exams. Educational Opportunity Program. Special admissions for those not normally admissable.
Student Life Student government. Newspaper, magazine. Several music & dance groups. Debate. Numerous academic, athletic, ethnic, honorary, professional, political, religious, and special interest clubs. 11 fraternities and 3 sororities. 5 coed dorms, 4 cafeterias. 5% of students live on campus. 10 intercollegiate sports for men, 9 for women; many intramurals. AIAW, NCAA, Far Western & Golden State Conferences. Student body composition: 7.8% Asian, 7% Black, 5.7% Hispanic, 1.7% Native American, 74% White, 3.8% Other. 4% from out of state.

■[1] HUMBOLDT STATE UNIVERSITY

Arcata 95521, (707) 826-3421
Dean of Admissions & Records: Robert L. Hannigan

- **Undergraduates: 3,311m, 2,898w; 7,228 total (including graduates)**
- **Tuition & Fees (1982/83): $462 (in-state), $4,404 (out-of-state)**
- **Room & Board: $2,700**
- **Degrees offered: BA, BS**
- **Mean ACT 22; mean SAT 495v, 525m**
- **Student-faculty ratio: 17 to 1**

A public university established in 1913. 142-acre rural campus overlooking a small seacoast town 275 miles north of San Francisco. Air and bus service.
Academic Character WASC and professional accreditation. Trimester system, summer terms. Over 70 majors offered in the areas of arts, business administration, environmental & natural resources, home economics, humanities, industrial arts, journalism, languages & literatures, nursing, oceanography, physical education, sciences, social sciences, social welfare, speech, and wildlife management. Special & self-designed majors. Distributive requirements. MA, MS, MBA, MFA granted. Independent study, honors program, pass/fail, cooperative work/study, internships. Preprofessional programs in dentistry, law, medicine, veterinary medicine. Indian Teacher Education Project, Native American Education Program in Natural Resources. National Student Exchange program. Study abroad in 24 locations. Elementary, secondary, services, and special education certification. Forest & marine science labs. Computer center, language lab. 280,000-volume library.
Financial CEEB CSS. University scholarships, BIA & Cal grants; PELL, SEOG, NSS, NDSL, GSL, NSL, CWS. Priority application deadline March 1.
Admissions High school graduation with college prep program recommended. SAT or ACT required. Minimum grades and test scores. $25 application fee. Rolling admissions; suggest applying soon after November 1, and before November 30. *Early Decision* and *Concurrent Enrollment* programs. Transfers accepted. Credit possible for CEEB AP and CLEP exams. Educational Opportunity Program. Special programs for Native Americans.
Student Life Student government. Newspaper, magazines, radio station. Music & theatre groups. Intercollegiate debate. Academic, athletic, ethnic, honorary, religious, social, and special interest clubs. Coed and single-sex dorms. No married-student housing. 15% of students live on campus. 6 intercollegiate sports for men, 6 for women; intramurals. NCAA, Northern California Athletic Conference. Student body composition: 2% Asian, 0.5% Black, 2.5% Hispanic, 1.5% Native American, 93.5% White. 2% from out of state.

■[1] SAN DIEGO STATE UNIVERSITY

5300 Campanile Drive, San Diego 92182, (714) 265-6871
Director of Admissions: Nancy C. Sprotte

- **Undergraduates: 8,920m, 9,300w; 31,265 total (including graduates)**
- **Tuition & Fees (1982/83): $400 (in-state), $2,750 (out-of-state)**
- **Room & Board: $2,266**
- **Degrees offered: BA, BS, BMus, BVEd**
- **Mean ACT 28**
- **Student-faculty ratio: 20 to 1**

A public university established in 1897. 300-acre urban residential campus 12 miles from the ocean. Imperial Valley campus 120 miles east in Calexico. Air, rail, and bus service.
Academic Character WASC and professional accreditation. Semester system, 3 summer terms. Over 70 majors offered in the areas of area studies, arts, business administration, child development, communications, computer science, criminal justice, engineering, health science, home economics, industrial arts, languages & literatures, music, nursing, recreation, sciences, social sciences, social welfare, speech, and vocational arts. Self-designed & special majors. Distributive requirements. MA, MS, MBA, MPA, MSW, PhD granted. Independent study, honors program, Phi Beta Kappa, pass/fail, cooperative work/study. Preprofessional programs in dentistry, law, medicine, veterinary medicine. Dual degree programs. Exchanges with other state schools and U of New Hampshire. Study abroad in 15 countries. Elementary, secondary, and special education certification. AFROTC, ROTC. Research, A-V, and computer centers, language lab. 767,730-volume library.
Financial CEEB CSS. University scholarships, loans; PELL, SEOG, NDSL, FISL, GSL, CWS. Scholarship application deadline February 1.
Admissions High school graduation with college prep program recommended. SAT or ACT required. Minimum grades and test scores. $30 application fee. Rolling admissions; suggest applying soon after November 1, and before November 30. Transfers accepted. Credit possible for CEEB AP and CLEP exams. Educational Opportunity Program.
Student Life Student government. Newspaper, yearbook. Several music & drama groups. Academic, athletic, religious, honorary, service, and special interest clubs. 15 fraternities and 10 sororities with houses. 3% of students join. Coed and single-sex dorms. No married-student housing. 17% of students live on campus. 2 semesters of phys ed required. 10 intercollegiate sports for men,

9 for women; intramurals. NCAA, Western Athletic Conference, Western Collegiate Athletic Association. Student body composition: 3.3% Asian, 3.7% Black, 7.1% Hispanic, 1.8% Native American, 76.3% White, 7.8% Other. 9% from out of state.

■[1] SAN FRANCISCO STATE UNIVERSITY
1600 Holloway Ave., San Francisco 94132, (415) 469-2141
Interim Director of Admissions & Records: Deanna T. Wong

- **Undergraduates: 5,038m, 6,521w; 23,227 total (including graduates)**
- **Tuition & Fees (1982/83): $444 (in-state), $3,594 (out-of-state)**
- **Room & Board: $2,400**
- **Degrees offered: BS, BS, BSBA, BMus, BVEd**
- **Student-faculty ratio: 17 to 1**

A public university established in 1899. 93-acre urban campus near Lake Merced. Air, rail, and bus service.
Academic Character WASC and professional accreditation. Semester system, summer terms. Over 80 majors offered in the areas of area studies, arts, biological & physical sciences, business, communications, computer science, engineering, film, health sciences, home economics, humanities, industrial arts, languages & literatures, music, recreation, social sciences, speech, and vocational education. Special majors. MA, MBA, MS, MSW, MSBA, MMus, MAEd granted. Independent study, Phi Beta Kappa, credit by exam, field work, internships. 3-2 engineering program with Columbia U. Several study abroad programs. Teacher training. ROTC. 500,000-volume library.
Financial CEEB CSS. University scholarships, Cal grants; PELL, SEOG, FISL, CWS. Application deadline April 1.
Admissions High school graduation with college prep program recommended. SAT or ACT required. Minimum grades and test scores. $25 application fee. Rolling admissions; suggest applying soon after November 1, and before November 30. *Early Entrance* Program. Transfers accepted. Credit possible for CEEB AP exams.
Student Life Student government. Newspaper, literary magazine. Music, drama, debate groups. Athletic, honorary, religious, social, and special interest clubs. 2 fraternities and 1 sorority without houses. Dorms for 1500 students. 8% of students live on campus. 13 intercollegiate sports for men; several intramurals for men & women. Far Western Athletic Conference. Student body composition: 15.1% Asian, 7.1% Black, 5.5% Hispanic, 1.8% Native American, 52.2% White, 18.3% Other. 5.8% from out of state.

■[1] SAN JOSE STATE UNIVERSITY
Washington Square, San Jose 95192, (408) 277-2000
Director of Admissions & Records: Edgar Chambers

- **Enrollment: 12,281m, 12,664w**
- **Tuition & Fees (1982/83): $294 (in-state), $3,224 (out-of-state)**
- **Room & Board: $2,306**
- **Degrees offered: BA, BS, BMus, BFA**
- **Mean ACT 21; mean SAT 435v, 500m**
- **Student-faculty ratio: 21 to 1**

A public university established in 1857. 134-acre urban campus 50 miles south of San Francisco. Air, rail, and bus service.
Academic Character WASC and professional accreditation. 4-1-4 system, 3 summer terms. Over 75 majors offered in the areas of advertising, aeronautics, arts, business administration, communications, criminal justice, design, engineering, humanities, industrial studies, languages & literatures, meteorology, music, nursing, occupational therapy, public relations, recreation, sciences, social sciences, speech. Special, double, self-designed majors. Minors in most major fields and 43 additional areas. Distributive requirements. Masters degrees granted. Independent study, honors programs, Phi Beta Kappa, cooperative work/study, pass/fail, internships. Preprofessional programs in dentistry, law, medicine, optometry, theology, and veterinary medicine. Exchanges with other state schools. Several study abroad programs. Elementary, secondary, and special education certification. AFROTC, ROTC. A-V center, language lab, computer. 713,000-volume library with microform resources.
Financial CEEB CSS. University scholarships, loans; PELL, SEOG, NDSL, NSL, FISL, CWS. Application deadline March 1.
Admissions High school graduation with college prep program recommended. Portfolio required for design applicants. SAT or ACT required. Minimum grades and test scores. $25 application fee. Rolling admissions; suggest applying soon after November 1, and before November 30. *Early Entrance* and *Early Decision* programs. Transfers accepted. Credit possible for CEEB AP, CLEP, and university exams. Educational Opportunity Program.
Student Life Student government. Newspapers, literary magazine, radio station. Several music and drama groups. Academic, athletic, honorary, religious, social, service, and special interest clubs. 8 fraternities and 6 sororities with houses. 3% of students join. Coed dorms, international house, married-student housing. 10% of students live on campus. 2 units of phys ed required. 13 intercollegiate sports for men, 6 for women; intramurals. NCAA, AIAW, Pacific Coast Athletic Association. Student body composition: 13.2% Asian, 6% Black, 8.3% Hispanic, 3.2% Native American, 63.7% White, 5.6% Other. 1.5% from out of state.

■[1] SONOMA STATE UNIVERSITY
1801 East Cotati Ave., Rohnert Park 94928, (707) 664-2880
Dean of Admissions & Records: Dr. Frank Tansey

- **Undergraduates: 1,296m, 1,580w; 5,300 total (including graduates)**
- **Tuition & Fees (1982/83): $430 (in-state), $3,261 (out-of-state)**
- **Room & Board: $2,800**
- **Degrees offered: BA, BS**
- **Student-faculty ratio: 15 to 1**

A public university founded in 1960. 220-acre rural campus 10 miles from Santa Rosa and 50 miles from San Francisco.
Academic Character WASC and professional accreditation. Semester system, 6-week summer term. Majors offered in Afro-American studies, anthropology, art (history, studio), biology, chemistry, criminal justice administration, economics, English, environmental studies/planning, French, geography, geology, German, history, India studies, liberal studies, management, mathematics (applied, computer, statistics), Mexican-American studies, music, philosophy, physical education, physics, political science, psychology, sociology, Spanish, theatre arts. Special and interdisciplinary majors. Nursing major for students with an RN. Distributive requirements. MA granted. Independent study, honors program. Preprofessional programs in counseling, criminal justice administration, education, management, nursing. National Student Exchange program. Several study abroad programs. Elementary and secondary education certification. ROTC at San Francisco State. Language lab. 300,000-volume library.
Financial CEEB CSS. University scholarships, loans; PELL, SEOG, NDSL, FISL, NSL, CWS.
Admissions High school graduation with college prep program recommended. SAT or ACT required. Minimum grades and test scores. $25 application fee. Rolling admissions; suggest applying soon after November 1, and before November 30. *Early Entrance* Program. Transfers accepted. Credit possible for CEEB AP and CLEP exams. Educational Opportunity Program.
Student Life Student government. Academic, athletic, drama, service, honorary, religious, and special interest groups. Dorms. 7% of students live on campus. 7 intercollegiate sports; intramurals. Far Western Conference. Student body composition: 2.2% Asian, 3.7% Black, 4.4% Hispanic, 1.4% Native American, 87.5% White, 0.8% Other. 3% from out of state.

[P] CALIFORNIA WESTERN SCHOOL OF LAW
350 Cedar Street, San Diego 92101

[J1] CANADA COLLEGE
4200 Farm Hill Blvd., Redwood City 94061

[J1] CANYONS, COLLEGE OF THE
25000 West Valencia Blvd., Valencia 91355

[J1] CERRITOS COLLEGE
11110 Alondra Blvd., Norwalk 90650

[J1] CERRO COSO COMMUNITY COLLEGE
3000 College Heights Blvd., Ridgecrest 93555

[J1] CHABOT COLLEGE
25555 Hesperian Blvd., Hayward 94545

[J1] CHAFFEY COLLEGE
5885 Haven Avenue, Alta Loma 91701

[1] CHAPMAN COLLEGE
333 N. Glassell St., Orange 92666, (714) 977-6711
Dean of Admissions: Anthony Garcia

- **Enrollment: 695m, 805w**
- **Tuition (1982/83): $5,570**
- **Room & Board: $2,500**
- **Degrees offered: BA, BS, BMus**
- **Mean SAT 455v, 426m**
- **Student-faculty ratio: 13 to 1**

A private college associated with the Christian Church (Disciples of Christ), established in 1861. 32-acre suburban campus 32 miles southeast of Los Angeles. Rail service; bus and helicopter to LA airport.
Academic Character WASC and professional accreditation. 4-1-4 system with optional January interterm, 2 6-week summer terms. Over 35 majors offered in the areas of arts, business administration, communications, communicative disorders, computer, criminal justice, education, English, ethnic studies, food science/nutrition, French, health sciences, humanities, international studies, mathematics, music, philosophy, physical education, psychology, recreation, religion, sciences, social sciences, social work, and Spanish. Interdepartmental and self-designed majors. Minors. Courses in 10 additional areas. Distributive requirements. MA, MS, MBA granted. Independent study, honors program, cooperative work/study, pass/fail, credit by exam, internships. Preprofessional programs in dentistry, law, medical technology, medicine, social service, teaching, theology, veterinary medicine. Several study abroad programs. Elementary, secondary, and special education certification. AFROTC at USC, Loyola Marymount. TV studio, computer, language lab. 170,000-volume library.
Financial CEEB CSS. College scholarships, grants, loans, church matching grants, ministerial grants & scholarships, family tuition discount, Cal grants, deferred payment. PELL, SEOG, NDSL, GSL, CWS. Application deadlines February 11 (Cal grants), March 1 (priority for other aid).
Admissions High school graduation with minimum 2.5 GPA expected. SAT, ACT, or CLEP General Exams required. $20 application fee. Rolling admissions; suggest applying before April 15. Deadline August 1. $100 deposit required on acceptance of admissions offer. *Early Decision, Early Admission, Concurrent Enrollment* programs. Transfers accepted. Credit possible for CEEB AP and CLEP exams. Provisional admission possible.

Student Life Student government. Newspaper, yearbook, radio station. Several music, drama, film groups. International Students Club, MECHA, Hillel, Black Student Alliance. Honorary, academic, religious, service, social, and special interest clubs. 3 fraternities and 2 sororities. Single students under 21 must live at home or on campus. Coed dorms. Apartments. Married-student housing. 60% of students live on campus. Class attendance required. 4 semesters of phys ed required. 6 intercollegiate sports for men, 4 for women; many intramurals. AIAW, CCAA, NCAA. Student body composition: 18% minority. 30% from out of state.

[1] CHRIST COLLEGE IRVINE

1530 Concordia, Irvine 92715, (714) 752-6222
Acting Director of Admissions: Mrs. Maureen Witte

- **Undergraduates: 105m, 107w; 226 total (including part-time)**
- **Tuition (1982/83): $3,000 (liberal arts), $2,220 (church workers)**
- **Room: $1,095; Fees: $240**
- **Degrees offered: BA, AA**
- **Student-faculty ratio: 8 to 1**

A private college founded in 1972, owned and operated by the Lutheran Church, Missouri Synod. 113-acre suburban campus in hills overlooking Orange County near U California, Irvine, and 45 miles southeast of Los Angeles.

Academic Character WASC accreditation. Trimester system, summer terms. Majors offered in behavioral science, Biblical languages, Director of Christian Education (evangelism/youth, choral music, organ music), evangelism, humanities, life science, mathematics & computer science, multiple subject, natural science (environmental), single subject, social science (composite, history, psychology, sociology), and social welfare. Minors in some majors and in art, biology, chemistry, communications, English, music, religion, Spanish, and youth. Distributives and 17 hours of religion required. AA offered in liberal arts and pre-deaconess studies. Independent study, pass/fail, credit by exam. Preprofessional programs in law, medicine, nursing, theology. Cross-registration with University of California, Irvine. Seminary extension courses offered in the summer for pastors and lay students. Lutheran Teacher's Certificate granted. 5-year elementary and secondary education certification. 60,000-volume library with access to area libraries.

Financial CEEB CSS. College & church scholarships, grants, Cal grants, deferred payment; PELL, SEOG, GSL, CWS, college work program.

Admissions High school graduation with college prep program required. GED accepted. SAT or ACT required. 2.0 GPA and 700 combined SAT required. $10 application fee. Priority application deadline June 1. $40 tuition and $50 housing deposits required. *Early Admission* Program. Transfers accepted. Provisional admission possible.

Student Life Living-Learning Center. Service and special interest groups. Single students must live at home, on campus, or in approved off-campus housing. Dorms to be built for fall 1983. Apartments for single and married students. No cafeteria/dining hall. 4 hours of phys ed required. Daily chapel services held. College encourages religious worship. Recreational sports.

[2] CHRISTIAN HERITAGE COLLEGE

2100 Greenfield Drive, El Cajon 92021

[J1] CITRUS COLLEGE

18824 East Foothill Blvd., Azusa-Glendora 91702

[G1] CLAREMONT, SCHOOL OF THEOLOGY AT

1325 North College Avenue, Claremont 91711

CLAREMONT COLLEGES

■[G1] CLAREMONT GRADUATE SCHOOL

Claremont 91711

■[1] CLAREMONT McKENNA COLLEGE

Claremont 91711, (714) 621-8088
Dean of Admission: Linda S. Davis

- **Undergraduates: 610m, 220w**
- **Tuition (1982/83): $7,200**
- **Room & Board: $2,820; Fees: $50**
- **Degree offered: BA**
- **Mean SAT 563v, 608m**
- **Student-faculty ratio: 11 to 1**

A private college established in 1946. Formerly Claremont Men's College, became coed in 1976. 40-acre suburban campus at foot of San Gabriel Mountains, 35 miles east of Los Angeles. Bus service. Rail 4 miles away. Airport 10 miles away.

Academic Character WASC accreditation. Semester system. Most students major in economics or political science. Majors also offered in American studies, Asian studies, biological sciences, chemistry, drama, European civilization, film studies, fine arts, history, international relations, Latin American studies, literature, management/engineering, mathematics, modern languages, philosophy/religion, physics, psychology, women's studies. Self-designed majors. Interdisciplinary programs. Courses in Black studies, Greek, Japanese, Latin, Mexican-American studies, phys ed, Russian, written/oral expression. Courses and majors available at other Claremont colleges. Distributives and senior thesis required for graduation. Independent study, honors program, Phi Beta Kappa, pass/fail. Political and economic internships. Preprofessional programs in business, foreign service, law. 3-2 engineering-management program with Stanford. 3-3 program with Columbia Law School. Study abroad. ROTC. AFROTC at USC. Research institutes, Black Studies and Chicano Studies Centers. Computer, language lab. Over 1,500,000-volume combined libraries.

Financial CEEB CSS. College scholarships, grants, loans, deferred payment; PELL, SEOG, FISL, NDSL, CWS. Scholarship application deadline February 15.

Admissions High school graduation with 16 units required. Interview recommended. SAT required, 3 ACH recommended. $25 application fee. Suggest applying between October 1 and February 15. $100 deposit required on acceptance of admissions offer. *Early Decision* and *Early Admission* programs. Admission deferral possible. Transfers accepted. Credit possible for CEEB AP exams or similar evidence.

Student Life Student governments. Newspaper, yearbook, radio station. Music, drama, debate groups. Honorary, religious, service, and special interest organizations. Freshmen must live on campus. Coed and special interest dorms. No married-student housing. 95% of students live on campus. 3 semesters of phys ed required. Gambling, firearms, and public possession of liquor on campus prohibited. 13 intercollegiate sports for men (with Harvey Mudd College), 6 for women (with Harvey Mudd & Scripps). Club and intramural sports. AIAW, NCAA, SCIAC. Student body composition: 9% Asian, 2% Black, 4% Hispanic, 81% White, 4% Other. 40% from out of state.

■[1] HARVEY MUDD COLLEGE

Claremont 91711, (714) 621-8000, ext. 3843
Dean of Admission & Financial Aid: Duncan C. Murdoch

- **Undergraduates: 425m, 75w**
- **Tuition (1982/83): $7,200**
- **Room & Board: $2,980-$3,180; Fees: $360**
- **Degree offered: BS**
- **Mean SAT 600v, 710m**
- **Student-faculty ratio: 11 to 1**

A private college established in 1955. 18-acre suburban campus at the foot of the San Gabriel Mountains, 35 miles east of Los Angeles. Bus service. Rail 4 miles away. Airport 10 miles away.

Academic Character WASC and professional accreditation. Semester system. Majors offered in chemistry, engineering, mathematics, physics. Self-designed majors, interdisciplinary programs. Courses in composition, drama, economics, English & American literature, government, history, philosophy, psychology. Courses available at other Claremont colleges. Distributive requirements. Independent study/original lab research in 3rd & 4th years. Pass/fail. 5-year MEng program. Program leading to FAA Private Pilot License. ROTC; AFROTC with USC. Engineering Clinic. Black Studies and Chicano Studies Centers. Over 1,500,000-volume combined libraries.

Financial CEEB CSS. College scholarships, grants, loans, deferred payment; PELL, SEOG, NDSL, FISL, GSL, CWS. File FAF (for scholarships) by February 1.

Admissions High school graduation with 16 units required. Interview encouraged. SAT and 3 ACH required. $25 application fee. Suggest applying between October 1 and February 15. $50 deposit required on acceptance of admissions offer. *Early Decision*, limited *Early Entrance* programs. Admission deferral possible. Few transfers accepted. Credit possible for CEEB AP exams.

Student Life Student government. Newspaper, yearbook. Music and drama groups. Debate. Political, athletic, service, and special interest organizations. Freshmen must live on campus. Coed dorms. Some women live at Scripps. 95% of students live on campus. Firearms, fireworks, and public possession of liquor prohibited. 3 semesters of phys ed required. 13 intercollegiate sports for men (with Claremont McKenna), 6 for women (with Scripps and Claremont McKenna); intramurals. AIAW, NCAA, SCIAC. Student body composition: 23% Asian, 1% Black, 2% Hispanic, 1% Native American, 73% White. 40% from out of state.

■[1] PITZER COLLEGE

Claremont 91711, (714) 621-8000
Dean of Admissions: Martin A. Tucker

- **Undergraduates: 317m, 346w**
- **Tuition (1982/83): $7,334**
- **Room & Board: $2,432; Fees: $364**
- **Degree offered: BA**
- **Mean SAT 550v, 550m**
- **Student-faculty ratio: 13 to 1**

A private college specializing in the social and behavioral sciences, established in 1963, became coed in 1970. 25-acre suburban campus at foot of San Gabriel Mountains, 35 miles from Los Angeles. Bus service. Rail 4 miles away. Airport 10 miles away.

Academic Character WASC accreditation. Semester system, summer term through other Claremont schools. Majors offered in American studies, anthropology, art, Asian studies, biology, chemistry, Chicano studies, classics, economics, English, environmental studies, European studies, film studies, folklore, French, German, history, human biology, Latin American studies, linguistics, mathematics, organizational studies, philosophy, physics, political studies, psychobiology, psychology, sociology, Spanish, and study of woman. Combined, interdisciplinary majors. Other majors with Claremont colleges. Courses in computer science, religion, and television. Interdisciplinary study stressed. Independent study, pass/fail, internships. New Resources program for post-college-age students. Preprofessional counseling. Combined degree programs in business administration, mathematics, and public policy with Claremont Graduate School. Exchange program with Colby College in Maine. Washington Semester. Several study abroad programs. ROTC at Claremont McKenna, Pomona. Several research centers, film & TV studios, computer. Over 1,500,000-volume combined libraries.

Financial CEEB CSS. College scholarships, grants, loans, Cal grants; PELL, SEOG, NDSL, FISL, GSL, CWS. Application deadline February 1.

Admissions High school graduation with minimum 13 units recommended. Interview encouraged. SAT or ACT required. 3 ACH urged. $25 application fee. Rolling admissions; suggest applying in summer or fall of 12th year. Priority application deadline February 1. $300 deposit required on acceptance of admissions offer. *Early Decision* and *Early Entrance* programs. Admission deferral possible. Transfers accepted. Credit possible for CEEB AP exams.
Student Life Student government, several publications. Music, drama, film, debate groups. Numerous student organizations within the 5 colleges. Students under 23 must petition to live off campus. Coed & single-sex dorms. Suite housing, thematic units. No married-student housing. 90% of students live on campus. Cars discouraged for freshmen. 11 intercollegiate sports for men, 5 for women, and coed badminton, fencing; all with Pomona. AIAW, NAIA, NCAA, SCIAC. Student body composition: 6% Asian, 8% Black, 8% Hispanic, 78% White. 57% from out of state.

■[1] POMONA COLLEGE
Claremont 91711, (714) 621-8134
Dean of Admissions: R. Fred Zuker

- **Undergraduates: 698m, 678w**
- **Tuition (1982/83): $7,200**
- **Room & Board: $3,000; Fees: $190**
- **Degree offered: AB**
- **Mean SAT 600v, 630m**
- **Student-faculty ratio: 11 to 1**

A private liberal arts college founded in 1887. 160-acre suburban campus 35 minutes from Los Angeles. Bus service. Rail 4 miles away. Airport 10 miles away.
Academic Character WASC accreditation. Semester system, limited summer term. Majors offered in American studies, anthropology, art, Asian studies, biology, chemistry, classics, economics, English, film studies, geology, government, history, international relations, linguistics, mathematics, modern languages & literature, music, philosophy, physics, psychology, religion, sociology, theater. Self-designed majors. Courses in astronomy, Black studies, Chicano studies, computer science, dance, education, military science, public policy, women's studies. Interdisciplinary courses. Distributive requirements. Senior project, thesis, or comprehensive exam required in major field. Independent study, Phi Beta Kappa, pass/fail, internships. Preprofessional programs in allied health fields, business, education, engineering, law, medicine, public affairs, social work, and theology. 3-2 engineering programs with Caltech and Washington U (St. Louis). Exchanges with Caltech, Colby (Maine), Smith, Swarthmore, and Fisk U (Tenn). Washington Semester. Several study abroad programs. Elementary and secondary education certification with Claremont Graduate School. ROTC. Research institutes, botanic garden, language lab, computer. Over 1,500,000-volume combined libraries.
Financial CEEB CSS. College scholarships, grants, loans, Cal grants, deferred payment; PELL, SEOG, NDSL, GSL, FISL, CWS. Application deadline February 1.
Admissions High school graduation with college prep program expected. Interview encouraged. SAT or ACT required. 3 ACH recommended. $25 application fee. Suggest applying early in 12th year; deadline February 1. $100 deposit required on acceptance of admissions offer. *Early Entrance* and *Early Decision* programs. Admission deferral possible. Transfers accepted. Credit possible for CEEB AP and CLEP exams.
Student Life Student government. Several publications. Radio station. Music, dance, drama groups. Political, honorary, religious, academic, service, and special interest organizations. 7 fraternities (3 coed) without houses. 25% of students join. Freshmen must live at home or on campus. Coed and single-sex dorms. Language clusters. No married-student housing. 90% of students live on campus. 1 semester of phys ed required. 11 intercollegiate sports for men, 6 for women; several club and intramural sports. AIAW, NAIA, NCAA, SCIAC. Student body composition: 12% Asian, 3% Black, 4% Hispanic, 81% White. 44% from out of state.

■[1] SCRIPPS COLLEGE
Claremont 91711, (714) 621-8000
Director of Admissions: Janet E. A. Burback

- **Undergraduates: 575w**
- **Tuition (1982/83): $7,130**
- **Room & Board: $3,250; Fees: $60**
- **Degree offered: AB**
- **Mean SAT 530v, 510m**
- **Student-faculty ratio: 11 to 1**

A private women's college established in 1926. 27-acre suburban campus at foot of San Gabriel Mountains, 35 miles from Los Angeles. Bus service. Rail 4 miles away. Airport 10 miles away.
Academic Character WASC accreditation. Semester system. Majors offered in American studies, American/British literature, art (2), Asian studies, biochemistry, biology, Black studies, chemistry, Chicano studies, classics, comparative literature, dance, European studies, foreign languages, French, German literature, Hispanic studies, history, international relations, Italian, Latin American studies, modern French civilization, music, philosophy, physics, psychobiology, psychology, religion, social studies, Spanish, and women's studies. Interdepartmental majors. Other majors available through Claremont Colleges. Distributives with humanities sequence and senior thesis required. Independent study, honors programs, Phi Beta Kappa, pass/fail, internships. Preprofessional advising. Dual degree programs in business, government, international studies, public policy studies, religion. BA/MS and BS/MS programs with Stanford. Exchange program with Caltech. Washington Semester. Several study abroad programs. Elementary and secondary education certification with Claremont Graduate School. ROTC at Claremont McKenna. Children's school, language labs. Over 1,500,000-volume combined libraries.
Financial CEEB CSS. College scholarships, grants, loans, Cal grants; PELL, SEOG, NDSL, GSL, CWS. Application deadline February 1.
Admissions High school graduation with at least 13 units recommended. SAT required. Interview encouraged. 2 ACH recommended. $25 application fee. Application deadline February 15. $150 deposit required on acceptance of admissions offer. *Early Entrance* Program. Admission deferral possible. Transfers accepted. Credit possible for CEEB AP exams.
Student Life Student government. Newspaper, literary magazine, yearbook. Several music, drama, dance groups. Debate, coffee house. Academic, service, and special interest organizations. Freshmen must live on campus. Women's dorms, special-interest houses. 90% of students live on campus. 6 intercollegiate sports for women; club and intramural sports. AIAW, NCAA, SCIAC. Student body composition: 5% Asian, 3% Black, 6% Hispanic, 86% White. 45% from out of state.

[P] CLEVELAND CHIROPRACTIC COLLEGE
590 North Vermont Avenue, Los Angeles 90004

[J1] COASTLINE COMMUNITY COLLEGE
10231 Slater Avenue, Fountain Valley 92708

[1 & J1] COGSWELL COLLEGE
600 Stockton Street, San Francisco 94108

[J1] COLUMBIA COLLEGE
PO Box 1849, Columbia 95310

[J1] COMPTON COMMUNITY COLLEGE
1111 East Artesia Blvd., Compton 90221

[J2] CONDIE COLLEGE
1 West Campbell Avenue, Campbell 95008

[J1] CONTRA COSTA COLLEGE
2600 Mission Bell Drive, San Pablo 94806

[J1] COSUMNES RIVER COLLEGE
8401 Center Parkway, Sacramento 95823

[J1] CRAFTON HILLS COLLEGE
11711 Sand Canyon Road, Yucaipa 92399

[J1] CUESTA COLLEGE
PO Box J, San Luis Obispo 93406

[J1] CUYAMACA COLLEGE
2950 Jamacha Road, El Cajon 92020

[J1] CYPRESS COLLEGE
9200 Valley View Street, Cypress 90630

■[J1] CYPRESS MORTUARY SCIENCE DEPARTMENT
9200 Valley View Street, Cypress 90630

[J1] DE ANZA COLLEGE
21250 Stevens Creek Blvd., Cupertino 95014

[J1] DEEP SPRINGS COLLEGE
Mailing address: Deep Springs via Dyer, Nevada 89010
Phone: (619) Deep Springs #2 Toll Station, Bishop CA
Associate Dean: George Newton

- **Undergraduates: 24m**
- **Tuition, Room & Board: full scholarship for all students**
- **Student-faculty ratio: 4 to 1**

A private men's junior college founded in 1917. 420-acre rural ranch campus in a desert valley 300 miles north of Los Angeles, and 28 miles from the nearest town (Big Pine, CA).
Academic Character WASC accreditation. Year round trimester system. No formal degrees granted; most students transfer with junior standing after 2-3 years of study to 4-year colleges/universities. Courses offered in art, biology, chemistry, computers, cultures, drama, ecology, English, French, German, history, literature, mathematics, music, photography, physics, political science, religion & philosophy, and Spanish. Seminars. Independent study, honors program. 20,000-volume library.
Financial All students receive a full scholarship, and work at least 20 hours per week running the ranch.
Admissions High school graduation required. GED accepted. Interview required. SAT or ACT required. Application deadline March 15. *Early Entrance* Program. Admission deferral possible. Transfers accepted.
Student Life Students govern college with nominal control by Board of Trustees. Students must live in ranch boarding house and remain on campus except for 6 vacation breaks. Liquor and drugs forbidden on campus. Recreational sports, college-sponsored hiking trips. Student body composition: 5% Asian, 95% White. 85% from out of state.

[J1] DESERT, COLLEGE OF THE
43-500 Monterey Avenue, Palm Desert 92260

[J1] DIABLO VALLEY COLLEGE
321 Golf Club Road, Pleasant Hill 94523

[1] DOMINICAN COLLEGE OF SAN RAFAEL
San Rafael 94901, (415) 457-4440
Director of Admissions & Financial Aid: Jan Tomsky

- **Enrollment: 123m, 355w; 694 total (including part-time)**
- **Tuition (1982/83): $4,450**
- **Room & Board: $3,500; Fees: $58**
- **Degrees offered: BA, BS, BMus**
- **Mean SAT 500**
- **Student-faculty ratio: 10 to 1**

An independent Catholic college founded in 1890, became coed in 1971. 80-acre wooded campus 17 miles north of San Francisco.
Academic Character WASC accreditation. Semester system, 10-week summer term. Majors offered in art, art history, biology, biology & movement education, business administration, dance, drama, English, English/writing, French studies, history, humanities, international business, international social services, Latin American studies, legal studies, mathematics, movement education, music, political science, psychology, political services, sociology, and business, psychology, & special education. 21 minors offered including philosophy, physical sciences. Courses in Spanish, German, Latin. Special humanities colloquia. Interdisciplinary and double majors. Cooperative program for a BS in Nursing is planned to begin in fall, 1983. Distributive requirements in the humanities and 6 units of religion required. Exam, project, or paper required in major field. Masters degrees granted. Legal studies certificate. Independent study, pass/fail, credit by exam, internships. Credit possible for independent work during January interim. Exchanges with Aquinas, Barry, St. Mary's (New Orleans), and St. Thomas Aquinas Colleges. Study abroad. Elementary, secondary and special education certification. AFROTC at San Francisco State; NROTC at UCal (Berkeley); ROTC at U of San Francisco. Observatory, art gallery. American Music Research Center. Learning Center. 80,875-volume library with microform resources.
Financial CEEB CSS. College scholarships, grants, loans, Cal grants, deferred payment; PELL, SEOG, NDSL, GSL, CWS. File FAF by February 1. Application deadline February 10.
Admissions High school graduation with 15 units required. Interview urged. SAT required. $20 application fee. Rolling admissions. $50 tuition and $50 room deposits required on acceptance of admissions offer. *Early Admission* and *Early Decision* programs. Admission deferral possible. Transfers accepted. Special program for re-entry students. College Credit possible for CEEB AP, CLEP, & ACT PEP exams, and for life/work experience. College exams used for placement.
Student Life Student government. Publications. Several music groups. Campus Ministry. Honorary societies. Special interest groups. 40% of full-time students live on campus. Coed and women's dorms. Honor code. 4 intercollegiate sports for men, 4 for women. Student body composition: 15% minority. Over 33% of students are older, re-entry students.

[1] DOMINICAN SCHOOL OF PHILOSOPHY AND THEOLOGY
2401 Ridge Road, Berkeley 94709

[J1] DON BOSCO TECHNICAL INSTITUTE
1151 San Gabriel Blvd., Rosemead 91770

[J1] D-Q UNIVERSITY
PO Box 409, Davis 95616, (916) 758-0470

- **Undergraduates: 44m, 32w; 190 total (including part-time)**
- **Tuition (1982/83): $2,940**
- **Room & Board: $2,849; Fees: $560**
- **Degrees offered: AA, AS**

A private junior college under American Indian control, founded in 1971. Formerly named Deganwidah-Quetzalcoatl University. Suburban campus. Air, rail, and bus nearby.
Academic Character WASC accreditation. Semester system. University emphasizes American Indian and Chicano cultures. Associate degrees offered with majors in appropriate technology, community development, fine arts, general agriculture, general education, humanities, indigenous studies, and social science. Certificate program in appropriate technology. Remedial math program.
Student Life Limited dormitory and dining facilities for students.

[J1] EARLY EDUCATION, CENTER FOR
563 Alfred Street, Los Angeles 90048, (213) 271-6853

- **Enrollment: 2m, 16w; 68 total (including part-time)**
- **Tuition (1982/83): $95 per credit unit**
- **Degrees offered: AA**

A private college of education. Urban campus. Air, rail, and bus service.
Academic Character WASC accreditation. Semester system. Associate degree offered in early childhood education. Graduate program towards California education credentials and MA in child development. Graduate tuition $105 per credit unit.
Admissions Admissions notification is done on a rolling basis.

[J1] EAST LOS ANGELES COLLEGE
1301 East Brooklyn Avenue, Monterey Park 91754

[J1] EL CAMINO COLLEGE
16007 South Crenshaw Blvd., via Torrance 90506

[J1] EVERGREEN VALLEY COLLEGE
3095 Yerba Buena Road, San Jose 95135

[J1] FASHION INSTITUTE OF DESIGN AND MERCHANDISING
818 West Seventh Street, Los Angeles 90017

[J1] FASHION INSTITUTE OF DESIGN AND MERCHANDISING
790 Market Street, San Francisco 94102

[J1] FASHION INSTITUTE OF DESIGN AND MERCHANDISING
13701 Riverside Drive, Sherman Oaks 91403

[J1] FEATHER RIVER COLLEGE
PO Box 1110, Quincy 95971

[G1] FIELDING INSTITUTE
226 East de la Guerra Drive, Santa Barbara 93101

[J1] FOOTHILL COLLEGE
12345 El Monte Road, Los Altos Hills 94022

[G1] FRANCISCAN SCHOOL OF THEOLOGY
1712 Euclid Avenue, Berkeley 94709

[J1] FRESNO CITY COLLEGE
1101 University Avenue, Fresno 93741

[1] FRESNO PACIFIC COLLEGE
1717 S. Chesnut St., Fresno 93702, (209) 251-7194

- **Enrollment: 191m, 246w; 824 total (including part-time)**
- **Tuition & Fees (1982/83): $1,900 per term**
- **Room & Board: $1,100 per term**
- **Degree offered: BA**

A private Christian liberal arts college founded in 1944, supported by the Mennonite Brethren Church but with a non-sectarian student body. Suburban campus.
Academic Character WASC accreditation. Trimester system, summer term. Bachelor's degree offered with majors in Biblical studies & religion, business administration (accounting, computer science, general), communications, contemporary Christian ministries, education, history, humanities, liberal arts, literature, mathematics, mathematics/computer science, music, natural science, physical education, psychology, social science, social services, and Spanish. MA granted in reading, mathematics, and administrative services. 5-year primary, secondary, and special education certification. 62,000-volume library.
Financial CEEB CSS. College scholarships, loans; PELL, SEOG, NDSL, GSL. Priority application deadline March 15.
Admissions High school graduation required. SAT or ACT required. Rolling admissions; suggest applying by March 15. Deadline 2 weeks before beginning of term.
Student Life Student residence halls and cafeteria available.

[G1] FULLER THEOLOGICAL SEMINARY
135 North Oakland Avenue, Pasadena 91101

[J1] FULLERTON COLLEGE
321 East Chapman Avenue, Fullerton 92634

[J1] GAVILAN COLLEGE
5055 Santa Teresa Blvd., Gilroy 95020

[J1] GLENDALE COMMUNITY COLLEGE
1500 North Verdugo Road, Glendale 91208

[1] GOLDEN GATE UNIVERSITY
536 Mission St., San Francisco 94105, (415) 442-7000
Dean of Admissions: Char Hamada

- **Enrollment: 6,922m, 3,838w**
- **Tuition (1982/83): $2,550**
- **Fees: $42**
- **Degrees offered: BA, BS, AA**
- **Student-faculty ratio: 20 to 1**

A private university established in 1901. Urban campus in downtown San Francisco. Air, rail, and bus service.

Academic Character WASC and professional accreditation. Semester system, 15-week summer term. Majors offered in accounting, administration of justice, administrative management, business economics, finance/financial planning, health services management, hotel/restaurant/institutional management, human relations, information science, insurance, management, marketing, medical record management, political science, pre-legal studies, public administration, security management, telecommunications management, and transportation & physical distribution management. AA in business administration, public administration. Certificates in administration of justice, advertising, applied politics, finance, information science, marketing, political science, real estate, and credit, general, health services, hotel/restaurant/institutional, medical record, office, record, security, telecommunications, and transportation & physical distribution managements. MA, MS, MBA, MPA, MSPA, JD, LLM granted. Day & evening classes. Directed study, pass/fail, cooperative work/study, internships. Off-campus study on military bases and in Sacramento, Santa Barbara, Monterey, and the South Bay Area. ROTC, NROTC at UC, Berkeley; AFROTC at San Francisco State. 325,000-volume library.
Financial CEEB CSS. University scholarships, grants, loans, Cal grants; PELL, SEOG, GSL, NDSL, FISL, CWS. Application deadline April 1.
Admissions High school graduation with college prep program expected. GED accepted. Interview encouraged. SAT, ACT, or SCAT recommended and sometimes required. $25 application fee. Rolling admissions; suggest applying by 4 weeks before beginning of semester. *Early Decision, Early Admission, Concurrent Enrollment* programs. Admission deferral possible. Transfers accepted. Credit possible for CEEB AP and CLEP exams.
Student Life Newspaper. Black Students' Association, International Club. Academic, athletic, professional, political, and special interest groups. No university housing. Intramural sports. 20% of students from out of state.

[J1] GOLDEN WEST COLLEGE
15744 Golden West Street, Huntington Beach 92647

[G1] GRADUATE THEOLOGICAL UNION
2465 Le Conte Avenue, Berkeley 94709

[J1] GROSSMONT COLLEGE
8800 Grossmont College Drive, El Cajon 92020

[J1] HARTNELL COLLEGE
156 Homestead Avenue, Salinas 93901

[1] HARVEY MUDD COLLEGE
Claremont — see Claremont Colleges

[P] HASTINGS COLLEGE OF THE LAW
San Francisco 94102
Affiliated with University of California, San Francisco.

[2] HEALD ENGINEERING COLLEGE
1215 Van Ness Avenue, San Francisco 94109

[1] HEBREW UNION COLLEGE — JEWISH INSTITUTE OF RELIGION
3077 University Avenue, Los Angeles 90007

[2] HEED UNIVERSITY/WEST
3923 West 6th Street, Los Angeles 90020

[1] HOLY FAMILY COLLEGE
Box 3248, Mission San Jose 94538

[1] HOLY NAMES COLLEGE
3500 Mountain Blvd., Oakland 94619, (415) 436-0111
Director of Admissions: Sister Jacquelyn Slater

- **Enrollment: 160m, 233w; 662 total (including part-time)**
- **Tuition (1982/83): $4,500**
- **Room & Board: $2,800**
- **Degrees offered: BA, BS, BFA, BMus, BSN**
- **Student-faculty ratio: 8 to 1**

A private, independent Roman Catholic college chartered in 1880, became coed in 1971. Operated by the Sisters of the Holy Names. 65-acre wooded campus in hills overlooking Oakland and San Francisco Bay. Bus and rapid transit service; air and rail nearby.
Academic Character WASC and professional accreditation. Semester system, 6-week summer term. Majors offered in American studies, art, biological science, business administration, chemistry, economics, English, English studies for internationals, French, history, international affairs, liberal studies, mathematics, music, philosophy, physical science, political science, psychology, recreation, religious studies, social science, social work, sociology, Spanish, and speech correction. Nursing major for students with an RN. Interdisciplinary and self-designed majors possible. Minors. Programs in administration, gerontology, laboratory technology. Core or Breadth Program in Humanistic Studies required. MA, MS, MBA, MEd, MMus granted. Independent study, pass/fail, credit by exam, internships. Preprofessional programs in dentistry, engineering, law, medicine, optometry, veterinary medicine. 3-2 dual degree programs in architecture and engineering with U California, Berkeley. Exchange with Anna Maria College (Mass). Cross-registration with California College of Arts & Crafts; Cal State U, Hayward; Graduate Theological Union; UCal, Berkeley; and Merritt, Mills, and St. Mary's Colleges. Study abroad in Japan. Elementary, secondary, and special education certification. ROTC at UCal, Berkeley. Kodaly Resource Center, Speech Center, Raskob Learning Institute. 91,600-volume library with microform resources.
Financial CEEB CSS. College scholarships, grants, loans, Cal grants, deferred payment; PELL, SEOG, NDSL, GSL, PLUS, CWS, college work program. Priority application deadline April 1; Cal grants deadline mid-February.
Admissions High school graduation with college prep program required. SAT or ACT required. $25 application fee. Rolling admissions. Application deadline August 1. $100 deposit required on acceptance of admissions offer. Transfers accepted. Credit possible for CEEB AP and CLEP exams.
Student Life Student government. Newspaper, yearbook. Music, dance, drama clubs. Campus Ministry. Academic, cultural, honorary, professional, recreational, religious, service, and special interest groups. Coed dorms with separate areas for men and women. Cafeteria. Regular class attendance expected. 4 intercollegiate sports; intramurals.

[G2] HUMANISTIC PSYCHOLOGY INSTITUTE
San Francisco — see Saybrook Institute

[1] HUMBOLDT STATE UNIVERSITY
Arcata — see California State University

[J1] HUMPHREYS COLLEGE
6650 Inglewood Ave., Stockton 95207, (209) 478-0800

- **Undergraduates: 28m, 116w; 215 total (including part-time)**
- **Tuition (1982/83): $1,964**
- **Degrees offered: AA, AS**

A private, independent junior college. Urban campus.
Academic Character WASC accreditation. Trimester system, summer term. AS offered with majors in the fields of business and technology (electronics). AA offered with majors in the liberal arts & sciences. Remedial math & English programs.
Admissions High school graduation required. Rolling admissions. Advanced placement credit possible.
Student Life Room and board reservations. Student body composition: 15% minority.

[J1] IMPERIAL VALLEY COLLEGE
PO Box 158, Imperial 92251

[J1] INDIAN VALLEY COLLEGES
1800 Ignacio Blvd., Novato 94947

[G2] INSTITUTE FOR CREATION RESEARCH GRADUATE SCHOOL
2100 Greenfield Drive, El Cajon 92021

[G1] JESUIT SCHOOL OF THEOLOGY
1735 LeRoy Avenue, Berkeley 94709

[1] JOHN F. KENNEDY UNIVERSITY
12 Altarinda Road, Orinda 94563

[1] JUDAISM, UNIVERSITY OF
15600 Mulholland Drive, Los Angeles 90077

[2] KENSINGTON UNIVERSITY
PO Box 2036, 512 East Wilson Avenue, Glendale 91206

[J1] KINGS RIVER COMMUNITY COLLEGE
995 North Reed Avenue, Reedley 93654, (209) 638-3641
Dean of Admissions & Records: Moire Charters

- **Undergraduates: 1,136m, 1,144w; 3,215 total (including evening)**
- **Tuition & Fees (1982/83): $20 (in-state); $2,270 (out-of-state)**
- **Room & Board: $2,540**
- **Degrees offered: AA, AS**

A public community college founded in 1926. Formerly Reedley College. 300-acre campus in the San Joaquin Valley midway between San Francisco and Los Angeles.
Academic Character WASC accreditation. Semester system, 6-week summer term. Terminal and transfer majors offered in administration of justice, agriculture (6), art, automotive technology, aviation maintenance technology, business (8), biological science, child development, computer science, dental assisting, drafting, English, fashion merchandising, fine arts, foreign languages, forest/park technology, general studies, home economics, industrial technology, information systems, landscape horticulture, liberal arts, mathematics, metal working (2), music (2), physical education, physical science, social science, and speech/theatre arts. Distributive requirements. Several certificate programs. Credit/no credit, credit by exam.

Preprofessional transfer programs in business administration, dentistry, engineering, law, medicine, medical technology, natural resources & forestry, nursing, optometry, pharmacy, physical therapy, and veterinary medicine. Credit for travel-study. Child care center. Over 26,000-volume library with microform and A—V resources.
Financial CEEB CSS. College scholarships, Cal grants; PELL, SEOG, EOPS, GSL, CWS. Application deadlines February 9 (scholarships), April 15 (federal programs).
Admissions Open admissions. High school graduation or equivalent required. Provisional admission for non-high school graduates over 18. *Concurrent Enrollment* Program. Transfers accepted. Credit possible for CEEB AP exams. College exams used for placement.
Student Life Student government. Newspaper. Music and drama groups. Circle K. Academic, athletic, ethnic, honorary, professional, religious, service, and special interest clubs. Dorm housing for 102 men and 102 women. Cafeteria. 2 phys ed classes required. 5 intercollegiate sports for men, 4 for women, and coed cross-country, golf, swimming; intramurals. Student body composition: 40% minority.

[1] LA VERNE, UNIVERSITY OF
1950 Third St., La Verne 91750, (714) 593-3511
Director of Admissions: Michael Welch

- **Undergraduates: 639m, 571w; 1,530 total (including graduates)**
- **Tuition (1982/83): $4,950**
- **Room & Board: $2,310-$2,960; Fees: $208**
- **Degrees offered: BA, BS, AA, AS**
- **Student-faculty ratio: 17 to 1**

A private university established in 1891, related to the Church of the Brethren. 27-acre suburban campus in San Gabriel Valley, 30 miles from Los Angeles. Air, rail, and bus service.
Academic Character WASC accreditation. 4-1-4 system, 3 4-week summer terms. 45 majors offered in the areas of accounting, arts, biological & physical sciences, business administration, child development, communications, computer science & engineering, criminal justice, environmental management, health care management, humanities, human services, industrial science, insurance, mathematics, physical education, psychology, public administration, recreation, social sciences, speech pathology. Self-designed majors encouraged. Undergraduate Record Exam and senior project required. Associate degrees in business, communications, criminal justice, digital technology, information systems, general studies, and paralegal studies. Graduate and professional degrees granted. Certificate programs. Each student may have a custom-tailored learning plan with internships, independent, off-campus, and foreign study encouraged. Pass/fail, credit by exam. Preprofessional programs in law, medicine, nursing, social service, theology. Exchanges with other Brethren Colleges. Study abroad, semester at sea. Elementary, secondary, reading, administrative, clinical/rehabilitative, early childhood, pupil personnel services, and special education certification. American Armenian International College, language lab. 195,000-volume library.
Financial CEEB CSS. University scholarships, grants, Church of Brethren grants, Cal grants, deferred payment; PELL, SEOG, NDSL, GSL, FISL, CWS, university work program. Priority application deadline April 1.
Admissions No required program; highly motivated students urged to apply. Interview encouraged. SAT or ACT required. $20 application fee. Rolling admissions; suggest applying before March 1. $100 deposit required on acceptance of admissions offer. *Early Decision* and *Early Entrance* programs. Transfers accepted. Credit possible for CEEB AP and CLEP exams.
Student Life Student government. Newspaper, literary magazine, yearbook. Drama, debate, several music groups. Athletic, academic, religious, and special interest organizations. First-year students under 18 must live at home or on campus. Coed and single-sex dorms. No married-student housing. 62% of students live on campus. Liquor, drugs, fireworks, and explosives prohibited on campus. Smoking prohibited in public areas. Class attendance expected, 2 phys ed classes required. 9 intercollegiate sports for men, 7 for women; several intramurals. AIAW, SCIAC. Student body composition: 2% Asian, 15% Black, 17% Hispanic, 1% Native American, 60% White, 5% Other. 16% from out of state.

[J1] LAKE TAHOE COMMUNITY COLLEGE
2659 Lake Tahoe Blvd., South Lake Tahoe 95702

[J1] LANEY COLLEGE
900 Fallon Street, Oakland 94607

[J1] LASSEN COLLEGE
Highway 139, PO Box 3000, Susanville 96130, (916) 257-6181

- **Enrollment: 2,478 total (including part-time)**
- **Tuition & Fees (1982/83): $15 (in-state); $2,415 (out-of-state)**
- **Degrees offered: AA**

A public community college established in 1925. New campus on Highway 139 north of Susanville.
Academic Character WASC accreditation. Semester system, 6-week summer term. Terminal and transfer majors offered in agriculture, art, automotive technology, business, construction trades, cosmetology, criminal justice, drafting technology, forestry, graphics technology, gunsmithing, liberal arts, math/science, media technology, physical education, vocational nursing, and welding technology. Distributive requirements. Certificate programs. Credit/no credit, credit by exam, cooperative work/study. Preprofessional transfer programs in business administration, dentistry, education, engineering, recreation/park/forest management, law, medicine, nursing, and wildlife management. Library with microform resources.
Financial College scholarships, loans; PELL, SEOG, EOPS, GSL, CWS.
Admissions Open admissions. High school graduation or equivalent required. Non-high school graduates over 18 accepted. *Early Admission* Program. Transfers accepted. Credit possible for CEEB AP exams. College exams used for placement. Extended Opportunity Programs and Services provides financial and academic support for disadvantaged students.
Student Life Student union. Newspaper. Debate. Academic, athletic, ethnic, professional, religious, and special interest groups. 1 sorority. Dorm housing for 128 men and women. Cafeteria. 4 semesters of phys ed required except for veterans. Regular class attendance required. 6 intercollegiate sports for men, 6 for women, and coed shooting; intramurals. Golden Valley Conference. Student body composition: 20% minority.

[P] LATIN AMERICA BIBLE COLLEGE
14209 East Lomitas Avenue, La Puente 91746

[P] L.I.F.E. BIBLE COLLEGE
1100 Glendale Blvd., Los Angeles 90026

[P] LIFE CHIROPRACTIC COLLEGE—WEST
2005 Via Barrett, San Lorenzo 94580
Formerly Pacific States Chiropractic College; alliance formed with Life Chiropractic College, Marietta, Georgia, in March, 1981.

[2] LINCOLN UNIVERSITY
281 Masonic Avenue, San Francisco 94118

[1] LOMA LINDA UNIVERSITY
Riverside 92515, (714) 785-2176
Professional schools: Loma Linda 92350, (714) 796-7311

- **Undergraduates: 2,024m, 1,883w; 5,000 total (including graduates)**
- **Tuition (1982/83): $5,220**
- **Room & Board: $2,343; Fees: $150**
- **Degrees offered: BA, BS, BMus, BSW, AS, AA**
- **Student-faculty ratio: 14 to 1**

A private university founded in 1905 and affiliated with the Seventh-Day Adventist Church. 5 miles from downtown Riverside and 55 miles east of Los Angeles, the suburban La Sierra campus houses the College of Arts & Sciences and the School of Education. The schools of Allied Health Professions, Dentistry, Health, Medicine, and Nursing are 17 miles away on the Loma Linda campus. Air, rail, and bus in Riverside.
Academic Character WASC and professional accreditation. Trimester system, 6- to 8-week summer term. Over 80 majors offered in the areas of administration of justice, agriculture, art, business, consumer related sciences, communication, education, English, modern languages, geology, industrial studies, liberal arts, mathematics/computer, music, religion, sciences, secretarial & business education, social work, speech, social sciences, and physical education, health, & recreation. Distributives, 16 units of religion, and religion course in major field required. Senior exams. Graduate & professional degrees granted. Independent study, internships. Preprofessional transfer programs with graduate schools in allied health fields, dentistry, education, medicine, and nursing. Study abroad in Europe. Elementary, secondary, and post-secondary education certification. Language lab, computer center. 453,000-volume combined libraries, plus access to UC (LA, Riverside, & Irvine) and U of Redlands libraries.
Financial CEEB CSS and ACT FAS. University scholarships, grants, loans, deferred payment; PELL, SEOG, NSS, NDSL, FISL, NSL, CWS, university work program. Application deadlines March 15 (FAF), May 1 (university applications).
Admissions High school graduation with 16 units required. GED accepted. ACT required. $10 application fee. Rolling admissions; suggest applying after January. Deadline August 15. $50 room deposit required on acceptance of admissions offer. *Early Entrance* Program. Transfers accepted. Credit possible for CEEB AP and CLEP exams, other courses, and university placement exams. Provisional admission possible.
Student Life Student government. Newspaper. Several music groups. Academic, athletic, ethnic, honorary, religious, service, and special interest clubs. Single students under 23 must live at home or on campus. No coed dorms. Married-student housing. 50% of students live on campus. Liquor, drugs, tobacco prohibited. Dress code. Students under 21 need permission to marry. Class and weekly chapel attendance required. 6 quarters of phys ed required. Intramural sports. Student body composition: 9.7% Asian, 10% Black, 8.3% Hispanic, 0.1% Native American, 64.8% White, 7.1% Other. 13% from out of state.

[J1] LONG BEACH CITY COLLEGE
4901 East Carson Street, Long Beach 90808

[1] LOS ANGELES BAPTIST COLLEGE
21726 W. Placerita Canyon Road, Newhall 91322-0878, (805) 259-3540
Director of Admissions: Randy Murphy

- **Undergraduates: 184m, 172w; 375 total (including part-time)**
- **Tuition (1982/83): $3,450**
- **Room & Board: $2,170; Fees: $150**
- **Degrees offered: BA, AA**
- **Student-faculty ratio: 15 to 1**

A private Baptist liberal arts college founded in 1927. 43-acre suburban campus 45 miles north of Los Angeles.

Academic Character WASC accreditation. Semester system. Majors offered in Bible (Biblical languages, Biblical ministries, Christian education, pre-theological, women's Biblical ministries), business administration, communications, English, general studies, history, music, natural science, physical education, and psychology. Minors in major fields and in Greek, mathematics, missions, political science. Distributives required. At least one Bible course required each semester for a minimum total of 23 units. Introduction to Christian Ministries course required of entering students. GRE or National Teacher Exam required for graduation. Terminal AA in Biblical studies, Christian education, and general studies. Cooperative program with College of the Canyons for AA in 9 fields. Study abroad in Israel. Elementary and secondary education certification. Computer center. 32,500-volume library with A-V resources.
Financial CEEB CSS. College scholarships, grants, Cal grants, deferred payment; PELL, SEOG, NDSL, GSL, CWS, college work program. Application deadline February 1 (Cal grants).
Admissions High school graduation with 15 units required. GED accepted. SAT or ACT required. $15 application fee. Rolling admissions. $100 reservation deposit required on June 15. Transfers accepted. Credit possible for CEEB AP exams. College exams used for placement. Probationary admission possible.
Student Life Yearbook, radio station. Drama and several music groups. Student Missionary Fellowship. Honorary society. Single students must live at home or on campus. Class and chapel attendance required. 2 units of phys ed required. 4 intercollegiate sports for men, 3 for women; intramurals. Athletic Gospel Team. NAIA, National Christian Athletic Association, National Little College Athletic Association. 21% of students from out of state.

[J1] LOS ANGELES CITY COLLEGE
855 North Vermont Avenue, Los Angeles 90029

[P] LOS ANGELES COLLEGE OF CHIROPRACTIC
PO Box 1166, Whittier 90609

[J1] LOS ANGELES HARBOR COLLEGE
1111 Figueroa Place, Wilmington 90744

[J1] LOS ANGELES METROPOLITAN COLLEGE
1212 South Flower Street, Los Angeles 90015

[J1] LOS ANGELES MISSION COLLEGE
1101 South San Fernando Road, San Fernando 91340

[J1] LOS ANGELES PIERCE COLLEGE
6201 Winnetka Avenue, Woodland Hills, 91371

[J1] LOS ANGELES SOUTHWEST COLLEGE
1600 West Imperial Highway, Los Angeles 90047

[J1] LOS ANGELES TRADE-TECHNICAL COLLEGE
400 West Washington Blvd., Los Angeles 90015

[J1] LOS ANGELES VALLEY COLLEGE
Fulton and Burbank Blvd., Van Nuys 91401

[J1] LOS MENDANOS COLLEGE
2700 East Leland Road, Pittsburg 94565

[1] LOYOLA MARYMOUNT UNIVERSITY
Loyola Blvd. at W. 80 St., Los Angeles 90045, (213) 642-2750
Director of Admissions: Michel E. L'Heureux

- **Undergraduates: 1,739m, 1,977w; 6,366 total (including graduates)**
- **Tuition (1982/83): $5,114**
- **Room & Board: $2,438-$2,548**
- **Degrees offered: BA, BS, BBA**
- **Mean SAT 460v, 500m**
- **Student-faculty ratio: 17 to 1**

An independent Roman Catholic university established in 1911, became coed in 1968. 100-acre suburban campus in southwest Los Angeles, 5 miles from the Pacific. Air, rail, and bus service.
Academic Character WASC and professional accreditation. Semester system, 6-week summer term. 21 majors offered by the College of Liberal Arts, 7 by the College of Fine & Communication Arts, 2 by the College of Business Administration, and 10 by the College of Science & Engineering. Self-designed majors. Minors. Courses in 7 additional areas. Special program in alcohol/drug studies. Distributives, 2 theology courses, and GRE required for graduation. Masters & professional degrees granted. Independent study, honors program, pass/fail, credit by exam, internships. Preprofessional programs in dentistry, law, medical technology, medicine, occupational therapy, optometry, pharmacy, physical therapy, podiatry, public health, and veterinary medicine. Several study abroad programs. Elementary, secondary, reading, administrative services, pupil personnel services, bilingual/cross-cultural emphasis, and special education certification. AFROTC; ROTC, NROTC at UCLA & USC. Language lab, computer center. Over 400,000-volume library with microform resources.
Financial CEEB CSS. University scholarships, grants, loans, Cal grants, deferred payment; PELL, SEOG, NDSL, FISL, GSL, CWS, university work program. Application deadline March 1.
Admissions High school graduation with 16 units recommended. Interview encouraged. SAT or ACT required. $25 application fee. Rolling admissions; suggest applying by January 1. Deadline August 1. $50 deposit required on acceptance of admissions offer. *Early Decision, Early Entrance, Concurrent Enrollment* programs. Admission deferral possible. Transfers accepted. Credit possible for CEEB AP and CLEP exams.
Student Life Student government. Newspaper, literary magazine, yearbook, radio station. Music, drama, debate clubs. Academic, ethnic, honorary, political, professional, religious, service, social, and special interest groups. 8 fraternities with houses, and 2 sororities. 10% of students join. Coed and single-sex dorms, student apartments. 45% of students live on campus. Class attendance required in 1st & 2nd years. Hazing prohibited. 10 intercollegiate sports for men, 7 for women; several intramurals. AIAW, NCAA, WCAC. Student body composition: 4% Asian, 7% Black, 8% Foreign, 13% Hispanic, 57% White, 11% Other. 13% from out of state.

[J1] MARIN, COLLEGE OF
Kentfield 94904

[J1] MARYMOUNT PALOS VERDES COLLEGE
30800 Palos Verdes Dr. E, Rancho Palos Verdes 90274, (213) 377-5501

- **Undergraduates: 184m, 245w; 450 total (including part-time)**
- **Tuition (1982/83): $3,600**
- **Degree offered: AA**

A private Roman Catholic junior college founded in 1932.
Academic Character WASC accreditation. 4-1-4 system. Transfer majors offered in the liberal arts. Career majors offered in the areas of business, communication arts, early childhood education, fashion merchandising, interior design, social service, studio arts, and theatre arts. Program in English as a second language for international students. Remedial math and English programs. College is affiliated with world-wide network of Marymount institutions.
Admissions High school graduation required. Students over 18 may be admitted without a diploma. Rolling admissions. *Early Admission* Program. Advanced placement credit possible.
Student Life Dorms for men and women located one mile from campus. Student body composition: 21% minority.

[P] McGEORGE SCHOOL OF LAW, UNIVERSITY OF THE PACIFIC
Sacramento 95817

[2] MELODYLAND SCHOOL OF THEOLOGY
1730 Clementine Street, Anaheim 92802

[J1] MENDOCINO COMMUNITY COLLEGE
PO Box 3000, Ukiah 95482

[1] MENLO COLLEGE
Menlo Park 94025, (415) 323-6141
Dean of Admissions: Douglas Walker

- **Enrollment: 487m, 154w**
- **Tuition & Fees (1982/83): $5,970**
- **Room & Board: $3,190**
- **Degrees offered: BSBA, AA**
- **Mean SAT 430v, 430m**
- **Student-faculty ratio: 15 to 1**

A private college founded in 1927, became coed in 1971. 62-acre suburban campus 30 miles from San Francisco. Rail and bus service; airport in San Francisco.
Academic Character WASC accreditation. 4-1-4 system, 2 4-week summer terms, 6-week Summer Study Skills Program. The 4-year School of Business Administration offers a BSBA with concentrations in accounting, finance, quantitative analysis, marketing, legal environment, and general business. The 2-year School of Letters and Sciences offers an AA with concentrations in biological & pre-medical sciences, engineering, liberal arts, managerial science, and mathematics & physical sciences. Distributive requirements in liberal arts for both degrees. Transfer possible from BSBA to AA program. AA students encouraged to continue studies at 4-year colleges. Member of Cooperative Information Network. 45,000-volume library.
Financial CEEB CSS. College scholarships, grants, loans, Cal grants; PELL, SEOG, NDSL, GSL, college work program.
Admissions High school graduation with 12 units with a minimum 2.0 GPA required. GED accepted. Interview encouraged. SAT or ACT required. $20 application fee. Rolling admissions; suggest applying early in 12th year. $150 tuition deposit required on acceptance of admissions offer. *Early Decision, Early Entrance, Concurrent Enrollment* programs. Admission deferral possible. Transfers accepted. Credit possible for CEEB AP and CLEP exams. College has own advanced placement program.
Student Life Student government. Newspaper, yearbook, radio station. Circle K, Women's Collective. Music and drama groups. Honorary, professional, social, and special interest organizations. Single students under 21 (except seniors) must live at home or on campus. Single-sex and coed dorms. No married-student housing. 75% of students live on campus. 2 semesters of phys ed required. Class attendance expected. 11 intercollegiate sports for men, 5 for women; many intramurals. Coastal Conference, West Coast Intercollegiate Soccer Association. Student body composition: 0.2% Asian, 0.5% Black, 23.9% Foreign, 1% Hispanic, 0.1% Native American, 74.3% White. 40% from out of state.

[G1] MENNONITE BRETHREN BIBLICAL SEMINARY
4824 East Butler, Fresno 93727

[J1] MERCED COLLEGE
3600 M Street, Merced 95340

[J1] MERRITT COLLEGE
12500 Campus Drive, Oakland 94619

[1] MILLS COLLEGE
Oakland 94613, (415) 430-2135
Director of Admissions: Gail Berson Weaver

- **Undergraduates: 737w; 924 total (including m & w graduates)**
- **Tuition (1982/83): $6,380**
- **Room & Board: $3,200; Fees: $220**
- **Degree offered: BA**
- **Mean SAT 518v, 502m**
- **Student-faculty ratio: 11 to 1**

A private women's college founded in 1852. Graduate programs coed. 127-acre urban campus 18 miles east of San Francisco and 8 miles south of Berkeley. Air, rail, and bus service.

Academic Character WASC accreditation. Semester system. Majors offered in administration & legal processes, American civilization, art, biochemistry, biology, chemistry, child development, communication, computer science, dance, dramatic arts, economics, English, ethnic studies, fine arts, French, French studies, general studies, German studies, government, Hispanic studies, history, international relations, mathematics, music, philosophy, physical science, psychology, sociology, western literature, and women's studies. Interdisciplinary & self-designed majors. MA, MFA granted. Independent study, honors program, Phi Beta Kappa, pass/fail, internships. Preprofessional programs in medicine, health sciences, law. 3-2 engineering programs with UCal (Berkeley), Stanford, Boston U, Washington U (St. Louis). 5-yr BA/MS in statistics or computer science with Stanford. Cross-registration with Berkeley, California College of Arts & Crafts, California State U (Hayward), College of Alameda, Graduate Theological Union, and Holy Names, Merritt, and St. Mary's Colleges. Exchanges with Fisk and Howard Universities, and Agnes Scott, Barnard, Hollins, Manhattanville, Mt. Holyoke, Simmons, Skidmore, Spelman, Swarthmore, Wellesley, and Wheaton Colleges. Washington Semester. Several study abroad programs. Early childhood, elementary, and secondary education certification. AFROTC, NROTC, ROTC at Berkeley. Art gallery, language lab. 185,000-volume library.

Financial CEEB CSS. College scholarships, grants, music & middle-income awards, loans, deferred payment; PELL, SEOG, Cal grants, NDL, FISL, CWS. Application deadline February 1.

Admissions HIgh school graduation with 16 units required. Interview encouraged. SAT or ACT required. 3 ACH recommended. $25 application fee. Suggest applying early in 12th year; deadline February 1. $200 deposit required on acceptance of admissions offer. *Early Decision* and *Early Admission* programs. Admission deferral possible. Transfers accepted. Credit possible for CEEB AP exams. Probationary admission possible for underqualified students.

Student Life Student government. Newspaper, literary magazine, yearbook. Music, dance, and drama groups. Academic, ethnic, political, professional, religious, women's, and special interest groups. Single students under 21 must live at home or on campus. Dorms & apartments. Some married-student housing. 80% of students live on campus. Honor system. 6 intercollegiate sports for women; intramurals. AIAW, Redwood Conference. Student body composition: 13.5% Asian, 11.5% Black, 4% Hispanic, 1% Native American, 68.5% White, 1.5% Other. 35% from out of state.

[J1] MIRA COSTA COLLEGE
One Barnard Drive, Oceanside 92056

[J1] MISSION COLLEGE
3000 Mission College Blvd., Santa Clara 95054

[J1] MODESTO JUNIOR COLLEGE
College Avenue, Modesto 95350

[1] MONTEREY INSTITUTE OF INTERNATIONAL STUDIES
425 Van Buren Street, Monterey 93940

[J1] MONTEREY PENINSULA COLLEGE
980 Fremont Blvd., Monterey 93940

[J1] MOORPARK COLLEGE
7075 Campus Road, Moorpark 93021

[1] MOUNT ST. MARY'S COLLEGE
12001 Chalon Road, Los Angeles 90049, (213) 476-2237
Doheny campus: 10 Chester Place, Los Angeles 90007, (213) 746-0450
Director of Admissions: Sister Helen Oswald

- **Undergraduates: 12m, 827w; 1,099 total (including graduates)**
- **Tuition (1982/83): $4,420**
- **Room & Board: $2,360-$2,870; Fees: $70**
- **Degrees offered: BA, BS, BFA, BMus, AA**
- **Mean SAT 413v, 437m**
- **Student-faculty ratio: 10 to 1**

A private Roman Catholic women's college founded in 1925. Conducted by the Sisters of Saint Joseph of Carondelet. Coed music, nursing, and graduate programs. 56-acre main campus in the Santa Monica Mountains above Los Angeles. Doheny estate campus for AA students is located in central LA. College provides transportation between campuses. Air, rail, and bus service in LA.

Academic Character WASC and professional accreditation. 4-1-4 system, 6-week summer term. Majors offered in American studies, art, biological sciences, biochemistry, business, chemistry, child development, English, French, gerontology, history, mathematics, music, nursing, philosophy, physical therapy, political science, psychology, religious studies, respiratory therapy, social science, sociology, and Spanish. Self-designed majors. Minors in most major fields. Terminal and transfer AA offered at Doheny campus in business, liberal studies, nursing, physical therapist assistant, pre-school teaching, respiratory therapy. Distributive requirements. 6 to 9 units of religious studies required. MA in RS, MSEd granted. Independent study, pass/fail, internships. Preprofessional programs in dentistry, medicine, medical technology, and law. Exchanges with 5 other Carondelet schools in the U.S. Study abroad. Elementary, secondary, and special education certification. ROTC at UCLA; AFROTC at Loyola Marymount. 132,060-volume library.

Financial CEEB CSS and ACT FAS. College scholarships, grants, loans, Cal grants, deferred payment; PELL, SEOG, NSS, NDSL, FISL, GSL, NSL, CWS. Priority application deadline March 1.

Admissions High school graduation required; college prep program recommended. GED accepted. Interview encouraged. SAT or ACT required. $25 application fee. Rolling admissions; suggest applying by March. Deadline in June. $100 tuition and $100 refundable room deposits required on acceptance of admissions offer. *Early Decision, Early Admission, Concurrent Enrollment* programs. Admission deferral possible. Transfers accepted. Credit possible for CEEB AP and CLEP exams, and for learning experience.

Student Life Student government, residence council. Newspaper, magazine, yearbook. Several music groups. Honorary, professional, religious, service, and special interest organizations. 1 social sorority without a house. 5% join. Women's dorm and apartment housing. No married-student housing. 50% of students live on campus. Intramural sports and phys ed courses. Student body composition: 9.1% Asian, 10.7% Black, 17.7% Hispanic, 1% Native American, 58.2% White, 3.3% Other. 3% from out of state.

[J1] MT. SAN ANTONIO COLLEGE
1100 North Grand Avenue, Walnut 91789

[J1] MT. SAN JACINTO COLLEGE
21-400 Highway 79, San Jacinto 92383

[J1] NAPA COMMUNITY COLLEGE
2277 Napa-Vallejo Highway, Napa 94558

[1] NATIONAL UNIVERSITY
4141 Camino del Rio South, San Diego 92108

[1 & G1] NAVAL POSTGRADUATE SCHOOL
Monterey 93940

[1] NEW COLLEGE OF CALIFORNIA
777 Valencia St., San Francisco 94110, (415) 626-1694
Director of Admissions: Mark Feldman

- **Enrollment: 100m, 200w; 330 total (including part-time)**
- **Tuition (1982/83): $1,500 per term**
- **Degrees offered: BA, AA**

A private, non-residential college of liberal arts and law established in 1971. Urban campus. Air, rail, and bus service.

Academic Character WASC accreditation. Trimester system. BA and AA offered in the Humanities. 200 students and 40 teachers are in the undergraduate program, which adapts to the personal educational needs & goals of each student. Small classes, tutorials, work/study, and independent study are the modes of instruction. MA in Poetics, MA in Psychology, law degrees granted. Weekend College offers a BA degree completion program for working adults with prior college credit. Science Institute offers non-matriculated, 6-week intensive weekend courses in biology & chemistry. Continuing Education and English as a Second Language programs. West Marin center.

Financial Financial aid available including Cal grants, PELL, GSL.

Admissions Open admissions policy. Rolling admissions. Credit possible for prior learning experience.

Student Life No college housing. Student body composition: 30% minority.

[2] NEWPORT UNIVERSITY
3720 Campus Drive, Newport Beach 92660

[P] NORTHERN CALIFORNIA COLLEGE OF CHIROPRACTIC
Sunnyvale - see Palmer College of Chiropractic—West

[1] NORTHROP UNIVERSITY
5800 West Arbor Vitae St., Inglewood 90306, (213) 641-3470
Director of Admissions: Judson W. Staples

- **Undergraduates: 1,058m, 49w; 1,850 total (including graduates)**
- **Tuition (1982/83): $4,950**
- **Room & Board: $3,492-$4,572**
- **Degrees offered: BS, BSBA, BSEng, BSME, AA, AAS**
- **Mean SAT 420v, 480m**
- **Student-faculty ratio: 17 to 1**

A private engineering university founded in 1943. 18-acre urban campus 10 miles southwest of Los Angeles. Air, rail, and bus in LA.

Academic Character WASC and professional accreditation. Trimester system, 11-week summer term. Majors offered in aerospace engineering, aircraft/avionics, aircraft maintenance, business administration, computer science, electronic engineering, engineering technology/manufacturing management, mechanical/civil engineering, mechanical/electrical engineering, mechanical/energy systems engineering, and mechanical engineering. Associate degrees in aircraft/avionics technology, aircraft maintenance technology, computer science technology. Technical certificate programs. Distributive requirements. Masters degrees granted. Honors program, cooperative work/study. Programs with NASA and others. AFROTC at Loyola Marymount, USC; NROTC, ROTC at UCLA. Several labs, workshops, computers. 63,802-volume library.

Financial CEEB CSS and ACT FAS. University scholarships, grants, loans, Cal grants; PELL, SEOG, NDSL, FISL, CWS. Priority application deadline April 30.

Admissions High school graduation required. GED accepted for certificate programs. SAT or ACT required. $25 application fee. Rolling admissions; suggest applying by June. Deadline in August. $75 deposit required on acceptance of admissions offer. *Early Decision* and *Early Entrance* programs. Transfers accepted. Credit possible for CEEB CLEP exams.

Student Life Student government. Newspaper, literary magazine. Flying, karate clubs. Professional, honorary, ethnic, international, religious, and special interest groups. 2 fraternities, 1 with house. 1% of men join. Coed, single-sex, and special interest housing. No married-student housing. 20% of students live on campus. Class attendance required. Intramurals. Student body composition: 17% Asian, 8% Black, 41% Foreign, 8% Hispanic, 1% Native American, 25% White. 80% from out of state.

[1] NOTRE DAME, COLLEGE OF
Belmont 94002, (415) 593-1601
Director of Admissions: Kris Zavoli

- **Undergraduates: 284m, 444w; 1,371 total (including graduates)**
- **Tuition (1982/83): $4,700**
- **Room & Board: $2,800**
- **Degrees offered: BA, BS, BFA, BMus, AA, AS**
- **Mean SAT 445v, 450m**
- **Student-faculty ratio: 15 to 1**

A private Catholic college founded in 1851, became coed in 1968. Conducted by the Sisters of Notre Dame de Namur. 80-acre suburban campus 25 miles south of San Francisco. Air, rail, and bus nearby.

Academic Character WASC and professional accreditation. 4-1-4 system, summer terms. Majors offered in art, behavioral science, biology, business administration, business & public administration, chemistry, economics, English, French, history, mathematics, mathematics/computer science, music, nutrition, philosophy, politics & government, psychology, religious studies, social science, social services, sociology, Spanish, and theatre arts. Interdisciplinary, self-designed majors. Distributives and 2 semesters of religion required. Masters degrees granted. Independent study, honors program, cooperative work/study, pass/fail, internships. Preprofessional programs in allied health fields, engineering, interior design, law, nutrition, and medicine. Exchange with Emmanuel College (Boston). Study abroad in Europe. Early childhood, elementary, secondary, administrative, and special education certification. Museum, language lab, computer. 92,897-volume library with microform resources.

Financial CEEB CSS and ACT FAS. College scholarships, grants; PELL, SEOG, NDSL, GSL, CWS. Application deadline March 1.

Admissions High school graduation with 13 units and minimum GPA of 2.5 recommended. GED accepted. Interview encouraged. SAT or ACT required. English ACH recommended. $25 application fee. Rolling admissions; suggest applying by March 1. Deadline August 1. $100 tuition and $50 room deposits required on acceptance of admissions offer. *Early Decision, Early Entrance, Concurrent Enrollment* programs. Admission deferral possible. Transfers accepted. Credit possible for CEEB AP and CLEP exams. Special admission possible for underprepared students.

Student Life Student government. Literary magazine, yearbook. Several music groups. Circle K, Campus Ministry. Honorary, religious, service, and special interest clubs. Coed and single-sex dorms. Married-student housing. 47% of students live on campus. Honor code. Class attendance expected. 2 intercollegiate sports for men, 2 for women; intramurals. NAIA. Student body composition: 9% Asian, 4.9% Black, 4.6% Hispanic, 0.7% Native American, 49.6% White, 31.2% Other. 30% from out of state.

[1] OCCIDENTAL COLLEGE
1600 Campus Road, Los Angeles 90041, (213) 259-2700
Director of Admission: James Montoya

- **Undergraduates: 858m, 792w; 1,650 total (including graduates)**
- **Tuition (1982/83): $6,852**
- **Room & Board: $3,000; Fees: $242**
- **Degree offered: BA**
- **Mean SAT 556v, 593m**
- **Student-faculty ratio: 12 to 1**

A private college founded in 1887. 120-acre suburban campus in hills of northeast LA. Air, rail, and bus service.

Academic Character WASC accreditation. Trimester system, 10-week and 2 5-week summer terms. Majors offered in American studies, art (2), biochemistry, biology, chemistry, comparative literature, diplomacy & world affairs, economics, English, French, geochemistry, geology, geophysics, German, history, languages/linguistics, marine biology, mathematics, music, philosophy, physical education, physics, political science, psychology, religious studies, sociology & anthropology, Spanish, and theatre arts/rhetoric. Self-designed and combined majors. Interdepartmental programs in computer science, health professions, and in Asian, Hispanic/Latin American, Soviet, urban, and women's studies. Minors. Distributive requirements. Comprehensive exam in major field and writing exam required for graduation. MA and MAT granted. Independent study, honors program, Phi Beta Kappa, pass/fail, internships. Preprofessional programs in business administration, dentistry, diplomacy, foreign service, engineering, government service, law, library science, medicine, music, personnel work, physical education, public administration, social work, theology, and writing. 3-2 and 4-2 programs in liberal arts & engineering/computer science with Caltech and Columbia University. Cooperative program with Columbia University Law School. Exchange with Caltech. Washington Semester. Study abroad in Europe and Japan. International Fellowships for independent study abroad. 5-year programs for elementary, secondary, and community college education certification. AFROTC at USC; ROTC at UCLA. Language lab. 500,000-volume library with extensive periodical resources.

Financial CEEB CSS and ACT FAS. College scholarships, grants, Cal grants, deferred payment; PELL, SEOG, NDSL, FISL, CWS. Application deadline February 15.

Admissions High school graduation with at least 14 academic units recommended. Interview encouraged. SAT or ACT required. 3 ACH strongly recommended. $30 application fee. Application deadline February 1. $200 deposit required on acceptance of admissions offer. *Early Decision* and *Early Entrance* programs. Admission deferral possible. Transfers accepted. Credit possible for CEEB AP exams.

Student Life Student government. Newspaper, literary magazine, yearbook, radio station. Several drama and music groups. Film series, debates. Food coop, Project Link. Asian, international, and women's groups. Honorary, academic, religious, athletic, political, and special interest organizations. 3 fraternities and 3 sororities, all with houses. 10% join. Freshmen must live on campus. Coed and single-sex dorms. Special-interest housing. 75% of students live on campus. Honor system. 12 intercollegiate sports for men, 9 for women, and coed badminton, sailing, skiing. Intramurals. AIAW, SCIAC, NCAA. Student body composition: 13% Asian, 3% Black, 7% Hispanic, 1% Native American, 74% White, 2% Other. 45% from out of state.

[J1] OHLONE COLLEGE
43600 Mission Blvd., PO Box 3909, Fremont 94537

[J1] ORANGE COAST COLLEGE
2701 Fairview Road, Costa Mesa 92626

[P] OSTEOPATHIC MEDICINE OF THE PACIFIC, COLLEGE OF
309 Pomona Mall East, Pomona 91766

[1] OTIS ART INSTITUTE OF PARSONS SCHOOL OF DESIGN
2401 Wilshire Blvd., Los Angeles 90057, (213) 387-5288
Director of Admissions: Waynna Kato

- **Enrollment: 158m, 242w; 662 total (including part-time)**
- **Tuition (1982/83): $4,680**
- **Room & Board: $3,130; Fees: $90**
- **Degree offered: BFA**
- **Mean SAT 510**

A private, professional art school founded in 1918, merged with Parsons School of Design in 1978. Urban campus in the heart of Los Angeles. Air, rail, and bus service.

Academic Character WASC and professional accreditation. Semester system. Majors offered in ceramics, communication design & illustration, environmental design, fashion design, and fine arts. Freshman year foundation program, 27 liberal arts credits, and 10 art history credits required for graduation. MFA granted. AAS offered by the Division of Continuing Education. Exchange with Parsons School of Design in New York City (courses available at New School for Social Research). Other exchanges with Cooper Union School of Art, Maryland Institute College of Art, Mass College of Art, Nova Scotia College of Art & Design, Philadelphia College of Art, Pratt Institute, Tyler School of Art, School of the Art Institute of Chicago, and Winchester School of Art in England. Summer programs in Paris and Japan. Study abroad in Paris. Sculpture workshops, foundry, ceramics building with multi-kiln firing installation, art galleries.

Financial CEEB CSS. Institute scholarships, Cal grants; PELL, SEOG, NDSL, GSL, PLUS, CWS, college work program. Part-time and free-lance work available off-campus. Application deadline April 1.

Admissions High school graduation required. College prep program recommended. Interview required for those living within 200 miles of Los Angeles; encouraged for others. Portfolio (for most programs) and home exam required. SAT or ACT required. $25 application fee. Rolling admissions; suggest applying in winter months. Deadline April 30 for aid applicants. $100 deposit required on acceptance of admissions offer (May 1). *Early Admission* Program. Admission deferral possible. Transfers accepted. Credit or placement possible for CEEB AP exams. Special summer programs for high school students.

Student Life Dorm for over 200 students located 2 blocks from campus. Student body composition: 37% minority.

[J1] OXNARD COLLEGE
4000 South Rose Avenue, Oxnard 93033

[G1] PACIFIC, CHURCH DIVINITY SCHOOL OF THE
2451 Ridge Road, Berkeley 94709

[1] PACIFIC, UNIVERSITY OF THE
Stockton 95211, (209) 946-2211
Dean of Admissions: E. Leslie Medford, Jr.

- **Undergraduates: 1,710m, 1,800w; 3,624 total (including graduates)**
- **Tuition (1982/83): $7,380**
- **Room & Board: $3,070; Fees: $235**
- **Degrees offered: BA, BS, BFA, BMus, BSEng, BSPharm, BSBA**
- **Mean SAT 460v, 510m**
- **Student-faculty ratio: 13 to 1**

A private university established in 1851. 150-acre suburban campus 85 miles east of San Francisco, and 85 miles from the High Sierras. Graduate School of Dentistry in San Francisco, McGeorge School of Law in Sacramento. Air, rail, and bus service.

Academic Character WASC and professional accreditation. 4-1-4 system, 2 5-week summer terms. 53 majors offered by the College of the Pacific, 6 by the Conservatory of Music, 1 by the School of Education, 6 by the School of Engineering, 1 by the School of Pharmacy, and 10 by the School of Business & Public Administration. Elbert Clovell Program provides a liberal arts education in Spanish for Latin American students and North American students who speak Spanish; majors available through other divisions of the University. Cross-disciplinary and self-designed majors. Distributive requirements vary with colleges. Graduate and professional degrees granted. Independent study, honors program, cooperative work/study, pass/fail, internships. Last 3 years of engineering spent in 8 months of study/4 months of paid work. Concurrent study at 2 University schools possible. Preprofessional programs in dentistry, law, medicine, nursing, and pharmacy. UN semester at Drew U (NJ). Several study abroad programs. Elementary, secondary, and special education certification. Language labs. 350,000-volume library with microform resources.

Financial CEEB CSS. University scholarships, grants, music & athletic awards, loans, Methodist loans, Cal grants, deferred payment; PELL, SEOG, GSL, NDSL, HPSL, CWS. Priority application deadline February 9.

Admissions High school graduation with college prep program required. Interview encouraged. Audition required for music students; portfolio for art students. SAT or ACT required. $25 application fee. Application deadlines February 9 (financial aid applicants), March 15 (non-aid applicants). $100 deposit required on acceptance of admissions offer. *Early Approval* and *Early Entrance* programs. Admission deferral possible. Transfers accepted. Special program for underprepared applicants.

Student Life Student government. Newspaper, yearbook, radio station. Drama, music, debate groups. YMCA/YWCA. Academic, honorary, professional, religious, service, and special interest clubs. 5 fraternities and 6 sororities, most with houses. 15% join. 1st & 2nd year students live on campus. Single-sex, coed, apartment, and language housing. 60% of students live on campus. Illegal drugs, firearms, and fireworks prohibited on campus. Honor system. 8 intercollegiate sports for men, 6 for women; several intramurals. PCAC, Northern Pacific Athletic Association. Student body composition: 11% Asian, 4% Black, 6% Hispanic, 77% White, 2% Other. 25% from out of state.

[1] PACIFIC CHRISTIAN COLLEGE
2500 East Nutwood Ave., Fullerton 92631, (714) 879-3901
Director of Admissions: Cathy L. Bodell

- **Enrollment: 185m, 251w; 461 total (including part-time)**
- **Tuition (1982/83): $2,570**
- **Room & Board: $1,710-$3,390; Fees: $210**
- **Degrees offered: BA, AA**

A private non-denominational Christian college founded in 1928. Metropolitan campus 30 miles from downtown Los Angeles.

Academic Character WASC and AABC accreditation. 4-1-4 system, summer term. Majors offered in child development, children's ministry, Christian education, cross-cultural mission, diversified general studies, human services, management, music, preaching, psychology, secondary social science, social science, social work, and youth ministries. Distributive requirements. 15 Bible & theology courses required for a BA; 8 for an AA. MA granted. AA in early childhood education. Pass/fail, credit by exam, internships. Cross-registration with California State University, Fullerton offers additional majors. Child Development Center. 40,000-volume library plus access to Cal State (Fullerton) and other libraries.

Financial College scholarships, grants, missionary's dependent & family tuition discounts, loans, Cal grants, deferred payment; PELL, SEOG, BIA, NDSL, GSL, CWS, college work program.

Admissions High school graduation with 2.0 GPA required. GED accepted. SAT or ACT required. $30 application fee. *Early Admission* and *Early Decision* programs. Transfers accepted. Credit possible for CEEB AP and CLEP exams, and for life/work experience. Special admission possible for underprepared students.

Student Life Student government. Newspaper, yearbook. Men's, women's, service, ethnic, evangelical, and special-interest groups. Single-sex dorms for 500 students with weekly devotions, Christian service projects. Cafeteria. Liquor, drugs, smoking, firearms, explosives prohibited on campus. 5 intercollegiate sports for men and women; intramurals.

[G2] PACIFIC GRADUATE SCHOOL OF PSYCHOLOGY
1631 El Camino Real, Palo Alto 94306

[P] PACIFIC LUTHERAN THEOLOGICAL SEMINARY
2770 Marin Avenue, Berkeley 94708

[1] PACIFIC OAKS COLLEGE AND CHILDREN'S PROGRAMS
5 Westmoreland Place, Pasadena 91103, (213) 795-9161

- **Enrollment: 9m, 101w; 271 total (including part-time)**
- **Tuition (1982/83): $160 per unit**
- **Fees: $10**
- **Degree offered: BA**
- **Student-faculty ratio: 9 to 1**

A private upper-division & graduate college founded by Quakers in 1945. 2 campuses in a residential area of urban Pasadena.

Academic Character WASC accreditation. Semester system, 6-week summer term, intensive January term. BA offered with a major in human development. BA ABLE program for students with 3-5 years work experience in human services. MA granted. Fieldwork, seminars, internships. Member of National Consortium for Early Childhood Education with Bank Street and Wheelock Colleges. Early childhood, elementary, learning handicapped, and severely handicapped education certification. Children's School and Day Care Center. Library with children's collection.

Financial CEEB CSS. College scholarships, fellowships, loans; PELL, SEOG, NDSL, GSL, CWS. Priority application deadline March 1.

Admissions Minimum of 60 transferable college semester units in general education subjects with a 2.0 GPA required. $25 application fee. Rolling admissions. Application deadline at least 3 months before registration.

Student Life Student Union. No college housing. Student body composition: 15% minority.

[G1] PACIFIC SCHOOL OF RELIGION
1798 Scenic Avenue, Berkeley 94709

[P] PACIFIC STATES CHIROPRACTIC COLLEGE
San Lorenzo — see Life Chiropractic College—West

[2] PACIFIC STATES UNIVERSITY
1516 South Western Avenue, Los Angeles 90006

[1] PACIFIC UNION COLLEGE
Angwin 94508, (707) 965-6336
Director of Admissions: Charles T. Smith

- **Undergraduates: 753m, 839w; 1,592 total (including graduates)**
- **Tuition (1982/83): $5,220**
- **Room & Board: $2,115**
- **Degrees offered: BA, BS, BSMT, BBA, BMus, BSW, AA, AS**
- **Mean ACT 19**
- **Student-faculty ratio: 13 to 1**

A private college established in 1882, controlled by the Seventh-Day Adventist Church. 200-acre rural campus on Howell Mountain with 1,800 acres of woodland. Bus 8 miles away in St. Helena; air and rail 2 hours away in San Francisco.

Academic Character WASC and professional accreditation. Trimester system, 8-week summer term. Over 60 majors offered by the departments of art, behavioral science, biology, business administration & economics, chemistry, communication, education, English, history & social studies, home economics, industrial education, mathematics, modern languages, music, nursing, office administration, physics & computer science, religion, and physical education, health & recreation. Interdisciplinary majors. Associate degrees in 20 areas. Certificate programs. Minors in most major fields and in Biblical languages, New Testament Greek. Courses in 10 additional areas. Distributive requirements. 18 hours of religion required. MA granted. Independent study, honors program, credit by exam. Preprofessional programs include allied health fields, architecture, dentistry, engineering, law, medicine, nursing, optometry, pharmacy, public health, and veterinary medicine. Adventist Colleges Abroad. Computer center. 145,000-volume library.

Financial CEEB CSS. College scholarships, grants, loans, Cal grants; PELL, SEOG, NDSL, GSL, NSL, CWS, college work program. Application deadlines February 9 (Cal grants), April 1 (priority for other aid).

Admissions High school graduation with 2.3 GPA required. GED or equivalent accepted. ACT required. $10 application fee. Rolling admissions; suggest applying as early as possible. No deadline. $50 room deposit required by July 31. *Early Entrance* Program. Admission deferral possible. Transfers accepted. Credit possible for CEEB AP and CLEP exams. Provisional admission possible.

Student Life Student association. Newspaper, yearbook. Several religious groups. Single students under 23 must live at home or on campus. Others may live in approved housing off campus. No coed dorms. Married-student apartments. 71% of students live on campus. Liquor, drugs, smoking, profanity, gambling, and dancing prohibited on campus. Attendance at daily religious services, chapel, and Sabbath services expected. 4 phys ed courses required. Several intramural sports. Student body composition: 12% Asian, 4% Black, 5% Hispanic, 75% White, 4% Other. 18% from out of state.

[P] PALMER COLLEGE OF CHIROPRACTIC—WEST
Formerly Northern California College of Chiropractic
1095 Dunford Way, Sunnyvale 94087

[J1] PALO VERDE COLLEGE
811 West Chanslorway, Blythe 92225

[J1] PALOMAR COLLEGE
1140 West Mission Road, San Marcos 92069

[J1] PASADENA CITY COLLEGE
1570 East Colorado Blvd., Pasadena 91106

[P] PASADENA COLLEGE OF CHIROPRACTIC
1505 North Marengo Avenue, Pasadena 91103

[1] PATTEN COLLEGE
2433 Coolidge Avenue, Oakland 94601

[1] PEPPERDINE UNIVERSITY
24255 Pacific Coast Highway, Malibu 90265, (213) 456-4392
Dean of Admissions: Robert L. Fraley

- **Undergraduates: 990m, 1,182w; 2,457 total (including graduates)**
- **Tuition (1982/83): $6,688**
- **Room & Board: $3,030; Fees: $30**
- **Degrees offered: BA, BS**
- **Mean ACT 23; mean SAT 492v, 510m**
- **Student-faculty ratio: 21 to 1**

A private university founded in 1937, affiliated with the Church of Christ. 819-acre rural Malibu campus, established in 1972, houses Seaver College and the School of Law in the mountains overlooking Malibu Beach. Graduate School of Education & Psychology and School of Business & Management located at Los Angeles campus. Air, rail, and bus 30 miles away in LA.
Academic Character WASC and professional accreditation. Trimester system, with optional 2-part spring term ending August 5. 2 majors offered by the business division, 10 by communication, 10 by humanities & fine arts, 8 by natural sciences, 1 by religion, and 8 by social science/teacher education. Distributives and 2 religion courses required. Undergraduate Assessment Exam required for seniors in their major field. Graduate and professional degrees granted. Independent study, credit by exam. Washington trimester. Year-in-Europe program. Elementary and secondary education certification. ROTC at UCLA; AFROTC at USC. Computer center. 403,657-volume libraries.
Financial CEEB CSS and ACT FAS. University scholarhips, loans, Cal grants, deferred payment; PELL, SEOG, NDSL, FISL, GSL, CWS. Application deadlines February 12 (Cal grants), April 1 (other aid).
Admissions High school graduation with 15 units required. Interview encouraged. SAT or ACT required. $25 application fee. Rolling admissions; deadline April 5. $250 deposit required on acceptance of admissions offer (May 1). *Early Decision* Program. Transfers accepted. Credit possible for CEEB AP, CLEP, and university exams.
Student Life Student government. Newspaper, magazines, yearbook, radio & TV stations. Debate, drama, music groups. Academic, service, and special interest clubs. 1st & 2nd-year students under 21 must live at home or on campus. No coed dorms. Apartments for upperclassmen. 60% of students live on campus. Liquor, drugs, firearms, gambling, profanity prohibited on campus. Weekly chapel attendance required. 4 trimesters of phys ed required. 6 intercollegiate sports for men, 3 for women; many intramurals. AIAW, NCAA, WCAC. Student body composition: 6% Asian, 11% Black, 5% Hispanic, 0.5% Native American, 76.5% White, 1% Other. 33% from out of state.

[1] PITZER COLLEGE
Claremont — see Claremont Colleges

[1] POINT LOMA COLLEGE
3900 Lomaland Drive, San Diego 92106, (619) 222-6474
Director of Admissions & Recruitment: William J. Young, Jr.

- **Undergraduates: 674m, 848w; 1,870 total (including part-time)**
- **Tuition & Fees (1982/83): $3,693**
- **Room & Board: $1,860**
- **Degrees offered: BA, BSN**
- **Student-faculty ratio: 18 to 1**

A private college established in 1902, conducted by the Church of Nazarene. 88-acre urban campus in San Diego. Air, rail, and bus service.
Academic Character WASC and professional accreditation. Trimester system, 3 summer terms. Majors offered in accounting, art (3), biology, business administration, business education, chemistry, child development, church music/youth ministries, computer science (4), economics, engineering/physics, fine arts, history/political science, home economics, liberal studies, literature, mathematics, music (7), nursing, office administration, philosophy, physical education (2), physics, psychology, religion (5), social science, sociology, Spanish studies, and speech communications (3). Several interdepartmental majors. Certificate programs include youth, pastoral, and children's ministries. Distributives and 12 religion units required. Masters degrees granted. Honors program, credit/no credit, Christian ministries internship. Preprofessional programs in dentistry, engineering, law, and medicine. Summer Field Biology Institute, summer ministries. Interfuture Scholars Program. Courses at Institute of Holy Land Studies in Jerusalem. Elementary, secondary, and special education certification. AFROTC & ROTC at San Diego State U. A-V center, computer, language lab. 176,000-volume library.
Financial CEEB CSS. College scholarships, grants, loans, Cal grants; PELL, SEOG, NSS, NDSL, GSL, NSL, CWS. Application deadlines February 9 (Cal grants), March 15 (priority for other aid).
Admissions High school graduation with 9 units and 2.5 GPA required. GED accepted. SAT required. $15 application fee. Rolling admissions; suggest applying early in 12th year. *Early Admission* and *Early Decision* programs. Transfers accepted. Credit possible for CEEB AP and CLEP exams. Provisional admission possible.
Student Life Associated students. Newspaper, yearbook. Music, debate, drama groups. Several religious, honorary, and professional clubs. Single students under 25 must live at home or on campus. No coed dorms. 68% live on campus. Liquor, drugs, smoking, profanity, gambling, and social dancing prohibited. Chapel and class attendance required. 3 phys ed courses required. 10 intercollegiate sports; intramurals. NAIA, NCCAA. Student body composition: 3% Asian, 2.6% Black, 2% Foreign, 4.7% Hispanic, 1.2% Native American, 86.5% White. 10% from out of state.

[1] POMONA COLLEGE
Claremont — see Claremont Colleges

[J1] PORTERVILLE COLLEGE
900 South Main Street, Porterville 93257

[J1] QUEEN OF THE HOLY ROSARY COLLEGE
PO Box 3508, Mission San Jose 94538

[G1] RAND GRADUATE INSTITUTE FOR POLICY STUDIES
1700 Main Street, Santa Monica 90406

[1] REDLANDS, UNIVERSITY OF
1200 East Colton Ave., Redlands 92373, (714) 793-2121
Dean of Admissions: C. Stephen Hankins

- **Undergraduates: 560m, 640w; 2,500 total (including graduates)**
- **Tuition (1982/83): $6,750**
- **Room & Board: $2,860; Fees: $115**
- **Degrees offered: BA, BS, BFA, BMus**
- **Mean SAT 523v, 530m**
- **Student-faculty ratio: 12 to 1**

A private university established in 1907. 130-acre small city campus 65 miles east of Los Angeles. Rail and bus service; airport nearby.
Academic Character WASC and professional accreditation. 4-1-4 system. Majors offered in accounting, art, biology, chemistry, child development, communications, communicative disorders, computer science, creative writing, economics, education, engineering, English, ethnic & women's studies, fine arts, French, geology, German, history, journalism, management, mathematics, music (5), musical theatre, philosophy, physical education, physics, political science/public relations, psychology, religion, sociology/anthropology, Spanish, speech, and theatre arts. Interdisciplinary majors in European studies, international relations, and modern languages. Self-designed majors. Minor required. Johnston Center for Individualized Learning offers a non-traditional approach with independent study, seminars, & tutorials, and without grades or requirements. Whitehead Center for Lifelong Learning offers non-degree, bachelors, and masters programs for adults. Distributive requirements. Masters degrees granted. Independent study, honors programs, Phi Beta Kappa, pass/fail, credit by exam, internships. Cooperative work/study required for engineering majors. Preprofessional programs in law, medicine. Washington and UN Semesters. Several study abroad programs. 5-year programs for elementary, secondary, pupil personnel, administrative, and special education certification. ROTC at Claremont McKenna; AFROTC at Loyola Marymount. Language lab. 300,000-volume library.
Financial CEEB CSS. University scholarships, grants, Cal grants; PELL, SEOG, NDSL, GSL, PLUS, CWS, university work program. Application deadlines February 9 (Cal grants), March 15 (priority for other aid).
Admissions High school graduation required; 16 units recommended. Interview encouraged. SAT or ACT required. $25 application fee. Rolling admissions; priority application deadline March 1. $150 deposit required on acceptance of admissions offer. Admission deferral possible. Transfers accepted. *Early Decision* and *Early Admissions* programs. Credit possible for CEEB AP exams.
Student Life Student government. 2 newspapers, yearbook, radio station. Several music groups, drama, intercollegiate debate. Ethnic, religious, and special interest clubs. 4 fraternities and 3 sororities. 15% of students join. Single students under 23 must live at home or on campus. Coed & single-sex dorms, married-student apartments. 85% of students live on campus. Gambling, drugs, and firearms prohibited. 4 units of phys ed required. 11 intercollegiate sports for men, 8 for women; several intramurals. AIAW, NCAA. Student body composition: 9% Asian, 6% Black, 60% White, 25% Other. 38% from out of state.

[J1] REDWOODS, COLLEGE OF THE
7351 Tompkins Hill Road, Eureka 95501-9302, (707) 443-8411

- **Undergraduates: 1,043m, 1,496w; 10,868 total (including part-time)**
- **Tuition (1982/83): $0 (in-state), $2,250 (out-of-state)**
- **Room & Board: $2,669**
- **Degree offered: AA**

A public community college controlled by the Redwood Community College District, founded in 1964. 275-acre campus 8 miles south of Eureka. 6 branch campuses.

Academic Character WASC and professional accreditation. Trimester system, 6-week summer term. Many terminal and transfer majors offered by the divisions of business & economics, creative arts, guidance & counseling, health occupations, humanities, public services, science & mathematics, vocational/technical, and health, physical education, & recreation. Distributive requirements. Numerous certificate programs. Credit/no credit, credit by exam, cooperative work/study. Planetarium. Regional Law Enforcement Center. Over 60,000-volume library.

Financial CEEB CSS. College scholarships, loans, Cal grants; PELL, SEOG, NSS, BIA, EOPS, GSL, CWS. Priority application deadline June 1.

Admissions High school graduation or equivalent required. Students over 18 without a diploma accepted. California residents from outside the district may need a permit to enroll. ACT or SAT recommended for placement. Transfers accepted. Credit possible for military training/service. Extended Opportunity Programs and Services provides economic and/or academic support for disadvantaged students.

Student Life Student government. Newspaper. Music and drama events. Academic, honorary, service, social, and special interest groups. Dorm housing for 160 men and women. Liquor and drugs prohibited on campus. Smoking restricted. Intercollegiate sports. Golden Valley Athletic Conference.

[J1] REEDLEY COLLEGE

Reedley — see Kings River Community College

[J1] RIO HONDO COLLEGE

3600 Workman Mill Road, Whittier 90608

[J1] RIVERSIDE CITY COLLEGE

4800 Magnolia Avenue, Riverside 92506

[G1] ROSEMEAD SCHOOL OF PSYCHOLOGY

Biola College, 13800 Biola Avenue, La Mirada 90639

[J1] SACRAMENTO CITY COLLEGE

3835 Freeport Blvd., Sacramento 95822

[J1] SADDLEBACK COMMUNITY COLLEGE

28000 Marguerite Parkway, Mission Viejo 92692

[1] ST. JOHN'S COLLEGE

5118 East Seminary Road, Camarillo 93010

[1] SAINT MARY'S COLLEGE OF CALIFORNIA

Moraga 94575, (415) 376-4411
Dean of Admissions: Peter J. Mohorko

- **Enrollment: 1,011m, 1,083w**
- **Tuition (1982/83): $5,050**
- **Room & Board: $2,745; Fees: $80**
- **Degrees offered: BA, BS, BSBA, AA, AS**
- **Mean SAT 1010**
- **Student-faculty ratio: 15 to 1**

A private Catholic college operated by the Brothers of the Christian schools. Founded in 1863, became coed in 1970. 450-acre suburban campus 20 minutes from Oakland and 30 minutes from San Francisco. Air, rail, and bus in Oakland.

Academic Character WASC accreditation. 4-1-4 system. Majors offered in accounting, American studies, art, biology, business administration, chemistry, classical languages, communications, cross-cultural studies, diversified liberal arts, economics, English & drama, European studies, French, government, health science, history, integral curriculum, Latin American studies, mathematics, philosophy, psychology, religious studies, Spanish, and health, physical education, & recreation. Interdisciplinary majors. Courses in 8 additional areas. Distributives and 2 religion courses required. Masters degrees granted. External degrees, 1-yr paralegal program. Independent study, pass/fail, credit by exam. Preprofessional programs in dentistry, medical technology, medicine, nursing, pharmacy, physical therapy. 4-year nursing program with Samuel Merritt Hospital School of Nursing. 3-2 engineering program with Washington U (St. Louis). Cross-registration with Holy Names and Mills Colleges. Study abroad in Europe. Elementary, secondary, and special education certification. NROTC at UCal (Berkeley). 140,000-volume library with microform resources.

Financial CEEB CSS. College scholarships, grants, loans, Cal grants; PELL, SEOG, NDSL, GSL, CWS. Application deadlines February 9 (Cal grants), May 1 (other aid).

Admissions High school graduation with 15 units required. GED accepted. SAT or ACT required. $20 application fee. Rolling admissions; suggest applying by March 1. Deadline May 1. $50 tuition and $50 room deposits required on acceptance of admissions offer. Admission deferral possible. Transfers accepted. *Early Decision, Early Admissions, Concurrent Enrollment* programs. Credit possible for CEEB AP and CLEP exams. Academic Amnesty and High Potential Program.

Student Life Student government. Newspaper, literary magazine, yearbook, radio station. Several music, drama, debate groups. Black Student Union, Chicano Student Organization. Campus Ministry. Outward Bound. Academic, ethnic, and special interest clubs. Coed and single-sex dorms, apartments, some married-student housing. 52% of students live on campus. Liquor restricted on campus. Class attendance required. 9 intercollegiate sports for men, 6 for women; intramurals. AIAW, WCAC. Student body composition: 9% Black, 10% Hispanic, 1% Native American, 80% White. 24% from out of state.

[1] ST. PATRICK'S COLLEGE

PO Box 151, Mountain View 94042

[J1] SAN BERNARDINO VALLEY COLLEGE

701 South Mount Vernon Avenue, San Bernardino 92410

[1] SAN DIEGO, UNIVERSITY OF

Alcala Park, San Diego 92110, (619) 291-6480
Director of Admissions: Mrs. Kathleen Estey

- **Undergraduates: 1,286m, 1,664w; 3,593 total (including graduates)**
- **Tuition (1982/83): $5,100**
- **Room & Board: $3,200; Fees: $30**
- **Degrees offered: BA, BS, BBA, BSN**
- **Mean SAT 463v, 487m**
- **Student-faculty ratio: 18 to 1**

An independent Catholic university established in 1952. 200-acre urban campus overlooking the Pacific. Air, rail, and bus service.

Academic Character WASC and professional accreditation. Semester system, optional January intersession, 6-week summer term. Majors offered in accounting, American studies, anthropology, art, behavioral science, biology, business administration, business economics, chemistry, computer science, diversified liberal arts, economics, English, European studies, French, Hispanic/Latin American studies, history, international relations, mathematics, music, non-western studies, philosophy, physics, political science, psychology, religious studies, sociology, Spanish. Major in nursing for students with an RN. Minors urged, offered in major fields and 10 additional areas. Distributives and 3 religion courses required. MA, MAT, MBA, MEd, EdD granted. Independent study, honors program, pass/fail. Preprofessional programs in dentistry, education, engineering, foreign service, law, medicine, optometry, pharmacy, public administration, and veterinary medicine. Study abroad in Mexico and Oxford. Elementary, secondary, and special education certification. NROTC; AFROTC & ROTC at San Diego State U. Language lab. 270,000-volume library with microform resources.

Financial CEEB CSS. University scholarships, grants, loans, religious scholarships, Cal grants; PELL, SEOG, NSS, NDSL, FISL, GSL, CWS, university work program. Application deadlines February 9 (Cal grants), March 1 (priority for other aid).

Admissions High school graduation with 16 units required. Interview encouraged. SAT or ACT (out-of-state only) required. $25 application fee. Rolling admissions; suggest applying as early as possible. Deadline in April. $50 tuition and $100 room deposits required on acceptance of admissions offer. Informal early decision. *Early Entrance* and *Concurrent Enrollment* programs. Admission deferral possible. Transfers accepted. Credit possible for CEEB AP and CLEP exams. Educational Opportunity Program.

Student Life Student government. Newspaper, yearbook. Film, drama, several music groups. Model UN. Mecha-Maya, Black Student's Union. Circle K. Academic, honorary, professional, religious, service, and special interest clubs. 2 fraternities and 2 sororities. Single freshmen under 21 must live at home or on campus. Dorms & apartments. 30% of students live on campus. 8 intercollegiate sports for men, 7 for women; intramurals. AIAW, NCAA. Student body composition: 4.1% Asian, 3.6% Black, 9.4% Hispanic, 0.2% Native American, 82.7% White. 33% from out of state.

[J1] SAN DIEGO CITY COLLEGE

1313 12th Avenue, San Diego 92101

[J1] SAN DIEGO MESA COLLEGE

7250 Mesa College Drive, San Diego 92111

[1] SAN DIEGO STATE UNIVERSITY

San Diego — see California State University

[G2] SAN FERNANDO VALLEY COLLEGE OF LAW

8353 Sepulveda Blvd., Sepulveda 91343

[J1] SAN FRANCISCO, CITY COLLEGE OF

50 Phelan Avenue, San Francisco 94112

[1] SAN FRANCISCO, UNIVERSITY OF

2130 Fulton St., San Francisco 94117, (415) 666-6563
Director of Admissions & Financial Aid: Gabriel P. Capeto

- **Undergraduates: 1,320m, 1,497w; 4,203 total (including graduates)**
- **Tuition (1982/83): $4,980**
- **Room & Board: $2,768-$3,512; Fees: $40**
- **Degrees offered: BA, BS, BSBA, BSN, BFA, BPA, BRehab Admin**
- **Mean SAT 510v, 530m**
- **Student-faculty ratio: 12 to 1**

A private Jesuit university founded in 1855, became coed in 1964. 53-acre urban residential campus, 20 blocks from center of San Francisco. Air, rail, and bus service.

Academic Character WASC and professional accreditation. 4-1-4 system, 6-week summer term. Majors offered in the areas of business administration, communication arts, computer science, engineering, English, French, hospitality management, mathematics, nursing, physical education, public administration, psychology, religious studies, sciences, social sciences, and Spanish. St. Ignatius Institute offers a 4-year integrated Catholic liberal arts program. Minors. Courses in many additional areas. Interdisciplinary programs. Distributives and 12 units of philosophy/religious studies required. Graduate and professional degrees granted. Independent study, honors program, pass/fail, internships. Preprofessional programs in dentistry, engineering, law, medicine, pharmacy, veterinary medicine. BFA program with San Francisco Academy of Art College. 6-year BS/JD program. Exchanges with Boston College, Fordham U. Study abroad. Elementary, secondary, supervisory, junior college, and special education certification. ROTC; AFROTC with San Francisco State. Tokyo campus. Computer center, language lab. 500,000-volume library.
Financial CEEB CSS. University scholarships, grants, Cal grants; PELL, SEOG, NSS, NDSL, NSL, GSL, CWS, university work program. Application deadline April 1.
Admissions High school graduation with 15 units required. SAT or ACT required. $20 application fee. Rolling admissions; suggest applying by March 15. $100 tuition and $100 room deposits required on acceptance of admissions offer (May 1). Transfers accepted. Credit possible for CEEB AP and CLEP exams and for life experience. Upward Bound.
Student Life Student government. Newspaper, literary magazine, yearbook, radio stations. Music, drama, debate groups. Campus Ministry. Academic, honorary, political, professional, social, and special interest groups. 15 fraternities. Freshmen and sophmores must live at home or on campus. Coed and single-sex dorms. 39% of students live on campus. No smoking in class. Gambling prohibited. 6 intercollegiate sports for men, 6 for women; intramurals. AIAW, NCAA, West Coast and Northern California Athletic Conferences. Student body composition: 11.9% Asian, 5.6% Black, 5.6% Hispanic, 0.3% Native American, 48.1% White, 28.5% Other. 20% from out of state.

[1] SAN FRANCISCO ART INSTITUTE
800 Chesnut Street, San Francisco 94133

[J1] SAN FRANCISCO COLLEGE OF MORTUARY SCIENCE
1450 Post Street, San Francisco 94109

[J1] SAN FRANCISCO COMMUNITY COLLEGE
33 Gough Street, San Francisco 94103

[1] SAN FRANCISCO CONSERVATORY OF MUSIC
1201 Ortega Street, San Francisco 94122

[1] SAN FRANCISCO STATE UNIVERSITY
San Francisco — see California State University

[G1] SAN FRANCISCO THEOLOGICAL SEMINARY
2 Kensington Road, San Anselmo 94960

[J1] SAN JOAQUIN DELTA COLLEGE
5151 Pacific Avenue, Stockton 95207

[P] SAN JOSE BIBLE COLLEGE
790 South 12th Street, San Jose 95108

[J1] SAN JOSE CITY COLLEGE
2100 Moorpark Avenue, San Jose 95128

[1] SAN JOSE STATE UNIVERSITY
San Jose — see California State University

[J1] SAN MATEO, COLLEGE OF
1700 West Hillsdale Blvd., San Mateo 94402

[J1] SANTA ANA COLLEGE
17th Street at Bristol, Santa Ana 92706

[J1] SANTA BARBARA CITY COLLEGE
721 Cliff Drive, Santa Barbara 93109

[1] SANTA CLARA, UNIVERSITY OF
Santa Clara 95053, (408) 984-4288
Director of Admissions: Daniel J. Saracino

- **Undergraduates: 1,778m, 1,691w; 7,231 total (including graduates)**
- **Tuition (1982/83): $5,190**
- **Room & Board: $2,697**
- **Degrees offered: BA, BS, BSC, BSChem, BCS**
- **Mean SAT 512v, 576m**
- **Student-faculty ratio: 18 to 1**

A private Jesuit university established in 1851, became coed in 1961. 67-acre suburban campus 46 miles south of San Francisco. Air, rail, and bus service.
Academic Character WASC and professional accreditation. Trimester system, 6-week summer term. The College of Arts & Sciences offers 14 majors for a BA and 11 majors for a BS, including a BSChem. The School of Business offers a BSCommerce in accounting, economics, finance, management, marketing, and quantitative methods. The School of Engineering offers a BS in civil engineering, computer science, engineering, electrical engineering, and mechanical engineering. Interdisciplinary and self-designed majors. Ethnic and women's studies programs. Distributives and 3 religion courses required. Thesis may be required. Masters, JD, PhD granted. 1-year paralegal certificate program. Independent study, honors program, Phi Beta Kappa, pass/fail, credit by exam. Preprofessional programs in dentistry, law, business, and medicine. Washington and UN Semesters. Study abroad in Europe and Asia. 5-year programs for elementary, secondary, and special education certification. ROTC. Language lab, computer, TV studio. 655,000-volume library.
Financial CEEB CSS. University scholarships, grants, loans, ROTC scholarships, Cal grants; PELL, SEOG, NDSL, GSL, FISL, CWS. Application deadline March 1.
Admissions High school graduation with 16 units required. Interview encouraged. SAT required. $25 application fee. Rolling admissions; deadline March 1. $100 deposit required on acceptance of admissions offer. Transfers accepted. Credit possible for CEEB AP exams.
Student Life Student government. Newspaper, literary magazine, yearbook, radio station. Dance, drama, several music groups. Intercollegiate debate. Academic, honorary, religious, service, and special interest clubs. 1 fraternity and 2 sororities. Coed and single-sex dorms, apartments. No married-student housing. 54% of students live on campus. Hazing prohibited. 12 intercollegiate sports for men, 7 for women; several intramurals. AIAW, NCAA, WCAC. Student body composition: 10% Asian, 2% Black, 6% Foreign, 5% Hispanic, 1% Native American, 76% White. 23% from out of state.

[J1] SANTA MONICA CITY COLLEGE
1900 Pico Blvd., Santa Monica 90405

[J1] SANTA ROSA JUNIOR COLLEGE
1501 Mendocino Avenue, Santa Rosa 95401

[G2] SAYBROOK INSTITUTE
1771 Vallejo Street, San Francisco 94123
Formerly Humanistic Psychology Institute

[1] SCRIPPS COLLEGE
Claremont — see Claremont Colleges

[J1] SEQUOIAS, COLLEGE OF THE
915 South Mooney Blvd., Visalia 93277

[J1] SHASTA COLLEGE
1065 North Old Oregon Trail, Redding 96099

[J1] SIERRA COLLEGE
5000 Rocklin Road, Rocklin 95677

[1] SIMPSON COLLEGE
801 Silver Avenue, San Francisco 94134, (415) 334-7400

- **Enrollment: 101m, 105w; 305 total (including off-campus)**
- **Tuition (1982/83): $2,800**
- **Room & Board: $2,000**
- **Degrees offered: BA, BS, BMus**
- **Mean ACT 18**

A private college founded in 1921, moved to San Francisco in 1955. Affiliated with the Christian and Missionary Alliance, but with an interdenominational staff and student body. Urban campus. Air, rail, and bus service.
Academic Character WASC and AABC accreditation. 4-1-4 system. Majors offered in Biblical literature, business administration, Christian education, communication, English, history, humanities, liberal studies/diversified, missions, music, psychology, and urban studies. Minors in major fields (except liberal arts/diversified and urban studies) and in pastoral studies. Courses in remedial English. MA in education and Bible theology granted. 1-year Biblical literature certificate program.
Financial $2,800 tuition guaranteed for four semesters. January interim is offered at no additional cost to full-time students.
Admissions Rolling admissions. *Early Decision* Program. Admission deferral possible. Advanced placement credit possible.
Student Life Dormitories and cafeteria available. Students who live on campus must also take their meals there.

[J1] SISKIYOUS, COLLEGE OF THE
800 College Avenue, Weed 96094, (916) 938-4462

- **Undergraduates: 544m, 697w; 1,726 total (including part-time)**
- **Tuition & Fees (1982/83): $30 (in-state), $1,830 (out-of-state)**
- **Room & Board: $1,500**
- **Degrees offered: AA, AS**

A public, district-controlled junior college established in 1957. Small town campus at the base of Mt. Shasta.

Academic Character WASC accreditation. Terminal and transfer majors offered in administration of justice, agriculture (6), auto mechanics, business (3), civil engineering technology, electronics technology, emergency medical technician, fire science technology, forestry (3), home economics (3), library technology, natural resources (2), nursing (LVN), real estate, recreation technology, ski patrol, and social welfare. 1- and 2-year certificate programs. Distributive requirements. Pass/fail. Work experience program. Learning Resources Center, A-V center, TV studio, computer, art gallery. Over 28,000-volume library.
Financial CEEB CSS. College scholarships, loans, Cal grants; PELL, SEOG, EOP, GSL, CWS. Cal grant application deadline February 12.
Admissions High school graduation or equivalent required. Non-graduates who demonstrate ability to profit from instruction accepted. $200 housing deposit (for boarders) required by August 1. *Concurrent Enrollment* Program. Transfers accepted. Credit possible for occupational experience. Extended Opportunity Programs and Services provides financial and/or academic support for disadvantaged students.
Student Life Student government. Student Center, cafeteria, snack bar. Academic, athletic, drama, and special interest groups. Men's and women's dorms. About 25% of students live on campus. Liquor & drugs prohibited on campus. No smoking in classrooms. Regular class attendance expected. Hazing prohibited. 3 intercollegiate sports for men, 3 for women, and coed cross-country, tennis, and track; intramurals. Golden Valley Conference.

[J1] SKYLINE COLLEGE
3300 College Drive, San Bruno 94066

[J1] SOLANO COMMUNITY COLLEGE
PO Box 246, Suisun Valley Road, Suisun City 94585

[1] SONOMA STATE UNIVERSITY
Rohnert Park — see California State University

[1] SOUTHERN CALIFORNIA, UNIVERSITY OF
University Park, Los Angeles 90007, (213) 743-2311
Dean of Admissions:Jay Berger

- **Undergraduates: 7,573m, 5,549w; 28,129 total (including graduates)**
- **Tuition (1982/83): $7,000**
- **Room & Board: $3,000; Fees: $88**
- **Degrees offered: AB, BS, BArch, BFA, BMus, BSN, BSDental Hygiene**
- **Mean SAT 475v, 535m**
- **Student-faculty ratio: 14 to 1**

A private university established in 1880. 150-acre urban campus. Air, rail, and bus service.
Academic Character WASC and professional accreditation. Semester system, summer terms. Over 70 majors offered in the areas of anthropology, architecture, area studies, arts, broadcasting, business administration, cinema, communication arts & sciences, computer science, dental hygiene, engineering, humanities, languages & literatures, mathematics, music, nursing, occupational therapy, physical education, psychology, public administration, sciences, social sciences, and sports information. Individual & interdepartmental majors. Courses in other areas including Arabic & Hebrew. Distributive requirements. Graduate & professional degrees granted. Independent study, honors programs, Phi Beta Kappa, pass/fail, internships. Theatre & cinema workshops. 3-2 AB/BS engineering program. Admission to School of Pharmacy after 2 undergraduate years. Concurrent enrollment with Hebrew Union College. Washington and other semester programs. Study abroad in Costa Rica, England, Israel, Japan, Spain. 5-year programs for elementary, secondary, and special education certification. AFROTC, NROTC, ROTC. Language labs. 2,105,389-volume library.
Financial CEEB CSS. University & ROTC scholarships, handicapped student scholarship, Cal grants, deferred payment; PELL, SEOG, NDSL, GSL, CWS, university work program. Priority application deadline January 1.
Admissions High school graduation with 12 units required. Auditions required for music & drama majors. SAT or ACT required. $35 application fee. Rolling admissions; priority application deadline December 31. Deadline May 1. $50 deposit required on acceptance of admissions offer (May 1). *Early Entrance* Program. Transfers accepted. Credit possible for CEEB AP and CLEP exams. Special program for promising students with low GPA/test scores.
Student Life Student Senate. Newspaper, magazines, yearbook, radio station. Numerous music groups. Debate & drama groups. Women's center. Academic, professional, service, and special interest clubs. 25 fraternities, 23 with houses, and 13 sororities with houses. 22% of students join. Coed, single-sex, special interest, and married-student housing. 33% of students live on campus. No liquor on campus. 17 intercollegiate sports; many intramurals. NCAA, WCAA. Student body composition: 5.8% Black, 5.4% Hispanic, 0.4% Native American, 65.1% White, 23.3% Other. 30% from out of state.

■[1] SOUTHERN CALIFORNIA, UNIVERSITY OF (IDYLLWILD CAMPUS)
PO Box 38, Idyllwild 92349

[1] SOUTHERN CALIFORNIA COLLEGE
55 Fair Drive, Costa Mesa 92626, (714) 556-3610
Director of Admissions: Wes Wick

- **Undergraduates: 325m, 302w**
- **Tuition (1982/83): $2,894**
- **Room & Board: $2,182; Fees: $198**
- **Degree offered: BA**
- **Student-faculty ratio: 17 to 1**

A private college founded in 1920, associated with the Assemblies of God Church. 40-acre suburban campus 40 miles southeast of Los Angeles. Air, rail, and bus service nearby.
Academic Character WASC accreditation. 4-1-4 calendar, 3 3-week summer terms. Majors offered in biology, business, communications, English, history/political science, music, physical education, religion (Biblical studies, church ministries, missions, youth education), science/chemistry, science/mathematics, and sociology. 16 hours of religion/theology required. Independent study, internships. 5-year program for elementary and secondary education certification. TV studio. 71,850-volume library.
Financial CEEB CSS. College scholarships, grants, loans, ministerial scholarships; PELL, SEOG, NDSL, GSL, CWS. Application deadline April 15.
Admissions High school graduation with 11 units recommended. GED accepted. Interview may be required. SAT or ACT required. ACH recommended. $15 application fee. Rolling admissions; suggest applying by March. Deadline July 30. Admission deferral possible. Transfers accepted. *Early Admission, Early Decision, Concurrent Enrollment* programs. Credit possible for CEEB AP and CLEP exams. Provisional admission possible.
Student Life Student government. Newspaper, yearbook. Music and drama groups. Ministries Assistance Program. Business, women's, and special interest clubs. Students must live at home or on campus. No coed dorms. Married-student housing. 70% of students live on campus. Liquor prohibited. Chapel attendance required. 2 semesters of phys ed required. Dress code. Students must consult with Dean before marrying during school year. 3 intercollegiate sports for men, 2 for women; intramurals. NAIA. Student body composition: 2% Asian, 1% Black, 7% Hispanic, 1% Native American, 89% White. 20% from out of state.

[1] SOUTHERN CALIFORNIA COLLEGE OF OPTOMETRY
2001 Associated Road, Fullerton 92631

[J1] SOUTHWESTERN COLLEGE
900 Otay Lakes Road, Chula Vista 92010

[P] SOUTHWESTERN UNIVERSITY SCHOOL OF LAW
675 South Westmoreland Avenue, Los Angeles 90005

[1] STANFORD UNIVERSITY
Stanford 94305, (415) 497-2091
Dean of Admissions: Fred A. Hargadon

- **Undergraduates: 3,726m, 2,864w; 12,092 total (including graduates)**
- **Tuition (1982/83): $8,220**
- **Room & Board: $3,423**
- **Degrees offered: AB, BS**
- **Mean SAT 615v, 665m**
- **Student-faculty ratio: 10 to 1**

A private university established in 1891. 3,800-acre campus in the small city of Palo Alto, 30 miles south of San Francisco. Rail and bus service; airport 18 miles away.
Academic Character WASC and professional accreditation. Trimester system, 8-week summer term. Majors offered in African & Afro-American studies, American studies, anthropology, applied earth sciences (3), art (2), biological sciences, chemistry, Chinese, classics, communication, comparative literature, drama, East Asian studies, economics, engineering (8), English, French, geology, geophysics, German studies, history, human biology, humanities, international relations, Italian, Japanese, Latin American studies, linguistics, mathematical sciences, mathematics, medical microbiology, medieval studies, music, philosophy, physics, political science, psychology, religious studies, Slavic languages & literatures, sociology, Spanish, statistics, and science, technology & society. Self-designed, combined, interdisciplinary majors. Courses in astronomy, British studies, computer science, feminist studies, modern thought & literature, Portuguese, social thought & institutions, urban studies. Distributive requirements. Graduate and professional degrees granted. Independent study, honors programs, Phi Beta Kappa, pass/fail, internships. Dual degree and 3-2 programs. Exchange with Howard U. Numerous study abroad programs. Elementary, secondary, and special education certification. AFROTC at San Jose State; NROTC at UCal (Berkeley); ROTC at Santa Clara. Food Research Institute, computer center. 4,700,000-volume library.
Financial CEEB CSS. University scholarships, grants, loans, deferred payment; PELL, SEOG, NDSL, FISL, CWS. Scholarship application deadline February 1.
Admissions Strong high school preparation recommended. SAT required; ACT may be accepted. ACH strongly recommended. $30 application fee. Suggest applying as early as possible. Deadline January 1. $125 deposit required on acceptance of admissions offer. Admission deferral possible. Transfers accepted. Credit possible for CEEB AP exams.
Student Life Student government. Newspaper, literary magazine, yearbook, radio station. Drama, debate, several music groups. Academic, honorary, political, and special interest groups. 13 fraternities with houses and 6 sororities without houses. 15% of men and 10% of women join. Freshmen must live on campus. Single-sex, coed, special-interest, cooperative housing. Married-student apartments. 80% of students live on campus. 14 intercollegiate sports for men, 9 for women; intramurals. AIAW, NCAA, Athletic Association of Western Universities. Student body composition: 6% Asian, 7% Black, 7% Hispanic, 1% Native American, 79% White. 55% from out of state.

[P] STARR KING SCHOOL FOR THE MINISTRY
2441 LeConte Avenue, Berkeley 94709

[J1] TAFT COLLEGE
29 Emmons Park Drive, Taft 93268, (802) 763-4282

- **Enrollment: 700m, 600w (including part-time)**
- **Tuition & Fees (1982/83): $30(in-state), $2,288 (out-of-state)**
- **Room & Board: $1,270-$1,630**
- **Degree offered: AA**

A public community college founded in 1922, operated by the West Kern Community College District.
Academic Character WASC accreditation. Semester system, 3- and 6-week summer terms. 33 transfer majors offered in the areas of liberal arts & sciences, business administration, computer science, early childhood education, electronics, engineering, forestry, industrial arts & technology, nursing, physical education, physical therapy, recreation, and social welfare. Terminal majors offered in the areas of business (5), technology (18), and arts (4). Distributive requirements. Certificate programs. Pass/fail, credit by exam, internships. Cooperative work-experience program. Preprofessional programs in dentistry, law, medicine, pharmacy. Evening program. Learning Resource Center.
Financial CEEB CSS. College scholarships, grants, loans; PELL, SEOG, EOPS, NDSL, GSL, CWS, college work program. Application deadlines August 2 (scholarships), September 7 (grants).
Admissions Open admissions. High school graduation or equivalent required. Provisional admission for non-high school graduates over 18. California residents outside the West Kern Community College District may need a permit to attend. Rolling admissions. *Early Admission, Concurrent Enrollment, Early Decision* programs. Transfers accepted. Credit possible for CEEB AP exams, military service. College exams used for placement. Extended Opportunities Programs and Services provides financial and academic support for disadvantaged students.
Student Life Student government. Newspaper, magazines. Drama & music groups. Athletic, social, honorary, and special interest clubs. Freshmen who are not district residents must live on campus. Dorms for men and women. Regular class attendance expected. 2 semesters of phys ed required for students under 22. Intercollegiate and intramural sports for men and women. Western State Conference. Student body composition: 12% minority.

[1] THOMAS AQUINAS COLLEGE
10000 North Ojai Road, Santa Paula 93060, (805) 525-4417
Director of Admissions & Financial Aid: Thomas J. Susanka

- **Undergraduates: 60m, 50w**
- **Tuition (1982/83): $4,940**
- **Room & Board: $2,540**
- **Degree offered: BA**
- **Mean ACT 26; mean SAT 580v, 550m**
- **Student-faculty ratio: 8 to 1**

A private, independent Catholic liberal arts college founded in 1971. 131-acre rural campus adjacent to the Los Padres National Forest, 36 miles from Santa Barbara and 80 miles northwest of Los Angeles.
Academic Character WASC accreditation. Semester system. Four-year non-elective Great Books curriculum consists of readings and discussion in the areas of philosophy, theology, mathematics, laboratory science, language, literature, history, and music theory. Work is done in seminars, laboratories, and tutorials. Several papers including a senior thesis are required.
Financial CEEB CSS and ACT FAS. College scholarships, grants, loans, college work program.
Admissions High school graduation with college prep program recommended. Essays required. Interview encouraged. SAT or ACT required. Rolling admissions. $100 deposit required on acceptance of admissions offer. *Early Admission* and *Early Decision* programs. Admission deferral possible.
Student Life 2 men's and 2 women's dorms which are off-limits to the opposite sex. Liquor and drugs prohibited on campus. Dress code. Regular class attendance expected. Daily Mass optional. Several intramural sports. 65% of students from out of state.

[1] UNITED STATES INTERNATIONAL UNIVERSITY
10455 Pomerado Road, San Diego 92131, (714) 569-4772
Dean of Admissions & Financial Aid: Donald E. Smith

- **Undergraduates: 1,725 men & women; 1,717 graduates**
- **Tuition (1982/83): $4,770**
- **Room & Board: $2,772; Fees: $255**
- **Degrees offered: BA, BS, BFA, AA**
- **Student-faculty ratio: 17 to 1**

A private multicampus university established in 1952. Campus on rolling, wooded land 20 minutes from downtown San Diego. Other campuses in London, Mexico City, and Nairobi, Kenya. Air, rail, and bus in San Diego.
Academic Character WASC and professional accreditation. Calendar quarter system with summer term. 5 majors offered by the School of Business Management, 5 by the School of Education, 5 by the School of Human Behavior, 1 by the School of International & Intercultural Studies, 14 by the School of Performing & Visual Arts, and 5 by the Division of Engineering, Science, & Mathematics. Middle University offers an AA in general studies. Interdepartmental majors. Distributive requirements. MA, MBA, MFA, MIBA, MS, DBA, EdD, PhD, PsyD granted. Independent & guided study, credit by exam. Preprofessional programs in dentistry, engineering, law, and medicine. Elementary and secondary education certification. Over 427,000-volume library with microform resources.
Financial CEEB CSS and ACT FAS. University achievement awards, merit grants, loans, Cal grants; PELL, SEOG, NDSL, GSL, CWS. Priority application deadline April 15.
Admissions High school graduation with 12 units required. GED accepted. Interview & biographical statement required. SAT or ACT required. $25 application fee. Rolling admissions; suggest applying early in 12th year. $100 tuition and $100 room deposits required on acceptance of admissions offer. *Early Decision* and *Early Entrance* programs. Admission deferral possible. Transfers accepted. Credit possible for CEEB AP, CLEP, and university exams. Conditional admission possible.
Student Life Student Activity Council. Newspaper, literary magazine, yearbook. Model UN. Cross-cultural program. Athletic and social clubs. Single freshmen under 21 and other students under 18 must live at home or on campus. 14% of students live on campus. Apartment-style dorms for men and women. Drugs, liquor, firearms prohibited on campus. Smoking restricted on campus. 9 intercollegiate sports for men, 7 for women; several intramurals. AIAW, NAIA. Student body composition: 23% minority. 48% of students from out of state.

[J1] VENTURA COLLEGE
4667 Telegraph Road, Ventura 93003

[J1] VICTOR VALLEY COLLEGE
18422 Bear Valley Road, Victorville 92392

[J1] VISTA COLLEGE
2020 Milvia Street, Berkeley 94704

[1] WEST COAST CHRISTIAN COLLEGE
6901 North Maple Avenue, Fresno 93710, (209) 299-7201
Registrar: Pamela Williams

- **Undergraduates: 110m, 110w**
- **Tuition (1982/83): $900**
- **Room & Board: $858**
- **Degrees offered: BA, AA**
- **Student-faculty ratio: 13 to 1**

A private Church of God college established in 1949 primarily to prepare students for Christian service. 21-acre campus 4 hours from Los Angeles and San Francisco. Air and bus service.
Academic Character WASC and AABC accreditation. 4-4-1 system. BA offered with majors in Bible, Christian ministries, Christian education, and music. Minors in business, Christian education, English, evangelism & missions, music, pastoral studies, psychology, and social science. 30 semester hours of Bible required. AA offered with majors in Bible, business, general studies, and music. Independent study, pass/fail, credit by exam. Additional majors offered through cross-registration at California State U, Fresno. AFROTC at Cal State, Fresno. 18,000-volume library.
Financial CEEB CSS and ACT FAS. College scholarships, ministerial & music scholarships, loans, 2nd-family-member discount; PELL, SEOG, NDSL, GSL, CWS, institutional work program. Priority application deadline April 1.
Admissions High school graduation required. GED accepted. ACT required. $15 application fee. *Early Admission* Program. Transfers accepted. Credit possible for CEEB AP exams, prior learning experience. Probationary admission possible for underprepared students.
Student Life Student Council. Yearbook. Music, debate groups. Academic, athletic, honorary, professional, religious, social, and special interest clubs. All students must live on campus. Dorms for men and women. Married-student apartments. Cafeteria. Liquor, drugs, smoking, immorality, and disrespect prohibited. Attendance required at Sunday evening and 3 morning chapels, and at Sunday morning services at a local church. Students attend a week-long religious convocation each semester. 2 years of phys ed required. Intercollegiate basketball for men, volleyball for women; intramural and recreational sports. Southern California Christian College Conference. Student body composition: 20% minority.

[1 & G1] WEST COAST UNIVERSITY
440 South Shatto Place, Los Angeles 90020

[J1] WEST HILLS COMMUNITY COLLEGE
300 Cherry Lane, Coalinga 93210, (209) 935-0801

- **Undergraduates: 766m, 992w; 2,600 total (including part-time)**
- **Fees (1982/83): $60**
- **Room & Board: $1,780-$2,190**
- **Degrees offered: AA, AS**

A public, district-controlled junior college. Formerly named Coalinga College.
Academic Character WASC accreditation. Semester system. Day and evening programs. University-parallel majors in agriculture, business administration, engineering, and liberal arts. Preprofessional terminal majors in auto mechanics, diesel mechanics, secretarial studies, and vocational agriculture. Remedial courses in math and English.
Admissions Open admissions.
Student Life College housing for 126 men and 56 women. Student body composition: 33% mincrity.

[2] WEST LOS ANGELES, UNIVERSITY OF
10811 Washington Blvd., Culver City 90230

[J1] WEST LOS ANGELES COLLEGE
4800 Freshman Drive, Culver City 90230

[J1] WEST VALLEY COLLEGE
14000 Fruitvale Avenue, Saratoga 95070

[G1] WESTERN STATE UNIVERSITY COLLEGE OF LAW
1111 North State College Blvd., Fullerton 92631

[1] WESTMONT COLLEGE
955 La Paz Road, Santa Barbara 93108, (805) 969-5051

- **Undergraduates: 497m, 568w**
- **Tuition (1982/83): $5,490**
- **Room & Board: $2,760**
- **Degree offered: BA**
- **Mean ACT 21; mean SAT 480v, 505m**
- **Student-faculty ratio: 17 to 1**

A private interdenominational Christian college founded in 1940. 140-acre suburban campus 4 miles from the center of Santa Barbara and 2 miles from the beach. Air and rail service.

Academic Character WASC accreditation. 4-1-4 system, 3 4-week summer terms. Majors offered in biology, chemistry, diversified liberal arts, economics & business, English, English/language, fine arts, history, mathematics, music, natural science, philosophy, physical education, physical science, political science, psychology, religious studies, social science, and sociology. Self-designed majors. Minors offered in major fields. Courses in 7 additional areas. Distributives, 16 semester hours of religious studies, and GRE required. Independent study, honors programs, pass/fail, cooperative work/study, internships. Preprofessional programs in dentistry, engineering, law, medicine, and missionary work. 3-2 engineering program. Christian College Consortium. Institute of Holy Land Studies. Study abroad. 5-year programs for elementary and secondary education certification. ROTC at UCal (Santa Barbara); AFROTC at Loyola. Language lab, observatory. 129,522-volume library.

Financial CEEB CSS. College scholarships, grants, loans, deferred payment; PELL, SEOG, NDSL, FISL, CWS. Application deadline March 1.

Admissions High school graduation with 16 units required. Interview required for California applicants. SAT or ACT required. Math ACH for math/science majors. $20 application fee. Rolling admissions; suggest applying early in 12th year and by March 1. $100 deposit required on acceptance of admissions offer. Transfers accepted. Credit possible for CEEB AP and CLEP exams.

Student Life Student government. Newspaper, literary magazine, yearbook. Drama and several music groups. Academic, honorary, religious service, and special interest clubs. Single students must live at home or on campus. 4 residence halls for men and women. No married-student housing. 95% of students live on campus. Liquor, smoking, gambling, drugs, and social dancing prohibited on campus. Students must inform dean 30 days before they marry. 2 years of phys ed required. Attendance required at daily chapel. 7 intercollegiate sports for men, 3 for women. AIAW, NAIA. Student body composition: 1.1% Asian, 0.7% Black, 1.8% Foreign, 2% Hispanic, 0.2% Native American, 94.2% White. 29% from out of state.

[1] WHITTIER COLLEGE
13406 East Philadelphia St., Whittier 90608, (213) 693-0771
Director of Admissions: Michael A. Adams

- **Undergraduates: 575m, 625w**
- **Tuition (1982/83): $5,700**
- **Room & Board: $2,440; Fees: $186**
- **Degree offered: BA**
- **Mean ACT 24; mean SAT 490v, 510m**
- **Student-faculty ratio: 13 to 1**

A private college founded by the Society of Friends in 1901. 105-acre suburban campus 18 miles east of Los Angeles. Rapid transit service.

Academic Character WASC and professional accreditation. 4-1-4 system, 3 summer terms. 34 majors offered in the areas of arts, business administration, child development, communication disorders, economics, English, environmental studies, geology, home economics, mathematics, modern languages, music, philosophy & religion, physical education & recreation, psychology, sciences, social sciences, social work, and urban studies. Self-designed majors. Distributive requirements. MA, MS, MEd, MBA, JD granted. Various grading options. Internships. Preprofessional & professional programs in athletic training, dentistry, law, medical technology, medicine, ministry, nursing, optometry, osteopathic medicine, pharmacy, religious education, social work, therapy, and veterinary science. 4-1 program in social work. 5-yr liberal arts/engineering programs with U of Southern California, Stanford, and Colorado State U. Exchange with Fisk and Howard Universities. Study abroad programs include Denmark & China. Elementary and secondary education certification. AFROTC at USC; ROTC at Claremont College. Laboratory pre-school, language lab, computer. 180,000-volume library.

Financial CEEB CSS. College scholarships, grants, loans, grants for ministers' children, deferred payment; PELL, SEOG, NDSL, FISL, CWS, college work program. Application deadline March 1 (scholarships & grants).

Admissions High school graduation required; 9 units recommended. Interview encouraged. SAT or ACT required. $25 application fee. Rolling admissions; suggest applying by February 15 of 12th year. $100 deposit required on acceptance of admissions offer. *Early Decision, Early Admission, Concurrent Enrollment* programs. Admission deferral possible. Transfers accepted. Credit possible for CEEB AP and CLEP exams, correspondence courses

Student Life Associated students. Newspaper, literary magazine, yearbook. Several music, drama, and debate groups. Hawaiian Club, Hispanic Students Association, Black Student Union. Academic, religious, service, and special interest clubs. 4 men's and 5 women's social societies. 15% of students join. Freshmen must live at home or on campus. Coed & single-sex dorms. 55% of students live on campus. Liquor in public, firearms, drugs, and hazing prohibited. 13 intercollegiate sports; several intramurals. SCIAC, NCAA. Student body composition: 4% Asian, 8% Black, 16% Hispanic, 1% Native American, 71% White. 40% from out of state.

[1] WOODBURY UNIVERSITY
1027 Wilshire Blvd., Los Angeles 90017, (213) 482-8491
Director of Admissions: Daniel T. Angelo

- **Enrollment: 589m, 611w**
- **Tuition (1982/83): $3,729**
- **Fees: $34**
- **Degrees offered: BS, AS**
- **Student-faculty ratio: 21 to 1**

A private university established in 1884. 2-acre urban campus in downtown Los Angeles. Air, rail, and bus service.

Academic Character WASC accreditation. Trimester system, 12-week summer term. Majors offered in accounting, computer science, economics, fashion design, fashion marketing, graphic design, information systems, interior design, international business, management, and marketing. Minor required; minors offered in accounting, fashion design, business computer applications, economics, international business, management, and marketing. Distributive requirements. Associate degrees in computer science, graphic design, fashion merchandising. MS, MBA granted. 9-month certificate programs. Independent study, honors program, Phi Beta Kappa, internships. Computer center. 50,000-volume library.

Financial CEEB CSS. University scholarships, grants, loans, deferred payment; PELL, SEOG, NDSL, FISL, GSL, CWS. Priority scholarship application deadline March 1.

Admissions High school graduation with at least 9 units and a 2.0 GPA required. GED accepted. Interview encouraged. SAT or ACT, and ACHs recommended. $20 application fee. Rolling admissions; suggest applying by January 1. Admission deferral possible. Transfers accepted. Credit possible for CEEB AP and CLEP exams.

Student Life Student government. Newspaper. Academic, professional, and special interest groups. No university housing. Liquor prohibited on campus. No organized sports. Student body composition: 10% minority. 10% of students from out of state.

[1] WORLD COLLEGE WEST
PO Box 3060, San Rafael 94912, (415) 332-4522

- **Undergraduates: 27m, 31w**
- **Tuition (1982/83): $3,810**
- **Room & Board: $2,700**
- **Degree offered: BA**
- **Mean ACT 22; mean SAT 1,000**

A private liberal arts college in operation since 1973. Residential college community 24 miles north of San Francisco.

Academic Character WASC accreditation. Trimester calendar. College offers unique opportunities to explore and develop capabilities through a unified, innovative program emphasizing lifework exploration, world study, and preparation for the future. Curriculum includes a transdisciplinary 1st-year program addressing the perennial problems of being human and living creatively with other people and the natural world; Lifework program in which students work 16-20 hours a week, and are enrolled in seminars which integrate work & academics; World study year including 6 months in a developing country; and an upper-division (3rd and 4th year) program incorporating internship specialization with academic courses in one of the following areas: applied environmental systems, human service, and international management & economics.

Financial Financial aid available.

Admissions Admission based on application, 5 references, and previous educational record. Interview urged. SAT or ACT accepted. Rolling admissions. *Early Decision* Program. Admission deferral possible. Transfers accepted.

Student Life Residence requirement for first year. Student body composition: 10% minority.

[G1] WRIGHT INSTITUTE, THE
2728 Durant Avenue, Berkeley 94704

[J1] YUBA COLLEGE
2088 North Beale Road, Marysville 95901

COLORADO (CO)

[1] ADAMS STATE COLLEGE OF COLORADO
Alamosa 81102, (303) 589-7321
Director of Admissions & Records: Wayne S. Farley

- **Undergraduates: 687m, 803w; 1,878 total (including graduates)**
- **Tuition (1982/83): $650 (in-state), $2,612 (out-of-state)**

• Room & Board: $2,136; Fees: $230
• Degrees offered: BA, BS, AA
• Mean ACT 19
• Student-faculty ratio: 19 to 1

A public university founded in 1921. 90-acre small city campus in San Luis Valley, bounded on the west by Continental Divide, 220 miles south of Denver and 200 miles north of Albuquerque. Air and bus service.
Academic Character NCACS and professional accreditation. Semester system, 7-week summer term. Over 40 majors offered in the areas of business & economics, cultural & sociological studies, fine arts, humanities, psychology, scientific & technological studies, special education, preprofessional studies, and history, government & philosophy. Self-designed majors. AA offered in liberal arts, behavioral science, industrial arts, secretarial administration, and teacher aides. Distributive requirements. MA granted. Independent study. Honors program. Credit by exam. Internships. Preprofessional programs in dentistry, engineering, law, medicine, optometry, osteopathy, pharmacy, physical therapy, and veterinary medicine. Study abroad. Elementary, secondary, and special education certification. Learning resources center. Planetarium-observatory. 250,000-volume library.
Financial ACT FAS. College scholarships, grants, loans, state grants; PELL, SEOG, NDSL, FISL, CWS. Mail FFS by March 1; priority application deadline April 15.
Admissions High school graduation with 15 units required. GED accepted. Interview encouraged. ACT required. $10 application fee. Rolling admissions. Suggest applying at least 30 days before semester starts. $75 deposit required on acceptance of offer of admission. *Early Entrance* and *Early Decision* programs. Admission deferral possible. Transfers accepted. Credit possible for CEEB AP, CLEP, and ACT English exams.
Student Life Student government, residence hall councils. Newspaper, creative writing magazine, radio station, closed-circuit TV station. Music and drama groups. Wide variety of outdoor activities. Religious, political, ethnic, service, and special interest groups. Single freshmen and sophomores must live at home or on campus. Coed and single-sex dorms, 3 with cooking facilities. Married-student housing. 40% of students live on campus. Class attendance expected. 2 years of phys ed required. 7 intercollegiate sports for men, 6 for women; several intramurals. Rocky Mountain Athletic Conference. Student body composition: 0.4% Asian, 1.9% Black, 23.2% Hispanic, 1% Native American, 61.9% White, 11.6% Other. 11% from out of state.

[J1] AIMS COMMUNITY COLLEGE
Greeley 80631

[J1] ARAPAHOE COMMUNITY COLLEGE
Littleton 80120

[J2] BLAIR JUNIOR COLLEGE
10 North Farragut Avenue, Colorado Springs 80909

[1] COLORADO, UNIVERSITY OF
Boulder 80309, (303) 492-6301
Director of Admissions: Millard Storey

• Undergraduates: 9,043m, 7,824w; 22,249 total (including graduates)
• Tuition (1982/83): $981 (in-state), $4,490 (out-of-state)
• Room & Board: $2,286; Fees: $220
• Degrees offered: BA, BS, BSEd, BSJour, BSE, BFA, BEnv De, BMus, BMus Ed, BPharm, BSRec, BSPhys Ed, BSN
• Student-faculty ratio: 17 to 1

A public university established in 1876. 600-acre campus in a small city environment 25 miles northwest of Denver. Bus to Denver.
Academic Character NCACS and professional accreditation. Semester system, 10-week summer term. 51 majors offered by the College of Arts and Sciences, 13 by the College of Business Administration, 3 by the School of Education, 11 by the College of Engineering and Applied Science, 3 by the School of Journalism, 15 by the College of Music, 1 by the College of Environmental Design, and 1 by the School of Pharmacy. Self-designed majors. Graduate & professional degrees granted. Independent study, honors program, Phi Beta Kappa, cooperative work/study, pass/fail. Preprofessional programs in child health, dentistry, journalism, medical technology, medicine, nursing, pharmacy, and physical therapy. Dual degree programs, including 5-year engineering/business BS. Study abroad. Elementary and secondary education certification. AFROTC, NROTC, ROTC. Computer center. Language lab. Planetarium. 1,880,000-volume library with microform resources.
Financial ACT FAS. University scholarships, grants, loans, state grants, deferred payment; PELL, SEOG, NDSL, GSL, CWS, university work-study program. Preferred application deadline March 1.
Admissions High school graduation with 15-16 units required. GED accepted. Audition required for College of Music. SAT or ACT required. $20 application fee. Rolling admissions. Apply between October 1 and May 1; nonresident quote usually filled by March. Confirmation deposit required. *Early Entrance* Program. Transfers accepted. Credit possible for CEEB AP and CLEP exams. EOP for minority students.
Student Life Student Union. Daily newspaper, yearbook, literary magazine. Several music, dance, and drama groups. Debate. Religious, service, academic, and special interest clubs. 18 fraternities and 11 sororities, all with houses. 10% of men and 15% of women join. Freshmen under 20 must live at home or on campus. 21 coed and single-sex dorms, some with language floors. 900 married-student apartments. 25% of students live on campus. One year of phys ed required. Large intercollegiate, club, and intramural sports programs. AIAW, NCAA, Big 8 Conference. Student body composition: 2% Asian, 2% Black, 3% Hispanic, 1% Native American, 85% White, 7% Other. 33% from out of state.

[1] COLORADO, UNIVERSITY OF
Denver 80202, (303) 629-2703
Director of Admissions & Records: George L. Burnham

• Undergraduates: 4,032m, 3,818w; 9,808 total (including graduates)
• Tuition (1982/83): $752 (in-state), $3,372 (out-of-state)
• Fees: $46
• Degrees offered: BA, BS, BFA, BMus
• Mean ACT 33; mean SAT 1000
• Student-faculty ratio: 18 to 1

A public university established in 1964. Urban campus. Air, rail, and bus service.
Academic Character NCACS and professional accreditation. Semester system, 8-week summer term. 14 majors offered by the College of Business Administration, 5 by the College of Engineering & Applied Sciences, 25 by the College of Liberal Arts & Sciences, 16 by the College of Music, and 2 by the School of Education. Self-designed majors. Masters degrees granted. Health Sciences Center, also located in Denver, offers bachelor's, master's, doctor's, and professional degrees. Independent study, honors program, cooperative work/study, pass/fail, internships. Preprofessional programs in health careers, journalism, law. Transfer programs in 4 engineering fields with U of Colorado, Boulder. Combined degree programs in business with engineering, pharmacy, and environmental design. Cross-registration with Metropolitan State and Community College of Denver-Auraria. Elementary and secondary education certification. ROTC, AFROTC. Over 600,000-volume library.
Financial ACT FAS (preferred) and CEEB CSS. University scholarships, grants, loans, state grants, deferred payment; PELL, SEOG, NDSL, FISL, GSL, CWS, Colorado Assistance Program. Preferred application deadline March 1.
Admissions High school graduation with 15 units (16 for engineering) required. GED accepted. Audition required for College of Music. ACT or SAT required. $10 application fee. Rolling admissions; suggest applying in fall of 12th year. Deadline August 1. Admission deferral possible. Transfers accepted. Credit possible for CEEB AP and CLEP exams. Minority assistance programs.
Student Life Newspaper, magazine. Music and drama groups. Debate. Religious, political, academic, ethnic, honorary, professional, and special interest groups. No campus housing. Liquor prohibited on campus. Intramural sports. Student body composition: 1.7% Asian, 2.5% Black, 1.9% Hispanic, 1% Native American, 84.9% White, 8% Other. 8% from out of state.

[1] COLORADO, UNIVERSITY OF
Colorado Springs 80907, (303) 593-3000
Director of Admissions & Records: Douglas R. Johnson

• Undergraduates: 1,035m, 994w; 5,288 total (including graduates)
• Tuition (1982/83): $757 (in-state), $2,996 (out-of-state)
• Fees: $47
• Degrees offered: BA, BS
• Mean ACT 23; mean SAT 1000
• Student-faculty ratio: 19 to 1

A public university established in 1965. 425-acre campus in a small city 60 miles from Denver. Air, rail, and bus service.
Academic Character NCACS and professional accreditation. Semester system, 8-week summer term. 10 majors offered by the College of Business & Administration, 3 by the College of Engineering & Applied Science, 16 by the College of Letters, Arts, & Sciences, and 2 by the School of Education. Courses in 7 additional areas. MA, MS, MPA, MBA, MBS granted. Independent study, honors program, pass/fail, internships. Preprofessional programs in dental hygiene, dentistry, environmental design, journalism, law, medicine, nursing, pharmacy, and physical therapy. Transfer programs in several engineering fields with U of Colorado, Boulder. Study abroad. Elementary, secondary, and special education certification. ROTC. 160,000-volume library plus access to UC Boulder and UC Denver libraries.
Financial ACT FAS. University scholarships, loans, deferred payment; PELL, SEOG, NDSL, GSL, CWS. File FFS by March 1. Priority application deadline April 1.
Admissions High school graduation with 15 units recommended. GED accepted. ACT or SAT required. $20 application fee. Rolling admissions; suggest applying between February and May. Deadline July 1. *Early Decision* Program. Transfers accepted. Credit possible for CEEB AP and CLEP exams; university has own advanced placement program. Project Equal Opportunity.
Student Life Joint Board. Newspaper, literary magazine. Choir. Theater group. Honorary, religious, academic, service, and special interest groups. No university housing. Intramural sports. Student body composition: 1.9% Asian, 2.7% Black, 3.8% Hispanic, 0.5% Native American, 91.1% White. 7% from out of state.

[1] COLORADO COLLEGE
Colorado Springs 80903, (303) 473-2233
Director of Admissions: Richard E. Wood

• Undergraduates: 972m, 946w
• Tuition & Fees (1982/83): $6,400
• Room & Board: $2,100
• Degree offered: AB
• Student-faculty ratio: 14 to 1

A private college founded in 1874. 79-acre urban campus 70 miles south of Denver. Air and bus service.
Academic Character NCACS and professional accreditation. Modular calendar (4 blocks first semester, 5 second), 8-week summer term. Majors offered in anthropology, art, biology, business economics, chemistry,

classics, economics, English, French, fine arts (drama), geology, German, history, liberal arts & sciences, mathematics, music, philosophy, physics, political economy, political science, psychology, religion, sociology, and Spanish. 3-1 medical technology major. Self-designed and double majors. Interdisciplinary programs. Courses in 6 additional areas. Distributive requirements. Exam and/or GRE required in some majors. MAT granted. Independent study, seminars, research stressed. Phi Beta Kappa, cooperative work/study, pass/no credit, internships. 3-2 program in forestry with Duke. 2-2 medical technology and nursing programs with Rush U. 5-yr engineering programs with 4 other colleges. 6-yr BA/JD program with Columbia U. Numerous cooperative programs with schools throughout the country. Study abroad. Elementary and secondary education certification. ROTC at U of Southern Colorado. Computer services. Language lab. 300,000-volume library.
Financial CEEB CSS and ACT FAS. College scholarships, grants, loans, deferred payment; PELL, SEOG, NDSL, GSL, CWS. Application deadline February 15.
Admissions High school graduation with minimum 15 units expected. ACT or SAT required. $20 application fee. Application deadline February 15. $100 tuition and $50 room deposits required on acceptance of admissions offer. *Early Action* decisions made on an individual basis. Admission deferral possible. Transfers accepted. Credit possible for CEEB AP exams.
Student Life Campus government. Newspaper, yearbook, literary magazine, radio station. Music and drama groups. Debate. Mountain Club. Women's Commission. Ethnic, honorary, academic, professional, political, and religious groups. 5 fraternities with houses; 4 sororities without houses. 33% of students join. Seniors, veterans, and married students may live off campus. Coed and single-sex dorms. Language houses. 70% of students live on campus. 3.2% beer allowed on campus. 14 intercollegiate sports for men, 9 for women; extensive intramural program. AIAW, NAIA, NCAA, WCHA. Student body composition: 2% Asian, 3% Black, 4% Hispanic, 1% Native American, 90% White. 63% from out of state.

[J2] COLORADO INSTITUTE OF ART
200 East 9th Avenue, Denver 80203

[J1] COLORADO MOUNTAIN COLLEGE/ALPINE CAMPUS
PO Box 775288, Steamboat Springs 80447

- **Enrollment: 4,500 men & women**
- **Tuition (1982/83): $810 (in-state), $2,835 (out-of-state)**
- **Room & Board: $689-$765**
- **Degrees offered: AA, AAS**

A public, coeducational junior college that is district controlled. Campus located in northwestern Colorado.
Academic Character NCACS accreditation. Trimester system. Transfer majors offered in liberal arts, business, community services, early childhood education, resort management, ski business management, and special education. Terminal programs offered in community services, early childhood education, electricity, guide & outfitting, resort management, ski business management, solar technology, special education, and welding. Remedial mathematics and English programs available.
Admissions Open admissions for Colorado residents. High school graduation with a satisfactory record required. Application deadlines August 31 for fall term, December 31 for winter, February 28 for spring.
Student Life Dormitory and dining facilities available. Intercollegiate skiing and soccer.

[J1] COLORADO MOUNTAIN COLLEGE/SPRING VALLEY CAMPUS
3000 County Road 114, Glenwood Springs 81601, (303) 945-7481

- **Enrollment: 249m, 299w; 700 total (including part-time)**
- **Tuition (1982/83): $381 (in-district), $810 (in-state), $2,835 (out-of-state)**
- **Degrees offered: AA, AGS, AAS**

A public, coeducational, junior college controlled by the district. Campus located about 75 miles east of Grand Junction.
Academic Character NCACS accreditation. Trimester system. Liberal arts, general studies, and preprofessional curricula offered. Terminal programs offered include animal health technology, business management, commercial art, farm ranch management, graphic communication, natural resources management, photography, solar energy, and secretarial science. Remedial mathematics and English programs available.
Admissions Open admissions for district/Colorado residents. Out-of-state applicants must rank in the upper 75% of their high school graduating class.
Student Life Intramural sports program available including basketball, football, soccer, and volleyball.

[J1] COLORADO MOUNTAIN COLLEGE/TIMBERLINE CAMPUS
Leadville 80461, (303) 486-2015

- **Enrollment: 151m, 81w; 669 total (including part-time)**
- **Tuition (1982/83): $810 (in-state), $2,835 (out-of-state)**
- **Degrees offered: AA, AAS**

A public, coeducational, junior college that is controlled by the district. Campus located in west central Colorado about 80 miles from Denver and 90 miles from Colorado Springs.
Academic Character NCACS accreditation. Trimester system. Transfer programs offered in liberal arts, art design, behavioral science, computer science, creative photography, fine arts, health science, music, and outdoor studies. Terminal/vocational programs in accounting & data processing, environmental protection, marketing management, secretarial science, ski-touring operations, and welding. Remedial mathematics and English programs available. Certificates granted.
Admissions Admissions notification on a rolling basis. Admission deferral possible. *Early Decision* Program. Advanced placement credit possible.
Student Life Housing available on campus. Student body composition: 18% minority.

[J1] COLORADO NORTHWESTERN COMMUNITY COLLEGE
Kennedy Drive, Rangeley 81648, (303) 675-2261
Director of Admissions: Gary KuyKendall

- **Undergraduates: 245m, 118w; 1,350 total (including part-time)**
- **Tuition (1982/83): $0 (in-district), $440 (in-state), $1,650 (out-of-state)**
- **Room & Board: $1,800**
- **Degrees offered: AA, AS, AAS, AGS**
- **Mean ACT 17**
- **Student-faculty ratio: 15 to 1**

A public college established in 1960. 110-acre rural campus, 300 miles northwest of Denver.
Academic Character NCACS and professional accreditation. Semester system. 2-year programs offered in aviation technology, construction technology, dental hygiene, instrumentation technology, office occupations, petroleum technology, general business, education, liberal arts, mathematics/physical sciences, physical education, and geology. Vocational certificate programs. Independent study. Limited pass/fail, credit by exam. Preprofessional programs in dentistry, medicine, veterinary medicine. Over 15,000-volume library.
Financial ACT FAS. College scholarships, grants, loans, state grants; PELL, SEOG, NDSL, GSL, CWS.
Admissions Open admissions. ACT required of students with no previous college work. $10 application fee. Rolling admissions. Credit possible for CLEP exams.
Student Life Student Senate. Recreational and social activities. Single-sex dormitories for 200 men and 136 women. 4 intercollegiate sports for men, 4 for women. Outdoor sports including skiing and hunting. NJCAA, NLCAC, 1-MCAC.

[1] COLORADO SCHOOL OF MINES
Golden 80401, (303) 279-0300
Director of Admissions: A. William Young

- **Undergraduates: 1,989m, 436w; 2,985 total (including graduates)**
- **Tuition (1982/83): $2,100 (in-state), $6,000 (out-of-state)**
- **Room & Board: $2,700; Fees: $280**
- **Degree offered: BS in engineering specialization**
- **Mean ACT 23e, 29m; mean SAT 560v, 665m**
- **Student-faculty ratio: 15 to 1**

A public college established in 1874. 207-acre campus in the small town of Golden, 13 miles west of Denver. Air, rail, and bus in Denver.
Academic Character NCACS and professional accreditation. Semester system, 6-week field summer term, 8-week academic summer term. Majors offered in chemical & petroleum-refining engineering, geological engineering, geophysical engineering, metallurgical engineering, mineral engineering (civil, electrical, mechanical), mineral engineering chemistry, mineral engineering mathematics, mineral engineering physics, mining engineering, and petroleum engineering. Minors offered in some major fields and in environmental science and mineral economics. Courses in area studies, economics, English, German, history, philosophy, psychology, Russian, sociology, Spanish. 30 hours in 300 and 400 series technical courses required. MS, ME, PhD granted. Honors program. Cooperative work/study. Geophysics field camp 90 miles away in Fairplay. Petroleum field camp 280 miles away in Rangeley. Experimental mine 25 miles away in Idaho Springs. Colorado Energy Research and other institutes. ROTC; AFROTC & NROTC at UCol, Boulder. Computer center. 215,000-volume library.
Financial ACT FAS. College scholarships, grants, loans; PELL, SEOG, NDSL, CWS, state work program. Preferred application deadline March 5.
Admissions High school graduation with 15½ units required. GED accepted. SAT or ACT required. $10 application fee for out-of-state students. Rolling admissions; suggest applying by April 1. Application deadline is 21 days before registration. $50 room deposit required on acceptance of admissions offer ($25 refundable until August 1). *Early Entrance* Program. Transfers accepted. Credit possible for CEEB AP and CLEP exams. Summer Intensive English program for foreign students.
Student Life Student government. Newspaper, yearbook, press club, radio club. Band and chorus. Ski club. Engineering societies. Religious, service, academic, and special interest groups. 6 fraternities, all with houses; 35% of men join. 2 sororities without houses. Coed and single-sex dorms. Married-student apartments. 25% of students live on campus. Class attendance required. 4 semesters of phys ed required. 14 intercollegiate sports for men, 2 for women; intramurals. AIAW, NAIA, NCAA, Rocky Mountain Athletic Conference. Student body composition: 2% Asian, 1% Black, 2% Hispanic, 95% White. 30% from out of state.

[1] COLORADO STATE UNIVERSITY
Fort Collins 80523, (303) 491-7201
Director of Admissions: John F. Kennedy

- **Undergraduates: 7,137m, 7,289w; 18,909 total (including graduates)**
- **Tuition & Fees (1982/83): $1,104 (in-state), $4,122 (out-of-state)**
- **Room & Board: $2,400-$2,600**
- **Degrees offered: BA, BS, BEd, BFA, BMus**
- **Mean ACT 22; mean SAT 474v, 522m**
- **Student-faculty ratio: 18 to 1**

A public land-grant university established in 1870. 400-acre campus in the small city of Fort Collins, 65 miles north of Denver. Rail and bus service.

Academic Character NCACS and professional accreditation. Semester system, 4-, 8-, and 12-week summer terms, interim. 91 majors offered by the colleges of Arts, Humanities & Social Science, Natural Science, Agriculture, Business, Engineering, Forestry & Natural Resources, Home Economics, Veterinary Medicine & Biomedical Sciences, and Professional Studies. Minors. Interdisciplinary programs in 8 areas. Distributive requirements. Graduate and professional degrees granted. Independent study, honors program, Phi Beta Kappa, cooperative work/study, pass/fail, internships. Preprofessional program in veterinary science. Study abroad. Elementary, secondary, art, music, and physical education certification. ROTC, AFROTC. Language lab. Computer center. Agricultural Experiment Station research done on campus with 8 off-campus stations in Colorado. 1,200,000-volume library.
Financial ACT FAS. University scholarships, grants, loans, state grants; PELL, SEOG, NDSL, GSL, CWS. Preferred application deadline April 1.
Admissions High school graduation with 15 units required. Additional requirements for some programs. GED accepted. SAT or ACT required. $15 application fee. Rolling admissions; suggest applying early in 12th year. *Early Admission* Program. Transfers accepted. Credit possible for CEEB AP and CLEP exams. Project GO for disadvantaged and minority students. Summer program for underprepared students.
Student Life Associated students. Newspaper, yearbook, radio station. Special events board. Over 200 campus groups in academic, political, recreational, religious, service, and special interest areas. 12 fraternities and 9 sororities, all with houses. 10% of men and women join. Freshmen under 21 must live at home or on campus. Coed dorms. Honors residence, special-interest corridors. Married-student apartments. 33% of students live on campus. 2 semesters of phys ed required. Many intercollegiate and intramural athletics for men and women. AIAW, NCAA, Western Athletic Conference. Student body composition: 1% Asian, 1% Black, 3% Hispanic, 1% Native American, 91% White, 3% Other. 25% from out of state.

[1] COLORADO TECHNICAL COLLEGE
655 Elkton Drive, Colorado Springs 80907

[1] COLORADO WOMEN'S COLLEGE
Denver — see University of Denver

[G1] DENVER CONSERVATIVE BAPTIST SEMINARY
PO Box 10 000, University Park Station, Denver 80210

[J1] DENVER, COMMUNITY COLLEGE OF
1600 Downing Street, Denver 80218

[1] DENVER, UNIVERSITY OF
2301 South Gaylord, Denver 80208, (303) 753-2036
Director of Admissions: N. Kip Howard

- **Undergraduates: 2,200m, 2,200w; 8,600 total (including graduates)**
- **Tuition (1982/83): $5,790**
- **Room & Board: $2,595-$2,700**
- **Degrees offered: BA, BS, BFA, BMus, BMus Ed, BSAT, BSBA, BSAcc, BSChem, BSN**
- **Mean SAT 482v, 521m**
- **Student-faculty ratio: 14 to 1**

A private university founded in 1864, affiliated with the Methodist Church. University acquired Colorado Women's College in 1982. Suburban main campus in a residential section of Denver, College of Law in the business district. Air, rail, and bus service.
Academic Character NCACS and professional accreditation. Trimester system, 9-week summer term, December interterm. 56 majors offered in the areas of accounting, animal technology, arts, area studies, business administration, computer science, education, engineering, hotel & restaurant, languages & literatures, music, philosophy/religion, physical education, real estate & construction, sciences, social sciences, speech/communications. Major in nursing for students who are RNs. Distributive requirements. Graduate and professional degrees granted. Independent study, honors program, Phi Beta Kappa, internships. Preprofessional programs in dentistry, engineering, law, librarianship, medicine, theology. 3-2 program in liberal arts/business. Clinical education for audiologists, speech & hearing therapists, psychologists, and special education teachers. Study abroad. Elementary, secondary, and special education certification. AFROTC, ROTC at University of Colorado. Language lab, computer center, A-V services, observatory. 1,300,000-volume library.
Financial CEEB CSS and ACT FAS. College scholarships, grants, loans, state grants, deferred payment; PELL, SEOG, NDSL, GSL, CWS. Preferred application deadline April 1.
Admissions High school graduation or 15 units required. Nursing applicants must be RNs. Interview encouraged. ACT or SAT required. $15 application fee. Rolling admissions; suggest applying by April 1. Deadline July 1. $100 tuition and $100 room deposits required on acceptance of admissions offer (both refundable until May 1). *Early Decision* and *Early Admission* programs. Admission deferral possible. Transfers accepted. Credit possible for CEEB AP and CLEP exams.
Student Life Student Senate. Newspaper, yearbook, radio station. Music groups. 5 major drama productions annually. Debate. Religious, academic, professional, and special interest groups. 10 fraternities and 6 sororities, all with houses. 17% of men and 13% of women join. Coed, special-interest dorms. Cooperative apartments for single and married students. 85% of freshmen live on campus. 3 quarters of phys ed required. 7 intercollegiate sports for men, 7 for women; extensive intramural program. AIAW, NAIA. Student body composition: 1.4% Asian, 1.9% Black, 2.1% Hispanic, 0.5% Native American, 87.4% White, 6.7% Other. 57% from out of state.

[P] DENVER BAPTIST BIBLE COLLEGE
1200 Miramonte Street, Broomfield 80020

[P] DENVER PARALEGAL INSTITUTE
908 Central Bank Building, 1108 15th Street, Denver 80202

[1] FORT LEWIS COLLEGE
Durango 81301, (303) 247-7185
Director of Admissions: Harlan L. Steinle

- **Undergraduates: 1,500m, 1,300w**
- **Tuition (1982/83): $658 (in-state), $2,896 (out-of-state)**
- **Room & Board: $1,822; Fees: $126**
- **Degrees offered: BA, BS, AA**
- **Student-faculty ratio: 20 to 1**

A public college established in 1933. 300-acre campus in a small city 200 miles from Albuquerque and 350 miles from Denver. Air and bus service.
Academic Character NCACS and professional accreditation. Trimester system, 3 5-week summer terms. Majors offered in the areas of accounting, agriculture, anthropology, biology, business administration, business education, chemistry, economics, education (elementary, secondary, physical), English, environmental science, foreign languages, geology, history, mathematics (computer science), music, physical sciences, political science, psychology, sociology & human services, southwest studies, and theatre. Self-designed majors. AA offered in secretarial science and agriculture. Minors offered by some departments. Courses in 8 additional areas. Distributive requirements. Independent study, honors program, credit by exam, cooperative work/study, pass/fail. Preprofessional programs in agriculture, dentistry, engineering, forestry, law, medical technology, medicine, and veterinary medicine. Programs in forestry, agriculture (1 to 3 years), and engineering (2-2 and 3-2) with Colorado State U. 2-year transfer program in engineering with Colorado School of Mines. 3-1 medical technology program with several hospitals. Programs with other schools. Exchange with Concordia College in Moorhead, Minnesota. Study abroad. Elementary and secondary education certification. Computer center. 120,000-volume library.
Financial ACT FAS. College scholarships and loans; PELL, SEOG, NDSL, CWS. Tuition waivers for American Indian students. Application deadline May 1.
Admissions High school graduation with 15 units recommended. ACT or SAT required. $10 application fee. Rolling admissions; suggest applying in fall of 12th year. Deadline 1 month before registration. $50-$100 room deposit required on acceptance of admissions offer (refundable up to one month before registration). *Early Entrance, Early Decision, Concurrent Enrollment* programs. Admission deferral possible. Transfers accepted. Credit possible for CEEB AP and CLEP exams, high ACT scores, and high school grades. College has special assistance programs for minorities.
Student Life Student Senate. Newspaper, literary magazine, radio station. Music and drama groups. Wambiodiota Club. Outdoor Pursuits Program. Athletic, academic, honorary, religious, service, and special interest groups. Dorms and apartments for 1,212 single men & women. Some married-student housing. 30% of students live on campus. Guns prohibited on campus. 2 terms of phys ed required. 6 intercollegiate sports for men, 4 for women; many intramurals. AIAW, NAIA, NCAA, Rocky Mountain Athletic Conference. Student body composition: 0.4% Asian, 0.7% Black, 3.9% Hispanic, 6.3% Native American, 87.8% White. 31% from out of state.

[G1] ILIFF SCHOOL OF THEOLOGY
2201 South University Blvd., Denver 80210

[2] INTERMOUNTAIN BIBLE COLLEGE
2101 Patterson Road, Grand Junction 81501

[J1] LAMAR COMMUNITY COLLEGE
2401 South Main Street, Lamar 81052, (303) 336-2248

- **Enrollment: 110m, 124w; 450 total (including part-time)**
- **Tuition (1982/83): $553 (in-state), $1,692 (out-of-state)**
- **Room & Board: $1,998**
- **Degrees offered: AA, AS, AAS**
- **Mean ACT 16.9**
- **Student-faculty ratio: 16 to 1**

A public college established in 1937. 115-acre small-town campus. Air, rail, and bus service.
Academic Character NCACS accreditation. Trimester system, December interim, summer term. 2-year transfer programs offered in the areas of liberal arts, agriculture, business, data processing, and math/science. Vocational certificate programs in auto mechanics, building trades, cosmetology, horse training & management, secretarial/clerical, and welding. Distributive requirements. Independent study, credit by exam. 30,000-volume library with microform resources.
Financial ACT FAS. College scholarships, loans, state grants; PELL, SEOG, NDSL, GSL, CWS. Scholarship application deadline April 15.
Admissions Open to high school graduates and to non-graduates 16 years or older. Rolling admissions. $70 room deposit (for boarders) due on acceptance of admissions offer. *Early Admission* and *Early Decision* programs. Transfers accepted. Credit possible for CLEP exams.
Student Life Student Senate. VICA. Rodeo Club. Horse Club. Saddle &

Sirloin Club. Skiing & Outing Club. Single-sex dorms. Cafeteria. 3 credits of phys ed required. 3 intercollegiate sports for men, 1 for women; intramurals. NJCAA.

[1] LORETTO HEIGHTS COLLEGE

3001 South Federal Blvd., Denver 80236, (303) 936-8441
Director of Admissions & Financial Aid: Connie Campbell

- **Undergraduates: 128m, 517w**
- **Tuition (1982/83): $4,900**
- **Room & Board: $2,700; Fees: $45**
- **Degrees offered: BA, BS, BSN, BFA**
- **Mean SAT 450v, 450m**
- **Student-faculty ratio: 10 to 1**

A private college founded in 1918, became coed in 1969. 104-acre suburban campus located 20 minutes from downtown Denver. Air, rail, and bus service.

Academic Character NCACS and professional accreditation. Semester system, summer term. Majors offered in art, behavioral sciences, biology, business, chemistry, dance, design/theatre technology, English, environmental sciences, French, history, humanities, interdisciplinary sciences, international relations, liberal arts, mathematics, modern foreign languages, music, musical theatre, natural science, nursing, philosophy, psychology, religious education, religious studies, social science, sociology, sociology/criminal justice, Spanish, special education, and theatre. 3-1 medical technology major. Self-designed majors. Minor in women's studies. Courses in 6 additional areas. Distributive requirements. Independent study, pass/fail, credit by exam, internships. Preprofessional programs in law and medicine. 2-2 program with Colorado Institute of Art. Off-campus and study abroad. Elementary, secondary, and special education certification. University Without Walls for people between 16 and 74. Language lab. Art gallery. Research Center on Women. 100,000-volume library; membership in 2,000,000-volume Bibliographical Center for Research of Rocky Mountain Region.

Financial ACT FAS. College scholarships, grants, loans, state grants, deferred payment; PELL, SEOG, NDSL, GSL, CWS. Suggest applying by January 1 for scholarships & grants. Preferred application deadline for loans April 1.

Admissions High school graduation with 16 units recommended. Biology, chemistry, math for nursing students. Interview recommended. $10 application fee. Rolling admissions; suggest applying early in the fall of 12th year. Deadline August 15. $150 deposit required on acceptance of admissions offer. *Early Admission* and *Early Decision* programs. Transfers accepted. Credit possible for CEEB AP and CLEP exams. Conditional admission possible.

Student Life Student Council. Student Life Committee. Newspaper, yearbook. Chorus & instrumental groups. Center for Religious Meaning. Academic, honorary, religious, and special interest groups. Veterans, seniors, and students over 21 may live off campus. Coed, women's, and cooperative dorms. No married-student housing. 40% of students live on campus. 8 intramural sports. Student body composition: 4% Asian, 4% Black, 5% Hispanic, 86% White, 1% Other. 40% from out of state.

[1] MESA COLLEGE

Grand Junction 81501, (303) 248-1020
Director of Admissions: C. A. Scott

- **Enrollment: 1,714m, 1,416w**
- **Tuition & Fees (1982/83): $918 (in-state), $3,226 (out-of-state)**
- **Room & Board: $1,944**
- **Degrees offered: BA, BS, BBA, BSN, AA, AS, AAS**
- **Student-faculty ratio: 30 to 1**

A public college established in 1925. 42-acre campus located in a small city in the Rocky Mountains.

Academic Character NCACS and professional accreditation. Semester system, 1 12-week & 2 6-week summer terms. Over 40 majors offered in the areas of accounting, business administration, English, fine arts, humanities, biological & agricultural sciences, physical & mathematical sciences, nursing, leisure & recreational services, selected studies, and social & behavioral sciences. Self-designed majors. Distributive requirements. 20 associate degree programs in the areas of accounting, agriculture, auto body mechanics, business, education, electronics, engineering, forestry, graphic communications, law enforcement, nursing, radiologic technology, secretarial/office administration, travel/recreation/hospitality, and welding. Certificate programs at Area Vocational School. Independent study, honors program, cooperative work/study. Cross-registration with Adams, Metropolitan, and Western State Colleges. Elementary education certification. ROTC. College farm. 100,000-volume library.

Financial ACT FAS. College scholarships, grants; PELL, SEOG, GSL, NDSL, CWS, Colorado Work-Study Program. Priority application deadline March 15.

Admissions Open to graduates of accredited Colorado high schools. GED accepted. ACT required. $10 application fee. Rolling admissions; suggest applying after first semester of 12th year. $100 room deposit required on acceptance of admissions offer (refundable up to 30 days before registration). *Early Decision* Program. Transfers accepted. Credit possible for above average ACT and CLEP exams; college has own advanced placement program.

Student Life Student Body Association. Newspaper, yearbook, radio station. Athletic, music, drama, debate, and religious groups. Fraternities and sororities. Freshmen under 21 must live at home or on campus. Dorms for men & women. Campus apartments available for upperclass students. Married-student housing. 25% of students live on campus. Class attendance required. 4 intercollegiate sports for men, 3 for women; intramurals. Student body composition: 0.4% Asian, 0.3% Black, 1.4% Hispanic, 0.7% Native American, 95% White, 2.2% Other. 16% from out of state.

[1] METROPOLITAN STATE COLLEGE

1006 11th Street, Denver 80204, (303) 629-3018
Director of Admissions & Records: Kenneth C. Curtis

- **Enrollment: 3,479m, 2,887w; 15,436 total (including part-time)**
- **Tuition (1982/83): $716 (in-state), 2,840 (out-of-state)**
- **Fees: $132**
- **Degrees offered: BA, BS**
- **Student-faculty ratio: 17 to 1**

A public college established in 1965. 169-acre urban campus located in downtown Denver. Air, rail, and bus service.

Academic Character NCACS and professional accreditation. Semester system, 10-week summer term. Over 60 majors offered by the schools of Business, Community & Human Services, Education, Engineering Technology, Liberal Arts, Professional Studies, and Science & Mathematics in the areas of accounting, Afro-American studies, anthropology, arts, aviation management, bilingual/Chicano studies, business, communications, computer, criminal justice, engineering technology, hospitality meeting/travel administration, human services, industrial/technical studies, languages & literatures, meteorology, music, philosophy, professional pilot, psychology, sciences, and social sciences. Upper-division majors in nursing (for RN's) and health care management. Minors offered in most major fields and in 24 additional areas. Distributive requirements. Honors program. Pass/no credit, internships, self-paced learning, major-minor contracts. Cross-registration with Adams, Mesa, and Western State Colleges. Off-campus study. Elementary, secondary, and early childhood education certification. ROTC; AFROTC at UCol (Boulder). Learning Resource Center. Computer center, 628,000-volume library.

Financial ACT FAS. College scholarships, grants, loans, state grants, athletic scholarships & loans; PELL, SEOG, NSS, NDSL, FISL, NSL, CWS. Application deadline March 15.

Admissions All Colorado accredited high school graduates eligible for admission. Out-of-state applicants must rank in upper 67% of their class. GED accepted. ACT or SAT recommended. $10 application fee. Rolling admissions; suggest applying 4 weeks before registration. *Early Decision* and *Concurrent Enrollment* programs. Transfers accepted. Credit possible for CLEP exams; college has own advanced placement program.

Student Life Student Center. Newspaper. Music, drama, and dance groups. Athletic, academic, political, service, and religious groups. No college housing. Food services in student center. Extensive intercollegiate and intramural sports programs for men and women. NAIA, AIAW. Student body composition: 1.6% Asian, 5.3% Black, 0.9% Foreign, 5.7% Hispanic, 0.4% Native American, 69.9% White, 16.2% Other. 5% from out of state.

[J1] MORGAN COMMUNITY COLLEGE

17800 County Road 20, Fort Morgan 80701

[2] NAROPA INSTITUTE

1111 Pearl Street, Boulder 80302

[P] NAZARENE BIBLE COLLEGE

PO Box 15749, Knob Hill Station, Colorado Springs 80935

[J1] NORTHEASTERN JUNIOR COLLEGE

Sterling 80751, (303) 522-6600
Director of Admissions: Tom Martin

- **Enrollment: 521m, 468w; 1,233 total (including part-time)**
- **Tuition (1982/83): $0 (in-county), $360 (in-state), $1,575 (out-of-state)**
- **Room & Board: $2,050; Fees: $423**
- **Degrees offered: AA, AAS**
- **Mean ACT 17.6**
- **Student-faculty ratio: 15 to 1**

A public college established in 1941. 25-acre small-town campus, 125 miles northeast of Denver.

Academic Character NCACS accreditation. Trimester system, summer term. 2-year transfer and terminal programs offered by the Divisions of Agriculture, Business, Health & Physical Education, Humanities, Science, and Social Science. Distributive requirements. Cooperative work/study. Preprofessional programs in education, medicine, nursing, pharmacy, veterinary medicine. 65,000-volume library with microform resources.

Financial ACT FAS. College scholarships, state grants; PELL, SEOG, NDSL, GSL, CWS. Priority application deadline April 1.

Admissions High school graduation required. GED accepted. ACT or SAT required. $10 application fee. Rolling admissions. *Early Admission* Program. Admission deferral possible. Transfers accepted. Credit possible for CLEP exams.

Student Life Student Government. Newspaper, literary magazine. Academic, honorary, religious, and special interest groups. Coed and single-sex dorms. 3 phys ed credits required. 5 intercollegiate sports for men, 6 for women; intramurals. JCLIC, ECC.

[1] UNIVERSITY OF NORTHERN COLORADO

Greeley 80639, (303) 351-2881
Director of Admissions: James Blackburn

- **Undergraduates: 3,687m, 4,701w; 9,543 total (including graduates)**
- **Tuition (1982/83): $834 (in-state), $3,558 (out-of-state)**
- **Room & Board: $2,268-$2,520; Fees: $240**
- **Degrees offered: BA, BS, BMus, BMus Ed**
- **Mean ACT 19; mean SAT 480v, 430m**
- **Student-faculty ratio: 18 to 1**

A public university established in 1890. 237-acre small-city campus, 52 miles northeast of Denver. Bus and rail service; air in Denver & Cheyenne.
Academic Character NCACS and professional accreditation. Trimester system, summer term. 31 majors offered by the College of Arts & Sciences, 10 by the College of Education, 16 by the School of Performing & Visual Arts, 7 by the School of Business, 9 by the College of Health & Human Services, and 8 by the School of Health, Physical Education, & Recreation. Self-designed and interdisciplinary majors. Minors offered in most major fields and in 4 other areas. Distributive requirements. MA, EdS, EdD, PhD, DA granted. Independent study, honors seminar, Phi Beta Kappa, pass/fail, internships. Preprofessional programs in dentistry, engineering, law, medicine. 4-year, year-round BA/MA option. 4-year medical technology program with Weld County General Hospital. Summer study abroad. Elementary, junior high, secondary, and special education certification. University Laboratory School. AFROTC, ROTC. Language lab. 691,570-volume library.
Financial ACT FAS. University scholarships, loans; PELL, SEOG, NSS, NDSL, GSL, NSL, CWS. Application deadlines March 1 (scholarships), March 31 (loans).
Admissions High school graduation with 15 units required. Audition required for music majors. ACT or SAT required. $15 application fee. Rolling admissions; suggest applying early in 12th year. $100 room deposit required on acceptance of admissions offer ($50 refundable until August 30). *Early Admission* and *Early Decision* programs. Admission deferral possible. Transfers accepted. Credit possible for CEEB AP, CLEP, and challenge exams. Center for Human Enrichment and special summer programs for underprepared students.
Student Life Associated Students. Associated Women Students. Newspaper, magazine, radio station. Music & drama groups. Debate. Honorary and service fraternities. Academic, political, religious, and special interest groups. 11 fraternities and 11 sororities, all with houses. 20% of men and 22% of women join. Single freshmen under 21 must live at home or on campus. Coed, single-sex, and special interest dorms. Married-student apartments. 40% of students live on campus. 3.2 beer allowed on campus. 10 intercollegiate sports for men, 9 for women; intramurals. NCAA, North Central Conference. Student body composition: 0.8% Asian, 1.9% Black, 4.1% Hispanic, 0.5% Native American, 90.6% White, 2.1% Other. 16% from out of state.

[J1] OTERO JUNIOR COLLEGE
La Junta 81050, (303) 384-8721

- **Enrollment: 255m, 244w; 823 total (including part-time)**
- **Tuition (1982/83): $771 (in-state), $2,055-2,370 (out-of-state)**
- **Room & Board: $1,980**
- **Degrees offered: AA, AS, AAS**
- **Mean ACT 18.5**
- **Student-faculty ratio: 17 to 1**

A public college established in 1941. Small-town campus in southeastern Colorado. Served by rail.
Academic Character NCACS accreditation. Trimester system, 2 5-week summer terms, December mini-term. 2-year transfer programs offered in agriculture, business, liberal arts, secretarial science, architectural technology, nursing, and early childhood education. Terminal programs in agriculture, business, data processing, drafting, engineering technology, machine shop, nursing, pre-school education, secretarial science, surveying, and welding. Distributive requirements. Certificates granted. Credit by exam. Preprofessional programs in law, medicine, medical technology, physical therapy, occupational therapy, pharmacy, veterinary medicine. Koshare Kiva. 32,000-volume library.
Financial ACT FAS. College scholarships, grants, loans, state grants; PELL, SEOG, NDSL, GSL, CWS, college job placement.
Admissions High school graduation required. GED accepted. ACT required. $10 application fee. Rolling admissions. Credit possible for CLEP exams.
Student Life Student government. Newspaper, literary magazine. Music & drama groups. VICA. Rodeo Club. Academic, professional, recreational, religious, and special interest groups. Single students under 21 must live at home or on campus. Single-sex dorms. 3 hours of phys ed required. 2 intercollegiate sports for men and women; intramurals. NJCAA. Student body composition: 30% minority.

[J2] PARKS COLLEGE
7350 North Broadway, Denver 80221

[J1] PIKES PEAK COMMUNITY COLLEGE
5675 South Academy Blvd., Colorado Springs 80906

[J1] PUEBLO COMMUNITY COLLEGE
Pueblo 81004

[1] REGIS COLLEGE
3539 West 50th Avenue, Denver 80221, (303) 458-4900
Director of Admissions: Domenic N. Teti

- **Undergraduates: 600m, 450w**
- **Tuition (1982/83): $5,160**
- **Room & Board: $2,820; Fees: $140**
- **Degrees offered: BA, BSChem, BSMath**
- **Mean ACT 23**
- **Student-faculty ratio: 15 to 1**

A private Roman Catholic college established in 1877 under the auspices of the Society of Jesus. Became coed in 1968. 90-acre suburban campus. Air, rail, and bus service.
Academic Character NCACS and professional accreditation. Semester system, 10-week summer term, summer workshops. Majors offered in accounting, biology, business administration, chemistry, ecology, economics, education, English, environmental studies/human ecology, French, history, mathematics, media studies, medical record administration, medical technology, philosophy, political science, psychology, religious studies, sociology, Spanish, theatre/English, and theater studies. Self-designed and interdivisonal majors. Courses offered in 15 additional areas. Distributives and 9 religious studies credits required. Independent study, honors program, pass/fail, extensive internships. Preprofessional programs in dentistry, law, medicine. 3-2 engineering program with Marquette and Washington Universities. Study abroad in Europe & Japan. Elementary and secondary education certification. AFROTC at University of Colorado. Seismic observatory. Language lab. 65,000-volume library.
Financial CEEB CSS and ACT FAS. College scholarships, loans; continuing education, state, and teacher grants; deferred payment; PELL, SEOG, NDSL, GSL, CWS. Application deadline April 1.
Admissions High school graduation with 15 units required. GED accepted. Interview encouraged. SAT or ACT required. $10 application fee. Rolling admissions; suggest applying by January. $100 ($50 for day student) deposit required on acceptance admissions offer. Credit possible for CEEB AP, CLEP, ACT PEP exams; college has own advanced placement program.
Student Life Student Senate. Newspaper, yearbook, radio station. Glee club. Debate. Theater Guild. Ski club. Academic, religious, service, and special interest groups. Academic and social fraternities and sororities without houses. Single freshmen and sophomores under 21 must live at home or on campus. Coed dorms. No married-student housing. 50% of students live on campus. 8 intercollegiate sports for men, 2 for women; intramurals. AIAW, NAIA, NCAA, Rocky Mountain Athletic Conference. 55% of students from out of state.

[1] ROCKMONT COLLEGE
8801 West Alameda Avenue, Lakewood 80226, (303) 238-5386
Director of Admissions: Jack Keat

- **Enrollment: 101m, 125w; 277 total (including part-time)**
- **Tuition (1982/83): $3,060**
- **Room & Board: $2,040; Fees: $171**
- **Degrees offered: BA, BChristian Ministries, AA**
- **Mean ACT 18.8**
- **Student-faculty ratio: 12 to 1**

A private, non-denominational Christian college established in 1914. 38-acre suburban campus, 15 minutes from downtown Denver. Air, rail, and bus service.
Academic Character NCACS accreditation. Quarter system, December interterm, summer term. Majors offered in art, biology, Biblical studies, business, Christian ministries, communications, elementary education, history, humanities, literature, music, music education, psychology, secretarial science, social science, and sociology. Minors in music and philosophy. Distributives and 28 hours of theology required. AA offered in general studies, lay counseling, early childhood education, and secretarial science. Preprofessional program in the ministry. Cooperative programs in art with Colorado Institute, in music education with Metropolitan State, in ecology with Rocky Mountain Nature Association, in elementary education with U Colorado at Denver. Elementary education certification. 30,000-volume library.
Financial ACT FAS. College scholarships; PELL, SEOG, NDSL, GSL, CWS. Application deadline March 1.
Admissions High school graduation with 15 units required. GED accepted. ACT (preferred) or SAT required. $15 application fee. Rolling admissions. $50 deposit due on acceptance of admissions offer. *Early Admission* and *Early Decision* programs. Admission deferral possible. Transfers accepted. Credit possible for CLEP exams and relevant life/work experience.
Student Life Student government. Newspaper, yearbook. Music & drama groups. Outdoor Fanatics Club. Ski club. Students under 25 must live at home or on campus. Apartment housing for single and some married students. Liquor, drugs, tobacco prohibited. Twice-weekly chapel attendance encouraged. 4 intercollegiate sports for men, 3 for women; intramurals. NAIA, NCCAA, ASCA, CICAL.

[1] ST. THOMAS SEMINARY
1300 South Steele Street, Denver 80210

[1] SOUTHERN COLORADO, UNIVERSITY OF
Pueblo 81001, (303) 549-0123
Director of Admissions: Jose A. Padilla

- **Undergraduates: 2,483m, 2,083w; 4,821 total (including gradutes)**
- **Tuition (1982/83): $974 (in-state), $3,604 (out-of-state)**
- **Room & Board: $1,340-$1,390**
- **Degrees offered: BA, BS, AA, AAS**
- **Mean ACT 16**
- **Student-faculty ratio: 21 to 1**

A public university established in 1933. 800-acre suburban campus in the small city of Pueblo, 110 miles from Denver. Air and bus service.
Academic Character NCACS and professional accreditation. Semester system, 5- and 8-week summer terms. 50 majors offered in the areas of applied sciences, arts, business, communications, computer science, education, engineering technologies, geology/geography, humanities, industrial engineering, languages, music, nursing, physical education, sciences, social sciences. Interdisciplinary and double majors. Distributive requirements. Associate degrees in 6 areas. MA granted. Independent study, honors program, cooperative work/study, internships. Experiential credit. Preprofessional program in medicine. Exchange program with Adams State.

Elementary education certification. ROTC. 210,000-volume library.
Financial CEEB CSS and ACT FAS. University scholarships, grants, loans; PELL, SEOG, NDSL, GSL, CWS. Application deadline March 1.
Admissions Open to graduates of accredited Colorado high schools. Out-of-state applicants must be in top 67% of their class. GED accepted. SAT or ACT required. $10 application fee. Rolling admissions; suggest applying by March 1. Deadline July 21. $100 room deposit required on acceptance of admissions offer (refundable up to 30 days before beginning of semester). *Early Entrance* and *Early Decision* programs. Transfers accepted. Credit possible for CEEB AP and CLEP exams; university has own advanced placement program.
Student Life Associated Student Government. Newspaper. Music and drama groups. Debate. Athletic, academic, political, religious, and special interest groups. 2 fraternities, one with house; 2 sororities without houses. Less than 5% of men and women join. Freshmen under 21 must live on campus. Residence halls & cafeteria. No married-student housing. 12% of students live on campus. 3.2% beer allowed on campus. 2 semester hours of phys ed required. 8 intercollegiate sports for men, 5 for women; intramurals. AIAW, NAIA, NCAA. Student body composition: 1% Asian, 4% Black, 18% Hispanic, 6% Native American, 64% White, 7% Other. 13% from out of state.

[J1] TRINIDAD STATE JUNIOR COLLEGE
Trinidad 81082, (303) 846-5011
Director of Admissions: Pete C. Deluca

- **Enrollment: 481m, 205w; 1,600 total (including part-time & evening)**
- **Tuition (1982/83): $620 (in-state), $1,861 (out-of-state)**
- **Room & Board: $2,100; Fees: $145**
- **Degrees offered: AA, AAS**
- **Mean ACT 15**
- **Student-faculty ratio: 25 to 1**

A public college established in 1925. Small-city campus.
Academic Character NCACS accreditation. Trimester system, 7-week summer term. 2-year transfer programs in liberal arts, anthropology, art, biology, business administration, chemistry, education, engineering, forestry, general office, geology, home economics, human ecology, industrial arts, interior design, journalism, mathematics, mining technology, music, nursing, physical education, speech & drama. Vocational programs offered in auto mechanics, auto body mechanics, building trades, civil technology, cosmetology, data processing, drafting, electronics, gunsmithing, law enforcement, industrial arts, law enforcement, mining technology, musical instrument repair, practical nursing, secretarial science, technologies, and welding. Distributive requirements. Preprofessional programs in dentistry, law, medicine, medical technology, nursing, pharmacy. 50,000-volume library.
Financial ACT FAS. College scholarships, state grants; PELL, SEOG, GSL, CWS. Application deadline June 1.
Admissions Open to all Colorado high school graduates. GED accepted. ACT required. Rolling admissions. $100 room deposit due on acceptance of admissions offer. Transfers accepted. Credit possible for CLEP exams.
Student Life Student association. Newspaper. Academic, honorary, professional, and special interest groups. Single-sex dorms. No married-student housing. Regular class attendance expected. 3 hours of phys ed required. 3 intercollegiate sports for men, 1 for women; intramurals. NJCAA. Student body composition: 43% minority.

[1] UNITED STATES AIR FORCE ACADEMY
USAFA 80840, (303) 472-2640
Director of Admissions: Colonel Warren L. Simmons

- **Undergraduates: 4,532m, 524w**
- **Degree offered: BS**
- **Mean ACT 24e, 29m; mean SAT 560v, 655m**
- **Student-faculty ratio: 8 to 1**

A United States Service Academy established in 1954 to train officers for the Air Force. Every cadet is commissioned as a 2nd lieutenant on graduation, and must serve 5 years in the Air Force. Became coed in 1976. 18,000-acre rural campus 8 miles north of Colorado Springs. Air and bus service.
Academic Character NCACS and professional accreditation. Semester system, 3 3-week summer terms for upperclass students, 6-week basic training for new students in June. Majors offered in aeronautical engineering, astronautical engineering, aviation sciences, basic sciences, behavioral sciences, biological sciences, chemistry, civil engineering, computer science, economics, electrical engineering, engineering, engineering mechanics, engineering sciences, geography, history, humanities, international affairs, management, mathematical sciences, operations research, physics, and social sciences. Program emphasizes leadership, academic, military, and athletic training. Distributive requirements. GRE required for graduation. Independent study, honors program, some pass/fail. Exchange programs with French Air Force Academy, other US service academies. Visits with Argentinian, British, and Canadian academies. Aeronautics, instrumentation, radio frequency, research, language labs. Computer center, observatory, planetarium. 2 3,500-foot parallel airstrip runways. 405,000-volume library with microform resources.
Financial Full 4-year government scholarships for all students including tuition, room, board, and medical care. $350 monthly pay for personal needs. $500 uniform deposit required of all first-year students.
Admissions High school graduation required; 15 units recommended. GED accepted. Applicants must be 17-21 years of age on admission, unmarried, US citizens. Interview required. Medical exam and candidate fitness test required. ACT or SAT required. Suggest filing Precandidate Questionnaire in spring of 11th year; deadline December of 12th year. Apply to Member of Congress for nomination by spring of 11th year. Candidate must accept offer by May 1. $500 uniform deposit due upon arrival. *Early Decision* Program. Transfers accepted as freshmen. Credit possible for CEEB AP exams; academy has own advanced placement program.
Student Life Air Force Cadet Wing. Newspaper, literary magazine, yearbook. Choir, drum & bugle corps. Debate. Drama group. Over 70 competitive, recreational, and professional activities; religious, support, and special interest groups. All cadets must live on campus. Coed dorms. Juniors and seniors may have cars. Liquor prohibited on campus. Class attendance required. Cadets may not marry. Honor code, military rules, uniforms required. 8 semesters of phys ed and intercollegiate/intramural sports participation required. 17 intercollegiate and 13 intramural sports. Western Athletic Conference. Student body composition: 3% Asian, 7% Black, 4% Hispanic, 1% Native American, 85% White. Students appointed from all states.

[P] WESTERN BIBLE COLLEGE
16075 West Belleview Avenue, Morrison 80465

[1] WESTERN STATE COLLEGE OF COLORADO
Gunnison 81230, (303) 943-2119
Director of Admissions: Stu Kaplan

- **Enrollment: 1,813m, 1,343w**
- **Tuition (1982/83): $678 (in-state), $2,950 (out-of-state)**
- **Room & Board: $1,792; Fees: $426**
- **Degree offered: BA**
- **Mean ACT 17**
- **Student-faculty ratio: 20 to 1**

A public college established in 1911. 228-acre small-city campus 200 miles southwest of Denver. Air and bus service; rail in Salida.
Academic Character NCACS and professional accreditation. Semester system, 2- and 8-week summer terms. Majors offered in accounting, applied music, art, biology, business administration, chemistry, economics, elementary education, English, French, geology, history, industrial education & technology, mass communications, mathematics, music education, physical education, physics, political science, recreation, sociology, and Spanish. Various emphases offered in several majors. Minors offered in most major fields and in 8 additional areas. Distributive requirements. MA, MBA granted. Independent study, field study, internships. Preprofessional programs in dentistry, environmental science, health fields, medicine, and veterinary medicine. Exchange programs with Adams, Mesa, and Metropolitan State Colleges. Study abroad. Elementary, secondary, and special education certification. 175,000-volume library.
Financial ACT FAS. College scholarships, grants, loans, state grants; PELL, SEOG, NDSL, FISL, GSL, CWS, state & institutional work programs. Application deadlines April 15 (scholarships & grants), June 1 (loans).
Admissions High school graduation with 15 units required. GED accepted. Interview recommended. ACT (preferred) or SAT required. $10 application fee. Rolling admissions; suggest applying early in 12th year. *Early Admission, Early Decision, Concurrent Enrollment* Programs. Admission deferral possible. Transfers accepted. Credit possible for CEEB AP and CLEP exams; college has own advanced placement program.
Student Life Student Senate. Newspaper, literary magazine, yearbook, radio station. Music & drama groups. Debate. Academic, political, religious, honorary, and athletic groups. 4 fraternities, 1 with house; 3 sororities without houses. Coed & single-sex dorms. Married-student housing. 50% of students live on campus. 10 intercollegiate sports for men, 7 for women; intramurals. AIAW, NAIA, Rocky Mountain Athletic Conference. Student body composition: 10% minority. 20% from out of state.

CONNECTICUT *(CT)*

[1] ALBERTUS MAGNUS COLLEGE
700 Prospect Street, New Haven 06511, (203) 777-6631

- **Undergraduates: 1m, 375w; 550 total (including part-time)**
- **Tuition (1982/83): $4,700**
- **Room & Board: $2,900; Fees: $130**
- **Degrees offered: BA, BFA, AA**
- **Mean SAT 450v, 450m**
- **Student-faculty ratio: 11 to 1**

A private Roman Catholic liberal arts college for women founded in 1925 by the Dominican Sisters of St. Mary of the Springs. Urban campus located near Yale University in New Haven. Air, rail, and bus service.
Academic Character NEASC accreditation. Semester system. Majors offered in accounting, art history, art/studio, art therapy, biology, biology/chemistry, business administration, chemistry, child care, community psychology, classics, communications, computer science, criminal justice, drama, economics, English, French, history, humanities, industrial engineering, industrial psychology, international business, Italian, mathematics, physical science, political science, psychology, public administration, secondary education, social gerontology, social welfare, sociology, Spanish, and urban studies. Preprofessional programs in law and medicine. Secondary education certification. 83,000-volume library.
Financial Financial aid available includes scholarships, grants, loans, campus work/study.
Admissions High school graduation with 16 units required. Interview encouraged. SAT required. Rolling admissions. *Early Admission* Program. Admission deferral possible. Transfers accepted. Advanced placement credit possible.

Student Life Student government. Publications. Campus theatre. Glee club. Academic, minority, and special interest groups. Women housed in 8 converted mansions on campus. Intercollegiate competition in cross-country, softball, tennis, and volleyball. Student body composition: 13% minority.

[J1] ASNUNTUCK COMMUNITY COLLEGE

Enfield 06082

[J1] BRIARWOOD COLLEGE

2279 Mount Vernon Road, Southington 06489, (203) 628-4751
Director of Admissions: Virginia P. Murray

- **Undergraduates: 350 men & women**
- **Tuition (1983/84): $3,450**
- **Room & Board: $1,596; Fees: $200**
- **Degree offered: AAS**

A private college composed primarily of women, established in 1966. 32-acre campus in Southington.
Academic Character NEASC and professional accreditation. Semester system. 2-year programs offered in accounting, broadcast secretary, broadcast specialist, business management, dental assistant/office manager, executive medical assistant, executive medical secretary, executive secretary, fashion merchandising-retailing, legal secretary, travel consultant. 1-year diploma programs in 8 additional areas. Double majors. Credit by exam, internships. Medical and dental labs. Travel and radio station work areas.
Financial College and state scholarships, parental loans, state grants; PELL, GSL, college work program. Application deadline April 30 (state funds).
Admissions High school graduation required. Interview encouraged. $20 application fee. Rolling admissions. $185 tuition and $100 room deposits (for boarders) required on acceptance of offer of admission. *Early Admission* Program. Transfers accepted. Credit possible for CLEP exams.
Student Life Student government. Apartment housing. Intramural sports. Limited class absences allowed.

[1] BRIDGEPORT, UNIVERSITY OF

Bridgeport 06602, (203) 576-4552
Director of Admissions: Richard D. Huss

- **Undergraduates: 1,681m, 1,370w; 6,733 total (including part-time/evening)**
- **Tuition (1982/83): $5,760**
- **Room & Board: $3,104; Fees: $183**
- **Degrees offered: BA, BS, BES, BFA, BMus, AA, AS**
- **Mean SAT 449v, 484m**
- **Student-faculty ratio: 13 to 1**

A private university established in 1927. 90-acre urban campus overlooking Long Island Sound, 55 miles from New York City. Served by bus, rail, air.
Academic Character NEASC and professional accreditation. Semester system, 2 5-week summer terms. 24 majors offered by the College of Arts & Humanities, 8 by the College of Business & Public Management, 11 by the College of Health Sciences, and 8 by the College of Science Engineering. Self-designed majors. Distributive requirements. MA, MS, JD granted. Independent study. Honors program. Cooperative work/study, pass/fail, internships. Dual degree programs. Elementary, secondary, and early childhood education certification. ROTC. Continuing Education Program. Computer center, language lab. 325,000-volume library.
Financial CEEB CSS. University scholarships, loans, deferred payment; PELL, SEOG, NSS, NDSL, NSL, CWS, work program at Conn. State. Application deadline April 1.
Admissions High school graduation with 16 units required. GED and State High School Equivalency certificates accepted. Audition required for music, art, theatre majors; recommended for cinema majors. SAT or ACT required. ACH recommended. $25 application fee. Rolling admissions; application deadline August 1. $200 tuition and $200 room deposits required on acceptance of admissions offer. *Early Decision* and *Early Admission* programs. Admission deferral possible. Transfers accepted. Credit possible for CEEB AP and CLEP exams; university exams used for placement. Basic Studies Program for underprepared students.
Student Life Student government. Newspaper, yearbook, magazine, radio station. Music and drama groups. Cultural activities. Service, academic, and special interest organizations. 4 fraternities and 3 sororities without houses. 3% of men and women join. Single freshmen and sophomores under 21, except veterans, must live at home or on campus. Coed and single-sex dorms. Married-student housing off campus. 50% of students live on campus. 8 intercollegiate sports for men, 7 for women; 9 intramurals. AIAW, EAIAW, ECAC, NCAA, New England College Athletic Conference. Student body composition: 1% Asian, 2% Black, 1% Hispanic, 1% Native American, 85% White, 10% Other. 39% from out of state.

[1] BRIDGEPORT ENGINEERING INSTITUTE

5229 Park Avenue, Bridgeport 06606

[1] CENTRAL CONNECTICUT STATE UNIVERSITY

New Britain 06050, (203) 827-7000
Director of Admissions: Johnie M. Floyd

- **Undergraduates: 3,454m, 3,145w; 12,487 total (including part-time)**
- **Tuition (1982/83): $931 (in-state), $1,931 (out-of-state)**
- **Room & Board: $2,156**
- **Degrees offered: BA, BS, BFA, BSN**
- **Mean SAT 403v, 442m**
- **Student-faculty ratio: 17 to 1**

A public college established in 1849. 140-acre suburban campus 9 miles from Hartford. Served by air, rail, bus.
Academic Character NEASC and professional accreditation. Semester system, 3- and 6-week summer terms. 57 majors offered by the schools of Arts & Sciences, Business, Education & Professional Studies, and Technology. Self-designed majors. Minors required for some majors. Concentrations offered in 17 additional areas. Associate degrees possible. Distributive requirements. MA, MS granted. Independent study. Honors program. Cooperative work/study, some pass/fail, internships, credit by exam. Cooperative library science certification program with Southern Conn State College. Cross-registration with other state colleges. International exchange program. Study abroad. Elementary, secondary, and special education certification. ROTC, AFROTC at UConn. Computer center, TV center, observatory, planetarium, language lab. 350,807-volume library with microform resources.
Financial CEEB CSS. University scholarships, grants, loans, state grants; PELL, SEOG, NDSL, GSL, PLUS, CWS, college has own work program. Application deadline March 15.
Admissions High school graduation with 16 units required. SAT required. $10 application fee. Rolling admissions; suggest applying by October 1. $100 deposit required on acceptance of offer of admission; $50 housing deposit due May 1. *Concurrent Enrollment* Program. Transfers accepted. Credit possible for CEEB AP exams and USAFI courses; college has own advanced placement program. EOP.
Student Life Student government. Newspaper, magazines, yearbook, afro-am publication, radio station. Music and drama groups. Religious, political, service, academic, social, and special interest groups. Coed and single-sex dorms. No married-student housing. 26% of students live on campus. 2 semester-hours of phys ed required. 11 intercollegiate sports for men, 8 for women; intramurals. AIAW, ECAC, NCAA, New England Intercollegiate Athletic Conference. Student body composition: 1.4% Asian, 2.4% Black, 1% Foreign, 1.4% Hispanic, 0.3% Native American, 93.5% White. 4% from out of state.

[J1] CONNECTICUT, JUNIOR COLLEGE OF

Bridgeport — see Bridgeport, University of

[1] CONNECTICUT, UNIVERSITY OF

Storrs 06268, (203) 486-3137
Director of Admissions: John W. Vlandis

- **Undergraduates: 8,480m, 7,826w; 21,988 total (including graduates)**
- **Tuition (1982/83): $1,225 (in-state), $4,305 (out-of-state)**
- **Room & Board: $2,245**
- **Degrees offered: BA, BS, BFA, BMus**
- **Student-faculty ratio: 25 to 1**

A public university established in 1881. 2,800-acre rural campus, 30 miles from Hartford. Served by bus. Air and rail in Hartford.
Academic Character NEASC and professional accreditation. Semester system, 2 6-week summer terms. 9 majors offered by the College of Agriculture & Natural Resources, 30 by the College of Liberal Arts & Sciences, 3 by the School of Allied Health Professions, 11 by the School of Business Administration, 12 by the School of Education, 7 by the School of Engineering, 17 by the School of Fine Arts, and 3 by the School of Home Economics & Family Studies; also majors in nursing and pharmacy. MA, MS, MD, DMD, JD, PhD granted. Phi Beta Kappa. 3-2 program in pharmacy. 2-2 program in nursing. Cooperative program with other New England state schools. Study abroad. Elementary, secondary, and early childhood education certification. ROTC, AFROTC. Research Institutes. Branch campuses throughout the state offer first 2 years of most programs. Computer center, language lab. 3,000,000-volume library with microform resources.
Financial CEEB CSS and ACT FAS. University scholarships, grants, loans; PELL, SEOG, NDSL, GSL, NSL, CWS. Scholarship application deadline February 15.
Admissions High school graduation with 16 units required. 10% quota on students from out of state. SAT required. $20 application fee. Rolling admissions; preferred deadlines March 1 (in-state), February 15 (out-of-state). $60 deposit required by May 1. *Early Admission* and *Early Decision* programs. Admission deferral possible. Transfers accepted in some programs. Credit possible for CEEB AP exams; university has own advanced placement program.
Student Life Student government. Newspaper, magazine, yearbook, radio & TV stations. Music, drama, debate groups. Many religious, academic, honorary, professional, service, and special interest groups. Freshmen under 21 must live at home or on campus. No married-student housing. 75% of students live on campus. Resident freshmen and sophomores may not have cars on campus. Many intercollegiate and intramural sports for men and women. AIAW, ECAC, NCAA, Yankee and Big East Conferences. Student body composition: 0.7% Asian, 3.5% Black, 1.1% Hispanic, 0.1% Native American, 94.6% White.

[1] CONNECTICUT COLLEGE

New London 06320, (203) 447-7511
Dean of Admissions: Jeanette B. Hersey

- **Undergraduates: 593m, 1,011w; 1,882 total (including graduates)**
- **Tuition (1982/83): $8,000**
- **Room & Board: $2,600**
- **Degree offered: BA**
- **Mean SAT 550v, 570m**
- **Student-faculty ratio: 12 to 1**

A private college established in 1911, became coed in 1969. 680-acre campus overlooking Long Island Sound, 2 miles from downtown New London, midway

between Boston & New York. Served by air, rail, and bus.
Academic Character NEASC accreditation. Semester system, 6-week summer term. 34 majors offered in the arts & sciences, classics, languages, mathematics, humanities, social sciences, and religion, plus 9 interdisciplinary majors. Self-designed majors. Courses in education. Distributive requirements. MA, MAT, MFA in Dance granted. Independent study. Honors program. Phi Beta Kappa. Pass/fail. Internships. Cross-registration with Trinity, Coast Guard Academy, Wesleyan. Programs with Institute for Architecture & Urban Studies (New York City), National Theatre Institute, and Mystic Seaport. 12-College Exchange. Washington Semester. Study abroad in 10 countries. Elementary, secondary, and special education certification. Computer center, botanic garden, 415-acre arboretum, observatory, language lab, children's school. 352,000-volume library.
Financial CEEB CSS. University scholarships, grants, loans, deferred payment; PELL, SEOG, GSL, NDSL, CWS. File FAF and application by February 15.
Admissions High school graduation with 16 units required. Interview encouraged. SAT or ACT, and 3 ACH required. $30 application fee. Application deadline February 1. $100 deposit required on acceptance of offer of admission. *Early Admission* and *Early Decision* programs. Admission deferral possible. Transfers accepted. Credit possible for CEEB AP exams; college has own advanced placement program.
Student Life Student government. Newspapers, magazine, Journal of Arts & Sciences, yearbook, radio station. Music, dance, drama groups. Religious, service, academic, and special interest groups. Students with parental consent may live off campus. 20 coed dorms including language, special interest, and cooperative housing. 96% of students live on campus. 8 intercollegiate sports for men, 9 for women; intramurals. New England Small College Athletic Conference. 72% from out of state.

[1] EASTERN CONNECTICUT STATE COLLEGE

Willimantic 06226, (203) 456-2331, ext. 286
Director of Admissions & Records: Arthur Forst, Jr.

- **Undergraduates: 1,084m, 1,227w; 3,250 total (including graduates)**
- **Tuition & Fees (1982/83): $738 (in-state), $1,563 (out-of-state)**
- **Room & Board: $2,096-$2,278**
- **Degrees offered: BA, BS, AS**
- **Student-faculty ratio: 15 to 1**

A public college established in 1889. 96-acre suburban campus, 28 miles from Hartford and New London. Served by bus. Air, bus, rail in Hartford.
Academic Character NEASC accreditation. Semester system, 2 4-week summer terms. Majors offered in biology, economics, English, environmental earth science, music, visual arts, history & social science, mathematics, psychology, public policy & government, education, sociology, Spanish, business administration, early childhood, elementary, physical education. Minors offered in all major fields and in 11 additional areas; courses in 3 additional areas. AS offered in general studies, and in athletic coaching, business administration, communications, computer & information science, law enforcement, and physical education. Distributive requirements. MS granted. Independent study. Honors program. Pass/fail. Preprofessional programs in dentistry, law, medicine. Cross-registration at other Conn. state colleges. Library science program at Southern Conn. State. Study abroad. Oceanic Island Ecology in Bermuda. Elementary and secondary education certification. ROTC, AFROTC at UConn. Computer center, media center, planetarium, language lab. 115,000-volume library.
Financial CEEB CSS. College scholarships, grants, loans, fee waivers for veterans, children of veterans, Conn. Tuition Waiver Program; PELL, SEOG, NDSL, CWS. Application deadline April 1.
Admissions High school graduation with 16 units required. SAT required. $10 application fee. Rolling admissions. $50 deposit required on acceptance of offer of admission. *Early Admission* and *Early Decision* programs. Admission deferral possible. Transfers accepted. Credit possible for CEEB AP and CLEP exams; college has own advanced placement program. Contract Admissions Program.
Student Life Student government. Newspaper, magazine, yearbook. Music, drama, outing clubs. Afro-am society. Women's center. Religious, service, academic, and special interest groups. Freshmen must live on campus. Coed dorms. No married-student housing. 50% of students live on campus. Class attendance required. 3 semester-hours of phys ed required. 7 intercollegiate sports for men, 5 for women; several intramural and club sports. AIAW, ECAC, NCAA, New England State Athletic Conference. Student body composition: 1% Asian, 5% Black, 2% Hispanic, 1% Native American, 91% White. 5% from out of state.

[1] FAIRFIELD UNIVERSITY

Fairfield 06430, (203) 255-5411
Dean of Admissions: David M. Flynn

- **Undergraduates: 1,381m, 1,450w; 5,131 total (including graduates)**
- **Tuition (1982/83): $5,025**
- **Room & Board: $2,815; Fees: $120**
- **Degrees offered: BA, BS, BSBA**
- **Mean SAT 517v, 558m**
- **Student-faculty ratio: 16 to 1**

A private Jesuit university established in 1942, became coed in 1970. 200-acre suburban campus 5 miles from Bridgeport, 50 miles from New York City. Served by bus and rail; air in Bridgeport.
Academic Character NEASC and professional accreditation. Semester system, 6-week summer term. Majors offered in American studies, economics, English, fine arts, history, biology, chemistry, mathematics, accounting, finance, management, marketing, modern languages, philosophy, politics, religious studies, sociology, nursing, physics, and psychology. Minors offered in all major fields and in several additional areas, including Latin American and Caribbean studies. Distributive requirements. MA, MS granted. Independent study. Honors program. Internships. Preprofessional programs in accounting, business, dentistry, law, and medicine. 3-2 program in engineering with UConn. Cross-registration with Sacred Heart and University of Bridgeport. Study abroad. Washington Semester. Secondary education, supervisory, administrative, and counseling certification. Computer center, language lab, TV studio. 300,000-volume library with microform resources.
Financial CEEB CSS. University scholarships, grants, loans, deferred payment; PELL, SEOG, NSL, NDSL, FISL, CWS, campus employment. Scholarship application deadline February 1.
Admissions High school graduation with 15 units required. SAT or ACT, and 3 ACH required. $25 application fee. Application deadline March 1. $100 tuition and $100 room deposits required on acceptance of offer of admission. *Early Decision* and *Early Admission* programs. Admission deferral possible. Transfers accepted. Credit possible for CEEB AP and CLEP exams.
Student Life Student government. Newspapers, magazine, yearbook, radio station. Music, debate, drama groups. Religious, political, service, honorary, academic, and special interest groups. Students live off campus when housing is unavailable. Some coed dorms. No married-student housing. 60% of students live on campus. Freshmen may not have cars on campus. Class attendance required for freshmen. 8 intercollegiate sports for men, 4 for women; 15 intramural and club sports. AIAW, NCAA. Student body composition: 2% Black, 1% Hispanic, 97% White. 53% from out of state.

[J1] GREATER HARTFORD COMMUNITY COLLEGE

61 Woodland Street, Hartford 06105

[J2] GREATER NEW HAVEN STATE TECHNICAL COLLEGE

222 Maple Avenue, North Haven 06473

[1] HARTFORD, UNIVERSITY OF

West Hartford 06117, (203) 243-4296
Director of Admissions: Walter M. Bortz, III

- **Undergraduates: 2,232m, 1,782w; 8,563 total (including part-time)**
- **Tuition (1982/83): $6,000**
- **Room & Board: $2,940; Fees: $350**
- **Degrees offered: BA, BS, BFA, BMus, BMus Ed, BSE, AA, AS**
- **Mean SAT 454v, 503m**
- **Student-faculty ratio: 16 to 1**

A private non-sectarian university established in 1877. 200-acre suburban campus in residential section of West Hartford, 4 miles from downtown. Served by air, rail, bus.
Academic Character NEASC and professional accreditation. Semester system, 2 6-week summer terms. 64 majors offered by the colleges of Arts & Sciences, Basic Studies, Business & Public Administration, Education & Allied Services, Engineering, Fine Arts, Music, and Technology. Self-designed majors. AA and AS offered in basic studies, communication, humanities, social sciences, biological sciences, physical sciences. Distributive requirements. Graduate and professional degrees granted. Independent study. Honors program. Cooperative work/study, pass/fail, internships. Preprofessional programs in dentistry, law, medicine, optometry, osteopathy, podiatry. 3-1 program in medical technology. 5-year programs for a BA/MBA, BS/MBA, BMus/MBA, BA/MPA, or BS/MPA. Cooperative program with 6 area schools. Study abroad. Early childhood, elementary, secondary, and special education certification. ROTC at UConn. Computer center, language lab, A-V center, environmental center. 280,000-volume library with microform resources.
Financial CEEB CSS. University scholarships, grants, athletic scholarships, loans, 2nd-family-member discount; PELL, SEOG, NDSL, CWS. Suggest applying as early as possible.
Admissions High school graduation with 16 units required. Portfolio review required for art majors; audition, music theory, and music aptitude tests for music majors. SAT or ACT required. $25 application fee. Rolling admissions; suggest applying early in 12th year, and by February 1 for housing and/or finanical aid. Application deadline June 1. $100 tuition and $100 room deposits required on acceptance of offer of admission. *Early Admission* and *Concurrent Enrollment* programs. Early notification. Admission deferral possible. Transfers accepted. Credit possible for CEEB AP and CLEP exams. College of Basic Studies for underprepared students.
Student Life Student associations. Newspaper, magazines, yearbook, radio station. Music and drama groups. Film series. Over 90 religious, academic, honorary, professional, and special interest groups. 1 fraternity and 3 sororities. 1% of men and women join. Freshmen must live at home or on campus. Coed and single-sex dorms, special interest housing. 47% of students live on campus. 6 intercollegiate sports for men, 6 for women; several intramural and club sports. AIAW, EAIAW, ECAC, NCAA, New England College Athletic Conference. Student body composition: 3% Asian, 5% Black, 2% Hispanic, 1% Native American, 89% White. 63% from out of state.

■[J1] SAMUEL I. WARD TECHNICAL COLLEGE

200 Bloomfield Avenue, West Hartford 06117

[J1] HARTFORD COLLEGE FOR WOMEN

1265 Asylum Avenue, Hartford 06105, (203) 236-1215

- **Undergraduates: 160w; 230 total (including part-time)**
- **Tuition (1982/83): $4,100**
- **Room & Board: $2,600**
- **Degree offered: AA**
- **Mean SAT 470v, 470m**

A private, liberal arts junior college for women founded in 1933. Campus in an urban residential environment. Air, rail, and bus service.

Academic Character NEASC accreditation. Semester system. Associate of Arts degree offered with majors that will transfer to 4-year colleges and universities. Cooperative work/study program provides paid employment and educational job experience. 50,000-volume library.
Financial Aid available including scholarships, loans, self-help, work/study. Application deadline April 1.
Admissions SAT required. ACH strongly recommended. Admissions notification on a rolling basis. Application deadline for those requiring housing and/or financial aid is April 1. *Early Admission* Program. Admission deferral possible. Advanced placement credit possible.
Student Life Dormitory space available for 70 students. Student body composition: 14% minority.

[G1] HARTFORD GRADUATE CENTER
Hartford 06120

[P] HARTFORD INSTITUTE OF ACCOUNTING
PO Box 012217, Hartford 06112

[J1] HARTFORD STATE TECHNICAL COLLEGE
Hartford 06106

[1] HOLY APOSTLES SEMINARY COLLEGE
Cromwell 06416

[J1] HOUSATONIC COMMUNITY COLLEGE
510 Barnum Avenue, Bridgeport 06608

[J1] MANCHESTER COMMUNITY COLLEGE
PO Box 1046, 60 Bidwell, Manchester 06040

[J1] MATTATUCK COMMUNITY COLLEGE
750 Chase Parkway, Waterbury 06708

[J1] MIDDLESEX COMMUNITY COLLEGE
100 Training Hill Road, Middletown 06457

[J1] MITCHELL COLLEGE
437 Pequot Avenue, New London 06320, (203) 443-2811
Director of Admissions: Edward F. O'Neill

- **Undergraduates: 303m, 226w; 914 total (including part-time)**
- **Tuition (1982/83): $5,200**
- **Room & Board: $2,500; Fees: $209**
- **Degrees offered: AA, AS**
- **Mean SAT 384v, 400m**

A private, non-denominational junior college established in 1938. 40-acre campus on west bank of Thames River in a residential section of New London, midway between Boston and New York. Served by air, rail, bus.
Academic Character NEASC accreditation. Semester system. Transfer and terminal programs with majors offered in business administration, science & engineering, liberal studies, public administration, political studies, gerontology, human services, early childhood studies, special education, physical education, recreation, and athletic training. Courses in 11 additional areas. Distributive requirements. Gerontology internships. Pre-engineering science program. Audio-visual center. 50,000-volume library.
Financial CEEB CSS. College grants, loans, state grants and scholarships, athletic grants; PELL, SEOG, GSL, college work program.
Admissions High school graduation required. Interview encouraged. SAT or ACT recommended. $20 application fee. Rolling admissions. *Early Decision* and *Early Admission* programs. Admission deferral possible. College has advanced placement program.
Student Life Student council. Newspaper, yearbook, radio station. Drama, writer's groups. International Students. Model UN. Special interest groups. 86% of students live on campus. 1 course in phys ed required. 3 intercollegiate sports for men, 2 for women, 1 coed; intramurals. NJCAA.

[J1] MOHEGAN COMMUNITY COLLEGE
Mahan Drive, Norwich 06360

[1] NEW HAVEN, UNIVERSITY OF
West Haven 06516, (203) 934-6321
Dean of Admissions & Financial Aid: John Benevento

- **Undergraduates: 1,644m, 1,010w; 7,531 total (including graduates)**
- **Tuition (1982/83): $4,500**
- **Room & Board: $5,100; Fees: $110**
- **Degrees offered: BA, BS, AS**
- **Student-faculty ratio: 17 to 1**

An independent university established in 1920. 56-acre urban campus in West Haven, 3 miles from New Haven. Air, rail, bus in New Haven.
Academic Character NEASC and professional accreditation. Semester system, 2 5-week summer terms. 22 majors offered by the School of Arts & Sciences, 26 by the School of Business Administration, and 6 by the School of Engineering. Division of Evening Studies offers majors in arson investigation, fire science, and occupational safety & health. Minors offered in most major fields and in 11 additional areas. Courses in 5 additional areas. Distributive requirements. Graduate degrees granted. Independent study. Honors program. Cooperative work/study, advanced study, internships. Credit by exam. Preprofessional programs in dentistry, medicine, veterinary medicine. Cross-registration with 4 area colleges. Computer center. 208,333-volume library with microform resources.
Financial CEEB CSS. University scholarships, grants, loans, state grants; PELL, SEOG, NDSL, GSL, CWS. Loan application deadline end of February.
Admissions High school graduation with 15 units required. GED accepted. SAT, ACT, or University Admission Test required. $15 application fee. Rolling admissions; deadline August 15. $50 fee and $100 room deposit (for boarders) required on acceptance of offer of admission. *Early Admission* Program. Admission deferral possible. Transfers accepted. Credit possible for CEEB AP, CLEP, and SAT exams. Conditional acceptance possible.
Student Life Student government. Newspapers, magazine, yearbook, radio station. Drama group. 40 academic, religious, professional, social, and special interest groups. 2 fraternities and 2 sororities without houses. 3% of men and 2% of women join. One coed dorm for 200 students. No married-student housing. 8% of students live on campus. Limited class absences allowed. 2 semesters of phys ed required. 10 intercollegiate sports for men, 6 for women; several intramural and club sports. AIAW, ECAC, NCAA. Student body composition: 13.8% Black, 2.6% Hispanic, 0.1% Native American, 76.5% White, 7% Other. 25% from out of state.

[J1] NORTHWESTERN CONNECTICUT COMMUNITY COLLEGE
Park Place, Winsted 06098

[J1] NORWALK COMMUNITY COLLEGE
333 Wilson Avenue, Norwalk 06854

[J1] NORWALK STATE TECHNICAL COLLEGE
South Norwalk 06854

[1] POST COLLEGE
800 Country Club Road, Waterbury 06708, (203) 755-0121
Dean of Admissions & Records: Erika V. Torres

- **Undergraduates: 203m, 380w**
- **Tuition: $4,000**
- **Room & Board: $2,500**
- **Degrees offered: BS, AS, AA**
- **Student-faculty ratio: 18 to 1**

A private, non-denominational college established in 1890. 65-acre suburban campus 89 miles from New York City. Served by bus and rail.
Academic Character NEASC accreditation. Semester system, 12-week summer term. Majors offered in accounting, management, marketing, marketing with fashion emphasis, office management, and general studies. Self-designed majors. Associate degrees offered in these and in administrative assistant, correspondence secretary, early childhood education, English, executive secretary, fashion merchandising, general business, history, horsemanship, interior design, legal assistant, legal secretary, liberal arts, medical secretary, psychology, sociology, and therapeutic recreation. Courses in additional areas. Distributive requirements. Independent study. Honors program. Phi Beta Kappa. Internships. Nursery school. Center for Learning Alternatives. 25,000-volume library with microform resources.
Financial CEEB CSS and ACT FAS. College scholarships, grants, athletic scholarships, loans, state grants & loans; PELL, SEOG, NDSL, FISL, GSL, CWS. Application deadline April 15.
Admissions High school graduation with 16 units required. GED accepted. Interview required. SAT required. $25 application fee. Rolling admissions; suggest applying by December. $100 tuition and $100 room (for boarders) deposits required on acceptance of offer of admission. *Early Admission* and *Early Decision* programs. Admission deferral possible. Transfers accepted. Credit possible for CLEP exams.
Student Life Student government. Student Activities Council. Campus pub. Yearbook. Black Student Organization. Special interest groups. No coed dorms. No married-student housing. 50% of students live on campus. 4 intercollegiate sports for men, 4 for women; intramurals. NJCAA, Connecticut Small College Conference. Student body composition: 7% Black, 1% Hispanic, 92% White. 20% from out of state.

[J1] QUINEBAUG VALLEY COMMUNITY COLLEGE
Danielson 06239

[1] QUINNIPIAC COLLEGE
Mount Carmel Avenue, Hamden 06518, (203) 288-5251
Director of Admissions: Russell J. Ryan

- **Undergraduates: 843m, 1,493w; 4,267 total (including graduates)**
- **Tuition (1982/83): $4,900**
- **Room & Board: $2,280-$2,750; Fees: $300**
- **Degrees offered: BA, BS, BSHealth Sci, AA, AS**
- **Mean ACT 18; mean SAT 450v, 510m**
- **Student-faculty ratio: 15 to 1**

A private college established in 1929. 126-acre suburban campus 8 miles from New Haven. Served by bus; air and rail in New Haven.
Academic Character NEASC and professional accreditation. Semester system, 2 5-week summer terms. 17 majors offered by the School of Allied Health & Natural Sciences, 18 by the School of Business, 10 by the School of Liberal Arts. 5 interschool majors. Self-designed and double majors. AS offered in accounting, cytotechnology, nuclear medicine technology,

nursing, radiologic technology, radiotherapy technology, music studies, administrative assistant, and data processing. Associate in Music Arts. Distributive requirements. MHS, MPS granted. Independent study. Honors program. Phi Beta Kappa. Pass/fail. Cooperative work/study. Internships, field study, credit for theatre workshops, radio station work. Cross-registration with Albertus Magnus, U New Haven. Computer center. 140,000-volume library with microform resources.
Financial CEEB CSS and ACT FAS. College scholarships, grants, minority tuition waivers, athletic grants, loans, deferred payment; PELL, SEOG, NSL, NDSL, GSL, CWS. Application deadline March 1.
Admissions High school graduation with 16 units required. GED accepted. Applicants must be in top half of class with 2.5 GPA. SAT or ACT required; ACH required for some majors. $15 application fee. Rolling admissions; application deadline June 30 (April 1 for boarders). $100 tuition and $250 room (for boarders) deposits required on acceptance of offer of admission. *Early Admission, Early Decision, Concurrent Enrollment* programs. Admission deferral possible. Transfers accepted. Credit possible for CEEB AP and CLEP exams. Academic Assistance Program.
Student Life Student government. Newspaper, yearbook, radio station. Music and drama groups. Black Student Union. Rathskellar. Religious, honorary, special interest groups. 20% of women join. 10 coed and single-sex dorms. No married-student housing. 56% of students live on campus. 1 semester-hour of phys ed required. 7 intercollegiate sports for men, 3 for women; 11 intramurals. AIAW, EAIAW, NCAA. Student body composition: 3% Black, 96% White, 1% Other. 36% from out of state.

[1] SACRED HEART UNIVERSITY
PO Box 6460, Bridgeport 06606, (203) 371-7999
Director of Admissions: Sharon Brennan Browne

- **Undergraduates: 677m, 1,022w**
- **Tuition (1982/83): $3,400**
- **Fees: $50**
- **Degrees offered: BA, BS, AA, AS**
- **Student-faculty ratio: 20 to 1**

A private university affiliated with the Roman Catholic Church, established in 1963. 69-acre suburban campus 55 miles from New York City. Served by air, bus, and rail.
Academic Character NEASC accreditation. Semester system, 2 5-week summer terms. Majors offered in accounting, art, biology, business administration, chemistry, computer science, criminal justice, economics, education, English, history, legal administration, mathematics, media studies, medical technology, operations research, philosophy, political science, psychology, religious studies, social work, sociology, and Spanish. Self-designed majors. Minors offered in most major fields and in 4 additional areas. 2-year programs in liberal studies, accounting, general business, secretarial science, data processing, and legal assistant. Courses in additional areas including Gaelic, Hungarian, Lithuanian, Slovak, and Ukranian. Distributives and 1 semester of religion required. MAT, MA in RS, MS, MBA granted. Independent study. Honors program. Cooperative work/study, internships. Credit for life/work experience. Study abroad. Elementary and secondary education certification. ROTC at U of Bridgeport. Computer center, Center for Ethnic Studies, art gallery, language lab. 120,000-volume library with microform resources.
Financial CEEB CSS. University scholarships, loans, 2nd-family-member tuition reduction, deferred payment; PELL, SEOG, NDSL, CWS. Scholarship application deadline May 1.
Admissions High school graduation with 16 units recommended. GED accepted. Interview required. SAT required. $15 application fee. Rolling admissions; application deadline May 1. $50 deposit required on acceptance of offer of admission. *Early Admission, Concurrent Enrollment, Early Decision* programs. Admission deferral possible. Transfers accepted. Credit possible for CEEB AP and CLEP exams; university has own advanced placement program. Developmental Studies Program.
Student Life Student government. Newspaper, magazine, yearbook, radio station. Music and drama groups. Religious, academic, service, and special interest organizations. 4 fraternities and 3 sororities. No on-campus housing. 6 intercollegiate sports for men, 4 for women; intramurals. AIAW, EAIAW, ECAC, NCAA. 1% of students from out of state.

[1] ST. ALPHONSUS COLLEGE
Suffield 06078

[1] ST. JOSEPH COLLEGE
West Hartford 06117, (203) 232-4571
Director of Admissions: Anne M. Murphy

- **Undergraduates: 760w; 1,204 total (including graduates)**
- **Tuition (1982/83): $4,500**
- **Room & Board: $2,750; Fees: $70**
- **Degrees offered: BA, BS**
- **Mean SAT 453v, 489m**
- **Student-faculty ratio: 12 to 1**

A private women's college controlled by the Sisters of Mercy, established in 1932. 84-acre suburban campus 3 miles from Hartford. Air, bus, and rail in Hartford.
Academic Character NEASC and professional accreditation. Semester system, 5½-week summer term. 30 majors offered by the departments of biology, chemistry, child study, economics/business administration, education, English/communication, fine arts, foreign languages, history, home economics, mathematics, nursing, performing arts, philosophy, physics, political science, psychology, religious studies, sociology/social work, and special education. Interdisciplinary and self-designed majors. Minors offered in most major fields and in 15 additional areas. Distributives and 6 credits in religious studies required. MA granted. Independent study. Pass/fail. Internships. Preprofessional programs in social work. 3-2 program in engineering with George Washington U. Member Greater Hartford Consortium. Study abroad. Elementary, secondary, and special education certification; art and music certification through Wesleyan. School for exceptional children, language lab. 91,423-volume library with microform resources.
Financial CEEB CSS. College scholarships, grants, loans, College Aid Plan; PELL, SEOG, NSS, GSL, NDSL, FISL, NSL, CWS. Application deadline January 31; interview required before March 15.
Admissions High school graduation with 16 units required. Some programs have additional requirements. Interview required. SAT or ACT required. $15 application fee. Rolling admissions; application deadline May 1. $100 deposit required on acceptance of offer of admission. *Early Admission* and *Early Decision* programs. Admission deferral possible. Transfers accepted. Credit possible for CEEB AP exams. College program for students not meeting admission requirements.
Student Life Student government. Newspaper, magazine, yearbook. Music and drama groups. Religious, service, academic, and special interest groups. 5 dorms. No married-student housing. 50% of students live on campus. 2 semesters of phys ed required. 4 intercollegiate sports; intramural and club sports. AIAW. Student body composition: 1.2% Black, 1.6% Hispanic, 97.2% White. 13% from out of state.

[J1] SOUTH CENTRAL COMMUNITY COLLEGE
60 Sargent Drive, New Haven 06511

[1] SOUTHERN CONNECTICUT STATE COLLEGE
501 Crescent Street, New Haven 06515, (203) 397-4000
Director of Admissions: Robert C. Porter

- **Enrollment: 2,200m, 4,400w; 11,400 total (including evening)**
- **Tuition (1982/83): $903 (in-state), $1,903 (out-of-state)**
- **Room & Board: $2,424**
- **Degrees offered: BA, BS**
- **Mean SAT 905**
- **Student-faculty ratio: 17 to 1**

A public college established in 1893. 200-acre urban campus overlooking New Haven. Served by air, rail, and bus.
Academic Character NEASC and professional accreditation. Semester system, 2 5-week summer terms. 40 majors offered in the areas of arts, sciences, communications, economics, education, languages, social studies, history, library science, nursing, mathematics, physical education, social & political sciences, and special education. Minors offered in most major fields and in 12 additional areas. Courses in 8 additional areas. MA, MS, diplomas in professional education granted. Vocational diploma programs. Independent study. Honors program. Cooperative work/study, pass/fail. Preprofessional programs in dentistry, medicine, social welfare. Study abroad. School librarian, art, health, physical, elementary, secondary and special education certification. Computer center, language lab, planetarium, observatory, closed-circuit TV center. 300,000-volume library with microform resources.
Financial CEEB CSS. College scholarships, grants, state grants, loans, tuition waivers; PELL, SEOG, NSS, NDSL, NSL, CWS, college has own work program. Application deadline April 15.
Admissions High school graduation with 16 units required. State Equivalency Diploma accepted. SAT required. $10 application fee. Application deadline March 1. $50 deposit required on acceptance of offer of admission. Transfers accepted. Credit possible for CEEB AP and CLEP exams; college has own advanced placement program.
Student Life Student government. Newspaper, magazine, yearbook, radio and TV stations. Music, drama, law, environmental groups. Over 100 religious, service, academic, political, and special interest groups. 5 fraternities and 4 sororities. 2 men's and 5 women's dorms. No coed dorms. 25% of students live on campus. Liquor and drugs prohibited on campus. 2 semesters of phys ed required. 11 intercollegiate sports for men, 10 for women. AIAW, ECAC, NCAA. 10% of students from out of state.

[J1] THAMES VALLEY STATE TECHNICAL COLLEGE
Norwich 06360

[1] TRINITY COLLEGE
Hartford 06106, (203) 527-3151
Director of Admissions: Donald Dietrich

- **Undergraduates: 889m, 756w; 2,000 total (including graduates)**
- **Tuition (1982/83): $7,100**
- **Room & Board: $2,850; Fees: $340**
- **Degrees offered: BA, BS**
- **Mean SAT 570v, 610m**
- **Student-faculty ratio: 12 to 1**

A private college established in 1823, became coed in 1969. 90-acre rural campus on hilltop away from Hartford's business center. Served by air, rail, and bus.
Academic Character NEASC accreditation. Semester system, 2 5-week summer terms. 32 majors offered in the areas of American studies, arts, classics, comparative literature, computer, economics, engineering, English, history, intercultural studies, languages, mathematics, music, philosophy, political science, psychology, religion, sociology, sciences, theatre, and urban/environmental studies. Interdisciplinary majors. MA, MLA, MS granted. Independent study. Phi Beta Kappa. Pass/fail. Internships. 3-2 BS/MS in engineering with Hartford Graduate Center. 12-College Exchange. Chinese literature & language at Central Conn State. Williams-Mystic Program in

Maritime Studies. Cooperative program in elementary education with St. Joseph's. Washington Semester. Off-campus study in the US. Study abroad. Language lab. 625,000-volume library.
Financial CEEB CSS. College scholarships, grants, scholarships for students preparing for the ministry, loans, deferred payment; PELL, SEOG, NSS, NDSL, CWS, college has own work program. Application deadline February 1.
Admissions High school graduation with 11 units required. SAT or ACT, and English ACH required. $30 application fee. Application deadline January 1. *Early Decision* and *Early Admission* programs. Admission deferral possible. Transfers accepted. Credit possible for CEEB AP exams.
Student Life Student government. Newspaper, magazine, yearbook, radio station. Music, drama, film, political groups. Religious, service, academic, and special interest groups. 6 coed fraternities with houses, and 2 sororities without houses. Coed dorms. Some married-student housing. 90% of students live on campus. 14 intercollegiate sports for men, 10 for women; intramurals. ECAC, NCAA. Student body composition: 3% Black, 1% Hispanic, 94% White, 2% Other. 75% from out of state.

[J1] TUNXIS COMMUNITY COLLEGE
Farmington 06032

[1] U.S. COAST GUARD ACADEMY
New London 06320, (203) 444-8503
Director of Admissions: Capt. R. T. Getman

- **Undergraduates: 811m, 124w**
- **Tuition (1982/83): full scholarship**
- **Room & Board: full scholarship**
- **Degree offered: BS**
- **Mean SAT 555v, 629m**
- **Student-faculty ratio: 8 to 1**

A public academy established in 1876 to train officers for the Coast Guard. Every cadet must serve 5 years as a commissioned officer following graduation. Became coed in 1976. 100-acre small-city campus on the banks of the Thames River, 50 miles from Hartford. Served by air, rail, and bus.
Academic Character NEASC and professional accreditation. Semester system, 6-week required summer term. Majors offered in civil engineering, electrical engineering, government, management, marine engineering, marine science, mathematical sciences, ocean engineering, and physical science. Courses in 11 additional areas. Independent study. Honors program. Academy Scholars Program. Summer training cruises. Summer programs in aviation orientation, and training in seamanship, navigation, damage control, and fire fighting. 124,000-volume library.
Financial Full 4-year government scholarship for all students. Monthly basic pay of $461. $300 uniform deposit.
Admissions High school graduation with 15 units required. Applicants must be 17-21 years of age on admission, unmarried, US citizens, without parental obligations. Appointments made on basis of nationwide competition. SAT or ACT required. Application deadline December 15. *Early Decision* Program. Transfers not accepted. Placement possible for CEEB AP exams.
Student Life Magazine, yearbook. Music, debate, drama, radio groups. Religious and special interest groups. Coed dorms. All cadets must live on campus. Only first class cadets (seniors) may have cars on campus. 8 semesters of phys ed required. 14 intercollegiate sports for men, 6 for women; women may participate in men's intercollegiates. Intramural and club sports. Intercollegiate or intramural participation required. ECAC, NCAA, NEIAA. Student body composition: 3% Asian, 2% Black, 2% Hispanic, 1% Native American, 92% White. 93% from out of state.

[J1] WATERBURY STATE TECHNICAL COLLEGE
1460 West Main Street, Waterbury 06708

[1] WESLEYAN UNIVERSITY
Middletown 06457, (203) 347-9411
Director of Admissions: Karl M. Furstenberg

- **Undergraduates: 1,345m, 1,207w**
- **Tuition (1982/83): $7,950**
- **Room & Board: $2,990-$3,190; Fees: $420**
- **Degree offered: BA**
- **Mean SAT 630v, 650m**
- **Student-faculty ratio: 11 to 1**

A private, non-sectarian university established in 1831, became coed in 1969. 100-acre small-city campus on the Connecticut River, 17 miles south of Hartford, 20 miles from New Haven. Served by air, rail, and bus.
Academic Character NEASC accreditation. Semester system. 37 majors offered in the areas of English language & composition, ancient & modern languages & literatures, philosophy & religion, arts, history & social sciences, mathematics, and natural sciences, including African, Russian, and East Asian studies and interdepartmental majors. Self-designed majors. Courses in urban and women's studies. Distributive expectations. MA, MALS, PhD granted. Independent study. Honors program. Phi Beta Kappa. Pass/fail. Apprentice program. Internships. Intensive Language Program. 3-2 programs in engineering with Caltech and Columbia. Concurrent BA/MA program. 12-College Exchange. Study abroad. Elementary, secondary, and special education certification. Computer, language lab, observatory. Center for Afro-American Studies. 900,000-volume library.
Financial CEEB CSS. University scholarships, grants, loans; PELL, SEOG, NDSL, FISL, CWS. Application deadline February 1.
Admissions High school graduation required. SAT or ACT, and 3 ACH required. $30 application fee. Application deadline January 15. $100 deposit required on acceptance of offer of admission. *Early Admission, Early Decision*, and *Concurrent Enrollment* programs. Admission deferral possible. Some transfers accepted. Credit possible for CEEB AP exams.
Student Life Newspapers, magazine, yearbook, radio stations. Music, drama, debate groups. Religious, political, social action, service, academic, and special interest groups. 9 fraternities with houses. 10% of men join. Freshmen must live on campus. Coed, single-sex, special interest, and coop housing. 95% of students live on campus. Scholarship students may not have cars on campus. 14 intercollegiate sports for men, 11 for women; extensive intramural program. AIAW, ECAC, NCAA, New England Small College Athletic Conference. Student body composition: 5% Asian, 8% Black, 3% Hispanic, 84% White. 83% from out of state.

[1] WESTERN CONNECTICUT STATE COLLEGE
Danbury 06810, (203) 797-4298
Director of Admissions: Delmore Kinney, Jr.

- **Undergraduates: 1,174m, 1,563w**
- **Tuition & Fees (1982/83): $931 (in-state), $1,931 (out-of-state)**
- **Room & Board: $2,128**
- **Degrees offered: BA, BS, BBA, BMus, AS**
- **Student-faculty ratio: 18 to 1**

A public college established in 1903. 28-acre urban campus, 315-acre west side campus in small city of Danbury, 65 miles from New York City.
Academic Character NEASC and professional accreditation. Semester system, 2 5-week summer terms. 45 majors offered in the areas of arts, sciences, English, political & social science, communication, computer, languages, education, history, library science, mathematics, medical technology, nursing, business, and music. Self-designed majors. AS offered in basic studies, criminal justice, and liberal arts. Minors offered in 7 additional areas. Distributive requirements. MA, MS, MSA granted. Independent study. Honors program. Cooperative work/study, pass/fail, internships. Preprofessional programs in dentistry, medicine, law. New England Regional Student Program. Consortium with Conn State, UConn. Elementary and secondary education certification. ROTC nearby. Computer center, language lab, observatory, TV studio. 170,000-volume library with microform resources.
Financial CEEB CSS. College scholarships, loans, tuition waiver; PELL, SEOG, NDSL, GSL, SSGP, NSL, CWS. Application deadline April 30.
Admissions High school graduation with 16 units required. Interview required for medical technology, nursing; audition required for music. SAT required. $10 application fee. Rolling admissions; application deadline August 15. $50 deposit required after May 1. *Early Admission* and *Early Decision* programs. Admission deferral possible. Transfers accepted. Credit possible for CEEB AP and CLEP exams.
Student Life Student government. Newspaper, magazine, yearbook, radio station. Music, drama, debate groups. Religious, service, academic, and special interest groups. 2 fraternities. Coed and single-sex dorms for 880 students. No married-student housing. 20% of students live on campus. 4 activity courses required. 7 intercollegiate sports for men, 7 for women; several intramural and club sports. AIAW, NCAA, New England Football Conference. Student body composition: 0.2% Asian, 2.7% Black, 1.3% Hispanic, 1.5% Native American, 91.6% White. 13% from out of state.

[1] YALE UNIVERSITY
1502A Yale Station, New Haven 06520, (203) 436-0300
Dean of Admissions: Worth David

- **Undergraduates: 2,958m, 2,170w; 9,558 total (including graduates)**
- **Tuition (1982/83): $8,190**
- **Room & Board: $3,600; Fees: $90**
- **Degrees offered: BA, BS**
- **Mean SAT 670v, 690m**
- **Student-faculty ratio: 7 to 1**

A private university established in 1701, became coed in 1969. 175-acre urban campus in center of New Haven. Served by air, bus, and rail.
Academic Character NEASC and professional accreditation. Semester system. 59 majors offered in the areas of languages & literatures, humanities, social sciences, and natural sciences, engineering, and mathematics. Self-designed majors. Courses in 31 additional areas. Senior general exam required in some fields. Graduate and professional degrees granted. Independent study. Phi Beta Kappa. Pass/fail. Accelerated degree, early concentration program. 5-year BA with junior year in underdeveloped country. Summer Language Institute. Study abroad. Computer center, observatory, accelerators, museums. Art gallery. Over 7.5 million-volume library.
Financial CEEB CSS. University scholarships, loans, Parent Loan Plan, Yale Bursary Program; PELL, SEOG, NDSL, FISL, CWS. Application deadline January 15.
Admissions High school graduation with 16 units recommended. SAT and 3 ACH required. $35 application fee. Application deadline January 2. *Early Action* and *Early Admission* programs. Admission deferral possible. Credit possible for CEEB AP exams.
Student Life Newspaper, magazines, yearbook, radio station. Music, debate, drama, film groups. Religious, service, language, academic, political, and special interest groups. 3 fraternities (2 coed) without houses; less than 5% join. Sophomores and juniors may live off campus with parental consent. Assigned housing in 12 residential colleges which provide dining, social, and athletic facilities. Married-student apartments. 89% of students live on campus. Many intercollegiate, intramural, and club sports for men and women. Ivy League. Student body composition: 6% Asian, 6% Black, 3% Hispanic, 79% White, 6% Other. 90% from out of state.

DELAWARE (DE)

[J1] BRANDYWINE COLLEGE

PO Box 7139, Concord Pike, Wilmington 19803, (302) 478-3000
Director of Admissions: Kenneth J. Oswald

- **Enrollment: 380m, 600w; 900 total (including part-time)**
- **Tuition (1982/83): $3,600**
- **Room & Board: $2,550-$2,880**
- **Degrees offered: AA, AS**
- **Student-faculty ratio: 25 to 1**

A private college established in 1965 and affiliated with Widener University. 40-acre campus 4 miles north of Wilmington. Train service; airport 30 minutes away in Philadelphia.
Academic Character MSACS accreditation. Semester system. 2-year programs offered in business administration (accounting, merchandising, management), general studies, liberal arts, law enforcement administration, restaurant & hotel management, office administration/secretarial science (executive, legal, medical), and travel & tourism. Remedial English program. 42,000-volume library with microform resources.
Financial CEEB CSS. College scholarships, grants, Girard Plan, deferred payment; PELL, SEOG, GSL, NDSL, CWS.
Admissions High school graduation required. Interview encouraged. $25 application fee. Rolling admissions. $100 deposit due on acceptance of admissions offer. *Early Admissions* Program. Admission deferral possible. Advanced placement credit possible.
Student Life Student Senate. Yearbook. National Leadership Conference. Circle K. Professional, recreational, and special interest groups. 3 fraternities and 3 sororities. Coed dorms. Townhouses. Freshmen may not use cars on campus. 4 intercollegiate sports for men, 5 for women; extensive intramurals. NJCAA. Student body composition: 10% minority.

[1] UNIVERSITY OF DELAWARE

Newark 19711, (302) 738-8123
Dean of Admissions: Douglas McConkey

- **Undergraduates: 5,441m, 6,917w; 18,243 total (including graduates)**
- **Tuition & Fees (1982/83): $1,255 (in-state), $3,335 minimum (out-of-state)**
- **Room & Board: $2,354**
- **Degrees offered: BA, BS, BFA, BALS, BBA, BCE, BChE, BME, BEE, BMus, BMus Ed, BSAg, BSEd, BSBus Ed, BSHEd, BSN, BSPEd**
- **Mean SAT 483v, 538m**
- **Student-faculty ratio: 17 to 1**

A public university established in 1743. 1,500-acre suburban campus in the town of Newark, 14 miles from Wilmington. Rail and bus in Wilmington.
Academic Character MSACS and professional accreditation. 4-1-4 system, summer terms. 9 majors offered by the College of Agricultural Sciences, 49 by the College of Arts & Sciences, 3 by the College of Business & Economics, 2 by the College of Education, 4 by the College of Engineering, 12 by the College of Human Resources, 1 by the College of Nursing, 3 by the College of Life & Health Sciences, and 2 by the College of Physical Education, Athletics, & Recreation. Associate, graduate, and professional degress granted. Honors program, Phi Beta Kappa. Preprofessional programs in dentistry, law, marine studies, medicine, theology, and veterinary science. 5-year liberal arts/engineering program. Elementary and secondary education certification. ROTC, AFROTC. Agricultural & experimental farm adjoining campus, experimental substation in Georgetown. Marine studies field station in Lewes. Language lab. 1,750,000-volume library.
Financial CEEB CSS. University scholarships, grants, loans; PELL, SEOG, NDSL, CWS. Application deadline May 1.
Admissions High school graduation with 11-16 units recommended. Specific course requirements for some programs. SAT required. ACH recommended. $25 application fee. Rolling admissions; application deadline March 1. Limited *Early Admission* Program. Admission deferral possible. Transfers accepted. Credit possible for CEEB AP; university has advanced placement program.
Student Life Student government. Newspaper, yearbook, radio station. Music & drama groups. Debate. Athletic, academic, ethnic, honorary, political, religious, service, and special interest groups. 16 fraternities with houses; 6 sororities without houses. 6% of men live in fraternities. Coed dorms. Apartments for single & married students. Special interest & language housing. 57% of students live on campus. Cars usually prohibited for boarders. 11 intercollegiate sports for men, 9 for women; intramurals. Student body composition: 0.4% Asian, 5% Black, 0.4% Hispanic, 0.1% Native American, 94.1% White. 44% from out of state.

[P] DELAWARE LAW SCHOOL

PO Box 7474, Concord Pike, Wilmington 19808

[1] DELAWARE STATE COLLEGE

Dover 19901, (302) 736-4917, 4918
Director of Admissions: Jethro C. Williams

- **Undergraduates: 961m, 1,167w**
- **Tuition (1982/83): $650 (in-state), $1,600 (out-of-state)**
- **Room & Board: $1,850**
- **Degrees offered: BA, BS, BTech**

A public college established in 1891. 400-acre suburban campus 1 mile north of the small city of Dover. Bus service.
Academic Character MCACS accreditation. Semester system, 1 6-week and 2 3-week summer terms. Over 45 majors offered in the areas of agriculture, business administration, education, engineering, home economics, languages & literatures, liberal arts, mathematics, nursing, psychology, recreation, sciences, secretarial science, and social sciences. Courses in 3 additional areas. Black studies program. Honors program. Preprofessional programs in dentistry, law, medicine, nursing, public health, pharmacy, social work, and veterinary science. Elementary, secondary, and special education certification. Computer center. Observatory. Language lab. 140,000-volume library.
Financial CEEB CSS. College scholarships, grants, loans; PELL, SEOG, NSS, NDSL, FISL, CWS. Limited number of Work-Aid assignments. Application deadlines July 15 (scholarships & grants), June 30 (loans).
Admissions High school graduation with 15 units required. GED accepted. ACT or SAT required. $10 application fee. Application deadline June 1. $25 ($50 out-of-state) deposit required on acceptance of admissions offer. *Early Admission* Program. Transfers accepted. Credit possible for CEEB AP exams.
Student Life Student government, Women's Senate, Men's Council. Newspaper, yearbook. Music and drama groups. Debate. Writers Club. Athletic, art, academic, service, and religious groups. 4 fraternities and 4 sororities without houses. 10% of students join. Single-sex dorms. 45% of students live on campus. Narcotics, profanity, liquor prohibited. Class attendance required. Women must have parental approval for overnight or weekend leaves. College must be informed of all marriages. 2 years of phys ed required. 8 intercollegiate sports; recreational sports. NAIA, NCAA, Mid-Eastern Athletic Conference. 33% of students from out of state.

[J1] DELAWARE TECHNICAL AND COMMUNITY COLLEGE

Georgetown 19947

[J1] DELAWARE TECHNICAL AND COMMUNITY COLLEGE

Stanton Campus, Newark 19711

[J1] DELAWARE TECHNICAL AND COMMUNITY COLLEGE

Terry Campus, Dover 19901

[J1] DELAWARE TECHNICAL AND COMMUNITY COLLEGE

Wilmington Campus, 333 Shipley Street, Wilmington 19801

[1] GOLDEY BEACOM COLLEGE

Pike Creek Valley Campus, 4701 Limestone Road, Wilmington 19808, (302) 998-8814
Director of Admissions: Susan E. Zawislak

- **Undergraduates: 229m, 767w**
- **Tuition & Fees (1982/83): $2,700**
- **Room: $1,650 (includes kitchen)**
- **Degrees offered: BS, AS**
- **Mean SAT 419v, 455m**
- **Student-faculty ratio: 22 to 1**

A private college established in 1886. 23-acre suburban campus 10 miles from downtown Wilmington. Air, rail, and bus service.
Academic Character MSACS accreditation. Semester system, summer workshops, optional winter interim. Majors in business administration with options of accounting, automated accounting, business information systems, management, marketing management, office administration, and business teacher education. AS degrees offered in most majors and in business administration, executive secretary, legal secretary, liberal studies/business, and medical secretary. Courses in 11 other areas. Distributive requirements. Certificate programs. Cooperative work/study, experiential credit, internships. Secondary education certification. 12,000 volume library.
Financial CEEB CSS. College scholarships, grants, loans, various state grants & loans; PELL, SEOG, FISL, GSL, NDSL, CWS. Priorty application deadline April 15.
Admissions High school graduation with algebra/geometry required. GED accepted. Interview recommended. CEEB Comparative Guidance & Placement Test (administered by college) required; SAT highly recommended. $20 application fee. Rolling admissions. $50 deposit required on acceptance of admissions offer. *Early Admission* and *Concurrent Enrollment* programs. Admission deferral possible. Transfers accepted. Credit possible for CLEP exams; college has own advanced placement program.
Student Life Student government. Newspaper, yearbook. Black Student Union. Foreign Students Association. Academic, music, religious, and special interest groups. 2 fraternities and 2 sororities without houses. 40% of men and 15% of women join. Coed and apartment-style dorms. No married-student housing. 25% of students live on campus. Class attendance required. 3 recreational league sports for men; 9 intramural sports for men and women. Student body composition: 0.5% Asian, 11% Black, 1% Hispanic, 87% White, 0.5% Other. 40% from out of state.

[1] WESLEY COLLEGE

Dover 19901, (302) 736-2300
Dean of Admissions: Doris M. Freeman

- **Undergraduates: 301m, 343w; 1,400 total (including graduates)**
- **Tuition (1982/83): $4,970**
- **Room & Board: $2,420; Fees: $260**
- **Degrees offered: BSBA, BSEnv Sc, BSMed Tech, BSCIS, AA**
- **Student-faculty ratio: 23 to 1**

A private college affiliated with the United Methodist Church, established in 1873. 16-acre small-town campus 45 miles from Wilmington, 76 miles from Philadelphia. Served by bus.
Academic Character MSACS and professional accreditation. Semester system. Majors offered in accounting, business administration, computer information systems, environmental sciences, and medical technology. AA offered in liberal arts, education, paralegal studies, marketing, science, nursing, engineering, business administration, secretarial, and medical secretarial. Courses offered in 8 areas of Arts & Humanities; 6 areas of Business; 6 areas of Natural Sciences & Mathematics; 7 areas of Social Sciences & Education, and in Nursing. Distributive requirements. Cooperative work/study, internships. Computer center. 45,000-volume library.
Financial CEEB CSS and ACT FAS. PELL, SEOG, NSS, NDSL, NSL, CWS, deferred payment. Application deadline March 15.
Admissions High school graduation with 16 units required. GED accepted. SAT or ACT recommended. $15 application fee. Rolling admissions; suggest applying early in 12th year. $85 deposit required on acceptance of admissions offer. *Early Admission* and *Early Decision* programs. Admission deferral possible. Transfers accepted. Credit possible for CEEB AP and CLEP exams.
Student Life Student government. Newspaper, yearbook, radio station. Music and drama groups. Bible study, fellowships, retreats. Ecological group. Afro-American Cultural Club. Academic, honorary, political, professional and special interest groups. Single students under 20 must live at home or on campus. 4 intercollegiate sports for men, 4 for women; several intramural and club sports. Student body composition: 7.7% Black, 0.1% Hispanic, 0.1% Native American, 92% White.

[1] WILMINGTON COLLEGE
320 DuPont Highway, New Castle 19720, (302) 328-9401

- **Enrollment: 157m, 105w; 786 total (including part-time)**
- **Tuition (1982/83): $3,160**
- **Room: $1,200**
- **Degrees offered: BA, BS, AA, AS**
- **Student-faculty ratio: 20 to 1**

A private, non-sectarian college of liberal arts and business founded in 1965. Suburban campus 6 miles south of Wilmington.
Academic Character MSACS accreditation. Trimester system, 8-week summer term. Programs offered for associate's, bachelor's, and master's degrees. Liberal arts majors include behavioral science, communication arts, criminal justice, early childhood education, and social work. Business administration majors include business management, aviation management, accounting, and advertising production. Remedial math and English programs. Weekend MBA program. Evening division.
Financial Aid available including scholarships based on need and academic standing; PELL, SEOG, GSL, PLUS.
Admissions Admissions notification is done on a rolling basis. *Early Admission* Program. Admission deferral possible. Advanced placement credit possible.
Student Life Off-campus apartments available for men and women. Intercollegiate and recreational sports. Student body composition: 12% minority.

DISTRICT OF COLUMBIA (DC)

[1] AMERICAN UNIVERSITY, THE
Washington 20016, (202) 686-2211
Dean of Admissions & Financial Aid: Rebecca R. Dixon

- **Undergraduates: 2,072m, 2,455w; 12,617 total (including graduates)**
- **Tuition (1982/83): $6,200**
- **Room & Board: $2,564-$3,472; Fees: $174**
- **Degrees offered: BA, BS, BFA, BGS, BMus, BSBA, BSTM, AA, AGS, AJ**
- **Mean SAT 510v, 510m**
- **Student-faculty ratio: 12 to 1**

A private university affiliated with the Methodist Church, established in 1893. 74-acre campus located in a residential section of urban Washington, which is served by air, rail, and bus.
Academic Character MSACS and professional accreditation. Semester system, 5 summer terms. 71 majors offered by the Colleges of Arts & Sciences, Public Affairs, and the Schools of Business Administration and Nursing. Self-designed majors. University also contains the Schools of Education, Government & Public Administration, International Service, Law, Justice, and the Wesley Theological Seminary, Center for Technology & Administration, and Division of Continuing Education. Distributive requirements. Graduate and professional degrees granted. Honors programs. Cooperative work/study, pass/fail, internships. Preprofessional programs in dentistry, law, medicine, secondary education, social work, theology. 3-2 engineering programs. Host for 140-member Washington Semester Program. Elementary, secondary, and special education certification. ROTC, AFROTC. Research centers. Language lab, computer center, radio & TV facilities. 400,000-volume library with microform resources.
Financial CEEB CSS. University scholarships, grants, loans, deferred payment; PELL, SEOG, NDSL, CWS. Application deadline March 1.
Admissions High school graduation with 16 units required. Equivalency diplomas accepted. SAT or ACT required; SAT preferred. English ACH required for placement. $20 application fee. Rolling admissions; deadline February 1. $100 deposit required on acceptance of offer of admission. University early decision and *Early Entrance* programs. Admission deferral possible. Transfers accepted. Credit possible for CEEB AP and CLEP exams. Special admission program for local and adult applicants.
Student Life Student government. Newspapers, literary magazine, yearbook, radio station. Music, drama, debate clubs. Service, professional, academic, religious organizations. 4 fraternities, 3 with houses, and 6 sororities without houses. 5% of undergraduates join. No married-student housing. Living-learning centers. 43% of students live on campus. Many intercollegiate and intramural sports for men and women. AIAW, ECC, EIAC, NAIA. Student body composition: 2% Asian, 10.1% Black, 2.4% Hispanic, 0.1% Native American, 72.8% White, 12.6% Other. 92% from outside the District.

[2] ANDREW JACKSON UNIVERSITY
4600 Connecticut Avenue N.W., Washington 20008

[G1] ANTIOCH SCHOOL OF LAW
Incorporating the Urban Law Institute
2633 16th Street and 1624 Crescent Place, N.W., Washington 20009

- **Enrollment: 450 men & women**
- **Tuition (1982/83): $5,750 for JD; $3,800 for MA**
- **Estimated living expenses: $6,800**
- **Degrees offered: MA in Legal Studies, JD**
- **Student-faculty ratio: 14 to 1**

A private cooperative law school opened in 1972 in the center of Washington. Part of Antioch University, which has campuses in Ohio and elsewhere. Affiliated with the Center for Legal Studies. Air, rail, and bus service.
Academic Character NCACS accreditation. Year-long MA in Legal Studies program is designed to train non-lawyer professionals in essential legal skills. Specialties include equal employment opportunity law, general legal skills program, insurance law, international trade law, labor relations law, telecommunications law. Doctoral preparation programs possible. Special 10-week class program for entering students. Part-time programs, independent study, internships. Comprehensive exams. 3-year JD program. Program includes required daily work/study with teaching law firm or neighborhood legal service. Emphasis on federal (legislative and executive) law. 14-18 month Legal Technician certification program designed for economically and academically disadvantaged and minority students. 54,000-volume library.
Financial Law School Financial Aid Service. College scholarships, part-time employment, and other types of aid available.
Admissions Law School Data Assembly Service. College degree and LSAT required for MLS, JD. High school graduation required for Certified Legal Technician. Writing sample may be required. Transfers accepted to fall session. MA credit for experience possible.
Student Life No dormitories in School of Law; school assists in locating housing. Center for Legal Studies has housing. Substantial enrollment of minority-group members.

[1] BEACON COLLEGE
2706 Ontario Road, N.W., Washington 20006

[2] BENJAMIN FRANKLIN UNIVERSITY
1100 16th Street, N.W., Washington 20036

[1] CATHOLIC UNIVERSITY OF AMERICA
4th Street & Michigan Avenue, N.E., Washington 20064, (202) 635-5305
Director of Admissions & Financial Aid: Robert J. Talbot

- **Undergraduates: 1,264m, 1,334w; 6,777 total (including graduates)**
- **Tuition (1982/83): $5,750**
- **Room & Board: $3,400; Fees: $120**
- **Degrees offered: BA, BS, BMus, BFA, BChE, BCE, BEE, BME**
- **Mean SAT 550v, 550m**
- **Student-faculty ratio: 12 to 1**

A private university established in 1887, affiliated with the Roman Catholic Church. Urban residential campus. Served by air, bus, and rail.
Academic Character MSACS and professional accreditation. Semester system, summer terms. 30 majors offered by the School of Arts & Sciences, 9 by the School of Engineering & Architecture, 6 by the School of Music, and 1 by the School of Nursing. Joint major programs. Distributives and 3-4 religion courses required for graduation. Graduate and professional degrees granted. Independent and accelerated study, honors program, Phi Beta Kappa. Cooperative work/study, pass/fail, internships. Preprofessional programs in business, dentistry, foreign service, law, medicine. Joint degree programs include BA/MA, BA/JD, BA/MSW, BS/MSLS, BSArch/BCE. Study abroad. Elementary, secondary, and special education certification. ROTC at Howard U; AFROTC at Georgetown. 1,000,000-volume library.
Financial CEEB CSS. University scholarships, grants, loans; Catholic scholarships, tuition discounts for simultaneously enrolled siblings. College Aid Plan, PELL, SEOG, NDSL, NSL, GSL, CWS. Application deadline February 1.
Admissions High school graduation with 15 units recommended. Audition required for music majors. SAT or ACT required; SAT preferred. $20 application fee. Rolling admissions; no deadline. $100 deposit required on acceptance of admissions offer (May 1). *Early Entrance* and University early decision programs. Admission deferral possible. Transfers accepted. Credit

possible for CEEB AP, CLEP, and ACH exams. University has own advanced placement program.
Student Life Student government. Newspaper, yearbook, radio station. Music groups. Debate. Academic, honorary, professional, special interest organizations. Partnership Program for minority students. 3 fraternities and 3 sororities without houses. 20% of men and 15% of women join. Coed, single-sex, and quiet dorms. 60% of students live on campus. 9 intercollegiate sports for men, 5 for women; intramurals. Student body composition: 1.3% Asian, 5.5% Black, 1.7% Hispanic, 0.2% Native American, 82.9% White, 8.4% Other. 70% of students from outside the District.

[2] CORCORAN SCHOOL OF ART
17th and New York Avenue, N.W., Washington 20006

[1] DE SALES HALL SCHOOL OF THEOLOGY
721 Lawrence Street, N.E., Washington 20064

[1] DISTRICT OF COLUMBIA, UNIVERSITY OF
Georgia Avenue and Harvard Street, Washington 20009, (202) 727-2270
Director of Admissions: LaHugh Bankston

- **Undergraduates: 2,103m, 1,894w; 13,705 total (including graduates)**
- **Tuition (1982/83): $364 (in-state), $1,614 (out-of-state)**
- **Degrees offered: BA, BS, BBA, BPA, AA, AAS**
- **Student-faculty ratio: 15 to 1**

A public university established in 1978. Campuses in northwest Washington, Mount Vernon Square, and at Connecticut Avenue and Van Ness Street; all reachable by public transportation. Air, rail, and bus service.
Academic Character MSACS and professional accreditation. Semester system, 3 summer terms. 67 majors offered by the Colleges of Business & Public Management, Education & Human Ecology, Liberal & Fine Arts, Life Science, and Physical Science, Engineering, & Technology. Over 25 associate degree programs. Certificate and diploma programs. Graduate and professional degrees granted. Member of the 9-institution Consortium of Universities of the Washington Metropolitan Area; courses and libraries open to all consortium member students. Elementary and special education certification. AFROTC at Howard U. 400,000-volume library.
Financial CEEB CSS and ACT FAS. University scholarships, grants, loans, deferred payment; PELL, SEOG, NSS, NDSL, FISL, NSL, CWS. Application deadline April 15.
Admissions Open admission. High school graduation or GED required. $10 application fee. Rolling admissions; deadline August 1. Informal early decision and *Concurrent Enrollment* programs. Transfers accepted. Credit possible for CEEB AP and CLEP exams.
Student Life Student government. Newspaper, yearbook. Music, art, dance groups. Political, academic, and special interest groups. 4 fraternities and 4 sororities. No university housing. 4 semesters of phys ed required. 7 intercollegiate and 6 intramural sports. Student body composition: 86.3% Black, 1% Hispanic, 1.4% Native American, 2.1% White, 9.2% Other. 10% from outside the District.

[1] DISTRICT OF COLUMBIA, UNIVERSITY OF MOUNT VERNON SQUARE CAMPUS
Washington 20005

[1] DISTRICT OF COLUMBIA, UNIVERSITY OF VAN NESS CAMPUS
929 E Street, N.W., Washington 20005
Formerly Federal City College

[G2] DISTRICT OF COLUMBIA LAW SCHOOL
Washington — see Northern Virginia Law School

[P] EMERSON INSTITUTE
1326 18th Street, N.W., Washington 20036

[2] FEDERAL CITY COLLEGE
Washington — see District of Columbia, University of

[1] GALLAUDET COLLEGE
Washington 20002, (202) 651-5000
Director of Admissions & Records: Jerald M. Jordan

- **Undergraduates: 425m, 520w; 1,436 total (including graduates)**
- **Tuition (1982/83): $984**
- **Room & Board: $2,267; Fees: $291**
- **Degrees offered: BA, BS, AA**
- **Student-faculty ratio: 6 to 1**

A private college established in 1864, it is the only liberal arts college in the world exclusively for the deaf. 92-acre urban campus. Air, rail, and bus service.
Academic Character MSACS and professional accreditation. Semester system, 2 3-week summer terms. Majors offered in American studies, art, biology, business administration, chemistry, computer mathematics, economics, education, English, general science, German, government, history, home economics, mathematics, philosophy, physical education, physics, psychology, romance languages, social work, and theatre arts. Associate degree in interpreting for the deaf. Distributive requirements. MA, MS, MBA, PhD granted. Independent study. Honors program. Pass/fail. Cooperative work/study, internships. Associate member of the 9-institution Consortium of Universities of the Washington Metropolitan Area. Exchange programs with Oberlin and Western Maryland Colleges. Study abroad. International Center on Deafness. Elementary, secondary, and special education certification. Demonstration elementary school and model secondary school for the deaf. TV studio. Computer center. Library of 397,000 print and non-print materials, and an extensive collection of materials on deafness.
Financial CEEB CSS. College scholarships, grants, grants-in-aid, loans; PELL, GSL, NDSL, CWS. Application deadlines April 1 (scholarships & grants) and May 1 (loans).
Admissions High school graduation required; college prep program with algebra recommended. GED accepted. Gallaudet entrance exam and proof of hearing impairment required. SAT or ACT accepted but not required. Application deadline January 1. $50 deposit required with acceptance of admissions offer (May 1). *Early Entrance* and *Early Decision* programs. Admission deferral possible. Transfers accepted. Credit possible for CEEB CLEP subject exams. Preparatory year and tutorial help for students accepted with academic deficiencies.
Student Life Student government. Newspaper, literary magazine, yearbook. Religious, athletic, ethnic, drama, and special interest groups. 3 fraternities and 3 sororities. 20% of men and 15% of women join. No single-sex dorms or married-student housing. 90% of students live on campus. Preparatory (pre-freshman) year students may not have cars. 4 semesters of phys ed required. 11 intercollegiate sports for men, 8 for women; intramurals. AIAW, NCAA. Student body composition: 1% Asian, 10% Black, 3% Hispanic, 1% Native American, 70% White, 15% Other. 96% from outside the District.

[1] GEORGE WASHINGTON UNIVERSITY
Washington 20052, (202) 676-6040
Director of Admissions: Joseph Y. Ruth

- **Undergraduates: 3,294m, 3,101w; 18,698 total (including graduates)**
- **Tuition (1982/83): $4,900 ($5,375 for engineering)**
- **Room & Board: $3,500; Fees: $111**
- **Degrees offered: BA, BS, BMus, BGS, AA, AS**
- **Mean SAT 550v, 550m**
- **Student-faculty ratio: 14 to 1**

A private university established in 1821 by an Act of Congress. 30-acre campus located in the federal section of Washington, close to the White House and Kennedy Center. Air, bus, and rail service.
Academic Character MSACS and professional accreditation. Semester system, 3 summer terms. Over 100 majors offered by the undergraduate divisions: Columbian College of Arts & Sciences, and the schools of Allied Health Science, Education & Human Development, Engineering & Applied Science, Government & Business Administration, and Public & International Affairs. Double, self-designed, and interdisciplinary majors. Distributive requirements. Graduate and professional degrees granted. Independent study, honors program. Phi Beta Kappa. Cooperative work/study in engineering. Internships. Preprofessional programs in law and medicine. 3-2 engineering programs. Member of 9-institution Consortium of Universities of the Washington Metropolitan Area; cross-registration possible. Study abroad. Exchange with American College (Paris). Elementary, secondary, and special education certification. AFROTC, ROTC. Computer center, language lab. 1,126,064-volume library.
Financial CEEB CSS. University scholarships, grants, loans, deferred payment; PELL, SEOG, NDSL, CWS. Application deadline February 1.
Admissions High school graduation with 15 units required. SAT or ACT required; SAT preferred. $20 application fee. Rolling admissions; deadline March 1. $200 tuition and $100 room deposits required on acceptance of offer of admission (May 1). *Early Entrance* Program. Transfers accepted. Credit possible for CEEB AP and CLEP exams, and for University's proficiency exams.
Student Life Student government. Newspaper, literary magazine, yearbook, radio station. Music, drama, dance, debate, and other special interest groups. 11 fraternities with houses, 4 sororities with club rooms. 5% of men and 3% of women join. Some university-owned apartments. 35% of students live in dorms. School of Education has phys ed requirements. 9 intercollegiate sports for men, 9 for women; intramurals. Student body composition: 3.5% Asian, 6.4% Black, 2.5% Hispanic, 0.3% Native American, 76.5% White, 9.8% Other. 95% from outside the District.

[1] GEORGETOWN UNIVERSITY
Washington 20057, (202) 625-3051
Director of Admissions: Charles A. Deacon

- **Undergraduates: 2,479m, 2,765w; 10,867 total (including graduates)**
- **Tuition (1982/83): $6,830**
- **Room & Board: $3,039; Fees: $880**
- **Degrees offered: AB, BS, BBA, BSN, BSFS, BSL**
- **Mean SAT 600v, 600m**
- **Student-faculty ratio: 15 to 1**

A private Roman Catholic university conducted by Jesuits, established in 1789, became coed in 1968. 110-acre campus in residential area of northwest Washington, overlooking the Potomac River and Virginia. Air, bus, and rail service.
Academic Character MSACS and professional accreditation. Semester system, 2 5-week summer terms. 40 majors offered by the College of Arts & Sciences and the schools of Business Administration, Foreign Service, and Languages & Linguistics. Distributives and 2 theology courses required. Graduate and professional degrees granted. Pre-Honors English and liberal arts seminar for selected freshmen. Independent study, honors program. Phi Beta Kappa. Internships. Pass/fail. Preprofessional programs in dentistry, law, medicine. 3-2 physics/engineering program with Catholic U. Member of 9-institution Consortium of Universities of the Washington Metropolitan Area;

cross-registration possible. Junior year and summer school abroad. ROTC; AFROTC at Howard U. Seismological observatory, computer center, language lab. 1,500,000-volume libraries plus access to 240 libraries in the area.
Financial CEEB CSS. University scholarships, grants, deferred payment; PELL, SEOG, NSS, NDSL, FISL, NSL, GSL, CWS. Application deadlines January 31 (scholarships & grants), January 15 (loans).
Admissions High school graduation with 16 units required. Interview strongly recommended. SAT or ACT required, 3 ACH recommended. $30 application fee. Application deadline January 15. $300 deposit required on acceptance of offer of admission (May 1). *Early Decision* and *Early Admission* programs. Admission deferral possible. Transfers accepted. Credit possible for CEEB AP exams.
Student Life Student government. Newspapers, literary magazines, yearbook. Music, drama, debate groups. Honorary, religious, political, special interest, community service organizations. Freshmen must live at home or on campus. Coed dorms. University-owned apartments, special interest housing. 60% of students live on campus. Class attendance required. 13 intercollegiate sports for men, 9 for women; intramurals. Student body compositon: 8% Black, 87% White, 5% Other. 90% from outside the District.

[1] HOWARD UNIVERSITY

2400 Sixth Street, N.W., Washington 20059, (202) 636-6200
Dean of Admissions & Records: William H. Sherrill

- **Undergraduates: 2,467m, 3,180w; 12,338 total (including graduates)**
- **Tuition (1982/83): $2,200**
- **Room & Board: $2,367; Fees: $325**
- **Degrees offered: BA, BS, BArch, BBA, BCP, BFA, BMus, BMus Ed, BSN, BSW, BSE's, BSTh's**
- **Student-faculty ratio: 13 to 1**

A private university established in 1867. 4 campuses: 89-acre main, 22-acre west, 108-acre Beltsville, and Divinity School Campus, in urban Washington. Air, rail, and bus service.
Academic Character MSACS and professional accreditation. Semester system, 2 summer terms. Over 90 majors offered by the Colleges of Allied Health Sciences, Fine Arts, Liberal Arts, Nursing, Pharmacy & Pharmacal Sciences, and the Schools of Architecture & Planning, Business & Public Administration, Communications, Education, Engineering, Human Ecology, Social Work. Minors. Over 65 graduate and professional degrees granted. Independent study, honors program. Phi Beta Kappa. Cooperative work/study, internships. University Without Walls. 3-3 bachelor's/JD and MBA/JD program with School of Law. Coordinated attendance program: courses available at American, Catholic, George Washington, and Georgetown Universities. Domestic exchange program, International Student Exchange Program. Elementary and secondary education certification. AFROTC, ROTC. Language labs, art gallery. 1,242,553-volume library.
Financial CEEB CSS. University scholarships, loans, grants, deferred payment; PELL, SEOG, SSIG, NSS, GSL, NSL, FISL, NDSL, HEAL, CWS. University has own work program. Application deadline April 1.
Admissions High school graduation required. Music majors must audition or submit tape; art majors must submit portfolio. SAT and 3 ACH required. $25 application fee. Rolling admissions; deadline April 1. $75 deposit required on acceptance of offer of admission. College of Liberal Arts has *Early Entrance* Program and may give credit for CEEB AP exams and college-level high school work. Transfers accepted. Center for Academic Reinforcement.
Student Life Student Council. Newspaper, magazines, yearbook, radio station. Music, drama, dance groups. Debate. Service fraternity, honor societies, International Club, special interest organizations. 4 fraternities, 4 sororities; 15% of Liberal Arts students join. University housing limited. 30% of students live on campus. Liquor, hazing prohibited. 4 semesters of phys ed required. 11 intercollegiate sports for men, 3 for women; intramurals. NCAA, Mid-Eastern Athletic Conference. Student body composition: 1% Asian, 79.6% Black, 16.5% Foreign, 0.4% Hispanic, 0.1% Native American, 2.4% White. 66% from outside District.

[1] MOUNT VERNON COLLEGE

2100 Foxhall Road, N.W., Washington 20007, (202) 331-3444
Director of Admissions: Elaine B. Liles

- **Enrollment: 500w**
- **Tuition (1982/83): $4,800**
- **Room & Board: $3,600**
- **Degrees offered: BA, AA**
- **Mean SAT 410v, 416m**

A private liberal arts college for women, founded in 1875. 26-acre campus in residential northwest Washington. Air, rail, and bus service.
Academic Character MSACS and professional accreditation. Trimester system, 2 6-week summer terms. Majors (all interdisciplinary) offered in business administration, communications, human development, interior design, and public affairs & government. Individualized majors. Minors in computer science & information management, and in historic preservation. Distributive requirements. Additional courses in anthropology/sociology, art, art history, arts & humanities, biology, chemistry, childhood education, economics, English, French, history, math, performing arts, philosophy, phys ed, political science, psychology, religion, Spanish. Special studies courses. Independent study, credit by exam, internships. Credit for work/study. Cross-registration with the 8 other member schools in the Consortium of Universities of the Washington Metropolitan Area. Washington Institute of Mount Vernon College offers winter, spring, and summer programs in public policy, business administration, and arts & humanities management. Study abroad.
Financial CEEB CSS. College and state scholarships & grants, deferred payment; PELL, SEOG, GSL, PLUS, CWS. College part-time employment. Application deadline March 1.
Admissions High school graduation with 16 units required. Interview recommended. SAT or ACT required. No application fee. Rolling admissions starting November 1. $100 deposit required on acceptance of offer of admission. *Early Admission, Concurrent Enrollment* programs. Admission deferral possible. Transfers accepted. Credit possible for CEEB AP and CLEP exams, and for life experiences.
Student Life Student government. Social, cultural, and recreational activities. Freshmen must live on campus or at home. About 65% of students live on campus. Intercollegiate tennis, field hockey, and basketball.

[G2] NORTHERN VIRGINIA LAW SCHOOL

PO Box 2532, Washington 20013

[1] OBLATE COLLEGE

391 Michigan Avenue, N.E., Washington 20017

[1 & J1] SOUTHEASTERN UNIVERSITY

501 Eye Street, S.W., Washington 20024, (202) 488-8162
Director of Admissions: John C. Carter

- **Undergraduates: 600m, 400w; 1,700 total (including graduates)**
- **Tuition (1982/83): $3,000**
- **Fees: $105**
- **Degrees offered: BS, BSBA, AS**
- **Student-faculty ratio: 14 to 1**

A private, non-sectarian university established in 1897 in Washington. Air, bus, and rail service.
Academic Character MSACS accreditation. Trimester system. Majors offered in business administration, computer science, economics, information systems management, legal support services, public administration, and small business management. Minors in accounting, finance, mathematics, management/marketing. AS in business administration, computer science, legal support services, small business management. Master's degrees granted. Independent study. Credit by exam. Cooperative work/study. Day, evening, and weekend programs. 20,000-volume library.
Financial CEEB CSS. University scholarships, tuition waivers, loans, state scholarships & grants, tuition assistance for staff dependents, deferred payment; PELL, SEOG, NDSL, FISL, GSL, CWS. FAF deadline is July 1.
Admissions High school graduation with 7 units of English and math required. GED accepted. Interview recommended. SAT required. $25 application fee. Rolling admissions; no deadline. *Early Entrance* Program. Admission deferral possible. Transfers accepted. Credit possible for CEEB CLEP exams, life/work experiences, and some non-collegiate educational programs. Developmental English & mathematics programs.
Student Life Student government. Newspaper, yearbook. Academic, honorary, social, special interest groups. No university housing. Class attendance expected. No sports program. Student body composition: 75% Black, 10% Hispanic, 10% White, 5% Other. 50% of students are foreign.

[1] STRAYER COLLEGE

D.C. campus: 601 Thirteenth Street, N.W., Washington 20005, (202) 783-5180
Virginia campus: 3045 Columbia Pike, Arlington, VA 22204, (703) 892-5100
Director of Admissions: Phillip Ramsey

- **Undergraduates: 634m, 1,139w**
- **Tuition (1982/83): $2,294**
- **Degrees offered: BS, AA**
- **Student-faculty ratio: 25 to 1**

A private college established in 1904. Urban D.C. and Virginia campuses in the metropolitan Washington area. Air, rail, and bus service.
Academic Character MSACS accreditation. Semester system, summer term. Majors offered in accounting, business administration, data processing management, and hospital & health care management. Associate degrees in accounting, business administration, computer programming, court & conference reporting, marketing & retailing, office administration (private, legal, medical), and word processing. Diploma and certificate programs. Liberal arts courses. Distributive requirements. Independent study. Internships, credit by exam, cooperative work/study. 18,000-volume library.
Financial CEEB CSS. College scholarships, loans, deferred payment; PELL, SEOG, GSL, NDSL, FISL, CWS. Application deadline July 1.
Admissions High school graduation required. GED accepted. SAT or ACT and interview recommended. $25 application fee. Rolling admissions; no deadline. *Early Entrance* Program. Admission deferral possible. Transfers accepted. Credit possible for CEEB CLEP exams and previous work experience. College has own advanced placement tests in math and English.
Student Life Student government. Newspaper. Academic clubs. International Club. No college housing. Liquor prohibited on campus. Regular class attendance required. Intercollegiate soccer; intramural soccer & volleyball. Student body composition: 10% Asian, 49% Black, 0.9% Hispanic, 0.1% Native American, 15% White, 25% Other. 20% from outside the District.

[1] TRINITY COLLEGE

Michigan Avenue & Franklin Street, N.E., Washington 20017, (202) 269-2000

- **Enrollment: 594w; 747 total (including part-time)**
- **Tuition (1981/82): $4,050**
- **Room & Board: $2,425**
- **Degrees offered: BA, BS**
- **Mean SAT 500v, 510m**

A private, Roman Catholic, liberal arts college for women founded in 1897, conducted by the Sisters of Notre Dame de Namur. Coed graduate school.

Campus in a suburban area of metropolitan Washington. Air, rail, and bus service.
Academic Character MSACS accreditation. Semester system. 18 majors offered in the areas of languages, history, social sciences, mathematics, natural sciences, music & history of arts, fine arts. Masters degrees granted. Preprofessional program in medicine. Teacher education preparation. 122,000-volume library.
Admissions High school graduation required. SAT required.

[2] WASHINGTON INTERNATIONAL COLLEGE
814 20th Street, N.W., Washington 20006

FLORIDA *(FL)*

[J2] ART INSTITUTE OF FORT LAUDERDALE
3000 East Las Olas Blvd., Fort Lauderdale 33316

[1] BAPTIST BIBLE INSTITUTE
1306 College Drive, Graceville 32440

[1] BARRY UNIVERSITY
11300 N.E. Second Ave., Miami Shores 33161, (305) 758-3392
Dean of Admissions: Debbie Iacono

- **Undergraduates: 447m, 720w; 3,018 total (including graduates)**
- **Tuition (1982/83): $4,400**
- **Room & Board: $2,150-$3,000**
- **Degrees offered: BA, BS, BFA, BM, BSN, BSW**
- **Mean SAT: 458v, 484m**
- **Student-faculty ratio: 14 to 1**

A public university controlled by the Adrian Dominican Sisters, established in 1940, became coed in 1975. 87-acre suburban campus located in village of Miami Shores, 10 miles north of Miami. Served by air, rail, bus.
Academic Character SACS and professional accreditation. Semester system, 6-week summer term and numerous summer workshops. 24 majors offered by School of Arts and Sciences, 5 by the School of Business, 4 by the School of Education, 1 by the School of Nursing, 1 by the School of Social Work, 3 by the School of Adult & Continuing Education. Minors in all major fields and in 5 additional areas. Courses in 8 other areas. Distribution requirements; 9 credits in religious studies and/or philosophy required. MA, MBA, MS, MSW granted. Independent study. Honors programs in some areas. Pass/fail, internships, credit by exam. 3-1 program in medical technology. Exchange program with 4 Catholic colleges. Consortium with Embry-Riddle Aeronautical. 4-year nursing program with 5 area hospitals. Legal Assistants Program. Study abroad in Europe. Elementary, secondary, and early childhood education certification. ROTC, AFROTC at University of Miami. Language lab. Over 125,000-volume library.
Financial CEEB CSS. University scholarships, grants, and loans, possible tuition reduction for 2nd family member, PELL, SEOG, FSAG, NSL NDSL, GSL, CWS, Florida Tuition Voucher Fund, Florida Academic Scholar's Fund. Application deadline April 1.
Admissions High school graduation with 16 units required. Interview optional. Audition required for music majors. SAT or ACT required. $20 application fee. Rolling admissions; suggest applying by April. $100 deposit required within 10 days of registration. *Early Admission* and *Early Decision* programs. Transfers accepted. Admission deferral possible. Credit possible for CEEB AP and CLEP exams.
Student Life Student government. Newspaper, yearbook. Music and drama groups. Black Students for Progress. Federation of Cuban Students. International Students Association. Departmental, honorary, recreational, religious, service, and special interest groups. Fraternities and sororities. Single-sex dorms. Married students may not live on campus. 25% of students live on campus. Intercollegiate and intramural softball and volleyball, 14 other sports in athletic program. Student body composition: 1% Asian, 5% Black, 17% Hispanic, 72% White, 5% Other. 22% from out of state.

[J2] BAUDER FASHION COLLEGE
100 Southeast Fourth Street, Miami 33131

[1] BETHUNE-COOKMAN COLLEGE
640 2nd Avenue, Daytona Beach 32015, (904) 255-1401
Director of Admissions: James C. Wymes, Sr.

- **Undergraduates: 676m, 960w; 1,636 total**
- **Tuition (1982/83): $3,162**
- **Room & Board: $2,096**
- **Degrees offered: BA, BS, BBA**
- **SAT: 321v, 344m**
- **Student-faculty ratio: 18 to 1**

A private college affiliated with the United Methodist Church, established in 1904. Became coed in 1923. 58-acre urban campus located in small city, 60 miles from Orlando. Served by air and bus; train in Deland.
Academic Character SACS accreditation. Semester system, 8-week summer term. Majors offered in arts, business, education, engineering, nursing, physical education, science. Minors offered in 10 additional areas, including criminal justice and police science. Distributive requirements; 2 semesters of religion required. Independent study. Honors program. Cooperative work/study. Internships. Dual degree in engineering offered with U of Florida and Tuskegee. Preprofessional programs in dentistry, medicine, engineering, law, optometry, pharmacy. Elementary and secondary education certification. ROTC, AFROTC at Embry-Riddle. 106,530-volume library.
Financial CEEB CSS and ACT FAS. College scholarships, grants, and loans, PELL, SEOG, NDSL, NSL, FISL, CWS. Application deadline March 1.
Admissions High school graduation with 15 units required. GED accepted. SAT or ACT required. $15 application fee. Application deadline June 1. Rolling admissions. $50 room deposit required on acceptance of offer of admission. *Early Admission* and *Early Decision* programs. Transfers accepted. Admission deferral possible. Credit possible for CEEB AP and CLEP exams.
Student Life Student government. Newspaper, yearbook. Music and drama groups. 4 fraternities and 4 sororities without houses. 2% of men and 5% of women join. Freshmen must live at home or on campus. No married-student housing. 68% of students live on campus. 2 semesters physical education required. 3 intercollegiate sports for men, 1 for women. MEAC. Student body composition: 1% Asian, 98% Black, 1% White. 11% from out of state.

[1] BISCAYNE COLLEGE
16400 Northwest 32nd Avenue, Miami 33054, (305) 625-6000
Director of Admissions: James Parker

- **Undergraduates: 1,340m, 1,420w**
- **Tuition (1982/83): $3,300**
- **Room & Board: $2,700; Fees: $150**
- **Degree offered: BA**
- **Mean SAT 435v, 450m**
- **Student-faculty ratio: 17 to 1**

A private college controlled by the Augustinian Fathers of Villanova, established in 1961, became coed in 1975. 130-acre suburban campus in large city. Served by air, rail, and bus.
Academic Character SACS accreditation. Semester system, 2 5-week summer terms. 4 majors offered in humanities, 3 in physical sciences and math, 7 in social sciences, 4 in business and economics and in religious studies, education, health management, public service, transportation/travel/tourism. Minors in some major fields. Distributive requirements; 9 hours of religious studies required. Independent and accelerated study. Honors program. Cooperative work/study, internships. Preprofessional programs in dentistry, law, medicine, veterinary medicine. Cross-registration with Barry. Elementary, secondary, and special education certification. ROTC at Miami-Dade North; AFROTC at University of Miami. 220,000-volume library with microform resources.
Financial CEEB CSS and ACT FAS. College scholarships, grants, and loans; PELL, SEOG, NDSL, FISL, CWS, deferred payment plan. No application deadline.
Admissions High school graduation with 16 units required. ACT or SAT required; English and math ACH recommended. $20 application fee. Rolling admissions; suggest applying by February 1. $100 tuition deposit and $200 room deposit required on acceptance of offer of admission. Credit possible for CEEB AP and CLEP exams, for life/work experience and for departmental proficiency exams.
Student Life Student government, student court. Newspaper, literary magazine, yearbook. Music and drama groups. Athletic, departmental, honorary, political, service, and special interest groups. Social activities with Barry University. 25% of students live on campus. Liquor prohibited for students under 19. Juniors and seniors with 3.0 GPA have privilege of not attending class. 7 intercollegiate and intramural sports. NCAA. Student body composition: 10% Black, 25% Hispanic, 65% White. 30% from out of state.

[1] BOCA RATON, COLLEGE OF
Boca Raton 33431, (305) 994-0770

- **Enrollment: 600**
- **Tuition (1982/83): $4,400**
- **Room & Board: $2,000**
- **Degrees offered: AA, AS**

A private college affiliated with the Roman Catholic Church, established in 1963. 123-acre suburban campus, 20 miles south of Palm Beach. Airport in Boca Raton.
Academic Character SACS accreditation. Semester system. 4-year programs offered in business administration, commercial art, communications, early childhood education, electronics, fashion merchandising, fine arts, hotel management, liberal arts, mortuary science, office systems, and theatre arts. Distributive requirements. Independent study. Learning resources center.
Financial CEEB CSS. State grants and loans, SEOG, NDSL, GSL, Tuition Plan, College Aid Plan, CWS. Preferred application deadline February 15.
Admissions High school graduation required. GED accepted. SAT or ACT required; SAT preferred. $20 application fee. Rolling admissions. *Early Admission* Program. Transfers accepted. Admission deferral possible. Credit possible for CEEB AP and CLEP exams.
Student Life Student government. Newspaper, yearbook. Music and drama groups. Cultural activities. Athletic and social events. Single-sex dorms. Liquor, drugs, firearms, fireworks prohibited. Attendance in class expected. 3 intercollegiate sports for men, 3 for women; intramurals. Student body composition: 10% minority.

[J1] BREVARD COMMUNITY COLLEGE
1519 Clearlake Road, Cocoa 32922

[J1] BROWARD COMMUNITY COLLEGE
225 East Las Olas Blvd., Fort Lauderdale 33301

[1] UNIVERSITY OF CENTRAL FLORIDA
Orlando 32816, (305) 275-2511
Director of Admissions: Ralph Boston

- **Undergraduates: 6,168m, 5,607w, 13,097 total (includes graduates)**
- **Tuition (1982/83): $750 (in-state), $1,980 (out-of-state)**
- **Room & Board: $2,408; Fees: $36**
- **Degrees offered: BA, BS, BFA, BEngTech, BSBA, BSE, BA or BS in General Studies**
- **Mean ACT 20.7 composite; mean SAT 450v, 504m**
- **Student-faculty ratio: 26 to 1**

A public university established in 1963. 1,227-acre campus 13 miles east of downtown Orlando. Served by air, rail, and bus.

Academic Character SACS and professional accreditation. Semester system, 2 6-week summer terms. 38 majors offered in arts and sciences, 6 in business administration, 12 in education, 11 in engineering, 6 in health; general studies program. Graduate degrees granted. Independent and accelerated study. Cooperative work/study, internships. Preprofessional programs in dentistry, medicine, optometry, pharmacy, podiatry, veterinary medicine. Environmental studies program required in all colleges. 3-1 programs may be arranged. Elementary and secondary education certification. ROTC, AFROTC. Media center. Language lab. 513,948-volume library with microform resources.

Financial CEEB CSS and ACT FAS. University scholarships, grants, loans; PELL, SEOG, FSAG, GAP, GSL, NDSL, FISL, CWS. Application deadline April 1.

Admissions High school graduation with 12 units required. GED accepted. SAT or ACT required. $15 application fee. Rolling admissions; fall application deadline June 14. *Early Admission* Program. Transfers accepted. Admission deferral possible. Credit possible for CEEB AP and CLEP exams; university has own advanced placement program.

Student Life Student government. Newspaper, literary magazine, yearbook, TV station. Music and drama groups. Debates. Chess club. Athletic, departmental, academic groups. 11 fraternities, 6 sororities. Cluster housing. Single-sex dorms. 6% of students live on campus. 5 intercollegiate sports for men, 4 for women; extensive intramural program. AIAW, NCAA. Student body composition: 1% Asian, 4% Black, 3% Hispanic, 89% White, 3% Other. 10% from out of state.

[2] CENTRAL FLORIDA BIBLE COLLEGE
PO Box 8023A, Orlando 32856

[J1] CENTRAL FLORIDA COMMUNITY COLLEGE
Ocala 32678

[J2] CHARRON-WILLIAMS COLLEGE
255 S.W. 8th Street, Miami 33130

[J1] CHIPOLA JUNIOR COLLEGE
Marianna 32446

[2] CLEARWATER CHRISTIAN COLLEGE
3400 Gulf to Bay, Clearwater 33519

[J1] DAYTONA BEACH COMMUNITY COLLEGE
Daytona Beach 32015

[1] ECKERD COLLEGE
PO Box 12560, St. Petersburg 33733, (813) 867-1166
Director of Admissions and Records: Richard R. Hallin, PhD

- **Undergraduates: 543m, 531w**
- **Tuition (1982/83): $5,495**
- **Room & Board: $2,465; Fees: $100**
- **Degrees offered: BA, BS**
- **Mean ACT 21.3 composite, Mean SAT 500v, 510m**
- **Student-faculty ratio: 14 to 1**

A private college affiliated with the Presbyterian Church, established in 1958. 281-acre subtropical suburban campus on Boca Ciega Bay. Air, rail, and bus in St. Petersburg.

Academic Character SACS accreditation. 4-1-4 calendar, 2 4-week summer modules. 31 majors offered in humanities, science, business, education. College organized by interdisciplinary subject groupings(collegia): Behavioral Science, Comparative Cultures, Creative Arts, Letters, Natural Sciences. 3-week freshman autumn term and first year make up Foundation Collegium, studying Western Heritage. 4 courses required of sophomores and juniors in areas of aesthetic, cross-cultural, environmental, and social relations perspective. Judeo-Christian Perspective course required of seniors plus senior seminar, thesis or comprehensive exam. Self-designed majors. Independent and accelerated study. Credit/no credit, internships. Women's Studies program. Preprofessional programs in many fields. 3-2 engineering program with Washington University, Auburn, Columbia, Georgia Tech. Extensive study abroad. Elementary, secondary, and early childhood education certification. ROTC. Primate lab. Language lab. 170,000-volume library.

Financial CEEB CSS. College scholarships, grants, loans; PELL, SEOG, GSL, NDSL, state grants and vouchers, installment and deferred payment plans. Application deadline April 1 for scholarships, none for loans.

Admissions High school graduation with 13 units recommended. GED accepted. Interview highly recommended. SAT or ACT required. $15 application fee. Rolling admissions; suggest applying by December. $100 deposit required on acceptance of admission. *Early Admission* and *Early Decision* programs. Transfers accepted. One-year admission deferral possible. Credit possible for CEEB AP and CLEP exams.

Student Life Association of Students. Newspaper, literary magazine, yearbook, radio station. Music and drama groups. Afro-American Society. Waterfront program: over 50 boats. Honorary and special interest groups. Students under 23 must live at home or on campus. Self-governing residential houses for 34-36 students. Coed and single-sex dorms. 85% of students live on campus. 8 intercollegiate sports for men, 8 for women; extensive intramural program. AIAW, NCAA, Sunshine State Conference. Student body composition: 1% Asian, 5% Black, 3% Hispanic, 84% White, 7% Other. 65% from out of state.

[J1] EDISON COMMUNITY COLLEGE
Fort Myers 33907

[J1] EDWARD WATERS COLLEGE
Jacksonville 32209

[1] EMBRY-RIDDLE AERONAUTICAL UNIVERSITY
Star Route, Box 540, Bunnell 32010, (904) 673-3180
Dean of Admissions: Peter Brooker

- **Undergraduates: 6,103m, 437w; 8,449 total (including graduates)**
- **Tuition (1982/83): $2,900**
- **Room & Board: $929-$1,088**
- **Degrees offered: BS, BProfAero**
- **Mean ACT 22 composite; mean SAT 905**
- **Student-faculty ratio: 30 to 1**

A private university established in 1926. 86-acre campus located at Daytona Beach Regional Airport; (see also Embry-Riddle, Prescott, AR). International campus: centers near airports in 80 U.S. and European areas.

Academic Character SACS and professional accreditation. Trimester system, 2 8-week summer terms. 11 majors offered in aeronautical engineering, science, studies; general and professional aeronautics; aviation administration, computer science, maintenance management, management, and technology. Areas of Concentration in all major fields and in 11 additional areas. Courses in humanities, social & physical sciences. Distributive requirements; Basic Skills Test required. MAS, MAM, MBA/A granted. Independent study. Cooperative work/study, internships. Non-degree programs. FAA exam preparation. Two degrees possible. 80 campuses at military bases abroad. Cross-registration with Barry. SOC. ROTC, AFROTC; NROTC at Pensacola, PLCP Marine Corps at Quantico. Late model, fully-equipped aircraft, "Gemini Flight" concept, training simulators. Computer center. 52,000-volume library.

Financial CSS FAF. University scholarships, grants, loans, tuition waivers; PELL, SEOG, NDSL, GSL, CWS; university has own work program. Early application recommended.

Admissions Open admissions. GED accepted. Interview required of handicapped students. E-RAU Medical Report, FAA Medical Certificate (Class I or II) required. SAT or ACT required. $25 application fee. Rolling admissions; apply at least 60 days before enrollment date. $150 tuition deposit and $95 room deposit required on acceptance of offer of admission, refundable 60 days before enrollment date. *Early Admission* Program. Transfers accepted. Credit possible for CEEB AP and CLEP exams, and for military, aeronautical, and professional experience.

Student Life Student government. Student representation on University Board of Trustees. Newspaper, yearbook. Professional, honorary, athletic, religious, and special interest groups. Several fraternities without houses. On-campus housing limited. Some coed dorms. 25% of students live on campus. Class attendance expected. Dorm regulations enforced. 8 intramural sports. Student body composition: 1.2% Asian, 3.2% Black, 1.1% Hispanic, 0.4% Native American, 89.4% White.

[J2] FASHION INSTITUTE OF FORT LAUDERDALE
3000 East Las Olas Blvd., Fort Lauderdale 33316

[1] FLAGLER COLLEGE
St. Augustine 32084, (904) 829-6481
Director of Admissions: William T. Abare, Jr.

- **Undergraduates: 315m, 488w**
- **Tuition (1982/83): $2,700**
- **Room & Board: $1,700**
- **Degree offered: BA**
- **Mean ACT: 18.1 composite; SAT: 430v, 454m**
- **Student-faculty ratio: 20 to 1**

A private college established in 1968, became coed in 1971. 29-acre campus located in historic town. Served by bus; airport and train 30 miles away in Jacksonville.

Academic Character SACS accreditation. Semester system, 1 3-week, 2 5-week summer terms. Majors offered in art, business administration, education, humanities, social sciences, physical education. Self-designed majors. Minors offered in most major fields and in 9 additional areas. Distributive requirements. Independent study. Internships. Preprofessional programs in business, education, human services, journalism, law, youth ministries. Study in Mexico. Elementary, secondary, and special education certification. ROTC. 61,000-volume library.

Financial CEEB CSS and ACT FAS. College scholarships, grants, loans,

deferred payment plan. PELL, SEOG, NDSL, FISL, CWS. Application deadline April 1.
Admissions High school graduation with 16 units required. GED accepted. Interview recommended. SAT or ACT required. $15 application fee. Rolling admissions; suggest applying by April 1. $100 tuition and $100 room deposits required on acceptance of offer of admission. *Early Admission* Program. Transfers accepted. Admission deferral possible. Credit possible for CEEB AP and CLEP exams.
Student Life Student government. Newspaper, literary magazine, yearbook. Extensive drama program. Academic, honorary, and service groups. Freshmen must live on campus. Limited dorm space; students urged to submit forms and payment before April 1. Single-sex dorms. No married-student housing. 56% of students live on campus. Liquor prohibited on campus. No interdorm visitation. Attendance in class regulated. 6 intercollegiate sports for men, 4 for women; 8 intramural sports. AIAW, NAIA. Student body composition: 4% Black, 93% White, 3% Other. 58% from out of state.

[1] FLORIDA, UNIVERSITY OF
Gainesville 32611, (904) 392-1365
Director of Admissions: James B. Parrish

- **Undergraduates: 15,680m, 11,987w; 33,056 total**
- **Tuition (1982/83): $750 (in-state), $1,980 (out-of-state)**
- **Room & Board: $2,186-$2,480**
- **Degrees offered: BA, BS, BDesign, BLA, BFA, BMus, BSN, many baccaulaureate education and engineering degrees**
- **Mean SAT: 507v, 561m**
- **Student-faculty ratio: 12 to 1**

A public university established in 1853. 1,800-acre suburban campus, served by air, rail, and bus.
Academic Character SACS and professional accreditation. Semester system, 2 5-week summer terms. 15 majors offered by the College of Agriculture, 3 by the College of Architecture, 7 by the College of Business Administration, 19 by the College of Education, 15 by the College of Engineering, 13 by the College of Fine Arts, 4 by the School of Forest Resources & Conservation, 5 by the College of Health Related Professions, 5 by the College of Journalism & Communications, 31 by the College of Liberal Arts & Sciences, 3 by the College of Physical Education, and 1 each by the School of Accounting, Center for Latin American Studies, College of Medicine, College of Nursing, and College of Pharmacy. Self-designed majors. Distributive requirements. Graduate degrees granted. Accelerated study. Honors programs. Phi Beta Kappa. Cooperative work/study, pass/fail, internships. Several preprofessional programs. Study abroad. Elementary, secondary, and special education certification. ROTC, AFROTC, NROTC. Computer center, language labs. Art gallery, museum. Broadcast facility. 2,600,000-volume library with microform resources.
Financial CEEB CSS. University scholarships, grants, loans; NSL, PELL, NDSL, GSL, deferred payment plan, CWS. Application deadline March 1.
Admissions High school graduation with 12-14 units required. SAT or ACT required. $15 application fee. Rolling admissions. Room deposit due when accept admissions offer. *Early Decision, Early Admission* programs. Transfers accepted. Credit possible for CEEB AP and CLEP exams.
Student Life Student government. Newspaper, radio and TV stations. Music, theatre, debate groups. Over 150 organizations. 30 fraternities, 20 sororities, most with houses; 20% join. Married-student housing. 27% of students live on campus. 8 intercollegiate sports for men, 7 for women; extensive intramurals. NCAA, SAC, AIAW. Student body composition: 0.8% Asian, 5.6% Black, 4.1% Hispanic, 0.1% Native American, 89.4% White. 10% from out of state.

[1] FLORIDA AGRICULTURAL AND MECHANICAL UNIVERSITY
Tallahassee 32307, (904) 599-3000
Director of Admissions: Samuel Washington, Jr.

- **Undergraduates: 2,077m, 2,047w**
- **Tuition (1982/83): $864 (in-state), $2,464 (out-of-state)**
- **Room & Board: $1,800**
- **Degrees offered: BA, BS, BTech, AA, AS**
- **Mean ACT 17 composite; mean SAT 840**
- **Student-faculty ratio: 30 to 1**

A public university established in 1887. 490-acre campus located in large city. Served by air and bus.
Academic Character SACS and professional accreditation. Semester system, 1 4-week and 1 8-week summer term. 50 majors offered by Colleges of Education, Humanities & Social Sciences, Science & Technology and by the Schools of Architecture, Business & Industry, Nursing, Pharmacy. Distributive requirements. Graduate degrees granted. Interdisciplinary studies program. Accelerated study. Honors program. Cooperative work/study, internships. Preprofessional programs in architecture, engineering, health. Elementary, secondary, and special education certification. ROTC, NROTC; AFROTC at Florida State. Computer center. TV studio. Black Archives. Research Center and Museum. 380,000-volume library with microform resources.
Financial CEEB CSS and ACT FAS. University scholarships, grants, loans, health profession loans. PELL, SEOG, NDSL, NSL, FISL, CWS, IWS, GWS. Application deadline April 1.
Admissions High school graduation with 16 units required. GED accepted. ACT or SAT required. $15 application fee. Rolling admissions; suggest applying 6 months before entrance. *Early Admission* and *Concurrent Enrollment* programs. Transfers accepted. Admission deferral possible. Credit possible for CEEB AP and CLEP exams, and for ACT PEP scores.
Student Life Student government. Newspaper, literary guild, yearbook, radio station. Music and drama groups. Political, service, religious, departmental, ethnic, and special interest groups. 5 fraternities and 5 sororities. 10% of men and 15% of women join. Single-sex dorms. Married-student housing. 40% of students live on campus. Liquor prohibited. Class attendance required. 3 terms phys ed required. 7 intercollegiate sports for men, 6 for women; intramural program. Student body composition: 85% Black, 1% Hispanic, 10% White, 4% Other. 15% from out of state.

[1] FLORIDA ATLANTIC UNIVERSITY
Boca Raton 33431, (305) 393-3000
Director of Admissions: D. Blair Thorburn

- **Total Enrollment: 8,300 (including graduates)**
- **Tuition (1982/83): $28 per credit hour (in-state), $91 (out-of-state)**
- **Room: $945**
- **Degrees offered: BA, BS, BBA, BFA, BHS, BPA, BSN, BSE's**
- **Student-faculty ratio: 20 to 1**

A public university established in 1961. Small-city campus. Served by air.
Academic Character SACS accreditation. Semester system, 8-, 10-, and 12-week summer terms. 86 majors offered by the Colleges of Business Administration, Education, Engineering, Humanities, and Science & Social Science. All courses are junior, senior, and graduate level. Independent study. Cooperative work/study, limited pass/fail. Preprofessional programs in dentistry, medicine, optometry, veterinary medicine. Early childhood, elementary, secondary, and special education certification. ROTC. University lab school. Environmental science center. Fish Research Lab. 1,000,000-volume library with microform resources.
Financial CEEB CSS. University scholarships, PELL, SEOG, FSAG, FASF, NDSL, FIGSL, CWS. Priority application deadline April 1.
Admissions AA degree or 60 semester hours of approved college or university work with 36 hours general education required. SAT or ACT scores required for education students. $15 application fee. Rolling admissions. *Early Decision* and *Early Admission* programs. Admission deferral possible. Credit possible for CLEP exams.
Student Life Student government. Newspaper. Academic, cultural, honorary, religious, service, social, and special interest groups. No married-student housing. Various meal plans available. 6 intercollegiate sports for men, 5 for women; intramurals. AIAW, NAIA.

[2] FLORIDA BIBLE COLLEGE
101 North Ocean Drive, Hollywood 33019

[J1] FLORIDA COLLEGE
Temple Terrace 33617, (813) 988-5131
Admissions Officer: Wayne C. Moody

- **Undergraduates: 239m, 221w**
- **Tuition (1982/83): $2,300**
- **Room & Board: $775**
- **Degrees offered: AA, AAMusic**
- **Mean SAT 450v, 460m**
- **Student-faculty ratio: 15 to 1**

A private college affiliated with the Church of Christ, established in 1944. 195-acre campus, 10 miles from Tampa. Served by air and bus.
Academic Character SACS accreditation. Semester system. 2-year programs offered in art, biology, business, chemistry, drama, education, English, home economics, humanities, industrial arts, mathematics, modern languages, music, philosophy, physical education, physics, psychology, religion, secretarial science, social sciences, and speech. Distributive requirements; daily Bible classes required. Preprofessional programs in agriculture, dental hygiene, dentistry, engineering, forestry, law, medical technology, medicine, nursing, optometry, pharmacy, veterinary medicine. Interchange programs with U Tampa and U Southern Florida. 27,000-volume library.
Financial College scholarships, grants, loans, PELL, BEOG, NDSL, FCL, college employment.
Admissions High school graduation with 12 units required. GED accepted. SAT required. Application fee. Rolling admissions. $50 tuition deposit ($200 for boarders) due on acceptance of admissions offer. Credit possible for CEEB AP and CLEP exams.
Student Life Student government. Newspaper, literary magazine, yearbook. Drama group. Honorary, religious, social, and special interest groups. Students under 21 must live at home or on campus. Single-sex dorms. Limited married-student housing. Liquor, drugs, firearms, fireworks prohibited. Restricted use of cars. Dress code. Marriage intentions require parents' and president's approval. Daily chapel attendance mandatory. Attendance in class required. 4 courses in phys ed required. 4 intercollegiate sports; intramurals.

[1] FLORIDA INSTITUTE OF TECHNOLOGY
150 West University, Melbourne 32901, (305) 723-3701
Director of Admissions: Robert S. Heidinger

- **Undergraduates: 2,584m, 579w; 4,344 total (including graduates)**
- **Tuition (1982/83): $3,825**
- **Room & Board: $2,205; Fees: $160**
- **Degrees offered: BS, BSEd, BTech, BAirCom**
- **Mean ACT: 24.5; Mean SAT 500v, 550m**
- **Student-faculty ratio: 20 to 1**

A private university established in 1958. 16-acre campus in beach community; branch campus 85 miles south at Jensen Beach. Served by air and bus.
Academic Character SACS and professional accreditation. Trimester system, summer term. 25 majors offered by School of Science & Engineering, 3 by School of Aeronautics, and 7 at Jensen Beach Campus. Distributive requirements. Graduate degrees granted. Some independent study. Phi Beta Kappa. Cooperative work/study. AS programs at Jensen Beach in oceangraphic, electronics, environmental, marine, medical, photographic, underwater, and petroleum technologies. 2-year program at Cape Kennedy Regional Airport for pilots and in air commerce. English training for foreign

students. Exchange program with High Point College. Study abroad. Secondary science education certification. ROTC. 120,000-volume library.
Financial CEEB CSS. University scholarships, grants, loans; PELL, SEOG, NDSL, FISL, CWS, deferred payment plan. Application deadline March 15.
Admissions High school graduation with 11 or more units required with more units in sciences expected. GED accepted. SAT or ACT required. $15 application fee. Rolling admissions; application deadline is June 30. $50 tuition and $100 room deposits required on acceptance of offer of admission. *Early Admission* Program. Transfers accepted. Admission deferral possible. Credit possible for CEEB AP and CLEP exams; university has own advanced placement program.
Student Life Student government. Newspaper, radio station. Stage band. Drama club. Volunteer ambulance. Athletic, departmental, honorary, religious, tutoring, service, and special interest groups. 10 fraternities and 1 sorority. Single students with less than 45 credit hours must live on campus. Coed and single-sex dorms. 60% of students live on campus. Class attendance is required. 10 intercollegiate sports for men, 6 for women; intramural and club sports. Student body composition: 0.7% Asian, 2.6% Black, 2.6% Hispanic, 80.3% White, 13.71% Other. 75% from out of state.

■[1] FLORIDA INSTITUTE OF TECHNOLOGY-SCHOOL OF APPLIED TECHNOLOGY
Jensen Beach — see Florida Institute of Technology

[1] FLORIDA INTERNATIONAL UNIVERSITY
Tamiami Trail & 107th Avenue, Miami 33199, (305) 554-2311
Director of Admissions, School and College Relations: William Brinkley

- **Enrollment: 1,956m, 1,918w; 11,441 total(includes part-time)**
- **Tuition (1982/83): $25 per semester hour (in-state), $66 (out-of-state)**
- **Degrees offered: BA, BS, BM, BFA, BBA, BTech, BSN**

A public university established as an upper-level institution in 1965. Became a 4-year college in 1981. 344-acre Tamiami campus and 200-acre Bay Vista campus. Both served by air, rail, and bus.
Academic Character SACS and professional accreditation. Semester system, 2 6-week summer terms. 30 majors offered by the College of Arts & Sciences, 10 by the School of Business & Organizational Sciences, 24 by the School of Education, 1 by the School of Hospitality Management, 1 by the School of Nursing, 4 by the School of Public Affairs & Services, and 20 by the School of Technology. Minors offered in 23 areas. Distributive requirements. Cooperative work/study. Credit by exam. Cross-registration with Broward and Miami-Dade. ROTC, AFROTC. International Banking Center. International Affairs Center. Women's Studies Center. 510,000-volume library with microform resources.
Financial ACT FAS. University scholarships, grants, loans, PELL, SEOG, FSAG, NDSL, GSL, ALAS, CWS.
Admissions High school graduation with 12 units required. ACT or SAT required. $15 application fee. Rolling admissions. *Early Admission* Program. Transfers accepted. Credit possible for CEEB AP and CLEP exams.
Student Life Student Government. Newspaper, magazine, yearbook. Departmental, professional, and special interest groups. No student housing. Intramural, club, and recreational sports.

[J1] FLORIDA JUNIOR COLLEGE AT JACKSONVILLE
Jacksonville 32205

[J1] FLORIDA KEYS COMMUNITY COLLEGE
Key West 33040

[1] FLORIDA MEMORIAL COLLEGE
15800 North West 42nd Street, Opa Locka 33054, (305) 625-4141
Director of Admissions: Roberto Barragan

- **Undergraduates: 339m, 377w**
- **Tuition (1982/83): $2,200**
- **Room & Board: $1,800; Fees: $340**
- **Degrees offered: BA, BS**
- **Student-faculty ratio: 15 to 1**

A private college affiliated with the Baptist Church, established 1879. 50-acre urban campus in large city of Miami. Served by air, bus, and rail.
Academic Character SACS accreditation. Semester system, 2 5-week summer terms. 4 majors offered in the Division of Business Administration, 4 in Education, 2 in Humanities, 3 in Natural Sciences & Math, 6 in Social Sciences. Minors offered in all major fields; courses in 11 additional areas. Distributive requirements. 2 semesters of religion required. GREs required for graduation. Exchange program with International College of the Cayman Islands. Summer courses in physics at Howard, in pre-medicine at Fisk. General Education Program divided into 3 ability levels. Elementary and secondary education certification. AFROTC through U of Miami. Reading lab. Language lab. 70,000-volume library.
Financial CEEB CSS and ACT FAS. College scholarships, grants, loans. Member United Negro College Fund. PELL, SEOG, FISL, CWS.
Admissions High school graduation with 16 units recommended. GED accepted. Interview recommended. $25 application fee. Rolling admissions; suggest applying by March. $50 room deposit required on acceptance of offer of admission. Transfers accepted.
Student Life Student government. Newspaper, literary magazine, yearbook. Choir, band, drama circle. Cultural arts program. Athletic, departmental, honorary, religious, service, and special interest groups. 4 fraternities and 4 sororities. All non-commuting students must live on campus except with permission of the Dean of Students. No married-student housing. 40% of students live on campus. 75% attendance minimum requirement for passing course. Drugs, liquor, and firearms prohibited. 4 semesters of phys ed required. Student body composition: 88.3% Black, 0.5% Hispanic, 11.2% Other.

[1] FLORIDA SOUTHERN COLLEGE
Lakeland 33802, (813) 683-5521
Director of Admissions: William B. Stephens, Jr.

- **Undergraduates: 900m, 1,000w**
- **Tuition (1982/83): $3,015**
- **Room & Board: $2,200; Fees: $345**
- **Degrees offered: BA, BS, BMus, BMusEd**
- **Student-faculty ratio: 19 to 1**

A private college affiliated with the Methodist Church, established in 1885. 100-acre campus designed by Frank Lloyd Wright and listed in National Historic Buildings Register, located in small city 30 miles from Tampa, 35 miles from Disney World. Served by bus and rail; air service available in Tampa and Orlando.
Academic Character SACS accreditation. Semester system, 2 4-week summer terms. 34 majors offered in the areas of arts, humanities, social sciences, natural sciences, education, business administration, nursing, physical education, communications, citrus/horticulture. Minor in secondary education. Distributive requirements; 6 hours of religion required. Core comprehension and senior exams required. Senior Honors. Pass/fail, internships, field experience. Acceleration possible. Preprofessional programs in dentistry, engineering, forestry, law, medicine, nursing, theology. 3-2 forestry program with Duke and U. of Florida; 3-1 medical technology with local hospitals. Study abroad. Washington and United Nations semesters. Elementary, secondary, and special education certification. ROTC. 170,000-volume library.
Financial CEEB CSS. College scholarships, grants, loans, 5% tuition reduction for simultaneously enrolled members of immediate family, discounts for ministers' children. PELL, SEOG, Florida Tuition Voucher, NDSL, Education Funds, Inc., Tuition Plan, Inc., monthly installment plan. Application deadline March 1.
Admissions High school graduation with 13 units required. GED accepted. Interview recommended. SAT (minimum 840 composite) or ACT (minimum 17 composite) required. $20 application fee. Rolling admissions; suggest applying 30 days before registration. $100 deposit required on acceptance of offer of admission. *Early Admission* Program. Transfers accepted. Admission deferral possible. Credit possible for CEEB AP, CLEP, and ACH exams.
Student Life Student government. Newspaper, yearbook. Music and drama groups. Honorary, political, civic, religious, and special interest groups. 10 fraternities and 6 sororities; members live in sections of college housing. 33% of men and 34% of women join. All students who live more than 35 miles away must live on campus. 93% of students live on campus. Liquor or illegal drugs forbidden on or off campus. Hazing prohibited. Dorm visitation regulations. Attendance in class and at weekly and special convocations required. Dress code. 2 hours of phys ed required. 5 intercollegiate sports for men, 4 for women; extensive intramural programs. NCAA. Composition of student body: 3% Black, 1% Hispanic, 95% White, 1% Other. 30% of students from out of state.

[1] FLORIDA STATE UNIVERSITY
Tallahassee 32306, (904) 644-6200
Director of Admissions: Peter F. Metarko

- **Enrollment: 10,668m, 11,720w (including graduates)**
- **Tuition (1982/83): $750 (in-state), $1,980 (out-of-state)**
- **Room & Board: $1,360; Fees: $46**
- **Degrees offered: BA, BS, BME, BFA**
- **Student-faculty ratio: 23 to 1**

A public university established in 1851. 343-acre urban campus. Served by air and bus.
Academic Character SACS and professional accreditation. Semester system. 28 majors offered by the College of Arts & Sciences, 10 by the College of Business, 2 by the College of Communication, 16 by the College of Education, 4 by the College of Social Science, 5 by the School of Home Economics, 6 by the School of Music, 3 by the School of Visual Arts, and 1 each by the Schools of Dance, Criminology, Nursing, Social Work, and Theatre. Interdisciplinary majors. Distributive requirements. Graduate degrees granted. Independent and accelerated study. Honors program. Cooperative work/study, limited pass/fail, credit by exam, internships. Cross-registration with area schools. Study abroad. Elementary, secondary, and special education certification. ROTC, AFROTC; NROTC at Florida A&M. Oceanographic Institute. Art gallery. Museum. Computer center. 1,393,156-volume library with microform resources.
Financial CEEB CSS and ACT FAS. University scholarships, grants, loans, out-of-state tuition waivers, PELL, SEOG, NDSL, CWS. Application deadline March 1.
Admissions High school graduation with 7 units, 2.5 GPA, and SAT 950 composite or ACT 21 composite (3.0 GPA and SAT 1000 composite or ACT 23 composite for out-of-state applicants) required. Audition required for music and dance. $15 application fee. Rolling admissions. *Early Admission* and *Concurrent Enrollment* programs. Transfers accepted. Credit possible for CEEB AP and CLEP exams. Horizons Unlimited Program for disadvantaged.
Student Life Student government. Newspaper, magazines, yearbook, radio and TV stations. Music, dance, and drama groups. Debates. Circus. Departmental, honorary, religious, and service groups. 20 fraternities and 20 sororities, all with houses. 25% of students join. Freshmen encouraged to live on campus. Married-student housing. Cooperative houses for academically talented. 25% live on campus. Liquor prohibited. Honor code. Attendance in class expected. 8 intercollegiate sports for men, 8 for women; extensive intramural and club sports program. 10% from out of state.

[2] FORT LAUDERDALE COLLEGE
1401 East Broward Blvd., Fort Lauderdale 33301
Director of Admissions: Ross Groat

- **Undergraduates: 717m, 216w**
- **Tuition (1982/83): $1,820**
- **No college housing**
- **Degrees offered: BS, BBA**
- **Student-faculty ratio: 15 to 1**

A private college established in 1962. Urban campus in large city. Served by air, rail, and bus.
Academic Character AICS accreditation. Quarter system. Majors offered in accounting, data processing, management, marketing, and business administration. Associate degrees in major areas and in hotel & restaurant administration and real estate; courses in 16 additional areas. Distributive requirements. Independent and accelerated study. Cooperative work/study. Campuses in Miami and West Palm Beach.
Financial Some gift aid, 10% discount on tuition paid year in advance. PELL, SEOG, NDSL, GSL, CWS, deferred payment plan.
Admissions High school graduation or equivalent required. GED accepted. $10 application fee. Rolling admissions; suggest applying early in 12th year. $75 deposit required on acceptance of offer of admission. Transfers accepted. Credit possible for CLEP exams; college has own advanced placement program.
Student Life International club. Academic and special interest groups. No college housing. Attendance in class required. Intercollegiate baseball and soccer for men. Student body composition: 0.5% Asian, 26.5% Black, 5.9% Hispanic, 64.8% White.

[J1] GULF COAST COMMUNITY COLLEGE
Panama City 32401

[G2] HEED UNIVERSITY/EAST
PO Box 311, Hollywood 33022

[J1] HILLSBOROUGH COMMUNITY COLLEGE
PO Box 22127, Tampa 33622

[2] HOBE SOUND BIBLE COLLEGE
PO Box 1065, Hobe Sound 33455

[J1] INDIAN RIVER COMMUNITY COLLEGE
Fort Pierce 33450

[P] INTERNATIONAL COLLEGE OF THE CAYMAN ISLANDS (Miami Center)
PO Box 593578, Miami 33159

[J1] INTERNATIONAL FINE ARTS COLLEGE OF FASHION
1737 North Bayshore Drive, Miami 33132, (305) 373-4684

- **Enrollment: 275 men & women**
- **Tuition (1982/83): $7,890 (including fees, texts, housing)**
- **Degree offered: AA**
- **Student-faculty ratio: 12 to 1**

A private college established in 1965. Urban building campus on Biscayne Bay. Served by air, rail, and bus.
Academic Character SACS accreditation. Trimester system, summer term. Majors offered in fashion merchandising, commercial art, and interior design. Courses in liberal arts. Internships. Field trips. Study abroad and travel-study tours to Europe, Mexico, and the Orient. Remedial tutoring. Library.
Financial Guaranteed tuition. Federal grants, loans, & other aid available.
Admissions High school graduation required. GED accepted. Interview recommended. Second-year by invitation only. $15 application fee. $300 deposit required on acceptance of admissions offer. *Early Admission* and *Early Decision* programs. Transfers accepted.
Student Life Student government. Special events are held throughout the year. Chateau Shannon and Villa Starr apartments for women, each with resident houseparents. Manor Lord apartments for men. Regular class attendance expected. Proper dress required. Student body composition: 28% minority.

[1] JACKSONVILLE UNIVERSITY
University Blvd. N, Jacksonville 32211, (904) 744-3950
Director of Admissions: J. Bradford Sargent

- **Undergraduates: 1,145m, 878w; 2,394 total (including graduates)**
- **Tuition (1982/83): $3,825**
- **Room & Board: $2,317; Fees: $160**
- **Degrees offered: BA, BS, BFA, BMus, BMus Ed, BArt Ed, BSN**
- **Mean SAT 450v, 489m**
- **Student-faculty ratio: 18 to 1**

A private university established in 1934. 273-acre suburban campus on St. John's River, 15 miles from downtown. Served by air, rail, and bus.
Academic Character SACS and professional accreditation. Modified trimester system, 6-week summer term. Over 35 majors offered in the areas of arts & sciences, engineering, education, marine science, music, nursing, physical education, theatre, urban studies, and business administration. Self-designed majors. MAT & MBA granted. Independent study. Honors program. Some pass/fail options. Credit by exam. Internships. Preprofessional programs in dentistry, engineering, law, medicine. 3-2 engineering programs with Columbia, U of Florida, Georgia Tech. Study abroad. Elementary, secondary, and special education certification. AFROTC, NROTC. 282,000-volume library.
Financial CEEB CSS and ACT FAS. University scholarships, grants, loans, state grants, payment plans; PELL, SEOG, NDSL, GSL, CWS. Application deadline March 15.
Admissions High school graduation with 14 units required. Interview encouraged. Audition required for music and dance majors. SAT or ACT required; ACH recommended. $25 application fee. Rolling admissions; suggest applying in fall of 12th year. $200 room deposit required on acceptance of offer of admission, half refundable until July 1. *Early Admission* and *Early Decision* programs. Admission deferral possible. Transfers accepted. Credit possible for CEEB AP, CLEP, and ACH exams; university has own advanced placement program. Jump Program for underprepared students.
Student Life Student government. Newspaper, literary magazine, yearbook. Music and drama groups. Academic, honorary, religious, service, and special interest groups. 6 fraternities and 4 sororities without houses. 18% of men and 21% of women join. Single students must live at home or on campus. No coed dorms. Special interest housing. No married-student housing. 39% of students live on campus. 2 semesters of phys ed required. 7 intercollegiate sports for men, 4 for women; intramurals. NCAA. Student body composition: 0.8% Asian, 5.4% Black, 4.6% Hispanic, 0.2% Native American, 84.3% White, 4.7% Other. 45% from out of state.

[2 & J2] JONES COLLEGE
5353 Arlington Expressway, Jacksonville 32211

[2] JONES COLLEGE
Orlando — see Orlando College

[J1] LAKE CITY COMMUNITY COLLEGE
Route 7, Box 42, Lake City 32055, (904) 752-1822

- **Enrollment: 776m, 540w; 3,192 total (including part-time)**
- **Tuition (1982/83): $0 (in-state), $18 per credit hour (out-of-state)**
- **Fees: $34**
- **Degrees offered: AA, AS**

A public, district-controlled junior college established in 1962, formerly named Lake City Junior College and Forest Ranger School.
Academic Character SACS accreditation. Semester system. Occupational, university-parallel/transfer, community service, special education, and adult education programs. Remedial math and English course work available.
Admissions Open admission for most programs.
Student Life Dormitory housing available. Student body composition: 19% minority.

[J2] LAKELAND COLLEGE
PO Box 3612, Lakeland 33802

[J1] LAKE-SUMTER COMMUNITY COLLEGE
Leesburg 32748

[2] LIBERTY BIBLE COLLEGE
Highway 98 West, PO Box 3138, Pensacola 32506

[P] LINDSEY HOPKINS TECHNICAL EDUCATION CENTER
1410 Northeast Second Avenue, Miami 33132

[J1] MANATEE JUNIOR COLLEGE
PO Box 1849, Bradenton 33506

[1] MIAMI, UNIVERSITY OF
Coral Gables 33124, (305) 284-4323
Director of Admissions: George F. Giampetro

- **Undergraduates: 7,404m, 4,947w**
- **Tuition (1982/83): $5,700**
- **Room & Board: $2,550; Fees: $196**
- **Degrees offered: BA, BS, BFA, BBA, BSEd, BSN, BMus, BArch, BSSysAnal, BGS, BSE's**
- **Mean SAT 471v, 513m**
- **Student-faculty ratio: 13 to 1**

A private university established in 1925. 260-acre suburban campus on southern side of small city, 15 minutes from downtown Miami. Served by air, bus, and rail.
Academic Character SACS and professional accreditation. Semester system, 2 6-week summer terms. 33 majors offered in the College of Arts & Sciences, 11 in the School of Business Administration, 7 in the School of Education & Allied Professions, 7 in the School of Engineering & Architecture, 8 in the School of Music; Nursing. Non-major program in Afro-American studies. Honors and Privileged Studies programs. Preprofessional programs in dentistry, law, medicine. Credit-only option; credit by examination. Study abroad. ROTC, AFROTC. Computer center. 1,132,000-volume library.
Financial CEEB CSS. University scholarships, grants, and loans; PELL, SEOG, NDSL, NSL, FISL, CWS. Application deadline March 1.
Admissions High school graduation with 16 units required. $25 application

fee. Rolling admissions; application deadline July 15. *Early Admission* Program. Transfers accepted. Credit possible for CEEB AP and CLEP exams.
Student Life Student government. Newspaper, magazine, 7 professional magazines, yearbook, radio station. Rathskeller. Drama. Over 200 honorary, professional, religious, special interest, and service groups. 12 fraternities, 7 with houses; 9 sororities, no houses. 8%-10% of men and 8% of women join. Freshmen live on campus. Limited housing for upperclass and married students. 42% live on campus. 6 intercollegiate sports for men, 6 for women; extensive intramural sports. AIAW. Student body composition: 2.3% Asian, 7.2% Black, 18.8% Hispanic, 0.4% Native American, 71.2% White.32% from out of state.

[P] MIAMI CHRISTIAN COLLEGE

2300 N.W. 135th Street, Miami 33167, (305) 685-7431
Admissions Counselor: William Brown

- **Enrollment: 162m, 94w**
- **Tuition (1982/83): $2,750**
- **Room & Board: $2,080**
- **Degrees offered: BA, BS**
- **Mean ACT 19.5 composite**
- **Student-faculty ratio: 14 to 1**

A private Bible college, established in 1949. 16-acre urban campus. Served by air, rail, and bus.
Academic Character Semester system. Majors offered in Biblical languages, Biblical studies, Christian communications, church ministries, elementary education, psychology, and sacred music. Distributive requirements. Radio station. 27,000-volume library.
Financial ACT FAS. College scholarships, loans, family tuition remission, PELL, SEOG, FSAG, FGSL, CWS.
Admissions High school graduation with 16 units recommended. ACT required. $20 application fee. Rolling admissions. $100 tuition and $50 room deposits due on acceptance of admissions offer. *Early Admissions* Program. Transfers accepted. Admission deferral possible. Credit possible for ACT PEP and CEEB CLEP exams.
Student Life Student Government. Newspaper, yearbook, radio station. Music groups. Daily chapel. Prayer meetings. Students encouraged to live on campus. Practical Christian Service assignments required. 4 intercollegiate sports for men, 3 for women; intramurals. FCCC, NCCAA.

[J1] MIAMI-DADE JUNIOR COLLEGE

Miami 33176

[J2] MORRIS COLLEGE OF BUSINESS

4635 North Harbor City Blvd., Melbourne 32935

[1] NEW COLLEGE OF THE UNIVERSITY OF SOUTH FLORIDA

5700 North Tamiami Trail, Sarasota 33580, (813) 355-7671, Ext.201
Director of Admissions: Roberto Noya

- **Enrollment: 250m, 250w**
- **Tuition (1982/83): $946 (in-state), $2,754 (out-of-state)**
- **Room & Board: $2,140**
- **Degree offered: BA**
- **Mean SAT 1200**
- **Student-faculty ratio: 10 to 1**

A public college established in 1964. Became a separate college of the University of South Florida in 1975. 100-acre suburban campus adjacent to the Ringling Museum of Art, and between the towns of Bradenton and Sarasota. Served by air, rail, and bus.
Academic Character SACS accreditation. Semester system. 22 majors offered in the humanities, natural sciences, and social sciences. Self-designed majors. 7 contracts, 3 independent study projects, thesis, and baccalaureate exam required. Independent study. Tutorials. No letter grades. Internships, field work. Classes at USF. Study abroad. Computer center. Electron microscope. 150,000-volume library with microform resources.
Financial College scholarships, grants, loans, merit awards, out-of-state tuition waivers, NDSL, FISL. Suggested application deadline is February 1.
Admissions High school graduation with college preparatory program recommended. Interview required for local residents. SAT or ACT required; SAT preferred. $15 application fee. Rolling admissions. *Early Decision* and *Early Admission* programs. Admission deferral possible.
Student Life Student government. Newspaper, literary magazine, yearbook. Music, dance, drama groups. Athletic, academic, special interest groups. Freshmen must live at school. Athletic activities. 50% of students from out of state.

[1] UNIVERSITY OF NORTH FLORIDA

4567 Saint Johns Bluff Road S, Jacksonville 32216

[J1] NORTH FLORIDA JUNIOR COLLEGE

Madison 32340

[G1] NOVA UNIVERSITY

3301 College Avenue, Fort Lauderdale 33314

[J1] OKALOOSA-WALTON JUNIOR COLLEGE

Niceville 32578

[2] ORLANDO COLLEGE

5500-5800 Diplomat Circle, Orlando 32810

[2] COLLEGE OF THE PALM BEACHES

660 Fern Street, West Palm Beach 33402

[1] PALM BEACH ATLANTIC COLLEGE

1101 South Olive Avenue, West Palm Beach 33401, (305) 833-8592

- **Full-time enrollment: 238m, 260w, 567 total (includes part-time)**
- **Tuition, room, board, and fees (1982/83): $4,700**
- **Degrees offered: BA, BS**
- **Mean ACT: 18; SAT: 800**

A private liberal arts college about 50 miles north of Ft. Lauderdale.
Academic Character SACS accreditation. Trimester system. Remedial math and English programs.
Admissions SAT or ACT required. Rolling admissions. *Early Admission* Program. Advanced placement possible.

[J1] PALM BEACH JUNIOR COLLEGE

Lake Worth 33461

[J1] PASCO-HERNANDO COMMUNITY COLLEGE

Dade City 33525

[J1] PENSACOLA JUNIOR COLLEGE

Pensacola 32504

[J1] POLK COMMUNITY COLLEGE

999 Avenue H, N.E., Winter Haven 33880

[1] RINGLING SCHOOL OF ART AND DESIGN

1191 27th Street, Sarasota 33580, (813) 355-9771
Director of Admissions and Registrar: Lisa Redling Kaplan

- **Full-time enrollment: 220m, 250w; 470 total (includes part-time)**
- **Tuition (1982/83): $3,200**
- **Room & Board: $2,100**
- **Degree offered: BFA**
- **Student-faculty ratio: 15 to 1**

A private college established in 1931. Urban campus. Served by air, rail, and bus.
Academic Character SACS and professional accreditation. Semester system. Majors offered in fine arts, graphic design, illustration, and interior design & space planning. Liberal arts requirements filled at college of student's choice with approval of registrar. 10,000-volume library.
Financial CEEB CSS. PELL, SEOG, GSLP, FSAG, Florida Tuition Vouchers, campus part-time employment program. Application deadline March 1.
Admissions High school graduation recommended. Visual presentation required. $25 application fee. Rolling admissions. $100 tuition deposit and $100 room deposit due on acceptance of admissions offer. Transfers accepted.
Student Life Student Government. Sidewalk Sale. Medieval Fair. Campus ministry. Single-sex dorms.

[1] ROLLINS COLLEGE

Winter Park 32789, (305) 646-2161
Director of Admissions: Julia H. Ingraham

- **Undergraduates: 638m, 724w; 2,153 total (including graduates)**
- **Tuition (1982/83): $5,710**
- **Room & Board: $2,640; Fees: $226**
- **Degree offered: BA**
- **Student-faculty ratio: 13 to 1**

A private college established in 1885. 65-acre suburban campus in small city, 5 miles from Orlando and 120 miles from Jacksonville. Air, rail, and bus in Orlando.
Academic Character SACS and professional accreditation. 4-1-4 system. Majors offered in the arts, education, languages, theatre, natural sciences, social studies, music. Minors offered in business administration, computer science, religion, Russian, speech. Area studies majors available. Independent study. Honors program. Preprofessional programs in business, dentistry, law, medicine, ministry. 4-1 program in business administration offered at Rollins' Crummer School of Finance and Business Administration. 3-2 engineering programs with Auburn, Columbia, Georgia Tech, Washington U. 3-2 forestry program with Duke and U of Florida. Study abroad. Elementary and secondary education certification. AFROTC at U of Central Florida. Merrill-Palmer Program. Computer and language labs. 223,721-volume library with microform resources.
Financial CEEB CSS. College scholarships, grants, loans; PELL, SEOG, NDSL, CWS, Tuition Plan, Inc. Application deadline March 1.
Admissions High school graduation with 15 units recommended. Interview recommended. Audition or tape required for music majors. SAT or ACT required; 3 ACH recommended. $20 application fee. Application deadline March 1. $100 tuition and $150 room deposits required on acceptance of offer of admission. *Early Admission* and *Early Decision* programs. Transfers accepted. Admission deferral possible. Credit possible for CEEB AP and CLEP exams.
Student Life Student government. Newspaper, literary magazine, yearbook, radio station. Music and drama groups. "Real World" program. Student pub. Honorary and special interest groups. 6 fraternities and 6 sororities; all have houses. 40% of students join. Most freshmen live on campus. 24-hour visitation. Coed dorms. No married-student housing. 75% of students live on campus. Narcotics prohibited on campus. 2 years phys ed required. 8

intercollegiate sports for men, 8 for women; intramurals. AIAW, NCAA, Sunshine State Conference. Student body composition: 0.3% Asian, 2.5% Black, 3% Hispanic, 94.2% White. 55% from out of state.

[J1] SAINT JOHN VIANNEY COLLEGE SEMINARY
Miami 33165

[J1] ST. JOHNS RIVER COMMUNITY COLLEGE
Palatka 32077

[1] SAINT LEO COLLEGE
Saint Leo 33574, (904) 588-8283
Director of Admissions: Reverend J. Dennis Murphy, OSB

- **Undergraduates: 600m, 550w**
- **Tuition (1982/83): $3,530**
- **Room & Board: $1,370-$1,840; Fees: $271**
- **Degrees offered: BA, BSMedTech, AA**
- **Student-faculty ratio: 17 to 1**

A private college affiliated with the Order of Saint Benedict. 50-acre rural campus 30 miles northeast of Tampa. College bus to Tampa on opening, closing, and vacation days.

Academic Character SACS accreditation. Semester system, 6-week summer term. Majors offered in accounting, art, art management, biology, business administration, business education, criminology, dance-theatre, early childhood education, elementary education, English, history, human resources administration, management, marketing, medical technology (3-1), music, physical education, political science, psychology, real estate, religious education, religious study, restaurant management, secondary education, social work, sociology, special education, theatre-dance, secretarial science. Associate degrees in criminal justice, real estate, liberal arts, and secretarial science. Distributive requirements; 3 courses in philosophy/theology required. Independent study. Research options. Internships. Preprofessional programs in dentistry, law, medicine, nursing, osteopathy, pharmacy, veterinary medicine. Study abroad. Early childhood, elementary, secondary, and special education certification. ROTC. Language lab. 90,000-volume library with microform resources.

Financial CEEB CSS and ACT FAS. College scholarships, grants, loans, tuition reduction for 2nd family member. PELL, SEOG, NDSL, GSL, CWS, Florida Tuition Voucher Program, Insured Tuition Payment Plan, Academic Management Services, Inc. Preferred application deadline April 15.

Admissions High school graduation with 16 units required. GED accepted. Interview recommended. SAT or ACT required. $15 application fee. Rolling admissions; suggest applying early in 12th year. $100 tuition deposit required on acceptance of offer of admission. *Early Admission* Program. Transfers accepted. Admission deferral possible. Credit possible for CEEB AP and CLEP exams.

Student Life Student government. Yearbook. Music and theatre groups. Dance. Honor Society. Academic, service, and special interest groups. Fraternities and sororities. Single freshmen and sophomores (except veterans) live at home or on campus. 85% live on campus. 4 hours of phys ed required. 7 intercollegiate sports for men, 5 for women; extensive intramural programs. AIAW, NCAA. Student body composition: 11% Black, 5% Hispanic, 70.1% White. 53% from out of state.

[J1] ST. PETERSBURG JUNIOR COLLEGE
PO Box 13489, St. Petersburg 33733

[1] ST. VINCENT DE PAUL, SEMINARY OF
Boynton Beach 33435

[J1] SANTA FE COMMUNITY COLLEGE
Gainesville 32602

[2] SARASOTA, THE UNIVERSITY OF
2080 Ringling Blvd., Sarasota 33577

[J1] SEMINOLE COMMUNITY COLLEGE
Sanford 32771

[1] THE UNIVERSITY OF SOUTH FLORIDA
Tampa 33620, (813) 974-3350
Director of Admissions: Linda E. Erickson

- **Undergraduates: 6,178m, 6,189w; 25,800 total (includes graduates)**
- **Tuition (1982/83): $750 (in-state), $1,980 (out-of-state)**
- **Room & Board: $2,200; Fees: $46**
- **Degrees offered: BA, BS, BFA, BET, BEngSci, BIndStud, BAMedTech, BSW**
- **Mean ACT 20.5 composite; mean SAT 562v, 499m**
- **Student-faculty ratio: 22 to 1**

A public university established in 1956. 1,672-acre urban campus in large city. Branch campuses in St. Petersburg, Fort Myers, and Sarasota. Tampa served by air, rail, and bus.

Academic Character SACS and professional accreditation. Semester system, 8-week summer term. 19 majors offered in the College of Arts & Letters, 6 in Business Administration, 23 in Education, 3 in Engineering, 4 in Fine Arts, 11 in Natural Science, 10 in Social & Behavioral Sciences; 1 in Nursing. External Degree Program offers Bachelor of Independent Studies. Minors offered in most major fields. Distributive requirements. Graduate and professional degrees granted. Independent study. Honors by contract course at New College. Cooperative work/study, pass/fail. Credit by exam. 3-2 BS/MS in engineering. Exchange program in education with U of Maine. Exchange with Florida College. National Student Exchange. Greek, Hebrew, Bible or religion courses at Florida College. Branch campus courses available for juniors, seniors, and for graduate study. Extensive study abroad. Elementary, secondary, and special education certification. ROTC, AFROTC. Upward Bound. Computer center. Over 790,000-volume library.

Financial CEEB CSS and ACT FAS. University scholarships, grants, loans, nursing scholarships and loans; PELL, SEOG, NDSL, FISL, CWS. Application deadline January 31.

Admissions High school graduation required; 12 units recommended. SAT or ACT required. Minimum C average and 850 SAT or 18 ACT composite required. $15 application fee. Rolling admissions. *Early Admission* and *Concurrent Enrollment* programs. Transfers accepted. Admission deferral possible. Credit possible for CEEB AP and CLEP exams; university has own credit by exam program. Special programs for students not normally admissible.

Student Life Student government. Newspaper, literary magazine. Music, drama, and dance groups. Afro-American Society. Athletic, departmental, honorary, political, religious, service, and special interest groups. 17 fraternities and 10 sororities, none have houses. Coed and single-sex dorms. 12% of students live on campus. Firearms, weapons, explosives prohibited. Beer and wine available in authorized areas to students over 19. 8 intercollegiate sports for men, 5 for women; intramurals. AIAW, NCAA, Sun Belt Conference. Student body composition: 0.7% Asian, 3.5% Black, 4.4% Hispanic, 89.5% White, 1.8% Other. 10% from out of state.

[J1] SOUTH FLORIDA JUNIOR COLLEGE
Avon Park 33825

[P] SOUTHEASTERN COLLEGE OF OSTEOPATHIC MEDICINE
1750 NE 168th St., North Miami Beach 33162

[P] SOUTHEASTERN COLLEGE OF THE ASSEMBLIES OF GOD
Lakeland 33801

[P] SOUTHERN COLLEGE
5600 Lake Underhill Road, Orlando 32807

[2] SPURGEON BAPTIST BIBLE COLLEGE
4440 Spurgeon Drive, Mulberry 33860

[1] STETSON UNIVERSITY
DeLand 32720, (904) 734-4121
Director of Admissions: Gary A. Meadows

- **Undergraduates: 997m, 1,004w; 3,007 total (including graduates)**
- **Tuition (1982/83): $4,200**
- **Room & Board: $1,850; Fees: $185**
- **Degrees offered: BA, BS, BBA, BM, BME**
- **Student-faculty ratio: 18 to 1**

A private university affiliated with the Baptist Church, established in 1883. 100-acre campus located in small city 20 miles west of Daytona Beach and 100 miles south of Jacksonville. Served by air, rail, and bus.

Academic Character SACS and professional accreditation. 4-1-4 system, 8-week summer term. 24 majors offered in the College of Liberal Arts, 5 in the School of Business Administration, 8 in the School of Music. Biblical studies and church leadership majors through Extension Division of Christian Education. Interdepartmental majors in social science and urban studies. Self-designed majors. Minors offered. Distributive requirements. 2 religion courses required. Independent and acceleratd study. Honors programs. "Music Only" program for faculty-approved musicians. Phi Beta Kappa. Some pass/fail options, internships. Preprofessional programs in dentistry, law, medical technology, medicine, ministry, nursing, veterinary medicine. 3-2 program in engineering with U of Florida, U of Central Florida, and Washington U (MO); in forestry with Duke. 3-1 program in medical technology. Cross-registration with 4 area colleges. Study abroad. Elementary, secondary, and special education certification. ROTC. United Nations Semester. Language lab. 300,000-volume library with microform resources.

Financial CEEB CSS. University scholarships, grants, loans; pre-ministerial, academic, athletic, music scholarships. PELL, SEOG, NDSL, FISL, CWS, Tuition Plan, Inc. Suggested application deadline March 1.

Admissions High school graduation with 14 units of a college-preparatory program required. Audition required for music majors. ACT or SAT required. 2 ACH recommended. $20 application fee. Rolling admissions; suggest applying by March 15. $100 deposit required on acceptance of offer of admission. *Early Admission* and *Early Decision* programs. Transfers accepted. Admission deferral possible. Credit possible for CEEB AP and CLEP exams. Credit also possible for summer *Advanced Study* Program.

Student Life Student government. Newspaper, literary magazine, yearbook. Music and drama groups. Debates. Departmental and special interest groups. 7 fraternities with houses; 7 sororities without houses. 42% of men and 36% of women join. Single freshmen and sophomores under 21 and all single financial aid recipients must live on campus or at home. No coed dorms. No married-student housing. 80% of students live on campus. Students must inform Dean before marriage. 3 semesters of phys ed required of liberal arts students under 30. 4 intercollegiate sports for men, 4 for women; extensive intramurals. AIAW, NCAA, Florida Intercollegiate Athletic Conference. Student body composition: 0.8% Asian, 2.6% Black, 1.2% Hispanic, 0.2% Native American, 95% White. 30% from out of state.

[G1] STETSON UNIVERSITY COLLEGE OF LAW
Gulfport, 61st Street & 15th Avenue S., St. Petersburg 33707

[J1] TALLAHASSEE COMMUNITY COLLEGE
Tallahassee 32304

[1] UNIVERSITY OF TAMPA
Tampa 33606, (813) 253-8861
Director of Admissions: Walter Turner

- **Undergraduates: 835m, 743w; 2,206 total (includes graduates)**
- **Tuition (1982/83): $5,036**
- **Room & Board: $2,400**
- **Degrees offered: BA, BS, BFA, BM**
- **Mean ACT 22.7 composite; SAT 465v, 507m**
- **Student-faculty ratio: 16 to 1**

A private university established in 1931. Campus in business area of large city. Served by air, rail, and bus.
Academic Character SACS accreditation and professional accreditation. 2-2-2-2-1 system, 2 5-week summer terms. Majors offered in English, French, history, philosophy, political science, sociology, Spanish, urban affairs, accounting, biology, business management, chemistry, criminology, economics, elementary education, finance, marine science, math, medical technology, physical education, social work, psychology, social sciences, writing, art, music. Minors in some majors and in 3 other areas. Distributive requirements. Independent and accelerated study. Limited pass/fail, internships. Medical technology students work 15 months in approved lab. Honors program. Preprofessional programs in dentistry, engineering, law, medicine, and veterinary science. Study abroad. Elementary, secondary, and speech education certification. ROTC; AFROTC through U of South Florida. Language lab. 208,000-volume library.
Financial CEEB CSS. University scholarships, grants, loans, state grants and tuition vouchers. PELL, SEOG, NDSL, GSL, CWS, College Aid Plan, Tuition Plan, Inc. Scholarship and grant application deadline March 1; loan deadline March 15.
Admissions High school graduation with 15 units required. GED accepted. SAT or ACT required. $30 application fee. Rolling admissions; suggest applying early in 12th year. $150 deposit required on acceptance of offer of admission. *Early Admission* Program. Transfers accepted. Admission deferral possible. Credit possible for CEEB AP and CLEP exams; entrance with sophomore standing possible.
Student Life Student Congress. Newspaper, literary magazine, poetry review, yearbook. Public service programs on radio and TV. Music groups and participation in Sun State Opera. Theatre. Film society. Honorary, religious, and special interest groups. 8 fraternities, 4 with houses; 3 sororities without houses. 10% of students join. Coed and single-sex dorms. No married-student housing. 71% of students live on campus. Firearms, fireworks prohibited. Attendance in class required. 9 intercollegiate sports for men, 8 for women; extensive intramurals. FIC, NCAA. Student body composition: 1% Asian, 4% Black, 10% Hispanic, 1% Native American, 84% White. 54% from out of state.

[1] TAMPA COLLEGE
2511 North Grady Avenue, Tampa 33607, (813) 879-6000
511 Rosary Road, NE, Largo 33450, (813) 585-4765
4950 34th Street North, St. Petersburg 33714, (813) 527-8464
2501 Kennedy Blvd., Tampa 33609, (813) 251-5425
Director of Admissions: Ted Whitworth

- **Undergraduates: 695m, 636w**
- **Tuition (1982/83): $1,620**
- **No college housing**
- **Degrees offered: BBA, BS**
- **Student-faculty ratio: 22 to 1**

A private college established 1890. Suburban campus in large city. Branch campuses in Largo, St. Petersburg, and Tampa.
Academic Character AICS accreditation. Quarter system, 10-week summer term. Majors offered in business administration, accounting, data processing, management, marketing. Courses in 9 additional business areas; 9 courses in liberal arts areas. Certification program in court reporting. Distributive requirements. Accelerated study. Honors program. Internships. Evening classes offered.
Financial Contact Office of Financial Aid for full information. PELL, SEOG, NDSL, GSL, CWS, deferred payment plan.
Admissions High school graduation required. GED accepted. $10 application fee. Rolling admissions. $100 deposit required on acceptance of offer of admission. *Early Admission* Program. Transfers accepted. Credit possible for CLEP exams; college has own advanced placement program.
Student Life Student government. Honor societies. Special interest groups. 1 fraternity and 1 sorority. No campus housing. Attendance in class required. No sports programs. Student body composition: 0.4% Asian, 8.7% Black, 2.1% Hispanic, 88.6% White.

[2] THOMAS A. EDISON COLLEGE
— Moved to Arkansas -

[J1] VALENCIA COMMUNITY COLLEGE
Orlando 32802

[1] WARNER SOUTHERN COLLEGE
5301 U.S. Highway 27S, Lake Wales 33853, (813) 638-1426
Director of Recruitment: Joe DeHart

- **Full-time enrollment: 141m 133w; 295 total (includes part-time)**
- **Tuition (1982/83): $2,970**
- **Room & Board: $1,650-$1,990; Fees:$98**
- **Degree offered: BA**
- **Student-faculty ratio: 11 to 1**

A private college controlled by the Church of God, established in 1968. 380-acre rural campus, 60 miles from Tampa. Air service in Tampa.
Academic Character SACS accreditation. Semester system, 2 6-week summer terms. Majors offered in Biblical studies, business administration, church ministries, communication/English, education, social sciences, and speech. Minors required. Self-designed majors. Distributive requirements; 16 hours of theology and philosophy required; GRE required. Elementary, secondary, and music education certification. 65,000-volume library.
Financial CEEB CSS and ACT FAS. College grants and loans, state grants, PELL, SEOG, NDSL, deferred payment plans, CWS. Priority application deadline April 1.
Admissions High school graduation with 13 units recommended. GED accepted. Interview sometimes required. SAT or ACT required. $10 application fee. Rolling admissions. *Early Admission* Program. Transfers accepted. Credit possible for CEEB AP and CLEP exams, and for college proficiency exams.
Student Life Service and special interest groups. Students under 21 must live on campus. Single-sex dorms. Married-student housing available. Use of cars must be approved by Dean. Dress code. Church and chapel attendance required; service projects mandatory. Attendance in class required.

[1] WEBBER COLLEGE
Babson Park 33827, (813) 638-1431
Dean of Student Services/Admissions: Thomas D. Creola

- **Full-time enrollment: 52m, 110w; 204 total (includes part-time)**
- **Tuition (1982/83): $3,090**
- **Room & Board: $1,750-$2,530; Fees: $43**
- **Degrees offered: BA, BS**
- **Student-faculty ratio: 10 to 1**

A private college established in 1927, became coed in 1971. 110-acre campus on Lake Caloosa in a small town 40 minutes south of Disney World.
Academic Character SACS accreditation. Semester system, 4-week intersession. Majors offered in accounting, business and finance, business computing, data processing, fashion retail management, hotel management, insurance, marketing, office management, personnel management, real estate, and travel & tourism. Minors. Distributive requirements. MBA granted. ADN program in nursing. Study abroad. Airline operations program with Lufthansa in Germany. ROTC at Florida Southern. 12,000-volume library with microform resources.
Financial CEEB CSS and ACT FAS. College scholarships, loans, PELL, SEOG, NDSL, FISL, GSL, FSAG, semester and monthly payment plans, CWS.
Admissions High school graduation required. GED accepted. SAT or ACT required. $20 application fee. Rolling admissions. $100 tuition and $50 room deposits due on acceptance of admissions offer. *Early Admission* and *Early Decision* programs. Transfers accepted. Credit possible for CLEP exams.
Student Life Newspaper, yearbook. Drama club. Honorary, professional, service, and special interest groups. Single-sex dorms. Class attendance expected. 4 semesters of phys ed required. Intercollegiate and intramural sports. NLCAA.

[1] WEST FLORIDA, THE UNIVERSITY OF
Pensacola 32404, (904) 476-9500
Director of Admissions: Edith Anne Cones

- **Enrollment: 2,608m, 2,738w**
- **Tuition (1982/83): $28 per credit hour (in-state), $91 (out-of-state)**
- **Room & Board: $1,965**
- **Degrees offered: BA, BS, BFA**
- **Student-faculty ratio: 17 to 1**

A public upper-level university established in 1963. 1,000-acre suburban campus. Served by air and bus.
Academic Character SACS and professional accreditation. Semester system, summer term. 41 majors offered by the Colleges of Arts & Sciences, Business, and Education. Graduate degrees granted. Credit by exam. Preprofessional programs in civil service, dentistry, law, medicine, ministry, veterinary science. Elementary and secondary education certification. ROTC. Computer center. Institute for Statistical and Mathematical Modeling. Cultural and Archeological Research Center. 400,000-volume library with microform resources.
Financial CEEB CSS. University scholarships, tuition waivers, PELL, SEOG, FSAG, NDSL, FGSL, CWS, OPS. Priority application deadline April 1.
Admissions AA or AS degree from Florida community college or 60 hours of college work required. $15 application fee. Rolling admissions.
Student Life Student Government. Newspaper. Music and drama activities. Honorary, professional, religious, and special interest groups. 4 fraternities and 4 sororities. 23 small residence halls. Married-student housing. 2 intercollegiate sports for men, 3 for women; intramurals. NAIA, FAIAW.

GEORGIA (GA)

[J1] ABRAHAM BALDWIN AGRICULTURAL COLLEGE
Box 4, ABAC Station, Tifton 31794, (912) 386-3236

- **Undergraduates: 2,400 men & women**

- **Tuition (1982/83): $652 (in-state), $1,956 (out-of-state)**
- **Room & Board: $1,460-$2,540; Fees: $63**
- **Degrees offered: AA, AS**
- **Mean SAT 397v, 408m**

A public junior college established in 1908. 390-acre campus in south central Georgia, 55 miles from Florida state line. Airport nearby.
Academic Character SACS and professional accreditation. Trimester system, summer term. Majors offered in agricultural engineering, agriculture, art, biology, business administration, chemistry, drama, elementary education, English, environmental health, forestry/wildlife management, history, home economics, junior high education, journalism, marketing & distributive education, mathematics, music, physical education, psychology, political science, recreation, secondary education, sociology, special education, and speech. 15 career technological programs. Distributive requirements. Cooperative work/study. Preprofessional programs in dental hygiene, dentistry, medicine, nursing, pharmacy, veterinary medicine. 200-acre experimental farm. Arts Experiment Station. 60,000-volume library.
Financial CEEB CSS. College and state scholarships, state grants; PELL, SEOG, NSS, NDSL, GSL, CWS, college has own work program. Application deadlines June 1 (FAF), April 1 (state scholarships).
Admissions High school graduation required. GED accepted. SAT required. $5 application fee. Rolling admissions. *Early Admission* and *Concurrent Enrollment* programs. Transfers accepted. Credit possible for CEEB AP, CLEP, and ACT PEP exams.
Student Life Student government. Newspaper, magazine, yearbook, radio station. Music groups. Academic, professional, religious, and special interest groups. No coed dorms. About 50% of students live on campus. 6 quarters of phys ed required. 4 intercollegiate sports; intramurals.

[1] AGNES SCOTT COLLEGE

Decatur 30030, (404) 373-2571
Director of Admissions: Judith Maguire Tindel

- **Undergraduates: 525w; 560 total (including part-time)**
- **Tuition (1982/83): $5,100**
- **Room & Board: $1,900; Fees: $75**
- **Degree offered: BA**
- **Mean ACT 25; mean SAT 530v, 540m**
- **Student-faculty ratio: 8 to 1**

A private college established in 1889. 100-acre suburban campus 1 mile from Atlanta. Air, rail, and bus service in Atlanta.
Academic Character SACS accreditation. Trimester system, 6-week holiday Thanksgiving - New Year. 28 majors offered in the areas of art, Bible & religion, classics, economics, English, history, international relations, languages, mathematics, music, philosophy, political science, psychology, sciences, social sciences, and theatre. Interdisciplinary and self-designed majors. Distributives and 5 quarter hours of Biblical literature required. Independent study. Phi Beta Kappa. Pass/fail. Internships. Preprofessional programs in dentistry, law, and medicine. 3-2 program with Georgia Tech in engineering, information & computer science, industrial management & management science. Washington Semester. Exchange program with Mills College. Study abroad. Elementary and secondary education certification. AFROTC & NROTC at Georgia Tech. Observatory, language lab. 165,500-volume library with microform resources.
Financial CEEB CSS and ACT FAS. College scholarships, grants, loans, deferred payment; PELL, GSL, ALAS. Priority application deadline February 15.
Admissions High school graduation with 16 units recommended. SAT or ACT required; SAT preferred. 3 ACH required. $25 application fee. Rolling admissions. $250 deposit required on acceptance of offer of admission. *Early Admission* and *Concurrent Enrollment* programs. Admission deferral possible. Transfers accepted. Credit possible for CEEB AP exams.
Student Life Student government. Newspaper, magazine, yearbook. Music, drama, dance groups. Students for Black Awareness. Religious, academic, service, and special interest groups. Students must live at home or on campus. Language halls. Married-student housing. 93% of students live on campus. Midnight curfew, class attendance requirement for fall-quarter freshmen. Attendance at 7 convocations required. 6 quarters of phys ed required. 3 intercollegiate sports; intramurals. AIAW. Student body composition: 0.9% Asian, 3.8% Black, 1.5% Hispanic, 0.4% Native American, 93.4% White. 53% from out of state.

[J1] ALBANY JUNIOR COLLEGE

2400 Gillionville Road, Albany 31707

[1] ALBANY STATE COLLEGE

Albany 31705, (912) 439-4234
Director of Admissions & Records: Dorothy B. Hubbard

- **Undergraduates: 547m, 917w**
- **Tuition (1982/83): $855 (in-state), $2,145 (out-of-state)**
- **Room & Board: $1,650; Fees: $210**
- **Degrees offered: BA, BS, BBA, BSN**
- **Student-faculty ratio: 12 to 1**

A public teacher-training college established in 1903. Unit of the University of Georgia. 128-acre urban campus on the Flint River. Served by bus.
Academic Character SACS and professional accreditation. Trimester system, 8-week summer term. Majors offered in art, biology, business administration, business education, chemistry, computer sciences, criminal justice, elementary education, English, health & physical education, history, mathematics, modern languages, music, nursing, political science, psychology, secondary education, secretarial science, sociology, special education, and speech & theatre. Minor required. Distributive requirements. Seniors required to take GRE, Regent's Test. MBA, MEd granted. Cooperative work/study. Preprofessional programs in law, medical technology, medicine, and pharmacy. Elementary, secondary, and special education certification. ROTC. Computer center. 150,000-volume library with microform resources.
Financial CEEB CSS. College scholarships, grants, athletic scholarships, loans, state scholarships & loans; PELL, SEOG, NSS, GSL, NDSL, CWS, college has own work program.
Admissions High school graduation with 15 units and a minimum 1.8 GPA required. GED accepted. SAT required. Rolling admissions; deadline 20 days before registration. $178 matriculation fee required before registration. *Early Admission* and *Concurrent Enrollment* programs. Transfers accepted. Credit possible for CEEB AP exams; college has own advanced placement program.
Student Life Student government. Publications. Music groups. Honor societies and special interest groups. 4 fraternities and 4 sororities. Students not living at home must live on campus. No coed dorms. Class attendance required. Intercollegiate and intramural sports. Student body composition: 0.1% Asian, 96.6% Black, 3.1% White.

[J1] ANDREW COLLEGE

Cuthbert 31740, (912) 732-2171
Dean of Student Development: James T. Gilbert

- **Undergraduates: 300 men and women**
- **Tuition (1982/83): $1,728**
- **Room & Board: $2,049; Fees: $216**
- **Degrees offered: AA, AS, AAS**

A private junior college affiliated with the United Methodist Church, established in 1854. Campus located in town of Cuthbert in southwest Georgia, 43 miles from Albany. Served by air and bus.
Academic Character SACS accreditation. Quarter system. Majors offered in humanities, business administration, business education, and applied music. Distributive requirements. Independent study. Honors program. Direct transfer programs with 17 colleges. Preprofessional programs in dentistry, medicine, pharmacy, medical technology, dental hygiene, nursing, others. Study abroad.
Financial CEEB CSS. College scholarships, grants, loans, music scholarships, Methodist loans, state grants; PELL, SEOG, NDSL, GSL, ALAS, CWS. Priority application deadline June 1.
Admissions High school graduation required. GED accepted. $10 application fee. Rolling admissions. $50 deposit required on acceptance of offer of admission. *Early Admission* Program. Transfers accepted. Credit possible for CEEB AP and CLEP exams; college has own advanced placement program.
Student Life Student government. Yearbook. Music group. Religious, honorary, and special interest groups. 21 fraternities and 2 sororities. Class attendance required. 6 hours of phys ed required. Intercollegiate tennis and soccer; intramurals. GJCAA, NJCAA. Student body composition: 10% minority.

[1] ARMSTRONG STATE COLLEGE

11935 Abercorn Street, Savannah 31406, (912) 927-5258
Director of Admissions: Thomas P. Miller

- **Undergraduates: 681m, 1,073w**
- **Tuition (1982/83): $750 (in-state), $2,040 (out-of-state)**
- **Degrees offered: BA, BS, BSN, BSW, BSEd, BMusEd, AA, AS**
- **Mean SAT 750 composite**
- **Student-faculty ratio: 17 to 1**

A public college established in 1935. 250-acre campus 10 miles from downtown Savannah. Served by air, rail, and bus.
Academic Character SACS and professional accreditation. Trimester system, 9-week summer term. Majors offered in English, history, music political science, psychology, art education, biology, chemistry, criminal justice, dental hygiene education, mathematical sciences, medical technology, early elementary education, health education & recreation, middle school education, and secondary education. Courses in 18 additional areas. Distributive requirements; reading and writing competency tests and exam in major required. MHS and ME granted. Independent study. Honors program. Preprofessional programs in dentistry, engineering, forestry, industrial management, law, medicine, optometry, pharmacy, veterinary medicine. 3-2 program in engineering with Georgia Tech. Cross-registration with Savannah State; business education, industrial arts education, and trade & industrial arts education through Savannah State. Courses at Marine Science Center. Elementary and secondary education certification. ROTC; NROTC at Savannah State. Computer center, language lab. 115,000-volume library with microform resources.
Financial CEEB CSS. College scholarships, grants, loans; PELL, SEOG, NSS, NDSL, NSL, CWS. Application deadline June 30.
Admissions High school graduation. GED accepted. SAT required. $10 application fee. Rolling admissions; application deadline September 1. *Early Admission* and *Concurrent Enrollment* programs. Transfers accepted. Credit possible for CEEB AP and CLEP exams; college has own advanced placement program. Special Studies Program.
Student Life Student government. Newspaper, yearbook. Music and drama groups. Religious, honorary, service, academic, and special interest groups. 4 fraternities with houses and 3 sororities without houses. 8% of men and 9% of women join. No dorms on campus. 6 hours of phys ed required. 5 intercollegiate sports for men and women; intramurals. AIAW, NAIA, NCAA, South Atlantic Conference. Student body composition: 0.5% Asian, 11.1% Black, 0.5% Hispanic, 0.2% Native American, 87.5% White. 7% from out of state.

[J2] ART INSTITUTE OF ATLANTA

3376 Peachtree Road, NE, Atlanta 30326

[P] ATLANTA CHRISTIAN COLLEGE
East Point 30344

[1] ATLANTA COLLEGE OF ART
Atlanta 30309

[J1] ATLANTA JUNIOR COLLEGE
1630 Stewart Avenue, SW, Atlanta 30310

[G1] ATLANTA UNIVERSITY
Atlanta 30314

[1] AUGUSTA COLLEGE
2500 Walton Way, Augusta 30910, (404) 828-3301
Director of Admissions: Donald L. Smith

- **Undergraduates: 934m, 1,150w; 3,836 total (includes graduates)**
- **Tuition (1982/83): $750 (in-state), $2,040 (out-of-state)**
- **Degrees offered: BA, BS, BBA, BFA, BMus, BSEd, AA, AAS**
- **Mean SAT 912**
- **Student-faculty ratio: 14 to 1**

A public college established in 1783. 80-acre campus overlooking downtown Augusta. Served by bus.
Academic Character SACS and professional accreditation. Quarter system. Majors offered in accounting, art, art education, biology, business education, chemistry, computer science, economics, elementary education, executive secretarial, finance/insurance/real estate, general business, history, management, marketing, mathematics, medical technology, music, music education, physical science, physics, political science, psychology, sociology, special education, and studio art. Minors offered in most major fields and in 10 additional areas. Distributive requirements. Regent's Test and comprehensive exam required. MBA, MEd, MS granted. Accelerated study. Cooperative work/study. Credit by exam. Internships. Preprofessional programs in allied health, clinical psychology, dentistry, engineering, forestry, law, medicine, optometry, pharmacy. Cross-registration with Paine College. Elementary, secondary, and special education certification. ROTC. Computer center. 260,000-volume library with microform resources.
Financial CEEB CSS. College and state scholarships, grants, loans; PELL, SEOG, NDSL, GSL, NSL, CWS; college has own work program. Application deadline April 1.
Admissions High school graduation with 8 units required. GED accepted. SAT required. $10 application fee. Rolling admissions; deadline 30 days before quarter begins. *Early Admission* and *Concurrent Enrollment* programs. Admission deferral possible. Transfers accepted. Credit possible for CEEB AP exams. Special Studies Program.
Student Life Student government. Newspaper, yearbook, magazine, radio station. Choir. Religious, academic, service, honorary, and special interest groups. Social fraternities and sororities. No college housing. 6 quarters of phys ed required. 6 intercollegiate sports for men, 3 for women; intramurals. South Atlantic Conference. Student body composition: 1.7% Asian, 13.2% Black, 1% Hispanic, 0.1% Native American, 84% White. 10% from out of state.

[J1] BAINBRIDGE JUNIOR COLLEGE
Bainbridge 31717

[J2] BAUDER FASHION COLLEGE
3355 Lenox Road, NE, Atlanta 30326

[1] BERRY COLLEGE
Mount Berry 30149, (404) 235-4494
Dean of Admissions: Thomas C. Glover

- **Undergraduates: 547m, 837w**
- **Tuition (1982/83): $3,300**
- **Room & Board: $2,100; Fees: $180**
- **Degrees offered: BA, BFA, BS, BMus, AS**
- **Mean SAT 981**
- **Student-faculty ratio: 16 to 1**

A private college established in 1902. 28,000-acre suburban campus bordering the small city of Rome, 65 miles from Atlanta. Served by bus.
Academic Character SACS and professional accreditation. Quarter system; December mini-term, summer quarter. 35 majors offered in the areas of business, agriculture, art, social sciences, science, education, English, foreign language, history, home economics, mathematics, music, physical education, religion & philosophy, speech & drama. Self-designed majors. Minor or double major required. Minors offered in most major fields and in 6 additional areas. Distributive requirements. 1 religion or philosophy course required. MEd, MBA granted. Independent study. Cooperative work/study, pass/fail, internships. Credit by exam. Preprofessional programs in allied health, dentistry, engineering, forestry, law, medicine, optometry, pharmacy, theology, veterinary medicine. 3-2 engineering program with Georgia Tech. Study abroad. Summer study at Gulf Coast Research Lab in Mississippi. Elementary and secondary education certification. ROTC. Language lab. 120,000-volume library with microform resources.
Financial CEEB CSS. College scholarships, grants, loans; PELL, SEOG, NDSL, Tuition Plan, Education Funds, CWS, Scholarship-Work-Loan Plan. Scholarship application deadline February 1.
Admissions High school graduation with 16 units required. SAT or ACT required. $15 application fee. Rolling admissions; suggest applying by February 1. $75 tuition and $50 room deposits required on acceptance of offer of admission. *Early Admission* and *Concurrent Enrollment* programs. Transfers accepted. Admission deferral possible. Credit possible for CEEB AP and CLEP exams.
Student Life Student government; all students join. Newspaper, magazine, yearbook. Music, debate, and drama groups. International Relations Club. Religious, service, academic, and special interest groups. Freshmen and sophomores must live at home or on campus. No coed dorms or married-student housing. 74% of students live on campus. Liquor prohibited on campus. 4 quarters of phys ed and 1 of first aid required. 5 intercollegiate sports for men, 5 for women; intramurals. AIAW, NAIA. Student body composition: 0.4% Asian, 2.7% Black, 0.7% Hispanic, 95.5% White. 26% from out of state.

[P] BEULAH HEIGHTS BIBLE COLLEGE
892-906 Berne Street, SE, Atlanta 30316

[1] BRENAU COLLEGE
Gainesville 30501, (404) 534-6100
Director of Admissions: Deborah S. Fennell

- **Enrollment: 796w; 955 men and women total (includes evening students)**
- **Tuition (1982/83): $2,976**
- **Room & Board: $2,824; Fees: $100**
- **Degrees offered: BA, BS, BMusEd, BSN**
- **Mean SAT 850**
- **Student-faculty ratio: 14 to 1**

A private college established in 1878. 52-acre suburban campus in foothills of Blue Ridge Mountains, 45 minutes from Atlanta. Served by rail and bus.
Academic Character SACS accreditation. Quarter system, 2 3-week summer terms. 16 majors offered by the Division of Fine Arts & Humanities, 6 by the Division of Education, 7 by the Division of Social & Behavioral Services, 6 by the Division of Natural Sciences, and 4 by the Community Services College (evenings). Self-designed majors. Distributive requirements. Comprehensive exams required. MEd, MBA granted. Independent study. Honors program. Pass/fail. Internships. Preprofessional programs in dentistry, laboratory technology, law, medicine, pharmacy, theology, veterinary medicine. Summer stock apprentice program. Study abroad. Elementary, secondary, and special education certification. Infant development center. 50,000-volume library with microform resources.
Financial CEEB CSS. College scholarships and loans; PELL, SEOG, NDSL, GSL, payment plans, CWS.
Admissions High school graduation with 16 units required. SAT or ACT required. $15 application fee. Rolling admissions; suggest filing by April 1. $100 deposit required on acceptance of offer of admission. *Early Decision, Early Admission,* and *Credit in Escrow* programs. Transfers accepted. Credit possible for CEEB AP and CLEP exams and for life/work experience.
Student Life Student government. Newspaper, journal, yearbook, radio station. Music and drama groups. Religious, academic, and special interest groups. 7 sororities with houses. 75% of women join. Students must live at home or on campus. 62% of students live on campus. College must be notified of student marriage. 6 quarter hours of phys ed required. 3 intercollegiate sports; intramurals. AIAW. Student body composition: 0.1% Asian, 4.6% Black, 0.1% Native American, 93.9% White. 33% from out of state. 159 men as evening students.

[J1] BREWTON—PARKER COLLEGE
Mount Vernon 30445, (912) 583-2241
Director of Admissions: David Currie

- **Enrollment: 724 men and women**
- **Tuition (1982/83): $2,080**
- **Room & Board: $1,840**
- **Degrees offered: AA, AS**

A private college controlled by the Georgia Baptist Convention, established in 1904. 137-acre campus located between the small towns of Mount Vernon and Ailey.
Academic Character SACS accreditation. Quarter system. Majors offered in art, biology, business administration, business education, criminal justice, economics, general studies, health/physical education/recreation, history, home economics, mathematics & statistics, music, physics, political science, psychology, religion, social science, sociology, teacher education, visual arts, business, ministry, secretarial, teacher aide, and trade & industries education. 1-year certificate programs in 7 areas. Distributive requirements. Independent study. Credit by exam. Preprofessional programs in dentistry, dental hygiene, law, medicine, ministry, occupational therapy, pharmacy, veterinary medicine, and other health fields. 27,500-volume library with microform resources.
Financial CEEB CSS. College scholarships and loans, day student scholarships, Baptist scholarships, ministerial scholarships, state grants; deferred payment plan, PELL, SEOG, NDSL, GSL, CWS. File FAF by June 1 for priority consideration.
Admissions High school graduation required. GED accepted. SAT recommended. $15 application fee. Rolling admissions. $50 room deposit required on acceptance of admission. *Early Admission* and *Concurrent Enrollment* programs. Transfers accepted. Credit possible for CLEP exams.
Student Life Student government. Newspaper, yearbook. Music, drama groups. Religious, academic, honorary, and special interest groups. Students must live at home or on campus. No coed dorms. Attendance in class and at chapel required. 6 hours of phys ed required. Intramurals.

[J1] BRUNSWICK JUNIOR COLLEGE
Brunswick 31520

[P] CARVER BIBLE INSTITUTE AND COLLEGE
PO Box 4335, Atlanta 30302

[1] CLARK COLLEGE

240 Chesnut Street, SW, Atlanta 30314, (404) 681-3080
Director of Admissions: Clifton B. Rawles

- **Undergraduates: 692m, 1,352w**
- **Tuition (1982/83): $2,900**
- **Room & Board: $1,750; Fees: $415**
- **Degrees offered: BA, BS, BFA**
- **Mean SAT 378v, 380m**
- **Student-faculty ratio: 14 to 1**

A private college established in 1869. Over 450-acre urban campus in downtown Atlanta. Served by air and bus.

Academic Character SACS and professional accreditation. Semester system. 42 majors offered by the divisions of Humanities, General Education, Natural Sciences & Mathematics, and Sociocultural Studies. Self-designed majors. Afro-American minor. Distributive requirements. Freshman seminars required. Independent study. Honors program. Cooperative work/study. Internships. 3-2 program in engineering with Georgia Tech. Cooperative program with Atlanta University Center. Preprofessional programs in dentistry, Christian education, engineering, law, library work, medical technology, ministry, nursing, pharmacy. Study abroad. Elementary and secondary education certification. ROTC, AFROTC, NROTC. Southern Center for Studies in Public Policy. Computer center, language lab. 67,289-volume library.

Financial CEEB CSS. College and state scholarships, grants, and loans; PELL, NDSL, FISL, USA Loan Fund, United Methodist Loan Fund, CWS; college has own work program. Member United Negro College Fund. Application deadline April 1.

Admissions High school graduation with 16 units recommended. GED accepted. SAT or ACT required. $15 application fee. Rolling admissions; application deadline August 1. *Early Admission* and *Concurrent Enrollment* programs. Transfers accepted.

Student Life Student government. Newspaper, yearbook, radio station. Music groups. Over 50 chartered organizations. Many special interest groups. 4 fraternities and 4 sororities; none have houses. Students must live at home or on campus. No coed dorms; some apartments. 40% of students live on campus. 2 semesters of phys ed required. 5 intercollegiate sports; intramural and recreational sports. SIAC. Student body composition: 0.1% Asian, 98.6% Black, 0.3% Hispanic, 0.1% White.

[J1] CLAYTON JUNIOR COLLEGE

PO Box 285, Morrow 30260

[P] COLUMBIA THEOLOGICAL SEMINARY

Decatur 30031

[1] COLUMBUS COLLEGE

Columbus 31993, (404) 568-2035
Director of Admissions: Carl Wallman

- **Undergraduates: 1,081m, 1,219w; 4,476 total (including graduates)**
- **Tuition (1982/83): $645 (in-state), $1,935 (out-of-state)**
- **Fees: $88**
- **Degrees offered: BA, BS, BBA, BMus, BSEd, AA, AS, AAS**
- **Mean SAT 424v, 437m**
- **Student-faculty ratio: 20 to 1**

A public college established in 1958. 130-acre campus in Columbus. Served by air and bus.

Academic Character SACS and professional accreditation. Quarter system, 11-week summer term. 33 majors offered by the schools of Business and Education and the divisions of Fine Arts, Health Sciences, Language & Humanities, and Science & Mathematics. Minors offered in 10 areas. Distributive requirements. Seniors must take GRE in some programs. Independent study. Cooperative work/study. Internships. Preprofessional programs in dentistry, engineering, forestry, medicine, pharmacy, and veterinary medicine. 3-2 program in engineering with Georgia Tech. Study abroad. Secondary and special education certification. ROTC. Computer center. 168,947-volume library.

Financial CEEB CSS. College and state scholarships, grants, loans; PELL, SEOG, NDSL, FISL, NSL, CWS, assistantships. Application deadlines May 1 (scholarships), June 1 (loans).

Admissions High school graduation with 17 units required. GED accepted. Interview required for some programs. SAT required. $10 application fee. Rolling admissions; suggest applying by March. *Early Admission* and *Concurrent Enrollment* programs. Transfers accepted. Admission deferral possible. Credit possible for CEEB AP and CLEP exams. Developmental Studies Program.

Student Life Student government. Newspaper. Music and drama groups. Academic, professional, and special interest organizations. 7 fraternities and 4 sororities. 7% of men and 3% of women join. No dormitories. Liquor prohibited on campus. 6 quarters of phys ed required. 6 intercollegiate sports for men, 3 for women; intramurals. AIAW, NAIA, NCAA. Student body composition: 1.2% Asian, 17.5% Black, 1.3% Hispanic, 0.2% Native American, 76.7% White, 3.2% Other. 12% from out of state.

[1] COVENANT COLLEGE

Mailing address: Lookout Mountain, Tennessee 37350, (404) 820-1560
Director of Admissions and Records: Rudolph F. Schmidt

- **Undergraduates: 264m, 265w**
- **Tuition (1982/83): $3,990**
- **Room & Board: $2,140-$2,520; Fees: $80**
- **Degrees offered: BA, BMus, AA**
- **Mean ACT 17 composite; mean SAT 486v, 502m**
- **Student-faculty ratio: 16 to 1**

A private college affiliated with the Presbyterian Church in America, established in 1955. Campus on Lookout Mountain in northwest Georgia, overlooking city of Chattanooga, Tennessee.

Academic Character SACS accreditation. Semester system, 3-week summer term. Majors offered in accounting, Biblical studies & missions, biology, business administration, chemistry, computer science, economics, education, English, history, interdisciplinary studies, music, applied music, natural science, philosophy, psychology, and sociology. Minors offered in most major fields and in 7 additional areas. Distributive requirements. 12 credits in Bible and Christian doctrine required. Independent study. Preprofessional programs in nursing, law, medicine, ministry. Dual-degree programs in engineering, computer science, physics with Georgia Tech. Study abroad. Elementary and secondary education certification. Language lab. 101,000-volume library.

Financial CEEB CSS. College scholarships and grants, state grants and loans; PELL, SEOG, NDSL, GSL, CWS. Priority application deadline March 31.

Admissions High school graduation with 15 units required. GED accepted. SAT or ACT required. $15 application fee. Rolling admissions. $100 deposit required on acceptance of offer of admission. Transfers accepted. Credit possible for CEEB AP and CLEP exams and for own placement exams.

Student Life Student government. Activities Board. Proto-Ministerial Club. Service groups. Underclassmen under 21 must live on campus. No coed dorms. No married-student housing. Liquor, tobacco, drugs, gambling, dancing prohibited. 4 credits in phys ed required. 4 intercollegiate sports for men, 2 for women; intramurals.

[J2] CRANDALL COLLEGE

1283 Adams Street, Macon 31201

[J1] DALTON JUNIOR COLLEGE

Dalton 30720

[J1] DEKALB COMMUNITY COLLEGE

955 North Indian Creek Drive, Clarkston 30021

[1] DEVRY INSTITUTE OF TECHNOLOGY

Atlanta 30341, (404) 452-0045
Director of Admissions: Marjory Coffing

- **Undergraduates: 1,800m, 200w**
- **Tuition (1982/83): $2,980**
- **Fees: $45**
- **Degrees offered: BS, AAS**
- **Student-faculty ratio: 56 to 1**

A private institute, established in 1931, controlled by the Bell & Howell Company. Institute is in 1 building in Atlanta. Served by air and bus.

Academic Character NCACS and professional accreditation. Trimester system. Majors offered in computer science for business and electronics engineering technology. Diploma programs in computer programming for business, digital electronics technician, electronics technician. Courses in 12 additional areas. Pass/fail option. Evening division. Computer center. Library.

Financial Institute scholarships, PELL, SEOG, NDSL, FISL, ALAS, GSL, revolving charge plan; institute has own work program.

Admissions High school graduation. GED accepted. SAT, ACT, or Institute Entrance exam required. $25 application fee. Rolling admissions. $50 deposit required on acceptance of offer of admission. Transfers accepted. Institute has own advanced placement program.

Student Life Student government. Newspaper. Radio club. Honorary fraternity. No dormitories. Special interest groups.

[J1] EMANUEL COUNTY JUNIOR COLLEGE

Swainsboro 30401

[J1] EMMANUEL COLLEGE

Franklin Springs 30639, (404) 245-7226
Admissions Counselors: Mike Hartsfield, Rick Reynolds

- **Undergraduates: 173m, 203w**
- **Tuition (1982/83): $1,770**
- **Room & Board: $1,560; Fees: $90**
- **Degree offered: AA**
- **Student-faculty ratio: 12 to 1**

A private college affiliated with the Pentecostal Holiness Church, established in 1919. Campus located in northeast Georgia, 100 miles from Atlanta. Train station 2 miles away in Royston.

Academic Character SACS accreditation. 3-term system. Majors offered in business, general education, music, and religion. Courses in art, Christian education, English, French, health/physical education/recreation, mathematics, psychology, science, social science, and Spanish. Distributive requirements. 12 credit hours in religion required. Independent study. Honors program. Preprofessional programs in pharmacy, optometry. ROTC. 28,000-volume library.

Financial CEEB CSS. College scholarships, grants, and loans, state grants and loans, ministerial scholarships, athletic grants; PELL, SEOG, NDSL, CWS, college has own work program. Priority application deadline June 10.

Admissions High school graduation with 16 units required. GED accepted. SAT or ACT required. $10 application fee. Rolling admissions. $50 deposit required on acceptance of offer of admission. *Early Admission* and *Concurrent Enrollment* programs. Transfers accepted. Credit possible for CEEB AP and CLEP exams, and for college advanced placement exams.

Student Life Student government. Newspaper, yearbook. Music and drama groups. Religious, service, missionary, honorary, and special interest organizations. No coed dorms. Married-student housing. Liquor, tobacco, illegal drugs, gambling, dancing, and card playing not allowed. Attendance in class, at twice-weekly chapel services, and at church services required. 3 credit hours in phys ed/activity required. 2 intercollegiate sports for men, 2 for women; intramurals.

[1] EMORY UNIVERSITY

Atlanta 30322, (404) 329-6036
Director of Admissions: Linda S. Davis

- **Undergraduates: 1,585m, 1,499w; 8,164 total (including graduates)**
- **Tuition (1982/83): $6,200**
- **Room & Board: $2,680**
- **Degrees offered: BA, BS**
- **Mean SAT 550v, 600m**
- **Student-faculty ratio: 12 to 1**

A private university affiliated with the Methodist Church, established in 1836; became coed in 1953. 600-acre suburban campus just outside Atlanta. Served by air, rail and bus.

Academic Character SACS and professional accreditation. Semester system. 5-, 6-, and 9-week summer terms. 34 majors offered by Emory College in the areas of Afro-American studies, art history, social & political sciences, science, classics, economics, education, English, foreign languages, history, international studies, mathematics, medieval & Renaissance studies, music, philosophy, religion. Other majors offered by the Schools of Business Administration and Nursing. Self-designed and joint majors. Dual degree programs in chemistry, English, history, math, math/computer science, philosophy, physics, psychology, political science, sociology. Distributive requirements. Graduate and professional degrees granted. Independent study. Honors program. Phi Beta Kappa. Pass/fail. Internships. Exchange program with 4 area schools. Washington Semester. Study abroad. Elementary and secondary education certification. ROTC at Georgia State; NROTC at Georgia Tech. Computer center, language lab. 1.8 million-volume library with microform resources.

Financial CEEB CSS. University scholarships, grants, courtesy scholarships, Methodist scholarships, loans; PELL, SEOG, NDSL, FISL, CWS. Application deadlines April 1 (scholarships), April 15 (loans).

Admissions High school graduation with 16 units required. SAT or ACT required; SAT preferred. $25 application fee. Application deadline February 15. $250 deposit required on acceptance of offer of admission. *Early Decision* and *Early Admission* programs. Transfers accepted. Admission deferral possible. Credit possible for CEEB AP and CLEP exams.

Student Life Student government. Newspaper, magazine, yearbook. Music, drama, debate groups. Black Student and Women's Liberation groups. Academic, religious, honorary, service, political, and special interest groups. 14 fraternities and 10 sororities; all have houses. 50% of students join. Freshmen must live at home or on campus. Coed and single-sex dorms. Married-student housing. 70% of students live on campus. Dormitory freshmen may not have cars on campus during weekday. 2 years of phys ed required. 5 intercollegiate sports for men, 4 for women; intramurals. AIAW, NCAA. Student body composition: 4% Asian, 6% Black, 2% Hispanic, 83% White, 5% Other. 80% from out of state.

■[J1] OXFORD COLLEGE

Oxford 30267

- **Undergraduates: 525men and women**
- **Tuition (1982/83): $4,900**
- **Room & Board: $2,294**
- **Degree offered: AA**
- **Mean SAT 493v, 510m**
- **Student-faculty ratio: 15 to 1**

A private junior college affiliated with the United Methodist Church. Suburban campus in Oxford, 38 miles from Emory University (Atlanta).

Academic Character SACS accreditation. Semester system, 6-week summer term. 2-year programs offered in the arts and sciences. Courses in humanities, natural sciences & mathematics, physical education & health, and history & social sciences. Distributive requirements. Transfer programs with Emory University's Emory College, the Division of Allied Health Professions, and the School of Business Administration. Pre-engineering program. Off-campus study/travel program.

Financial CEEB CSS. College scholarships, Methodist scholarships, state grants; college work program. Application deadline April 1.

Admissions High school graduation with 16 units required. SAT or ACT required. $25 application fee. Rolling admissions; suggest applying soon after completing junior year. $100 deposit required on acceptance of offer of admission. *Early Admission* and *Concurrent Enrollment* programs. Transfers accepted. Credit possible for CEEB AP and CLEP exams.

Student Life Student government. Students must live with relatives or on campus. No coed dorms. 1 hour of phys ed per term required. Student body composition: 15% minority.

[J2] FASHION INSTITUTE OF ATLANTA

3376 Peachtree Road, Atlanta 30326

[J1] FLOYD JUNIOR COLLEGE

PO Box 789, Rome 30161

[1] FORT VALLEY STATE COLLEGE

State College Drive, Fort Valley 31030, (912) 825-6211
Director of Admissions: Lawrence W. Young

- **Undergraduates: 684m, 850w**
- **Tuition (1982/83): $855 (in-state), $2,145 (out-of-state)**
- **Room & Board: $1,650**
- **Degrees offered: BA, BS, BBA, BSAgr, BSBEd, BSEd, BSEE, BSHomeEc, BSMusEd, AS**
- **Student-faculty ratio: 8 to 1**

A public college established in 1895. 630-acre campus in the small town of Fort Valley, southwest of Macon.

Academic Character SACS and professional accreditation. Quarter system, 8-week summer term. 34 majors offered by the divisions of Agriculture, Business & Economics, Education, Home Economics, Humanities, Science & Mathematics, and Social Sciences. Minors offered in most major fields and in library science for education majors. Distributive requirements. Exam in major required for seniors. MS granted. Cooperative work/study. Internships. Preprofessional programs in agricultural engineering, veterinary medicine, dentistry, medicine. 3-2 programs with Georgia Tech. Cooperative physics program with Howard U. Summer exchange program with International College of the Cayman Islands. ROTC. Computer center. Experimental agricultural land. 137,000-volume library with microform resources.

Financial CEEB CSS. State scholarships and loans, NDSL, CWS; college has own work program.

Admissions High school graduation with 16 units required. GED accepted. Auditions required for music major or minor. SAT required. Application deadline 20 days before enrollment. $20 room deposit required on acceptance of offer of admission. *Early Admission* Program. Transfers accepted. Credit possible for CLEP exams; college has own advanced placement program. Talent Search Program.

Student Life Student government. Student publication. Drama guild. Academic clubs, honor societies. 4 fraternities and 5 sororities. Students must live at home or on campus. 6 quarters of phys ed required. 5 intercollegiate sports; intramurals. NCAA, NCIA, Southern Intercollegiate Athletic Association. Student body composition: 0.1% Asian, 91.3% Black, 0.2% Hispanic, 6.7% White.

[J1] GAINESVILLE JUNIOR COLLEGE

Gainesville 30503

[1 & G1] GEORGIA, MEDICAL COLLEGE OF

Augusta 30912, (404) 828-2725
Director of Admissions: Elizabeth Griffin

- **Undergraduates: 104m, 705w; 2,000 total (including graduates)**
- **Tuition (1982/83): $1,014 (in-state), $2,724 (out-of-state)**
- **Room: $765.**
- **Degrees offered: BS, BSN, AS**
- **Student-faculty ratio: 3 to 1**

A public college established in 1828. 78-acre urban campus in downtown Augusta. Served by air, rail, and bus.

Academic Character SACS and professional accreditation. Quarter system, 10-week summer term. Majors offered in dental hygiene, medical record administration, medical technology, nuclear medicine technology, nursing, occupational therapy, physical therapy, physician's assistant, radiologic technology, and respiratory therapy. Distributive requirements. MD, DMD, PhD, and MS granted. General education courses at Augusta College; for nursing students at U of Georgia, Savannah State-Armstrong State. Teaching and clinical research facilities at 9 major hospitals. Computer center. 117,700-volume library with microform resources.

Financial CEEB CSS. College scholarships, grants, loans; PELL, SEOG, NSL, NDSL, CWS. Application deadline April 1.

Admissions High school graduation with 16 units required. GED accepted. Interview required for most programs. SAT or ACT required; SAT preferred. Rolling admissions; preferred application deadline April 15. $50 tuition and $50 room deposits required on acceptance of offer of admission. Transfers accepted for fall admission. Credit possible for CEEB CLEP exams.

Student Life Student government. Newspaper, yearbook. Professional and special interest groups. Limited housing in coed and single-sex dorms and apartments. 2 intercollegiate sports for men; 4 intramurals for men and women. Student body composition: 1% Asian, 7% Black, 1% Hispanic, 0.5% Native American, 90% White. 5% from out of state.

[1] GEORGIA, UNIVERSITY OF

Athens 30602, (404) 453-5187
Director of Admissions: M. Overton Phelps

- **Undergraduates: 8,729m, 9,144w; 23,806 total (including graduates)**
- **Tuition (1982/83): $1,107 (in-state), $2,817 (out-of-state)**
- **Room & Board: $1,683-$2,202**
- **Degrees offered: AB, BS, BFA, BMus, BBA, BLA, ABJ**
- **Mean SAT 1000**
- **Student-faculty ratio: 12 to 1**

A public university established in 1785. 3,500-acre campus in Athens, 80 miles from Atlanta. Served by air, rail, and bus.

Academic Character SACS and professional accreditation. Trimester system, summer term. 24 majors offered by the College of Agriculture, 49 by the Franklin College of Arts & Sciences, 15 by the College of Business Administration, 24 by the College of Education, 16 by the College of Home Economics, 1 by the School of Environmental Design, 5 by the School of Forest Resources, 8 by the Henry Grady School of Journalism, 1 by the School of Pharmacy, and 1 by the School of Social Work. Self-designed majors. Graduate and professional degrees granted. Independent study. Honors program. Phi Beta Kappa. Pass/fail. Internships. Preprofessional programs in allied health, dentistry, forest resources, medicine, optometry, veterinary

medicine, and for all professional schools and colleges in the University. 3-2 program in engineering with Georgia Tech. 3-1 programs in medicine, dentistry, veterinary medicine. Study abroad. Elementary, secondary, and special education certification. ROTC, AFROTC. Language lab, gerontology center, museum. 2,062,499-volume library with microform resources.
Financial CEEB CSS. University scholarships and loans, health professions loans; PELL, SEOG, NDSL, GSL, CWS. Scholarship application deadline April 15.
Admissions High school graduation with 16 units required. SAT required. $15 application fee. Rolling admissions; suggest applying by end of 1st semester. $50 room deposit required on acceptance of offer of admission. *Early Admission* and *Early Decision* programs. Transfers accepted. Credit possible for CEEB AP and CLEP exams; University has own advanced placement program.
Student Life Student government. Newspaper, yearbook, other publications. Music, debate, drama groups. 370 registered religious, honorary, academic, and special interest groups. 30 fraternities and 19 sororities, all with houses. 21% of men and 26% of women join. Coed and single-sex dorms; married-student apartments. 30% of students live on campus. Phys ed required for freshmen and sophomores. Many intercollegiate and intramural sports. Southeastern Conference. Student body composition: 0.4% Asian, 4.5% Black, 0.5% Hispanic, 0.1% Native American, 90.1% White, 4.4% Other. 17% from out of state.

[1] GEORGIA COLLEGE

Milledgeville 31061, (912) 453-5187
Director of Admissions: R. Linton Cox, Jr.

- **Undergraduates: 826m, 1,277w**
- **Tuition (1982/83): $645 (in-state), $1,935 (out-of-state)**
- **Room & Board: $1,440; Fees: $126**
- **Degrees offered: BA, BS, BBA, BSN, BMus, BMus Ed, BMus Ther, AS**
- **Mean SAT 435v, 438m**
- **Student-faculty ratio: 20 to 1**

A public college established in 1889. 43-acre campus in small town of Milledgeville, 30 miles from Macon and 100 miles from Atlanta.
Academic Character SACS and professional accreditation. Trimester system, 2 4-week summer terms. 40 majors offered by the Schools of Arts & Sciences, Business, and Education. Minors offered in all major courses and in library science and philosophy. Distributive requirements. Graduate and professional degrees granted. Independent study. Honors program. Cooperative work/study, internships. Preprofessional programs in dentistry, engineering, health therapy, law, medical technology, medicine, optometry, pharmacy, and veterinary medicine. 3-2 program in engineering with Georgia Tech. Study abroad. Elementary and secondary education certification. ROTC. Language lab, nursery school, Home Management House. 132,000-volume library with microform resources.
Financial CEEB CSS. College scholarships, grants, loans, deferred payment; PELL, SEOG, NDSL, NSL, CWS. Application deadlines March 15 (scholarships), April 1 (loans).
Admissions High school graduation with 16 units required. GED accepted. SAT required. $10 application fee. Rolling admissions; application deadline September 1. $35 room deposit required on acceptance of offer of admission. *Early Admission* and *Concurrent Enrollment* programs. Transfers accepted. Credit possible for CEEB AP and CLEP exams.
Student Life Student government. Newspaper, yearbook, radio station. Music, theatre, dance groups. Academic, honorary, religious, service, and special interest organizations. 5 fraternities and 5 sororities. Freshmen and sophomores must live at home or on campus. Single-sex dorms. Married-student housing. 30% of students live on campus. Liquor prohibited on campus. Limited class absences allowed. 6 hours of phys ed required. 7 intercollegiate sports for men, 3 for women; intramurals. NAIA, GIAC. Student body composition: 0.1% Asian, 18% Black, 0.1% Hispanic, 81.1% White, 0.7% Other. 5% from out of state.

[1] GEORGIA INSTITUTE OF TECHNOLOGY

Atlanta 30332, (404) 894-4154
Director of Admissions: Jerry L. Hitt

- **Undergraduates: 6,985m, 1,768w; 11,396 total (including graduates)**
- **Tuition (1982/83): $855 (in-state), $2,088 (out-of-state)**
- **Room & Board: $2,160; Fees: $231**
- **Degrees offered: BS, BE**
- **Mean SAT 534v, 636m**
- **Student-faculty ratio: 22 to 1**

A public institute established in 1885, became coed in 1952. 300-acre urban campus in downtown Atlanta. Served by air, rail, and bus.
Academic Character SACS and professional accreditation. Trimester system, 11-week summer term. BS offered in applied biology, applied mathematics, applied physics, applied psychology, architecture, building construction, chemistry, economics, health physics, health systems, industrial design, industrial management, information & computer science, management science, physics, textile chemistry, and textiles; BE offered in aerospace, ceramic, chemical, civil, electrical, industrial, mechanical, nuclear, and textile engineering, and in engineering science and mechanics. Self-designed majors. Dual degree programs. Courses offered in languages and social sciences. Distributive, English proficiency, and major area exam requirements. MS, PhD granted. Honors program. Cooperative work/study, internships. Pass/fail. 3-2 program in engineering with 100 institutions. Study abroad. ROTC, NROTC, AFROTC. Secondary education certification. Computer center. Experimental centers for engineering, health systems, water resources, nuclear research, environmental resources, bioengineering, radiological protection. 1,300,000-volume library with microform resources.
Financial CEEB CSS. Institute scholarships, grants, loans, deferred payment; PELL, SEOG, NDSL, FISL, CWS; institute has own work program. Application deadline February 15.
Admissions High school graduation with 10-11 units required. SAT required. $15 application fee. Rolling admissions; application deadlines April 1 (in-state), January 1 (out-of-state). $100 tuition and $75 room deposits required on acceptance of offer of admission. *Early Decision* and *Early Admission* programs. Admission deferral possible. Transfers accepted. Credit possible for CEEB AP exams.
Student Life Student government. Newspaper, technical publication, yearbook, radio station. Music, debate, drama groups. Religious, political, and special interest groups. 29 fraternities and 4 sororities, all with houses. 35% of men and 25% of women join. Single freshmen must live at home or on campus. N coed dorms. Cooperative dorms. Married-student housing. 45% of students live on campus. Liquor at student functions, gambling, drugs, hazing prohibited on campus. 3 hours of phys ed, including swimming, required. Several intercollegiate sports for men, 5 for women; intramurals for men. ACC. Student body composition: 4% Asian, 6% Black, 3% Hispanic, 1% Native American, 86% White. 47% from out of state.

■[1] SOUTHERN TECHNICAL INSTITUTE

Marietta 30060, (404) 424-7212
Director of Admissions: Gini Smith

- **Undergraduates: 1,650m, 250w**
- **Tuition (1982/83): $744 (in-state), $2,034 (out-of-state)**
- **Room & Board: $1,920**
- **Degrees offered: BEng Tech, AEng Tech, ATex Mgmt**
- **Student-faculty ratio: 19 to 1**

A public institute established in 1948. 180-acre campus, 15 miles from Atlanta. Air, rail, and bus in Atlanta.
Academic Character SACS and professional accreditation. Trimester system, 11-week summer term. Majors offered in apparel, architectural, civil, electrical, industrial, mechanical, and textile engineering technology. Distributive requirements. Regent's Test and comprehensive exam required. Cooperative work/study. ROTC; AFROTC & NROTC at Georgia Tech. Computer center. 76,000-volume library.
Financial CEEB CSS. Institute scholarships, grants, loans, state scholarships; PELL, SEOG, GSL, NDSL, FISL, CWS. Application deadline April 1.
Admissions High school graduation with 15 units required. GED accepted. SAT required. Rolling admissions; suggest applying by March 1. *Early Decision, Early Admission, Concurrent Enrollment* programs. Admission deferral possible. Transfers accepted. Credit possible for CEEB CLEP exams.
Student Life Student government. Newspaper, yearbook, radio station. Band. Black Student Association. Professional, academic, religious, and special interest organizations. 7 fraternities, one with house, and 2 sororities without houses. 10% of men and women join. Single-sex dorms. No married-student housing. 20% of students live on campus. 3 intercollegiate sports for men; intramurals. NAIA, GIAC. Student body composition: 8% Black, 90% White, 2% Other. 12% from out of state.

[J1] GEORGIA MILITARY COLLEGE

Milledgeville 31601, (912) 453-3481

- **Full-time enrollment: 173m, 98w, 327 total (includes part-time)**
- **Tuition & fees (1982/83): $2,850 (estimate); does not include uniform deposit for 1st-year cadets**
- **Degrees offered: AA, AS, ABA**

A private, coeducational junior college. Private secondary school on campus.
Academic Character SACS accreditation. Trimester system. Majors offered include most preprofessional and college-parallel curricula. Credit possible for ROTC.
Admissions SAT required.
Student Life Dormitory and dining facilities maintained. Intercollegiate and recreational sports, many intramurals offered.

[1] GEORGIA SOUTHERN COLLEGE

Statesboro 30460, (912) 681-5611
Director of Admissions and Registrar: Don Coleman

- **Undergraduates: 2,425m, 3,241w; 6,626 total (including graduates)**
- **Tuition (1982/83): $645 (in-state), $1,935 (out-of-state)**
- **Room & Board: $1,590; Fees: $210**
- **Degrees offered: BA, BS, BBA, BMus, BSEd, BSN, BSTech, BET, AS**
- **Mean SAT 416v, 448m**
- **Student-faculty ratio: 21 to 1**

A public college established in 1906. 300-acre small-town campus, 50 miles from Savannah. Served by air and bus.
Academic Character SACS and professional accreditation. Trimester system, summer term. 39 majors offered by the School of Arts & Sciences, 13 by the School of Business, 10 by the School of Education, and 7 by the School of Technology. Minors, interdisciplinary minors. Distributive requirements. Senior exit exams required. Graduate and professional degrees granted. Cooperative work/study. Preprofessional programs in dentistry, forestry, law, medicine, optometry, pharmacy, physical therapy, veterinary medicine. 3-1 program in medical technology. Cooperative program in agriculture with U of Georgia. Elementary, secondary, and special education certification. ROTC. Computer center, language lab, laboratory school. Institute of Arthropodology and Parasitology. 660,000-volume library with microform resources.
Financial CEEB CSS. College scholarships and grants, health career, Methodist, nursing scholarships and loans; PELL, SEOG, NDSL, FISL, HELP, Tuition Plan, deferred payment plan, CWS; college has own work program. Preferred application deadline March 1.

Admissions High school graduation with 16 units required. GED accepted. SAT required. Interview may be required. Rolling admissions; application deadline September 1. $25 room deposit due 20 days before registration. *Early Admission* and *Concurrent Enrollment* programs. Transfers accepted. Credit possible for CEEB AP and CLEP exams; college has own advanced placement program. Special studies program.
Student Life Student government. Newspaper, yearbook. Music, drama, debate groups. Academic, religious, service, and special interest groups. 14 fraternities and 9 sororities; none have houses. 14% of men and women join. Single freshmen and sophomores under 21 must live at home or on campus. Special interest houses. Married-student housing. 52% of students live on campus. 5 hours of phys ed and 2 of health required. 8 intercollegiate sports for men, 4 for women; intramurals. AIAW, NCAA. Student body composition: 8% Black, 0.3% Hispanic, 90.8% White, 0.9% Other. 7% from out of state.

[1] GEORGIA SOUTHWESTERN COLLEGE

Americus 31709, (912) 928-1279
Director of Admissions: Ronald J. DeValinger

- **Undergraduates: 638m, 1,045w; 2,221 total (including graduates)**
- **Tuition (1982/83): $645 (in-state), $1,935 (out-of-state)**
- **Room & Board: $1,545-$1,920; Fees: $189**
- **Degrees offered: BA, BS, BBA, BSEd, AA**
- **Mean SAT 842**
- **Student-faculty ratio: 15 to 1**

A public college established in 1906. 187-acre campus in a small town 135 miles from Atlanta. Served by bus.
Academic Character SACS and professional accreditation. Trimester system, 10-week summer term. 41 majors offered in the areas of art, biology, business administration, chemistry, education, English, geology, history, mathematics, nursing, office administration, political science, psychology, and sociology. Distributive requirements; exit exam required. Honors program. Cooperative work/study, internships. Credit by exam. Preprofessional programs in art, dentistry, law, medical record administration, medicine, pharmacy, veterinary medicine. 3-2 engineering program with Georgia Tech. Elementary, secondary, and special education certification. ROTC. Computer center. 160,000-volume library with microform resources.
Financial CEEB CSS. College scholarships and grants; Regent's, state scholarships; PELL, SEOG, NSP, NDSL, GSL, NSL, CWS. Preferred application deadline April 1.
Admissions High school graduation with 16 units required. GED accepted. SAT required. Interview may be required. Application deposit $15 (day students), $25 (boarders). Rolling admissions; suggest applying by spring. *Early Admission* and *Concurrent Enrollment* programs. Transfers accepted. College has own advanced placement program.
Student Life Student government. Newspaper, magazine, yearbook. Music, drama groups. Association for Women Students, Student Association for Black Unity. Religious, honorary, political, academic, outing, and special interest groups. 5 fraternities and 5 sororities. Freshmen and sophomores must live at home or on campus. No coed dorms. 40% of students live on campus. 6 courses of phys ed required. 4 intercollegiate sports for men, 3 for women; intramurals. Student body composition: 22% Black, 78% White. 3% from out of state.

[1] GEORGIA STATE UNIVERSITY

University Plaza, Atlanta 30303, (404) 658-2000
Dean of Admissions: George W. Stansbury, Jr., PhD

- **Undergraduates: 3,825m, 4,516w; 20,333 total (including graduates)**
- **Tuition (1982/83): $855 (in-state), $2,880 (out-of-state)**
- **Fees: $60**
- **Degrees offered: BA, BS, BBA, BMus, BSEd, BSN, BVisArts, AA, AS**
- **Mean SAT 962**
- **Student-faculty ratio: 24 to 1**

A public university established in 1913. Urban campus in Atlanta. Served by air, bus, rail.
Academic Character SACS and professional accreditation. Trimester system, summer term. 6 majors offered by the College of Allied Health Sciences, 24 by the College of Arts & Sciences, 10 by the College of Business Administration, 12 by the College of Education, and 7 by the College of Urban Life. Distributive requirements. Senior exam required. Graduate and professional degrees granted. Independent study. Preprofessional program in medicine. Study abroad. Elementary and secondary education certification. ROTC. Computer center, language lab. Art gallery. 571,505-volume library.
Financial University scholarships, grants, and loans; PELL, SEOG, NDSL, CWS; university has own work program. Application deadline April 1.
Admissions High school graduation with 16 units required. Interview may be required. Audition and theory placement test required for music majors. SAT required. $10 application fee. Rolling admissions; application deadline 20 days before trimester begins. *Early Decision* and *Concurrent Enrollment* programs. Transfers accepted. Admission deferral possible. Credit possible for CEEB AP and CLEP exams; university has own advanced placement program. Division of Development program.
Student Life Student government. Newspaper, magazine, radio station, yearbook. Georgia State Players. Recreation program for urban students. Academic, religious, service, and special interest groups. 11 fraternities with social rooms and 8 sororities. No on-campus housing. Gambling, hazing, weapons, liquor, and drugs prohibited on campus. 6 intercollegiate sports for men, 4 for women, 2 coed; intramurals and club sports. NCAA. 12% of students from out of state.

[J1] GORDON JUNIOR COLLEGE

Barnesville 30204, (404) 358-1700

- **Full-time enrollment: 258m, 404w, 1,412 total (includes part-time)**
- **Tuition (1982/83): $489**
- **Room & Board: $1,380-$1,680; Fees: $60**
- **Degrees offered: AA, AAS**

A public junior college established in 1852. 125-acre suburban campus, in a small city 1 hour from Atlanta and Macon.
Academic Character SACS accreditation. Trimester system, summer term. Majors offered in agricultural engineering, agriculture, art, biological sciences, business administration/industrial management/economics, chemistry, computer science, criminal justice, dental hygiene, English, foreign language, forestry, general studies, geology, health & physical education, history, home economics, journalism, mathematics, medical illustration, medical records administration, medical technology, music, nursing, physical therapy, physics, political science, psychology, radiologic technology, secretarial studies, sociology/anthropology, speech & drama, teacher education, technology, and urban life. Career programs in 11 fields. AAS with vocational technical schools in 21 areas. Distributive requirements. Preprofessional programs in dentistry, law, medicine, pharmacy, and veterinary medicine.
Financial CEEB CSS. State scholarships and loans; PELL, SEOG, NDSL, CWS. Application deadline May 1.
Admissions High school graduation required. GED accepted. SAT required. Rolling admissions. *Early Admission* and *Concurrent Enrollment* programs. Transfers accepted. Credit possible for CLEP exams.
Student Life Student Affairs Committee. Cultural events. Single students under 21 must live at home or on campus. Intercollegiate and intramural sports.

[P] INTERDENOMINATIONAL THEOLOGICAL CENTER

Atlanta 30314

[P] JOHN MARSHALL LAW SCHOOL

Atlanta 30308

[1] KENNESAW COLLEGE

PO Box 444, Marietta 30061, (404) 422-8770
Registrar and Director of Admissions: Thomas H. Rogers

- **Enrollment: 1,841m, 2,293w**
- **Tuition (1982/83): $684 (in-state), $1,974 (out-of-state)**
- **Degrees offered: BA, BS**
- **Mean SAT 442v, 431m**
- **Student-faculty ratio: 14 to 1**

A public college established in 1963. 152-acre campus 20 miles from Atlanta. Served by bus. Air and rail in Atlanta.
Academic Character SACS accreditation. Trimester system. Majors offered in biology, business administration, chemistry, education, English, history, mathematics, music, music education, political science, and psychology. Double majors in business fields. Courses in 14 additional areas. Distributive requirements. Exit exam required. Independent study. Internships, cooperative work study. Credit by exam. Member of a consortium with other Atlanta area colleges; cross-registration possible. Elementary and secondary education certification. Study abroad. ROTC. Computer facilities. 101,000-volume library with microform resources.
Financial CEEB CSS. College scholarships, grants, and loans; PELL, SEOG, NSP, GSL, NDSL, FISL, NSL, CWS. Priority application deadline March 15.
Admissions High school graduation with 15 units required. GED accepted. SAT required. Rolling admissions; application deadline 20 days before trimester begins. *Early Admission* and *Concurrent Enrollment* programs. Transfers accepted. Credit possible for CEEB AP and CLEP exams. Special Studies Program.
Student Life Student government. Newspaper, magazine, yearbook. Music, art groups. Black Student Alliance. Academic, honorary, religious, service, and special interest groups. 1 social fraternity. No on-campus housing. Liquor prohibited on campus. 6 hours of phys ed required. Intramural and club sports. Student body composition: 0.2% Asian, 1.2% Black, 0.5% Hispanic, 0.1% Native American, 95.6% White. 5% from out of state.

[1] LA GRANGE COLLEGE

La Grange 30240, (404) 882-2911
Director of Admissions: John T. Helton

- **Undergraduates: 271m, 416w; 996 total (including graduates)**
- **Tuition (1982/83): $2,355**
- **Room & Board: $1,515; Fees: $60**
- **Degrees offered: BA, BBA, AA**
- **Mean SAT 412v, 429m**
- **Student-faculty ratio: 16 to 1**

A private college affiliated with the First United Methodist Church, established in 1831; became coed in 1951. 19-acre campus in small city 40 miles from Columbus and 70 miles from Atlanta.
Academic Character SACS accreditation. Trimester system, 2 4-week summer terms. Majors offered in art, biology, business administration, chemistry, Christian education, early childhood education, economics, elementary education, English, environmental management, general science, health & physical education, history, mathematics, middle childhood education, political science, psychology, recreational management, religion, social work, Spanish, and speech & drama. Minors. Distributive requirements. MBA, MEd granted. Independent study. Honors program in some fields. Joint

enrollment in engineering with Georgia Tech, Auburn. Preprofessional programs in dentistry, engineering, law, medicine, optometry, paramedicine, pharmacy, social work, theology. Study abroad for religion, foreign language majors. Elementary and secondary education certification. ROTC. Language lab. 70,000-volume library with microform resources.
Financial CEEB CSS. College scholarships and loans, Methodist loans; PELL, SEOG, NDSL, Tuition Plan, CWS, College Student Aid Program. Application deadline May 1.
Admissions High school graduation with 11 units required. GED accepted. SAT or ACT required. $10 application fee. Rolling admissions. $50 room deposit required on acceptance of offer of admission. *Early Admission* and *Concurrent Enrollment* programs. Transfers accepted. Credit possible for CEEB AP and CLEP exams.
Student Life Student government, membership on faculty committees. Newspaper, magazine, yearbook. Music and drama groups. Association of Black Collegians. Academic, religious, service, honorary, and special interest groups. 3 fraternities with houses and 4 sororities without houses. 50% of men and women join. Seniors and students over 21 may live off campus. No married-student housing. 48% of students live on campus. Liquor and drugs prohibited on campus. 3 trimesters of phys ed required. 6 intercollegiate sports, 5 intramurals. NAIA, GIAC. 10% of students from out of state.

[P] LIFE CHIROPRACTIC COLLEGE
1269 Barclay Circle, Marietta 30060

[J1] MACON JUNIOR COLLEGE
Macon 31297

[1] MERCER UNIVERSITY
Macon 31207, (912) 744-2700, ext. 253, 254
Director of Admissions: Joseph S. McDaniel

- **Undergraduates: 1,369m, 1,139w; 2,972 total (including graduates)**
- **Tuition (1982/83): $3,321 (in-county), $4,119 (others)**
- **Room & Board: $1,994**
- **Degrees offered: AB, BS, BBA**
- **Mean SAT 490v, 510m**
- **Student-faculty ratio: 16 to 1**

A private university affiliated with Baptist Convention of Georgia, established in 1833. 130-acre urban campus in Macon, 85 miles from Atlanta. Served by air and bus.
Academic Character SACS and professional accreditation. Trimester system, 2 5-week summer terms. Majors in accounting, Afro-American studies, art, biology, business, chemistry, Christianity, economics, English, finance, French, German, health/physical education/recreation, history, Latin, law, management, mathematics, music, philosophy, physics, political science, psychology, sociology, Spanish, and speech & dramatic art. Special and self-designed majors. Minors offered in most major fields and in 6 additional areas. Distributive requirements. MEd granted. Independent study. Pass/fail. Internships. 3-2 programs in engineering, forestry, pharmacy. 3-1 program in medical technology. Exchange programs with other southeastern schools. Fine arts summer tour in Europe. ROTC. Computer center. 240,000-volume library.
Financial CEEB CSS. University scholarships and grants, state grants, incentive scholarships, fund for students preparing for church work; PELL, SEOG, NDSL, FISL, Tuition Plan, deferred payment, CWS. Application deadline May 1; file FAF by April 1.
Admissions High school graduation with 16 units required. SAT or ACT required. $10 application fee. Rolling admissions; application deadline 2 weeks before trimester begins. $25 tuition deposit and $75 room deposit required on acceptance of offer of admission. *Early Admission* Program. Transfers accepted. Admission deferral possible. Credit possible for CEEB AP and CLEP exams.
Student Life Student government; women's student government. Newspaper, magazine, yearbook. Music, drama, debate groups. Black Student Alliance. Honorary, religious, service, and special interest groups. 10 fraternities, 8 with houses, and 7 sororities, 4 with dorm suites. 35% of men and women join. Students under 21 must live at home or on campus. Some married-student housing. 65% of students live on campus. Liquor, gambling, hazing prohibited. 5 intercollegiate sports for men, 2 for women; several intramural sports for men, 4 for women. AIAW, NCAA. Student body composition: 12% Black, 1% Hispanic, 87% White. 24% from out of state.

■[1] MERCER UNIVERSITY AT ATLANTA
Atlanta 30303

■[1] and [G1] SOUTHERN SCHOOL OF PHARMACY OF MERCER UNIVERSITY
Atlanta 30303

[J1] MIDDLE GEORGIA COLLEGE
Cochran 31014

[1] MOREHOUSE COLLEGE
Atlanta 30314, (404) 681-2800
Director of Admissions: Robert E. Miller

- **Undergraduates: 1,841m**
- **Tuition (1982/83): $2,900**
- **Room & Board: $2,060; Fees: $356**
- **Degrees offered: BA, BS**
- **Mean SAT 374v, 408m**
- **Student-faculty ratio: 17 to 1**

A private college established in 1867. 40-acre urban campus in Atlanta. Served by air, bus, and rail.
Academic Character SACS accreditation. Semester system, 8-week summer term. 33 majors offered by the departments of English, Foreign Languages, Philosophy & Religion, Music, Art, Drama, Biology, Chemistry, Mathematics, Physics, Psychology, Engineering, Economics & Business Administration, Computer Science, History, Political Science, Sociology, Teacher Education, and Health & Physical Education. Minors offered in African studies, Afro-American studies, Caribbean studies, and library science. Courses in non-Western studies, Russian, Swahili. Distributive requirements. 1 religion course and senior comprehensive exam required. Phi Beta Kappa. Internships. Preprofessional programs in dentistry, medicine, pharmacy. Cooperative programs with Interdenominational Theological Center, Clark, Morris Brown, Spelman. 3-2 program in engineering with Georgia Tech. Early childhood, elementary, and secondary education certification. ROTC, AFROTC, NROTC at Georgia Tech. 300,000-volume library serves all members of Atlanta U. Center.
Financial CEEB CSS. College scholarships, Georgia incentive grants, loans; PELL, SEOG, GSL, NDSL, CWS. Member United Negro College Fund. Application deadline April 15 (scholarships, loans), June 1 (Georgia incentive grants). $80 acceptance fee required within 20 days of award.
Admissions High school graduation with 12 units required. GED accepted. SAT required. $15 application fee. Rolling admissions; application deadline April 15. $80 deposit required on acceptance of offer of admission. *Early Admission* Program. Transfers accepted.
Student Life Newspaper, yearbook. Music, debate, drama groups. Honorary, academic, and special interest groups. 4 fraternities; all have houses. 16% join. Freshmen must live on campus. 50% of students live on campus. Liquor and weapons prohibited on campus. Attendance in class and at weekly chapel required. Phys ed required for freshmen. 5 intercollegiate sports; intramurals. NCAA, SIAC. Student body composition: 100% Black. 70% from out of state.

[1] MORRIS BROWN COLLEGE
Atlanta 30314, (404) 525-7831
Director of Admissions: Lucille S. Williams

- **Undergraduates: 610m, 953w**
- **Tuition (1982/83): $2,900**
- **Room & Board: $1,726-$1,760; Fees: $316**
- **Degrees offered: BA, BS**
- **Student-faculty ratio: 15 to 1**

A private college affiliated with the African Methodist Episcopal Church, established in 1881. 18-acre urban campus in Atlanta. Served by air, rail, and bus.
Academic Character SACS accreditation. Semester system, 8-week summer term. 50 majors offered by the departments of Education & Psychology, Health & Physical Education, Foreign Language, Music, Art, English, Biology, Chemistry, Mathematics, Social Relations, and Business. Minors offered in all major fields except education and in 8 additional areas. Distributive requirements. GRE required for graduation. 1 religion course required. Preprofessional programs in business, medicine, ministry, social work. 3-3 program in engineering with Georgia Tech. Member Atlanta U. Center. Elementary, secondary, and special education certification. NROTC. Computer center, language lab. 56,000-volume library; use of Atlanta U. Center facilities.
Financial CEEB CSS. College scholarships, grants, music scholarships, loans; PELL, SEOG, NDSL, FISL, deferred payment plan, CWS. Application deadlines: May 15 (scholarships), June 1 (loans).
Admissions High school graduation with 15 units required. SAT or ACT required. $20 application fee. Rolling admissions; suggest applying in fall. $50 tuition and $50 room deposits required on acceptance of offer of admission. *Early Admission* Program. Transfers accepted.
Student Life Student government. Newspaper. Music, debate, drama groups. Academic, religious, honorary, and special interest groups. 4 fraternities and 5 sororities. Students may live off campus. No married-student housing. 45% of students live on campus. Attendance at daily chapel, Sunday service required. Liquor, weapons prohibited on campus. 2 semesters of phys ed required. 5 intercollegiate sports for men and women; intramurals. NCAA, SIAC. Student body composition: 0.1% Asian, 97.9% Black, 0.1% White. 24% from out of state.

[P] NATIONAL CENTER FOR PARALEGAL TRAINING
3376 North Peachtree Road, Atlanta 30326

[1] NORTH GEORGIA COLLEGE
Dahlonega 30597, (404) 864-3391
Director of Admissions: Gary R. Steffey

- **Undergraduates: 657m, 766w**
- **Tuition (1982/83): $645 (in-state), $1,935 (out-of-state)**
- **Room & Board: $1,410; Fees: $156**
- **Degrees offered: BA, BS, BBA, BSW, AS**
- **Mean SAT 420v, 430m**
- **Student-faculty ratio: 18 to 1**

A public military college established in 1873. 150-acre rural campus in small town 70 miles from Atlanta. Bus and airport in Gainesville.
Academic Character SACS and professional accreditation. Quarter system, 9-week summer term. 33 majors offered in the areas of allied health, biology, business administration, chemistry, education, English, fine arts, mathematics, modern languages, physical education, physics, psychology, and social sciences. Minor required; offered in most major fields. Exit exams required. MEd granted. Independent study. Internships. Preprofessional

programs in dental hygiene, dentistry, forestry, law, medical records, medical technology, medicine, pharmacy, physical therapy. 3-2 programs in engineering, industrial management, and information & computer science with Georgia Tech, Clemson. Elementary, secondary, and special education certification. ROTC. 130,000-volume library with microform resources.
Financial CEEB CSS. College scholarships, grants, Georgia Incentive Scholarships, loans; PELL, SEOG, GSL, FISL, NDSL, CWS. Scholarship application deadline July 1.
Admissions High school graduation with 16 units required. GED accepted. SAT required. $10 application fee. Rolling admissions; suggest filing in fall. $25 deposit required on acceptance of offer of admission. *Early Decision, Early Admission,* and *Concurrent Enrollment* programs. Transfers accepted. Admission deferral possble. Credit possible for CEEB AP and CLEP exams; college has own advanced placement program. Developmental Studies Program for academically disadvantaged students.
Student Life Student government. Newspaper, yearbook. Music, drama groups. Parachutist club. Honorary, military, and special interest groups. 4 fraternities and 2 sororities; none have houses. 10% of men and women join. Unmarried students under 23 must live on campus or at home. No married-student housing or coed dorms. 60% of students live on campus. Curfews. Liquor prohibited on campus. Military science required for men; cadets must wear uniforms. 6 quarters of phys ed required. 4 intercollegiate sports for men, 4 for women, 1 coed; intramurals. AIAW, NAIA. Student body composition: 4% Black, 95% White, 1% Other. 6% from out of state.

[1] OGLETHORPE UNIVERSITY
4484 Peachtree Road, NE, Atlanta 30319, (404) 233-6864
Director of Admissions: James A. Nesbitt

- **Undergraduates: 433m, 450w**
- **Tuition (1982/83): $3,990**
- **Room & Board: $2,190**
- **Degrees offered: BA, BS, BBA**
- **Mean SAT 505v, 538m**
- **Student-faculty ratio: 19 to 1**

A private university established in 1835, became coed in 1910. 160-acre suburban campus 8 miles from downtown Atlanta. Served by air, rail, and bus.
Academic Character SACS accreditation. Semester system, 2 5-week summer terms. Majors offered in accounting, American studies, biology, business administration, chemistry, economics, education, English, general studies, history, international studies, mathematics, philosophy, physics, political studies, psychology, sociology, and social work. Distributive requirements. MA granted. Independent study. Internships. Preprofessional programs in allied health, dentistry, law, medicine, ministry. 3-2 program in engineering with Auburn, Georgia Tech. 2-3 program in art with Atlanta College of Art. 3-1 program in medical technology. Study abroad. Early childhood, middle, and secondary education certification. ROTC, NROTC, AFROTC at Georgia Tech. Language lab. 183,000-item library with microform resources.
Financial CEEB CSS. University scholarships, grants, loans; PELL, SEOG, FISL, NDSL, College Aid Plan, CWS. Application deadline May 1.
Admissions High school graduation with 15 units required. ACT or SAT required. $20 application fee. Rolling admissions; application deadline July 1. $100 tuition and $100 room deposits required on acceptance of offer of admission. *Early Decision* and *Early Admission* programs. Some transfers accepted. Admission deferral possible. Credit possible for CEEB AP and CLEP exams.
Student Life Student government. Newspaper, magazine, yearbook. Music, drama, photography groups. Black Student Caucus. Honorary, political, religious, service, social, and special interest groups. 3 fraternities and 2 sororities. Students may live off campus. No coed dorms. 55% of students live on campus. 5 intercollegiate sports for men, 4 for women; intramural and club sports. GAIAW, NAIA, NCAA. Student body composition: 1% Asian, 9% Black, 5% Hispanic, 82% White, 3% Other. 48% from out of state.

[1] PAINE COLLEGE
1235 15th Street, Augusta 30910, (404) 722-4471
Coordinator of Admissions: Edythe G. Dimond

- **Undergraduates: 230m, 533w**
- **Tuition (1982/83): $2,535**
- **Room & Board: $1,500; Fees: $195**
- **Degrees offered: BA, BS, BSBA, BSEd**
- **Mean SAT 308v, 337m**
- **Student-faculty ratio: 15 to 1**

A private college affiliated with Christian Methodist Episcopal and United Methodist churches, established in 1882. 43-acre urban campus in downtown Augusta. Served by air and bus.
Academic Character SACS accreditation. Trimester system, 5-week summer term. Majors offered in biology, accounting, business administration, management, chemistry, elementary education, English, history, mass communications, mathematics, music education, religion/philosophy, and sociology. Minors, offered in most major fields and in 8 additional areas. Distributive requirements. 1 trimester of religion required. Independent study. Honors program. Cooperative work/study, internships. Credit for life/work experience. Preprofessional programs in dentistry, medicine, pharmacy, veterinary science. Transfer programs in engineering, nursing. Consortium with Augusta College, Medical College of Georgia. Elementary and secondary education certification. ROTC. Early Childhood Development Center. 74,196-volume library.
Financial CEEB CSS. College scholarships, grants, Methodist and athletic scholarships, state grants, loans; PELL, SEOG, NDSL, GSL, CWS. Application deadline March 15 (scholarships), July 15 (loans).
Admissions High school graduation with 15 units recommended. GED accepted. SAT or ACT required. Rolling admissions; suggest applying by March. $25 deposit required on acceptance of offer of admission. *Early Admission* and *Concurrent Enrollment* programs. Transfers accepted. Admission deferral possible. Credit possible for CEEB CLEP and for college placement exams. Upward Bound pre-college program.
Student Life Student government. Newspaper, yearbook. Music, drama, forensic groups. Academic, religious, and special interest organizations. 8 fraternities, 4 with houses, and 4 sororities with houses. 20% of men and 30% of women join. Students must live at home or on campus. No coed dorms. No married-student housing. 55% of students live on campus. Liquor prohibited on campus. Attendance in class and at weekly assemblies required. 2 trimesters of phys ed required. 2 intercollegiate sports for men; intramurals. NAIA. Student body composition: 99% Black, 0.5% Hispanic, 0.5% White.

[1] PIEDMONT COLLEGE
Demorest 30535, (404) 778-8033
Registrar: Nolan Nix

- **Undergraduates: 500 men and women**
- **Tuition (1982/83): $1,575**
- **Room & Board: $2,075; Fees: $83**
- **Degrees offered: BA, BS, BFA**

A private college affiliated with the Congregational Christian Churches of America, established in 1897. 250-acre rural campus 85 miles from Atlanta. Bus nearby.
Academic Character SACS accreditation. Quarter system, 5½-week summer term. Majors offered in art, accounting, business administration, English, history, psychology, social work, sociology, Spanish, biology, chemistry, mathematics, early childhood education, middle grades education, and in 7 secondary education areas. Minors offered in all major fields and in 7 additional areas. Distributive requirements. Accelerated study. Preprofessional programs in medical sciences, forestry, wildlife management. ROTC. Language lab. 70,000-volume library.
Financial CEEB CSS. College scholarships, grants, music and art scholarships, athletic grants, state grants; PELL, SEOG, NDSL, GSL, FISL, CWS; college has own work program.
Admissions High school graduation with 16 units required. GED accepted. SAT required. $10 application fee. Rolling admissions. $50 tuition and $75 room deposits required on acceptance of offer of admission. *Early Admission* and *Concurrent Enrollment* programs. Transfers accepted. Credit possible for CEEB AP and CLEP exams; college has own advanced placement program.
Student Life Student government. Newspaper, yearbook. Music and drama groups. Religious, honorary, professional, and special interest organizations. Single students must live at home or on campus. No coed dorms. Married-student housing. Liquor, drugs, weapons, hazing prohibited on campus. Attendance in class, and at chapels, assemblies, lyceums, and Sunday vespers required. 5 intercollegiate sports; intramurals. GAIAW, GIAA.

[J1] REINHARDT COLLEGE
Waleska 30183
Director of Admissions: David J. Tucker

- **Undergraduates: 450 men and women**
- **Tuition (1983/84): $50 per quarter hour**
- **Room & Board: $600-$675; Fees: $75**
- **Degrees offered: AA, ABA, AFA, AS**
- **Mean SAT 750 composite**
- **Student-faculty ratio: 12 to 1**

A private junior college affiliated with the United Methodist Church. 600-acre campus 40 miles from Atlanta.
Academic Character SACS accreditation. Quarter system, summer quarter. Majors offered in English, behavioral science, social science, natural science, mathematics, business administration, music, art, criminal justice, horticulture, and secretarial science. Distributive requirements. 5 hours of religion/philosophy required. Preprofessional programs in dental hygiene, dentistry, education, engineering, forestry/fish & wildlife, law, medical technology, medicine, nursing, pharmacy, veterinary medicine. Cooperative program with vocational-technical schools. Banking program with American Institute of Banking. 40,000-volume library.
Financial CEEB CSS. College scholarships, state grants and loans, Methodist scholarships and loans; PELL, SEOG, NDSL, FISL, CWS.
Admissions High school graduation required with 10 units recommended. GED accepted. SAT required. $10 application fee. *Early Admission* and *Concurrent Enrollment* programs. Transfers accepted. Credit possible for CEEB CLEP exams; college has own advancement placement program.
Student Life No coed dorms.

[1] SAVANNAH COLLEGE OF ART AND DESIGN
342 Bull Street, Savannah 31401, (912) 236-7458

- **Undergraduates: 180m, 204w**
- **Tuition (1982/83): $3,150**
- **Room & Board: $1,650; Fees: $210**
- **Degree offered: BFA**
- **Mean ACT 20, mean SAT 500v, 500m**
- **Student-faculty ratio: 8 to 1**

A private college established in 1976. Urban campus located in the center of Savannah. Served by bus.
Academic Character Professional accreditation. Quarter system, 2 5-week summer terms. Majors offered in photography, painting, interior design, graphic design, illustration, and historic preservation. Distributive requirements. Internships. Study trips. Summer terms in New York and Europe. Gallery. 24,000-volume library.
Financial College scholarships and loans, state grants and loans; PELL,

SEOG, NDSL, FISL, CWS.
Admissions High school graduation required. SAT or ACT required. $25 application fee. Rolling admissions. *Early Admission, Early Decision,* and *Concurrent Enrollment* programs. Transfers accepted.
Student Life Monthly receptions for area artists. Limited housing. No coed dorms.

[1] SAVANNAH STATE COLLEGE
Savannah 31404, (912) 356-2240
Director of Admissions: David Foye

- **Undergraduates: 1,100m, 1,200**
- **Tuition (1982/83): $645 (in-state), $1,935 (out-of-state)**
- **Room & Board: $1,560; Fees: $270**
- **Degrees offered: BA, BBA, BS, BSW, AS**
- **Student-faculty ratio: 14 to 1**

A public college established in 1890. 136-acre suburban campus in Savannah.
Academic Character SACS and professional accreditation. Quarter system. Majors offered in accounting, economics, finance, business administration, information systems, management, marketing, office administration, criminal justice, English language and literature, history, music, political science, social sciences, sociology, biology, chemistry, civil engineering technology, dietetics & institutional management, electronics engineering technology, environmental studies, marine biology, mathematics, mechanical engineering technology, and textiles & clothing. Minors offered in some major fields and in 18 additional areas. Distributive requirements. Competency and senior exams required. MBA granted. Honors program. Cooperative work/study, internships. Preprofessional programs in 12 areas. 3-2 programs in engineering with Georgia Tech. ROTC, NROTC. Computer center, nursery school. 138,000-volume library
Financial CEEB CSS. College scholarships, grants, loans, one-year merit scholarships; PELL, SEOG, NDSL, FISL, CWS. Application deadline August 18.
Admissions High school graduation required. GED accepted. SAT required. $10 application fee. Rolling admissions; application deadline 20 days before registration. Transfers accepted. Credit possible for CEEB AP and CLEP exams, military service. Special Studies Program for applicants with below minimum required test scores.
Student Life Student government. Newspaper, yearbook, radio station. Music and special interest groups. 6 fraternities and 4 sororities. Students must live at home or on campus. No coed dorms. Married-student housing. Class attendance required. 6 hours of phys ed/health required. Intercollegiate and intramural sports. NAIA, NCAA, SIAC. Student body composition: 88.9% Black, 0.6% Native American, 6.5% White.

[1] SHORTER COLLEGE
Rome 30161, (404) 291-2121
Director of Admissions: Pat Hart

- **Undergraduates: 298m, 475w**
- **Tuition (1982/83): $2,700**
- **Room & Board: $1,650**
- **Degrees offered: BA, BS, BM, BChurchMus, BMusEd, BSEd, BFA**
- **Student-faculty ratio: 15 to 1**

A private college affiliated with the Baptist Church, established in 1873. 150-acre small-city campus, 90 miles from Atlanta. Served by bus.
Academic Character SACS and professional accreditation. Semester system, summer term. 38 majors offered in the areas of arts, sciences, humanities, business, mathematics, recreation management, education, music, church music, and music education. Special majors. Distributive requirements. Progress exams. Independent study. Internships. Some pass/fail grading. Preprofessional programs in allied health sciences, dentistry, law, medicine, ministry. Elementary and secondary education certification. TV studio, music library. Area libraries available totaling 304,000 volumes and microform resources.
Financial CEEB CSS. College scholarships, ministerial scholarships, state grants, loans; PELL, SEOG, NDSL, deferred payment; college has own work program.
Admissions High school graduation. Audition required for music majors. ACT or SAT required. $10 application fee. Rolling admissions; suggest applying by early spring. $150 deposit required on acceptance of offer of admission. *Early Admission* and *Concurrent Enrollment* programs. Transfers accepted. College has own advanced placement program.
Student Life Student government. Newspaper, magazine, yearbook. Music, drama, art groups. Religious, honorary, and special interest groups. 3 fraternities and 3 sororities. Single students under 23 must live at home or on campus. No coed dorms. Some married-student housing. 65% of students live on campus. Attendance required at convocations. Phys ed required for freshmen. 4 intercollegiate sports for men, 3 for women; intramural and club sports. Student body composition: 4.5% Black, 95% White. 10% from out of state.

[J1] SOUTH GEORGIA COLLEGE
Douglas 31533 (912) 384-1100

- **Full-time enrollment: 365m, 393w, 1,074 total (includes part-time)**
- **Tuition and fees (1982/83): $181 per quarter (in-state), $314 per quarter (out-of-state)**
- **Room & Board: $450 (in-state), $464 (out-of-state)**
- **Degrees offered: AA, AS**

A public coeducational junior college about 100 miles south of Macon and 60 west of Savannah.
Academic Character SACS accreditation. Quarter system. College offers more than 100 college parallel and career programs including accounting, agribusiness, agriscience, autoparts management, banking, business, computer science, criminal justice, education, industrial technology, nursing (RN), secretarial science, and word processing. Remedial math and English programs.
Admissions High school graduation required. GED accepted. SAT required. Rolling admissions. *Early Decision* Program. Admission deferral possible. Credit possible for CEEB AP exams.
Student Life Dormitories available for 300 men and 200 women. Student body composition: 20% minority.

[1] SOUTHERN TECHNICAL INSTITUTE
Marietta — see Georgia, University of

[1] SPELMAN COLLEGE
Atlanta 30314, (404) 681-3643, ext. 300
Director of Admissions: Juanita Wallace Dillard

- **Undergraduates: 1,450w**
- **Tuition (1982/83): $2,900**
- **Room & Board: $2,245; Fees: $350**
- **Degrees offered: BA, BS**
- **Student-faculty ratio: 15 to 1**

A private college established in 1881. 32-acre urban campus in Atlanta. Served by air and bus.
Academic Character SACS accreditation. Semester system, 8-week summer term with Atlanta U. Majors offered in art, biochemistry, biology, chemistry, child development, computer sciences, drama, economics, English, French, German, health/physical education, history, mathematics, music, natural sciences, philosophy, physics, political science, psychology, sociology, and Spanish. Distributive requirements. Independent study. Honors program. Phi Beta Kappa. Pass/fail. Internships. Member Atlanta U. Center. 3-2 program in engineering with Georgia Tech or Boston U. 3-1 program in medicine. Preprofessional program in medicine. Exchange with Mount Holyoke, Simmons, Smith, and Wellesley Colleges. Study abroad. ROTC, AFROTC; NROTC through Morehouse College. Elementary, secondary, and special education teacher training. Nursery-Kindergarten school, language lab. 553,197-volume library; 250,000-volume library with microform resources available through Atlanta U. Center.
Financial CEEB CSS. College scholarships and loans; PELL, SEOG, NDSL, deferred payment plan, CWS. Application deadline April 1.
Admissions High school graduation with 15 units required. SAT or ACT required. Interview may be required. $20 application fee. Application deadline January 15. Notification by March 1. $100 deposit required on acceptance of offer of admission. *Early Decision* and *Early Admission* programs. Transfers accepted. Admission deferral possible. Credit possible for CEEB AP and CLEP exams.
Student Life Student government. Newspaper, magazine, yearbook. Music, drama, dance groups. Academic, political, religious, service, and special interest groups. Students may live off campus. Honors dorm. No married-student housing. 58% of students live on campus. Juniors and seniors may have cars on campus. Liquor and illegal drugs prohibited on campus; cigarette smoking allowed in some areas. Limited class absences. Attendance at biweekly convocations required. 4 semesters of phys ed required. 2 intercollegiate and 6 intramural sports. Student body composition: 100% Black. 66% from out of state.

[1] TIFT COLLEGE
Forsyth 31029, (912) 994-2515

- **Full-time enrollment: 400 men and women**
- **Tuition, room & board (1982/83): $4,380**
- **Degrees offered: AB, BS**
- **Mean SAT 890 composite**
- **Student-faculty ratio: 15 to 1**

A private, primarily women's, liberal arts college chartered in 1849 and supported by the Southern Baptist Church. Campus in the small town of Forsyth, located between Macon and Atlanta.
Academic Character SACS accreditation. Major programs in liberal arts (AB) and in elementary education (BS). Graduate degrees granted in cooperation with Mercer University. Remedial math and English programs. 59,000-volume library.
Financial CEEB CSS. Approximately 80% of students receive financial aid, which is awarded on the basis of need. Awards are usually granted in a package of scholarship, loan, and work grant, and range from $200 to $2,100 per year.
Admissions High school graduation required. SAT required. Rolling admissions. *Early Admission* and *Early Decision* programs. Transfers accepted. Admission deferral possible. Credit possible for CEEB AP exams.
Student Life Dormitories on campus, one dining hall. No sororities.

[P] TOCCOA FALLS COLLEGE
Toccoa Falls 30598, (404) 886-6831
Admissions-Registrar: Michael G. Scales

- **Undergraduates: 324m, 337w**
- **Tuition (1982/83): $2,500**
- **Room & Board: $1,850-$1,970**
- **Degrees offered: BA, BS, ThB, AA**
- **Mean SAT 411v, 416m**
- **Student-faculty ratio: 14 to 1**

A private college established in 1907. 1,100-acre rural campus 2 miles from Toccoa and 100 miles from Atlanta. Served by bus and rail.
Academic Character Semester system, 2 4½-week summer terms. Majors offered in Bible-theology, Christian education, church music, communication, elementary education, missiology, music education, and general studies. Minors offered in most major fields and in 13 additional areas.

Distributive requirements. 30 hours of Bible-theology required. GRE required. Independent study. Pastoral internships. Elementary education certification. 55,000-volume library with microform resources.
Financial CEEB CSS. College scholarships and loans, state grants; PELL, SEOG, NDSL, GSL, deferred payment plan, CWS.
Admissions High school graduation required. GED accepted. SAT or ACT required. $20 application fee. Rolling admissions. $100 deposit required on acceptance of offer of admission. *Early Admission* and *Early Decision* programs. Transfers accepted. Admission deferral possible. Credit possible for CEEB CLEP exams.
Student Life Student government. Newspapers, yearbook. Music groups. Religious and service organizations. Single students must live at home or on campus. No coed dorms. Limited married-student housing. Dress code. Attendance in class required. 2 hours of phys ed required. 4 intercollegiate sports for men, 2 for women; intramurals. NAIA, NCCAA.

[J1] TRUETT McCONNELL COLLEGE
Cleveland 30528 (404) 865-2134
- **Full-time enrollment: 261m, 260w, 746 total (includes part-time)**
- **Tuition, room, and board (1982/83): $3,510**
- **Degrees offered: AA, AS**
- **Mean SAT 750 composite**

A private, coeducational, liberal arts college in Cleveland.
Academic Character SACS and professional accreditation. Summer term. Remedial math and English programs.
Admissions High school graduation required. SAT required. *Early Admission* Program. Advanced placement possible.
Student Life Dormitories. Intercollegiate athletics.

[1] VALDOSTA STATE COLLEGE
Valdosta 31601, (912) 247-3233
Director of Admissions: Gary L. Bass
- **Undergraduates: 1,556m, 1,813w; 4,909 total (including graduates)**
- **Tuition (1982/83): $849 (in-state), $2,139 (out-of-state)**
- **Room & Board: $1,377-$1,497**
- **Degrees offered: BA, BS, BSN, BBA, BFA, BMus, BSCrimJus, BSEd**
- **Student-faculty ratio: 20 to 1**

A public college established in 1912, became coed in 1950. 165 acres of urban campuses in Valdosta, near Florida line. Bus and rail nearby.
Academic Character SACS and professional accreditation. Quarter system, 12-week summer quarter. 15 majors offered by the School of Arts & Sciences, 5 by the School of Business Administration, 9 by the School of Education, 8 by the Division of Fine Arts, and 1 by the Division of Nursing. Distributive requirements. Exit exams. MA, MS, MEd, MFA granted. Independent study. Honors program. Internships. Preprofessional programs in health fields, law, theology. 3-2 program in engineering with Georgia Tech. Elementary, secondary, and special education certification. AFROTC. Computer center. 222,000-volume library with microform resources.
Financial CEEB CSS. College and state scholarships and loans; PELL, SEOG, GSL, FISL, NDSL, NSL, CWS, and college work program.
Admissions High school graduation with 15 units required. GED and state certificates accepted from students over 21. Interview may be required. SAT required. $10 application fee. Rolling admissions; application deadline 20 days before registration. $75 deposit required on acceptance of offer of admission. Transfers accepted. Credit possible for CEEB AP and CLEP exams; college has own advanced placement program.
Student Life Student government. Newspaper, yearbook. Music and drama groups. 12 religious groups. Honorary, service, and special interest groups. 7 fraternities and 3 sororities. Freshmen must live at home or on campus. No coed dorms. Married-student and special interest housing. 38% of students live on campus. 3 hours of phys ed required. 7 intercollegiate sports for men, 4 for women. NCAA, GSC. Student body composition: 0.5% Asian, 13% Black, 0.4% Hispanic, 0.1% Native American, 86% White. 10% from out of state.

[J1] WAYCROSS JUNIOR COLLEGE
2007 Francis Sreet, Waycross 31501

[1] WESLEYAN COLLEGE
4760 Forsyth Road, Macon 31297, (912) 477-1110
Dean of Admissions: Herbert Mudie
- **Undergraduates: 530w**
- **Tuition (1982/83): $3,600**
- **Room & Board: $2,100; Fees: $130**
- **Degrees offered: AB, BBA, BMus, BS, BFA**
- **Mean SAT 483v, 498m**
- **Student-faculty ratio: 10 to 1**

A private women's college affiliated with the United Methodist Church, established in 1836. 240-acre suburban campus in residential section of Macon.
Academic Character SACS and professional accreditation. Semester system, 4-week May term. 30 majors offered for the AB degree, 3 for the BBA, 10 for the BFA, 4 for the BMus, and 7 for the BS. Distributive requirements. Independent study. Honors program. Pass/fail grading option, internships. Preprofessional programs in engineering, dentistry, medicine, veterinary science, health sciences, medical technology, law, social work. Cooperative engineering program with Georgia Tech. Study abroad. Exchange program with International Christian University in Japan. Elementary, secondary, and physical education certification. Gallery. 115,000-volume library with microform resources.
Financial CEEB CSS. College scholarships, grants, and loans, state grants and loans, Methodist scholarships and loans; PELL, SEOG, GSL, FISL, NDSL, PLUS, CWS. Application deadline April 1.
Admissions High school graduation with 10 units required. Interview encouraged. Audition required for music majors. SAT or ACT required. $15 application fee. Rolling admissions. $125 deposit required on acceptance of offer of admission. *Early Admission* Program. Transfers accepted. Admission deferral possible. Credit possible for CEEB AP and CLEP exams.
Student Life Student government. Newspaper, magazine, yearbook. Music and drama groups. Black Student's Alliance. Religious, professional, honorary, service, and special interest groups. Students must live at home or on campus. Class attendance required. 2 intercollegiate sports; intramurals. Student body composition: 15% minority.

[1] WEST GEORGIA COLLEGE
Carrollton 30118, (404) 834-1290
Director of Admissions: C. Doyle Bickers
- **Undergraduates: 1,970m, 2,307w; 6,050 total (including graduates)**
- **Tuition (1982/83): $645 (in-state), $1,935 (out-of-state)**
- **Room & Board: $1,716; Fees: $189**
- **Degrees offered: AB, BS, BBA, BMus, BSEarthSci, BSEd, BSRec, AA, AS**
- **Mean SAT 419v, 443m**
- **Student-faculty ratio: 20 to 1**

A public college established in 1906. 400-acre campus in Carrollton, 45 miles from Atlanta. Bus service nearby; air and rail in Atlanta.
Academic Character SACS and professional accreditation. Quarter system. 46 majors offered by the schools of Arts & Sciences, Business, and Education. Minors offered in most major fields and in 9 additional areas. Distributive requirements. Exit exams required. Independent study. Honors program. Cooperative work/study, pass/fail, internships. Preprofessional programs in agriculture, forestry, law, medicine, pharmacy. 2-year transfer program in medical record administration with Medical College of Georgia. 3-2 program in engineering with Auburn, Georgia Tech, Southern Tech. Study abroad. Early childhood, middle, secondary, and special education certification. Computer center, observatory. 250,700-volume library with microform resources.
Financial CEEB CSS and ACT FAS. College and state scholarships, grants, nursing scholarships, loans; PELL, SEOG, FISL, NDSL, NSL, CWS, student assistantships. Application deadline April 1.
Admissions High school graduation with 16 units recommended. GED accepted. SAT required. $10 application fee. Rolling admissions; suggest applying by January 1. $40 room deposit required on acceptance of offer of admission. *Early Admission* and *Concurrent Enrollment* programs; Superior Junior Program. Transfers accepted. Credit possible for CEEB AP and CLEP exams.
Student Life Student government. Newspaper, magazine, yearbook, radio station. Music and debate groups. Honorary, academic, religious, and special interest groups. 10 fraternities, 2 with houses, and 8 sororities without houses. 25% of men and 25% of women join. Freshmen and sophomores must live at home or on campus. Coed and single-sex dorms. Special academic and athletic housing. 45% of students live on campus. 6 quarters of phys ed required. 8 intercollegiate sports for men, 6 for women; intramurals. AIAW, NCAA, SAC. Student body composition: 1% Asian, 13% Black, 1% Hispanic, 1% Native American, 87% White. 3% from out of state.

[J1] YOUNG HARRIS COLLEGE
Young Harris 30582, (404) 379-3185
Director of Admissions: George L. Dyer, Jr.
- **Undergraduates: 496 men and women**
- **Tuition (1983/84): $1,935**
- **Room & Board: $1,860-$1,920; Fees: $85**
- **Degrees offered: AA, AS, AFA**
- **Student-faculty ratio: 14 to 1**

A private junior college affiliated with the United Methodist Church, established in 1886. 30-acre campus in small town of Young Harris. 700 acres of college-owned mountain land adjoins the campus.
Academic Character SACS accreditation. Quarter system, summer quarter. Majors offered in history, political science, sociology, psychology, philosophy, religion, English, language, journalism, art, music, theatre, theatre education, science, business, education, recreation. Distributive requirements. Independent study. Internships. Study abroad. Planetarium, language lab. 36,000-volume library with microform resources.
Financial CEEB CSS. Scholarships, grants, loans, Methodist scholarships and loans, state grants; PELL, NDSL, CWS. Scholarship application deadline February 1.
Admissions High school graduation required. SAT or ACT required. $15 application fee. Rolling admissions; suggest applying soon after 1st semester. $100 deposit required on acceptance of offer of admission. *Early Admission* and *Concurrent Enrollment* programs. Transfers accepted. Credit possible for CEEB AP and CLEP exams; college has own advanced placement program.
Student Life Student government. Newspaper, magazine, yearbook. Music, art, drama groups. Religious, honorary, academic, and special interest groups. 3 fraternities and 3 sororities. Students must live at home or on campus. No coed dorms. Attendance in class and at several convocations required. 3 quarter hours of phys ed required. Intercollegiate tennis for men and women.

HAWAII (HI)

[1] BRIGHAM YOUNG UNIVERSITY (HAWAII CAMPUS)
Laie, Oahu 96762, (808) 293-3211
Director of Admissions: Charles W.H. Goo

- **Enrollment: 865m, 1,080w**
- **Tuition (1982/83): $1,050 (for members of the Church of Latter-Day Saints), $1,576 (for others)**
- **Room & Board: $1,800**
- **Degrees offered: BA, BS, BSW, AA, AS**
- **Student-faculty ratio: 22 to 1**

A private university affiliated with the Church of Jesus Christ of Latter-Day Saints (Mormons). Established in 1955, affiliated with Brigham Young University in 1974. 60-acre small-town campus 38 miles from Honolulu on the island of Oahu.
Academic Character WASC accreditation. Trimester system, 2 4-week summer terms. Majors offered in art, biological sciences, business management (accounting, restaurant/food service, travel/tourism), elementary education, English, executive secretary, family living, government, history, industrial education & technology, math, music, office management, physical education & recreation, physical science, physics, social work, and vocational management. Several minors or related concentrations offered. 14 hours of religion required. Home study possible. Credit by exam. Pass/fail option. 5th-year teaching certificate offered. Pacific Institute and Museum conducts research and offers course work relating to the Pacific Islands area. ROTC. 100,000-volume library.
Financial ACT FAS. Brigham Young University scholarships and grants-in-aid; PELL, SEOG, NDSL, FISL. Application deadline July 15. Work/study program with college employing 1,100 students each year.
Admissions High school graduation with 12 units required. GED accepted. Interview required. SAT or ACT required. $10 application fee. Rolling admissions; deadline 30 days before registration. $30 tuition deposit required on acceptance of offer of admission. *Early Entrance* and *Early Decision* programs. Admission deferral possible. Transfers accepted. Credit possible for university placement exams, and for CLEP results.
Student Life Student government. Newspaper, yearbook. Music and drama groups. Athletic, academic, honorary, religious, service, and special interest groups. Single students with loans and single foreign students must live on campus. Married-student housing. 60% of students live on campus. Pledge of conduct required including promise to abstain from tobacco, liquor, tea, and coffee. Class attendance expected. Dress and hair code. 2 hours of phys ed required. 3 intercollegiate sports for men, 3 for women; intramurals. Student body composition: 64% minority.

[1] CHAMINADE UNIVERSITY OF HONOLULU
3140 Waialae Avenue, Honolulu 96816, (808) 735-4735
Director of Admissions: William F. Murray, Jr.

- **Undergraduates: 484m, 475w; 1,091 total (including graduates)**
- **Tuition & Fees (1982/83): $2,980**
- **Room & Board: $2,352-$2,910**
- **Degrees offered: BA, BS, BBA, BFA, BGS, AA, AS, AGS**
- **Mean SAT 427v, 433m**
- **Student-faculty ratio: 14 to 1**

A private university founded in 1955 by the Roman Catholic Marianist order. 67-acre campus in residential St. Louis Heights area of Honolulu, overlooking Diamond Head and Waikiki.
Academic Character WASC accreditation. Semester system, 2 6-week summer terms; accelerated semester system in evening and off-campus programs. Majors in accounting, American studies, applied math, art, behavioral sciences, biology, business administration, chemistry, computer science, criminal justice, education, English, general business, general psychology, history, humanities, international studies, management science, marketing science, philosophy, political science, psychology, religious studies, social studies, sociology, and studio art. Special majors. Minors in most major areas and in anthropology, drama, physics, speech communications. Associate degrees in business management, history, leadership management, criminal justice, social studies. Distributives and 6 semester hours of religious studies required. MBA granted. Directed independent reading and research. Internships. Credit/no credit option, credit by exam. Preprofessional programs in biomedical sciences and law. Concurrent enrollment possible with UHawaii at Manoa, Brigham Young U in Hawaii, Hawaii Loa, Hawaii Pacific. Semester at Sea. Provisional early childhood (Montessori), elementary, and secondary education certification; 5th-Year Certificate Program. ROTC and AFROTC through UHawaii at Manoa. 55,000-volume library.
Financial CEEB CSS. University scholarships and grants, state grants & loans; PELL, SEOG, NDSL, GSL, CWS. Application deadline March 15.
Admissions High school graduation with 15 units required. Interview recommended. SAT or ACT required. $25 application fee. Rolling admissions; deadline August 1. $25 tuition and $50 room deposits required on acceptance of offer of admission. *Early Decision, Early Entrance, Concurrent Enrollment* programs. Admission deferral possible. Transfers accepted. Credit possible for CEEB AP and CLEP exams, and for life/work experience. College prep program in reading, English, and math.
Student Life Student government. Newspaper, literary magazine, yearbook. Drama groups. Honor societies. Special interest clubs. Coed, single-sex, and special interest housing. Apartments. 25% of students live on campus. Class attendance expected. 4 intercollegiate sports for men and women; intramurals. NAIA, NCAA. Student body composition: 54% Asian, 3% Black, 1% Hispanic, 1% Native American, 41% White. 43% of students from out of state.

[1] HAWAII, UNIVERSITY OF
Honolulu 96822, (808) 948-8207

- **Enrollment: 10,205m, 10,628w**
- **Degrees offered: BA, BS, BBA, BEd, BFA, BMus, BArch, BSW**

A public university started in 1907. Urban residential environment. Includes campuses of Hilo, Manoa, West Oahu College, and 7 community colleges.
Academic Character WASC accreditation. Semester system, 2 summer terms. Numerous majors offered by the Colleges of Arts & Sciences, Architecture, Business Administration, Education, Engineering, Tropical Agriculture, and Health Sciences & Social Welfare (which includes the Schools of Medicine, Nursing, Public Health, and Social Work). University also contains the School of Law, Graduate Division, and Graduate School of Library Studies. Graduate and professional degrees granted in many areas. 2-year certificate program in dental hygiene. Phi Beta Kappa. 5-year education certification. UHawaii at Hilo offers lower division courses and West Oahu College offers upper division courses. Continuing Education & Community Resources Service. Research institutes in many fields including agriculture, astronomy, biomedical science, education, engineering, geophysics, industrial relations, marine biology, social sciences, social welfare, and water resources. Computer center. Arboretum. 1,530,000-volume library.
Financial Aid available includes University scholarships (most for Hawaii residents), federal grants & loans.
Admissions High school graduation required. SAT required. Transfers accepted.
Student Life Some dorm housing for men and women, including YMCA dorm (for men). Cafeteria. Intercollegiate sports include football, baseball, and basketball.

■[1] HAWAII, UNIVERSITY OF, AT HILO
1400 Kapiolani Street, Hilo 96720, (808) 961-9311
Admissions Coordinator: Peggy Yorita

- **Enrollment: 1,675m, 1,792w**
- **Tuition (1982/83): $110 (in-state), $900 (out-of-state)**
- **Room & Board: $1,498-$1,914**
- **Degrees offered: BA, BS, BBA, AA, AS**
- **Mean SAT 399v, 456m**
- **Student-faculty ratio: 20 to 1**

A public university organized in 1970 and including Hawaii Community College, Center for Continuing Education, College of Agriculture, and College of Arts & Sciences. 2 campuses comprising 80 acres in Hilo on Hawaii, 200 air miles from Honolulu. Airport, bus station.
Academic Character WASC and professional accreditation. Semester system, 6-week summer term. Majors in animal husbandry, general agriculture, tropical crop production (BS); anthropology, biology, business administration, chemistry, economics, English, geography, Hawaiian studies, history, liberal studies, linguistics, math, music, philosophy, physics, political science, psychology, social science, sociology, speech (BA, BBA); AA, AS, and certificates in 18 vocational-technical areas. Individual programs possible. Distributive requirements. Inter-college registration possible. 2-year transfer programs in engineering, nursing; 1-year transfer program in home economics. Biomedical research program, Marine Option Program. Study abroad. Provisional elementary and secondary education certification. Farm laboratory. Computer center. 160,000-volume library with microform resources.
Financial CEEB CSS. University scholarships and loans, state scholarships and loans; PELL, SEOG, NSS, NDSL, GSL, NSL, PLUS, CWS. Application deadline March 1.
Admissions High school graduation with 15 units required for 4-year programs; age of 18 required for 2-year programs. GED accepted. SAT or ACT required. $10 application fee for out-of-state applicants. Rolling admissions; deadline July 15. *Early Admission* Program. Transfers accepted. Credit possible for CEEB AP and CLEP exams, and for university language placement tests.
Student Life Student government. Newspaper. Music and drama organizations. Academic, honorary, religious, political, and special interest groups. Limited on-campus housing. Married-student housing. Coed dorms. 13% of students live on campus. Limited parking on campus. Permission required for liquor at campus activities. No lethal weapons allowed in or around dorms. 5 intercollegiate sports for men, 3 for women; intramurals. AIAW, NAIA, NCAA. Student body composition: 56% Asian/Pacific, 7% Foreign, 6% Hispanic, 22% White, 9% Other. 12% from out of state.

■[1] HAWAII, UNIVERSITY OF, AT MANOA
2530 Dole Street, C-200, Honolulu 96822, (808) 948-8111
Director of Admissions: Donald R. Fukuda

- **Enrollment: 7,093m, 7,750w**
- **Tuition (1982/83): $450 (in-state), $1,125 (out-of-state)**
- **Room & Board: $1,830-$2,268; Fees: $31**
- **Degrees offered: BA, BS, BBA, BFA, BSW, BArch, BEd, BMus, AS**
- **Student-faculty ratio: 9 to 1**

A public university established in 1907. 300-acre campus in Oahu Island's residential Manoa Valley, between downtown Honolulu and Waikiki.
Academic Character WASC and professional accreditation. Semester system, 2 6-week summer terms. Over 110 majors offered by the Colleges of Arts & Sciences, Business Administration, Education, Engineering, Health Sciences & Social Welfare, Tropical Agriculture & Human Resources, and the Schools of Architecture, Law, Library Studies. College of Health Sciences & Social Welfare includes Schools of Medicine, Nursing, Public Health, Social Work. Courses in ethnic and women's studies. Graduate and professional degrees granted. Independent study. Phi Beta Kappa. Credit by exam possible; some credit/no credit options. Numerous research and science centers, including marine biological, astronomical, geophysical, biomedical centers. Population genetics lab. Environmental, Water Resources Research, and Cancer Research centers. Urban & Regional Planning Program. Language lab. Computer center. ROTC, AFROTC. 1,750,000-volume library.
Financial CEEB CSS. University, state, medical, AFROTC scholarships; short-term, state, and health professions loans; PELL, SEOG, NSS, NDSL, NSL, GSL, CWS, university work program.
Admissions High school graduation with 15 units required. Admission standards higher for out-of-state applicants. SAT or ACT required. $10 fee for out-of-state applicants. Rolling admissions. Application deadline May 1; later applications considered if space available. Partial tuition deposit required with acceptance of offer of admission. *Early Admission* for local students. Transfers accepted. Credit possible for CEEB AP and CLEP exams. Trio Project for disadvantaged students.
Student Life Student government. Newspaper, literary magazine, yearbook. Debate. Drama & music groups. Numerous special interest, academic, and honorary groups. Fraternities and sororities. Limited campus housing; state residents receive priority. Some off-campus university housing. 28% of students live on campus. 10 intercollegiate sports for men, 8 for women; intramurals. Student body composition: 73.1% Asian, 0.4% Black, 1.3% Hispanic, 0.1% Native American, 20.4% White, 4.7% Other. 17% from out of state.

[J1] HAWAII COMMUNITY COLLEGE
Hilo — see University of Hawaii at Hilo

[1] HAWAII LOA COLLEGE
45045 Kamehameha Highway, Kaneohe, Oahu 96744, (808) 235-3641

- **Undergraduates: 135m, 144w; 297 total (including part-time)**
- **Tuition (1982/83): $3,200**
- **Room & Board: $2,600**
- **Degrees offered: BA, BSN**
- **Student-faculty ratio: 10 to 1**

An independent liberal arts college founded in 1963, sponsored by the United Church of Christ, United Methodist, United Presbyterian, and Episcopal Churches. Campus on the Windward side of Oahu, 15 minutes from downtown Honolulu.
Academic Character WASC accreditation. 4-1-4 system, summer term with open admissions policy. Majors offered include American culture, anthropology, art, Asian history, Asian studies, biology, chemistry, Chinese, computer science, economics, European/American history, French, Japanese, literature, mathematics, music, ocean studies, philosophy, physics, political science, psychology, religion, and theatre. Second-step BS in Nursing program. Interdisciplinary academic instruction stresses intercultural themes. Independent & directed study, tutorials. Preprofessional programs in business, health sciences, law, theology.
Admissions High school graduation required. SAT or ACT required. Rolling admissions. *Early Admission* and *Early Decision* programs. Admission deferral possible. Transfers accepted. Advanced placement credit possible.
Student Life Student body composition: 51% minority.

[1] HAWAII PACIFIC COLLEGE
1060 & 1164 Bishop Street, Honolulu 96813, (808) 521-3881

- **Undergraduates: 286m, 133w; 1,508 total**
- **Tuition & Fees (1982/83): $2,680**
- **Degrees offered: BA, BS**
- **Student-faculty ratio: 15 to 1**

A private, coeducational college of liberal arts and business, founded in 1953. Campus located in downtown Honolulu.
Academic Character WASC accreditation. Semester system, summer term. Majors offered for a BA in the liberal arts and for a BS in business administration. Cooperative work/study provides curriculum-related work experience and helps to defray the cost of education. Special program in English as a second language. Remedial math and English programs.
Financial Financial aid available.
Admissions Admissions notification is done on a rolling basis. *Early Admission* and *Early Decision programs. Advanced placement credit possible.*
Student Life Student body composition: 55% minority.

[J1] HONOLULU COMMUNITY COLLEGE
874 Dillingham Blvd., Honolulu 96817

[P] INTERNATIONAL COLLEGE
20 Dowsett Avenue, PO Box 235, Honolulu 96817

[J1] KAPIOLANI COMMUNITY COLLEGE
620 Pensacola Street, Honolulu 96822

[J1] KAUAI COMMUNITY COLLEGE
3-1901 Kaumualii Highway, Lihu, Kauai 96766

[J1] LEEWARD COMMUNITY COLLEGE
96-045 Ala Ike, Pearl City 96782

[J1] MAUI COMMUNITY COLLEGE
310 Kaahumanu Avenue, Kahului 96732

[J1] WINDWARD COMMUNITY COLLEGE
45-720 Keaahala Road, Kaneohe 96744

IDAHO (ID)

[J1 & 1] BOISE STATE UNIVERSITY
Boise 83725, (208) 385-1156
Dean of Admissions: Guy L. Hunt

- **Undergraduates: 3,554m, 3,182w; 11,363 total (including graduates)**
- **Tuition & Fees (1982/83): $801 (in-state), $2,701 (out-of-state)**
- **Room & Board: $2,100**
- **Degrees offered: BA, BS, BBA, BFA, BMus, AA**
- **Mean ACT 19.1**
- **Student-faculty ratio: 19 to 1**

A public university established in 1932. 120-acre campus in downtown Boise, the capital city of Idaho. Boise has air, bus, and railroad services.
Academic Character NASC and professional accreditation. Semester system, 4 summer terms. 60 majors offered by the School of Arts & Sciences, 25 by the School of Business, 9 by the School of Education, 9 by the School of Health Sciences, and 8 by the Area Vocational-Technical School. Interdisciplinary humanities program. Certificate and diploma programs. Minors possible. Distributive requirements. Masters degrees granted. Independent study. Honors program. Credit by exam. Internships. Preprofessional programs in architecture, dentistry, medicine, veterinary medicine. 2-2 dental hygiene, 3-2 pharmacy programs with Idaho State U. 2-2 or 3-2 engineering program with U of Idaho. Member of 55-institution National Student Exchange. Study abroad in England, France, Germany; branch campus in Spain. Early childhood, elementary, secondary, and special education certification. ROTC. Data processing center. 260,000-volume library.
Financial CEEB CSS. University scholarships, loans, state scholarships; PELL, SEOG, BIA, NSS, SSIG, NDSL, GSL, FISL, NSL, CWS, university work program. FAF application deadline is March 1.
Admissions Open admission to Idaho residents. Graduation from high school required. GED or equivalent accepted. ACT, SAT, or equivalent required. $10 application fee. Rolling admissions; deadline August 15. $60 room deposit required on acceptance of offer of admission. *Early Decision* and *Concurrent Enrollment* programs. Transfers accepted. Credit possible for CEEB AP, CLEP, and university advanced placement program. Provisional acceptance possible for academically disadvantaged students.
Student Life Student government. Newspaper, yearbook, radio and TV stations. Music groups. Debate. Numerous academic, athletic, honorary, religious, service, and special interest groups. 4 fraternities and 4 sororities with houses. 3% of men and 2% of women join. Coed and single-sex dorms. Married-student housing. 8% of students live on campus. Liquor prohibited in public areas of campus. 7 intercollegiate sports for men, 7 for women; intramurals. AIAW, NCAA, Big Sky, Northwest College Women's Sports Association. Student body composition: 1% Asian, 1% Black, 1% Hispanic, 1% Native American, 95% White, 1% Other. 5% from out of state.

[1] IDAHO, COLLEGE OF
2112 Cleveland, Caldwell 83605, (208) 459-5011
Dean of Admissions & External Affairs: Brett S. Harrell

- **Enrollment: 237m, 193w; 708 total (including part-time)**
- **Tuition (1981/82): $4,600**
- **Room & Board: $2,012-$2,515; Fees: $269**
- **Degrees offered: BA, BS, BBA**
- **Mean ACT 21.5**
- **Student-faculty ratio: 13 to 1**

A private college affiliated with the United Presbyterian Church, and founded in 1891. Campus in the small town of Caldwell, 25 miles west of Boise. Bus and train stations in Caldwell, airport in Boise.
Academic Character NASC accreditation. 4-1-4 system, 6-week summer term. Majors offered in American studies, art, biology, business administration, chemistry, elementary education, English literature, English teaching, history, human ecology, human services, math, math/computer science, math teaching, music, philosophy, phys ed, political science, psychology, religion, social studies teaching, sociology, zoology. J.A. Albertson School of Business offers a BBA in accounting, business administration, computer information systems. Minors possible in most major

areas. Distributives and 1 Biblical literature course required. MAEd, MEd granted; Planned Fifth-Year Program offers advanced (non-Master's) education certification. Interdisciplinary study. Independent study. Honors programs. Pass/fail, credit by exam. Internships. Preprofessional programs in dentistry, medicine, optometry, physical therapy, seminary studies, veterinary medicine. 3-2 engineering program with Columbia, U of Idaho, Washington U (MO), Stanford. Study abroad. Elementary and secondary education certification. Computer system. 155,000-volume library.
Financial CEEB CSS (preferred) and ACT FAS. College scholarships, grants, loans; Presbyterian scholarships, grants, and loans; Native American Education Grants; PELL, SEOG, SSIG, PLUS, FISL, GSL, NDSL, CWS, college part-time employment. Budgeted tuition payment plan. File application with application for admission.
Admissions High school graduation required with 12 units recommended. GED accepted. Interview suggested. ACT or SAT required. $15 application fee. Rolling admissions. Apply any time after beginning of 11th year. $45 deposit required on acceptance of offer of admission. Non-degree-credit *Concurrent Enrollment* Program. Transfers accepted. Credit possible for CEEB AP and CLEP exams. Probational, provisional, and conditional admission possible.
Student Life Student government. Newspaper, yearbook. Literary, drama, music, religious, and political groups. Special academic societies. Honorary service societies. 3 fraternities and 4 sororities without houses. Single freshmen & sophomores under 21 must live at home or on campus. Dorms for men and women. Dining hall. Class attendance expected. 3 phys ed courses required. 2 intercollegiate sports for men, 2 for women; intramural and club sports.

[1] IDAHO, UNIVERSITY OF

Moscow 83843, (208) 885-6326
Director of Admissions & Registrar: Matt Telin

- **Undergraduates: 3,820m, 2,306w; 8,129 total (including graduates)**
- **Tuition (1982/83): $0 (in-state), $1,800 (out-of-state)**
- **Room & Board: $1,870; Fees: $701**
- **Degrees offered: BA, BS, BArch, BDan, BFA, BGS, BLArch, BMus, BNS, BApplPhys, BTech, BSE's**
- **Mean ACT 21; mean SAT 450v, 489m**
- **Student-faculty ratio: 18 to 1**

A public university established in 1889. 1,450-acre campus and college farm in the small city of Moscow, 85 miles from Spokane, WA and 310 miles from Boise, ID.
Academic Character NASC and professional accreditation. Semester system, 8-week summer term. 132 majors offered by the Colleges of Agriculture, Art & Architecture, Business & Economics, Education, Engineering, Letters & Sciences, Mines & Earth Resources, and Forestry, Wildlife, & Range Sciences. Combined programs possible. 1- and 2-year pre-nursing programs. Distributive requirements. Graduate & professional degrees granted. Honors program; Phi Beta Kappa. Pass/fail. Study abroad. Elementary, secondary, and special education certification. ROTC, NROTC; AFROTC at Washington State. Language labs. 975,000-volume library.
Financial CEEB CSS. University and merit scholarships, deferred payment; PELL, SEOG, SSIG, NDSL, FISL, GSL, CWS. Application deadline March 1.
Admissions High school graduation with 15 units required. Out-of-state applicant must graduate in top 50% of class. SAT or ACT required. $10 application fee. Rolling admissions; deadline August 1. $25 deposit required on acceptance of offer of admission. *Early Decision* and *Early Entrance* programs. Admission deferral possible. Transfers accepted. Credit possible for CEEB AP and CLEP exams. Students with academic deficiencies may be considered for admission.
Student Life Student government. Newspaper, yearbook, radio & TV stations. Music and debate groups. Dance and drama productions. Young Democrats, Young Republicans. Many academic, athletic, honorary, service, and special interest groups. 18 fraternities and 9 sororities; all with houses. 16% of men and 22% of women join. Married-student housing. Men's and women's co-op dorms. 45% of students live on campus. Class attendance expected. 2 semesters of phys ed required; freshman women must complete one course in healthful living. 8 intercollegiate sports for men, 8 for women; intramurals. AIAW, NCAA, Big Sky, Northwest College Women's Sports Association. Student body composition: 1% Asian, 0.5% Black, 0.6% Hispanic, 0.6% Native American, 94.6% White, 2.7% Other. 20% from out of state.

[1] IDAHO STATE UNIVERSITY

Pocatello 83209, (208) 236-0211
Director of Admissions: Tim Hayhurst

- **Enrollment: 10,804 men and women**
- **Tuition (1982/83): $805 (in-state), $2,605 (out-of-state)**
- **Room & Board: $1,840**
- **Degrees offered: BA, BS, BBA, BFA, BMus Ed, BMus, BSPharm, BUniversity Studies, BVTTE, BSN, AA, AS**
- **Mean ACT 18.4**
- **Student-faculty ratio: 15 to 1**

A public university established in 1901, and located in the eastern residential section of Pocatello. Air and bus services in Pocatello.
Academic Character NASC and professional accreditation. Semester system, 8-week summer term. 6 majors offered by College of Business, 7 by College of Education, 6 by College of Health-Related Professions, 32 by College of Liberal Arts, 21 by School of Vocational-Technical Education. Other divisions are College of Pharmacy, School of Engineering, School of Graduate Studies. Distributive requirements. Graduate degrees granted. Noncredit independent study. Honors program. Pass/fail option. Preprofessional programs in dental hygiene, dentistry, law, optometry, osteopathy, medicine, pharmacy, veterinary medicine. 3-2 engineering, 2-2 agriculture and forestry, and 3-1 medical technology programs. Cooperative program in dentistry with Creighton U. Radiation protection "training-study" program. Elementary and secondary education certification. ROTC. 1,000,000-volume library.
Financial CEEB CSS. University scholarships, grants, loans; state scholarships, health professional loans, non-resident fee waivers; PELL, SSIG, SEOG, GSL, NDSL, NSL, CWS. Application deadlines in April (scholarships, grants) and May 1 (loans).
Admissions Open admission to high school graduates who specify ISU as a choice on their ACT form. ACT required for placement and counseling. No application fee. Application deadline August 1. $35 housing reservation deposit required. *Early Entrance* Program. Transfers accepted (minimum out-of-state GPA of 2.0 required). Credit possible for CEEB AP exams.
Student Life Student government. Newspaper, yearbook. University Bank. Music groups. Honorary drama group. Young Democrats, Young Republicans. Crafts workshop. Honorary, professional, religious, special interest groups. 5 fraternities, 4 with houses, and 3 sororities with a shared dorm. 10% of men and women join. Dorms for men & women. Some married-student apartments. 20% of students live on campus. Liquor not allowed on campus. Class attendance expected. 10 intercollegiate sports for men; intramurals. NCAA, Big Sky. Student body composition: 1.3% Asian, 0.7% Black, 1% Hispanic, 0.5% Native American, 96.5% White. 8% from out of state.

[1] LEWIS-CLARK STATE COLLEGE

Lewiston 83501, (208) 746-2341
Director of Admissions: Reid Bailey

- **Enrollment: 588m, 571w; 1,951 total (including part-time)**
- **Tuition (1982/83): $640 (in-state), $2,340 (out-of-state)**
- **Room & Board: $1,970**
- **Degrees offered: BA, BS, BSN, AA, AS, AAS**
- **Student-faculty ratio: 18 to 1**

A public college established in 1894. 44-acre small-city campus on Normal Hill, in northern part of state 100 miles from Spokane, WA. Lewiston served by air and bus; train in Spokane.
Academic Character NASC and professional accreditation. Semester system, 8-week summer term. Majors offered in business administration, criminal justice (corrections, law enforcement), drama/speech, elementary education, English, general studies, history, management technology, mathematics, natural sciences (biology, chemistry, earth sciences-geology), nursing, physical education, social science. Associate degrees in the above areas and in autobody repair & auto mechanics, behavioral science, drafting technology, general electronics, graphic arts, industrial mechanics, lab science, legal and medical secretary, mid-management, welding technology. Self-designed majors possible. Diploma programs. Distributive requirements. Independent study, pass/fail. Honors program. Internships, cooperative work/study. Preprofessional programs in agriculture, engineering, forestry, law, medicine, veterinary medicine. Elementary, secondary, and special education certification. Computer center, language lab, museum/gallery. ROTC; NROTC & AFROTC at U of Idaho. 100,000-volume library.
Financial CEEB CSS. College scholarships, grants, loans, tuition and fee waivers; PELL, SEOG, NSS, NDSL, GSL, NSL, CWS, veteran's work-study, work-scholarship program. Application deadline March 15.
Admissions Open admission to high school graduates. GED accepted. Admission to vocational programs on a space-available basis; interview required. Nursing program admission competitive. ACT, SAT, or Washington Pre-College Test required for guidance and placement; ACT preferred. Nursing application fee $10; none for other programs. Rolling admissions; deadline August 15. $50 room reservation deposit required on acceptance of offer of admission. *Early Entrance, Concurrent Enrollment,* and informal early decision programs. Admission deferral possible. Transfers accepted. Credit possible for CEEB AP, CLEP, and departmental exams. Provisional enrollment possible.
Student Life Student government. Newspaper. Music and drama groups. Political and religious organizations. Native American Indian Club. Meditation Society. Men's and Women's Associations. Cheerleaders. Professional and special interest groups. No coed dorms or married-student housing. 10% of students live on campus. Liquor prohibited on campus. 4 intercollegiate sports for men, 4 for women; intramurals. AIAW, NAIA. Student body composition: 1% Black, 1% Hispanic, 5% Native American, 92% White, 1% Other. 10% from out of state.

[J1] NORTH IDAHO COLLEGE

1000 West Garden Avenue, Coeur D'Alene 83814, (208) 667-7422
Director of Admissions: Itsuko Nishio

- **Enrollment: 2,081 men & women**
- **Tuition & Fees (1981/82): $530 (in-state), $1,170 (out-of-state)**
- **Room & Board: $1,780**
- **Degrees offered: AA, ALA, AS, AAS**
- **Student-faculty ratio: 22 to 1**

A public community college established in 1933. Wooded 40-acre campus at the junction of Lake Coeur D'Alene and the Spokane River.
Academic Character NASC and professional accreditation. Semester system. 51 college transfer majors offered in the divisions of applied sciences, business administration, communication arts, English & foreign languages, home economics & hospitality services, physical sciences, social sciences, and life sciences, forestry, & health. Paraprofessional programs in 15 areas including advertising, and medical, business, secretarial, and educational areas. Vocational-technical programs in 19 areas. Distributive requirements for transfer programs. Credit by exam. Preprofessional programs. Evening classes. 30,000-volume library.
Financial CEEB CSS. College scholarships, activity grants, loans; PELL,

Key to ratings [1, 2, J1, J2, G, P, R, S] and list of abbreviations start on page 120

SEOG, SSIG, NSS, NDSL, FISL, GSL, college part-time employment. Application deadline April 15. Notification by July 15.
Admissions High school graduation with 11 or 12 units required. GED accepted. $5 application fee. Rolling admission; deadline August 20. *Concurrent Enrollment* Program. Provisional acceptance for non-high school graduates over 18.
Student Life Student government. Newspaper, literary magazine. Drama, music, and debate groups. Forums and convocations. Honorary societies. Many academic groups and associations. 1 coed dorm. 4 semesters of phys ed required. 5 intercollegiate sports for men, 5 for women; intramurals. NJCAA, NCWSA.

[1] NORTHWEST NAZARENE COLLEGE

Nampa 83651, (208) 467-8011
Director of Admissions: Bruce Webb

- **Undergraduates: 585m, 668w; 1,352 total (including graduates)**
- **Tuition (1982/83): $3,240**
- **Room & Board: $1,875; Fees: $240**
- **Degrees offered: AB, BS, AA**
- **Mean ACT 16**
- **Student-faculty ratio: 19 to 1**

A private college operated by the Church of the Nazarene, established in 1913. 64-acre campus adjacent to the small agricultural and industrial city of Nampa, 20 miles west of Boise. Air and bus service in Nampa.
Academic Character NASC and professional accreditation. Trimester system, 2 4-week summer terms. Departmental majors include art, biological science, business, chemistry, education, engineering physics, English, history, home economics, math, music, philosophy, physics, psychology, recreation, religion, social work, speech & hearing pathology, and speech/communication. Divisional, interdisciplinary, and self-designed majors. Distributives and 4 religion & philosophy courses required. GRE required for graduation. MEd granted. Independent study. Internships. Preprofessional programs in agriculture, dentistry, engineering, forestry, law, medical technology, medicine, ministry, nursing, optometry, pharmacy, physical therapy, veterinary medicine. Exchange program with College of Idaho. Elementary, secondary, and special education certification. ROTC. Computer center. 97,081-volume library with microform resources.
Financial CEEB CSS. College scholarships, awards, loans; veteran's, handicapped, and missionary grants; PELL, SEOG, BIA, NDSL, GSL, CWS. Priority application deadline April 1.
Admissions High school graduation with at least a 2.0 GPA required. ACT required. $10 application fee. Rolling admissions. $40 tuition deposit required on acceptance of offer of admission. *Early Entrance* and *Early Decision* programs. Transfers accepted. Credit possible for CEEB AP, CLEP, and college placement exams. Provisional acceptance possible for academically disadvantaged applicants.
Student Life Student government. Newspaper, yearbook. Music groups. Debate. Community tutoring program. Model UN. Circle K. Athletic, honorary, professional, political, religious, special interest groups. Single students under 21 must live at home or on campus. Use of liquor, illegal drugs, tobacco prohibited. Attendance in class and 3 convocations per week required; attendance at Sunday church services expected. 3 phys ed courses required. 7 intercollegiate sports for men, 4 for women; intramurals. AIAW, NAIA. Student body composition: 0.5% Asian, 1% Black, 1% Hispanic, 0.5% Native American, 95.5% White, 1.5% Other. 68% from out of state.

[J1] RICKS COLLEGE

Rexburg 83440, (208) 356-2011
Director of Admissions: Hal C. Barton

- **Enrollment: 1,964m, 3,006w; 6,500 total (including part-time)**
- **Tuition (1982/83): $1,140 (for Church of Latter-Day Saints members), $1,600 (for others)**
- **Room & Board: $1,980**
- **Degrees offered: AA/AS, AS**
- **Mean ACT 16.8**

A private college founded in 1888 and operated by The Church of Jesus Christ of Latter-Day Saints (Mormons). 255-acre campus in Rexburg, in the Upper Snake River Valley.
Academic Character NASC and professional accreditation. Semester system, 3 5-week summer terms. 2-year transfer and terminal programs. Majors in agricultural business & mechanics, art, automotive, biology, business administration, chemistry, communication, dairy production management, design & drafting technology, economics, education areas, engineering areas, English, family development, farm crop management, foreign language, geology, geography, health science, history, home economics, humanities, industrial arts & building construction, landscape horticulture, livestock production management, math, music, nursing, political science, physics, religion, sociology & law enforcement, theatre arts, and welding. One-year certificates in mid-management, office education, small business management. Distributives and 8 credit hours of religion required. Mid-semester class registration possible. Honors program. Pass/fail, credit by exam. "Forum" discussion series for students and faculty. Correspondence courses possible. Preprofessional programs in architecture, dentistry, forestry, law, medicine, physical therapy, veterinary medicine. Study abroad. Learning Assistance Labs. 75,000-volume library.
Financial College scholarships, loans, honors scholarships, Brigham Young University loans; PELL, BIA, GSL. Application deadline March 1.
Admissions High school graduation required. GED accepted. Non-high school graduates with 3.0 GPA are considered. ACT required. Some programs require special admissions forms and have special requirements. $13 application fee. Rolling admissions; deadline August 1 (October 1 for mid-semester registration). $50 deposit required on acceptance of offer of admission. Transfers accepted. Credit possible for CEEB AP and CLEP exams.
Student Life Student government. Yearbook. Over 45 student clubs. Service, academic, religious, and special interest organizations. No coed dorms. Women's coop dorms. Trailer court space for married students. Use of alcohol, tobacco, and narcotics prohibited. Dress code. Class attendance expected. 1 credit of phys ed required. 6 intercollegiate sports for men, 4 for women. NJCAA, ICAC.

[J1] SOUTHERN IDAHO, COLLEGE OF

PO Box 1238, Twin Falls 83301, (208) 733-9554
Director of Admissions & Records: John R. Sims

- **Enrollment: 1,500m, 1,300w**
- **Tuition (1982/83): $224 (in-state), $675 (out-of-state)**
- **Room & Board: $1,700-$1,910; Fees: $387**
- **Degrees offered: AA, AS, AAS**
- **Mean ACT 20**

A public college established in 1964 in residential Twin Falls, located in the Magic Valley. Campus is barrier-free to handicapped. Airport, bus and train stations.
Academic Character NASC accreditation. Semester system, summer term. Transfer and terminal programs in agriculture, auto body repair, auto mechanics, business, commercial culinary arts, consumer electronics, diesel & agricultural mechanics, English & foreign languages, fine arts, fire service training, home economics, industrial plant maintenance mechanics, law enforcement training, library science, marketing & distributive education, mathematics & engineering, nursing (PN, RN), physical education, science, small engine mechanics, social & behavioral sciences, welding, and air conditioning, refrigeration, & heating. Certificates granted. Distributive requirements. Internships. Credit by exam. Programs for physically handicapped and for deaf and hard-of-hearing students. Continuing education program. Senior citizens programs. Library.
Financial CEEB CSS. College scholarships and loans, state loans; SSIG, PELL, SEOG, NDSL, CWS. Application deadlines vary for different programs.
Admissions High school graduation and ACT required. GED accepted. Applicants without high school diploma must be 18 or over. Nursing applicants must fulfill more specific requirements. Rolling admissions. $50 room deposit required on acceptance of offer of admission. *Early Decision, Early Admission* programs. Admission deferral possible. Transfers accepted. Credit possible for CEEB AP and CLEP exams, for advanced high school courses.
Student Life Student government. Newspaper, bulletin. Band, choir. Academic, honorary, cheerleading, and other athletic clubs. 1 coed dorm. No gambling, firearms, or liquor allowed on campus. Smoking allowed only in designated areas. 2 phys ed activities required. 3 intercollegiate sports for men, 2 for women; coed intramurals. NJCAA.

ILLINOIS *(IL)*

[G1] ADVANCED MANAGEMENT INSTITUTE

Lake Forest — see Lake Forest School of Management

[2] AERO—SPACE INSTITUTE

57 West Grand Avenue, Chicago 60610

[G1] ALFRED ADLER INSTITUTE

159 North Dearborn Street, Chicago 60601

[P] AMERICAN CONSERVATORY OF MUSIC

116 South Michigan Avenue, Chicago 60603

[1] ART INSTITUTE OF CHICAGO, SCHOOL OF THE

Michigan Avenue at Adams Street, Chicago 60603, (312) 443-3700
Director of Admissions: Nicole Rae Brown

- **Undergraduates: 304m, 407w; 1,509 total (including graduates)**
- **Tuition (1982/83): $4,950**
- **Fees: $101**
- **Degree offered: BFA**
- **Student-faculty ratio: 10 to 1**

A private college established in 1866. Campus on lake front in downtown Chicago. Served by air, rail, and bus.
Academic Character NCACS and professional accreditation. Semester system, 8-week summer term. Studio concentrations in ceramics, design, fashion, fabrics, filmmaking, painting & drawing, photography, printmaking, sculpture, sound/music, video. Major not required; students develop own programs. 30 hours of liberal arts required. Courses offered in English, humanities, history, natural sciences, social sciences. MFA granted. Cooperative work/study, pass/fail. Off-campus study program. Exchange program with 9 colleges of art and design. Study abroad. Elementary and secondary education, and art therapy certification. Museum. 15,455-volume library.
Financial CEEB CSS and ACT FAS. School scholarships, grants, loans, deferred payment; PELL, SEOG, NDSL, FISL, CWS.
Admissions High school graduation required. As much art experience as possible recommended. GED accepted. Interview recommended. Portfolio recommended. SAT or ACT required. $15 application fee. Rolling admissions;

suggest applying by March 1. Deadline July 15. $100 deposit required on acceptance of offer of admission. *Concurrent Enrollment* Program. Credit possible for CEEB AP and CLEP exams.
Student Life Student government. Newspaper, literary magazine. Music groups. Cultural and special interest groups. No campus housing, but coop dorms and other housing available through nearby schools. Housing referral service. Extracurricular sports. Student body composition: 6% Asian, 11% Black, 2.8% Hispanic, 0.1% Native American, 67% White, 13% Other. 40% from out of state.

[1] AUGUSTANA COLLEGE

639 38th Street, Rock Island 61201, (309) 794-7341
Vice-President for Admissions & Financial Aid: Ralph Starenko

- **Undergraduates: 1,060m, 1,190w**
- **Tuition (1982/83): $4,704**
- **Room & Board: $2,157; Fees: $39**
- **Degrees offered: BA, BMus, BMus Ed, BSMed Tech**
- **Mean ACT 24; mean SAT 1,100**
- **Student-faculty ratio: 17 to 1**

A private college established in 1860, affiliated with the Lutheran Church. 110-acre urban campus in a small city overlooking the Mississippi River, 165 miles from Chicago. Served by air, rail, and bus.
Academic Character NCACS and professional accreditation. Trimester system, 7 3- to 9-week summer terms. Over 40 majors offered in the areas of liberal arts, sciences, education, engineering, computer science, medical technology, medicine, music, physical education, public administration, religion, urban studies, Scandinavian, Spanish, and speech. Distributives and 12 credits in religion required. Masters degrees granted. Interdisciplinary studies and special sequences. Journalism concentration. Independent study. Honors program. Phi Beta Kappa. Pass/fail, internships. Preprofessional programs in law, ministry, pharmacy, physiotherapy, veterinary medicine. 3-2 engineering program with U of Illinois, Northwestern, Purdue. 3-2 forestry and environmental management programs with Duke. Washington Semester. Study abroad. Elementary and secondary education certification. Speech and Hearing Center. Computer center. Language lab. Planetarium. 230,000-volume library.
Financial CEEB CSS and ACT FAS. College scholarships, grants, loans, state grants, pre-ministerial loans, tuition reduction for 2nd family member, deferred payment. PELL, SEOG, NDSL, CWS.
Admissions High school graduation with 16 units recommended. GED accepted. Interview encouraged. SAT or ACT required. $15 application fee. Rolling admissions; suggest applying early in 12th year. $100 deposit required on acceptance of offer of admission. *Early Decision* Program. Transfers accepted. Credit possible for CEEB AP exams; college has own advanced placement program.
Student Life Student Union. Newspaper, literary magazines, yearbook, radio station. Music and drama groups. Handel Oratorio Society. Debate. Black Student Union. Cheerleaders. Feminist forum. Athletic, academic, honorary, political, religious, service, and social groups. 6 fraternities and 6 sororities without houses. 40% of men and 35% of women join. Students must live at home or on campus. Single-sex dorms. No married-student housing. 65% live on campus. Liquor and gambling prohibited. 4 activity courses required. 9 intercollegiate sports for men, 7 for women; extensive intramural program. AIAW, College Conference of Illinois and Wisconsin. Student body composition: 0.2% Asian, 7% Black, 0.5% Hispanic, 92.3% White. 16% from out of state.

[1] AURORA COLLEGE

Aurora 60507, (312) 892-6431
Director of Admissions: John Seveland

- **Undergraduates: 307m, 387w**
- **Tuition (1982/83): $3,900**
- **Room & Board: $2,400; Fees: $75**
- **Degrees offered: BA, BS, BSN**
- **Mean ACT 19**
- **Student-faculty ratio: 20 to 1**

A private college established in 1893, affiliated with the Advent Christian Church. 26-acre suburban campus, 40 miles west of Chicago. Served by rail and bus in Aurora; airport in Chicago.
Academic Character NCACS accreditation. Trimester system, 6-week summer term. 36 majors offered in the areas of humanities, science, business, Christian studies, computer science, criminal justice management, education, engineering, medical technology, nursing, physical education, and public administration. Self-designed majors. Minors offered in 24 areas. Management development programs. Distributive requirements. Masters degrees granted. Independent study. Honors program. Pass/fail. Internships and other off-campus experiences. Preprofessional programs in dentistry, law, medicine, and veterinary medicine. Cross-registration with 3 area colleges. Study abroad. Washington Semester. Elementary and secondary education certification. Computer center. 111,000-volume library with microform resources.
Financial CEEB CSS and ACT FAS. College scholarships, grants, loans, deferred payment; PELL, SEOG, NSS, NDSL, CWS.
Admissions High school graduation required. GED accepted. Interview recommended. SAT or ACT required. $15 application fee. Rolling admissions. $50 tuition and $50 room deposits required on acceptance of offer of admission. Admission deferral possible. Transfers accepted. Credit possible for CEEB AP, CLEP, and ACT PEP exams, and for life/work experience.
Student Life Student Association. Newspaper, literary magazine, yearbook. Music and drama groups. Black Student Association. Religious groups. Chess Club. Academic, political, and special interest groups. 2 fraternities and 1 sorority without houses. 10% of men and 5% of women join. Single-sex dorms. No married-student housing. 48% of students live on campus. Liquor prohibited. Class attendance expected. 6 intercollegiate sports for men, 4 for women; intramurals. NAIA, NCAA. Student body composition: 10% Black, 5% Hispanic, 85% White. 7% from out of state.

[1] BARAT COLLEGE

Lake Forest 60045, (312) 234-3000
Director of Admissions: Carol L. McCart

- **Enrollment: 705w**
- **Tuition (1982/83): $4,800**
- **Room & Board: $2,300**
- **Degrees offered: BA, BFA**
- **Mean ACT 22; mean SAT 460v, 440m**
- **Student-faculty ratio: 11 to 1**

A private Roman Catholic women's college founded in 1858 by the Society of the Sacred Heart. Men admitted to evening programs and the Performing Arts Center .30-acre suburban campus 29 miles north of downtown Chicago. Served by air, rail, and bus.
Academic Character NCACS accreditation. Semester system, summer term. 16 majors offered by the Centers of Arts & Sciences, Human Sciences & Services, Management & Business, Performing Arts, Public Policy, and Studio Arts; 20 interdisciplinary concentrations. Self-designed majors. Independent study. Internships. Preprofessional programs in dentistry, health-related areas, law, medicine. 2-2 nursing program with Northwestern. Cooperative management program with Lake Forest. Cross-registration with Lake Forest. Study abroad. Elementary, secondary, and special education certification. Evening programs. Computer center. Language lab. Art gallery. Drake Repertory Theatre. 84,000-volume library.
Financial College scholarships, grants, state grants; PELL, SEOG, NDSL, GSL, CWS, college work program.
Admissions High school graduation with college prep program required. GED accepted. Interview required. ACT or SAT required. $15 application fee. Rolling admissions. $100 deposit due on acceptance of admissions offer. *Early Decision* and *Early Admission* programs. Admission deferral possible. Transfers accepted. Credit possible for CEEB AP exams.
Student Life Student Governing Board. Music, dance, and drama groups. Academic, religious, social activities. Single-sex dorms. 53% of students live on campus. Intercollegiate and intramural sports. Student body composition: 25% minority.

[J1] BELLEVILLE AREA COLLEGE

2500 Carlyle Road, Belleville 62221

[G1] BETHANY THEOLOGICAL SEMINARY

Butterfield and Meyers Road, Oak Brook 60521

[J1] BLACK HAWK COLLEGE

6600 34th Avenue, Moline 61265

[J1] BLACK HAWK EAST COLLEGE

Kewanee 61443

[1] BLACKBURN COLLEGE

Carlinville 62626, (217) 854-3231

- **Enrollment: 173m, 192w; 376 total (including part-time)**
- **Tuition (1982/83): $3,160**
- **Room & Board: $1,340**
- **Degree offered: AB**
- **Mean ACT 24; mean SAT 500v, 500m**
- **Student-faculty ratio: 12 to 1**

A private liberal arts college founded in 1857, associated with the Presbyterian Church. Small-city campus located 40 miles south of Springfield.
Academic Character NCACS accreditation. Semester system. Majors offered include art, art history, biology, business administration, chemistry, economics, elementary education, English, mathematics, music, political science, psychology, sociology, Spanish, special education, speech & theatre, and theatre arts. Washington Semester. Study abroad in Mexico. Elementary and secondary education certification.
Financial CEEB CSS. Aid available including College scholarships & loans.
Admissions High school graduation in upper quarter of class recommended. SAT or ACT required. Rolling admissions. *Early Admission* Program. Admission deferral possible. Advanced placement credit possible.
Student Life Dormitories and dining hall available. 90% of students live on campus. Each student contributes 15 hours per week on the work plan to help keep college costs low. 6 intercollegiate sports; intramurals. Student body composition: 12% minority.

[1] BRADLEY UNIVERSITY

Peoria 61625, (309) 676-7611
Director of Admissions: Robert G. Voss

- **Undergraduates: 2,627m, 1,964w; 5,658 total (including graduates)**
- **Tuition (1982/83): $4,590**
- **Room & Board: $2,176; Fees: $10**
- **Degrees offered: BA, BS, BFA, BMus, BMus Ed, BSEng, BSTech**
- **Mean ACT 23; mean SAT 480v, 530m**
- **Student-faculty ratio: 16 to 1**

A private university established in 1897. 65-acre urban residential campus halfway between St. Louis and Chicago.

Academic Character NCACS and professional accreditation. Semester system, 2 5-week summer terms, 3-week interim term. 7 majors offered by the College of Business Administration, 26 by Communications & Fine Arts, 10 by Education, 10 by Engineering & Technology, 2 by Health Sciences, 26 by Liberal Arts & Sciences, and 2 by the Institute of International Studies. Minors offered. Academic Exploration Program. Black studies program. Masters degrees granted. Phi Beta Kappa. Cooperative work/study, pass/fail, internships, credit by exam. Preprofessional programs in allied health, law. 3-1 program in medical technology. 5-year liberal arts & MBA program. Washington semester. Study abroad. Elementary, secondary, and special education certification. ROTC. Urban Studies Institute. College of Continuing Education. Computer center. Language labs. Over 350,000-volume library with microform resources.
Financial CEEB CSS. University scholarships, grants, loans, deferred and monthly payment plans; PELL, SEOG, NSS, NDSL, CWS. Priority to early applicants; notification starts January 15.
Admissions High school graduation with 9 units required. GED accepted. Interview highly recommended. Requirements vary for individual majors. Audition required for music majors. SAT or ACT required. $20 application fee. Rolling admissions; apply between August 1 and June 1. $100 tuition deposit required on acceptance of offer of admission; $50 room deposit due on registration. *Early Admission* Program. Bradley Preference Plan. Admission deferral possible. Transfers accepted. Credit possible for CEEB AP and CLEP exams.
Student Life Student Senate and Supreme Court. AWS. Newspaper, yearbook, radio and TV stations. Many music groups. Debate, discussion, oratory. Theatre. Athletic, honorary, professional, religious, and special interest groups. 17 fraternities, 10 sororities; all with houses. 30% of men and 26% of women join. Juniors and seniors may live off campus. Single-sex and coed dorms. Student apartments. 90% of students live on campus. 3 hours of phys ed required of all education students. 7 intercollegiate sports for men, 5 for women; several club and intramural sports. AIAW, NCAA, Missouri Valley Athletic Conference. Student body composition: 8% Black, 2% Hispanic, 90% White. 21% from out of state.

[J1] CARL SANDBURG COLLEGE
Galesburg 61401

[G1] CATHOLIC THEOLOGICAL UNION
5402 South Cornell, Chicago 60615

[J1] CENTRAL YMCA COMMUNITY COLLEGE
211 West Wacker Drive, Chicago 60606

[1] CHICAGO, THE UNIVERSITY OF
Chicago 60637, (312) 753-1234
Dean of Admissions & Financial Aid: Dan Hall

- **Undergraduates: 1,870m, 986w; 7,930 total (including graduates)**
- **Tuition (1982/83): $7,065**
- **Room & Board: $3,550; Fees: $114**
- **Degrees offered: BA, BS**
- **Mean ACT 28; mean SAT 1,265**
- **Student-faculty ratio: 8 to 1**

A private university established in 1890. 171-acre urban campus. Served by air, rail, and bus.
Academic Character NCACS and professional accreditation. Trimester system, 10-week summer term. 13 majors offered by the division of Biological Sciences, 19 by Humanities, 6 by Physical Sciences, and 12 by Social Sciences. New Collegiate Division offers interdisciplinary programs in arts and sciences. Common core program required of all freshmen. Graduate and professional degrees granted. Independent study. Honors program. Phi Beta Kappa. Pass/fail. Preprofessional programs in business, law, library science, social work. BA/MA, BS/MS programs in several areas. Study abroad. Many research labs and institutes. Language lab. 3,500,000-volume library with microform resources.
Financial CEEB CSS. University scholarships, grants, loans, monthly payment plans; PELL, SEOG, NDSL, FISL, CWS. Scholarship application deadline January 15.
Admissions High school graduation required. Interview strongly recommended. SAT or ACT required. $20 application fee. Application deadline January 15. $50 class and $50 room deposits due on acceptance of admissions offer (May 1). *Early Notification* and *Early Admission* programs. Admission deferral possible. Transfers accepted. Credit possible for CEEB AP and university placement tests.
Student Life Student Government. Newspaper, magazines, yearbook, radio station. Music and drama groups. Debate. Over 100 student organizations. 5 fraternities. 10% of men join. Freshmen must live at home or on campus. Married-student housing. 65% of students live on campus. 1 year of phys ed required. Extensive intercollegiate and intramural sports. AIAW. Student body composition: 7.4% Asian, 5.3% Black, 3.2% Hispanic, 0.1% Native American, 84% White. 67% from out of state.

[J1] CHICAGO CITY-WIDE COLLEGE
185 North Wabash Avenue, Chicago 60601

[P] CHICAGO COLLEGE OF OSTEOPATHIC MEDICINE
5200 South Ellis Avenue, Chicago 60615

[P] CHICAGO MEDICAL SCHOOL
2020 West Ogden, Chicago 60612

[2] CHICAGO NATIONAL COLLEGE OF NAPRAPATHY
3330 North Milwaukee Avenue, Chicago 60641

[1] CHICAGO STATE UNIVERSITY
95th Street and King Drive, Chicago 60628, (312) 995-2000
Dean of Admissions: Dr. Walter Heinzel

- **Enrollment: 2,585m, 4,856w**
- **Tuition (1982/83): $690 (in-state),$2,070 (out-of-state)**
- **Fees: $98**
- **Degrees offered: BA, BS**
- **Student-faculty ratio: 27 to 1**

A public university established in 1938. 161-acre urban campus. Served by air, rail, and bus.
Academic Character NCACS and professional accreditation. Trimester system. 3 majors offered by the colleges of Allied Health, 26 by Arts & Sciences, 5 by Business Administration, 19 by Education, and in Nursing. Self-designed majors and University Without Walls program. Preprofessional programs in dentistry, medicine, optometry, pharmacy, podiatry, veterinary science. Elementary and secondary education certification. ROTC. Art gallery. 250,000-volume library.
Financial ACT FAS. Aid available includes Illinois State Scholarships, PELL. Application deadline July 11.
Admissions High school graduation required. GED accepted. ACT required. No application fee. Rolling admissions; deadline August 1. *Early Decision* Program. Transfers accepted. College advanced placement program.
Student Life Student government. Publications, television. Academic, music, social, and special interest groups. No student housing. Intercollegiate and intramural sports for men and women. Student body composition: 0.4% Asian, 84.6% Black, 2.1% Hispanic, 0.1% Native American, 12.4% White.

[G1] CHICAGO THEOLOGICAL SEMINARY
5757 University Avenue, Chicago 60637

[1] COLUMBIA COLLEGE
600 South Michigan Avenue, Chicago 60605, (312) 663-1600
Director of Admissions: Don Warzeka

- **Undergraduates: 2,025m, 1,939w**
- **Tuition (1982/83): $3,500 (est.)**
- **Fees: $30**
- **Degree offered: BA**
- **Student-faculty ratio: 10 to 1**

A private college established in 1890. Urban campus in downtown Chicago. Served by air, rail, and bus.
Academic Character NCACS accreditation. Semester system, 10-week summer term, 3-week January interim. Individualized programs in advertising/journalism, television/radio, dance, film, graphic/fine arts, interior design, photography, theatre/music, entertainment management, humanities/literature, and writing/English. Distributive requirements. Independent study. Cooperative work/study, pass/fail, internships. Student-at-large and professional apprentice programs. Exchange programs with several Chicago cultural and educational facilities. Cross-registration through Associated Colleges of the Midwest. Theatre/Music Center. Dance Center. TV studio. Film facilities. 40,000-volume library.
Financial CEEB CSS and ACT FAS. College scholarships, grants, loans, state scholarships & loans, payment plan; PELL, SEOG, CWS, college work program. Suggested applying for scholarships by May 1.
Admissions High school graduation required; college prep program preferred. GED accepted. Interview and SAT or ACT recommended. No application fee. Rolling admissions; suggest applying in fall of 12th year. $20 deposit required on acceptance of offer of admission. *Concurrent Enrollment* Program. Transfers accepted. Credit possible for CEEB AP and CLEP exams.
Student Life Student government. Newspaper, arts magazine, radio station. Rock Band. Filmmakers festival. Art galleries. Dance groups. Extensive theatre activities. No campus housing, but rooms available at nearby colleges. Liquor prohibited on campus. Intramural sports. Student body composition: 1.7% Asian, 36.3% Black, 5.4% Hispanic, 0.4% Native American, 56.2% White. 18% from out of state.

[1] CONCORDIA COLLEGE
River Forest 60305, (312) 771-8300
Director of Admissions: Robert A. Preloger

- **Undergraduates: 368m, 724w; 1,274 total (including graduates)**
- **Tuition (1982/83): $3,000**
- **Room & Board: $2,001; Fees: $45**
- **Degrees offered: BA, BS, BMus, BMus Ed**
- **Mean ACT 22**
- **Student-faculty ratio: 16 to 1**

A private college affiliated with the Lutheran church, established in 1864. 40-acre suburban campus, less than 30 minutes from Chicago. Air, rail, and bus service in Chicago.
Academic Character NCACS and professional accreditation. Trimester system, 3-week winter miniterm, 2-5 week summer terms. Over 35 majors offered in the areas of early childhood, elementary, & secondary education, business, computer science, church careers, nursing, liberal arts & sciences, music. Minor offered in most major fields and in Biblical languages, foreign languages, physics. Courses in 6 additional areas. Interdisciplinary majors. Distributives and 12 hours of theology required. Masters degrees granted. Independent study, pass/fail, internships. Preprofessional programs in dentistry, law, medicine, seminary studies. Exchange program with Chicago

Consortium, Associated Colleges, and Rosary College. Elementary and secondary education certification. Computer. 130,000-volume library.
Financial CEEB CSS. College scholarships, grants, loans, deferred payment; PELL, SEOG, NDSL, CWS. Application deadline July 15.
Admissions High school graduation with 15 units required. GED accepted. Interview required for nursing students. ACT required. Rolling admissions; deadline September 1. $50 tuition deposit required on acceptance of offer of admission; $25 room deposit due July 1, refundable until August 10. Transfers accepted. Credit possible for CEEB AP and CLEP exams; college has own advanced placement program. Pre-Admission College Skills Program.
Student Life Student government. Newspaper, yearbook. Many music groups. Theatre. Academic, service, and religious groups. Single students (except seniors) must live at home or on campus. Single-sex dorms. No married-student housing. 85% of students live on campus. Cars discouraged. Liquor prohibited on campus. 5 hours of phys ed required. 7 intercollegiate sports for men, 6 for women; intramurals. AIAW, NAIA, NCAA. Student body composition: 2% Black, 98% White. 55% from out of state.

[J1] DANVILLE AREA COMMUNITY COLLEGE
Danville 61832

[P] DeANDREIS INSTITUTE OF THEOLOGY
511 East 127th Street, Lemont 60439

[1] DePAUL UNIVERSITY
25 East Jackson Blvd., Chicago 60604, (312) 321-7600
Dean of Undergraduate Assessment & Admissions: Dr. L. Edward Allemand

- **Undergraduates: 2,599m, 2,567w; 13,300 total (including graduates)**
- **Tuition (1982/83): $4,260**
- **Room & Board: $2,580-$2,847; Fees: $15**
- **Degrees offered: BA, BS, BFA, BMus, BSCom, BSEd, BSMed Tech, BSN, BSRad Tech**
- **Student-faculty ratio: 21 to 1**

A private, Roman Catholic university controlled by the Vincentian Fathers. Established in 1898, became coed in 1911. 30-acre urban Lincoln Park Campus located 15 minutes from the Loop; 3-building Lewis Center at Jackson and Wabash Avenues. Served by air, rail, and bus.
Academic Character NCACS and professional accreditation. Trimester system, 2 day and 2 evening summer terms. 6 majors offered by the College of Commerce, 28 by the College of Liberal Arts & Sciences, 6 by the Goodman School of Drama, 8 by the School of Education, and 11 by the School of Music. Minors offered in some major fields. Distributives, and religion & philosophy courses required. Graduate and professional degrees granted. Independent study. Honors program. Some pass/fail, internships, credit by exam. Preprofessional program in law. 3-2 program in engineering with Urbana, Notre Dame, USC; 3-2 or 2-3 programs with Detroit, U of Illinois (Chicago), Northwestern, Iowa State, Ohio State. Early admission to graduate schools possible. Study abroad. Elementary and secondary education certification. ROTC. Language lab. 446,410-volume library.
Financial CEEB CSS. University scholarships, grants, loans, state grants, deferred payment; PELL, SEOG, NSS, NDSL, GSL, NSL, CWS. Recommended application deadline May 1.
Admissions High school graduation with 16 units recommended. Interview recommended. Audition required for music and drama majors. SAT or ACT required. $20 application fee. Rolling admissions; suggest applying early in 12th year. Deadline July 1. *Early Admission, Early Decision, Concurrent Enrollment* programs. Transfers accepted. Credit possible for CEEB AP, CLEP, and University exams.
Student Life Student government. Programming Board. Newspaper, literary magazine, radio station. Music and drama groups. College Democrats. Academic, honorary, religious, and special interest groups. 8 fraternities and 4 sororities without houses. Coed dorms. Married-student housing. 5% of students live on campus. Liquor and gambling prohibited. 6 intercollegiate sports for men, 4 for women; intramurals. AIAW, NCAA. Student body composition: 2.8% Asian, 10.4% Black, 3.7% Hispanic, 0.1% Native American, 81.9% White, 1.1% Other. 5.4% from out of state.

[1] DeVRY INSTITUTE OF TECHNOLOGY
3300 North Campbell Avenue, Chicago 60618, (312) 929-8500
Director of Admissions: Lawrence E. McHugh

- **Undergraduates: 4,212m, 700w**
- **Tuition (1982/83): $2,980**
- **Fees: $45**
- **Degrees offered: BS, AS**
- **Student-faculty ratio: 49 to 1**

A private institute established in 1931 as one of Bell & Howell Education Group. Campus in downtown Chicago. Served by air, rail, and bus.
Academic Character NCACS and professional accreditation. Trimester system. Majors offered in computer science for business and in electronics engineering technology. Diploma and certificate programs. Credit by exam. Electronics labs. Computer center.
Financial CEEB CSS. Institute scholarships, grants, loans; 60 Bell and Howell full scholarships, limited-tuition fellowships, payment plans. PELL, SEOG, NDSL, GSL, FISL, institute has own work program. Application deadline March 31 (scholarships & grants).
Admissions High school graduation required. GED accepted. Interview recommended. SAT or ACT recommended. $25 application fee. Rolling admissions. $50 registration fee required on acceptance of offer of admission. *Concurrent Enrollment* Program. Transfers accepted. Institute has own advanced placement program.
Student Life Student Association. Newspaper. Professional and special interest groups. No student housing. Liquor prohibited. Attendance in class and reasonable dress expected. Intramural sports. Student body compositon: 5.4% Asian, 19.4% Black, 5.6% Hispanic, 0.2% Native American, 68.4% White. 16% from out of state.

[J1] DuPAGE, COLLEGE OF
22nd Street & Lambert Road, Glen Ellyn 60137

[J1] EAST SAINT LOUIS, STATE COMMUNITY COLLEGE OF
East St. Louis 62201

[2] EAST-WEST UNIVERSITY
816 South Michigan Avenue, Chicago 60605

[1] EASTERN ILLINOIS UNIVERSITY
Chicago 61920, (217) 581-2223
Director of Admissions: John E. Beacon

- **Undergraduates: 4,020m, 5,083w; 10,016 total (including graduates)**
- **Tuition & Fees (1982/83): $1,123 (in-state), $2,671 (out-of-state)**
- **Room & Board: $1,930**
- **Degrees offered: BA, BS, BSEd, BSBus, BMus**
- **Mean ACT 20.4**
- **Student-faculty ratio: 20 to 1**

A public university established in 1895. 314-acre rural campus located in a small town 175 miles south of Chicago and 135 miles east of St. Louis. Air, rail, and bus service nearby.
Academic Character NCACS and professional accreditation. Semester system, 5- and 8-week summer terms. Over 45 majors offered by the College of Arts & Sciences, the schools of Business, Education, Fine Arts, Home Economics, Technology, and Health, Physical Education & Recreation. Minors offered in some areas. Distributive requirements. Masters degrees granted. Independent study. Phi Beta Kappa. Cooperative work/study, pass/fail, internships. Preprofessional programs in dentistry & medicine. 3-1 medical technology program. 3-2 program in engineering with U of Illinois. Study abroad. Elementary, secondary, and special education certification. ROTC. Art gallery, TV studio. 480,000-volume library with microform resources.
Financial CEEB CSS and ACT FAS. University scholarships, grants, loans, state scholarships & grants; PELL, SEOG, NDSL, FISL, CWS. Application deadline October 1.
Admissions High school graduation with 16 units recommended. GED accepted. SAT or ACT required. Rolling admissions. *Early Admission* and *Concurrent Enrollment* programs. Admission deferral possible. Transfers accepted. Credit possible for CEEB AP and CLEP exams; university has own advanced placement program.
Student Life Student government. Newspaper, literary magazine, yearbook, radio station. Music and drama groups. Debate. Black Student Union. Academic, honorary, professional, political, religious, and special interest groups. 15 fraternities, 10 with houses, and 11 sororities, 7 with houses. 8% of men and 6% of women join. Single freshmen & sophomores must live on campus. Attendance in class expected. 10 intercollegiate sports for men, 8 for women; many intramurals. AIAW, NCAA, Mid-Continent Conference. Student body composition: 0.2% Asian, 0.5% Black, 0.3% Hispanic, 0.1% Native American, 91.9% White. 4% from out of state.

[J1] ELGIN COMMUNITY COLLEGE
Elgin 60120

[1] ELMHURST COLLEGE
190 Prospect, Elmhurst 60126, (312) 279-4100
Director of Admissions: Michael E. Dessimoz

- **Undergraduates: 850m, 1,100w; 3,630 total (including part-time)**
- **Tuition (1982/83): $4,248**
- **Room & Board: $2,200; Fees: $90**
- **Degrees offered: BA, BS, BMus**
- **Mean ACT 20**
- **Student-faculty ratio: 16 to 1**

A private college established in 1871, affiliated with the United Church of Christ. 35-acre suburban campus, 16 miles west of Chicago. Rail and bus service to Chicago and O'Hare Airport.
Academic Character NCACS and professional accreditation. 4-1-4 system, 8-week summer term. 42 majors offered in the areas of liberal arts, computer science, education, health, business, music, physical education, speech, theology, and transportation. Minors offered in all major fields. Distributives and 1 course in religion required. Independent and interdisciplinary study. Honors program. Limited pass/fail, internships. Preprofessional programs in dentistry, education, engineering, law, medical technology, medicine, social work, theology, veterinary medicine. 3-2 program in engineering. Study abroad. Washington Semester. Elementary, secondary, and special education certification. AFROTC at Illinois Tech. Facilities available at Institute of Nuclear Science and Argonne Labs. Language lab. 150,000-volume library.
Financial CEEB CSS. College scholarships, grants, loans, payment plans; PELL, SEOG, NDSL, CWS. On- and off-campus work available. Application deadline March 1.
Admissions High school graduation with 16 units required. GED accepted. Interview recommended. Audition required for music majors. SAT or ACT required. $15 application fee. Rolling admissions; application deadline August 15. $50 tuition deposit and $50 refundable room deposit required on

acceptance of offer of admission. *Early Admission, Early Decision, Concurrent Enrollment* programs. Admission deferral possible. Transfers accepted. Credit possible for CEEB AP and CLEP exams, and for life/work experience.
Student Life Student government. Newspaper, yearbook, radio station. Music and theatre groups. Creative Writer's Association. Academic, honorary, professional, religious, and special interest groups. 6 fraternities and sororities. All students must have Dean's permission to live off campus. Coed and single-sex dorms. No married-student housing. 40% of students live on campus. Class attendance expected. 4 phys ed courses required. 9 intercollegiate sports for men, 5 for women; intramurals. AIAW, NAIA, NCAA, College Conference of Illinois and Wisconsin. Student body composition: 2% Asian, 5% Black, 5% Hispanic, 1% Native American, 87% White. 5% from out of state.

[1] EUREKA COLLEGE
Eureka 61530, (309) 467-3721

- **Undergraduates: 210m, 200w**
- **Tuition, Room, & Board (1982/83): $6,450**
- **Degrees offered: AB, BS**
- **Mean ACT 20**
- **Student-faculty ratio: 13 to 1**

A private college related to the Disciples of Christ Church. Small-town campus 20 miles east of Peoria.
Academic Character NCACS accreditation. Intensive Study Plan system of 4 8-week quarters. Majors offered in the areas of accounting, art, art therapy, biology, business, chemistry, education, humanities, liberal arts, mathematics, medical technology, music, philosophy, physical education, psychology, religious studies, sciences, social sciences, sociology, and speech & theatre. Preprofessional majors in engineering, law, medicine, and social work. Tutoring available. 75,000-volume library.
Financial College scholarships, state grants; PELL SEOG, NDSL, GSL.
Admissions High school graduation required. ACT or equivalent required. Rolling admissions. *Early Admission* and *Early Decision* programs. Transfers accepted.
Student Life 2 fraternities and 2 sororities. Students with sophmore standing may live in chapter houses. 8 dormitories for men, 4 for women. Dining hall. Student body composition: 10% minority.

[J1] FELICIAN COLLEGE
3800 Peterson Avenue, Chicago 60659

[J2] FRONTIER COMMUNITY COLLEGE
Fairfield 62837

[G1] GARRETT EVANGELICAL THEOLOGICAL SEMINARY
2121 Sheridan Road, Evanston 60201

[1] GEORGE WILLIAMS COLLEGE
555 31st Street, Downers Grove 60515, (312) 964-3100
Director of Admissions: Donald Weiss

- **Enrollment: 234m, 435w; 1,258 total (including part-time)**
- **Tuition (1982/83): $4,575**
- **Room & Board: $2,070**
- **Degrees offered: BA, BS, BSN, BSW**
- **Student-faculty ratio: 15 to 1**

A private college affiliated with the YMCA, established in 1915. 200-acre suburban main campus 20 miles west of Chicago. 148-acre Lake Geneva campus, 90 minutes away in Williams Bay, Wisconsin, for special and continuing educational activities.
Academic Character NCACS and professional accreditation. Trimester system, summer programs. 52 majors offered by the divisions of Applied Behavioral Sciences, Humanities, Leisure & Environmental Resources Administration, Natural & Health Sciences, Physical Education, and Social Sciences. Self-designed majors. Distributive requirements. Masters degrees granted. Independent study. Honors program. Pass/no credit. Preprofessional programs in business, dentistry, law, library science, medicine, nursing, social services, teaching, theology, veterinary science. Cooperative programs with Argonne National Lab. Cross-registration with Aurora, Illinois Benedictine, North Central. Study abroad. Institute for Environmental Awareness. 93,000-volume library.
Financial CEEB CSS. College scholarships, loans, discount for children of YMCA directors; PELL, SEOG, NDSL, GSL, CWS.
Admissions High school graduation with 12 units recommended. GED accepted. ACT or SAT required. $15 application fee. Rolling admissions. $50 tuition and $50 room deposits due on acceptance of admissions offer. *Early Admission* Program. Admission deferral possible. Transfers accepted. Credit possible for CEEB AP, CLEP, and departmental proficiency exams.
Student Life Student Union Board. Newspaper, literary magazine, yearbook. Black Student Alliance. International Student Association. Model UN. Academic, recreational, religious, and special interest groups. 2 fraternities and 2 sororities. Single-sex dorms. Married-student housing. 6 quarter hours of phys ed and studio courses required. 6 intercollegiate sports for men and women; intramurals. Student body composition: 30% minority.

[1] GOVERNORS STATE UNIVERSITY
Park Forest South 60466, (312) 534-5000
Director, Admissions & Student Recruitment: Richard S. Pride

- **Undergraduates: 890m, 1,044w; 5,017 total (including graduates)**
- **Tuition (1982/83): $852 (in-state), $2,496 (out-of-state)**
- **Room & Board: $3,720 (est.)**
- **Degrees offered: BA, BHS, BSN**
- **Student-faculty ratio: 20 to 1**

A public upper-division university established in 1971. 753-acre campus, 35 miles from Chicago.
Academic Character NCACS accreditation. Year-round trimester system, 8-week summer term. 2-year upper-level programs. 13 majors offered by the College of Business & Public Administration, 15 by the College of Arts & Sciences, 10 by the College of Human Learning & Development, and 6 by the School of Health Professions. Distributive requirements. Graduate degrees granted. Independent study. Pass/fail. Cooperative work/study. Early childhood, bilingual, elementary, secondary, and special education certification. ROTC. Instructional Communications Center. Office of Experiential Assessment. 192,000-volume library with microform resources.
Financial CEEB CSS. University scholarships, loans, state grants & loans; PELL, SEOG, NDSL, GSL, CWS. Priority application deadline May 1.
Admissions AA or AS degree, or 60 semester hours from an accredited college or university required. Rolling admissions. Application deadline 1 month prior to registration. Admission deferral possible. Transfers accepted. Credit possible for life/work experience.
Student Life Student government. Newspaper. Music and drama groups. YMCA. Professional, religious, and special interest groups. No campus housing. Cafeteria. Student body composition: 24% minority.

[1] GREENVILLE COLLEGE
Greenville 62246, (618) 664-1840
Director of Admissions & Enrollment Development: Dr. Thomas Morgan

- **Undergraduates: 314m, 407w**
- **Tuition (1982/83): $4,290**
- **Room & Board: $2,060**
- **Degrees offered: AB, BS, BMus Ed**
- **Mean ACT 21.5**
- **Student-faculty ratio: 16 to 1**

A private college affiliated with the Free Methodist Church, established in 1892. 40-acre rural campus located in a small town 50 miles east of St. Louis. Bus service; air and rail service in St. Louis.
Academic Character NCACS and professional accreditation. 4-1-4 system, 8-week summer term, 2-week intensive summer pre-term. 33 majors offered in the areas of arts, sciences, business, education, physical education, religion, social work, speech. Self-designed majors. Courses in 3 additional areas. Distributives, 2 semesters of religion, and 2 January interims required. Independent study. Cooperative work/study. Credit by exam. Preprofessional programs in business, education, law, medicine, ministry, social work. 3-2 program in engineering with U of Illinois. 3-1 medical technology program. Exchange with Christian College Consortium. Summer Spanish program in Santiago, Spain. Washington seminar program. Elementary, secondary, and special education certification. 95,000-volume library.
Financial CEEB CSS. College scholarships, grants, loans, ministerial grants, deferred payment; PELL, SEOG, NDSL, GSL, CWS. Application deadline June 1.
Admissions High school graduation with 16 units expected. GED accepted. Interview may be required. SAT or ACT required. $10 application fee. Rolling admissions; application deadline September 8. $50 tuition deposit required on acceptance of offer of admission, refundable to July 15. *Early Admission* and *Early Decision* programs. Admission deferral possible. Transfers accepted. Credit possible for CEEB AP and CLEP exams. Developmental Learning Program for below-C students.
Student Life Student association and senate. Newspaper, creative writing anthology, yearbook, radio station. Numerous music groups. Debate. Academic, honorary, religious, service, and special interest groups. Single students under 21 expected to live on campus. Dorms for men and women. Spanish house. No married-student housing. 70% of students live on campus. Liquor, tobacco, drugs prohibited. Dancing and questionable forms of amusement discouraged. Attendance at chapel, vespers, and Sunday services encouraged. 1 full course of phys ed required. 7 intercollegiate sports for men, 5 for women; intramurals. NAIA, Prairie College Conference. Student body composition: 1% Asian, 4% Black, 0.1% Hispanic, 92.9% White, 2% Other. 32% from out of state.

[J] HARPER COLLEGE
Algonquin & Roselle Roads, Palatine 60067
Also known as William Rainey Harper College.

[J2] HARRINGTON INSTITUTE OF INTERIOR DESIGN
410 South Michigan Avenue, Chicago 60605

[J1] HARRY S. TRUMAN COLLEGE, CITY COLLEGES OF CHICAGO
1145 Wilson Avenue, Chicago 60640

[J1] HIGHLAND COMMUNITY COLLEGE
Freeport 61032

[1] ILLINOIS, UNIVERSITY OF

■[1] CHICAGO, UNIVERSITY OF ILLINOIS AT

Box 38, Chicago 60680, (312) 996-4388
Director of Admissions: William H. Bain

- **Undergraduates: 7,798m, 5,926w; 20,600 total (including graduates)**
- **Tuition (1982/83): $1,200 (in-state), $2,844 (out-of-state)**
- **Degrees offered: BA, BS, BArch, BSW**
- **Mean ACT 18**
- **Student-faculty ratio: 16 to 1**

A public university established in 1965. Urban campus created by merger of Chicago Circle and Medical Center campuses, located a few blocks from the Loop in downtown Chicago. Served by air, rail, and bus.
Academic Character NCACS and professional accreditation. Trimester system, 8-week summer term. 9 majors offered by the College of Architecture, Art, & Urban Sciences, 6 by Business Administration, 2 by Education, 19 by Engineering, 30 by Liberal Arts & Sciences, 1 by Health, Physical Education, & Recreation, and 1 by Social Work. Self-designed majors. Courses in 9 additional areas, including Arabic, Chinese, Japanese, Swahili, Yiddish. Distributive requirements. Graduate degrees granted. Independent study. Honors program. Phi Beta Kappa. Cooperative work/study, pass/fail. Preprofessional programs in medical dietetics, medical laboratory sciences, medical record administration, occupational therapy, physical therapy, dentistry, law, medicine, nursing, pharmacy, veterinary medicine. Dual-degree programs. Cross-registration at other U of Illinois campuses. Study abroad. Elementary, secondary, and special education certification. ROTC, NROTC, AFROTC. Computer. Center for Research in Criminal Justice, Energy Resources Center, Urban Systems Laboratory. 1,120,335-volume library with microform resources.
Financial ACT FAS. University scholarships, grants, loans, state grants, teacher education grants; PELL, SEOG, NDSL, GSL, CWS, university work program. Application deadline May 1.
Admissions High school graduation with 16 units required. SAT or ACT required. $20 application fee. Rolling admissions; suggest applying by July 1. *Early Admission* and *Concurrent Enrollment* programs. Transfers accepted. Credit possible for CEEB AP and CLEP exams; university has own advanced placement program.
Student Life Extensive program of extracurricular activities. No student housing. 9 intercollegiate sports for men, 8 for women; intramurals. Student body composition: 9.8% Asian, 15.5% Black, 8% Hispanic, 0.5% Native American, 64.3% White, 1.9% Other. 12% from out of state.

■[1] URBANA—CHAMPAIGN CAMPUS

Urbana 61801, (217) 333-1000
Director of Admissions: Gary R. Engelgau

- **Undergraduates: 14,495m, 10,914w; 35,152 total (including graduates)**
- **Tuition (1982/83): $822 (in-state), $2,466 (out-of-state)**
- **Room & Board: $2,670; Fees: $388**
- **Degrees offered: AB, BS, BFA, BMus, BSW, BArch, BLand Arch, BUrb Plan**
- **Mean ACT 26; mean SAT 517v, 585m**
- **Student-faculty ratio: 13 to 1**

A public university established in 1867. 703-acre campus, 130 miles south of Chicago. Served by air, rail, and bus.
Academic Character NCACS and professional accreditation. Semester system, 8-week summer term. 20 majors offered by the College of Agriculture, 3 by Applied Life Studies, 3 by Commerce & Business Administration, 3 by Communications, 7 by Education, 16 by Engineering, 23 by Fine & Applied Arts, 46 by Liberal Arts & Sciences. Self-designed majors. Minors in some fields. Distributive requirements. Graduate and professional degrees granted. Independent study. Honors program. Phi Beta Kappa. Cooperative work/study in industrial education and engineering. Pass/fail, internships. Many preprofessional programs. 5-year engineering/agricultural science, engineering/liberal arts & sciences programs. 5-year BS/MS in accountancy program. 2-year programs in aviation. Medical Center in Chicago. Study abroad & exchange programs in Colombia, England, Europe, Japan, Mexico, Puerto Rico, Russia. Elementary, secondary, and special education certification. ROTC, NROTC, AFROTC. 9,599,336-volume library with microform resources.
Financial CEEB CSS and ACT FAS. University scholarships, grants, loans; PELL, SEOG, NDSL, GSL, CWS. Priority application deadline March 14.
Admissions High school graduation with 15 units required. Interview or audition required for some majors. SAT or ACT required. $20 application fee. Priority application deadline November 15. Later applications as space is available; deadline 2 weeks before registration. *Early Admission* and *Concurrent Enrollment* programs. Admission deferral possible. Transfers accepted. Credit possible for CEEB AP and CLEP exams; university placement exams. Educational Opportunities Program.
Student Life 550 academic, political, professional, religious, social, and special interest groups. 48 fraternities and 24 sororities with houses. 16% of men and 11% of women join. Single students under 21 or with less than 60 credit hours must live off campus. Coed and single-sex dorms. French & coop houses. Beckwith Living Center for handicapped students. Married-student apartments. 52% of students live on campus. 12 intercollegiate sports for men, 8 for women; many intramural & recreational sports. AIAW, NCAA, Big Ten. Student body composition: 3% Asian, 3% Black, 1% Hispanic, 0.3% Native American, 87% White, 5.7% Other. 3% from out of state.

[1] ILLINOIS BENEDICTINE COLLEGE

5700 College Road, Lisle 60532, (312) 968-7270
Director of Admissions: Thomas F. Rich

- **Enrollment: 836m, 788w**
- **Tuition (1982/83): $4,100**
- **Room & Board: $2,320; Fees: $101**
- **Degrees offered: BA, BS, BMus**
- **Mean ACT 21.2**
- **Student-faculty ratio: 15 to 1**

A private college founded in 1887, conducted by the Benedictine Monks. Became coed in 1968. 108-acre suburban campus 25 miles southwest of Chicago. Rail service; O'Hare Airport nearby.
Academic Character NCACS and professional accreditation. Semester system, 2 4-week summer terms. Majors offered in accounting, biochemistry, biology, business economics, chemistry, computer science, economics, elementary education, engineering science, health sciences, history, international business & economics, literature & communications, mathematics, music, nutrition, philosophy, physical education, physics, political science, psychology, religious studies, social science, sociology. Nursing major for RNs only. Minors in most major fields and in language, visual arts. Courses in 5 additional areas. Distributives, 6 hours of religion, 3 of philosophy required. MBA granted. Independent study, internships. Preprofessional programs in dentistry, law, medicine, nursing, optometry, pharmacy, podiatry, veterinary medicine. 3-1 medical records administration and medical technology programs. Nursing, occupational therapy, physical therapy programs with U of Illinois. 2-2 program in nursing with Rush. 3-2 dual degree and 2-2 engineering programs with several schools. Exchange programs with Aurora, George Williams, North Central colleges. Elementary and secondary education certification. ROTC at Wheaton. Language lab. 174,000-volume library.
Financial CEEB CSS and ACT FAS. College scholarships, loans, deferred payment; PELL, SEOG, NDSL, GSL, CWS. Application deadline April 15.
Admissions High school graduation with 16 units required. GED accepted. Interview urged. SAT or ACT required. $10 application fee. Rolling admissions; suggest applying early in 12th year. $100 deposit required on acceptance of admissions offer. *Concurrent Enrollment* Program. Admission deferral possible. Transfers accepted. Credit possible for CEEB AP & CLEP exams and for life experience.
Student Life Student government. Newspaper, yearbook. Music and theatre groups. Campus ministry, Circle K. Black Student Association. Academic, honorary, service, and special interest groups. Students must have parental consent to live off campus. Coed and single-sex dorms. No married-student housing. 60% of students live on campus. 9 intercollegiate sports for men, 6 for women; intramurals. AIAW, NAIA, NCAA, NIIC. Student body composition: 0.4% Asian, 3.3% Black, 0.4% Hispanic, 95.7% White, 0.2% Other. 2% from out of state.

[J1] ILLINOIS CENTRAL COLLEGE

East Peoria 61635

[1] ILLINOIS COLLEGE

Jacksonville 62650, (217) 245-7126
Director of Admissions: Martha V. Clark

- **Undergraduates: 414m, 350w**
- **Tuition (1982/83): $3,075**
- **Room & Board: $1,915**
- **Degrees offered: BA, BS**
- **Mean SAT 500v, 510m**
- **Student-faculty ratio: 16 to 1**

A private college affiliated with the United Presbyterian Church and the United Church of Christ. Established in 1829, became coed in 1903. 62-acre suburban campus 35 miles west of Springfield. Served by air and bus.
Academic Character NCACS accreditation. Semester system. Majors offered in accounting, art, biology, chemistry, economics & business administration, elementary education, English, fine arts, French, German, history, history/political science, interdisciplinary studies, mathematics, music, philosophy, philosophy/religion, physical education, physics, psychology, religious studies, sociology, Spanish, and speech communications & theatre. Courses in Asian studies, education, journalism, technical drawing. Distributives and 2 religion courses required. Independent and interdisciplinary studies. Phi Beta Kappa. Limited pass/fail, internships. Preprofessional programs in communications, dentistry, law, medicine, ministry, optometry, pharmacy, physical therapy, veterinary medicine. 3-2 programs in engineering with U of Missouri, U of Illinois, Washington U. 3-2 home economics program with U of Illinois. 2-2 program in nursing with Rush Medical Center. Study abroad. Elementary, secondary, and physical education certification. Chicago Urban Studies Program. Language lab. 100,000-volume library.
Financial CEEB CSS. College scholarships, grants, grants for ministers' children and ministerial candidates, payment plans; PELL, SEOG, NDSL, GSL, CWS.
Admissions High school graduation with 15 units required. Interview may be required. SAT or ACT required. $10 application fee. Rolling admissions. $50 tuition and $50 room deposits required on acceptance of offer of admission. *Early Admission* and *Early Decision* programs. Transfers accepted. Credit possible for CEEB AP and CLEP exams.
Student Life Student forum. Newspaper, literary magazine, yearbook, radio station. Music and drama groups. Intercollegiate debate. Honorary, religious, service, and special interest groups. 4 literary/social societies for men and 3 for women; all with chapter rooms. 40% of men and 35% of women join. Freshmen must live at home or on campus. Single-sex dorms. No married-student housing. 80% of students live on campus. Liquor prohibited. Attendance in class required on introductory levels. Weekly convocation required. 7 intercollegiate sports for men, 5 for women; intramurals. AIAW, NCAA. Student body composition: 4% Black, 1% Hispanic, 95% White. 10% from out of state.

[1] ILLINOIS COLLEGE OF OPTOMETRY

3241 South Michigan Avenue, Chicago 60616

[P] ILLINOIS COLLEGE OF PODIATRIC MEDICINE
Chicago — see Scholl College of Podiatric Medicine

[J2] ILLINOIS COMMERCIAL COLLEGE
207 West Elm, Urbana 61801

[J1] ILLINOIS EASTERN COMMUNITY COLLEGE
Olney 62450

[1] ILLINOIS INSTITUTE OF TECHNOLOGY
3300 South Federal Street, Chicago 60616, (312) 567-3025
Director of Admissions: Dr. Ron Koger

- **Undergraduates: 2,293m, 494w; 7,103 total (including graduates)**
- **Tuition (1982/83): $5,700**
- **Room & Board: $2,730**
- **Degrees offered: BA, BS, BArch, BBA**
- **Student-faculty ratio: 13 to 1**

A private institute established in 1892. 120-acre urban campus, 3 miles south of the Loop in Chicago. Buses and elevated trains to downtown Chicago.
Academic Character NCACS and professional accreditation. Semester system, 8-week summer term. 25 majors offered by the College of Architecture, Planning & Design, the College of Engineering, the College of Sciences & Letters, and the School of Business Administration. Specialized minors offered in most major fields. Distributive requirements. Graduate degrees granted. Independent study. Honors program. Phi Beta Kappa. Cooperative work/study, pass/fail, internships. Preprofessional programs in dentistry, law, medicine, opthalmology. 5-year architecture program; 6-year architecture-MBA program. 3-2 program in engineering/business; 3-3 program in engineering/law. Exchange program abroad. Secondary education certification. ROTC, NROTC, AFROTC. Environment center. Computer center. Extrusion press. 1,400,000-volume library.
Financial CEEB CSS and ACT FAS. Institute scholarships, grants, loans; PELL, SEOG, NDSL, CWS.
Admissions High school graduation with 16 units required. Interview recommended. SAT or ACT required; ACH recommended. $20 application fee. Rolling admissions; deadline August 1. $50 deposit required on acceptance of offer of admission. *Early Admission* Program. Transfers accepted. Credit possible for CEEB AP and CLEP exams.
Student Life Student government. 2 newspapers, yearbook, radio station. Jazz band. Ethnic, honorary, professional, and religious groups. 9 fraternities with houses; 2 sororities. 20% of men and 10% of women join. Freshmen must live on campus. Coed and single-sex dorms. Married-student housing. 45% of students live on campus. Attendance in class expected. 1 year phys ed required. 8 intercollegiate sports for men, 2 for women; intramurals. NCAA, AIAW. Student body composition: 9% Asian, 16% Black, 1% Hispanic, 61% White, 13% Other. 20% from out of state.

■[P] CHICAGO-KENT COLLEGE OF LAW
77 South Wacker Drive, Chicago 60606

[1] ILLINOIS STATE UNIVERSITY
Normal 61761, (309) 438-2111
Director of Admissions: Wilbur Venerable

- **Undergraduates: 7,055m, 9,028w; 19,479 total (including graduates)**
- **Tuition (1982/83): $780 (in-state), $2,340 (out-of-state)**
- **Room & Board: $2,088; Fees: $299**
- **Degrees offered: BA, BS, BFA, BMus, BMus Ed, BSEd**
- **Mean ACT 20.2**
- **Student-faculty ratio: 18 to 1**

A public university established in 1857. 711-acre small-city campus, 130 miles from Chicago. Air, rail, and bus service in twin city of Bloomington.
Academic Character NCACS and professional accreditation. Semester system, 8-week summer term plus 3-week pre-term. 55 majors offered in the areas of agriculture, computer science, criminal justice, health, physical education, recreation, dance, home economics, industrial technology, social work, speech, business, education, fine arts, and liberal arts & sciences. Self-designed majors. Minors offered in all major fields and in 11 additional areas, including consumer education, ethnic studies, Latin American studies, and Russian. Graduate degrees granted. Independent study. Honors program. Cooperative work/study, pass/fail, internships. Preprofessional programs in dentistry, engineering, law, medicine, social work, veterinary medicine. 3-2 program in engineering with U of Illinois. Exchange program with other state universities. Study abroad. Elementary, secondary, and special education certification. ROTC. Language lab. 1,181,947-volume library.
Financial ACT FAS. University scholarships, grants, loans; PELL, SEOG, NDSL, GSL, CWS. Application deadline April 1.
Admissions High school graduation required. ACT required; SAT may be substituted by out-of-state applicants. Rolling admissions. *Early Admission, Concurrent Enrollment, Early Decision* programs. Transfers accepted. Credit possible for CEEB AP and CLEP exams. High Potential Student Program for disadvantaged students.
Student Life Student Association. Newspaper, literary magazine, radio & TV stations. Music and drama groups. Film society. ACLU. Gay Alliance. Friends of Old Time Music. Debate. Athletic, academic, service, political, religious, and special interest groups. 18 fraternities and 15 sororities, most with houses. 2 coed social organizations. 4-semester residency required of all freshmen. Coed and single-sex dorms. International House. Married-student housing. 39% of students live on campus. Attendance in class expected. 3 hours of phys ed required for education majors. 11 intercollegiate sports for men, 11 for women; intramurals. Golf course. AIAW, Missouri Valley Athletic Conference. Student body composition: 2% Asian, 7% Black, 0.5% Hispanic, 82.5% White, 8% Other. 2% from out of state.

[J1] ILLINOIS VALLEY COMMUNITY COLLEGE
Oglesby 61348

[1] ILLINOIS WESLEYAN UNIVERSITY
PO Box 2900, Bloomington 61701, (309) 556-3031
Director of Admissions: James R. Ruoti

- **Undergraduates: 750m, 900w**
- **Tuition (1982/83): $5,295**
- **Room & Board: $2,280; Fees: $52**
- **Degrees offered: BA, BS, BFA, BMus, BMus Ed, BSacred Mus, BSN**
- **Mean ACT 24.1**
- **Student-faculty ratio: 13 to 1**

A private university affiliated with the Methodist Church, established in 1850. 47-acre suburban campus, 130 miles southwest of Chicago. Served by air, rail, and bus.
Academic Character NCACS and professional accreditation. 4-1-4 system, summer term. Majors offered in accounting, American studies, art, art education, arts management, biology, business administration, chemistry, drama, economics, elementary education, English, finance & insurance, fine arts, French, German, history, math, math/computer science, music (7), music education, music theatre, natural sciences, nursing, philosophy, physics, political science, psychology, religion, sacred music, sociology, and Spanish. Self-designed majors. Distributives and 1 course in religion required. Independent study. Honors program. Limited credit/no credit, internships. Preprofessional programs in journalism, ministry, nursing, social work, veterinary medicine. Combined liberal arts-professional programs in dentistry, law, medical technology, medicine, osteopathy. Cooperative program in forestry & environmental management with Duke. 3-2 programs in engineering with Northeastern, Washington U, Case Western Reserve. Credit for travel programs in US and abroad. Study abroad. UN and Washington semesters. Elementary and secondary education certification. Summer stock and music programs. Computer center, observatory, language lab. Music library. 145,000-volume library.
Financial CEEB CSS. University scholarships, grants, loans; tuition reduction possible for Methodist ministers' children and ministerial students; payment plans. PELL, SEOG, NSS, NDSL, NSL, GSL, CWS. Application deadlines March 1 (scholarships), April 1 (loans).
Admissions High school graduation with college prep program and in top 40% of class required. GED accepted. Interview recommended. Audition required for music and drama majors; portfolio recommended for art. SAT or ACT required. Rolling admissions. $100 deposit required on acceptance of offer of admission. *Early Admission* and *Early Decision* programs. Transfers accepted, except in nursing. Credit possible for CEEB AP and CLEP exams; university has own advanced placement program.
Student Life Student Senate. Newspaper, literary magazine, yearbook, radio station. Choirs, bands, opera theatre, symphony. Debate, oratory. Masquers. Black Student Union. Contemporary dance. Drama, honorary, professional, religious, service, and special interest groups. 6 fraternities and 5 sororities, all with houses. 38% of men and 30% of women join. Freshmen and others under 21 must live on campus. Coed and single-sex dorms. No married-student housing. 85% of students live on campus. Liquor prohibited. Attendance in class required. 2 semesters of phys ed required. 8 intercollegiate sports for men, 5 for women; intramurals. AIAW, NAIA, NCAA, College Conference of Illinois & Wisconsin. Student body composition: 0.6% Asian, 4.3% Black, 0.4% Hispanic, 94.1% White. 8% from out of state.

[J1] JOHN A. LOGAN COLLEGE
Carterville 62918

[P] JOHN MARSHALL LAW SCHOOL
315 South Plymouth Court, Chicago 60604

[J1] JOHN WOOD COMMUNITY COLLEGE
1919 North 18th Street, Quincy 62301

[J1] JOLIET JUNIOR COLLEGE
Joliet 60436

[1] JUDSON COLLEGE
1151 North State Street, Elgin 60120, (312) 695-2500
Director of Enrollment Services: Richard Mitchell

- **Undergraduates: 191m, 208w; 426 total (including part-time)**
- **Tuition (1982/83): $3,420**
- **Room & Board: $2,100; Fees:$130**
- **Degree offered: BA**
- **Mean ACT 20**
- **Student-faculty ratio: 11 to 1**

A private college controlled by the Baptist church, established in 1963. 75-acre suburban campus on the Fox River, 40 miles west of Chicago.
Academic Character NCACS accreditation. 4-1-4-1 system. Majors offered by the divisions of Christian Religion & Philosophy, Communication Arts, Human Institutions, Human Relations, Fine Arts, Science & Mathematics, and Physical Education/Teaching. Distributives and 2 religion courses required. Independent study. Honors program. Preprofessional programs in

law and medicine. ROTC with Wheaton. 77,000-volume library with microform resources.
Financial College scholarships, grants, scholarships for ministers' children, state grants; PELL, SEOG, NDSL, GSL, CWS.
Admissions High school graduation with 15 units recommended. GED accepted. Interview encouraged. ACT required. $15 application fee. Rolling admissions. $50 deposit due on acceptance of admissions offer. *Early Admission* and *Early Decision* programs. Admission deferral possible. Transfers accepted. Credit possible for CEEB CLEP exams.
Student Life Student Senate. Newspaper, yearbook. Music and drama activities. Academic, religious, social, and special interest groups. Single students under 22 must live at home or on campus. Liquor, tobacco, and dancing prohibited. 3 hours of phys ed required. 5 intercollegiate sports for men, 3 for women; intramurals. NAIA, NCCAA, NIIC.

[J1] KANKAKEE COMMUNITY COLLEGE
Kankakee 60901

[J1] KASKASKIA COLLEGE
Centralia 62801

[G1] KELLER GRADUATE SCHOOL OF MANAGEMENT
10 South Riverside Plaza, Chicago 60606

[1] KENDALL COLLEGE
2408 Orrington Avenue, Evanston 60201, (312) 866-1300
Director of Admissions & Financial Aid: Michael J. Alexander

- **Enrollment: 132m, 213w; 417 total (including part-time)**
- **Tuition (1982/83): $3,710**
- **Room & Board: $2,288**
- **Degrees offered: BA, BSBA, BSN, AA**
- **Student-faculty ratio: 16 to 1**

A private college affiliated with the United Methodist Church, established in 1934. Urban campus. Served by air, rail, and bus.
Academic Character NCACS accreditation. 4-1-4 system, summer term. Majors offered in business studies (accounting, data processing, finance, management, marketing), early childhood education, human services, American studies, applied social sciences, and nursing. AA in art & photography, business studies, early childhood education, human services, liberal studies, and pre-health. Distributive requirements. Independent study. Cooperative work/study, internships. Preprofessional program in law. Mitchell Indian Museum.
Financial CEEB CSS. College scholarships, loans, state and federal grants, student employment.
Admissions High school graduation with 10 units recommended. GED accepted. Interview recommended. ACT or SAT required. $15 application fee. Rolling admissions. Tuition and room deposits due on acceptance of admissions offer. *Early Admission* Program. Admission deferral possible. Transfers accepted. Credit possible for CEEB AP exams.
Student Life Newspaper. Music and drama groups. Cultural and social activities. Single-sex and coed dorms. Intramural sports. Student body composition: 23% minority.

[J1] KENNEDY-KING COLLEGE, CHICAGO CITY COLLEGE
6800 South Wentworth, Chicago, 60621

[J1] KISHWAUKEE COLLEGE
Malta 60150

[1] KNOX COLLEGE
Galesburg 61401, (309) 343-0112
Director of Admissions: David C. Tilley

- **Undergraduates: 533m, 458w**
- **Tuition (1982/83): $6,350**
- **Room & Board: $2,260; Fees: $85**
- **Degree offered: BA**
- **Mean ACT 25; mean SAT 520v, 550m**
- **Student-faculty ratio: 11 to 1**

A private college established in 1837. 60-acre urban campus, 200 miles north of St. Louis & 180 miles southwest of Chicago. Served by air, rail, and bus.
Academic Character NCACS and professional accreditation. Trimester system. Majors offered in American studies, art (2), biology, chemistry, classics, computer science, economics & business administration, education (2), English (2), French, geology, German, German area studies, history, international relations, mathematics, music, philosophy, physics, political science, psychology, Russian, Russian area studies, sociology & anthropology, Spanish, and theatre. Self-designed, interdepartmental, interdisciplinary majors. Distributives and 2 terms of freshman preceptorials required. Independent study. Senior honors program. Phi Beta Kappa. Limited pass/fail, internships. Preprofessional programs in dentistry, medical technology, medicine, nursing, veterinary medicine. 3-2 programs in engineering with Columbia, Stanford, Washington, Illinois, and RPI. 3-2 forestry & environmental management program with Duke. 3-3 programs in law with Chicago, Columbia. 3-2 MBA program with Washington. Physical education, medical technology, and nursing programs with Rush. Social work program with U of Chicago. Member of Associated Colleges of the Midwest. Special prorgams include the Oak Ridge Science Semester, Chicago Urban Education Semester, Rocky Mountains Geology Semester, Newberry Library Humanities Seminar, Washington Semester. Study in Europe, Costa Rica, Japan, India, and Hong Kong. Elementary and secondary education certification. ROTC. Language lab. Wilderness Research Station. 200,000-volume library with microform resources.
Financial CEEB CSS. College scholarships, grants, loans, payment plans; PELL, SEOG, NDSL, work program.
Admissions High school graduation with 15 units required. Interview recommended. SAT or ACT required. $15 application fee. Rolling admissions. $100 deposit required on acceptance of offer of admission; refundable at commencement or end of academic year. Limited *Early Admission* Program. Admission deferral possible. Transfers accepted. Credit possible for CEEB AP and CLEP exams. Special admissions program for minority students.
Student Life Student-faculty government. Newspaper, literary magazine, yearbook, radio station. Music and drama groups. Art exhibits. Academic, ethnic, political, service, and special interest groups. 5 fraternities with houses; 3 sororities with joint recreational building. 25% of students join. Most students required to live on campus. Coed and single-sex dorms. 1 cooperative and some special interest houses. 99% of students live on campus. Many intercollegiate and intramural sports. AIAW, Midwest Athletic Conference. Student body composition: 1.5% Asian, 3% Black, 1% Hispanic, 0.1% Native American, 94.4% White. 18% from out of state.

[J1] LAKE COUNTY, COLLEGE OF
19351 West Washington Street, Grayslake 60030

[1] LAKE FOREST COLLEGE
Lake Forest 60045, (312) 234-3100
Dean of Admissions: Francis B. Gummere, Jr.

- **Undergraduates: 520m, 530w**
- **Tuition (1982/83): $6,665**
- **Room & Board: $2,225; Fees: $130**
- **Degree offered: AB**
- **Student-faculty ratio: 11 to 1**

A private college affiliated with the Presbyterian Church, established in 1857. 107-acre suburban campus on the shores of Lake Michigan, 32 miles north of Chicago. Served by air, rail, and bus.
Academic Character NCACS accreditation. Flexible semester system: 15-week fall semester, spring semester of 2 7-week terms. 7-week summer term. Majors offered in art history, biology, business, chemistry, computer studies, economics, education, English, French, German, history, mathematics, music, philosophy, physics, politics, psychology, sociology/anthropology, and Spanish. Interdisciplinary majors offered in American studies, area studies, behavioral science, comparative world literature, environmental studies, health services, humanistic inquiry, international relations, local & regional studies, and scientific inquiry. Self-designed majors. Courses in 7 additional areas, including ancient Mediterranean civilizations, Black, urban, and women's studies. Freshman Interdisciplinary Seminar. Independent study. Honors program. Phi Beta Kappa. Credit/no credit, internships. Preprofessional programs in law, medicine, dentistry, and veterinary medicine. 3-2 programs in social service and in public policy with U of Chicago. 3-2 program in engineering with Washington. Cooperative medical technology and nursing programs with Rush. Cross-registration in creative arts and women's studies with Barat. Marine biology program in Florida. Study abroad. Elementary and secondary education certification. Computer center. Language lab. Member Associated Colleges of the Midwest. Institute for Local and Regional Studies. 200,000-volume library with microform resources.
Financial College scholarships, grants, loans, payment plan; PELL, SEOG, GSL, NDSL, CWS. Application deadlines February 1 (scholarships), March 1 (loans).
Admissions High school graduation with 16 units recommended. Interview suggested. SAT or ACT required. $15 application fee. Preferred application deadline March 1. $100 deposit required on acceptance of offer of admission. *Early Admission* and *Early Decision* programs. Admission deferral possible. Transfers accepted. Credit possible for CEEB AP exams.
Student Life Student government. Newspaper, literary & foreign language magazines, yearbook, radio station. Music, film, & theatre groups. Outing club. Black Student group. Academic, religious, service, political, honorary, social, and special interest groups. 3 fraternities and 1 sorority without houses. All freshmen and most upperclassmen live at home or on campus. Coed and single-sex dorms. Special interest housing. Coop dorms. 84% of students live on campus. Liquor prohibited to students under 21. 8 intercollegiate sports for men, 6 for women; many intramural and club sports. Midwest Collegiate Athletic Conference. Student body composition: 1% Asian, 8% Black, 2% Hispanic, 88% White. 65% from out of state.

[G1] LAKE FOREST SCHOOL OF MANAGEMENT
Lake Forest 60045

[J1] LAKE LAND COLLEGE
Mattoon 61938

[J1] LEWIS AND CLARK COMMUNITY COLLEGE
Godfrey 62035

[1] LEWIS UNIVERSITY
Route 53, Romeoville 60441, (815) 838-0500
Director of Admissions: Irish O'Reilly

- **Undergraduates: 914m, 685w; 2,747 total (including graduates)**
- **Tuition (1982/83): $4,580**
- **Room & Board: $2,696; Fees: $140**
- **Degrees offered: BA, BS, BElected Studies, BSN, AS**

- **Mean ACT 18**
- **Student-faculty ratio: 18 to 1**

A private university controlled by the Brothers of the Christian Schools, established in 1939. 250-acre suburban campus, 5 miles north of Joliet and 20 miles southwest of Chicago. Bus to Chicago, which has air and rail service.
Academic Character NCACS and professional accreditation. Semester system, 6- and 8-week summer terms. 33 majors offered in the areas of the accounting, art, athletics, aviation maintenance, biology, business administration, chemistry, computer science, economics, education, English, finance, fire science, history, journalism, liberal arts, management, marketing, math, medical technology, music, music merchandising, nursing, philosophy, physics, political science, psychology, public administration, religious studies, social justice, social work, sociology, speech/drama. Self-designed majors. Distributives and 2 religion courses required. Masters degrees granted. Independent study. Honors program. Pass/fail, internships. Preprofessional programs in dentistry, medicine, engineering, law, meteorology, optometry, pharmacy, and veterinary medicine. Elementary and secondary education certification. ROTC at Wheaton; AFROTC at Illinois Tech. Over 155,788-volume library.
Financial CEEB CSS and ACT FAS. University scholarships, grants, loans, athletic grants, payment plan; PELL, SEOG, NSS, NDSL, GSL, NSL, CWS. Scholarship application deadline April 1.
Admissions High school graduation with 15 units required. ACT or SAT required; ACT preferred. Rolling admissions. *Early Decision* and *Early Admission* programs. Admission deferral possible. Transfers accepted. Credit possible for CEEB CLEP exams, competence, and experience. Success Program for underprepared students.
Student Life Student government. Newspaper, yearbook, radio station. Music and theatre groups. Young Democrats. Academic, honorary, religious, and special interest groups. 9 fraternities and 5 sororities without houses. 3 dormitories. Dining hall. 25% of students live on campus. 8 intercollegiate sports for men, 5 for women; intramurals. Student body composition: 1% Asian, 11% Black, 1% Foreign, 3% Hispanic, 84% White. 1% from out of state.

[P] LINCOLN CHRISTIAN COLLEGE
Limit at Keokuk Streets, Lincoln 62656

[J1] LINCOLN COLLEGE
Lincoln 62656, (217) 732-3155
Director of Admissions: Mary McLaughlin

- **Enrollment: 396m, 218w; 1,116 total (including part-time)**
- **Tuition (1983/84): $4,300**
- **Room & Board: $2,040; Fees: $235**
- **Degrees offered: AA, AAS, AGS**
- **Student-faculty ratio: 23 to 1**

A private college established in 1865. 40-acre small city campus, 175 miles south of Chicago. Served by rail and bus; air service 30 miles away in Springfield.
Academic Character NCACS accreditation. 4-4-1-1 system. 2-year programs in agriculture, American studies, art, biology, business, chemistry, criminology, economics, English, geography, history, human services, mathematics, media, music, physical education, political science, psychology, sociology, and speech. Honors program. Cooperative work/study. Study abroad. Performing arts center. Lincoln Museum. Natatorium. 30,000-volume library.
Financial ACT FAS. College scholarships, loans, state grants, payment plans; PELL, SEOG, NDSL, GSL, CWS, college employment.
Admissions Open admission to students with ACT score of 15 or higher. $25 application fee. Rolling admissions. $100 deposit due on acceptance of admissions offer. *Early Admission* and *Early Decision* programs. Admission deferral possible. Transfers accepted. Academic Enrichment Program for academically-deficient students.
Student Life Student government. Music, drama, literary groups. Interfaith committee. Students under 21 must live on campus. Dorms for men and women. No married-student housing. Liquor, drugs, gambling prohibited. Class attendance required. 6 intercollegiate sports for men, 5 for women; intramurals. Student body composition: 25% minority.

[J1] LINCOLN LAND COMMUNITY COLLEGE
Springfield 62708

[J1] LINCOLN TRAIL COLLEGE
Robinson 62454

[J1] LOOP COLLEGE, CHICAGO CITY COLLEGE
30 East Lake Street, Chicago 60601

[1] LOYOLA UNIVERSITY
820 North Michigan Avenue, Chicago 60611, (312) 670-2900
Director of Admission Counseling: John W. Christian

- **Undergraduates: 2,951m, 3,690w; 16,140 total (including graduates)**
- **Tuition (1982/83): $4,170**
- **Room & Board: $2,550-$2,878**
- **Degrees offered: BA, BS, BAClassics, BBA, BSN, BSDent Hyg, BSEd**
- **Mean ACT 23**
- **Student-faculty ratio: 13 to 1**

A private, Roman Catholic university controlled by the Society of Jesus, established in 1870. 27-acre urban main campus on the shore of Lake Michigan, 20 minutes from downtown Chicago. 3 other campuses in the area house various Schools & Colleges of the University. Served by air, rail, and bus.
Academic Character NCACS and professional accreditation. Semester system, 1 9-week and 2 5-week summer terms. 41 majors offered in the areas of arts, sciences, business, computer science, criminal justice, dental hygiene, education, nursing, public affairs, social work, theatre, theology. Programs in Afro-American, socio-legal, women's studies. Additional courses in Arabic, Chinese, Japanese, Polish, Russian language & literature. 9 hours of theology required. Graduate and professional degrees granted. Freshman tutorials. Independent study. Honors program. Limited pass/fail. Preprofessional programs in business, dentistry, industrial relations, law, medicine, social work. Study abroad in Rome. Elementary, secondary, and special education certification. ROTC. Language lab. 796,000-volume library with microform resources.
Financial CEEB CSS. University scholarships, grants, loans, payment plans; PELL, SEOG, NSS, NDSL, CWS. Application deadline June 1.
Admissions High school graduation with 15 units required. GED accepted. SAT or ACT required. $15 application fee. Rolling admissions. $50 deposit required on acceptance of offer of admission. Transfers accepted. Credit possible for CEEB AP, CLEP, and ACT PEP exams; university has own advanced placement program.
Student Life Student government, activities board. Newspaper, literary quarterly, yearbook, radio station. Theatre group. Debate. Athletic, academic, social, and special interest groups. 11 fraternities, 2 with houses; 3 sororities without houses. 14% of men and 16% of women join. Coed and single-sex dorms. 33% of students live on campus. 7 intercollegiate sports for men, 4 for women; intramural and club sports. AIAW. Student body composition: 3.5% Asian, 8.3% Black, 4.7% Hispanic, 0.1% Native American, 82.9% White, 0.5% Other. 10% from out of state.

[P] LUTHERAN SCHOOL OF THEOLOGY AT CHICAGO
1100 East 55th Street, Chicago 60615

[J1] MacCORMAC JUNIOR COLLEGE
Downtown Center: 327 South LaSalle Street, Chicago 60604
West Suburban Campus: 5825 St. Charles Road, Berkeley 60163

[1] MacMURRAY COLLEGE
Jacksonville 62650, (217) 245-6151, (800) 252-7485 (Illinois only)
Director of Admissions: Joe Rigell

- **Undergraduates: 221m, 397w**
- **Tuition (1982/83): $4,470**
- **Room & Board: $2,020**
- **Degrees offered: BA, BS, BMus, AS, AAS**
- **Mean ACT 20; mean SAT 1,000**
- **Student-faculty ratio: 12 to 1**

A private college affiliated with the United Methodist Church, established in 1846, became coed in 1969. 60-acre rural campus in a college town 35 miles from Springfield and 80 miles northwest of St. Louis, MO. Served by air and bus in Jacksonville, rail in Springfield.
Academic Character NCACS and professional accreditation. 4-1-4 system, 6-week summer term. 42 majors offered in the areas of business, computer science, education, music, nursing, labor relations, physical education, religion, social work, special education, theatre arts, justice, journalism, industrial management, Russian & East European studies, urban studies, and liberal arts & sciences. Interdisciplinary and self-designed majors. AA offered in business, AAS in administration of justice. Distributive requirements: Liberal Education Profile includes 3 skill areas and 8 awareness areas. Requirements may be met through majors, course work, self-designed projects, and exams. 4 hours of religion/philosophy required. Independent study. Honors program. Pass/fail, internships. Preprofessional programs in dentistry, engineering, law, medicine, veterinary medicine. 3-1 program in engineering with Columbia and Illinois; 3-2 with Washington U. Study abroad. Elementary, secondary, and special education certification. Computer center. Language lab. Art gallery. 145,000-volume library with microform resources.
Financial CEEB CSS and ACT FAS. College scholarships, grants, loans, United Methodist scholarships, payment plan; PELL, SEOG, NSS, NDSL, FISL, NSL, CWS.
Admissions High school graduation with 16 units recommended. GED accepted. Interview recommended. SAT or ACT required. $10 application fee. Rolling admissions. $200 deposit required on acceptance of offer of admission. *Early Admission, Early Decision, Concurrent Enrollment* programs. Admission deferral possible. Transfers accepted. Credit possible for CEEB AP, CLEP, and college exams.
Student Life Student Association. Newspaper, journals, yearbook. Music and drama groups. Mortar Board. Black Student Union. Young Democrats, Young Republicans. Religious and special interest groups. Students must live at home or on campus. Coed and single-sex dorms. Special interest houses. 91% of students live on campus. Liquor prohibited to students under 21. Competence in 2 recreational areas required. 8 intercollegiate sports for men, 7 for women; many intramurals. NCAA, IAAIW, Prairie College Conference. Student body composition: 8% Black, 2% Hispanic, 90% White. 13% from out of state.

[J1] MALCOLM X COLLEGE, CHICAGO CITY COLLEGE
2250 West Van Buren Street, Chicago 60612

[J1] MALLINCKRODT COLLEGE
1041 Ridge Road, Wilmeltte 60091

[G1] McCORMICK THEOLOGICAL SEMINARY
5555 South Woodlawn Avenue, Chicago 60637

[J1] McHENRY COUNTY COLLEGE
Highway 14, Crystal Lake 60014

[1] McKENDREE COLLEGE
Lebanon 62254, (618) 537-4481
Director of Admissions: Steve Jackson

- **Undergraduates: 489m, 311w**
- **Tuition (1982/83): $3,600**
- **Room & Board: $1,900; Fees: $190**
- **Degrees offered: BA, BS, BBA, BFA, BSEd, BSN**
- **Mean ACT 20**
- **Student-faculty ratio: 13 to 1**

A private college affiliated with the United Methodist Church, established in 1828. 32-acre rural campus in a small town 25 miles east of St. Louis. Bus service to St. Louis.

Academic Character NCACS accreditation. Semester system, summer terms. 35 majors offered in the areas of liberal arts & sciences, business, fine arts, education, physical education, medical technology, and religion. Major in nursing for students with an RN. Self-designed majors. Minors in coaching, computer science, gerontology, journalism, and music. Distributive requirements. Independent study, honors courses. Credit by exam, pass/fail, cooperative work/study, internships. Preprofessional programs may be arranged. Aerospace studies with Southern Illinois U. Exchange program with 9 area colleges. Elementary, secondary, and special education certification. AFROTC; ROTC & NROTC at Belleville and Southern Illinois. 100,000-volume library.

Financial CEEB CSS. College scholarships, grants, loans, state & athletic scholarships; PELL, SEOG, GSL, NDSL, FISL, CWS.

Admissions High school graduation with 16 units required. GED accepted. Interview recommended. ACT required. $15 application fee. Rolling admissions. $100 deposit required on acceptance of offer of admission. *Early Decision, Early Admission, Credit in Escrow* programs. Admission deferral possible. Transfers accepted. Credit possible for CEEB AP and CLEP exams; college has own advanced placement program.

Student Life Student government. Newspaper, literary magazine, yearbook. Music and drama groups. Investment league. Academic, religious, and special interest groups. 5 fraternities and 3 sororities without houses. 48% of men and 38% of women join. Students under 21 must live at home or on campus. Single-sex dorms. No married-student housing. 33% of students live on campus. Liquor prohibited. 2 hours of phys ed required of students under 23. 4 intercollegiate sports for men, 3 for women; intramurals. AIAW, NAIA. Student body composition: 5% Black, 80% White, 15% Other. 22% from out of state.

[P] MEADVILLE/LOMBARD THEOLOGICAL SCHOOL
5701 South Woodlawn Avenue, Chicago 60637

[2] MIDSTATE COLLEGE
244 Southwest Jefferson Avenue, Peoria 61602

[1] MIDWEST COLLEGE OF ENGINEERING
PO Box 127, Lombard 60148

[1] MILLIKIN UNIVERSITY
Decatur 62522, (217) 424-6211
Dean of Admissions & Records: Jack C. Allen

- **Undergraduates: 731m, 768w**
- **Tuition (1982/83): $4,800**
- **Room & Board: $2,120; Fees: $57**
- **Degrees offered: BA, BS, BFA, BMus, BSN**
- **Mean ACT 21; mean SAT 431v, 489m**
- **Student-faculty ratio: 14 to 1**

A private university affiliated with the United Presbyterian Church, established in 1901. 40-acre suburban campus, 40 miles east of Springfield. Air and bus service.

Academic Character NCACS and professional accreditation. 4-1-4 system, summer term. 28 majors offered by the College of Arts & Sciences, 8 by the School of Business & Engineering, 6 by the School of Music, and 1 by the School of Nursing. Special majors. Minors offered in some major fields. Distributives, 7 winter term units, and some comprehensive exams required. Independent study. Honors programs in some areas. Pass/fail, internships. Preprofessional programs in dentistry, law, medical technology, medicine, ministry, occupational therapy, and physical therapy. Engineering program with U of Illinois, Urbana. Washington Semester. Study abroad. Elementary and secondary education certification. Language lab. 154,000-volume library.

Financial CEEB CSS. University scholarships, grants, loans, payment plans; PELL, SEOG, NDSL, GSL, PLUS, CWS.

Admissions High school graduation with 15 units required, 16 preferred. GED accepted. Audition required for music majors. ACT or SAT required. $15 application fee. Rolling admissions. $50 deposit required on acceptance of offer of admission. *Early Decision* and *Early Admission* programs. Admission deferral possible. Transfers accepted. Credit possible for CEEB AP and CLEP exams; university has own advanced placement program.

Student Life Student Senate. Newspaper, literary magazine, yearbook, radio station. Music and drama groups. Debate. Photography Club. Academic, athletic, honorary, religious, and special interest groups. 6 fraternities and 4 sororities with houses. 42% of men and 39% of women join. Freshmen must live at home or on campus. Dorms and dining facilities. 80% of students live on campus. 7 intercollegiate sports for men, 4 for women, and 2 coed; many intramurals. AIAW, NCAA, College Conference of Illinois. Student body composition: 0.1% Asian, 6.3% Black, 0.7& Hispanic, 0.1% Native American, 92.8% White. 6% from out of state.

[1] MONMOUTH COLLEGE
Monmouth 61462, (309) 457-2131
Director of Admissions: John M. Fettig

- **Undergraduates: 350m, 325w**
- **Tuition (1982/83): $5,140**
- **Room & Board: $2,160; Fees: $195**
- **Degree offered: BA**
- **Student-faculty ratio: 11 to 1**

A private college affiliated with the United Presbyterian Church, established in 1853. 36-acre small-town campus, 60 miles west of Peoria and 16 miles from Galesburg. Air, rail, and bus service nearby.

Academic Character NCACS and professional accreditation. Trimester system, summer term. Majors offered in accounting, art, biology, chemistry, classics, computer science, economics & business administration, education, English, French, geology, government, history, mathematics, music, philosophy, physical education, physics, psychology, religious studies, sociology, Spanish, and speech/communication arts. 3-1 medical technology program. Interdisciplinary, self-designed, and general studies majors. Distributive requirements, freshman seminar. Independent study. Honors program. Credit by exam, pass/fail, internships. Preprofessional programs include dentistry, journalism, law, library science, medicine, ministry, veterinary medicine. 3-2 program in engineering with Case Western, U of Illinois, and Washington U. 2-2 programs in medical technology and nursing with Rush. Exchange programs with Knox. Many special programs through the Associated Colleges of the Midwest. Washington Semester. Study abroad. Independent study in Europe with the Experiment in International Living. Elementary, secondary, and special education certification. ROTC. 185,000-volume library.

Financial CEEB CSS. College scholarships, state grants, payment plan; PELL, SEOG, GSL, NDSL, CWS. Recommended loan application deadline March 15.

Admissions High school graduation with 15 units required. Interview encouraged. SAT or ACT required. $15 application fee. Rolling admissions. $100 deposit required on acceptance of offer of admission. *Early Decision, Early Admission, Concurrent Enrollment* programs. Admission deferral possible. Transfers accepted. Credit possible for CEEB AP and CLEP exams; college has own advanced placement program.

Student Life Student Association. Newspaper, literary magazine, yearbook, radio station. Music and drama groups. Cultural activities. Association of Women Students, International Club. Black Action & Affairs Council. Academic, honorary, religious, and special interest groups. 6 fraternities with houses and 4 sororities without houses. 50% of men and women join. Single students live at home or on campus. Single-sex dorms. 95% of students live on campus. 10 intercollegiate sports for men, 8 for women; many intramurals. AIAW, MIAC, MACW. Student body composition: 5% Asian, 2% Black, 91% White, 2% Other. 15% from out of state.

[P] MOODY BIBLE INSTITUTE
820 North LaSalle Drive, Chicago 60610

[J1] MORAINE VALLEY COMMUNITY COLLEGE
10900 South 88th Avenue, Palos Hills 60495

[J1] MORTON COLLEGE
Cicero 60650

[1] MUNDELEIN COLLEGE CHICAGO
6363 North Sheridan Road, Chicago 60660, (312) 262-8100
Director of Admissions: Betty Miller

- **Undergraduates: 77m, 1,354w**
- **Tuition (1982/83): $4,140**
- **Room & Board: $2,175; Fees: $15**
- **Degrees offered: BA, BS, BFA**
- **Mean ACT 18; mean SAT 900**
- **Student-faculty ratio: 12 to 1**

A private college primarily for women, controlled by the Sisters of Charity of the Blessed Virgin Mary, established in 1929. 6-acre suburban campus on the shore of Lake Michigan. Served by train and bus from downtown Chicago.

Academic Character NCACS and professional accreditation. Trimester system, summer term. Majors offered in art, Asian studies, bilingual/bicultural studies, biology, chemistry, communications, early childhood education, English, French, history, home economics, humanities, management, math, music, philosophy, psychology, religious studies, social science, Spanish, and speech & language disorders. Inter- and multidisciplinary majors. Weekend College offers majors in Community Studies and Personal Universe. Physics major with Loyola U; Judaic studies major with Spertus. Courses in journalism and theatre. Intensive language training in Chinese, German, and Japanese. Distributive requirements. MA in Religious Studies granted. Independent study. Cooperative work/study, pass/fail, internships. Preprofessional programs in law and medicine. 3-2 program in engineering with Georgia Tech. 3-1 medical technology programs with area hospitals. Exchange programs with Columbia, Clarke, Loyola. Central States College Consortium. Study abroad. Elementary, secondary, and special education

certification. Language Labs. Center for Religious Education. Hispanic Institute. Institute in Creation-Centered Spirituality. 128,000-volume library.
Financial CEEB CSS. College scholarships, loans, state grants, payment plans; PELL, SEOG, NDSL, CWS.
Admissions High school graduation required; college prep program recommended. GED accepted. Interview required. SAT or ACT required. $15 application fee. Rolling admissions. $50 tuition and $50 room (for boarders) deposits required on acceptance of offer of admission. *Early Admission* Program. Admission deferral possible. Transfers accepted. Credit possible for CEEB AP and CLEP exams; college has own advanced placement program.
Student Life Commuter Council. Community Government. Magazine. College Women in Broadcasting. United Black Students Association. Music and dance groups. Athletic, academic, honorary, political, religious, and service groups. 18% of students (47% of freshmen) live on campus. Student body composition: 1.7% Asian, 17.3% Black, 5.7% Hispanic, 0.4% Native American, 72.5% White, 2.4% Other. 9% from out of state.

[P] NATIONAL COLLEGE OF CHIROPRACTIC
200 East Roosevelt Road, Lombard 60148

[1] NATIONAL COLLEGE OF EDUCATION
2840 North Sheridan Road, Evanston 60201, (312) 256-5150
Director of Admissions: Gail Kligerman Straus

- **Enrollment: 45m, 518w; 1,417 (including part-time)**
- **Tuition (1982/83): $4,665**
- **Room & Board: $2,565-$3,090**
- **Degree offered: BA**
- **Mean ACT 20; mean SAT 463v, 474m**
- **Student-faculty ratio: 12 to 1**

A private college established in 1886. Urban campus north of Chicago; branch campuses in Chicago and Lombard. Served by air, rail, and bus.
Academic Character NCACS accreditation. Trimester system, 8-week summer term, December interim. Programs in human services, instructional technologies, liberal arts studies, radiation therapy technologies, urban education, early childhood, elementary, middle school and special education. Minor in legal assistance. 2-year diploma in early childhood education offered at Chicago campus. Distributive requirements. Graduate degrees granted. Credit by exam. Field training. Bilingual early childhood program (Chicago campus only). Computer center. Children's Library and Media Center. 95,000-volume library with microform resources.
Financial CEEB CSS. College scholarships, grants, state grants; PELL, SEOG, NDSL, GSL, CWS.
Admissions High school graduation required; 12 units recommended. Interview recommended. SAT or ACT required. $15 application fee. Rolling admissions. $75 deposit due on acceptance of admissions offer. *Early Admission* Program. Admission deferral possible. Advanced placement credit possible.
Student Life Student government. Newspaper, literary magazine, yearbook. Music and drama activities. United Black Students. Honorary, professional, religious, service, and special interest groups. Single students under 21 must live at home or on campus. Dormitories for men & women on Evanston campus. 6 credits of phys ed required. 2 intercollegiate sports for women; intramurals. Student body composition: 25% minority.

[1] NORTH CENTRAL COLLEGE
Naperville 60566, (312) 420-3414
Director of Admissions: Rick Spencer

- **Undergraduates: 650m, 550w**
- **Tuition (1982/83): $4,689**
- **Room & Board: $2,325; Fees: $75**
- **Degree offered: BA**
- **Mean ACT 22.5**
- **Student-faculty ratio: 16 to 1**

A private college affiliated with the United Methodist Church, established in 1861. 53-acre suburban campus 28 miles from downtown Chicago. Rail and bus service to Chicago.
Academic Character NCACS accreditation. Trimester December interim, summer term. Majors offered in accounting, art, bank management, biology, business, chemistry, classics, computer science, economics, education, English, French, general studies, German, history, mathematics, metropolitan studies, music, philosophy, physical education, physics, political science, psychology, recreation, religious studies, social studies, sociology/anthrolpology, Spanish, and speech communications/theatre. Self-designed majors. Curriculum has 3 areas: Foundations, Explorations, and Concentration. Close faculty-student work, no class division by year. Independent study. Honors program. Cooperative work/study, internships. Preprofessional programs in dentistry, law, medicine, medical technology. 3-2 program in engineering with Washington. 2-2 program with Illinois Tech. 3-2, 2-2 nursing programs with Rush. Cross-registration with 3 area schools. Study abroad. Washington and UN semesters. Elementary and secondary education certification. ROTC at Wheaton. Gulf Coast Research Lab. Language lab. 100,000-volume library.
Financial CEEB CSS. College scholarships, grants, loans, deferred payment; PELL, SEOG, NDSL, CWS. Application deadline August 15 (scholarships), August 1 (loans).
Admissions High school graduation with 15 units required. SAT or ACT required. $15 application fee. Rolling admissions. $100 deposit required on acceptance of offer of admission. Credit possible for CEEB AP and CLEP exams; college has own advanced placement program.
Student Life Student Senate. House Councils. Black Student Association. Newspaper, literary magazine, yearbook, radio station. Music and drama groups. Debate. Academic, honorary, political, religious, and special interest groups. 55% of students live on campus; 25% in nearby housing. 3 terms of phys ed required. 10 intercollegiate sports for men, 7 for women; intramurals. AIAW, NCAA, CCIW. Student body composition: 3% Black, 95% White, 2% Other. 5% from out of state.

[1] NORTH PARK COLLEGE
5125 North Spaulding Avenue, Chicago 60625, (312) 583-2700
Director of Admissions: James Lundeen

- **Total enrollment: 559m, 683w (including graduates)**
- **Tuition (1982/83): $4,365**
- **Room & Board: $2,166; Fees: $359**
- **Degrees offered: BA, BS, BMus, BSMed Tech, BSN**
- **Mean ACT 21; SAT 470v, 510m**
- **Student-faculty ratio: 14 to 1**

A private college affiliated with the Evangelical Covenant Church, established in 1891. 25-acre suburban campus 7 miles from downtown Chicago. Served by air, rail, bus, and rapid transit.
Academic Character NCACS and professional accreditation. Trimester system, 8-week summer term. 37 majors offered in the areas of liberal arts & sciences, business, computer science, education, medical technology, music, nursing, physical education, religion, speech. Self-designed majors. Minor required in most fields; offered in Latin and interdisciplinary area studies. Distributive requirements; 2 religion courses required; comprehensive exams in some departments. Independent study. Limited pass/fail, internships. Preprofessional programs in dentistry, law, medicine, ministry. 3-1 medical technology program with area hospitals. Swedish exchange program. Study abroad in cooperation with Schiller College. Computer center. Language lab. 150,000-volume library.
Financial CEEB CSS. College scholarships and loans, tuition reduction for clergy families, travel discounts; PELL, SEOG, NDSL, deferred payment plans, CWS. Application deadline May 1.
Admissions High school graduation with 15 units required. Interview encouraged. SAT or ACT required. $20 application fee. Rolling admissions. $100 tuition and $75 room deposits required on acceptance of offer of admission. *Early Admission* Program. Transfers accepted. Credit possible for CEEB AP and CLEP exams and for college proficiency exams.
Student Life Student Association. Newspaper, literary magazine, yearbook. Music and drama groups. Debates. Black Student Association. Missions Fellowship. Christian service teams. Political, religious, service, and tutoring groups. Students live at home, or in college apartments or single-sex dorms. 60% live on campus. 3 terms of phys ed required. Dancing and smoking prohibited. Convocation attendance required on certain occasions. 9 intercollegiate sports for men, 6 for women; extensive intramurals. AIAW, NCAA, CCIW. Student body composition: 1.93% Asian, 5.02% Black, 2.16% Hispanic, 0.3% Native American, 89.71% White, 0.85% Other. 35% from out of state.

[1] NORTHEASTERN ILLINOIS UNIVERSITY
5500 North St. Louis Avenue, Chicago 60625, (312) 583-4050
Director of Admissions: Eric B. Moch

- **Undergraduates: 2,025m, 2,650w; 10,045 total (including graduates)**
- **In-state Tuition (1982/83): $774 (1st & 2nd years), $822 (3rd & 4th years)**
- **Out-of-state Tuition (1982/83): $1,161 (1st & 2nd years), $1,233 (3rd & 4th years)**
- **Fees: $134**
- **Degrees offered: BA, BS**
- **Student-faculty ratio: 22 to 1**

A public university established in 1961. 67-acre urban campus. Served by air, rail, and bus.
Academic Character NCACS and professional accreditation. Trimester system, 2 8-week summer terms. 28 majors offered by the College of Arts & Sciences, 7 by the College of Education. Special Majors. Courses in German, Italian, and Russian. Distributive requirements. Independent study. Women's studies. Pass/fail. Program for Interdisciplinary Education to develop new curricula, some off-campus. English Trimester Project. Creative Writing Program center off-campus. Field centers in Chicago for community study and service. Internships. Pre-professional programs in dentistry, medicine, and others. National Student Exchange. Study abroad. Elementary, secondary, and special education certification. ROTC at Loyola, AFROTC at Illinois Tech. Learning Center: audio-visual, multi-media, film, TV, language lab. 397,661-volume library.
Financial ACT FAS. University scholarships, grants, and loans, PELL, SEOG, NDSL, FISL, CWS. Priority application deadline May 1.
Admissions High school graduation with 11 units recommended. GED accepted. ACT required. Rolling admissions. Transfers accepted. Credit possible for CEEB CLEP exam; Project Success for disadvantaged students, Proyecto Pa'lante recruiting program for bilingual Spanish-Americans.
Student Life Student Government. Newspaper, literary magazine, yearbook. Music groups. Academic, athletic, honorary, religious, service, and special interest groups. 1 fraternity, 2 sororities. No university housing. 3 semesters of phys ed required of education majors. Attendance in class required. 6 intercollegiate sports for men, 4 for women; intramurals. NAIA, AIAW. Student body composition: 6.9% Asian, 12.1% Black, 11.1% Hispanic, 0.4% Native American, 67.5% White, 2% Other. 1% from out of state.

[G1] NORTHERN BAPTIST THEOLOGICAL SEMINARY
660 East Butterfield Road, Lombard 60148

Key to ratings **[1, 2, J1, J2, G, P, R, S]** *and list of abbreviations start on page 120*

[1] NORTHERN ILLINOIS UNIVERSITY
DeKalb 60115, (815) 753-1000
Director of Admissions: Daniel S. Oborn

- **Undergraduates: 7,670m, 9,188w; 25,428 total (including graduates)**
- **Tuition (1982/83): $1,114 (in-state), $2,674 (out-of-state)**
- **Room & Board: $1,050-$1,080**
- **Degrees offered: BA, BS, BFA, BGS, BMus, BSEd**
- **Mean ACT 20.9**
- **Student-faculty ratio: 18 to 1**

A public university established in 1895. 449-acre campus in small city 65 miles from Chicago. Served by bus.

Academic Character NCACS and professional accreditation. Semester system, 3 4-week module summer terms. 5 majors offered by the College of Business, 4 by the College of Education, 23 by the College of Liberal Arts & Sciences, 10 by the College of Professional Studies, 7 by the College of Visual & Performing Arts. Interdisciplinary minors offered in 9 areas. Programs in environmental, foreign, Latin American, minority, and medieval studies. Distributive requirements. Graduate degrees granted. Independent study. Honors program. Pass/fail, internships. 3-2 engineering program with U of Illinois at Urbana-Champaign. Preprofessional programs in dentistry, engineering, law, medicine, optometry, pharmacy, podiatry, veterinary medicine. Study abroad. ROTC. Elementary, secondary, and special education certification. 1,000,000-volume library.

Financial CEEB CSS. University scholarships, grants, and loans, PELL, SEOG, NSS, SMA, NDSL, GSL, CWS. Application deadline March 1.

Admissions High school graduation; college-prep program recommended. GED accepted. ACT required. Rolling admissions. *Concurrent Enrollment* Program. Transfers accepted. Credit possible for CEEB AP; university has own advanced placement program. CHANCE program for disadvantaged students.

Student Life Student Association. Newspaper, literary magazine, yearbook, radio station. Music, drama, and speaking groups. Academic, athletic, community service, honorary, political, religious, and special interest groups. 16 fraternities, 14 sororities. Freshmen must live at home or on campus. Coed and single-sex dorms. Special interest housing. Some married-student housing. 33% of students live on campus. 3 semesters of phys ed required for teaching certificate. 12 intercollegiate sports for men, 12 for women; extensive intramurals. AIAW, NAIA, NCAA, Mid-America Conference. Student body composition: 1.2% Asian, 5% Black, 1.4% Hispanic, 0.3% Native American, 92.1% White. 2% from out of state.

[1] NORTHWESTERN UNIVERSITY
633 Clark Street, Evanston 60201, (312) 492-7456
Dean of Admissions: William Ihlanfeldt, PhD

- **Enrollment: 7,028m, 5,090w**
- **Tuition (1982/83): $8,085**
- **Room & Board: $2,800**
- **Degrees offered: BA, BMus, BMus Ed, BS, BSE, BSEng, BSJourn, BSSpeech**
- **Mean ACT 28; mean SAT 575v, 625m**
- **Student-faculty ratio: 6 to 1**

A private university established in 1851. 170-acre suburban campus on shore of Lake Michigan, 12 miles north of Chicago. Served by air, rail, and bus.

Academic Character NCACS and professional accreditation. Trimester system, 8-week summer term. 56 majors offered by the College of Arts & Sciences, 2 by the School of Education, 3 by the School of Journalism, 6 by the School of Music, 10 by the School of Speech, 13 by the Technological Institute. Self-designed majors. Special programs in American culture, comparative literature, neuroscience, urban affairs. African, Asian, and women's studies. Distributive requirements. Graduate degrees granted. Writer's workshop. Independent study; voluntary tutorials. Honors program. Phi Beta Kappa. Cooperative education in Technological Institute. Pass/no credit, internships. Preprofessional programs in law, medicine, management, and others. 3-year degree program in Arts & Sciences; 4-year master's program in 5 areas. 3-2 management program. 2-4 honors program with Northwestern Medical School. Integrated Science Program. Combined BA-professional degree program from Northwestern Dental or Medical School. Medical technology and physical therapy programs with Medical School. Thematic residential colleges in commerce & industry, community studies, and philosophy & religion. Study abroad. Education certification. NROTC. English Curriculum and Social Studies Curriculum Study Centers. Transportation Center. Traffic Institute. Archaeological Field School. 2,900,000-volume library with microform resources.

Financial CEEB CSS. University scholarships, grants, and loans, PELL, SEOG, NDSL, CWS. Application deadline February 1.

Admissions High school graduation with 16 units required. Interview encouraged. SAT or ACT, and 3 ACH required. $25 application fee. Application deadline February 15; suggest filing before January 1. $200 deposit required on acceptance of admissions offer. *Early Notification* Program. Transfers accepted. Admission deferral possible. Credit possible for CEEB AP and ACH exams, and for university placement exams.

Student Life Student government. Newspaper, literary magazine, yearbook, radio station. Debates. Music and drama groups. NOVA (mental-health volunteers). Students for a Better Environment. 29 fraternities and 17 sororities; all have houses. 30% of students join. Freshmen must live on campus. Thematic dorms. 80% of students live on campus. Freshmen not permitted cars. Extensive intercollegiate and intramural sports programs. AIAW, Western Big Ten Conference. Student body composition: 2% Asian, 8.7% Black, 1.2% Hispanic, 0.1% Native American, 85.7% White. 67% from out of state.

[J1] OAKTON COMMUNITY COLLEGE
7900 North Nagle Avenue, Morton Grove 60053

[J1] OLIVE—HARVEY COLLEGE, CHICAGO CITY COLLEGE
10001 South Woodlawn Avenue, Chicago 60628

[1] OLIVET NAZARENE COLLEGE
Kankakee 60901, (815) 939-5011
Director of Development and Admissions: Roy F. Quanstrom

- **Enrollment: 753m, 1,037w**
- **Tuition (1982/83): $3,210**
- **Room & Board: $1,916; Fees: $130**
- **Degrees offered: BA, BS, ThB**
- **Mean ACT 18.4**
- **Student-faculty ratio: 19 to 1**

A private college affiliated with the Nazarene Church, established in 1907. 160-acre suburban campus, 60 miles from Chicago. Served by rail and bus.

Academic Character NCACS and professional accreditation. Semester system, January interim, 2 3-week and 1 5-week summer terms. 38 majors offered in the liberal arts & sciences, business, Christian education, computer science, education, home economics, medical technology, music, nursing, physical education, religion, speech. 5 associate degree programs. Self-designed majors. Minors. 12 hours of religion required. Honors program. Limited pass/fail. Preprofessional programs in astronomy, biochemistry, biophysics, chemical physics, counseling psychology, dietetics, engineering, geochemistry, geology, geophysics, guidance & counseling, law, mathematical physics, medicine, physical therapy, social work. Some use of Argonne National Labs possible. Elementary and secondary education certification. TV and A-V labs. 120,000-volume library.

Financial CEEB CSS. College scholarships, grants, and loans, PELL, SEOG, NSS, NDSL, FISL, CWS. Preferred application deadline March 1.

Admissions High school graduation with 15 units required. GED accepted. ACT required. Interview recommended. Rolling admissions. $30 room deposit required on acceptance of admissions offer. Transfers accepted. Credit possible for CEEB AP and CLEP exams.

Student Life Student Council. Newspaper, yearbook. Music and drama groups. Community service. Public Affairs Club. Academic, honorary, political, religious, and special interest groups. Students not living at home must live and board on campus. Single-sex dorms. Married-student housing. 70% live on campus. 2 hours of phys ed required. Thrice-weekly chapel attendance required. Liquor, tobacco, narcotics, gambling, hazing, firearms, dancing, movies, and profanity prohibited. Marriage discouraged during school year; notification of Dean required. Overnight absences must be approved. 7 intercollegiate sports for men, 4 for women; extensive intramurals. NAIA, NIIC. Student body compositon: 0.4% Asian, 4.1% Black, 0.4% Hispanic, 0.2% Native American, 94.1% White, 0.8% Other. 65% from out of state.

[J1] OLNEY CENTRAL COLLEGE
Olney 62450

[J1] PARKLAND COLLEGE
Champaign 61820

[1] PARKS COLLEGE OF SAINT LOUIS UNIVERSITY
Cahokia 62206, (618) 337-7500
Director of Admissions: John Wilbur

- **Enrollment: 983m, 89w**
- **Tuition (1982/83): $3,240**
- **Room & Board: $2,130**
- **Degrees offered: BS, AS**
- **Mean ACT 21 composite; mean SAT 445v, 518m**
- **Student-faculty ratio: 20 to 1**

A private college established in 1927, one of the eleven colleges of St. Louis University, controlled by the Jesuits. 113-acre campus 5 miles from St. Louis. Served by air, rail, and bus in St. Louis.

Academic Character NCACS and professional accreditation. Trimester system. Majors offered in aeronautical administration, aerospace engineering, aircraft maintenance engineering, aircraft maintenance engineering technology, aircraft maintenance management, aircraft maintenance management technology, aviation flight technology, aviation management, aviation science/professional pilot, meterology, and transportation, travel, & tourism. Airframe and Powerplant Technician certificate. FAA-approved flight programs. Some pass/fail. AFROTC. Aerodynamics, meterology, and other labs. Computer center. College-owned single-engine and twin-engine planes. 35,076-volume library.

Financial CEEB CSS. College scholarships, grants, and loans, state grants, PELL, SEOG, NDSL, GSL, Tuition Plan, deferred payment plans, CWS. Application deadline April 1.

Admissions High school graduation with 15 units recommended. GED accepted. Interview recommended. SAT or ACT required. $25 application fee. Rolling admissions. $400 deposit required on acceptance of admissions offer. *Concurrent Enrollment* Program. Transfers accepted. Admission deferral possible. Credit possible for CEEB AP and CLEP exams, and for college placement exams.

Student Life Student government. Newspaper, radio station. Black Student Alliance. Athletic, honorary, professional, religious, service, and special interest groups. 5 fraternities and 1 sorority, none with houses. Students must live at home or on campus. Single-sex dorms. 60% live on campus. Liquor prohibited. 4 intercollegiate sports; intramurals. NLCAA, St. Louis Area College Athletic Association. Student body composition: 1% Asian, 6% Black, 1% Hispanic, 92% White. 65% from out of state.

[J1] PRAIRIE STATE COLLEGE
Halsted and 197th Streets, Chicago Heights 60411

[1] PRINCIPIA COLLEGE
Elsah 62028, (618) 374-2131
Director of Admissions: Martha Green Quirk

- **Undergraduates: 367m, 481w**
- **Tuition (1982/83): $5,616**
- **Room & Board: $3,180; Fees: $60**
- **Degrees offered: BA, BS**
- **Mean SAT 485v, 520m**
- **Student-faculty ratio: 11 to 1**

A private college for Christian Scientists, established in 1910. 2,800-acre campus overlooking the Mississippi River, 10 miles from Alton. Public transportation to St. Louis, 40 miles away.

Academic Character NCACS accreditation. Trimester system, 3-week December term. 22 majors in liberal arts & sciences, business, education, religion, and special studies. Self-designed majors. 1-2 religion courses required. Courses in 8 additional areas. Independent and accelerated study. Honors program in some departments. Internships. 2-year pre-engineering program. Special studies off-campus; study abroad. Elementary and secondary education certification. Language lab. 135,000-volume library.

Financial CEEB CSS. College scholarships and loans, PELL, International scholarships, Tuition Plan, deferred payment plans.

Admissions High school graduation with 16 units recommended. Interview recommended. SAT or ACT required; foreign language ACH required for placement. $25 application fee. Rolling admissions. $100 deposit required on acceptance of offer of admission. Transfers accepted. Admission deferral possible. Credit possible for CEEB AP, International Baccalaureate, and CLEP exams.

Student Life Student government. Newspaper, yearbook, radio station. Music and drama groups. Academic, honorary, service, and special interest groups. 98% of students live on campus. No married-student housing. 6 quarters of phys ed required. Liquor, drugs, and tobacco prohibited. 10 intercollegiate sports for men, 8 for women; extensive intramurals. AIAW, NCAA. Student body composition: 1% Black, 99% White. 95% from out of state.

[1] QUINCY COLLEGE
Quincy 62301, (217) 222-8020, Ext. 321,322
Director of Admissions: Richard J. Smith

- **Undergraduates: 604m, 661w; 1,940 total (including graduates)**
- **Tuition (1982/83): $3,950**
- **Room & Board: $2,000; Fees: $80**
- **Degrees offered: BA, BS, BFA, AS**
- **Mean ACT 21.5; mean SAT 452v, 482m**
- **Student-faculty ratio: 16 to 1**

A private college controlled by the Franscisean Friars, established in 1858. 26-acre campus in a small city 120 miles northwest of St. Louis. Served by air, rail, and bus.

Academic Character NCACS and professional accreditation. Semester system, 4- and 8-week summer terms. 36 majors offered in liberal arts & sciences, alcohol education, business, communications, computer science, education, Japanese studies, music, nursing, physical education, social work, and theology. Self-designed and interdisciplinary majors. Associate degree offered in chemical technology, data processing. Minors. Distributive requirements; 2 courses in theology required. Independent study. Limited pass/fail. Preprofessional programs in dentistry, engineering, law, medicine, pharmacy, physical therapy, and veterinary medicine. Study abroad. Elementary, secondary, and special education certification. 210,000-volume library.

Financial CEEB CSS and ACT FAS. College scholarships, grants, and loans, tuition reduction for 2nd family member, PELL, SEOG, NDSL, GSL, CWS. Application deadline February 1; recommend filing with admission application.

Admissions High school graduation with 14 units recommended. SAT or ACT required. Interview recommended. Rolling admissions. $50 deposit required on acceptance of offer of admission. *Early Decision* Program. Transfers accepted. Deferred admission possible. Credit possible for CEEB AP, ACH, and CLEP exams. College has program for disadvantaged students.

Student Life Student government. Newspaper, yearbook, radio station. Music and drama groups. Black Student Organization. Cheerleaders. Academic, athletic, religious, service, and special interest groups. Fraternities and sororities. Seniors may live off campus. Married-student housing. 60% of students live on campus. 1 semester hour of phys ed required. 5 intercollegiate sports for men, 5 for women; intramurals. NAIA, MIAC. Student body composition: 3.5% Black, 1.1% Hispanic, 91% White, 4.4% Other. 25% from out of state.

[J1] REND LAKE COLLEGE
Route 1, Ina 62846

[J1] RICHARD J. DALEY COLLEGE, CHICAGO CITY COLLEGE
3939 West 79th Street, Chicago 60652

[J1] RICHLAND COMMUNITY COLLEGE
100 North Water Street, Decatur 62523

[J2] ROBERT MORRIS COLLEGE
College Avenue, Carthage 62321

[J1] ROCK VALLEY COLLEGE
Rockford 61101

[1] ROCKFORD COLLEGE
Rockford 61101, (815) 226-4000, (800) 892-2984 (from Illinois only)
Dean of Enrollment Planning: Charles B. Wharton

- **Undergraduates: 331m, 366w; 1,400 total (including graduates)**
- **Tuition (1982/83): $4,390**
- **Room & Board: $2,100; Fees: $100**
- **Degrees offered: BA, BS, BFA, BSGS, BSN**
- **Mean ACT 24; mean SAT 510v, 540m**
- **Student-faculty ratio: 13 to 1**

A private college established in 1847. 304-acre suburban campus, a 75-minute drive from O'Hare Airport, 90 minutes from Chicago. Also served by rail and bus.

Academic Character NCACS accreditation. 4-1-4 system, 8-week summer term. Majors offered in anthropology/sociology, art, biology, business administration, chemistry, classics, computer science, dance, economics, education, English, French, German, Greek, history, humanities, Latin, math, music, nursing, philosophy/religion, physical education, political science, psychology, recreation, religion, sociology, Spanish, theatre arts. Divisional and interdivisional majors. Minors. Distributive requirements; major seminars required of seniors. 3 interims required. Graduate degrees granted. Independent study. Honors program. Phi Beta Kappa. Internships. Preprofessional programs in dentistry, engineering, law, medicine, medical technology, physical therapy, optometry, and veterinary medicine. 3-1 enigineering program with U of Illinois. Study abroad. Urban semesters. Elementary and secondary education certification. Language lab. 120,000-volume library.

Financial CEEB CSS and ACT FAS. College scholarships, grants, and loans, PELL, state aid, GSL, Education Funds. Application deadine August 1.

Admissions High school graduation with 15 units recommended. SAT or ACT required. $15 application fee. Rolling admissions. *Early Admission* Program. Transfers accepted. Credit possible for CEEB AP and CLEP exams.

Student Life Student government. Newspaper, literary magazine, yearbook, radio station. Music, drama, and dance groups. Community Volunteer Services. Academic, athletic, political, religious, and special interest groups. Students must live at home or on campus. Coed and single-sex dorms. No married-student housing. 80% of students live on campus. 2 semesters of phys ed required. 7 intercollegiate sports for men, 4 for women; intramurals. AIAW, NAIA, NCAA, NIIC. Student body composition: 2.1% Asian, 4% Black, 2.1% Hispanic, 91.8% White. 20% from out of state.

[1] ROOSEVELT UNIVERSITY
430 South Michigan Avenue, Chicago 60605, (312) 341-3500
Director of Admissions: Lily S. Rose

- **Undergraduates: 1,914m, 2,532w; 6,683 total (including graduates)**
- **Tuition (1982/83): $3,870**
- **Room & Board: $2,880**
- **Degrees offered: BA, BS, BAEd, BFA, BSBA, BMus, BGS**
- **Mean ACT 21**
- **Student-faculty ratio: 16 to 1**

A private university established in 1945. Lakefront campus in downtown Chicago. Served by air, rail, and bus.

Academic Character NCACS and professional accreditation. Semester system, 3-week pre-summer term, 2 6-week day summer terms and 2 8-week evening summer terms. 48 majors offered by the College of Arts & Sciences, 8 by the College of Business Administration, 4 by the College of Education, 11 by the Chicago Music College, 31 by the College of Continuing Education. Interdepartmental and self-designed majors. Distributive requirements. Graduate degrees granted. Independent and accelerated study. Honors program. Pass/fail, internships, correspondence study. 2-2 and 3-2 programs in engineering. 3-1 medical technology program with area hospitals. Courses at School of the Art Institute of Chicago and Spertus College of Judaica. Elementary, secondary, and special education certification. Language lab. 350,000-volume library.

Financial CEEB CSS. University scholarships, grants, and loans, PELL, SEOG, GSL, NDSL, deferred payment plans, CWS. Applications may be filed from October 15 to May 1.

Admissions High school graduation with 15 units required. SAT, ACT, or university entrance exam required. Theory test and audition required of music applicants. $20 application fee. Rolling admissions. *Early Admission* and *Concurrent Enrollment* programs. Transfers accepted. Admission deferral possible. Credit possible for CEEB AP and CLEP exams, and for university placement exams.

Student Life Student government. Newspaper, literary magazine, radio workshop. Music and theatre groups. Student center and coed dorm for 350 students; 5% live on campus. 3 credits of phys ed required for music education majors. Liquor prohibited. 3 intercollegiate sports; club and intramural programs. Chicagoland Collegiate Athletic Conference. Student body composition: 4.5% Asian, 30.3% Black, 3.7% Hispanic, 0.2% Native American, 51.8% White, 9.5% Other. 12% from out of state.

■[1] CHICAGO MUSICAL COLLEGE OF ROOSEVELT UNIVERSITY
430 South Michigan Avenue, Chicago 60605

[1] ROSARY COLLEGE
7900 West Division Street, River Forest 60305, (312) 366-2490
Dean of Admissions: John Ballhein

- **Undergraduates: 130m, 556w; 1,692 total (including graduates)**
- **Tuition (1982/83): $4,300**
- **Room & Board: $2,400; Fees: $50**
- **Degrees offered: AB, BMus Ed**
- **Mean ACT 21**
- **Student-faculty ratio: 10 to 1**

A private college controlled by the Dominican Sisters of Sinsinawa, established in 1901, became coed in 1970. 30-acre campus in a suburb 10 miles west of downtown Chicago. Served by air, rail, and bus in Chicago.
Academic Character NCACS accreditation. Semester system, 2 6-week summer terms. Majors offered in accounting, American studies, art, biology, biology-chemistry, British studies, business administration, chemistry, clothing & textiles, communication arts & sciences, computer science, economics, English, fashion design, fashion merchandising, fine arts, foods & nutrition, gerontology, history, home economics, home economics education, international business, math, modern foreign languages (4), music, music education, philosophy, political science, psychology, religious studies, social science, sociology, women's studies. Self-designed interdepartmental majors. Graduate degrees granted. Independent and accelerated study. Honors program. Pass/fail, internships. 4-year BA/MA programs in English, French, and history. 5-year BA/MBA program. Preprofessional programs in law and medicine. Exchange program with Concordia College in River Forest. Study abroad. Semesters at U of Chicago and in New Mexico. Elementary, secondary, and special education certification. Argonne National Lab. Radio workshop. Language, computer labs. 250,000-volume library.
Financial CEEB CSS. College scholarships, grants, and loans; state scholarships, PELL, SEOG, NDSL, FISL, GSL, monthly payment plan, CWS, institutional work program. Preferred application deadline January 15.
Admissions High school graduation with 16 units expected. GED accepted. SAT or ACT required. Interview encouraged. $15 application fee. Rolling admissions. $10 matriculation fee and $50 room deposit required on acceptance of admissions offer. *Early Admission* Program. Transfers accepted. Admission deferral possible. Credit possible for CEEB AP, ACH, and CLEP exams, and for college placement tests. Special programs for disadvantaged and minority students.
Student Life Student government. Newspaper, literary magazine. Music, dance, and drama groups. Black and Latino Student Organizations. Community service. Academic, honorary, political, and religious groups. Special interest housing. 30% of students live on campus. 4 semester hours of phys ed required. 3 intercollegiate sports for men, 4 for women; club and intramural sports. Student body composition: 1% Asian, 7% Black, 3% Hispanic, 89% White. 10% from out of state.

[G1] RUSH UNIVERSITY
Chicago 60612

[1] ST. FRANCIS, COLLEGE OF
500 Wilcox Street, Joliet 60435, (815) 740-3400
Director of Admissions: Chuck Beutel

- **Enrollment: 250m, 400w; 1,166 total**
- **Tuition (1982/83): $3,560**
- **Room & Board: $2,084; Fees: $60**
- **Degrees offered: BA, BS, BBA**
- **Mean ACT 21.3**
- **Student-faculty ratio: 13 to 1**

A private college controlled by the Sisters of St. Francis of Mary; established in 1920, became coed in 1970. 15-acre campus in a suburb 35 miles from Chicago. Served by rail and bus; air service in Chicago.
Academic Character NCACS and professional accreditation. Semester system, 6-week summer term. Majors offered in accounting, biology, business administration, computer science, creative arts, elementary education, English, health arts, history, journalism/communications, management, mathematics, political science, professional arts, psychology, religious studies, social work, and therapeutic recreation. 3-1 majors in cytotechnology, medical technology, and nuclear medicine with area hospitals. Contract and self-designed majors possible. Minors offered in coaching, library science, and philosophy. Distributive requirements. 2 semesters of religion required; some departments require senior thesis. Independent and accelerated study. Pass/fail, internships. Preprofessional programs in dentistry, law, medicine, and veterinary medicine. Elementary and secondary education certification. 130,000-volume library.
Financial CEEB CSS. College scholarships, grants, and loans, state grants, PELL, SEOG, NDSL, GSL, College Aid Plan, CWS. Application deadline for scholarships May 1.
Admissions High school graduation with 16 units required. SAT or ACT required. $15 application fee. Rolling admissions. $50 tuition and $50 room deposits required on acceptance of admissions offer. *Early Decision* Program. Transfers accepted. Deferred admission possible. Credit possible for CEEB AP exams and for college advanced placement tests.
Student Life Student government. Newspaper, literary magazine, yearbook, radio station. Musical groups. Community Action Program. Academic, honorary, religious, service, and special interest groups. 2 sororities without houses. Coed dorms. No married-student housing. 40% of students live on campus. 5 intercollegiate sports for men, 4 for women; extensive intramurals. NAIA, Chicago Collegiate Athletic Conference. Student body composition: 1% Asian, 3% Black, 1% Hispanic, 1% Native American, 94% White. 8% from out of state.

[1] SAINT XAVIER COLLEGE
3700 West 103rd Street, Chicago 60655, (312) 779-3300
Director of Admissions: Robert J. Schwendau

- **Undergraduates: 570m, 1,600w**
- **Tuition (1982/83): $4,050**
- **Room & Board: $2,380; Fees: $25**
- **Degrees offered: BA, BS**
- **Mean ACT 21; mean SAT 450v, 450m**
- **Student-faculty ratio: 13 to 1**

A private college controlled by the Sisters of Mercy; established in 1847, became coed in 1969. 47-acre campus in a southwest suburb of Chicago. Served by air, rail, and bus.
Academic Character NCACS and professional accreditation. 4-1-4 system, 4- and 6-week summer terms. Majors offered in art, biology, business & administration, chemistry, criminal justice, early childhood education, early childhood studies, education, English, family studies, French, history, international studies, mass communications, math, music, nursing, philosophy, political science, psychology, religious studies, social science, Spanish, speech/language pathology. Special majors. Minors. Distributive requirements; 6 semester hours of religion required. Independent study. Some pass/fail, credit by exam, senior seminars. Preprofessional programs in dentistry, law, medicine, and veterinary medicine. Science courses through Associated Colleges of Chicago. Study abroad. Early childhood, elementary, and secondary education certification. AFROTC at Illinois Tech. Computer center. Argonne National Lab. Language lab. 75,000-volume library.
Financial CEEB CSS. College scholarhips, grants, and loans, PELL, SEOG, NDSL, GSL, NSL, CWS, service assistantships. Application deadline March 1.
Admissions High school graduation with 16 units required. SAT or ACT accepted. Interview recommended. $10 application fee. Rolling admissions. $75 deposit required on acceptance of offer of admission. *Early Admission* and *Early Decision* programs. Transfers accepted. Admission deferral possible. Credit possible for CEEB AP and CLEP exams; college recognizes Acceleration Program grades of C or better.
Student Life Student government. Magazines, yearbook. Choral and drama groups. Honorary and religious groups. Students must live at home or on campus. 10% live on campus. 2 semester hours of phys ed required. Class attendance expected; no cuts. 3 intercollegiate sports for men, 3 for women; intramurals. AIAW, NAIA. Student body composition: 10% Black, 5% Hispanic, 85% White. 1% from out of state.

[1] SANGAMON STATE UNIVERSITY
Springfield 62708

- **Enrollment: 3,500**
- **Tuition (1982/83): $390 (in-state), $1,170 (out-of-state)**
- **Degrees offered: BA, BS**
- **Student-faculty ratio: 17 to 1**

A public upper division university established in 1969. 740-acre suburban campus; Capital campus 4 blocks from Capitol complex.
Academic Character NCACS accreditation. Early semester system, 8-week summer term. Majors offered in accounting, biology, chemistry, community services, communication, computer science, creative arts, economics, environmental studies, health administration, history, labor, legal studies, literature, management, mathematical systems, nursing, political studies, psychology, sociology, and social justice. Self-designed majors. 6 hours in Public Affairs colloquia required. Masters degrees granted. Cooperative work/study. Credit/no credit. Center for Legal Studies. Illinois Legislative Studies Center. Policy Studies Center. Community and Regional Studies Center. Computer center. 250,000-volume library.
Financial ACT FAS. University scholarships, loans, education waivers, PELL, SEOG, NDSL, GSL, CWS. Application deadline April 1.
Admissions Admissions open to community college graduates and college transfers at junior level (60 semester hours of credit, with a C average).
Student Life Student Senate. Radio station. Music, dance, and drama groups. Residential apartments available. Cafeteria. Intercollegiate soccer and tennis; recreational sports. NAIA, AIAW.

[J1] SAUK VALLEY COLLEGE
Rural Route #1, Dixon 61021

[P] SCHOLL COLLEGE OF PODIATRIC MEDICINE
1001 North Dearborn Street, Chicago 60610
Formerly Illinois College of Podiatric Medicine

[1] SEABURY—WESTERN THEOLOGICAL SEMINARY
Evanston 60201

[J1] SHAWNEE COLLEGE
Ullin 62992

[P] SHERWOOD MUSIC SCHOOL
1014 South Michigan Avenue, Chicago 60605

[2] SHIMER COLLEGE
438 North Sheridan Road, Waukegan 60085, (312) 623-8400

- **Enrollment: 45m, 55w**
- **Tuition (1982/83): $3,500**
- **Room & Board: $2,300**

- **Degrees offered: BA, BS**
- **Mean ACT 26; mean SAT 590v, 550m**
- **Student-faculty ratio: 8 to 1**

A private college established in 1853. Campus in the suburbs 50 miles north of Chicago.
Academic Character Integrative core curriculum including the humanities, social sciences, and natural sciences required of students and faculty. Other concentrations may be arranged with faculty members or in cooperation with other accredited institutions. Discussion method centered on great books approach and utilization of original source readings. Special emphasis placed on developing reading, speaking, and writing skills. Semester paper, basic skills comprehensive exam, area comprehensive exam, and thesis required. Honors program. Independent study can lead to graduation in less than 4 years. Study abroad. 250,000-volume library.
Financial Early entrants receive $1,200 Robert Maynard Hutchins scholarships. Other college and federal aid available. CWS.
Admissions Open to high school sophomores, juniors, and seniors. Placement exams administered on entry determine level at which each student begins studies. ACT or SAT required. 2 personal essays required. $10 application fee.
Student Life Apartment-style housing with private kitchens and baths. Extracurricular activities organized according to interest.

[J1] SOUTHEASTERN ILLINOIS COLLEGE
Rural Route #4, College Drive, Harrisburg 62946

[1] SOUTHERN ILLINOIS UNIVERSITY
Carbondale 62901, (618) 453-2121
Director of Admissions: Jerre C. Pfaff

- **Total enrollment: 11,855m, 6,262w**
- **Tuition (1982/83): $810 (in-state), $2,430 (out-of-state)**
- **Room & Board: $2,236; Fees: $400**
- **Degrees offered: BA, BS, BMus, BMus Ed, AS**
- **Student-faculty ratio: 16 to 1**

A public university established in 1869. 4,000-acre campus in a small city 100 miles from St. Louis. Served by air, rail, and bus.
Academic Character NCACS and professional accreditation. Semester system, 8-week summer term. 7 majors offered by the School of Agriculture, 6 by the College of Business Administration, 8 by the College of Communications & Fine Arts, 33 by the College of Education, 3 by the College of Engineering & Technology, 7 by the College of Human Resources, 21 by the College of Liberal Arts, and 10 by the College of Science. Self-designed majors. Minors. Associate degree programs offered by the School of Technical Careers. Distributive requirements. Graduate and professional degrees granted. Independent and accelerated study. Honors program. Some pass/fail. Cooperative work/study, internships. 3-1 programs in dentistry, law, medical technology, pharmacy, physical therapy, public health, theology, veterinary medicine. 3-2 business administration program. 2-year associate programs in School of Technical Careers. Elementary, secondary, and special education certification. ROTC, AFROTC. Museum. Language lab. 1,700,000-volume library with microform resources.
Financial ACT FAS. University scholarships, grants, and loans, state grants, payment plan; PELL, SEOG, NDSL, FISL, CWS, extensive institutional employment program. Scholarship application deadline April 1.
Admissions High school graduation with 16-18 units required. GED accepted. ACT required. Rolling admissions. *Early Admission* Program. Transfers accepted. Credit possible for CEEB AP, and CLEP exams and for university proficiency exams. Special Supportive Services Program for selected students.
Student Life Student government. Newspaper, literary magazine, yearbook, TV and radio stations. Music and theatre groups. Debate. Academic, athletic, honorary, religious, service, and special interest groups. 16 fraternities, 12 with houses; 10 sororities, 6 with houses. Juniors and seniors may live off campus. Coed dorms. Married-student housing. 25% of students live on campus. 4 semester hours of phys ed or health required. Liquor prohibited. 10 intercollegiate sports for men, 11 for women; intramurals. NCAA, AIAW, Missouri Valley Conference. Student body compositon: 1.1% Asian, 8.6% Black, 1.1% Hispanic, 76.4% White, 12.3% Other. 12% from out of state.

[1] SOUTHERN ILLINOIS UNIVERSITY
Edwardsville 62026, (618) 692-2720
Director of Admissions: Eugene J. Magac

- **Undergraduates: 2,871m, 3,152w; 10,205 total (including graduates)**
- **Tuition (1982/83): $798 (in-state), $2,394 (out-of-state)**
- **Room & Board: $2,000-$2,200; Fees: $297**
- **Degrees offered: BA, BFA, BS, BSEng, BLS, BMus**
- **Student-faculty ratio: 14 to 1**

A public university established in 1869; Edwardsville campus opened in 1965. 2,600-acre campus in small town 20 miles from St. Louis. Air, rail, and bus in St. Louis.
Academic Character NCACS and professional accreditation. Trimester system, 8- and 12-week summer terms. 44 majors offered by the Schools of Business, Education, Fine Arts & Communications, Humanities, Nursing, Science & Technology, and Social Sciences. Minors offered in 10 additional areas, including aerospace, Black American, classical, peace, and women's studies. Distributive requirements. Graduate degrees granted. Independent and accelerated study. Dean's College for outstanding students. Cooperative work/study, pass/fail. Preprofessional programs in dentistry, medicine, veterinary medicine. Student Colloquia. BS in agriculture or home economics by transfer to Carbondale. 3-1 medical technology program. Elementary, secondary, and special education certification. AFROTC. Language lab. 780,000-volume library.
Financial CEEB CSS. University scholarships, grants, and loans, PELL, SEOG, NDSL, NSL, CWS. Application deadline May 1.
Admissions High school graduation with 16 units required. GED accepted. ACT required. Rolling admissions. *Early Admission* Program. Transfers accepted. ACT APP. Credit possible for CEEB AP and CLEP exams, and for university's advanced placement exams.
Student Life Student government. Newspaper, literary magazine, radio station. Community Involvement Project. Ethnic groups. Academic, athletic, honorary, political, religious, service, and special interest groups. 11 fraternities, 7 sororities, 2 coed social clubs. Limited housing. Some married-student housing. 15% of students live on campus. 8 intercollegiate sports for men, 6 for women; intramurals. AIAW, NCAA. Student body composition: 2% Asian, 15% Black, 1% Hispanic, 0.5% Native American, 80% White, 1.5% Other. 9% from out of state.

[1] SPERTUS COLLEGE OF JUDAICA
618 South Michigan Avenue, Chicago 60605

[J1] SPOON RIVER COLLEGE
Canton 61520

[J1] SPRINGFIELD COLLEGE IN ILLINOIS
Springfield 62702

[J1] THORNTON COMMUNITY COLLEGE
South Holland 60473

[1] TRINITY CHRISTIAN COLLEGE
6601 West College Drive, Palos Heights 60463, (312) 597-3000

- **Enrollment: 166m, 196w; 429 total (including part-time)**
- **Tuition, Room, Board, & Fees (1982/83): $3,750**
- **Degrees offered: BA, BS**
- **Mean ACT 22; mean SAT 500**

A private liberal arts college connected with the Christian Reformed Church.
Academic Character NCACS accreditation. Semester system. 24 majors and 11 minors offered with 1-semester internships in most areas. One-semester transcultural programs in Paris, Vienna, Madrid, and the Yucatan in association with other colleges. Remedial English program.
Admissions High school graduation with 16 units required. Rolling admissions. *Early Admission* Program. Admission deferral possible. Advanced placement possible.
Student Life Dormitory for 220 students on campus. Dining facilities.

[1] TRINITY COLLEGE
2077 Half Day Road, Deerfield 60015, (312) 948-8980
Vice President and Dean of Admissions: Dr. John B. Aker

- **Undergraduates: 314m, 373w**
- **Tuition (1982/83): $4,300**
- **Room & Board: $2,190; Fees: $50**
- **Degree offered: BA**
- **Mean ACT 20**
- **Student-faculty ratio: 14 to 1**

A private college affiliated with the Evangelical Free Church of America, established in 1897. 105-acre campus in the suburbs 25 miles north of Chicago. Served by train and bus; airport 15 miles away.
Academic Character NCACS accreditation. Semester system, 4 3-week summer modules. Majors in accounting, Biblical studies, biological science, business administration, chemistry, computer & information science, economics, economics & management, elementary education, English, English communications, general studies, history, human resources/organizational development, humanities, math, music, natural science, philosophy, physical education, psychology, secondary education, social science, and sociology. Distributives and 12 hours of Bible required. Independent study. Honors program. Internships. Preprofessional programs in dentistry, law, medicine, ministry, nursing. 3-1 program in medical technology. Cooperative Bible courses program with American Institute of Holy Land Studies in Jerusalem. Christian College Consortium. Psychology and sociology externships in San Francisco. Study at other American schools and abroad. Elementary and secondary education certification. 79,000-volume library.
Financial CEEB CSS. College scholarships, grants, and loans, payment plans; PELL, SEOG, NDSL, FISL, CWS.
Admissions High school graduation with 15 units. Interview encouraged. SAT or ACT required; ACT preferred. $15 application fee. Rolling admissions. $100 deposit required on acceptance of offer of admission. Limited *Early Admission* Program. Transfers accepted. Credit possible for CEEB AP and CLEP exams, and for college's proficiency exams.
Student Life Newspaper, yearbook. Music and drama groups. Community service. Academic, honorary, religious, and special interest groups. Students under 21 must live at home or on campus. Single-sex dorms. No married-student housing. 75% live on campus. 2 hours of phys ed required. Mandatory chapel attendance. 4 semesters of Christian service assigned. Liquor, drugs, gambling, and smoking prohibited. 7 intercollegiate sports for men, 4 for women; extensive intramurals, Venture program. AIAW, NAIA, NIIC, NCCAA. Student body composition: 3% Black, 1% Hispanic, 92% White, 4% Other. 26% from out of state.

[G1] TRINITY EVANGELICAL DIVINITY SCHOOL
Deerfield 60015

[J1] TRITON COLLEGE
2000 Fifth Avenue, River Grove 60171

[G1] VANDER COOK COLLEGE OF MUSIC
3209 South Michigan Avenue, Chicago 60616

[J1] WABASH VALLEY COLLEGE
Mt. Carmel 62863

[J1] WAUBONSEE COMMUNITY COLLEGE
Route 47 at Harter Road, Sugar Grove 60554

[1] WESTERN ILLINOIS UNIVERSITY
900 W. Adams St., Macomb 61455, (309) 295-1414, (800) 322-3902 (in IL)
Dean of Admissions and Records: Dr. F.E. Fess

- **Undergraduates: 5,081m, 4,417w; 12,411 total (including graduates)**
- **Tuition (1982/83): $774 (in-state), $2,322 (out-of-state)**
- **Room & Board: $1,950; Fees: $308**
- **Degrees offered: BA, BS, BB**
- **Mean ACT 18.5**
- **Student-faculty ratio: 16 to 1**

A public university established in 1899. 1,054-acre campus in small city. Served by rail and bus; airport 70 miles away in Peoria.
Academic Character NCACS and professional accreditation. Semester system, summer term. 50 majors offered by the colleges of Applied Sciences, Arts & Sciences, Business, Education, Fine Arts, and Health, Physical Education & Recreation. Self-designed majors. Minors offered in most major fields. Distributive requirements. Graduate degrees granted. Experimental Studies Program. Independent and accelerated study. Some pass/fail. Honors program. Cooperative work/study, internships. Preprofessional programs in agricultural engineering, architecture, dentistry, engineering, forestry, medicine, nursing, optometry, pharmacy, and veterinary medicine. Arts & sciences and professional dual-degree programs. Study abroad. Elementary, secondary, and special education certification. ROTC. 516,000-volume library.
Financial ACT FAS. University scholarships, grants, and loans, Talent Grants, state grants; PELL, SEOG, NDSL, FISL, CWS.
Admissions High school graduation with 16 units recommended. GED accepted. ACT or SAT required. Rolling admissions. $50 room deposit required on acceptance of admissions offer. Transfers accepted. Credit possible for CEEB AP and CLEP exams, and for university's proficiency exams. Multicultural student recruitment and supportive services program.
Student Life Student government. Newspaper, yearbook, radio station. Extensive music activities. Debates. Religious, service, and special interest groups. 19 fraternities, 14 with houses, and 10 sororities, 6 with houses. 17% of men and 11% of women join. Juniors and seniors may live off campus. Coed and single-sex dorms. Married-student housing. 55% of students live on campus. 2 hours of phys ed required in teacher education program. Beer and wine permitted for students over 21. 9 intercollegiate sports for men, 10 for women; intramurals. AIAW, Mid-Continent Conference. Student body composition: 1% Asian, 9% Black, 1% Hispanic, 85% White, 4% Other. 3% from out of state.

[1] WHEATON COLLEGE
Wheaton 60187, (312) 682-5000
Director of Admissions: Stuart O. Michael

- **Enrollment: 1,012m, 1,060w**
- **Tuition (1982/83): $4,780**
- **Room & Board: $2,500**
- **Degrees offered: AB, BS, BMus, BMus Ed**
- **Mean ACT 25; mean SAT 543v, 588m**
- **Student-faculty ratio: 16 to 1**

A private college established in 1860. 70-acre suburban campus 25 miles west of Chicago.
Academic Character NCACS and professional accreditation. Semester system; special summer programs. 32 majors offered in ancient languages, archeology, art, Biblical studies, biology, chemistry, Christian education, economics, education, ethnomusicology, French, geology, German, history, liberal arts/engineering, literature, math, medical technology, music, nursing, philosophy, physical education, physics, political science, psychology, religious studies, social science, sociology, Spanish, speech. Conservatory of Music. Distributive requirement. 5 Bible and apologetics courses required. Internships. Accelerated study. Some pass/fail. Preprofessional programs in business, education, engineering, government service, law, medicine, ministry, nursing, and science. Christian College Consortium. Study abroad. Several specialized summer programs off-campus. Washington Semester. ROTC. Computer. Observatory. Language lab. 155,000-volume library.
Financial CEEB CSS. College scholarships, grants, and loans, payment plans; PELL, SEOG, NDSL. Application deadline February 10.
Admissions High school graduation with 16 units required. Interview required. SAT or ACT required; accepted applicant must take ACH. Conservatory of Music has additional requirements. $20 application fee. Application deadline January 15. $100 deposit required on acceptance of admissions offer. Transfers accepted. Credit possible for CEEB AP and CLEP exams. Special programs for disadvantaged and minority students.
Student Life Student government. Newspaper, literary magazine, yearbook, radio station. Music groups. Intercollegiate debate. Inner-city tutorials. Gospel teams. Academic, professional, and special interest activities. Freshmen must live on campus. No coed dorms. College-owned residence halls, apartments, and houses. Some married-student housing. 85% of students live on campus. 6 trimesters of phys ed required. Students must agree to abstain from alcohol, tobacco, gambling, occult practices, and social dancing, and to use discretion in use of folk and interpretive dance, movies, radio, television, and theatre. Class attendance regulations. 13 intercollegiate sports for men, 7 for women; extensive intramurals. AIAW, NCAA, College Conference of Illinois and Wisconsin. Student body compositon: 2.6% Asian, 0.5% Black, 0.6% Hispanic, 0.2% Native American, 95% White, 1.5% Other. 70% from out of state.

[J1] WILBUR WRIGHT COLLEGE, CHICAGO CITY COLLEGE
3400 North Austin Avenue, Chicago 60634

[P] WORSHAM COLLEGE OF MORTUARY SCIENCE
3701 West Davis, Skokie 60076

INDIANA (IN)

[J1] ANCILLA COLLEGE
Donaldson 46513

[1] ANDERSON COLLEGE
Anderson 46012, (317) 649-9071
Director of Admissions: George Nalywaiko

- **Undergraduates: 981m, 1,051w**
- **Tuition (1982/83): $3,840**
- **Room & Board: $1,540**
- **Degrees offered: BA, AA, AS**
- **Mean ACT 21; mean SAT 450v, 460m**
- **Student-faculty ratio: 17 to 1**

A private college affiliated with the Church of God, established in 1917. 77-acre campus in a small city 40 miles from Indianapolis. Served by air and bus.
Academic Character NCACS and professional accreditation. Semester system, 3 summer terms totaling 15 weeks. 51 majors offered in the areas of art, American studies, business, religion, languages, computer science, criminal justice, science, education, political & social sciences, environmental science, history, mathematics, music, philosophy, physical education, and speech. Self-designed majors. Minor required. Distributives and 9 hours of religion/Bible required. MDiv, MRE, MARel granted. Independent study. Honors program. Pass/fail. Internships. Preprofessional programs in allied health, dentistry, law, medicine, ministry, public service. Transfer program in engineering. 2-2 BS program in nursing with Ball State. 3-1 program in medical technology with St. John's Medical Center. Study abroad. Elementary, secondary, and special education certification. Computer center, language lab, Center for Public Service. 150,000-volume library.
Financial CEEB CSS. College scholarships, grants, and loans, payment plan; PELL, SEOG, NDSL, CWS. Priority application deadline March 15 (scholarships); recommended deadline April 1 (loans).
Admissions High school graduation with 16 units recommended. SAT or ACT required. $10 application fee. Rolling admissions; suggest applying in fall. $100 deposit required on acceptance of offer of admission. Transfers accepted. Credit possible for CEEB AP and CLEP exams.
Student Life Student government. Newspaper, magazine, yearbook. Music, drama, debate organizations. Religious, honorary, political, social, and special interest groups. 5 social clubs for men and 5 for women, none with houses. 21% of men and 23% of women join. Students under 24 must live at home or on campus. No coed dorms. Married-student housing. 80% of students live on campus. Cheating, gambling, liquor, drugs prohibited. Smoking, dancing prohibited on campus. Attendance at bi-weekly convocation required. 3-4 hours of phys ed required. 8 intercollegiate sports for men, 6 for women; intramural and club sports. NAIA, NCCAA, ICAC, Hoosier-Buckeye College Conference. Student body compositon: 0.2% Asian, 5.3% Black, 0.3% Hispanic, 0.4% Native American, 92.5% White. 55% from out of state.

[G1] ASSOCIATED MENNONITE BIBLICAL SEMINARIES
Elkhart 46517

[1] BALL STATE UNIVERSITY
Muncie 47306, (317) 289-1241
Director of Pre-Admissions Services: Charles E. Kaufman

- **Undergraduates: 6,337m, 8,010w; 18,541 total (including graduates)**
- **Tuition (1982/83): $1,275 (in-state), $2,880 (out-of-state)**
- **Room & Board: $1,818-$1,854**
- **Degrees offered: BA, BS, BFA, BMus, BArch, BLA, AA, AS**
- **Student-faculty ratio: 20 to 1**

olic university established in 1918. 945-acre campus in residential section Muncie, 56 miles from Indianapolis. Served by air, rail, and bus.
Academic Character NCACS and professional accreditation. Trimester system, 2 5-week summer terms. 4 majors offered by the College of Architecture & Planning, 9 by the College of Business, 11 by the College of Fine & Applied Arts, 32 by the College of Sciences & Humanities, and 3 by Teachers College. Special majors. Minors offered in Afro-Asian studies, astronomy, Russian. Distributive requirements. Graduate and professional degrees granted. Independent study. Honors program. Cooperative work/study, internships. Pass/fail. Credit by exam. Preprofessional programs in dentistry, engineering, law, medicine, pharmacy. 3-2 program in engineering with Purdue. Study abroad. Elementary, secondary, and special education certification. ROTC. Computer center, language lab, physical therapy lab, weather station, museum. 1,006,906-volume library with microform resources.
Financial CEEB CSS. University scholarships, grants, and loans; PELL, SEOG, NDSL, GSL, NSL, CWS, college work program. Application deadline March 1.
Admissions High school graduation with college prep program required. GED accepted. SAT, PSAT, or ACT required; SAT preferred. $15 application fee. Rolling admissions; suggest applying by January 1. $25 deposit required on acceptance of offer of admission. Transfers accepted. Credit possible for CEEB AP and CLEP exams; university has own advanced placement program.
Student Life Student government. Newspaper, magazine, yearbook, radio and TV stations. Music, drama, debate groups. International and Black Student groups. Over 250 academic, honorary, religious, service, and special interest groups. 17 fraternities and 3 sororities. Juniors and seniors may live off campus. Coed and single-sex dorms. Freshmen dorms, language houses, married-student housing. 41% of students live on campus. Class attendance required. 6 hours of phys ed required. 12 intercollegiate sports for men, 12 for women; intramural and club sports. Mid-America Conference. Student body compositon: 0.2% Asian, 4.7% Black, 0.4% Hispanic, 0.2% Native American, 94.3% White. 7% from out of state.

[1] BETHEL COLLEGE
Mishawaka 46545, (219) 259-8511

- **Enrollment: 176m, 185w; 431 total (including part-time)**
- **Tuition (1982/83): $3,255**
- **Room & Board: $1,900; Fees: $70**
- **Degrees offered: BA, BS, AA**

A private, coeducational, non-sectarian liberal arts college founded in 1947 and affiliated with the Missionary Church.
Academic Character NCACS accreditation. Semester system. Eleven associate of arts degree programs. MMin granted. Music preparation for full-time Christian service. Two-year cooperative nursing program with Ball State University. Five-year engineering program in cooperation wtih the University of Notre Dame. Remedial programs in math and English. 57,000-volume library.
Financial Student loan fund averages $300 per applicant. College employs 95 to 100 students who work eight to ten hours weekly on grants-in-aid appointments, earning an average of $400 to $500 per semester. NDEA, PELL, SEOG.
Admissions High school graduation or equivalent required. Rolling admissions. *Early Admission* Program. Transfers accepted.
Student Life College maintains dormitories and a dining hall.

[1] BUTLER UNIVERSITY
46th at Sunset Avenue, Indianapolis 46208, (317) 283-9255
Dean of Admissions: Stephen Bushouse

- **Undergraduates: 851m, 1,229w**
- **Tuition (1982/83): $4,440**
- **Room & Board: $2,100; Fees: $25**
- **Degrees offered: BA, BS, BFA, BMus, AA, AS**
- **Mean SAT 500v, 530m**
- **Student-faculty ratio: 15 to 1**

A private university established in 1855. 300-acre campus 5 miles from downtown Indianapolis. Served by air, rail, and bus.
Academic Character NCACS and professional accreditation. Semester system, 7- and 3-week summer terms. 5 majors offered by the College of Business Administration, 19 by the College of Education, 30 by the College of Liberal Arts & Sciences, 1 by the College of Pharmacy, and 11 by the Jordan College of Fine Arts. Distributive requirements. Graduate and professional degrees granted. Honors program. Cooperative work/study, internships. Pass/fail. Preprofessional programs in dentistry, medicine, medical technology, nursing, engineering, forestry, law, ministry, dietetics. Member Consortium for Urban Education. Elementary, secondary, and special education certification. AFROTC at Indiana U-Purdue U (Indianapolis), and Indiana U (Bloomington). Observatory/planetarium. 350,000-volume library.
Financial CEEB CSS. University and state scholarships, grants, and loans; PELL, SEOG, NDSL, GSL, USAF, deferred payment plan.
Admissions High school graduation with 15 units required. Audition required for music, dance, radio/TV, and theatre majors. SAT or ACT required. $15 application fee. Rolling admissions; suggest applying during 1st semester. $150 deposit required on acceptance of offer of admission. *Early Admission* and *Concurrent Enrollment* programs. Admission deferral possible. Transfers accepted. Credit possible for CEEB AP exams.
Student Life Student government. Newspaper, magazine, special interest publications, yearbook, radio station. Many music groups. Debate, ballet, drama groups. Honorary, academic, service, religious, and special interest organizations. 7 fraternities and 7 sororities with houses. 34% of men and 35% of women join. Coed and single-sex dorms. 77% of students live on campus. 2 semesters of phys ed, dance, or marching band required. 8 intercollegiate sports for men, 5 for women; intramurals. AIAW, NCAA, Heartland Collegiate, Midwestern City Conferences. Student body composition: 5% Black, 2% Oriental, 92% White, 1% Other. 23% from out of state.

[1] CALUMET COLLEGE
2400 New York Avenue, Whiting 46394

[G1] CHRISTIAN THEOLOGICAL SEMINARY
1000 West 42nd Street, Indianapolis 46208

[G1] CONCORDIA THEOLOGICAL SEMINARY
6600 North Clinton Street, Fort Wayne 46825

[1] DEPAUW UNIVERSITY
Greencastle 46135, (317) 658-4006
Director of Admissions: David C. Murray

- **Undergraduates: 1,050m, 1,280 w**
- **Tuition (1982/83): $6,100**
- **Room & Board: $2,600; Fees: $150**
- **Degrees offered: BA, BMus, BSN**
- **Mean SAT 515v, 560m**
- **Student-faculty ratio: 15 to 1**

A private university established in 1837. 116-acre campus in small city 45 miles from Indianapolis. Served by bus; airport in Indianapolis.
Academic Character NCACS and professional accreditation. 4-1-4 system. Majors offered in anthropology, art, botany/bacteriology, chemistry, classical languages, communication, earth sciences, elementary education, English, German, health, history, mathematics, music, nursing, philosophy/religion, physics, political science, psychology, Romance languages, Russian, sociology, and zoology. Self-designed majors. Minors offered in all major fields and computer science. Distributive requirements; writing competency requirement. MA, MAT granted. Honors program. Phi Beta Kappa. Pass/fail for juniors, seniors. Internships. Cooperative engineering programs with 6 schools. Washington, UN Semesters. Study abroad. Elementary and secondary education certification. ROTC; AFROTC at Indiana U. Computer center, observatory, language lab, anthropology museum, art center. 360,000-volume library.
Financial CEEB CSS. University scholarships, grants, and loans, deferred payment plan; PELL, SEOG, NDSL, FISL, NSL, CWS, and college work program.
Admissions High school graduation with 12 units recommended. Audition required for music majors. SAT or ACT required. $20 application fee. Application deadlines December 1, February 15. $200 tuition and $100 room deposits required on acceptance of offer of admission. *Early Admission* Program. Transfers accepted. Credit possible for CEEB AP and CLEP exams and for university placement exams.
Student Life Student government. Newspaper, magazine, yearbook, radio station, TV workshop. Several music, debate, and drama organizations. Religious, academic, and special interest groups. 13 fraternities and 9 sororities with houses. 70% of students join. Coed and single-sex dorms. No married-student housing. 95% of students live on campus. Liquor, weapons prohibited on campus. Class attendance required. ½ credit in activity required. 12 intercollegiate and 10 intramural sports for men and women. AIAW, NCAA, ICC. Student body composition: 1% Asian, 2% Black, 1% Hispanic, 1% Native American, 95% White. 58% from out of state.

[1] EARLHAM COLLEGE
Richmond 47374, (317) 962-6561
Dean of Admissions: Lynette Robinson-Weening

- **Undergraduates: 529m, 604w**
- **Tuition (1982/83): $6,333**
- **Room & Board: $2,180; Fees: $187**
- **Degree offered: AB**
- **Mean SAT 520v, 540m**
- **Student-faculty ratio: 12 to 1**

A private college affiliated with the Society of Friends (Quakers), established in 1847. 800-acre campus 70 miles from Indianapolis, near Ohio line. Served by air, rail, and bus.
Academic Character NCACS accreditation. Trimester system. Majors offered in African studies, biology, chemistry, classics, economics, elementary education, English, environmental studies, fine arts, French, geology, German, history, human development/social relations, Japanese studies, Latin American studies, mathematics, music, peace and conflict studies, philosophy, physical education, physics/astronomy, political science, psychology, religion, sociology/anthropology, and Spanish. Self-designed majors. Distributives senior exams, and 2 courses in religion/philosophy required. Internships. Preprofessional programs in business, engineering, environmental education, law, medicine, ministry, nursing. 3-2 programs in engineering with 5 schools, in nursing with Case Western Reserve. Several special interest study terms. Study abroad. Observatory/planetarium, computer center, East Asian center, language labs, museum. 230,000-volume library.
Financial CEEB CSS. College scholarships, grants, loans, deferred payment; PELL, SEOG, FISL, CWS, college work program. Scholarship application deadline January 1.
Admissions High school graduation with 15 units required. SAT or ACT required, SAT preferred. $15 application fee. Application deadline March 15. $100 deposit required on acceptance of offer of admission. *Early Decision* Program. Admission deferral possible. Transfers accepted. Credit possible for CEEB AP and CLEP exams.

Key to ratings **[1, 2, J1, J2, G, P, R, S]** *and list of abbreviations start on page 120*

Student Life Student government. Newspaper, magazine, yearbook, radio station. Music, drama groups. Meditation Society. Black Leadership Action Committee. Women's Center. Service, honorary, and special interest groups. Seniors may live off campus. Coed dorms. Coop, living-learning, special interest houses. Vegetarian meals offered. Married-student housing. 90% of students live on campus. Freshmen may not have cars on campus. Liquor prohibited on campus; smoking restricted. 2 years of phys ed required. 8 intercollegiate sports for men, 7 for women, 3 coed; intramurals. AIAW, NAIA, NCAA, Hoosier Buckeye Conference, Indiana Intercollegiate Athletic Association. Student body composition: 10% minority. 80% of students from out of state.

[P] EARLHAM SCHOOL OF RELIGION
Richmond 47374

[1] EVANSVILLE, UNIVERSITY OF
Evansville 47702, (812) 479-2468
Director of Admissions: Steve Grissom

- **Undergraduates: 1,242m, 1,698w**
- **Tuition (1982/83): $4,188**
- **Room & Board: $1,953-$2,127; Fees: $90**
- **Degrees offered: BA, BS, BFA, BMus, BMus Ed, BLS, AA**
- **Mean SAT 450v, 490m**
- **Student-faculty ratio: 15 to 1**

A private school affiliated with the United Methodist Church, established in 1854. 75-acre urban campus in Southwestern Indiana, close to the Illinois and Kentucky borders. Served by air and bus.

Academic Character NCACS and professional accreditation. Trimester system, 2 5-week summer terms. 32 majors offered by the College of Arts & Sciences, 11 by the College of Fine Arts, 11 by the School of Business Administration, 5 by the School of Education, 7 by the School of Engineering & Applied Science, and 2 by the School of Nursing. Self-designed majors. Distributive requirements. Graduate and professional degrees granted. Independent study. Honors program. Cooperative work/study, internships. Pass/fail for juniors, seniors. Preprofessional programs in medicine, theology, dentistry, law, optometry, pharmacy, physical therapy, veterinary medicine. Elementary, secondary, and special education certification. Study abroad. Language lab. Gerontology center. 290,000-volume library.

Financial CEEB CSS. University scholarships, grants, and loans, deferred payment; PELL, SEOG, GSL, NDSL, FISL, HELP, NSL, CWS. Application deadline March 1.

Admissions High school graduation with 16 units required. SAT or ACT required. Interview required for some majors. $15 application fee. Rolling admissions. $100 enrollment deposit due May 1; $50 room deposit due on acceptance of offer of admission. *Early Admission* Program. Transfers accepted. Credit possible for CEEB AP and CLEP exams, and for university advanced placement tests. Conditional admission and summer probationary programs.

Student Life Student government. Newspaper, magazine, yearbook, radio station. Music, drama groups. Black Student Union. Religious and special interest groups. 8 fraternities, 5 with houses, and 5 sororities with dorm suites. 30% of men and women join. Freshmen must live at home or on campus. Coed and single-sex dorms. Married-student housing. 50% of students live on campus. Liquor prohibited on campus. 4 hours of phys ed required. 9 intercollegiate sports for men, 8 for women; 15 intramurals for men and women. AIAW, NCAA, IIAA, Heartland and Midwest City Conferences. Student body composition: 1% Asian, 4% Black, 1% Hispanic, 93% White, 1% Other. 25% from out of state.

[P] FORT WAYNE BIBLE COLLEGE
Fort Wayne 46807

[1] FRANKLIN COLLEGE
Franklin 46131, (317) 736-8441
Vice President for Student Services: Nolan C. Cooper

- **Undergraduates: 274m, 277w**
- **Tuition (1982/83): $4,730**
- **Room & Board: $2,120; Fees: $60**
- **Degree offered: BA**
- **Mean SAT 429v, 479m**
- **Student-faculty ratio: 11 to 1**

A private college affiliated with the American Baptist Convention, established in 1834. 74-acre campus in rural town 20 miles from Indianapolis. Served by bus. Air and rail in Indianapolis.

Academic Character NCACS and professional accreditation. 4-1-4 system, 8-week summer term. Majors offered in accounting, American studies, art, biology, business, chemistry, economics, elementary education, English, French, history, journalism, mathematics/computing, philosophy, physical education, physics, political science, psychology, religion/history, sociology, and Spanish. Minors. Distributive requirements. Senior exams. Independent study. Honors program. Some pass/fail. Internships. 3-2 programs in engineering with Purdue, Washington U. 3-1 program in medical technology. 2-2 nursing program with DePauw. Study abroad. Washington, UN Semesters. Elementary, secondary, and special education certification. ROTC at Indiana U-Purdue. 97,000-volume library.

Financial CEEB CSS. College scholarships, grants, grants to children of ABC ministers, and loans, Tuition Exchange; PELL, SEOG, NDSL, GSL, CWS. Loan application deadline March 15.

Admissions High school graduation with 15 units required. GED accepted. SAT or ACT required. Rolling admissions; deadline August 1. $100 deposit required on acceptance of offer of admission. *Early Admission* and *Early Decision* programs. Transfers accepted. Credit possible for CEEB AP and CLEP exams and for college language placement exams.

Student Life Student government. Newspaper, magazine, yearbook. Music, debate, drama groups. Academic, political, honorary, religious, and special interest organizations. 4 fraternities, 2 with houses, and 4 sororities without houses. 33% of men and 44% of women join. Students under 21 must live at home or on campus. Single-sex dorms. No married-student housing. 82% of students live on campus. First-semester freshmen may not have cars on campus. Liquor prohibited on campus. 8 intercollegiate sports for men, 7 for women; intramurals. AIAW, NAIA, NCAA, Heartland Conference. Student body composition: 1% Asian, 1% Black, 1% Hispanic, 97% White. 7% from out of state.

[G1] GOSHEN BIBLICAL SEMINARY
Elkhart — see Associated Mennonite Biblical Seminaries

[1] GOSHEN COLLEGE
Goshen 46526, (219) 533-3161
Director of Admissions: Dennis Koehn

- **Undergraduates: 454m, 626w; 1,208 total (including graduates)**
- **Tuition (1982/83): $4,165**
- **Room & Board: $1,925**
- **Degrees offered: BA, BSN**
- **Mean SAT 528v, 534m**
- **Student-faculty ratio: 14 to 1**

A private college affiliated with the Mennonite Church, established in 1894. 135-acre campus in a small town 25 miles from South Bend, 120 miles from Chicago. Served by bus. Airport in South Bend.

Academic Character NCACS and professional accreditation. Trimester system, 3 3½-week summer terms. 32 majors offered in the areas of business, arts, religion, sciences, communication, education, economics, English, family life, nutrition, foreign languages, history, ministries, mathematics, physical education, political and social sciences. Self-designed majors. Minors. Distributives and 8 hours of religion required. Trimester of international studies or study abroad required. Independent study. Honors program. Pass/fail. Credit for church-related work. Preprofessional programs in dentistry, law, nursing, medical technology, medicine, ministry, social work. 3-2 engineering program with Purdue. 2-3 pharmacy program. Elementary and secondary education certification. Many study abroad programs. Computer center. Laboratory kindergarten for education majors. Over 105,365-volume library.

Financial CEEB CSS and ACT FAS. College scholarships, grants, and loans, payment plans; PELL, SEOG, NSS, NDSL, FISL, NSL, CWS, college work program. Application deadlines March 1 (scholarships), April 1 (loans).

Admissions High school graduation with 16 units required. GED accepted. SAT or ACT required. $10 application fee. Rolling admissions. *Early Admission* Program. Transfers accepted. Credit possible for CEEB AP and CLEP exams and for college advanced placement tests.

Student Life Student government. Newspaper, magazine, yearbook, radio station. Music, drama, speaking, debate, poetry reading groups. Peace, cross-cultural societies. Black and International student groups. Academic, honorary, religious, service, and special interest groups. Seniors and students over 21 may live off campus. Coed and single-sex dorms. Small group housing. Married-student housing. 68% of students live on campus. Liquor, smoking, dancing prohibited on campus. Attendance at biweekly chapel required. 1 term of phys ed required. 7 intercollegiate sports for men, 5 for women; intramurals. NAIA, AIAW, Mid-Central Conference. Student body compositon: 1% Asian, 2% Black, 6% Foreign, 4% Hispanic, 87% White. 68% from out of state.

[1] GRACE COLLEGE
Winona Lake 46590, (219) 267-8191
Director of Admissions: Ron Henry

- **Undergraduates: 359m, 453w**
- **Tuition (1982/83): $3,286**
- **Room & Board: $2,186**
- **Degrees offered: BA, BS, AA**
- **Mean ACT 18.9**
- **Student-faculty ratio: 17 to 1**

A private college affiliated with the Fellowship of Grace Brethren Churches, established in 1948. 150-acre campus in a rural town 45 miles from Fort Wayne. Bus nearby; air and rail service in Fort Wayne.

Academic Character NCACS accreditation. Semester system, 2 4-week summer terms. 35 majors offered by the divisions of Languages & Literature, Religion & Philosophy, Teacher Education, Social Sciences, Natural Sciences, and Fine Arts. Interdisciplinary majors. Minors required in some fields. Distributives and 16 hours of religion required. Preprofessional programs in dentistry, medicine, pharmacy, physical therapy, veterinary medicine. 2-2 programs in home economics, industrial technology, and nursing with Ball State. Study abroad. Elementary and secondary education certification. Art gallery, language lab. 143,000-volume library system.

Financial CEEB CSS and ACT FAS. College and state scholarships, grants, and loans, deferred payment; PELL, SEOG, GSL, NDSL, CWS. Application deadline June 1.

Admissions High school graduation with 16 units required. GED accepted. ACT required. Portfolio required for art majors; audition for music majors. $10 application fee. Rolling admissions; suggest applying by June 1. $125 deposit required on acceptance of offer of admission. *Early Admission* Program. Admission deferral possible. Transfers accepted. Credit possible for CEEB AP and CLEP exams. Restricted admission and special orientation programs.

Student Life Student government. Newspaper, magazine, yearbook. Music, a groups. Special interest organizations. Single students under 23 must at home or on campus. No coed dorms or married-student housing. 73% of students live on campus. Liquor, tobacco, gambling, social dancing, movies, blue jeans prohibited on campus. Attendance at daily chapel and at assemblies and convocations required. 2 semesters of phys ed required. 7 intercollegiate sports for men, 5 for women; intramural and club sports. AIAW, NAIA, NCCA, Mid-Central Conference. Student body compositon: 1.5% Black, 97.5% White, 1% Other. 55% from out of state.

[1] HANOVER COLLEGE
Hanover 47243, (812) 866-2151
Director of Admissions: C. Eugene McLemore

- **Undergraduates: 510m, 490w**
- **Tuition (1982/83): $3,440**
- **Room & Board: $1,840; Fees: $160**
- **Degree offered: AB**
- **Mean SAT 510v, 520m**
- **Student-faculty ratio: 13 to 1**

A private college affiliated with the Presbyterian Church, established in 1827. 550-acre campus in a small town 40 miles from Louisville, 60 miles from Cincinnati. Served by bus. Airports in Louisville and Cincinnati.
Academic Character NCACS accreditation. 4-4-1 system. Majors offered in art, biology, business administration, chemistry, communication, economics, elementary education, English, French, geology, German, history, international studies, mathematics, music, philosophy, physical education, physics, political science, psychology, sociology, Spanish, theatre, theology. Minors. Distributive requirements. Hebrew-Christian thought course and senior exam required. Independent study. Honors program. Pass/fail. Internships. 3-2 program in engineering with Washington U. Double degree programs in nursing, medical technology with Rush. Several off-campus and exchange programs. Study abroad. Elementary and secondary education certification. Observatory, geological museum, computer center. 220,000-volume library.
Financial CEEB CSS. College scholarships, grants, and loans, deferred payment; PELL, GSL, CWS. Preferred application deadline (scholarships) February 1; deadline for loans March 1.
Admissions High school graduation with 16 units required. SAT or ACT required. $10 application fee. Rolling admissions; suggest applying in fall. $100 deposit required on acceptance of offer of admission. *Early Decision* Program. Transfers accepted. Credit possible for CEEB AP, CLEP, and ACH exams.
Student Life Student government. Newspaper, magazine, yearbook, radio and TV productions. Music, debate, drama, dance groups. Many honorary, religious, professional, service, and special interest groups. 5 fraternities and 4 sororities; all have houses. 62% of men and 61% of women join. Students must live at home or on campus. 95% of students live on campus. Parietal rules. Liquor, drugs, hazing, gambling, fireworks, firearms prohibited. No sports on Sunday. Dress code. Attendance at chapel and convocation required. 4 activity courses required. 8 intercollegiate sports for men, 5 for women; several intramural and club sports. Hoosier-Buckeye Conference. Student body composition: 3% Asian, 2% Black, 95% White. 45% from out of state.

[1] HERRON SCHOOL OF ART
Indianapolis 46219

[J2] HOLY CROSS JUNIOR COLLEGE
Notre Dame 46556

[1] HUNTINGTON COLLEGE
Huntington 46750, (219) 356-6000

- **Enrollment: 200m, 210w; 498 total (including part-time)**
- **Tuition (1982/83): $3,180**
- **Typical expenses: $5,000**
- **Degrees offered: AB, BS, AA**
- **Mean SAT 430v, 467m**

A private college operated by the United Brethren Church. Campus is in a small city about 25 miles southwest of Fort Wayne.
Academic Character NCACS accreditation. 4-1-4 system, 3 summer terms. Majors offered in liberal arts and theology. Through accelerated study, student may earn degree in three years and two months. Master of Christian Ministries degree granted.
Financial Tuition scholarships, awarded on basis of upper-level academic performance in high school. Twenty-three other scholarships. $60,000 loan fund; average loan is $500.
Admissions High school graduation required. SAT required.
Student Life Open fraternities and sororities. College operates on-campus dormitories and dining facilities. Married students may rent space in college-owned trailer park; college also has some trailers for rent. Intercollegiate sports for men and women, including soccer.

[1] INDIANA CENTRAL UNIVERSITY
Indianapolis 46227, (317) 788-3216
Director of Admissions: David J. Huffman

- **Undergraduates: 430m, 828w**
- **Tuition (1982/83): $4,100**
- **Room & Board: $2,050**
- **Degrees offered: BA, BS, AA, AS**
- **Mean SAT 413v, 453m**
- **Student-faculty ratio: 14 to 1**

A private university affiliated with the United Methodist Church, established in 1902. 60-acre campus in the suburbs 5 miles from Indianapolis. Served by air, rail, and bus.
Academic Character NCACS and professional accreditation. Semester system, 2 7-week summer terms, 4 week "fleximester" in the spring. Majors offered in art, biology, business administration, business education, chemistry, criminal justice, earth/space science, economics, elementary education, English language & literature, French, general science (teaching), history, law enforcement, math, medical technology, mortuary science, music, music education, nursing, philosophy, phys ed, physics, political science, psychology, religion, social studies, sociology, Spanish, speech-theatre, youth agency administration. Minors. Distributive requirements. 3 religion courses required. Senior exams. MA, MS, MBA granted. Independent study. Honors program. Some pass/fail. Internships. Preprofessional programs in engineering, forestry, law, medicine, dentistry, veterinary medicine. 3-2 engineering program with Purdue. 3-2 forestry program with Duke. Member of an 8-college consortium; cross-registration possible. Study abroad. Elementary, secondary, and special education certification. Language lab, computer center. 106,000-volume library.
Financial CEEB CSS. University scholarships, grants, ministerial discounts, and loans; PELL, SEOG, NDSL, FISL, NSL, deferred payment. Application deadlines March 1 (scholarships), April 1 (loans).
Admissions High school graduation with 16 units required. SAT or ACT required. $10 application fee. Rolling admissions; suggest applying in 1st semester of 12th year. $100 deposit required on acceptance of admissions offer. *Early Admission* and *Concurrent Enrollment* programs. Transfers accepted. Admission deferral possible. Credit possible for CEEB AP and CLEP exams. Special admission program.
Student Life Student government. Newspaper, magazine, yearbook, radio station. Music, drama groups. Academic, honorary, religious, and special interest groups. Students may live off campus. Liquor, gambling, immorality prohibited. 17 of 24 convocations required per semester. 4 semesters of phys ed required. 9 intercollegiate sports for men, 5 for women; intramurals. AIAW, NCAA, IIAA, GLVC, Heartland Conference. Student body composition: 0.6% Asian, 2.7% Black, 0.4% Hispanic, 0.4% Native American, 95.8% White. 5% from out of state.

[J2] INDIANA COLLEGE OF MORTUARY SCIENCE
3111 Hanburg Pike, Jeffersonville 47130

[1] INDIANA INSTITUTE OF TECHNOLOGY
1600 East Washington Blvd., Fort Wayne 46803, (219) 422-5561

- **Undergraduates: 367m, 110w; 800 total (including part-time)**
- **Tuition (1982/83): $3,510**
- **Room & Board: $2,200-$2,820**
- **Degrees offered: BA, AS**

A private institute established in 1930. 25-acre urban campus in the large city of Fort Wayne.
Academic Character NCACS accreditation. Semester system, summer term. Baccalaureate degree offered in engineering (aerospace, chemical, civil, computer, electrical, mechanical), engineering management, accounting, business administration, computer science, data processing, secretarial science. Associate degree offered in accounting, business administration, data processing, secretarial science. Independent study. Cooperative work/study. Competency-based education program. 50,000-volume library.
Financial CEEB CSS. Institute scholarships, state scholarships and grants; PELL, SEOG, NDSL, GSL, CWS; institute work program. Priority application deadline April 1.
Admissions High school graduation required. Interview encouraged. SAT or ACT recommended. $25 application fee. Rolling admissions. $75 tuition and $100 room deposits required on acceptance of offer of admission. *Early Decision* and *Early Admission* programs. Admission deferral possible. Advanced placement.
Student Life Student activities club. Malaysian Student Organization. 5 fraternities with houses. Single students must live at home or on campus. 3 intercollegiate sports for men, 1 for women; intramurals. NAIA.

[G2] INDIANA NORTHERN GRADUATE SCHOOL OF PROFESSIONAL MANAGEMENT
PO Box 1000, Gas City 46933

[1] INDIANA STATE UNIVERSITY
Evansville 47712, (812) 464-1765
Director of Admissions: Timothy K. Buechner

- **Enrollment: 1,649m, 2,015w**
- **Tuition (1982/83): $1,116 (in-state), $2,604 (out-of-state)**
- **Degrees offered: BA, BS, AS**
- **Student-faculty ratio: 18 to 1**

A public university established in 1965. 300-acre campus midway between the cities of Mount Vernon and Evansville. Served by bus.
Academic Character NCACS accreditation. Semester system, 2 5-week summer terms. 43 majors offered by the divisions of Allied Health Sciences, Business, Education, Engineering Technology, General Studies, Humanities, Science & Mathematics, and Social Sciences. Double bachelor's degree possible. Minors. Distributive requirements. Cooperative work/study, internships. Pass/fail. Preprofessional programs in cytotechnology, dentistry, forestry, medicine, occupational therapy, osteopathy, pharmacy, physical therapy, podiatry, veterinary science. Elementary and secondary education certification. 141,265-volume library with microform resources.
Financial University scholarships, grants, loans, state loans; PELL, SEOG,

NDSL, FISL, CWS. Recommended scholarships application deadline March 1.
Admissions High school graduation required. GED accepted. SAT required. Rolling admissions; deadline August 15. *Early Admission* and *Concurrent Enrollment* programs. Transfers accepted. Credit possible for CEEB AP and CLEP exams, and for university advanced placement tests.
Student Life Student government. Newspaper, magazine, yearbook. Academic, religious, service, honorary, social, and special interest groups. No student housing. 2 hours of phys ed required. Intercollegiate and intramural sports for men and women. 10% of students from out of state.

[1] INDIANA STATE UNIVERSITY

Terre Haute 47809, (812) 232-6311
Director of Admissions: John Bush

- **Undergraduates: 4,782m, 4,602w**
- **Tuition (1982/83): $1,318 (in-state), $3,147 (out-of-state)**
- **Room & Board: $1,734**
- **Degrees offered: BA, BS, BFA, AA**
- **Mean ACT 17.5; mean SAT 375v, 410m**
- **Student-faculty ratio: 15 to 1**

A public university established in 1865. 72-acre urban campus, 74 miles from Indianapolis. Served by air, rail, and bus.
Academic Character NCACS and professional accreditation. Semester system, 2 5-week summer terms. 43 majors offered by the College of Arts & Sciences, 3 by the School of Business, 3 by the School of Education, 4 by the School of Health, Physical Education, & Recreation, 1 by the School of Nursing, and 6 by the School of Technology. Minors. Distributive requirements. MA, MS, MBA, MFA granted. Independent study. Honors program. Phi Beta Kappa. Cooperative work/study, internships. Pass/fail. Preprofessional programs in dental hygiene, dentistry, engineering, law, medicine, medical technology, optometry, pharmacy, ministry, veterinary medicine. Elementary, secondary, and special education certification. ROTC. Audio-visual center, language lab. 878,812-volume library.
Financial CEEB CSS. University scholarships, grants, and loans; PELL, SEOG, NDSL, NSL, FISL, CWS. Priority application deadline March 1.
Admissions High school graduation. GED accepted. SAT or ACT required. $10 application fee. Rolling admissions; application deadline August 15. *Early Admission* Program. Transfers accepted. Credit possible for CEEB AP and CLEP exams and for university advanced placement tests. Freshman Opportunity Program.
Student Life Student government. Newspaper, magazine, yearbook, radio station. Music, speech, debate, drama groups. Academic, religious, and special interest organizations. 18 fraternities, 10 with houses, and 14 sororities without houses. 12% of men and 10% of women join. Students under 20 must live at home or on campus. Coed and single-sex dorms. Married-student housing. 52% of students live on campus. 2 hours of phys ed required. 8 intercollegiate sports for men, 9 for women, 1 coed; intramurals. AIAW, NCAA. Student body composition: 0.7% Asian, 9.1% Black, 0.5% Hispanic, 0.2% Native American, 85% White, 4.5% Other. 20% from out of state.

[1] INDIANA UNIVERSITY

Bloomington 47405, (812) 335-0661
Director of Admissions: Robert S. Magee

- **Undergraduates: 13,699m, 12,749w; 32,000 total (including graduates)**
- **Tuition (1982/83): $1,300 (in-state), $3,470 (out-of-state)**
- **Room & Board: $1,977**
- **Degrees offered: BA, BS, BFA, BMus, BMus Ed, AS**
- **Mean SAT 471v, 543m**
- **Student-faculty ratio: 16 to 1**

A public university established in 1820. 3,200-acre campus 50 miles from Indianapolis. Served by air and bus.
Academic Character NCACS and professional accreditation. Semester system, 6-week, 8-week, and 5 2-week summer terms. 45 majors offered by the College of Arts & Sciences, 11 by the Division of Allied Health Services, 16 by the School of Business, 7 by the School of Education, 4 by the School of Health, Physical Education, & Recreation, 16 by the School of Music, and 13 by the School of Public & Environmental Affairs. Self-designed majors. Programs in 11 additional areas. Senior thesis and exam required. Graduate and professional degrees granted. Independent study. Honors program. Phi Beta Kappa. Cooperative work/study, internships. Pass/fail. Study abroad. Elementary, secondary, and special education certification. ROTC, AFROTC. Computer center, language lab. 3,600,000-volume library.
Financial CEEB CSS. University scholarships, grants, loans, state grants; PELL, SEOG, NDSL, GSL, CWS. Application deadline February 15.
Admissions High school graduation with 15 units required. Audition required for music, ACH required for foreign language study. SAT or ACT required. $20 application fee. Rolling admissions; deadline July 15. $5 housing application fee. *Early Decision* and *Early Admission* programs. Admission deferral possible. Transfers accepted. Credit possible for CEEP AP and CLEP exams, and for university advanced placement tests. Program for Indiana minority students.
Student Life Student government. Newspaper, magazine, yearbook, radio and TV stations. Over 40 music groups. 200 special interest organizations. 32 fraternities and 19 sororities; most have houses. 10% of men and 8% of women join. Coed and single-sex dorms; special interest housing. 50% of students live on campus. Freshmen may not have cars. Many intercollegiate and intramural sports for men and women. AIAW, Big Ten, NCAA. Student body composition: 6% Black, 1% Hispanic, 92% White, 1% Other. 30% from out of state.

■[1] INDIANA UNIVERSITY AT KOKOMO

2300 South Washington Street, Kokomo 46901, (317) 453-2000
Director of Admissions & Financial Aids: Gerald B. Wesoloski

- **Enrollment: 1,123m, 1,685w**
- **Tuition (1982/83): $1,118 (in-state), $2,730 (out-of-state)**
- **Degrees offered: BA, BS, BGS**
- **Student-faculty ratio: 30 to 1**

A public university established in 1820. 24-acre urban campus in Kokomo.
Academic Character NCACS accreditation. Semester system, 2 7-week summer terms. 11 majors offered in humanities, 7 in social & behavioral sciences, 11 in biological & physical sciences; others in medical technology, business, general studies, and education. Self-designed majors. Distributive requirements. MS granted. Independent study. Cooperative work/study. Some pass/fail. Preprofessional programs in dentistry, law, medicine. Study abroad in 20 cities. ROTC at Indiana U/Purdue U (Indianapolis). 100,000-volume library.
Financial CEEB CSS. University scholarships, grants, loans; PELL, SEOG, NDSL, FISL, NSL, CWS, university work program. Priority application deadline February 15.
Admissions High school graduation with 13 units required. SAT or ACT required. $20 application fee. Rolling admissions; priority application deadline July 1. *Early Decision* and *Concurrent Enrollment* programs. Transfers accepted. Credit possible for CLEP exams and for university advanced placement tests. Venture Program for academically deficient students with potential.
Student Life Student government. Theatre, speech groups. Political, religious, service, and special interest groups. No university housing. Intramural sports. Student body composition: 0.1% Asian, 2% Black, 0.4% Hispanic, 0.2% Native American, 97.2% White.

■[1] INDIANA UNIVERSITY AT SOUTH BEND

1700 Mishawaka Avenue, South Bend 46634, (219) 237-4455
Director of Admissions: Connie Horton-Neville

- **Undergraduates: 1,611m, 2,310w; 6,116 total (including graduates)**
- **Tuition (1982/83): $1,118 (in-state), $2,730 (out-of-state)**
- **Degrees offered: AB, BS, BGS, BMus, BMus Ed, BSEd, BSN, AS**
- **Mean ACT 20; mean SAT 900**
- **Student-faculty ratio: 28 to 1**

A public university established in 1962. 17-acre campus overlooking St. Joseph River in large city of South Bend. Served by air and bus.
Academic Character NCACS and professional accreditation. Semester system, 2 6-week summer terms. 48 majors offered by the divisions of Arts & Sciences, Business & Economics, Education, Music, Public & Environmental Affairs, the School of Nursing, and in general studies. Interdepartmental and double majors. Minors. Distributive requirements. MS granted. Honors program. Pass/fail, credit by exam. Internships. Preprofessional programs in dentistry, engineering, law, medicine, optometry, pharmacy. Member of a 5-college consortium; cross-registration possible. Medical technology in cooperation with Indiana U/Purdue U (Indianapolis). Elementary, secondary, and music education certification. Study abroad. ROTC, AFROTC, NROTC at Notre Dame. Language lab. 200,050-volume library with microform resources.
Financial CEEB CSS. University scholarships, loans, Merit scholarships; PELL, SEOG, NDSL, CWS. Application deadline February 15.
Admissions High school graduation with 13 units required. Audition required for music, ACH required for foreign language. SAT or ACT required. $20 application fee. Rolling admissions; suggest applying by June 15. Admission deferral possible. Transfers accepted. Credit possible for CEEB CLEP exams and for university advanced placement tests. Special services program for academically disadvantaged students.
Student Life Student government. Newspaper, magazine. Music, debate, drama groups. Academic, honorary, religious, service, and special interest groups. 4 fraternities with houses and 4 sororities, 3 with houses. 3% of students join. No university housing. Liquor prohibited on campus. Intramural and club sports. Student body composition: 0.38% Asian, 5.45% Black, 0.78% Hispanic, 0.23% Native American, 87.08% White, 5.8% Other. 7% from out of state.

■[J1] INDIANA UNIVERSITY EAST

Richmond 47374

■[1] INDIANA UNIVERSITY NORTHWEST

3400 Broadway, Gary 46408, (219) 980-6500
Director of Admissions: Bill Lee

- **Undergraduates: 1,164m, 2,782w**
- **Tuition (1982/83): $1,118 (in-state), $2,730 (out-of-state)**
- **Degrees offered: BA, BS, BGS, BSN**
- **Mean SAT 400v, 420m**
- **Student-faculty ratio: 24 to 1**

A public university established in 1922. 240-acre campus in the large city of Gary. Served by air, rail, and bus.
Academic Character NCACS and professional accreditation. Semester system, 6- and 8-week summer terms. 16 majors offered by the College of Arts & Sciences, 7 by the School of Business, 2 by the School of Continuing Studies, 3 by the School of Public & Environmental Affairs, and 2 by the Division of Education. Distributive requirements. MS, MSBA, MPA granted. Independent study. Honors program. Pass/fail for juniors and seniors, credit by exam. Internships. 3-1 program in medical technology with local hospitals. Preprofessional programs in dentistry, law, medicine, optometry, pharmacy. Study abroad. Elementary, secondary, reading, bilingual, and special education certification. 550,000-volume library.
Financial CEEB CSS. University scholarships, loans, grants; PELL, SEOG, NSS, NDSL, CWS. Priority application deadline February 15.
Admissions High school graduation with 13 units required. SAT or ACT required; foreign language and chemistry ACH recommended. $20 application fee. Rolling admissions; suggest applying by January 15. Transfers accepted. Credit possible for CEEB AP and CLEP exams.

Life Student government. Newspaper. Music, drama groups. Black and women's groups. Academic, political, religious, honorary, and ...l interest groups. 2 fraternities and 2 sororities without houses. No ...ersity housing. Liquor prohibited on campus. Class attendance required. ...amural basketball. Student body composition: 0.5% Asian, 25.8% Black, ... Hispanic, 0.1% Native American, 66.4% White. 3% from out of state.

■[1] INDIANA UNIVERSITY SOUTHEAST

4201 Grant Line Road, New Albany 47150, (812) 945-2731
Director of Admissions: Kela O. Adams

- **Undergraduates: 1,522m, 2,093w**
- **Tuition (1982/83): $934 (in-state),$2,224 (out-of-state)**
- **Degrees offered: BA, BS, BGS, AAS, AGS**
- **Student-faculty ratio: 28 to 1**

A public university established in 1941. 180-acre campus in suburban New Albany, just outside Louisville, Kentucky. Air, rail, and bus service in Louisville.
Academic Character NCACS accreditation. Semester system, 2 6-week summer terms. Majors offered in accounting, biology, business economics/public policy, business management, chemistry, economics, elementary education, English, fine arts, general studies, history, mathematics, nursing, philosophy, political science, psychology, secondary education, sociology, special education, and speech/theatre. Interdepartmental majors. Preprofessional programs in dentistry, law, medicine, optometry, pharmacy, veterinary medicine. Several transfer programs. 3-1 program in medical technology. Member of the Kentuckiana Metroversity. Elementary and secondary education certification. ROTC; AFROTC at Metroversity schools. Computer center, language lab. 113,000-volume library.
Financial CEEB CSS. University scholarships, grants, and loans; PELL, SEOG, NSS, NDSL, FISL, NSL, CWS. Scholarship application deadline March 1; priority application deadline for loans February 15.
Admissions High school graduation with 13 units required. SAT or ACT required. $20 application fee. Rolling admissions; suggest applying in fall. *Early Admission* Program. Transfers accepted. Credit possible for CEEB AP and CLEP exams, and for university advanced placement tests.
Student Life Student government. Newspaper. Music, drama groups. Social committee. Honorary, professional, religious, and special interest groups. 3 fraternities and 3 sororities. No university housing. Liquor, drugs, firearms prohibited on campus. Class attendance required. 3 intercollegiate sports for men, 3 for women, 1 coed; intramurals. Student body composition: 0.2% Asian, 2.2% Black, 0.2% Hispanic, 0.4% Native American, 96.8% White. 3% from out of state.

[1] INDIANA UNIVERSITY-PURDUE UNIVERSITY AT FORT WAYNE

Fort Wayne 46805, (219) 482-5626
Office of Admissions: Phillip A. Kennell, Carol Isaacs, Karl Zimmerman

- **Undergraduates: 4,304m, 4,849w; 10,150 total (including graduates)**
- **Tuition (1982/83): $1,156 (in-state), $2,836 (out-of-state)**
- **Fees: $45**
- **Degrees offered: BA, BS, BFA, BGS, BMus, BMus Ed, BSEd, AAS, AS**
- **Mean SAT 425v, 472m**
- **Student-faculty ratio: 21 to 1**

A public university established by merger in 1964. 412-acre campus in Fort Wayne. Served by air, rail, and bus.
Academic Character NCACS and professional accreditation. Semester system, 2 6-week summer terms. Majors offered in anthropology, biology, business, chemistry, engineering, English, fine arts, French, general science, general studies, geology, German, history, interpersonal & public communication, math, music, music therapy, nursing, philosophy, physics, political science, psychology, public affairs, radio-TV-film, sociology, Spanish, supervision, 10 teaching areas, theatre, and in computer, construction, electrical, industrial engineering, mechanical, and medical technologies. Self-designed majors. Distributive requirements. Graduate and professional degrees granted. Independent study. Honors program. Pass/fail, credit by exam. Internships. 3-1 program in dentistry, medicine, optometry. Transfer programs with other IU-Purdue campuses in 15 areas. National Student Exchange. Study abroad. Elementary and secondary education certification. ROTC. 280,000-volume library with microform resources.
Financial CEEB CSS. University scholarships, grants, loans; PELL, SEOG, NDSL, GSL, NSL, CWS. Application deadline March 1.
Admissions High school graduation with 13 units required. GED accepted. SAT or ACT required. $20 application fee. Rolling admissions; deadline August 1. *Early Admission* and *Concurrent Enrollment* programs. Transfers accepted. Credit possible for CEEB AP exams.
Student Life Student government. Newspaper, yearbook. Music, drama, debate groups. Academic, honorary, religious, service, and special interest groups. Social fraternities and sororities. University has housing agreement with adjacent college. 1% of students live on campus. 5 intercollegiate sports for men, 3 for women; intramurals. NCAA (Division III). Student body composition: 0.6% Asian, 3.4% Black, 0.5% Hispanic, 0.1% Native American, 94.1% White, 1.3% Other. 3% from out of state.

[1] INDIANA UNIVERSITY-PURDUE UNIVERSITY AT INDIANAPOLIS

Indianapolis 46202, (317) 264-4591

- **Undergraduates: 4,231m, 4,966w; 23,477 total (including part-time)**
- **Tuition (1982/83): $1,207 (in-state), $3,172 (out-of-state)**
- **Room: $945; Fees: $29**
- **Degrees offered: BA, BS, BSW, BFA, BSEd**
- **Student-faculty ratio: 15 to 1**

A public university established by merger in 1969. Urban campus in Indianapolis. Served by air, bus, and rail.
Academic Character NCACS and professional accreditation. Semester system, 2 6-week summer terms. 60 majors offered in the areas of fine & applied arts, allied health fields, business, science, engineering, education, English, foreign languages, history, metropolitan studies, philosophy, religious studies, social sciences, and communications. Self-designed majors. Distributive requirements. Graduate and professional degrees granted. Independent study. Honors program. Limited pass/fail, internships. Cooperative programs with 6 area schools and community agencies. Study abroad. Elementary, secondary, and middle education certification. ROTC. 1,144,533-volume library.
Financial CEEB CSS. University scholarships, grants, loans; PELL, SEOG, NDSL, CWS. Scholarship application deadline March 1.
Admissions High school graduation with 7 units required. SAT or ACT required. $20 application fee. Rolling admissions. *Early Admission* and *Early Decision* programs. Admission deferral possible. Transfers accepted. Credit possible for CEEB AP exams. Guided Study Program.
Student Life Student government. Newspaper. Music, debate, drama groups. Academic, special interest organizations and scholastic societies. Limited university housing. Some married-student housing. 5% of students live on campus. Liquor prohibited on campus. 4 intercollegiate sports for men, 3 for women; intramurals. AIAW, NAIA. Student body composition: 0.6% Asian, 11.1% Black, 0.4% Hispanic, 0.2% Native American, 86.7% White. 32% from out of state.

■[J1] INDIANA VOCATIONAL TECHNICAL COLLEGE

646 Franklin Street, Columbus 47201

■[J1] INDIANA VOCATIONAL TECHNICAL COLLEGE

3501 First Avenue, Evansville 47710

■[J1] INDIANA VOCATIONAL TECHNICAL COLLEGE

3800 North Anthony Blvd, Fort Wayne 46805

■[J1] INDIANA VOCATIONAL TECHNICAL COLLEGE

5221 Ivy Tech Drive, Indianapolis 46268

■[J1] INDIANA VOCATIONAL TECHNICAL COLLEGE

1815 East Morgan Street, Kokomo 46901

■[J1] INDIANA VOCATIONAL TECHNICAL COLLEGE

PO Box 6299, Lafayette 47903

■[J1] INDIANA VOCATIONAL TECHNICAL COLLEGE

Madison 47250

■[J1] INDIANA VOCATIONAL TECHNICAL COLLEGE

2325 Chester Blvd., Richmond 47374

■[J1] INDIANA VOCATIONAL TECHNICAL COLLEGE

8204 Highway 311, Sellersburg 47172

■[J1] INDIANA VOCATIONAL TECHNICAL COLLEGE

1534 West Sample Street, South Bend 46619

■[J1] INDIANA VOCATIONAL TECHNICAL COLLEGE

7377 Dixie Bee Highway, Terre Haute 47802

■[J1] INDIANA VOCATIONAL TECHNICAL COLLEGE

4100 Cowan Road, Muncie 47302

■[J1] INDIANA VOCATIONAL TECHNICAL COLLEGE-NORTHWEST TECHNICAL INSTITUTE

1440 East 35th Avenue, Gary 46409

[P] INTERNATIONAL BUSINESS COLLEGE

3811 Old Illinois Road, Fort Wayne 46804

[J2] LOCKYEAR COLLEGE

Northwest Fifth Street, Evansville 47706

[1] MANCHESTER COLLEGE

604 College Avenue, North Manchester 46962, (219) 982-2141

- **Undergraduates: 577m, 612w**
- **Tuition (1982/83): $4,050**
- **Room & Board: $1,850; Fees: $200**
- **Degrees offered: BA, BS, AA**
- **Mean SAT 441v, 497m**
- **Student-faculty ratio: 15 to 1**

A private college affiliated with the Church of the Brethren, established in 1889. 200-acre small-town campus, one mile from downtown North Manchester, 40 miles from Fort Wayne.
Academic Character NCACS and professional accreditation. 4-1-4 system, 3 3-week summer terms. 48 majors offered in the areas of arts, sciences, business, education, English, foreign languages, home economics, mathematics, peace studies, political & social science, and communication. Self-designed majors. Minors offered in most major fields. Distributive requirements. 1 religion course required. Senior exams. MA granted.

Independent study. Honors program. Limited pass/fail. Cooperative work/study, internships. Preprofessional programs in dentistry, law, library science, medical technology, medicine, ministry. 3-2 program in engineering science. Study abroad. Elementary, secondary, music supervision, and special education certification. Language lab, observatory, psychological lab. 154,000-volume library with microform resources.
Financial CEEB CSS. College scholarships, grants, loans, state awards, payment plan; PELL, SEOG, NDSL, GSL, CWS. Preferred application deadline March 1.
Admissions High school graduation. GED accepted. SAT or ACT required; SAT preferred. $10 application fee. Rolling admissions. $50 deposit required on acceptance of offer of admission. *Early Decision* and *Concurrent Enrollment* programs. Transfers accepted. Credit possible for CEEB AP and CLEP exams.
Student Life Student council. Newspaper, magazine, yearbook, radio station. Music, drama, debate, speaking groups. Religious, academic, and special interest groups. Single students under 21 must live at home or on campus. Coed and single sex dorms; AAFRO House. Married-student housing. 75% of students live on campus. Liquor prohibited on campus; smoking restricted. Attendance required at 30 of 45 convocations. 4 terms of phys ed required. 8 intercollegiate sports for men, 5 for women; intramurals. Hoosier-Buckeye Conference. Student body composition: 0.2% Asian, 2.6% Black, 0.4% Hispanic, 0.1% Native American, 94.9% White, 1.8% Other. 18% from out of state.

[1] MARIAN COLLEGE
3200 Cold Spring Road, Indianapolis 46222, (317) 924-3291

- **Enrollment: 178m, 453w; 879 total (including part-time)**
- **Tuition (1982/83): $3,200**
- **Room & Board: $1,800; Fees: $95**
- **Degrees offered: BA, BS, BSN, AA, ADN**
- **Mean ACT 18; mean SAT 400v, 400m**
- **Student-faculty ratio: 10 to 1**

A private, coeducational, liberal arts college founded by the Sisters of St. Francis of Oldenburg, Indiana, in 1851. 114-acre campus in residential area of a large city in the center of the state.
Academic Character NCACS and professional accreditation. Semester plan. Majors offered include accounting, art, art therapy, business administration, biology, chemistry, dietetics, economics, English & literature, French, German, history, home economics, math, music, philosophy, physical education, psychology, religious education, sociology, theatre & drama, Spanish. Minors possible in most major fields and in physics and theology. 3-1 medical technology program with St. Vincent Hospital awards BS and MT degrees. Nursing program with Indiana University Medical Center offers 2-2 BSN, LPN-ADN, and RN-BSN programs. Preprofessional programs in medicine, dentistry, law, and engineering. Independent study. Honors program. Early childhood, elementary, and secondary education certification.
Financial Aid is available to all students. Scholarships, tuition grants, loans, PELL, campus employment.
Admissions High school graduation required. SAT required. Rolling admissions. Advanced placement possible.
Student Life Indoor and outdoor swimming pools and golf course adjacent to campus. Intercollegiate sports include basketball, baseball, volleyball, softball, tennis, and golf; intramurals for both men and women. Student body composition: 10% minority.

[1] MARION COLLEGE
Marion 46952, (317) 674-6901
Director of Admissions: James C. Blackburn

- **Enrollment: 336m, 471w; 1,096 total (including part-time)**
- **Tuition (1982/83): $3,650**
- **Room & Board: $2,000; Fees: $310**
- **Degrees offered: BA, BS, AA, AS**
- **Mean SAT 410v, 425m**
- **Student-faculty ratio: 14 to 1**

A private college affiliated with the Wesleyan Church, established in 1920. 50-acre campus in a small city 50 miles from Fort Wayne and 65 miles from Indianapolis. Served by air and bus.
Academic Character NCACS and professional accreditation. Semester system, 2 5-week summer terms. 34 majors offered by the divisions of Education & Psychology, Fine Arts, Modern Languages & Literature, Natural Science & Mathematics, Nursing Education, Religion & Philosophy, and Social Science. Minors. Distributive requirements. 6 hours of Bible required. MME granted. Independent and accelerated study. Honors program. Pass/fail. Preprofessional programs in dentistry, engineering, law, medicine, optometry, veterinary medicine. 3-1 program in medical technology. Exchange program with Taylor U. Study abroad; American Institute of Holy Land Studies. Elementary and secondary teacher training. Language lab. 100,000-volume library.
Financial CEEB CSS (preferred) and ACT FAS. College scholarships, grants, loans, ministerial loans; PELL, SEOG, NSS, NSL, NDSL, CWS. Priority scholarship application deadline May 1.
Admissions High school graduation with 10 units required. Interview recommended. SAT or ACT required. $10 application fee. Rolling admissions; application deadline August 15. $50 deposit required on acceptance of offer of admission. *Early Admission* and *Credit in Escrow* programs. Transfers accepted. Credit possible for CEEB AP and CLEP exams.
Student Life Student government. Newspaper, magazine, yearbook. Music, debate, drama groups. Academic, religious, honorary, and special interest organizations. Single students must live at home or on campus. Some married-student housing. 45% of students live on campus. Liquor, immorality, obscenity, tobacco, cards, gambling, dancing, secret societies prohibited. Attendance at 3 weekly chapel services and at convocations required. 3 courses of phys ed required. 7 intercollegiate sports for men, 4 for women; intramurals. NAIA, IIAA. Student body composition: 7% Black, 92% White, 1% Other. 30% from out of state.

[G1] MENNONITE BIBLICAL SEMINARY
Elkhart — see Associated Mennonite Biblical Seminaries

[1] NORTHWOOD INSTITUTE
West Baden 47469, (812) 936-9971

- **Enrollment: 62m, 37w; 104 total (including part-time)**
- **Tuition (1982/83): $3,075**
- **Room & Board: $1,860; Fees: $120**
- **Degree offered: AA**
- **Student-faculty ratio: 15 to 1**

A private, coeducational, business management college located in a rural environment about 50 miles northwest of Louisville.
Academic Character NCACS accreditation. Trimester system. Majors in business management, food & equipment distribution management, hotel & restaurant management. Certificate program in culinary arts. 17,000-volume library.
Financial Complete financial aid program.
Admissions High school graduation required. SAT or ACT recommended. Rolling admissions.
Student Life Social and service clubs. Intramural sports.

[1] NOTRE DAME, UNIVERSITY OF
Notre Dame 46556, (219) 239-5000
Director of Admissions: John T. Goldrick

- **Undergraduates: 5,266m, 1,882w; 9,023 total (including graduates)**
- **Tuition (1982/83): $5,950**
- **Room & Board: $2,100; Fees: $70**
- **Degrees offered: BA, BS, BArch, BBA, BFA, BMus, BSEngr, BSMet**
- **Mean SAT 1250**
- **Student-faculty ratio: 12 to 1**

A private university affiliated with the Congregation of Holy Cross, established in 1842, became coed in 1972. 1,250-acre suburban campus just outside South Bend, 90 miles from Chicago. Served by air, rail, and bus.
Academic Character NCACS and professional accreditation. Semester system, 6-week summer term. 22 majors offered by the College of Arts & Letters, 4 by the College of Business Administration, 8 by the College of Engineering, 6 by the College of Science. Distributive requirements. 6 credits in theology required. MS, MA, MBA, JD, PhD granted. Honors program. Phi Beta Kappa. Pass/fail. Preprofessional programs in dentistry, medicine, veterinary studies combined with liberal arts studies. Dual-degree programs in arts & letters/engineering. Exchange with St. Mary's College. Study abroad. Elementary, secondary, and special education certification. ROTC, AFROTC, NROTC. Many centers, laboratories, institutes. Art museum, computer center, language lab. 1,500,000-volume library with microform resources.
Financial CEEB CSS. Scholarships, grants, loans, deferred payment; PELL, SEOG, NDSL, GSL, CWS. Application deadline March 1.
Admissions High school graduation with 16 units required. SAT and 3 ACH required. $25 application fee. Rolling admissions beginning in February; application deadline March 1. $100 deposit required on acceptance of offer of admission. Transfers accepted. Credit possible for CEEB AP exams, and for university placement tests.
Student Life Student government. Newspaper, magazines, yearbook, radio and TV stations. Music, debate, drama groups. Religious, academic, and service organizations; special interest groups. Freshmen must live on campus. No coed dorms. Married-student housing. 82% of students live on campus. Class attendance required. 2 semesters of phys ed or ROTC required. 11 intercollegiate sports for men, 6 for women; intramural and club sports. AIAW, NCAA. Student body composition: 3% Asian, 3% Black, 3% Hispanic, 0.2% Native American, 90% White, 0.8% Other. 92% from out of state.

[1] OAKLAND CITY COLLEGE
Oakland City 47660
Director of Admissions: Donald F. Brown

- **Undergraduates: 366m, 228w**
- **Tuition (1982/83): $3,300**
- **Room & Board: $2,106; Fees: $25**
- **Degrees offered: BA, BS, AA, AS, AAS**
- **Mean SAT 400v, 440m**
- **Student-faculty ratio: 18 to 1**

A private college controlled by the General Baptists, established in 1885. Rural campus in small town 30 miles from Evansville. Served by bus; airport in Evansville.
Academic Character NCACS and professional accreditation. Trimester system, mini-term, 5- and 10-week summer terms. Majors offered in accounting, Biblical studies, biology, business administration, business education, Christian education, Christian missions, elementary education, English, English/secondary education, humanities, music, physical education, science, and visual arts. Minors. Distributive requirements. 10 hours of religion/philosophy required. Independent study. Pass/no fail. Credit by exam. Preprofessional programs in law, medicine, dentistry, nursing. Cooperative program in general studies with Indiana U. Elementary and secondary education certification. 61,000-volume library.
Financial CEEB CSS. College scholarships, grants, and loans, ministerial grants, state scholarships and grants; PELL, SEOG, NDSL, GSL, CWS; college

work program. Application deadline May 1.
Admissions High school graduation required. GED accepted. SAT or ACT required. $75 application fee/tuition deposit required with application. Rolling admissions. *Early Admission* Program. Transfers accepted. Credit possible for CEEB AP and CLEP exams, and for college placement exams.
Student Life Student government. Newspaper, yearbook. Music, drama groups. Religious, honorary, professional, service, and special interest groups. Single freshmen under 21 must live at home or on campus. Married-student housing. Liquor, gambling, drugs, weapons prohibited on campus. Attendance in class required. 3 intercollegiate sports for men, 4 for women; intramurals. NLCAA.

[1] PURDUE UNIVERSITY

West Lafayette 47907, (317) 494-1776
Director of Admissions: James Kraynak

- **Undergraduates: 16,253m, 11,703w; 32,797 total (including graduates)**
- **Tuition (1982/83): $1,350 (in-state), $3,800 (out-of-state)**
- **Room & Board: $2,100 average**
- **Degrees offered: BA, BS, BPhys Ed**
- **Mean SAT 465v, 544m**
- **Student-faculty ratio: 15 to 1**

A public university established in 1869. 516-acre campus across the Wabash River from small city of Lafayette, 60 miles from Indianapolis. Served by air, rail, and bus.
Academic Character NCACS and professional accreditation. Semester system, 8-week summer term. 35 majors offered in agriculture, 13 in engineering, 11 in management, 3 in pharmacy, nursing, & health sciences, 45 in science, 19 in consumer science, 52 in humanities, social science, & education, 13 in technology, and 6 in physical education. Self-designed majors. Distributive requirements. Graduate and professional degrees granted. Independent study. Honors program. Phi Beta Kappa. Cooperative work/study, internships. Pass/fail. Preprofessional programs in dentistry, law, medicine, veterinary science. Study abroad. Elementary, secondary, and special education certification. ROTC, AFROTC, NROTC. TV unit, A-V center. 1,700,000-volume library with microform resources.
Financial CEEB CSS. University scholarships, grants, loans, payment plan; PELL, SEOG, NDSL, FISL. Scholarship application deadline February 15.
Admissions High school graduation with 15 units required. SAT or ACT required. Interview recommended. Rolling admissions; suggest applying in early fall. $50 deposit required on acceptance of offer of admission. *Early Admission* Program. Transfers accepted. Credit possible for CEEB AP, CLEP, and ACH exams.
Student Life Student government. Newspaper, magazines, yearbook, radio station. Music, debate, and theatre programs. Many special interest groups. 41 fraternities and 18 sororities. Limited housing. Coed and single-sex dorms. 52% of students live on campus. Freshmen and sophomores may not have cars on campus. No liquor allowed. Many intercollegiate and intramural sports for men and women. AIAW, NCAA, Big Ten. Student body composition: 2.5% Asian, 5% Black, 0.5% Hispanic, 92% White. 30% from out of state.

■[1 & J1] CALUMET CAMPUS

Hammond 46323, (219) 844-0520
Director of Admissions: John P. Fruth

- **Undergraduates: 1,410m, 2,353w; 7,230 total (including graduates)**
- **Tuition (1982/83): $1,119 (in-state), $2,745 (out-of-state)**
- **Fees: $52**
- **Degrees offered: BA, BS, BPhys Ed, BSEng, BSInd Mgmt, AAS**
- **Mean SAT 975**
- **Student-faculty ratio: 20 to 1**

A public university established in 1946. 167-acre campus in Hammond, 26 miles from Chicago. Served by air, rail, and bus.
Academic Character NCACS and professional accreditation. Semester system, 8-week summer term. 42 majors offered by the schools of Science & Nursing; General Studies & Community Services; Engineering, Management, & Technology; and Humanities, Education, & Social Sciences. Independent study. Some pass/fail. Preprofessional programs in pharmacy, forestry, veterinary medicine, dentistry, medicine. Elementary and secondary education certification. AFROTC, NROTC at West Lafayette Campus. A-V services. Urban Development Institute. 125,000-volume library.
Financial CEEB CSS and ACT FAS. University scholarships, grants, loans; PELL, SEOG, NSS, NDSL, FISL, NSL, CWS. FAF deadline March 1.
Admissions High school graduation with 15 units required. SAT required; ACT may be substituted by out-of-state students. Rolling admissions; suggest applying in fall. Transfers accepted. Credit possible for CEEP AP and CLEP exams, and for university placement exams. General Studies Division program.
Student Life Student government. Newspaper. Music organizations. Academic, honorary, religious, service, and special interest groups. No university housing. 2 intercollegiate sports for men, 3 for women. Student body composition: 11% Black, 8% Hispanic, 80% White, 1% Other. 12% from out of state.

■[J1] NORTH CENTRAL CAMPUS

Westville 46391

[G2] ROGER WILLIAMS UNIVERSITY

29 North Grant Avenue, Indianapolis 46201

[1] ROSE-HULMAN INSTITUTE OF TECHNOLOGY

Terre Haute 47803, (812) 877-1511
Dean of Admissions: Charles G. Howard

- **Undergraduates: 1,270m**
- **Tuition (1982/83): $4,740**
- **Room & Board: $2,240; Fees: $49**
- **Degree offered: BS**
- **Mean ACT 31.5; mean SAT 544v, 671m**
- **Student-faculty ratio: 15 to 1**

A private men's institute established in 1874. 123-acre campus in the suburbs 5 miles from Terre Haute. Served by air and bus.
Academic Character NCACS and professional accreditation. Trimester system. Majors offered in chemical engineering, chemistry, civil engineering, computer sciences, electrical engineering, mathematics, mathematical economics, mechanical engineering, physics. 1 year of academic ROTC required. MS granted. Independent study. Technical translation program in German, Russian. Consortium with Indiana State and Saint Mary-of-the-Woods. Academic ROTC; AFROTC at Indiana State. Observatory, computer center. 55,000-volume library.
Financial CEEB CSS. Scholarships, grants, loans, payment plan; PELL, SEOG, NDSL, FISL, CWS. Priority application deadline April 1.
Admissions High school graduation with 16 units required. ACT or SAT required. $20 application fee. Rolling admissions; application deadlines December 1 (priority) and May 1. $100 deposit required on acceptance of admissions offer. Transfers accepted. Credit for CEEB AP exams and for institute placement exams.
Student Life Student government. Newspaper, magazine, yearbook, radio station. Music groups, debate teams. Honorary, technical, special interest groups. 6 fraternities with houses. 42% of men join. Freshmen must live at home or on campus. 70% of students live on campus. 10 intercollegiate sports; intramurals. NCAA, College Athletic Conference. Student body composition: 2% Asian, 1% Black, 1% Hispanic, 95% White, 1% Other. 41% from out of state.

[1] ST. FRANCIS COLLEGE

2701 Spring Street, Fort Wayne 46808, (219) 432-3551
Director of Admissions: V. Peter Pitts

- **Undergraduates: 440m, 360w; 1,300 total (including graduates)**
- **Tuition (1982/83): $3,178**
- **Room & Board: $2,100; Fees: $130**
- **Degrees offered: BA, BBA, BS, BSEd, BSW, AA**
- **Mean SAT 470v, 440m**
- **Student-faculty ratio: 14 to 1**

A private Roman Catholic college controlled by the Sisters of St. Francis of Perpetual Adoration, established in 1890. 70-acre suburban campus on the western edge of Fort Wayne.
Academic Character NCACS and professional accreditation. Semester system, 3-, 5-, and 8-week summer terms. Majors offered in accounting, American studies, business administration, English, fine arts, fine/commercial art, psychology, social studies, biology, chemistry, general science, health & safety, mathematics, social work, medical technology, nursing home administration, office administration, and elementary, secondary, & special education. Minors offered in most major fields and in 16 additional areas. Distributives and 6 hours of religious studies required. MS, MBA, MSEd granted. Honors program. Preprofessional programs in dentistry, law, medicine, veterinary medicine. Cooperative nursing program with Ball State. Elementary, secondary, and special education certification. 79,000-volume library with microform resources.
Financial CEEB CSS. College scholarships and grants, state scholarships and grants, payment plan; PELL, SEOG, NDSL, GSL, CWS, college has own work program.
Admissions High school graduation required. GED accepted. SAT or ACT required. $20 application fee. Rolling admissions. $30 tuition and $70 room deposits required on acceptance of offer of admission. Transfers accepted. Credit possible for CLEP exams.
Student Life Student government. Newspaper, magazine. Professional, religious, service, honorary, and special interest organizations. 1 fraternity and 1 sorority. 43% of students live on campus. 2 hours of phys ed required. 6 intercollegiate sports for men, 3 for women, 2 coed; coed intramurals. NAIA, AIAW, MCC.

[1] ST. JOSEPH'S COLLEGE

Rensselaer 47978, (219) 866-7111
Director of Admissions: William T. Craig

- **Undergraduates: 605m, 388w**
- **Tuition (1982/83): $3,950**
- **Room & Board: $2,325; Fees: $140**
- **Degrees offered: BA, BS, BBA, AA, AS**
- **Mean SAT 443v, 474m**
- **Student-faculty ratio: 16 to 1**

A private Roman Catholic college controlled by the Society of Precious Blood, established in 1889, became coed in 1967. 1,500-acre campus in small town of Rensselaer, 75 miles from Chicago.
Academic Character NCACS and professional accreditation. Semester system, 5-week spring and summer terms. 33 majors offered in the areas of accounting, business, science, arts, education, English, history, international studies, mathematics, philosophy/religion, social & political sciences, and physical education. Minor or group major required. Minors offered in most major fields and in 8 additional areas. Distributive requirements. MA in music granted. Independent study. Pass/fail. Internships. 3-2 programs in engineering. 3-2 program in agriculture with Purdue. Field work at Gulf Coast Research Lab. Study abroad. Elementary and secondary education certification. ROTC, AFROTC at Purdue. Computer center. 200,000-volume library.

Financial CEEB CSS. College scholarships, grants, loans, tuition reduction for 2nd sibling, payment plans; PELL, SEOG, NDSL, FISL, NSL, CWS, college has own work program. Application deadline March 15.
Admissions High school graduation with 15 units required. SAT or ACT required. $10 application fee. Rolling admissions. $100 deposit required on acceptance of offer of admission. *Early Admission* and *Early Decision* programs. Admission deferral possible. Transfers accepted. Credit possible for CEEB AP and CLEP exams; college has own advanced placement program.
Student Life Student government. Newspaper, magazine, yearbook. Chorus groups. Academic and special interest organizations. Students must live at home or on campus. Single-sex dorms. 93% of students live on campus. Class attendance required. 8 intercollegiate sports for men, 4 for women; intramurals. Great Lakes Valley, Heartland Conferences, IWISO. Student body composition: 5% Black, 3% Hispanic, 1% Native American, 91% White. 50% from out of state.

[1] SAINT MARY-OF-THE-WOODS COLLEGE
Saint Mary-of-the-Woods 47876, (812) 535-4141

- **Undergraduates: 340w; 690 total (including external degree)**
- **Tuition & Fees (1982/83): $4,010**
- **Room & Board: $1,910**
- **Degrees offered: BA, BS, AA**
- **Mean ACT 20; mean SAT 850**

A private Roman Catholic liberal arts college for women operated by the Sisters of Providence. Established in 1840. Suburban campus located northwest of Terre Haute.
Academic Character NCACS and professional accreditation. Semester system. Bachelor's degree programs offered in accounting, art, biology, chemistry, early childhood education, elementary education, special education, secondary education, English, fine arts, French, general science, political science, history, home economics, humanities, journalism, management, marketing, mathematics, medical technology, music, psychology, religion, social gerontology, social work, Spanish, theater & allied arts, and French & Spanish translation. AA in food management, general business, speech & drama, and Spanish translation (for native Spanish speakers). English Language Institute. Women's External Degree Program. 132,000-volume library.
Financial CEEB CSS. College scholarships awarded on basis of academic excellence and need. College grants, PELL, SEOG, NDSL, GSL, college on-campus employment.
Admissions Admission notification on a rolling basis. *Early Admission* and *Early Decision* programs. Advanced placement credit possible.
Student Life Dormitories and dining hall on campus. Student body composition: 10% minority.

[1] ST. MARY'S COLLEGE
Notre Dame 46556, (219) 284-4305
Director of Admissions: Mary Ann Rowan

- **Undergraduates: 1,800w**
- **Tuition (1982/83): $4,930**
- **Room & Board: $2,500; Fees: $370**
- **Degrees offered: BA, BS, BMus, BBA, BFA**
- **Mean ACT 24; mean SAT 493v, 521m**
- **Student-faculty ratio: 14 to 1**

A private Roman Catholic women's college controlled by the Sisters of the Holy Cross, established in 1844. 275-acre suburban campus near South Bend. Air and rail in South Bend.
Academic Character NCACS and professional accreditation. Semester system. 21 majors offered in the liberal arts, sciences, and education, 6 in allied health fields & sciences, 6 in music; also in business administration & studio art. Courses in 4 additional areas. 3 semester hours of theology required. Interdisciplinary urban studies program. Pass/fail. Preprofessional programs in medicine and law. Exchange program with Notre Dame. Study abroad. Elementary and secondary education certification; endorsements in kindergarten and reading. ROTC, AFROTC, NROTC at Notre Dame. Language lab. 154,000-volume library.
Financial CEEB CSS. College scholarships and grants; PELL, SEOG, NDSL, College Aid Plan, some on-campus employment. Application deadline February 1.
Admissions High school graduation with 16 units required. Interview recommended. Audition required for music majors, portfolio for art majors. SAT or ACT required. $25 application fee. Modified rolling admissions; deadline March 1. *Early Admission* Program. Admission deferral possible. Transfers accepted to sophomore, junior years. Credit possible for CEEB AP, CLEP, and ACH exams.
Student Life Student government. Newspaper, magazine, yearbook. Music, drama groups. Religious, academic, service, and special interest organizations. Students expected to live on campus. Dorms and dining hall. No married-student housing. 90% of students live on campus. 13 intercollegiate sports; intramurals. AIAW. Student body composition: 1% Asian, 0.5% Black, 2% Hispanic, 96.5% White. 84% from out of state.

[1] SAINT MEINRAD COLLEGE
Saint Meinrad 47577, (812) 357-6575
Coordinator of Recruitment: Rev. Jonathan Fassero

- **Undergraduates: 180m**
- **Tuition (1982/83): $2,470**
- **Room & Board: $2,818; Fees: $40**
- **Degrees offered: BA, BS**
- **Mean SAT 430v, 431m**
- **Student-faculty ratio: 4 to 1**

A private Roman Catholic liberal arts college for men preparing for the priesthood. Controlled by the Benedictine Monks of St. Meinrad Archabbey. Established in 1857. 350-acre rural campus in Saint Meinrad, 50 miles northeast of Evansville. Bus service nearby.
Academic Character NCACS accreditation. Semester system. Majors offered in biology, classics, English, history, philosophy, psychology, Spanish, chemistry. Minor required. Minors offered in all major fields and in 9 additional areas. Courses in 20 additional areas. Distributive requirements. 30 semester hours in religion and philosophy required. Independent study. Honors program. Secondary education certification. Ministerial Experience Program. 120,000-volume library.
Financial College scholarships, state grants; PELL, SEOG, NDSL, GSL, CWS. Scholarship application deadline June 15.
Admissions High school graduation with 15 units required. Pastor's recommendation required. SAT or ACT required. Rolling admissions; application deadline July 30. Transfers accepted. Credit possible for CEEB AP and CLEP exams.
Student Life Student government. Religious and service programs. Dormitories and dining hall available. 2 semester hours of phys ed required. 4 intercollegiate sports; intramurals.

[G1] ST. MEINRAD SCHOOL OF THEOLOGY
St. Meinrad 47577

[1] TAYLOR UNIVERSITY
Upland 46989, (317) 998-2751
Director of Admissions: Ronald L. Keller

- **Undergraduates: 648m, 755w; 1,470 total (including graduates)**
- **Tuition (1982/83): $4,424**
- **Room & Board: $2,038; Fees: $90**
- **Degrees offered: AB, BS, BMus, AA**
- **Mean SAT 460v, 496m**
- **Student-faculty ratio: 18 to 1**

A private interdenominational Christian university established in 1846. 240-acre rural campus in Upland, 13 miles southeast of Marion. Air and bus in Marion.
Academic Character NCACS and professional accreditation. 14-4-14 system, 5-week summer term, 4-week presession. 32 majors offered in the areas of business, liberal arts, art & music, education, religious studies, physical education, and sciences. Self-designed majors. Distributive requirements. 2 Bible courses, 1 philosophy and Christian thought course required. Senior exams. Independent study. Honors program. Pass/fail. Preprofessional programs in business, engineering, law, medical technology, medicine, natural resources, nursing, theology. 3-2 program in engineering with Purdue. 3-1 medical technology program. 2-2 program in nursing with Ball State. Elementary, secondary, early childhood, and special education certification. Research under Atomic Energy Commission. Consortium with Christian colleges. Study abroad. ROTC, AFROTC, NROTC at Ball State, Purdue. Language lab. 131,000-volume library.
Financial CEEB CSS. University scholarships, grants, loans, Methodist loans, state grants, payment plan; PELL, SEOG, NDSL, GSL, PLUS, CWS, college employment program. Preferred application deadline for scholarships April 1.
Admissions High school graduation with 15 units required. Interview may be required. SAT or ACT required. $15 application fee. Rolling admissions; suggest applying before March 1. $150 deposit required on acceptance of offer of admission. Credits-in-Escrow Program. Transfers accepted. Credit possible for CEEB AP and CLEP exams.
Student Life Student government. Newspaper, magazine, yearbook. Music, drama groups. Religious and special interest groups. Students must live at home or on campus. Single-sex dorms. Married-student housing. 95% of students live on campus. Liquor, drugs, dancing, gambling, smoking, hazing prohibited. Attendance at 3 chapel services per week, church and campus services on Sunday required. 2 courses in phys ed required. 8 intercollegiate sports for men, 6 for women; intramurals. NAIA, Hoosier-Buckeye Collegiate Conference. Student body composition: 0.7% Asian, 1.1% Black, 0.2% Hispanic, 0.1% Native American, 97.1% White, 0.8% Other. 59% from out of state.

[1] TRI-STATE UNIVERSITY
Angola 46703, (219) 665-3141
Director of Admissions: Kent D. Myers

- **Undergraduates: 926m, 242w**
- **Tuition (1982/83): $3,981**
- **Room & Board: $1,950**
- **Degrees offered: BA, BS, AS**
- **Mean ACT 21; mean SAT 420v, 530m**
- **Student-faculty ratio: 13 to 1**

A private university established in 1884. 400-acre campus in small town of Angola, 45 miles from Fort Wayne. Air, rail, and bus service in Fort Wayne.
Academic Character NCACS and professional accreditation. Trimester system, 2 5-week summer terms. Majors offered in accounting, business & arts, computer science, criminal justice, elementary education, engineering administration, English & humanities, information processing, management, marketing, mathematics, office administration, physical education, science, secondary education, social studies, technical management, transportation, and aerospace, chemical, civil, electrical, and mechanical engineering. AS offered in drafting & design, accounting, secretarial science, industrial technology, criminal justice, computer technology. Cooperative work/study.

Credit by exam. Year-round operation permits completion of degree in 36 months. Elementary and secondary education certification. Computer center. 91,000-volume library.
Financial CEEB CSS and ACT FAS. University scholarships, grants, loans, payment plans; PELL, SEOG, FISL, CWS. Scholarship application deadline April 1.
Admissions High school graduation with 16 units required. GED accepted. SAT or ACT recommended. $15 application fee. Rolling admissions. $40 tuition and $50 room deposits (for boarders) required on acceptance of offer of admission. *Early Admission* Program. Admission deferral possible. Transfers accepted. Credit possible for CEEB AP and CLEP exams; university has own advanced placement program.
Student Life Student government. Newspaper, yearbook, radio station. Music and drama groups. Honorary, professional, religious, and special interest groups. 8 fraternities with houses and 2 sororities without houses. 21% of men and 11% of women join. Freshmen must live at home or on campus. Single-sex dorms. 80% of students live on campus. Class attendance required. 6 hours of phys ed required. 8 intercollegiate sports for men and women; intramurals. NAIA, NCAA. Student body composition: 1% Asian, 6% Black, 1% Hispanic, 86% White, 6% Other. 58% from out of state.

[P] VALPARAISO TECHNICAL INSTITUTE
PO Box 490, Valparaiso 46383, (219) 462-2191

- **Undergraduates: 175 men & women**
- **Tuition (1982/83): $2,520**
- **Room: $666-$756; Fees: $40**
- **Degrees offered: BS, AEE**
- **Student-faculty ratio: 14 to 1**

A private technical institute established in 1874. 30-acre small-town campus, 40 miles southeast of Chicago. Served by air, bus, and rail.
Academic Character Semester system, 12-week summer term. Electronic engineering offered for the BS degree. Associate degree programs (5 terms) in electronic engineering technology and electronic technology. Senior associate degree program (6 terms) in electronic engineering technology. Diploma program in electronic technology. Summer employment program. 2,500-volume library.
Financial Institute scholarships, work program. Application deadline March 15.
Admissions High school graduation with 1 year of algebra required. Rolling admissions. *Early Decision* and *Early Admission* programs. Admission deferral possible. Institute has own advanced placement program. Summer term program for students with academic deficiencies or for those who have been out of school for over 2 years.
Student Life Student government. Radio stations. Professional and special interest groups. Dormitories. Married-student housing. Class attendance required. Intercollegiate basketball; intramurals. Institute is coed but most students are male.

[1] VALPARAISO UNIVERSITY
Valparaiso 46383, (219) 464-5000
Dean of Admissions: Warren Muller

- **Enrollment: 1,785m, 2,001w; 3,900 total (including part-time)**
- **Tuition (1982/83): $4,610**
- **Room & Board: $2,140; Fees: $172**
- **Degrees offered: BA, BMus, BMus Ed, BSW, BSBA, BSN, BSEd, BSFA, BSHome Ec, BSPhys Ed, BSCE, BSEE, BSME, AS**
- **Mean ACT 26; mean SAT 500v, 550m**
- **Student-faculty ratio: 12 to 1**

A private university affiliated with the Lutheran Church, established in 1859. 310-acre semi-rural campus in small city of Valparaiso, 44 miles southeast of Chicago. Served by air, rail, and bus.
Academic Character NCACS and professional accreditation. Semester system, 8-week summer term, 4-week intensive study term. 46 majors offered by the colleges of Arts & Sciences, Business Administration, Engineering, and Nursing, and by Christ College (honors). Minors offered in computer science, Hebrew, Russian. Interdepartmental and Black studies courses. Distributive requirements including courses in religion. Masters and professional degrees granted. Independent study. Honors program. Pass/fail. Preprofessional programs in allied health sciences, dentistry, engineering, foreign service, law, medical technology, medicine, seminary education. Deaconess Training program. Merrill-Palmer Institute. Washington, UN Semesters. Urban affairs semester. Study abroad at Cambridge on Reutlingen. Elementary and secondary education certification, and special education endorsement. Computer center. Audio-visual lab, language lab. 300,000-volume library with 75,000-volume law library and microform resources.
Financial CEEB CSS. University scholarships, grants, loans, payment plans; PELL, SEOG, NDSL, CWS.
Admissions High school graduation with 15 units required. Interview encouraged. SAT or ACT required; SAT strongly preferred. $15 application fee. Rolling admissions. *Early Admission* and *Early Decision* programs. Admission deferral possible. Transfers accepted. Credit possible for CEEB AP and CLEP exams; university has own advanced placement program.
Student Life Student government. Newspaper, magazine, yearbook, radio station. Choirs, band, debate, drama clubs. Women's tutoring group. Service, academic, honorary, and special interest organizations. 12 fraternities with houses and 8 sororities in dorm. 33% of students join. Seniors, veterans, and students over 21 may live off campus. 3 dorms for men, 6 for women; 6 cafeterias. No married-student housing. 85% of students live on campus. Liquor, firearms, explosives prohibited. Honor system. Daily chapel attendance urged. 1 year of phys ed required. 9 intercollegiate sports for men, 6 for women; intramural and club sports. ICC, IIAA, AIAW, NCAA. Student body composition: 0.4% Asian, 3% Black, 0.4% Hispanic, 0.2% Native American, 95% White. 70% from out of state.

[J1] VINCENNES UNIVERSITY
1002 North First Street, Vincennes 47591, (812) 882-3350
Director of Admissions: Stephen Simonds

- **Undergraduates: 2,661m, 1,538w; 5,662 total (including part-time)**
- **Tuition (1982/83): $950 (in-county), $2,640 (out-of-state)**
- **Room & Board: $1,792; Fees: $15**
- **Degrees offered: AA, AS, AAS**

A public junior college established in 1801. Campus located in city of Vincennes on the Wabash River. Airport 18 miles away.
Academic Character NCACS and professional accreditation. Semester system, 2 5-week summer terms. 59 college transfer programs and 55 occupational programs offered by the divisions of Business, Health Occupations, Humanities, Public Service, Science & Mathematics, Social Science, Technology, and Health, Physical Education & Recreation. Distributive requirements. Independent study. Cooperative work/study, pass/fail, internships. Preprofessional programs in engineering, dental hygiene, dentistry, law, medical records, medical technology, medicine, occupational therapy, optometry, pharmacy, and veterinary medicine. Banking program with American Institute of Banking. Evening program sponsored with Indiana State U. ROTC. 37,000-volume library with microform resources.
Financial CEEB CSS. University scholarships, state grants; PELL, SEOG, NDSL, GSL, NSL, CWS. Priority application deadline March 1.
Admissions High school graduation required. GED accepted. SAT or ACT required. $20 application fee. Rolling admissions. *Early Decision* and *Early Admission* programs. Transfers accepted. Credit possible for CLEP exams; university has own advanced placement program.
Student Life Student government. Newspapers. Music, art, drama, dance groups. International Students. Academic, honorary, religious, and special interest organizations. 4 fraternities and 1 sorority. Single students under 21 must live at home or on campus. Coed and single sex dorms. Class attendance required. 2 hours of phys ed required. 7 intercollegiate sports for men, 7 for women; intramurals.

[1] WABASH COLLEGE
Crawfordsville 47933, (317) 362-1400
Director of Admissions: Paul M. Garman

- **Undergraduates: 789m**
- **Tuition (1982/83): $5,200**
- **Room & Board: $2,300; Fees: $80**
- **Degree offered: AB**
- **Mean SAT 500v, 590m**
- **Student-faculty ratio: 10 to 1**

A private men's college established in 1832. 50-acre campus in small city of Crawfordsville, 45 miles northwest of Indianapolis. Served by bus and rail.
Academic Character NCACS and professional accreditation. Semester system. Majors offered in biology, chemistry, classical civilization, economics, English, French, German, Greek, history, humanities, Latin, mathematics, music, philosophy, physics, political science, psychology, religion, Russian, Spanish/French, speech, theatre. Self-designed majors. Minor required. Minors offered in most major fields and in art. Distributive requirements. Comprehensive and oral exams required. Independent study. Phi Beta Kappa. Pass/fail. Internships. Preprofessional programs in medicine, dentistry, law, optometry, veterinary science. Cooperative engineering programs with Columbia U and Washington U (St. Louis). 3-3 law program with Columbia. Member Great Lakes College Association. Oak Ridge, Washington Semesters. New York arts program. Newberry Library Humanities Program. Marine biology summer terms. Study abroad in 12 countries. ROTC at Purdue. Language lab, computer center. Over 225,000-volume library.
Financial CEEB CSS. College scholarships, grants, and loans; PELL, FISL.
Admissions High school graduation with 15 units required. SAT or ACT required. $15 application fee. Rolling admissions after 15th of each month. $100 deposit required on acceptance of offer of admission. Admission deferral possible. Transfers accepted. Credit possible for CEEB AP and CLEP exams.
Student Life Student government. Newspaper, magazine, yearbook, radio station. Music, drama groups. Speakers Bureau. Malcolm X Institute. Political, religious, service, and special interest organizations. 9 fraternities with houses. 75% of men join. Freshmen and sophomores must live on campus. Dormitories and dining facilities. 95% of students live on campus. 10 intercollegiate, several intramural and club sports. NCAA. Student body composition: 2% Asian, 4% Black, 1% Hispanic, 93% White. 20% from out of state.

IOWA (IA)

[1] BRIAR CLIFF COLLEGE
Sioux City 51104, (712) 279-5321
Director of Admissions: James Hoffman

- **Enrollment: 328m, 491w; 1,293 total (including part-time)**
- **Tuition (1982/83): $3,300**
- **Room & Board: $1,750; Fees: $150**
- **Degrees offered: BA, BS, BSMT, BSRT, BSN**

• **Mean ACT 20.5**
• **Student-faculty ratio: 16 to 1**

A private Roman Catholic college, established in 1930 and became coed in 1966. 70-acre urban campus in Sioux City, with city bus service at campus and airport nearby.

Academic Character NCACS and professional accreditation. Trimester system, 2 6-week summer terms. Majors offered in accounting, art, biology, business administration, chemistry, English, history, mass communications, math, math/computer science, music, psychology, social work, sociology, Spanish, theology, and phys ed, health, & recreation. Self-designed, divisional, interdivisional, and interdisciplinary majors. Distributive requirements. CLEP, GRE required. Interdivisional seminar courses required in junior and senior years. Independent study. Course credit by correspondence possible. Pass/fail. Honors program. 3-2 cooperative engineering program with Iowa State U, Ames; 3-1 program in medical technology. 5-year physical therapy program with U of Iowa. Cooperative RN program with local hospitals. Urban semester in Chicago or St. Paul. Study abroad. Elementary and secondary education certification. Language lab, writing lab. 83,900-volume library.

Financial CEEB CSS and ACT FAS. College scholarships, grants, loans, church scholarships, payment plans; PELL, SEOG, FISL, NDSL, CWS, college work program. Scholarships/grants application deadline January 31.

Admissions High school graduation required with 17 units suggested. Interview recommended. ACT (preferred) or SAT required. $15 application fee. Rolling admissions; no deadline. $50 deposit required on acceptance of offer of admission. *Early Decision* and *Early Entrance* programs. Admission deferral possible. Transfers accepted. Credit possible for CEEB AP and CLEP exams.

Student Life Student government. Newspaper, literary magazine, yearbook. Athletic, academic, and special interest organizations. Seniors may live off campus. No married-student housing. 45% of students live on campus. Class attendance required. 5 intercollegiate sports for men, 5 for women; intramurals. AIAW. Student body composition: 0.5% Asian, 2% Black, 1% Hispanic, 0.5% Native American, 96% White. 15% from out of state.

[1] BUENA VISTA COLLEGE

Storm Lake 50588, (712) 749-2235, (800) 792-6822 (toll-free in IA)
Director of Admissions: Kent McElvania

• **Undergraduates: 480m, 435w; 1,386 total (including part-time)**
• **Tuition (1982/83): $4,910**
• **Room & Board: $1,945**
• **Degrees offered: BA, BS**
• **Mean ACT 22**
• **Student-faculty ratio: 19 to 1**

A private college affiliated with the General Assembly Presbyterian Church, established in 1891. 30-acre campus in the small town of Storm Lake, northwest of Des Moines and 75 miles east of Sioux City. Bus service.

Academic Character NCACS and professional accreditation. 4-1-4 system, 2 4½-week summer terms, workshops and special classes. Majors offered in accounting, art, biology, business, business education, chemistry, computer science, corporate communications, economics, elementary education, English, finance & banking, German, health & physical education, history, library science, management systems & personnel, mass communications, mathematics, mathematics/physics, music, politico-economic systems, psychology, religion & philosophy, science, small business management, social science, social work, sociology, Spanish, special education, and speech & drama. Self-designed majors. Minors usually required; offered in most major fields and in physics, political science, recreation, other career areas. GRE and area exam required for graduation. Seminars, independent study, honors program. Internships. Honors/pass/no credit option. Preprofessional programs in dentistry, engineering, law, medicine, optometry, theology, veterinary medicine. 3-1 programs in medical technology, physical therapy. Off-campus and foreign study. Elementary, secondary, and special education certification. Language lab. 83,000-volume library with computer information services.

Financial CEEB CSS and ACT FAS. College and state scholarships, grants, loans; PELL, SEOG, NDSL, GSL, CWS, academic assistanceships. Application deadline March 1.

Admissions High school graduation required, with 11 units recommended. Interview recommended. ACT or SAT required. $15 application fee. Rolling admissions; suggest applying any time after first semester of 3rd year. $100 deposit required on acceptance of offer of admission. *Early Decision, Early Admission* programs. Admission deferral possible. Transfers accepted. Credit possible for CEEB AP and CLEP exams, and for life experience.

Student Life Student Council. Newspaper, literary magazine, yearbook, radio station. Music, drama, debate groups. Religious and political organizations. Special interest, service, and honorary groups. 6 fraternities and sororities without houses. Single students must live at home or on campus. Coed and single-sex dorms. No married-student housing. 80% of students live on campus. Explosives, firearms, fireworks, gambling prohibited on campus. 9 intercollegiate sports for men, 8 for women; intramurals. NCAA, Iowa Intercollegiate Athletic Conference, Io-Kota Conference. Student body composition: 1% Asian, 1% Black, 98% White. 8% from out of state.

[1] CENTRAL COLLEGE

Pella 50219, (515) 628-4151
Director of Admissions: Garrett Knoth

• **Enrollment: 681m, 821w**
• **Tuition (1982/83): $4,650**
• **Room & Board: $1,851; Fees: $72**
• **Degree offered: BA**
• **Mean ACT 22; mean SAT 1000**
• **Student-faculty ratio: 17 to 1**

A private college sponsored by the Reformed Church in America, established in 1853. 75-acre small-town campus, 40 miles southeast of Des Moines. Served by bus; college transportation to air, bus, and train services.

Academic Character NCACS and professional accreditation. Trimester system, 10-week summer term. Majors offered in accounting, Afro-American studies, art, biology, business management, chemistry, communication/theatre, economics, elementary education, English, French, general studies, German, history, home economics, international management, Latin American studies, linguistics, mathematics, mathematics/computer science, music, natural science education, philosophy, physical education, physics, political science, psychology, recreation, religion, social science education, sociology, Spanish, systems management, urban studies. Preprofessional major in medicine. Interdisciplinary majors. Minors. Distributive requirements. Honors programs. Student-faculty research encouraged. Internships. Off-campus work-study and independent research for qualified upperclassmen. Some pass/no record grading. Credit by exam. Preprofessional programs in law and ministry. BA/MBA program with U of Iowa. 3-1 Associate in Church Work program with Western Theological Seminary. 2-2 and 3-1 home economics programs with Iowa State U at Ames. Chicago Urban Term. Study abroad. Elementary, secondary, and special education certification. Home economics and language labs. Art gallery, drama and music centers. 200,000-volume library.

Financial CEEB CSS and ACT FAS. College scholarships, grants, loans, activity awards, state grants & loans, Reformed Church grants, 2nd-sibling tuition discounts; PELL, SEOG, NDSL, GSL, CWS, college work program. Application deadline March 1.

Admissions High school graduation with 15 units and rank in upper 50% of class recommended. Interview recommended. ACT or SAT required. $20 application fee. Rolling admissions; deadline August 1. $100 deposit required on acceptance of offer of admission. *Early Decision* and *Early Entrance* programs. Admission deferral possible. Transfers accepted. Requirements may be waived without credit for CEEB AP exams. Credit possible for CLEP exams. Guided Studies and Special Services programs for older, disadvantaged, and minority students.

Student Life Student government. Newspaper, literary magazine, yearbook, radio station. Music, speech, and theatre groups. Religious, service, honorary, academic, athletic, and special interest groups. 3 fraternities with houses and 2 sororities without houses. 10% of men, 4% of women join. Coed, single-sex, language, and married-student housing. 87% of students live on campus. Liquor prohibited on campus. Class attendance expected. One physical education orientation course required. 8 intercollegiate sports for men, 8 for women; intramurals. AIAW, NCAA, Iowa Intercollegiate Athletic Conference. Student body composition: 0.8% Asian, 2.1% Black, 0.9% Hispanic, 0.1% Native American, 93.2% White, 2.9% Other. 28% from out of state.

[1] CLARKE COLLEGE

Clarke Drive, Dubuque 52001, (319) 588-6316
Director of Admissions: Edwin Reger

• **Enrollment: 73m, 488w; 848 total (including part-time)**
• **Tuition (1982/83): $4,150**
• **Room & Board: $1,830**
• **Degrees offered: BA, BS, BFA, AA**
• **Student-faculty ratio: 10 to 1**

A private Roman Catholic college established in 1843, college instruction started in 1901, became coed in 1979. Conducted by the Sisters of Charity, BVM. Campus in Dubuque, 180 miles from Chicago and 190 from Des Moines. Airport, bus and train stations in Dubuque.

Academic Character NCACS accreditation. Semester system, 3 summer terms. Majors offered in allied health, art, biology, business, chemistry/physical science, communication, computer sciences, drama/speech, education/special education, English, foreign languages, history/political science, math, music, nursing, psychology, religious studies/philosophy, sociology/social work. Minors. Distributives and 6 semester hours of religion required. MA granted. Credit for learning experiences. Internships. Preprofessional health programs. Cross-registration with Loras College and U of Dubuque. Exchange program with Mundelein College, Chicago. Study abroad. Continuing Education. 120,000-volume library with microform resources.

Financial CEEB CSS. College scholarships and tuition grants, state scholarships and grants; PELL, SEOG, NDSL, GSL, CWS. Apply with admissions application.

Admissions High school graduation with 16 units and rank in upper 50% of class required. SAT or ACT required. $15 application fee. Rolling admissions; suggest applying late in 11th or early in 12th year. $50 deposit required on acceptance of offer of admission. *Early Admission* program. Admission deferral possible. Transfers accepted. Credit possible for CEEB AP and CLEP exams.

Student Life Newspaper, magazine. Theatre and music clubs. Volunteer groups. Circle K. Leo Club. Academic organizations. International Student Leadership Institute. Cultural Events Committee. Single students must live at home or on campus. Dorms and dining hall. 2 intercollegiate sports for men, 3 for women; intramurals.

[J1] CLINTON COMMUNITY COLLEGE

Clinton 52732
Part of the Eastern Iowa Community College District

[1] COE COLLEGE

Cedar Rapids 52402, (319) 399-8500, (800) 332-8404 (toll-free in Iowa)
Dean of Admissions: Peter D. Feickert

• **Undergraduates: 600m, 600w**

- **Tuition (1982/83): $5,280**
- **Room & Board: $1,805; Fees: $90**
- **Degrees offered: BA, BMus, BSN**
- **Mean ACT 23; mean SAT 1075**
- **Student-faculty ratio: 13 to 1**

A private college affiliated with the United Presbyterian Church, established in 1851. 26-acre campus in residential section of Cedar Rapids 8 blocks from the central business district. Airport and bus station in Cedar Rapids.

Academic Character NCACS and professional accreditation. 4-1-4 system, 2 5-week summer terms. Majors offered in accounting, Afro-American studies, American studies, art, Asian studies, biology, bio-social science, business administration, chemistry, economics, English, environmental studies, French, general science, German, history, humanities, literature, mathematics, music, nursing, philosophy, philosophy/religion, physical education, physics, political science, psychology, religion, sociology, Spanish, speech, teacher education, and theatre arts. Major in computer science in cooperation with Mount Mercy and Cornell Colleges. Self-designed majors. 3- and 5-year programs in allied health sciences. Program in computer applications. Minors optional. Community service certificate program. Two courses required. Pass/fail. Accelerated study, honors program, Phi Beta Kappa. Work/service terms, internships. Independent study, sponsored team research. Cooperative work/study. Preprofessional programs in business, church service, college teaching, dentistry, government service, law, medicine. 3-1 program in medical technology, 3-2 engineering program with Washington U, 3-1 and 3-2 social service administration programs with U of Chicago. Cross-registration with Mount Mercy. Numerous exchange programs and off-campus semesters. Study abroad. Elementary and secondary education certification. Computer center, language lab. ROTC at U of Iowa. 180,000-volume library.

Financial CEEB CSS (preferred) and ACT FAS. College scholarships and grants, state scholarships and tuition grants, merit scholarships, Presbyterian scholarships, 2nd-sibling tuition reductions, payment plans; PELL, SEOG, NDSL, FISL, GSL, CWS. March 1 deadline for state grant application.

Admissions High school graduation required with 15 units recommended. SAT or ACT required; ACH recommended. Interview recommended. $15 application fee. Rolling admissions; recommended application deadline May 1. $100 deposit required on acceptance of offer of admission. *Early Entrance* Program. Admission deferral possible. Transfers accepted. Credit possible for CEEB AP and CLEP exams.

Student Life Student government. Newspaper, literary magazines, yearbook, radio station. Music, debate, drama groups. Affiliate artist program. Varsity lettermen's group. Ethnic organizations, International Club. Many academic, honorary, special interest clubs. 5 fraternities and 3 sororities without houses. 30% of men, 25% of women join. Most single students live on campus or at home. Single-sex and coed dorms. Married-student housing. 85% of students live on campus. 10 intercollegiate sports for men, 8 for women; intramurals. AIAW, NCAA. Student body composition: 1% Asian, 3% Black, 96% White. 45% from out of state.

[1] CORNELL COLLEGE

Mount Vernon 52314, (319) 895-8811
Dean of Admissions: Frank G. Krivo

- **Enrollment: 480m, 426w**
- **Tuition (1982/83): $5,330**
- **Room & Board: $2,044; Fees: $286**
- **Degrees offered: BA, BS, BMus, BPh, BSpecialStudies**
- **Mean ACT 24-26; mean SAT 1000-1100**
- **Student-faculty ratio: 12 to 1**

A private college established in 1853. Wooded 125-acre campus in small town of Mount Vernon, 20 minutes from Cedar Rapids and Iowa City. Bus station; airport in Cedar Rapids. Campus is a national historic district.

Academic Character NCACS and professional accreditation. One-course-at-a-time calendar of 9 3½-week terms. Majors offered in American studies, art, biology, chemistry, computer science, economics/business, elementary education, English, environmental studies, French, geology, German, German studies, Greek, health/physical education, history, math, medieval & Renaissance studies, music, origins of behavior, philosophy, physics, politics, psychology, religion, Russian, Russian studies, sociology, Spanish, theatre/speech. Double, triple, interdisciplinary, and self-designed majors. BPhilosophy curriculum has no set requirements except comprehensive exam in field; BSS includes independent study, field work, audited and credited class work. Distributive requirements. Masters degrees granted. Accelerated study, honors program, Phi Beta Kappa. Interdepartmental study. Internships. Preprofessional programs in dentistry, engineering, journalism, law, medicine, sociology, theology. 3-2 health & hospital administration and accelerated MBA programs with U of Iowa. Cooperative nursing, allied health sciences programs with Rush U. Combined degree programs in engineering (with Washington U), social service administration (U of Chicago), forestry, environmental management (Duke U), and in medical technology with 2 Cedar Rapids hospitals. Exchange program with Fisk U, U of Puerto Rico, Rust College. Numerous off-campus study opportunities. Study abroad. Kindergarten through secondary education certification. Computer center, geology center and museum. 185,000-volume library.

Financial CEEB CSS and ACT FAS. College scholarships, grants, loans; state grants and scholarships, United Methodist scholarships, 50% tuition awards for children of ordained ministers; PELL, SEOG, NDSL, GSL, PLUS, CWS.

Admissions High school graduation and SAT or ACT required. Interview recommended. $15 application fee. Rolling admissions; no deadline. $100 deposit required on acceptance of offer of admission. *Early Acceptance* and *Early Decision* programs. Admission deferral possible. Transfers accepted in all 9 terms. Credit possible for CEEB AP and CLEP exams, and for college tests.

Student Life Student government. Newspaper, literary magazine, yearbook, radio station. Music groups, various public speaking organizations. Campus theatre. Writer's Club. Students for Black People. Religious, honorary, academic, and special interest groups. 7 social clubs for men, 3 for women; none have houses. 30% of men, 20% of women join. Students must live on campus. Coed and single-sex dorms that are student-managed. Married-student housing. 99% of students live on campus. One course in health and physical education sometimes required. 10 intercollegiate sports for men, 7 for women; intramurals. AIAW, NCAA, Midwest Athletic Conference. Student body composition: 5% Black, 89% White, 6% Other. 71% from out of state.

[J1] DES MOINES AREA COMMUNITY COLLEGE, ANKENY CAMPUS

2006 Ankeny Blvd., Ankeny 50021

[J1] DES MOINES AREA COMMUNITY COLLEGE, BOONE CAMPUS

Boone 50036

[1] DIVINE WORD COLLEGE

Epworth 52045

[1] DORDT COLLEGE

Sioux Center 51250, (712) 722-3771
Director of Admissions & Financial Aid: Howard Hall

- **Enrollment: 526m, 617w**
- **Tuition (1982/83): $3,850**
- **Room & Board: $1,540**
- **Degrees offered: AB, AA**
- **Mean ACT 20**
- **Student-faculty ratio: 16 to 1**

A private college established 1955, affiliated with the Christian Reformed Church. 40-acre campus in Sioux Center, 45 miles from Sioux City and 55 from Sioux Falls.

Academic Character NCACS accreditation. Semester system. Majors offered in accounting, agri-business, agriculture, art, astronomy-physics, biology, business administration, business education, chemistry, classical studies, communication, Dutch, early childhood education, elementary education, engineering science, English, German, general studies, history, individual studies, math, mechanical engineering, music, natural sciences, philosophy, physical education, physics, political science, psychology, secretarial science, social sciences, social work, sociology, Spanish, special education aid, speech, teacher aid, theatre arts, theology. Church music minor. Distributives and 2 semesters of theology or one theology & one philosophy required. Independent study. Some pass/fail. Preprofessional programs in allied health, dentistry, law, medicine, pharmacy, seminary studies; combined transfer programs arrangeable in dentistry, law, medicine. 3-1 medical technology program. First year of 5-year BA/RN nursing program offered. Iowa Legislative Internship Program, Chicago Metropolitan Center Program. Study abroad. Elementary and secondary education certification. ROTC. Language lab, observatories. 110,000-volume library.

Financial CEEB CSS and ACT FAS. College scholarships, grants, loans; Canadian student aids, state scholarships and grants, grants-in-aid to dependents of Church members; PELL, SEOG, NDSL, FISL, CWS. Application deadlines August 29 (scholarships, grants) and May 15 (loans).

Admissions High school graduation with 15 units required. ACT required. $10 application fee. Rolling admissions; no deadline. *Early Admission* Program. $30 room deposit required on acceptance of offer of admission. Transfers accepted. Advanced placement credit possible. Probational enrollment possible.

Student Life Newspaper, literary magazine, yearbook, radio. Music groups and ensembles, debate and drama activities. Athletic, political, special interest clubs. Freshmen must live at home or on campus. Dorms. Married-student housing. 80% of students live on campus. No liquor allowed on campus. Attendance at chapel twice a week and at church twice on Sunday expected. 4 semesters of phys ed required. 7 intercollegiate sports for men, 6 for women; intramural and club sports. AIAW, NAIA, Tri-State Conference. 70% of students from out of state.

[1] DRAKE UNIVERSITY

Des Moines 50311, (515) 271-3182
Toll-free from IA: (800) 362-2416; from IL, MN, MO, NE, SD, WI: (800) 247-2135
From other states: (515) 271-3181 (call collect)
Executive Director of Admissions: Everett Hadley

- **Enrollment: 2,210m, 2,650w; 6,627 total (including graduates)**
- **Tuition (1982/83): $5,230**
- **Room & Board: $2,380**
- **Degrees offered: BA, BS, BJourn, BFA, BMus, BMus Ed, BSBA, BSEd, BSPharm, BGS**
- **Mean ACT 22.1**
- **Student-faculty ratio: 18 to 1**

A private university established in 1881 in Des Moines. 79-acre urban campus. Airport and bus station in Des Moines.

Academic Character NCACS and professional accreditation. Semester system, 2 5-week summer terms, many workshops and short-term courses. 10 majors offered by the College of Business Administration, 7 by the College of Education, 19 by the College of Fine Arts, 26 by the College of Liberal Arts, 8 by the School of Journalism. Graduate and professional degrees granted.

Honors program. Phi Beta Kappa. Some pass/fail. Cooperative work/study. Preprofessional programs in allied health, dentistry, divinity, engineering, law, medicine, social work. 5-year program in College of Pharmacy. 4-year BA/MA program. Marine science program with Southampton College. 3-1 degree programs with Drake Law School, any approved college of medicine or dentistry, Mercy and Methodist Hospital Schools of Medical Technology. 2-2, 3-2 engineering with Cornell U, Washington U. Campus afloat. Study in Appalachia. Washington and UN semesters. Study abroad. Elementary and secondary education certification. ROTC. Language lab, media service center, computer center. 481,601-volume library.
Financial CEEB CSS (preferred) and ACT FAS. University scholarships and loans, merit scholarships, state scholarships and grants, athletic grants; PELL, SEOG, NDSL, FISL, GSL, HEAL, CWS. File FAF between January 1 and March 1 for grants and loans; by March 1 for scholarships.
Admissions High school graduation with at least 11 academic units required. GED accepted. Interview encouraged. SAT or ACT required; aptitude and ACH may be requested. $25 application fee. Rolling admissions; deadline August 15. $100 housing deposit required on acceptance of offer of admission. *Early Decision, Early Admission, Concurrent Enrollment* programs. Admission deferral possible. Transfers accepted. Advanced placement credit possible. Transitional Services Program for those not granted regular admission.
Student Life Student government. Newspaper, literary magazine. Music groups. Speech team. Theatre. Student Volunteer Programs Office. Athletic, academic, special interest, religious, honorary, and professional organizations. 9 fraternities and 6 sororities, all with houses. 19% of men and 20% of women join. Single freshmen under 19 must live at home or on campus. Coed and single-sex dorms. Married-student housing. 50% of students live on campus. Liquor limited to dorms and the University Center. 8 intercollegiate sports for men, 5 for women; intramurals. AIAW, Missouri Valley Athletic Conference. Student body composition: 1.3% Asian, 6.1% Black, 0.6% Hispanic, 0.1% Native American, 90% White. 60% from out of state.

[1] DUBUQUE, UNIVERSITY OF
Dubuque 52001, (319) 589-3200
Director of Student Services & Admissions: Clifford Bunting

- **Enrollment: 597m, 497w**
- **Tuition (1982/83): $4,200**
- **Room & Board: $1,700; Fees: $75**
- **Degrees offered: BA, BS, BMus, BSN, BBA, AA**
- **Mean ACT 19**
- **Student-faculty ratio: 14 to 1**

A private university affiliated with the United Presbyterian Church, established in 1852. 50-acre campus in residential Dubuque, on the Bluffs West bank of the Mississippi River, 180 miles west of Chicago. Airport and bus station in Dubuque.
Academic Character NCACS and professional accreditation. Semester system, 3 3-week summer terms. Majors offered in accounting, aviation management, biology, business administration, chemistry, computer science, earth science, economics, education, English, environmental science, flight operations, foreign language, general science, history, marketing, math, music, music education, occupational safety & health, philosophy, physical education, physics, political science, psychology, religious studies, safety education, social work, sociology, Spanish, special administration, special education, speech. 3-1 medical technology major. Nursing major for students with an RN. Art major possible through cross-registration. Self-designed majors. Distributive requirements. Honors semester, accelerated study. Independent reading and research for upperclassmen. Credit by exam, some credit/no credit. Internships, cooperative work/study. Preprofessional courses in dentistry, engineering, law, medicine, veterinary medicine, and research. Graduate Theological Seminary in Dubuque offers combined 6-year plan for undergraduates. Member of the Tri-College Cooperative Program with Clarke and Loras; cross-registration also possible with 3 local theological schools. 2-2 nursing program. 2-2 and 3-2 engineering programs. Combined programs possible with dental, medical, law, or veterinary schools. Off-campus studies. Study abroad. Elementary, secondary, and special education certification. ROTC. Language labs. Art gallery. 131,000-volume libraries with microform resources.
Financial CEEB CSS (preferred) and ACT FAS. University scholarships, grants, loans; state scholarships and tuition grants, Presbyterian scholarships and grants-in-aid; PELL, SEOG, NDSL, FISL, GSL, PLUS, CWS, part-time University employment. Application deadline August 15.
Admissions High school graduation with 15 units required. ACT or SAT required. $15 application fee. Rolling admissions; deadline August 15. $50 deposit required on acceptance of offer of admission. *Early Admission* Program. Admission deferral possible. Transfers accepted. Credit possible for CEEB AP and CLEP subject exams.
Student Life Student government. Newspaper, yearbook, radio station. Music, drama, debate groups. Political, religious, academic, honorary, and professional groups. 5 fraternities and 4 sororities, none with houses. 20% of men and women join. First-year students must live at home, with relatives, or on campus. Dormitories, one with a coed floor. Married-student housing. 55% of students live on campus. Freshmen may not have cars on campus. Liquor prohibited on campus. 8 intercollegiate sports for men, 5 for women; intramurals. AIAW, NCAA, Iowa Intercollegiate Athletic Conference. Student body composition: 5% Asian, 2% Black, 0.5% Hispanic, 0.5% Native American, 92% White. 56% from out of state.

[G1] DUBUQUE THEOLOGICAL SEMINARY
Dubuque 52001

[J1] ELLSWORTH COMMUNITY COLLEGE
1100 College Avenue, Iowa Falls 50126, (515) 648-4611
Admissions Counselor & Registrar: Phil Rusley

- **Enrollment: 490m, 410w; 1,375 total (including evening)**
- **Tuition (1982/83): $620 (in-state), $1,240 (out-of-state)**
- **Room & Board: $1,740**
- **Degrees offered: AA, AAS**
- **Mean ACT 19.6**

A public community college founded in 1890. Campus in Iowa Falls next to the Iowa River.
Academic Character NCACS accreditation. Semester system, summer term. Typical transfer programs include liberal arts, business administration, pre-mortuary science, teacher education, engineering, science & humanities, pre-medicine, pre-dentistry, pre-nursing, physical therapy, pre-agriculture, pre-veterinary medicine, home economics. Career option programs in accounting, clerical, illustration & design, industrial lab technology, minicomputer & electronic accounting systems, and secretarial studies. Diplomas and certificates granted. Distributive requirements. Credit by exam. 76-acre campus farm. 44,000-volume library.
Financial College scholarships, state scholarships and grants, deferred tuition plan; PELL, SEOG, NDSL, GSL, CWS.
Admissions High school graduation required. GED accepted. ACT required. Rolling admissions. Admission deferral possible. Transfers accepted. Credit possible for CEEB CLEP exams, and for departmental exams.
Student Life Student government. Newspaper, yearbook. Social Program, wildlife club. Music, drama organizations. Art Club. Cheerleaders. Special interest clubs. Full-time students under 21 must live on campus or at home. No coed dorms. 2 semester hours of phys ed required. 5 intercollegiate sports for men, 3 for women; intramurals. NJCAA.

[P] FAITH BAPTIST BIBLE COLLEGE
1900 North 4th Street, Ankeny 50021

[1] GRACELAND COLLEGE
Lamoni 50140, (515) 784-5000
Director of Admissions: Robert L. Watts

- **Enrollment: 574m, 594w**
- **Tuition (1982/83): $4,060**
- **Room & Board: $1,710; Fees: $30**
- **Degrees offered: BA, BS**
- **Mean ACT 20; mean SAT 915**
- **Student-faculty ratio: 15 to 1**

A private college founded in 1895 and sponsored by the Reorganized Church of Jesus Christ of Latter-Day Saints (Mormons). 175-acre rural campus on the Missouri state border about 75 miles south of Des Moines. Bus station.
Academic Character NCACS and professional accreditation. 4-1-4 system, 4-6 week summer term. Majors offered in art, biology, business, chemistry, computer, economics, education, English, German, health, history, international studies, liberal studies, math, medical technology, music, nursing, phys ed, psychology, religious studies, science, social studies, sociology, Spanish, special studies, and theatre & speech. Minors. Distributive requirements. Interdisciplinary honors program. Independent study. Credit by exam. Internships. Cooperative medical technology program with any approved hospital school. Cooperative education program with Drake U. Member of the Kansas City Regional Council for Higher Education consortium. Study abroad. Elementary, secondary, and special education certification. 91,114-volume library.
Financial CEEB CSS. College scholarships, grants, and loans, Canadian Student Loans; PELL, SEOG, NDSL, GSL, CWS, college part-time employment. Application deadline February 15 for some aids, none for others.
Admissions High school graduation with 12 units required. GED accepted. ACT or SAT required. $60 application fee required, $40 of which is an enrollment deposit refundable until July 1. Rolling admissions; deadline the summer before entrance. *Early Decision* and *Early Entrance* programs. Transfers accepted. Credit possible for CEEB AP and CLEP exams, and for college language placement exams. Applicants with 15 academic units but no high school diploma are considered for admission.
Student Life Student government. Newspaper, yearbook. Music groups. Religious organizations. Honor societies. Freshmen, sophomores, and financial aid students must live on campus or at home. Single-sex dorms. Some married-student housing. 78% of students live on campus. Gambling, possession of liquor, and smoking prohibited; firearms not allowed in dorms and must be registered with college. Class attendance expected; some instructors set dress codes. 4 semester hours of phys ed required. 8 intercollegiate sports, intramurals. NAIA, Heart of America Conference. Student body composition: 1% Black, 1% Hispanic, 1% Native American, 92% White, 5% Other. 76% from out of state.

[1] GRAND VIEW COLLEGE
Des Moines 50316, (515) 263-2800
Director of Admissions: Jerry Slater

- **Enrollment: 427m, 457w; 1,247 total (including part-time)**
- **Tuition (1982/83): $3,390**
- **Room & Board: $1,700**
- **Degrees offered: BA, BSN, AA**
- **Mean ACT 19**
- **Student-faculty ratio: 16 to 1**

A private college affiliated with the Lutheran Church in America, established in 1896. 25-acre campus in Des Moines. Airport, bus and train stations.

Academic Character NCACS and professional accreditation. 4-4-1 system, 2 4-week summer terms. Majors offered in American studies, applied computer science, art, business administration, creative & performing arts, English, general social sciences, human behavior, human services, humanities, journalism, nursing, philosophy, radio & television. AA offered in biology, chemistry, foreign language, history, mathematics, music, philosophy, physics, political science, psychology, religion, sociology. Interdisciplinary majors. Distributives and 2 religion or philosophy courses required. Independent study. Pass/fail. Internships, cooperative work/study. Preprofessional programs in law, medicine, theology. Courses may be taken at Des Moines Art Center. Cross-registration with Drake College, Des Moines Area Community College. Study abroad. AFROTC at Iowa State; ROTC at Drake. 72,000-volume library.
Financial CEEB CSS and ACT FAS. College scholarships, grants, loans, and activity awards; Lutheran scholarships, state scholarships and grants; PELL, SEOG, NSS, NDSL, GSL, CWS, college part-time employment. Application deadline March 1.
Admissions High school graduation with 15 units required. GED (45-point average) accepted. ACT or SAT required. $15 application fee. Rolling admissions. Suggested application deadlines March 1 (nursing), June 1 (other). $50 tuition and $25 room deposits due on acceptance of offer of admission. *Early Admission, Early Entrance, Concurrent Enrollment* programs. Transfers accepted. Credit possible for CEEB AP and CLEP subject exams, prior service-related experience, and departmental exams. Challenge program for nursing students.
Student Life Student government. Newspaper, radio and TV stations. Music, dance, drama, and sports clubs. Art club, literary criticism group. Honor societies. International Students Club. Concerned Black Students. Nursing clubs. Student Chapel Organization. Single-sex dorms. No married-student housing. 12% of students live on campus. 4 intercollegiate sports for men, 5 for women; intramurals. Club soccer. NAIA. Student body composition: 4% Asian, 4% Black, 1% Native American, 88% White, 3% Other. 4% from out of state.

[1] GRINNELL COLLEGE
Grinnell 50112, (515) 236-7545
Director of Admissions & Student Financial Aid: John R. Hopkins

- **Enrollment: 657m, 573w**
- **Tuition (1982/83): $6,522**
- **Room & Board: $2,000; Fees: $188**
- **Degree offered: BA**
- **Mean SAT 580v, 590m**
- **Student-faculty ratio: 11 to 1**

A private college established in 1846 in Grinnell. 90-acre small-town campus 300 miles west of Chicago and 55 miles east of Des Moines. Bus station. Airport 60 miles away in Cedar Rapids and in Des Moines.
Academic Character NCACS and professional accreditation. Semester system. Majors offered in American studies, anthropology, art, biology, chemistry, classics, economics, English, French, general science, German, history, mathematics, music, philosophy, physics, political science, psychology, religious studies, Russian, sociology, Spanish, theatre. Self-designed, interdepartmental, and interdisciplinary majors. General literary studies. No required courses except freshman tutorial. Pass/fail. Accelerated study. Internships. Phi Beta Kappa. Preprofessional programs in business, dentistry, government service, journalism, law, medicine, nursing, social work, theology. 3-2 engineering programs with CalTech, Columbia, RPI, Washington U (St. Louis). 3-3 law program with Columbia. Cooperative programs in nursing and medicine with Rush U; in special education certification with Drake U. Member of the Associated Colleges of the Midwest. Over 40 domestic and foreign off-campus programs. Exchange programs in Georgia and in Japan. 365-acre environmental research area, language lab, computer services, and art galleries. Over 250,000-volume library.
Financial CEEB CSS. College scholarships and loans, payment plan; PELL, SEOG, NDSL, FISL, GSL, college part-time employment program. Priority application deadline January 15 for scholarships and grants.
Admissions High school graduation with 16 units required. SAT or ACT required. $20 application fee. Application deadline February 15. Notification of admission March 1. $100 deposit required on acceptance of offer of admission. *Early Decision* and *Early Admission* programs. Admission deferral possible. Transfers accepted. Credit possible for CEEB AP exams.
Student Life Student government. Newspaper, literary magazine, yearbook, radio station. Music and dance groups. PIRG. Audubon Society. Women's group, Concerned Black Students. Outdoor Recreation Program. Athletic, academic, religious, service, and special interest groups. Some off-campus living allowed. Single-sex, coed, coop, and special interest housing. 92% of students live on campus. Financial aid recipients may not have cars; cars are discouraged in general. Liquor not permitted outside Pub or residence halls. Firearms prohibited in dorms. 11 intercollegiate sports for men, 8 for women; intramurals. AIAW, NCAA, Midwest Collegiate Athletic Conference. Student body composition: 2.5% Asian, 5% Black, 1.5% Hispanic, 0.2% Native American, 86% White, 4.8% Other. 89% from out of state.

[J1] HAWKEYE INSTITUTE OF TECHNOLOGY
Waterloo 50704

[J1] INDIAN HILLS COMMUNITY COLLEGE
Centerville 52544

■[J1] INDIAN HILLS COMMUNITY COLLEGE (IOWA TECHNICAL CAMPUS)
9th and College Streets, Ottumwa 52501

[1] IOWA, UNIVERSITY OF
Iowa City 52242, (319) 353-3976
Director of Admissions: John E. Moore

- **Undergraduates: 8,487m, 8,408w; 28,140 total (including graduates)**
- **Tuition (1982/83): $1,040 (in-state), $2,580 (out-of-state)**
- **Room & Board: $1,912**
- **Degrees offered: BA, BS, BMus, BFA, BGS, BLS, BBA, BSPharm, BSN, BSE in 6 areas**
- **Mean ACT 23**
- **Student-faculty ratio: 17 to 1**

A public university founded in 1847 in the small town of Iowa City. 1,375-acre campus on the Iowa River, 24 miles from Cedar Rapids. Airport, bus station.
Academic Character NCACS and professional accreditation. Semester system, 8-week summer term. 85 majors offered by the colleges of Liberal Arts, Business Administration, Dentistry, Education, Engineering, Law, Medicine, Nursing, Pharmacy. College of Liberal Arts includes the schools of Fine Arts, Journalism, Letters, Library Science, Mathematical Sciences, Religion, and Social Work. Self-designed majors. Distributive requirements. Graduate and professional degrees granted. Independent study. Honors program. Phi Beta Kappa. Pass/fail. Internships. Accelerated study. 5-year BA/BS engineering program. Cooperative program in medical technology. 3-2 physical therapy, 2-2 physician's assistant programs. Exchange with Iowa State and Northern Iowa U. Study abroad. Elementary, secondary, and special education certification. ROTC, AFROTC. Newspaper production lab, TV lab, language labs. Natural history museum. Iowa Geological Survey research facilities. Hospital School for severely handicapped children. 2,400,000-volume libraries.
Financial CEEB CSS and ACT FAS. University scholarships, grants, and loans; NSS, PELL, SEOG, NDSL, FISL, NSL, CWS, university part-time employment. Priority application deadline March 1.
Admissions High school graduation with 17 units required. ACT required. $10 application fee. Application deadlines March 1 (business, pharmacy, dental hygiene), January 15 (nursing), February 1 (physical therapy), 10 days before registration (liberal arts, engineering). Rolling admissions. Admission deferral possible. Transfers accepted. Credit possible for CEEB AP and CLEP exams, and for university departmental exams. Special admission programs for minority, disadvantaged, and non-high school graduate applicants.
Student Life Student government. Newspaper, 2 radio stations. Numerous clubs, including music, drama, debate, and religious groups. 18 fraternities and 15 sororities, all with chapter houses. 18% of men and 13% of women join. Coed and women's dorms. Married-student housing. Language houses. 26% of students live on campus. Parking on campus limited. 4 semester hours of phys ed required. Intercollegiate and intramural sports for men and women. Big Ten, AIAW. Student body composition: 1.1% Asian, 2% Black, 0.9% Hispanic, 0.3% Native American, 90.9% White, 4.8% Other. 28% from out of state.

[J1] IOWA CENTRAL COMMUNITY COLLEGE
330 Avenue M, Fort Dodge 50501, (800) 362-2793

- **Enrollment: 965m, 877w; 2,833 total (including part-time)**
- **Tuition (1982/83): $620 (in-state), $930 (out-of-state)**
- **Room & Board: $1,725**
- **Degrees offered: AA, AS, AAS, AGS**

A public college established in 1966. 3 campuses comprising 131 acres, in Eagle Grove, Fort Dodge, and Webster City. Rural area.
Academic Character NCACS accreditation. Semester system; 1 arts & sciences summer term and 5 voc-tech summer terms. 2-year transfer programs offered include agriculture, art, business administration, computer science, dental hygiene, education, engineering, food technology, home economics, hotel & restaurant management, liberal arts, library science, medical technology, nursing, physical therapy, physician's assistant. Career Option Programs (conferring AS degree or Certificate of Graduation) in community services, data processing, educational aide, environmental control technology, horticulture, law enforcement, supervision & administrative management. Vocational Technical Programs in agriculture, health occupations, marketing, office occupations, trades & industries. Secondary career programs for students still enrolled in high school. Numerous programs for the handicapped. Most students with Associates degrees transfer to senior college; those with Certificate of Graduation find jobs. Pass/fail. Preprofessional programs in chiropractice, dentistry, law, medicine, mortuary science, optometry, osteopathic medicine, pharmacy, veterinary medicine. Computer system, Instructional Materials Center (non-print resources). 60,000-volume library.
Financial CEEB CSS and ACT FAS. College scholarships, state vocational-technical tuition grants. PELL, SEOG, NDSL, GSL, NSL, CWS. Suggest applying early; first come-first served decisions.
Admissions Open admission to high school graduates; non-high school graduates and those still in high school may apply. $20 application fee. Rolling admissions; no deadline. *Early Admission, Early Decision* programs. Transfers accepted. Credit possible for CEEB AP and CLEP exams, college proficiency exams, and educational experience in the armed services.
Student Life Student government. Newspaper, yearbook. Music and drama groups. Special interest clubs. Single students under 20 must live at home or in college-approved housing. Dorms and dining facilities at Fort Dodge Center. Class attendance expected. 2 semester hours of phys ed required. 7 intercollegiate sports; intramurals. Iowa Area Community College Athletic Association.

[J1] IOWA LAKES COMMUNITY COLLEGE
Estherville 51334, (712) 362-2601

- **Undergraduates: 708m, 575w; 1,470 total (including part-time)**

• **Tuition (1982/83): $700**
• **Degrees offered: AA, AS, AAS**

A public junior college with campuses located in Estherville and Emmetsburg.
Academic Character NCACS accreditation. Trimester system, summer term. College transfer, vocational-technical, and adult education programs. Preprofessional, one- and two-year terminal, and career-option curricula. Diploma programs. Remedial mathematics and English programs.
Admissions Open admissions policy.
Student Life Student housing available both on and off campus. Full food service available on both campuses.

[1] IOWA STATE UNIVERSITY OF SCIENCE AND TECHNOLOGY

Ames 50011, (515) 294-5836
Dean of Admissions & Records: Fred C. Schlunz

• **Undergraduates: 13,118m, 8,224w; 24,906 total (including graduates)**
• **Tuition & Fees (1982/83): $1,040 (in-state), $2,580 (out-of-state)**
• **Room & Board: $1,762**
• **Degrees offered: BA, BS, BBA, BFA, BLA, BLS, BMus**
• **Mean ACT 23.4**
• **Student-faculty ratio: 19 to 1**

A public university established in 1858. 1,000-acre campus in a small city 30 miles north of Des Moines.
Academic Character NCACS and professional accreditation. Semester system, 8-week summer term. 124 majors offered by colleges of Agriculture, Design, Education, Engineering, Home Economics, and Science & Humanities. University also contains Veterinary Medicine and Graduate Colleges, and School of Business Administration. Preprofessional studies majors. Self-designed majors. Distributed Studies major may be departmental or interdepartmental. Optional minors. Distributive requirements. Graduate and professional degrees granted. Honors program, independent study. Phi Beta Kappa. Some pass/fail. Internships, cooperative work/study. International Service Program. Exchange with Regents Universities. Study abroad. Elementary, secondary, and special education certification. AFROTC, NROTC, ROTC. Many research centers, service agencies, and institutes on campus. Computation center. 1,413,991-volume library.
Financial CEEB CSS and ACT FAS. University scholarships, grants, and loans, state scholarships; PELL, SEOG, NDSL, GSL, CWS. Priority application deadline March 1.
Admissions High school graduation required; rank in upper 50% of class recommended. ACT or SAT required. $10 application fee. Rolling admissions; no deadline. *Concurrent Enrollment* and *Early Entrance* programs. Admission deferral possible. Transfers accepted. Credit possible for CEEB AP, CLEP subject, and university placement exams.
Student Life Student government. Newspaper, magazines, yearbook, radio and TV stations. Music, debate, and drama organizations. Special interest, service, professional, and honorary groups. 32 fraternities and 16 sororities, all with houses. 14% of men and 12% of women join. Married-student housing. 50% of students live on campus. Cars discouraged. Some departments have physical education requirements. 9 intercollegiate sports for men, 8 for women; intramurals. AIAW, NCAA, Big Eight. Student body composition: 0.8% Asian, 1.9% Black, 7.1% Foreign, 0.8% Hispanic, 0.1% Native American, 89.2% White. 27% from out of state.

[1] IOWA WESLEYAN COLLEGE

601 Main Street, Mount Pleasant 52641, (319) 385-8021, Toll-free to Admissions: (800) 582-2383
Director of Admissions: Laurie A. Wolf

• **Undergraduates: 185m, 386w; 720 total (including part-time)**
• **Tuition (1982/83): $4,600**
• **Room & Board: $1,670; Fees: $25**
• **Degrees offered: BA, BS, BSN, BMus Ed, AA, AFA**
• **Mean ACT 18**
• **Student-faculty ratio: 11 to 1**

A private college related to the United Methodist Church, established in 1842. 60-acre campus in small city of Mount Pleasant, 28 miles northwest of Burlington and the Mississippi River. Train and airport in Mount Pleasant.
Academic Character NCACS and professional accreditation. 4-1-4 system, summer term. 38 majors offered in areas of accounting, art, business, criminal justice, education, English, health sciences, history, home economics, math, music, natural sciences, philosophy, psychology, physical education, religion, and social sciences. Major in business education offered in cooperation with Southeastern Community College. BGS degree offered by continuing education program. Self-designed majors. Minors offered in most major fields and in communications. Independent study. Satisfactory/unsatisfactory grading and credit by exam possible. Cooperative work/study. Responsible Social Involvement Program offered by Center for Participative Learning for academic credit. Legislative Internship Program. Preprofessional programs in dentistry, law, library science, medicine, ministry, physical therapy, scientific research. 3-2 BS/MS forestry programs with Duke and Iowa State U. 3-1 medical technology program with Ottumwa School of Medical Technology; other 3-1 programs may be arranged. Accelerated admission possible to U of Iowa's MBA program. Study abroad. Elementary, secondary, and special education certification. Computer center. 105,000-volume library.
Financial CEEB CSS and ACT FAS. College scholarships, grants, and loans; ministerial and pre-theological assistance, United Methodist scholarships & loans, state tuition grants; PELL, SEOG, NSS, NDSL, GSL, NSL, CWS, college campus employment. Application deadline June 15.
Admissions High school graduation with 15 units required. GED accepted. SAT or ACT required. $15 application fee. Rolling admissions; no deadline. $100 deposit required on acceptance of offer of admission. *Early Admission* and *Early Decision* programs, summer program for advanced high school students for college credit. Admission deferral possible. Transfers accepted. Credit possible for CEEB AP and CLEP subject exams.
Student Life Student government. Newspaper, yearbook. Music, drama, and professional organizations. Honorary societies. Black Awareness Board. Many religious activities and groups. 2 fraternities and 3 sororities, all with houses. 18% of men and 27% of women join. All students live at home, on campus, or work for room and board in approved houses. Seniors with a 3.0 GPA may live off campus. Single-sex dorms with a visitation policy. No married-student housing. 80% of students live on campus. Class attendance expected. Swimming test or one semester of swimming instruction required; some majors require 2-4 terms of phys ed. 8 intercollegiate sports for men, 8 for women; intramurals. AIAW, NAIA. Student body composition: 1% Asian, 6% Black, 1% Hispanic, 1% Native American, 91% White. 46% from out of state.

[J1] IOWA WESTERN COMMUNITY COLLEGE

Clarinda 51632

[J2] IOWA WESTERN COMMUNITY COLLEGE

Council Bluffs 51502

[J1] KIRKWOOD COMMUNITY COLLEGE

6301 Kirkwood Blvd., SW, Cedar Rapids 52406, (319) 398-5411
Associate Head of Admissions: James Miller

• **Undergraduates: 1,595m, 1,865w; 5,437 total (including part-time)**
• **Tuition (1982/83): $585 (in-state), $1,170 (out-of-state)**
• **Degrees offered: AA, AS, AGS**
• **Mean ACT 19.1**

A public community college serving the counties of Benton, Linn, Jones, Iowa, Johnson, Cedar, Washington, and adjacent counties. Established in 1965. 315-acre countryside campus on the south edge of Cedar Rapids.
Academic Character NCACS accreditation. Trimester system, summer term. College parallel programs in accounting, agricultural science, anthropology, art, biochemistry, biology, biophysics, broadcasting, business administration, chemistry, computer science, economics, education, engineering, English, environmental studies, finance, foreign language, forestry, history, journalism, liberal arts, literature, math, music, nursing, physical education, political science, psychology, recreation, sociology, speech, statistics. College parallel/career option programs in aide for the handicapped, communications media & technology, criminal justice, fire science, human services, international trade, legal assistant, purchasing, teacher associate, pre-environmental science & forestry. Several vocational-technical, diploma, and certificate programs. Distributive requirements. Credit by exam possible. Community Education Division with several centers throughout the area. Vocational programs for high school students. Correspondence studies. Several remedial learning centers and programs. Library on campus.
Financial College scholarships and loans, state scholarships and loans; PELL, SEOG, NSS, NDSL, GSL. Apply between January 1 and June 1.
Admissions High school graduation or GED required. Mature adults who have not completed high school may be admitted on an individual basis. Admission to the college does not insure admission to all programs offered. Interview and tests may be required. ACT recommended for Arts & Science applicants. Rolling admissions; suggest applying during senior year. *Early Decision, Early Admission* programs. Transfers accepted. Credit possible for CEEB AP and CLEP exams.
Student Life Student government. Newspaper. Several academic and special interest clubs. No college on-campus housing, but approved housing available. 3 intercollegiate sports for men, 3 for women; intramurals. Iowa Area Community College Athletic Association.

[1] LORAS COLLEGE

Dubuque 52001, (319) 588-7100
Director of Admissions: Daniel P. Conry

• **Enrollment: 1,050m, 815w**
• **Tuition (1982/83): $4,000**
• **Room & Board: $1,990; Fees: $200**
• **Degrees offered: BA, BS, BMus, AA, AS**
• **Mean ACT 22.5**
• **Student-faculty ratio: 17 to 1**

A private Roman Catholic college conducted by the Archdiocese of Dubuque; established in 1839 and became coed in 1971. 60-acre campus in residential Dubuque. Airport, bus and train stations in Dubuque.
Academic Character NCACS and professional accreditation. Semester system, 3 3-week summer terms. 34 majors offered by the divisions of Humanities, Social & Behavioral Studies, Natural Science, Philosophy & Religious Studies, and Professional Studies. 4 education majors possible through Tri-College Cooperative (cross-registration with Clarke College, U of Dubuque). Self-designed majors. Distributives and 12 hours of theology/philosophy required. Thesis or comprehensives required in some majors. Masters degrees granted. Independent study, internships. Accelerated study. Honors program. Credit by exam, pass/fail. St. Pius X Seminary located on campus. Preprofessional programs in dentistry, ecclesiastical areas, engineering, law, medicine, mortuary science. 3-1 medical technology program, other 3-1 programs may be arranged with recognized professional schools. 2-4 architecture program. 2-2 and 3-2 engineering with Iowa State, U of Iowa, U of Illinois, Notre Dame. 2-3 nursing with U of Iowa. Junior year abroad. Elementary, secondary, and special education certification. Language lab, computer facilities. 259,000-volume library.
Financial ACT FAS. College scholarships, loans, athletic grants-in-aid; state scholarships, grants, loans; PELL, SEOG, FISL, GSL, NDSL, CWS, college

part-time employment. Priority application deadline April 1.
Admissions High school graduation required; 16 units recommended. GED accepted. ACT or SAT required. $15 application fee. Rolling admissions; application deadline August 15. $65 deposit due on acceptance of offer of admission. *Early Admission* and *Early Decision* programs. Admission deferral possible. Transfers accepted. Credit possible for CEEB SAT, AP, CLEP, and ACT exams.
Student Life Student government. Newspaper, yearbook. Honor societies. Music groups. Numerous athletic, professional, and special interest clubs. Freshmen and sophomores must live at home or on campus. Coed and single-sex dorms. 65% of students live on campus. Class attendance expected. 9 intercollegiate sports for men, 8 for women; intramurals. AIAW, NAIA. Student body composition: 1% Black, 98% White, 1% Other. 40% from out of state.

[1] LUTHER COLLEGE
Decorah 52101, (319) 387-1287
Dean of Admissions & Financial Aid: David J. Roslien

- **Enrollment: 932m, 1,178w**
- **Tuition (1982/83): $5,225**
- **Room & Board: $1,675**
- **Degree offered: BA**
- **Mean SAT 525v, 560m**
- **Student-faculty ratio: 15 to 1**

A private Lutheran Church-affiliated college established in 1861. 800-acre small-town campus in the northeast corner of Iowa 15 miles south of Minnesota. Airport and bus depot in Decorah, train station in LaCrosse, WI.
Academic Character NCACS and professional accreditation. 4-1-4 system, 2 4-week summer terms. Over 35 majors offered by the divisions of mathematics & science, social sciences, and humanities, including computer science, nursing, Black studies, Scandinavian studies, political science, classical languages, and linguistics. Interdisciplinary majors offered in health education, psychobiology, and sociology-political science. Distributive requirements. Senior research paper and 3 religion or philosophy courses required for graduation. Independent study allows credit by exam. Honors program. Pass/fail. Preprofessional programs in most fields. 3-2 program in engineering with Washington U. 3-1 program in medical technology arrangeable with 8 affiliated hospitals. 3-1 medical programs possible. 2-2 or 3-2 nursing programs. 2-3 pharmacy program. Iowa General Assembly Legislative Intern Program, Washington Semester. Study abroad. Primary and secondary education certification. Planetarium, museum. Computer center, language lab. 250,000-volume library.
Financial CEEB CSS and ACT FAS. College scholarships and grants; church scholarships, state scholarships and grants; PELL, SEOG, NDSL, FISL, GSL, CWS. Application deadline May 1.
Admissions High school graduation with 15 units required. SAT, ACT, or PSAT required. $20 application fee. Rolling admissions; no deadline. $100 deposit required on acceptance of offer of admission. *Early Admission* Program. Admission deferral possible. Transfers accepted. Credit possible for CEEB AP and CLEP subject exams. Upward Bound summer project for financially disadvantaged high school students.
Student Life Student government. Newspaper, literary magazine, yearbook. Radio station. Music, debate, drama clubs. Black Student Union, Black Cultural Center. Social and academic organizations. 11 fraternities and 4 sororities. 50% of men and 45% of women join. All students live at home or on campus. Coed and single-sex dorms. Married-student housing. 95% of students live on campus. Academic honor system. 2 phys ed courses required. 12 intercollegiate sports for men, 8 for women. AIAW, NCAA, Iowa Conference. Student body composition: 4% Black, 94% White, 2% Other. 48% from out of state.

[1] MAHARISHI INTERNATIONAL UNIVERSITY
Fairfield 52556, (515) 472-5031

- **Undergraduates: 314m, 196w; 562 total (including part-time)**
- **Tuition (1982/83): $4,320**
- **Room & Board: $1,755-$2,160**
- **Degrees offered: BA, BS**

A private university founded in 1972 by Maharishi Mahesh Yogi to offer education based on the principles that knowledge is structured in consciousness and higher education is for higher consciousness. Small-town campus 110 miles southwest of Des Moines.
Academic Character NCACS accreditation. Semester system. Undergraduate study begins with the Science of Creative Intelligence course, which offers instruction in Transcendental Meditation (a mental technique for experiencing pure creative intelligence and developing the student's full potential) and provides knowledge of the source, course, and goal of creative intelligence, the impelling force in the universe which continually gives rise to new expressions of life and order. This course provides the foundation of the MIU education, since at MIU each discipline is studied in the light of the Science of Creative Intelligence. 1st-year comprehensive interdisciplinary studies program of 24 core courses; each course is studied intensively for one week at a time, and presents the traditional academic disciplines in the light of the universal principles of orderliness and evolution developed within the Science of Creative Intelligence. 2nd-year one-month core courses in biology, mathematics, and physics; electives may be selected from art, business administration, literature, philosophy, psychology. Major begins in the 3rd year; majors currently offered are in business administration, computer science, law, government, and public affairs. Curriculum also includes a series of 8 one-month courses: Themes of Human Development, which are taken at regular intervals throughout the 4 years of study. They examine selected topics of human development and provide students with extended periods for practice of the Transcendental Meditation Technique which gives increased knowledge and experience of the field of pure creative intelligence. MIU is the only University in the world to offer the TM-Sidhi program. MA granted. Remedial math and English programs. 51,000-volume library with access to over 8,000,000 volumes.
Financial Iowa Tuition Grants, PELL, SEOG, NDSL, GSL, CWS.
Admissions All applicants considered on individual merit. Applications accepted for any semester. CEEB SAT required. Admission deferral possible.
Student Life Dorms and dining hall on campus.

[J1] MARSHALLTOWN COMMUNITY COLLEGE
3700 South Center Street, Marshalltown 50158

[1] MARYCREST COLLEGE
1607 West 12th Street, Davenport 52804, (319) 326-9226

- **Enrollment: 83m, 359w; 1,295 total (including part-time)**
- **Tuition (1982/83): $4,140**
- **Room & Board: $1,880-$2,490; Fees: $80**
- **Degrees offered: BA, BS, BASpecial Studies, BSN**
- **Mean ACT 18**

A private college founded in 1939 by the Congregation of the Humility of Mary. 20-acre urban campus in southwestern Davenport overlooking the Mississippi River. Airport, bus and train stations in Davenport.
Academic Character NCACS and professional accreditation. Semester system, 3 summer terms. Broad major areas cover art, biology, business administration, chemistry, communication & theatre arts, computer science/math, education, English, French, general science, history, home economics, humanities, library science, music, nursing, philosophy, pre-law, religious studies, social work, Spanish. Distributives and 5 semester hours of religious studies and/or philosophy required. MA granted. Independent study. Pass/no pass and satisfactory/unsatisfactory grading options. Preprofessional programs include dentistry, law, medicine. 80,000-volume library.
Financial CEEB CSS and ACT FAS. College and state scholarships and grants; PELL, SEOG, NDSL, GSL, NSL, CWS, deferred payment plan. Application deadline May 1.
Admissions High school graduation required. GED accepted. ACT or SAT required. $15 application fee. Rolling admissions; suggest applying at beginning of 12th year. $35 tuition and $50 room deposits required on acceptance of offer of admission. *Concurrent Enrollment* Program. Transfers accepted. Credit possible for CEEB CLEP and for departmental exams.
Student Life Student government. Newspaper, magazine. Several academic organizations. Coffeehouse. Underclassmen under 21 must live on campus or at home. 3 dorms. 2 intercollegiate sports for men, 2 for women; club and intramural sports.

[1] MORNINGSIDE COLLEGE
Sioux City 51106, (712) 274-5111
Director of Admissions: Fred Erbes

- **Enrollment: 603m, 763w**
- **Tuition (1982/83): $4,650**
- **Room & Board: $1,660; Fees: $130**
- **Degrees offered: BA, BS, BSN, BMus, BMus Ed, AA**
- **Mean ACT 22**
- **Student-faculty ratio: 16 to 1**

A private college established in 1894, related to United Methodist Church. 27-acre campus in suburban Sioux City, on the Missouri River. Airport, bus and train stations in Sioux City.
Academic Character NCACS and professional accreditation. Semester system, 2 5-week summer terms. 41 majors offered in the areas of art, business, communication, computers, criminal justice, drama, education, health, history, math, modern languages, music, natural science, philosophy, physics, political science, psychology, religion, social work, sociology, speech. Divisional majors in humanities, natural sciences, and social sciences. Minor required; possible in most major areas and in American Indian studies. Distributives and 1 philosophy/religion course required. Oral and written language proficiency required for graduation. MAT granted. Independent study. Departmental tutorials for juniors and seniors. Interdepartmental Honors Program. Some pass/fail. Preprofessional programs in many areas. Cooperative program in home economics with Iowa State. 3-3 and 4-3 law and medicine programs may be arranged. 2-3 engineering with U of Iowa, Iowa State. 2-2 nursing with U of Iowa. United Nations and Washington Semesters. Study abroad. Elementary and secondary education certification. Observatory, computer center. 135,000-volume library.
Financial ACT FAS (preferred) and CEEB CSS. College scholarships and grants, talent grants, ministry and ministerial rebates, state tuition grants, Methodist loans, vocational rehabilitation grants; PELL, SEOG, NDSL, GSL, CWS, college part-time employment. Application deadlines June 1 (college aid), March 1 (federal aid).
Admissions High school graduation with 16 units required. GED accepted. ACT or SAT required. Interview recommended. No application fee. Rolling admissions; application deadline August 15. $50 deposit required on acceptance of offer of admission. *Early Admission* and *Early Decision* programs. Admission deferral possible. Transfers accepted. Credit possible for CEEB AP and CLEP general exams.
Student Life Student government. Newspaper, literary magazine, yearbook, radio station. Music and drama organizations. Outing center. Cultural and convocation series. Honor societies. 3 fraternities and 2 sororities. 16% of men and 18% of women join. Seniors may live off campus. Dorms for men and women. Married-student housing. Non-prescription or illegal drugs prohibited. Liquor allowed in dorm rooms only. 7 intercollegiate sports for men, 3 for women; intramurals. AIAW, NAIA, NCAA, North Central

Intercollegiate Conference. Student body composition: 1% Asian, 2% Black, 0.4% Hispanic, 1% Native American, 93.5% White. 20% from out of state.

[1] MOUNT MERCY COLLEGE
1330 Elmhurst Drive NE, Cedar Rapids 52402, (319) 363-8213
Director of Admissions: Donald McCormick

- **Enrollment: 321m, 800w**
- **Tuition & Fees (1982/83): $3,970**
- **Room & Board: $1,750-$2,340**
- **Degrees offered: BA, BS, BAA, BAS**
- **Mean ACT 20**
- **Student-faculty ratio: 13 to 1**

A private college operated by the Sisters of Mercy. Established in 1928 and became coed in 1969. 30-acre campus in urban Cedar Rapids, 230 miles from Chicago. Airport and bus station in Cedar Rapids.
Academic Character NCACS and professional accreditation. 4-1-4 system, 2 5- or 6-week and 1 10- or 12-week summer terms. Majors offered in accounting, art, biology, business administration, business education, computer science, criminal justice administration, elementary education, English, history, math, music, music education, nursing, piano pedagogy, political science, psychology, public relations, religious studies, social work, sociology, speech & drama. Self-designed majors. Minors. Distributives and 1 religious studies course required. Independent study. Pass/fail, credit by exam. Preprofessional programs in agriculture, environmental sciences, health sciences, law, mortuary science, and theology. 3-1 medical technology program with any AMA-approved hospital. Cross-registration with Coe College. Elementary and secondary education certification. Computer center. 65,000-volume library.
Financial CEEB CSS (preferred) and ACT FAS. College scholarships, state scholarships and grants; PELL, SEOG, NDSL, GSL, NSL, CWS, college part-time employment. Application deadline March 1.
Admissions High school graduation with 16 units required. GED accepted. Interview encouraged. ACT, PSAT, or SAT required. $10 application fee. Rolling admissions; suggest applying early in 12th year. $50 housing deposit due on acceptance of offer of admission. *Concurrent Enrollment* Program. Admission deferral possible. Transfers accepted. Credit possible for CEEB AP and CLEP exams, and for college advanced placement program in English.
Student Life Student government. Drama, music, and art productions. Speaker, film series. Major area clubs. Contemporary issues, voluntary projects, and international living organizations. Freshmen may not have cars without college's permission. Single underclassmen under 21 must live at home, on campus, or work in an approved home for room & board. Liquor prohibited in dorms. Modified honor system. 3 intercollegiate sports for men, 4 for women; intramurals. NAIA. Student body composition: 5% Black, 95% White. 8% from out of state.

[1] MOUNT SAINT CLARE COLLEGE
400 North Bluff Blvd., Clinton 52732, (319) 242-4023
Director of Admissions: Sister Evelyn McKenna

- **Tuition (1982/83): $2,450**
- **Room & Board: $1,950; Fees: $75**
- **Degrees offered: BA, AA, AAS**
- **Mean ACT 19**

A private college operated by the Sisters of St. Francis. Founded in 1895 and became coed in 1967. Small-city campus on the west bank of the Mississippi River 150 miles west of Chicago.
Academic Character NCACS accreditation. Semester system, summer term. Transfer and terminal programs available. BA offered in business administration, accounting, and business administration/accounting. AAS offered in clerical assistant, early childhood education, executive secretary, medical secretary. AA offered in accounting, art, biology, business, chemistry, cytotechnology, early childhood education, elementary & secondary education, English, French, history, liberal arts, math, medical technology, music, philosophy, psychology, secretarial science, Spanish, speech therapy, theology. Several pre-professional programs in biomedical sciences and in law. Distributives and 2 semester hours of theology required. Credit by exam possible. English as a second language program. 23,000-volume library.
Financial CEEB CSS and ACT FAS. College and state scholarships, local scholarships and grants, state grants; PELL, SEOG, GSL, NDSL, CWS, campus employment. Application deadline is March 1.
Admissions High school graduation required, with 3 English units and college-prep distribution of courses. Applicants to a science/health programs should have more science & math. GED accepted. SAT or ACT required. $15 application fee. Rolling admissions. *Early Admission, Early Decision, Concurrent Enrollment* programs. Admission deferral possible. Transfers accepted. Credit possible for CEEB CLEP exams, non-traditional and experiential learning (PENTEL), military courses, and college placement exams.
Student Life Student government. Several academic clubs. Honor societies. Freshmen and sophomores must live at home or on campus. 1 coed dorm. Honor code. Liquor and smoking allowed only in dorm rooms and in student lounge. Neither use nor abuse of drugs allowed on campus. 2 semester hours of phys ed required. Intercollegiate basketball for men and women. Intramural and recreational sports offered. Iowa-Illinois College Conference.

[J1] MUSCATINE COMMUNITY COLLEGE
Muscatine 52761

[J1] NORTH IOWA AREA COMMUNITY COLLEGE
500 College Drive, Mason City 50401, (515) 421-4399
Director of Admissions & Counseling: Joseph V. Critelli

- **Enrollment: 854m, 833w**
- **Tuition & Fees (1982/83): $670 (in-state), $960 (out-of-state)**
- **Room & Board: $1,750**
- **Degrees offered: AA, AS, AAS, AGS, AS in Business**

A public community junior college and vocational technical school founded in 1966. Campus 4 miles east of downtown Mason City.
Academic Character NCACS accreditation. Semester system, summer term. 2-year, 1-year, and 9-month programs in accounting, ag-power mechanics, agricultural business, automotive service, building trades, clerical, electronics technology, electronics, farm management, general business, horticulture, industrial maintenance/electrician, law enforcement, mechanical design technology, medical assistant, nursing, optometric assistant, refrigeration-air conditioning, retail merchandising, secretarial, welding, wholesale marketing. College transfer programs in agriculture, architecture, business, computer science, education, social work, engineering, health-related program, home economics, journalism, law, mortuary science, phys ed, psychology, social work, veterinary medicine. Diploma and certificate programs. Extensive evening school programs. 30,000-volume library.
Financial CEEB CSS and ACT FAS. College and state scholarships and loans; PELL, SEOG, NSS, NDSL, GSL, NSL, CWS, college part-time employment.
Admissions High school graduation or GED required. ACT required for nursing; recommended for transfer programs. Interview may be required. Apply any time after junior year of high school. Rolling admissions. Credit possible for CEEB CLEP exams, proficiency exams, and education received while in the armed forces.
Student Life Student government. Newspaper. Theatre and music clubs. Honorary, academic, special interest organizations. Religious and political groups. Students under 21 must live on campus or at home. 3 intercollegiate sports for men, 3 for women. Iowa Athletic and Activity Association of Community and Junior Colleges.

[J1] NORTHEAST AREA ONE VOCATIONAL SCHOOL
PO Box 400, Calmar 52132

[1] NORTHERN IOWA, UNIVERSITY OF
Cedar Falls 50614, (319) 273-2281
Director of Admissions: Jack Wielenga

- **Undergraduates: 3,585m, 4,624w; 10,900 total (including graduates)**
- **Tuition (1982/83): $1,990 (in-state), $2,040 (out-of-state)**
- **Room & Board: $1,648**
- **Degrees offered: BA, BFA, BLS, BMus, BT**
- **Mean ACT 21**
- **Student-faculty ratio: 16 to 1**

A public university established in 1876. 723-acre campus in small city of Cedar Falls, seven miles from Waterloo. Airport and bus station.
Academic Character NCACS and professional accreditation. Semester system, 2 4-week summer terms. 79 majors offered by the colleges of Education, Humanities & Fine Arts, Natural Sciences, Social & Behavioral Sciences, and the schools of Business and Music. Self-designed individual and general studies majors. Minors. Distributive requirements. Graduate and professional degrees granted. Independent study. Credit by exam, pass/no credit. Internships, cooperative work/study. Preprofessional programs in dentistry, engineering, law, medicine, osteopathy, podiatry. Cooperative nursing program. Exchange programs with U of Iowa, Iowa State U. Study abroad. Elementary, secondary, and special education certification. ROTC. Lakeside biology lab and field lab. Educational media center. Curriculum lab. Museum, lab school. 550,000-volume library.
Financial CEEB CSS and ACT FAS. University scholarships, athletic grants-in-aid, loans; PELL, SEOG, NDSL, FISL, CWS. Application deadline March 1.
Admissions High school graduation with 12 units required. ACT required. $10 application fee. Rolling admissions; deadline August 1. *Concurrent Enrollment* and university early decision programs. Admission deferral possible. Transfers accepted. Credit possible for CEEB AP and CLEP exams, and for university proficiency exams. Center for Urban Education, Educational Talent Search Program, EOP for academically disadvantaged applicants.
Student Life Student government. Newspaper, other student publications, radio station. Music, drama, and debate organizations. Special interest groups. Honorary clubs. Religious activities. Annual Artists Series. 6 fraternities with houses, and 6 sororities, some with houses. Coed and single-sex dorms. Married-student housing. 45% of students live on campus. 2 to 4 semester hours of phys ed required. 10 intercollegiate sports for men, 9 for women; intramurals. NCAA, AIAW, Mid-Continent Conference. Student body composition: 2% Black, 97% White, 1% Other. 3% from out of state.

[J1] NORTHWEST IOWA TECHNICAL COLLEGE
Highway 18 West, Sheldon 51201

[1] NORTHWESTERN COLLEGE
Orange City 51041, (712) 737-4821
Director of Admissions: Ronald K. DeJong

- **Enrollment: 410m, 461w**
- **Tuition (1982/83): $3,900**
- **Room & Board: $1,780**
- **Degree offered: BA**
- **Mean ACT 22**
- **Student-faculty ratio: 16 to 1**

A private college established in 1882, sponsored by the Reformed Church in

America. 35-acre rural campus 40 miles from Sioux City. Airport and bus station.

Academic Character NCACS and professional accreditation. Semester system, 2- and 6-week summer terms. Majors offered in art, behavioral sciences, biology, business/economics, chemistry, communications, education, English, French, history, humanities, library science, math, math/physics, music, natural science, philosophy, physical education, political science teaching, psychology, religion, social science, social work, sociology, Spanish, theatre, theatre/speech. Self-designed majors. Minors. Distributives and 3 religion courses required. Independent and directed study. Internships. Pass/fail. Junior year cross-cultural experience. Undergraduate Record Exams may be required. Preprofessional programs in 20 areas, including agriculture, art, mortuary science, music. Cooperative 3-2 physical therapy program. 3-1 medical technology program. Member of Colleges of Mid-America and Christian College Coalition. Chicago Urban Semester, Washington Semester. Study abroad. Library science, elementary, secondary, and special education certification. Language lab. 75,000-volume library.

Financial CEEB CSS and ACT FAS. College scholarships, grants, loans, state grants; PELL, SEOG, NDSL, FISL, college part-time employment. Suggest applying early.

Admissions High school graduation with 15 units required. GED accepted. ACT or SAT required. Interview encouraged. $15 application fee. Rolling admissions; suggest applying early. $40 general deposit required on acceptance of offer of admission. *Early Decision* Program. Admission deferral possible. Transfers accepted. Credit possible for CEEB AP and CLEP exams, and for college proficiency exams. Provisional and probational enrollment possible.

Student Life Student government. Newspaper, literary magazines, yearbook. Art, music, and drama organizations. Religious and political clubs. Academic clubs. Black Student Union. Special interest and athletic groups. Students must live on campus or at home. Single-sex dorms. Parietals. 85% of students live on campus. Liquor and unauthorized drugs not allowed. Class attendance required. 2 semester hours of physical education required. Attendance at chapel 3 times a week required. 9 intercollegiate sports for men, 7 for women; intramurals. AIAW, NAIA. Student body composition: 1% Asian, 2% Black, 97% White. 30% from out of state.

[P] OPEN BIBLE COLLEGE
2633 Fleur Drive, Des Moines 50321

[P] OSTEOPATHIC MEDICINE SCIENCES, UNIVERSITY OF
3200 Grand Avenue, Des Moines 50312

[P] OTTUMWA SCHOOL OF MEDICAL TECHNOLOGY
1005 East Pennsylvania, Ottumwa 52501

[P] PALMER COLLEGE OF CHIROPRACTIC
1000 Brady Street, Davenport 52803

[1] ST. AMBROSE COLLEGE
Davenport 52803, (319) 383-8888
Dean of Admissions: James T. Barry

- **Enrollment: 1,146m, 913w**
- **Tuition (1982/83): $4,350**
- **Room & Board: $1,900; Fees: $60**
- **Degrees offered: BA, BS, BMus, BMus Ed, BSpecial & BElected Studies**
- **Mean ACT 18**
- **Student-faculty ratio: 16 to 1**

A private college affiliated with the Roman Catholic Church. Founded in 1882 and became coed in 1968. 23-acre campus in Davenport, part of Quad Cities. Airport, bus and train stations.

Academic Character NCACS accreditation. Semester system. Majors offered in accounting, art, biology, business administration, chemistry, classical/modern languages, computer science, criminal justice, criminalistics, criminology, economics, elementary education, English, history, industrial engineering, management science/statistics, mass communication, mathematics, mathematics education, music, music education, natural science, philosophy, phys ed/recreation, physics, political science, psychology, public administration, sociology, speech & theatre, theology. Special studies and elected studies. Minors in the above and in geography, justice, peace, women's studies. MBA granted. Distributives and 9 semester hours of philosophy or theology required. Independent study, seminars. Internships, cooperative work/study. Honors program. Pass/fail. Undergraduate Record Exams required for graduation. Preprofessional programs in chiropractic, law, theology. 2-year pre-engineering transfer program. 2-3 engineering with U of Detroit. Study abroad. Elementary and secondary education certification. Observatory, language lab. 110,000-volume library.

Financial CEEB CSS and ACT FAS. College scholarships and grants, state tuition grants; PELL, SEOG, NDSL, GSL, FISL, CWS, college part-time employment. Application deadline March 1.

Admissions High school graduation required with 15 units recommended. GED accepted. SAT or ACT required. $15 application fee. Rolling admissions. $100 deposit required on acceptance of offer of admission. *Early Decision* and *Concurrent Enrollment* programs. Admission deferral possible. Transfers accepted. Credit possible for CEEB AP and CLEP exams. Special admission programs for disadvantaged and minority students.

Student Life Student government. Newspaper, yearbook, radio and TV stations. Music groups. Black Student Union. Veterans Club. Political, religious, and academic groups. Community service, athletic, honorary, and special interest groups. 4 fraternities and 4 sororities. 5% of men and women join. Students not from Quad Cities must live and board on campus. Dorms for men and women. No married-student housing. 30% of students live on campus. 1 semester of phys ed required. 5 intercollegiate sports for men, 4 for women; intramurals. Student body composition: 0.1% Asian, 2.4% Black, 0.2% Native American, 96.6% White. 30% from out of state.

[J1] SCOTT COMMUNITY COLLEGE
Bettendorf 52722

[1] SIMPSON COLLEGE
Indianola 50125, (515) 961-6251
Director of Admissions: John Kellogg

- **Undergraduates: 345m, 375w; 1,065 total (including part-time)**
- **Tuition (1982/83): $4,980**
- **Room & Board: $1,795; Fees: $55**
- **Degrees offered: BA, BMus**
- **Mean ACT 22**
- **Student-faculty ratio: 14 to 1**

A private college established in 1860 and affiliated with the Methodist Church. 61-acre campus in suburban Indianola, 12 miles south of Des Moines. Bus station in Indianola, airport in Des Moines.

Academic Character NCACS and professional accreditation. 4-1-4 system, 2 6-week summer terms. Majors offered in accounting, agricultural resources management, American studies, applied music, art, biology, chemistry, computer science, corrections, criminal justice, economics, early childhood education, education, English, environmental studies, French, German, health care administration, history, international management, international relations, management, math, music, music education, natural science & management, philosophy, phys ed, political science, psychology, religion, social work, sociology, Spanish, special education, speech communication, theatre arts. Special majors, minors. Distributive requirements. Independent study. Honors programs. Pass/fail. Preprofessional programs in dentistry, engineering, law, medicine, nursing, theology. Cooperative programs with 8 colleges and 2 hospitals. Washington and UN Semesters. Study abroad. Elementary, secondary, and special education certification. 120,000-volume library.

Financial CEEB CSS and ACT FAS. College scholarships and grants, state tuition grants, ministerial grants, multi-dependency grants, Methodist loans; PELL, SEOG, NDSL, GSL, CWS, college part-time employment. Application deadline June 1.

Admissions High school graduation required with 14 units recommended. GED accepted. SAT or ACT required. Interview recommended. No application fee. Rolling admissions; application deadline August 1. $100 deposit required on acceptance of offer of admission. College early decision and *Early Entrance* programs. Admission deferral possible. Transfers accepted. Credit possible for CEEB AP and CLEP exams.

Student Life Student government. Newspaper, literary magazine, yearbook. Music and debate organizations. Campus Activity board. Concerned Black Students. Honor societies. 3 fraternities and 3 sororities, all with houses. 35% of men and 28% of women join. Students must live at home or on campus. Coed and single-sex dorms. Married-student housing. 70% of students live on campus. 7 intercollegiate sports for men, 6 for women; intramurals. AIAW, NCAA. Student body composition: 1% Asian, 5% Black, 1% Hispanic, 90% White, 3% Other. 20% from out of state.

IA-52

[J2] SIOUX EMPIRE COLLEGE
Hawarden 51031

[J1] SOUTHEASTERN COMMUNITY COLLEGE
Drawer F, Highway 406, West Burlington 52655

[J1] SOUTHWESTERN COMMUNITY COLLEGE
Creston 50801

[J2] UNITED ELECTRONICS INSTITUTE
1119 Fifth Street, West Des Moines 50265

[1] UPPER IOWA UNIVERSITY
Fayette 52142, (800) 632-5954 in Iowa, or (800) 553-4152, 4155
Director of Admissions: Paul H. Jones

- **Enrollment: 275m, 200w**
- **Tuition (1982/83): $4,100**
- **Room & Board: $1,900; Fees: $220**
- **Degrees offered: BA, BS, BAS, BGS, BSN**
- **Mean ACT 20**
- **Student-faculty ratio: 10 to 1**

A private university founded in 1857. 10-acre campus in Fayette, about 50 miles northeast of Waterloo. Branch campus in Mason City.

Academic Character NCACS accreditation. 4-4-2 system, summer terms. Majors offered in art, biology, business administration, chemistry, education, English, history, mathematics/computer science, music, political science, psychology, sociology, speech & theatre, and health, physical education, & recreation. Nursing major for students with an RN. BAS degree combines liberal arts and vocational-technical programs, and is offered to students with an AAS. Some majors are offered in conjunction with Hawkeye Institute of Technology. Minor required with education and mortuary science; possible in

all major areas and in French. Additional courses in geography, German, philosophy/religion, physics. Pass/fail. Coordinated Off-Campus Degree Program: BA in public or business administration. 3-1 medical technology program may be arranged with an approved school. Preprofessional programs in chiropractic, dentistry, law, medicine, medical technology, nursing, optometry, osteopathy, pharmacy, physical therapy, physician's assistant (with U of Iowa), podiatry. ROTC. 100,000-volume library.
Financial University scholarships and loans, sibling grants, various federal and state programs, NDSL, FISL, CWS, university part-time employment.
Admissions High school graduation with 16 units required. ACT or SAT required. Interview recommended. $25 application fee. Rolling admissions; suggest applying between October and July. $100 tuition deposit required on acceptance of offer of admission. *Concurrent Enrollment, Early Decision, Early Admission* programs. Admission deferral possible. Transfers accepted. Credit possible for CLEP exams. Conditional enrollment possible.
Student Life Student government. Newspaper, yearbook. Academic clubs, honor societies. Political and expressive arts organizations. Religious groups. Social fraternities. All students must live on campus (off-campus living may be approved). Dorms. Married-student housing. 1 semester hour of phys ed required. 8 intercollegiate sports for men, 5 for women; intramurals. IIAA, NCAA. Student body composition: 10% minority.

[P] VENNARD COLLEGE
University Park 52595

[J1] WALDORF COLLEGE
Forest City 50436, (515) 582-2450
Director of Admissions: Steve Lovik

- **Enrollment: 228m, 176w; 411 total (including part-time)**
- **Tuition & Fees (1982/83): $4,150**
- **Room & Board: $2,020**
- **Degrees offered: AA, ABusiness Studies, AAS**
- **Student-faculty ratio: 13 to 1**

A private college owned and operated by the American Lutheran Church. Campus of 10 buildings in small town of Forest City, midway between Minneapolis-St. Paul and Des Moines. Airport.
Academic Character NCACS accreditation. Semester system. Majors in art, biology, business, chemistry, computer science, English, foreign languages, history, human services, industrial education, math, music, parish ministries, phys ed, science, sociology, speech. Transfer and terminal degree programs. First 2 years of a 4-year program offered in agriculture, home economics, journalism, law, political science, social science. Distributives and 6 semester credits of religion required. Independent study. Honors programs. Cooperative work/study. 29,000-volume library.
Financial CEEB CSS and ACT FAS. College scholarships and grants, state scholarships and grants; PELL, SEOG, NDSL, GSL, university part-time employment. Apply with admissions application.
Admissions High school graduation required. ACT, SAT, or PSAT required. $15 application fee. Rolling admissions; no deadline. *Early Admission* Program. $50 deposit required on acceptance of offer of admission.
Student Life Student government. Newspaper, yearbook. Musical activities. Educational and social organizations. Religious and political activities and groups. Black Student Union. Ski club. Students must live at home or on campus. Dorms. Parietals. Liquor and illegal drugs prohibited on campus. Class attendance and 3 semester credits of phys ed required. 5 intercollegiate sports for men, 3 for women; intramurals. NJCAA, Iowa Area Community College Athletic Association.

[1] WARTBURG COLLEGE
Waverly 50677, (319) 352-1200
Director of Admissions: Drew Boster

- **Enrollment: 475m, 603w**
- **Tuition (1982/83): $4,600**
- **Room & Board: $1,880; Fees: $150**
- **Degrees offered: BA, BSMus, BMus Ed**
- **Mean ACT 21.8**
- **Student-faculty ratio: 15 to 1**

A private college, established in 1852 and affiliated with the American Lutheran Church. 83-acre campus in Waverly, 100 miles from Des Moines, 20 miles from Waterloo. Shuttle to and from airports; train and bus stations within an hour from school.
Academic Character NCACS and professional accreditation. 4-4-1 system. 2 6-week summer terms. Majors offered in accounting, art, art education, biology, business administration, business education, chemistry, communication arts, computer science/math, economics, elementary education, English, French, German, history, leisure services, math, music, philosophy, phys ed, physics, political science, psychology, religion, social studies teaching, social work, sociology, Spanish. Individual and interdepartmental majors. 3-1 medical technology, 3-2 physical therapy programs. Minors. Chrysalis program for 60 freshmen: integrated humanities program. Distributives and 2 religion courses required. Independent study. Honors program. Pass/fail. Preprofessional programs in many areas. Cooperative corrections, law enforcement programs with Hawkeye Institute. 2-2 nursing with U of Iowa, 3-2 engineering with Iowa State, U of Iowa, U of Illinois (Urbana). Member of Spring Term Consortium. UN Semester. Urban internships in Chicago; legislative internships. Gulf Coast Research Lab (Mississippi) available for marine biological study. Study abroad. Elementary, secondary, and special education certification. 130,000-volume library.
Financial CEEB CSS and ACT FAS. College scholarships and grants, state scholarships and tuition grants; PELL, SEOG, NDSL, GSL, CWS. Application deadline March 1.
Admissions High school graduation required with 12 units recommended. GED accepted. SAT or ACT required. Interview recommended. $15 application fee. Rolling admissions; suggest applying early in 12th year. $100 deposit required on acceptance of offer of admission. College early decision and *Early Entrance* programs. Admission deferral possible. Transfers accepted. Credit possible for CEEB AP and CLEP exams, and for college exams.
Student Life Student government. Newspaper, literary magazine, yearbook, radio station. Music and drama groups. Black Culture Center. Sierra Club. Special interest, religious, honorary, and service organizations. Students live at home, on campus, or work in local homes for room & board. Coed and single-sex dorms. College-operated trailer court for married students with trailers. 1 phys ed course required. 9 intercollegiate sports for men, 7 for women; intramurals. AIAW, NCAA, Iowa Intercollegiate Athletic Conference. 35% of students are from out of state.

[G1] WARTBURG THEOLOGICAL SEMINARY
331 Wartburg Place, Dubuque 52001

[J1] WESTERN IOWA TECH
Sioux City 51106

[1] WESTMAR COLLEGE
Le Mars 51031, (712) 546-7081

- **Undergraduates: 287m, 223w; 600 total (including part-time)**
- **Tuition (1982/83): $4,060**
- **Room & Board: $2,600**
- **Degrees offered: BA, BMus Ed**
- **Mean ACT 20**
- **Student-faculty ratio: 18 to 1**

A private liberal arts college founded in 1890 and affiliated with the United Methodist Church.
Academic Character NCACS accreditation. 4-1-4 system, 4- and 5-week summer terms. Majors offered by 30 departments including art, accounting, computer science, business administration, music, industrial arts, home economics, and teacher education. Student-designed majors possible. Remedial mathematics and English programs. Evening workshops offered. 90,000-volume library.
Financial Private scholarships and loans; government grant and loan programs.
Admissions ACT required. Admission notification on a rolling basis. *Early Admission* Program. Admission deferral possible.
Student Life Dormitories and dining halls for men and women. Apartments available for married students.

[1] WILLIAM PENN COLLEGE
Oskaloosa 52577, (515) 673-8311
Director of Admissions: Eric Otto

- **Enrollment: 285m, 188w**
- **Tuition (1982/83): $4,880**
- **Room & Board: $1,670; Fees: $230**
- **Degree offered: BA**

A private Quaker college established in 1873. 40-acre small-city campus in Oskaloosa, located southeast of Des Moines.
Academic Character NCACS and professional accreditation. Semester system, 2 summer terms. Majors offered in accounting, biology, business management, chemistry, economics, elementary education, English, history, home economics, human relations, industrial arts, math, music, phys ed, religion, sociology. Composite majors. Minor required. Distributive requirements. 4 semester hours of religion required. Independent study. Internships. Pass/fail option. Freshman Development Program. Preprofessional programs in health-related and biomedical fields, engineering, journalism, law, social welfare, agriculture, theology. Experimental College. 75,000-volume library.
Financial CEEB CSS. College scholarships and grants, state grants, loans; PELL, SEOG, NDSL, GSL, work grant program. Application deadline July 15.
Admissions High school graduation with 15 units required. ACT, PSAT, or SAT required. Rolling admissions. $50 deposit required on acceptance of offer of admission. *Early Admission* and *Early Decision* programs. Transfers accepted. Credit possible for CEEB AP and CLEP exams.
Student Life Student government. Newspaper, literary magazine, yearbook. Radio station. Academic and honorary clubs. Black Student Union. Music groups. Writer's club. Fraternities and sororities. Dorms for men and women. Married-student housing. Abstinence from any forms of liquor, tobacco, or drugs strongly encouraged. 2 semester hours of phys ed required. Intercollegiate and intramural sports for men and women. IIAC, NCAA, AIAW. Student body composition: 12% minority.

KANSAS *(KS)*

[J1] ALLEN COUNTY COMMUNITY JUNIOR COLLEGE
Iola 66749

[1] BAKER UNIVERSITY

Baldwin City 66006, (913) 594-6451
Dean of Admissions: Kenneth Snow

- **Undergraduates: 406m, 455w**
- **Tuition (1982/83): $3,300**
- **Room & Board: $1,990; Fees: $75**
- **Degrees offered: BA, BS, BMus Ed**
- **Student-faculty ratio: 14 to 1**

A private university affiliated with the United Methodist Church, established in 1858. 26-acre campus in small town of Baldwin City, 45 miles from Kansas City and Topeka. Served by bus. Airport in Kansas City.
Academic Character NCACS and professional accreditation. 4-1-4 system, 2 6-week summer terms. 34 majors offered by the departments of Art, English, Foreign Language, History & Political Science, Music, Philosophy & Religion, Theatre, Communications, Education, Home Economics, Physical Education, Psychology, Sociology, Biology, Chemistry, Business & Economics, Mathematics, and Physics. Distributive requirements. MLA granted in conjunction with SMU. Independent study. Honors program. Cooperative work/study, pass/fail, internships in religion. Preprofessional programs in allied health, dentistry, law, medicine, veterinary medicine. 3-2 programs in forestry with Duke, in engineering with Washington U, Kansas State, and U of Kansas. 2-2 and 3-2 programs in nursing. Cross-registration with 14 regional schools. Study abroad. Experiment in International Living Program. Elementary and secondary education certification. ROTC at U of Kansas. Language lab. 90,000-volume library with microform resources.
Financial CEEB CSS and ACT FAS. University scholarships, grants, loans, Kansas tuition grants, Methodist and valedictorian scholarships, payment plans; PELL, SEOG, FISL, GSL, NDSL, HELP, CWS. Priority application deadline March 1.
Admissions High school graduation required. GED accepted. Interview encouraged. SAT or ACT required. $15 application fee. Rolling admissions. $75 deposit required on acceptance of offer of admission. *Early Admission* and *Early Decison* programs. Admission deferral possible. Transfers accepted. Credit possible for CEEB AP and CLEP exams.
Student Life Student Senate. Newspaper, magazine, yearbook, radio station. Music groups. Cheerleaders. Black Students Organization, Native American Club, International Club. Several honorary, religious, academic, and special interest organizations. 4 fraternities with houses and 5 sororities, 4 with houses. 35% of men and 52% of women join. Freshmen must live at home or on campus. Single-sex dorms. No married-student housing. 71% of students live on campus. Liquor prohibited on campus. 4 hours of phys ed required. 8 intercollegiate sports for men, 7 for women; several intramural and club sports. AIAW, NAIA, Heart of America Conference. Student body composition: 1% Asian, 7% Black, 1% Hispanic, 1% Native American, 89% White, 1% Other. 36% from out of state.

[J1] BARTON COUNTY COMMUNITY COLLEGE

Great Bend 67530, (316) 792-2701

- **Enrollment: 293m, 372w; 2,022 total (including part-time)**
- **Tuition (1982/83): $12 per semester hour, with some additional fees**
- **Degrees offered: AA, AS**

A public coeducational junior college.
Academic Character NCACS and professional accreditation. Semester system. 2-year transfer programs in liberal arts and sciences; terminal programs in vocational technical areas.
Admissions Rolling admissions.
Student Life Dormitories on campus. Intercollegiate cross-country running; intramural basketball, track, baseball, volleyball, and tennis.

[1] BENEDICTINE COLLEGE

Atchison 66002, (913) 367-5340
Director of Admissions: Ronald W. Lehmann

- **Undergraduates: 482m, 497w**
- **Tuition (1982/83): $3,700**
- **Room & Board: $1,880; Fees: $47**
- **Degrees offered: BA, BMus, BMus Ed, AA**
- **Mean ACT 21; mean SAT 1050**
- **Student-faculty ratio: 14 to 1**

A private college controlled by the Benedictines, established in 1971 through merger of St. Benedict's College and Mount St. Scholastica College. 2 campuses of 225 acres in residential section of Atchison, 50 miles from Kansas City, MO, 60 miles from Topeka. Served by bus. Airport in Kansas City.
Academic Character NCACS and professional accreditation. 4-4-1 system, 8-week summer term. Majors offered in accounting, art, arts management, biology, business administration, chemistry, communications, costume design, day care, economics, elementary education, English, fashion merchandising, French, history, home economics/community service, Latin, liberal studies, mathematics, music, music education, music marketing, natural science, philosophy, physical education, physics, political science, psychology, religious studies, restaurant management, social science, sociology, Spanish, theatre arts, theatre arts management, and youth ministries. Special, double majors. Minors offered. Courses in 9 additional areas. Distributives and 9 hours of religious studies required. Independent study. Cooperative work/study, pass/fail, internships. Preprofessional programs in dentistry, divinity, dramatics, engineering, journalism, law, medicine, nursing, pharmacy, veterinary medicine. Member Kansas City Consortium. 3-2 program in engineering with U of Kansas, several others. 3-1 medical technology program. Study abroad. Elementary, secondary, and special education certification. ROTC at Missouri Western State College; AFROTC at U of Kansas. Language, special ed labs. 284,000-volume library.
Financial ACT FAS preferred. College scholarships, grants, loans, tuition discount for 2nd family member, payment plans; PELL, SEOG, NDSL, FISL, CWS, college work program. Priority application deadline March 1.
Admissions High school graduation with 16 units required. Interview encouraged. ACT or SAT required; ACT preferred. $10 application fee. Rolling admissions, beginning November 1; suggest applying in September. $50 deposit required on acceptance of offer of admission. *Early Decision, Early Admission, Concurrent Enrollment* programs. Admission deferral possible. Transfers accepted. Credit possible for CEEB AP and CLEP exams; college has own advanced placement program. Conditional admission program.
Student Life Student government. Newspaper, magazine, yearbook, TV station. Music groups, including participation with St. Joseph (MO) Symphony. Political, religious, service, social, and special interest groups. Single students must live at home or on campus. Single-sex dorms. Some married-student housing. 96% of students live on campus. Class attendance required. 2 courses in phys ed required. 8 intercollegiate sports for men, 5 for women; several intramurals. AIAW, NAIA. Student body composition: 7% Black, 2% Hispanic, 90% White, 1% Other. 60% from out of state.

[R] BEREAN CHRISTIAN COLLEGE

Wichita — Institution moved to California

[1] BETHANY COLLEGE

Lindsborg 67456, (913) 227-3312, ext. 32
Dean of Admissions: Leon Burch

- **Undergraduates: 394m, 374w**
- **Tuition (1982/83): $3,090**
- **Room & Board: $1,985; Fees: $65**
- **Degree offered: BA**
- **Mean ACT 20**
- **Student-faculty ratio: 16 to 1**

A private college affiliated with the Lutheran Church in America, established in 1881. 40-acre campus in small town of Lindsborg, 20 miles south of Salina and 70 miles north of Wichita. Served by bus and rail. Airport in Salina.
Academic Character NCACS and professional accreditation. 4-1-4 system, 2 3-week summer terms. Majors offered in art, biology, chemistry, economics & business, English, health & physical education, history & political science, mathematics, music, psychology, recreation, science, social work, and sociology; 10 teaching majors. Self-designed majors. Courses in 9 additional areas. Distributives and one religion course required. Independent study. Cooperative work/study. Credit by exam. Internships. Preprofessional programs in Christian service, dentistry, law, medicine. Member 6-college Central Kansas Consortium. Study abroad in Sweden. Elementary, secondary, and special education certification. Art gallery. 98,000-volume library.
Financial CEEB CSS and ACT FAS. College scholarships, grants, loans, state programs, payment plan; PELL, SEOG, NDSL, GSL, HELP, PLUS, CWS. Priority application deadline February 1.
Admissions High school graduation with 16 units required. Interview encouraged. Audition encouraged for music majors, portfolio for art majors. ACT or SAT required. $10 application fee. Rolling admissions; suggest applying by June 1. $120 deposit required on acceptance of offer of admission. *Early Admission* and informal early decision programs. Transfers accepted. Credit possible for CEEB AP and CLEP exams, and for experience.
Student Life Student government. Newspaper, yearbook. Several bands and music societies. Dramatics. Honor societies and special interest groups. 3 fraternities and 3 sororities without houses. 20% of men and 25% of women join. Students must live at home or on campus. Coed and single-sex dorms. 90% of students live on campus. Attendance required at some convocations. 7 intercollegiate sports for men, 5 for women; intramurals. AIAW, NAIA, Kansas College Athletic Conference. Student body composition: 2% Black, 1% Hispanic, 95% White, 2% Other. 32% from out of state.

[1] BETHEL COLLEGE

North Newton 67117, (316) 283-2500
Director of Admissions: Diana Torline

- **Undergraduates: 282m, 337w; 748 total (including part-time)**
- **Tuition (1982/83): $3,400**
- **Room & Board: $1,970; Fees: $120**
- **Degrees offered: BA, BS, AA**
- **Mean ACT 21**
- **Student-faculty ratio: 14 to 1**

A private college affiliated with the General Conference Mennonite Church, established in 1887. 40-acre suburban campus in small city of West Newton, 22 miles north of Wichita. Bus and rail stations in Newton, airport in Wichita.
Academic Character NCACS and professional accreditation. 4-1-4 system, 3 4-week summer terms. 12 majors for the BA degree offered by the divisions of Fine Arts, History-Social Sciences, Liberal Arts, and Natural Sciences, and 14 for the BS degree offered by the Division of Natural Sciences. Divisional and self-designed majors. Minors offered in all major fields and in political science and secretarial studies. Distributives, GRE, senior exams, and 4 hours of religion required. Independent study. Cooperative work/study, pass/fail, internships. Preprofessional programs in agriculture, dentistry, engineering, law, medicine, ministry, nursing. 3-2 programs in agriculture, engineering, and home economics with Kansas State. Member Associated Colleges of Central Kansas. Cross-registration with Hesston Junior College and Wichita State. Study abroad in Europe and Japan. Elementary, secondary, and special education certification. Computer center, language lab, museum. 78,800-volume library with microform resources.
Financial CEEB CSS and ACT FAS. College scholarships, grants, grants-in-aid, loans; PELL, SEOG, GSL, FISL, NDSL, CWS, college has own work program.

Admissions High school graduation with 17 units required. GED accepted. Interview encouraged. SAT or ACT required. $10 application fee. Rolling admissions; application deadline August 15. *Early Admission* and *Concurrent Enrollment* programs. Admission deferral possible. Transfers accepted. Credit possible for CEEB AP and CLEP exams, and for experience. College has own advanced placement program.
Student Life Student government. Newspaper, magazine, yearbook, radio station. Music, drama, debate groups. Peace club. Political, service, and special interest organizations. Single students under 23 must live at home or on campus. Single-sex and upperclass coed dorms. Married-student housing. 75% of students live on campus. Liquor, drugs prohibited; smoking restricted. Attendance at 2 convocations per week required. 2 hours of phys ed required. 7 intercollegiate sports for men, 4 for women; intramurals. NAIA, NCAA. Student body composition: 1% Asian, 3% Black, 1% Hispanic, 1% Native American, 89% White, 5% Other. 36% from out of state.

[J1] BUTLER COUNTY COMMUNITY COLLEGE
Haverhill Road and Towanda Avenue, El Dorado 67042, (316) 321-5083
Director of Admissions & Records: Everett Kohls

- **Enrollment: 473m, 358w; 2,300 total (including part-time)**
- **Tuition (1982/83): $14.50 per credit hour (in-state), $48.83 (out-of-state)**
- **Degrees offered: AA, AS, AAS**
- **Student-faculty ratio: 18 to 1**

A public junior college. 80-acre campus located in city of El Dorado near Wichita. Served by air and bus.
Academic Character NCACS accreditation. Semester system, 8-week summer term. 2-year programs offered by the departments of Agriculture, Business, Data Processing, Marketing & Distributive Education, Fine Arts, Industrial Education, and Health, Physical Education & Recreation. Certificate programs. Distributive requirements. Independent study. Cooperative work/study. Preprofessional programs in law, engineering, health fields. Cooperative vocational-technical programs with area schools. Day and evening programs. 30,000-volume library with microform resources.
Financial ACT FAS. College scholarships, PELL, SEOG, NDSL, NSL, GSL, CWS.
Admissions High school graduation required. GED accepted. ACT required. Rolling admissions. Transfers accepted. Credit possible for CEEB CLEP exams.
Student Life Student Activities Council. Newspaper, yearbook. Music, drama groups. Religious, honorary, professional, and special interest groups. Limited college housing. Class attendance required. 2 semesters of phys ed required. 7 intercollegiate sports for men, 4 for women; intramurals. Jayhawk JC Conference, NJCAA.

[G1] CENTRAL BAPTIST THEOLOGICAL SEMINARY
Kansas City 66102

[J1] CENTRAL COLLEGE
McPherson 67460, (316) 241-0723, (800) 835-0078
Director of Admissions & Financial Aid: Don Munce

- **Undergraduates: 141m, 158w**
- **Tuition (1982/83): $3,150**
- **Room & Board: $1,750**
- **Degrees offered: AA, AGS**

A private junior college affiliated with the Free Methodist Church, established in 1884. 16-acre campus located in small city of McPherson, 60 miles from Wichita.
Academic Character NCACS accreditation. 4-1-4 system. 2-year transfer programs in art, business administration, Christian education, dentistry, economics, education, home economics, industrial education, law, library, medical, medical technology, ministry, nursing, social work, and veterinary medicine. Career programs in auto mechanics, library technology, agri-business, data processing, legal secretary, medical secretary, executive secretary, business management, carpentry, aviation, food-service management, child care, Christian service, social service, recreation leadership, piano instruction, accounting technician. Independent study. Cooperative work/study.
Financial ACT FAS. College scholarships, loans, PELL, college work program.
Admissions High school graduation required. $5 application fee. Admission notification on a rolling basis. Admission deferral possible. Advanced placement credit possible.
Student Life Student government. Newspaper, yearbook. Music groups. Special interest organizations. Dormitories for men and women; dining hall. Liquor, tobacco, gambling, dancing prohibited on campus. 7 intercollegiate sports for men, 5 for women; intramurals.

[J1] CLOUD COUNTY COMMUNITY COLLEGE
Concordia 66901

[J1] COFFEYVILLE COMMUNITY COLLEGE
11th and Willow, Coffeyville 67337, (316) 251-7700
Dean of Student Services: Ty Patterson

- **Undergraduates: 226m, 203w; 1,441 total (including part-time)**
- **Tuition (1982/83): $10 per credit hour (in-state), $44.50 (out-of-state)**
- **Fees: $40**
- **Degrees offered: AA, AS, AAS**

A public junior college established in 1923.
Academic Character NCACS accreditation. Semester system, 6-week summer term. Transfer, technical, terminal, and preprofessional programs. 2-year programs offered in agriculture, art, biology, chemistry, drama, economics, engineering, English, foreign language, government, history, home economics, humanities, journalism, literature, mathematics, military science, music, physical science, psychology, reading, sociology, speech, and health, physical education, & recreation. 14 occupational programs. Distributive requirements. Remedial math and English courses. Evening program. ROTC.
Financial Guaranteed tuition. College scholarships, PELL, SEOG, GSL, CWS.
Admissions High school graduation required. GED accepted. Rolling admissions. *Early Admission* and *Early Decision* programs. Admission deferral possible. Transfers accepted. Credit possible for CEEB CLEP exams.
Student Life Student government. Newspaper. Music and drama groups. Religious, professional, and special interest groups. 1 dorm. Class attendance required. 7 intercollegiate sports. Kansas Jayhawk Conference, NJCAA. Student body composition: 18% minority.

[J1] COLBY COMMUNITY COLLEGE
Colby 67701

[J1] COWLEY COUNTY COMMUNITY COLLEGE
Arkansas City 67005, (316) 442-1990
Registrar: Walter L. Mathiasmeier

- **Enrollment: 260m, 208w; 1,767 total (including part-time)**
- **Tuition (1982/83): $15 per semester hour (in-state), $49.33 (out-of-state)**
- **Degrees offered: AA, AAS**
- **Mean ACT 17.6**
- **Student-faculty ratio: 27 to 1**

A public junior college established in 1922. Main campus in Arkansas City, 50 miles from Wichita. Served by air, rail, and bus.
Academic Character NCACS accreditation. Semester system, 6-week summer term. Liberal arts/transfer, preprofessional, and occupational programs. 2-year programs offered by the departments of Business Technology, Humanities, Industrial Technology, Natural Sciences, Service Technology, and Social Sciences. Distributive requirements. Independent study. Preprofessional programs in nursing, chiropractic, cytotechnology, dentistry, engineering, medicine, mortuary science, osteopathy, pharmacy, physical therapy, veterinary medicine, x-ray technician. Certificate programs. 18,000-volume library with microform resources.
Financial ACT FAS. College scholarships, grants, loans; PELL, SEOG, GSL, CWS. Application deadline April 1.
Admissions High school graduation required. GED accepted. ACT recommended. Rolling admissions. *Early Admission* Program. Transfers accepted. Credit possible for CEEB CLEP exams.
Student Life Student government. Newspaper, magazine, yearbook. Music groups. Academic, honorary, religious, professional, and special interest groups. Limited college housing. Dormitory and dining hall. Class attendance required. Liquor prohibited on campus. Smoking restricted. Dress code. 7 intercollegiate sports; intramurals. Kansas Jayhawk Conference, NJCAA. Student body composition: 10% minority.

[J1] DODGE CITY COMMUNITY COLLEGE
Dodge City 67801

[J1] DONNELLY COLLEGE
608 North 18th Street, Kansas City 66102

[1] EMPORIA STATE UNIVERSITY
Emporia 66801, (316) 343-1200
Director of Admissions: Jan Jantzen

- **Undergraduates: 1,625m, 1,990w; 5,768 total (including graduates)**
- **Tuition (1982/83): $756 (in-state), $1,550 (out-of-state)**
- **Room & Board: $1,870**
- **Degrees offered: BA, BS, BFA, BGS, BMus, BMus Ed, BSBus, BSEd, BSMed Tech, AS, AA**
- **Mean ACT 18**
- **Student-faculty ratio: 24 to 1**

A public university established in 1863. 200-acre campus in small city of Emporia, 55 miles southwest of Topeka. Served by bus and rail. Airport in Topeka.
Academic Character NCACS and professional accreditation. Semester system, 2 5-week summer terms. 43 majors offered in the areas of arts, sciences, business, education, language, general studies, health & recreation, home economics, industrial education, mathematics, political & social sciences, retailing, and speech. Self-designed majors. Minor required for business majors. Distributive requirements. Masters degrees granted. Independent study. Honors program. Phi Beta Kappa. Limited pass/fail. Internships. Credit by exam. Cooperative work/study. Preprofessional programs in agriculture, dentistry, law, medicine, nursing, occupational therapy, optometry, osteopathic medicine, pharmacy, physical therapy, veterinary medicine. 2-2 program in engineering. 3-2 engineering program with Kansas State and U of Kansas. 2-2 programs in journalism and social work with U of Kansas. Study abroad. Early childhood, elementary, secondary, and special education certification. ROTC. Language lab, laboratory school, planetarium. 644,810-volume library.
Financial CEEB CSS and ACT FAS. University scholarships, grants, loans, payment plan; PELL, SEOG, NDSL, GSL, CWS. Priority application deadline March 15.
Admissions High school graduation required. GED accepted. ACT

required; SAT accepted for out-of-state students. Rolling admissions; suggest applying by August 15. *Early Admission* and *Concurrent Enrollment* programs. Admission deferral possible. Transfers accepted. Credit possible for CEEB AP, CLEP, and ACT PEP exams; university has own advanced placement program.
Student Life Student government. Newspaper, magazine, yearbook, radio station. Several music groups. Debate team, drama groups. Special interest groups. 9 fraternities, 6 with houses, and 8 sororities, 5 with houses. 12% of men and 9% of women join. Freshmen must live at home or on campus. Coed and single-sex dorms. Married-student housing. 22% of students live on campus. Only 3.2 liquor permitted on campus. 2 hours of phys ed required. 8 intercollegiate sports for men, 10 for women; intramurals. AIAW, NAIA, CSIC. Student body composition: 0.1% Asian, 2.7% Black, 0.8% Hispanic, 0.2% Native American, 92.6% White, 3.6% Other. 10% from out of state.

[P] FLINT HILLS AREA VOCATIONAL-TECHNICAL SCHOOL
3301 West 18th Avenue, Emporia 66801

[1] FORT HAYS STATE UNIVERSITY
600 Park Street, Hays 67601-4099
(913) 628-4000 or toll free (800) 432-0248
Director of Admissions: James V. Kellerman

- **Undergraduates: 1,637m, 1,710w; 5,513 total (including graduates)**
- **Tuition (1982/83): $833 (in-state), $1,628 (out-of-state)**
- **Room & Board: $1,790**
- **Degrees offered: BA, BS, BFA, BGS, BMus, BSN, AA, AS**
- **Mean ACT 18**
- **Student-faculty ratio: 25 to 1**

A public university established in 1902. 200-acre campus in Hays, 160 miles from Wichita, and midway between Kansas City and Denver on Interstate 70. Served by air and bus.
Academic Character NCACS and professional accreditation. Semester system, 8-week summer term. 44 majors offered by the schools of Arts & Sciences, Business, Education, and Nursing. AA in humanities, social sciences, natural sciences, and mathematics. AS in data processing, radiological technology, secretarial administration, and nursing. Courses in 7 additional areas. Distributive requirements; GRE required for graduation. Masters degrees granted. Independent study. Pass/fail. Internships. Cooperative work/study. Preprofessional programs in forestry, pharmacy. Cooperative justice program with Wichita State. Cooperative program in social work with Kansas State U. 3-1 programs in 11 fields. Participation in National Student Exchange with over 40 schools. Study abroad through International Student Exchange. Elementary, secondary, and special education certification. ROTC. Art gallery, media center, Museum of High Plains, paleontology museum, computer center. 615,000-volume library with microform resources.
Financial CEEB CSS and ACT FAS (preferred). University scholarships, grants, loans; PELL, SEOG, NSS, FISL, NDSL, HELP, NSL, CWS. Priority application deadlines March 1 (scholarships), July 1 (loans).
Admissions High school graduation required. GED accepted. ACT or SAT required. Rolling admissions. *Early Decision* and *Concurrent Enrollment* programs. Admission deferral possible. Transfers accepted. Credit possible for CEEB AP, CLEP, and ACT PEP exams; university has own advanced placement program.
Student Life Student government. Newspaper, magazine, yearbook, radio and TV stations. Music, debate, drama groups. Black, Chinese, Hispanic, Nigerian student associations. Academic, honorary, political, religious, and special interest groups. 5 fraternities and 4 sororities with houses. 10% of men and women join. Single freshmen must live on campus. Coed and single-sex dorms. Married-student housing. Coop dorms. 25% of students live on campus. Beer allowed only in some locations. Attendance in class required. 4 semesters of phys ed required. 9 intercollegiate sports for men, 6 for women; several intramural and club sports. NAIA, CSIC. Student body composition: 1% Asian, 2% Black, 0.8% Hispanic, 0.4% Native American, 95.8% White. 7% from out of state.

[J1] FORT SCOTT COMMUNITY JUNIOR COLLEGE
Fort Scott 66701, (316) 223-2700

- **Undergraduates: 283m, 202w; 1,278 total (including part-time)**
- **Tuition (1982/83): $10 per hour (in-state), $650 per semester (out-of-state)**
- **Degree offered: AA**

A public, district-controlled junior college.
Academic Character NCACS accreditation. Semester system. Terminal and transfer programs. Diplomas granted. Remedial mathematics and English programs. Evening program.
Admissions High school graduation required.
Student Life Dormitories for men and women. Cafeteria.

[P] FRIENDS BIBLE COLLEGE
Haviland 67059

[1] FRIENDS UNIVERSITY
Wichita 67213, (316) 261-5800
Dean of Admissions: George D. Potts

- **Undergraduates: 320m, 300w; 822 total (including part-time)**
- **Tuition (1982/83): $3 540**
- **Room & Board: $1,650; Fees: $115**
- **Degrees offered: BA, BS, BMus, ThB, AA, AS**
- **Mean ACT 17.5**
- **Student-faculty ratio: 14 to 1**

A private university affiliated with the Society of Friends (Quakers), established in 1898. 54-acre urban campus in Wichita. Served by air, bus, and rail.
Academic Character NCACS and professional accreditation. Semester system with 2-week January term, 2 5-week summer terms. Majors offered in agri-business, agri-science, art, biology, business administration, chemistry, communications, elementary education, English, environmental studies, history, human services, mathematics, Spanish, music, philosophy, physical education, political science, religion, secretarial science, and sociology. AA in accounting, secretarial science, data processing. Courses offered in peace studies. Distributives and 6 hours of religion/philosophy required. Independent study. Honors program. Pass/fail. Internships. Preprofessional programs in agriculture, business administration, dentistry, engineering, law, medical technology, medicine, nursing, optometry, podiatry, theology, veterinary medicine. Cooperative programs in psychology with Kansas Newman, in vocational agriculture with Kansas State. Cross-registration with Kansas Newman. Elementary and secondary education certification. Museum. 88,200-volume library.
Financial ACT FAS. University scholarships, grants, loans; achievement, honor, ministerial scholarships, Kansas Tuition Grants; PELL, SEOG, NDSL, GSL, CWS. Priority application deadline for scholarships May 1.
Admissions High school graduation with 13 units required. GED accepted. Interview encouraged. ACT required. $10 application fee. Rolling admissions; suggest applying by May 1. *Early Admission* Program. Admission deferral possible. Transfers accepted. Credit possible for CEEB AP and CLEP exams, for life, work, & military experience; university has own advanced placement program.
Student Life Student government. Newspaper, yearbook. Music and drama groups. Volunteer opportunities. Religious, honorary, service, academic, and special interest groups. Dorms for men and women. Married-student housing. 21% of students live on campus. Liquor, smoking prohibited on campus. Class attendance required. 3 intercollegiate sports for men, 3 for women. NAIA, KCAC. Student body composition: 1% Asian, 7% Black, 1% Hispanic, 1% Native American, 89% White, 1% Other. 24% from out of state.

[J1] GARDEN CITY COMMUNITY JUNIOR COLLEGE
801 Campus Drive, Garden City 67846, (316) 276-7611

- **Undergraduates: 346m, 305w; 1,112 total (including part-time)**
- **Tuition & Fees (1981/82): $358**
- **Degrees offered: AA, AS**

A public, coed, district-controlled junior college.
Academic Character NCACS accreditation. Semester system. 2-year general education and preprofessional programs offered for students planning to transfer to four-year colleges. 2-year terminal/career programs also available. Certificates granted. Evening adult program.
Admissions High shcool graduation with 15 units required.
Student Life Dormitories and dining hall available.

[J1] HASKELL INDIAN JUNIOR COLLEGE
Lawrence 66044

[J1] HESSTON COLLEGE
Box 3000, Hesston 67062, (316) 327-4221, (800) 835-2026 (toll-free)
Registrar: Erna E. Saltzman

- **Enrollment: 277m, 302w; 657 total (including part-time)**
- **Tuition (1982/83): $3,400**
- **Room & Board: $1,900; Fees: $100**
- **Degrees offered: AA, ALA**
- **Student-faculty ratio: 13 to 1**

A private junior college affiliated with the Mennonite Church, established in 1909. 50-acre campus located in the small town of Hesston, 35 miles from Wichita. Airport nearby.
Academic Character NCACS accreditation. 4-1-4 system. 2-year programs offered in agriculture, automotive service, aviation, Bible, business (management, data processing, secretarial), education, electronics, liberal arts, and nursing. Distributive requirements. 2 hours of religion required. Independent study. Cooperative work/study. Credit by exam. Cooperative programs with Goshen and Eastern Mennonite colleges. Travel in US, Mexico, and the Middle East. 30,000-volume library.
Financial ACT FAS. College scholarships, grants, loans, state scholarships and grants; family grants, minority grants, church worker grants; PELL, SEOG, NDSL, GSL. College has own work program.
Admissions High school graduation required. GED accepted. ACT or SAT required. $10 application fee. Rolling admissions. Advanced placement credit possible for CEEB CLEP exams.
Student Life Yearbook. Music and drama groups. Service projects, special interest clubs. Single students under 21 must live at home or on campus. Dormitories and dining hall. Liquor, tobacco, dancing prohibited on campus. Attendance in class and at chapel and convocations required. 1 hour of phys ed required. Intercollegiate and intramural sports. 72% of students from out of state.

[J1] HIGHLAND COMMUNITY COLLEGE
Highland 66035, (913) 442-3238
Dean of Student Affairs: Douglas L. Fitch

- **Undergraduates: 253m, 199w; 1,374 total (including part-time)**
- **Tuition (1982/83): $430 (in-state), $1,330 (out-of-state)**
- **Room & Board: $1,500; Fees: $120**
- **Degrees offered: AA, AGS, AAS**
- **Mean ACT 18.3**

- **Student-faculty ratio: 12 to 1**

A public junior college established in 1858. Rural campus located in the town of Highland, 10 miles from Nebraska state line, 25 miles from St. Joseph, Missouri.
Academic Character NCACS accreditation. Semester system, summer term. 61 2-year programs offered in the areas of humanities, social science, mathematics-natural science, and career studies. Cooperative programs in vocational-technical areas. 1-year certificate programs. Distributive requirements. Independent study. Internships. Language labs, TV studio. Early Childhood Experimental Center. 28,000-volume library with microform resources.
Financial College scholarships and loans, state scholarships; PELL, SEOG, BIA, GSL, CWS.
Admissions High school graduation required. ACT recommended. Rolling admissions. *Early Admission* Program. Credit possible for CEEB AP and CLEP exams; college has own advanced placement program. Non-high school graduates over 21 admitted to some programs.
Student Life Student government. Newspaper, yearbook. Music groups. Religious, professional, and special interest organizations. Single students under 21 must live at home or on campus. Dormitories for men and women. Class attendance required. 2 hours of phys ed required. 4 intercollegiate sports for men, 4 for women; intramurals. Student body composition: 12% minority.

[J1] HUTCHINSON COMMUNITY COLLEGE
1300 North Plum, Hutchinson 67501, (316) 665-3500
Director of Admissions & Records: Deborah S. Brown

- **Undergraduates: 682m, 589w; 2,918 total (including part-time)**
- **Tuition (1982/83): $12 per credit hour (in-state), $1,330 per year (out-of-state)**
- **Room & Board: $1,700; Fees: $51**
- **Degrees offered: AA, ATech Ed**
- **Student-faculty ratio: 15 to 1**

A private college established in 1928. 47-acre campus located in the small city of Hutchinson.
Academic Character NCACS and professional accreditation. Semester system, 2 4-week summer terms. 2-year transfer and terminal programs offered in agriculture, architecture, art, banking, broadcasting, business, chemistry, chiropractic, computer science, cytotechnology, data processing, dental hygiene, dentistry, education, engineering, engineering technology, English, fire science, forestry, mortuary science, geology, home economics, industrial arts education, journalism, public administration, legal assistant, liberal arts, library science, mathematics, medical record administration, medical technology, medicine, modern language, music education, nursing, occupational therapy, optometry, pharmacy, physical therapy, physics, psychology, recreation, sociology, speech & drama, sports medicine, and veterinary medicine. Vocational-technical programs offered. Distributive requirements. Computer center. 40,000-volume library with microform resources.
Financial ACT FAS. College scholarships, grants, loans; PELL, SEOG, NDSL, GSL, CWS. Application deadline March 1.
Admissions High school graduation required. GED accepted. ACT recommended. Rolling admissions. *Early Decision* and *Early Admission* programs. Transfers accepted. Credit possible for CEEB AP and CLEP exams.
Student Life Student government. Newspaper, literary annual, yearbook, radio station. Music and drama groups. Honorary, academic, religious, and special interest groups. Single freshmen must live at home or on campus. Limited college housing. Dining facilities. Dress code. Class attendance required. 2 credit hours of phys ed required. 8 intercollegiate sports for men, 4 for women. Kansas Jayhawk Conference, NJCAA. Student body composition: 17% minority.

[J1] INDEPENDENCE COMMUNITY COLLEGE
Independence 67301

[J1] JOHNSON COUNTY COMMUNITY COLLEGE
12345 College Blvd., Overland Park 66210

[1] KANSAS, UNIVERSITY OF
Lawrence 66043, (913) 864-3911
Toll free: (800) 332-6332 (in-state), (800) 255-6322 (out-of-state)
Dean of Admissions & Records: Gil Dyck

- **Enrollment: 11,020m, 9,024w; 26,367 total (including part-time)**
- **Tuition (1982/83): $904 (in-state), $2,220 (out-of-state)**
- **Room & Board: $1,860; Fees: $5-$50**
- **Degrees offered: BA, BS, BArch, BEd, BFA, BGS, BMus Ed, BSEd, BSW, BE's**
- **Mean ACT 23**
- **Student-faculty ratio: 16 to 1**

A public university established in 1866. 930-acre urban campus in Lawrence, 40 miles from Kansas City.
Academic Character NCACS and professional accreditation. Semester system, 8-week summer term. 44 majors offered by the College of Liberal Arts & Sciences, 5 by the School of Allied Health, 2 by the School of Architecture & Urban Design, 2 by the School of Business, 10 by the School of Education, 8 by the School of Engineering, 18 by the School of Fine Arts, 7 by the School of Journalism, and in nursing, pharmacy, and social welfare. Distributive requirements. Graduate and professional degrees granted. Honors program. Phi Beta Kappa. Preprofessional programs in dentistry, journalism, law, medicine, nursing, pharmacy. Study abroad. Language Institute Programs. ROTC, AFROTC, NROTC. 2,250,000-volume library.
Financial CEEB CSS. University scholarships, grants, loans, freshman engineering grants; PELL, SEOG, NDSL, CWS. Application deadline March 1.
Admissions High school graduation with 13½ units recommended. ACT required. Rolling admissions. *Early Admission* and *Early Decision* programs. Transfers accepted. Credit possible for CEEB AP exams.
Student Life Student government. Music, debate, speech, drama groups. Academic, honorary, religious, and special interest organizations. 23 fraternities and 13 sororities with houses. 12% of men and 9% of women join. Housing in scholarship halls, rooming houses, homes, dormitories, married-student apartments. 40% of students live on campus. Intercollegiate and intramural sports for men and women. Student body composition: 0.7% Asian, 3.5% Black, 1.1% Hispanic, 0.5% Native American, 87.3% White, 6.9% Other. 25% from out of state.

[J1] KANSAS CITY KANSAS COMMUNITY JUNIOR COLLEGE
7250 State Avenue, Kansas City 66112

[1] KANSAS NEWMAN COLLEGE
3100 McCormick Avenue, Wichita 67213, (316) 942-4291

- **Undergraduates: 204m, 273w; 700 total (including part-time)**
- **Tuition (1982/83): $3,317**
- **Room & Board: $1,890**
- **Degrees offered: BA, BS, BSN, AA, AS, ASN**
- **Mean ACT 20**
- **Student-faculty ratio: 20 to 1**

A private, Roman Catholic college owned and operated by the Sisters A.S.C., founded in 1933. Suburban campus.
Academic Character NCACS and professional accreditation. Semester system, summer term. Majors offered include accounting, biology, business, business administration, chemistry, cytotechnology, education, English, fine arts, history, industrial management, management science, math, medical technology, nuclear medicine technology, nurse anesthesia, nursing, political science, psychology, sociology. Remedial mathematics and English programs. 60,000-volume library with 450 periodicals.
Financial College scholarships, including academic, athletic, and music awards; Kansas Tuition Grant; PELL, SEOG, NDSL, GSL, CWS.
Admissions High school graduation required. ACT required. Admission notification is done on a rolling basis. *Early Admission* Program. Advanced placement credit possible.
Student Life Residence halls on main campus.

[1] KANSAS STATE UNIVERSITY
Manhattan 66506, (913) 532-6250
Director of Admissions: Richard N. Elkins

- **Undergraduates: 8,563m, 6,464w; 19,497 total (including graduates)**
- **Tuition & Fees (1982/83): $898 (in-state), $2,214 (out-of-state)**
- **Room & Board: $1,740**
- **Degrees offered: BA, BS, BSBA, BSMus Ed, BMus, BArch**
- **Mean ACT 22**
- **Student-faculty ratio: 19 to 1**

A public land-grant university established in 1863. 325-acre campus located in the small city of Manhattan, 50 miles west of Topeka and 120 miles from Kansas City. Served by air and bus.
Academic Character NCACS and professional accreditation. Semester system, 8-week summer term. 17 majors offered by the College of Agriculture, 3 by the College of Architecture & Design, 39 by the College of Arts & Sciences, 10 by the College of Engineering, 4 by the College of Home Economics, and majors in business administration and education. Special and self-designed majors. Courses in 8 additional areas. Distributive requirements. Graduate and professional degrees granted. Independent study. Honors program. Phi Beta Kappa. Pass/fail. Cooperative work/study, internships. Preprofessional programs in law, dentistry, forestry, medical technology, medicine, nursing, optometry, pharmacy, physical therapy, social work, veterinary medicine. 5-year dual degree program in engineering. 6-year veterinary medicine program. Study abroad, exchange program with Justus Liebig University in Germany. Elementary, secondary, and special education certification. South Asian center. Computer center, language lab. 900,000-volume library.
Financial ACT FAS. University scholarships, grants, loans, athletic grants-in-aid; PELL, SEOG, NDSL, GSL, PLUS, CWS, college work program. Application deadlines January 15 (scholarships), March 15 (loans).
Admissions High school graduation required. ACT required; SAT accepted. Rolling admissions. Transfers accepted. Credit possible for CEEB AP and CLEP exams; university has own advanced placement program.
Student Life Student government. Newspaper, magazine, yearbook, radio station. Several music groups. Academic, religious, service, and special interest groups. 28 fraternities and 13 sororities, most with houses. Single students under 21 must live at home or on campus. Coed, single-sex, and coop dorms. Married-student housing includes trailer area and apartments. 40% of students live on campus. Liquor prohibited, except for 3.2 beer in dorms. 2 semesters of phys ed required. 7 intercollegiate sports for men, 7 for women; intramurals. AIAW, NCAA, Big Eight. Student body composition: 1% Asian, 5% Black, 1% Hispanic, 92% White, 1% Other. 15% from out of state.

[J1] KANSAS TECHNICAL INSTITUTE
2409 Scanlan Avenue, Salina 67401, (913) 825-0275
Dean of Student Services: Herbert F. Petracek

- **Undergraduates: 340m, 80w; 582 total (including part-time)**
- **Tuition (1982/83): $300 (in-state), $900 (out-of-state)**
- **Room & Board: $1,500; Fees: $45**

• **Degree offered: AT**

A public technical college established in 1965.
Academic Character NCACS and professional accreditation. 2-year programs for an Associate of Technology degree offered in aeronautical engineering, civil engineering, computer science, electronic engineering, general engineering, and mechanical engineering technologies. Certificate programs. Credit by exam.
Financial ACT FAS. College scholarships, emergency loans; PELL, SEOG, HEAF, CWS. Application deadline April 15.
Admissions High school graduation required. GED accepted. ACT or SAT required. $25 application fee. Rolling admissions. Transfers accepted. Credit possible for CEEB CLEP exams.
Student Life Student government. Honorary, professional, and special interest groups. Single freshmen males must live at home or on campus. Dormitories for men. No women's or married-student housing. Intramural sports.

[1] KANSAS WESLEYAN
Salina 67401, (913) 827-5541
Director of Admissions: Jack Ropp

• **Undergraduates: 180m, 156w; 427 total (including part-time)**
• **Tuition (1982/83): $3,568**
• **Room & Board: $1,983**
• **Degrees offered: BA, BS, AA**
• **Student-faculty ratio: 16 to 1**

A private college affiliated with the United Methodist Church, established in 1886. Campus located in the small city of Salina.
Academic Character NCACS accreditation. 4-1-4 system, 2 4-week summer terms. Majors offered in speech & drama, English, music, religion & philosophy, Spanish, business administration & economics, accounting, history, behavioral sciences, biology, chemistry, computer science, mathematics, physics, education, home economics, and health, physical education, & recreation. AA offered in business administration and criminal justice. Minor offered in art. Distributives and 1 course in religion required. Independent study. Preprofessional programs include dentistry, engineering, law, medicine, medical technology, theology. Preprofessional programs in technical drafting and mechanical detailing with Kansas Technical Institute. Dual-degree programs in agriculture, home economics, engineering. Washington, UN Semesters. Summer in Europe program. 70,000-volume library.
Financial College scholarships, loans, work program, 2nd-sibling discount.
Admissions High school graduation required. GED accepted. ACT required. $15 application fee. Rolling admissions. Transfers accepted. Credit possible for CEEB AP and CLEP exams; college has own advanced placement program.
Student Life Honorary societies. 3 sororities without houses. Cafeteria operated. 4 intercollegiate sports for men, 4 for women; intramurals. Student body composition: 30% minority.

[J1] LABETTE COMMUNITY COLLEGE
Parsons 67357

[P] MANHATTAN CHRISTIAN COLLEGE
1407 Anderson, Manhattan 66502

[1] MARYMOUNT COLLEGE OF KANSAS
Salina 67401, (913) 825-2101
Admissions Coordinator: Clare Schulte

• **Undergraduates: 143m, 341w; 758 total (including part-time)**
• **Tuition (1982/83): $3,225**
• **Room & Board: $1,825**
• **Degrees offered: BA, BS, BMus, BMus Ed, BSN, AS**
• **Student-faculty ratio: 12 to 1**

A private college controlled by the Sisters of Saint Joseph, established in 1922, became coed in 1968. 28-acre wooded campus overlooking the small city of Salina. Served by air and bus.
Academic Character NCACS and professional accreditation. 4-1-4 system, summer term. Majors offered in accounting, art, biology, business administration, chemistry, elementary education, English, French, graphic design, history, mathematics, medical record administration, medical technology, music, music-religious studies, nuclear medicine technology, nursing, photography, physical education, psychology, recreation, speech & drama, philosophy, and religious studies. Distributives, senior exam, UGRE, and 6 hours of religious studies required. Pass/fail. Credit by exam. Preprofessional programs in dentistry, medicine, optometry, pharmacy, physical therapy, veterinary medicine. Elementary and secondary education certification. Audio-visual and computer centers. 63,000-volume library.
Financial CEEB CSS and ACT FAS. College scholarships, grants, state scholarships & grants, health careers loans; PELL, SEOG, NDSL, NSL, GSL, PLUS, CWS. Application deadline April 1.
Admissions High school graduation required. GED accepted. ACT required. $10 application fee. Rolling admissions. $50 room deposit (for boarders) required on acceptance of offer of admission. *Early Admission* and *Early Decision* programs. Admission deferral possible. Transfers accepted. Credit possible for CEEB AP and CLEP exams.
Student Life Student government. Music and drama groups. Academic, religious, and special interest organizations. Single students under 21 must live with relatives or on campus. Single-sex dorms. 4 intercollegiate sports for men, 5 for women. NAIA, AIAW.

[1] McPHERSON COLLEGE
McPherson 67460, (316) 241-0731
Director of Admissions: Connie S. Andes

• **Undergraduates: 236m, 230w**
• **Tuition (1982/83): $3,330**
• **Room & Board: $1,900; Fees: $160**
• **Degrees offered: BA, BS, AT**
• **Student-faculty ratio: 13 to 1**

A private college affiliated with the Church of the Brethren. Campus located in the small city of McPherson, 60 miles northwest of Wichita.
Academic Character NCACS accreditation. 4-1-4 system, 4-week summer term. Majors offered in physical education, physical sciences, music, English, education, speech/theatre, foreign language, behavioral sciences, industrial education, biology, home economics, art, philosophy & religion, math, computer science, audio visual, business, and history. Distributives and 3 hours of philosophy/religion required. Independent study. Cooperative work/study. Credit by exam. Preprofessional programs in engineering, law, library/media science, medicine & osteopathy, dentistry, physical therapy, nursing, medical technology, veterinary medicine, pharmacy, physician assistant, optometry, forestry. Member Associated Colleges of Central Kansas. Urban teacher program. Study abroad. Elementary, secondary, and special education certification.
Financial ACT FAS. College scholarships, grants, loans, state grants; PELL, SEOG, NDSL, GSL, CWS; college has own work program. Application deadline March 15.
Admissions High school graduation required. GED accepted. Interview encouraged. ACT required. $15 application fee. Rolling admissions. $75 deposit required on acceptance of admissions offer. Transfers accepted. Credit possible for CEEB CLEP exams.
Student Life Student government. Newspaper, yearbook. Music, debate, drama groups. International Students. Intercultural Forum. Academic, religious, service, political, honorary, and special interest groups. Single students must live at home or on campus. Single-sex dorms. Married-student housing. Liquor, gambling prohibited; smoking restricted. Attendance in class and at convocations required. 6 intercollegiate sports for men, 6 for women; intramural and club sports. NAIA, AIAW, KCAC.

[1] MID-AMERICA NAZARENE COLLEGE
2030 College Way, Olathe 66061, (913) 782-3750
Director of Admissions & Student Financial Services: Barth Smith

• **Undergraduates: 651m, 703w**
• **Tuition (1982/83): $2,394**
• **Room & Board: $1,998; Fees: $120**
• **Degrees offered: AB, BSN, AA**
• **Mean ACT 19.4**
• **Student-faculty ratio: 19 to 1**

A private college affiliated with the International Church of the Nazarene, established in 1966. 112-acre campus 19 miles southwest of Kansas City, Missouri. Air, bus, and rail service nearby.
Academic Character NCACS accreditation. 4-1-4 system, 6-week summer term. 37 majors offered by the divisions of Business Administration, Communication, Education & Psychology, Fine Arts, Nursing, Religion & Philosophy, Science & Mathematics, and Social Sciences. Double majors. Courses in French, Spanish. Distributives and 4 courses in religion required. Independent study. Pass/fail. Dual degree program in vocational agriculture, home economics with Kansas State. 3-1 program in medical technology with Trinity Lutheran. Elementary and secondary education certification. ROTC, AFROTC, NROTC at U of Kansas. 89,000-volume library with microform resources.
Financial CEEB CSS and ACT FAS. College scholarships, grants, loans, state grants, payment plan; PELL, SEOG, NSS, NDSL, GSL, FISL, NSL, CWS. Application deadlines March 1 (PELL), September 1 (SEOG & loans), June 1 (priority for other aid).
Admissions High school graduation with 15 units required. GED accepted. SAT or ACT required. $20 application fee. Rolling admissions; suggest applying by May 1. $40 deposit required on acceptance of offer of admission. Informal early decision, *Early Admission*, and *Concurrent Enrollment* programs. Admission deferral possible. Transfers accepted. Credit possible for CEEB AP and CLEP exams.
Student Life Student government. Newspaper, yearbook. Music, drama, debate groups. Academic and special interest groups. Students under 23 must live at home or on campus. No married-student housing. 72% of students live on campus. Liquor, tobacco, drugs, gambling, movies, dances prohibited. Dress code. Attendance required in class and at 2 chapel services weekly. ½ course of phys ed required. 5 intercollegiate sports for men, 5 for women; intramural and club sports. NAIA, Heart of America. Student body composition: 2% Black, 98% White. 50% from out of state.

[J1] NEOSHO COUNTY COMMUNITY COLLEGE
1000 South Allen, Chanute 66720, (316) 431-2820
Dean of Students: Homer F. Bearrick

• **Enrollment: 162m, 173w; 713 total (including part-time)**
• **Tuition (1982/83): $10 per credit hour (in-state), $36.50 (out-of-state)**
• **Room & Board: $1,200; Fees: $70**
• **Degrees offered: AA, AGS**

A public junior college established in 1936. 50-acre campus located in the city of Chanute.
Academic Character NCACS accreditation. Semester system. 2-year transfer and terminal programs offered in aeronautical science, art, biological science, building trades, business & office education, chemistry, distributive

education, education, English, graphic arts, health care, home economics, humanities, industrial arts, mathematics, modern language, music, physical education, physical science, police science, psychology, social science, speech & drama, and technology. Preprofessional programs in law, medicine, nursing, mortuary science, optometry, pharmacy, physical therapy, veterinary medicine. Credit by exam. Study abroad. 23,000-volume library with microform resources.
Financial ACT FAS. College scholarships, athletic scholarships; PELL, SEOG, FISL, GSL, CWS.
Admissions High school graduation required. GED accepted. Rolling admissions. *Early Admission* Program. Transfers accepted.
Student Life Student government. Newspaper, yearbook. Professional, honorary, and special interest organizations. Single students under 21 must live at home or on campus. One dormitory with men's and women's wings. Dining hall. Class attendance required. 5 intercollegiate sports. KJCCC, NJCAA.

[1] OTTAWA UNIVERSITY
Ottawa 66067, (913) 242-5200, ext. 225
Director of Admissions: Daniel B. Baker

- **Undergraduates: 227m, 174w; 742 total (including part-time)**
- **Tuition (1982/83): $3,390**
- **Room & Board: $2,000**
- **Degree offered: BA**
- **Mean ACT 19; mean SAT 800 composite**
- **Student-faculty ratio: 16 to 1**

A private university affiliated with the American Baptist Churches, established in 1860. Small-city campus in Ottawa, 50 miles southwest of Kansas City.
Academic Character NCACS accreditation. Semester system with flexible terms. Majors offered in accounting, art, biology, business administration, chemistry, computer systems, economics, English, history, human services, management, mathematics, music, philosophy, physical education, political science, psychology, religion, and sociology. Self-designed and interdepartmental majors. Minors offered in 18 additional areas. Distributive requirements. Graduate courses offered. Independent study. Internships. Preprofessional programs in law, medicine, dentistry, allied health, medical technology. Dual-degree programs with Kansas State in agronomy/business administration, agronomy/physical science, engineering, and home economics. Dual degree program in forestry with Duke. Elementary, secondary, and middle school education certification. 91,000-volume library.
Financial CEEB CSS and ACT FAS. University scholarships, grants, loans, state scholarships & grants, athletic grants, payment plan; PELL, SEOG, NDSL, GSL.
Admissions High school graduation required. Interview encouraged. SAT or ACT required. $15 application fee. Rolling admissions. Transfers accepted. Credit possible for CEEB AP and CLEP exams.
Student Life Religious, honorary, and academic organizations. 5 social clubs for men, 6 for women. Single students must live at home or on campus. Single-sex dorms. No married-student housing. Liquor, drugs, gambling prohibited on campus. Class attendance required. 2 activity courses required. 4 intercollegiate sports for men, 3 for women, 2 coed. KCAC. Student body composition: 40% minority.

[1] PITTSBURG STATE UNIVERSITY
Pittsburg 66762, (316) 231-7000
Director of Admissions: James E. Parker

- **Undergraduates: 1,687m, 1,487w; 5,438 total (including graduates)**
- **Tuition & Fees (1982/83): $726 (in-state), $1,520 (out-of-state)**
- **Room & Board: $2,056**
- **Degrees offered: BA, BS, BFA, BMus, BMus Ed, BSG, BSMT, BSET, BSVTEd, BSEd, BSN, BST, BSBA, BBA, AA, AS**
- **Student-faculty ratio: 20 to 1**

A public university established in 1903. 125-acre campus in small city of Pittsburg, 100 miles from Kansas City. Bus nearby; airport 30 miles away in Joplin, Missouri.
Academic Character NCACS and professional accreditation. Semester system, 8-week summer term. 53 majors offered by the School of Arts & Sciences, 10 by the Gladys A. Kelce School of Business & Economics, 4 by the School of Education, and 25 by the School of Technology & Applied Science. Self-designed majors. Minors required. Minors offered in most major fields. Distributive requirements. Masters degrees granted. Independent study. Honors program. Cooperative work/study, pass/fail, internships. Preprofessional programs in dentistry, engineering, forestry, health science, law, medicine, mortuary science, optometry, pharmacy, physical therapy, theology, veterinary medicine. 3-2 programs in chemistry, physics, engineering with Kansas State and U of Kansas. Study abroad. Elementary, secondary, and special education certification. ROTC. Computer center. 450,000-volume library.
Financial ACT FAS. University scholarships; PELL, SEOG, NSS, NDSL, FISL, CWS. Scholarship application deadline March 15.
Admissions High school graduation required. GED accepted. ACT required. $25 application fee for foreign students. Rolling admissions. *Concurrent Enrollment* Program. Admission deferral possible. Transfers accepted. Credit possible for CEEB AP and CLEP exams; university has own advanced placement program.
Student Life Student government. Newspaper, magazine, yearbook. Special interest groups. 8 fraternities, 7 with houses, and 4 sororities, 3 with houses. 10% of men and women join. Freshmen under 21 must live on campus. Coed and single-sex dorms. Married-student housing. 20% of students live on campus. Only 3.2 beer allowed on campus. 4 intercollegiate sports for men, 5 for women; intramurals. NAIA, CSIC. Student body composition: 0.5% Asian, 2% Black, 1% Hispanic, 0.5% Native American, 95% White, 1% Other. 15% of students from out of state.

[J1] PRATT COMMUNITY COLLEGE
Pratt 67124, (316) 672-5641
Dean of Admissions and Registrar: Ray O. McKinney

- **Undergraduates: 178m, 164w; 1,201 total (including part-time)**
- **Tuition (1982/83): $384 (in-state), $1,330 (out-of-state)**
- **Room & Board: $1,585-$1,685; Fees: $130**
- **Degrees offered: AS, AA, AAS**
- **Mean ACT 18.3**
- **Student-faculty ratio: 16 to 1**

A public college established in 1891. Campus located in small city of Pratt.
Academic Character NCACS accreditation. Semester system. 2-year programs offered in agriculture, science & math, social & behavioral science, fine arts & humanities, business & education, and health, physical education, & recreation. Technical programs in 41 subjects for AAS or certificate. Preprofessional programs in forestry, engineering, social work, chiropractic, cytotechnology, dentistry, medicine, dental hygiene, medical technology, optometry, pharmacy, physical therapy, nursing, respiratory therapy. Transfer programs with U of Kansas and Wichita State in physical therapy, with St. Mary of the Plains in respiratory therapy.
Financial College scholarships; PELL, SEOG, NDSL, HELP, CWS. Priority application deadline April 15.
Admissions High school graduation required. GED accepted. ACT recommended. Rolling admissions. Transfers accepted. Advanced placement credit possible.
Student Life Student government. Newspaper, yearbook. Music, drama, arts groups. International Student Association. Religious, honorary, academic, and special interest groups. Limited college housing in one dorm. Class attendance required. 2 credit hours of phys ed required. 4 intercollegiate sports for men, 3 for women; intramurals. Kansas Jayhawk Conference, NJCAA. Student body composition: 10% minority. 17% of students from out of state.

[1] ST. JOHN'S COLLEGE
Winfield 67156, (316) 221-4000

- **Undergraduates: 83m, 115w; 212 total (including part-time)**
- **Tuition, Room & Board (1982/83): $4,700 avg.**
- **Degrees offered: BA, BS, ADN, AA**

A private college controlled by the Lutheran Church-Missouri Synod.
Academic Character NCACS accreditation. 4-1-4 system. Majors offered in the areas of business administration, liberal arts, nursing. Terminal programs include secretarial studies with special emphasis on preparation for church secretaries. Remedial mathematics and English programs.
Admissions High school graduation with C average or in upper 60% of graduating class required. GED accepted. Rolling admissions. Admission deferral possible. Advanced placement credit possible.
Student Life Dormitories and dining hall.

[1] SAINT MARY COLLEGE
Leavenworth 66048, (913) 682-5151

- **Undergraduates: 65m, 299w; 845 total (including part-time)**
- **Tuition & Fees (1982/83): $2,850**
- **Typical Expenses: $5,450**
- **Degrees offered: BA, BS, BMus, BMus Ed, AA**
- **Mean ACT 19.1**
- **Student-faculty ratio: 12 to 1**

A private Roman Catholic liberal arts college primarily for women, founded in 1923, controlled by the Sisters of Charity of Leavenworth. Suburban campus in the small city of Leavenworth, located in northeastern Kansas.
Academic Character NCACS and professional accreditation. Semester system, 6-week summer term. Majors offered in fields including liberal arts, music, and education. Remedial mathematics and English programs. 120,000-volume library.
Financial Limited college scholarships available up to approximately $1000. PELL, SEOG, NDSL, FISL.
Admissions Admission notification on a rolling basis. *Early Decision* and *Early Admission* programs. Admission deferral possible. Advanced placement credit possible.
Student Life Dormitories and dining halls.

[1] SAINT MARY OF THE PLAINS COLLEGE
Dodge City 67801, (316) 225-4171
Dean of Admissions: Maurice Werner

- **Undergraduates: 204m, 388w**
- **Tuition (1982/83): $3,000**
- **Room & Board: $2,000; Fees: $90**
- **Degrees offered: BA, BS, BMus Ed, BSN, BSW**
- **Mean ACT 22**
- **Student-faculty ratio: 10 to 1**

A private Roman Catholic college controlled by the Sisters of St. Joseph of Wichita, established in 1952. 60-acre suburban campus in Dodge City, which is located in southwestern Kansas.
Academic Character NCACS and professional accreditation. Semester system, flexible summer terms. Majors offered in agribusiness, biology, business administration, business education, chemistry, computer/business, criminal justice, elementary education, English, government, history, human behavior, journalism, mathematics, medical technology, music, nursing, physical education, psychology, religious studies, social work, sociology, Spanish, and speech & theatre. Interdisciplinary, self-designed majors. Minors offered in all major fields and in art, economics, library science, philosophy, and physics. Distributives and 1 course in Christian morality or

ethics required. Independent study. Honors program. Internships. Preprofessional programs in agriculture, dentistry, engineering, law, medicine, optometry, physical therapy. Elementary and secondary education certification. Study abroad. 70,960-volume library.
Financial ACT FAS. College scholarships, grants, loans, state grants, Black and Mexican-American student scholarships, payment plan; PELL, SEOG, NDSL, GSL, NSL, CWS. Application dates January 1 to April 1.
Admissions High school graduation required. GED accepted. ACT or SAT required. $20 application fee. Rolling admissions. $25 deposit required on acceptance of offer of admission. Transfers accepted. Credit possible for CEEB AP and CLEP exams; college has own advanced placement program.
Student Life Student government. Newspaper, yearbook. Music, drama, criminal justice groups. Spanish-American club. Honorary and special interest organizations. Freshmen and sophomores must live at home or on campus. Dorms for men and women. No married-student housing. 75% of students live on campus. Phys ed required for teaching majors. 3 intercollegiate sports for men, 3 for women; intramurals. AIAW, KAIAW, KCAC, NAIA. Student body composition: 4% Black, 12% Hispanic, 84% White. 14% from out of state.

[J1] SEWARD COUNTY COMMUNITY COLLEGE
Box 1137, Liberal 67901, (316) 624-1951
Registrar: Larry Kruse

- **Undergraduates: 134m, 159w; 1,560 total (including part-time)**
- **Tuition (1982/83): $300 (in-state); $1,330 (out-of-state)**
- **Fees: $120**
- **Degrees offered: AA, AS, AAS**

A public college established in 1969. Campus located in Liberal. Airport nearby.
Academic Character NCACS and professional accreditation. Semester system, 6- and 8-week summer terms. Liberal arts, preprofessional, and terminal programs offered, with 30 programs for the AA, 18 for the AS, and 24 for the AAS. Certificate programs in 18 areas. Pass/fail. Internships. Credit by exam. Preprofessional programs in law, forestry, engineering, medical technology, medicine, and nursing. Cooperative programs with area vocational-technical school. Learning Resource Center.
Financial College scholarships; PELL, SEOG, NDSL, GSL, CWS; college has own work program.
Admissions High school graduation required. GED accepted. ACT recommended. Rolling admissions. *Early Admission* Program. Transfers accepted. College has own advanced placement program.
Student Life Student government. Academic and special interest groups. 1 coed dorm. Cafeteria. Class attendance required. 2 hours of phys ed required. 5 intercollegiate sports; intramurals. Kansas Jayhawk JC Conference.

[1] SOUTHWESTERN COLLEGE
100 College Street, Winfield 67156, (316) 221-4150, ext. 233
Director of Admissions: Carl A. Pagles

- **Undergraduates: 311m, 345w**
- **Tuition (1982/83): $2,960**
- **Room & Board: $1,895; Fees: $90**
- **Degrees offered: BA, BMus, BS, BBA, BPh**
- **Mean ACT 21.5**
- **Student-faculty ratio: 13 to 1**

A private college affiliated with the United Methodist Church, established in 1885. Suburban campus in small city of Winfield, southeast of Wichita.
Academic Character NCACS and professional accreditation. 4-1-4 system, 3 3-week summer terms. 41 majors offered by the divisions of Fine Arts, Humanities, Management, Natural Science, Professional Service Programs, and Social Science. Distributives and 1 course in religion/philosophy required. Independent study. Honors program. Cooperative work/study, internships. Preprofessional programs in nursing, physical therapy, medical technology, special education, medicine, law, divinity, psychology, religious education. Urban Teacher Education program. Study abroad. Exchange program with International Christian U. Washington, UN Semesters. Elementary and secondary education certification. Media center, greenhouses. 100,000-volume library with microform resources.
Financial ACT FAS. College scholarships, grants, loans, state grants, activity scholarships, family plan; PELL, SEOG, NDSL, GSL, USAF, CWS. Preferred application deadline April 15.
Admissions High school graduation required. GED accepted. Interview encouraged. ACT or SAT required. $10 application fee. Rolling admissions. $50 deposit required on acceptance of offer of admission. *Early Decision* and *Early Admission* programs. Admission deferral possible. Transfers accepted. Credit possible for CEEB AP and CLEP exams, and for experience; college has own advanced placement program.
Student Life Student government. Newspaper, yearbook, radio station. Music, drama groups. Debate fraternity. Academic, honorary, religious, service, and special interest groups. Single freshmen and sophomores must live at home or on campus. Dorms for men and women. Honors housing. 77% of students live on campus. 7 intercollegiate sports; intramural and club sports. KCAA.

[1] STERLING COLLEGE
Sterling 67579, (316) 278-2173
Director of Admissions & Enrollment Development: Janet L. Splitter

- **Undergraduates: 240m, 260w**
- **Tuition (1982/83): $3,350**
- **Room & Board: $1,850**
- **Degrees offered: BA, BS**
- **Mean ACT 19.2; mean SAT 900**
- **Student-faculty ratio: 14 to 1**

A private college operated by the United Presbyterian Church, established in 1887. Campus located in Sterling, northwest of Hutchinson.
Academic Character NCACS and professional accreditation. 4-1-4 system. Majors offered in art, English, music, religious & philosophic studies, speech & theatre arts, natural sciences, mathematics, biology, chemistry, behavioral science, business, history & government, education, health & physical education, home economics, and youth leadership. Minors offered in most major fields. Distributives and 5 courses in Bible/church required. Honors program. Pass/fail. Preprofessional programs in medicine, dentistry, pharmacy, nursing, medical technology, law, ministry, engineering. Agronomy program with Kansas State. Elementary and secondary education certification. 80,000-volume library.
Financial ACT FAS. College scholarships, state grants, Presbyterian scholarships, payment plans; PELL, SEOG, BIA, NDSL, GSL, CWS.
Admissions High school graduation required. GED accepted. ACT or SAT required. $10 application fee. Rolling admissions. $100 deposit required on acceptance of admissions offer. Transfers accepted. Credit possible for CEEB AP and CLEP exams; college has own advanced placement program.
Student Life Religious, social, cultural activities. Single students must live at home or on campus. Dorms for men and women. No married-student housing. Liquor, tobacco, gambling prohibited on campus. Class attendance required. 1 phys ed course required. 5 intercollegiate sports for men, 4 for women; intramurals. NAIA, AIAW, KCAC. Student body composition: 10% minority.

[J1] TABOR COLLEGE
Hillsboro 67063, (316) 947-3121, ext. 221
Director of Admissions: Barry Jackson

- **Undergraduates: 203m, 235w**
- **Tuition (1982/83): $3,200**
- **Room & Board: $1,950-$2,500; Fees: $120**
- **Degrees offered: BA, BMus Ed, AA**
- **Student-faculty ratio: 15 to 1**

A private college controlled by the Mennonite Brethren, established in 1908. 26-acre campus located in small town of Hillsboro, 50 miles from Wichita. Air, rail, and bus service nearby.
Academic Character NCACS accreditation. 4-1-4 system, summer term. Majors offered in humanities, contemporary church ministries, Christian studies, English, English/communications, music, natural & mathematical sciences, agriculture, biology, chemistry, computer science, mathematics, mathematical sciences, medical technology, social sciences, social work, business administration & economics, accounting, business education, office administration, secretarial science, health & physical education, and teacher education. Self-designed majors. Distributives and 8 credit hours of religion required. Independent study. Cooperative work/study. Preprofessional programs in medicine, dentistry, optometry, veterinary medicine, nursing, engineering, foreign service, law, seminary. Member Associated Colleges of Central Kansas. Cooperative agriculture and home economics programs with Kansas State. Environmental Studies program in Michigan. Urban teaching program. Study abroad. Elementary, secondary, and special education certification. 60,000-volume library with microform resources.
Financial ACT FAS. College scholarships, state scholarships and grants; PELL, SEOG, NDSL, GSL, CWS, assistantships. Application deadline May 1.
Admissions High school graduation required. GED accepted. ACT or SAT required. $16 application fee. Rolling admissions. $50 deposit required on acceptance of offer of admission. Transfers accepted. Advanced placement credit possible for CEEB AP and CLEP exams.
Student Life Student government. Newspaper, yearbook. Music and drama groups. Minority Student Union, International Student Club. Religious, academic, service, and special interest groups. Single students must live at home or on campus. Single-sex dorms. Liquor, tobacco prohibited on campus. Attendance in class and at 15 convocations per semester required. 3 credit hours in phys ed and activity required. 6 intercollegiate sports for men, 3 for women; intramurals. NAIA, KCAC.

[G1] UNITED STATES ARMY COMMAND AND GENERAL STAFF COLLEGE
Fort Leavenworth 66027

[1] WASHBURN UNIVERSITY OF TOPEKA
Topeka 66621, (913) 295-6300
Director of Admissions Process: John E. Triggs

- **Undergraduates: 2,225m, 2,657w**
- **Tuition (1982/83): $1,360 (in-state), $1,770 (out-of-state)**
- **Room & Board: $2,100; Fees: $204**
- **Degrees offered: BA, BS, BBA, BBus Ed, BFA, BMus, BEd, AA, AS**
- **Student-faculty ratio: 25 to 1**

A public university established in 1865. 160-acre urban campus in Topeka, 60 miles from Kansas City. Served by air, rail, and bus.
Academic Character NCACS and professional accreditation. Semester system, 13-week summer term. 43 majors offered in the areas of business, American citizenship, arts, sciences, communication & languages, criminal justice, education, general studies, home economics, medicine & health, philosophy, and social & political sciences. Distributive requirements. JD, MEd, MPsy granted. Honors program. Pass/fail. Internships. Credit by exam. Preprofessional programs in aviation technology, dentistry, engineering, journalism, law, medicine, medical technology, nursing, physical education, recreation, social work, teaching, theology. Study abroad. Elementary and secondary education certification. AFROTC. Computer center, language lab. 203,000-volume library.
Financial University scholarships, grants, loans, payment plan; PELL, SEOG, NDSL, FISL, CWS. Priority application deadline March 15.

Admissions High school graduation required. GED accepted. ACT highly recommended. Rolling admissions. *Early Admission* and *Early Decision* programs. Transfers accepted. Credit possible for CEEB AP and CLEP exams.
Student Life Student government. Newspaper, yearbook, TV station. Music, dance, drama, debate groups. Black Student Alliance. Latin American Student Service Organization. Academic, political, religious, and special interest groups. 5 fraternities and 5 sororities with houses. Coed dorms. Married-student housing. Liquor prohibited on campus. 2 semesters of phys ed required. 8 intercollegiate sports for men and women; intramurals. AIAW, NAIA. Student body composition: 0.4% Asian, 7.4% Black, 2.9% Hispanic, 0.7% Native American, 88% White, 0.6% Other. 5% from out of state.

[1] WICHITA STATE UNIVERSITY
Wichita 67208, (316) 689-3085
Director of Admissions: Stanley E. Henderson

- **Undergraduates: 3,444m, 3,156w; 16,954 total (including graduates)**
- **Tuition (1982/83): $930 (in-state), $2,245 (out-of-state)**
- **Room & Board: $2,000**
- **Degrees offered: BA, BBA, BFA, BAE, BMus, BMus Ed, BGS, BSMT, BSE's,**
- **Student-faculty ratio: 18 to 1**

A public university established in 1895. 320-acre urban campus in northeast Wichita. Served by air, rail, and bus.
Academic Character NCACS and professional accreditation. Semester system, 2 4-week and 1 8-week summer terms. 90 majors offered by the colleges of Business Administration, Education, Engineering, Fine Arts, Health Related Professions, and Liberal Arts & Sciences. Distributive requirements. Graduate and professional degrees granted. Independent study. Honors program. Cooperative work/study, pass/fail, internships. Credit by exam. Preprofessional programs in law, medicine, optometry, pharmacy, public service, theology, veterinary medicine. Study abroad in France, Mexico. Elementary, secondary, and special education certification. ROTC. Computer center, museum, gerontology center. Over 662,675-volume library with microform resources.
Financial University scholarships, grants, loans; PELL, SEOG, NSS, NDSL, HELP, NSL, CWS. Application deadline February 15.
Admissions High school graduation with 12½ units required. GED accepted. Interview encouraged. ACT required. Rolling admissions; application deadline June 1 (out-of-state), August 1 (in-state). Transfers accepted. Credit possible for CEEB AP and CLEP exams; university has own advanced placement program.
Student Life Student government. Association of Women Students. Newspaper, magazine, yearbook, radio station. Music, debate, drama groups. International Students Club. Academic, religious, political, honorary, and special interest groups. 9 fraternities, with dorm facilities, and 8 sororities with houses. 5% of men and 8% of women join. Single freshmen under 21 must live at home or on campus. Coed and single-sex dorms. 5% of students live on campus. 3.2 beer allowed on campus. 8 intercollegiate sports for men, 7 for women; several intramural and club sports. AIAW, MVAC. Student body composition: 5.6% Asian, 6.1% Black, 1.8% Hispanic, 0.8% Native American, 85.7% White. 7% from out of state.

KENTUCKY (KY)

[1] ALICE LLOYD COLLEGE
Pippa Passes 41844, (606) 368-2101
Director of Admissions: Billy C. Melton

- **Enrollment: 167m, 235w; 418 total (including part-time)**
- **Tuition (1982/83): $2,245**
- **Room & Board: $1,550**
- **Degrees offered: BA, BS, BSMed Tech, AA, AS, AAS**
- **Mean ACT 18**
- **Student-faculty ratio: 7 to 1**

A private college established in 1923 and sustained by the Caney Creek Community Center, Inc. 175-acre rural campus 100 miles from Huntington, West Virginia.
Academic Character SACS accreditation. Semester system, 6-week summer term. Majors offered in biology, business administration, elementary education, mathematics/physical science, medical technology, physical education, and social studies. Courses in 14 additional areas. Distributive requirements. Independent study. Elementary and secondary education certification. Appalachian Oral History Project. 45,000-volume library.
Financial Students required to apply for financial aid. CEEB CSS (KFAF) for in-state applicants; CEEB CSS or ACT FAS for others. College scholarships and grants, state grants, Regional Opportunity Program; PELL, SEOG, NDSL, GSL, CWS. All students required to work. Application deadline August 15.
Admissions High school graduation required. GED accepted. ACT required. Financial Aid form required. *Concurrent Enrollment* Program. Transfers accepted.
Student Life Student government. Newspaper, literary magazine, yearbook. Voices of Appalachia. Drama productions. Crafts program. Academic, honorary, recreational, religious, service, and special interest groups. Single-sex dorms. 4 intercollegiate sports for men, 4 for women; extensive intramural program. NAIA, KIAC, KWIC.

[1] ASBURY COLLEGE
201 North Lexington Avenue, Wilmore 40390, (606) 858-3511
Director of Admissions: William E. Eddy

- **Undergraduates: 558m, 646w**
- **Tuition (1982/83): $2,959**
- **Room & Board: $2,109; Fees: $259**
- **Degrees offered: BA, BS, BSEd**
- **Mean ACT 18; mean SAT 800 composite**
- **Student-faculty ratio: 16 to 1**

A private college established in 1890. 400-acre campus in a small town 20 miles from Lexington. Bus service to Lexington.
Academic Character SACS accreditation. Trimester system, 2 4-week, 1 8-week summer terms. 31 majors offered by the divisions of education & psychology, English & speech, fine arts, foreign languages, philosophy & religion, science & mathematics, social services and health, physical education, & recreation. Minors offered in most major fields and in 11 additional areas. Distributives and 3 quarters of religion or theology required. Preprofessional programs in dentistry, engineering, medicine, and nursing. 3-1 medical technology program. Exchange with Christian College Consortium. Study in France and Germany. Elementary and secondary education and library science certification. 100,000-volume library.
Financial CEEB CSS and ACT FAS. College scholarships, grants, loans, payment plan; PELL, SEOG, NDSL, CWS. Application deadline May 1.
Admissions High school graduation with 15 units required. GED accepted from veterans. Interview recommended. SAT or ACT required. $25 application fee. Rolling admissions. $100 tuition and $30 room deposits required on acceptance of offer of admission. *Early Admission* Program. Transfers accepted. Credit possible for CEEB AP, CLEP, and ACT PEP exams. Probationary acceptance possible.
Student Life Newspaper, yearbook. Music groups. Ministerial Association. Women in Service for Christ. Christian Education Association. Foreign Missions Fellowship. Fellowship of Christian Athletes. Foreign Students Clubs. Academic, political, and service groups. Students must live on campus or at home. Single-sex dorms. Married-student housing. 89% of students live on campus. 4 quarters of phys ed required. Liquor, drugs, and smoking prohibited. Dress code. Attendance in class required. Parental permission necessary for off-campus weekends. 5 intercollegiate sports for men, 5 for women; intramurals. NAIA. Student body composition: 0.1% Asian, 0.6% Black, 0.6% Hispanic, 97.7% White, 1% Other. 89% from out of state.

[P] ASBURY THEOLOGICAL SEMINARY
Wilmore 40390

[1] BELLARMINE COLLEGE
Newburg Road, Louisville 40205, (502) 452-8160
Dean of Admissions: Robert G. Pfaadt

- **Undergraduates: 580m, 576w; 2,585 total (including graduates)**
- **Tuition (1982/83): $3,350**
- **Room: $750**
- **Degrees offered: BA, BS, BSN**
- **Mean ACT 22; mean SAT 970**
- **Student-faculty ratio: 19 to 1**

A private college affiliated with the Archdiocese of Louisville, established in 1968. 115-acre suburban campus. Served by air, rail, and bus.
Academic Character SACS accreditation. Semester system, 2 5-week summer terms (day and evening) and a 10-week evening summer term. Majors offered in accounting, business administration, elementary education, kindergarten, learning & behavior disorders, secondary education, speech & communication disorders, art, English, music, philosophy, theology, biology, chemistry, computer science, mathematics, economics, history, political science, psychology, and sociology. Major in nursing for students with an RN. Major in engineering in cooperation with U of Louisville. Minors offered in all major fields. Courses in 4 additional areas. Associate programs in data processing and theology. Distributives and 9 hours of theology required; seniors must take comprehensive exams. MBA granted. Independent and accelerated study. Honors program. Cooperative work/study, limited pass/fail, internships. Preprofessional programs in engineering, law, medicine, pharmacy, veterinary medicine. Member Kentuckiana Metroversity. Elementary, secondary, and special education certification. AFROTC through Metroversity. Thomas Merton Studies Center. 99,000-volume library.
Financial CEEB CSS. College scholarships, grants, loans, payment plans; PELL, SEOG, NDSL, FISL, CWS. Application deadlines March 1 (scholarships), May 1 (grants & loans).
Admissions High school graduation or equivalent required. SAT or ACT required. $10 application fee. Rolling admissions. $50 room deposit required on acceptance of offer of admission. *Early Admission* and *Early Decision* programs. Admission deferral possible. Transfers accepted. Credit possible for CEEB AP, CLEP, and course exams.
Student Life Student Senate. Newspaper, literary magazine, yearbook. Pep band. College chorus. Debate. Honorary, religious, service, and special interest groups. Single freshmen and sophomores must live at home or on campus. Single-sex dorms. No married-student housing. 25% of students live on campus. Food purchased by meal ticket or cash. Honor code. Limited class absences. 7 intercollegiate sports for men, 6 for women; extensive intramurals. AIAW, NCAA, Great Lakes Valley Conference. Student body composition: 1% Asian, 5% Black, 3% Hispanic, 85% White, 6% Other. 22% from out of state.

[1] BEREA COLLEGE
Berea 40404, (606) 986-9341
Director of Admissions: John S. Cook

- **Undergraduates: 697m, 853w**

- **Tuition (1982/83): $0**
- **Room & Board: $1,629; Fees: $118**
- **Degrees offered: BA, BSAg, BSHEc, BSBA, BSIndus Arts, BSN**
- **Student-faculty ratio: 12 to 1**

A private college established in 1855 to provide Christian education opportunities for young people of the mountain region of the South. 160-acre campus with 1,100 acres of farmland in the foothills of the Cumberland Mountains, 40 miles south of Lexington. Served by bus.
Academic Character SACS and professional accreditation. 4-1-4 system, 8-week summer term. 23 majors offered in the areas of liberal arts & sciences, 10 in agriculture, business, home economics, industrial arts, and nursing. Self-designed majors. Courses offered in 6 additional areas. Distributives and 8 hours of religious and historical perspectives required. Each student works a minimum of 10 hours per week in college labor program. Independent and accelerated study. Phi Beta Kappa. Cooperative work/study, internships. Preprofessional programs in law, medicine, veterinary science. Exchange programs with various small colleges. Language majors may take junior year abroad. Elementary and secondary teacher certification. Nursery school lab. Appalachian museum. Computer, language lab. Over 230,000-volume library.
Financial CEEB CSS, ACT FAS, and state financial aid service. College scholarships, grants, loans, payment plan; PELL, SEOG, NSS, NDSL, FISL, NSL, CWS. Each student works at least 10 hours a week in a college department or in one of the student industries (bakery, tavern hotel, broomcraft, fireside weaving, needlecraft, woodcraft). Preferred application deadline is early spring.
Admissions High school graduation. Interview encouraged. SAT or ACT required. $5 application fee. Rolling admissions. $35 confirmation deposit required on acceptance of offer of admission, refundable up to 30 days before registration. *Early Admission* and *Concurrent Enrollment* programs. Transfers accepted. Credit possible for CEEB AP and CLEP exams; college has own placement program.
Student Life Student Association. Newspaper, Black student literary magazine, yearbook, radio stations. Music, drama, and dance groups. Black Student Union. Academic, honorary, religious, and special interest groups. Students must live at home or in single-sex dorms. Limited married-student housing. 80% of students live on campus. Dormitory students may not have cars on campus. 3 terms of phys ed and 1 term of health required. Regular class attendance expected. Attendance at 10 convocations each term mandatory. Liquor and narcotics prohibited. Committee of deans must approve student marriages. 8 intercollegiate sports for men, 6 for women; many intramurals. AIAW, NAIA, KIAC. Student body composition: 1% Asian, 10% Black, 89% White. 80% of students are from the mountain counties of Kentucky, Alabama, Georgia, N. Carolina, Ohio, S. Carolina, Tennessee, Virginia, and W. Virginia. 60% from out of state.

[1] BRESCIA COLLEGE

120 West 7th Street, Owensboro 42301, (502) 685-3131
Dean of Admissions: Sister Annalita Lancaster

- **Enrollment: 182m, 306w; 890 total (including part-time)**
- **Tuition (1982/83): $2,700**
- **Room & Board: $1,815**
- **Degrees offered: BA, BS, BMus, BMus Ed, AA, AS**
- **Mean ACT 18.3**
- **Student-faculty ratio: 16 to 1**

A private college controlled by the Ursuline Sisters of Mount Saint Joseph, established in 1925. Urban campus 125 miles west of Louisville. Served by air and bus.
Academic Character SACS and professional accreditation. Semester system, 2 4½-week summer terms. 26 majors offered by the Divisions of Business, Educational Services, Fine Arts, Humanities, Mathematics & Natural Sciences, and Social & Behavioral Sciences. Self-designed majors. Minors offered in most major fields. Courses offered in 14 additional areas. Distributives and 6 hours of religion required. Independent study. Pass/fail, credit by exam. Preprofessional programs in dentistry, engineering, law, medicine, optometry, pharmacy, veterinary science. Early childhood, elementary, secondary, and special education certification. Language lab. Speech and hearing clinic. 100,000-volume library.
Financial College scholarships, loans, state grants; PELL, SEOG, NDSL, GSL, CWS, college employment. Priority application deadline March 31.
Admissions High school graduation required. GED accepted. ACT or SAT required; ACT preferred. $15 application fee. Rolling admissions. Transfers accepted. Credit possible for CEEB CLEP exams.
Student Life Student government. Newspaper, literary magazine, yearbook. Music and drama groups. Circle K. Union of Black Identity, Christian Student Union. Honorary, professional, service, and special interest groups. Students not living at home expected to live on campus. Single-sex dorms. 2 intercollegiate sports; intramurals.

[P] CALVARY COLLEGE

Letcher 41832

[1] CAMPBELLSVILLE COLLEGE

Campbellsville 42718, (505) 465-8158
Director of Admissions: James C. Coates

- **Undergraduates: 268m, 323w**
- **Tuition (1982/83): $2,500**
- **Room & Board: $1,970; Fees: $140**
- **Degrees offered: BA, BS, BMus, BSMT**
- **Mean ACT 16.5**
- **Student-faculty ratio: 15 to 1**

A private college affiliated with the Kentucky Baptist Convention, established in 1906. 30-acre small-town campus. Served by air, rail, and bus.
Academic Character SACS accreditation. Semester system, 8-week summer term. Majors offered in art, basic business, biology, business, chemistry, Christian studies, church music, church recreation, economics, elementary education, English, history, math, medical technology, music, physical education, political science, psychology, secretarial studies, social work, and sociology. Minors offered in most major fields and in 7 additional areas. Distributives, 6 hours of Christian studies, and Correlated Studies Program required. GRE required of all seniors. Independent study. Pass/fail. Preprofessional programs in dentistry, engineering, law, medicine, ministry, nursing, and pharmacy. 3-1 medicine and dentistry programs with Georgia Tech. 3-2 programs in computer science, economics, engineering, industrial management, management science, and physics with Georgia Tech. Western Kentucky University Consortium. Study in Israel. Elementary and secondary education certification. 90,000-volume library.
Financial CEEB CSS. College scholarships, grants, loans, academic and church-related awards, payment plan; PELL, SEOG, GSL, NDSL, CWS. Application deadline April 15.
Admissions High school graduation or equivalent required. GED accepted. ACT or SAT required; ACT preferred. No application fee. Rolling admissions. $100 deposit required on acceptance of offer of admission. *Concurrent Enrollment* Program. Credit possible for CEEB AP, CLEP, and ACT exams.
Student Life Student government. Newspaper, literary magazine, yearbook. Music groups. Baptist Student Union. Baptist Young Women. Ministerial Association. Retreats, vespers, youth teams, service projects, dorm devotions. Circle K. Academic and political groups. Students must live at home or on campus. Single-sex dorms. Married-student housing. 54% of students live on campus. 3 hours of phys ed required. Liquor and social dancing prohibited. Regular class attendance expected. Dress code. Weekly chapel attendance required. 4 intercollegiate sports for men, 4 for women; intramurals. KIAC. Student body composition: 1% Asian, 2% Black, 97% White. 20% from out of state.

[1] CENTRE COLLEGE OF KENTUCKY

Danville 40422, (606) 236-5211
Director of Admissions: Steve Grissom

- **Undergraduates: 419m, 325w**
- **Tuition (1982/83): $5,100**
- **Room & Board: $2,275; Fees: $275**
- **Degrees offered: AB, BS**
- **Mean ACT 25; mean SAT 530v, 550m**
- **Student-faculty ratio: 12 to 1**

A private college established in 1819. 75-acre small-city campus, 35 miles southwest of Lexington. Served by bus.
Academic Character SACS accreditation. 4-2-4 system, 6-week summer term. Majors offered in applied math, art, biochemistry, biology, chemical physics, chemistry, dramatic art, economics, elementary education, English, environmental science, French, German, government, history, management, math, molecular biology, music, philosophy, physics, psychobiology, psychology, religion, and Spanish. Self-designed majors. Minors offered in some major fields. Courses in 3 additional areas. Distributives and 2 courses in religious studies required; major program exams required of seniors. Independent research. Honors program. Phi Beta Kappa. 3-2 program in engineering with Columbia, Georgia Tech, Kentucky, Vanderbilt, and Washington U. Math and science term at Oak Ridge. Junior year abroad. Elementary and secondary education certification. ROTC. Language lab. Regional Arts Center. Over 125,000-volume library.
Financial CEEB CSS. College scholarships, grants, loans, payment plan; PELL, SEOG, NDSL, CWS. Application deadline March 15.
Admissions High school graduation with 15 units required. Interview urged. SAT or ACT required. $15 application fee. Rolling admissions. $150 deposit required on acceptance of offer of admission. *Early Admission* Program. Admission deferral possible. Transfers accepted. Credit possible for CEEB AP and CLEP exams.
Student Life Student Congress, Student Judicial System. Newspaper, magazines, yearbook. Association for Centre Women. Music and drama groups. Big Brother and Sister Program. Black Student Union. Academic, honorary, professional, religious, service, and special interest groups. 6 fraternities with houses, 3 sororities. 70% of men and 39% of women join. Freshmen and sophomores must live at home or on campus. Dormitories. 95% of students live on campus. 2 years of phys ed required. 8 convocations per year required. Intoxication and disorderly conduct prohibited. Class attendance expected. 5 intercollegiate sports for men, 6 for women; coed and intramural sports. AIAW, NCAA, CAC. Student body composition: 0.3% Asian, 2.5% Black, 0.3% Hispanic, 96.4% White. 40% from out of state.

[1] CUMBERLAND COLLEGE

Williamsburg 40769, (606) 549-2683
Director of Admissions: Michael B. Colegrove

- **Undergraduates: 658m, 903w**
- **Tuition & Fees (1982/83): $2,380**
- **Room & Board: $1,576**
- **Degrees offered: BA, BS, BMus**
- **Mean ACT 16**
- **Student-faculty ratio: 16 to 1**

A private college affiliated with the Kentucky Baptist Convention, established in 1889. 20-acre campus located in a small town 80 miles north of Knoxville. Bus to Williamsburg; airport at London, Kentucky.
Academic Character SACS and professional accreditation. Semester system, 2 5-week summer terms. Majors offered in accounting, art, biology, business, chemistry, data processing, education, English, health, history, political science, math, medical technology, music, physical education,

psychology, religion, secretarial practice, and sociology. Minors offered in most major fields and in 10 additional areas. Distributives and 6 hours of religion or theology required. Area of concentration, 2 majors, 1 major & 2 minors, or 1 major & 1 minor required. Honors program. Preprofessional programs in agriculture, dentistry, engineering, forestry, journalism, law, library science, medical records, medicine, optometry, pharmacy, religious vocations, social work, and veterinary medicine. 3-2 engineering program with Kentucky. 3-1 program in medical technology with area hospital. Elementary, secondary, and special education certification. ROTC. Language lab. Access to Lockheed Dialogue for computer base reference. 130,000-volume library with microform resources.
Financial CEEB CSS and ACT FAS. College scholarships, loans, payment plans; PELL, SEOG, NDSL, GSL, CWS. Priority application deadline April 1.
Admissions High school graduation with 16 units required. GED accepted. ACT required. $5 application fee. Rolling admissions. $10 room deposit required on acceptance of offer of admission. *Early Admission* and *Early Decision* programs. Admission deferral possible. Transfers accepted. Credit possible for CEEB AP and CLEP exams; college has own advanced placement program. One-term conditional admittance for students with less than a C average.
Student Life Student Government Association. Newspaper, yearbook. Music and theatre groups. Baptist Student Union. Black Student Union. Student Artists Collective. Athletic, academic, honorary, religious, and special interest groups. Dorms for men and women. 50% of students live on campus. 2 hours of phys ed required. Attendance in all classes and at one chapel period a week required. Liquor prohibited. Deans must be notified of students intending to marry. 7 intercollegiate sports; intramurals. KAIA, NAIA. Student body composition: 4.4% Black, 94.1% White, 1.5% Other. 34% from out of state.

[1] EASTERN KENTUCKY UNIVERSITY
Richmond 40475, (606) 622-2106
Dean of Admissions: Charles Ambrose

- **Undergraduates: 4,678m, 5,788w; 13,394 total (including graduates)**
- **Tuition (1982/83): $362 (in-state), $1,036 (out-of-state)**
- **Room & Board: $1,906**
- **Degrees offered: BA, BS, BBA, BFA, AA, AS**
- **Mean ACT 18.3**
- **Student-faculty ratio: 15 to 1**

A public university established in 1906. 325-acre campus located in a small city 26 miles southeast of Lexington. Served by rail and bus.
Academic Character SACS and professional accreditation. Semester system, 8-week summer term. 21 majors offered by the College of Applied Arts & Technology, 40 by the College of Arts & Sciences, 14 by the College of Business, 8 by the College of Education, 5 by the College of Law Enforcement, Traffic Safety, & Fire Science, and 3 by the School of Allied Health & Nursing. Central University College advises freshmen and sophomores undecided about their major. Masters degrees granted. Cooperative work/study, credit by exam, limited pass/fail. Preprofessional programs in dentistry, engineering, law, medical technology, medicine, ministry, and social work. Elementary, secondary, and special education certification. 662,000-volume library.
Financial CEEB CSS and ACT FAS. University scholarships, grants, loans; PELL, SEOG, NDSL, NSL, CWS.
Admissions High school graduation required. GED accepted. ACT required. Rolling admissions. $50 room deposit required on acceptance of offer of admission. *Early Admission* and *Early Decision* programs. Transfers accepted. Credit possible for CEEB AP and CLEP exams.
Student Life Student government. Newspaper, literary magazine, yearbook. University Players. Academic, honorary, religious, service, and special interest groups. 14 fraternities and 12 sororities without houses. 10% of students join. Students live at home or on campus. Dorms for men and women. Married-student housing. 71% of students live on campus. 2 semesters of phys ed required. 4 semesters of military science or academic options required of all male students. Freshmen must attend 6 assemblies. 10 intercollegiate sports for men, 5 for women; intramurals. AIAW, NCAA, Ohio Valley Athletic Conference. 16% of students from out of state.

[1] GEORGETOWN COLLEGE
Georgetown 40324, (502) 863-8011
Director of Admissions: Don DeBorde

- **Undergraduates: 508m, 541w; 1,263 total (including graduates)**
- **Tuition & Fees (1982/83): $3,306 (in-state), $3,404 (out-of-state)**
- **Room & Board: $2,146**
- **Degrees offered: BA, BS, BSMT, BME**
- **Mean ACT 19.6; mean SAT 900**
- **Student-faculty ratio: 14 to 1**

A private college affiliated with the Kentucky Baptist Convention. Started as a school in 1727, chartered as a college in 1829. 52-acre campus in a small town 12 miles from Lexington. Served by rail and bus; airport in Lexington.
Academic Character SACS accreditation. Semester system, 2 7-week summer terms. 31 majors offered in the areas of liberal arts & sciences, business administration, education, engineering, physical education, home economics, medical technology, music, religion, secretarial science, and social work. Self-designed majors. 2 majors or major & minor required. Distributives and 1 or 2 semesters of religion required. Seniors take comprehensive exams. Graduate degrees granted. Independent study. Honors program. Limited pass/fail. Internships. Preprofessional programs in dentistry, law, medicine, ministry, and pharmacy. 3-1 medical technology program. 3-2 engineering program with Georgia Tech and Kentucky. Kindergarten, elementary, and secondary education certification. ROTC; AFROTC at U of Kentucky. Planetarium. Over 110,000-volume library with microform resources.
Financial CEEB CSS. College scholarships, grants, loans, payment plans, athletic and Christian service grants; PELL, SEOG, NDSL, FISL, CWS, institutional work program. Recommended application deadline April 1.
Admissions High school graduation with 16 units required. GED accepted. Interview recommended. ACT required. $15 application fee. Rolling admissions. $100 tuition deposit required on acceptance of offer of admission. *Early Admission* Program. Transfers accepted. Credit possible for CEEB AP, CLEP, and ACT exams.
Student Life Student government. Newspaper, literary magazine, yearbook. Music and theatre groups. Debate. Athletic, academic, honorary, religious, service, and special interest groups. 5 fraternities and 3 sororities with houses. 35% of students join. Students live at home or on campus. Single-sex dorms with no visitation. 90% of students live on campus. 2 semesters of phys ed required. 10 co-curricular events required each term. 10 assemblies required each semester. Liquor and narcotics prohibited. Regular class attendance expected. 7 intercollegiate sports for men, 4 for women; many intramurals. AIAW, NAIA, KIAC, NCAA. Student body composition: 3% Black, 96% White, 1% Other. 30% from out of state.

[1] KENTUCKY, UNIVERSITY OF
Lexington 40506, (606) 258-9000
Director of Admissions & Registrar: Elbert W. Ockerman

- **Undergraduates: 8,335m, 7,068w; 23,047 total (including graduates)**
- **Tuition (1982/83): $846 (in-state), $2,470 (out-of-state)**
- **Room & Board: $2,220**
- **Degrees offered: BA, BS, BArch, BBA, BAEd, BFA, BGS, BHealth Sci, BMus, BMus Ed, BSN, BASW**
- **Mean ACT 19.9**
- **Student-faculty ratio: 15 to 1**

A public university established in 1865. 700-acre urban campus. Served by air, rail, and bus.
Academic Character SACS and professional accreditation. Semester system, 8-week summer term, 4-week spring intersession. 13 majors offered by the College of Agriculture, 4 by the College of Allied Health Professions, 35 by the College of Arts & Sciences, 3 by the College of Business & Economics, 4 by the College of Communications, 23 by the College of Education, 8 by the College of Engineering, 7 by the College of Fine Arts, 8 by the College of Home Economics; also Colleges of Architecture, Nursing, Pharmacy, and Social Professions. Self-designed majors. Interdepartmental majors. Courses in library science and public service. Distributive requirements. Graduate and professional degrees granted. Independent and accelerated study. Honors program. Phi Beta Kappa. Cooperative work/study, pass/fail. Preprofessional programs in dentistry, pharmacy, recreation & parks administration, veterinary medicine. 3-1 and 3-2 programs in law, medicine, dentistry, forestry, and engineering. Summer Study Abroad Program. Elementary, secondary, and special education certification. ROTC, AFROTC. University operates several community colleges. Experimental Education Program. Art gallery, museum. Language lab. Nuclear reactor. 1,800,000-volume library with microform resources.
Financial CEEB CSS. University scholarships, grants, loans; PELL, SEOG, NSS, NDSL, CWS. Preferred application deadline March 15.
Admissions High school graduation required. GED accepted. ACT required. Rolling admissions; deadline June 1. *Early Admission* and *Credit in Escrow* programs. Transfers accepted. Credit possible for CEEB AP and CLEP exams.
Student Life Student government. Newspaper, literary magazine, yearbook, radio station. Music, dance, and theatre groups. Debate. Numerous academic, honorary, religious, service, and special interest groups. 24 fraternities and 16 sororities with houses. 15% of men and 17% of women join. Coed and single-sex dorms. Apartments. Married-student housing. 25% of students live on campus. 12 intercollegiate sports for men, 10 for women; many intramurals. AIAW, NCAA, Southeastern Conference. Student body composition: 1% Asian, 3% Black, 1% Hispanic, 1% Native American, 92% White, 2% Other. 14% from out of state.

■[J1] ASHLAND COMMUNITY COLLEGE
Ashland 41101

■[J1] ELIZABETHTOWN COMMUNITY COLLEGE
Elizabethtown 42701

■[J1] HAZARD COMMUNITY COLLEGE
Hazard 41701

■[J1] HENDERSON COMMUNITY COLLEGE
Henderson 42420

■[J1] HOPKINSVILLE COMMUNITY COLLEGE
Hopkinsville 42240

■[J1] JEFFERSON COMMUNITY COLLEGE
Louisville 40201

■[J1] LEXINGTON TECHNICAL INSTITUTE
Lexington 40506

■[J1] MADISONVILLE COMMUNITY COLLEGE
University Drive, Madisonville 42431

■[J1] MAYSVILLE COMMUNITY COLLEGE
Maysville 41056

■[J1] PADUCAH COMMUNITY COLLEGE
PO Box 7380, Alben Barkley Drive, Paducah 42001

■[J1] PRESTONBURG COMMUNITY COLLEGE
Prestonburg 41653

■[J1] SOMERSET COMMUNITY COLLEGE
Somerset 42501

■[J1] SOUTHEAST COMMUNITY COLLEGE
Cumberland 40823

[P] KENTUCKY CHRISTIAN COLLEGE
Grayson 41143

[J2] KENTUCKY COLLEGE OF TECHNOLOGY
3947 Park Drive, Louisville 40216

[1] KENTUCKY STATE UNIVERSITY
Frankfort 40601, (502) 564-2550
Director of Admissions: Charles A. Edington

- **Undergraduates: 654m, 546w; 2,342 total (including graduates)**
- **Tuition (1982/83): $674 (in-state), $1,670 (out-of-state)**
- **Room & Board: $1,670; Fees: $54**
- **Degrees offered: BA, BS, BMus, BPublic Affairs**
- **Student-faculty ratio: 13 to 1**

A public university established in 1886. 344-acre campus located in a small city 25 miles from Lexington. Airport and bus station in Lexington.
Academic Character SACS and professional accreditation. Semester system, 8-week summer term. 39 majors offered in the areas of liberal arts & sciences, business, computer science, criminal justice, education, health & physical education, home economics, industrial education, management, manufacturing technology, medical technology, music, and public affairs. Minors offered in some major fields and in 4 additional areas. Distributive requirements. Masters degrees granted. Independent study. Honors Seminars. Cooperative work/study, internships. 3-2 program in engineering with Kentucky. Elementary and secondary education certification. ROTC, AFRTOC nearby. Computer center. Language lab. 188,000-volume library with microform resources.
Financial CEEB CSS. University scholarships, grants, loans, payment plans; PELL, SEOG, NSS, NDSL, FISL, NSL, CWS, institutional employment program. Suggest applying by March.
Admissions High school graduation with 17 units required. ACT required. Rolling admissions. *Concurrent Enrollment* Program. Transfers accepted. Credit possible for CEEB AP and CLEP exams; university has own proficiency exams.
Student Life Student government. Newspaper, yearbook. Jazz ensemble. Theatre group. Debate. Black Student Union. Tutoring service. Athletic, academic, honorary, religious, service, and special interest groups. 4 fraternities and 3 sororities. Coed and single-sex dorms. 28% of students live on campus. 4 semesters of phys ed required. Intercollegiate and intramural sports for men and women. AIAW. Student body composition: 51% Black, 46% White, 3% Other. 22% from out of state.

[1] KENTUCKY WESLEYAN COLLEGE
3000 Frederica Street, Owensboro 42301, (502) 926-3111
Director of Admissions: Richard Button

- **Undergraduates: 305m, 392w; 938 total (including part-time)**
- **Tuition (1982/83): $3,200**
- **Room & Board: $1,700; Fees: $230**
- **Degrees offered: BA, BS, BMus, BMus Ed, AA, AS**
- **Mean ACT 21**
- **Student-faculty ratio: 14 to 1**

A private college affiliated with the United Methodist Church, established in 1858. 60-acre suburban campus on the Ohio River.
Academic Character SACS accreditation. Semester system, 2 5-week summer terms. 33 majors offered in the liberal arts & sciences, business administration, telecommunications, criminal justice, education, physical education, library science, medical technology, music, nursing, and religion. Distributives and 6 hours of religion required. Associate degree programs in 18 fields. Independent study. Honors program. Phi Beta Kappa. Limited pass/fail. Preprofessional programs in dentistry, law, medicine, ministry, optometry, pharmacy, physical therapy, veterinary medicine. 3-1 medical technology program. 3-2 engineering program with Kentucky and Auburn. Kindergarten, elementary, and secondary education certification. Television studio. 150,000-volume library.
Financial CEEB CSS. College scholarships, grants, loans, athletic and performance grants-in-aid, church-related tuition remission, Kentucky tuition grants; PELL, SEOG, SSIG, NDSL, GSL, CWS, institutional work program.
Admissions High school graduation required. Interview recommended. ACT required; SAT accepted. $15 application fee. Rolling admissions. $100 deposit required on acceptance of offer of admission. Credit possible for CEEB AP and CLEP exams; college has own advanced placement program.
Student Life Student government. Newspaper, literary magazine. Music and drama groups. Debate. Religious organizations. 3 fraternities and 2 sororities. Students live at home or on campus. Single-sex dorms. 30% of students live on campus. 6 intercollegiate sports for men, 4 for women; many intramurals. Student body composition: 0.1% Asian, 5% Black, 0.3% Hispanic, 93.9% White, 0.7% Other. 18% from out of state.

[J1] LEES JUNIOR COLLEGE
Jackson 41339, (606) 666-7521

- **Undergraduates: 111m, 160w; 347 total (including part-time)**
- **Tuition (1982/83): $2,400**
- **Fees: $50**
- **Degrees offered: AA, AS**

A private junior college affiliated with the Presbyterian Church.
Academic Character SACS accreditation. Semester system. 2-year transfer programs offered in the liberal arts and preprofessional fields. 2-year terminal programs in business, electronics, human services, media, mining technology, and secretarial science. Remedial mathematics and English programs offered.
Financial Guaranteed tuition.
Admissions High school graduation or equivalent required.
Student Life Dormitories and dining hall available.

[P] LEXINGTON THEOLOGICAL SEMINARY
Lexington 40508

[J1] LINDSEY WILSON COLLEGE
210 Lindsey Wilson Street, Columbia 42728, (502) 384-2126, ext. 223
Director of Admissions: Linda McKinley

- **Enrollment: 137m, 121w; 418 total (including part-time)**
- **Tuition (1982/83): $2,400**
- **Room & Board: $1,045**
- **Degrees offered: AA, ASS**
- **Student-faculty ratio: 23 to 1**

A private college affiliated with the United Methodist Church, established in 1903.
Academic Character SACS accreditation. Semester system, 4-week summer term, 1½-week spring intersession. 2-year transfer programs offered in agriculture, art, biology, business, chemistry, communications, economics, education, English, geography, history, mathematics, music, physical education, physical science, physics, political science, psychology, religion, and sociology. Distributives and 3 hours of religion required. Phi Theta Kappa. Preprofessional programs offered in forestry, law, and medical fields. 21,000-volume library.
Financial Guaranteed tuition. College scholarships, grants, loans; ministerial & state grants; PELL, SEOG, NDSL, GSL, CWS. Priority application deadline April 15.
Admissions Open admissions policy. GED accepted. ACT required. Rolling admissions. $25 room deposit due on acceptance of admissions offer. Transfers accepted.
Student Life Newspaper, yearbook, radio station. Drama club. Black Student Union. Christian Students Association. Academic and special interest groups. Students not living at home must live on campus. Single-sex dorms. Weekly chapel attendance required. Intercollegiate basketball; intramurals.

[1] LOUISVILLE, UNIVERSITY OF
Louisville 40292, (502) 588-6531
Director of Admissions: Ray A. Stines

- **Undergraduates: 4,725m, 4,163w; 20,059 total (including graduates)**
- **Tuition (1982/83): $852 (in-state), $2,476 (out-of-state)**
- **Room & Board: $1,839**
- **Degrees offered: AB, BS, BLS, BSBA, BSPolice Ad, BMus, BMus Ed, BAS, AA, AS, AAS, ASN**
- **Mean ACT 19**
- **Student-faculty ratio: 12 to 1**

A public university established in 1798. 140-acre urban campus. Served by air, rail, and bus.
Academic Character SACS and professional accreditation. Semester system, 2 summer terms. 39 majors offered by the Arts & Sciences School, 6 by the School of Business, 3 by the School of Dentistry, 4 by the School of Education, 2 by the School of Justice Administration, 3 by the School of Medicine, 9 by the School of Music, 8 by the Speed Scientific School, and 5 by the University College. Minors offered in some major fields. Distributive requirements. Graduate and professional degrees granted. Independent study. Honors program. Phi Beta Kappa. Cooperative internship in Speed School. Limited pass/fail. Preprofessional programs in optometry, pharmacy, and veterinary medicine. Cross-registration with Bellarmine, Indiana University-Southeast, Louisville Presbyterian Theological Seminary, Southern Baptist Theological Seminary, and Spalding College. Study abroad. Elementary, secondary, and special education certification. Numerous institutes and centers. Planetarium. 905,511-volume library.
Financial CEEB CSS and ACT FAS. University scholarships, grants, loans; PELL, SEOG, FISL, CWS. Application deadline April 1.
Admissions High school graduation with 15 units recommended. Audition required for music majors. ACT required. Rolling admissions. *Early Admission* and *Concurrent Enrollment* programs. Transfers accepted. Credit possible for CEEB AP and CLEP exams.
Student Life Student government. Newspaper, literary magazine, yearbook, radio station. Numerous music groups. Debate. Theatre. Athletic, academic, religious, service, and special interest groups. 10 fraternities and 9 sororities with houses. 15% of men and women join. 3 dorms. Married-student housing. 8% of students live on campus. 2 semesters of phys ed required. Freshmen may not have cars on campus. 28 sports for men, 24 for women. NCAA, Metro Conference. Student body composition: 1.3% Asian, 8.4% Black, 0.6% Hispanic, 0.1% Native American, 88.3% White, 1.3% Other. 6% from out of state.

[2] LOUISVILLE SCHOOL OF ART
806 East Chestnut Street, Louisville 40204

[J1] MIDWAY COLLEGE
Midway 40347, (606) 846-4421
Director of Admissions: Elaine E. Larson

- **Enrollment: 249w; 338 total (including part-time)**
- **Tuition (1982/83): $2,700**
- **Room & Board: $1,050-$1,200**
- **Degrees offered: AA, ASMLT, ADN**
- **Student-faculty ratio: 9 to 1**

A private college affiliated with the Christian Churches, established in 1847. 105-acre rural campus 10 miles from Lexington. Served by air and bus.

Academic Character SACS accreditation. Semester system, 5-week summer term. 2-year transfer programs offered in business administration, home economics, general studies, and teacher education. 2-year terminal programs in equine office administration, fashion merchandising, interior design, medical technology, nursing, paralegal studies, secretarial administration. Distributive requirements. Phi Theta Kappa. Learning lab. 31,000-volume library.

Financial CEEB CSS. College scholarships, grants, loans, state grants; PELL, SEOG, NDSL, GSL, CWS, college work program. Application deadline August 1.

Admissions High school graduation with 11 units and a C average recommended. GED accepted. ACT or SAT required. Rolling admissions. *Early Admission* and *Early Decision* programs. Admission deferral possible. Transfers accepted. Credit possible for ACT PEP and CEEB CLEP exams.

Student Life Student government. Newspaper, yearbook. Music and drama groups. Religious Activities Committee. Academic, honorary, and special interest groups. Students under 21 must live at home or on campus. Dorms and dining facilities. 2 hours of phys ed required. 4 intercollegiate sports; intramurals.

[1] MOREHEAD STATE UNIVERSITY
Morehead 40351, (800) 262-7474 (in KY),
(800) 354-2090 (from states near KY)
Director of Admissions: Rondal D. Hart

- **Undergraduates: 2,229m, 2,475w; 6,739 total (including graduates)**
- **Tuition (1982/83): $714 (in-state), $2,062 (out-of-state)**
- **Room & Board: $1,860; Fees: $40**
- **Degrees offered: BA, BS, BBA, BMus, BMus Ed, BSW, BUniv Studies, AA, AS, AAS**
- **Student-faculty ratio: 22 to 1**

A public university established in 1923. Rural campus northeast of Lexington.

Academic Character SACS and professional accreditation. Semester system, 2 5-week summer terms. 10 majors offered by the School of Applied Sciences & Technology, 11 by the School of Business & Economics, 8 by the School of Education, 16 by the School of Humanities, 8 by the School of Sciences & Mathematics, and 8 by the School of Social Science. Minors required; offered in most major fields. Distributive requirements. Graduate and professional degrees granted. Independent study. Honors program. Cooperative work/study, pass/fail, internships, field career experiences program. Preprofessional programs in chiropractic medicine, dentistry, engineering, forestry, law, medicine, optometry, pharmacy, physical therapy, and veterinary medicine. 3-2 program in engineering with U of Kentucky. Elementary, secondary, and special education certification. ROTC. Agriculture complex. 850,000-volume capacity library.

Financial CEEB CSS. University scholarships, grants, loans; PELL, SEOG, NDSL, NSL, GSL, part-time employment.

Admissions High school graduation required. GED accepted for in-state students. Interview may be required for marginal students. ACT required. Rolling admissions. Admission deferral possible. Transfers accepted. Advanced placement credit possible.

Student Life Student government. Several publications. Academic, musical, religious, social, and special interest groups. Single-sex dorms. 4 hours of health/phys ed required. Class attendance required. Liquor prohibited. Intramural sports. Student body composition: 0.3% Asian, 3% Black, 0.3% Hispanic, 0.3% Native American, 95% White, 1.1% Other. 18% from out of state.

[1] MURRAY STATE UNIVERSITY
15th and Main Streets, Murray 42071, (502) 762-3741, (800) 592-3977 (in KY only)
Dean of Admissions & Registrar: Wilson Gantt

- **Enrollment: 2,616m, 2,876w**
- **Tuition & Fees (1982/83): $714 (in-state), $2,062 (out-of-state)**
- **Room & Board: $1,440-$1,890**
- **Degrees offered: BA, BS, BFA, BMus, BMus Ed, BSAg, BSBus, BSHome Ec, BSVTE, BSN, AA, AS**
- **Mean ACT 18.5**
- **Student-faculty ratio: 18 to 1**

A public university established in 1922. 238-acre campus in a small city in West Kentucky's lake country.

Academic Character SACS and professional accreditation. Semester system, 2 5-week summer terms. 14 majors offered by the College of Business & Public Affairs, 6 by the College of Creative Expression, 11 by the College of Environmental Sciences, 19 by the College of Human Development & Learning, 7 by the College of Humanistic Studies, 9 by the College of Industry & Technology, and 1 by the Department of Library Science. Area of concentration or major and minor required. Minors offered in most major fields and in 12 additional areas. Distributive requirements. Graduate degrees granted. Accelerated study. Cooperative work/study, limited pass/fail, internships. Preprofessional programs in dentistry, engineering, forestry, law, medical technology, medicine, optometry, pharmacy, speech/hearing, theology, and veterinary medicine. 3-1 bachelor degrees in dentistry, medicine, and theology. Study abroad. Semester at Sea. Elementary, secondary, and special education certification. ROTC. Biological station. Agricultural lab farms. Language lab. 354,000-volume library.

Financial University scholarships, grants, loans, state grants & loans; PELL, SEOG, NDSL, GSL, NSL, CWS, university employment. Application deadline April 1.

Admissions High school graduation required. GED accepted. ACT required. Rolling admissions. $50 housing deposit required on acceptance of offer of admission. *Early Admission* Program. Admission deferral possible. Transfers accepted. University has own advanced placement program.

Student Life Student government. Newspaper, yearbook, radio and TV stations. Numerous music groups. Debate. Academic, honorary, political, religious, and special interest groups. 14 fraternities and 9 sororities. Single freshmen and sophomores under 21 and students with out-of-state tuition waivers must live on campus or at home. Single-sex dorms. Married-student housing. 50% of students live on campus. Class attendance expected. 6 intercollegiate sports for men, 4 for women; extensive club and intramural sports program. AIAW, NCAA, Ohio Valley Conference, Kentucky Women's Intercollegiate Conference. Student body composition: 0.2% Asian, 5% Black, 0.2% Hispanic, 0.1% Native American, 93% White, 1.5% Other. 20% from out of state.

[1] NORTHERN KENTUCKY UNIVERSITY
Highland Heights 41076, (606) 572-5220
Director of Admissions: Dr. Joe Griffin

- **Enrollment: 2,403m, 2,080w**
- **Tuition & Fees (1982/83): $714 (in-state), $2,062 (out-of-state)**
- **Room & Board: $1,100**
- **Degrees offered: BA, BS, BFA, BMus, BMus Ed, BSW, AA, AS**
- **Student-faculty ratio: 25 to 1**

A public university established in 1968. 300-acre suburban campus, 7 miles from Cincinnati. Airport, rail and bus stations nearby in Kentucky and Ohio.

Academic Character SACS and professional accreditation. Semester system, 1 3-week, 2 5-week, and 1 8-week summer terms. 39 majors offered by the divisions of arts & sciences, business administration, communications, education & health/physical education, industrial & technical education, nursing & allied health, public administration, and experimental & interdisciplinary programs. Minors offered in most major fields. Graduate degrees granted. Cooperative work/study. Preprofessional programs in dentistry, engineering, forestry, medicine, optometry, pharmacy, veterinary science, and wildlife management. Elementary, secondary, and special education certification. ROTC; AFROTC at U of Cincinnati. 135,000-volume library with microform resources.

Financial CEEB CSS. University scholarships, grants, loans, state grants; PELL, SEOG, NSS, FISL, GSL, NDSL, NSL, CWS. Application deadline March 1.

Admissions High school graduation required. GED accepted. ACT required. Rolling admissions. $240 tuition deposit required on acceptance of offer of admission. *Early Admission* and *Concurrent Enrollment* programs. Transfers accepted. Credit possible for CEEB AP and CLEP exams. Educational Talent Search and Special Services Program for students needing assistance.

Student Life Student government. Newspaper, literary magazine, yearbook. Music groups. Debate. Minority Student Union. Academic, religious, and special interest groups. 5 fraternities and 3 sororities without houses. Dormitories. Liquor prohibited. 5 intercollegiate sports for men, 4 for women; intramurals. Student body composition: 0.2% Asian, 1.1% Black, 98.1% White. 9% from out of state.

[J2] OWENSBORO JUNIOR COLLEGE OF BUSINESS
1926 Triplett Street, Owensboro 42301

[P] PASSIONIST SEMINARY COLLEGE
1924 Newburg Road, Louisville 40205

[1] PIKEVILLE COLLEGE
Pikeville 41501, (606) 432-9319
Dean of Admissions: William Little

- **Enrollment: 229w, 261m; 650 total (including part-time)**
- **Tuition (1982/83): $2,825**
- **Room & Board: $1,920-$2,050**
- **Degrees offered: BA, BS, BMus Ed, BBA**
- **Student-faculty ratio: 13 to 1**

A private college affiliated with the United Presbyterian Church, established in 1889. Rural campus in the Cumberland Mountains. Served by bus.

Academic Character SACS accreditation. Semester system, 2 5½-week summer terms, May minimester. Majors offered in accounting, art, biology, business administration, general business, chemistry, English, economics, history, math, medical technology, music, psychology, sociology, political science, mine management, mining technology, and art, music, physical, secondary, and exceptional child education. Minors offered in most major fields. Distributives, 3 hours of religion, and 3 hours of Appalachian studies required. Independent study. Credit by exam. Preprofessional programs. Appalachian Graduate Consortium. 80,000-volume library with microform resources.

Financial CEEB CSS. College scholarships, loans, church scholarships, performance scholarships, state grants; PELL, SEOG, NDSL, GSL, CWS,

campus employment. Priority application deadline March 30.
Admissions High school graduation required. GED accepted. Interview recommended. ACT or SAT required; ACT preferred. $10 application fee. Rolling admissions. $50 room deposit due on acceptance of admissions offer. *Early Decision* and *Early Admission* programs. Transfers accepted. Credit possible for CEEB AP and CLEP exams.
Student Life Student government. Newspaper, yearbook. Music, dance, and drama groups. Appalachian Studies Society. Academic, honorary, religious, and special interest groups. Non-commuting students must live on campus. Dorms. 5 hours of phys ed required. 4 intercollegiate sports; intramurals. NAIA, KIAC.

[G1] PRESBYTERIAN THEOLOGICAL SEMINARY
1044 Alta Vista, Louisville 40205

[J1] SAINT CATHERINE COLLEGE
St. Catherine 40061, (606) 336-9304
Registrar & Admissions Officer: Sister Ann Bell

- **Enrollment: 85m, 86w; 246 total (including part-time)**
- **Tuition (1982/83): $2,000**
- **Room & Board: $1,650; Fees: $100**
- **Degrees offered: AA, AS, AAS**
- **Student-faculty ratio: 10 to 1**

A private college controlled by the Sisters of Saint Dominic. Established in 1931, became coed in 1951. 10-acre campus 1 hour from Louisville. Served by bus.
Academic Character SACS accreditation. Semester system, 6-week summer term. 2-year degree programs offered in business administration, secretarial science (general, legal, medical), biological science, farm management, humanities, and vocational education. Distributive requirements. 4 hours of religion required for Catholic students, 3 hours of philosophy for all others. Phi Theta Kappa. Preprofessional programs in agriculture, business, engineering, physical education, medical fields & allied health, nursing, pharmacy. 16,000-volume library with microform resources.
Financial Guaranteed tuition. College scholarships, grants, loans, state grants; PELL, SEOG, NDSL, GSL, CWS. Priority application deadline March 1.
Admissions High school graduation recommended. GED accepted. ACT or SAT required. $10 application fee. Rolling admissions. Transfers accepted. Credit possible for CEEB CLEP exams.
Student Life Student government. Academic, religious, service, and social groups. Bertrand Hall for resident students. 2 hours of phys ed required. Intercollegiate basketball and tennis; intramurals. NJCAA, KJCAC. Student body composition: 13% minority.

[1] SOUTHERN BAPTIST THEOLOGICAL SEMINARY
Louisville 40280

[1] SPALDING COLLEGE
851 South 4th Street, Louisville 40203, (502) 585-9911
Director of Admissions: Mary Pat Nolan

- **Enrollment: 52m, 384w; 1,005 total (including part-time)**
- **Tuition (1982/83): $2,900**
- **Room & Board: $1,850**
- **Degrees offered: BA, BS**
- **Student-faculty ratio: 7 to 1**

A private college controlled by the Sisters of Charity of Nazareth, established in 1814. Urban campus. Served by air, rail, and bus.
Academic Character SACS and professional accreditation. Semester system, 3 summer terms. Majors offered in art, business, biology, chemistry, communications, education, English, history, home economics, library science, liberal studies, mathematics, media librarianship, medical technology, nursing, philosophy, psychology, religious studies, social sciences, sociology, social work, Spanish, and speech. Minors offered in most major fields. Distributives and 6 hours of religion required. Master's and specialist degrees granted. Independent study. Cooperative work/study, pass/fail. Preprofessional programs in law and medicine. Cross-registration with Bellarmine, Indiana University-Southeast, U of Louisville, Louisville Presbyterian, Southern Baptist Theological Seminary. Study abroad. Elementary, secondary, and special education certification. AFROTC at U of Louisville. Preschool Learning Center. Art gallery, language lab. Recording studio. 106,000-volume library with microform resources.
Financial CEEB CSS. College scholarships, grants, loans, tuition waiver for families, state grants; PELL, SEOG, NSS, NDSL, GSL, CWS. Application deadlines March 1 (scholarships), March 15 (loans & grants).
Admissions High school graduation with 12 units recommended. GED accepted. SAT or ACT required. $15 application fee. Rolling admissions. $50 tuition and $50 room deposits due on acceptance of admissions offer. *Early Admission* Program. Transfers accepted. Credit possible for CEEB AP, CLEP, and college exams.
Student Life Student government. Professional and special interest groups. Freshmen and sophomores must live at home or on campus. Coed dormitory. Cafeteria.

[J1] SUE BENNETT COLLEGE
London 40741, (606) 864-2238

- **Enrollment: 89m, 126w; 315 total (including part-time)**
- **Tuition (1982/83): $1,200**
- **Room & Board: $1,570**
- **Degree offered: AA**
- **Mean ACT 16**

A private, coeducational junior college related to the Board of Global Ministries of the United Methodist Church.
Academic Character SACS accreditation. Semester system. Programs offered in liberal arts, teacher education, and business. Diploma programs for those who follow the core curriculum with additional courses to make a total of 64 hours. Preprofessional programs in several areas.
Admissions High school graduation suggested. ACT required. Rolling admissions. *Early Admission* Program.
Student Life Dormitory and dining facilities on campus.

[J1] SULLIVAN JUNIOR COLLEGE OF BUSINESS
3101 Bardstown Road, Louisville 40205

[1] THOMAS MORE COLLEGE
Covington 41042, (606) 341-5800
Director of Admissions: Catherine M. Grady

- **Undergraduates: 402m, 344w; 1,300 total (including part-time)**
- **Tuition (1982/83): $3,680**
- **Room & Board: $2,260; Fees: $200**
- **Degrees offered: AB, BSN, BElected Studies, AA, AES**
- **Mean ACT 21**
- **Student-faculty ratio: 20 to 1**

A private college affiliated with the Catholic Church, established in 1945. 330-acre suburban campus 10 miles south of Cincinnati. Air, rail, and bus service in Cincinnati.
Academic Character SACS and professional accreditation. Semester system, 2 7-week summer terms. Majors offered in accounting, art, banking, biology, business, chemistry, computer science, criminal justice, drama, economics, education, English, history, insurance, mathematics, medical technology, nuclear medicine technology, nursing, philosophy, physics, psychology, social work, and theology. Special majors. Double majors encouraged. Associate degrees and 30-hour certificates awarded by evening division. Courses in 8 additional areas. Distributives and 3-6 hours of religion required. Independent study. Cooperative work/study, pass/fail, internships. Preprofessional programs in dentistry, engineering, law, medicine, pharmacy, and veterinary medicine. 3-1 medical technology program. 3-2 engineering programs with the universities of Notre Dame, Dayton, Detroit, and Kentucky. Cross-registration with 12 area colleges. Study abroad. Elementary and secondary education certification. AFROTC, ROTC, NROTC at U of Cincinnati. Computer center. 88,000-volume library.
Financial CEEB CSS. College scholarships, grants, loans, payment plan; PELL, SEOG, NDSL, FISL, CWS, institutional employment. Application deadline March 1.
Admissions High school graduation with 16 units required. GED accepted. Interview recommended. SAT or ACT required. $25 application fee. Rolling admissions. $50 deposit required on acceptance of offer of admission. *Early Admission* Program. Transfers accepted. Credit possible for CEEB AP, CLEP, and ACT PEP exams; college has own advanced placement program.
Student Life Student government. Newspaper, literary magazine, yearbook. Afro-American Student Association. Music and drama groups. Academic, professional, and special interest groups. 2 fraternities without houses; 1 sorority with house. Seniors may live off campus; others must live at homeor on campus. 3 coed dorms. No married-student housing. 20% of students live on campus. 4 intercollegiate sports for men, 4 for women; intramurals. NAIA, KIAC. Student body composition: 0.7% Asian, 1.8% Black, 0.4% Hispanic, 0.1% Native American, 94.4% White, 1.5% Other. 35% from out of state.

[1] TRANSYLVANIA UNIVERSITY
Lexington 40508, (606) 233-8242
Acting Director of Admissions: Wendy S. Warner

- **Enrollment: 343m, 371w**
- **Tuition (1982/83): $5,100**
- **Room & Board: $2,280; Fees: $220**
- **Degree offered: AB**
- **Mean ACT 23; mean SAT 490v, 520m**
- **Student-faculty ratio: 13 to 1**

A private university affiliated with the Christian Church (Disciples of Christ), established in 1780. 32-acre urban campus. Served by air and bus.
Academic Character SACS accreditation. 4-4-1 system, 2 4-week summer terms. 31 majors offered in the areas of liberal arts & sciences, business, computer science, education, fine arts, medical technology, physical education, public administration, and religion. Distributive requirements. Honors program. Internships. Preprofessional programs in engineering, medicine, and veterinary medicine. 3-2 program in engineering with U of Kentucky and Washington U. 3-1 medical technology program. Study abroad. Secondary education certification. ROTC, AFROTC at U of Kentucky. Computer center. Language lab. 110,000-volume library.
Financial CEEB CSS. University scholarships, grants, loans, payment plan; PELL, SEOG, NDSL, GSL, CWS. Recommended applying by March 15.
Admissions High school graduation with 12 units required. Interview required. SAT or ACT required. $15 application fee. Rolling admissions. $125 deposit required on acceptance of offer of admission. *Early Admission* and *Early Decision* programs. Transfers accepted. Credit possible for CEEB AP and CLEP exams.
Student Life Student government. Newspaper, literary magazine, yearbook, radio station. Music and drama groups. Athletic, academic, honorary, religious, service, and special interest groups. 4 fraternities and 4 sororities; all have dormitory chapter suites. 42% of men and 49% of women join. Single underclass students must live at home or on campus. Dorms for men and women. No married-student housing. 72% of students live on campus. 3 activity courses required. 6 intercollegiate sports for men, 6 for women; extensive intramurals. NAIA, NCAA, KWIC. Student body composition: 2% Black, 94% White, 4% Other. 40% from out of state

[1] UNION COLLEGE
Barbourville 40906, (606) 546-4151
Director of Admissions: James Garner

- **Undergraduates: 188m, 248w; 1,030 total (including part-time)**
- **Tuition (1982/83): $3,500**
- **Room & Board: $1,760**
- **Degrees offered: BA, BS**
- **Student-faculty ratio: 15 to 1**

A private college affiliated with the Methodist Episcopal Church, established in 1879. Small-town campus midway between Lexington and Knoxville. Served by bus; airport 30 miles away.
Academic Character SACS accreditation. Semester system, 2 5-week summer terms, May interim. 32 majors offered by the Departments of Business & Economics, Education, Health & Physical Education, Fine Arts, Languages, Religion & Philosophy, Natural Sciences, and Social Sciences. Self-designed majors. Minors offered in most major fields. Distributive requirements. MAEd granted. Independent study. Cooperative work/study, limited pass/fail, credit by exam, internships. Preprofessional programs offered in dentistry, law, medicine, optometry, theology, veterinary medicine. 3-1 medical technology program with U of Louisville. 3-2 engineering program with U of Kentucky and Auburn U. Elementary and secondary education certification. ROTC. Appalachian Semester. Dramatic Arts Center. Oak Ridge seminars. 70,000-volume library.
Financial CEEB CSS. College scholarships, loans, grants, ministerial grants, state grants; PELL, SEOG, NDSL, CWS, college work/grant. Application deadline March 15.
Admissions High school graduation with 16 units required. GED accepted. Interview recommended. SAT or ACT required. $15 application fee. Rolling admissions. *Early Decision* and *Early Admission* programs. Transfers accepted. Credit possible for CEEB AP exams. Developmental Studies Program.
Student Life Newspaper, yearbook. Circle K. Academic, honorary, recreational, social, and special interest groups. Single-sex dorms. Married-student housing. Liquor, drugs, gambling, firearms prohibited. Class attendance required. 7 intercollegiate sports for men, 5 for women; intramurals. NAIA, KIAC.

[J2] WATTERSON COLLEGE
440 Breckinridge Lane, Louisville 40218

[1] WESTERN KENTUCKY UNIVERSITY
Bowling Green 42101, (502) 745-2551
Director of Admissions: Cheryl Chambless

- **Undergraduates: 4,431m, 4,726w; 13,105 total (including graduates)**
- **Tuition (1982/83): $714 (in-state), $2,062 (out-of-state)**
- **Room & Board: $1,340-$1,400**
- **Degrees offered: BA, BS, BFA, BSN, BMus, AS, ASN**
- **Student-faculty ratio: 16 to 1**

A public university established in 1906. 1,000-acre campus located in a small city 65 miles from Nashville. Served by air, rail, and bus.
Academic Character SACS and professional accreditation. Semester system, 8-week summer term. 81 majors offered in the areas of liberal arts & sciences, business, computer science, education, health, home economics, industrial technology, institution management, journalism, library science, mass communications, medical technology, music, nursing, physical education, and religion. Double major, 60-hour major, major/minor, or area of concentration required. Distributives and GRE required. Master's degrees granted. Accelerated and independent study. Honors program. Pass/fail, internships. Several preprofessional programs. Exchange programs with Brescia, Murray, and Kentucky Wesleyan. Study abroad. Elementary, secondary, and special education certification. ROTC. 785-acre university farm. Kentucky Museum. 825,000-volume library with microform resources.
Financial CEEB CSS. University scholarships, grants, loans; PELL, SEOG, SSIG, NSS, FISL, NDSL, CWS, institutional work program. Application deadlines March 1 (scholarships), May 1 (loans).
Admissions High school graduation required. GED accepted. ACT required. Rolling admissions. $40 room deposit due on acceptance of offer of admission. *Early Decision, Junior Scholars, Concurrent Enrollment* programs. Admission deferral possible. Transfers accepted. Credit possible for CEEB AP and CLEP exams; university has own advanced placement program.
Student Life Newspaper, literary magazine, yearbook, radio station. United Black Students. International Club. Western Religions Council. Athletic, academic, honorary, political, professional, service, and special interest groups. 16 fraternities, 9 with houses, and 11 sororities, 2 with houses. 10% of men and 7% of women join. Freshmen must live on campus for first 4 semesters. Single-sex dorms. 50% of students live on campus. 2-3 hours of phys ed required. Liquor prohibited. 9 intercollegiate sports; intramurals. NCAA, Ohio Valley Conference. Student body composition: 0.2% Asian, 6.8% Black, 0.2% Hispanic, 0.1% Native American, 89.9% White, 2.8% Other. 16% from out of state.

LOUISIANA (LA)

[2] ANDREW JACKSON COLLEGE
PO Box 14891, Baton Rouge 70898

[2] ANDREW JACKSON UNIVERSITY
4816 Jamestown Avenue, Baton Rouge 70808

CENTENARY COLLEGE OF LOUISIANA
Shreveport 71104, (318) 869-5131
Director of Admissions: John Lambert

- **Undergraduates: 413m, 396w; 1,492 total (including part-time)**
- **Tuition (1982/83): $3,040**
- **Room & Board: $2,140; Fees: $120**
- **Degrees offered: BA, BS, BMus**
- **Mean ACT 23; mean SAT 1050**
- **Student-faculty ratio: 12 to 1**

A private college affiliated with the United Methodist Church. Established in 1825. 93-acre campus in suburban Shreveport. Air and bus service.
Academic Character SACS and professional accreditation. 4-1-4 system, 8-week summer term. 30 majors offered in the areas of arts, humanities, math, sciences, social sciences, education, religion & religious education, business, and accounting. Interdisciplinary major offered in liberal arts. Distributive requirements. MEd, MBA granted. Honors program, independent study. Pass/fail, internships. Professional programs offered in church careers, computer science, journalism, accounting, business/Spanish, dance, general business, petroleum land management, public administration, teacher/coach. Preprofessional programs offered in church careers, dentistry, engineering, forestry, law, math/computer science, medical technology, medicine, pharmacy, physical therapy, theology, veterinary medicine. 3-2 programs in engineering, forestry, math/computer science. 3-1 programs in medicine and medical technology. Dual degree programs with Case Western and Southern Methodist U. Oak Ridge, Washington Semesters. Study abroad. Pre-school, elementary, secondary, and special education certification. ROTC. Language lab. 144,000-volume library.
Financial CEEB CSS and ACT FAS. University scholarships, grants, loans; PELL, SEOG, NDSL, GSL, CWS. Application deadline April 15.
Admissions High school graduation with 15 units required. GED accepted. Audition required for music majors. SAT or ACT required. $10 application fee. Rolling admissions. $50 tuition and $50 room deposits required on acceptance of offer of admission. *Early Admission* and *Concurrent Enrollment* programs. Admission deferral possible. Transfers accepted. Credit possible for CEEB AP and CLEP exams.
Student Life Student government. Newspaper, yearbook, radio station. Choir, band, drama clubs. Religious, academic, and special interest groups. 4 fraternities and 2 sororities with houses. 32% of men and 24% of women join. Single students must live at home or on campus. Single-sex dorms. No married-student housing. 60% of students live on campus. Liquor prohibited on campus. Class attendance expected. Convocation attendance strongly encouraged. 9 intercollegiate sports for men and women; several intramurals. AIAW, NCAA, Trans-America Athletic Conference. Student body composition: 3% Asian, 7% Black, 90% White. 32% from out of state.

[J1] DELGADO COLLEGE
615 City Park Avenue, New Orleans 70119

[1] DILLARD UNIVERSITY
New Orleans 70122, (504) 283-8822
Director of Admissions: Vernese B. O'Neal

- **Undergraduates: 333m, 903w**
- **Tuition (1982/83): $2,600**
- **Room & Board: $1,900**
- **Degrees offered: BA, BS, BSN**
- **Mean SAT 380v, 360m**
- **Student-faculty ratio: 14 to 1**

A private university affiliated with the United Church of Christ and the United Methodist Church. Established in 1869. 62-acre urban campus in New Orleans, served by air, bus, and rail.
Academic Character SACS and professional accreditation. Semester system, 1 summer term. Majors offered in art, biology, business administration/accounting, chemistry, drama, early childhood education, economics, elementary education, English, French, Spanish, health & physical education, history, mathematics, music, nursing, philosophy, physics, political science, psychology, religion, secondary education, social welfare, sociology & anthropology, special education, and speech. Distributive requirements. Honors programs. Independent study, directed study. Preprofessional programs in dentistry, law, medicine. Nursing major offered with Flint-Goodridge Hospital. Elementary and secondary education certification. ROTC at Tulane. 120,000-volume library.
Financial CEEB CSS and ACT FAS. University scholarships and grants; PELL, SEOG, NDSL, NSL, CWS. Application deadline June 1.
Admissions High school graduation with 15 units required. SAT or ACT required. $5 application fee. Rolling admissions; application deadline July 1. $50 tuition and $50 room deposits required on acceptance of offer of admission. *Early Admission* and *Concurrent Enrollment* programs. Transfers accepted. Credit possible for CEEB AP and CLEP exams.
Student Life Student government. Newspaper, yearbook. Music, debate, and drama groups. Academic, political, athletic, honorary, and service clubs. 8 fraternities and sororities without houses. Dorms for men and women. Dining hall. No married-student housing. 51% of students live on campus. Liquor prohibited on campus. Class attendance expected. 4 semesters of phys ed required. Intercollegiate and intramural sports. Student body composition: 99% Black, 1% Other. 44% from out of state.

[1] GRAMBLING STATE UNIVERSITY

Grambling 71242, (318) 247-6941
Director of Admissions: Irene S. A. Thomas

- **Undergraduates: 1,626m, 1,612w; 3,549 total (including graduates)**
- **Tuition (1982/83): $744 (in-state), $1,374 (out-of-state)**
- **Room & Board: $1,664; Fees: $22**
- **Degrees offered: BA, BS, BPA, AS, AA**
- **Mean ACT 11.1**
- **Student-faculty ratio: 23 to 1**

A public university established in 1901. Campus located in rural Louisiana, 5 miles west of Ruston and 60 miles east of Shreveport. Rail service in Ruston.
Academic Character SACS and professional accreditation. Semester system, 9-week summer term. 33 majors offered by the College of Arts & Sciences, 16 by the College of Business & Applied Programs, 15 by the College of Education. MS, MA granted. Honors programs. Cooperative work/study. Credit by exam. Preprofessional programs in dentistry, law, medicine, nursing. Elementary and secondary education certification. AFROTC. Audio-visual and television center. 159,148-volume library.
Financial ACT FAS. University scholarships, grants, tuition waivers, loans; PELL, SEOG, NDSL, GSL, PLUS, CWS. Application deadline June 1.
Admissions High school graduation with 16 units recommended. ACT required. $5 application fee. Rolling admissions; application deadline 30 days prior to enrollment. $50 room deposit required on acceptance of offer of admission. *Early Admission* program. Transfers accepted.
Student Life Student government. Newspaper, magazine, yearbook. Music, drama, debate, athletic, academic, honorary, religious, service, and special interest groups. 4 fraternities and 4 sororities without houses. 5% of men and women join. Single students must live at home or on campus as long as space is available. Freshmen may not have cars on campus. Class attendance required for freshmen and sophomores. 4 hours of phys ed required. Intercollegiate and intramural sports for men and women. Southwestern Athletic Conference, AIAW. Student body composition: 99% Black, 1% Other. 20% from out of state.

[1] LOUISIANA COLLEGE

Pineville 71360, (318) 487-7011
Director of Admissions: Wayne Ryan

- **Undergraduates: 398m, 470w**
- **Tuition (1982/83): $1,664**
- **Room & Board: $1,570; Fees: $290**
- **Degrees offered: BA, BS, BMus, BGS, BSMed Tech, BSPublic Admin, AS**
- **Mean ACT 18.9**
- **Student-faculty ratio: 17 to 1**

A private college owned by the Louisiana Baptist Convention. Established in 1906 at Pineville. 81-acre suburban campus, 1½ miles from Alexandria business district. Air, bus, and rail service.
Academic Character SACS accreditation. Semester system, 2 6-week summer terms. Majors offered in art, business, science, humanities, social sciences, music, math, education, religion, medicine, communications, criminal studies. Interdisciplinary concentration. Minors required. Minors offered in most fields. Distributives and 9 hours of religion required. Independent study. Honors programs. Pass/fail. Credit by exam. Preprofessional programs in medicine, dentistry, veterinary medicine, law, architecture, engineering, pharmacy, forestry. Study abroad. Elementary and secondary education certification. ROTC. Language lab. Over 100,000-volume library.
Financial ACT FAS. University scholarships, grants, loans; PELL, SEOG, NDSL, GSL, CWS. Application deadline May 1.
Admissions High school graduation with 17 units required. GED accepted. Various acceptance criteria offered. Additional requirements include: rank in upper 50% of class, C or better average in academic course, 18 or better composite ACT score, 800 or better composite SAT score. Rolling admissions; suggest applying in fall of 12th year. Deadline 4 months before registration. $50 room deposit required on acceptance of offer of admission. *Early Admission, Early Decision, Concurrent Enrollment* programs. Transfers accepted. Credit possible for CEEB CLEP exams.
Student Life Student government. Newspaper, yearbook. Music, debate, drama clubs. Honorary, professional, religious, service, and social groups. Single students required to live on campus on space-available basis, unless living at home. Dorms for men and women. Married-student housing. 42% of students live on campus. Class attendance expected. Attendance at weekly chapel required. Intercollegiate baseball, basketball, tennis; intramural sports. 6% of students from out of state.

[1] LOUISIANA STATE UNIVERSITY AND AGRICULTURAL AND MECHANICAL COLLEGE

Baton Rouge 70803, (504) 388-1686
Director of Academic Services for Admissions: Ordell Griffith

- **Undergraduates: 12,549m, 10,638w; 28,673 total (including graduates)**
- **Tuition (1982/83): $798 (in-state), $2,128 (out-of-state)**
- **Room & Board: $1,424-$2,002**
- **Degrees offered: BA, BS, BArch, BEng Tech, BFA, BLArch, BMus, BMus Ed, BCJ, BID**
- **Mean ACT 19.6**
- **Student-faculty ratio: 18 to 1**

A public university established in 1860. 300-acre urban campus in Baton Rouge. Air and bus service.
Academic Character SACS and professional accreditation. Semester system, 9-week summer term. 30 majors offered by the College of Agriculture, 31 by the College of Arts & Sciences, 16 by the College of Business Administration, 13 by the College of Chemistry & Physics, 21 by the College of Education, 8 by the College of Design, 11 by the College of Engineering, 3 by the General College, and 9 by the School of Music. Minors offered in some major fields. Distributive requirements. Graduate and professional degrees granted. Independent study. Honors program. Phi Beta Kappa. Cooperative work/study, pass/fail, internships. Preprofessional programs in dentistry, law, library science, medicine, nursing, social welfare, veterinary medicine, optometry, pharmacy, nuclear science, environmental studies, wetland resources. Junior Division for underprepared students. Organization for Tropical Studies. Oak Ridge Associated Universities. Exchange program with Southern University in Baton Rouge. Study abroad. Elementary, secondary, and special education certification. AFROTC & ROTC: NROTC at Southern University. Departmental libraries. Several research institutes and museums. Nuclear Science Center. Computer center, language lab. 1,844,656-volume library with microform resources and access to other area libraries.
Financial University scholarships, grants, loans. PELL, SEOG, SSIG, NDSL, CWS. Application deadlines March 31 (scholarships), June 1 (loans).
Admissions High school graduation required; college prep program suggested. ACT required. $20 application fee. Rolling admissions; application deadline July 1. $75 room reservation fee required with application. Informal early decision, *Early Admission,* and *Concurrent Enrollment* programs. Admission deferral possible. Transfers accepted. Credit possible for CEEB AP and CLEP exams. Special admission requirements for gifted & talented students. Advanced-standing program.
Student Life Student government. Newspaper, magazine, yearbook, radio station. Music, drama, academic, honorary, religious, political, and special interest groups. 23 fraternities, most with houses; 17 sororities, some with houses. 20% of men and 35% of women join. Single undergraduates with less than 30 semester hours live on campus or at home. Married-student housing. 32% of students live on campus. Drunkeness, disorderly conduct, gambling, dishonesty, hazing, rioting, possession of firearms, fireworks, or other explosives forbidden. Phys ed required of freshmen in some colleges. Class attendance expected. Numerous intercollegiate and intramural sports. AIAW, NCAA, Southeastern Conference. Student body composition: 0.2% Asian, 5.9% Black, 1.5% Hispanic, 86% White, 6.4% Other. 14% from out of state.

[J1] LOUISIANA STATE UNIVERSITY AT ALEXANDRIA

Alexandria 71301

[J1] LOUISIANA STATE UNIVERSITY AT EUNICE

PO Box 1129, Eunice 70535

[1] LOUISIANA STATE UNIVERSITY IN SHREVEPORT

Shreveport 71115, (318) 797-5207
Director of Admissions & Records: Betty B. Crippen

- **Undergraduates: 966m, 1,049w; 4,280 total (including graduates)**
- **Tuition (1982/83): $580 (in-state), $1,610 (out-of-state)**
- **Degrees offered: BA, BS, BGS, BCJ, AS, ASCJ**
- **Mean ACT 19**
- **Student-faculty ratio: 21 to 1**

A public university established in 1965. 200-acre campus in Shreveport. Served by air and bus.
Academic Character SACS and professional accreditation. Semester system, 8-week summer term. Over 30 majors offered in the areas of arts, education, business, humanities, social sciences, sciences, public administration, medical technology, criminal studies, mathematics. Minors offered in communication/information processing skills, business administration, urban studies. MBA, MEd granted. Independent study. Honors programs. Pass/fail. Internships. Preprofessional programs in agriculture, animal science, forestry & wildlife, law, occupational therapy, pharmacy, physical therapy, respiratory therapy, veterinary medicine, vocational education. 6-year BS/MD program. Exchange program with Southern U in Shreveport. Study abroad. Elementary, secondary, and special education certification. ROTC. 140,839-volume library.
Financial ACT FAS. University scholarships and loans. PELL, SEOG, SSIG, NDSL, GSL, CWS. Scholarship application deadline December 1. Suggested application date for loans April 1.
Admissions High school graduation with college prep program recommended. ACT required. Rolling admissions. *Early Admission* and *Concurrent Enrollment* programs. Educational Enrichment Program. Transfers accepted. Credit possible for CEEB AP and CLEP exams.
Student Life Student government. Newspaper, magazine, yearbook. Debate, drama clubs. Academic, political, religious, special interest groups. 3 fraternities and 2 sororities without houses. 3% of men and 6% of women join. Intramural sports. Student body composition: 1% Asian, 8% Black, 1% Hispanic, 90% White. 11% from out of state.

[1] LOUISIANA STATE UNIVERSITY MEDICAL CENTER

New Orleans 70122

[1] LOUISIANA TECH UNIVERSITY

Ruston 71272, (318) 257-3036
Director of Admissions: Patsy Lewis

- **Enrollment: 5,199m, 3,353w; 11,000 total (including part-time)**
- **Tuition (1982/83): $744 (in-state), $1,380 (out-of-state)**
- **Room & Board: $1,782; Fees: $19**
- **Degrees offered: BA, BS, BFA, BArch, AS**
- **Mean ACT 19**
- **Student-faculty ratio: 26 to 1**

A public university established 1894 in Ruston. Rural 891-acre campus, 68 miles from Shreveport. Ruston served by bus and rail.

Academic Character SACS and professional accreditation. Trimester system, 2 6-week summer terms. 12 majors offered by the College of Administration & Business, 23 by the College of Arts & Sciences, 16 by the College of Education, 12 by the College of Engineering, 6 by the College of Home Economics, and 10 by the College of Life Sciences. Minors required in some programs. Graduate and professional degrees granted. Associate degrees and preprofessional programs offered in several fields. Independent study. Cooperative work/study, pass/fail, internships. 2-year pre-nursing program with Northwestern State. 3-1 medical technology program. 5-year Master of Professional Accountancy program. 3-1 programs with dental, law, medical schools. Student and faculty exchange with Grambling State. Study abroad. Elementary, secondary, and special education certification. AFROTC. Computer, nuclear, water resources, dairy testing, speech & hearing, and summary tape processing centers. Soils testing lab. Observatory and planetarium. 1,003,237-volume library.
Financial ACT FAS. University scholarships, grants, loans. PELL, SEOG, SSIG, NDSL, GSL. Application deadline April 1.
Admissions High school graduation or equivalent required with 18-20 units suggested. GED accepted. ACT required; composite score of 20 required for applicants from out of state (except Arkansas, Mississippi, Texas). $5 application fee. Rolling admissions; deadline August 15. $50 room deposit required on acceptance of offer of admission. *Early Admission* Program. Summer Enrichment Program for high school students. Transfers accepted. Credit possible for CEEB AP and CLEP exams. University has own advanced placement program.
Student Life Student government. Newspaper, yearbook, radio & television stations. Music, debate, drama, public speaking groups. Athletic, academic, religious, special interest clubs. 11 fraternities, 9 with houses; 9 sororities with lodges. 16% of men and 22% of women join. Single students must live at home or on campus, as long as space permits. Dorms for men and women. Married-student housing. 46% of students live on campus. Liquor prohibited on campus. Class attendance required. 4 hours phys ed required in some courses. 7 intercollegiate sports for men, 3 for women; intramurals. NCAA, Southland Conference. Student body composition: 0.4% Asian, 8.8% Black, 0.5% Hispanic, 0.2% Native American, 87.3% White. 14% from out of state.

[1] LOYOLA UNIVERSITY

New Orleans 70118, (504) 865-3240
Director of Admissions: Dr. Rebecca Brechtel

- **Enrollment: 1,072m, 1,374w; 4,347 total (including part-time)**
- **Tuition (1982/83): $3,650**
- **Room & Board: $2,544-$2,622; Fees: $68**
- **Degrees offered: BA, BS, BBA, BPA, BMus, BMus Ed, BCJ, BLS, BSocial Studies, BPA, AA, AS, ASDen Hyg**
- **Mean ACT 21.5; mean SAT 458v, 479m**
- **Student-faculty ratio: 16 to 1**

A private Roman Catholic university conducted by the Jesuits, established in 1912. 19-acre campus in a residential section of New Orleans. Air, rail, and bus service.
Academic Character SACS and professional accreditation. Semester system, 2 5-week summer terms. 28 majors offered by the College of Arts, 8 by the College of Business Administration, and 14 by the College of Music. City College (evening) offers 4 majors. Weekend College. Drama therapy and dance program. Associates degrees include business administration, criminal justice, dental hygiene. Six hours of religion/theology required. Graduate and professional degrees granted. Independent study. Honors programs. Pass/fail, cooperative work/study. Internships. Preprofessional programs in dentistry, engineering, law, medicine, pharmacy, veterinary medicine. 3-2 engineering program with U of Notre Dame. Cross-registration with St. Mary's Dominican, Xavier Universities. Exchange with Tulane. Study abroad. Elementary and secondary education certification. ROTC. AFROTC at U of New Orleans. NROTC at Tulane. Computer center. 305,000-volume library.
Financial CEEB CSS and ACT FAS. University scholarships, grants, 2nd-family-member discounts, payment plan; PELL, SEOG, NDSL, GSL, FISL, CWS. Priority application deadline April 1.
Admissions High school graduation required. GED accepted. Campus visit urged. SAT (minimum 770) or ACT (minimum 17) required. $15 application fee. Rolling admissions; deadline August 1. $50 room deposit required on acceptance of offer of admission. *Early Admission, Early Decision, Concurrent Enrollment* programs. Admission deferral possible. Transfers accepted. Credit possible for CEEB AP, CLEP, ACT, and university exams. Special admission and academic support for underprepared students.
Student Life Student government. Newspaper, magazine, yearbook. Music, drama, ballet groups. Black Student Union, International Student Association, Community Action Program. Honorary, professional, social, and special interest groups. 4 fraternities, 1 with house; 5 sororities without houses. Freshmen must live on campus or at home. Single-sex dorms. No married-student housing. 36% of students live on campus. Freshmen may not have cars on campus. Intramural sports for men and women. Student body composition: 0.7% Asian, 14% Black, 6.3% Hispanic, 0.4% Native American, 72.1% White, 6.1% Other. 28% from out of state.

[1] McNEESE STATE UNIVERSITY

Lake Charles 70609, (318) 477-2520
Admissions Counselor: Mrs. Barbara Breedlove

- **Undergraduates: 2,220m, 2,484w; 7,351 total (including graduates)**
- **Tuition (1982/83): $556 (in-state), $1,186 (out-of-state)**
- **Room & Board: $1,480; Fees: $555**
- **Degrees offered: BA, BS, BMus, BMus Ed, AA, AS**

A public university established in 1939. 99-acre urban campus in Lake Charles. Bus and rail service.
Academic Character SACS and professional accreditation. Semester system, 8-week summer term. 8 majors offered by the College of Business, 6 by the College of Education, 9 by the College of Engineering & Technology, 29 by the College of Liberal Arts, and 24 by the College of Science. Associate degree programs. Masters degrees granted. Honors programs. Accelerated study possible. Cooperative work/study. Elementary, secondary, and special education certification. ROTC. Computer center. Over 300,000-volume library.
Financial ACT FAS. University scholarships, grants. PELL, SSIG, SEOG, NSS, NDSL, NSL, FISL, CWS. Application deadline May 1.
Admissions High school graduation required. ACT required. $5 application fee. Rolling admissions. *Early Admission* and *Concurrent Enrollment* programs. Transfers accepted. Credit possible for CEEB AP and CLEP exams, and for ACT scores. Admission possible by university entrance exam.
Student Life Student government. Newspaper, magazine, yearbook. Music, academic, special interest groups. Honorary and professional societies. Student Congress for Afro-American Culture. 9 fraternities and 6 sororities. Single students must live at home or on campus. Single-sex dorms. Married-student apartments. 17% of students live on campus. 6 intercollegiate sports for men, 4 for women; intramurals. NCAA, Southland Conference. Student body composition: 0.5% Asian, 16% Black, 0.5% Hispanic, 0.1% Native American, 82.9% White. 5% from out of state.

[1] NEW ORLEANS, UNIVERSITY OF

New Orleans 70148, (504) 286-6000
Director of Admissions: S. Mark Strickland

- **Undergraduates: 4,236m, 3,960w; 15,901 total (including graduates)**
- **Tuition & Fees (1982/83): $624 (in-state), $1,654 (out-of-state)**
- **Room & Board: $1,880**
- **Degrees offered: BA, BS, BGS, AS**
- **Mean ACT 17**
- **Student-faculty ratio: 23 to 1**

A public university established in 1958. 195-acre campus in New Orleans. Air, bus, rail service.
Academic Character SACS and professional accreditation. Semester system, 7-week summer term. 14 majors offered by the College of Liberal Arts, 13 by the College of Sciences, 11 by the College of Education, 8 by the College of Business Administration, and 4 by the School of Engineering. Distributive requirements. Graduate degrees granted. Independent study. Honors programs. Phi Beta Kappa. Interdisciplinary courses, honors projects. Pass/fail, internships. 5-year cooperative work/study program. 2-year transfer programs in inhalation therapy, physical therapy, 3-year programs in dentistry, law, medicine. Preprofessional programs in dental hygiene, dentistry, inhalation therapy, law, medicine, nursing, pharmacy, physical therapy, veterinary medicine. Exchange program with Southern U in New Orleans. Study abroad. Elementary, secondary, and special education certification. AFROTC & ROTC; NROTC at Tulane. A-V, computer, special education centers. 998,000-volume library with microform resources.
Financial ACT FAS. University scholarships, grants, loans, payment plan; PELL, SEOG, SSIG, NDSL, FISL, CWS. Application deadline May 1.
Admissions High school graduation recommended. GED accepted. ACT or SAT required. $10 application fee. Rolling admissions; suggest applying early in 12th year. Deadline July 1. *Early Admission* and *Concurrent Enrollment* programs. Transfers accepted. Credit possible for CEEB AP, ACT, and departmental exams; university has own placement programs.
Student Life Student government. Newspaper, magazine, yearbook, radio station. Music, drama groups. Academic, honorary, political, professional, religious, service, special interest groups. Fraternities and sororities. Single-sex dorms. Married-student housing. 5% of students live on campus. Phys ed required for some courses. Class attendance required. 6 intercollegiate sports for men, 4 for women; intramurals. AIAW, NCAA. Student body composition: 3% Asian, 16% Black, 1.5% Foreign, 4% Hispanic, 0.2% Native American, 75.3% White. 5% from out of state.

[G1] NEW ORLEANS BAPTIST THEOLOGICAL SEMINARY

3939 Gentilly Blvd., New Orleans 70126

[1] NICHOLLS STATE UNIVERSITY

Thibodaux 70310, (504) 446-8111
Dean of Admissions & Registrar: S. Dan Montz, Jr.

- **Undergraduates: 2,318m, 2,364w; 7,248 total (including graduates)**
- **Tuition (1982/83): $541 (in-state), $1,171 (out-of-state)**
- **Room & Board: $1,440**
- **Degrees offered: BA, BS, BMus, BMus Ed, AS**
- **Mean ACT 15.1**
- **Student-faculty ratio: 17 to 1**

A public university established in 1948. 166-acre campus in rural Thibodaux, 60 miles southwest of New Orleans. Bus service to Nicholls.
Academic Character SACS and professional accreditation. Semester system, 8½-week summer term. 8 majors offered by the College of Business Administration, 15 by the College of Education, 12 by the College of Liberal Arts, 14 by the College of Life Sciences & Technology, and 5 by the College of Sciences. Minors required in some areas. Associate degrees offered. Distributive requirements. Masters degrees granted. Cooperative work/study, internships, independent study. Credit by exam. Preprofessional programs in agricultural engineering, engineering, law, optometry, veterinary medicine. 3-1 programs in dentistry, medicine, physical therapy. Study abroad. Library science, nursery, kindergarten, elementary, secondary, and special education certification. ROTC. Computer center, film center. 250,000-volume library with microform resources.
Financial ACT FAS. University scholarships. PELL, SEOG, SSIG, NDSL, GSL, NSL, CWS, college work program.
Admissions Open admission for in-state high school graduates. High

school graduation required for out-of-state. GED accepted. ACT required. $5 application fee. Rolling admissions. $50 room deposit required on acceptance of offer of admission. *Early Admission* and *Concurrent Enrollment* programs. Transfers accepted. Credit possible for CEEB AP and ACT exams. Entrance by exam possible for non-high school graduates over 18.
Student Life Student government. Newspaper, magazine, yearbook. Music, drama, debate groups. Academic, honorary, religious, special interest groups. 9 fraternities and 5 sororities without houses. Single students must live at home or on campus. Coed, single-sex, and athletic dorms. Married-student housing. 20% of students live on campus. Class attendance required of freshmen and sophomores. 2 semesters of phys ed required (4 for education majors). 10 intercollegiate sports for men, 3 for women; intramurals. AIAW, NCAA. Student body composition: 1% Asian, 14.8% Black, 1% Hispanic, 0.6% Native American, 82.6% White. 3% from out of state.

[1] NORTHEAST LOUISIANA UNIVERSITY
Monroe 71209, (318) 342-4170
Director of Admissions: Barry M. Delcambre

- **Undergraduates: 3,574m, 4,104w; 11,300 total (including graduates)**
- **Tuition & Fees (1982/83): $527 (in-state), $1,127 (out-of-state)**
- **Room & Board: $1,564**
- **Degrees offered: BA, BS, BBA, BFA, BMus, BMus Ed, AA, AS**
- **Student-faculty ratio: 20 to 1**

A public university established 1931 in Monroe. 192-acre campus in an urban area 250 miles northwest of New Orleans, 100 miles west of Jackson. Air and bus service.
Academic Character SACS and professional accreditation. Semester system, 2 6-week summer terms. 9 majors offered by the College of Business Administration, 28 by the College of Education, 16 by the College of Liberal Arts, 6 by the College of Pharmacy & Health Sciences, 23 by the College of Pure & Applied Sciences. Distributive requirements. Associate degrees offered. Graduate degrees granted. Credit by exam. Preprofessional programs in dental hygiene, dentistry/medicine, engineering, forestry, law, nursing, occupational therapy, radiologic technology, veterinary science. Elementary, secondary, and special education certification. ROTC. Computer center. Educational Media Center. Agricultural farm lab. Center for Business & Economic Research. Pre-school child lab, reading lab. 412,666-volume library with microform resources.
Financial ACT FAS. University scholarships. PELL, NDSL, NSL, HPL, CWS. Application deadlines December 15 (scholarships), July 15 (loans).
Admissions High school graduation required. GED accepted. ACT required. $5 application fee. Rolling admissions; deadline 30 days prior to registration. $25 room deposit required on acceptance of offer of admission. *Early Admission* and *Concurrent Enrollment* programs. Transfers accepted. Credit possible for CEEB AP and ACT exams.
Student Life Student government. Residence Hall Council. Newspaper, magazine, yearbook, radio station. Music and drama groups. Academic, honorary, religious, special interest groups. 9 fraternities, 4 with houses; 7 sororities with Panhellenic dorm. 10% of men and women join. Single students must live on campus or at home. Coed and single-sex dorms. No married-student housing. 36% of students live on campus. 9 intercollegiate sports for men, 3 for women; intramurals. AIAW, LAIAW, NCAA. Student body composition: 22% minority. 8% of students from out of state.

[1] NORTHWESTERN STATE UNIVERSITY OF LOUISIANA
Natchitoches 71457, (318) 357-6011
Director of Admissions: Curtis Wester

- **Undergraduates: 1,195m, 1,244w; 6,722 total (including graduates)**
- **Tuition & Fees (1982/83): $746 (in-state), $1,376 (out-of-state)**
- **Room & Board: $1,590**
- **Degrees offered: BA, BS, BMus, AS**
- **Student-faculty ratio: 21 to 1**

A public university established in 1884. 900-acre campus in the small town of Natchitoches, 70 miles southeast of Shreveport. Bus service from Shreveport.
Academic Character SACS and professional accreditation. Semester system, 9-week summer term. 10 majors offered by the College of Business, 40 by the College of Education, 25 by the College of Liberal Arts, 1 by the College of Nursing, and 26 by the College of Science & Technology. College of Basic Studies curricula lead to Associate & Bachelor of Arts in General Studies. Distributive requirements. Graduate degrees granted. Associate degrees offered. Non-traditional education. Self-designed majors possible. Honors program. Phi Beta Kappa. Pass/fail. Cooperative work/study. Preprofessional programs in dentistry, engineering, forestry, law, medicine, ministry, pharmacy, physical therapy, radiologic technology, speech pathology, veterinary medicine, vocational agricultural education. 3-1 professional programs offered. Elementary, secondary, and special education certification. ROTC. American Language & Orientation Center, Computer Center, Center for Continuing Education & Community Services, Meat Technology Facility, Television Center, Williamson Museum, Southern Studies Institute, Center for History of Louisiana Education, Lignite Research & Development Institute, School Planning Lab. NSU Center at Fort Polk, NSU College of Nursing in Shreveport. 256,524-volume library with microform resources.
Financial CEEB CSS and ACT FAS. University scholarships, grants, loans. PELL, SEOG, SSIG, NSS, NDSL, NSL, CWS. Application deadline May 1.
Admissions High school graduation required. GED accepted. ACT required. $5 application fee. Rolling admissions; deadline 30 days prior to registration. *Early Admission* Program. Transfers accepted. Credit possible for CEEB CLEP exams; university has own advanced placement program. Special programs for students with special academic needs.
Student Life Student government. Newspaper, magazine, yearbook, radio station. Music and drama groups. Honorary, academic, religious, professional, political, special interest groups. 10 fraternities and 7 sororities, some with houses. Single students must live on campus or at home. Single-sex, coed, and special interest dorms. Married-student housing. 23% of students live on campus. Class attendance required. Intercollegiate baseball, basketball, football, badminton, golf, swimming, tennis, track. AIAW, TACC, LAIAW. Student body composition: 0.6% Asian, 19.3% Black, 2.2% Hispanic, 0.5% Native American, 74.8% White, 2.6% Other. 6.2% from out of state.

[G1] NOTRE DAME SEMINARY
2901 South Carrollton Avenue, New Orleans 70118

[1] OUR LADY OF HOLY CROSS COLLEGE
4123 Woodland Drive, New Orleans 70114

[J2] PHILLIPS COLLEGE
1333 South Clearview Parkway, New Orleans 70121

[2] ST. JOHN'S UNIVERSITY
Edgard 70064

[1] ST. JOSEPH SEMINARY COLLEGE
St. Benedict 70457

[1] ST. MARY'S DOMINICAN COLLEGE
7214 St. Charles Avenue, New Orleans 70118, (504) 865-7761

- **Undergraduates: 8m, 396w; 867 total (including part-time)**
- **Tuition (1981/82): $3,100**
- **Room & Board: $1,830**
- **Degrees offered: BA, BS, AA**

A private Roman Catholic college primarily for women, established in 1861. Urban campus. Airport, bus and rail stations nearby.
Academic Character SACS and professional accreditation. Semester system, 3- and 6-week summer terms. Majors offered in the liberal arts and sciences by the divisions of Humanities, Natural Science, Philosophy & Religion, Social Science & Community Service, and Business. Member of a consortium with Loyola and Xavier Universities. 80,000-volume library.
Financial Financial aid available includes 10 competitive scholarships.
Admissions High school graduation required. ACT or SAT required. Students accepted for admission in September and at mid-year.
Student Life 3 sororities. Dormitory housing available for 340 women.

[1] SOUTHEASTERN LOUISIANA UNIVERSITY
Hammond 70402, (504) 549-2187
Director of Admissions: Iris S. Wiggins

- **Undergraduates: 3,513m, 5,476w**
- **Tuition (1982/83): $684 (in-state), $1,364 (out-of-state)**
- **Room & Board: $1,410; Fees: $20**
- **Degrees offered: BA, BS, BMus, BMus Ed, AS**
- **Student-faculty ratio: 30 to 1**

A public university established in 1925. 365-acre campus in the small city of Hammond, 50 miles northwest of New Orleans. Bus and rail service.
Academic Character SACS and professional accreditation. Semester system, 7-week summer term. 6 majors offered by the College of Business, 26 by the College of Education, 16 by the College of Humanities, 17 by the College of Science & Technology, and 1 by the School of Nursing. Associate degrees offered in automotive technology, computer science, drafting technology, law enforcement, office administration. Masters degrees granted. Honors program. Cooperative work/study, pass/fail. Preprofessional programs in dentistry, engineering, forestry, medicine, optometry, pharmacy, physical therapy, veterinary medicine, vocational agricultural education. Study abroad. Elementary and secondary education certification. ROTC. 225,000-volume library.
Financial CEEB CSS and ACT FAS. University scholarships, PELL, SEOG, NDSL, NSL, FISL, CWS, work program. Application deadline May 1.
Admissions High school graduation with 20 units required. GED accepted. ACT required. $5 application fee. Rolling admissions; deadline 30 days prior to start of semester. $50 room deposit required on acceptance of offer of admission. Transfers accepted. Credit possible for CEEB AP and CLEP exams; university has own placement program.
Student Life Student government. Newspaper, yearbook. Music, debate, drama groups. Academic and special interest groups. 9 fraternities, 4 with houses, and 6 sororities without houses. 9% of men and 8% of women join. Dorms for men and women. Married-student housing. 25% of students live on campus. No liquor on campus. 2 semesters of phys ed required in most courses. 8 intercollegiate sports, 4 intramural sports. Student body composition: 0.1% Asian, 10% Black, 0.3% Hispanic, 0.2% Native American, 87.6% White, 1.8% Other. 4% from out of state.

[G2] SOUTHEASTERN UNIVERSITY
5163 General de Gaulle Drive, New Orleans 70114

[1] SOUTHERN UNIVERSITY AND AGRICULTURAL AND MECHANICAL COLLEGE
Baton Rouge 70813, (504) 771-4500
Director of Admissions & Recruitment: Colonel Johnson

- **Undergraduates: 3,571m, 3,362w**
- **Tuition (1982/83): $672 (in-state), $730 (out-of-state)**

- **Room & Board: $2,710**
- **Degrees offered: BS, BA, BMus, BArch, AS**
- **Student-faculty ratio: 20 to 1**

A public university established in 1879. 592-acre suburban campus 2 miles north of Baton Rouge. Airport and bus station.
Academic Character SACS and professional accreditation. Semester system, 9-week summer term. 4 majors offered by the College of Agriculture, 15 by the College of Arts & Humanities, 4 by the College of Business, 13 by the College of Education, 7 by the College of Engineering, 7 by the College of Home Economics, and 11 by the College of Science. Associate degrees offered. Distributive requirements. Graduate and professional degrees granted. Independent study. Honors program. Preprofessional programs in dentistry, veterinary medicine, law, medicine, ministry. Remedial programs; Bureau of Developmental Studies. Cross-registration with LSU Baton Rouge. Elementary and secondary education certification. NROTC, ROTC. Jazz Institute. 287,272-volume library with microform resources.
Financial CEEB CSS. University scholarships, loans. PELL, SEOG, SSIG, NDSL, GSL, CWS. Application deadline April 15.
Admissions High school graduation or equivalency diploma recommended. GED accepted. ACT required. Rolling admissions; deadline July 1. $50 room deposit required on acceptance of offer of admission. *Early Decision* and *Early Admission* programs. Transfers accepted. Credit possible for CEEB AP, CLEP, university, and departmental exams.
Student Life Student government, residence hall councils. Newspaper, magazine, yearbook. Music, debate, drama clubs. Academic, honorary, religious, political, special interest groups. 4 fraternities and 4 sororities without houses. Single students must live on campus or at home. Dormitories. Married-student housing. 33% of students live on campus. Class attendance and 4 hours of phys ed required. Intercollegiate basketball, football, golf, swimming, tennis, track; numerous intramural sports. Student body composition: 95.7% Black, 1.4% White, 2.9% Other. 17% from out of state.

[1] SOUTHERN UNIVERSITY IN NEW ORLEANS
New Orleans 70126

[J1] SOUTHERN UNIVERSITY AT SHREVEPORT
Shreveport-Bossier City Campus
3050 Martin Luther King, Jr. Drive, Shreveport 71107

[1] SOUTHWESTERN LOUISIANA, UNIVERSITY OF
Lafayette 70504, (318) 264-6000
Director of Admissions: Leroy Broussard, Jr.

- **Undergraduates: 5,058m, 4,859w**
- **Tuition (1982/83): $552 (in-state), $1,182 (out-of-state)**
- **Room & Board: $1,464**
- **Degrees offered: BA, BS, BArch, BFA, BGS, BMus, BMus Ed, BSBA, AS, AA**
- **Mean ACT 16.6**
- **Student-faculty ratio: 21 to 1**

A public university established in 1898. 735-acre campus in the small city of Lafayette, 50 miles from Baton Rouge. Air, bus, rail service.
Academic Character SACS and professional accreditation. Semester system, 9-week summer term. 12 majors offered by the College of Agriculture, 12 by the College of Business Administration, 21 by the College of Education, 7 by the College of Engineering, one by the College of General Studies, one by the College of Nursing, 13 by the College of Sciences, and 33 by the College of Arts, Humanities, Behavioral Sciences. Associate degrees in criminal justice, general studies, office administration, petroleum technology, secretarial science; certificate in office administration. Distributive requirements. Graduate and professional degrees granted. Honors program. Credit by exam. 3-1 programs in medical technology, physical therapy, pre-law. 2 year preprofessional programs in forestry, pharmacy. DOORS program. Elementary, secondary, and special education certification. AFROTC. Computer center, Conference center, Office of Research & Sponsored Programs, Center of Louisiana Studies. 500,000-volume library with microform resources and Horticulture Library.
Financial ACT FAS. University scholarships, loans; PELL, SEOG, SSIG, NDSL, NSL, FISL, CWS. Loan application deadline February 15.
Admissions High school graduation required. Equivalency degree or GED accepted. ACT required. $5 application fee. Rolling admissions; deadline 30 days prior to start of semester. $50 room deposit on acceptance of offer of admission. *Early Decision, Early Admission, Concurrent Enrollment* programs. Admission deferral possible. Transfers accepted. Credit possible for CEEB AP, CLEP, and ACT PEP exams; university has own advanced placement.
Student Life Student government. Newspaper, magazine, yearbook, radio & TV stations. Music, debate, drama groups. Academic, honorary, political, professional, service, and social organizations. Special interest groups. 15 fraternities, 11 with houses; 10 sororities, 7 with houses. 12% of men and 10% of women join. Single students must live on campus or at home. Dorms for men and women. Married-student housing. 25% of students live on campus. Class attendance and 4 hours of phys ed required. 7 intercollegiate sports for men, 3 for women; extensive intramural sports. AIAW, LIAW, NCAA, Southland Conference. Student body composition: 0.2% Asian, 14.6% Black, 0.2% Hispanic, 0.1% Native American, 75.3% White, 9.6% Other. 15% from out of state.

[1] TULANE UNIVERSITY OF LOUISIANA
New Orleans 70118, (504) 865-5731
Tulane Director of Admissions: Jillinda G. Jonker
Newcomb Director of Admissions: Lois V. Conrad

- **Undergraduates: 3,117m, 1,751w; 10,000 total (including part-time)**
- **Tuition (1982/83): $5,934**
- **Room & Board: $2,555-$2,960; Fees: $616**
- **Degrees offered: BA, BS, BArch, BFA, BSE's**
- **Mean SAT 1152**
- **Student-faculty ratio: 13 to 1**

A private university containing the College of Liberal Arts and Sciences for men, Newcomb College for women, and coed undergraduate Schools of Architecture and Engineering. Established in 1834. 110-acre campus in a residential area 5 miles from downtown New Orleans. Airport, bus and rail stations nearby.
Academic Character SACS and professional accreditation. Semester system, 2 5½-week and one 8-week summer terms. 46 majors offered in the areas of art, humanities, math, science, social sciences, economics, engineering, management, physical education, education, and communications. Programs in Afro-American studies and international affairs. Distributive requirements. Graduate and professional degrees granted. Independent study. Honors programs. Phi Beta Kappa. Preprofessional programs in business administration, dentistry, law, medicine, social work. Washington Semester. Domestic interchange program. Study abroad. Pre-school, elementary, and secondary education certification. AFROTC, NROTC, ROTC. Newcomb Women's Center. Several research centers. Computer lab, language lab. 1,350,000-volume library with departmental libraries and microform resources.
Financial CEEB CSS. University scholarships, grants, loans, payment plan; PELL, SEOG, NDSL, CWS. Application deadline for scholarships and grants March 1.
Admissions High school graduation with 15 units required. SAT or ACT required. $25 application fee. Rolling admissions; deadline February 1. $100 deposit required on acceptance of offer of admission. *Early Decision, Early Admission, Concurrent Enrollment* programs. Admission deferral possible. Transfers accepted. Credit possible for CEEB AP and CLEP exams; university has own advanced placement programs.
Student Life Student government. Newspaper, yearbook, radio station. Music, debate, public speaking, drama groups. Community service, academic, religious, special interest groups. 18 fraternities with houses, 7 sororities with non-residential houses. 35% of men and 45% of women join. Freshmen must live on campus. Dorms for men and women. Married-student apartments. 60% of students live on campus. 2 years of phys ed required for Newcomb students; one year for Arts & Sciences students. Many intercollegiate, intramural, and club sports for men and women. Student body composition: 1% Asian, 4.2% Black, 4.7% Hispanic, 0.5% Native American, 83.4% White, 6.2% Other. 76% from out of state.

[1] XAVIER UNIVERSITY OF LOUISIANA
New Orleans 70125, (504) 486-7411
Dean of Arts & Sciences and Admissions: Alfred J. Guillame, Jr.

- **Undergraduates: 735m, 1,491w**
- **Tuition (1982/83): $3,000**
- **Room & Board: $1,950**
- **Degrees offered: BA, BS, BMus**
- **Mean ACT 17.6**
- **Student-faculty ratio: 15 to 1**

A private Catholic university founded in 1915 by the Sisters of the Blessed Sacrament. 22-acre campus in New Orleans. Airport, bus and rail stations nearby.
Academic Character SACS and professional accreditation. 4-1-4 system, 8-week summer term. 38 majors offered in the areas of art, education, humanities, social sciences, math, science, communications, music, business, medicine, computer science, and pharmacy. Distributives and 6 hours of religion/theology required. Masters degrees granted. Honors program. Cooperative work/study. Preprofessional preparation including accounting, engineering, government service, law, management, medical technology, medicine, social work. 3-3 business administration and law programs with Tulane. Consortium with Loyola, St. Mary's Dominican College, Notre Dame. Elementary and secondary education certification. ROTC; NROTC & AFROTC at Tulane. Computer center. 100,000-volume library with microform resources.
Financial CEEB CSS and ACT FAS. University scholarships, grants, loans, health professions loan; PELL, SEOG, NDSL, GSL, CWS. Application deadlines March 30 (scholarships), May 15 (loans).
Admissions High school graduation with 16 units required. GED accepted. SAT or ACT required. $10 application fee. Rolling admissions; deadline August 1. $20 tuition and $40 room deposits required on acceptance of offer of admission. *Concurrent Enrollment* Program. Transfers accepted. Credit possible for CEEB AP and CLEP exams; university has own placement program.
Student Life Student government. Music, religious, honorary, academic, special interest groups. 3 fraternities and 3 sororities without houses. 40% of men and 25% of women join. Single-sex dorms. No married-student housing. 35% of students live on campus. Attendance in class and at 2 convocations required. Liquor prohibited on campus. Dress restrictions for class and dining hall. Intercollegiate basketball for men; 8 intramural sports. NAIA. Student body composition: 0.6% Asian, 90% Black, 0.5% Hispanic, 1.3% White, 7.6% Other. 37% from out of state.

MAINE *(ME)*

[J2] ANDOVER COLLEGE
335 Forest Avenue, Portland 04101

[1] ATLANTIC, COLLEGE OF THE

Bar Harbor 04609, (207) 288-5015
Director of Admissions: James Frick

- **Undergraduates: 80m, 90w; 200 total (including part-time)**
- **Tuition (1982/83): $4,850**
- **Room & Board: $1,800-$1,950**
- **Degree offered: BA in Human Ecology**
- **Student-faculty ratio: 11 to 1**

A private college of human ecology established in 1969 in rural Bar Harbor, on Mount Desert Island. Acadia National Park is ½ mile away. Airport and bus station in Bar Harbor.
Academic Character NEASC accreditation. Trimester system. Majors in environmental science, environmental design, human studies, public policy & social change, ecological education, and writing & literature. Courses in art, music, and dance also offered. Curriculum is problem-oriented. Internship and senior project required for graduation. Independent study. Grades optional, course credit by 3-part teacher evaluation and student self-evaluation. Exchange programs with UMaine at Orono, Marlboro College, and Huxley College of Environmental Studies. Art gallery. 16,000-volume library.
Financial CEEB CSS. College awards financial assistance based on need and merit.
Admissions Decisions based on essay questions, references, academic records, required personal interview, and optional standardized test scores. Application deadline May 1. Rolling admission with notification within a month of receipt of application. Admission deferral possible. Transfers accepted. Credit possible for CEEB AP and CLEP exams.
Student Life Student government. Student activities committee. Literary and art magazine. Community service groups. Surrounding community offers a wide selection of cultural opportunities. 5 dorms on campus reserved for entering students. 75% of students live in off-season housing in Bar Harbor. Students have full privileges at the Mt. Desert Island YMCA.

[G1] BANGOR THEOLOGICAL SEMINARY

Bangor 04401

[1] BATES COLLEGE

Lewiston 04240, (207) 784-0181
Dean of Admissions: William Hiss

- **Undergraduates: 745m, 725w**
- **Tuition, Room, & Board (1982/83): $10,500**
- **Degrees offered: BA, BS**
- **Mean SAT 566v, 596m**
- **Student-faculty ratio: 13 to 1**

A private college established in 1864. 125-acre campus in a suburban residential area at the edge of Lewiston, 35 miles northeast of Portland and 145 miles from Boston. 600-acre Bates-Morse Mountain Conservation Area near Bath. Airport and bus station in Lewiston.
Academic Character NEASC accreditation. 4-4-1 system. Majors offered in anthropology, art, biology, chemistry, economics, English, French, geology, German, history, math, music, philosophy, physics, political science, psychology, religion, rhetoric, sociology, Spanish, theatre arts. Self-designed, interdisciplinary, and double majors. Minors. Distributive requirements. Comprehensive exam and/or thesis required for graduation. Independent study. Honors program. Phi Beta Kappa. Internships, job placement for students taking leave of absence. 3-2 engineering programs with RPI and Columbia. Washington Semester, City Semester, Mystic Seaport Maritime Studies Semester. Study abroad. Secondary education certification. Language labs, computer center. 330,000-volume library with microform resources.
Financial CEEB CSS. College scholarships, loans; PELL, SEOG, NDSL, GSL, CWS. Application deadline March 1.
Admissions High school graduation required; 16 units recommended. SAT or ACT, and 3 ACH required. Interview suggested. $25 application fee. Application deadline February 1. Notification in mid-April. $200 deposit required on acceptance of admissions offer (May 1). *Early Decision* and *Early Admission* programs. Admission deferral possible. Transfers accepted. Credit possible for CEEB AP exams.
Student Life Student government. Newspaper, literary magazine, yearbook, radio station. Intercollegiate debate. Music, drama, and dance groups. Community activities club. Afro-American Society. Outing club. Political and special interest groups. Students must live at home or on campus. Dorms for men and women. 97% of students live on campus. Scholarship students must have permission to have cars on campus. One year of phys ed required. 11 intercollegiate sports for men, 10 for women; intramurals. CBB, ECAC, NCAA, NESCAC. Student body composition: 2% Black, 96% White, 2% Other. 88% from out of state.

[J2] BEAL COLLEGE

629 Main Street, Bangor 04401, (800) 432-7351
Director of Admissions: Patti Le Blanc

- **Undergraduates: 96m, 360w; 1,367 total (including part-time)**
- **Tuition & Fees (1982/83): $2,850**
- **Room: $1,600**
- **Degrees offered: Associate**
- **Student-faculty ratio: 20 to 1**

A private junior college of business, founded in 1891 in the small city of Bangor. Other campuses in Brunswick and Skowhegan.
Academic Character AICS accreditation; candidate for NEASC accreditation. Semester system. Majors offered in accounting, business management, data processing, medical assisting, office management, paralegal studies, secretarial science (executive, legal, medical), travel & airline careers, word processing. Certificates in general business. Diploma courses in secretarial science and typing-clerical. 4-day (Monday-Thursday) week. Accounting courses offered to all degree candidates. Beal Early Experience Program provides graduating student with field experience in major. Computer center. 8,746-volume library, plus access to libraries at U of Maine and Husson College.
Financial CEEB CSS. College scholarships, state scholarships, payment plan; PELL, SEOG, NDSL, GSL. Application deadline May 1.
Admissions High school graduation required. GED accepted. 2 recommendations required. SAT and interview recommended. $15 application fee. Rolling admissions; no deadline. $100 tuition and $100 room deposits required on acceptance of offer of admission. All incoming students must take Beal's math and language skills tests before matriculation. Transfers and special students accepted.
Student Life Student government. Dorms for men and women. Class attendance expected.

[1] BOWDOIN COLLEGE

Brunswick 04011, (207) 725-8731
Director of Admissions: William R. Mason

- **Enrollment: 759m, 621w**
- **Tuition (1982/83): $7,600**
- **Room & Board: $2,880; Fees: $65**
- **Degree offered: AB**
- **Mean SAT 600v, 629m**
- **Student-faculty ratio: 13 to 1**

A private college, established in 1794 and became coed in 1970. 110-acre campus in the small town of Brunswick, 25 miles northeast of Portland. Bus station in Brunswick, airport in Portland.
Academic Character NEASC and professional accreditation. Semester system. Majors offered in Afro-American studies, archaeology-classics, art, biology, chemistry, classics, economics, English, environmental studies, German, government & legal studies, history, math, music, philosophy, physics & astronomy, psychology, religion, Romance languages, sociology & anthropology. Self-designed, interdepartmental, joint, and double majors possible. Distributive requirements. Senior comprehensive exams in some majors. Independent study, honors programs and projects. Senior research fellowships. Phi Beta Kappa. Preprofessional programs in law, medicine. 3-2 engineering programs with CalTech, Columbia; 3-2 law with Columbia. 12-College Exchange with New England colleges; exchanges with Tougaloo and U of Dundee, Scotland. Many domestic and foreign off-campus study programs. Elementary and secondary education certification. Biological field station in New Brunswick. 4 research centers. Art museum, computing center. 650,000-volume library with microform resources.
Financial CEEB CSS. College scholarships and loans; PELL, SEOG, NDSL, CWS. Application deadline January 15.
Admissions High school graduation with 16 units required. SAT and ACH may be submitted but not required. Interview recommended. $25 application fee. Application deadline January 15. Notification in mid-April. Acceptance of offer of admission and $100 fee required by May 1. *Early Decision* and *Early Entrance* programs. Admission deferral possible. Some transfers accepted; freshmen may enter only in fall. Credit possible for CEEB AP and departmental exams.
Student Life Student government and admissions interviewing board. Newspapers, literary magazine, yearbook, radio station. Music, drama, dance groups. Religious and social service organizations. Franco-American, Afro-American societies. Women's Association. Gay-Straight Alliance. 10 coed fraternities. 45% of students join. Dorms, college-owned apartments and houses. 90% of students live on campus. Honor system. 16 intercollegiate sports for men, 9 for women; intramurals. Student body composition: 0.7% Asian, 3% Black, 0.3% Hispanic, 94.3% White, 1.7% Other. 85% from out of state.

[2] CASCO BAY COLLEGE

477 Congress Street, Portland 04101

[J1] CENTRAL MAINE MEDICAL CENTER SCHOOL OF NURSING

300 Main Street, Lewiston 04240, (207) 795-2477, 2308
Director: Fay E. Ingersoll

- **Enrollment: 6m, 99w**
- **Tuition & Fees (1982/83): $3,800**
- **Room & Board: $2,443**
- **Degree offered: AAS in Nursing**
- **Student-faculty ratio: 6 to 1**

A private nursing school founded in 1891 in Lewiston. Lewiston-Auburn area served by bus.
Academic Character NEASC and professional accreditation. 22-month program offered leading to an Associate in Applied Science of Nursing degree. Courses offered in English, nursing, psychology, science, sociology. Some biology, psychology, English and microbiology courses may be taken at any regionally accredited college or university. School's rationale for teaching and learning process is based on concepts from Abraham Maslow and Malcolm Knowles. Health Science library at the Central Maine Medical Center.
Financial CEEB CSS. School scholarships and loans; federal scholarships and loans.
Admissions High school graduation with 15 units required. GED accepted. SAT required. $10 application fee. Rolling admissions; application deadline in July 31. *Early Admission* and *Early Decision programs.*
Student Life Maine State Nursing Students' Association, National Nursing Students' Association. 2 coed dorms. Some class and seminar rooms in dorms. Cafeteria, meal tickets at reduced price.

[J1] CENTRAL MAINE VOCATIONAL-TECHNICAL INSTITUTE
Auburn 04210

[1] COLBY COLLEGE
Waterville 04901, (207) 873-1131
Dean of Admissions: Robert P. McArthur

- **Enrollment: 875m, 800w**
- **Tuition (1982/83): $7,290**
- **Room & Board: $2,800; Fees: $260**
- **Degree offered: BA**
- **Mean SAT 570v, 610m**
- **Student-faculty ratio: 13 to 1**

A private college founded in 1813. 900-acre semi-rural campus on a hill 2 miles from downtown Waterville, about 75 miles north of Portland. Airport, bus station in Waterville.

Academic Character NEASC and professional accreditation. 4-1-4 system. Majors offered in administrative science, art, biology, chemistry, classics, economics, English, French, geology, German, government, history, math, music, philosophy, physics, psychology, religion, sociology, and Spanish. Several combined and interdisciplinary majors. Self-designed majors. Distributive requirements. Senior comprehensive exams in some majors. Accelerated study. Honors and Senior Scholars programs. Phi Beta Kappa. Independent study. Pass/fail, credit possible for field experience. Preprofessional programs in administrative science, dentistry, engineering, government, law, medicine, theology, veterinary science. 3-2 engineering programs with U of Rochester, Case Western Reserve. Exchanges with Fisk, Pomona, Pitzer, Howard. Washington and Mystic Seaport Semesters, Sea Semester. Secondary education certification. Language lab, computer center. 365,000-volume library with microform resources.

Financial CEEB CSS. College scholarships and loans, payment plan; PELL, SEOG, GSL, NDSL, FISL, CWS. Application deadline for scholarships and grants March 15. Deadline for loans varies.

Admissions High school graduation with 16 units required. SAT or ACT, 3 ACH, and English teacher's recommendation required. $30 application fee. Application deadline February 1. Notification about April 15. Acceptance of offer and $200 tuition deposit required by May 1. *Early Decision* and *Early Entrance* programs. Admission deferral possible. Transfers accepted. Credit possible for CEEB AP and departmental exams.

Student Life Student government. Newspaper, literary magazine, yearbook, radio station. Music, drama, and public speaking groups. Student Arts Festival. Outing Club. Student Organization for Black Unity. Women's Group. Community service, religious, and special interest groups. 8 fraternities with houses, 2 sororities with chapter rooms. 35% of men and 8% of women join. Coed and single-sex dorms. No married-student housing. 92% of students live on campus. 3 semester hours of phys ed required. 12 intercollegiate sports for men, 11 for women; intramurals, club rugby for men and women. AIAW, ECAC, NCAA, NESCAC. Student body composition: 1% Asian, 2% Black, 1% Hispanic, 95% White, 1% Other. 86% from out of state.

[J1] EASTERN MAINE VOCATIONAL-TECHNICAL INSTITUTE
354 Hogan Road, Bangor 04401

[1] HUSSON COLLEGE
College Circle, Bangor 04401, (207) 947-1121
Director of Admissions: Paul E. Husson

- **Undergraduates: 367m, 322w; 1,563 total (including graduates)**
- **Tuition (1982/83): $4,200**
- **Room & Board: $2,500**
- **Degrees offered: BS, AS**
- **Mean SAT 384v, 445m**
- **Student-faculty ratio: 19 to 1**

A private college of business established 1898. 250-acre campus in the small city of Bangor. Airport, bus station in Bangor.

Academic Character NEASC accreditation. Semester system, 2 6-week summer terms. Majors offered in the divisions of accounting, business administration, business teacher education, court reporting, and office administration. Minors in behavioral science, economics, English, history, media communications, psychology. Distributive requirements. MS in business granted. Independent and directed study. Cooperative work/study. Secondary education certification. International Center for Language Studies. Computer center. ROTC, AFROTC at U of Maine. 28,500-volume library.

Financial CEEB CSS. College scholarships and grants, payment plans; PELL, SEOG, SSIG, NDSL, GSL, PLUS, CWS. No application deadline.

Admissions High school graduation with 16 units required. GED accepted. SAT or ACT and interview recommended. $10 application fee. Rolling admission; no deadline. $125 deposit required within 30 days of acceptance of offer of admission. *Early Entrance, Concurrent Enrollment*, and informal early decision programs. Admission deferral possible. Transfers accepted. Credit possible for CEEB AP and CLEP exams, and for college challenge exams. Conditional acceptance and supplemental education programs for students not normally admissable. Special (non-degree) enrollment possible.

Student Life Student government. Newspaper, yearbook, radio station. Music and drama organizations. Political groups. Ebony club. Outing club. Over 25 other organizations. 5 fraternities and 3 sororities without houses. 35% of men and 25% of women join. Students must live at home or on campus. Single-sex dorms. No married-student housing. 70% of students live on campus. Regular class attendance required. 4 intercollegiate sports for men, 3 for women; intramurals. AIAW, NAIA, NCAA, Northeastern College Conference. Student body composition: 2% Black, 2% Native American, 96% White. 30% from out of state.

[J1] KENNEBEC VALLEY VOCATIONAL-TECHNICAL INSTITUTE
Gilman Street, Waterville 04901

[J1] MAINE, UNIVERSITY OF, AT AUGUSTA
University Heights, Augusta 04330

[1] MAINE, UNIVERSITY OF, AT FARMINGTON
Farmington 04938, (207) 778-9521
Director of Admissions: J. Anthony McLaughlin

- **Undergraduates: 406m, 1,138w**
- **Tuition (1982/83): $1,320 (in-state), $3,630 (out-of-state)**
- **Room & Board: $2,210; Fees: $65**
- **Degrees offered: BA, BS, BGS, AA, AS**
- **Mean SAT 427v, 456m**
- **Student-faculty ratio: 16 to 1**

A public university established in 1864. Small-town campus in Farmington, 80 miles north of Portland and 35 miles northwest of Augusta in the mountain and lake region. Bus station in Farmington.

Academic Character NEASC and professional accreditation. Semester system, 3 summer terms. Majors offered in the areas of biology, community health education, elementary education (2), English, geography, history, home economics education (5), math, psychology, rehabilitation work, secondary education, and special education (5). Interdisciplinary and self-designed majors. Associate degrees in liberal arts, early childhood education, dietary technology, land planning technology. Certificate program in athletic coaching. Distributive requirements. Independent study, group and individual research. Honors program. Internships, cooperative work/study. Credit for dance and music and for field work. Pass/fail. Preprofessional programs in law, medicine, optometry, veterinary medicine. 1-3 engineering and life science & agriculture programs with U of Maine, Orono. Member of consortiums with U of Maine, Augusta, the Auburn and Waterville Vocational-Technical Institutes, and with nine other colleges in Maine. Student may enroll in other New England state universities for programs not offered at Farmington for in-state costs. Exchange with Glassboro State and U of South Florida. Study abroad. Elementary, secondary, and special education certification. 90,000-volume library.

Financial CEEB CSS. University scholarships, loans; PELL, SEOG, NDSL, GSL, CWS. Application deadline March 15.

Admissions High school graduation with 16 units required. SAT or ACT (Canadians may substitute SACU), and 2 ACH required. AA, AS degree candidates may be exempt. Student Descriptive Questionnaire required. Interview recommended. Special consideration for non-high school graduate veterans. $10 application fee. Rolling admission; no deadline. $25 registration fee and $50 room deposit due on acceptance of offer of admission. *Early Decision* and *Early Entrance* programs. Admission deferral possible. Transfers accepted. Credit possible for CEEB AP, CLEP, and departmental exams.

Student Life Student government. Newspaper, yearbook, radio station. Music, dance, and theatre groups. Community service groups. Maine PIRG. Outing club. Many special interest, athletic, academic, religious and honorary groups. 2 fraternities and 3 sororities. Coed and single-sex dorms. No married-student housing. 60% of students live on campus. Class attendance expected. 4 semesters of phys ed and health required. 13 intercollegiate sports for men, 10 for women; intramurals. AIAM, ECAC, NAIA, NCAA, Northeast College Conference. Student body composition: 0.5% Black, 0.5% Hispanic, 1% Native American, 98% White. 20% from out of state.

[1] MAINE, UNIVERSITY OF, AT FORT KENT
Pleasant Street, Fort Kent 04743, (207) 834-3162
Director of Admissions: Glenys M. Sayward

- **Enrollment: 290m, 280w**
- **Tuition (1982/83): $1,170 (in-state), $3,270 (out-of-state)**
- **Room & Board: $2,250; Fees: $85**
- **Degrees offered: BA, BSEd, BSN, BS in Env Studies, BUniv Studies, AA**
- **Mean SAT 406v, 436m**
- **Student-faculty ratio: 18 to 1**

A public university established in 1878 and located in far northern Maine at the end of U.S. Route 1. 52-acre campus five minutes from St. John River and Canadian Border. 16-acre biological park on campus.

Academic Character NEASC accreditation. Semester system, summer term. Majors include bilingual/bicultural studies, biology, business, English, environmental studies, French, history, nursing. Minors in some major areas and in art, behavioral science, computer science, geography, math, music, social science, theatre. Minor required. AA in bicultural studies, business management, criminal justice, forestry, gerontology, teacher's aide. Distributive requirements. Honors program. Cooperative work/study. 1- or 2-year transfer programs include engineering, social welfare, industrial arts in education, agricultural mechanization, agricultural & resource economics, animal & veterinary sciences, biochemistry. National Student Exchange, New England Regional Student Program. Elementary education certification. 41,000-volume library with microform resources.

Financial CEEB CSS. University scholarships, state scholarships and loans, Indian Scholarship Program; PELL, SEOG, NDSL, CWS. Application deadline April 1.

Admissions Open admission to BUniversity Studies and AA programs. High school graduation with 10 units required. Interview recommended. SAT or ACT required. $10 application fee. Rolling admissions; no deadline. $25 tuition and $25 room deposits required on acceptance of offer of admission. *Early Decision* and *Early Admission* programs. Admission deferral possible. Transfers accepted. Credit possible for CEEB AP and CLEP exams, and for French equivalency exam.

Student Life Student government. Newspaper, yearbook, radio station. Drama, music, photography clubs. Sporting clubs. Campus Fellowship. Friends of the Handicapped. 1 fraternity. 2 dorms house 150 students. 2 semester hours of phys ed required. 4 intercollegiate sports for men and women; intramurals, club ice hockey. NAIA, NCC.

[1] MAINE, UNIVERSITY OF, AT MACHIAS

Machias 04654, (207) 255-3313

- **Undergraduates: 185m, 243w; 626 total (including part-time)**
- **Tuition (1982/83): $1,320 (max. in-state), $3,770 (max. out-of-state)**
- **Room & Board: $2,250; Fees: $150**
- **Books: $250**
- **Degrees offered: BA, BS, AA, AS**
- **Mean SAT 435v, 460m**

A public, independently accredited unit of the University of Maine system.

Academic Character NEASC accreditation. Semester system, summer term. Baccalaureate degree programs offered in early childhood education, elementary education, junior high education, business education, business administration, accounting, marketing, biological technology, recreation management, and environmental studies. Associate degrees offered in liberal arts, recreation management, secretarial science, small business management, and in business technology in accounting and marketing. Remedial mathematics and English programs.

Admissions Admission notification is done on a rolling basis. Students accepted for admission in September and at mid-year. *Early Admission* and *Early Decision* programs. Admission deferral possible. Advanced placement credit possible.

[1] MAINE, UNIVERSITY OF, AT ORONO

Orono 04469, (207) 581-7568
Director of Admissions: William J. Munsey

- **Undergraduates: 5,345m, 4,379w; 11,315 total (including graduates)**
- **Tuition (1982/83): $1,410 (in-state), $4,200 (out-of-state)**
- **Room & Board: $2,680; Fees: $70**
- **Degrees offered: BA, BS, BSEd, BMus, BET, AS**
- **Mean SAT 470v, 520m**
- **Student-faculty ratio: 15 to 1**

A public university established in 1865. Suburban main campus in Orono. University also owns 900 acres of farmland, 2,000 acres of forest, 360 acres of bog, 33 acres of woodland preserve. 2-year branch campus, airport, and bus station 9 miles away in Bangor.

Academic Character NEASC and professional accreditation. Semester system, 4 3-week and 3 6-week summer terms. Over 70 majors offered by the Colleges of Arts & Sciences, Business Administration, Education, Engineering & Science, Forest Resources, Life Sciences & Agriculture. Double, self-designed, and interdisciplinary concentrations possible. Many minors offered. Distributive requirements. Graduate degrees granted. Independent and accelerated study. Honors program. Phi Beta Kappa. Cooperative work/study, internships. Pass/fail. Preprofessional programs in dentistry, medicine. Registration for courses at Bangor Theological Seminary possible. Living/Learning program. Study abroad. Elementary, secondary, and special education certification. ROTC, AFROTC. Several centers and institutes on campus. Northeast Archive of Folklore and Oral History, art collection, museum. Computer center, farm. 551,000-volume libraries.

Financial CEEB CSS. University scholarships, loans, payment plan; PELL, SEOG, NDSL, CWS. Application deadline March 1.

Admissions High school graduation with 16 units required; some programs have additional requirements. SAT and 2 ACH required. $10 application fee. Rolling admissions; application deadline March 1. $25 tuition and $50 room deposits required on acceptance of offer of admission. *Early Admission* Program. Transfers accepted. Credit possible for CEEB AP, CLEP, and departmental exams.

Student Life Student government. Newspaper, magazines, yearbook, radio & TV stations. Music, drama, dance, and speaking groups. Debate. Athletic, academic, religious, service, and special interest groups. 16 fraternities, 15 with houses, and 10 sororities. Coed and single-sex dorms. 70% of students live on campus. 16 intercollegiate sports for men and women; intramurals. AIAW. Student body composition: 1.6% Minorities, 98.4% White. 25% from out of state.

■[J1] BANGOR COMMUNITY COLLEGE

Bangor 04401

[1] MAINE, UNIVERSITY OF, AT PRESQUE ISLE

181 Main Street, Presque Isle 04769, (207) 764-0311
Director of Admissions: Steven E. Crouse

- **Undergraduates: 385m, 425w; 1,280 total (including part-time)**
- **Tuition (1982/83): $1,320 (in-state), $3,630 (out-of-state)**
- **Room & Board: $2,437; Fees: $70**
- **Degrees offered: BA, BS, AA, AS**
- **Mean SAT 425v, 460m**
- **Student-faculty ratio: 18 to 1**

A public university established in 1903 in Presque Isle. 150-acre campus 195 miles north of Bangor. Airport, bus station.

Academic Character NEASC accreditation. Semester system, 6 summer terms. Majors offered in art, behavioral science, business management, criminal justice, education areas, English, environmental science, French, history, humanities, library technology, life sciences, management science, math, medical laboratory technician, political studies, recreation-leisure, social science, speech-communication, theatre & drama, and health, physical education & recreation. Minors in most major areas and in teaching exceptional children, geology, music, Soviet area studies. Associate degrees include recreation, criminal justice, and medical lab technology. Independent and directed study. Pass/fail, cooperative work/study. 2-year transfer programs with U of Southern Maine and U of Maine at Orono in the areas of engineering, geology, nursing, life sciences, and agriculture. Certificate programs in real estate, recreation, teacher's aide. Elementary, secondary, and physical education certification. Language lab. 69,000-volume library.

Financial CEEB CSS. University scholarships, loans, Indian Scholarship Program, state scholarships; PELL, SEOG, NDSL, GSL, CWS, university work program. Recommended application deadline March 1.

Admissions High school graduation with 16 units required. Interview recommended. SAT and 2 ACH required. $10 application fee. Rolling admissions; no application deadline. $25 tuition and $50 room deposits required on acceptance of offer of admission. *Early Admission* and *Early Decision* programs. Admission deferral possible. Transfers accepted. Credit possible for CEEB AP and CLEP exams.

Student Life Student government. Literary magazine, yearbook, radio station. Music, drama clubs. Tutorial program. Community service, athletic, academic, religious, and special interest groups. 2 fraternities and 2 sororities. 15% of men and women join. Freshmen must live on campus. 4 residence halls. No married-student housing. 33% of students live on campus. Liquor allowed in dorm rooms. 5 intercollegiate sports for men, 5 for women; intramurals. AIAW, NAIA, NCAA, NCC. Student body composition: 1% Black, 98% White, 1% Other. 15% from out of state.

[1] MAINE MARITIME ACADEMY

Castine 04421, (207) 326-4311
Director of Admissions: Leonard H. Tyler

- **Enrollment: 625m, 20w**
- **Tuition (1982/83): $2,120 (in-state), $3,885 (out-of-state)**
- **Room & Board: $2,745; Fees: $360**
- **Degree offered: BS**
- **Mean SAT 450v, 530m**
- **Student-faculty ratio: 15 to 1**

A public academy founded in 1941, became coed in 1974. 30-acre campus in the small coastal town of Castine. Airport and bus station 38 miles away in Bangor.

Academic Character NEASC accreditation. Year-round trimester system. Mandatory freshmen indoctrination in August. Majors in marine engineering and nautical science. Minors in business transportation, engineering science, humanities, marine industrial management, natural science, ocean engineering, oceanography, social science. Independent study. Merchant Marine Licensing Program qualifies student for Merchant Marine Officer's License and a Reserve Commission in USNR or Coast Guard Reserve. Required program for first-year students. Training cruise required after freshman and junior years. Cadet Shipping Training Program after sophomore year. Tanker simulator, several labs and sailing vessels. NROTC. 51,000-volume library with microform resources; 1,000-volume shipboard library. Maritime history collection.

Financial CEEB CSS. Academy scholarships and loans, state scholarships, payment plan; PELL, SEOG, GSL, NDSL, FISL, CWS. Application deadline April 15.

Admissions High school graduation with 12 units required. US citizenship and sound mental and physical health required. Interview recommended. SAT or ACT required. $25 application fee. Rolling admissions. Application deadline June 1 for Maine residents, April 15 for others. $50 room deposit required on acceptance of admissions offer. Informal early decision program. Transfers accepted. Credit possible for CEEB AP and CLEP exams.

Student Life Student government. Newspaper, yearbook, radio station. Music and singing groups. Service fraternity. Karate, radio, propellor, scuba, and yacht clubs. One social fraternity. Students must live on campus or on board the training ship during mandatory cruises. Coed and single-sex dorms. Freshmen may not have cars. Liquor prohibited on campus. Mandatory class attendance. Honor code. Uniforms required at all times while at the Academy. 3 terms of phys ed required. 6 intercollegiate sports for men; club rugby and intramurals. NAIA, NCAA, NCC. Student body composition: 1% Black, 1% Native American, 98% White. 30% of students are from out of state.

[1] NASSON COLLEGE

Springvale 04083, (207) 324-5340
Director of Admissions: Richard Lolatte

- **Undergraduates: 275m, 225w; 600 total (including part-time)**
- **Tuition (1982/83): $5,195**
- **Room & Board: $2,550 (average); Fees: $210**
- **Degrees offered: BA, BS, AA**
- **Mean SAT 460v, 430m**
- **Student-faculty ratio: 14 to 1**

A private college established in 1912, became coed in 1935. 240-campus in a small town 14 miles from the Atlantic Ocean, 35 miles southwest of Portland, and 90 miles from Boston. 130-acre environmental studies tract on campus. Bus station in Springvale, airport in Boston.

Academic Character NEASC accreditation. Semester system. Majors in accounting, biology, business management, chemistry, communications, English, environmental science, finance, government, history, human services, journalism, marine science, marketing, medical technology, laboratory science, pre-engineering, psychology. Concentrated study in art, literature, music, philosophy, religion, drama, physics, linguistics, math, gerontology. BS in nursing major for registered nurses. Minors in some of the above and in math, music, small business, sociology. Self-designed majors. Distributive requirements. Accelerated study. Independent study. Honors program. Internships. Interdisciplinary seminars. Preprofessional programs

in dentistry, engineering, law, medicine, veterinary studies. Study abroad. Member of the International Studies Consortium of Central College (Iowa). Language lab. ROTC at UNH. 130,000-volume library with microform resources.
Financial CEEB CSS and ACT FAS. College scholarships, grants, and loans, state scholarships; PELL, SEOG, NDSL, GSL, CWS. Application deadline March 1.
Admissions High school graduation with 16 units required. ACT or SAT required. English ACH and interview recommended. $15 application fee. Application deadline February 1. Notification of admission on rolling basis starting October 15. $200 tuition deposit required on acceptance of offer of admission. *Early Entrance* and *Early Decision* programs. Admission deferral possible. Transfers accepted. Credit possible for CEEB AP and CLEP exams.
Student Life Student government. Newspaper, literary magazines, yearbook, radio station. Music and drama organizations. Theatre company. Big Brother, Big Sister. Special interest clubs. Coffeehouse. Honorary and religious organizations. Single students must live at home or on campus. 7 residence halls. International house. 95% of students live on campus. 6 intercollegiate sports for men, 5 for women; club lacrosse, intramurals. MAIAW, MAPEIAW, NAIA, NCAA. Student body composition: 0.5% Black, 94% White, 4.5% Other. 85% from out of state.

[1] NEW ENGLAND, UNIVERSITY OF

11 Hills Beach Road, Biddeford 04005, (207) 283-0171
Director of Admissions: Judith L. Evrard

- **Enrollment: 368m, 230w; 661 total (including part-time)**
- **Tuition (1982/83): $4,725**
- **Room & Board: $2,670; Fees: $60**
- **Degrees offered: BA, BS, BSN**
- **Mean SAT 430v, 465m**
- **Student-faculty ratio: 15 to 1**

A private university established in 1978 by merger of Saint Francis College and New England College of Osteopathic Medicine. Campus in the small coastal town of Biddeford, between Portland and Maine's southern border.
Academic Character NEASC accreditation. 4-1-4 system. University consists of Saint Francis College and College of Health Sciences. Majors offered in business administration, chemistry-toxicology, environmental analysis, general biology, human services, marine biology, medical biology, occupational therapy, physical therapy, teacher preparation. Division of Liberal Learning offers program leading to a BLS. Nursing major for students with an RN. Concentration in gerontology. Distributive requirements. College of Osteopathic Medicine grants doctoral degree. Pass/fail. Cooperative work/study. January term of concentrated study. Clinical experience available. 2-3 pharmacy program with Massachusetts College of Pharmacy and Allied Health Sciences. Cross-registration with Nasson College. Elementary, secondary, and special education certification.
Financial CEEB CSS. University scholarships and grants, state scholarships, payment plans; PELL, SEOG, NDSL, CWS.
Admissions High school graduation with 13 units required. GED accepted. SAT or ACT required. 2 recommendations required. $15 application fee. Application deadline January 15 for College of Health Sciences; notification by mid-February. Rolling admissions for Saint Francis College applicants. $100 deposit required on acceptance of offer of admission. *Early Admission* and *Early Decision* programs. Admission deferral possible. Transfers accepted. Credit possible for CEEB AP and CLEP exams. Conditional acceptance possible.
Student Life Student government. Radio station. Chapel Council. Theatre productions. Single students must live at home or on campus. Dorms and dining hall. 80% of students live on campus. 5 intercollegiate sports for men, 3 for women; club and intramural sports. NAIA, NCAA.

[J1] NORTHERN MAINE VOCATIONAL-TECHNICAL INSTITUTE

33 Edgemont Drive, Presque Isle 04769

[1] PORTLAND SCHOOL OF ART

97 Spring Street, Portland 04101

[1] ST. JOSEPH'S COLLEGE

North Windham 04062, (207) 892-6766

- **Undergraduates: 113m, 270w; 500 total (including part-time)**
- **Tuition (1982/83): $3,700**
- **Room & Board: $2,000; Fees: $175**
- **Degrees offered: BA, BS, BSN, BSBA, BSPA**

A private Roman Catholic liberal arts college. Rural campus located 16 miles west of Portland.
Academic Character NEASC accreditation. Semester system. Majors offered in business administration (accounting, marketing & management), biology, English, education (elementary & secondary), French, history, mathematics, nursing, communications/broadcasting, environmental science, liberal arts, sociology. Preprofessional majors in dentistry, law, and veterinary science. Bachelor of Science in Professional Arts program for registered nurses. 2-year Bachelor degre completion program for radiologic technologist. 65,000-volume library.
Financial Financial aid available including scholarships.
Admissions Competitive admission based on high school graduation, secondary school record, and SAT scores. Admission notification on a rolling basis. *Early Admission* Program. Admission deferral possible. Advanced placement credit possible.
Student Life Intercollegiate and intramural sports for men and women.

[1] SOUTHERN MAINE, UNIVERSITY OF

Gorham 04038, (207) 780-5215
Director of Admissions: Dennis J. Farrell

- **Undergraduates: 3,456m, 4,747w; 8,454 total (including part-time)**
- **Tuition (1982/83): $1,410 (in-state), $4,200 (out-of-state)**
- **Room & Board: $2,315; Fees: $60**
- **Degrees offered: BA, BS, BFA, BSN, BSBA, AS**
- **Mean SAT 473v, 520m (for 4-year degree)**
- **Mean SAT 402v, 420m (for 2-year degree)**
- **Student-faculty ratio: 18 to 1**

A 2-campus public university established in 1970 by a merger of U Maine and Gorham State. Total campus area of 150 acres in Portland and in Gorham, ten minutes drive from Sebago Lake. Airport, bus station.
Academic Character NEASC and professional accreditation. Semester system, several 3- to 8-week summer terms. 38 majors offered by the Colleges of Arts & Sciences and Education, and the Schools of Business & Education and Nursing. Self-designed and double majors. Certificate programs. Distributive requirements. Graduate and professional degrees granted. Independent study. Honors program. Credit by exam, pass/fail. Cooperative work/study. Internships. Preprofessional programs in dentistry, medicine, veterinary medicine. 1-3 engineering with U Maine, Orono. 2-2 engineering program. Study abroad. Elementary and secondary education certification. ROTC; AFROTC at U of New Hampshire. Writing lab, language lab, planetarium. 500,000-volume library.
Financial CEEB CSS. University scholarships, Indian scholarships and tuition waivers; PELL, SEOG, NSS, NDSL, NSL, GSL, CWS. Suggest applying as soon as possible after January 1.
Admissions High school graduation with 13 units required. Specific programs may have additional requirements. SAT or ACT required. Interview required for music, industrial arts, and voc-tech programs. $15 application fee. Rolling admissions; suggest applying in fall of 12th year. $25 tuition and $50 room deposits required on acceptance of offer of admission. *Early Admission* and informal early decision programs. Admission deferral possible. Transfers accepted. Credit possible for CEEB AP and CLEP exams. Conditional Admission Program.
Student Life Student government. Newspaper, literary magazine, yearbook, radio station. Music and drama organizations. Political and religious clubs. Many special interest groups. 5 fraternities, 3 with houses, and 3 sororities without houses. 8% of men and 10% of women join. Coed and single-sex dorms. No married-student housing. 15% of students live on campus. Boarding freshmen may not have cars on campus. Liquor allowed only in dorms. 2 semesters of phys ed required for College of Education. 6 intercollegiate sports for men, 9 for women; intramurals. AIAW, ECAC, NAIA, NCAA, NECAC. Student body composition: 1% Asian, 1% Black, 1% Hispanic, 1% Native American, 96% White. 15% from out of state.

[J1] SOUTHERN MAINE VOCATIONAL-TECHNICAL INSTITUTE

Fort Road, South Portland 04106

[1 & J1] THOMAS COLLEGE

Waterville 04901, (207) 873-0771
Dean of Admissions: L. Lincoln Brown, Jr.

- **Enrollment: 362m, 512w**
- **Tuition (1982/83): $4,560**
- **Room & Board: $2,550-$2,650; Fees: $105**
- **Degrees offered: BS, AA, AS**
- **Mean SAT 383v, 460m**
- **Student-faculty ratio: 18 to 1**

A private college established in 1894. 70-acre campus by the Kennebec River in the small city of Waterville, 75 miles north of Portland. Airport, bus station.
Academic Character NEASC accreditation. Semester system. Majors offered in accounting, applied business, banking, business, business administration, computer information systems, executive and legal secretarial, liberal arts, management, marketing-management, medical assistant, professional studies, real estate, retail management, retail merchandising. Minors. AA offered in liberal arts. AS in secretarial science, banking, real estate, business, and retail merchandising. MS granted. Exchange program with Colby College. Computer center. 18,000-volume library.
Financial CEEB CSS. College scholarships and grants, state aid, payment plans; PELL, SEOG, NDSL, GSL, CWS.
Admissions High school graduation required. Interview recommended. SAT or ACT required for bachelor's degree candidates. $15 application fee. Rolling admissions. *Early Acceptance* and *Early Decision* programs. Admission deferral possible. Transfers accepted. Credit possible for CEEB AP and CLEP exams.
Student Life Student government. Newspaper, yearbook, *Thomas Business Review*. Academic clubs. Newman Council. Honorary societies. Chorus. Circle K. Special interest clubs. 3 fraternities and 3 sororities without houses. Freshmen and sophomores live at home or on campus. Dorms for men and women. Dining hall and student union. 5 intercollegiate sports for men, 5 for women; club hockey, intramurals. NCAA, NAIA, ECAC, MAIA.

[1] UNITY COLLEGE

Unity 04988, (207) 948-3131
Director of Admissions: F. Edward Hinkley

- **Enrollment: 225m, 100w**
- **Tuition (1982/83): $4,200**
- **Room & Board: $2,600; Fees: $240**
- **Degrees offered: BA, BS, AA, AS, AAS**

- **Student-faculty ratio: 14 to 1**

A private college founded in 1965 in the small town of Unity. 185-acre rural campus overlooking Lake Winnecook, within 30 miles of Augusta and Bangor, and about 200 miles north of Boston. Airport and bus station in Waterville.
Academic Character NEASC accreditation. 4-1-4-1 (January and May terms) system. Summer terms. Majors offered in conservation law enforcement, environmental science, forest technology, interdisciplinary studies, outdoor recreation, wildlife & fisheries technology. Associate degree programs are self-designed in the areas of general studies, forest technology, conservation law enforcement, wildlife & fisheries technology. Distributive requirements, including senior seminar, internships, or thesis for bachelor's degree candidates. Courses in administrative science, anthropology, biology, ceramics, chemistry, developmental skills, drawing, economics, education, English, environmental science, forestry, French, geology, history, humanities, learning resources, math, outdoor recreation, painting, philosophy, photography, physics, political science, psychology, religion, sculpture, sociology, visual studies, wildlife & fisheries. Independent and directed study. Internships, cooperative work/study. Washington Center for Learning Alternatives: internships and colloquia in D.C. for students and faculty. Center for Human Ecology Studies internship in Freeport. 40,000-volume library.
Financial CEEB CSS. College scholarships and grants, state scholarships, payment plans; PELL, SEOG, NDSL, GSL, PLUS, CWS. Application deadline June 1.
Admissions High school graduation required. GED accepted. SAT or ACT should be submitted if available. Interview strongly recommended. Rolling admissions. Suggested application deadline (for financial aid applicants) June 1. $100 enrollment and $50 housing deposits required on acceptance of offer of admission. Admission deferral possible. Transfers accepted. Credit possible for CEEB AP, CLEP, and college placement exams.
Student Life Student government. Newspaper, literary magazine, yearbook. Several special interest clubs. American Fisheries Society chapter. Forest fire crew. Full-time single freshmen must live on campus. 3 dorms. 4 intercollegiate sports; intramurals, club sports. Woodsmen's team. NAIA, NCC, AIAW.

[1 & J1] WESTBROOK COLLEGE
Portland 04103, (207) 797-7261
Director of Admissions: Ruth Ann Brooks

- **Enrollment: 80m, 548w; 935 total (including part-time)**
- **Tuition (1982/83): $4,960**
- **Room & Board: $2,675; Fees: $355**
- **Degrees offered: BA, BS, AA, AS**
- **Student-faculty ratio: 14 to 1**

A private college established in 1831 in Portland. 40-acre suburban campus with 25-acre wooded area adjoining. Airport and bus station in Portland.
Academic Character NEASC and professional accreditation. Semester system. Bachelors degrees offered in business administration and medical technology, and in nursing for RNs. Associates in business administration, dental hygiene, environmental studies, executive secretary, fine arts, general studies, legal secretary, liberal arts, medical assistant, merchandising & retailing, nursing education. BBA for holders of associate degrees. Maine Printmaking Workshop. Lifelong external degree program. Continuing education. Art gallery. 24,900-volume library.
Financial CEEB CSS. College scholarships, state grants and scholarships, dental hygiene loans, PELL, SEOG, NSS, NDSL, GSL, NSL, CWS, college part-time employment.
Admissions 3-4 years of high school college-prep subjects required. Most programs have specific requirements. Audition or portfolio required for fine arts. SAT, ACH, and interview recommended. $25 application fee. Rolling admissions; no deadline. $150 tuition and $150 room deposits required on acceptance of offer of admission. *Early Decision* and *Early Entrance* programs. Admission deferral possible.
Student Life Student government. Newspaper, newsletter, yearbook. Activities and cultural affairs committees. 5 professional organizations. Music groups, theatre company. Outing committee. Intercollegiate sports clubs. Student body composition: 0.3% Black, 99.7% White.

MARYLAND *(MD)*

[J1] ALLEGANY COMMUNITY COLLEGE
Cumberland 21502

[2] ANDREW JACKSON UNIVERSITY
10106 Georgia Avenue, Silver Spring 20902

[J1] ANNE ARUNDEL COMMUNITY COLLEGE
101 College Parkway, Arnold 21012

[J1] BALTIMORE, COMMUNITY COLLEGE OF
Baltimore 21215

■[J1] BALTIMORE, COMMUNITY COLLEGE OF
Harbor Campus, Baltimore 21202

[1] BALTIMORE, UNIVERSITY OF
1420 North Charles Street, Baltimore 21201

[1] BALTIMORE HEBREW COLLEGE
5800 Park Heights, Baltimore 21215

[1] BOWIE STATE COLLEGE
Bowie 20715, (301) 464-3000
Director of Admissions: Patricia A. Wilson

- **Undergraduates: 1,243m, 1,636w**
- **Tuition (1982/83): $960 (in-state), $2,000 (out-of-state)**
- **Room & Board: $2,425; Fees: $300**
- **Degrees offered: BA, BS**
- **Student-faculty ratio: 28 to 1**

A public college established in 1865. 237-acre campus located 18 miles from Washington, DC. Served by air, rail, and bus.
Academic Character MSACS and professional accreditation. Semester system, 2 6-week summer terms. 26 majors offered in the areas of liberal arts & sciences, business, communications, education, engineering, music, nursing, physical education, social work, theatre. Distributive requirements. Graduate degrees granted. Independent study. Honors program. Phi Beta Kappa. Cooperative work/study, internships. 5-year dual degree program in engineering with George Washington U and U of Maryland. Exchange program with Anne Arundel Community College. Elementary, secondary, and special education certification. ROTC at Howard; AFROTC at U of Maryland. 149,603-volume library.
Financial CEEB CSS. College scholarships, grants, loans, Maryland Other Race Grants (for minorities); PELL, SEOG, NDSL, FISL, CWS. Application deadline July 1.
Admissions High school graduation with 20 units required. Interview recommended. SAT required. $10 application fee. Rolling admissions. $35 deposit required on acceptance of offer of admission. *Early Admission* and *Early Decision* programs. Transfers accepted. Credit possible for CEEB AP and CLEP exams.
Student Life Student government. Newspaper, literary magazine, yearbook. Music and drama groups. Veterans Club. Respond Center. Academic and special interest groups. 5 fraternities and 3 sororities. No married-student housing. 25% of students live on campus. 2 semesters of phys ed required. Disciplinary action for alcohol abuse. 5 intercollegiate sports for men, 5 for women; intramurals. CIAA, NAIA, NIAA, PIC. Student body composition: 0.1% Asian, 78.7% Black, 0.3% Hispanic, 0.2% Native American, 15.3% White, 5.4% Other. 15% from out of state.

[1] CAPITOL INSTITUTE OF TECHNOLOGY
10335 Kensington Parkway, Kensington 20895

[J1] CATONSVILLE COMMUNITY COLLEGE
Catonsville 21228

[J1] CECIL COMMUNITY COLLEGE
North East 21901

[J1] CHARLES COUNTY COMMUNITY COLLEGE
La Plata 20646

[J1] CHESAPEAKE COLLEGE
Wye Mills 21679

[1] COLUMBIA UNION COLLEGE
7600 Flower Avenue, Takoma Park 20912, (302) 891-4120
Director of Admissions: Connie Hovanic

- **Undergraduates: 294m, 399w**
- **Tuition (1982/83): $4,770**
- **Room & Board: $2,400; Fees: $164**
- **Degrees offered: BA, BS, BSW, AA**
- **Student-faculty ratio: 10 to 1**

A private college controlled by the Seventh-Day Adventist Church, established in 1904. 19-acre suburban campus 7 miles from Washington, DC. Airport, rail and bus stations in DC.
Academic Character MCACS and professional accreditation. Semester system, 12-week summer term. 34 majors offered in the areas of liberal arts & sciences, business, communication, computer science, education, medical technology, mental health, music, religion, respiratory therapy, and social work. Minor required for BA. Minors offered in most majors and in 7 additional areas. Distributives and 12 hours of religious studies required. Senior Comprehensive Exam. Independent study. Cooperative work/study, pass/fail. Preprofessional programs in dental hygiene, dentistry, law, medical records, medicine, physical and occupational therapy, optometry, pharmacy, veterinary medicine, and x-ray. Study abroad. Student Missionary Program. Elementary and secondary education certification. 105,665-volume library with microform resources.
Financial CEEB CSS. PELL, SEOG, NSS, NDSL, FISL, GSL, NSL, CWS, college employment program. Application deadline June 1.

Admissions High school graduation with 2.0 GPA required. GED accepted. SAT or ACT required. $15 application fee. Rolling admissions. $75 room deposit required on acceptance of offer of admission. *Early Admission, Early Decision, Concurrent Enrollment* programs. Admission deferral possible. Transfers accepted. Credit possible for CEEB AP and CLEP exams; college has own advanced placement program.
Student Life Student Association. Newspaper, literary magazine, yearbook. Radio Club. Spiritual emphasis weeks. Academic, religious, service, and special interest groups. Single students under 23 must live at home or on campus. Single-sex dorms. Married-student housing. 4 hours of phys ed required. Attendance at chapel, assemblies, and daily group worship mandatory. Liquor and tobacco prohibited. Dress code. Class attendance required. Intramural sports. Student body composition: 3.8% Asian, 24.8% Black, 4.5% Hispanic, 0.1% Native American, 63.6% White.

[1] COPPIN STATE COLLEGE
2500 West North Avenue, Baltimore 21216, (301) 383-5990
Director of Admissions: Clyde Hatcher

- **Undergraduates: 367m, 1,112w; 2,100 total (including graduates)**
- **Tuition (1982/83): $1,135 (in-state), $2,175 (out-of-state)**
- **Degrees offered: BA, BS**
- **Mean SAT 340v, 329m**
- **Student-faculty ratio: 14 to 1**

A public college established in 1900. 29-acre urban campus. Served by air, rail, and bus.
Academic Character MSACS and professional accreditation. Semester system, 2 summer terms. Majors offered in adapted physical education, adult education, alcoholism counseling, applied psychology, biology, chemistry, criminal justice, early childhood education, elementary education, English, general science, history, industrial arts education, management science, math, nursing, social science, special education. Minors in most major fields and in 11 additional areas. MEd granted. Courses in 7 other areas. Distributive requirements; Undergraduate Record Exam required. Independent study. Honors program. Preprofessional programs in dentistry and medicine. Elementary, secondary, and special education certification. Language lab. 78,000-volume library.
Financial CEEB CSS. College scholarships, grants, loans, state loans, PELL, SEOG, NDSL, GSL, NSL, student employment program. Application deadline May 1.
Admissions High school graduation required. GED accepted. SAT required. $10 application fee. Rolling admissions. $15 acceptance fee required. *Early Admission* and *Early Decision* programs. Transfers accepted. Credit possible for CEEB AP and CLEP exams.
Student Life Student government. Newspaper, yearbook. Music, dance, and drama groups. Academic, honorary, professional, and special interest groups. 3 fraternities and 4 sororities. Housing for nursing students. Class attendance required. 1 course in phys ed required. 6 intercollegiate sports; intramurals. NAIA. Student body composition: 94% Black, 4% White, 2% Other. 4% from out of state.

[J1] DESALES HALL SCHOOL OF THEOLOGY
Hyattsville — located in District of Columbia

[J1] DUNDALK COMMUNITY COLLEGE
Baltimore 21222

[2] EASTERN CHRISTIAN COLLEGE
PO Box 629, Bel Air 21014

[J1] ESSEX COMMUNITY COLLEGE
Baltimore County 21237

[J1] FREDERICK COMMUNITY COLLEGE
Frederick 21701

[1] FROSTBURG STATE COLLEGE
Frostburg 21532, (301) 689-4201
Dean of Admissions: David L. Sanford

- **Undergraduates: 1,430m, 1,482w; 3,100 total (including graduates)**
- **Tuition (1982/83): $1,231 (in-state), $2,271 (out-of-state)**
- **Room & Board: $1,870-$2,060**
- **Degrees offered: BA, BS**
- **Student-faculty ratio: 17 to 1**

A public college established in 1902. 220-acre small town campus 11 miles from Cumberland. Served by bus; airport in Cumberland.
Academic Character MSACS and professional accreditation. Semester system, 3 4½-week summer terms. 33 majors offered in the liberal arts & sciences, business, education, engineering, physical education, music, reclamation, speech/theatre, and wildlife/fisheries. Minors in most major fields and in 2 additional areas. Distributive requirements. Masters degrees granted. Independent study. Honors program. Limited pass/fail, internships. Preprofessional programs in dentistry, law, medicine, pharmacy, physical therapy, medical technology, nursing, and other areas. 2-2 nursing, 2-3 pharmacy, and 3-2 engineering programs with U of Maryland. 2-2 medical technology, 3-2 physical therapy, and 3-2 dental hygiene programs. Exchange program with St. Mark and St. John Colleges in England. Study abroad. Elementary and secondary education certification. ROTC. Computer center. 391,000-volume library.
Financial CEEB CSS. College scholarships, grants, loans, state and minority grants, payment plans; PELL, SEOG, NDSL, GSL, FISL, ALAS, CWS. Application deadline March 1 (scholarships).
Admissions High school graduation required; recommend background in English, math, and science. GED accepted. Interview recommended. SAT required. $20 application fee. Rolling admissions. $100 deposit due on acceptance of offer of admission. *Concurrent Enrollment* Program. Transfers accepted. Credit possible for CEEB AP and CLEP exams; college has own advanced placement program.
Student Life Student government. Newspaper, literary magazine, yearbook, radio station. Music and drama groups. Debate. Ski Club. Academic, honorary, service, social, and special interest groups. 9 fraternities and 11 sororities without houses. 9% of men and 8% of women join. Coed and single-sex dorms. No married-student housing. 70% of students live on campus. 1 semester of phys ed required. 8 intercollegiate sports for men, 6 for women; extensive intramurals. ECAC, NCAA. Student body composition: 1.5% Asian, 11.5% Black, 1% Hispanic, 87% White. 13% from out of state.

[J1] GARRETT COMMUNITY COLLEGE
McHenry 21541

[1] GOUCHER COLLEGE
Dulaney Valley Road, Towson 21204, (301) 337-6000
Director of Admissions: Janis Boster

- **Undergraduates: 1,087w**
- **Tuition (1982/83): $6,150**
- **Room & Board: $3,100; Fees: $250**
- **Degree offered: BA**
- **Mean SAT 530v, 530m**
- **Student-faculty ratio: 11 to 1**

A private college established in 1885. 330-acre suburban campus 8 miles north of Baltimore. Served by air and rail in Baltimore, which is 20 minutes away by bus.
Academic Character MSACS. Semester system. 33 majors offered by the Faculty of Languages, Literature, Philosophy, Religion & the Arts, the Faculty of History & the Social Sciences, and the Faculty of the Natural Sciences & Mathematics. Self-designed and combined majors. Interdepartmental programs in public affairs, and in Black and women's studies. Distributive requirements; one off-campus experience required. Senior thesis option. MA granted. Independent study. Phi Beta Kappa. Limited pass/fail for freshmen and sophomores, unlimited for upperclasses. 5-year BA/MHS with Johns Hopkins. Field Politics Center. Center for Sociological Study. Computer center. Language house. 197,149-volume library with microform resources.
Financial CEEB CSS. College scholarships, grants, loans, PELL, SEOG, NDSL, GSL, CWS. Application deadline March 1.
Admissions High school graduation with 16 units required. Interview required. SAT or ACT required. $25 application fee. Rolling admissions. $150 deposit required on acceptance of offer of admission. *Early Admission* and *Early Decision* programs. Admission deferral possible. Transfers accepted. Credit possible for CEEB AP exams.
Student Life Student government. Newspaper, literary magazine, yearbook. Dance group. Riding club. Newman Club. Jewish Student's Association. Black Student's Association. International Club. Christian Fellowship. Students must live at home or on campus. Special interest housing, language floors. 70% of students live on campus. 3 semesters of phys ed required. 10 intercollegiate sports; extensive intramurals. AIAW, EAIAW, MAIAW. Student body composition: 2.8% Asian, 6.8% Black, 2.1% Hispanic, 0.2% Native American, 86% White, 2.1% Other. 70% from out of state.

[J1] HAGERSTOWN JUNIOR COLLEGE
Hagerstown 21740

[J1] HARFORD COMMUNITY COLLEGE
Bel Air 21014

[1] HOOD COLLEGE
Frederick 21701, (301) 663-3131
Director of Admissions & Financial Aid: Diane R. Wilson

- **Undergraduates: 90m, 1,035w; 1,823 total (including graduates)**
- **Tuition (1982/83): $5,510**
- **Room & Board: $2,765; Fees: $75**
- **Degrees offered: AB, BS**
- **Mean SAT 460v, 465m**
- **Student-faculty ratio: 12 to 1**

A private college established in 1893, male commuting students accepted since 1971. 100-acre suburban campus, 45 miles northwest of Washington, DC, 45 miles west of Baltimore. Served by bus.
Academic Character MSACS accreditation. Semester system. 33 majors offered in the areas of liberal arts & sciences, education, environmental studies, home economics, computer science, management, medical technology, music, radiologic technology, recreation, religion, and social work. Special and self-designed majors. Double majors. Courses in 7 additional areas. Distributive requirements. MA, MS granted. Independent study. Honors program. Pass/fail, students may schedule own exams. Internships, field projects. Preprofessional programs in the health professions and law. 3-1 programs in medical and radiological technology. 3-2 engineering program with George Washington U. Cross-registration with Frederick and Hagerstown. Study abroad. Elementary, secondary, and special education certification. Nursery school. Observatory. Language lab. Computer center. Art gallery. 140,000-volume library.
Financial CEEB CSS. College scholarships, grants, loans, academic and

state scholarships, PELL, SEOG, NDSL, GSL, CWS, student employment program. Preferred application deadline March 31.
Admissions High school graduation with 16 units expected. Interview recommended. SAT or ACT required. $20 application fee. Rolling admissions. $150 deposit ($100 for commuters) required on acceptance of offer of admission. *Early Admission* and *Early Decision* programs. Admission deferral possible. Transfers accepted. Credit possible for CEEB AP and CLEP results; college has own advanced placement program. Some conditional admissions.
Student Life Student government. Newspaper, literary magazine, yearbook. Choral, dance, and drama groups. Black Student Union. Outing club. Big Sister Program. Honorary, political, professional, and religious groups. Students must live at home or on campus. Single-sex dorms. Language and home economics residences. 63% of students live on campus. 2 semesters of phys ed required. Honor system. 6 intercollegiate sports; intramurals. Student body composition: 1% Asian, 3% Black, 2% Hispanic, 94% White. 41% from out of state.

[J1] HOWARD COMMUNITY COLLEGE
Little Patuxent Parkway, Columbia 21044

[1] JOHNS HOPKINS UNIVERSITY
Baltimore 21218, (301) 338-8171
Director of Admissions: Jerome D. Schnydman

- **Undergraduates: 1,553m, 692w; 3,159 total (including graduates)**
- **Tuition (1982/83): $6,700**
- **Room & Board: $3,000 (estimate); Fees: $220**
- **Degrees offered: BA, BS, BEng Sci**
- **Mean SAT 626v, 677m**
- **Student-faculty ratio: 10 to 1**

A private university established in 1876, became coed in 1970. 140-acre campus located in residential section of northern Baltimore. Served by air, rail, and bus.
Academic Character MSACS and professional accreditation. 4-1-4 system, 6- to 8-week summer term. 22 majors offered by the School of Arts & Sciences, 8 by the School of Engineering. Interdepartmental liberal arts major. 5 area majors. Self-designed majors. Courses in 3 additional areas. Distributive requirements. Graduate degrees granted. Individual study, research. Honors program in humanistic studies. Phi Beta Kappa. Limited pass/fail, internships. Preprofessional programs in engineering, foreign service, law. BA/MD Human Biology program. 7-year medical program with medical school. BA/PhD psychology program. 5-year BA/MA international studies program. Evening college. Cross-registration with Goucher, Maryland Institute of Art, Peabody Conservatory of Music, and other area schools. Study abroad. Elementary and secondary education certification. ROTC; AFROTC at Maryland. 4 major research centers. 2,000,000-volume library with microform resources; specialized libraries available to students.
Financial CEEB CSS. University scholarships, grants, loans, PELL SEOG, NDSL, FISL, GSL, PLUS, ALAS, CWS. Application deadline February 1.
Admissions High school graduation with 17 units strongly recommended. Interview highly recommended. SAT or ACT required; SAT preferred. 3 ACH required. $30 application fee. Application deadline January 15. $200 deposit required on acceptance of admissions offer. *Early Admission* and *Early Decision* programs. Admission deferral possible. Transfers accepted. Credit possible for CEEB AP exams.
Student Life Student Council. Student Activities Committee. Newspaper, literary magazines, departmental journals, handbook, yearbook, radio station. Music and theatre groups. Debating Council. International Student Association. Young Democrats, Young Republicans. Tutoring. Community service. Black Students' Union. Women's Center. Rathskellar. Honorary and special interest groups. 8 fraternities, 5 with houses; 3 sororities. 20% of students join. Freshmen must live at home or in dorms. Coed and single-sex housing. Married-student apartments. 25% of students live on campus. 12 intercollegiate sports for men, 8 for women; extensive intramurals. AIAW, NCAA, MAC. Student body composition: 6.3% Asian, 2.8% Black, 1.3% Hispanic, 0.2% Native American, 89.4% White. 50% from out of state.

[1] LOYOLA COLLEGE
Baltimore 21210, (301) 323-1010
Director of Admissions: Martha Gagnon

- **Undergraduates: 1,293m, 1,061w; 5,906 total (including graduates)**
- **Tuition (1982/83): $3,950**
- **Room & Board: $2,250; Fees: $130**
- **Degrees offered: BA, BS**
- **Mean SAT 508v, 550m**
- **Student-faculty ratio: 18 to 1**

A private college controlled by the Society of Jesus (Jesuits) and the Sisters of Mercy, established in 1852, became coed in 1971. 63-acre campus in suburban Baltimore. Served by air, rail, and bus.
Academic Character MSACS accreditation. 4-1-4 system, 2 6-week summer terms. Majors offered in accounting, biology, business administration, chemistry, computer science, economics, education, English/fine arts, French, German, history, Latin, math, medical technology, philosophy, physics, political science, psychology, sociology, Spanish, speech, and theology. Interdisciplinary majors. Courses in Greek, Italian, and Russian. Distributives and 2 semesters of theology required. Masters degrees granted. Independent study. Honors program. Limited pass/no credit, internships. Preprofessional programs in dentistry, engineering, law, medicine, ministry. 3-1 medical technology program with Mercy Hospital. 3-2 program in education; 5-year program in speech pathology. Music courses at Peabody Conservatory. Exchange program with 5 area schools. Study abroad. Elementary and secondary education certification. ROTC; AFROTC nearby. 195,000-volume joint Loyola-Notre Dame library with microform resources.
Financial CEEB CSS. College scholarships, grants, loans, state scholarships, National Direct Education loans, tuition reduction for siblings, deferred payment; PELL, SEOG, NDSL, CWS. Application deadline February 1 (scholarships), March 1 (other aid).
Admissions High school graduation with 16 units required. GED accepted. Interview recommended. SAT required. $15 application fee. Rolling admissions. $200 deposit due on acceptance of admission offer. *Early Admission* Program. Admission deferral possible. Transfers accepted. Credit possible for CEEB AP and CLEP exams; college has own advanced placement program.
Student Life Student government. Newspaper, literary magazine, yearbook, radio station. Music and drama groups. Debate. Academic, athletic, honorary, religious, and volunteer groups. Freshmen and sophomores must live at home or on campus. No married-student or transfer housing. 53% of students live on campus. 8 intercollegiate sports for men, 6 for women; intramurals. AIAW, ECAC, NCAA. Student body composition: 6% Black, 88% White, 6% Other. 15% from out of state.

[1] MARYLAND, UNIVERSITY OF
College Park 20742, (301) 454-5550
Director of Undergraduate Admissions: Dr. Linda Clement

- **Enrollment: 14,764m, 13,042w**
- **Tuition (1982/83): $1,185 (in-state), $3,303 (out-of-state)**
- **Room & Board: $2,650**
- **Degrees offered: BA, BS, BMus, BArch, BGS**
- **Mean SAT 457v, 513m**
- **Student-faculty ratio: 16 to 1**

A public university established in 1812. 300-acre suburban campus outside of Washington, DC. Served by air, rail, and bus.
Academic Character MSACS and professional accreditation. Semester system, 2 6-week summer terms. 93 majors offered by the Divisions of Agricultural & Life Science, Arts & Humanities, Behavioral & Social Sciences, Human & Community Resources, Mathematical & Physical Sciences, and Engineering. Distributive requirements. Individual Study Program. Freshman honors program. Some pass/fail, credit by exam. Preprofessional programs in numerous areas. Binary programs with University Schools of Dentistry, Law, and Medicine. Elementary, secondary, and special education certification. AFROTC. 2,000-acre University farms. Many scientific research facilities. 1,563,000-volume library with microform resources.
Financial CEEB CSS. University scholarships, grants, National Achievement program; PELL, SEOG, NDSL, GSL, CWS. Application deadline February 15.
Admissions High school graduation required. SAT required. $20 application fee. Rolling admissions. $100 deposit required with housing contract. *Early Decision* Program for Maryland residents only. *Early Admission* and *Concurrent Enrollment* programs. Transfers accepted. Credit possible for CEEB AP exams.
Student Life Student government. Newspaper, magazines, yearbook, radio station. Music and drama groups. Debate. Black Student Union. Academic, honorary, religious, service, and special interest groups. 29 fraternities, 22 with houses; 22 sororities, 18 with houses. 8,100 housing spaces available. Graduate married-student housing. 33% of students live on campus. Freshmen and sophomores may not have cars on campus. 12 intercollegiate sports for men, 9 for women; extensive intramurals. AIAW, NCAA, Atlantic Coast Conference. Student body composition: 4.1% Asian, 7.6% Black, 1.9% Hispanic, 0.3% Native American, 80.4% White. 24% from out of state.

[1] MARYLAND, UNIVERSITY OF, BALTIMORE COUNTY
5401 Wilkens Avenue, Catonsville 21228, (301) 455-2291
Director of Academic Services: Donald W. Griffin

- **Undergraduates: 2,257m, 2,617w; 6,753 total (including part-time)**
- **Tuition (1982/83): $1,224 (in-state), $3,340 (out-of-state)**
- **Room & Board: $2,430**
- **Degrees offered: BA, BS**
- **Mean SAT 422v, 477m**
- **Student-faculty ratio: 17 to 1**

A public university established in 1963. 474-acre suburban campus. Served by air, rail, and bus.
Academic Character MSACS and professional accreditation. Semester system, 1 8-week and 2 4-week summer terms, January interim. 32 majors offered in the areas of the liberal arts, sciences, preprofessional, and professional studies. Self-designed majors. Programs in 3 additional areas. Distributive requirements. Independent study. Honors program. Cooperative work/study, some pass/fail, internships, credit by exam. Preprofessional programs in several biomedical areas, and in engineering, law, social work. Exchange program with 5 area schools. Early childhood, elementary, secondary, and special education certification. AFROTC through cooperative program. 500,000-volume library.
Financial CEEB CSS. University scholarships, loans, PELL, SEOG, NSS, NDSL, GSL, NSL, CWS.
Admissions High school graduation required. GED accepted. SAT required. $15 application fee. Rolling admissions. *Early Admission* Program. Transfers accepted. Credit possible for CEEB AP and CLEP exams; university has own advanced placement program.
Student Life Student government. Newspaper, magazine, yearbook. Music and drama groups. Debate. Black Student Union. Academic, honorary, religious, service, and special interest groups. 1 fraternity and 1 sorority. Coed dorms. No married-student housing. 23% of students live on campus. 2 semesters of phys ed required. 8 intercollegiate sports for men, 7 for women; intramurals. AIAW, NCAA, Mason-Dixon and Potomac Intercollegiate Conferences. Student body composition: 3.6% Asian, 14.8% Black, 1.3% Hispanic, 0.3% Native American, 74.5% White, 5.5% Other. 3% from out of state.

[1] MARYLAND, UNIVERSITY OF, BALTIMORE
Baltimore 21201

[1] MARYLAND, UNIVERSITY OF, EASTERN SHORE
Princess Anne 21853, (301) 651-2200
Director of Admissions & Registrations: James B. Ewers

- **Undergraduates: 504m, 507w**
- **Tuition (1982/83): $968 (in-state), $2,716 (out-of-state)**
- **Room & Board: $2,176; Fees: $15**
- **Degrees offered: BA, BS**
- **Student-faculty ratio: 13 to 1**

A public university established in 1886. 536-acre rural campus. Bus service; airport 45 minutes away in Ocean City.

Academic Character MSACS accreditation. Semester system, 3-week and 6-week summer terms. 31 majors offered in the areas of agriculture, art, business, education, English & languages, experimental studies, human ecology, hotel & restaurant management, industrial education & technology, mathematics & computer science, music, natural sciences, physical education, and social sciences. Minors offered in most major fields and in 5 other areas. Courses in 6 additional fields. 10 concentrations in General Agriculture. Distributive requirements. Independent study. Honors program. Cooperative work/study, internships. Preprofessional programs in community planning, dentistry, law, medicine, nursing, pharmacy, and social work; entrance into corresponding U of Maryland professional school guaranteed. 2-2 nursing, physical therapy, and radiological technology and 2-3 pharmacy programs with U Maryland, Baltimore. 2-2 engineering with U Maryland, College Park. Cross-registration with Salisbury State. Cooperative program with Cornell, Duke, MIT, U of Pittsburgh, Princeton. Research programs with NASA at Wallops Island, National Marine Labs, and National Resources Labs. Elementary, secondary, and special education certification. ROTC. Early Childhood Research Center. 100,000-volume library with microform resources.

Financial CEEB CSS. University scholarships, grants, loans, Methodist loans, payment plan; PELL, SEOG, NDSL, GSL, CWS. Application deadline April 1.

Admissions Open admission to Maryland high school graduates in upper half of class with a C average; those in lower half may be admitted on basis of Predictive Index, SAT, and GPA; those in lower half with below C average may be admitted to Academic Development Program. Admission for out-of-state students competitive. GED accepted. SAT required. $25 application fee. Rolling admissions. $75 deposit due on acceptance of admissions offer. *Early Admission* and *Concurrent Enrollment* programs. Admission deferral possible. Transfers accepted. Credit possible for CEEB AP and CLEP exams; university has own advanced placement program.

Student Life Student government. Literary magazine, yearbook. Music and drama groups. Black Awareness Movement, NAACP. Athletic, academic, honorary, religious, service, and special interest groups. 10 fraternities and sororities. Coed and single-sex dorms. No married-student housing. 49% of students live on campus. 2 semester hours of phys ed required. Liquor restricted to certain areas of campus. Narcotics prohibited. Class attendance required in lower division courses. 6 intercollegiate sports for men, 2 for women; intramurals. Mid-Eastern Conference. Student body composition: 1.6% Asian, 74.4% Black, 3.8% Foreign, 0.2% Hispanic, 20% White. 27% from out of state.

[J2] MARYLAND COLLEGE OF ART AND DESIGN
10500 Georgia Avenue, Silver Spring 20902

[1] MARYLAND INSTITUTE COLLEGE OF ART
1300 Mount Royal Avenue, Baltimore 21217, (301) 669-9200
Director of Admissions: Theresa M. Lynch

- **Undergraduates: 390m, 460w**
- **Tuition (1982/83): $4,850**
- **Room & Board: $2,750 (estimate); Fees: $100**
- **Degree offered: BFA**
- **Student-faculty ratio: 13 to 1**

A private college established in 1826. Downtown campus. Served by air, rail, and bus.

Academic Character MSACS and professional accreditation. Semester system, summer term. Majors offered in art teacher education, ceramics, crafts, drawing, general fine arts, graphic design/illustration, interior design, painting, photography, printmaking, and sculpture. Liberal arts requirements; first-year foundation courses. MFA granted. Independent study. Exchange programs with Goucher, Johns Hopkins, Peabody, 16 other US schools, and one in England. Member of Union of Independent Colleges of Art and East Coast Art Schools. Elementary and secondary teacher certification. Exhibition Galleries. 36,000-volume library with collection of 65,000 color slides.

Financial CEEB CSS. Institute scholarships, grants, state scholarships and grants; PELL, SEOG, NDSL, CWS. Application deadline March 15.

Admissions High school graduation required. Interview and 8-12 piece portfolio, including 3 drawings, required. SAT required. $20 application fee. Rolling admissions. $100 tuition deposit due on acceptance of admissions offer. *Early Admission* and *Concurrent Enrollment* programs. Admission deferral possible. Transfers accepted. Institute has own advanced placement program.

Student Life Newspaper. Galleries. Special interest groups. Limited on-campus housing. Student body composition: 1.2% Asian, 9.9% Black, 0.5% Hispanic, 87.7% White.

[J1] MONTGOMERY COLLEGE
Rockville 20850
Additional campuses in Germantown (20874) and Takoma Park (20912)

[1] MORGAN STATE UNIVERSITY
Baltimore 21239, (301) 444-3000
Director of Admissions: Chelseia Harold

- **Undergraduates: 1,591m, 2,027w; 4,685 total (including graduates)**
- **Tuition (1982/83): $1,216 (in-state), $2,271 (out-of-state)**
- **Room & Board: $2,615**
- **Degrees offered: BA, BS**
- **Mean SAT 800 composite**
- **Student-faculty ratio: 15 to 1**

A public university established in 1867. 120-acre campus in northeast Baltimore. Served by air, rail, and bus.

Academic Character MSACS and professional accreditation. Semester system, 7-week summer term. 55 majors offered by the College of Arts & Sciences, the School of Business & Management, the School of Education, and the School of Urban Studies & Human Development. Minors offered in some major fields. Distributive requirements. Graduate degrees granted. Independent study. Honors program. Cooperative work/study, some pass/no credit, internships. Preprofessional programs in dentistry, engineering, law, medicine, pharmacy, physical therapy. 3-2 and 4-1 engineering programs with U of Pennsylvania. Exchange programs with 6 colleges. Cross-registration with 6 area schools. Cooperative program with Notre Dame, Goucher, Johns Hopkins, Loyola, and Towson State. Elementary and secondary education certification. ROTC. 579,000-volume library.

Financial Guaranteed tuition. University scholarships, grants, loans, state scholarships, minority-student grants, payment plans; PELL, SEOG, NDSL, FISL, CWS. Application deadline April 1.

Admissions High school graduation required. GED accepted. SAT required. $20 application fee. Rolling admissions. $25 tuition deposit due on acceptance of offer of admission. *Early Admission* and *Early Decision* programs. Transfers accepted. Credit possible for CEEB AP and CLEP exams.

Student Life Student government. Newspaper, yearbook. Music, dance, and drama groups. Several academic, honorary, social work, and special interest groups. 6 fraternities and 6 sororities. Single-sex dorms. 15% of students live on campus. 2 semesters of phys ed required. Most courses require class attendance. 5 intercollegiate sports for men, 4 for women; intramurals. AIAW, ECAC, NAIA, NCAA. Student body composition: 0.3% Asian, 89% Black, 0.2% Hispanic, 0.1% Native American, 4.1% White, 6.3% Other. 20% from out of state.

[1] MOUNT ST. MARY'S COLLEGE
Emmitsburg 21727, (301) 447-6122
Director of Admissions: Larry J. Riordan

- **Undergraduates: 812m, 708w**
- **Tuition (1982/83): $4,300**
- **Room & Board: $2,200**
- **Degrees offered: BA, BS**
- **Mean SAT 470v, 500m**
- **Student-faculty ratio: 19 to 1**

A private Catholic college established in 1808, became coed in 1972. 1,400-acre small town campus 12 miles from Gettysburg. Served by bus.

Academic Character MSACS accreditation. Semester system, limited summer term, optional January term. Majors offered in accounting, biology, business, chemistry, economics, education, English, fine arts, history, languages, mathematics, medical technology, philosophy, political science, pre-dental, pre-law, pre-medical, psychology, sociology. Self-designed majors. Interdepartmental concentrations in American, Catholic, and international studies. Courses in 8 additional areas, including Greek. Distributives and 6 credits of theology required. MBA granted. Independent study. Cooperative work/study, limited pass/fail, internships. Degree completion program for nurses. Elementary and secondary education certification. ROTC. 135,000-volume library with microform resources.

Financial CEEB CSS. College scholarships, grants, loans, payment plans; PELL, SEOG, NDSL, GSL, CWS. Application deadlines March 1 (scholarships), April 1 (loans).

Admissions High school graduation with 16 units required. Interview recommended. SAT or ACT required. $20 application fee. Rolling admissions. $150 deposit required on acceptance of admissions offer. *Early Admission* and *Early Decision* programs. Admission deferral possible. Transfers accepted. Credit possible for CEEB AP and CLEP exams.

Student Life Student Council. Newspaper, literary magazine, yearbook, radio and TV stations. Music and drama groups. Honor societies. Athletic, academic, religious, and special interest groups. Upperclass students may live off campus with parental permission. Coed and single-sex dorms. 85% of students live on campus. 10 intercollegiate sports for men, 6 for women; many intramurals. NCAA. Student body composition: 0.6% Asian, 3% Black, 0.2% Hispanic, 96% White, 0.2% Other. 60% from out of state.

[1] NOTRE DAME OF MARYLAND, COLLEGE OF
4701 North Charles Street, Baltimore 21210, (301) 435-0100
Dean of Admissions: Michael L. Mahoney

- **Enrollment: 1m, 559w; 1,632 total (including part-time)**
- **Tuition (1982/83): $3,800**
- **Room & Board: $2,500**
- **Degree offered: BA**
- **Mean SAT 420v, 430m**
- **Student-faculty ratio: 12 to 1**

A private college controlled by the School Sisters of Notre Dame, established in 1873. Suburban campus. Served by air, rail, and bus.
Academic Character MSACS accreditation. 4-1-4 system. Majors offered in art, biology, chemistry, communications, economics, education, English, history, management, mathematics, modern languages, music, physics, political science, psychology, religion, and an interdisciplinary major in liberal arts. Distributives and 2 courses in religion required. Independent study. Honors program. Pass/fail, internships. Preprofessional programs in dentistry, engineering, law, medicine, nursing, pharmacy. 3-2 engineering program with U of Maryland. 2-2 nursing program with Georgetown. Cross-registration with Loyola, Johns Hopkins, Morgan, Towson, Goucher, and Coppin. Study abroad. Elementary, secondary, and special education certification. ROTC at Loyola. Writing lab. 310,000-volume library with microform resources.
Financial CEEB CSS. College scholarships, grants, loans, state scholarships; PELL, SEOG, NDSL, GSL, PLUS, CWS, campus employment. Application deadline February 15.
Admissions High school graduation with 18 units required. SAT required. $15 application fee. Rolling admissions. $100 deposit ($50 for day students) due on acceptance of admissions offer. *Early Decision* and *Early Admission* programs. Transfers accepted. Credit possible for CEEB AP exams.
Student Life Student government. Newspaper, literary magazine, yearbook. Music and drama groups. Black student's organization. Academic, recreational, service, and special interest groups. 4 semesters of phys ed required. 6 intercollegiate sports.

[P] OSCAR B. HUNTER SCHOOL OF MEDICAL TECHNOLOGY
6935 Arlington Road, Bethesda 20014

[1] PEABODY INSTITUTE OF THE JOHNS HOPKINS UNIVERSITY
1 East Mount Vernon Place, Baltimore 21202, (301) 659-8100
Director of Admissions: Edward J. Weaver, III

- **Enrollment: 148m, 171w; 420 total (including part-time)**
- **Tuition (1982/83): $5,750**
- **Room & Board: $2,550**
- **Degree offered: BMus**
- **Mean SAT 510v, 540m**
- **Student-faculty ratio: 4 to 1**

A private institute established in 1857. Campus in downtown Baltimore. Served by air, rail, and bus.
Academic CharacterNASM and MSACS accreditation. Majors offered in keyboard, string, wind, and percussion instruments; voice, composition, and music education. Minors offered. Degree recitals required. Graduate degrees granted. Artist diplomas awarded. Cross-registration with Johns Hopkins, Loyola, Maryland Art Institute. Recording studios. Electronic and computer music studios. Digital facilities. 55,000-volume library plus library of 14,500 recordings.
Financial CEEB CSS. Institute and state scholarships, undergraduate and graduate teaching assistantships, PELL, SEOG, NDSL, GSL, campus employment. Application deadlines January 15 (scholarships), February 15 (state scholarships), March 15 (PELL), April 15 (SEOG, NDSL, employment), June 1 (GSL).
Admissions High school graduation required. GED accepted. Personal audition required; other audition requirements. SAT or ACT required. $35 application fee. Application deadline January 15 for scholarship students; May 1 for others. $100 tuition and $150 room deposits due on acceptance of admissions offer.
Student Life Freshmen required to live at school or with family. Single-sex dorms. Recreational facilities available.

[J1] PRINCE GEORGE'S COMMUNITY COLLEGE
301 Largo Road, Largo 20870

[1] ST. JOHN'S COLLEGE
Annapolis 21404, (301) 263-2371
Director of Admissions: John Christensen

- **Undergraduates: 225m, 169w**
- **Tuition (1982/83): $6,700**
- **Room & Board: $2,600**
- **Degree offered: BA**
- **Mean SAT 611v, 583m**
- **Student-faculty ratio: 8 to 1**

A private college established in 1696, became coed in 1951. 36-acre campus in the historic district, 30 miles from Washington, DC. Served by bus; air service at Baltimore-Washington International Airport, 20 miles away.
Academic Character MSACS accreditation. Semester system, 10-week summer term. No majors or electives. 4-year study sequence of great books from Homer to present in conjunction with programs in language, mathematics, laboratory science, and 1 year of music theory. Classes organized around discussion. Academic year has 6 divisions: seminars, language, mathematics, and music tutorials, laboratory, and formal lectures. Oral exams at end of each semester; comprehensive orals in fall of senior year. Senior thesis defended in oral examination. Students may spend one or more years at Santa Fe campus. Masters degrees granted. 80,000-volume library.
Financial CEEB CSS. College scholarships, grants, payment plan; PELL, SEOG, NDSL, FISL, CWS. Scholarship application deadline January 31.
Admissions High school graduation with college-prep courses advised. Interview encouraged, sometimes required. Rolling admissions. $200 deposit due on acceptance of admissions offer. *Early Decision* and *Early Admission* programs. Admission deferral possible. Students accepted only as freshmen.
Student Life Student Polity regulates dorms and activities. Newspaper, literary magazine. Music and drama groups. Chess club. Extracurricular classes. Arts, crafts, religious, and special interest groups. Single students not living at home usually live and board on campus. Coed and single-sex dorms. No married-student housing. 75% of students live on campus. Illegal drugs prohibited. Extensive intramural sports program. Student body composition: 1% Asian, 1% Black, 1% Hispanic, 1% Native American, 96% White. 85% from out of state.

[1] ST. MARY'S COLLEGE OF MARYLAND
St. Mary's City 20686, (301) 863-7100
Director of Admissions: Susan Silanskis

- **Undergraduates: 503m, 619w**
- **Tuition (1982/83): $1,120 (in-state), $2,120 (out-of-state)**
- **Room & Board: $2,680; Fees: $275**
- **Degrees offered: BA, BS**
- **Mean SAT 478v, 492m**
- **Student-faculty ratio: 17 to 1**

A public college established in 1839. 270-acre campus on St. Mary's River, 68 miles northeast of Washington, DC. Airport and bus station nearby.
Academic Character MSACS accreditation. Semester system. 23 majors offered in anthropology/sociology, art, biology, drama, economics/business, engineering, English, history, human development, mathematics, music, natural science, political science, public policy, and social science. Self-designed majors. Courses in 9 additional areas, including Chinese. Distributive requirements; seniors take comprehensive exams. Independent study. Honors program. Limited pass/fail, internships. 3-2 engineering dual-degree program with U of Maryland and George Washington U. Exchange program with Evergreen State. Study abroad. Elementary and secondary education certification. 100,000-volume library with microform resources.
Financial CEEB CSS. College scholarships, grants, state loans, payment plans; PELL, SEOG, FISL, NDSL, CWS. Preferred application deadlines March 1 (scholarships), April 1 (loans).
Admissions High school graduation with 18 units required. GED accepted. Interview recommended. SAT required. $20 application fee. Rolling admissions. $200 deposit required on acceptance of admissions offer. *Early Decision, Early Admission, Concurrent Enrollment* programs. Admission deferral possible. Transfers accepted. Credit possible for CEEB AP and CLEP exams.
Student Life Student government. Newspaper, literary magazine, yearbook, radio station. Music and drama groups. Special interest activities. Coed and single-sex dorms. No married-student housing. 70% of students live on campus. Liquor and firearms prohibited. Honor code. 8 intercollegiate sports for men and women; intramurals. AIAW, NCAA. Student body composition: 0.5% Asian, 6.8% Black, 0.7% Hispanic, 0.1% Native American, 91.2% White, 0.7% Other. 10% from out of state.

[1] SALISBURY STATE COLLEGE
Salisbury 21801, (301) 546-3261
Director of Admissions: M. P. Minton III

- **Undergraduates: 1,410m, 1,540w; 4,300 total (including graduates)**
- **Tuition (1982/83): $960 (in-state), $2,000 (out-of-state)**
- **Room & Board: $2,320; Fees: $236**
- **Degrees offered: BA, BS,**
- **Student-faculty ratio: 16 to 1**

A public college established in 1925. 140-acre suburban campus 115 miles southeast of Baltimore. Served by air and bus.
Academic Character MSACS and professional accreditation. Semester system, 2 6-week summer terms. Majors offered in art, biology, business, chemistry, communications, economics, education, English, French, geography, history, leisure studies, liberal studies, mathematics, medical technology, nursing, philosophy, physical education, physical science, psychology, respiratory therapy, social science, social work, sociology, and Spanish. Self-designed majors. Interdisciplinary programs in American, European, Latin American, and urban studies and in earth sciences. Courses in 4 additional areas. Distributive requirements. Masters degrees granted. Independent study. Honors program. Limited pass/fail, internships. Preprofessional programs in dentistry, law, medicine, and veterinary medicine. 3-2 engineering programs with Old Dominion and U of Maryland. Exchange program with U of Maryland, Eastern Shore. Elementary, secondary, and special education certification. ROTC. 200,000-volume library with microform resources.
Financial CEEB CSS. College scholarships, grants, loans; PELL, SEOG, NSS, NDSL, FISL, HELP, NSL, CWS, Work Learning program. Application deadlines March 1 (scholarships), February 15 (loans).
Admissions High school graduation required. GED accepted. SAT required. $15 application fee. Rolling admissions. $110 deposit required on acceptance of offer of admission. *Early Admission* Program. Transfers accepted. Credit possible for CEEB AP, CLEP, and ACT PEP exams; college has own advanced placement program.
Student Life Student government. Newspaper, literary magazine, yearbook, radio station. Music, dance, and theatre groups. NAACP. Circle K. Academic, honorary, religious, and special interest groups. 10 fraternities and 5 sororities. 22% of men and 12% of women join. Coed and single-sex dorms. No married-student housing. 47% of students live on campus. 3 phys ed courses required. 11 intercollegiate sports for men, 8 for women; intramurals. AIAW, NCAA. Student body composition: 9% Black, 91% White. 15% from out of state.

[1] SOJOURNER-DOUGLAS COLLEGE
500 North Caroline Street, Baltimore 21205

[1] TOWSON STATE UNIVERSITY
Towson 21204, (301) 321-2112
Director of Admissions: Linda J. Collins

- **Undergraduates: 4,163m, 5,246w; 15,107 total (including graduates)**
- **Tuition (1982/83): $960 (in-state), $2,000 (out-of-state)**
- **Room & Board: $2,400; Fees: $260**
- **Degrees offered: BA, BS**
- **Mean SAT 430v, 460m**
- **Student-faculty ratio: 19 to 1**

A public university established in 1866. 324-acre suburban campus 5 miles from Baltimore. Air, rail, and bus service nearby.

Academic Character MSACS and professional accreditation. 4-1-4 system, 2 6-week summer terms. 40 majors offered in the areas of liberal arts, natural & physical sciences, business, education, instructional technology, mass communication, medical technology, nursing, occupational therapy, physical education, speech, and theatre. Special and double majors. Minors offered in some major fields and in 2 additional areas. Courses in many foreign languages and in special education. General studies program with 11 options. Distributive requirements. Masters degrees granted. Independent study. Cooperative work/study, limited pass/fail, internships. Honors program. Preprofessional programs in dentistry, law, medicine, and pharmacy. 3-1 program in medical technology. 3-2 engineering program with U of Maryland. Exchange program with 29 colleges. Cooperative programs with several state colleges, and with Baltimore, Maryland, Goucher, Loyola, Johns Hopkins, Notre Dame, American Institute of Banking. Study abroad. Elementary and secondary education certification. AFROTC at U of Maryland. 374,000-volume library.

Financial CEEB CSS. University scholarships, grants, loans, PELL, SEOG, NDSL, FISL, CWS, Job Location Program. Application deadlines March 2 (scholarships), April 1 (grants & loans).

Admissions High school graduation with 23 units recommended. GED accepted. SAT required. $20 application fee. Rolling admissions. $150 deposit due on acceptance of offer of admission. *Early Admission* and *Concurrent Enrollment* programs. Admission deferral possible. Transfers accepted. Credit possible for CEEB AP and CLEP exams.

Student Life Student government. Music groups. Public speaking. Honorary, religious, service, and special interest groups. 12 fraternities and 7 sororities. Coed and single-sex dorms. Academic emphasis areas. No married-student housing. 13% of students live on campus. 1 semester hour of phys ed required. Liquor permitted only during licensed activities. 12 intercollegiate sports for men, 9 for women; intramurals. AIAW, ECAC, NCAA. Student body composition: 0.9% Asian, 11.7% Black, 0.6% Hispanic, 0.2% Native American, 85% White, 2% Other. 5% from out of state.

[1] UNITED STATES NAVAL ACADEMY
Annapolis 21402, (301) 267-6100
Director of Admissions: Rear Adm. Robert W. McNitt, USN (Ret.)

- **Undergraduates: 4,262m, 308w**
- **Tuition (1982/83): full scholarship**
- **Room & Board: full scholarship**
- **Degrees offered: BS, BSE**
- **Mean ACT 24e, 31m; mean SAT 572v, 656m**
- **Student-faculty ratio: 8 to 1**

A public service academy, established in 1845, became coed in 1976. On graduation, each midshipman is commissioned an ensign in the Navy or a 2nd Lieutenant in the Marine Corps and is required to serve 5 years active duty. 329-acre campus, 30 miles from Washington, DC, and Baltimore. Served by bus; air and rail in Baltimore.

Academic Character MSACS and professional accreditation. Semester system, mandatory 2-month summer term. Majors offered in aerospace engineering, electrical, general, marine, mechanical, ocean, and systems engineering, and in naval architecture, English, history, applied science, chemistry, mathematics, oceanography, physical science, physics, economics, and political science. Courses in 7 additional areas, including Chinese and Russian. Trident Scholars Program offers independent research and study for superior firstclassmen. Professional training program includes physical education, practical training, and drills. Distributive requirements. Plebe (1st-year) summer: instruction in seamanship, navigation, signaling, infantry drill, and physical conditioning. Third class summer: 6-8 weeks training at sea. Second class summer: training in warfare specialties. First class summer: training at sea as junior officers. Exchange programs with Air Force, Coast Guard, and military (West Point) academies. Educational Resource Center. Computer Center. Fleet of over 100 small craft. 515,000-volume library.

Financial Full 4-year government scholarships for all students. Midshipmen receive $461 basic pay per month to cover uniform and book costs, personal expenses, etc.

Admissions High school graduation with 15 units recommended. GED considered. Interview recommended. All applicants must be between 17 and 21 on July 1 of admission year, unmarried US citizens with no parental responsibilities. Nomination by a member of Congress, the Vice-President, or the President necessary. Rolling admissions; suggest applying by September. $500 deposit required on entrance. Transfers accepted as first-year students (Plebes) only. Credit possible for CEEB AP and ACH exams; Naval Academy Preparatory School Program has 1-year training to prepare unsuccessful nominees.

Student Life Magazine, yearbook, radio station. Music and drama groups. Debate. Cultural Affairs Program. Yard Patrol Squadron. Aviation Training. Big Brothers. Academic, honorary, professional, religious, service, and special interest groups. All students live on campus. Some coed dorms. 8 semesters of phys ed required. Only seniors may have cars. Liquor permitted only at Officers Club or in private homes. Mandatory dismissal for drug involvement. Uniforms required. Class attendance required. Honor Code. Marriage not permitted. 18 intercollegiate sports for men, 7 for women; intramurals. Student body composition: 4% Asian, 4.4% Black, 3.7% Hispanic, 0.5% Native American, 87.3% White. 94% from out of state.

[J1] VILLA JULIE COLLEGE
Green Spring Valley Road, Stevenson 21153

[P] WASHINGTON BIBLE COLLEGE
6511 Princess Garden Parkway, Lanham 20706

[1] WASHINGTON COLLEGE
Chestertown 21620, (301) 778-2800
Director of Admissions: A. M. DiMaggio

- **Undergraduates: 359m, 305w**
- **Tuition (1982/83): $4,650**
- **Room & Board: $2,250; Fees: $171**
- **Degrees offered: BA, BS**
- **Mean SAT 492v, 509m**
- **Student-faculty ratio: 12 to 1**

A private college established in 1782. 100-acre small town campus, 71 miles east of Baltimore.

Academic Character MSACS accreditation. Semester system. Majors offered in art, biology, chemistry, drama, economics, English, French, German, history, mathematics, music, philosophy, physics, political science, psychology, sociology, Spanish, American studies, humanities, and international studies. Special majors. Minors. Distributives and senior exam required. Independent study. Honors program. Limited pass/fail, internships, apprenticeships, field-work programs. 3-2 programs arranged in dentistry, engineering, law, medical technology, medicine, nursing, veterinary medicine. Washington Semester. Study abroad. Secondary education certification. ROTC at U of Delaware. Computer center. Language labs. Over 135,000-volume library.

Financial CEEB CSS and ACT FAS. College scholarships, grants, loans, merit awards, payment plans; PELL, SEOG, NDSL, CWS. Application deadline February 15.

Admissions High school graduation with 16 units required. Interview recommended. SAT or ACT required; ACH optional. $15 application fee. Rolling admissions. $100 deposit due on acceptance of admissions offer. *Early Admission* and *Early Decision* programs. Admission deferral possible. Transfers accepted. Credit possible for CEEB AP and CLEP exams.

Student Life Student Council. Newspaper, literary magazine, yearbook. Music, dance, and drama groups. Film society. Debate, Writers Union. Academic, honorary, political, religious, and special interest groups. 4 fraternities with houses, 3 sororities without housing. 21% of men and women join. Permission required to live off campus. Coed and single-sex dorms. Language halls. No married-student housing. 95% of students live on campus. 8 intercollegiate sports for men, 4 for women; intramurals. NCAA, Middle Atlantic Conference, Mason-Dixon Conference. Student body composition: 2% Black, 98% White. 49% from out of state.

[G1] WASHINGTON THEOLOGICAL SEMINARY
9001 New Hampshire Avenue, Silver Spring 20910

[1] WESTERN MARYLAND COLLEGE
Westminster 21157, (301) 848-7000
Dean of Admissions & Financial Aid: L. Leslie Bennett

- **Undergraduates: 585m, 675w**
- **Tuition (1982/83): $5,200**
- **Room & Board: $2,075**
- **Degree offered: BA**
- **Mean SAT 500v, 530m**
- **Student-faculty ratio: 14 to 1**

A private college established in 1867. 160-acre small town campus, 28 miles from Baltimore. Served by bus; air and rail facilities in Baltimore and Washington.

Academic Character MSACS and professional accreditation. 4-1-5 system, 2 5-week summer terms. Majors offered in American studies, art, biology, business, chemistry, comparative literature, drama, economics, English, French, German, history, mathematics, music, philosophy-religion, physics, political science, psychobiology, psychology, social work, sociology, and Spanish. Special majors. Distributive requirements. Graduate degrees granted. Honors program. Phi Beta Kappa. Limited pass/fail, internships. Preprofessional programs in dentistry, law, medicine, the ministry. 3-2 engineering program with U of Maryland and Washington U. 3-2 forestry program with Duke. 2-2 nursing program with Emory. Study abroad. Elementary, secondary, and deaf education certification. ROTC; AFROTC & NROTC at Maryland. Language labs. 130,000-volume library.

Financial CEEB CSS. College scholarships, grants, loans, payment plan; PELL, SEOG, NDSL, CWS. Application deadline March 15.

Admissions High school graduation with 16 units recommended. Interview desirable. SAT required; language ACH required for placement. $15 application fee. Rolling admissions. $150 deposit due on acceptance of admissions offer. *Early Admission* Program. Admission deferral possible. Transfers accepted. Credit possible for CEEB AP and CLEP exams.

Student Life Student government. Newspaper, literary magazine, yearbook. Black Student Union. Music and drama groups. Academic, honorary, political, religious, and service organizations. 4 fraternities and 4 sororities. 30% of men and women join. Students must live on campus or at home. Coed and single-sex dorms. 90% of students live on campus. 3 semester hours of phys ed required. Honor system. Class attendance expected. 8 intercollegiate sports for men, 5 for women; many intramurals. AIAW, NCAA, Penn-Mar and Middle Atlantic Athletic Conferences. Student body composition: 1% Asian, 7% Black, 90% White, 2% Other. 30% from out of state.

[J1] WOR-WIC TECHNICAL COMMUNITY COLLEGE
1202 Old Ocean City Road, Salisbury 21801

MASSACHUSETTS (MA)

[1] AMERICAN INTERNATIONAL COLLEGE
Springfield 01107, (413) 737-7000
Dean of Admissions: John R. Fallon

- **Undergraduates: 885m, 690w; 2,150 total (including graduates)**
- **Tuition & Fees (1982/83): $4,215**
- **Room & Board: $2,285**
- **Degrees offered: BA, BSBA, BSEd, BSHS, BSN, BLS, BAMT, BSCrim Just**
- **Mean SAT 462v, 468m**
- **Student-faculty ratio: 16 to 1**

A private college founded in 1885. 52-acre campus in residential area of metropolitan Springfield, 90 miles from Boston. Rail and bus service.
Academic Character NEASC and professional accreditation. Semester system, 3 6-week summer terms (2 evening, 1 day). 33 majors offered in the areas of accounting, arts & humanities, business, criminal justice, education, human services, information systems, languages, liberal studies, nursing, psychology, public administration, sciences, and social sciences. Self-designed majors. Minors in most major fields and in journalism. Distributive requirements. MA, MBA, MEd granted. Coaching certificate program. Associate and other degrees offered in evening school. Independent study, pass/fail, internships. Preprofessional programs in dentistry, law, medicine, optometry, veterinary medicine. Cross-registration through Cooperating Colleges of Greater Springfield. Elementary and secondary education certification. ROTC at Western New England College. Child development center, Center for Human Relations and Community Affairs. 125,000-volume library.
Financial CEEB CSS. College scholarships, grants, loans, payment plan; PELL, SEOG, NDSL, FISL, GSL, NSL, CWS. Scholarship application deadline April 1.
Admissions High school graduation with 16 units required. GED accepted. Interview encouraged. SAT or ACT required. $15 application fee. Rolling admissions; suggest applying early in 12th year. *Early Entrance* and *Early Decision* programs. Admission deferral possible. Transfers accepted. Credit possible for CEEB AP and CLEP exams. Supportive Service Program.
Student Life Student government. Newspaper, literary magazine, yearbook. Music, dance, drama groups. Outdoor club. Academic, athletic, honorary, religious, service, and special interest organizations. 4 fraternities with houses, 4 sororities without houses. 25% of men and 15% of women join. Veterans and students over 24 may live off campus. Coed and single-sex dorms. 55% of students live on campus. 4 semesters of phys ed required. 7 intercollegiate sports for men, 3 for women; several intramurals. AIAW, ECAC, NCAA, Northeast 8. Student body composition: 2% Asian, 7% Black, 91% White. 38% from out of state.

[1] AMHERST COLLEGE
Amherst 01002, (413) 542-2328
Dean of Admission: Henry F. Bedford

- **Undergraduates: 921m, 613w**
- **Tuition (1982/83): $8,150**
- **Room & Board: $2,750; Fees: $105**
- **Degree offered: BA**
- **Mean SAT 617v, 654m**
- **Student-faculty ratio: 10 to 1**

A private college established in 1821, became coed in 1975. 1,000-acre small-town campus, 90 miles west of Boston and 150 miles north of New York. Served by bus; 5-college exchange bus.
Academic Character NEASC accreditation. 4-1-4 system. Majors offered in American studies, anthropology, Asian studies, astronomy, biology, Black studies, chemistry, classics, dramatic arts, economics, English, European studies, fine arts, French, geology, German, Greek, history, Latin, mathematics, music, neuroscience, philosophy, physics, political science, psychology, religion, Romance languages, Russian, sociology, and Spanish. Self-designed and interdisciplinary majors. Required freshman year program. Comprehensive exams required. Independent study and honors programs. Phi Beta Kappa, pass/fail, internships. Preprofessional program in medicine. 5-college cooperation with Hampshire, Mt. Holyoke, Smith, and UMass provides cross-registration, shared facilities & programs. 12-college exchange with other northeastern schools. Numerous study abroad programs. ROTC at UMass. Museums. 584,684-volume library.
Financial CEEB CSS. College scholarships, loans, payment plan; PELL, SEOG, NDSL, FISL, CWS. Application deadline January 15 (November 15 for early decision).
Admissions Sound high school preparation required. Interview urged. SAT & 3 ACH, or ACT required. $30 application fee (waiver possible). Application deadline January 15. $200 deposit required on acceptance of admissions offer. *Early Decision* and *Early Entrance* programs. Admission deferral possible. Transfers accepted. Placement possible for CEEB AP exams.
Student Life Newspaper, literary magazine, yearbook, radio station. Music & drama groups. Debate. Academic, honorary, special interest groups. Numerous activities with 5-college exchange. 6 fraternities with houses. Upperclass students may live off campus with permission. Coed dorms, special interest & language houses. 95% of students live on campus. 15 intercollegiate sports for men, 11 for women; intramurals. AIAW, ECAC, NCAA, NESCAC. Student body composition: 4% Asian, 6% Black, 2% Foreign, 2% Hispanic, 86% White. 82% from out of state.

[G1] ANDOVER NEWTON THEOLOGICAL SCHOOL
Newton Centre 02159

[1] ANNA MARIA COLLEGE
Paxton 01612, (617) 757-4586
Director of Admissions: Paul Lynskey

- **Enrollment: 133m, 324w; 1,609 total (including part-time)**
- **Tuition (1982/83): $3,600**
- **Room & Board: $2,360; Fees & Books: $200-$250**
- **Degrees offered: BA, BS, BBA, BMus, AA, AS**
- **Mean SAT 460v, 460m**
- **Student-faculty ratio: 15 to 1**

A private Roman Catholic liberal arts college established in 1946 by the Sisters of Saint Anne. Became coed in 1973. 180-acre suburban campus 8 miles northwest of downtown Worcester, and one hour from Boston, Hartford, and Providence.
Academic Character NEASC and professional accreditation. 4-1-4 system. Majors offered in art, art education, biology, chemistry, computer science, elementary education, engineering, French, music, psychology, social relations, social work, accounting, management, marketing, music education, music therapy, performance, health studies, medical lab science, medical technology, nuclear medicine technology. Interdisciplinary major in liberal studies. Nursing major for RNs. AA in paralegal studies, AS in medical lab technology. Distributives, 3 religion, and 3 philosophy courses required. Thesis, senior exam or project may be required. Masters degrees, CAGS granted. Independent study, pass/fail, internships. Preprofessional programs in medicine, dentistry, optometry, allied health fields. 3-1 medical technology program. 3-2 liberal arts & engineering program with Worcester Polytechnic. New England-Quebec Student Exchange. Exchange with Holy Names College (CA). Cross-registration and special gerontology program through Worcester Consortium. Study abroad. Elementary, secondary, and special education certification. ROTC at WPI; AFROTC & NROTC at Holy Cross. Continuing education. Language lab. 54,000-volume library.
Financial CEEB CSS and ACT FAS. College scholarships, grants, state scholarships; PELL, SEOG, NDSL, GSL, CWS. Priority application deadline February 15.
Admissions High school graduation with 16 units required. GED accepted. Interview strongly recommended. Audition required for music majors; portfolio for art majors. SAT required; 3 ACH urged. $15 application fee. Rolling admissions. $50 tuition and $100 room deposits required on acceptance of admissions offer. *Early Decision* and *Early Admission* programs. Admission deferral possible. Transfers accepted. Credit possible for CEEB AP and CLEP exams.
Student Life Student government. Newspaper, literary magazine, yearbook. Art club. Chorus. Christian Forum. Honorary groups. Pub. Dormitory with separate wings for men and women. Parietals. 60% of students live on campus. 3 intercollegiate sports for men and women; intramural & recreational sports. MAIAW, NCAA.

[J1] AQUINAS JUNIOR COLLEGE
303 Adams Street, Milton 02186

[J1] AQUINAS JUNIOR COLLEGE
15 Walnut Park, Newton 02158

[G1] ARTHUR D. LITTLE MANAGEMENT EDUCATION INSTITUTE
Cambridge 02140

[1] ASSUMPTION COLLEGE
500 Salisbury Street, Worcester 01609, (617) 752-5615
Dean of Admissions & Financial Aid: Thomas E. Dunn

- **Undergraduates: 710m, 825w; 1,969 total (including graduates)**
- **Tuition (1982/83): $4,830**
- **Room & Board: $2,580; Fees: $100**
- **Degree offered: BA**
- **Mean SAT 465v, 485m**
- **Student-faculty ratio: 16 to 1**

A private college established in 1904, became coed in 1969. Sponsored by the Assumptionist Fathers. Over 175-acre suburban campus located 3 miles from downtown Worcester, 40 miles west of Boston. Air and bus service.
Academic Character NEASC accreditation. Semester system, 2 6-week summer terms. Majors offered in accounting, biology, biology/medical technology, chemistry, economics, economics/business, English, foreign

affairs, foreign languages, French, history, management, mathematics, natural sciences, philosophy, politics, psychology, religious studies, social & rehabilitation services, sociology, and Spanish. Self-designed majors. Minors in most major fields and in 10 additional areas. Foundations of Western Civilization program of interdisciplinary studies for 1st- and 2nd-year students. Community studies program. Distributive requirements. MA, MAT, MBA, CAGS granted. Independent study, honors program, Phi Beta Kappa, pass/fail, internships. Preprofessional programs in dentistry, law, medicine, medical technology. 3-2 BA/BSE program with Worcester Polytechnic. Cross-registration through Worcester Consortium for Higher Education. Study abroad. Elementary education certification. ROTC at WPI; NROTC & AFROTC at Holy Cross. Religious Studies and Social & Rehabilitation Services institutes. Media and computer centers, language lab. 155,820-volume library plus access to area libraries.
Financial CEEB CSS. College scholarships, loans, ROTC scholarships, 2nd-family-member discount; PELL, SEOG, NDSL, GSL, CWS, college work program. Application deadline February 1.
Admissions High school graduation with 15 units required. GED accepted. Interview suggested. SAT required. 3 ACH recommended. $20 application fee. Rolling admissions; suggest applying by January of 12th year. Deadline March 1. *Early Decision* and *Early Admission* programs. Transfers accepted. Credit possible for CEEB AP, CLEP, ACT, and college exams.
Student Life Student government. Newspaper, arts magazine, yearbook. Drama, film, & music groups. Campus Ministry. Academic, ethnic, honorary, professional, service, social, and special interest groups. Coed and single-sex dorms. Language, special interest, and townhouse/apartment housing. 75% of students live on campus. 9 intercollegiate sports for men, 9 for women; club and intramural sports. AIAW, ECAC, NCAA, New England Conference. Student body composition: 1% Asian, 1% Black, 2% Hispanic, 96% White. 35% from out of state.

[1] ATLANTIC UNION COLLEGE

Main Street, South Lancaster 01561, (617) 365-4561
Director of Admissions: Ronna Archbold

- **Undergraduates: 232m, 348w; 700 total (including graduates)**
- **Tuition (1982/83): $5,010**
- **Room & Board: $1,950-$2,450; Fees: $160**
- **Degrees offered: BA, BS, BMus, AS**
- **Student-faculty ratio: 10 to 1**

A private college founded in 1882, affiliated with the Seventh-day Adventist Church. 200-acre rural campus, 45 miles west of Boston. Air, rail, and bus 15 miles away in Worcester.
Academic Character NEASC and professional accreditation. Semester system, 3 4-week summer terms. Majors offered in accounting, art, biology, business administration, business education, chemistry, computer science, elementary education, engineering, English, foods & nutrition, French, history, home economics, interior design, mathematics, medical technology, music, music education, music performance, nursing, personal ministries, physical education, psychology, religion, social work, Spanish, and theology. Distributives and 9 hours of religion required. Graduate degrees granted. Associate degrees in business computer programming, early childhood education, nursing, office administration (4), personal ministries. Adult degree program. Independent study, honors program, pass/fail. Preprofessional programs in dentistry, law, medicine, dietetics. Dual-degree programs in engineering and architecture. Study abroad. Elementary and secondary education certification. Museum, language lab, computer. 96,000-volume library.
Financial CEEB CSS. College & denominational scholarships, state grants, payment plan; PELL, SEOG, NSS, NDSL, GSL, NSL, CWS, college work program. Application deadline March 1.
Admissions High school graduation with minimum of 11 units required. GED accepted. Interview encouraged. ACT required. $15 application fee. Rolling admissions; suggest applying by February 1. $100 deposit required on acceptance of admissions offer. *Early Decision* and *Concurrent Enrollment* programs. Admission deferral possible. Transfers accepted. Credit possible for CEEB CLEP and ACT PEP exams. College has own advanced placement program. Headstart Program.
Student Life Student government. Newspaper, literary magazine, yearbook. Music & drama groups. Ethnic, religious, service, and special interest clubs. Students must live at home or on campus. Single-sex dorms. Language and married-student housing. 40% of students live on campus. Liquor, smoking, drugs, gambling prohibited on campus. 2 hours of phys ed required. Class and twice-weekly chapel attendance required. Student body composition: 1% Asian, 24% Black, 10% Hispanic, 1% Native American, 64% White.

[1] BABSON COLLEGE

Babson Park 02157, (617) 235-1200
Director of Admissions: Joseph B. Carver

- **Undergraduates: 913m, 470w; 3,100 total (including graduates)**
- **Tuition (1982/83): $6,176**
- **Room & Board: $2,530-$3,280; Fees: $188**
- **Degree offered: BS**
- **Mean SAT 500v, 590m**
- **Student-faculty ratio: 22 to 1**

A private college of management founded in 1919, became coed in 1968. 450-acre suburban campus in Wellesley, 12 miles from Boston. Air, rail, and bus service.
Academic Character NEASC and professional accreditation. Semester system, 2 6-week summer terms. Majors offered in accounting/law, American studies, communication, economics, entrepreneurial studies, finance, investments, management & organizational behavior, marketing, quantitative methods (with economics, finance, investments, marketing), and society & technology. Self-designed majors. Courses in humanities and social sciences. Distributive requirements. MBA granted. Independent study, honors program, internships. Cross-registration with Pine Manor and Regis colleges, and Brandeis U. Study abroad. Computer center, management lab. 81,000-volume library with microform resources.
Financial CEEB CSS. College scholarships, grants, loans, state scholarships, payment plan; PELL, SEOG, NDSL, GSL, CWS, college work program. Suggest filing FAF in early January; application deadline February 15.
Admissions High school graduation with college prep program required. SAT or ACT required. ACHs and interview recommended. $25 application fee. Application deadline February 1. $100 deposit required on acceptance of admissions offer (May 1). *Early Decision* Program. Admission deferral possible. Transfers accepted. Credit possible for CEEB AP and CLEP exams, and for life/work experience.
Student Life Student government. Newspaper, yearbook. Drama, film, and music groups. Student businesses & Chamber of Commerce. Circle K. Black Society. Academic, athletic, honorary, outing, professional, and special interest clubs. 2 fraternities and 2 sororities. Coed and single-sex dorms. Married-student housing. 70% of students live on campus. 2 semesters of phys ed required. 12 intercollegiate sports for men, 9 for women; club and intramural sports. AIAW, ECAC, NCAA. Student body composition: 1% Black, 92% White, 7% Other. 39% from out of state.

[J1] BAY PATH JUNIOR COLLEGE

588 Longmeadow Street, Longmeadow 01106, (413) 567-0621
Director of Admissions: James M. Skinner

- **Undergraduates: 684w**
- **Tuition (1982/83): $3,700**
- **Room & Board: $3,300; Fees: $200**
- **Degrees offered: AA, AS**

A private junior college for women established in 1897. Suburban campus in a town near Springfield. Bus and rail stations in Springfield. Airport 15 miles away.
Academic Character NEASC and professional accreditation. Semester system. Career and transfer programs offered in arts & sciences, accounting, business administration-management, certified professional secretary, computer science, executive assistant, executive secretary, fashion merchandising & retail management, legal assistant-paralegal, legal secretary, medical assistant, travel administration, word processing management. Distributive requirements. Directed study, internships. Cross-registration through Cooperating Colleges of Greater Springfield. ROTC at Western New England College. Continuing education. Theater and ceramics studies, fashion lab. Learning Resources Center. 29,000-volume library.
Financial CEEB CSS. College and state scholarships, payment plans; PELL, SEOG, NDSL, GSL, PLUS, CWS. Suggest filing FAF by February 15.
Admissions High school graduation required. Interview required. SAT or equivalent urged. $25 application fee. Rolling admissions. $200 tuition and $100 room deposits required on acceptance of admissions offer. *Early Admission* and *Early Decision* programs. Transfers accepted. Credit possible for CEEB AP and CLEP exams. Paths to Academic Success program for underprepared students.
Student Life Student government. Yearbook. Music and theater groups. College-sponsored spring Bermuda trip. Outing & ski club. Interfaith Council. Honorary, social, service, and professional groups. Student center. 8 women's dorms. 80% of students live on campus. Liquor & illegal drugs prohibited. Regular class attendance expected. Recreational sports.

[P] BAY STATE JUNIOR COLLEGE OF BUSINESS

122 Commonwealth Avenue, Boston 02116, (617) 266-0220

- **Undergraduates: 30m, 704w; 744 total (including part-time)**
- **Tuition (1982/83): $3,100**
- **Room & Board: $3,150**
- **Degree offered: AAS**

A private, coed junior college of business. Campus located in the Back Bay area of Boston. Air, rail, bus, and subway service.
Academic Character AICS and professional accreditation; candidate for NEASC accreditation. Semester system. 2-year programs offered in fashion retailing-merchandising, business administration, medical laboratory technician, airline & transportation secretary, legal secretary, medical secretary, environmental health technician. 1-year diploma programs in secretarial science (legal, medical, travel, executive), general clerical, and medical assistant. Remedial mathematics and English programs.
Financial Aid available includes PELL, SEOG, NDSL, CWS.
Admissions Admission notification is done on a rolling basis. *Early Decision* Program. Admission deferral possible.
Student Life Dormitories available. Student body composition: 31% minority.

[J1] BECKER JUNIOR COLLEGE—WORCESTER CAMPUS

61 Sever Street, Worcester 01609, (617) 791-9241
Dean of Admissions: Thomas J. Redman

- **Undergraduates: 94m, 408w; 710 total (including part-time)**
- **Tuition (1982/83): $2,750**
- **Room & Board: $2,150; Fees: $111**
- **Degree offered: AS**

A private, non-denominational junior college founded in 1887. Becker Junior College and Leicester Junior College merged to become a 2-campus college in 1977. Campus in a residential area of Worcester a short walk from downtown. Air, rail, and bus service nearby.
Academic Character NEASC accreditation. Semester system. Career and

transfer majors offered in general studies, occupational therapy assistant, interior design, social worker assistant, physical therapist assistant, secretarial (general, legal/paralegal, medical, executive), medical assistant, accounting, management/administrative assistant, retail fashions, retail management, business administration, computer management, word processing administration. Distributive requirements. Internships. Cooperative work/study. Cross-registration through Worcester Consortium for Higher Education.
Financial CEEB CSS. College scholarships & grants, athletic grants, state scholarships; PELL, SEOG, NDSL, GSL, PLUS, CWS. Priority application deadline April 1.
Admissions High school graduation required. Special requirements for some majors. Interview encouraged. SAT or ACT recommended. $20 application fee. Rolling admissions. $100 tuition and $100 room deposits required on acceptance of admissions offer. *Early Admission* and *Early Decision* programs. Admission deferral possible. Transfers accepted. Credit possible for CEEB AP and CLEP exams.
Student Life Student government. Newspaper, yearbook. Student Center. Social activities. Film series, drama club. Athletic, professional, service, honorary, and special interest groups. Single students must live at home or on campus. 18 dorms that have been converted from private homes. Boarding freshmen may not have cars on campus.

■[J1] BECKER JUNIOR COLLEGE—LEICESTER CAMPUS
1003 Main Street, Leicester 01524, (617) 892-8122
Dean of Admissions: Thomas J. Redman

- **Undergraduates: 500 men & women**
- **Tuition (1982/83): $2,750**
- **Room & Board: $2,150; Fees: $111**
- **Degree offered: AS**

A private junior college founded in 1784, became coed in 1969. Becker Junior College and Leicester Junior College merged to become a 2-campus college in 1977. Suburban campus in a small town near Worcester, 50 miles from Boston. Air, rail, and bus service nearby.
Academic Character NEASC and professional accreditation. Semester system. Transfer and terminal majors offered in liberal arts, travel & tour services, business administration (accounting, management, marketing), early childhood education, horticulture (landscape/nursery, floral shop), sports administration, recreational leadership, physical education, veterinary assistant, animal care, nursing. Distributive requirements. Field experience, internships. Cross-registration through Worcester Consortium for Higher Education. Animal Health Center, Nursing Center. 25,000-volume library.
Financial CEEB CSS. College scholarships & grants, athletic grants, state scholarships; PELL, SEOG, NDSL, GSL, PLUS, CWS. Priority application deadline April 1.
Admissions High school graduation required. Special requirements for some majors. Interview encouraged. SAT or ACT recommended. $20 application fee. Rolling admissions. $100 tuition and $100 room deposits required on acceptance of admissions offer. *Early Admission* and *Early Decision* programs. Admission deferral possible. Transfers accepted. Credit possible for CEEB AP and CLEP exams.
Student Life Student government. Newspaper. Film series. Social activities. Athletic, service, honorary, special interest groups. Student Center. Single students must live at home or on campus. Dorms and dining hall. Regular class attendance expected. 4 intercollegiate sports for men, 6 for women; intramurals. NJCAA.

[1] BENTLEY COLLEGE
Waltham 02254, (617) 891-2244
Dean of Admissions & Financial Aid: Kent P. Ericson

- **Undergraduates: 2,070m, 1,588w; 10,500 total (including evening division)**
- **Tuition (1982/83): $5,100**
- **Room & Board: $2,800**
- **Degrees offered: BA, BS, AS**
- **Mean SAT 468v, 544m**
- **Student-faculty ratio: 22 to 1**

A private college founded in 1917. 100-acre suburban campus 9 miles from Boston. Air, rail, and bus service nearby.
Academic Character NEASC and professional accreditation. Semester system, 2 summer terms. BS offered with majors in accountancy, business communication, computer information systems, economics, economics/finance, finance, general business, management, marketing management, public administration, quantitative analysis. BA offered with self-designed and interdisciplinary majors in areas including behavioral sciences, communications, environmental studies, history & government, legal studies, literature, philosophy, and psychology. AS offered with majors in accountancy, management, and paralegal studies. Distributive requirements. Directed study, honors program, internships. Cross-registration with Regis College. AFROTC at U of Lowell. Computer center. 102,000-volume library.
Financial CEEB CSS and ACT FAS. College scholarships, grants, minority grants-in-aid, payment plan; PELL, SEOG, NDSL, GSL, PLUS, CWS. File FAF by February 1; application deadline March 1.
Admissions High school graduation with 16 units required. GED accepted. Interview recommended. SAT or ACT required. $25 application fee. Application deadline March 10. $100 tuition and $200 room deposits required on acceptance of admissions offer (May 1). *Early Decision, Early Entrance, Concurrent Enrollment* programs. Admission deferral possible. Transfers accepted. Credit possible for CEEB AP and CLEP exams; college has own advanced placement program.
Student Life Student government. Newspaper, yearbook. Music, debate, and drama groups. Academic, athletic, professional, religious, service, and special interest groups. 6 fraternities and 3 sororities. 6% of men and 4% of women join. Coed dorms, apartments. No married-student housing. 59% of students live on campus. 2 semesters of phys ed required. 9 intercollegiate sports for men, 5 for women; intramurals. AIAW, ECAC, NCAA. Student body composition: 1% Black, 97% White, 2% Other. 40% from out of state.

[1] BERKLEE COLLEGE OF MUSIC
1140 Boylston Street, Boston 02215, (617) 266-1400
Director of Admissions: Steven Lipman

- **Undergraduates: 2,097m, 366w**
- **Tuition (1983/84): $3,700**
- **Room & Board: $2,710; Fees: $120**
- **Degree offered: BMus**
- **Student-faculty ratio: 12 to 1**

A private professional college founded in 1945. Campus in Back Bay section of Boston. Air, rail, and bus service.
Academic Character NEASC accreditation. Semester system, 12-week for-credit summer term, 2 non-credit 7-week summer terms. Majors offered in arranging, composition, electronic music, film scoring, jazz composition & arranging, music education, music production & engineering, performance, professional music, and traditional performance. Self-designed majors. 5-year dual major in music education with one of above fields. Courses in art, English, French, history, music reviewing, political science, psychology, religion & philosophy, and Spanish. Required first-year program. 4-yr professional and artist's diploma, 2-year certificate programs. International Jazz Program and Visting Artist Series bring foreign students and music professionals to campus for study & teaching. Elementary and secondary education certification. Electronic music lab, 3 recording studios, film scoring & editing studio, performance center. 38,193-volume library with ensemble library.
Financial CEEB CSS and ACT FAS. College scholarships, grants, state awards, loans; PELL, SEOG, GSL, NDSL, CWS. Suggested application deadline March 31.
Admissions High school graduation required; 16 units recommended. GED accepted. Minimum 2 years of musical study and/or experience expected. Interview encouraged. SAT or ACT required. $25 application fee. Rolling admissions; suggest applying as early as possible. $100 tuition and $75 room deposits required before registration. 7-week Career Exploration Program for high school students. Admission deferral possible. Transfers accepted. Credit possible for CEEB AP and CLEP exams. College placement exams required of all entering students.
Student Life Student-faculty committee. Numerous instrumental & vocal groups. Student theater. Over 500 ensembles, 650 performances annually. Students under 21 must live at home or on campus for first year. Coed dorms. No married-student housing. 30% of students live on campus. Liquor prohibited on campus. Boarders may not have cars on campus. Class attendance required. 81% of students from out of state.

[P] BERKSHIRE CHRISTIAN COLLEGE
200 Stockbridge Road, Lenox 01240

[J1] BERKSHIRE COMMUNITY COLLEGE
Pittsfield 01201

[J1] BLUE HILLS REGIONAL TECHNICAL INSTITUTE
100 Randolph Street, Canton 02021

[P] BOSTON ARCHITECTURAL CENTER
320 Newbury Street, Boston 02115

[1] BOSTON COLLEGE
Chesnut Hill 02167, (617) 969-0100
Director of Admissions: Charles Nolan

- **Undergraduates: 3,855m, 5,125w; 14,166 total (including graduates)**
- **Tuition (1982/83): $6,000**
- **Room & Board: $3,100-$3,480; Fees: $300**
- **Degrees offered: AB, BS**
- **Mean SAT 507v, 555m**
- **Student-faculty ratio: 16 to 1**

A private Catholic college conducted by Jesuits, founded in 1863, became coed in 1947. 200-acre suburban campus in Chesnut Hill area of Newton, 6 miles from Boston, plus 40-acre Newton College campus. Rapid transit to Boston, airport, rail and bus stations.
Academic Character NEASC and professional accreditation. Semester system, 6-week summer term. Majors offered in accounting, American studies, art (2), biology, chemistry, classical studies, computer science, economics, education (4), English, finance, geology & geophysics, Germanic studies, history, linguistics, management, marketing, mathematics, modern languages (5), nursing, organizational studies, philosophy, physics, political science, psychology, quantitative analysis, Slavic studies, speech communication, speech/theatre, and theology. Double majors. Interdepartmental programs in 7 areas. 2 theology courses required; other requirements vary with programs. Graduate and professional degrees granted. Independent study, honors programs, Phi Beta Kappa, pass/fail, internships. Preprofessional programs in dentistry, law, medicine. PULSE combines community work with study of philosophy & theology. Bachelors/Masters programs. Cross-registration at BU, Brandeis, Tufts, and Hebrew, Pine Manor, and Regis colleges. New England Consortium on Environmental Protection. Study abroad. Elementary, secondary, and special education certification. ROTC, AFROTC, & NROTC at Northeastern. Computer center. Over 1,000,000-volume library.

Financial CEEB CSS. College scholarships, grants; PELL, SEOG, NSS, NDSL, NSL, GSL, CWS. Application deadline February 1.
Admissions High school graduation with minimum of 11½ units (more for nursing) recommended. Interview urged. 5-8 slides of work for studio art majors. ACT or SAT, and 3 ACH required. $30 application fee. Application deadline January 15. $100 tuition and $100 room deposits required on acceptance of admissions offer (May 1). *Early Decision* and *Early Entrance* programs. Admission deferral possible. Transfers accepted. Credit possible for CEEB AP and CLEP exams. Options Through Education Program.
Student Life Campus Council. Radio station, magazines. Music, drama, debate groups. PIRG, Hillel, Black Forum. Academic, ethnic, honorary, political, professional, religious, service, and special interest clubs. Coed, single-sex, honors, and language dorms. Apartments. No married-student housing. 75% of students live on campus. No cars for resident freshmen & sophomores. 11 intercollegiate sports for men, 10 for women; many intramural & club sports. Student body composition: 3% Asian, 2% Black, 5% Hispanic, 1% Native American, 88% White, 1% Other. 52% from out of state.

[1] BOSTON CONSERVATORY OF MUSIC
8 The Fenway, Boston 02215, (617) 536-6340
Director of Admissions & Public Relations: Margaret Mary Haley

- **Enrollment: 126m, 274w; 450 total (including part-time)**
- **Tuition (1982/83): $4,290**
- **Room & Board: $2,735-$2,995**
- **Degrees offered: BFA, BMus**
- **Mean SAT 500**

A private college of music, drama, and theatre, founded in 1867. Urban campus located in the Fenway section of Boston's Back Bay. Air, rail, bus, and subway service.
Academic Character NEASC and professional accreditation. Semester system, 6- & 8-week summer terms. BMus granted with majors in composition, guitar, piano, organ, music education, opera preparation, strings & harp, voice, winds & percussion. BFA granted with majors in dance, acting/directing, and musical theatre. 2-year liberal arts core. Performance requirements. Diplomas offered in several areas. MMus and Artist Diploma granted. Evening programs. Music Education Curriculum Lab with A-V facilities. Concert halls, theatre, studios. 40,000-volume library.
Financial CEEB CSS (preferred) and ACT FAS. Conservatory scholarships, work-assistantships, emergency loans, payment plan; PELL, SEOG, GSL, PLUS, CWS. Application deadline April 15.
Admissions High school graduation (or equivalent) with 16 units required. Audition required. Specific requirements for particular programs. SAT or ACT required. $45 application fee. Rolling admissions; suggest applying as early as possible. Deadline April 15. $50 tuition and $100 room (for boarders) deposits required on acceptance of admissions offer. *Early Admission* and *Early Decision* programs. Admission deferral possible. Transfers accepted. Advanced placement credit possible.
Student Life Student government. Film series. Many performing groups give over 250 performances a year. 3 music fraternities (for men & women) without houses. Coed and single-sex dorms. Dining hall. Regular class and public performance attendance required.

[1] BOSTON STATE COLLEGE
Boston — see University of Massachusetts, Boston

[1] BOSTON UNIVERSITY
Commonwealth Avenue, Boston 02215, (617) 353-2000
Director of Admissions: Anthony T. G. Pallett

- **Undergraduates: 6,076m, 6,573w; 28,157 total (including graduates)**
- **Tuition (1982/83): $7,175**
- **Room & Board: $3,400; Fees: $100**
- **Degrees offered: BA, BS, BFA, BSBA, BMus, BSEd, BAA, AAA**
- **Mean SAT 538v, 582m**
- **Student-faculty ratio: 14 to 1**

A private university established in 1869. 68-acre urban campus on the Charles River. Air, rail, and bus service.
Academic Character NEASC and professional accreditation. Semester system, 2 summer terms. 8 majors offered by the College of Engineering, 46 by the College of Liberal Arts, 5 by the Program in Artisanry, 6 by Sargent College of Allied Health Professions, 13 by the School for the Arts, 15 by the School of Education, 7 by the School of Management, 1 by the School of Nursing, and 6 by the School of Public Communication. The College of Basic Studies offers a 2-year, non-traditional liberal arts program for transfer within the University. University Professors Program offers independent study, tutorials, self-designed majors for exceptional students. Self-designed majors. Minors. Distributive requirements. Graduate and professional degrees granted. Independent study, honors program, Phi Beta Kappa, credit by exam, internships. Preprofessional programs in allied health fields, dentistry, medicine, veterinary medicine. 4-yr BA/MA, 5-yr MBA, 6-yr BA/MD & BA/DMD programs. 8-yr program for a BA/MD. Cross-registration with Boston College, Brandeis, Tufts. Study abroad. Elementary, secondary, and special education certification. ROTC, AFROTC, NROTC at Northeastern. Labs and research institutes. Computer center. 1,347,000-volume library with microform resources.
Financial CEEB CSS. University scholarships, grants; PELL, SEOG, NSS, NDSL, GSL, NSL, CWS. Application deadline March 1.
Admissions High school graduation with 16 units required. Audition required for music & theatre majors, portfolio for visual arts & program in artisanry. SAT or ACT required. ACH for some programs. $30 application fee. Application deadline February 15. $200 deposit required on acceptance of admissions offer. *Early Admission* and *Early Decision* programs. Admission deferral possible. Transfers accepted. Credit possible for CEEB AP, CLEP, & ACH exams. Minority Application Program.
Student Life Student government. Newspapers, magazines, radio & TV stations. Music, drama, debate, film groups. Honorary, ethnic, professional, religious, political, academic, and special interest clubs. 2 fraternities, 1 with house; 3 sororities without houses. 5% of students join. Single freshmen under 21 must live at home or on campus. Coed, single-sex, married-student housing. 60% of students live on campus. No cars for boarding freshmen & sophomores. Many intercollegiate and intramural sports. Student body composition: 2% Asian, 5% Black, 2% Hispanic, 83% White, 8% Other. 75% from out of state.

[1] BRADFORD COLLEGE
Bradford 01830, (617) 372-7161
Associate Director of Admissions: Laura Wallingford

- **Undergraduates: 170m, 230w**
- **Tuition (1982/83): $5,800**
- **Room & Board: $3,150**
- **Degrees offered: BA, AA**
- **Mean SAT 400v, 400m**
- **Student-faculty ratio: 13 to 1**

A private college founded in 1803, became coed in 1971. 70-acre suburban campus located 35 miles north of Boston.
Academic Character NEASC accreditation. Semester system. Interdisciplinary BA degree programs offered in liberal arts, creative arts, administration & management, human studies (social sciences), and individual studies. AA degree in liberal arts conferred within BA structure. Writing requirement. Independent study, pass/fail, service activities, field work, internships. College Learning Program for students with moderate learning disabilities. Cross-registration with Northern Essex Community College and Merrimack College. Language lab. 57,000-volume library with microform resources.
Financial CEEB CSS. Financial aid available. Application deadline March 15.
Admissions High school graduation required; college prep program recommended. SAT or ACT required. Rolling admissions. $100 tuition and $150 room deposits required on acceptance of admissions offer. *Early Admission* and *Early Decision* programs. Admission deferral possible. Transfers accepted. Credit possible for CEEB AP and CLEP exams.
Student Life Student government. Publications. Theatre, dance, music, athletic groups. Cultural activities. Intercollegiate volleyball for men and women; intramurals. Student body composition: 10% minority.

[1] BRANDEIS UNIVERSITY
Waltham 02154, (617) 647-2878
Dean of Admissions: David L. Gould

- **Undergraduates: 1,149m, 1,338w; 3,354 total (including graduates)**
- **Tuition (1982/83): $7,650**
- **Room & Board: $3,355; Fees: $180**
- **Degree offered: BA**
- **Mean SAT 580v, 620m**
- **Student-faculty ratio: 10 to 1**

A private university founded under Jewish auspices in 1948. 250-acre suburban campus on the banks of the Charles River, 10 miles from Boston. Rail and bus to Boston.
Academic Character NEASC accreditation. Semester system, limited summer term. Majors offered in African & Afro-American studies, American studies, anthropology, biochemistry, biology, chemistry, Classical & Oriental studies, comparative literature, computer science, economics, English & American literature, English & Classics, fine arts, French, general science, German, history, history of western thought, Italian, Latin American studies, linguistics, mathematics, music, Near Eastern & Judaic studies, philosophy, physics, politics, psychology, Russian, sociology, Spanish, theatre arts. Independent majors. Distributive requirements. MA, MFA, PhD granted. Independent study, honors program, Phi Beta Kappa, pass/fail, internships. 4-year BA/MA programs. Cross-registration with Boston College, Boston and Tufts Universities. Washington Semester. Study abroad in Israel and other countries. International Coordinate Degree Program with up to 2 years of foreign study. Elementary and secondary education certification. Research institutes. Computer center, language lab. Over 816,270-volume library.
Financial CEEB CSS. University scholarships, grants, deferred payment; PELL, SEOG, NDSL, GSL, CWS. Application deadline February 1.
Admissions High school graduation with 15-16 units required. SAT and 3 ACH required. $25 application fee. Application deadline February 1. $150 deposit required on acceptance of admissions offer (May 1). *Early Decision* and *Early Entrance* programs. Admission deferral possible. Transfers accepted. Credit possible for CEEB AP exams. University has own advanced placement program. Transitional Year Program for students not normally admissable.
Student Life Student government. Newspaper, literary magazine, yearbook, radio station. Music, dance, drama, photography groups. Debate. Hillel, Amnesty International. African Circle, Gay Alliance, Women's Coalition. Academic, outing, political, professional, religious, service, and special interest groups. Dorms coed by floor. 83% of students live on campus. 1 year of phys ed required. 9 intercollegiate sports for men, 9 for women, and coed sailing; intramurals. AIAW, ECAC, NAIA, NCAA. Student body composition: 11% minority. 80% from out of state.

[1] BRIDGEWATER STATE COLLEGE
Bridgewater 02324, (617) 697-8321, ext. 215
Director of Admissions: James F. Plotner, Jr.

- **Enrollment: 1,703m, 2,763w**

- **Tuition (1982/83): $845 (in-state), $2,800 (out-of-state)**
- **Room & Board: $2,106-$2,164; Fees: $261**
- **Degrees offered: BA, BS, BSEd**
- **Mean SAT 420v, 440m**
- **Student-faculty ratio: 19 to 1**

A public college established in 1840. Small-town campus 28 miles south of Boston. Air, rail, and bus in Boston.

Academic Character NEASC and professional accreditation. Semester system, 2 summer terms in Bridgewater, Buzzards Bay, and West Barnstable. Majors offered in anthropology, art, aviation science, biology, chemistry, chemistry-geology, chemistry-professional, communication arts & sciences (3), computer science, early childhood education, earth science, elementary education, English, French, geography, history, management science, mathematics, philosophy, physical education, physics, political science, psychology, social work, sociology, Spanish, and special education. Minors in some major fields and 20 additional areas. Distributive requirements. CAGS and masters degrees granted. Independent study, honors program, internships. Preprofessional programs in dentistry, medicine, veterinary medicine. Cross-registration through New England Regional Student Program, College Academics Program Sharing, and Southeastern Association for Cooperation of Higher Education in Mass. Elementary, secondary, and special education certification. 195,165-volume library with microform resources.

Financial CEEB CSS. PELL, SEOG, NDSL, GSL, CWS, college work program. Application deadline April 15.

Admissions High school graduation required. GED accepted. SAT required. Rolling admissions; deadline March 1. *Early Admission* Program. Admission deferral possible. Transfers accepted. Credit possible for CEEB AP and CLEP exams. Conditional admission possible. PROGRESS program for minority & economically disadvantaged students.

Student Life Coed and single-sex dorms, student apartments. Housing limited. No cars on campus for freshmen & sophomores. 5 intercollegiate and 2 club sports; intramurals include modern dance, gymnastics, swimming. AIAW, ECAC, NAIA, NCAA. Student body composition: 0.5% Asian, 1.5% Black, 0.2% Hispanic, 0.3% Native American, 96.5% White, 1% Other.

[J1] BRISTOL COMMUNITY COLLEGE
777 Elsbree Street, Fall River 02720

[J1] BUNKER HILL COMMUNITY COLLEGE
Boston 02129

[G1] CAMBRIDGE COLLEGE/INSTITUTE OF OPEN EDUCATION
Cambridge 02138

[J1] CAPE COD COMMUNITY COLLEGE
West Barnstable 02668

[1] CENTRAL NEW ENGLAND COLLEGE
Worcester 01610

■[2] CENTRAL NEW ENGLAND COLLEGE OF TECHNOLOGY
Worcester 01610

■[J1] WORCESTER JUNIOR COLLEGE
Worcester 01610

[J2] CHAMBERLAYNE JUNIOR COLLEGE
128 Commonwealth Avenue, Boston 02116, (617) 536-4500
Director of Admissions: James F. Mulligan

- **Undergraduates: 452m, 545w; 1,149 total (including part-time)**
- **Tuition (1982/83): $3,300**
- **Room & Board: $3,050; Fees: $40**
- **Degree offered: AAS**

A private junior college founded in 1892, became coed in 1950. Urban campus located in Boston's Back Bay. Air, rail, bus, and subway service.

Academic Character AICS accreditation; NEASC accreditation candidate. 2-year programs offered in interior design, fashion design, fashion illustration, advertising design/commercial art, accounting, business administration, data processing, marketing, advertising & sales, retail merchandising, hotel & institutional management, executive secretary/office manager, medical/dental office assistant, general college, general technician, and technical electricity. One-year program in secretarial/data management. 3-year interior design program for professional certification. Internships. Continuing Education. Studios. Computer terminals. Over 20,000-volume library.

Financial CEEB CSS. State scholarships; PELL, SEOG, NDSL, GSL, PLUS, CWS. Application deadline August 1.

Admissions High school graduation required. GED accepted. Interview recommended. $20 application fee. Rolling admissions. $100 tuition and $100 room deposits required on acceptance of admissions offer. Credit possible for CEEB AP and CLEP exams.

Student Life Academic and professional groups. Social activities. 2 dorms. Dining facilities. Class attendance required. Intramural sports for men and women. Student body composition: 13% minority.

[1] CLARK UNIVERSITY
Worcester 01610, (617) 793-7431
Dean of Admissions: Richard W. Pierson

- **Undergraduates: 950m, 1,075w; 2,595 total (including graduates)**
- **Tuition (1982/83): $6,980**
- **Room & Board: $2,430; Fees: $276**
- **Degrees offered: AB, BFA**
- **Mean SAT 550v, 580m**
- **Student-faculty ratio: 14 to 1**

A private university founded in 1887. 50-acre urban campus located 40 miles west of Boston. Air, rail, and bus service.

Academic Character NEASC and professional accreditation. Semester system, optional May/June term, summer term. Majors offered in art (fine, history, studio), biochemistry, biology, business-management, chemistry, comparative literature, computer science, economics, English, French, geography, German, government-international relations, history, international development-social change, mathematics, music, philosophy, physics, psychology, Romance languages, sociology-social anthropology, Spanish, theatre arts, and science, technology, & society. Self-designed majors. Interdisciplinary programs. Distributive requirements. MA, MBA, MAEd, EdD, PhD granted. Independent study, honors program, Phi Beta Kappa, pass/fail, internships. 4- or 5-year BA/MA programs in several areas. 5-year BA/MBA program. Cross-registration through Worcester Consortium for Higher Education. Washington Semester. Study abroad. Elementary, secondary, and special education certification. AFROTC & ROTC at Worcester Polytechnic; NROTC at Holy Cross. Language lab. 400,000-volume library with microform resources.

Financial CEEB CSS. University scholarships, payment plan; PELL, SEOG, NDSL, GSL, CWS. File FAF by February 15.

Admissions High school graduation with 16 units required. Interview urged. Portfolio required for art majors. SAT and 3 ACH required. $25 application fee. Application deadline February 15. $100 tuition and $100 room deposits required on acceptance of admissions offer (May 1). *Early Decision* and *Early Entrance* programs. Admission deferral possible. Transfers accepted. Credit possible for CEEB AP exams.

Student Life Student government. Newspaper, magazine, yearbook, radio station. Drama and several music groups. Debate. Third World Cultural Center. Academic, honorary, religious, service, and special interest groups. One fraternity with house. 7% of men join. Freshmen must live at home or on campus. Coed, single-sex, language dorms. 75% of students live on campus. 9 intercollegiate sports for men, 6 for women; many intramurals. ECAC, MAIAW, NCAA, NECAC. Student body composition: 94% White, 6% Other. 70% from out of state.

[1] CURRY COLLEGE
1071 Blue Hill Avenue, Milton 02186, (617) 333-0500
Director of Admissions: Dana Denault

- **Undergraduates: 380m, 398w; 868 total (including part-time)**
- **Tuition (1982/83): $5,750**
- **Room & Board: $3,300; Fees: $185**
- **Degrees offered: BA, BS**
- **Mean SAT 455v, 470m**
- **Student-faculty ratio: 13 to 1**

A private, preprofessional liberal arts college established in 1879. 120-acre suburban campus 7 miles from downtown Boston. Bus service to Boston, airport, and rail station.

Academic Character NEASC accreditation. Semester system, 6-week summer term. Majors offered in biology, chemistry, communication arts & sciences (radio & TV, speech), elementary education (learning disabilities), English, fine arts (art, music), management, moderate special needs education, nursing, philosophy, physics, political & historical studies, psychology, socio-cultural studies. Interdisciplinary and self-designed majors. Minors in most major fields and in computer science, dance, theatre, and visual arts. Courses in Spanish. Independent study, pass/fail. Exchange programs with Johnston College and U of Redlands in California. Credit for foreign study. Elementary and secondary education certification. Language lab. Over 100,000-volume library.

Financial CEEB CSS. College scholarships, payment plan; PELL, SEOG, NDSL, GSL, CWS. Priority application deadline March 1.

Admissions High school graduation with 16 units required. Interview urged. SAT or ACT required. $15 application fee. Rolling admissions; suggest applying by February 15. $50 tuition and $50 room deposits required on acceptance of admissions offer (May 1). *Early Decision* and *Early Entrance* programs. Admission deferral possible. Transfers accepted. Credit possible for CEEB AP and CLEP exams, and for life/work experience.

Student Life Student government. Newspaper, arts magazine, yearbook, radio station. Music, dance, drama groups. Athletic, professional, religious, and special interest clubs. Students must live at home or on campus. Coed dorms. No married-student housing. 70% of students live on campus. 6 intercollegiate sports for men, 4 for women; intramurals. NCAA, New England Football Conference. Student body composition: 2.9% Black, 94.1% White, 3% Other. 40% from out of state.

[J1] DEAN JUNIOR COLLEGE
99 Main Street, Franklin 02038, (617) 528-9100
Director of Admissions: Steven T. Briggs

- **Undergraduates: 423m, 567w; 2,160 total (including part-time)**
- **Tuition (1982/83): $4,845**
- **Room & Board: $2,410; Fees: $135**
- **Degrees offered: AA, AS**
- **Student-faculty ratio: 14 to 1**

A private junior college founded in 1865. Suburban campus 30 miles southwest of Boston. Bus and train service to Boston.

Academic Character NEASC accreditation. Semester system, 2 summer

terms. Majors offered in building construction, business administration, child studies, communication arts, computer science/systems management, dance, fashion merchandising, humanities, human services, interior merchandising, law enforcement, liberal studies, math/science, medical assisting, music, music/theatre/dance, physical education, recreational leadership, retailing, secretarial science (executive, legal, medical), small business management, social science, theatre arts, visual arts, and corrections, probation, & parole. 6 English credits required. Independent study, honors program, cooperative work/study, internships, practicums. Continuing Education. Learning Lab. Computer center. A-V facilities. 37,000-volume library with microform resources.
Financial CEEB CSS. College grants & loans, state scholarships, payment plans; PELL, SEOG, NDSL, GSL, PLUS, CWS, college workship program. File FAF by February 10. Priority application deadline March 15.
Admissions High school graduation required. Interview recommended. SAT or ACT urged. $20 application fee. Rolling admissions. $200 deposit (refundable to May 1) required on acceptance of admissions offer. *Early Admission* Program. Admission deferral possible. Transfers accepted. Credit possible for CEEB AP and CLEP exams. College exams used for placement.
Student Life Student government. Newspaper, yearbook, radio station. Music and dance groups. Community service. Honorary, athletic, and special interest clubs. 1 fraternity and 1 sorority. Students usually must live at home or on campus. Coed and single-sex dorms. 90% of students live on campus. 2 phys ed credits required. 6 intercollegiate sports for men, 4 for women; intramural & recreational sports. NJCAA. Facilities for boarding & training horses available off-campus.

[P] DIMAN REGIONAL TECHNICAL INSTITUTE
Stonehaven Road, Fall River 02723

[1] EASTERN NAZARENE COLLEGE
Wollaston Park, Quincy 02170, (617) 773-6350
Director of Admissions: Donald A. Yerxa

- **Undergraduates: 375m, 527w**
- **Tuition & Fees (1982/83): $3,326**
- **Room & Board: $2,050**
- **Degrees offered: BA, BS, AA**
- **Mean SAT 412v, 446m**
- **Student-faculty ratio: 13 to 1**

A private college founded in 1900, affiliated with the Church of the Nazarene. 15-acre suburban campus south of Boston, 2 blocks from the Atlantic Ocean. Subway to Boston, airport, rail and bus stations.
Academic Character NEASC accreditation. 4-1-4 system, 2 4-week summer terms. Majors offered in biology, chemistry, Christian education, communication arts, computer science, early childhood education, economics/business administration, elementary education, engineering physics, English, general science, history, math, modern languages, music (4), philosophy, physical education, physics, psychology, religion, social studies, social work, sociology, and Spanish. AA in general studies, early childhood education, Biblical studies, and youth & Christian education ministry. Courses in German & Greek. Distributives, 3 semesters of religion/philosophy, and comprehensive exam in major required for graduation. MA granted. Independent study, pass/fail. Preprofessional programs in engineering, medical technology, medicine, nursing. 3-2 engineering program with Boston U. 2-3 pharmacy program with Mass College of Pharmacy. Transfer program in nursing with BU. Elementary and secondary education certification. 90,000-volume library.
Financial CEEB CSS. University scholarships, grants, loans, athletic & honor scholarships, payment plan; PELL, SEOG, NDSL, GSL, CWS. Application deadline March 1.
Admissions High school graduation with 16 units required. GED accepted. Interview urged. Music majors must show talent & accomplishment. SAT or ACT required. $20 application fee. Rolling admissions. $100 deposit required on acceptance of admissions offer (May 1). Transfers accepted. Credit possible for CEEB AP exams; college has own advanced placement program. College Achievement Program for underprepared students.
Student Life Student Council. Newspaper, yearbook. Several music groups. Student Ministerial Association. Circle K. Academic, honorary, religious, service, social, and special interest clubs. Non-veteran students under 23 must live at home or on campus. Single-sex dorms. Married-student apartments. Juniors, seniors, and those over 20 may have cars on campus. No liquor or smoking. 2 semesters of phys ed required. Class and thrice-weekly chapel attendance required. 5 intercollegiate sports for men, 5 for women. Student body composition: 0.6% Asian, 3.5% Black, 0.8% Hispanic, 93% White, 2.1% Other.

[1] ELMS COLLEGE
291 Springfield Street, Chicopee 01013, (413) 598-8351
Director of Admissions: Peter J. Miller

- **Undergraduates: 525w; 727 total (including part-time)**
- **Tuition (1982/83): $3,950**
- **Room & Board: $2,250; Fees :$110**
- **Degrees offered: AB, BS, BSN, BSMT**
- **Mean SAT 430v, 440m**
- **Student-faculty ratio: 9 to 1**

A private, Catholic liberal arts college for women, founded by the Sisters of Saint Joseph in 1928. Urban campus in Chicopee, 2 miles north of downtown Springfield, 1½ hours from Boston and 3 hours from New York City. Bus service in Springfield; airport nearby.
Academic Character NEASC accreditation. Semester system. Majors offered in American studies, art, biology, business management, chemistry, communication disorders, education, English, French, history, math, medical technology, modern language, natural science, nursing, social work, sociology, Spanish. Interdepartmental & self-designed majors. Minors in media communications, music, philosophy, and religious studies. Distributives and 3 religious studies courses required. Independent study, pass/fail, credit by exam, internships. Preprofessional programs in medicine, dentistry, optometry, veterinary medicine. 3-1 medical technology program. Cross-registration through Cooperating Colleges of Greater Springfield. Study abroad. Art, elementary, and secondary education certification. Continuing Education. Art gallery. Over 75,000-volume library with A-V resources.
Financial CEEB CSS. College scholarships and grants, state scholarships, 2nd-family-member grant, payment plan; PELL, SEOG, NSS, NDSL, GSL, NSL, PLUS, CWS, college working grants. Application deadline April 1.
Admissions High school graduation with 16 units required. Interview recommended. SAT required. Rolling admissions. $100 tuition and $50 room deposits required on acceptance of admissions offer. *Early Admission* and *Early Decision* programs. Admission deferral possible. Transfers accepted. Credit possible for CEEB AP and CLEP exams.
Student Life Faculty-Student Senate. Yearbook. Cultural and social activities. Campus Ministry. Professional and academic groups. 2 women's dorms. 60% of students live on campus. Class attendance required for freshmen and sophomores. Phys ed courses offered.

[1] EMERSON COLLEGE
Boston 02116, (617) 262-2010
Director of Admissions: Anne Heller

- **Undergraduates: 699m, 881w**
- **Tuition (1982/83): $5,650**
- **Room & Board: $3,670; Fees:$240**
- **Degrees offered: BA, BS, BFA, BSSpeech, BMus, BLiterary Interpretation**
- **Mean SAT 485v, 460m**
- **Student-faculty ratio: 15 to 1**

A private college founded in 1880. Urban campus in Boston's Back Bay. Air, rail, bus, and subway service.
Academic Character NEASC accreditation. Semester system, 6-week summer term. Majors offered in acting, business & organizational communications, communication disorders, creative writing, directing, film, mass communications (broadcast, film, journalism, radio, TV), musical theatre, oral interpretation, orchestral instrumentation, piano/organ, public relations & advertising, speech/communications studies, technical theatre, theatre arts, theatre education, and voice. Interdisciplinary and self-designed majors. Courses in additional areas. Distributive requirements. MA, MS in Speech granted. Honors program, internships. Cross-registration with Boston Museum School, Longy School of Music, Suffolk U. Elementary, secondary, and special education certification. Radio/TV studios, speech/hearing clinic, pre-school deaf nursery. Member Fenway Library Consortium. 87,750-volume library.
Financial CEEB CSS. College scholarships, grants, state grants, payment plan; PELL, SEOG, NDSL, GSL, PLUS, CWS. Application deadline March 1.
Admissions High school graduation with 12 units required. Creative writing sample required of all applicants, plus audition for BFA in theatre majors, portfolio for BFA in technical theatre majors. SAT or ACT required. $25 application fee. Rolling admissions; suggest applying by March 1. $125 tuition and $125 room deposits required on acceptance of admissions offer, refundable to May 15. *Early Decision* and *Early Entrance* programs. Admission deferral possible. Transfers accepted. Credit possible for CEEB AP and CLEP exams. 6-week Communications Skills summer program for underprepared students.
Student Life Student government. Newspaper, magazines, yearbook, radio station, closed-circuit TV. Music, arts, drama, film, TV groups. Intercollegiate debate. Ethnic, honorary, professional, religious, service, and special interest groups. 3 fraternities and 2 sororities. Freshmen under 21 must live at home or on campus. Coed and single-sex dorms. 40% of students live on campus. 9 intercollegiate sports; intramurals. Student body composition: 1.5% Asian, 8% Black, 2% Hispanic, 1% Native American, 87.5% White. 60% from out of state.

[1] EMMANUEL COLLEGE
400 The Fenway, Boston 02115, (617) 277-9340
Director of Admissions: Tina Segalla

- **Undergraduates: 687w; 1,065 total (including part-time)**
- **Tuition (1982/83): $4,950**
- **Room & Board: $2,600; Fees: $200**
- **Degrees offered: BA, BS, BFA, BSN, AA**
- **Mean SAT 435v, 450m**
- **Student-faculty ratio: 13 to 1**

A private Roman Catholic women's college established in 1919. Conducted by the Sisters of Notre Dame of Namur. 17-acre urban campus in Boston's Back Bay. Air, rail, bus, and subway service.
Academic Character NEASC accreditation. Semester system, 2 3-week summer terms. Majors offered in art (education, history, studio, therapy), biochemistry, biology, business management, chemistry, communication arts, economics, education (elementary, secondary), engineering, English, French, German, gerontology, history, Italian, math, medical technology, music education, music therapy, philosophy, physics, political science, psychology, rehabilitation counseling, sociology, Spanish, and theological studies. BS in Nursing for students with an RN. AA degrees through continuing education. Distributives, 2 semesters of theology, 1 of philosophy required. MA granted. Independent study, internships. Biology research internships. Preprofessional programs in dentistry, law, medicine, veterinary medicine. Program in early childhood & family intervention with Tufts NE

Medical Center. 3-2 engineering programs with Columbia, Northeastern, and Worcester Polytechnic Institute. Cross-registration with Simmons. Washington Semester. Study abroad. Elementary and secondary education certification. ROTC at Northeastern. Language lab. Member Fenway Library Consortium. 123,040-volume library.
Financial CEEB CSS. College scholarships, grants, state grants, payment plan; PELL, SEOG, NDSL, GSL, CWS. Application deadline February 15.
Admissions High school graduation with 16 units recommended. Interview required. SAT required. $20 application fee. Rolling admissions; suggest applying in fall of 12th year. $200 tuition and $100 room deposits required on acceptance of admissions offer (May 1). *Early Decision* and *Early Entrance* programs. Admission deferral possible. Transfers accepted. Credit possible for CEEB AP exams.
Student Life College Council. Newspaper, yearbook. Music and drama groups. Cultural program with Simmons & Wheelock Colleges. Academic, honorary, religious, service, and special interest groups. Women's dorms. 70% of students live on campus. Senior boarders and commuters may have cars on campus. Honor system. 6 intercollegiate sports; intramurals. Student body composition: 0.3% Asian, 3% Black, 2% Hispanic, 0.2% Native American, 89% White, 5.5% Other. 26% from out of state.

[J1] ENDICOTT COLLEGE
376 Hale Street, Beverly 01915, (617) 927-0585
Dean of Admissions: Harry C. Biser

- **Undergraduates: 800w**
- **Room & Board: $2,750-$2,950; Fees: $100-$150**
- **Degrees offered: AA, AS**
- **Student-faculty ratio: 12 to 1**

A private junior college for women, founded in 1939. 160-acre suburban campus with 3 private beaches on Massachusetts Bay, 20 miles from Boston. Bus service, train nearby, airport in Boston.
Academic Character NEASC accreditation. Trimester system, 4-week December internship term. Terminal & transfer AS offered with majors in advertising, apparel design, business administration (general & accounting), commercial art, computer science/business, crafts, day care, early childhood education, fashion merchandising, gerontology, hotel-restaurant management, interior design, medical assistant, office management, photography, radio-TV, retailing, secretarial (executive, bilingual, legal, medical, technical), and travel & tourism. AA offered in arts & sciences, elementary/secondary education, humanities, natural sciences/mathematics, social sciences, and social service. AS offered with an individual student program. Distributives and 1 phys ed credit required. 4-week December internship in major field required. Honors program. Consortium (NECCUM) with Salem State, Gordon, & Merrimack Colleges, Middlesex, North Shore, & Northern Essex Community Colleges, Montserrat School of Art, and U of Lowell provides cross-registration, shared facilities & programs. Radio/TV studios, art gallery, computer, A-V center, language lab. 48,000-volume library.
Financial CEEB CSS. College scholarships, grants, state scholarships, payment plan; PELL, SEOG, NDSL, GSL, PLUS, CWS, college work program. File FAF by February 15 (Mass residents by Feb. 1). Application deadline March 15.
Admissions High school graduation with 16 units required. Interview encouraged. SAT or ACT required. $25 application fee. Rolling admissions beginning in mid-October. $175 deposit required on acceptance of admissions offer, refundable to April 15; additional $225 deposit due by May 1. Transfers accepted. Credit possible for CEEB AP and CLEP exams. Women 23 or older with high school diploma or equivalent may enroll full-time or in Continuing Education.
Student Life Student government. Yearbook. Music and drama groups. Christian fellowship. Hiking, skiing, women's, honorary, and international groups. Single students must live at home or on campus. 13 women's dorms. 90% of students live on campus. 6 intercollegiate sports; sports clubs, dance classes. Student body composition: 2% minority. 65% of students from out of state.

[P] EPISCOPAL DIVINITY SCHOOL
Cambridge 02138

[J1] ESSEX AGRICULTURAL AND TECHNICAL INSTITUTE
Hawthorne 01937

[J1] FISHER JUNIOR COLLEGE
118 Beacon Street, Boston 02116, (617) 262-3240
Director of Admissions: Peter Burke

- **Undergraduates: 550w**
- **Tuition (1982/83): $3,950**
- **Room & Board: $3,650-$3,850; Fees: $250**
- **Degrees offered: AA, AS**

A private junior college for women founded in 1903. Urban campus located in Boston's Back Bay. Air, rail, bus, and subway service.
Academic Character NEASC and professional accreditation. Semester system. Terminal and transfer majors offered in business administration, accounting, business computer programming, business assistant, travel & tourism administration, fashion merchandising, interior design/retailing, executive secretarial, legal secretarial, medical secretarial, medical assistant (pediatric speciality option), social service/child development, and liberal arts. 8-month secretarial certificate program. Distributive requirements. Coed continuing education. A-V and information processing facilities. Library.
Financial CEEB CSS. College and state scholarships, payment plan; PELL, SEOG, NDSL, GSL, PLUS, CWS. Priority application deadline February 15.
Admissions High school graduation or GED required. Interview recommended. SAT suggested. No application fee. Rolling admissions. *Early Admission* and *Early Decision* programs. Admission deferral possible. Transfers accepted. Advanced placement credit possible. Non-high school graduates may be accepted; they must receive their h.s. diploma before college graduation.
Student Life Student government. Magazine, yearbook. Drama and music groups. Professional, academic, special interest, service groups. Cultural, social, and athletic activities. College-sponsored spring tour. 6 women's dorms. Over 50% of students live on campus.

[1] FITCHBURG STATE COLLEGE
Fitchburg 01420, (617) 345-2151, ext. 3144
Director of Admissions: Joseph A. Angelini

- **Undergraduates: 1,454m, 2,294w; 6,609 total (including graduates)**
- **Tuition (1982/83): $850 (in-state), $2,792 (out-of-state)**
- **Room & Board: $1,718-$2,048; Fees: $246**
- **Degrees offered: BA, BS, BSEd, BSN, AS**
- **Mean SAT 440v, 465m**
- **Student-faculty ratio: 16 to 1**

A public college established in 1894. 92-acre campus in a small city 55 miles west of Boston. College owns 120 acres of conservation land nearby. Bus to Worcester and Boston.
Academic Character NEASC and professional accreditation. Semester system, 6-week summer term. Majors offered in biology, business administration, chemistry, communications/media, computer science, early childhood education, elementary education, English, geography, history, human services, industrial arts, industrial science, math, medical technology, nursing, psychology, secondary education, sociology, special education, special needs teacher for young children. Distributive requirements. Masters degrees granted. Independent study, honors program, field work, internships. Cross-registration with other Mass state schools. Elementary, secondary, and special education certification. ROTC. Continuing education, evening division. Campus school. Computer center, language lab. Art gallery. 170,000-volume library.
Financial CEEB CSS. College scholarships, tuition waivers, state scholarships; PELL, SEOG, NSS, NDSL, GSL, NSL, CWS. Application deadline April 15.
Admissions High school graduation (or equivalent) with 16 units required. Interview recommended. SAT required; ACH recommended. $18 (in-state), $25 (out-of-state) application fees. Rolling admissions; deadline March 1. $50 tuition and $50 room deposits required on acceptance of admissions offer. Transfers accepted. Credit possible for CEEB AP and CLEP exams. Alternatives for Individual Development Program for economically/academically disadvantaged students.
Student Life Student government. Newspaper, literary magazine, yearbook. Several music groups. Theatre and debate clubs. Hiking Club. Academic, athletic, religious, special interest, and service groups. One fraternity. 1% of men join. Coed and single-sex dorms. Apartments. No married-student housing. 30% of students live on campus. Boarders may not drive cars on campus. One semester of phys ed required. 8 intercollegiate sports for men, 6 for women; intramurals. AIAW, ECAC, NCAA, Mass State College Athletic Conference. Student body composition: 4% Black, 1% Hispanic, 94% White, 1% Other. 1% from out of state.

[1] FRAMINGHAM STATE COLLEGE
Framingham 01701, (617) 620-1220
Director of Admissions: Philip M. Dooher

- **Undergraduates: 1,031m, 2,094w**
- **Tuition (1982/83): $845 (in-state), $2,792 (out-of-state)**
- **Room & Board: $1,585-$1,785; Fees: $280**
- **Degrees offered: BA, BS, BSEd**
- **Mean SAT 423v, 455m**
- **Student-faculty ratio: 19 to 1**

A public college established in 1839, became coed in 1964. 71-acre suburban campus 20 miles west of Boston. Rail and bus to Boston.
Academic Character NEASC and professional accreditation. Semester system, 6-week summer term. Majors offered in art (history, studio), biology, chemistry, clothing & textiles, computer science, dietetics, earth science, economics, education (early childhood, elementary), English, food & nutrition, food science, French, geography, history, home economics, mathematics, media/communications, medical technology, philosophy, political science, psychology, sociology, and Spanish. Self-designed liberal studies major. Minors in major fields and in 11 additional areas. Distributive requirements. Independent study, honors program, pass/fail, internships. Preprofessional program in medicine. 3-1 medical technology program with area hospitals. Cross-registration with other state schools. Study abroad. Elementary and secondary education certification. Language lab. 200,000-volume library.
Financial CEEB CSS. College scholarships, grants, loans, state grants; PELL, SEOG, NDSL, GSL, CWS, college work program. Application deadline April 15.
Admissions High school graduation with 16 units recommended. Special requirements for some majors; portfolio for art. SAT required; 3 ACH suggested. $18 application fee. Rolling admissions; suggest applying early in 12th year. Deadline March 1. *Early Entrance* Program. Admission deferral possible. Transfers accepted. Credit possible for CEEB AP and CLEP exams. Alternative for Individual Development program for economically/academically disadvantaged students.
Student Life Student government. Newspaper, arts magazine, yearbook, radio station. Music and drama groups. Academic, athletic, political, service,

and special interest clubs. Coed and women's dorms. 46% of students live on campus. 7 intercollegiate sports for men, 6 for women; intramurals. NCAA, ECAC, NEFC, MASCAC, AIAW. Student body composition: 1% Asian, 2% Black, 2% Hispanic, 1% Native American, 94% White. 3% from out of state.

[J1] FRANKLIN INSTITUTE OF BOSTON

41 Berkeley Street, Boston 02116, (617) 423-4635

- **Undergraduates: 500m, 50w**
- **Tuition (1982/83): $3,950**
- **Room & Board: $3,520; Fees: $50-$200**
- **Degree offered: AE**

A private institute of engineering and technology founded in 1908. Institute is affiliated with Boston University. Urban campus. Air, rail, bus, and subway service.
Academic Character NEASC and professional accreditation. Semester system. Majors offered in architectural, civil, computer, electrical, electronic, energy systems, mechanical, and medical electronics engineering technologies. Curriculum includes lab work and practical design applications. 2-year certificate program in automotive technology. 1-year certificate programs in architectural & structural drafting, computer service technology, electro-mechanical drafting, photography, and practical electricity. Transfer program with BU's College of Engineering. Cross-registration with BU's Metropolitan College. Access to BU library.
Financial CEEB CSS. Scholarships, grants, and loans available.
Admissions High school graduation with English, math, and science preparation recommended. SAT urged. Rolling admissions; no deadline. 1-year preparatory for engineering technology program for students with deficient preparation; completion prepares students for admission to degree program.
Student Life Dorm housing available at Boston University.

[1] GORDON COLLEGE

Wenham 01984, (617) 927-2300
Dean of Admissions: Ted Rodgers

- **Undergraduates: 435m, 588w; 1,060 total (including graduates)**
- **Tuition (1982/83): $5,010**
- **Room & Board: $2,349; Fees: $237**
- **Degrees offered: AB, BS, BMus, BMus Ed**
- **Mean SAT 486v, 502m**
- **Student-faculty ratio: 20 to 1**

A private, evangelical, non-denominational Protestant college established in 1889. 800-acre suburban campus 25 miles north of Boston. Rail to Boston.
Academic Character NEASC and professional accreditation. Trimester system. Majors offered in Bible, biology, business administration, chemistry, computer science, economics, education (early childhood, elementary, middle school, music, physical), English, foreign language-linguistics, history, mathematics, music, philosophy, physics, political science, psychology, and sociology. American studies, urban studies, social services programs. 3 Bible courses required for graduation. Honors exams in some majors. Independent study, honors program, pass/fail, cooperative work/study, internships. Urban internship program with Westmont College (CA). Preprofessional programs in engineering, law, medicine. Member of Christian College Consortium and Northeast Consortium of Colleges and Universities. American studies program in Washington, urban studies program in San Francisco. Summer study abroad. Elementary and secondary education certification. Language lab. Computer & media centers. 152,000-volume library.
Financial CEEB CSS. College scholarships, grants, loans, payment plan; PELL, SEOG, NDSL, GSL, CWS. File FAF by February 15. Application deadline March 15.
Admissions High school graduation with 15 units required. Interview required. Audition required for music majors. SAT or ACT required. $25 application fee. Rolling admissions; suggest applying before January 1. $150 deposit required on acceptance of admissions offer (May 1). *Early Entrance, Early Decision, Immediate Decision* programs. Admission deferral possible. Transfers accepted. Credit possible for CEEB AP and CLEP exams.
Student Life Student government. Newspaper, arts magazine, yearbook. Music and drama groups. Honorary, political, religious, service, and special interest clubs. Students must live at home or on campus. Coed & single-sex dorms. Special interest housing. No married-student housing. 80% of students live on campus. Liquor, drugs, smoking, social dancing prohibited on campus. Chapel attendance required 3 times a week. 6 terms of phys ed required. 5 intercollegiate sports for men, 5 for women; intramurals. NAIA, AIAW, Seaboard Conference. Student body composition: 3% Black, 1% Hispanic, 95% White, 1% Other. 63% from out of state.

[R] GORDON-CONWELL THEOLOGICAL SEMINARY

South Hamilton 01982

[J1] GREENFIELD COMMUNITY COLLEGE

1 College Drive, Greenfield 01301

[1] HAMPSHIRE COLLEGE

Amherst 01002, (413) 549-4600
Director of Admissions: Robert L. deVeer

- **Undergraduates: 558m, 682w**
- **Tuition (1982/83): $8,495**
- **Room & Board: $2,595; Fees: $300**
- **Degree offered: BA**
- **Mean SAT 565v, 550m**
- **Student-faculty ratio: 13 to 1**

A private college established in 1969. 550-acre rural campus 90 miles west of Boston. Bus to Springfield.
Academic Character NEASC accreditation. 4-1-4 system. 15 areas of concentration are offered by the School of Humanities & Arts, 12 by Language & Communications, 13 by Natural Science, and 8 by Social Science. All majors are self-designed; several interdisciplinary programs are possible. Students must pass one exam in each school at the Basic Studies level, one exam in the concentration, and one in advanced study. Students direct their own study, help fashion their own exams, and are graded by written personal evaluations. They learn through courses, independent reading & study, and field study. 5-College Consortium allows cross-registration with Amherst, Mount Holyoke, Smith, and UMass. Study abroad. Elementary and secondary education certification. ROTC & AFROTC at UMass (Amherst). Arts village, computer. 65,000-volume library plus access to 5-College libraries.
Financial CEEB CSS. College scholarships, grants, loans, payment plan; PELL, SEOG, NDSL, GSL, PLUS, CWS. Application deadline February 15.
Admissions High school graduation required; college prep program recommended. Interview strongly recommended. SAT or ACT accepted. $30 application fee. Application deadline February 15. $200 deposit required on acceptance of admissions offer (May 1). *Early Entrance, Early Decision, Early Action* programs. Admission deferral possible. Transfers accepted. Credit possible for CEEB AP and college exams.
Student Life Student government. Newspaper, arts magazine, radio. Third World group. Women's Center. Coed & single-sex dorms and houses. Student apartments. No married-student housing. 95% of students live on campus. Outdoor Program, several intramural sports. Student body composition: 2% Asian, 4% Black, 2% Hispanic, 92% White. 87% from out of state.

[1] HARVARD AND RADCLIFFE COLLEGES

Cambridge 02138, (617) 495-1551
Acting Director of Admissions: William R. Fitzsimmons

- **Undergraduates: 4,062m, 2,432w; 15,611 total (including graduates)**
- **Tuition (1982/83): $8,195**
- **Room & Board: $3,280; Fees: $625**
- **Degree offered: AB, SB**
- **Student-faculty ratio: 10 to 1**

A private university established in 1636. Radcliffe, an affiliated, independent women's college, was founded in 1879. Classes became coed in 1943. Facilities, organizations, most athletics, and housing are coed. Urban campus across the Charles River from Boston. Air, rail, bus, and subway service.
Academic Character NEASC and professional accreditation. Semester system, 6- and 8-week summer terms. Majors offered in over 60 areas including Afro-American studies, anthropology, archaeology, astronomy, classics, East Asian studies, economics, engineering, environmental sciences, fine arts, folklore & mythology, languages & literatures, linguistics, math, philosophy & religion, Portuguese-Brazilian, Sanskrit & Indian Studies, sciences, Slavic languages & literatures, social sciences, statistics, and visual & environmental studies. Self-designed and interdepartmental majors. 10 graduate schools offer numerous graduate & professional degrees. Independent study, Phi Beta Kappa. Tutorial method of instruction. Study abroad. AFROTC, NROTC, ROTC at MIT. Many research centers, museums, and other facilities. Extension and summer schools. Language labs, computer. Over 10,260,571-volume library with microform resources.
Financial CEEB CSS. College scholarships, loans, payment plan; PELL, SEOG, NDSL, GSL, CWS. Application deadlines January 1 (scholarships), September 1 (loans).
Admissions Applicants chosen by a joint Harvard/Radcliffe Admissions Committee. High school graduation with 16 units recommended. Interview required; local alumni interviews possible. SAT and 3 ACH required. $30 application fee. Suggest applying by November 15 of 12th year. Deadline January 1. Notification in mid-April; candidate must accept offer by May 1. *Early Action* Program. Admission defferal possible. Transfers accepted. Credit possible for CEEB AP, CLEP, and university exams. Admission program for students without a high school diploma.
Student Life Newspapers, magazines, yearbook, radio station. Many music and drama groups. Debate. Special interest, social, athletic, academic, political, religious, and service clubs. Freshmen live at home or in coed dorms. Upperclass students live in Houses with their own libraries, dining, social, cultural, and athletic facilities. Cooperative and married-student housing. 92% of students live on campus. 19 intercollegiate sports for men, 15 for women; intramural & club sports. ECAC, Ivy League. Student body composition: 16% minority. 80% of students from out of state.

[1] HEBREW COLLEGE

43 Hawes Street, Brookline 02146

[1] HELLENIC COLLEGE

50 Goddard Avenue, Brookline 02146

[1] HOLY CROSS, COLLEGE OF THE

Worcester 01610, (617) 793-2443
Director of Admissions: James R. Halpin

- **Enrollment: 1,312m, 1,182w**
- **Tuition (1982/83): $6,200**
- **Room & Board: $3,000; Fees: $140**
- **Degree offered: AB**
- **Mean SAT 560v, 580m**
- **Student-faculty ratio: 14 to 1**

A private Jesuit college founded in 1843, became coed in 1972. 174-acre urban campus, 40 miles west of Boston. Air, rail, and bus service.

Academic Character NEASC accreditation. Semester system. Majors offered in biology, chemistry, classics, economics, economics-accounting, English, European literature studies, French, German, history, math, music, philosophy, physics, political science, psychology, religious studies, Russian, Russian studies, sociology, Spanish, and visual arts. Self-designed and interdisciplinary majors. Courses in 4 additional areas. MS granted. Independent study, honors programs, Phi Beta Kappa, pass/fail, internships. Preprofessional programs in dentistry, law, medicine. 3-2 dual degree program in engineering with Worcester Polytechnic Institute. Worcester Consortium for Higher Education provides extensive cross-registration opportunities and cooperative gerontology studies program. Washington Semester. Study abroad. AFROTC & NROTC; ROTC at WPI. Institute of Industrial Relations. Computer. 390,000-volume library.
Financial CEEB CSS. College scholarships, grants, loans, payment plan; PELL, SEOG, NDSL, FISL, CWS. Application deadline February 1.
Admissions High school graduation with at least 14 units recommended. SAT and 3 ACH required. $25 application fee. Suggest applying by December 1. Deadline February 1. $200 deposit required on acceptance of admissions offer (May 1). *Early Decision* and *Early Entrance* programs. Admission deferral possible. Transfers accepted. Credit possible for CEEB AP exams.
Student Life Student government. Newspapers, literary magazine, yearbook, radio station. Several music, drama, debate groups. Black Student Union. Athletic, professional, religious, service, and special interest clubs. Coed dorms. No married-student housing. 80% of students live on campus. No cars for resident freshmen & sophomores. 17 intercollegiate sports for men, 7 for women; several intramurals. AIAW, ECAC, NCAA, NECAC. Student body composition: 95% White, 5% Other. 52% from out of state.

[G2] HOLY CROSS GREEK ORTHODOX SCHOOL OF THEOLOGY
Brookline — see Hellenic College

[J1] HOLYOKE COMMUNITY COLLEGE
303 Homestead Avenue, Holyoke 01040

[1] JACKSON COLLEGE FOR WOMEN
Medford — see Tufts University

[P] KATHARINE GIBBS SCHOOL
21 Marlborough Street, Boston 02116

[J1] LABOURE JUNIOR COLLEGE
2120 Dorchester Avenue, Boston 02124, (617) 296-8300, ext. 4016
Director of Admissions: Elizabeth Fleming

- **Enrollment: 33m, 302w; 586 total (including part-time)**
- **Tuition (1982/83): $100 per credit**
- **Room: $1,800; Fees: $275**
- **Degree offered: AS**
- **Student-faculty ratio: 12 to 1**

A private, Roman Catholic junior college of nursing and allied health, opened in 1972 under the auspices of the Daughters of Charity of St. Vincent de Paul. Urban campus. Air, rail, bus, and subway service.
Academic Character NEASC and professional accreditation. Flexible system of 15-week semesters and 6- or 7-week modules. Summer term. Associate of Science degrees offered in dietetic technology, electroencephalographic technology, medical record technology, nursing, radiation therapy technology, and respiratory therapy. Distributive requirements. Independent study. Learning Activity Packages in nursing and dietetics programs allows students to learn at their own level of understanding. Clinical experience available through affiliation with Carney Hospital and 27 other Boston-area institutions. Evening and other part-time programs. Over 10,000- volume library with audiovisual resources.
Financial CEEB CSS. College and state scholarships, PELL, SEOG, GSL, work program. File FAF by March 1.
Admissions High school graduation or equivalent required. College prep program recommended. Interview recommended; required for radiation therapy program. $20 application fee. Rolling admissions. $100 deposit required on acceptance of admissions offer; $100 room deposit required in mid-May. Credit possible for prior learning and for work experience.
Student Life Student government. Yearbook. Cultural, social, and religious activities. Limited dorm space for women only. Dining facilities next door at Carney Hospital. Average age of Laboure students is 29.

[J1] LASELL JUNIOR COLLEGE
1844 Commonwealth Avenue, Newton 02166, (617) 243-2225

- **Undergraduates: 2m, 585w; 650 total (including part-time)**
- **Tuition (1981/82): $4,695**
- **Room & Board: $2,873; Fees: $220-$260**
- **Degree offered: AA, AS**

A private junior college for women with a coed nursing program, founded in 1851. 60-acre suburban campus located along the Charles River in the Auburndale section of Newton, 8 miles west of Boston. Nearby subway to Boston, airport, rail and bus stations.
Academic Character NEASC and professional accreditation. Semester system, summer term. Majors offered in nursing, physical therapy assistant, medical laboratory assistant, medical assistant, human services (recreation leadership, mental retardation, general), business management, retailing-merchandising, accounting, computer science, executive secretarial, legal secretarial, administrative assistant, medical secretarial, open studies, liberal arts, early childhood education, and art (fashion design, interior design, fine arts, advertising design, and jewelry, ceramics, & photography). Internships. Clinical experience through affiliations with area hospitals. Model nursery school. Language lab. Over 55,000-volume library with microform resources.
Financial CEEB CSS. College and state scholarships; PELL, SEOG, NSS, NDSL, NSL, GSL, CWS. File FAF by February 15 for Mass state scholarships.
Admissions High school graduation or equivalent required. Specific course requirements for some programs. Interview urged; required for nursing majors. SAT usually required. $20 application fee. Rolling admissions. $100 tuition and $100 room deposits required on acceptance of admissions offer. *Early Admission* and *Early Decision* programs. Admission deferral possible.
Student Life Student government. Newspaper. Music, dance, and drama clubs. Outing Club. International, professional, and special interest clubs. Athletic, cultural, and social activities. Single students must live at home or on campus, unless they are financially independent. Dorms for women. 80% of students live on campus. One year of phys ed required. 4 intercollegiate sports for women.

[1] LESLEY COLLEGE
29 Everett Street, Cambridge 02238, (617) 868-9600
Director of Admissions: Martha B. Ackerson

- **Undergraduates: 625w; 2,100 total (including graduates)**
- **Tuition (1982/83): $5,400**
- **Room & Board: $3,405; Fees: $40**
- **Degrees offered: BS, BSEd, AAS**
- **Mean SAT 400v, 420m**
- **Student-faculty ratio: 18 to 1**

A private women's teacher-training college established in 1909. 7-acre urban campus adjacent to Harvard University, 3 miles from downtown Boston. Subway to Boston, airport, rail and bus stations.
Academic Character NEASC accreditation. Semester system, 6-week summer term for graduate students. Majors offered for a BS in child & community, or a BSEd in education with an early childhood, elementary, or middle school concentration and optional specializations in day care/preschool, economics, mathematics resource personnel, multicultural teaching, reading, moderate special, and special education. Minor required. Minors in art, computer science, environmental studies, literature, guidance, history, mathematics, music, psychology, social science. Distributive requirements. Graduate degrees granted in education. AAS & BS offered through continuing education division. Independent study, honors program, pass/fail. All students work with children as part of their major. Exchange with U of Arizona (Tucson). Washington Semester. Study abroad. Exchange with Bradford and Hull Colleges in England. 76,000-volume library.
Financial CEEB CSS. College scholarships, grants, state scholarships, payment plan; PELL, SEOG, NDSL, GSL, PLUS, ALAS, CWS, college work program. Application deadline March 1.
Admissions High school graduation with 15 units required. Interview required. SAT required. $25 application fee. Rolling admissions; suggest applying by December of 12th year. Deadline March 15. $100 tuition and $100 room deposits required on acceptance of admissions offer (May 1). Admission deferral possible. Transfers accepted. Credit possible for CEEB AP and CLEP exams.
Student Life Student government. Newspaper, literary magazine, yearbook. Music, dance, drama, film groups. Professional, religious, service, and special interest clubs. Students under 21 must live at home or on campus. Special-interest housing. No coed dorms or married-student housing. 81% of students live on campus. Cars discouraged. 3 hours of phys ed required. Intercollegiate soccer & softball; intramurals. Student body composition: 0.6% Asian, 6% Black, 1.4% Hispanic, 91% White, 1% Other. 45% from out of state.

[1] LOWELL, UNIVERSITY OF
Lowell 01854, (617) 452-5000, ext. 2214
Director of Admissions: Lawrence R. Martin, Jr.

- **Undergraduates: 5,556m, 3,231w; 9,723 total (including graduates)**
- **Tuition (1982/83): $986 (in-state), $3,242 (out-of-state)**
- **Room & Board: $2,144; Fees: $193**
- **Degrees offered: BA, BS, BFA, BMus, BMus Ed**
- **Mean SAT 476v, 544m**
- **Student-faculty ratio: 16 to 1**

A public university established by the merger of Lowell State College and Lowell Technological Institute in 1974. 100-acre urban campus on both sides of the Merrimac River, 25 miles northwest of Boston. Bus to Boston, which has air, rail, and bus service.
Academic Character NEASC and professional accreditation. Semester system, 2 6-week summer terms. Over 35 majors offered in the areas of American studies, art, biology, business, chemistry, computer science, earth science, engineering, English, environmental science, health, industrial management & technology, math, medical technology, meterology, modern languages, nursing, philosophy, physical therapy, physics, political science, psychology, radiological health, and sociology. Distributive requirements. Graduate degrees granted. Independent study, pass/fail. 5-year cooperative work/study in several majors. Preprofessional programs in dentistry, engineering, medicine, technology. 3-2 liberal arts & engineering program. Consortium with NECCUM. AFROTC. Language lab, computers, media & A-V centers. 320,000-volume library.
Financial CEEB CSS. University, state, AFROTC scholarships; PELL, SEOG, NSS, NDSL, NSL, GSL, CWS. Application deadline April 1.
Admissions High school graduation required; 16 units recommended with requirements for specific majors. GED accepted. Music test required for music majors; portfolio for art majors. Interview and SAT required. $10 (in-state), $25 (out-of-state) application fees. Rolling admissions; suggest applying after 1st marking period in 12th year. Deadline April 1. $50 tuition and $50 room deposits required on acceptance of admissions offer. *Early Admission*

Program. Admission deferral possible. Transfers accepted. Credit possible for CEEB AP and CLEP exams. University placement exams. AID program, Educational Opportunity Program. Second Chance program for adults.
Student Life Student government. Newspaper, yearbook, radio station. Music, art, drama groups. PIRG. Academic, ethnic, honorary, literary, political, professional, religious, service, and special interest clubs. 7 fraternities with houses and 5 sororities without houses. Dorms. Married-student housing for graduate students. 22% of students live on campus. Liquor prohibited. 1 year of phys ed required. Over 20 intercollegiate sports for men & women; intramurals. Student body composition: 1.9% Asian, 0.6% Black, 0.6% Hispanic, 0.1% Native American, 95.6% White, 1.2% Other. 7% from out of state.

[1] LOWELL TECHNOLOGICAL INSTITUTE
Lowell — see University of Lowell

[J2] MARIAN COURT JUNIOR COLLEGE OF BUSINESS
35 Littles Point Road, Swampscott 01907

[1] MASSACHUSETTS, UNIVERSITY OF (Amherst)
Amherst 01003, (413) 545-0222
Director of Freshman Admissions: David Taggart

- **Undergraduates: 9,901m, 9,048w; 24,243 total (including graduates)**
- **Tuition (1982/83): $1,150 (in-state), $4,150 (out-of-state)**
- **Room & Board: $1,154; Fees: $300**
- **Degrees offered: BA, BS, BFA, BMus, BSEng**
- **Mean SAT 470v, 513m**
- **Student-faculty ratio: 20 to 1**

Academic Character NEASC and professional accreditation. Semester system, 2 5-week summer terms. Over 100 majors offered by the colleges of Arts & Sciences and of Foods & Natural Resources, and by the schools of Business Administration, Education, Engineering, Health Sciences, and Physical Education. Double and self-designed majors. Interdisciplinary programs. Distributive requirements. Graduate and professional degrees granted. Independent study, honors program, Phi Beta Kappa, pass/fail, cooperative work/study, internships. 5-college cooperation with Smith, Mount Holyoke, Amherst, and Hampshire provides cross-registration and shared programs & facilities. Regional exchange with other New England state schools allows special programs at in-state tuition. National Student Exchange. Elementary and secondary education certification. ROTC, AFROTC; NROTC in Worcester. Child Guidance Center, Population Research Institute. Computer center, language lab. Over 3,000,000-volume library.
Financial CEEB CSS. University scholarships, tuition waivers, state scholarships; PELL, SEOG, NDSL, GSL, CWS. Application deadline March 15.
Admissions High school graduation with 16 units required. Specific requirements for some programs. Audition required for music and dance majors; portfolio for art majors. SAT required; 3 ACH recommended. $18 (in-state), $25 (out-of-state) application fees. Rolling admissions; application deadline March 1. $62 deposit required on acceptance of admissions offer (May 1). Early entrance for exceptional high school juniors possible. Admission deferral possible. Transfers accepted. Credit possible for CEEB AP and CLEP exams; placement for ACH and departmental exams. University Without Walls, Upward Bound, special programs for minority and low-income applicants.
Student Life Student government. Newspaper, magazines, yearbook, radio station. Several music groups. Theatre, debate clubs. Mass PIRG. Over 500 student organizations. 15 fraternities and 9 sororities with houses. 1 coed fraternity. 8% of men and 14% of women join. Single freshmen and sophomores, except veterans, must live on campus or at home. Coed and single-sex dorms. Special interest and some married-student housing. 57% of students live on campus. 15 intercollegiate sports for men, 14 for women; intramurals. ECAC, NCAA, Yankee Conference. Student body composition: 10-12% minority. 15% from out of state.

[1] MASSACHUSETTS, UNIVERSITY OF (Boston)
Boston 02125, (617) 287-1900
Director of Admissions: Ronald E. Ancrum

- **Enrollment: 6, 125m, 6,375w**
- **Tuition (1982/83): $1,129 (in-state), $3,686 (out-of-state)**
- **Fees: $150**
- **Degree offered: BA**
- **Mean SAT 440v, 480m**
- **Student-faculty ratio: 17 to 1**

A public university established in 1965, merged with Boston State College in 1982. New urban harbor campus which houses the John F. Kennedy Presidential Library and Museum. Air, rail, and bus service.
Academic Character NEASC accreditation. Semester system, 2 6-week summer terms. Majors offered include anthropology, art, biology, Black studies, chemistry, classics, computer science, economics, engineering, English, French, German, Greek, history, Italian, Latin, math, music, philosophy, physics, political science, psychology, regional studies, Russian, sociology, Spanish, theatre arts, accounting, criminal justice, elementary education, health services administration, human resource management, management information systems, management science, public management, marketing, medical technology, nursing, operations management, physical education, public/private financial management, and public policy analysis. Interdisciplinary programs. Masters degrees granted. Independent study, honors program, pass/fail, internships. Preprofessional programs in dentistry, medicine, law, veterinary medicine. 2-2 engineering program with UMass (Amherst). Semester program on Nantucket. Elementary and secondary education certification. AFROTC, ROTC at Northeastern. Evening division. Language lab. 350,000-volume library.
Financial CEEB CSS. University and state scholarships, PELL, SEOG, NDSL, GSL, CWS. Application deadline March 1.
Admissions High school graduation with 16 units required. GED accepted. SAT required. $18 (in-state), $25 (out-of-state) application fees. Rolling admissions; suggest applying in fall of 12th year. *Early Entrance* Program. Transfers accepted. Credit possible for CEEB AP, CLEP, and departmental exams. Developmental studies program for economically and academically disadvantaged students.
Student Life Student government. Newspaper, literary magazine, yearbook, radio station. Music, dance, drama groups. Mass PIRG. Afro-American Club, Club Ohray, Gay Pride. Academic, athletic, religious, honorary, special interest, political, and service groups. No university housing. 4 intercollegiate sports for men, 2 for women. Student body composition: 2% Asian, 9% Black, 3% Hispanic, 1% Native American, 85% White. 4% from out of state.

[J1] MASSACHUSETTS BAY COMMUNITY COLLEGE
50 Oakland Street, Wellesley 02181

[1] MASSACHUSETTS COLLEGE OF ART
Boston 02215, (617) 731-2340
Director of Admissions: Kay Ransdell

- **Undergraduates: 468m, 572w; 1,100 total (including graduates)**
- **Tuition (1982/83): $845 (in-state), $2,750 (out-of-state)**
- **Fees: $250**
- **Degree offered: BFA**
- **Mean SAT 440v, 420m**
- **Student-faculty ratio: 16 to 1**

A public college founded in 1873. Urban campus in Boston, near Fenway park. Air, rail, and bus service.
Academic Character NEASC and professional accreditation. Semester system, summer terms. Majors offered in architectural design, art education, art history, ceramics, fashion design, fibers, film, glass, graphic design, illustration, industrial design, metals, painting, photography, printmaking, sculpture, and studio interrelated media. Independent study, internships. Courses graded honors/pass/no credit. Consortia with East coast art schools provides cross-registration. Exchanges with Roxbury Community College, Elma Lewis School of Fine Arts, Boston Opera Company, Open Door Theatre, MIT, Wentworth Institute & College, School of the Museum of Fine Arts, and with the Ruskin School at Oxford, England. Elementary and secondary education certification. TV resource center, 60,000-slide & 180-film collections. 50,000-volume library.
Financial CEEB CSS. College scholarships, loans; PELL, SEOG, NDSL, GSL, CWS. Application deadline May 1.
Admissions High school graduation with strong college prep & art program preferred. GED accepted. Statement of purpose and portfolio required. SAT required. $18 (in-state), $25 (out-of-state) application fees; waiver possible. Rolling admissions; application deadlines February 1 for March notification, April 1 for May notification, June 1 for July notification. Admission deferral possible. Transfers accepted. Credit possible for CEEB AP and CLEP exams. Enrichment Program.
Student Life Student government. Academic-professional groups in art, art education, design, graphics, performance, photography, and sculpture & crafts. Black Artists' Union, Women's Group. Student housing available at nearby colleges. Liquor allowed only at registered events. Basketball, ice hockey for men. Greater Boston Small College Conference. Student body composition: 3% Asian, 4% Black, 1% Hispanic, 89% White, 3% Other. 15% from out of state.

[1] MASSACHUSETTS COLLEGE OF PHARMACY AND ALLIED HEALTH SCIENCES
179 Longwood Avenue, Boston 02115

[2] MASSACHUSETTS COLLEGE OF PHARMACY AND ALLIED HEALTH SCIENCES/HAMPDEN CAMPUS
24 Bellamy Road, Springfield 01119

[1] MASSACHUSETTS INSTITUTE OF TECHNOLOGY
Cambridge 02139, (617) 253-4791
Director of Admissions: Peter H. Richardson

- **Undergraduates: 3,550m, 950w; 9,000 total (including graduates)**
- **Tuition (1982/83): $8,700**
- **Room & Board: $3,550**
- **Degree offered: SB**
- **Mean SAT 630v, 725m**
- **Student-faculty ratio: 4 to 1**

A private institute founded in 1861. 130-acre urban campus across the Charles River from Boston. Subway and bus to Boston, airport, rail and bus stations.
Academic Character NEASC and professional accreditation. 4-1-4 system, 10-week summer term. 4 majors offered by the School of Architecture & Planning, 10 by the School of Engineering, 18 by the School of Humanities & Social Sciences, 4 by the School of Management, and 7 by the School of Science. Self-designed and interdepartmental majors. Distributive requirements. Graduate and professional degrees granted. Independent study, Phi Beta Kappa, cooperative work/study, internships. Freshmen graded pass/fail only. Preprofessional programs in law and medicine. Undergraduate research opportunities program encourages student-faculty research. 5-year BS/MS programs in aeronautics & astronautics, electrical engineering, mechanical engineering. Cross-registration with Wellesley College and Harvard. Programs with Harvard and Woods Hole Oceanographic Institute.

Study abroad. Elementary and secondary education certification. AFROTC, NROTC, ROTC. Numerous research labs, nuclear reactor, computer center. Over 1,750,000-volume library.
Financial CEEB CSS. Institute scholarships, grants, loans, payment plan; PELL, SEOG, NDSL, GSL, CWS, institutional work program. Application deadline January 1.
Admissions High school graduation with math & science background required. Interview required. SAT and 3 ACH required. $30 application fee. Application deadline January 1. *Early Action* and *Early Entrance* programs. Admission deferral possible. Transfers accepted. Credit possible for CEEB AP exams. University has own advanced standing exams.
Student Life Student government. Newspapers, magazines, yearbook, radio stations. Music, drama, debate groups. Outing Club. Academic, athletic, political, professional, religious, service, social, and special interest clubs. 35 fraternities (4 coed). 40% of students join. Freshmen must live at home, on campus, or in fraternities. Coed, single-sex, language, cooperative, married-student, and special interest housing. 85% of students live on campus or in fraternities. 8 points of phys ed required. 20 intercollegiate sports for men, 12 for women; numerous intramurals. AIAW, ECAC, NCAA, NECAC. Student body composition: 3.1% Asian, 3.6% Black, 19.2% Foreign, 1.5% Hispanic, 0.2% Native American, 72.4% White. 89% from out of state.

[1] MASSACHUSETTS MARITIME ACADEMY
Buzzards Bay 02532, (617) 759-5761
Director of Admissions: William F. Shanahan

- **Undergraduates: 801m, 49w**
- **Expenses (1982/83): $5,400**
- **Degree offered: BS**
- **Mean SAT 470v, 530m**
- **Student-faculty ratio: 16 to 1**

A public service academy preparing men and women to become officers in the Merchant Marine. 12-acre campus on a peninsula adjacent to Cape Cod at the western tip of the Canal, 60 miles from Boston. Rail and bus service; airport in Hyannis.
Academic Character NEASC accreditation. Semester system, required summer sea term. BS offered with majors in marine engineering and marine transportation. Courses offered in naval science which qualify students for the Naval Reserve. Students must apply for and accept (if offered) a commission as Ensign in the Naval Reserve. US Coast Guard exam for Merchant Marine Officers' license and minimum of 180 days of sea-time training required for graduation. Academy prepares students to become Third Assistant Engineers or Third Mates in the USMM. Computer, TV studio. 65,000-volume library with microform resources.
Financial CEEB CSS. Academy and state scholarships, federal grants; PELL, SEOG, NDSL, GSL, CWS, academy work program. Application deadline May 1.
Admissions High school graduation with 16 units required. GED accepted. Interview recommended. Applicant must be US citizen or non-immigrant alien, and must pass a USCG physical. SAT required. $18 application fee. Rolling admissions; suggest applying by January. Deadline March 1. $100 deposit required on acceptance of admissions offer. *Early Admission* Program. Some transfers accepted. Credit possible for CEEB AP and CLEP exams.
Student Life Student government. Yearbook, drama, several music groups. Cadet Corps. Circle K. Athletic, religious, and special interest groups. Students must live on campus. Coed and single-sex dorms. No married-student housing. Alcohol prohibited on campus. Military discipline. Uniforms and class attendance required. 4 semesters of phys ed required for graduation. 8 intercollegiate sports for men, 2 for women; numerous intramurals. ECAC, NCAA, Colonial Intercollegiate Lacrosse, New England Football, and Mass State College Athletic Conferences. Student body composition: 1.6% minority. 10% of students from out of state.

[2] MASSACHUSETTS SCHOOL OF PROFESSIONAL PSYCHOLOGY
785 Centre Street, Newton 02158

[J1] MASSASOIT COMMUNITY COLLEGE
1 Massasoit Blvd., Brocton 02402

[1] MERRIMACK COLLEGE
North Andover 01845, (617) 683-7111, ext. 121
Dean of Admissions: E. Joseph Lee

- **Undergraduates: 1,238m, 967w**
- **Tuition (1982/83): $4,750**
- **Room & Board: $3,000; Fees: $100**
- **Degrees offered: BA, BS**
- **Mean SAT 492v, 516m**
- **Student-faculty ratio: 16 to 1**

A private Roman Catholic college established in 1947, conducted by the Order of St. Augustine. 220-acre rural suburban campus 25 miles north of Boston. Bus to Lawrence and Boston.
Academic Character NEASC and professional accreditation. Semester system, 2 5-week summer terms. Majors offered in accounting, American studies, biology, business/economics, chemistry, civil engineering, computer science, economics, electrical engineering, English, finance, health science, history, management, marketing, mathematics, philosophy, physics, political science, psychology, religious studies, secondary education, and sociology. Interdepartmental, double, and self-designed majors. Courses in 5 additional areas. Distributives and 6 semesters of religion/philosophy required. Division of Continuing Education offers Bachelor's and Associate's degrees. Independent study, pass/fail, internships. 5-year cooperative work/study programs in engineering, computer science, and business. Preprofessional programs in dentistry, law, medicine. 3-1 program in medical technology. Member Northeast Consortium of Colleges and Universities in Massachusetts. Study abroad. Secondary education certification. Computer, language lab. 91,300-volume library.
Financial CEEB CSS. College & state scholarships, 2nd-family-member discount; PELL, SEOG, NDSL, GSL, CWS. File FAF to arrive at Merrimack by March 1.
Admissions High school graduation with 16 units required. SAT or ACT required; 3 ACH suggested. $20 application fee. Rolling admissions. Deadlines: January 15 (scholarship applicants), February 15 (boarders), June 30 (commuters). $100 deposit and $35 fee required on acceptance of admissions offer (May 1). *Early Decision* and *Early Admission* programs. Admission deferral possible. Transfers accepted. Credit possible for CEEB AP exams. Special minority admission program.
Student Life Student Council. Newspaper, literary magazine, yearbook. Music, film, drama groups. Academic, honorary, religious, service, and special interest groups. 5 fraternities and 1 sorority without houses. 50% of men join fraternities. Students must live at home or on campus. Coed and single-sex dorms. No married-student housing. 50% of students live on campus. 7 intercollegiate sports for men, 4 for women, and coed skiing; several intramurals. AIAW, ECAC, NCAA, New England College Athletic Conference. Student body composition: 1% Black, 1% Hispanic, 98% White. 30% from out of state.

[J1] MIDDLESEX COMMUNITY COLLEGE
Springs Road, Bedford 01730

[1] MOUNT HOLYOKE COLLEGE
South Hadley 01075, (617) 538-2000
Director of Admissions: Susan P. Staggers

- **Undergraduates: 1,903w; 1,948 total (including graduates)**
- **Tuition (1982/83): $7,750**
- **Room & Board: $2,950; Fees: $84**
- **Degree offered: AB**
- **Mean SAT 590v, 570m**
- **Student-faculty ratio: 11 to 1**

A private women's college founded in 1837. 800-acre campus in a rural residential area, 90 miles from Boston. Bus service, airport and rail station nearby.
Academic Character NEASC accreditation. 4-1-4 system. Majors offered in anthropology, art (2), astronomy, biological sciences, Black studies, chemistry, classics, dance, economics, English (3), French, geography, geology, German, Greek, history, Italian, Latin, mathematics, music (2), philosophy, physics, politics, psychology, religion, Russian, sociology, Spanish, and theatre arts. Interdisciplinary majors in biochemistry, international relations, psychobiology, psychology & education, Romance languages & literature, and American, Asian, Latin American, medieval, urban, and women's studies. Special majors. Courses include computer science, education. Distributives and 2 interims required. Graduate degrees granted. Independent study, honors program, Phi Beta Kappa, pass/fail, internships. 5-college cooperation provides cross-registration with Amherst, Hampshire, Smith, and U of Mass. 12-college exchange for a year at Amherst, Bowdoin, Connecticut, Dartmouth, Mount Holyoke, Trinity, Vassar, Wellesley, Wesleyan, Wheaton, Williams. Study abroad in Europe, India, Japan, the Philippines. Elementary and secondary education certification. AFROTC & ROTC at UMass. Child study, A-V centers. 471,734-volume library.
Financial CEEB CSS. College scholarships, grants, state grants, loans, payment plan; PELL, SEOG, NDSL, FISL, GSL, PLUS, CWS. Application deadline February 1 (November 15 for Early Decision).
Admissions High school graduation with solid college prep work recommended. Interview expected for those within 200 miles; urged for others. SAT and 3 ACH required. $25 application fee. Suggest applying early in 12th year. Deadline February 1. $300 deposit required on acceptance of admissions offer (May 1). *Early Decision, Early Evaluation, Early Entrance* programs. Admission deferral possible. Transfers accepted. Credit possible for CEEB AP exams; departments give placement exams.
Student Life Student government. Newspaper, literary magazine, yearbook, radio station. Several music groups. Academic, ethnic, political, religious, service, and special interest clubs. Students must live at home or on campus. Women's dorms, international residence hall. 95% live on campus. Honor code. 1½ years of phys ed required. 11 intercollegiate sports; intramurals. NCAA. Student body composition: 4% Asian, 4% Black, 4% Foreign, 2% Hispanic, 86% White. 79% from out of state.

[J1 & 1] MOUNT IDA COLLEGE
777 Dedham Street, Newton Centre 02159, (617) 969-7000
Director of Admissions: Kenneth C. Barone

- **Undergraduates: 40m, 765w**
- **Tuition (1982/83): $4,290**
- **Room & Board: $3,130; Fees: $95-$150**
- **Degrees offered: AA, AS**
- **Mean SAT 420v, 410m**
- **Student-faculty ratio: 13 to 1**

A private junior college primarily for women, founded in 1899. Senior college division opened in 1982. 85-acre suburban campus set on a former estate, 11 miles from Boston. Subway service nearby to Boston, airport, rail and bus stations.
Academic Character NEASC and professional accreditation. 4-2-4

system. Transfer and career majors offered in fine arts, fashion design, fashion illustration, fashion merchandising, graphic design, interior design, business administration, accounting, executive secretarial, legal secretarial, travel & tourism, education, communication, human services, child study, individualized studies, liberal arts, paralegal studies, dental assistant/office management, medical assistant, science, medical technology, environmental services, biological & chemical technology, selected science, and veterinary technician. Externships.
Financial CEEB CSS. College scholarships, grants, athletic scholarships, state grants, payment plans; PELL, SEOG, NDSL, GSL, CWS.
Admissions Open admission for high school graduates until programs are filled. College prep program and SAT or ACT required for admission to transfer programs. SAT or ACT recommended for others. Interview recommended. $25 application fee. $100 tuition and $250 room deposits required on acceptance of admissions offer. *Early Admissions* Program. Transfers accepted. Credit possible for CEEB CLEP exams.
Student Life Student government. Cultural, social, outdoor, and community service activities. 4 women's dorms. Cooperative program in surrounding communities provides housing in exchange for light housekeeping & child care. 2 leisure skills (phys ed) credits required. 4 intercollegiate sports for women; intramural & recreational sports. NJCAA.

[J1] MOUNT WACHUSETT COMMUNITY COLLEGE
Green Street, Gardner 01440

[P] MUSEUM OF FINE ARTS, SCHOOL OF THE
Boston 02115

[1] NEW ENGLAND COLLEGE OF OPTOMETRY
424 Beacon Street, Boston 02115

[1] NEW ENGLAND CONSERVATORY OF MUSIC
290 Huntington Avenue, Boston 02115, (617) 262-1120
Director of Admissions: Lawrence Eric Murphy

- **Undergraduates: 252m, 177w**
- **Tuition (1982/83): $6,250**
- **Room & Board: $3,425-$3,975; Fees: $225**
- **Degree offered: BMus**
- **Mean SAT 512v, 524m**
- **Student-faculty ratio: 10 to 1**

A private college of music established in 1867. Urban campus in downtown Boston. Air, rail, and bus service.
Academic Character NEASC and professional accreditation. Semester system, 6-week summer term. Majors offered in composition, jazz studies, music education (2), music history, theoretical studies, third stream studies, and performance in 30 areas including early music (3), guitar, orchestral instruments, organ, piano, and voice. 5-year double majors in performance with composition, music education, or music theory. Courses include economics, English, film, French, German, Italian, political science, psychology. Distributives, participation in ensembles, and annual promotional audition required. Recital or comprehensive exam required for graduation. 3-year diploma programs in orchestral instruments, organ, piano, voice. Masters degrees granted. Independent study. 5-year BA/BMus or BS/BMus program with Tufts. Cross-registration with Simmons and Tufts. Secondary education certification. Studios, concert halls, rare instrument collection. 50,000-volume and 15,000-recording library.
Financial CEEB CSS. College scholarships, loans, payment plan; PELL, SEOG, NDSL, GSL, ALAS, CWS. Application deadline February 15.
Admissions High school graduation with 16 units recommended. GED accepted. Audition and SAT required. Composition applicants must submit several original compositions. $35 application fee. Suggest applying by January 1. Deadline February 15. $200 tuition and $100 refundable room deposits required on acceptance of admissions offer. *Early Admission* Program. Transfers accepted. Credit possible for CEEB AP and college exams.
Student Life Student government. Music groups include choir, choruses, ensembles, bands, orchestras, opera. Ethnic, international, religious, and special interest groups. Freshmen must live at home or on campus. Coed dorms. No married-student housing. 22% of students live on campus. Student body composition: 2.2% Asian, 4.3% Black, 2.6% Hispanic, 87.6% White, 3.3% Other. 77% from out of state.

[J1] NEW ENGLAND INSTITUTE OF APPLIED ARTS & SCIENCES
656 Beacon Street, Boston 02215

[P] NEW ENGLAND SCHOOL OF LAW
154 Stuart Street, Boston 02116

[J1] NEWBURY JUNIOR COLLEGE (Boston Campus)
921 Boylston Street, Boston 02115, (617) 262-9350
Director of Admissions: Gerard Gignac

- **Undergraduates: 248m, 630w; 3,000 total (including evening students)**
- **Tuition (1982/83): $3,950**
- **Room & Board: $2,600-$3,300; Fees: $108**
- **Degree offered: AAS**
- **Mean SAT 560v, 580m**
- **Student-faculty ratio: 14 to 1**

A private junior college. Urban campus in Boston, with branch campuses in suburban Brookline and rural Holliston. Air, rail, bus, and subway service nearby.
Academic Character NEASC and professional accreditation. Semester system, summer term. Career and transfer majors offered in accounting, administrative assistant, audiovisual technology, computer science, executive secretary, fashion design, fashion merchandising, finance, hotel & restaurant management, interior design, legal secretary, management, marketing, medical assistant, medical secretary, ophthalmic dispensing, retail management, travel secretary, travel & tourism management, and word processing specialist. Additional majors in the areas of allied health, animal health science, and culinary arts offered on branch campuses. Distributive requirements. One-year certificates granted. Internships. Library with A-V department.
Financial CEEB CSS. College scholarships, state scholarships; PELL, SEOG, NDSL, GSL, PLUS, CWS, part-time employment.
Admissions High school graduation or equivalent required. Interview strongly recommended. $20 application fee. Rolling admissions. $100 tuition and $150 room deposits required on acceptance of admissions offer. Admission deferral possible. Transfers accepted. Credit possible for CEEB CLEP exams. College Educational Planning Program for pre-entrance counseling.
Student Life Student government. Yearbook. Drama society. Black Student Union. Academic, athletic, special interest, and professional groups. Single students under 21 must live at home or on Boston campus, which has dorms and apartments for men and women. Students in Brookline may live in dorms on campus; Holliston campus has no college housing. Liquor and drugs prohibited on campus. Student body composition: 30% minority.

■[J1] NEWBURY JUNIOR COLLEGE (Brookline Campus)
129 Fisher Avenue, Brookline 02146

■[J1] NEWBURY JUNIOR COLLEGE (Holliston Campus)
100 Summer Street, Holliston 01746

[1] NICHOLS COLLEGE
Dudley 01570, (617) 943-1560
Director of Admissions: Thomas J. McGinn, III

- **Undergraduates: 478m, 236w**
- **Tuition (1982/83): $4,330**
- **Room & Board: $2,500; Fees: $60**
- **Degrees offered: BA, BSBA, BSPA**
- **Mean SAT 400v, 460m**
- **Student-faculty ratio: 21 to 1**

A private college established in 1815, became coed in 1971. 200-acre rural campus, 45 miles from Boston and Hartford. Bus service in Worcester.
Academic Character NEASC and professional accreditation. Semester system, 2 6-week summer terms. Majors offered with a BA in history, psychology, and social service; with a BSBA in accounting, economics, finance, general business, management, management information systems, and marketing; and with a BSPA in public administration. Courses in computer science, English, environmental science, humanities, mathematics, political science, and sociology. Distributive requirements. MBA granted. Independent study, internships. Secondary education certification. ROTC. Computer center. Member of Worcester Area Cooperating Libraries. 60,000-volume library.
Financial CEEB CSS. College scholarships, grants, loans, state & ROTC scholarships, payment plan, half-tuition for additional family members; PELL, SEOG, NDSL, FISL, GSL, CWS, college work program. Application deadline April 1.
Admissions High school graduation with 16 units recommended. GED accepted. Interview encouraged. SAT or ACT required. $15 application fee. Rolling admissions; suggest applying by December 1. Deadline August 1. $50 tuition and $50 room deposits required on acceptance of admissions offer, refundable to May 1. *Early Entrance, Early Decision, Concurrent Enrollment* programs. Admission deferral possible. Transfers accepted. Credit possible for CEEB AP, CLEP, ACT PEP, and DANTES exams, and for correspondence courses.
Student Life Student government. Newspaper, yearbook, radio station. Drama club. Women's organization. Academic, athletic, business, honorary, professional, and special interest groups. Single students must live at home or on campus. No coed dorms. 75% of students live on campus. 7 intercollegiate sports for men, 3 for women, and 3 coed (golf, track, tennis); intramurals. AIAW, ECAC, NCAA, New England Football Conference. Student body composition: 2% Black, 1% Hispanic, 95% White, 2% Other. 42% from out of state.

[1] NORTH ADAMS STATE COLLEGE
North Adams 01247, (413) 664-4511, ext. 241, 242
Director of Admissions: William T. West, Jr.

- **Enrollment: 1,048m, 1,280w**
- **Tuition (1982/83): $845 (in-state), $2,792 (out-of-state)**
- **Room & Board: $2,080; Fees: $255**
- **Degrees offered: BA, BS**
- **Mean SAT 460v, 490m**
- **Student-faculty ratio: 19 to 1**

A public college founded in 1894. 100-acre campus in the Berkshires of western Massachusetts, 40 miles from Albany and 120 miles from Boston. Air and bus service.
Academic Character NEASC and professional accreditation. 4-1-4 system, summer term. Majors offered in biology, business administration (4), chemistry, computer science, early childhood education, elementary education, English (3), history, mathematics, medical technology,

philosophy, physics, psychology, and sociology. Interdisciplinary and self-designed majors. Minors in art, economics, geography, history of civilization, music. Courses in 6 other areas. Distributive requirements. Masters degrees granted. Independent study, honors program, pass/fail, cooperative work/study, internships. 52-acre farm houses Center for Resourceful Living Program. Special program for BA in psychology with an education minor for teaching disturbed/learning disabled children. Dual degree in biology/medical technology. Cross-registration with other state schools. Exchange programs with Southern U (New Orleans) and Williams. Study in Canada. Elementary, secondary, and special education certification. Computer center. Over 125,000-volume library.
Financial CEEB CSS. College scholarships, state grants, tuition waivers; PELL, SEOG, NDSL, GSL, PLUS, CWS. Application deadline May 1.
Admissions High school graduation with minimum C+ average recommended. Interview encouraged. SAT required. $18 application fee. Rolling admissions; suggest applying before December 1. Deadline March 1. $50 tuition and $50 room deposits required on acceptance of admissions offer. *Early Decision* and *Early Entrance* programs. Admission deferral possible. Transfers accepted. Credit possible for CEEB AP, CLEP, some SAT/ACH exams, and for military & life experience. College has own placement program. Individual review for minority and disadvantaged applicants.
Student Life Student government. Newspaper, magazine, yearbook, radio station. Dance, drama, music groups. Academic, athletic, religious, service, and special interest clubs. 2 fraternities and 2 sororities. Non-area freshmen must live on campus. Coed and single-sex dorms, apartments. 65% of students live on campus. No cars for 1st and 2nd-year students living on campus. 2 semesters of phys ed required. 5 intercollegiate sports for men, 5 for women, and coed cross-country & golf; several intramurals. AIAW, ECAC, NCAA. Student body composition: 0.8% Asian, 1.2% Black, 0.6% Hispanic, 0.4% Native American, 96.3% White, 0.7% Other. 5% from out of state.

[J1] NORTH SHORE COMMUNITY COLLEGE
3 Essex Street, Beverly 01915

[1] NORTHEASTERN UNIVERSITY
Boston 02115, (617) 437-2200
Dean of Admissions: Philip R. McCabe

- **Undergraduates: 13,144m, 7,790w; 42,406 total (including evening)**
- **Tuition (1982/83): $4,725-$5,100 (1st-year)**
- **Room & Board: $3,600; Fees: $300**
- **Degrees offered: BA, BS, BSEd, BSBA, BSN, BSEng Tech, BSE's, AA, AS, AEng**
- **Mean SAT 485v, 500m**
- **Student-faculty ratio: 11 to 1**

A private university founded in 1898. 50-acre urban campus in the Back Bay section of Boston. Air, rail, bus, and subway service.
Academic Character NEASC and professional accreditation. Trimester system, summer term. 27 majors offered by the College of Arts & Sciences, 9 by the College of Business Administration, 1 by the College of Criminal Justice, 10 by the College of Engineering, 1 by the College of Nursing, 5 by the College of Pharmacy & Allied Health Professions, and 14 by the Boston-Bouve College of Human Development Professions. Lincoln College offers 5-day cooperative programs in engineering technology, and University College offers adult degree programs at Burlington branch campus and off-campus centers. Distributive requirements. Graduate and professional degrees granted. Certificate program. Honors programs, pass/fail. Beginning in 2nd year, 5-year cooperative education plan alternates classroom study and work in various fields, provides work experience, and defrays education costs. 3-2 programs with professional schools. 2-year AS/certificate program with Forsyth School for Dental Hygienists. Study abroad. Early childhood, elementary, and secondary education certification. AFROTC, ROTC. Computer center. 857,000-volume library.
Financial CEEB CSS. University scholarships, loans, state grants, payment plan; PELL, SEOG, NSS, NDSL, GSL, PLUS, NSL, CWS. University cooperative work/study plan. Application deadline February 15.
Admissions High school graduation required. Courses required vary with programs. SAT or ACT, and 3 ACH required. $25 application fee. Rolling admissions; suggest applying early in 12th year. $100 tuition and $100 room deposits required on acceptance of admissions offer (May 1). *Early Entrance* and *Concurrent Enrollment* programs. Admission deferral possible. Transfers accepted. Credit possible for CEEB AP and CLEP exams.
Student Life Student Council. Newspaper, literary magazine, yearbook, radio station. Music & arts groups. Debate. Academic, ethnic, honorary, political, professional, religious, and special interest clubs. 14 fraternities with houses and 5 sororities without houses. 5% of men and 2% of women join. Coed and single-sex dorms, student apartments. No married-student housing. 50% of freshmen live on campus. No cars on campus for boarding freshmen. 10 intercollegiate sports for men, 9 for women; several intramurals. AIAW, ECAC, NCAA. Student body composition: 4% Black, 1% Hispanic, 46% White, 49% Unknown. 35% from out of state.

[J1] NORTHERN ESSEX COMMUNITY COLLEGE
100 Elliott Street, Haverhill 01830

[1] PINE MANOR COLLEGE
400 Heath Street, Chesnut Hill 02167, (617) 731-7104
Director of Admissions: Gillian M. Lloyd

- **Undergraduates: 540w**
- **Tuition (1982/83): $6,600**
- **Room & Board: $3,900; Fees: $150-$370**
- **Degrees offered: BA, AA, AS**

A private college for women with coed summer terms, established in 1911. 79-acre campus located 5 miles west of Boston. Subway nearby to Boston, airport, rail and bus stations.
Academic Character NEASC accreditation. Semester system, 2 5-week coed summer terms. Majors offered for a BA in American studies, art history (general, interior design, textiles), biological psychology, business management, developmental psychology (child study, adult psychology), English: writing & literature, history & government, French, and visual arts. Individualized major. All students receive the AA after their first two years of study. AA offered in liberal studies, art history, biology, business management, child study, English, history & government, psychology, theatre arts, visual arts; AS in health sciences. Minors offered in major fields and in biology, drama & speech, economics, history, Italian, Spanish, music, politics, sociology. Courses in Japanese, Chinese, modern dance. Distributive requirements. Independent study & research, credit/no credit, internships. Cross-registration with Babson and Boston Colleges. Member Marine Studies Consortium. Model UN. Study abroad. Open College for continuing education. International Language Institute. Child Study Center. American Institute of Textile Arts. Computer terminals, language labs. 40,000-volume library with microform resources.
Financial CEEB CSS. College scholarships, grants, state scholarships, payment plan; PELL, SEOG, NDSL, GSL, ALAS, CWS. File FAF by February 15. Application deadline March 15.
Admissions High school graduation with college prep program of 16 units recommended. Interview encouraged. SAT or ACT required. $15 application fee. Rolling admissions; suggest applying as early as possible. $500 deposit required on acceptance of admissions offer (May 1). *Early Admission* and *Early Decision* programs. Admission deferral possible. Transfers accepted. Credit possible for CEEB AP and CLEP exams. Students over 22 with an educational gap of 3 or more years may have open admission to The Open College; after successful completion of 2 courses they may be admitted to degree programs.
Student Life 1st and 2nd-year students must live at home or on campus. Dorms. French, quiet, and international houses. No married-student housing. About 90% of students live on campus. 4 intercollegiate sports; phys ed courses. 78% of students from out of state. 23% come from 35 foreign countries.

[J1] QUINCY JUNIOR COLLEGE
34 Coddington Street, Quincy 02169

[J1] QUINSIGAMOND COMMUNITY COLLEGE
670 West Boylston Street, Worcester 01606

[1] RADCLIFFE COLLEGE
Cambridge 02138

A private college of arts & sciences for women, affiliated with Harvard University. Founded in 1879, adopted present name in 1894. Classes became coed with Harvard in 1943. Today women are admitted to Radcliffe by a joint Harvard/Radcliffe Admissions Committee. Classes, facilities, organizations, housing, and most athletics are coed. (See listing for Harvard and Radcliffe Colleges). Radcliffe independently undertakes programs (seminars, conferences, advanced scholarly research, fellowships, etc.) of special interest to women. These include the Arthur and Elizabeth Schlesinger Library on the History of Women in America; the Mary Ingraham Bunting Institute (a center for postdoctoral research by women scholars), the Henry A. Murray Center for the Study of Lives; the Radcliffe seminars (a continuing education program that serves 1,000 adult students each year); the Radcliffe Publishing Procedures Course; the Radcliffe Career Services.

[1] REGIS COLLEGE
235 Wellesley Street, Weston 02193, (617) 893-1820
Director of Admissions: Julie O'Connor

- **Undergraduates: 859w; 1,191 total (including graduates)**
- **Tuition (1982/83): $4,700**
- **Room & Board: $3,025; Fees: $255**
- **Degrees offered: AB, BS**
- **Mean SAT 430v, 434m**
- **Student-faculty ratio: 14 to 1**

A private, Roman Catholic women's college established in 1927. Conducted by the Sisters of Saint Joseph of Boston. 168-acre suburban campus 12 miles west of Boston. College bus to rapid transit. Air, rail, and bus service in Boston.
Academic Character NEASC and professional accreditation. 4-1-4 system, coed summer terms. Majors offered in art, biology, chemistry, classics, economics, English, French, German, history, management, mathematics, medical technology, music, political science, psychology, sociology/social work, and Spanish. Self-designed majors. Programs in art therapy, American studies, communications, education, Greek studies, legal studies, management studies, social work, and women's studies. Distributive requirements. Masters in special education granted. Honors program, pass/fail, internships. Preprofessional programs in medicine and law. 3-2 AB/BS or MS program with Worcester Polytechnic Institute. Cross-registration with Babson, Bentley, and Boston Colleges. Study abroad. Elementary and secondary education certification. Language lab. 124,000-volume library.
Financial CEEB CSS. College and state scholarships, payment plan; PELL, SEOG, NDSL, GSL, PLUS, CWS. Application deadline March 1.
Admissions High school graduation with 15 units required. Interview encouraged. SAT required. $20 application fee. Rolling admissions; suggest applying in fall of 12th year. Deadline September 1. $100 tuition and $100 room

deposits required on acceptance of admissions offer (May 1). *Early Admission* Program. Admission deferral possible. Transfers accepted. Credit possible for CEEB AP exams. College has own placement tests.
Student Life Student government. Newspaper, literary magazine, yearbook. Music, drama, film groups. Academic, athletic, honorary, political, religious, and special interest clubs. 4 women's dorms. No married-student housing. 79% of students live on campus. 6 intercollegiate sports; intramurals. MAIAW, New England Women's Intercollegiate Swim Association. Student body composition: 2% Asian, 2% Black, 5% Hispanic, 91% White. 19% from out of state.

[J1] ROXBURY COMMUNITY COLLEGE
Roxbury 02119

[1] ST. HYACINTH COLLEGE AND SEMINARY
Granby 01033

[1] ST. JOHN'S SEMINARY
Brighton 02135

[1] SALEM STATE COLLEGE
Salem 01970, (617) 745-0556
Director of Admissions: David Sartwell

- **Undergraduates: 2,032m, 3,091w; 5,680 total (including graduates)**
- **Tuition (1982/83): $845 (in-state), $2,688 (out-of-state)**
- **Room & Board: $1,822; Fees: $205**
- **Degrees offered: BA, BS, BSEd, BSBA, BSBus Ed, BSN, BSW, BGS**
- **Mean SAT 410v, 420m**
- **Student-faculty ratio: 19 to 1**

A public college established in 1854. 62-acre suburban campus 18 miles northeast of Boston. Bus to Boston.
Academic Character NEASC and professional accreditation. Semester system. Majors offered in art, aviation science, biology, business administration, business education, chemistry, early childhood education, earth science, economics, elementary education, English, general studies, geography, history, mathematics, nursing, political science, psychology, social work, sociology, theatre arts, and sports, fitness, & leisure. Self-designed majors. Minors in 26 and courses in 15 additional areas. Distributive requirements. MS granted. Independent & directed study, field work, internships. Member Northeast Consortium of Colleges and Universities. Study abroad in England. Elementary and secondary education certification. ROTC. TV studio, media center. 300,000-volume library.
Financial CEEB CSS. University and state scholarships; PELL, SEOG, NSS, NDSL, NSL, CWS. Application deadline March 1.
Admissions High school graduation with 16 units recommended. GED accepted. SAT required. $18 application fee. Rolling admissions; deadline March 1. $50 tuition deposit required on acceptance of admissions offer (May 1). *Early Entrance* and *Early Decision* programs. Transfers accepted. Credit possible for CEEB AP and CLEP exams. Alternatives for Individual Development Program for underprepared students.
Student Life Student government. Newspaper, literary magazine, yearbook, radio station. Several music & arts groups. Academic, athletic, political, religious, service, and special interest clubs. 2 fraternities and 1 sorority without houses. 3% of men and women join. Coed and single-sex dorms. No married-student housing. 15% of students live on campus. Class attendance required. 1 year of phys ed required. 8 intercollegiate sports for men, 7 for women; intramurals. AIAW, ECAC, NCAA, Mass State College Athletic Conference. Student body composition: 0.2% Asian, 2.7% Black, 1% Hispanic, 0.1% Native American, 96% White. 2% from out of state.

[1] SIMMONS COLLEGE
300 The Fenway, Boston 02115, (617) 738-2000
Director of Admissions: Linda Cox Maguire

- **Undergraduates: 1,916w; 2,766 total (including graduates)**
- **Tuition (1982/83): $6,464**
- **Room & Board: $3,364; Fees: $194**
- **Degrees offered: BA, BS**
- **Mean SAT 480v, 490m**
- **Student-faculty ratio: 12 to 1**

A private women's college with coed graduate programs, founded in 1899. Urban campus in Boston. Air, rail, bus, and subway service.
Academic Character NEASC and professional accreditation. Semester system, 7-week summer term. Majors offered in applied computer science, art, biology, communications (4), chemistry, economics, education, English, French, government, history, human services, international relations, management (3), mathematics, music, nursing, nutrition (2), philosophy, physics, psychology, sociology, and women's studies. Prince Program in Retail Management. Self-designed, interdepartmental, and double majors. Distributive requirements. Graduate degrees granted. Independent study, honors programs, pass/fail, field work, internships. 4-year BA/MA in English. 4½-year BS in physical therapy with Children's Medical Center. 4-year BS in medical technology with Lynn Hospital. Graphic & publishing arts major with School of Museum of Fine Arts. 5½-year dual degree program in chemistry & pharmacy with Mass College of Pharmacy. 5-year dual degree engineering programs with Dartmouth and Boston U. Cross-registration with Emmanuel and Hebrew Colleges, New England Conservatory of Music, School of Museum of Fine Arts. Exchanges with Mills, Fisk, Johnston (U of Redlands), and Spelman Colleges. Washington Semester. Study abroad. Early childhood, elementary, secondary, and special education certification. ROTC at Northeastern. 200,000-volume library plus access to 10 area libraries.
Financial CEEB CSS. College scholarships, grants, loans, state grants; PELL, SEOG, NDSL, GSL, PLUS, CWS. Application deadline March 1.
Admissions High school graduation with strong college prep program recommended. Interview strongly encouraged. SAT or ACT, and 3 ACH required. $25 application fee. Rolling admissions; deadline March 15. $100 tuition and $150 room deposits required on acceptance of admissions offer (May 1). *Early Entrance* Program. Admission deferral possible. Transfers accepted. Credit possible for CEEB AP exams.
Student Life Student government. Newspaper, literary magazine, yearbook, radio station. Music, dance, drama groups. Outing Club. Academic, cultural, ethnic, religious, and special interest clubs. Women's dorms. 75% of students live on campus. Honor code. 1 year of phys ed required. 5 intercollegiate sports for women. AIAW. Student body composition: 2.3% Asian, 8.6% Black, 1.3% Hispanic, 84% White, 3.8% Other. 50% from out of state.

[1] SIMON'S ROCK OF BARD COLLEGE
Great Barrington 01230, (413) 528-0771

- **Undergraduates: 159m, 131w**
- **Tuition (1982/83): $7,450**
- **Room & Board: $2,650; Fees: $140**
- **Degree offered: BA, AA**

A private liberal arts institution designed to provide a collegiate program for students 15 to 20 years old. Founded in 1964, became a part of Bard College in 1979.
Academic Character NEASC accreditation. Semester system. 7 interdisciplinary liberal arts majors offered leading to a BA. Other majors offered leading to an AA; students with these majors may transfer to Bard or another college to complete their bachelor's degree. Transitional Studies Program for students who have completed one year of high school.
Financial Financial aid available.
Admissions Students admitted after their 9th, 10th, 11th, and 12th years of high school. Admission is based on interview, questionnaires, recommendations, school records, and SAT, PSAT, or SSAT scores. A strong academic record and evidence of self-motivation and self-discipline are essential for admission. Rolling admissions. *Early Decision* Program.

[1] SMITH COLLEGE
Northampton 01063, (413) 584-2700
Director of Admissions: Lorna R. Blake

- **Undergraduates: 2,650w; 2,880 total (including graduates)**
- **Tuition (1982/83): $7,750**
- **Room & Board: $3,100; Fees: $75**
- **Degree offered: BA**
- **Mean SAT 606v, 601m**
- **Student-faculty ratio: 10 to 1**

A private women's college established in 1875. 125-acre campus in a small city 18 miles from Springfield. Rail and bus service.
Academic Character NEASC and professional accreditation. 4-1-4 system. Majors offered in Afro-American studies, art, astronomy, biological sciences, chemistry, economics, education & child study, geology, government, Hispanic studies, history, languages & literatures (classical, English, French, German, Italian, & Russian), mathematics, music, philosophy, physics, psychology, religion/Biblical literature, sociology/anthropology, and theatre. Interdepartmental majors in biochemistry, comparative literature, computer science, and American, ancient, & medieval studies. Self-designed majors. Graduate degrees granted. Independent study, honors program, Phi Beta Kappa, pass/fail, internships. Preprofessional programs in law and medicine. 5-year AB/BS or MS in engineering program with U of Mass. 5-college cooperation provides cross-registration with Amherst, Hampshire, Smith, and UMass. 12-college exchange allows for year exchange at Amherst, Bowdoin, Connecticut, Dartmouth, Mount Holyoke, Trinity, Vassar, Wellesley, Wesleyan, Wheaton, Williams. Semester in Washington. Numerous study abroad programs. Elementary, secondary, and special education certification. AFROTC & ROTC at UMass. Observatory, language lab, museum. 950,000-volume library.
Financial CEEB CSS. College grants, loans, state grants, payment plan; PELL, SEOG, GSL, CWS, college work program. Application deadline February 1 (November 15 for Early Decision).
Admissions High school graduation with 16 units required. Interview encouraged. SAT and 3 ACH required. $25 application fee. Suggest applying early in 12th year. Deadline February 1. $300 deposit required on acceptance of admissions offer (May 1). *Early Decision, Early Evaluation, Early Admission* programs. Admission deferral possible. Transfers accepted. Credit possible for CEEB AP exams. Ada Comstock Program for adults.
Student Life Student government. Newspaper, magazine, yearbook, radio station. Several music, drama, dance groups. Black Students Alliance. Academic, athletic, political, religious, service, and special interest clubs. Married students and Northampton residents may live off campus. Residential houses with dining facilities. 99% live on campus. No cars for 1st-year and financial aid students. 15 intercollegiate sports; intramurals. AIAW, NCAA. Student body composition: 5% Asian, 4% Black, 4% Foreign, 2% Hispanic, 85% White. 75% from out of state.

[1] SOUTHEASTERN MASSACHUSETTS UNIVERSITY
North Dartmouth 02737, (617) 999-8605

- **Undergraduates: 2,433m, 2,493w; 5,364 total (including graduates)**
- **Tuition (1982/83): $939 (in-state), $3,090 (out-of-state)**
- **Room & Board: $3,100; Fees: $181**
- **Degrees offered: BA, BS, BFA, BMus, BSN**
- **Mean SAT 450v, 500m**
- **Student-faculty ratio: 15 to 1**

A public university established in 1964. 710-acre large-town campus on Buzzard's Bay, 60 miles south of Boston. Air and bus service.

Academic Character NEASC and professional accreditation. Semester system. 18 majors offered by the College of Arts & Sciences, 8 by the College of Business & Industry, 7 by the College of Engineering, 1 by the College of Nursing, and 10 by the College of Visual & Performing Arts. Interdisciplinary and self-designed majors. Women's studies program. Distributive requirements. MA, MS, MBA, MFA granted. Independent study, honors program, internships. BS/MS program in chemistry. Consortium with Bridgewater State, Dean Junior, Stonehill Colleges, Mass Maritime Academy, Swain School of Design, and Bristol, Cape Cod, and Massasoit Community Colleges. Elementary and secondary education certification. TV studio, computer center. 250,000-volume library.

Financial CEEB CSS. College & state grants; PELL, SEOG, NSS, NDSL, GSL, NSL, CWS. Some students may qualify for in-state tuition through New England Regional Student Program.

Admissions High school graduation with 12 units expected. Other requirements for specific programs. Portfolio required for arts majors; audition for music majors. SAT required. ACH recommended. $18 (in-state), $25 (out-of-state) application fees. Rolling admissions; suggest applying after 1st marking period of 12th year. $50 fee required on acceptance of admissions offer. *Early Entrance* Program. Transfers accepted. Credit possible for CEEB AP and CLEP exams. College Now program provides alternative admission for academically disadvantaged students.

Student Life Student government. Academic, athletic, honorary, service, and special interest clubs. Coed dorms with suites for 10-12 people. 32% of students live on campus. 10 intercollegiate sports for men, 9 for women; intramurals. AIAW, NCAA, New England Conferences. Student body composition: 1% Asian, 4% Black, 1% Hispanic, 94% White. 4% from out of state.

[1] SPRINGFIELD COLLEGE

Springfield 01109, (413) 787-2030

- **Undergraduates: 1,000m, 1,050w; 2,450 total (including graduates)**
- **Tuition (1982/83): $4,500**
- **Room & Board: $2,380**
- **Degrees offered: BA, BS, BPhys Ed**
- **Mean SAT 425v, 470m**
- **Student-faculty ratio: 18 to 1**

A private college established in 1885. 156-acre suburban residential campus on Lake Massasoit, 90 miles west of Boston and 150 miles north of New York City. Air, rail, and bus service.

Academic Character NEASC and professional accreditation. Semester system, 3- and 6-week summer terms. Over 40 majors offered in the areas of art in urban life, biology, business management, chemistry, community service, education, English, environmental studies, health education, history, mathematics, medical technology/lab science, physical education, political science, psychology, recreation & leisure services, rehabilitation services, social services, and sociology. Double majors. Minors. Programs in Afro-American, American, and international studies. Distributive requirements; 2 years of foreign language required for BA. Graduate degrees granted. Independent research, pass/fail, internships. Preprofessional programs in dentistry, law, medicine, theology. Courses at Morven Park Equestrian Institute in Virginia. Cross-registration through Cooperative Colleges of Greater Springfield. Cooperative programs with YMCA. Study abroad. Elementary and secondary education certification. ROTC at Western New England College. International center, language lab, summer day camp. 115,000-volume library.

Financial CEEB CSS. College scholarships, state grants, payment plan; PELL, SEOG, NDSL, GSL, CWS, college work program. File FAF by February 15. Application deadline April 1.

Admissions High school graduation with college prep program required. Portfolio required for art in urban life majors. Interview & SAT required. $25 application fee. Rolling admissions; suggest applying in fall of 12th year. Deadline April 1. $100 deposit required on acceptance of admissions offer (May 1). *Early Entrance* and *Concurrent Enrollment* programs. Admission deferral possible. Transfers accepted. Credit possible for CEEB AP and CLEP exams.

Student Life Student government. Newspaper, magazine, yearbook, radio station. Drama & music groups. Performing dance & gymnastics groups. Academic, athletic, religious, service, and special interest clubs. Freshmen must live on campus. Coed and single-sex dorms. 75% of students live on campus. Juniors and seniors may have cars on campus. 4 semester hours of health/phys ed required. 13 intercollegiate sports for men, 12 for women; many intramurals. AIAW, ECAC, NCAA, New England Conference on Athletics. 66% of students from out of state.

[J1] SPRINGFIELD TECHNICAL COMMUNITY COLLEGE

Springfield 01105

[1] STONEHILL COLLEGE

North Easton 02356, (617) 238-1081

- **Undergraduates: 815m, 918w**
- **Tuition (1982/83): $4,750**
- **Room & Board: $2,700; Fees: $90**
- **Degrees offered: AB, BS, BSBA**
- **Mean SAT 470v, 510m**
- **Student-faculty ratio: 14 to 1**

A private Roman Catholic college conducted by the Holy Cross Fathers. Established in 1948, became coed in 1951. 558-acre small-town campus 20 miles south of Boston. Bus to Boston.

Academic Character NEASC and professional accreditation. Semester system, 3- and 6-week summer terms. Majors offered in accounting, American studies, biology, chemistry, college studies, criminal justice, economics, education (2), English, health care administration, history (3), human resource management, international studies, marketing management, mathematics, medical technology, modern languages, philosophy, political science, psychology, public administration, religious studies, and sociology. Self-designed majors. Minors, courses in additional areas. Distributives and 2 religious studies courses required. Independent study, pass/fail, internships. Preprofessional programs in dentistry, engineering, law, medicine. 3-2 engineering program with Notre Dame. 3-1 programs in medicine and dentistry. Exchange program with Wheaton College. Cross-registration with 9 area schools. Study abroad in Ireland and elsewhere. Elementary education certification. ROTC. Laboratory school. Language lab. 110,000-volume library with access to area libraries.

Financial CEEB CSS. College scholarships, loans, state grants, ROTC scholarships, payment plan; PELL, SEOG, NDSL, GSL, CWS. Priority application deadline February 1; deadline March 1.

Admissions High school graduation with 16 units required. Interview urged. SAT or ACT required. ACH recommended. $20 application fee. Rolling admissions. Application deadlines: March 1 (boarders), May 1 (commuters). $50 tuition and $100 room deposits required on acceptance of admissions offer (May 1). *Early Entrance* and *Early Decision* programs. Admission deferral possible. Transfers accepted. Credit possible for CEEB AP and CLEP exams.

Student Life Student government. Newspaper, magazine, yearbook, radio station. Drama, dance, music groups. Intercollegiate debate. Academic, athletic, religious, service, and special interest clubs. Coed and single-sex dorms. No married-student housing. 66% of students live on campus. 7 intercollegiate sports for men, 6 for women; club and intramural sports. Tri-State Conference. Student body composition: 1% Black, 99% White. 28% of students from out of state.

[1] SUFFOLK UNIVERSITY

8 Ashburton Place, Boston 02108, (617) 723-7000
Director of Admissions: William F. Coughlin

- **Undergraduates: 1,787m, 1,630w; 6,181 total (including graduates & evening)**
- **Tuition (1982/83): $3,630**
- **Fees: $25**
- **Degrees offered: BA, BS, BSBA, BSGS, AA, AS**
- **Mean SAT 430v, 450m**
- **Student-faculty ratio: 17 to 1**

A private university established in 1906. Urban campus on Beacon Hill near State House. Air, rail, bus, subway service.

Academic Character NEASC and professional accreditation. Semester system, 2 6-week day and 2 7-week evening summer terms. Majors offered in the areas of accounting, biology (6), chemistry (4), communication & speech (8), computer information systems, economics (2), education (2), English (2), finance, French, government (2), history, humanities (2), journalism (8), management, marketing, math & computer science (3), philosophy, physics (2), psychology, sociology (4), and Spanish. Graduate and professional degrees granted. BSGS granted by evening division. Pass/fail, cooperative work/study. Preprofessional programs in child care, crime & delinquency, dentistry, law, medical technology, medicine, optometry, social work, veterinary medicine. 3-2 programs in computer and electrical engineering with Notre Dame. 6-year BA/JD degree program. Cooperative program with Emerson College for journalism/speech majors. Elementary and secondary education certification. ROTC. Language lab. 92,460-volume library.

Financial CEEB CSS. University and state scholarships, payment plan; PELL, SEOG, NDSL, GSL, CWS, university work program. Application deadline March 1.

Admissions High school graduation with 16 units required. SAT required; English ACH recommended. $15 application fee. Rolling admissions; suggest applying in November. Deadline May 1. $100 deposit required on acceptance of admissions offer (May 1). *Early Decision* and *Early Entrance* programs. Admission deferral possible. Transfers accepted. Credit possible for CEEB AP and CLEP exams.

Student Life Student government. Newspaper, magazines, yearbook, radio & TV stations. Drama group. Intercollegiate debate. Afro-American, academic, service, and special interest clubs. 4 fraternities and 2 sororities without houses. 11% of men and 7% of women join. No university housing. Cafeteria. 5 intercollegiate sports for men, 2 for women; club and intramural sports. AIAW, ECAC, NCAA. Student body composition: 0.8% Asian, 4% Black, 0.2% Hispanic, 0.2% Native American, 92.1% White, 2.7% Other. 15% from out of state.

[P] SWEDENBORG SCHOOL OF RELIGION

48 Sargent Street, Newton 02158

[1] TUFTS UNIVERSITY

Medford 02155, (617) 628-0990
Dean of Undergraduate Admissions: Michael C. Behnke

- **Undergraduates: 2,162m, 2,152w; 6,778 total (including graduates)**
- **Tuition (1982/83): $7,650**
- **Room & Board: $3,880; Fees: $60**
- **Degrees offered: BA, BS, BFA, BMus, BSEd, BSEng Sci, BSE's**
- **Mean SAT 575v, 625m**
- **Student-faculty ratio: 14 to 1**

A private university established in 1852. 150-acre suburban campus 6 miles from Boston. Bus to Boston.

Academic Character NEASC and professional accreditation. Semester system, 6-week summer term. Over 45 majors offered in the areas of area studies, archaeology, arts, child study, education, engineering, humanities, languages & literatures, mental health, occupational therapy, psychology, sciences, and social sciences. Self-designed majors. Experimental College for innovative & student-designed courses. Distributive requirements. Graduate and professional degrees granted. Independent study, honors program, Phi Beta Kappa, pass/fail, internships. BA/MA and BS/MS programs. 4-yr program for a BS in Occupational Therapy. 5-yr BA/BS in liberal arts & engineering. 5-yr BA/MA in international affairs with Fletcher School of Law & Diplomacy. BFA, BSEd, BA/BFA, BS/BFA programs with School of Museum of Fine Arts; BA/BMus, BS/BMus with New England Conservatory of Music. Cross-registration with Boston College, Brandeis, Boston U. Washington and Maritime Studies programs. Exchange with Swarthmore College. Several study abroad options. Elementary and secondary education certification. AFROTC, NROTC, ROTC at MIT. Computer center, language lab, research labs. 584,000-volume library with microform resources

Financial CEEB CSS. University scholarships, payment plan; PELL, SEOG, NDSL, CWS. Application deadline February 1.

Admissions High school graduation with college prep program recommended. SAT or ACT, and 3 ACH required. $30 application fee. Application deadline January 15. $200 deposit required on acceptance of admissions offer (May 1). *Early Admission* and *Early Decision* programs. Admission deferral possible. Transfers accepted. Credit possible for CEEB AP exams.

Student Life Student government. Newspapers, magazines, yearbook, radio & TV stations. Several music, dance, drama, film groups. Debate. African American Center. Mountain Club. Numerous academic, athletic, ethnic, political, professional, religious, and special interest groups. 10 fraternities and 3 sororities with houses. 10% of students join. Freshmen and sophomores must live at home or on campus. Coed & single-sex dorms, special interest houses, coop apartments. 75% of stuents live on campus. No cars for freshmen. 14 intercollegiate sports for men, 12 for women; intramural & club sports. AIAW, ECAC, NESCAC. Student body composition: 4% Asian, 6% Black, 2% Hispanic, 88% White. 65% from out of state.

[1] WELLESLEY COLLEGE

Wellesley 02181, (617) 235-0320
Director of Admissions: Mary Ellen Ames

- **Undergraduates: 2,060w; 2,167 total (including part-time)**
- **Tuition (1982/83): $7,430**
- **Room & Board: $3,460; Fees: $80**
- **Degree offered: BA**
- **Mean SAT 610v, 610m**
- **Student-faculty ratio: 11 to 1**

A private women's college established in 1875. 600-acre suburban campus 12 miles west of Boston. Bus to Boston.

Academic Character NEASC accreditation. Semester system. Over 35 majors offered in the areas of area studies, anthropology, arts, astronomy, biology, chemistry, classics, economics, geology, history, humanities, languages & literatures, mathematics, music, philosophy, political science, psychobiology, psychology, religion, social sciences, and theatre. Self-designed and interdisciplinary majors. Distributive requirements. Independent study, honors program, Phi Beta Kappa, pass/fail, internships. Cross-registration with MIT. 12-college exchange with Amherst, Bowdoin, Connecticut, Dartmouth, Mount Holyoke, Smith, Trinity, Vassar, Wesleyan, Wheaton, Williams. Exchange with Spelman College in Atlanta. Summer urban studies program. Study abroad in several countries. Secondary education certification. AFROTC, NROTC, ROTC at MIT. Computer center, observatory, language lab, child study center. Over 600,000-volume library.

Financial CEEB CSS. College scholarships, grants, payment plan; PELL, SEOG, NDSL, GSL, CWS. Application deadline February 1 (November 15 for early decision).

Admissions High school graduation with college prep program expected. Interview required. SAT and 3 ACH required. $25 application fee. Application deadline February 1. $300 deposit required on acceptance of admissions offer (May 1). *Early Entrance* and *Early Decision* programs. Admission deferral possible. Transfers accepted. Credit possible for CEEB AP exams. College has departmental exams.

Student Life Student government. Newspaper, magazines, yearbook, radio station. Music & theatre groups. Black and Jewish Community Centers. Academic, athletic, ethnic, honorary, professional, religious, and special interest clubs. Women's dorms, special interest & language housing. 96% live on campus. Honor system. 1 year of phys ed required. 11 intercollegiate sports; intramurals. AIAW, NIAC. Student body composition: 7% Asian, 6.3% Black, 3.2% Hispanic, 0.1% Native American, 78.1% White, 5.3% Other. 75% from out of state.

[1 & J1] WENTWORTH INSTITUTE OF TECHNOLOGY

550 Huntington Avenue, Boston 02115, (617) 442-9010
Dean of Admissions: Charles P. Uppvall

- **Undergraduates: 2,900m, 210w; 3,468 total (including part-time)**
- **Tuition (1982/83): $3,990**
- **Room & Board: $2,935; Fees: $120**
- **Degrees offered: BSEng Tech, AEng, AAS**
- **Student-faculty ratio: 17 to 1**

A private institute established in 1904, became coed in 1972. 9-acre urban campus. Air, rail, and bus service.

Academic Character NEASC and professional accreditation. Semester system, 12-week summer term. Majors offered in architectural, civil, electronic, manufacturing, & mechanical engineering technologies, building construction technology, and technical science. Associate degrees in most of above and in architectural technology, computer science, and computer, electrical, mechanical design, & mechanical power engineering technologies. AAS programs in aeronautical, building construction, electronic, manufacturing, mechanical design, mechanical power, and welding technologies. Certificate programs in aircraft maintenance, architectural drafting, building, civil construction, dental laboratory, electronic maintenance, and mechanical drafting technologies. Several of the 2-year programs lead into BSEng Tech degree programs. Extensive cooperative work/study program. ROTC at Northeastern U. 53,000-volume library.

Financial CEEB CSS. Institute and state scholarships, payment plan; PELL, SEOG, NDSL, GSL, CWS. Application deadline May 15 (February 15 for early decision).

Admissions High school graduation with 9 or more units required. GED accepted. Interview encouraged. SAT or ACT recommended. $25 application fee. Rolling admissions; suggest applying by July 1. $150 tuition and $200 room deposits required on acceptance of admissions offer (May 1). Transfers accepted. Credit possible for CEEB AP and CLEP exams.

Student Life Student government. Newspaper, yearbook. Academic, drama, honorary, professional, and special interest groups. Dorms, apartments, married-student housing 22% of students live on campus. Class attendance required. 3 intercollegiate sports for men; club and intramural sports. Greater Boston College Conference. Student body composition: 1.9% Asian, 3.2% Black, 1.4% Hispanic, 0.7% Native American, 84.7% White, 8.1% Other. 15% from out of state.

[1] WESTERN NEW ENGLAND COLLEGE

Springfield 01119, (413) 782-3111
Dean of Admissions: Rae J. Malcolm

- **Undergraduates: 1,341m, 773w; 5,454 total (including graduates)**
- **Tuition (1982/83): $3,840**
- **Room & Board: $2,450; Fees: $278**
- **Degrees offered: BA, BS, BSBA, BSW, BSEng's**
- **Mean SAT 430v, 510m**
- **Student-faculty ratio: 20 to 1**

A private college established in 1919. 94-acre residential campus 90 miles west of Boston. Air, rail, and bus service.

Academic Character NEASC and professional accreditation. Semester system, 5-week summer terms (day & evening). Majors offered in biology, chemistry, computer science, economics, English, government, history, mathematics, philosophy, psychology, social work, sociology; accounting, computer system, finance, general business, human resources management, management, marketing, quantitative methods, technical business; and biomedical, computer, electrical, environmental, industrial, management, and mechanical engineering. BA in Liberal Studies offered through Continuing Education. Evening programs. Courses in 11 additional areas. Distributive requirements. Independent study, internships. 5-year program with Mass College of Pharmacy & Allied Health Sciences for a BS in Pharmacy. Cross-registration through Cooperating Colleges of Greater Springfield. Washington Semester. Study abroad in Europe, South America. Secondary education certification. ROTC. Computer center. 90,500-volume library.

Financial CEEB CSS. College scholarships, grants, loans, state grants, payment plan; PELL, SEOG, NDSL, GSL, PLUS, CWS. Application deadline April 1.

Admissions High school graduation required. Specific units required vary with programs. Interview urged. SAT required. $20 application fee. Rolling admissions; suggest applying early in 12th year. $100 tuition and $100 room deposits required on acceptance of admissions offer. *Early Enrollment* and *Early Decision* programs. Admission deferral possible. Transfers accepted. Credit possible for CEEB AP and CLEP exams, and for non-traditional education.

Student Life Student government. Newspaper, literary magazine, yearbook, radio station. Film club. Rathskellar. Academic, athletic, honorary, professional, religious, service, and special interest groups. Students live at home or on campus. Dorms and apartments. 47% live on campus. 2 semesters of phys ed required. 14 intercollegiate sports for men & women; intramurals. AIAW, ECAC, NAIA, NCAA. Student body composition: 0.8% Asian, 3% Black, 0.9% Hispanic, 0.2% Native American, 94.6% White, 0.5% Other. 36% from out of state.

[1] WESTFIELD STATE COLLEGE

Westfield 01085, (413) 568-3311
Director of Admissions: William E. Crean

- **Enrollment: 1,250m, 1,650w**
- **Tuition (1982/83): $845 (in-state), $2,792 (out-of-state)**
- **Room & Board: $1,836; Fees: $250**
- **Degrees offered: BA, BS, BSEd**
- **Mean SAT 453v, 482m**
- **Student-faculty ratio: 19 to 1**

A public college established in 1838. 228-acre campus in a small city 10 miles from Springfield. Bus service; airport and rail station in Springfield.

Academic Character NEASC and professional accreditation. Semester system, 6-week summer term. Majors offered in art, biology, business management, computer science, criminal justice, education (early childhood, elementary, special), English, environmental urban & regional analysis, French, general science, general studies, history, mathematics, media systems & management, music, physical education, political science, psychology, social sciences, and Spanish. Minors in most major fields and 7 other areas. Distributive requirements. MA and EdM granted. Independent study, honors program, Phi Beta Kappa, internships. Cross-registration and library privileges through Cooperating Colleges of Greater Springfield. Study and student teaching abroad. Elementary, secondary, and special education certification. ROTC. Language lab, TV studio, computer. 130,000-volume library with microform resources.

Financial CEEB CSS. College scholarships; PELL, SEOG, NDSL, GSL, CWS. Preferred application deadline March 1.
Admissions High school diploma or equivalent required. Interview encouraged. Portfolio required for art majors, audition for music majors. SAT required. $18 application fee. Rolling admissions; suggest applying by December 1. $50 tuition and $50 room deposits required on acceptance of admissions offer (within 30 days for boarders; commuters may wait until May 1). *Early Admission* and *Early Decision* programs. Admission deferral possible. Transfers accepted. Credit possible for CEEB AP and CLEP exams. Urban Education Program for economically/culturally deprived students provides 6-week remedial summer school, self-paced program.
Student Life Student government. Newspaper, magazine, yearbook, radio station. Several music, drama, film groups. Academic, athletic, religious, service, and special interest groups. Coed and single-sex dorms. No married-student housing. 60% of students live on campus. 12 intercollegiate sports for men, 7 for women; several intramurals. AIAW, ECAC, NCAA, Mass State Athletic Conference. Student body composition: 1% Asian, 2.3% Black, 0.5% Hispanic, 0.1% Native American, 96.1% White. 5% from out of state.

[P] WESTON SCHOOL OF THEOLOGY
3 Phillips Place, Cambridge 02138

[1] WHEATON COLLEGE
Norton 02766, (617) 285-7722
Director of Admissions: Andronike Janus

- **Undergraduates: 1,222w**
- **Tuition (1982/83): $7,750**
- **Room & Board: $3,125; Fees: $75**
- **Degree offered: BA**
- **Mean SAT 530v, 540m**
- **Student-faculty ratio: 10 to 1**

A private women's college established in 1834. 300-acre campus in a small town 35 miles southwest of Boston, and 15 miles from Providence, RI. Rail and bus service.
Academic Character NEASC accreditation. Semester system. Majors offered in American history & literature, anthropology, art, Asian studies, biochemistry, biology, chemistry, classical civilization, classics (Greek, Latin), economics, English, French, German, government, history, Italian studies, mathematics, music, philosophy, physics, psychobiology, psychology, religion, Russian, Russian studies, sociology, and Spanish. Interdepartmental and self-designed majors. Courses in 7 additional areas. Departmental proficiency exams. Independent study, Phi Beta Kappa, career exploration internships. Preprofessional programs in law, medicine. Dual-degree programs in computer science, engineering, health systems, management science with Georgia Tech. Programs in business & management with Tuck School of Dartmouth College, and with U of Rochester. Program in religion & theology with Andover-Newton Theological Seminary. Cross-registration with Stonehill College. Exchange program with Mills College (CA), and through 12-college exchange. Washington, Mystic Seaport, National Theatre Institute semester programs. Study abroad. Preschool and secondary education certification possible. ROTC at Stonehill. Language lab, observatory, computer. 220,000-volume library.
Financial CEEB CSS. College scholarships, grants, payment plan; PELL, SEOG, NDSL, GSL, CWS. Application deadline February 1.
Admissions High school graduation with 16 units required. Interview encouraged. SAT and 2 ACH required. $25 application fee. Application deadline February 1. $300 deposit required on acceptance of admissions offer (May 1). *Early Admission* and *Early Decision* programs. Transfers accepted. Admission deferral possible. Credit possible for CEEB AP exams.
Student Life Student government. Newspaper, literary magazine, yearbook, radio station. Music, theatre, dance groups. Crafts Center. Black Student Society. Academic, professional, religious, service, and special interest clubs. Women's dorms & houses. 98% of students live on campus. Honor code. 2 semesters of phys ed required. 9 intercollegiate sports for women; intramurals. AIAW. Student body composition: 2% Asian, 3% Black, 2% Hispanic, 93% White. 66% from out of state.

[1] WHEELOCK COLLEGE
200 Riverway, Boston 02215, (617) 734-5200
Dean of Admissions: Joan Wexler

- **Enrollment: 10m, 550w; 810 total (including graduates)**
- **Tuition (1982/83): $5,550**
- **Room & Board: $3,000; Fees: $175**
- **Degree offered: BSEd, ASEd**
- **Mean SAT 440v, 450m**
- **Student-faculty ratio: 12 to 1**

A private college established in 1888, became coed in 1972. 5-acre residential urban campus on the Riverway in Boston. Air, rail, and bus service.
Academic Character NEASC and professional accreditation. Semester system. Majors offered in teaching children, children in health care settings, and social services for children & families. Programs in infants & toddlers and their families; young children & their families; children in day care & their families; multicultural settings; primary classrooms; museum as a learning center; young children with special needs; moderate special needs; special needs in family & clinical settings. Liberal arts minors offered in art, English, history, music, philosophy, psychology, sociology, science, and theater arts. Courses in economics, math, political science, Spanish. Distributive requirements. MSEd and CAGS granted. ASEd offered on a part-time basis. Independent study, pass/fail, internships. Field work and student teaching stressed. Combined BS/MS program. Study abroad. Early childhood and special education certification. Member Fenway Library Consortium. 65,000-volume library with children's literature collection.

Financial CEEB CSS and ACT FAS. College scholarships, grants, loans, state grants, payment plan; PELL, SEOG, NDSL, GSL, PLUS, CWS. Application deadline March 1 (December 1 for Early Decision).
Admissions High school graduation required. 16 units and child care experience recommended. Interview required. SAT or ACT required. Application deadline February 15. $100 tuition and $100 room deposits required on acceptance of admissions offer (May 1). *Early Decision* Program. Transfers accepted. Admission deferral possible. Credit possible for CEEB AP and CLEP exams.
Student Life Student Board. Newspaper, yearbook. Music, drama, dance groups. Black Student Organization. Women's Center. Academic, professional, and special interest clubs. Freshmen must live at home or on campus. Coed and single-sex dorms. No married-student housing. 70% of students live on campus. Cars discouraged on campus. Regular class attendance expected. One health & phys ed course required. Intercollegiate field hockey and tennis. Recreational sports. Student body composition: 6% Black, 92% White, 2% Other. 48% from out of state.

[1] WILLIAMS COLLEGE
Williamstown 01267, (413) 597-2211
Director of Admissions: Philip F. Smith

- **Undergraduates: 1,132m, 873w**
- **Tuition (1982/83): $6,950**
- **Room & Board: $2,825; Fees: $70**
- **Degree offered: BA**
- **Mean SAT 633v, 655m**
- **Student-faculty ratio: 12 to 1**

A private college established in 1793, became coed in 1970. 450-acre small-town campus in the Berkshire hills, 140 miles from Boston. Bus service to Pittsfield, Boston, and New York.
Academic Character NEASC accreditation. 4-1-4 system. Majors offered in American studies, art (2), astronomy & physics, biology, chemistry, classics (2), economics, English, French, geology, German, history, history of ideas, math/computer science, music, philosophy, physics, political economy, political science, psychology, religion, Russian, sociology, Spanish, theatre. Double, self-designed majors. Distributive requirements. Interdisciplinary programs. Independent study, honors program, Phi Beta Kappa, internships. Several research programs. 3-2 engineering program with Columbia U. Maritime studies term at Mystic Seaport (CT). Cross-registration at North Adams State and Bennington Colleges. 12-college and other exchange programs. Study abroad in Spain, Japan, and elsewhere. Center for Developmental Economics. Computer, museums, observatory & planetarium. 489,000-volume library.
Financial CEEB CSS. College and state scholarships, payment plan; PELL, SEOG, NDSL, PLUS, GSL, CWS. Application deadline January 15 (November 15 for early decision).
Admissions High school graduation with strong college prep program recommended. Interview encouraged. SAT or ACT, and 3 ACH required. $30 application fee. *Early Decision* and *Early Entrance* programs. Admission deferral possible. Transfers accepted. Credit possible for CEEB AP exams.
Student Life Student government. Newspapers, literary magazine, yearbook, radio station. Several music, drama, film, and dance groups. Intercollegiate debate. Black Student Union, women's and gay student groups. Academic, honorary, outing, service, and special interest organizations. Coed and single-sex dorms for freshmen and residential houses for upperclass students. 94% of students live on campus. No cars for 1st-semester freshmen. 2 years of phys ed required. Honor system. 14 intercollegiate sports for men, 10 for women; club and intramural sports. AIAW, NCAA, NESCAC. Student body composition: 2.5% Asian, 5.3% Black, 1.9% Hispanic, 0.5% Native American, 89.8% White. 87% from out of state.

[G2] WOODS HOLE OCEANOGRAPHIC INSTITUTION
Woods Hole 02543

[P] WORCESTER ART MUSEUM, SCHOOL OF THE
55 Salisbury Street, Worcester 01608

[1] WORCESTER POLYTECHNIC INSTITUTE
Worcester 01609, (617) 793-5286
Director of Admissions: Roy A. Seaberg, Jr.

- **Undergraduates: 1,950m, 450w; 2,600 total (including graduates)**
- **Tuition (1982/83): $6,700**
- **Room & Board: $2,625**
- **Degree offered: BS**
- **Mean SAT 540v, 650m**
- **Student-faculty ratio: 12 to 1**

A private institute established in 1865, became coed in 1968. 56-acre campus in a residential area of Worcester, 45 miles west of Boston. Additional 227-acre research & lab facilities in nearby Holden. Air and bus service.
Academic Character NEASC and professional accreditation. 4-term system, optional summer term. WPI Plan provides student-designed programs that stress projects, individualized study, and tutorials with self-paced learning that balances classroom and real-life experience. Degrees awarded on basis of demonstrated competence rather than specific course credits. Calendar permits flexibility for acceleration, employment, or internship experiences. Majors include applied mathematics, biology-biotechnology, chemistry, computer science, economics, humanities-technology, management, management-engineering, mathematics, physics, social science-technology, urban-environmental planning, and biomedical, chemical, civil, computer, electrical, environmental, materials, mechanical, & nuclear engineering. Minor, humanities sufficiency, and independent study

requirements. MS and PhD granted. Internships. 5-year cooperative work/study option. 16 off-campus project centers. 3-2 dual degree programs with Holy Cross, St. Lawrence, 6 other schools. Study abroad in England and Switzerland. ROTC; AFROTC & NROTC at Holy Cross. Many research labs. Computer center, nuclear reactor. 165,000-volume library.
Financial CEEB CSS. Institute scholarships, grants, loans, state scholarships; PELL, SEOG, NDSL, GSL, CWS. Suggest filing FAF in early February. Application deadline March 1.
Admissions High school graduation with a college prep program required. Interview strongly recommended. SAT & 3 ACH, or ACT required. $25 application fee. Application deadline Feburary 15. $200 deposit required on acceptance of admissions offer (May 1). *Early Entrance* and *Early Decision* programs. Admission deferral possible Transfers accepted. Credit possible for CEEB AP exams.
Student Life Student government. Newspaper, yearbook, radio station. Music and drama groups. Professional, academic, honorary, religious, women's, and special interest groups. 12 fraternities with houses. 35% of men join. Freshmen encouraged to live on campus. Coed and men's dorms. 70% of students live on campus. Freshmen may not keep cars on campus. 2 years of phys ed required. 10 intercollegiate sports for men, 5 for women; many club & intramural sports. AIAW, NCAA, ECAC, NECAC. Student body composition: 3% Asian, 2% Black, 2% Hispanic, 1% Native American, 92% White. 50% from out of state.

[1] WORCESTER STATE COLLEGE
Worcester 01602-2597, (617) 793-8000
Acting Director of Admissions: E. Jay Tierney

- **Undergraduates: 1,267m, 1,549w; 5,363 total (including graduates)**
- **Tuition (1982/83): $885 (in-state), $2,792 (out-of-state)**
- **Room & Board: $1,790; Fees: $182**
- **Degrees offered: BA, BS, BSEd**
- **Mean SAT 396v, 427m**
- **Student-faculty ratio: 16 to 1**

A public college established in 1874. 50-acre urban campus 40 miles west of Boston. Air, rail, and bus service.
Academic Character NEASC and professional accreditation. Semester system, 2 6-week summer terms. Majors offered in biology (6), chemistry (3), communication disorders, early childhood education, economics, elementary education (7), English, (1), French, geography (3), health studies, history (3), management (4), math (5), media (4), natural science (5), nursing, physics (1), psychology (5), sociology (1), Spanish (1), and urban studies (4). Minors in most major fields and 12 additional areas. Distributive requirements. EdM, MA, MS, CAGS granted. Independent study, honors program, pass/fail, internships. Preprofessional programs in dentistry, law, medicine, and veterinary medicine. Cross-registration through Worcester Consortium for Higher Education. Year exchanges with other state schools. Transfer programs in architecture, engineering. Marine sciences program at Mass Maritime. Study abroad. Elementary, secondary, and special education certification. AFROTC at Holy Cross, ROTC at Worcester Polytechnic. Language lab. 151,733-volume library.
Financial CEEB CSS. State scholarships; PELL, SEOG, NDSL, GSL, NSL, CWS. Scholarship application deadline May 1.
Admissions High school graduation with college prep program recommended. SAT required. $18 (in-state), $25 (out-of-state) application fees. Rolling admissions; suggest applying in fall of 12th year. Deadline March 1. $50 tuition and $50 room deposits required on acceptance of admissions offer (May 1). Transfers accepted. Credit possible for CEEB AP and CLEP exams. Special Academic Assistance and AID programs for disadvantaged students.
Student Life Student government. Newspaper, literary magazine, yearbook. Debate and drama groups. Academic, religious, service, and special interest clubs. Student apartments. 15% of students live on campus. 3 semester hours of phys ed required. 9 intercollegiate sports for men, 6 for women; intramurals. ECAC, NCAA. Student body composition: 2% Black, 1% Hispanic, 97% White. 2% from out of state.

MICHIGAN *(MI)*

[1] ADRIAN COLLEGE
Adrian 49221, (517) 265-5161
Director of Admissions: Thomas Williams

- **Undergraduates: 544m, 517w**
- **Tuition (1982/83): $4,776**
- **Room & Board: $2,022; Fees: $198**
- **Degrees offered: BA, BS, BFA, BMus, BMus Ed, BBA, AA**
- **Mean ACT 22; mean SAT 460v, 500m**
- **Student-faculty ratio: 14 to 1**

A private college affiliated with the United Methodist Church, established in 1859. 200-acre campus located in the small city of Adrian, 25 miles from Toledo, Ohio. Served by air and bus.
Academic Character NCACS and professional accreditation. Semester system, 3- and 6-week summer terms. Majors offered in accounting, art, biology, business administration, chemistry, earth science, economics, English, French, history, home economics, interior design, mathematics, music, philosophy-religion, physics, political science, psychology, sociology-anthropology, Spanish, speech communication-broadcasting-theatre, and health, physical education, & recreation. Distributives and 3 hours of religion or philosophy required. Independent study. Honors program. Internships. Preprofessional programs in dentistry, law, medical technology, medicine, ministry. 3-2 programs in engineering, veterinary science. Consortium with 8 area schools. Cooperative programs in Appalachia with Union College (KY), in fashion design in London, New York City. Study abroad. Elementary and secondary education certification. ROTC, NROTC at U of Michigan. Observatory, planetarium, language lab. 125,000-volume library with microform resources.
Financial CEEB CSS. College scholarships and loans, National Methodist loans, payment plans; PELL, SEOG, NDSL, CWS.
Admissions High school graduation with 15 units required. ACT or SAT required; ACT preferred. $15 application fee. Rolling admissions. $100 deposit required on acceptance of offer of admission. *Early Admission* Program. Admission deferral possible. Transfers accepted. Credit possible for CEEB AP exams; college has own advanced placement program. Learning development program.
Student Life Newspaper, yearbook, radio & TV stations. Music, drama, debate, and special interest groups. 5 fraternities and 5 sororities with houses. 17% of men and 21% of women join. Freshmen must live at home or on campus. Coed and single-sex dorms. Co-op dorm. 73% of students live on campus. 2 semesters of phys ed required. 8 intercollegiate sports for men, 6 for women; intramurals. AIAW, MIAA. Student body composition: 1.8% Asian, 3.4% Black, 94.4% White, 0.4% Other. 18% from out of state.

[1] ALBION COLLEGE
Albion 49224, (517) 629-5511
Director of Admissions: Frank Bonta

- **Undergraduates: 982m, 934w**
- **Tuition (1982/83): $5,152**
- **Room & Board: $2,492; Fees: $394**
- **Degrees offered: AB, BFA**
- **Mean SAT 530v, 580m**
- **Student-faculty ratio: 15 to 1**

A private college affiliated with the Methodist Church, established in 1835. 181-acre small-city campus, 15 miles from Jackson and 20 miles from Battle Creek. Served by rail; airport in Jackson.
Academic Character NCACS and professional accreditation. Semester system, 7-week summer term. Majors offered in anthropology & sociology, biology, chemistry, economics & management, English, French, geological sciences, German, history, home economics, mathematics, physics, music, philosophy, physical education, political science, psychology, religious studies, Spanish, speech communication & theatre, and visual arts. Distributive requirements. Honors program. Phi Beta Kappa. Some pass/fail. Internships. Preprofessional programs in dentistry, engineering, medical technology, law, medicine, nursing. Business management program. 3-2 programs in engineering, forestry, wildlife management. 3-1 program in medical technology. Member association with 11 area schools. Philadelphia, Oak Ridge, Washington Semesters. New York arts program. Study abroad. Elementary and secondary education certification. Language house, computer center, nature center. 220,000-volume library.
Financial CEEB CSS. College scholarships, grants, loans, state scholarships and grants, payment plan; PELL, SEOG, GSL, NDSL, CWS. Application deadline March 15.
Admissions High school graduation with 15 units required. Interview encouraged. SAT or ACT required. $15 application fee. Rolling admissions; application deadline April 1. $150 deposit required on acceptance of offer of admission. Admission deferral possible. Transfers accepted. Credit possible for CEEB AP and CLEP exams; college has own advanced placement program.
Student Life Student government. Newspaper, magazine, yearbook. Music, debate, speaking, drama groups. Tutorial association. Religious, academic, honorary, service, and special interest groups. 6 fraternities with houses and 6 sororities without houses. 60% of men and 40% of women join. Single students must live with relatives or on campus. Dorms for men & women, co-op women's dorm. Married-student housing. 96% of students live on campus. Freshmen may not have cars on campus. Liquor, drugs prohibited on campus. Class attendance required. 10 intercollegiate sports for men, 10 for women; intramurals. MIAA. Student body composition: 2% Black, 98% White. 12% from out of state.

[1] ALMA COLLEGE
Alma 48801, (800) 292-9078 (in-state); (800) 248-9267 (out-of-state)
Director of Admissions: Ted C. Rowland

- **Undergraduates: 547m, 553w**
- **Tuition (1982/83): $5,544**
- **Room & Board: $2,446; Fees: $88**
- **Degrees offered: BA, BS, BFA, BMus, BSW**
- **Mean ACT 24.1; mean SAT 528v, 581m**
- **Student-faculty ratio: 16 to 1**

A private college affiliated with the Presbyterian Church of USA, established in 1886. 80-acre campus in residential section of Alma, 120 miles from Detroit. Served by bus.
Academic Character NCACS and professional accreditation. 4-4-1 system. Majors offered in art, biology, business administration, chemistry, computer studies, economics, education, English, foreign service, French, German, history, international business, mathematics, music, philosophy, physical education, physics, political science, psychology, public service, religion, social work, sociology, Spanish, speech/theatre, and theatre/dance.

Self-designed majors. Courses in 7 additional areas. Distributives, GRE, and senior exams required. Independent study. Honors program. Phi Beta Kappa. Pass/fail. Preprofessional programs in dentistry, engineering, foreign service, law, medicine, public service, social work, theology. 3-1 program in medical technology. 3-2 programs in engineering, natural studies with U Michigan. Cooperative programs with Merrill-Palmer Institute, Wayne State. Consortium with 7 area schools. Princeton Critical Language Program. Washington workshop. Elementary, secondary, and bilingual education certification. Study abroad. Teaching program in Nigeria. ROTC at Central Michigan. Language lab. 150,000-volume library.

Financial CEEB CSS and ACT FAS. College scholarships, grants, loans, state scholarships and grants, payment plan; PELL, SEOG, NDSL, CWS. Application deadlines March 1 (scholarships), June 1 (loans).

Admissions High school graduation with 16 units required. Interview encouraged. SAT or ACT required. $10 application fee. Rolling admissions; suggest applying soon after October 1. *Early Decision* and *Early Admission* programs. Admission deferral possible. Transfers accepted. Credit possible for CEEB AP and CLEP exams.

Student Life Student government. Newspaper, magazine, yearbook, radio & TV stations. Music, debate, oratory, drama groups. Afro-American society. College quiz bowl. Academic, honorary, religious, and special interest groups. 4 fraternities and 3 sororities with houses. 38% of men and 35% of women join. Students must live at home or on campus. Coed and single-sex dorms and cottages. 90% of students live on campus. Gambling and drugs prohibited on campus. Attendance required at 2 convocations per year. 10 intercollegiate sports for men, 9 for women; intramurals. AIAW, MIAC. Student body composition: 1% Black, 1% Hispanic, 97% White, 1% Other. 5% from out of state.

[J1] ALPENA COMMUNITY COLLEGE

Alpena 49707

[1] ANDREWS UNIVERSITY

Berrien Springs 49104, (616) 471-7771
Toll-free: (800) 632-2248 (in-state), (800) 253-2874 (out-of-state)
Director of Admissions & Records: Douglas K. Brown

- **Undergraduates: 926m, 1,073w; 3,083 total (including graduates)**
- **Tuition (1982/83): $4,950**
- **Room & Board: $2,670; Fees: $25**
- **Degrees offered: BA, BS, BMus, BSW, BBA, BFA, BArch Tech, BET, BInd Tech, AA, AS, AArch Tech, AET, AInd Tech**
- **Mean ACT 18.6**
- **Student-faculty ratio: 14 to 1**

A private university affiliated with the Seventh-day Adventist Church, established in 1874. 1,000-acre rural campus in small town of Berrien Springs, 20 miles from South Bend, Indiana. Served by bus.

Academic Character NCACS and professional accreditation. Trimester system, 8-week summer term. 86 majors offered in the areas of arts & sciences, agriculture, engineering & technology, business & economics, education, health, home economics, communication, and physical education. Minor or interdisciplinary major required. Minors offered in most major fields and in 20 additional areas. Distributives, comprehensive exams, and 18 credits in religion required. Graduate and professional degrees granted. Independent study. Honors program. Cooperative work/study, pass/fail, internships. Preprofessional programs in 19 areas. 2-2 engineering program with Walla Walla. Cooperative programs with Loma Linda U in dental assistant, dental hygiene, medical record administration, occupational therapy, physical therapy, respiratory therapy. Study abroad. Elementary, secondary, and special education certification. A-V center, lab school. 777,847-volume library with microform resources.

Financial CEEB CSS and ACT FAS. University and state scholarships, grants, loans, grants-in-aid, tuition discounts for siblings; PELL, SEOG, NSS, NDSL, FISL, NSL, CWS; university has own work program. Recommended application deadline June 1.

Admissions High school graduation with 10 units required. GED accepted with restrictions. Interview recommended. ACT required. $15 application fee. Rolling admissions; suggest applying 9 months before intended date of entrance. $50 deposit required on acceptance of offer of admission. Admission deferral possible. Transfers accepted. Credit possible for CEEB AP and CLEP exams; university has own advanced placement program.

Student Life Student government. Newspaper, yearbook, radio station. Music groups. Academic, honorary, religious, service, and special interest groups. Single students under 25 must live at home or on campus. Single-sex dorms. Some married-student housing. 71% of students live on campus. First term freshmen may not have cars on campus. Liquor, tobacco, drugs, card playing, dancing, profanity, obscene materials, improper associations prohibited. Class, chapel, and convocation attendance required. 3 credits of phys ed required. Intramural and club sports. Student body composition: 3% Asian, 13% Black, 6% Hispanic, 1% Native American, 57% White, 20% Other. 58% from out of state.

[1] AQUINAS COLLEGE

Grand Rapids 49506, (616) 459-8281
Dean of Admissions: James L. Schultz

- **Enrollment: 1,197m, 1,526w**
- **Tuition (1982/83): $4,498**
- **Room & Board: $2,314**
- **Degrees offered: BA, BS, BAGen Ed, BFA, BMus, BMus Ed, BSBA, AA**
- **Student-faculty ratio: 16 to 1**

A private college controlled by the Dominican Sisters of Grand Rapids, established in 1923. 70-acre wooded campus in Grand Rapids. Served by air, rail, and bus.

Academic Character NCACS accreditation. Semester system, 4-week spring term, 8-week summer term. 40 majors offered in the areas of art, sciences, business, communication, information systems, environmental studies, humanities, music, physical education, and urban studies. Self-designed majors. Teaching minors offered in all major fields. Distributive requirements. Senior exams in some departments. Masters degrees granted. Independent study. Cooperative work/study, pass/fail. Preprofessional programs in dentistry, law, medicine, social work. 2-year transfer program in engineering with U of Detroit. Exchange programs with schools in Miami, San Rafael, New Orleans, New York state. Study abroad. Elementary and secondary education certification. 140,000-volume library.

Financial CEEB CSS. College scholarships, grants, loans, state tuition grants, payment plan; PELL, SEOG, NDSL, GSL, CWS; college has own work program. Priority application deadline for scholarships February 1.

Admissions High school graduation with 15 units required. SAT or ACT required. $15 application fee. Rolling admissions. $50 deposit required on acceptance of offer of admission. *Early Admission* Program. Admission deferral possible. Transfers accepted. Credit possible for CEEB AP and CLEP exams, and for life/work experience.

Student Life Student government. Newspaper, magazine, yearbook. Music clubs. Academic, service, honorary, and special interest groups. Freshmen and sophomores must live at home or on campus. Coed and single-sex dorms, special interest housing. 35% of students live on campus. 7 intercollegiate sports for men, 6 for women; several intramurals. Student body composition: 3% Black, 1.3% Hispanic, 0.4% Native American, 87.5% White, 7.8% Other. 2% from out of state.

[J1] BAY DE NOC COMMUNITY COLLEGE

Escanaba 49829

[1] CALVIN COLLEGE

3201 Burton Street, SE, Grand Rapids 49506, (616) 949-4000
Director of Admissions: Donald Lautenbach

- **Undergraduates: 1,921m, 2,052w**
- **Tuition (1982/83): $3,950**
- **Room & Board: $1,850**
- **Degrees offered: AB, BS, BFA**
- **Mean ACT 22; mean SAT 485v, 525m**
- **Student-faculty ratio: 19 to 1**

A private college affiliated with the Christian Reformed Church, established in 1876. 181-acre suburban campus in Grand Rapids. Served by air, rail, and bus.

Academic Character NCACS accreditation. 4-1-4 system, 3 4-week summer terms. Majors offered in art, biology, chemistry, computer science, economics, education, engineering, English, French, geology, German, Greek, history, Latin, mathematics, music, nursing, philosophy, physical education, physics, political science, psychology, recreation, religion & theology, sociology, Spanish, special education, and speech. Courses in Dutch, geography. Distributives and 2 religion courses required. Masters degrees granted. Honors programs. Credit by exam. Preprofessional programs in agriculture, architecture, business administration, dentistry, engineering, forestry, home economics, law, librarianship, medical technology, medicine, nursing, occupational therapy, theology. 3-2 programs in engineering, 3-1 programs in dentistry, law, medical technology, medicine. 3-year Masters program with U of Michigan, U of Chicago. Urban internship in Chicago. Washington Semester. Study abroad. Elementary and secondary education certification. Teacher-Learning Materials Center, language lab. 330,000-volume library.

Financial CEEB CSS. College scholarships, grants, loans, grants-in-aid for children of CRC members; PELL, SEOG, CWS. Application deadlines February 1 (scholarships), July 1 (loans).

Admissions High school graduation with 16 units required. SAT or ACT required. Rolling admissions; application deadline July 1. *Early Admission* Program. Admission deferral possible. Transfers accepted. Credit possible for CEEB AP and CLEP exams; college has own advanced placement program.

Student Life Student government. Associated Women Students. Newspaper. Social action groups. Music and drama organizations. Religious, literary, and special interest groups. Freshmen and sophomores must live on campus. Single-sex dorms, some college apartments. 60% of students live on campus. Attendance expected in class, at church of choice, and at chapel services. 2 years of phys ed required. 10 intercollegiate sports for men, 8 for women. AIAW, MIAA. Student body composition: 0.3% Asian, 0.6% Black, 0.2% Hispanic, 0.2% Native American, 87.4% White, 11.3% Other. 43% from out of state.

[P] CALVIN THEOLOGICAL SEMINARY

Grand Rapids 49506

[1] CENTER FOR CREATIVE STUDIES—COLLEGE OF ART AND DESIGN

245 East Kirby, Detroit 48202, (313) 872-3118

- **Enrollment: 320m, 253w; 856 total (including part-time)**
- **Tuition (1982/83): $4,300**
- **Room & Board: $2,900**
- **Degree offered: BFA**
- **Mean ACT 17.6; SAT 480v, 450m**
- **Student-faculty ratio: 12 to 1**

A private, coeducational college of art and design founded in 1926 and located in the large city of Detroit.

Academic Character NCACS and professional accreditation. Semester system, 8-week summer term. Majors offered in fine arts, photography, industrial design, advertising design, and crafts. Certificates in the above also awarded. Students work with professional artists active in their fields. Private studio space is available in most majors. Pre-college programs are available. Accelerated study. Internships. 15,000-volume library with 25,000 slides and 100 periodicals.
Financial CEEB CSS. Scholarships range from $500 to full tuition, and are based on need. 75% of the student body is on some type of financial aid. GSL available.
Admissions High school graduation with 2.5 GPA required. SAT or ACT required. Rolling admissions; application deadline June 1. *Early Admission* Program. Admission deferral possible. Transfers accepted. Advanced placement credit possible.
Student Life Dormitories and apartments are available but not owned or operated by the college. Married-student housing. No intercollegiate or intramural athletics.

[1] CENTRAL MICHIGAN UNIVERSITY
Mount Pleasant 48859, (517) 774-3151
Director of Admissions: Michael A. Owens

- **Undergraduates: 6,137m, 7,828w; 16,477 total (including graduates)**
- **Tuition (1982/83): $1,287 (in-state), $3,286 (out-of-state)**
- **Room & Board: $2,140; Fees: $50**
- **Degrees offered: BA, BS, BFA, BMus, BMus Ed, BSBA, BSEd, BSW, BAA, BInd St**
- **Mean ACT 20**
- **Student-faculty ratio: 21 to 1**

A public university established in 1892. 850-acre campus located in small city of Mount Pleasant, 70 miles from Lansing. Served by air and bus.
Academic Character NCACS and professional accreditation. Semester system, 3-, 6-, and 8-week summer terms. 75 majors offered by the Schools of Arts & Sciences, Business Administration, Education, Fine & Applied Arts, and Health, Physical Education, & Recreation. Interdisciplinary and self-designed majors and minors. Distributive requirements. Graduate and professional degrees granted. Independent study. Honors program. Some pass/fail. Internships. Credit by exam. Preprofessional programs in 22 areas. 3-1 program in medical technology. Elementary, secondary, and special education certification. ROTC. Language lab, Instructional Materials Center, observatory. 675,000-volume library with microform resources.
Financial CEEB CSS and ACT FAS. University scholarships, grants, loans; PELL,SEOG, NDSL, CWS.
Admissions High school graduation required. ACT required for placement. Rolling admissions. $60 deposit required on acceptance of offer of admission. *Early Admission* Program. Admission deferral possible. Transfers accepted. Credit possible for CEEB AP and CLEP exams.
Student Life Student government. Newspaper, magazine, yearbook. Music, debate, drama groups. Tenants union. Volunteer programs. Women's Health and Information Project. Organization for Black Unity. Chicanos Organized for Progress and Action. Academic, honorary, political, religious, professional, service, and special interest groups. 12 fraternities, 7 with houses, and 10 sororities, 4 with houses. 5% of men and 4% of women join. Freshmen and sophomores must live at home or on campus. Coed and single-sex dorms. Married-student housing. 40% of students live on campus. Freshmen and students on academic probation may not have cars on campus. Liquor, hazing prohibited. 4 activity courses required. 9 intercollegiate sports for men, 8 for women; intramurals. AIAW, Mid-American Conference. Student body composition: 0.2% Asian, 1.3% Black, 0.6% Hispanic, 0.3% Native American, 97.3% White, 0.3% Other. 2% from out of state.

[J1] CHARLES STEWART MOTT COMMUNITY COLLEGE
1401 East Court Street, Flint 48503

[2] CLEARY COLLEGE
Washtenaw Avenue, Ypsilanti 48197

[1] CONCORDIA COLLEGE
Ann Arbor 48105

[1] CRANBROOK ACADEMY OF ART
Bloomfield Hills 48013, (313) 645-3300

- **Enrollment: 76m, 74w**
- **Tuition (1982/83): $4,350**
- **Room & Board: $2,200**
- **Degrees offered: MFA, MArch**

A private professional graduate school of art with a limited enrollment. Campus located in a rural environment northwest of Detroit.
Academic Character NCACS and professional accreditation. Semester system. Major programs include architecture, design, ceramics, painting, printmaking, photography, sculture, metalsmithing, and fiber.
Financial Typical annual expenses average $8,200.
Admissions Students are not accepted directly from high school. Portfolio required. Students admitted only in September.
Student Life Dormitory facilities available for unmarried students.

[J1] DAVENPORT COLLEGE OF BUSINESS
415 East Fulton Street, Grand Rapids 49503, (616) 451-3511, (800) 632-9569
Director of Admissions: Bill Kingma

- **Undergraduates: 1,484m, 2,798w**
- **Tuition (1982/83): $81 per credit hour**
- **Room: $1,425**
- **Degree offered: AS**

A private college established in 1866. Urban campus in Grand Rapids with branches in Lansing and Kalamazoo.
Academic Character NCACS accreditation. Trimester system, 2 5-week summer terms. Majors offered in accounting, general business, business management, computer programming, fashion merchandising, sales & marketing, retail management, transportation & distribution management, hospitality management, emergency medical services systems management, and administrative services. Double majors. Diploma programs in 8 additional areas. Credit by exam. Cooperative work/study at Walt Disney World. Cooperative BS program with Detroit College of Business.
Financial CEEB CSS. College scholarships, state scholarships and grants, Indiana grants; PELL, SEOG, NDSL, GSL, CWS.
Admissions High school graduation required. GED accepted. $20 application fee; $30 room deposit required with application. Rolling admissions. *Early Admission* and *Early Decision* programs. Admission deferral possible. Transfers accepted. Credit possible for CEEB CLEP exams.
Student Life Student Activities Board. Newspaper. Minority Student Union. Religious and professional groups. Single-sex dorms. Class attendance required. Club sports.

[J1] DELTA COLLEGE
University Center 48710, (515) 686-9000
Director of Admissions: Richard L. Wirtz

- **Undergraduates: 1,989m, 2,431w**
- **Tuition (1982/83): $25 per credit hour (in-state); $60 per credit hour (out-of-state)**
- **Room & Board: $1,045-$1,068**
- **Degrees offered: AA, ABS, AS, AAS, AGS**

A public junior college established in 1922. 640-acre campus in Bay County located between the cities of Saginaw, Bay City, and Midland. Served by bus.
Academic Character NCACS accreditation. Trimester system, 2 7½-week summer terms. 38 liberal arts and preprofessional transfer programs offered, as well as 45 occupational degree programs, and 21 certificate programs. Courses offered in 40 additional areas. Distributive requirements. Independent study. Pass/fail, credit by exam. Criminal Justice Training Center. Audio-visual labs, TV station, planetarium. 80,000-volume library.
Financial College scholarships, state scholarships, Native American scholarships and grants; PELL, NDSL, GSL, NSL, CWS; college has own work program.
Admissions High school graduation required. GED accepted. Rolling admissions; suggest applying by November. *Concurrent Enrollment* Program. Transfers accepted. Credit possible for CEEB CLEP exams.
Student Life Student government. Newspaper, literary publication, yearbook. Music, drama, film groups. Ethnic and cultural organizations. Professional, honorary, religious, and special interest groups. Limited college housing. Single-sex dorms. No married-student housing. 2 hours of phys ed required. 4 intercollegiate sports for men, 3 for women; intramurals. Student body composition: 0.5% Asian, 8.8% Black, 2.7% Hispanic, 0.4% Native American, 87.5% White, 0.1% Other. 0.4% from out of state.

[1] DETROIT, UNIVERSITY OF
4001 West McNichols Road, Detroit 48221, (313) 927-1245
Director of Admissions: James M. Masuga

- **Undergraduates: 1,550m, 950w; 6,375 total (including graduates)**
- **Tuition (1982/83): $4,770 ($5,130 for architecture majors)**
- **Room & Board: $2,560; Fees: $20**
- **Degrees offered: AB, ABClass, BS, BSAnes, BSMed Tech, BBA, BSW, BTA, BSEd, BEng, BArch**
- **Student-faculty ratio: 15 to 1**

A private Roman Catholic university controlled by the Jesuits, established in 1877. 70-acre urban campus in a residential section of Detroit. Served by air, rail, and bus.
Academic Character NCACS and professional accreditation. Trimester system, 6-week summer term. 24 majors offered by the College of Liberal Arts, 7 by the College of Business & Administration, 14 by the College of Engineering & Science, and 8 by the School of Education & Human Services. Self-designed majors. Distributive requirements. Graduate and professional degrees granted. Independent study. Honors programs. Cooperative work/study, some pass/fail. Internships. Preprofessional programs in medicine, dentistry. 5-year architecture program. Cross-registration with other Detroit area Catholic colleges. Study abroad. Elementary, secondary, and special education certification. ROTC. Computer center. 515,000-volume library.
Financial CEEB CSS. University scholarships, grants, loans, state scholarships, payment plan; PELL, SEOG, NDSL, CWS. Application deadlines February 15 (academic scholarships), March 31 (other aid).
Admissions High school graduation required. Interview encouraged. SAT or ACT required. $20 application fee. Rolling admissions; application deadline August 1. $100 deposit required on acceptance of offer of admission. *Early Admission* Program. Transfers accepted. Credit possible for CEEB AP and CLEP exams; university has own advanced placement program. Project One Hundred, Educational Opportunity Program for academically disadvantaged.
Student Life Student government, student court. Newspapers, magazine, yearbook, radio station. Music, drama, debate groups. Many academic, honorary, religious, service, and special interest organizations. 14 fraternities and 6 sororities; 2 have houses. Coed and single-sex dorms. Married-student housing. 36% of students live on campus. 6 intercollegiate sports for men, 3 for women; several intramural and club sports. AIAW, NCAA. Student body composition: 2% Asian, 15% Black, 2% Hispanic, 1% Native American, 55% White, 25% Other. 21% from out of state.

[P] DETROIT BIBLE COLLEGE
Farmington Hills — see William Tyndale College

[P] DETROIT COLLEGE OF BUSINESS
4801 Oakman Blvd., Dearborn 48126, (313) 582-6983
Director of Admissions: Judy Broderick

- **Undergraduates: 840m, 1,949w**
- **Tuition (1982/83): $2,496 ($2,592 for data processing and word processing**
- **Fees: $45**
- **Degrees offered: BBA, ABA, AA**
- **Student-faculty ratio: 20 to 1**

A private college established in 1962. 12-acre suburban campus in Dearborn. Served by bus.
Academic Character AICS and professional accreditation; NCACS accreditation candidate. Trimester system, 8-week summer term. Majors offered in accounting, accounting-data processing, data processing, industrial management, information management, management, marketing, and office administration. Courses in 9 additional areas. Independent study. Cooperative work/study. Credit by exam. 20,000-volume library.
Financial CEEB CSS. College scholarships, grants, loans, state grants and loans; PELL, Tuition Differential Grants, CWS.
Admissions High school graduation required. GED accepted. $15 application fee. Rolling admissions. $50 deposit required on acceptance of offer of admission. *Concurrent Enrollment* Program. Admission deferral possible. Transfers accepted. Credit possible for CEEB AP and CLEP exams, and for life/work experience. College has own advanced placement program.
Student Life Student government. Newspaper. Accounting Aid Society. Honorary and professional societies. One fraternity and one sorority. No student housing. Liquor, drugs prohibited on campus. Intercollegiate golf; intramural and club sports. NAIA. Student body composition: 0.3% Asian, 41.2% Black, 0.1% Foreign, 1.4% Hispanic, 0.7% Native American, 56.3% White.

[P] DETROIT COLLEGE OF LAW
130 East Elizabeth Street, Detroit 48201

[1] EASTERN MICHIGAN UNIVERSITY
Ypsilanti 48197, (313) 487-3060
Director of Admissions: Don Kajcienski

- **Undergraduates: 6,537m, 8,351w; 19,306 total (including graduates)**
- **Tuition (1982/83): $1,252 (in-state), $3,060 (out-of-state)**
- **Room & Board: $2,270; Fees: $71**
- **Degrees offered: BA, BS, BFA, BSN, BArt Ed, BBus Ed, BBA, BMus, BMus Ther, BMus Ed**
- **Mean ACT 18.5; mean SAT 450v, 443m**
- **Student-faculty ratio: 20 to 1**

A public university established in 1849. 460-acre campus in small city of Ypsilanti, 7 miles from Ann Arbor. Served by rail and bus. Airport 30 miles away in Detroit.
Academic Character NCACS and professional accreditation. Semester system, 6- and 7½-week summer terms. 72 majors offered by the College of Arts & Sciences, 11 by the College of Business, 10 by the College of Education, 14 by the College of Human Services, and 14 by the College of Technology. Minors offered in 15 additional areas. Distributive requirements. Graduate and professional degrees granted. Independent study. Honors program. Some pass/fail. Credit by exam. Preprofessional programs in applied science, architecture, dentistry, engineering, forestry, law, medicine, mortuary science, osteopathy, pharmacy, religious careers, social work. 3-1 medical technology program with area hospitals. Study abroad. Tropical biology program in the Bahamas. Elementary and secondary education certification. ROTC; AFROTC & NROTC at U of Michigan, Ann Arbor. 555,614-volume library with microform resources.
Financial CEEB CSS and ACT FAS. University scholarships, grants, loans, Michigan Competitive Scholarships, state loans; PELL, SEOG, NDSL, GSL, CWS. Recommended application deadline for scholarships December 15.
Admissions High school graduation required. GED accepted. SAT or ACT required of students under 21. Rolling admissions; suggest applying by December 1. *Early Admission* and *Concurrent Enrollment* programs. Transfers accepted. Credit possible for CEEB AP and CLEP exams; university has own advanced placement program.
Student Life Student government. Newspaper, magazine, yearbook. Debate group. Black, Chicano, Chinese, gay student associations. Adult Returning Student Organization. Academic, professional, honorary, religious, service, and special interest groups. 13 fraternities and 11 sororities. Freshmen and sophomores must live at home or on campus. Dorms & apartments for men and women. Married-student housing. 48% of undergraduates live on campus. 2 hours of phys ed required. 10 intercollegiate sports for men, 9 for women; several intramural and club sports. AIAW, NCAA, Mid-America Conference. Student body composition: 1% Asian, 10% Black, 3% Foreign, 1% Hispanic, 85% White. 5% from out of state.

[1] FERRIS STATE COLLEGE
Big Rapids 49307, (616) 796-9971
Director of Admissions: Karl S. Walker

- **Undergraduates: 6,061m, 3,796**
- **Tuition (1982/83): $1,419 (in-state), $3,126 (out-of-state)**
- **Room & Board: $2,190; Fees: $45**
- **Degree offered: BS**
- **Student-faculty ratio: 19 to 1**

A public college established in 1884. 650-acre campus located in small town of Big Rapids, 1 hour from Grand Rapids. Air, rail, and bus in Grand Rapids.
Academic Character NCACS and professional accreditation. Trimester system, 10-week summer term. 6 majors offered by the School of Allied Health, 26 by the School of Business, 11 by the School of Education & Learning Resources, 5 by the School of General Education, 1 by the School of Pharmacy, and 5 by the School of Technical & Applied Arts. Dual degrees possible. Independent study. Cooperative work/study. Internships. Secondary education certification. Art gallery, computer center. 210,000-volume library with microform resources.
Financial College scholarships, grants, loans, athletic scholarships, health professions loans, state loans; PELL, SEOG, NSS, NDSL, CWS. Application deadline 2 months before beginning of term.
Admissions High school graduation required. GED accepted. ACT required. Rolling admissions. $130 deposit required on acceptance of offer of admission. Transfers accepted. Credit possible for CEEB AP and CLEP exams; college has own advanced placement program.
Student Life Student government. Newspaper, magazine, yearbook, radio station. Music, drama, debate groups. Academic, religious, honorary, professional, service, and special interest organizations. 14 fraternities and 8 sororities. Coed and single-sex dorms. Married-student housing. 50% of students live on campus. Boarding freshmen may not have cars on campus. 3 hours of phys ed required. 10 intercollegiate sports for men, 6 for women; intramurals. NAIA, AIAW, NCAA. Student body composition: 3.8% Black, 0.2% Hispanic, 0.3% Native American, 95% White, 0.7% Other. 3.6% from out of state.

[1] GMI
Formerly General Motors Institute
1700 West 3rd Avenue, Flint 48502, (313) 762-7865
Toll-free: (800) 572-9908 (in-state), (800) 521-7436 (out-of-state)
Associate Dean of Admissions, Records, & Financial Aid: Dr. Fern Ramirez

- **Undergraduates: 1,609m, 780w**
- **Tuition (1982/83): $1,800**
- **Room & Board: $1,650; Fees: $64**
- **Degrees offered: BMech Eng, BInd Eng, BElec Eng, BInd Admin**
- **Mean ACT 28; mean SAT 572v, 675m**
- **Student-faculty ratio: 14 to 1**

A private institute established in 1919, became coed in 1965. 45-acre campus located in residential section of Flint. Served by air, rail, and bus.
Academic Character NCACS and professional accreditation. Semester system. Majors offered in electrical engineering, industrial engineering, industrial administration, and mechanical engineering. All are 5-year, cooperative work/study programs. Courses in 10 additional areas. Thesis required. Independent study. Dual degree programs with several graduate schools. 6-week overseas work periods at General Motors units. Resources of over 140 cooperative units available. Extensive engineering labs. 90,000-volume library.
Financial All students are employees of a sponsoring GM unit and draw salaries. Institute loans; PELL, CWS.
Admissions High school graduation with 16 units required. SAT or ACT required; SAT preferred. 2 ACH required for placement. $10 application fee. Rolling admissions; application deadline January 18. $100 deposit required on acceptance of offer of admission. *Early Decision* Program. Transfers accepted. Credit possible for CEEB AP and CLEP exams; institute has own advanced placement program.
Student Life Student government. Newspaper, magazine, yearbook, radio station. Music, drama, photography groups. Black Unity Congress, International Club. Honor societies. Professional, religious, and special interest groups. 17 fraternities, 12 with houses, 5 sororities, 3 with houses. Single freshmen must live in dorms on campus. Limited upperclass housing. 40% of students live on campus. Class attendance required. Intramural and club sports. Student body composition: 6% Asian, 10% Black, 3% Hispanic, 1% Native American, 80% White. 56% from out of state.

[J1] GLEN OAKS COMMUNITY COLLEGE
Centreville 49032

[J1] GOGEBIC COMMUNITY COLLEGE
Ironwood 49938

[P] GRACE BIBLE COLLEGE
1011 Aldon Street, SW, Grand Rapids 49509

[1] GRAND RAPIDS BAPTIST COLLEGE AND SEMINARY
Grand Rapids 49505

[J1] GRAND RAPIDS JUNIOR COLLEGE
Grand Rapids 49503

[1] GRAND VALLEY STATE COLLEGES
College Landing, Allendale 49401, (616) 895-6611
Director of Admissions: Carl Wallman

- **Enrollment: 1,733m, 1,930w**
- **Tuition (1982/83): $1,350 (in-state), $3,150 (out-of-state)**
- **Room & Board: $2,290; Fees: $30**
- **Degrees offered: BA, BFA, BSW, BS, BMus, BMus Ed, BAS, BBA**
- **Mean ACT 19**
- **Student-faculty ratio: 20 to 1**

A public college established in 1960. 876-acre rural campus in Allendale, 12

miles from Grand Rapids. Served by bus. Air and rail in Grand Rapids.
Academic Character NCACS accreditation. Semester system, 12-week summer term. 61 majors offered by the College of Arts & Sciences, William James College (liberal arts), Kirkhof College (business & professional skills), and the Seidman College of Business. Self-designed majors. Distributive requirements. Independent study. Honors program in Arts and Sciences. Cooperative work/study, pass/fail, internships. Preprofessional programs in engineering, law. 2-2, 3-2 programs in engineering, forestry, fisheries & wildlife management. Study abroad. Elementary, secondary, and special education certification. Computer center, A-V center, Urban and Environmental Studies Institute. 293,000-volume library with microform resources.
Financial CEEB CSS and ACT FAS. College scholarships and loans, payment plan; PELL, SEOG, NDSL, FISL, HELP, NSL, CWS. Application deadlines February 15 (FAF, FFS), April 1 (loans).
Admissions High school graduation with 9 units required. Personal essay required for William James College. Interview encouraged. ACT required. $15 application fee. Rolling admissions; suggest applying before April 1. $90 deposit required on acceptance of admissions offer. *Early Admission, Early Decision, Concurrent Enrollment* programs. Admission deferral possible. Transfers accepted. Credit possible for CEEB AP and CLEP exams; colleges have own advanced placement programs. Developmental Skills Institute.
Student Life Newspaper, magazine, yearbook, radio & TV stations. Music, drama groups. Afro-American Association, Native American group. Jewish Students Organization, Muslim Students Association. Women's Information Bureau. Academic, service, and special interest groups. 2 fraternities without houses. 2% of men join. Single-sex & co-op dorms. 20% of students live on campus. Liquor prohibited. 9 intercollegiate sports for men, 7 for women; intramurals. NAIA, AIAW, Great Lakes Association. Student body composition: 5% Black, 1% Hispanic, 0.5% Native American, 89% White, 4.5% Other. 3% from out of state.

[P] GREAT LAKES BIBLE COLLEGE
PO Box 40060, Lansing 48901

[J2] GREAT LAKES MARITIME ACADEMY
Traverse City — see Northwestern Michigan College

[J1] HENRY FORD COMMUNITY COLLEGE
5101 Evergreen Road, Dearborn 48128

[J1] HIGHLAND PARK COMMUNITY COLLEGE
Glendale Avenue at Third Street, Highland Park 48203

[1] HILLSDALE COLLEGE
Hillsdale 49242, (517) 437-7341
Director of Admissions: Russell L. Nichols

- **Undergraduates: 540m, 510w**
- **Tuition (1982/83): $5,200**
- **Room & Board: $2,620; Fees: $170**
- **Degrees offered: BA, BS, BLS**
- **Mean SAT 501v, 516m**
- **Student-faculty ratio: 14 to 1**

A private college established in 1844. 200-acre campus located in small city of Hillsdale, 100 miles from Detroit, 70 miles from Toledo. Served by air and bus.
Academic Character NCACS accreditation. Semester system, 2 3-week and 1 6-week summer terms. Majors offered in accounting, American studies, art, biology, business administration, chemistry, communication arts, comparative literature, early childhood education, economics, education, English, environmental business, European studies, French, German, history, humanities, international business, math, music, philosophy-religion, physical education/health, physics, political economy, psychology, sociology, social work, Spanish, speech, and theatre arts. Minors offered in all major fields. Distributive requirements. Paralegal certification. Independent study. Honors program. Journalism internships. Preprofessional programs in forestry, nursing, osteopathy. 3-1 programs in allied health, dentistry, engineering, law, medicine, medical technology. 3-2 and 4-2 programs in engineering with Northwestern Tech. Study abroad. Early childhood, elementary, and secondary education certification. Preschool lab, psychology lab, language lab. 100,000-volume library.
Financial CEEB CSS. College scholarships, grants, loans; PELL, GSL, NDSL. Application deadline March 15.
Admissions High school graduation required. Interview encouraged. SAT or ACT required; ACH encouraged. $15 application fee. Rolling admissions; suggest applying at end of 11th year. $150 deposit required on acceptance of offer of admission. *Early Admission* Program. Admission deferral possible. Transfers accepted. Credit possible for CEEB AP and CLEP exams.
Student Life Student government. Newspaper, magazine, yearbook. Music, debate, film, theatre groups. Blacks United. Academic, honorary, political, religious, and special interest groups. 6 fraternities and 3 sororities with houses. 52% of men and 40% of women join. Freshmen must live at home or in dorms. Single-sex dorms. 80% of students live on campus. 1 year of phys ed required. 7 intercollegiate sports for men, 6 for women; intramurals. NAIA, Great Lakes Conference. Student body composition: 0.3% Asian, 3.1% Black, 0.2% Hispanic, 95.7% White. 51% from out of state.

[1] HOPE COLLEGE
Holland 49423, (616) 392-5111
Director for Admissions: James R. Bekkering

- **Undergraduates: 1,077m, 1,119w; 2,458 total (including part-time)**
- **Tuition (1982/83): $4,980**
- **Room & Board: $2,290; Fees: $30**
- **Degrees offered: AB, BS, BMus, BSN**
- **Mean ACT 23; mean SAT 490v, 540m**
- **Student-faculty ratio: 15 to 1**

A private college affiliated with the Reformed Church in America, established in 1844. 45-acre campus in Holland, 25 miles from Grand Rapids. Airport and bus station in Grand Rapids.
Academic Character NCACS and professional accreditation. Semester system, 6-week summer term, 2 3-week spring terms. 42 majors offered in the areas of arts & sciences, business, communication, international studies, languages, music, nursing, and physical education. Self-designed and interdepartmental majors. Courses in Greek, linguistics, Russian. Distributives and 2 religion courses required. Independent study. Phi Beta Kappa. Pass/fail. Internships. 3-2, 4-1 programs in engineering with Case Western Reserve, Columbia, U of Michigan, Michigan State, RPI, USC, Washington U (St. Louis). Area studies and foreign language studies with Great Lakes Colleges Association. Member of Associated Colleges of the Midwest. Study abroad in over 20 countries. Washington Semester. Fine Arts semester in New York City, urban semesters in Chicago and Philadelphia. Oak Ridge Semester. Elementary, secondary, and special education certification. Computer center, language lab. 192,000-volume library with microform resources.
Financial CEEB CSS (preferred) and ACT FAS. College and state scholarships and grants, college loans, National Merit scholarships, payment plan; PELL, SEOG, NDSL, GSL, CWS. Application deadline March 1.
Admissions High school graduation with 16 units required. Interview encouraged. SAT or ACT required; ACT preferred. $15 application fee. Rolling admissions. $100 deposit required by May 1. *Early Admission* and *Early Decision* programs. Admission deferral possible. Transfers accepted. Credit possible for CEEB AP and CLEP exams; college has own advanced placement program. FOCUS program.
Student Life Student government. Newspaper, magazine, yearbook, radio station. Several music, debate, speaking, reading, drama groups. Religious, academic, honorary, and special interest groups. 5 fraternities with houses and 5 sororities with rooms; 25% of students join. Students must live with relatives or on campus. Coed and single-sex dorms, language houses. 75% of students live on campus. Limited visiting hours in houses. Liquor prohibited. Class attendance required. 2 semesters of phys ed required. 10 intercollegiate sports for men, 9 for women; intramurals. AIAW, NCAA, MIAA. Student body composition: 0.5% Asian, 1% Black, 1% Hispanic, 0.2% Native American, 94.3% White. 27% from out of state.

[P] JACKSON BUSINESS UNIVERSITY
234 South Mechanic Street, Jackson 49201

[J1] JACKSON COMMUNITY COLLEGE
Jackson 49201

[1] KALAMAZOO COLLEGE
Kalamazoo 49007, (616) 383-8408
Toll-free: (800) 632-5757 (in-state), (800) 253-3602 (out-of-state)
Director of Admissions: David M. Borus

- **Undergraduates: 650m, 650w**
- **Tuition (1982/83): $6,492**
- **Room & Board: $2,430**
- **Degree offered: AB**
- **Mean ACT 26; mean SAT 540v, 565m**
- **Student-faculty ratio: 16 to 1**

A private college affiliated with the American Baptist Churches, USA, established in 1833. 60-acre suburban campus within walking distance of downtown Kalamazoo, 140 miles from Chicago and Detroit. Served by air and bus.
Academic Character NCACS accreditation. Trimester system, 9½-week summer term. Majors offered in anthropology, anthropology-sociology, art, art history, biology, chemistry, computer science, economics-business administration, English, French, German, health sciences, history, mathematics, music, philosophy, physics, political science, psychology, religion, sociology, and theatre-communication arts. Self-designed majors. Special programs in 9 additional areas including African studies. Neglected language program in Japanese, Mandarin Chinese, Portuguese, Swahili. Distributive requirements. Senior exams. Independent study. Phi Beta Kappa. Internships. Pass/fail. 3-1 programs in dentistry, medicine, optometry, osteopathy, podiatry. 3-2 programs in engineering with Georgia Tech, U of Michigan, Washington U. Consortium with Western Michigan. Member Great Lakes College Association. Washington, New York, Philadelphia, Oak Ridge Semesters. Newberry Library term. Outward Bound. Study abroad. Secondary education certification. Computer center, language lab. 250,000-volume library with microform resources.
Financial CEEB CSS (preferred) and ACT FAS. College scholarships, grants, loans, state scholarships & grants, payment plans; PELL, SEOG, NDSL, CWS. Scholarship application deadline March 15.
Admissions High school graduation with 16 units preferred. Interview encouraged. ACT or SAT, and 3 ACH required. $20 application fee. Rolling admissions; suggest applying by March 15. $125 deposit required by May 1. *Early Admission* Program. Admission deferral possible. Transfers accepted. Credit possible for CEEB AP exams; college has own advanced placement program.
Student Life Student government. Newspaper, magazine, yearbook, radio station. Music, speech, drama groups. Women's Interest Group, Black Student Organization, Jewish fellowship organization. Religious, service, academic, and special interest groups. Seniors may live off-campus; others must live on

campus or with relatives. Coed and single-sex dorms, small houses, language houses. Married-student housing. 92% of students live on campus. Freshmen may not have cars on campus. 6 quarters of phys ed required. 9 intercollegiate sports for men, 8 for women; several intramural and club sports. NCAA, MIAA. Student body composition: 2% Asian, 2% Black, 1% Hispanic, 95% White. 25% from out of state.

[J1] KALAMAZOO VALLEY COMMUNITY COLLEGE
6767 West O Avenue, Kalamazoo 49009

[J1] KELLOGG COMMUNITY COLLEGE
Battle Creek 49016

[J1] KENDALL SCHOOL OF DESIGN
Grand Rapids 49503

[J1] KIRTLAND COMMUNITY COLLEGE
Roscommon 48653

[J1] LAKE MICHIGAN COLLEGE
Benton Harbor 49022

[1] LAKE SUPERIOR STATE COLLEGE
Sault Sainte Marie 49783, (906) 635-2231
Dean of Admissions: James E. Honkanen

- **Undergraduates: 1,104m, 879w; 2,559 total (including graduates)**
- **Tuition (1982/83): $1,320 (in-state), $2,509 (out-of-state)**
- **Room & Board: $2,295**
- **Degrees offered: BA, BS, AA**
- **Mean ACT 19.2**
- **Student-faculty ratio: 19 to 1**

A public college established in 1946. 115-acre campus in Sault Sainte Marie, 350 miles from Detroit. Airport 20 miles away.

Academic Character NCACS and professional accreditation. Trimester system, 5- and 10-week summer terms. Majors offered in accounting, biological science, biology, business administration, chemistry, criminal justice, earth science, economics-finance, engineering technology, English language & literature, environmental science, fisheries & wildlife, history, human services, industrial technology, math, medical technology, nursing, parks & recreation management, political science, psychology, social science, sociology, and sport & recreation management. Geology major in cooperation with Sault College in Ontario. Minors offered in several major fields and in French, geography, journalism, physics, and public administration. Associate degree in 20 areas. Certificate programs. Distributive requirements. Honors program. Pass/fail. Internships. Preprofessional programs in dentistry, education, law, medicine, pharmacy. ROTC. 117,000-volume library.

Financial CEEB CSS and ACT FAS. College scholarships, grants, loans, Native American grants, state loans; PELL, SEOG, NSS, NDSL, FISL, GSL, NSL, CWS. Application deadline April 1.

Admissions High school graduation with 15 units required. GED accepted. ACT required. $15 application fee. Rolling admissions; suggest applying by February 15. $50 deposit required on acceptance of offer of admission. *Concurrent Enrollment* Program. Transfers accepted. Credit possible for CEEB AP and CLEP exams; college has own advanced placement program.

Student Life Student government. Newspaper, magazine, radio station. Bands, debate, speaking, drama groups. Religious, professional, and special interest groups. Freshmen and sophomores must live at home or on campus. Coed and single-sex dorms. Married-student housing. 44% of students live on campus. 6 quarters of phys ed required. 7 intercollegiate sports for men, 6 for women; intramurals. AIAW, NAIA, NCAA, Central Collegiate Hockey Association, Great Lakes Intercollegiate Athletic Conference. 13% of students from out of state.

[J1] LANSING COMMUNITY COLLEGE
419 North Capitol, Lansing 48914

[1] LAWRENCE INSTITUTE OF TECHNOLOGY
21000 West Ten Mile Road, Southfield 48075, (313) 356-0200
Director of Admissions: Stanley F. Harris

- **Undergraduates: 2,826m, 548w; 5,703 total (including part-time)**
- **Tuition (1982/83): $1,830**
- **Room & Board: $2,200; Fees: $60**
- **Degrees offered: BS, BArch, AS, AEng**
- **Student-faculty ratio: 20 to 1**

A private institute established in 1932. 85-acre suburban campus in city of Southfield, 10 miles from Detroit. Served by bus. Air and rail in Detroit.

Academic Character NCACS and professional accreditation. Trimester system, 7-week summer term. Majors offered in architecture, business administration, chemistry, construction engineering, electrical engineering, humanities, industrial management, interior architecture, mathematics, computer science, mechanical engineering, and physics-computer science. Business administration and industrial management majors offer several options within their programs. Associate degrees offered in chemical technology, data processing, construction engineering, electrical engineering, industrial engineering, and mechanical engineering technologies. Accelerated study. Cooperative work/study in engineering and business. Credit by exam. "Two in Four" AS/BS program in management. ROTC at U of Detroit. 60,000-volume library with microform resources.

Financial CEEB CSS and ACT FAS. Institute scholarships, grants, loans, state scholarships and grants, payment plan; PELL, SEOG, NDSL, FISL, GSL, CWS. Scholarship application deadline March 1.

Admissions High school graduation with 16 units required. GED accepted. SAT or ACT recommended. $15 application fee. Rolling admissions; application deadline 30 days before term starts. $50 room deposit required on acceptance of offer of admission. *Early Admission* and *Concurrent Enrollment* programs. Admission deferral possible. Transfers accepted. Credit possible for CEEB AP, CLEP, and ACT PEP exams.

Student Life Student government. Newspaper, magazine, yearbook. Association of Black Students. Arab Student Association. Academic, honorary, professional, religious, and special interest groups. 3 fraternities, 2 with houses, and 2 sororities without houses. 2% of men and 5% of women join. Limited on-campus housing. Married-student housing. 7% of students live on campus. Public possession of liquor prohibited. Fireworks, firearms, drugs prohibited on campus. Intercollegiate golf; intramural and club sports. Student body composition: 7.3% Black, 1% Hispanic, 0.5% Native American, 84% White, 7.2% Other. 11% from out of state.

[J1] LEWIS COLLEGE OF BUSINESS
17370 Meyers Road, Detroit 48235

[J1] MACOMB COUNTY COMMUNITY COLLEGE—CENTER CAMPUS
Mt. Clemens 48044

[J1] MACOMB COUNTY COMMUNITY COLLEGE—SOUTH CAMPUS
Warren 48093

[1] MADONNA COLLEGE
36600 Schoolcraft, Livonia 48150, (313) 591-5052
Director of Admissions: Louis E. Brohl, III

- **Undergraduates: 804m, 2,581w**
- **Tuition (1982/83): $1,950**
- **Room & Board: $2,030; Fees: $20**
- **Degrees offered: BA, BS, BSN, BSW, AA, AS**
- **Student-faculty ratio: 20 to 1**

A private college controlled by the Felician Sisters, established in 1947. 49-acre suburban campus 20 miles from Detroit. Air, rail, and bus in Detroit.

Academic Character NCACS and professional accreditation. Trimester system. 17 majors offered by the Division of Humanities, 18 by the Division of Natural Science & Mathematics, and 37 by the Division of Social Sciences. Minors offered in most major areas. Distributive requirements. Independent study. Cooperative work/study, internships. Cross-registration through Detroit Area Consortium of Catholic Colleges. Credit from 4 area institutes. Study abroad. Elementary, secondary, and special education certification. Computer center, Psycho-educational Center. 100,000-volume library with microform resources.

Financial CEEB CSS. College scholarships, grants, loans; PELL, SEOG, NSS, NDSL, FISL, NSL, CWS. Application deadline March 1.

Admissions High school graduation required. GED accepted. ACT required. $15 application fee. Rolling admissions. Transfers accepted. Credit possible for CEEB AP and CLEP exams; college has own advanced placement program.

Student Life Student government. Newspaper. Music, drama groups. Deaf & hearing impaired club. Professional, religious, and special interest groups. 1 residence hall. 16% of students live on campus. Liquor, drugs, gambling prohibited on campus. Class attendance required. 3 intercollegiate sports for women, intercollegiate basketball for men; intramurals. Student body composition: 0.3% Asian, 9.3% Black, 0.7% Hispanic, 0.3% Native American, 84.9% White, 1.7% Other, 2.8% Unknown.

[1] MARYGROVE COLLEGE
8425 West McNichols Road, Detroit 48221, (313) 862-8000
Director of Undergraduate Admissions: Charles P. Donaldson

- **Undergraduates: 123m, 566w**
- **Tuition (1982/83): $3,787**
- **Room & Board: $2,100-$2,700**
- **Degrees offered: BA, BFA, BS, BSW, BMus, AA**
- **Student-faculty ratio: 16 to 1**

A private college conducted by the Sisters, Servants of the Immaculate Heart of Mary, established in 1905. Wooded 68-acre campus in Detroit. Served by air, rail, and bus.

Academic Character NCACS and professional accreditation. Semester system. 4 majors offered by the Education Division, 11 by the Letters Division, 5 by the Natural Science & Mathematics Division, 10 by the Professional Studies Division, 9 by the Social Science Division, and 20 by the Visual & Performing Arts Division. Minors required; minors offered in most major fields. Distributives and 6 hours of philosophy-religion required. MEd and MA in pastoral ministry granted. Independent study. Pass/fail. Cooperative work/study. Preprofessional programs in chiropractic studies, dentistry, law, medicine. 3-2 program in engineering and engineering technology with Georgia Tech. Member consortium with 5 area Catholic colleges. Elementary, secondary, and special education certification. Computer center, media center, continuing education center. 171,000-volume library with microform resources.

Financial CEEB CSS. College scholarships, grants, loans, room fee waivers, family tuition discounts, achievement scholarships, payment plan; PELL,

SEOG, GSL, NDSL, CWS, service grant employment. Application deadline March 1.
Admissions High school graduation required. GED accepted. Audition required for music, drama majors; interview, portfolio for art majors. SAT or ACT required. $15 application fee. Rolling admissions; suggest applying by 2 months before beginning of term. $50 deposit required on acceptance of offer of admission. *Early Admission* Program. Admission deferral possible. Transfers accepted. Credit possible for CEEB AP, CLEP, and ACT PEP exams; college has own advanced placement program.
Student Life Student government. Yearbook. Music groups. Religious, honorary, and special interest organizations. Coed dorms. 2 intercollegiate sports for men, 3 for women; intramurals. Student body composition: 54.1% Black, 0.6% Hispanic, 43.8% White, 0.7% Other.

[1] MERCY COLLEGE OF DETROIT

8200 West Outer Drive, Detroit 48219, (313) 531-7820
Director of Admissions: Jeanne Umholtz

- **Undergraduates: 238m, 1,156w**
- **Tuition (1982/83): $3,140**
- **Room & Board: $1,450-$2,150; Fees: $60**
- **Degrees offered: BA, BS, BSN, AA, AS**
- **Mean ACT 18**
- **Student-faculty ratio: 15 to 1**

A private college controlled by the Sisters of Mercy, established in 1941. 40-acre urban, residential campus in northwest Detroit. Served by air, rail, and bus.
Academic Character NCACS and professional accreditation. Semester system, 2 5-week and 1 11-week summer terms. 36 majors offered in the areas of business, alcoholism & drug abuse studies, health sciences, art, natural sciences, legal studies, education, English, history, home economics, industrial & institutional security, mathematics, philosophy, political & social sciences, Spanish, and speech & drama. Minor required. Minors offered in anthropology, dance, ethics, family life education, gerontology, music. Distributives and 2 hours of religion required. Independent study. Cooperative work/study. Pass/fail. Washington internships. Preprofessional programs in law, medicine. 3-2 program in engineering with U of Detroit. Member consortium with 5 area Catholic colleges. Study abroad. Elementary and secondary education certification. 100,000-volume library.
Financial CEEB CSS and ACT FAS. College scholarships, grants, and loans, Tuition Differential Grants; PELL, SEOG, GSL, NDSL, FISL, NSL, CWS. Suggested application deadlines April 1 (scholarships), January (loans).
Admissions High school graduation with 16 units required. GED accepted. SAT or ACT required. $15 application fee. Rolling admissions; suggest applying by January 1. $100 deposit required on acceptance of offer of admission. *Concurrent Enrollment* Program. Transfers accepted. Credit possible for CEEB AP and CLEP exams; college has own advanced placement program. Summer College Preparatory Program.
Student Life Student Planning Board. Newspaper, magazine. League of Black Students. Religious, academic, service, and special interest groups. Dorms. No married-student housing. 10% of students live on campus. Liquor prohibited on campus. Intercollegiate basketball for men and women, volleyball for women. Student body composition: 1.1% Asian, 32.1% Black, 0.9% Hispanic, 0.1% Native American, 65.7% White. 3% from out of state.

[1] MICHIGAN, THE UNIVERSITY OF

Ann Arbor 48109, (313) 764-7433
Director of Admissions: Cliff Sjogren

- **Undergraduates: 12,000m, 10,000w; 45,000 total (including graduates)**
- **Tuition (1982/83): $2,020 (est. in-state), $5,760 (est. out-of-state)**
- **Room & Board: $2,500**
- **Degrees offered: AB, BS, BSEng, BGS, BSMed Chem, BFA, BBA, BSEd, BMus, BMA, BSForestry, BSN**
- **Student-faculty ratio: 17 to 1**

A public university established in 1817. 2,542-acre campus in small city of Ann Arbor, 35 miles from Detroit.
Academic Character NCACS and professional accreditation. Trimester system, summer half term. 12 majors offered by the College of Engineering, 2 by the College of Pharmacy, 8 by the School of Art, 1 by the School of Business Administration, 8 by the School of Education, 12 by the School of Music, 7 by the School of Natural Resources, 1 by the School of Nursing, and 70 by the College of Literature, Science, & the Arts. Self-designed majors. Distributives and GRE required. Graduate and professional degrees granted. Honors program, Phi Beta Kappa. Pass/fail. Internships. Preprofessional programs in business administration, dentistry, law, education, medical technology, medicine, physical therapy, social work. 3-2 program with College of Engineering, 2-2 program with School of Business Administration. Study abroad. Elementary, secondary, and special education certification. ROTC, AFROTC, NROTC. Biological station, Fresh Air Camp (education, psychology, sociology, social work), geology, music, speech correction camps. Museums, computer center, A-V center. 5,800,000-volume library with microform resources.
Financial CEEB CSS and ACT FAS. University scholarships, grants, loans, athletic grants; PELL, SEOG, NDSL, GSL, HPL, CWS.
Admissions High school graduation with 16 units required. Portfolio required for art majors, audition for music majors. ACT or SAT required. $20 application fee. Rolling admissions; equal consideration deadline March 1. $100 deposit required on acceptance of offer of admission. *Early Admission* Program. Admission deferral possible. Transfers accepted. Credit possible for CEEB AP and CLEP exams.
Student Life Student government. Radio and TV stations. Music and dance groups. Over 500 student organizations. 36 fraternities, most with houses, and 19 sororities with houses. 10% of men and 13% of women join. Freshmen expected to live with relatives or on campus. Coed and single-sex dorms, co-op dorms, special interest housing. Married-student housing. 65% of students live on campus. Several intercollegiate and intramural sports for men and women. Student body composition: 3% Asian, 6% Black, 2% Hispanic, 1% Native American, 88% White. 32% from out of state.

■[1] MICHIGAN-DEARBORN, UNIVERSITY OF

4901 Evergreen Road, Dearborn 48128, (313) 593-5100
Director of Admissions: Edward J. Bagale

- **Undergraduates: 1,911m, 1,587w; 6,575 total (including graduates)**
- **Tuition (1982/83): $2,190 (in-state), $6,730 (out-of-state)**
- **Fees: $138**
- **Degrees offered: BA, BS, BBA, BGS, BSA, BSEng**
- **Student-faculty ratio: 24 to 1**

A public university established in 1959. 202-acre campus in small city of Dearborn. Served by air, rail, and bus.
Academic Character NCACS and professional accreditation. Trimester system, 2 7½-week summer terms. 7 majors offered by the Division of Education, 4 by the School of Engineering, 4 by the Division of Interdisciplinary Studies, 2 by the School of Management, and 22 by the College of Arts, Sciences, & Letters. 8 management and 6 administration concentrations. College of Arts, Sciences, & Letters offers courses in 10 additional areas. Distributive requirements. Graduate and professional degrees granted. Independent study. Honors program. Cooperative work/study in engineering, liberal arts. Internship required for BBA. Some pass/fail. Preprofessional programs in dentistry, law, medicine. 3-2 engineering programs. Study abroad. Elementary and secondary education certification. ROTC, NROTC, AFROTC at UMI-Ann Arbor. 225,000-volume library with microform resources.
Financial ACT FAS. University scholarships, grants, loans, payment plan; PELL, SEOG, NDSL, CWS. Application deadlines March 1 (scholarships), May 1 (loans).
Admissions High school graduation with 15 units required. Interview encouraged. SAT or ACT required; ACT preferred. $20 application fee. Rolling admissions; suggest applying by December 1. $50 deposit required on acceptance of offer of admission. *Early Decision* and *Early Admission* programs. Admission deferral possible. Transfers accepted. Credit possible for CEEB AP and CLEP exams; university has own advanced placement program.
Student Life Student government. Newspaper, magazine. Academic and honorary societies. Special interest groups. Limited university housing in apartments for single and married students. 1% live on campus. 3 intercollegiate sports for men, 2 for women; intramurals. NAIA, AIAW. 1% of students from out of state.

■[1] MICHIGAN-FLINT, UNIVERSITY OF

1321 East Court Street, Flint 48503, (313) 762-3300
Director of Admissions: Charles E. Rickard

- **Undergraduates: 1,129m, 1,246w; 4,609 total (including graduates)**
- **Tuition (1982/83): $1,180 (in-state), $3,820 (out-of-state)**
- **Degrees offered: AB, BS, BApp Sci, BBA, BGS, BMus Ed, BSN**
- **Mean SAT 451v, 514m**
- **Student-faculty ratio: 18 to 1**

A public university established in 1956. 42-acre riverfront campus in downtown Flint. Served by air, rail, and bus.
Academic Character NCACS and professional accreditation. Semester system, 7-week spring and summer terms. 36 majors offered in the areas of arts & sciences, business, education, and health fields; African/Afro-American studies majors. Self-designed majors. Special courses and programs. Distributive requirements. MLS, MPA, MBA granted. Independent study in some departments. Honors program. Limited pass/fail. Internships. Credit by exam. Joint program in medicine-liberal arts. Nursing program in cooperation with UMI-Ann Arbor for RNs. Elementary and secondary education certification; urban education preparation. Planetarium, natatorium, handicapped facilities, language lab, TV studio. 124,895-volume library.
Financial ACT FAS. University scholarships, grants, loans; PELL, SEOG, NDSL, CWS. Application deadlines May 1 (scholarships), April 1 (loans).
Admissions High school graduation with 15 units recommended. SAT or ACT required. $20 application fee. Rolling admissions; suggest applying by March 1. $50 deposit required on acceptance of offer of admission. *Early Admission* and *Concurrent Enrollment* programs. Admission deferral possible. Transfers accepted. Credit possible for CEEB AP exams. Challenge Scholar Program.
Student Life Student government. Newspaper, magazine. Music groups. Organization for Women Students. Students for Black Action. El Movimiento Estudiantil Chicano. Academic, honorary, religious, service, and special interest groups. No university housing. Intramural and club sports. Student body composition: 1% Asian, 12% Black, 1% Hispanic, 1% Native American, 84% White, 1% Other. 1% from out of state.

[J1] MICHIGAN CHRISTIAN COLLEGE

800 West Avon Road, Rochester 48063, (313) 651-5800
Director of Admissions: Larry Stewart

- **Undergraduates: 135m, 164w**
- **Tuition (1982/83): $2,325**
- **Room & Board: $2,000; Fees: $160**
- **Degrees offered: BRE, AA, AS, AAS**
- **Mean ACT 15.4**
- **Student-faculty ratio: 16 to 1**

A private junior college established in 1959. 91-acre suburban campus in Rochester, a suburb of Detroit.
Academic Character NCACS accreditation. Semester system. Majors

offered in Christian ministry, Biblical studies, art, Bible, business administration, education, English, history, home economics, journalism, law, music, psychology, sociology, speech, biology, chemistry, engineering, environmental sciences, mathematics, medicine, nursing, physical education, secretarial science, and legal assistantship. Minor required. Distributive requirements. Bible class required each semester. Credit by exam. Legal assistant internships. 49,200-volume library with microform resources.
Financial ACT FAS. College scholarships, state grants and loans, family discounts; PELL, SEOG, NDSL, GSL, CWS.
Admissions High school graduation required. GED accepted. ACT required. $15 application fee and $25 room deposit. Rolling admissions. *Early Admission* Program. Admission deferral possible. Transfers accepted. Credit possible for CEEB AP and CLEP exams; college has own advanced placement program.
Student Life Student government. Yearbook. Music and drama groups. Service and special interest groups. 4 social clubs for men and 4 for women. Single students must live at home or on campus. Single-sex dorms. No married-student housing. Limited class absences allowed; daily chapel required. 1 phys ed course required. 2 intercollegiate sports for men, 2 for women; intramural and club sports.

[1] MICHIGAN STATE UNIVERSITY
East Lansing 48824, (517) 355-8332
Director of Admissions: Charles Seeley

- **Undergraduates: 15,253m, 15,428w; 42,094 total (including graduates)**
- **In-state Tuition (1982/83): $1,610 (1st & 2nd years), $1,782 (3rd & 4th years)**
- **Out-of-state Tuition (1982/83): $3,564 (1st & 2nd years), $3,663 (3rd & 4th years)**
- **Room & Board: $2,281; Fees: $58**
- **Degrees offered: BA, BS, BMus, BFA, BLA**
- **Student-faculty ratio: 12 to 1**

A public university established in 1855. 5,320-acre suburban campus outside of Lansing, 82 miles from Detroit. Served by air and bus.
Academic Character NCACS and professional accreditation. Trimester system. Over 100 majors offered by the Colleges of Agriculture & Natural Resources, Arts & Letters, Business, Communication Arts & Sciences, Education, Engineering, Human Ecology, Natural Science, Nursing, Social Science, Veterinary Medicine, and the Colleges of James Madison and Lyman J. Briggs. Distributive requirements. Graduate and professional degrees granted. Independent study. Honors program, honors college, Phi Beta Kappa. Pass/fail, internships, credit by exam. Preprofessional programs in dentistry, law, medicine, optometry, osteopathy, theology, veterinary medicine. 5-year engineering programs for international service. 40 overseas programs. Elementary, secondary, and special education certification. ROTC, AFROTC. China Relations Center, Mathematics Teaching Center. Several research centers. Botanical garden, experimental farm. Planetarium, cyclotron, museum, language labs. Audio library, Broadcasting Service Division. 2,650,000-volume library.
Financial CEEB CSS and ACT FAS. University and state scholarships, grants, loans, payment plan; PELL, SEOG, NSS, NDSL, FISL, NSL, CWS. Suggest filing FAF or FFS by February.
Admissions High school graduation with 16 units required. ACT or SAT required. $20 application fee. Rolling admissions; suggest applying before January. Limited *Concurrent Enrollment* Program. Admission deferral possible. Transfers accepted. Credit possible for CEEB AP exams; university has own advanced placement program. Special admission programs.
Student Life Student government. Newspaper, magazine, yearbook, radio and TV stations. Music, debate, speaking, drama groups. 450 honorary, professional, religious, and special interest groups. 26 fraternities and 15 sororities; most have houses. 6% to 8% of men and women join. Freshmen and sophomores under 20 must live at home or on campus. Coed and single-sex dorms; honors, quiet houses. Co-op dorms. Married-student housing. 41% of students live on campus. Freshmen may not have cars on campus. Many intercollegiate, intramural, and club sports. NCAA, Big Ten. Student body composition: 0.9% Asian, 5.6% Black, 0.9% Hispanic, 0.2% Native American, 86.6% White, 6% Other. 14% from out of state.

[1] MICHIGAN TECHNOLOGICAL UNIVERSITY
Houghton 49931, (906) 487-1885
Director of Admissions: Ernest R. Griff

- **Enrollment: 5,414m, 1,616w; 7,640 total (including graduates)**
- **Tuition (1982/83): $1,512 (in-state), $3,246 (out-of-state)**
- **Room & Board: $2,209**
- **Degrees offered: BA, BS, AAS**
- **Mean ACT 25**
- **Student-faculty ratio: 19 to 1**

A public university established in 1885. 240-acre campus in small city of Houghton on Michigan's Upper Peninsula, 325 miles from Milwaukee. Served by air and bus.
Academic Character NCACS and professional accreditation. Trimester system, 2 6-week summer terms. Majors offered in liberal arts and theater technology (BA), and in applied geophysics, applied physics, biological sciences, business administration, chemistry, computer science, engineering administration, forestry, geology, interdisciplinary engineering, land surveying, mathematics, medical technology, physics, social sciences, scientific & technical communication, wood & fiber utilization, and in chemical, civil, electrical, geological, mechanical, metallurgical, and mining engineering. Self-designed majors. Associate degrees in civil engineering technology, electrical engineering technology, electromechanical engineering technology, forest technology, general studies, mechanical design engineering technology. Distributive requirements. Graduate and professional degrees granted. Independent study. Internships, cooperative work/study. Preprofessional programs in dentistry, law, medicine. Cooperative programs in business administration, computer sciences, engineering, forestry. Dual degree programs in engineering and forestry with several colleges. Secondary school science education certification. ROTC, AFROTC. 4,000-acre forestry center, simulation lab. Computer center, language lab. 543,590-volume library with microform resources.
Financial CEEB CSS and ACT FAS. University scholarships, grants, loans, state scholarships, tuition waivers for children of deceased veterans, aid for physically handicapped; PELL, SEOG, GSL, NDSL, FISL, CWS. Application deadline March 1.
Admissions High school graduation with 15 units required. Interview encouraged. ACT required for counseling purposes. $20 application fee. Rolling admissions; suggest applying after October 1. $50 deposit required on acceptance of offer of admission. *Early Admission* Program. Admission deferral possible. Transfers accepted. Credit possible for CEEB AP and CLEP exams; university has own advanced placement program.
Student Life Student government. Newspaper, yearbook, radio stations. Music and drama groups. 125 academic, professional, religious, service, and special interest groups. 12 fraternities with houses and 3 sororities, 1 with house. 6% of men and 4% of women join. Single freshmen and sophomores must live at home or on campus. Coed and single-sex dorms and apartments, special interest houses. 43% of students live on campus. 6 quarters of phys ed required. 7 intercollegiate sports for men, 4 for women; intramurals. AIAW, NCAA, CCHA, Great Lakes Intercollegiate Athletic Conference. Student body composition: 0.6% Asian, 0.5% Black, 0.5% Hispanic, 0.3% Native American, 95.2% White, 2.9% Other. 12% from out of state.

[J1] MID-MICHIGAN COMMUNITY COLLEGE
Harrison 48625

[J1] MONROE COUNTY COMMUNITY COLLEGE
Monroe 48161

[J1] MONTCALM COMMUNITY COLLEGE
Sidney 48885

[P] MUSKEGON BUSINESS COLLEGE
145 Apple Avenue, Muskegon 49441

[J1] MUSKEGON COMMUNITY COLLEGE
Muskegon 49442

[1] NAZARETH COLLEGE
Nazareth 49074, (616) 349-7783

- **Enrollment: 53m, 287w; 528 total (including part-time)**
- **Tuition & Fees (1982/83): $4,790**
- **Room & Board: $2,370**
- **Degrees offered: BA, BBA, BS, BSN, BSW**
- **Mean ACT 21**

A private, coeducational college for human service professions.
Academic Character NCACS and professional accreditation. Semester system. Majors offered in elementary education, accounting, managerial accounting, management of health care agencies, gerontology, learning disabilities, nursing, medical technology, management, social work, criminal justice, interdisciplinary studies. Innovative learning techniques are available to all students. Independent study. Learning contracts. Field work. Remedial mathematics and English programs.
Financial Financial aid is available for all students, and includes college scholarships and grants, PELL, NDSL, GSL, NSL, CWS, and on-campus employment.
Admissions ACT required. Rolling admissions policy. *Early Admission* and *Early Decision* programs. Admission deferral possible. Advanced placement possible.
Student Life Dormitories and dining hall maintained on campus.

[J1] NORTH CENTRAL MICHIGAN COLLEGE
1515 Howard Street, Petoskey 49770, (616) 347-3973

- **Enrollment: 279m, 395w; 1,957 total (including part-time)**
- **Tuition (1982/83): $21 per semester hour (in-county), $27 (out-of-county)**
- **Fees & Books: $340**
- **Degrees offered: AA, AS, AES, ASN**
- **Mean ACT 18**

A public, coeducational junior college offering college-level evening programs.
Academic Character NCACS and professional accreditation. Semester system. College parallel courses offered in general education, pre-science, pre-engineering, and general business. Terminal programs offered in small engines, nursing, respiratory therapy, and secretarial science.
Admissions College maintains an open-door admissions policy. ACT required.
Student Life No student housing.

[1] NORTHERN MICHIGAN UNIVERSITY
Marquette 49855, (906) 227-2650
Director of Admissions: Jack M. Kunkel

- **Undergraduates: 3,212m, 2,850w; 8,352 total (including graduates)**
- **Tuition (1982/83): $1,344 (in-state), $3,088 (out-of-state)**

- **Room & Board: $2,198; Fees: $55**
- **Degrees offered: BA, BS, BFA, BMus Ed, BSN, BSW**
- **Student-faculty ratio: 20 to 1**

A public university established in 1899. 300-acre campus in small city of Marquette. Served by air and bus.
Academic Character NCACS and professional accreditation. Semester system, 6- to 8-week summer term. 77 majors offered by the Schools of Arts & Science, Business & Management, Education, and Nursing & Allied Health Sciences. Minor required. Courses in 7 additional areas. Distributive requirements. Graduate and professional degrees granted. Honors program. Preprofessional programs in dentistry, law, medicine. Study abroad. Elementary, secondary, and special education certification. ROTC. Over 1,000,000-volume library.
Financial CEEB CSS and ACT FAS. University scholarships, grants, and loans, state loans; PELL, SEOG, NDSL, FISL, NSL, CWS. Application deadline February 1.
Admissions High school graduation with 16 units required. School of Nursing requires 2.0 GPA. GED accepted. ACT required. $15 application fee. Rolling admissions; suggest applying by February 1. $50 deposit required on acceptance of offer of admission. *Early Admission* and *Concurrent Enrollment* programs. Admission deferral possible. Transfers accepted. Credit possible for CEEB AP and CLEP exams; university has own advanced placement program.
Student Life Student associations. Newspaper. Music, debate groups. Academic, honorary, religious, service, and special interest groups. 6 fraternities, 2 with houses, and 1 sorority without house. 1% of men of women join. Freshmen and sophomores must live at home or on campus. Coed and single-sex dorms, special-interest housing, apartments. Married-student housing. 50% of students live on campus. 4 hours of phys ed required. 7 intercollegiate sports for men, 5 for women; intramurals. NCAA, CCHA. Student body composition: 2% Black, 1% Hispanic, 1% Native American, 96% White. 6% from out of state.

[J1] NORTHWESTERN MICHIGAN COLLEGE
Traverse City 49684

■[J2] GREAT LAKES MARITIME ACADEMY
Traverse City 49684

[1] NORTHWOOD INSTITUTE
Midland 48640, (517) 631-1600
Dean of Admissions: Jack S. King

- **Undergraduates: 1,200m, 700w**
- **Tuition (1982/83): $3,645**
- **Room & Board: $2,130; Fees: $120**
- **Degrees offered: BBA, associate degrees**
- **Mean ACT 18**
- **Student-faculty ratio: 35 to 1**

A private institute established in 1959. 268-acre suburban campus in Midland, 170 miles from Detroit. Additional campuses in West Baden, Indiana, and Cedar Hill, Texas. Air, rail, and bus nearby.
Academic Character NCACS accreditation. Trimester system, 3 3-week summer terms. BBA offered in accounting, computer science-management, management, management-economics, and marketing. Associate degree programs in accounting, advertising, computer science-management, automotive marketing, automotive replacement management, business management, executive secretarial, fashion marketing merchandising, hotel & restaurant management, residential & commercial design management, and retailing management. 2 minors required. Courses in 15 additional areas. Distributive requirements. Cooperative work/study, internships. Member Associated Independent Colleges of Michigan. Study abroad. Computer center, TV studio, museum. 40,000-volume library with microform resources.
Financial CEEB CSS. Scholarships, grants, loans, athletic grants, payment plan; PELL, SEOG, NDSL, GSL, CWS.
Admissions High school graduation with 18 units and 2.0 GPA required. GED accepted. Interview encouraged. ACT or SAT required. $15 application fee. Rolling admissions; suggest applying by January 1. $150 tuition and $50 room deposits required on acceptance of admissions offer. *Early Admission* and *Early Decision* programs. Transfers accepted. Credit possible for CEEB AP, CLEP, and ACT PEP exams.
Student Life Student government. Newspapers, yearbook, radio station. Music and drama groups. United Black Students. Academic, political, religious, service, and special interest groups. 10 fraternities, 4 with houses, and 4 sororities, 2 with houses. 35% of men and 45% of women join. Single freshmen must live on campus. Single-sex dorms. 70% of students live on campus. 6 intercollegiate sports for men, 2 for women; intramurals. NCAA. Student body composition: 7% Black, 1% Hispanic, 90% White, 2% Other. 37% from out of state.

[J1] OAKLAND COMMUNITY COLLEGE
2480 Opdyke Road, Bloomfield Hills 48013

[J1] OAKLAND COMMUNITY COLLEGE—AUBURN HILLS CAMPUS
Auburn Heights 48057

[J1] OAKLAND COMMUNITY COLLEGE—HIGHLAND LAKES CAMPUS
7350 Cooley Lake Road, Union Lake 48085

[J1] OAKLAND COMMUNITY COLLEGE—ORCHARD RIDGE CAMPUS
Farmington 48024

[1] OAKLAND UNIVERSITY
Rochester 48063, (313) 377-3360
Director of Admissions: Jerry W. Rose

- **Undergraduates: 2,633m, 3,642w; 11,614 total (including graduates)**
- **Tuition (1982/83): $1,312 (in-state), $3,520 (out-of-state)**
- **Room & Board: $2,345; Fees: $135**
- **Degrees offered: BA, BS, BMus, BSN**
- **Mean ACT 21**
- **Student-faculty ratio: 22 to 1**

A public university established in 1957. 1,500-acre suburban campus located in Rochester, 30 miles from Detroit. Rail and bus nearby. Airport in Detroit.
Academic Character NCACS and professional accreditation. Semester system, 2 8-week summer terms. 58 majors offered by the College of Arts & Sciences, and the Schools of Economics & Management, Engineering, Human & Educational Services, Nursing, and Performing Arts. Self-designed and double majors. Minors offered in most major fields and in 27 additional areas. Distributive requirements. Graduate and professional degrees granted. Independent study. Honors program. Cooperative work/study, pass/fail, internships. Preprofessional programs in dentistry, law, medicine, optometry. Study abroad. Elementary and secondary education certification. 462,000-volume library with microform resources.
Financial CEEB CSS and ACT FAS. University scholarships, grants, loans; PELL, SEOG, NSS, NDSL, FISL, NSL, CWS. Application deadline March 1.
Admissions High school graduation with 12 units required. GED accepted. ACT required for counseling. $15 application fee. Rolling admissions. *Early Admission* and *Concurrent Enrollment* programs. Transfers accepted. Credit possible for CEEB AP and CLEP exams; university has own advanced placement program.
Student Life Student government. Newspaper, yearbook, radio station. Several music and drama groups. Over 70 academic, political, religious, and special interest groups. 1 fraternity and 1 sorority. Less than 1% of men and women join. Freshmen and sophomores must live at home or on campus. Coed and single-sex dorms, married-student housing. 20% of students live on campus. 9 intercollegiate sports for men, 10 for women; intramurals. AIAW, NCAC, Great Lakes Conference. Student body composition: 8% Black, 1% Hispanic, 1% Native American, 86% White, 4% Other. 2% from out of state.

[1] OLIVET COLLEGE
Olivet 49076, (616) 749-7000
Director of Admissions: John J. Bart

- **Undergraduates: 417m, 212w**
- **Tuition (1982/83): $5,080**
- **Room & Board: $2,350**
- **Degree offered: BA**
- **Mean ACT 18**
- **Student-faculty ratio: 13 to 1**

A private college affiliated with the United Church of Christ, established in 1844. 45-acre rural campus located in the small town of Olivet, 30 miles from Lansing. Served by bus. Rail 22 miles away in Battle Creek.
Academic Character NCACS accreditation. Semester system. Majors offered in art, communications, music, biology, mathematics, business administration, economics, history, philosophy, political science, psychology, religion, social studies, sociology. Special majors, trial majors. Courses in astronomy, experimental courses. Distributive requirements. Independent study. Honors program. Credit by exam. Professional semester. Study abroad. Elementary and secondary education certification. Language lab. 82,000-volume library.
Financial CEEB CSS. College scholarships, grants, loans, UCC grants; PELL, SEOG, NDSL, CWS. Scholarship application deadline March 15.
Admissions High school graduation with 16 units recommended. Interview encouraged. ACT or SAT required. $10 application fee. Rolling admissions. $50 deposit required on acceptance of offer of admission. *Early Decision* Program. Transfers accepted. Credit possible for CEEB AP and CLEP exams; college has own advanced placement program.
Student Life Student government. Newspaper, yearbook, radio station. Music, art, debate, theatre groups. Academic, religious, and special interest organizations. 3 fraternities and 3 sororities with houses. 40% of men and 45% of women join. Seniors and students over 21 may live off campus. Dorms for men and women. Married-student housing. 87% of students live on campus. Limited dorm visitation. Several intercollegiate and intramural sports for men, 6 intercollegiate sports for women. AIAW, NCAA, MIAC. Student body composition: 6.1% Black, 93.2% White. 2% from out of state.

[P] REFORMED BIBLE COLLEGE
1869 Robinson Road, SE, Grand Rapids 49506

[1] SACRED HEART SEMINARY COLLEGE
2701 Chicago Blvd., Detroit 48206

[1] SAGINAW VALLEY STATE COLLEGE
University Center 48710, (517) 790-4200
Director of Admissions: Richard P. Thompson

- **Undergraduates: 942m, 1,058w; 4,355 total (including graduates)**
- **Tuition (1982/83): $1,395 (in-state), $2,635 (out-of-state)**
- **Room & Board: $2,256; Fees: $93**

- **Degrees offered: BA, BS, BBA, BSN**
- **Student-faculty ratio: 20 to 1**

A public college established in 1963. 780-acre suburban campus between the cities of Midland, Saginaw, and Bay City. Served by bus.
Academic Character NCACS and professional accreditation. Trimester system, 7½-week spring and summer terms. 14 majors offered by the School of Arts & Behavioral Sciences, 7 by the School of Business & Management, 13 by the School of Education, 2 by the School of Nursing & Allied Health Sciences, and 17 by the School of Science, Engineering, & Technology. Self-designed majors. Minor or double major required. Minors offered in most major fields and in 7 additional areas. Distributive requirements. MAT, MBA granted. Independent study. Honors program. Cooperative work/study, limited pass/fail. Preprofessional programs in dentistry, law, medicine, theology. 2- and 3-year transfer programs in engineering. Study abroad. Elementary and secondary education certification; bilingual endorsement possible. Institute of Polish Studies. 100,000-volume library with microform resources.
Financial CEEB CSS. College scholarships, grants, loans, state scholarships; PELL, SEOG, NSS, NDSL, GSL, PLUS, CWS. Application deadline April 15.
Admissions High school graduation with 7 units required. GED accepted. ACT or SAT required; ACT preferred. Rolling admissions. $225 deposit required by June 15. *Early Admission* and *Concurrent Enrollment* programs. Transfers accepted. Credit possible for CEEB AP and CLEP exams; college has own advanced placement program.
Student Life Student government. Newspaper. Music and drama groups. Honorary, service, religious, and special interest organizations. Fraternities and sororities. Freshmen must live at home or on campus. Single-sex dorms. 11% of students live on campus. 8 intercollegiate sports for men, 6 for women; intramurals. AIAW, NAIA, NCAA, Great Lakes Conference. Student body composition: 1% Asian, 6% Black, 5% Hispanic, 0.7% Native American, 87.3% White. 1% from out of state.

[J1] ST. CLAIR COUNTY COMMUNITY COLLEGE
Port Huron 48060

[1] ST. JOHN'S PROVINCIAL SEMINARY
44011 Five Mile Road, Plymouth 48170

[1] ST. MARY'S COLLEGE
Orchard Lake 48033, (313) 682-1885
Director of Admissions: Randall J. Berd

- **Undergraduates: 82m, 49w; 260 total (including part-time)**
- **Tuition (1982/83): $2,100**
- **Room & Board: $2,100**
- **Degrees offered: BA, BS, AA**
- **Student-faculty ratio: 6 to 1**

Private Roman Catholic college established in 1885. 120-acre suburban campus in Orchard Lake, 17 miles from Detroit. Airport, rail and bus stations nearby.
Academic Character NCACS accreditation. Semester system. Majors offered in communication arts, English, Polish studies, philosophy, theology, religious education, social science, business administration, and natural science. Minor required. Distributives and 15 hours of philosophy-theology required. Independent study. Member Detroit Consortium of Catholic Colleges. Study abroad in Poland. 50,000-volume library.
Financial CEEB CSS. State scholarships, grants, and loans, Polish studies subsidies; PELL, SEOG, GSL, PLUS, CWS; college has own work program.
Admissions High school graduation with 16 units required. GED accepted. Interview encouraged. ACT or SAT required. $10 application fee. Rolling admissions. *Early Admission* Program. Admission deferral possible. Transfers accepted. Credit possible for CEEB CLEP exams; college has own advanced placement program.
Student Life Student government. Newspaper. Music and drama groups. Academic, service, and special interest organizations. 2 fraternities. Single-sex dorms. Intercollegiate basketball; intramurals. NAIA.

[J1] SCHOOLCRAFT COLLEGE
Haggerty Road, Livonia 48152

[2] SHAW COLLEGE AT DETROIT
7351 Woodward, Detroit 48202

[1] SIENA HEIGHTS COLLEGE
1247 East Siena Heights Drive, Adrian 49221
Dean of Admissions: Norman Bukwaz

- **Undergraduates: 316m, 439w; 1,517 total (including graduates)**
- **Tuition (1982/83): $3,300**
- **Room & Board: $2,000**
- **Degrees offered: BA, BS, BFA, BAS, AA, AS, AAS, AFA**
- **Student-faculty ratio: 15 to 1**

A private college controlled by the Dominicans, established in 1919, became coed in 1969. 140-acre rural campus located in the small city of Adrian, 35 miles from Toledo, Ohio. Air, rail, and bus in Toledo.
Academic Character NCACS accreditation. Semester system, 2 3½-week summer terms. Majors offered in accounting, American studies, art, banking & finance, biology, business administration, business education, English-communication, fashion merchandising, institutional management, general studies, history, home economics, home economics education, humanities, human services, medical technology, music, natural science, office administration, philosophy, religious studies, social science, and theatre & speech communications. Self-designed majors. Minors offered in most major fields and in 8 additional areas. Distributive requirements. MA granted. Independent study. Cooperative work/study, pass/fail, internships. Credit by exam. Preprofessional programs in chiropractic, dentistry, medicine, mortuary science, osteopathy, pharmacy, physical therapy, veterinary medicine. Study abroad. Elementary, secondary, and vocational education certification. Computer center, language lab, TV studio. 81,567-volume library with microform resources.
Financial CEEB CSS. College scholarships, grants, loans, state scholarships and grants, payment plan; PELL, SEOG, GSL, CWS; college has own work program.
Admissions High school graduation required. GED accepted. Interview encouraged. SAT or ACT required. $15 application fee. Rolling admissions; application deadline August 15. $100 tuition and $50 room deposits required 1 month after offer of admission. *Early Admission* and *Concurrent Enrollment* programs. Admission deferral possible. Transfers accepted. Credit possible for CEEB AP and CLEP exams; college has own advanced placement program.
Student Life Student government. Newspaper, magazine, yearbook. Music, drama groups. Coed and single-sex dorms. 40% of students live on campus. 8 intercollegiate sports for men, 6 for women; intramurals. AIAW, NAIA, SWAC. Student body composition: 6.5% Black, 2.5% Hispanic, 85% White, 6% Other. 18% from out of state.

[J1] SOUTHWESTERN MICHIGAN COLLEGE
Cherry Grove Road, Dowagiac 49047

[1] SPRING ARBOR COLLEGE
Spring Arbor 49283, (517) 750-1200
Director of Enrollment & College Relations: Richard H. Bailey

- **Undergraduates: 302m, 373w**
- **Tuition (1982/83): $4,400**
- **Room & Board: $1,800; Fees: $45**
- **Degrees offered: BA, AA**
- **Mean ACT 18.3**
- **Student-faculty ratio: 18 to 1**

A private college affiliated with the Free Methodist Church, established in 1873. 70-acre campus located in the village of Spring Arbor, 9 miles from Jackson. Air, rail, and bus in Jackson.
Academic Character NCACS accreditation. 14-4-14 system, 2 4-week summer terms. Majors offered in art, biology, business administration, chemistry, contemporary ministries, economics & business administration, English, English-speech, French, history, mathematics, music, philosophy, philosophy-religion, physical education, physics, physics-mathematics, psychology, social science, social work, sociology, and Spanish. Courses in computer science, geography, political science, speech. 3 courses in Christianity, 2 in religion/philosophy required. Independent study. Limited pass/fail. Internships. Preprofessional programs in dentistry, law, medicine. 3-2 program in engineering with U of Michigan. Member Wesleyan Urban Coalition. January exchange with several colleges. Chicago Urban Life Center, American Studies Program. Environmental semester. Study abroad. Elementary and secondary education certification. 69,832-volume library.
Financial CEEB CSS. College scholarships, grants, and loans, state grants, payment plans; PELL, SEOG, NDSL, FISL, CWS. Application deadline August 1.
Admissions High school graduation required. GED accepted. ACT required. $15 application fee. Rolling admissions; suggest applying by April 1. $50 tuition and $50 room deposits required on acceptance of offer of admission. *Early Admission* and *Credit in Escrow* programs. Admission deferral possible. Transfers accepted. Credit possible for CEEB AP and CLEP exams.
Student Life Student government. Newspaper, yearbook, radio station. Music, drama, photography groups. Academic, religious, service, and special interest organizations. Students must live at home or on campus. Single-sex dorms. Married-student housing. 80% of students live on campus. Freshmen may not have cars on campus. Liquor, tobacco, drugs prohibited. Attendance at chapel twice weekly required. 1 semester of phys ed required. 7 intercollegiate sports for men, 5 for women; intramural and club sports. AIAW, NAIA. Student body composition: 3% Black, 93% White, 4% Other. 16% from out of state.

[J1] SUOMI COLLEGE
Hancock 49930, (906) 482-5300
Director of Admissions: John Hilpert

- **Enrollment: 219m, 279w; 510 total (including part-time)**
- **Tuition (1982/83): $5,500**
- **Room & Board: $2,400**
- **Degrees offered: AA, AAS, AGS**
- **Student-faculty ratio: 12 to 1**

A private junior college affiliated with the Lutheran Church, established in 1896. Rural campus in town of Hancock on Michigan's upper peninsula. Served by air and bus.
Academic Character NCACS accreditation. Semester system. 2-year programs offered in English, fine arts, general education, human services, physical education, education, religious studies, accounting, business administration, criminal justice, data processing, general business, marketing, recreational leadership, travel services, medical administrative assistant, and executive secretarial studies. Distributive requirements. Independent study. Cooperative work/study. Credit by exam. Preprofessional programs in law, medicine. Learning center.

Key to ratings **[1, 2, J1, J2, G, P, R, S]** *and list of abbreviations start on page 120*

Financial CEEB CSS. College scholarships, grants, and loans, state grants and loans, family discounts; PELL, SEOG, NDSL, GSL, CWS.
Admissions High school graduation with 15 units required. GED accepted. ACT recommended. Rolling admissions. *Early Decision* and *Early Admission* programs. Admission deferral possible. Transfers accepted. Credit possible for CEEB AP and CLEP exams.
Student Life Student government. Newspaper, yearbook. Music and drama groups. Special interest clubs. Students must live at home or on campus. Dorms for men and women. Class attendance required. 2 semester hours of phys ed required. Intercollegiate basketball; intramurals. NJCAA. Student body composition: 10% minority.

[P] THOMAS M. COOLEY LAW SCHOOL
217 South Capitol Avenue, Lansing 48910

[1] WALSH COLLEGE OF ACCOUNTANCY AND BUSINESS ADMINISTRATION
3838 Livernois Road, Troy 48084

[J1] WASHTENAW COMMUNITY COLLEGE
Ann Arbor 48106

[J1] WAYNE COUNTY COMMUNITY COLLEGE
4612 Woodward Avenue, Detroit 48201

[1] WAYNE STATE UNIVERSITY
5980 Cass Avenue, Detroit 48202, (313) 577-3577
Director of Admissions: Ronald C. Hughes

- **Undergraduates: 6,025m, 6,560w; 32,543 total (including graduates)**
- **Tuition (1982/83): $1,760 (in-state), $3,860 (out-of-state)**
- **Room: $982-$1,414**
- **Degrees offered: BA, BS, BFA, BMus, BSEd, BSN, BSW**
- **Mean SAT 440v, 490m**
- **Student-faculty ratio: 18 to 1**

A public university established in 1933. 180-acre urban campus in Detroit. Served by air, rail, and bus.
Academic Character NCACS and professional accreditation. Semester system, spring and summer terms. 52 majors offered by the College of Liberal Arts, 5 by the School of Business Administration, 15 by the College of Education, 12 by the College of Engineering, 6 by the College of Pharmacy & Allied Health Professions; additional majors in nursing, social work. Distributive requirements. Graduate and professional degrees granted. Independent study. Honors program. Phi Beta Kappa. Cooperative work/study in engineering. Pass/fail. Preprofessional programs in business administration, dentistry, education, law, library science, medicine, medical technology, mortuary science, occupational therapy, optometry, osteopathy, pharmacy, physical therapy, radiation therapy, social work. Dual degree programs in allied health, business administration, distributive education, engineering technology. Study abroad. Elementary, secondary, and special education and library science certification. ROTC at U of Detroit; AFROTC at U Michigan-Ann Arbor. Language lab, computer center. Black studies, cognitive processes, engineering, gerontology, health, labor, peace, urban centers. 1,839,429-volume library with microform resources.
Financial University scholarships, grants, loans; PELL, SEOG, NDSL, GSL, CWS.
Admissions High school graduation required. SAT or ACT required for students not meeting minimum requirements and for Liberal Arts applicants. $15 application fee. Rolling admissions. *Early Decision* Program. Transfers accepted. Credit possible for CEEB AP and CLEP exams; university has own advanced placement program. PROJECT 350.
Student Life Student government. Publications. Music groups. Academic, religious, service, and special interest groups. 14 fraternities and 13 sororities; some have houses. Limited university housing. No married-student housing. 2% of students live on campus. Intercollegiate and intramural sports for men and women. NCAA, GLIAC. Student body composition: 2.5% Asian, 22.5% Black, 1.7% Hispanic, 0.9% Native American, 72.7% White. 30% from out of state.

[J1] WEST SHORE COMMUNITY COLLEGE
Scottville 49454

[1] WESTERN MICHIGAN UNIVERSITY
Kalamazoo 49008, (616) 383-1950
Director of Admissions: Duncan A. Clarkson

- **Undergraduates: 6,890m, 6,020w; 18,965 total (including graduates)**
- **Tuition (1982/83): $1,283 (in-state), $3,083 (out-of-state)**
- **Room & Board: $2,138; Fees: $66**
- **Degrees offered: BA, BS, BFA, BBA, BMus, BSE, BSMed, BSW**
- **Mean ACT 19.7**
- **Student-faculty ratio: 17 to 1**

A public university established in 1903. 400-acre suburban campus in Kalamazoo, 145 miles from Chicago and Detroit. Served by air, rail, and bus.
Academic Character NCACS and professional accreditation. Semester system, 7½-week spring and summer terms. 37 majors offered by the College of Applied Science, 36 by the College of Arts & Sciences, 15 by the College of Business Administration, 8 by the College of Education, 24 by the College of Fine Arts, and 7 by the College of Health & Human Services. Self-designed majors. Dual degrees in manufacturing, health studies, applied liberal studies. Minor required. Courses in area and cultural studies. Distributive requirements. Graduate and professional degrees granted. Independent study. Honors program. Pass/fail. Internships, cooperative work/study. Preprofessional programs in architecture, engineering, medical technology, social work, speech pathology. 3-1 program in medical technology, 3-2 program in occupational therapy with area hospitals. Member consortium with Kalamazoo, Kalamazoo Valley, Nazareth colleges. Study abroad. Elementary, secondary, and special education certification. ROTC. Language labs. 1,677,248-volume library with microform resources.
Financial CEEB CSS. University scholarships, grants, loans, payment plans; PELL, SEOG, NDSL, FISL, CWS; university has own work program. Application deadlines February 15 (scholarships), March 15 (loans).
Admissions High school graduation with 3 units in English required. ACT required; ACH recommended. Audition required for music. $15 application fee. Rolling admissions; suggest applying after October 1. $50 deposit required on acceptance of offer of admission. Transfers accepted. Credit possible for CEEB AP, CLEP, and ACT PEP exams. Martin Luther King Program for minority applicants.
Student Life Student government. Newspaper, magazine, radio station. Music, debate, drama groups. Several academic, honorary, political, professional, religious, and special interest organizations. 17 fraternities and 10 sororities. Coed and single-sex dorms. Married-student housing. 31% of students live on campus. Liquor prohibited. 2 hours of phys ed required (ROTC students excepted). 14 intercollegiate sports; intramurals. AIAW, CCAC, Mid-American Athletic Conference. Student body composition: 0.3% Asian, 5.3% Black, 0.5% Hispanic, 0.2% Native American, 89.1% White, 4.6% Other. 11% from out of state.

[P] WESTERN THEOLOGICAL SEMINARY
Holland 49423

[P] WILLIAM TYNDALE COLLEGE
35700 West 12 Mile Road, Farmington Hills 48018
Formerly Detroit Bible College

MINNESOTA (MN)

[J1] ALEXANDRIA AREA TECHNICAL INSTITUTE
Alexandria 56308

[J1] ANOKA-RAMSEY COMMUNITY COLLEGE
Coon Rapids 55433

[J1] ARROWHEAD COMMUNITY COLLEGE, HIBBING CAMPUS
Hibbing 55746

[J1] ARROWHEAD COMMUNITY COLLEGE, ITASCA CAMPUS
Grand Rapids 55744

[J1] ARROWHEAD COMMUNITY COLLEGE, MESABI CAMPUS
Virginia 55792

[J1] ARROWHEAD COMMUNITY COLLEGE, RAINY RIVER CAMPUS
International Falls 56649

[J1] ARROWHEAD COMMUNITY COLLEGE, VERMILION CAMPUS
Ely 55731

[1] AUGSBURG COLLEGE
731 21st Avenue South, Minneapolis 55454, (612) 330-1000
Director of Admissions: John Hjelmeland

- **Undergraduates: 653m, 771w**
- **Tuition (1982/83): $4,820**
- **Room & Board: $2,038-$4,673**
- **Degrees offered: BA, BS, BMus**
- **Mean ACT 20; mean SAT 976**
- **Student-faculty ratio: 14 to 1**

A private college founded by and affiliated with the American Lutheran Church; established in 1869, became coed in 1922. 22-acre campus in metropolitan Minneapolis. Airport, bus and train stations.
Academic Character NCACS and professional accreditation. 4-1-4 system, 2 summer terms. 40 majors offered by the Divisions of Humanities, Natural Science & Mathematics, Social & Behavioral Sciences, and Professional Studies, including East Asian, metro-urban, Russian area, and Scandinavian area studies, and Norwegian. Interdisciplinary majors. Minors in most major areas. Distributives and 3 religious studies courses required. Honors program. Independent and directed study. Internships, cooperative work/study. Pass/no credit. Preprofessional programs in health fields, engineering, law, seminary studies. 3-1 medical technology and 3-2

engineering programs. Cross-registration with the Associated Colleges of the Twin Cities, and with U Minnesota. Computer programming courses at Control Data. Classes in prisons and other institutions. Study abroad. Early childhood, elementary, and secondary education certification. AFROTC at College of Saint Thomas. 145,345-volume library.
Financial CEEB CSS and ACT FAS. College and state scholarships and grants, Lutheran scholarships, BIA scholarships and grants, payment plan; PELL, SEOG, NSS, NDSL, GSL, NSL, PLUS, CWS. State work-study, Lutheran work service programs. Application deadline March 1.
Admissions High school graduation with 12 units required. GED accepted. PSAT, SAT, or ACT required. Interview encouraged. $15 application fee. Rolling admissions; application deadline August 1. *Early Decision* and *Early Entrance* programs. Admission deferral possible. Transfers accepted. Credit possible for CEEB AP and CLEP exams. Project Ahead for Army students.
Student Life Student government. Newspaper, magazine, yearbook. Radio station. Music and drama groups. Black Student Union. Community service, academic, political, religious, and special interest clubs. Freshmen and sophomores must live at home or on campus. Married-student, special interest, and cooperative housing. 56% of students live on campus. Liquor allowed only in dorms. No gambling. Class attendance required. Proficiency or participation in 2 lifetime sports required. 9 intercollegiate sports for men, 6 for women; intramurals. MIAC, AIAW, NAIA, NCAA. Student body composition: 1% Asian, 4% Black, 0.4% Hispanic, 1% Native American, 93.6% White. 12% from out of state.

[J1] AUSTIN COMMUNITY COLLEGE
Austin 55912

[1] BEMIDJI STATE UNIVERSITY
Bemidji 56601, (218) 755-2040
Dean of Admissions: Dr. Fulton Gallagher

- **Undergraduates: 2,088m, 1,964w; 4,429 total (including graduates)**
- **Estimated Tuition (1982/83): $846 (in-state), $1,686 (out-of-state)**
- **Room & Board: $1,365**
- **Degrees offered: BA, BS, BSEd, BFA, AA, AS**
- **Mean ACT 19.6**
- **Student-faculty ratio: 20 to 1**

A public university founded in 1919, became coed in 1952. 89-acre lakeside campus in Bemidji, 150 miles west of Duluth. Airport, bus and train stations.
Academic Character NCACS and professional accreditation. Trimester system, 2 5-week summer terms. 45 majors offered by the Divisions of Humanities & Fine Arts, Professional & Applied Studies, Science & Mathematics, Social & Behavioral Sciences, and by Library & Library Services. Minor or comprehensive major required. Distributive requirements. Masters degrees granted. Licensure programs in educational and vocational areas. Honors program, accelerated study. Independent study. Masters degrees granted. Internships. Pass/no pass option. Extension and correspondence credits. Preprofessional programs in agriculture, dentistry, home economics, nursing. Study at other Minnesota universities possible. External Studies Program. Study abroad. ROTC. Center for Environmental and Outdoor Education, aquatics lab. Over 205,000-volume library.
Financial ACT FAS. College scholarhips and loans, PELL, SEOG, NDSL, GSL, CWS, college part-time employment. Recommended application deadline April 15.
Admissions High school graduation required. GED accepted. Interview recommended. ACT, SAT, SCAT, or PSAT required. Rolling admissions; deadline 3 weeks before graduation (March 15 for financial aid applicants). *Early Entrance* and *Concurrent Enrollment* programs. Admission deferral possible. Transfers accepted. Credit possible for CEEB AP and CLEP exams.
Student Life Student government. Newspaper, literary magazine, radio station, TV studio. Music and debate groups. Political and community service organizations. Over 50 other student groups. 5 fraternities and 4 sororities. 6% of men and 7% of women join. Coed dorms. No married-student housing. 52% of students live on campus. Liquor prohibited on campus. 5 terms of phys ed required. 9 intercollegiate sports for men, 7 for women; intramurals. AIAW, NAIA, NCHC, NIC, NSC. Student body composition: 0.3% Asian, 0.4% Black, 0.1% Hispanic, 4.3% Native American, 93% White, 1.9% Other. 8% from out of state.

[J1] BETHANY LUTHERAN COLLEGE
734 Marsh Street, Mankato 56001, (507) 625-2977
Director of Admissions: Michael W. Butterfield

- **Undergraduates: 127m, 129w**
- **Tuition & Fees (1983/84): $3,170**
- **Room & Board: $2,010**
- **Degree offered: AA**
- **Mean ACT 21**
- **Student-faculty ratio: 11 to 1**

A private junior college supported by the Evangelical Lutheran Synod, and founded in 1927. Small campus overlooking the Minnesota river valley 80 miles southwest of the Twin Cities, 80 miles west of Rochester, and 50 miles north of Iowa.
Academic Character NCACS accreditation. Semester system. Transfer programs in art, business, conservation & natural resources, health science, home economics, humanities, library science/media, liberal arts, medical technology, music, natural sciences/math, physical therapy, physical education, social science, social work, teacher education. Preprofessional transfer majors in engineering, law, medicine, dentistry, nursing, pharmacy, ministry, theology, and veterinary medicine. Career education program in secretarial science-business education. Distributive requirements. 1 religion course required each semester. Diplomas granted. Pre-ministerial program is in cooperation with the Wisconsin Evangelical Lutheran Seminary. Credit by exam possible for work done outside the classroom. Several microcomputers on campus. Library with microform resources.
Financial CEEB CSS and ACT FAS. College and state scholarships and grants; PELL, SEOG, NDSL, GSL, PLUS, campus part-time employment. Priority application period January 1 to March 1.
Admissions High school graduation required. ACT, SAT, or PSAT/MSAT required. $10 application fee. Rolling admissions. *Early Admission* Program. $50 tuition and $35 room deposits required on acceptance of offer of admission. Transfers accepted.
Student Life Student government. Newspaper, yearbook. Music and drama groups. Several annual guest artist programs. Many volunteer and religious organizations. Single students must live at home or on campus. Single-sex dorms. No liquor or illegal drugs allowed on campus. Daily chapel attendance expected. 2 phys ed credits required. 3 intercollegiate sports for men, 2 for women; intramurals.

[1] BETHEL COLLEGE
3900 Bethel Drive, St. Paul 55112, (612) 638-6242
Director of Admissions: Philip Kimball

- **Enrollment: 966m, 1,220w**
- **Tuition (1982/83): $4,550**
- **Room & Board: $2,240; Fees: $850**
- **Degrees offered: BA, AA**
- **Mean ACT 20; mean SAT 951**
- **Student-faculty ratio: 20 to 1**

A private college owned and operated by the Baptist General Conference, established in 1871. 220-acre campus in a residential area of St. Paul. Airport, bus and train stations.
Academic Character NCACS and professional accreditation. 4-1-4 system, 4- and 7-week summer terms. 40 majors offered by the Divisions of Humanities, Social & Behavioral Sciences, Mathematics & Natural Sciences, Nursing, Fine & Performing Arts, and Education & Physical Education. Interdepartmental majors, general arts major arrangeable. Distributives, 3 Biblical studies courses, and senior comprehensive exam required. Directed and independent study. Internships, cooperative work/study through Christian College Consortium. Preprofessional programs in medicine, seminary, social work. 3-1 medical technology, 3-2 engineering programs. American studies program in Washington, D C Study abroad. Elementary and secondary education certification. ROTC at Saint Thomas. Media center, art gallery. 115,000-volume library. 70,000-volume Theological Seminary library nearby.
Financial CEEB CSS and ACT FAS. College scholarships, grants, loans; state scholarships & grants; PELL, SEOG, NDSL, GSL, CWS, college part-time employment. Application deadline March 1.
Admissions High school graduation in upper half of class required. ACH and interview recommended. SAT, ACT, or PSAT required. $10 application fee. Rolling admissions; application deadline August 1. $100 enrollment deposit required on acceptance of offer of admission. *Early Entrance*, informal early decision programs. Admission deferral possible. Transfers accepted. Credit possible for CEEB AP, CLEP, and college exams.
Student Life Student government. Newspaper, literary magazine, yearbook. Radio & TV studios. Musical and dramatic productions. Speaking clubs and teams. Religious, athletic, academic, and special interest groups. Freshmen must live in college housing or at home. Single-sex dorms. Some married-student housing. 85% of students live in college housing. 6 components of phys ed required. Daily chapel attendance expected. 10 intercollegiate sports for men, 5 for women; intramurals. AIAW, MIAC, NAIA. Student body composition: 0.4% Asian, 0.7% Black, 0.3% Hispanic, 0.4% Native American, 97.4% White. 40% from out of state.

[G1] BETHEL THEOLOGICAL SEMINARY
3949 Bethel Drive, St. Paul 55112

[J1] BRAINERD COMMUNITY COLLEGE
Brainerd 56401

[1] CARLETON COLLEGE
Northfield 55057, (507) 663-4190
Dean of Admissions: Richard E. Steele

- **Enrollment: 941m, 813w**
- **Tuition (1982/83): $6,900**
- **Room & Board: $2,309; Fees: $51**
- **Degree offered: BA**
- **Mean SAT 607v, 627m**
- **Student-faculty ratio: 11 to 1**

A private college established in 1866 in the small town of Northfield. 950-acre campus 40 miles south of Minneapolis/St. Paul. 450-acre arboretum on campus. Bus station in Northfield.
Academic Character NCACS accreditation. Trimester system. Majors offered in American studies, art, biology, Black studies, chemistry, classical languages, classical studies, economics, English, geology, history, Latin American studies, math, modern languages (French, German, Hebrew, Japanese, Russian, Spanish), music, philosophy, physics & astronomy, political science, psychology, religion, and sociology & anthropology. 13 interdepartmental programs include Asian, computer, environmental, film, Russian, theatre, urban, and women's studies. Self-designed majors. Distributive requirements. Independent study. Phi Beta Kappa. Credit by exam and for directed summer reading, satisfactory/unsatisfactory option.

Internships, cooperative work/study. 3-2 engineering with Columbia and Washington U (St. Louis); 3-3 law with Columbia. Several off-campus study opportunities. Study abroad. Secondary education certification. Computer, language labs. 310,000-volume library.
Financial ACT FAS (for Minnesota residents) and CEEB CSS. College scholarships and grants, payment plan; PELL, SEOG, NDSL, FISL, GSL, CWS and college part-time employment. Application deadline February 15.
Admissions High school graduation with 15 units required. ACH and interview recommended. SAT or ACT required. $25 application fee. Application deadline February 1. Notification by April 15. $100 deposit required on acceptance of offer of admission. *Early Admission, Early Decision* programs. Admission deferral possible. Transfers accepted. Credit possible for CEEB AP exams. Applicants who do not meet academic admission standards, but who show unusual ability and interest, are considered.
Student Life Student government. Newspaper, magazines, photo journal, yearbook. Radio station. Music, dance, and drama groups. Coffeehouse. Many community service programs. Amnesty International. All students must live at least one year on campus. 11 dorms and 22 student houses; most are coed. Special interest housing. No married-student housing. 95% of students live on campus. Permission required to have a car or motorcycle in Northfield. Hazing and firearms forbidden. Intercollegiate, intramural, and recreational sports. MCAC, AIAW, NCAA. Student body composition: 3% Asian, 3% Black, 2% Hispanic, 0.5% Native American, 91.5% White. 70% from out of state.

[1] CONCORDIA COLLEGE

South Eighth Street, Moorhead 56560, (218) 299-3066
Dean of Admissions & Financial Aids: James L. Hausmann

- **Enrollment: 1,134m, 1,491w**
- **Tuition (1982/83): $4,760**
- **Room & Board: $1,645; Fees: $45**
- **Degrees offered: BA, BMus**
- **Mean ACT 22**
- **Student-faculty ratio: 16 to 1**

A private college established in 1891 and affiliated with the American Lutheran Church. 120-acre campus on the Red River 7 blocks from the center of Moorhead, across from Fargo, North Dakota. Airport, bus and train stations in Moorhead and Fargo.
Academic Character NCACS and professional accreditation. Semester system, 2 4-week summer terms. Majors in art, biology, business administration, business education, chemistry, classical languages, communications, computer science, economics, education, English, French, German, history, history-political science, home economics, humanities, international relations, Latin, math, music, philosophy, physical education, physics, political science, psychology, religion, science education, social studies education, social work (long term care administration), sociology, Spanish, and speech & drama. 3-1 medical technology major. Minors. Distributives and 2 religion courses required. Independent study. Honors programs. Pass/fail. Cooperative work/study, internships. Preprofessional programs in business, medicine, law, theology. Exchange program with Moorhead and Dakota State Universities, Fort Lewis College, and Virginia Union U. 2-2 nursing program. Semesters in New York, Chicago, and Washington, D C Study abroad. Elementary and secondary education certification. Kevatron Linear Accelerator (for atomic studies), computer center, language lab. AFROTC & ROTC. 253,000-volume library.
Financial CEEB CSS and ACT FAS. College scholarships, grants, loans; NDSL, GSL, CWS. Application deadline April 1.
Admissions High school graduation required. ACT, SAT or Minnesota State Program test required. $10 application fee. Rolling admissions; application deadline July 1. $50 advanced payment required on acceptance of offer of admission. *Early Decision, Early Entrance* programs. Admission deferral possible. Transfers accepted. Credit possible for CEEB AP and CLEP exams, and on basis of high school performance.
Student Life Student government. Newspaper, yearbook, radio & TV stations. Music, drama, debate, and political groups. Religious, honorary, academic, and special interest clubs. 3 men's and 3 women's societies. 16% of students join. Freshmen and sophomores must live at home or on campus. Single-sex dorms. 70% of students live on campus. Students on financial aid may not have cars. Daily class and chapel attendance required. Freshman phys ed required. 10 intercollegiate sports for men, 9 for women; intramurals. MIAC, AIAW, NAIA, NCAA. Student body composition: 1% Asian, 1% Black, 1% Hispanic, 1% Native American, 96% White. 35% from out of state.

[1] CONCORDIA COLLEGE

St. Paul 55104, (612) 641-2878
Director of Admissions: Myrtle Shira

- **Enrollment: 361m, 340w; 747 total (including part-time)**
- **Tuition (1982/83): $3,450**
- **Room & Board: $1,710**
- **Degrees offered: BA, AA**
- **Mean ACT 21.5**
- **Student-faculty ratio: 6 to 1**

A private college owned by the Lutheran Church-Missouri Synod. Established in 1893 and became coed in 1950. 26-acre urban campus in St. Paul. Air, rail, and bus service.
Academic Character NCACS and professional accreditation. Trimester system, 2 5-week summer terms. Majors in director of Christian education, director of evangelism, early childhood education, elementary teacher education, liberal education, physical education, secondary education, and special education. Distributives, 12 religion and theology credits required. Orientation required of entering students. Independent study. Internships. Preprofessional programs in education, law, medicine, theology; others may be self-designed. Concurrent enrollment possible with other accredited colleges. Member of the Higher Education Consortium for Urban Affairs which sponsors several urban semesters. Study abroad. ROTC at U of Minnesota. Library with microform resources.
Financial CEEB CSS and ACT FAS. College and state scholarships and grants, minority student grants, church vocation grants; PELL, SEOG, NDSL, FISL, GSL, PLUS, ALAS, CWS and college part-time employment. Application deadine April 1.
Admissions High school graduation with 12 units required. ACT, SAT, or PSAT required. $10 application fee. Rolling admissions. *Early Admission, Early Decision, Concurrent Enrollment* programs. Admission deferral possible. Transfers accepted. Credit possible for CEEB AP, CLEP, and ACT PEP exams. M-TEPS program for minority students.
Student Life Student government. Music, drama, and special interest groups and clubs. Students under 21 must live at home or on campus. Married-student housing. Class attendance expected. 3 phys ed and health credits required. 7 intercollegiate sports for men, 4 for women; intramurals. Cheerleaders, drill team. AIAW, NLCAA, UMCC, MLNCC, MAIAW. Student body composition: 0.3% Asian, 10% Black, 0.3% Native American, 87.8% White, 1.6% Other.

[J1] CROSIER SEMINARY

Onamia 56359

[J2] DAKOTA COUNTY AREA VOCATIONAL TECHNICAL INSTITUTE

County Road 42, Rosemount 55068

[1] DR. MARTIN LUTHER COLLEGE

College Heights, New Ulm 56073, (507) 354-8221
Director of Admissions: Lloyd O. Huebner

- **Enrollment: 223m, 551w**
- **Tuition (1982/83): $1,320**
- **Room & Board: $1,270; Fees: $300**
- **Degree offered: BSEd**
- **Mean ACT 21.8**
- **Student-faculty ratio: 11 to 1**

A private college established in 1884 and affiliated with the Wisconsin Evangelical Lutheran Synod. 50-acre rural campus 100 miles southwest of Minneapolis. Bus station in Mankato; airport and train station in Minneapolis.
Academic Character NCACS accreditation. Semester system, 5-week summer term. Major in elementary education with concentrations in English, math, music, science, social studies. College exists to prepare teachers for the Synod's Christian day schools. Required 4-year program. Independent and accelerated study. Study abroad. 77,874-volume library with microform resources.
Financial CEEB CSS and ACT FAS. College scholarships and grants, state loans, payment plan; PELL, SEOG, GSL, FISL, NDSL, CWS. Application deadline April 30.
Admissions High school graduation with 10 units and minimum GPA of C- required. GED accepted. ACT required. $10 application fee. Rolling admissions; deadline is 2nd full week of semester. Admission deferral possible. Transfers accepted. Credit possible for CEEB AP exams.
Student Life Student government. Newspaper, yearbook. Music and drama groups. Current events group. Religious, special interest, and speaking clubs. Winter Carnival. Students less than 4 years out of high school must live on campus or at home. Single-sex dorms. No married-student housing. 93% of students live on campus. Liquor prohibited. Dress code. Marriage regulations. 4 semesters of phys ed required. 6 intercollegiate sports for men, 6 for women; intramurals. AIAW, NAIA, several regional conferences. Student body composition: 0.2% Asian, 0.1% Black, 0.4% Native American, 99.3% White. 82% from out of state.

[J1] FERGUS FALLS COMMUNITY COLLEGE

Fergus Falls 56537

[J1] GOLDEN VALLEY LUTHERAN COLLEGE

6125 Olson Highway, Minneapolis 55422, (612) 542-1201

- **Enrollment: 254m, 271w; 539 total (including part-time)**
- **Tuition & Fees (1982/83): $1,518 per quarter**
- **Room & Board: $680 per quarter**
- **Degree offered: AA**
- **Student-faculty ratio: 15 to 1**

A private junior college affiliated with the Lutheran Church. Campus in the city of Minneapolis. Air, rail, and bus service.
Academic Character NCACS accreditation. Quarter system. Programs offered include 32 liberal arts majors; training programs in church staff work, parish secretary, parish education director, youth work director, social service, recreational leadership; YMCA, community action, and other community-related programs; career programs in law enforcement, secretarial, electronic technician, and computer. Junior College and Vocational Certificates granted. Remedial math and English programs.
Financial Academic, athletic, music, and drama scholarships; grants and loans available.
Admissions High school graduation or equivalent required. Counselor's and pastor's recommendations required. All applications are considered individually and no set cut off points are determined. Rolling admissions. *Early Admissions* Program.
Student Life Men's football, track, cross-country, basketball, baseball, and wrestling. Women's volleyball, track, cross-country, basketball, and softball.

[1] GUSTAVUS ADOLPHUS COLLEGE
St. Peter 56082, (507) 931-7676
Director of Admissions: Owen Sammelson

- **Enrollment: 987m, 1,263w**
- **Tuition (1982/83): $5,350**
- **Room & Board: $1,900**
- **Degree offered: BA**
- **Mean ACT 24.2; mean SAT 510v, 558m**
- **Student-faculty ratio: 14 to 1**

A private college established in 1862 and affiliated with the Lutheran Church in America. 246-acre campus overlooking the small city of St. Peter, 65 miles southwest of Minneapolis. Bus station in St. Peter. Airport in Mankato and Minneapolis, train in Minneapolis.

Academic Character NCACS and professional accreditation. 4-1-4 system, 4-week summer term. Majors offered in accounting, art, biology, business, chemistry, computer science, economics, education, English, French, geography, geology, German, Greek, health education, history, Latin, math, music, nursing, philosophy, physics, political science, psychology, religion, sociology/anthropology, Spanish, speech, theatre, and phys ed, health, & athletics. Interdisciplinary programs. Self-designed majors. Distributives, 1 religion course, and senior comprehensive exam required. Independent study, honors program. Internships, cooperative work/study. Preprofessional programs in accounting, architecture, arts administration, many health fields, church work, theology, engineering, communications, law, forestry, social work, and veterinary medicine. 3-2 engineering with Washington U and other schools. 3-1 medical technology program. Cross-registration with Mankato State. Many study abroad and off-campus programs. Elementary and secondary education certification. ROTC with Mankato State. Language lab. 289,000-volume library.

Financial Guaranteed tuition. CEEB CSS and ACT FAS. College scholarships & grants; state scholarships, grants, and loans; payment plans; PELL, SEOG, NDSL, GSL, NSL, CWS. Application deadline March 1.

Admissions High school graduation required with 13 units recommended. Interview recommended. SAT, ACT, or PSAT required. $15 application fee. Suggest applying by February 1; deadline April 1. Notification on Dec. 1, Feb. 15, Mar. 15, or Apr. 15. $100 deposit required on acceptance of offer of admission. *Early Decision, Early Entrance* programs. Admission deferral possible. Transfers accepted. Credit possible for CEEB AP and CLEP exams.

Student Life Student government. Newspaper, literary magazine, yearbook. Music, drama, and speaking clubs. International Students organization. Coffeehouse. Academic, honorary, special interest groups. 8 fraternities and 6 sororities; about 25% of students join. No married-student housing. Special interest housing, coed and single-sex dorms. 95% of students live on campus. Liquor allowed only in dorm rooms of students of legal age. 1 phys ed course required. 12 intercollegiate sports for men, 10 for women; intramurals. AIAW, MIAC. Student body composition: 1% Black, 98% White, 1% Other. 24% from out of state.

[1] HAMLINE UNIVERSITY
St. Paul 55104, (612) 641-2207
Director of Admissions: Daniel J. Murray

- **Undergraduates: 643m, 582w; 1,863 total (including graduates)**
- **Tuition (1982/83): $5,350**
- **Room & Board: $2,140; Est. Fees: $100**
- **Degree offered: BA**
- **Mean ACT 22.8; mean SAT 510v, 580m**
- **Student-faculty ratio: 14 to 1**

A private university established in 1854, affiliated with the United Methodist Church. 37-acre campus in Midway district of St. Paul. Airport, bus and train stations in St. Paul.

Academic Character NCACS and professional accreditation. 4-1-4 system, 2 4-week, one 6-week, and one 8-week summer terms. Majors in American studies, anthropology, art, art history, biology, business administration, chemistry, East Asian Studies, economics, English, environmental studies, French, German, history, international business administration, international relations, Latin American Studies, legal studies, math, music, music education, philosophy, phys ed, physics, political science, psychology, religion, science education, social studies, sociology, Spanish, theatre, and urban studies. Other majors possible through exchange with the Associated Colleges of the Twin Cities: Augsburg, Macalester, St. Catherine, and St. Thomas. Distributive requirements. MALS and JD granted. 3 different curriculum offerings to choose from. Interdepartmental and open courses available. Independent, accelerated study. Phi Beta Kappa, honors program. Grade/no grade option. Internships. Preprofessional training in law, engineering, dentistry, medicine, ministry. 3-2 engineering with Washington U. Several exchange programs and urban semesters. Study abroad. AFROTC at St. Thomas. Elementary and secondary education certification. 155,000-volume library.

Financial CEEB CSS and ACT FAS. University scholarships and grants, payment plan; PELL, SEOG, NDSL, GSL, PLUS, CWS.

Admissions High school graduation with 15 units required. SAT, ACT, or PSAT required. $15 application fee. Rolling admission; application deadline August 1. $100 comprehensive and $50 room deposits required on acceptance of offer of admission. *Early Entrance*, informal early decision programs. Admission deferral possible. Transfers accepted. Credit possible for CEEB AP, CLEP, and university exams. Graduates from unaccredited high schools and non-graduates may be admitted by examination.

Student Life Student government. Newspaper, literary magazine, yearbook, radio station. Music, drama, debate, religious, and political groups. Black Student group. PIRG. Academic, athletic, service, and special interest clubs. 2 fraternities with houses; 10% of men join. Students must live on campus or at home. Coed and single-sex dorms. Some married-student and special interest housing. 70% of students live on campus. 11 intercollegiate sports for men, 7 for women; intramurals. AIAW, NCAA, NAIA, MIAC. Student body composition: 0.2% Asian, 2% Black, 0.5% Hispanic, 0.5% Native American, 96.8% White. 20% from out of state.

[J1] HIBBING COMMUNITY COLLEGE
Hibbing — see Arrowhead Community College, Hibbing Campus

[J1] INVER HILLS STATE COMMUNITY COLLEGE
Inver Grove Heights 55075

[J1] ITASCA COMMUNITY COLLEGE
Grand Rapids — see Arrowhead Community College, Itasca Campus

[J1] LAKEWOOD COMMUNITY COLLEGE
3401 Century Avenue, White Bear Lake 55110

[G1] LUTHER/NORTHWESTERN THEOLOGICAL SEMINARY
2481 Como Avenue, St. Paul 55108

[1] MACALESTER COLLEGE
St. Paul 55105, (612) 696-6357
Dean of Admissions: William M. Shain

- **Enrollment: 875m, 855w**
- **Tuition (1982/83): $6,225**
- **Room & Board: $2,080; Fees: $55**
- **Degree offered: BA**
- **Mean ACT 26.1; mean SAT 545v, 565m**
- **Student-faculty ratio: 14 to 1**

A private college established in 1874 and related to the United Presbyterian Church. 50-acre campus in a residential area of St. Paul. Airport, bus and train stations.

Academic Character NCACS and professional accreditation. 4-1-4 system, 8-week summer term. Majors offered in anthropology, art, biology, chemistry, classics, computer studies, dramatic arts, East Asian studies, economics & business, English, environmental studies, French, general science, geography, geology, German, history, humanities, international studies, Japan studies, law & society, library science, linguistics, math, music, philosophy, phys ed, physics, political science, psychology, religious studies, Russian, Russian area studies, social science, sociology, Spanish, speech communications, and urban studies. Interdepartmental, self-designed majors, minors. Distributive requirements. Independent study, internships. Credit by exam. Satisfactory/D/No credit grading option. Honors program. Phi Beta Kappa. Preprofessional programs in several areas. Many exchange programs, urban studies programs. Study abroad. ROTC with St. Thomas. Elementary and secondary education certification. Observatory/planetarium, electron microscope, language lab, computer. Natural history area, Arizona geology center. Over 290,000-volume library.

Financial CEEB CSS and ACT FAS. College and state scholarships, loans, and grants, Presbyterian scholarships, payment plan; PELL, SEOG, NDSL, GSL, PLUS, CWS. Application deadline March 1.

Admissions High school graduation with 13 units expected. SAT or ACT required; state residents may substitute PSAT. 3 ACH suggested. $20 application fee. Application deadline March 15. Notification on March 1 or April 1. $50 tuition and $50 room deposits required on acceptance of offer of admission. *Early Decision, Early Entrance, Concurrent Enrollment* programs. Admission deferral possible. Transfers accepted. Credit possible for CEEB AP exams. Minority admissions program.

Student Life Student government. Newspaper, literary quarterly, radio station. Music, dance, drama, and debate clubs. Community Involvement Program. Political, athletic, academic, and special interest groups. Scottish Country Fair in May. Coed dorms, special interest and language housing. No married-student housing. 65% of students live on campus. Intercollegiate and intramural sports for men and women. AIAW, MIAC. Student body composition: 1% Asian, 3% Black, 3% Hispanic, 1% Native American, 92% White. 65% from out of state.

[1] MANKATO STATE UNIVERSITY
Mankato 56001, (507) 389-2422 or (800) 722-0544
Director of Admissions: Jack Parkins

- **Undergraduates: 4,613m, 4,825w; 12,271 total (including graduates)**
- **Tuition (1982/83): $847 (in-state), $1,687 (out-of-state)**
- **Room & Board: $1,408; Fees: $144**
- **Degrees offered: BA, BS, BFA, BMus, AA, AS**
- **Mean ACT 19.2**
- **Student-faculty ratio: 19 to 1**

A public university established in 1867. 400-acre campus in the small city of Mankato, 75 miles southwest of Minneapolis. Bus station in Mankato.

Academic Character NCACS and professional accreditation. Trimester system, 2 4-week summer terms. Over 60 majors offered by the Colleges of Arts & Humanities, Business, Education, Natural Science, Math & Home Economics, Social & Behavioral Science, and Health, Phys Ed, & Nursing. Self-designed majors. Minors. Distributive requirements. MA, MS granted. Independent study. Honors program. Phi Beta Kappa. Pass/no credit, credit by exam, internships, cooperative work/study. Preprofessional programs in several areas. Exchange with other state universities. Friday College for working students. Study abroad. ROTC. Elementary, secondary, and special education certification. 600,000-volume library.

Financial CEEB CSS and ACT FAS. University scholarships and loans, state

scholarships and grants; PELL, SEOG, NSS, GSL, NDSL, PLUS, NSL, CWS. Application deadline April 23.
Admissions High school graduation with GPA or test scores placing student in upper 2/3 of students. GED accepted. Mankato area students given priority. SAT, ACT, or PSAT required. $10 application fee. Applications accepted up to registration. Room deposit required on acceptance of offer of admission. *Early Admission* and *Early Decision* programs. Admission deferral possible. Transfers accepted. Credit possible for CEEB CLEP exams.
Student Life Student government. Newspaper, radio stations. Several music groups. Speaking and drama groups. Special interest, political, professional, academic, and service clubs. Fraternities and sororities. Coed, single-sex, language, and special interest housing. 26% of students live on campus. Liquor prohibited on campus. 4 hours of activity courses and 3 hours of health science/recreation required. 11 intercollegiate sports for men, 9 for women; intramurals. Student body composition: 0.3% Asian, 1% Black, 0.5% Hispanic, 0.5% Native American, 95.7% White, 2% Other. 12% from out of state.

[J1] MESABI COMMUNITY COLLEGE
Virginia — see Arrowhead Community College, Mesabi Campus

[1] METROPOLITAN STATE UNIVERSITY
7th and Roberts Streets, St. Paul 55101

[1] MINNEAPOLIS COLLEGE OF ART AND DESIGN
200 East 25th Street, Minneapolis 55404, (612) 870-3161
Director of Admissions: Tom Reeve

- **Enrollment: 228m, 299w**
- **Tuition (1982/83): $4,070**
- **Room (with kitchen): $1,040-$1,680**
- **Degree offered: BFA**
- **Student-faculty ratio: 13 to 1**

A private professional school of art established in 1886 in Minneapolis. Airport, bus and train stations in Minneapolis.
Academic Character NCACS and professional accreditation. Semester system, 4- and 8-week summer terms. Majors offered in design: architecture, clothing, environmental, furniture, graphic, illustration, interior, photography, product, theory & methodology, typography, urban, visual communication; and in fine arts: critical studies, drawing, film, painting, photography, printmaking, sculpture, video. Distributive requirements; one-third of all work must be in liberal arts. Independent study. Internships. Exchange programs with 9 other art schools. Active Visiting Artist Program. Gallery. 46,000-volume library with extensive slide and cassette resources. Access to library at Minneapolis Institute of Art.
Financial CEEB CSS and ACT FAS. College scholarships, payment plan; PELL, SEOG, GSL, CWS, college part-time employment. Application deadline March 1.
Admissions High school graduation and 2 recommendations required. GED accepted. Interview recommended. $15 application fee. Rolling admissions; suggest applying early in 12th year. Deadline August 1. $100 tuition deposit and $50 matriculation fee required on acceptance of offer of admission. Informal early decision program. Admission deferral possible. Transfers accepted. SAT and ACT used only for advising.
Student Life Student Council. Student-initiated special interest groups. Coed dorms. Apartments. 25% of students live on campus. No formal meal plan. No sports program. Student body composition: 0.4% Asian, 3.5% Black, 0.6% Hispanic, 2.1% Native American, 92.1% White, 1.3% Other.

[J1] MINNEAPOLIS COMMUNITY COLLEGE
1501 Hennepin Avenue, Minneapolis 55403

[1] MINNESOTA, UNIVERSITY OF, TWIN CITIES
Minneapolis 55455, (612) 373-2144
Director of Admissions: Leo D. Abbott

- **Enrollment: 22,226m, 17,395w; 47,386 total (including graduates)**
- **Tuition (1982/83): $1,515 (WI, SD, ND, and MN residents), $3,771 (others)**
- **Room & Board: $2,217-$2,875; Fees: $224**
- **Degrees offered: BA, BS, BFA, BMus, BIindividualized Studies, ALA**
- **Mean ACT 22.6; mean SAT 1051**
- **Student-faculty ratio: 16 to 1**

A public university established in 1851. 280-acre campus in Minneapolis, with additional 70 acres in northern St. Paul. Airport, bus and train stations in Minneapolis/St. Paul.
Academic Character NCACS and professional accreditation. Trimester system, 2 summer terms. Over 140 majors offered by the Colleges of Agriculture, Biological Sciences, Business Administration, Education, Forestry Home Economics, Liberal Arts, and Pharmacy, and by the General College, the Institute of Technology, the School of Nursing, and the Department of Mortuary Science. Self-designed interdepartmental majors. Distributive requirements. Graduate and professional degrees granted. Independent study, honors programs. Phi Beta Kappa. Pass/fail, cooperative work/study. Preprofessional programs in architecture, dentistry, medicine, social work. 2-2, 3-1, and 1-3 transfer programs from College of Liberal Arts to other Colleges within the University. Study abroad. Elementary, secondary, and special education certification. ROTC, AFROTC, NROTC. Language lab. 4,030,654-volume library.
Financial ACT FAS. University scholarships, grants, and loans, Martin Luther King Fund; PELL, SEOG, NDSL, GSL, CWS. Application deadline March 1.
Admissions High school graduation required; unit requirements vary with Colleges. ACT, PSAT, or SAT required. General College admissions open to MN, WI, ND, and SD residents. $15 application fee. Rolling admissions; suggest applying before April of 12th year. Deadline July 15. *Early Entrance* Program. Transfers accepted to most colleges. Credit possible for CEEB AP and CLEP exams.
Student Life 400 student activities groups. 28 fraternities and 13 sororities with houses. 4% of students join. Coed and single-sex dorms. Married-student and special interest housing. 10% of students live on campus. Intercollegiate and intramural sports. AIAW, Big Ten. Student body composition: 2.4% Asian, 2% Black, 1% Hispanic, 0.5% Native American, 94.1% White. 10% of freshmen from out of state.

■[1] MINNESOTA, UNIVERSITY OF
Duluth 55812, (218) 726-8000
Director of Admissions: Gerald R. Allen

- **Enrollment: 3,536m, 3,070w (including graduates)**
- **Tuition (1982/83): $1,538 (MN, ND, SD, WI residents), $3,875 (others)**
- **Room & Board: $2,310**
- **Degrees offered: BA, BS, BAA, BAS, BBA, BFA, BOA, BSD, BAC, BMus, AA, AS**
- **Student-faculty ratio: 13 to 1**

A public university established in 1947. 240-acre campus in Duluth. Airport, bus and train stations in Duluth.
Academic Character NCACS and professional accreditation. Trimester system, 2 5-week summer terms. Majors offered in accounting, art, art education, biology, business administration, business & office education, chemistry, commercial art, communication, communication disorders, computer science, dental hygiene, early child care & development, earth science, economics, education, English, French, geography, geology, German, health education, history, home economics, industrial technology, interdisciplinary studies, liberal arts, math, music, office administration, philosophy, phys ed, physics, political science, psychology, social development, sociology-anthropology, Spanish, theatre, urban studies, vocational teacher education. Minors. Master's degrees granted. Cross-college curriculums. Independent study. Honors programs. Off-campus field study. 2-year basic sciences medical school program leads to MD at U Minnesota Medical School. Several preprofessional programs in biomedical fields, engineering, agricultural & forestry areas, journalism, and law. Elementary, secondary, and special education certification. AFROTC. Art museum, computer center, Lake Superior Basin Studies Area. 240,000-volume library.
Financial ACT FAS. University scholarships, grants, and loans; PELL, SEOG, NDSL, GSL, CWS. Application deadline March 1.
Admissions High school graduation and SCAT, ACT, SAT, or PSAT required. Open admission to all students ranked in upper ½ of class. $10 application fee. Rolling admissions. *Early Entrance,* informal early decision programs. Admission deferral possible. Transfers accepted. Credit possible for CEEB AP and CLEP exams.
Student Life Student government. Newspaper, radio station. Music and drama groups. Several academic, athletic, religious, and special interest groups. 5 fraternities, 4 sororities. Dorms & apartments. No married-student housing. 25% of students live on campus. 11 intercollegiate sports for men, 9 for women. AIAW, NAIA, NCAA. Student body composition: 0.9% Asian, 0.6% Black, 0.3% Hispanic, 0.8% Native American, 96% White, 1.4% Other. 10% from out of state.

■[1] MINNESOTA, UNIVERSITY OF
Morris 56267, (612) 589-2211
Director of Admissions: Robert J. Vikander

- **Enrollment: 849m, 841w**
- **Tuition (1982/83): $1,260 (in-state), $3,780 (out-of-state)**
- **Room & Board: $2,100; Fees: $195**
- **Degree offered: BA**
- **Mean ACT 22; mean SAT 420v, 502m**
- **Student-faculty ratio: 14 to 1**

A public university founded in 1959. 130-acre campus in the small city of Morris, 150 miles west of Minneapolis–St. Paul. Airport, bus and train stations.
Academic Character NCACS and professional accreditation. Trimester system, 2 summer terms. Majors offered in art history, biology, business-economics, chemistry, economics, elementary education, English, European studies, French, geology, German, health education, history, human services/liberal arts, Latin American area studies, math, music, philosophy, phys ed, physics, political science, psychology, social science, sociology, Spanish, speech communication, studio art, theatre arts. Cross-college curriculums. Self-designed majors. Minors. Distributive requirements. Independent study. Pass/no record, credit by exam. Internships. 26 preprofessional programs. Several 1-, 2-, and 3-year transfer programs with Twin Cities campus. Elementary and secondary education certification. University Without Walls. Computer center, art gallery. 120,000-volume library.
Financial No tuition for students who are at least ¼ American Indian. ACT FAS. University scholarships, grants, and loans; PELL, SEOG, NDSL, GSL, CWS. Application deadline April 23.
Admissions High school graduation required. Admission by exam possible. ACT, PSAT, or SAT required. $15 application fee. Rolling admissions; application deadline September 15. *Early Entrance,* informal early decision programs. Transfers accepted. Credit possible for CEEB AP and CLEP exams.
Student Life Student government. Newspaper, literary magazine, radio station. Music, debate, and drama groups. Minority group organizations. Sports clubs. Academic, honorary, and special interest groups. 2 fraternities and 1 sorority with houses. Freshmen encouraged to live on campus first term. Coed dorms. Apartments on campus, married-student housing. 85% of students live on campus. Liquor use restricted. 7 intercollegiate sports for

men, 4 for women; intramurals. AIAW, NCAA, NIC, NSC. Student body composition: 0.3% Asian, 3.8% Black, 0.2% Hispanic, 0.7% Native American, 95% White. 13% from out of state.

■[J1] MINNESOTA, UNIVERSITY OF, TECHNICAL COLLEGE
Crookston 56716

■[J1] MINNESOTA, UNIVERSITY OF, TECHNICAL COLLEGE
Waseca 56093

- **Undergraduates: 409m, 418w; 1,101 total (including part-time)**
- **Tuition (1982/83): $370 per quarter**
- **Degree offered: AAS**

A public junior college, part of a state university. Campus located in the small city of Waseca which is situated in a rich agricultural area of southern Minnesota.
Academic Character NCACS accreditation. Quarter system. 2-year terminal programs offered in agricultural/technical education, in the areas of agricultural business, agricultural industries & services, agricultural production, animal health technology, food industry & technology, home & family services, and horticultural technology. Remedial mathematics and English programs available.
Admissions High school graduation or equivalent required.
Student Life Residence halls and food service available. Intercollegiate and intramural athletic programs for men and women.

[P] MINNESOTA BIBLE COLLEGE
920 Mayowood Road, SW, Rochester 55901

[1] MOORHEAD STATE UNIVERSITY
1104 7th Avenue South, Moorhead 56560, (218) 236-2161
Director of Admissions: Floyd Brown

- **Enrollment: 2,669m, 3,326w; 6,206 total (including part-time)**
- **Tuition (1982/83): $842 (in-state), $1,687 (out-of-state)**
- **Room & Board: $1,400; Fees: $151**
- **Degrees offered: BA, BS, BFA, BSN, BSW, AA, AS**
- **Mean ACT 21.1**
- **Student-faculty ratio: 23 to 1**

A public university established in 1885. 104-acre campus in the small city of Moorhead, adjacent to Fargo, ND. Bus station in Moorhead, airport and train station in Fargo.
Academic Character NCACS and professional accreditation. Trimester system, 2 5-week summer terms. Majors offered in accounting, American studies, anthropology, art, biology, business administration, chemistry, computer science, criminal justice, education, economics, English, finance, French, geography, German, health education, history, hotel-motel-restaurant management, industrial areas, languages, legal assistant, management, marketing, mass communications, math, medical technology, music, office administration, philosophy, phys ed, physics, political science, psychology, social work, sociology, Spanish, speech, theatre arts, and vocational rehabilitation therapy. Nursing major for students with an RN. Self-designed majors. Distributive requirements. MSEd, MBA, MS granted. Honors program. Pass/fail, internships. Many preprofessional programs. Exchange programs with North Dakota State U, Concordia (Moorhead), and through National Student Exchange. Study abroad. Elementary, secondary, and special education certification. AFROTC, ROTC. 271,643-volume library.
Financial ACT FAS. University and state scholarships and grants; PELL, SEOG, NDSL, FISL, CWS. Application deadline April 16.
Admissions High school graduation required. GED accepted. SAT, ACT, or PSAT required. High school rank in upper ½ suggested. $10 application fee. Rolling admissions; application deadline August 15. $30 room deposit required on acceptance of offer of admission. Informal early decision program. Transfers accepted. Credit possible for CEEB AP and CLEP exams. Center for Multidisciplinary Studies may accept academically disadvantaged applicants.
Student Life Student government. Newspaper, literary magazine. Academic, honorary, special interest, and other organizations. 5 fraternities, 4 with houses, and 5 sororities, 4 with houses. 4% of men and women join. Coed and single-sex dorms. No married-student housing. 38% of students live on campus. Liquor prohibited on campus. 8 intercollegiate sports for men, 9 for women; intramurals. NAIA, NCAA, NIC, NSC. Student body composition: 99% White, 1% Other. 39% from out of state.

[J1] NORMANDALE COMMUNITY COLLEGE
Bloomington 55431

[P] NORTH CENTRAL BIBLE COLLEGE
910 Elliot Avenue, Minneapolis 55404

[J1] NORTH HENNEPIN COMMUNITY COLLEGE
Minneapolis 55445

[J1] NORTHLAND COMMUNITY COLLEGE
Thief River Falls 56701

[1] NORTHWESTERN COLLEGE
3003 Snelling Avenue North, Roseville 55113, (612) 636-4840
Director of Admissions: Dr. Donald G. Lindahl

- **Enrollment: 433m, 397w**
- **Tuition (1982/83): $3,900**
- **Room & Board: $1,905**
- **Degrees offered: BA, BS, AA**
- **Mean ACT 18.6**
- **Student-faculty ratio: 19 to 1**

A private independent Christian college established in 1902. Suburban 95-acre campus beside Lake Johanna, 20 minutes from Minneapolis & St. Paul. Airport, bus and train stations in Minneapolis.
Academic Character NCACS accreditation. Trimester system, summer term. Majors offered in art, Biblical studies, broadcasting, business administration, business education, church music & Christian education, commercial art, elementary education, ministries, music, office administration, pastoral studies, phys ed, recreation, social science, communication (literature), and youth ministries. 5-year major offered in music education. 3-year majors (AA) in arts & Bible, and arts, vocational studies & Bible. All bachelor's degree programs include a major in Bible, Ministries requires a minor. Distributives, 45 credits of religion, and Bible knowledge exam required for graduation. Independent and directed study, credit by exam. Internships. Study abroad. Elementary and secondary education certification. 64,196-volume library.
Financial ACT FAS and CEEB CSS. College and state scholarships and grants, payment plan; PELL, SEOG, GSL, NDSL, CWS. Recommended application deadline April 23.
Admissions Modified open admissions policy. High school graduation required. GED accepted. ACT (preferred), PSAT, or SAT accepted. Interview recommended. $15 application fee. Rolling admissions; application deadline one month before entrance date. Informal early decision,*Early Entrance, Concurrent Enrollment* programs. Admission deferral possible. Transfers accepted. Credit possible for CEEB AP and CLEP exams, and for ACT scores.
Student Life Student government. Newspaper, yearbook. College owns and operates a non-commerical, Christian network of radio stations. Music and drama clubs. Student Missionary Fellowship. Rotaract Service Club. Cheerleaders. Special interest and academic organizations. Students must live at home or on campus. Single-sex dorms. 80% of students live on campus. Liquor, tobacco, illegal drugs, gambling, and dancing absolutely prohibited both on and off campus. Class attendance mandatory. 3 credits of phys ed required. 9 intercollegiate sports for men, 6 for women; intramurals. AIAW, NCCAA, Upper Midwest Football, Twin River Collegiate Conferences. Student body composition: 0.3% Asian, 0.2% Black, 0.1% Hispanic, 0.5% Native American, 98.9% White. 40% from out of state.

[P] NORTHWESTERN COLLEGE OF CHIROPRACTIC
1834 South Mississippi River Blvd., St. Paul 55116

[P] NORTHWESTERN LUTHERAN THEOLOGICAL SEMINARY
1501 Eulham Street, St. Paul 55108

[P] OAK HILLS BIBLE INSTITUTE
Bemidji 56601

[J1] RAINY RIVER COMMUNITY COLLEGE
International Falls — see Arrowhead Community College, Rainy River Campus

[J1] ROCHESTER COMMUNITY COLLEGE
Rochester 55901

[1] SAINT BENEDICT, COLLEGE OF
Saint Joseph 56374, (612) 363-5308
Director of Admissions: Richard J. Manderfeld

- **Undergraduates: 1,750w**
- **Tuition (1982/83): $4,390**
- **Room & Board: $1,830; Fees: $100**
- **Degrees offered: BA, BS, BMus, AA**
- **Mean ACT 22**
- **Student-faculty ratio: 17 to 1**

A private women's college established in 1858 and conducted by the Sisters of the Order of Saint Benedict. Coordinate with Saint John's University for men. 700-acre campus 6 miles from Saint Cloud, 65 miles northwest of Minneapolis. Bus and train stations in Saint Joseph.
Academic Character NCACS and professional accreditation. 4-1-4 system. Majors offered in accounting, art, art history, biology, business administration, chemistry, classics, consumer home economics, dietetics, early childhood development, economics, elementary education, English, family studies, French, German, government, history, home economics, horsemanship, humanities, Latin, liberal studies, liturgical music, math, Medieval studies, music, natural science, nursing, nutrition science, philosophy, physics, psychology, religious education, social science, social work, sociology, Spanish, textiles-clothing-housing, theatre, and theology. 3-1 major in medical technology, 3-2 in physical therapy. Individualized and interdepartmental majors. AA offered in music and English. Minors. Distributives and 1 theology course required. Tutorials, directed & independent study. Honors program. Satisfactory/unsatisfactory option, credit by exam. Field work, internships. Preprofessional programs in biomedical fields, divinity, engineering, forestry, law. Optional Christian Service Semester. Study abroad. ROTC at St. John's. Elementary and secondary education certification. 200,000-volume St. Benedict library; additional 300,000-volumes at St. John's.
Financial CEEB CSS and ACT FAS. College and state scholarships and

grants, sibling discounts, payment plan; PELL, SEOG, NSS, NDSL, GSL, FISL, PLUS, NSL, CWS. File FAF or FFS by March 1.
Admissions High school graduation with GPA or test scores placing student in upper 2/3 of students required. GED accepted. Mankato area students given priority. SAT, ACT, or PSAT required. $10 application fee. Applications accepted up to registration. Room deposit required on acceptance of offer of admission. *Early Admission* Program. Admission deferral possible. Transfers accepted. Credit possible for CEEB CLEP exams.
Student Life Student government. Newspapers, literary magazine, yearbook, radio station. Music and drama clubs. Forum discussion group. Community service, religious, athletic, academic, and special interest groups. Dorms and apartments. 90% of students live on campus. Class attendance expected. One phys ed or dance course required. 5 intercollegiate sports, intramurals. AIAW. Student body composition: 0.3% Asian, 0.3% Black, 0.2% Hispanic, 0.2% Native American, 97.7% White, 1.3% Other. 14% from out of state.

[1] SAINT CATHERINE, COLLEGE OF

2004 Randolph Street, St. Paul 55105, (612) 690-6000
Director of Admissions: Lorraine Jensen

- **Enrollment: 2,498w**
- **Tuition (1982/83): $4,480**
- **Room & Board: $2,200; Fees: $55**
- **Degree offered: BA**
- **Mean ACT 22.6; mean SAT 500v, 510m**
- **Student-faculty ratio: 13 to 1**

A private women's college conducted by the Sisters of St. Joseph of Carondelet, established in 1905. 110-acre wooded campus in a residential area midway between St. Paul and Minneapolis. Airport, rail and bus stations nearby.
Academic Character NCACS and professional accreditation. 4-1-4 system, 3 4-week summer terms, workshops. Majors offered in art, biology, business administration, chemistry, classics, communication & theatre, communication, economics, education, English, French, German, history, home economics, humanities, languages, Latin, library science, mathematical sciences, music, nursing, occupational therapy, philosophy, phys ed, physics, political science, psychology, Russian area studies, social studies, social work, sociology, Spanish, theology. Majors offered through cooperative programs with other area colleges in American studies, anthropology, art history, East Asian studies, environmental studies, general science, geography, geology, health education, international relations, journalism, Latin American studies, linguistics, quantitative methods & computer science, and urban studies. Certificates granted. Distributives and 4 religion & theology courses required; student may plan own core program with approval. Honors program. Phi Beta Kappa. Credit by exam, pass/no credit. Preprofessional programs in health fields, engineering, law. 3-2 engineering with Washington U. Member of the Associated Colleges of the Twin Cities. Study abroad. Elementary and secondary education certification. AFROTC, ROTC. Montessori school on campus. Experimental psychology lab, language lab. Weekend College. Over 200,000-volume library.
Financial CEEB CSS and ACT FAS. College scholarships and loans, payment plans; PELL, SEOG, NSS, NDSL, FISL, NSL, CWS. Application deadline February 15.
Admissions High school graduation with college prep courses required. Nursing applicants should take biology, chemistry, physics. Interview encouraged. SAT or ACT required; PSAT may be substituted. $15 application fee. Rolling admissions beginning in October. $50 tuition and $100 room deposits required on acceptance of offer of admission. *Early Decision, Early Entrance* programs. Admission deferral possible. Transfers accepted. Credit possible for CEEB AP, CLEP, and college placement exams.
Student Life Student government. Newspaper, literary magazine, yearbook. Many music groups; some with College of St. Thomas. Drama group. Religious, political, athletic, academic, service, and special interest clubs. Traditional dorms and on-campus apartments. 52% of students live on campus. Class attendance expected. 2 semesters of phys ed required. 6 intercollegiate sports; intramurals. AIAW. Student body composition: 1% Black, 1% Hispanic, 0.6% Native American, 96.5% White, 0.9% Other. 30% from out of state.

[1] ST. CLOUD STATE UNIVERSITY

St. Cloud 56301, (612) 255-2111
Director of Admissions: Keith Rauch

- **Enrollment: 4,690m, 4,825w; 11,651 total (including part-time)**
- **Tuition (1982/83): $847 (in-state), $1,687 (out-of-state)**
- **Room & Board: $1,431; Fees: $146**
- **Degrees offered: BA, BS, BFA, BMus, BElective Studies, AA, AS, AElective Studies**
- **Mean ACT 19.6**
- **Student-faculty ratio: 23 to 1**

A public university established in 1869. Urban campus in St. Cloud, 75 miles from Minneapolis & St. Paul. Bus and train stations in St. Cloud.
Academic Character NCACS and professional accreditation. Trimester system, 2 5-week summer terms. 65 majors offered by the Colleges of Business, Education, Fine Arts, Industry, and Liberal Arts & Sciences. Elective Studies is an intercollege major. Distributive requirements. Master's degrees, 5th- and 6th-year, and specialist programs in education. Independent study, honors program. Pass/fail, internships. 18 preprofessional programs in biomedical fields, agriculture, engineering, home economics, law, fisheries management, forestry, horticulture, wildlife management. Cross-registration with other state universities and with St. Benedict/St. John's. Study abroad. Elementary, secondary, and special education certification. ROTC at St. John's. Computer center. 1,508,153-volume library.
Financial ACT FAS. University scholarships, grants, and loans; PELL, SEOG, NDSL, FISL, CWS, college part-time employment. Application deadline May 15.
Admissions High school graduation required. GED accepted. Applicant must rank in upper 2/3 of high school class. School of Business has more stringent requirements. Interview recommended. ACT, PSAT, or SAT required. $10 application fee. Rolling admissions; application deadline August 15. *Early Entrance, Concurrent Enrollment,* and informal early decision programs. Admission deferral possible. Transfers accepted. Credit possible for CEEB AP, CLEP, and university placement exams.
Student Life Newspaper, yearbook. Several academic, honorary, and special interest organizations. Coed and single-sex dorms. 25% of students live on campus. No liquor allowed on campus. 9 intercollegiate sports for men, 7 for women; intramurals. NCAC, Northern Sun Conference. Student body composition: 0.5% Asian, 0.2% Black, 0.3% Hispanic, 0.3% Native American, 97.1% White, 1.6% Other. 3% from out of state.

[1] SAINT JOHN'S UNIVERSITY

Collegeville 56321, (612) 363-2196
Director of Admissions: Roger C. Young

- **Enrollment: 1,850m**
- **Tuition (1982/83): $4,365**
- **Room & Board: $2,165; Fees: $50**
- **Degrees offered: BA, BS**
- **Mean ACT 24; mean SAT 510v, 560m**
- **Student-faculty ratio: 16 to 1**

A private men's university founded by the Order of Saint Benedict in 1857. Coordinate with College of Saint Benedict for women. 2,400-acre campus in a rural area 12 miles west of Saint Cloud and 80 miles northwest of Minneapolis. Bus station in Collegeville.
Academic Character NCACS and professional accreditation. 4-1-4 system, graduate summer term. Majors offered in accounting, art, art history, biology, business administration, chemistry, classics, computer science, dietetics, early childhood education, economics, elementary education, English, family life education, family studies, French, German, government, history, home economics, home economics education, humanities, math, medical technology, Medieval studies, music, natural science, nursing, nutrition science, occupational food service, philosophy, physical therapy, physics, psychology, religious education, social science, social work, sociology, Spanish, textiles/clothing, theatre, theology. Minors. Distributives, 1 theology course, and comprehensive exams required for graduation. Graduate school of theology grants MATheology. Honors programs and sections, pass/fail. Tutorials. Preprofessional programs in health fields, law; 2-year pre-forestry. Faculty and student exchange among members of the Central States College Association. Tri-College Great Issues Program: joint discussions. 3-2 divinity program. 2-3 and 3-3 engineering programs; 3-1 dentistry and medicine arrangeable. Study abroad. Secondary education certification. ROTC. Computer center, journalism and language labs. 320,000-volume library.
Financial CEEB CSS. University scholarships, grants, and loans, payment plan; PELL, SEOG, NDSL, GSL, CWS. Application deadline April 1.
Admissions High school graduation required; 10 units recommended. Interview encouraged. PSAT, ACT, or SAT required. $15 application fee. Rolling admissions; suggest applying by April 15. $100 deposit required on acceptance of offer of admission. *Early Decision* and *Early Entrance* programs. Admission deferral possible. Transfers accepted. Credit possible for CEEB AP exams.
Student Life Undergraduate student government. Newspaper, literary quarterly, yearbook, radio stations. Music and debate organizations. Religious and political groups. Film Society. Honorary and academic groups. Freshmen must live at home or on campus. Men's dorms. 80% of students live on campus. 1 phys ed activity required. 14 intercollegiate sports, intramurals. MIAC. 25% of students are from out of state.

[1] SAINT MARY'S COLLEGE

Winona 55987, (507) 452-4430
Director of Admissions: Anthony M. Piscitiello

- **Undergraduates: 627m, 577w; 1,404 total (including graduates)**
- **Tuition (1982/83): $4,300**
- **Room & Board: $1,960; Fees: $40**
- **Degree offered: BA**
- **Mean ACT 21; mean SAT 911**
- **Student-faculty ratio: 15 to 1**

A private Catholic college conducted by the Brothers of the Christian Schools. Established in 1912 and became coed in 1969. 350-acre suburban campus on the upper Mississippi River, 110 miles southeast of Minneapolis-St. Paul. Airport, bus and train stations.
Academic Character NCACS accreditation. Semester system, graduate summer term. Majors in art, biology, business administration, chemistry, classics, communication arts, computer science, criminal justice, economics, education, English, environmental biology, history, humanities, human services, journalism, math, medical technology, modern languages, music, music merchandising, natural sciences, nature interpretation, nuclear medical technology, philosophy, physical therapy, physics, political science, psychology, public administration, public relations, religious education, religious studies (youth ministries), sociology-anthropology, statistics. Self-designed majors. Minors. Distributive requirements. Master's degrees granted. Independent study, honors program. Pass/fail, cooperative work/study, internships. Preprofessional programs in dentistry, law, medicine, physical therapy. Cross-registration with Winona State, Saint Teresa. 3-2 engineering. Study abroad. Elementary and secondary education certification; certification at Cardinal Stritch in early childhood, special

education. ROTC at Winona State. Language and psychology labs. 156,100-volume library.
Financial CEEB CSS and ACT FAS. College scholarships, state scholarships and grants, payment plan; PELL, SEOG, GSL, NDSL, PLUS, CWS. Priority application deadline March 1; deadline May 1.
Admissions High school graduation with 16 units required. ACT (preferred) or SAT required. $15 application fee. Rolling admissions; application deadline in February. *Early Entrance* and *Early Decision* programs. Admission deferral possible. Transfers accepted. Credit possible for CEEB AP and CLEP exams.
Student Life Student government. Newspapers, literary journal, yearbook, radio station. Music and drama groups. Special interest, honorary, service, and academic groups. Fraternities & sororities. Students must live at home or on campus. Coed and single-sex dorms. 87% of students live on campus. 2 semesters of phys ed required. 7 intercollegiate sports for men, 6 for women; intramurals. AIAW, NAIA, MIAC. Student body composition: 0.1% Asian, 0.7% Black, 0.3% Hispanic, 0.3% Native American, 98.1% White, 0.5% Other. 63% from out of state.

[J1] SAINT MARY'S JUNIOR COLLEGE
2500 South Sixth Street, Minneapolis 55454, (612) 332-5521, ext. 305
Director of Admissions: Rebecca Innocent

- **Undergraduates: 36m, 444w; 789 total (including part-time)**
- **Tuition (1982/83): $3,690**
- **Room & Board: $1,179**
- **Degree offered: AAS**
- **Student-faculty ratio: 10 to 1**

A private junior college founded in 1964 by the Sisters of St. Joseph of Carondelet. Campus in the Cedar-Riverside area of Minneapolis, overlooking the Mississippi River. Airport, bus and train stations in Twin Cities.
Academic Character NCACS and professional accreditation. Trimester system, summer term. Majors in medical lab technician, medical record technician, nursing, occupational therapy assistant, physical therapy assistant, respiratory therapy, special education associate. Certificate in chemical dependency family treatment. Distributives and 4 credits of religion required. Support services for hearing and visually impaired students. Over 26,000-volume library.
Financial Private loans and grants, state grants-in-aid, PELL, NSS, NDSL, GSL, work/study.
Admissions High school graduation required. GED accepted. Evidence of achievement, including class rank, test results, or recommendations may be required. $20 application fee. Rolling admissions beginning in January. Suggest applying early for priority consideration. Extended Program for students unprepared for full-time study.
Student Life Educational Planning Committee, Judicial Committee. Professional interest groups. Extracurricular activities. Religious events and activities are offered by the campus ministry throughout the year. Student chorus. Housing for men and women. Intramural sports.

[1] ST. OLAF COLLEGE
Northfield 55057, (507) 663-2222
Director of Admissions: Bruce K. Moe

- **Enrollment: 1,395m, 1,640w**
- **Tuition (1982/83): $5,335**
- **Room & Board: $1,915**
- **Degrees offered: BA, BSN, BMus**
- **Mean ACT 25.5; mean SAT 540v, 585m**
- **Student-faculty ratio: 15 to 1**

A private college established in 1874 and affiliated with the American Lutheran Church. Wooded 350-acre campus 1 mile west of the small town of Northfield, and 40 miles south of Minneapolis-St. Paul. Bus station in Northfield.
Academic Character NCACS and professional accreditation. 4-1-4 system, 2 5½-week summer terms. Majors in American minority studies, American studies, ancient & Medieval studies, art, art history, Asian studies, biology, chemistry, classics, dance, economics, English, fine arts, French, German, health studies, Hispanic studies, history, home economics, literature, math, music, Norwegian, nursing, philosophy, phys ed, physics, political science, psychology, religion, Russian, Russian studies, social studies education, sociology, Spanish, speech-theatre, urban studies. Self-designed majors. Concentrations in computer science, statistics, and in Afro-American, American Indian, Latin American, Western European, and women's studies. Distributives and 3 religion courses required. Independent study and research, Phi Beta Kappa. Pass/no credit, credit by exam, internships. Several alternate study selections for qualified students. Cross-registration with Carleton; exchange with Fisk. Art courses through Union of Independent Colleges of Art. 3-2 engineering programs. Several off-campus and study abroad programs. Summer natural sciences program at wilderness station. Secondary education certification; elementary certification possible through Augsburg. Computer center, language labs. 325,000-volume library.
Financial CEEB CSS and ACT FAS. College scholarships, grants, and loans, PELL, SEOG, NDSL, GSL, NSL, CWS.
Admissions High school graduation required, with 15 units recommended. ACT, SAT, or PSAT required. $15 application fee. Rolling admissions; application deadline February 15. $100 deposit required on acceptance of offer of admission. *Early Decision* and *Early Entrance* programs. Transfers accepted. Credit possible for CEEB AP and CLEP exams, and for extracurricular academic work.
Student Life Student government. Newspaper, literary magazine, yearbook, radio station. Music, debate, and drama groups. Academic clubs and honorary fraternities. Political and volunteer groups. Coed, single-sex, and language dorms. No married-student housing. Off-campus students must eat one meal a day in the dining hall. 99% of students live on campus. Students may not have cars on campus. Honor system. Liquor prohibited on campus. 2 phys ed courses required. 12 intercollegiate sports for men, 9 for women; many intramurals. AIAW, NAIA, NCAA, MIAC. Student body composition: 97% White, 3% Other. 35% from out of state.

[1] ST. PAUL BIBLE COLLEGE
Bible College 55275, (612) 446-1411
Director of Admissions: Richard D. Porter

- **Enrollment: 267m, 344w**
- **Tuition (1982/83): $2,335**
- **Room & Board: $2,170; Fees: $245**
- **Degrees offered: BA, BS, BS in Missions, BReligious Ed, AA in Bible, AA, AS**
- **Mean ACT 18; mean SAT 470v, 440m**
- **Student-faculty ratio: 20 to 1**

A private college established in 1916, and affiliated with the Christian and Missionary Alliance. 173-acre campus in suburban St. Bonifacius, 23 miles from Minneapolis/St. Paul. Airport, bus and train stations in Twin Cities.
Academic Character NCACS and AABC accreditation. Semester system, 2 4-week summer terms. Majors offered in Bible & theology, Christian education, communications, elementary education, history, missionary nursing, missiology, music, teacher education. Minors. Diploma program in evangelical teacher training, Bible certificates. Distributives and 30 semester hours of theology required. Independent study. Honors program. Internships. Christian service program. Study abroad in the Holy Land. Elementary education certification. Language lab. 70,000-volume library with microform resources.
Financial ACT FAS. College and state scholarships & grants, college loans; PELL, SEOG, GSL, FISL, NDSL, PLUS, CWS. Application deadline March 15.
Admissions High school graduation required. Rank in upper 75% of class recommended. GED accepted. Interview recommended. SAT, ACT, or PSAT required. $20 application fee. Rolling admissions; application deadine August 15. Admission deferral possible. Transfers accepted. Credit possible for CEEB AP and CLEP exams. Conditional admission possible for academically disadvantaged applicants.
Student Life Student government. Newspaper, yearbook. Several religious groups. Music groups. Student Wives Organization. Annual missionary conference. Student must live at home or in college housing. Single-sex dorms; no married-student housing. 75% of students live on campus. Liquor, illegal drugs, tobacco, gambling prohibited. Dress code. Marriage regulations. 2 hours of phys ed required. Attendance at chapel four days a week required. 5 intercollegiate sports for men, 4 for women; intramurals. Northern Intercollegiate Christian Conference. Student body composition: 1.7% Asian, 0.5% Black, 0.9% Hispanic, 0.2% Native American, 96.7% White. 50% from out of state.

[G1] ST. PAUL SEMINARY
St. Paul 55101

[1] SAINT SCHOLASTICA, COLLEGE OF
Duluth 55811, (218) 723-6046
Director of Admissions: Thomas Kotulak

- **Enrollment: 187m, 720w; 1,048 total (including part-time)**
- **Tuition (1982/83): $4,149**
- **Room & Board: $2,079; Fees: $121**
- **Degree offered: BA**
- **Mean ACT 21.7**
- **Student-faculty ratio: 12 to 1**

A private college conducted by the Benedictine Sisters. Founded in 1910 and became coed in 1968. 160-acre campus in an urban residential section of Duluth. Airport, bus and train stations in Duluth.
Academic Character NCACS and professional accreditation. Trimester system, 2 3-week and 1 6-week summer terms. Majors in American Indian studies, biology, chemistry, computer information systems, dietetics, English, history, home economics, humanities, intermediate science education, management, math, media arts, medical record administration, music, music-drama, music-management, natural sciences, physical science education, physical therapy, preschool education, social work, sociology, and youth ministry. 3-1 medical technology major. Self-designed majors. Minors. Distributives, Direct Action Project required. Master's degrees granted. Independent study, honors program, pass/fail, internships. Preprofessional programs in dietetics, engineering, law, medicine. Professional certification programs in medical fields and in social work. Clinical experience at St. Mary's Hospital. Lake Superior Association of Colleges and Universities. 3-2 engineering program. 3-1 cytotechnology program arrangeable. Study abroad. Nursery, elementary, and secondary education certification. AFROTC at U Minnesota. American Indian Cultural Resource Center. 87,000-volume library.
Financial CEEB CSS and ACT FAS. College and state scholarships and grants, Native Americans scholarships, 2nd-family-member discount, payment plan; PELL, SEOG, NSS, NDSL, GSL, PLUS, CWS. Application deadline March 1.
Admissions High school graduation with 10 units recommended. GED accepted. Interview strongly recommended. SAT, ACT, or PSAT required. $10 application fee. Rolling admissions; suggested deadline one month before classes begin, earlier for some programs. $50 fee and $50 room deposit required on acceptance of offer of admission. *Early Admission,* informal early decision programs. Admission deferral possible. Transfers accepted. Credit possible for CEEB AP and CLEP exams, for evidence of high academic achievement in high school, and for correspondence courses. Second Chance Program for students who have done unsatisfactory work at another college, but who show potential.
Student Life Student government. Newspaper, literary magazine, yearbook,

radio station. Music and drama groups. 32 other stuaents clubs and organizations. Freshmen encouraged but not required to live on campus. Coed dorms, on-campus apartments. No married-student housing. 44% of students live on campus. Liquor allowed only in dorms. 5 intercollegiate sports for men, 4 for women; intramurals. Independent Conference, NAIA, MAIAW. Student body composition: 0.5% Black, 0.5% Hispanic, 2% Native American, 97% White. 15% from out of state.

[1] SAINT TERESA, COLLEGE OF

Winona 55987, (507) 454-2930
Director of Admissions: Sister Katarina Schuth

- **Enrollment: 18m, 774w**
- **Tuition (1982/83): $4,500**
- **Room & Board: $1,800; Fees: $90**
- **Degrees offered: BA, BS, BSW**
- **Mean ACT 17; mean SAT 827**
- **Student-faculty ratio: 10 to 1**

A private college founded in 1907 under the auspices of the Sisters of Saint Francis. 75-acre campus in the Mississippi Valley, 120 miles from Twin Cities and 300 miles from Chicago. Bus and train stations in Winona.

Academic Character NCACS and professional accreditation. Trimester system. BA offered in accounting, art, art education, art therapy, biology, business management, church music, communicative disorders, computer science, criminal justice, dance performance, dance therapy, educational studies, English, English for secondary education, French, German, history, humanities, journalism & media communications, management, math, music, political science, psychology, religious studies, social science, social work, sociology, Spanish, statistics, theatre. BS offered in business education, dietetics, elementary education, home economics, home economics education, medical technology, middle school science education, nursing, physical therapy. Self-designed majors. Minors in chemistry, gerontology, philosophy. Distributives, 4 credits of religion, and senior seminar required. Independent study. Internships, cooperative work/study. Preprofessional programs in law, medicine, pahrmacy, veterinary medicine. 3-2 engineering with Georgia Tech. Cross-registration with St. Mary's and Winona State Colleges. Study abroad. Elementary, secondary, and special education certification. 150,000-volume library.

Financial CEEB CSS and ACT FAS. College scholarships, PELL, SEOG, NDSL, FISL, GSL, NSL, CWS. Recommended application deadline March 2.

Admissions High school graduation with college prep courses required. Interview recommended. SAT, ACT, or PSAT/NMSQT required. $15 application fee. Rolling admissions. $100 commitment fee required on acceptance of offer of admission. *Early Admission* and *Early Decision* programs. Transfers accepted. Credit possible for CEEB CLEP exams and for life experiences.

Student Life Student government. Newspaper, literary magazine, yearbook. Music, drama, and dance groups. American Indian Student Association. Political, religious, academic, and special interest groups. Students expected to live on campus or at home. Women's dorms. 85% of students live on campus. 4 credits of phys ed required. 4 intercollegiate sports, intramurals. Student body composition: 0.2% Asian, 0.6% Black, 2.7% Hispanic, 0.2% Native American, 93.6% White, 2.7% Other. 50% from out of state.

[1] ST. THOMAS, COLLEGE OF

2115 Summit Avenue, St. Paul 55105
Director of Admissions: Charles E. Murphy

- **Enrollment: 1,936m, 1,291w; 5,630 total (including part-time)**
- **Tuition (1982/83): $4,160**
- **Room & Board: $1,975; Fees: $80**
- **Degree offered: BA**
- **Mean SAT 460v, 520m**
- **Student-faculty ratio: 19 to 1**

A private Catholic college established in 1885, became coed in 1977. 50-acre suburban wooded campus midway between St. Paul and Minneapolis. Airport, bus and train stations nearby.

Academic Character NCACS and professional accreditation. 4-1-4 system, 3 6-week summer terms. Majors offered in art history, biology, business administration, chemistry, communication & theatre, criminal justice, economics, education, English, foreign language, geology, history, international studies, journalism, math, music, philosophy, phys ed, physics, political science, psychology, public administration, public relations, quantitative methods & computer science, social work, sociology, theology. Majors offered through the Associated College of the Twin Cities consortium: American studies, anthropology, art, elementary education, environmental studies, geography, home economics, international relations, Latin American studies, library science, linguistics, music therapy, Russian, urban studies. Self-designed majors. Distributives and 3 courses in theology required. Masters degrees granted. Independent study. Aquinas Scholars Program. Pass/fail, cooperative work/study. Preprofessional programs in dentistry, engineering, law, medicine. 2-2 and 3-2 engineering programs. Cross-registration with other members of the Twin Cities consortium. Urban semester. Study abroad. Elementary and secondary certification. AFROTC. Computer center. 195,000-volume library.

Financial CEEB CSS and ACT FAS. College scholarships, state scholarships and grants; PELL, SEOG, GSL, NDSL, CWS, MN work-study, college part-time employment. Application deadline March 1.

Admissions High school graduation with 15 units required. SAT, PSAT, or ACT required. $15 application fee. Rolling admissions; priority application deadline November 1. $50 tuition and $50 housing deposits required on acceptance of offer of admission. Informal early decision. Admission deferral possible. Transfers accepted. Credit possible for CEEB AP, CLEP, ACT PEP, and college placement exams, and for experiential learning.

Student Life Student government. Newspaper, yearbook. Music, drama, and debate organizations. Film series. Professional, service, and social fraternities & sororities. Several academic honor societies. Students may live on or off campus. Dorms and dining halls. Class attendance expected. 1 semester of phys ed required. 11 intercollegiate sports for men, 8 for women; intramurals. AIAW, NCAA, NAIA. Student body composition: 0.5% Black, 0.7% Hispanic, 0.3% Native American, 97.9% White, 0.6% Other.

[2] SCHOOL OF THE ASSOCIATED ARTS

344 Summit Avenue, St. Paul 55102

[1] SOUTHWEST STATE UNIVERSITY

Marshall 56258, (507) 537-6286
Director of Admissions & Orientation: Philip M. Coltart

- **Enrollment: 919m, 762w; 2,082 total (including part-time)**
- **Tuition (1982/83): $700 (in-state), $850 (out-of-state)**
- **Room & Board: $1,500**
- **Degrees offered: BA, BS, BEng Tech, AS, AEng Tech**
- **Student-faculty ratio: 18 to 1**

A public university established in 1963. 216-acre rural, barrier-free campus in the small town of Marshall, 90 miles from Sioux Falls and 150 miles southwest of Minneapolis. Airport, bus and train stations nearby.

Academic Character NCACS and professional accreditation. Trimester system, 2 5-week summer terms. 50 majors offered by the School of Business, Science, & Technology and by the School of Humanities, Social Science, & Education. Individualized interdisciplinary majors. Minors. Distributive requirements, including general studies and rural studies courses. Graduate studies available through consortium with Mankato State and St. Cloud State. Independent study, honors program. Pass/fail, cooperative work/study, internships. Preprofessional programs in 13 areas. 4-year Institution Management program. Cooperative baccalaureate program with Worthington Community College. External studies and continuing education programs. Study abroad. Elementary and secondary education certification. Computer center, greenhouse, planetarium, museums, art gallery. 135,000-volume library with microform resources.

Financial ACT FAS. University and state scholarships and grants, PELL, SEOG, BIA, NDSL, FISL, CWS. Application deadline March 1. Notification in April and May.

Admissions High school graduation with rank in top 50% of class required. SAT, ACT, or PSAT required. Rolling admissions; application deadline one month before registration. Informal early decision. Transfers accepted. Credit possible for CEEB CLEP and departmental exams, and for military and non-collegiate post-secondary credit.

Student Life Student government. Newspaper, yearbook, radio and TV stations. Music, drama, and debate groups. Coffeehouses. Film series. Several special interest and volunteer organizations. Coed and single-sex dorms, special interest housing. 55% of students live on campus. Regular class attendance expected. 7 credit hours of phys ed required. 6 intercollegiate sports for men, 6 for women; intramurals. AIAW, NAIA, NCAA, NIC, NSC. Student body composition: 0.9% Asian, 0.7% Black, 0.4% Hispanic, 0.3% Native American, 97.7% White.

[G1] UNITED THEOLOGICAL SEMINARY OF THE TWIN CITIES

New Brighton 55112

[J1] VERMILION COMMUNITY COLLEGE

Ely — see Arrowhead Community College, Vermilion Campus

[P] WILLIAM MITCHELL COLLEGE OF LAW

875 Summit Avenue, St. Paul 55105

[J1] WILLMAR COMMUNITY COLLEGE

Willmar 56201, (612) 231-5102

- **Enrollment: 399m, 424w**
- **Tuition (1982/83): $840 (MN, WI, SD, ND residents), $1,680 (others)**
- **Fees: $15**
- **Degrees offered: AA, AS, AAA**
- **Student-faculty ratio: 25 to 1**

A public liberal arts community college in Willmar, west of the Twin Cities.

Academic Character NCACS accreditation. Trimester system, summer term. Transfer & preprofessional programs offered in agriculture business, agriculture, accounting, art, architecture, biology, business, business administration, executive secretary, chemistry, dentistry, economics, elementary education, secondary education, engineering, forestry, home economics, journalism, law, law enforcement, liberal arts, math, medical technology, medicine, physical medicine, music, mortuary science, nursing, optometry, pharmacy, social service, speech & theatre, veterinary science. Career programs in law enforcement, nursing, human services, community services. Self-designed majors. Independent study. Extension courses. Cooperative work/study. Evening program. 20,000-volume library with microform resources.

Financial ACT FAS. College scholarships and loans, state grants-in-aid; PELL, SEOG, NDSL, GSL, CWS, state and college work-study. Application deadline is May 1.

Admissions High school graduation, GED, or evidence of a reasonable chance of success required. ACT or PSAT required. Non-resident applications must achieve a minimum score on the exam and show scholastic aptitude. $15 application fee. Application deadline 2 weeks before term begins. Late applications considered. *Early Admissions* Program. Transfers accepted. Credit possible for CEEB CLEP exams.

Student Life Student government. Newspaper. Music and drama organizations. Circle K (Kiwanis). Religious and political groups. Ski club. Veteran's club. Cheerleaders. No housing on campus. $2,300 average for room & board off campus. Intercollegiate and intramural sports for men and women. Minnesota Community College Conference.

[1] WINONA STATE UNIVERSITY

Winona 55987, (507) 457-2065
Director of Admissions: Dr. J. A. Mootz

- **Undergraduates: 2,000m, 2,500w; 5,000 total (including graduates)**
- **Tuition (1982/83): $850 (in-state) ,$1,700 (out-of-state)**
- **Room & Board: $1,450; Fees: $160**
- **Degrees offered: BA, BS, AA, AS**
- **Mean ACT 19; mean SAT 902**
- **Student-faculty ratio: 19 to 1**

A public university established in 1858. 40-acre small-city campus on the Mississippi River, 110 miles from Minneapolis/St. Paul. Bus and train stations in Winona; airport in LaCrosse, WI.

Academic Character NCACS and professional accreditation. Trimester system, 2 5-week summer terms. Majors offered in accounting, art, biology, business administration, business education, chemistry, communication, computer, criminal justice, earth science, economics, elementary education, English, general education, general studies, geography, geology, German, history, industrial education, industry, mass communications, math, medical assistant, medical technician, medical technology, music, nursing, paralegal, phys ed, physical science, physical therapy, physics, political science, psychology, public administration, recreational/leisure studies, school/community health education, social science, sociology, theatre arts, veterinary medical technician, and vocational education. Cooperative majors (with other area colleges) offered in French, Spanish, speech pathology. Self-designed majors. Minors. Distributive requirements. Masters degrees granted. One-year and certificate programs. Honors programs, pass/no credit, internships. Preprofessional programs in 12 areas. Cooperative programs in engineering. Exchange with other state universities. Study abroad. Elementary, secondary, and special education certification. 250,000-volume library.

Financial CEEB CSS and ACT FAS. University scholarships, grants, and loans; PELL, SEOG, NSS, NDSL, FISL, NSL, CWS. Application deadlines January 15 (scholarships), March 1 (loans).

Admissions High school graduation required, with 16 units recommended. Rank in upper 50% of class suggested. GED accepted. SAT, ACT, or PSAT required. $10 application fee. Rolling admissions; application deadline one week before registration. $50 room deposit required on acceptance of offer of admission. *Early Entrance, Concurrent Enrollment*, informal early decision programs. Admission deferral possible. Transfers accepted. Credit possible for CEEB AP, CLEP, and university placement exams.

Student Life Student government. Newspaper, literary magazine, radio and TV stations. Music, drama, and dance groups. Cultural activities committee. 4 fraternities and 3 sororities without houses. 3% of student join. Coed and single-sex dorms. 45% of students live on campus. Liquor prohibited on campus. 2 terms of phys ed required. 11 intercollegiate sports. Northern Intercollegiate Conference, Sun Conference. Student body composition: 1% Asian, 1% Black, 1% Hispanic, 1% Native American, 96% White. 25% from out of state.

[J1] WORTHINGTON COMMUNITY COLLEGE

1450 Collegeway, Worthington 56187, (507) 372-2107

- **Enrollment: 203m, 174w; 680 total (including part-time)**
- **Tuition (1982/83): $888 (MN, SD, ND, WI, & areas of Iowa), $1,776 (others)**
- **Degrees offered: AA, AS, AAS, AES**
- **Student-faculty ratio: 20 to 1**

A public community college established in 1936. 70-acre campus on the north shore of Lake Okabena, in southwest Minnesota. Extended centers in Windom and Luverne.

Academic Character NCACS accreditation. Trimester system, summer term. Transfer programs include accounting, agriculture, art, biology, business administration, chemistry, computer science, economics, elective studies, elementary education, English, forestry, geography, history, math, music, physical education, physics, psychology, political science, pre-dentistry, pre-engineering, pre-law, pre-medicine, pre-pharmacy, secretarial science, social work, sociology, speech. Career programs in agproduction management, agribusiness, business management, human services, practical nursing. Vocational certificates and certificates of attendance also offered, including nursing, secretarial, and clerical certificates. Independent study. Evening classes. Continuing education program. 29,000-volume library.

Financial ACT FAS. College scholarships and loans, state scholarships and grants-in-aid, PELL grants. File application with admissions application.

Admissions Open admission to applicants who show evidence of high school graduation, GED, or whose high school class has graduated. ACT encouraged. Requirements for admission to nursing program are more stringent. $15 application fee. *Concurrent Enrollment* Program. Transfers accepted.

Student Life Student government. Newspaper. Music, drama, and special interest organizations. Cheerleading. No dorms; Star Student Village (a mobile home complex) adjacent to campus. Dining hall. 4 intercollegiate sports for men, 3 for women; intramurals. Minnesota Community College Conference.

MISSISSIPPI *(MS)*

[1] ALCORN STATE UNIVERSITY

Lorman 39096, (601) 877-6100, (800) 222-6970 (in-state)
Director of Admissions: Alice Davis-Gill

- **Undergraduates: 801m, 1,086w**
- **Tuition (1982/83): $825 (in-state), $1,757 (out-of-state)**
- **Room & Board: $1,475**
- **Degrees offered: BA, BS, BMus**
- **Mean ACT 15**
- **Student-faculty ratio: 11 to 1**

A public university established in 1871. 244-acre campus located in the small town of Lorman, 45 miles from Vicksburg, 90 miles from Jackson. Served by rail and bus. Airport in Vicksburg.

Academic Character SACS accreditation. Semester system, 2 6-week summer terms. 34 majors offered by the divisions of Arts & Sciences, Business, Education & Psychology, Agriculture & Applied Science, and Nursing. Distributive requirements, senior exam or project required. MS granted. Honors program. Cooperative work/study. Preprofessional programs in allied health, dentistry, engineering, forestry, medical records administration, medical technology, medicine, nursing, optometry, pharmacy, veterinary medicine. Cooperative program in physics with Howard U. Elementary and secondary education certification. ROTC. Computer center. 175,000-volume library with microform resources.

Financial CEEB CSS. University scholarships, grants, and loans, athletic and music scholarships; PELL, SEOG, NDSL, FISL, CWS. Preferred application deadline April 15.

Admissions High school graduation with 15 units required. GED accepted. ACT required. Rolling admissions. $20 deposit required on acceptance of offer of admission. Transfers accepted. University has own advanced placement program.

Student Life Student government. Newspapers, yearbook. Music and drama groups. Religious, honorary, academic, and special interest groups. 5 fraternities and 4 sororities without houses. Students must live at home or on campus. Single-sex dorms. No married-student housing. Attendance in class and at assemblies required. 4 hours of phys ed required. Intercollegiate and intramural sports. NAIA, NCAA. Student body composition: 0.2% Asian, 96.3% Black, 3.5% White.

[1] BELHAVEN COLLEGE

1500 Peachtree Street, Jackson 39202
Director of Admissions: R. Doug Mickey

- **Undergraduates: 260m, 290w; 1,021 total (including special students)**
- **Tuition (1982/83): $1,500**
- **Room & Board: $1,640; Fees: $50**
- **Degrees offered: BA, BS, BBA, BMus**
- **Mean ACT 20.8**
- **Student-faculty ratio: 18 to 1**

A private college affiliated with the Presbyterian Church, established in 1883. 42-acre urban campus in large city of Jackson.

Academic Character SACS and professional accreditation. Semester system, 2 5-week summer terms. Majors offered in art, Bible, Christian ministries, classical languages, English, Greek, history, modern languages, philosophy-Bible, political science-history, psychology, speech-English, accounting, biology, business administration, business education, chemistry, elementary education, health-physical education, home economics-art, mathematics, secretarial science, music (4 areas), finance, general business, and marketing. Distributives and 3 Bible courses required. Pass/fail. Internships. Preprofessional programs in ministry, medicine, dentistry, nursing, law. Cooperative program with Millsaps College. 60,229-volume library with microform resources.

Financial CEEB CSS. College scholarships & loans, state grants, athletic grants, music and ministerial scholarships; PELL, SEOG, NDSL, FISL, GSL, CWS; college has own work program. Priority application deadline May 1.

Admissions High school graduation with 16 units required. ACT or SAT required; ACT preferred. $10 application fee. Rolling admissions. $30 room deposit required on acceptance of offer of admission. *Early Admission* Program. Transfers accepted. Credit possible for CEEB AP and CLEP exams.

Student Life Student government. Newspaper, magazine, yearbook. Religious, honorary, academic, professional, and special interest groups. Dorms and dining hall. Attendance at weekly chapel required. 4 intercollegiate sports for men, 3 for women; intramurals. 16% of students from out of state.

[1] BLUE MOUNTAIN COLLEGE

PO Box 338, Blue Mountain 38610, (601) 685-4771

- **Enrollment: 81m, 199w; 356 total (including part-time)**
- **Tuition & Fees (1982/83): $2,130**

- **Typical expenses: $3,680**
- **Degrees offered: BA, BS, BMus, BSEd**
- **Student-faculty ratio: 11 to 1**

A private college operated by the State Baptist Convention primarily for women; men are admitted if they are professional religious workers and/or summer school students.
Academic Character SACS accreditation. Semester system, 2 5-week summer terms. Programs offered leading to majors in liberal arts, education, and music. 44,000-volume library.
Financial College scholarships and loans, PELL grants, CWS.
Admissions High school graduation and recommendation required. Entrance test required of non-accredited high school graduates. Rolling admissions policy. *Early Admission* Program. Transfers accepted.
Student Life Social societies. Dormitories and dining hall maintained.

[J1] CLARKE COLLEGE
PO Box 440, Newton 39345, (601) 683-2061
Director of Admissions & Public Relations: Joseph Dow Ford

- **Undergraduates: 73m, 48w; 149 total (including part-time)**
- **Tuition (1982/83): $1,560**
- **Room & Board: $1,410; Fees: $120**
- **Degree offered: AA**
- **Student-faculty ratio: 16 to 1**

A private junior college controlled by the Mississippi Baptist Convention, established in 1907. 245-acre campus in the small town of Newton in east central Mississippi. Served by air and bus.
Academic Character SACS accreditation. Semester system, 2 5-week summer terms. Majors offered in art, English, foreign language, music, speech & drama, Bible, philosophy, religious education, biology, chemistry, mathematics, physics, business, economics, history, psychology, secretarial science, sociology, elementary education, and physical education & recreation. Distributives and 6 hours of Bible required. Credit by exam. Preprofessional programs in health sciences, medicine, nursing. Language lab. 18,000-volume library.
Financial CEEB CSS. College scholarships, music and athletic scholarships, payment plan; PELL, SEOG, NDSL, FISL, CWS; college has own work program. Priority application deadline April 1.
Admissions High school graduation required. ACT required. $15 application fee. Rolling admissions. $25 room deposit ($40 for apartment) required on acceptance of offer of admission. *Early Admission* Program. Transfers accepted. Credit possible for CEEB AP and CLEP exams; college has own advanced placement program.
Student Life Student Personnel Committee. Baptist Student Union. Quarterly, yearbook. Music and drama groups. Religious, academic, and special interest groups. Single students under 21 must live at home or on campus. Single-sex dorms. Married-student housing. Liquor, drugs, gambling prohibited on campus. Attendance in class, at chapel and church services, and at convocations required. 2 courses in phys ed required. 2 intercollegiate sports; intramurals.

[J1] COAHOMA JUNIOR COLLEGE
Route 1, Box 616, Clarksdale 38614

[J1] COPIAH-LINCOLN JUNIOR COLLEGE
Wesson 39191

[1] DELTA STATE UNIVERSITY
Cleveland 38733, (601) 843-4073
Director of Admissions: Robert A. Bain

- **Boarding undergraduates: 960m, 1,268w; 3,193 total (including grads and commuters)**
- **Tuition (1982/83): $770 (in-state), $926 (out-of-state)**
- **Room & Board: $1,096**
- **Degrees offered: BA, BS, BSEd, BMus, BMus Ed, BSCrim Jus, BSGS, BBA, BFA, BSN, BSW**
- **Mean ACT 18.4**
- **Student-faculty ratio: 21 to 1**

A public university established in 1924. 275-acre small-city campus in the Mississippi delta.
Academic Character SACS and professional accreditation. Semester system, 2 5-week summer terms. 49 majors offered by the schools of Arts & Sciences, Business, Education, and Nursing. Minors offered in most major fields and in business administration, geography, media-library science, philosophy. Distributive requirements. MEd granted. Independent study. Honors program. Cooperative work/study, internships. Preprofessional programs in engineering, dentistry, medicine. Semester exchange with Westfield State (MA). Elementary, secondary, and special education certification. ROTC on campus, AFROTC at Mississippi Valley State. Language lab. 231,668-volume library with microform resources.
Financial University scholarships, grants, loans; PELL, SEOG, NDSL, FISL, CWS; university has own work program. Application deadline April 1.
Admissions High school graduation with 15 units required. GED accepted. Portfolio required for art majors; performance in ensemble activities for music. ACT required. $25 room deposit required with application. Rolling admissions; application deadline August 5. *Early Admission* and *Early Decision* programs. Transfers accepted. Credit possible for CEEB AP and CLEP exams; university has own advanced placement program.
Student Life Student government. Newspaper, magazine, yearbook. Music, debate, drama groups. Black Student Organization, Ebony Woman's Association, Circulo Hispanico. Honorary, religious, academic, and special interest groups. 6 fraternities and 5 sororities. Single-sex dorms. Married-student housing. 50% of students live on campus. 2 hours of phys ed required. 8 intercollegiate sports for men, 2 for women; intramurals. AIAW, NCAA. Student body composition: 0.7% Asian, 18% Black, 81% White, 0.3% Other. 6% from out of state.

[J1] EAST CENTRAL JUNIOR COLLEGE
Decatur 39327, (601) 635-2126, ext. 206
Dean of Admissions & Records: Frank Rives

- **Undergraduates: 456m, 377w; 1,089 total (including part-time)**
- **Tuition (1982/83): $380**
- **Room & Board: $1,070; Fees: $38**
- **Degrees offered: AA, AS, AAS**
- **Mean ACT 15**
- **Student-faculty ratio: 15 to 1**

A public junior college established in 1928. 200-acre campus in Decatur.
Academic Character SACS accreditation. Semester system, 2 5-week summer terms. Majors offered in agriculture, business, education (6 areas), home economics, liberal arts, music. Technical and vocational programs offered in intensive business, secretarial science, drafting, technical data processing, cosmetology, auto mechanics, body and fender, electricity, refrigeration/air conditioning, machine shop, radio/TV repair, welding, carpentry & cabinet making, and masonry. Honors program. Preprofessional programs in dentistry, medicine, law, forestry, engineering, nursing, pharmacy, optometry, veterinary medicine, ministry. 50,000-volume library with microform resources.
Financial College scholarships; athletic, band, and cheerleader scholarships; PELL, FISL, CWS; college has own work program.
Admissions High school graduation with 15 units required. GED accepted. ACT required. Rolling admissions. $25 room deposit required with application. *Early Enrollment* Program. Transfers accepted. Credit possible for CEEB CLEP exams.
Student Life Student government. Newspaper, yearbook. Music groups. Religious, academic, honorary, and special interest groups. Students must live at home or on campus. Single-sex dorms. Married-student housing. Class attendance required. Intercollegiate and intramural sports. Student body composition: 25% minority.

[J1] EAST MISSISSIPPI JUNIOR COLLEGE
Scooba 39358, (601) 476-2111

- **Enrollment: 403m, 305w; 1,095 total (including part-time)**
- **Tuition (1980/81): $90 (out-of-district), $300 (out-of-state)**
- **Room & Board: $315**
- **Degree offered: AA**

A coeducational junior college under county control in Scooba.
Academic Character SACS and professional accreditation. Semester system. Programs offered include 13th and 14th grades for transfer and a nine-month business program. Vocational-technical programs available.
Admissions Character reference from five graduates of the institution required for entrance or registration.
Student Life Two dormitories for men and one for women. Dining hall available.

[J1] HINDS JUNIOR COLLEGE
Raymond 39154, (601) 857-5261
Director of Admissions & Records: Billy T. Irby

- **Undergraduates: 3,956m, 4,251w**
- **Tuition (1982/83): $370 (in-state), $1,290 (out-of-state)**
- **Room & Board: $980-$1,160**
- **Degrees offered: AA, AAS**

A public junior college established in 1922. 1,000-acre main campus in Raymond with branches in Jackson and Vicksburg. Served by air and bus.
Academic Character SACS accreditation. Semester system, 2 4-week summer terms. Majors offered in accounting, agriculture, architecture, art, business, criminal justice, education, engineering, forestry, geology, home economics, industrial education, industrial technology, institutional management-dietetics, journalism, music, nursing science, physical education, physical science, public administration, and speech. 41 technical programs offered. Distributive requirements. Cooperative work/study. Preprofessional programs in dentistry, law, medical technology, medicine, pharmacy, veterinary medicine. ROTC. Computer center. 73,000-volume library.
Financial Aid is available; contact Financial Aid Office for further details.
Admissions High school graduation required. GED accepted. Interview required for technical and vocational programs. ACT required. $50 room deposit required with application. Rolling admissions. Transfers accepted. Credit possible for CEEB AP and CLEP exams; college has own advanced placement program.
Student Life Student government. Newspaper, yearbook. Music groups. Black Student Association. Religious, academic, service, and special interest groups. Single-sex dorms. Liquor, gambling prohibited on campus. Limited class absences allowed. 2 hours of phys ed, ROTC, or marching band required. 6 intercollegiate sports; intramurals. MJCAA.

[J1] HOLMES JUNIOR COLLEGE
Goodman 39079

[J1] ITAWAMBA JUNIOR COLLEGE
Fulton 38843

[1] JACKSON STATE UNIVERSITY
Jackson 39217, (601) 968-2323
Dean of Admissions & Records: Haskell S. Bingham

- **Undergraduates: 3,021m, 4,078w**
- **Tuition (1982/83): $416 (in-state), $2,080 (out-of-state)**
- **Room & Board: $1,557-$1,656**
- **Degrees offered: BA, BS, BMus, BMus Ed, BSEd, BSW**
- **Student-faculty ratio: 19 to 1**

A public university established in 1877. 120-acre urban campus located 1 mile from downtown Jackson. Served by air and bus.
Academic Character SACS and professional accreditation. Semester system, 2 5-week summer terms. 51 majors offered in the areas of business, art, science & technology, education, humanities, fire science, health, industrial arts & sciences, communication, meteorology, music, and recreation. Minors offered. Courses in 7 additional areas. MS granted. Honors program. Cooperative work/study. Preprofessional programs in engineering, health careers. Medical technology/medical record administration program with U of Mississippi Medical Center. National Student Exchange. Elementary and secondary education certification. ROTC. Computer center. 400,000-volume library with microform resources.
Financial CEEB CSS. University scholarships, grants, loans, state grants; PELL, SEOG, NDSL, FISL, CWS; university has own work program. Application deadline April 1.
Admissions High school graduation required. GED accepted. SAT or ACT required. Rolling admissions; application deadline August 1. $20 room deposit required 15 days before entrance. *Early Admission, Early Decision, Concurrent Enrollment* programs. Admission deferral possible. Transfers accepted. Credit possible for CEEB CLEP exams.
Student Life Student government. Newspaper, yearbook, radio station. Music and drama groups. Academic, honorary, professional, religious, and special interest groups. 4 fraternities and 4 sororities. Campus housing available. Class attendance required. 2-4 hours of health or phys ed required. Intercollegiate and intramural sports. AIAW, NAIA, NCAA, SAC. Student body composition: 0.1% Asian, 94.9% Black, 0.2% Native American, 3.2% White.

[J1] JONES COUNTY JUNIOR COLLEGE
Ellisville 39437
Director of Student Recruiting: Richard Hoyt Walley

- **Enrollment: 921m, 1,164w; 2,340 total (including part-time)**
- **Tuition (1982/83): $600 (in-state), $1,500 (out-of-state)**
- **Room & Board: $609**
- **Degrees offered: AA, ATech**
- **Student-faculty ratio: 15 to 1**

A public junior college established in 1927. 360-acre campus located in the small city of Ellisville, 20 miles from Hattiesburg. Served by rail.
Academic Character SACS accreditation. Semester system, 2 5-week summer terms. 42 majors offered by the divisions of Business, Fine Arts, Music, Humanities, Mathematics & Science, Nursing, Social Science, Vocational-Technical Education, and Health & Physical Education & Recreation. 12 certificate programs; other training programs possible. Preprofessional programs in engineering, medicine, dentistry, nursing, pharmacy, and veterinary medicine. 300-acre farm. 40,000-volume library with microform resources.
Financial College scholarships, grants, loans; PELL, NDSL, NSL, CWS; college has own work program. Application deadline June 15.
Admissions High school graduation with 15 units required. GED accepted. Interview required for nursing, cosmetology students. ACT required. $15 room deposit required with application. Rolling admissions. Transfers accepted. Credit possible for CEEB CLEP exams.
Student Life Student government. Newspaper, yearbook. Religious, professional, honorary, and special interest groups. Single-sex dorms. No married-student housing. 20% of students live on campus. Liquor, gambing, hazing prohibited on campus. Class attendance required. 6 intercollegiate sports; intramurals.

[2] MAGNOLIA BIBLE COLLEGE
PO Box 655, Kosciusko 39090

[J1] MARY HOLMES COLLEGE
West Point 39773
Director of Admissions & Records: Clyde Leggette

- **Enrollment: 197m, 224w; 447 total (including part-time)**
- **Tuition (1982/83): $1,250**
- **Room & Board: $1,650-$1,900**
- **Degrees offered: AS, AA**
- **Student-faculty ratio: 20 to 1**

A private college affiliated with the United Presbyterian Church USA, established in 1892. 192-acre rural campus just west of the town of West Point. Served by air and bus.
Academic Character SACS accreditation. Semester system, 8-week summer terms. Majors offered in accounting, business administration, data processing, business education, business management, computer science, secretarial science, education, criminal justice, economics, physical education, psychology, social science, liberal arts, music, chemical technology, mathematics & physics, and medical technology. Distributive requirements. Independent study. Honors program. Cooperative work/study, internships. Credit by exam. Preprofessional programs in theology, engineering, nursing, science, medicine, veterinary science. Computer lab. 23,058-volume library.
Financial CEEB CSS. College scholarships and grants, state grants; PELL, SEOG, NDSL, GSL, FISL, CWS; college has own work program. Application deadline April 1.
Admissions High school graduation with 15 units required. GED accepted. ACT or SAT recommended. $35 room deposit required. Transfers accepted. Credit possible for CEEB AP and CLEP exams. Talent Search, Upward Bound, and Special Service programs.
Student Life Student government. Choir. Academic, honorary, religious, and special interest groups. Students encouraged to live on campus or at home. Phys ed required for freshmen. 2 intercollegiate sports. NLCC.

[J1] MERIDIAN JUNIOR COLLEGE
Meridian 39301

[1] MILLSAPS COLLEGE
Jackson 39210, (601) 354-5201
Director of Admissions: John H. Christmas

- **Undergraduates: 456m, 390w**
- **Tuition (1982/83): $4,100**
- **Room & Board: $1,700; Fees: $120**
- **Degrees offered: AB, BMus, BBA, BS, BSEd**
- **Mean ACT 24.3**
- **Student-faculty ratio: 14 to 1**

A private college affiliated with the United Methodist Church, established in 1892. 100-acre urban campus in the center of Jackson, 180 miles from New Orleans, 190 miles from Memphis. Served by air and rail.
Academic Character SACS accreditation. Semester system, 2 5-week summer terms. Majors offered in accounting, administration, art, biology, chemistry, church music, economics, elementary education, English, French, geology, German, history, mathematics, music, music education, philosophy, physical education, physics, political science, psychology, psychology-sociology, religion, sociology-anthropology, Spanish, and theatre. Courses in 7 additional areas. Distributive requirements, senior exams, 6 credits in religion/philosophy required. Independent study, honors program. Internships. Preprofessional programs in medicine, law, ministry, education. 3-2 programs in engineering with Auburn, Columbia, Georgia Tech, Vanderbilt, Washington U. 3-1 medical technology and medical records librarianship programs. Member Southern College and University Union. Study abroad. UN, Washington, London, Oak Ridge semesters. Elementary and secondary education certification. ROTC at Jackson State. Computer center. 155,000-volume library.
Financial CEEB CSS. University scholarships, grants, loans, Methodist and ministerial grants and loans, payment plans; PELL, SEOG, NDSL, FISL, CWS. Application deadline April 1.
Admissions High school graduation with 12 units required. GED accepted. Interview encouraged. ACT or SAT required. $10 application fee. Rolling admissions. $25 tuition and $50 room deposits required on acceptance of offer of admission. *Early Admission* Program. Transfers accepted. Credit possible for CEEB AP and CLEP exams; college has own advanced placement program.
Student Life Student government. Newspaper, magazine, yearbook. Music, debate, drama groups. Black Students Association. Academic, honorary, religious, and special interest groups. 4 fraternities with houses, and 4 sororities without houses. 38% of men and 35% of women join. Freshmen and sophomores must live at home or on campus. Some married-student housing. 72% of students live on campus. Liquor, gambling prohibited. 1 hour of phys ed required. 5 intercollegiate sports for men, 2 for women; intramurals. AIAW, NCAA. Student body composition: 6% Black, 1% Hispanic, 93% White. 28% from out of state.

[1] MISSISSIPPI, UNIVERSITY OF
University 38677, (601) 232-7226, in MS: (800) 222-5102
Director of Admissions & Records: Kenneth L. Wooten

- **Undergraduates: 3,918m, 3,454w**
- **Tuition (1982/83): $1,165 (in-state), $2,091 (out-of-state)**
- **Room & Board: $1,828**
- **Degrees offered: BA, BS, BMus, BBA, BFA, BSW, BPA, BRec Leadership, BEng, BSB, BAccountancy, BEd**
- **Student-faculty ratio: 17 to 1**

A public university established in 1848. Campus of 640 acres adjacent to Oxford, in the northern part of the state 75 miles from Memphis.
Academic Character SACS and professional accreditation. Semester system, 2 5½-week summer terms. 55 majors offered by the College of Liberal Arts, 1 by the School of Accountancy, 13 by the School of Business Administration, 22 by the School of Education, 9 by the School of Engineering, 1 by the School of Pharmacy, and 4 by the School of Health Related Professions. Minor required in some divisions. Distributive requirements. Graduate and professional degrees granted. Independent study. Honors program. Limited pass/fail. Cooperative work/study, internships. 2-3 program in pharmacy. 3-1 programs in medicine, dentistry. Study abroad. Elementary, secondary, and special education certification. ROTC, AFROTC, NROTC. Computer center, Engineering Experiment Station, center for women's studies, center for Southern culture. 6 libraries comprising 1,750,000 volumes; all have microform resources.
Financial CEEB CSS. University scholarships and loans; PELL, SEOG, NDSL, FISL. File FAF by March 1; application deadline April 1.
Admissions High school graduation with 15 units required. ACT required; SAT may be substituted by out-of-state applicants. Rolling admissions; suggest applying soon after mid-year. *Early Admission* Program. Transfers accepted. Credit possible for CEEB AP and CLEP exams.
Student Life Student government. Newspaper, magazine, yearbook, radio station. Music, debate, drama groups. Academic, honorary, and special

interest organizations. 21 fraternities, 16 with houses, and 14 sororities, 11 with houses. 40% of men and 45% of women join. Freshmen must have permission to live off campus. Dorms for men and women. Cafeteria. Married-student housing. 60% of students live on campus. Cars discouraged. Activity courses for freshmen and sophomores required by some divisions. 7 intercollegiate sports; intramurals. Southeastern Conference. Student body composition: 8% Black, 90% White, 2% Other. 28% from out of state.

■[1 & G1] MISSISSIPPI, UNIVERSITY OF, MEDICAL CENTER
Jackson 39216

[1] MISSISSIPPI COLLEGE
Clinton 39058, (601) 924-6082
Dean of Admissions: Buddy Wagner

- **Undergraduates: 681m, 751w; 2,763 total (including graduates)**
- **Tuition (1982/83): $2,250**
- **Room & Board: $1,580; Fees: $210**
- **Degrees offered: BA, BS, BSEd, BSN, BMus, BMus Ed, BSBA**
- **Mean ACT 20**
- **Student-faculty ratio: 17 to 1**

A private college affiliated with the Mississippi Baptist Convention, established in 1826. 320-acre campus in the small town of Clinton, 10 miles from Jackson. Served by air, rail, and bus.

Academic Character SACS and professional accreditation. Semester system, 2 5½-week summer terms. 43 majors offered in the areas of fine arts, humanities, religion, science & mathematics, social studies, business, education, and nursing. Distributives and 6 hours of Bible required. Graduate and professional degrees granted. Honors program. Cooperative work/study, internships. Preprofessional programs in allied health, dentistry, law, medicine, medical records administration, medical technology, pharmacy, theology, veterinary medicine. 3-2 programs in engineering with Auburn, U of Mississippi. Dual-degree engineering and physical therapy/medical records programs. Study abroad. Exchange program with Gutenberg U in Germany. Elementary, secondary, and special education certification. ROTC at Jackson State. Language lab. 185,000-volume library.

Financial CEEB CSS. College scholarships and loans, ministerial grants, payment plans; PELL, SEOG, GSL, NDSL, NSL, CWS; college has own work program. Preferred application deadline April 1.

Admissions High school graduation required. GED accepted. ACT or SAT required. 2 recent photographs required with application. $15 application fee. Rolling admissions; suggest applying in 1st semester of 12th year. $50 refundable room deposit required on acceptance of offer of admission. *Early Admission* Program. Transfers accepted. Credit possible for CEEB AP and CLEP exams.

Student Life Student government. Newspaper, magazine, yearbook, radio station. Music, debate, drama groups. Academic, honorary, religious, and special interest groups. 4 social clubs for women. Single students must live at home or on campus. Single-sex dorms. Married-student housing. 50% of students live on campus. Liquor prohibited; women not allowed to smoke. Attendance in class and at 5 semesters of twice-weekly chapel required. 4 hours of phys ed required. 8 intercollegiate sports for men, 6 for women; intramurals. AIAW, NCAA, Gulf South Conference. Student body composition: 1% Asian, 7% Black, 0.1% Hispanic, 1% Native American, 90.9% White. 10% from out of state.

[J1] MISSISSIPPI DELTA JUNIOR COLLEGE
Moorhead 38761
Dean of Student Affairs: Travis Thornton

- **Undergraduates: 696m, 835w; 1,674 total (including part-time)**
- **Tuition (1982/83): $360 (in-state), $960 (out-of-state)**
- **Room & Board: $950**
- **Degrees offered: AA, AS**
- **Mean ACT 16.5**
- **Student-faculty ratio: 5 to 1**

A public junior college established in 1926. Campus located in town of Moorhead near the center of the Mississippi delta. Served by rail and bus.

Academic Character SACS and professional accreditation. Semester system, 3 3-week summer terms. Programs offered in business, education, fine arts, home economics, liberal arts, science, and technology. Certificate programs in 14 areas. Preprofessional programs in architecture, engineering, forestry, medicine, dentistry, nursing, pharmacy, physical therapy. Cooperative program in practical nursing. 375-acre farm, art gallery. 29,000-volume library.

Financial ACT FAS. College scholarships; PELL, SEOG, CWS.

Admissions High school graduation or 15 units required. GED accepted. ACT required. $10 room deposit required with application. Rolling admissions; application deadline 7 days before semester starts. Transfers accepted.

Student Life Student government. Newspaper, magazine, yearbook. Music groups. Drama club. Religious, honorary, professional, service, and special interest groups. Single-sex dorms. No married-student housing. Liquor, gambling, hazing prohibited on campus. Class attendance required. 5 intercollegiate sports; intramurals. NJCAA, MJCA. Student body composition: 30% minority.

[J1] MISSISSIPPI GULF COAST JUNIOR COLLEGE
PO Box 47, Perkinston 39573

- **Enrollment: 1,847m, 2,332w; 5,965 total (including part-time)**
- **Estimated Fees & Expenses: $1,515-$1,605**
- **Degrees offered: AA, AAS**

A public junior college established in 1911. 3 campuses totaling 900 acres in the Mississippi Gulf Coast region.

Academic Character SACS accreditation. Semester system, 2 5-week and 1 10-week summer terms. 25 college transfer programs, 21 career programs, and 25 vocational-technical programs offered. Distributive requirements. Cooperative work/study. Internships in some programs. Combined library facilities of 74,800 volumes.

Financial ACT FAS and CEEB CSS. College scholarships and loans, PELL grants, college has own work program.

Admissions High school graduation with 15 units required. GED accepted. ACT required. $20 application fee. Rolling admissions. Transfers accepted. Credit possible for CEEB CLEP exams. Special Services Program.

Student Life Student government. Newspapers, magazines, yearbooks. Music groups. Black Culture Society. Honorary, professional, academic, religious, service, and special interest groups. Single-sex dorms. Liquor prohibited on campus. 2 hours of phys ed required. 6 intercollegiate sports; intramurals. JCAC.

■[J1] JACKSON COUNTY CAMPUS
Gautier 39553

■[J1] JEFFERSON DAVIS CAMPUS
Gulfport 39501

[1] MISSISSIPPI STATE UNIVERSITY
Mississippi State 39762, (601) 325-2224
Director of Admissions: Jerry B. Inmon

- **Undergraduates: 6,219m, 4,112w; 11,531 total (including graduates)**
- **Tuition (1982/83): $1,142 (in-state), $2,068 (out-of-state)**
- **Room & Board: $1,820; Fees: $170**
- **Degrees offered: BA, BS, BArch, BLA, BMus Ed, BPA, BBA, BSurveying**
- **Mean ACT 19.5**
- **Student-faculty ratio: 22 to 1**

A public university established in 1878. 4,200-acre suburban campus adjoining the city of Starkville, 20 miles from Columbus, 120 miles from Jackson. Served by air and bus.

Academic Character SACS and professional accreditation. Semester system, 2 5-week and 2 3-week summer terms. 28 majors offered by the College of Agriculture & Home Economics, 29 by the College of Arts & Sciences, 12 by the College of Business & Industry, 19 by the College of Engineering, 3 by the College of Forest Resources, 1 by the School of Architecture, 1 by the College of Veterinary Medicine, and over 17 by the College of Education. Graduate and professional degrees granted. Independent study. Honors program. Cooperative work/study, limited pass/fail, internships. 3-2 programs in agriculture, engineering, business. 3-1 medical technology program. Study abroad in agriculture in Central and South America; in architecture at University of Jordan. Elementary, secondary, and special education certification. ROTC, AFROTC. Computer center, language lab. 8,000-acre experimental forest. 755,437-volume library with microform resources.

Financial CEEB CSS and ACT FAS (preferred). University scholarships, grants, loans, industrial scholarships, payment plan; PELL, SEOG, NDSL, FISL, CWS. Application deadline April 1.

Admissions High school graduation with 15 units required. GED accepted. ACT or SAT required. File application in April. *Early Decision* and *Early Admission* programs. Transfers accepted. Credit possible for CEEB AP and CLEP exams. Provisional admission granted.

Student Life Student government. Newspaper, yearbook. Music groups. Academic, religious, service, and special interest groups. 21 fraternities with houses and 12 sororities without houses. 16% of men and 21% of women join. Single-sex dorms. Married-student housing. 45% of students live on campus. Liquor, drugs, gambling prohibited. 7 intercollegiate sports for men, 3 for women; intramurals. AIAW, Southeastern Conference. Student body composition: 11% Black, 89% White. 16% from out of state.

[1] MISSISSIPPI UNIVERSITY FOR WOMEN
Columbus 39701, (601) 328-5891
Director of Admissions: James B. Alinder

- **Undergraduates: 1,856w**
- **Tuition (1982/83): $800 (in-state), $926 (out-of-state)**
- **Room & Board: $1,580**
- **Degrees offered: BA, BS, BSMed Tech, BSN, BMus, BMus Ed, BFA, BSW, AS**
- **Mean ACT 20**
- **Student-faculty ratio: 10 to 1**

A public university for women established in 1884; men are admitted to the nursing program. 110-acre campus located in the small city of Columbus, 120 miles from Birmingham. Served by air and bus; rail nearby.

Academic Character SACS and professional accreditation. Semester system, 2 5-week summer terms. Majors offered in art, art history, biology, broadcast journalism, broadcasting, business administration, chemistry, education, English, French, history, 5 home economics areas, journalism, mathematics, microbiology, music, nursing, paralegal studies, physical sciences, political science, psychology, social sciences, social work, Spanish, speech communication, speech pathology, and theatre. Distributive requirements. MA, MS, MEd granted. Independent study. Honors program. Cooperative work/study, pass/fail, internships. Preprofessional programs in dentistry, law, medicine, pharmacy, physical therapy, veterinary medicine. 3-2 program in engineering with Auburn, Mississippi State. Elementary, secondary, and special education certification. AFROTC. Computer center, language lab, museum, TV studio. 200,000-volume library with microform resources.

Financial CEEB CSS. University scholarships, grants, and loans; athletic, ROTC scholarships, music scholarships, state loans, payment plan; PELL,

SEOG, NDSL, FISL, CWS. Application deadline June 1.
Admissions High school graduation with 15 units and ACT score of 15 required. $10 application fee. Rolling admissions; suggest applying by July 15. $25 deposit required on acceptance of offer of admission. *Early Admission,* Pre-College Enrichment programs. Admission deferral possible. Transfers accepted. Credit possible for CEEB AP and CLEP exams; university has own advanced placement program.
Student Life Student government. Newspaper, magazine, yearbook, radio station. Music, mime, dance, comic groups. Black, Chinese culture organizations. Honorary, religious, academic, and special interest groups. 17 social clubs. 30% of women join. Students must live at home or on campus. Dormitories. Married-student and single-parent housing. 60% of students live on campus. Liquor prohibited. 2 semesters of phys ed required. 7 intercollegiate sports; intramurals. AIAW. Student body composition: 0.4% Asian, 19.7% Black, 0.1% Hispanic, 0.4% Native American, 77.9% White. 18% from out of state.

[1] MISSISSIPPI VALLEY STATE COLLEGE
Itta Bena 38941, (601) 254-9041
Director of Recruitment: Macon Steward

- **Undergraduates: 1,030m, 1,233w**
- **Tuition (1982/83): $810**
- **Room & Board: $1,457 (all expenses may have increased)**
- **Degrees offered: BA, BS, BMus, BSInd Ed**
- **Student-faculty ratio: 13 to 1**

A public college established in 1950. 450-acre rural campus located northeast of Itta Bena, 100 miles from Jackson.
Academic Character SACS and professional accreditation. Semester system, 2 5-week summer terms. 30 majors offered by the Division of Arts & Sciences, 4 by the Division of Business, 3 by the Division of Education, and 4 by the Division of Technical Education. Music minor. Distributives and senior recital, project, or exam required. Honors program. Cooperative work/study. Member consortium with 5 area colleges. Study abroad. Elementary and secondary teacher training. AFROTC. 160,000-volume library.
Financial CEEB CSS. College scholarships, grants, loans; PELL, SEOG, GSL, NDSL.
Admissions High school graduation with 15 units required. GED accepted. ACT or SAT required. Rolling admissions. $25 room deposit required on acceptance of offer of admission. *Early Decision* Program. Admission deferral possible. Transfers accepted. College has own advanced placement program. Upward Bound, Special Services, Talent Search programs.
Student Life Student government. Music, drama groups. Service programs. Academic, professional, and special interest groups. Fraternities and sororities. Single-sex dorms. Class attendance required. 1 hour phys ed required. 2 intercollegiate sports; intramurals. Student body composition: 99.2% Black, 0.8% White.

[J1] NORTHEAST MISSISSIPPI JUNIOR COLLEGE
Booneville 38829, (601) 728-7751

- **Enrollment: 739m, 942w; 1,843 total (including part-time)**
- **Tuition (1982/83): $480 (in-district), $1,080 (out-of-district), $1,580 (out-of-state)**
- **Degree offered: AA**

A state-appropriated, coeducational college operated by the Prentiss, Alcorn, Tishomingo, Tippah, and Union counties.
Academic Character SACS and professional accreditation. Semester system, 2 summer terms totaling 12 weeks. First and second years of most college parallel programs offered. Terminal programs offered in agriculture, business, engineering, health-related programs, child care, and development technology. Remedial mathematics and English programs available for all students.
Admissions High school graduation required. Rolling admissions. *Early Admission* and *Early Decision* programs.
Student Life Dormitories and complete dining facilities are maintained. Student body composition: 10% minority.

[J1] NORTHWEST MISSISSIPPI JUNIOR COLLEGE
Senatobia 38668, (601) 562-5262

- **Enrollment: 2,762 total**
- **Tuition (1981/82): $400 (out-of-state)**
- **Room & Board: $296; Fees: $101**
- **Degrees offered: AA, AS**

A district-controlled, coeducational college.
Academic Character SACS and professional accreditation. Semester system. Majors offered in arts, business, education, science, and applied science (technical). Certificates awarded in intensive secretarial training, intensive junior executive training, and cosmetology. 11,000-volume library.
Admissions High school graduation required. GED accepted. ACT required.
Student Life Dormitories and dining facilities for men and women are maintained.

[J1] PEARL RIVER JUNIOR COLLEGE
Station A, Poplarville 39470, (601) 795-4558
Director of Admissions: Willis Lott

- **Enrollment: 649m, 817w; 1,600 total (including part-time)**
- **Tuition (1982/83): $350**
- **Room & Board: $934-$1,070**
- **Degrees offered: AA, AAS**
- **Student-faculty ratio: 12 to 1**

A public junior college established in 1909. 350-acre rural campus in the small town of Poplarville. Served by rail and bus.
Academic Character SACS accreditation. Semester system, 2 4-week summer terms. 42 majors offered by the departments of Business, Fine Arts, Humanities, Mathematics, Nursing, Science, Social Science, Vocational & Technical Education, and Health, Physical Education, & Recreation. Distributive requirements. Preprofessional programs in engineering, nursing, veterinary medicine, pharmacy, dentistry, law. Elementary and secondary teacher training. ROTC. Farm, automotive mechanics lab. 37,000-volume library with microform resources.
Financial ACT FAS. College scholarships; PELL, SEOG, NSS, GSL, NSL, CWS.
Admissions High school graduation required. GED accepted. Interview required for nursing and respiratory therapy programs. Rolling admissions. Admission deferral possible. Transfers accepted. Credit possible for CEEB CLEP exams.
Student Life Student government. Newspaper, yearbook. Music groups. Afro-American Cultural Society. Religious, academic, professional, and special interest groups. Single-sex dorms. Married-student housing. 36% of students live on campus. Liquor, drugs, gambling, hazing prohibited. Class attendance required. 6 credits in phys ed required. Intercollegiate and intramural sports. Student body composition: 25% minority.

[2] PHILLIPS COLLEGE
0942 East Beach Blvd., Gulfport 39501

[G1] REFORMED THEOLOGICAL SEMINARY
5422 Clinton Blvd., Jackson 39209

[1] RUST COLLEGE
Holly Springs 38635, (601) 252-4661

- **Enrollment: 301m, 370w; 704 total (including part-time)**
- **Tuition, Room, & Board (1982/83): $3,609 (estimate)**
- **Degrees offered: BA, BS, AS**
- **Mean ACT 12.5**

A private, coeducational liberal arts college controlled by the Methodist Church, and founded in 1866. Campus is in the rural northern part of the state, 45 miles southeast of Memphis, TN.
Academic Character SACS accreditation. Modified semester system, 2 5-week summer terms. Majors offered in elementary and secondary education, early childhood education, secretarial science, and business administration. Divisions of the college are business & economics, humanities, science & mathemtics, and social & behavioral sciences. Courses offered include elementary and secondary education, psychology, sociology, social work, public service, history, politics, law, public administration, music education, and mass communication.
Financial College scholastic, music, and athletic scholarships. Work-aid program.
Admissions ACT required.
Student Life Dormitories and dining facilities are maintained. Intercollegiate basketball, track, tennis, and baseball.

[1] SOUTHERN MISSISSIPPI, UNIVERSITY OF
Southern Station Box 5011, Hattiesburg 39406, (601) 266-5555
Director of Admissions: Charles McNeil

- **Undergraduates: 3,675m, 4,245w; 10,222 total (including graduates)**
- **Tuition (1982/83): $1,040 (in-state), $1,966 (out-of-state)**
- **Room & Board: $1,650**
- **Degrees offered: BA, BS, BFA, BMus, BMus Ed, BSBA**
- **Mean ACT 15**
- **Student-faculty ratio: 19 to 1**

A public university established in 1910. 840-acre campus located in the small city of Hattiesburg, 85 miles from Jackson. Served by air, rail, and bus.
Academic Character SACS and professional accreditation. Semester system, 10-week summer term. 8 majors offered by the College of Business Administration, 11 by the College of Education & Psychology, 6 by the College of Fine Arts, 28 by the College of Liberal Arts, 20 by the College of Science & Technology, 8 by the School of Home Economics, 1 by the School of Library Science, 1 by the School of Nursing, and 4 by the School of Health, Physical Education, & Recreation. Distributive requirements. Graduate and professional degrees granted. Independent study. Honors program. Cooperative work/study, internships, pass/fail. Preprofessional programs in dentistry, dental hygiene, law, medicine, medical records, optometry, physical therapy, veterinary medicine. Study abroad. Elementary, secondary, and special education certification. ROTC, AFROTC. Computer center. Latin American Institute. Microbiology, Psychological institute. Language lab. 1,300,000-volume library.
Financial ACT FAS. University scholarships, grants, loans, payment plan; PELL, SEOG, SSIG, NSS, NDSL, FISL, NSL, CWS. Priority application deadline March 15.
Admissions High school graduation required. GED accepted. ACT required. Rolling admissions; suggest applying in January. $40 room deposit required on acceptance of offer of admission. *Early Admission* Program. Transfers accepted. Credit possible for CEEB CLEP exams; university has own advanced placement program.
Student Life Student government. Newspaper, magazine, yearbook, radio station. Music, debate, drama groups. Academic, service, honorary, religious, and special interest groups. 11 fraternities with houses, and 12 sororities without houses. 12% of men and women join. Single-sex dorms. Married-student housing. 40% of students live on campus. Liquor prohibited at

university functions. 2 semesters of phys ed required. 8 intercollegiate sports for men, 2 for women; intramurals. NCAA. Student body composition: 1% Asian, 11.5% Black, 0.4% Hispanic, 0.4% Native American, 86.7% White. 10% from out of state.

[J1] SOUTHWEST MISSISSIPPI JUNIOR COLLEGE

Summit 39666, (601) 684-0411
Registrar: Charles R. Breeland

- **Undergraduates: 554m, 729w**
- **Tuition (1982/83): $350**
- **Room & Board: $1,000**
- **Degrees offered: AA, AS, ASN**
- **Student-faculty ratio: 21 to 1**

A public junior college established in 1918. 680-acre rural campus 1 mile from the town of Summit. Served by rail and bus.
Academic Character SACS accreditation. Semester system, 2 4½-week summer terms. Majors offered in business education, business administration, education, English, history, mathematics, music, physical education, chemistry, chemical engineering, general science, medical technology, physics, forestry, wood science & technology, and nursing. Vocational-technical program. Preprofessional programs in engineering, dentistry, law, medicine, nursing, pharmacy, veterinary medicine. ROTC. 28,000-volume library with microform resources.
Financial ACT FAS. College scholarships, medical scholarships, PELL grants.
Admissions High school graduation with 15 units required. GED accepted. ACT required for some programs. Rolling admissions. Transfers accepted.
Student Life Student government. Newspaper, yearbook. Drama groups. Religious, professional, honorary, and special interest organizations. Single-sex dorms. Married-student housing. Liquor, gambling, weapons, drugs prohibited on campus. Class attendance required. 2 intercollegiate sports; intramurals. Junior College Conference. Student body composition: 24% minority.

[1] TOUGALOO COLLEGE

Tougaloo 39174, (601) 956-4951
Director of Admissions & Academic Records: Halbert E. Dockins

- **Undergraduates: 348m, 684w**
- **Tuition (1982/83): $2,350**
- **Room & Board: $1,330; Fees: $100**
- **Degrees offered: BA, BS, AA**
- **Student-faculty ratio: 12 to 1**

A private college affiliated with the United Christian Missionary Society and American Missionary Association, established in 1869. 500-acre campus located in the small town of Tougaloo at city line of Jackson. Served by air and rail.
Academic Character SACS accreditation. Semester system. Majors offered in accounting-economics, Afro-American studies, art, biology, chemistry, economics, early childhood education, elementary education, English, English-journalism, health & physical education, history, humanities, mathematics, mathematics-computer science, music, political science, physics, psychology, psychology-mental health, sociology. Interdisciplinary majors. Distributive requirements. GRE, senior exam, or paper required for some majors. Independent study. Cooperative work/study, pass/fail, internships. Preprofessional programs in dentistry, engineering, laboratory technology, law, medicine, ministry, nursing, social work, veterinary medicine. 3-2 programs in engineering with Brown, Georgia Tech, Howard, U of Mississippi, Tuskegee, U of Wisconsin. 3-1 medical technology program. Student Exchange program. Intensive Summer Studies Program at Harvard, Yale, Columbia. Study abroad, work/study in Africa. Washington, Brookhaven semesters. Elementary, secondary, early childhood education certification. ROTC. 99,000-volume library.
Financial CEEB CSS and ACT FAS. College scholarships, grants, and loans, payment plans; PELL, SEOG, NDSL, FISL, CWS, Work Aid. Application deadlines April 15 (scholarships), May 15 (loans).
Admissions High school graduation with 16 units required. GED accepted. Interview encouraged. SAT or ACT required. $12 room deposit required with application. Rolling admissions; suggest applying in early spring. *Early Admission* Program. Transfers accepted. College has own advanced placement program. Upward Bound, Talent Search, Special Services programs.
Student Life Student government. Newspaper, magazine. Music, debate, art, drama groups. Public speaking contests. Academic and honorary organizations. 4 fraternities and 3 sororities without houses. 25% of men and 30% of women join. Students must live at home or on campus. Dormitories for men and women. Dining hall. 80% of students live on campus. Liquor prohibited. Class attendance required. 2 hours of phys ed required. 2 intercollegiate sports for men, 1 for women; intramurals. AIAW, NAIA, Gulf Coast Conference. Student body composition: 98% Black, 2% Other. 18% from out of state.

[J1] UTICA JUNIOR COLLEGE

Utica 39175

[2] WHITWORTH COLLEGE

Brookhaven 39601

[1] WILLIAM CAREY COLLEGE

Hattiesburg 39401, (601) 582-5051, ext. 210
Director of Admissions: Antonio R. Pascale

- **Undergraduates: 470m, 531w**
- **Tuition (1982/83): $2,100**
- **Room & Board: $1,810; Fees: $90**
- **Degrees offered: BA, BS, BFA, BMus, BSN**
- **Student-faculty ratio: 16 to 1**

A private college affiliated with the Mississippi Baptist Convention, established in 1906. 64-acre campus located in the small city of Hattiesburg, 85 miles from Jackson, 100 miles from New Orleans. 20-acre beachfront campus in Gulfport. Served by air and rail.
Academic Character SACS and professional accreditation. Semester system, 2 5-week summer terms. 32 majors offered by the Schools of Arts & Sciences, Music, and Nursing. Minor required. Minors offered in all major fields and in coaching, German, journalism, philosophy, political science, secondary education, special education. Courses in 4 additional areas. 6 hours of Bible, junior English exam required. MMus, MEd granted. Independent study. Honors program. Internships. Preprofessional programs in engineering, optometry, pharmacy. 3-2 program in forestry with LSU. 6-year law program. 7-year programs in dentistry, medicine, theology. 5-year optometry, pharmacy programs. Elementary and secondary education certification. AFROTC; ROTC nearby. 82,650-volume library.
Financial CEEB CSS. College scholarships, grants, loans; PELL, SEOG, NDSL, FISL, NSL, CWS. Loan application deadline August 15.
Admissions High school graduation with 15 units. GED accepted. ACT, SAT, or Iowa Test required. $10 application fee. Rolling admissions; suggest applying during fall. $50 room deposit required on acceptance of offer of admission. *Early Admission* Program. Transfers accepted. Credit possible for CEEB AP and CLEP exams.
Student Life Student government. Newspaper, yearbook, magazine. Music, debate, drama groups. Academic, honorary, religious, and special interest groups. Single students must live at home or on campus. Dormitories. Married-student housing. 30% of students live on campus. Liquor prohibited on campus. Attendance at Tuesday chapel required; church and Sunday school attendance encouraged. 2 semesters of phys ed required. 3 intercollegiate sports; intramurals. NAIA. Student body composition: 19.8% Black, 0.2% Hispanic, 0.1% Native American, 77.2% White, 2.7% Other. 25% from out of state.

[J1] WOOD JUNIOR COLLEGE

Mathiston 39752, (601) 263-5352
Admissions Coordinator: Bobbie Shaw

- **Enrollment: 116m, 143w; 371 total (including part-time)**
- **Estimated Fees & Expenses: $3,200**
- **Degrees offered: AA, AAS**
- **Mean ACT 18**
- **Student-faculty ratio: 15 to 1**

A private junior college affiliated with the North Mississippi Conference of the United Methodist Church. 400-acre rural campus in the small town of Mathiston in southern Appalachia.
Academic Character SACS accreditation. Semester system, 2 5-week summer terms. 2-year programs offered in business, elementary education, secondary education, physical education, special education, liberal arts, music, horsemanship, secretarial science. Courses in 25 areas. Distributives and 3 hours of Bible required. Preprofessional programs in ministry, dentistry, medicine.
Financial ACT FAS. College scholarships and loans, PELL, FISL, CWS; college has own work program.
Admissions High school graduation with 15 units required. GED accepted. ACT required. $10 application fee. Rolling admissions. $25 deposit required on acceptance of offer of admission. *Early Admission* and *Early Decision* programs. Transfers accepted. Credit possible for CEEB CLEP exams.
Student Life Student government. Newspaper, yearbook. Music and drama groups. International club. Honorary, academic, professional, and special interest groups. Students under 21 must live at home or on campus. Single-sex dorms. 2 hours of phys ed required. Club sports. Student body composition: 10% minority.

MISSOURI (MO)

[1] AQUINAS INSTITUTE

3642 Lindell, St. Louis 63108

[G1] ASSEMBLIES OF GOD GRADUATE SCHOOL

1445 Boonville Avenue, Springfield 65802

[1] AVILA COLLEGE

11901 Wornall Road, Kansas City 64145, (816) 942-8400
Director of Admissions: Gary Forney

- **Undergraduates: 211m, 651w; 1,974 total (including graduates)**

- **Tuition (1982/83): $3,500**
- **Room & Board: $1,800; Fees: $50**
- **Degrees offered: BA, BS, BABus, BFA, BMus, BSW, BSN**
- **Mean ACT 21.5; mean SAT 460v, 450m**
- **Student-faculty ratio: 14 to 1**

A private college controlled by the Sisters of St. Joseph of Carondelet, established in 1916, became coed in 1969. Suburban campus, 10 miles from Kansas City. Airport, rail and bus stations in Kansas City.
Academic Character NCACS and professional accreditation. Semester system, 8-week summer term. 37 majors offered in the areas of the humanities, social & behavioral sciences, natural sciences & mathematics, business, corrections & justice, education, medical records & technology, music, nursing, pre-medicine, recreation, religious studies, social work, and speech. Minors offered in most major fields and in 8 additional areas, including women's studies and gerontology. Distributive requirements. Graduate degrees granted. Cooperative work/study, pass/fail, internships. Member of Federation of Carondelet Colleges. Study abroad. Elementary, secondary, and special education certification. ROTC at Central Missouri. 65,000-volume library.
Financial CEEB CSS and ACT FAS. College scholarships, grants, loans, payment plan; PELL, SEOG, GSL, FISL, CWS. Preferred application deadline March 31.
Admissions High school graduation with 16 units required. GED accepted. ACT or SAT required; ACT preferred. $20 application fee. Rolling admissions. $125 deposit due on acceptance of offer of admission. *Early Admission* and *Concurrent Enrollment* programs. Admission deferral possible. Transfers accepted. Credit possible for CEEB AP and CLEP exams; college has own advanced placement program. Provisional admission possible.
Student Life Student Union Board. Newspaper, yearbook. Academic, honorary, and special interest groups. Coed dorms. No married-student housing. 12% of students live on campus. 3 intercollegiate sports for men, 3 for women; intramurals. NAIA. Student body composition: 0.7% Asian, 8% Black, 2% Hispanic, 0.4% Native American, 86% White, 0.8% Other. 10% from out of state.

[P] BAPTIST BIBLE COLLEGE
628 East Kearney Street, Springfield 65802

[P] CALVARY BIBLE COLLEGE
Kansas City 64147

[1] CARDINAL GLENNON COLLEGE
5200 Glennon Drive, St. Louis 63119, (314) 644-0266
Chairman, Committee on Admissions: Harold B. Persich

- **Enrollment: 88m; 93 total (including part-time)**
- **Expenses: $1,000**
- **Degree offered: AB**
- **Student-faculty ratio: 2 to 1**

A private college controlled by the Roman Catholic Archdiocese of St. Louis, and operated by the Vincentian Fathers of the Western Province. Formerly St. Louis Preparatory Seminary.
Academic Character NCACS accreditation. Semester system. Liberal arts curriculum, with emphasis on philosophy, for students entering the priesthood. Distributives, 8 hours of theology, 3 hours of catechetics, and 3 hours of philosophy required. Independent study.
Admissions High school graduation with 16 units required. ACT required. $10 registration fee. Students make application through the representative of the Bishop or Provincial Superior. $50 room deposit due on acceptance of admissions offer.

[1] CARDINAL NEWMAN COLLEGE
7701 Florissant Road, St. Louis 63121, (314) 261-2600
Director of Admissions: John E. Herriage

- **Enrollment: 52m, 41w**
- **Tuition (1983/84): $3,900**
- **Room & Board: $2,330**
- **Degrees offered: BA, BS**
- **Student-faculty ratio: 11 to 1**

A private Roman Catholic college established in 1976. Suburban campus. Served by air, rail, and bus.
Academic Character NCACS accreditation. Semester system. Majors offered in biology, business administration, English, history, humanities, languages, media arts, philosophy, political science, and theology. Distributives and 12 hours of theology required. Career apprenticeships. Preprofessional programs in business, dentistry, government, law, medicine, religion, veterinary medicine. Focus courses. Weekly seminar. Senior seminar. Education certification possible. 25,000-volume library.
Financial CEEB CSS and ACT FAS. College scholarships, state grants, PELL, SEOG, GSL, CWS.
Admissions High school graduation with 16 units required. GED accepted. ACT or SAT required. $15 application fee. Rolling admissions; deadline August 1. $100 tuition deposit due on acceptance of admissions offer. Transfers accepted. Credit possible for CEEB AP and CLEP exams.
Student Life Associated Students. Newspaper, yearbook. Newman Chorale. Special interest groups. Single students under 21 live at home or on campus. 2 men's dorms, 2 women's dorms. Intercollegiate basketball and soccer; intramurals. NAIA.

[P] CENTRAL BIBLE COLLEGE
3000 North Grant Avenue, Springfield 65802

[1] CENTRAL METHODIST COLLEGE
Fayette 65248, (816) 248-3391
Exec. Director of New Student Relations & Financial Aid: Anthony J. Boes

- **Undergraduates: 327m, 281w**
- **Tuition (1982/83): $3,790**
- **Room & Board: $1,760; Fees: $50**
- **Degrees offered: BA, BS, BSEd, BMus, BMus Ed**
- **Student-faculty ratio: 6 to 1**

A private college affiliated with the United Methodist Church, established in 1853. Small-town campus. Bus service nearby.
Academic Character NCACS and professional accreditation. 4-1-4 system, 5-week summer term. 21 majors offered in liberal arts & sciences, 3 in business, 3 in education, 3 in music. Special majors. Distributives and 6 hours of religion required. Independent study. Honors program. Cooperative work/study, credit by exam. Preprofessional programs in dental hygiene, dentistry, engineering, home economics, journalism, law, library science, medical technology, medicine, the ministry, occupational & physical therapy, pharmacy, nursing, religious education, social work. 3-2 physical therapy program. 2-2 engineering program at Rolla. 3-2 engineering programs at Rolla, Columbia, Stanford. 3-3 law program with Missouri. Mid-Missouri Associated Colleges Exchange Program. Cross-registration with Columbia, U Missouri-Columbia, and Stevens and William Woods colleges. Elementary and secondary education certification. ROTC. Language lab. Observatory. Museums. 100,000-volume library with microform resources.
Financial CEEB CSS. College scholarships, grants, loans, merit and talent awards, payment plan; PELL, SEOG, NDSL, CWS.
Admissions High school graduation with 13 units recommended. GED accepted. Interview recommended. ACT required. $10 application fee. Rolling admissions. $100 deposit due on acceptance of admissions offer. *Early Admission* Program. Transfers accepted. Credit possible for CEEB CLEP and challenge exams.
Student Life Student government. Music and drama groups. Several religious organizations. International Student Organization. 5 fraternities and 4 sororities. Students under 21 must live on campus or at home. Single-sex dorms. Married-student housing. 4 hours of phys ed required. Attendance in class, at church, and at 6 convocations per year required. Liquor, gambling, hazing, and immoral practices prohibited. Dean's permission necessary to operate cars. 10 intercollegiate sports for men and women; intramurals. Student body composition: 0.8% Asian, 2.9% Black, 96.3% White.

[1] CENTRAL MISSOURI STATE UNIVERSITY
Warrensburg 64093, (816) 429-4111
Dean of Admissions: A. Lewis Sosebee

- **Undergraduates: 4,035m, 4,129w; 9,887 total (including graduates)**
- **Tuition (1982/83): $630 (in-state), $1,305 (out-of-state)**
- **Room & Board: $1,842-$1,902**
- **Degrees offered: BA, BS, BFA, BMus, BMus Ed, BSBA, BSED, AA, AS**
- **Student-faculty ratio: 19 to 1**

A public university established in 1871. 940-acre campus in a small city 50 miles from Kansas City. Served by air, rail, and bus.
Academic Character NCACS and professional accreditation. Trimester system, 3-week, 8-week, and 11-week summer terms. 36 majors offered by the College of Applied Science & Technology, 39 by the College of Arts & Sciences, 9 by the College of Business & Economics, 18 by the College of Education & Human Services. Special majors. Minors offered in most major fields. Distributive requirements. Graduate degrees granted. Independent study. Honors program. Cooperative work/study, limited pass/fail, internships. Preprofessional programs in dentistry, law, medicine, optometry, osteopathy, pharmacy, physical therapy, veterinary medicine, wildlife biology & forestry. 3-2 program in engineering with U Missouri in Rolla or Columbia, and U of Kansas. Study abroad. Elementary, secondary, and special education certification. ROTC. Language lab. Traffic Management Institute. 188-acre farm. Airport for aviation program. 500,000-volume library with microform resources.
Financial ACT FAS. University scholarships, grants, loans; PELL, SEOG, NDSL, FISL, CWS. Application deadline is the last day before beginning of classes.
Admissions High school graduation required. GED accepted. ACT required. Rolling admissions. $25 room deposit required on acceptance of admissions offer. *Early Admission* Program. Admission deferral possible. Transfers accepted. Credit possible for CEEB AP and CLEP exams. College Skills Program for non-qualifying applicants.
Student Life Student government. Newspaper, literary magazine, yearbook. Association of Black Collegiates. Numerous athletic, academic, honorary, religious, service, and special interest groups. 15 fraternities, 8 with chapter wings in special dorm; 14 sororities, 8 with chapter wings. 15% of men and 10% of women join. Unmarried students under 21 with less than 30 semester hours required to live on campus. Coed, single-sex, language, and special-interest dorms. Family and married-student housing. 45% of students live on campus. 3 hours of phys ed required. Liquor prohibited. 8 intercollegiate sports for men, 8 for women; intramurals. AIAW, NCAA, MIAA. Student body composition: 0.3% Asian, 6.6% Black, 0.3% Hispanic, 91% White, 1.9% Other. 5% from out of state.

[P] CHRIST SEMINARY—SEMINEX
539 North Grand Blvd., St. Louis 63103

[2] CLAYTON UNIVERSITY
PO Box 16150, St. Louis 63105

[G2] CLEVELAND CHIROPRACTIC COLLEGE
6401 Rockhill Road, Kansas City 64131

[1] COLUMBIA COLLEGE
10th and Rogers, Columbia 65216, (314) 875-7352
Dean of Admissions: John J. Bart

- **Undergraduates: 331m, 410w**
- **Tuition (1982/83): $3,975**
- **Room & Board: $2,000; Fees: $70**
- **Degrees offered: BA, BS, BFA, BSW, AA**
- **Student-faculty ratio: 13 to 1**

A private college affiliated with the Christian Church (Disciples of Christ), established in 1851, became coed in 1970. Coordinate with U of Missouri. 20-acre suburban campus, 125 miles from St. Louis and Kansas City. Served by air and bus; rail service in Jefferson City.
Academic Character NCACS accreditation. Semester system, 6-week summer term. Majors offered in art, business/travel administration, commercial art, criminal justice, education, English, fashion, history/government, music, psychology, public administration, and social work. Special majors. Minors offered in all major fields. Distributive requirements. Independent study. Honors program. Limited pass/fail, internships. Cross-registration with Mid-Missouri Associated Colleges, Central Methodist, Stephens, U of Missouri-Columbia, and William Woods. Elementary and secondary education certification. ROTC, AFROTC, NROTC at Columbia. Computer center. 60,000-volume library.
Financial CEEB CSS and ACT FAS. College scholarships, grants, loans, payment plans; PELL, SEOG, NDSL, FISL, GSL, CWS. Priority application deadline March 15.
Admissions High school graduation with 15 units required. GED accepted. Interview recommended. ACT required. $15 application fee. Rolling admissions. $100 deposit required on acceptance of admissions offer. *Early Admission* Program. Admission deferral possible. Transfers accepted. Credit possible for CEEB AP, CLEP, and ACT PEP exams; college has own advanced placement program. Special arrangements possible for students not normally admissable.
Student Life Student government. Newspaper, literary magazine, yearbook. Music groups. Minority Student Organization. Travel Center Organization. Fashion Group, Ltd. Modeling Board. Honorary, political, and special interest groups. Freshmen must live at home or on campus. Coed and single-sex dorms. 52% of students live on campus. Liquor prohibited. Excessive class absences not permitted. 2 intercollegiate sports for men, 2 for women; intramurals. AIAW, NAIA, Ozark Collegiate Conference. Student body composition: 1% Asian, 18% Black, 1% Hispanic, 80% White. 50% from out of state.

[1] CONCEPTION SEMINARY COLLEGE
Conception 64433

[G1] CONCORDIA SEMINARY
Clayton, St. Louis 63105

[J1] COTTEY COLLEGE
Nevada 64772, (417) 667-8181

- **Undergraduates: 306w**
- **Tuition & Fees: $2,200**
- **Room & Board: $1,800**
- **Degree offered: AA**
- **Student-faculty ratio: 10 to 1**

A private college established in 1884. Owned by the P.E.O. Sisterhood, a secular group dedicated to providing educational opportunities for women.
Academic Character NCACS accreditation. Semester system. 2-year transfer programs offered in fine arts, humanities, physical education, science and mathematics, social sciences. Independent study. Phi Theta Kappa.
Financial ACT FAS. College scholarships, PELL, SEOG, NDSL, CWS. Application deadline March 1.
Admissions High school graduation required. ACT or SAT required. $15 application fee. Rolling admissions. $50 tuition and $50 room deposits due on acceptance of admissions offer. *Early Admission* and *Early Decision* programs. Admission deferral possible. Credit possible for CEEB AP exams.
Student Life Student government. Honorary societies. 4 social societies. 3 dorms composed of suites housing 10-14 women. Intramural sports.

[G1] COVENANT THEOLOGICAL SEMINARY
12330 Conway Road, St. Louis 63141

[J1] CROWDER COLLEGE
Neosho 64850

[1] CULVER-STOCKTON COLLEGE
Canton 63435, (314) 288-5221
Director of Admissions: Richard D. Valentine

- **Enrollment: 296m, 273w; 644 total (including part-time)**
- **Tuition (1982/83): $3,270**
- **Room & Board: $1,750; Fees: $80**
- **Degrees offered: BA, BS, BFA, BMus, AS**
- **Mean ACT 17; mean SAT 345v, 392m**
- **Student-faculty ratio: 10 to 1**

A private college affiliated with the Christian Church (Disciples of Christ), established in 1853. 111-acre small-town campus, 20 miles from Quincy. Served by air, rail, and bus in Quincy.
Academic Character NCACS accreditation. Semester system, 5-week summer term, spring interim. 30 majors offered by the divisions of Education-Psychology, Fine Arts, Humanities, Natural Science, and Social Science. Self-designed majors. Distributives and 3 hours of religion required. Honors program. Pass/fail, credit by exam, life-experience degree, internships. Preprofessional programs in dentistry, law, library science, medicine, theology, veterinary medicine. 3-1 medical technology program. 3-2 engineering program with Washington U. 2-2 agriculture program with U of Missouri. Cross-registration with 7 area schools. Study abroad. Elementary, secondary, and special education certification. 100,000-volume library.
Financial CEEB CSS and ACT FAS. College scholarships, grants, loans, payment plans; PELL, SEOG, NDSL, GSL, CWS.
Admissions High school graduation with 13 units recommended. Interview recommended. SAT or ACT required. $10 application fee. Rolling admissions. $50 tuition and $50 room deposits due on acceptance of admissions offer. Transfers accepted. Credit possible for CEEB AP and CLEP exams.
Student Life Student government. Newspaper, yearbook. Music groups. Academic, honorary, professional, religious, service, and special interest groups. 4 fraternities, 3 with houses; 3 sororities with dorm space. Students under 21 must live at home or on campus. Liquor, drugs, firearms, fireworks prohibited. Extensive intramural sports program.

[1] DRURY COLLEGE
900 Benton Avenue, Springfield 65802, (417) 862-0541
Director of Admissions: Eltjen Flikkema

- **Undergraduates: 494m, 618w; 1,386 total (including graduates)**
- **Tuition (1982/83): $3,550**
- **Room & Board: $1,810; Fees: $120**
- **Degrees offered: AB, BMus, BMus Ed, BSN**
- **Mean SAT 476v, 502m**
- **Student-faculty ratio: 15 to 1**

A private college affiliated with the United Church of Christ and the Disciples of Christ, established in 1873. 40-acre urban campus. Served by air and bus.
Academic Character NCACS and professional accreditation. 4-1-4 system, 2 5-week summer terms. 34 majors offered in the liberal arts & sciences, business, criminology, education, physical education, music, nursing, and religion. Special majors. Minors offered in all major fields and in 3 others. Distributives, 3 hours of religion, and senior seminar required. Graduate degrees granted. Independent study. Honors program. Internships. Credit by exam. Optional senior year Try-Out Experience. 3-1 medical technology program with area hospitals. 3-2 engineering program with Washington U. 3-1 professional school programs arranged. 4½-year international management program with American Institute in Arizona. Exchange program with Grambling State. Extensive study abroad. International Education program in England. Washington Semester. Elementary, secondary, and special education certification. ROTC at Southwest Missouri. Geological field station. Computer center. 170,000-volume library.
Financial CEEB CSS and ACT FAS. College scholarships, grants, loans, honor scholarships, payment plan; PELL, SEOG, NDSL, GSL, CWS.
Admissions High school graduation with college prep program encouraged. Interview desirable. SAT or ACT required. $15 application fee. Rolling admissions. $100 deposit due on acceptance of admissions offer. *Early Decision* Program. Admission deferral possible. Transfers accepted. Credit possible for CEEB AP and CLEP exams.
Student Life Student Senate. Newspaper, literary magazine, yearbook, radio and TV stations. Music and drama groups. Environmental action group. Black United Independent Collegiates. Academic, community action, honorary, political, and special interest groups. 6 fraternities with houses, 5 sororities without houses. 45% of men and women join. Permission required to live off campus. Single-sex dorms. 65% of students live on campus. 2 hours of phys ed required. Class attendance expected. 4 intercollegiate sports for men, 2 for women; intramurals. AIAW, NAIA, NCAA. Student body composition: 1% Asian, 3% Black, 0.5% Hispanic, 0.5% Native American, 95% White. 30% from out of state.

[J1] EAST CENTRAL MISSOURI COLLEGE
Union 63084

[G1] EDEN THEOLOGICAL SEMINARY
Webster Groves 63119

[1] EVANGEL COLLEGE
1111 North Glenstone, Springfield 65802, (417) 865-2811
Director of Admissions: Carol Duncan

- **Undergraduates: 754m, 978w**
- **Tuition (1982/83): $2,380**
- **Room & Board: $1,870; Fees: $67**
- **Degrees offered: BA, BS, BBA, BMus Ed, AA**
- **Student-faculty ratio: 22 to 1**

A private college affiliated with the Assemblies of God, established in 1955. 80-acre urban campus. Served by air, rail, and bus.
Academic Character NCACS and professional accreditation. Semester system, 2 5-week summer terms. 34 majors offered by the departments of Communications & Art, Music, Biblical Studies & Philosophy, Science & Technology, Education, Social Sciences, Behavioral Sciences, Business & Economics, and Health, Physical Education, & Recreation. Special majors. Major/minor, double major, double concentration, or concentration/2 minors required. Minors offered in most major fields and in 16 additional areas.

Distributives and 16 hours of Biblical studies required. Independent study. Internships. Christian College Consortium. Elementary and secondary education certification. ROTC. 90,000-volume library.
Financial CEEB CSS. College scholarships, grants, loans; athletic, academic, music, valedictorian scholarships; payment plan; PELL, SEOG, NDSL, GSL, CWS.
Admissions High school graduation with 15 units required. GED accepted. Interview recommended. ACT required. $25 application fee. Rolling admissions. *Early Admission* Program. Admission deferral possible. Transfers accepted. Credit possible for CEEB AP and CLEP exams.
Student Life Student government. Newspaper, yearbook, radio station. Music groups. Circle K. Student Corps of Pentecostal Endeavor. Academic, honorary, political, service, and special interest groups. Students must live on campus or at home. Coed and single-sex dorms. Married-student housing. 90% of students live on campus. 2 semesters of phys ed required. Honor code. Tobacco and liquor prohibited. Daily chapel attendance mandatory. 3 intercollegiate sports for men, 3 for women; intramurals. NAIA. Student body composition: 0.3% Asian, 1.3% Black, 1.8% Hispanic, 0.7% Native American, 93.7% White, 2.2% Other. 75% from out of state.

[1] FONTBONNE COLLEGE
6800 Wydown Blvd., St. Louis 63105, (314) 862-3436, ext. 208
Director of Admissions: Charles E. Beech

- **Undergraduates: 99m, 488w; 882 total (including graduates)**
- **Tuition (1982/83): $4,100**
- **Room & Board: $2,100; Fees: $55**
- **Degrees offered: BA, BS, BMus, BFA, BSMT**
- **Mean ACT 21**
- **Student-faculty ratio: 11 to 1**

A private college conducted by the Sisters of St. Joseph of Carondelet, established in 1917, became coed in 1970. 13-acre suburban campus. Served by air, rail, and bus.
Academic Character NCACS and professional accreditation. Semester system, 1-, 2-, 3-, 4-, 6-, and 8-week summer terms. 54 majors offered in the areas of art, business, communication disorders, deaf education, education, English, general studies, home economics, mathematics, music, natural sciences, social sciences, and theatre. Special majors. Distributive requirements. Graduate degrees granted. Independent study. Cooperative work/study, pass/unsatisfactory, internships, experiential credit. Cross-registration with Lindenwood, Maryville, and Webster colleges. Carondelet exchange program. Study abroad. Elementary, secondary, and special education certification. ROTC at Washington U. 85,600-volume library.
Financial CEEB CSS. College scholarships, grants, loans, 2nd-family-member discount, payment plan; PELL, SEOG, NDSL, FISL, GSL, CWS. Application deadline April 1; February 15 for academic scholarships.
Admissions High school graduation with 16 units required. GED accepted. Interview recommended. SAT or ACT required. $15 application fee. Rolling admissions. $75 room deposit due on acceptance of admissions offer. *Early Admission* Program. Admission deferral possible. Transfers accepted. Credit possible for CEEB AP and CLEP exams; college has own advanced placement program.
Student Life Student government. Newspaper, literary magazine. Music and drama groups. Association of Black Collegians, Social Action on Campus, and Community Organization. Athletic, academic, honorary, religious, and special interest groups. Dorms and dining hall on campus. No married-student housing. 25% of students live on campus. Liquor prohibited to students under 21. Varsity, intramural, and club sports. Student body composition: 1% Asian, 15% Black, 1% Hispanic, 1% Native American, 78% White, 4% Other. 20% from out of state.

[1] HANNIBAL-LAGRANGE COLLEGE
Hannibal 63401, (314) 221-3675

- **Enrollment: 150m, 162w; 496 total (including part-time)**
- **Approximate annual fees: $4,112**
- **Degrees offered: BSBA, BSEd, ThB, BCM, BRE, AA, AS**
- **Mean ACT 17.3**

A private, coeducational college controlled by the Missouri Baptist Convention.
Academic Character NCACS accreditation. Semester system, 2 2-week and 2 5-week summer terms. Courses offered in liberal arts, fine arts, business administration, secretarial science, and church-related vocations. Preprofessional programs in agriculture, dentistry, education, engineering, journalism, law, medicine, nursing, pharmacy, social science, veterinary science.
Admissions Graduation in upper 50% of high school class required. ACT required. *Early Admission* Program. Transfers accepted. Advanced placement possible.
Student Life Dormitories and dining hall for men and women maintained.

[1] HARRIS-STOWE STATE COLLEGE
3026 Laclede Avenue, St. Louis 63103

[G2] INTERNATIONAL GRADUATE SCHOOL
27 Maryland Plaza, St. Louis 63108

[J1] JEFFERSON COLLEGE
Hillsboro 63050

[1] KANSAS CITY ART INSTITUTE
4415 Warwick Blvd., Kansas City 64111, (816) 561-4852
Director of Admissions: William Wolkersz

- **Enrollment: 245m, 231w; 518 total (including part-time)**
- **Tuition (1981/82): $5,100**
- **Room & Board: $2,030-$2,650**
- **Degree offered: BFA**
- **Student-faculty ratio: 12 to 1**

A private institute established in 1885. Urban campus. Served by air, rail, and bus.
Academic Character NCACS accreditation. Semester system, 8½-week summer term. Majors offered in crafts, design, painting & printmaking, photography, and sculpture. 42 credits of liberal arts required. Independent study. Foundation Studio. Sophomore review. Cooperative programs with 8 art colleges and 17 area schools. Field programs. Gallery. Photo labs. Media center. 46,000-slide library and 30,000-volume library.
Financial CEEB CSS. Institute scholarships, state grants, payment plan; PELL, SEOG, NDSL, GSL, PLUS, CWS. Preferred application deadline February 15.
Admissions High school graduation required. GED accepted. Interview strongly recommended. Portfolio of 15 samples required. SAT or ACT required. $20 application fee. Rolling admissions. $100 deposit due on acceptance of admissions offer. *Early Admission* Program. Admission deferral possible. Transfers accepted. Credit possible for CEEB AP and ACT PEP exams.

[P] KANSAS CITY COLLEGE OF OSTEOPATHIC MEDICINE
Kansas City — see University of Health Sciences

[J1] KEMPER MILITARY SCHOOL AND COLLEGE
706 Third Street, Boonville 65233, (816) 882-5623
Director of Admissions: Lt. Col. John S. Daniel, USA (Ret)

- **Enrollment: 112m, 6w**
- **Tuition (1982/83): $2,800**
- **Room & Board: $2,300**
- **Degrees offered: AA, AMS, AJJ**
- **Mean ACT 18; mean SAT 400v, 400m**
- **Student-faculty ratio: 14 to 1**

A private college established in 1844. Prep school for grades 7-12 also on campus; dorms and programs are separate. 120-acre small-town campus, 100 miles east of Kansas City.
Academic Character NCACS accreditation. Semester system, 6-week summer advanced camp at Fort Riley. General courses in liberal arts; military science and leadership courses lead to 2nd Lieutenant commission. Distributive requirements. ROTC. 20,000-volume library with microform resources.
Financial College scholarships, state grants, PELL, SEOG, NDSL, FISL, PLUS, CWS.
Admissions High school graduation required. SAT, ACT, or ROTC GST required. $50 application fee. Rolling admissions. $1,000 deposit due by July 15 if admissions offer accepted. *Early Admission* Program.
Student Life Newspaper, yearbook. Marching band and drill team. Flying program. ROTC students must live on campus. Dorms. Class attendance required. 2 hours of phys ed required. 7 intercollegiate sports. Student body composition: 40% minority.

[G1] KENRICK SEMINARY
St. Louis 63119

[P] KIRKSVILLE COLLEGE OF OSTEOPATHIC MEDICINE
Kirksville 63501

[1] LINCOLN UNIVERSITY
Jefferson City 65102, (314) 751-2325
Director of Admissions & Financial Aid: Charles E. Glasper

- **Undergraduates: 971m, 745w; 2,657 total (includes graduates)**
- **Tuition (1982/83): $525 (in-state), $965 (out-of-state)**
- **Room & Board: $1,650**
- **Degrees offered: BA, BS, BSEd, BMus Ed**
- **Student-faculty ratio: 20 to 1**

A public university established in 1866. 547-acre urban campus located between St. Louis and Kansas City. Airport 30 miles away.
Academic Character NCACS accreditation. Semester system, 8-week summer term. 9 majors offered by the College of Applied Science & Technology, 25 by the College of Arts & Sciences, 8 by the College of Business & Economics. Minors offered in most major fields. Distributive requirements. Graduate degrees granted. Independent study. Freshman honors program. Cooperative work/study, credit by exam. Preprofessional programs in dentistry, law, medicine, pharmacy, veterinary medicine. Elementary, secondary, and special education certification. ROTC. Ethnic Studies Center. 124,000-volume library with microform resources.
Financial CEEB CSS and ACT FAS. University scholarships, grants, loans, state loans, payment plan; PELL, SEOG, BIA, NDSL, FISL, NSL, CWS. Application deadline April 30.
Admissions Open admission for Missouri high school graduates; out-of-state applicants must have a minimum C average. GED accepted. SAT, ACT, or SCAT required. $12 application fee. Rolling admissions. *Early Admission* and *Concurrent Enrollment* programs. Transfers accepted. Credit possible for CEEB CLEP exams; university has own advanced placement program.

Student Life Student government. Newspaper, yearbook, radio station. Music and drama groups. Academic, honorary, and special interest groups. 4 fraternities and 4 sororities, none with houses. All students with less than 60 credit hours must live on campus or at home, except veterans, married students, and students over 21. 25% of students live on campus. 4 semesters of phys ed required. Compulsory attendance for some courses. 7 intercollegiate sports; intramurals. AIAW, MIAA. Student body composition: 8% Asian, 40% Black, 2% Hispanic, 50% White.

[1] LINDENWOOD COLLEGES, THE

St. Charles 63301, (314) 723-7152
Director of Admissions: Sarah Fulton

- **Undergraduates: 308m, 460w; 1,916 total (including graduates & part-time)**
- **Tuition (1982/83): $4,600**
- **Room & Board: $2,700-$3,200**
- **Degrees offered: BA, BS, BFA, BMus, BMus Ed, BSN**
- **Mean SAT 420v, 460m**
- **Student-faculty ratio: 12 to 1**

A private college established in 1827, became coed in 1969. 140-acre suburban campus, 20 miles west of St. Louis. Served by air, rail, and bus.
Academic Character NCACS and professional accreditation. 4-1-4 system, 4-, 6-, and 8-week summer terms. 27 majors offered in the areas of art, biology, business, chemistry, education, English, French, history, international studies, mass communications, mathematics, medical technology, music, physical education, political science, psychology, public affairs, sociology, Spanish, and theatre. Self-designed majors. Distributive requirements. Honors program. Independent study. Pass/fail, internships. Preprofessional programs in dentistry, engineering, law, medical technology, medicine, social service, veterinary medicine. 3-2 engineering and social work programs with Washington U. Cross-registration with Fontbonne, Maryville, and Webster Colleges. Merrill-Palmer Institute, UN, and Washington Semesters. Study abroad. Elementary, secondary, and special education certification. 112,000-volume library.
Financial CEEB CSS and ACT FAS. College scholarships, grants for children of Presbyterian ministers and alumni, academic and athletic scholarships, state grants, payment plan; PELL, SEOG, BIA, NDSL, FISL, GSL, CWS. Application deadline 2 weeks before term begins.
Admissions High school graduation with college prep program in upper 50% class required. Interview recommended. SAT or ACT required. $25 application fee. Rolling admissions. $100 deposit due on acceptance of admissions offer. *Early Admission* Program. Admission deferral possible. Transfers accepted. Credit possible for CEEB AP and CLEP exams.
Student Life Student Association. Newspaper, literary magazine, yearbook, radio station. Music and drama groups. Athletic, academic, honorary, religious, and special interest groups. Students must live at home or on campus. Coed and single-sex dorms. 35% of students live on campus. Class attendance expected. Honor code. 2 semesters of phys ed required. 9 intercollegiate sports; recreational activities. Student body composition: 10% Black, 85% White, 5% Other. 25% from out of state.

[P] LOGAN COLLEGE OF CHIROPRACTIC

1851 Schoettler Road, PO Box 100, Chesterfield 63017

[1] MARYVILLE COLLEGE

13550 Conway Road, St. Louis 63141, (314) 576-9350
Director of Admissions: Michael J. Gillick

- **Undergraduates: 412m, 1,276w**
- **Tuition (1982/83): $4,100**
- **Room & Board: $2,160; Fees: $45**
- **Degrees offered: BA, BS, BFA, BSN, BPhys Ther, BSMed Tech**
- **Mean ACT 20; mean SAT 455v, 425m**
- **Student-faculty ratio: 14 to 1**

A private college established in 1872, became coed in 1969. 300-acre suburban campus, 20 miles from downtown St. Louis. Airport, rail and bus stations nearby.
Academic Character NCACS and professional accreditation. Semester system, 3-, 4-, and 5-week summer terms. 31 majors offered in the humanities, science, social science, fine arts, actuarial science, communications, health, interior design, legal administration, management, medical technology, nursing, physical therapy, and therapeutic art. Minors in economics and physics. Distributive requirements. Independent study. Honors program. Pass/fail, internships. Several preprofessional programs. 3-2 medical technology program. Cross-registration with Fontbonne, Lindenwood, Missouri Baptist, Webster Colleges. Elementary, secondary, and special education certification. 90,000-volume library.
Financial CEEB CSS and ACT FAS. College scholarships, state grants, payment plans; PELL, SEOG, NDSL, FISL, NSL, CWS. Application deadline March 1.
Admissions High school graduation with 16 units required. GED accepted. Interview recommended; required for physical therapy students. Audition required for musical therapy program. $10 application fee. Rolling admissions. $135 deposit required on acceptance of admissions offer. *Concurrent Enrollment* Program. Transfers accepted. Credit possible for CEEB AP and CLEP exams.
Student Life Student government. Newspaper, literary magazine, yearbook. Music groups. Campus ministry. Academic and special interest activities. Coed dorms. No married-student housing. 30% of students live on campus. 2 intercollegiate sports for men, 2 for women. Student body composition: 0.4% Asian, 12.7% Black, 0.4% Hispanic, 0.1% Native American, 85.6% White. 5% from out of state.

METROPOLITAN COMMUNITY COLLEGES

■[J1] LONGVIEW COMMUNITY COLLEGE

500 Longview Road, Lee's Summit 64063

■[J1] MAPLE WOODS COMMUNITY COLLEGE

2601 NE Barry Road, Kansas City 64165

■[J1] PENN VALLEY COMMUNITY COLLEGE

3201 Southwest Trafficway, Kansas City 64111

■[J1] PIONEER COMMUNITY COLLEGE

560 Westport Road, Kansas City 64111

[G1] MIDWESTERN BAPTIST THEOLOGICAL SEMINARY

5001 North Oak Street, Kansas City 64118

[J1] MINERAL AREA COLLEGE DISTRICT

Flat River 63601

[1] MISSOURI, UNIVERSITY OF

Columbia 65201, (314) 882-2121
Director of Admissions & Registrar: Gary L. Smith

- **Undergraduates: 9,060m, 8,669w; 24,774 total (including graduates)**
- **Tuition (1982/83): $1,068 (in-state), $3,108 (out-of-state)**
- **Room & Board: $1,650**
- **Degrees offered: AB, BS, BES, BFA, BGS, BMus, BSBA, BSEd, BSN, BSW, BSE's, BJournalism, BHealth Sci**
- **Median ACT 21-25; median SAT 950-1150**

A public university established in 1839. Urban campus. Served by air and bus.
Academic Character NCACS and professional accreditation. Semester system, 4-, 6-, and 8-week summer terms. 17 majors offered by the College of Agriculture, 36 by the College of Arts & Sciences, 13 by the College of Business & Public Administration, 35 by the College of Education, 13 by the College of Engineering, 3 by the School of Forestry, Fisheries, & Wildlife, 6 by the School of Health-Related Professions, 6 by the College of Home Economics, 6 by the School of Journalism, 1 by the School of Nursing, and 2 by the College of Public & Community Services. Self-designed majors. Distributive requirements. Graduate and professional degrees granted. Independent study. Honors program. Phi Beta Kappa. Limited pass/fail, internships. Cross-registration with U Nebraska, U Kansas at Lawrence and at Manhattan, and Wichita State in certain programs. Study abroad. Elementary, secondary, and special education certification. ROTC, AFROTC, NROTC. Computer center. Museums. Language lab. 1,000,000-volume library with microform resources.
Financial CEEB CSS. PELL, SEOG, NSS, NDSL, FISL, NSL, CWS. Application deadline April 1.
Admissions High school graduation with 20 units required. GED accepted. SAT, ACT, or SCAT required. Rolling admissions. $20 deposit due on acceptance of admissions offer. *Early Admission* Program. Admission deferral possible. Transfers accepted. Credit possible for CEEB AP, CLEP, and university exams.
Student Life Student government. Newspaper, yearbook, radio and TV stations. Music and theatre groups. Debate. Athletic, academic, honorary, religious, service, and special interest groups. 29 fraternities and 18 sororities, all with houses. Coed and single-sex dorms. Co-op women's dorms. Married-student housing. 25% of students live on campus. Many intercollegiate and intramural sports for men and women. Student body composition: 1% Asian, 4% Black, 1% Hispanic, 1% Native American, 88% White, 5% Other. 16% from out of state.

■[1] MISSOURI, UNIVERSITY OF, KANSAS CITY

5100 Rockhill Road, Kansas City 64110, (816) 932-4444
Director of Admissions: Leo J. Sweeney

- **Enrollment: 3,596m, 2,519w**
- **Tuition (1982/83): $1,110 (in-state), $3,150 (out-of-state)**
- **Room & Board: $1,668-$1,968**
- **Degrees offered: BA, BS, BBA, BMus Ed, BSN, BSP**
- **Student-faculty ratio: 17 to 1**

A public university established in 1929. 100-acre urban campus. Served by air, rail, and bus.
Academic Character NCACS and professional accreditation. Semester system, 8-week summer term. 27 majors offered by the College of Arts & Sciences, 8 by the Conservatory of Music, 5 by the School of Administration, 6 by the School of Dentistry, 2 by the School of Education, and one each by the Schools of Medicine, Nursing, and Pharmacy. Special majors. Minors offered in many major fields. Distributive requirements. Graduate degrees granted. Independent study. Honors program. Credit by exam. Exchange programs in engineering with U Missouri-Columbia. Interstate exchange with Kansas and Nebraska. Elementary and secondary education certification. Computer center. Language lab. Animal center lab. 421,234-volume general library with microform resources; specialized libraries.
Financial ACT FAS. PELL, SEOG, NDSL, GSL, CWS. Apply between January 1 and March 15.
Admissions High school graduation with 15 units required. GED accepted. ACT, SAT, PSAT/NMSQT, or Ohio State Psychological Exam required. Rolling admissions. *Early Admission, Concurrent Enrollment, Early Decision* programs. Admission deferral possible. Transfers accepted. Credit possible for CEEB AP and CLEP exams.
Student Life Student government. Newspaper, literary magazine, yearbook, radio station. Debate. Theatre. Academic, political, religious, service, and

special interest groups. 6 fraternities and 3 sororities. 3% of students join. Freshmen must live at home or in dorms when space available. Coed dorm with separate floors for men & women. Limited married-student housing. 3% of students live on campus. Liquor prohibited. Regular class attendance required of freshmen. 4 intercollegiate sports; intramurals. NAIA. Student body composition: 0.8% Asian, 7.8% Black, 1.1% Hispanic, 0.7% Native American, 87.6% White. 20% from out of state.

■[1] MISSOURI, UNIVERSITY OF, ROLLA

Rolla 65401, (341) 341-4164
Director of Admissions: Robert B. Lewis

- **Undergraduates: 4,122m, 1,163w; 5,686 total (including graduates)**
- **Tuition (1982/83): $1,219 (in-state), $3,259 (out-of-state)**
- **Room & Board: $2,114-$2,349**
- **Degrees offered: BA, BS**
- **Mean ACT 25; mean SAT 490v, 575m**
- **Student-faculty ratio: 14 to 1**

A public university established in 1870. 70-acre small-city campus, 100 miles southwest of St. Louis.

Academic Character NCACS and professional accreditation. Semester system, 8-, 6-, and 4-week summer terms. 51 majors offered in arts & sciences; aerospace, ceramic, chemical, civil, electrical, geological, mechanical, metallurgical, mining, nuclear, and petroleum engineering. Minors offered in some fields. Distributives and comprehensive exams required. Graduate and professional degrees granted. Independent study. Honors program. Phi Beta Kappa. Cooperative work/study, pass/fail, internships. Preprofessional programs in law, medicine, nursing. 5- and 6-year double engineering degree programs. Interstate exchange with Kansas and Nebraska. Cross-registration with U Missouri-Columbia. Secondary education certification. ROTC, AFROTC. Computer center. Geophysical Observatory. Water, environmental, industrial, and rock mechanics research centers. Nuclear reactor. 410,000-volume library.

Financial ACT FAS. University scholarships and loans, state grants, payment plan; PELL, SEOG, GSL, NDSL, FISL, CWS. Freshman scholarship application deadline March 1.

Admissions High school graduation with 15 units required. GED accepted. ACT or SAT required. $20 application fee (in-state), $40 (out-of-state). Rolling admissions. *Early Admission* and *Concurrent Enrollment* programs. Transfers accepted. Credit possible for CEEB AP and CLEP exams; university has own advanced placement program. Special admissions for veterans and older students. Minority engineering program.

Student Life Student government. Association of Women Students. Association of Black Students. Newspaper, engineering magazine, radio station. Numerous music groups. Chinese, Latin American, Indian, Muslim, and Arabian student organizations. Athletic, academic, honorary, political, religious, service, and special interest groups. 20 fraternities and 3 sororities with houses. Coed and single-sex dorms. Married-student housing. 25% of students live on campus. 12 intercollegiate sports; extensive intramurals. MIAA, NAIA. Student body composition: 2.1% Asian, 3.4% Black, 1.2% Hispanic, 0.3% Native American, 88.8% White, 4.2% Other. 10% from out of state.

■[1] MISSOURI, UNIVERSITY OF, ST. LOUIS

St. Louis 63121, (314) 553-5451
Director of Admissions & Registrar: Hilbert E. Mueller

- **Undergraduates: 5,250m, 4,935w; 12,048 total (including graduates)**
- **Tuition (1982/83): $1,104 (in-state), $3,144 (out-of-state)**
- **Degrees offered: BA, BS, BMus, BGS, BSN, BSW**
- **Student-faculty ratio: 26 to 1**

A public university established in 1963. 114-acre urban campus. Served by air, rail, and bus.

Academic Character NCACS and professional accreditation. Semester system, 3 4-week and 1 8-week summer terms. Majors offered in administration of justice, anthropology, applied math, art history, biology, business administration, business education, chemistry, early childhood education, elementary education, economics, English, French, general studies, German, history, math, music, music education, music history & literature, philosophy, physical education, physics, political science, psychology, social work, sociology, Spanish, special education, speech communication. Self-designed majors. Minors offered in some fields. Interdisciplinary programs. Distributive requirements. Independent study. Honors program. Limited pass/fail, internships. Preprofessional programs in dentistry, engineering, journalism, law, medicine, pharmacy, veterinary medicine. Interstate exchange with Kansas and Nebraska. Exchange with Washington and St. Louis. Elementary, secondary, and special education certification. ROTC; AFROTC at St. Louis. Language and writing labs. International Studies, Urban Journalism, Metropolitan Studies centers. Computer center. 362,000-volume library with microform resources.

Financial ACT FAS. University scholarships, PELL, SEOG, NDSL, FISL, CWS. Recommended application deadline March 1 (scholarships).

Admissions High school graduation with 15 units required. GED accepted. ACT, SAT, or SCAT required. Rolling admissions. *Concurrent Enrollment* Program. Transfers accepted. Credit possible for CEEB AP and CLEP exams; university has own advanced placement program. Special admissions for veterans, older students, and disadvantaged.

Student Life Student government. Radio station. Minority Student Service Coalition. Women's Center. Disabled Students Union. Athletic, academic, and special interest groups. No university housing. 7 intercollegiate sports for men, 5 for women; intramurals. AIAW, NAIA, NCAA. Student body composition: 1.1% Asian, 10.7% Black, 0.6% Hispanic, 0.3% Native American, 87% White, 0.3% Other. 3.7% from out of state.

[1] MISSOURI BAPTIST COLLEGE

12542 Conway Road, St. Louis 63141

[2] MISSOURI INSTITUTE OF TECHNOLOGY

9001 State Line Road, Kansas City 64114

[G2] MISSOURI SCHOOL OF RELIGION

100 Hitt Street, Columbia 65201

[1] MISSOURI SOUTHERN STATE COLLEGE

Joplin 64801, (417) 624-8100
Director of Admissions: Richard D. Humphrey

- **Undergraduates: 2,000m, 2,400w**
- **Tuition (1982/83): $610 (in-state), $1,190 (out-of-state)**
- **Room & Board: $1,365; Fees: $150**
- **Degrees offered: BA, BS, BSBA, BSEd, BSG**
- **Student-faculty ratio: 27 to 1**

A public college established in 1938. 350-acre suburban campus in southwest corner of state. Served by air and bus; rail service in Kansas City.

Academic Character NCACS and professional accreditation. Semester system, 8-week summer term. 38 majors offered by the Schools of Arts & Sciences, Business Administration, Education & Psychology, and Technology. Minors offered in some fields. Distributive requirements. Independent study. Credit/no credit. Preprofessional programs in agriculture, dentistry, engineering, journalism, medicine, optometry, pharmacy. Elementary, secondary, and special education certification. ROTC. 104,000-volume library.

Financial ACT FAS. College scholarships, grants, loans, payment plan; PELL, SEOG, NSS, NDSL, FISL, NSL, CWS, Student Help Employment. Priority application deadline April 30.

Admissions High school graduation required. GED accepted. ACT required. $10 application fee. Rolling admissions. $75 room deposit due on acceptance of admissions offer. *Early Admission* and *Early Decision* programs. Admission deferral possible. Transfers accepted. Credit possible for ACT and CLEP exams.

Student Life Student Senate. Newspaper, literary magazine, arts magazine, yearbook. Music and drama groups. Debate. Afro-American Society. Class, academic, honorary, political, service, and special interest groups. 2 fraternities with houses, 3 sororities without houses. 2% of students join. Juniors and seniors may live off campus. Dorms for men and women. No married-student housing. 18% of students live on campus. Liquor prohibited. Class attendance expected. Appropriate dress expected. 4 hours of phys ed required. 9 intercollegiate sports; intramurals. AIAW, NAIA, Central State Intercollegiate Council. Student body composition: 2% Black, 2% Hispanic, 16% Native American, 70% White, 10% Other. 2% from out of state.

[1] MISSOURI VALLEY COLLEGE

Marshall 65340, (816) 886-6924, ext. 115
Director of Admissions: Kenneth V. Sibert, Jr.

- **Enrollment: 275m, 162w; 482 total (including part-time)**
- **Tuition (1982/83): $3,050**
- **Room & Board: $1,750; Fees: $50**
- **Degrees offered: BA, BS**
- **Student-faculty ratio: 12 to 1**

A private college controlled by the United Presbyterian Church, established in 1888. 40-acre small-town campus, 70 miles east of Kansas City.

Academic Character NCACS accreditation. Semester system, 2- and 5-week summer terms. Majors offered in accounting, agribusiness, art, biology, business administration, chemistry, computer science, economics, elementary education, English, history, human service management, interdisciplinary science, mass communications, mathematics, physical education, political science, psychology, government management, religion & philosophy, social work, sociology, special education, and speech & theatre. Distributive requirements. Independent study. Honors program. Cooperative work/study, limited pass/fail, internships. Preprofessional programs in dentistry, medicine, theology, veterinary medicine. Elementary, secondary, and special education certification. 100,000-volume library.

Financial CEEB CSS and ACT FAS. College scholarships, grants, loans; PELL, SEOG, NDSL, GSL, CWS.

Admissions High school graduation with 12 units recommended. Interview strongly recommended. SAT or ACT required. $10 application fee. Rolling admissions. $50 deposit due on acceptance of admissions offer. *Early Admission* and *Early Decision* programs. Admission deferral possible. Transfers accepted. Credit possible for CEEB AP, CLEP, and ACT PEP exams.

Student Life Music and drama activities. Special interest groups. 3 fraternities with space in residence halls. Single-sex dorms. Sports facilities.

[1 & J1] MISSOURI WESTERN STATE COLLEGE

4525 Downs Drive, St. Joseph 64507, (816) 271-4200
Director of Admissions: George M. Ashworth

- **Undergraduates: 2,013m, 2,258w**
- **Tuition (1982/83): $780 (in-state), $1,360 (out-of-state)**
- **Room & Board: $1,460**
- **Degrees offered: BA, BS, BSBA, BSEd, BST, BSW, AA, AS**
- **Student-faculty ratio: 18 to 1**

A public college established in 1969. 744-acre suburban campus, 40 miles from Kansas City. Served by rail and bus; airport in Kansas City.

Academic Character NCACS and professional accreditation. Semester system, 2 4-week and 1 8-week summer terms. 52 majors offered in the

departments of Agriculture, Business & Economics, Criminal Justice, Engineering Technology, Education, Psychology, and Health, Physical Education, & Recreation, and in the Division of Liberal Arts & Sciences. Minors offered in many major fields. Distributive requirements. Pass/fail, internships. Elementary and secondary education certification. ROTC. 130,000-volume library with microform resources.
Financial ACT FAS (preferred) and CEEB CSS. College scholarships, grants, loans; PELL, SEOG, NSS, GSL, NDSL, FISL, NSL, CWS. Application deadline May 1.
Admissions High school graduation required. GED accepted. ACT required. $5 application fee. Rolling admissions. $50 room deposit due on acceptance of admissions offer. *Early Admission* and *Concurrent Enrollment* programs. Admission deferral possible. Transfers accepted. Credit possible for CEEB CLEP and college proficiency exams.
Student Life Student government. Newspaper, literary magazine, yearbook. Music, drama, debate, and dance groups. International Students. Circle K. Academic, honorary, religious, and special interest clubs. 4 fraternities, 2 with houses; 3 sororities without houses. 6% of men and 4% of women join. 17% of students live on campus. Liquor prohibited. Class attendance required. 4 semester hours of phys ed required. 6 intercollegiate sports for men, 4 for women; intramurals. NAIA, Central States Conference. Student body composition: 4% Black, 1% Hispanic, 1% Native American, 94% White. 7% from out of state.

[J1] MOBERLY JUNIOR COLLEGE
Moberly 65270

[G2] NATIONAL GRADUATE SCHOOL-NATIONAL UNIVERSITY
St. Louis — see Roger Williams University-National Graduate School

[P] NAZARENE THEOLOGICAL SEMINARY
1700 East Meyer Blvd., Kansas City 64131

[1] NORTHEAST MISSOURI STATE UNIVERSITY
Kirksville 63501, (816) 785-4000
Director of Admissions: Terry Taylor

- **Enrollment: 2,922m, 3,702w**
- **Tuition (1982/83): $520 (in-state), $1,000 (out-of-state)**
- **Room & Board: $1,330**
- **Degrees offered: BA, BS, BMus, BMus Ed, BSEd, BSN**
- **Mean ACT 19**
- **Student-faculty ratio: 19 to 1**

A public university established in 1867. 90-acre urban campus.
Academic Character NCACS and professional accreditation. Semester system, 2 5-week summer terms. 110 majors offered by the divisions of Business, Education, Fine Arts, Health/Physical Education/Recreation, Home Economics, Language & Literature, Mathematics, Nursing, Practical Arts, Science, and Social Science. Areas of concentration required in some majors. Distributive requirements. Independent study. Internships. Preprofessional programs in dentistry, dietetics, engineering, law, medical technology, medicine, osteopathy, pharmacy, physical therapy, social work, veterinary medicine. 3-2 engineering program with U Missouri. Exchange programs with 54 schools. Study abroad. Elementary and secondary education certification. ROTC. Child Development lab schools. Greenhouse. 240,000-volume library with microform resources.
Financial CEEB CSS and ACT FAS; FAF preferred. University scholarships, grants, loans; academic, athletic, talent scholarships, agricultural loans, state grants; PELL, SEOG, NDSL, FISL, NSL, CWS. Scholarship application deadline June 1.
Admissions High school graduation with 15 units required. GED accepted. Interview recommended. SAT, ACT, PSAT, or SCAT recommended. Rolling admissions. $40 room deposit required on acceptance of admissions offer. *Early Admission* and *Concurrent Enrollment* programs. Admission deferral possible. Transfers accepted. Credit possible for CEEB AP, CLEP, college exams, and military service. Applicants not meeting admissions requirements will be considered.
Student Life Student Senate. Newspaper, yearbook, radio station. Many honorary, service, social, and special interest groups. 26 fraternities and sororities. Single-sex dorms. Married-student housing. 53% of students live on campus. Intercollegiate and intramural sports. Student body composition: 1% Asian, 6% Black, 1% Hispanic, 1% Native American, 89% White, 2% Other. 29% from out of state.

[1] NORTHWEST MISSOURI STATE UNIVERSITY
Maryville 64468, (816) 582-7141
Director of Admissions: James Goff

- **Enrollment: 2,400m, 2,600w**
- **Tuition (1982/83): $720 (in-state), $1,120 (out-of-state)**
- **Room & Board: $1,410-$1,790; Fees: $60**
- **Degrees offered: BA, BS, BFA, BSEd**
- **Student-faculty ratio: 20 to 1**

A public university established in 1905. 175-acre campus, 90 miles from Kansas City. Served by bus in Maryville.
Academic Character NCACS and professional accreditation. Semester system, 2 5-week summer terms. Over 85 majors offered in the areas of business & management, agriculture & natural resources, biological sciences, communications, computer & information services, education, fine & applied arts, foreign languages, health professions, home economics, interdisciplinary studies, letters, library science, mathematics, physical sciences, psychology, public affairs, and social sciences. Minors offered in most fields. Distributives, and minor or comprehensive major required. Graduate degrees granted. Independent study. Honors program. Cooperative work/study, pass/fail, internships. Preprofessional programs in engineering, forestry, medicine, veterinary medicine. Elementary, secondary, and special education certification. ROTC. Computer center. Learning Resources Center. 315,000-volume library.
Financial CEEB CSS and ACT FAS. University scholarships, grants, loans, state grants; PELL, SEOG, NDSL, FISL, CWS. Application deadlines April 1 (loans), April 30 (scholarships).
Admissions High school graduation required. GED accepted. ACT required. Rolling admissions. $50 room deposit due on acceptance of admissions offer. *Early Admission* and *Concurrent Enrollment* programs. Transfers accepted. Credit possible for ACT and CEEB CLEP exams.
Student Life Student government. Newspaper, yearbook. Academic and special interest groups. 6 fraternities with houses, 5 sororities without houses. 8% of men and 6% of women join. Freshmen under 21 must live on campus. Coed and single-sex dorms; special interest housing. 60% of students live on campus. Liquor prohibited. 4 semesters of phys ed required. Intercollegiate and intramural sports. NCAA, MIAA. Student body composition: 2% Asian, 3% Black, 1% Hispanic, 94% White. 45% from out of state.

[1] OZARKS, SCHOOL OF THE
Point Lookout 65726, (417) 334-6411
Director of Admissions: Darella Banks

- **Undergraduates: 675m, 618w**
- **Tuition (1982/83): $1,950 (day students only); resident students pay fees through required campus work and scholarships**
- **Degrees offered: BA, BS**
- **Student-faculty ratio: 14 to 1**

A private college established in 1906. 930-acre rural campus, 40 miles from Springfield. Served by air, rail, and bus in Springfield.
Academic Character NCACS and professional accreditation. Semester system, 10-week summer term. Majors offered in agriculture, art, aviation science, biology, business, chemistry, computer science, criminal justice administration, education, English, graphic arts, history, home economics, industrial education, mass media, math, modern foreign languages, music, philosophy & religion, physical education, political science, psychology, sociology, speech communication. Minors offered in many fields. Distributives and one religion course per semester required. Independent study. Internships, cooperative work/study. Credit by exam. Preprofessional programs in engineering, law, medicine, nursing, pharmacy, medical technology, veterinary medicine. Elementary and secondary education certification. Computer center. Language lab. 90,000-volume library with microform resources.
Financial ACT FAS. All boarding students pay for room and board through college's Work Program. Each student works 20 hours per week during semester and 3 40-hour weeks during term breaks. Employment is both on campus and in small local industries. Work grades reported. College scholarships and grants also available. PELL, state grants, and other forms of aid.
Admissions High school graduation with 20 units recommended and rank in top 25% of class. GED accepted. Interview recommended. ACT required. Rolling admissions. $80 deposit due on acceptance of admissions offer. *Early Admission* and *Concurrent Enrollment* programs. Transfers accepted. Credit possible for CEEB CLEP exams.
Student Life Student Senate. Newspaper, literary magazine, yearbook, radio station. Music and drama groups. Volunteer fire department. Academic, political, religious, and special interest groups. Students must live at home or on campus. Single-sex dorms. No married-student housing. 80% of students live on campus. Liquor and drugs prohibited. Class attendance mandatory. 2 semesters of phys ed required. Attendance at chapel and convocations required 7 times each semester. 4 intercollegiate sports for men, 6 for women; intramurals. NAIA, Ozark Collegiate Council. Student body composition: 1% Asian, 2% Black, 1% Hispanic, 1% Native American, 95% White. 25% from out of state.

[1] PARK COLLEGE
Parkville 64152, (816) 741-2000

- **Enrollment: 2,411 men & women total**
- **Tuition, Room, Board, & Fees (1982/83): $4,500**
- **Degree offered: BA**
- **Student-faculty ratio: 14 to 1**

A private college established in 1875, and affiliated with the Reorganized Church of Jesus Christ of the Latter-Day Saints (Mormons). Campus is in a rural suburban area 9 miles north of Kansas City, which is served by air, rail, and bus.
Academic Character NCACS accreditation. 4-1-4 system. 20 majors offered by the divisions of liberal studies, life science, social sciences, math sciences, communications & performing arts. Interdepartmental and self-designed majors possible. Oral and/or written senior comprehensive exams required. Preprofessional programs in medicine, dentistry, law, nursing. Internships for credit possible. Military degree completion program for service personnel. Portfolio and degree completion program for adults. Washington and UN Semesters. 150,000-volume library.
Financial In a typical year, 200 students receive scholarships totaling $75,000. $500 sibling tuition grants. $80,000 loan fund; average loan is $450. PELL, SEOG, NDSL. Employment possible both on campus and in the surrounding community.
Admissions Rolling admissions. Transfers accepted. Special services for the disadvantaged.
Student Life Social clubs. Coed and single-sex dorms. Some married-student housing. Dining hall. 7 intercollegiate sports for men, women's sports.

[1] PLATT COLLEGE
St. Joseph 64501

[1] ROCKHURST COLLEGE
Kansas City 64110, (816) 926-4100
Director of Admissions: Thomas J. Audley

- **Undergraduates: 665m, 610w; 1,925 total (including graduates)**
- **Tuition (1982/83): $3,840**
- **Room & Board: $2,400; Fees: $130**
- **Degrees offered: BA, BS, BSBA**
- **Mean ACT 22**
- **Student-faculty ratio: 14 to 1**

A private college controlled by the Society of Jesus (Jesuits), established in 1917, became coed in 1969. 25-acre urban campus. Served by air, rail, and bus.
Academic Character NCACS and professional accreditation. Semester system, 2 5-week summer terms. 34 majors offered in the areas of arts & sciences, communications, education, industrial relations, theology, medical technology, nursing, and business administration. Minors offered in 4 fields. Distributives and 9 hours of theology required. Senior comprehensive exam required in some departments. MBA granted. Independent study. Honors program. Cooperative work/study. Preprofessional programs in dentistry, engineering, journalism, law, medicine, optometry, pharmacy, veterinary medicine. Cooperative program in engineering. BSN offered with Research Medical Center. Jesuit Colleges and Universities of America consortiums. Cross-registration with 16 area schools. Social work semester. Study abroad. Urban teacher program. Elementary and secondary education certification. Computer center. Language lab. 100,000-volume library.
Financial CEEB CSS. College scholarships, grants, loans, payment plan; PELL, SEOG, NSS, NDSL, FISL, CWS. Application deadline March 1.
Admissions High school graduation with 16 units required. Interview recommended. ACT required. Rolling admissions. $100 deposit due on acceptance of admissions offer. *Early Decision* and *Early Admission* programs. Admission deferral possible. Transfers accepted. Credit possible for CEEB AP, CLEP, and college's proficiency exams.
Student Life Student Senate. Newspaper, literary magazine, yearbook, radio station. Music and drama groups. Debate. Black Student Union. Veterans Club. Academic, honorary, language, political, preprofessional, religious, and special interest groups. 3 fraternities and 1 sorority, all without houses. Students must live on campus or with relatives, unless they are in the Cooperative Education Program. Coed and single-sex dorms. Special interest housing. 50% of students live on campus. Class attendance required. 4 intercollegiate sports for men, 4 for women; intramurals. AIAW, NAIA. Student body composition: 10% Black, 2.3% Hispanic, 86.7% White, 1% Other. 33% from out of state.

[G2] ROGER WILLIAMS UNIVERSITY-NATIONAL GRADUATE SCHOOL
123 West Clinton Place, St. Louis 63122
Formerly National Graduate School

[P] ST. LOUIS CHRISTIAN COLLEGE
Florissant 63033

[1] ST. LOUIS COLLEGE OF PHARMACY
St. Louis 63110

[J1] ST. LOUIS COMMUNITY COLLEGE
5801 Wilson Avenue, St. Louis 63110

■[J1] ST. LOUIS COMMUNITY COLLEGE AT MERAMEC
11333 Big Bend, Kirkwood 63122
Formerly Meramec Community College

■[J1] FLORISSANT VALLEY, ST. LOUIS COMMUNITY COLLEGE AT
3400 Pershall Road, St. Louis 63135

■[J1] FOREST PARK COMMUNITY COLLEGE
5600 Oakland, St. Louis 63110

[P] ST. LOUIS CONSERVATORY OF MUSIC
560 Trinity Avenue, St. Louis 63130

[1] SAINT LOUIS UNIVERSITY
221 North Grand Blvd., St. Louis 63103, (314) 658-2500
Dean of Admissions: Louis A. Menard

- **Undergraduates: 2,749m, 2,079w; 10,596 total (including graduates)**
- **Tuition (1982/83): $4,690**
- **Room & Board: $2,432-$2,850**
- **Degrees offered: AB, ABClass, BS, BSBA, BSMed Rec Ad, BSMed Tech, BSNurs, BSPhys Ther, BSW**
- **Mean ACT 22; mean SAT 525v, 510m**
- **Student-faculty ratio: 12 to 1**

A private university controlled by the Society of Jesus (Jesuits), established in 1818. 50-acre urban campus. Served by air, rail, and bus.
Academic Character NCACS and professional accreditation. Semester system, 8-week and 6-week summer terms. 65 majors offered by the College of Arts & Sciences, the School of Business Administration, the School of Nursing, the School of Allied Health Professions, the School of Social Service, and the College of Philosophy & Letters. Self-designed majors. Area requirements in communication, areas of concentration in at least 2 departments, and 9 semester hours of theology required. Graduate and professional degrees granted. Independent study. Honors program. Phi Beta Kappa. Limited pass/fail, credit by exam, internships. Preprofessional programs in dentistry, law, medicine, social work. 3-2 engineering and exchange programs with Washington U. Study abroad. Elementary, secondary, and special education certification. AFROTC; ROTC nearby. Computer center. Language lab. 1,238,487-volume libraries.
Financial CEEB CSS. University scholarships, grants, loans, payment plans; PELL, SEOG, NSS, NDSL, FISL, NSL, CWS. Application deadlines March 1 (scholarships), May 1 (loans).
Admissions High school graduation with 15 units recommended. ACT or SAT required. $20 application fee. Rolling admissions. Housing deposit due on acceptance of offer of admission. *Early Admission* Program. Admission deferral possible. Transfers accepted. Credit possible for CEEB AP, ACH, and CLEP exams. Special 6-week summer term for students not normally admissable.
Student Life Student government. Newspaper, yearbook, radio station. Music and drama groups. Academic, honorary, religious, and special interest groups. 4 fraternities and 3 sororities without houses. 10% of men and 11% of women join. Coed and single-sex dorms. 35% of students live on campus. 6 intercollegiate sports for men, 6 for women; intramurals. AIAW, NCAA. Student body composition: 11% Black, 0.5% Hispanic, 0.5% Native American, 86% White, 2% Other. 35% from out of state.

[J1] ST. MARY'S COLLEGE OF O'FALLON
200 North Main Street, O'Fallon 63366

[1] ST. MARY'S SEMINARY AND COLLEGE
Perryville 63775

[G1] ST. PAUL SCHOOL OF THEOLOGY
5123 Truman Road, Kansas City 64127

[J1] SAINT PAUL'S COLLEGE
Concordia 64020, (816) 463-2238
Director of Admissions: Daniel Frerking

- **Enrollment: 38m, 41w; 137 total (including part-time)**
- **Tuition (1982/83): $2,370**
- **Room & Board: $2,066**
- **Degrees offered: AA, AS, AAS**
- **Mean ACT 22**
- **Student-faculty ratio: 5 to 1**

A private college controlled by the Lutheran Church-Missouri Synod, established in 1905. 80-acre small-town campus.
Academic Character NCACS accreditation. Semester system, January interim. 2-year programs offered in art, business, education, liberal arts, music, physical education, religion, sciences, and social sciences. Distributives and 6 hours of religion required. Independent study. Preprofessional programs in law, medicine, nursing, teaching, theology. 31,000-volume library.
Financial CEEB CSS. College scholarships, grants, PELL, SEOG, GSL, FISL, CWS, college part-time employment.
Admissions High school graduation with 17 units recommended. ACT required. $10 application fee. Rolling admissions; application deadline August 15. $50 deposit due on acceptance of admissions offer. *Early Decision* and *Early Admission* programs. Admission deferral possible. Transfers accepted. Advanced placement possible.
Student Life Student government. Music groups. Religious activities. Special interest groups. 2 residence halls. 2 hours of phys ed required. Intercollegiate and intramural sports.

[1] SOUTHEAST MISSOURI STATE UNIVERSITY
Cape Girardeau 63701, (314) 651-2255
Director of Admissions: John Behrens

- **Undergraduates: 4,194m, 4,823w; 9,020 total (including graduates)**
- **Tuition (1982/83): $550 (in-state), $1,050 (out-of-state)**
- **Room & Board: $1,475**
- **Degrees offered: BA, BS, BGS, BMus, BMus Ed, BSN, BSBA, BSEd, BSInter Studies, BSVoc Home Ec Ed**
- **Student-faculty ratio: 24 to 1**

A public university established in 1873. 200-acre campus in a small city 120 miles from St. Louis. Airport and bus station nearby.
Academic Character NCACS and professional accreditation. Semester system, 2 summer terms. 75 majors offered by the colleges of Applied Arts & Sciences, Business, Education, Humanities, Sciences, Social Sciences, and in interdisciplinary studies. Self-designed majors. Minors in most major fields and in 16 additional areas. Distributive requirements. Independent study. Limited pass/fail. Internships, cooperative work/study. Preprofessional programs in agriculture, architecture, dentistry, engineering, medicine, optometry, pharmacy, physical therapy, veterinary science. 4-year programs in agriculture and engineering with U Missouri. 3-1 medical technology and 3-2 law programs. Early childhood, elementary, secondary, and special education certification. AFROTC. Institute of Environmental Studies. 290,000-volume library with microform resources.
Financial ACT FAS. University scholarships, grants, loans, state grants; PELL, SEOG, NSS, NDSL, FISL, NSL, CWS. Loan application deadline July 1.

Admissions High school graduation with 16 units recommended. GED accepted. ACT required. $10 application fee. Rolling admissions. $75 room deposit due on acceptance of admissions offer. *Early Admission* and *Concurrent Enrollment* programs. Transfers accepted. Credit possible for CEEB AP, CLEP, and university proficiency exams.
Student Life Student government. Newspaper, literary magazine, yearbook, radio and TV stations. Music and drama groups. Athletic, academic, honorary, and special interest groups. 6 fraternities and 5 sororities without houses. Freshmen and students with less than 57 credit hours must live on campus or at home. Single-sex dorms. 34% of students live on campus. Liquor prohibited. 3 absences allowed in each course. 4 semesters of phys ed required. 7 intercollegiate sports for men, 7 for women; intramurals. AIAW, MIAA, NCAA. Student body composition: 4% Black, 95% White, 1% Other. 4% from out of state.

[1] SOUTHWEST BAPTIST UNIVERSITY
Bolivar 65613, (417) 326-5281
Vice President for Admissions & Student Development: Jerald L. Andrews

- **Enrollment: 4,194m, 4,823w**
- **Tuition (1982/83): $3,015**
- **Room & Board: $1,385; Fees: $60**
- **Degrees offered: BA, BS, BMus, BGS**
- **Student-faculty ratio: 15 to 1**

A private university affiliated with the Missouri Baptist Convention, established in 1878. 123-acre small-town campus, 28 miles north of Springfield. Bus station.
Academic Character NCACS accreditation. 4-1-4 system, 2 4-week and 1 8-week summer terms. 26 majors offered in art, biology, business, chemistry, church recreation, church secretarial science, education, English, physical education, history, home economics, mathematics, medical technology, music, political science, psychology, religious studies, social science, speech. Self-designed majors. Minors offered in most major fields and in 9 additional areas. Distributives, GRE, and 6 hours of Biblical studies required. Independent study. Honors program. Phi Beta Kappa. Preprofessional programs in dentistry, law, medicine, optometry, pharmacy. 2-year transfer programs in engineering and nursing. Elementary, secondary, and special education certification. Language lab. 80,000-volume library.
Financial ACT FAS. University scholarships, grants, loans; scholarships for families of Baptist ministers, ministry scholarships, payment plans; PELL, SEOG, NDSL, GSL, CWS. Application deadlines April 1 (full-tuition scholarships), August 1 (other scholarships), April 30 (loans).
Admissions High school graduation with C average or rank in top 50% of class required. GED accepted. SAT or ACT required; ACT preferred. $10 application fee. Rolling admissions. $75 deposit due on acceptance of offer of admission. *Early Admission* and *Credit in Escrow* programs. Admission deferral possible. Transfers accepted. Credit possible for CEEB AP, CLEP, and school proficiency exams.
Student Life Student government. Newspaper, yearbook. Extensive musical activities. Debate. Theatre. Honorary, political, religious, and special interest groups. Students under 23 live at home or on campus. Single-sex apartment-style housing. 83% of students live on campus. Liquor, hazing, gambling, obscenity, profanity, dancing, tobacco prohibited. Attendance in class required. Students must inform school of marriage intentions. Attendance required at ¾ of chapel services. 1 hour of phys ed required. 5 intercollegiate sports for men, 5 for women; club and intramural sports. AIAW, NAIA. Student body composition: 0.2% Asian, 0.8% Black, 0.1% Native American, 98% White, 0.9% Other. 20% from out of state.

[1] SOUTHWEST MISSOURI STATE UNIVERSITY
901 South National, Springfield 65804, (417) 836-5000
Director of Admissions: Edward Pierce

- **Undergraduates: 4,921m, 5,042w; 15,015 total (including graduates)**
- **Tuition (1982/83): $650 (in-state), $1,300 (out-of-state)**
- **Room & Board: $1,340**
- **Degrees offered: BA, BS, BFA, BMus, BSEd, BSN**
- **Student-faculty ratio: 20 to 1**

A public university established in 1905. 120-acre urban campus. Served by air and bus.
Academic Character NCACS and professional accreditation. Semester system, 8-week summer term. 77 majors offered by the schools of Arts & Humanities, Business, Education & Psychology, and Science & Technology. Special majors. Minors required in some areas. Courses in Greek, Italian, Hebrew. Distributive requirements. Independent study. Cooperative work/study, pass/fail. Preprofessional programs in health, law, environment, veterinary medicine. 2-2 engineering programs with U Missouri at Rolla or Columbia. Elementary, secondary, and special education certification. ROTC. 375,000-volume library with microform resources.
Financial CEEB CSS. University scholarships, grants, loans, state grants; PELL, SEOG, NDSL, FISL, CWS. Application deadline March 31.
Admissions High school graduation with 10 units recommended. GED accepted. ACT required; SAT, SCAT, PSAT may be substituted. $20 application fee. Rolling admissions; apply by March 1 if interested in housing on campus. $75 room deposit due on acceptance of admissions offer. *Early Decision* Program. Transfers accepted. Credit possible for CEEB CLEP exams.
Student Life Student government. Newspaper, literary magazine, yearbook, radio station. Music and drama groups. Debate. Academic, honorary, political, professional, and service groups. 12 fraternities, 11 with houses, and 5 sororities with houses. 9% of students join. Freshmen and sophomores must live at home or on campus. Single-sex dorms. 20% of students live on campus. 3 semesters of phys ed required. 11 intercollegiate sports for men, 8 for women; intramurals. NCAA, Gateway Collegiate Athletic Conference, Association of Mid-Continent Universities. Student body composition: 98% White, 2% Other. 3% from out of state.

[J1] STATE FAIR COMMUNITY COLLEGE
1900 Clarendon Road, Sedalia 65301

[1] STEPHENS COLLEGE
Columbia 65215, (314) 442-2211
Dean of Admissions: Martha G. Wade

- **Undergraduates: 22m, 1,265w**
- **Tuition (1982/83): $5,175**
- **Room & Board: $2,325**
- **Degrees offered: BA, BS, BFA, AA**
- **Student-faculty ratio: 11 to 1**

A private college established in 1833. 325-acre campus in a small city 125 miles from St. Louis. Airport, bus station.
Academic Character NCACS accreditation. Quarter system, 7-week summer term. 27 majors offered in the areas of fine arts, business, communications, equestrian science, fashion, humanities, and physical education. Self-designed majors. Minors offered in most major fields. Distributive requirements. Independent study. Honors program. Pass/fail, internships. "House Plan" study course for freshmen. Preprofessional programs in law and medicine. 3-2 engineering programs with Georgia Tech, Washington U. Animal science and engineering programs with U Missouri at Columbia. Mid-Missouri Association of Colleges and Universities. Study abroad. Elementary and special education certification. ROTC, NROTC, AFROTC at Columbia. 125,000-volume library.
Financial CEEB CSS and ACT FAS. College scholarships, grants, loans, payment plan; PELL, SEOG, NDSL, FISL, CWS. Application deadline March 15 (scholarships), May 1 (loans).
Admissions High school graduation with 12 units in college prep program recommended. Interview recommended. ACT or SAT required. $25 application fee. Rolling admissions. $275 deposit due on acceptance of admissions offer. *Early Admission* Program. Admission deferral possible. Transfers accepted. Credit possible for CEEB AP and CLEP exams.
Student Life Student government. Students serve on faculty and administrative committees. Newspaper, literary magazine, yearbook, radio and TV stations. Music and theatre groups. Honorary, political, service, and special interest groups. 4 sororities without houses. 20% of women join. Except for a special group of seniors, students must live at home or on campus. 95% of students live in residence halls. Juniors and seniors may have cars on campus. 4 terms of phys ed required. 5 intercollegiate sports; intramurals. Student body composition: 0.8% Asian, 6% Black, 1% Hispanic, 0.2% Native American, 92% White. 80% from out of state.

[1] TARKIO COLLEGE
Tarkio 64491, (816) 736-4131

- **Enrollment: 219m, 132w; 386 total (including part-time)**
- **Tuition & Fees (1982/83): $3,550**
- **Room & Board: $1,900**
- **Degree offered: BA**
- **Mean ACT 15**
- **Student-faculty ratio: 12 to 1**

A private institution affiliated with the United Presbyterian Church, established in 1883. Campus is in a small town north of Kansas City in the northwest corner of the state.
Academic Character NCACS accreditation. 4-1-4 system. 22 major programs offered. Remedial mathematics and English programs. 80,000-volume library.
Admissions ACT required. Application deadline is September 1. *Early Decision* and *Early Admission* programs. Advanced placement possible.
Student Life Dining hall and dormitories for men and women are maintained.

[J1] THREE RIVERS COMMUNITY COLLEGE
Three Rivers Blvd., Poplar Bluff 63901

[J2] TRENTON JUNIOR COLLEGE
Trenton 64683

[P] UNIVERSITY OF HEALTH SCIENCES
2105 Independence Avenue, Kansas City 64124
Formerly Kansas City College of Osteopathic Medicine

[1] WASHINGTON UNIVERSITY
St. Louis 63130, (314) 889-6000
Director of Admissions: William H. Turner

- **Undergraduates: 2,670m, 1,308w; 8,454 total (including graduates)**
- **Tuition (1982/83): $7,125**
- **Room & Board: $3,193; Fees: $54**
- **Degrees offered: BA, BS, BFA, BSBA**
- **Mean SAT 563v, 613m**
- **Student-faculty ratio: 14 to 1**

A private university established in 1853. 176-acre suburban campus. Served by air, rail, and bus.
Academic Character NCACS and professional accreditation. Semester system, 4 summer terms. 38 majors offered by the College of Arts & Sciences, 1 by the School of Architecture, 4 by the School of Business Administration, 8 by the School of Engineering & Applied Science, 9 by the School of Fine Arts, and 2 by the School of Medicine. Self-designed majors. Distributive requirements. Graduate and professional degrees granted. 4-year program combines 2 years

of Common Studies and 2 years of Independent Studies. Honors programs. Phi Beta Kappa. Limited pass/fail. Internships. Preprofessional programs in architecture, business, dentistry, health administration, law, medicine, occupational therapy, physical therapy, social work, teaching the deaf. Study abroad. Elementary, secondary, and special education certification. ROTC, AFROTC. Language lab. 1,800,000-volume library with microform resources.
Financial Guaranteed tuition. CEEB CSS. University scholarships, grants, loans, payment plans; PELL, SEOG, NDSL, FISL, CWS.
Admissions High school graduation with high academic performance required. Interview encouraged. SAT or ACT required; ACH encouraged. $20 application fee. Rolling admissions. $200 deposit due on acceptance of admissions offer. *Early Decision* Program. Admission deferral possible. Transfers accepted. Credit possible for CEEB AP exams and for university placement exams.
Student Life Student Senate. Newspaper, literary magazine, journals, yearbook. Music and drama groups. Opera Workshop. Dance theatre. Honorary, religious, social, and special interest groups. 10 fraternities with houses. 6 sororities. 10% of students join. Freshmen must live at home or on campus. Coed and single-sex dorms. Special interest houses. 75% of students live on campus. 10 intercollegiate sports for men, 3 for women; intramurals. AIAW, NCAA. Student body composition: 3% Asian, 9% Black, 0.5% Hispanic, 0.5% Native American, 87% White. 77% from out of state.

[1] WEBSTER COLLEGE
470 East Lockwood, Webster Groves 63119, (314) 968-6985
Director of Admissions & Financial Aid: Michael S. Newman

- **Undergraduates: 1,095m, 698w**
- **Tuition (1982/83): $3,900**
- **Room & Board: $2,130; Fees: $75**
- **Degrees offered: BA, BFA, BMus, BMus Ed, BSN**
- **Mean SAT 491v, 462m**
- **Student-faculty ratio: 12 to 1**

A private college established in 1915. 20-acre campus in suburban St. Louis. Served by air and rail.
Academic Character NCACS and professional accreditation. Semester system; some half-semester classes available. 24 majors offered in anthropology, art, biology, child study, dance, fine arts, languages, science, history/political science, literature/language, management, mathematics, media, music, music education, philosophy, psychology, religion, social sciences, and theatre. Self-designed majors. Minors offered in many fields. Senior comprehensive exam required in some areas. Graduate degrees granted. Independent study. Credit/no credit. Nursing program in cooperation with St. Luke's Hospital, Kansas City. Cross-registration with Fontbonne, Lindenwood, Maryville Colleges. Study abroad. Elementary, secondary, and special education certification. Multi-media center. Language lab. Theatre. 162,000-volume library.
Financial CEEB CSS. College scholarships, grants, loans, fine arts grants, payment plan; PELL, SEOG, NDSL, FISL, CWS. Scholarship application deadline April 30.
Admissions High school graduation with 16 units recommended. GED accepted. Interview recommended. Art and music students should submit tapes or portfolios. SAT or ACT required. $20 application fee. Rolling admissions. $100 deposit required on acceptance of offer of admission. *Early Admission* Program. Admission deferral possible. Transfers accepted. Credit possible for CEEB AP and CLEP exams.
Student Life Student Association. Newspaper, literary magazine. Numerous music groups. Professional resident repertory company. Academic, religious, and special interest groups. Freshmen must live at home or on campus. 2 dorms, dining hall. 30% of students live on campus. Intramural sports. Student body composition: 0.3% Asian, 20% Black, 0.7% Hispanic, 0.4% Native American, 78% White. 30% from out of state.

[J1] WENTWORTH MILITARY ACADEMY AND JUNIOR COLLEGE
Lexington 64076
Dean of Admissions: Lt. Col. Robert M. Martin

- **Enrollment: 147 men, 40w; 232 total (including part-time)**
- **Expenses (1982/83): $6,570**
- **Degrees offered: AA, AS**

A private academy established in 1880. 137-acre small-town campus, one hour from Kansas City. Served by rail and bus.
Academic Character NCACS accreditation. Semester system. 2-year programs in liberal arts, physical education. Preparation programs for West Point and Annapolis military academies, and Air Force Academy. Distributive requirements. ROTC. 20,000-volume library.
Financial Academy scholarships, state grants, PELL, SEOG, ROTC contract, CWS.
Admissions High school graduation required. ACT required. $25 application fee. Rolling admissions. $400 deposit due on acceptance of admissions offer.
Student Life Newspaper. Flight training. Military Band. Intercollegiate and intramural sports.

[1] WESTMINSTER COLLEGE
Fulton 65251, (314) 642-3361
Dean of Admissions: Thomas King

- **Undergraduates: 581m, 133w**
- **Tuition (1982/83): $4,300**
- **Room & Board: $2,200; Fees: $100**
- **Degrees offered: BA, BFA**
- **Mean ACT 23; mean SAT 483v, 528m**
- **Student-faculty ratio: 14 to 1**

A private college established in 1851, became coed in 1979. 253-acre small-town campus, 80 miles west of St. Louis.
Academic Character NCACS accreditation. 5-4-1 system. Majors offered in accounting, art, biology, chemistry, computer science, economics, education, English, French, history, mathematics, music, philosophy, physical education, physics, political science, psychology, religion, sociology/anthropology, Spanish, speech, and theatre. Self-designed majors. Pass/fail, internships. Preprofessional programs in commerce & finance, dentistry, engineering, journalism, law, medicine, ministry, veterinary medicine. 4-2 engineering program with Stanford. 3-2 engineering and MBA programs with Washington U. Cooperative programs in fine arts with William Woods. Study abroad. Washington and UN Semesters. Elementary, secondary, and special education certification. ROTC. Computer center. Language lab. 80,000-volume library.
Financial CEEB CSS. College scholarships, grants, loans, payment plans; PELL, SEOG, NDSL, FISL, NSL, CWS. Application deadlines February 15 (scholarships), registration day (loans).
Admissions High school graduation with 15 units required. SAT or ACT required. $15 application fee. Rolling admissions. $200 deposit due on acceptance of admissions offer. *Early Admission* and *Early Decision* programs. Transfers accepted. Credit possible for CEEB AP, CLEP, and college proficiency exams.
Student Life Student government. Newspaper, literary magazine, yearbook. Music and drama groups. Debate. Big Brother Program. Academic, honorary, political, religious, and special interest groups. 7 fraternities with houses, 2 sororities. 65% of men and 50% of women join. All freshmen must live on campus; upperclassmen live at home or at school. Single-sex dorms. Married-student apartments available. 98% of students live on campus. Phys ed required for freshmen. 9 intercollegiate sports for men, 5 for women; extensive intramurals. NAIA, NCAA. Student body composition: 3% Black, 96% White, 1% Other. 50% from out of state.

[1] WILLIAM JEWELL COLLEGE
Liberty 64068, (816) 781-3806
Director of Admissions & Student Records: Harley Wyatt, Jr.

- **Undergraduates: 800m, 600w**
- **Tuition (1982/83): $3,370**
- **Room & Board: $1,790; Fees: $210**
- **Degrees offered: AB, BS**
- **Student-faculty ratio: 16 to 1**

A private college affiliated with the Baptist Church, established in 1849. 106-acre suburban campus, 15 minutes from downtown Kansas City. Bus to Kansas City.
Academic Character NCACS and professional accreditation. 4-1-4 system, 8-week summer term. 37 majors offered in the areas of the humanities, arts, science, business, education, music, public relations, religion, and social sciences. Self-designed majors. Distributives, 1 Bible course, and senior comprehensive exam required. Independent study. Honors program. Cooperative work/study, limited pass/fail, internships. Preprofessional programs in dentistry, journalism, law, medicine, ministry. 3-2 engineering program with Columbia, Washington, and U Missouri at Rolla or Columbia. 3-2 forestry program with Duke. Cross-registration at 16 schools. Study abroad. Washington and UN Semesters. Elementary and secondary education certification. Language labs. 140,000-volume library.
Financial CEEB CSS and ACT FAS. College scholarships, grants, loans, tuition grants to candidates for ministry, their wives, and unmarried children of ministers; state grants, payment plans; PELL, SEOG, GSL, NDSL, FISL, HELP, CWS. Recommended loan application deadline March 15.
Admissions High school graduation with 16 units recommended. Interview recommended. ACT required. $10 application fee. Rolling admissions. $50 room deposit due on acceptance of admissions offer. *Concurrent Enrollment* Program. Admission deferral possible. Transfers accepted. Credit possible for CEEB AP, CLEP, and departmental exams.
Student Life Student Senate. Newspaper, yearbook, radio station. Music and drama groups. Debate. Christian Student Ministries Program. Academic, honorary, political, religious, service, and special interest groups. 4 fraternities with houses, 4 sororities without houses. 45% of men and 40% of women join. Students must live at home or on campus. Single-sex dorms. Married-student housing. 80% of students live on campus. Liquor prohibited. 1 absence per credit hour permitted in each course. 1 phys ed course and 1 activity required. 10 intercollegiate sports for men, 5 for women; many intramurals. AIAW, Heart of America Conference. Student body composition: 2% Asian, 3% Black, 2% Hispanic, 1% Native American, 91% White, 1% Other. 30% from out of state.

[1] WILLIAM WOODS COLLEGE
Fulton 65251, (314) 642-2251
Acting Director of Admissions: Janet White

- **Undergraduates: 67m, 748w**
- **Tuition (1982/83): $4,540**
- **Room & Board: $1,985; Fees: $175**
- **Degrees offered: BA, BS, BFA**
- **Student-faculty ratio: 13 to 1**

A private college established in 1870. 160-acre small-town campus, 20 miles east of Columbia, 80 miles west of St. Louis. Airport, bus station.
Academic Character NCACS and professional accreditation. 5-4-1 system plus 3-week post session. 64 majors offered by the Divisions of Fine Arts, Humanities, Natural & Applied Sciences, Social Sciences, and Administrative & Consumer Services. Minors offered in many fields. Distributive requirements. Independent study. Internships. Advanced projects. 3-3

program in law with Duke. 3-2 engineering program with USC, Washington U, Georgia Tech. 3-1 medical technology program. Cooperative programs with 5 area schools. Cooperative nursing program. Study abroad. Broadway semester. Early childhood, elementary, secondary, and special education certification. ROTC at Westminster. Computer center. Language lab. 152,000-volume joint library with Westminster; microform resources.
Financial CEEB CSS. College scholarships, grants, loans, 2nd-family-member discount (applicable at Woods or Westminster), athletic scholarships, state grants, payment plans; PELL, SEOG, GSL, PLUS, NDSL, FISL, CWS.
Admissions High school graduation with 16 units required. Interview recommended. SAT or ACT required. $25 application fee. Rolling admissions. $250 deposit required on acceptance of offer of admission. *Early Admission* and *Early Decision* programs. Admission deferral possible. Transfers accepted. Credit possible for CEEB AP and CLEP exams; college has own advanced placement program.
Student Life Student government. Newspaper, yearbook. Art, music, drama, and dance groups. Athletic, academic, honorary, political, professional, religious, and special interest groups. 4 sororities with houses. 40% of women join. Single students must live at home or in dorms. 95% of students live on campus. Attendance at 3 convocations a year required. Liquor and drugs prohibited. Academic honor code. Regular class attendance required. 6 intercollegiate sports; intramurals. NAIA. Student body composition: 0.2% Asian, 2% Black, 0.5% Hispanic, 96.8% White, 0.5% Other. 55% from out of state.

MONTANA *(MT)*

[1] CARROLL COLLEGE

Helena 59625, (406) 442-3450, ext. 286
Director of Admissions: Allen Kohler

- **Undergraduates: 457m, 641w**
- **Tuition (1982/83): $2,700**
- **Room & Board: $1,960; Fees: $178**
- **Degrees offered: BA**
- **Mean ACT 23**
- **Student-faculty ratio: 16 to 1**

A private Roman Catholic college controlled by the Diocese of Helena, established in 1909. 55-acre urban campus in capital of Montana, located in the Rocky Mountains. Served by air, bus, and rail.
Academic Character NASC and professional accreditation. Semester system, 6-week summer term. Majors offered in American studies, biology, business administration (3 areas), classical languages, communication arts, dental hygiene, economics, elementary education, English, French, history, mathematics, medical records administration, medical technology, nursing, philosophy, physical education (K-12), political science, psychology, religious education, sciences, social sciences, social work, Spanish, and theology. Interdepartmental majors. Minors offered in most major fields and in art, chemistry, physics, secondary education. Courses in German, Greek, music. Comprehensive exam required. Independent study. Honors program. Limited pass/fail. Preprofessional programs in dentistry, engineering, law, medicine, pharmacy, seminary, veterinary medicine. 3-2 engineering programs with 6 schools including Notre Dame, Columbia, and USC. Affiliation with 3 area hospitals. Study in Mexico, France. Elementary and secondary education certification. Observatory, seismograph, language lab, computer center. 100,000-volume library.
Financial CEEB CSS. College scholarships, grants, loans, family discounts, payment plan; PELL, SEOG, SSIG, NDSL, FISL, NSL, CWS. Application deadlines March 1 (scholarships), April 1 (loans).
Admissions High school graduation with 15 units required. Interview encouraged. ACT or SAT required. $20 application fee. Rolling admissions; suggest applying at least 3 weeks before registration. $50 deposit required on acceptance of offer of admission. *Early Admission* Program. Admission deferral possible. Transfers accepted. Credit possible for CEEB AP exams.
Student Life Student government. Newspaper, magazine, yearbook. Music, debate, drama groups. Academic, religious, and special interest organizations. Students must live at home or on campus. Dormitories and dining hall. Married-student housing available near campus. 61% of students live on campus. 2 courses in phys ed required. 7 intercollegiate sports for men, 2 for women; intramurals. AIAW, NAIA, Frontier Conference. Student body composition: 1.4% Asian, 0.4% Black, 0.5% Hispanic, 1.5% Native American, 95.6% White, 0.6% Other. 34% from out of state.

[J1] DAWSON COLLEGE

PO Box 421, 300 College Drive, Glendive 59330, (406) 365-3396
Registrar: Jeanne Moran

- **Enrollment: 112m, 108w; 608 total (including part-time)**
- **Tuition & Fees (1982/83): $375 (in-district), $525 (out-of-district), $825 (out-of-state)**
- **Room: $900**
- **Degrees offered: AA, AAS**
- **Mean ACT 17.9**
- **Student-faculty ratio: 23 to 1**

A public junior college established in 1940. Campus located in the small town of Glendive in Dawson County. Served by air and rail.
Academic Character NASC accreditation. Trimester system, 7-week summer term. 2-year transfer and terminal programs offered in agriculture, business, business administration, business management, secretarial science, land surveying technology, general education, art, English, foreign languages, humanities, journalism, music, religious studies, speech & drama, biology, chemistry, physics, mathematics, health & physical education, and social and behavioral sciences. Certificate programs in 7 areas. Independent study. Internships. Preprofessional programs in allied health professions, engineering. 18,000-volume library.
Financial College scholarships, state grants and loans, athletic scholarships; PELL, SEOG, NDSL, GSL, CWS.
Admissions High school graduation required. GED accepted. ACT required. $10 application fee. Rolling admissions. *Early Admission* Program. Admission deferral possible. Transfers accepted. Credit possible for CEEB CLEP exams.
Student Life Student government. Newspaper, yearbook. Band. Religious, cultural, and special interest groups. Limited college housing. Apartment-style dorms for men & women. Liquor allowed only in dorms. Class attendance required. 2 intercollegiate sports for men and women; rodeo club. Empire and Mon-Dak Conferences, NJCAA. Student body composition: 10% minority.

[1] EASTERN MONTANA COLLEGE

Billings 59101, (406) 657-2158
Director of Admissions: Victor M. Signori

- **Undergraduates: 1,059m, 1,616w; 4,177 total (including gradutes)**
- **Tuition & Fees (1982/83): $628 (in-state), $1,758 (out-of-state)**
- **Room & Board: $2,200**
- **Degrees offered: BA, BS, BABA, BSBA, BSEd, BSHum Ser, BSRehab, AA, AS**
- **Student-faculty ratio: 18 to 1**

A public college established in 1927. 92-acre urban campus in Billings. Served by air, bus, and rail.
Academic Character NASC and professional accreditation. Trimester system, 2 4½-week summer terms. Majors offered in art, biology, business administration (in 14 areas), chemistry, communication arts, economics, elementary education, English, German, health, history, human services, mathematics, music, psychology, rehabilitation, secondary education, social science education, sociology, Spanish, and special education. Minor required. Minors offered in most major fields and in 17 additional areas. Courses in Norwegian, women's studies. Distributive requirements. Masters degrees granted. Cooperative work/study, internships. Pass/withdraw. Preprofessional programs in agriculture, dentistry, engineering, forestry, law, medical technology, medicine, nursing, wildlife management, veterinary medicine. National Student Exchange. Study abroad. Elementary, secondary, and special education certification. Crow Indian Teacher Training Program. ROTC. 300,000-volume library with microform resources.
Financial CEEB CSS. College scholarships, grants, loans, fee waivers, payment plan; PELL, SEOG, SSIG, BIA, GSL, NDSL, CWS, college has own work program. Priority application deadline March 1.
Admissions High school graduation with 16 units required. GED or state certificate accepted. ACT recommended. $20 application fee. Rolling admissions. $25 room deposit (for boarders) required on acceptance of offer of admission. *Early Admission* and *Concurrent Enrollment* programs. Admission deferral possible. Transfers accepted. Credit possible for CEEB CLEP exams; college has own advanced placement program.
Student Life Student government. Newspaper, radio station. Music, drama groups. Rodeo club. Indian and Hispanic groups. Religious, academic, honorary, and special interest organizations. 1 fraternity with house. 1% of men join. Coed dorms, co-op dorms. No married-student housing. 25% of students live on campus. Liquor prohibited on campus. 3 credits of phys ed required. 7 intercollegiate sports for men, 8 for women; intramurals. AIAW, NCAA, Frontier Conference. Student body composition: 0.1% Asian, 0.1% Black, 0.2% Hispanic, 1.8% Native American, 97.8% White. 5% from out of state.

[J1] FLATHEAD VALLEY COMMUNITY COLLEGE

Kalispell 59901

[1] GREAT FALLS, COLLEGE OF

1301 20th Street S, Great Falls 59405, (406) 761-8210
Director of Admissions: Bruce N. Day

- **Enrollment: 192m, 235w; 1,201 total (including part-time)**
- **Tuition (1982/83): $2,850**
- **Room & Board: $1,410-$2,050; Fees: $30**
- **Degrees offered: BA, BS, AA, AS**
- **Mean ACT 20**
- **Student-faculty ratio: 10 to 1**

A private Roman Catholic college controlled by the Sisters of Providence, established in 1932. Urban campus located in the city of Great Falls.
Academic Character NASC accreditation. Semester system, 12-week summer term. Majors offered in accounting, biology, broadcast communication, business administration, chemistry, elementary education, English, history, history & political science, liberal arts, mathematics, physical education, public administration, social sciences, sociology, and teaching. Associate degrees in some major fields and in other areas, including Native American studies. Minors offered in most major fields and in 12 additional areas. Distributive requirements. Master of Human Services granted. Independent study. Cooperative work/study, pass/fail. Preprofessional programs in chiropody, dentistry, law, medical technology, medicine, nursing, optometry, pharmacy, physical therapy, veterinary science. Graduate

program with MSU. 5-year teaching programs. Elementary and secondary education certification. 80,000-volume library.
Financial CEEB CSS. College scholarships, short-term loans, family plan; PELL, SEOG, GSL, NDSL, CWS. Application deadline April 1.
Admissions High school graduation required. GED accepted. ACT or SAT required. $20 application fee. Rolling admissions; application deadline registration day. Transfers accepted. Credit possible for CEEB CLEP exams.
Student Life Student government. Newspaper, literary publication. Music and drama groups. Native American Students. Honorary, service, academic, and special interest groups. Freshmen under 21 must live on campus. On-campus dorm. Off-campus college housing for married and single upperclass students. Intercollegiate basketball; intramural and club sports. Frontier Conference. 56% of students are non-Catholics.

[J1] MILES COMMUNITY COLLEGE
Miles City 59301

[1] MONTANA, UNIVERSITY OF
Missoula 59812, (406) 243-6266
Director of Admissions: Michael Akin

- **Undergraduates: 3,415m, 3,102w; 9,101 total (including graduates)**
- **Tuition (1982/83): $825 (in-state), $2,265 (out-of-state)**
- **Room & Board: $2,081**
- **Degrees offered: BA, BS, BFA, BMus, BMus Ed, AA**
- **Mean ACT 20.3**
- **Student-faculty ratio: 20 to 1**

A public university established in 1893. 201-acre campus in the Rocky Mountain town of Missoula. Served by air and bus.
Academic Character NASC and professional accreditation. Trimester system, 4- and 8-week summer terms. 39 majors offered by the College of Arts & Sciences, 4 by the School of Business Administration, 6 by the School of Education, 5 by the School of Fine Arts, 4 by the School of Forestry, 2 by the School of Journalism, and 4 by the School of Pharmacy & Allied Health Sciences. Courses in Chinese. Distributive requirements. Graduate and professional degrees granted. Independent study. Honors program. Cooperative work/study, pass/fail/internships. Preprofessional program in medical sciences. National Student Exchange Program. Study abroad in Europe, Russia, New Zealand, Taiwan. Elementary, secondary, and special education certification. ROTC. Biological station, experimental forestry lab. 675,000-volume library with microform resources.
Financial CEEB CSS. University scholarships and loans; PELL, SEOG, SSIG, GSL, NDSL, FISL, CWS. Application deadlines March 1 (scholarships), April 1 (NDSL).
Admissions High school graduation with 4 units required. GED accepted. ACT or SAT required. $20 application fee. Rolling admissions; application deadline September 1. $100 room deposit (for boarders) required on acceptance of offer of admission. *Early Admission* Program. Transfers accepted. Credit possible for CEEB AP and CLEP exams.
Student Life Student association. Newspaper, magazines. Music, drama groups. Religious, honorary, professional, service, and special interest organizations. 7 fraternities and 5 sororities, all with houses. 3% of men and 2% of women join. Coed and single-sex dorms. Coop dorm for women. Married-student apartments. 28% of students live on campus. 7 intercollegiate sports for men, 7 for women; intramurals. AIAW, NCAA, Big Sky, Mountain West. Student body composition: 1% Asian, 0.7% Black, 1% Hispanic, 3% Native American, 94.3% White. 28% from out of state.

[1] MONTANA COLLEGE OF MINERAL SCIENCE AND TECHNOLOGY
Butte 59701, (406) 496-4101
Director of Admissions: Rich Meredith

- **Undergraduates: 1,101m, 413w**
- **Tuition & Fees (1982/83): $616 (in-state), $2,056 (out-of-state)**
- **Estimated Room & Board: $2,145**
- **Degrees offered: BA, BS, AA, AS**
- **Mean ACT 20**
- **Student-faculty ratio: 20 to 1**

A public college established in 1900. 130-acre urban campus in Butte, 60 miles from Helena. Served by air and bus.
Academic Character NASC and professional accreditation. Semester system, 13-week summer term. Majors offered in business administration, chemistry, computer science, engineering science, mathematics, occupational safety & health, society & technology, and in environmental, geological, geophysical, metallurgical, mineral processing, mining, and petroleum engineering. Courses in 10 additional areas. Masters degrees granted. Independent study. Honors program. Cooperative work/study. Internships. Credit by exam. Preprofessional programs in biological sciences, economics, education, general studies, geology, health, humanities/social science, physics. 3-2 liberal arts-engineering program with Carroll College. Computer center, mineral museum, mining museum. 75,000-volume library with microform resources.
Financial CEEB CSS and ACT FAS. College scholarships, grants, loans, payment plan; PELL, SEOG, SSIG, NDSL, GSL, CWS. Scholarship application deadline March 1.
Admissions High school graduation with 16 units required. GED accepted. ACT or SAT required; ACT preferred. $20 application fee. Rolling admissions; suggest applying by May 30. $100 deposit required on acceptance of offer of admission. *Early Admission, Early Decision, Concurrent Enrollment* programs. Admission deferral possible. Transfers accepted. Credit possible for CEEB AP and CLEP exams.
Student Life Student association. Newspaper, yearbook, radio station. Music, debate, drama, dance, speaking groups. Society of Women Engineers. Academic, professional, and special interest groups. 2 fraternities, 1 with house. 3% of men join. Students under 20 must live at home or on campus. Coed dorms, special interest housing. Married-student housing. 14% of students live on campus. 2 hours of phys ed required. 2 intercollegiate sports for men, 2 for women; several intramural and club sports. NAIA. Student body composition: 0.2% Asian, 0.6% Black, 0.2% Hispanic, 1% Native American, 87% White, 11% Other. 17% from out of state.

[1] MONTANA STATE UNIVERSITY AT BOZEMAN
Bozeman 59717, (406) 994-2452
Director of Admissions: Jaynee Drange Groseth

- **Undergraduates: 5,547m, 3,996w; 11,187 total (including graduates)**
- **Tuition & Fees (1982/83): $728 (in-state), $2,168 (out-of-state)**
- **Room & Board: $2,143**
- **Degrees offered: BA, BS, BArch, BMus Ed**
- **Student-faculty ratio: 18 to 1**

A public university established in 1893. 1,170-acre campus in the small city of Bozeman, 90 miles north of Yellowstone Park. Served by air and bus.
Academic Character NASC and professional accreditation. Trimester system, one 9- and 2 4½-week summer terms. 6 majors offered by the College of Agriculture, 5 by the College of Arts & Architecture, 4 by the College of Education, 11 by the College of Engineering, 27 by the College of Letters and Science, 7 by the School of Business, and 1 by the School of Nursing. Self-designed majors. Distributive requirements. Graduate degrees granted. Independent study. Honors program. Internships. Pass/fail. Preprofessional programs in dentistry, medicine, optometry. Consortium with U of Washington Medical School. National Student Exchange, WICHE programs. Study abroad in England. Elementary, secondary, and special education certification. ROTC, AFROTC. Museum of the Rockies, Water Resources Center, nature area, computer center. 622,000-volume library with microform resources.
Financial CEEB CSS. University scholarships, grants, loans; PELL, SEOG, NDSL, GSL, CWS. Application deadline September 1.
Admissions High school graduation with 16 units recommended. GED accepted. SAT or ACT required. $20 application fee. Rolling admissions; suggest applying at least 30 days before registration. $100 deposit required on acceptance of offer of admission. *Early Admission* and *Concurrent Enrollment* programs. Transfers accepted. Credit possible for CEEB AP and CLEP exams; university has own advanced placement program.
Student Life Student government. Newspaper, magazines, yearbook, radio station, Music, debate, and drama groups. Honorary, professional, and special interest organizations. 11 fraternities and 7 sororities, all with houses. 11% of men and 22% of women join. Coed and single-sex dorms. Coop men's dorm. Family housing. 40% of students live on campus. Liquor prohibited except in private rooms. 7 intercollegiate sports for men, 6 for women; many intramurals. AIAW, Big Sky Conference. Student body composition: 2% Native American, 96% White, 2% Other. 18% from out of state.

[1] NORTHERN MONTANA COLLEGE
Haure 59501, (406) 265-7821
Director of Admissions: Ralph Brigham

- **Undergraduates: 737m, 514w; 1,584 total (including graduates)**
- **Tuition (1982/83): $597 (in-state), $2,082 (out-of-state)**
- **Room & Board: $1,950**
- **Degrees offered: BA, BS, BTech, AA, AS**
- **Mean ACT 16**
- **Student-faculty ratio: 14 to 1**

A public college established in 1929. 105-acre small-city campus in north central Montana, 50 miles from the Canadian border. Served by air and rail.
Academic Character NASC accreditation. Trimester system, 10-week summer term. Majors offered in change & values, elementary education, secondary education (7 areas), vocational-technical education (5 areas), and in automotive, business, construction, diesel, drafting, electronics, farm mechanics, mechanical, and trade & technical technology. Self-designed majors. Minor required for traditional majors. Minors offered in some major fields and in biology, Canadian studies, chemistry, French, Native American studies. Associate degrees offered in terminal & transfer fields. Distributive requirements. MS granted. Independent study. Cooperative work/study. Credit by exam. 1- and 2-year transfer programs in agriculture, engineering, fish & wildlife management, forestry, health, home economics, law, medical technology, pharmacy. Elementary and secondary education certification. Language lab. 86,000-volume library.
Financial CEEB CSS. College scholarships, grants, loans, fee waivers, payment plan; PELL, SEOG, SSIG, BIA, NSS, NDSL, FISL, GSL, NSL, CWS. Application deadline March 1.
Admissions High school graduation required. GED accepted. ACT required. $20 application fee. Rolling admissions. $50 deposit required on acceptance of offer of admission. *Concurrent Enrollment* Program. Admission deferral possible. Transfers accepted. Credit possible for CEEB AP exams.
Student Life Student associations. Newspaper, yearbook, radio station. Music, drama groups. Academic, honorary, religious, service, and special interest groups. Single students under 21 must live on campus. Dorms for men and women. Married-student housing. 33% of students live on campus. Liquor allowed only in dorm rooms. 5 intercollegiate sports for men, 5 for women; intramurals. AIAW, NAIA, Frontier Conference. Student body composition: 1% Black, 10% Native American, 89% White. 4% from out of state.

[1] ROCKY MOUNTAIN COLLEGE

1511 Poly Drive, Billings 59102, (406) 245-6151
Director of Admissions: Steven F. Olson

- **Enrollment: 186m, 153w; 450 total (including part-time)**
- **Tuition (1982/83): $3,124**
- **Room & Board: $2,044; Fees: $120**
- **Degrees offered: BA, BS, AA**
- **Student-faculty ratio: 16 to 1**

A private college established in 1878 and affiliated with the United Methodist Church, United Church of Christ, and United Presbyterian Church USA. 135-acre campus in a residential area of the small city of Billings.

Academic Character NASC accreditation. Semester system, 6- and 8-week summer terms. Majors offered in art, biology, chemistry, Christian thought, economics & business administration, elementary education, English, English-drama, geology, history, history of ideas, history-political science, mathematics, music, music education, natural science & mathematics, philosophy, physical education, psychology, and sociology-anthropology. Minors offered in all major fields. Distributive requirements. Independent study. Honors program. Cooperative work/study, pass/fail. Preprofessional programs include medicine, nursing, dentistry, law, medical technology, physical therapy, engineering, ministry, social service. Study abroad. Secondary education certification. 65,000-volume library.

Financial CEEB CSS. College scholarships, grants, and loans; athletic, music, & drama grants, church scholarships; PELL, SEOG, NDSL, FISL, CWS; college has own work program.

Admissions High school graduation with 11 units required. GED accepted. ACT or SAT required. $15 application fee. Rolling admissions. $52 deposit required on acceptance of offer of admission. *Early Decision* and *Early Admission* programs. Admission deferral possible. Transfers accepted. Credit possible for CEEB AP and CLEP exams.

Student Life Student government. Newspaper, yearbook. Music, drama, debate groups. Honorary, service, academic, and special interest groups. Single students must live with relatives or on campus. Coed and single-sex dorms. 2 intercollegiate sports for men, 2 for women; intramurals. Frontier Conference.

[1] WESTERN MONTANA COLLEGE

Dillon 59725, (406) 683-7251

- **Undergraduates: 381m, 369w**
- **Tuition & Fees (1982/83): $633 (in-state), $1,713 (out-of-state)**
- **Room & Board: $2,012**
- **Degrees offered: BA, BS, AA, AS**
- **Mean ACT 16.7**
- **Student-faculty ratio: 20 to 1**

A coed, public college located in southwestern Montana. Rural campus in a mountainous recreational area south of Butte.

Academic Character NASC accreditation. Semester system; 4½- and 9-week summer terms. Summer enrollment is approximately 525 students. BS offered in elementary education, secondary education, human resource management, and in natural heritage, which is a special liberal arts program involving outdoor experience in natural areas. Associate degrees offered in all academic areas. MS in education granted. Remedial mathematics and English programs. 60,000-volume library.

Financial Scholarships, grants, loans, and work-study available. Some high school honor scholarships.

Admissions Admissions notification on a rolling basis. *Early Admission* Program. Transfers accepted. College exams used for guidance purposes.

Student Life No fraternities or sororities. College residence halls for men and women.

NEBRASKA *(NE)*

[1] BELLEVUE COLLEGE

Bellevue 68005

[J1] CENTRAL TECHNICAL COMMUNITY COLLEGE

PO Box 1204, Hastings 68901

[1] CHADRON STATE COLLEGE

Chadron 69337, (308) 432-4451
Director of Admissions: Randy Bauer

- **Undergraduates: 617m, 636w; 1,979 total (including graduates)**
- **Tuition (1982/83): $736 (in-state), $1,280 (out-of-state)**
- **Room & Board: $1,666; Fees: $96**
- **Degrees offered: BA, BSEd, AA**
- **Mean ACT 18**
- **Student-faculty ratio: 16 to 1**

A public college established in 1911. 213-acre small-town campus, 100 miles from Rapid City, SD. Served by air, rail, and bus.

Academic Character NCACS and professional accreditation. Semester system, 2 4-week summer terms, workshops. 38 majors offered by the Divisions of Business, Education & Psychology, Fine Arts, Language & Literature, Science & Mathematics, Social Science, Vocational & Technical Education, and Health, Physical Education & Recreation. Minors required in some departments. Minors offered in some major fields and in 4 other areas. Distributive requirements. Masters degrees granted. 2-year certificate programs available. Independent study. Cooperative work/study, internships. Preprofessional programs in allied health, architecture, dentistry, engineering, forestry/wildlife, journalism, law, medicine, mortuary science, nursing, optometry, pharmacy, physical therapy, range management, veterinary science. 3-1 medical technology program. Summer study abroad. Elementary and secondary education certification. 180,000-volume library with microform resources.

Financial CEEB CSS and ACT FAS. College scholarships, grants, loans, payment plan; PELL, SEOG, SSIG, NDSL, FISL, CWS. Scholarship application deadline January 15.

Admissions Open admission to graduates of Nebraska high schools. 15 high school units required. GED accepted. Interview recommended. ACT required. $10 application fee. Rolling admissions. $25 room deposit due with housing contract. Transfers accepted. Credit possible for CEEB CLEP exams.

Student Life Student Senate. Newspaper, yearbook. Music and drama groups. Debate. Unified campus ministries. Native American Student Association. Honorary fraternities. Circle K. Academic, political, and special interest groups. 3 fraternities and 2 sororities without houses. 5% of students join. Freshmen must live at home or on campus. Coed and single-sex dorms. Married-student housing. 60% of students live on campus. Liquor prohibited. 3 hours of phys ed required. 5 intercollegiate sports for men, 4 for women; intramurals. NAIA, NCC. Student body composition: 0.5% Asian, 0.5% Black, 0.5% Hispanic, 0.5% Native American, 98% White. 17% from out of state.

[1] CONCORDIA TEACHERS COLLEGE

800 North Columbia Avenue, Seward 68434, (402) 643-3651
Admissions Counselors: Courtney A. Meyer, Kathy Soyk

- **Undergraduates: 435m, 535w; 1,067 total (including part-time)**
- **Tuition (1982/83): $3,010**
- **Room & Board: $1,980; Fees: $253**
- **Degrees offered: BA, BSEd, BMus**
- **Mean ACT 21**
- **Student-faculty ratio: 16 to 1**

A private college controlled by the Lutheran Church-Missouri Synod, established in 1894. Campus in a small town 30 minutes from Lincoln. Airport, rail and bus stations in Lincoln.

Academic Character NCACS and professional accreditation. Semester system, 2 summer terms. 20 majors offered in elementary education, 16 in secondary education, 15 in liberal arts, and 1 each in Christian education, pre-seminary pastoral, social work, and theology. Divisions include humanities, natural science & math, physical education, theology, social science, music, and education & psychology. Minors offered in some fields. Courses in 12 additional areas, including Greek and Hebrew. Distributives and 11-12 hours of religion required. Independent study. Honors program. Pass/fail. Preprofessional programs in dentistry, law, medicine, nursing, pharmacy. Elementary and secondary education certification. ROTC. 127,000-volume library.

Financial CEEB CSS and ACT FAS. College scholarships, state grants, PELL, NDSL, CWS, college part-time employment. Application deadline April 15.

Admissions High school graduation with 16 units required. ACT required. Rolling admissions. $50 deposit due on acceptance of admissions offer. *Early Admission* and *Early Decision* programs. Transfers accepted. Credit possible for CEEB AP exams; college has own advanced placement program.

Student Life Student Activities Committee. Newspaper. Music and drama groups. Academic, social, and special interest groups. Single students must live at home or on campus. 12 dorms for women, 9 for men. No married-student housing. Approved off-campus housing. 3 hours of phys ed required. Class attendance expected. 7 intercollegiate sports for men, 6 for women; intramurals. Student body composition: 0.2% Asian, 2.9% Black, 0.1% Hispanic, 0.9% Native American, 91.8% White, 4.1% Other.

[1] CREIGHTON UNIVERSITY

2500 California Street, Omaha 68178, (402) 280-2703
Director of Admissions: Howard Bachman

- **Undergraduates: 1,825m, 1,678w; 5,776 total (including graduates)**
- **Tuition & Fees (1982/83): $4,070**
- **Room & Board: $2,100**
- **Degrees offered: BA, BS, BFA, BSChem, BSMed Tech, BSN, BSRad Tech, BSBA**
- **Mean ACT 23**
- **Student-faculty ratio: 14 to 1**

A private Roman Catholic university conducted by the Society of Jesus, established in 1878. 85-acre suburban campus, 10 minutes from downtown Omaha. Served by air, rail, and bus.

Academic Character NCACS and professional accreditation. Semester system; 11-week, 3-term summer semester. 30 majors offered by the College of Arts & Sciences, 7 by the College of Business Administration, 1 by the School of Nursing, and concentrations in communication arts, natural science, social sciences, social work, and education. Minors offered in some fields. Distributives and 6 hours of theology required. Graduate & professional degrees granted. Independent study. Greek honors program. Pass/fail, internships. Preprofessional programs in architecture, dentistry, engineering,

law, librarianship, medicine, mortuary science, occupational therapy, optometry, pharmacy, physical therapy, veterinary medicine. 3-1 medical technology program. 2-2 radiologic technology program. 2-3 engineering program with U of Detroit. Elementary and secondary education certification. ROTC, AFROTC. Educational television. Observatory. Language lab. 457,911-volume library.
Financial CEEB CSS and ACT FAS. University scholarships, grants, loans, 2nd-family-member discount; PELL, SEOG, NDSL, FISL, HELP, CWS. Application deadline March 1.
Admissions High school graduation with 15 units required. ACT required. $20 application fee. Rolling admissions. $100 deposit due on acceptance of admissions offer. *Early Decision* Program. Admission deferral possible. Transfers accepted. Credit possible for CEEB AP and CLEP exams, and for high ACT scores.
Student Life Student Union. Newspaper, literary magazine, yearbook, radio & TV stations. Music, drama, and literary groups. Honorary, service, and special interest clubs. 6 fraternities, one with house, and 5 sororities. 25% of men and 17% of women join. Juniors and seniors may live off campus. Coed and single-sex dorms. No married-student housing. 60% of students live on campus. 5 intercollegiate sports for men, 4 for women; club & intramural sports. AIAW. Student body composition: 3% Asian, 3% Black, 2% Hispanic, 92% White. 60% from out of state.

[1] DANA COLLEGE
2848 College Drive, Blair 68008, (402) 426-4101
Director of Admissions: Lee E. Johnson

- **Undergraduates: 299m, 266w**
- **Tuition (1982/83): $3,800**
- **Room & Board: $1,655; Fees: $220**
- **Degrees offered: BA, BS**
- **Mean ACT 21**
- **Student-faculty ratio: 10 to 1**

A private college affiliated with the American Lutheran Church, established in 1884. Campus in a small town 20 miles north of Omaha.
Academic Character NCACS and professional accreditation. 4-1-4 system, 3- and 6-week summer terms. 41 majors offered in the areas of art, biology, broadcasting, business, chemistry, community planning, corrections, economics, English, environmental studies, foreign language, general science, humanities, mathematics, medical arts, music, psychology, physical education, religion, social sciences, speech, and teaching. Distributives and 6 hours of religion required. Preprofessional programs in agriculture, dentistry, engineering, law, medicine, nursing, pharmacy, seminary. Cross-registration with area schools. Exchange program with U Copenhagen. Elementary and secondary education certification.
Financial College scholarships, grants, PELL, SEOG, NDSL, GSL, CWS. Application deadline March 1.
Admissions High school graduation required. SAT or ACT required. $10 application fee. Rolling admissions. $50 room deposit due on acceptance of admissions offer. *Early Admission* Program. Admission deferral possible. Transfers accepted. Credit possible for CEEB AP and CLEP exams.
Student Life Student government. Newspaper, literary magazine, yearbook, radio station. Music and drama groups. Athletic, academic, honorary, religious, political, and special interest groups. Fraternities & sororities. Single students must live at home or on campus. Dorms and dining halls for men and women. Chapel and class attendance expected. 4 hours of phys ed required. 8 intercollegiate sports for men, 7 for women; many intramurals. NIAC.

[1] DOANE COLLEGE
Crete 68333, (402) 826-2161
Director of Admissions: Steve Rasmussen

- **Undergraduates: 276m, 336w**
- **Tuition & Fees (1982/83): $4,100**
- **Room & Board: $1,580**
- **Degree offered: BA**
- **Mean ACT 20.9**
- **Student-faculty ratio: 14 to 1**

A private college affiliated with the Congregational Church, established in 1872. 350-acre small-town campus, 25 miles southwest of Lincoln and 75 miles from Omaha.
Academic Character NCACS and professional accreditation. 4-1-4 system, 3-, 4-, and 5-week summer terms. Majors offered in accounting, art, biology, business administration, chemistry, communication, computer science, economics, elementary education, English, English-language arts, environmental studies, fine arts, history, humanities, international studies, math, music, natural science, philosophy-religion, physical education, physical science, political science, psychology, public administration, social science, special education, and theatre-drama. Self-designed majors. Minors offered in most fields and in 5 additional areas. Distributive requirements. Independent study. Honors program. Limited pass/fail, cooperative work/study, internships. Preprofessional programs in engineering, forestry, law, nursing, medicine, medical technology, ministry, social work, music therapy. 3-1 medical technology program. 3-2 and 4-2 engineering programs with Columbia and Washington U. 3-2 forestry program with Duke and Iowa. 4-2 music therapy program with SMU. Study in Copenhagen, Spain, Germany, and Colombia. Washington Semester. Elementary and secondary education certification. ROTC. Language lab. 133,779-volume library.
Financial CEEB CSS and ACT FAS. College scholarships, loans; athletic, music, drama, art scholarships; payment plans; PELL, SEOG, SSIG, NDSL, GSL, CWS. Scholarship application deadline May 1.
Admissions High school graduation required; college prep program recommended. Interview sometimes required. SAT or ACT required. $10 application fee. Rolling admissions. $60 deposit due on acceptance of admissions offer. *Early Decision* and *Early Entrance* programs. Admissions deferral possible. Transfers accepted. Credit possible for CEEB AP and CLEP exams; college has own advanced placement program. Teaching Learning Center for underprepared students.
Student Life Student government. Newspaper, literary magazine, yearbook. Music and drama groups. Debate. Women's Study Group. AFFRO. Honorary, religious, service, and special interest groups. 5 fraternities and 4 sororities without houses. 35% of students join. Single students must live at home or on campus. Coed and single-sex dorms. 90% of students live on campus. 2 terms of phys ed required. 7 intercollegiate sports for men, 7 for women; many intramurals. NIAC, NAIA. Student body composition: 0.6% Asian, 0.8% Black, 0.6% Hispanic, 92% White, 6% Other. 18% from out of state.

[P] GRACE COLLEGE OF THE BIBLE
1515 South 10th Street, Omaha 68108

[1] HASTINGS COLLEGE
Hastings 68901, (402) 463-2402
Director of Admissions: Judy Uerling

- **Undergraduates: 342m, 438w**
- **Tuition (1982/83): $3,590**
- **Room & Board: $1,760; Fees: $230**
- **Degrees offered: AB, BMus**
- **Mean ACT 21**
- **Student-faculty ratio: 13 to 1**

A private college affiliated with the United Presbyterian Church, established in 1882. 80-acre small-city campus, 150 miles west of Omaha. Served by air, rail, and bus.
Academic Character NCACS and professional accreditation. 4-1-4 system, 6-week summer term. Majors offered in art, art education, biology, business administration, chemistry, computer science, economics, elementary education, English, English-journalism, German, history, human services administration, math, music (3), philosophy, physical education, physics, political science, psychology, religion, social science education, sociology, Spanish, speech, and theatre. Self-designed majors. Distributives and 1 course in religion required. Independent study. Honors program. Limited pass/fail, internships, cooperative work/study, credit by exam. Preprofessional programs in church education, dentistry, engineering, journalism, law, medical technology, medicine, ministry, mortuary science, pharmacy, physical therapy, social work. 1-4 nursing program. 3-2 engineering programs with Georgia Tech, Columbia, Washington U. Study abroad. Washington Semester. Elementary and secondary education certification. Language lab. 100,000-volume library.
Financial CEEB CSS and ACT FAS. College scholarships, grants, special skills, academic, & Presbyterian scholarships; PELL, SEOG, NDSL, GSL, CWS. Application deadline May 1.
Admissions High school graduation with 15 units required. GED accepted. Interview recommended. Audition required for music, speech, & drama majors; portfolio for art majors. SAT or ACT required. $15 application fee. Rolling admissions. $50 deposit due on acceptance of admissions offer. *Early Decision* and *Early Admission* programs. Admission deferral possible. Transfers accepted. Credit possible for CEEB AP and CLEP exams.
Student Life Student government. Newspaper, literary magazine, yearbook. Music and drama groups. Debate. International Relations Club. Academic, honorary, religious, and special interest groups. 3 social societies for men and 4 for women, all without houses; societies are open to all students. 40% of men and 60% of women join. Students must live at home or on campus. Coed and single-sex dorms. 65% of students live on campus. Liquor and hazing prohibited. Honor system. Class attendance required. 1 hour of phys ed required in core program. Intercollegiate and intramural sports. AIAW, NAIA, NIAC. Student body composition: 1% Asian, 1% Black, 1% Hispanic, 97% White. 15% from out of state.

[1] KEARNEY STATE COLLEGE
905 West 25th Street, Kearney 68847, (308) 236-4141
Director of Admissions: Wayne Samuelson

- **Undergraduates: 2,174m, 2,583w; 7,200 total (including graduates)**
- **Tuition (1982/83): $800 (in-state), $1,320 (out-of-state)**
- **Room & Board: $1,538; Fees: $115**
- **Degrees offered: BA, BS, BFA, BAEd, BSEd**
- **Mean ACT 21**
- **Student-faculty ratio: 22 to 1**

A public college established in 1903. 235-acre small-city campus, 150 miles from Lincoln. Airport and bus station; train station nearby.
Academic Character NCACS and professional accreditation. Semester system, 4- and 8-week summer terms. 40 majors offered by the schools of Business & Technology, Education, Fine Arts & Humanities, and Natural Sciences & Social Sciences. Self-designed majors. Minors offered. Distributive requirements. MSEd granted. Independent study. Honors program. Pass/fail, internships. Preprofessional programs in architecture, engineering, law. 3-1 programs in medical technology, nuclear medicine technology, and physical therapy. Cross-registration with 54 state-supported institutions. Study abroad. Elementary, secondary, and special education certification. ROTC. Computer center. Art gallery. Language lab. 192,341-volume library with microform resources.
Financial CEEB CSS and ACT FAS. College scholarships, grants, loans, PELL, SEOG, SSIG, NDSL, FISL, GSL, CWS. Application deadline April 15 for grants and loans; scholarship deadlines vary.
Admissions Open admission for Nebraska high school graduates. 15 secondary school units required. GED accepted. ACT or SAT recommended. $10 application fee. Rolling admissions. $45 room deposit due on acceptance

of admissions offer. *Early Admission* and *Concurrent Enrollment* programs. Transfers accepted. Credit possible for CEEB AP, CLEP, and departmental exams.
Student Life Student Senate. Newspaper, literary magazine, yearbook, radio & TV stations. Music and drama groups. Debate. Academic, religious, and special interest groups. 7 fraternities with houses, 5 sororities without houses. Freshmen under 21 must live at home or on campus. Coed and single-sex dorms. Married-student housing. 25% of students live on campus. Liquor prohibited. Class attendance expected. 8 intercollegiate sports for men, 7 for women; intramurals. NAIA, CIC. Student body composition: 0.2% Asian, 0.1% Black, 0.6% Hispanic, 0.2% Native American, 98.2% White, 0.7% Other. 2% from out of state.

[J1] McCOOK COMMUNITY COLLEGE

1205 East 3rd Street, McCook 69001, (308) 345-6303

- **Enrollment: 131m, 103w; 549 total (including part-time)**
- **Tuition (1982/83): $225 (in-state), $292 (out-of-state)**
- **Room & Board: $631**
- **Degrees offered: AA, AGS, AAS**
- **Mean ACT 19**
- **Student-faculty ratio: 10 to 1**

A public college established in 1926. Small-town campus, 290 miles southwest of Omaha. Served by air, rail, and bus.
Academic Character NCACS accreditation. Semester system, 4-week summer term. 2-year transfer, vocational, and preprofessional programs in the areas of liberal arts, agriculture, business, and home economics. Distributive requirements. One-year diploma programs. Independent study. Credit by exam. Internships. 27,000-volume library with microform resources.
Financial College scholarships, grants, loans, state grants; PELL, GSL, CWS. Application deadline June 1.
Admissions High school graduation required. GED accepted. ACT or SAT required. $10 application fee. Rolling admissions. $35 room deposit due on acceptance of admissions offer. *Early Admission* Program. Transfers accepted. Credit possible for CEEB CLEP exams.
Student Life Student Senate. Music groups. Circle K. Honorary and professional groups. Coed dorm. 2 intercollegiate sports for men, 2 for women; intramurals. NJCAA, NTCCAC.

[J1] METROPOLITAN TECHNICAL COMMUNITY COLLEGE

PO Box 3777, Omaha 68103

[1] MIDLAND LUTHERAN COLLEGE

720 East 9th Street, Fremont 68025, (402) 721-5480
Director of Admissions: Roland R. Kahnk

- **Undergraduates: 400m, 451w**
- **Tuition (1982/83): $3,850**
- **Room & Board: $1,790**
- **Degrees offered: BA, AA**
- **Mean ACT 21**
- **Student-faculty ratio: 13 to 1**

A private college affiliated with the Lutheran Church in America, established in 1883. 27-acre small-city campus 36 miles northwest of Omaha, 51 miles north of Lincoln.
Academic Character NCACS and professional accreditation. 4-1-4 system, 7-week summer term, 3-week post-session. Majors offered in art, behavioral sciences, biology, business, chemistry, communication, education, English, history, language arts, mathematics/computer science, music, natural science, nursing, performing arts, physical education, physical science, psychology, religion-philosophy, social science, sociology, and special studies. Special majors. Minors offered in all major fields and 7 additional areas. Courses in Greek, library science. Distributives and 6 hours of religion required. Independent study. Honors program. Pass/fail, credit by exam, internships. Preprofessional programs in architecture, forestry, law, library science, medical technology, medicine, ministry, mortuary science, optometry, parish work, physical therapy, podiatry, social work, veterinary medicine. 3-1 respiratory therapy program. Cooperative interim programs with 300 colleges. Study abroad. Elementary, secondary, and special education certification. Observatory. Planetarium. 105,000-volume library with microform resources.
Financial CEEB CSS and ACT FAS. College scholarships, grants, loans, special aid for Lutheran students, payment plan; PELL, SEOG, NDSL, FISL, CWS, institutional employment. Application deadline May 1.
Admissions High school graduation with 15 units required. Open admission for students in upper 50% of class. ACT required. $10 application fee. Rolling admissions. $50 deposit due on acceptance of admissions offer. *Early Admission* Programs. Transfers accepted. Credit possible for CEEB AP, CLEP, and ACT PEP exams.
Student Life Student Senate. Newspaper, creative writing magazine, yearbook. Music and drama groups. Debate. International Relations Club. Honorary, service, religious, and special interest groups. 5 fraternities and 5 sororities without houses. 30% of men and 40% of women join. Seniors and veterans may live off campus. Dorms and dining hall for men and women. No married-student housing. 70% of students live on campus. Dorms. Liquor prohibited. 7 intercollegiate sports for men, 6 for women; many intramurals. AIAW, NIAC. Student body composition: 2.4% Black, 0.1% Native American, 96.3% White, 1.2% Other. 30% from out of state.

[J2] MID-PLAINS COMMUNITY COLLEGE

North Platte 69101

[1] NEBRASKA, UNIVERSITY OF

Lincoln 68508, (402) 472-3601
Director of Admissions: Al Papik

- **Undergraduates: 10,273m, 8,212w; 25,102 total (including graduates)**
- **Tuition (1982/83): $967 (in-state), $2,633 (out-of-state)**
- **Room & Board: $1,825; Fees: $160**
- **Degrees offered: BA, BS, BFA, BMus, BMus Ed, BSAS**
- **Student-faculty ratio: 18 to 1**

A public university established in 1869. 556-acre urban campus. Airport, bus station.
Academic Character NCACS and professional accreditation. Semester system, 2 5-week summer terms. 15 majors offered by the College of Agriculture, 1 by the College of Architecture, 42 by the College of Arts & Sciences, 8 by the College of Business Administration, 9 by the College of Engineering & Technology, 1 by the College of Nursing, 37 by the Teachers College, and 6 by the College of Home Economics. Self-designed majors. Graduate and professional degrees granted. Independent study. Honors program. Phi Beta Kappa. Cooperative work/study, pass/fail, internships. Preprofessional programs in chemistry, geology, microbiology, social work, government. Cooperative engineering program. Several study abroad programs. Elementary, secondary, and special education certification. ROTC, AFROTC, NROTC. Art galleries. State museum. Recital hall, theatres. 1,160,000-volume library with microform resources.
Financial CEEB CSS. University scholarships, loans, athletic grants, state grants; PELL, SEOG, NDSL, GSL, CWS. Application deadlines February 1(scholarships), March 1 (loans).
Admissions High school graduation with 16 units required. Interview required for nursing students. Audition for music majors. ACT required; SAT may be substituted. $10 (in-state), $25 (out-of-state) application fees. Rolling admissions. *Early Admissions* Program. Transfers accepted. Credit possible for CEEB AP and CLEP exams; departmental advanced placement program.
Student Life Student government. Associated Women Students. Newspaper, literary magazine, yearbook, educational TV station. Academic, ethnic, honorary, and special interest groups. 26 fraternities, 24 with houses; 15 sororities with houses. 25% of men and 33% of women join. Freshmen under 20 must live at home or on campus. Coed, single-sex, coop dorms. Special-interest houses. Limited married-student housing. 45% of students live on campus. Liquor prohibited. 1 year of phys ed required. Extensive intercollegiate and intramural sports program. AIAW, NCAA, Big Eight Conference. Student body composition: 0.7% Asian, 1.6% Black, 0.9% Hispanic, 96.8% White. 9% from out of state.

■[1] NEBRASKA, UNIVERSITY OF, AT OMAHA

Wayne 68182

■[1] NEBRASKA, UNIVERSITY OF, MEDICAL CENTER

42nd and Dewey Avenue, Omaha 68105

■[J1] NEBRASKA, UNIVERSITY OF, SCHOOL OF TECHNICAL AGRICULTURE

Curtis 69015

[J2] NEBRASKA INDIAN COMMUNITY COLLEGE

PO Box 752, Winnebago 68071

[1] NEBRASKA WESLEYAN UNIVERSITY

50th and St. Paul, Lincoln 68504, (402) 466-2371
Director of Admissions: Kendal E. Sieg

- **Enrollment: 542m, 665w**
- **Tuition (1982/83): $3,990 ($4,140 for music)**
- **Room & Board: $1,790-$2,070; Fees: $148**
- **Degrees offered: BA, BS, BLA, BMus, BSN**
- **Mean ACT 24.6**
- **Student-faculty ratio: 13 to 1**

A private university affiliated with the United Methodist Church, established in 1887. 44-acre suburban campus. Served by air, rail, and bus.
Academic Character NCACS and professional accreditation. Semester system, 3-, 5-, and 8-week summer terms. 40 majors offered by the Divisions of the Humanities, Social Sciences, Natural Sciences, Professional Education, and Fine & Applied Arts. Self-designed majors. Minor required. Courses in astronomy, library science. Distributive requirements. Independent study. Cooperative work/study, pass/fail, credit by exam, internships. Preprofessional programs in dentistry, law, medicine, ministry. 3-2 programs in engineering with Columbia, Georgia Tech, Washington U. Exchange program with Union. Study in Europe, Latin America. UN Semester. Washington Semester. Library science, elementary, secondary, and special subject education certification. ROTC, AFROTC, NROTC at U Nebraska-Lincoln. Language labs. Observatory. Brownville Village Theatre. 190,000-volume library.
Financial CEEB CSS. University scholarships, grants, loans, tuition reduction for clergy children, payment plans; PELL, SEOG, NDSL, GSL, CWS.
Admissions High school graduation required; placement in top 50% of class preferred. Interview recommended. ACT or SAT required. $10 application fee. Rolling admissions. $100 deposit due on acceptance of admissions offer. *Early Decision* and *Early Admission* programs. Admission deferral possible. Transfers accepted. Credit possible for CEEB AP and CLEP exams.
Student Life Student government. Newspaper, yearbook, radio station. Music and theatre groups. Debate. Academic, honorary, religious, and special interest groups. 5 fraternities and 4 sororities, all with houses. 36% of men and 42% of women join. Freshmen must live at home or on campus. Upperclassmen may live off campus in approved housing. Coed and single-sex dorms. No married-student housing. 71% of students live on campus.

Liquor allowed only in dorm rooms. Firearms prohibited. Class attendance usually required. 1 year of phys ed required. 7 intercollegiate sports for men, 5 for women; intramurals. NCAA. 17% of students from out of state.

[J1] NEBRASKA WESTERN COLLEGE

1601 East 27th Street, NE, Scottsbluff 69361, (308) 635-3606

- **Undergraduates: 195m, 306w; 1,434 total (including part-time)**
- **Tuition (1982/83): $540 (in-state), $810 (out-of-state)**
- **Estimated Room & Board: $1,625**
- **Degrees offered: AA, AS, AAS**
- **Mean ACT 19.8**
- **Student-faculty ratio: 17 to 1**

A public junior college, formerly known as Scottsbluff County Junior College. 44-acre small-city campus.

Academic Character NCACS accreditation. Semester system, summer term. 2-year programs offered in business, elementary education, nursing, language & arts, science & mathematics, social science, and vocational areas. Distributive requirements. Certificate programs. Independent study. Preprofessional programs in dentistry, education, law, liberal arts, pharmacy. 21,500-volume library.

Financial College scholarships, grants, state grants; PELL, SEOG, NDSL, GSL, CWS. Application deadline July 1.

Admissions High school graduation required. GED accepted. ACT required. Rolling admissions. *Early Admissions* Program. $50 room deposit due on acceptance of admissions offer.

Student Life Student government. Newspaper. Music and drama groups. Circle K. Athletic, honorary, professional, religious, and special interest groups. Coed dorm. 3 intercollegiate sports; intramurals. Empire Conference.

[J1] NORTHEAST TECHNICAL COMMUNITY COLLEGE

Norfolk 68701

[1] PERU STATE COLLEGE

Peru 68421, (402) 872-3815
Director of Admissions: Kenneth L. Steidle

- **Undergraduates: 291m, 289w; 767 total (including part-time)**
- **Tuition (1982/83): $736 (in-state), $1,280 (out-of-state)**
- **Room & Board: $1,748; Fees: $124**
- **Degrees offered: BA, BS, BTech, BAEd, BSEd, BFAEd, AA**
- **Student-faculty ratio: 15 to 1**

A public college established in 1867. 100-acre rural campus in a small town 65 miles from Omaha. Airport and train station nearby. Bus station in Auburn.

Academic Character NCACS and professional accreditation. Semester system, 2 5-week summer terms. Majors offered in accounting, art, biological science, biology, business administration, business education, computer science, early childhood development, elementary education, general science, geography, geology, industrial arts, industrial management technology, language arts, manual arts therapy, math, music, physical education, psychology-sociology, retail merchandising, social science, and special education. Self-designed majors. AA offered in early childhood education. Distributive requirements. Independent study. Cooperative work/study, internships. Elementary, secondary, and special education certification. ROTC. Computer center. TV studio. 90,000-volume library.

Financial CEEB CSS and ACT FAS. College scholarships, grants, loans, special activity tuition waivers, payment plan; PELL, SEOG, NDSL, CWS. Scholarship application deadline April 1.

Admissions Guaranteed admission for Nebraska high school graduates. GED accepted. ACT required. $10 application fee. Rolling admissions. $50 room deposit due on acceptance of admissions offer. Transfers accepted. Credit possible for CEEB CLEP and ACT exams.

Student Life Student government. Newspaper. Music and drama groups. Religious, service, and special interest groups. 1 fraternity. 2% of men join. Students must live at home or on campus. Coed and single-sex dorms. Married-student apartments. 50% of students live on campus. 2 semesters of phys ed required. 8 intercollegiate sports for men, 8 for women; intramurals. Student body composition: 1% Asian, 9% Black, 1% Native American, 89% White. 10% from out of state.

[J1] PLATTE TECHNICAL COMMUNITY COLLEGE

Box 1027, Columbus 68601

[1] SAINT MARY, COLLEGE OF

1901 South 72nd Street, Omaha 68124, (402) 399-7446
Director of Admissions: Gary Johnson

- **Enrollment: 1,040w**
- **Tuition & Fees (1982/83): $3,546**
- **Room & Board: $1,576**
- **Degrees offered: BA, BS, AA, AS**
- **Student-faculty ratio: 15 to 1**

A private women's college affiliated with the Roman Catholic Church, established in 1923. 31-acre urban campus southwest of downtown Omaha. Served by air, rail, and bus.

Academic Character NCACS and professional accreditation. Semester system, 6-week summer term, 3-week January interim. Majors offered include accounting, art, biology, business administration, business education, chemistry, computer information management, early childhood education, elementary and secondary education, English, history, human resource management, human services, humanities, medical records administration, medical technology, recreation, respiratory therapy, and social science. Minors required; offered in 23 areas. Associate degrees in computer information management, early childhood education, nursing, respiratory therapy, accounting, business, therapeutic recreation, and recreation. Distributives and 8 hours of theology required. Limited pass/fail, credit by exam. Cooperative nursing program with U Nebraska, Creighton, and local hospitals. Elementary and secondary education certification. 65,000-volume library.

Financial CEEB CSS. College scholarships, grants, loans, state grants, payment plan; PELL, SEOG, NSS, NDSL, GSL, CWS, college work program. Application deadline April 15.

Admissions High school graduation with 16 units required. GED accepted. ACT or SAT required. $15 application fee. Rolling admissions. $50 tuition and $15 room deposits (for boarders) due on acceptance of admissions offer. Transfers accepted. Credit possible for CEEB CLEP exams; college has own advanced placement program.

Student Life Student Senate. Newspaper, yearbook. Campus Ministry. Academic, honorary, social, and special interest groups. Students under 23 required to live on campus. Dorms. Liquor permitted only at special functions approved by Dean and President. Drugs prohibited. Proper dress required. Class attendance required. Student body composition: 11% minority.

[J1] SOUTHEAST COMMUNITY COLLEGE

924 K Street, Fairbury 68352

[J1] SOUTHEAST COMMUNITY COLLEGE—LINCOLN CAMPUS

8800 O Street, Lincoln 68520

[J1] SOUTHEAST COMMUNITY COLLEGE—MILFORD CAMPUS

Buena Vista, SE, Milford 68405

[1] UNION COLLEGE

3800 South 48th Street, Lincoln 68506, (402) 488-2331
Director of Admissions: Leona Murray

- **Undergraduates: 463m, 461w**
- **Tuition (1982/83): $4,950**
- **Room & Board: $1,565-$1,845**
- **Degrees offered: BA, BATheo, BMus, BS, BSW, AS**
- **Mean ACT 17.8**
- **Student-faculty ratio: 15 to 1**

A private college conducted by the Seventh-day Adventist Church, established in 1891. Suburban campus. Served by air, rail, and bus.

Academic Character NCACS and professional accreditation. Semester system, 4 summer terms. 36 majors offered in the areas of business, education & psychology, fine arts, history & social work, home economics, language arts, mathematics, nursing, physical education, religion, and sciences. Self-designed majors. Associate degrees offered in art, business, business computer programming, early childhood education, engineering, foods & nutrition, health science, home economics, secretarial science, social services. Distributive requirements. Honors program. Credit for missionary work. Limited credit/no credit. Preprofessional programs in allied health, dentistry, medicine. Cross-registration with Nebraska Wesleyan and U Nebraska-Lincoln. Study abroad. Elementary, secondary, and special education certification. 116,014-volume library.

Financial Guaranteed tuition. College scholarships, grants, loans, payment plan; PELL, SEOG, NSS, NDSL, FISL, GSL, NSL, CWS. Scholarship application deadline June 15.

Admissions High school graduation with 18 units required. GED accepted. ACT required. $10 application fee. Rolling admissions. $100 deposit due on acceptance of admissions offer. Transfers accepted. Credit possible for CEEB CLEP exams; college has own advanced placement program. Freshman Development Program for students not normally admissable.

Student Life Student government. Newspaper. Music groups. Union for Christ. Campus ministry. Academic, social, religious, recreational, and special interest groups. Students under 24 must live at home or on campus. Single-sex dorms. Married-student housing. 74% of students live on campus. Attendance at 12 religious services and 3 convocations required in each 2-week period. Dress code. Curfew. 2 phys ed courses required. Intramural sports. Student body composition: 5% Black, 11% Foreign, 2% Hispanic, 0.3% Native American, 81.7% White. 78% from out of state.

[1] WAYNE STATE COLLEGE

Wayne 68787, (402) 375-2200
Director of Admissions: Jimmy D. Hummel

- **Enrollment: 823m, 1,142w; 2,384 total (including graduates)**
- **Tuition (1982/83): $690 (in-state), $1,200 (out-of-state)**
- **Room & Board: $1,716; Fees: $131**
- **Degrees offered: BA, BS, BAEd, BFAEd, BSEd**
- **Student-faculty ratio: 17 to 1**

A public college established in 1901. 135-acre small-city campus in northeastern Nebraska, near Omaha, Lincoln, and Sioux City. Bus station; airport nearby.

Academic Character NCACS and professional accreditation. Semester system, 2 5-week summer terms. 40 majors offered in the areas of liberal arts & sciences, business, communications, community service, criminal justice, education, fashion, home economics, industrial management, interior design, medical technology, mortuary science, physical education, and technology, trades, & industry. Major/minor, 2 majors, or 50-hour majors required. Minors offered in many major fields and in 9 additional areas. Distributive requirements. Masters degrees granted. Independent study. Honors program.

Cooperative work/study, pass/fail, internships, credit by exam. Preprofessional programs in agriculture, dentistry, engineering, forestry, medicine, nursing, oceanography, optometry, pharmacy, physical therapy, physician's assistant, veterinary medicine. Study in Denmark. Elementary and secondary education certification. Fine Arts Center. 160,000-volume library with microform resources.
Financial College scholarships, grants, loans; PELL, SEOG, NDSL, GSL, CWS. Application deadline April 30.
Admissions High school graduation with 16 units required. SAT or ACT required; ACT preferred. $10 application fee. Rolling admissions. $25 room deposit required on acceptance of offer of admission. *Early Entrance, Concurrent Enrollment, Early Decision* programs. Admission deferral possible. Transfers accepted. Credit possible for CEEB AP and CLEP exams.
Student Life Student Senate. Newspaper, literary magazine, radio and TV stations. Music and drama groups. Debate. Academic, honorary, political, religious, and special interest groups. 3 fraternities and 3 sororities. Single freshmen under 20 must live at home or on campus. Dorms for men and women. Liquor, narcotics, firearms prohibited. 4 hours of phys ed required. 4 intercollegiate sports for men, 4 for women; intramurals. AIAW, NAIA, CSIC. Student body composition: 1.2% Asian, 0.2% Hispanic, 1% Native American, 97.3% White. 13% from out of state.

[J1] YORK COLLEGE
York 68467, (402) 362-4441
Director of Admissions: Elton W. Albright

- **Enrollment: 185m, 224w**
- **Tuition (1982/83): $2,170**
- **Room & Board: $2,150**
- **Degrees offered: AA, AS, AAABus**
- **Mean ACT 18.6**
- **Student-faculty ratio: 13 to 1**

A private college established in 1890, operated by members of the Churches of Christ since 1956. 15-acre small-town campus, 50 miles west of Lincoln.
Academic Character NCACS accreditation. Semester system. 2-year transfer programs offered by the divisions of Bible & Related Subjects, Humanities, Natural Sciences, and Social Sciences. Majors offered include Greek, art, English, music, speech, math, chemistry, business administration, education, history, physical education. Distributives and 7 hours of religion required. Independent study. Honors program. Preprofessional programs in agriculture, dentistry, engineering, journalism, law, medical technology, medicine, nursing, optometry, pharmacy, veterinary medicine. 28,000-volume library.
Financial ACT FAS. College scholarships, loans, ministerial scholarships, discount for simultaneously-enrolled siblings, PELL, SEOG, NDSL, GSL, student employment. Scholarship application deadline August 25.
Admissions High school graduation required. ACT required. $10 application fee. Rolling admissions. $25 tuition and $50 room (for boarders) deposits due on acceptance of admissions offer. *Early Admission* Program. Admission deferral possible. Transfers accepted. Credit possible for CEEB CLEP exams.
Student Life Student Association. Newspaper, yearbook. Music and drama groups. Academic, honorary, professional, social, and special interest groups. Single students must live at home or on campus. Single-sex dorms. Married-student apartments. Liquor, drugs, tobacco, gambling, profanity, firearms prohibited. Church attendance expected. Class and daily chapel attendance required. 2 hours of phys ed required. 5 intercollegiate sports; intramurals. PJCC.

NEVADA (NV)

[1] NEVADA, UNIVERSITY OF
Reno 89557, (702) 784-6865
Director of Admissions: Jack H. Shirley

- **Undergraduates: 2,998m, 2,541w; 10,441 total (including graduates)**
- **Tuition (1982/83): $992 (in-state), $2,992 (out-of-state)**
- **Room & Board: $2,200**
- **Degrees offered: BA, BS, BACrimJus, BAEcon, BAJourn, BSBA, BSEng**
- **Mean ACT 19.5**
- **Student-faculty ratio: 21 to 1**

A public university established in 1874. 195-acre hillside campus overlooking the cities of Reno and Sparks. Served by air, rail, and bus.
Academic Character NASC and professional accreditation. Semester system, 2 5-week summer terms, 3-week minisession. 16 majors offered by the College of Agriculture, 32 by the College of Arts & Sciences, 9 by the College of Business Administration, 25 by the College of Education, 4 by the College of Engineering, 6 by the College of Home Economics, 2 by the College of Medical Sciences, 7 by the College of Mines, and 1 by the School of Nursing. Special majors. Minors offered in many fields. Distributive requirements. Independent study. Honors program. Pass/fail, internships, credit by exam. Preprofessional programs in dentistry, law, medicine, pharmacy, physical therapy. National Student Exchange program. Study abroad. Congressional Intern Program. Elementary, secondary, and special education certification. ROTC. Planetarium. Desert Research Institute. Seismological lab. 705,533-volume libraries with microform resources.
Financial ACT FAS. University scholarships, grants, loans, agricultural & home economics loans, payment plan; PELL, SEOG, NDSL, FISL, NSL, CWS.
Admissions High school graduation with 2.3 GPA required; Nevada residents with 2.0 admitted on probation. ACT required; SAT may be substituted. $5 application fee. Rolling admissions. *Early Decision, Early Admission, Concurrent Enrollment* programs. Transfers accepted. Credit possible for CEEB AP, CLEP, ACT PEP, and departmental exams.
Student Life Associated Students. Newspaper, literary magazine, yearbook, radio station. Music and drama groups. Debate. Academic, honorary, and special interest groups. 7 fraternities and 5 sororities with houses. 10% of men and 13% of women join. Coed and single-sex dorms. Special interest wings. Married-student housing. 11% of students live on campus. Liquor prohibited for students under 21. 9 intercollegiate sports for men, 7 for women; many intramurals. NCAA, Big Sky Conference. Student body composition: 2% Asian, 2% Black, 2% Hispanic, 1% Native American, 90% White, 3% Other. 12% from out of state.

■[J1] CLARK COUNTY COMMUNITY COLLEGE
3200 East Cheyenne Avenue, Las Vegas 89030

■[1] NEVADA, UNIVERSITY OF, LAS VEGAS
4505 South Maryland Parkway, Las Vegas 89154, (702) 739-3443
Director of Admissions: Joeanne Adler

- **Undergraduates: 2,998m, 2,541w; 9,064 total (including graduates)**
- **Tuition (1982/83): $930 (in-state), $2,930 (out-of-state)**
- **Room & Board: $2,414**
- **Degrees offered: BA, BS, BAEcon, BAEd, BFA, BSBA, BSEd, BSEng, BSHotel Admin, AA, AS**
- **Mean ACT 19; mean SAT 410v, 456m**
- **Student-faculty ratio: 18 to 1**

A public university established in 1955. 355-acre suburban campus. Airport, bus station.
Academic Character NASC accreditation. Semester system, 2 5-week summer terms, January mini-term. 3 majors offered by the College of Allied Health Professions, 19 by the College of Arts & Letters, 6 by the College of Business & Economics, 4 by the College of Education, 1 by the College of Hotel Administration, and 8 by the College of Science, Mathematics, & Engineering. Self-designed majors. Minors in 6 areas. Masters degrees granted. Limited pass/fail, internships, credit by exam. Preprofessional programs in dentistry, medicine, veterinary medicine. Study abroad. Elementary, secondary, and special education certification. ROTC. Computer center. Environmental Protection Agency Monitoring and Support Lab. Desert Research Institute. 750,000-volume library.
Financial ACT FAS. University scholarships, loans; PELL, SEOG, BIA, NDSL, GSL, NSL, CWS. Application deadline April 1.
Admissions High school graduation with 2.3 GPA required. ACT or SAT required. $5 application fee. Rolling admissions; application deadline one week before start of classes. *Early Decision* and *Concurrent Enrollment* programs. Transfers accepted. Credit possible for CEEB AP and CLEP exams. Acceptance on probation possible for students not normally admissible.
Student Life Student government. Newspaper, radio station. Music, film, and drama groups. Academic, ethnic, political, service, and special interest groups. 7 fraternities and 2 sororities. Single-sex dorms & one coed dorm; some have air-conditioning. No married-student housing. 2% of students live on campus. Liquor restrictions. 10 intercollegiate sports for men, 5 for women; intramurals. NCAA, PCAA. Student body composition: 2% Asian, 5.6% Black, 3% Hispanic, 0.4% Native American, 87.1% White. 14% from out of state.

■[J1] WESTERN NEVADA COMMUNITY COLLEGE
Carson City 89701

[J1] NORTHERN NEVADA COMMUNITY COLLEGE
Elko 89801

[1] SIERRA NEVADA COLLEGE
Incline Village 89450

[J1] TRUCKEE MEADOWS COMMUNITY COLLEGE
7000 Dandini Blvd., Reno 89512

NEW HAMPSHIRE (NH)

[J2] CASTLE JUNIOR COLLEGE
Searles Road, Windham 03087

[J1 & 1] COLBY-SAWYER COLLEGE
New London 03257, (603) 526-2010
Dean of Admissions & Financial Aid: Peter R. Dietrich

- **Undergraduates: 650w**

- **Tuition (1982/83): $6,120**
- **Room & Board: $2,600; Fees: $270**
- **Degrees offered: BA, BS, BFA, BSN, AA, AS**
- **Mean SAT 432v, 427m**
- **Student-faculty ratio: 13 to 1**

A private women's liberal arts college established in 1837 in rural New London. 40-acre campus 100 miles from Boston. Bus service; airport 30 minutes away in Lebanon.

Academic Character NEASC and professional accreditation. 4-1-4 system. Majors offered in American studies, art, biology, business administration, child study, health records administration, medical technology, nursing, orthoptics, and theatre (acting, dancing, design). Self-designed majors. Courses offered in 13 additional areas. Associate degrees in liberal arts, recreation leadership, administrative services, and science-medical fields. Distributive requirements. Independent study. Phi Beta Kappa. Pass/fail, internships. Consortium with other New Hampshire colleges. Study abroad. Pre-school and kindergarten education certification. 60,000-volume library with microform resources.

Financial CEEB CSS. College scholarships, loans, grants, payment plan; PELL, SEOG, NDSL, GSL, CWS. Preferred application deadline February 15.

Admissions High school graduation with 15 units required. GED accepted. Interview recommended. SAT or ACT required. $25 application fee. Rolling admissions; suggest applying by January 1. *Early Decision, Early Admission* programs. Admission deferral possible. Transfers accepted. Credit possible for CEEB AP and CLEP exams, and for professional experience. College has own placement program.

Student Life Student government. Newspaper, magazine, yearbook. Music, drama, dance, art, athletic, outing, religious, academic, special interest groups. 98% of students live on campus. Women's dorms. 4 semesters of phys ed required. 8 intercollegiate sports, 13 intramural sports. AIAW, EIAW. Student body composition: 93% White, 7% Other. 84% from out of state.

[1] DANIEL WEBSTER COLLEGE

University Drive, Nashua 03063, (603) 883-3556
Director of Admissions: David T. Leach

- **Undergraduates: 360m, 90w**
- **Tuition (1982/83): $4,990**
- **Room & Board: $2,600; Fees: $90**
- **Degrees offered: BS, AS**
- **Mean SAT 380v, 460m**
- **Student-faculty ratio: 19 to 1**

A private college established in 1965 in Nashua. 60-acre suburban campus in a rural area 45 miles north of Boston. Bus service.

Academic Character NEASC accreditation. Semester system, 2 8-week summer terms. Majors offered in air traffic control management, aviation management/flight training, aviation management, business management, and computer systems. Associate degrees in accounting, aeronautical engineering, computer systems, engineering, engineering science, general studies, marketing, travel management. Courses in behavioral & social sciences, humanities & fine arts, science, math. Distributive requirements. Independent study, honors program, internships. Preprofessional program in engineering. Member of New Hampshire College and University Council. New flight center on campus located adjacent to Nashua Municipal Airport. Computer center. Flight students may earn their private, instrument, commercial instructor, and multi-engine ratings. AFROTC. 21,500-volume library with microform resources.

Financial CEEB CSS. College scholarships, state grants, payment plan; PELL, SEOG, NDSL, GSL, CWS.

Admissions High school graduation with 16 units required. GED accepted. SAT or ACT required. Interview recommended; required for students pursuing the Aviation Consumer Management curriculum. Rolling admissions; application deadline June 1. $100 room and $100 tuition deposits required on acceptance of offer of admission. *Early Decision, Early Admission, Concurrent Enrollment* programs. Admission deferral possible. Transfers accepted. Credit possible for CEEB AP, CLEP exams, and for life experience.

Student Life Student government. Newspaper, yearbook. Academic, religious, service, special interest groups. Aero club. Freshmen and sophomores must live on campus or at home. Single-sex dorms. No married-student housing. 65% of students live on campus. Class attendance required. 5 intercollegiate sports for men, 3 for women; many intramurals. Greater Boston Small College Conference, New Hampshire Women's Athletic Conference. Student body composition: 1% Asian, 6% Black, 4% Hispanic, 1% Native American, 88% White. 80% of students from out of state.

[1] DARTMOUTH COLLEGE

Hanover 03755, (603) 646-1110
Director of Admissions: Alfred T. Quirk

- **Undergraduates: 2,548m, 1,398w; 4,759 total (including graduates)**
- **Tuition & Fees (1982/83): $8,190**
- **Room & Board: $3,307**
- **Degree offered: AB**
- **Mean SAT 640v, 690m**
- **Student-faculty ratio: 12 to 1**

A private college established in 1769, became coed in 1972. 175-acre small-town campus on the Connecticut River. Bus service; airport and rail station nearby.

Academic Character NEASC and professional accreditation. Year-round system of four 10-week terms. Freshmen attend fall/winter/spring. Students plan their own enrollment patterns, usually including 11 study terms, with 1 summer & 6 on-campus terms required. Majors offered in anthropology, art, Asian studies, biochemistry, biology, chemistry, classics, comparative literature, drama, earth sciences, economics, education, engineering sciences, English, French, geography, German, government, history, Italian, mathematics, math & social sciences, music, philosophy, physics/astronomy, policy studies, psychology, religion, Russian, sociology, and Spanish. Special majors. Interdisciplinary programs. Distributive requirements. Graduate and professional degrees granted. Independent study, honors programs, Phi Beta Kappa, pass/fail and non-recording option. Extensive internship program. Combined programs with graduate schools of business, engineering, and medicine. 12-college exchange, exchange with UCalifornia San Diego and other schools. Numerous language and other study abroad programs. Elementary and secondary education certification. ROTC at Norwich U. Public Affairs Center. Computer center, observatory. Over 1,500,000-volume library with microform resources.

Financial CEEB CSS. College scholarships, grants, loans, payment plans; PELL, SEOG, NDSL, GSL, CWS. Application deadline January 15.

Admissions High school graduation with strong college prep program recommended. SAT and 3 ACH required. Alumni interview in applicant's home area required. $30 application fee. Application deadline January 1. *Early Decision* Program. Transfers not accepted. Credit possible for CEEB AP, ACH, and college exams. Intensive Academic Support/Equal Opportunity Programs.

Student Life Student government. Newspapers, magazines, yearbook, radio station. Several music and drama groups, film society, intercollegiate debate. Outing club. Academic, ethnic, honorary, political, professional, religious, service, women's, and special interest groups. 22 fraternities (4 coed) with houses, and 4 sororities, 1 with house. 50% of students join. Freshmen must live on campus. Coed and single-sex dorms. Apartment, language, and married-student housing. 92% of students live on campus. No cars for 1st- and 2nd-term freshmen. Honor code. 3 terms of phys ed required. 15 intercollegiate sports for men, 14 for women, and 3 coed; several intramural and club sports. EAIAW, NCAA, ECAC, Ivy League. Student body composition: 1.1% Asian, 7.5% Black, 0.5% Hispanic, 0.9% Native American, 87.2% White, 2.8% Other. 95% from out of state.

[1] FRANKLIN PIERCE COLLEGE

Rindge 03461, (603) 899-5111
Director of Admissions: Thomas E. Desrosiers

- **Undergraduates: 520m, 430w**
- **Tuition (1982/83): $5,400**
- **Room & Board: $2,475; Fees: $100**
- **Degrees offered: BA, BS**
- **Mean SAT 421v, 433m**
- **Student-faculty ratio: 15 to 1**

A private college established in 1962. 720-acre rural campus in the small town of Rindge, 50 miles northwest of Boston. Airport and bus service in nearby Keene.

Academic Character NEASC accreditation. 4-1-4 system, 2 4-week summer terms. Majors offered in the areas of anthropology, business administration, creative & performing arts, education, English, history, psychology, social work & counseling, and sociology. Interdisciplinary-Independent major. Courses offered in chemistry, geology, math, modern languages, philosophy, religion, physics, political science; concentrations in mass communication, recreation management, computer science. Distributive requirements. Independent and directed study, pass/fail, internships. Preprofessional programs in law, medicine, dentistry, veterinary medicine. New Hampshire College and University Council exchange program. Study abroad. Elementary and secondary education certification. Computer lab, learning materials lab. 42,500-volume library; Human Relations Area File is a 50,000-piece microform resource dealing mainly with anthropology.

Financial CEEB CSS. College scholarships, grants; PELL, SEOG, NDSL, GSL, CWS. Application deadline March 31.

Admissions High school graduation with 16 units required. Interview recommended. ACT or SAT required. Rolling admissions. $100 tuition deposit required on acceptance of offer of admission. *Early Admission* and *Early Decision* programs. Admission deferral possible. Transfers accepted. Credit possible for CEEB AP and CLEP exams. Provisional acceptance possible.

Student Life Student government. Newspaper, magazine, yearbook, radio station. Music, drama groups. Athletic, outing, academic, honorary, religious, and special interest groups. Single freshmen must to live on campus or at home. Coed and single-sex dorms. No married-student housing. 85% of students live on campus. Lakeshore waterfront, on-campus ski facility. 10 intercollegiate sports for men, 5 for women; intramurals. NAIA, AIAW, NEHAC. Student body composition: 9% Black, 1% Hispanic, 90% White. 88% from out out of state.

[P] FRANKLIN PIERCE LAW CENTER

Concord 03301

[1] HAWTHORNE COLLEGE

Antrim 03440, (603) 588-6341
Director of Admissions: Ronald K. Cooper

- **Undergraduates: 307m, 59w; 900 total (including extension)**
- **Tuition, Room & Board (1982/83): $6,700**
- **Degrees offered: BS, AA, AS**
- **Mean SAT 420v, 430m**
- **Student-faculty ratio: 13 to 1**

A private college founded in 1962. Rural campus in the small town of Antrim, 30 minutes from Concord and 1½ hours from Boston. College airport located 10 minutes from campus.

Academic Character NEASC accreditation. Semester system, summer term. Majors offered for a BS in aeronautics, aviation management, biological sciences, business administration, computer engineering, computer science, computer technology, electrical engineering, general studies, mechanical engineering, and recreation management. Associate degrees in aeronautics, business administration, computer programming, general studies, and recreation management. Minors. Distributive requirements in the liberal arts & humanities. Flight training sequence leads to Commercial Pilot Certificate with instrument rating. 2-year pre-engineering program; cooperative program for transfer with Florida Institute of Technology. Cross-registration and exchanges possible through New Hampshire College & University Council. ROTC & AFROTC at U of New Hampshire. Extension program. 50,000-volume library.
Financial CEEB CSS. College scholarships, loans, ROTC scholarships; PELL, SEOG, NDSL, GSL, CWS. File FAF by February 15.
Admissions High school graduation required. Interview recommended. SAT or ACT required. $15 application fee. Rolling admissions. $150 deposit required on acceptance of admissions offer. *Early Admissions* Program. Transfers accepted. Credit possible for CEEB AP and CLEP exams.
Student Life Student government. Newspaper, yearbook. International, drama, ski, and outing clubs. 2 fraternities. Freshmen must live on campus. Men's and coed dorms. 98% of students live on campus. 2 semesters of phys ed required. 5 intercollegiate sports for men, 3 for women; intramurals. NAIA.

[J2] HESSER COLLEGE
25 Lowell Street, Manchester 03101, (603) 668-6660
Vice President, Director of Admissions: J. Donovan Mills

- **Undergraduates: 466m, 691w; 1,584 total (including part-time)**
- **Tuition & Fees (1982/83): $3,040-$3,340**
- **Room (1983/84): $1,100**
- **Degrees offered: ABusiness Science, AComputer Science**

A private, coed junior college established in 1900. Urban campus in downtown Manchester, 1¼ hours from Boston.
Academic Character AICS accreditation. Semester system. Majors offered include accounting, management, retailing & fashion merchandising, airline & travel careers, office administration, digital electronics technician, computer science programming, medical administrative assistant, and executive, medical, and legal secretarial. Distributive requirements. Internships and externships. Computer.
Financial CEEB CSS and ACT FAS. Scholarships, grants, loans, state grants; PELL, SEOG, NDSL, CWS. Application deadlines March 15 (scholarships), May 15 (preferred for other aid).
Admissions High school graduation or equivalent required. Interview recommended. $10 application fee. Rolling admissions. $50 tuition and $50 room (for boarders) deposits required on acceptance of admissions offer. *Early Decision* Program. Admission deferral possible. Transfers accepted. Credit possible for college exams and life/work experience.
Student Life Student government. Newspaper, yearbook. Professional groups. Dorms with kitchens for men and women; refrigerators provided in each room. Intercollegiate basketball for men; softball and volleyball for women. NJCAA, Northern New England Small College Conference.

[J2] LEBANON COLLEGE
PO Box 481, Lebanon 03766

[J2] MERRIMACK VALLEY COLLEGE
Manchester 03102

[1] NATHANIEL HAWTHORNE COLLEGE
Antrim — see Hawthorne College

[1] NEW ENGLAND COLLEGE
Henniker 03242, (603) 428-2211
Director of Admissions: Theodor F. Stoerker, Jr.

- **Undergraduates: 740m, 479w**
- **Tuition (1982/83): $5,900**
- **Room & Board: $2,390; Fees: $90**
- **Degrees offered: BA, BS**
- **Mean SAT 400v, 440m**
- **Student-faculty ratio: 14 to 1**

A private college established in 1946. 210-acre small-town campus, 60 miles northwest of Boston and 15 miles west of Concord.
Academic Character NEASC accreditation. 4-1-4 system, 6-week summer term. Majors offered in American studies, biology, business administration, communications, economics, education, engineering, English, environmental studies, geology, history, international administration, math, natural sciences, philosophy, physical education, political science, psychology, public administration, sociology, theatre, visual arts, women's studies. Self-designed majors. Courses in chemistry, ecology, British studies, folklore, communications skills, foreign languages & literature, humanities, music, physics, religion. Independent study. Honors program. Pass/fail, internships. Branch campus in Arundel, England (55 miles south of London) with 300 students. New Hampshire College and University Council exchange program. Study abroad. Elementary and secondary education certification. Communication skills center, math learning center, computer center and lab. 80,000-volume library with microform resources.
Financial CEEB CSS. College scholarships. PELL, SEOG, NDSL, GSL, CWS. Application deadline April 15.
Admissions High school graduation with 12 units required. Interview recommended. SAT or ACT required. $20 application fee. Rolling admissions. $100 tuition deposit required on acceptance of offer of admission. *Early Admission* and *Early Decision* programs. Admission deferral possible. Transfers accepted. Credit possible for CEEB AP and CLEP exams.
Student Life Student government and residence hall council. Newspaper, newsletter, magazine, yearbook, radio station. Music and drama clubs. Academic, honorary, religious, and special interest groups. 3 fraternities with houses, one sorority without house. Freshmen and sophomores must live on campus or at home. Coed dorms. Special interest housing. No married-student housing. 60% of students live on campus. 10 intercollegiate sports for men, 8 for women; 8 intramural sports. AIAW, ECAC, NAIA, NCAA. Student body composition: 0.9% Black, 0.1% Hispanic, 0.1% Native American, 88.7% White, 10.2% Other. 90% from out of state.

[1] NEW HAMPSHIRE, UNIVERSITY OF
Durham 03824, (603) 862-1360
Director of Admissions: Stanwood C. Fish

- **Enrollment: 5,366m, 5,156w; 12,175 total (including evening)**
- **Tuition (1982/83): $1,550 (in-state), $4,400 (out-of-state)**
- **Room & Board: $2,264**
- **Degrees offered: BA, BS, BFA, BMus, BEng Tech, BSForestry, AA, AAS**
- **Mean SAT 480v, 540m**
- **Student-faculty ratio: 16 to 1**

A public university established in 1866. 188-acre rural campus in Durham, 15 miles from the seacoast and 50 miles north of Boston.
Academic Character NEASC and professional accreditation. Semester system, summer terms. 29 majors offered by the College of Liberal Arts, 18 by the College of Life Sciences & Agriculture, 20 by the College of Engineering & Physical Sciences, 3 by the Whittemore School of Business & Economics, and 7 by the School of Health Studies. University also contains Thompson School of Applied Science and Graduate School. Self-designed and interdepartmental majors. Minors offered. Associate degrees available in 17 areas. Distributive requirements. Graduate degrees granted. Independent study. Honors program. Phi Beta Kappa. Pass/fail, internships. Preprofessional programs in law, medicine, dentistry, optometry, osteopathy, podiatry, pharmacy, physician assistant. 4-year program leads to BS/MT; 5-year programs lead to BA/MBA, BS/MBA, BA/ME, BS/ME. New Hampshire College and University Council exchange program. New England Regional Student Program. California Exchange Program. Study abroad. Elementary and secondary education certification. AFROTC, ROTC. Computer center, language lab. 813,785-volume library with microform resources.
Financial CEEB CSS. University scholarships, grants, loans; PELL, SEOG, NDSL, CWS. Application deadline February 1.
Admissions High school graduation with 16 units required. SAT required. Application fees $10 (in-state), $25 (out-of-state). Application deadline February 1 (March 1 for transfers). $100 (in-state), $300 (out-of-state) tuition deposit required on acceptance of offer of admission; $50 room deposit required with housing application. *Early Decision* Program. Admission deferral possible. Transfers accepted. Credit possible for CEEB AP exams.
Student Life Student government. Newspaper, yearbook, TV and radio stations. Music, drama, cultural, political, academic, honorary, international, women's, religious, service, and special interest groups. 12 fraternities and 5 sororities, all with houses. 8% of men and 4% of women join. Dorms and dining halls. Limited married-student housing. 43% of students live on campus. Freshmen and sophomores may not have cars on campus without permission. 16 intercollegiate sports for men, 10 for women; many intramural sports. NCAA, Yankee Athletic Conference, ECAC. Student body composition: 0.3% Asian, 0.3% Black, 0.3% Hispanic, 0.2% Native American, 98.1% White, 0.7% Other. 30% from out of state.

■[1] KEENE STATE COLLEGE
Keene 03431, (603) 352-1909
Director of Admissions: John J. Cunningham

- **Undergraduates: 1,150m, 1,550w**
- **Tuition (1982/83): $935 (in-state), $2,835 (out-of-state)**
- **Room & Board: $2,096; Fees: $258**
- **Degrees offered: BA, BS, BMus, BGS, BSEd, BSInd Tech, AA, AS**
- **Mean SAT 420v, 450m**
- **Student-faculty ratio: 18 to 1**

A public college established in 1909. 58-acre small-city campus in southwestern New Hampshire, 50 miles northwest of Boston. Airport, bus service.
Academic Character NEASC and professional accreditation. Semester system, 2 6-week summer terms. 44 majors offered in the areas of arts, humanities, math, sciences, social sciences, economics, communications, industrial technology, education, music. Independent and self-designed majors. Associate degrees offered in computer studies, early childhood development, general studies, safety studies, drafting, design technology, industrial electronics, manufacturing technology. Distributive requirements. Masters degrees granted. Independent study. Internships. New Hampshire College and University Council exchange program. Exchange program with Merrill-Palmer Institute in Detroit. Study abroad. Elementary, secondary, and special education certification. Computer center, Reading Development Lab, Wheelock School, Safety Center, Reading Clinic. ROTC at U of New Hampshire. 160,000-volume library with microform resources.
Financial CEEB CSS. University scholarships, grants, loans. PELL, SEOG, NDSL, FISL, GSL, CWS. Preferred application deadline March 1.
Admissions High school graduation required. SAT required. Application fees $10 (in-state), $20 (out-of-state). Rolling admissions; application deadline June 1 (July 1 for transfers). $85 tuition deposit required on acceptance of offer of admission. *Early Admission* Program. Admission deferral possible.Transfers accepted. Credit possible for CEEB AP and CLEP exams.

Student Life Student government. Newspaper, yearbook, radio station. Music, drama, film groups. Academic, political, religious, service, special interest clubs. 5 fraternities and 4 sororities. Coed, single-sex, special interest, and married-student housing. 60% of students live on campus. 6 intercollegiate sports for men, 10 for women. intramurals. AIAW, ECAC, NAIA, NCAA, NEAC. Student body composition: 99% White, 1% Other. 45% from out of state.

■[1] PLYMOUTH STATE COLLEGE
Plymouth 03264, (603) 536-1550
Director of Admissions: Clarence W. Bailey, Jr.

- **Undergraduates: 1,350m, 1,350w**
- **Tuition (1982/83): $1,100 (in-state), $3,000 (out-of-state)**
- **Room & Board: $2,062; Fees: $197**
- **Degrees offered: BA, BS, BFA, AA, AS, ASec Sc**
- **Mean SAT 900**
- **Student-faculty ratio: 21 to 1**

A public college established in 1871. 96-acre campus in Plymouth, 40 miles north of Concord. Served by bus; airport in Laconia.
Academic Character NEASC and professional accreditation. Semester system, 3 summer terms. 70 majors offered in the areas of arts, humanities, education, math, sciences, social sciences, music, economics, business, interdisciplinary studies. Minors in most major fields. Associate degrees offered. Distributive requirements. MBA, MEd granted. Independent study. Honors programs. Pass/fail, credit by exam, internships. Preprofessional program in law. 3-2 MBA program. Cross-registration and exchanges possible through New Hampshire College and University Council. New England Regional Student Program. Study abroad. Elementary and secondary education certification. ROTC & AFROTC at U of New Hampshire. Computer Services Center, Reading lab, Institute for New Hampshire Studies, Environmental Studies Center. 300,000-volume library.
Financial CEEB CSS and ACT FAS. College scholarships and loans; PELL, SEOG, NDSL, FISL, GSL, CWS. Application deadline March 1.
Admissions High school graduation or equivalent required. Audition required for music majors. SAT or ACT required. Application fees $10 (in-state), $20 (out-of-state). Rolling admissions; application deadline June 1. $60 tuition and $50 room deposits required on acceptance of offer of admission. Transfers accepted. Credit possible for CEEB AP and CLEP exams. College has own placement exams; proficiency exams in math and English required. Special Services program for underprepared students.
Student Life Student government. Newspaper, magazine, yearbook. Music, drama, athletic, academic, honorary, religious, service, and special interest groups. 5 fraternities with houses and 4 sororities, 3 with houses. 15% of men and 10% of women join. Students must live at home or on campus. Dorms for men and women. Married-student housing. 75% of students live on campus. 2 semesters of phys ed required. 11 intercollegiate sports for men, 6 for women; many intramurals. New Hampshire Interscholastic Athletic Association. Student body composition: 99% White, 1% Other. 35% from out of state.

[1] NEW HAMPSHIRE COLLEGE
2500 North River Road, Manchester 03104, (603) 668-2211
Director of Admissions: Michael L. DeBlasi

- **Undergraduates: 900m, 775w**
- **Tuition (1982/83): $5,454**
- **Room & Board: $3,126**
- **Degrees offered: BS, AS**
- **Mean SAT 850**
- **Student-faculty ratio: 11 to 1**

A private college established in 1932. 700-acre dual-site campus located on the outskirts of Manchester, 50 miles north of Boston. Air and bus service.
Academic Character NEASC accreditation. Semester system, 2 5-week summer terms. Majors offered in accounting, business communications, business/distributive teacher education, economics/finance, hotel/restaurant management, human services, management, management advisory systems, management information systems, marketing, office administration, and retailing. Techni-business major for transfers with non-business associate degrees to earn a BBus. Associate degrees offered in accounting, administrative assistant/word processing specialist, electronic data processing, executive secretarial, fashion merchandising, general studies, legal secretarial, and management. Courses in English, fine art, government, history, math, philosophy, psychology, science. Masters degrees granted; evening MBA program. Independent study. Cooperative work/study, pass/fail, internships. New Hampshire College and University Council exchange program. Secondary education certification. AFROTC at U of Lowell; ROTC at U of New Hampshire. Continuing education program at 10 locations in NH, Maine, and Puerto Rico, with enrollment over 4,000. Computer center. Language lab. Over 67,000-volume library with microform resources.
Financial CEEB. CSS. College scholarships, state grants; PELL, SEOG, NDSL, GSL, CWS. Application deadline March 15.
Admissions High school graduation required. GED accepted. Interview recommended. SAT required. Rolling admissions; suggest applying by March 1. $100 room and $100 tuition deposits required on acceptance of offer of admission. *Early Entrance* Program. Admission deferral possible. Transfers accepted. Credit possible for CEEB AP, CLEP and ACT PEP exams; departmental testing for placement. Freshman Entrance Program for underprepared students; students complete a 3-course summer program before admission to regular degree program.
Student Life Student government. Newspaper, yearbook, radio station. Religious, outing, honorary, academic, and special interest groups. 3 fraternities and 3 sororities, without houses. Students must live on campus or at home. Coed and single-sex dorms; apartments and townhouses. No married-student housing. 80% of students live on campus. Class attendance required. 6 intercollegiate sports for men, 5 for women; 17 intramural sports for men & women. AIAW, ECAC, NAIA, NCAA, NECAC. Student body composition: 1% Asian, 5% Black, 90% White, 4% Other. 75% from out of state.

[J1] NEW HAMPSHIRE TECHNICAL INSTITUTE
Fan Road, Concord 03301, (603) 271-2531

- **Enrollment: 376m, 432w; 981 total (including part-time)**
- **Tuition & Fees (1981/82): $992 (in-state), $3,442 (out-of-state)**
- **Room & Board: $1,760-$1,860**
- **Degrees offered: AS, AE**

A public technical institute opened in 1965. 225-acre campus on the Merrimack River near downtown Concord.
Academic Character NEASC and professional accreditation. Semester system, summer term. Majors offered in architectural engineering technology, electronic engineering technology, mechanical engineering technology, computer information systems, business administration (banking & finance option), nursing, dental assisting, dental hygiene, emergency medical care/paramedic, radiological technology, human services/mental health, human services/alcoholism counseling, and general science. ASN/RN program for LPNs. Certificates granted. One-year Pre-tech program teaches basic skills to prepare students for college-level work. Independent study, credit by exam, internships. Transfer programs with U of New Hampshire in electronic and mechanical engineering technologies. New England Regional Student Program. Many lab facilities including computer, engineering, electricity, and metallurgy labs. 20,000-volume library.
Financial CEEB CSS and ACT FAS. College loans, state grants & loans; PELL, SEOG, NSS, NDSL, GSL, NSL, CWS. Suggest applying by January 1; deadline April 1.
Admissions High school graduation or equivalent required. SAT or ACT strongly recommended. Students apply to particular programs; courses, testing, and/or interview may be required. No application fee. Application deadline for health-related programs January 15. $50 tuition deposit required on acceptance of admissions offer. Transfers accepted. Credit possible for CEEB CLEP exams, life/work experience, and military training.
Student Life Student government. Newspaper, yearbook. Music groups. Outing Club. Academic, honorary, social, professional, cultural, and athletic groups. Students not living at home live on campus as long as space is available. Single-sex dorms for 100 men and 100 women. Cafeteria. Regular class attendance expected. Intercollegiate and intramural sports for men & women. Northern New England Small College Conference.

[J1] NEW HAMPSHIRE VOCATIONAL-TECHNICAL COLLEGE
Milan Road, Berlin 03570

[J1] NEW HAMPSHIRE VOCATIONAL-TECHNICAL COLLEGE
Hanover Street Extension, Claremont 03743

[J1] NEW HAMPSHIRE VOCATIONAL-TECHNICAL COLLEGE
Prescott Hill, Laconia 03246

[J1] NEW HAMPSHIRE VOCATIONAL-TECHNICAL COLLEGE
1066 Front Street, Manchester 03102

[J1] NEW HAMPSHIRE VOCATIONAL-TECHNICAL COLLEGE
505 Amherst Street, Nashua 03063

[J1] NEW HAMPSHIRE VOCATIONAL-TECHNICAL COLLEGE
Portsmouth 03801

[1 & J1] NOTRE DAME COLLEGE
2321 Elm Street, Manchester 03104, (603) 669-4298

- **Undergraduates: 47m, 377w; 740 total (including part-time)**
- **Tuition (1982/83): $3,100**
- **Room & Board: $2,100; Fees: $150-$220**
- **Degrees offered: BA, BS, BMus, BSMT, AA, AS**
- **Student-faculty ratio: 10 to 1**

A private, Roman Catholic, liberal arts college primarily for women, owned and operated by the Sisters of Holy Cross and founded in 1950. Campus in residential north end of Manchester, 60 miles from Boston. Airport, bus station in Manchester.
Academic Character NEASC accreditation. Semester system, summer term. Majors offered in behavioral science, biology, business education, commercial art, elementary education, English, fine art, French, history, Latin, music education, music performance, paralegal studies, religious studies, secretarial sciences, and Spanish. Concentrations in art education, bio-secondary education, early childhood education, microbiology, special education. 3-1 and 4-1 cytotechnology majors with Boston School of Cytotechnology and Northeastern U. 4-1 medical technology program. Associate degrees in early childhood education, music performance, pre-pharmacy, and general, legal, and medical secretarial sciences. Distributives and 4 religious studies-philosophy courses required. Masters in education granted. Internships, field work. Cross-registration and exchanges through New Hampshire College and University Council. Cross-registration possible with Manchester Institute of Art & Sciences. Summer programs in Appalachia. Quebec-New England Exchange. ROTC through NHCUC; AFROTC at U of

New Hampshire and U of Lowell. Continuing education. Learning Resource Center. 44,000-volume library.
Financial CEEB CSS. College scholarships, state scholarships and grants; PELL, SEOG, NDSL, GSL, CWS. Priority application deadline March 1.
Admissions High school graduation or equivalent required. GED accepted. At least 16 secondary school units expected. Interview strongly recommended; required for pre-pharmacy. Audition required for music majors; portfolio for art majors. SAT or ACT optional. $15 application fee. Rolling admissions; suggest applying as early as possible. $100 tuition and $50 room (for boarders) deposits required by May 1. *Early Admission* and *Early Decision* programs. Admission deferral possible. Transfers accepted. Credit possible for CEEB AP exams.
Student Life Student government. Music groups. Campus Ministry. Outing Club. Special interest groups. Student Center. 8 converted homes house 149 students. Many intramural sports.

[1] RIVIER COLLEGE
Nashua 03060, (603) 888-1311
Director of Admissions: Diane Hewitt

- **Undergraduates: 576w; 2,035 total (including part-time & graduates)**
- **Tuition (1982/83): $3,500**
- **Room & Board: $2,400; Fees: $120**
- **Degrees offered: BA, BS, BFA, AA, AMus, AS**
- **Mean SAT 454v, 446m**
- **Student-faculty ratio: 17 to 1**

A private women's college founded by the Sisters of the Presentation of Mary in 1933. Men accepted for part-time, graduate, and special programs. 45-acre suburban campus, one mile from downtown Nashua and 35 miles from Boston. Airport, bus station.
Academic Character NEASC and professional accreditation. Semester system, 2 6-week summer terms. Over 45 majors offered in the areas of art, biology, business, chemistry, computer science, education, English, home economics, math, modern languages, music, paralegal studies, political science, psychology, sociology/social work, and liberal studies. Minors offered in most major fields. Associate degrees offered in art, business, chemical laboratory technician, home economics, human services, liberal arts, medical laboratory technician, music, and secretarial science. Distributives and 3 religion courses required. Masters degrees granted. Certificate programs in education and paralegal studies. Preprofessional programs in art therapy, medicine, dentistry, law. Internships. Member of New Hampshire College and University Council. Study abroad. Early childhood, elementary, secondary, and special education certification. AFROTC at U of New Hampshire and U of Lowell. 100,000-volume library.
Financial CEEB CSS. College scholarships, grants, loans; PELL, SEOG, NDSL, GSL, CWS. Application deadline February 15.
Admissions High school graduation with 16 units required. Interview strongly recommended; required for paralegal and medical lab technician programs. Music majors must audition. SAT required. $15 application fee. Rolling admissions; suggest applying by January 1. *Early Decision* and *Concurrent Enrollment* programs. Admission deferral possible. Transfers accepted. Credit possible for CEEB AP and CLEP exams; college has own placement exams.
Student Life Student Council. Newspaper, magazine, yearbook. Music, drama, athletic, academic, honorary, service, political, and special interest groups. 2 dorms house 300 women. No married-student housing. 50% of students live on campus. Class attendance expected. Intercollegiate and intramural sports. Student body composition: 1% Black, 2% Hispanic, 94% White, 3% Other. 45% from out of state.

[1] ST. ANSELM COLLEGE
Manchester 03102, (603) 669-1030
Director of Admissions: Donald E. Healy

- **Undergraduates: 840m, 790w**
- **Tuition (1982/83): $4,750**
- **Room & Board: $2,450**
- **Degrees offered: BA, BSN, BSCrim Jus, AS**
- **Mean SAT 480v, 510m**
- **Student-faculty ratio: 13 to 1**

A private Roman Catholic college founded in 1889 by the Benedictines of St. Mary's Abbey. 300-acre suburban campus in Manchester, 50 miles north of Boston. Airport, bus station.
Academic Character NEASC and professional accreditation. Semester system, 2-, 3- and 2 4-week summer terms. Majors offered in biology, business, chemistry, classical languages, computer science, criminal justice, economics, English, French, history, math, natural science, nursing, philosophy, politics, psychology, sociology, Spanish, and theology. Combined and interdisciplinary studies. Soviet Studies Program. AS in criminal justice. Distributive requirements. 3 theology courses required of Catholic students. Independent study, internships. Preprofessional programs in dentistry, engineering, law, medicine, theology. Member of New Hampshire College and University Council. Study abroad. Secondary education certification. ROTC & AFROTC at U of New Hampshire and U of Lowell. 145,000-volume library with microform resources.
Financial CEEB CSS. College scholarships, grants, loan;. PELL, SEOG, NSS, NDSL, GSL, NSL, CWS. Application deadline April 15.
Admissions High school graduation with 16 units required. Interview recommended. SAT required. $15 application fee. Application deadline February 15 for nursing program. Rolling admissions. $100 tuition deposit required on acceptance of offer of admission. *Early Decision* and *Early Entrance* programs. Admission deferral possible. Transfers accepted. Credit possible for CEEB AP and CLEP exams.
Student Life Student government. Newspaper, periodical. Debate, drama, political, academic, honorary, religious, service, and special interest groups. Freshmen and sophomores must live on campus or at home. 11 single-sex dorms. No married-student housing. 65% of students live on campus. Class attendance expected. 8 intercollegiate sports for men, 6 for women; 3 club sports and several intramurals. NCAA, ECAC, AIAW. Student body composition: 1% Black, 1% Hispanic, 97% White, 1% Other. 83% from out of state.

[1 & J1] SCHOOL FOR LIFELONG LEARNING
Durham 03824

[J1] WHITE PINES COLLEGE
Chester 03036, (603) 887-4401
Director of Admissions: Kevin K. Hill

- **Undergraduates: 71 men & women; 193 total (including part-time)**
- **Tuition (1982/83): $3,400**
- **Room & Board: $2,100; Fees & Bookstore Deposit: $350**
- **Degree offered: AA**
- **Student-faculty ratio: 15 to 1**

A private, coed junior college founded in 1965. 80-acre rural campus located in a small town in southern New Hampshire, 15 miles southeast of Manchester and one hour from Boston.
Academic Character NEASC accreditation. 4-1-4 system. Terminal and transfer programs offered in business administration, liberal arts, professional photography, photojournalism, journalism, social work, gerontology, and child welfare. Photography concentration. Courses offered in liberal arts & sciences. Distributive requirements. Independent & directed study, honors seminar, winter term projects Photography lab & studio. Continuing education program for adults. Summer Elderhostel program. Over 20,000-volume library with children's literature collection and A-V resources.
Financial CEEB CSS. College scholarships, grants, state scholarships; PELL, SEOG, NDSL, GSL, CWS. File FAF by March 15. Application deadline April 15.
Admissions High school graduation or equivalent required. Interview and tour strongly recommended. SAT or ACT recommended. $20 application fee. Rolling admissions. $100 tuition and $200 room (for boarders) deposits required on acceptance of admissions offer (April 15). Admission deferral possible. Transfers accepted. Advanced placement credit possible. Non-high school graduates over 25 may be accepted.
Student Life Student Association. Student Center. Students must live at home or on campus. 2 men's and 2 women's dorms. Cafeteria. Liquor, drugs, and narcotics prohibited. Financial aid students may not have cars on campus. Regular class attendance expected. Honor code. Intramural and recreational sports. Student body composition: 10% minority.

NEW JERSEY (NJ)

[1] ASSUMPTION COLLEGE FOR SISTERS
Mendham 07945

[J1] ATLANTIC COMMUNITY COLLEGE
Mays Landing 08330

[J1] BERGEN COMMUNITY COLLEGE
400 Paramus Road, Paramus 07652

[J2] BERKELEY SCHOOL
Drawer F, Little Falls 07424

[1] BLOOMFIELD COLLEGE
Bloomfield 07003, (201) 748-9000
Vice President of Admissions: Nancy M. Wolcott

- **Undergraduates: 394m, 680w; 1,898 total (including evening & part-time)**
- **Tuition (1982/83): $4,350**
- **Room & Board: $2,380; Fees: $140**
- **Degrees offered: BA, BS**
- **Mean SAT 370v, 380m**
- **Student-faculty ratio: 11 to 1**

A private college affiliated with the United Presbyterian Church, established in 1868. 13-acre suburban campus located in Bloomfield, 15 miles from New York City. Served by rail and bus.
Academic Character MSACS accreditation. 4-1-4 system, 1 3-week and 2 5-week summer terms. Majors offered in accounting, biology, business administration, chemistry, economics, English, fine arts, French, history, nursing, philosophy, political science, psychology, religion, sociology, and Spanish. Self-designed majors. Africana studies. Distributive requirements.

Independent study. Honors program. Pass/fail. Internships. Preprofessional programs in law, medicine, ministry. Pre-chiropractic program with New York Chiropractic College. ROTC at Seton Hall. 86,500-volume library.
Financial CEEB CSS. College scholarships, loans, athletic and academic scholarships; PELL, SEOG, NDSL, NSL, CWS, work grants.
Admissions High school graduation with 15 units required. GED accepted. Interview encouraged. SAT or ACT required. $20 application fee. Rolling admissions; suggest applying in fall. $100 tuition and $50 room deposits required on acceptance of offer of admission. *Early Admission* Program. Admission deferral possible. Transfers accepted. Credit possible for CEEB AP and CLEP exams. Upward Bound program.
Student Life Student government. Newspaper, yearbook. Music, drama clubs. Black Student Union. Women's Community Center. Academic, service, and special interest groups. 3 fraternities with houses, 1 sorority, and 1 coed fraternity. 15% of men join fraternities. Coed and single-sex dorms. No married-student housing. 33% of students live on campus. Hazing prohibited. 5 intercollegiate sports; intramurals. NAIA, Central Atlantic College Conference. Student body composition: 0.5% Asian, 35.5% Black, 1% Hispanic, 63% White. 10% from out of state.

[J1] BROOKDALE COMMUNITY COLLEGE
765 Newman Springs Road, Lincroft 07738

[J1] BURLINGTON COUNTY COLLEGE
Pemberton-Browns Mills Road, Pemberton 08068

[1] CALDWELL COLLEGE
Caldwell 07006, (201) 228-4424

- **Enrollment: 455w; 766 total (including part-time)**
- **Tuition (1982/83): $115 per credit**
- **Room & Board: $2,250**
- **Degrees offered: BA, BS, BFA**
- **Mean SAT 435v, 440m**

A private Roman Catholic liberal arts college for women, established in 1939 and operated by the Sisters of Saint Dominic. Campus is in a suburban area northwest of Newark.
Academic Character MSACS accreditation. Semester system. Majors offered in art, biology, business, chemistry, early childhood education, elementary education, English, history, mathematics, music, social studies, Spanish, psychology, sociology, medical technology. Courses in library science, secondary education. Preprofessional programs in law, medicine. 99,200-volume library.
Financial Financial aid program available.
Admissions SAT required. Rolling admissions. *Early Admission* and *Early Decision* programs. Admission deferral possible. Advanced placement credit possible.
Student Life Sororities. Dormitory and dining hall. Student body composition: 11% minority.

[J1] CAMDEN COUNTY COLLEGE
PO Box 200, Blackwood 08012

[J1 & 1] CENTENARY COLLEGE
Hackettstown 07840, (201) 852-1400
Director of Admissions: Cynthia Rowan

- **Undergraduates: 681w; 700 total (including part-time)**
- **Tuition (1982/83): $4,000**
- **Room & Board: $3,250; Fees: $105**
- **Degrees offered: BA, BS, BFA, AA, AS**
- **Student-faculty ratio: 12 to 1**

A private women's college established in 1867. Campus in Hackettstown, 34 miles from New York City.
Academic Character MSACS accreditation. Semester system. Majors offered in art & design, business/stable management, business administration/management, communications, computer technology, dance, education, equine studies, fashion design, fashion merchandising/retailing, individualized studies, interior design, journalism, liberal arts, office administration, and performing & visual arts. Self-designed majors. Independent study. Pass/fail. Internships. Credit for employment, extracurricular activities. Study abroad for equine studies majors. Elementary and special education certification. 47,500-volume library.
Financial CEEB CSS. College scholarships, state scholarships, Tuition Aid Grants; PELL, SEOG, NDSL, GSL, CWS, college work program.
Admissions High school graduation required. Interview encouraged; required for equine studies majors. $20 application fee. Rolling admissions. $100 tuition and $50 room deposits required on acceptance of offer of admission. *Early Admission* Program. Admission deferral possible. Transfers accepted. Credit possible for CEEB AP and CLEP exams. Developmental Studies Program.
Student Life Publications. Drama, dance groups. Special interest organizations. Freshmen and sophomores must live at home or on campus. 80% of students live on campus. 8 intercollegiate sports. Student body composition: 15% Black, 85% White. 40% from out of state.

[J1] CUMBERLAND COUNTY COLLEGE
PO Box 517, Vineland 08360

[1] DON BOSCO COLLEGE
Newton 07860

[1] DREW UNIVERSITY
Madison 07940, (201) 377-3000
Director of Admissions: Daniel R. Boyer

- **Undergraduates: 615m, 850w; 1,578 total (including graduates)**
- **Tuition (1982/83): $6,430**
- **Room & Board: $2,380; Fees: $220**
- **Degree offered: BA**
- **Mean SAT 523v, 536m**
- **Student-faculty ratio: 15 to 1**

A private university established in 1866. 186-acre suburban-rural campus located in Madison, 27 miles from New York City. Served by train. Airport and bus station in New York City.
Academic Character MSACS accreditation. 4-1-4 system, 6-week summer term. Majors offered in anthropology, art, behavioral science, biology, botany, chemistry, classics, economics, English, French, German, history, mathematics, music, philosophy, physics, political science, psychobiology, psychology, religion, Russian, Russian studies, sociology, Spanish, theatre arts, zoology. Special, double, self-designed majors. Distributives and senior comprehensive project required. Graduate and professional degrees granted. Independent study. Honors program. Phi Beta Kappa. Cooperative work/study, pass/fail, internships. 3-2 program in engineering and technology with Georgia Tech, Washington U. 5-year forestry, environmental management program with Duke. Study abroad. Marine biology semester. Washington, London, Brussels, UN semesters. New York art semester. Elementary and secondary education certification with College of St. Elizabeth. Computer center, language lab, instructional services center. 440,000-volume library.
Financial CEEB CSS. University scholarships, loans, Methodist scholarships and loans, payment plans; PELL, SEOG, NDSL, CWS. Application deadline March 1.
Admissions High school graduation with 16 units required. Interview encouraged. SAT or ACT required. $20 application fee. Application deadline March 1. $300 deposit required on acceptance of offer of admission. *Early Decision, Early Admission* programs. Admission deferral possible. Transfers accepted. Credit possible for CEEB AP and CLEP exams. EOF Program.
Student Life Student government. Newspaper, magazine, yearbook, radio station. Music, debate, drama groups. Women's Resource Center. Minority, international students' organizations. Religious, honorary, special interest groups. Students must live at home or on campus. Coed and single-sex dorms. No married-student housing. 90% of students live on campus. Only seniors and commuters may have cars. 7 intercollegiate sports for men, 6 for women; intramural and club sports. AIAW, ECAC, NCAA, Mid-Atlantic Conference. Student body composition: 1.4% Asian, 4.5% Black, 1.5% Foreign, 2.7% Hispanic, 89.8% White, 1.9% Other. 50% from out of state.

[J1] ESSEX COUNTY COLLEGE
303 University Avenue, Newark 07102

[1] FAIRLEIGH DICKINSON UNIVERSITY
Rutherford 07070, (201) 460-5181
Dean of University Admissions, Financial Aid & Enrollment Services: Thomas Heaton

- **Enrollment: 3,520m, 3,055w; 11,158 total (including part-time)**
- **Tuition (1982/83): $4,576**
- **Room & Board: $2,633; Fees: $200-$250**
- **Degrees offered: BA, BS, AA, AS**
- **Student-faculty ratio: 14 to 1**

A private university established in 1942 with 3 undergraduate campuses. 15-acre Rutherford campus is 9 miles from Manhattan. 115-acre Teaneck campus is 5 miles from New York. 187-acre Florham-Madison campus is 35 miles from New York City and served by rail. Airport and bus station in New York City.
Academic Character MSACS and professional accreditation. Semester system, 2 6-week summer terms. 27 majors offered by the College of Arts & Sciences, 5 by the College of Business Administration, 10 by the College of Education, 17 by the College of Science & Engineering, and majors in dentistry and recreation & leisure studies. Not all majors offered on all campuses. Double majors. Graduate and professional degrees granted. Independent study. Honors program. Pass/fail. Credit by exam. 3-4 BS/DMD program. Preprofessional programs in dentistry, law, medicine, veterinary medicine, medical technology. Study abroad. Elementary and secondary education certification. ROTC nearby. Psychological Research Center, West Indies Laboratory, language labs. Libraries of 243,000 volumes (Teaneck), 161,000 volumes (Rutherford), 146,000 volumes (Madison).
Financial CEEB CSS. University scholarships and loans, Family Plan, payment plan; PELL, SEOG, NSS, NDSL, GSL, NSL, CWS. Application deadlines April 15 (FAF), April 1 (loans).
Admissions High school graduation with 16 units required. Interview encouraged. SAT required; ACH recommended. $20 application fee. Rolling admissions; suggest applying by March 1. Application deadline February 1 for dental hygiene program. $100 tuition and $50 room deposits required on acceptance of offer of admission. *Early Decision, Early Admission, Concurrent Enrollment* programs. Admission deferral possible. Transfers accepted. Credit possible for CEEB AP and CLEP exams; university has own advanced placement program.
Student Life Student government. Newspaper, magazines, yearbook, radio and TV stations. Music, debate, drama groups. Service and special interest organizations. Social fraternities and sororities. Coed dorms. 35% of undergraduates live on campus at Rutherford, 50% at Madison, 40% at Teaneck. 1 semester of phys ed required for liberal arts freshmen. 11 intercollegiate sports for men, 11 for women; intramural and club sports. AIAW, ECAC, NCAA, NIWFA, IHSA. Student body composition: 13% minority. 15% of students from out of state.

■[J1] EDWARD WILLIAMS COLLEGE
150 Kotte Place, Hackensack 07601
Acting Dean: Kenneth T. Vehrkens

- **Enrollment: 700 men & women**
- **Tuition (1982/83): $3,496**
- **Degree offered: AA**
- **Mean SAT 350v, 360m**

A private 2-year college affiliated with Fairleigh Dickinson University, established in 1964. Located at the Teaneck-Hackensack campus of Fairleigh Dickinson, 20 minutes from New York City.
Academic Character MSACS accreditation. 2-year program in liberal arts. Courses offered in business, literature, mathematics & logic, philosophy, psychology, sociology, history. Electives in accounting, business law, art, economics, communication, cultural arts, government, child development, and group dynamics. Additional courses at other Fairleigh Dickinson colleges. Distributive requirements. Independent study. Cooperative work/study. Saturday college. 9,000-volume library.
Financial College scholarships and grants, state scholarships and grants, family plan, payment plan; PELL, NDSL
Admissions High school graduation with 16 units required. GED accepted. Interview required in some cases. SAT and ACH required. Rolling admissions. Credit possible for CEEB CLEP exams.
Student Life Activities and housing shared with Fairleigh Dickinson.

[1] FELICIAN COLLEGE
Lodi 07644

[1] GEORGIAN COURT COLLEGE
Lakewood 08701, (201) 367-4400
Director of Admissions: John P. Burke

- **Undergraduates: 168m, 1,231w**
- **Tuition (1982/83): $3,100**
- **Room & Board: $2,000; Fees: $100**
- **Degrees offered: BS, BA, BSW**
- **Mean SAT 446v, 443m**
- **Student-faculty ratio: 12 to 1**

A private college affiliated with the Sisters of Mercy, established in 1908. Undergraduate school is for women; evening program is coeducational. 152-acre campus in Lakewood in central New Jersey.
Academic Character MSACS accreditation. Semester system, 2-week June intersession, 6-week summer term. Majors offered in art, biology, biochemistry, business administration, chemistry, elementary education, English, French, German, history, mathematics, music, physics, psychology, religious studies, social work, sociology, Spanish, and special education. Minors offered in some major fields. Distributives and 1 religious studies course required. MEd granted. Independent study. Field studies. Preprofessional programs in medicine, dentistry. 3-2 program in engineering with George Washington U. Study abroad. Member College Consortium for International Studies. Elementary and secondary education certification. 75,000-volume library.
Financial CEEB CSS. College scholarships, state scholarships and grants, payment plan; PELL, SEOG, NDSL, GSL, CWS, college has own work program.
Admissions High school graduation with 16 units required. Interview required. SAT required. $20 application fee. Rolling admissions. $100 deposit required on acceptance of offer of admission. *Early Decision, Early Admission* programs. Admission deferral possible. Transfers accepted. Credit possible for CEEB AP and CLEP exams.
Student Life Student government. Newspaper, magazine, yearbook. Music and drama groups. Black Women's League. Academic, honorary, service, and special interest organizations. 1 course in phys ed required. 3 intercollegiate sports; intramurals. Student body composition: 18% minority.

[1] GLASSBORO STATE COLLEGE
Glassboro 08028, (609) 445-5346
Director of Admissions: John G. Davies

- **Undergraduates: 2,629m, 3,341w; 9,558 total (including graduates)**
- **Tuition (1982/83): $1,164 (in-state), $1,668 (out-of-state)**
- **Room & Board: $2,050**
- **Degrees offered: BA, BS**
- **Mean SAT 430v, 470m**
- **Student-faculty ratio: 18 to 1**

A public college established in 1923. 180-acre campus in Glassboro, 20 miles from Philadelphia. Air, rail, and bus in Philadelphia.
Academic Character MSACS and professional accreditation. Semester system, 2 5-week summer terms. 9 majors offered by the Division of Administrative Studies, 4 by the Division of Fine & Performing Arts, 14 by the Division of Liberal Arts & Sciences, and 13 by the Division of Professional Studies. Programs in 12 additional areas. Distributive requirements. MA granted. Independent study. Cooperative work/study, pass/fail, internships. Preprofessional program in engineering. Study abroad. Early childhood, elementary, kindergarten, secondary, reading, speech correction education and teacher/librarian certification. ROTC at UPenn. Elementary school, early childhood center. Learning resource center. Animal studies center. Observatory, greenhouse. 300,000-volume library.
Financial CEEB CSS and ACT FAS. College scholarships and loans, Martin Luther King Scholars Program, Tuition Aid Grants; PELL, SEOG, NDSL, GSL, CWS, college work program. Application deadline April 30.
Admissions High school graduation with 16 units required. Portfolio required for art majors, audition for music, theatre art, and dance majors. SAT or ACT required; English ACH recommended. $10 application fee. Rolling admissions; suggest applying by January 15. $50 tuition and $50 room deposits required on acceptance of offer of admission. *Early Admission* Program. Admission deferral possible. Transfers accepted. Credit possible for CEEB AP and CLEP exams. Educational Opportunity Program.
Student Life Student government. Newspaper, magazine, yearbook. Music, dance, drama, debate groups. Puerto Rican Students in Action. Afro-American, Black culture groups. Academic, honorary, religious, service, and special interest organizations. 5 fraternities and 4 sororities. 35% of men and 40% of women join. 7 single-sex and coed dorms. No married-student housing. 30% of students live on campus. Liquor prohibited in dorms. 2 semesters of phys ed required. Several intercollegiate sports for men, 11 for women. AIAW, ECAC, NCAA, NJSCC. Student body composition: 0.5% Asian, 10% Black, 6% Hispanic, 83% White, 0.5% Other. 2% from out of state.

[J1] GLOUCESTER COUNTY COLLEGE
Sewell 08080

[J1] HUDSON COUNTY COMMUNITY COLLEGE
168 Sip Avenue, Jersey City 07306

[G1] IMMACULATE CONCEPTION SEMINARY
671 Ramapo Valley Road, Mahwah 07430

[1] JERSEY CITY STATE COLLEGE
2039 Kennedy Memorial Blvd., Jersey City 07305, (201) 547-3234
Director of Admissions: Samuel T. McGhee

- **Undergraduates: 2,317m, 2,296w; 7,511 total (including graduates)**
- **Tuition & Fees (1982/83): $34 per credit (in-state), $54 (out-of-state)**
- **Room: $1,350**
- **Degrees offered: BA, BS, BSN**
- **Mean SAT 400v, 400m**
- **Student-faculty ratio: 16 to 1**

A public college established in 1929. 17-acre urban campus in Jersey City, 15 miles from New York City. Airport and bus station nearby.
Academic Character MSACS and professional accreditation. Semester system, 3- and 6-week summer terms. Majors offered in art, biology, chemistry, computer science, economics, English, geoscience, history, mathematics, music, performing arts, philosophy, political science, psychology, sociology, Spanish, business administration, criminal justice-fire safety-security administration, early childhood education, elementary education, health sciences, media arts, nursing, and special education. Minors offered in most major fields and in 23 additional areas. Distributive requirements. MA, MS granted. Independent study. Honors program. Cooperative work/study, pass/fail, internships. Preprofessional programs in law, medicine. Elementary, secondary, and special education certification. ROTC; AFROTC at NJ Tech. 350,000-volume library with microform resources.
Financial CEEB CSS. College scholarships and loans, payment plan; PELL, SEOG, NDSL, NDEA, CWS. Preferred application deadlines June 1 (scholarships), May 1 (loans).
Admissions High school graduation with 16 units required. GED accepted. Audition required for music majors. SAT or ACT required. $10 application fee. Rolling admissions; suggest applying by May 1. $50 deposit required on acceptance of offer of admission. *Early Admission* Program. Admission deferral possible. Transfers accepted. Credit possible for CEEB AP and CLEP exams.
Student Life Student government. Newspaper, magazine, yearbook. Music and drama groups. Black Freedom Society. Women's Student Collective. Academic and special interest groups. 8 fraternities and 6 sororities without houses. Limited college housing. Coed dorm. 2% of students live on campus. Liquor restricted on campus. Class attendance required. 2 hours of phys ed required. 10 intercollegiate sports for men and women; intramurals. NJSCAC. Student body composition: 3% Asian, 21% Black, 15% Hispanic, 1% Native American, 56% White, 4% Other. 5% from out of state.

[P] KATHARINE GIBBS SCHOOL
33 Plymouth Street, Montclair 07042

[1] KEAN COLLEGE OF NEW JERSEY
Morris Avenue, Union 07083, (201) 527-2195
Director of Admissions: E. Theodore Stier

- **Undergraduates: 2,580m, 3,537w; 13,237 total (including graduates)**
- **Tuition (1982/83): $864 (in-state), $1,504 (out-of-state)**
- **Room & Board: $2,000; Fees: $170**
- **Degrees offered: BA, BS, BSN, BSW**
- **Mean SAT 410v, 420m**
- **Student-faculty ratio: 20 to 1**

A public college established in 1855. 128-acre suburban campus in Union, 12 miles from New York City. Served by air, rail, and bus.
Academic Character MSACS and professional accreditation. 4-1-4 system, 6-week summer term. 27 majors offered for the BA degree in liberal arts areas, and in education, speech & hearing, and public administration, 7 for the BS in the areas of computer science, industrial technology, management science, medical records administration, medical technology, occupational therapy, and physical therapy, and majors in nursing and social work. Distributive requirements. MA granted. Independent study. Honors program. Cooperative work/study, pass/fail. Study abroad. Nursery and elementary education certification, and certification in 19 additional areas. ROTC at Seton Hall; AFROTC at NJ Tech. 241,611-volume library.

Key to ratings **[1, 2, J1, J2, G, P, R, S]** *and list of abbreviations start on page 120*

Financial CEEB CSS and ACT FAS. State scholarships and loans; PELL, SEOG, NDSL, FISL, CWS.
Admissions High school graduation with 16 units required. SAT required; ACT may be substituted. $10 application fee. Rolling admissions; suggest applying by February 15. $50 tuition and $50 room deposits required on acceptance of offer of admission. *Early Admission* Program. Transfers accepted. Credit possible for CEEB AP and CLEP exams.
Student Life Student government. Newspaper, magazine, yearbook. Music and drama groups. Political, religious, service, and special interest groups. Fraternities and sororities. Dorms for men and women. No married-student housing. 12% of students live on campus. Liquor prohibited on campus. Class attendance required for freshmen. 12 intercollegiate sports. NCAA, New Jersey State Athletic Conference. Student body composition: 0.6% Asian, 12.6% Black, 7.1% Hispanic, 0.3% Native American, 77.8% White. 2% from out of state.

[J1] MERCER COUNTY COMMUNITY COLLEGE
Trenton 08690

[J1] MIDDLESEX COUNTY COLLEGE
Edison 08817

[1] MONMOUTH COLLEGE
West Long Branch 07764, (201) 222-6600
Director of Admissions: Robert N. Cristadoro

- **Undergraduates: 1,550m, 1,600w; 4,100 total (including graduates)**
- **Tuition (1982/83): $4,972**
- **Room & Board: $2,480; Fees: $210**
- **Degrees offered: BA, BS, BFA, BSN, BSW**
- **Mean SAT 440v, 470m**
- **Student-faculty ratio: 15 to 1**

A private college established in 1933. 125-acre campus in West Long Branch, 50 miles from New York City. Served by rail and bus.
Academic Character MSACS and professional accreditation. Semester system, 7 summer terms. 51 majors offered in the areas of business, humanities, art, education, sciences, communication, media studies, and music. Interdisciplinary study. Distributive requirements. Masters degrees granted. Independent study. Honors program. Internships, cooperative work/study. Preprofessional programs in dentistry, law, medicine, veterinary science. Study abroad. Elementary and secondary education certification. ROTC, AFROTC. Language and computer labs. 229,000-volume library.
Financial CEEB CSS. College scholarships, grants, and loans, payment plans; PELL, SEOG, NDSL, GSL, CWS. Application deadline March 1.
Admissions High school graduation with 16 units required. Interview encouraged. SAT required. $20 application fee. Rolling admissions; suggest applying early in 12th year. $100 tuition and $150 room deposits required on acceptance of offer of admission. *Early Admission, Credit in Escrow* programs. Admission deferral possible. Transfers accepted. Credit possible for CEEB AP and CLEP exams; college has own advanced placement program. Educational Opportunity Program.
Student Life Student government. Newspaper, magazine, yearbook, radio station. Music groups. Black Student Union. Academic, honorary, religious, service, and special interest groups. 6 fraternities, 3 with houses, and 4 sororities, some with houses. 15% of men and 5% of women join. Single freshmen under 21 must live at home or on campus. Coed and single-sex dorms. No married-student housing. 35% of students live on campus. 2 hours of phys ed required. 10 intercollegiate sports for men, 9 for women; intramurals. AIAW, NAIA, NCAA. Student body composition: 2% Asian, 3% Black, 2% Hispanic, 92% White, 1% Other. 11% from out of state.

[1] MONTCLAIR STATE COLLEGE
Upper Montclair 07043, (201) 893-4444
Director of Admissions: Alan Buechler

- **Undergraduates: 3,000m, 4,500w**
- **Tuition (1982/83): $1,133 (in-state), $1,733 (out-of-state)**
- **Room & Board: $3,268**
- **Degrees offered: BA, BS, BFA, BMus**
- **Student-faculty ratio: 16 to 1**

A public college established in 1908. 200-acre campus in Upper Montclair, 14 miles from New York City. Airport, rail and bus stations.
Academic Character MSACS and professional accreditation. Semester system, one 6-week and 2 2-week summer terms. 44 majors offered in the areas of allied health, social sciences, Asian studies, sciences, business, humanities, communication, dance, fine arts, home economics, industrial studies, Latin American studies, music, physical education, and transcultural studies. Minors offered in some major areas and in archaeology, paralegal studies, reading, women's studies. Distributive requirements. MA, MBA granted. Independent study. Cooperative work/study, pass/fail, internships. Study abroad. Secondary education certification. ROTC at Seton Hall; AFROTC at NJ Tech. Computer center. 311,000-volume library with microform resources.
Financial CEEB CSS. College scholarships and loans, state scholarships; PELL, SEOG, NDSL, CWS, Student Assistance Program. Application deadline February 15.
Admissions High school graduation with 16 units required. Tests, auditions, interviews required for fine arts, music, speech/theatre programs. SAT required. $10 application fee. Rolling admissions; application deadline March 1. $50 deposit required on acceptance of offer of admission. Admission deferral possible. Transfers accepted. Credit possible for CEEB AP and CLEP exams; college has own advanced placement program. Educational Opportunity Program.
Student Life Student government. Newspaper, magazine, yearbook, radio station. Music, drama, debate, groups. Black Student Cooperative Union. Latin American Student Organization. Human Relations Organization. Religious and special interest groups. Students must live at home or on campus. Coed and single-sex dorms. No married-student housing. 30% of students live on campus. 1 hour of phys ed required. 12 intercollegiate sports for men, 8 for women; intramurals. AIAW, ECAC, NCAA. Student body composition: 0.6% Asian, 4.7% Black, 6.5% Hispanic, 86.3% White. 2% from out of state.

■[1] PANZER SCHOOL OF PHYSICAL EDUCATION AND HYGIENE AT MONTCLAIR STATE COLLEGE
Upper Montclair 07043

- **Undergraduates: 123m, 150w**
- **Tuition & Fees (1981/82): $247**
- **Degree offered: BA**

A coeducational school in a suburban environment 12 miles from New York City. Originally founded in 1917 as the Newark Normal School of Physical Education and Hygiene; merged with Montclair State College in 1958.
Academic Character MSACS accreditation. Curriculum includes a broad program of general education. Summer camping and outdoor education experience included in the curriculum.
Admissions Students may enter only in September. Institutional entrance exam must be taken in January. SAT recommended.
Student Life Limited dormitory space available; rooms in private houses are available near campus. Regulation uniforms must be worn by students.

[J1] MORRIS, COUNTY COLLEGE OF
Randolph Township, Dover 07801

[P] NEW BRUNSWICK THEOLOGICAL SEMINARY
New Brunswick 08901

[P] NEW JERSEY COLLEGE OF MEDICINE AND DENTISTRY—RUTGERS MEDICAL SCHOOL
PO Box 101, Piscataway 08854

[1] NEW JERSEY INSTITUTE OF TECHNOLOGY
Newark 07102, (201) 645-5321
Director of Admissions: Neil Holtzman

- **Undergraduates: 2,964m, 340w**
- **Tuition (1982/83): $1,110 (in-state), $2,220 (out-of-state)**
- **Room & Board: $2,380; Fees: $240**
- **Degrees offered: BS, BSET, BArch**
- **Mean SAT 450v, 550m**
- **Student-faculty ratio: 14 to 1**

A public institute established in 1881. 25-acre urban campus in Newark, less than an hour from New York City. Airport, rail and bus stations.
Academic Character MSACS and professional accreditation. Semester system, 10- to 15-week summer term. Majors offered in architecture, computer science, engineering science, engineering technology, industrial administration, man & technology, surveying, and chemical, civil, electrical, industrial, and mechanical engineering. MS, DEngSci granted. Independent study. Honors program. Cooperative work/study. Cross-registration with Rutgers-Newark, Essex County College, New Jersey College of Medicine and Dentistry. ROTC, AFROTC. Computer center. 127,000-volume library.
Financial CEEB CSS. Institute scholarships, grants, and loans, payment plan; PELL, SEOG, NDSL, CWS. Scholarship application deadline March 1.
Admissions High school graduation with 16 units required. GED accepted. Interview may be required. SAT required; ACH required for some majors. $10 application fee. Rolling admissions; suggest applying by March 1. $50 deposit ($100 for out-of-state students) required on acceptance of offer of admission. *Early Admission* Program. Admission deferral possible. Transfers accepted. Credit possible for CEEB AP and CLEP exams; institute has own advanced placement program. Educational Opportunity Program.
Student Life Student government. Newspaper, magazine, yearbook. Debate, drama groups. Society of Women Engineers. Honorary, professional, and special interest groups. 13 fraternities. Coed dorms house 210 students. Cafeteria. 9% of students live on campus. Freshmen must attend class. 2 semesters of phys ed required. 19 intercollegiate sports; intramurals. NCAA. Student body composition: 7% Black, 5% Hispanic, 83% White, 5% Other. 3% from out of state.

[1 & G1] NEW JERSEY UNIVERSITY OF MEDICINE AND DENTISTRY—NEW JERSEY MEDICAL SCHOOL
100 Bergen Street, Newark 07103

[1] NORTHEASTERN BIBLE COLLEGE
Essex Fells 07021

[J1] OCEAN COUNTY COLLEGE
Toms River 08753

[J1] PASSAIC COUNTY COMMUNITY COLLEGE
College Blvd., Paterson 07509

[1] PRINCETON THEOLOGICAL SEMINARY
Princeton 08540

[1] PRINCETON UNIVERSITY
Princeton 08544, (609) 452-3060
Dean of Admissions: James W. Wickenden

- **Undergraduates: 2,747m, 1,713w; 6,000 total (including graduates)**
- **Tuition (1982/83): $8,380**
- **Room & Board: $3,150**
- **Degrees offered: BA, BSEng**
- **Mean SAT 639v, 680m**
- **Student-faculty ratio: 7 to 1**

A private university established in 1746, became coed in 1969. 2,200-acre campus in the small city of Princeton, 50 miles from New York City, 45 miles from Philadelphia. Served by rail and bus.

Academic Character MSACS and professional accreditation. Semester system. 42 majors offered in the areas of science, social science, arts & letters, and in history, philosophy, religion; 11 engineering majors. Self-designed majors. Senior comprehensive exam and thesis required. Graduate and professional degrees granted. Woodrow Wilson School of Public and International Affairs admits students in junior year. Independent study. Honors program. Phi Beta Kappa. Limited pass/fail. Study abroad. ROTC; AFROTC. Secondary education certification. Computer center, language lab. 3,000,000-volume library with microform resources.

Financial CEEB CSS. Scholarships, grants, and loans, payment plan; PELL, SEOG, NDSL, FISL, PLUS, CWS. Application deadline January 10.

Admissions High school graduation with 16 units required. SAT and 3 ACH required. $35 application fee. Application deadline January 1. *Early Decision* Program. Admission deferral possible. Transfers accepted for September admission. Credit possible for CEEB AP exams; university has own advanced placement program.

Student Life Student government. Newspaper, magazines, yearbook. Music, drama groups. Religious, service, and special interest groups. Upperclass eating clubs. Residential colleges. Freshmen and sophomores must live on campus. Coed and single-sex dorms. 98% of students live on campus. Games required for freshmen. 17 intercollegiate sports for men, 13 for women; intramurals. Student body composition: 3.2% Asian, 7.5% Black, 4.4% Hispanic, 0.3% Native American, 84.6% White. 87% from out of state.

[1] RAMAPO COLLEGE OF NEW JERSEY
Mahwah 07430, (201) 825-2800
Director of Admissions: Wayne C. Marshall

- **Undergraduates: 2,000m, 2,300w**
- **Tuition (1982/83): $1,125 (in-state), $1,725 (out-of-state)**
- **Room & Board: $2,410**
- **Degrees offered: BA, BS, BSW**
- **Mean SAT 440v, 470m**
- **Student-faculty ratio: 17 to 1**

A public college established in 1969. 350-acre suburban campus located in Mahwah, 35 miles from New York City. Served by rail and bus; airport in Newark.

Academic Character MSACS accreditation. Semester system, several summer terms. Majors offered in American/international studies, anthropology/sociology, biology, business administration, chemistry, communication arts, computer science, contemporary arts, economics, environmental science, environmental studies, fine arts, history, human ecology, literature, math, math/physics, metropolitan studies, philosophy, political science, psychology, social work, and sociology. Self-designed majors. Distributive requirements. Independent study. Honors program. Cooperative work/study, interships, field work, pass/fail. Preprofessional programs in dentistry, law, medicine, veterinary medicine. Member College Consortium for International Studies. Study abroad. Elementary education certification. Computer center, media center. 150,000-volume library with microform resources.

Financial CEEB CSS. Scholarships and loans; PELL, SEOG, NDSL, GSL, CWS. Loan application deadline May 1.

Admissions High school graduation required; 16 units recommended. GED accepted. Interview encouraged. SAT or ACT required. $10 application fee. Rolling admissions; application deadline March 15. $50 tuition and $100 room deposits required on acceptance of offer of admission. *Early Admission, Concurrent Enrollment* programs. Admission deferral possible. Transfers accepted. Credit possible for CEEB AP and CLEP exams. Educational Opportunity Program.

Student Life Student government. Newspaper, magazine, yearbook, radio station. Music and drama groups. Black Student Union. Jewish Student Union. Academic and special interest groups. Coed and single-sex dorms, barrier-free dorm. Married-student housing. 20% of students live on campus. Liquor and illegal drugs prohibited on campus. 12 intercollegiate sports for men, 9 for women; intramural and club sports. AIAW, NCAA. Student body composition: 6% Black, 4% Hispanic, 90% White. 10% from out of state.

[1] RIDER COLLEGE
PO Box 6400, Lawrenceville 08648, (609) 896-0800
Director of Admissions & Financial Aid: Earl L. Davis

- **Undergraduates: 1,586m, 1,739w; 5,699 total (including grads & part-time)**
- **Tuition (1982/83): $4,000**
- **Room & Board: $2,248; Fees: $35**
- **Degrees offered: BA, BS, BSComm, BSEd, AA**
- **Mean SAT 430v, 480m**
- **Student-faculty ratio: 17 to 1**

A private college established in 1863. 340-acre suburban campus located in Lawrenceville, 3 miles from Trenton, 60 miles from New York City. Served by bus; rail nearby.

Academic Character MSACS and professional accreditation. Semester system, 2 5-week summer terms. 9 majors offered by the School of Business Administration, 9 by the School of Education, and 26 by the School of Liberal Arts & Sciences. Intercultural program possible in conjunction with major. Minors offered. Distributive requirements; oral and written exams required for some majors. MA, MBA granted. Independent study in most majors. Honors program. Phi Beta Kappa. Internships. Preprofessional programs in dentistry, law, medicine, secondary education, and social work. Study abroad. Elementary and secondary education certification. ROTC; AFROTC at Rutgers. Computer center, language lab. 340,000-volume library.

Financial CEEB CSS and ACT FAS. College scholarships, grants-in-aid, loans, payment plans; PELL, SEOG, NDSL, GSL, CWS.

Admissions High school graduation with 16 units required. Interview encouraged. SAT or ACT required. $20 application fee. 6 application deadlines and notification dates throughout year. $200 tuition and $150 room deposits required on acceptance of offer of admission. *Early Decision* Program. Admission deferral possible. Transfers accepted. Credit possible for CEEB AP and CLEP exams. Educational Opportunity Program, Summer Trial Program.

Student Life Student government. Newspaper, magazine, yearbook, radio station. Music, debate groups. Organization of Black Collegians. Academic, religious, service, and special interest groups. 4 fraternities and 4 sororities with houses. 12% of men and 15% of women join. Coed and single-sex dorms. Language and special interest housing. No married-student housing. 66% of students live on campus. 9 intercollegiate sports for men, 4 for women, 2 coed; intramurals. AIAW, ECAC, NCAA, MASCC. Student body composition: 1% Asian, 5% Black, 2% Foreign, 1% Hispanic, 1% Native American, 90% White. 20% from out of state.

[P] RIDGEWOOD SCHOOL OF ART
83 Chestnut Street, Ridgewood 07450

[1] RUTGERS, THE STATE UNIVERSITY OF NEW JERSEY
New Brunswick 08903, (201) 932-1766

A public, coeducational university with campuses in Camden, New Brunswick, and Newark, consisting of 13 undergraduate and graduate colleges.

■[1] CAMDEN COLLEGE OF ARTS AND SCIENCES
Camden 08102, (609) 757-6104
University Director of Undergraduate Admissions: Natalie Aharonian

- **Undergraduates: 1,152m, 1,095w**
- **Tuition (1982/83): $1,330 (in-state), $2,660 (est. out-of-state)**
- **Fees: $275**
- **Degrees offered: BA, BS**
- **Student-faculty ratio: 17 to 1**

An undergraduate college of a public university, established in 1927. 16-acre campus in Camden, across the Delaware River from Philadelphia. Served by rail and bus.

Academic Character MSACS and professional accreditation. Semester system, 3 4-week summer terms. Majors offered in accounting, Afro-American studies, art, biology, business administration, chemistry, economics, English, French, general science, German, history, mathematics, music, nursing, philosophy, physics, political science, psychology, social work, sociology, Spanish, theatre arts, urban studies. Self-designed and independent majors. Minors offered in some major fields and in 11 additional areas. Distributive requirements. Independent study. Honors programs. Pass/fail. Preprofessional programs in dentistry, law, library science, medicine, veterinary medicine. 2-2 and 3-2 programs in engineering with College of Engineering. 3-1 program in medical technology. Study abroad. Elementary and secondary education certification. ROTC & NROTC at U of Pennsylvania; AFROTC at St. Joseph's. 170,000-volume library; 2,580,000 volumes in university library.

Financial CEEB CSS. Scholarships, grants, loans, state scholarships and loans, payment plan; PELL, SEOG, NSS, NDSL, NSL, CWS. Application deadline March 1.

Admissions High school graduation with 16 units required. SAT required. $15 application fee ($20 for 2 Rutgers colleges, $25 for 3). Rolling admissions; application deadline March 15. *Early Admission* Program. Admission deferral possible. Transfers accepted. Credit possible for CEEB AP exams; college has own advanced placement program. Educational Opportunity Program.

Student Life Student government. Newspaper, magazine, yearbook, radio station. Music, drama, debate, groups. Academic, honorary, religious, service, and special interest organizations. 4 fraternities and 2 sororities. No college housing. 9 intercollegiate sports for men, 4 for women. AIAW, NCAA. Student body composition: 1% Asian, 12% Black, 2% Hispanic, 84% White, 1% Other. 2% from out of state.

■[1] COLLEGE OF ENGINEERING
New Brunswick 08903, (201) 932-3770
University Director of Undergraduate Admissions: Natalie Aharonian

- **Undergraduates: 2,155m, 457w**
- **Tuition (1982/83): $1,330 (in-state), $2,660 (out-of-state)**
- **Room & Board: $2,140; Fees: $275**
- **Degree offered: BS**
- **Student-faculty ratio: 13 to 1**

Engineering college of a public university, established in 1864. Suburban campus in the Piscataway/Brunswick area, 33 miles from New York City. Airport in Newark, bus and rail stations in New Brunswick.

Academic Character MSACS and professional accreditation. Semester system, 3 4-week summer terms. Majors offered in agricultural, applied science, ceramic, chemical, biochemical, civil, electrical, industrial, and mechanical engineering. Distributive requirements. Independent study.

Honors program. Pass/fail. Credit by exam. 3-2 BA-BS programs with other university colleges. ROTC, AFROTC. Engineering labs, computer center, language labs. 2,580,000-volume university library.
Financial CEEB CSS. University and state scholarships, grants, loans, payment plan; PELL, SEOG, NDSL, GSL, CWS. Scholarship application deadline March 1.
Admissions High school graduation with 16 units required. SAT required. $15 application fee ($20 for 2 Rutgers colleges, $25 for 3). Rolling admissions; application deadline February 1. *Early Admission* Program. Admission deferral possible. Transfers accepted. Credit possible for CEEB AP and CLEP exams; college has own advanced placement program. Educational Opportunity Program.
Student Life Student activities through university liberal arts colleges. Technical societies. Minority Engineering Educational Task Organization. Students live at liberal arts colleges. 54% of students live on campus. Sports through liberal arts colleges. 14 intercollegiate sports for men, 13 for women; intramurals. AIAW, NCAA, Eastern Eight. Student body composition: 5% Asian, 4% Black, 3% Hispanic, 83% White, 4% Other. 12% from out of state.

■[1] COLLEGE OF NURSING
Newark 07102, (201) 648-5205
University Director of Undergraduate Admissions: Natalie Aharonian

- **Undergraduates: 566 men & women (total)**
- **Tuition (1982/83): $1,110 (in-state), $2,220 (out-of-state)**
- **Fees: $177**
- **Degree offered: BS**
- **Student-faculty ratio: 6 to 1**

An undergraduate college of a public university, established in 1956. 22-acre urban campus in Newark. Served by air, rail, and bus.
Academic Character MSACS and professional accreditation. Semester system, 3 4-week summer terms. Major offered in nursing. Minors available through Newark College of Arts and Sciences. Courses in anatomy & physiology, anthropology, chemistry, history, nutrition, microbiology, nursing intervention, trends in delivery of health care. Distributive requirements. Honors program. Clinical experience integrated with course work. Learning laboratory. 2,580,000-volume university library.
Financial CEEB CSS. University and state scholarships, grants, loans; PELL, SEOG, NSS, NDSL, NSL, CWS. Application deadline March 1.
Admissions No upper age limit. High school graduation with 16 units required. GED accepted. SAT and ACH required. $15 application fee ($20 for 2 Rutgers colleges, $25 for 3). Rolling admissions; application deadline March 15. Admission deferral possible. Transfers accepted. Credit possible for CEEB AP and CLEP exams. Educational Opportunity Program.
Student Life Student government. Newspaper, yearbook, radio station. The Organization of Registered Nurses. Music groups. Political, service, religious, and special interest clubs. Housing at Newark YWCA/YMCA. Class attendance required. Uniforms required in clinical courses. 6 intercollegiate sports for men, 4 for women, 2 coed; intramural and club sports. Student body composition: 1% Asian, 18% Black, 5% Hispanic, 75% White. 2% from out of state.

■[1] COLLEGE OF PHARMACY
New Brunswick 08903, (201) 932-3770
University Director of Undergraduate Admissions: Natalie Aharonian

- **Undergraduates: 325m, 439w**
- **Tuition (1982/83): $1,330 (in-state), $2,660 (out-of-state)**
- **Room & Board: $2,140; Fees: $275**
- **Degree offered: BS**
- **Mean SAT 470v, 530m**
- **Student-faculty ratio: 13 to 1**

A five-year college of pharmacy that is part of a public university, founded in 1897. Suburban campus in Piscataway, near New Brunswick, 33 miles from New York City. Served by bus and rail; airport in Newark.
Academic Character MSACS and professional accreditation. Semester system, 3 4-week summer terms. 5-year major in pharmacy offered. Distributive requirements. Honors program. Pass/fail. Internships. Cross-registration with other university colleges. ROTC, AFROTC. Museum, computer center, TV studio, language lab. 2,580,000-volume university library.
Financial CEEB CSS. University and state scholarships, grants, loans; PELL, SEOG, NSS, GSL, NDSL, NSL, CWS. Application deadline March 1.
Admissions High school graduation with 16 units required. SAT required. $15 application fee ($20 for 2 Rutgers colleges, $25 for 3). Rolling admissions; application deadline February 1. *Early Admission* Program. Admission deferral possible. Transfers accepted. Credit possible for CEEB AP and CLEP exams. Educational Opportunity Program.
Student Life Student activities through university liberal arts colleges. Housing at liberal arts colleges. 53% of students live on campus. 14 intercollegiate sports for men, 13 for women; intramurals. NCAA, AIAW, Eastern Eight. Student body composition: 4% Asian, 3% Black, 5% Hispanic, 86% White, 1% Other. 9% from out of state.

■[1] COOK COLLEGE
New Brunswick 08903, (201) 932-3770
University Director of Undergraduate Admissions: Natalie Aharonian

- **Undergraduates: 1,425m, 1,253w**
- **Tuition (1982/83): $1,330 (in-state), $2,660 (out-of-state)**
- **Room & Board: $2,140; Fees: $275**
- **Degrees offered: BA, BS**
- **Mean SAT 510v, 570m**
- **Student-faculty ratio: 17 to 1**

An undergraduate college of a public university, established in 1973. Suburban campus at edge of New Brunswick, 33 miles from New York City. Served by rail and bus.
Academic Character MSACS and professional accreditation. Semester system, 3 4-week summer terms. Majors offered in agricultural engineering, agricultural sciences, animal science, biology, chemistry, computer science, earth/atmospheric sciences, environmental/business economics, environmental planning/design, environmental studies, food science, geography, geology, home economics, human ecology, natural resources management, physical education, plant science, public health, vocational-technical education, and chemistry, food & nutrition. Self-designed majors. Distributive requirements. Independent study. Honors program. Cooperative work/study, pass/fail, internships. Preprofessional programs in dentistry, law, medicine, veterinary medicine. Study abroad. Secondary, agricultural science, and professional-occupational education certification. ROTC, AFROTC. 2,580,000-volume university library.
Financial CEEB CSS. University and state scholarships, grants, loans, payment plan; PELL, SEOG, NDSL, GSL, CWS. Scholarship application deadline March 1.
Admissions High school graduation with 16 units required. SAT required. $15 application fee ($20 for 2 Rutgers colleges, $25 for 3). Rolling admissions; application deadline February 1. *Early Decision* and *Early Admission* programs. Admission deferral possible. Transfers accepted. Credit possible for CEEB AP exams; college has own advanced placement program. Educational Opportunity Program.
Student Life Student government. Newspaper, yearbook, radio station. Music, debate groups. Academic, professional societies. Religious, service, and special interest groups. 27 fraternities and 10 sororities; all have houses at other colleges. Coed and single-sex dorms and apartments. Married-student housing. Co-op dorm for men. 65% of students live on campus. Freshmen and sophomores living on campus may not have cars. 14 intercollegiate sports for men, 13 for women; intramural and club sports. AIAW, NCAA, Eastern Eight. Student body composition: 3% Asian, 8% Black, 3% Hispanic, 85% White, 1% Other. 12% from out of state.

■[1] DOUGLASS COLLEGE
New Brunswick 08903, (201) 932-3770
University Director of Undergraduate Admissions: Natalie Aharonian

- **Undergraduates: 3,492w**
- **Tuition (1982/83): $1,330 (in-state), $2,660 (out-of-state)**
- **Room & Board: $2,140**
- **Degrees offered: BA, BS**
- **Mean SAT 490v, 510m**
- **Student-faculty ratio: 16 to 1**

An undergraduate women's college of a public university, established in 1918. Suburban campus on the edge of New Brunswick, 33 miles from New York City. Served by rail and bus.
Academic Character MSACS and professional accreditation. Semester system, 3 4-week summer terms. 60 majors offered in the areas of cultural & area studies, political & social sciences, arts, archaeology, sciences, business, languages & literature, ecology, humanities, communication, physical education, and mathematics. Special programs in education. Distributive requirements. Independent study. Honors program, Phi Beta Kappa. Pass/fail, internships. Preprofessional programs in dentistry, law, medicine. 2-3 program with College of Engineering. 3-1 program in medical technology. Students may take courses at other New Brunswick colleges. Study abroad. ROTC, AFROTC. Several education certification programs. 2,580,000-volume university library.
Financial CEEB CSS. College and state scholarships, grants, loans; PELL, SEOG, NDSL, GSL, CWS. FAF deadline March 1.
Admissions High school graduation with 16 units required. SAT required. $15 application fee ($20 for 2 Rutgers colleges, $25 for 3). Rolling admissions; application deadline February 1. *Early Decision* and *Early Admission* programs. Admission deferral possible. Transfers accepted. Credit possible for CEEB AP and CLEP exams; college has own advanced placement program. Educational Opportunity Program.
Student Life Student government. Newspaper, magazine, yearbook, radio station. Music and drama groups. Black Students Congress. United Puerto Rican Students. Sophia group for women out of school 4 or more years. Several academic, religious, service, political, and special interest groups. Sororities at other university colleges. Freshmen must live at home or on campus. Language houses. Afro-American, Puerto Rican houses. 62% of students live on campus. Only commuters and seniors may have cars on campus. 13 intercollegiate sports; intramurals. AIAW, NCAA. Student body composition: 2% Asian, 10% Black, 3% Hispanic, 83% White, 1% Other. 6% from out of state.

■[1] LIVINGSTON COLLEGE
New Brunswick 08903, (201) 932-3770
University Director of Undergraduate Admissions: Natalie Aharonian

- **Undergraduates: 1,962m, 1,275w**
- **Tuition (1982/83): $1,330 (in-state), $2,660 (out-of-state)**
- **Room & Board: $2,140; Fees: $275**
- **Degrees offered: BA, BS**
- **Mean SAT 450v, 500m**
- **Student-faculty ratio: 15 to 1**

A liberal arts college of a public university, established in 1969. Modern campus in Piscataway, near New Brunswick, 33 miles from New York City. Served by rail and bus.
Academic Character MSACS and professional accreditation. Semester system, 3 4-week summer terms. 63 majors offered in the areas of business, area & cultural studies, political & social sciences, arts, sciences, urban & community studies, languages & literatures, ecology, humanities, communications, and health. Self-designed majors. Distributive requirements. Independent study. Honors program. Internships. Preprofessional programs in law, medicine, dentistry. 2-3 program with

College of Engineering. 3-1 program in medical technology. Elementary, secondary, and preschool education certification. ROTC, AFROTC. 2,580,000-volume university library.
Financial CEEB CSS. College and state scholarships, grants, loans; PELL, SEOG, NDSL, GSL, CWS. FAF deadline March 1.
Admissions High school graduation with 16 units required. Interview encouraged. SAT required. $15 application fee ($20 for 2 Rutgers colleges, $25 for 3). Rolling admissions; application deadline February 1. *Early Decision* and *Early Admission* programs. Admission deferral possible. Transfers accepted. Credit possible for CEEB AP and CLEP exams, and for life/work experience. College has own advanced placement program. Educational Opportunity Program.
Student Life Student government. Newspaper, yearbook, radio station. Music groups. Academic, religious, service, and special interest groups. Coed and single-sex dorms. Special interest housing. 52% of students live on campus. 14 intercollegiate sports for men, 13 for women; several intramural and club sports. AIAW, AAU, NCAA, AAHPER, Eastern Eight. Student body composition: 2% Asian, 24% Black, 5% Hispanic, 67% White, 1% Other. 12% from out of state.

■[1] MASON GROSS SCHOOL OF THE ARTS
New Brunswick 08903, (201) 932-3770
University Director of Undergraduate Admissions: Natalie Aharonian

- **Undergraduates: 104m, 166w**
- **Tuition (1982/83): $1,330 (in-state), $2,660 (out-of-state)**
- **Room & Board: $1,140; Fees: $275**
- **Degree offered: BFA**
- **Mean SAT 480v, 490m**
- **Student-faculty ratio: 3 to 1**

A professional school of a public university, established in 1976. Suburban campus in New Brunswick, 33 miles from New York City. Served by rail and bus.
Academic Character MSACS accreditation. Semester system, 3 4-week summer terms. Majors offered in dance, theatre arts (acting, design, production), and visual arts (drawing, graphics, painting, sculpture). Self-designed majors. Independent study. Honors program. Pass/fail. Cross-registration with other university colleges. ROTC, AFROTC. Arts computer center, language lab, museum, TV studio. 2,580,000-volume university library.
Financial CEEB CSS. College scholarships, grants, and loans, state scholarships & loans; PELL, SEOG, NDSL, GSL, CWS. Application deadline March 1.
Admissions High school graduation with 16 units required. Portfolio required for visual arts majors; audition for theatre, dance majors. SAT required. $15 application fee ($20 for 2 Rutgers colleges, $25 for 3). Rolling admissions; application deadline March 15. *Early Decision* and *Early Admission* programs. Admission deferral possible. Transfers accepted. Credit possible for CEEB AP and CLEP exams. Educational Opportunity Program.
Student Life Student government. Student activities and housing at liberal arts colleges. 14 intercollegiate sports for men, 13 for women; intramurals. Sports through liberal arts colleges. AIAW, NCAA, Eastern Eight. Student body composition: 6% Black, 2% Hispanic, 1% Native American, 90% White. 7% from out of state.

■[1] NEWARK COLLEGE OF ARTS AND SCIENCES
Newark 07102, (201) 648-5205
University Director of Undergraduate Admissions: Natalie Aharonian

- **Undergraduates: 1,888m, 1,423w**
- **Tuition (1982/83): $1,330 (in-state), $2,660 (out-of-state)**
- **Fees: $275**
- **Degrees offered: BA, BS**
- **Mean SAT 460v, 510m**
- **Student-faculty ratio: 18 to 1**

An undergraduate college of a public university, became part of the university in 1946. 22-acre urban campus in Newark, the largest business community in the state. Served by rail and bus.
Academic Character MSACS and professional accreditation. Semester system, 3 4-week summer terms. 37 majors offered in the areas of business, cultural & area studies, social sciences, arts, natural sciences, and humanities. Self-designed majors. Minors offered in some major fields and in women's studies. Distributive requirements. Independent study. Honors program. Phi Beta Kappa. Pass/fail. Internships. Preprofessional programs in dentistry, law, medicine. 3-2 program with College of Engineering. Cross-registration with NJ Tech. Study abroad. Elementary and secondary education certification. AFROTC at NJ Tech. Computer center. 2,580,000-volume university library.
Financial CEEB CSS. College and state scholarships and grants, college loans; PELL, SEOG, NDSL, GSL, CWS. Application deadline March 1.
Admissions High school graduation with 16 units required. SAT required. $15 application fee ($20 for 2 Rutgers colleges, $25 for 3). Rolling admissions; application deadline March 15. *Early Decision* and *Early Admission* programs. Admission deferral possible. Transfers accepted. Credit possible for CEEB AP and CLEP exams. Educational Opportunity Program.
Student Life Newspaper, magazine, yearbook, radio station. Music and drama groups. Volunteer program. Academic, honorary, religious, service, and special interest groups. No college housing. 8 intercollegiate sports for men and women. AIAW, NCAA. Student body composition: 2% Asian, 16% Black, 12% Hispanic, 69% White, 1% Other. 2% from out of state.

■[1] RUTGERS COLLEGE
New Brunswick 08903, (201) 932-3770
University Director of Undergraduate Admissions: Natalie Aharonian

- **Undergraduates: 4,442m, 3,665w**
- **Tuition (1982/83): $1,330 (in-state), $2,660 (out-of-state)**
- **Room & Board: $2,140; Fees: $275**
- **Degrees offered: BA, BS**
- **Mean SAT 500v, 560m**
- **Student-faculty ratio: 17 to 1**

An undergraduate college of a public university, established in 1766, became coed in 1972. Campus in and around New Brunswick, 33 miles from New York City. Served by rail and bus.
Academic Character MSACS and professional accreditation. Semester system, 3 4-week summer terms. 56 majors offered in the areas of cultural & area studies, social & political sciences, arts, natural sciences, business, languages & literatures, humanities, and communication. Self-designed majors. Minor required; double major and additional minors encouraged. Distributive requirements. Independent study. Honors programs, Phi Beta Kappa. Pass/fail. Preprofessional programs in dentistry, law, library & information studies, medicine, social work. 2-3 engineering program with College of Engineering. National Student Exchange. Study abroad. Elementary, secondary, and special education certification. ROTC, AFROTC. Language lab. 2,580,000-volume university library.
Financial CEEB CSS. College and state scholarships, grants, loans; PELL, SEOG, NDSL, GSL, CWS. FAF deadline March 1.
Admissions High school graduation with 16 units required. SAT required. $15 application fee ($20 for 2 Rutgers colleges, $25 for 3). Rolling admissions; application deadline February 1. *Early Decision* and *Early Admission* programs. Admission deferral possible. Transfers accepted. Credit possible for CEEB AP and CLEP exams; college has own advanced placement program. Educational Opportunity Program.
Student Life Student government. Newspaper, magazine, yearbook, radio station. Music, drama, debate groups. Honorary, academic, professional, religious, and special interest groups. 27 fraternities and 10 sororities. 10% of students join. Coed and single-sex dorms. Special interest housing. Married-student housing. 54% of students live on campus. 14 intercollegiate sports for men, 13 for women; intramural and club sports. NCAA, AIAW, Eastern Eight. Student body composition: 3% Asian, 8% Black, 4% Hispanic, 83% White, 1% Other. 8% from out of state.

■[1] UNIVERSITY COLLEGE—CAMDEN
Camden 08102, (609) 757-6057
Coordinator of Admissions: Joanne Robinson

- **Enrollment: 1,076 men & women**
- **Tuition (1982/83): $47 per credit hour (in-state), $94 (out-of-state)**
- **Fees: $40-$50**
- **Degrees offered: BA, BS**

An evening college of Rutgers University.
Academic Character MSACS accreditation. Semester system. Majors offered in computer science, English, history, political science, psychology, social work. Distributive requirements. Independent study. Honors program. Pass/fail. Credit by exam. Vocational-technical education program. Cross-registration with other Rutgers University colleges. Secondary education certification. 2,580,000-volume university library with microform resources.
Financial CEEB CSS. College scholarships and loans, state grants and loans; PELL, SEOG, NDSL, GSL, CWS. Application deadline March 1.
Admissions High school graduation with 16 units required. GED accepted. $10 application fee. Rolling admissions; application deadline August 1. Transfers accepted. Credit possible for CEEB CLEP exams.
Student Life Student government. Honorary societies. No college housing. Student body composition: 25% minority.

■[1] UNIVERSITY COLLEGE—NEWARK
Newark 07102

- **Enrollment: 1,997 men & women**
- **Degrees offered: BA, BS**

An evening college of Rutgers University.
Academic Character MSACS accreditation. Semester system. Programs offered in accountancy, criminal justice, economics, English, history, labor studies management, marketing, mathematics, philosophy, political science, psychology, social welfare, sociology, Spanish, urban studies. Vocational technical education program. Remedial mathematics and English programs. Cross-registration with other Rutgers University colleges. University library of 2,580,000 volumes with microform resources.
Financial CEEB CSS. College scholarships and loans, state grants and loans; PELL, SEOG, NDSL, GSL, CWS. Application deadline March 1.
Admissions Entrance requirements are flexible. Application deadline is July 30.
Student Life No college housing. Student body composition: 65% minority.

■[1] UNIVERSITY COLLEGE—NEW BRUNSWICK
New Brunswick 08903

- **Enrollment: 3,400 men & women**
- **Degrees offered: BA, BS**

An evening college of Rutgers University.
Academic Character MSACS accreditation. Semester system. Programs offered in accounting, chemistry, computer science, criminal justice, economics, English, French, German, history, home economics, labor studies, management, marketing, mathematics, philosophy, political science, psychology, sociology, statistics, vocational-technical education. Remedial mathematics and English programs. Cross-registration with other Rutgers University colleges. Education certification in several areas. University library of 2,580,000 volumes with microform resources.
Financial CEEB CSS. College scholarships and loans, state grants and loans; PELL, SEOG, NDSL, GSL, CWS. Application deadline March 1.
Admissions Flexible entrance requirements. Rolling admissions; application deadline July 30. *Early Admission* Program. Admission deferral possible. Transfers accepted. Advanced placement credit possible.
Student Life No college housing. Student body composition: 13% minority.

[1] SAINT ELIZABETH, COLLEGE OF
Convent Station 07961, (201) 539-1600
Director of Admissions: Sister Maureen Sullivan

- **Undergraduates: 517w**
- **Tuition (1982/83): $4,000**
- **Room & Board: $2,200; Fees: $200**
- **Degrees offered: BA, BS, BSN**
- **Student-faculty ratio: 10 to 1**

A private Roman Catholic college for women conducted by the Sisters of Charity, established in 1899. 400-acre campus in Convent Station, 35 miles from New York City. Served by rail; airport and bus 2 miles away in Morristown.
Academic Character MSACS accreditation. Semester system, 4-week summer term. Majors offered in art, biology, business administration, chemistry, economics, education, English, French, gerontology, history, home economics, mathematics, music, nursing, philosophy, psychology, sociology, and Spanish. Double majors. Minors offered. Distributive requirements. Independent study. Honors program. Pass/fail. Internships. Cross-registration with Drew and Fairleigh Dickinson. Exchange program with 6 Seton Colleges. Study abroad. Elementary, secondary, and special education certification. Shakespeare garden, Greek theatre, educational resource center. 151,000-volume library with microform resources.
Financial CEEB CSS. College scholarships, grants, and loans, payment plan; PELL, SEOG, NDSL, GSL, CWS. Scholarship application deadline February 15.
Admissions High school graduation with 16 units required. GED accepted. Interview encouraged. SAT required. $15 application fee. Rolling admissions; suggest applying by February 1. $100 deposit required on acceptance of offer of admission. *Early Decision, Early Admission, Concurrent Enrollment* programs. Admission deferral possible. Transfers accepted. Credit possible for CEEB AP and CLEP exams; college has own advanced placement program. Educational Opportunity Program.
Student Life Student government. Newspaper, magazine, yearbook. Glee club. International Intercultural Club. Black, Hispanic student organizations. Religious, service, academic, and special interest groups. Students must live at home or on campus. Women's dorms. No married-student housing. 65% of students live on campus. 2 semesters of phys ed required. 6 intercollegiate sports; intramurals. Student body composition: 9% Black, 7% Hispanic, 66% White, 18% Other. 10% from out of state.

[1] SAINT PETER'S COLLEGE
2641 Kennedy Blvd., Jersey City 07306
Director of Admissions: Robert J. Nilan

- **Undergraduates: 1,402m, 1,259w**
- **Tuition (1982/83): $3,828**
- **Fees: $219**
- **Degrees offered: BA, BS**
- **Mean SAT 390v, 410m**
- **Student-faculty ratio: 17 to 1**

A private Catholic college controlled by the Society of Jesus (Jesuits). Established in 1872, became coed in 1966. 8-acre urban campus in Jersey City, ½ hour from Manhattan and Newark. Served by bus; airport and rail station in Newark.
Academic Character MSACS accreditation. Semester system, 2 5-week summer terms. 30 majors offered in the areas of humanities, theology, natural sciences, social sciences, business, and health. Special majors. Distributives and 2 semesters of religion required. Independent study. Honors program. Cooperative work/study, pass/fail, internships. Preprofessional programs in dentistry, law, medicine, veterinary medicine. Member Georgetown University International Student Exchange; study abroad in 12 countries. Elementary and secondary education certification. ROTC; AFROTC nearby. Computer center, language lab, museum. 240,000-volume library.
Financial CEEB CSS. College scholarships, grants, and loans, state grants and loans; PELL, SEOG, NDSL, CWS. Application deadline March 1.
Admissions High school graduation with 16 units required. GED accepted. Interview encouraged. SAT recommended. $15 application fee. Rolling admissions; suggest applying by March 1. *Early Decision, Early Admission, Concurrent Enrollment* programs. Admission deferral possible. Transfers accepted. Credit possible for CEEB AP, CLEP, and ACT PEP exams, and for life/work experience.
Student Life Student government. Newspaper, magazine. Music, drama groups. Black Student Association. Hispanic Cultural Society. Academic, service, and special interest groups. 4 fraternities and 3 sororities. 5% of men and 8% of women join. No college housing. Liquor permitted on campus only with permission. 14 intercollegiate sports; intramurals. AIAW, ECAC, NCAA. Student body composition: 10% Black, 15% Hispanic, 70% White, 5% Other. 10% from out of state.

■[1] ST. PETER'S COLLEGE (ENGLEWOOD CLIFFS CAMPUS)
Englewood Cliffs 07632

[J1] SALEM COMMUNITY COLLEGE
PO Box 551, Penns Grove 08069

[1] SETON HALL UNIVERSITY
South Orange 07079, (201) 761-9332
Director of Admissions: Lee W. Cooke

- **Undergraduates: 2,756m, 2,937w; 10,248 total (including grads & part-time)**
- **Tuition (1982/83): $4,096**
- **Room & Board: $2,550; Fees: $200**
- **Degrees offered: BA, BS, BSN, BSMed Tech**
- **Mean SAT 450v, 480m**
- **Student-faculty ratio: 17 to 1**

A private Roman Catholic university controlled by the Archdiocese of Newark, established in 1856, became coed in 1968. 56-acre campus in the village of South Orange, 14 miles from New York City. Served by bus and rail.
Academic Character MSACS and professional accreditation. Semester system, 2 4-week summer terms, 3-week May term. 39 majors offered in the areas of business, cultural studies, social & political sciences, arts, natural sciences, communication, education, health, and humanities. Distributive requirements. Religious studies required for Catholic students. Graduate and professional degrees granted. Independent study. Honors program in College of Arts and Sciences. Internships. Study abroad. Elementary, secondary, and special education certification. ROTC; AFROTC at NJ Tech. Computer center, art gallery, language lab. 325,000-volume library with microform resources.
Financial CEEB CSS. University scholarships, grants, loans, athletic & debate scholarships, state scholarships, payment plan; PELL, SEOG, NSS, NDSL, NSL, CWS. Scholarship application deadline April 15.
Admissions High school graduation with 16 units required. SAT or ACT required. $25 application fee. Rolling admissions; preferred application deadline March 1. $100 deposit required on acceptance of offer of admission. *Early Admission* Program. Admission deferral possible. Transfers accepted. Credit possible for CEEB AP and CLEP exams. Educational Opportunity Program.
Student Life Student government. Newspaper, magazine, yearbook, radio station, TV studios. Music, debate, drama groups. Black Studies Center. Puerto Rican Institute. Honorary, professional, religious, academic, and special interest organizations. 10 fraternities and 5 sororities. Coed dorms. No married-student housing. 22% of students live on campus. 11 intercollegiate sports for men, 6 for women; intramural and club sports. AIAW, ECAC, NCAA. Student body composition: 1% Asian, 13% Black, 3% Hispanic, 82% White, 1% Other. 10% from out of state.

[J1] SOMERSET COUNTY COLLEGE
Somerville 08876

[1] STEVENS INSTITUTE OF TECHNOLOGY
Hoboken 07030, (201) 420-5194
Director of Admissions: Robert H. Seavy

- **Enrollment: 1,355m, 250w**
- **Tuition (1982/83): $6,500**
- **Room & Board: $2,550; Fees: $100**
- **Degrees offered: BS, BEng**
- **Mean SAT 510v, 620m**
- **Student-faculty ratio: 11 to 1**

A private institute established in 1870. 55-acre suburban campus in Hoboken, across the Hudson River from New York City. Airport, bus and rail stations in New York City.
Academic Character MSACS and professional accreditation. Semester system, 6-week summer term. Majors offered in applied psychology, biology, chemical engineering, chemistry, civil engineering, computer science, electrical engineering, engineering, engineering physics, industrial engineering, management science, materials/metallurgical engineering, materials science, mathematics, mechanical engineering, ocean engineering, and physics. Distributive requirements. MS, MEng, PhD granted. Independent study. Honors program. Pass/fail, internships, credit by exam. Dual degree programs. Mini-graduate program. ROTC at St. Peter's; AFROTC at NJ Tech. Computer center, hydrodynamics lab, psychology lab, energy center. 190,000-volume library.
Financial CEEB CSS. Institute scholarships and loans, payment plan; PELL, SEOG, NDSL, GSL, CWS. Application deadline February 1.
Admissions High school graduation with 12 units required. Interview encouraged. SAT and 3 ACH required. $25 application fee. Rolling admissions; suggest applying late in 11th year or early in 12th. $100 tuition and $100 room deposits required on acceptance of offer of admission. *Early Decision* Program. Admission deferral possible. Transfers accepted. Credit possible for CEEB AP and CLEP exams; institute has own advanced placement program.
Student Life Student government. Newspaper, yearbook, radio station. Music and drama groups. Black Student Union, Latin American Club, Chinese Association, India Student Association. Honorary, political, religious, and special interest organizations. 10 fraternities with houses, and 1 sorority with rooms. 35% of students join. Freshmen must live at home or on campus. Single-sex dorms. Married-student housing. 80% of students live on campus. 3 hours of phys ed a week for 3 years required. 12 intercollegiate sports for men, 3 for women; intramurals. AIAW, ECAC, NCAA. Student body composition: 3.8% Asian, 2.8% Black, 5.2% Hispanic, 84% White. 40% from out of state.

[1] STOCKTON STATE COLLEGE
Pomona 08240, (609) 652-1776
Director of Admissions: Pat Hall-Miller

- **Undergraduates: 2,666m, 2,275w**
- **Tuition (1982/83): $800 (in-state), $1,515 (out-of-state)**
- **Room & Board: $2,260; Fees: $312**
- **Degrees offered: BA, BS, BSN, BSW**
- **Mean SAT 450v, 450m**
- **Student-faculty ratio: 21 to 1**

A public college established in 1969. 1,600-acre rural campus in Pomona, 12 miles from Atlantic City. Bus nearby. Airport and rail station in Philadelphia.
Academic Character MSACS and professional accreditation. Semester system, 8-week summer term. Majors offered in applied physics, biology,

biomedical communications, business studies, chemistry, criminal justice, economics, environmental studies, geology, historical studies, information & systems sciences, liberal studies, literature & language, marine science, mathematics, nursing, philosophy & religion, political science, psychology, public health, social work, sociology & anthropology, and studies in the arts. Self-designed majors. Distributive requirements. Independent study. Cooperative work/study, pass/fail, internships. Study abroad in Europe, Israel, Australia. Secondary education certification. Computer center, observatory. 180,000-volume library with microform resources.
Financial CEEB CSS. College scholarships, grants, loans, state scholarships; PELL, SEOG, NDSL, GSL, CWS. FAF deadline March 1.
Admissions High school graduation with 14 units required. GED accepted. SAT or ACT required. $10 application fee. Rolling admissions; application deadline June 1. $50 tuition and $50 room deposits required on acceptance of offer of admission. *Early Decision* and *Early Admission* programs. Admission deferral possible. Transfers accepted. Credit possible for CEEB AP and CLEP exams; college has own advanced placement program.
Student Life Student government. Newspapers, magazine. Music, film groups. Los Latinos Unidos, Unified Black Student Society, Women's Union. Academic, service, religious, political, and special interest groups. 7 fraternities and 2 sororities without houses. Coed dorms. Handicapped-student housing. 40% of students live on campus. 5 intercollegiate sports for men, 3 for women; intramurals. AIAW, ECAC, NCAA. Student body composition: 0.7% Asian, 7% Black, 0.9% Hispanic, 0.1% Native American, 91% White. 2% from out of state.

[1] THOMAS A. EDISON COLLEGE
101 West State Street, Trenton 08625

[1] TRENTON STATE COLLEGE
Hillwood Lakes, CN550, Trenton 08625, (609) 771-2131
Director of Admissions: Alfred W. Bridges

- **Undergraduates: 3,950m, 5,762w**
- **Tuition (1982/83): $1,200 (in-state), $1,800 (out-of-state)**
- **Room & Board: $2,600; Fees: $277**
- **Degrees offered: BA, BS**
- **Mean SAT 460v, 480m**
- **Student-faculty ratio: 19 to 1**

A public college established in 1855. 210-acre suburban campus in Ewing Township, 4 miles from Trenton. Airport, rail and bus stations nearby.
Academic Character MSACS and professional accreditation. Semester system, 2 6-week summer terms. 47 majors offered by the schools of Arts & Sciences and Education, and by the divisions of Business & Economics and Industrial Education & Technology. Minor encouraged. Distributive requirements. MA, MS granted. Independent study. Honors program, Phi Beta Kappa. Cooperative work/study, internships. Preprofessional programs in medicine, dentistry, pharmacy, podiatry, and optometry. National Student Exchange. New Jersey Marine Biology Consortium. Study abroad. Early childhood, elementary, and secondary education certification. ROTC; AFROTC & NROTC at Rutgers. Media center. 375,000-volume library.
Financial CEEB CSS. College scholarships and loans, state scholarships and grants, payment plans; PELL, SEOG, NSS, NDSL, GSL, NSL, CWS; college has own work program. Application deadline April 1.
Admissions High school graduation with 16 units required. State equivalency certificate accepted. Interview recommended; required for some programs. SAT or ACT required. $10 application fee. Rolling admissions, suggest applying by March 1. *Early Decision, Early Admission, Concurrent Enrollment* programs. Admission deferral possible. Transfers accepted. Credit possible for CEEB AP and CLEP exams. College has own advanced placement program. Project CHANCE.
Student Life Student government. Newspapers, magazine, yearbook, radio station. Music, drama, debate groups. Over 100 special interest groups. 15 fraternities and 13 sororities without houses. 25% of men and women join. Coed and single-sex dorms. No married-student housing. 40% of students live on campus. Boarders, except for student teachers and nursing students, may not have cars on campus. 10 intercollegiate sports for men, 11 for women; intramurals. NCAA. Student body composition: 1% Asian, 11% Black, 1% Hispanic, 87% White. 12% from out of state.

[J1] UNION COLLEGE
Cranford 07016

[1] UPSALA COLLEGE
East Orange 07019, (201) 266-7191
Director of Admissions: Barry Abrams

- **Undergraduates: 694m, 463w; 1,207 total (including graduates)**
- **Tuition (1982/83): $4,718**
- **Room & Board: $2,320-$2,740; Fees: $150**
- **Degrees offered: BA, BS**
- **Mean SAT 450v, 460m**
- **Student-faculty ratio: 16 to 1**

A private college affiliated with the Lutheran Church in America, established in 1893. 48-acre suburban campus in East Orange, 15 miles from New York City. Served by air, rail, and bus.
Academic Character MSACS accreditation. 4-1-4 system, 2 6-week and 2 1-month summer terms. Majors offered in accounting, anthropology, art, biochemistry, biology, business administration, public service, chemistry, cytotechnology, economics, English, French, German translating, history, human resources management, mathematics, multinational corporate studies, music, philosophy, physics, political science, psychology, religion, Scandinavian studies, social work, sociology, Spanish, and theatre. Self-designed majors. Distributive requirements. MS granted. Independent study. Honors program. Pass/fail. Internships. Preprofessional programs in business, dentistry, law, medicine, parish work, seminary, veterinary science. 3-2 engineering program with NJ Tech. 3-2 bachelor's-master's program in forestry and environmental science with Duke. 1-4 architecture program with NJ Tech. Study abroad. UN Semester. Preschool, elementary, and secondary education certification. ROTC at Seton Hall. Computer center. 142,872-volume library with microform resources.
Financial CEEB CSS. College scholarships and loans, Lutheran scholarships, pre-ministerial loans, payment plan; PELL, SEOG, NDSL, GSL, CWS. Application deadline August 15.
Admissions High school graduation with 16 units required. Interview encouraged. SAT required. $20 application fee. Rolling admissions; suggest applying after October 1. $100 deposit required by May 1. *Early Decision* and *Early Admission* programs. Admission deferral possible. Transfers accepted. Credit possible for CEEB AP and CLEP exams. Timothy J. Still Program for disadvantaged students.
Student Life Student government. Newspaper, magazine, yearbook, radio station. Music, drama groups. Debate. Service, honorary, and special interest groups. 4 fraternities and 3 sororities without houses. 15% of men and women join. Students expected to live at home or on campus. Coed and single-sex dorms. 60% of students live on campus. 8 intercollegiate sports for men, 4 for women, 3 coed; intramurals. AIAW, ECAC, MAC, NCAA. Student body composition: 2% Asian, 22% Black, 5% Hispanic, 1% Native American, 69% White. 10% from out of state.

[1] WESTMINSTER CHOIR COLLEGE
Princeton 08540, (609) 921-7100

- **Enrollment: 194m, 229w; 470 total (including part-time)**
- **Tuition (1982/83): $5,075**
- **Room & Board: $2,460**
- **Degrees offered: BMus, BMus Ed**
- **Mean SAT 460v, 470m**
- **Student-faculty ratio: 8 to 1**

A private professional college founded in 1926. Campus located in a suburban university community.
Academic Character MSACS and professional accreditation. 4-1-4 system. Majors offered in vocal, choral, and keyboard music. MMus granted. Programs offered which prepare for church music vocations, music education in public schools, and performance in voice, organ, and piano. 35,000-volume library.
Financial College scholarships, trustee grants, talent awards for freshmen in voice, organ, and piano. PELL, SEOG, NDSL and other loans, CWS. 128 weekend church positions.
Admissions ACT or SAT and audition required. Rolling admissions. *Early Admission* and *Early Decision* programs. Admission deferral possible. Advanced placement possible.
Student Life 2 residence halls for women, 1 for men, 3 coed.

[1] WILLIAM PATERSON COLLEGE OF NEW JERSEY, THE
Wayne 07470, (201) 595-2000
Director of Admissions: Joseph McNally

- **Undergraduates: 3,212m, 3,612w; 12,517 total (including gradutes)**
- **Tuition (1982/83): $810 (in-state), $1,410 (out-of-state)**
- **Room & Board: $2,545; Fees: $255**
- **Degrees offered: BA, BS, BFA, BMus**
- **Mean SAT 850**
- **Student-faculty ratio: 23 to 1**

A public college established in 1855. 250-acre campus in Wayne, 20 miles from New York City. Served by rail and bus.
Academic Character MSACS and professional accreditation. Semester system, 4-week and 6-week summer terms. 35 majors offered by the schools of Arts & Communication, Education & Community Service, Health Professions & Nursing, Humanities, Management, Science, and Social Science. Distributive requirements. Graduate and professional degrees granted. Independent study. Honors program. Pass/fail. Credit by exam. Preprofessional programs in dentistry, law, medicine, veterinary science. National and International Student Exchange. Study abroad. Elementary and secondary education certification. AFROTC nearby. A-V center, nursing lab, learning center, film library, language lab. 230,000-volume library.
Financial CEEB CSS. College scholarships, grants, loans, state grants, health profession loans; PELL, SEOG, NSS, NDSL, GSL, NSL, CWS. Scholarship application deadline April 15.
Admissions High school graduation with 16 units required. GED accepted. Audition required for music majors. SAT required. $10 application fee. Rolling admissions; application deadline March 1. $50 tuition and $90 room deposits required on acceptance of offer of admission. *Early Admission* Program. Admission deferral possible. Transfers accepted. Credit possible for CEEB AP and CLEP exams; college has own advanced placement program.
Student Life Student government. Newspaper, magazines, yearbook, radio and TV stations. Music, debate, dance, theatre groups. Veteran's, women's groups. Academic, honorary, political, religious, and special interest organizations. 10 fraternities and 8 sororities without houses. No married-student housing. 8% of students live on campus. 12 intercollegiate sports for men, 9 for women; intramurals. AIAW, ECAC, NCAA, NJCAC. Student body composition: 0.4% Asian, 5.6% Black, 2% Hispanic, 0.1% Native American, 91.9% White. 2% from out of state.

NEW MEXICO (NM)

[1] ALBUQUERQUE, UNIVERSITY OF

Albuquerque 87140, (505) 831-1111
Director of Admissions: Steve Gutknecht

- **Undergraduates: 1,007m, 1,054w**
- **Tuition (1982/83): $2,910 ($97 per credit hour)**
- **Room & Board: $1,860; Fees: $30**
- **Degrees offered: BA, BS, BFA, BBA, BSCorrec, BSCrim, BSEd, BUniv Studies**
- **Mean ACT 19**
- **Student-faculty ratio: 22 to 1**

A private university founded by the Sisters of St. Francis; established in 1920 and became coed in 1982. 68-acre campus on the Rio Grande River. Served by air, rail, and bus.
Academic Character NCACS and professional accreditation. Semester system, 2 7-week summer terms. Majors offered in art, bilingual education, 5 business administration areas, corrections, criminology, economics, elementary education, English, finance, health science administration, history, marketing, medical technology, Native American education, natural science, nursing, office management, philosophy, political science, psychology, religious studies, secondary education, social work, sociology, special education, theatre. Distributive requirements. Independent study. Honors program. Cooperative work/study, limited pass/fail, internships, credit by exam. Preprofessional programs in law, medicine, veterinary medicine. Exchange programs with Albuquerque Technical-Vocational, Southwest Indian Polytechnic, College of Santa Fe. Study in Mexico. Elementary, secondary, and special education certification. ROTC; AFROTC & NROTC at U of New Mexico. 78,000-volume library.
Financial CEEB CSS and ACT FAS. University scholarships, grants, loans, payment plan; PELL, SEOG, SSIG, BIA, NSS, NDSL, FISL, NSL, CWS. Application deadline March 1.
Admissions Open admissions. High school graduation required. Interview recommended. $15 application fee. Rolling admissions. *Early Admission* and *Concurrent Enrollment* programs. Admission deferral possible. Transfers accepted. Credit possible for CEEB AP and CLEP exams; university has own advanced placement program.
Student Life Student Senate. Newspaper, yearbook. Music and drama groups. Ecology and International Clubs. MECHA. Black Student Union. Native American Student Organization. Athletic, honorary, religious, and special interest groups. No married-student housing. 20% of students live on campus. 2 hours of phys ed required. Numerous sports and outdoor activities. Student body composition: 7% Asian, 6% Black, 31% Hispanic, 5% Native American, 51% White. 25% from out of state.

[2] ARTESIA CHRISTIAN COLLEGE

PO Box 9, 13th Street & Richey Avenue, Artesia 88210

[1] EASTERN NEW MEXICO UNIVERSITY

Portales 88130, (505) 562-2178
Director of Admissions: Larry Fuqua

- **Undergraduates: 1,334m, 1,338w; 3,634 total (including graduates)**
- **Tuition (1982/83): $698 (in-state), $1,985 (out-of-state)**
- **Room & Board: $1,570**
- **Degrees offered: BA, BS, BMus, BBA, BBus Ed, BFA, BAEd, BSEd, BSIndus Ed, BUniv Studies**
- **Mean ACT 20**
- **Student-faculty ratio: 20 to 1**

A public university established in 1934. 400-acre small-town campus, 120 miles from Lubbock and Amarillo, Texas. Served by bus in Portales; airport in Clovis.
Academic Character NCACS and professional accreditation. 4-1-4 system, 8-week summer term. 13 majors offered by the College of Education & Technology, 21 by the College of Fine Arts, and 34 by the College of Liberal Arts & Sciences. Self-designed and interdepartmental majors. Minors in 11 additional areas. Interdisciplinary and special programs. Distributive requirements. Graduate degrees granted. Independent study. Honors program. Cooperative work/study. Preprofessional programs in agriculture, dentistry, engineering, forestry, law, medicine, nursing, pharmacy, social work, veterinary medicine. Elementary, secondary, and special education certification. ROTC. A-V center. Archaeological and natural history museums. Natatorium. 368,100-volume library with microform resources.
Financial CEEB CSS and ACT FAS. University scholarships, grants, loans; PELL, SEOG, GSL, NDSL, CWS. Preferred application deadline March 1.
Admissions High school graduation with 15 units required. ACT or SAT required. $10 application fee. Rolling admissions. *Early Admission* and *Early Decision* programs. Admission deferral possible. Transfers accepted. Credit possible for CEEB AP, CLEP, and university exams.
Student Life Student government. Newspaper, literary magazine, yearbook. Music, art, and drama groups. Debate. Academic, ethnic, honorary, professional, and special interest groups. 7 fraternities with chapter houses, 3 sororities without houses. 17% of men and 6% of women join. Coed and single-sex dorms. Language and special interest residences. Married-student housing. 34% of students live on campus. Liquor, gambling, drugs, firearms prohibited. Class attendance required. 2 hours of phys ed required. 5 intercollegiate sports for men, 3 for women; intramurals. AIAW, NAIA. Student body composition: 0.5% Asian, 4.8% Black, 14% Hispanic, 1.4% Native American, 74.9% White. 21% from out of state.

■[J2] EASTERN NEW MEXICO UNIVERSITY—CLOVIS

Clovis 88101

■[J1] ROSWELL CAMPUS

PO Box 6761, Roswell 88201

■[J2] TUCUMCARI COMMUNITY COLLEGE

Tucumcari 88401

[J2] INSTITUTE OF AMERICAN INDIAN ARTS

College of Santa Fe Campus, St. Michael's Drive, Santa Fe 87501
(505) 988- 6493
Director of Admissions: Ramona M. Tse Pe'

- **Degree offered: AFA**

A public institute established in 1962. Part of the comprehensive Indian Education Program under the direction of the Bureau of Indian Affairs. Served by air, rail, and bus.
Academic Character Trimester system. Majors offered in two-dimensional and three-dimensional arts, museum training, dance, drama, and creative writing. Museum training program provides actual experience in exhibition, preservation, and restoration of artifacts, and sponsors ongoing museum shows. Arts Division offers courses in drawing, commercial illustration, ceramic pottery, jewelry, photography & printmaking, Indian art history, painting with oils, acrylic & watercolors, and sculpture in wood, stone, and clay. Certificates and diplomas granted. Liberal arts programs. Remedial mathematics and English programs. 15,000-volume library.
Financial No room, board, tuition, or fees for students who are ¼ or more Indian, and who are living on campus. Students living off campus must apply for financial assistance before enrolling. PELL, BIA, CWS. Contact Financial Aids Counselor for more information.
Admissions High school graduation or GED required. Personal written statement of interest with samples of work may be required if appropriate. Rolling admissions. Refundable room deposit of $32 due on acceptance of admissions offer. *Early Admission* Program. Admission deferral possible. Advanced placement possible.
Student Life Varied student-organized activities. Coed dorm. Liquor, drugs, and weapons prohibited on campus. Class attendance required. Sports programs. The student population often represents as many as 80 tribes and 26 states.

[1] NEW MEXICO, UNIVERSITY OF

Albuquerque 87131, (505) 277-0111
Dean of Admissions & Records: Robert M. Weaver

- **Undergraduates: 6,097m, 5,853w; 22,902 total (including graduates)**
- **Tuition (1982/83): $768 (in-state), $2,448 (out-of-state)**
- **Room & Board: $1,936**
- **Degrees offered: BA, BS, BBA, BAS, BFA**
- **Mean ACT 18.4**
- **Student-faculty ratio: 24 to 1**

A public university established in 1889. 600-acre campus overlooking the Rio Grande River. Served by air, rail, and bus.
Academic Character NCACS and professional accreditation. Semester system, 8-week summer term. 36 majors offered by the College of Arts & Sciences, 22 by the College of Education, 6 by the College of Engineering, 7 by the College of Fine Arts, 1 by the College of Nursing, 3 by the College of Pharmacy, 2 by the School of Architecture & Planning, and 8 by the School of Management. All freshmen enroll in University College. Sophomores enroll in other Colleges. Juniors select major/minor, 2 majors, or a special curriculum. Graduate degrees granted. Independent study. Honors programs. Phi Beta Kappa. Cooperative work/study, limited pass/fail, credit by exam. Preprofessional programs in dentistry, forestry, medicine. Programs in physical therapy and medical technology with area hospitals. 3-2 business-economics program. Elementary, secondary, and special education certification. ROTC, NROTC. Anthropological, art, biological, geological museums. Computer center. 1,043,936-volume library with microform resources.
Financial CEEB CSS. University scholarships, grants, loans; PELL, SEOG, NSS, NDSL, FISL, NSL, CWS. Application deadline March 1.
Admissions High school graduation with 13 units required. ACT required. $15 application fee. Rolling admissions. $25 room deposit due on acceptance of admissions offer. *Early Admission* and *Early Decision* programs. Transfers accepted. Credit possible for CEEB AP and CLEP exams.
Student Life Student government. Newspaper, literary magazine. Music and theatre groups. Women's Center. Academic, ethnic, honorary, religious, service, and special interest groups. 9 fraternities and 8 sororities, all with houses. 5% of men and 4% of women join. Coed and single-sex dorms. Limited married-student housing. 9% of students live on campus. Liquor prohibited. 13

intercollegiate sports; extensive intramurals. AIAW, IAC, NCAA, WAC. Student body composition: 1% Asian, 2% Black, 2.5% Foreign, 22% Hispanic, 3.5% Native American, 69% White. 8% from out of state.

■[J1] NEW MEXICO, UNIVERSITY OF, GALLUP BRANCH
Gallup 87301

■[J1] NEW MEXICO, UNIVERSITY OF—LOS ALAMOS
Los Alamos 87544

■[J2] NEW MEXICO, UNIVERSITY OF, NORTHERN BRANCH
Espando 87532

[1] NEW MEXICO HIGHLANDS UNIVERSITY
Las Vegas 87701, (505) 425-7511
Director of Admissions: Stanley J. Hipwood

- **Enrollment: 806m, 753w**
- **Tuition (1982/83): $510 (in-state), $1,796 (out-of-state)**
- **Room & Board: $1,510-$1,750**
- **Degrees offered: BA, BS**
- **Mean ACT 14**
- **Student-faculty ratio: 18 to 1**

A public university established in 1893. Campus in a small southwestern city in the Sangre de Cristo mountains, 70 miles east of Santa Fe and 70 miles south of Taos. Served by rail.

Academic Character NCACS and professional accreditation. Semester system, 8-week summer term. 32 majors offered in the areas of the arts, business, Chicano & Native American studies, education, home economics, humanities, industrial arts, library science, physical education, sciences, social sciences, and Spanish. Minor required. Minors offered in 10 additional areas. Distributive requirements. Graduate degrees granted. Independent study. Cooperative work/study. Preprofessional programs in dentistry, engineering, forestry, law, library science, medicine, optometry, pharmacy, social service, veterinary medicine. 3-1 medical technology program. Elementary, secondary, and administrative education certification. Computer center. Language lab. 235,000-volume library with microform resources.

Financial CEEB CSS. University scholarships, grants, loans; PELL, SEOG, NDSL, FISL, CWS.

Admissions High school graduation with 15 units required. ACT required. Rolling admissions. $20 room deposit due on acceptance of admissions offer. *Early Decision* and *Early Admission* programs. Transfers accepted. Credit possible for CEEB AP and CLEP exams.

Student Life Student Senate. Newspaper, yearbook. Music groups. Debate. Chicano Associated Student Organization. Organization of Concerned Black Students. Ecology Club. Karate Club. Athletic, academic, honorary, political, religious, service, and special interest groups. 5 fraternities and 2 sororities without houses. 10-15% of students join. Students not living at home are encouraged to live in dorms. Married-student housing. 35% of students live on campus. Liquor prohibited. 3 health and phys ed courses required. 6 intercollegiate sports for men, 3 for women; intramurals. AIAW, NAIA, RMAC. Student body composition: 0.4% Asian, 2.3% Black, 72.2% Hispanic, 2.8% Native American, 20.7% White. 7% from out of state.

[1] NEW MEXICO INSTITUTE OF MINING AND TECHNOLOGY
Socorro 87801, (505) 835-5424
Director of Admissions: Louise E. Chamberlin

- **Undergraduates: 712m, 256w; 1,292 total (including graduates)**
- **Tuition (1982/83): $421 (in-state), $2,105 (out-of-state)**
- **Room & Board: $2,160; Fees: $261**
- **Degrees offered: BA, BS, BGS, AGS**
- **Mean ACT 25**
- **Student-faculty ratio: 15 to 1**

A public institute established in 1889. 320-acre campus (with 7,000 additional acres for research) in a small city in the Rio Grande Valley, 75 miles south of Albuquerque. Served by bus.

Academic Character NCACS and professional accreditation. Semester system, 8-week summer term. Majors offered in basic sciences, biology, chemistry, computer science, general studies, geology, geophysics, history, mathematics, medical technology, physics, psychology, social science, and in environmental, geological, material, metallurgical, mining, and petroleum engineering. Distributive requirements. Independent study. On-site mining experience possible. Cooperative work/study, limited pass/fail. Preprofessional programs in dentistry, law, medical technology, medicine, nursing, optometry, physical therapy, pharmacy, veterinary science. 3-2 programs with Reed and SUNY College at New Paltz. WICHE Program. Secondary education certification. Computer center. Observatory. Mineral museum. Scanning electron microscope facility. 90,000-volume library with microform resources.

Financial CEEB CSS and ACT FAS. Institute scholarships, grants, loans, state loans; PELL, SEOG, SSIG, NDSL, FISL, GSL, CWS, honors work program, industrial work/study program.

Admissions High school graduation with 15 units required. Open admission to students with appropriate secondary school background, 2.0 GPA, and ACT 19 composite. GED accepted. Interview recommended. ACT required. $10 application fee. Rolling admissions. $50 tuition and $55 room deposits due on acceptance of admissions offer. *Early Admission* Program. Transfers accepted. Credit possible for CEEB AP exams; institute has own advanced placement program.

Student Life Student government. Newspaper. Music and drama groups. Professional, community, and special interest groups. Coed and single-sex dorms. Married-student housing. 47% of students live on campus. Liquor prohibited. Informal club sports with area schools; intramurals. Student body composition: 2% Asian, 1% Black, 8% Hispanic, 1% Native American, 83% White, 5% Other. 27% from out of state.

[J1] NEW MEXICO JUNIOR COLLEGE
Lovington Highway, Hobbs 88240

[J1] NEW MEXICO MILITARY INSTITUTE
Roswell 88201, (505) 622-6250, ext. 203
Director of Admissions: Major William C. Wyles

- **Enrollment: 457m, 52w; 765 total (including part-time)**
- **Tuition (1982/83): $325 (in-state), $1,035 (out-of-state)**
- **Room & Board: $1,500; Fees: $288**
- **Personal Account Deposit: $1,750 (for uniforms, etc.)**
- **Degree offered: AA**
- **Mean ACT 18.6**
- **Student-faculty ratio: 18 to 1**

A public junior college with a 2-year high school college-preparatory division, established in 1915. Campus in a small city in the southeast part of the state. Served by air, rail, and bus.

Academic Character NCACS accreditation. Semester system. 2-year transfer programs offered in agriculture, biology, business, chemistry, engineering, fine arts, liberal arts, medical careers, and physical education. Distributives and 8-12 hours of military science required. Credit by exam. ROTC.

Financial College scholarships, state grants and loans; PELL, SEOG, NDSL, GSL, PLUS, CWS. Application deadlines January 31 (scholarships), April 1 (loans).

Admissions High school graduation required. GED accepted. ACT or SAT required. $60 application fee. *Early Admission* and *Early Decision* programs. Transfers accepted. Credit possible for CEEB CLEP exams.

Student Life All students live and board on campus. Honor code. Furloughs. Uniforms must be worn. Phys ed required. 6 intercollegiate sports; intramurals. NJCAA. Student body composition: 30% minority.

[1] NEW MEXICO STATE UNIVERSITY
Las Cruces 88003, (505) 646-3121
Director of Admissions & Records: Billy J. Bruner

- **Undergraduates: 5,060m, 3,951w; 12,512 total (including graduates)**
- **Tuition (1982/83): $798 (in-state), $2,480 (out-of-state)**
- **Room & Board: $1,482-$1,642**
- **Degrees offered: BA, BS, BBA, BFA, BMus, BMus Ed, BSN, BSW, BSAg, BSEd, BSHome Ec, BSMT, BAcc, BCom Health, BGeo Sci, BPolice Sci, BIndivid Studies**
- **Student-faculty ratio: 21 to 1**

A public university established in 1888. 6,250-acre campus on the eastern mesa of the Rio Grande Valley, 40 miles from El Paso. Served by air, rail, and bus.

Academic Character NCACS and professional accreditation. 4-4-1 system, 2 6-week summer terms. 24 majors offered by the College of Agriculture & Home Economics, 30 by the College of Arts & Sciences, 8 by the College of Business Administration & Economics, 20 by the College of Education, 8 by the College of Engineering, and 4 by the College of Human & Community Services. Self-designed majors. Minors offered in most major fields. Distributive requirements. Graduate degrees granted. Independent study. Honors program. Cooperative work/study, pass/fail, internships, credit by exam. Preprofessional programs in dentistry, forestry, law, medicine, veterinary medicine. 3-1 medical technology program. National Student Exchange Program. Elementary, secondary, and special education certification. ROTC, AFROTC. Computer center. Physical Science Lab. Language lab. 650,000-volume library.

Financial CEEB CSS. University scholarships, grants, loans; PELL, SEOG, NDSL, CWS. Application deadline March 1.

Admissions High school graduation with 15 units required. GED accepted. ACT required. $10 application fee. Rolling admissions. $50 room deposit required with housing application. *Early Admission* Program. Transfers accepted. Credit possible for CEEB AP and CLEP exams, and for ACT scores; university has own advanced placement program. Provisional admission possible.

Student Life Associated Students. Associated Women Students. Newspaper, yearbook, radio and TV stations. Music and drama groups. Black, Chicano, and Native American organizations. Athletic, academic, honorary, political, religious, and special interest groups. 9 fraternities and 5 sororities, all with houses. 5% of students join. Single-sex dorms. Handicapped-student housing. Married-student apartments and houses. 30% of students live on campus. Liquor, drugs, and gambling prohibited. Class attendance expected. 11 intercollegiate sports; intramurals. NCAA, Missouri Valley Conference. Student body composition: 1% Black, 24% Hispanic, 2% Native American, 73% White. 12% from out of state.

■[J1] NEW MEXICO STATE UNIVERSITY AT ALAMOGORDO
PO Box 477, Alamogordo 88310

■[J1] NEW MEXICO STATE UNIVERSITY AT CARLSBAD
Carlsbad 88220

■[J1] NEW MEXICO STATE UNIVERSITY AT GRANTS
Grants 87020

■[J1] NEW MEXICO STATE UNIVERSITY-SAN JUAN COLLEGE
Farmington — see San Juan College

[J2] NEW MEXICO TECHNICAL VOCATIONAL SCHOOL
Espanola — see Northern New Mexico Community College—Espanola Campus

[J2] NORTHERN NEW MEXICO COMMUNITY COLLEGE
El Rito 87530

[J2] NORTHERN NEW MEXICO COMMUNITY COLLEGE—ESPANOLA CAMPUS
Espanola 87632
Formerly New Mexico Technical Vocational School

[1] ST. JOHN'S COLLEGE
Santa Fe 87501, (505) 982-3691
Director of Admissions: Mary McCormick Freitas

- **Undergraduates: 155m, 130w; 343 total (including graduates)**
- **Tuition (1982/83): $6,700**
- **Room & Board: $2,600**
- **Degree offered: BA**
- **Mean SAT 611v, 564m**
- **Student-faculty ratio: 8 to 1**

A private college established in 1964, as a sister campus of St. John's College of Annapolis, MD. 330-acre suburban campus, 60 miles from Albuquerque. Served by bus. Rail service 20 miles away in Lamy; airport in Albuquerque.
Academic Character NCACS accreditation. Semester system, 10-week summer term for students who entered in January. 4-year sequential study of great books from Homer to present combined with language, mathematics, laboratory science, and 1 year of music theory. Discussion classes. Academic year consists of 6 divisions: seminars, language, mathematics, and music tutorials, laboratory, and formal lecture. Oral exam at the end of each semester; comprehensive exam in fall of senior year. Senior thesis defended in oral examination. Students may spend one or more years at Annapolis campus. MLA granted. Art gallery. 52,600-volume library.
Financial CEEB CSS. College scholarships, grants, payment plans; PELL, SEOG, NDSL, FISL, CWS, student aid program. Scholarship application deadline in early February.
Admissions High school graduation with college prep program expected. Interview encouraged; may be required. SAT or ACT recommended. Rolling admissions. $200 deposit due on acceptance of admissions offer. *Early Decision* and *Early Admission* programs. Admission deferral possible. Transfers accepted, but enter as freshmen.
Student Life Literary magazine. Music, film, and drama groups. Search-and-rescue team. Art, athletic, crafts, service, and special interest groups. Single students not living at home live on campus. Seniors may live off campus. Coed dorms. Limited married-student housing. 80% of students live on campus. Intercollegiate fencing and soccer; individual and intramural sports programs. Student body composition: 2% Asian, 2% Hispanic, 96% White. Freshmen range in age from 16 to 30 years old. 90% from out of state.

[J1] SAN JUAN COLLEGE
Farmington 87401
Formerly New Mexico State College, San Juan College Branch

[1] SANTA FE, COLLEGE OF
Santa Fe 87501, (505) 473-6131
Director of Admissions: Mary Bacca

- **Undergraduates: 328m, 380w; 1,105 total (including part-time)**
- **Tuition (1982/83): $3,200 (approximate)**
- **Room & Board: $1,950; Fees: $100 (approximate)**
- **Degrees offered: BA, BS, BFA, BAcc, BBA, BCollege Studies, AS, ASecretarial Admin**
- **Mean ACT 17**
- **Student-faculty ratio: 18 to 1**

A private college controlled by the Christian Brothers of New Mexico, established in 1874, became coed in 1966. 120-acre small-city campus. Served by air, rail, and bus.
Academic Character NCACS and professional accreditation. Semester system, 4-, 6-, and 8-week summer terms. 32 majors offered by the divisions of Business Administration, Humanities, Nursing, Performing Arts, Sciences & Mathematics, Social Sciences, and Education, Physical Education, & Recreation. Self-designed majors. Minors offered in some major fields and in 3 additional areas. Distributives and 6 semester hours of religion required. Independent study. Honors program. Cooperative work/study, internships, credit by exam. Preprofessional programs in dentistry, law, medicine, physical therapy. Cooperative programs in corrections, criminology, and police science with U of Albuquerque. 3-1 medical technology program. Elementary and secondary education certification. Theatre Center. Art gallery. 87,000-volume library.
Financial CEEB CSS and ACT FAS. College scholarships, grants, loans, state grants and loans; PELL, SEOG, NSS, NDSL, FISL, NSL, CWS.
Admissions High school graduation with 16 units required. Interview and physical exam required for nursing applicants. ACT required. $16 application fee. Rolling admissions. $100 deposit required on acceptance of admissions offer. *Early Admission* and *Concurrent Enrollment* programs. Admission deferral possible. Transfers accepted. Credit possible for CEEB AP and CLEP exams. Center for Academic Development for underprepared students.
Student Life Student government. Music and drama groups. Black Student Union. Hispanic Club. Four Winds Indian Club. Cultural, educational, honorary, religious, social, and special interest groups. 2 fraternities and 1 sorority without houses. 20% of men join fraternities. Freshmen must live at home or on campus. Coed and single-sex dorms. No married-student housing. 30% of students live on campus. Class attendance expected. 4 hours of phys ed required. 3 intercollegiate sports for men, 3 for women; intramurals. AIAW, NAIA. Student body composition: 3% Black, 37% Hispanic, 12% Native American, 47% White, 1% Other. 23% from out of state.

[1] SOUTHWEST, COLLEGE OF THE
Lovington Highway, Hobbs 88240

[1] WESTERN NEW MEXICO UNIVERSITY
Silver City 88061, (505) 538-6441

- **Undergraduates: 637m, 852w**
- **Tuition (1982/83): $530 (in-state), $1,816 (out-of-state)**
- **Room & Board: $1,658**
- **Degrees offered: BA, BS, BAcad Stud, BSCrim Jus**
- **Student-faculty ratio: 20 to 1**

A public university established in 1893. 80-acre campus in a small city in the southwestern part of the state, 100 miles from El Paso. Train and bus stations nearby; airport in El Paso.
Academic Character NCACS and professional accreditation. Semester system, 2 6-week summer terms. 32 majors offered in the areas of business administration, criminal justice, education, fine arts, home economics, liberal arts, management, physical education, public administration, sciences, social sciences, and Spanish. Minors offered in most major fields and in 9 other areas. Distributive requirements. Internships. Preprofessional programs in dentistry, engineering, forestry, law, medicine, nursing, pharmacy, social work. Elementary and secondary education certification. Fine Arts Center. Police Training Academy. 117,000-volume library with microform resources, and access to over 1,500 other libraries through the Ohio College library's central terminal.
Financial CEEB CSS and ACT FAS. University scholarships, grants, loans, state grants, payment plans; PELL, SEOG, NDSL, GSL, FISL, CWS. Application deadlines March 30 (scholarships), April 1 (loans).
Admissions High school graduation with 9 units recommended. GED accepted. ACT required. $10 application fee. Rolling admissions. $50 tuition deposit due on acceptance of admissions offer. *Early Admission, Early Decision, Concurrent Enrollment* programs. Admission deferral possible. Transfers accepted. Credit possible for CEEB AP and CLEP exams.
Student Life Associated Students. Newspaper, yearbook. Music and drama groups. Academic, honorary, religious, service, and special interest groups. Dorms for men and women. Married-student housing. Liquor, drugs, firearms prohibited. 2 semesters of phys ed required. 5 intercollegiate sports. NAIA, Rocky Mountain Athletic Association. Student body composition: 1% Asian, 4.2% Black, 42% Hispanic, 6% Native American, 46.8% White. 10% from out of state.

NEW YORK *(NY)*

[1] ADELPHI UNIVERSITY
Garden City 11530, (516) 294-8700
Director of Admissions: Susan Reardon

- **Undergraduates: 1,470m, 3,074; 11,836 total (including graduates)**
- **Tuition (1982/83): $4,650**
- **Room & Board: $2,850; Fees: $380**
- **Degrees offered: BA, BS, BFA, BBA, AS**
- **Mean SAT 490v, 474m**
- **Student-faculty ratio: 16 to 1**

A private university established in 1896. 75-acre campus in suburban Garden City, Long Island, 20 miles from Manhattan. Air, bus, rail service.
Academic Character MSACS and professional accreditation. Semester system, 2 4-week summer terms. 30 majors offered by the College of Arts & Sciences, 5 by the School of Business, and one each by the schools of Nursing and Social Work. Associate degrees granted. Minors offered in most areas. Courses in 10 additional areas. Distributive requirements. Graduate and professional degrees granted. Independent study. Honors program. Pass/fail, internships. Preprofessional programs in dentistry, engineering, law, medicine, physical therapy, veterinary medicine. 3-2 programs in social welfare and business. 5-year BA/BS engineering (through other universities). Study abroad. "Adelphi-On-Wheels" commuter classroom School of Business. PRIDE program for underqualified students. Member of Long Island Regional Advisory Council on Higher Education. ROTC at Hofstra. Computing Center, language lab. 377,941-volume library with microform resources; departmental libraries and research facilities.
Financial CEEB CSS. University scholarships, grants. PELL, SEOG, NSS, NDSL, NSL, CWS, state programs. Application deadline April 15. HEOP.
Admissions High school graduation with 16 units required. SAT or ACT required. $20 application fee. Rolling admissions; application deadline for financial aid applicants February 1. $200 tuition and $100 room deposits required on acceptance of offer of admission. *Early Admission* and *Concurrent Enrollment* programs. Admission deferral possible. Transfers accepted. Credit possible for CEEB AP and CLEP exams.
Student Life Student government. Newspaper, magazine, yearbook, radio

station. Music, drama, dance groups. Academic, honorary, religious, language, special interest clubs. 6 fraternities, 5 sororities without houses. 7% of students join. Community housing available on request. Coed and women's dorms. Special interest housing. 20% of students live on campus. 12 intercollegiate sports for men, 5 for women; 11 intramurals. AIAW, ECAC, ICYA, NAIA, NCAA. Student body composition: 1% Asian, 13% Black, 4% Hispanic, 0.2% Native American, 75% White, 6.8% Other. 13% from out of state.

[J1] ADIRONDACK COMMUNITY COLLEGE
Glens Falls 12801

[J1] AERONAUTICS, ACADEMY OF
La Guardia Airport, New York 11371

[1] ALFRED UNIVERSITY
Alfred 14802, (607) 871-2115
Director of Admissions: Paul P. Piggon

- **Undergraduates: 984m, 895w**
- **Private Tuition (1982/83): $6,450**
- **Public Tuition (1982/83): $1,900 (in-state), $2,850 (out-of-state)**
- **Room & Board: $2,500**
- **Degrees offered: BA, BS, BFA**
- **Mean SAT 500v, 535m**
- **Student-faculty ratio: 13 to 1**

A private university, including public New York State College of Ceramics, established in 1836. 232-acre rural campus in Alfred, 70 miles south of Rochester. Air, bus, rail service.
Academic Character MSACS and professional accreditation. Semester system, 2 summer terms. 11 majors offered by the College of Ceramics, 25 by the College of Liberal Arts & Sciences, 2 by the College of Nursing & Health Care, 7 by the College of Business & Administration, and a Division of Industrial Engineering major. Self-designed major. Distributive requirements. Graduate and professional degrees granted. Independent study. Honors program. Cooperative work study, pass/fail, internships. Preprofessional programs in dentistry, law, medical laboratory technology, medicine, veterinary medicine. 3-2 program in forestry and environmental studies with Duke. 4-1 MBA with Clarkson College. 5-year program in engineering with Columbia. Member consortium with Rochester Area Colleges. United Nations Semester. Washington Semester. World Campus Afloat. Study abroad. Elementary and secondary education certification. ROTC at St. Bonaventure. Computer Center, language lab. 210,000-volume library.
Financial CEEB CSS. University scholarships, grants, state programs; PELL, SEOG, NDSL, NSL, CWS. Priority application deadline February 15.
Admissions High school graduation with 16 units required. Portfolio required of Ceramic Art and Design applicants. Interview recommended. SAT or ACT required. $20 application fee. Rolling admissions; application deadline February 1. $200 tuition deposit required on acceptance of offer of admission. *Early Decision* and *Early Admission* programs. Admission deferral possible. Transfers accepted. Credit possible for CEEB AP and CLEP exams.
Student Life Student government. Student assembly. Newspaper, literary review, yearbook, radio station. Music, drama, religious, and special interest groups. 5 fraternities and 3 sororities with houses. 25% of men and 20% of women join. Freshmen and sophomores live in dormitories. Coed and single-sex dorms. 85% of students live on campus. 2 phys ed courses required. 10 intercollegiate sports for men, 7 for women. Extensive intramural program. ECAC, NCAA, ICAC. Student body composition: 2% Black, 0.5% Hispanic, 0.5% Native American, 97% White. 30% from out of state.

[G1] BANK STREET COLLEGE OF EDUCATION
610 West 112th Street, New York 10009

[1] BARD COLLEGE
Annandale-on-Hudson 12504, (914) 758-6822
Director of Admissions: Karen G. Wilcox

- **Undergraduates: 352m, 448w**
- **Tuition (1982/83): $8,700**
- **Room & Board: $2,800; Fees: $250**
- **Degree offered: BA**
- **Mean SAT 570v, 540m**
- **Student-faculty ratio: 10 to 1**

A private college established in 1860, became coed in 1944. 1,000-acre rural campus in Annandale-on-Hudson, 100 miles north of New York City.
Academic Character MSACS accreditation. Semester system. 31 majors offered in the areas of arts, sciences, math, music, humanities, social sciences, religion, women's studies, and economics through four college divisions: the Arts, Languages & Literature, Natural Sciences & Mathematics, Social Sciences. Distributive requirements. MFA degree program. Independent study. Honors program. Internships, honors/pass/fail. Preprofessional programs in medicine, law. 3-2 engineering program with Columbia; BA/MS in forestry and environmental studies at Duke. "Professional Option" allows entrance to approved graduate school after 3 years at Bard. Bard/Hudson Valley Studies. Individual study. Winter field Period. Study abroad. Workshop in Language and Thinking. Senior Project. Ecology field station. Language lab. Performing arts complex, art institute. 155,000-volume library with microform resources.
Financial CEEB CSS. College scholarships, awards, prizes; PELL, SEOG, NDSL, GSL, CWS. Application deadline March 15.
Admissions High school graduation with 16 units required. SAT or ACT recommended. GED accepted. Interview recommended. $20 application fee. Regular application deadline March 15. $250 tuition deposit required on acceptance of offer of admission. *Immediate Decision Plan;* one-day program on campus where applicant is told whether or not he or she is accepted. *Early Admission* and *Concurrent Enrollment* programs. Admission deferral possible. Transfers accepted. Credit possible for CEEB AP exams. HEOP.
Student Life Student government. Newspapers, literary magazines, journals. Music, drama, religious, academic, special interest groups. Coed and women's dorms. 85% of students live on campus. Firearms and pets prohibited. Intercollegiate soccer, cross-country, basketball, tennis for men; basketball, cross-country, volleyball, softball, tennis for women. Club sports and intramural program. NEAC, NAIA. Student body composition: 0.3% Asian, 7.5% Black, 3% Hispanic, 0.1% Native American, 88.6% White, 2.5% Other. 57% from out of state.

[1] BORICUA COLLEGE
3755 Broadway, New York City 10032, (212) 865-9000

- **Undergraduates: 358m, 511w**
- **Tuition (1982/83): $3,500**
- **Degrees offered: BS, AA**

A private, nontraditional, bilingual college established in 1980. Urban campus in Manhattan. Brooklyn Learning Center nearby.
Academic Character MSACS accreditation. Trimester system. Majors offered in business administration, elementary education, human services. Associate of Arts offered in major areas. Courses in 10 additional fields. Distributive requirements. Independent study. Individualized curriculum. Field internships. Multimedia programs of instruction. Colloquia. Evening classes.
Financial Financial aid programs available to all students. State aid, PELL, SEOG, NDSL, GSL.
Admissions High school graduation recommended. GED accepted. $5 application fee. Knowledge of English and Spanish required of applicant; 2-3 recommendations, and photos of applicant also required. Minimum age of applicant 17 years. Essay with application recommended. Students encouraged to apply their education to the needs of their community. Rolling admissions. Transfers accepted. Credit possible for CEEB CLEP exams and life/work experience. HEOP, SEEK, College Discovery programs.
Student Life The college is designed to serve the needs of Puerto Rican and other Spanish-speaking people in the United States. Student body composition: 5.1% Black, 94.9% Hispanic.

[P] BROOKLYN LAW SCHOOL
250 Joralemon Street, Brooklyn 11201

[J1] BROOME COMMUNITY COLLEGE
Binghamton 13902

[1] CANISIUS COLLEGE
Buffalo 14208, (716) 883-7000
Director of Admissions: Penelope Lips

- **Undergraduates: 1,432m, 1,031w; 3,746 total (including graduates)**
- **Tuition (1982/83): $4,100**
- **Room & Board: $2,280; Fees: $60**
- **Degrees offered: BA, BS, BSBA**
- **Mean SAT 474v, 530m**
- **Student-faculty ratio: 18 to 1**

A private college founded by the Society of Jesus, established 1870. College became coed in 1966. 18-acre campus in Buffalo. Airport, bus and train stations nearby.
Academic Character MSACS and professional accreditation. Semester system, 2 summer terms. 29 majors offered in the areas of business, education, communications, computer science, sciences, math, humanities, social sciences, physical education, religious studies, medical technology. Masters degrees granted. Independent study. Honors program. Pass/fail, internships. Preprofessional programs in dentistry, law, forestry, medicine, veterinary medicine. Federal College Internship Program. 3-2 engineering program with U of Detroit. 2-2 program at SUNY College of Environmental Science and Forestry in Syracuse. BA cooperative program in fashion merchandising with Fashion Institute in New York City. Engineering programs at some New York State schools. Secondary education certification. Member of consortium with 18 western New York colleges. ROTC. Language lab. 210,000-volume library.
Financial University scholarships, grants, loans; PELL, SEOG, NDSL, GSL, CWS. Priority application deadline March 1.
Admissions High school graduation with 16 units required. Interview recommended. SAT or ACT required. $15 application fee. Rolling admissions. $50 tuition and $100 room deposits required on acceptance of offer of admission. *Early Admission* Program. Admission deferral possible. Transfers accepted. Credit possible for CEEB AP and CLEP exams. HEOP, COPE.
Student Life Student government. Newspaper, magazine, yearbook. Music, drama, debate clubs. Religious, academic, honorary, service, special interest groups. Students live at home or in dorms. Single-sex dorms. 25% of students live on campus. Class attendance expected. 2 phys ed courses required. 13 intercollegiate sports for men, 6 for women; intramurals. AIAW. Student body composition: 0.4% Asian, 4.1% Black, 0.7% Hispanic, 0.5% Native American, 94% White, 0.2% Other. 3% from out of state.

[P] CARDOZO SCHOOL OF LAW
New York — see Yeshiva University.

[1] CATHEDRAL COLLEGE OF THE IMMACULATE CONCEPTION
7200 Douglaston Parkway, Douglaston 11362

[J1] CAYUGA COMMUNITY COLLEGE
Franklin Street, Auburn 13021

[J1] CAZENOVIA COLLEGE
Cazenovia 13035, (315) 655-3466

- **Residential Undergraduates: 585w**
- **Tuition (1982/83): $4,465**
- **Room & Board: $2,340**
- **Degrees offered: AA, AS, AAS**
- **Mean SAT 380v, 400m**

A private junior college for women established in 1824.
Academic Character MSACS accreditation. Semester system. Programs offered in liberal arts, studio arts, administrative secretarial services, fashion design, fashion merchandising, interior design, medical office assistant, nursing (RN), human services, merchandising, advertising design, day care services, early childhood education, business management, social services for children, special education assistant, equine studies, and horsemanship.
Financial Financial aid available.
Admissions High school graduation required. SAT required. Admission decision is based on academic performance and test data. Rolling admissions. *Early Admission* Program. Admission deferral possible. Advanced placement program.

[G1] CHRIST THE KING SEMINARY
East Aurora 14052

[1] CITY UNIVERSITY OF NEW YORK
Headquarters: 535 East 80th Street, New York 10021, (212) 794-5317

A public university composed of nine senior colleges, eight community colleges, and the Graduate School and University Center; affiliated with the Mount Sinai School of Medicine.
Academic Character MSACS and professional accreditation. All units are coed. Graduate study is conducted on the campuses of the senior colleges and at the University Graduate School. The master's degree is offered by the senior colleges, and the doctorate in 27 fields by the University.
Financial The University is financed by the City of New York, the State of New York, tuition, fees, and miscellaneous income. Some funds for research and special purposes provided by the federal government.
Admissions Under open admissions program initiated in 1970, all graduates of New York City high schools are eligible for admission. Undergraduates are admitted in September and February through the University Applications Processing Center. Graduates of the community colleges may transfer to the senior colleges of the University as juniors. Programs for disadvantaged students include SEEK (Search for Education, Elevation, and Knowledge) at the senior colleges, and the College Discovery Program at the community colleges.

■[1] BERNARD M. BARUCH COLLEGE (CUNY)
17 Lexington Avenue, New York 10010, (212) 725-3000
Director of Admissions: Patricia Hassett

- **Undergraduates: 12,300 men & women; 15,000 total (including graduates)**
- **Tuition (1982/83): $1,075 (in-state), $1,575 (out-of-state)**
- **Degrees offered: BA, BBA, BSEd**
- **Student-faculty ratio: 22 to 1**

A public college established as an independent school in 1968. Urban campus in New York City. Air, rail, bus, and subway service.
Academic Character MSACS and professional accreditation. Semester system. Over 35 majors offered in the areas of accounting, art administration, biology, education, English, finance, Hebrew, industrial psychology, management, marketing, mathematics, music, office administration, philosophy/religion, public administration, social sciences, Spanish, and statistics. Ad Hoc majors in art, liberal arts, natural science, Romance languages. Interdisciplinary and dual majors. Minor or equivalent required. Minor in most majors and in 16 additional areas. Distributive requirements. MBA, MPA, MSEd granted. Independent study, honors programs, pass/fail, internships. Preprofessional programs in law, medicine, translation. Cooperative training for business students. 4½-year BBA/MBA in accounting. 4-year BBA/MS in statistics, operations research, or computer methodology. Early childhood, elementary, secondary, and special education certification. 265,000-volume library with microform resources.
Financial Application procedures vary with programs. College scholarships, loans, state scholarships, grants, loans, aid to Native Americans; PELL, SEOG, GSL, NDSL, PLUS, CWS.
Admissions High school graduation required. GED accepted. Students with a GPA of 80%, total SAT of at least 900, or in top 30% of class are eligible. SAT or ACT recommended. $20 application fee. Rolling admissions; suggest applying as soon as possible. *Early Admission* and *Concurrent Enrollment* programs. Admission deferral possible. Transfers accepted. Credit possible for CEEB CLEP and ACT PEP exams; college has own advanced placement program. SEEK program for the academically/economically disadvantaged.
Student Life Student government. Several music groups. Athletic, honorary, political, professional, social, and special interest groups. No college housing. 1 semester of phys ed required. Class attendance expected. 9 intercollegiate and several intramural sports for men & women. NCAA. Student body composition: 9% Asian, 28% Black, 12% Hispanic, 0.4% Native American, 40% White, 10.6% Other. 5-10% from out of state.

■[J1] BRONX COMMUNITY COLLEGE (CUNY)
University Avenue & West 181st Street, Bronx 10453, (212) 220-6450

- **Undergraduates: 1,787m, 2,795w; 6,719 total (including part-time)**
- **Tuition (1982/83): $X,XXX**
- **Degrees offered: AA, AS, AAS**

A public junior college. First class entered in 1959.
Academic Character MSACS and professional accreditation. Semester system, summer term. Transfer programs offered in liberal arts & sciences, engineering, teaching of business subjects, business administration, pharmacy, music, and education. Career programs offered in accounting, audiovisual technology, marketing, management, sales, secretarial studies (executive, legal, medical, and school secretary), data processing, electrical technology, paralegal studies, medical laboratory technology, nuclear medicine technology, and nursing. Centers for nursing curriculum are Bronx Municipal Hospital Center, Montefiore Hospital, Bronx-Lebanon Hospital, and Bronx Psychiatric Center. Remedial mathematics and English programs.
Admissions High school graduation required.
Student Life Student body composition: 80% minority.

■[1] BROOKLYN COLLEGE (CUNY)
Bedford Avenue & Avenue H, New York 11210, (212) 780-5485
Dean of Admissions: Rose C. Erwin

- **Enrollment: 4,830m, 5,729w**
- **Tuition (1982/83): $925 (in-state), $1,425 (out-of-state)**
- **Fees: $77**
- **Degrees offered: BA, BS**
- **Student-faculty ratio: 14 to 1**

A public college established in 1930 by merger of men's branch of CUNY Brooklyn and women's branch of Hunter College. Urban campus in Flatbush section of Brooklyn. Air, rail, bus, and subway service.
Academic Character MSACS and professional accreditation. Semester system, 6- and 8-week summer terms. Over 50 majors offered by the schools of Education, Humanities, Liberal Arts, Performing Arts, Science, Social Science, and Contemporary Studies. Interdisciplinary programs include Carribean, Italian-American, Middle East/North African, Russian/East European, and African studies. Courses in Arabic, Chinese, Polish, Swahili, Yiddish. Distributive requirements. Masters degrees granted. Certificate programs. Honors programs, Phi Beta Kappa, pass/fail, internships. Preprofessional preparation in dentistry, engineering, medicine, nursing, health professions. BA/MA in biology, chemistry, information science, physics, political science, psychology. 4½-year BS/MPS in economics/computer information science. 7-year BA/MD. Elementary and secondary education certification. Research institutes. TV studio, computer center, language lab. Over 800,000-volume library.
Financial Application procedures vary with programs. College scholarships, grants, loans, state scholarships, grants, loans, aid to Native Americans; PELL, SEOG, GSL, NDSL, PLUS, college work program.
Admissions High school graduation or equivalent required. 16 units recommended. Audition required for music majors. SAT recommended. Rolling admissions; suggest applying as soon as possible. *Early Admission* and *Concurrent Enrollment* programs. Transfers accepted. Credit possible for CEEB AP, CLEP, ACT PEP and college exams. SEEK program for the academically/economically disadvantaged. Provisional admission possible.
Student Life Student government. Newspapers, magazine, radio station. Honorary societies. Numerous student organizations. No college housing. Class attendance expected. 15 intercollegiate and several intramural sports for men & women. Student body composition: 4.1% Asian, 20% Black, 8.2% Hispanic, 1.2% Native American, 66.5% White.

■[1] CITY COLLEGE, THE (CUNY)
Covenant Avenue & West 138 Street, New York 10031, (212) 690-6977
Director of Admissions: Dr. Saul Friedman

- **Undergraduates: 6,846m, 4,277w; 13,389 total (including graduates)**
- **Tuition (1982/83): $925 (in-state), $1,425 (out-of-state)**
- **Fees: $66**
- **Degrees offered: BA, BS, BArch, BSArch, BSEd, BEng, BTech**
- **Student-faculty ratio: 15 to 1**

A public college founded in 1847. Urban campus in Manhattan. Air, rail, bus, and subway service.
Academic Character MSACS and professional accreditation. Semester system, 7½-week summer term. Over 55 majors offered in the areas of architecture, area studies, arts, computer, education, engineering, English, Hebrew, languages & literatures, linguistics, mathematics, meteorology, nursing, oceanography, psychology, sciences, social sciences, and speech/pathology. Programs in dance, film, music, and theatre. Masters degrees granted. Phi Beta Kappa. Preprofessional programs in dentistry, journalism, medicine. 6-year BS/JD program. 7-year BS/MD program. Elementary, secondary, and special education certification. Center for the Performing Arts. 937,000-volume library.
Financial Application procedures vary with programs. College grants, loans, state scholarships, grants, loans, aid to Native Americans, payment plan; PELL, SEOG, GSL, NDSL, NSL, PLUS, CWS. Application deadline January 15 for scholarships & grants.
Admissions High school graduation or equivalent required. GED accepted. SAT or ACT recommended. $20 application fee. Rolling admissions; suggest applying by January 15. *Early Entrance* Program. Transfers accepted. Credit possible for CEEB AP and CLEP exams.
Student Life Student government. Newspaper, yearbook. Academic, service, social, and special interest groups. Fraternities. No college housing. 2 semesters of phys ed required. Class attendance required. 19 intercollegiate and several intramural sports for men & women. CUNY Conference. Student body composition: 13% Asian, 34% Black, 21% Hispanic, 1% Native American, 31% White.

■[J1] EUGENIO MARIA DE HOSTOS COMMUNITY COLLEGE (CUNY)
475 Grand Concourse, Bronx 10451, (212) 960-1200

- **Enrollment: 1,230m, 2,166w**
- **Tuition (1982/83): $X,XXX**

• **Degrees offered: AA, AS, AAS**

A public junior college.
Academic Character MSACS and professional accreditation. Semester system. Transfer programs offered in the liberal arts. Career programs in allied health sciences, dental hygiene, early childhood education, medical laboratory technology, medical secretarial sciences, radiological technology, accounting, and civil & public service. Remedial mathematics and English programs available.
Admissions High school graduation, medical exam, and proof of New York City residency required. Rolling admissions. Advanced placement program.
Student Life No campus housing. Cafeteria operated on campus.

■[1] GRADUATE SCHOOL AND UNIVERSITY CENTER (CUNY)
33 West 42 Street, New York 10036, (212) 790-4395

• **Enrollment: 1,282m, 1,106w (all graduates)**

A public graduate school of the City University of New York, with the first PhD granted in 1965. Urban campus across from the New York Public Library. Air, rail, bus, and subway service.
Academic Character MSACS accreditation. The school conducts 5 masters programs and the CUNY doctoral programs in the humanities, social sciences, mathematics, and education, and it administers the other CUNY doctoral programs in the fields of sciences, engineering, business, and criminal justice, for a total of 28 doctoral programs. It also serves as the center for many other university-wide academic programs, research centers, summer institutes, and continuing education programs. Total university library of over 3,750,000 volumes with microform resources.
Financial Financial aid available includes grants, loans, work-study, and fellowships.

■[1] HERBERT H. LEHMAN COLLEGE (CUNY)
Bedford Park Blvd. West, Bronx 10468, (212) 960-8000
Director of Admissions: Dr. Ann Quinley

• **Undergraduates: 1,931m, 3,379w; 9,351 total (including graduates)**
• **Tuition (1982/83): $925 (in-state), $1,425 (out-of-state)**
• **Fees: $51**
• **Degrees offered: BA, BS, BFA**
• **Student-faculty ratio: 18 to 1**

A public college founded in 1931, established as an independent school in 1968. 38-acre campus in an urban residential area of the Bronx. Air, rail, bus, and subway service.
Academic Character MSACS and professional accreditation. Semester system, 6-week summer term. Over 60 majors offered in the areas of accounting, area studies, arts, business education, classics, dance, English, geography, geology, health services, Hebrew/Judaic studies, humanities, languages & literatures, linguistics, math/computer science, music, nursing, physical/recreation education, psychology, sciences, social sciences, speech, and theatre. Distributive requirements. MA, MS, MFA granted. Independent study, Phi Beta Kappa, pass/fail, cooperative work/study. Curriculum for Self-Determined Studies provides honors work & seminars. 4-year BA/MA programs. Study abroad. Elementary, secondary, and special education certification. ROTC at Fordham. Computer center, language lab. 380,000-volume library.
Financial Application procedures vary with programs. State scholarships, grants, loans, aid to Native Americans; PELL, SEOG, GSL, NDSL, FISL, NSL, PLUS, CWS, work incentive program.
Admissions High school graduation with solid preparation recommended. GED accepted. Applicants with a GPA of 80% or in the top 33% of their class are eligible. SAT recommended. $20 application fee. Rolling admissions; suggest applying before June 15. *Early Entrance* and *Concurrent Enrollment* programs. Admission deferral possible. Transfers accepted. Credit possible for CEEB AP, CLEP, PEP, and college exams. SEEK program for the academically/economically disadvantaged.
Student Life Student government. Newspaper, magazine, yearbook, radio station. Music, drama, debate groups. Ethnic, honorary, political, religious, service, social, and special interest clubs. 1 fraternity and 1 sorority. No college housing. Cafeteria. 2 semesters of phys ed required. 9 intercollegiate sports for men, 6 for women; intramurals. ECAC, NCAA, CUNY Conference. Student body composition: 70% minority. 1% of students from out of state.

■[1] HUNTER COLLEGE (CUNY)
659 Park Avenue, New York 10021, (212) 570-5483
Director of Admissions: William DiBrienza

• **Undergraduates: 2,300m, 7,100w; 17,990 total (including evening)**
• **Tuition (1982/83): $1,270 (in-state), $1,724 (out-of-state)**
• **Room: $1,050**
• **Degrees offered: BA, BS, BFA, BMus, BSN**
• **Student-faculty ratio: 18 to 1**

A public college established in 1870. Urban campus of 3 blocks in New York City. Air, rail, bus, and subway service.
Academic Character MSACS and professional accreditation. Semester system, 6-week summer term. Over 65 majors offered in the areas of accounting, anthropology, archaeology, area studies, arts, Chinese, classics, communications, community health education, computer, dance, education, energy policy studies, environmental health/science, film production, geography, geology, Hebrew, home economics, humanities, languages & literatures, math, medical lab sciences, Medieval studies, music, nursing, philosophy/religion, physical therapy, psychology, sciences, social sciences, statistics, theatre/cinema, urban studies, and women's studies. Double majors. Minor required. Distributive requirements in liberal arts. MA, MS, MSW, MUP granted. Independent study, honors program, Phi Beta Kappa, credit/no credit, cooperative work/study, internships. Preprofessional programs in dentistry, engineering, law, medicine, optometry, pharmacy, social work, veterinary medicine. Transfer programs in dentistry, medicine, veterinary medicine. 4- and 5-year BA/MA, BS/MS programs. Cross-registration with Marymount-Manhattan and Yivo Institute. Elementary and secondary education certification. Art gallery, language lab. 456,618-volume library.
Financial Application procedures vary with programs. College scholarships, loans, state scholarships, grants, loans, aid to Native Americans, payment plan; PELL, SEOG, NDSL, FISL, NSL, PLUS, CWS. Application deadline April 30 for scholarships & grants.
Admissions High school graduation with at least 10 units required. GED accepted. Applicants with a GPA of 80%, combined SAT of 900, or in the top 33% of their class are eligible. SAT recommended. $20 application fee. Rolling admissions; deadline January 15. *Early Entrance* Program. Admission deferral possible. Transfers accepted. Credit possible for CEEB AP, CLEP, state, and college exams.
Student Life Student government. Newspaper, literary paper, yearbook, radio station. Music & drama groups. Academic, ethnic, honorary, professional, religious, and special interest clubs. Fraternities and sororities. Limited dorm space for scholarship, health science, and nursing students. 1 semester of phys ed required. 9 intercollegiate sports for men, 7 for women; intramurals. AIAW, NCAA, CUNY Conference. Student body composition: 4.5% Asian, 29.7% Black, 15.1% Hispanic, 0.9% Native American, 48.4% White, 1.4% Other.

■[1] JOHN JAY COLLEGE OF CRIMINAL JUSTICE (CUNY)
445 West 59 Street, New York 10019, (212) 489-5080
Director of Admissions: Francis M. McHugh

• **Undergraduates: 1,920m, 1,832w; 5,900 total (including graduates)**
• **Tuition (1982/83): $1,075 (in-state), $1,575 (out-of-state)**
• **Fees: $65**
• **Degrees offered: BA, BS, AS**
• **Student-faculty ratio: 17 to 1**

A public college established in 1964. Urban campus near Lincoln Center in Manhattan. Air, rail, bus, and subway service.
Academic Character MSACS accreditation. Semester system, summer term. Majors offered in correction administration, criminal justice, criminal justice administration/planning, deviant behavior & social control, fire service administration, forensic pathology, forensic science, government/public administration, and police science. Courses include anthropology, art, communications, economics, English, foreign languages & literatures, government, history, law, mathematics, music, philosophy, psychology, sciences, sociology, speech, and theatre. Puerto Rican and Afro-American studies programs. Associate degrees offered in correction administration, government/public administration, police science, and security administration. Distributive requirements. MPA, MACJ, MAFD, MSFS granted. Independent study, honors program, pass/fail, cooperative work/study, internships. BA/MA program. Cross-registration with other CUNY colleges. Study abroad in England, Ireland. Computer center. Research centers. 130,000-volume library.
Financial Application procedures vary with programs. State scholarships, grants, loans, aid to Native Americans; PELL, SEOG, NDSL, GSL, FISL, CWS, college work program.
Admissions High school graduation or equivalent required. GPA of 75% or placement in top 50% of class required for 4-year programs. $20 application fee. Rolling admissions; suggest applying by January 15. *Early Entrance* and *Concurrent Enrollment* programs. Transfers accepted. Credit possible for CEEB AP, CLEP, and college exams.
Student Life College Council. Newspaper, literary magazine, yearbook, radio station. Music, drama, & dance groups. Women's Coalition. Outdoor Recreation Club. Academic, ethnic, professional, and special interest clubs. No college housing. 7 intercollegiate sports for men, 3 for women; intramurals & coed cheerleading. AIAW, ECAC, NCAA, CUNY Conference. Student body composition: 32% Black, 20% Hispanic, 48% White. 50% of full-time students are over 21. Many students already work in the criminal justice system. 3% of students are from out of state.

■[J1] KINGSBOROUGH COMMUNITY COLLEGE (CUNY)
2001 Oriental Blvd., Brooklyn 11235, (212) 934-5109

• **Undergraduates: 2,123m, 3,396w; 8,425 total (including part-time)**
• **Tuition (1982/83): $????? (in-state), $????? (out-of-state)**
• **Degrees offered: AA, AS, AAS**

A public junior college, first class admitted in 1964. Urban campus. Air, rail, bus, and subway service.
Academic Character MSACS and professional accreditation in nursing. System of fall and spring semesters, 6-week winter & summer modules. Day and evening programs in accounting, art, biology, business administration, chemistry, child care, community mental health, computer science, data processing, liberal arts, mathematics, music, nursing, physics, pre-physical therapy, recreation leadership, retail business management (supermarket management concentration), secretarial science, and theatre arts (radio broadcasting concentration). Continuing Education program. 81,333-volume library.
Financial Financial aid available.

■[J1] LA GUARDIA COMMUNITY COLLEGE (CUNY)
31-10 Thomson Avenue, Long Island City, Queens 11101, (212) 626-2700

• **Undergraduates: 1,936m, 3,980w; 6,926 total (including part-time)**
• **Tuition (1982/83): $X,XXX**
• **Degrees offered: AA, AS, AAS**

A public junior college.
Academic Character MSACS accreditation. Quarter system. Career and transfer programs offered in business, secretarial science, data processing,

occupational therapy, liberal arts & sciences, accounting, mortuary science, and education. College is run on a cooperative work/study program. Each student interns for three 13-week quarters during a two year period of study.
Admissions Open admissions program.
Student Life No college dormitories. Small cafeteria operated on campus. Intramural athletics program.

■[J1] MANHATTAN, BOROUGH OF, COMMUNITY COLLEGE (CUNY)

199 Chambers Street, New York 10007, (212) 262-5460

- **Undergraduates: 2,290m, 3,476w; 8,950 total (including part-time)**
- **Tuition (1982/83): $????? (in-state), $????? (out-of-state)**
- **Degrees offered: AA, AAS**

A public junior college. Urban campus. Air, rail, bus, and subway service.
Academic Character MSACS and professional accreditation. Semester system. Terminal/career and 4-year college transfer programs available. Majors offered with an AA in business administration (transfer), dance, fine arts, liberal arts (transfer), performing arts/music, physical education, recreation leadership, social service, and urban planning. Majors for an AAS in accounting, business management (advertising, banking & finance, marketing), community mental health assistant, data processing (programming, operations), inhalation therapy, medical emergency technology, medical record technology, nursing, respiratory therapy technology, and secretarial science (bilingual, executive, legal, New York City school secretary). Cooperative work/study program for students in career programs. Remedial mathematics and English programs.
Admissions Admissions notification is done on a rolling basis.
Student Life Student body composition: 70% minority.

■[1] MEDGAR EVERS COLLEGE (CUNY)

1150 Carroll Street, Brooklyn 11225, (212) 735-1947
Director of Admissions: Roberta Dannenfelser

- **Undergraduates: 727m, 1,512w; 2,988 total (including graduates)**
- **Tuition (1982/83): $925 (in-state), $1,425 (out-of-state)**
- **Fees: $51**
- **Degrees offered: BS, AA, AS, AAS**
- **Student-faculty ratio: 23 to 1**

A public college established in 1969, opened in 1971. One-acre urban campus in New York City. Air, rail, bus, and subway service.
Academic Character MSACS and professional accreditation. Semester system, 6-week summer term. Majors offered in accounting, biology, business administration, early childhood & elementary education, and public administration. Major in nursing for students with an RN. Terminal and transfer majors offered for an associate degree in business administration, computer applications, elementary education, liberal arts, public administration, science, and secretarial science. Courses in 20 additional areas including advertising design, communications, and urban planning. Common Core program for freshmen. Independent study, honors program, cooperative work/study, pass/fail, credit by exam, internships. Cross-registration with other CUNY colleges. Elementary education certification. Community Education program. Language lab, computer center. 77,568-volume library.
Financial Application procedures vary with programs. State scholarships, grants, loans, aid to Native Americans; PELL, SEOG, NSS, NDSL, GSL, NSL, CWS. Application deadline April 15 for scholarships & grants.
Admissions High school graduation required. GED accepted. $20 application fee. Rolling admissions; suggest applying as soon as possible. Admission deferral possible. Transfers accepted. Credit possible for CEEB CLEP exams.
Student Life Student government. Newspaper, yearbook, radio station. Drama and dance groups. Ethnic, religious, and special interest clubs. Food service. 1 semester of phys ed required. Regular class attendance required. 4 intercollegiate sports for men, 3 for women. NCAA, CUNY Conference. Student body composition: 89% Black, 5% Hispanic, 5% White, 1% Other. 70% of undergraduates are over 21. 3% from out of state.

■[2] MOUNT SINAI SCHOOL OF MEDICINE (CUNY)

One Gustave L. Levy Place, New York 10029, (212) 650-6500

- **Enrollment: 301m, 158w**
- **Tuition (1982/83): $10,400**
- **Degrees offered: MD, PhD**

A privately supported institution affiliated with the City University of New York. First class was graduated in 1970.
Academic Character Professional accreditation in medicine and health services administration. 4-year program of medical education offered leading to an MD. PhD offered in Biomedical Science. First two years of MD program conducted primarily on campus. 3rd and 4th years are pursued in the school's major teaching hospital, Mount Sinai Hospital, which is located on campus, and in four other affiliated hospitals located in New York City. Field work opportunities for medical students in public and private health care institutions and community-based projects.
Financial Aid including scholarships and loans available.
Student Life One dorm on campus. School aids students in finding adequate housing.

■[J1] NEW YORK CITY TECHNICAL COLLEGE (CUNY)

300 Jay Street, Brooklyn 11201, (212) 643-8595

- **Undergraduates: 7,250 men & women (day), 6,920 (evening)**
- **Tuition (1982/83): $????? (in-state), $????? (out-of-state)**
- **Degrees offered: AA, AS, AAS**

A public junior college. Urban campus. Additional Voorhees Campus located at 450 West 41st Street. Air, rail, bus, and subway service.
Academic Character MSACS and professional accreditation. Semester system, 6-week summer term. Terminal/career and college transfer programs available. Majors offered with an AA/AS in liberal arts and sciences. Other programs include accountancy, art & advertising design, data processing, dental hygiene, hotel & restaurant management, human services, marketing, nursing, ophthalmic dispensing, secretarial science, and architectural, automotive, chemical, construction, dental laboratory, design drafting, electrical/electronics, electromechanical, environmental control, graphic arts & advertising, lithographic offset, machine tool, mechanical, medical laboratory, and radiologic technologies. Remedial mathematics and English programs.
Admissions High school graduation or equivalent required. Admissions notification is done on a rolling basis.
Student Life No dormitories. Student body composition: 50% minority.

■[1] QUEENS COLLEGE (CUNY)

65-30 Kissena Blvd., Flushing 11367, (212) 520-7323
Director of Pre-Admissions: Richard Bory

- **Undergraduates: 6,576m, 8,791w; 17,500 total (including part-time)**
- **Tuition (1982/83): $925 (in-state), $1,425 (out-of-state)**
- **Fees: $142**
- **Degrees offered: BA, BMus, BSHealth & Phys Ed**

A public college established in 1937. 76-acre campus in an urban, residential section of Flushing. Air, rail, and bus service nearby.
Academic Character MSACS and professional accreditation. Semester system, 3-week June & 6-week summer terms. Over 40 majors offered in the areas of accounting, anthropology, art, biology, chemistry, communications, comparative literature, computer science, earth sciences, economics, education, English, film, geology, history, home economics, languages & literatures, linguistics, math, music, philosophy, physical education, physics, political science, psychology, sociology, urban studies, Yiddish, and drama, theatre, & dance. Interdisciplinary & individual majors. Many area studies programs. MA, MLS, MSEd granted. Independent study, honors program, Phi Beta Kappa, credit by exam. Preprofessional programs in accounting, dentistry, education, engineering, law, medicine, pharmacy, and veterinary medicine. BA/MA programs in 6 fields. Study abroad. Early childhood, elementary, and secondary education preparation. Evening College. Performing arts center. TV studio. 500,000-volume library with microform resources.
Financial Application procedures vary with programs. College scholarships, state scholarships, grants, loans, aid to Native Americans; PELL, SEOG, NDSL, FISL, CWS.
Admissions High school graduation required. GED accepted. SAT required (combined score of 900 recommended). $20 application fee. Rolling admissions; suggest applying as soon as possible. *Early Admission* and *Concurrent Enrollment* programs. Transfers accepted. Credit possible for CEEB CLEP, ACT PEP, and college exams.
Student Life Student government. Newspapers, literary magazine, radio station. Several music groups & drama productions. Academic, ethnic, political, religious, and special interest clubs. No college housing. Dining facilities. Intercollegiate and intramural sports for men and women. Student body composition: 4.4% Asian, 14.2% Black, 8.3% Hispanic, 1.1% Native American, 70.4% White, 1.6% Other.

■[J1] QUEENSBOROUGH COMMUNITY COLLEGE (CUNY)

Springfield Blvd. & 56 Avenue, Bayside 11364, (212) 631-6262

- **Undergraduates: 3,550m, 3,379w; 12,000 total (including part-time)**
- **Tuition (1982/83): $X,XXX**
- **Degrees offered: AA, AS, AAS**

A public junior college.
Academic Character MSACS and professional accreditation. 2-year transfer programs offered in liberal arts & sciences, business administration, environmental health, and pre-engineering. 2-year career programs in accounting, marketing management, transportation management, electrical technology (electronic and computer), mechanical technology, medical laboratory technology, nursing, and design-drafting technology. Certificate programs offered in data processing, photography, word processing, and medical office technology. Remedial mathematics and English programs.
Admissions High school graduation required. Rolling admissions. *Early Admission* and *Early Decision* programs. Advanced placement program.

■[1] STATEN ISLAND COLLEGE (CUNY)

715 Ocean Terrace, Staten Island 10301, (212) 390-7940
Assistant Dean of Admissions & Recruitment: Ann Merlino

- **Undergraduates: 2,825m, 2,817w; 10,416 total (including graduates)**
- **Tuition (1982/83): $872 (in-state), $1,372 (out-of-state)**
- **Fees: $53**
- **Degrees offered: BA, BS**
- **Student-faculty ratio: 29 to 1**

A public college established in 1976 by the union of Staten Island Community and Richmond Colleges. 36-acre Sunnyside campus plus high-rise St. George campus in the middle of the Civic Center. Ferry to New York City, which has air, rail, and bus service.
Academic Character MSACS accreditation. Semester system. Over 40 majors offered in the areas of anthropology, area studies, art, cinema, computer, drama, economics, education, engineering, English, history, international studies, math, medical technology, music, philosophy, political science, psychology, Romance languages, sciences, sociology, women's studies, and science, letters, & society. Major in nursing for students with an RN. Transfer AA/AS offered in business, pre-architecture, community service assistant, environmental health, computer science, liberal arts & sciences, and engineering science. Terminal degrees in business, nursing, industrial

technology/management; civil, electrical, mechanical, science lab, medical lab, computer, and electro-mechanical technologies. Distributive requirements. GRE required for graduation. Independent study, honors program, internships. Preprofessional programs in dentistry, law, medicine, veterinary medicine. Off-campus study. Cross-registration with other CUNY colleges. Early childhood, elementary, and secondary education certification. Continuing Education program. Computer, film studio. Over 165,000-volume library with microform resources.
Financial Application procedures vary with programs. State scholarships, grants, loans, aid to Native Americans; PELL, SEOG, NSS, NDSL, GSL, CWS.
Admissions High school graduation or equivalent required. GED accepted. Applicants with a GPA of 80% or in the top 33% of their class are eligible. Open admission with high school diploma or equivalent for associate's programs. $20 application fee. Rolling admissions; suggest applying as early as possible. *Early Entrance* Program. Transfers accepted. Credit possible for CEEB CLEP and college exams. SEEK program for the academically/economically disadvantaged.
Student Life Student government. Newspaper, literary magazines, radio station, TV studio. Honorary and special interest groups. No college housing. Cafeterias on both campuses. 2 semesters of phys ed required. 5 intercollegiate sports for men, 3 for women. ECAC, NCAA, CUNY Conference. Student body composition: 3.8% Asian, 17.1% Black, 7.9% Hispanic, 0.8% Native American, 69.3% White, 1.1% Other.

■[1] YORK COLLEGE (CUNY)

Jamaica 11451, (212) 969-4040
Director of Admissions: Ronnie Levitt

- **Undergraduates: 999m, 1,475w**
- **Tuition (1982/83): $1,075 (in-state), $1,575 (out-of-state)**
- **Fees: $55**
- **Degrees offered: BA, BS**
- **Student-faculty ratio: 17 to 1**

A public college established in 1966. Campus in Jamaica, New York. Air, rail, bus, and subway nearby.
Academic Character MSACS accreditation. Semester system, summer term. Majors offered in the areas of accounting, Afro-American studies, anthropology, biology, business administration, chemistry, community health education, economics, elementary education, English, environmental health science, fine arts, French, geology, gerontology, health education, history, information systems management, Italian, marketing, math, medical technology, music, occupational therapy, philosophy, physical education, physics, political science, psychology, social work, sociology, Spanish, and speech. Self-designed majors. Certificate programs in Judaic, Latin American, Puerto Rican studies. Courses in 13 other areas including Chinese, Greek, Hebrew, Russian, Swahili, and Yiddish. Distributive requirements. Independent study, honors program, pass/fail, internships. Cooperative work/study in business administration, computer studies, and gerontology. Preprofessional programs in architecture, dentistry, engineering, medicine. Elementary and secondary education certification. Computer. 160,000-volume library.
Financial Application procedures vary with programs. State scholarships, grants, loans, aid to Native Americans; PELL, SEOG, NDSL, GSL, CWS.
Admissions High school graduation or equivalent required. GED accepted. Additional requirements for health majors. $20 application fee. Rolling admissions; suggest applying as early as possible. *Early Decision, Early Admission, Concurrent Enrollment* programs. Transfers accepted. Credit possible for CEEB CLEP and ACT PEP exams; college has own advanced placement program. SEEK program for academically/economically disadvantaged students. Flexible admissions for veterans & adults.
Student Life Student government. Music groups. Cultural activities. Academic, athletic, political, and special interest clubs. No college housing. 2 credits of phys ed required. 8 intercollegiate sports for men, 1 for women; intramurals. AIAW, NCAA, ECAC, CUNY Conference. Student body composition: 10% Asian, 50% Black, 20% Hispanic, 20% White. 5% from out of state.

[1] CLARKSON COLLEGE OF TECHNOLOGY

Potsdam 13676, (315) 268-6400
Director of Freshman Admissions: Robert A. Croot

- **Undergraduates: 2,876m, 788; 3,867 total (including graduates)**
- **Tuition (1982/83): $6,120**
- **Room & Board: $2,879; Fees: $200**
- **Degrees offered: BS, BProf Studies**
- **Mean SAT 530v, 640m**
- **Student-faculty ratio: 20 to 1**

A private college established in 1896. 650-acre small-city campus in Potsdam, 140 miles north of Syracuse. Bus service.
Academic Character MSACS and professional accreditation. Semester system, 2 5-week summer terms. Majors offered in accounting, biology, chemistry, computer science, economics & finance, engineering, history, humanities, industrial distribution, industrial hygiene/environmental toxicology, management & marketing, mathematics, physics, psychology,, social sciences, sociology, technical communications. Self-designed & interdisciplinary studies. Distributive requirements. Graduate and professional degrees granted. Independent study. Pass/fail. Preprofessional programs in law, dentistry, medicine. 3-2 programs in engineering with several New York state colleges. Cross-registration with SUNY College at Potsdam and St. Lawrence U. Member of Associated Colleges of St. Lawrence Valley consortium. STRETCH Program. Study abroad. ROTC, AFROTC. Institute of Colloid and Surface Science. Division of Research. Educational Resources Center, incorporating computer center, technologically-assisted education, and library with microform resources.
Financial CEEB CSS. College scholarships, grants, loans, state aid; PELL, SEOG, NDSL, GSL, CWS. Application deadline February 1.
Admissions High school graduation with 16 units required. Interview and 3 ACH recommended. SAT or ACT required. $25 application fee. Rolling admissions; application deadline April 1. $50 tuition and $100 room deposits required on acceptance of offer of admission. *Early Decision, Early Admission, Concurrent Enrollment* programs. Admission deferral possible. Transfers accepted. Credit possible for CEEB AP and CLEP exams; college has own placement exams.
Student Life Student government. Newspaper, magazine, yearbook, radio and TV stations. Music, drama, athletic, academic, honorary, professional, religious, special interest groups. 13 fraternities with houses. 20% of men join. Students live on campus unless living at home. 84% of students live on campus. 11 intercollegiate sports for men, 9 for women. Intramural sports program. ECAC, ICAC, NCAA, AIAW. Student body composition: 0.2% Black, 0.3% Hispanic, 0.2% Native American, 96% White, 3.3% Other.

[J1] CLINTON COMMUNITY COLLEGE

Plattsburgh 12901

[P] COLGATE ROCHESTER/BEXLEY HALL/CROZER

Rochester 14620

[1] COLGATE UNIVERSITY

Hamilton 13346, (315) 824-1000
Director of Admissions: David S. Perham

- **Enrollment: 1,500m, 1,100w**
- **Tuition (1982/83): $7,410**
- **Room & Board: $2,785; Fees: $80**
- **Degree offered: BA**
- **Mean SAT 579v, 621m**
- **Student-faculty ratio: 13 to 1**

A private university established in 1819. University became coed in 1970. 1,400-acre rural campus, 40 miles southeast of Syracuse. Bus service.
Academic Character MSACS accreditation. 4-1-4 system. 36 majors offered in the areas of fine arts, music, humanities, math, sciences, social sciences, economics, religion, peace studies, international relations, political science. Minors offered in all fields. Distributive requirements. MA, MAT granted. Independent study. Honors program. Phi Beta Kappa. Pass/fail, internships. Preprofessional programs in engineering, theology, law, medicine, government service, business and management. 3-2, 3-3 programs in engineering, management engineering with Carnegie-Mellon, Columbia, Dartmouth, RPI, U of Rochester. Colgate Visiting Student Program. Off-Campus, Study Group Programs. Sea Semester. Washington Semester. January Special Studies Period. Study abroad. Secondary education certification. Observatory, Computer Center, Dana Arts Center. Eric Ryan Studio. 360,000-volume library with microform resources; departmental libraries.
Financial CEEB CSS. University scholarships, grants, loans, state aid; PELL, SEOG, NDSL, CWS. Application deadline February 1.
Admissions High school graduation with 16 units required. SAT and ACH, or ACT required. Campus visit recommended. $35 application fee. Application deadline January 15. $300 deposit required on acceptance of offer of admission. *Early Decision* and *Early Admission* programs. Admission deferral possible. Transfers accepted. Credit possible for CEEB AP, CLEP, state, departmental exams. University has own placement program. HEOP; University Scholars Program.
Student Life Student government. Newspapers, magazines, yearbook, radio and TV stations. Music, debate, drama, outing, service, academic, religious, athletic, honorary, special interest groups. 10 fraternities, 2 sororities, 1 coed fraternity. Students live on campus. Coed, single-sex, language, and special interest housing. 87% of students live on campus. 8 units of phys ed and survival swim test required. 11 intercollegiate sports for men, 8 for women; many intramural and club sports. AIAW, ECAC, NCAA. Student body composition: 3% Asian, 6% Black, 2% Hispanic, 89% White. 50% from out of state.

[1] COLUMBIA UNIVERSITY

Broadway & West 116 Street, New York 10027, (212) 280-2521

- **Undergraduates: 2,800m; 17,000 men & women total (including graduates)**
- **Tuition (1982/83): $7,894**
- **Room & Board: $3,554**
- **Degree offered: AB**
- **Mean SAT 630v, 650m**
- **Student-faculty ratio: 5 to 1**

A private university including the undergraduate Columbia College for men, which is coordinate with Barnard College for women. Established in 1754. Urban campus in Morningside Heights area of New York City. Air, rail, bus, and subway service.
Academic Character MSACS and professional accreditation. Semester system, 2 6-week summer terms. Over 45 majors offered in the areas of ancient studies, anthropology, architecture, art history, computer, East Asian studies, geography, geology, geophysics, history, 10 languages & literatures, linguistics, math, Medieval-Renaissance studies, Middle East studies, music, philosophy, psychology, religion, sciences, social sciences, statistics, and urban studies. Interdepartmental and self-designed majors. Special programs in chemistry. Courses in other areas including film, Korean, Portuguese. Distributive requirements. Graduate and professional degrees granted. Independent study, Phi Beta Kappa, pass/fail, internships. Seminar institute for some junior and seniors, who take one intensive course per semester. Preprofessional programs in medicine and dentistry. Cross-registration with Barnard and other University divisions. 5-year programs with University

graduate schools including Arts, Engineering, International Affairs, and Teachers College. Study abroad. Numerous research institutes and centers. Computer Center. Language lab. Over 5,000,000-volume library.
Financial CEEB CSS. University scholarships, grants, loans, payment plans; PELL, SEOG, NDSL, GSL, part-time employment. Application deadlines February 16 (scholarships & grants), August 1 (loans).
Admissions High school graduation with college prep program recommended. SAT and 3 ACH required. $30 application fee. Application deadline January 1; notification in mid-April. *Early Admission* and *Early Decision* programs. Transfers accepted. Credit possible for CEEB AP exams.
Student Life Student government. Newspaper, magazines, yearbook, radio & TV stations. Several music groups. Drama groups, Gilbert and Sullivan Society. Debate. Asian Student Union, Black Student Union, Chicano Caucus. Service, academic, athletic, religious, special interest, and political clubs. 18 fraternities, most with houses. 16% of men join. Freshmen must live at home or on campus. Men's and coed dorms. 85% of students live on campus. Class attendance required for freshmen. 2 terms of phys ed required. Many intercollegiate and intramural sports. Ivy League. Student body composition: 10% Asian, 8% Black, 6% Hispanic, 75% White, 1% Other. 62% from out of state.

■[1] BARNARD COLLEGE
606 West 120th Street, New York 10027, (212) 280-2014
Director of Admissions: R. Christine Royer

- **Undergraduates: 2,500w**
- **Tuition & Fees (1982/83): $8,142**
- **Room & Board: $3,830**
- **Degree offered: BA**
- **Mean SAT 620v, 600m**
- **Student-faculty ratio: 11 to 1**

A private women's college coordinate with undergraduate Columbia College for men. Established in 1889, joined Columbia University in 1900. 4-acre urban campus in Morningside Heights area of New York City. Air, rail, bus, and subway service.
Academic Character MSACS accreditation. Semester system, 2 6-week summer terms. Over 50 majors offered in the areas of American studies, ancient studies, anthropology, architecture, art history, biopsychology, computer, education, English, foreign area studies, French translation & literature, geography, geology, history, languages & literatures, linguistics, maths, Medieval & Renaissance studies, music, Oriental studies, philosophy, psychology, religion, sciences, social sciences, urban studies, and women's studies. Program in the arts for students gifted in dance, music, theatre, visual arts, writing. Self-designed majors. Programs in health & society, humanities, experimental studies. Distributive requirements; GRE required in some majors. Independent study, Phi Beta Kappa, pass/fail, internships. Senior Scholar Program. Cross-registration with Columbia College and other University divisions. 5-year programs with University graduate schools including schools of Engineering and International Affairs. 3-3 program with Law School. Study possible at Jewish Theological Seminary, Manhattan School of Music. Study abroad. Elementary and secondary education certification. Language lab, theatre. 150,000-volume library plus access to University library of over 5,000,000 volumes.
Financial CEEB CSS. College scholarships, grants, loans, payment plans; PELL, SEOG, NDSL, GSL, CWS, institutional work program. Application deadline February 1 (scholarships & grants).
Admissions High school graduation with college prep program recommended. Interview strongly recommended. SAT and 3 ACH required. $25 application fee. Application deadline January 15; notification in mid-April. *Early Decision* and *Early Admission* programs. Admission deferral possible. Transfers accepted. Credit possible for CEEB AP exams. HEOP for New York State residents.
Student Life Student Council. Newspaper, literary magazine, yearbook, radio station. Several music groups. Drama groups, Gilbert and Sullivan Society. Debate. Women's Center. Service, academic, religious, pre-professional, special interest, and political clubs. Women's, coed, and apartment-style dorms. 58% of students live on campus. Honor system. Regular class attendance expected. 2 years of phys ed required. 9 intercollegiate sports; intramural & club sports. Student body composition: 10% Asian, 5% Black, 5% Hispanic, 80% White. 65% from out of state.

■[1] COLUMBIA UNIVERSITY SCHOOL OF GENERAL STUDIES
Lewisohn Hall, New York 10027

[J1] COLUMBIA-GREENE COMMUNITY COLLEGE
PO Box 1000, Hudson 12534

[1] CONCORDIA COLLEGE
171 White Plains Road, Bronxville 10708, (914) 337-9300
Director of Admissions: John Bahr

- **Enrollment: 192m, 212w; 443 total (including part-time)**
- **Tuition (1982/83): $3,170**
- **Room & Board: $2,055; Fees: $515**
- **Degrees offered: BA, BS, AA, AAS**
- **Student-faculty ratio: 11 to 1**

A private college controlled by the Lutheran Church-Missouri Synod, established in 1881. Suburban campus.
Academic Character MSACS and professional accreditation. Semester system. Majors offered in behavioral sciences, biology, business education, education, educational services, English, environmental science, history, interdisciplinary studies, Judeo-Christian heritage, mathematics, music, and social work. Minors required. Associate degrees in liberal arts, and in terminal programs for business and medical secretaries. Distributives and 9 hours of religion required. Independent study. Preprofessional programs in business, journalism, law, medicine, nursing, seminary. Elementary, secondary, and special education certification. Language lab. 40,000-volume library.
Financial College scholarships, grants, loans, Lutheran grants, payment plans; PELL, SEOG, GSL, CWS.
Admissions High school graduation with 16 units recommended. SAT or ACT required. $15 application fee. Rolling admissions. $150 deposit due on acceptance of admissions offer. *Early Admission* Program. Credit possible for CEEB AP, CLEP, and ACT PEP exams.
Student Life Student government. Cultural, religious, social, and special interest activities. Students must live at home or on campus. Dorms for men and women. No married-student housing. Daily chapel. 2 hours of phys ed required. Intercollegiate and intramural sports.

[1] COOPER UNION
New York 10003, (212) 254-6300
Director of Admissions: Herbert Liebeskind

- **Undergraduates: 572m, 277w**
- **Tuition (1982/83): None**
- **Fees: $300**
- **Degrees offered: BS, BFA, BEng, BArch**
- **Mean SAT 561v, 577m**
- **Student-faculty ratio: 6 to 1**

A private college established in New York City in 1859. City campus of 3 buildings in Cooper Square. Air, bus, rail service.
Academic Character MSACS and professional accreditation. Semester system. Majors offered in architecture, drawing, graphic design, painting, photography, sculpture, chemical engineering, civil engineering, electrical engineering, mechanical engineering. Certificates offered in art. Courses in liberal arts. Distributive requirements. Graduate degrees granted. Independent study. Honors program. Pass/fail, internships. Exchange program with 6 East Coast schools, 1 West Coast school, 4 European schools for art majors. Joint BS/BE, BS/ME programs with New York U. Cross-registration with Parsons School of Design. Interim Year offered at School of Architecture. 95,000-volume library; access to other area libraries.
Financial No tuition charges; admission to Cooper Union constitutes a full tuition scholarship. CEEB CSS. College grants, awards, state aid; PELL, SEOG, NDSL, GSL, CWS. FAF application deadline March 30.
Admissions High school graduation with 16 units required. Home project required of applicant to schools of art or architecture. SAT required; also 2 ACH for engineering applicants. $10 application fee. Application deadlines January 1 for art and architecture, February 1 for engineering. $300 deposit required on acceptance of offer of admission. *Early Admission* program. Admission deferral possible. Transfers accepted. Credit possible for CEEB AP and CLEP exams.
Student Life Student councils. Newspaper, literary and graphics magazine, yearbook. Music, drama, honorary, academic, professional, special interest groups. No student housing; 80% of students live at home. Class attendance required. Intercollegiate bowling; intramural programs. Student body composition: 7.4% Asian, 1.5% Black, 3.4% Hispanic, 86.4% White, 1.3% Other. 20% from out of state.

[1] CORNELL UNIVERSITY
Ithaca 48103, (607) 256-1000
Dean of Admissions: James Scannell

- **Undergraduates: 6,943m, 4,844w; 16,340 total (including graduates)**
- **Public School Tuition (1982/83): $3,300 (in-state), $5,350 (out-of-state)**
- **Private School Tuition (1982/83): $7,950**
- **Room & Board: $3,050; Fees: $50**
- **Degrees offered: BA, BS, BArch, BFA**
- **Mean SAT 589v, 647m**
- **Student-faculty ratio: 6 to 1**

A private university established in 1865. 3 divisions are New York State colleges. 734-acre campus in Ithaca, 45 miles from Syracuse. Air and bus service.
Academic Character MSACS and professional accreditation. Semester system, 3-, 6-, and 8-week summer terms. 38 majors offered by the College of Arts & Sciences, 40 by the College of Agriculture & Life Sciences, 8 by the College of Architecture, Art, & Planning, 11 by the College of Engineering, 9 by the College of Human Ecology, and majors in the schools of Hotel Administration and Industrial & Labor Relations. Self-designed majors. Interdisciplinary programs and courses. Distributive requirements. Graduate and professional degrees granted. Independent study. Honors programs. Phi Beta Kappa. Cooperative work/study, pass/fail, internships. Preprofessional programs in business, law, dentistry, medicine, veterinary medicine. 5-year BA/MA programs in business administration, public administration, hospital and health services administration. 6-year BS/MBA/ME. Study abroad. Cornell-in-Washington Program. Program on Science, Technology, and Society. Secondary education certification. AFROTC, NROTC, ROTC. Computer Services. Language labs. Remedial education programs. Observatory. Research facilities. Herbert F. Johnson Museum of Art. 16 libraries with 4,500,000 volumes and microform resources.
Financial CEEB CSS. University scholarships, grants, loans, state aid; PELL, SEOG, NDSL, GSL, CWS. Application deadline January 15.
Admissions High school graduation with 16 units required. College of Architecture, Art, and Planning, School of Industrial & Labor Relations, and School of Hotel Management require interviews. SAT or ACT required; some colleges require ACH exams. $30 application fee. Application deadline January 1. $200 deposit required on acceptance of offer of admission. *Early Decision* and *Early Admission* programs. Admission deferral possible. Transfers accepted. Credit possible for CEEB AP programs and CLEP exams;

some departmental advanced placement exams. COSEP, HEOP, EOP.
Student Life Student government. Newspapers, magazines, yearbook, radio station. Music, debate, drama, service, religious, academic, honorary, political, special interest groups. 48 fraternities, 12 sororities all with houses; 37% of men and 22% of women join. Coed and non-coed dorms, cooperative, special interest, married-student housing; 50% of students live on campus. 2 semesters of phys ed required. 20 intercollegiate sports for men, 16 for women; 19 intramurals. Ivy League. Student body composition: 4% Asian, 7% Black, 2% Hispanic, 85% White. 46% from out of state.

[J1] CORNING COMMUNITY COLLEGE
Spencer Hill, Corning 14830

[J2] CULINARY INSTITUTE OF AMERICA, THE
PO Box 53, Hyde Park 12538, (914) 452-9600
Director of Admissions: Wayne J. Berning

- **Enrollment: 1,750**
- **Estimated Expenses (1982/83): $5,906**
- **Degree offered: AOS**
- **Student-faculty ratio: 20 to 1**

A private school established in 1946. 75-acre campus, 3 miles north of Poughkeepsie. Served by air, rail, and bus.
Academic Character NYSBR accreditation. 4 terms, 1 externship. Progressive curriculum in culinary arts and professional food service development. Baking majors program. Cross-registration with 4 area colleges. 4 public restaurants. Learning resources center. 20,000-volume library.
Financial Scholarships, grants, loans, PELL, SEOG, NDSL, GSL, PLUS, CWS, fellowships.
Admissions High school graduation required. Equivalency diplomas accepted. 4-months food service employment recommended. Employer references. Interview recommended. $25 application fee. 72 students admitted 16 times each year. Transfers accepted.
Student Life Student government. Newspaper, television station. Professional and social activities. Class attendance mandatory. Sports facilities. Student body composition: 29% minority.

[1] DAEMEN COLLEGE
Amherst 14226, (716) 839-3600
Vice President for Admissions: Peter W. Stevens

- **Undergraduates: 468m, 854w**
- **Tuition (1982/83): $4,090**
- **Room & Board: $2,200; Fees: $185**
- **Degrees offered: BA, BS, BFA, BMus**
- **Mean SAT 480v, 490m**
- **Student-faculty ratio: 13 to 1**

A private college founded by the Order of St. Francis. 37-acre campus established 1947 in Amherst, a suburb of Buffalo. Air, bus, rail service.
Academic Character MSACS and professional accreditation. Semester system, 4- and 6-week summer terms. 41 majors offered in the areas of arts, sciences, math, computer science, humanities, social sciences, business, education, music, nursing, medical technology, physical therapy, administration, management. Certificate programs. Distributives and 6 hours of religion or philosophy required. Independent study. Cooperative work/study, pass/fail, internships. Preprofessional programs in law, medicine. Member of Western New York Consortium of Higher Education with area schools. Study abroad. Elementary, secondary, special education certification. ROTC at Canisius College. Teaching Resource Center. Language lab. 108,198-volume library.
Financial CEEB CSS. College scholarships, grants, loans, state aid; PELL, SEOG, NDSL, GSL, FISL, CWS. Application deadline March 1.
Admissions High school graduation with 16 units required. GED accepted. Interview recommended; required of theatre arts applicants. Portfolio required of art applicants; music applicants must audition. SAT or ACT required. $15 application fee. Rolling admissions. $50 tuition and $50 room deposits required on acceptance of offer of admission. *Early Decision, Early Admission, Concurrent Enrollment* programs. Admission deferral possible. Transfers accepted. Credit possible for CEEB AP and CLEP exams. HEOP.
Student Life Student government. Newspaper, magazine, yearbook. Music, drama, service, athletic, academic, honorary, special interest organizations. 2 fraternities and 2 sororities without houses. Single-sex dorms. No married-student housing. 44% of students live on campus. Class attendance expected. 3 intercollegiate sports for men, 3 for women; intramurals. NAIA, AIAW. Student body composition: 0.4% Asian, 2.3% Hispanic, 17.6% Black, 1% Native American, 78.5% White, 0.2% Other.

[1] DOMINICAN COLLEGE
Western Highway, Orangeburg 10962

[1] DOWLING COLLEGE
Oakdale 11769, (516) 589-6100
Dean of Admissions: William B. Galloway

- **Undergraduates: 868m, 717w**
- **Tuition (1982/83): $3,480**
- **Room: $1,400; Fees: $270**
- **Degrees offered: BA, BS, BBA**
- **Student-faculty ratio: 7 to 1**

A private college established in 1959. 65-acre campus in Oakdale, Long Island, 60 miles from New York City. Bus and rail stations.
Academic Character MSACS accreditation. 4-1-4 system, 2 6-week summer terms. 25 majors offered in areas of art, music, speech, humanities, science, math, aeronautics, medical technology, economics, business, social sciences, education. Certificates in foreign language proficiency or writing offered. Distributive requirements. MBA, MSEd offered. Independent study. Internships, pass/fail. Preprofessional programs in law, dentistry, medicine, veterinary science. MAEd in cooperation with Adelphi. Elementary, secondary, special education certification. Weekend College. Reading and Learning Clinic. Peter Hausman Resource Center. 90,000-volume library with microform resources; access to other area libraries.
Financial CEEB CSS. College scholarships, grants, loans, state aid; PELL, SEOG, NDSL, CWS. Application deadline May 1.
Admissions High school graduation with 16 units required. GED accepted. Interview required. SAT or ACT required. $20 application fee. Rolling admissions. $150 tuition and $150 room deposits required on acceptance of offer of admission. *Early Admission* and *Concurrent Enrollment* programs. Transfers accepted. Credit possible for CEEB AP, CLEP, USAFI, DANTES exams; college has own departmental exams. HEOP.
Student Life Student government. Newspaper, magazine, yearbook. Drama, music, aviation, academic, honorary, special interest groups. Apartment-style residences for men and women. Class attendance expected. Intercollegiate and intramural sports for men and women. NCAA, ECAC, NAIA.

[J1] DUTCHESS COMMUNITY COLLEGE
Pendell Road, Poughkeepsie 12601

[1] D'YOUVILLE COLLEGE
Buffalo 14201, (716) 886-8100
Director of Admissions and Financial Aid: Linda L. Nissen-McQueen

- **Undergraduates: 141m, 1,008w**
- **Tuition (1982/83): $3,900**
- **Room & Board: $2,180**
- **Degrees offered: BA, BS, BSN**
- **Mean ACT 19.6**
- **Student-faculty ratio: 12 to 1**

A private college founded by the Grey Nuns of the Sacred Heart in 1908. College became coed in 1971. Urban campus in Buffalo served by air, bus, rail.
Academic Character MSACS and professional accreditation. Semester system, 2 3-week and one 6-week summer terms. Majors offered in biology, business, education, English, history, math, medical technology, nursing, philosophy, sociology. General studies. Programs in management, accounting, blind and partially-sighted. Self-designed majors. Courses in other areas. Distributive requirements. Independent study. Cooperative work/study, pass/fail, internships. 3-1 medical technology program with E.J. Meyer leading to BS and certification. Member of Colleges of Western New York Consortium. Semester exchange with area schools. Study abroad. Elementary, secondary, special, and bilingual education certification. ROTC at Canisius. Language lab. Special Service Programs. 125,000-volume library with microform resources.
Financial CEEB CSS. College scholarships, state aid; PELL, SEOG, NSS, NDSL, GSL, NSL, CWS. Application deadline April 1.
Admissions High school graduation with 16 units required. GED accepted. Interview recommended. SAT or ACT required. $15 application fee. Rolling admissions; application deadline July 1. $75 tuition and $100 room deposits required on acceptance of offer of admission. *Concurrent Enrollment* and *Early Admission* programs. Admission deferral possible. Transfers accepted. Credit possible for CEEB AP, CLEP, and ACT PEP exams.
Student Life Student government. Newspaper, yearbook, TV studio. Music, academic, political, honorary, religious, special interest groups. All students (except seniors) must live on campus or at home. Dorms for men and women. No married-student housing. 25% of students live on campus. Limited visitation hours between opposite sexes. Class attendance expected. 3 intercollegiate sports for men, 4 for women; jogging, ski, swim clubs. AIAW, Little League Athletic Association. 4% of students from out of state.

[J1] ELIZABETH SETON COLLEGE
1061 North Broadway, Yonkers 10701, (914) 969-4000
Dean of Admissions: Barbara C. Sweeney

- **Undergraduates: 312m, 690w; 1,249 total (including part-time)**
- **Tuition (1983/84): $3,100**
- **Room & Board: $2,600; Fees: $100**
- **Degrees offered: AA, AS, AAS, AOS**
- **Student-faculty ratio: 17 to 1**

A private college affiliated with the Sisters of Charity, established in 1960, became coed in 1972. Suburban campus. Served by rail.
Academic Character MSACS and professional accreditation. Trimester system. 2-year transfer programs offered in child study, humanities & social science, and natural science. Programs also in general studies, art, business, retail merchandising, radio & television broadcasting, secretarial science, legal assistant training, and practical nursing. Distributives and 9 credits of religion required. Independent study. Internships, credit by exam. Cooperative programs with American Institute of Banking and Cochran School of Nursing. 2-2 journalism and media programs with Mercy. Learning Resources Center. 44,000-volume library.
Financial CEEB CSS. College scholarships, grants, PELL, SEOG, NDSL, GSL, PLUS, ALAS, CWS.
Admissions High school graduation required. State equivalency diploma accepted. Interview required. $20 application fee. Rolling admissions. $80 deposit due on acceptance of admissions offer. *Early Admission* and *Early Decision* programs. Admission deferral possible. Transfers accepted. Credit possible for CEEB AP exams. Admission on probation possible.
Student Life Student government. Newsletter, literary magazine, yearbook, radio station. Chorus, dancers, players. Special interest groups. 4 phys ed courses required. 2 intercollegiate sports for men, 2 for women. NYJCAA. Student body composition: 25% minority.

[1] ELMIRA COLLEGE
Elmira 14901, (607) 734-3911
Director of Admissions: John H. Zeller

- **Undergraduates: 439m, 576w; 2,932 total (including graduates)**
- **Tuition (1982/83): $5,325**
- **Room & Board: $2,200; Fees: $125**
- **Degrees offered: BA, BS, AA, AAS**
- **Mean SAT 430v, 477m**
- **Student-faculty ratio: 16 to 1**

A private college established in 1855. College became coed in 1969. 38-acre campus in residential area of Elmira. Airport, bus service.
Academic Character MSACS accreditation. 4-4-1 system, 6-week summer term. 41 majors offered in the areas of arts, sciences, math, business, social sciences, humanities, music, nursing, medical technology, speech & hearing, dance, theatre, education, computer science. Self-designed majors. Associate degrees granted in liberal arts, business, computer systems and programming, human services, mechanical technology. Minors in 21 areas. Distributive requirements. MSEd granted. Independent study. Honors program. Phi Beta Kappa. Cooperative work/study, pass/fail, internships. Preprofessional programs in law, medicine, dentistry, osteopathy. 3-2 engineering programs with Georgia Tech and Worcestor Polytech. 3-1 medical technology program with approved hospital. Spring Term Consortium. 13-13-6 system. Washington Semester. United Nations Semester. Junior Year Study in the United States. Washington Center for Learning Alternatives. Critical Languages study. Study abroad. San Salvador campus. Elementary and secondary education certification. ROTC at Cornell. 135,000-volume library with microform resources.
Financial CEEB CSS. College scholarships, awards, loans, prizes, state aid; PELL, SEOG, NSS, NDSL, GSL, CWS. Application deadlines March 1 (scholarships), February 1 (loans). $100 tuition discount for each enrolled sibling.
Admissions High school graduation with 17 units required. Interview recommended. SAT or ACT recommended. $20 application fee. Rolling admissions. $100 deposit required on acceptance of offer of admission. *Early Decision* and *Early Admission* programs. Admission deferral possible. Transfers accepted. Credit possible for CEEB AP, CLEP, and ACT PEP exams; some departmental exams. HEOP.
Student Life Student government. Newspaper, magazine, yearbook, radio station. Music, drama, dance, outing, ski, international relations clubs. Academic, political, religious, special interest groups. Freshmen and sophomores are required to live on campus or at home. Coed dorms. Single-sex dorms with overnight visitation restrictions. 80% of students live on campus. Class attendance expected. Two phys ed activities required. 5 intercollegiate sports for men, 5 for women; intramural and club sports. AIAW, ECAC, NAIA, NCAA, Private College Athletic Conference. 42% of students from out of state.

[J1] ERIE COMMUNITY COLLEGE
4140 Southwestern Blvd.,Buffalo 14127

[1 & J1] FASHION INSTITUTE OF TECHNOLOGY
227 West 27 Street, New York 10011, (212) 760-7675
Director of Admissions: James C. Pidgeon

- **Undergraduates: 600m, 3,000w**
- **Tuition (1982/83): $1,050 (in-state), $2,100 (out-of-state)**
- **Room & Board: $2,500; Fees: $110**
- **Degrees offered: BS, BFA, AAS**
- **Mean SAT 800 composite**
- **Student-faculty ratio: 6 to 1**

A public institute under SUNY supervision, established in 1944 in Manhattan. Air, bus, rail service.
Academic Character MSACS accreditation. Semester system, summer term. Majors offered in advertising design, packaging design, interior design, apparel and accessories, textiles, fashion and related industries, apparel management, textiles management. Associate degree programs in 16 areas. 3-year certificate in illustration. Courses in English, humanities, educational skills, math, phys ed, social sciences. Distributive requirements. Cooperative work/study, pass/fail, internships. 1-year AAS programs. Study abroad. Technical classrooms, production and design labs, studios. Fashion and art galleries, fashion sketchbook and clothing/fabric collections. 1,250,000-volume library.
Financial CEEB CSS. Institute honor scholarships, emergency loans; PELL, SEOG, NDSL, CWS. Application deadline March 1.
Admissions High school graduation or equivalent required. GED accepted. Applicants to arts or design programs should supply examples of their work. Interview recommended; required in some areas. SAT or ACT required. $10 application fee. Rolling admissions; application deadline March 15. $50 tuition and $100 room deposits required on acceptance of offer of admission. Transfers accepted. Credit possible for CEEB AP, CLEP, and ACT PEP exams.
Student Life Student government. Newspaper, magazine, yearbook, radio station, TV studio. Athletic, religious, academic, drama, music, special interest groups. Institute housing for 750. Coed and women's dorms. 20% of students live on campus. Class attendance expected. 2 semesters of phys ed required. Intercollegiate bowling, basketball, tennis, softball. Student body composition: 5.8% Asian, 17% Black, 7.4% Hispanic, 0.1% Native American, 68.4% White, 1.3% Other. 18% from out of state.

[J1] FINGER LAKES, COMMUNITY COLLEGE OF THE
Canandaigua 14424

[J2] FIVE TOWNS COLLEGE
2350 Merrick Avenue, Merrick 11566

[1] FORDHAM UNIVERSITY
New York 10458, (212) 933-2233
Director of Admissions: R.T. Waldron

- **Undergraduates: 3,180m, 2,812w; 14,653 total (including part-time)**
- **Tuition (1982/83): $4,950**
- **Room & Board: $2,650; Fees: $90**
- **Degrees offered: BA, BS, BSBA**
- **Mean SAT 525v, 550m**
- **Student-faculty ratio: 17 to 1**

A private Roman Catholic university established by the Society of Jesus in 1841. University became coed in 1974. 86-acre campus in the Bronx. Air, bus, rail service.
Academic Character MSACS and professional accreditation. Semester system, 3- and 6-week summer terms. 56 majors offered in the areas of arts, sciences, math, humanities, communications, social sciences, religion, computer science, education, business. Self-designed majors. Interdisciplinary studies. Minors in most areas. Distributive requirements. Graduate and professional degrees granted. Independent study. Honors program. Phi Beta Kappa. Pass/fail, internships. Preprofessional programs in law, medicine, dentistry. 3-2 program in engineering with Columbia. 3-3 program in law. Junior year exchange with other schools. Study abroad. Early childhood, elementary, secondary, special education, bilingual education certification. ROTC. Lincoln Center campus, computer center, language lab, conservation and ecology center in Armonk. 1,309,264-volume library with microform resources.
Financial CEEB CSS. University scholarships, grants, state aid; PELL, SEOG, NDSL, GSL, CWS. Application deadline February 15.
Admissions High school graduation with 16 units required. SAT or ACT required. $20 application fee. Rolling admissions; application deadline February 15. $50 deposit required on acceptance of offer of admission. *Early Decision* and *Early Admission* programs. Admission deferral possible. Transfers accepted. Credit possible for CEEB AP and CLEP exams. HEOP.
Student Life Student government. Newspapers, magazine, yearbook, radio station. Music, drama, debate groups. Service, academic, honorary, religious, athletic, recreational, special interest organizations. Dorms for men and women. Apartment-style housing. 40% of students live on campus. Class attendance expected. 19 intercollegiate sports for men, 7 for women. Intramural sports program. AIAW, NCAA, ECAC. Student body composition: 1% Asian, 12% Black, 12% Hispanic, 0.2% Native American, 74.8% White. 25% from out of state.

[J1] FULTON-MONTGOMERY COMMUNITY COLLEGE
Johnstown 12095

[G1] GENERAL THEOLOGICAL SEMINARY
175 Ninth Avenue, New York 10011

[J1] GENESEE COMMUNITY COLLEGE
Batavia 14020

[1] HAMILTON COLLEGE
Clinton 13323, (315) 859-4421
Dean of Admissions: Douglas C. Thompson

- **Undergraduates: 979m, 672w**
- **Tuition (1982/83): $7,950**
- **Room & Board: $2,650**
- **Degree offered: BA**
- **Mean SAT 590v, 610m**
- **Student-faculty ratio: 12 to 1**

A private college established in 1812. College became coed in 1978. 15-acre campus in Clinton, 11 miles from Utica. Air, bus, rail service to Utica; bus to Clinton.
Academic Character MSACS accreditation. 4-1-4 system. 28 majors offered in areas of arts, sciences, math, social sciences, humanities, religion, economics, theatre, music, writing, government. Self-designed majors. Interdisciplinary studies. Distributive requirements. Independent study. Honors programs. Phi Beta Kappa. Pass/fail, internships. Preprofessional programs in law, veterinary medicine, dentistry, medicine. 3-2 engineering program with Columbia, U of Rochester, Washington U; 3-3 program with RPI. 3-3 law program with Columbia. Cross-registration with Colgate, Syracuse, Utica. Winter Term. Hamilton College Term in Washington. Williams College Mystic Seaport program. Study abroad. Afro-Latin Cultural Center. Computer Center. List Art Center. Observatory. 360,000-volume library with microform resources.
Financial CEEB CSS and ACT FAS. College scholarships, loans, state aid; PELL, SEOG, NDSL, GSL, FISL, CWS. Application deadline February 1.
Admissions High school graduation with 16 units required. Interview recommended. SAT or ACT required. Application fee $30. Application deadline January 15. $100 deposit required on acceptance of offer of admission. *Early Decision, Early Admission* programs. Admission deferral possible. Transfers accepted. Credit possible for CEEB AP exams. HEOP.
Student Life Student government. Newspaper, magazine, yearbook, radio station. Music, debate, drama clubs. Outing, academic, honorary, service, special interest groups. 8 fraternities with houses. 40% of men and some women join. Coed dorms. Language and special interest housing. Some married-student housing. 98% of students live on campus. Class attendance expected. Swimming and physical fitness test, 2 seasonal sports required. 12

intercollegiate sports for men, 9 for women; intramurals. AIAW, ECAC, NCAA, NESCAC. Student body composition: 1% Asian, 3% Black, 1% Hispanic, 95% White. 45% from out of state.

[1] HARTWICK COLLEGE

Oneonta 13820, (607) 432-4200
Dean of Admissions: John Muyskens

- **Undergraduates: 596m, 856w**
- **Tuition (1982/83): $6,150**
- **Room & Board: $2,450; Fees: $275**
- **Degrees offered: BA, BS**
- **Mean SAT 487v, 514m**
- **Student-faculty ratio: 14 to 1**

A private college established in 1928. 175-acre campus in Oneonta, 180 miles northwest of New York City. 1,100-acre environmental studies campus in Pine Lake, 8 miles from Oneonta. Airport, bus station nearby.

Academic Character MSACS and professional accreditation. 4-1-4 system, 5-week summer term. 27 majors offered in the areas of arts, sciences, math, humanities, medical technology, music, nursing, social sciences, religion, theatre arts, computer science, economics, management. Minors in most major areas. Self-designed majors. Distributive requirements. Independent study. Internships. Preprofessional programs in engineering, law, medicine, dentistry, veterinary medicine, osteopathy, optometry, podiatry. 3-2 engineering program with Clarkson, Georgia Tech, Columbia. Member consortium with Elmira, Corning Community College to form College Center of the Finger Lakes. Washington Semester. United Nations Semester. Philadelphia Urban Semester. Study abroad. Elementary and secondary education, provisional certification. Anderson Center for the Arts. 168,000-volume library with microform resources.

Financial CEEB CSS. College scholarships, grants, state aid; PELL, SEOG, NSS, NDSL, GSL, NSL, CWS. Application deadline April 1.

Admissions High school graduation with 16 units required. SAT or ACT required. Interview recommended. $20 application fee. Application deadline March 1. $200 deposit required on acceptance of offer of admission. *Early Decision* and *Early Admission* programs. Admission deferral possible. Transfers accepted. Credit possible for CEEB AP and CLEP exams; college has own placement program.

Student Life Student government. Newspaper, magazine, yearbook, radio station. Music, drama, outing clubs. Honorary, professional, religious, special interest groups. 4 fraternities, 4 sororities with houses. 25% of students join. Freshmen and sophomores must live on campus or at home. Coed, single-sex, language, special interest housing. No married-student housing. 90% of students live on campus. Class attendance expected. Students must inform Student Affairs Office concerning marriage. 4 skill courses in phys ed required. 9 intercollegiate sports for men, 9 for women; intramurals. ECAC, NCAA, AIAW. Student body composition: 1% Asian, 1% Black, 1% Hispanic, 97% White. 47% from out of state.

[1] HEBREW UNION COLLEGE—JEWISH INSTITUTE OF RELIGION

One West 4th Street, New York 10012

[J1] HERKIMER COUNTY COMMUNITY COLLEGE

Reservoir Road, Herkimer 13350

[J1] HILBERT COLLEGE

5200 South Park Avenue, Hamburg 14075, (716) 649-7900, ext. 211
Director of Admissions: Robert W. Laskie

- **Enrollment: 630 men & women**
- **Tuition (1982/83): $2,650**
- **Room & Board: $2,050-$2,320; Fees: $170**
- **Degrees offered: AA, AAS**
- **Student-faculty ratio: 14 to 1**

A private college affiliated with the Franciscan Sisters of St. Joseph, established in 1957. 40-acre small-town campus, 10 miles south of Buffalo. Served by bus.

Academic Character MSACS accreditation. Semester system, 7-week summer term. 2-year transfer programs offered in the areas of business & economics, criminal justice, human services, and liberal arts. Distributives and 6 hours of philosophy/religion required. 43,000-volume library with microform resources.

Financial CEEB CSS. College scholarships, state aid, PELL, SEOG, NDSL, CWS.

Admissions High school graduation required. GED accepted. SAT or ACT required. $15 application fee. Rolling admissions. $50 deposit due on acceptance of admissions offer. *Early Admissions* Program. Transfers accepted. Credit possible for CEEB AP and CLEP exams.

Student Life Student government. Literary magazine. Honorary, professional, recreational, and special interest groups. Coed dorm. Class attendance expected. 2 intercollegiate sports for men, 3 for women; NJCAC, P-YAC.

[1] HOBART AND WILLIAM SMITH COLLEGES

Geneva 14456, (315) 789-5500
Hobart Director of Admissions: Leonard A. Wood, Jr.
William Smith Director of Admissions: Mara O'Laughlin

- **Undergraduates: 1,070m, 700w**
- **Tuition (1982/83): $7,200**
- **Room & Board: $2,730; Fees: $125**
- **Degrees offered: BA, BS**
- **Mean SAT 530v, 590m (Hobart); 550v, 550m (William Smith)**
- **Student-faculty ratio: 14 to 1**

Private coordinate colleges located in Geneva. Hobart College for men established in 1822, William Smith College for women established in 1908. 17-acre campus on shore of Seneca Lake, 40 miles southeast of Rochester and 50 miles west of Syracuse.

Academic Character MSACS accreditation. Trimester system. 27 majors offered in areas of art, humanities, science, math, social sciences, religion, music, economics. Student-designed majors. General education and interdisciplinary courses. 3-part program: First Year (general education), the Middle Years (Baccalaureate Essay), the Baccalaureate year (Baccalaureate Colloquium). Distributive requirements. Independent study. Honors programs. Phi Beta Kappa. Internships. Preprofessional programs in law, dentistry, medicine. 3-2 engineering programs with Columbia, U of Rochester, RPI. 4-1 BA/MBA with Clarkson. Member of 15-college Rochester Area College Consortium. Washington Semester. Philadelphia Urban Semester. United Nations Semester. Art term in New York City. Visiting Student Program. Study abroad. Elementary and secondary education certification. Developmental Learning Center. Computing system. 225,000-volume library with microform resources.

Financial CEEB CSS. College scholarships, state aid; PELL, SEOG, NDSL, FISL, CWS. Application deadline March 1.

Admissions High school graduation with 16 units required. Interview recommended. SAT and English ACH, or ACT required. $20 application fee. Application deadline February 15. $250 tuition and $100 room deposits required on acceptance of offer of admission. *Early Decision* and *Early Acceptance* programs. Admission deferral possible. Transfers accepted. Credit possible for CEEB AP, CLEP, and departmental exams. HEOP.

Student Life Student government. Newspaper, yearbook, magazines, radio station. Music, drama, community service, honorary, special interest groups. 9 fraternities with houses; 35% of men join. Single-sex, coed, and co-op housing. Class attendance required. Swimming test required. 12 intercollegiate sports for men, 6 for women. Intramural programs and club sports. NCAA, USILA, AIAW, ICAC. Student body composition: 0.2% Asian, 3.3% Black, 2.5% Hispanic, 94% White. 52% from out of state.

[1] HOFSTRA UNIVERSITY

Hempstead 11550, (516) 560-6600
Director of Admissions: Joan E. Isaac

- **Undergraduates: 3,259m, 2,727w; 10,500 total (including graduates)**
- **Tuition (1982/83): $4,600**
- **Room & Board: $2,360-$2,900; Fees: $350**
- **Degrees offered: BA, BBA, BE, BFA, BS, BSEd, AAS**
- **Mean SAT 1,026**
- **Student-faculty ratio: 17 to 1**

A private university established in 1935. 238-acre campus in Hempstead, Long Island, 25 miles east of New York City. Bus and rail service.

Academic Character MSACS and professional accreditation. Semester system, 2 5-week summer terms. 47 majors offered by the College of Liberal Arts & Sciences, 5 by the School of Business, 17 by the School of Education. New College liberal arts programs. Interdisciplinary studies. Self-designed majors. Minors in most fields. AAS specialization in elementary education. Distributive requirements. Graduate and professional degrees granted. Independent study. Honors programs. Phi Beta Kappa. Pass/fail, internships. Preprofessional programs in dentistry, forestry, law, medicine, veterinary medicine. Cooperative program with Jewish Theological Seminary. 3-2 BA/BS and 4-1 BS/MS engineering programs with Columbia. Visiting Student program. Study abroad. Elementary, secondary, and special education certification. Computer center, language lab. Center for cultural and Intercultural Studies, Emily Lowe Gallery. ROTC. 930,000-volume library with microform resources.

Financial CEEB CSS. University scholarships, grants, loans, state aid; PELL, SEOG, NDSL, CWS. Application deadline February 15.

Admissions High school graduation with 16 units required. Interview recommended. SAT or ACT required; ACH recommended. $20 application fee. Rolling admissions; preferred application deadline February 15. $100 tuition and $100 room deposits required on acceptance of offer of admission. *Early Decision* and *Early Admission* programs. Admission deferral possible. Transfers accepted. Credit possible for CEEB AP, CLEP, and state exams; university has own advanced placement program. Army Cooperative Education Program.

Student Life Student government. Newspaper, magazine, yearbook, radio station. Music, debate, drama clubs. Service, athletic, dance, academic, honorary, special interest organizations. 11 fraternities and 4 sororities. 15% of men and women join. Coed and single-sex dorms. Special interest housing. 45% of students live on campus. 8 intercollegiate sports for men, 8 for women; intramurals. Student body composition: 0.2% Asian, 6.2% Black, 2.1% Hispanic, 0.2% Native American, 89.6% White, 1.7% Other. 20% from out of state.

[1] HOUGHTON COLLEGE

Houghton 14744, (716) 567-2211
Director of Admissions: Wayne A. MacBeth

- **Undergraduates: 468m, 645w**
- **Tuition (1982/83): $3,987**
- **Room & Board: $1,978; Fees: $220**
- **Degrees offered: BA, BS, BMus, AA, AAS**
- **Mean SAT 505v, 535m**
- **Student-faculty ratio: 15 to 1**

A private college directed by the Wesleyan church of America, established in 1883. 50-acre campus in Houghton, 65 miles southeast of Buffalo. Buffalo

Suburban Campus in West Seneca. Bus service.
Academic Character MSACS and professional accreditation. Semester system, 3 3-week and 2 4-week summer terms. 3 majors offered by the Division of English & Speech, 4 by Foreign Languages, 4 by History & Social Science, 22 by Psychology & Education, 5 by Science & Mathematics, 7 by Religion & Philosophy, and 5 by Fine Arts. Interdisciplinary studies. AA in liberal arts, AAS in Christian Ministries. Minors offered in most major areas. Distributives, minor, and 4 hours of Bible Literature, 3 hours of Ethics required. Honors program. Independent study. Internships, pass/fail. Preprofessional programs in law, health services, seminary, engineering. Cooperative engineering program with New York U. Member of Western New York Consortium and Christian College Consortium. Study abroad. Elementary and secondary education certification. ROTC at St. Bonaventure. Computing facilities. 145,000-volume library.
Financial CEEB CSS. College scholarships, grants, loans, state aid; PELL, SEOG, NDSL, GSL, PLUS, CWS. Preferred application deadline March 15.
Admissions High school graduation with 16 units required. GED accepted. ACT or SAT required. $15 application fee. Rolling admissions. $100 deposit required on acceptance of offer of admission. *Early Decision* and *Early Admission* programs. Admission deferral possible. Transfers accepted. Credit possible for CEEB AP, CLEP, state exams.
Student Life Student government. Newspaper, magazine, yearbook, 2 radio stations, TV studio. Music, drama, debate, service, athletic, academic, honorary, religious, special interest groups. Freshmen and sophomores must live at home or on campus. Single-sex dorms. Limited married-student housing. 62% of students live on campus. 2/3 class attendance required. Chapel attendance required 4 times weekly. No dancing, card playing, illegal drugs, tobacco, alcohol. 2 semesters of phys ed required. 6 intercollegiate sports for men, 5 for women; 11 intramurals. Student body composition: 1% Asian, 1% Hispanic, 2% Black, 96% White. 39% of students from out of state.

[J1] HUDSON VALLEY COMMUNITY COLLEGE
Troy 12180

[2] HUMAN SERVICES, COLLEGE FOR
345 Hudson Street, New York 10014

[G1] IMMACULATE CONCEPTION, SEMINARY OF THE
Huntington 11743

[1] INSURANCE, COLLEGE OF THE
123 William Street, New York 10038

[1] IONA COLLEGE
New Rochelle 10801, (914) 636-3100
Director of Admissions: Francis I. Offer, C.F.C.

- **Undergraduates: 2,153m, 1,464w; 6,300 total (including graduates)**
- **Tuition (1982/83): $4,200**
- **Room & Board: $2,700; Fees: $80**
- **Degrees offered: BA, BS, BBA**
- **Mean SAT 407v, 467m**
- **Student-faculty ratio: 20 to 1**

A private college founded in 1940 by the Congregation of the Christian Brothers of Ireland. Suburban campus in New Rochelle. Rail and bus stations in New Rochelle; airport in nearby New York City.
Academic Character MSACS accreditation. Semester system, 2 5-week summer terms. 37 majors offered in the areas of humanities, communications, business, science, math, social sciences, gerontology, speech & dramatic arts, computer & information sciences, education, religious studies. Interdisciplinary studies. Minors in most fields. Distributives and 6 credits in religion required. Masters degrees granted. Independent study. Honors program. Pass/fail, internships. Preprofessional programs in law, dentistry, medicine, veterinary medicine, engineering. Coop work/study BE in engineering program at U of Detroit. Cross-registration with area colleges. Elementary, secondary, special, and bilingual education certification. ROTC at Fordham. Language lab, computer center. 191,000-volume library; access to other area libraries.
Financial CEEB CSS. College scholarships, grants, state aid; PELL, SEOG, NDSL, GSL, CWS. Application deadline April 15.
Admissions High school graduation with 16 units required. Interview recommended. SAT or ACT required. $15 application fee. $100 deposit required on acceptance of offer of admission. Rolling admissions. *Early Decision* and *Early Admission* programs. Transfers accepted. Credit possible for CEEB AP and CLEP exams. HEOP.
Student Life Student government. Academic, honorary, religious, service, athletic, journalism, special interest groups. Social fraternities and sororities. 1 coed dorm. 5% of students live on campus. Intercollegiate and intramural sports programs. Student body composition: 0.5% Asian, 3.7% Black, 3.4% Hispanic, 91% White, 1.4% Other. 80% from out of state.

[1] ITHACA COLLEGE
Ithaca 14850, (607) 274-3124
Director of Admissions: Peter A. Stace

- **Undergraduates: 2,070m, 2,650w**
- **Tuition (1982/83): $5,526**
- **Room & Board: $2,487; Fees: $70**
- **Degrees offered: BA, BS, BFA, BMus**
- **Student-faculty ratio: 15 to 1**

A private college established in 1892. 250-acre campus on Cayuga Lake in Ithaca, 50 miles south of Syracuse. Air and bus service.
Academic Character MSACS and professional accreditation. Semester system, 3 4-week summer terms. 5 majors offered by the School of Allied Health Professions, 4 by the School of Business, 5 by the School of Communications, 3 by the School of Health, Physical Education, & Recreation, 25 by the School of Humanities & Science, and 7 by the School of Music. Self-designed majors. Interdisciplinary majors. Minors offered in most major areas. Distributive requirements. Independent study. Internships, pass/fail. Preprofessional programs in law, medicine, veterinary medicine, dentistry. 3-2 engineering programs and cross-registration with Cornell. Study abroad. Elementary and secondary education certification. ROTC, NROTC, AFROTC at Cornell. Instructional Resources Center. Reading and Writing labs. Computer services. 207,000-volume library with microform resources.
Financial CEEB CSS. University scholarships, awards, state aid; PELL, SEOG, NDSL, GSL, CWS. Application deadline March 1.
Admissions High school graduation with 16 units required. Auditions required of music and theatre arts applicants. SAT required; English ACH recommended. $20 application fee. Rolling admissions; preferred application deadline March 1. $100 deposit required on acceptance of offer of admission. *Early Decision* and *Early Admission* programs. Admission deferral possible. Transfers accepted. Credit possible for CEEB AP and state exams. HEOP/EOP.
Student Life Student government. Newspaper, magazine, yearbook, TV and radio stations. Music, drama, academic, religious, special interest groups. 6 fraternities, 2 sororities housed in dorms. Students under 21 required to live on campus or at home. Coed and single-sex dorms. Some married-student housing. 80% of students live on campus. 13 intercollegiate sports for men, 12 for women; club and intramural sports. AIAW, ECAC, NCAA. Student body composition: 0.4% Asian, 2% Black, 1% Hispanic, 0.3% Native American, 96.3% White. 50% from out of state.

[J1] JAMESTOWN COMMUNITY COLLEGE
525 Falconer Street, Jamestown 14701

[J1] JEFFERSON COMMUNITY COLLEGE
Outer Coffeen Street, Watertown 13601

[1] JEWISH THEOLOGICAL SEMINARY OF AMERICA
3080 Broadway, New York 10027

[1] JUILLIARD SCHOOL
New York 10023, (212) 799-5000
Registrar: Mary H. Smith

- **Undergraduates: 304m, 341w; 1,320 total (including graduates)**
- **Tuition (1982/83): $4,600**
- **Degrees offered: BFA, BMus**
- **Student-faculty ratio: 5 to 1**

A private college established in 1905. Campus at Lincoln Center in New York City. Air, bus, rail service.
Academic Character MSACS accreditation. Semester system. Majors offered in ballet, modern dance, drama, brass, composition, conducting, harp, harpsicord, organ, percussion, piano, strings, voice, woodwinds. Interdepartmental studies. Diploma courses in all majors and in choral conducting. Distributive requirements. Graduate degrees offered. Member of Lincoln Center for the Performing Arts. Lincoln Center Program. Juilliard String Quartet. 12,000-volume library with 38,000 musical scores.
Financial CEEB CSS. College scholarships, fellowships, apprenticeships, state aid; PELL, SEOG, NDSL, CWS. Application deadline February 15.
Admissions High school graduation or equivalent required. Evidence for sufficient prior preparation in major study required. Performance exam in major study required. $50 application and $35 examination fees. Application deadlines January 15, April 15, July 1 for entrance exams given in March, May, September, respectively. $100 deposit required on acceptance of offer of admission. Transfers accepted. All admissions for fall semester only. Credit possible for CEEB AP and state exams; college has own placement exams.
Student Life News bulletin. Large and small ensembles, chorus, 4 symphony orchestras. Drama groups. Dances, concerts, lectures, film series. Special student rates through Juilliard Concert Office on productions in New York City. No institutional dorms but several residence clubs for women and the International House for men & women are used by out-of-town students. Class attendance required. Student body composition: 15% Asian, 3% Black, 4% Hispanic, 78% White.

[J2] KATHARINE GIBBS SCHOOL
535 Broad Hollow Road, Huntington 11747

[J2] KATHARINE GIBBS SCHOOL
200 Park Avenue, New York 10017

[1] KEUKA COLLEGE
Keuka Park 14478, (315) 536-4411

- **Undergraduates: 2m, 493w; 539 total (including part-time)**
- **Tuition, Room & Board (1982/83): $6,780**
- **Degrees offered: BA, BS**
- **Median SAT 450v, 474m**
- **Student-faculty ratio: 13 to 1**

A private college founded in 1890. Campus located at Keuka Lake in the Finger Lakes Region of New York, four miles from Penn Yan.

Academic Character MSACS and professional accreditation. Quarter system, field period. Majors offered in biochemistry, biology, dramatic literature & theatre arts, English, fine arts (art, dance, music options), history, mathematics, philosophy & religion, political science, public administration-management, psychology, social studies, sociology, business administration-management, elementary education, medical technology, nursing, social work, special education. Student-initiated majors. Field Period provides opportunity for off-campus work/study for credit. Summer program allows students to earn credit abroad in work/study. 95,186-volume library.
Financial Financial aid based on need. Loan funds available.
Admissions SAT required. Rolling admissions. *Early Admission* and *Early Decision* programs. Admission deferral possible. Advanced placement program.
Student Life Dormitories and dining hall maintained.

[1] KING'S COLLEGE

Briarcliff Manor 10510, (914) 941-7200
Director of Admissions: Roy McCandless

- **Undergraduates: 283m, 513w**
- **Tuition (1982/83): $4,100**
- **Room & Board: $2,200; Fees: $100**
- **Degrees offered: BA, BS, AA**
- **Mean SAT 430v, 470m**
- **Student-faculty ratio: 16 to 1**

A private Christian liberal arts college, established in 1938. 69-acre campus in the village of Briarcliff Manor, Westchester County. Train service to New York City.
Academic Character MSACS accreditation. Semester system, 3 summer terms. Applied music, biology, business administration & economics, chemistry, elementary education, English, history, math, medical technology, modern foreign languages (French, Spanish), music education, philosophy, psychology, physical education, psychology, religion (Biblical studies, religious education), sociology. Interdepartmental studies. Minors. Associate degrees in pre-dental hygiene, pre-nursing, pre-therapy (occupational, physical). Distributives and 16 semester hours of Bible required. Independent study. Pass/fail, internships. Seniors must take GRE. Preprofessional programs in law, medicine, theology. Elementary and secondary education certification. Study abroad. Institute of Holy Land Studies affiliate. American Studies Program of the Christian College Consortium/Coalition offers work/study in Washington, DC. Language lab. 87,000-volume library with microform resources.
Financial CEEB CSS. College scholarships, grants, loans, ministerial & missionary scholarships; PELL, SEOG, NSS, NDSL, GSL, CWS. Application deadline March 15.
Admissions High school graduation with 16 units required. Equivalency certificate and GED accepted. Interview recommended. Audition required of music major. SAT or ACT required. $10 application fee. Rolling admissions. $100 reservation fee required on acceptance of offer of admission; $50 room damage deposit required by registration date. *Early Admission* and *Early Decision* programs. Admission deferral possible. Transfers accepted. Credit possible for CEEB AP and CLEP exams.
Student Life Student government. Newspaper, news bulletin, yearbook. Music, service, honorary, religious, special interest groups. Single students must live on campus or at home. Single-sex dorms. No married-student housing. 89% of students live on campus. Alcohol, tobacco, gambling, card playing, illegal drugs, dancing, participation in oath-bound secret societies, attendance of commericial stage and motion picture productions prohibited. Class and daily chapel attendance expected. 7 intercollegiate sports for men, 7 for women; intramurals. NAIA, SAC, CACC, NCCAA. Student body composition: 1% Asian, 6% Black, 5% Hispanic, 88% White. 54% from out of state.

[2 & J1] LABORATORY INSTITUTE OF MERCHANDISING

12 East 53rd Street, New York 10022

[1] LE MOYNE COLLEGE

Syracuse 13214, (315) 446-2882
Director of Admissions: Edward J. Gorman

- **Undergraduates: 911m, 901w; 2,022 total (including part-time)**
- **Tuition (1982/83): $4,250**
- **Room & Board: $2,200; Fees: $110**
- **Degrees offered: BA, BS**
- **Mean SAT 520v, 560m**
- **Student-faculty ratio: 16 to 1**

A private college affiliated with the Society of Jesus, established in 1945. 150-acre campus in Le Moyne Heights, a suburb of Syracuse. Air, bus, and rail service.
Academic Character MSACS accreditation. Semester system, 2 5-week summer terms. 29 majors offered in areas of biology, business, chemistry, computer science, humanities, history, math, psychology, political science, physics, sociology, religious studies. Interdepartmental and self-designed majors. Minors in most areas. Distributives and 6 hours of religious studies required. Independent study. Honors programs. Pass/fail, internships. Preprofessional programs in law, dentistry, medicine, veterinary science. 3-2 engineering program with Manhattan College; 2-2 program with SUNY College of Environmental Science and Forestry. Member of Consortium for the Cultural Foundation of Medicine with Upstate Medical Center. Exchange programs with several schools. Study abroad. Secondary education certification. ROTC & AFROTC at Syracuse U. Political internships in Washington, DC, and Albany. Computer Center. Writing Center. 158,000-volume library with microform resources.
Financial CEEB CSS. College scholarships, grants, state aid; PELL, SEOG, NDSL, GSL, FISL, CWS. Application deadine March 1.
Admissions High school graduation with 16 units required. Interview recommended. SAT or ACT required. $15 application fee. Rolling admissions. $50 tuition and $50 room deposits required on acceptance of offer of admission. *Early Decision* and *Early Admission* programs. Admission deferral possible. Transfers accepted. Credit possible for CEEB AP and CLEP exams. HEOP, HEPP.
Student Life Student government. Newspaper, literary journal, yearbook. Music, debate, drama clubs. Political, service, honorary, religious, special interest groups. Students must live on campus or at home. Coed and single-sex dorms. 70% of students live on campus. Class attendance expected. One year of phys ed required. 7 intercollegiate sports for men, 6 for women; intramurals. ECAC, NCAA. Student body composition: 4% Black, 2% Hispanic, 92% White, 2% Other. 16% from out of state.

[1] LONG ISLAND UNIVERSITY

Greenvale 11548, (516) 299-2501

- **Enrollment: 23,000 men & women**
- **Degrees offered: BA, BS, AA, AAS**

An independent university comprised of four main units: Brooklyn Center, C.W. Post Center, Southampton Center, and the Arnold and Marie Schwartz College of Pharmacy and Health Sciences; branches also located in Suffolk, Westchester, and Rockland counties.
Academic Character MSACS and professional accreditation. In addition to undergraduate degrees, the University grants the MA, MS, MBA, MPA, MPS, PhD degrees. Special features include honors study program, 3-year accelerated program for students in good standing, and special educational services program for students with physical disabilities.
Financial Financial aid available through Federal, University, and state programs up to full tuition & fees on both need and achievement bases. CWS.

■[1] ARNOLD AND MARIE SCHWARTZ COLLEGE OF PHARMACY AND HEALTH SCIENCES

95 Dekalb Avenue, Brooklyn 11201, (212) 834-6046
Director of Admissions: Fran A. Mantovani

- **Enrollment: 1,200 men & women**
- **Tuition (1982/83): $4,800**
- **Room & Board (1980/81): $2,520-$3,040**
- **Degree offered: BSPharm**
- **Student-faculty ratio: 28 to 1**

A five-year college established in 1886. Urban campus.
Academic Character MSACS and professional accreditation. Semester system, 2 summer terms. 2-year preprofessional and 5-year professional program in pharmacy and hospital pharmacy administration and general pharmaceutical training. MS granted. Drug Information Center. Museum. Drug Archives. Research unit.
Financial CEEB CSS. College scholarships, state aid; PELL, SEOG, NDSL, NSL, HPL, PLUS, ALAS, CWS. Application deadline May 15.
Admissions High school graduation with 16 units required. SAT or ACT required. $20 application fee. Rolling admissions. $100 deposit due on acceptance of admissions offer. Transfers accepted.
Student Life Yearbook. Asian Students Association. Professional and recreational activities. Honorary fraternities. Single and married-student housing available. Intramural sports.

■[1] BROOKLYN CENTER OF LONG ISLAND UNIVERSITY

University Plaza, Brooklyn 11201, (212) 834-6049
Director of Admissions: Alan B. Chaves

- **Undergraduates: 2,100m, 2,322w; 6,800 total (including graduates)**
- **Tuition (1982/83): $4,590**
- **Room & Board: $2,520-$3,040; Fees: $160**
- **Degrees offered: BA, BS, AA, AAS**
- **Mean SAT 500v, 482m**
- **Student-faculty ratio: 9 to 1**

A private university established in 1926. 22-acre campus in downtown Brooklyn. Air, bus, rail, and subway service.
Academic Character MSACS accreditation. Semester system, 2 6-week summer terms. 32 majors offered in the areas of business, sciences, math, computer science, humanities, music, art, health sciences, education, social sciences, speech & theatre, and communications. Associate degrees in business administration, social sciences, humanities, allied health, and others. The Center houses Richard L. Connolly College (liberal arts), School of Business Administration, and the Arnold and Marie Schwartz College of Pharmacy & Health Sciences. Courses in linguistics. Certificates in criminal justice, international studies, social welfare. Paralegal studies. Graduate degrees granted. Honors programs. Internships, pass/fail, cooperative work/study. Preprofessional programs in dentistry, law, medicine. 3-1 cytotechnology and medical technology programs. 5-year BA/MBA; 6-year BSPharm/MBA. Elementary, secondary, and special education certification. SALENA Library Learning Center. Communications center, Computer Center, Developmental Skills Center, English Language Institute, Academic Readiness Program, Special Educational Services Program. ROTC nearby. 290,000-volume library with microform resources.
Financial CEEB CSS. University scholarships, state aid, payment plans; PELL, SEOG, NSS, NDSL, NSL, CWS. Application deadlines May 1 (loans), May 15 (scholarships).
Admissions High school graduation with 16 units required. GED accepted. SAT or ACT preferred. $20 application fee. Rolling admissions. Preferred application deadline June 1. $100 deposit required on acceptance of admissions offer. *Early Decision* and *Early Entrance* programs. Transfers accepted. Credit possible for CEEB AP, CLEP, and state exams. HEOP,

Guided Studies Program for students with low GPAs. Martin Luther King and Albizu Campos Programs for Black and Spanish-speaking students from the New York City area.
Student Life Student government. Newspaper, magazine, yearbook, radio station. Music, drama, academic, political, religious, honorary, special interest groups. Dorms for men and women. Limited married-student housing. 6% of students live on campus. Class attendance regulations for freshmen. 7 intercollegiate sports for men, 3 for women; intramurals. AIAW, NCAC, NCAA. Student body composition: 5% Asian, 33% Black, 10% Hispanic, 44% White, 8% Other. 8% from out of state.

■[1] C.W. POST CENTER OF LONG ISLAND UNIVERSITY

Greenvale 11548, (516) 299-0200
Director of Admissions: James F. Reilly

- **Undergraduates: 5,099m, 2,684w; 11,168 total (including graduates)**
- **Tuition (1982/83): $4,736**
- **Room & Board: $2,720; Fees: $320**
- **Degrees offered: BA, BS, BFA, BProf Studies**
- **Mean SAT 432v, 469m**
- **Student-faculty ratio: 12 to 1**

A private university established in 1954. 350-acre campus in suburban Greenvale, Long Island. Rail service to New York City. Suffolk Campus, 200-acre facility at nearby Brentwood.
Academic Character MSACS and professional accreditation. Semester system, 3 summer terms. 75 majors offered in the areas of art, sciences, math, humanities, business, criminal studies, international studies, education, social sciences, medical studies, speech, theatre, communications, computer, music, management, economics. Interdisciplinary studies. Minors and areas of specialization offered. Distributive requirements. Masters degrees granted. Independent study. Cooperative work/study, pass/fail, internships. Honors programs. Preprofessional programs include law, dentistry, medicine, business, foreign service, library science, allied health fields, social work, theology, veterinary medicine. 3-2 MBA, MPA, MPS programs. Member of Nassau Higher Education Consortium. Elementary, secondary, and special education certification. ROTC at Hofstra. Evening and week-end programs. Computer center. Communication center, speech & hearing center, art gallery. 960,000-volume library.
Financial CEEB CSS. University scholarships, awards, grants, state aid; PELL, SEOG, NSS, NDSL, GSL, NSL, CWS. Priority application deadline March 1 for loans.
Admissions High school graduation with 16 units required. GED accepted. Art, music, theatre applicants must audition. SAT or ACT required. $20 application fee. Rolling admissions. $75 deposit required on acceptance of admissions offer. *Early Admission* Program. Admission deferral possible. Transfers accepted. Credit possible for CEEB AP and CLEP exams. HEOP.
Student Life Student government. Newspaper, magazine, yearbook, radio station. Music, theatre, political, religious, social, honorary, special interest groups. 3 fraternities and 2 sororities without houses. Less than 10% of students join. Coed and single-sex dorms. 25% of students live on campus. 10 intercollegiate sports for men, 5 for women. Intramural sports program. Student body composition: 2% Asian, 11% Black, 3% Hispanic, 1% Native American, 83% White. 10% from out of state.

■[1] SOUTHAMPTON COLLEGE OF LONG ISLAND UNIVERSITY

Southampton 11968, (516) 283-4000
Director of Admissions: Kevin Coveney

- **Undergraduates: 608m, 520w; 1,316 total (including graduates)**
- **Tuition (1982/83): $5,000**
- **Room & Board: $3,000; Fees: $200**
- **Degrees offered: BA, BS, BFA**
- **Mean SAT 465v, 487m**
- **Student-faculty ratio: 17 to 1**

A private university established in 1963. 110-acre campus in Southampton on Long Island. Bus and rail service to New York City, which is 90 miles west of campus.
Academic Character MSACS accreditation. 4-1-4 system, several summer terms. Majors offered in art, art education, biology, business administration, chemistry, elementary education, English/writing, environmental science, environmental studies, geology, history & politics, psychology/biology, marine science, pre-law, psychology, sociology, social science. Interdisciplinary and self-designed majors. Courses in 20 additional areas. Distributive requirements. MS in Elem Ed granted. Independent study, cooperative work/study, pass/fail, internships, credit by exam. Coordinate programs with Long Island University campuses. Study abroad. Elementary, secondary, and special education certification. Summer Art Workshop, Major Writers Conference. Seamester. InterFuture. Winter session. Marine Station. Study Center for underprepared students. Computer center. 128,000-volume library with microform resources.
Financial CEEB.CSS. University scholarships, awards, grants, loans; state aid; PELL, SEOG, NDSL, GSL, CWS. Application deadline June 1.
Admissions High school diploma or equivalent required. SAT or ACT required. Satisfy 3 of 4 admission criteria: 1) SAT 350v, 2) combined SAT 800, 3) 80 GPA, 4) class rank in top 60%. Interview strongly recommended. $20 application fee. Rolling admissions. $100 tuition and $100 room deposits required on acceptance of admissions offer. *Early Admissions* and *Concurrent Enrollment* programs. Admission deferral possible. Transfers accepted. Credit possible for CEEB AP, CLEP, and state exams, and for life experience. HEOP. Freshman year developmental program.
Student Life Student government. Newspaper, magazine, yearbook, radio station. Music, drama, reading, sailing, scuba, athletic, academic, religious, service, special interest groups. Freshmen and sophomores under 21 must live on campus or at home. Coed and single-sex dorms. 60% of students live on campus. Class attendance expected. 10 intercollegiate sports; intramural sports program. NCAA, ECAC. Student body composition: 0.5% Asian, 10% Black, 5% Hispanic, 0.5% Native American, 84% White. 29% from out of state.

[1] MANHATTAN COLLEGE

Manhattan College Parkway & West 242nd Street, Riverdale 10471, (212) 920-0100
Director of Admissions: Brother C. William Batt, F.S.C.

- **Enrollment: 2,745m, 971w; 5,006 total (including part-time & graduates)**
- **Tuition (1982/83): $4,200**
- **Room & Board: $3,000; Fees: $100**
- **Degrees offered: BA, BS, BEng, BSBA, BSGS, BSRHS**
- **Mean SAT 490v, 540m**
- **Student-faculty ratio: 15 to 1**

A private college controlled by the Brothers of Christian Schools, founded in 1853. Suburban campus. Served by subway, bus, rail, and air.
Academic Character MSACS and professional accreditation. Semester system, 2 3-week and 2 4-week summer terms. 31 majors offered by the School of Arts & Sciences, 6 by the School of Business, 23 by the School of Engineering, 1 by the School of General Studies, and 13 by the School of Teacher Preparation. Minors offered in all major fields. Distributives and 3 hours of religion required. Masters degrees granted. Liberal Arts Curriculum I: study of Western civilization divided into 4 historical periods; Curriculum II: selected courses from humanities, sciences, and social sciences. Honors programs. Cooperative work/study, pass/no credit, internships. Preprofessional programs in dentistry, law, medicine, physical therapy. Cooperative program with NY College of Podiatry. 3-2 engineering programs with La Moyne, Saint John Fisher, and Siena. Cross-registration with Mount St. Vincent. Study abroad. Nursery, elementary, and secondary education certification. AFROTC. 228,458-volume library with microform resources.
Financial CEEB CSS. College scholarships, grants, loans, state aid; PELL, SEOG, NSS, NDSL, PLUS, ALAS, CWS, college employment program. Application deadline March 1.
Admissions High school graduation with 16 units required. GED accepted. Interview recommended. SAT or ACT required; SAT preferred. $20 application fee. Rolling admissions. $100 tuition and $200 room deposits due on acceptance of admissions offer. *Early Admission* Program. Admission deferral possible. Transfers accepted. Credit possible for CEEB AP, CLEP, and state exams.
Student Life Student government. Newspaper, professional journals. Athletic, cultural, academic, honorary, religious, social, and special interest groups. Freshmen must live at home or on campus. Upperclassmen required to live at school while space permits. Dormitories and dining hall. Regular class attendance required. 9 intercollegiate sports for men, 3 for women; many club and intramural sports. Student body composition: 10% minority.

[1] MANHATTAN SCHOOL OF MUSIC

120 Claremont Avenue, New York 10027

[1] MANHATTANVILLE COLLEGE

Purchase 10577, (914) 694-2200
Dean of Admissions: Marshall Raucci

- **Undergraduates: 350m, 650w; 1,900 total (including graduates)**
- **Tuition (1982/83): $6,400**
- **Room & Board: $3,170; Fees: $40**
- **Degrees offered: BA, BFA, BMus, BSacred Mus**
- **Mean SAT 530v, 520m**
- **Student-faculty ratio: 11 to 1**

A private college established in 1841, became coed in 1971. 220-acre campus in suburban Purchase, 24 miles from New York City. Bus service.
Academic Character MSACS and professional accreditation. Semester system, 2 summer terms. Majors offered in art, art history, biochemistry, biology, business management, chemistry, classics, computer science, economics, English, environmental studies, French, history, math, music, philosophy, physics, political science, psychobiology, psychology, religion, Romance languages, Russian, sociology, Spanish. Interdisciplinary and self-designed majors. Certificate programs. Courses in several areas. Distributive requirements. Masters degrees granted. Independent study. Honors programs. Cooperative work/study, internships, pass/fail. Pre-law program. Portfolio evaluation required of seniors. Exchanges with SUNY College at Purchase, Mills College (CA). Visiting Student Program. 6-year BA/JD with New York Law School. 5-year BA/MBA and 5-year BA/MS computer science with New York U. Washington Semester. Study abroad. Elementary and secondary education certification. College Skills Center. Learning Center. Language Resource Center. English Language Institute. 250,000-volume library.
Financial CEEB CSS and ACT FAS. College scholarships, grants, state aid; PELL, SEOG, NDSL, FISL, GSL, CWS. Priority application deadline March 1.
Admissions High school graduation required. Two admission plans: 1) submit letters of recommendation, transcripts, SAT or ACT scores or 2) submit letters of recommendation, transcripts, examples of academic work. Interview recommended, required in some cases. Audition required for music candidates, portfolio for art candidates. $20 application fee. Rolling admissions; preferred deadline March 1. $100 tuition and $100 room deposits required on acceptance of offer of admission. *Early Decision* and *Early Acceptance* programs. Admission deferral possible. Transfers accepted. Credit possible for CEEB AP exams. HEOP.
Student Life Student government. Newspaper, magazine, yearbook. Music, drama, academic, special interest groups. Weekly socials. 88% of students live on campus. 9 intercollegiate sports; intramurals. Student body composition: 0.4% Asian, 11.2% Black, 3.7% Hispanic, 0.1% Native American, 84.6% White. 54% from out of state.

[1] MANNES COLLEGE OF MUSIC
157 East 74th Street, New York 10021

[J1] MARIA COLLEGE OF ALBANY
Albany 12208

[J1] MARIA REGINA COLLEGE
1024 Court Street, Syracuse 13208, (315) 474-4891
Director of Admissions: Michael McCann

- **Enrollment: 399w**
- **Tuition (1982/83): $2,200**
- **Room & Board: $1,700; Fees: $250**
- **Degrees offered: AA, AS, AAS**
- **Student-faculty ratio: 14 to 1**

A private Roman Catholic college for women, affiliated with the Sisters of the Third Order of St. Francis, founded in 1963. Suburban campus. Served by air and bus.

Academic Character MSACS accreditation. Semester system, winter interim. 2-year programs offered in business, child development, liberal arts, library science, merchandising, occupational therapy, pre-nursing, religious education, science, secretarial, and social & community service. 3-year religious studies program. Distributives and 6 hours of religion required. Practicum program. Media center. 35,000-volume library.

Financial CEEB CSS. College grants, state aid; PELL, SEOG, GSL, NDSL, CWS.

Admissions High school graduation required. Interview recommended. SAT or ACT required. $15 application fee. Rolling admissions. $100 deposit due on acceptance of admissions offer. *Early Admission* and *Concurrent Enrollment* programs. Transfers accepted. Credit possible for CEEB AP, CLEP, and state exams.

Student Life Student government. Newspaper, yearbook. Music and drama groups. Art club. Ski club. Campus residence recommended. Dormitories and dining hall. Marriage intentions must be reported to Vice-president for student services. 1 hour of phys ed required. Student body composition: 19% minority.

[1] MARIST COLLEGE
Poughkeepsie 12601, (914) 471-3240
Dean of Admissions: James E. Daly

- **Undergraduates: 900m, 900w**
- **Tuition (1982/83): $4,430**
- **Room & Board: $2,860; Fees: $150**
- **Degrees offered: BA, BS, BProf Studies**
- **Mean SAT 475v, 515m**
- **Student-faculty ratio: 18 to 1**

A private college established in 1929, became coed in 1968. 100-acre campus in Poughkeepsie, 75 miles north of New York City. Air, bus, rail service.

Academic Character MSACS accreditation. 4-1-4 system, summer terms. Majors offered in accounting, American studies, biology, business administration, chemistry, communication arts, computer math, computer science, criminal justice, economics, English, environmental science, fashion design/retail, fine arts, French history, juvenile justice, math, medical technology, political science, psychology, Russian, social work, Spanish. Interdisciplinary studies. Distributive requirements. Masters degrees granted. Independent study. Honors program. Cooperative work/study, pass/fail, internships. 2-3 engineering program with U of Detroit. Preprofessional programs in law, allied health, engineering. Member Associated Colleges of Mid-Hudson Area. Visiting Student Program. Upward Bound Program. Science of Man Program. Franklin D. Roosevelt Studies. Marist Research Institute. Marist Institute for Local Government. Richmond Center. Cary Arboretum. Special Academic and Special Services programs. Learning Center. Center for Estuarine and Environmental Studies. Computer Center. 90,000-volume library.

Financial CEEB CSS. College scholarships, grants, state aid; PELL, SEOG, NDSL, GSL, CWS. Application deadline March 1.

Admissions High school graduation with 16 units required. GED accepted. Interview recommended. SAT or ACT required. $15 application fee. Application deadline April 1. $25 tuition and $150 room deposits required on acceptance of admissions offer. *Early Decision, Early Admission, Concurrent Enrollment* programs. Credit possible for CEEB AP, CLEP, and state exams. HEOP.

Student Life Student government. Newspaper, quarterlies, yearbook, TV center. Music, drama, political, athletic, academic, honorary, special interest groups. Students must live at home or on campus. Coed dorms. 65% of students live on campus. 11 intercollegiate sports for men, 6 for women; intramurals. AIAW, ECAC, NCAA. Student body composition: 1.5% Asian, 5% Black, 3% Hispanic, 0.5% Native American, 90% White. 35% from out of state.

[1] MARYKNOLL SCHOOL OF THEOLOGY
Maryknoll 10545

[1] MARYMOUNT COLLEGE
Tarrytown 10591, (914) 631-3200
Director of Admissions: Micheileen J. Doran

- **Undergraduates: 821w; 1,271 total (including part-time)**
- **Tuition (1982/83): $4,725**
- **Room & Board: $3,090; Fees: $170**
- **Degrees offered: BA, BS, BSW**
- **Mean SAT 450v, 450m**
- **Student-faculty ratio: 10 to 1**

A private women's college with a coed weekend program. Established by the Religious of the Sacred Heart of Mary in 1907. 25-acre campus in Tarrytown, 20 miles north of New York City.

Academic Character MSACS accreditation. Semester system, summer term. 32 majors offered in the areas of art, science, math, home economics, design, fashion, business, humanities, religious studies, social sciences, journalism, speech & drama, and international careers. Interdisciplinary studies. Self-designed majors. Distributive requirements. Independent study. Honors program. Pass/fail, internships. 3-1 program in medical technology with local hospital. MBA program with Fordham. Member of Westchester Consortium. Visiting Student Program. Study abroad. Elementary, secondary, and special education certification. Language lab. Computer center. Learning Center. Coeducational Weekend College. 103,000-volume library with microform resources.

Financial CEEB CSS. College scholarships, state aid; PELL, SEOG, NDSL, GSL, CWS. Application deadline May 30.

Admissions High school graduation with 16 units required. Interview recommended. SAT required. $20 application fee. Rolling admissions; deadline March 1. $100 tuition and $150 room deposits required on acceptance of admissions offer. *Early Entrance* Program. Admission deferral possible. Transfers accepted. Credit possible for CEEB AP and CLEP exams. HEOP.

Student Life Newspaper, magazine, yearbook. Music, drama, dance clubs. Service and special interest groups. Students must live in dorms or at home. 75% of students live on campus. 2 years of phys ed required. 7 intercollegiate sports; intramurals. Student body composition: 6.1% Black, 8.2% Hispanic, 85.7% White. 40% from out of state.

[1] MARYMOUNT MANHATTAN COLLEGE
221 East 71st Street, New York City 10021
Director of Admissions: Catherine O'Rourke

- **Undergraduates: 61m, 741w; 2,214 total (including part-time)**
- **Tuition (1982/83): $3,990**
- **Room: $2,590**
- **Degrees offered: BA, BS, BFA**
- **Mean SAT 453v, 451m**
- **Student-faculty ratio: 18 to 1**

A private college established in 1936. Urban campus in midtown Manhattan. Air, bus, rail, subway service.

Academic Character MSACS accreditation. Semester system, 2 4-week summer terms. 26 majors offered in the areas of art, business, communications, dance, education, humanities, international studies, math, music, religion, sciences, social sciences, theatre. Courses in data processing, religious studies, reading. Certificate programs in several areas. Interdepartmental studies. Language study possible at area schools. Independent study. Honors program. Pass/fail, internships. Cooperative programs: AAS or BFA at New York School of Interior Design, BA at Laboratory Institute of Merchandising, BS at New York Botanical Garden, BABM at Cornell & with Mannes College of Music. Study abroad. Early childhood, elementary, secondary, and special education certification. 70,000-volume library.

Financial CEEB CSS. College scholarships, grants, loans, state aid; PELL, SEOG, NDSL, GSL, CWS. Application deadline March 1.

Admissions High school graduation with 16 units required. GED accepted. Interview recommended. Audition required of acting, dance, music applicants. SAT or ACT, and 2 ACH recommended. $15 application fee. Rolling admissions; preferred deadline March 15. $50 tuition and $100 room deposits required on acceptance of admissions offer. *Early Decision, Early Admission, Concurrent Enrollment* programs. Admission deferral possible. Transfers accepted. Credit possible for CEEB AP, CLEP, and state exams, and for life experience. Community Leadership Program.

Student Life Student-faculty-administration committee. Yearbook. Drama, international relations, academic, special interest groups. No campus housing. 5% live in college off-campus housing. Student body composition: 5% Asian, 19% Black, 16% Hispanic, 60% White. 10% from out of state.

[J1] MATER DEI COLLEGE
Riverside Drive, Ogdensburg 13669, (315) 393-5930
Director of Admissions: William G. Powers

- **Undergraduates: 96m, 242w**
- **Tuition (1982/83): $2,000**
- **Room & Board: $1,800; Est. Fees: $150**
- **Degrees offered: AA, AS, AAS**
- **Student-faculty ratio: 16 to 1**

A private college founded by the Sisters of St. Joseph, established in 1960. 211-acre rural campus, 130 miles north of Syracuse. Served by air and bus.

Academic Character MSACS accreditation. Semester system, 6-week summer term. 2-year transfer and career programs offered in alcohol & chemical dependence studies, community residence management, liberal arts, nursery education, ophthalmic dispensing, rehabilitative criminal justice, religious studies, social services paraprofessional, and teaching assistant programs. Certificate programs in business, court reporting, and secretarial science. Distributives and 3 hours of religion required. 50,000-volume library with microform resources.

Financial College scholarships, grants, state aid; PELL, SEOG, CWS.

Admissions High school graduation with 16 units required. GED accepted. Interview recommended. SAT or ACT required. $25 application fee. Rolling admissions. *Early Admission* and *Early Decision* programs. Admission deferral possible. Transfers accepted. Credit possible for CEEB AP, CLEP,

and state exams.
Student Life Student government. Catholic Club. Professional groups. Dorms. Drugs and firearms prohibited. Class attendance expected. Student body composition: 21% minority.

[1] MEDAILLE COLLEGE
18 Agassiz Circle, Buffalo 14031

[1] MERCY COLLEGE
Dobbs Ferry 10522

[J1] MOHAWK VALLEY COMMUNITY COLLEGE
1101 Sherman Drive, Utica 13501, (315) 797-9530
Director of Admissions: Ian B. Lindsey

- **Enrollment: 8,500 men & women (including part-time)**
- **Tuition (1983/84): $1,000 (in-state), $2,000 (out-of-state)**
- **Room & Board: $1,810-$2,670; Fees: $277**
- **Degrees offered: AA, AS, AAS, AOS**

A public college established in 1946, part of the New York State University system. Suburban campus; branch in Rome. Served by air, rail, and bus.
Academic Character MSACS and professional accreditation. Semester system. 2-year transfer programs offered in biology, business administration, chemistry, engineering, fine arts, general studies, geology, international studies, liberal arts, mathematics, physical education, physics, and science. 39 career programs available. Distributive requirements. ROTC at Syracuse U, Utica. Computer center. 60,000-volume library.
Financial CEEB CSS. College scholarships, loans, state aid; PELL, SEOG, NSS, GSL, NDSL, ALAS, CWS. Priority deadline May 1.
Admissions High school graduation required. Equivalency diploma accepted. Campus visit strongly recommended. $10 application fee. Rolling admissions. $30 tuition and $35 room deposits due on acceptance of admissions offer. *Concurrent Enrollment* Program. Admission deferral possible. Credit possible for CEEB AP, CLEP, and state exams.
Student Life Student government. Newspaper, literary magazine, yearbook, radio station. Minority Student Union. Academic, honorary, religious, social, and special interest groups. 4 dormitories. Cafeteria. Freshmen have first chance at on-campus housing. Student Life Office assists with off-campus residences. 2 hours of phys ed required. 5 intercollegiate sports for men, 5 for women, 4 coed; intramurals. NJCAA.

[1] MOLLOY COLLEGE
1000 Hempstead Avenue, Rockville Centre 11570

[J1] MONROE COMMUNITY COLLEGE
Box 9892, Rochester 14623

[1] MOUNT ST. ALPHONSUS SEMINARY
Esopus 12429

[1] MOUNT SAINT MARY COLLEGE
Newsburgh 12550, (914) 561-0800
Director of Admissions: James P. Christy

- **Undergraduates: 139m, 876w**
- **Tuition (1982/83): $3,660 ($122 per credit hour)**
- **Room & Board: $2,200**
- **Degrees offered: BA, BSN, BSEd**
- **Student-faculty ratio: 14 to 1**

A private liberal arts college established in 1959, became coed in 1968. 73-acre campus in Newburgh, 58 miles from New York City. Bus and rail service.
Academic Character MSACS and professional accreditation. 4-1-4 system, 5-week summer term. Majors offered in biology, business administration & management, chemistry, communication arts, education (elementary, secondary, special), English, history/political science, interdisciplinary studies, math, media studies, medical technology, nursing, psychology, public relations, sociology, social science, theatre arts. Minors in most major areas. Courses in 15 additional areas. Bilingual education program. Distributive requirements. Independent study. Honors program. Preprofessional programs in medicine, dentistry, law. Cross-registration with Associated Colleges of the Mid-Hudson Area. Visiting Student Program. Study abroad. Elementary, secondary, and special education certification. Developmental Skills Center. 89,845-volume library with microform resources.
Financial CEEB CSS. College scholarships, grants, state aid; PELL, SEOG, NSS, NDSL, NSL, CWS. Application deadline March 1.
Admissions High school graduation with 17 units required. Interview recommended. SAT or ACT required. $15 application fee. Rolling admissions. deadline 2 weeks prior to start of semester. $50 tuition and $50 room deposits required on acceptance of admissions offer. *Early Admission, Early Decision, Concurrent Enrollment* programs. Admission deferral possible. Transfers accepted. Credit possible for CEEB AP and CLEP exams, and for life experience. HEOP.
Student Life Student government. Newspaper, yearbook. Ecology, Latin American clubs. Academic, service, special interest groups. 50% of students live on campus. Single-sex facilities. No married-student housing. First semester freshmen may not have cars on campus. Intercollegiate basketball and tennis. Intramural sports program. Student body composition: 8.5% Black, 3.1% Hispanic, 88.3% White, 0.1% Other. 16.2% from out of state.

[1] MOUNT SAINT VINCENT, COLLEGE OF
Riverdale 10471, (212) 549-8000
Director of Admissions: Margaret Sawicki

- **Undergraduates: 48m, 711w; 1,147 total (including part-time)**
- **Tuition & Fees(1982/83): $4,400**
- **Room & Board: $2,800**
- **Degrees offered: BA, BS, AA, AAS**
- **Mean SAT 453v, 477m**
- **Student-faculty ratio: 12 to 1**

A private college founded by the Sisters of Charity of New York in 1847. College became coed in 1974. 70-acre campus in residential Riverdale. Subway, bus, and train to Manhattan.
Academic Character MSACS and professional accreditation. Semester system, 3 summer terms, 2 miniterms (January & June). Majors offered in biochemistry, biology, chemistry, communication arts, computer science, economics & business, English, fine arts, French, German, health education, history/political science, Italian, Latin, liberal arts, math, modern foreign languages, nursing, physics, psychology, sociology, Spanish. Majors in American studies, peace studies, philosophy, religious studies, urban affairs through cooperative program with Manhattan College. Self-designed majors. Distributives and one religion course required. Independent study. Honors program. Cooperative work/study, pass/fail, internships. Preprofessional programs in dentistry, law, medicine. Cross-registration at Manhattan College. Exchange with other Seton colleges. Study abroad. June intersession at Institute for Aquatic Biology, Nassau. Elementary, secondary, and special education certification. Language lab. 125,000-volume library.
Financial CEEB CSS. College scholarships, state aid; PELL, SEOG, NSS, NDSL, GSL, NSL, PLUS, CWS. Scholarship & grant application deadline February 1.
Admissions High school graduation with 16 units required. Interview recommended. SAT required. $20 application fee. Rolling admissions. $250 deposit ($50 for commuters) required on acceptance of admissions offer. *Early Decision, Early Admission, Concurrent Enrollment* programs. Admission deferral possible. Transfers accepted. Credit possible for CEEB AP, CLEP, and state exams. HEOP.
Student Life Student government. Newspaper, magazine, yearbook. Music, drama, radio, film groups. Athletic, service, academic, professional, special interest groups. Coed and single-sex dorms. No married-student housing. 60% of students live on campus. 5 intercollegiate sports. Club sports & intramurals. Hudson Valley Women's Athletic Conference. Student body composition: 1% Asian, 6% Black, 8% Hispanic, 85% White. 12% from out of state.

[J1] NASSAU COMMUNITY COLLEGE
Garden City 11530

[1] NAZARETH COLLEGE OF ROCHESTER
Rochester 14610, (716) 586-2525
Director of Admissions: Paul Buntich

- **Undergraduates: 270m, 1,100w; 3,134 total (including graduates)**
- **Tuition (1982/83): $4,200**
- **Room & Board: $2,500; Fees: $50**
- **Degrees offered: BA, BS**
- **Mean SAT 950**
- **Student-faculty ratio: 12 to 1**

A private college established by the Sisters of St. Joseph in 1924. College became coed in 1973. 75-acre suburban campus 7 miles from center of Rochester. Air, bus, and rail service.
Academic Character MSACS accreditation. Semester system, 6-week summer term. 39 majors offered in the areas of art, accounting, business, humanities, sciences, math, computer science, social sciences, religious studies, music, music therapy, theatre, fine arts, and speech pathology. Nursing major for RNs. Minors offered in major areas and in computer science and women's studies. Distributive requirements. Masters degrees granted. Independent study. Honors program. Pass/fail, internships. Preprofessional programs in dentistry, law, medicine, library science, social work. Member of Rochester Area Colleges Consortium. Study abroad. Visiting Student Program. Elementary, secondary, and special education certification. ROTC & NROTC at nearby schools. Language lab. 200,000-volume library.
Financial CEEB CSS. College scholarships, grants, state aid; PELL, SEOG, NSS, NDSL, GSL, NSL, CWS. Application deadline March 30 for scholarships; varies for loans.
Admissions High school graduation with 16 units required. GED accepted. Interview recommended. Music applicants must audition. SAT or ACT required. $20 application fee. Rolling admissions; application deadline in August. $100 tuition and $50 room deposits required on acceptance of admissions offer. *Early Admission* Program. Admission deferral possible. Transfers accepted. Credit possible for CEEB AP, CLEP, and state exams. HEOP.
Student Life Student government. Newspaper, magazine, yearbook. Music, drama, philosophy, language clubs. Athletic, academic, religious, special interest groups. Coed, single-sex, language housing. No married-student housing. 65% of students live on campus. One year of phys ed required. 6 intercollegiate sports for men, 6 for women; intramurals. AIAW, ECAC, NCAA, NAIA, Rochester Area Athletic Association. Student body composition: 6% Black & Hispanic, 94% White. 6% from out of state.

[1] NEW ROCHELLE, COLLEGE OF
New Rochelle 10801, (914) 632-5300
Director of Admissions: Lynn McCaffrey

- **Undergraduates: 1,303w; 4,485 total (including part-time)**

- **Tuition (1982/83): $4,110 (Arts & Sciences), $4,170 (Nursing)**
- **Room & Board: $2,840**
- **Degrees offered: BA, BS, BFA, BSN**
- **Mean SAT 483v, 482m**
- **Student-faculty ratio: 14 to 1**

A private college founded by the Ursuline Order in 1904. School of Arts & Sciences admits women only; School of Nursing is coed. 30-acre suburban campus in New Rochelle, 15 miles north of New York City. Bus and rail service to Manhattan.

Academic Character MSACS and professional accreditation. Semester system, 4- and 6-week summer terms. Majors offered in applied design, art, biology, business, chemistry, classics, communication arts, economics, English, French, history, interdisciplinary studies, Italian, math, nursing, philosophy, physics, political science, psychology, religion, social work, sociology, Spanish. Self-designed majors. Distributive requirements. Masters degrees granted. Independent study, honors programs. Internships, pass/fail. Preprofessional program in medicine, law, veterinary medicine, dentistry. 5-year MS in community psychology. Member Westchester Social Work Consortium. Visiting Student Program. Washington Semester. UN Semester. Study abroad. Elementary, secondary, and special education certification. School of New Resources for adult men & women. Media Center. Learning Skills Center. 168,515-volume library with microform resources.

Financial CEEB CSS. College scholarships, grants, state and city aid; PELL, SEOG, NSS, NDSL, FISL, NSL, CWS. Application deadline March 1.

Admissions High school graduation with 15 units required (16 for nursing). Interview preferred. SAT or ACT required. $15 application fee. Rolling admissions; preferred application deadline April 1. $100 tuition and $50 room deposits required on acceptance of admissions offer. *Early Decision* and *Early Admission* programs. Admission deferral possible. Transfers accepted. Credit possible for CEEB AP and CLEP exams. HEOP.

Student Life College Council. Newspaper, magazine, yearbook. Music, drama, international students' organizations. Athletic, service, academic, special interest groups. Single-sex dorms. 55% of students live on campus. Class attendance required. 2 years of phys ed required. 4 intercollegiate sports, 3 intramurals. Hudson Valley Women's Athletic Conference. Student body composition: 1% Asian, 11% Black, 9% Hispanic, 79% White. 35% from out of state.

[1] NEW SCHOOL FOR SOCIAL RESEARCH

66th West 12th Street, New York City 10011, (212) 741-5665
Director of Admissions: Michael Parlapiano

- **Undergraduates: 52m, 74w; 2,434 total (including graduates)**
- **Tuition (1982/83): $5,260**
- **Room & Board: $3,200; Fees: $120**
- **Degree offered: BA**
- **Median SAT 600v, 580m**
- **Student-faculty ratio: 6 to 1**

A private, non-traditional university established in 1919 as the first university in America for adults. Five divisions: Undergraduate, Adult, Graduate Faculty of Political & Social Science, Graduate School of Management & Urban Professions, Parsons School of Design (see separate entry). 5-building urban campus in Greenwich Village, New York City. Air, bus, rail, subway service.

Academic Character MSACS and professional accreditation. Semester system, 6-week summer term. All majors are self-designed. The undergraduate division of the New School is subdivided into the Seminar College and the Senior College. Seminar College has a 1st-year program of colloquia in humanities, social sciences, sciences, and math; after freshman year students may enroll in the Senior College or continue studies in the Seminar College until graduation. Senior College enables undergraduates to utilize the curriculum of the Adult Division. Graduate degrees granted. Independent study, honors programs. BA/MA programs in economics & political economy, human resources management, media studies, and urban affairs & policy analysis. Visiting Student Program. Computer center. Museum/gallery. Member of library consortium with Cooper Union and New York U for a total of 2,500,000 volumes plus microform resources.

Financial CEEB CSS. University scholarships, awards, state aid; PELL, SEOG, NDSL, GSL, FISL, CWS.

Admissions High school graduation required. Interview recommended. SAT required. $25 application fee. Rolling admissions; deadline August 15. $100 tuition and $100 room deposits required on acceptance of offer of admission. *Early Decision* and *Early Admission* programs. Admission deferral possible. Transfers accepted. Credit possible for CEEB AP and CLEP exams.

Student Life Newspaper, magazine. Music and drama groups. Exhibits & lectures. Coed dorms. No married-student housing. 25% of students live on campus. Student body composition: 5% Black, 3% Hispanic, 92% White. 50% from out of state.

[1] NEW YORK, POLYTECHNIC INSTITUTE OF

333 Jay Street, Brooklyn 11201, (212) 643-2150
Director of Admissions: Elizabeth Sharp Ross

- **Undergraduates: 1,842m, 211w; 4,828 total (including graduates)**
- **Tuition (1982/83): $6,300**
- **Room & Board: $2,500; Fees: $10**
- **Degrees offered: BS, BEng**
- **Mean SAT 498v, 618m**
- **Student-faculty ratio: 14 to 1**

A private institute founded in 1854. Merged with New York University School of Engineering & Science in 1973. Main campus in Brooklyn. Long Island campus in Farmingdale (Rt. 110, Farmingdale 11735). Graduate center in White Plains. Air, rail, and bus service.

Academic Character MSACS and professional accreditation. Semester system, 2 6-week summer terms. Majors offered in engineering (areospace. chemical, electrical, industrial, mechanical, metallurgical, nuclear), humanities, social sciences, computer science, operations research, information management, chemistry, life sciences, math, physics, and science, technical, and financial writing. Distributive requirements. Graduate degrees granted. Independent study. Honors program. Cooperative work/study, pass/fail, credit by exam. Preprofessional program in medicine. 5-year BS/MS in engineering with bioengineering or life sciences. Research institutes and labs. Center for Urban Environmental Studies. Computer center. 265,000-volume library with microform resources.

Financial CEEB CSS. Institute scholarships, grants, state aid; PELL, SEOG, NDSL, GSL, CWS.

Admissions High school graduation with 16 units preferred. Interview recommended. SAT or ACT, and 3 ACH required. $20 application fee. Rolling admissions. $50 deposit required on acceptance of admissions offer. *Early Decision, Early Admission, Concurrent Enrollment* programs. Transfers accepted. Credit possible for CEEB AP exams.

Student Life Student government. Newspaper, magazines, yearbook, radio station. Debate. Academic, honorary, professional, and special interest groups. 6 fraternities with houses. 15-20% of men join. Coed and single-sex dorms. 2% of students live on campus. Phys ed required of freshmen & sophomores. 9 intercollegiate sports; intramurals. Metropolitan Conference. Student body composition: 19% Asian, 8% Black, 5% Hispanic, 68% White. 11% from out of state.

[1] NEW YORK, STATE UNIVERSITY OF

Central Administrative Office, University Plaza, Albany 12246, (518) 473-1011

Academic Character A state supported university system composed of 64 colleges and centers including 4 university centers, 4 medical centers, 13 colleges of arts & sciences, Empire State College (the University's non-residential college), 4 specialized colleges, 5 statutory colleges (located on the campuses of Cornell and Alfred Universities), and 30 locally sponsored 2-year community colleges. The University furthur comprises a network of Educational Opportunity Centers, providing occupational and academic training for the educationally and culturally disadvantaged and identifying students with college potential for preparation and matriculation into the State's public and private colleges. Graduate study at the Master's level is offered by the State University at 25 of the campuses, and graduate work at the doctoral level at 12. Several campuses offer time-shortened degree programs. Total course enrollment of the entire University is 379,741 with 241,389 full-time and 138,352 part-time students, including 92,702 full-time and 88,889 part-time students in locally sponsored community colleges. Most colleges have summer sessions of varying length. Libraries have more than 12,700,000 bound volumes. For more information on state-operated schools see listings below. For more information on locally-sponsored community colleges see individual listings throughout New York State.

Financial Yearly tuition and fees for New York State residents at the state-operated units are $1,075 (undergraduate), $1,725 (graduate), $2,325 (pharmacy), $2,525 (law), $4,325 (medicine, optometry, dentistry). For out of state students the tuition and fees are $1,775 (undergraduate), $2,410 (graduate), $3,475 (pharmacy), $3,775 (law), $6,325 (medicine, optometry, dentistry). Financial aid available varies with schools; it includes state aid, PELL, SEOG, NDSL, GSL, CWS.

Admissions Campuses of SUNY offer a broad range of undergraduate admissions opportunities from very selective to open; generally the most competitive campuses are the University centers and health sciences centers, the specialized and statutory colleges, and certain four-year schools; campuses requiring pre-admissions exams will accept the SAT or ACT. All of the community colleges in the system guarantee admission to all high school graduates within their sponsorship areas through the Full Opportunity Program.

The University includes:

University and Medical Centers: State University at Albany (1844); State University at Binghamton (1946); State University at Buffalo (1946); State University at Stony Brook (1957); Downstate Medical Center at Brooklyn (1860); Upstate Medical Center at Syracuse (1834).

Colleges of Arts and Sciences: College at Brockport (1841); College at Buffalo (1869); College at Cortland (1863); Empire State College, with headquarters at Saratoga Springs (1971); College at Fredonia (1867); College at Geneseo (1867); College at New Paltz (1886); College at Old Westbury (1968); College at Oneonta (1887); College at Oswego (1861); College at Plattsburgh (1889); College at Potsdam (1834); College at Purchase (1965).

Specialized Colleges: College of Environmental Science and Forestry (1911); Maritime College at Fort Schuyler, Bronx (1874); College of Optometry at New York City (1971); College of Technology at Utica/Rome (1966).

Agricultural and Technical Colleges: at Alfred (1908); at Canton (1906); at Cobleskill (1911); at Delhi (1915); at Farmingdale (1916); at Morrisville (1908).

Statutory: College of Ceramics at Alfred University (1900); College of Agriculture and Life Sciences at Cornell University (1904); College of Human Ecology at Cornell (1908); School of Industrial and Labor Relations at Cornell (1945); and College of Veterinary Medicine at Cornell (1894).

Community Colleges For information on the 30 two-year community colleges under the program of SUNY, see individual listings throughout New York State. Following is a list of these colleges and the year they were established:

Adirondack Community College at Glens Falls (1960)
Broome Community College at Binghamton (1953)
Cayuga Community College at Auburn (1953)
Clinton Community College at Plattsburgh (1966)
Columbia-Greene Community College at Hudson (1966)
Community College of the Finger Lakes at Canandaigua (1966)
Corning Community College at Corning (1956)
Dutchess Community College at Poughkeepsie (1957)
Erie Community College at Buffalo (1953)
Fashion Institute of Technology at New York City (1951)
Fulton-Montgomery Community College at Johnstown (1963)
Genesee Community College at Batavia (1966)
Herkimer County Community College at Herkimer (1966)
Hudson Valley Community College at Troy (1953)
Jamestown Community College at Jamestown (1950)
Jefferson Community College at Watertown (1959)
Mohawk Valley Community College at Utica (1953)
Monroe Community College at Rochester (1961)
Nassau Community College at Garden City (1959)
Niagara County Community College at Sanborn (1962)
North Country Community College at Saranac Lake (1966)
Onondaga Community College at Syracuse (1961)
Orange County Community College at Middletown (1950)
Rockland Community College at Suffern (1959)
Schenectady County Community College at Schenectady (1967)
Suffolk County Community College at Selden (1959)
Sullivan County Community College at Lock Sheldrake (1962)
Tompkins Cortland Community College at Dryden (1966)
Ulster County Community College at Stone Ridge (1961)
Westchester Community College at Valhalla (1953)

■[J1] SUNY AGRICULTURAL AND TECHNICAL COLLEGE AT ALFRED

Alfred 14802, (607) 871-6288

- **Undergraduates: 2,466m, 1,646w; 4,284 total (including part-time)**
- **Tuition (1982/83): $1,075 (in-state), $1,775 (out-of-state)**
- **Typical Annual Expenses: $4,455**
- **Degrees offered: AAS, AOS**

A public junior college established in 1908. Campus in a small village 12 miles southwest of Hornell and 74 miles south of Rochester.
Academic Character MSACS and professional accreditation. AAS curricula include animal husbandry, general agriculture, agricultural business, agricultural engineering technology, floriculture merchandising & production, landscaping, agricultural science, agronomy; business (accounting, data processing, computer science, business administration, marketing, secretarial science, court reporting, retail management); construction technology, internal combustion engine technology, electrical technology, engineering science, electromechanical technology, air-conditioning technology, design & drafting, product & machine design, architectural technology, industrial electronics technology, chemical technology, surveying; nursing, medical laboratory technology, medical assistant, and medical records technology. Wellsville Vocational Training Division offers AOS degree programs including drafting, auto specialist, food service management, building construction, plumbing & heating, and electrical service. 53,000-volume library.
Financial College scholarships, state aid; PELL, SEOG, NDSL, CWS.
Admissions Rolling admissions. Advanced placement program.
Student Life Dormitories and dining halls available. 7 intercollegiate sports for men, 7 for women; intramurals.

■[J1] SUNY AGRICULTURAL AND TECHNICAL COLLEGE AT CANTON

Canton 13617

- **Undergraduates: 1,352m, 1,046w**
- **Tuition (1982/83): $1,075 (in-state), $1,775 (out-of-state)**
- **Typical Annual Expenses: $4,700**
- **Degrees offered: AA, AS, AAS**

A public junior college established in 1906. Campus in a small town 120 miles north of Syracuse.
Academic Character MSACS and professional accreditation. Semester system. AA and AS offered in liberal arts and science, AS also in engineering science. AAS in agricultural engineering, agricultural science, agronomy, animal husbandry, dairy & food science, general agriculture, veterinary science technology, mortuary science, medical laboratory technology, science laboratory technology (biology and chemistry options), accounting, banking insurance & real estate, business administration, data processing, restaurant management, criminal justice, hotel technology, retail business management, secretarial science, air-conditioning technology, automotive technology, civil technology, construction technology, electrical technology (power & electronics option), mechanical technology, industrial technology, and nursing (RN). One-year certificate conferred in individual studies, building construction-maintenance, electrical construction-maintenance, heating & plumbing services, and auto mechanics. 39,000-volume library.
Financial College scholarships, state aid; PELL, SEOG, NDSL, GSL, CWS.
Admissions Rolling admissions. *Early Admission* Program. Admission deferral possible. Advanced placement program.
Student Life College housing, apartments, and private homes available to house students. Intercollegiate and intramural athletics.

■[J1] SUNY AGRICULTURAL AND TECHNICAL COLLEGE AT COBLESKILL

Cobleskill 12043, (518) 234-5011

- **Undergraduates: 1,122m, 1,376w**
- **Tuition (1982/83): $1,075 (in-state), $1,775 (out-of-state)**
- **Degree offered: AAS**
- **Mean SAT 850**

A public junior college established in 1911. Campus in a small town 40 miles southwest of Albany.
Academic Character MSACS and professional accreditation. Semester system. AAS offered in business, agricultural engineering technology, agricultural science, agronomy, animal husbandry, fisheries & wildlife technology, science-laboratory technology, medical laboratory technology, early childhood education, ornamental horticulture, accounting, business administration, data processing, computer science, landscape development, secretarial science, food-service administration, and liberal arts. One-year certificate programs in commercial cooking and secretarial studies. Remedial math and English programs. One-plus-one in Forest tech., floriculture, data processing. Study abroad in England in food services curriculum. Continuing education. Special facilities include a computer center, meat processing labs, art gallery, on-campus nursery school, food laboratories, science labs. 64,000-volume library.
Financial College scholarships, state aid; PELL, SEOG, NDSL, GSL, CWS.
Admissions Rolling admissions. *Early Admission* Program. Admission deferral possible. Advanced placement program. EOP.
Student Life Residence halls for men and women. Dining hall. 13 intercollegiate sports; intramurals. Indoor riding arena, ski slope, Olympic size swimming pool, bowling alley.

■[J1] SUNY AGRICULTURAL AND TECHNICAL COLLEGE AT DELHI

Delhi 13753, (607) 746-4100

- **Undergraduates: 1,370m, 1,017w**
- **Tuition (1982/83): $1,075 (in-state), $1,775 (out-of-state)**
- **Degrees offered: AA, AS, AAS**

A public junior college established in 1915. Campus in a village located northeast of Binghamton.
Academic Character MSACS accreditation. Quarter system. Curricula offered in agricultural sciences, business, engineering technologies, individual studies, parks & recreation management, and hotel, restaurant & food services management. Two-year university-parallel transfer programs in liberal arts and engineering science. One-year diploma programs in vocational education. Remedial mathematics and English programs. 48,317-volume library.
Financial State aid, student loans; PELL, SEOG, NDSL, GSL, CWS.
Admissions Rolling admissions. *Early Admission* Program. Admission deferral possible. Advanced placement program.
Student Life Residence halls for men and women. Dining hall. 10 intercollegiate sports; intramurals.

■[J1] SUNY AGRICULTURAL AND TECHNICAL COLLEGE AT FARMINGDALE

Farmingdale 11735, (516) 420-2000

- **Undergraduates: 3,229m, 3,025w; 13,264 total (including part-time)**
- **Tuition (1982/83): $1,075 (in-state), $1,775 (out-of-state)**
- **Estimated Resident Expenses: $4,460**
- **Estimated Commuter Expenses: $2,800**
- **Degree offered: AA, AAS**

A public junior college established in 1916. Campus in a small suburban area 30 miles east of New York City.
Academic Character MSACS and professional accreditation. Semester system. AAS offered in agriculture, ornamental horticulture, advertising art & design, air-construction technology, construction technology, architectural technology, civil technology-highway, aerospace technology, electrical technology, automotive technology, mechanical technology, food processing technology, business administration, medical laboratory technology, dental hygiene, early childhood education. AA offered in liberal arts & sciences. Continung education division. Remedial math and English programs. 93,867-volume library.
Financial Scholarships, emergency short-term loans, state aid; PELL, SEOG, NDSL, GSL, CWS.
Admissions Students admitted in September on rolling admissions except for dental hygiene applicants (Dec. 15). *Early Admission* Program. Advanced placement program.
Student Life Dormitory rooms available. 8 intercollegiate sports; intramurals. Student body composition: 10% minority.

■[J1] SUNY AGRICULTURAL AND TECHNICAL COLLEGE AT MORRISVILLE

Morrisville 13408, (315) 684-7000

- **Undergraduates: 2,840m, 1,700w**
- **Tuition (1982/83): $1,075 (in-state), $1,775 (out-of-state)**
- **Room & Board: $2,200**
- **Degrees offered: AA, AS, AAS**

A public junior college established in 1908. Campus in a village located southeast of Syracuse.
Academic Character MSACS and professional accreditation. Semester system. Curricula offered in agricultural business, agricultural engineering, agricultural science, agronomy, animal husbandry-dairy, animal husbandry-horses, horticulture, natural resources conservation, accounting, business administration, data processing, secretarial science, plastics technology, mechanical technology, journalism, food processing technology, medical laboratory technology, nursing, agricultural mechanics, general agriculture, design & drafting, musical instrument technology, food service administration, liberal arts. Vocational programs in agricultural mechanics, clerical skills, general agriculture, automotive mechanics, secretarial studies. Remedial math and English programs. Evening division. 65,000-volume library.
Financial Guaranteed tuition. College scholarships, loans, assistantships, state aid; PELL, SEOG, NDSL, GSL, CWS.
Admissions Rolling admissions. *Early Admission* and *Early Decision* programs. Admission deferral possible. Advanced placement program.
Student Life Residence halls for men and women. Dining hall. Intercollegiate and intramural athletics. Student body composition: 12% minority.

■[1] STATE UNIVERSITY OF NEW YORK AT ALBANY

Western & Washington Avenues, Albany 12222, (518) 457-3300
Director of Admissions & Records: Rodney A. Hart

- **Undergraduates: 5,500m, 5,700w; 16,730 total (including graduates)**
- **Tuition (1982/83): $1,050 (in-state), $1,750 (out-of-state)**
- **Room & Board: $2,020; Fees: $250**
- **Degrees offered: BA, BS**
- **Mean SAT 521v, 580m**
- **Student-faculty ratio: 18 to 1**

A public university founded in 1844, joined SUNY in 1948. 350-acre urban main campus with 284-acre Mohawk River campus 15 miles away and 800-acre recreational Adirondack campus 75 miles north. Air, rail, and bus service.
Academic Character MSACS and professional accreditation. Semester system, 3- & 6-week summer terms. Over 50 majors offered by the Schools & Colleges of Business, Education, Humanities & Fine Arts, Science & Mathematics, Social & Behavioral Science, Social Welfare, Criminal Justice, and Public Affairs. Self-designed majors. Distributive requirements. Graduate and professional degrees granted. Independent study, honors program, Phi Beta Kappa, pass/fail, credit by exam, internships. Preprofessional programs include dentistry, law, medicine. BA/MA, BS/MS programs in 6 fields. Exchange with 60 schools in NY state through Visting Student Program. Cross-registration with 8 area schools. Over 80 study abroad programs. Secondary education certification. ROTC. AFROTC & NROTC nearby. Computer center, meteorological lab. Art gallery. 1,000,000-volume library.
Financial CEEB CSS. College scholarships, loans, state scholarships, grants, loans, aid to Native Americans; PELL, SEOG, NSS, NDSL, NSL, GSL, CWS, work incentive program. Application deadline April 25.
Admissions High school graduation with 18 units required. Portfolio required for art majors; audition for music majors. Interview for some programs. SAT or ACT required. $10 application fee. Rolling admissions; suggest applying by January 5. $50 tuition deposit required on acceptance of admissions offer (May 1). *Early Entrance* and *Concurrent Enrollment* programs. Admission deferral possible. Transfers accepted. Credit possible for CEEB AP, CLEP, and state exams. Talented Student Admission Program. Educational Opportunity Program.
Student Life Student government. Newspaper, arts magazine, yearbook, radio station. Music & drama groups. Many academic, honorary, political, religious, service, and special interest groups. 7 fraternities and 4 sororities. 12% of men and 5% of women join. Coed and single-sex dorms. No married-student housing. 59% of students live on campus. 11 intercollegiate sports for men, 9 for women; many intramurals. AIAW, ECAC, SUNY Conference. Student body composition: 1.4% Asian, 2.9% Black, 2.7% Foreign, 1.7% Hispanic, 0.3% Native American, 91% White. 1% from out of state.

■[1] STATE UNIVERSITY OF NEW YORK AT BINGHAMTON

Binghamton 13901, (607) 798-2171
Asst. Vice President for Admissions & Financial Aid: Geoffrey Gould

- **Undergraduates: 3,535m, 4,226w; 8,934 total (including graduates)**
- **Tuition (1982/83): $1,050 (in-state), $1,750 (out-of-state)**
- **Room & Board: $2,540; Fees: $130**
- **Degrees offered: BA, BS, BTech**
- **Mean SAT 527v, 579m**
- **Student-faculty ratio: 20 to 1**

A public university established in 1946. 606-acre suburban campus 185 miles northwest of New York City, and one hour from 225-acre recreation & field study area. Air and bus service.
Academic Character MSACS and professional accreditation. Semester system, 4- & 6-week summer terms. Over 45 majors offered by the Harpur College (of Arts & Sciences), schools of Management, Nursing, and General Studies & Professional Education (for adult/evening programs). Many area studies programs. Self-designed majors. Distributive requirements. Graduate degrees granted. Independent, group, field study. Honors program, Phi Beta Kappa, internships. Preprofessional programs in dentistry, engineering, health sciences, law, medicine. 3-2 program in management. 3-2 engineering programs with 5 schools. Exchanges with 60 schools in NY state through Visting Student Program. Cross-registration with Broome Community College. Many study abroad programs. AFROTC, NROTC, ROTC at Cornell. Center for Medieval & Renaissance Studies. Computer, language lab. 1,017,000-volume library with microform resources.
Financial CEEB CSS. College scholarships, grants, loans; state scholarships, grants, loans, aid to Native Americans; PELL, SEOG, NDSL, NSL, GSL, CWS. Application deadlines February 1 (scholarships & grants), April 1 (loans).
Admissions High school graduation required. Course requirements vary with program. SAT or ACT required. $10 application fee. Rolling admissions; suggest applying in October or November. Deadline February 15. $50 tuition deposit required on acceptance of admissions offer (May 1); $125 room deposit by July 1. *Early Entrance* and *Concurrent Enrollment* programs. Admission deferral possible. Transfers accepted. Credit possible for CEEB AP, CLEP, and university exams. Talented Student Admission Program. Educational Opportunity Program.
Student Life Student government. Newspaper, journals, yearbook, radio station. Several music groups. Drama club. Many ethnic, academic, honorary, religious, service, women's, and special interest groups. Single freshmen must live at home or on campus. University composed of 1 commuter's & 5 residential colleges. Coed dorms. No married-student housing. 52% of students live on campus. Class attendance required. 2 semesters of phys ed required. 8 intercollegiate sports for men, 7 for women; many intramurals. AIAW, ECAC, NCAA, SUNY Conference. 4% of students from out of state.

■[1] STATE UNIVERSITY OF NEW YORK AT BUFFALO

Buffalo 14214, (716) 831-2000
Director of Admissions: Kevin Durkin

- **Undergraduates: 8,682m, 5,912w; 27,400 total (including graduates)**
- **Tuition (1982/83): $1,050 (in-state), $1,750 (out-of-state)**
- **Room & Board: $2,300; Fees: $187**
- **Degrees offered: BA, BS, BFA, BPS, BSEd**
- **Student-faculty ratio: 17 to 1**

A public university established in 1846. 178-acre urban Buffalo campus and 1,200-acre suburban campus in Amherst. Air, rail, and bus service in Buffalo.
Academic Character MSACS and professional accreditation. Semester system, 3 6-week summer terms. Over 60 majors offered by the divisions of Architecture & Environmental Design, Arts & Letters, Engineering & Applied Sciences, Health Sciences, Management, Natural Sciences & Mathematics, and Social Studies Administration. Programs in communications, humanities, mathematical sciences, modern education, social theory, urban poor, and environmental, health, and women's studies. Self-designed and double majors. Distributive requirements. Graduate & professional degrees granted. Independent study, honors program, Phi Beta Kappa, pass/fail, credit by exam. Exchanges with other schools in NY state. Study abroad in Europe. Elementary, secondary, art, music, and physical education certification. ROTC nearby. Research institutes. Computer, language lab. 2,003,090-volume library.
Financial CEEB CSS. College scholarships, grants, loans; state scholarships, grants, loans, aid to Native Americans; PELL, SEOG, NDSL, CWS. File FAF by February 28.
Admissions High school graduation with 16 units required. GED accepted. SAT or ACT required. $10 application fee. Rolling admissions; suggest applying early in 12th year. Priority deadline January 5. $50 tuition and $100 room deposits required on acceptance of admissions offer (May 1). *Early Entrance* Program. Transfers accepted. Credit possible for CEEB AP, CLEP, and university exams, and for Regents External Degree Programs. Educational Opportunity Program. Individualized admission possible for students without traditional requirements.
Student Life Student government. Newspaper, magazines, yearbook, radio station. Music, drama, dance groups. Athletic, academic, religious, service, and special interest clubs. Social fraternities & sororities. Dorm housing available. No married-student housing. 18% of students live on campus. 2 credit hours of phys ed required. 9 intercollegiate sports for men, 5 for women. AIAW, SUNY Conference. Student body composition: 3% Asian, 6% Black, 1% Hispanic, 1% Native American, 74% White, 15% Other. 4% of students from out of state.

■[1] STATE UNIVERSITY OF NEW YORK AT STONY BROOK

Stony Brook 11794, (516) 246-5126
Director of Admissions: Daniel M. Frisbie

- **Undergraduates: 5,725m, 4,561w; 15,415 total (including graduates)**
- **Tuition (1982/83): $1,050 (in-state), $1,750 (out-of-state)**
- **Room & Board: $2,340; Fees: $80**
- **Degrees offered: BA, BS, BEng**
- **Mean SAT 480v, 560m**
- **Student-faculty ratio: 15 to 1**

A public university established in 1957. 1,100-acre suburban campus, 60 miles east of New York City. Bus and rail service to New York.
Academic Character MSACS and professional accreditation. Semester system, 2 summer terms. Over 40 majors offered by the colleges of Arts & Sciences, Engineering & Applied Sciences, the Health Sciences Center, and the schools of Nursing and Social Welfare. 5-year BA/MS program offered by the W. Averill Harriman College of Urban & Policy Sciences. Interdisciplinary, self-designed, and double majors. Graduate & professional degrees granted. Independent study, honors program, Phi Beta Kappa, pass/fail, credit by exam. Preprofessional programs in business, dentistry, law, medicine. 5-year dual-degree program in engineering/liberal arts. Exchange with 60 other NY state schools through Visiting Student Program. Many study abroad programs. Secondary education certification. Research centers. Computer, language lab. 1,275,000-volume library.
Financial CEEB CSS. College scholarships, grants, loans; state scholarships, grants, loans, aid to Native Americans; PELL, SEOG, NDSL, GSL, CWS. File FAF by February 19.

Admissions High school graduation or equivalent required. SAT or ACT required. $10 application fee. Rolling admissions; suggest applying in fall of 12th year. $50 tuition and $75 room deposits required on acceptance of admissions offer. *Early Admission* Program. Admission deferral possible. Transfers accepted. Credit possible for CEEB AP exams. Talented Student Admission Program. Advancement on Individual Merit Program for disadvantaged students.
Student Life Student government. Publications, radio station. Music & drama groups, coffeehouse. Black Students Union. Academic, political, religious, service, and special interest clubs. Dorms and married-student housing. 50% of students live on campus. 9 intercollegiate sports for men, 7 for women. ECAC, SUNY Conference. Student body composition: 7% Asian, 5% Black, 3% Foreign, 4% Hispanic, 1% Native American, 80% White. 3% of students from out of state.

■[1] STATE UNIVERSITY OF NEW YORK AT BROCKPORT

Brockport 14420, (716) 395-2751
Director of Admissions: Marsha R. Gottovi

- **Undergraduates: 2,717m, 2,740w; 7,402 total (including graduates)**
- **Tuition (1982/83): $1,050 (in-state), $1,750 (out-of-state)**
- **Room & Board: $2,350; Fees: $110**
- **Degrees offered: BA, BS, BSN, BPS**
- **Mean SAT 480v, 490m**
- **Student-faculty ratio: 16 to 1**

A public university established in 1948. 591-acre campus in Brockport, 16 miles from Rochester. Air, rail, and bus service in Rochester.
Academic Character MSACS and professional accreditation. Semester system, 3 summer terms. Majors offered in African/Afro-American studies, American studies, anthropology, art, art history, arts for children, biological sciences, chemistry, communications, computer sciences, criminal justice, dance, earth science, economics, English, French, geology, global studies, health science, history, liberal studies, math, meteorology, philosophy, physical education, physics, political science, psychology, recreation/leisure studies, sociology, Spanish, speech, theatre. Junior-entry majors in business administration, nursing, and social work. Self-designed majors. Minors in most majors and 6 other areas. Courses in several languages. Distributive requirements. MA, MS granted. Independent study, honors program, pass/fail, cooperative work/study, internships. Year for Action Program for independent work, study, and seminars in low-income communities. Program in recreation & parks. 3-2 engineering with SUNY Buffalo and Stony Brook. Rochester Area Colleges Consortium. Washington Semester. Many study abroad programs. Elementary, secondary, special, health, and physical education certification. ROTC; NROTC at U of Rochester. Computer, language lab, audio-visual and TV facilities. 404,617-volume library.
Financial CEEB CSS. College scholarships, grants, loans; state scholarships, grants, loans, aid to Native Americans; PELL, SEOG, NSS, NDSL, GSL, NSL, CWS. Application deadline May 1.
Admissions High school graduation with 14-16 units required. Interview encouraged. SAT or ACT required. $10 application fee. Rolling admissions; suggest applying in fall of 12th year. $50 tuition and $50 room deposits required on acceptance of admissions offer (May 1). *Early Admission* Program. Admission deferral possible. Transfers accepted. Credit possible for CEEB AP exams. Talented Student Admission Program. Educational Opportunity Program.
Student Life Student government. Newspaper, magazine, yearbook. Several music groups. Drama & debate. Academic, athletic, women's, honorary, religious, and special interest clubs. Freshmen must live at home or on campus. Coop, single-sex, coed, and special interest dorms. Apartments for upperclass single & married students. 45% of students live on campus. 8 intercollegiate sports for men, 6 for women. ECAC, AIAW, NCAA, SUNY Conference. Student body composition: 1% Asian, 7% Black, 1% Hispanic, 0.5% Native American, 90.5% White. 1% of students from out of state.

■[1] STATE UNIVERSITY OF NEW YORK COLLEGE AT BUFFALO

1300 Elmwood Avenue, Buffalo 14222, (716) 878-5511
Director of Admissions: Kevin Durkin

- **Undergraduates: 3,787m, 4,739w; 11,782 total (including graduates)**
- **Tuition (1982/83): $1,050 (in-state), $1,750 (out-of-state)**
- **Room & Board: $2,450; Fees: $105**
- **Degrees offered: BA, BS, BFA, BSEd, BEng Tech**
- **Mean SAT 428v, 464m**
- **Student-faculty ratio: 19 to 1**

A public college established in 1871. 110-acre urban campus in Buffalo. Air, rail, and bus service.
Academic Character MSACS and professional accreditation. Semester system, 3 6-week and 1 3-week summer terms. 29 majors offered for a BA, 26 for a BSEd, 14 for a BS, 3 for a BEng Tech, and 4 for a BFA. Courses in Hebrew, Latin, Polish, Portuguese, Russian, Swahili, and Ukranian. Distributive requirements. MA, MS, MSEd granted. Independent study, pass/fail, credit by exam, cooperative work/study, internships. 3-2 engineering program with SUNY at Buffalo. Cross-registration through Western New York Consortium. National and International Student Exchange Programs. Study abroad. Elementary, secondary, and special education certification. ROTC at Canisius College. Language lab. 500,000-volume library.
Financial CEEB CSS. College scholarships, grants, loans; state scholarships, grants, loans, aid to Native Americans; PELL, SEOG, NDSL, CWS. Application deadline March 15.
Admissions High school graduation with 16 units required. Interview & portfolio required for design & fine arts majors. ACT or SAT recommended. $10 application fee. Rolling admissions; suggest applying in fall of 12th year. Deadline August 1. $50 tuition deposit required on acceptance of admissions offer (May 1). *Early Entrance* Program. Admission deferral possible. Transfers accepted. Credit possible for CEEB AP and CLEP exams. Educational Opportunity Program.
Student Life Student government. Newspaper, arts magazine, yearbook, radio station. Drama and several music groups. Athletic, political, religious, honorary, service, and special interest clubs. Coed and single-sex dorms. No married-student housing. 20% of students live on campus. 2 semesters of phys ed required. 10 intercollegiate sports for men, 10 for women; intramural & club sports. AIAW, NCAA, ECAC, SUNY Conference. Student body composition: 0.4% Asian, 9.3% Black, 1.4% Hispanic, 0.5% Native American, 88.4% White. 3% of students from out of state.

■[1] STATE UNIVERSITY OF NEW YORK COLLEGE AT CORTLAND

PO Box 2000, Cortland 13045, (607) 753-2011
Director of Admissions: Thomas A. Syracuse

- **Enrollment: 2,126m, 3,155w**
- **Tuition (1982/83): $1,050 (in-state), $1,750 (out-of-state)**
- **Room & Board: $2,190; Fees: $125**
- **Degrees offered: BA, BS, BSEd**
- **Mean SAT 425v, 481m**
- **Student-faculty ratio: 19 to 1**

A public college established in 1868. 140-acre small-city campus, 30 miles from Syracuse. Bus service.
Academic Character MSACS and professional accreditation. Semester system, 6-week summer term. Majors offered in anthropology, art, biology, Black studies, chemistry, cinema study, education (early-secondary, elementary, health, physical, recreation), economics, English, French, general studies, geography, geology, geology/chemistry, German, health science, history, math, math/physics, music, philosophy, physics, political science, psychology, recreation, social studies, sociology, Spanish, speech, speech pathology & audiology. Programs in arts management, computer, geophysics, journalism, management, public administration & policy, psychology of exceptional children, social gerontology, and Asian, international, Russian, and urban studies. Self-designed majors. Distributive requirements. MA, MAT, MSEd granted. Independent study, pass/fail, internships. Preprofessional preparation in dentistry, law, medicine, physical therapy. 3-2 programs with several schools in engineering, environmental studies, and languages. Study abroad in Europe. Elementary, secondary, and special education certification. ROTC; AFROTC & NROTC at Cornell. 250,000-volume library with microform resources.
Financial CEEB CSS. College scholarships, grants, loans; state scholarships, grants, loans, aid to Native Americans; PELL, SEOG, NDSL, GSL, CWS. File FAF by March 15. Application deadline May 1.
Admissions High school graduation with college prep program recommended. SAT or ACT required. $10 application fee. Rolling admissions; suggest applying by January 1. $50 tuition and $50 room deposits required on acceptance of admissions offer. *Early Entrance* Program. Admission deferral possible. Transfers accepted. Credit possible for CEEB AP, CLEP, and state exams; college has own advanced placement program. Talented Student Admission Program. Educational Opportunity Program.
Student Life Student Association. Newspaper, magazine, yearbook, radio station. Several music groups. Drama & debate clubs. About 100 other special interest groups. 2 fraternities and 2 sororities, all with houses. 4% of men and 5% of women join. Quiet and coed dorms. Apartments. 55% of students live on campus. 14 intercollegiate sports for men, 14 for women; many intramurals. ECAC, AIAW, NCAA, SUNY Conference. Student body composition: 0.3% Asian, 2% Black, 0.9% Hispanic, 0.2% Native American, 96.8% White. 2% of students from out of state.

■[1] STATE UNIVERSITY OF NEW YORK COLLEGE AT FREDONIA

Fredonia 14063, (716) 673-3251
Director of Admissions: William S. Clark

- **Enrollment: 2,379m, 2,521w; 5,192 total (including part-time)**
- **Tuition (1982/83): $1,050 (in-state), $1,750 (out-of-state)**
- **Room & Board: $2,408; Fees: $110**
- **Degrees offered: BA, BS, BMus, BSEd, BFA**
- **Mean SAT 465v, 517m**
- **Student-faculty ratio: 19 to 1**

A public college established in 1826. 230-acre campus in a residential community near Lake Erie, 45 miles from Buffalo. Bus service.
Academic Character MSACS and professional accreditation. Semester system, 2 5-week summer terms. Over 35 majors offered in the areas of accounting, arts, business administration, communications, education, engineering, English, geology, geophysics, history, languages, math & computer science, medical technology, music, music education, music therapy, musical theatre, philosophy, physics, psychology, sciences, social sciences, sound recording, speech pathology & audiology, theatre. Special & self-designed majors. Distributive requirements. Masters degrees granted. Independent study, Phi Beta Kappa, pass/fail, internships. Preprofessional programs in dentistry, law, medicine, theology. Cooperative programs in agriculture with Cornell; in special education with SUNY Buffalo & D'Youville; in engineering with 11 schools including Cornell, Columbia, RPI, Ohio State, Clarkson. Consortium with other western NY schools. Study abroad, exchange programs in Europe. Early childhood, elementary, secondary, and special education certification. ROTC. Education research centers. Computer. 300,000-volume library.
Financial CEEB CSS. College scholarships, grants, loans, state aid; PELL, SEOG, NDSL, GSL, CWS. File FAF by April 1.
Admissions High school graduation with 16 units recommended. Specific

requirements for some programs. Music majors must audition. SAT or ACT required. $10 application fee. Rolling admissions; suggest applying by May 1. $100 deposit required on acceptance of admissions offer (May 1). *Early Entrance, Early Decision, Concurrent Enrollment* programs. Admission deferral possible. Transfers accepted. Credit possible for CEEB AP, CLEP, and college exams. Nontraditional applicants accepted. Educational Development Program.
Student Life Student government. Newspaper, literary magazine, yearbook, radio station. Many music groups. Drama & dance groups. Honorary, academic, religious, special interest, and service groups. 2 fraternities and 2 sororities. Freshmen must live on campus. Single-sex and coed dorms. No married-student housing. 60% of students live on campus. 8 intercollegiate sports for men, 5 for women; intramurals. ECAC, NAIA, AIAW, NCAA, SUNY Conference. Student body composition: 3% minority. 5% of students from out of state.

■[1] STATE UNIVERSITY OF NEW YORK COLLEGE AT GENESEO

Geneseo 14454, (716) 245-5571
Dean of Admissions: William L. Caren

- **Undergraduates: 1,793m, 2,689w; 4,900 total (including graduates)**
- **Tuition (1982/83): $1,050 (in-state), $1,750 (out-of-state)**
- **Room & Board: $2,000; Fees: $95**
- **Degrees offered: BA, BS, BSEd**
- **Mean ACT 25; mean SAT 515v, 545m**
- **Student-faculty ratio: 19 to 1**

A public college established in 1867. Campus in a small town 30 miles south of Rochester. Bus to Rochester.
Academic Character MSACS and professional accreditation. Semester system, 2 3- and one 5-week summer terms. Over 35 majors offered in the areas of American civilization, arts, Black studies, comparative literature, computer, drama, education, English, geography, geology, languages, management, math, medical technology, music, philosophy, psychology, sciences, social sciences, and speech. Double majors. Minors in 13 additional areas. Distributive requirements. Masters degrees granted. Independent study, honors program, pass/fail, internships. Preprofessional programs in dentistry, law, medicine, medical technology, nursing, planning, public service, theology, veterinary medicine. 3-2 MBA program. 3-2 program in engineering with 8 schools; in environmental science & forestry with SUNY-Syracuse. Visting Student Program. Washington Semester. Cross-registration with area colleges. Many study abroad programs. Elementary, secondary, and special education certification. ROTC at Rochester Institute of Technology. Computer center. 342,000-volume library with microform resources.
Financial CEEB CSS and ACT FAS. College scholarships, grants, loans, state aid; PELL, SEOG, NDSL, GSL, CWS. File FAF by February 1.
Admissions High school graduation with 18 units recommended. Interview urged. SAT or ACT required. $10 application fee. Rolling admissions; suggest applying in November of 12th year. Priority application deadline March 15. $50 tuition and $50 room deposits required on acceptance of admissions offer (May 1). *Early Entrance* Program. Admission deferral possible. Transfers accepted. Credit possible for CEEB AP, CLEP, and college exams, and for military learning experience. Talented Student Admission Program. Educational Opportunity Program.
Student Life Student Association. Newspaper, literary magazine, yearbook, radio station. Music, debate, and drama groups. Special interest clubs. 6 fraternities and 7 sororities. Freshmen must live at home or on campus. Coed, single-sex, special interest, language dorms. 65% of students live on campus. 4 semesters of phys ed required. 7 intercollegiate sports for men, 6 for women; many intramurals. ECAC, AIAW, NCAA, SUNY Conference. Student body composition: 0.3% Asian, 2.1% Black, 0.8% Hispanic, 0.2% Native American, 96.6% White. 2% from out of state.

■[1] STATE UNIVERSITY OF NEW YORK COLLEGE AT NEW PALTZ

New Paltz 12562, (914) 257-2414
Dean of Admissions: Robert Seaman

- **Enrollment: 2,064m, 2,374w**
- **Tuition (1982/83): $1,050 (in-state), $1,750 (out-of-state)**
- **Room & Board: $2,200; Fees: $130**
- **Degrees offered: BA, BS, BFA**
- **Mean SAT 500v, 500m**
- **Student-faculty ratio: 18 to 1**

A public college established in 1828. 100-acre campus in a small village 75 miles north of New York City and 70 miles south of Albany. College has 375-acre camp in the Catskills. Bus service.
Academic Character MSACS and professional accreditation. Semester system, 6-week summer term. Majors offered in anthropology, art education, art history, Asian studies, biology, business administration, chemistry, economics, English, French, geography, geology, German, history, math, music, philosophy, physics, political science, psychology, Russian studies, sociology, Spanish, speech communication, studio art (7), and theatre arts. Nursing major for RNs. Self-designed majors. Minors in 20 areas. Courses in Arabic, Chinese, Swahili. Distributive requirements. MA, MFA, MAT, MSEd granted. Independent study, honors program, pass/fail, field work, cooperative work/study, internships. Preprofessional programs in law, medicine. 3-2 programs in geology and engineering. Visting Student Program. Cross-registration with 6 area schools. Many study abroad programs. Early childhood, elementary, secondary, and special education certification. Planetarium, art gallery, language labs. Over 345,000-volume library with microform resources.
Financial CEEB CSS. College scholarships, grants, loans; state aid; PELL, SEOG, NDSL, GSL, CWS. Application deadline March 1.
Admissions High school graduation with 16 units recommended. GED or equivalent accepted. Audition required for music majors; portfolio for art majors. Interview sometimes required. SAT or ACT required. $10 application fee. Rolling admissions; suggest applying in fall of 12th year. Deadline July 1. $50 tuition and $50 room deposits required on acceptance of admissions offer (May 1). *Early Entrance* Program. Admission deferral possible. Transfers accepted. Credit possible for CEEB AP, CLEP, and college exams. Educational Opportunity Program.
Student Life Student government. Newspapers, yearbook, radio station. Many music, dance, and drama groups. Black Student Union. Political, religious, academic, special interest, and women's organizations. Freshmen & sophomores under 21 must live on campus or at home. Special interest, coed, and women's dorms. Married-student housing. 50% of students live on campus. 2 semesters of phys ed required. 9 intercollegiate sports for men, 7 for women, and coed track & field; many intramurals. ECAC, AIAW, NCAA, SUNY Conference. Student body composition: 1.3% Asian, 11.1% Black, 3.6% Hispanic, 79.7% White, 4.3% Other. 5% from out of state.

■[1] STATE UNIVERSITY OF NEW YORK COLLEGE AT OLD WESTBURY

Box 210, Old Westbury 11568, (516) 876-3073
Acting Director of Admissions: James W. Gathard

- **Undergraduates: 1,500m, 1,700w**
- **Tuition (1982/83): $1,110 (in-state), $1,810 (out-of-state)**
- **Room & Board: $2,250; Fees: $60**
- **Degrees offered: BA, BS, BProfessional Studies**
- **Student-faculty ratio: 20 to 1**

A public college established in 1968. 600-acre suburban estate campus on Long Island, 20 miles from New York City. Airport, rail and bus stations nearby.
Academic Character MSACS accreditation. Semester system, 4-week summer term. Majors offered in American studies, bilingual & bicultural studies, biological sciences, business & management, chemistry & physics, communicative & creative arts (performing, visual), computer science, elementary & early childhood education, labor studies, mathematics, psychology, sociology, urban studies; comparative history, ideals, & cultures; and politics, economics, & society. Distributive and proficiency exam requirements. Independent study, pass/fail, internships. Alternative to Classroom Study Program. Exchanges with other SUNY schools. Cross-registration with area colleges. Study abroad. Elementary education certification. Museum. Computer center, language lab, TV studio. 150,000-volume library.
Financial CEEB CSS. State scholarships, grants, loans, aid to Native Americans, payment plans; PELL, SEOG, NDSL, GSL, CWS.
Admissions High school graduation or equivalent required. GED accepted. Interview urged; sometimes required. $10 application fee. Rolling admissions. $50 room deposit required on acceptance of admissions offer. Admission deferral possible. Transfers accepted. Credit possible for CEEB CLEP exams, and for military and life/work experience. Educational Opportunity Program.
Student Life Student government. Newspaper. Special interest groups. Coed dorms. 5% of students live on campus. Intercollegiate basketball and soccer for men; intramurals for men and women. Student body composition: 36% Black, 4% Hispanic, 60% White. 1% from out of state.

■[1] STATE UNIVERSITY OF NEW YORK COLLEGE AT ONEONTA

Oneonta 13820, (607) 431-3500
Director of Admissions: Richard H. Burr

- **Undergraduates: 2,331m, 3,300w**
- **Tuition (1982/83): $1,050 (in-state), $1,750 (out-of-state)**
- **Room & Board: $2,150; Fees: $423**
- **Degrees offered: BA, BS, BSEd**
- **Mean SAT 471v, 519m**
- **Student-faculty ratio: 18 to 1**

A public college established in 1889. 217-acre campus in a small city 75 miles from Albany and 175 miles northwest of New York City. Air and bus service.
Academic Character MSACS and professional accreditation. Semester system, 5- and 6-week summer terms. Over 40 majors offered in the areas of anthropology, arts, Black-Hispanic studies, dietetics, economics, education, food & business, general studies, geography, geology, history, home economics, languages, literature, math, meteorology, music, philosophy, psychology, sciences, school nurse, social sciences, speech, statistics, theatre, and water resources. Dual majors. MA, MS, MSEd granted. Independent study, honors program, pass/fail, internships. Preprofessional programs in accounting, business, dentistry, law, medicine, veterinary medicine. Cooperative home economics programs with Fashion Institute of Technology (NYC) and Merrill-Palmer Institute (Detroit). 3-2 programs in business, accounting; and in engineering with 5 schools including Clarkson, Georgia Tech, SUNY-Buffalo. Cross-registration with Hartwick College. Exchange program in Germany. Many study abroad programs. Elementary and secondary education certification. 383,000-volume library.
Financial CEEB CSS. College scholarships, grants, loans, state grants & loans; PELL, SEOG, NDSL, GSL, CWS. File FAF by February 1. Application deadlines April 15 (scholarships & grants), May 1 (loans).
Admissions High school graduation with 18 units recommended. Interview recommended. SAT or ACT required. $10 application fee. Rolling admissions; suggest applying in fall of 12th year. Application deadline May 1. $50 tuition and $50 room deposits required on acceptance of admissions offer (May 1). *Early Entrance* Program. Admission deferral possible. Transfers accepted. Credit possible for CEEB AP exams. College has own advanced placement program. Educational Opportunity Program.
Student Life Student Association. Newspaper, literary magazine, yearbook, radio station. Several music groups. Academic, religious, honorary, athletic, and special interest clubs. Fraternities and sororities. Coed dorms. No married-student housing. 65% of students live on campus. Boarding freshmen

and sophomores may not have cars on campus. 9 intercollegiate sports for men, 8 for women; many intramurals. ECAC, AIAW, NCAA, SUNY Conference. Student body composition: 0.2% Asian, 4.7% Black, 1% Hispanic, 0.1% Native American, 94% White. 2% from out of state.

■[1] STATE UNIVERSITY OF NEW YORK COLLEGE AT OSWEGO

Oswego 13126, (315) 341-2250
Director of Admissions: Joseph F. Grant, Jr.

- **Undergraduates: 3,347m, 3,343w; 7,500 total (including graduates)**
- **Tuition (1982/83): $1,050 (in-state), $1,750 (out-of-state)**
- **Room & Board: $2,290; Fees: $120**
- **Degrees offered: BA, BS**
- **Mean ACT 23.8; mean SAT 480v, 532m**
- **Student-faculty ratio: 20 to 1**

A public college established in 1861. 696-acre rural campus in a small town on Lake Ontario, 35 miles northwest of Syracuse. Bus service.

Academic Character MSACS and professional accreditation. Semester system, 4 3-week summer terms. Over 30 majors offered in the areas of American studies, anthropology, arts, business/accounting, communications, computer, economics, education, geochemistry, geology, history, industrial arts, languages, math, meteorology, music, philosophy, political science, psychology, public justice, sciences, sociology, theatre, vocational technology, and zoology. Self-designed majors. Minors. Distributive requirements. MA, MS, CAS granted. Independent study, honors program, pass/fail, cooperative work/study, internships. Pre-environmental science with SUNY ESF. 3-2 engineering with Clarkson. 2-2 environmental science & forestry with SUNY-Syracuse. Exchanges to Puerto Rico, St. Etienne. Many study abroad programs. Elementary and secondary education certification. ROTC. Learning Resources and computer centers. TV studio. 457,542-volume library with microform resources.

Financial CEEB CSS and ACT FAS. College scholarships, grants, loans, state aid; PELL, SEOG, NDSL, GSL, CWS. Application deadline March 1.

Admissions High school graduation or equivalent required. Interview urged. SAT or ACT required. $10 application fee. Rolling admissions; suggest applying by January 15. Deadline April 1. $50 tuition and $50 room deposits required on acceptance of admissions offer (May 1). *Early Entrance* and *Concurrent Enrollment* programs. Admission deferral possible. Transfers accepted. Credit possible for CEEB AP, CLEP, and state exams; college has own placement program. Educational Opportunity Program. Regional Service Program for county residents.

Student Life Student Association. Newspaper, literary magazine, yearbook, radio stations. Many music, dance, and drama groups. Women's Center. Academic, special interest, religious, honorary, and political clubs. 7 fraternities and 5 sororities with houses. 10% of men and 12% of women join. Freshmen must live at home or on campus. Coed and single-sex dorms. No married-student housing. 65% of students live on campus. Class attendance required. 11 intercollegiate sports for men, 8 for women; club and intramural sports. ECAC, AIAW, NCAA, SUNY Conference. Student body composition: 0.4% Asian, 2.3% Black, 0.7% Hispanic, 0.1% Native American, 95.6% White. 4% from out of state.

■[1] STATE UNIVERSITY OF NEW YORK COLLEGE AT PLATTSBURGH

Plattsburgh 12901, (518) 564-2040
Director of Admissions: David E. Traux

- **Undergraduates: 2,268m, 3,077w; 6,266 total (including graduates)**
- **Tuition (1982/83): $1,050 (in-state), $1,750 (out-of-state)**
- **Room & Board: $2,165; Fees: $105**
- **Degrees offered: BA, BS**
- **Mean ACT 21; mean SAT 450v, 500m**
- **Student-faculty ratio: 20 to 1**

A public college established in 1889. 150-acre small-city campus 45 miles from Lake Placid and 60 miles from Montreal. Air, rail, and bus service.

Academic Character MSACS and professional accreditation. Semester system, 6-week summer term, workshops. Over 40 majors offered in the areas of arts, biology-environmental science, business, Canadian studies, child-family services, communications, computer, food-nutrition, hearing-speech, languages, Latin American studies, math, medical technology, music, nursing, philosophy, psychology, sciences, social sciences, theatre, and elementary, health, home economics, secondary, speech, & speech-hearing handicapped education. Self-designed majors. Distributive requirements. MA, MS granted. Independent study, honors program, pass/fail, cooperative work/study, internships. 3-2 engineering with Clarkson, SUNY Buffalo, Stonybrook, Binghamton. Albany Semester. Many study abroad programs. Elementary, secondary, and special education certification. Special facilities with Miner Inst. in Chazy for educational research and innovation with emphasis in environmental sciences. 350,000-volume library.

Financial CEEB CSS. College scholarships, grants, loans, state aid; PELL, SEOG, NSS, NDSL, GSL, NSL, CWS. Priority application deadline April 1.

Admissions High school graduation required. Specific courses for some programs. Interview urged. Music majors must audition. SAT or ACT required. $10 application fee. Rolling admissions; suggest applying in October of 12th year. $50 tuition and $50 room deposits required on acceptance of admissions offer (May 1). *Early Entrance* Program. Admission deferral possible. Transfers accepted. Credit possible for CEEB AP and CLEP exams; college has own placement program. Educational Opportunity Program.

Student Life Student Association. Newspaper, literary magazine, yearbook, radio & TV stations. Music, drama, debate groups. Academic, special interest, religious, honorary, and service clubs. 5 fraternities and 4 sororities, some with houses. 10% of men and 11% of women join. Students under 21 must live on campus for 2 years. Coed dorms, single-sex floors. No married-student housing. 47% of students live on campus. 2 semesters of phys ed required. 7 intercollegiate sports for men, 8 for women; intramurals. ECAC, AIAW, NCAA, SUNY Conference. Student body composition: 0.4% Asian, 1.7% Black, 1% Hispanic, 0.5% Native American, 80.6% White, 15.8% Other. 1% from out of state.

■[1] STATE UNIVERSITY OF NEW YORK COLLEGE AT PURCHASE

Purchase 10577, (914) 253-5046
Acting Director of Admissions: T.R. Phillips

- **Undergraduates: 895m, 1,298w; 3,653 total (including part-time)**
- **Tuition (1982/83): $1,050 (in-state), $1,750 (out-of-state)**
- **Room & Board: $1,966; Fees: $235**
- **Degrees offered: BA, BFA**
- **Mean SAT 550v, 550m**
- **Student-faculty ratio: 15 to 1**

A public college established in 1971. 550-acre country estate campus in Westchester county, 3 miles from White Plains. Air, rail, and bus service nearby.

Academic Character MSACS accreditation. Semester system, 6-week summer term. Majors offered in acting, anthropology, art history, biology, chemistry, culture & society, dance, economics, environmental science, film, history, language & culture, literature, math, music, philosophy, physics, political science, psychobiology, psychology, sociology, theatre design & technology, urban studies, and visual arts. Individually-planned programs stressing independent research and tutorials. Preprofessional programs in visual and performing arts. Performing Arts Center. Museum. 200,000-volume library.

Financial CEEB CSS. College scholarships, grants, loans, state aid; PELL, SEOG, NDSL, GSL, CWS. Application deadlines February 15 (scholarships), March 15 (loans).

Admissions High school graduation with 16 units required. Interview urged. SAT or ACT required; English ACH recommended. $9 application fee. Application deadline January 5. $50 tuition and $100 room deposits required on acceptance of admissions offer (May 1). Transfers accepted. Credit possible for CEEB AP and CLEP exams; college has own advanced placement program. Educational Opportunity Program.

Student Life Student government. Newspapers, literary magazine, yearbook. Several music and drama groups. Women's Union. Academic, ethnic, and special interest clubs. Student dorms and apartments. 65% of students live on campus. 3 intercollegiate sports; intramurals. Student body composition: 0.1% Asian, 9.9% Black, 1.2% Hispanic, 87% White, 1.8% Other. 17% from out of state.

■[1] SUNY COLLEGE OF AGRICULTURE AND LIFE SCIENCES AT CORNELL UNIVERSITY

Ithaca 14853, (607) 256-1000

- **Undergraduates: 1,500m, 1,500w; 16,340 (total Cornell enrollment)**
- **Tuition & Fees (1982/83): $3,300 (in-state), $5,350 (out-of-state)**
- **Room & Board: $3,050**
- **Degree offered: BS**
- **Mean SAT 585v, 635m**
- **Student-faculty ratio: 8 to 1**

A public college established in 1904, supported by the state and operated by Cornell University. Small-city campus.

Academic Character MSACS and professional accreditation. Semester system. Major fields include agricultural and biological engineering, animal sciences, applied economics and business management, behavioral and social sciences, biological sciences, environmental studies, food science, and plant science. Program with Cornell College of Engineering for a BS in agricultural engineering. 5-year BS/MBA and BS/MPA programs with Cornell School of Business & Public Administration. Combined program with Cornell College of Veterinary Medicine can lead to a BS and DVM in a minimum of 7 years. Program with Cornell Division of Nutritional Science. About 8,100 acres used for instruction and research. 525,000-volume library shared with the College of Human Ecology.

Financial Scholarships and other aid through Cornell University; state aid; PELL, SEOG, NDSL, GSL, CWS.

Admissions New York State Regents diploma required. SAT required. Rolling admissions; application deadline January 1. *Early Admission* and *Early Decision* programs. Admission deferral possible. Transfers accepted. Advanced placement program.

Student Life Numerous student clubs & activities at Cornell. Dormitories and dining facilities available. Student body composition: 20% minority.

■[1] SUNY COLLEGE OF CERAMICS, ALFRED UNIVERSITY

Alfred 14802, (607) 871-2111

- **Full-time Enrollment: 394m, 278w**
- **Tuition (1982/83): $1,900 (in-state), $2,850 (out-of-state)**
- **Typical Annual Expenses: $4,350-$5,350**
- **Degrees offered: BS, BFA**
- **Mean Engr SAT 522v, 635m; mean Art SAT 483v, 474m**
- **Student-faculty ratio: 15 to 1**

A public college established in 1900, supported by the state and operated by Alfred University. Rural campus located 70 miles south of Rochester.

Academic Character MSACS and professional accreditation. Four-year program in ceramic engineering and sciences leads to a BS. Four-year program in art and design leads to a BFA. MS, MFA, PhD in ceramics granted. 45,100-volume library.

Financial Aid available including state aid, PELL, SEOG, NDSL, GSL, CWS.

Admissions SAT or ACT required. Rolling admission. *Early Admission* and *Early Decision* programs. Admission deferral possible. Advanced placement program.

Student Life Several student clubs and activities available at Alfred U. Fraternities and sororities with housing. Freshmen must live in residence halls and board on campus. University residence halls. Off-campus apartments available.

■[1] SUNY COLLEGE OF ENVIRONMENTAL SCIENCE AND FORESTRY

Syracuse 13210, (315) 470-6600

- **Enrollment: 1,043m, 334w; 1,738 total (including part-time)**
- **Tuition (1982/83): $1,050 (in-state), $1,750 (out-of-state)**
- **Room & Board: $2,720**
- **Typical Expenses: $4,710 (in-state), $5,360 (out-of-state)**
- **Degrees offered: BS, BLands Arch, AAS**

An upper-division public college established in 1911. 12-acre campus adjacent to Syracuse U campus. 7 regional campuses & field stations totaling 25,000 acres.

Academic Character MSACS and professional accreditation. Semester system, 5-week summer term in the Adirondacks for forest biology and forestry students. Undergraduate degrees offered in chemistry, environmental & forest biology, environmental studies, forest engineering, paper science & engineering, wood products engineering, resource management, and landscape architecture. AAS offered in forest technology. MS, MLand Arch, PhD granted. Internships in industry for paper science and engineering students. 5-year BLandscape Architecture program. 4-1 BS in forest engineering, BCivil Engineering program with SUNY Buffalo and Syracuse U. Off-campus and foreign study possible for landscape architecture majors. Students use facilities and participate in programs of Syracuse U, including ROTC & AFROTC. 6 forest properties (25,000 acres) used for field studies, research, and demonstration. Numerous research institutes. 105,000-volume library plus Syracuse U library of over 1,500,000 volumes.

Financial College scholarships, loans, state aid; PELL, SEOG, NDSL, GSL, CWS.

Admissions Completion of 2 years of college required; specific course requirements vary with programs. Rolling admissions. Cooperative transfer programs with over 53 schools. Advanced *Early Admission* Program for motivated high school seniors, who are guaranteed admission after they successfully complete prerequisite two years of college. *Early Decision* Program. Admission deferral possible. Transfers accepted. Advanced placement program.

Student Life Many students clubs and activities at Syracuse U. Dormitories and dining facilities through Syracuse.

■[1] SUNY COLLEGE OF HUMAN ECOLOGY AT CORNELL UNIVERSITY

Ithaca 14853, (607) 256-1000
Director of Admissions: Brenda H. Bricker

- **Undergraduates: 219m, 959w; 1,428 total (including graduates)**
- **Tuition & Fees (1982/83): $3,300 (in-state), $5,350 (out-of-state)**
- **Room & Board: $3,050**
- **Degree offered: BS**
- **Mean SAT 560v, 600m**
- **Student-faculty ratio: 6 to 1**

A public college supported by New York State and operated by Cornell University. Small city environment.

Academic Character MSACS and professional accreditation. Semester system. With a blend of interdisciplinary coursework, research, and practical study, students develop expertise in critical areas of contemporary concern: nutrition, textiles, social work, adult education, child, adolescent or adult development, biology & society, social planning, public policy, apparel & textile management, consumer economics, human-environment relations, housing, interior design, apparel design, or home economics education. Graduate degrees granted. Preparation for law, medicine, business, or graduate school, or for professional employment in the areas of consumer & public affairs, marketing, advertising design, banking, real estate, counseling, dietetics, public health, social work, home economics education, nutrition education, research & product development, biochemistry, toxicology, economics, textile chemistry, and statistics. 525,000-volume library shared with College of Agriculture and Life Sciences. University library system of over 4,400,000 volumes open to students.

Financial College and Cornell University scholarships, grants, loans; state aid; PELL, SEOG, NDSL, GSL, CWS.

Admissions Completion of 16 secondary school units required. SAT or ACT required. Application deadline January 15. *Early Decision* Program. Admission deferral possible. Transfers accepted. Credit possible for CEEB AP, CLEP, and departmental exams. Cornell University Minority Student Program (COSEP). EOP.

Student Life Numerous student clubs and activities through Cornell U. Coed, single-sex, co-op, and special interest housing. 92-97% of freshmen live on campus. Meal plans are optional. Numerous intercollegiate and intramural sports through Cornell University.

■[G1] SUNY COLLEGE OF OPTOMETRY

100 East 24th Street, New York 10010

■[1] SUNY COLLEGE OF TECHNOLOGY

811 Court Street, Utica 13502, (315) 792-3450

- **Full-time Enrollment: 850m, 550w; 3,500 total (including part-time)**
- **Tuition (1982/83): $1,050 (in-state), $1,750 (out-of-state)**
- **Room & Board: $1,800-$2,000**
- **Degrees offered: BA, BS, BTech, BProfessional Studies**
- **Student-faculty ratio: 20 to 1**

A public upper-division college of technology established in 1973. Urban campus located 70 miles west of Albany.

Academic Character MSACS and professional accreditation. Semester system, 6- to 8-week day & evening summer terms. Majors offered include business/public management, nursing, human services, general studies, behavioral sciences, natural sciences, mechanical technology, industrial technology, computer & information science, medical record technology, electrical technology, vocational education, health services management. MS granted. Internships in health services technologies, human services, and criminal justice. Small Business Management Institute, Institute for the Aging, Rural & Urban Crime Studies Institute. 100,000-volume library.

Financial CEEB CSS. College scholarships, emergency loans, state aid; PELL, SEOG, NDSL, GSL, NSL, CWS.

Admissions Completion of two years of college required. Rolling admissions. Admission deferral possible. Transfers accepted. Advanced placement program.

Student Life No dormitories, but off-campus housing available. Intercollegiate basketball for men, basketball and softball for women; intramurals.

■[1] STATE OF NEW YORK COLLEGE OF VETERINARY MEDICINE

Ithaca 14853, (607) 256-1000

- **Full-time Enrollment: 385 men & women**
- **Tuition & Fees (1982/83): $5,600 (in-state), $6,700 (out-of-state)**
- **Room & Board: $3,400**
- **Other Expenses: $3,200**
- **Degree offered: DVM**
- **Student-faculty ratio: 4 to 1**

A public college housed on the campus of Cornell University. Small-city campus in a farming area.

Academic Character MSACS and professional accreditation. Semester system. 4-year program offered leading to a DVM degree. MS, PhD, DSc granted in veterinary medicine sciences. 133-acre farm used to maintain herds and flocks for experimental purposes. 58,200-volume library.

Admissions Completion of at least 3 years of college study required. Prerequisite courses include 6 hours each of English, physics, inorganic chemistry, organic chemistry, and biology or zoology, 4 hours of biochemistry, and 3 hours of microbiology. Experience with animals also required. GRE required. DVM application deadline October 15. Application for non-DVM graduate study is made through Cornell University.

■[1] SUNY DOWNSTATE MEDICAL CENTER

450 Clarkson Avenue, Brooklyn 11203, (212) 270-1000

- **Enrollment: 741m, 573w; 1,424 total (including part-time)**
- **Undergraduate Tuition (1982/83): $1,075 (in-state), $1,775 (out-of-state)**
- **Degrees offered: BS, BSN**

A public college of medicine, nursing, and health related professions. Urban campus. Air, rail, and bus service.

Academic Character MSACS and professional accreditation. Undergraduate programs offered for degrees in nursing, medical record administration, occupational therapy, physical therapy, radiologic sciences & technology. Certificate program in nurse-midwifery. PhD in anatomy & cell biology, biological psychology, biophysics, microbiology & immunology, neuroscience, pathology, pharmacology, physical & organic chemistry, and physiology; DMSc in psychiatry; and MD granted. Academic and clinical facilities include Basic Sciences Building, 350-bed State University Hospital (opened in 1966), and 13 affiliated hospitals. 230,530-volume library.

Financial Aid available including scholarships and loans.

Admissions SAT required for admission to Colleges of Nursing and Health Related Professions. Physical exam also required. Admission for September entrance only.

Student Life 2 residence halls. Cafeteria. Student Center.

■[1] SUNY—EMPIRE STATE COLLEGE, COORDINATING CENTER AT SARATOGA SPRINGS

Saratoga Springs 12866

■[1] STATE UNIVERSITY OF NEW YORK MARITIME COLLEGE

Fort Schuyler, Bronx 10465, (212) 892-3000
Director of Admissions: R. Thomas Cerny

- **Undergraduates: 860m, 68w; 1,108 total (including graduates)**
- **Tuition (1982/83): $1,075 (in-state), $1,775 (out-of-state)**
- **Room, Board, & Summer Sea Term: $2,750; Fees: $125**
- **Uniforms: $1,000**
- **Degrees offered: BS, BEng**
- **Mean ACT 26; mean SAT 500v, 580m**
- **Student-faculty ratio: 15 to 1**

A public college established in 1874 to train students for employment as licensed officers in the Merchant Marine and in professional positions in maritime & related industries. Became coed in 1972. 56-acre urban residential campus on Throgs Neck Peninsula of the Bronx, 10 miles from New York City. Air, rail, and bus service.

Academic Character MSACS and professional accreditation. Semester system, required 2-month summer term. Majors offered in computer science & mathematics, electrical engineering, humanities concentration, marine engineering, marine transportation (economics, management), meteorology & oceanography, naval architecture, nuclear science & engineering, and ocean engineering. Courses offered in naval science which qualify students for the Naval Reserve. Courses also offered in liberal arts & sciencesand additional areas. 3 summer sea terms on training vessel EMPIRE STATE required. NROTC. Extensive lab facilities for engineering, sciences,

computer. 66,000-volume library with non-print resources.
Financial CEEB CSS. College and state aid; PELL, SEOG, NDSL, GSL, CWS. US citizens who are qualified for original license as an Merchant Marine officer may receive a federal Incentive Payment of $1,200 per year; but must agree to sail on their license for 3 years after graduation. Application deadline December 1 (scholarships & grants). Suggest applying for loans by March 1.
Admissions High school graduation with 16 units required. GED accepted. Interview urged. SAT or ACT required; ACH recommended. $10 application fee. Rolling admissions; suggest applying by January 1. Deadline May 1. $50 tuition and $50 room deposits required on acceptance of admissions offer. *Early Entrance* Program. Admission deferral possible. Transfers accepted. Credit possible for CEEB AP and CLEP exams.
Student Life Student Council. Regiment of Cadets. Newspaper, literary magazine, yearbook. Radio club. Music groups. International Relations Club. Eagle Scout fraternity. Academic, special interest, religious, and professional clubs. Students must live on campus. Dorms for men and women. No married-student housing. Class attendance required. Liquor restricted. Uniforms required. 8 semesters of phys ed required. 13 intercollegiate sports for men, 2 for women; many club and intramural sports. ECAC, NCAA. Student body composition: 1% Asian, 2% Black, 2% Hispanic, 94% White. 15% from out of state.

■[1] STATE UNIVERSITY OF NEW YORK—POTSDAM COLLEGE OF ARTS & SCIENCES

Potsdam 13676, (315) 267-2185
Director of Admissions: Ross Pfeiffer

- **Undergraduates: 1,921m, 2,136w; 4,901 total (including graduates)**
- **Tuition (1982/83): $1,050 (in-state), $1,750 (out-of-state)**
- **Room & Board: $2,146-$2,296; Fees: $105**
- **Degrees offered: BA, BMus**
- **Mean ACT 24; mean SAT 475v, 555m**
- **Student-faculty ratio: 20 to 1**

A public college established in 1866. 240-acre campus in a small college town near the St. Lawrence River, 150 miles north of Syracuse.College Star Lake Camp in the Adirondacks.
Academic Character MSACS and professional accreditation. Semester system. Majors offered for a BA in anthropology, art history, art-studio, biology, chemistry, computer, drama, economics, English, French, geography, geology, history, math, music history & literature, music theory, philosophy, physics, political science, psychology, religious studies, sociology, and Spanish; for a BMus in church music, composition, music education, musical studies, and music performance. Self-designed and double majors. Many liberal arts and career courses offered. Distributives or School-Within-a-School program required. MA, MSEd, MMus granted. Independent study, honors program, pass/fail, cooperative work/study, internships. Preprofessional programs in law and health sciences. Cooperative programs in business administration, computer science, engineering. Cross-registration with Clarkson, St. Lawrence U, and SUNY Ag-Tech College at Canton. National Student Exchange. Washington Semester. Many study abroad programs. Music, elementary, and secondary education certification. ROTC & AFROTC at Clarkson. Campus School. Computer center, language lab. 300,000-volume library with access to area libraries.
Financial CEEB CSS. College scholarships, grants, loans, state aid, payment plan; PELL, SEOG, NDSL, GSL, CWS, college work program. Priority application deadline March 1.
Admissions High school graduation with 16 units required. Interview required. Audition required for music majors; scores & tapes for composition majors. SAT or ACT required. $10 application fee. Rolling admissions; suggest music students apply by January 5. Deadline March 1. $100 deposit required on acceptance of admissions offer (May 1). *Early Entrance* Program. Admission deferral possible. Transfers accepted. Credit possible for CEEB AP exams; college has own placement program. Educational Opportunity Program.
Student Life Student government. Newspaper, literary magazine, yearbook, radio stations. Several music groups. Dance, debate, and theatre groups. Academic, special interest, religious, service, and athletic clubs. 4 fraternities and 6 sororities. Students must live on campus for one year. Coed and single-sex dorms. 75% of students live on campus. 4 semesters of phys ed required. 7 intercollegiate sports for men, 6 for women; many intramurals. ECAC, AIAW, NCAA, SUNY Conference. Student body composition: 0.5% Asian, 1% Black, 1% Hispanic, 0.5% Native American, 97% White. 2% from out of state.

■[1 & J1] SUNY REGENTS EXTERNAL DEGREE PROGRAM

Cultural Education Center, Albany 12230

- **Enrollment: 20,000 men & women**
- **Degrees offered: BS, BS, BSN, BSBA, AA, AS, AASN**

A public external-degree college with no campus. More than 15,000 individuals have earned degrees since 1972.
Academic Character MSACS and professional (National League for Nursing) accreditation The program is registered (approved) by the Board of Regents of the State University of New York. College provides a non-traditional educational program providing an alternate route to undergraduate degrees in liberal arts & sciences, nursing, and business. University itself provides no instruction but rather assesses the academic accomplishments of students it has not taught. There are no classroom attendance or residence requirements. The program emphasizes independent study and the philosophy that what a person knows is more important than how or when the knowledge was acquired. Students proceed at their own pace. Degree requirements may be met in a variety of ways, including courses taken at regionally accredited colleges, recognized proficiency exams, military service school, and special courses offered by business, industry, and government. Requirements for all degrees may be completed entirely by examination. Students outside of New York State who wish to take the Regents own examinations may do so through the American College Testing Program which administers most of the exams throughout the US and in some foreign countries. Nursing graduates are eligible to be licensed as registered nurses in most states.
Financial The cost of earning a RED varies with the amount of previously earned credit and methods chosen to satisfy requirements; average cost of earning a degree entirely by exam $400-$900. Financial aid (state grants, SEOG, PELL), available to qualified individuals.
Admissions Students may enroll at any time. The program is open to all. SAT or ACT not required. Rolling admissions.
Student Life Most of the approximately 20,000 enrolled students are employed full-time and are over 30 years of age, about 33% live in New York State.

■[1] SUNY SCHOOL OF INDUSTRIAL AND LABOR RELATIONS AT CORNELL UNIVERSITY

Ithaca 14853, (607) 256-1000

- **Full-time Enrollment: 384m, 256w**
- **Tuition (1982/83): $3,300 (in-state), $5,350 (out-of-state)**
- **Room & Board: $3,050; Fees: $50**
- **Degree offered: BS**
- **Median SAT 628v, 640m**
- **Student-faculty ratio: 9 to 1**

A public school established in 1945, supported by the state and operated by Cornell University. Small city campus.
Academic Character MSACS accreditation. Majors offered by the departments of Economics & Social Statistics, International & Comparative Labor Relations, Labor Economics, Organizational Behavior, Personnel & Human Resource Studies, and Collective Bargaining, Labor Law, and Labor History. Graduate degrees granted. Directed study
, internships. 5-year BS/MS program. Dual degree program with Graduate School of Business and Public Administration. Off-campus and foreign study possible. Over 100,000-volume library.
Financial School and Cornell University scholarships, grants, state aid; PELL, SEOG, NDSL, GSL, CWS.
Admissions Completion of 16 secondary school units required. SAT and 2 ACH, or ACT required. Freshmen accepted for September entrance only. Application deadline January 15. Transfers accepted for September or February entrance.
Student Life Numerous student clubs and activities through Cornell. Fraternities and sororities with housing. Coed, single-sex, co-op, and special interest housing. Many intercollegiate and intramurals sports for men and women with Cornell.

■[1] SUNY UPSTATE MEDICAL CENTER

155 Elizabeth Blackwell Street, Syracuse 13210

[P] NEW YORK CHIROPRACTIC COLLEGE

PO Box 167, Glen Head 11545

[P] NEW YORK COLLEGE OF PODIATRIC MEDICINE

53 East 124th Street, New York 10035

[1 & J1] NEW YORK INSTITUTE OF TECHNOLOGY

Old Westbury 11568

Three campuses: Old Westbury Campus (750-acre suburban setting, 25 miles east of New York City); Commack College Center (6350 Jericho Turnpike, Commack 11725, 10-acre suburban setting 35 miles east of New York City); Metropolitan Center (1855 Broadway at 61st Street, New York 10023).

[P] NEW YORK LAW SCHOOL

57 Worth Street, New York 10013

[P] NEW YORK MEDICAL COLLEGE

Elmwood Hall, Valhalla 10595

[P] NEW YORK SCHOOL OF INTERIOR DESIGN

155 East 56th Street, New York 10022

[P] NEW YORK THEOLOGICAL SEMINARY

5 West 29th Street, New York 10001

[1] NEW YORK UNIVERSITY

25 West 4th Street, New York 10012, (212) 598-3591
Director of Admissions: Harold R. Doughty

- **Undergraduates: 8,363m, 6,886w; 45,524 total (including part-time & grads)**
- **Tuition (1982/83): $6,634**
- **Room & Board: $2,900-$3,339**
- **Degrees offered: BA, BS, BFA, AA, AAS**
- **Mean SAT 544v, 565m**
- **Student-faculty ratio: 13 to 1**

A private university established in 1831. Urban campus surrounds Washington Square in New York City. Additional centers: Institute of Fine Arts (1 E. 78th St.), Medical Center (550 First Ave.), Brookdale Dental Center (421 First Ave.), Graduate Business Center (100 Trinity Place). Air, bus, rail, subway service.
Academic Character MSACS and professional accreditation. Semester system, 2 6-week summer terms. 52 majors offered by the College of Arts & Sciences, 13 by the College of Business & Public Administration, 10 by the

School of Arts, 35 by the School of Education, Health, Nursing, and Arts Professions, and one by the School of Social Work. Self-designed majors. Joint degree programs. Distributive requirements. Graduate and professional degrees granted. AA and AS granted by School of Continuing Education. Independent study, honors programs, Phi Beta Kappa. Cooperative work/study, internships, pass/fail. Preprofessional programs in law, dentistry, medicine, optometry, podiatry. Joint bachelor's/master's degree programs. BS/BEng, BS/MEng programs with Cooper Union. Elementary, secondary, and special education certification. Visiting Students. Study abroad. Computer center, language lab. Several libraries with over 3,000,000 volumes and microform resources.
Financial CEEB CSS. University scholarships, grants, state aid; PELL, SEOG, NDSL, CWS. Application deadline February 15.
Admissions High school graduation with 16 units required. Interview recommended; audition, interview, portfolio required in some cases. SAT or ACT required; ACH sometimes required. $25 application fee. Rolling admissions; application deadline February 1. $200 tuition and $200 room deposits required on acceptance of admissions offer. *Early Decision, Early Admission, Concurrent Enrollment* programs. Admission deferral possible. Transfers accepted. Credit possible for CEEB AP and CLEP exams. Special programs for disadvantaged students.
Student Life Student government. 4 newspapers, 2 radio stations. Over 160 student clubs. 9 fraternities, 3 sororities. 11% of men and 4% of women join. Single-sex dorms, French House, German House house 2,000 students. 30% of students live on or near campus. 10 intercollegiate sports for men, 4 for women. Intramurals. Student body composition: 8% Asian, 8% Black, 6% Hispanic, 75% White, 3% Other. 35% from out of state.

[J1] NIAGARA COUNTY COMMUNITY COLLEGE
3111 Saunders Settlement Road, Sanborn 14132

[1] NIAGARA UNIVERSITY
Niagara University 14109, (716) 285-1212
Dean of Admissions: George C. Pachter

- **Undergraduates: 1,300m, 1,600w; 4,028 total (including graduates)**
- **Tuition (1982/83): $4,170**
- **Room & Board: $2,650; Fees: $200**
- **Degrees offered: BA, BS, BBA, AS, AA, AAS**
- **Mean SAT 450v, 500m**
- **Student-faculty ratio: 16 to 1**

A private university founded in 1856 by Vincentian Congregation of the Mission of the Roman Catholic Church. 160-acre suburban campus in Niagara Falls, 20 miles north of Buffalo. 50-acre DeVeaux campus nearby. Air, bus, and rail service in Buffalo.
Academic Character MSACS and professional accreditation. Semester system, 8-week summer term. 24 majors offered by the College of Arts & Sciences, 8 by the College of Business Administration, 2 by the School of Education, and majors by the College of Nursing and the Institute of Transportation, Travel, & Tourism. Courses in modern languages. Minority group studies program. Associate degrees granted by Evening Division. Distributives and 3 religion courses required. Masters degrees granted. Independent study. Internships. Preprofessional programs in law, engineering, medicine, dentistry. 3-2 engineering program with U of Detroit. Member Western New York Consortium. Visiting Student Program. Study abroad. Secondary education certification. ROTC. Computer center. Art gallery. 200,000-volume library with microform resources.
Financial CEEB CSS. University scholarships, grants, awards, state aid; PELL, SEOG, NSS, NDSL, GSL, NSL, CWS. Scholarship application deadline February 15. Deadline varies for loans.
Admissions High school graduation with 16 units required. GED accepted. SAT or ACT required. $15 application fee. Rolling admissions; deadline August 1. $50 tuition and $50 room deposits required on acceptance of admissions offer. *Early Decision, Early Admission, Concurrent Enrollment* programs. Admission deferral possible. Transfers accepted. Credit possible for CEEB AP, CLEP, and state exams; departmental challenge exams offered.
Student Life Student government. Newspaper, magazines, yearbook, radio stations. Music, drama, ski, cinema, athletic clubs. Religious, academic, service, special interest groups. Students under 21 must live on campus or at home. Single-sex dorms; no visitation in rooms. No married-student housing. 65% of students live on campus. Freshmen may not have cars on campus. 6 intercollegiate sports for men, 5 for women; club and intramural sports. AIAW, ECC, NCAA. Student body composition: 0.2% Asian, 4.6% Black, 0.7% Hispanic, 0.5% Native American, 94% White. 15% from out of state.

[J1] NORTH COUNTRY COMMUNITY COLLEGE
20 Winona Avenue, Saranac Lake 12983

[1] NYACK COLLEGE
Nyack 10960, (914) 358-1710
Director of Admissions: Dan Rinker

- **Enrollment: 229m, 293w**
- **Tuition (1982/83): $3,460**
- **Room & Board: $2,115; Fees: $250**
- **Degrees offered: BA, BS, BMus, BSacred Mus, AA, AS**
- **Mean SAT 478v, 450m**

A private college sponsored by the Christian and Missionary Alliance, established in 1882. 65-acre suburban campus at Nyack-on-Hudson. Air, bus, and rail service in New York City, which is 25 miles south.
Academic Character MSACS and professional accreditation. Semester system, 2 3-week summer terms. Majors offered in Bible, Christian education, elementary education, English, history, missions, music, pastoral ministries, philosophy, psychology, religion, social science. Associate degree programs. Distributive requirements. GRE required of BA graduates. 2 Winterims required. Independent study, internships, pass/fail. Preprofessional program in nursing. Post-baccalaureate one-year program in the Alliance School of Theology and of Missions. Study abroad. Elementary and secondary education certification. 66,000-volume library.
Financial CEEB CSS. College scholarships, loans, state aid; PELL, SEOG, NDSL, CWS.
Admissions High school graduation with 16 units required. GED accepted. Interview recommended. Audition required of music applicants. "Candidates's own testimony of Christian experience" required. SAT or ACT required. $15 application fee (no fee for applications filed before January 31). Rolling admissions. $50 deposit required on acceptance of admissions offer. *Early Admission* and *Concurrent Enrollment* programs. Admission deferral possible. Transfers accepted. Credit possible for CEEB AP and CLEP exams. HEOP.
Student Life Student government. Newspaper, magazine, yearbook, radio station. Music, drama, religious, service, special interest groups. Students must live on campus or at home. Single-sex dorms. Married-student housing. Alcohol, tobacco, narcotics, illegal drugs, dancing prohibited. Class attendance expected. Christian service and field work, daily chapel attendance, Sunday worship required. 2 credits in phys ed required. 6 intercollegiate sports for men, 5 for women. Intramurals. NAIA, NCCAA, SAC, ECVL, HVWAC. Student body composition: 2.8% Asian, 5.8% Black, 3.9% Hispanic, 0.1% Native American, 87.4% White. 56% from out of state.

[J1] ONONDAGA COMMUNITY COLLEGE
Syracuse 13215

[J1] ORANGE COUNTY COMMUNITY COLLEGE
Middletown 10940

[1] PACE UNIVERSITY IN NEW YORK
Pace College Plaza, New York 10038, (212) 285-3323
Director of Admissions: Stuart L. Medow

- **Undergraduates: 1,969m, 2,195w; 14,335 total (including graduates)**
- **Tuition (1982/83): $4,340**
- **Room & Board: $1,950-$2,850; Fees: $180**
- **Degrees offered: BA, BS, BBA, BPS, AA, AS, AAS**
- **Mean SAT 440v, 490m**
- **Student-faculty ratio: 22 to 1**

A private university established in 1906. 3-acre urban main campus in New York City; branch campuses in Pleasantville/Briarcliffe and the College of White Plains (see White Plains). Air, bus, rail service.
Academic Character MSACS and professional accreditation. Semester system, 2 6-week summer terms. 52 majors offered in the areas of arts, sciences, math, humanities, social sciences, communications, education, computer science, medical fields, accounting, business, professional studies. Associate degrees in arts & sciences, theatre, general science, early childhood education, industrial relations, and business fields. Certificate programs. Distributive requirements. Graduate degrees granted. Independent study. Honors program. Cooperative work/study, internships, pass/fail. BBA/MBA, BA/BS-MBA programs. Cross-registration at White Plains and Pleasantville/Briarcliff campuses. Visiting Student Program. Open Curriculum Program. Study abroad. Elementary and secondary education certification. InterFuture. Institute for Sub/Urban Governance. Math lab, language lab, computer center. 293,000-volume library with microform resources.
Financial CEEB CSS. University scholarships, grants, state aid; PELL, SEOG, NSS, NDSL, FISL, NSL, CWS. Application deadline March 15.
Admissions High school graduation with 16 units required. GED accepted. Interview recommended. SAT or ACT required; ACH recommended. $15 application fee. Rolling admissions; deadline August 15. $100 deposit required on acceptance of admissions offer. *Early Decision* and *Early Admission* programs. Admission deferral possible. Transfers accepted. Credit possible for CEEB AP, CLEP, and ACT PEP exams, and for life experience. University has own advanced placement program. CAP program for underprepared students.
Student Life Student government. Newspapers, magazine, yearbook, radio station. Music, drama, political, religious, service, special interest groups. Coed dorms. 7% of students live on campus. 3 fraternities, 3 sororities. 10 intercollegiate sports for men, 9 for women. Intramurals. NCAA, ECAC, NAIAW. Student body composition: 6% Asian, 19% Black, 1% Foreign, 13% Hispanic, 1% Native American, 60% White. 11% from out of state.

■[1] PACE UNIVERSITY—PLEASANTVILLE/BRIARCLIFF CAMPUS
Pleasantville 10570, (914) 769-3788
Director of Admissions: Richard A. Avitable

- **Undergraduates: 1,158m, 1,426w; 4,829 total (including graduates)**
- **Tuition (1982/83): $4,340**
- **Room & Board: $1,950-$2,850**
- **Degrees offered: BA, BS, BBA, BPS, AA, AS, AAS**
- **Mean SAT 456v, 506m**
- **Student-faculty ratio: 18 to 1**

A private university established in 1962. Suburban 200-acre campus in Pleasantville, 50 miles north of New York City. Air, bus, rail service in New York City.
Academic Character MSACS and professional accreditation. 4-1-4 system, 2 6-week summer terms. 51 majors offered in the areas of arts, sciences, math, accounting, business, humanities, communications, social

sciences, nursing, education, computer, criminal justice. Associate degrees in many areas. Distributive requirements. Masters degrees granted. Independent study, honors program. Cooperative work/study, pass/fail, credit by exam, internships. Preprofessional programs in medicine, law, dentistry. Cross-registration with White Plains and New York City campuses. Open Curriculum Program. Study abroad. Elementary and secondary education certification. Institute for Sub/Urban Governance. InterFuture. Math lab. Writing Center and workshop referral. Computer center. 203,000-volume library with microform resources.
Financial CEEB CSS. University scholarships, grants, state aid; PELL, SEOG, NSS, NDSL, FISL, GSL, CWS. Application deadline March 15.
Admissions High school graduation with 16 units required. GED accepted. Interview recommended. Portfolio required of art applicants. SAT or ACT required. $15 application fee. Rolling admissions; deadline August 1. $100 deposit required on acceptance of offer of admission. *Early Decision* and *Early Admission* programs. Admission deferral possible. Transfers accepted. Credit possible for CEEB AP, CLEP, and state exams.
Student Life Student government. Newspaper, magazine, yearbook, radio station. Music, drama, political, religious, service, special interest organizations. One fraternity and one sorority. Coed dorms. No married-student housing. 39% of students live on campus. 10 intercollegiate sports for men, 9 for women. Intramurals. ECAC, NAIAW, NCAA. Student body composition: 1% Asian, 5% Black, 2% Hispanic, 1% Native American, 91% White. 13% from out of state.

[1] PARSONS SCHOOL OF DESIGN
New York 10011, (212) 741-8910
Associate Director of Admissions: Catherine Kent Chase

- **Undergraduates: 555m, 945w**
- **Tuition (1982/83): $5,640**
- **Room & Board: $3,000**
- **Degrees offered: BFA, AAS**
- **Mean SAT 500v, 490m**
- **Student-faculty ratio: 8 to 1**

A private college established in 1896. Affiliated with the New School of Social Research since 1970; merged with Otis Art Institute of Los Angeles in 1979 to form the Otis Art Institute of Parsons School of Design, Los Angeles. Urban campus in Greenwich Village. Air, bus, rail, subway service.
Academic Character MSACS and professional accreditation. Semester system, 5-week summer term. Majors offered in art education, ceramics, communication design, environmental design, fashion design, fashion illustration, fiber arts, illustration, industrial design, interior design, jewelry, metals, painting, photography, product design, sculpture. Courses offered in the liberal arts & sciences. AAS and certificate programs available for adults. Distributive requirements. Foundation Year for freshmen. MFA granted. Apprenticeships. Member East Coast Consortium of art schools; term exchanges. American College in Paris program. Study abroad in Europe and Japan. Fifth Avenue Campus. Fashion Education Center. 32,000-volume library; 35,000-picture collection; library consortium with area libraries.
Financial CEEB CSS and ACT FAS. School scholarships, awards, state aid; PELL, SEOG, NDSL, GSL, CWS. Application deadline March 1 (Parsons).
Admissions High school graduation with 16 units required. GED accepted. Interview required for nearby residents, recommended for others. Portfolio and home-art test required. SAT or ACT required. $25 application fee. Rolling admissions. $100 deposit required on acceptance of admissions offer. *Early Admission* and *Early Decision* programs. Transfers accepted. Credit possible for CEEB AP exams. HEOP.
Student Life Student government. Newspaper, yearbook. Film society, exhibition committee, annual exhibition/fashion show. Dorms for men & women. No married-student housing. 20% of students live on campus. Class attendance required. Student body composition: 15% Black, 8% Hispanic, 1% Native American, 76% White. 63% from out of state; 13% foreign enrollment.

[J1] PAUL SMITH'S COLLEGE
Paul Smiths 12970, (518) 327-6227

- **Enrollment: 805m, 314w**
- **Tuition (1982/83): $3,200**
- **Room & Board: $2,250; Fees: $80**
- **Degrees offered: AA, AS, AAS**
- **Student-faculty ratio: 12 to 1**

A private college established in 1946. 170-acre rural campus in the Adirondack mountains, 22 miles from Lake Placid. Served by bus; airport nearby.
Academic Character MSACS accreditation. Semester system, summer terms. 2-year programs offered in ecology & environmental technology, forestry, hotel & restaurant management, and liberal arts. Distributive requirements for AA degree. Cooperative work/study. Experimental forest. 37,000-volume library.
Financial State aid, PELL, SEOG, GSL, CWS.
Admissions High school graduation required. Interview required. SAT or ACT required. $20 application fee. Rolling admissions. $100 deposit due on acceptance of admissions offer. *Early Decision* and *Early Admission* programs. Admission deferral possible. Transfers accepted. Advanced placement program.
Student Life Student Council. Newspaper, yearbook, radio station. Drama club. Academic, professional, religious, service, social, and special interest groups. Dorms and dining hall for men and women. Class attendance expected. 2 hours of phys ed required of all freshmen. 6 intercollegiate sports for men, 5 for women.

[1] PRATT INSTITUTE
Brooklyn 11205, (212) 636-3669
Director of Admissions: Daniel S. Kimball

- **Undergraduates: 2,050m, 1,124w; 4,320 total (including graduates)**
- **Tuition (1982/83): $5,200**
- **Room & Board: $2,950; Fees: $210**
- **Degrees offered: BS, BFA, BID, BPS, BArch, BEng, AAS, AOS**
- **Mean SAT 485v, 525m**
- **Student-faculty ratio: 14 to 1**

A private institute established in 1887. 25-acre urban campus in Brooklyn. Air, rail, bus service.
Academic Character MSACS and professional accreditation. Semester system, 2 summer terms. Majors offered in architecture, art & design, construction, drawing, engineering, environmental design, fashion design, fashion merchandising, film, food service/management, industrial design, interior design, nutrition/dietetics, painting, photography, printmaking, science, sculpture. Self-designed majors. Interdisciplinary studies. Distributive requirements. Graduate degrees granted. Independent study. Cooperative work/study, pass/fail, internships. 6-year program leads to BArch/MS (planning) or BArch/MS (urban design). 5-year engineering/science program. Member consortium with East Coast Schools of Art. Study abroad. Elementary and secondary art education certification. ROTC at St. John's U. Computer center. 220,000-volume library with microform resources.
Financial CEEB CSS. Institute scholarships, grants, awards, loans, state aid; PELL, SEOG, NDSL, CWS. Application deadline February 1.
Admissions High school graduation with 16 units required. Interview & portfolio may be required; home exam required of art & design applicants. SAT or ACT required; ACH required in some cases. $25 application fee. Rolling admissions; deadline April 1. $100 deposit required on acceptance of offer of admission. *Early Decision* and *Early Admission* programs. Admission deferral possible. Transfers accepted. Credit possible for CEEB AP and CLEP exams. HEOP.
Student Life Student government. Newspaper, yearbook, radio station. Student gallery. Honorary, professional, religious, and special interest groups. 1 fraternity with house, 1 sorority. 22% of students live on campus in coed and single-sex dorms. Married-student housing. 7 intercollegiate sports for men, 5 for women. ECAC, NCAA. Student body composition: 5.7% Asian, 15% Black, 6% Hispanic, 63.7% White, 9.6% Other. 31% from out of state.

[1] RENSSELAER POLYTECHNIC INSTITUTE
Troy 12181, (518) 270-6216
Dean of Admissions & Financial Aid: Christopher Small

- **Undergraduates: 3,558m, 756w; 6,185 total (including graduates)**
- **Tuition (1982/83): $7,540**
- **Room & Board: $2,750; Fees: $250**
- **Degrees offered: BS, BArch**
- **Mean SAT 566v, 675m**
- **Student-faculty ratio: 12 to 1**

A private institute established in 1824. 260-acre urban campus overlooking the Hudson River, 15 miles from Schenectady and Albany. Served by air, bus, and rail.
Academic Character MSACS and professional accreditation. Semester system, 8-week summer term. Majors offered in aeronautical engineering, architecture, biology, biomedical engineering, building science, chemical engineering, chemistry, civil engineering, communication, computer & systems engineering, computer science, economics, electrical engineering, electrical power engineering, engineering science, environmental engineering, geology, German, interdisciplinary science, management, management engineering, materials engineering, mathematics, mechanical engineering, nuclear engineering, philosophy, physics, and psychology. Distributive requirements. MS, MArch, PhD granted. Independent study. Honors program. Cooperative work/study, pass/fail, internships. Pre-medical program. 3-2 programs with 15 liberal arts colleges. 6-year biology-medicine program with Albany Medical College; biology-dentistry program with U of Penn; management-law with Albany Law. Member Hudson-Mohawk Consortium. Study abroad. ROTC, NROTC, AFROTC. Fresh Water Institute, computer center.
Financial CEEB CSS. Institute scholarships and grants, payment plan; PELL, SEOG, NDSL, campus employment. Scholarship application deadline January 31.
Admissions High school graduation with 10 units required. Interview encouraged. ACT or SAT, and 3 ACH required. $25 application fee. Application deadline January 1. $100 deposit required on acceptance of offer of admission. *Early Decision* and *Early Admission* programs. Admission deferral possible. Transfers accepted. Credit possible for CEEB AP exams. HEOP.
Student Life Student government. Newspaper, magazines, yearbook, radio station. Music and drama groups. Several academic and special interest groups. 24 fraternities (some coed) and 2 sororities; some have houses. 35% of students join. Freshmen must live at home or on campus. Coed and single-sex dorms. Married-student apartments. 80% of students live on campus. 1½ years of phys ed required. 15 intercollegiate sports for men, 4 for women; intramurals. AIAW, ECAC, NCAA. Student body composition: 5% Asian, 3% Black, 4% Hispanic, 87% White, 1% Other. 60% from out of state.

[1] ROBERTS WESLEYAN COLLEGE
2301 Westside Drive, Rochester 14624, (716) 594-9471
Director of Admissions: Karl G. Somerville

- **Undergraduates: 183m, 392w**
- **Tuition (1982/83): $3,930**
- **Room & Board: $2,150; Fees: $109**
- **Degrees offered: BA, BS**
- **Student-faculty ratio: 13 to 1**

A private college affiliated with the Free Methodist Church, established in 1866. Rural suburban campus, 10 miles west of Rochester.

Academic Character MSACS and professional accreditation. Semester system, summer term. Majors offered in art, biology, business administration, chemistry, comprehensive science, comprehensive social studies, elementary education, English, fine arts, history, humanities, mathematics, music, music education, natural science, nursing, physical science, physics, psychology, religion, religion/philosophy, sociology, and social work. Minors. Distributives and 3 hours of religion required. Independent and directed study. Tutorials. Preprofessional programs in business, computer science, engineering, dentistry, law, library science, medicine, medical technology, pharmacy, theology, and veterinary medicine. Davis Bristol Mountain campus. 82,000-volume library.
Financial CEEB CSS. College scholarships, ministerial and ministers' dependent grants, clergy discounts, 2nd-family member discounts, state aid; PELL, SEOG, GSL, NDSL, campus employment program.
Admissions High school graduation with 12 units required. SAT or ACT required. $10 application fee. Rolling admissions. $100 deposit due on acceptance of admissions offer. *Concurrent Enrollment* Program. Transfers accepted. Credit possible for CEEB AP, CLEP, and state exams.
Student Life Student Association. Newspaper, yearbook. Academic, cultural, religious, and social activities. Dorms for men and women. Dining hall. Married-student housing. Liquor, drugs, tobacco, and social dancing prohibited. Class attendance expected. Twice-weekly chapel attendance mandatory. 3 hours of phys ed required. 6 intercollegiate sports; intramurals.

[1] ROCHESTER, UNIVERSITY OF

Rochester 14627, (716) 275-3221
Dean of Admissions & Student Aid: Timothy Scholl

- **Undergraduates: 2,656m, 1,847w; 8,829 total (including graduates)**
- **Tuition (1982/83): $6,850**
- **Room & Board: $3,152; Fees: $210**
- **Degrees offered: BA, BS, BMus, BSGS**
- **Student-faculty ratio: 11 to 1**

A private university established in 1850. Campus in residential section of Rochester. Served by air, bus, and rail.
Academic Character MSACS and professional accreditation. Semester system, optional May term, summer term. Divisions include College of Arts & Science, Graduate School of Education & Human Development, College of Engineering & Architecture, School of Medicine & Dentistry, School of Nursing, Eastman School of Music, Graduate School of Management. 30 majors offered for the BA degree, 14 for the BS, 5 for the BMus, and part-time general studies major. Offers only undergraduate degree in optics in U.S. Self-designed majors. Distributive requirements. Graduate and professional degrees granted. Independent study. Honors program. Phi Beta Kappa. Pass/fail. Internships in some majors. 3-2 bachelor's-master's programs in human development, management, optics, political science, biology-geology, community health. Dual-degree program in liberal arts and engineering. 8-year medical school program. Cross-registration with Rochester Area Colleges Consortium. Washington Semester. Study abroad. Politics, fine arts semesters in Britain. Internships in London, St. Croix. NROTC. Centers for Brain Research, Visual Science. Laser lab. Observatory. Space Science Center. Computer Center. Over 1,956,000-volume library with microform resources.
Financial CEEB CSS. University scholarships, grants, loans, payment plans; PELL, SEOG, NDSL, NSL, FISL, CWS. Application deadline January 31.
Admissions High school graduation with 16 units required. Interview encouraged. Audition required for BA in Music applicants. SAT or ACT required; 3 ACH recommended. $25 application fee. Preferred application deadline January 15. $200 deposit required on acceptance of offer of admission. *Early Decision* and *Early Admission* programs. Admission deferral possible. Transfers accepted. Credit possible for CEEB AP exams; unversity has own advanced placement program.
Student Life Student government. Newspaper, magazine, yearbook, radio station. Music, drama, dance, film groups. Black Student Union. Spanish and Latin American Student Association. 90 religious, academic, service, and special interest groups. 11 fraternities, 7 with houses, and 5 sororities. Coed and single-sex dorms. Special interest housing. Married-student housing. 85% of students live on campus. 10 intercollegiate sports for men, 7 for women, 1 coed; intramurals. AIAW, ECAC, NCAA. Student body composition: 3% Black, 1% Hispanic, 89% White, 7% Other. 44% from out of state.

■[1] EASTMAN SCHOOL OF MUSIC

26 Gibbs Street, Rochester 14604, (716) 275-3003
Director of Admissions: Charles Krusenstjerna

- **Enrollment: 400 men & women; 650 total (including graduates)**
- **Tuition (1982/83): $6,850**
- **Room & Board: $2,625; Fees: $454**
- **Degrees offered: BA, BMus**
- **Student-faculty ratio: 7 to 1**

The music college of the University of Rochester, established in 1921.
Academic Character MSACS and professional accreditation. Semester system, 6-week summer term. Majors offered in applied music, composition, history of music, music education, and theory. Distributive requirements. Graduate degrees granted. Theatre. Recital halls. Electronic music facilities. Instrument collection. Music library has over 500,000 items; collection of 60,000 records & tapes.
Financial CEEB CSS. School scholarships, grants, loans, state aid; PELL, SEOG, NDSL, GSL, CWS, school employment. Application deadline February 15.
Admissions High school graduation with 16 units required. Audition and supporting samples of work in chosen major required. SAT or ACT helpful, but not required. $25 application fee. Application deadline February 20. $200 deposit due on acceptance of admissions offer.
Student Life Student association. Honorary and professional groups. Professional sororities and fraternity. All U Rochester facilities available to Eastman students. Dorms with dining facilities.

[P] ROCHESTER BUSINESS INSTITUTE

107 Clinton Avenue North, Rochester 14604

[1 & J1] ROCHESTER INSTITUTE OF TECHNOLOGY

Rochester 14623, (716) 475-6631
Director of Admissions: E. Louis Guard

- **Enrollment: 6,200m, 2,800w**
- **Tuition (1982/83): $5,084**
- **Room & Board: $2,904; Fees: $120**
- **Degrees offered: BFA, BS, BTech, AS, AAS**
- **Mean SAT 473v, 553m**
- **Student-faculty ratio: 18 to 1**

A private institute established in 1829. 1,300-acre suburban campus in Henrietta, 5 miles from Rochester. Air, bus, and rail in Rochester.
Academic Character MSACS and professional accreditation. Trimester system, 2 5-week summer terms. 20 majors offered by the College of Applied Science & Technology, 4 by the College of Business, 5 by the College of Engineering, 10 by the College of Fine & Applied Arts, 2 by the College of General Studies, 11 by the College of Graphic Arts & Photography, 11 by the College of Science, and 4 by the National Technical Institute for the Deaf. Distributive requirements. ME, MS, MST, MBA, MFA granted. Cooperative work/study, internships. Member Rochester Area Colleges Consortium. Dual-degree program with Mass. College of Pharmacy. Study abroad in Scandinavia. ROTC; NROTC at U of Rochester. Media Resource Center, TV Center, Graphic Arts Center. 194-000-volume library.
Financial CEEB CSS. Institute scholarships, grants, loans, state grants, payment plans; PELL, SEOG, NDSL, FISL, CWS, institute has own work program. Priority application deadline for scholarships March 1.
Admissions High school graduation with 16 units required. Interview encouraged. Portfolio required for College of Fine & Applied Arts. SAT or ACT required; ACH recommended. $25 application fee. Rolling admissions; suggest applying early in fall. $200 deposit required on acceptance of offer of admission. *Early Decision* and *Early Admission* programs. Admission deferral possible. Transfers accepted. Credit possible for CEEB AP, CLEP, and state exams; university has own advanced placement program. HEOP.
Student Life Student government. Newspaper, magazine, yearbook. Drama, debate groups. Black Awareness Coordinating Committee. Academic, religious, honorary, service, and special interest organizations. 10 fraternities and 3 sororities, all with houses. 10% of men and 1% of women join. Freshmen must live at home or on campus. Coed and single-sex dorms. Special interest housing. Married-student housing. Coop dorms. 50% of students live on campus. 6 quarters of phys ed required. 9 intercollegiate sports for men, 4 for women; intramurals. AIAW, ECAC, NCAA, ICAC. Student body composition: 12% minority. 45% from out of state.

[J1] ROCKLAND COMMUNITY COLLEGE

145 College Road, Suffern 10901

[1] RUSSELL SAGE COLLEGE

Troy 12180, (518) 270-2000
Director of Admissions: Janice Johnston

- **Undergraduates: 1,400w**
- **Tuition (1982/83): $5,200**
- **Room & Board: $2,496-$2,672**
- **Degrees offered: BA, BS**
- **Mean SAT 456v, 501m**
- **Student-faculty ratio: 12 to 1**

A private women's college established in 1916. 10-acre urban campus in Troy, 15 miles from Albany and Schenectady. Served by air, rail, and bus.
Academic Character MSACS and professional accreditation. 4-1-4 system. Majors offered in biochemistry, biology, chemistry, criminal science, economics/business, education, English/journalism, French, German, history, health education, international studies, mathematics, medical technology, nursing, nutrition, philosophy, physical education, physical therapy, political science, psychology, public administration, public service, sociology, Spanish, and visual & performing arts. Self-designed majors. Distributive requirements. MS granted. Independent study. Honors program. Internships. Preprofessional program in medicine. 3-1 medical technology program. 3-2 mathematics/engineering program with Rensselaer. Cross-registration with Hudson-Mohawk Consortium (14 schools). Visiting Student Program with 50 other colleges. Washington Semester. Study abroad. Early childhood, elementary, secondary, and special education certification. ROTC, AFROTC, NROTC at Rensselaer. Language labs, child study center. 180,000 volume library.
Financial CEEB CSS. College scholarships, grants, loans, state grants & scholarships, Native American grants, payment plan; PELL, SEOG, GSL, NDSL, NSL, CWS. Application deadline March 1.
Admissions High school graduation with 16 units required. Interview encouraged. SAT or ACT required. $20 application fee. Rolling admissions; suggest applying in fall. $150 deposit required on acceptance of offer of admission. Admission deferral possible. Transfers accepted. Credit possible for CEEB AP and state exams. HEOP.
Student Life Student government. Newspaper, yearbook. Music, dance, drama groups. Academic, religious, service, and special interest groups. Students live at home or on campus. Language housing. No married-student housing. 66% of students live on campus. Parietals for first semester freshmen. 1 year of phys ed required. 7 intercollegiate sports; intramurals. AIAW. Student body composition: 3% Black, 2% Hispanic, 95% White. 40% from out of state.

■[J1] ALBANY, JUNIOR COLLEGE OF
140 New Scotland Avenue, Albany 12208

[1] ST. BONAVENTURE UNIVERSITY
St. Bonaventure 14778, (716) 375-2400
Director of Admissions: Donald C. Burkard

- **Undergraduates: 1,162m, 1,098w**
- **Tuition & Fees (1982/83): $4,250**
- **Room & Board: $2,390-$2,540**
- **Degrees offered: BA, BS, BBA**
- **Mean ACT 24**
- **Student-faculty ratio: 15 to 1**

A private university established in 1856 by the Franciscan Fathers. 500-acre campus in small city of Saint Bonaventure, 65 miles from Buffalo. Served by bus; air nearby.

Academic Character MSACS accreditation. Semester system, 4- and 5-week summer terms. Majors offered in classical languages, English, history, mass communications, modern languages, philosopy, psychology, social science, sociology, theology, biology, chemistry, computer science, economics, elementary education, mathematics, medical technology, physical education, physics, psychology, accounting, finance, management sciences, and marketing. Interdisciplinary majors. Graduate degrees granted. Senior exams, 9 hours of theology, 9 of philosophy required. Honors program. Pass/fail, internships. Preprofessional programs in dentistry, engineering, law, medicine, osteopathy, pharmacy, veterinary medicine. 2-3 engineering program with U of Detroit. Member Western NY Consortium, Visiting Student Program. Study abroad. Elementary and secondary education certification. ROTC. Computer center, language lab. 253,000 volume library.

Financial CEEB CSS. University scholarships, grants, loans, state grants, loans, scholarships, payment plan; PELL, SEOG, GSL, NDSL, FISL, CWS. Application deadlines March 1 (scholarships), April 30 (loans).

Admissions High school graduation with 16 units required. GED accepted. Interview encouraged. SAT or ACT required. $20 application fee. Rolling admissions. $125 deposit required on acceptance of offer of admission. *Early Decision, Concurrent Enrollment, Early Admission* programs. Admission deferral possible. Transfers accepted. Credit possible for CEEB AP, CLEP, and ACT PEP exams. HEOP.

Student Life Student government. Newspaper, magazine, yearbook, radio station. Music, drama groups. Women's Council. Academic, honorary, religious, service, and special interest groups. Single students under 21 must live at home or on campus. Single-sex dorms. No married-student housing. 84% of students live on campus. 10 intercollegiate sports for men, 6 for women; intramurals. AIAW, ECAC, NCAA, Little 3. Student body composition: 1% Black, 99% White. 20% from out of state.

[1 & J1] ST. FRANCIS COLLEGE
180 Remsen Street, Brooklyn 11201, (212) 522-2300
Director of Admissions: Brother George Larkin

- **Undergraduates: 1,077m, 802w; 2,996 total**
- **Tuition (1982/83): $3,000**
- **Fees: $150**
- **Degrees offered: BA, BS, AS, AAS**
- **Mean SAT 420v, 520m**
- **Student-faculty ratio: 41 to 1**

A private college controlled by the Franciscan Brothers, established in 1884, became coed in 1969. 2-acre urban campus in Brooklyn. Served by air, bus, and rail.

Academic Character MSACS accreditation. Semester system, 2 5-week summer terms. Majors offered in accounting, accounting & business practice, biology, chemistry, economics, English, French, health care management, health science, health service administration, history, management, mathematics, medical technology, philosophy, physical education, political science, psychology, religious studies, social studies, sociology, Spanish, special studies, and urban studies. Distributives and 3 hours of religion required. Independent study. Pass/fail, internships. Preprofessional programs in dentistry, medicine, ophthalmology, veterinary medicine. 3-1 program in medical technology. Study abroad. Elementary and secondary education certification. ROTC. Institute for Local Historical Studies. Computer center. 125,000-volume library with microform resources.

Financial CEEB CSS and ACT FAS. College scholarships, grants, loans, athletic scholarships, family discounts; PELL, SEOG, GSL, NDSL, CWS. Application deadline February 15.

Admissions High school graduation with 16 units required. GED accepted. Interview encouraged. SAT and ACH, or ACT recommended. $20 application fee. Rolling admissions. $55 deposit required on acceptance of offer of admission. *Early Admission* and *Early Decision* programs. Admission deferral possible. Transfers accepted. Credit possible for CEEB AP and CLEP exams.

Student Life Student government. Newspaper, magazine, yearbook. Music, drama groups. Black Students organization. Academic, religious, and special interest groups. 13 fraternities, 2 with houses, and 6 sororities without houses. 5% of men and 3% of women join. No college housing. Liquor prohibited on campus. 1 semester of phys ed required. 7 intercollegiate sports for men, 4 for women; intramurals. Student body composition: 17% Black, 8% Hispanic, 70% White, 5% Other. 1% from out of state.

[1] ST. JOHN FISHER COLLEGE
3690 East Avenue, Rochester 14618, (716) 586-4140
Diean of Admissions: Jay S. Valentine

- **Undergraduates: 1,020m, 869w**
- **Tuition (1982/83): $4,624**
- **Room & Board: $2,623; Fees: $100**
- **Degrees offered: BA, BS, BBA**
- **Mean SAT 430v, 470m**
- **Student-faculty ratio: 18 to 1**

A private college established in 1948, became coed in 1971. 125-acre suburban campus in Rochester. Served by air, bus, and rail.

Academic Character MSACS and professional accreditation. Semester system, 6- and 3-week summer terms. Majors offered in anthropology, biology, chemistry, communication/journalism, economics, English, French, German, gerontology, history, Italian, liberal studies, mathematics, philosophy, physics, political science, psychology, religious studies, sociology, Spanish, accounting, computer science, industrial/commercial accounting, and management. Minor required for most majors; offered in most major fields and in 9 additional areas. Distributive requirements. Independent study. Pass/fail, internships. Preprofessional programs in allied health, dentistry, law, medicine, pharmacy, veterinary science. 3-2 computer science, computer systems management programs with RIT. 2-3 engineering programs with several colleges. Language programs with Nazareth College and U of Rochester. Member Rochester Area Colleges Consortium, Visiting Student Program. Washington Semester. Study abroad. Elementary and secondary education certification. ROTC at RIT; NROTC at U of Rochester. Language labs, computer center. 135,000-volume library.

Financial CEEB CSS and ACT FAS. College scholarships, grants, loans, state grants & scholarships, payment plan; PELL, SEOG, NDSL, FISL, GSL, CWS; college has own work program. Application deadline March 1.

Admissions High school graduation with 16 units required. Interview encouraged. SAT or ACT required. Rolling admissions. *Early Decision, Early Admission, Concurrent Enrollment* Programs. Admission deferral possible. Transfers accepted. Credit possible for CEEB AP and CLEP exams.

Student Life Student government. Newspaper, magazine, yearbook. Music, drama groups. Academic, political, honorary, service, and special interest groups. Students must live at home or on campus. Single-sex dorms. No married-student housing. 50% of students live on campus. 7 intercollegiate sports for men, 5 for women; intramural & club sports. ECAC, CWAA, NCAA. Student body composition: 0.1% Asian, 1.9% Black, 0.7% Hispanic, 0.1% Native American, 96.9% White. 2% from out of state.

[1] ST. JOHN'S UNIVERSITY
Jamaica 11439, (212) 990-6161
Director of Admissions: Henry F. Rossi

- **Undergraduates: 6,347m, 5,048w**
- **Tuition (1982/83): $3,400**
- **Degrees offered: BA, BS, BFA, BSEd, BSMed Tech, BSPhar, AA, AS**
- **Mean SAT 440v, 475m**
- **Student-faculty ratio: 20 to 1**

A private university controlled by the Congregation of the Mission (Vincentian Fathers), established in 1820. 95-acre urban campus in Jamaica, Queens, New York, and 16 acres on Staten Island.

Academic Character MSACS and professional accreditation. Semester system, 2 5-week summer terms. 71 majors offered in the areas of business, area studies, social sciences, arts, education, science, religion & philosophy, communication, criminal & legal sciences, humanities, environment, funeral service administration, political sciences, human service, library studies, health & medical science, and government. Distributives and 3 semesters of theology required. Graduate and professional degrees granted. Honors program. Pass/fail, internships. 3-2 programs in library science, pharmaceutical science, sociology, Spanish. Study abroad. Consortiums with International Association of Universities and International Council on Education for Teaching. Elementary, secondary, and special education certification. ROTC. 1,091,393-volume library with microform resources.

Financial CEEB CSS. University scholarships, grants, loans, health professions loans; PELL, SEOG, NDSL, FISL, CWS. Preferred application deadline April 1.

Admissions High school graduation with 16 units required. GED accepted. SAT or ACT required; SAT preferred. $10 application fee. Rolling admissions; suggest applying by March 1. $100 deposit required on acceptance of offer of admission. *Early Admission* and *Concurrent Enrollment* programs. Admission deferral possible. Transfers accepted. Credit possible for CEEB AP and CLEP exams.

Student Life Student government. Newspaper, magazine, yearbook. Music and drama groups. Academic, cultural, political, service, and special interest groups. 18 fraternities and 10 sororities. No university housing. 9 intercollegiate sports for men, 4 for women; intramurals. AIAW, ECAC, NCAA, MCTC, MITFA, Tri State Soccer Conference, Big East. Student body composition: 1.1% Asian, 3.8% Black, 2.1% Hispanic, 0.3% Native American, 87.3% White. 8% from out of state.

[1] ST. JOSEPH'S COLLEGE
245 Clinton Avenue, Brooklyn 11205, (212) 622-4696
Director of Admissions: Sherri Van Arham

- **Undergraduates: 198m, 1,047w**
- **Tuition (1982/83): $2,900**
- **Fees: $110**
- **Degrees offered: BA, BS**
- **Mean SAT 448v, 458m**
- **Student-faculty ratio: 7 to 1**

A private college established in 1916, became coed in 1970. 2-acre urban campus in Brooklyn, 8 miles from Manhattan. Served by air, bus, and rail.

Academic Character MSACS accreditation. 4-1-4 system, 5-week summer term. Majors offered in biology, business administration, chemistry, child study, English, French, history, mathematics, psychology, recreation, social

sciences, Spanish, and speech communications. Distributive requirements. Independent study. Pass/fail. 2-4 program with New York College of Podiatric Medicine. Elementary, secondary, and special education certification. Child Study Center, laboratory school, language lab. 132,000-volume library with microform resources.
Financial CEEB CSS. College scholarships, state scholarships, loans; PELL, SEOG, NDSL, GSL, CWS; college has own work program. Application deadline February 25.
Admissions High school graduation with 16 units required. GED accepted. Interview encouraged. SAT or ACT required. $15 application fee. Rolling admissions; suggest applying by March 15. $50 deposit required on acceptance of offer of admission. *Early Decision, Early Admission, Concurrent Enrollment* programs. Admission deferral possible. Transfers accepted. Credit possible for CEEB AP and CLEP exams.
Student Life Student government. Newspaper, yearbook. Music and drama groups. Political, ethnic, religious, and special interest organizations. 1 sorority. 5% of women join. No college housing. 2 hours of physical education required. Intercollegiate basketball for men and women; intramurals. Hudson Valley Conference. Student body composition: 3% Asian, 25% Black, 12% Hispanic, 60% White. 3% from out of state.

[1] ST. JOSEPH'S SEMINARY
Dunwoodie, Yonkers 10704

[1] ST. LAWRENCE UNIVERSITY
Canton 13617, (315) 379-5261
Director of Admissions: Conrad J. Sharrow

- **Undergraduates: 1,169m, 1,102w**
- **Tuition (1982/83): $6,800**
- **Room & Board: $2,410; Fees: $100**
- **Degrees offered: BA, BS**
- **Mean SAT 530v, 580m**
- **Student-faculty ratio: 14 to 1**

A private university established in 1856. 1,000-acre campus located in small town of Canton in St. Lawrence River Valley, 80 miles from Syracuse and Montreal. Served by bus.
Academic Character MSACS and professional accreditation. 4-1-4 system, 2 5-week summer terms. Majors offered in Canadian studies, economics, English, fine arts, French, German, government, history, modern languages, music, philosophy, religious studies, sociology, Spanish, theatre arts, biology, biochemistry, biophysics, chemistry, environmental studies, geology, geophysics, mathematics, physical education, physics, psychology. Self-designed majors. Distributive requirements. Masters degrees granted. Independent study. Honors programs. Phi Beta Kappa. Pass/fail, internships. 3-2 engineering programs with Clarkson, Columbia, Rensselaer, U of Rochester, others. 4-1 MBA program with Clarkson. 3-1 programs in dentistry, law, medicine. Cross-registration with area colleges. Study abroad in Canada, Europe, Kenya. Secondary education certification. ROTC; AFROTC at Clarkson. Computer lab, language lab. 310,000-volume library with microform resources.
Financial CEEB CSS. University scholarships and loans, state scholarships, payment plan; PELL, SEOG, NDSL, GSL, CWS. Scholarship application deadline February 15.
Admissions High school graduation required. Interview encouraged. SAT and 3 ACH, or ACT required. $30 application fee. Application deadline February 1. $500 deposit required on acceptance of offer of admission (May 1). *Early Decision* Program. Admission deferral possible. Transfers accepted. Credit possible for CEEB AP, CLEP, and state exams.
Student Life Student government. Newspaper, magazine, yearbook, radio stations. Music, speaking, drama groups. Black Student Union. Native American, Jewish organizations. Honorary, tutoring groups. 7 fraternities and 5 sororities; all have houses. 40% of men and 35% of women join. Students must live on campus. Coed and single-sex dorms. Special interest housing. 99% of students live on campus. Cars discouraged. 1 year of phys ed required. 12 intercollegiate sports for men, 9 for women, 1 coed; intramurals. AIAW, ICAC. Student body composition: 1% Black, 1% Native American, 98% White. 50% from out of state.

[1] SAINT ROSE, COLLEGE OF
432 Western Avenue, Albany 12203, (518) 454-5150
Director of Admissions: Genevieve Flaherty

- **Undergraduates: 240m, 912w; 2,728 total (including part-time)**
- **Tuition (1982/83): $3,900**
- **Room & Board: $2,200; Fees: $90**
- **Degrees offered: BA, BS**
- **Student-faculty ratio: 13 to 1**

A private college established in 1920, became coed in 1970. 22-acre urban campus in residential section of Albany. Served by air, bus, and rail.
Academic Character MSACS accreditation. 5-1-5 system, 2 6-week summer terms. Majors offered in advertising design, American studies, art education, biology, biology-chemistry, business administration, chemistry, computer science, elementary education, English, fine arts, history, history-political science, mathematics, medical technology, music, music education, music in special education, public communication, religious studies, social sciences, sociology, Spanish, special education, special studies, and studio art. Distributive requirements. MA, MS, MSEd granted. Independent study. Pass/fail, internships. Credit by exam. BA/MA program in communication disorders. Cross-registration with area colleges. Exchanges with Avila, Fontbonne, Mount St. Mary's, and College of St. Catherine. Visiting Student Program. Study abroad. Elementary, secondary, art, music, and special education certification. ROTC, NROTC, AFROTC at Siena College or Rensselaer. Art gallery. 138,000-volume library with microform resources.
Financial CEEB CSS and ACT FAS. College scholarships, grants, parental loans, state scholarships & grants, payment plan; PELL, SEOG, NDSL, GSL, CWS. Application deadline for scholarships March 1.
Admissions High school graduation with 16 units required. Interview encouraged. Audition required for music majors. SAT required; ACT accepted. $15 application fee. Rolling admissions; suggest applying by December 15. $50 tuition and $50 room (for boarders) deposits required on acceptance of offer of admission. *Early Admission* and *Concurrent Enrollment* programs. Admission deferral possible. Transfers accepted. Credit possible for CEEB AP, CLEP, and state exams.
Student Life Student government. Newspaper, magazine, yearbook. Music and drama groups. Single-sex dorms. No married-student housing. 47% of students live on campus. 2 semesters of phys ed required. 9 intercollegiate and intramural sports. NAC, AIAW, NAIA. Student body composition: 0.3% Asian, 2.1% Black, 0.3% Hispanic, 0.1% Native American, 97.2% White. 2% from out of state.

[1] ST. THOMAS AQUINAS COLLEGE
Sparkhill 10976, (914) 359-9500
Director of Admissions: Andrea Kraeft

- **Undergraduates: 793m, 847w**
- **Tuition (1982/83): $3,000**
- **Room & Board: $1,900**
- **Degrees offered: BA, BS, BSEd**
- **Mean SAT 487v, 480m**
- **Student-faculty ratio: 20 to 1**

A private college established in 1952, became coed in 1969. 24-acre rural campus in Sparkhill, 13 miles from New York City. Air and rail in New York City.
Academic Character MSACS accreditation. 4-1-4 system, 3 summer terms. Majors offered in accounting, art, bilingual education, business administration, communication arts, criminal justice, elementary education, English, finance, gerontology, history, marketing, mathematics, natural sciences, philosophy & religious studies, psychology, recreation & leisure, Romance languages, social science, Spanish, and special education. Distributives and GRE required. Independent study. Pass/fail, internships. Preprofessional programs in medicine, law, nursing. 3-2 math/engineering program with George Washington U. 3-1 medical technology program. Child care/mental health offered in cooperation with State Association of Child Care Workers. Campus interchange program with Barry (FL), Dominican (CA), St. Mary's Dominican (LA), Aquinas (MI). Study abroad. Elementary, secondary, and special education certification. AFROTC at Manhattan College. 104,000-volume library with microform resources.
Financial CEEB CSS. College scholarships, state grants, bilingual education and gerontology grants, payment plans; PELL, SEOG, NDSL, GSL, CWS. Priority application deadline March 1.
Admissions High school graduation with 16 units required. GED accepted. Interview encouraged. SAT or ACT required. $15 application fee. Rolling admissions; suggest applying by February 28. $75 tuition and $50 room (for boarders) deposit required on acceptance of offer of admission. *Early Admission* Program. Admission deferral possible. Transfers accepted. Credit possible for CEEB AP and CLEP exams. HEOP.
Student Life Student government. Newspaper, magazine, yearbook, radio station. Music, drama groups. Academic, professional, and special interest groups. Single-sex dorms. No married-student housing. 10% of students live on campus. 3 intercollegiate sports for men, 3 for women; intramurals. NAIA, CACC, Hudson Valley Conference, AIAW. Student body composition: 0.1% Asian, 5.3% Black, 10.2% Hispanic, 84.4% White. 35% from out of state.

[P] ST. VLADIMIR'S ORTHODOX THEOLOGICAL SEMINARY
575 Scarsdale Road, Crestwood, Tuckahoe 10707

[1] SARAH LAWRENCE COLLEGE
Bronxville 10708, (914) 793-4242
Director of Admissions: Dudley F. Blodget

- **Undergraduates: 158m, 685w; 955 total (including graduates)**
- **Tuition (1982/83): $8,150**
- **Room & Board: $3,600**
- **Degree offered: BA**
- **Student-faculty ratio: 9 to 1**

A private college established in 1928, became coed in 1968. 35-acre suburban campus in Bronxville, 15 miles north of New York City. Served by bus and rail.
Academic Character MSACS accreditation. Semester system. Self-designed majors. Courses in anthropology, architecture, art, Asian studies, biology, chemistry, classical languages, dance, economics, film, French, German, history, international studies, Italian, Latin, literature, mathematics, music, philosophy, physics, political science, psychology, religion, Russian, sociology, Spanish, theatre, women's studies, and writing. MA, MFA, MS, MPS granted. Independent study. Pass/fail, internships. Preprofessional programs in medicine, human genetics. Study abroad in cooperation with U of Michigan. Early Childhood Center. 166,000-volume library with microform resources.
Financial CEEB CSS. College scholarships and loans, state grants, Native American aid, payment plan; PELL, SEOG, NDSL, GSL, CWS; college has own work program. Application deadline February 1.
Admissions High school graduation with 16 units required. Interview encouraged. SAT, ACT, or 3 ACH required. $25 application fee. Application deadline February 15. $250 deposit required on acceptance of offer of admission. *Early Admission* and *Early Decision* programs. Admission deferral possible. Transfers accepted in January. Credit possible for CEEB AP exams.
Student Life Student government. Newspaper, magazine. Music, dance groups. Political, academic, environmental, and special interest clubs. Coed and single-sex dorms. 80% of students live on campus. 1 year of phys ed

required. 4 intercollegiate sports; intramurals. Student body composition: 3% Asian, 5% Black, 1% Hispanic, 91% White. 65-70% from out of state.

[J1] SCHENECTADY COUNTY COMMUNITY COLLEGE
Washington Avenue, Schenectady 12305

[P] SEMINARY OF THE IMMACULATE CONCEPTION
Huntington 11743

[1] SIENA COLLEGE
Loudonville 12211, (518) 783-2423
Director of Admissions: Harry W. Wood

- **Undergraduates: 1,399m, 1,204w; 3,331 total (including part-time)**
- **Tuition (1982/83): $4,000**
- **Room & Board: $2,650; Fees: $155**
- **Degrees offered: BA, BS, BBA**
- **Mean SAT 498v, 554m**
- **Student-faculty ratio: 18 to 1**

A private college affiliated with the Franciscan Fathers, established in 1937. 120-acre suburban campus in Loudonville, 2 miles from Albany. Served by air, bus, and rail.

Academic Character MSACS accreditation. Semester system, 6-week summer term. Majors offered in American studies, classical languages, English, French, history, international studies, mathematics, philosophy, political science, psychology, religious studies, sociology, Spanish, biology, chemistry, computer science, mathematics, physics, accounting, economics, finance, and marketing/management. Distributives and 6 credits in religious studies required. Independent study. Honors program. Pass/fail, internships. Preprofessional programs in dentistry, law, medicine, veterinary medicine. 3-2 engineering programs with Manhattan College, Clarkson, Catholic U. 2-2 environmental science and forestry programs with SUNY-Syracuse. Member Hudson-Mohawk Council. Study abroad. Secondary education certification. ROTC; AFROTC, NROTC at RPI. 175,000-volume library with microform resources.

Financial CEEB CSS. College scholarships, state aid, payment plan; PELL, SEOG, NDSL, GSL, college has own work program. Application deadline February 15.

Admissions High school graduation with 16 units required. Interview encouraged. SAT or ACT required. $15 application fee. Rolling admissions; suggest applying in December. $100 deposit required on acceptance of offer of admission. *Early Admission* and *Early Decision* programs. Admission deferral possible. Transfers accepted. Credit possible for CEEB AP and CLEP exams. HEOP.

Student Life Student government. Newspaper, magazines, yearbook, radio station. Music, debate, speaking, drama groups. Religious, service, honorary, political, academic, and special interest organizations. Fraternities. Undergraduates must live at home or on campus. Coed and single-sex dorms. No married-student housing. 60% of students live on campus. 8 intercollegiate sports for men, 7 for women; intramural & club sports. AIAW, ECAC, NCAA, MECAC. Student body composition: 0.6% Asian, 2.2% Black, 1% Hispanic, 96.2% White. 5% from out of state.

[P] SIMMONS SCHOOL OF MORTUARY SCIENCE
Syracuse 13207

[1] SKIDMORE COLLEGE
Saratoga Springs 12866, (518) 584-5000
Director of Admissions: Louise B. Wise

- **Undergraduates: 700m, 1,450w**
- **Tuition (1982/83): $7,310**
- **Room & Board: $3,290; Fees: $110**
- **Degrees offered: BA, BS**
- **Mean SAT 530v, 540m**
- **Student-faculty ratio: 13 to 1**

A private college established in 1922, became coed in 1971. 650-acre wooded campus in Saratoga Springs, 2 hours from Lake Placid, 34 miles from Albany. Served by bus and rail; airport in Albany.

Academic Character MSACS and professional accreditation. 4-1-4 system, 6-week summer term. 21 majors offered for the BA, 8 for the BS, 20 interdepartmental. Self-designed programs. Courses in Asian or Russian studies, computer applications. Senior exam or project required. Independent study. Honors program. Phi Beta Kappa. Pass/fail, internships. Preprofessional programs in art, business, law, medicine, physical education, theatre. 3-2 engineering program with Dartmouth. 4-1 MBA program with Clarkson. BS-RN program. Exchange with Colgate, 6 others. Washington Semester, New York City year. Hudson-Mohawk Association. Study abroad. Early childhood, elementary, and secondary education certification. Computer center, language lab, art gallery. 290,000-volume library.

Financial CEEB CSS. College scholarships, grants, loans, payment plan; PELL, SEOG, NSS, NDSL, NSL, CWS. Scholarship application deadline February 1.

Admissions High school graduation required with 16 units recommended. Interview encouraged. SAT required; ACT accepted. 3 ACH recommended. $30 application fee. Application deadline February 1. $300 deposit required on acceptance of offer of admission. *Early Admission* and *Early Decision programs. Admission deferral possible. Transfers accepted. Credit possible for CEEB AP and CLEP exams. HEOP.*

Student Life Student government. Newspaper, magazines, yearbooks, radio station. Music, dance, film, drama groups. Black, Latin, International Student organizations. Academic, religious, service, and special interest groups. Freshmen must live on campus. Coed and single-sex dorms. Special interest housing. No married-student housing. 85% of students live on campus. 8 intercollegiate sports for men, 12 for women, 1 coed; intramurals. AIAW, NAIA, NAC, NIAC, Mayflower Conference. Student body composition: 1% Asian, 2.6% Black, 1.3% Hispanic, 0.1% Native American, 90% White, 5% Other. 64% from out of state.

[J1] SUFFOLK COUNTY COMMUNITY COLLEGE
533 College Road, Selden, Long Island 11784

[J2] SUFFOLK COUNTY COMMUNITY COLLEGE, EASTERN CAMPUS
Riverhead 11901

[J1] SUFFOLK COUNTY COMMUNITY COLLEGE, WESTERN CAMPUS
Brentwood 11717

[J1] SULLIVAN COUNTY COMMUNITY COLLEGE
Loch Sheldrake 12759

[1] SYRACUSE UNIVERSITY
Syracuse 13210, (315) 423-3611
Dean of Admissions & Financial Aid: Thomas F. Cummings, Jr.

- **Undergraduates: 6,097m, 5,276w**
- **Tuition (1982/83): $6,220**
- **Room & Board: $3,050**
- **Degrees offered: AB, BS, BArch, BFA, BLA, BInd Des, BMus**
- **Mean SAT 512v, 546m**
- **Student-faculty ratio: 14 to 1**

A private university established in 1870. 200-acre main campus in residential section of Syracuse. Served by air, bus, and rail.

Academic Character MSACS and professional accreditation. Semester system, 2 6-week summer terms. 39 majors offered by the College of Arts & Sciences, 8 by the School of Education, 12 by the L.C. Smith College of Engineering, 7 by the SUNY College of Environmental Science & Forestry, 6 by the College for Human Development, 12 by the School of Management, 8 by the School of Public Communications, 33 by the College of Visual & Performing Arts, and majors in architecture, computer science, nursing, and social work. Graduate and professional degrees granted. Honors program. Phi Beta Kappa. Dual degree programs in most colleges. 3-year degree programs. 3-2 engineering program. 3-1 medicine, dentistry programs. 6-year AB-MArch program. Study abroad. ROTC, AFROTC. Special Education Center, nursery school, audio-visual center. Language labs, computer center. 2,000,000-volume library with microform resources.

Financial CEEB CSS. University scholarships, grants, loans, payment plan; PELL, SEOG, NDSL, CWS. Scholarship application deadline February 1.

Admissions High school graduation with 16 units required. Interview encouraged. Audition or portfolio required for arts majors. SAT or ACT required. $25 application fee. Suggested application deadline February 1. $150 tuition and $100 room (for boarders) deposits required on acceptance of offer of admission. *Early Decision* and *Early Admission* programs. Admission deferral possible. Transfers accepted. Credit possible for CEEB AP, CLEP, and state exams. HEOP.

Student Life Student government. Newspaper, magazine, yearbook, radio & TV stations. Music, drama, debate groups. Political, religious, and special interest organizations. 30 fraternities and 25 sororities; all have houses. 12% of men and 8% of women join. Freshmen must live on campus. Married-student housing. Coop dorms. 82% of students live on campus. Freshmen and sophomores may not have cars or motorcycles. Intercollegiate and intramural sports. Student body composition: 1% Asian, 10% Black, 2% Hispanic, 0.2% Native American, 86.8% White. 55% from out of state.

[J2] TOBE-COBURN SCHOOL FOR FASHION CAREERS
686 Broadway, New York 10012

[J1] TOMPKINS-CORTLAND COMMUNITY COLLEGE
170 North Street, Dryden 13053

[1] TOURO COLLEGE
226 West 26th Street, New York 10001, (212) 620-0090
Dean of Admissions: Norman Twersky

- **Undergraduates: 581m, 1,093w; 2,289 total (including graduates)**
- **Tuition (1982/83): $3,250**
- **Room & Board: $1,200 (men), $1,800 (women); Fees: $40**
- **Degrees offered: BA, BS, AA, AS**
- **Mean SAT 520v, 490m**
- **Student-faculty ratio: 8 to 1**

A private college established in 1971. Urban campus in midtown New York City. Served by air, bus, and rail.

Academic Character MSACS and professional accreditation. Semester system, summer term. Majors offered in accounting, biology, chemistry, economics & business, finance, health sciences, history, Judaic studies, language & literature, management, mathematics & computer science, philosophy, political science, psychology, and sociology. Self-designed majors. Distributive requirements. Senior thesis or project required. Graduate degrees granted. Independent study. Honors program. Pass/fail, internships. Preprofessional programs in accounting, business, elementary education,

dentistry, law, medicine. Study abroad in Israel. Provisional elementary education certification. 130,000-volume library. Interlibrary access.
Financial College scholarships and loans, state scholarships and loans, payment plan; PELL, SEOG, FISL, NDSL, CWS. Scholarship application deadline May 1.
Admissions High school graduation required with 16 units recommended. Interview encouraged. SAT recommended; ACT accepted. $20 application fee. Rolling admissions. $50 tuition deposit and $10 room deposit (for boarders) required on acceptance of offer of admission. *Early Admission* Program. Admission deferral possible. Transfers accepted. Credit possible for CEEB AP and CLEP exams.
Student Life Student government. Newspaper, magazine, yearbook. Choir. Academic clubs. Single-sex dorms. No married-student housing. 20% of students live on campus. Liquor prohibited in dorms. Student body composition: 2.5% Asian, 36% Black, 9.6% Hispanic, 0.3% Native American, 49.1% White. 35% from out of state.

[J1] TROCAIRE COLLEGE
Buffalo 14220

[J1] ULSTER COUNTY COMMUNITY COLLEGE
Stone Ridge 12484

[1] UNION COLLEGE AND UNIVERSITY
Schenectady 12308, (518) 370-6112
Dean of Admissions: Kenneth A. Nourse

- **Undergraduates: 1,300m, 700w; 3,394 total**
- **Tuition (1982/83): $7,300**
- **Room & Board: $2,600; Fees: $99**
- **Degrees offered: AB, BS, BCE, BEE, BME**
- **Mean SAT 560v, 610m**
- **Student-faculty ratio: 13 to 1**

A private college established in 1795, became coed in 1970. 100-acre urban campus, 15 miles from Albany. Served by air, bus, and rail.
Academic Character MSACS and professional accreditation. Trimester system, summer term. Majors offered in art, biology, chemistry, classics, computer science, drama, economics, engineering (5 areas), English, general science, general social science, history, mathematics, medical education, modern languages, music, philosophy, physics, political science, psychology, and sociology. Self-designed majors. Distributive requirements. MA, MS, PhD granted. Independent study. Honors program. Phi Beta Kappa. Pass/fail, internships. 3-2 BA-MA programs. 2-4 medical and 3-3 law programs with Albany Medical and Law schools. Cross-registration with 16 area schools. Study abroad. International exchange programs. Secondary education certification. ROTC at Siena, RPI; AFROTC, NROTC at RPI. Horticultural garden, language lab, computer center. 400,000-volume library with microform resources.
Financial CEEB CSS. University scholarships, grants, loans, payment plan; NDSL, GSL, CWS; university has own work program. Scholarship application deadline February 1.
Admissions High school graduation with 16 units required. Interview encouraged. SAT and 3 ACH, or ACT required. $30 application fee. Application deadline February 1. $200 deposit required on acceptance of offer of admission. *Early Decision* and *Early Admission* programs. Admission deferral possible. Transfers accepted. Credit possible for CEEB AP, CLEP, and state exams. EOP.
Student Life Student government. Newspaper, magazine, yearbook, radio stations. Music, speaking, drama, film groups. Political, religious, academic, professional, service, and special interest organizations. 16 fraternities and 3 sororities. 36% of men and 19% of women join. Freshmen must live on campus. Coed and single-sex dorms. 75% of students live on campus. 12 intercollegiate sports for men, 10 for women; intramural & club sports. AIAW, ECAC, NCAA. Student body composition: 1.8% Black, 94.4% White, 3.8% Other. 40% from out of state.

■[1] ALBANY COLLEGE OF PHARMACY, UNION UNIVERSITY
106 New Scotland Avenue, Albany 12208

■[1] ALBANY LAW SCHOOL, UNION UNIVERSITY
80 New Scotland Avenue, Albany 12208

■[1] ALBANY MEDICAL COLLEGE, UNION UNIVERSITY
47 New Scotland Avenue, Albany 12208

[1] UNION THEOLOGICAL SEMINARY
3041 Broadway at West 120 Street, New York 10027

[1] UNITED STATES MERCHANT MARINE ACADEMY
Kings Point, Great Neck 11024, (516) 482-8200
Director of Admissions: Emmanuel L. Jenkins

- **Enrollment: 1,100 men & women**
- **Fees: $600 uniform deposit (1st year)**
- **Degree offered: BS**
- **Mean SAT 520v, 620m**
- **Student-faculty ratio: 13 to 1**

A federal academy controlled by the Department of Commerce, established in 1943, became coed in 1974. 68-acre suburban campus in Kings Point, 20 miles from New York City.
Academic Character MSACS accreditation. Quarter system. Majors offered in marine engineering, nautical science, and a dual license. Minors offered in 15 areas. Courses in humanities, management, science. 4-year program leading to license as merchant marine deck or engineering officer and commission as Ensign in Naval Reserve. Distributive requirements. Independent study. Junior year spent on merchant vessels. Maritime Research Center, Operations Research Facility. Over 80 vessels, small craft. 100,000-volume library.
Financial 4-year government scholarship covers expenses. $461 monthly salary.
Admissions High school graduation with 15 units required. Candidates must be US citizens between 17 and 25 years of age. Congressional nomination required. SAT or ACT required. Application deadline March 1.
Student Life Regiment organization under senior class. Newspaper, yearbook. Music, debate groups. Professional, honorary, and special interest societies and clubs. Students must live on campus. Upperclassmen may have cars. Class attendance required. Military rules. Midshipmen may not marry. Weekend liberty and holiday leaves granted. Phys ed required each semester. 15 intercollegiate sports for men and women; intramurals. Students from each state; quota system.

[1] UNITED STATES MILITARY ACADEMY
West Point 10996, (914) 938-4041
Director of Admissions: Col. Manley E. Rogers

- **Enrollment: 4,103m, 426w**
- **Degree offered: BS**
- **Mean ACT 26; mean SAT 550v, 620m**
- **Student-faculty ratio: 7 to 1**

A public service academy established in 1802, became coed in 1976. On graduation cadets are commissioned as 2nd Lieutenants and must serve five years in the army. 16,000-acre campus on Hudson River near small town of Highland Falls, 50 miles from New York City. Rail station nearby; airport and bus station in New York City.
Academic Character MSACS accreditation. Semester system, 2-month summer term. 9 concentrations offered in applied sciences & engineering, 4 in basic sciences, 10 in humanities, 9 in national security & public affairs, and 2 interdisciplinary. Double majors. Distributive requirements. Independent study. Honors program. Summer military training programs in US and abroad. Exchange programs with Air Force, Coast Guard, Naval Academies. Science Research Lab, computer center, TV system, military museum. 400,000-volume library.
Financial No tuition, room & board, or fees. Cadets receive $5,536 salary per year for expenses. Free medical and dental care.
Admissions High school graduation with 13 units required. GED accepted. Applicants must be unmarried US citizens between 17 and 22 years of age, and without parental responsibilities. Nomination from approved source required. SAT or ACT required. Rolling admissions; suggest applying by September of 12th year. $500 deposit required on entrance. *Early Decision* Program. Admission deferral possible. Transfers accepted as first-semester freshmen. Credit possible for CEEB AP and CLEP exams.
Student Life Military structure. Newspaper, magazine, yearbook, radio station. Music, debate, art, film, drama groups. Academic, religious, and special interest organizations. Students must live on campus. Seniors may keep cars on campus. Class attendance required. Honor code. Leaves granted. 8 semesters of phys ed and intercollegiate or intramural sports required. 22 intercollegiate sports for men, 9 for women; several intramural and club sports. AIAW, NCAA. Student body composition: 2.9% Asian, 6.3% Black, 3.8% Hispanic, 0.3% Native American, 86.7% White. 88% from out of state.

[1] UTICA COLLEGE OF SYRACUSE UNIVERSITY
Burrstone Road, Utica 13502, (315) 792-3006
Director of Admissions: Dominic Passalacqua

- **Undergraduates: 714m, 806w; 2,465 total (including part-time)**
- **Tuition & Fees (1982/83): $4,800**
- **Room & Board: $2,260**
- **Degrees offered: BA, BS, AS**
- **Student-faculty ratio: 15 to 1**

A college of a private university established in 1946. College has its own admissions office and is financially independent of the University. 210-acre suburban campus, 50 miles from Syracuse. Served by air, bus, and rail.
Academic Character MSACS accreditation. Semester system, summer terms. 30 majors offered in the areas of business & economics, public and social studies, arts, humanities, science & mathematics, medicine & health, and communication. Minors in some major fields and in 7 additional areas. Distributive requirements. Independent study. Pass/fail, internships. Preprofessional programs in certified public accounting, dentistry, engineering, law, medicine, teaching. 2-2, 3-2 engineering programs with Syracuse. Member Gerontology Consortium of Utica. Study abroad. Provisional secondary education certification. ROTC; AFROTC at Syracuse. Language lab, writing and media center. 123,134-volume library with microform resources.
Financial CEEB CSS. College scholarships and grants, state aid, payment plan; PELL, SEOG, NDSL, GSL, CWS. Application deadlines March 15 (FAF), July 1 (loans)
Admissions High school graduation with 16 units required. Interview encouraged. SAT or ACT required. $15 application fee. Rolling admissions; suggest applying by February 1. $50 deposit required on acceptance of offer of admission. *Early Decision* and *Early Admission* programs. Admission deferral possible. Transfers accepted. Credit possible for CEEB AP, CLEP, and state exams; college has own advanced placement program. HEOP.
Student Life Student government. Newspaper, magazines, yearbook, radio station. Music, drama, debate groups. Black, Latin American Student Unions. Religious, honorary, service, academic, and special interest groups. 5

fraternities with some housing, and 5 sororities. Coed and single-sex dorms. No married-student housing. 40% of students live on campus. Liquor restricted. Gambling prohibited. 8 intercollegiate sports for men, 4 for women; intramurals. AIAW, ECAC, NCAA. Student body composition: 0.6% Asian, 9.4% Black, 1.8% Hispanic, 0.1% Native American, 86.5% White, 1.5% Other. 16% from out of state.

[1] VASSAR COLLEGE

Poughkeepsie 12601, (914) 452-7000
Director of Admissions: Fred R. Brooks, Jr.

- **Undergraduates: 929m, 1,290w**
- **Tuition (1982/83): $7,400**
- **Room & Board: $3,100**
- **Degree offered: AB**
- **Median SAT 600v, 600m**
- **Student-faculty ratio: 11 to 1**

A private college established in 1861, became coed in 1969. 1,000-acre rural campus outside the small city of Poughkeepsie, 75 miles north of New York City. Served by air, bus, and rail.

Academic Character MSACS accreditation. Semester system. Concentrations offered in Africana studies, American culture, anthropology, art, astronomy, biochemistry, biology, biopsychology, chemistry, classics, computer science, drama, East Asian studies, economics, English, environmental science, French, geography-anthropology, geology, German, Greek, Hispanic studies, history, Italian, Latin, mathematics, music, philosophy, physics, political science, psychology, religion, Russian, sociology, and science, technology & society. Self-designed majors. MA, MS granted. Independent study. Honors programs. Phi Beta Kappa. Pass/fail, internships. 4-year AB-MA programs in chemistry, French, Hispanic studies. 12-College Exchange. College Venture program. Washington Semester, theatre semester, Mystic Seaport semester. Study abroad. Elementary and secondary education certification. 543,125-volume library.

Financial CEEB CSS. College scholarships, state grants, payment plan; PELL, SEOG, NDSL, FISL, GSL, CWS; college has own work program. File FAF by February 1.

Admissions High school graduation required. Interview encouraged. SAT and 3 ACH required. $20 application fee. Application deadline February 1. $200 deposit required on acceptance of offer of admission. *Early Decision* and *Early Admission* programs. Admission deferral possible. Transfers accepted. Credit possible for CEEB AP, CLEP, and state exams.

Student Life Student government. Newspaper, magazines, yearbook, radio station. Music, dance, drama, film groups. 33 academic, honorary, political, religious, service, and special interest organizations. Coed and women's dorms. Married-student housing. Coop and apartment housing. 97% of students live on campus. Attendance at Fall Convocation required. 6 intercollegiate sports for men, 7 for women, 1 coed; intramural and club sports, ECAC, AIAW. Student body composition: 3% Asian, 5% Black, 6% Hispanic, 86% White. 60% from out of state.

[J1] VILLA MARIA COLLEGE OF BUFFALO

240 Pine Ridge Road, Buffalo 14225

[1] VISUAL ARTS, SCHOOL OF

209 East 23rd Street, New York 10010

[1] WADHAM'S HALL COLLEGE

Riverside Drive, Ogdensburg 13669

[1] WAGNER COLLEGE

631 Howard Avenue, Staten Island 10301, (212) 390-3011
Director of Admissions: James Keating

- **Undergraduates: 746m, 902w; 2,314 total (including graduates & part-time)**
- **Tuition (1982/83): $4,800**
- **Room & Board: $2,880; Fees: $100**
- **Degrees offered: AB, BS, BSEd**
- **Mean SAT 450-500v, 450-500m**
- **Student-faculty ratio: 20 to 1**

A private college affiliated with the Lutheran Church in America, established in 1883. 86-acre suburban campus. Served by ferry and bus.

Academic Character MSACS and professional accreditation. Semester system, 11 summer terms of varying lengths. 34 majors offered in the areas of Afro-American studies, art, business, criminal justice, education, forensic chemistry, humanities, mathematics, medical technology, music, nuclear medical technology, nursing, religion, science, social sciences, and theatre. Self-designed majors. Minors offered. Courses in Italian and social welfare. Distributive requirements. Masters degrees granted. Independent study. Honors program. Limited pass/fail, internships. Preprofessional programs in dentistry, engineering, journalism, law, medicine, ministry, optometry, pharmacy, social work, theology, veterinary medicine. 2-2 engineering programs with Valparaiso. Cooperative engineering program with NY Polytechnic. 3-2 Lutheran Deaconess training program. Exchange program with California Lutheran. Study in Austria. Elementary, secondary, and special education certification. ROTC at St. John's; AFROTC at Rutgers; NROTC nearby. Marine Corps Platoon Leaders' Class. College Nursery School. Language labs. 261,000-volume library with microform resources.

Financial CEEB CSS. College scholarships, grants, loans, loans for Lutheran pre-ministerial students, state aid; PELL, SEOG, NNS, NSL, NDSL, CWS, campus employment. Application deadlines April 1 (scholarships), August 1 (loans).

Admissions High school graduation with 16 units required. Interview recommended. SAT or ACT required. $15 application fee. Rolling admissions. $100 tuition and $50 room deposits due on acceptance of admissions offer. *Early Decision* and *Early Admission* programs. Admission deferral possible. Transfers accepted. Credit possible for CEEB AP and CLEP exams. Conditional admission may be arranged.

Student Life Student government. Newspaper, literary magazine, yearbook. Music and drama groups. Academic, honorary, religious, service, social, and special interest groups. 6 fraternities and 4 sororities without housing. 35% of men and 30% of women join. Students live at home, on campus, or in college-approved housing. Coed and single-sex dorms. 50% of students live on campus. Freshmen may not have cars. Drugs, firearms, fireworks, gambling, liquor prohibited, except for beer available at snack bar. Students under 21 must notify Dean of marriage intentions. 8 intercollegiate sports for men, 5 for women; intramurals. AIAW, NCAA, MASCAC. Student body composition: 0.2% Asian, 6.6% Black, 2.2% Hispanic, 84.9% White. 21% from out of state.

[1] WEBB INSTITUTE OF NAVAL ARCHITECTURE

Glen Cove 11542, (516) 671-2213
Registrar: William G. Murray

- **Enrollment: 77m, 5w**
- **Tuition: none**
- **Room & Board: $2,400; Fees: $60**
- **Degrees offered: BSNA, BSME**
- **Mean SAT 610v, 710m**
- **Student-faculty ratio: 7 to 1**

A private institute established in 1894. 26-acre suburban campus on Long Island, 30 miles from New York City. Served by train.

Academic Character MSACS and professional accreditation. Semester system. Majors offered for a BS in naval architecture and marine engineering. Courses offered in humanities, mathematics, science, electrical engineering, mechanical engineering, naval architecture, and marine engineering. Distributives, senior thesis and seminar required. 8-week winter practicum required of all students. Computer center. Center for Maritime Studies. Model Testing Basin. Library.

Financial Admission to the Institute constitutes a four-year full tuition scholarship. Other aid available.

Admissions High school graduation with 16 units required; calculus and mechanical drawing recommended. SAT and 3 ACH required. Interview recommended. $25 application fee. Rolling admissions. $50 tuition and $25 room deposits due on acceptance of admissions offer.

Student Life Student government. Social and recreational activities. Students are required to live on campus. Dormitory and dining hall. Honor system. 3 intercollegiate sports; intramurals. Sailing fleet; waterfront.

[1] WELLS COLLEGE

Aurora 13026, (315) 364-3360
Director of Admissions: Joan Irving

- **Undergraduates: 500w**
- **Tuition, Room & Board (1982/83): $9,470**
- **Degree offered: BA**
- **Mean ACT 25; mean SAT 550v, 550m**
- **Student-faculty ratio: 9 to 1**

A private women's college established in 1870. 360-acre rural campus, 25 miles north of Ithaca. Served by bus.

Academic Character MSACS accreditation. 4-1-4 system. 29 majors offered in the areas of American studies, art, classics, humanities, mathematics, modern languages, music, philosophy-religion, Russian studies, science, social science, and theatre. Minors offered in most major fields. Self-designed majors. Independent and interdepartmental study. Phi Beta Kappa. Pass/fail, internships. Preprofessional programs in dentistry, law, medicine, veterinary science. 3-2 engineering programs with Columbia, Washington U, Texas A&M. 3-2 business administration program with U Rochester. Cooperative education with Elmira. Science, technology, & society program with Cornell. Other off-campus programs arranged. Study abroad. Washington Semester. Elementary and secondary education certification. ROTC, AFROTC, NROTC at Cornell. Art gallery. Computer facilities. Public Leadership Education Network. 201,000-volume library with microform resources.

Financial CEEB CSS. College scholarships, grants, state aid; PELL, SEOG, NDSL, GSL, ALAS, CWS. Priority application deadline February 15.

Admissions High school graduation with 14 units recommended. Interview required. SAT or ACT required. $20 application fee. Rolling admissions. *Early Decision* and *Early Admission* programs. Admission deferral possible. Transfers accepted. Credit possible for CEEB AP, CLEP, state, and college challenge exams.

Student Life Collegiate Association. Newspaper, literary magazine, yearbook. Music, dance, and drama groups. Black and Latin Women's Society. Academic, professional, and special interest groups. Honor code. 5 intercollegiate sports; club and intramural sports.

[J1] WESTCHESTER COMMUNITY COLLEGE

Valhalla 10595

[1] WHITE PLAINS, COLLEGE OF, OF PACE UNIVERSITY

78 North Broadway, White Plains 10603, (914) 682-7070
Director of Admissions: Mark J. Brooks

- **Undergraduates: 545m, 1,006w**
- **Tuition & Fees (1982/83): $4,340**
- **Room & Board: $2,850**

- **Degrees offered: BA, BS, BBA, BPS, AAS**
- **Median SAT 480v, 525m**
- **Student-faculty ratio: 19 to 1**

A private college established in 1923, joined Pace University in 1975. 32-acre urban campus in White Plains, 23 miles north of New York City. Served by bus and rail.
Academic Character MSACS and professional accreditation. 4-1-4 system, 2 6-week summer terms. Majors offered in accounting (information systems, taxation, managerial, public), business, business education, children's studies, community development, education, English, finance, French, health sciences, history, human services, international management, journalism, liberal studies, management, management information systems, marketing, mathematics-computer science, performing arts, retail management, science-physics, social science, and Spanish. AAS in general business, acounting concepts & techniques, marketing, and accounting & information systems. Independent study. Honors program. Pass/fail, internships. BBA-MBA program in public accounting. Cross-registration with other Pace colleges. Study abroad, language tours. Elementary and secondary education certification. Language labs. 94,500-volume library with microform resources.
Financial CEEB CSS. College scholarships and grants, state aid, Native American grants, payment plan; PELL, SEOG, NDSL, GSL, CWS, campus work/study, off-campus employment. Application deadline March 15.
Admissions High school graduation required with 13 units recommended. GED accepted. Interview encouraged. SAT or ACT recommended. $15 application fee. Rolling admissions; suggest applying in fall. Deadline August 15. $100 deposit required on acceptance of offer of admission. *Early Decision* and *Early Admission* programs. Admission deferral possible. Transfers accepted. Credit possible for CEEB AP and CLEP exams.
Student Life Student government. Newspaper, magazine, yearbook. Music, debate, drama groups. Academic, honorary, service, and special interest organizations. Students must live at home or on campus. Dormitory and dining facilities. No married-student housing. 20% of full-time students live on campus. 10 intercollegiate sports for men, 9 for women; intramurals. NCAA, ECAC, AIAW. Student body composition: 1.5% Asian, 9.2% Black, 3.8% Hispanic, 0.6% Native American, 84.8% White. 13% from out of state.

[1] WILLIAM SMITH COLLEGE
Geneva — see Hobart and William Smith Colleges

[1] YESHIVA UNIVERSITY
500 West 185 Street, New York 10033, (212) 960-5400
Director of Admissions: Paul S. Glasser

- **Undergraduates: 796m, 500w; 6,640 total (including graduates)**
- **Tuition (1982/83): $5,050**
- **Room & Board: $2,925; Fees: $175**
- **Degrees offered: BA, BS, AA**
- **Mean SAT 540v, 580m (men); 523v, 524m (women)**
- **Student-faculty ratio: 8 to 1**

A private university under Jewish auspices with coordinate undergraduate colleges and coed graduate schools. Established in 1886. Urban campus with Stern College for Women at 245 Lexington Avenue and branch campus in the Bronx. Air, bus, and rail service.
Academic Character MSACS accreditation. Semester system. Majors offered in accounting, biology, chemistry, computer sciences, economics, English, history, mathematics, political science, pre-health, psychology, sociology, and speech-drama. Yeshiva College also offers classics, French, Hebrew, music, philosophy, physics, pre-engineering, and pre-law. Stern College also offers education, Hebraic studies, and nursing. Minors offered. Distributives, comprehensive major exam, and Jewish studies required. Graduate and professional degrees granted. Independent study. Honors program. Men's college has 3-2 engineering program with NY Polytechnic and Columbia; 3-4 program with NY College of Podiatry. Women's college has cooperative programs in art, design, and fashion with Fashion Institute; Shanah program of intensive Jewish studies. Year in Israel. Language labs. Museum. 850,000-volume library with microform resources.
Financial CEEB CSS. University scholarships, grants, loans, state aid; PELL, SEOG, NDSL, FISL, work/study contracts.
Admissions High school graduation with 16 units required. GED accepted. Interview required. SAT required; Hebrew ACH required. $25 application fee. Rolling admissions. *Early Admission* and *Concurrent Enrollment* programs. Admission deferral possible. Transfers accepted. Credit possible for CEEB AP, CLEP, ACT PEP, and state exams. Conditional admission may be arranged.
Student Life College Senates. Newspapers, yearbooks, publications. Drama groups. Academic, service, and special interest groups. Students not living with relatives live in residence halls. 85% of men and 90% of women live on campus. 2 hours of phys ed required. 5 intercollegiate sports for men, 1 for women; intramurals. NCAA, ECAA. Yeshiva College student body composition: 0.3% Asian, 0.1% Black, 95.7% White. 46% of Yeshiva students from out of state; 66% of Stern students from out of state.

NORTH CAROLINA *(NC)*

[J1] ALAMANCE, TECHNICAL COLLEGE OF
PO Box 623, Haw River 27258

[J1] ALBEMARLE, COLLEGE OF THE
Riverside Avenue, Elizabeth City 27909

[J1] ANSON TECHNICAL COLLEGE
Ansonville 28007

[1] APPALACHIAN STATE UNIVERSITY
Boone 28608, (704) 262-2000
Director of Admissions: T. Joe Watts

- **Enrollment: 4,687m, 5,003w (including graduates)**
- **Tuition (1982/83): $733 (in-state), $2,521 (out-of-state)**
- **Room & Board: $1,460**
- **Degrees offered: BA, BS, BMus, BSBA, BTech**
- **Mean SAT 900**
- **Student-faculty ratio: 16 to 1**

A public university established in 1889. 75-acre small-town campus, 95 miles from Asheville. Served by bus; air service in Asheville.
Academic Character SACS and professional accreditation. Semester system, 4- and 6-week summer terms, summer semester. 23 majors offered by the College of Arts & Sciences, 14 by the College of Business, 17 by the College of Fine & Applied Arts, and 13 by the College of Learning & Human Development. Minors required in some programs. Minors offered in most major fields and in 10 others. Distributive requirements. Graduate degrees granted. Independent study. Honors program. Cooperative work/study, limited pass/fail, internships, credit by exam. Preprofessional programs in dentistry, law, medicine, theology. 3-2 engineering program with Auburn. 2-year transfer programs in engineering, forestry, nursing, pharmacy. Appalachian Consortium. Study abroad. Elementary, secondary, library science, and special education certification. ROTC. Computer center. Language lab. 412,000-volume library with microform resources.
Financial CEEB CSS and ACT FAS. University scholarships, grants, loans, payment plan; PELL, SEOG, NDSL, CWS, self-help program. Application deadline March 15.
Admissions High school graduation with 16 units required. GED accepted. Audition required for music majors. SAT or ACT required. $15 application fee. Rolling admissions. $200 deposit due on acceptance of admissions offer. *Early Admission* Program. Admission deferral possible. Transfers accepted. Credit possible for CEEB AP, CLEP, and departmental exams.
Student Life Student government. Newspaper, literary magazine, yearbook. Music groups. Debate. Student Research Union. Academic, honorary, religious, service, and special interest groups. Fraternities and sororities. Single freshmen live at home or on campus. Married-student housing. 49% of students live on campus. Freshmen may not have cars on campus. Class attendance expected. 2 semesters of phys ed required. 12 intercollegiate sports for men, 8 for women, and one coed; intramurals. AIAW, NCAA, SC. Student body composition: 0.1% Asian, 2.4% Black, 0.2% Hispanic, 0.1% Native American, 96.9% White. 7% from out of state.

[J1] ASHEVILLE-BUNCOMBE TECHNICAL INSTITUTE
Asheville 28801

[1] ATLANTIC CHRISTIAN COLLEGE
Wilson 27893, (919) 237-3161
Director of Admissions: James D. Daniell

- **Undergraduates: 556m, 993w**
- **Tuition (1982/83): $2,850**
- **Room & Board: $1,440; Fees: $144**
- **Degrees offered: BA, BS, BFA**
- **Mean SAT 840**
- **Student-faculty ratio: 15 to 1**

A private college controlled by the Christian Church (Disciples of Christ), established in 1902. 50-acre small-city campus, 40 miles from Raleigh. Airport.
Academic Character SACS and professional accreditation. Semester system, 2 6-week summer terms. 30 majors offered in the areas of art, business, drama, education, English, foreign languages, health & physical education, history, mathematics, medical technology, music, nursing, psychology, religion/philosophy, science, social science, and social studies. Distributives and 6 hours of religion required. Independent study. Honors seminars. Internships, credit by exam. Preprofessional programs in dentistry, medicine, veterinary medicine. Study abroad in England. Elementary,

secondary, and special education certification. Media center. Learning resource center. 157,097-volume library with microform resources.
Financial CEEB CSS and ACT FAS. College scholarships, grants, loans, ministerial grants, state grants, payment plans; PELL, SEOG, NSS, NDSL, GSL, FISL, CWS.
Admissions High school graduation with 16 units required. Interview recommended. SAT or ACT required. $10 application fee. Rolling admissions. $100 deposit due on acceptance of admissions offer. *Early Admission* and *Concurrent Enrollment* programs. Admission deferral possible. Transfers accepted. Credit possible for CEEB AP and CLEP exams.
Student Life Student government. Newspaper, literary magazine, yearbook. Music and drama groups. Afro-American Awareness Society. Campus Christian Association. Academic, honorary, political, and special interest groups. 4 fraternities with houses; 3 sororities without housing. 10% of students join. Students not living at home must live on campus. Married-student housing available. Single-sex dorms. 53% of students live on campus. Liquor, drugs, gambling, hazing prohibited. Class attendance required. 3 semesters of phys ed required. 7 intercollegiate sports for men, 3 for women; intramurals. AIAW, CC. Student body composition: 0.2% Asian, 12% Black, 1.5% Foreign, 0.1% Hispanic, 0.3% Native American, 85.9% White. 17% from out of state.

[1] BARBER-SCOTIA COLLEGE
Concord 28025, (704) 786-5171

- **Undergraduates: 141m, 204w**
- **Tuition & Fees (1980/81): $1,829**
- **Room & Board: $1,329**
- **Typical extra expenses: $950**
- **Degrees offered: BA, BS, AA**

A private, coed, liberal arts and teacher's college established in 1867 and controlled by the United Presbyterian Church, USA. Small-city campus.
Academic Character SACS accreditation. Semester system. BA or BS offered with majors in early childhood education, intermediate education, biology education, business education, social science education, medical technology, sociology, and business administration. AA offered in secretarial science and accounting. 30,000-volume library.
Financial Financial aid available including limited number of college scholarships, small loan fund, NDSL.
Admissions High school graduation or equivalent required. SAT required.
Student Life Dormitories for men and women. Dining hall on campus.

[J1] BEAUFORT COUNTY TECHNICAL INSTITUTE
Washington 27889

[1] BELMONT ABBEY COLLEGE
Belmont 28012, (704) 825-3711
Director of Admissions: Robin R. Roberts

- **Undergraduates: 473m, 337w**
- **Tuition (1982/83): $2,850 (in-state), $3,500 (out-of-state)**
- **Room & Board: $1,680; Fees: $110**
- **Degrees offered: AB, BS**
- **Mean SAT 900**
- **Student-faculty ratio: 17 to 1**

A private college founded by Benedictine Monks, established in 1876, became coed in 1972. 650-acre campus, 10 miles west of Charlotte. Served by air, rail, and bus.
Academic Character SACS accreditation. Semester system. Majors offered in accounting, art education, biology, business, chemistry, distribution management, economics, English, environmental science, history, medical technology, natural science, political science, recreation, religion, and sociology. Majors in art, education, psychology, and special education offered with Sacred Heart. Distributives, 6 hours of theology, and senior comprehensive exam required. Independent study. Honors program. Pass/fail, internships. Preprofessional programs in dentistry, law, medicine, pharmacy, veterinary medicine. Cross-registration with Sacred Heart, 10 area schools, and 20 state schools. Study in France. Elementary and special education certification. ROTC, AFROTC at UNC Charlotte. Language lab. 100,000-volume library with microform resources.
Financial CEEB CSS. College scholarships, grants, loans, payment plan; PELL, SEOG, NDSL, CWS. Application deadlines April 1 (scholarships), March 15 (loans).
Admissions High school graduation with 16 units required. Interview recommended. SAT or ACT required. $15 application fee. Rolling admissions. $150 deposit due on acceptance of admissions offer. *Early Admission* and *Early Decision* programs. Admission deferral possible. Transfers accepted. Credit possible for CEEB AP and CLEP exams.
Student Life Student government. Newspaper, literary magazine, yearbook, radio station. Drama group. Campus ministry. Honorary, political, professional, religious, and special interest groups. 3 fraternities with houses. 70% of men join. Students must live at home or on campus. 77% of students live on campus. Beer permitted in dorms. Class attendance required of freshmen. 4 intercollegiate sports for men, 2 for women; intramurals. Student body composition: 2% Asian, 7% Black, 3% Foreign, 1% Hispanic, 87% White. 67% from out of state.

[1] BENNETT COLLEGE
Greensboro 27420, (919) 273-4431
Registrar: Mary M. Eady

- **Undergraduates: 605w**
- **Tuition (1982/83): $2,700**
- **Room & Board: $1,500; Fees: $25**
- **Degrees offered: BA, BS, BFA, BASIS**
- **Student-faculty ratio: 11 to 1**

A private women's college affiliated with the United Methodist Church, established in 1873. Small urban campus.
Academic Character SACS accreditation. Semester system, 2 5-week summer terms. Majors offered in accounting, art, biology, business, chemistry, dietetics, education, English, history, home economics, mathematics, music education, physical education, political science, psychology, social sciences, social welfare, sociology, and women's studies. Majors in drama, French, and Spanish with Greensboro Consortium. Self-designed majors. Distributives and 3 hours of religion required. Independent study. Honors program. Preprofessional programs in dentistry, medicine. 3-1 medical technology program with Howard and School of Medical Technology, Washington. 3-2 nursing program with UNC Greensboro. 5-year engineering program with NC A&T State. Communications Media and Public Relations program with UNC and NC A&T. Elementary and special education certification. ROTC at NC A&T. Computer center. 80,000-volume library with microform resources.
Financial CEEB CSS. College scholarships, grants, payment plans; PELL, SEOG, NDSL, CWS, college work program.
Admissions High school graduation with 16 units required. SAT or ACT required. $10 application fee. Rolling admissions. $75 deposit due on acceptance of admissions offer. *Early Admission* Program. Transfers accepted. Credit possible for CEEB AP and CLEP exams. Non-admissible students may apply for special student status.
Student Life Student government. Honor societies. Students must live at home or on campus. Permission required to keep car on campus. 1 class absence per semester allowed. 4 hours of phys ed required. Intercollegiate basketball and volleyball; intramurals.

[J1] BLADEN TECHNICAL INSTITUTE
Dublin 28332

[J1] BLUE RIDGE TECHNICAL COLLEGE
Flat Rock 28731

[J1] BREVARD COLLEGE
Brevard 28712, (704) 883-8292
Dean of Admissions: Robert G. McLendon

- **Enrollment: 750 men & women**
- **Tuition & Fees (1982/83): $2,620**
- **Room & Board: $1,870**
- **Degrees offered: AA, AFA**
- **Mean ACT 18; mean SAT 870**
- **Student-faculty ratio: 11 to 1**

A private college controlled by the Western North Carolina Annual Conference of the United Methodist Church, established in 1934. Rural campus in the Blue Ridge Mountains, 33 miles south of Asheville. Airport in Asheville.
Academic Character SACS and professional accreditation. Semester system, 5-week summer term. 2-year programs offered in agriculture, American studies, art, architecture, business, forestry, journalism, liberal arts, mathematics, medical & life sciences, music, recreation, social sciences, social work, and teaching. Distributive requirements. Preprofessional programs in dentistry, engineering, forestry, law, medicine, nursing, theology. 36,000-volume library with microform resources.
Financial CEEB CSS and ACT FAS. College scholarships, Methodist ministers scholarships, state grants and loans; PELL, SEOG, NDSL, GSL, CWS.
Admissions High school graduation required. SAT or ACT required. $10 application fee. Rolling admissions. $100 deposit due on acceptance of admissions offer. *Early Admission* and *Early Decision* programs. Admission deferral possible. Transfers accepted. Credit possible for CEEB AP and CLEP exams. Special admissions for underprepared students.
Student Life Student government. Newspaper, literary magazine, yearbook. Music and drama groups. Circle K. Mentors. Honorary, religious, and special interest groups. Single-sex dorms. 3 hours of phys ed required. 5 intercollegiate sports for men, 4 for women; intramurals. Student body composition: 10% minority.

[J1] CALDWELL COMMUNITY COLLEGE AND TECHNICAL INSTITUTE
Lenoir 28645

[J1 & 1] CAMPBELL UNIVERSITY
Buies Creek 27506, (919) 893-4111
Director of Admissions: Winslow Carter

- **Undergraduates: 1,075m, 879w; 3,100 total (including graduates)**
- **Tuition & Fees (1982/83): $3,790 (in-state), $3,840 (out-of-state)**
- **Room & Board: $1,716**
- **Degrees offered: BA, BS, BBA, BME, BHS, BSS, AA**
- **Mean SAT 800 composite**
- **Student-faculty ratio: 19 to 1**

A private university affiliated with the North Carolina Baptist Convention, established in 1887. 850-acre rural campus, 30 miles from Raleigh. Served by air, rail, and bus.
Academic Character SACS and professional accreditation. Semester system, 2 5-week summer terms. 33 majors offered in the areas of business,

church ministries, communications, data processing, education, home economics, humanities, modern languages, mathematics, music, natural sciences, physical education, physical sciences, religion, social sciences, and trust management. Distributives and 6 hours of religion required. Graduate degrees granted. Independent study. Honors program. Internships. 3-1 medical technology program. Exchange program with Baptist College in Wales. Pre-school, elementary, and secondary education certification. ROTC. 160,000-volume library.
Financial CEEB CSS and ACT FAS. University scholarships, loans, payment plans; PELL, SEOG, NDSL, GSL, CWS. Scholarship application deadline April 15.
Admissions High school graduation with 18 units required. Interview recommended. SAT or ACT required. $15 application fee. Rolling admissions. $100 deposit due on acceptance of admissions offer. *Early Decision, Early Admission, Concurrent Enrollment* programs. Admission deferral possible. Transfers accepted. Credit possible for CEEB AP and CLEP exams.
Student Life Student government. Newspaper, literary magazine, yearbook, radio station. Music and drama groups. Academic, honorary, religious, and special interest groups. Students must live at home or on campus. Single-sex dorms. Married-student housing. 70% of students live on campus. Liquor prohibited. Class attendance expected. Attendance at biweekly convocations required. 2 hours of phys ed required. 8 intercollegiate sports for men, 4 for women; intramurals. AIAW, NCAA. Student body composition: 10% Black, 87% White, 3% Other. 20% from out of state.

[J1] CAPE FEAR TECHNICAL INSTITUTE
Wilmington 28401

[J1] CARTERET TECHNICAL COLLEGE
Morehead City 28557

[1] CATAWBA COLLEGE
Salisbury 28144, (704) 637-4111
Dean of Admissions: J. William Hall

- **Undergraduates: 516m, 423w**
- **Tuition (1982/83): $3,510**
- **Room & Board: $1,830; Fees: $250**
- **Degrees offered: AB, BSW**
- **Mean SAT 410v, 444m**
- **Student-faculty ratio: 17 to 1**

A private college affiliated with the United Church of Christ, established in 1851. 210-acre small-city campus, 50 miles from Charlotte. Served by rail and bus.
Academic Character SACS and professional accreditation. Semester system, 2 5-week summer terms. 34 majors offered in the areas of business, computer science, corrective therapy, drama, education, humanities, mathematics, modern languages, music, physical education, recreation, religion, science, social sciences, and speech. Minors in most major fields. Distributive requirements. Independent study. Internships. Preprofessional programs in dentistry, law, medicine. 3-1 medical technology and physician assistant programs with Wake Forest. 3-2 forestry program with Duke. Study abroad. Elementary, secondary, and special education certification. Language lab. 175,000-volume library with microform resources.
Financial CEEB CSS. College scholarships, grants, loans, tuition reduction for UCC ministers' children, payment plans; PELL, SEOG, NDSL, CWS. Loan application deadline February 15.
Admissions High school graduation with 16 units required. Interview recommended. SAT required; ACT may be substituted. 3 ACH recommended. $15 application fee. Rolling admissions. $100 ($50 for day students) deposit due on acceptance of admissions offer. *Credit in Escrow* Program. Transfers accepted. Credit possible for CEEB AP and CLEP exams.
Student Life Student government. Newspaper, literary magazine, yearbook, radio station. Music and drama groups. Debate. Academic, ethnic, honorary, religious, and special interest groups. Freshmen and sophomores under 21 must live at home or on campus. Married-student housing. 75% of students live on campus. Gambling, hazing, fireworks prohibited. Dean must be notified of marriage intentions. Class attendance strongly recommended. 8 intercollegiate sports for men, 5 for women; many intramurals. AIAW, NAIA, CIAC, SAC. Student body composition: 10% Black, 90% White. 45% from out of state.

[J1] CATAWBA VALLEY TECHNICAL COLLEGE
Highway 64-70, Hickory 28601

[J1] CENTRAL CAROLINA TECHNICAL COLLEGE
1105 Kelly Drive, Sanford 27330

[J1] CENTRAL PIEDMONT COMMUNITY COLLEGE
1141 Elizabeth Avenue, Charlotte 28235

[J1] CHOWAN COLLEGE
Murfreesboro 27855, (919) 398-4101
Director of Admissions: Bennett J. Utley

- **Undergraduates: 736m, 379w**
- **Tuition (1983/84): $1,900**
- **Room & Board: $1,875; Fees: $715**
- **Degrees offered: AA, AS**
- **Student-faculty ratio: 19 to 1**

A private college controlled by the Baptist State Convention, established in 1848. 289-acre campus.
Academic Character SACS accreditation. Semester system. 2-year programs offered by the departments of Business, Fine Arts, Graphic Communications, Health & Physical Education, Language & Literature, Mathematics, Religion & Philosophy, Science, and Social Science. Distributives and 6 hours of religion required. Preprofessional programs in agriculture, cytotechnology, dental hygiene, dentistry, education, engineering, forestry, health & physical education, journalism, law, medical illustration, medical technology, medicine, nursing, optometry, pharmacy, physical therapy, pulp & paper science, religion, sports medicine, veterinary medicine. 75,000-volume library.
Financial CEEB CSS and ACT FAS. College scholarships, grants, loans, church-vocation grants, reduction for ministers' families, state grants and loans; PELL, SEOG, NSS, NDSL, GSL, CWS. Application deadline March 15.
Admissions High school graduation with 18 units required. Interview strongly recommended. SAT required; ACT accepted. $10 application fee. Rolling admissions. $100 deposit due on acceptance of admissions offer. *Early Admission* Program. Transfers accepted. Credit possible for CEEB AP and CLEP exams.
Student Life Student government. Newspaper, yearbook. Music and drama groups. Circle K. Honorary, religious, service, social, and special interest groups. Students must live at home or on campus. Single-sex dorms. Liquor, drugs, gambling, firearms prohibited. Class and chapel attendance required. 2 hours of phys ed required. 6 intercollegiate sports for men, 5 for women. NJCAA, TJCAC, CFC. Student body composition: 18% minority.

[J1] CLEVELAND TECHNICAL COLLEGE
137 South Post Road, Shelby 28150

[J1] COASTAL CAROLINA COMMUNITY COLLEGE
Jacksonville 28540

[J1] CRAVEN COMMUNITY COLLEGE
New Bern 28560

[1] DAVIDSON COLLEGE
Davidson 28036, (704) 892-2000
Director of Admissions & Financial Aid: John V. Griffith

- **Undergraduates: 900m, 490w**
- **Tuition (1982/83): $5,310**
- **Room & Board: $2,190; Fees: $270**
- **Degrees offered: AB, BS**
- **Mean SAT 605v, 620m**
- **Student-faculty ratio: 13 to 1**

A private college affiliated with the Presbyterian Church, established in 1837, became coed in 1972. 450-acre small-town campus, 20 miles north of Charlotte. Served by bus; air and rail service in Charlotte.
Academic Character SACS accreditation. Trimester system. Majors offered in art, biology, chemistry, classics, economics, English, French, German, history, mathematics, music, philosophy, physics, political science, medicine, psychology, religion, sociology, Spanish, and theatre. Preprofessional pre-medicine major offered. Distributives, 3 religion and philosophy courses, and GRE, comprehensive exam, or research project required. Independent study. Honors program. Phi Beta Kappa. Pass/fail. 3-2 engineering program with Columbia, NC State, Georgia Tech, Washington U. Several study abroad programs. Washington Semester. Foreign Policy Semester. Secondary education certification. ROTC. Computer facilities. Language lab. Center for Special Studies. 270,000-volume library with microform resources.
Financial CEEB CSS. College scholarships, grants, loans, payment plan; PELL, SEOG, NDSL, GSL, CWS. Application deadline February 15.
Admissions High school graduation with 16 units required. Interview encouraged. SAT required; 3 ACH recommended. $25 application fee. Application deadline February 15. $200 deposit due on acceptance of admissions offer. *Early Decision* and *Early Admission* programs. Transfers accepted. Credit possible for CEEB AP exams.
Student Life Student government. Newspaper, literary magazine, yearbook, radio station. Music and drama groups. Debate. Black Student Coalition. Academic, honorary, political, religious, service, and special interest groups. 4 fraternities and 6 social-eating clubs; all without housing. 70% of students join. Coed and single-sex dorms. Limited married-student housing. 87% of students live on campus. Honor code. 2 team sports and 3 individual sports required. 12 intercollegiate sports for men, 5 for women; many intramurals. AIAW, NCAA, SC. Student body composition: 5% Black, 93% White, 2% Other. 64% from out of state.

[J1] DAVIDSON COUNTY COMMUNITY COLLEGE
Lexington 27292

[1] DUKE UNIVERSITY
Durham 27706, (919) 684-8111
Director of Undergraduate Admissions: Jean A. Scott

- **Enrollment: 5,448m, 3,921w (including graduates)**
- **Tuition (1982/83): $6,210**
- **Room & Board: $2,930; Fees: $240**
- **Degrees offered: AB, BS, BSE**
- **Mean SAT 1285**
- **Student-faculty ratio: 9 to 1**

A private university established in 1838. 800-acre suburban campus, 25 miles northwest of Raleigh.
Academic Character SACS and professional accreditation. Semester system, 3 5-week summer terms. 36 majors offered by the College of Arts & Sciences, and 4 by the School of Engineering. Courses include African and Asian languages. Distributive requirements in Program I; seminars, tutorials, or independent study required during first two years; two small group courses required during junior and senior years. Program II allows self-designed majors with possible credit for off-campus work. Graduate and professional degrees granted. Honors program. Phi Beta Kappa. Pass/fail, internships. 3-1 programs in business, forestry/environmental studies, law, medicine with graduate school. Reciprocal enrollment with UNC, NC State, and NC Central. Several study abroad programs. Education certification. ROTC, AFROTC, NROTC. Computer center. Language lab. Record library. Duke Forest. 2,800,000-volume library with microform resources.
Financial CEEB CSS. University scholarships, grants, loans, payment plans; PELL, SEOG, NDSL, FISL, CWS, university work program. Recommended application deadline February 1.
Admissions High school graduation with at least 12 units in college prep program. SAT required; ACT accepted. 3 ACH required. $30 application fee. Application deadline January 15. $130 deposit due on acceptance of admissions offer. *Early Decision* and *Early Admission* programs. Admission deferral possible. Transfers accepted. Credit possible for CEEB AP and departmental exams; university has own advanced placement program.
Student Life Student government. Newspaper, 3 magazines, yearbook, radio and television stations. Music and drama groups. Black Students Alliance. Elcirculo Hispano. Jewish Forum. Circle K. Academic, honorary, professional, political, religious, service, and special interest groups. 16 fraternities and 8 sororities without houses. 45% of men and 42% of women join. Freshmen must live on campus. 70% of students live on campus. 12 intercollegiate sports for men, 8 for women; many club and intramural sports. AIAW, ACC. Student body composition: 1.2% Asian, 4.8% Black, 0.6% Hispanic, 0.1% Native American, 91.1% White. 85% from out of state.

[J1] DURHAM TECHNICAL INSTITUTE
1637 Lawson Street, Durham 27703

[1] EAST CAROLINA UNIVERSITY
East Fifth Street, Greenville 27834, (919) 757-6131
Director of Admissions: Walter M. Bortz, II

- **Enrollment: 5,682m, 7,582w (including graduates)**
- **Tuition (1982/83): $668 (in-state), $2,456 (out-of-state)**
- **Room & Board: $1,870**
- **Degrees offered: BA, BS, BFA, BMus, BSAC, BSB, BSBA, BSBE, BSMT, BSN, BSPT**
- **Mean SAT 876**
- **Student-faculty ratio: 15 to 1**

A private university established in 1907. 600-acre small-city campus, 85 miles east of Raleigh. Airport 30 miles away in Kinston.
Academic Character SACS and professional accreditation. Semester system, 2 5½-week summer terms. 112 majors offered by the College of Arts & Sciences and by the schools of Allied Health & Social Professions, Art, Business, Education, Home Economics, Medicine, Music, Nursing, and Technology. Minors required in some areas and recommended in others. Distributive requirements. Graduate degrees granted. Independent study. Honors seminars. Cooperative work/study, internships, credit by exam. Preprofessional programs in dentistry, law, medicine, optometry, pharmacy, veterinary medicine. 2-2 engineering program with NCSU Raleigh. Cooperative programs in agriculture, forestry, pulp and paper technology, wood science with NCSU. Study in Costa Rica. Elementary, secondary, special, and library science education certification. AFROTC. Estuarine lab. Health Sciences Library. Computer center. Language labs. 655,205-volume library with microform resources.
Financial CEEB CSS. University scholarships, grants, loans, PELL, SEOG, MPGP, NDSL, FISL, NSL, CWS. Application deadline March 1.
Admissions High school graduation with 16 units required. Audition required for music majors. SAT or ACT required. $10 application fee. Rolling admissions. $25 deposit due on acceptance of admissions offer. *Early Decision* Program. Transfers accepted. Credit possible for CEEB AP and CLEP exams.
Student Life Student government. Newspaper, minority newspaper, literary magazine, yearbook, radio and television stations. Music, opera, and drama groups. Crafts center. Athletic, academic, honorary, political, professional, religious, and special interest groups. 6 fraternities and 8 sororities, most with houses. 11% of men and 8% of women join. International House. Coed and single-sex dorms. 41% of students live on campus. Freshmen may use cars only on weekends. Liquor use limited on campus. 3 hours of phys ed required. 8 intercollegiate sports for men, 6 for women; club and intramural sports. AIAW, ECAC, NCAA. Student body composition: 0.5% Asian, 10.1% Black, 0.3% Hispanic, 0.5% Native American, 88.2% White, 0.4% Other. 11% from out of state.

[J1] EDGECOMB TECHNICAL INSTITUTE
PO Box 550, Tarboro 27886

[1] ELIZABETH CITY UNIVERSITY
PO Box 172, Elizabeth City 27909, (919) 335-3400
Director of Admissions: Wanda E. McLean

- **Undergraduates: 579m, 727w; 1,488 total (including part-time)**
- **Tuition (1982/83): $782 (in-state), $1,900 (out-of-state)**
- **Room & Board: $1,780**
- **Degrees offered: BA, BS, BSE**
- **Student-faculty ratio: 15 to 1**

A public university established in 1891. 87-acre campus in the Albermarle Sound area. Served by bus.
Academic Character SACS accreditation. Semester system, summer term. 26 majors offered in the areas of business, criminal justice, education, fine arts, humanities, industrial arts & technology, mathematics & natural science, physical education, and social & behavioral sciences. Minors offered in some major fields and in 10 others. Distributive requirements. Honors program in English. Independent study. Cooperative work/study, internships. Preprofessional programs in dentistry, medicine, speech pathology. Elementary and secondary education certification. ROTC. Computer center. Laboratory school. 150,000-volume library.
Financial PELL, SEOG, PTSL, MPG, NDSL, GSL, CWS.
Admissions High school graduation with 16 units required. GED accepted. SAT required. $10 application fee. Rolling admissions. $25 tuition and $25 room deposits due on acceptance of admissions offer. Transfers accepted. Credit possible for CEEB CLEP exams. Upward Bound program for disadvantaged.
Student Life Student government. Newspaper, literary magazine, yearbook. Music groups. Academic, religious, and special interest groups. Fraternities and sororities. Single-sex dorms. Most students live on campus. Class attendance expected. 2 hours of phys ed required. 5 intercollegiate sports for men, 4 for women; intramurals. AIAW, NCAA, NCAIAW, CIAC. Student body composition: 91.8% Black, 0.1% Native American, 7.3% White.

[1] ELON COLLEGE
Elon College 27244, (919) 584-9711
Director of Admissions: Marydell R. Bright

- **Undergraduates: 1,468m, 1,157w (including part-time)**
- **Tuition (1982/83): $2,700**
- **Room & Board: $1,740; Fees: $40**
- **Degrees offered: AB, BS, BAA, BAS, AA**
- **Mean SAT 390v, 425m**
- **Student-faculty ratio: 24 to 1**

A private college affiliated with the United Church of Christ, established in 1889. 145-acre rural campus, 17 miles east of Greensboro. Served by bus and rail; airport in Greensboro.
Academic Character SACS and professional accreditation. 4-1-4 system, 2 5-week summer terms. Majors offered in accounting, biology, business, chemistry, computer information science, cytotechnology, economics, education, English, history, human resources, mathematics, medical technology, music, philosophy, physical education, physics, political science, radiologic technology, religion, secretarial studies, and social sciences. Self-designed majors. Distributives and 2 courses in religion required. Independent study. Honors program. Cooperative work/study, limited pass/fail, internships. Preprofessional programs in dentistry, law, medicine, nursing. Study abroad. Elementary, secondary, and special education certification. ROTC. Language lab. 150,000-volume library.
Financial CEEB CSS and ACT FAS. College scholarships, grants, loans, discounts for ministers' children; PELL, SEOG, NDSL, FISL, CWS. Scholarship application deadline May 1.
Admissions High school graduation with 16 units required. Interview recommended. SAT or ACT required. $10 application fee. Rolling admissions. $125 ($50 for day students) deposit due on acceptance of admissions offer. *Early Decision, Early Admission, Credit-in-Escrow* programs. Transfers accepted. Credit possible for CEEB AP, CLEP, and ACT PEP exams. Conditional admission possible.
Student Life Student government. Newspaper, literary magazine, yearbook, radio station. Music groups. Academic, honorary, and service groups. 7 fraternities and 4 sororities; 8 have houses. 20% of students join. Single-sex dorms. 64% of students live on campus. Honor system. Class attendance required. 2 semesters of phys ed required. 8 intercollegiate sports for men, 3 for women; many intramurals. AIAW, NAIA, CIAC, SAC. Student body composition: 9% Black, 90% White, 1% Other. 41% from out of state.

[1] FAYETTEVILLE STATE UNIVERSITY
Fayetteville 28301, (919) 486-1141
Director of Admissions: Charles Darlington

- **Undergraduates: 1,062m, 1,252w**
- **Tuition (1982/83): $689 (in-state), $2,271 (out-of-state)**
- **Room & Board: $1,150-$1,700**
- **Degrees offered: BA, BS**
- **Student-faculty ratio: 16 to 1**

A public university established in 1867. 150-acre urban campus. Served by air, rail, and bus.
Academic Character SACS and professional accreditation. Semester system, 2 5-week summer terms. Majors offered in biology, Black studies, business, chemistry, education, economics, English, geography, history, mathematics/computer science, medical technology, physical education, police science, political science, psychology, reading, sociology, and speech/theatre. Minors available in most major fields and in 3 others. Masters degrees granted. Independent study. Honors program. Cooperative work/study, internships. 2-2 programs with NCSU Raleigh in several areas of technology. Study in Taiwan. Elementary, secondary, and special education certification. ROTC, AFROTC. Language lab. 134,605-volume library.
Financial CEEB CSS and ACT FAS. University scholarships, grants, loans, payment plans; PELL, SEOG, NDSL, CWS. Application deadlines July 1 (scholarshps), March 1 (loans).
Admissions High school graduation with 16 units recommended. SAT required. $10 application fee. Rolling admissions. $10 room deposit required. *Early Admission* Program. Admission deferral possible. Transfers accepted.

Credit possible for CEEB AP and CLEP exams. Upward Bound program.
Student Life Student government. Newspaper, yearbook. Music and drama groups. Afro-American Society. Academic, honorary, and special interest groups. 4 fraternities and 4 sororities. 5% of men and 7% of women join. Coed and single-sex dorms. 38% of students live on campus. Liquor prohibited. Class attendance expected. Dean must be notified of marriage intentions. 3 hours of phys ed required. 6 intercollegiate sports for men, 1 for women; intramurals. AIAW, NAIA, CIAA. Student body composition: 0.8% Asian, 79.6% Black, 1.2% Hispanic, 0.5% Native American, 17.6% White. 18% from out of state.

■[1] FAYETTEVILLE STATE UNIVERSITY, FORT BRAGG BRANCH
Fort Bragg 28307

[J1] FAYETTEVILLE TECHNICAL INSTITUTE
PO Box 35236, Fayetteville 28303

[J1] FORSYTH TECHNICAL INSTITUTE
2100 Silas Creek Parkway, Winston-Salem 27103

[1 & J1] GARDNER-WEBB COLLEGE
Boiling Springs 28017, (704) 434-2361
Director of Admissions: Richard M. Holbrook

- **Enrollment: 818m, 916w (including graduates)**
- **Tuition (1982/83): $3,260**
- **Room & Board: $1,730-$1,990; Fees: $150**
- **Degrees offered: BA, BS, BSN, AA**
- **Mean SAT 400v, 400m**
- **Student-faculty ratio: 17 to 1**

A private college affiliated with the Baptist State Convention, established in 1905. 200-acre campus, 50 miles from Charlotte. Airport and train station in Charlotte; bus service nearby in Shelby.
Academic Character SACS and professional accreditation. Semester system, 2 5-week summer terms. Majors offered in Biblical literature & languages, biology, business, chemistry, education, English, French, general science, health & physical education, history, mathematics, music, nursing, psychology, religion, social science, and Spanish. Distributives and 6 hours of religion required. Independent study. 3-1 medical technology program with Bowman Gray. 3-2 engineering program with Auburn. Study abroad. Early childhood, elementary, and secondary education certification. 200,000-volume library.
Financial CEEB CSS and ACT FAS. College scholarships, loans, state grants, payment plans; PELL, SEOG, NDSL, GSL, CWS, college work program. Application deadline April 1.
Admissions High school graduation with 16 units required. GED accepted. Interview recommended. SAT required; ACT accepted. $15 application fee. Rolling admissions. $100 deposit due on acceptance of admissions offer. *Early Decision* and *Early Admission* programs. Admission deferral possible. Transfers accepted. Credit possible for CEEB AP and CLEP exams. SAT may be waived for deaf students.
Student Life College is specially equipped for hearing-impaired students. Dormitories have visual fire alarms, doorbell lights, and TTY's. Qualified interpreters and tutors available. Tape recorders, sound amplification equipment, and speech analyzers available. Hearing students designated as notetakers in each class. Special study areas. Full-time counselor proficient in sign language present. Student government. Newspaper, literary magazine, yearbook, radio station. Music and drama groups. Athletic, academic, honorary, religious, service, and special interest groups. Single students must live at home or on campus. Single-sex dorms. Married-student housing. 70% of students live on campus. Liquor, gambling, hazing prohibited. Class and weekly convocation attendance required. 2 semesters of phys ed required. 6 intercollegiate sports for men, 4 for women; intramurals. AIAW, NAIA. Student body composition: 0.3% Asian, 9.6% Black, 0.2% Hispanic, 0.2% Native American, 88.4% White, 1.3% Other. 30% from out of state.

[J1] GASTON COLLEGE
Dallas 28034

[1] GREENSBORO COLLEGE
Greensboro 27420, (919) 272-7102
Director of Admissions: James M. Tucker, Jr.

- **Undergraduates: 221m, 429w**
- **Tuition (1982/83): $3,200**
- **Room & Board: $1,960; Fees: $210**
- **Degrees offered: BA, BS, BFA, BMus, BMus Ed**
- **Student-faculty ratio: 14 to 1**

A private college affiliated with the United Methodist Church, established in 1838, became coed in 1954. 35-acre suburban campus. Served by air, rail, and bus.
Academic Character SACS and professional accreditation. Semester system, 2 5-week summer terms. 36 majors offered by the departments of Accounting, Business, Legal Administration, Social Work, & Sociology; Art; Behavioral Science & Education; English; Foreign Languages; History & Political Science; Music; Physical Education & Recreation; Religion & Philosophy; Science & Mathematics; and Speech & Drama. Distributives, 2 semesters of religion, and senior comprehensive exams required. Independent study. Honors program. Limited pass/fail, internships. Preprofessional programs in dentistry, law, medicine, theology. 2-2 radiology program; 3-2 physician's assistant program; 3-1 medical technology program. Cross-registration with UNC Greensboro, A&T State, High Point, Bennett, and Guilford. Study abroad. Elementary, secondary, and special education certification. ROTC nearby. Language lab. Museum. 73,000-volume library with microform resources.
Financial CEEB CSS and ACT FAS. College scholarships, grants, loans; PELL, SEOG, NDSL, FISL, CWS, college employment program. Application deadline May 15.
Admissions High school graduation with 16 units required. GED accepted. Interview recommended. Audition encouraged for music students. SAT or ACT required; ACH recommended. $10 application fee. Rolling admissions. $100 deposit due on acceptance of offer of admission. *Early Decision* and *Early Admission* programs. Admission deferral possible. Transfers accepted. Credit possible for CEEB AP and CLEP exams.
Student Life Student government. Newsletter, newspaper, literary magazine, yearbook. Music and drama groups. Afro-American Society. Political, religious, service, and special interest groups. Single students must live at home or on campus. Single-sex dorms. 80% of students live on campus. Freshmen must have permission to use cars. Liquor prohibited. Honor code. Class attendance expected. 4 semesters of phys ed required. 5 intercollegiate sports for men, 4 for women; several intramurals. NCAA, DAC. Student body composition: 18% minority. 40% from out of state.

[1] GUILFORD COLLEGE
5800 Friendly Avenue, Guilford College 27410, (919) 292-5511
Director of Admissions: Herbert Poole

- **Undergraduates: 611m, 494w**
- **Tuition (1982/83): $4,320**
- **Room & Board: $2,030; Fees: $225**
- **Degrees offered: AB, BS, BAS, BFA, BMus, BMus Ed, AA**
- **Mean SAT 1050**
- **Student-faculty ratio: 16 to 1**

A private college affiliated with the Society of Friends, established in 1837. 290-acre suburban campus in Greensboro. Served by air, rail, and bus.
Academic Character SACS accreditation. Semester system, 2 5-week summer terms. Majors offered in accounting, administration of justice, biology, chemistry, drama/speech, economics, education, English, French, geology, history, humanistic studies, management, mathematics, philosophy, physical education, physics, political science, psychology, religion, sociology, Spanish, sports management, and sports medicine. Majors in art, art education, German, music, music education, and special education offered through cooperative consortium program. Distributive requirements. Independent study. Honors program. Limited pass/fail, internships. Preprofessional programs in dentistry, law, medicine, ministry, veterinary medicine. 3-2 engineering program with Georgia Tech. BS/MS forestry and environmental science program with Duke. 3-1 medical technology and physician's assistant programs with Bowman Gray. Cross-registration with A&T State, Bennett, Greensboro, High Point, UNC Greensboro. Study abroad. New York, Philadelphia, Washington, Florida seminars. Geology field trips. Elementary, secondary, and special education certification. ROTC, AFROTC, NROTC at A&T State. Computer center. Language lab. 190,000-volume library with microform resources.
Financial ACT FAS. College scholarships, grants, loans, grants for Quaker students, payment plan; PELL, SEOG, NDSL, employment opportunities. Application deadline April 15.
Admissions High school graduation with 16-18 units recommended. Interview encouraged. SAT or ACT required. $15 application fee. Rolling admissions; preferred application deadline April 1. $100 deposit due on acceptance of admissions offer. *Early Decision* and *Early Admission* programs. Admission deferral possible. Transfers accepted. Credit possible for CEEB AP and CLEP exams; college has own advanced placement program.
Student Life Student government. Newspaper, literary magazine, journals, yearbook, radio station. Music and drama groups. Debate. Academic, ethnic, religious, service, and special interest groups. Single students under 21 live on campus. Married-student housing. 85% of students live on campus. Gambling and firearms prohibited. Honor code. 9 intercollegiate sports for men, 5 for women; several intramurals. AIAW, NAIA, CC. Student body composition: 0.2% Asian, 6% Black, 0.7% Hispanic, 0.1% Native American, 93% White. 60% from out of state.

[J1] GUILFORD TECHNICAL INSTITUTE
PO Box 309, Jamestown 27282

[J1] HALIFAX COMMUNITY COLLEGE
Weldon 27890

[J2] HAMILTON COLLEGE
Charlotte — see Rutledge College of Charlotte

[J1] HAYWOOD TECHNICAL COLLEGE
Clyde 28721

[1] HIGH POINT COLLEGE
High Point 27262, (919) 885-5101
Director of Admissions: Al Hassell

- **Undergraduates: 695m, 745w**
- **Tuition (1982/83): $3,000**
- **Room & Board: $1,410; Fees: $330**
- **Degrees offered: BA, BS**
- **Mean SAT 410v, 460m**

• **Student-faculty ratio: 17 to 1**

A private college affiliated with the United Methodist Church, established in 1924. 75-acre suburban campus, 12 miles from Greensboro. Served by air, rail, and bus.

Academic Character SACS and professional accreditation. Semester system, 2 5-week summer terms. 30 majors offered in the areas of business, Christian education, communications, education, fine arts, gerontology, human relations, humanities, religion, social & behavioral sciences, physical education, and science. Minors offered. Self-designed majors. Distributive requirements. Independent study. Honors program. Limited pass/fail, internships. Preprofessional programs in dentistry, engineering, forestry, law, medicine, theology. 2-2 forestry program with Duke. Programs in air commerce, computers, environment, oceanography, photography, and applied math with Florida Tech. Elementary and secondary education certification. ROTC, AFROTC. Language lab. 91,500-volume library.

Financial CEEB CSS and ACT FAS. College scholarships, grants, loans, payment plan; PELL, SEOG, NDSL, FISL, CWS, college work program. Application deadline April 15.

Admissions High school graduation with 16 units required. Interview recommended. SAT required. $10 application fee. Rolling admissions. $100 deposit due on acceptance of admissions offer. *Early Decision* and *Early Admission* programs. Admission deferral possible. Transfers accepted. Credit possible for CEEB AP, CLEP, and college proficiency exams.

Student Life Student government. Newspaper, literary magazine, yearbook. Music and drama groups. Religious, service, and special interest groups. 6 fraternities and 5 sororities; all have chapter rooms. 33% of students join. Students must live with family or on campus. 75% of students live on campus. 2 hours of phys ed required. 6 intercollegiate sports for men, 4 for women; intramurals. AIAW, CIAC. Student body composition: 6.1% Black, 0.8% Hispanic, 91.4% White. 45% from out of state.

[P] HOOD THEOLOGICAL SEMINARY
Salisbury 28144

[J1] ISOTHERMAL COMMUNITY COLLEGE
PO Box 804, Spindale 28160

[J1] JAMES SPRUNT TECHNICAL COLLEGE
PO Box 398, Kenansville 28349

[J2] JEFFERSON COLLEGE
Greensboro — see Rutledge College

[2] JOHN WESLEY COLLEGE
924 Eastchester Drive, High Point 27260

[1] JOHNSON C. SMITH UNIVERSITY
100 Beatties Ford Road, Charlotte 28216, (704) 378-1000
Director of Admissions: Moses W. Jones

• **Undergraduates: 607m, 703w**
• **Tuition (1982/83): $2,420**
• **Room & Board: $1,600; Fees: $280**
• **Degrees offered: BA, BS, BSW**
• **Student-faculty ratio: 14 to 1**

A private university affiliated with the United Presbyterian Church, established in 1867. 85-acre urban campus. Served by air, rail, and bus.

Academic Character SACS accreditation. Semester system, 2 5-week summer terms. 5 majors offered by the Department of Education, Physical Education, Health & Psychology, 4 by the Department of the Humanities, 5 by the Department of Mathematics & Science, and 10 by the Department of Social Sciences. Distributives and 6 hours of religion and philosophy required. Seniors must take an interdisciplinary seminar. Departmental honors program. Cooperative work/study, internships. Preprofessional programs in law and medicine. 3-2 engineering program. Cross-registration with 9 area schools. Study abroad. Elementary and secondary education certification. AFROTC at UNC Charlotte. Language lab. 97,000-volume library.

Financial CEEB CSS. United Negro College Fund. University scholarships, grants, loans, payment plans; PELL, SEOG, NDSL, GSL, CWS. Application deadline April 15.

Admissions High school graduation with 16 units required. Interview recommended. SAT required. $10 application fee. Rolling admissions; suggest applying in December. $50 room deposit due on acceptance of admissions offer. Admission deferral possible. Transfers accepted. Special Service Program for students not normally admissible.

Student Life Student government. Newspaper, yearbook, radio station. Music and drama groups. Debate. Student Christian Association. Academic, honorary, and special interest groups. 4 fraternities and 4 sororities without houses. 20% of men and 25% of women join. Single-sex dorms. 55% of students live on campus. 4 hours of phys ed required; swimming requirement. 6 intercollegiate sports for men, 4 for women; intramurals. AIAW, NAIA, NCAA, CIAA. Student body composition: 2.1% African, 97.5% Black, 0.4% White. 55% from out of state.

[J1] JOHNSTON TECHNICAL COLLEGE
Smithfield 27577

[J1] LEES-McRAE COLLEGE
Banner Elk 28604, (704) 898-5241
Director of Admissions: Gina Berini

• **Enrollment: 735**
• **Tuition (1983/84): $2,312**
• **Room & Board: $1,722; Fees: $450**
• **Degrees offered: AA, AS**
• **Student-faculty ratio: 16 to 1**

A private college affiliated with the United Presbyterian Church, established in 1900. Rural campus in the Blue Ridge Mountains.

Academic Character SACS accreditation. Semester system, 2 5-week summer terms. 2-year programs offered in agriculture, biology, business, chemistry, engineering education, English, executive secretary, fine arts, forestry, French, journalism, mathematics, medical technology, optometry, pharmacy, physics, physical education, physical therapy, political science, psychology, religion, sociology, and Spanish. Distributives and 2 semesters of religion required. Preprofessional programs in dentistry, law, medicine, nursing, theology. Internships. 60,000-volume library with microform resources.

Financial CEEB CSS. College scholarships, state grants and loans; PELL, SEOG, NDSL, GSL, CWS, assistantships.

Admissions High school graduation with 16 units recommended. GED accepted. SAT or ACT required. $15 application fee. Rolling admissions. $200 deposit due on acceptance of admissions offer. *Early Decision* and *Early Admission* programs. Transfers accepted.

Student Life Student government. Drama group. Circle K. Wilderness Society. Honorary, professional, religious, and special interest groups. Single-sex dorms. 2 semesters of phys ed required. 4 intercollegiate sports; intramurals.

[J2] LAFAYETTE COLLEGE
Fayetteville — see Rutledge College

[J1] LENOIR COMMUNITY COLLEGE
PO Box 188, Kinston 28501

[1] LENOIR-RHYNE COLLEGE
Hickory 28603, (704) 328-1741, ext. 250
Dean of Admissions: Richard P. Thompson

• **Undergraduates: 531m, 893w; 1,386 total (including graduates)**
• **Tuition (1982/83): $3,895**
• **Room & Board: $1,610; Fees: $265**
• **Degrees offered: AB, BS, BMus**
• **Student-faculty ratio: 14 to 1**

A private college controlled by the North Carolina Synod of the Lutheran Church in America, established in 1891. 100-acre small-city campus, 50 miles from Charlotte. Served by air and bus.

Academic Character SACS and professional accreditation. Semester system, 2 5-week summer terms. 36 majors offered by the divisions of Humanities, Natural Science & Mathematics, Social & Behavioral Sciences, and Professional Programs. Minors offered in most major fields. Self-designed majors. Distributive requirements. Graduate degrees granted. Honors program. Experiential education program. Limited pass/fail, internships. Preprofessional programs in law, medicine, parish work, seminary studies, and social work. 3-1 medical technology program. 2-3 pharmacy program. 3-2 engineering programs with Georgia Tech, Duke, NCS. 3-2 forestry and environmental management programs with Duke. Elementary, secondary, and hearing-impaired education certification. ROTC at Davidson. Washington Semester. Computer center. Language lab. Observatory. 107,390-volume library.

Financial CEEB CSS. College scholarships, grants, oans, ministerial scholarships, payment plans; PELL, SEOG, NSS, NDSL, FISL, CWS. Application deadline March 15.

Admissions High school graduation with 16 units recommended. Interview recommended. SAT or ACT required. $15 application fee. Rolling admissions. $100 ($50 for day students) deposit required on acceptance of admissions offer. *Early Decision* and *Early Admission* programs. Admission deferral possible. Transfers accepted. Credit possible for CEEB AP, CLEP, and departmental proficiency exams.

Student Life Student government. Newspaper, literary magazines, yearbook, radio and television stations. Music and drama groups. Debate. Academic, honorary, political, religious, service, and special interest groups. 4 fraternities and 4 sororities. 22% of men and 25% of women join. Special facilities for hearing-impaired students. Single-sex dorms. No married-student housing. 65% of students live on campus. Drugs and firearms prohibited. Monthly convocation mandatory. Phys ed required of freshmen. 6 intercollegiate sports for men, 4 for women; many intramurals. AIAW, NAIA, SAC. Student body composition: 6% Black, 93% White, 1% Other. 30% from out of state.

[1] LIVINGSTONE COLLEGE
Salisbury 28144, (704) 633-7960
Director of Admissions: Edward Clemmons

• **Undergraduates: 422m, 291w**
• **Tuition (1982/83): $2,200**
• **Room & Board: $1,686; Fees: $410**
• **Degrees offered: BA, BS, BSW**
• **Student-faculty ratio: 13 to 1**

A private college affiliated with the African Methodist Episcopal Zion Church, established in 1879. 272-acre small-city campus, 45 miles from Charlotte. Served by rail and bus.

Academic Character SACS accreditation. Semester system, 6-week summer term. Majors offered in accounting, biology, business, chemistry,

education, English, French, history, mathematics, music, office administration, physical education, political science, psychology, secretarial science, social studies, social welfare, and sociology. English proficiency exams required of juniors; GRE required of seniors; 2 courses in Bible required. Independent study. Honors program. Cooperative work/study. Preprofessional programs in dentistry, law, medicine, music, pharmacy, social work. Dual degree program in engineering. Cross-registration with 20 area colleges. Elementary and secondary education certification. Language lab. Hood Theological Seminary. 61,001-volume library.
Financial CEEB CSS and ACT FAS. College scholarships, grants, loans, payment plan; PELL, SEOG, NDSL, CWS. Application deadline June 15. Member United Negro College Fund.
Admissions High school graduation with 16 units required. SAT required. $10 application fee. Rolling admissions. *Early Decision* Program. Admission deferral possible. Transfers accepted. Credit possible for CEEB AP exams. Special admissions for students not meeting requirements.
Student Life Student government. Newspaper, yearbook. Music and drama groups. Debate. Academic, religious, and special interest groups. 8 fraternities and 6 sororities without houses. 20% of men and 30% of women join. No married-student housing. 85% of students live on campus. Liquor, firearms, and hazing prohibited. Class attendance expected. Sunday Vesper Hour and assemblies mandatory. 1 year of phys ed required. 6 intercollegiate sports; intramurals. CIAA, NAIAA. Student body composition: 99% Black, 1% White. 51% from out of state.

[J1] LOUISBURG COLLEGE
501 North Main Street, Louisburg 27549, (919) 496-2521
Director of Admissions: Steven E. Brooks

- **Enrollment: 725**
- **Tuition (1982/83): $2,500**
- **Room & Board: $1,550; Fees: $225**
- **Degrees offered: AA, AS**
- **Mean SAT 350v, 380m**
- **Student-faculty ratio: 15 to 1**

A private college controlled by the North Carolina Conference of the United Methodist Church, established in 1805. 75-acre campus. Served by bus; airport 45 minutes away in Raleigh.
Academic Character SACS accreditation. Semester system, 2 3-week summer terms. 2-year transfer programs offered in business administration, education, general college, general science, liberal arts, medical arts, social work, recreation, and religion. Distributives and 6 hours of religion required. Independent study. Cooperative work/study. Fine arts center. 49,000-volume library.
Financial College scholarships, loans, state grants and loans; PELL, SEOG, NDSL, GSL, CWS, college employment.
Admissions High school graduation with 16 units required. SAT required. $15 application fee. Rolling admissions. Transfers accepted. Credit possible for CEEB CLEP exams. Conditional admission possible.
Student Life Student government. Newspaper, literary magazine, yearbook. Music and drama groups. Athletic, honorary, political, religious, and special interest groups. Single-sex dorms. Liquor prohibited. Class attendance required. Regular chapel, convocation, and assembly participation encouraged. 2 hours of phys ed required. 4 intercollegiate sports for men, 4 for women; intramurals. NJCAA, ETHC. Student body composition: 11% minority.

[1] MARS HILL COLLEGE
Mars Hill 27854, (704) 689-1201
Director of Admissions: Smith Goodrum

- **Undergraduates: 763m, 1,145w**
- **Tuition (1982/83): $3,235**
- **Room & Board: $1,460; Fees: $215 (commuter), $245 (boarder)**
- **Degrees offered: BA, BS, BMus, BSW, BMTP**
- **Mean SAT 422v, 447m**
- **Student-faculty ratio: 15 to 1**

A private college affiliated with the North Carolina Baptist Convention, established in 1856. 150-acre rural campus, 18 miles from Asheville. Served by air and bus in Asheville.
Academic Character SACS and professional accreditation. 4-1-4 system, 2 5-week summer terms. 34 majors offered in the areas of liberal arts & sciences, business, education, fine arts, home economics, medical technology, physical education, secretarial administration, and social work. Appalachian Studies Concentration. Independent study. Internships. Preprofessional programs in dentistry, law, and medicine. 3-1 medical technology program with Bowman Gray. 2-3 nursing programs. Cooperative allied health programs. Cross-registration with UNC Asheville and 5 other area schools. Study abroad. Elementary and secondary education and library science certification. Language lab. 100,000-volume library with microform resources.
Financial CEEB CSS and ACT FAS. College scholarships, discounts for ministers' children and ministerial students, payment plans; PELL, SEOG, NDSL, FISL, SISL, CWS. Application deadlines March 1 (scholarships), May 1 (loans).
Admissions High school graduation with 16 units required. Interview recommended. SAT or ACT required. $15 application fee. Rolling admissions. $150 deposit due on acceptance of admissions offer. *Early Admission* and *Concurrent Enrollment* programs. Transfers accepted. Credit possible for CEEB AP and CLEP exams.
Student Life Student government. Newspaper, literary magazine, yearbook, radio station. Music and drama groups. Christian Student Movement. Academic, honorary, professional, service, and special interest groups. Fraternities and sororities. Students under 21 must live with families or in dorm. Married-student housing. 75% of students live on campus. Liquor, drugs, hazing prohibited. 4 hours of phys ed required. 5 intercollegiate sports for men, 4 for women; intramurals. AIAW, NAIA. Student body composition: 0.1% Asian, 5% Black, 0.2% Hispanic, 1.1% Native American, 93.6% White. 46% from out of state.

[J1] MARTIN COMMUNITY COLLEGE
Kehukee Park Road, Williamston 27892

[J1] MAYLAND TECHNICAL COLLEGE
PO Box 547, Spruce Pine 28777

[J1] MCDOWELL TECHNICAL COLLEGE
Marion 28752

[1] MEREDITH COLLEGE
3800 Hillsborough Street, Raleigh 27607, (919) 833-6461
Director of Admissions: Mary Bland Josey

- **Undergraduates: 1,418w; 1,486 total (including part-time)**
- **Tuition (1982/83): $3,050**
- **Room & Board: $1,350**
- **Degrees offered: BA, BS, BMus**
- **Mean SAT 443v, 473m**
- **Student-faculty ratio: 17 to 1**

A private women's college affiliated with the North Carolina Baptist Convention, established in 1891. 225-acre suburban campus. Served by air, rail, and bus.
Academic Character SACS and professional accreditation. Semester system, 3 3-week summer terms. Majors offered in American civilization, applied music, art, biology, business administration, chemistry, economics, English, French, history, home economics, mathematics, music, music education, non-Western civilizations, political studies, psychology, religion, sociology, and Spanish. Minors offered in most major fields and in 12 others. Distributives and 6 hours of religion required. Individual study. Limited pass/fail. Preprofessional programs in many areas. Cross-registration with 5 area schools. Washington Semester. United Nations Semester. Study abroad. Art, music, early childhood, elementary, and secondary education certification. ROTC, AFROTC at NCS. Language lab. 100,000-volume library.
Financial CEEB CSS. College scholarships, loans, grants, payment plans; PELL, SEOG, NDSL, GSL, CWS. Application deadline February 15.
Admissions High school graduation with 16 units required. Interview desirable. Audition required for music majors. SAT required; ACT accepted. $15 application fee. Rolling admissions after December 1; suggest applying by February 15. $100 deposit due on acceptance of admissions offer. *Early Decision* and *Early Admission* programs. Admission deferral possible. Transfers accepted. Credit possible for CEEB AP, CLEP, and departmental challenge exams.
Student Life Student government. Newspaper, literary magazine, yearbook. Music and drama groups. Academic, honorary, political, religious, service, and special interest groups. Students must live at home or on campus. Limited married-student housing. 86% of students live on campus. Upperclassmen may have cars. Freshman curfew. Honor code. Liquor prohibited. 2 years of phys ed required. 5 intercollegiate sports; intramurals. Dance, gymnastics, and synchronized swimming groups. AIAW. Student body composition: 0.5% Asian, 1.5% Black, 0.4% Hispanic, 97% White, 0.6% Other. 15% from out of state.

[1] METHODIST COLLEGE
Raleigh Road, Fayetteville 28301, (919) 488-7110
Director of Admissions: Tommy Dent

- **Undergraduates: 393m, 351w**
- **Tuition (1982/83): $3,140**
- **Room & Board: $1,970; Fees: $140**
- **Degrees offered: BA, BS, BAS, AA**
- **Student-faculty ratio: 16 to 1**

A private college affiliated with the United Methodist Church, established in 1956. 600-acre rural campus, 100 miles east of Charlotte. Served by air, rail, and bus.
Academic Character SACS accreditation. Semester system, summer term. Majors offered in art, biology, business, chemistry, education, English, French, history, mathematics, music, physical education, political science, psychology, religion, science, social work, sociology, and Spanish. Minors required and offered in most major fields and in 6 others. Distributive requirements. Honors program. Internships. Preprofessional programs in 12 disciplines. 3-2 engineering programs with NCS, Georgia Tech, U of Southern California. Elementary and secondary education certification. ROTC. Language lab. 65,840-volume library.
Financial CEEB CSS. College scholarships, grants, loans, tuition reduction for ministerial students and dependents of ministers, payment plans; PELL, SEOG, NDSL, GSL, FISL, CWS. Recommended application deadline April 1.
Admissions High school graduation with 16 units required. GED accepted. SAT or ACT required. $15 application fee. Rolling admissions; suggest applying in October-November. $50 deposit due on acceptance of admissions offer. *Early Admission* Program. Admission deferral possible. Transfers accepted. Credit possible for CEEB AP and CLEP exams.
Student Life Student government. Newspaper, literary magazine, yearbook. Drama group. Academic, honorary, religious, and special interest groups. Fraternities and sororities. Students must live at home or on campus. Married-student housing. 45% of students live on campus. Liquor and hazing prohibited. Attendance in class and at assemblies required. 2 hours of phys ed required. 7 intercollegiate sports for men, 5 for women; intramurals. AIAW,

NCAA, NCAIAW, DIAC. Student body composition: 18% Black, 1% Hispanic, 76% White, 5% Other. 13% from out of state.

[J1] MITCHELL COMMUNITY COLLEGE
Statesville 28677

[J1] MONTGOMERY TECHNICAL INSTITUTE
PO Drawer 487, Troy 27371

[J1] MONTREAT-ANDERSON COLLEGE
Montreat 28757, (704) 669-8011, ext. 31
Director of Admissions: Charles A. Lance

- **Enrollment: 400 men & women**
- **Tuition (1982/83): $2,384**
- **Room & Board: $2,030; Fees: $198**
- **Degrees offered: AA, AS**
- **Student-faculty ratio: 16 to 1**

A private college controlled by the Presbyterian Church, established in 1916. Rural campus, 15 miles east of Asheville.
Academic Character SACS accreditation. Semester system, summer term. 2-year transfer programs offered in agriculture, Bible, biology, business, Christian education, communications, drama, education, English, environmental studies, foreign languages, forestry, history, journalism, medical technology, music, nursing, philosophy, public administration, physical education, speech therapy, and youth ministry. Distributives and 6 hours of Bible required. Preprofessional programs in dentistry, law, medicine, ministry, optometry, veterinary medicine. Mountain Retreat Association. Historical Foundation of the Presbyterian Church. 45,000-volume library.
Financial ACT FAS. College scholarships, state scholarships, grants, and loans; PELL, SEOG, NDSL, GSL, CWS.
Admissions High school graduation required. GED accepted. SAT or ACT required. $15 application fee. Rolling admissions. $100 ($50 for day students) deposit due on acceptance of admissions offer. *Early Admission* and *Concurrent Enrollment* programs. Transfers accepted. Credit possible for CEEB AP, CLEP, ACT PEP, and departmental proficiency exams.
Student Life Student government. Newspaper, yearbook. Music and drama groups. Special interest groups. Single-sex dorms. Chapel and convocation attendance mandatory. 2 hours of phys ed required. 4 intercollegiate sports for men, 3 for women.

[J1] MOUNT OLIVE COLLEGE
Mount Olive 28365, (919) 658-2502
Director of Admissions: Nancy Sampsell

- **Enrollment: 400 men & women**
- **Tuition (1982/83): $2,250**
- **Room & Board: $1,600**
- **Degrees offered: AA, AS**
- **Student-faculty ratio: 10 to 1**

A private college controlled by the North Carolina Convention of Original Free Will Baptists, established in 1951. 100-acre small-town campus, 60 miles southeast of Raleigh.
Academic Character SACS accreditation. Semester system, 2- and 4-week summer terms. 2-year transfer programs offered in the areas of agriculture, art, biology, business, chemistry, economics, education, fine arts, geography, history, journalism, mathematics, music, natural science, nursing, physical education, physical science, political science, psychology, recreation, religion, secretarial science, sociology, and Spanish. Distributives and 6 hours of religion required. Independent study. Cooperative work/study. Preprofessional programs in commercial art, dentistry, engineering, law, medicine, pharmacy, theology. Paul Palmer Institute of Christian Study. 29,000-volume library.
Financial College scholarships, ministerial grants, church-member grants, state scholarships, grants, loans; PELL, SEOG, NDSL, GSL, CWS.
Admissions High school graduation with 10 units required. GED accepted. Interview encouraged. SAT recommended. $10 application fee. Rolling admissions. $50 tuition and $25 room deposits due on acceptance of admissions offer. *Early Admission* and *Concurrent Enrollment* programs. Transfers accepted. Credit possible for CEEB AP, CLEP, and departmental exams.
Student Life Student government. Yearbook. Religious and special interest groups. Students must live at home or on campus. Single-sex dorms. Class attendance expected. Weekly chapel services mandatory. Intercollegiate sports.

[J1] NASH TECHNICAL COLLEGE
Rocky Mount 27801

[1] NORTH CAROLINA, UNIVERSITY OF, AT CHAPEL HILL
Chapel Hill 27514, (919) 966-3621
Director of Undergraduate Admissions: Richard Cashwell

- **Undergraduates: 6,096m, 7,999w; 21,575 total (including graduates)**
- **Tuition (1982/83): $436 (in-state), $2,260 (out-of-state)**
- **Room & Board: $2,050 (average); Fees: $257**
- **Degrees offered: AB, BS, BAL, BFA, BMus, BSBA, BAEd, BMus Ed, BSSciTeach, BAJ, BSN, BSPharm**
- **Mean SAT 510v, 552m**
- **Student-faculty ratio: 14 to 1**

A public university established in 1789. 622-acre small-city campus, 30 miles from Raleigh. Served by air, rail, and bus.
Academic Character SACS and professional accreditation. Semester system, 2 6-week summer terms. 61 majors offered by the College of Arts & Sciences, 1 by the School of Business Administration, 4 by the School of Education, 3 by the School of Journalism, 3 by the School of Medicine, 1 by the School of Nursing, 1 by the School of Pharmacy, 5 by the School of Public Health, and 1 by the Division of Health Affairs. Courses in 9 additional areas, including Arabic, Celtic, Chinese, Hebrew, and Sanskrit. Self-designed majors. Freshmen and sophomores enroll in General College. Graduate degrees granted. Independent study. Honors programs. Phi Beta Kappa. Pass/fail, internships. Many study abroad programs. Elementary and secondary education certification. AFROTC, NROTC. Institutes of Latin American Studies, Fisheries Research, Natural Science, Anthropology, Folk Music. Communications center. Language lab. 3,000,000-volume library with microform resources.
Financial CEEB CSS and ACT FAS. University scholarships, grants, loans, state grants; PELL, SEOG, NDSL, GSL, CWS, departmental work. Application deadline March 1.
Admissions High school graduation with 16 units required. Auditions required for performance majors in drama and music. SAT required; ACH or AP exams recommended for placement. $15 application fee. Rolling admissions. Room deposit due with housing application. Transfers accepted. Credit possible for CEEB AP and challenge exams. Special admissions possible for disadvantaged.
Student Life Student government. Newspaper, magazines, radio station. Music, dance, drama, and film groups. Debate. Numerous academic, honorary, political, religious, social, service, and special interest groups. 24 fraternities and 4 sororities, all with houses. 22% of men and 17% of women join. Freshmen must live at home or on campus. Coed and single-sex dorms. Academic floors. Limited married-student housing. 45% of students live on campus. Freshmen may not have cars on campus; upperclassmen with C average may have cars. Honor Code. Campus Code. 1 year of phys ed required. Intercollegiate sports; several intramurals. AIAW. Student body composition: 8.4% Black, 90% White, 1.6% Other. 15% from out of state.

■[1] NORTH CAROLINA, UNIVERSITY OF, AT ASHEVILLE
Asheville 28814, (704) 258-6481
Director of Admissions: Kendall Rice

- **Undergraduates: 979m, 1,287w**
- **Tuition (1982/83): $628 (in-state), $2,210 (out-of-state)**
- **Room & Board: $1,670**
- **Degrees offered: BA, BS**
- **Student-faculty ratio: 16 to 1**

A public university established in 1927. 200-acre urban campus. Served by air and bus.
Academic Character SACS accreditation. Semester system, 2 5½-week summer terms. Majors offered in accounting, art, biology, chemistry, classics, communications, drama, economics, environmental studies, French, German, history, literature, management, mathematics, meteorology, philosophy, physics, political science, psychology, social science, sociology, and Spanish. Self-designed majors. Distributive requirements. Independent study. Honors program. Internships. Preprofessional programs in dentistry, law, medicine, pharmacy. Pre-engineering, chemistry, forestry, and textile chemistry with NCS Raleigh. Nursing program with WCU. Cross-registration with Mars Hill. Study abroad. Elementary, secondary, and special education certification. Computer center. Botanical gardens, theatre. Southern Highlands Research Center. 125,000-volume library with microform resources.
Financial CEEB CSS. University scholarships, grants, loans, state grants; PELL, SEOG, MPG, NDSL, GSL, FISL, CWS. Grants-in-aid application deadline March 1.
Admissions High school graduation with 13 units required. SAT required. $15 application fee. Rolling admissions. *Early Decision* and *Early Admission* programs. Admission deferral possible. Transfers accepted. Credit possible for CEEB AP, CLEP, and departmental exams. Developmental studies program for students not normally admissible.
Student Life Student government. Newspaper, literary magazine, yearbook. Theatre. Black Student Association. Athletic, academic, honorary, political, religious, service, and special interest groups. 5 fraternities and 3 sororities without houses. 13% of men and 1% of women join. Coed and single-sex dorms. No married-student housing. 10% of students live on campus. Class attendance expected. 4 semesters of phys ed required. 3 intercollegiate sports for men, 2 for women; intramurals. AIAW, NAIA. Student body composition: 1% Asian, 4% Black, 1% Hispanic, 0.1% Native American, 93.9% White. 5% from out of state.

■[1] NORTH CAROLINA, UNIVERSITY OF, AT CHARLOTTE
UNCC Station, Charlotte 28223, (704) 597-2211
Director of Admissions: Kathi M. Baucom

- **Undergraduates: 3,505m, 3,039w; 9,574 total (including graduates)**
- **Tuition (1983/84): $626 (in-state), $2,414 (out-of-state)**
- **Room & Board: $1,744-$2,160**
- **Degrees offered: BA, BS, BArch, BCreative Arts, BET, BSE, BSN**
- **Mean SAT 917**
- **Student-faculty ratio: 16 to 1**

A public university established in 1946. 1,000-acre suburban campus. Served by bus.
Academic Character SACS and professional accreditation. Semester system, 3-week, 2 6-week, and 8-week summer terms. 42 majors offered by the colleges of Arts & Sciences, Business Administration, Engineering, Human Development & Learning, and Nursing. Self-designed majors. Distributive requirements. Graduate degrees granted. Independent study. Honors program. Cooperative work/study, limited pass/fail, credit by exam, internships. Preprofessional programs in chemical engineering, dentistry,

forestry, journalism, law, medical technology, medicine, optometry, pharmacy, social work, veterinary medicine. Study abroad. Elementary and secondary education certification. ROTC, AFROTC. Computer center. Language lab. Ecological reserve. 313,792-volume with microform resources.
Financial CEEB CSS and ACT FAS. University scholarships, grants, loans, state grants and loans, payment plan; PELL, SEOG, NDSL, FISL, CWS. Priority application deadline April 15.
Admissions High school graduation with 16 units required. Interview required of architecture and creative arts students; portfolio or audition required. SAT or ACT required. $15 application fee. Rolling admissions. $100 deposit due on acceptance of admissions offer. *Early Admission* and *Credit-in-Escrow* programs. Transfers accepted. Credit possible for CEEB AP exams.
Student Life Student government. Newspaper, literary magazine, yearbook, radio and TV studios. Music groups. Black Student Union. Academic, honorary, political, religious, service, and special interest groups. 11 fraternities and 5 sororities, 2 with houses. Coed and single-sex dorms. No married-student housing. 29% of students live on campus. Drugs and firearms prohibited. Class attendance required. 6 intercollegiate sports for men, 4 for women; intramurals. AIAW, NCAA, SBC. Student body composition: 0.9% Asian, 8% Black, 0.6% Hispanic, 0.1% Native American, 87.9% White, 2.5% Other. 9% from out of state.

■[1] NORTH CAROLINA, UNIVERSITY OF, AT GREENSBORO
Greensboro 27412, (919) 379-5243
Director of Admissions: Robert Hites

- **Undergraduates: 1,766m, 4,461w; 10,390 total (including graduates)**
- **Tuition (1982/83): $436 (in-state), $2,260 (out-of-state)**
- **Room & Board: $1,640-$1,750; Fees: $308**
- **Degrees offered: BA, BS, BFA, BMus, BSN, BSHE, BSMT**
- **Mean SAT 469v, 481m**
- **Student-faculty ratio: 15 to 1**

A public university established in 1892, became coed in 1963. 141-acre campus. Served by air, rail, and bus.
Academic Character SACS and professional accreditation. Semester system, 12-week summer term. 37 majors offered by the College of Arts & Sciences, 6 by the School of Business & Economics, 2 by the School of Education, 5 by the School of Health, Physical Education, & Recreation, 5 by the School of Home Economics, 6 by the School of Music, and 1 by the School of Nursing. Minors in most major fields and in 6 others. Self-designed majors. Distributive requirements. Honors program. Phi Beta Kappa. Internships, credit by exam. Preprofessional programs in dentistry, law, medicine, pharmacy, physical therapy. 3-1 or 5-year medical technology program. 2-year engineering transfer program. Cross-registration with 5 area colleges. Study abroad. Elementary and secondary education certification. ROTC, AFROTC at NC A&T. Art gallery. Computer center. Language lab. Observatory. 1,250,000-volume library with microform resources.
Financial CEEB CSS and ACT FAS. University scholarships, grants, loans, state grants; PELL, SEOG, NDSL, GSL, CWS. Application deadline March 1.
Admissions High school graduation with 15 units required. Interview required for interior design students. Audition required of music and drama students. SAT or ACT required; 3 ACH recommended. $15 application fee. Rolling admissions. $150 room deposit due on acceptance of admissions offer. *Early Decision, Concurrent Enrollment, Early Admission* programs. Transfers accepted. Credit possible for CEEB AP and CLEP exams. Conditional admission possible for academically deficient students.
Student Life Student government. Newspaper, literary magazine, yearbook, radio and TV stations. Music, dance, opera, and drama groups. Debate. Academic, honorary, religious, service, and special interest groups. Fraternities and sororities. Coed and single-sex dorms. International house. Residential college for 110 freshmen. No married-student housing. 51% of students live on campus. Dorm residents may not have cars on campus. 4 intercollegiate sports for men, 3 for women; intramurals. NCAA, DIAC. Student body composition: 0.6% Asian, 10% Black, 1.5% Foreign, 0.4% Hispanic, 0.2% Native American, 87.3% White. 11% from out of state.

■[1] NORTH CAROLINA, UNIVERSITY OF, AT WILMINGTON
PO Box 3725, 601 South College Road, Wilmington 28406, (919) 791-4330
Dean of Admissions: Ralph H. Parker

- **Undergraduates: 2,002m, 2,058w; 5,106 total (including graduates)**
- **Tuition (1982/83): $645 (in-state), $2,227 (out-of-state)**
- **Room & Board: $1,945-$2,145**
- **Degrees offered: BA, BS**
- **Student-faculty ratio: 17 to 1**

A public university established in 1947. 610-acre suburban campus. Served by air and bus.
Academic Character SACS accreditation. Semester system, 2 5½-week summer terms. 33 majors offered by the College of Arts & Sciences, the School of Business Administration, and the School of Education. Distributive requirements. Graduate degrees granted. Independent study. Honors program. Internships. Preprofessional programs in dentistry, engineering, forestry, law, medicine, pharmacy, veterinary medicine. Associate nursing program. 2-2 and 3-2 engineering programs. Marine biology program. Near Eastern Archaeology Seminar. Elementary, secondary, and special education certification. ROTC. Art gallery. Computer center. Wildflower preserve. 210,000-volume library with microform resources.
Financial CEEB CSS and ACT FAS. University scholarships, grants, loans, state loans; PELL, SEOG, NSS, NDSL, FISL, CWS, college work program. Application deadline March 15.
Admissions High school graduation with 11 units required. Interview recommended. SAT required. $15 application fee. Rolling admissions. $50 room deposit due on acceptance of admissions offer. *Concurrent Enrollment* Program. Transfers accepted. Credit possible for CEEB AP, CLEP, and departmental exams.
Student Life Student government. Newspaper, literary magazine, marine science journal, yearbook. Music and theatre groups. Black Student Union. Academic, honorary, religious, service, and special interest groups. 8 fraternities and 4 sororities. 5% of men and 2% of women join. Coed and single-sex dorms. No married-student housing. 27% of students live on campus. 2 semesters of phys ed required. 7 intercollegiate sports for men, 7 for women; intramurals. AIAW, NCAA. Student body composition: 0.4% Asian, 6.3% Black, 0.4% Hispanic, 0.2% Native American, 92.4% White, 0.3% Other. 7% from out of state.

■[1] NORTH CAROLINA STATE UNIVERSITY
Raleigh 27650, (919) 737-2434
Director of Admissions: Anna P. Keller

- **Undergraduates: 9,864m, 4,661w; 22,468 total (including graduates)**
- **Tuition (1982/83): $436 (in-state), $2,260 (out-of-state)**
- **Room & Board: $1,990; Fees: $234**
- **Degrees offered: BA, BS, BE, BSW**
- **Mean SAT 466v, 538m**
- **Student-faculty ratio: 14 to 1**

A public university established in 1889. Urban campus. Served by air, rail, and bus.
Academic Character SACS and professional accreditation. Semester system, 2 5-week summer terms. 16 majors offered by the School of Agricultural & Life Sciences, 3 by the School of Design, 9 by the School of Education, 11 by the School of Engineering, 5 by the School of Forest Resources, 13 by the School of Humanities & Social Sciences, 7 by the School of Physical & Mathematical Sciences, and 4 by the School of Textiles. Self-designed majors. Distributive requirements. Graduate degrees granted. Independent study. Honors programs. Cooperative work/study, limited pass/fail, internships. 2-2 engineering program with UNC Asheville; dual degree engineering program with Shaw. Cross-registration with 4 area schools. National and international student exchange program. International program for agriculture students. Secondary and middle grades education certification. ROTC, AFROTC; NROTC at UNC Chapel Hill. 2-year Agricultural Institute. Computer center. Language labs. Biological Field Lab. Water Resources Research Institute. Electron microscope center. 1,000,000-volume library with microform resources.
Financial CEEB CSS. University scholarships, loans, state grants; PELL, SEOG, MIG, NDSL, GSL, CWS, university employment. Scholarship application deadline February 1.
Admissions High school graduation with 11 units required. Interview required for School of Design. SAT or ACT required. $15 application fee. Rolling admissions. Room deposit required. *Early Admission* and *Early Decision* programs. Admission deferral possible. Transfers accepted. Credit possible for CEEB AP and CLEP exams. Special admissions for disadvantaged.
Student Life Student government. Newspaper, magazines, yearbook, radio and TV stations. Music and drama groups. Academic, honorary, professional, and technical groups. 22 fraternities, 9 with houses; 5 sororities, 2 with houses. 12% of men and 5% of women join. Coed and single-sex dorms. Special interest housing. Married-student housing. Living-learning program for freshmen. Transition residence for 60 freshmen. 30% of students live on campus. Boarding freshmen may not have cars. Phys ed required of freshmen and sophomores. 14 intercollegiate sports for men, 8 for women; intramurals. AIAW, NCAA, ACC. Student body composition: 1.6% Asian, 7.4% Black, 3.7% Foreign, 0.7% Hispanic, 0.3% Native American, 86.3% White. 14% from out of state.

[1] NORTH CAROLINA AGRICULTURAL AND TECHNICAL STATE UNIVERSITY
Greensboro 27411, (919) 379-7946
Director of Admissions: Clenton Blount

- **Undergraduates: 3,125m, 2,325w**
- **Tuition (1982/83): $819 (in-state), $2,607 (out-of-state)**
- **Room & Board: $1,774**
- **Degrees offered: AB, BS, BSN**
- **Student-faculty ratio: 16 to 1**

A public university established in 1891. Urban campus. Served by air and bus.
Academic Character SACS and professional accreditation. Semester system, 12-week summer term. 11 majors offered by the School of Agriculture, 29 by the School of Arts & Sciences, 6 by the School of Business, 7 by the School of Education, 4 by the School of Engineering, and 1 by the School of Nursing. Graduate degrees granted. Secondary education certification. ROTC, AFROTC. 300,000-volume library.
Financial CEEB CSS and ACT FAS. University scholarships, grants, loans; PELL, SEOG, NDSL, FISL, NSL, CWS. Scholarship application deadline May 15.
Admissions High school graduation with 16 units required. GED accepted. Interview recommended. SAT required. $10 application fee. Rolling admissions. $50 room deposit due on acceptance of admissions offer. *Early Admission* and *Concurrent Enrollment* programs. Admission deferral possible. Transfers accepted. Credit possible for CEEB AP, CLEP, and university exams.
Student Life Student government. Newspaper, yearbook. Music and drama groups. Academic and religious groups. 10 fraternities and 11 sororities. 15% of men and 12% of women join. Single-sex dorms. No married-student housing. 59% of students live on campus. 2 semesters of phys ed required. 8 intercollegiate sports; intramurals. Student body composition: 92.8% Black, 0.1% Hispanic, 3.1% White. 20% from out of state.

[1] NORTH CAROLINA CENTRAL UNIVERSITY
Durham 27707, (919) 683-6298
Director of Admissions: Mrs. Nancy R. Rowland

- **Enrollment: 5,000 (including graduates)**
- **Tuition (1982/83): $685 (in-state), $2,473 (out-of-state)**
- **Room & Board: $1,796; Fees: $125**
- **Degrees offered: BA, BS, BBA, BMus ,BSN**
- **Student-faculty ratio: 16 to 1**

A public university established in 1910. 110-acre urban campus. Served by air, rail, and bus.
Academic Character SACS and professional accreditation. Semester system, 2 6-week summer terms. Majors offered in the areas of commerce, home economics, liberal arts, and nursing. Distributive requirements. Graduate degrees granted. Honors program. Cooperative work/study, internships. 3-2 engineering program. Cross-registration with U Wisconsin. Elementary, secondary, and special education certification. AFROTC with Duke. Computer center. Museum.
Financial ACT FAS. University scholarships, PELL, SEOG, CWS. Application deadline March 1.
Admissions High school graduation with 16 units recommended. GED accepted. SAT or ACT required. $15 application fee. Rolling admissions. $50 room deposit due on acceptance of admissions offer. Transfers accepted. Credit possible for CEEB AP and CLEP exams. Admission deferral possible. Academic Skills Area for underprepared students.
Student Life Student government. Newspaper, literary magazine, yearbook. Music and drama groups. 11 fraternities, 1 with house; 11 sororities without houses. Single-sex dorms. 70% of students live on campus. 2 semesters of health or 2 semesters of phys ed and 1 semester of health required. 6 intercollegiate sports for men, 5 for women; intramurals. NAIA, CIAA. Student body composition: 90% Black, 8% White, 2% Other. 16% from out of state.

[1] NORTH CAROLINA SCHOOL OF THE ARTS
200 Waughtown Street, Winston-Salem 27117, (919) 784-7170
Director of Admissions: Dirk Dawson

- **Undergraduates: 281m, 224w**
- **Tuition (1982/83): $666 (in-state), $2,190 (out-of-state)**
- **Room & Board: $1,692; Basic Fees: $324**
- **Degrees offered: BMus, BFA**
- **Mean SAT 434v, 452m**
- **Student-faculty ratio: 7 to 1**

A public school established in 1965, became part of the University of North Carolina system in 1971. Urban campus.
Academic Character SACS accreditation. Trimester system, 5-week summer term. High school and college-level courses offered in dance, design & production, drama, music, visual arts, and general studies. Requirements for each discipline. Graduate degrees granted. Dance theatre. Television, film, and recording studios. Artist-in-residence program. League of Professional Theatre Training Programs. Shakespeare Festival. Chamber orchestra. Opera theatre. 65,000-volume library with 26,000 recordings and 25,500 scores.
Financial NCSA scholarships, awards; PELL, MPG, NDSL, GSL, FISL, CWS. Preferred application deadline March 1.
Admissions High school graduation required. Auditions and portfolios required; audition dates sent upon request. SAT required. $15 audition fee. Rolling admissions. $100 deposit due on acceptance of admissions offer. Transfers accepted. Credit possible for CEEB AP and CLEP exams.
Student Life More than 350 performances scheduled each year. School-arranged trips to off-campus events. Single full-time students required to live on campus. Coed dorms. Attendance in class and at rehearsals and performances required. Recreational facilities. Student body composition: 10% minority.

[1] NORTH CAROLINA WESLEYAN COLLEGE
Rocky Mount 27801, (919) 442-7121
Director of Admissions: R. Richard Davis

- **Undergraduates: 482m, 435w**
- **Tuition (1982/83): $3,500**
- **Room & Board: $4,220; Fees: $110**
- **Degrees offered: BA, BS**
- **Mean SAT 390v, 470m**
- **Student-faculty ratio: 18 to 1**

A private college affiliated with the United Methodist Church, established in 1958. 200-acre suburban campus.
Academic Character SACS accreditation. Semester system, 2 5-week summer terms, spring interim. Majors offered in behavioral studies, biology business administration, chemistry, criminal justice, economics, education, English, environmental science, fish & wildlife management, mathematics, music, philosophy-religion, physical education, politics, psychology, religion, sociology & anthropology, and theatre. Distributives and 6 hours of religion-philosophy required. Independent study. Contract learning. Cooperative work/study, internships, credit by exam. Elementary and secondary education certification. Theatre. Art gallery. Music library. 58,000-volume library with microform resources.
Financial CEEB CSS. College scholarships, grants, loans, ministers' children grants, state grants and loans; PELL, SEOG, NDSL, GSL, CWS. Application deadline April 1.
Admissions High school graduation with 16 units recommended. GED accepted. SAT or ACT required. $15 application fee. Rolling admissions. $100 deposit due on acceptance of admissions offer. *Early Admission* Program. Admission deferral possible. Transfers accepted. Advanced placement possible.
Student Life Student government. Newspaper, literary magazine, yearbook. Music and drama groups. Black Student Alliance. Academic, honorary, professional, political, religious, social, and special interest groups. Single-sex dorms. Class and convocation attendance required. 2 hours of phys ed required. 5 intercollegiate sports for men, 3 for women; intramurals. NCAA, DIAC. Student body composition: 22% minority.

[J1] PAMLICO TECHNICAL COLLEGE
Grantsboro 28529

[J1] PEACE COLLEGE
Raleigh 27604, (919) 832-2881
Director of Admissions: Cynthia Wyatt

- **Undergraduates: 501w**
- **Expenses: $1,750 (in-state day students), $3,710-$3,820 (in-state resident students), $4,470 (out-of-state)**
- **Degrees offered: AA, AFAM, ASB**
- **Mean SAT 865**
- **Student-faculty ratio: 15 to 1**

A private women's college affiliated with the Presbyterian Church, established in 1857. 15-acre downtown campus. Served by air, rail, and bus.
Academic Character SACS accreditation. Semester system. 2-year transfer programs offered in art, business, communications, drama, education, history, home economics, languages/literature, mathematics, philosophy, physical education, religion, sciences, and social sciences. Distributives and 6 hours of religion required. Special Studies program. Preprofessional programs in dentistry, medical technology, medicine, nursing, pharmacy. Cross-registration with Cooperating Raleigh Colleges. Study abroad.
Financial CEEB CSS. College scholarships, grants, loans, discounts for ministers' children and simultaneously-enrolled siblings, state grants and loans; PELL, SEOG, NDSL, GSL.
Admissions High school graduation with 13 units recommended. Interview recommended. SAT required. $15 application fee. Rolling admissions. $100 room deposit due on acceptance of admissions offer. Transfers accepted. Credit possible for CEEB AP exams.
Student Life Student government. Newspaper, literary magazine, yearbook. Music and drama groups. Academic, religious, and special interest groups. Students must live with family or on campus. Honor code. Class attendance required. 3 hours of phys ed required. Intercollegiate basketball and tennis.

[1] PEMBROKE STATE UNIVERSITY
Pembroke 28372, (919) 521-4214
Director of Admissions: Warren Baker

- **Undergraduates: 925m, 1,262w**
- **Tuition (1982/83): $582 (in-state), $2,164 (out-of-state)**
- **Room & Board: $1,220-$1,490**
- **Degrees offered: BA, BS, BSAS**
- **Mean SAT 810**
- **Student-faculty ratio: 16 to 1**

A public university established in 1887. 90-acre small-town campus, 30 miles from Fayetteville. Served by bus; airport in Fayetteville.
Academic Character SACS and professional accreditation. Semester system, 2 5-week summer terms. 23 majors offered in the areas of art, biology, business, communication, chemistry, economics, education, history, mathematics, music, philosophy/religion, physical education, political science, psychology, and sociology. Minors in 16 areas, including American Indian studies. Distributive requirements. Independent study. Honors program. Experiential Learning Program. Cooperative work/study, internships. Preprofessional programs in dentistry, law, medical technology, medicine, veterinary science. 3-4 program in podiatric medicine with Pennsylvania College. Elementary, secondary, and special education certification. ROTC, AFROTC. 186,000-volume library.
Financial CEEB CSS and ACT FAS. University scholarships, grants, loans; PELL, SEOG, NDSL, FISL, CWS, university self-help program. Application deadline April 15.
Admissions High school graduation with 16 units recommended. GED accepted. Interview recommended. SAT or ACT required; SAT preferred. $15 application fee. Rolling admissions. $25 room deposit due on acceptance of admissions offer. Transfers accepted. Credit possible for CEEB AP and CLEP exams. Opportunity Program for students not normally admissible.
Student Life Student government. Newspaper, literary magazine, yearbook. Music and drama groups. Art shows. American Indian Student Association. Black Student Organization. Honorary, religious, and special interest groups. 5 fraternities, 4 with chapter houses; 3 sororities without houses. 3% of men and women join. Freshmen and sophomores live at home or on campus. 31% of students live on campus. 8 intercollegiate sports for men, 4 for women; intramurals. NAIA, NCAA, AIAW. Student body composition: 0.3% Asian, 12% Black, 0.5% Hispanic, 24% Native American, 62% White, 1.2% Other. 4% from out of state.

[1] PFEIFFER COLLEGE
Misenheimer 28109, (704) 463-7343
Director of Admissions: Kenneth D. Sigler

- **Undergraduates: 368m, 329w**
- **Tuition (1982/83): $3,450**
- **Room & Board: $1,715**
- **Degrees offered: AB, BS**
- **Student-faculty ratio: 13 to 1**

A private college affiliated with the United Methodist Church, established in 1885. Rural campus, 40 miles from Charlotte. Served by bus. Airport in Charlotte; train station 18 miles away in Salisbury.
Academic Character SACS and professional accreditation. Semester system, 2 4½-week summer terms. 4 majors offered in business, 6 in education & physical education, 3 in fine arts, 8 in humanities, 7 in natural sciences &

mathematics, and 10 in social sciences. Minors offered. Distributives, English competency, and GRE required. Self-paced program. Independent study. Honors program. Internships. Preprofessional programs in diplomacy, government, law, medical technology, ministry, missions, social work. 2-3 nursing program with Emory. 3-3 nursing program with Case. 3-2 engineering programs with Georgia Tech and Auburn. Study-travel tours and study abroad. Elementary and secondary education certification. ROTC at Davidson. Computer center. Language lab. 93,000-volume library.
Financial CEEB CSS. College scholarships, Methodist grants and loans, discounts for siblings, payment plans; PELL, SEOG, NDSL, GSL, CWS. Application deadline May 1.
Admissions High school graduation with 12 units required; college prep program recommended. SAT or ACT required. $15 application fee. Rolling admissions. $100 deposit due on acceptance of admissions offer. *Early Admission* and *Concurrent Enrollment* programs. Admission deferral possible. Transfers accepted. Credit possible for CEEB AP and CLEP exams.
Student Life Student government. Newspaper, yearbook, radio station. Music and drama groups. Debate. Academic, political, religious, service, and special interest groups. Students must live at home or on campus. Single-sex dorms. Married-student housing. 72% of students live on campus. Liquor, drugs, firearms, gambling, profanity prohibited. Administrative convocations and attendance at one cultural event per week required. 4 credits of phys ed required. 7 intercollegiate sports for men, 5 for women; several intramurals. AIAW, CIAC. Student body composition: 0.1% Asian, 8% Black, 0.8% Hispanic, 89% White, 2.1% Other. 23% from out of state.

[P] PIEDMONT BIBLE COLLEGE
716 Franklin Street, Winston-Salem 27101

[J1] PIEDMONT TECHNICAL COLLEGE
PO Box 1197, Roxboro 27573

[J1] PITT COMMUNITY COLLEGE
PO Drawer 7007, Greenville 27834

[1] QUEENS COLLEGE
1900 Selwyn Avenue, Charlotte 28274, (704) 332-7121
Director of Admissions: Eugenia H. Burton

- **Enrollment: 1,000w**
- **Expenses: $5,460**
- **Board: $1,020-$1,100**
- **Degrees offered: BA, BS, BSN, BMus, BGS**
- **Mean SAT 900**
- **Student-faculty ratio: 10 to 1**

A private women's college affiliated with the Presbyterian Church, established in 1857. Suburban campus.
Academic Character SACS and professional accreditation. 4-1-4 system. 32 majors offered in the areas of art, business, computer science, education, liberal arts, mathematics, museums, music, science, and social sciences. Self-designed majors. Minors offered. Distributive requirements. MBA granted. Independent study. Internships, limited pass/fail. Preprofessional programs in dentistry, law, medicine, physical therapy. 4½-year music therapy program. Cooperative nursing program with Presbyterian Hospital. 3-2 BA/MA program with Presbyterian School of Christian Education. Junior-year exchange with Davidson. Cross-registration with 11 area schools. Washington Semester. Study abroad. Early childhood, elementary, and secondary education certification. Fine Arts Center. 88,000-volume library with microform resources.
Financial CEEB CSS. College scholarships, discounts for ministers' dependants, state grants and loans, payment plans; PELL, SEOG, NDSL, GSL, PLUS, CWS.
Admissions High school graduation with 11 units recommended. Interview recommended. SAT or ACT required. $15 application fee. Rolling admissions. $150 deposit ($50 for day students) due on acceptance of admissions offer. *Early Admission* Program. Transfers accepted. Credit possible for CEEB AP and CLEP exams.
Student Life Student government. Newspaper, literary magazine, yearbook. Honorary and special interest groups. 4 sororities. Single students live with families or on campus. Honor code. Class attendance expected. Attendance at twice-yearly convocations expected. 2 hours of phys ed required. 2 intercollegiate sports; intramurals.

[J1] RANDOLPH TECHNICAL INSTITUTE
PO Box 1009, Asheboro 27203

[J1] RICHMOND TECHNICAL INSTITUTE
Rockingham 28379

[P] ROANOKE BIBLE COLLEGE
Elizabeth City 27909

[J1] ROANOKE-CHOWAN TECHNICAL COLLEGE
Ahoskie 27910

[J1] ROBESON TECHNICAL INSTITUTE
Lumberton 28358

[J1] ROCKINGHAM COMMUNITY COLLEGE
Wentworth 27375

[J1] ROWAN TECHNICAL COLLEGE
I-85 at Klumac Road, Salisbury 28144

[J2] RUTLEDGE COLLEGE OF CHARLOTTE
610 East Morehead Street, Charlotte 28202
Formerly Hamilton College

[J2] RUTLEDGE COLLEGE OF GREENSBORO
PO Box 21266, 617 West Market Street, Greensboro 27420
Formerly Jefferson College

[J2] RUTLEDGE COLLEGE OF FAYETTEVILLE
603 Country Club Drive, Fayetteville 28301
Formerly Lafayette College

[J2] RUTLEDGE COLLEGE OF DURHAM
410 West Chapel Hill Street, Durham 27701

[J2] RUTLEDGE COLLEGE OF WINSTON-SALEM
820 West Fourth Street, Winston-Salem 27102
Formerly Winsalm College

[1] SACRED HEART COLLEGE
Belmont 28012, (704) 825-5146

- **Undergraduates: 91m, 266w; 405 total (including part-time)**
- **Expenses (1980/81): $3,760 (boarders), $2,360 (commuters)**
- **Degrees offered: BA, BS, AA**
- **Mean ACT 18; mean SAT 800 composite**
- **Student-faculty ratio: 15 to 1**

A private Roman Catholic college primarily for women.
Academic Character SACS accreditation. Semester system, summer term. Programs offered in psychology, early childhood education, intermediate education, social work, art, biology, special education, art education, accounting, chemistry, criminal justice, economics & business, English, environmental science, general studies, history, management, medical technology, political science, recreation, and sociology. AA offered in church music. English as a second language program for foreign students.
Financial Strong financial aid program with over 80% of students receiving assistance.
Admissions High school graduation with a minimum C- average required. No test score cutoff; high school record most important factor in admissions decision.

[1] ST. ANDREWS PRESBYTERIAN COLLEGE
Laurinberg 28352, (919) 276-3652
Director of Admissions: Peggy Anderson

- **Undergraduates: 354m, 351w**
- **Tuition (1982/83): $4,650**
- **Room & Board: $2,200**
- **Degrees offered: BA, BS**
- **Student-faculty ratio: 15 to 1**

A private college affiliated with the Presbyterian Synod of North Carolina, established in 1961. 280-acre campus. Served by bus; airport nearby.
Academic Character SACS and professional accreditation. 4-1-4 system, 2½-week and 5-week summer terms. 9 majors offered by the Division of Humanities & the Fine Arts, 7 by the Division of Mathematical, Natural, & Health Sciences, and 9 by the Division of Social & Behavioral Sciences. Self-designed majors. Distributive requirements. Independent study. Pass/fail, internships. Preprofessional programs in dentistry, law, medicine, ministry, pharmacy, veterinary medicine. 3-2 engineering program with Georgia Tech. Study abroad. Elementary, secondary, and special education certification. 93,000-volume library with microform resources 1,600 music scores and 2,150 records.
Financial CEEB CSS and ACT FAS. College scholarships, grants, loans, payment plans; PELL, SEOG, NDSL, GSL, college work program.
Admissions High school graduation with 15 units recommended. Interview recommended. SAT or ACT required. $15 application fee. Rolling admissions. $100 room deposit due on acceptance of admissions offer. *Early Admission* Program. Transfers accepted. Credit possible for CEEB AP and CLEP exams.
Student Life Student government. Newspaper, literary magazine, yearbook, radio station. Music and drama groups. Religious and special interest groups. Students live at home or on campus. Coed and single-sex dorms. 75% of students live on campus. Honor code. 2 courses of phys ed required. 7 intercollegiate sports for men, 5 for women; intramurals. AIAW, NCAA. Student body composition: 0.1% Asian, 10.9% Black, 0.9% Hispanic, 0.8% Native American, 85.7% White, 1.6% Other. 38% from out of state.

[1] SAINT AUGUSTINE'S COLLEGE
Raleigh 27611, (919) 828-4451
Director of Admissions: Igal E. Spraggins

- **Undergraduates: 738m, 942w**
- **Tuition (1982/83): $2,700**
- **Room & Board: $1,500**
- **Degrees offered: BA, BS**

- **Student-faculty ratio: 24 to 1**

A private college affiliated with the Episcopal Church. Urban campus. Served by air, rail, and bus.
Academic Character SACS accreditation. Semester system, 6-week summer term. Majors offered in the areas of art, biology, business, chemistry, criminal justice, education, engineering, English, history, industrial hygiene, industrial mathematics, mathematics & physics, modern languages, music, physical education, social studies, and sociology. Distributives and 3 semesters of ethics required. Juniors take URE and ECE; seniors take oral and written comprehensive exams. Independent study. Honors program. Cooperative work/study. Preprofessional programs in dentistry, lab technology, law, medicine, nursing, pharmacy, physical therapy, social work, theology, veterinary medicine. Cross-registration with 5 area schools. Elementary and secondary education certification. ROTC. 100,000-volume library with microform resources.
Financial CEEB CSS. College scholarships, loans, state aid; PELL, SEOG, NDSL, GSL, CWS.
Admissions High school graduation with 16 units required. SAT required. Rolling admissions. $25 room deposit due on acceptance of admissions offer. Transfers accepted.
Student Life Student government. Newspaper, yearbook. Music and drama groups. Athletic, academic, honorary, religious, service, and special interest groups. 7 fraternities and sororities. Students must live at home or on campus. Single-sex dorms. 75% class attendance required. Attendance at daily and Sunday church services encouraged. 2 years of phys ed required. 7 intercollegiate sports for men; intramurals for men and women. NAIA, NCAA. Student body composition: 95.8% Black, 0.1% Hispanic, 0.1% Native American, 0.3% White

[J1] ST. MARY'S COLLEGE

900 Hillsborough Street, Raleigh 27611, (919) 828-2521
Director of Admissions & Financial Aid: Robert T. Simpson

- **Enrollment: 490w**
- **Tuition (1982/83): $3,470**
- **Room & Board: $2,780**
- **Degrees offered: AA, ABA**
- **Student-faculty ratio: 10 to 1**

A private women's college affiliated with the Episcopal Church, established in 1842. 23-acre urban campus. Served by air, rail, and bus.
Academic Character SACS accreditation. Semester system. 2-year transfer programs offered in art, drama, English, foreign languages, mathematics, music, physical education, religion & philosophy, sciences, and social studies. Distributives and 6 hours of religion & philosophy required. Internships. Cross-registration with 5 area schools. Summer in England. 33,500-volume library.
Financial CEEB CSS and ACT FAS. College scholarships, reduction for clergy daughters, state grants and loans; PELL, SEOG, CWS. Application deadline March 1.
Admissions High school graduation with 12 units required. Interview encouraged. SAT required. $15 application fee. Rolling admissions. $100 deposit due on acceptance of admissions offer. *Early Decision* and *Early Admission* programs. Admission deferral possible. Credit possible for CEEB AP exams.
Student Life Student government. Newspaper, literary journal, yearbook. Music and drama groups. Honorary, religious, physical education, and special interest groups. Seniors and day students may have cars. Curfew during week. Liquor and drugs prohibited. Honor system. 4 semesters of phys ed required. 5 intercollegiate sports; 2 club sports.

[1] SALEM COLLEGE

PO Box 10548, Winston-Salem 27108, (919) 721-2600
Director of Admissions: Jeannie Dorsey

- **Undergraduates: 686w**
- **Expenses: $7,000**
- **Degrees offered: BA, BS, BMus**
- **Student-faculty ratio: 9 to 1**

A private women's college affiliated with Moravian Church, established in 1772. 56-acre urban campus. Served by air and bus.
Academic Character SACS and professional accreditation. 4-1-4 system. 32 majors offered by the departments of American studies, art, biology, chemistry & physics, classics, economics & management, education, English & drama, history & political science, home economics, mathematics, modern languages, music, physical education, psychology, religion & philosophy, and sociology. Self-designed majors. Distributive requirements. 1 course in religion/philosophy required for BA. Independent study. Honors program. Pass/fail, internships, credit by exam. Preprofessional programs in dentistry, law, medicine, veterinary science. Cross-registration with 3 area schools. United Nations Semester. Washington Semester. Study abroad. Elementary, secondary, art, music, and special education certification. ROTC at Wake Forest. Computer facilities. Language lab. 106,528-volume library; music library.
Financial CEEB CSS and ACT FAS. College scholarships, grants, loans, payment plan; PELL, SEOG, NDSL, GSL, CWS. File FAF/FAS by March 1.
Admissions High school graduation with 12 units required. Interview recommended. Audition required of music majors. SAT or ACT required. $20 application fee. Rolling admissions. $250 room deposit due on acceptance of admissions offer. Admission deferral possible. Transfers accepted. Credit possible for CEEB AP and CLEP exams. Special admissions for disadvantaged students.
Student Life Student government. Newspaper, literary magazine, yearbook. Music and drama groups. Academic, honorary, religious, and special interest groups. Students must live on campus or at home. Single-sex dorms. 85% of students live on campus. Honor code. 4 terms of phys ed required. Intramural sports. Student body composition: 2% Black, 97% White, 1% Other. 47% from out of state.

[J1] SAMPSON TECHNICAL COLLEGE

Clinton 28328

[J1] SANDHILLS COMMUNITY COLLEGE

Carthage 28327

[1] SHAW UNIVERSITY

Raleigh 27611, (919) 755-4800
Director of Admissions: James Mitchell

- **Undergraduates: 747m, 692w**
- **Tuition (1982/83): $2,150**
- **Room & Board: $1,350; Fees: $300**
- **Degrees offered: BA, BS**
- **Mean SAT 664 composite**
- **Student-faculty ratio: 18 to 1**

A private university affiliated with the Baptist Church, established in 1865. 18-acre urban campus. Served by air, rail, and bus.
Academic Character SACS accreditation. Semester system, 3- and 5-week summer terms. 30 majors offered by the divisions of Business & Public Administration, Communications, Education, Preprofessional Studies, and Human Resources & Human Development. Distributive requirements. Independent study. Internships. Preprofessional programs in dentistry, medical technology, medicine, osteopathy, podiatry, pharmacy, theology, veterinary science. Cooperative engineering program with NCS. Cross-registration with 3 area schools. Elementary and secondary education certification. ROTC. AFROTC nearby. Computer center. 79,374-volume library.
Financial CEEB CSS and ACT FAS. University scholarships, grants, loans, state grants and loans, payment plan; PELL, SEOG, NDSL, FISL, GSL, CWS, university work/aid programs. Priority application deadline for scholarships June 15.
Admissions High school graduation with 15 units required. GED accepted. SAT or ACT recommended. $10 application fee. Rolling admissions. $20 room deposit due on acceptance of admissions offer. Admission deferral possible. Transfers accepted. Credit possible for CEEB CLEP exams. Upward Bound Program for disadvantaged.
Student Life Student government. Newspaper, yearbook, radio station. Television and film production. Music and drama groups. Debate. Black Scientists of America. Academic and religious groups. 11 fraternities and 4 sororities without houses. Co-op dorms. No married-student housing. 68% of students live on campus. Liquor prohibited. Class attendance required. 1 semester of phys ed required. 7 intercollegiate sports; intramurals. CIAA, NAIA, NAIWA, NCAA. Student body composition: 93.6% Black, 0.2% Hispanic, 0.1% Native American, 1.4% White. 56% from out of state.

[G1] SOUTHEASTERN BAPTIST THEOLOGICAL SEMINARY

Wake Forest 27587

[J1] SOUTHEASTERN COMMUNITY COLLEGE

Whiteville 28472

[J1] SOUTHWESTERN TECHNICAL COLLEGE

PO Box 67, Sylva 28779

[J1] STANLY TECHNICAL INSTITUTE

Albemarle 28001

[J1] SURRY COMMUNITY COLLEGE

Dobson 27017

[J1] TRI-COUNTY COMMUNITY COLLEGE

Murphy 28906

[J1] VANCE-GRANVILLE COMMUNITY COLLEGE

Henderson 27536

[1] WAKE FOREST UNIVERSITY

Winston-Salem 27109, (919) 761-5201
Director of Admissions: William G. Starling

- **Undergraduates: 1,862m, 1,214w; 4,485 total (including graduates)**
- **Tuition (1982/83): $4,700**
- **Room & Board: $2,050**
- **Degrees offered: BA, BS**
- **Student-faculty ratio: 14 to 1**

A private university affiliated with the North Carolina Baptist Convention, established in 1834. 470-acre urban campus. Served by bus.
Academic Character SACS and professional accreditation. Semester system, 2 5-week summer terms. 36 majors offered in the areas of anthropology, art, biology, business, chemistry, classics, economics, education, English, history, mathematics, medical sciences, modern languages, music, philosophy, physical education, physics, politics, psychology, religion, sociology, and speech. Courses in 8 additional areas,

including Hindi and Norwegian. Distributives, senior exams, 1 course in religion, and English competency exam required. Graduate degrees granted. Honors programs. Phi Beta Kappa. Limited pass/fail. Cooperative programs in law, medical science, medical technology, microbiology, and physician's assistant with Wake Forest. 3-2 engineering program with NCSU. 3-2 forestry program with Duke. Study abroad. Elementary and secondary education certification. ROTC. Computer center. Fine Arts Center. 818,711-volume library with microform resources.
Financial CEEB CSS. University scholarships, grants, loans, ministerial grants, payment plans; PELL, SEOG, NDSL, FISL, CWS, university work program. Preferred application deadline February 1.
Admissions High school graduation with 16 units required. Interview recommended. SAT required. $20 application fee. Preferred application deadline January 15. $200 deposit due on acceptance of admissions offer. *Early Decision* and *Early Admission* programs. Admission deferral possible. Transfers accepted. Credit possible for CEEB AP and CLEP exams.
Student Life Student government. Newspaper, literary magazine, yearbook, radio station. Music and drama groups. Extensive debate program. Afro-American Society. Academic, honorary, and special interest groups. 10 fraternities with chapter rooms; 6 sororities. 40% of men and 60% of women join. Freshmen not living at home live on campus. Coed and single-sex dorms. Married-student housing. Language dorms. 85% of students live on campus. Honor system. Class attendance expected. 1 year of phys ed required. 8 intercollegiate sports for men, 6 for women; many club and intramural sports. AIAW, NCAA, ACC. Student body composition: 0.3% Asian, 3.7% Black, 0.5% Hispanic, 0.2% Native American, 94.5% White, 0.8% Other. 55% from out of state.

[J1] WAKE TECHNICAL COLLEGE
9101 Fayetteville Road, Raleigh 27603

[1] WARREN WILSON COLLEGE
Swannanoa 28778, (704) 298-3325
Director of Admissions: Robert Glass

- **Enrollment: 525 men & women**
- **Tuition (1982/83): $3,900**
- **Room & Board: $1,608; Fees: $450**
- **Degree offered: BA**
- **Student-faculty ratio: 10 to 1**

A private college affiliated with the United Presbyterian Church in the USA, established in 1894. 1,000-acre rural campus in the Blue Ridge Mountains.
Academic Character SACS and professional accreditation. 2-2 modular calendar. Majors offered in applied mathematics, behavioral sciences, biological sciences, chemistry, economics, education, English, fine arts, environmental studies, general studies, history & political science, humanities, intercultural studies, music, sociology, and social work. Minors offered in 6 additional areas. Distributives and 4 credits of religion required. 15-hour per week work requirement. Service project required. Seminar for all freshmen. Masters degree granted. Independent study. Cross-registration with Appalachian State, DuPage, and Washington U. Elementary, middle, secondary, and music education certification. Craft shop. Appalachian Museum. Archaeological dig. 75,000-volume library.
Financial CEEB CSS and ACT FAS. College scholarships, loans, state grants; PELL, SEOG, NDSL, GSL, CWS. Students earn room and board by working 15 hours a week for the school. Additional employment possible. Application for financial aid should be made with admission application. Deadline April 1.
Admissions High school graduation with 12 units required. SAT or ACT required. $10 application fee. Application deadline December 15. $150 deposit due on acceptance of admissions offer. *Early Admission* Program. Admission deferral possible. Transfers accepted. Credit possible for CEEB AP exams.
Student Life Student Caucus. Newspaper, literary magazine, yearbook. Music and drama groups. Dance program. Campus life is dormitory centered. 4 intercollegiate sports; intramurals.

[J1] WAYNE COMMUNITY COLLEGE
PO Box 8002, Goldsboro 27530

[1] WESTERN CAROLINA UNIVERSITY
Cullowhee 28723, (704) 227-7317
Director of Admissions: Tyree H. Kiser, Jr.

- **Undergraduates: 2,756m, 2,675w; 6,366 total (including graduates)**
- **Tuition (1982/83): $783 (in-state), $2,571 (out-of-state)**
- **Room & Board: $1,634**
- **Degrees offered: BA, BS, BSBA, BSE, BFA, BSN, BSMed Rec Ad, BSMT**
- **Mean SAT 394v, 422m**
- **Student-faculty ratio: 15 to 1**

A public university established in 1889. 400-acre small-town campus, 50 miles from Asheville. Served by air, rail, and bus in Asheville.
Academic Character SACS and professional accreditation. Semester system, 2 4½-week summer terms. 70 majors offered by the schools of Arts & Sciences, Business, Education & Psychology, Nursing & Health Sciences, and Technology & Applied Science. Minors offered in most major fields and in 9 others, including Cherokee studies. Distributive requirements. Graduate degrees granted. Honors program. Cooperative work/study, internships, credit by exam. Preprofessional programs in dentistry, law, medicine, occupational therapy, optometry, pharmacy, veterinary medicine. Cross-registration with UNC Asheville. Elementary, secondary, special, and vocational education certification. ROTC. Computer center. Fine Arts Center. Speech & Hearing Center. Mountain Heritage Center. 318,000-volume library with microform resources.
Financial CEEB CSS. University scholarships, grants, loans, state grants, payment plan; PELL, SEOG, MSF, NDSL, FISL, CWS. Application deadlines February 15 (scholarships), March 1 (loans).
Admissions High school graduation with 15 units recommended. GED accepted. SAT required. $15 application fee. Rolling admissions. $75 room deposit due on acceptance of admissions offer. *Pre-University Honors* Program. Admission deferral possible. Transfers accepted. Credit possible for CEEB AP and CLEP exams. Transitional Admissions Program for underprepared students.
Student Life Student government. Newspaper, literary magazine, yearbook. Music, film, and drama groups. Debate. Special interest groups. 11 fraternities, 7 with houses; 5 sororities without housing. 10% of men and 7% of women join. Single freshmen live with families or on campus. Married-student housing. 52% of students live on campus. 4 semesters of phys ed required. 12 intercollegiate sports for men, 7 for women; several intramurals. AIAW, NCAA, SC. Student body composition: 0.3% Asian, 5% Black, 0.4% Hispanic, 1.5% Native American, 92.2% White, 0.6% Other. 11% from out of state.

[J1] WESTERN PIEDMONT COMMUNITY COLLEGE
Morganton 28655

[J1] WILKES COMMUNITY COLLEGE
Wilkesboro 28697

[J1] WILSON COUNTY TECHNICAL INSTITUTE
902 Herring Avenue, Wilson 27893

[1] WINGATE COLLEGE
Wingate 28174, (704) 233-4061
Director of Student Recruitment & Financial Aid: Dan M. Shive

- **Undergraduates: 766m, 670w**
- **Tuition (1982/83): $2,600**
- **Room & Board: $1,700**
- **Degrees offered: BA, BS, BMus, BMus Ed**
- **Mean SAT 800 composite**
- **Student-faculty ratio: 18 to 1**

A private college affiliated with the Baptist Church, established in 1896. Small-town campus, 30 miles from Raleigh.
Academic Character SACS accreditation. Semester system, 6-week summer term. 6 majors offered by the Division of Business & Economics, 15 by the Division of Education & Social Sciences, 5 by the Division of Fine Arts, 2 by the Division of Humanities, and 2 by the Division of Science & Mathematics. Minors offered in 22 additional areas. Distributives, 6 hours of religion, and "life ISSUES" program required. Independent study. Honors program. Pass/fail, internships. Cross-registration with 10 area schools. Elementary and secondary education certification. ROTC at Davidson. Fine Arts Center. 82,000-volume library with microform resources.
Financial CEEB CSS and ACT FAS. College scholarships, PELL, SEOG, NDSL, GSL, CWS. Application deadline May 1.
Admissions High school graduation required. SAT or ACT required. $15 application fee. Rolling admissions. $50 deposit due on acceptance of admissions offer. Credit possible for CEEB AP, CLEP, and departmental exams.
Student Life Student government. Newspaper, literary magazine, yearbook. Black Awareness Club. Christian Student Union. Academic, honorary, political, and special interest groups. Students live with families or at school. Single-sex dorms. 3 hours of phys ed required. 5 intercollegiate sports for men, 4 for women; intramurals. AIAW, NAIA. Student body composition: 8.6% Black, 0.2% Hispanic, 0.3% Native American, 89.4% White, 0.1% Other. 11% from out of state.

[J2] WINSALM COLLEGE
Winston-Salem — see Rutledge College of Winston-Salem

[1] WINSTON-SALEM STATE UNIVERSITY
Winston-Salem 27102, (919) 761-2070
Director of Admissions: Emily H. Harper

- **Undergraduates: 768m, 1,139w; 2,294 total (including graduates)**
- **Tuition (1982/83): $738 (in-state), $2,320 (out-of-state)**
- **Room & Board: $1,625; Fees: $420**
- **Degrees offered: BA, BS, BSAS**
- **Student-faculty ratio: 15 to 1**

A public university established in 1892. 8-acre campus. Served by air, rail, and bus.
Academic Character SACS and professional accreditation. Semester system, 2 4-week summer terms. 22 majors offered in the areas of applied science, art, biology, business, computer science, education, English, health/physical education, history, mathematics, medical technology, music education, nursing, political science, psychology, sociology, and urban affairs. Minors offered in 11 additional areas. Distributive requirements. Graduate degrees granted. Independent study. Honors program. Cooperative work/study, internships. Preprofessional programs in dentistry and medicine. Elementary, secondary, and special education certification. ROTC at Wake Forest. 153,791-volume library.
Financial CEEB CSS and ACT FAS. University scholarships, grants, loans, state grants, payment plan; PELL, SEOG, NDSL, NSL, CWS, university employment program. Application deadline May 15.
Admissions High school graduation with 16 units required. GED accepted. SAT required. Interview recommended. $15 application fee. Rolling

admissions. $25 room deposit due on acceptance of admissions offer. Transfers accepted. Credit possible for CEEB AP, CLEP, and departmental proficiency exams. Supplemental Education Program for academically underprepared.
Student Life Student government. Newspaper, literary magazine, yearbook. Music and drama groups. Circle K. Academic, honorary, religious, and special interest groups. 8 fraternities and 9 sororities without houses. 45% of men and 50% of women join. Students live at home or at school. Single-sex dorms. No married-student housing. 49% of students live on campus. Liquor and hazing prohibited. Class attendance required for freshmen. 2 semesters of phys ed required. 10 intercollegiate sports; intramurals. AIAW, CIAA, NAIA, NCAA. Student body composition: 85% Black, 14% Hispanic, 1% Other. 9% from out of state.

NORTH DAKOTA *(ND)*

[J1] BISMARCK JUNIOR COLLEGE
Bismarck 58501, (701) 224-5429
Associate Director of Admissions: Jason Karch

- **Enrollment: 1,975 men & women**
- **Tuition & Fees (1982/83): $790 (in-state), $910-$1,120 (out-of-state)**
- **Room & Board: $1,230**
- **Degrees offered: AA, AAS**
- **Student-faculty ratio: 22 to 1**

A public junior college established in 1939. 95-acre campus in Bismarck.
Academic Character NCACS accreditation. Semester system, 8-week summer term. 39 transfer programs offered in liberal arts and pre-professional areas. 15 vocational-technical programs offered in secretarial, agricultural, engineering & technology, business & management, medical lab technology, and data processing areas. Certificate programs. Distributive requirements. Internships, field experience, credit by exam. Preprofessional programs in education, business, medicine, law, nursing, medical technology. Audio-visual center. 33,000-volume library.
Financial ACT FAS. College scholarships, tuition waivers, talent awards, state grants and waivers, Native American scholarships; PELL, SEOG, BIA, NSS, NDSL, FISL, NSL, CWS.
Admissions High school graduation required. GED accepted. Interview required for voc-tech programs. ACT recommended for college transfer programs. $10 application fee. Rolling admissions. Transfers accepted. Credit possible for CEEB CLEP exams; college has own advanced placement program.
Student Life Student government. Music and drama groups. Professional and special interest organizations. Student Center. Single-sex dorms. 10% of students live on campus. Intercollegiate and intramural sports. Student body composition: 10% minority.

[1] DICKINSON STATE COLLEGE
Dickinson 58601, (701) 227-2326
Director of Admissions & Registrar: Neil Ableidinger

- **Undergraduates: 436m, 553w**
- **Tuition (1982/83): $735 (in-state), $1,296 (out-of-state)**
- **Room & Board: $1,539**
- **Degrees offered: BA, BS, BCS, AS, ACS**
- **Student-faculty ratio: 13 to 1**

A public college established in 1918. Campus located in the small city of Dickinson, 100 miles west of Bismarck. Served by air and bus.
Academic Character NCACS and professional accreditation. Trimester system, summer terms. Majors offered in art, art education, biology, business administration, business education, chemistry, communications education, composite science, earth science/geography, elementary education, English, environmental science, fine arts, history, language arts, mathematics, medical technology, music, physical education, political science, secondary education, social/behavioral science, Spanish, speech, and theatre. Self-designed majors. Minors offered in most major fields. Distributive requirements. Independent study. Honors program. Pass/fail. Internships. Preprofessional programs in agriculture, dentistry, engineering, health sciences, home economics, law, life & environmental sciences, medicine, mortuary science, physics/astronomy, social science, theology. 3-2 chemical engineering and BSW programs with UND. Member Northern Plains Consortium. Primary and secondary education certification. Language lab, art gallery. 70,000-volume library with microform resources.
Financial ACT FAS. College scholarships and loans, state grants; PELL, SEOG, NDSL, FISL, NSL, CWS.
Admissions High school graduation required. ACT required. $15 application fee. Rolling admissions; suggest applying by spring. $25 room deposit required on acceptance of offer of admission. Transfers accepted. Credit possible for CEEB CLEP exams; college has own advanced placement program.
Student Life Student government. Newspaper, magazine, yearbook. Music, debate, drama groups. Honorary, professional, religious, and special interest groups. 2 fraternities and 1 sorority without houses. Students under 21 must live at home or on campus. Single-sex dorms. Married-student housing. 7 intercollegiate sports for men, 3 for women; intramurals. NAIA, NDCAC, NIRA. Student body composition: 1% Black, 1.5% Native American, 97.5% White. 7% from out of state.

[1] JAMESTOWN COLLEGE
Jamestown 58401, (701) 253-2550

- **Undergraduates: 275m, 250w; 625 total (including part-time)**
- **Tuition (1982/83): $4,400**
- **Room & Board: $1,575**
- **Degree offered: BA**
- **Student-faculty ratio: 12 to 1**

A private college related to the United Presbyterian Church, USA, founded in 1883. Small city campus located between Fargo and Bismarck.
Academic Character NCACS and professional accreditation. 4-1-4 system. Majors offered by the departments of art, biology, chemistry, business administration & economics, education, English, history & political science, math, computer science, music, philosophy, physical education-health-recreation, psychology, religion, sociology, and theatre. Nursing major leads to an RN in 4 years. Several preprofessional programs. 3-2 pre-engineering program. 80,000-volume library.
Financial College honor and achievement scholarships, loans, state aid; PELL, SEOG, NDSL, GSL, part-time employment.
Admissions High school graduation required; rank in upper 50% of class suggested. ACT or SAT required. Rolling admissions. *Early Admission* and *Early Decision programs. Admission deferral possible. Transfers accepted.*
Student Life Single-sex and coed dorms. Dining hall. 8 intercollegiate sports for men, 5 for women; intramurals.

[J1] LAKE REGION COMMUNITY COLLEGE
Devils Lake 58301, (701) 662-8683
Director of Admissions: Daniel Johnson

- **Enrollment: 500 men & women; 900 total (including part-time)**
- **Tuition (1982/83): $22 per credit hour (in-district); $31 (out-of-state)**
- **Room & Board: $1,390-$1,720; Fees: $55**
- **Degrees offered: AA, AAS**
- **Student-faculty ratio: 11 to 1**

A public junior college established in 1941. 2-building campus in Devils Lake in northeastern North Dakota.
Academic Character NCACS accreditation. Semester system. 2-year programs offered in accounting, agriculture, anthropology, art, banking, biology, business administration, business education, chemistry, chiropractic, computer science, criminal justice, nursing, economics, education, engineering, English, forestry & wildlife, general business, history, home economics, law, mathematics, medical technology, music, optometry, pharmacy, physics, political science, police science, psychology, public administration, social science, social work, sociology, speech & drama, and health, physical education & recreation. Distributive requirements. Terminal certificate programs. Cooperative work/study and internships in some programs. Preprofessional programs in dentistry, medicine, seminary studies.
Financial ACT FAS. College scholarships, state grants and loans, Native American grants, scholarships, and loans; PELL, SEOG, NDSL, GSL, CWS.
Admissions High school graduation required. GED accepted. ACT required. Rolling admissions. *Early Admission* and *Early Decision* programs. Transfers accepted. Credit possible for CEEB CLEP exams.
Student Life Student government. Professional, religious, political, and special interest groups. Single-sex dorms. Married-student housing. Class attendance required. 2-4 credits in phys ed required. Intercollegiate basketball and baseball; intramurals. AIAW, NJCAA.

[1] MARY COLLEGE
Apple Creek Road, Bismarck 58501, (701) 255-4681
Director of Admissions: Leland D. Nagel

- **Undergraduates: 232m, 569w; 1,003 total (including part-time)**
- **Tuition (1982/83): $2,690**
- **Room & Board: $1,520; Fees: $200**
- **Degrees offered: BA, BS, BColl Studies, AA, AS**
- **Mean ACT 19.5**
- **Student-faculty ratio: 14 to 1**

A private college controlled by the Benedictine Sisters, established in 1959, became coed in 1968. 200-acre campus 7 miles south of Bismarck. Air, bus, and rail service nearby.
Academic Character NCACS and professional accreditation. 4-4-1 system, 2 4-week summer terms. Majors offered in accounting, business administration, Christian ministry, communications, early childhood education, elementary education, English, music (4 areas), natural science/mathematics, nursing, physical education & health, social & behavioral sciences, social work, special education, and secondary education in 7 areas. Double majors. Minors offered in some major fields and in 17 additional areas. Courses in art, Native American languages. AA in mental health technician, AS in respiratory therapy. Distributives and 3 semesters of religion & philosophy required. Independent study. Pass/fail. Credit by exam. Preprofessional programs in dentistry, law, medicine, mortuary science, optometry, pharmacy, occupational therapy, physical therapy, veterinary medicine. Member Northern Plains Consortium, Missouri Valley Consortium for Addiction Training. Study abroad. Kindergarten, elementary, and secondary education certification. 50,000-volume library.
Financial CEEB CSS and ACT FAS. College scholarships and loans, state grants, athletic, music, honor scholarships, family discounts; PELL, SEOG, NSS, GSL, NDSL, NSL, CWS. State aid application deadline April 15.

Admissions High school graduation with 16 units recommended. GED accepted. SAT or ACT required. $15 application fee. Rolling admissions; suggest applying by April 1. $100 tuition deposit and $25 room deposit (for boarders) required on acceptance of offer of admission. *Early Admission* and *Concurrent Enrollment* programs. Admission deferral possible. Transfers accepted. Credit possible for CEEB AP, CLEP, and ACT PEP exams; college has own advanced placement program.
Student Life Student government. Newspaper, magazine, yearbook. Music groups. Indian club. Service, professional, and special interest organizations. Freshmen and sophomores must live at home or on campus. Single-sex dorms. 40% of students live on campus. Liquor prohibited on campus. 1 intercollegiate sport for men, 3 for women; intramurals. NAIA, WACND. Student body composition: 0.2% Asian, 0.2% Black, 0.1% Hispanic, 8.4% Native American, 91% White. 12% from out of state.

[1] MAYVILLE STATE COLLEGE

Mayville 58257, (701) 786-2301
Director of Admissions: Ronald G. Brown

- **Undergraduates: 260m, 375w**
- **Tuition & Fees (1982/83): $702 (in-state), $1,263 (out-of-state)**
- **Room & Board: $1,344**
- **Degrees offered: BA, BSEd, BSComp Stud, BSGS, AA**
- **Student-faculty ratio: 15 to 1**

A public college established in 1889. 60-acre rural campus in Mayville, 45 miles from Grand Forks. Air, bus, and rail nearby.
Academic Character NCACS and professional accreditation. Trimester system, 2 4-week summer terms. Majors offered in art, business, computer science, elementary education, English, general studies, health education, mathematics, music, physical education, science, and social science. Self-designed majors. Minor required; minors offered in most major fields and in 7 additional areas. Distributive requirements. Independent study. Cooperative work/study, pass/fail, internships. Preprofessional programs in agriculture, chiropractic, criminal justice, dentistry, engineering, home economics, law, medicine, medical technology, mortuary science, nursing, optometry, pharmacy, veterinary medicine, wildlife management. Elementary, secondary, and special education certification. Computer center, reading lab. 75,000-volume library with microform resources.
Financial CEEB CSS and ACT FAS. College scholarships, grants, loans; PELL, SEOG, FISL, GSL, NDSL, CWS; college has own work program. Scholarship application deadline April 15.
Admissions High school graduation with 18 units recommended. Interview encouraged. ACT or SAT strongly encouraged; ACH recommended. $10 application fee. Rolling admissions; suggest applying by August 15. $15 room deposit (for boarders) required on acceptance of offer of admission. *Early Admission* and *Early Decision* programs. Admission deferral possible. Transfers accepted. Credit possible for CEEB CLEP exams.
Student Life Student government. Newspaper, magazine, yearbook. Music, debate groups. Religious, political, academic, honorary, and special interest groups. Single students must live at home or on campus. Coed and single-sex dorms. Married-student housing. 77% of students live on campus. Liquor prohibited on campus. 6 quarters of phys ed required. 7 intercollegiate sports for men, 7 for women; intramurals. NDCAC, WACND. Student body composition: 0.9% Black, 3.1% Native American, 96% White. 17% from out of state.

[1] MINOT STATE COLLEGE

Minot 58701, (701) 857-3340
Director of Admissions & Assistant Registrar: Dawn Evenson

- **Undergraduates: 693m, 1,314w**
- **Tuition (1982/83): $681 (in-state), $1,242 (out-of-state)**
- **Room & Board: $1,278**
- **Degrees offered: BA, BS, BSW, AS, AA**
- **Mean ACT 18**
- **Student-faculty ratio: 12 to 1**

A public college established in 1913. Campus located in the small city of Minot. Served by air, bus, and rail.
Academic Character NCACS and professional accreditation. Trimester system, 8-week and 2 4-week summer terms. 32 majors offered in the areas of fine arts, business, education & psychology, health, physical education & recreation, literature & language, music, nursing, science & mathematics, social science, and special education. Interdisciplinary majors. Minors offered in most major fields and in 10 additional areas. Distributive requirements. MS granted. Pass/fail. Preprofessional programs in business personnel, chiropractics, clergy, dental hygiene, dentistry, dietetics, engineering, home economics, law, medicine, occupational therapy, optometry, pharmacy, physical therapy, seminary, teaching, veterinary medicine. Classes at Northwest Bible College. Elementary and secondary education certification. 100,000-volume library.
Financial ACT FAS. College scholarships, grants, and loans, state grants; PELL, SEOG, NDSL, FISL, GSL, CWS. Application deadline March 1.
Admissions High school graduation with 17 units required. GED accepted. ACT, SAT, or PSAT recommended. $10 application fee. Rolling admissions; suggest applying early in 12th year. *Concurrent Enrollment* Program. Transfers accepted. Credit possible for CEEB CLEP exams; college has own advanced placement program.
Student Life Student government. Newspaper, magazine, yearbook. Music and drama groups. Academic, political, religious, and special interest groups. 3 fraternities and 4 sororities. Limited housing; dorms for men and women. Married-student housing. Liquor, drugs prohibited. Some phys ed required. 9 intercollegiate sports for men, 6 for women; intramurals. NAIA, NDCAC. Student body composition: 0.3% Asian, 1.6% Black, 0.2% Hispanic, 1.7% Native American, 94.5% White.

[1] NORTH DAKOTA, UNIVERSITY OF

Box 8135, University Station, Grand Forks 58202, (701) 777-2011
Director of Admissions & Records: D.J. Wermers

- **Enrollment: 5,450m, 5,081w**
- **Tuition (1982/83): $804 (in-state), $1,572 (out-of-state)**
- **Room & Board: $1,550**
- **Degrees offered: BA, BFA, BSN, BBA, BPA, BS in 14 areas**
- **Mean ACT 22**
- **Student-faculty ratio: 18 to 1**

A public university established in 1883. 472-acre campus in the small city of Grand Forks. Served by air, bus, and rail.
Academic Character NCACS and professional accreditation. Semester system, mini-semester in May & June, 8-week summer term. 41 majors offered by the College of Arts & Sciences, 11 by the College of Business & Public Administration, 7 by the College of Engineering, 4 by the College of Fine Arts, 9 by the College for Human Resources Development, 3 by the School of Medicine, 24 by the Center for Teaching & Learning, and 1 in nursing. Composite majors. Minors offered in most major subjects and in 4 additional areas. Distributive requirements. Graduate and professional degrees granted. Honors program. Phi Beta Kappa. Pass/fail. Preprofessional programs in dentistry, law, medicine, optometry. Study abroad. Elementary and secondary education certification. ROTC. Language lab. 592,923-volume library with microform resources.
Financial ACT FAS. University scholarships, loans; PELL, SEOG, NDSL, FISL, CWS. Application deadline March 15.
Admissions High school graduation with 14 units required. GED accepted. Interview encouraged. ACT, SAT, or PSAT required. $20 application fee. Application deadline July 1. *Early Decision* and *Early Admission* programs. Admission deferral possible. Transfers accepted. Credit possible for CEEB AP and CLEP exams.
Student Life Student government. Newspaper, yearbook, radio and TV stations. Music, debate, drama groups. Women's organizations. Academic, professional, religious, honorary, and special interest groups. 13 fraternities and 8 sororities; all have houses. 22% of men and 24% of women join. Dorms for men and women. Married-student housing. 60% of students live on campus. Liquor prohibited on campus. 11 intercollegiate sports for men, 10 for women, wheelchair basketball; intramurals. Student body composition: 0.4% Asian, 0.5% Black, 0.2% Hispanic, 1.9% Native American, 96.2% White. 25% from out of state.

■[J1] WILLISTON CENTER

Williston 58801

[J1] NORTH DAKOTA STATE SCHOOL OF SCIENCE

Wahpeton 58075, (701) 671-1130
Director of Admissions & Records: Richard L. Holm

- **Enrollment: 2,327m, 1,013w; 3,400 total (including part-time)**
- **Tuition (1982/83): $570 (in-state), $1,131 (out-of-state)**
- **Fees: $60**
- **Degrees offered: AA, AS, AAS**
- **Mean ACT 17.5**
- **Student-faculty ratio: 17 to 1**

A public junior college established in 1903. Campus in the small city of Wahpeton, 1 hour from Fargo. Air and bus service.
Academic Character NCACS and professional accreditation. Trimester system, 4-, 8-, and 10-week summer terms. 21 programs offered by the Arts, Science, & Preprofessional Division, 25 by the Business Division, 15 by the Technical Division, and 23 by the Trades Division. Distributive requirements. Independent study. Pass/fail. Graduation by Work Experience Program. 90,000-volume library.
Financial ACT FAS. School scholarships and loans, state scholarships, Native American scholarships; PELL, SEOG, NSS, NDSL, GSL, NSL, CWS; school has own work program. Application deadline April 15.
Admissions High school graduation required. GED accepted. Some programs require interview. ACT required; SAT or PSAT accepted. $20 application fee. Rolling admissions. *Early Admission* and *Early Decision* programs. Transfers accepted. Credit possible for CEEB CLEP exams; school has own advanced placement program.
Student Life Student government. Newspaper, yearbook. Music and drama groups. Religious, academic, political, and special interest groups. Students expected to live on campus. Coed and single-sex dorms. Married-student housing. About 50% of students live on campus. Liquor prohibited on campus. 3 hours of health and phys ed required for college transfer programs. 7 intercollegiate sports for men, 6 for women; intramurals. NDCAC, NJCAA.

[1] NORTH DAKOTA STATE UNIVERSITY

Fargo 58105, (701) 237-8643
Director of Admissions: George H. Wallman

- **Undergraduates: 5,228m, 3,008w; 8,923 total (including graduates)**
- **Tuition (1982/83): $732 (in-state), $1,500 (out-of-state)**
- **Room & Board: $1,593**
- **Degrees offered: BA, BS, BArch, BFA**
- **Mean ACT 21**
- **Student-faculty ratio: 22 to 1**

A public university established in 1890. 2,300-acre urban campus in Fargo, at the eastern edge of the state. Served by air, bus, and rail.
Academic Character NCACS and professional accreditation. Trimester system, 2 5-week summer terms. 13 majors offered by the College of Agriculture, 20 by the College of Humanities & Social Sciences, 14 by the College of Science & Mathematics, 10 by the College of Engineering & Architecture, 8 by the College of Home Economics, and 3 by the College of

Pharmacy. Self-designed majors. Distributive requirements. Graduate degrees granted. Independent study. Honors program. Cooperative work/study, pass/fail, internships. Preprofessional programs in law, medicine, dentistry. Pre-engineering program with area schools. 3-1 medical technology program, 2-2 physical therapy program. Cross-registration with Concordia, Moorhead State. Elementary and secondary education certification. ROTC, AFROTC. Genetics institute. Language lab. 358,960-volume library.
Financial CEEB CSS and ACT FAS. University scholarships, grants, loans; PELL, SEOG, NDSL, FISL, NSL, HPL, CWS. Application deadline April 15.
Admissions High school graduation with 15 units required. GED accepted. ACT, SAT, or PSAT required; ACT preferred. $20 application fee. Rolling admissions. *Early Admission* Program. Transfers accepted. Credit possible for CEEB AP, CLEP, and ACT PEP exams; university has own advanced placement program.
Student Life Student government. Newspaper, radio station. Music and drama groups. Academic, service, and special interest groups. 11 fraternities and 6 sororities; all have houses. Freshmen under 19 must live on campus or at home. Coed and single-sex dorms. Married-student housing. 35% of students live on campus. Liquor prohibited on campus. 3 terms of phys ed required for non-ROTC students. 9 intercollegiate sports for men, 6 for women; intramurals. NCIAC, NCAA. Student body composition: 1.1% Asian, 0.6% Black, 0.1% Native American, 96% White, 2.2% Other. 29% from out of state.

[J1] NORTH DAKOTA STATE UNIVERSITY—BOTTINEAU BRANCH AND INSTITUTE OF FORESTRY
Bottineau 58318, (701) 228-2277
Admissions & Placement Officer: Kenneth Kostad

- **Enrollment: 137m, 134w; 417 total (including part-time)**
- **Tuition (1982/83): $570 (in-state), $1,131 (out-of-state)**
- **Room & Board: $1,407; Fees: $128**
- **Degrees offered: AA, AS, AAS**
- **Student-faculty ratio: 15 to 1**

A public junior college established in 1894. 35-acre campus on northern edge of city of Bottineau at base of Turtle Mountains.
Academic Character NCACS accreditation. Trimester system, 8-week summer term. 2-year programs offered in agriculture, art, biology, business administration, business aviation, chemistry, elementary education, engineering, English, forestry, health professions, history, home economics, horticulture, journalism, mathematics, music, parks & recreation, pharmacy, physical education, secondary education, secretarial science, social science, special education, and wildlife management. 16 vocational-technical programs. Certificate programs. Distributive requirements. Cooperative work/study, field experience. Preprofessional programs in law, veterinary medicine. Cooperative programs with Turtle Mountain School of ParaMedical Technique. 26,000-volume library.
Financial ACT FAS. College scholarships, state grants; PELL, SEOG, NDSL, FISL, CWS. Application deadline April 15.
Admissions High school graduation required. GED accepted. ACT or SAT required; ACT preferred. $10 application fee. Rolling admissions. *Early Admission* Program. Transfers accepted. Credit possible for CEEB CLEP exams.
Student Life Student government. Newspaper, newsletter. Music groups. Professional, honorary, service, and special interest clubs. Single students under 21 must live at home or on campus. Coed and single-sex dorms. 73% of students live on campus. 3 credits of phys ed required. 3 intercollegiate sports for men, 3 for women; intramurals. NJCAA, Mon-Dak JC Conference, Southwest Canadian Hockey League.

[P] NORTHWEST BIBLE COLLEGE
Minot 58701

[P] TRINITY BIBLE INSTITUTE
Ellendale 58436

[1] VALLEY CITY STATE COLLEGE
Valley City 58072, (701) 845-7990
Director of Admissions: David A. Nelson

- **Undergraduates: 435m, 515w**
- **Tuition (1982/83): $572 (in-state), $1,132 (out-of-state)**
- **Room & Board: $1,621; Fees: $135**
- **Degrees offered: BA, BS, BSEd, BColl Studies, AA**
- **Student-faculty ratio: 17 to 1**

A public college established in 1890. 94-acre wooded campus in small city of Valley City, 60 miles west of Fargo. Bus and rail nearby; airport 30 miles away.
Academic Character NCACS and professional accreditation. Trimester system, 5-week summer term. Majors offered in business administration, business education, executive secretarial service, communications education, earth & environmental science, English, human resources administration & management, history, Spanish, education, health education, physical education, art, art education, biology, chemistry, mathematics, and mathematics education. Special majors. Minor required. Distributive requirements. Independent study. Pass/fail. Internships. Preprofessional programs in law, medicine, dentistry, optometry, veterinary medicine, and other areas. Elementary and secondary education certification. ROTC. Museum. 78,000-volume library.
Financial CEEB CSS and ACT FAS. College scholarships, grants, loans; PELL, SEOG, NDSL, FISL, GSL, CWS. Priority application deadline April 15.
Admissions High school graduation required. GED accepted. ACT required. $10 application fee. Rolling admissions. $35 deposit required on acceptance of offer of admission. *Concurrent Enrollment* Program. Transfers accepted. Credit possible for CEEB CLEP exams; college has own advanced placement program.
Student Life Student government. Music, drama groups. Honorary, religious, service organizations. 9 fraternities and sororities; 2 have houses. Single students under 21 must live at home or on campus. Single-sex dorms. 6 hours of phys ed required. 8 intercollegiate sports for men, 7 for women; intramurals. AIAW, NAIA, NDCAC. Student body composition: 1% Black, 1% Native American, 98% White. 7% from out of state.

OHIO *(OH)*

[1] AIR FORCE INSTITUTE OF TECHNOLOGY
Wright-Patterson Air Force Base, Dayton 45433

[1] AKRON, UNIVERSITY OF
302 East Buchtel Avenue, Akron 44325, (216) 375-7100
Director of Admissions: John W. Owen

- **Undergraduates: 6,873m, 6,395w; 25,820 total (including graduates)**
- **Tuition (1982/83): $3,062 (in-state), $4,352 (out-of-state)**
- **Room & Board: $2,130**
- **Degrees offered: BA, BS, BMus, BFA, BSN, BAEd, BSEd, BSMed Tech, BSEng**
- **Mean ACT 19**
- **Student-faculty ratio: 24 to 1**

A public university established in 1870. 140-acre urban campus. Served by air and bus.
Academic Character NCACS and professional accreditation. Semester system, 2 5-week summer terms. 39 majors offered by the College of Arts & Sciences, 6 by the College of Business Administration, 13 by the College of Education, 7 by the College of Engineering, 33 by the College of Fine & Applied Arts, 1 by the College of Nursing, 2 by the Community & Technical College. Self-designed majors. Distributive requirements. Graduate degrees granted. Independent study. Honors program. Phi Beta Kappa. Cooperative work/study, pass/fail, internships, credit by exam. Study abroad. Elementary, secondary, and special education certification. ROTC, AFROTC. Computer center. Learning Resources Center. 1,164,375-volume library with microform resources.
Financial CEEB CSS. University scholarships, grants, loans, state grants, payment plans; PELL, SEOG, NSS, GSL, NDSL, NSL, CWS. Primary application deadline February 1.
Admissions High school graduation with 10 units required. Interview recommended. SAT or ACT required. $25 application fee. Rolling admissions. $100 room deposit required on acceptance admissions offer. *Early Admission* Program. Admission deferral possible. Transfers accepted. Credit possible for CEEB AP and CLEP exams.
Student Life Student council. Newspaper, literary magazine, yearbook, 2 radio stations. Music, dance, and drama groups. Academic, honorary, religious, and special interest groups. 13 fraternities, 12 with houses; 11 sororities, most with houses. 8% of men and 5% of women join. 2.5 GPA required for residence on campus. Single-sex dorms. No married-student housing. 11% of students live on campus. Class attendance expected. 1 hour of phys ed required. 10 intercollegiate sports for men, 6 for women; club and intramural sports. AIAW, Ohio Valley Conference. Student body composition: 0.5% Asian, 7% Black, 2.3% Foreign, 0.3% Hispanic, 0.3% Native American, 89.6% White. 2% from out of state.

[2] ALLEGHENY WESLEYAN COLLEGE
2161 Woodsdale Road, Salem 44460

- **Undergraduates: 75 men & women**
- **Tuition (1982/83): $1,296**
- **Room & Board: $1,200**
- **Typical Expenses: $2,676**
- **Degrees offered: AB, BRE**
- **Mean ACT 17.3**

A private college controlled by a denominational private board, organized in 1956 and merged with Allegheny Wesleyan Methodist Connection (original Allegheny Conference) in 1973. Rural campus located 3 miles south of the small industrial city of Salem.
Academic Character Trimester system, 2 6-week summer terms. The College prepares ministers, missionaries, and Christian Day School teachers. Departments include Christian Ministry, Missions, and Christian Teacher Education. 8,000-volume library.
Financial Limited scholarship and self-help aid available.
Admissions ACT used for admission. Rolling admissions. Admission deferral possible. Students admitted in August, November, and January.
Student Life Dormitories for men and women. Cafeteria.

[1] ANTIOCH COLLEGE
Yellow Springs 45387, (513) 767-7331
Director of Admissions: Benjamin F. Thompson

- **Undergraduates: 331m, 364w**
- **Tuition (1982/83): $6,170**
- **Room & Board: $2,510; Fees: $160**
- **Degrees offered: BA, BS, BFA**
- **Student-faculty ratio: 11 to 1**

A private college established in 1852. 100-acre small-town campus with 1,000-acre adjacent nature preserve, 18 miles east of Dayton. Programs also in Los Angeles, San Francisco, Venice, Honolulu, Seattle, Denver, Philadelphia, Chicago, Keene (NH), and Fairbault (MN).

Academic Character NCACS accreditation. Trimester system. Majors offered in arts, humanities, social sciences, and environmental studies & urban studies, with concentrations in 22 areas and interdisciplinary programs in 5 additional disciplines. Major plus concentration required. Distributive requirements. 6 quarters of co-op jobs and community participation required; approximately 50% of students are on co-op jobs each term. University emphasizes rigorous scholarship, practical work experience, and leadership development. Undergraduate, graduate, and professional degrees offered at other University centers. Written evaluations of course work; letter grades upon request. Preprofessional programs in dentistry, law, medicine, veterinary science. Joint programs with over 20 colleges. 3-2 engineering with Boston U, Washington U (St. Louis), Georgia Inst. of Technology. 3-2 nursing with Case Western Reserve (Cleveland). Study in Asia, Europe, South America. Elementary and secondary education certification. Computer Activities Center. Environmental Studies Center. Language lab. 250,000-volume library.

Financial CEEB CSS. College scholarships, grants, loans; PELL, SEOG, NDSL, CWS, co-op job program required. Application deadline March 1.

Admissions High school graduation required; college prep program recommended. Interview recommended. ACT or SAT recommended. $20 application fee for out-of-state students. Rolling admissions. $150 deposit due on acceptance of admissions offer. *Early Admission, Early Decision, Concurrent Enrollment* programs. Admission deferral possible. Transfers accepted. Credit possible for CEEB AP, CLEP, and college's proficiency exams.

Student Life Community Council. Newspaper, radio station. Music, dance, drama, and film groups. Gay Center. Women's Center. Third World Alliance. Academic, political, professional, social, service, and special interest groups. Single students expected to live on campus. Coed dorms. Married-student housing. 90% of students live on campus. 4 hours of phys ed required. Extensive intramural, individual, and recreational sports programs. Student body composition: 1% Asian, 12% Black, 1% Hispanic, 1% Native American, 83% White, 2% Other. 89% from out of state.

[1] ASHLAND COLLEGE
Ashland 44805, (419) 289-5079
Director of Admissions: Carl Gerbasi, Jr.

- **Undergraduates: 660m, 593w; 2,757 total (including graduates)**
- **Tuition (1982/83): $5,166**
- **Room & Board: $2,230; Fees: $120**
- **Degrees offered: BA, BS, BMus, BSBA, BSCrim Jus, BSEd, BSHum Dev, BSN, BSW, AA**
- **Mean ACT 18.5; mean SAT 440v, 400m**
- **Student-faculty ratio: 17 to 1**

A private college affiliated with the Brethren Church, established in 1878. 67-acre suburban campus, 60 miles south of Cleveland. Served by bus.

Academic Character NCACS and professional accreditation. 4-1-4 system, 2 5-week summer terms. 65 majors offered in the areas of art, biology, business administration, chemistry, earth science, economics, education, English, foreign language, home economics, mathematics, music, nursing, philosophy, physical & health education, physics, psychology, radio/television, religion, social science, and speech. Minor required. Minors offered in most major fields and in 6 additional areas. Distributives and 3-4 hours of religion required. Graduate degrees granted. Independent study. Honors seminar. Limited pass/fail. Preprofessional programs in dentistry, engineering, law, medical technology, medicine, nursing, pharmacy, theology, veterinary medicine. 2-2 program in broadcast technology with Hocking. 2-2 and 3-2 engineering programs with U Detroit, Washington U. 3-3 nursing program with Case Western Reserve. Cooperative programs with 7 area schools. Northwest Ohio Consortium. Study in England, Vienna, Hong Kong. Elementary, secondary, and special education certification. AFROTC at Bowling Green. 166,505-volume library.

Financial CEEB CSS. College scholarships, grants, loans, state grants, tuition reduction for children of Brethren Church ministers, payment plans; PELL, SEOG, NDSL, CWS, institutional work/study program. Application deadline April 15.

Admissions High school graduation with 16 units required. GED accepted. Interview strongly recommended. SAT or ACT required. $15 application fee. Rolling admissions. $100 room deposit due on acceptance of admissions offer. *Early Decision* Program. Admission deferral possible. Transfers accepted. Credit possible for CEEB AP, CLEP, and college exams.

Student Life Student Senate. Newspaper, literary magazine, yearbook. Music groups. Debate. Council for Black Minority Edification. Academic, honorary, religious, and service groups. 6 fraternities and 5 sororities; all have houses. 25% of men and 28% of women join. Unmarried students live at home or on campus. Coed and single-sex dorms. 85% of students live on campus. 2 hours of phys ed required. 12 intercollegiate sports for men, 6 for women; intramurals. AIAW, NCAA. Student body composition: 1% Asian, 3% Black, 96% White. 20% from out of state.

[P] ASHLAND THEOLOGICAL SEMINARY
Ashland 44805

[1] ATHENAEUM OF OHIO, THE
Norwood, Cincinnati 45230, (513) 731-2630

- **Enrollment: 150 men & women**
- **Tuition (1982/83): $45 per credit hour**
- **Room & Board: $1,510**
- **Degree offered: BA**

A private institution for the training of candidates for the priesthood of the Roman Catholic Church and training of men and women for Catholic Lay Ministry. Founded in 1829.

Academic Character NCACS accreditation. Divisions include School of Theology (Mt. St. Mary's Seminary) and Lay Pastoral Ministry Program. BA offered in theology. MA in Theology, MA in Biblical Theology, MA in Religion, and MDiv granted. 70,000-volume library.

Admissions Rolling admissions. Transfers accepted. Students enter in September.

Student Life Housing available only for candidates for the priesthood.

[1] BALDWIN-WALLACE COLLEGE
Berea 44017, (216) 826-2424
Director of Admissions: John T. Amy

- **Undergraduates: 958m, 990w; 3,505 total (including graduates)**
- **Tuition (1982/83): $4,953; $5,397 (for music majors)**
- **Room & Board: $2,829; Fees: $228**
- **Degrees offered: BA, BS, BMus, BMus Ed, BSEd**
- **Mean ACT 20; mean SAT 450v, 450m**
- **Student-faculty ratio: 15 to 1**

A private college affiliated with the Methodist Church, established in 1845. 52-acre suburban campus, 15 miles southwest of Cleveland. Served by bus.

Academic Character NCACS and professional accreditation. Trimester system, 2 5-week summer terms. 43 majors offered in the areas of business, education, health & physical education, humanities, music, science & mathematics, and social sciences. Minors offered in most major fields. Distributives and senior comprehensive exams required. Graduate degrees granted. Independent reading program. Honors program. Limited pass/fail. Preprofessional programs in dentistry, engineering, forestry, government service, law, library science, medicine, medical technology, ministry. 3-2 engineering program with Columbia, Washington U, Case Western Reserve; 3-2 biology with Case; 3-2 forestry with Duke. 2-2 programs in dental hygiene, respiratory therapy, radiologic technology, and physician's surgical assistance with area community colleges. Washington Semester. UN Semester. Extensive study abroad program. Elementary and secondary education certification. Observatory. Learning center. Language lab. 200,000-volume library.

Financial CEEB CSS. College scholarships, grants, loans, state grants, payment plan; PELL, SEOG, NDSL, FISL, CWS.

Admissions High school graduation with 16 units required. SAT or ACT required. Interview desirable. Audition required for music majors. SAT or ACT required. $15 application fee. Rolling admissions. $100 deposit due on acceptance of admissions offer. *Early Admission* and *Concurrent Enrollment* programs. Admission deferral possible. Transfers accepted. Credit possible for CEEB AP and CLEP exams.

Student Life Student Senate. Women's Self-Governing Association. Newspaper, literary magazine, yearbook, radio station. Music, dance, and drama groups. Debate. Black Student Alliance. Academic, honorary, religious, and special interest groups. 7 fraternities and 7 sororities; all have suites. 35% of men and 25% of women join. Coed and single-sex dorms. 70% of students live on campus. 1 year of phys ed required. 9 intercollegiate sports for men, 6 for women; many intramural and club sports. AIAW, OAC. Student body composition: 7% Black, 1% Hispanic, 92% White. 12% from out of state.

[J1] BELMONT TECHNICAL COLLEGE
68094 Hammond Road, St. Clairsville 43950

[1] BLUFFTON COLLEGE
Bluffton 45817, (419) 358-8015

- **Undergraduates: 307m, 353w**
- **Tuition (1982/83): $4,320**
- **Room & Board: $1,760**
- **Degrees offered: BA, BSN**
- **Mean ACT 18; mean SAT 436v, 493m**
- **Student-faculty ratio: 13 to 1**

A private college controlled by the General Conference Mennonite Church, established in 1899. 234-acre small-town campus, halfway between Lima and Findley. Served by bus; rail service at Lima; air service 90 minutes away in Toledo and Dayton.

Academic Character NCACS accreditation. 1-3-3-2 system. 27 majors offered by the departments of art, economics & business, education, English & speech, foreign language, home economics, mathematics, music, nursing, psychology-sociology-social work, sciences, and health, physical education & recreation. Self-designed and special majors. Distributives, 2 units of religion, and junior oral & senior comprehensive exams required. Independent study. Honors program. Credit/no credit, credit by exam. Preprofessional programs in law and medicine. Study abroad. Elementary, secondary, and special education certification. Cooperative program in MR and LD/BD education with Bowling Green. Mennonite Historical Library. Computer center. 94,000-volume library with microform resources.

Financial CEEB CSS. College scholarships, grants, loans, discount for ministers' children, church-member scholarships; PELL, SEOG, NSS, NDSL, NDSL, NSL, CWS, student employment. Preferred application deadline April 1.

Admissions High school graduation with 16 units recommended. GED

accepted. ACT or SAT required. Interview recommended. Rolling admissions. $50 tuition and $25 room (for boarders) deposits due on acceptance of admissions offer. *Early Admission* Program. Transfers accepted. Credit possible for CEEB AP and CLEP exams.
Student Life Student government. Newspaper, yearbook, radio station. Music and drama groups. Black Student Union. PEACE. Academic, professional, service, and special interest groups. Students live at home or on campus. Single-sex dorms. Liquor, drugs, smoking, gambling, profanity prohibited. Honor system. 8 intercollegiate sports for men, 5 for women; intramurals. NAIA, OAISW, AIAW, HBCC. Student body composition: 13% minority.

[1] BORROMEO COLLEGE OF OHIO
28700 Euclid Avenue, Wickliffe 44012, (216) 943-3888

- **Undergraduates: 90m**
- **Tuition, Room & Board (1982/83): $3,000**
- **Degree offered: BA**

A private Romacn Catholic college for men.
Academic Character NCACS accreditation. Bachelor's degrees offered in liberal arts and general programs. Remedial mathematics and English programs available.
Admissions Rolling admissions. *Early Admission* and *Early Decision* programs. Advanced placement program.

[1] BOWLING GREEN STATE UNIVERSITY
Bowling Green 43403, (419) 372-2086
Director of Admissions: John W. Martin

- **Undergraduates: 6,059m, 8,187w; 17,080 total (including graduates)**
- **Tuition (1982/83): $1,473 (in-state), $3,228 (out-of-state)**
- **Room & Board: $1,756 (minimum)**
- **Degrees offered: BA, BS, BACom, BFA, BLib Studies, BMus, BS in 20 areas, AAB**
- **Mean ACT 21.2; mean SAT 451v, 484m**
- **Student-faculty ratio: 17 to 1**

A public university established in 1910. 1,250-acre suburban campus, 25 miles south of Toledo. Served by air and bus.
Academic Character NCACS and professional accreditation. Trimester system, 2 summer terms. 122 majors offered by the Colleges of Arts & Sciences, Business Administration, Education, Musical Arts, Health & Community Services; the Schools of Journalism, Technology, Nursing, and Health, Physical Education & Recreation; and the Department of Home Economics. Self-designed majors. Minors offered in some major fields. Distributive requirements. Graduate degrees granted. Independent study. Honors program. Cooperative work/study, pass/fail, internships. Preprofessional programs in dentistry, engineering, home economics, law, library science, mathematics, medicine, mortuary science, occupational therapy, optometry, osteopathy, pharmacy, religion, veterinary medicine. National Student Exchange. Washington Semester. Study abroad. Elementary, secondary, and special education certification. ROTC, AFROTC. Computer center. Language lab. 694,000-volume library with microform resources.
Financial CEEB CSS and ACT FAS. University scholarships, grants, loans, special talent grants, payment plans; PELL, SEOG, NSS, NDSL, NSL, CWS. Scholarship application deadline February 1.
Admissions High school graduation with 16 units required. GED accepted. Audition required for music majors. ACT or SAT required. $25 application fee. Rolling admissions. $100 room deposit due on acceptance of offer of admission. *Early Admission* and *Concurrent Enrollment* programs. Transfers accepted. Credit possible for CEEB AP and CLEP exams. Project Search minority recruitment.
Student Life Student government. Newspaper, yearbook, radio and TV stations. Music and theatre groups. Debate. Black Student Union. Spanish Student Union. 17 fraternities and 12 sororities; all have houses. 20% of students join. Juniors and seniors may live off campus. Coed and single-sex dorms. Special interest housing. 56% of students live on campus. 3 quarters of phys ed required. Several intercollegiate and intramural sports. AIAW, NCAA, MAC. Student body composition: 0.6% Asian, 4.1% Black, 0.6% Hispanic, 93.9% White, 0.8% Other. 8% from out of state.

■[J1] BOWLING GREEN STATE UNIVERSITY, Firelands Campus
Huron 44839

[1] CAPITAL UNIVERSITY
Columbus 43209, (614) 236-6101
Director of Admissions: Diane Kohlmeyer

- **Undergraduates: 638m, 834w; 2,569 total (including graduates)**
- **Tuition (1982/83): $5,350, $5,650 (music majors)**
- **Room & Board: $2,240**
- **Degrees offered: BA, BFA, BGS, BMus, BSN, BSW**
- **Mean SAT 490v, 520m**
- **Student-faculty ratio: 16 to 1**

A private university owned and maintained by the American Lutheran Church, established in 1850. 48-acre urban campus in Bexley, 4 miles from downtown Columbus. Served by air and bus.
Academic Character NCACS and professional accreditation. Semester system, 4- and 6-week summer terms, optional 8-week modules. 32 majors offered in the areas of art, business, education, humanities, music, nursing, physical education, religion, sciences, social work, and speech. Special majors. Minors offered in most major fields and in 9 additional areas. Distributive requirements. Graduate and professional degrees granted. Limited independent study. Honors program. Pass/fail, internships. Preprofessional programs in allied health, dentistry, law, medicine, pharmacy, theology. 3-2 engineering program with Washington U. Study abroad. Elementary, secondary, and special education certification. AFROTC. Art gallery. Language lab. 150,000-volume library.
Financial CEEB CSS. University scholarships, grants, loans, Lutheran grants, payment plan; PELL, SEOG, NDSL, GSL, CWS. Scholarship application deadline March 15.
Admissions High school graduation with 12 units required. Interview recommended. Audition required for music majors. SAT or ACT required. $15 application fee. Rolling admissions. $100 deposit due on acceptance of admissions offer. *Early Admission* and *Concurrent Enrollment* programs. Admission deferral possible. Transfers accepted. Credit possible for CEEB AP and CLEP exams.
Student Life Student government. Newspaper, literary magazine, yearbook. Music and drama groups. Debate. Students for Advancement of Afro-American Culture. Honorary, political, professional, religious, and service groups. 5 fraternities and 4 sororities without houses. 25% of students join. Students under 23 must live at home or on campus. 2 dorms for men, 3 for women. No married-student housing. 62% of students live on campus. 2 hours of phys ed required. 9 intercollegiate sports for men, 5 for women; intramurals. AIAW, NCAA, OC. Student body composition: 0.5% Asian, 12.5% Black, 0.2% Native American, 86.1% White, 0.7% Other. 13% from out of state.

[1] CASE WESTERN RESERVE UNIVERSITY
University Circle, Cleveland 44106, (216) 368-4450
Assoc. Dean of Student Affairs & Undergraduate Admissions: Donald W. Chenelle

- **Undergraduates: 2,121m, 818w; 8,488 total (including graduates)**
- **Tuition (1982/83): $6,200**
- **Room & Board: $2,940; Fees: $246**
- **Degrees offered: BSScience & Math (Case); BA, BS, BFA (Western Reserve)**
- **Mean SAT 549v, 654m (Case); 539v, 581m (Western Reserve)**
- **Student-faculty ratio: 9 to 1**

A private university established in 1967 by the federation of Case Institute of Technology (est.1880) and Western Reserve University (est.1826). 125-acre and 500-acre campuses, 20 minutes from downtown Cleveland. Served by air and bus.
Academic Character NCACS and professional accreditation. Semester system, 6-week summer term. Case offers 22 majors in mathematics & sciences. Western Reserve offers 43 majors in liberal arts & sciences, accounting, gerontology, legal studies, music & art education, nutrition, and theatre. Minors in most major fields. Special majors. Distributive requirements. Graduate degrees granted. Independent study. Undergraduate Scholars Program. Phi Beta Kappa. Cooperative work/study at Case, pass/fail, credit by exam. Preprofessional programs in dentistry, law, library science, management, medicine, nursing, social work. Case offers 3-2 engineering program with 32 colleges. 6-year dental program. Cross-registration with 6 area schools. Washington Semester. Study abroad. Art and music education certification. NROTC; ROTC at John Carroll, AFROTC at Akron. Computer center, observatories, biological research station. 1,613,000-volume library with microform resources.
Financial CEEB CSS. University scholarships, grants, loans, payment plans; PELL, SEOG, NDSL, FISL, GSL, CWS. Application deadline February 1.
Admissions High school graduation with 16 units required. Interview recommended. Audition required for music applicants; portfolio for art students. ACT or SAT required; 3 ACH recommended. $20 application fee. Rolling admissions. $150 deposit due on acceptance of offer of admission. Admission deferral possible. Transfers accepted. Credit possible for CEEB AP and departmental exams.
Student Life Student government. Newspaper, magazines, yearbook, radio station. Music, film, and drama groups. Afro-American Society. Women's Center. Commuter Club. Academic, honorary, professional, religious, and special interest groups. 16 fraternities, all with houses; 3 sororities with limited housing. 20% of students join. Single students live at home or on campus. Coed and single-sex dorms. Married-student apartments. 85% of students live on campus. 1 year of phys ed required for freshmen. 6 intercollegiate sports for men, 6 for women; many club and intramural sports. PAC, AIAW. Student body composition: 3.2% Asian, 3.9% Black, 0.8% Hispanic, 0.3% Native American, 91.8% White. 48% from out of state.

[1] CEDARVILLE COLLEGE
Cedarville 45314, (513) 766-2211
Director of Admissions: David M. Ormsbee

- **Undergraduates: 717m, 868w; 1,657 total (including part-time)**
- **Tuition (1982/83): $2,976**
- **Room & Board: $2,085; Fees: $231**
- **Degree offered: BA, BSN**
- **Mean ACT 20.5**
- **Student-faculty ratio: 22 to 1**

A private college controlled by the Baptist Church, established in 1887. 180-acre small-town campus, 45 miles southwest of Columbus.
Academic Character NCACS accreditation. Trimester system, 2 5-week summer terms. Majors offered in accounting, behavioral science, Bible, biology, broadcasting, business, chemistry, education, English, history, mathematics, medical technology, music, nursing, physical education, political science, psychology, social science, sociology, Spanish, and speech. Special majors. Minors offered in 6 areas. Distributives, 24 credit hours of Biblical education, and GRE required. Independent study. Cooperative work/study, pass/fail, internships, credit by exam. Preprofessional programs in dentistry, medicine, veterinary medicine. Pharmacy program with Ohio State. Transfer programs in engineering, nursing, physical therapy. Study abroad. Elementary and secondary education certification; special education

with Wright State. ROTC at Central; AFROTC at Wright. 95,000-volume library with microform resources.
Financial CEEB CSS. College scholarships, grants, loans, state grants, payment plans; PELL, SEOG, NDSL, GSL, FISL, job opportunities. Scholarship application deadline April 1.
Admissions High school graduation with 15 units required. ACT or SAT required; ACT preferred. $15 application fee. Rolling admissions. $250 deposit ($125 for commuters) required on acceptance of admissions offer. *Early Admission* Program. Admission deferral possible. Transfers accepted. Credit possible for CEEB AP, CLEP, and ACT PEP exams. Educational Development Program for underprepared students.
Student Life Student Senate. Newspaper, yearbook, radio station. Music and drama groups. Debate. Missionary Internship. Honorary and special interest groups. Single-sex dorms. Married-student housing nearby. 85% of students live on campus. First-quarter freshmen may not have cars. Liquor, tobacco, narcotics, gambling, dancing, movies prohibited. Dress code. Daily chapel required. Church attendance 3 times per week mandatory. 3 phys ed courses required. 8 intercollegiate sports for men, 6 for women; intramurals. NAIA, NCAA, AIAW, MOC. Student body composition: 1.5% Black, 97% White, 1.5% Other. 63% from out of state.

[J1] CENTRAL OHIO TECHNICAL COLLEGE
Newark 43055

[1] CENTRAL STATE UNIVERSITY
Wilberforce 45384, (513) 376-1351
Director of Admissions: Edith W. Johnson

- **Undergraduates: 1,117m, 1,074w**
- **Tuition (1982/83): $1,290 (in-state), $2,301 (out-of-state)**
- **Room & Board: $2,607; Fees: $240**
- **Degrees offered: BA, BS, BSEd**
- **Student-faculty ratio: 15 to 1**

A public university established in 1887. 550-acre rural campus, 18 miles east of Dayton. Served by air and bus in Dayton.
Academic Character NCACS accreditation. Trimester system, 8-week summer term. 33 majors offered by the College of Arts & Sciences, 20 by the College of Education, and 9 by the College of Business Administration. Minors required in some departments. Distributive requirements. Honors program. Cooperative work/study, credit by exam. Preprofessional programs in allied health, dentistry, law, medicine, theology. 3-1 medical technology program. 2-2 and 3-2 engineering programs with Wright. Cross-registration with 15 area schools. Elementary, secondary, and special education certification. ROTC. Performing arts center. Language lab. Computer center. 146,000-volume library with microform resources.
Financial CEEB CSS. University scholarships, grants, loans; PELL, SEOG, NDSL, GSL, CWS. Scholarship application deadline May 15.
Admissions High school graduation required. Open admissions for Ohio residents. GED accepted. ACT required. $15 application fee. Rolling admissions. $60 room deposit due on acceptance of admissions offer. *Early Admission* and *Concurrent Enrollment* programs. Admission deferral possible. Transfers accepted. Credit possible for CEEB CLEP exams.
Student Life Student government. Newspaper, yearbook, radio and TV stations. Music and drama groups. Interfaith Campus Ministry. Honorary, service, and special interest groups. 4 fraternities and 3 sororities without houses. 10% of students join. Juniors and seniors may live off campus. Single-sex dorms. No married-student housing. 49% of students live on campus. 5 hours of phys ed required. 7 intercollegiate sports for men, 4 for women; intramurals. AIAW, NAIA, NCAA. Student body composition: 0.1% Asian, 85.2% Black, 0.1% Hispanic, 10.2% White. 27% from out of state.

[J1] CHATFIELD COLLEGE
St. Martin 45118

[J1] CHILLICOTHE BRANCH (Ohio University)
Chillicothe 45601

[2] CINCINNATI, ART ACADEMY OF
Eden Park, Cincinnati 45202

[1] CINCINNATI, UNIVERSITY OF
Cincinnati 45221, (513) 475-3427
Director of Admissions: Robert W. Neel

- **Undergraduates: 10,105m, 8,467w; 38,895 total (including graduates)**
- **Tuition (1982/83): $1,479 (in-state), $3,444 (out-of-state)**
- **Room & Board: $2,316**
- **Degrees offered: BA, BS, BBA, BFA, BGS, BMus, BSEd, BSIn Man, AA, AS**
- **Mean ACT 22; SAT 434v, 495m**
- **Student-faculty ratio: 17 to 1**

A public university established in 1819. 200-acre urban campus, 2 miles from downtown Cincinnati. Served by air, rail, and bus.
Academic Character NCACS and professional accreditation. Trimester system, 3 summer term totaling 10 weeks. 36 majors offered in the arts & sciences, 4 in applied sciences, 9 in business, 4 in community service, 20 in music, 9 in design, architecture, & art, 10 in education, 8 in engineering, and majors in nursing and pharmacy. Self-designed majors. Distributive requirements. Senior comprehensive exams required in some departments. Graduate degrees granted. Independent study. Honors program. Phi Beta Kappa. Cooperative work/study, pass/fail, internships. Exchange programs with Art Academy and Hebrew Union. Cincinnati Consortium of Colleges. Washington Semester. Study abroad. Elementary, secondary, and special education certification. ROTC, AFROTC. Language lab. 1,600,000-volume library with microform resources.
Financial CEEB CSS. University scholarships, grants, loans, state grants & loans, payment plan; PELL, SEOG, NSS, NDSL, NSL, CWS, college has own work program. Application deadline February 1.
Admissions High school graduation with 12 units required for Arts & Sciences. Specific course requirements for professional colleges. Audition required for music and dance majors. 2 letters of professional recommendation necessary for broadcasting majors. SAT or ACT required. $25 application fee. Rolling admissions. $75 deposit required on acceptance of offer of admission. Transfers accepted. Credit possible for CEEB AP and CLEP exams.
Student Life Student government. Newspaper, literary magazine. Music and drama groups. Debate. Student Community Involvement Program. Athletic, academic, honorary, political, special interest, and vocational groups. 21 fraternities and 15 sororities, all with houses. 7% of men and 9% of women join. Freshmen & sophomores under 21 must live at home or on campus as long as space is available. Coed, single-sex, and special interest dorms. Married-student housing. 7% of students live on campus. 11 intercollegiate sports; intramural & club sports. AIAW, NCAA, MCAC. Student body composition: 1% Asian, 10% Black, 80% White, 9% Other. 14% from out of state.

■[J1] CLERMONT GENERAL AND TECHNICAL COLLEGE OF THE UNIVERSITY OF CINCINNATI
College Drive, Batavia 45103

[P] CINCINNATI BIBLE SEMINARY
2700 Glenway Avenue, Cincinnati 45204

[P] CINCINNATI COLLEGE OF MORTUARY SCIENCE
Cincinnati 45206

[J1] CINCINNATI STATE TECHNICAL COLLEGE
3520 Central Parkway, Cincinnati 45223

[P] CIRCLEVILLE BIBLE COLLEGE
Lancaster Pike East, PO Box 458, Circleville 43113

[J1] CLARK TECHNICAL COLLEGE
570 East Leffels Lane, PO Box 570, Springfield 45501

[1] CLEVELAND INSTITUTE OF ART
11141 East Blvd., Cleveland 44106, (216) 421-4322

- **Undergraduates: 251m, 265w**
- **Tuition & Fees (1982/83): $4,000**
- **Room & Board: $2,650**
- **Total Costs: $8,000**
- **Degree offered: BFA**
- **Median ACT 20; median SAT 450v, 450m**
- **Student-faculty ratio: 10 to 1**

A private college of art founded in 1882. Campus located in University Circle (a group of 35 educational, cultural, medical, religious, and social service organizations), 4 miles east of downtown Cleveland.
Academic Character NCACS and professional accreditation. Semester system. Five-year program offered leading to the Bachelor of Fine Arts degree. Majors include ceramics, enameling, drawing, glassblowing, graphic design & illustration, industrial design, medical illustration & photography, painting, photography, printmaking, sculpture, silversmithing, textile design, and weaving. Art teacher education program offered in conjunction with Case Western Reserve University. Remedial English program. 40,000-volume library with a 45,000-slide collection, print & cassette collections, and other resources.
Financial CEEB CSS. Aid available including NDSL, GSL, and student employment.
Admissions High school graduation required. GED accepted. Portfolio required. SAT or ACT required. Rolling admissions; application deadline July 29. *Early Admission* and *Early Decision* programs. Admission deferral possible. Advanced placement program.
Student Life Dormitories and dining halls available.

[1] CLEVELAND INSTITUTE OF MUSIC
11021 East Blvd., Cleveland 44106

[1] CLEVELAND STATE UNIVERSITY
Euclid Avenue at East 24th Street, Cleveland 44115, (216) 687-3755
Director of Admissions: Dr. Richard C. Dickerman

- **Enrollment: 10,532m, 8,617w**
- **Tuition (1982/83): $1,377 (in-state), $2,754 (out-of-state)**
- **Room: $630**
- **Degrees offered: BA, BS, BSEd, BMus, BSN, BBA, BSBus Ed, BSTech, 7 BSEngs**
- **Mean ACT 17; mean SAT 433v, 469m**
- **Student-faculty ratio: 21 to 1**

A public university established in 1964. 44-acre urban campus. Served by air, rail, and bus.
Academic Character NCACS and professional accreditation. Trimester

system, 5½-, 8-, and 11-week summer terms. 56 majors offered by the colleges of Arts & Sciences, Business Administration, Education, Engineering, and Urban Affairs. Distributive requirements. Graduate degrees granted. Independent study. Honors program. Cooperative work/study, pass/fail, credit by exam. Preprofessional programs in dentistry, medicine, veterinary medicine. 3-1, 4-1 medical technology programs. Study abroad. Elementary, secondary, and special education certification. ROTC. Computer center, media services. 660,000-volume library with microform resources.
Financial CEEB CSS. University scholarships, grants, loans; PELL, SEOG, NSS, NDSL, FISL, NSL, CWS. Application deadline April 15.
Admissions High school graduation with 12 units recommended. Open admission to Ohio students. GED accepted. SAT or ACT required. $25 application fee. Rolling admissions. *Early Admission* and *Early Decision* programs. Admission deferral possible. Transfers accepted. Credit possible for CEEB AP and CLEP exams; university has own advanced placement program.
Student Life Student government. Newspaper, literary magazine, radio station. Music, dance, and drama groups. Social, political, professional, recreational, and religious groups. 8 fraternities, 4 with houses; 5 sororities without houses. Less than 1% of students join. Limited dorm facilities for men and women. 1% of students live on campus. No meal plans; cafeteria service only. 3 hours of phys ed required. 11 intercollegiate sports for men, 6 for women; intramurals. AIAW, NCAA. Student body composition: 17% minority. 1% of students from out of state.

■[P] CLEVELAND-MARSHALL COLLEGE OF LAW
Cleveland 44115

[2] COLUMBUS COLLEGE OF ART AND DESIGN
47 North Washington Avenue, Columbus 43215, (614) 224-9101
Directors of Admissions: Laurie Clements, Patrick Marion

- **Undergraduates: 335m, 359w**
- **Tuition (1982/83): $3,750**
- **Room: $1,200; Fees: $390**
- **Degree offered: BFA**
- **Student-faculty ratio: 10 to 1**

A private college established in 1879. Urban campus in downtown Columbus. Served by air, rail, and bus.
Academic Character Professional accreditation; NCACS accreditation candidate. Semester system, summer term. Majors offered in advertising design, art therapy, ceramics, fashion illustration, fine arts, glassblowing, industrial design, illustration, interior design, packaging, painting, photography, printmaking, retail advertising, and sculpture. Dual majors possible. Foundation first year. Independent study. Library including print and slide collections.
Financial CCAD National Scholarship Competition; apply by April 1. NDSL, GSL, CWS.
Admissions High school graduation required. Portfolio of 7-14 pieces required. SAT or ACT required. $25 application fee. Rolling admissions. $100 deposit due on acceptance of admissions offer. *Concurrent Enrollment* Program. Transfers accepted.
Student Life Student-produced publications. Special interest groups. Dorm housing only for freshmen. No meal plan. Student body composition: 1% Asian, 6.1% Black, 0.6% Hispanic, 0.3% Native American, 90.5% White, 1.5% Other.

[J1] COLUMBUS TECHNICAL INSTITUTE
PO Box 1609, Columbus 43216

[J1] CUYAHOGA COMMUNITY COLLEGE
2900 Community College Avenue, Cleveland 44115

■[J1] CUYAHOGA COMMUNITY COLLEGE—EASTERN CAMPUS
4250 Richmond Road, Warrensville Township 44240

■[J1] CUYAHOGA COMMUNITY COLLEGE—METROPOLITAN CAMPUS
2900 Community College Avenue, Cleveland 44115

■[J1] CUYAHOGA COMMUNITY COLLEGE—WESTERN CAMPUS
11000 Pleasant Valley Road, Parma 44130

[1] DAYTON, UNIVERSITY OF
300 College Park Avenue, Dayton 45469, (513) 229-4411
Director of Admissions: Myron H. Achbach

- **Undergraduates: 3,520m, 2,823w; 10,870 total (including graduates)**
- **Tuition (1982/83): $3,700**
- **Room & Board: $2,240; Fees: $210**
- **Degrees offered: BA, BS, BFA, BMus, BSBA, BSArt Ed, BSEd, BSHom Econ Ed, BSMus Ed, BE, BCE, BChE, BEE, BME, BGS, BTech, ABA, ATech**
- **Mean ACT 22; mean SAT 467v, 523m**
- **Student-faculty ratio: 18 to 1**

A private university controlled by the Society of Mary, established in 1850. 76-acre suburban campus. Served by air and bus.
Academic Character NCACS and professional accreditation. Semester system, 2 6-week summer terms. 41 majors offered by the College of Arts & Sciences, 5 by the School of Business Administration, 10 by the School of Education, and 10 by the School of Engineering. Special majors. Minors offered in some major fields and in 4 other areas. Distributive requirements. Graduate degrees granted. Independent study. Honors program. Cooperative work/study, limited pass/fail, internships in some areas. Preprofessional programs in dentistry, law, medicine. 2-2 medical technology program with Kettering. 3-1 cytotechology program with Miami Valley. Cross-registration with 13 area schools. Consortium for Higher Education Religion Studies. Study abroad. Kindergarten, elementary, secondary, and special education certification. ROTC. Computer center. Center for Afro-American Affairs. 800,000-volume library with microform resources.
Financial CEEB CSS. University scholarships, grants, loans, academic scholarships, tuition reduction for 2nd family member, state grants; PELL, SEOG, NDSL, GSL, USAF, CWS, institutional work program. Application deadlines January 15 (freshman scholarships), April 30 (other aid).
Admissions High school graduation with 15-18 units preferred. GED accepted. Interview recommended. SAT or ACT required; ACH optional. $15 application fee. Rolling admissions. $120 deposit due on acceptance of admissions offer. *Early Admission, Concurrent Enrollment, Early Decision* programs. Admission deferral possible. Transfers accepted. Credit possible for CEEB AP, ACH, and CLEP exams.
Student Life Student government. Newspaper, literary magazine, yearbook, radio and TV stations. Music and drama groups. Debate. Veterans Club. Women's Center. International Club. Noon Forums. Academic, professional, and service groups. 16 fraternities and 5 sororities. Freshmen and sophomores under 21 must live at home or on campus. Single-sex dorms. 45% of students live on campus. Limited class absences for freshmen. 8 intercollegiate sports for men, 5 for women; intramurals. AIAW. Student body composition: 0.4% Asian, 4.3% Black, 1.1% Hispanic, 0.1% Native American, 89.1% White, 5% Other. 42% from out of state.

[1] DEFIANCE COLLEGE
Defiance 43512, (419) 784-4010
Director of Admissions: Brian Kesse

- **Undergraduates: 322m, 293w**
- **Tuition (1982/83): $3,930**
- **Room & Board: $1,980; Fees: $200**
- **Degrees offered: BA, BS, AA**
- **Mean SAT 470v, 460m**
- **Student-faculty ratio: 14 to 1**

A private college affiliated with the United Church of Christ, established in 1850. 159-acre suburban campus. Served by bus; airport 1 hour away in Toledo.
Academic Character NCACS and professional accreditation. 4-1-4 system, 4- and 7-week summer terms. 38 majors offered in the areas of business administration, Christian education, communication arts, computer science, criminal justice, education, fine arts, liberal arts, mathematics, medical technology, physical education, religion, science, and social sciences. Self-designed majors. Distributives and 6 hours of religion & philosophy required. Independent study. Cooperative work/study, pass/fail, internships. Preprofessional programs in dentistry, law, medicine, nursing, theology, veterinary medicine. Cooperative program in special education with Bowling Green. Washington Semester. Study abroad. Operations Crossroads Africa. Elementary, secondary, and special education certification. Art gallery. Genetics center. 80,000-volume library.
Financial Guaranteed tuition. CEEB CSS. College scholarships, grants, loans, church vocation scholarships, state scholarships & grants, payment plans; PELL, SEOG, NDSL, PLUS, CWS.
Admissions High school graduation with 14 units required. SAT or ACT required. $20 application fee. Rolling admissions. $100 tuition and $25 room deposits due on acceptance of admissions offer. *Early Admission* Program. Transfers accepted. Credit possible for CEEB CLEP exams.
Student Life Student government. Newspaper, literary magazine, yearbook. Music and drama groups. Honorary, ethnic, religious, and special interest groups. 3 fraternities with houses; 3 sororities without housing. 30% of students join. Single-sex dorms. 70% of students live on campus. Liquor, drugs, gambling prohibited. 1 semester of phys ed required. 7 intercollegiate sports for men, 3 for women; intramurals. AIAW, H-BCC. Student body composition: 5% Black, 2% Hispanic, 0.5% Native American, 90% White, 2.5% Other. 10% from out of state.

[1] DENISON UNIVERSITY
Granville 43023, (614) 587-0810
Director of Admissions: Richard F. Boyden

- **Undergraduates: 1,054m, 1,048w**
- **Tuition (1982/83): $6,320**
- **Room & Board: $2,360; Fees: $350**
- **Degrees offered: BA, BS, BFA, BMus**
- **Mean SAT 500v, 540m**
- **Student-faculty ratio: 13 to 1**

A private university established in 1831. 1,000-acre small-town campus, 27 miles east of Columbus. Airport in Columbus.
Academic Character NCACS and professional accreditation. 4-1-4 system. 33 majors offered in the areas of art, dance, English, history, mathematics, modern languages, music, philosophy, physical education, political science, psychology, religion, science, sociology, speech, and several area studies. Self-designed majors. Minors offered in most major fields. Distributives, 2 January terms, and 1 credit in philosophy or religion required. Senior comprehensive exams required in some areas. Independent study. Honors program. Phi Beta Kappa. Pass/fail, internships. Preprofessional programs in business, dentistry, law, medicine. 3-1 medical technology program. 3-2 engineering program with Case Western Reserve, Columbia, Rensselaer, U Rochester. 3-2 programs in forestry and natural resources with Duke and U Michigan. Cross-registration with 12 midwestern

liberal arts colleges. Black College Student Exchange Program. New York City Arts Program. Human development semester at Merrill-Palmer. Management semester at Keller. Urban semester in Philadelphia. Oak Ridge Semester. Washington Semester. Newberry Library Semester. Study abroad. Secondary education certification. Computer center. Language lab. 248,000-volume library.

Financial CEEB CSS. University scholarships, grants, loans, state grants, payment plan; PELL, SEOG, NDSL, GSL, CWS. Scholarship application deadline February 15.

Admissions High school graduation with 16 units expected. Interview recommended. ACT or SAT required; ACH recommended. $20 application fee. Application deadline February 1. $200 deposit due on acceptance of offer of admission. *Early Decision* and *Early Admission* programs. Admission deferral possible. Transfers accepted. Credit possible for CEEB AP, CLEP, and university exams. Special attention to minority groups.

Student Life Student government. Newspaper, literary magazine, yearbook, radio station. Music, dance, and drama groups. Black Student Union. Academic, political, religious, service, and special interest groups. 10 fraternities with houses, 5 sororities with non-residential chapter houses. 60% of men and 46% of women join. All freshmen live on campus. Coed and single-sex dorms. Some married-student housing. 91% of students live on campus. Upperclassmen may have cars. 10 intercollegiate sports for men, 10 for women; several intramurals. AIAW, NCAA, OAC. Student body composition: 4% Black, 95% White, 1% Other. 74% from out of state.

[1] DYKE COLLEGE
1375 East 6th Street, Cleveland 44114

[2] EDGECLIFF COLLEGE
2220 Victory Parkway, Cincinnati 45206

- **Enrollment: 900 men & women**
- **Tuition (1981/82): $2,016**
- **Room & Board: $1,420**
- **Degrees offered: BA, BS, AA, AS**
- **Student-faculty ratio: 16 to 1**

A private, Roman Catholic college established in 1935; formerly Our Lady of Cincinnati College. Campus in suburban Cincinnati.

Academic Character Semester system. 5- and 8-week summer terms. Majors offered in the humanities and social sciences. AA offered in humanities and social sciences, AS in child care. Acceleration permits earning the degree in less than four years. Academic cooperation with 12 area colleges. Pre-college program for high school seniors. Primary level Montessori Teacher Training available on campus. 80,000-volume library.

Financial CEEB CSS. College scholarships & grants, academic & art scholarships, state grants; PELL, SEOG, NDSL, CWS.

Admissions High school graduation required. GED accepted. SAT and ACT accepted. Transfers accepted. Credit possible for CEEB CLEP exams.

Student Life On-campus housing for men and women. No married-student housing. Cafeteria available. Limited athletics programs available.

[J1] EDISON STATE COMMUNITY COLLEGE
Piqua 45356

[1] FINDLAY COLLEGE
Findlay 45840, (419) 422-8313
Director of Admissions: J. Michael Turnbull

- **Undergraduates: 531m, 510w**
- **Tuition (1982/83): $4,380**
- **Room & Board: $1,970; Fees: $45**
- **Degrees offered: BA, BS, AA**
- **Student-faculty ratio: 15 to 1**

A private college affiliated with the Churches of God, General Conference; established in 1882. 25-acre small-town campus, 46 miles from Toledo. Served by air, rail, and bus.

Academic Character NCACS and professional accreditation. Semester system, 2 5-week summer terms. 36 majors offered by the divisions of Business & Economics, Education, Fine Arts, Humanities, Natural Science, Social Science, and Health, Physical Education, & Recreation. Special majors. Distributives and 18 credits of religion required. Seniors take Undergraduate Record Exam. Independent study. Honors program. Limited pass/fail, credit by exam. Preprofessional programs in law, medicine, theology. 2-2 programs in nursing and physical therapy. 3-1 medical technology program. 3-2 engineering program. Study abroad. Elementary and secondary education certification. Computer center. Spanish lab. 90,000-volume library.

Financial CEEB CSS. College scholarships, grants, loans, state grants, payment plans; PELL, SEOG, NDSL, GSL, CWS. Application deadline April 1.

Admissions High school graduation with 10-13 units recommended. Interview recommended. SAT or ACT required; ACH required for placement. Rolling admissions. $100 deposit due on acceptance of admissions offer. *Early Decision* Program. Transfers accepted. Credit possible for CEEB AP, CLEP, and college proficiency exams.

Student Life Student government. Newspaper, yearbook, radio station. Music and drama groups. Black Student Union. Athletic, academic, honorary, political, professional, religious, service, and special interest groups. 4 fraternities and 3 sororities, all with houses. Students under 22 must live at home or on campus. Single-sex dorms. Visitation hours. 60% of students live on campus. Liquor prohibited. 5 terms of phys ed required. 9 intercollegiate sports for men, 5 for women; intramurals. AIAW, NAIA, HBCC. Student body composition: 7.2% Black, 0.2% Hispanic, 90% White. 15% from out of state.

[1] FRANKLIN UNIVERSITY
201 South Grant Avenue, Columbus 43215

[G1] HEBREW UNION COLLEGE—JEWISH INSTITUTE OF RELIGION
Clifton Avenue, Cincinnati 45220

[1] HEIDELBERG COLLEGE
Tiffin 44883, (419) 448-2000
Director of Admissions: Anne Kear

- **Undergraduates: 353m, 340w**
- **Tuition (1982/83): $5,550**
- **Room & Board: $2,270; Fees: $70**
- **Degrees offered: AB, BS, BMus**
- **Mean ACT 20**
- **Student-faculty ratio: 12 to 1**

A private college affiliated with the United Church of Christ, established in 1850. 100-acre campus in a small city 52 miles from Toledo. Served by bus; rail station in Toledo.

Academic Character NCACS and professional accreditation. Semester system, 2 summer terms. 31 majors offered in the areas of American studies, business administration, communication/theatre, computer science, education, foreign languages, humanities, physical education, medieval studies, music, politics, psychology, religion, science, and sociology. Self-designed majors. Independent study. Honors program. Home study—on campus consultation program. Cooperative programs in agriculture (Ohio State), forestry (Duke), engineering, medical technology, nursing, (Case), Japanese (SUNY). Washington, United Nations, Merrill-Palmer, Argonne Lab semesters. Study abroad. Elementary and secondary education certification. Water Quality Lab. 139,000-volume library.

Financial CEEB CSS. College scholarships, grants, loans, grants for ministers' children and UCC members, payment plans; PELL, SEOG, NDSL, CWS. Application deadline April 1.

Admissions High school graduation required. Interview recommended. Music majors must audition. SAT or ACT required. $15 application fee. Rolling admissions. $100 room deposit due on acceptance of admissions offer. *Early Decision* and *Early Admission* programs. Admission deferral possible. Transfers accepted. Credit possible for CEEB AP and CLEP exams.

Student Life Student participation in faculty committees, college council. Newspaper, literary magazine, yearbook, radio station. Athletic, academic, honorary, musical, religious, and special interest groups. 4 fraternities and 5 sororities without housing. 35% of students join. Seniors may live off campus if dorms are full. 4 dorms for men, 4 for women. Married-student housing available. 85% of students live on campus. Drugs and gambling prohibited. Class attendance expected. 2 years of phys ed required. 10 intercollegiate sports for men, 7 for women; intramurals. AIAW, NCAA, OAC. Student body composition: 0.2% Asian, 5.7% Black, 0.2% Hispanic, 93.8% White. 25% from out of state.

[1] HIRAM COLLEGE
Hiram 44234, (216) 569-3211
Dean of Admissions: John P. Pirozzi

- **Undergraduates: 600m, 550w**
- **Tuition (1982/83): $5,970**
- **Room & Board: $1,905; Fees: $80**
- **Degree offered: BA**
- **Mean SAT 500v, 480m**
- **Student-faculty ratio: 12 to 1**

A private college affiliated with the Disciples of Christ, established in 1850. 145-acre rural campus, 35 miles southeast of Cleveland.

Academic Character NCACS and professional accreditation. Trimester system, November interterm, 3- and 6-week summer terms. 32 majors offered in the areas of liberal arts & sciences, computer science, education, management, physical education, and religion. Special and self-designed majors. Minors offered in most major fields and in 12 other areas. Courses in Arabic, Greek, Latin. Distributives and 1 religion or philosophy course required. Some independent study. Honors program. Phi Beta Kappa. Limited pass/fail, internships. Preprofessional programs in dentistry, medicine, optometry, podiatry, veterinary medicine. 3-1 medical technology program. 3-2 nursing program with Case Western Reserve. 3-2 engineering with Case Western, Washington U. 3-2 agriculture and home economics programs with Ohio State. Many study abroad programs. United Nations Semester. Washington Semester. Elementary, secondary, and special education certification. AFROTC; ROTC at Kent State. Computer center. Art and music centers. Observatory. Language lab. 150,000-volume library.

Financial CEEB CSS. College scholarships, grants, loans, chemistry and music scholarships, payment plan; PELL, SEOG, NDSL, GSL, CWS.

Admissions High school graduation with 16 units recommended. Interview recommended. SAT or ACT required. $15 application fee. Rolling admissions. $100 deposit due on acceptance of offer of admission. *Early Admission* Program. Admission deferral possible. Transfers accepted. Credit possible for CEEB AP and CLEP exams; college has own advanced placement program.

Student Life Student government. Newspaper, literary magazine, yearbook, radio station. Music and drama groups. Alliance for Black Consciousness. Academic, honorary, tutoring, and special interest groups. 3 social clubs for men, 3 for women. 20% of students join. Freshmen must live at home or on campus. Coed and single-sex dorms. Special interest houses. Married-student housing. 90% of students live on campus. 6 activity units, including 3 in phys ed, required. 8 intercollegiate sports for men, 5 for women, 3 coed; club & intramural sports. AIAW, NCAA, PAC, WRAC. Student body composition: 0.6% Asian, 9.1% Black, 0.4% Hispanic, 89.8% White. 35% from out of state.

[J1] HOCKING TECHNICAL COLLEGE
Nelsonville 45764, (614) 753-3591
Director of Admissions: Candace S. Vancko

- **Enrollment: 4,200 men & women**
- **Tuition & Fees (1982/83): $846 (OH & Appalachian residents), $1,692 (others)**
- **Estimated Room & Board: $1,900**
- **Degree offered: AS**

A public college established in 1969. Small-town campus, 60 miles southeast of Columbus.
Academic Character NCACS accreditation. 2-year terminal and transfer mprograms offered in business technologies, engineering technologies, health career technologies, natural resources technologies, and public service technologies. General studies programs.
Financial CEEB CSS. State grants, PELL, SEOG, NSS, GSL, CETA, CWS, Earn & Learn.
Admissions Open admissions. High school transcript or equivalent required. Interview recommended. $10 application fee. Rolling admissions. Admission deferral possible. Transfers accepted. Credit possible for experience and departmental exams.
Student Life Student Senate. Social events. Privately-owned dorm available on campus. Information on available housing from Admissions Office. Intramural sports.

[J1] JEFFERSON TECHNICAL COLLEGE
4000 Sunset Blvd., Steubenville 43952

[1] JOHN CARROLL UNIVERSITY
20700 North Park Blvd., University Heights 44118, (216) 491-4911
Director of Admissions: John P. Sammon

- **Undergraduates: 1,404m, 1,196w**
- **Tuition (1982/83): $3,968**
- **Room & Board: $2,250**
- **Degrees offered: AB, ABClassics, BS, BSBA**
- **Mean SAT 502v, 534m**
- **Student-faculty ratio: 15 to 1**

A private Roman Catholic university conducted by the Society of Jesus. Established in 1886, became coed in 1968. 66-acre suburban campus, 12 miles southeast of downtown Cleveland. Served by air, rail, and bus.
Academic Character NCACS and professional accreditation. Semester system, 2 5-week summer terms. 20 majors offered in the arts & humanities, 7 in sciences, and 6 in business. Self-designed majors. Minors in some major fields and in 4 other areas. Distributives, 2 religion courses, and senior comprehensive exams required. Graduate degrees granted. Independent study. Honors program. Cooperative work/study, pass/fail, internships. Preprofessional programs in dentistry, law, medicine. 3-2 engineering programs with Case Western Reserve, Washington U; 2-2 with Case, U Detroit. 3-3 nursing program with Case. Study abroad. Kindergarten, elementary, and secondary education certification. ROTC. Language lab. Computer center. Institute on Violence and Aggression. Seismological observatory. 325,000-volume library.
Financial CEEB CSS. University scholarships, grants, loans, Presidential Honor Awards, American Values Scholarships, payment plans; PELL, SEOG, NDSL, GSL, CWS. Application deadline March 1.
Admissions High school graduation with 16 units required. Interview recommended. SAT or ACT required; 3 ACH required for advanced standing. $20 application fee. Rolling admissions. $110 deposit ($50 for commuters) due on acceptance of admissions offer. *Early Decision, Early Admission, Concurrent Enrollment* programs. Admission deferral possible. Transfers accepted. Credit possible for CEEB AP exams; university has own advanced placement program.
Student Life Student government. Newspaper, literary magazine, yearbook, radio station. Music and drama groups. Debate. Afro-American Society. Hillel. Academic, honorary, military, religious, service, and special interest groups. Students live at home, on campus, or in university-arranged housing. 55% of students live on campus. Freshmen and sophomores required to attend classes. Freshmen may not have cars on campus. 10 intercollegiate sports for men, 4 for women, coed rifle team; club & intramural sports. AIAW, NCAA, PAC. Student body composition: 0.7% Asian, 4.3% Black, 0.4% Hispanic, 94.2% White, 0.4% Other. 30% from out of state.

[1] KENT STATE UNIVERSITY
Kent 44242, (216) 672-2444
Director of Admissions: Bruce L. Riddle

- **Undergraduates: 6,313m, 6,813w; 19,660 total (including graduates)**
- **Tuition (1982/83): $1,712 (in-state), $2,912 (out-of-state)**
- **Room & Board: $1,700-$1,980**
- **Degrees offered: BA, BS, BGS, BBA, BFA, BMus, BArch, BMus Ed, BSN**
- **Mean ACT 19**
- **Student-faculty ratio: 19 to 1**

A public university established in 1910. 1,200-acre small-city campus with a 232-acre airport, 12 miles east of Akron. Served by bus.
Academic Character NCACS and professional accreditation. Semester system, 2 5-week and one 8-week summer terms. 37 majors offered by the College of Arts & Sciences, 13 by the College of Business Administration, 27 by the College of Education, 3 by the College of Fine & Professional Arts, 6 by the School of Art, 7 by the School of Home Economics, 6 by the School of Journalism, 8 by the School of Music, 5 by the School of Speech, 8 by the School of Technology, 3 by the School of Physical Education, Recreation, & Dance, and 1 by the School of Nursing. Self-designed majors. Minors required in some departments. Minors offered in most major fields. Distributive requirements. Graduate degrees granted. Independent study. Honors program. Phi Beta Kappa. Cooperative work/study, pass/fail, internships, credit by exam. Preprofessional programs in dentistry, legal professions, medicine, pharmacy, osteopathy, veterinary medicine. 3-1 programs in medical technology and in natural resources areas. Many international study programs. Honors and Experimental Colleges. Elementary, secondary, and special education certification. ROTC, AFROTC. Computer center. Center for Peaceful Change. World Music Center. Liquid Crystal Institute. Arboretum. 1,500,000-volume library with microform resources.
Financial CEEB CSS and ACT FAS. University scholarships, grants, loans, state grants, payment plans; PELL, SEOG, NSS, NDSL, GSL, NSL, CWS. Application deadline June 1.
Admissions Ohio residents admitted unconditionally with either a 16-unit college preparatory program or a 2.5 GPA and ACT 19 composite. Out-of-state students must have a college preparatory curriculum, satisfactory GPA, and ACT 19 or SAT 900. Audition required for music applicants. ACT or SAT accepted; ACT preferred. $25 application fee. Rolling admissions. $50 room deposit due on acceptance of admissions offer. *Early Admission* and *Concurrent Enrollment* programs. Transfers accepted. Credit possible for CEEB AP, CLEP, and departmental exams.
Student Life Student government. Newspaper, literary magazine, yearbook, radio and TV studios. Numerous student organizations. 15 fraternities and 10 sororities, most with houses. 5% of students join. Juniors and seniors may live off campus. Coed and single-sex dorms. Special interest housing. Married-student housing. 40% of students live on campus. 10 intercollegiate sports for men, 9 for women; several intramurals. NCAA, MAC. Student body composition: 1% Asian, 9% Black, 1% Hispanic, 0.1% Native American, 85.9% White, 3% Other. 8% from out of state.

■[J1] KENT STATE UNIVERSITY ASHTABULA REGIONAL CAMPUS
Ashtabula 44004

■[J1] KENT STATE UNIVERSITY EAST LIVERPOOL REGIONAL CAMPUS
East Liverpool 43920

■[J1] KENT STATE UNIVERSITY SALEM REGIONAL CAMPUS
2491 St. Rt. 45, Salem 44460

■[J1] KENT STATE UNIVERSITY STARK CAMPUS
North Canton 44720

■[J1] KENT STATE UNIVERSITY TRUMBULL CAMPUS
Warren 44483

■[J1] KENT STATE UNIVERSITY TUSCARAWAS CAMPUS
New Philadelphia 44663

[1] KENYON COLLEGE
Gambier 43022, (614) 427-2244
Director of Admissions: John D. Kushan

- **Undergraduates: 801m, 643w**
- **Tuition (1982/83): $6,800**
- **Room & Board: $2,455; Fees: $290**
- **Degree offered: AB**
- **Mean SAT 580v, 590m**
- **Student-faculty ratio: 13 to 1**

A private college affiliated with the Episcopal Church, established in 1824, became coed in 1969. 600-acre rural campus, 50 miles north of Columbus.
Academic Character NCACS accreditation. Semester system. Majors offered in anthropology, art, biology, chemistry, classics, drama, economics, English, French studies, German studies, history, mathematics, modern foreign languages & literature, music, philosophy, physics, political science, psychology, religion, Russian studies, sociology, and Spanish studies. Self-designed majors. Distributive requirements. Independent study. Honors program. Phi Beta Kappa. Pass/fail. Preprofessional programs in law and medicine. 3-2 engineering program with Case Western Reserve and Washington U. Urban semester in Philadelphia. Newberry Library Semester. Oak Ridge Lab Semester. Study in Africa, Colombia, Hong Kong, India, Japan, Europe. Computer center. 286,000-volume library with microform resources.
Financial CEEB CSS. College scholarships, grants, loans, honor scholarships, payment plan; PELL, SEOG, NDSL, CWS. Scholarship application deadline March 1.
Admissions High school graduation with 15 units required. Interview urged. SAT or ACT required. $20 application fee. Rolling admissions. $200 deposit due on acceptance of admissions offer. *Early Decision* Program. Admission deferral possible. Transfers accepted. Credit possible for CEEB AP exams.
Student Life Student Council. Student-faculty Senate. Newspaper, journal, photographic publications, yearbook, radio station. Music and drama groups. Debate. Poetry Society. Kenyon Wilderness Experience. Women's Center. Athletic, academic, religious, service, and special interest groups. 10 fraternities housed in dorms. 40% of men join. All students live on campus. Coed and single-sex dorms. Language houses. 10 intercollegiate sports for men, 8 for women; many intramural & club sports. AIAW, NCAA, OAC. Student body composition: 0.7% Asian, 0.9% Black, 0.3% Hispanic, 97.1% White. 71% from out of state.

[J1] KETTERING COLLEGE OF MEDICAL ARTS
Kettering 45429

[1] LAKE ERIE COLLEGE FOR WOMEN
Painesville 44077, (216) 352-3361
Director of Admissions: Frances J. Cook

- **Enrollment: 400w**
- **Approximate Fees (1982/83): $7,995**
- **Degrees offered: BA, BFA**
- **Mean ACT 21; median SAT 490v, 490m**
- **Student-faculty ratio: 18 to 1**

A private college established in 1856. 57-acre suburban campus, 30 miles east of Cleveland. Airport in Cleveland.
Academic Character NCACS and professional accreditation. Trimester system, 2 6-week summer terms. 31 fields of concentration offered in the areas of business administration, equestrian studies, fine & performing arts, human development, languages & literatures, physician's assistant, sciences & mathematics, and social studies. Self-designed majors. Distributive requirements. MSEd granted. Independent study. Internships. 3-3 Doctor of Nursing program. All students participate in an academic term abroad at no extra cost. Elementary and secondary education certification. Learning Resource Center.
Financial CEEB CSS. College scholarships, grants, loans, state grants; PELL, SEOG, NDSL, GSL, work scholarships.
Admissions High school graduation with 16 units required. Interview advised. SAT or ACT required. Rolling admissions. $150 deposit due on acceptance of admissions offer. *Early Admission* Program. Admission deferral possible. Transfers accepted. Credit possible for CEEB AP and CLEP exams.
Student Life Students live at home or on campus. Women's dorms.

[J1] LAKELAND COMMUNITY COLLEGE
Mentor 44060

[J1] LIMA TECHNICAL COLLEGE
Lima 45804

[J1] LORAIN COUNTY COMMUNITY COLLEGE
1005 North Abbe Road, Elyria 44035

[J1] LOURDES COLLEGE
6832 Convent Blvd., Sylvania 43560

[1] MALONE COLLEGE
515 25th Street NW, Canton 44709, (216) 489-0800
Director of Admissions: Lee Sommers

- **Undergraduates: 380m, 400w**
- **Tuition (1982/83): $4,216**
- **Room & Board: $2,064; Fees: $90**
- **Degrees offered: BA, BSEd, AA**
- **Mean ACT 22**
- **Student-faculty ratio: 16 to 1**

A private college affiliated with the Evangelical Friends Church—Eastern Region, established in 1892. 78-acre suburban campus, 15 miles south of Akron. Served by air, rail, and bus.
Academic Character NCACS accreditation. Semester system, 2 5-week summer terms. Majors offered in accounting, allied health, art, biology, business administration, chemistry, Christian ministries or education, communications, elementary education, English, history, liberal arts, mathematics, music, physical education, psychology, social science, social work, and sociology. AA in early childhood education. Distributives, 9 Bible & philosophy credits, and GRE required. Independent study. Credit by exam. Preprofessional programs in dentistry, engineering, medicine, nursing, veterinary medicine. 3-1 medical technology program. Study abroad. Kindergarten, elementary, and secondary education certification. 100,000-volume library.
Financial Guaranteed tuition. CEEB CSS and ACT FAS. College scholarships, grants, loans, state grants, payment plan; PELL, SEOG, NDSL, CWS. Application deadline February 1.
Admissions High school graduation with 16 units required. GED accepted. Interview recommended. ACT required. $20 application fee. Rolling admissions. $50 deposit due on acceptance of offer of admission. *Early Admission* and *Concurrent Enrollment* programs. Transfers accepted. Credit possible for CEEB AP and CLEP exams.
Student Life Student government. Newspaper, literary magazine, yearbook. Music and drama groups. Academic, honorary, political, and religious groups. Students must live at home or on campus. Single-sex dorms. 60% of students live on campus. Dancing, liquor, smoking prohibited. Attendance at 2 chapel services per week required. 3 hours of phys ed required for freshmen and sophomores. 8 intercollegiate sports; many intramurals. NAIA, MOIAC. 6.3% of students from out of state.

[1] MARIETTA COLLEGE
Marietta 45750, (614) 373-4600
Director of Admissions: Daniel J. Jones

- **Undergraduates: 841m, 445w**
- **Tuition (1982/83): $5,900**
- **Room & Board: $2,090**
- **Degrees offered: AB, BS, BFA, BSPetro Eng**
- **Mean ACT 23; mean SAT 479v, 537m**
- **Student-faculty ratio: 13 to 1**

A private college founded in 1835. 60-acre campus in a small city 200 miles east of Cincinnati. Served by bus; airport and train station in West Virginia.
Academic Character NCACS accreditation. Semester system, 2 3-week and 1 5-week summer terms. 34 majors offered in the areas of art, computer science, drama, finance, humanities, journalism, management, marketing, mathematics, music, petroleum engineering, physical education, radio/television, religion, and sports medicine. Special majors. Distributive requirements. Independent study. Honors program. Phi Beta Kappa. Limited pass/fail, internships. Preprofessional programs in dentistry, law, medical technology, medicine, veterinary medicine. 3-2 engineering programs with Case Western Reserve, Columbia, U Penn. 3-2 forestry program with Duke. 3-2 natural resources program with U Michigan. Nursing program with Case Western Reserve. Cross-registration with 6 colleges. Washington Semester. Study abroad. Elementary, secondary, art, music, and physical education certification. Language lab. Observatory. 248,000-volume library.
Financial Guaranteed tuition. CEEB CSS. College scholarships, grants, loans, academic scholarships, payment plan; PELL, SEOG, NDSL, CWS. Scholarship application deadline April 15.
Admissions High school graduation with 16 units recommended. Interview encouraged. SAT or ACT required. $15 application fee. Rolling admissions. $100 deposit due on acceptance of offer of admission. *Early Admission* and *Early Decision* programs. Admission deferral possible. Transfers accepted. Credit possible for CEEB AP, CLEP, and ACT PEP exams.
Student Life Student government. Newspaper, literary magazine, yearbook, radio and TV stations. Music and drama groups. Academic, honorary, political, religious, service, and special interest groups. 7 fraternities and 5 sororities, all with houses. 35% of students join. Seniors may live off campus. 95% of students live in dorms. Gambling, drugs, firearms prohibited. Dean of Students must be notified of intention to marry. 2 semesters of phys ed required. 11 intercollegiate sports for men, 7 for women; intramurals. AIAW, NCAA, OAC. Student body composition: 0.2% Black, 0.2% Hispanic, 98% White, 1.6% Other. 65% from out of state.

[J1] MARION TECHNICAL COLLEGE
Marion 43302

[1] MEDICAL COLLEGE OF OHIO
Toledo 43699

[G1] METHODIST THEOLOGICAL SCHOOL IN OHIO
Delaware 43015

[1] MIAMI UNIVERSITY
Oxford 45056, (513) 529-2531
Director of Admissions: Charles R. Schuler

- **Undergraduates: 6,604m, 7,204w; 14,803 total (including graduates)**
- **Tuition (1982/83): $2,090 (in-state), $4,090 (out-of-state)**
- **Room & Board: $2,050**
- **Degrees offered: AB, BS, BArch, BInt Studies, BEnv Des, BFA, BMus, BPhil, BS in ASc, BSBus, BSEd, BSHome Ec, BSPaper Tech**
- **Mean ACT 24; mean SAT 500v, 560m**
- **Student-faculty ratio: 23 to 1**

A public university established in 1809. 1,100-acre rural campus, 35 miles north of Cincinnati. Served by bus.
Academic Character NCACS and professional accreditation. Semester system, summer term. 47 majors offered by the College of Arts & Sciences, 5 by the School of Applied Science, 9 by the School of Business Administration, 16 by the School of Education & Allied Professions, 6 by the School of Fine Arts, and several by the School of Interdisciplinary Studies. Self-designed majors. Minors offered in many major fields. Courses in Chinese, Hebrew, Japanese. Distributive requirements; senior comprehensive exam required. Graduate degrees granted. Independent study. Honors program. Phi Beta Kappa. Pass/fail, internships. Preprofessional programs in dentistry, law, medicine, physical therapy, veterinary medicine. 3-2 engineering programs with Case Western Reserve, Columbia. 3-2 forestry program with Duke. 3-1 medical technology program with area hospitals. Cross-registration with many area colleges. Study abroad. Elementary, secondary, and special education certification. AFROTC, NROTC. Computer center. Art Museum. 1,100,000-volume library with microform resources.
Financial CEEB CSS. University scholarships, grants, loans, athletic scholarships, payment plan; PELL, SEOG, NSS, NDSL, GSL, CWS. Application deadlines February 1 (scholarships), March 1 (grants & loans).
Admissions High school graduation with 16 units required. ACT or SAT required. $15 application fee. Rolling admissions. $110 deposit ($60 for commuters) due on acceptance of offer of admission. Admission deferral possible. Transfers accepted. Credit possible for CEEB AP and CLEP exams; university has own advanced placement program. EOP for disadvantaged students.
Student Life Student government. Newspaper, literary magazine, yearbook, radio station. Music and drama groups. Debate. Professional, academic, honorary, political, religious, service, and special interest groups. 24 fraternities with houses; 22 sororities with suites. 35% of men and 30% of women join. Juniors and seniors may live off campus. Coed and single-sex dorms. Language residences. Married-student housing. 58% of students live on campus. Cars prohibited. Many intercollegiate, club, and intramural sports. AIAW, NCAA, MAC. Student body composition: 3% Black, 96% White, 1% Other. 20% from out of state.

■[J1] MIAMI UNIVERSITY—HAMILTON CAMPUS
Hamilton 45011

■[J1] MIAMI UNIVERSITY—MIDDLETOWN CAMPUS
Middletown 45042

■[J1] MIAMI UNIVERSITY—OXFORD CAMPUS
Oxford 45056

[J1] MICHAEL J. OWENS TECHNICAL COLLEGE
Caller No. 10,000, Toledo 43699

[1] MOUNT ST. JOSEPH-ON-THE-OHIO, COLLEGE OF
5701 Delhi Road, Mount St. Joseph 45051, (513) 244-4531
Director of Admissions: Domenic N. Teti

- **Undergraduates: 165m, 960w; 1,865 total (including graduates)**
- **Tuition (1982/83): $3,970**
- **Room & Board: $1,825; Fees: $50**
- **Degrees offered: BA, BS, BFA, BLib Studies, BSN**
- **Mean SAT 423v, 436m**
- **Student-faculty ratio: 13 to 1**

A private college controlled by the Sisters of Charity of Cincinnati, established in 1890, became coed in 1981. 325-acre suburban campus, 7 miles from downtown Cincinnati. Served by air, rail, and bus.
Academic Character NCACS and professional accreditation. Semester system. Majors offered in accounting, art, biology/chemistry, business management, chemistry, communication, dietetics, education, English, food service management, health, history, home economics, human services, liberal studies, music, natural science, nursing, physical education, religion, sociology, and speech. Self-designed majors. Distributives and 12-16 hours in religion-philosophy required. MA granted. Independent study. Cooperative work/study, pass/fail, internships, credit by exam. Preprofessional programs in allied health, law, medicine. 3-1 medical technology program. Cross-registration with 26 area schools. Study abroad. Elementary, secondary, and special education certification. ROTC at Xavier; AFROTC at U Cincinnati. 140,000-volume library.
Financial CEEB CSS. College scholarships, grants, loans, art scholarships; PELL, SEOG, NSS, NDSL, GSL, CWS. Scholarship application deadline February 1.
Admissions High school graduation with 16 units required. GED accepted. Interview recommended. SAT or ACT required. $15 application fee. Rolling admissions. $100 deposit due on acceptance of admissions offer. *Early Admission* and *Concurrent Enrollment* programs. Transfers accepted. Credit possible for CEEB AP and CLEP exams.
Student Life Student government. Newspaper, yearbook. Music groups. Art gallery. Black Student Association. Academic, honorary, service, and special interest groups. Students under 22 live at home or on campus. Single-sex dorms. 42% of students live on campus. 2 hours of phys ed required. 5 intercollegiate sports; several intramurals. AIAW. Student body composition: 4% Black, 1% Hispanic, 95% White. 20% from out of state.

[P] MOUNT SAINT MARY'S SEMINARY OF THE WEST
Cincinnati 45212

[1] MOUNT UNION COLLEGE
Alliance 44601, (216) 821-5320
Director of Admissions: W. Edwin Seaver, III

- **Undergraduates: 584m, 478w**
- **Tuition (1982/83): $5,625**
- **Room & Board: $1,860; Fees: $420**
- **Degrees offered: BA, BS, BMus, BMus Ed**
- **Mean SAT 480v, 510m**
- **Student-faculty ratio: 13 to 1**

A private college affiliated with the Methodist Church, established in 1846. 72-acre city campus in a small city 55 miles south of Cleveland. Airport, rail and bus stations nearby.
Academic Character NCACS and professional accreditation. Semester system. 31 majors offered in the areas of business, communications, drama, interdisciplinary studies, music, physical education & health, religion, social services, speech, and liberal arts & sciences. Self-designed majors. Distributives and 1 religion course required. Independent study. Honors program. Cooperative work/study, limited pass/fail, internships. Preprofessional programs in dentistry, law, medicine, ministry. 3-1 medical technology program. 3-2 programs in engineering and nursing. Study abroad. Elementary, secondary, and special education certification. Computer center. 200,000-volume library.
Financial CEEB CSS. College scholarships, grants, loans, tuition discounts for clergy children, payment plan; PELL, SEOG, NDSL, work grants. Application deadline March 31.
Admissions High school graduation with 15 units required. Interview required. SAT or ACT required. $15 application fee. Rolling admissions. $100 room deposit due on acceptance of admissions offer. *Early Decision* and *Early Admission* programs. Transfers accepted. Credit possible for CEEB AP and CLEP exams.
Student Life Student Senate. Men's and Women's Independent Student Associations. Newspaper, literary magazine, yearbook, radio station. Music and drama groups. Debate. Athletic, academic, ethnic, honorary, religious, and service groups. 4 fraternities with houses; 4 sororities with non-residential houses. 30% of men and 35% of women join. Students live at home or on campus. Single-sex dorms. Special interest houses. 90% of students live on campus. 3 terms of phys ed required. 12 intercollegiate sports for men, 7 for women; many intramurals. Student body composition: 1% Asian, 8% Black, 88% White, 3% Other. 20% from out of state.

[1] MOUNT VERNON NAZARENE COLLEGE
800 Martinsburg Road, Mount Vernon 43050, (614) 397-1244
Director of Enrollment Development: Dr. Ron J. Phillips

- **Undergraduates: 505m, 522w**
- **Tuition (1982/83): $2,813**
- **Room & Board: $1,777; Fees: $238**
- **Degree offered: BA**
- **Student-faculty ratio: 18 to 1**

A private college controlled by the Church of the Nazarene, established in 1964. 210-acre small-town campus. Bus service nearby.
Academic Character NCACS accreditation. Semester system, 6-week summer term. Majors offered in art, biology, business, chemistry, Christian education, communications, computer science, education, English, history, home economics, journalism, mathematics, music, office administration, philosophy/humanities, physical education, psychology, religion, sociology, and Spanish. Distributives and 10 hours of religion/philosophy required. Independent study. Cooperative work/study, internships, credit by exam. Preprofessional programs in agriculture, engineering, law, medicine. Elementary and secondary education certification. 75,000-volume library.
Financial CEEB CSS. Activity, athletic, ministerial, and Christian service scholarships, state grants, payment plans; PELL, SEOG, NDSL, FISL, GSL, CWS. Application deadline April 15.
Admissions High school graduation with 15 units required. ACT required. $20 application fee. Rolling admissions. $30 housing deposit due within 30 days of admissions offer. Transfers accepted. Credit possible for CEEB AP, CLEP, and general exams. EGP Program for disadvantaged students.
Student Life Associated Students. Student Council. Newspaper, yearbook. Music and drama groups. Living Witness. Christian Ministries. Honorary and special interest groups. Students must live at home or on campus. Single-sex dorms. Liquor, tobacco, dancing, movies prohibited. Dress code. Cars disencouraged. Chapel attendance 3 times per week required. 3 hours of phys ed required. 4 intercollegiate sports for men, 3 for women; intramurals. Student body composition: 1% Black, 1% Hispanic, 98% White.

[J1] MUSKINGUM AREA TECHNICAL COLLEGE
1555 Newark Road, Zanesville 43701

[1] MUSKINGUM COLLEGE
New Concord 43762, (614) 826-8137
Director of Admissions: Jay R. Leiendecker, Jr.

- **Undergraduates: 527m, 492w**
- **Tuition (1982/83): $5,444**
- **Room & Board: $2,106; Fees: $175**
- **Degrees offered: BA, BS**
- **Mean ACT 21; mean SAT 460v, 509m**
- **Student-faculty ratio: 15 to 1**

A private college affiliated with the United Presbyterian Church, established in 1837. 215-acre small-town campus, 70 miles east of Columbus. Served by air and bus.
Academic Character NCACS and professional accreditation. Semester system, 8-week summer term. 31 majors offered in the areas of business, communication, education, humanities, music, physical education, psychology, public affairs, science, religion, sociology, and theatre. Self-designed majors. Minors offered; required for elementary education majors. Distributives and 1 religion course required. Independent study. Honors program. Cooperative work/study, limited pass/fail, internships, credit by exam. Preprofessional programs in dentistry, law, medicine, ministry, physical therapy, veterinary science. 3-1 medical technology program. 3-3 nursing program with Case. East Central College Consortium. Washington Semester. Merrill-Palmer terms for psychology and sociology students. Critical Languages Program at Princeton. Study abroad. Elementary, secondary, and special education certification. ROTC at Ohio U. Language lab. 172,000-volume library.
Financial CEEB CSS. College scholarships, grants, loans, Presbyterian tuition allowances, 2nd-family-member discounts, payment plans; PELL, SEOG, NDSL, CWS. Recommended scholarship application deadline April 15.
Admissions High school graduation with 15 units required. Interview recommended. SAT or ACT required. $15 application fee. Rolling admissions. $100 deposit due on acceptance of offer of admission. *Early Admission* Program. Admission deferral possible. Transfers accepted. Credit possible for CEEB AP, CLEP, and college proficiency exams.
Student Life Student Senate. Newspaper, literary magazine, yearbook, radio and TV stations. Music and drama groups. Debate. Academic, honorary, political, religious, and special interest groups. 2 fraternities and 3 social clubs for men; limited housing. 4 social clubs, with houses, for women. 65% of men and 70% of women join. Students live at home or on campus. Single-sex dorms. Special interest houses. 95% of students live on campus. Liquor restricted. Smoking prohibited in some areas. Students must notify Personnel Office of marriage plans. 3 hours of phys ed required. 10 intercollegiate sports for men, 9 for women; intramurals. AIAW, OAISW, NCAA, OAC. Student body composition: 2% Black, 1% Hispanic, 95% White, 2% Other. 25% from out of state.

[J1] NORTH CENTRAL TECHNICAL COLLEGE
PO Box 698, Mansfield 44901

[P] NORTHEASTERN OHIO UNIVERSITIES COLLEGE OF MEDICINE
4209 State Route 44, Rootstown 44272

[J1] NORTHWEST TECHNICAL COLLEGE
Archbold 43502

[1] NOTRE DAME COLLEGE OF OHIO
4545 College Road, Cleveland 44121, (216) 381-1680

- **Enrollment: 600w**
- **Tuition (1982/83): $3,250**
- **Room & Board: $2,070**
- **Degrees offered: BA, BS**
- **Student-faculty ratio: 10 to 1**

A private, Roman Catholic college for women, operated by the Sisters of Notre Dame, established in 1922. 52-acre suburban campus. Served by air and bus.
Academic Character NCACS accreditation. Semester system, 5-week summer term. Majors offered in accounting, art, biology, catechetics, chemistry, communications, design merchandising, elementary education, English, French, German, home economics, management, mathematics, medical technology, physical education, psychology, social science, sociology, and Spanish. Distributives and 4 courses in theology required. Cooperative work/study, internships. Preprofessional programs in dentistry, law, medicine, pharmacy, scientific research. 3-1 medical technology program with area hospitals. 3-2 dietetic and engineering programs with Case Western Reserve. Study abroad. Elementary, secondary, and special education certification. Professional translator certification. 82,000-volume library.
Financial CEEB CSS (preferred) or ACT FAS. College scholarships. Other aid available include work/study. Application deadlines May 1 (scholarships), March 1 (other aid).
Admissions High school graduation with 15 units required. Interview recommended. SAT or ACT required. $20 application fee. Rolling admissions. $100 deposit due on acceptance of admissions offer. *Early Admission* Program. Admission deferral possible. Transfers accepted. Credit possible for CEEB AP and CLEP exams. Conditional admission possible.
Student Life Student government. Campus ministry. Cultural, religious, social, and special interest groups. Single students live at home or on campus. Attendance at school functions and in class expected. 2 phys ed courses required. 2 intercollegiate sports; intramurals. Student body composition: 12% minority.

[1] OBERLIN COLLEGE
Oberlin 44074, (216) 775-8411
Director of Admissions: Carl W. Bewig

- **Undergraduates: 1,251m, 1,432w**
- **Tuition (1982/83): $7,505**
- **Room & Board: $2,855; Fees: $250**
- **Degrees offered: AB, BMus, BFA in Music**
- **Mean SAT 1191**
- **Student-faculty ratio: 13 to 1**

A private college established in 1833. 440-acre small-town campus, 34 miles southwest of Cleveland. Air, rail, and bus service nearby.
Academic Character NCACS and professional accreditation. 4-1-4 system. 41 majors offered by the College of Arts & Sciences and 9 by the Conservatory of Music. Special majors. Minors offered. Distributive guidelines, no requirements. Independent study. Honors Program. Phi Beta Kappa. Senior Scholars Program. Experimental College. Choice of letter grades or credit/no credit. Some internships. 3-2 engineering programs with Case, U Penn, Washington U. Exchange programs with Tougaloo, Fisk, Gallaudet, and 11 colleges of the Great Lakes Association. Philadelphia Urban Semester. New York Arts Semester. Oak Ridge Science Semester. Wharton Business Semester. Newberry Library Program. Music education certification. Computer center. Isotope lab. Language labs. 800,000-volume library.
Financial CEEB CSS. College scholarships, grants, loans, state grants, payment plan; PELL, SEOG, NDSL, GSL, CWS. Application deadline February 15.
Admissions High school graduation with 15-18 units recommended. Interview strongly encouraged. Audition required for Conservatory applicants. SAT or ACT required; ACH recommended for foreign languages. $25 application fee. Application deadline February 15 (Feb. 1 for *Early Decision*); urge applying early in 12th year. $200 deposit due on acceptance of offer of admission. *Early Decision* and *Early Admission* programs. Admission deferral possible. Transfers accepted. Credit possible for CEEB AP exams.
Student Life Student Senate. Student representation on most faculty committees. Newspaper, magazines, yearbook, radio station. Several music groups. Dance and drama groups. Debate. Honorary, language, political, religious, and special interest organizations. Freshmen and sophomores must live on campus. Coed and single-sex dorms. Co-op dorms. Special interest and language houses. Married-student housing. 80% of students live on campus. Freshmen may not have cars; upperclassmen must have Dean's permission. Illegal possession of drugs, liquor, firearms, firecrackers prohibited. Honor system. 9 intercollegiate sports for men, 9 for women; intramurals. AIAW, OAC, Centennial Conference. Student body composition: 3.7% Asian, 8.6% Black, 1.3% Hispanic, 0.1% Native American, 86.3% White. 87% from out of state.

[P] OHIO, MEDICAL COLLEGE OF, AT TOLEDO
CS 10008, Toledo 43699

[P] OHIO COLLEGE OF PODIATRIC MEDICINE
10515 Carnegie Avenue, Cleveland 44106

[1] OHIO DOMINICAN COLLEGE
1216 Sunbury Road, Columbus 43219, (614) 253-2741
Director of Admissions: James L. Sagona

- **Undergraduates: 251m, 365w**
- **Tuition (1982/83): $3,990**
- **Room & Board: $2,280**
- **Degrees offered: BA, BS, BSEd, AA, AS**
- **Mean ACT 18.5**
- **Student-faculty ratio: 13 to 1**

A private Roman Catholic college controlled by the Dominican Sisters of St. Mary of the Springs, established in 1911, became coed in 1964. 43-acre suburban campus, 4 miles from downtown Columbus. Served by air, rail, and bus.
Academic Character NCACS accreditation. Semester system, 7-week summer term, 2-week pre-summer and post-summer terms. 28 majors offered in the areas of arts, business, criminal justice, education, fashion merchandising, home economics, humanities, library science, physical education, religion, science, social science, and theatre. Distributives, 1 semester of religion, and senior research project required. Independent study. Honors program. Limited pass/fail, internships. Preprofessional programs in dentistry, engineering, law, pharmacy, medical technology, medicine, veterinary science. Study abroad. Elementary, secondary, and special education certification. ROTC and NROTC at Ohio State; AFROTC at Capital. 98,845-volume library.
Financial CEEB CSS and ACT FAS. College scholarships, grants, loans, payment plans; PELL, SEOG, NDSL, CWS. Application deadlines March 1 (scholarships), March 15 (loans).
Admissions High school graduation with 15 units required. GED accepted. Interview required for in-state applicants. SAT or ACT required. Rolling admissions. $100 deposit due on acceptance of offer of admission. *Early Admission, Early Decision, Concurrent Enrollment* programs. Admission deferral possible. Transfers accepted. Credit possible for CEEB AP and CLEP exams.
Student Life College Council. Newspaper, magazine, yearbook, radio station. Music and drama groups. Shades of Black. International Students Club. Prayer group. Service and special interest groups. Students live at home or on campus. Coed and single-sex dorms. 33% of students live on campus. 1 semester of phys ed required. 2 intercollegiate sports for men, 3 for women; intramurals. AIAW, NAIA, MOC. Student body composition: 13% Black, 1% Hispanic, 72% White, 14% Other. 15% from out of state.

[1] OHIO NORTHERN UNIVERSITY
Ada 45810, (419) 634-9921
Director of Admissions: Ronald L. Knoble

- **Undergraduates: 1,238m, 944w; 2,759 total (including part-time)**
- **Tuition (1982/83): $4,710**
- **Room & Board: $2,010**
- **Degrees offered: BA, BS, BFA, BMus, BSBA, BSCE, BSEE, BSME, BSMed Tech, BSPharm**
- **Mean ACT 22; mean SAT 451v, 514m**
- **Student-faculty ratio: 16 to 1**

A private university affiliated with the United Methodist Church, established in 1871. 187-acre small-town campus, 14 miles from Lima. Airport in Lima.
Academic Character NCACS and professional accreditation. Trimester system, 3 3-week summer terms. 30 majors offered by the College of Arts & Sciences, 5 by the College of Business Administration, 3 by the College of Engineering, and 1 by the College of Pharmacy. Distributives and 1 religion course required. JD in law granted. Independent study. Pass/fail, internships, credit by exam. Preprofessional programs in dentistry, law, medicine, theology. Study abroad. Elementary, secondary, and special education certification. ROTC at Bowling Green. Computer center. Language lab. 320,100-volume library.
Financial CEEB CSS. University scholarships, grants, loans, tuition discount for siblings; PELL, SEOG, NDSL, CWS. Scholarship application deadline February 1.
Admissions High school graduation with 16 units required. ACT or SAT required. $20 application fee. Rolling admissions. $200 deposit required on acceptance of admissions offer. *Early Decision* and *Early Admission* programs. Transfers accepted. Credit possible for CEEB AP, CLEP, and university proficiency exams.
Student Life Newspaper, literary magazine. Music and drama groups. Debate. Academic, honorary, professional, and religious groups. 8 fraternities with houses, 4 sororities with non-residential houses. 46% of men and 27% of women join. Single students live at home or on campus. Coed and single-sex dorms. Honors houses. 63% of students live on campus. Liquor prohibited. 1 year of phys ed required. 10 intercollegiate sports for men, 6 for women; many club and intramural sports. AIAW, NCAA, CAC, OAC. Student body composition: 0.6% Asian, 2% Black, 0.5% Hispanic, 0.1% Native American, 94.6% White, 2.2% Other. 23% from out of state.

[1] OHIO STATE UNIVERSITY, THE
Columbus 43210, (614) 422-3980
Director of Admissions: James J. Mager

- **Undergraduates: 22,141m, 18,712w; 57,604 total (including graduates)**
- **Tuition (1982/83): $1,455 (in-state), $3,750 (out-of-state)**
- **Room & Board: $2,504**
- **Degrees offered: BA, BS, BAg, BArch, BArt Ed, BBA, BEd, 12 BEngs, BFA, BLArch, BMus, BMus Ed, BSN, BPharm, BSW, BAllied Health Prof, BAud**

Record, BComp & Info Sc, BFood Sc, BFood Tech, BHEc, BJourn, BInd Des, BLabor & Human Resources, BNat Res, BNutr, BRest Man, BSurveying
- **Mean ACT 21.2**
- **Student-faculty ratio: 16 to 1**

A public university established in 1870. 3,251-acre suburban campus. Served by air, rail, and bus.
Academic Character NCACS and professional accreditation. Trimester system, summer term. 201 programs and 6,700 courses offered by 211 divisions. Self-designed majors. Distributive requirements. Graduate degrees granted. Independent study. Honors program. Phi Beta Kappa. Cooperative work/study, limited pass/fail, internships. Professional schools of dentistry, law, medicine, optometry, veterinary medicine. Study abroad. Elementary, secondary, and special education certification. ROTC, AFROTC, NROTC. Planetarium. Art gallery. 3,615,108-volume library with microform resources.
Financial CEEB CSS. University scholarships, grants, loans; PELL, SEOG, NDSL, CWS. Scholarship application deadline March 1.
Admissions High school graduation with 15 units recommended. SAT or ACT required. $10 application fee. Rolling admissions. $40 deposit due on acceptance of admissions offer. *Early Admission* Program. Admission deferral possible. Transfers accepted. Credit possible for CEEB AP, CLEP, and departmental exams. Freshman Foundation Program offered by Minority Affairs Office.
Student Life Student government. Newspaper, radio and TV stations. Music, dance, and drama groups. Over 500 athletic, academic, honorary, political, service, and special interest groups. 39 fraternities, 36 with houses; 21 sororities, 18 with houses. 9% of students join. Single freshmen must live on campus or at home. Special-interest houses. Coed and single-sex dorms. Married-student housing. 25% of students live on campus. 18 intercollegiate sports for men, 15 for women; intramurals. AIAW, NCAA, NAIA, Big Ten Conference. Student body composition: 1% Asian, 4% Black, 1% Hispanic, 1% Native American, 93% White. 11% from out of state.

■[J1] OHIO STATE UNIVERSITY—AGRICULTURAL TECHNICAL INSTITUTE
Wooster 44691

■[1] OHIO STATE UNIVERSITY—LIMA CAMPUS
4240 Campus Drive, Lima 45804

■[1] OHIO STATE UNIVERSITY—MANSFIELD CAMPUS
Mansfield 44906

■[1] OHIO STATE UNIVERSITY—MARION CAMPUS
Marion 43302

■[1] OHIO STATE UNIVERSITY—NEWARK CAMPUS
Newark 43055

[1] OHIO UNIVERSITY
Athens 45701, (614) 594-5174
Director of Admissions: James C. Walters

- **Enrollment: 7,811m, 6,604w**
- **Tuition (1982/83): $1,692 (est. in-state), $3,483 (est. out-of-state)**
- **Room & Board: $2,409**
- **Degrees offered: AB, BS, BBA, BFA, BGS, BMus, BSJ, BSEd, BSC, BSN, BSEng & Tech, AA**
- **Mean SAT 435v, 468m**
- **Student-faculty ratio: 14 to 1**

A public university established in 1804. 600-acre campus in a small city 76 miles southeast of Columbus. Served by rail and bus.
Academic Character NCACS and professional accreditation. Trimester system, 2 5-week summer terms. 28 majors offered by the College of Arts & Sciences, 12 by the College of Business Administration, 14 by the College of Communication, 28 by the College of Education, 6 by the College of Engineering & Technology, 12 by the College of Fine Arts, 28 by the College of Health & Human Services, and 1 by the College of Osteopathic Medicine. Honors Tutorial College: selective program with 1-to-1 student-faculty relationship; 20 majors offered. University College offers an AA in general studies for students with undeclared majors. Minors required in some majors; offered in most major fields. Distributive requirements. Graduate degrees granted. Phi Beta Kappa. Limited pass/fail, credit by exam. Senior *in absentia* possible. Preprofessional programs include agri-business, criminology, dentistry, environmental studies, foreign service, law, medicine, optometry, pharmacy, physical therapy, public administration, theology, urban planning, veterinary medicine. Cooperative forestry programs with U Michigan, North Carolina, Duke. 3-1 medical technology program. Study abroad. Elementary, secondary, and special education certification. ROTC, AFROTC. Computer center. Center for International Studies. Language labs. 1,107,000-volume library with microform resources.
Financial CEEB CSS. University scholarships, grants, loans, special talent & corporate scholarships, state grants, payment plans; PELL, SEOG, NSS, NDSL, FISL, CWS. Application deadlines February 15 (scholarships), April 1 (loans).
Admissions High school graduation required. GED accepted. ACT or SAT required; ACT preferred. $25 application fee. Rolling admissions. $100 room deposit due on acceptance of admissions offer. *Early Admission* Program. Admission deferral possible. Transfers accepted. Credit possible for CEEB AP and CLEP exams.
Student Life Student Senate. Newspaper, magazines, yearbook, radio & TV stations. Music, dance, and drama groups. International houses. Academic, honorary, professional, recreational, volunteer, and special interest groups. 18 fraternities and 12 sororities; most with houses. Students with less than 90 quarter hours must live on campus. Coed and single-sex dorms. Married-student housing. 50% of students live on campus. Hazing prohibited. 9 intercollegiate sports for men, 8 for women; many club and intramural programs. NCAA, AIAW, MAC. Student body composition: 0.3% Asian, 4.9% Black, 0.3% Hispanic, 0.3% Native American, 84.2% White, 10% Other. 19% from out of state.

■[J1] BELMONT COUNTY CAMPUS
45425 National Road, St. Clairsville 43950

■[J1] CHILLICOTHE CAMPUS
571 West Fifth Street, Chillicothe 45601

■[J1] LANCASTER CAMPUS
Lancaster 43130

■[J1] ZANESVILLE CAMPUS OF OHIO UNIVERSITY
Zanesville 43701

[1] OHIO WESLEYAN UNIVERSITY
Delaware 43015, (614) 369-4431, ext. 550
Dean of Admissions: Fred E. Weed

- **Undergraduates: 1,199m, 1,059w**
- **Tuition (1982/83): $6,300**
- **Room & Board: $2,570**
- **Degrees offered: AB, BFA, BMus, BSN**
- **Mean ACT 21; mean SAT 461v, 499m**
- **Student-faculty ratio: 13 to 1**

A private university controlled by the United Methodist Church, established in 1842. 200-acre campus in a small city 20 miles north of Columbus. Served by bus; airport in Columbus.
Academic Character NCACS and professional accreditation. Trimester system, 6-week summer term. 41 majors offered in the areas of the arts, Black studies, business, education, humanities, journalism, music, nursing, physical education, religion, sciences, social sciences, and urban studies. Self-designed majors. Minors offered. Distributive requirements. Independent study. Honors program. Phi Beta Kappa. Limited pass/fail, internships, credit by exam. Preprofessional programs in art therapy, dentistry, law, medicine, music therapy, occupational therapy, optometry, pharmacy, public administration, theology, veterinary medicine. 3-2 engineering program with Case, Rensselaer, Washington U, California Tech, Georgia Tech, NY Polytechnic. 3-1 medical technology program. 3-2 physical therapy program. Exchange programs with Hampton, Spelman, Fisk. United Nations, Washington, Oak Ridge, Newberry Library semesters. New York art program. Philadelphia urban studies program. Human development at Merrill-Palmer. Study abroad. Elementary and secondary education certification. AFROTC at Ohio State. Computer center. Drama center. Observatory. 450,000-volume library with microform resources.
Financial CEEB CSS. University scholarships, grants, loans, Methodist scholarships, payment plans; PELL, SEOG, NDSL, GSL, CWS. Suggested scholarship application deadline February 1.
Admissions High school graduation with 16 units recommended. Interview strongly recommended. Audition required for music majors. SAT or ACT required; ACH recommended. $20 application fee. Application deadline March 1. $200 deposit due on acceptance of admissions offer. *Early Decision* and *Early Admission* programs. Admission deferral possible. Transfers accepted. Credit possible for CEEB AP exams; university offers credit for own exams and for off-campus experience.
Student Life Student government. Newspaper, literary magazine, yearbook, radio station. Music and drama groups. Orchesis. Academic, professional, religious, tutorial, social action, and special interest groups. 11 fraternities with houses; 8 sororities with non-residential houses. 45% of men and 40% of women join. Seniors may live off campus. Special interest houses. One single-sex and 6 coed dorms. No married-student housing. 95% of students live on campus. Financial aid recipients may not have cars. 12 intercollegiate sports for men, 11 for women. AIAW, NCAA, OAC. Student body composition: 1% Asian, 6% Black, 1% Hispanic, 92% White. 64% from out of state.

[1] OTTERBEIN COLLEGE
Westerville 43081, (614) 890-3000
Dean of Admissions: Morris Briggs

- **Undergraduates: 591m, 709w**
- **Tuition (1982/83): $5,364**
- **Room & Board: $2,166**
- **Degrees offered: BA, BS, BMus Ed, BFA, BSEd, BSN, ASN**
- **Mean ACT 21; mean SAT 460v, 500m**
- **Student-faculty ratio: 15 to 1**

A private college affiliated with the United Methodist Church, established in 1847. 70-acre suburban campus, 20 minutes from downtown Columbus. Served by air and rail.
Academic Character NCACS and professional accreditation. Trimester system, 8-week summer term. 34 majors offered by the divisions of Fine Arts, Language & Literature, Professional Studies, Science & Mathematics, and Social Studies. Self-designed majors. Minors offered in most major fields and in geology and athletic training. Distributive requirements. MEd granted with Ashland; MBA with Dayton. Honors program. Cooperative work/study, internships. Preprofessional programs in dentistry, law, medicine, theology. 3-2 programs in forestry and environmental management with Duke. 2-3 architecture program with Ohio State. Engineering programs with New York U and Ohio State. 3-1 medical and radiological technology programs. Interpretive Naturalist Program with Ohio Natural Resources Department.

Study in Dijon, Bonn, Segovia. Washington Semester. Semester at Sea. Teaching semester in New Mexico. Elementary and secondary education certification. AFROTC at Ohio State. Language lab. 120,000-volume library.
Financial CEEB CSS and ACT FAS. College scholarships, grants, loans, state grants, Methodist loans, payment plan; PELL, SEOG, NDSL, FISL, CWS. Academic Scholarship deadline July 1.
Admissions High school graduation with 16 units required. Interview desirable. SAT or ACT required; English Comp ACH recommended. Rolling admissions. $100 deposit due on acceptance of admissions offer. *Early Admission* Program. Admission deferral possible. Transfers accepted. Credit possible for CEEB AP and CLEP exams.
Student Life Campus government. Newspaper, literary magazine, yearbook, radio station. Music, dance, and drama groups. Debate. Urban civic projects. Athletic, academic, honorary, political, religious, and special interest groups. 6 fraternities and 6 sororities, all with houses. 48% of men and 55% of women join. Single freshmen, sophomores, & juniors under 22 must live on campus or at home. Dorms for men and women. 55% of students live on campus. Liquor prohibited. Class attendance expected. Freshmen must take phys ed. 7 intercollegiate sports for men, 6 for women; intramurals. AIAW, NCAA, OAC. Student body composition: 4% Black, 1% Hispanic, 94% White, 1% Other. 12% from out of state.

[P] PAYNE THEOLOGICAL SEMINARY
PO Box 474, Wilberforce 45384

[1] PONTIFICAL JOSEPHINUM COLLEGE, THE
Columbus 43085

[J1] RAYMOND WALTERS COLLEGE
9555 Plainfield Road, Cincinnati 45236
Part of the University of Cincinnati.

[1] RIO GRANDE COLLEGE/COMMUNITY COLLEGE
Rio Grande 45674, (614) 245-5353
Director of Admissions & Records: Dean S. Brown

- **Undergraduates: 503m, 722w**
- **Tuition & Fees (1982/83): $855-$1,035 (in-state), $3,030 (out-of-state)**
- **Room & Board: $1,920**
- **Degrees offered: BA, BS, AS, AAS**
- **Student-faculty ratio: 20 to 1**

A private college established in 1876 with a coordinate public community college, established in 1974. 178-acre small-town campus, 96 miles south of Columbus.
Academic Character NCACS and professional accreditation. Trimester system, 2 5-week summer terms. Majors offered in acccounting, art, biology, business, chemistry, communications, economics, education, English, history, humanities, mathematics, physical education, physical science, recreation, social science, social work, and speech. Special majors. Minors required in some areas and offered in others. Associate degrees offered in most majors and in computer technology, drafting, medical lab technology, electronics, manufacturing technology, automotive/diesel technology, secretarial technology, nursing, agriculture. Distributive requirements. English and senior comprehensive exams required. Independent study. Pass/fail, internships. Preprofessional programs in engineering, law, medicine, ministry. Study abroad. Elementary and secondary education certification. ROTC. 68,000-volume library with microform resources.
Financial CEEB CSS. College scholarships, grants, loans, state grants, payment plan; PELL, SEOG, GSL, NDSL, CWS. Scholarship application deadline April 15.
Admissions Open admissions. GED required for students over 18. Interview recommended. ACT required for nursing applicants. $15 application fee. Rolling admissions. $110 room deposit due on acceptance of admissions offer. *Early Admission* Program. Transfers accepted. Credit possible for CEEB AP and CLEP exams.
Student Life Student Senate. Newspaper, yearbook, radio workshop. Music and drama groups. Debate. Chess Club. Honorary, professional, religious, service, and special interest groups. 4 fraternities and 4 sororities. 15% of students join. Students must live at home or on campus. Dorms for men and women. Married-student housing off-campus. Co-op dorms. 56% of students live on campus. Liquor restricted to dorm rooms. Class attendance expected. 3 hours of phys ed required. 4 intercollegiate sports for men, 4 for women; intramurals. AIAW, NAIA, MOC. Student body composition: 0.1% Asian, 1.5% Black, 0.2% Hispanic, 0.2% Native American, 94.9% White. 2% from out of state.

[G1] SAINT MARY'S SEMINARY
Cleveland 44108

[J1] SHAWNEE STATE COMMUNITY COLLEGE
940 Second Street, Portsmouth 45662

[J1] SINCLAIR COMMUNITY COLLEGE
444 West Third Street, Dayton 45402

[J1] SOUTHERN STATE COMMUNITY COLLEGE
Hillsboro 45133

[J1] STARK TECHNICAL COLLEGE
6200 Frank Avenue, Canton 44720

[1] STEUBENVILLE, UNIVERSITY OF
Steubenville 43952, (614) 283-3771
Director of Admissions: David Skiviat

- **Undergraduates: 265m, 359w; 926 total (including graduates)**
- **Tuition (1982/83): $4,170**
- **Room & Board: $2,500; Fees: $60**
- **Degrees offered: BA, BS, BSN**
- **Mean ACT 20; mean SAT 441v, 463m**
- **Student-faculty ratio: 15 to 1**

A private, Roman Catholic university conducted by the Franciscan Friars, established in 1946. 100-acre suburban campus, 42 miles west of Pittsburgh.
Academic Character NCACS accreditation. Semester system, 2 5-week summer terms. Majors offered in the areas of business, criminal justice, education, engineering, humanities, mental health, nursing, public administration, science, sociology, and theology. Distributive requirements. Masters degrees granted. Minors offered. Independent study. Pass/fail, internships. Preprofessional programs in dentistry, law, medicine, pharmacy, veterinary medicine. 3-1 medical technology program. 2-2 criminal justice program. Elementary, secondary, and special education certification. 170,000-volume library with microform resources.
Financial CEEB CSS. University scholarships, grants, loans, academic & athletic scholarships, state grants; PELL, SEOG, NSS, NDSL, GSL, CWS.
Admissions High school graduation with 15 units required. SAT or ACT required. $15 application fee. Rolling admissions. $150 deposit due on acceptance of admissions offer. *Early Decision* and *Early Admission* programs. Credit possible for CEEB AP and CLEP exams.
Student Life Student government. Newspaper, yearbook. Music and drama groups. Academic, honorary, religious, and special interest groups. 3 fraternities and 3 sororities. Married students and seniors may live off campus. Single-sex dorms. Small-group houses. Intramural sports. Student body composition: 0.4% Asian, 4.3% Black, 0.9% Hispanic, 0.4% Native American, 92.7% White.

[J1] TERRA TECHNICAL COLLEGE
1220 Cedar Street, Fremont 43420

[2 & J2] TIFFIN UNIVERSITY
155 Miami Street, Tiffin 44883, (419) 447-6442
Dean of Enrollment Services: John J. Millar

- **Enrollment: 163m, 172w; 475 total (including part-time)**
- **Estimated Tuition (1982/83): $2,400**
- **Estimated Room & Board: $1,520**
- **Degrees offered: BBA, BCS, ABus Tech**
- **Student-faculty ratio: 20 to 1**

A private university established in 1918. Small-town campus, 50 miles south of Toledo.
Academic Character AICS accreditation. Trimester system, 2 5-week summer terms. Majors offered in accounting, data processing, business management, hotel & restaurant management, criminal justice, and office administration. Distributive requirements. One-year certificate programs offered. Credit by exam. Library with microform resources.
Financial CEEB CSS. University scholarships, state grants; PELL, SEOG, NDSL, GSL, PLUS, CWS. Recommended application deadline April 15.
Admissions High school graduation with 16 units recommended. GED accepted. SAT or ACT required. $15 application fee. Rolling admissions. $50 tuition fee and $50 room deposit due on acceptance of admissions offer. *Early Admission* and *Early Decision* programs. Admission deferral possible. Transfers accepted. Credit possible for CEEB AP and CLEP exams.
Student Life Student Council. Newspaper, yearbook. Christian Fellowship. Academic, social, and special interest groups. 2 fraternities and 2 sororities. Honors residence. 4 intercollegiate sports for men, 2 for women; intramurals. NAIA, MOC.

[1] TOLEDO, THE UNIVERSITY OF
Toledo 43606, (419) 537-2696
Director of Admissions: Richard J. Eastop

- **Undergraduates: 9,298m, 8,990w; 21,400 total (including graduates)**
- **Tuition (1982/83): $1,359 (in-state), $3,114 (out-of-state)**
- **Room & Board: $2,031-$2,844**
- **Degrees offered: BA, BS, BMus, BFA, BBA, BEd**
- **Mean SAT 436v, 502m**
- **Student-faculty ratio: 19 to 1**

A public university established in 1872. 487-acre suburban campus. Served by air, rail, and bus.
Academic Character NCACS and professional accreditation. Trimester system, 2 5½-week, one 8-week summer terms. 36 majors offered by the College of Arts & Sciences, 5 by the College of Business Administration, 39 by the College of Education, 8 by the College of Engineering, and 1 by the College of Pharmacy. Self-designed majors. Distributive requirements. Graduate and professional degrees granted. Community and Technical College offers associate degrees. Honors program. Phi Beta Kappa. Pass/fail, internships. Preprofessional programs in business, law, librarianship, social work. Cooperative art program with Toledo Museum. Study abroad. Elementary, secondary, and special education certification. ROTC; AFROTC at Bowling Green State U. Computer center. Planetarium. Language lab. 1,000,000-volume library with microform resources.
Financial CEEB CSS. University scholarships, grants, loans, state grants; PELL, SEOG, NSS, NDSL, HPL, CWS. Application deadline March 1.
Admissions High school graduation with 16 units required. Audition required for music majors. ACT or SAT required. $20 application fee. Rolling admissions. *Early Admission* Program. Admission deferral possible. Transfers

accepted. Credit possible for CEEB AP and CLEP exams.
Student Life Student Senate. Newspaper, radio & TV stations. Music and drama groups. Debate. Academic, ethnic, honorary, religious, and special interest groups. 12 fraternities, 9 with houses; 9 sororities, 6 with apartments. 10% of men and 14% of women join. Freshmen live at home or on campus. Coed and single-sex dorms. 9% of students live on campus. Gambling and hazing prohibited. 3 quarter hours of phys ed or ROTC required. 12 intercollegiate sports for men, 5 for women; intramurals. AIAW, NCAA, M-AAC. Student body composition: 0.6% Asian, 8.5% Black, 1% Hispanic, 1% Native American, 88% White, 0.9% Other. 10% from out of state.

[G1] TRINITY LUTHERAN SEMINARY
2199 East Main Street, Columbus 43209

[P] TRI-STATE BIBLE COLLEGE
PO Box 445, South Point 45680

[J1] TUSCARAWAS REGIONAL CAMPUS
New Philadelphia 44663

[2] UNION FOR EXPERIMENTING COLLEGES AND UNIVERSITIES, THE
PO Box 85315, Provident Bank Building, Cincinnati 45201
Formerly University Without Walls.

[G1] UNITED THEOLOGICAL SEMINARY
1810 Harvard Blvd., Dayton 45406 **CR**

[2] UNIVERSITY WITHOUT WALLS
Cincinnati — see Union for Experimenting Colleges and Universities, The

[1] URBANA COLLEGE
Urbana 43078, (513) 652-1301
Director of Admissions: William E. Riska

- **Undergraduates: 446m, 248w**
- **Tuition (1982/83): $3,300**
- **Room & Board: $2,040; Fees: $177**
- **Degrees offered: BA, BS**
- **Mean ACT 15**
- **Student-faculty ratio: 15 to 1**

A private college affiliated with the Swedenborgian Church, established in 1850. 128-acre small-town campus, 45 miles from Dayton. Air, rail, and bus service nearby.
Academic Character NCACS accreditation. Trimester system, summer term. Majors offered in accounting, business administration, economics, general marketing, personnel management, small business enterprise, comprehensive science (biology, chemistry, physics), education/physical education, philosophy/religion, child-family services, corrections, health care, law enforcement, and psychological services. Self-designed majors. Independent study. Pass/fail, internships. Cross-registration with Dayton-Miami Valley Consortium schools. Elementary and secondary education certification. Off-campus centers at Bellefontaine, Cincinnati, Dayton, Mansfield. 58,000-volume library with microform resources.
Financial CEEB CSS and ACT FAS. College scholarships, grants, loans, state grants; PELL, SEOG, GSL, NDSL, CWS. Scholarship application deadline in July.
Admissions High school graduation with 16 units recommended. GED accepted. Interview encouraged. SAT or ACT required for applicants 3 years out of school. $10 application fee. Rolling admissions. $100 deposit due on acceptance of admissions offer. *Early Admission* and *Concurrent Enrollment* programs. Admission deferral possible. Transfers accepted. Credit possible for CEEB AP and CLEP exams.
Student Life Student government. Newspaper, yearbook. Music and drama groups. Volunteer service club. Students must live at home or on campus. Coed and single-sex dorms. 26% of students live on campus. 4 intercollegiate sports for men, 3 for women; intramurals. NAIA, OAISW, MOC. Student body composition: 19% Black, 78% White, 3% Other. 1% from out of state.

[1] URSULINE COLLEGE
2550 Lander Road, Pepper Pike 44124, (216) 449-4200
Director of Admissions: David Dalsky

- **Enrollment: 1,166w**
- **Tuition & Fees (1982/83): $3,150; $3,750 (for nursing)**
- **Room & Board: $1,700-$2,000**
- **Degrees offered: BA, BSN, AA**
- **Mean SAT 450v, 450m**
- **Student-faculty ratio: 11 to 1**

A private, Roman Catholic college for women, operated by the Ursuline Nuns, established in 1871. Suburban campus, ½ hour from Cleveland. Served by bus and rapid transit; airport in Cleveland.
Academic Character NCACS and professional accreditation. Semester system. 26 majors offered by the divisions of Applied Sciences, Education, Humanities, Fine Arts, Natural Sciences, Social Sciences, and the Center for Nursing. Distributives and 6 credits in religious studies required. MA granted. Independent study. Pass/no credit. 3-2 dietetics program with Case and Akron. Study abroad. Kindergarten, elementary, and secondary education certification. Media center. Curriculum library. 72,000-volume library.
Financial College scholarships, state grants; PELL, SEOG, NDSL, GSL, CWS.
Admissions High school graduation with 15 units required. SAT or ACT required. $15 application fee. Rolling admissions. $50 tuition and $50 room deposits due on acceptance of admissions offer. *Early Admission* and *Concurrent Enrollment* programs. Admission deferral possible. Transfers accepted. Credit possible for CEEB AP, CLEP, and departmental exams.
Student Life Student government. Newspaper, literary magazine. Music and drama groups. Honorary, professional, religious, service, and special interest groups. 2 residence halls. Intramural sports.

[1] WALSH COLLEGE
2020 Easton Street, NW, Canton 44720

[J1] WASHINGTON TECHNICAL COLLEGE
State Route 676 (Route 2), Marietta 45750

[J1] WAYNE GENERAL AND TECHNICAL COLLEGE
Orrville 44667

[1] WILBERFORCE UNIVERSITY
Wilberforce 45384, (513) 376-2911
Associate Director of Admissions: Sheila L. Brown

- **Undergraduates: 492m, 542w**
- **Tuition (1982/83): $3,280**
- **Room & Board: $1,770; Fees: $132**
- **Degrees offered: BA, BS, BSEd**
- **Student-faculty ratio: 17 to 1**

A private university affiliated with the African Methodist Episcopal Church, established in 1856. 65-acre small-town campus, 5 miles from Xenia, 18 miles east of Dayton. Air, rail, and bus service in Dayton.
Academic Character NCACS accreditation. Trimester system. Majors offered in accounting, art, biology, business administration, chemistry, communications & literature, economics, engineering, liberal studies, mathematics, music, political science, rehabilitation, science, and sociology. 9 specialized interdisciplinary studies. Distributive requirements; 36 hours of cooperative work/study required. Independent study. Honors program. Preprofessional programs in law, medicine, ministry. 3-1 engineering program with Dayton. Cross-registration with 15 area schools through the Dayton-Miami Valley Consortium. Early childhood and elementary education certification. Special education programs at Central State. ROTC at Central. 50,000-volume library.
Financial CEEB CSS. University scholarships, grants, loans; PELL, SEOG, NDSL, CWS.
Admissions High school graduation with 15 units required. GED accepted. Interview strongly recommended. ACT required for placement only. $10 application fee. Rolling admissions. $25 deposit due on acceptance of admissions offer. *Early Decision* Program. Transfers accepted. Credit possible for CEEB AP and CLEP exams; university has own advanced placement program. PEP program for academically deficient students.
Student Life Student Council. Newspaper. Music and drama groups. Awareness Series. Academic, honorary, religious, and special interest groups. 4 fraternities and 4 sororities. 25% of men and 30% of women join. Students live at home or on campus. 95% of students live on campus. Liquor and drugs prohibited. 2 phys ed credits required. Intercollegiate basketball, volleyball, and softball for men and women. NAIA, NCAA. Student body composition: 99% Black, 1% Other. 80% from out of state.

[1] WILMINGTON COLLEGE
Wilmington 45177, (513) 382-6661
Director of Admissions: Rhonda A. Inderhees

- **Undergraduates: 500m, 275w**
- **Tuition (1982/83): $4,185**
- **Room & Board: $2,040; Fees: $240**
- **Degrees offered: AB, BS**
- **Mean ACT 19; mean SAT 450v, 450m**
- **Student-faculty ratio: 15 to 1**

A private college affiliated with the Society of Friends (Quakers), established in 1870. 88-acre rural campus with a 1,000-acre farm, 30 miles from Dayton and Springfield, 50 miles from Cincinnati and Columbus. Airport in Cincinnati, Columbus, and Dayton.
Academic Character NCACS accreditation. Trimester system, 2 5-week summer terms. Majors offered in agriculture, art, biology, chemistry, communication, economics, education, French, German, history, industrial education, language/literature, management, mathematics, music, peace studies, political science, psychology, religion/philosophy, sociology, Spanish, theatre, and health, physical education, & recreation. Individualized Educational Planning: students work out curriculum with faculty advising team. Minors offered. General guidelines for academic breadth. Independent study. Cooperative work/study, credit by exam, limited pass/fail. Preprofessional programs in dentistry, law, medicine, theology, veterinary medicine. 3-1 medical technology program. Cross-registration with 15 area colleges. Washington Semester. Study abroad. Elementary and secondary education certification. Language labs. 3 farms. 100,000-volume library.
Financial CEEB CSS. College scholarships, grants, loans; PELL, SEOG, NDSL, CWS. Application deadline April 30.
Admissions High school graduation with 16 units required. GED accepted. Interview recommended. SAT or ACT required. Rolling admissions. $115 deposit due on acceptance of admissions offer. Admission deferral possible. Transfers accepted. Credit possible for CEEB AP and CLEP exams; college has own advanced placement program.

Student Life Student government. Newspaper, literary magazine, yearbook. Music and drama groups. Athletic, academic, honorary, religious, and special interest groups. 4 fraternities and 3 sororities without houses. 12% of men and 8% of women join. Freshmen live at home or on campus. Dorms for men and women. 68% of students live on campus. 9 intercollegiate sports for men, 5 for women; intramurals. AIAW, NAIA, NCAA, HBC. Student body composition: 0.1% Asian, 18.9% Black, 1.2% Hispanic, 75.5% White, 4.3% Other. 14% from out of state.

[1] WITTENBERG UNIVERSITY

Springfield 45501, (800) 762-5911 (in Ohio), (800) 543-5977 (elsewhere)
Director of Admissions: Kenneth G. Benne

- **Undergraduates: 1,037m, 1,217w**
- **Tuition (1982/83): $6,000**
- **Room & Board: $2,385; Fees: $311**
- **Degrees offered: BA, BFA, BMus, BMus Ed**
- **Student-faculty ratio: 16 to 1**

A private university supported by the Ohio and Indiana-Kentucky Synods of the Lutheran Church in America, established in 1845. 70-acre suburban campus, 45 miles west of Columbus. Served by bus; airport 25 miles away in Dayton.

Academic Character NCACS and professional accreditation. Trimester system, 6-week summer term. 48 majors offered in the areas of business administration, education, fine & applied arts, foreign languages, humanities, mathematics & sciences, music, physical education, radiation & laboratory medicine, sociology; American, East Asian, future, and urban studies. Special majors. Minors offered. Courses in 6 additional areas, including Chinese. Distributives and one religion course required. MSacred Music granted. Independent study. Honors program. Cooperative work/study, limited pass/fail, internships. Preprofessional programs in dentistry, law, medicine, pharmacy, veterinary medicine. 3-2 engineering programs with Case, Columbia, Georgia Tech, Washington U. 3-2 nursing program with Case. 3-2 forestry and environmental programs with Duke. Cross-registration with 15 area schools. Exchange programs in Great Britain. Study abroad. Elementary, secondary, and special education certification. ROTC, AFROTC, NROTC nearby. Language lab. 500,000-volume library.

Financial CEEB CSS. University scholarships, grants, loans, tuition reduction for children of Lutheran pastors; PELL, SEOG, NDSL, CWS. Application deadline March 1.

Admissions High school graduation with 12 units required. Interview recommended. Audition required for music students. SAT or ACT required; ACH used for placement. $20 application fee. Rolling admissions. $100 deposit due on acceptance of admissions offer. *Early Admission* Program. Admission deferral possible. Transfers accepted. Credit possible for CEEB AP, CLEP, and university's proficiency exams.

Student Life Student government. Newspaper, literary magazines, yearbook, radio station. Music and drama groups. Debate. Concerned Black Students. Academic, honorary, religious, service, and special interest groups. 8 fraternities and 9 sororities, all with houses. 42% of men and 46% of women join. Freshmen live at home or on campus. Coed and single-sex dorms. Language houses. Married-student housing. 61% of students live on campus. Freshmen may not have cars. 3 phys ed courses required. 10 intercollegiate sports for men, 10 for women; intramurals. NCAA, OAC. Student body composition: 0.2% Asian, 5% Black, 0.1% Hispanic, 0.1% Native American, 94.1% White, 0.5% Other. 47% from out of state.

[1] WOOSTER, THE COLLEGE OF

Wooster 44691, (800) 362-7386 (in Ohio), (800) 321-9885 (elsewhere)
Dean of Admissions: Samuel Barnett

- **Tuition, Room, Board, & Fees (1982/83): $8,820**
- **Degrees offered: BA, BMus, BMus Ed**
- **Mean ACT 24; SAT 528v, 510m (women); 499v, 532m (men)**
- **Student-faculty ratio: 13 to 1**

A private college affiliated with the Presbyterian Church, established in 1866. 320-acre small-city campus, 60 miles from Cleveland. Airports, bus stations in Cleveland and Akron.

Academic Character NCACS and professional accreditation. Trimester system, 6-week summer term. 43 majors offered in the areas of art, Black studies, computer science, cultural area studies, foreign languages, the humanities, international relations, music, physical education, science, social science, religion, theatre, and urban studies. Special and self-designed majors. Courses include archaeology, Hebrew, Russian. Distributives and one religion course required. Independent study. Phi Beta Kappa. Limited pass/fail, internships. Preprofessional programs in law, medicine, religion, and business. 3-2 engineering programs with Case, U Michigan, Washington U. 3-year special law program with Columbia. 3-2 social work program with Case. 3-year graduate school programs in economics, math, physics with U Michigan. 3-2 nursing program with Case. 3-2 forestry and environmental studies program with Duke. Washington, UN, Oak Ridge, Newberry Library semesters. Many study abroad programs. Elementary and secondary education certification. Computer center. Language lab. Art center. 525,000-volume library.

Financial CEEB CSS. College scholarships, grants, loans, Presbyterian Church grants, payment plans; PELL, SEOG, NDSL, FISL, CWS. Application deadline April 15.

Admissions High school graduation with 15 units required. Interview recommended. SAT or ACT required. $15 application fee. Rolling admissions. $100 deposit due on acceptance of admissions offer. *Early Admission* and *Early Decision* programs. Admission deferral possible. Transfers accepted. Credit possible for CEEB AP and CLEP exams.

Student Life Student government. Newspaper, magazine, yearbook, radio station. Music, dance, and drama groups. Debate. Japan Association. Black Student Association. International Student Association. Academic, religious, and special interest groups. 7 social clubs for men and 4 for women; housed as units in dorms. 30% of men and 24% of women join. Freshmen live on campus. Coed and single-sex dorms. Special interest housing. 90% of students live on campus. Cars permitted after 1st quarter of 1st year. 11 intercollegiate sports for men, 9 for women; many intramurals. AIAW, NCAA, OAC. Student body composition: 1% Asian, 5% Black, 1% Hispanic, 86% White, 7% Other. 55% from out of state.

[1] WRIGHT STATE UNIVERSITY

Dayton 45435, (513) 873-2211
Registrar: Louis Falkner

- **Undergraduates: 3,551m, 3,236w; 15,635 total (including graduates)**
- **Tuition (1982/83): $1,470 (in-state), $2,940 (out-of-state)**
- **Room & Board: $2,075**
- **Degrees offered: BA, BS, BFA, BMus, BSBus, BSEd, BSMed Tech, BSN, AA, AAS, AAS**
- **Mean ACT 21.15**
- **Student-faculty ratio: 20 to 1**

A public university established in 1964. 618-acre suburban campus. Served by air, rail, and bus.

Academic Character NCACS and professional accreditation. Trimester system, summer term. 6 majors offered by the College of Business & Administration, 25 by the College of Education & Human Services, 27 by the College of Liberal Arts, 16 by the College of Science & Engineering, and 1 by the School of Nursing. AA offered in law enforcement technology, AAS in business areas, AAS in electronics technology, mechanical drafting design technology. Self-designed majors. Distributive requirements. Independent study. Honors programs. Cooperative work/study, pass/fail, internships, credit by exam. Preprofessional programs include dentistry, law, medicine. Cross-registration with 15 area schools. Elementary, secondary, and special education certification. ROTC, AFROTC. Computer center. Black Cultural Resources Center. 362,000-volume library with microform resources.

Financial University scholarships, grants, loans; PELL, SEOG, NSS, NDSL, NSL, CWS. Application deadlines April 1 (scholarships), March 1 (loans).

Admissions Open admission to Ohio high school graduates and to out-of-state students who evidence above-average ability. GED accepted. ACT required. $25 application fee. Rolling admissions. *Early Decision* Program. Admission deferral possible. Transfers accepted. University has own advanced placement program.

Student Life Student government. Newspaper, literary magazine, radio station. Music and drama groups. Athletic, academic, religious, and special interest groups. 14 fraternities and sororities. Limited campus housing. University apartments near campus. 2% of students live on campus. 7 intercollegiate sports for men, 5 for women; intramurals. AIAW, NCAA, IWA. Student body composition: 1.1% Asian, 6.1% Black, 0.7% Hispanic, 0.1% Native American, 90.3% White, 1.7% Other. 5% from out of state.

[1] XAVIER UNIVERSITY

Victory Parkway, Cincinnati 45207, (513) 745-3301
Dean of Admissions: Rene A. Durand, Jr.

- **Undergraduates: 1,338m, 1,218w; 7,023 total (including graduates)**
- **Tuition (1982/83): $3,800**
- **Room & Board: $2,210-$2,370; Fees: $350**
- **Degrees offered: BA, BS, BSBA, BFA**
- **Mean SAT 466v, 492m**
- **Student-faculty ratio: 16 to 1**

A private, Roman Catholic university operated by the Society of Jesus, established in 1831, became coed in 1969. 65-acre suburban campus. Served by air, rail, and bus.

Academic Character NCACS and professional accreditation. Semester system, 2 5-week summer terms. 28 majors offered by the College of Arts & Sciences, 7 by the College of Business Administration, and 8 by Edgecliff College. Self-designed majors. Distributives, 12 theology, and 12 philosophy credits required. Masters degrees granted. Honors program. Pass/fail, internships, credit by exam. Preprofessional programs in dentistry, law, medicine, pharmacy. 3-3 engineering program with Cincinnati. 3-1 medical and nuclear medical technology programs. Study abroad. Elementary, secondary, and special education certification. ROTC; AFRTOC at Cincinnati. Computer center. Language lab. 350,000-volume library with microform resources.

Financial CEEB CSS. University scholarships, grants, loans, payment plans; PELL, SEOG, NDSL, GSL, CWS. Application deadlines February 1 (scholarships), April 15 (loans).

Admissions High school graduation with 15 units required. Interview recommended. SAT or ACT required. $15 application fee. Rolling admissions. $125 deposit due on acceptance of admissions offer. *Early Admission* Program. Admission deferral possible. Transfers accepted. Credit possible for CEEB AP exams. Programs for disadvantaged students.

Student Life Student Senate. Newspaper, literary magazine, yearbook, radio station. Debate. Afro-American Student Association. Academic, honorary, religious, service, and special interest groups. Fraternities and sororities. Juniors and seniors with permission may live off campus. Coed and single-sex dorms. No married-student housing. 40% of students live on campus. Intoxication and drug possession prohibited. 7 intercollegiate sports for men, 5 for women; intramurals. AIAW, NCAA. Student body composition: 5% Black, 1% Hispanic, 93% White, 1% Other. 20% from out of state.

[1] YOUNGSTOWN STATE UNIVERSITY

Youngstown 44555, (216) 742-3150
Director of Admissions: William Livosky

- **Undergraduates: 5,286m, 4,613w; 15,644 total (including graduates)**
- **Tuition (1982/83): $1,050 (in-state), $1,950 (out-of-state)**
- **Room & Board: $1,995; Fees: $195**
- **Degrees offered: AB, BS, BSin AS, BSEd, BSBA, BEng, BFA, BMus, BSN, BSBA, AA, AAS, ALS, AApp Bus**
- **Mean ACT 17**
- **Student-faculty ratio: 21 to 1**

A public university established in 1908. 120-acre urban campus. Served by air, rail, and bus.
Academic Character NCACS and professional accreditation. Trimester system, 2 5-week summer terms. 36 majors offered by the College of Arts & Sciences, 14 by the College of Fine & Performing Arts, 4 by the School of Education, 6 by the School of Engineering, 11 by the College of Applied Science & Technology, and 14 by the School of Business Administration. Self-designed majors. Minors offered. Distributive requirements. Masters degrees granted. Pass/fail, credit by exam. Elementary, secondary, and special education certification. ROTC. 455,460-volume library.
Financial CEEB CSS. University scholarships, grants, loans, payment plan; PELL, SEOG, NSS, NDSL, some student employment. Application deadline April 1.
Admissions High school graduation with 16 units required. GED accepted. Interview recommended. SAT or ACT required. $20 application fee. Rolling admissions. $50 room deposit due on acceptance of admissions offer. *Early Admission* Program for local residents. Transfers accepted. Credit possible for CEEB AP and CLEP exams; university has own advanced placement program.
Student Life Student government. Newspaper, literary magazine, yearbook. Music and drama groups. Afro-American Chorale. Special interest groups. 10 fraternities, 7 with houses; 4 sororities with houses. 7% of students join. Coed dorm. 1% of students live on campus. 6 quarter hours of phys ed required. 9 intercollegiate sports for men, 7 for women; intramurals. NCAA, AIAW, OVC, POC. Student body composition: 0.2% Asian, 6.9% Black, 0.5% Hispanic, 0.1% Native American, 90.3% White, 2% Other. 10% from out of state.

OKLAHOMA *(OK)*

[J1] BACONE COLLEGE
Muskogee 74401, (918) 683-4581

- **Undergraduates: 94m, 226w; 398 total (including part-time)**
- **Tuition (1981/82): $50 per credit hour**
- **Room & Board: $1,400**
- **Degrees offered: AA, AAN**
- **Mean ACT 14.5**

A private coed college founded for the education of American Indians, affiliated with the American Baptist Churches, USA, and governed by a 36-member Board of Trustees.
Academic Character NCACS and professional accreditation. Semester system. Terminal and transfer programs offered in liberal arts, preprofessional fields, fine arts, business, home economics, journalism, music, physical education, social science, nursing, and physical science. One-year certificate programs offered in business areas: general business, secretarial science, mid-management.
Student Life Dormitories and dining hall for men and women.

[1] BARTLESVILLE WESLEYAN COLLEGE
2201 Silver Lake Road, Bartlesville 74003, (918) 333-6151
Director of Recruitment: Wendell Rovenstine

- **Undergraduates: 820 men & women**
- **Tuition (1982/83): $2,760**
- **Room & Board: $1,950**
- **Degrees offered: BA, BS, AA**
- **Student-faculty ratio: 13 to 1**

A private college owned by the Wesleyan Church, established in 1972. 36-acre suburban campus, 50 miles north of Tulsa.
Academic Character NCACS accreditation. Semester system, 6-week summer term. Majors offered in accounting, behavioral science, biology, business, business education, Christian education, church music, elementary education, history/political science, missions, music education, music performance, physical education, religion, science education, and social science. Minors offered in some major fields. Distributives and 9 hours of religion required. Preprofessional programs in engineering, nursing, paramedical fields. Elementary and secondary education certification. 100,000-volume library.
Financial ACT FAS. College scholarships, grants, loans, ministerial grants, state grants & loans, payment plan; PELL, SEOG, NDSL, GSL, CWS. Application deadline April 1.
Admissions High school graduation with 16 units required. ACT required. Rolling admissions. $60 room deposit due on acceptance of admissions offer. *Early Admission* and *Early Decision* programs. Transfers accepted. Credit possible for CEEB CLEP exams.
Student Life Student government. Newspaper, yearbook. Music and drama groups. Campus ministries. Professional, service, social, and special interest groups. Single students live at home or on campus. No married-student housing. Church, chapel, and vespers attendance required. 4 hours of phys ed required. 5 intercollegiate sports for men, 2 for women; intramurals. NAIA, NCCAA.

[1] BETHANY NAZARENE COLLEGE
Bethany 73008, (405) 789-6400
Director of Admissions: Vernon A. Snowbarger

- **Undergraduates: 473m, 606w; 1,364 total (including graduates)**
- **Tuition (1982/83): $2,450**
- **Room & Board: $1,890; Fees: $138**
- **Degrees offered: AB, BS, BMus Ed, BSN, AA**
- **Mean ACT 18.1**
- **Student-faculty ratio: 18 to 1**

A private college controlled by the Church of the Nazarene, established in 1899. 40-acre suburban campus, 30 minutes from downtown Oklahoma City. Served by air, rail, and bus.
Academic Character NCACS accreditation. Semester system, 4-week summer term. 33 majors offered in the areas of business, education, humanities, home economics, modern languages, music, physical education, religion, science, social science, and speech. Self-designed majors. Minors required of AB candidates. Distributives and 3 religion courses required. Graduate degrees granted. Independent study. Limited pass/fail, internships, credit by exam. Preprofessional programs in allied health, dentistry, engineering, law, medicine, theology. 3-1 medical technology program. Christian College Consortium. Elementary and secondary education certification. ROTC at Central State. Language lab. 104,399-volume library.
Financial CEEB CSS. College scholarships, grants, loans, music scholarships, payment plans; PELL, SEOG, NDSL, CWS, assistantships. Scholarship application deadline May 1.
Admissions High school graduation required. GED accepted. ACT required. $35 application fee. Rolling admissions; suggest applying in March. *Early Admission* Program. Transfers accepted. Credit possible for CEEB AP and CLEP exams; college has own advanced placement program.
Student Life Student government. Newspaper, yearbook. Music groups. Circle K. Ecology Club. Academic, honorary, religious, service, and special interest groups. Upperclassmen may live in approved off-campus houses if dorm space is unavailable. Single-sex dorms. 62% of students live on campus. Liquor, tobacco, dancing, gambling, loose conduct, hazing, profanity prohibited. Dress code. Permission to marry required. Attendance in class and at chapel services required. 2 hours of phys ed required. 5 intercollegiate sports for men, 4 for women; intramurals. NAIA, SC. Student body composition: 1.5% Asian, 3% Black, 4% Hispanic, 1.5% Native American, 82% White, 8% Other. 75% from out of state.

[1] CAMERON UNIVERSITY
Lawton 73505, (405) 248-2200
Director of Admissions & Records: Raymond Chapman

- **Undergraduates: 1,391m, 1,432w; 5,077 total (including part-time)**
- **Tuition (1982/83): $490 (in-state), $1,400 (out-of-state)**
- **Room & Board: $1,700-$2,000**
- **Degrees offered: BA, BS, BSN, AA**
- **Mean ACT 18**
- **Student-faculty ratio: 25 to 1**

A public university established in 1909. 160-acre suburban campus, 100 miles from Oklahoma City. Served by air, rail, and bus.
Academic Character NCACS and professional accreditation. Semester system, summer term. Majors offered in accounting, agriculture, art, biology, business, chemistry, computer science, education, English, health & physical education, history, home economics, mathematics, music, natural science, nursing, physics, political science, Romance languages, sociology, speech/drama, and technology. Minors required and offered in most major fields and in 29 others. Distributive requirements. Independent study. Honors program. Phi Beta Kappa. Cooperative work/study, credit by exam. Preprofessional programs in dentistry, engineering, law, medicine, pharmacy, veterinary medicine. 3-1 medical technology program. Elementary and secondary education certification. ROTC. 152,000-volume library.
Financial University scholarships, grants, loans; PELL, SEOG, NSS, NDSL, FISL, NSL, CWS.
Admissions High school graduation in upper ¾ of class for in-state, upper ½ for out-of-state applicants required. GED accepted. ACT required. Rolling admissions. $20 room deposit due on acceptance of admissions offer. *Concurrent Enrollment* Program. Transfers accepted. Credit possible for CEEB CLEP exams; university has own advanced placement program.
Student Life Student government. Newspaper, yearbook. Music groups. Debate. Academic, honorary, political, religious, and social organizations. Single-sex dorms. 8% of students live on campus. Class attendance expected. 8 intercollegiate sports; intramurals. AIAW, NAIA. Student body composition: 2% Asian, 14% Black, 3% Hispanic, 3% Native American, 77% White, 1% Other. 1% from out of state.

[J1] CARL ALBERT JUNIOR COLLEGE
Poteau 74953

[1] CENTRAL STATE UNIVERSITY
Edmond 73034, (405) 341-2980
Director of Admissions: Jack Beeson

- **Enrollment: 5,243m, 6,761w**
- **Tuition (1982/83): $500 (in-state), $1,320 (out-of-state)**
- **Room & Board: $1,400**
- **Degrees offered: BA, BS, BBA, BMus, BMus Ed, BAEd, BSEd**
- **Student-faculty ratio: 25 to 1**

A public university established in 1891, became coed in 1981. 200-acre suburban campus, 12 miles from Oklahoma City. Served by bus; airport and rail station nearby.
Academic Character NCACS and professional accreditation. Semester system, 9-week summer term, May, August and December interims. 23 majors offered by the School of Business, 10 by the School of Education, 44 by the School of Liberal Arts, 26 by the School of Mathematics & Science, and 19 by the School of Special Arts & Sciences. Minors offered in most major fields. Distributive requirements. Graduate degrees granted. Independent study. Pass/fail. Preprofessional programs in dentistry, dietetics, engineering, law, medical fields. Early childhood, elementary, secondary, and special education certification. ROTC. Computer center. Language lab. Museum. 400,000-volume library with microform resources.
Financial ACT FAS. University scholarships, grants, loans, freshman tuition waivers; PELL, SEOG, BIA, NDSL, GSL, NSL, CWS. Application deadline March 1.
Admissions High school graduation with 10 units recommended. GED accepted. ACT required; SAT accepted from out-of-state applicants. Rolling admissions; suggest applying by March 1. *Concurrent Enrollment* Program. Transfers accepted. Credit possible for CEEB AP and CLEP exams; university has own advanced placement program.
Student Life Student government. Newspaper, literary magazine, yearbook, radio station. Music, dance, and drama groups. Afro-American Student Union. Native American Club. Chinese Student Union. Rodeo Club. Academic, honorary, and special interest groups. 3 fraternities, 2 with houses, and 3 sororities with houses. 3% of men and 8% of women join. Students under 23 live at home or on campus. Single-sex dorms. Married-student housing. 10% of students live on campus. Liquor prohibited. Class attendance expected. 4 hours of phys ed required. 7 intercollegiate sports for men, 6 for women; many intramurals. NAIA. Student body composition: 1.5% Asian, 9.5% Black, 0.7% Hispanic, 1.9% Native American, 80.4% White. 5% from out of state.

[J1] CLAREMORE JUNIOR COLLEGE
Claremore — see Rogers State College

[J1] CONNORS STATE COLLEGE
Warner 74469, (918) 463-2931

- **Enrollment: 346m, 401w; 1,192 total (including part-time)**
- **Tuition (1982/83): $13 per semester hour (in-state), $33 (out-of-state)**
- **Room & Board: $1,158-$1,370**
- **Degrees offered: AA, AS**
- **Mean ACT 15.9**
- **Student-faculty ratio: 20 to 1**

A public college established in 1908. 35-acre small-town campus.
Academic Character NCACS accreditation. Semester system. 2-year programs offered in business, communications & fine arts, physical education, mathematics & science, and practical & technical arts. Distributive requirements. Preprofessional programs in chemistry, dentistry, education, journalism, law, medicine, medical technology, nursing, optometry, and pharmacy. 27,102-volume library.
Financial ACT FAS. College scholarships, state grants & loans; PELL, SEOG, BIA, NDSL, FISL. Application deadline April 15.
Admissions High school graduation required. GED accepted. ACT required. Rolling admissions. Transfers accepted. Credit possible for challenge exams.
Student Life Student government. Newspaper, magazine. Music and drama groups. Speech team. Black Student Society. Rodeo club. Academic, honorary, professional, and special interest groups. Single students must live at home or on campus. Single-sex dorms. Married-student housing. 5 intercollegiate sports. OJCC. Student body composition: 12% minority.

[1] EAST CENTRAL OKLAHOMA STATE UNIVERSITY
Ada 74820, (405) 332-8000
Registrar & Director of Admissions: Merle Boatwright

- **Undergraduates: 1,264m, 1,599w; 3,940 total (including graduates)**
- **Tuition (1982/83): $500 (in-state), $1,170 (out-of-state)**
- **Room & Board: $1,650; Fees: $100**
- **Degrees offered: BA, BS, BAEd, BSEd**
- **Mean ACT 16**
- **Student-faculty ratio: 20 to 1**

A public university established in 1909. 130-acre campus in a small city 86 miles from Oklahoma City. Served by air and bus.
Academic Character NCACS and professional accreditation. Semester system, 8-week summer term. 35 majors offered by the divisions of Allied Health, Applied Sciences, Arts & Letters, Business, Education, Human Resources, Mathematics & Sciences, Nursing, Social Sciences, and Health, Physical Education, & Recreation. Minors required for some majors. Minors offered in most major fields and in 8 other areas. Courses in humanities, French, Seminole-Creek. Distributive requirements. Masters degrees granted. Exchange program with Westfield State, MA. Elementary, secondary, and special education certification. ROTC. 200,000-volume library.
Financial ACT FAS. University scholarships, grants, loans; PELL, SEOG, NDSL, NSL, GSL, FISL, CWS.
Admissions High school graduation required. GED accepted. ACT required; SAT may be substituted by non-residents. Rolling admissions. $50 room deposit due on acceptance of admissions offer. Limited *Early Admission* and *Concurrent Enrollment* programs. Transfers accepted. Credit possible for CEEB CLEP exams; university has own advanced placement program. Special admissions program.
Student Life Student government. Newspaper, yearbook. Music groups. Debate. Black Student Union. Educational, honorary, political, professional, religious, and service groups. 3 fraternities and 3 sororities with lounges. 6% of men and 7% of women join. Single students must live in university-approved housing. Coed and single-sex dorms. 50% of students live on campus. 2 semesters of phys ed required. 5 intercollegiate sports; intramurals. NAIA, OAC. Student body composition: 0.4% Asian, 6.2% Black, 0.4% Hispanic, 5.9% Native American, 86.7% White, 0.4% Other. 1% from out of state.

[J1] EASTERN OKLAHOMA STATE COLLEGE
Wilburton 74578, (918) 465-2361
Director of Admissions: J.C. Hunt

- **Enrollment: 709m, 743w; 2,400 total (including part-time)**
- **Tuition (1982/83): $348 (in-state), $960 (out-of-state)**
- **Room & Board: $1,430-$1,578**
- **Degrees offered: AA, AS**
- **Student-faculty ratio: 34 to 1**

A public college established in 1927. Small-town campus. Served by bus.
Academic Character NCACS accreditation. Semester system, 8-week summer term. 2-year transfer programs offered in the areas of agriculture, art, business, computer science, education, engineering, forestry, horticulture, industrial education, journalism, liberal arts, mathematics, music, science, social science, speech, and vocational home economics. Distributive requirements. Preprofessional programs in nursing, medicine, pharmacy, veterinary science. 33,000-volume library.
Financial College scholarships, state loans; PELL, SEOG, BIA, NDSL, GSL, CWS, college work program.
Admissions High school graduation required. ACT required. $20 application fee. Rolling admissions. *Early Admission, Early Decision, Concurrent Enrollment* programs. Transfers accepted. Credit possible for CEEB CLEP and departmental exams.
Student Life Student government. Newspaper, yearbook. Music groups. Debate. Religious activities. Single students live at home or on campus. Single-sex dorms. Married-student housing. 6 intercollegiate sports; intramurals.

[J1] EL RENO COLLEGE
El Reno 73036

[1] LANGSTON UNIVERSITY
Langston 73050, (405) 466-2231
Director of Admissions: Willie L. Lawrence

- **Undergraduates: 826m, 515w; 1,512 total (including part-time)**
- **Tuition (1982/83): $380 (in-state), $743 (out-of-state)**
- **Room & Board: $1,702; Fees: $60**
- **Degrees offered: BA, BS, BAEd, BSEd, AS**
- **Student-faculty ratio: 23 to 1**

A public university established in 1897. 40-acre rural campus, 42 miles northeast of Oklahoma City. Served by rail and bus.
Academic Character NCACS and professional accreditation. Semester system, 8-week summer term. 51 majors offered by the divisions of Arts & Sciences, Applied Sciences, Education & Behavioral Sciences, and Nursing. Minor required. Minors offered in all major fields and in 4 other areas. Cooperative work/study. Preprofessional programs in law, library science, social work. Elementary and secondary education certification. Language lab. 147,000-volume library.
Financial CEEB CSS. University scholarships, loans, payment plans; PELL, SEOG, NDSL, CWS. Application deadline April 15.
Admissions High school graduation required. GED accepted. ACT required; SAT accepted from out-of-state students. Rolling admissions; suggest applying by March 1. *Early Admission* Program. Transfers accepted. Advanced placement program.
Student Life Student government. Newspaper, yearbook. Music groups. Debate. Honorary, political, religious, and special interest groups. 8 fraternities and 8 sororities without houses. 10% of men and 15% of women join. Students not at home live on campus when space is available. Dormitories for men and women. Married-student housing. 44% of students live on campus. Liquor prohibited. 4 hours of phys ed required. 4 intercollegiate sports for men, 2 for women; intramurals. AIAW, NAIA. Student body composition: 61% Black, 21% White, 18% Other. 33% from out of state.

[P] MIDWEST CHRISTIAN COLLEGE
6600 North Kelley Avenue, Oklahoma City 73111

[J1] MURRAY STATE COLLEGE
Tishomingo 73460, (405) 371-2371
Director of Admissions: Harold W. Slack

- **Enrollment: 310m, 294w; 1,400 total (including part-time)**
- **Tuition (1982/83): $378 (in-state), $990 (out-of-state)**
- **Degrees offered: AS, AAT, AB, AET, AHT, AIT, AN**
- **Mean ACT 14.5**

A public college established in 1908. Small-town campus.
Academic Character NCACS and professional accreditation. Semester system, 8-week summer term. 2-year programs in agriculture, business, engineering, general education, home economics, nursing, physical education, science, secretarial administration, teaching, and technology.

Preprofessional programs in dentistry, law, medicine, optometry, pharmacy, veterinary medicine. Library/learning resource center.
Financial College scholarships, state grants & loans; PELL, SEOG, BIA, NSS, NDSL, NSL, GSL, student employment.
Admissions High school graduation required. ACT required. Rolling admissions. *Concurrent Enrollment* Program. Transfers accepted.
Student Life Student government. Newspaper. Drama Club. Academic, honorary, professional, and special interest groups. Dorms for men and women. Co-op dorms. Intercollegiate and intramural sports. Student body composition: 20% minority.

[J1] NORTHEASTERN OKLAHOMA A&M COLLEGE
Miami 74354

[1] NORTHEASTERN OKLAHOMA STATE UNIVERSITY
Tahlequah 74464, (918) 456-5511
Director of Admissions/Registrar: James A. Watkins

- **Enrollment: 2,273m, 2,975w; 5,741 total (including part-time)**
- **Tuition (1982/83): $545 (in-state), $1,337 (out-of-state)**
- **Room & Board: $1,648-$2,008**
- **Degrees offered: BA, BS, BAEd, BSEd, BS Optom Ed, BSCrim J**
- **Student-faculty ratio: 18 to 1**

A public university established in 1846. 160-acre small-town campus, 30 miles from Muskogee. Served by bus; airport in Tulsa.
Academic Character NCACS and professional accreditation. Semester system, 7-week summer term. 66 majors offered in the areas of agriculture, allied health, art, business, Cherokee, criminal justice, education, health/physical education, humanities, home economics, Indian studies, industrial arts, journalism, mathematics & sciences, music, optometry, safety, social sciences, speech, and touristry management. Minor required. Courses include tribal management. Distributive requirements. Graduate degrees granted. Preprofessional programs in allied health, dentistry, dietetics, engineering, law, medicine, nursing, optometry, pahrmacy, veterinary medicine. 3-1 medical technology program. Elementary, secondary, and special education certification. ROTC at U of Arkansas. 150,000-volume library with microform resources.
Financial CEEB CSS. University scholarships, grants, loans, state grants & loans; PELL, SEOG, BIA, NDSL, GSL, CWS. Priority application deadline April 1.
Admissions High school graduation required. GED accepted. ACT required. Rolling admissions; suggest applying by January. *Early Decision, Early Admission, Concurrent Enrollment* programs. Admission deferral possible. Transfers accepted. Credit possible for CEEB CLEP exams; university has own advanced placement program.
Student Life Student government. Newspaper, yearbook. Music groups. Debate. Academic, honorary, service, and special interest groups. 4 fraternities, 2 with houses, and 3 sororities without houses. 10% of men and women join. Single students under 21 live at home or on campus. Campus apartments, married-student housing. 20% of students live on campus. Liquor and drugs prohibited. Class attendance expected. 4 hours of phys ed required. 5 intercollegiate sports for men, 3 for women; intramurals. OIC. Student body composition: 0.2% Asian, 6.8% Black, 0.4% Hispanic, 16.6% Native American, 74.8% White. 5% from out of state.

[J1] NORTHERN OKLAHOMA COLLEGE
Tonkawa 74653, (405) 628-2581
Assistant Dean for Admissions, Records, & Research: Ronald E. Appleman

- **Enrollment: 445m, 545w; 1,700 total (including part-time)**
- **Tuition (1982/83): $10.50 per credit hour (in-state), $28.25 (out-of-state)**
- **Degrees offered: AA, AB, AS, AAS**
- **Mean ACT 16.8**
- **Student-faculty ratio: 30 to 1**

A public college established in 1901. 30-acre small-town campus, 90 miles north of Oklahoma City.
Academic Character NCACS accreditation. Semester system, 9-week summer term. 2-year programs offered in the areas of the arts, applied sciences, business, and science. Distributive requirements. Preprofessional programs in computer science, dentistry, engineering, medicine, nursing, optometry, osteopathy, pharmacy, secondary education, veterinary medicine. Museum. Library.
Financial ACT FAS. College scholarships, loans, state grants; PELL, SEOG, BIA, NDSL, GSL, NSL, CWS.
Admissions High school graduation required. ACT required. Rolling admissions. Credit possible for proficiency exams.
Student Life Newspaper, yearbook, radio station. Music groups. Indian Cultural Society. Academic, honorary, political, professional, religious, and special interest groups. Single-sex dorms. Class attendance expected. Athletics programs.

[1] NORTHWESTERN OKLAHOMA STATE UNIVERSITY
Alva 73717, (405) 327-1700
Registrar: Doris Blue

- **Undergraduates: 919m, 871w; 2,081 total (including graduates)**
- **Tuition (1982/83): $534 (in-state), $683 (out-of-state)**
- **Room & Board: $1,368; Fees: $10**
- **Degrees offered: BA, BS, BAEd, BSEd**
- **Mean ACT 19**
- **Student-faculty ratio: 15 to 1**

A public university established in 1897. Small-town campus, located northwest of Enid.
Academic Character NCACS and professional accreditation. Semester system, 2 5-week summer terms. 37 majors offered in the areas of agriculture, art, business, conservation law enforcement, education, home economics, humanities, journalism, library science, music, science, social science, social work, and speech. Double majors or major/2 minors required. Distributive requirements. Masters degrees granted. Independent study. Honors program. Credit by exam. Preprofessional programs in agriculture, ecology, business, dentistry, engineering, home economics, industrial technology, law enforcement, medical technology, medicine, nursing, occupational therapy, optometry, osteopathy, pharmacy, and physician's associate. Elementary, secondary, and special education certification. ROTC. Education Center.200,000-volume library with microform resources.
Financial University scholarships, loans, PELL, SEOG, NDSL, CWS.
Admissions High school graduation required. GED accepted. ACT required. Rolling admissions; suggest applying in spring. Transfers accepted. University has own advanced placement program.
Student Life Student government. Newspaper, yearbook, radio station. Music and drama groups. Athletic, academic, honorary, political, religious, service, and special interest groups. 1 fraternity and 1 sorority. Students under 22 live at home or on campus. Single-sex dorms. Liquor prohibited on campus. Class attendance expected. 3 hours of phys ed required. Intercollegiate and intramural sports. Student body composition: 0.6% Asian, 3.4% Black, 1% Hispanic, 1% Native American, 92% White, 2% Other.

[1] OKLAHOMA, UNIVERSITY OF
Norman 73019, (405) 325-2251
Director of Admissions: Barbara Cousins

- **Undergraduates: 9,648m, 7,018w; 20,552 total (including graduates)**
- **Tuition (1982/83): $650 (in-state), $1,970 (out-of-state)**
- **Room & Board: $2,074; Fees: $100**
- **Degrees offered: BA, BS, BBA, BFA, BMus, BMus Ed, BAcct, BArch, BLib Studies**
- **Mean ACT 21**
- **Student-faculty ratio: 21 to 1**

A public university established in 1890. 2,695-acre suburban campus, 15 miles south of Oklahoma City. Served by bus; airport in Oklahoma City.
Academic Character NCACS and professional accreditation. Semester system, 8-week summer term. 65 majors offered by the College of Arts & Sciences, 8 by the College of Business Administration, 19 by the College of Education, 18 by the College of Engineering, 3 by the College of Environmental Design, 26 by the College of Fine Arts, and 1 each in the colleges of Liberal Studies, Nursing, and Pharmacy. Special majors. Distributive requirements; freshmen take at least 2 semesters in University College. Graduate degrees granted. Honors program. Phi Beta Kappa. Some cooperative work/study, pass/fail, credit by exam. Preprofessional programs. Study abroad. Elementary, secondary, and special education certification. ROTC, AFROTC, NROTC. Computer center. Hacienda El Cobano. Art museum. Science and history museum. Language lab. 1,800,000-volume library with microform resources.
Financial CEEB CSS. University scholarships, grants, loans; PELL, SEOG, NSS, NDSL, FISL, NSL, GSL, CWS. Application deadlines March 1 (scholarships), May 1 (loans).
Admissions High school graduation required. ACT required for in-state students. $10 application fee for out-of-state students. Rolling admissions. Transfers accepted. Credit possible for CEEB AP, CLEP, ACT PEP, and departmental exams. Special admissions program.
Student Life Student government. Newspaper, yearbook, radio and TV stations. Music and drama groups. Debate. Model UN. Academic, political, and volunteer groups. 22 fraternities and 15 sororities; most have houses. 11% of men and 15% of women join. Single students under 21 live at home or on campus. Coed and single-sex dorms. Special-interest housing. Married-student housing. 27% of students live on campus. Liquor prohibited. Several intercollegiate and intramural sports. AIAW, Big Eight Conference. Student body composition: 4% Black, 1% Hispanic, 3% Native American, 80% White, 12% Other. 19% from out of state.

[1] OKLAHOMA, UNIVERSITY OF SCIENCE AND ARTS OF
Chickasha 73018, (405) 224-3140
Director of Admissions: Jack D. Hudson

- **Undergraduates: 262m, 423w; 1,343 total (including part-time)**
- **Tuition (1982/83): $659 (in-state), $1,773 (out-of-state)**
- **Room & Board: $1,400; Fees: $45**
- **Degrees offered: BA, BS**
- **Student-faculty ratio: 14 to 1**

A public university established in 1908, became coed in 1965. 75-acre suburban campus, 50 miles southwest of Oklahoma City. Served by rail and bus.
Academic Character NCACS and professional accreditation. Trimester system, 10-week summer term. 30 majors offered in the areas of business, communications, education, fine arts, home economics, humanities, Indian studies, physical education, science, social science, and Spanish. Distributive requirements. Independent study. Honors program. Tutorial Scholar Program. Pass/fail. Preprofessional programs in dentistry, law, medicine, nursing, pharmacy, veterinary science. 3-1 medical technology program. Early childhood, elementary, secondary, and special education certification. ROTC nearby. Speech and Hearing Clinic. Language lab. 85,000-volume library.
Financial ACT FAS. University scholarships, loans, 3rd trimester tuition waiver for in-state students in good academic standing, payment plan; PELL, SEOG, NDSL, CWS. Loan application deadline July 1.
Admissions High school graduation with 16 units recommended. GED accepted. ACT required. Rolling admissions; suggest applying by June. $25

deposit due with housing application. Transfers accepted. Credit possible for CEEB AP and CLEP exams.
Student Life Student government. Newspaper, yearbook, TV station. Music, dance, and drama groups. Inter-tribal Heritage Club. Model UN. Academic, honorary, religious groups. 3 social clubs for men and 5 for women without houses. 30% of men and 35% of women join. Students live at home or on campus. Dorms for men and women. 30% of students live on campus. Liquor prohibited. Class attendance expected. 4 activity courses required. 3 intercollegiate sports; intramurals. AIAW. Student body composition: 1.5% Asian, 8.4% Black, 0.9% Hispanic, 11.6% Native American, 68.5% White. 5% from out of state.

[1] OKLAHOMA BAPTIST UNIVERSITY

Shawnee 74801, (405) 275-2850
Director of Admissions: John Fluke

- **Undergraduates: 671m, 817w**
- **Tuition (1982/83): $2,400**
- **Room & Board: $1,430; Fees: $255**
- **Degrees offered: BA, BS, BBA, BFA, BMus, BMus Ed, BHumanities, BSN**
- **Mean ACT 20.8**
- **Student-faculty ratio: 13 to 1**

A private university controlled by the Baptist General Convention, established in 1910. 125-acre campus in a small city 35 miles southeast of Oklahoma City. Served by bus.
Academic Character NCACS and professional accreditation. 4-1-4 system, 8-week summer term. 79 majors offered by the School of Christian Service, College of Arts & Sciences, School of Business & Administration, School of Nursing, and College of Fine Arts. Self-designed majors. Distributives and 2 religion courses required. GRE required in some programs. Independent study. Honors program. Cooperative work/study, pass/fail, internships, credit by exam. Preprofessional programs in dentistry, law, medicine, pharmacy, theology. 3-1 medical technology and engineering programs. Exchange program with St. Gregory's. Study abroad. Elementary and secondary education certification. Computer center. Learning center with talk-back closed circuit TV. 170,000-volume library with microform resources.
Financial ACT FAS. University scholarships, grants, loans, religious vocation scholarships, payment plans; PELL, SEOG, NSS, NDSL, GSL, NSL, CWS. Preferred application deadlines April 15 (scholarships), April 1 (loans).
Admissions High school graduation with 16 units required. GED accepted. ACT required. $25 application fee. Rolling admissions; suggest applying by February 1. $25 room deposit due on acceptance of admissions offer. *Concurrent Enrollment* Program. Transfers accepted. Credit possible for CEEB AP and CLEP exams; university has own advanced placement program. Conditional admission program.
Student Life Student government. Newspaper, yearbook. Music and drama groups. Debate. Special Services Program. Academic, honorary, political, professional, religious, and special interest groups. 4 fraternities and 4 sororities without houses. 7% of men and 8% of women join. Students under 21 live at home or on campus. Single-sex dorms. Limited married-student housing. 70% of students live on campus. Liquor, drugs, gambling, hazing, firearms, and dancing prohibited. Class, weekly chapel, and assembly attendance required. 2 semesters of phys ed required. 5 intercollegiate sports for men, 3 for women; intramurals. NAIA, SAC. Student body composition: 1% Asian, 2.3% Black, 1% Hispanic, 3.1% Native American, 90.6% White, 2% Other. 29% from out of state.

[1] OKLAHOMA CHRISTIAN COLLEGE

PO Box 141, Memorial at Eastern Ave., Oklahoma City 73111, (405) 478-1661
Dean of Admissions & Registrar: Bob D. Smith

- **Undergraduates: 716m, 828w; 1,721 total (including part-time)**
- **Tuition (1982/83): $2,250**
- **Room & Board: $1,673; Fees: $30**
- **Degrees offered: BA, BS, BMus Ed, BSEd**
- **Student-faculty ratio: 27 to 1**

A private college controlled by the Church of Christ, established in 1950. 200-acre suburban campus. Served by air, rail, and bus.
Academic Character NCACS and professional accreditation. Trimester system, 3-week and 2 5-week summer terms. 55 majors offered by the divisions of Bible, Business, Communication & Fine Arts, Education & Psychology, Language & Literature, Physical Education, Science, and Social Science. Minor required. Distributives and 8 semesters of Bible required. Independent study. Internships. Preprofessional programs in engineering, law, medical fields. Study abroad. Primary, secondary, and special education certification. ROTC, AFROTC nearby. 75,794-volume library.
Financial ACT FAS. College scholarships, grants, loans; PELL, SEOG, NDSL, FISL, CWS. Scholarship application deadline June 1.
Admissions High school graduation with 15 units required. GED accepted. ACT required. $10 application fee. Rolling Admissions; suggest applying by January. $35 room deposit requried on acceptance of admissions offer. *Early Admission* and *Concurrent Enrollment* programs. Transfers accepted. Credit possible for CEEB AP and CLEP exams; college has own advanced placement program.
Student Life Student government. Newspaper, yearbook, radio station. Music and drama groups. Debate. Academic, political, religious, and special interest groups. Single students live at home or on campus. Single-sex dorms. Married-student housing. 84% of students live on campus. Liquor and gambling prohibited. Dress code. Daily chapel attendance required. 1 semester of phys ed required. 7 intercollegiate sports; intramurals. NAIA. Student body composition: 0.6% Asian, 5.9% Black, 0.3% Hispanic, 1.2% Native American, 91.3% White, 0.8% Other. 54% from out of state.

[1] OKLAHOMA CITY UNIVERSITY

Oklahoma City 73106, (405) 521-5032
Director of Admissions: Kenneth Doake

- **Enrollment: 917m, 677w; 3,044 total (including part-time)**
- **Tuition (1982/83): $2,672**
- **Room & Board: $1,780-$2,010; Fees: $25**
- **Degrees offered: BA, BS, BMus, BSBus, BPerforming Arts**
- **Mean ACT 24; mean SAT 1,030**
- **Student-faculty ratio: 15 to 1**

A private university affiliated with the United Methodist Church, established in 1904. 64-acre urban campus. Served by air, rail, and bus.
Academic Character NCACS and professional accreditation. Semester system, 4- and 6-week summer terms. 42 majors offered by the College of Arts & Sciences, the School of Management & Business Sciences, the School of Music & Performing Arts, the School of Religion & Church Vocations, and the School of Law. Distributives and 6 hours of religion required; attendance at 1 Mid-Year Institute required. Graduate degrees granted. Honors program. Limited pass/fail, internships. Several preprofessional programs. 3-3 programs in dentistry, medicine, medical technology. Study abroad. UN and Washington Semesters. Primary and secondary education certification. AFROTC, NROTC, ROTC at U Oklahoma, ROTC at Central State. Audio-visual center. History center. Language lab. 202,000-volume library.
Financial CEEB CSS. University scholarships, grants, loans; PELL, SEOG, NDSL, CWS. Scholarship application deadline March 1.
Admissions High school graduation with 14 units recommended. Interview recommended. ACT or SAT required. $20 application fee. Rolling admissions; suggest applying before March 15. *Early Admission* Program. Admission deferral possible. Transfers accepted. Credit possible for CEEB AP, ACH, and CLEP exams.
Student Life Student government. Newspaper. Athletic, academic, honorary, political, religious, and special interest groups. 4 fraternities with houses, 4 sororities with apartments. 20% of men and 35% of women join. Single students live at home or on campus. Dorms for men and women. Married-student housing. 40% of undergraduates live on campus. Liquor prohibited. Class attendance expected. 2 phys ed courses required. 5 intercollegiate sports for men; intramurals for men. NCAA. Student body composition: 8.1% Black, 1.7% Hispanic, 2.1% Native American, 80.3% White. 30% from out of state.

[P] OKLAHOMA INSTITUTE OF OSTEOPATHIC MEDICINE AND SURGERY

PO Box 2280, 1111 West 17th Street, Tulsa 74101

[1] OKLAHOMA PANHANDLE STATE UNIVERSITY OF AGRICULTURE AND APPLIED SCIENCES

Goodwell 73939, (405) 349-2611
Director of Admissions: Jack V. Begley

- **Undergraduates: 582m, 521w; 1,392 total (including graduates)**
- **Tuition (1982/83): $603 (in-state), $1,586 (out-of-state)**
- **Room & Board: $835; Fees: $114**
- **Degrees offered: BA, BS, BMus Ed**
- **Mean ACT 17**
- **Student-faculty ratio: 24 to 1**

A public university established in 1909. 120-acre rural campus, 275 miles from Oklahoma City. Train and bus stations 10 miles away in Guymon.
Academic Character NCACS and professional accreditation. Semester system, 2 5-week summer terms. 31 majors offered in the areas of agriculture, business administration, education, library science, liberal arts, medical technology, music, science, secretarial science, social sciences, and vocational home economics. Minor required. Minors offered in most major fields and in 12 other areas. Distributive requirements. Independent study. Preprofessional programs in dentistry, engineering, forestry, law, medical fields, nursing, pharmacy, veterinary medicine. Elementary and secondary education certification. ROTC. Agricultural Research Station. Computer center. Language lab. 82,600-volume library with microform resources.
Financial ACT FAS. University scholarships, grants; PELL, SEOG, NDSL, GSL, CWS, college work program. Scholarship application deadline April 1.
Admissions High school graduation required. GED accepted. ACT required; SAT accepted. Rolling admissions; suggest applying by July 1. $20 room deposit due on acceptance of admissions offer. *Early Admission* and *Concurrent Enrollment* programs. Admission deferral possible. Transfers accepted. Credit possible for ACT PEP and CEEB CLEP exams.
Student Life Student government. Newspaper, yearbook, radio station. Music and drama groups. Academic, religious, and special interest groups. Single-sex dorms. Co-op dorms. Married-student housing. 45% of students live on campus. Liquor prohibited. Dress code for cafeteria and library. 2 hours of phys ed required. 3 intercollegiate sports for men, 3 for women; intramurals. Student body composition: 4% Black, 6% Hispanic, 1% Native American, 87% White, 2% Other. 7% from out of state.

[1] OKLAHOMA STATE UNIVERSITY

Stillwater 74078, (405) 624-6384
Director of Admissions: Raymond Girod

- **Undergraduates: 11,380m, 8,024w; 22,490 total (including graduates)**
- **Tuition (1982/83): $539 (in-state), $1,199 (out-of-state)**
- **Room & Board: $1,588-$1,852; Fees: $105**
- **Degrees offered: BA, BS, BMus, BMus Ed, BFA, BAEd, BUniv Studies**
- **Mean ACT 20**
- **Student-faculty ratio: 20 to 1**

A public university established in 1890. 150-acre campus in a small city 70 miles from Oklahoma City. Airport nearby.

Academic Character NCACS and professional accreditation. Semester system, 8-week summer term. 12 majors offered by the College of Agriculture, 47 by the College of Arts & Sciences, 10 by the College of Business Administration, 6 by the College of Education, 18 by the College of Engineering, and 6 by the College of Home Economics. Distributive requirements. Graduate degrees granted. Honors program. Pass/fail. Several preprofessional programs. Early childhood, elementary, secondary, and special education certification. ROTC, AFROTC. Performing arts center. 1,250,000-volume library with microform resources.
Financial University scholarships, grants, loans; PELL, SEOG, NDSL, GSL, CWS. Scholarship application deadline March 1.
Admissions High school graduation required. ACT required; SAT accepted from out-of-state students. $10 application fee for out-of-state applicants. Rolling admissions; suggest applying by March 1. *Concurrent Enrollment* Program. Transfers accepted. Credit possible for CEEB AP exams; university has own advanced placement program. Probationary admission possible.
Student Life Student government. Newspaper, literary magazine, yearbook. Music and drama groups. Debate. Academic, ethnic, honorary, religious, and special interest groups. 25 fraternities, 22 with houses; 14 sororities, 10 with houses. 20% of men and 25% of women join. Freshmen live on campus. Single-sex dorms. Co-op dorms. Married-student housing. 32% of students live on campus. Liquor prohibited. 12 intercollegiate sports; many intramurals. Big Eight Conference. Student body composition: 7% Asian, 3% Black, 1% Hispanic, 2% Native American, 87% White. 14% from out of state.

[1] ORAL ROBERTS UNIVERSITY
7777 South Lewis Avenue, Tulsa 74171, (918) 495-6518
Director of Admissions: Tim Cameron

- **Undergraduates: 1,468m, 1,578w; 4,184 total (including graduates)**
- **Tuition (1982/83): $3,550**
- **Room & Board: $2,198; Fees: $60**
- **Degrees offered: BA, BS, BMus, BMus Ed**
- **Mean SAT 460v, 500m**
- **Student-faculty ratio: 11 to 1**

A private university established in 1963. 500-acre suburban campus. Served by air and bus.
Academic Character NCACS and professional accreditation. Semester system, 3 summer terms. 44 majors offered in the areas of the arts, business administration, education, engineering, humanities, music, nursing, physical education, science, and theology. Self-designed majors. Minor required. Distributives and religion courses required; senior paper required in most disciplines. Graduate degrees granted. Independent study. Pass/fail, internships. Preprofessional programs in business, dentistry, law, medicine. 3-2 business program. Study in France and Germany. Elementary, secondary, and special education certification. Closed circuit TV. Programmed learning facilities. 1,000,000-volume library with microform resources.
Financial CEEB CSS. University scholarships, grants, loans, payment plans; PELL, SEOG, GSL, NDSL, FISL, CWS, university work program.
Admissions High school graduation with 16 units required. Interview recommended. Minister's recommendation required. ACT or SAT required. $15 application fee. Rolling admissions; suggest applying by end of 11th year. *Early Decision, Early Admission, Concurrent Enrollment* programs. Credit possible for CEEB AP and CLEP exams; university has own advanced placement program.
Student Life Student government. Academic, religious, and special interest groups. Students live at home or on campus. Single-sex dorms. Married-student housing. 82% of students live on campus. Liquor prohibited. Dress code. Attendance in class, at church, and at twice-weekly chapel required. Physical Activity and Aerobics program required. 6 intercollegiate sports for men, 4 for women; many intramurals. AIAW, NCAA, MCC. Student body composition: 1.5% Asian, 4.5% Black, 1.5% Hispanic, 0.5% Native American, 88% White, 4% Other. 90% from out of state.

[J1] OSCAR ROSE JUNIOR COLLEGE
6420 Southeast 15th Street, Midwest City 73110

[1] PHILLIPS UNIVERSITY
Enid 73701, (405) 237-4433
Director of Admissions: Rick Ziegler

- **Enrollment: 392m, 311w; 1,177 total (including part-time)**
- **Tuition (1982/83): $3,000**
- **Room & Board: $1,950; Fees: $144**
- **Degrees offered: BA, BS, BFA, BMus, BMus Ed, BMus Therapy, AA**
- **Mean ACT 22.5**
- **Student-faculty ratio: 16 to 1**

A private university affiliated with the Disciples of Christ, established in 1906. 140-acre campus in a small city 93 miles northwest of Oklahoma City. Served by air and bus.
Academic Character NCACS and professional accreditation. Semester system, 3 4-week summer terms. 52 majors offered by the centers of Arts & Humanities, Business & Communication, Human Development, and Systems (math & science). Self-designed majors. Distributives and 6 hours of religion, and senior project required. Graduate degrees granted. Independent study. Limited pass/fail, credit by exam. Preprofessional programs in dentistry, law, medical technology, medicine, osteopathy. 2-year pre-nursing program. 3-2 engineering program with Washington U. Phillips University in Sweden. Study in Europe. Elementary and secondary education certification. Language labs. 166,000-volume library with microform resources.
Financial CEEB CSS. University scholarships, grants, loans, Church-related grants, state grants & loans; PELL, SEOG, NDSL, GSL, CWS. Scholarship application deadline April 1.
Admissions High school graduation with college prep curriculum required. GED accepted. ACT or SAT required. $10 application fee. Rolling admissions; suggest applying in December. $50 deposit due on acceptance of admissions offer. *Early Decision, Early Admission, Concurrent Enrollment* programs. Admission deferral possible. Transfers accepted. Credit possible for CEEB AP and CLEP exams; college has own advanced placement program.
Student Life Student government. Newspaper, yearbook. Music and drama groups. Debate. Academic, honorary, religious, and social service groups. 6 fraternities and sororities. Single students live at home or on campus. Dorms for men and women. Married-student housing. 50% of students live on campus. Phys ed required for freshmen. 3 intercollegiate sports for men, 2 for women; intramurals. AIAW, NAIA, OIC. Student body composition: 0.6% Asian, 3.8% Black, 0.7% Hispanic, 1% Native American, 86.9% White. 50% from out of state.

[J1] ROGERS STATE COLLEGE
Claremore 74017, (918) 341-7510
Registrar: Shirley McClurg

- **Enrollment: 760m, 495w; 2,000 total (including part-time)**
- **Tuition (1982/83): $13.35 per semester hour (in-state), $33.75 (out-of-state)**
- **Room & Board: $920-$1,090**
- **Degrees offered: AA, AS, AAS, AT**
- **Mean ACT 17.1**
- **Student-faculty ratio: 20 to 1**

A public college, formerly Claremore College, established in 1909. Small-town campus, 25 miles from Tulsa.
Academic Character NCACS accreditation. Semester system, 8-week summer term. 2-year transfer programs offered in broadcasting, business, computer science, criminal justice, education, fine arts, interior design, journalism, liberal arts, Native American studies, physical education, science, and social science. Occupational-technical programs. Distributive requirements. Cooperative work/study. Preprofessional programs in dentistry, engineering, law, medicine, nursing, pharmacy. ROTC. Radio station and music hall. Learning Resource Center.
Financial College scholarships, state grants and loans; PELL, SEOG, BIA, NDSL, CWS.
Admissions High school graduation required. GED accepted. Any student over 19 admitted. ACT required. Rolling admissions. Transfers accepted. Credit possible for CEEB CLEP exams.
Student Life Student Activites Board. Afro-American Club. Baptist Student Union. Rodeo Club. Academic, honorary, and special interest groups. 4 hours of phys ed required. 5 intercollegiate sports; intramurals.

[J1] SAINT GREGORY'S COLLEGE
Shawnee 74801, (405) 273-9870
Director of Admissions: Gary Salwierak

- **Enrollment: 171m, 129w; 318 total (including part-time)**
- **Tuition (1982/83): $1,975**
- **Room & Board: $1,845**
- **Degrees offered: AA, AS**
- **Student-faculty ratio: 8 to 1**

A private college operated by Saint Gregory's Benedictine Abbey, established in 1916. Suburban campus, 35 miles east of Oklahoma City.
Academic Character NCACS accreditation. Semester system. 2-year programs offered in liberal arts, business, natural sciences, and social sciences. Distributives, 3 hours of religion, and sophomore comprehensive exam required. Preprofessional programs in engineering, medical technology, nursing. Museum. 40,000-volume library with microform resources.
Financial ACT FAS. College scholarships, grants, loans, state grants; PELL, SEOG, NDSL, GSL, CWS.
Admissions High school graduation required. ACT required. $10 application fee. Rolling admissions. $50 tuition and $50 room deposits due on acceptance of admissions offer. *Early Decision* and *Early Admission* programs. Admission deferral possible. Transfers accepted. Credit possible for CEEB AP and CLEP exams.
Student Life Student government. Various clubs, social and academic groups. Students not living with family must live on campus. Intercollegiate and intramural sports. Student body composition: 16% minority.

[J1] SEMINOLE JUNIOR COLLEGE
Seminole 74868

[J1] SOUTH OKLAHOMA CITY JUNIOR COLLEGE
Oklahoma City 73159

[1] SOUTHEASTERN OKLAHOMA STATE UNIVERSITY
Durant 74701, (405) 924-0121, ext. 381
Director of Admissions: Lisa Kutait

- **Undergraduates: 1,504m, 1,129w; 4,332 total (including graduates)**
- **Tuition (1982/83): $500 (in-state), $1,242 (out-of-state)**
- **Room & Board: $1,604-$2,160; Fees: $30**
- **Degrees offered: BA, BS, BAEd, BSEd**
- **Mean ACT 17**
- **Student-faculty ratio: 22 to 1**

A public university established in 1909. 120-acre rural campus, 90 miles from Dallas. Served by air and bus.

Key to ratings **[1, 2, J1, J2, G, P, R, S]** *and list of abbreviations start on page 120*

Academic Character NCACS and professional accreditation. Semester system, 8-week summer term. 60 majors offered in the areas of art, aviation, business, conservation, criminal justice, education, home economics, humanities, medical technology, music, physical education, science, social science, and technology. Minor required. Distributives and GRE required. Graduate degrees granted. Independent study. Cooperative work/study. Preprofessional programs in engineering, health, law, veterinary medicine. Biomedical Sciences Program for minority students. Choctaw Bilingual Education Program. Elementary, secondary, and special education certification. Computer center. Language lab. 134,560-volume library.
Financial ACT FAS. University scholarships, grants, loans, state grants & loans, payment plan; PELL, SEOG, BIA, FISL, GSL, NDSL, CWS, university employment. Application deadline May 1.
Admissions High school graduation required. GED accepted. ACT required. Rolling admissions; suggest applying by June 1. $50 room deposit required on acceptance of admissions offer. *Early Decision, Early Admission, Concurrent Enrollment* programs. Admission deferral possible. Transfers accepted. Credit possible for CEEB CLEP and ACT exams, and for life experience. Upward Bound Program for disadvantaged students.
Student Life Student government. Newspaper, yearbook, radio station. Music and drama groups. Afro-American Student Union. Los Pan Americanos Club. Native American Council. Academic, honorary, political, religious, and special interest groups. 4 fraternities and 2 sororities without houses. 8% of men and 4% of women join. Coed and single-sex dorms. Married-student housing. 25% of students live on campus. Liquor prohibited. 80% class attendance required. 3 semesters of phys ed required. 7 intercollegiate sports for men, 5 for women; intramurals. NAIA. Student body composition: 3% Asian, 4% Black, 1% Hispanic, 8% Native American, 74% White, 10% Other. 19% from out of state.

[J1] SOUTHWESTERN COLLEGE OF CHRISTIAN MINISTRIES
Bethany 73008

[1] SOUTHWESTERN OKLAHOMA STATE UNIVERSITY
Weatherford 73096, (405) 772-6611
Director of Admissions: Bob Klaassen

- **Undergraduates: 1,950m, 2,248w**
- **Tuition (1982/83): $517 (in-state), $1,309 (out-of-state)**
- **Room & Board: $1,080-$1,130**
- **Degrees offered: BA, BS, BAEd, BAMus, BMus Ed, BSEd, BSN, BSPharm**
- **Student-faculty ratio: 19 to 1**

A public university established in 1901. 73-acre small-town campus, 65 miles from Oklahoma City. Served by bus; airport in Oklahoma City.
Academic Character NCACS and professional accreditation. Semester system, 8-week summer term. 43 majors offered by the schools of Arts & Sciences, Business, Education, and Health Sciences. Minors offered in 11 fields. Distributive requirements. Graduate degrees granted. Independent study. Preprofessional programs in dentistry, law, medicine, osteopathy, pharmacy, veterinary medicine. 2-2 engineering program. 3-1 medical technology program. Elementary, secondary, and special education certification. ROTC. Language lab. 205,620-volume library with microform resources.
Financial CEEB CSS and ACT FAS. University scholarships, grants, loans; PELL, SEOG, BIA, NSS, NDSL, CWS. Application deadlines March 1 (scholarships), June 1 (loans).
Admissions High school graduation with 18 units required. ACT required. Rolling admissions; suggest applying in March. *Early Admission* Program. Admission deferral possible. Transfers accepted. Credit possible for CEEB CLEP exams.
Student Life Student government. Newspaper, yearbook. Ebony United. Indian Heritage Club. Sombreros Y Mantillas. Academic, honorary, professional, religious, service, and special interest groups. Fraternities and sororities, some with houses. 2% of students join. Coed and single-sex dorms. Married-student housing. 30% of students live on campus. Liquor prohibited. 4 hours of phys ed required. 8 intercollegiate sports for men, 5 for women; intramurals. AIAW, OIC. Student body composition: 2% Asian, 3% Black, 2% Hispanic, 3% Native American, 88% White, 2% Other. 7% from out of state.

[1] TULSA, UNIVERSITY OF
Tulsa 74104, (918) 592-6000
Dean of Records & Admissions: Charles Malone

- **Undergraduates: 2,276m, 1,857w; 6,382 total (including graduates)**
- **Tuition (1982/83): $3,200**
- **Room & Board: $1,970; Fees: $70**
- **Degrees offered: BA, BS, BFA, BMus, BMus Ed, BSBA, BSN**
- **Mean ACT 22; mean SAT 471v, 520m**
- **Student-faculty ratio: 17 to 1**

A private university founded in 1894. 115-acre urban campus, 2 miles from downtown Tulsa. Served by air and bus.
Academic Character NCACS and professional accreditation. 4-4-1 system, 12-week summer flexterm. 28 majors offered by the College of Arts & Sciences, 5 by the College of Business Administration, 11 by the College of Education, 11 by the College of Engineering, and 1 by the College of Nursing. Self-designed majors. Distributive requirements. Graduate degrees granted. Independent study. Honors program. Pass/fail, internships. Preprofessional programs in dentistry, law, medicine, optometry, osteopathy, pharmacy, physical therapy, social service, veterinary medicine. Study abroad. Elementary, secondary, and special education certification. Computer center. Language labs. 1,000,000-volume library with microform resources.
Financial ACT FAS. University scholarships, grants, loans, athletic and performance scholarships, state grants and loans; PELL, SEOG, NDSL, NSL, FISL, GSL, CWS. Priority application deadline March 1.
Admissions High school graduation with 15 units required. Interview encouraged. Audition required for music majors. SAT or ACT required. $10 application fee. Rolling admissions. $25 tuition deposit and $100 room deposit (for boarders) due on acceptance of admissions offer. *Early Admission* Program. Admission deferral possible. Transfers accepted. Credit possible for CEEB AP, CLEP, and university exams.
Student Life Student government. Newspaper, literary magazine, yearbook, radio and TV stations. Music and drama groups. Art competition. Academic, ethnic, honorary, professional, religious, and special interest groups. 6 fraternities and 8 sororities, all with houses. 15% of men and 20% of women join. Coed and single-sex dorms. Athletic and honors houses. 36% of students live on campus. Firearms and hazing prohibited. 7 intercollegiate sports for men, 7 for women; intramurals. AIAW, MVC. Student body composition: 0.4% Asian, 3% Black, 1% Hispanic, 1.8% Native American, 85% White, 8.8% Other. 41% from out of state.

[J1] TULSA JUNIOR COLLEGE
Tulsa 74102

[J1] WESTERN OKLAHOMA STATE COLLEGE
2801 North Main Street, Altus 73521

OREGON *(OR)*

[J1] BASSIST COLLEGE
2000 Southwest 5th Street, Portland 97201

[J1] BLUE MOUNTAIN COMMUNITY COLLEGE
Pendleton 97801

[J1] CENTRAL OREGON COMMUNITY COLLEGE
Collegeway 97701,(503) 382-6112

- **Undergraduates: 558m, 535w; 2,025 total (including part-time)**
- **Tuition & Fees (1982/83): $643**
- **Degrees offered: AA,AS**

A public junior college established in 1949. Small-city campus in central Oregon.
Academic Character NASC accreditation. Quarter system. 2-year programs offered in liberal arts, preprofessional, and vocational areas, including nurses' training, electronics, automotive, secretarial, office machine repair, industrial mechanics, business,and forestry.
Admissions Advanced placement program.
Student Life Dormitory and dining hall available.

[J1] CHEMEKETA COMMUNITY COLLEGE
Salem 97309

[J1] CLACKAMAS COMMUNITY COLLEGE
Oregon City 97045

[J1] CLATSOP COMMUNITY COLLEGE
Astoria 97103

[1] COLUMBIA CHRISTIAN COLLEGE
200 Northeast 91st Avenue, Portland 97220, (503) 255-7060
Director of Admissions: Paul King

- **Enrollment: 350 men & women**
- **Tuition (1982/83): $2,928**
- **Room & Board: $1,989; Fees: $150**
- **Degrees offered: BA, AA**
- **Student-faculty ratio: 12 to 1**

A private college established in 1956. 8-acre urban campus in downtown Portland. Served by air, rail, and bus.
Academic Character NASC accreditation. Quarter system. Majors offered in Bible, business, counseling education, education, interdisciplinary studies, music, and psychology. Distributives and 24 credits of Biblical Life Core required. Cooperative secondary education program with Warner. Elementary and music education certification. School of Preacher Training. 56,000-volume library with microform resources.
Financial ACT FAS. College scholarships, loans, ACT/SAT scholarships, state grants; PELL, SEOG, NDSL, GSL, CWS, GSP. Application deadline September 1.
Admissions High school graduation required. SAT or ACT required. $20 application fee. Rolling admissions. $50 room deposit required before registration. *Early Admission* Program. Transfers accepted. Advanced

placement possible.
Student Life Student government. Music groups. Drama Club. Missions Club. Spiritual Emphasis Week. Service and social groups. Single students live on campus. Liquor, drugs, tobacco prohibited. Dress code. Cars must be registered with college. Attendance in class, Bible classes and at church expected. 4 intercollegiate sports for men, 3 for women; intramurals. NAIA, NCCAA.

[1] CONCORDIA COLLEGE
2811 Northeast Holman, Portland 97211, (503) 288-9371
Dean of Admissions: William Cullen

- **Undergraduates: 123m, 150w**
- **Tuition (1982/83): $3,360**
- **Room & Board: $2,205; Fees: $280**
- **Degrees offered: BA, AA**
- **Mean ACT 20.5**
- **Student-faculty ratio: 8 to 1**

A private college controlled by the Lutheran Church-Missouri Synod, established in 1905, became coed in 1954. 10-acre suburban campus. Served by air, rail, and bus.
Academic Character NASC accreditation. Trimester system, 7-week summer term. Majors offered in business, Christian education, elementary education, liberal arts, parish music, pre-theology, and social work. Minors offered in some major fields and in 8 others. Distributives and 15 hours of religion required. Cooperative business program with City College of Seattle. 2-2 nursing program with U Portland. Cooperative secondary education program with Warner. Elementary education certification. AFROTC at U Portland. 45,000-volume library.
Financial CEEB CSS. College scholarships, loans, professional church work aid, student employment. Application deadline May 1.
Admissions High school graduation with 17 units recommended. SAT, ACT, or WPCT required. $25 application fee. Rolling admissions. $40 room deposit due on acceptance of admissions offer. Transfers accepted. Credit possible for CEEB CLEP exams.
Student Life Student government. Music and drama groups. Cultural, service, and social activities. Full-time students required to live on campus. Freshmen not encouraged to use cars; cars must be registered with college. Dress code. Chapel attendance expected. 4 intercollegiate sports for men, 4 for women; intramural and club sports. NAIA.

[1] EASTERN OREGON STATE COLLEGE
La Grande 97850, (503) 963-2171
Director of Admissions: Terral Schut

- **Undergraduates: 776m, 815w; 1,793 total (including graduates)**
- **Tuition (1982/83): $1,365**
- **Room & Board: $2,200**
- **Degrees offered: BA, BS, AA**
- **Mean SAT 836**
- **Student-faculty ratio: 18 to 1**

A private college established in 1929. 121-acre small-town campus, 260 miles from Portland. Served by air and bus.
Academic Character NASC and professional accreditation. Trimester system, 2 4-week summer terms. Majors offered in agriculture/business, anthropology/sociology, art, biology, business/economics, chemistry, community service, education, English, general studies, history, mathematics, music, physics, and psychology. Distributive requirements. Graduate degrees granted. Independent study. Cooperative work/study, pass/fail, internships, credit by exam. Preprofessional programs in dentistry, dental hygiene, medicine, nursing, pharmacy, veterinary medicine. 3-1 medical technology program. 3-2 engineering program with Oregon State. 2-year preprofessional programs in agriculture, computer science, home economics; 1-year programs in fisheries & wildlife, forestry, geology, oceanography. Cross-registration with area schools. Elementary and secondary education certification. ROTC. Computer center. Indian Education Institute. Language lab. Wallowa Mountain field station. 89,000-volume library.
Financial CEEB CSS. College scholarships, grants, loans, payment plan; PELL, SEOG, NDSL, FISL, GSL, CWS. Recommended application deadline March 1.
Admissions High school graduation required. GED accepted. SAT or ACT required. $20 application fee. Rolling admissions; suggest applying after October 15. $50 room deposit due on acceptance of admissions offer. Admission deferral possible. Transfers accepted. Credit possible for CEEB AP and CLEP exams; college has own advanced placement program. Provisional admission possible.
Student Life Student government. Newspaper, literary magazine, yearbook, radio station. Music and drama groups. Debate. Native American Student Club. Academic, athletic, professional, religious, service, and special interest groups. Married-student housing. 25% of students live on campus. 6 intercollegiate sports for men, 4 for women, 2 coed; several intramurals. NAIA, Evergreen Conference. Student body composition: 1.4% Asian, 1.6% Black, 1.9% Hispanic, 1.5% Native American, 86.3% White. 20% from out of state.

[1] GEORGE FOX COLLEGE
414 North Meridian, Newberg 97132, (503) 538-8383
Director of Admissions: James Settle

- **Undergraduates: 283m, 412w**
- **Tuition (1982/83): $4,860**
- **Room & Board: $2,200; Fees: $110**
- **Degrees offered: BA, BS**
- **Mean SAT 435v, 456m**
- **Student-faculty ratio: 16 to 1**

A private college controlled by the Northwest Yearly Meeting of Friends (Quakers), established in 1891. 60-acre small-town campus, 23 miles from Portland. Served by air, rail, and bus.
Academic Character NASC accreditation. Trimester system, 1-week September mini-term. 35 majors offered by the divisions of Education, Fine & Applied Arts, Communication & Literature, Natural Science, Religion, and Social Science. Self-designed majors. Minors offered. Distributives and 6-9 hours of religion required. Independent study. Intensified Studies Program. Honors program. Limited pass/fail, credit by exam, internships. Preprofessional programs in dentistry, law, medical technology, medicine, nursing, physical therapy, religion, veterinary science. Cross-registration with 12 colleges of Christian Consortium and 16 of Oregon Independent Colleges Association. Washington Semester. Study abroad. Elementary and secondary education certification. Language lab. Television center. Retreat center. 75,000-volume library.
Financial CEEB CSS and ACT FAS. College scholarships, grants, loans, payment plans; PELL, SEOG, NDSL, FISL, GSL, CWS. Preferred scholarship application deadline March 1.
Admissions High school graduation with 16 units required. GED accepted. Interview recommended. SAT, ACT, or WPCT required. $15 application fee. Rolling admissions. $75 deposit due on acceptance of admissions offer. *Concurrent Enrollment* Program. Admission deferral possible.Transfers accepted. Credit possible for CEEB AP and CLEP exams. Provisional admissions program.
Student Life Student government. Newspaper, yearbook, radio station. Music, theatre, and film groups. Minority Student Union. Academic, honorary, professional, religious, and special interest groups. Single students under 23 must live on campus. Single-sex dorms. Married-student housing. 85% of students live on campus. Liquor, drugs, gambling, tobacco, social dancing prohibited. Marriage during school year discouraged. Class attendance expected. Chapel attendance 3 times per week mandatory. 6 hours of phys ed required. 5 intercollegiate sports for men, 6 for women; several intramurals. AIAW, NAIA, IC. Student body composition: 0.3% Asian, 0.5% Black, 0.9% Hispanic, 0.9% Native American, 97.4% White. 32% from out of state.

[1] JUDSON BAPTIST COLLEGE
400 East Scenic Drive, The Dalles 97058, (503) 298-4455
Director of Admissions: Andrea Cook

- **Enrollment: 132m, 132w; 300 total (including part-time)**
- **Tuition (1982/83): $3,600**
- **Room & Board: $2,400**
- **Degrees offered: BA, BS, AA, AS**
- **Student-faculty ratio: 9 to 1**

A private college controlled by the Baptist Church, established in 1956. 65-acre small-town campus, 90 minutes from Portland. Served by bus.
Academic Character NACS accreditation. Quarter system. 10 majors offered by the divisions of Biblical Studies, Business Administration, Communications, Education, Fine Arts, Interdisciplinary Studies, Physical Education, Social & Behavioral Sciences, and Teacher Education. Minor offered in visual arts. Distributives and 15 credits of Bible required. Preprofessional programs in engineering, forestry, medicine, nursing, physical therapy. Cooperative program in physical education with Eastern Oregon. Elementary and secondary education certification.
Financial CEEB CSS. College scholarships, grants, loans, state grants; PELL, SEOG, NDSL, GSL, CWS, college work program. Priority application deadline March 1.
Admissions High school graduation required. SAT, ACT, or WPCT required. $20 application fee. Rolling admissions. $40 deposit required on acceptance of admissions offer. Transfers accepted.
Student Life Student government. Newspaper, yearbook. Music and drama groups. Honor society. Students under 21 live at home or on campus. Church attendance strongly encouraged. 4 intercollegiate sports; intramurals. NAIA.

[J1] LANE COMMUNITY COLLEGE
Eugene 97405

[1] LEWIS AND CLARK COLLEGE
0615 SW Palatine Hill Road, Portland 97219, (503) 244-6161
Director of Admissions: Robert H. Loeb, III

- **Enrollment: 1,501m, 1,687w**
- **Tuition (1982/83): $5,978**
- **Room & Board: $2,603; Fees: $505**
- **Degrees offered: BA, BS, BMus**
- **Mean SAT 510v, 530m**
- **Student-faculty ratio: 14 to 1**

A private college affiliated with the United Presbyterian Church, established in 1867. 130-acre suburban campus, 6 miles from downtown Portland. Served by air, rail, and bus.
Academic Character NASC and professional accreditation. Trimester system, 2 4½-week summer terms. 26 majors offered in the areas of liberal arts & sciences, business, education, fine arts, physical education, and religion. Self-designed majors. Distributive requirements. Graduate degrees granted. Independent study. Honors program. Pass/fail, internships. Preprofessional programs in dentistry, law, medicine. 3-2 engineering program with Columbia and Washington U. Washington term. Theatre term in New York City. Study abroad. Elementary and secondary education certification. Computer center. Language labs. Concert hall and theatre. 200,000-volume library with microform resources.
Financial CEEB CSS. College scholarships, grants, loans, family plan; PELL, SEOG, NDSL, GSL, CWS. Application deadline February 15.

Admissions High school graduation with 15 units recommended. Interview encouraged. SAT or ACT required. $25 application fee. Application deadline March 1. $100 deposit ($50 for commuters) due on acceptance of admissions offer. *Early Decision* and *Early Admission* programs. Admission deferral possible. Transfers accepted. Credit possible for CEEB AP exams.
Student Life Student government. Newspaper, literary magazine, radio station. Music and drama groups. Debate. Model UN. Black Student Union. Athletic, academic, ethnic, professional, service, and special interest groups. 3 fraternities without houses. Freshmen under 21 live at home or on campus. Coed and single-sex dorms. Co-op dorms. 65% of students live on campus. 1 term of phys ed required. 9 intercollegiate sports for men, 8 for women; intramurals. AIAW, PNIAC. Student body composition: 1% Black, 2% Hispanic, 1% Native American, 83% White, 13% Other. 65% from out of state.

[P] LEWIS AND CLARK LAW SCHOOL
10015 SW Terwilliger Boulevard, Portland 97219
Formerly Northwestern School of Law of Lewis and Clark College.

[1] LINFIELD COLLEGE
McMinnville 97128, (503) 472-4121
Dean of Admissions: Thomas Meicho

- **Undergraduates: 617m, 634w**
- **Tuition (1982/83): $4,940**
- **Room & Board: $2,170; Fees: $90**
- **Degrees offered: AB, BS**
- **Mean SAT 500v, 525m**
- **Student-faculty ratio: 14 to 1**

A private college affiliated with the Baptist Church, established in 1849. 90-acre small-town campus, 38 miles southwest of Portland. Served by air and bus.
Academic Character NASC and professional accreditation. 4-1-4 system, 2 5-week summer terms. 48 majors offered in the areas of art, business, education, home economics, humanities, music, physical education, religion, science, and social science. Self-designed and special majors. Minors offered. Distributives and GRE required. Independent study. Honors program. Cooperative work/study, pass/fail, internships. Preprofessional programs in dentistry, law, medicine, veterinary medicine. 3-1 medical technology program. 3-2 engineering programs with USC, Oregon State, Washington State. Study abroad. Elementary and secondary education certification. Linfield Research Institute. Computer center. Language lab. Environmental field station. 120,000-volume library with microform resources.
Financial CEEB CSS. College scholarships, grants, loans, family plan, payment plans; PELL, SEOG, NDSL, GSL, CWS. Preferred FAF deadline March 15.
Admissions High school graduation with 17 units recommended. Interview recommended. SAT or ACT required; WPCT accepted. $15 application fee. Rolling admissions; suggest applying by March 1. $100 deposit due on acceptance of admissions offer. *Early Decision, Early Admission, Concurrent Enrollment* programs. Admission deferral possible. Transfers accepted. Credit possible for CEEB AP and CLEP exams.
Student Life Student government. Newspaper, yearbook, radio station. Music and drama groups. Debate. Black Student Union. Academic, honorary, service, religious, and special interest groups. 3 fraternities and 3 sororities with rooms. 30% of men and 40% of women join. Seniors may live off campus. Coed and single-sex dorms. Special interest housing. Married-student housing. 78% of students live on campus. 2 hours of phys ed required. 9 intercollegiate sports for men, 7 for women; several intramurals. AIAW, NC. Student body composition: 4% Asian, 2% Black, 1% Hispanic, 1% Native American, 88% White, 4% Other. 54% from out of state.

[J1] LINN-BENTON COMMUNITY COLLEGE
6500 Southwest Pacific Blvd., Albany 97321

[1] MARYLHURST EDUCATION CENTER
Marylhurst 97036

[1] MOUNT ANGEL SEMINARY
St. Benedict 97373

[J1] MOUNT HOOD COMMUNITY COLLEGE
Gresham 97030

[P] MULTNOMAH SCHOOL OF THE BIBLE
8435 Northeast Glisan Street, Portland 97220

[1] NORTHWEST CHRISTIAN COLLEGE
Eugene 97401

[1] OREGON, UNIVERSITY OF
Eugene 97403, (503) 686-3201
Director of Admissions: James R. Buch

- **Undergraduates: 6,219m, 6,185w; 17,200 total (including graduates)**
- **Tuition (1982/83): $1,400 (in-state), $3,800 (out-of-state)**
- **Room & Board: $2,200**
- **Degrees offered: BA, BS, BArch, BInt Arch, BLand Arch, BFA, BBA, BEd, BPhys Ed, BMus**
- **Mean ACT 22; mean SAT 468v, 492m**
- **Student-faculty ratio: 19 to 1**

A public university established in 1872. 187-acre urban campus. Served by air, bus, and rail.
Academic Character NASC and professional accreditation. Trimester system, 8- and 11-week summer terms. 6 majors offered by the School of Architecture & Allied Arts, 9 by the College of Business Administration, 2 by the School of Community Service & Public Affairs, 3 by the College of Education, 4 by the College of Health, Physical Education & Recreation, 1 by the School of Journalism, 34 by the College of Liberal Arts, and 5 by the School of Music. Special majors. Distributive requirements. Graduate degrees granted. Independent study. Honors College. Phi Beta Kappa. Pass/fail, internships. Preprofessional programs in 13 areas. 3-2 medical technology program. 2-2 dental hygiene program. Member National Student Exchange. Study in Europe, Japan, Mexico. Elementary, secondary, and special education certification. ROTC. Computer center. Art and natural history museums. Language lab. 2,100,000-volume library with microform resources.
Financial CEEB CSS. University scholarships, grants, loans; PELL, SEOG, NDSL, GSL, CWS. Scholarship application deadline March 1.
Admissions High school graduation with 12-14 units recommended. Music majors must audition. SAT or ACT required. $25 application fee. Rolling admissions. $50 room deposit due on acceptance of admissions offer. Transfers accepted. Credit possible for CEEB AP, CLEP, and challenge exams. EOP.
Student Life Student government. Newspaper, literary magazine, yearbook, radio station. Music, dance, and drama groups. Debate. PIRG. PLUS. Women's Resource Service. Academic, ethnic, honorary, religious, service, and special interest groups. 14 fraternities and 12 sororities, all with houses. 15% of undergraduates join. Coed and single-sex dorms. Special interest and co-op dorms. Married-student housing. 20% of students live on campus. Liquor prohibited in dorms. 1 course in health education required. 8 intercollegiate sports for men, 8 for women; intramurals. AIAW, NCAA, NCWSA, Pac-10. Student body composition: 2% Asian, 2% Black, 1% Hispanic, 1% Native American, 93% White, 1% Other. 25% from out of state.

■[G1] OREGON, UNIVERSITY OF, HEALTH SCIENCES CENTER
Portland 97201

[G1] OREGON GRADUATE CENTER
Beaverton 97006

[1] OREGON INSTITUTE OF TECHNOLOGY
Klamath Falls 97601, (503) 882-6321
Director of Admissions: Al Roberson

- **Undergraduates: 1,797m, 853w**
- **Tuition (1982/83): $1,401 (in-state), $4,059 (out-of-state)**
- **Room & Board: $2,195**
- **Degrees offered: BS, BSMT, BSInd Mgmt, AAS, AE**
- **Mean SAT 416v, 463m**
- **Student-faculty ratio: 15 to 1**

A public institute established in 1947. 158-acre suburban campus, 270 miles from Portland. Served by air, rail, and bus.
Academic Character NASC and professional accreditation. Trimester system, 8- to 10-week summer term. 18 majors offered in the areas of allied health technology, engineering technology, industrial management, and industrial technology. Associate degrees in 17 other fields. Courses in 21 additional areas. Self-designed majors. Distributive requirements. Cooperative work/study, limited pass/fail, credit by exam. ROTC. Computer center. Geo-Heat Center. 60,000-volume library with microform resources.
Financial CEEB CSS and ACT FAS. Institute scholarships, grants, loans, payment plan; PELL, SEOG, GSL, FISL, NDSL, CWS. Application deadline March 1.
Admissions High school graduation with 12 units recommended. GED accepted. SAT or ACT required. $25 application fee. Rolling admissions. *Concurrent Enrollment* Program. Transfers accepted. Credit possible for CEEB AP, CLEP, and challenge exams.
Student Life Student government. Newspaper, yearbook, radio station. Craft center. Outdoor program. Academic, honorary, professional, and special interest groups. 4 fraternities and 1 sorority. About 1% of students join. Single-sex dorms. 21% of students live on campus. Liquor prohibited. 3 semesters of phys ed required. 4 intercollegiate sports for men, 3 for women; intramurals. AIAW, NAIA, NCWSA, NCAA. Student body composition: 2.5% Asian, 0.9% Black, 1.1% Hispanic, 1.5% Native American, 94% White. 7% from out of state.

[1] OREGON STATE UNIVERSITY
Corvallis 97331, (503) 754-4411
Director of Admissions: Wallace E. Gibbs

- **Undergraduates: 8,120m, 5,895w; 17,460 total (including graduates)**
- **Tuition (1982/83): $1,389 (in-state), $4,014 (out-of-state)**
- **Room & Board: $2,100**
- **Degrees offered: BA, BS, BFA, BAg**
- **Mean SAT 1,000**
- **Student-faculty ratio: 17 to 1**

A public university established in 1868. 397-acre campus in a small city 85 miles south of Portland. Served by bus; airport 40 miles away in Eugene.
Academic Character NASC and professional accreditation. Trimester system, 8- and 11-week summer terms. 13 majors offered by the School of Agriculture, 9 by the School of Business, 3 by the School of Education, 14 by the School of Engineering, 4 by the School of Forestry, 2 by the School of Health & Physical Education, 13 by the School of Home Economics, 20 by the College of Liberal Arts, 3 by the School of Pharmacy, and 19 by the College of

Science. Self-designed majors. Minors offered in many major fields. Distributive requirements. Graduate degrees granted. Independent study. Honors program. Phi Beta Kappa. Cooperative work/study, limited pass/fail, internships. Preprofessional programs in dentistry, dental hygiene, medicine, medical technology, nursing, optometry, physical therapy, podiatry, veterinary medicine. Cooperative mining engineering program with Idaho. WICHE exchange program with schools in the 13 Western states. National Student Exchange Program with 53 state schools. Several study abroad programs. Elementary and secondary education certification. ROTC, AFROTC, NROTC. Language lab. Marine Science Center. Natural History Museum. Art gallery. 919,789-volume library with microform resources.
Financial CEEB CSS. University scholarships, grants, loans; PELL, SEOG, GSL, NDSL, CWS. Preferred application deadline February 1.
Admissions High school graduation required. SAT or ACT required. $25 application fee. Rolling admissions. $50 room deposit due on acceptance of admissions offer. *Early Admission* and *Early Decision* programs. Transfers accepted. Credit possible for CEEB AP and CLEP exams. EOP.
Student Life Student government. Newspaper, yearbook. Music and drama groups. Debate. Academic, political, service, tutorial, and special interest groups. 28 fraternities and 15 sororities, all with houses. Single freshmen live on campus. Coed and single-sex dorms. Co-op houses. Married-student housing. 40% of students live on campus. Liquor prohibited. 3 hours of phys ed required. 8 intercollegiate sports for men, 9 for women; club and intramural sports. AIAW, NCAA, AAWU, PTC. Student body composition: 4% Asian, 1.4% Native American, 87.5% White, 7.1% Other. 18% from out of state.

[1] PACIFIC NORTHWEST COLLEGE OF ART

Portland 97205
Formerly Museum Art School.

[1] PACIFIC UNIVERSITY

Forest Grove 97116, (503) 357-6151
Director of Admissions: Marie B. Williams

- **Enrollment: 603m, 428w**
- **Tuition (1982/83): $5,505**
- **Room & Board: $2,295; Fees: $105**
- **Degrees offered: BA, BS, BMus, BMus Ed**
- **Mean SAT 450v, 480m**
- **Student-faculty ratio: 11 to 1**

A private university affiliated with the United Church of Christ, established in 1849. Rural campus, 25 miles from Portland. Served by bus; airport and rail station in Portland.
Academic Character NASC and professional accreditation. 7-7-3 system, 3 3-week summer terms. 48 majors offered in the areas of communications, education, fine arts, humanities, legal services, mathematics, medical technology, music, physical education, physical therapy, religion, science, social science, and speech. Special majors. Distributive requirements. Graduate degrees granted. Independent study. Honors program. Limited pass/fail, internships, credit by exam. Preprofessional programs in dentistry, law, medicine, nursing, optometry, pharmacy, physical therapy, theology, veterinary medicine. 3-1 medical technology program. 3-2 engineering programs with Georgia Tech, Oregon State, Washington State, Washington U. Study abroad. Elementary, secondary, and special education certification. Media center. Language lab. 128,000-volume library with microform resources.
Financial CEEB CSS. University scholarships, grants, loans; PELL, SEOG, NDSL, GSL, FISL, CWS. Preferred application deadline April 15.
Admissions High school graduation with 18 units recommended. Interview recommended. SAT or ACT required. $15 application fee. Rolling admissions; suggest applying by February 1. $100 deposit due on acceptance of admissions offer. *Early Admission* Program. Admission deferral possible. Transfers accepted. Credit possible for CEEB AP and CLEP exams.
Student Life Student government. Newspaper, literary magazine, yearbook, radio and TV studios. Music and drama groups. Debate. 1 fraternity and 2 sororities without houses. Juniors and seniors may live off campus. Dorms for men and women. Married-student housing. 40% of students live on campus. 10 intercollegiate sports for men, 9 for women; intramurals. WCIC, NC. Student body composition: 14.5% Asian, 4.3% Black, 1.5% Hispanic, 2.4% Native American, 76.5% White. 65% from out of state.

[1] PORTLAND, UNIVERSITY OF

5000 North Willamette Blvd., Portland 97203, (503) 283-7147
Director of Admissions: Daniel B. Reilly

- **Undergraduates: 878m, 838w; 2,800 total (including graduates)**
- **Tuition (1982/83): $4,350**
- **Room & Board: $2,260; Fees: $100-$250**
- **Degrees offered: BA, BS, BBA, BMus, BMus Ed, BSEE, BSEng, BSGE, BSN, BSAJ, BSCE**
- **Student-faculty ratio: 17 to 1**

A private university controlled by the Congregation of the Holy Cross, established in 1901, became coed in 1954. 92-acre suburban campus, 4 miles from downtown Portland. Served by air, rail, bus, and ship.
Academic Character NASC and professional accreditation. Semester system, 8-week summer term. 24 majors offered by the College of Arts & Sciences, 3 by the School of Business Administration, 2 by the School of Education, 6 by the School of Engineering, and 1 by the School of Nursing. Self-designed and special majors. Distributives and 9 hours of theology required. Graduate degrees granted. Independent study. Honors program. Cooperative work/study, limited pass/fail, internships. Preprofessional programs in dentistry, law, medicine. 3-1 medical technology program. Study abroad. Elementary, secondary, and special education certification. AFROTC. Computer center. Language lab. 200,000-volume library with microform resources.
Financial CEEB CSS and ACT FAS. University scholarships, grants, loans, payment plans; PELL, SEOG, NDSL, FISL, NSS, CWS. Application deadlines February 1 (scholarships), August 15 (loans).
Admissions High school graduation required. Interview encouraged. SAT, ACT, or WPTC required. $25 application fee. Rolling admissions. $25 tuition deposit and $50 room deposit (for boarders) due on acceptance of admissions offer. *Early Admission* Program. Admission deferral possible. Transfers accepted. Credit possible for CEEB AP and CLEP exams.
Student Life Student government. Newspaper, literary magazine, yearbook, radio and TV stations. Music and drama groups. Black Student Union. Hispanic fraternity. Hawaiian club. Academic, honorary, service, and special interest groups. 7 fraternities and sororities without houses. Single students under 21 live at home or on campus. Coed and single-sex dorms. 50% of students live on campus. Liquor prohibited. Class attendance required. 7 intercollegiate sports for men, 4 for women; intramurals. NCAA, AIAW, WCAA, PAC. Student body composition: 2.2% Black, 1.1% Hispanic, 0.7% Native American, 75.5% White, 20.5% Other. 39% from out of state.

[J1] PORTLAND COMMUNITY COLLEGE

12000 Southwest 49th Avenue, Portland 97219

[1] PORTLAND STATE UNIVERSITY

PO Box 751, Portland 97207, (503) 229-3511
Director of Admissions: Eileen M. Rose

- **Undergraduates: 3,380m, 2,904w; 15,500 total (including graduates)**
- **Tuition (1982/83): $1,480 (in-state), $4,514 (out-of-state)**
- **Room: $1,200**
- **Degrees offered: BA, BS**
- **Mean SAT 570v, 610**
- **Student-faculty ratio: 18 to 1**

A public university established in 1946. 26-block urban campus. Served by air, rail, and bus.
Academic Character NASC and professional accreditation. Trimester system, 1- to 11-week summer terms. 55 majors offered by the colleges of Arts & Letters, Science, Social Science, Business Administration, Education, Social Work, and Engineering & Applied Science. Self-designed and special majors. Distributive requirements. Graduate degrees granted. Independent study. Honors program. Cooperative work/study, pass/fail, internships, credit by exam. Preprofessional programs in 23 areas. Exchange programs through NICSA consortium and with other state schools. Study abroad. Elementary, secondary, and special education certification. AFROTC at U Portland. Learning Lab. Audio-visual center. 621,352-volume library with microform resources.
Financial CEEB CSS. University scholarships, grants, loans, state grants, payment plan; PELL, SEOG, NDSL, FISL, GSL, CWS. Priority application deadline March 1.
Admissions High school graduation required. GED accepted. SAT or ACT required. $25 application fee. Rolling admissions; suggest applying by June. *Early Admission* and *Concurrent Enrollment* programs. Transfers accepted. Credit possible for CEEB AP, CLEP, and university exams. Special admissions programs for disadvantaged students.
Student Life Student government. Newspaper, literary magazine, yearbook. Music, drama, and theatre groups. Debate. Academic, honorary, religious, service, and special interest groups. 3 fraternities and 2 sororities, all with houses. Housing arranged through Portland Student Services or privately. Married-student housing. 5 terms of phys ed required. 6 intercollegiate sports for men, 6 for women; intramurals. PCAC. Student body composition: 4.9% Asian, 2.3% Black, 7.3% Foreign, 1.3% Hispanic, 0.9% Native American, 83.3% White. 11% from out of state.

[1] REED COLLEGE

3203 Southeast Woodstock Blvd., Portland 97202, (503) 777-7511
Dean of Admissions: Robin Cody

- **Undergraduates: 656m, 498w**
- **Tuition (1982/83): $7,060**
- **Room & Board: $2,630; Fees: $100**
- **Degree offered: BA**
- **Mean SAT 621v, 630m**
- **Student-faculty ratio: 10 to 1**

A private college established in 1909. 100-acre suburban campus, 5 miles from downtown Portland. Served by air, rail, and bus.
Academic Character NASC accreditation. Semester system, January interim. 21 majors offered by the divisions of Humanities; Arts; History & Social Sciences; Literature & Languages; Mathematics & Natural Sciences; Philosophy , Education, Religion, & Psychology; and in 13 interdisciplinary fields. Self-designed majors. Distributive requirements. Junior Qualifying Exam. Independent research, oral exam, original work, and thesis required of seniors. Independent study. Phi Beta Kappa. Limited pass/fail. Internships. Preprofessional program in medicine. 3-2 engineering programs with Cal Tech, Columbia, Rensselaer. 3-2 forestry program with Duke. 3-2 computer science program with U Washington. 3-2 applied physics program with Oregon Graduate Center. Exchange program with Howard U. Study abroad. Computer center. Nuclear reactor. Language lab. Studio arts center. 300,000-volume library.
Financial CEEB CSS. College scholarships, grants, loans, payment plans; PELL, SEOG, NDSL, GSL, CWS. Application deadlines February 1 (FAF), March 1 (scholarships).
Admissions High school graduation with 14 units recommended. SAT required; ACT accepted. 3 ACH recommended. $20 application fee. Rolling

admissions; application deadline February 15. $100 deposit due on acceptance of admissions offer. *Early Decision* and *Early Admission* programs. Admission deferral possible. Transfers accepted. Credit possible for CEEB AP exams; college has own advanced placement program.
Student Life Community government. Newspaper, literary magazine, yearbook, radio station. Music, dance, and drama groups. Educational Policy Committee. Ethnic, religious, and special interest groups. Coed and single-sex dorms. Language houses. No married-student housing. 49% of students live on campus. 3 semesters of phys ed required. Several personal sports programs, club sports. Student body composition: 8% Asian, 1% Black, 3% Hispanic, 1% Native American, 87% White. 85% from out of state.

[J1] ROGUE COMMUNITY COLLEGE
Grants Pass 97526

[1] SOUTHERN OREGON STATE COLLEGE
Ashland 97520, (503) 482-6411
Director of Admissions: Allen H. Blaszak

- **Undergraduates: 1,967m, 1,967w; 4,710 total (including graduates)**
- **Tuition (1982/83): $1,260 (in-state), $3,425 (out-of-state)**
- **Room & Board: $2,150**
- **Degrees offered: BA, BS, BFA**
- **Mean SAT 850-900**
- **Student-faculty ratio: 20 to 1**

A public college established in 1926. 150-acre campus in a small city 15 miles from Medford. Airport and bus station nearby.
Academic Character NASC and professional accreditation. Trimester system, 8-week summer term. 34 majors offered by the schools of Humanities, Science & Mathematics, Social Science, Business, Education & Psychology, and Health & Physical Education. Special majors. Minors offered in many major fields. Distributive requirements. Graduate degrees granted. Honors program. Limited pass/fail, internships. Preprofessional programs in chiropractic medicine, dentistry, law, medicine, pharmacy, podiatry, theology, wildlife management. Cooperative programs with Oregon State in agriculture, computer science, pharmacy. Programs in dental hygiene with U Oregon. Nursing with Oregon Health Sciences U; optometry and physical therapy with Pacific U. Cooperative veterinary medicine programs with Washington and Idaho. Study abroad. Elementary and secondary education certification. Art gallery. Computer center. Drama lab. 180,000-volume library with microform resources.
Financial CEEB CSS and ACT FAS. College scholarships, grants, loans, state grants, payment plan; PELL, SEOG, NDSL, FISL, GSL, NSL, CWS. Application deadline February 15.
Admissions High school graduation with 15 units recommended. GED accepted. Interview recommended. Specific tests required of nursing applicants. SAT or ACT required. $25 application fee. Rolling admissions. $50 room deposit due on acceptance of admissions offer. *Early Admission* and *Concurrent Enrollment* programs. Admission deferral possible. Transfers accepted. Credit possible for CEEB AP and CLEP exams; college has own advanced placement program. Probationary admission possible.
Student Life Student government. Newspaper, yearbook, radio station. Music and drama groups. Debate. Common Cause. Outdoor Program. Academic, honorary, professional, religious, service, and special interest groups. Freshmen live at home or on campus. Limited married-student housing. Special-interest houses. 25% of students live on campus. 8 intercollegiate sports for men, 6 for women; intramurals. NCAA, NAIA, NCWSA, AIAW, Evergreen Conference. Student body composition: 1% Black, 1% Hispanic, 1% Native American, 96% White, 1% Other. 10% from out of state.

[J1] SOUTHWESTERN OREGON COMMUNITY COLLEGE
Coos Bay 97420

[J1] TREASURE VALLEY COMMUNITY COLLEGE
Ontario 97914

[J1] UMPQUA COMMUNITY COLLEGE
PO Box 967, Roseburg 97470

[1] WARNER PACIFIC COLLEGE
2219 Southeast 68th Avenue, Portland 97215, (503) 775-4368

Enrollment: 189m, 151w; 500 total (including part-time)
- **Tuition & Fees (1982/83): $3,915**
- **Room & Board: $1,905**
- **Degrees offered: BA, BS, BTh**
- **Mean SAT 450**
- **Student-faculty ratio: 12 to 1**

A private college controlled by the Church of God. Campus in residential section of Portland.
Academic Character NASC accreditation. Quarter system. Majors offered in Bible, theology, Christian education, music, history, philosophy, English, sociology, psychology, biological sciences, economics, business, health & physical education, literature, pastoral ministries, and social casework. MRel granted. 52,000-volume library.
Financial College loans, NDSL, work program.
Admissions High school graduation required. SAT required. Rolling admissions. *Early Admission* Program. Transfers accepted.
Student Life Single-sex dorms. Dining hall.

[1] WESTERN BAPTIST COLLEGE
5000 Deer Park Drive, SE, Salem 97301, (503) 581-8600

- **Enrollment: 172m, 150w; 350 total (including part-time)**
- **Tuition (1982/83): $3,600**
- **Room & Board: $2,160; Fees: $164**
- **Degrees offered: BA, BS, ThB, BRE, BE, AA**
- **Student-faculty ratio: 11 to 1**

A private college controlled by the Regular Baptists, established in 1935. Suburban campus, 1 hour from Portland.
Academic Character NASC accreditation. Quarter system. 33 majors offered in the areas of Bible study, business, church education, education, humanities, missions, music, pastoral ministries, psychology, social science, and youth ministry. Minors offered in 14 additional areas. Distributive requirements. Pre-seminary program. 5-year programs in Bible, pastoral education, missions, theology, Christian education. Dual-degree programs in education. 40,000-volume library.
Financial CEEB CSS. College scholarships, PELL, SEOG, NDSL, GSL, CWS. Application deadline May 1.
Admissions High school graduation required. GED accepted. SAT, ACT, or WPCAT required. $20 application fee. Rolling admissions. *Early Admission* Program.Transfers accepted. Credit possible for CEEB AP and CLEP exams.
Student Life Student government. Music groups. Student Missionary Fellowship. Single-sex dorms. Married-student housing. 3 intercollegiate sports; intramurals. NAIA.

[G1] WESTERN CONSERVATIVE BAPTIST SEMINARY
Portland 97215

[G1] WESTERN EVANGELICAL SEMINARY
Portland 97222

[1] WESTERN OREGON STATE COLLEGE
Monmouth 97361, (503) 838-1220
Director of Admissions: Barbara Gianneschi

- **Enrollment: 1,124m, 2,005w**
- **Tuition (1982/83): $1,376 (in-state), $3,404 (out-of-state)**
- **Room & Board: $2,145; Fees: $20**
- **Degrees offered: BA, BS, AA**
- **Mean SAT 900**
- **Student-faculty ratio: 15 to 1**

A public college established in 1882, formerly Oregon College of Education. 120-acre small-town campus, 15 miles southwest of Salem.
Academic Character NSAC and professional accreditation. Trimester system, 2 4-week summer terms. Majors offered in art, biology, corrections, drama, economics, education, fire services, geography, history, humanities, law enforcement, mathematics, music, natural sciences, psychology, social sciences, and interdisciplinary studies. Minors offered in most major fields. Distributive requirements. Graduate degrees granted. Independent study. Honors program. Pass/fail, internships. Preprofessional programs in dentistry, dental hygiene, journalism, medicine, nursing, pharmacy, physical therapy, podiatry, veterinary medicine. 3-1 medical technology program. Transfer programs in agriculture, atmospheric science, biochemistry & biophysics, chemistry, engineering, food science, forestry, geology, home economics, microbiology, physics. Study abroad. Elementary and secondary education certification. ROTC. Campus elementary school. Media center. 163,000-volume library with microform resources.
Financial CEEB CSS. College scholarships, grants, loans, state scholarships and loans, payment plan; PELL, SEOG, GSL, NDSL, CWS. Application deadline February 1.
Admissions High school graduation required. GED accepted. SAT or ACT required. $20 application fee. Rolling admissions. $50 room deposit due on acceptance of admissions offer. *Concurrent Enrollment* and *Early Admission* programs. Transfers accepted. Credit possible for CEEB AP and CLEP exams; college has own advanced placement program.
Student Life Student government. Newspaper, literary magazine. Music and drama groups. Debate. Athletic, academic, and religious groups. Single-sex dorms. No married-student housing. Phys ed required. 10 intercollegiate sports; 3 intramurals. Student body composition: 2% Asian, 1.4% Black, 0.3% Hispanic, 1% Native American, 94.8% White.

[P] WESTERN STATES CHIROPRACTIC COLLEGE
2900 Northeast 132nd Avenue, Portland 97230

[1] WILLAMETTE UNIVERSITY
Salem 97301, (503) 370-6300
Director of Admissions: Franklin D. Meyer

- **Undergraduates: 668m, 638w; 1,907 total (including graduates)**
- **Tuition (1982/83): $5,500**
- **Room & Board: $2,350; Fees: $70**
- **Degrees offered: BA, BS, BMus, BMus Ed, BMus Therapy, BTheatre**
- **Mean ACT 24; mean SAT 500v, 540m**
- **Student-faculty ratio: 13 to 1**

A private university affiliated with the United Methodist Church, established in 1842. 60-acre urban campus, 45 miles south of Portland. Served by air, rail, and bus.
Academic Character NASC and professional accreditation. Semester system. 31 majors offered in the areas of American studies, art, computer science, environmental science, humanities, international studies, languages, mathematics, music, physical education, religion, science, social science, and

Key to ratings **[1, 2, J1, J2, G, P, R, S]** *and list of abbreviations start on page 120*

theatre. Distributive requirements. Graduate degrees granted. Independent study. Limited pass/fail, internships. Preprofessional programs in business, dentistry, government, law, medical technology, medicine, religion, nursing, social service. 3-2 management program with Atkinson Graduate School. 3-2 engineering programs with Columbia and Stanford. 3-2 forestry program with Duke. Combined education program with Western Oregon. UN and Washington Semesters. Study in Europe, Japan, Mexico. Secondary education certification. AFROTC at U Portland. Art gallery. Playhouse. Language lab. 236,035-volume library with microform resources.

Financial CEEB CSS. University scholarships, grants, loans, state grants, payment plan; PELL, SEOG, NDSL, FISL, GSL, CWS. Recommended application deadline February 1.

Admissions High school graduation with 16 units required. GED accepted. Interview recommended. Audition required for music majors. SAT, ACT, or WPCT required. $20 application fee. Recommended application deadline March 1. $100 deposit due on acceptance of admissions offer. *Early Decision* and *Early Admission* programs. Admission deferral possible. Transfers accepted. Credit possible for CEEB AP and departmental exams.

Student Life Student government. Newspaper, literary magazine, yearbook. Music, dance, drama groups. Debate. Minority Student Union. Professional, religious, service, and special interest groups. 6 fraternities and 3 sororities, all with houses. Juniors and seniors may live off campus. Coed and single-sex dorms. Special interest houses. No married-student housing. 75% of students live on campus. Some phys ed recommended. 12 intercollegiate sports for men, 10 for women; several intramurals. AIAW, WCIC, NC. Student body composition: 4% Asian, 1% Black, 2% Hispanic, 88% White, 5% Other. 47% from out of state.

PENNSYLVANIA *(PA)*

[1] ALBRIGHT COLLEGE
PO Box 516, Reading 19604, (215) 921-2381
Director of Admissions: Dale H. Reinhart

- **Undergraduates: 667m, 753w**
- **Tuition (1982/83): $5,660**
- **Room & Board: $2,090; Fees: $75**
- **Degrees offered: BA, BS**
- **Mean SAT 520v, 570m**
- **Student-faculty ratio: 14 to 1**

A private college affiliated with the United Methodist Church, established in 1856. 80-acre suburban campus at base of Mount Penn in Reading, one hour from Philadelphia. Served by air, bus, and rail.

Academic Character MSACS accreditation. 4-1-5 system, summer terms. Majors offered in American studies, art, economics, English, French, German, government service, history, home economics, philosophy, political science, psychology, religion, social welfare, sociology, Spanish, accounting, biochemistry, biology, business administration, chemistry, computer science, home economics, math, medical technology, nursing, physics, and psychobiology. Self-designed and interdisciplinary majors. Distributives and 9 hours of philosophy/religion required. Independent study in languages. Pass/fail. Internships. Preprofessional programs in dentistry, dietetics, medicine, veterinary medicine, Christian education, law, social welfare, theology. 3-2 engineering programs with Penn State, U Penn. 4-1 engineering program with U Penn. 3-2 program in forestry and environmental management with Duke. Washington, NY semesters. Study abroad. Secondary education certification. Computer center, language lab. 155,000-volume library with microform resources.

Financial CEEB CSS. College scholarships, grants, loans, state grants, payment plan; PELL, SEOG, NSS, NDSL, GSL, FISL, PLUS, CWS. Application deadlines April 1 (scholarships), May 1 (loans).

Admissions High school graduation with 15 units required. Interview encouraged. SAT or ACT, and 3 ACH required. $15 application fee. Rolling admissions; suggest applying by March 15. $100 deposit required on acceptance of offer of admission. *Early Decision* and *Early Admission* programs. Admission deferral possible. Transfers accepted. Credit possible for CEEB AP and CLEP exams.

Student Life Student government. Newspaper, magazine, yearbook, radio station. Music, drama, oratory activities. Women's Resource Committee. Service, religious, academic, honorary, and special interest groups. 5 fraternities with houses, and 5 sororities without houses. 20% of students join. Freshmen must live on campus. Coed and single-sex dorms, senior houses. 80% of students live on campus. Freshmen may not have cars on campus. Liquor prohibited; gambling, drinking, immorality, narcotics cause for suspension or expulsion. 4 semesters of phys ed required. 9 intercollegiate sports for men, 8 for women; intramurals. AIAW, ECAC, NCAA, WAA, MASCAC. Student body composition: 1% Black, 97% White, 2% Other. 52% out of state.

[1] ALLEGHENY COLLEGE
Meadville 16335, (814) 724-4351
Dean of Admissions: Richard A. Stewart

- **Undergraduates: 964m, 935w**
- **Tuition (1982/83): $5,835**
- **Room & Board: $2,150**
- **Degrees offered: BA, BS**
- **Mean SAT 535v, 570m**
- **Student-faculty ratio: 15 to 1**

A private college established in 1815. 165-acre campus in small city of Meadville, 90 miles from Pittsburgh and Cleveland. Served by air and bus.

Academic Character MSACS accreditation. Trimester system, 2 5-week summer terms. Majors offered in aquatic environments, art, biology, chemistry, comparative literature, computer science, dramatic art, economics, English, French, geology, German, history, international studies, mathematics, music, philosophy, physics, political science, psychology, religious studies, Russian, sociology, Spanish, speech communication. Special majors. Distributive requirements. MA granted. Independent study. Phi Beta Kappa. Pass/fail. Preprofessional programs in 16 areas. 3-2 engineering programs with Case Western Reserve, Columbia. Cooperative programs in forestry, resource management, environmental protection with Duke, U of Michigan; in medical technology with Case Western Reserve; in nursing with U of Rochester, Case Western Reserve. Exchange programs. Washington, Appalachian semesters. Study abroad. Elementary and secondary education certification. Observatory, language lab, planetarium. 300,000-volume library.

Financial College scholarships, awards, loans, state aid, payment plans; PELL, SEOG, NDSL, FISL, CWS. Application deadline March 1.

Admissions High school graduation with 12 units required. Interview encouraged. SAT or ACT required; 3 ACH recommended. $20 application fee. Rolling admissions; suggest applying in fall. $150 deposit required on acceptance of offer of admission. *Early Decision* and *Early Admission* programs. Admission deferral possible. Transfers accepted. Credit possible for CEEB AP and CLEP exams. Project 101.

Student Life Student government. Newspaper, magazine, yearbook, radio station. Music, debate, drama groups. Association of Black Collegians. Honorary, academic, political, religious, and special interest groups. 8 fraternities with houses, and 4 sororities without houses. 40% of upperclass men and 35% of upperclass women join. Freshmen must live on campus. Coed and single-sex dorms; language and special interest housing. Freshmen, students receiving financial aid may not have cars on campus. Phys ed required for freshmen, sophomores; swimming test required. 11 intercollegiate sports for men, 7 for women; intramural and club sports. AIAW, NCAA, PAC, KAC. Student body composition: 1% Asian, 4% Black, 1% Hispanic, 92% White, 2% Other. 50% from out of state.

[J1] ALLEGHENY COUNTY, COMMUNITY COLLEGE OF
Monroeville 15146

[J1] ALLEGHENY COUNTY, COMMUNITY COLLEGE OF
808 Ridge Avenue, Pittsburgh 15212

[J1] ALLEGHENY COUNTY, COMMUNITY COLLEGE OF
West Mifflin 15122

[J1] ALLEGHENY COUNTY—NORTH, COMMUNITY COLLEGE OF
1130 Perry Highway, Pittsburgh 15044

[1] ALLENTOWN COLLEGE OF ST. FRANCIS DE SALES
Center Valley 18034, (215) 282-1100
Director of Admissions: George C. Kelly, Jr.

- **Undergraduates: 343m, 366w**
- **Tuition (1982/83): $4,060**
- **Room & Board: $2,420; Fees: $30**
- **Degrees offered: BA, BS, BSN**
- **Student-faculty ratio: 16 to 1**

A private, Roman Catholic college controlled by the Oblates of St. Francis de Sales, established in 1965, became coed in 1970. 300-acre rural campus in Center Valley, 8 miles from Bethlehem. Air, bus, and rail service nearby.

Academic Character MSACS and professional accreditation. Semester system, 3-, 6-, and 8-week summer terms. Majors offered in accounting & business, biology, business management, chemistry, computer science, criminal justice, dance, English, foreign languages, liberal studies, mathematics, nursing, politics, psychology, theatre, and theology. Distributives and 2 semesters of theology required. Independent study. Pass/fail. Credit by exam. Preprofessional programs in dentistry, law, medicine. Cross-registration with 5 area colleges. Harrisburg Urban Semester. Study abroad. Secondary education certification. ROTC, AFROTC at Lehigh. Computer center, language lab. 103,226-volume library with microform resources.

Financial CEEB CSS (out-of-state), state application (in-state). College scholarships, grants, loans, payment plan; PELL, SEOG, NSS, NDSL, FISL, NSL, CWS. Loan application deadline September 1.

Admissions High school graduation with 16 units recommended. GED accepted. SAT or ACT, and 3 ACH recommended. $10 application fee. Rolling admissions; suggest applying by December. $50 tuition deposit and $50 room deposit (for boarders) required on acceptance of offer of admission. *Early Admission, Early Decision, Concurrent Enrollment* programs. Admission

deferral possible. Transfers accepted. Credit possible for CEEB AP and CLEP exams; college has own advanced placement program.
Student Life Student government. Newspaper, magazine, yearbook, radio station. Music, drama activities. Political, service, religious, and special interest groups. One sorority. Single-sex dorms. 65% of students live on campus. Class attendance required for freshmen. 2 semesters of phys ed required. 5 intercollegiate sports for men, 5 for women; intramurals. AIAW, NCAA, PIAW. Student body composition: 1.5% Black, 1% Hispanic, 0.5% Native American, 96.5% White, 0.5% Other. 24% from out of state.

[1] ALLIANCE COLLEGE

Cambridge Springs 16403, (814) 398-4611

- **Undergraduates: 129m, 79w; 255 total (including part-time)**
- **Tuition (1982/83): $2,800**
- **Room & Board: $2,050; Fees: $260**
- **Degrees offered: BA, BS, AS**
- **Mean SAT 860**
- **Student-faculty ratio: 13 to 1**

A private college with support from the Polish National Alliance, established in 1912. Small-town campus, 25 miles south of Erie.
Academic Character MCACS accreditation. Semester system. 4-year majors offered in accounting, management, international business & Slavic area studies, English, communications, biology, chemistry, mathematics, psychology, sociology, history, Polish, and Russian. 2-year degree programs in tool design and technical drafting. 2-year certificates in general business and accounting. Remedial mathematics and English programs. 80,000-volume library.
Admissions SAT or ACT recommended. Rolling admissions. *Early Admission* and *Early Decision* programs. Admission deferral possible. Transfers accepted. Advanced placement program.
Student Life 3 fraternities. One dorm for men, one for women. Dining hall. Varsity baseball, basketball, and soccer.

[1] ALVERNIA COLLEGE

Reading 19607, (215) 777-5411
Director of Admissions: James A. Ford

- **Enrollment: 133m, 150w; 800 total (including part-time)**
- **Tuition (1982/83): $2,200**
- **Room & Board: $1,900**
- **Degrees offered: BA, BS, AVA, ANurs**
- **Mean SAT 450v, 500m**
- **Student-faculty ratio: 10 to 1**

A private, Roman Catholic college controlled by the Bernardine Sisters, established in 1926. 85-acre campus, 3 miles from the center of Reading.
Academic Character MSACS accreditation. Semester system, 5-week summer term. Majors offered in accounting, alcohol & drug abuse counseling, banking & finance, business management & administration, communications, criminal justice systems administration, education, English, French, history, music, political science, psychology, social studies, social work, sociology, Spanish, theology/philosophy, biology, chemistry, biochemistry, general science, and mathematics. Distributives and 12 credits in philosophy and theology required. Independent study. Cooperative work/study. Credit by exam. Elementary and secondary education certification. 66,000-volume library.
Financial CEEB CSS. College scholarships and grants, state scholarships; PELL, SEOG, NSS, NDSL, GSL, CWS. Application deadline April 1.
Admissions High school graduation with 16 units required. Interview required for nursing majors. SAT or ACT required. $10 application fee. Rolling admissions. $100 deposit required by May 1. *Early Admission* Program. Admission deferral possible. Transfers accepted. Credit possible for CEEB AP and CLEP exams; college has own advanced placement program.
Student Life Student government. Newspaper, magazine, yearbook. Music and drama groups. Religious, honorary, academic, professional, and special interest groups. One dorm. 3-4 credits in phys ed required. 4 intercollegiate sports for men, 1 for women; intramurals. NAIA, Keystone Conference.

[G1] AMERICAN COLLEGE

Bryn Mawr 19010

[J2] ART INSTITUTE OF PHILADELPHIA

1622 Chestnut Street, Philadelphia 19103

[J2] ART INSTITUTE OF PITTSBURGH

526 Penn Avenue, Pittsburgh 15222, (412) 263-6600
Director of Admissions: Janet Stevens

- **Undergraduates: 845m, 1,002w**
- **Tuition (1982/83): $4,650**
- **Fees: $810**
- **Degree offered: ASpecialized Tech**
- **Student-faculty ratio: 21 to 1**

A private institute established in 1921. 10-story building in center of Pittsburgh. Served by air, rail, and bus.
Academic Character Trimester system, summer term. 2-year programs offered in visual communication (commercial art), fashion illustration, interior design, photography/multimedia, and fashion merchandising. Cooperative work/study. Informal workshops. Affiliation with art institutes of Atlanta, Fort Lauderdale, Houston, Philadelphia, Seattle, Colorado. Audio-visual, computer graphics, photography labs. Gallery.
Financial College scholarships, state grants and loans, parental loans; PELL, SEOG, NDSL, FISL, CWS. Application deadline for college scholarships March 1.
Admissions High school graduation required. Portfolio recommended. Rolling admissions. *Early Decision* Program. Admission deferral possible. Transfers accepted.
Student Life American Society of Interior Designers. Dorms and dining facilities for men and women. Housing at Duquesne. Student body composition: 15% minority.

[P] BAPTIST BIBLE COLLEGE

Clarks Summit 18411

[1] BEAVER COLLEGE

Glenside 19038, (215) 884-3500
Director of Admissions: T. Edwards Townsley

- **Undergraduates: 146m, 575w; 2,177 total (including part-time)**
- **Tuition (1982/83): $5,400**
- **Room & Board: $2,400; Fees: $110-$120**
- **Degrees offered: BA, BS, BFA**
- **Student-faculty ratio: 12 to 1**

A private college affiliated with the United Presbyterian Church, established in 1853, became coed in 1973. 55-acre suburban campus in Glenside, 25 minutes from Philadelphia. Served by rail.
Academic Character MSACS and professional accreditation. 4-1-4 system, 2 4-week summer terms. 23 majors offered in the liberal arts & sciences, 8 offered in fine arts, and majors offered in computer science, medical technology, and physical therapy. Self-designed majors. Masters degrees granted. Evening/Weekend College offers AA, AS, BS. Independent study. Honors program. Cooperative work/study, limited pass/fail, internships. Preprofessional programs in law, medicine, social work. 2-2 program in nursing with U of Pennsylvania School of Nursing. 3-2 engineering program with Columbia, Washington, Widener; 3-3 engineering program with Drexel. Marine biology in cooperation with Stockton Institute. Limited cross-registration with U Penn. Washington, Harrisburg semesters. Study abroad. Elementary and secondary education certification. ROTC at Temple and LaSalle. Language lab. 122,000-volume library with microform resources.
Financial CEEB CSS. College scholarships and loans, payment plan; PELL, SEOG, NDSL, GSL, PLUS, CWS. Preferred application deadline for scholarships February 1.
Admissions High school graduation with 16 units recommended. Interview encouraged. SAT or ACT required. $15 application fee. Rolling admissions; recommended application deadline February 1. $100 deposit required on acceptance of offer of admission. *Early Decision* and *Early Admission* programs. Admission deferral possible. Transfers accepted. Credit possible for CEEB AP and CLEP exams.
Student Life Student government. Newspaper, magazine, yearbook. Music, drama groups. Association of Beaver College Blacks. Academic, professional, honorary and special interest groups. Students must live at home or on campus. Coed and single-sex dorms. No married-student housing. 61% of students live on campus. 2 semesters of phys ed required. 8 intercollegiate sports; intramurals. KAC, AIAW. Student body composition: 2% Asian, 14% Black, 1% Hispanic, 81% White, 2% Other. 40% from out of state.

[J1] BEAVER COUNTY, COMMUNITY COLLEGE OF

Monaca 15061

[1] BLOOMSBURG STATE COLLEGE

Bloomsburg 17815, (717) 389-3316
Director of Admissions: T.L. Cooper

- **Undergraduates: 1,964m, 2,978w; 6,339 total (including graduates)**
- **Tuition (1982/83): $1,480 (in-state), $2,590 (out-of-state)**
- **Room & Board: $1,434; Fees: $40**
- **Degrees offered: BA, BS, BSBA, BSEd, BSN, BSOA, AS**
- **Mean SAT 462v, 508m**
- **Student-faculty ratio: 18 to 1**

A public college established in 1839. 173-acre campus in small town of Bloomsburg, 80 miles from Harrisburg. Served by bus. Airport 1 hour away in Wilkes-Barre/Scranton.
Academic Character MSACS and professional accreditation. Semester system, 7 3- and 6-week summer terms. 25 majors offered by the School of Arts & Sciences, 10 by the School of Professional Studies, and 10 by the School of Business. Distributive requirements. MA, MS, MBA, MEd granted. Independent study. Honors program. Cooperative work/study, limited pass/fail, internships. Preprofessional programs in dentistry, law, medicine, optometry, pharmacy, veterinary medicine, allied health sciences. 3-2 engineering program with Penn State. Marine Science summer courses. Student teaching in South America, England. Study abroad. Elementary, secondary, and special education certification. ROTC at Wilkes College; AFROTC at Bucknell. Center for Learning & Communication Disorders, language lab, computer center. 300,000-volume library with microform resources.
Financial CEEB CSS. College scholarships, grants, loans, state aid; PELL, SEOG, NSS, NDSL, FISL, CWS. Scholarship application deadline April 1.
Admissions High school graduation with 16 units required. SAT required. $10 application fee. Rolling admissions; suggest applying by December 31. $80 activities deposit and 10% of Basic Fee required on acceptance of offer of admission. *Early Admission* Program. Admission deferral possible. Transfers accepted. Credit possible for CEEB AP and CLEP exams; college has own advanced placement program. Center for Academic Development Program.

Student Life Student government. Newspaper, magazine, yearbook. Music, debate, drama groups. Literary and film society. Academic, honorary, religious, service, and special interest organizations. 9 fraternities and 8 sororities. 15% of men and women join. Freshmen under 21 must live at home or on campus. Seniors must live off campus. Coed and single-sex dorms. 45% of students live on campus. Freshmen and sophomores may not have cars on campus. Liquor prohibited. 4 hours of phys ed required. 10 intercollegiate sports for men, 9 for women; many intramural and club sports. NCAA, ECAC, AIAW, PSAC, EWL. Student body composition: 0.4% Asian, 2.3% Black, 0.4% Hispanic, 0.2% Native American, 96.3% White, 0.3% Other. 6% from out of state.

[1] BRYN MAWR COLLEGE
Bryn Mawr 19010, (215) 645-5152
Director of Admissions: Elizabeth G. Vermey

- **Undergraduates: 1,118w; 1,815 total (including graduates)**
- **Tuition (1982/83): $7,725**
- **Room & Board: $3,385; Fees: $150**
- **Degree offered: BA**
- **Student-faculty ratio: 9 to 1**

A private women's college with coed graduate programs, established in 1885. 125-acre suburban campus in residential Bryn Mawr, 11 miles west of Philadelphia. Served by rail. Airport and bus station in Philadelphia.
Academic Character MSACS accreditation. Semester system. Majors offered in anthropology, astronomy, biology, chemistry, classical & Near Eastern archaeology, classical languages, economics, English, fine art, French, geology, German, Greek, growth & structure of cities, Hispanic & Hispanic/American studies, history, history of art, history of religion, Italian, Latin, mathematics, music, philosophy, physics, political science, psychology, religion, Romance languages, Russian, Russian studies, sociology, Spanish. Special majors. Courses in performing arts, education. Senior Conference in major required. MA, MSS, PhD granted. Independent study, honors program. Pass/fail, internships. Self-scheduled examinations. Premedical program. 3-2 engineering program with Caltech. BA/MD program for PA residents with Medical College of Pennsylvania. 4-college program with Haverford, Swarthmore, U of Pennsylvania. Study abroad. Secondary education certification. ROTC at U Penn. Computer center, language lab. 750,000-volume library with microform resources.
Financial CEEB CSS. College scholarships, grants, loans, state grants; PELL, SEOG, NDSL. Scholarship application deadline January 15.
Admissions High school graduation with 16 units required. Interview encouraged. SAT and 3 ACH required. $25 application fee. Application deadline February 1. $100 deposit required on acceptance of offer of admission. *Early Decision* and *Early Admission* programs. Admission deferral possible. A few transfers accepted. Credit possible for CEEB AP exams; college has own advanced placement program.
Student Life Student government. Newspaper, literary review. Music, drama, debate groups. Religious and special interest groups. Activities with Haverford students. Upperclass students may live off campus with permission. Single-sex dorms; coed and co-op dorms with Haverford. 96% of students live on campus. 2 years of phys ed required. Intercollegiate and intramural sports. AIAW, NCAA. Student body composition: 4.6% Asian, 3% Black, 2.1% Hispanic, 0.1% Native American, 90.2% White. 87% from out of state.

[1] BUCKNELL UNIVERSITY
Lewisburg 17837, (717) 524-1101
Director of Admissions: Richard C. Skelton

- **Undergraduates: 1,650m, 1,350w**
- **Tuition (1982/83): $7,350**
- **Room & Board: $2,000**
- **Degrees offered: BA, BS, BMus, BSBA, BSEd, BSE**
- **Mean SAT 554v, 620m**
- **Student-faculty ratio: 14 to 1**

A private university established in 1846. 300-acre rural campus in the small town of Lewisburg, 60 miles from Harrisburg and 160 miles from Philadelphia. Served by bus and air.
Academic Character MSACS and professional accreditation. 4-1-4 system, 6-week summer term. 27 majors offered for a BA degree, 8 for a BS, 7 for a BMusic, 7 for a BS Business Administration, 4 for a BS in Education, and 6 for a BS in Engineering. Self-designed majors. Distributive requirements. MA, MS granted. Independent study. Honors program. Phi Beta Kappa. Internships. Dual degree program in engineering. BS-MS programs in biology, chemistry, engineering. Exchange program with Penn State. Washington Semester. Study abroad in Europe, Japan; students may study abroad at any accredited university. Elementary, secondary, and early childhood education certification. ROTC; AFROTC at Penn State. Computer center, observatory, language lab, environmental science center, greenhouse. 450,000-volume library.
Financial CEEB CSS. University scholarships, grants, loans, payment plan; PELL, SEOG, NDSL, CWS. Application deadline January 15.
Admissions High school graduation required. Interview encouraged. Audition required for BMus candidates, recommended for BA music majors. SAT and 3 ACH required. $20 application fee. Application deadline January 1. $200 deposit required on acceptance of offer of admission. *Early Decision* and *Early Admission* programs. Admission deferral possible. Transfers accepted. Credit possible for CEEB AP and CLEP exams; university has own advanced placement program.
Student Life Student government. Newspaper, magazines, yearbook, radio station. Music, debate, dance, drama groups. Honorary, religious, service, professional, and special interest organizations. 14 fraternities with houses and 8 sororities with suites. 60% of men and 50% of women join. Freshmen must live at home or on campus. Coed and single-sex dorms, language houses. 90% of students live on campus. First-semester freshmen may not have cars on campus. Liquor prohibited on campus. 2 years of phys ed required. Several intercollegiate and intramural sports for men and women. AIAW, ECAC, MAC. Student body composition: 5% Asian, 4% Black, 1% Hispanic, 1% Native American, 89% White. 70% from out of state.

[J1] BUCKS COUNTY COMMUNITY COLLEGE
Newtown 18940

[J1] BUTLER COUNTY COMMUNITY COLLEGE
Butler 16001

[1] CABRINI COLLEGE
Radnor 19087, (215) 687-2100
Director of Admissions: Frank Willard

- **Undergraduates: 120m, 429w; 750 (including part-time)**
- **Tuition (1982/83): $3,850**
- **Room & Board: $2,650; Fees: $305-$425**
- **Degrees offered: BA, BS, BSEd**
- **Mean SAT 450v, 450m**
- **Student-faculty ratio: 18 to 1**

A public college affiliated with the Catholic Church, established in 1957 by the Missionary Sisters of the Sacred Heart. Became coed in 1970. 110-acre suburban campus in Radnor, 18 miles from Philadelphia. Served by bus and rail; airport in Philadelphia.
Academic Character MSACS accreditation. Semester system, 2 6-week summer terms. Majors offered in accounting, American studies, arts administration, biology, business administration, chemistry, community agency management, computer science, early childhood education, elementary education, English & communications, French, history, individualized studies, mathematics, philosophy, psychology, religion, social science, social work, secondary education, Spanish, and studio art. Self-designed majors. Minors offered. Distributives and 6 hours of religion required. Independent study. Honors program. Cooperative work/study, pass/fail, internships. Preprofessional programs in nursing, pharmacy, physical therapy. Exchange programs with Eastern College, Rosemont, Villanova. Study abroad. Elementary, secondary, and special education certification. Evening Programs. Children's School. Communications center. Computer center, language lab, TV studio. 69,000-volume library with microform resources.
Financial CEEB CSS. College scholarships, grants, loans, state grants, payment plans; PELL, SEOG, NDSL, FISL, GSL, CWS, college has own work program. Application deadline April 1.
Admissions High school graduation with 16 units required. GED accepted. Interview encouraged. SAT or ACT required. $20 application fee. Rolling admissions. $50 deposit required on acceptance of offer of admission. *Early Admission* Program. Admission deferral possible. Transfers accepted. Credit possible for CEEB AP, CLEP, and ACT PEP exams. College has own advanced placement program.
Student Life Student government. Newspaper, magazine, yearbook, radio station. Music, drama groups. Black Student Union. Women's groups. Council for Exceptional Children, Special Olympics. Several academic, service, and special interest groups. Single-sex dorms. No married-student housing. 68% of students live on campus. 2 hours of phys ed required. 3 intercollegiate sports for men, 5 for women; intramurals possible. NAIA, AIAW. Student body composition: 1% Asian, 7% Black, 1% Hispanic, 91% White. 32% from out of state.

[1] CALIFORNIA STATE COLLEGE
California 15419, (412) 938-4000
Dean of Admissions: Norman G. Hasbrouck

- **Enrollment: 2,384m, 2,032w**
- **Tuition (1982/83): $1,480 (in-state), $2,190 (out-of-state)**
- **Room & Board: $1,630; Fees: $172**
- **Degrees offered: BA, BS, BSEd, AS**
- **Student-faculty ratio: 14 to 1**

A public college established in 1852. 148-acre campus in small town of California, 40 miles south of Pittsburgh.
Academic Character MSACS and professional accreditation. Semester system, 2 5-week summer terms. 76 majors offered in the areas of business, humanities, arts, natural sciences, writing, technology, environment, mathematics, area studies, communication, health, and education. Distributive requirements. MA, MS, MEd granted. Independent study. Honors program. Phi Beta Kappa. Cooperative work/study, pass/fail, internships. Preprofessional programs in engineering, law. Study abroad. Elementary, secondary, special, and highway safety/driver education certification. ROTC. Computer center, language lab, elementary school. 481,000-volume library.
Financial CEEB CSS. College scholarships, grants, loans, state grants; PELL, SEOG, NDSL, GSL, CWS. Scholarship application deadline April 1.
Admissions High school graduation with 12 units required. SAT required. $15 application fee. Rolling admissions; suggest applying by March 1. $75 tuition deposit and $75 room deposit (for boarders) required on acceptance of offer of admission. *Early Decision* and *Early Admission* programs. Admission deferral possible. Transfers accepted. Credit possible for CEEB AP and CLEP exams; college has own advanced placement program. Special admissions programs for disadvantaged students.
Student Life Student government. Newspaper, magazine, yearbook. Music, debate, drama groups. Academic, honorary, religious, service, and special interest groups. 8 fraternities, 5 with houses, and 8 sororities, 5 with houses.

10% of men and 20% of women join. Single-sex dorms. 30% of students live on campus. Liquor, gambling prohibited on campus. 9 intercollegiate sports for men, 7 for women; intramurals. NAIA, NCAA, PSCC. Student body composition: 8.5% Black, 2.1% Hispanic, 0.6% Native American, 85.7% White, 3.1% Other. 6.5% from out of state.

[1] CARLOW COLLEGE

3333 Fifth Avenue, Pittsburgh 15213, (412) 578-6000
Director of Admissions & Financial Aid: John P. Hine, Jr.

- **Undergraduates: 29m, 698w; 1,013 total (including graduates)**
- **Tuition (1982/83): $4,790**
- **Room & Board: $2,520**
- **Degrees offered: BA, BS, BSN**
- **Median SAT 420v, 440m**
- **Student-faculty ratio: 14 to 1**

A private college controlled by the Sisters of Mercy, established in 1929. 13-acre urban campus in Oakland section of Pittsburgh. Served by air, bus, and rail.

Academic Character MSACS and professional accreditation. Semester system, 4-, 6-, and 8-week summer terms. Majors offered in art, art therapy, biology, business management, comprehensive social studies, English, history, liberal studies, mathematics, ministry, music, music therapy, nursing, political science, psychology, sociology/anthropology, speech pathology, theology, and speech, communication, & theatre. Self-designed and double majors. Distributives and 1 course in religious studies required. Graduate and professional degrees granted. Independent study. Honors program. Pass/fail. Internships. Preprofessional programs in business, law, medicine. Cross-registration with 9 area schools. Study abroad. Early childhood, elementary, secondary, special, art, and music education certification. AFROTC; ROTC nearby. Language lab, media center. 107,572-volume library.

Financial CEEB CSS. College scholarships, grants, loans, state grants; PELL, SEOG, NDSL, NSL, CWS.

Admissions High school graduation with 16 units required. Interview encouraged. Audition required for music majors. SAT or ACT required. Rolling admissions; suggest applying in early fall. $75 tuition deposit and $75 room deposit (for boarders) required on acceptance of offer of admission. *Early Decision* and *Early Admission* programs. Admission deferral possible. Transfers accepted. Credit possible for CEEB AP and CLEP exams. Academic Achievement Program.

Student Life Student government. Newspaper, yearbook. Music groups. United Black Students. Religious, academic, honorary, service, and special interest groups. Over 50% of students live on campus. Boarders may not have cars on campus. Liquor prohibited on campus. Intercollegiate basketball, volleyball; intramural and club sports. Pennwood West Conference. Student body composition: 0.5% Asian, 10.6% Black, 0.8% Hispanic, 0.7% Native American, 87.4% White. 8% from out of state.

[1] CARNEGIE—MELLON UNIVERSITY

5000 Forbes Avenue, Pittsburgh 15213, (412) 578-2000
Vice President for Enrollment: William F. Elliott

- **Undergraduates: 2,702m, 1,373w; 5,791 total (including graduates)**
- **Tuition (1982/83): $6,300**
- **Room & Board: $2,800; Fees: $50**
- **Degrees offered: BA, BS, BFA, BArch**
- **Mean SAT over 1200**
- **Student-faculty ratio: 9 to 1**

A private university established in 1900. 100-acre campus 4 miles from downtown Pittsburgh. Served by air, bus, and rail.

Academic Character MSACS and professional accreditation. Semester system, 6- and 8-week summer terms. 8 majors offered by the Carnegie Institute of Technology, 17 by the College of Fine Arts, 16 by the College of Humanities & Social Sciences, 21 by the Mellon College of Science, and 2 by the School of Industrial Administration. Self-designed and double majors. Distributive requirements in some colleges. MA, MFA, MS, ME, PhD granted. Independent study. Honors program. Cooperative work/study. Internships. Cross-registration with 5 Pittsburgh schools. 6-year BS-JD program with Duquesne. 5 year bachelor's-master's in social science/public policy & engineering/urban-public affairs. Washington Semester. Study abroad. Early childhood education certification at Chatham College. ROTC, AFROTC. Computer center. 604,128-volume library.

Financial CEEB CSS. University scholarships, grants, loans, state grants, music scholarships, payment plans; PELL, SEOG, NDSL, GSL, FISL, CWS, Rent-a-Tech Program. Scholarship application deadline March 1.

Admissions High school graduation with 16 units required. Interview encouraged. Audition required for music and drama; portfolio for arts; other requirements for specific programs. SAT and 3 ACH required. $25 application fee. Application deadline March 1. $200 tuition and $100 room (for boarders) deposits required on acceptance of offer of admission. *Early Decision* and *Early Admission* programs. Transfers accepted. Credit possible for CEEB AP exams. Academic preview programs for high school students. Carnegie-Mellon Action Program.

Student Life Student government. Newspaper, magazines, yearbook, radio station. Music groups. Several professional, service, and special interest groups. 12 fraternities and 5 sororities with houses. 11% of men and 6% of women join. Freshmen must live at home or on campus. Coed and single-sex dorms. No married-student housing. 80% of students live on campus. Several intercollegiate and intramural sports. NCAA, PAC. Student body composition: 1% Asian, 9% Black, 1% Hispanic, 1% Native American, 81% White, 7% Other. 62% from out of state.

[1] CEDAR CREST COLLEGE

Allentown 18104, (215) 437-4471
Director of Admissions: Dana Lim Laus

- **Undergraduates: 800w**
- **Tuition (1982/83): $5,100**
- **Room & Board: $2,340**
- **Degrees offered: BA, BS**
- **Student-faculty ratio: 13 to 1**

A private women's college affiliated with the United Church of Christ, established in 1867. 100-acre rural/suburban campus 3 miles from Allentown, 55 miles from Philadelphia. Served by air and bus.

Academic Character MSACS accreditation. Semester system, 2 5-week summer terms. Majors offered in art, biology, chemistry, communications, comparative literature, drama & speech, engineering/applied science, English, fine arts, foreign languages & literature, history, management studies, mathematics, medical technology, music, nuclear medicine technology, nursing, philosophy, politics, psychology, social work, sociology, and movement, health, & leisure services. Self-designed majors. Distributive requirements. Independent study. Pass/fail. Internships. 3-2 physical education program with Boston U. 3-2 engineering programs with Georgia Tech, Washington U. Washington, Harrisburg semesters. Study abroad. India semester. Elementary and secondary education certification. ROTC at Lehigh. Computer center. 108,000-volume library with microform resources.

Financial CEEB CSS. College scholarships, grants, loans, payment plans; PELL, SEOG, NDSL, NSL, campus employment. Scholarship application deadline February 1.

Admissions High school graduation with 15 units required. Interview encouraged; requried for nursing and nucler medicine technology. SAT or ACT required. $20 application fee. Rolling admissions; sugget applying in fall. $150 deposit required on acceptance of offer of admission. *Early Admission* Program. Admission deferral possible. Transfers accepted. Credit possible for CEEB AP and CLEP exams.

Student Life Student government. Newspaper, magazine, yearbook. Music, ballet groups. Afro-American Society. Honorary, service, and special interest groups. Students must live at home or on campus. Women's dorms. 85% of students live on campus. 6 intercollegiate sports; intramural and club sports. Student body composition: 1% Asian, 2% Black, 2% Hispanic, 0.1% Native American, 94.9% White. 55% from out of state.

[J2] CENTER FOR DEGREE STUDIES

Scranton 18515

[J1] CENTRAL PENNSYLVANIA BUSINESS SCHOOL

College Hill, Summerdale 17093, (717) 732-0702
Toll-free in-state: (800) 292-9639
Director, Admission Services: Pauline M. Wilson

- **Enrollment: 99m, 631w; 776 total (including part-time)**
- **Tuition (1983/84): $2,370**
- **Room & Board: $1,380; Fees: $80**
- **Degree offered: ASpecialized Bus**
- **Student-faculty ratio: 14 to 1**

A private junior college established in 1922. 9-acre wooded campus located in Summerdale, 5 miles from Harrisburg.

Academic Character MSACS and professional accreditation. Semester system, 15-week summer term. 2-year programs offered by the divisions of Allied Medical Health, Computer-Accounting, Court Reporting, Legal Studies, Media Studies, Management-Marketing, Office Communications, and Travel. Theatre, photography studio, store.

Financial State grants and loans, PELL, SEOG, GSL.

Admissions High school graduation required. GED accepted. $25 application fee. Rolling admissions. $100 deposit required on acceptance of offer of admission. *Early Decision* and *Early Admission* programs. Admission deferral possible. Transfers accepted. Credit possible for CEEB CLEP exams; college has own advanced placement program.

Student Life Student government. Yearbook, radio station. Music group. Religious, professional, and special interest groups. Apartment housing. 54% of students live on campus. Dress code. Class attendance required. Club and individual sports.

[1] CHATHAM COLLEGE

Woodland Road, Pittsburgh 15232, (412) 441-8200
Acting Director of Admissions: Kathy F. Williams

- **Undergraduates: 625w**
- **Tuition (1982/83): $5,425**
- **Room & Board: $2,645; Fees: $80**
- **Degrees offered: BA, BS**
- **Student-faculty ratio: 9 to 1**

A private women's college established in 1869. 55-acre wooded campus in residential section of Pittsburgh. Served by air, bus, and rail.

Academic Character MSACS and professional accreditation. 4-1-4 system. Majors offered in drama, art, music, English, modern languages, philosophy & religion, economics, history, political science, psychology, sociology-anthropology, biology, and chemistry. Courses in communication, administration & management, Black Studies, information science, and education. Independent study. Honors program. Phi Beta Kappa. Pass/fail, internships. Preprofessional programs in law, medicine, management, communication, education, health professions. Cross-registration with 11 Pittsburgh colleges and universities. Washington Semester. Study abroad. Elementary and secondary education certification. Computer center, art gallery, language labs. 120,000-volume library.

Financial CEEB CSS. College scholarships and grants, state grants; PELL, SEOG, NDSL, FISL, CWS.

Admissions High school graduation required. Interview encouraged. SAT or ACT recommended. $15 application fee. Rolling admissions. $150 deposit

required on acceptance of offer of admission. *Early Admission* Program. Admission deferral possible. Transfers accepted. Credit possible for CEEB AP exams.
Student Life Student government. Newspaper, magazine, yearbook. Music and drama groups. Academic, service, and special interest groups. Students must live at home or on campus. 5 intercollegiate sports; intramurals. Pennwood West Conference. Student body composition: 18% minority. 44% of students from out of state.

[1] CHESTNUT HILL COLLEGE
Chestnut Hill, Philadelphia 19118, (215) 248-7000
Director of Admissions: Sister Robert Archibald

- **Undergraduates: 642w**
- **Tuition (1982/83): $3,100**
- **Room & Board: $2,350**
- **Degrees offered: BA, BS**
- **Mean SAT 500v, 500m**
- **Student-faculty ratio: 10 to 1**

A private women's college controlled by the Sisters of St. Joseph, established in 1924. 45-acre suburban campus located in Chestnut Hill, outside Philadelphia. Served by bus and rail; airport in Philadelphia.
Academic Character MSACS accreditation. Semester system, 2 6-week summer terms. Majors offered in American studies, art, art history, biochemistry, biological sciences, biology, chemistry, classical civilization, early childhood/Montessori education, economics, elementary education, English, French, German, history, Latin, mathematics, music, music education, philosophy, political science, psychology, sociology, and Spanish. Self-designed majors. Comprehensive senior exams, 6 hours of theology required. Independent study. Honors program. Cooperative work/study, off-campus projects. Cross-registration with LaSalle. Medical technology program with Thomas Jefferson U. Nursing program with local hospitals. Marine ecology at St. Thomas Institute in Florida. Study abroad. Elementary and secondary education certification. Language lab, observatory. 88,000-volume library.
Financial CEEB CSS. College scholarships, grants, loans, payment plan; PELL, SEOG, NDSL, CWS. Scholarship application deadline May 1.
Admissions High school graduation with 16 units required. Interview encouraged. ACT or SAT required. $15 application fee. Rolling admissions; suggest applying by May 1. $100 deposit required on acceptance of offer of admission. *Early Decision* and *Early Admission* programs. Admission deferral possible. Transfers accepted. Credit possible for CEEB AP exams.
Student Life Student government. Newspaper, yearbook. Music groups. Professional, cultural, honorary, and special interest groups. Students must live at home or on campus. 58% of students live on campus. Liquor prohibited on campus. 2 years of phys ed required. 7 intercollegiate sports; intramurals. Student body composition: 5.3% Black, 5.8% Hispanic, 87.4% White, 1.5% Other. 27% from out of state.

[1] CHEYNEY STATE COLLEGE
Cheyney 19319, (215) 758-2000
Director of Admissions: Christopher Roulhac

- **Undergraduates: 1,264m, 1,239w**
- **Tuition (1982/83): $1,480 (in-state), $2,590 (out-of-state)**
- **Room & Board: $1,660; Fees: $160**
- **Degrees offered: BA, BS, BSEd**
- **Student-faculty ratio: 12 to 1**

A public college established in 1837. 275-acre suburban campus in Cheyney, 24 miles from Philadelphia. Served by rail; airport and bus station in Philadelphia.
Academic Character MSACS and professional accreditation. Semester system, 3- and 6-week summer terms. 25 majors offered for the BA degree, 19 for the BS, and 17 for the BSEd. MA, MS, MSEd granted. Independent study. Honors program in biological sciences. Internships, field work. Preprofessional programs in medicine, dentistry, nursing, medical technology. BA-DPM program in podiatric medicine. Cross-registration with West Chester State. Elementary and secondary education certification. ROTC at Widener. Computer center, Ethnic Study Center, Head Start Training Office. 160,000-volume library.
Financial CEEB CSS and ACT FAS. College scholarships, grants, loans, state grants, tuition waivers; PELL, SEOG, NDSL, CWS. Priority application deadline May 1.
Admissions High school graduation required. GED accepted. Interview encouraged. SAT or ACT required. $10 application fee. Rolling admissions; application deadline July 1. $35 tuition deposit and $50 room deposit required on acceptance of offer of admission. *Early Decision* Program. *Early Admission* Program for pre-med students. Admission deferral possible. Transfers accepted. Credit possible for CEEB CLEP exams. ACT 101 Program.
Student Life Student government. Newspaper, magazine, yearbook, radio station. Music, drama groups. Ethnic Cultural Society. Academic, professional, and special interest groups. 5 fraternities and 4 sororities without houses. 4% of men and 3% of women join. Housing by major. Co-op dorms. No married-student housing. 60% of students live on campus. Liquor, drugs prohibited on campus. Class attendance required for freshmen. Dress code. 2 hours of phys ed required. 6 intercollegiate sports for men, 5 for women; intramurals. AIAW, ECAC, NCAA. Student body composition: 0.3% Asian, 95.3% Black, 0.4% Hispanic, 0.8% Native American, 3.2% White. 17% from out of state.

[1] CLARION STATE COLLEGE
Clarion 16214, (814) 226-2306
Director of Admissions: John S. Shropshire

- **Enrollment: 2,300m, 2,900w**
- **Tuition (1982/83): $1,600 (in-state), $2,000 (out-of-state)**
- **Room & Board: $1,600; Fees: $120**
- **Degrees offered: BA, BS, BFA, BMus, BSBA, BSEd, BSComm, BSSp Path, AS**
- **Mean ACT 19; mean SAT 980**
- **Student-faculty ratio: 17 to 1**

A public college established in 1867. 100-acre campus located in small town of Clarion, 85 miles from Pittsburgh. Served by bus.
Academic Character MSACS and professional accreditation. Semester system, 2 5-week summer terms. 35 majors offered by the School of Arts & Sciences, 9 by the School of Business Administration, 3 by the School of Library Science, and 22 by the School of Professional Studies. Distributive requirements. Masters degrees granted. Independent study. Honors program. Limited pass/fail, cooperative work/study, internships. Preprofessional programs in dentistry, engineering, law, medicine, pharmacy, theology, veterinary medicine. 3-1 medical technology programs with 5 area hospitals. Study abroad in Europe, Mexico. Elementary, secondary, special, environmental education, and school librarian certification. ROTC. Computer center, closed circuit TV center. 425,000-volume library.
Financial CEEB CSS and ACT FAS. College scholarships, grants, loans, payment plan; PELL, SEOG, FISL, GSL, NDSL, NSL, CWS, State Employment Program. Application deadline in April.
Admissions High school graduation with 12 units recommended. GED accepted. Interview encouraged; required for nursing students. Audition required for music majors. SAT or ACT required; ACH required for foreign language majors. $10 application fee. Rolling admissions; suggest applying by October 1. $50 tuition deposit and $50 room deposit (for boarders) required on acceptance of offer of admission. *Early Admission, Early Decision, Concurrent Enrollment* programs. Admission deferral possible. Transfers accepted. Credit possible for CEEB AP and CLEP exams; college has own advanced placement program. EOP and ACT 101.
Student Life Student government. Newspaper, magazine, yearbook, TV and radio stations. Music, debate, drama groups. Black and Jewish Student Unions. Religious, honorary, professional, and special interest groups. 10 fraternities and 10 sororities. 20% of men and 25% of women join. Coed and single-sex dorms. No married-student housing. 55% of students live on campus. Liquor prohibited on campus. 2 hours of phys ed required. 8 intercollegiate sports for men, 8 for women, 3 coed; several intramural and club sports. AIAW, NAIA, NCAA. Student body composition: 1% Asian, 5% Black, 1% Hispanic, 90% White, 3% Other. 18% from out of state.

[1] COLLEGE MISERICORDIA
Dallas 18612, (717) 675-2181
Dean of Admissions: David M. Payne

- **Undergraduates: 155m, 732w; 1,233 total (including graduates)**
- **Tuition (1982/83): $3,465; $3,650 (for nursing and music)**
- **Room & Board: $2,100**
- **Degrees offered: BA, BS, BMus, BSN, BSOcc Ther, BSW, AAS**
- **Student-faculty ratio: 12 to 1**

A private college sponsored by the Religious Sisters of Mercy, established in 1924, became coed in 1970. 100-acre suburban campus in Dallas, 9 miles from Wilkes-Barre. Airport and bus station nearby.
Academic Character MSACS and professional accreditation. Semester system, 4 4-week summer terms. Majors offered in art, art education, biology, business administration, computer science, early childhood education, elementary education, English, foods & nutrition, history, information systems, mathematics, medical technology, merchandising, music, music education, music therapy, nursing, occupational therapy, psychology, radiologic technology, social work, sociology, and special education. Self-designed majors. Concentration in 9 additional areas. AAS in radiologic technology. Gerontology certificate program. Distributives and 6 hours of religion required. MSN, MHSA granted. Independent study. Honors program. Cooperative work/study, internships. 5-year bachelor's-master's programs with U of Scranton. MSW program with Marywood. Cross-registration with King's College. Consortium of Northeastern Pennsylvania Independent Colleges. Study abroad. Early childhood, elementary, secondary, special education, and school nurse certification. ROTC at U of Scranton; AFROTC at Wilkes. 67,350-volume library; access to 12 area libraries.
Financial CEEB CSS. College scholarships, grants, loans, state aid, payment plan; PELL, SEOG, NSS, NDSL, NSL, CWS. Scholarship application deadline March 1.
Admissions High school graduation with 15 units recommended. GED accepted. Interview encouraged; required for radiologic technology. Audition required for music majors. SAT or ACT required. $15 application fee. Rolling admissions; suggest applying by December 31. $100 room deposit (for boarders) required on acceptance of offer of admission. *Early Admission, Early Decision, Concurrent Enrollment* programs. Admission deferral possible. Transfers accepted. Credit possible for CEEB AP and CLEP exams.
Student Life Student government. Newspaper, magazine, yearbook. Music, dance, drama groups. Honorary, political, religious, service, academic, and special interest groups. Single-sex dorms. 53% of students live on campus. 2 semesters of phys ed required. 4 intercollegiate sports for men, 7 for women; intramurals. NPWIAA, NAIA, KAC. Student body composition: 1% Asian, 2% Black, 97% White. 30% from out of state.

[1] COMBS COLLEGE OF MUSIC
100 Pelham Road, Philadelphia 19119, (215) 951-2250
Director of Admissions: Morton Berger

- **Enrollment: 48m, 39w; 99 total (including part-time)**
- **Tuition (1982/83): $3,600**

- **Room: $1,000; Fees: $40**
- **Degrees offered: BMus, BMus Ed, BMus Therapy**
- **Mean SAT 400-499**
- **Student-faculty ratio: 8 to 1**

A private college established in 1885. Campus located in city of Philadelphia. Served by bus and rail; airport nearby.

Academic Character MSACS and professional accreditation. Semester system, 8-week summer term. Majors offered in piano, organ, voice, orchestral instruments, music theory/composition, music education, and music therapy. Courses in liberal arts and sciences. Distributive requirements. Graduate degrees granted. Internships. Conservatory department, which is non-collegiate and gives no credit, offers instruction in all instruments. Library with microform resources.

Financial College scholarships and grants, federal and state aid.

Admissions High school graduation with 16 units required. Audition required. $25 application fee. Rolling admissions. *Early Admission* and *Early Decision* programs. Transfers accepted. College has own advanced placement program.

Student Life Music fraternity. Coed dorm. Class attendance required. Student body composition: 30% minority.

[2] CURTIS INSTITUTE OF MUSIC
Rittenhouse Square, Philadelphia 19103

[J1] DELAWARE COUNTY COMMUNITY COLLEGE
Media 19063

[1] DELAWARE VALLEY COLLEGE OF SCIENCE AND AGRICULTURE
Doylestown 18901, (215) 345-1500
Director of Admissions: H. William Craver

- **Undergraduates: 940m, 454w**
- **Tuition (1982/83): $4,180**
- **Room & Board: $2,100; Fees: $215**
- **Degree offered: BS**
- **Mean SAT 418v, 466m**
- **Student-faculty ratio: 17 to 1**

A private college established in 1896, became coed in 1978. 725-acre rural campus in Doylestown, 30 miles from Philadelphia. Served by bus and rail; airport in Philadelphia.

Academic Character MSACS and professional accreditation. Semester system, 2 6-week summer terms. Majors offered in agronomy, animal husbandry, biology, business administration, chemistry, dairy husbandry, food industry, horticulture, and ornamental horticulture. Courses in 19 additional areas. Distributive requirements. 24-week work experience in major required. 850 acres of farms. Dairy processing plant, greenhouse and nursery labs, poultry diagnostic lab. 84,000-volume library.

Financial CEEB CSS. College scholarships, grants, loans, payment plan; PELL, SEOG, NDSL, FISL, CWS, college has own work program. Application deadline April 1.

Admissions High school graduation with 15 units required. GED accepted. Interview required. SAT or ACT required. $15 application fee. Rolling admissions; suggest applying early in 12th year. $100 tuition deposit and $50 room deposit (for boarders) required on acceptance of offer of admission. *Early Admission* Program. Transfers accepted. Credit possible for CEEB AP and CLEP exams.

Student Life Student government. Newspaper, magazine, yearbook, radio station. Music groups. Dairy livestock and soil judging teams. Religious, academic, professional, and special interest groups. Single-sex dorms. No married-student housing. 65% of students live on campus. Gambling, hazing prohibited. Class attendance required. 2 semesters of phys ed required. 8 intercollegiate sports for men, 4 for women, 3 coed; intramural and club sports. ECAC, NCAA, MAC. Student body composition: 2.1% Black, 0.7% Hispanic, 97.2% White. 32% from out of state.

[1] DICKINSON COLLEGE
Carlisle 17013, (717) 245-1231
Director of Admissions: J. Larry Mench

- **Undergraduates: 805m, 940w**
- **Tuition (1982/83): $6,635**
- **Room & Board: $2,360; Fees: $80**
- **Degrees offered: AB, BS**
- **Mean SAT 539v, 571m**
- **Student-faculty ratio: 12 to 1**

A private college established in 1773. 48-acre campus in small city of Carlisle, 18 miles from Harrisburg.

Academic Character MSACS accreditation. Semester system, summer terms. Majors offered in American studies, anthropology, biology, chemistry, computer science, economics, English, fine arts, French & Italian, geology, German, Greek, history, international studies, Judaic studies, Latin, mathematics, music, philosophy, physics, policy & management studies, political science, psychology, religion, Russian & Soviet area studies, sociology, Spanish, theatre & dramatic literature, and Western social & political thought. Self-designed majors. Independent study. Honors program. Phi Beta Kappa. Pass/fail. Credit by exam. Internships. Preprofessional programs in dentistry, law, medicine, optometry, osteopathy, podiatry, social work, theology. Central PA Consortium. 3-1 Asian studies program with U Penn. 3-2 engineering programs with Case Western Reserve, Rensselaer, and U Penn. Harrisburg, India, Washington, Appalachian semesters. Several programs for study abroad. ROTC. Plantarium, observatory. 3,800-acre wildlife sanctuary. Language lab. 328,303-volume library.

Financial CEEB CSS. College scholarships, grants, loans, state aid, payment plans; PELL, SEOG, NDSL, GSL, PLUS, CWS. Application deadline February 15.

Admissions High school graduation with 16 units required. SAT or ACT required; ACH recommended. $20 application fee. Preferred application deadline March 1. $200 deposit required on acceptance of offer of admission. *Early Decision* and *Early Admission* programs. Admission deferral possible. Transfers accepted. Credit possible for CEEB AP exams.

Student Life Student government. Newspaper, magazine, yearbook, radio station. Music, debate, literary, drama groups. Afro-American Society. Service, professional, academic, honorary, and special interest groups. 10 fraternities with houses and 4 sororities without houses. 50% of men and 45% of women join. Freshmen must live at home or on campus. Coed and single-sex dorms; language and special interest houses. No married-student housing. 3 units of phys ed required. 10 intercollegiate sports for men, 8 for women; intramural and club sports. AIAW, ECAC, NCAA, MACAC. Student body composition: 1% Asian, 1% Black, 1% Hispanic, 96% White, 1% Other. 53% from out of state.

[P] DICKINSON SCHOOL OF LAW
Carlisle 17013

[1] DREXEL UNIVERSITY
Philadelphia 19104, (215) 895-2400
Director of Admissions: John R. McCullough

- **Undergraduates: 5,095m, 2,156w; 11,953 total (including graduates)**
- **Tuition (1982/83): $4,402**
- **Room & Board: $2,435-$2,735; Fees: $318**
- **Degrees offered: BS, BSBA, BSE**
- **Median SAT 500v, 580m**
- **Student-faculty ratio: 20 to 1**

A private university established in 1891. 40-acre urban campus in University City, west of Philadelphia. Served by air, bus, and rail.

Academic Character MSACS and professional accreditation. Trimester system, 11-week summer term. 10 majors offered by the College of Business & Administration, 6 by the College of Engineering, 17 by the Nesbitt College of Design, Nutrition, Human Behavior, Home Economics, 3 by the College of Humanities & Social Sciences, and 7 by the College of Science. Distributive requirements. MS, MBA, PhD granted. Independent study in some departments. Honors programs. Extensive cooperative work/study program. Elementary education certification. ROTC; AFROTC, NROTC nearby. Evening College. Computer center, audio-visual center, TV studio. 409,000-volume library.

Financial CEEB CSS. University scholarships and loans, payment plan; PELL, SEOG, NDSL, FISL, GSL, CWS. Application deadlines March 1 (scholarships), April 1 (loans).

Admissions High school graduation with 16 units recommended. Interview encouraged. SAT or ACT required; 3 ACH required by some colleges. $10 application fee. Rolling admissions; application deadline April 1. $50 tuition deposit and $50 room deposit (for boarders) required on acceptance of offer of admission. *Early Admission* Program. Transfers accepted. Credit possible for CEEP AP and CLEP exams; university has own advanced placement program.

Student Life Student government. Newspaper, magazine, yearbook, radio station. Music, drama groups. Over 50 honorary and professional societies; religious, service, and special interest clubs. 12 fraternities with houses and 4 sororities with apartments. 20% of men and 25% of women join. Freshmen must live at home or on campus. No married-student housing. 45% of students live on campus. 2 quarters of phys ed required. Several intercollegiate and intramural sports for men and women. AIAW, NCAA, ECAA, MASCAA. Student body composition: 13% minority. 31% from out of state.

[G1] DROPSIE UNIVERSITY
Philadelphia 19132

[1] DUQUESNE UNIVERSITY
Pittsburgh 15282, (412) 434-6220
Director of Admissions: Frederick H. Lorensen

- **Undergraduates: 2,101m, 2,475w; 6,703 total (including graduates)**
- **Tuition (1982/83): $4,500**
- **Room & Board: $2,247; Fees: $330**
- **Degrees offered: BA, BS, BMus, BSBA, BSEd, BSN**
- **Mean SAT 450v, 550m**
- **Student-faculty ratio: 15 to 1**

A private, Roman Catholic university operated by the Holy Ghost Fathers, established in 1878. 38-acre urban campus overlooking downtown Pittsburgh. Served by air, rail, and bus.

Academic Character MSACS and professional accreditation. Semester system, summer terms. 40 majors offered by the College of Liberal Arts & Sciences, 7 by the School of Business Adminstration, 4 by the School of Education, 5 by the School of Music, and 3 by the School of Pharmacy. Minor required in most fields. Distributives and 3 religion/philosophy credits required. Graduate and professional degrees granted. Independent study. Honors program. Cooperative work/study, pass/fail, internships. Preprofessional programs in dentistry, engineering, law, medicine, speech pathology/audiology, theology, veterinary medicine. 3-2 engineering program with Case Western Reserve. Cross-registration with 9 Pittsburgh institutions. Study abroad. Elementary, secondary, special, and music education certification. ROTC; AFROTC at U of Pittsburgh. Language labs. 402,000-volume library.

Financial CEEB CSS. University scholarships, grants, loans, PELL, SEOG, NSS, NDSL, GSL, NSL, HPL, CWS. Application deadline May 1.
Admissions High school graduation with 16 units required. Interview encouraged. Audition and music theory test required by School of Music. SAT or ACT required. $20 application fee. Rolling admissions; application deadline July 1. Deposit required by May 1. *Early Decision* and *Early Admission* programs. Admission deferral possible. Transfers accepted. Credit possible for CEEB AP and CLEP exams.
Student Life Student government. Newspaper, magazine, yearbook, radio station, TV studio. Music, dance, drama, debate groups. Professional, honorary, service, religious, and academic organizations. 19 fraternities and 12 sororities without houses. 15% of men and women join. Freshmen and sophomores must live at home or on campus. Coed and single-sex dorms; special interest housing. 55% of students live on campus. 8 intercollegiate sports for men, 5 for women; intramurals. AIAW, NCAA, EAA. Student body composition: 10% minority. 20% from out of state.

[1] EAST STROUDSBURG STATE COLLEGE
East Stroudsburg 18301, (717) 424-3542
Director of Admissions: Alan T. Chesterton

- **Undergraduates: 1,600m, 2,000w; 3,900 total (including graduates)**
- **Tuition (1982/83): $1,600 (in-state), $2,590 (out-of-state)**
- **Room & Board: $1,674; Fees: $120**
- **Degrees offered: BA, BSEd, BSN, AS**
- **Student-faculty ratio: 17 to 1**

A public college established in 1893. 140-acre campus in a small city 75 miles from New York City. Served by bus; airport in Allentown, rail station in Bethlehem.
Academic Character MSACS and professional accreditation. Semester system, 3 summer terms. 13 majors offered by the School of Art & Sciences, 19 by the School of Professional Studies, 5 by the School of Health Sciences & Physical Education, 14 by the Faculty of Science, and 6 by the Faculty of Social Sciences. Distributive requirements. MA, MS, MEd granted. AS in media. 3-2 engineering program with Penn State. 5-year pharmacy program with Temple. 5-year master's program in clinical chemistry. 7-year doctoral program in podiatric medicine with Penn. College of Podiatric Medicine. Member Marine Science Consortium. Elementary, secondary, special, and physical education certification. ROTC; AFROTC at Lehigh. Computer center, TV studios. 300,032-volume library with microform resources.
Financial CEEB CSS. College scholarships, grants, loans; PELL, SEOG, NSS, NDSL, NSL, CWS. Application deadline March 31.
Admissions High school graduation required. Interview encouraged. SAT or ACT required. $10 application fee. Rolling admissions; suggest applying by January 1 (February 1 for health professions majors). $100 deposit required on acceptance of offer of admission. Transfers accepted. Credit possible for CEEB AP and CLEP exams.
Student Life Student government. Newspaper, magazine, yearbook, radio station. Music, debate, drama groups. Black Student Movement. Service, honorary, political, academic, and special interest groups. 5 fraternities, 3 with houses, and 4 sororities without houses. Freshmen must live at home or on campus. Coed and single-sex dorms. No married-student housing. 50% of students live on campus. Freshmen and sophomores may not have cars on campus. Liquor prohibited on campus. 3 hours of phys ed required. 13 intercollegiate sports for men, 10 for women, 1 coed; intramurals. AIAW, NCAA. Student body composition: 2% Asian, 10% Black, 5% Hispanic, 83% White. 25% from out of state.

[G1] EASTERN BAPTIST THEOLOGICAL SEMINARY
Overbrook, City Line, and Lancaster Avenue, Philadelphia 19151

[1] EASTERN COLLEGE
St. Davids 19087, (215) 688-3300
Dean of Admissions: William A. Zulker

- **Enrollment: 199m, 383w; 723 total (including part-time)**
- **Tuition (1982/83): $4,470**
- **Room & Board: $1,880; Fees: $330**
- **Degrees offered: BA, BS, BSW**
- **Mean SAT 440v, 440m**
- **Student-faculty ratio: 14 to 1**

A private college affiliated with the American Baptist Convention, established in 1932, became coed in 1951. 92-acre suburban campus at edge of town of Wayne, 30 minutes from Philadelphia. Served by rail.
Academic Character MSACS accreditation. 4-1-4 system, 2 4½-week summer terms. Majors offered in accounting, American studies, biology, business administration, chemistry, economics, elementary education, English (4 areas), French, health, history, math, math/computer science, medical technology, philosophy, psychology, religion, school nursing, social work, sociology, Spanish, and youth ministries. Self-designed majors. Minors offered in most major fields and in 11 additional areas. Distributives and 9 hours of religion required. MBA granted. World Language and Bilingual Business programs. Pass/fail. Preprofessional programs in dentistry, law, medicine, nursing. Research program at Argonne National Laboratory. Study abroad. Elementary and secondary education certification. Planetarium, computer centers. 80,000-volume library with microform resources.
Financial CEEB CSS. College scholarships and grants, athletic grants, family grants, state and out-of-state grants; PELL, SEOG, NDSL, GSL, PLUS, CWS; college has own work program. Suggest applying soon after January 1.
Admissions High school graduation with 15 units required. Interview encouraged. ACT or SAT required. $10 application fee. Rolling admissions; suggest applying at end of junior year. *Early Admission* and *Early Decision* programs. Transfers accepted. Credit possible for CEEB AP and CLEP exams. CCAS program.
Student Life Student government. Newspaper, magazine, yearbook. Music and drama groups. Black Student League, International Students. Honorary, academic, professional, religious, service, and special interest groups. 4 fraternities and 3 sororities. Coed and single-sex dorms. Liquor prohibited on campus. 5 intercollegiate sports for men, 5 for women; intramurals. NAIA, NCCAA. Student body composition: 19% minority.

[1] EDINBORO STATE COLLEGE
Edinboro 16444, (814) 732-2000
Dean of Admissions: Harold Umbarger

- **Undergraduates: 1,951m, 2,467w; 5,848 total (including graduates)**
- **Tuition (1982/83): $1,250 (in-state), $2,190 (out-of-state)**
- **Room & Board: $1,460; Fees: $150**
- **Degrees offered: BA, BS, BFA, BSEd, BSArt Ed, AA, AS**
- **Median SAT 416v, 429m**
- **Student-faculty ratio: 17 to 1**

A public college established in 1857. 585-acre campus located in small town of Edinboro, 18 miles from Erie. Served by air, bus, and rail.
Academic Character MSACS and professional accreditation. Semester system, 6-week and 2 3-week summer terms. 79 majors offered by the schools of Arts & Humanities, Behavioral & Social Sciences, Education, Nursing, and Science & Mathematics. Self-designed majors. AA, AS in general business administration, secretarial science, pre-school education, human services, computer technology, criminal justice, medical lab technology. Distributive requirements. Masters degrees granted. Independent study. Honors program. Limited pass/fail, internships. Preprofessional programs in gerontology, journalism, law, medicine, pharmacy, dentistry, and engineering. 3-2 engineering program with Penn State. Wildlife biology program with Penn State. Criminal justice consortium with Mercyhurst. Marine Science consortium. Elementary, secondary, and special education certification. ROTC. Computer center. 337,000-volume library with microform resources.
Financial College scholarships and loans, payment plan; PELL, SEOG, NDSL, FISL, CWS. Recommended application deadline March 15.
Admissions High school graduation required. SAT or ACT required. $10 application fee. Rolling admissions. $100 deposit required on acceptance of offer of admission. *Early Admission* and *Early Decision* programs. Admission deferral possible. Transfers accepted. Credit possible for CEEB AP and CLEP exams; college has own advanced placement program. Pre-college summer program for "high risk" students.
Student Life Student government. Newspaper, yearbook. Music groups. Association of Black Collegians. Campus Feminist Club. Professional, religious, honorary, and special interest organizations. 21 fraternities and sororities. Single-sex dorms. Some special interest housing. 42% of students live on campus. 3 hours of phys ed required. 11 intercollegiate sports for men, 6 for women. AIAW, ECAC, NCAA. Student body composition: 0.5% Asian, 3.8% Black, 0.2% Hispanic, 0.5% Native American, 94.2% White, 0.8% Other. 9% from out of state.

■[J1] WARREN CENTER
Warren 16365

[1] ELIZABETHTOWN COLLEGE
Elizabethtown 17022, (717) 367-1151, ext. 166
Director of Admissions: Sandra L. Zerby

- **Undergraduates: 571m, 844w**
- **Tuition (1982/83): $4,740**
- **Room & Board: $2,300; Fees: $135**
- **Degrees offered: BA, BS, AS**
- **Mean SAT 436v, 480m**
- **Student-faculty ratio: 14 to 1**

A private college affiliated with the Church of Brethren, established in 1899. 110-acre campus in Elizabethtown, 100 miles from Philadelphia, Washington, and Baltimore. Served by rail; airport 8 miles away in Middletown.
Academic Character MSACS and professional accreditation. Semester system, 2 5-week summer terms. 37 majors offered in the areas of communication, business, languages, history, music, political & social sciences, religion/philosophy, natural sciences, computer science, and education. Self-designed majors. Distributives and 6 hours of religion or philosophy required. Independent study. Limited pass/fail. Cooperative work/study, credit by exam, internships. Preprofessional programs in dentistry, law, medicine, ministry, osteopathy, pharmacy, veterinary medicine. 3-2 program in engineering with Penn State, in forestry and environmental management with Duke. 3-1 medical technology program. Nursing program with Georgetown. Urban Seminar. Study abroad; England semester. Early childhood, elementary, and secondary education certification. Language labs. 165,000-volume library.
Financial CEEB CSS. College scholarships, grants, loans, state grants; PELL, SEOG, NDSL, GSL, PLUS, CWS, college has own work program. Application deadlines March 1 (scholarships), April 1 (loans).
Admissions High school graduation required. GED accepted. Interview encouraged. SAT required. $15 application fee. Rolling admissions after October 1; suggest applying by February. $100 deposit required on acceptance of offer of admission. *Early Decision* and *Early Admission* programs. Admission deferral possible. Transfers accepted. Credit possible for CEEB AP and CLEP exams; college has own advanced placement program. Developmental Studies Program.
Student Life Student government. Newspaper, magazine, yearbook, radio station. Music, drama groups. Men's and women's affairs committees. Race relations committee. Academic, religious, honorary, service, and special interest groups. Students must live at home or on campus. Dorms for men and

women. Co-op and honors housing. No married-student housing. 85% of students live on campus. 4 semester hours of phys ed required. 7 intercollegiate sports for men, 7 for women; intramurals. AIAW, ECAC, NCAA, MAC. Student body composition: 1.5% Asian, 1.5% Black, 1% Hispanic, 96% White. 35% from out of state.

[1] FRANKLIN AND MARSHALL COLLEGE

Lancaster 17604, (717) 291-3951
Director of Admissions: Ronald D. Potier

- **Undergraduates: 1,129m, 928w**
- **Tuition (1982/83): $6,550**
- **Room & Board: $2,350**
- **Degree offered: BA**
- **Mean SAT 1200**
- **Student-faculty ratio: 16 to 1**

A private college established in 1787, became coed in 1969. 102-acre campus in a residential section of Lancaster, 60 miles from Philadelphia. Served by air, bus, and rail.

Academic Character MSACS accreditation. Semester system, 10-week summer term. Majors offered in American studies, anthropology, art, biology, business administration, chemistry, classics, drama, economics, English, European studies, French, geology, German, government, history, mathematics, philosophy, physics, psychology, religious studies, sociology, and Spanish. Self-designed majors. Distributive requirements. Independent study. Honors program. Phi Beta Kappa. Pass/fail. Internships. Credit by exam. Member Central Penn. Consortium. 3-2 engineering programs with Case Western, Columbia, Georgia Tech, Rensselaer. 3-2 forestry program with Duke. Washington, Harrisburg semesters. Archaeological field work. Study abroad. Secondary education certification. ROTC at Millersville State. Psychology lab, language lab, museum, observatory/planetarium, computer center. 188,000-volume library.

Financial CEEB CSS. College scholarships, grants, loans; PELL, SEOG, CWS. FAF deadline March 1.

Admissions High school graduation with 16 units recommended. Interview encouraged. SAT or ACT required; SAT preferred. English composition ACH required. $25 application fee. Application deadline February 10. $200 tuition deposit required on acceptance of offer of admission. *Early Decision* and *Early Admission* programs. Admission deferral possible. Transfers accepted. Credit possible for CEEB AP and CLEP exams. College has own advanced placement program.

Student Life Student-faculty government. Newspaper, magazine, yearbook, radio stations. Music, literary, film, drama groups. Black Student Union. Honorary, academic, political, and special interest organizations. 10 fraternities with houses and 2 sororities. 35% of men and 1% of women join. Freshmen must live at home or on campus. Coed dorms, language houses. 72% of students live on campus. Students receiving financial aid may not have cars on campus. 12 intercollegiate sports for men, 11 for women; intramural and club sports. AIAW, EIWA, NCAA, MAC. Student body composition: 1% Asian, 4% Black, 1% Hispanic, 92% White, 2% Other. 68% from out of state.

[1] GANNON UNIVERSITY

Perry Square, Erie 16541, (814) 871-7000
Director of Admissions: Richard E. Sukitsch

- **Undergraduates: 1,400m, 1,200w; 4,000 total (including graduates)**
- **Tuition (1982/83): $3,400**
- **Room & Board: $1,750**
- **Degrees offered: BA, BS, BEEng, BMEng, BSIM, AS, AA**
- **Mean ACT 19.2; mean SAT 900**
- **Student-faculty ratio: 17 to 1**

A private Roman Catholic university controlled by the Diocese of Erie, established in 1944, became coed in 1964. One-acre urban campus in downtown Erie. Served by air, rail, and bus.

Academic Character MSACS and professional accrediation. Semester system, May intersession, 2 5-week summer terms. 7 majors offered by the College of Business Administration, 22 by the College of Humanities, and 14 by the College of Science & Engineering. Some majors in cooperation with Mercyhurst and/or Villa Maria Colleges. 6 semesters of theology required. Pass/fail. Internships in business. Preprofessional programs in dentistry, law, medicine, optometry, osteopathy, pharmacy, podiatry, ministry. 5-year bachelor's-master's program. 7-year MD program. Seminary program with St. Mark's of Erie, PA. Study abroad. Elementary, secondary, and special education certification. ROTC. Language lab. 360,000-volume library with microform resources.

Financial CEEB CSS and ACT FAS. University scholarships and loans, payment plan; PELL, SEOG, NDSL, FISL, CWS. Suggested scholarship application deadline March 1.

Admissions High school graduation with 16 units required. SAT or ACT required. $15 application fee. Rolling admissions; suggest applying between September and April. $100 deposit required on acceptance of offer of admission. *Early Admission* and *Early Decision* programs. Transfers accepted. Credit possible for CEEB AP and CLEP exams. EOP.

Student Life Student government. Newspaper, yearbook, radio station. Music, debate, drama groups. Model UN. International Relations Club. Academic, honorary, professional, religious, service, and special interest groups. 7 fraternities with houses and 2 sororities. 15% of men join fraternities. Single freshmen and sophomores must live at home or on campus. 2 dorms, 4 university-owned apartments. Dining hall. 40% of students live on campus. Liquor prohibited. Limited class absences allowed. 9 intercollegiate sports; intramurals. AIAW, NCAA. Student body composition: 6% Black, 3% Hispanic, 1% Native American, 85% White, 5% Other. 15% from out of state.

[1] GENEVA COLLEGE

Beaver Falls 15010, (412) 846-5100
Director of Admissions: Paul E. Sutcliffe

- **Undergraduates: 649m, 500w**
- **Tuition (1982/83): $4,000**
- **Room & Board: $2,175; Fees: $220**
- **Degrees offered: BA, BS, BSEd, BSBA, BSCE, BSEE, BSIE, BSME**
- **Mean SAT 440v, 470m**
- **Student-faculty ratio: 17 to 1**

A private college affiliated with the Reformed Presbyterian Church, established in 1848. 52-acre campus in a small city 30 miles from Pittsburgh. Served by bus and rail. Pittsburgh airport 25 miles away.

Academic Character MSACS accreditation. Semester system, 2 5-week summer terms. 32 majors offered in the areas of business, science, engineering, education, communications, counseling, liberal arts, music, and social sciences. Minors offered in 9 additional areas. 9 hours of Bible required. Independent study. Honors program. Limited pass/fail. Preprofessional programs in medical science and ministerial studies. Affiliate degree programs in life support technology, medical technology, nursing. Study abroad in Spain. Elementary and secondary education certification. Language lab. 125,000-volume library with microform resources.

Financial CEEB CSS. College scholarships, grants, loans, church grants, clergy grants, payment plan; PELL, SEOG, NDSL, CWS. Application deadline March 15.

Admissions High school graduation with 16 units required. Interview encouraged. SAT or ACT required. $10 application fee. Rolling admissions; suggest applying between October and April. $25 tuition deposit and $75 room deposit (for boarders) required on acceptance of offer of admission. *Early Admission* and *Early Decision* programs. Admission deferral possible. Transfers accepted. Credit possible for CEEB AP and CLEP exams.

Student Life Student government. Newspaper, magazine, quarterly, yearbook, radio station. Music, debate, drama groups. Service, religious, academic, and special interest groups. Students must live at home or on campus. Single-sex dorms. 80% of students live on campus. Liquor, tobacco, drugs, profanity, gambling, social dancing prohibited on campus. Attendance at weekly chapel, monthly convocation required. 2 semesters of phys ed required. 7 intercollegiate sports for men, 4 for women; intramurals. AIAW, NCAA. Student body composition: 5% Black, 1% Hispanic, 94% White. 35% from out of state.

[1] GETTYSBURG COLLEGE

Gettysburg 17325, (717) 334-3131
Director of Admissions: Delwin K. Gustafson

- **Undergraduates: 927m, 957w**
- **Tuition (1982/83): $6,000**
- **Room & Board: $2,160**
- **Degrees offered: BA, BSMus Ed**
- **Mean SAT 540v, 575m**
- **Student-faculty ratio: 14 to 1**

A private college affiliated with the Lutheran Church in America, established in 1832. 200-acre campus in Gettysburg, 36 miles from Harrisburg. Served by bus. Harrisburg airport 45 miles away.

Academic Character MSACS accreditation. 4-1-4 system, summer term. Majors offered in art, biology, business administration, chemistry, classical studies, economics, English, French, German, Greek, health & physical education, history, Latin, mathematics, music, philosophy, physics, political science, psychology, religion, sociology & anthropology, Spanish, and theatre arts. Self-designed majors. Distributives and one religion course required. Independent study. Honors program. Phi Beta Kappa. Pass/fail. Member Central Penn. Consortium. Asian studies program in cooperation with U Penn. 5-year forestry program with Duke, 5-year engineering programs with Penn State, RPI, Washington U. CPA program. Washington, Colombia, India, UN, Harrisburg semesters. Study abroad. Elementary and secondary education certification. ROTC. Computer center, planetarium/observatory, language lab, electron microscopy lab. 250,000-volume library.

Financial CEEB CSS. College scholarships, grants, loans; PELL, SEOG, NDSL, CWS. FAF deadline February 1.

Admissions High school graduation required. Interview encouraged; required for music, art, physical education majors. SAT or ACT required; SAT preferred. $20 application fee. Application deadline February 15. $200 deposit required by May 1. *Early Decision* and *Early Admission* programs. Admission deferral possible. Transfers accepted. Credit possible for CEEB AP exams.

Student Life Student government. Newspaper, magazine, yearbook, radio station. Music, dance, drama groups. Service, political, academic, religious, and special interest groups. 11 fraternities with houses, and 7 sororities without houses. 75% of men and 50% of women join. Freshmen must live on campus. Coed and single-sex dorms, special interest houses. 85% of students live on campus. Quiet hours, parietals enforced. Liquor restricted. 2 years of phys ed required. 8 intercollegiate sports for men, 7 for women; intramurals. ECAC, NCAA, MASC. Student body composition: 0.5% Black, 0.5% Hispanic, 99% White. 70% from out of state.

[1] GRATZ COLLEGE

10th Street and Tabor Road, Philadelphia 19141

[1] GROVE CITY COLLEGE

Grove City 16127, (412) 458-6600
Director of Admissions: John H. Moser

- **Undergraduates: 1,171m, 1,085w**
- **Tuition (1982/83): $2,620 (for AB degree), $2,770 (for BS and BMus)**
- **Room & Board: $1,650**

- **Degrees offered: AB, BS, BMus**
- **Median SAT 492v, 553m**
- **Student-faculty ratio: 20 to 1**

A private college affiliated with the United Presbyterian Church, established in 1876. 150-acre rural campus in a small city 60 miles from Pittsburgh. Served by bus. Airport and rail station in Pittsburgh.

Academic Character MSACS accreditation. Semester system. Majors offered in accounting, biology, business administration, business education, Christian ministries, chemistry, communication arts, computer systems, economics, elementary education, French, German, history, international business, literature, mathematics, music, music education, philosophy, political science, psychology, religion, social work, sociology, and chemical, electrical, management, mechanical, metallurgical engineering, and engineering physics. Self-designed majors. Distributive requirements. Independent study. Honors program. Internships. Preprofessional programs in business, dentistry, law, medicine, ministry. Preprofessional Option Plan: students receive bachelor's degree after 1st year in professional school. Study abroad. Provisional elementary and secondary education certification. AFROTC. Computer center, language lab. 142,750-volume library.

Financial CEEB CSS. College scholarships, grants, loans; payment plan. Application deadlines March 15 (scholarships), April 15 (loans).

Admissions High school graduation with 13 units required. Interview encouraged. SAT or ACT required. $15 application fee. Rolling admissions; application deadline March 31. $100 deposit required on acceptance of offer of admission. *Early Decision* Program. Admission deferral possible. Transfers accepted. Credit possible for CEEB AP and CLEP exams; college has own advanced placement program.

Student Life Student government. Newspaper, yearbook, journals, radio station. Music, drama groups. Academic, honorary, religious, and special interest groups. 11 fraternities and 9 sororities without houses. 45% of men and 50% of women join. Students must live at home or on campus. Single-sex dorms. No married-student housing. 96% of students live on campus. Freshmen may not have cars on campus. Liquor, drugs, gambling, dishonesty, harmful conduct prohibited. Some departments have dress code. Class, lab, and weekly convocation attendance required. 2 hours of phys ed required. 9 intercollegiate sports for men, 4 for women; intramurals. AIAW, NCAA. Student body composition: 0.5% Asian, 1% Black, 97.5% White, 1% Other. 26% from out of state.

[1] GWYNEDD—MERCY COLLEGE

Gwynedd Valley 19437, (215) 641-5510
Director of Admissions: Sister Helen Cahill

- **Undergraduates: 358m, 1,702w; 2,200 total (including graduates)**
- **Tuition (1982/83): $3,450; $3,800 (for nursing)**
- **Room & Board: $2,300; Fees: $15-$45**
- **Degrees offered: BA, BS, AS**
- **Mean ACT 21; mean SAT 450v, 461m**
- **Student-faculty ratio: 11 to 1**

A private Roman Catholic college affiliated with the Congregation of the Religious Sisters of Mercy, established in 1948, became coed in 1973. 300-acre suburban campus in Gwynedd Valley, 20 miles from Philadelphia. Served by rail. Airport in Philadelphia.

Academic Character MSACS and professional accreditation. Semester system, 2 5-week summer terms. Majors offered in biology, English, French, history, mathematics, psychology, sociology, behavioral & social gerontology, accounting, busines administration, business education, computer-based business systems, elementary education, legal secretarial, medical technology, nursing, special education, clinical lab science (chemistry, hematology, microbiology), and in teacher education for allied health professionals, management for allied health professionals. Double majors. AS in business and health care areas. Distributives and 6 semester hours of religious studies required. MSN granted. Independent study. Honors program. Pass/fail. Computer systems internships. Certificate programs in gerontology, nurse practitioner (BSN required). Masters in education program with Chesnut Hill College. Early childhood, elementary, and secondary education certification. 70,000-volume library and access to Tri-State College Library Cooperative.

Financial CEEB CSS. College scholarships, grants, loans, Catholic grants, state aid, payment plans; PELL, SEOG, NDSL, FISL, GSL, NSL, CWS. Application deadline March 1.

Admissions High school graduation with 16 units required. Interview encouraged. SAT or ACT required; 3 ACH recommended. $20 application fee. Rolling admissions; suggest applying in fall. $100 tuition deposit and $50 refundable room deposit (for boarders) required on acceptance of offer of admission. *Early Admission* and *Early Decision* programs. Admission deferral possible. Transfers accepted. Credit possible for CEEB AP and CLEP exams; college has own advanced placement program.

Student Life Student government. Newspaper, magazine, journal, yearbook. Music and drama groups. Academic, honorary, religious, service, and special interest groups. Single-sex dorms. No married-student housing. About 10% of students live on campus. 2 semesters of phys ed required. 6 intercollegiate sports; intramurals. AIAW. Student body composition: 3% Asian, 2% Black, 3% Hispanic, 1% Native American, 91% White. 20% from out of state.

[1 & G1] HAHNEMANN COLLEGE OF ALLIED HEALTH PROFESSIONS

230 North Broad Street, Philadelphia 19102, (215) 448-8288
Director of Admissions: Arlene Willis Carpel

- **Undergraduates: 109m, 559w**
- **Tuition, Room, & Fees (1982/83): $12,320**
- **Degrees offered: BS, AS**
- **Student-faculty ratio: 2 to 1**

A private college established in 1968. Urban campus in downtown Philadelphia. Served by bus and rail; airport nearby.

Academic Character MSACS and professional accreditation. Trimester system, 12-week summer term. Majors offered in medical technology, mental health technology, nursing, physician assistant, and respiratory therapy. Associate degree program required for high school graduates before beginning BS program. AS programs in general studies, medical laboratory technology, mental health, nursing, physician assistance, radiologic technology, and respiratory therapy. Cooperative work/study, internships (required), pass/fail. Certification in child psychiatry (for RNs), nuclear medicine technology, radiologic technology, radiation therapy. 66,000-volume library and access to several area libraries.

Financial CEEB CSS. College scholarships, grants, loans, state grants; PELL, SEOG, GSL, NDSL, NSL, CWS. Application deadlines April 1 (scholarships), June 15 (loans).

Admissions High school graduation with 16 units required. GED accepted. Interview required. SAT or ACT required. $15 application fee. Rolling admissions. $100 deposit required on acceptance of offer of admission. Transfers accepted for fall term. Credit possible for CEEB AP and CLEP exams. Academic Re-enforcement Program.

Student Life Student Affairs Committee. Newspaper, yearbook. Music organization. Special interest groups. High-rise apartments on campus. Married-student housing. Cafeteria service; no meal plan. 8 intercollegiate sports. Student body composition: 0.8% Asian, 20.1% Black, 0.4% Hispanic, 77.4% White. 22% from out of state.

[J1] HARCUM JUNIOR COLLEGE

Bryn Mawr 19010, (215) 525-4100
Toll-free out-of-state: (800) 345-2600
Director of Admissions: Helen R. Gallagher

- **Enrollment: 7m, 843w**
- **Tuition (1968/83): $3,100**
- **Room & Board: $2,200**
- **Degrees offered: AA, AS**
- **Student-faculty ratio: 18 to 1**

A private women's junior college established in 1915. 15-acre suburban campus in Bryn Mawr, 11 miles from Philadelphia. Served by rail; airport in Philadelphia.

Academic Character MSACS accreditation. Semester system. Programs offered in allied health sciences, animal center management, animal health technician, art, business administration, child study, computer science technology, dental assistant/expanded functions, special education, fashion design, general studies, illustration & graphic design, interior design, laboratory animal science, liberal arts, medical assistant, medical lab technician, optometric technician, performing arts, physical therapy assistant, public relations, recreational leadership, retail merchandising, secretarial studies, tourism/travel, word processing, and equine studies. Distributive requirements. Independent study. Cooperative work/study. Hospital Cooperative Program. 31,000-volume library.

Financial CEEB CSS. College scholarships and grants, state grants; PELL, SEOG, NDSL, GSL, CWS. Application deadline April 15.

Admissions High school graduation required. Interview encouraged. SAT required. $10 application fee. Rolling admissions. *Early Admission* Program. Transfers accepted. Credit possible for CEEB AP and CLEP exams.

Student Life Student government. Newspaper, magazine, yearbook. Drama, music, dance groups. Organization of Black Students. Religious, honorary, and special interest groups. Students must live with relatives or on campus. 61% of students live on campus. 4 semesters of phys ed required. Intercollegiate volleyball; intramurals. Student body composition: 12% minority. 23% from out of state.

[J1] HARRISBURG AREA COMMUNITY COLLEGE

3300 Cameron Street Road, Harrisburg 17110

[1] HAVERFORD COLLEGE

Haverford 19041, (215) 896-1000
Director of Admissions: William W. Ambler

- **Undergraduates: 752m, 283w**
- **Tuition (1982/83): $8,000**
- **Room & Board: $2,820; Fees: $80**
- **Degrees offered: BA, BS**
- **Student-faculty ratio: 12 to 1**

A private college established in 1833, became coed in 1977. 226-acre suburban campus in village of Haverford, 15 minutes from Philadelphia by train.

Academic Character MSACS accreditation. Semester system. Majors offered in astronomy, biology, chemistry, classics, economics, English, fine arts, French, German, history, mathematics, music, philosophy, physics, political science, psychology, religion, Russian, sociology & anthropology, and Spanish. Self-designed and double majors. 5 additional majors offered at Bryn Mawr. Distributive requirements. Independent study. Phi Beta Kappa. 4-year bachelor's-master's programs. 3-2 engineering with U Penn. Cross-registration with Bryn Mawr, Swarthmore, U Penn. Off-campus study in the U.S. and abroad. Computer center, observatory, art gallery, language lab. 425,000-volume library with microform resources, interlibrary loan facilities.

Financial CEEB CSS. College scholarships, grants, loans, payment plan; PELL, SEOG, NDSL, CWS. Application deadlines January 31 (scholarships), January 15 (loans).

Admissions High school graduation with 12 units required. Interview advised. SAT and 3 ACH required. $25 application fee. Application deadline January 31. *Early Decision* and *Early Admission* programs. Admission deferral possible. Transfers accepted. Credit possible for CEEB AP exams.
Student Life Student government. All activities are with Bryn Mawr. Newspaper, magazine, yearbook, radio station. Music, drama, debate groups. Academic, honorary, service, and special interest organizations. Students must live at home or on campus. Dorm exchange with Bryn Mawr. Coed dorms, single-sex floors, campus apartments. Language houses at Bryn Mawr. 95% of students live on campus. Gambling prohibited. Honor code. 6 quarters of phys ed required. 11 intercollegiate sports for men, 5 for women; intramural and club sports. AIAW, NCAA, MAAC. Student body composition: 9.7% minority. 80% from out of state.

[1] HOLY FAMILY COLLEGE

Frankford Avenue at Grant Avenue, Torresdale, Philadelphia 19114

[1] IMMACULATA COLLEGE

Immaculata 19345, (215) 296-9067
Director of Admissions: Sister Maria Claudia

- **Undergraduates: 800w; 1,567 total (including part-time)**
- **Tuition (1983/84): $3,250**
- **Room & Board: $2,500; Fees: $97**
- **Degrees offered: BA, BMus, BS**
- **Median SAT 440v, 450m**
- **Student-faculty ratio: 18 to 1**

A private, Roman Catholic women's college controlled by the Sisters, Servants of the Immaculate Heart of Mary, established in 1906. 373-acre suburban campus overlooking Chester Valley, 20 miles from Philadelphia.
Academic Character MSACS accreditation. Semester system, 2 6½-week summer terms. Majors offered in biology (5 areas), chemistry, education, English, history & politics, home economics, math/computer science & physics, language (4 areas), music & related arts, philosophy, physical education, psychology, sociology, theology, and economics, accounting, & business. Distributives and 9 credits in philosophy & theology required. MA in bicultural/bilingual studies granted. Independent study. Honors program. Pass/fail, internships. Credit by exam. Premedical program. Study abroad. Elementary, secondary, and early childhood education certification. 122,000-volume library with microform resources.
Financial CEEB CSS. College scholarships and grants, state grants, family plan; PELL, SEOG, NDSL, GSL, ALAS, CWS.
Admissions High school graduation with 16 units required. GED accepted. Audition required for music majors. Interview encouraged. SAT or ACT required. $20 application fee. Rolling admissions. *Early Decision* and *Early Admission* programs. Admission deferral possible. Transfers accepted. Credit possible for CEEB AP and CLEP exams.
Student Life Student government. Newspaper, magazine, yearbook. Music and drama groups. Service, international, academic, and special interest organizations. Single students must live on campus. 3 credits in phys ed required. Individual sports. Student body composition: 10% minority.

[1] INDIANA UNIVERSITY OF PENNSYLVANIA

Indiana 15705, (412) 357-2230
Dean of Admissions: Fred Dakak

- **Undergraduates: 4,441m, 6,115w; 12,399 total (including part-time)**
- **Tuition (1982/83): $1,480 (in-state), $2,590 (out-of-state)**
- **Room & Board: $1,672; Fees: $150**
- **Degrees offered: BA, BS, BFA, BSEd, AA**
- **Mean SAT 1050**
- **Student-faculty ratio: 19 to 1**

A public university established in 1875. 95-acre campus in a small city 50 miles northeast of Pittsburgh. Served by bus. Airport and rail station in Pittsburgh.
Academic Character MSACS and professional accreditation. Semester system, 6-week and 2 3-week summer terms. 9 majors offered by the School of Business, 8 by the School of Education, 7 by the School of Fine Arts, 5 by the School of Health Services, 6 by the School of Home Economics, 11 by the School of Natural Sciences & Mathematics, and 18 by the School of Social Sciences & Humanities. Distributive requirements. Graduate degrees granted. Independent study. Limited pass/fail. Internships, cooperative work/study. Joint programs with other schools in engineering, medical technology, medicine, respiratory therapy, forestry, environmental studies. Marine Science Consortium. Commercial art at Art Institute of Pittsburgh. Study abroad in Europe, Asia, Africa, South America. Elementary, secondary, and special education certification. ROTC. Computer center, language lab. University School, lodge, farm. 510,000-volume library with microform resources.
Financial Penn. Higher Education Assistance Service Agency. University scholarships, grants, loans, state aid; PELL, SEOG, NSS, NDSL, NSL, CWS, university has own work program. Application deadlines March 1 (scholarships), May 1 (loans).
Admissions High school graduation required. GED accepted. Interview required. Portfolio required for art majors, audition for music majors. SAT required; ACT accepted. $10 application fee. Rolling admissions; application deadline May 1. $15 registration fee, $50 tuition deposit, and $50 room deposit (for boarders) required on acceptance of offer of admission. *Early Decision, Early Admission, Concurrent Enrollment* programs. Transfers accepted. Credit possible for CEEB AP and CLEP exams; university has own advanced placement program. EOP.
Student Life Student government. Newspaper, yearbook. Music, debate, drama groups. Black Student League. Academic, honorary, religious, service, and special interest groups. 14 fraternities with houses, and 13 sororities without houses. 18% of men and 12% of women join. Freshmen encouraged to live on campus. Coed and single-sex dorms, special interest housing. 33% of students live on campus. Freshmen residents may not have cars on campus. Liquor, gambling, weapons prohibited on campus. 2 semesters of phys ed required except for men in ROTC. 12 intercollegiate sports for men, 11 for women; intramurals. AIAW, ECAC, NAIA, NCAA. Student body composition: 0.2% Asian, 5% Black, 0.3% Hispanic, 0.1% Native American, 93% White, 1.4% Other. 3% from out of state.

[P] JEFFERSON MEDICAL COLLEGE OF THOMAS JEFFERSON UNIVERSITY

1025 Walnut Street, Philadelphia 19107

[1] JUNIATA COLLEGE

Huntingdon 16652, (814) 643-4310
Associate Dean/Director of Admissions: Gayle W. Kreider

- **Undergraduates: 703m, 590w**
- **Tuition (1982/83): $5,361**
- **Room & Board: $2,235**
- **Degrees offered: BA, BS**
- **Mean SAT 500v, 540m**
- **Student-faculty ratio: 17 to 1**

A private college established in 1876. 100-acre small-town campus, 30 miles from Altoona and State College. Served by rail.
Academic Character MSACS accreditation. Trimester system, 2 5-week summer terms. Students design own majors in such areas as business, arts & sciences, communications, community service, ecology, education, international studies, peace & conflict, social sciences, language. Core requirements. Independent study. Cooperative work/study. Internships. Preprofessional programs in engineering, forestry, law, medicine. 3-2 engineering programs with Columbia, Georgia Tech, Penn State, Washington U. 3-2 forestry program with Duke. 3-1 medical technology program, 2-2 nursing, allied health programs. Environmental science program with Duke and American U. Washington UN, urban semesters. Many study abroad programs. Elementary and secondary education certification. Computer center, early childhood center, human interaction lab, scientific field station, electron microscope. 2 libraries with 200,000 volumes.
Financial CEEB CSS. College scholarships, grants, loans, state aid, payment plans; PELL, SEOG, CWS. Scholarship application deadline March 1.
Admissions High school graduation with 16 units required. Interview encouraged. SAT required; ACT accepted. $20 application fee. Rolling admissions. $100 deposit required on acceptance of offer of admission. *Early Decision* Program. Admission deferral possible. Transfers accepted. Credit possible for CEEB AP exams; college has own advanced placement program.
Student Life Student government. Newspaper, magazine, yearbook, radio station. Music, drama groups. International Cultural Relations group. Honorary, professional, religious, service, and special interest organizations. Students expected to live on campus. Coed and single-sex dorms. 92% of students live on campus. 11 intercollegiate sports for men, 6 for women; intramurals. AIAW, ECAC, NCAA, MAAC. Student body composition: 0.4% Black, 0.7% Hispanic, 96% White, 2.9% Other. 24% from out of state.

[J1] KEYSTONE JUNIOR COLLEGE

La Plume 18440, (717) 945-5141
Director of Admissions: Daniel M. Rosenfield

- **Enrollment: 307m 374w; 750 total (including part-time)**
- **Tuition & Fees (1982/82): $3,750**
- **Room & Board: $2,350**
- **Degrees offered: AA, AAS, AFA, AS**
- **Student-faculty ratio: 19 to 1**

A private junior college established in 1868. 200-acre rural campus in La Plume, 15 miles north of Scranton. Airport and bus station in Scranton.
Academic Character MSACS accreditation. Semester system, summer terms. 2-year career and transfer programs offered in allied health, art, biology, biochemistry, business, chemistry, computer management, computer science, dietetic technician, early childhood education, economics, English, engineering, fashion merchandising, food technology, general studies, hospitality management, human services, liberal arts, pre-environmental science & forestry, psychology, science, secretarial science, textile design, and textile management. Distributive requirements. Cooperative work/study. Credit by exam. ROTC at U of Scranton; AFROTC at Wilkes. Environmental Education Center. Learning Center offers tutorial assistance. Language lab, observatory. 34,000-volume library.
Financial CEEB CSS. College grants and loans, state grants and loans; PELL, SEOG, NDSL, CWS, college has own work program. Application deadline May 1.
Admissions High school graduation with 16 units required. GED accepted. SAT or ACT required. $15 application fee. Rolling admissions. $200 deposit required on acceptance of offer of admission. *Early Admission* Program. Admission deferral possible. Transfers accepted. Credit possible for CEEB AP and CLEP exams; college has own advanced placement program.
Student Life Student government. Newspaper, yearbook. Music, art, drama groups. Multi-Ethnic association. Professional, honorary, and special interest groups. Dorms and dining hall for men and women. About 33% of students live on campus. 2 credits in phys ed required. 7 intercollegiate sports; intramurals. NJCAA.

[1] KING'S COLLEGE

Wilkes-Barre 18711, (717) 826-5900
Director of Admissions: George J. Machinchick

- **Undergraduates: 1,059m, 867w**
- **Tuition (1982/83): $4,100**
- **Room & Board: $2,200**
- **Degrees offered: BA, BS**
- **Mean SAT 440v, 470m**
- **Student-faculty ratio: 17 to 1**

A private, Roman Catholic college controlled by the Congregation of Holy Cross, established in 1946, became coed in 1970. 11-acre urban campus in city of Wilkes-Barre, 100 miles from Philadelphia. Served by air and bus.

Academic Character MSACS and professional accreditation. Semester system, 2 5-week summer terms. Majors offered in biology, communications, criminal justice, economics, English, French, German, government & politics, history, mathematics, philosophy, psychology, sociology, Spanish, theatre, theology, accounting, business administration, chemistry, general science, gerontology, health services administration, computer & information systems, marketing, medical technology, physician's assistant, physics, psychology, and social work. Special and self-designed majors. Minors offered in most major fields and in theatre and theology. Courses in anthropology, fine arts. 6 hours of theology required. Independent study. Honors program. Pass/fail. Internships. Preprofessional programs in dentistry, law, medicine, ministry, pharmacy, veterinary medicine, engineering. Dual degree physician's assistant and pre-dental programs. Exchange programs with area schools. Study abroad. Elementary, secondary, and special education certification. ROTC, AFROTC. Computer center. 154,000-volume library with microform and interlibrary resources.

Financial CEEB CSS. College grants and loans, state aid; PELL, SEOG, NDSL, GSL, CWS, college has own work program. Application deadline for scholarships and FAF March 1.

Admissions High school graduation with 15 units required. Interview encouraged. SAT or ACT required for placement. $15 application fee. Rolling admissions; suggest applying in fall. $50 deposit required on acceptance of offer of admission. *Early Admission* and *Early Decision* programs. Transfers accepted. Credit possible for CEEP AP, CLEP, and ACT PEP exams.

Student Life Student government. Newspaper, fine arts magazine, yearbook, radio station. Music, drama, debate groups. Film society. Political, service, honorary, religious, and special interest groups. Students under 21 must live at home or on campus. Single-sex dorms. 36% of students live on campus. Freshmen discouraged from bringing cars on campus. Liquor prohibited. 9 intercollegiate sports for men, 4 for women; intramural and club sports. ECAC, NCAA, MAAC, NPWIAA. Student body composition: 2.5% Asian, 1% Black, 2.5% Hispanic, 94% White. 36% from out of state.

[1] KUTZTOWN STATE COLLEGE

Kutztown 19530, (215) 683-4060
Director of Admissions: George McKinley

- **Enrollment: 2,340m, 3,343w**
- **Tuition (1982/83): $1,400 (in-state), $2,862 (out-of-state)**
- **Room & Board: $1,530; Fees: $150**
- **Degrees offered: BA, BS, BFA, BSEd**
- **Mean SAT 430v, 455m**
- **Student-faculty ratio: 15 to 1**

A public college established in 1866. 325-acre small-town campus located between Reading and Allentown. Served by bus; rail station in Reading, airport in Allentown.

Academic Character MSACS and professional accreditation. Semester system, 2 5-week summer terms. Majors offered in American studies, anthropology, art education, biology, business administration, chemistry, communication design, computer/information science, criminal justice, economics, elementary education, English, environmental science, fine arts (5 areas), French, general studies, geography, geology, German, history, library science, marine science, math, medical technology, music, philosophy, physics, political science, psychology, public administration, related arts, Russian, Russian/Slavics studies, secondary education, social welfare, sociology, Spanish, special education, speech theatre, and telecommunications. Nursing major for RNs. Distributive requirements. Masters degrees granted. Honors program. Pass/fail. Internships. Credit by exam. 3-2 engineering program. Study abroad in England. Elementary, secondary, and special education certification. ROTC; AFROTC at Lehigh. 281,068-volume library with microform resources.

Financial CEEB CSS. College scholarships and loans; PELL, SEOG, NDSL, FISL, CWS. Application deadline March 1.

Admissions High school graduation with 16 units required. GED accepted. SAT required. $10 application fee. Rolling admissions; application deadline August 15. $50 tuition deposit and $60 room deposit required on acceptance of offer of admission. Transfers accepted. Credit possible for CEEB AP and CLEP exams.

Student Life Student government. Newspaper, magazine, yearbook. Music, drama groups. Black Theatre League. Professional and special interest groups. 2 fraternities and 2 sororities. Coed and single-sex dorms, special interest housing. Married-student housing. 60% of students live on campus. Freshmen and sophomores may not have cars on campus. Liquor prohibited on campus. 2 semesters of phys ed required. 12 intercollegiate sports for men, 7 for women; intramurals. AIAW, NCAA. Student body composition: 0.1% Asian, 6.5% Black, 0.7% Hispanic, 0.1% Native American, 92.6% White. 18% from out of state.

[1] LA ROCHE COLLEGE

9000 Babcock Blvd., Pittsburgh 15237, (412) 367-9300
Director of Admissions: Valerie C. Donohue

- **Undergraduates: 275m, 398w; 1,548 total (including part-time)**
- **Tuition (1982/83): $3,170**
- **Room & Board: $2,320**
- **Degrees offered: BA, BS, BSN**
- **Student-faculty ratio: 21 to 1**

A private college affiliated with the Roman Catholic Church, established in 1963, became coed in 1969. 160-acre suburban campus in the North Hills area, 10 miles from Pittsburgh center. Air, bus, and rail nearby.

Academic Character MSACS accreditation. Semester system. Majors offered in accounting, administration, management, communications, graphic arts, graphic design, interior design, English, religious studies, religious education/catechesis, anesthesia for nurses, biology, chemistry, mathematics, medical technology, medical technology/chemistry, natural sciences, nursing, radiography, history, psychology, and sociology. Self-designed majors. Masters degrees granted. Independent study. Honors program. Pass/fail, internships. Preprofessional programs in dentistry, law, medicine, podiatry, veterinary medicine. Cross-registration with 9 area schools. Study abroad. Secondary education certification with Carlow College. ROTC at Duquesne; AFROTC at U of Pittsburgh. Design complex. 500,000-volume library.

Financial CEEB CSS. College scholarships and grants, state aid, payment plan; PELL, SEOG, NDSL, GSL, CWS. Application deadline June 30.

Admissions High school graduation with 14-16 units required. GED accepted. Interview encouraged. SAT or ACT recommended. Rolling admissions. *Early Admission* Program. Admission deferral possible. Transfers accepted. Credit possible for CEEB AP and CLEP exams; college has own advanced placement program.

Student Life Student government. Newspaper, yearbook. Art, literary clubs. Academic and special interest groups. Coed dorms, student apartments. 16% of students live on campus. Intercollegiate basketball for men; intramurals for men and women. NAIA. Student body composition: 0.6% Asian, 4.2% Black, 94% White, 1.2% Other.

[1] LA SALLE COLLEGE

Olney Avenue and 20th Street, Philadelphia 19141, (215) 951-1500
Director of Admissions: Brother Lewis Mullin

- **Undergraduates: 1,987m, 1,834w; 6,180 total (including graduates)**
- **Tuition (1982/83): $4,150**
- **Room & Board: $2,750; Fees: $150 (for science majors)**
- **Degrees offered: BA, BS, BSW**
- **Mean SAT 490v, 530m**
- **Student-faculty ratio: 17 to 1**

A private college controlled by the Brothers of the Christian Schools, established in 1863, became coed in 1967. 60-acre campus in Philadelphia. Served by air, bus, and rail.

Academic Character MSACS and professional accreditation. Semester system, 2 6-week summer terms. Majors offered in art history, biology, chemistry, classical languages, computer science, criminal justice, economics, English, geology, history, international studies, mathematics, military science, modern languages, music, philosophy, physics, political science, psychology, religion, secondary education, social work, sociology, special education, accounting, finance, management, marketing, personnel/labor relations, quantitative analysis, and special options. Minors offered in international and urban studies. Distributives and 2 semesters of religious studies required. Independent study. Honors program. Cooperative work/study, limited pass/fail. Preprofessional programs in correctional work, dentistry, law, medicine, social work, veterinary science. Cooperative nursing program with area hospitals. Cross-registration with Chestnut Hill College. Study abroad. Secondary and special education certification. ROTC; AFROTC at St. Joseph's. Day care center. Evening, Weekend, Continuing Education programs. Urban Studies Center, language lab, art gallery. 350,000-volume library.

Financial CEEB CSS. College scholarships, grants, loans, state aid, payment plan; PELL, SEOG, NDSL, GSL, CWS. Application deadlines February 15 (state forms), February 1 (loans).

Admissions High school graduation with 16 units required. Interview encouraged. SAT or ACT required. $20 application fee. Rolling admissions; priority application deadline April 1. $100 deposit required on acceptance of offer of admission. *Early Decision* and *Early Admission* programs. Admission deferral possible. Transfers accepted. Credit possible for CEEB AP and CLEP exams. Academic Opportunity Program.

Student Life Student government. Newspaper, magazine, yearbook. Music, debate, drama groups. Black Student Union. Academic, religious, honorary, service, and special interest groups. Fraternities and sororities. Students must live with relatives or on campus. Coed dorms, student apartments. Married-student housing. 4 cafeterias and snack bar. 28% of students live on campus. Class attendance required. 11 intercollegiate sports for men, 10 for women; intramurals. East Coast Conference. Student body composition: 0.5% Asian, 11% Black, 0.5% Foreign, 0.5% Hispanic, 0.5% Native American, 87% White. 32% from out of state.

[J1] LACKAWANNA JUNIOR COLLEGE

901 Prospect Avenue, Scranton 18503

[1] LAFAYETTE COLLEGE

Easton 18042, (215) 250-5000
Director of Admissions: Richard W. Haines

- **Undergraduates: 1,184m, 863w**
- **Tuition (1982/83): $7,025**
- **Room & Board: $2,555**
- **Degrees offered: AB, BS**
- **Mean SAT 560v, 620m**
- **Student-faculty ratio: 13 to 1**

A private college affiliated with United Presbyterian Church, established in 1826, became coed in 1970. 100-acre urban campus overlooking city of Easton, 80 miles from New York City. Served by bus; airport 20 minutes away.
Academic Character MSACS and professional accreditation. Semester system, 6-week summer term. Majors offered in American civilization, anthropology & sociology, art, biology, chemistry, classics, comparative literature, economics & business, engineering (5 areas), English, French, German, geology, government & law, history, international affairs, mathematics, music, philosophy, physics, psychology, religion, Russian, Spanish. Self-designed majors. Minor required in some departments. Distributive requirements. Honors program. Phi Beta Kappa. Pass/fail. Internships. 5-year AB?BS programs. Cross-registration with area colleges. Consortium with 5 area schools. Washington Semester. Study abroad in several countries. Elementary and secondary education certification. ROTC; AFROTC at Lehigh. 370,000-volume library with microform resources.
Financial CEEB CSS. College scholarships, grants, loans, payment plans; PELL, SEOG, NDSL, GSL, FISL, PLUS, CWS. FAF deadline February 1.
Admissions High school graduation with 16 units required. Interview encouraged. SAT and 3 ACH required. $25 application fee. Application deadline February 15. $100 deposit required on acceptance of offer of admission. *Early Decision* and *Early Admission* programs. Admission deferral possible. Transfers accepted. Credit possible for CEEB AP exams.
Student Life Student government. Newspaper, magazine, yearbook, radio station. Music, drama groups. Association of Black Collegians. Women's Caucus. Academic, professional, religious, service, and special interest groups. 17 fraternities, 5 sororities, 2 coed social dorms. 60% of men and 30% of women join. Freshmen must live on campus. Coed and single-sex dorms. Honors and international housing. No married-student housing. 95% of students live on campus. Freshmen and sophomores may not have cars on campus. Liquor prohibited in dorms. Gambling, hazing prohibited. 12 intercollegiate sports for men, 8 for women; intramural and club sports. AIAW, ECAC, NCAA, NC, ECC. Student body composition: 0.7% Asian, 3.4% Black, 1.9% Foreign, 0.6% Hispanic, 93.4% White. 74% from out of state.

[1] LANCASTER BIBLE COLLEGE
Lancaster 17601

[G1] LANCASTER THEOLOGICAL SEMINARY OF THE UNITED CHURCH OF CHRIST
Lancaster 17603

[1] LEBANON VALLEY COLLEGE
Annville 17003, (717) 867-4411
Director of Admissions: Gregory Stanson

- **Undergraduates: 460m, 460w**
- **Tuition (1982/83): $4,650**
- **Room & Board: $2,185; Fees: $140**
- **Degrees offered: BA, BS, BSMed Tech, BSChem**
- **Mean SAT 487v, 524m**
- **Student-faculty ratio: 11 to 1**

A private college affiliated with the United Methodist Church, established in 1866. 80-acre small-town campus 85 miles from Philadelphia.
Academic Character MSACS and professional accreditation. Semester system, 8-week summer term. Majors offered in accounting, actuarial science, biochemistry, biology, business administration, chemistry, computer science, economics, elementary education, English, foreign languages, history, international business, mathematics, medical technology, music, nuclear medicine technology, nursing, operations research, philosophy, physics, political science, psychology, religion, social sciences, social service, and sociology. Self-designed majors. Distributive requirements. Independent study. Honors program. Cooperative work/study, pass/fail, internships. 3-2 program in forestry with Duke, in engineering with U Penn and others. 2-2 health programs with Thomas Jefferson College of Allied Health Sciences. Marine biology program with U of Delaware and U of Georgia. Washington, Germantown, Merill-Palmer semesters. Study abroad. Elementary and secondary education certification. ROTC at Dickinson. Language lab. 160,000-volume library.
Financial CEEB CSS. College scholarships, grants, loans, state aid, payment plan; PELL, SEOG, NDSL, GSL, CWS, college work program. Application deadline March 1.
Admissions High school graduation with 16 units required. GED accepted. Interview required. Audition required for music majors. SAT required; ACT accepted. ACH recommended. $20 application fee. Rolling admissions; application deadline May 1. $100 deposit required on acceptance of offer of admission. *Early Decision* and *Early Admission* programs. Admission deferral possible. Transfers accepted. Credit possible for CEEB AP and CLEP exams; college has own advanced placement program.
Student Life Student government. Newspaper, yearbook, radio station. Music, drama groups. Academic, honorary, religious, and special interest groups. 3 fraternities and 2 sororities. 50% of men and women join. Students must live with relatives or on campus. 6 single-sex dorms. 90% of students live on campus. Liquor, gambling, hazing prohibited on campus. Phys ed required for freshmen. 10 intercollegiate sports for men, 3 for women; intramurals. ECC, NCAA, MSCAC. Student body composition: 2% Asian, 3% Black, 95% White. 34% from out of state.

[J1] LEHIGH COUNTY COMMUNITY COLLEGE
2370 Main Street, Schnecksville 18078

[1] LEHIGH UNIVERSITY
Bethlehem 18015, (215) 691-7000
Director of Admissions: Samuel H. Missimer

- **Undergraduates: 3,140m, 1,180w; 6,056 total (including graduates)**
- **Tuition (1982/83): $7,200**
- **Room & Board: $2,620**
- **Degrees offered: AB, BS, BSEng, BSBA**
- **Mean SAT 560v, 640m**
- **Student-faculty ratio: 14 to 1**

A private university established in 1865, became coed in 1971. 700-acre urban campus in Bethlehem, 50 miles from Philadelphia. Served by air, bus, and rail.
Academic Character MSACS and professional accreditation. Semester system. 34 majors offered by the College of Arts & Sciences, 5 by the College of Business & Economics, and 11 by the College of Engineering & Physical Sciences. Minors in education, law, Russian studies, technology & human values. Distributive requirements; senior exams. Graduate degrees granted. Independent study, honors program. Phi Beta Kappa. Pass/fail. Internships. Cooperative work/study. 5-year, dual-degree programs. Cross-registration with 5 area schools. 6-year BA-MD program with Medical College of PA. 7-year program with U of Penn. Dental School. 5-year teaching program. Harrisburg, Washington Semesters. Marine science program. Study abroad. ROTC, AFROTC. Center for Information Sciences. 730,000-volume library with microform resources.
Financial CEEB CSS. University scholarships, grants, loans; PELL, SEOG, NDSL, CWS. Application deadline January 31.
Admissions High school graduation with 16 units required. Interview encouraged. SAT and 3 ACH required. $25 application fee. Application deadline March 1. $50 deposit required on acceptance of offer of admission. *Early Admission* and *Early Decision* Program. Admission deferral possible. Transfers accepted. Credit possible for CEEB AP exams; university has own advanced placement program.
Student Life Student government. Newspaper, yearbook. Music and drama groups. Academic, honorary, professional, and special interest groups. 32 fraternities, 27 with houses. 50% of upperclass men join. Students must live at home or on campus. Coed and single-sex dorms, special interest housing. No married-student housing. 90% of students live on campus. Only upperclass students may have cars. Intercollegiate and intramural sports. AIAW, NCAA. Student body composition: 4% Asian, 3% Black, 1% Hispanic, 92% White. 64% from out of state.

[1] LINCOLN UNIVERSITY
Chester County 19352, (215) 932-8300
Director of Admissions: Darrell C. Davis

- **Undergraduates: 537m, 523w; 1,405 total (including part-time)**
- **Tuition (1982/83): $1,930 (in-state), $2,130 (out-of-state)**
- **Room & Board: $1,850; Fees: $220**
- **Degrees offered: BA, BS, AA**
- **Mean SAT 400v, 350m**
- **Student-faculty ratio: 15 to 1**

A public university established in 1854, became coed in 1965. 442-acre campus in Chester County, 40 miles from Philadelphia. Airport in Philadelphia, rail station 20 miles away in Wilmington, Delaware.
Academic Character MSACS accreditation. Trimester system. Majors offered in anthropology & sociology, biology, Black studies, business administration, chemistry, classical languages, computer science, economics, education, English, French, history, human services, mathematics, modern language education, music, philosophy, physical education/health, physics, political science, psychology, public affairs, recreation leadership, religion, science, social welfare, Spanish, and therapeutic recreation. GRE required. Independent study. Honors program. Cooperative work/study, pass/fail, internships. Preprofessional programs in engineering, law, medicine, theology. 3-2 program in internation service with American U. 5- and 6-year BA-BS programs with Drexel, Lafayette, Penn State. Exchange of students and faculty with Colgate. Work/study in Africa. Study abroad. Elementary and secondary education certification. Language lab, community affairs institute. 160,000-volume library with microform resources.
Financial CEEB CSS. University scholarships, grants, and loans; PELL, NDSL, GSL, CWS. Preferred application deadline for scholarships March 15.
Admissions High school graduation with 15 units required. GED accepted. SAT required; 3 ACH recommended. $10 application fee. Rolling admissions; recommended deadline March 1. $75 deposit required on acceptance of offer of admission. *Early Decision* and *Early Admission* programs. Admission deferral possible. Transfers accepted. Credit possible for CEEB AP and CLEP exams. Project Good Neighbor.
Student Life Student government, Women's Student Government. Newspaper, journal, yearbook. Music, drama groups. Honorary, religious, and special interest groups. 5 fraternities and 3 sororities without houses. Students under 21 must live at home or on campus. Dorms and dining hall. No married-student housing. 97% of students live on campus. Firearms, drugs, hazing, gambling prohibited. 1 year of phys ed required. 7 intercollegiate sports for men, 2 for women; intramurals. ECAC, NAIA, NCAA. Student body composition: 97% Black, 3% White. 40% from out of state.

[1] LOCK HAVEN STATE COLLEGE
Lock Haven 17745, (800) 332-8900 (in-state), (800) 233-8978 (out-of-state)
Director of Admissions: Joseph A. Goldren

- **Undergraduates: 1,100m, 1,312w**
- **Tuition (1982/83): $1,480 (in-state), $2,584 (out-of-state)**
- **Room & Board: $1,648; Fees: $124**
- **Degrees offered: BA, BS**

- **Mean SAT 410v, 450m**
- **Student-faculty ratio: 15 to 1**

A public college established in 1870. 135-acre campus in a small city 30 miles from Williamsport. Served by bus; rail in Harrisburg.
Academic Character MSACS and professional accreditation. Semester system, 2 5-week summer terms. Majors offered in English, fine arts, foreign languages, general studies, history, humanities, international studies, journalism/media studies, Latin American studies, mathematics, natural science, philosophy, political science, psychology, social sciences, social welfare, sociology, speech communications, biology, business computer science, chemistry, chemistry/biology, education (5 areas), management science, mathematical/computer science, physics, social work. Self-designed majors. Distributive requirements. Independent study. Pass/fail. Internships. Preprofessional programs in dentistry, law, medicine. 3-2 program in engineering/arts & sciences with Penn State. Special degree program in chemistry/biology for medical technology certification. Study abroad in Australia, England, Poland. Elementary, secondary, special, health, and physical education certification. ROTC. 300,000-volume library.
Financial CEEB CSS. College scholarships and loans; PELL, SEOG, NDSL, CWS. Application deadline April 15.
Admissions High school graduation required. Interview encouraged. SAT required; ACT accepted. $10 application fee. Rolling admissions; suggest applying before December 1. Deadline June 1. $35 tuition deposit and $50 room deposit (for boarders) required on acceptance of offer of admission. *Early Admission* Program. Admission deferral possible. Transfers accepted. Credit possible for CEEB AP and CLEP exams. EOP.
Student Life Student government. Newspaper, magazine, yearbook. Music, drama groups. Academic, education, and special interest groups. 6 fraternities with houses and 5 sororities without houses. 15% of men and women join. Dorms for men and women. No married-student housing. 64% of students live on campus. Only students with 64 credits may have cars on campus. Liquor prohibited. 3 hours of phys ed required. 9 intercollegiate sports for men, 9 for women; intramurals. AIAW, ECAC, NCAA, PSCC. Student body composition: 0.2% Asian, 4.1% Black, 0.2% Hispanic, 0.1% Native American, 92.2% White. 18% from out of state.

[G1] LUTHERAN THEOLOGICAL SEMINARY
Gettysburg 17325

[G1] LUTHERAN THEOLOGICAL SEMINARY
7301 Germantown Avenue, Philadelphia 19119

[J1] LUZERNE COUNTY COMMUNITY COLLEGE
Nanticoke 18634

[1] LYCOMING COLLEGE
Williamsport 17701, (717) 326-1951
Director of Admissions: Marshall Raucci

- **Undergraduates: 627m, 576w**
- **Tuition (1982/83): $4,980**
- **Room & Board: $2,200**
- **Degrees offered: BA, BFA, BSN**
- **Mean SAT 475v, 500m**
- **Student-faculty ratio: 15 to 1**

A private college affiliated with the Methodist Church, established in 1812. 35-acre urban campus in residential section of Williamsport, 182 miles from Philadelphia. Served by air and bus.
Academic Character MSACS accreditation. 4-4-1 system, 6-week summer term. Majors offered in accounting, accounting/mathematics, American studies, art, astronomy, biology, business administration, chemistry, computer science, criminal justice, economics, English, French, German, history, international studies, literature, mass communications, mathematics, music, Near Eastern culture & archaeology, nursing, philosophy, physics, political science, psychology, religion, sculpture, sociology & anthropology, Spanish, and theatre. Self-designed majors. Distributives and 2 courses in religion/philosophy required. Independent study. Honors program. Pass/fail, internships. Preprofessional programs in dentistry, law, medicine, veterinary medicine. 3-2 engineering programs with Bucknell, Penn State. 3-2 forestry program with Duke. 3-1 medical technology and nuclear medical technology programs. 3-4 program with PA College of Podiatric Medicine. Washington, UN, Harrisburg, London semesters. Student Enrichment Semester at Bucknell. Study abroad. Elementary and secondary education certification. ROTC at Bucknell. Language lab. 142,000-volume library.
Financial CEEB CSS. College scholarships, grants, ministerial grants, state aid, payment plan; PELL, SEOG, NDSL, CWS. Application deadline April 15.
Admissions High school graduation with 16 units required. Interview encouraged. Portfolio required for BFA candidates. SAT or ACT required. $15 application fee. Rolling admissions; application deadline April 1. $100 deposit required on acceptance of offer of admission. *Early Decision* and *Early Admission* programs. Admission deferral possible. Transfers accepted. Credit possible for CEEB AP and CLEP exams.
Student Life Student government. Literary review, yearbook, radio station. Music, drama groups. Art and lecture series. Academic, honorary, religious, and special interest groups. 6 fraternities with houses and 2 sororities. Single students under 23 must live at home or on campus (including fraternities). Coed and single-sex dorms. No married-student housing. 80% of students live on campus. Visitation restricted. 2 semesters of phys ed required. 7 intercollegiate sports for men, 3 for women, coed swimming; intramurals. ECAC, NCAA, MAC. Student body composition: 2% Black, 98% White. 40% from out of state.

[J2] LYON SCHOOL OF BUSINESS
316 Rhodes Place, New Castle 16101

[J1] MANOR JUNIOR COLLEGE
Fox Chase Road & Forest Avenue, Jenkintown 19046, (215) 885-2360
Dean of Admissions: Sister Anthony Ann

- **Enrollment: 400w**
- **Tuition (1982/83): $2,950-$3,400**
- **Room & Board: $2,200; Fees: $60**
- **Degrees offered: AA, AS**
- **Mean SAT 400v, 400m**
- **Student-faculty ratio: 9 to 1**

A private Catholic junior college for women, controlled by the Byzantine Ukrainian Sisters of St. Basil the Great, established in 1947. Suburban campus in Fox Chase Manor adjacent to Jenkintown and Huntingdon Valley, 15 miles from downtown Philadelphia. Air, bus, and rail service in Philadelphia.
Academic Character MSACS accreditation. Semester system. 2-year programs offered in allied health, dental assisting, medical assisting, medical laboratory technology, liberal arts, mental health/human services, accounting, administrative assistant, business administration, court reporting, executive secretarial, legal secretarial, medical secretarial, word processing, and optometric technician. Certificate and diploma programs. Courses in Ukrainian. Distributives and 6 credit hours of religious studies required. Independent study. Pass/fail, internships. Preprofessional programs in allied health fields. Ukrainian Studies Center, Dental Health Center. 26,500-volume library.
Financial CEEB CSS. College scholarships and grants, state grants; PELL, SEOG, GSL, CWS. Application deadline March 15.
Admissions High school graduation with 16 units required. GED accepted. Interview encouraged. SAT or ACT required. $10 application fee. Rolling admissions. *Early Admission* Program. Admission deferral possible. Transfers accepted. Credit possible for CEEB AP and CLEP exams, and for life experience.
Student Life Student government. Newspaper, magazine, yearbook. Honorary organizations. Women's dorm. 22% of students live on campus.

[1] MANSFIELD STATE COLLEGE
Mansfield 16933, (717) 662-4243
Director of Admissions: John J. Abplanalp

- **Enrollment: 1,000m, 1,350w**
- **Tuition (1982/83): $1,250 (in-state), $2,190 (out-of-state)**
- **Room & Board: $1,626; Fees: $116**
- **Degrees offered: BA, BS, BSEd, BMus, AS**
- **Student-faculty ratio: 14 to 1**

A public college established in 1857. 175-acre small-town campus, 50 miles from Williamsport. Air and bus service in Williamsport.
Academic Character MSACS and professional accreditation. Semester system, summer term. 41 majors offered in the areas of art, natural sciences, business, communication, criminal justice, education, humanities, home economics, music, social sciences, theatre, and travel/tourism. Self-designed majors. Distributive requirements. MA, MEd granted. Independent study. Honors program. Cooperative work/study, pass/fail, internships. 3-2 pre-engineering program. Exchange program with Bloomsburg State, Bucknell, Lock Haven, Lycoming, Susquehanna, and Williamsport. Elementary, secondary, and special education certification. ROTC. 200,000-volume library with microform resources.
Financial College scholarships, grants, loans; NDSL, CWS.
Admissions High school graduation with 16 units required. Audition required for music majors, interview and portfolio for art majors. SAT or ACT required. $10 application fee. Rolling admissions. $50 tuition deposit and $50 room deposit (for boarders) required on acceptance of offer of admission. *Early Decision* and *Early Admission* programs. Admission deferral possible. Transfers accepted. Credit possible for CEEB AP exams; college has own advanced placement program. EOP.
Student Life Music, drama, debate groups. Academic, honorary, service, and special interest groups. Coed and single-sex dorms. 70% of students live on campus. 6 intercollegiate sports for men, 5 for women; intramurals. Student body composition: 1% Asian, 5% Black, 1% Hispanic, 93% White. 10% from out of state.

[G1] MARY IMMACULATE SEMINARY
Northampton 18067

[1] MARYWOOD COLLEGE
2300 Adams Avenue, Scranton 18509, (717) 348-6234
Director of Admissions: Sister M. Gabriel Kane, IHM

- **Undergraduates: 420m, 1,680w; 3,100 total (including graduates)**
- **Tuition (1982/83): $2,820**
- **Room & Board: $2,000; Fees: $150**
- **Degrees offered: AB, BS, BMus, BFA, BSN, BSW**
- **Mean SAT 465v, 475m**
- **Student-faculty ratio: 16 to 1**

A private college controlled by the Sisters, Servants of the Immaculate Heart of Mary, established in 1915, became coed in 1981. 180-acre suburban campus in Scranton, 100 miles from Philadelphia and New York City. Air, bus, and rail nearby.
Academic Character MSACS and professional accreditation. Semester system, 2 summer terms. 48 majors offered in the areas of art, business, humanities, education, sciences, home economics, communication, health

services, legal studies, physical education, library studies, social sciences, and theatre. Self-designed and double majors. Distributives and 3 semesters of theology required. MA, MS, MBA, MSW, MFA granted. Independent study. Honors program. Cooperative work/study, pass/fail, internships. Preprofessional programs in dentistry, law, medicine, veterinary medicine. Cross-registration with U of Scranton. 3-2 math/engineering program with George Washington U. Study abroad. Elementary, secondary, and special education certification. ROTC at U of Scranton; AFROTC at Wilkes. Art gallery, communications center, TV studio, electronic learning lab, center for Justice and Peace. 160,000-volume library.
Financial CEEB CSS and ACT FAS. College scholarships and loans, talent scholarships, payment plan; PELL, SEOG, NDSL, FISL, NSL, CWS. Scholarship application deadline February 15.
Admissions High school graduation with 16 units required. GED accepted. Interview encouraged. Audition required for music majors. SAT or ACT required. $20 application fee. Rolling admissions; suggest applying by October. $100 deposit required on acceptance of offer of admission. *Early Decision, Early Admission, Special Acceleration* programs. Admission deferral possible. Transfers accepted. Credit possible for CEEB AP and CLEP exams. ACT 101.
Student Life Student government. Newspaper, magazine, yearbook, radio station. Music, art, literary, drama organizations. Black Cultural Society. Academic, political, religious, and special interest groups. Freshmen must live on campus. Single-sex dorms. Language and special interest housing. 40% of students live on campus. 4 terms of phys ed required. 5 intercollegiate sports for women; individual and club sports. Student body composition: 1% Asian, 2% Black, 1% Hispanic, 96% White. 40% from out of state.

[P] MEDICAL COLLEGE OF PENNSYLVANIA
Philadelphia 19129

[1] MERCYHURST COLLEGE
Glenwood Hills, Erie 16546, (814) 825-4000
Director of Admissions: Thomas A. Billingsley

- **Undergraduates: 559m, 882w**
- **Tuition (1982/83): $4,200**
- **Room & Board: $1,900; Fees: $125**
- **Degrees offered: BA, BSN, BMus, AS**
- **Student-faculty ratio: 17 to 1**

A private college affiliated with the Sisters of Mercy, established in 1962, became coed in 1969. 75-acre campus in suburban Erie, 100 miles from Buffalo, Cleveland, Pittsburgh. Served by air, bus, and rail.
Academic Character MSACS and professional accreditation. 4-3-3 system, 2 summer terms. 57 majors offered in the areas of business, art, science, communications, computer science, criminal justice, dance, education, English & modern languages, fashion, foods & nutrition, hotel & restaurant management, human ecology, interior design, mathematics, health sciences, music, political & social sciences, and religion. Self-designed majors. Minors offered in some major fields and in 9 additional areas. Distributives and one religion course required. MS granted. Independent study. Honors program. Cooperative work/study, pass/fail, internships. Preprofessional programs in dentistry, law, medicine. Member consortium with Gannon, Villa Maria. Study abroad. Early childhood, elementary, secondary, and special education certification. ROTC at Gannon. 80,000-volume library.
Financial CEEB CSS and ACT FAS. College scholarships, grants, loans, academic, athletic, talent scholarships, payment plan; PELL, SEOG, NSS, NDSL, FISL, GSL, CWS; college has own work program. Application deadline March 15.
Admissions High school graduation with 16 units required. Interview encouraged. Audition required for music and dance majors. SAT or ACT required; ACH recommended. $20 application fee. Rolling admissions. $100 tuition deposit and $150 room deposit required on acceptance of offer of admission. *Early Decision* and *Early Admission* programs. Admission deferral possible. Transfers accepted. Credit possible for CEEB AP and CLEP exams.
Student Life Student government. Newspaper, magazine, yearbook, radio station. Music and drama groups. Religious, service, and special interest groups. Coed and single-sex dorms. 60% of students live on campus. 10 intercollegiate sports; intramurals. AIAW, NCAA, Keystone Conference. Student body composition: 7% Black, 0.5% Hispanic, 92% White, 0.5% Other. 15% from out of state.

[1] MESSIAH COLLEGE
Grantham 17027, (717) 766-2511
Director of Admissions & Financial Aid: Ron E. Long

- **Undergraduates: 566m, 899w**
- **Tuition (1982/83): $4,000**
- **Room & Board: $2,240; Fees: $50**
- **Degrees offered: BA, BS, BSN, BSHE, BSMus**
- **Mean ACT 22; mean SAT 502v, 528m**
- **Student-faculty ratio: 18 to 1**

A private college affiliated with the Brethren in Christ Church, established in 1909. 310-acre rural campus in Grantham, 11 miles from Harrisburg. Served by air, bus, and rail. Urban campus in Philadelphia.
Academic Character MSACS accreditation. 4-1-3 system, summer term. 58 majors offered in the areas of behavioral science, education, health & recreation, history & political science, home & family, language & literature, fine arts, management & business, mathematical sciences, music, natural sciences, nursing, and religion & philosophy. Self-designed majors. Courses in Greek. Distributives and 12 units of Bible & religion required. Independent study. Honors program. Cooperative work/study, pass/fail, internships. Preprofessional programs in dentistry, law, medicine, ministry. Member Christian College Consortium. Cooperative medical technology and nursing programs with local hospitals. Study abroad in several countries. Elementary and secondary education certification. Language lab. 120,000-volume library with microform resources.
Financial CEEB CSS. College scholarships, grants, loans, state aid, payment plan; PELL, SEOG, NDSL, GSL, CWS. Application deadline April 1.
Admissions High school graduation with 16 units required. Interview encouraged. Audition required for music majors. ACT or SAT required. $15 application fee. Rolling admissions; application deadline June 1. $100 deposit required on acceptance of offer of admission. *Early Admission* Program. Admission deferral possible. Transfers accepted. Credit possible for CEEB AP and CLEP exams.
Student Life Student government. Newspaper, yearbook, radio station. Music and drama groups. Religious, academic, professional, and special interest groups. Single students must live at home or on campus. Single-sex dorms. Married-student housing. 92% of students live on campus. Freshmen may not have cars on campus. Liquor, tobacco, dancing, obscenity, profanity, hazing, secret societies prohibited on campus. Class and chapel attendance required. 3 semester hours of phys ed required. 6 intercollegiate sports for men, 4 for women; intramurals. NAIA, NCAA, Penn-Mar. Student body composition: 1% Asian, 3% Black, 2% Hispanic, 94% White. 40% from out of state.

[1] MILLERSVILLE STATE COLLEGE
Millersville 17551, (717) 872-3371
Director of Admissions: Blair E. Treasure

- **Undergraduates: 2,096m, 2,498w; 6,178 total (including part-time)**
- **Tuition (1982/83): $1,480 (in-state), $2,590 (out-of-state)**
- **Room & Board: $1,710; Fees: $163**
- **Degrees offered: BA, BS, BSEd, AS**
- **Mean SAT 459v, 502m**
- **Student-faculty ratio: 19 to 1**

A public college established in 1855. 225-acre small-town campus, 4 miles from Lancaster. Air, bus, and rail service in Lancaster.
Academic Character MSACS and professional accreditation. Semester system, 2 5-week summer terms. 17 majors offered for the BS degree, 24 for the BA, and 5 for the BSEd with 25 additional concentrations. Nursing major for RNs. Courses in Greek, speech/drama. Distributive requirements. MEd granted. Independent study. Honors program. Cooperative work/study, pass/fail, internships. Prepodiatry program. Physics-engineering in cooperation with Penn State, U Penn. Cross-registration with Franklin and Marshall, Lancaster Theological Seminary. Marine science consortium. Study abroad. Elementary, secondary, special education, and educational media certification. ROTC. Computer center. 379,000-volume library.
Financial CEEB CSS and ACT FAS. College and state scholarships, grants, loans, state aid; PELL, SEOG, NDSL, GSL, CWS, state work program. Application deadlines February 15 (scholarships), May 1 (loans).
Admissions High school graduation required. Interview encouraged. Audition required for music majors. SAT or ACT required. $15 application fee. Rolling admissions. $75 tuition deposit and $75 room deposit (for boarders) required on acceptance of offer of admission. *Early Entrance* and *Early Decision* programs. Admission deferral possible. Transfers accepted. Credit possible for CEEB AP and CLEP exams. ACT 101 Program.
Student Life Student government. Newspaper, magazine, yearbook, radio station. Music and drama groups. Over 100 special interest groups. 12 fraternities and 10 sororities without houses. 18% of men and 21% of women join. Freshmen must live at home or on campus. Coed and single-sex dorms. Special interest housing. No married-student housing. 60% of students live on campus. Freshmen and sophomores may not have cars on campus. Liquor prohibited on campus. 2 semesters of phys ed required. 10 intercollegiate sports for men, 7 for women, 2 coed; intramurals. Student body composition: 1% Asian, 6% Black, 1% Hispanic, 92% White. 7% from out of state.

[J1] MONTGOMERY COUNTY COMMUNITY COLLEGE
Blue Bell 19422

[1] MOORE COLLEGE OF ART
20th and the Parkway, Philadelphia 19103, (215) 568-4515
Dean of Admissions & Records: Delores Lewis

- **Enrollment: 442w; 600 total (including part-time)**
- **Tuition (1982/83): $4,600**
- **Room & Board: $2,350; Fees: $75**
- **Degrees offered: BSArt Ed, BFA**
- **Student-faculty ratio: 10 to 1**

A private women's college established in 1844. Urban campus in center of Philadelphia. Served by air, bus and rail.
Academic Character MSACS and professional accreditation. Majors offered in advertising design, fashion design, fashion illustration, illustration, interior design, photography, textile design, ceramics, jewelry & metal smithing, painting, printmaking, and sculpture. Distributive requirements. Pass/fail. Elementary, secondary, and art education certification. Galleries. 31,000-volume library with 73,000 slides and over 188,000 pictures.
Financial CEEB CSS. College scholarships and grants, state grants; PELL, SEOG, NDSL, CWS. Application deadline April 1.
Admissions High school graduation required. GED accepted. Portfolio required. SAT or ACT required. $20 application fee. Rolling admissions; suggest applying by April 1. *Early Admission* Program. Transfers accepted.
Student Life Student government. Student exhibitions, fashion shows. Dorms and dining hall. About 48% of students live on campus. Sports in cooperation with nearby schools.

[1] MORAVIAN COLLEGE
Bethlehem 18018, (215) 861-1320
Director of Admissions: John T. McKeown

- **Undergraduates: 678m, 632w**
- **Tuition (1982/83): $5,660**
- **Room & Board: $2,205**
- **Degrees offered: BA, BS**
- **Mean SAT over 1000**
- **Student-faculty ratio: 16 to 1**

A private college affiliated with the Moravian Church, established in 1742. 2 suburban campuses of 70 acres in Lehigh Valley, 1½ hours from Philadelphia. Served by air, bus, and rail.

Academic Character MSACS and professional accreditation. 4-1-4 system, 6- and 4-week summer terms. Majors offered in accounting, American studies, art, criminal justice, economics/business, English, foreign languages, history, journalism, management, music, philosophy, political science, psychology, religion, social science, social work, sociology, biology, chemistry, computer science, mathematics, and physics. Self-designed majors. 4 additional majors offered cooperatively. Distributives and one religion course required. Independent study. Honors program. Cooperative work/study, pass/fail, internships. Preprofessional programs in dentistry, law, medicine, theology. 5-year BA/BMus program. 3-2 programs in engineering & geology with Lafayette, U Penn; in forestry with Duke. 3-1 medical technology program. Cross-registration with 5 area schools. Washington and Harrisburg semesters. Study abroad. Elementary, secondary, and music education certification. AFROTC, ROTC at Lehigh. Language labs. 185,000-volume library.

Financial CEEB CSS. College scholarships, grants, loans; PELL, SEOG, NDSL, FISL. Application deadlines March 1 (scholarships), March 15 (loans).

Admissions High school graduation with 16 units required. Interview recommended. Audition required for music majors, portfolio for art majors. SAT or ACT required. $25 application fee. Rolling admissions; application deadline March 15. $100 tuition deposit and $100 room deposit (for boarders) required on acceptance of offer of admission. *Early Decision* and *Early Admission* programs. Admission deferral possible. Transfers accepted. Credit possible for CEEB AP and CLEP exams.

Student Life Student government. Newspaper, magazine, yearbook, radio station. Music and drama groups. Academic, religious, political, service, and special interest groups. 3 fraternities and 3 sororities, all with houses. 23% of men and 23% of women. Freshmen and sophomores must live at home or on campus. Coed and single-sex dorms. No married-student housing. 70% of students live on campus. Hazing, gambling prohibited. Phys ed required for freshmen and sophomores. 8 intercollegiate sports for men, 6 for women; intramurals. ECAC, NCAA, MAC. Student body composition: 1% Black, 1% Hispanic, 95% White, 3% Other. 40% from out of state.

■[1] MORAVIAN THEOLOGICAL SEMINARY
Bethlehem 18018

[J1] MOUNT ALOYSIUS JUNIOR COLLEGE
Cresson 16630, (814) 886-4131
Director of Admissions: Marianne Shertzer

- **Enrollment: 85m, 334w; 518 total (including part-time)**
- **Tuition (1982/83): $3,750-$4,550**
- **Room & Board: $2,150**
- **Degrees offered: AA, AS, AFA**
- **Mean ACT 15; SAT 794 composite**
- **Student-faculty ratio: 11 to 1**

A private Catholic junior college controlled by the Religious Sisters of Mercy, established in 1939. 125-acre wooded campus in Cresson between Altoona and Johnstown.

Academic Character MSACS accreditation. Semester system. 2-year programs offered in art education, art therapy aide, commerical art, fine arts, business administration, data processing, executive secretarial, legal secretarial, medical secretarial, merchandising, micro-computer science, medical assistant, medical laboratory technician, nursing, surgical technology, occupational therapy assistant, interpreter training, liberal arts, criminology, general studies, and pre-mortuary science. Certificate programs. Distributive requirements. Resources for deaf. Audio-visual center. Library consortium. 30,000-volume library.

Financial College scholarships, state grants; PELL, SEOG, NDSL, NSL, PLUS, CWS. Application deadlines April 1 (college aid), May 1 (state grants).

Admissions High school graduation required. GED accepted. SAT or ACT required. $15 application fee. Rolling admissions; suggest applying in fall. $100 deposit due on acceptance of offer of admission. *Early Admission* Program. Transfers accepted. Credit possible for CEEB CLEP exams. Educational Enrichment Program.

Student Life Student government. Newspaper, yearbook. Art, music groups. Professional, honorary, and special interest groups. Single-sex dorms. 1 intercollegiate sport for men, 3 sports for women; intramurals.

[1] MUHLENBERG COLLEGE
Allentown 18104, (215) 433-3191
Dean of Admissions & Freshmen: George W. Gibbs

- **Undergraduates: 811m, 727w**
- **Tuition (1982/83): $5,975**
- **Room & Board: $1,975**
- **Degrees offered: AB, BS**
- **Mean SAT 540v, 590m**
- **Student-faculty ratio: 12 to 1**

A private college affiliated with the Lutheran Church, established in 1848, became coed in 1957. 75-acre campus in residential section of Allentown, 55 miles from Philadelphia.

Academic Character MSACS and professional accreditation. Semester system, 2 summer terms. Majors offered in accounting, American studies, art, biology, business administration, chemistry, classics, communications studies, drama, economics, English, French, German, Greek, history, humanity, Latin, mathematics, music, natural sciences/mathematics, philosophy, physics, political science, psychology, Russian studies, social science, social work, sociology, and Spanish. Self-designed majors. Minors in some major fields and in computer science, religion. Distributives and 2 semesters of religion required. Independent study. Honors program. Phi Beta Kappa. Pass/fail, internships. 3-2 and 4-2 engineering programs with Columbia and Washington U. 3-2 forestry program with Duke. Cross-registration with 5 area schools. Study abroad. Elementary and secondary education certification. AFROTC, ROTC at Lehigh. 180,000-volume library.

Financial CEEB CSS. College scholarships and loans, state aid, payment plans; PELL, SEOG, NDSL, FISL, CWS. Application deadlines February 15 (scholarships), February 1 (loans).

Admissions High school graduation with 16 units required. Interview encouraged. SAT and 3 ACH required. $25 application fee. Application deadline February 15. $100 tuition deposit and $200 room deposit (for boarders) required on acceptance of offer of admission. *Early Decision* and *Early Admission* programs. Admission deferral possible. Transfers accepted. Credit possible for CEEB AP and CLEP exams and ACH test scores.

Student Life Student government. Newspaper, magazine, yearbook, radio stations. Music, debate, drama groups. International Students. Environmental Action. Religious, academic, service, professional, honorary, and special interest groups. 5 fraternities with houses. 40% of men join. Coed and single-sex dorms, college-owned houses, special interest houses. 90% of full-time single students (not in fraternities) live on campus. Freshman boarders may not have cars on campus. 4 semesters of phys ed required. 9 intercollegiate sports for men, 5 for women; intramural and club sports. NCAA, ECAC, MAC. 66% of students from out of state.

[1] NEUMANN COLLEGE
Aston 19014

[J2] NEW CASTLE BUSINESS COLLEGE
New Castle — see Lyon School of Business

[1] NEW CHURCH, ACADEMY OF THE
Bryn Athyn 19009

[P] NEW KENSINGTON COMMERCIAL SCHOOL
945 Greensburg Road, New Kensington 15068

[1] NEW SCHOOL OF MUSIC
301 South 21 Street, Philadelphia 19103

[J1] NORTHAMPTON COUNTY AREA COMMUNITY COLLEGE
Bethlehem 18017

[J1] NORTHEASTERN CHRISTIAN JUNIOR COLLEGE
1860 Montgomery Avenue, Villanova 19085
Director of Admissions: Douglas P. Edwards

- **Undergraduates: 91m, 100w**
- **Tuition (1982/83): $2,800**
- **Room & Board: $2,400**
- **Degrees offered: AA, AS**
- **Mean SAT 396v, 432m**
- **Student-faculty ratio: 6 to 1**

A private Christian junior college established in 1959. 24-acre campus in Villanova, near Philadelphia.

Academic Character MSACS accreditation. Semester system, 2 7-week summer terms. 2-year programs offered in art, Biblical studies, business, education, English & literature, foreign language, history/social studies, home economics, human services/sociology, industrial technology, mathematics, music, natural sciences, psychology, science, secretarial studies, speech, and health, physical education, & recreation. Career programs offered in human services, secretarial skills, data processing. Certificate programs. Distributives and 10 hours of Biblical studies required. Credit by exam. Preprofessional programs in agriculture, engineering, medical technology, mental health technology, nursing. 3-year Bible program. Music camp.

Financial CEEB CSS. College scholarships, loans, ministerial scholarships, state grants; PELL, SEOG, NDSL, GSL, CWS.

Admissions High school graduation required. GED accepted. SAT required. $15 application fee. Rolling admissions. $50 tuition deposit and $10 room deposit (for boarders) required on acceptance of offer of admission. *Early Decision* and *Early Admission* programs. Admission deferral possible. Transfers accepted. College has own advanced placement program.

Student Life Student government. Magazine, yearbook. Music and drama groups. Preprofessional, religious, service, and special interest groups. Single-sex dorms. Curfew. Liquor, smoking, dancing, gambling prohibited. Attendance in class and at assemblies required. 2 hours of phys ed required. 3 intercollegiate sports for men, 3 for women; intramurals. AIAW, EPCCC. Student body composition: 21% minority.

[J1] PEIRCE JUNIOR COLLEGE
1420 Pine Street, Philadelphia 19102

[P] PENN TECHNICAL INSTITUTE
Pittsburgh 15222

[1] PENNSYLVANIA, UNIVERSITY OF
Philadelphia 19104, (215) 243-7507
Director of Admissions: Willis J. Stetson, Jr.

- **Undergraduates: 5,285m, 3,433w; 16,132 total (including graduates)**
- **Tuition & Fees (1982/83): $8,000**
- **Average Room & Board: $3,700**
- **Degrees offered: AB, BS, BFA**
- **Mean SAT 610v, 660m**
- **Student-faculty ratio: 7 to 1**

A private university established in 1740. 147-acre urban campus in West Philadelphia, on Schuylkill River. Served by air, bus, and rail.
Academic Character MSACS and professional accreditation. Semester system, 2 6-week summer terms. 44 majors offered by the College of Arts & Sciences, 9 by the College of Engineering & Applied Sciences, 1 by the School of Nursing, and 14 by the Wharton School of Business. Self-designed and double majors. Distributive requirements. Graduate and professional degrees granted. Independent study. Honors programs. Phi Beta Kappa. Pass/fail. Preprofessional programs in city regional planning, dentistry, foreign service, government, law, medicine, theology, veterinary medicine. AB-AM program in museum curatorship. 3-2 liberal arts/engineering and business/engineering programs. 3-4 dual degree program with School of Veterinary Medicine. Dual degree architecture and landscape architecture programs. Consortium with Bryn Mawr, Haverford, Swarthmore. Study abroad; exchange with U of Edinburgh, French language exchange. Teacher certification. NROTC, ROTC; AFROTC at St. Joseph's. Several research institutes. Computer center, language lab, observatory. 3,000,000-volume library with microform resources.
Financial CEEB CSS. University scholarships and loans; PELL, SEOG, NDSL, GSL, FISL, CWS. Application deadline January 1.
Admissions High school graduation with 16 units required. Interview required by the School of Nursing. SAT and 3 ACH required. $30 application fee; fee waiver possible. Application deadline January 1. $50 deposit, refundable at graduation, required on acceptance of offer of admission. *Early Decision* and *Early Admission* programs. Admission deferral possible. Transfers accepted. Credit possible for CEEB AP exams.
Student Life Student government. Newspaper, magazine, yearbook, radio and TV stations. Music, debate, and drama groups. Women's Liberation. Ethnic associations. Academic, religious, and special interest groups. 30 fraternities with houses and 2 sororities, 1 with house. 30% of students join. Coed dorms, special interest houses. Married-student housing. 80% of students live on campus. 21 intercollegiate sports for men, 13 for women. Ivy League. Student body composition: 3.9% Asian, 5.3% Black, 2% Hispanic, 0.2% Native American, 87% White. 75% from out of state.

[P] PENNSYLVANIA ACADEMY OF THE FINE ARTS
Broad and Cherry Streets, Philadelphia 19102

[1] PENNSYLVANIA COLLEGE OF OPTOMETRY
1200 West Godfrey Avenue, Philadelphia 19141

[P] PENNSYLVANIA COLLEGE OF PODIATRIC MEDICINE
Eighth at Race Street, Philadelphia 19107

[1] PENNSYLVANIA STATE UNIVERSITY
University Park 16802, (814) 865-4700
Dean of Admissions: Donald G. Dickason

- **Undergraduates: 28,101m, 18,719w; 63,800 total (including graduates)**
- **Estimated Tuition (1982/83): $2,000 (in-state), $4,000 (out-of-state)**
- **Room & Board: $2,274**
- **Degrees offered: BA, BS, BArch, BArch Eng, BFA, BLA, BMus, BPhil**
- **Mean SAT 509v, 564m**
- **Student-faculty ratio: 22 to 1**

A public university established in 1855. 5,005-acre campus in small city of University Park, 70 miles from Harrisburg.
Academic Character MSACS and professional accreditation. 4-term system, 10-week summer terms. 18 majors offered by the College of Agriculture, 10 by the College of Arts & Architecture, 8 by the College of Business Administration, 10 by the College of Earth & Mineral Sciences, 8 by the College of Education, 11 by the College of Engineering, 3 by the College of Health, Physical Education, Recreation, 7 by the College of Human Development, 35 by the College of Liberal Arts, and 12 by the College of Science. Graduate and professional degrees granted. Independent study. Honors program. Phi Beta Kappa. Cooperative work/study, internships. 3-2 liberal arts programs with engineering or earth/mineral sciences. Medical program with Thomas Jefferson U. Study abroad. Elementary, secondary, and special education certification. ROTC, AFROTC, NROTC. Computer center, language lab. 2,380,215-volume library with microform resources.
Financial CEEB CSS. University scholarships, grants, and loans; PELL, SEOG, NDSL, GSL, CWS. Application deadlines February 15 (scholarships), April 1 (loans).
Admissions High school graduation with 15 units required. SAT required. $20 application fee. Rolling admissions; suggest applying by November 30. $102 tuition deposit and $45 deposit (for boarders) required on acceptance of offer of admission. Transfers accepted. Credit possible for CEEB AP and CLEP exams; university has own advanced placement program. EOP.
Student Life Student government. Newspaper, magazine, yearbook. Music, debate, drama groups. Many religious, academic, honorary, professional, service, and special interest groups. 50 fraternities with houses and 19 sororities without houses. 13% of men and 8% of women join. Freshmen under 21 must live at home or on campus. Freshmen may not have cars on campus. 4 hours of phys ed required. 16 intercollegiate sports for men, 14 for women; several intramural sports. Student body composition: 0.9% Asian, 2.4% Black, 0.6% Hispanic, 0.1% Native American, 94.2% White, 1.8% Other. 10% from out of state.

■**[J1] ALLENTOWN CAMPUS**
Fogelsville 18051

■**[J1] ALTOONA CAMPUS**
Altoona 16603

■**[J1] BEAVER CAMPUS**
Brodhead Road, Monaca 15061

■**[1] BEHREND COLLEGE**
Erie 16510

■**[J1] BERKS CAMPUS**
RD #5, Reading 19608

■**[1] CAPITOL CAMPUS**
Middletown 17057

■**[J1] DELAWARE COUNTY CAMPUS**
Media 19063

■**[J1] DUBOIS CAMPUS**
DuBois 15801

■**[J1] FAYETTE CAMPUS**
PO Box 519, Uniontown 15401

■**[J1] HAZLETON CAMPUS**
Hazleton 18201

■**[J1] McKEESPORT CAMPUS**
McKeesport 15132

■**[G1] MILTON S. HERSHEY MEDICAL CENTER**
Hershey 17033

■**[J1] MONT ALTO CAMPUS**
Mont Alto 17237

■**[J1] NEW KENSINGTON CENTER**
New Kensington 15068

■**[J1] OGONTZ CAMPUS**
1600 Woodland Road, Abington 19001

■**[G1] RADNOR GRADUATE CENTER**
Radnor 19087

■**[J1] SCHUYLKILL CAMPUS**
Schuylkill Haven 17972

■**[J1] SHENANGO VALLEY CAMPUS**
Sharon 16146

■**[J1] WILKES-BARRE CAMPUS**
Wilkes-Barre 18708

■**[J1] WORTHINGTON SCRANTON CAMPUS**
Dunmore 18512

■**[J1] YORK CAMPUS**
York 17403

[J1] PHILADELPHIA, COMMUNITY COLLEGE OF
34 South 11th Street, Philadelphia 19107

[1] PHILADELPHIA COLLEGE OF ART
Broad and Spruce Streets, Philadelphia 19104, (215) 893-3174
Director of Admissions: Caroline Kelsey

- **Undergraduates: 446m, 608w; 1,800 total (including part-time)**
- **Tuition (1982/83): $5,800**
- **Room: $1,900; Fees: $10**
- **Degrees offered: BFA, BS**
- **Student-faculty ratio: 11 to 1**

A private college established in 1876. 4-block urban campus in Philadelphia. Served by air, bus, and rail.

Academic Character MSACS and professional accreditation. Semester system. Majors offered in crafts. (4 areas), design, environmental design, fine arts, graphic design, illustration, industrial design, painting, photography/film, printmaking, and sculpture. Courses in art history, foreign languages, literature, philosophy, science, and social studies. Art therapy program. MA in Art Education granted. Independent study, honors program. Pass/fail, internships. Consortium with 9 art and design colleges. Elementary and secondary education certification. Gallery, slide library. 45,000-volume library.
Financial CEEB CSS. College scholarships; PELL, SEOG, NDSL, FISL, CWS. Application deadlines February 15 (scholarships), March 15 (NDSL).
Admissions High school graduation with 8 units required. GED accepted. Interview encouraged. Portfolio required. SAT required. $20 application fee. Rolling admissions; recommended application date February 1. $100 tuition deposit and $200 room deposit (for boarders) required on acceptance of offer of admission. *Early Admission* Program. Admission deferral possible. Transfers accepted. Credit possible for CEEB AP and CLEP exams.
Student Life Student government. Newspaper, yearbook. Music/film events. Arts council. Coed dorms. No married-student housing. Intramural basketball. Student body composition: 0.7% Asian, 11.4% Black, 1% Hispanic, 0.3% Native American, 84.3% White. 30% from out of state.

[1] PHILADELPHIA COLLEGE OF BIBLE
Langhore Manor, Langhore 19047, (215) 752-5800

- **Undergraduates: 252m, 229w; 572 total (including part-time)**
- **Tuition (1982/83): $3,200**
- **Room & Board: $2,155**
- **Degrees offered: BS, BMus, BSW**
- **Mean ACT 17.9**

A private, denominationally unaffiliated, racially non-discriminatory college. Suburban campus.
Academic Character MSACS and professional accreditation. Semester system. College offers majors for the degrees of BS in Bible, BMusic, and BSocial Work. Remedial English program available. Evening and non-credit adult education programs.
Financial College scholarships, loans, state aid, PELL, SEOG, CWS, on- and off-campus employment.
Admissions Rolling admissions, with entrance in September and at mid-year. *Early Admission* and *Early Decision* programs. Advanced placement program.
Student Life Student body composition: 12% minority.

[P] PHILADELPHIA COLLEGE OF OSTEOPATHIC MEDICINE
4150 City Avenue, Philadelphia 19131

[1] PHILADELPHIA COLLEGE OF PHARMACY AND SCIENCES
43rd Street and Kingsessing Mau, Philadelphia 19104, (215) 596-8800
Director of Admissions: Richard C. Kent

- **Undergraduates: 518m, 489w**
- **Tuition (1982/83): $4,400**
- **Room: $1,200; Fees: $20**
- **Degree offered: BS**
- **Mean SAT 490v, 545m**
- **Student-faculty ratio: 12 to 1**

A private college established in 1821. 10-acre urban campus in University City area of Philadelphia. Served by air, bus, and rail.
Academic Character MSACS and professional accreditation. Semester system, 2 4-week summer terms. Majors offered in biology, chemistry, medical technology, pharmacy (5-year), physical therapy, and toxicology. Graduate and professional degrees granted. Internships. Affiliation with Jefferson Medical College, Medical Center of Jefferson U, 7 clinical teaching facilities. Member University City Science Center Corporation. Summer ecology program in the Poconos. ROTC. 73,500-volume library.
Financial CEEB CSS. College scholarships, grants, loans, state aid, payment plans; PELL, SEOG, NDSL, FISL, HPL, CWS. Application deadline April 1.
Admissions High school graduation with 16 units required. GED accepted. Interview encouraged. SAT required; 3 ACH recommended. $15 application fee. Rolling admissions; suggest applying by January. $150 deposit required on acceptance of offer of admission. Transfers accepted. Credit possible for CEEB AP and CLEP exams.
Student Life Student government. Newspaper, magazine, yearbook, radio station. Drama groups. Black Academic Achievement Society. International Student Association. Professional and religious organizations. 6 fraternities, 5 with houses, and 3 sororities without houses. Coed dorms. No married-student housing. 66% of students live on campus. Dress code. 2 semesters of phys ed required. 6 intercollegiate sports for men, 5 for women; intramurals. NAIA. Student body composition: 2% Asian, 2% Black, 1% Hispanic, 95% White. 36% from out of state.

[1] PHILADELPHIA COLLEGE OF TEXTILES AND SCIENCE
Henry Avenue and School House Lane, Philadelphia 19144, (215) 951-2800
Director of Admissions: Mott R. Linn

- **Undergraduates: 820m, 867w; 1,900 total (including graduates)**
- **Tuition (1982/83): $4,000**
- **Room & Board: $2,350**
- **Degree offered: BS**
- **Mean ACT 20; mean SAT 486v, 512m**
- **Student-faculty ratio: 16 to 1**

A private college established in 1884. 86-acre suburban campus 8 miles from the center of Philadelphia. Served by air, bus, and rail.
Academic Character MSACS and professional accreditation. Semester system, 2 6-week summer terms. Majors offered in accounting, apparel management, chemistry, computer management, computer science, fashion merchandising, finance, life science, management, marketing, retail management, and in textile chemistry, design, engineering, management/marketing, and technology. Minors offered in history, literature, political science, psychology, sociology. MBA granted. Independent study. Cooperative work/study, pass/fail, internships. Credit by exam. Study abroad. ROTC, NROTC nearby. Fabric collection, Learning Resource Center, photography lab, TV studio. 67,000-volume library.
Financial CEEB CSS and ACT FAS. College scholarships, grants, loans, state grants, payment plan; PELL, SEOG, FISL, GSL, NDSL, CWS. Scholarship application deadline May 1.
Admissions High school graduation with 16 units required. GED accepted. SAT or ACT required. $20 application fee. Rolling admissions; suggest applying in fall. $200 tuition deposit and $100 room deposit (for boarders) required on acceptance of offer of admission. *Early Decision, Early Admission, Concurrent Enrollment* programs. Admission deferral possible. Transfers accepted. Credit possible for CEEB AP and CLEP exams.
Student Life Student government. Newspaper, yearbook, radio station. Drama guild. Black Student Union. International Club. Professional groups. 3 fraternities and 1 sorority. 35% of men and 10% of women join. Coed and single-sex dorms. No married-student housing. 53% of students live on campus. 3 class absences allowed per credit for underclassmen. 2 semesters of phys ed required. 8 intercollegiate sports; intramural and club sports. Student body composition: 11% minority. 44% of students from out of state.

[1] PHILADELPHIA COLLEGE OF THE PERFORMING ARTS
250 South Broad Street, Philadelphia 19102

[1] PITTSBURGH, UNIVERSITY OF
4200 Fifth Avenue, Pittsburgh 15260, (412) 624-4141
Director of Admissions & Student Aid: Joseph A. Merante

- **Undergraduates: 8,772m, 10,204w; 29,206 total (including graduates)**
- **Tuition (1982/83): $2,210 (in-state), $4,420 (out-of-state)**
- **Room & Board: $2,450; Fees: $108**
- **Degrees offered: BA, BS, BASW, BSE, BSHRP, BSPharm, BSN**
- **Student-faculty ratio: 14 to 1**

A private, state-related university established in 1787. 125-acre urban campus in Pittsburgh. Served by air, bus, and rail.
Academic Character MSACS and professional accreditation. 3-term system. Freshmen may enter the College of Arts & Sciences, College of General Studies, School of Engineering, and School of Nursing; upon earning required distribution credits they may then make application to other schools of the University. 45 majors offered by the College of Arts & Sciences, 35 by the College of General Studies, 6 by the School of Education, 7 by the School of Engineering, 7 by the School of Health-Related Professions; also majors offered by the schools of Library & Information Science, Nursing, Pharmacy, and Social Work. Self-designed and interschool majors. Minor required. Courses in astronomy, several languages. Distributive requirements. Graduate and professional degrees granted. Independent study. Honors program. Phi Beta Kappa. 5-year liberal arts/engineering dual degree program. Member consortium with other Pittsburgh schools. Study abroad. AFROTC, ROTC. Language labs. 3,721,596-volume library with microform resources.
Financial CEEB CSS. University scholarships, grants, loans, pharmacy student loans, payment plan; PELL, SEOG, NSS, NDSL, NSL, CWS. Application deadline March 1.
Admissions High school graduation with 15 units required. Interview encouraged. SAT or ACT required. $15 application fee. Rolling admissions; suggest applying in fall. $50 deposit required on acceptance of offer of admission. *Early Admission, Concurrent Enrollment* programs. Admission deferral possible. Transfers accepted. Credit possible for CEEB AP exams; university has own advanced placement program. UCEP.
Student Life Student government. Newspaper, magazine, yearbook, radio station. Music and drama groups. Many academic, service, and special interest groups. 22 fraternities, 15 with houses, and 15 sororities, 10 with suites, 2 with houses. 10% of students join. Coed and single-sex dorms. 22% of students live on campus. Many intercollegiate and intramural sports. AIAW, ECAC, ICAAAA, NCAA, CCIEE, ISL. Student body composition: 1% Asian, 9% Black, 90% White. 13% from out of state.

■[1] PITTSBURGH, UNIVERSITY OF, AT BRADFORD
Campus Drive, Bradford 16701-0990, (814) 362-3801
Director of Admissions: Michael L. Mulvihill

- **Undergraduates: 600m, 500w**
- **Tuition (1982/83): $2,120 (in-state), $4,240 (out-of-state)**
- **Room & Board: $2,500; Fees: $100**
- **Degrees offered: BA, BS, AAS**
- **Mean SAT 450v, 500m**
- **Student-faculty ratio: 18 to 1**

A public university established in 1963. 125-acre suburban campus in Bradford, 80 miles from Buffalo. Served by air and bus.
Academic Character MSACS accreditation. 3-term system. Majors offered in administrative science, earth & environmental science, environmental biology, writing, history & philosophy of the Western World, human relations, human relations/gerontology, literature, math/computer science, physical sciences, public relations, and social science. Majors in areas of education, engineering, engineering technology, health-related professions, pharmacy,

and social work possible by transfer to other University campuses after 2 years. Self-designed majors. Distributive requirements. Independent study. Honors program. Pass/fail, internships. Preprofessional programs in dentistry, engineering, health fields, medicine, pharmacy, social work. Cross-registration with other U of Pittsburgh campuses. Study abroad in Europe, Japan, Russia, Latin America. Semester at sea. Elementary and secondary education certification. ROTC, AFROTC. Computer center. 65,000-volume library with microform resources.
Financial CEEB CSS and ACT FAS. University scholarships, grants, loans, state aid, payment plan; PELL, SEOG, NDSL, GSL, CWS, university has own work program. Application deadline March 1.
Admissions High school graduation with 15 units required. GED accepted. Interview encouraged. SAT or ACT required. $15 application fee. Rolling admissions; suggest applying by December 31. $50 deposit required on acceptance of offer of admission. *Early Decision, Early Admission, Concurrent Enrollment* programs. Admission deferral possible. Transfers accepted. Credit possible for CEEB AP and CLEP exams; university has own advanced placement program.
Student Life Student government. Newspaper, magazine, yearbook, radio station. Music and drama groups. Black Action Society. Professional, service, and special interest groups. 1 fraternity. 1% of men join. 1st and 2nd-year students under 21 must live at home or on campus. Coed and single-sex apartments. 55% of students live on campus. 2 intercollegiate sports for men, 3 for women; intramurals. NAIA. Student body composition: 1% Asian, 6% Black, 1% Hispanic, 92% White. 15% from out of state.

■[1] PITTSBURGH, UNIVERSITY OF, AT GREENSBURG
1150 Mt. Pleasant Road, Greensburg 15601

■[1] PITTSBURGH, UNIVERSITY OF, AT JOHNSTOWN
Johnstown 15904, (814) 266-9661
Director of Admissions: Thomas J. Wonders

- **Undergraduates: 1,215m, 1,185w**
- **Tuition (1982/83): $2,210 (in-state), $4,420 (out-of-state)**
- **Room & Board: $2,150; Fees: $70**
- **Degrees offered: BA, BS, BSEng Tech**
- **Mean SAT 505v, 560m**
- **Student-faculty ratio: 20 to 1**

A public university established in 1927. 635-acre suburban campus in Johnstown, 70 miles from Pittsburgh. Served by air, bus, and rail.
Academic Character MSACS and professional accreditation. 3-term system. Majors offered in American studies, biology, business/economics, chemistry, composite writing, computer science, creative writing, ecology, economics, education, engineering technology, English literature, government & politics, history, humanities, journalism, mathematics, natural sciences, psychology, social sciences, sociology, speech/communications, and theatre arts. Cooperative majors with Pittsburgh campus. Self-designed majors. Minor required. Minors offered in most major fields and in 4 additional areas. Distributive requirements. Independent study. Honors program. Pass/fail. Internships. Preprofessional programs in health-related professions. Study abroad. Elementary and secondary education certification. Computer center, language lab. 80,000-volume library.
Financial CEEB CSS. University scholarships, grants, loans, state aid, payment plan; PELL, SEOG, NDSL, FISL, CWS, university has own work program. Application deadline March 1.
Admissions High school graduation with 15 units required. GED accepted. Interview encouraged. SAT or ACT required. $15 application fee. Rolling admissions; suggest applying by March 1. $50 deposit required on acceptance of offer of admission. *Early Decision, Early Admission, Concurrent Enrollment* programs. Admission deferral possible. Transfers accepted. Credit possible for CEEB AP exams; university has own advanced placement program.
Student Life Student government. Newspaper, magazine, yearbook, radio station. Music and drama groups. Religious, academic, political, ethnic, and special interest organizations. 4 fraternities, 1 with house, and 3 sororities without houses. 10% of men and 7% of women join. Freshmen must live at home or on campus. Single-sex dorms. No married-student housing. 60% of students live on campus. 2 terms of phys ed required for some majors. 7 intercollegiate sports for men, 4 for women; intramurals. AIAW, NAIA, NCAA. Student body composition: 1% Asian, 4% Black, 1% Hispanic, 1% Native American, 93% White. 9% from out of state.

■[J1] PITTSBURGH, UNIVERSITY OF, AT TITUSVILLE
Brown and Main Streets, Titusville 16354, (814) 827-2702
Director of Admissions, Student Aid, & Veterans Affairs: John B. Ague

- **Enrollment: 300 men & women; 500 total (including part-time)**
- **Tuition (1982/83): $2,995 (in-state), $5,910 (out-of-state)**
- **Room & Board: $2,670; Fees: $90**
- **Degrees offered: AA, AS**
- **Student-faculty ratio: 11 to 1**

A junior college operated by the University of Pittsburgh, established in 1963. Campus in city of Titusville, 40 miles from Erie, 90 miles from U of Pittsburgh campus.
Academic Character MCACS accreditation. Trimester system, 7-week summer term. Majors offered in classics, English, fine arts, Spanish, music, philosophy, speech, theatre arts, studio arts, anthropology, economics, geography, history, political science, sociology, biological sciences, chemistry, computer science, geology & planetary science, mathematics, physics, psychology. Self-designed majors. Other 2-year departmental programs in communications, accounting, education, engineering, general studies, health professions, pharmacy, social work. Pass/fail. Credit by exam. Preprofessional programs in dentistry, medicine, law. ROTC at Pittsburgh. 30,000-volume library with microform resources.
Financial CEEB CSS. University scholarships, state grants, PELL, SEOG, NDSL, CWS.
Admissions High school graduation with 15 units required. SAT or ACT required. $15 application fee. Rolling admissions. *Early Decision* and *Early Admissions* programs. Admission deferral possible. Transfers accepted. Credit possible for CEEB AP exams.
Student Life Student government. Dorms and town houses. 84% of full-time students live on campus. Some programs require phys ed. Intramural sports.

[J2] PITTSBURGH, ART INSTITUTE OF
Pittsburgh — see Art Institute of Pittsburgh

[G1] PITTSBURGH THEOLOGICAL SEMINARY
616 North Highland Avenue, Pittsburgh 15206

[1] POINT PARK COLLEGE
Blvd. of Allies & Wood Street, Pittsburgh 15222, (412) 391-4100
Dean of Enrollment Planning: Richard K. Watson

- **Undergraduates: 651m, 530w; 2,595 total (including graduates)**
- **Tuition (1982/83): $4,000**
- **Room & Board: $2,250; Fees: $335**
- **Degrees offered: BA, BFA, BS, AA, AS**
- **Mean SAT 425v, 435m**
- **Student-faculty ratio: 16 to 1**

A private college established in 1960. Urban campus in Pittsburgh. Served by air, bus, and rail.
Academic Character MSACS accreditation. Semester system, 2 6-week summer terms. Majors offered in accounting, banking, behavioral sciences, biological sciences, business management, chemistry, cinema, computer sciences, dance, early childhood education, elementary education, engineering technology, English, health services, history, journalism/communications, mathematics, medical technology, modern languages, mortuary sciences, philosophy, photography, political science, psychology, public administration, social sciences, theatre arts, and visual arts & design. Self-designed majors. Minors offered in all major fields. Distributive requirements. MA granted. Independent study. Cooperative work/study, pass/fail, internships. Preprofessional programs in dentistry, law, medicine, veterinary medicine. Cross-registration with 9 area schools. Cooperative medical technology program. Secondary education certification. ROTC at Duquesne; AFROTC at U of Pittsburgh. 101,000-volume library with microform resources.
Financial CEEB CSS. College scholarships, grants, and loans; dance, journalism, and theatre scholarships; state aid, payment plans; PELL, SEOG, NDSL, FISL, CWS.
Admissions High school graduation required. GED accepted. Interview encouraged. SAT required; ACT accepted. $15 application fee. Rolling admissions; suggest applying in October or November. $100 tuition deposit and $50 room deposit (for boarders) required on acceptance of offer of admission. *Early Admission* Program. Transfers accepted. Credit possible for CEEB AP, CLEP, and USAFI exams; college has own advanced placement program.
Student Life Student government. Newspapers, radio and TV stations. Music groups. Veterans organization. Academic, honorary, religious, service, and special interest groups. Coed and single-sex dorms. 35% of students live on campus. Liquor, drugs prohibited on campus. 2 intercollegiate sports for men, 2 for women; intramural and club sports. NAIA, Penn Wood West. Student body composition: 3% Asian, 10% Black, 0.5% Hispanic, 0.5% Native American, 79% White, 7% Other. 19% from out of state.

[J1] READING AREA COMMUNITY COLLEGE
2nd and Penn, Reading 19603

[J1 & 1] ROBERT MORRIS COLLEGE
Fifth Avenue at Sixth, Pittsburgh 15219, and Coraopolis 15108, (412) 264-9300
Director of Admissions: Helen Mullen

- **Enrollment: 1,396m, 1,734w; 5,964 total (including part-time)**
- **Tuition (1982/83): $2,880**
- **Room & Board: $2,000**
- **Degrees offered: BSBA, AS, AA**
- **Student-faculty ratio: 28 to 1**

A private college established in 1921. 230-acre suburban campus in Coraopolis, 15 miles from Pittsburgh. Urban campus in Pittsburgh. Airport nearby; bus and rail stations in Pittsburgh.
Academic Character MSACS accreditation. Semester system, 2 6-week summer terms. Majors offered in accounting, administration management, business information systems, business teacher education, economics, finance, industrial communications, management, marketing, sports management, and transportation. MS granted. Internships. Pass/fail for juniors and seniors. Member of Pittsburgh Council on higher education with 9 colleges and universities. Secondary education certification. ROTC at Duquesne; AFROTC at U of Pittsburgh. 93,005-volume library with microform resources.
Financial CEEB CSS. College scholarships, grants, loans, state grants, family discounts; PELL, SEOG, NDSL, FISL, GSL, CWS, college work program. Application deadline May 1.
Admissions High school graduation with 16 units recommended. GED accepted. Interview encouraged. SAT or ACT required for enrollment only. $20 application fee. Rolling admissions. $50 deposit required on acceptance

of offer of admission. *Early Admission* and *Concurrent Enrollment* programs. Admission deferral possible. Transfers accepted. Credit possible for CEEB AP, CLEP, and ACT PEP exams; college has own advanced placement program.
Student Life Student government. Newspaper, yearbook. Drama, dance groups. Black Student Union. Religious, honorary, professional, and special interest groups. 5 fraternities, 1 with house, and 3 sororities without houses. 30% of men and 40% of women join. Freshmen and sophomores must live at home or on campus. Liquor prohibited on campus. 2 semesters of sports and recreation required. 9 intercollegiate sports for men, 6 for women; intramurals. AIAW, ECAC, NCAA. 10% of students from out of state.

[1] ROSEMONT COLLEGE

Rosemont 19010, (215) 525-6420
Director of Admissions: Jane Maloney

- **Undergraduates: 650w**
- **Tuition (1982/83): $4,550**
- **Room & Board: $2,960; Fees: $165**
- **Degrees offered: BA, BFA, BS**
- **Mean SAT 450v, 450m**
- **Student-faculty ratio: 12 to 1**

A private women's college controlled by the Society of the Holy Child Jesus, established in 1921. 56-acre suburban campus in Rosemont, near Philadelphia. Served by air, rail, and bus.
Academic Character MSACS accreditation. Semester system. Majors offered in studio art, art history, English, theatre, French, German, Spanish, history, philosophy, religious studies, biology, chemistry, mathematics, economics, political science, psychology, and sociology. Interdisciplinary majors in American studies, humanities, Italian studies, and social sciences. Self-designed majors. Minors offered in all major fields. Distributives, 2 units of religion, and senior exam required. Independent study. Cooperative work/study, pass/fail. Preprofessional programs in medicine and law. Exchange programs with Villanova, 8 design schools. Washington Semester. Study abroad. Summer study in Italy. Elementary, secondary, foreign language, and art education certification. Language labs, art gallery, computer center. 139,000-volume library with microform resources.
Financial CEEB CSS. College scholarships, grants, art scholarships, state grants, parental loans; PELL, SEOG, NDSL, GSL, CWS.
Admissions High school graduation with 16 units required. Interview encouraged. SAT required. $15 application fee. Rolling admissions. $150 deposit required on acceptance of offer of admission. Admission deferral possible. Transfers accepted. Credit possible for CEEB AP exams.
Student Life Student government. Newspaper, magazine, yearbook. Music and drama groups. International Students. Academic, service, and special interest groups. Students expected to live at home or on campus. Most students live on campus; some Villanova women live on campus. 2 semesters of phys ed required. 6 intercollegiate sports; intramural and club sports. AIAW.

[1] ST. CHARLES BORROMEO SEMINARY

Overbrook, Philadelphia 19151

[1] SAINT FRANCIS COLLEGE

Loretto 15940, (814) 472-7000
Director of Admissions: Edward E. Kale, Jr.

- **Undergraduates: 594m, 531w; 1,656 total (including graduates)**
- **Tuition (1982/83): $3,840**
- **Room & Board: $2,200; Fees: $310**
- **Degrees offered: BA, BS, BSN, AS**
- **Mean SAT 450v, 460m**
- **Student-faculty ratio: 15 to 1**

A private college controlled by the Franciscan Order, established in 1847. 600-acre rural campus in small town of Loretto, 85 miles from Pittsburgh. Served by bus.
Academic Character MSACS and professional accreditation. Semester system, 2 5-week summer terms. Majors offered in American studies, anthropology, art, behavioral sciences, biology, business administration, chemistry, comparative literature, commerce/modern languages, criminal justice, elementary education, English, French, history, mathematics, medical technology, nursing, philosophy, physician assistant, podiatric science, psychology, public administration & government service, religious studies, social work, sociology, Spanish, and theatre. Concentrations in 6 additional areas. Self-designed majors. Distributives and 2 semesters of religious studies required. MA, MEd granted. Independent study. Pass/fail. Internships. Preprofessional programs in law, medicine. 3-2 engineering program with Penn State. 3-4 podiatric science program with Philadelphia College of Podiatric Medicine. Study abroad. Elementary and secondary education and library science certification. 165,000-volume library.
Financial CEEB CSS and ACT FAS. College scholarships, grants, loans; PELL, SEOG, NDSL, GSL, PLUS, CWS. Scholarship application deadline March 15.
Admissions High school graduation with 16 units required. Interview encouraged. SAT or ACT required. $15 application fee. Rolling admissions; suggest applying by January. $200 deposit required on acceptance of offer of admission. *Early Admission* and *Early Decision* programs. Transfers accepted. Credit possible for CEEB AP and CLEP exams. Freshman Achievement Program.
Student Life Student government. Newspaper, magazine, yearbook. Academic, religious, and special interest organizations. 4 fraternities with houses, 2 sororities without houses. Single-sex dorms. Married-student housing. Boarding freshmen may not have cars on campus first semester. 6 intercollegiate sports for men, 5 for women; intramural and club sports. ECAC, NCAA, Pennwood West. Student body composition: 0.5% Asian, 1.2% Black, 1.1% Hispanic, 97.2% White. 45% from out of state.

[1] SAINT JOSEPH'S UNIVERSITY

City Avenue and 54th Street, Philadelphia 19131, (215) 879-7400
Director of Admissions: Randy H. Miller

- **Undergraduates: 1,274m, 1,056w; 3,591 total (including graduates)**
- **Tuition (1982/83): $4,110-$4,400**
- **Room & Board: $2,700**
- **Degrees offered: AB, BS**
- **Mean SAT 520v, 528m**
- **Student-faculty ratio: 15 to 1**

A private university controlled by the Society of Jesus, established in 1851, became coed in 1970. 47-acre suburban campus in residential section of Philadelphia. Served by air, bus, and rail.
Academic Character MSACS accreditation. Semester system, 2 6-week summer terms. Majors offered in economics, English, French, German, history, international relations, philosophy, politics, psychology, sociology, Spanish, theology, accounting, biology, chemistry, computer science, engineering physics, finance, food marketing, industrial relations, information systems, management, marketing, mathematics, physics, and public administration. Special majors. Distributives and 9 credits in theology required. Masters degrees granted. Independent study. Honors program. Pass/fail, cooperative work/study, internships. Preprofessional programs in dentistry, law, medicine. Institute of Latin American Studies. Jesuit Student Exchange. Washington, Appalachian, Mexico City semesters. Study abroad. Brazilian Institute. Elementary and secondary education certification. AFROTC; NROTC at Villanova and U Penn; ROTC at Drexel. Computer center, language lab. 190,412-volume library with microform resources.
Financial CEEB CSS. University scholarships, grants, loans, payment plan; PELL, SEOG, NDSL, GSL, CWS. Application deadline March 1; FAF deadline February 1.
Admissions High school graduation with 15 units required. Interview encouraged. SAT required. $20 application fee. Rolling admissions beginning March 15; suggest applying by March 1. $100 tuition deposit and $150 room deposit required on acceptance of offer of admission. *Early Decision* and *Early Admission* programs. Admission deferral possible. Transfers accepted. Credit possible for CEEB AP exams.
Student Life Student association. Newspaper, quarterly, yearbook, radio station. Music, drama, debate groups. Black Awareness Society. International Student Association. Religious, service, academic, honorary, and special interest groups. Fraternities. Students must live with relatives or on campus. Coed and single-sex dorms, special interest houses. No married-student housing. 41% of students live on campus. 7 intercollegiate sports for men, 5 for women; intramural and club sports. AIAW, ECAC, NCAA, ECCC. Student body composition: 5% Black, 2% Hispanic, 92% White, 1% Other. 30% from out of state.

[1] SAINT VINCENT COLLEGE

Latrobe 15650, (412) 539-9761, ext. 305
Director of Admissions: Earl J. Henry, OSB

- **Undergraduates: 842m**
- **Tuition (1982/83): $3,875**
- **Room & Board: $1,950; Fees: $434**
- **Degrees offered: BA, BS**
- **Student-faculty ratio: 12 to 1**

A private men's college that will become coed in 1983. Controlled by the Benedictine Order, established in 1846. 100-acre campus in small city of Latrobe in foothills of the Alleghenies, 35 miles from Pittsburgh. Served by air and rail.
Academic Character MSACS accreditation. Semester system, 3-, 4-, 6-, and 7-week summer terms. Majors offered in biology, business administration, chemistry, economics, English, history, liberal arts, mathematics, modern languages, philosophy, physics, political science, psychology, religious education, and sociology. 7 additional majors offered in cooperation with Seton Hill. Self-designed, double majors. Minors offered in some major fields and in computer science, merchandising, and nutrition. Distributives and 9 hours of religion required. Independent study. Honors program. Cooperative work/study, internships, pass/fail. Preprofessional programs in dentistry, engineering, medicine, law, and education. Cooperative engineering program. 3-4 program with Penn. College of Podiatric Medicine. Study abroad. Secondary education certification. AFROTC at U of Pittsburgh. 215,527-volume library with microform resources.
Financial CEEB CSS. College scholarships, grants, loans, payment plan; PELL, SEOG, NDSL, GSL, CWS, college work program. Scholarship application deadline May 1.
Admissions High school graduation with 15 units required. Interview encouraged. SAT or ACT required. $15 application fee. Rolling admissions; suggest applying between October and November. $50 tuition deposit and $50 room deposit (for boarders) required on acceptance of offer of admission. *Early Admission* and *Early Decision* programs. Admission deferral possible. Transfers accepted. Credit possible for CEEB AP, CLEP, and ACT PEP exams; college has own advanced placement program. Special admissions program.
Student Life Student government. Newspaper, magazine, yearbook, radio station. Music, debate groups. Professional, social action, and special interest groups. Students must live at home or on campus. Special interest housing. 79% of students live on campus. Underclassmen may not have cars on campus. Liquor prohibited on campus. 8 intercollegiate sports; intramural and club sports. NAIA. Student body composition: 0.2% Asian, 2.5% Black, 0.6% Hispanic, 96% White. 20% from out of state.

[G1] SAINT VINCENT SEMINARY
Latrobe 15650

[1] SCRANTON, UNIVERSITY OF
Scranton 18510, (717) 961-7540
Dean of Admissions: Bernard R. McIlhenny, SJ

- **Undergraduates: 1,700m, 1,200w; 4,500 total (including graduates)**
- **Tuition (1982/83): $3,520**
- **Room & Board: $2,040; Fees: $150**
- **Degrees offered: AB, BS**
- **Mean SAT 470v, 520m**
- **Student-faculty ratio: 20 to 1**

A private university controlled by the Jesuit order, established in 1888, became coed in 1972. 37-acre urban campus in residential section of Scranton. Served by air, bus, and rail.

Academic Character MSACS and professional accreditation. 4-1-4 system, 10-week summer term. 35 majors offered in the areas of liberal arts, social sciences, natural sciences, business & education, and health & human services. Self-designed majors. Distributives and 18 credits in philosophy & religion required. MA, MS granted. Independent study. Honors program. Internships, pass/fail. Preprofessional programs in dentistry, law, medicine, veterinary medicine. 4- and 5-year master's programs. 2-3 engineering program with U of Detroit, Widener College. Cross-registration with Marywood College. Semester possible at any of 27 Jesuit schools. Study abroad. Secondary education certification. 210,000-volume library.

Financial CEEB CSS. University scholarships, grants, loans, state aid, payment plans; PELL, SEOG, NDSL, FISL, CWS, university work program. Application deadline February 15.

Admissions High school graduation with 16 units required. SAT or ACT required. $15 application fee. Rolling admissions; application deadline July 1. $25 tuition deposit and $50 room deposit (for boarders) required on acceptance of offer of admission. *Early Decision* and *Early Admission* programs. Admission deferral possible. Transfers accepted. Credit possible for CEEB AP and CLEP exams.

Student Life Student government. Newspaper, magazine, journals, yearbook. Service, academic, religious, political, and special interest groups. Students must live with relatives or on campus. Single-sex dorms. No married-student housing. 55% of students live on campus. Phys ed required for freshmen and sophomores. 8 intercollegiate sports for men, 7 for women; intramural and club sports. AIAW, NCAA, ECAC, MAC. Student body composition: 1% Asian, 1% Black, 1% Hispanic, 97% White. 34% from out of state.

[1] SETON HILL COLLEGE
Greensburg 15601, (412) 834-2200
Director of Admissions: Sister Jean Boggs

- **Enrollment: 770 w**
- **Tuition (1982/83): $4,260**
- **Room & Board: $2,300; Fees: $50**
- **Degrees offered: BA, BSHome Ec, BSMed Tech, BMus, BFA**
- **Mean SAT 480v, 480m**
- **Student-faculty ratio: 13 to 1**

A private women's college conducted by the Sisters of Charity, established in 1912. 200-acre suburban campus in the small city of Greensburg, 30 miles from Pittsburgh. Served by bus and rail, airport in Pittsburgh.

Academic Character MSACS and professional accreditation. Semeste sytem, 3-, 6-, and 8-week summer terms. Majors offered in accounting, American studies, art (9 areas), biochemistry, biology, chemistry, communication, economics, education, English, finance, French, history, home economics (9 areas), management, mathematics, medical technology, music, philosophy, physics, political science, psychology, social work, sociology, Spanish, theatre/communication, and theology. Some majors through St. Vincent College. Self-designed majors. Distributives, 2 courses in theology, and senior exam required. Honors program. Pass/fail, field work. Preprofessional programs in engineering, law, medicine, dentistry, social service, dietetics, veterinary medicine. 2-2 nursing program. Washington, UN Semesters. Study abroad. Early childhood, elementary, and secondary education certification. Child development center, language lab. 67,000-volume library.

Financial CEEB CSS. College scholarships, grants, loans, academic and professional scholarships, payment plans; PELL, SEOG, NDSL, GSL, CWS. Application deadlines June 1 (scholarships), May 1 (loans).

Admissions High school graduation with 15 units required. Interview encouraged. Audition required for music majors, portfolio recommended for art majors. SAT or ACT required. $10 application fee. Rolling admissions; application deadline July 1. $50 deposit required on acceptance of offer of admission. *Early Admission* Program. Admission deferral possible. Transfers accepted. Credit possible for CEEB AP and CLEP exams.

Student Life Student government. Newspaper, magazine, yearbook. Music groups. International Relations Club. Professional, academic, honorary, and special interest groups. Students must live with relatives or on campus. Women's dorms. Freshman hours restrictions. 6 intercollegiate sports; intramurals. AIAW. Student body composition: 0.5% Asian, 4.5% Black, 2.1% Hispanic, 92.9% White. 20% from out of state.

[1] SHIPPENSBURG STATE COLLEGE
Shippensburg 17257, (717) 532-9121
Dean of Admissions: Albert Drachbar

- **Enrollment: 2,050m, 2,405w**
- **Tuition (1982/83): $1,480 (in-state), $2,590 (out of state)**
- **Room & Board: $1,620; Fees: $164**
- **Degrees offered: BA, BS, BSBA, BSEd**
- **Mean SAT 460v, 510m**
- **Student-faculty ratio: 20 to 1**

A public college established in 1871. 200-acre campus located in small town of Shippensburg. Bus and rail service nearby.

Academic Character MSACS and professional accreditation. Semester system, 3-week and 2 5-week summer terms. 38 majors offered by the schools of Education & Professional Studies, Arts & Sciences, and Business. Interdisciplinary majors. Distributive requirements. Masters degrees granted. Independent study. Pass/fail, internships. Advanced specializations. Preprofessional programs in dentistry, law, medicine, ministry. 3-2 engineering program. Marine science consortium. Professional semester. Study abroad. Elementary and secondary education and library science certification. ROTC. 352,920-volume library with microform resources.

Financial College scholarships and loans, state grants; PELL, SEOG, NDSL, CWS. Application deadline May 1.

Admissions High school graduation required. SAT required. $15 application fee. Rolling admissions; suggest applying early in fall. $35 tuition deposit and $50 room deposit required on acceptance of offer of admission. *Early Admission* Program. Admission deferral possible. Transfers accepted. Credit possible for CEEB AP and CLEP exams. ACT 101 Program.

Student Life Student government. Newspaper, magazines, yearbook, radio station. Music and drama groups. International Students. Academic, honorary, religious, and special interest groups. 8 fraternities and 2 sororities. Coed and single-sex dorms. 56% of students live on campus. 10 intercollegiate sports for men, 7 for women; intramurals. AIAW, NAIA, NCAA. Student body composition: 0.4% Asian, 5% Black, 0.4% Hispanic, 94.2% White. 8% from out of state.

[1] SLIPPERY ROCK STATE COLLEGE
Slippery Rock 16057, (412) 794-7203
Director of Admissions: Elliott G. Baker

- **Undergraduates: 2,283m, 2,417w; 5,715 total (including graduates)**
- **Tuition (1982/83): $1,480 (in-state), $2,590 (out-of-state)**
- **Room & Board: $1,582; Fees: $190**
- **Degrees offered: BA, BS, BFA, BSEd, BSN, BSBA, BMus, BSApp Sc**
- **Mean SAT 385v, 425m**
- **Student-faculty ratio: 17 to 1**

A public college established in 1889. 600-acre rural campus located in small town of Slippery Rock, 50 miles from Pittsburgh. Served by bus; airport and rail station in Pittsburgh.

Academic Character MSACS and professional accreditation. Semester system, 3-, 7-, and 2 5-week summer terms. 4 majors offered by the School of Education, 8 by the School of Health, Physical Education, & Recreation, 7 by the School of Humanities & Fine Arts, 8 by the School of Natural Sciences & Mathematics, and 11 by the School of Social & Behavioral Sciences. Distributive requirements. MA, MEd, MS granted. Independent study. Pass/fail, internships. Preprofessional programs in dentistry, engineering, law, medicine, veterinary medicine, physical therapy. 3-2 engineering program with Penn State, U. of Pittsburgh. Marine science at Delaware Bay, Wallops Station. Member Council for International Education. Study abroad, summer in Salzburg. Certification in elementary, secondary, and special education, and in library science. ROTC, AFROTC. School for Exceptional Children. Computer center. 500,000-volume library.

Financial College scholarships, grants, loans, academic and athletic scholarships, state aid, payment plans; PELL, SEOG, NDSL, FISL, CWS. Application deadline May 1.

Admissions High school graduation with 17 units required. Interview recommended. Audition required for music, music therapy majors. SAT or ACT required. $10 application fee. Rolling admissions; suggest applying by February. $75 deposit required on acceptance of offer of admission. *Early Admission* Program. Admission deferral possible. Transfers accepted. Credit possible for CEEB AP and CLEP exams; college has own advanced placement program. EOP.

Student Life Student government. Newspaper, magazine, yearbook, radio station. Music, debate groups. Academic, religious, honorary, service, and special interest groups. 7 fraternities, 2 with houses, 8 sororities with rooms in dorms. 10% of men and women join. Coed and single-sex dorms. 50% of students live on campus. Liquor prohibited on campus. Conduct code. 3 semesters of phys ed required. 13 intercollegiate sports for men, 13 for women; intramurals. AIAW, ECAC, NCAA, PSAA. Student body composition: 0.5% Asian, 4.2% Black, 0.3% Hispanic, 94.1% White, 0.9% Other. 25% from out of state.

[1] SPRING GARDEN COLLEGE
102 East Mermaid Lane, Chestnut Hill 19118, (215) 242-3700
Director of Admissions: Peter J. Bonasto

- **Undergraduates: 590m, 158w; 1,427 total (including graduates)**
- **Tuition (1982/83): $3,950**
- **Degrees offered: BA, BArch, BS, BST, AS**
- **Mean SAT 400v, 450m**
- **Student-faculty ratio: 15 to 1**

A private college established in 1851, became coed in 1968. 7-acre suburban campus 12 miles from downtown Philadelphia. Served by air, bus, and rail.

Academic Character MSACS and professional accreditation. 4-1-4 system, 2 6-week summer terms. Majors offered in interior design, architecture, accounting, chemistry, computer systems, life sciences & administration, management, medical technology, biochemical technology, and in civil, computer, construction, electronic, energy, industrial/manufacturing, and mechanical engineering technology. Courses in humanities and social sciences. Distributive requirements. AS programs in

most majors and in medical lab technology. Diploma programs in 11 additional areas. Freshmen enroll in AS programs. Independent study. ROTC at Drexel. Computer center, several electronics and technical labs. Member of 2,000,000-volume Tri-State College Library Cooperative.
Financial CEEB CSS. College scholarships and loans, payment plan; PELL, SEOG, NDSL, CWS. Application deadline May 1.
Admissions High school graduation with 15 units required. GED accepted. Interview encouraged. SAT required; ACT accepted. $20 application fee. Rolling admissions; suggest applying by March 15. $100 deposit required on acceptance of offer of admission. *Early Decision, Early Admission Concurrent Enrollment* programs. Admission deferral possible. Transfers accepted. Credit possible for CEEB AP and CLEP exams.
Student Life Student government. Newspaper, magazine, yearbook, radio station. Drama, photography clubs. Black Student Union. Women's, foreign students' associations. Religious, professional, honorary, and special interest groups. 4 fraternities and 2 sororities. No college housing. Liquor prohibited on campus. Class absences limited. 3 intercollegiate sports for men, 1 for women; intramurals. AIAW, NAIA, NCAA. 10% of students from out of state.

[1] SUSQUEHANNA UNIVERSITY

Selinsgrove 17870, (717) 374-0101
Director of Admissions: Paul W. Beardslee

- **Undergraduates: 769m, 710w**
- **Tuition (1982/83): $5,136**
- **Room & Board: $2,200; Fees: $160**
- **Degrees offered: BA, BSBus, BMus**
- **Mean SAT 470v, 520m**
- **Student-faculty ratio: 15 to 1**

A private university affiliated with the Lutheran Church in America, established in 1858. 185-acre campus located in small town of Selinsgrove, 50 miles from Harrisburg. Airport in Harrisburg.
Academic Character MSACS and professional accreditation.Trimester system, 6-week summer term. Majors offered in biology, chemistry, classics, communications & theatre arts, computer & information science, economics, elementary education, English, French, geology, German, Greek, history, Latin, mathematics, philosophy, physics, politicial science, psychology, religion, sociology, Spanish, and 5 business majors and 4 music majors. Self-designed and double majors. Many minors offered. Courses in art, secondary education. Anesthesia major for RNs. Distributive requirements. 1 course in religion/philosophy required. Independent study. Honors program. Pass/fail, internships. Preprofessional programs in dentistry, engineering, law, medicine, ministry, music, optometry, teaching, veterinary medicine. 3-2 and 4-2 engineering programs with U Penn. 3-2 forestry program with Duke. Washington, UN, Appalachian, Baltimore semesters. Study abroad. Elementary and secondary education certification. ROTC at Bucknell. Language lab. 125,000-volume library with microform resources.
Financial CEEB CSS. University scholarships, grants, loans, Lutheran grants, payment plans; PELL, SEOG, NDSL, FISL, CWS. Application deadline May 1.
Admissions High school graduation with 17 units required. Interview encouraged, required for *Early Decision* and transfer applicants. Audition required for music majors. SAT or ACT required. $20 application fee. Rolling admissions; application deadline March 15. $200 deposit required on acceptance of offer of admission. *Early Decision* and *Early Admission* programs. Admission deferral possible. Transfers accepted. Credit possible for CEEB AP and CLEP exams; university has own advanced placement program.
Student Life Student government. Newspaper, magazine, yearbook, radio station. Music, drama groups. Religious, honorary, and special interest organizations. 5 fraternities with houses and 4 sororities without houses. 32% of students join. Freshmen must live at home or on campus. Coed and single-sex dorms, language houses. 82% of students live on campus. 4 terms of phys ed required. 10 intercollegiate sports for men, 7 for women; intramurals. NCAA, ECAC, MAC. 55% of students from out of state.

[1] SWARTHMORE COLLEGE

Swarthmore 19081, (215) 447-7300
Dean of Admissions: Robert A. Barr, Jr.

- **Undergraduates: 684m, 573w**
- **Tuition (1982/83): $7,130**
- **Room & Board: $3,000; Fees: $540**
- **Degrees offered: AB, BSEng**
- **Mean SAT 650v, 670m**
- **Student-faculty ratio: 10 to 1**

A private college established in 1864. 300-acre suburban campus in small town of Swarthmore, 30 minutes from Philadelphia. Air, bus, and rail service in Philadelphia.
Academic Character MSACS and professional accreditation. Semester system. Majors offered in art, art history, astronomy, biology, chemistry, economics, engineering (5 areas), English literature, French, German, Greek, history, Latin, linguistics, literature, mathematics, medieval studies, music, philosophy, physics, political science, psychology, religion, Russian, sociology/anthropology, Spanish, and theatre/dramatics. Self-designed majors. Minor required. Distributive requirements. MA granted (rarely). Independent study. Honors program. Phi Beta Kappa. First semester is pass/fail. Cooperative program with Bryn Mawr, Haverford, U Penn. Exchanges with Middlebury, Mills, Pomona, Rice, Tufts. Study abroad in France, Spain, Taiwan. Employment exchange program abroad for engineering/science majors. Secondary education certificiation. Observatory, computer center, language lab. 750,000-volume library.
Financial CEEB CSS. College scholarships, grants, loans, payment plan; PELL, SEOG, NDSL, CWS. Scholarship application deadline January 15.
Admissions High school graduation required. SAT and 3 ACH required. $25 application fee. Application deadline February 1. $100 deposit required on acceptance of offer of admission. Fall and Winter *Early Decision* Programs. Admission deferral possible. Transfers accepted. Credit possible for CEEB AP exams.
Student Life Extracurricular activities are an integral part of a sound Swarthmore education; they include: Student government. Newspaper, magazine, yearbook, radio station. Music, debate, drama, folk dance groups. Academic, honorary, religious, service, political, senior, and special interest groups. 3 fraternities with nonresidential houses. 15% of men join. Special permission needed to live off campus. Coed and single-sex dorms, special interest housing. 90% of students live on campus. Cars on campus limited. 2 semesters of phys ed required. 12 intercollegiate sports for men, 9 for women; intramurals. AIAW, NCAA, MACC. Student body composition: 15% minority. 80% of students from out of state.

[1] TEMPLE UNIVERSITY

Philadelphia 19122, (215) 787-7000
Director of Admissions: R. Kenneth Haldeman

- **Undergraduates: 8,530m, 8,438w; 31,442 total (including part-time)**
- **Tuition (1982/83): $2,616 (in-state), $4,800 (out-of-state)**
- **Room & Board: $2,850**
- **Degrees offered: BA, BS, BArch, BBA, BFA, BMus, BMus Ed, BSE, BSEd, BSW**
- **Mean SAT 994**
- **Student-faculty ratio: 8 to 1**

A public university established in 1888. 233-acre urban campus in Philadelphia. Served by air, bus, and rail.
Academic Character MSACS and professional accreditation. Semester system, 3 summer terms. 5 majors offered by the College of Allied Health Professions, 14 by the College of Education, 9 by the College of Engineering Technology, 4 by the College of Health, Physical Education, Recreation, & Leisure Studies, 36 by the College of Liberal Arts, 7 by the College of Music, 1 by the Department of Criminal Justice, 13 by the School of Business Administration, 3 by the School of Communications & Theater, 1 by the School of Pharmacy, 2 by the School of Social Administration, and 8 by the Tyler School of Art. Graduate and professional degrees granted. Honors program. Cooperative work/study. Study abroad. ROTC; AFROTC at St. Joseph's. Computer center, several special facilities. 1,800,000-volume library with microform resources.
Financial CEEB CSS. University scholarships, grants, loans, state aid, payment plan; PELL, SEOG, NDSL, GSL. Application deadline May 1.
Admissions High school graduation with 16 units required. GED accepted. SAT or ACT required. $15 application fee. Rolling admissions; suggest applying in September. $50 deposit required on acceptance of offer of admission. *Early Admission* and *Early Decision* programs. Admission deferral possible. Transfers accepted. Credit possible for CEEB AP and CLEP exams. Special Recruitment and Admissions Program.
Student Life Student government. Newspaper, magazine, yearbook, radio station. Music and drama groups. Business, professional, and special interest groups. 12 fraternities with houses and 7 sororities with nonresidential houses. 10% of men and women join. 18% of students live on campus. Liquor, gambling, firearms prohibited on campus. 14 intercollegiate sports for men, 14 for women; intramurals. AIAW, NCAA, ECAC. Student body composition: 22% minority.

■[1] AMBLER CAMPUS OF TEMPLE UNIVERSITY

Ambler 19002, (215) 643-1200
Acting Dean: Walter J. Gershenfeld

- **Enrollment: 2,581 men & women; 9,319 total (including evening and summer)**
- **Tuition (1982/83): $2,616 (in-state), $4,800 (out-of-state)**
- **Room: $2,834**
- **Degrees offered: BA, BBA, BS, AS**
- **Student-faculty ratio: 14 to 1**

Extension campus of public university, established in 1910. 187-acre campus in Montgomery county, 18 miles from Philadelphia. Served by bus and rail.
Academic Character MSACS accreditation. Semester system. Majors offered in accounting, American studies, art history, business administration, criminal justice, early childhood education, economics, elementary education, engineering technology, English, English education, geography, health education, history, industrial relations, journalism, law, liberal arts, management, mathematics, mathematics education, political science, psychology, religion, science education, secondary education, social studies education, sociology. Distributive requirements. Graduate and professional degrees granted. Honors program. Cooperative work/study. Preprofessional programs in allied health, dentistry, law, medicine, pharmacy. Elementary, secondary, and early childhood education certification. University resources available to Ambler students.
Financial University scholarships and grants, state grants, PELL, SEOG, NDSL. Application deadline May 1.
Admissions High school graduation with 16 units required. SAT or ACT required. Rolling admissions; application deadline June 15. $50 tuition deposit and $250 room deposit (for boarders) required on acceptance of offer of admission. *Early Admission* Program. Transfers accepted. Credit possible for CEEB CLEP exams.
Student Life Coed dorms. 5% of students live on campus. University programs and activities available.

■[1] COLLEGE OF ENGINEERING TECHNOLOGY OF TEMPLE UNIVERSITY

12th and Norris Streets, Philadelphia 19122

[1] THIEL COLLEGE
Greenville 16125, (412) 588-7700
Director of Admissions: John R. Hauser

- **Undergraduates: 468m, 453w**
- **Tuition (1982/83): $4,866**
- **Room & Board: $2,353; Fees: $80**
- **Degrees offered: BA, AA**
- **Student-faculty ratio: 14 to 1**

A private college affiliated with the Lutheran Church in America, established in 1866. 135-acre campus in small city of Greenville, 75 miles from Pittsburgh and Cleveland. Bus 15 minutes away in Mercer; airport 30 miles away in Youngstown.
Academic Character MSACS accreditation. 4-1-4 system, 2 4-week summer terms. Majors offered in accounting, actuarial studies, art, biology, business administration, chemistry, computer science, cytotechnology, economics, English, environmental science, French, geology, history, mathematics, medical technology, philosophy, physics, political science, psychology, religion, sociology, Spanish, and speech & hearing science. Distributives and senior comprehensive exams required. Independent study. Honors program. Pass/fail, internships. 3-2 program in engineering with Case Western Reserve. 2-2 nursing program with Widener; 3-1, 3-3 nursing programs with Case Western. 3-2 forestry program with Duke. 3-1 cytotechnology, medical technology programs. 3-1, 2-2 programs with Art Institute of Pittsburgh. Washington, UN, Drew U (art), Argonne, Appalachian semesters. Study abroad. Marine Corps Officer Candidate program. Language labs. 107,644-volume library.
Financial CEEB CSS. College scholarships, grants, loans, family grants, state aid, payment plan; PELL, SEOG, NDSL, CWS. FAF deadline April 1.
Admissions High school graduation with 16 units required. Interview encouraged. SAT or ACT required. $15 application fee. Rolling admissions; suggest applying in fall. $100 deposit required on acceptance of offer of admision. *Early Admission* Program. Admission deferral possible. Transfers accepted. Credit possible for CEEB AP and CLEP exams.
Student Life Student government. Newspaper, yearbook, radio station. Music, debate, drama groups. Organization of Black Collegiates. Honorary, academic, service, and special interest groups. 4 fraternities with houses, and 5 sororities without houses. Single students must live at home or on campus. 94% of students live on campus. 7 intercollegiate sports for men, 4 for women, 1 coed; intramurals. AIAW, NCAA, PAC. Student body composition: 1% Asian, 2% Black, 97% White. 30% from out of state.

[1 & G1] THOMAS JEFFERSON UNIVERSITY
11th & Walnut Streets, Philadelphia 19107, (215) 928-6000

- **Enrollment: 802m, 601w; 1,780 total (including part-time)**
- **Tuition (1982/83): $5,400**
- **Degrees offered: BS, BSN, BSDH**

A private, health-related university. Campus in an urban, center-city environment. Air, bus, and rail service nearby.
Academic Character MSACS and professional accreditation. 3-3-3 system. All BS degree programs are upper-division (junior & senior years); they include cytotechnology, dental hygiene, medical technology, nursing, radiologic technology. Advanced placement program for RNs seeking BSN. Post-certificate program for licensed dental hygienists seeking BDSH. Upper-division program in occupational therapy and physical therapy will start in September, 1983. Associate, graduate, and professional degrees granted. 120,000-volume library.
Financial CEEB CSS. College grants, loans, state aid; PELL, SEOG, NDSL, CWS, college employment.
Admissions Rolling admissions. New students admitted for September entrance only.
Student Life Student publications. Student activities include choir, drama club, scuba club. Intramural athletics. Recreational facilities include pool, gymnasium, sauna, game rooms, raquetball/squash court. Student body composition: 13% minority.

[2 & J2] UNITED WESLEYAN COLLEGE
1414 East Cedar Street, Allentown 18103

[1] URSINUS COLLEGE
Collegeville 19426, (215) 489-4111
Dean of Admissions: Kenneth L. Schaefer

- **Undergraduates: 601m, 523w**
- **Tuition (1982/83): $4,950-$5,150**
- **Room & Board: $2,300; Fees: $300**
- **Degrees offered: AB, BS**
- **Mean SAT 540v, 590m**
- **Student-faculty ratio: 12 to 1**

A private college affiliated with the United Church of Christ, established in 1869. 140-acre campus in small town of Collegeville, 25 miles from Philadelphia. Served by bus; rail station in Norristown; airport in Philadelphia.
Academic Character MSACS and professional accreditation. Semester system, 12-week summer term. Majors offered in American public policy, applied mathematics/economics, biology, chemistry, classical studies, economics & business administration, English, German, health/physical education, history, international relations, mathematics, philosophy-religion, physics, political science, psychology, and Romance languages. Self-designed majors. Distributive requirements. AA, AS, BBA offered in evening school. Independent study. Honors program. Preprofessional programs in law, medicine. 3-2 engineering programs with Georgia Tech, U Penn, USC. Study abroad. Secondary and physical education certification. Computer center, language labs. 136,000-volume library with microform resources.
Financial CEEB CSS. College scholarships, grants, loans, state aid, payment plan; PELL, SEOG, NDSL, FISL, PLUS, CWS. Application deadline March 1.
Admissions High school graduation with 16 units required. Interview required. SAT required; 3 ACH recommended. $20 application fee. Rolling admissions. $200 deposit required on acceptance of offer of admission. *Early Decision* and *Early Admission* programs. Admission deferral possible. Transfers accepted. Credit possible for CEEB AP and CLEP exams.
Student Life Student government. Newspaper, magazine, journal, yearbook, radio station. Music, drama groups. Academic, honorary, religious, and special interest organizations. 8 fraternities and 5 sororities. 45% of students join. Students must live at home or on campus. Single-sex dorms. No married-student housing. 92% of students live on campus. Financial aid recipients may not have cars on campus. 2 semesters of phys ed required. 10 intercollegiate sports for men, 9 for women; intramurals. AIAW, ECAC, NCAA. Student body composition: 1% Asian, 2% Black, 2% Hispanic, 95% White. 35% from out of state.

[J2] VALE TECHNICAL INSTITUTE/AUTO/DIESEL SCHOOL
135 West Market Street, Blairsville 15717

[P] VALLEY FORGE CHRISTIAN COLLEGE
Charlestown Road, Phoenixville 19460

[J1] VALLEY FORGE MILITARY JUNIOR COLLEGE
Wayne 19087, (215) 688-3151
Director of Admissions: Frank H. Schoendorfer

- **Enrollment: 120m**
- **Tuition (1982/83): $3,440**
- **Room & Board: $3,850**
- **Degrees offered: AA, AS, ABA**
- **Median SAT 410v, 450m**
- **Student-faculty ratio: 4 to 1**

A private men's junior college. 130-acre campus in Wayne, 15 miles from Philadelphia. Served by rail. Airport in Philadelphia.
Academic Character MSACS accreditation. 4-1-4 system. 2-year programs offered in business administration, liberal arts, science, criminal justice, and military science. Distributive requirements. Independent study. Internships. 2-year AROTC. 58,000-volume library.
Financial College scholarships, state grants, ROTC scholarships, payment plan; PELL, GSL, CWS. Application deadline for state grants August 1.
Admissions High school graduation required. Interview required. SAT or ACT required. $25 application fee. Rolling admissions. $500 deposit required on acceptance of offer of admission. *Early Admission* Program. Admission deferral possible. Credit possible for CEEB AP and CLEP exams.
Student Life Newspaper, yearbook. Music, arts groups. Honorary, military, religious, academic, service, and special interest groups. Students live on campus. Dorm and dining hall. Chapel attendance required. 2 years of physical training and 2 years of ROTC required. 6 intercollegiate sports. Student body composition: 10% minority.

[1] VILLA MARIA COLLEGE
2551 West 8th Street, Erie 16505, (814) 838-1966

- **Undergraduates: 525w**
- **Tuition, Room & Board (1982/83): $5,960**
- **Degrees offered: BA, BS, BSN, AA, AS, ASN**
- **Student-faculty ratio: 12 to 1**

A private, Roman Catholic women's college founded in 1925 by Sisters of St. Joseph. Suburban residential campus, equidistant from Pittsburgh, Buffalo, and Cleveland.
Academic Character MSACS and professional accreditation. 4-1-4 system. Majors offered in accounting, biology, chemistry, dietetics, early childhood education, elementary education, English/communications, home economics merchandising & retailing, marketing, math, medical technology, nursing, management/personnel administration, psychology, social work, sociology, Spanish, special education, therapeutic recreation. Associate degrees offered in nursing, early childhood education, public relations, advertising, and information. 43,000-volume library.
Financial CEEB CSS. State aid, service scholarships; PELL, SEOG, NDSL, NSS, NSL, CWS.
Admissions High school graduation required. SAT or ACT required. Rolling admissions. Transfers accepted. Advanced placement program.
Student Life Residence halls and dining halls.

[1] VILLANOVA UNIVERSITY
Villanova 19085, (215) 645-4000
Director of Admissions: Rev. Harry J. Erdlen, OSA

- **Undergraduates: 3,653m, 2,450w; 7,620 total (including graduates)**
- **Tuition (1982/83): $5,000**
- **Room & Board: $3,100**
- **Degrees offered: BA, BS, BChEng, BCE, BEE, BFA, BME, BSBA, BSEcon, BSA, BSEd, AA**
- **Mean SAT 520v, 580m**
- **Student-faculty ratio: 15 to 1**

A private, Roman Catholic university started by the Augustinian Fathers, established in 1842, became coed in 1965. 240-acre suburban campus in Villanova, 6 miles from Philadelphia. Served by bus and rail; airport in Philadelphia.

Academic Character MSACS and professional accreditation. Semester system, 2 5-week summer terms. 8 majors offered by the College of Commerce & Finance, 4 by the College of Engineering, 23 by the College of Liberal Arts & Sciences, and 1 by the College of Nursing. 6 additional concentrations offered. Distributives and 9 credits in religious studies required. Graduate degrees granted. Honors program. Pass/fail, internships. Study abroad. Elementary, secondary, and special education certification. NROTC; AFROTC at St. Joseph's. Computer center, language lab, Augustinian Historical Institute. 453,750-volume library with microform resources.
Financial CEEB CSS. University scholarships, and loans; PELL, SEOG, NSS, NDSL, CWS. Application deadlines March 1 (FAF), March 15 (loans).
Admissions High school graduation with 16 units required. Interview encouraged. SAT or ACT required; foreign language ACH required for Arts & Sciences. $20 application fee. Application deadline February 15. $200 deposit required on acceptance of offer of admission. *Early Decision* Program. Transfers accepted. Credit possible for CEEB AP and CLEP exams; university has own advanced placement program.
Student Life Student government. Newspaper, magazines, yearbook. Music, debate, and drama groups. Political, service, academic, professional, and special interest organizations. 16 fraternities and sororities without houses. 20% of students join. Limited university housing. Single-sex dorms. 43% of students live on campus. Junior and senior residents may have cars on campus. 11 intercollegiate sports for men, 11 for women; intramurals. NCAA. 65% of students from out of state.

[1] WASHINGTON AND JEFFERSON COLLEGE
Washington 15301, (412) 222-4400
Director of Admissions: Thomas P. O'Connor

- **Undergraduates: 654m, 404w**
- **Tuition (1982/83): $5,900**
- **Room & Board: $2,190; Fees: $210**
- **Degree offered: BA**
- **Mean ACT 24; mean SAT 500v, 550m**
- **Student-faculty ratio: 11 to 1**

A private college established in 1781, became coed in 1970. 30-acre campus located in small city of Washington, 30 miles from Pittsburgh. Served by bus; airport and rail station in Pittsburgh.
Academic Character MSACS accreditation. 4-1-4 system, 8-week summer term. Majors offered in art, biology, chemistry, economics & business, English, French, German, history, industrial chemistry/management, mathematics, philosophy, physics, political science, psychology, sociology, and Spanish. Self-designed majors. Distributive requirements. Independent study. Honors program. Phi Beta Kappa. Pass/fail, internships. 3-2 engineering programs with Case Western Reserve, Washington U. 3-1 medical technology program. Cooperative 3-4 podiatry and optometry programs. Washington Semester. Study abroad. Secondary education certification. ROTC. 185,000-volume library.
Financial CEEB CSS. College scholarships, grants, loans, state aid, payment plan; PELL, SEOG, NDSL, GSL, CWS. FAF deadline March 15.
Admissions High school graduation with 15 units required. Interview encouraged. SAT and 3 ACH, or ACT required. $15 application fee. Application deadline March 1. $100 deposit required on acceptance of offer of admission. *Early Decision* and *Early Admission* programs. Admission deferral possible. Transfers accepted. Credit possible for CEEB AP and CLEP exams.
Student Life Student government. Newspaper, magazine, yearbook, radio station. Music, literary, debate, drama groups. Academic, religious, honorary, and special interest organizations. 11 fraternities with houses and 2 sororities. 55% of men join fraternities. Students must live at home or on campus. Coed dorms. 90% of students live on campus. Limited class absences allowed. 1 year of phys ed (except for ROTC students) required. 12 intercollegiate sports for men, 5 for women; intramurals. AIAW, ECAC, NCAA, PAC, Penn Wood West. 35% of students from out of state.

[1] WAYNESBURG COLLEGE
Waynesburg 15370, (412) 627-8191
Director of Admissions: Ronald L. Shunk

- **Undergraduates: 470m, 304w**
- **Tuition (1982/83): $4,600**
- **Room & Board: $2,120; Fees: $160**
- **Degrees offered: BA, BS, BSBA, AA, AS**
- **Mean SAT 450v, 450m**
- **Student-faculty ratio: 14 to 1**

A private college affiliated with the United Presbyterian Church, USA, established in 1849. 30-acre small-town campus 50 miles from Pittsburgh. Air, bus, and rail service in Pittsburgh.
Academic Character MSACS and professional accreditation. Semester system, 2 5-week summer terms. Majors offered in economics, elementary education, English, English-communications, fine arts, French, history, psychology, public service administration, social science, Spanish, visual arts, biology, chemistry, earth-space science, geology, management science, mathematics, mathematics-computer science, medical technology, mine management, accounting, finance, general business, management, marketing, and small business administration. Distributive requirements. Independent study. Honors program. Pass/fail. CPA, government, psychology internships. Preprofessional programs in dentistry, engineering, law, medicine, ministry, nursing. Study abroad. Member Regional Council for International Education. Elementary and secondary education certification. ROTC. Arboretum, 174-acre farm, geology field station in Colorado, language lab. 115,000-volume library.
Financial CEEB CSS. College scholarships, loans, Presbyterian scholarships, state aid; PELL, SEOG, GSL, FISL, NDSL, CWS. Application deadlines May 1 (scholarships), March 1 (loans).
Admissions High school graduation with 16 units required. Interview encouraged. ACT or SAT required. $15 application fee. Rolling admissions. $100 deposit required on acceptance of offer of admission. *Early Admission* and *Early Decision* programs. Admission deferral possible. Transfers accepted. Credit possible for CEEB AP and CLEP exams.
Student Life Student government. Newspaper, magazine, yearbook, radio station. Music, drama groups. Academic, professional, service, honorary, and special interest organizations. 4 fraternities with houses and 4 sororities without houses. 32% of men and 33% of women join. Seniors may live off campus. Single-sex dorms. Married-student housing. 63% of students live off campus. Boarding freshmen may not have cars on campus. Liquor prohibited on campus. 7 intercollegiate sports for men, 3 for women; several intramural and club sports. AIAW, NAIA. Student body composition: 9% Black, 91% White. 23% from out of state.

[1] WEST CHESTER STATE COLLEGE
West Chester 19380, (215) 436-1000
Director of Admissions: William E. Kipp

- **Undergraduates: 2,586m, 3,696w; 9,700 total (including graduates)**
- **Tuition (1982/83): $1,480 (in-state), $2,420 (out-of-state)**
- **Room & Board: $1,750; Fees: $124**
- **Degrees offered: BA, BS, BSEd, BMus**
- **Student-faculty ratio: 18 to 1**

A public college established in 1871. 385-acre suburban campus in small city of West Chester, 25 miles west of Philadelphia. Air, bus, and rail service nearby.
Academic Character MSACS and professional accreditation. Semester system, 6-week and 2 3-week summer terms. 28 majors offered for the BA degree, 19 for the BS, 23 for the BS in Education, and 1 each for the BS in Nursing and the BMusic. Self-designed majors. Distributive and human relations requirements. Masters degrees granted. Independent study. Honors program. Phi Beta Kappa. Pass/fail, internships. Preprofessional programs in health fields, law, theology. 3-2 engineering program with Penn State. 2-2 dental hygiene program. Member Marine Science Consortium with 14 schools. Exchange program with 50 U.S. schools. Study abroad in Austria, France. ROTC; AFROTC at St. Joseph's. Computer center, art gallery, herbarium. 500,000-volume library with microform resources and music library.
Financial CEEB CSS. College scholarships, state aid; PELL, SEOG, NDSL, NSL, CWS. Application deadline May 1.
Admissions High school graduation required. GED accepted. SAT or ACT required. $15 application fee. Rolling admissions. $100 deposit required on acceptance of offer of admission. *Early Admission* Program. Admission deferral possible. Credit possible for CEEB AP and CLEP exams. ACT 101 Program.
Student Life Student government. Newspaper, magazine, yearbook, radio station. Music, dance, drama, debate groups. Black Student Union. Religious, service, and special interest groups. 8 fraternities and 7 sororities. Coed and single-sex dorms; honors and special interest housing. 50% of students live on campus. Limited class absences allowed. 11 intercollegiate sports for men, 11 for women; intramurals. Student body composition: 0.2% Asian, 8.1% Black, 0.7% Hispanic, 0.8% Native American, 90.2% White. 20% from out of state.

[1] WESTMINSTER COLLEGE
New Wilmington 16142, (412) 946-8761
Director of Admissions: Edwin G. Tobin

- **Undergraduates: 630m, 690w; 1,590 total (including graduates)**
- **Tuition (1982/83): $4,900**
- **Room & Board: $2,006**
- **Degrees offered: BA, BS, BMus**
- **Median SAT 459v, 502m**
- **Student-faculty ratio: 14 to 1**

A private college affiliated with the United Presbyterian Church USA, established in 1852. 300-acre campus in residential town of New Wilmington, 60 miles from Pittsburgh. Airport in Pittsburgh.
Academic Character MSACS and professional accreditation. 4-1-4 system, 6- and 3-week summer terms. Majors offered in art, art education, applied music, biology, business administration, chemistry, Christian education, church music, computer information systems, computer science, economics, elementary education, English, French, German, history, Latin, mathematics, music, music education, physics, philosophy, political science, psychology, religion, sociology, Spanish, speech, and theatre. 7 interdisciplinary majors. Intercultural majors. Self-designed majors. Distributives and one religion course required. MEd granted. Independent study. Honors program. Pass/fail, internships. Credit for field experience. Preprofessional programs include dentistry, law, medicine, theology. 3-2 engineering programs with Penn State, Washington, Lafayette. Member consortium with 6 colleges. Washington, East Asian semesters. Study abroad. ROTC at Youngstown State. Language lab, computer center. 200,000-volume library.
Financial CEEB CSS. College scholarships, grants, loans; PELL, SEOG, NDSL, CWS. Application deadline May 1.
Admissions High school graduation with 15 units required. Interview encouraged. SAT or ACT required. $15 application fee. Rolling admissions. $100 deposit required on acceptance of offer of admission. *Early Decision* and *Early Admission* programs. Admission deferral possible. Transfers accepted. Credit possible for CEEB AP and CLEP exams.
Student Life Student government. Newspaper, magazine, yearbook, radio station. Music, debate, drama groups. Film series. Academic, service, tutoring religious, and special interest groups. 5 fraternities with houses and 5 sororities without houses. 46% of men and 45% of women join. Except junior and senior men, students must live at home or on campus. Single-sex dorms.

90% of students live on campus. Liquor, drugs prohibited. 2 years of phys ed required. 8 intercollegiate sports for men, 5 for women; intramurals. AIAW, NAIA, KCWIA. Student body composition: 2% Black, 97% White, 1% Other. 28% from out of state.

[1] WESTMINSTER THEOLOGICAL SEMINARY
Chestnut Hill, Philadelphia 19118

[J1] WESTMORELAND COUNTY COMMUNITY COLLEGE
Armbrust Road, Youngwood 15697

[J2] WHEELER SCHOOL
212 Ninth Street, Pittsburgh 15222

[1] WIDENER UNIVERSITY
Chester 19013, (215) 499-4126
Dean of Admissions: Vincent F. Lindsley

- **Undergraduates: 1,243m, 1,100w**
- **Tuition (1982/83): $5,100**
- **Room & Board: $2,240-$2,665; Fees: $220**
- **Degrees offered: BA, BS, BSEng, BSBA, BSN, BSW**
- **Student-faculty ratio: 12 to 1**

A private university established in 1821. Suburban campus in Chester, 15 miles from Philadelphia. Air, bus, and rail service nearby.
Academic Character MSACS and professional accreditation. Semester system, 3- and 2 5-week summer terms. Majors offered in behavioral science, biology, chemistry, community psychology, computer science, English, history, humanities, international affairs, mathematics, modern languages, physics, political science, psychology, radiologic technology, science administration, science education, social work, sociology, engineering, accounting, economics, management, and nursing. Self-designed majors. Distributive requirements. Graduate degrees granted. Independent study. Cooperative work/study, pass/fail, internships. Preprofessional programs in law, medicine. Study abroad in several countries. Elementary and secondary education certification. ROTC. Museum, gallery. 160,000-volume library with microform resources.
Financial CEEB CSS. University scholarships, music scholarships, state grants, payment plan; PELL, SEOG, NSS, NDSL, GSL, CWS. Priority application deadline February 1.
Admissions High school graduation required with 14 units recommended. GED accepted. Interview encouraged. CEEB SAT, CLEP, or AP required. $15 application fee. Rolling admissions. $150 deposit required on acceptance of offer of admission. *Early Decision, Early Admission, Concurrent Enrollment* programs. Transfers accepted. Credit possible for CEEB AP and CLEP exams; university has own advanced placement program. Project Prepare.
Student Life Newspaper, magazine, yearbook, radio station. Music, drama groups. Hispanic-American Society. International Club. Religious, honorary, academic, and special interest groups. 5 fraternities, 2 sororities. Single students under 21 must live at home or on campus. 13 intercollegiate sports for men, 6 for women; women may compete on men's teams. Intramurals. AIAW, ECAC, NCAA, MASCAC. Student body composition: 0.4% Asian, 8.5% Black, 0.3% Hispanic, 0.1% Native American, 90.7% White.

[1] WILKES COLLEGE
170 South Franklin Street, Wilkes-Barre 18766, (717) 824-4651
Dean of Admissions: G.K. Wuori

- **Undergraduates: 1,096m, 991w**
- **Tuition (1982/83): $4,650**
- **Room & Board: $2,350; Fees: $50**
- **Degrees offered: BA, BS**
- **Mean SAT 430v, 480m**
- **Student-faculty ratio: 13 to 1**

A private college established in 1933. Urban campus in Wilkes-Barre, 20 miles from Scranton, 100 miles from Philadelphia. Served by air and bus.
Academic Character MSACS and professional accreditation. Semester system, 2 5-week summer terms. Majors offered in art, biology, chemistry, computer science, earth & environmental sciences, economics, elementary education, English, foreign languages, history, individualized studies, international studies, mathematics, music, philosophy, physics, political science, psychology, social science, sociology/anthropology, business education, commerce & finance, engineering, and nursing. Courses in Russian, speech. Distributive requirements. MA, MBA granted. Independent study. Honors program. Cooperative work/study, internships. Preprofessional programs in engineering, dentistry, optometry, podiatry, medicine, pharmacy, business administration, education, library science, law, and theology. 5-year pharmacy program with Temple. 5-year BS/MS mathematics program. 3-4 programs with Pennsylvania College of Optometry and College of Podiatric Medicine. Elementary and secondary education certification. AFROTC. Language lab, Institute for Regional Affairs, art gallery. 200,000-volume library.
Financial CEEB CSS. College scholarships, grants, loans, state aid, payment plans; PELL, SEOG, NSS, NDSL, NSL, CWS. Application deadlines February 1 (FAF), April 1 (loans).
Admissions High school graduation with 15 units required. Interview encouraged. Audition required for music majors. SAT required. $15 application fee. Rolling admissions; suggest applying by April 1. $100 deposit required on acceptance of offer of admission. *Early Decision* and *Early Admission* programs. Transfers accepted. Credit possible for CEEB AP and CLEP exams. ACT 101.
Student Life Student government. Newspaper, magazine, yearbook, radio station. Music, debate, drama groups. Film society. Service, professional, and special interest groups. Freshmen under 18 must live at home or on campus. Dorms for men and women. No married-student housing. 43% of students live on campus. 2 years of phys ed required. 9 intercollegiate sports for men, 6 for women; intramurals. AIAW, ECAC, NCAA, MAAC. Student body composition: 0.4% Asian, 0.7% Black, 0.2% Hispanic, 97.6% White, 1.1% Other. 25% from out of state.

[J1] WILLIAMSPORT AREA COMMUNITY COLLEGE
1005 West Third Street, Williamsport 17701

[1] WILSON COLLEGE
Chambersburg 17201, (717) 264-4141
Director of Admissions: Peter T. Sealy

- **Undergraduates: 240w**
- **Tuition (1982/83): $5,220**
- **Room & Board: $2,413; Fees: $65**
- **Degrees offered: BA, BS, AS**
- **Mean SAT 460v, 445m**
- **Student-faculty ratio: 6 to 1**

A private women's college affiliated with the Presbyterian Church, established in 1869. 300-acre campus in a small city southwest of Harrisburg.
Academic Character MSACS accreditation. Semester system, optional January term. Majors offered in American studies, behavioral sciences, business & economics, communications, creative arts, elementary education, international studies, literature & language studies, physical & life sciences, social & political institutions, and sources of Western culture. Special majors. AS offered in veterinary medical technology. Distributive requirements. Independent study, honors programs. Pass/fail, internships. Preprofessional programs in health sciences, law, medicine. Dual degree programs with Penn State in earth and mineral sciences, with Clarkson and Georgia Tech in engineering or industrial management. Medical technology programs with local hospitals. Exchange program with Shippensburg State. Washington, UN, Harrisburg semesters. Study abroad. Semester in South India. Elementary and secondary education certification. ROTC. 150,000-volume library.
Financial CEEB CSS. College scholarships, alumnae sponsorships, state grants; PELL, SEOG, NDSL, GSL, PLUS, CWS.
Admissions High school graduation required. SAT or ACT required. $15 application fee. Rolling admissions. $100 deposit required on acceptance of offer of admission. *Early Admission* Program. Admission deferral possible. Transfers accepted. Credit possible for CEEB AP and CLEP exams.
Student Life Student government. Newspaper, magazine, yearbook. Drama, music, dance groups. Afro-American Society. Religious, service, academic, outing, and special interest organizations. Full-time students must live on campus. Women's dorms. Language houses. 1 year of phys ed required. 6 intercollegiate sports; intramurals. EAIAW, USFHA, USLA, USGF.

[1 & J1] YORK COLLEGE OF PENNSYLVANIA
York 17405, (717) 846-7788
Director of Admissions: Nancy Clingan

- **Undergraduates: 930m, 1,309w; 4,277 total (including graduates)**
- **Tuition (1982/83): $2,670**
- **Room & Board: $1,770; Fees: $126**
- **Degrees offered: BA, BS, AA, AS**
- **Mean SAT 412v, 445m**
- **Student-faculty ratio: 24 to 1**

A private college established in 1873. 60-acre suburban campus located in city of York, 45 miles from Baltimore. Served by bus.
Academic Character MSACS and professional accreditation. Semester system, 3- and 2 5-week summer terms. Majors offered in accounting, art, behavioral science, biology, computer information systems, criminal justice, elementary education, engineering management, English, government/public administration, health records administration, history, humanities, international studies, long-term care administration, management, marketing, medical technology, music, nursing, psychology, recreation, secondary education, sociology, and speech. Minors offered in most major fields and in 15 additional areas. Distributive requirements. MBA granted. Independent study. Pass/fail, internships. Credit by exam. Elementary and secondary education certification. ROTC. Computer center. 100,000-volume library with microform resources.
Financial CEEB CSS and ACT FAS. College scholarships, grants, loans, payment plans; PELL, SEOG, NDSL, FISL, NSL, CWS. Scholarship application deadline May 1.
Admissions High school graduation with 15 units required. GED accepted. Interview encouraged. SAT or ACT required. $15 application fee. Rolling admissions; application deadline March 1 (for boarders). $100 tuition deposit and $100 room deposit (for boarders) required on acceptance of offer of admission. *Early Admission* and *Concurrent Enrollment* programs. Admission deferral possible. Transfers accepted. Credit possible for CEEB AP and CLEP exams.
Student Life Student government. Newspaper, yearbook. Music, debate, drama groups. Afro-American club. Deaf awareness group. Academic, professional, honorary, religious, and special interest groups. 4 fraternities without houses and 4 sororities, 1 with house. 2% of men and women join. Students must live at home or in college housing. Coed and single-sex dorms. Off-campus apartments. No married-student housing. 50% of students live on campus. Liquor prohibited on campus. 4 semesters of phys ed required. Student body composition: 3.1% Black, 0.4% Hispanic, 0.4% Native American, 83.1% White, 12.9% Other. 30% from out of state.

RHODE ISLAND (RI)

[1] BARRINGTON COLLEGE
Barrington 02806, (401) 246-1200
Director of Admissions & Church Relations: Donald Anderson

- **Enrollment: 520 men & women**
- **Tuition (1982/83): $4,820**
- **Room & Board: $2,475; Fees: $265**
- **Degrees offered: BA, BS, BMus, AS**
- **Student-faculty ratio: 12 to 1**

A private evangelical Christian college founded in 1900. 100-acre campus 7 miles from Providence on Narragansett Bay, one hour's drive from Boston. Bus and train stations in Providence.
Academic Character NEASC and professional accreditation. 4-1-4 system, 2 summer terms. Majors offered in American studies, Biblical studies, biology, business, business administration, chemistry, computer science, elementary education, liberal arts, marine biology, math, music, office administration, philosophy, pre-allied health, psychology, recreation, social work, youth ministries. AS offered in accounting, church or executive secretarial, pre-allied health. One-year concentrated Bible program can be applied to bachelor's degree. Distributives and 12 credit hours of Biblical study required. January Winterim involves all students and faculty in 4 interdisciplinary courses studying Culture, Nature, Man, Society. Honors program. Credit by exam possible. Field experience. Preprofessional programs in dentistry, medicine, optometry, veterinary medicine. Elementary and secondary education certification. ROTC at Providence College. 62,000-volume library.
Financial CEEB CSS. College and state scholarships and grants, payment plans; PELL, SEOG, NDSL, GSL, CWS, part-time and summer employment. Application deadline February 28.
Admissions High school graduation or GED required. SAT or ACT, 2 references, essay, interview, and audition (for music majors) required. $15 application fee. Rolling admissions. $150 enrollment deposit required on acceptance of offer of admission. *Early Decision* and *Early Admission* programs. Admission deferral possible. Transfers accepted. Credit possible for CEEB AP and CLEP exams.
Student Life Student government. Newspaper, yearbook, radio station. Musical, vocational, and professional organizations. Single students under 23 must live on campus or at home. Practices that are specifically proscribed in the Bible, in addition to the use of liquor, tobacco products, and illegal drugs, are not condoned. Dancing not permitted. 5 intercollegiate sports for men, 4 for women; intramurals. AIAW, NCCAA, NAIA, Seaboard Athletic Conference. Student body composition: 10% minority.

[1] BROWN UNIVERSITY
79 Waterman Street, Providence 02912, (401) 863-2378
Director of Admissions: James H. Rogers

- **Undergraduates: 2,668m, 2,564w; 6,655 total (including graduates)**
- **Tuition (1982/83): $8,200**
- **Room & Board: $3,135; Fees: $180**
- **Degrees offered: BA, ScB**
- **Mean SAT 636v, 685m**
- **Student-faculty ratio: 12 to 1**

A private university established in 1764, became coed in 1971 by merging with coordinate Pembroke College. 150-acre main campus on the East Side of Providence. Airport in Warwick, bus and train stations in Providence.
Academic Character NEASC and professional accreditation. Semester system. Majors offered in American civilization, ancient & Medieval cultures, anthropology, applied math, aquatic biology, art, biochemistry, biological & medical sciences, biology, biomedical ethics, biophysics, chemistry, classics, comparative literature. computer science, economics, engineering, English, French studies, geological sciences, German, Hispanic studies, history, human biology, international relations, Italian studies, Latin American studies, linguistics, math, modernization, music, operations reserach, organizational behavior, philosophy, physics, political science, Portuguese & Brazilian studies, psychology, religious studies, Renaissance studies, Russian studies, science education for the inner city, semiotics, Slavic languages, sociology, urban society. Combined and self-designed majors. Graduate and professional degrees granted. Flexible grading system. Independent study. Honors program. Phi Beta Kappa. Undergraduate research. Medical Education Program leads to BA in 4 years and MD in 7. Exchange program with Dartmouth Medical School. Member of Ivy League consortium. Study abroad. Secondary education certification. Language lab, computer. 2,600,000-volume library.
Financial CEEB CSS. University scholarships, grants, loans, payment plan; PELL, SEOG, FISL, CWS. Application deadline January 1.
Admissions High school graduation with at least 10 units required. Other course requirements for ScB candidates. SAT and 3 ACH required. Interview recommended. $35 application fee. Application deadline January 1; notification in mid-April. $50 committment deposit required on acceptance of offer of admission (May 1). *Early Action* and *Early Admission* programs. Admission deferral possible. Transfers accepted. Credit possible for CEEB AP, CLEP, ACH, and university placement exams.
Student Life Student government. Newspaper, literary magazines, yearbook, radio station. Music, debate, and drama groups. Over 100 students organizations and groups. 6 fraternities with houses, 1 sorority. 15% of men join fraternities. Permission required to live off campus. Coed and single-sex dorms. Special interest housing. Many intercollegiate and intramural sports for men and women. ECAC, NCAA, AIAW, Ivy League. Student body composition: 6% Asian, 9% Black, 1% Hispanic, 82.5% White, 1.5% Other. 90% from out of state.

[1] BRYANT COLLEGE
Smithfield 02917, (401) 231-1200
Dean of Admissions: Roy A. Nelson

- **Enrollment: 1,684m, 1,334w; 6,287 total (including evening)**
- **Tuition & Fees (1982/83): $3,750**
- **Room & Board: $2,780**
- **Degrees offered: BS, BSBA**
- **Mean SAT 480v, 540m**
- **Student-faculty ratio: 30 to 1**

A private college established in 1863. 295-acre suburban campus 12 miles from Providence. Bus and train stations in Providence, airport in Warwick.
Academic Character NEASC accreditation. 4-1-4-1 system, 3- and 5-week summer terms. Majors offered in business administration (accounting, applied actuarial math, business communications, computer information systems, economics, finance, management marketing, and hotel, restaurant, & institutional management) and in criminal justice. Distributive requirements. MBA, MS granted. Courses offered in the liberal arts. Political science internships. Study abroad. ROTC. Evening division. Center for Management Development. Computer center. Over 100,000-volume library.
Financial CEEB CSS. College scholarships and loans, sibling tuition discounts, payment plan; PELL, SEOG, NDSL, GSL, CWS. Application deadlines February 15 (scholarships & grants), February 1 (loans).
Admissions High school graduation with 16 units required. GED accepted. SAT or ACT required. Interview recommended. $20 application fee. Rolling admissions; no deadline. $100 tuition and $100 room deposits required on acceptance of offer of admission. *Early Decision* and *Early Entrance* programs. Admission deferral possible. Transfers accepted. Credit possible for CEEB AP, CLEP, and college proficiency exams.
Student Life Student government. Newspaper, yearbook, radio station. Music and drama groups. Student Services Foundation. Big Brothers. Religious, special interest, and professional groups. 8 fraternities and 6 sororities. 34% of men, 31% of women join. Single students under 20 live on campus. Coed and single-sex dorms. Townhouse apartments on campus. 61% of students live on campus. 8 intercollegiate sports for men, 7 for women; intramurals. AIAW, ECAC, Northeast 7, and 8 other associations. Student body composition: 0.5% Asian, 0.5% Black, 99% White. 75% from out of state.

[2 & J2] JOHNSON & WALES COLLEGE
Abbott Park Place, Providence 02903, (401) 456-1000
Director of Admissions: Manuel Pimentel, Jr.

- **Enrollment: 2,052m, 1,698w**
- **Tuition (1982/83): $3,825**
- **Room & Board: $2,247; Fees: $120**
- **Degrees offered: BS, AS**
- **Mean SAT 390v, 422m**
- **Student-faculty ratio: 20 to 1**

A private college established in 1914. 3 campuses in Providence and Warwick. Bus and train stations in Providence, airport in Warwick.
Academic Character AICS accreditation. Trimester system, summer term. Majors offered in accounting, administrative management, computer systems management, fashion/retailing management, food service management, hospitality management, hotel-restaurant institutional management, management, marketing, travel-tourism management. Additional AS programs in administrative assistant, advertising/public relations, business administration, computer administrative assistant, conference reporting, court reporting, culinary arts, equine studies, executive-management secretarial, fashion merchandising, finance/investment, hotel administrative assistant, insurance/real estate, legal secretarial, medical assistant, medical secretarial, pastry arts, retailing, travel administrative assistant, word processing secretarial. Diploma and certificate programs. All BS candidates receive AS after 2 years. Distributive requirements. Accelerated degree honor programs. Honors programs. Internships, cooperative work/study. RI State Government Intern Program. Exchange study abroad. ROTC with Providence College. Data processing and hotel, restaurant, & travel centers. Retailing and secretarial science labs. Computer center. 22,400-volume library.
Financial Guaranteed tuition for 3rd & 4th years. College & state scholarships, grants; PELL, SEOG, NDSL, GSL, CWS. File FAF by January 1.
Admissions High school graduation or GED required. SAT or ACT and interview recommended. $20 application fee. Rolling admissions; no deadline. $100 tuition and $100 room deposits required on acceptance of offer of admission. *Concurrent Enrollment* and *Early Admission* programs. Admission deferral possible. Transfers accepted. Credit possible for CEEB AP, CLEP, and ACT exams, and for life experiences.
Student Life Student government. Newspaper. Jazz/rock band, drama club. Travel club. Honor societies. Several special interest clubs. 2 fraternities (1 coed) and 1 sorority. Single freshmen must live at home or on campus. Coed and women's dorms. Language, special interest dorms. 55% of students live on campus. Class attendance expected. Intramural sports for men and women, dance and horsemanship programs. Student body composition: 0.5% Asian, 7.3% Black, 1.2% Hispanic, 91% White, 1% Other. 87% from out of state.

[1] NEWPORT COLLEGE-SALVE REGINA
Newport 02840, (401) 847-6650
Director of Admissions: Sister Mary Audrey, RSM

- **Full-time enrollment: 133m, 806w; 1,719 total (including graduates)**
- **Tuition (1982/83): $4,800**
- **Room & Board: $2,800; Fees: $50**
- **Degrees offered: AB, BS, AA, AS**
- **Student-faculty ratio: 19 to 1**

A private Roman Catholic college sponsored by the Religious Sisters of Mary, established in 1947 in the small city of Newport. 55-acre campus facing the ocean on Cliff Walk. Bus station in Newport, train station in Providence, airport in Warwick.
Academic Character NEASC and professional accreditation. 4-1-4 system, 2 summer terms. Majors offered in accounting, American studies, art, biology, business management, chemistry, computer science, criminal justice, education, English, French, history, horticulture, management, math, medical technology, music, nursing, philosophy, politics, psychology, religious studies, social work, sociology, Spanish, special education. Minors. AA offered in general studies; AS in criminal justice and management. MA, MS granted. Independent study. Credit by exam possible. 3-1 medical technology program with RI and CT hospitals. Study abroad. Elementary, secondary, art, and special education training; interstate certification on elementary and special education levels. ROTC at Providence College. 79,700-volume library.
Financial CEEB CSS. College grants, state scholarships & grants; PELL, SEOG, NDSL, NSL, CWS. Application deadline March 1.
Admissions High school graduation with 16 units required. Interview recommended. SAT required, 3 ACH required for placement. $20 application fee. Rolling admissions; no deadline. $100 commitment fee required on acceptance of offer of admission. *Early Decision, Early Entrance, Credit-in-Escrow* programs. Admission deferral possible. Transfers accepted. Credit possible for CEEB AP and CLEP exams.
Student Life Student government. Newspaper, literary magazine, yearbook. Music and drama groups. Community service, athletic, academic, honorary, religious, and service clubs. Single-sex dorms. Married students may not live on campus. 4 intercollegiate and intramural sports. NCAA. Student body composition: 0.1% Asian, 1.6% Black, 1% Hispanic, 0.3% Native American, 97% White. 60% from out of state.

[1] PROVIDENCE COLLEGE
River Avenue and Eaton Street, Providence 02918, (401) 865-2141
Director of Admissions: Michael Backes

- **Undergraduates: 2,602m, 1,989w; 6,503 total (including graduates)**
- **Tuition (1982/83): $5,278**
- **Room & Board: $3,100; Fees: $75**
- **Degrees offered: BA, BS**
- **Mean SAT 490v, 520m**
- **Student-faculty ratio: 16 to 1**

A private Roman Catholic college conducted by the Dominican Fathers. Established in 1917, became coed in 1971. 92-acre campus in Providence, which has train and bus stations. Airport in Warwick.
Academic Character NEASC and professional accreditation. Semester system, 6-week summer term. Majors offered in art & art history, biology, business, chemistry, clinical chemistry, economics, education, English, general social studies, health service administration, humanities, Latin American studies, math, modern languages, music, philosophy, physics, political science, psychology, religious studies, theatre arts, and sociology, anthropology, & social work. Self-designed majors. 6 hours of religious studies required. Graduate degrees granted. Honors program. Tutorials, research. Pass/fail, internships. 3-2 engineering with Columbia, Notre Dame, Washington U. Study abroad. Secondary and special education certification. ROTC. Language labs, computer center. 236,311-volume library.
Financial CEEB CSS. College scholarships, state scholarships and grants, Martin Luther King Program for minority students, payment plans; PELL, SEOG, NDSL, PLUS. Application deadline February 15.
Admissions High school graduation required, with 15 units recommended. 3 ACH and interview recommended. ACT or SAT required. $25 application fee. Application deadline February 15. $100 tuition and $100 room deposits required on acceptance of offer of admission. *Early Decision* and *Early Entrance* programs. Admission deferral possible. Transfers accepted. Credit possible for CEEB AP and CLEP exams.
Student Life Student government. Newspaper, magazine, yearbook, radio station. Music and debate groups. International clubs. Academic, honorary, service, and special interest groups. Single-sex dorms. 70% of freshmen, 51% of students live on campus. 10 intercollegiate sports for men, 9 for women; intramurals and club sports. AIAW, ECAC, NCAA, NECAC, RIRW. Student body composition: 2% Black, 1% Hispanic, 1% Native American, 95% White, 1% Other. 66% from out of state.

[1] RHODE ISLAND, UNIVERSITY OF
Kingston 02881, (401) 792-2164
Director of Admissions: Richard A. Edwards

- **Undergraduates: 4,378m, 4,138w; 10,580 total (including graduates)**
- **Tuition (1982/83): $1,311 (in-state), $4,085 (out-of-state)**
- **Room & Board: $2,856; Fees: $412**
- **Degrees offered: AB, BS, BFA, BMus, BGS, AS**
- **Mean SAT 450v, 505m**
- **Student-faculty ratio: 14 to 1**

A public university established in 1892. 1,200-acre main campus 5 miles from ocean, 30 miles from Providence. 165-acre Graduate School of Oceanography campus at Narragansett Bay and 2,300-acre W. Alton Jones Campus Research & Conference Center at West Greenwich. Bus and train stations available.
Academic Character NEASC and professional accreditation. Semester system, 2 5-week summer terms. 70 majors offered by the colleges of Arts & Sciences, Business Administration, Engineering, Human Science & Services, Nursing, Pharmacy, and Resource Development. Interdepartmental and interdisciplinary programs. Distributive requirements. MA, MS, PhD granted. Independent study. Honors program. Phi Beta Kappa. Pass/fail. Internships, Year for Action. Regional Cooperative Program with other New England land grant colleges. Preprofessional programs in dentistry, law, medicine, social work, veterinary medicine. Study abroad. Sea semester. Living/learning project. Elementary and secondary education certification. ROTC. Several research labs and centers for research and development. Over 1,300,000 volumes and microform items in several libraries.
Financial CEEB CSS. University scholarships, grants and loans, payment plan; PELL, SEOG, NSS, NDSL, GSL, NSL, HPL, CWS. File FAF by February 15.
Admissions High school graduation with 16 units required. Audition required of music applicants, DHAT of dental hygiene applicants. SAT required. $15 application fee. Rolling admissions; application deadline March 1. $50 deposit and $100 housing deposit required on acceptance of offer of admission. *Early Decision, Early Entrance, Concurrent Enrollment* programs. Admission deferral possible. Transfers accepted. Credit possible for CEEB AP and CLEP exams. Special Program for Talent Development for minority and disadvantaged applicants.
Student Life Student government. Newspaper, gazette, magazine, yearbook, radio and shortwave stations. Music, drama, and debate groups. Over 120 other student organizations. 17 fraternities, 9 sororities. About 1,300 students join. Coed, women's, and married-student housing. 60% of students live on campus. Limited parking space. Intercollegiate and intramural sports for men and women. AIAW, ECAC, NCAA, New England Conference of State Universities.

[1] RHODE ISLAND COLLEGE
Providence 02908, (401) 456-8000
Director of Admissions: James W. Colman

- **Undergraduates: 1,529m, 2,847w; 9,177 total (including grads & part-time)**
- **Tuition (1982/83): $812 (in-state), $2,994 (out-of-state)**
- **Room & Board: $2,470-$2,824; Fees: $126**
- **Degrees offered: BA, BS, BGS, BMus Performance, BSW**
- **Mean SAT 412v, 435m**
- **Student-faculty ratio: 17 to 1**

A public college established in 1854. 125-acre campus in suburban Providence. Bus and train stations in Providence, airport in Warwick.
Academic Character NEASC and professional accreditation. Semester system, summer terms. BA or BS possible in Afro-American studies, art, biology, business, chemistry, classical area studies, communications, computer science, economics, education areas, film studies, French, general science, geography, history, industrial technology, Latin American studies, management, math, medical technology, music, nursing, philosophy, physical science, political science, psychology, radiologic technology, social science, sociology, Spanish, urban studies, women's studies. Several combined majors. Minors. Distributive requirements. Master's degrees granted. Independent study. Honors program. Credit/no credit, internships, cooperative work/study. Preprofessional programs in medicine, law. Cross-registration with URI and Community College of Rhode Island. Learning Center provides clinical, internship, and lab experience for education majors. Elementary, secondary, and special education certification. ROTC. Several education centers, computer center, language lab. Elementary school on campus. 280,000 volume library.
Financial CEEB CSS. College scholarships and loans; PELL, SEOG, NSS, GSL, FISL, NDSL, NSL, CWS. Application deadline February 28.
Admissions High school graduation with 15 units required. GED accepted. SAT required. $15 application fee. Rolling admissions; application deadline May 1. *Early Decision, Early Admission, Concurrent Enrollment* programs. Transfers accepted. Credit possible for CEEB AP and CLEP exams. Preparatory Enrollment Program for disadvantaged RI residents; performance-based admission for those applicants returning to school after interruption.
Student Life Student government. Newspaper, literary magazine, yearbook, radio and TV stations. Music, dance, and drama groups. Coffeehouse. Handicapped students organization. Women's Center. Several special interest clubs. 2 fraternities and 5 sororities without houses. No married-student housing. Coed and single-sex dorms. 15% of students live on campus. 7 intercollegiate sports for men, 8 for women; intramurals. ECAC, NCAA. Student body composition: 1% Asian, 3% Black, 2% Hispanic, 1% Native American, 92% White, 1% Other. 9% from out of state.

[J1] RHODE ISLAND, COMMUNITY COLLEGE OF
400 East Avenue, Warwick 02886

■[J1] RHODE ISLAND, COMMUNITY COLLEGE OF
Lincoln 02865

[1] RHODE ISLAND SCHOOL OF DESIGN
2 College Street, Providence 02903, (401) 331-3511
Director of Admissions: Edward Newhall

- **Enrollment: 721m, 918w**
- **Tuition (1982/83): $6,770**
- **Room & Board: $2,880**
- **Degrees offered: BFA, BArch, BLA, BInterior Arch, BIndustrial Design**
- **Mean SAT 500v, 525m**
- **Student-faculty ratio: 11 to 1**

A private college established in 1877. Campus covers 2 city blocks in Providence. Bus and train stations in Providence, airport in Warwick.
Academic Character NEASC and professional accreditation. 4-1-4 system, 4 6-week summer terms. Majors offered in apparel design, architecture, ceramics, film/video, glass, graphic design, industrial design, illustration, interior architecture, painting, photography, printmaking, sculpture, textile design. Fifth-year architectural program leads to professional degree. Courses offered in liberal arts. Freshmen must take foundation courses. Senior project required. Master's degrees granted. Letter grades are accompanied by written evaluations. Cross-registration with Brown. European Honors Program. Summer workshops. Museum of Art with 50 galleries. 33-acre farm on Narragansett Bay. 60,500-volume library with 87,000 slides and 30,000 mounted photographs.
Financial CEEB CSS. School scholarships and loans, payment plan; PELL, SEOG, FISL, GSL, NDSL, CWS. Application deadline February 15.
Admissions High school graduation with courses in art and art history required. GED accepted. Portfolio required. Interview recommended. SAT required. Application deadline January 21. $300 matriculation fee required on acceptance of offer of admission. *Early Entrance* program. Admission deferral possible. Transfers accepted. Placement possible for CEEB AP exams.
Student Life Student government. Newspaper, literary magazine (with Brown), yearbook. 42 artistic student clubs on campus. Third World Coalition. International Club. Freshmen under 21 must live at home or on campus. Coed and single-sex dorms. No married-student housing. 30% of students live on campus. Liquor prohibited in dorms. 2 intercollegiate sports, intramurals. Student body composition: 2% Asian, 2% Black, 2% Hispanic, 1% Native American, 93% White. 89% from out of state.

[1 & J1] ROGER WILLIAMS COLLEGE
Old Ferry Road, Bristol 02809, (401) 255-2151
Dean of Admissions & Financial Aid: Robert P. Nemec

- **Enrollment: 1,400m, 1,000w; 4,300 total (including evening)**
- **Tuition (1982/83): $4,496**
- **Room & Board: $2,842; Fees: $171**
- **Degrees offered: BA, BS, BFA, AA, AS, AET**
- **Student-faculty ratio: 20 to 1**

A private college founded in 1919. 88-acre campus overlooking Mount Hope Bay in Bristol, 18 miles from Providence and Newport. Served by bus. Train in Providence, airport in Warwick.
Academic Character NEASC accreditation. 4-1-4 system, 6-week summer term. Majors offered in accounting, administration of justice, American studies, architectural engineering technology, art, biology, business administration, career writing, chemistry, civil engineering technology, creative writing, electrical engineering technology, engineering technology, environmental chemistry, fine arts, historic preservation, history, humanities, literature, management, marine biology, marketing, math/computer science, mechanical engineering technology, paralegal studies, philosophy, political studies, psychology, social science, sociology-anthropology, theatre, and urban & environmental planning. Self-designed majors. Minors. Historic preservation program is interdisciplinary. Distributive requirements. Independent study, directed readings. Honors program. Cooperative work/study, internships, apprenticeships. Open Division for working adults. Pass/fail option. Elementary and secondary education certification. ROTC at Providence College. 80,000-volume library.
Financial CEEB CSS. College scholarships and loans, payment plan; PELL, SEOG, NDSL, GSL. Application deadline February 15.
Admissions High school graduation required, with 16 units recommended. Interview recommended. $20 application fee. Open, rolling admissions; no deadline. $50 tuition and $100 room deposits required on acceptance of offer of admission. *Early Decision, Early Entrance, Concurrent Enrollment* programs. Transfers accepted. Credit possible for CEEB AP, CLEP, and college placement tests, and for job experience, life experiences, personal enrichment activities.
Student Life Student government. Newspaper, literary magazine, yearbook. Coffeehouse, theatre club, film society. Campus pub. Several special interest clubs. Coed, single-sex, and special interest housing. No married-student housing on campus. 50% of students live on campus; 18% live in college-supervised off-campus housing. 11 intercollegiate sports for men, 7 for women; intramurals. NAIA. Student body composition: 0.2% Asian, 5.5% Black, 0.7% Hispanic, 91.1% White, 2.5% Other. 85% from out of state.

SOUTH CAROLINA (SC)

[J1] AIKEN TECHNICAL COLLEGE
PO Drawer 696, Aiken 29801

[2] ALLEN UNIVERSITY
Columbia 29204

- **Undergraduates: 410 men & women**
- **Tuition (1982/83): $2,510**
- **Room & Board: $1,700**
- **Degrees offered: BA, BS**

A private university founded and supported by the A.M.E. Church. Urban campus.
Academic Character Semester system, summer term. BA and BS degrees offered with majors in the liberal arts and sciences, and in education. Remedial mathematics and English programs available.
Financial University scholarships, PELL, SEOG, NDSL, GSL, university part-time employment.
Admissions Rolling admissions. *Early Admission* and *Early Decision* programs. Admission deferral possible.
Student Life 4 fraternities and 4 sororities. Dormitories for men and women. Cafeteria.

[J1] ANDERSON COLLEGE
Anderson 29621, (803) 226-6181
Director of Admissions: Philip A. Nall

- **Enrollment: 1,000 men & women**
- **Tuition (1982/83): $2,370**
- **Room & Board: $1,790; Fees: $150**
- **Degrees offered: AA, AFA, AAFM, AAID, AARM, ABE**
- **Student-faculty ratio: 16 to 1**

A private college controlled by the South Carolina Baptist Convention, established in 1848. 44-acre campus.
Academic Character SACS and professional accreditation. Semester system, 3- and 5-week summer terms. 2-year programs offered in art, allied health, business, education, fashion merchandising, home economics, interior design, journalism, liberal arts, ministry, music, physical education, retail merchandising, and theatre & speech. Distributives, 6 hours of religion, and Contemporary Religious Experience required. Independent study. Preprofessional programs offered in dentistry, engineering, law, medicine, nursing, pharmacy, social service, and textile technology. Study abroad. ROTC and AFROTC at Clemson. Fine Arts Center.
Financial College scholarships, ministerial scholarships, discount for simultaneously-enrolled siblings, PELL, SEOG, NDSL, work grants.
Admissions High school graduation required. SAT or ACT required. $15 application fee. Rolling admissions. $100 ($50 for commuters) deposit due on acceptance of admissions offer. Transfers accepted. Conditional admission possible.
Student Life Student government. Newspaper, literary journal, annual. Music groups. Honorary, recreational, religious, and service groups. Students under 21 live at home or on campus. Single-sex dorms. Liquor, drugs, firearms, fireworks, gambling prohibited. Chapel programs mandatory. 1 hour of phys ed required. 2 intercollegiate sports; intramurals.

[1] BAPTIST COLLEGE AT CHARLESTON
Charleston 29411, (803) 797-4011
Director of Admissions: Barbara C. Mead

- **Undergraduates: 733m, 857w; 2,444 total (including graduates)**
- **Tuition (1982/83): $3,356**
- **Room & Board: $2,374; Fees: $594**
- **Degrees offered: BA, BS, BGen Studies**
- **Mean ACT 18; mean SAT 700 composite**
- **Student-faculty ratio: 10 to 1**

A private college controlled by the South Carolina Baptist Convention, established in 1960. 500-acre suburban campus, 16 miles from downtown Charleston. Served by air, rail, and bus.
Academic Character SACS and professional accreditation. Semester system, 2 5-week summer terms. 20 majors offered in the areas of fine & liberal arts and religion; 18 offered in the areas of business, education, science, and social science; 24 offered as general studies in humanities, fine arts, natural sciences, and social studies. Minor required. Senior comprehensive exams and 6 hours of religion required. Independent study. Honors program. President's Scholars. Cooperative work/study. Preprofessional programs in dentistry, engineering, law, medicine, theology. BApplied Science in Allied Health available with the Medical University of SC. Study abroad. Early childhood, elementary, and secondary education certification. AFROTC. 106,000-volume library.
Financial CEEB CSS. College scholarships, grants, loans, scholarships for church professions and ministers' families, payment plans; PELL, SEOG, NSS, NDSL, FISL.
Admissions High school graduation with 18 credits recommended. GED accepted. SAT or ACT required. $20 application fee. Rolling admissions. $100 deposit due on acceptance of admissions offer. *Early Admission* and *Concurrent Enrollment* programs. Transfers accepted. Credit possible for CEEB AP, CLEP, and college challenge exams. Foundation Studies Program for non-admissable applicants.
Student Life Student government. Newspaper, literary magazine, yearbook. Music groups. Academic, honorary, religious, and service groups. Single students under 25 must live at home or on campus. Class attendance required. Weekly convocation mandatory. 3 hours of phys ed required. 8 intercollegiate sports; intramurals. NCAA, SCIAW. Student body composition: 0.4% Asian, 28.1% Black, 70.3% White.

[J1] BEAUFORT TECHNICAL COLLEGE
100 South Ribaut Road, Beaufort 29902

[1] BENEDICT COLLEGE

Columbia 29204, (803) 256-0461
Director of Admissions & Records: Harrison F. DeShields, Jr.

- **Undergraduates: 555m, 1,058w**
- **Tuition (1982/83): $2,800**
- **Room & Board: $1,600; Fees: $136**
- **Degrees offered: BA, BS, BSW**
- **Student-faculty ratio: 16 to 1**

A private college affiliated with the Baptist Church, established in 1870. 20-acre urban campus. Served by air, rail, and bus.
Academic Character SACS accreditation. Semester system, 2 5-week summer terms. 36 majors offered by the divisions of Business & Administrative Services, Education & Recreation Services, Health & Science Services, Information & Cultural Services, and Social Services. Distributive requirements. Internships. Preprofessional programs in dentistry, forestry, optometry, veterinary science. 3-2 engineering program with Georgia Tech and Southern Technical Institute. Minority biomedical support program. Language lab. 148,536-volume library.
Financial CEEB CSS. College scholarships, grants, loans; PELL, SEOG, NDSL, FISL, CWS, college work aid. Application deadline March 15.
Admissions High school graduation with 18 units recommended. GE acceted. SAT or ACT required. $10 application fee. Rolling admissions. $50 deposit due on acceptance of admissions offer. *Early Admission* Program. Transfers accepted. Upward Bound Program for disadvantaged students.
Student Life Student government. Newspaper, yearbook. Music and drama groups. Academic, religious, service, and special interest groups. 4 fraternities and 4 sororities. Students live at home or on campus. Dorms for men and women. 80% of students live on campus. Liquor prohibited. Class attendance required. 4 intercollegiate sports for men, 3 for women; intramurals. AIAW, NAIA, NCAA, SIAC. Student body composition: 100% Black. 15% from out of state.

[2] BOB JONES UNIVERSITY

Greenville 29614, (803) 242-5100
Director of Admissions: David Christ

- **Tuition (1982/83): $1,836**
- **Room & Board: $2,268; Fees: $180**
- **Degrees offered: BA, BS, BSN, BSBA, BSEd, AAA, AAS**

A private Christian university, established in 1927. 200-acre urban campus.
Academic Character Semester system, 2 4-week summer terms. 27 majors offered by the College of Arts & Sciences, 8 by the School of Religion, 15 by the School of Fine Arts, 12 by the School of Education, and 4 by the School of Business. Minors required. Graduate degrees granted. AA and AS degrees granted by School of Applied Studies with courses in church-vocations and technical fields. Preprofessional programs offered in dentistry, law, medicine. Elementary and secondary education certification. 170,000-volume library.
Financial University scholarships, grants, loans, payment plan, work program.
Admissions High school graduation with 16-18 units required. GED accepted. ACT required. $25 application fee. Rolling admissions. *Early Decision* Program. Transfers accepted.
Student Life Yearbook. Music groups. Debate. Professional, religious, social groups. Single students under 23 live at home or on campus. Class attendance required. Church attendance required. 4 semesters of phys ed required. Intramural sports.

[1] CENTRAL WESLEYAN COLLEGE

Central 29630, (803) 639-2453
Director of Admissions: Lillian Robbins

- **Enrollment: 425 men & women**
- **Tuition (1982/83): $3,520**
- **Room & Board: $1,930**
- **Degree offered: AB**
- **Mean ACT 19; mean SAT 800**
- **Student-faculty ratio: 13 to 1**

A private college controlled by the Wesleyan Church, established in 1909. Small-town campus.
Academic Character SACS accreditation. Semester system, 2 4-week summer terms. Majors offered in accounting, business, biology, chemistry, church music, criminal justice, education, English, history, mathematics, medical technology, music education, physical education, psychology, religion, social studies, and special education. Minors offered. Distributives and 12 hours of religion & philosophy required. Independent study. Honors program. Pass/fail. Cross-registration with Clemson. Cooperative criminal justice program with Tri-County and Greenville Tech. 3-1 medical technology program. 2-2 nursing program with Clemson. Early childhood, elementary, secondary, and special education certification. ROTC and AFROTC at Clemson. 60,000-volume library.
Financial CEEB CSS. College scholarships, grants, discount for Wesleyan Church members, reduction for simultaneously-enrolled siblings, state grants; PELL, SEOG, NDSL, GSL, CWS.
Admissions High school graduation with 16 units required. SAT or ACT required. $25 room deposit required with application. Rolling admissions. $50 tuition deposit due on acceptance of admissions offer. Transfers accepted. Credit possible for CEEB AP and CLEP exams.
Student Life Numerous co-curricular activities. Class attendance required. Missions convention and spiritual emphasis services required each semester. Daily chapel and weekly church attendance expected. 3 hours of phys ed required.

[1] CHARLESTON, COLLEGE OF

Charleston 29424, (803) 792-5670
Dean of Admissions: Frederick W. Daniels

- **Undergraduates: 1,501m, 2,350w; 5,394 total (including graduates)**
- **Tuition (1982/83): $1,120 (in-state), $2,020 (out-of-state)**
- **Room & Board: $2,840**
- **Degrees offered: BA, BS, BSDentistry, BSMedicine**
- **Mean SAT 470v, 490m**
- **Student-faculty ratio: 19 to 1**

A public college established in 1770. Urban campus. Served by air, rail, and bus.
Academic Character SACS accreditation. Semester system, 2 5-week summer terms. Majors offered in biology, business, chemistry, classical studies, computer science, economics, education, English, fine arts, French, geology, German, history, marine biology, mathematics, philosophy, physical education & health, physics, political science, psychology, sociology, Spanish, and urban studies. Distributive requirements. Independent study. Honors program. Cooperative work/study, internships. 5-year biochemistry, biometry, and chemistry programs with Medical U of SC. 3-1 programs in dentistry and medicine. Cross-registration with Citadel, MUSC, Baptist, and Trident Technical. SEA semester. Study abroad. Elementary, secondary, and special education certification. AFROTC at Baptist. Marine biological research station. 216,000-volume library.
Financial CEEB CSS. College scholarships, grants, loans; PELL, SEOG, NDSL, FISL, CWS. Application deadlines January 15 (scholarships), April 1 (loans).
Admissions High school graduation with 18 units recommended. GED accepted. Interview encouraged. SAT required. $20 application fee. Rolling admissions. $100 deposit due on acceptance of admissions offer. *Early Admission* Program. Admission deferral possible. Transfers accepted. Credit possible for CEEB AP, CLEP, and college exams. Summer session for non-admissable students.
Student Life Student government. Newspaper, literary magazine, yearbook. Music and drama groups. Academic, honorary, literary, professional, religious, and special interest groups. 9 fraternities and 6 sororities, all with chapter rooms. 15% of students join. Students live at home or on campus. Coed and single-sex dorms. No married-student housing. 38% of students live on campus. Hazing prohibited. Honor system. Class attendance expected. 6 intercollegiate sports for men, 5 for women; many intramurals. AIAW, NAIA. Student body composition: 0.5% Asian, 7.1% Black, 0.3% Hispanic, 90.2% White, 1.7% Other. 14% from out of state.

[J1] CHESTERFIELD-MARLBORO TECHNICAL COLLEGE

Cheraw 29520

[1] CITADEL, THE

Charleston 29409, (803) 792-5230
Director of Admissions: Capt. Wallace I. West

- **Undergraduates: 2,000m; 3,439 total (including graduates)**
- **Expenses (1982/83): $4,370 (in-state), $5,770 (out-of-state)**
- **Degrees offered: BA, BS, BSBA, BSEng**
- **Mean ACT 23; mean SAT 456v, 510m**
- **Student-faculty ratio: 13 to 1**

A public college established in 1842. 110-acre urban campus. Served by air, rail, and bus.
Academic Character SACS and professional accreditation. Semester system, 2 5-week summer terms. Majors offered in biology, business administration, chemistry, civil engineering, computer science, education, electrical engineering, English, history, mathematics, modern languages, physical education, physics, political science, and psychology. Masters degrees granted. Phi Beta Kappa. Elementary, secondary, and special education certification. ROTC, AFROTC, NROTC required. Computer center. Language lab. 250,000-volume library with microform resources.
Financial CEEB CSS. College scholarships, grants, loans, payment plans; PELL, SEOG, NDSL, GSL, FISL. Application deadlines February 1 (scholarships), March 15 (loans).
Admissions High school graduation with 15 units required. Interview recommended. SAT or ACT required; English and math ACH recommended. $15 application fee. Rolling admissions. $100 deposit due on acceptance of admissions offer. Transfers accepted. Credit possible for CEEB AP and CLEP exams.
Student Life Newspaper, literary magazine, yearbook. Music and drama groups. Yacht Club. Literary, military, professional, and recreational clubs. All cadets live on campus. Freshmen may not have cars. Liquor prohibited. Daily room inspection. Uniforms must be worn at all times. Honor code. Cadets may not marry while in school. Class attendance mandatory. 4 semesters of phys ed required. 11 intercollegiate sports; many intramurals. NCAA. Student body composition: 4.5% Black, 94% White, 1.5% Other. 59% from out of state.

[1] CLAFLIN COLLEGE

Orangeburg 29115, (803) 534-2710
Director of Admissions: Leone M. Young

- **Undergraduates: 248m, 470w**
- **Tuition (1982/83): $2,552**
- **Room & Board: $1,480; Fees: $22**
- **Degrees offered: BA, BS, BSEd**
- **Student-faculty ratio: 13 to 1**

A private college affiliated with the Methodist Episcopal Church, established in 1869. 25-acre suburban campus. Served by air, rail, and bus nearby.

Academic Character SACS accreditation. Semester system, 8-week summer term. Majors offered in art, biology, business administration, chemistry, education, English, health & physical education, mathematics, music education, recreation, religion & philosophy, and social sciences. Minor required. Distributives, yearly comprehensive exams, and 6 hours of religion or philosophy required. Preprofessional programs in law and medicine. Elementary and secondary education certification. ROTC at South Carolina State. 43,240-volume library.
Financial CEEB CSS. College scholarships, loans, state grants; PELL, SEOG, NDSL, GSL, CWS. Application deadline April 1.
Admissions High school graduation with 16-18 units required. GED accepted. Interview recommended. SAT or ACT required. $10 application fee. Rolling admissions. $15 room deposit due on acceptance of admissions offer. Transfers accepted. Credit possible for CEEB CLEP exams. Conditional admission for academically deficient students.
Student Life Student government. Newspaper, yearbook. Music, dance, drama groups. NAACP. Student Christian Association. Academic, honorary, service, and special interest groups. 4 fraternities and 4 sororities. Single-sex dorms. Liquor prohibited. Class attendance required. Chapel, vespers, prayer meetings, and special occasions designated by college required. 3 hours of phys ed required. 4 intercollegiate sports; intramurals. Student body composition: 99.2% Black, 0.8% White.

[1] CLEMSON UNIVERSITY
Clemson 29631, (803) 656-2287
Director of Admissions: W. Richard Mattox

- **Undergraduates: 5,697m, 4,014w; 11,618 total (including graduates)**
- **Tuition (1982/83): $1,350 (in-state), $2,778 (out-of-state)**
- **Room & Board: $1,830**
- **Degrees offered: BA, BS, BArch, BSN, BText Tech**
- **Mean SAT 475v, 530m**
- **Student-faculty ratio: 12 to 1**

A public university established in 1889. 600-acre small-town campus. Served by rail and bus.
Academic Character SACS and professional accreditation. Semester system, one 9-week summer term. 12 majors offered by the College of Agricultural Sciences, 6 by the College of Education, 9 by the College of Engineering, 3 by the College of Forest & Recreation Resources, 8 by the College of Industrial Management/Textile Science, 6 by the College of Liberal Arts, 1 by the College of Nursing, 11 by the College of Sciences, and 2 by the School of Architecture. Minor required in liberal arts. Distributive requirements. Graduate degrees granted. Independent study, honors program. Cooperative work/study, pass/fail, internships. Study abroad. Elementary, secondary, and special education certification. ROTC, AFROTC. 801,023-volume library with microform resources.
Financial CEEB CSS. University scholarships, grants, loans; PELL, SEOG, NDSL, CWS. Application deadlines February 15 (scholarships), April 1 (loans).
Admissions High school graduation required. SAT required; math ACH required. $15 application fee. Rolling admissions. $80 deposit due on acceptance of admissions offer. *Early Entrance* program. Transfers accepted. Credit possible for CEEB AP exams.
Student Life Student government. Newspaper, literary journal, yearbook, radio station. Music and drama groups. Debate. Honorary, religious, and special interest groups. 15 fraternities and 8 sororities, most with dorm floors. 12% of men and 20% of women join. Coed and single-sex dorms. Married-student housing. 60% of students live on campus. 8 intercollegiate sports; many intramurals. AIAW, NCAA, ACC. Student body composition: 0.4% Asian, 3.5% Black, 0.2% Hispanic, 0.1% Native American, 96% White. 25% from out of state.

[1] COKER COLLEGE
Hartsville 29550, (803) 332-1381
Director of Admissions & Financial Aid: Charles F. Geren

- **Enrollment: 300 men & women**
- **Tuition (1982/83): $3,930**
- **Room & Board: $2,014-$2,364**
- **Degrees offered: BA, BS**
- **Student-faculty ratio: 10 to 1**

A private college established in 1894, became coed in 1969. 15-acre small-town campus.
Academic Character SACS and professional accreditation. Semester system. 32 majors offered in the areas of business administration, communications, education, fine arts, liberal arts, physical education, religion, science, and social sciences. Self-designed majors. Minors offered in most major fields. Distributives and 3 hours of religion or philosophy required. Independent study. Honors program. Internships. Preprofessional programs in dentistry, medicine, medical technology, nursing, pharmacy. Cooperative equestrian studies with Meredith Manor. Study abroad. Early childhood, elementary, secondary, and special education certification. 60,000-volume library with microform resources.
Financial College scholarships, loans, state grants; PELL, SEOG, NDSL, GSL, CWS.
Admissions High school graduation required. SAT or ACT required. $15 application fee. Rolling admissions. $50 tuition and $25 room deposits due on acceptance of admissions offer. Transfers accepted. Credit possible for CEEB CLEP exams. Probationary acceptance possible.
Student Life Student government. Newspaper, yearbook. Academic, professional, religious, social, and special interest groups. Students under 22 live at home or on campus. Dorms and dining hall. 1 year of phys ed required. 3 intercollegiate sports for men, 3 for women; intramurals. NAIA. Student body composition: 23% minority.

[P] COLUMBIA BIBLE COLLEGE
Columbia 29203

[1] COLUMBIA COLLEGE
Columbia 29203, (803) 786-3871
Dean of Admissions: Joe Mitchell

- **Undergraduates: 920w; 1,045 total (including graduates)**
- **Tuition (1982/83): $3,700**
- **Room & Board: $2,100**
- **Degrees offered: BA, BMus**
- **Mean SAT 410v, 430m**
- **Student-faculty ratio: 14 to 1**

A private women's college affiliated with the United Methodist Church, established in 1854. 32-acre urban campus. Served by air, rail, and bus.
Academic Character SACS and professional accreditation. Semester system, 2 4-week summer terms. 44 majors offered by the departments of Art, Biology, Business & Economics, Education, English & Germanic Language & Literature, History & Political Science, Human Relations, Intercultural & Language Center, Mathematics, Music, Physical Education, Physical Science, Religion, and Speech & Drama. Minors offered in 22 fields. Distributives and 6 hours of religion required. Independent study. Pass/fail, internships. Preprofessional programs in law and medicine. Study abroad. Elementary, secondary, and special education certification. ROTC; AFROTC at U South Carolina. Language lab. 145,000-volume library.
Financial CEEB CSS and ACT FAS. Scholarships, grants, loans, state grants, payment plans; PELL, SEOG, NDSL, FISL, CWS. Application deadline April 1.
Admissions High school graduation with 18 units recommended. Interview recommended. SAT or ACT required. $15 application fee. Rolling admissions. $100 ($50 for commuters) deposit due on acceptance of admissions offer. *Early Admission* and *Concurrent Enrollment* programs. Transfers accepted. Credit possible for CEEB AP and departmental exams.
Student Life Student government. Newspaper, literary magazine, yearbook. Music and drama groups. Academic, honorary, religious, and special interest groups. Women's dorms. 70% of students live on campus. Liquor prohibited. 80% class attendance required. 3 hours of phys ed required. 3 intercollegiate sports; intramurals. AIAW. Student body composition: 15% minority. 11% of students from out of state.

[J2] COLUMBIA JUNIOR COLLEGE
3810 North Main Street, Columbia 29203

[1] CONVERSE COLLEGE
Spartenburg 29301, (803) 585-6421
Director of Admissions: Margaret Printz

- **Undergraduates: 987w**
- **Expenses: $6,920**
- **Degrees offered: BA, BMus, BFA**
- **Mean ACT 19**
- **Student-faculty ratio: 11 to 1**

A private women's college established in 1889. 70-acre urban campus. Served by air, rail, and bus.
Academic Character SACS and professional accreditation. 4-2-4 system, 2 5-week summer terms. 29 majors offered by the College of Arts & Sciences, and 6 by the School of Music. Distributives and senior comprehensive exams required. Graduate degrees granted. Independent study. Internships. 3-2 engineering programs with Georgia Tech and Auburn. 6-year medical program with USC. Cooperative program in deaf and blind education with SC school for the Deaf and Blind. Study abroad. Elementary, secondary, and special education certification. Language lab. Music Hall. 114,000-volume library with microform resources.
Financial CEEB CSS. College scholarships, grants, loans, state grants; PELL, SEOG, NDSL, GSL, CWS. Application deadline March 15.
Admissions High school graduation with 16 units recommended. Interview recommended. Audition required for music students. SAT or ACT required. $20 application fee. Rolling admissions. $200 deposit due on acceptance of admissions offer. *Early Admission* Program. Transfers accepted. Credit possible for CEEB AP exams.
Student Life Student government. Newspaper, literary magazine, yearbook. Music, dance, and drama groups. Student Christian Association. Academic, honorary, religious, service, and special interest groups. Students live at home or on campus. Women's dorms. 90% of students live on campus. Liquor permitted only in the "Sneakers". Honor Pledge required. Class attendance expected. 2 semesters of phys ed required. 3 intercollegiate sports; intramurals. AIAW. Student body composition: 0.4% Asian, 2.6% Black, 97% White. 60% from out of state.

[J1] DENMARK TECHNICAL EDUCATION CENTER
PO Box 327, Denmark 29042

[1] ERSKINE COLLEGE
Due West 29639, (803) 379-8838
Director of Admissions: Phyllis E. Meredith

- **Undergraduates: 364m, 325w**
- **Tuition (1982/83): $3,850**
- **Room & Board: $1,850; Fees: $450**
- **Degrees offered: BA, BS**
- **Mean SAT 451v, 477m**
- **Student-faculty ratio: 13 to 1**

A private college affiliated with the Associated Reformed Presbyterian Church, established in 1839. 85-acre rural campus, 40 miles from Greenville. Served by bus; airport and rail service 20 miles away.
Academic Character SACS accreditation. 4-1-4 system, 2 5½-week summer terms. Majors offered in behavioral science, Bible, biology, business, Christian education, elementary education, English, French, German, history, mathematics, medical technology, modern languages, music, natural science, physical education, physics, psychology, social services, Southern studies, and Spanish. Self-designed majors. Courses in art. 2 semesters of religion and GRE required. Independent study. Honors program. Scholars Program. Limited pass/fail, cooperative work/study, internships. 3-2 engineering program with Georgia Tech. 2-2 early childhood education program with Spartanburg Methodist. Study abroad. Elementary, secondary, and special education certification. ROTC. Language lab. 110,000-volume library.
Financial CEEB CSS. College scholarships, loans, grants, discount for ministers' children and simultaneously-enrolled siblings, state aid, payment plan; PELL, SEOG, NDSL, GSL, CWS. Application deadlines March 1 (scholarships), July 1 (loans).
Admissions High school graduation with 14 units required. SAT required; ACT may be substituted. $15 application fee. Rolling admissions. $75 room deposit due on acceptance of admissions offer. *Early Decision, Early Admission, Credit-in-Escrow* programs. Admission deferral possible. Transfers accepted. Credit possible for CEEB AP, CLEP, and college proficiency exams. Learning Disabilities Program for non-admissable students.
Student Life Student government. Newspaper, literary magazine, yearbook. Music and drama groups. Academic, honorary, religious, and special interest groups. Local fraternities and sororities. Single-sex dorms. Married-student housing. 90% of students live on campus. Twice-weekly assembly attendance expected. Honor code. 4 terms of phys ed required. 6 intercollegiate sports for men, 4 for women; intramurals. NAIA. Student body composition: 5% Black, 1% Foreign, 94% White. 30% from out of state.

[J1] FLORENCE DARLINGTON TECHNICAL COLLEGE
PO Box 8000, Florence 29501

[1] FRANCIS MARION COLLEGE
PO Box F7500, Florence 29501, (803) 669-4121
Director of Admissions: Marvin W. Lynch

- **Undergraduates: 930m, 960w; 2,728 total (including graduates)**
- **Tuition (1982/83): $860 (in-state), $1,720 (out-of-state)**
- **Room & Board: $2,040**
- **Degrees offered: BA, BS, BGS, AA**
- **Student-faculty ratio: 19 to 1**

A public college established in 1970. 309-acre small-city campus. Served by air, rail, and bus.
Academic Character SACS accreditation. Semester system, 2 5½-week summer terms. Majors offered in biology, business, chemistry, economics, elementary education, English, French, health, physics, history, mathematics, political science, psychology, sociology, and Spanish. Minors offered. Distributive requirements. Graduate degrees granted. Independent study. Honors program. Cooperative work/study, internships. Pre-professional programs offered in dentistry, engineering, law, medicine and related fields, nursing, veterinary medicine. Cooperative programs in administrative technology, civil engineering, and electronic engineering technology with Florence-Darlington; anthropology, art, computer science, geography, geology with USC; engineering, forest management with Clemson; medical technology with McLeod. Elementary and secondary education certification. ROTC. Media center. Fine arts center. 231,431-volume library with microform resources.
Financial CEEB CSS. College scholarships, grants, loans; PELL, SEOG, NDSL, FISL, CWS. Applicants for scholarships and grants have personal interview in March. Loan application deadline April 1.
Admissions High school graduation with 20 units recommended. SAT required; ACT may be substituted. $10 application fee. Rolling admissions. $75 room deposit due on acceptance of admissions offer. *Early Admission* and *Concurrent Enrollment* programs. Admission deferral possible. Transfers accepted. Superior Student Program. Credit possible for CEEB AP, CLEP, and departmental exams.
Student Life Student government. Newspaper, yearbook. Music and drama groups. Academic, honorary, political, religious, and special interest groups. 7 fraternities, 3 with houses; 5 sororities. 12% of men and 6% of women join. Coed apartments. No married-student housing. 13% of students live on campus. Class attendance required. 6 intercollegiate sports for men, 4 for women; intramurals. AIAW, NAIA. Student body composition: 0.2% Asian, 11.1% Black, 0.2% Hispanic, 0.1% Native American, 88.4% White. 2% from out of state.

[1] FURMAN UNIVERSITY
Greenville 29613, (803) 294-2034
Director of Admissions: Charles E. Brock

- **Undergraduates: 1,251m, 1,130w; 2,850 total (including graduates)**
- **Tuition (1982/83): $4,256**
- **Room & Board: $2,664; Fees: $28**
- **Degrees offered: BA, BS, BGS, BMus**
- **Mean SAT 550v, 560m**
- **Student-faculty ratio: 14 to 1**

A private university affiliated with the South Carolina Baptist Convention, established in 1826. 750-acre suburban campus. Served by air, rail, and bus.
Academic Character SACS and professional accreditation. Trimester system, 6- and 4-week summer terms. 30 majors offered in the areas of classical languages, computer science, economics, education, fine arts, humanities, modern languages, physical education, sciences, and social sciences. Self-designed majors. Distributive requirements. Graduate degrees granted. Independent study. Phi Beta Kappa. Limited pass/fail, credit by exam, internships. 3-2 engineering program with Georgia Tech. 3-2 forestry programs with Duke and Clemson. 3-1 programs arranged in dentistry, law, medical technology, medicine, physical therapy, religion, social service. Study abroad. Pre-school, elementary, and secondary education certification. ROTC. Language labs. 450,000-volume library.
Financial CEEB CSS. University scholarships, grants, loans, discount for children of missionaries and Baptist ministers, payment plan; PELL, SEOG, NDSL, GSL, CWS. Application deadline February 1.
Admissions High school graduation with college prep program and B average expected. Interview recommended. Music students should audition. SAT required. $20 application fee. Rolling admissions. $100 deposit due on acceptance of admissions offer. *Early Decision* and *Early Admission* programs. Transfers accepted. Credit possible for CEEB AP exams.
Student Life Student government. Newspaper, literary magazine, yearbook, radio station. Music and drama groups. Academic, honorary, professional, religious, service, and special interest groups. 4 fraternities without houses. 10% of men join. Single freshmen and sophomores live at home or on campus. Single-sex dorms. 68% of students live on campus. Liquor prohibited. One phys ed course required. 11 intercollegiate sports for men, 7 for women; several intramurals. AIAW, NCAA, SAC. Student body composition: 1% Asian, 3% Black, 1% Hispanic, 95% White. 59% from out of state.

[J1] GREENVILLE TECHNICAL COMMUNITY COLLEGE
Greenville 29606

[J1] HORRY-GEORGETOWN TECHNICAL EDUCATION CENTER
PO Box 1966, Conway 29526

[1] LANDER COLLEGE
Greenwood 29646, (803) 229-8307
Director of Admissions: Jacquelyn DeVore Roark

- **Undergraduates: 755m, 1,203w**
- **Tuition (1982/83): $1,150 (in-state), $1,750 (out-of-state)**
- **Room & Board: $2,890; Fees: $20**
- **Degrees offered: BA, BS, BSBA, BMus Ed, ASN**
- **Student-faculty ratio: 23 to 1**

A public college established in 1872. 75-acre campus in a small city 50 miles from Greenville. Served by bus; airport and rail station in Greenville.
Academic Character SACS accreditation. Semester system, 2 4-week summer terms. Majors offered in art, biology, business administration & education, chemistry, computer science, education, English, French, history, home economics, mathematics, medical technology, music education, political science, psychology, sociology, and speech & theatre. Self-designed majors. Distributive requirements. Independent study. Limited pass/fail. Cooperative work/study. 3-2 dual-degree engineering program with Clemson. Study abroad. Elementary and secondary education certification. ROTC. Media center. Reading, writing, and math labs. 135,871-volume library.
Financial CEEB CSS and ACT FAS. College scholarships, grants, loans, state grants, payment plans; PELL, SEOG, NSS, NDSL, FISL, CWS. Application deadline April 15.
Admissions High school graduation required. GED accepted. Interview recommended. SAT or ACT required. $15 application fee. Rolling admissions. $175 housing deposit required on acceptance of admissions offer. *Early Admission, Early Decision, Concurrent Enrollment* programs. Admission deferral possible. Transfers accepted. Credit possible for CEEB AP and CLEP exams.
Student Life Student government. Newspaper, literary magazine, yearbook. Music, dance, and drama groups. Academic, honorary, professional, service, and special interest groups. 4 fraternities, 2 with houses, 4 sororities, one with house. 11% of men and 10% of women join. Single-sex dorms. 45% of students live on campus. 2 semesters of phys ed required. 3 intercollegiate sports; intramurals. NAIA. Student body composition: 0.2% Asian, 14% Black, 0.3% Hispanic, 0.3% Native American, 84.3% White, 0.9% Other. 2.5% from out of state.

[1] LIMESTONE COLLEGE
Gaffney 29340, (803) 489-7151
Director of Admissions: Anslie J. Waters

- **Undergraduates: 791m, 724w**
- **Tuition (1982/83): $3,940**
- **Room & Board: $1,960**
- **Degrees offered: BA, BS**
- **Student-faculty ratio: 12 to 1**

A private college established in 1845. 115-acre suburban campus, 50 miles from Charlotte. Served by bus.
Academic Character SACS and professional accreditation. Semester system, 2 5-week summer terms. Majors offered in art, art education, biology, business administration, chemistry, elementary education, English, guidance, history, mathematics, music, music education, physical education, psychology, religion, social work, and theatre. Self-designed majors. Distributive requirements. Independent study. Pass/fail, internships. Preprofessional programs offered in dentistry, law, medicine, nursing, pharmacy, religion, veterinary medicine. Elementary and secondary education certification. Computer center. Language lab. 60,000-volume library.
Financial CEEB CSS and ACT FAS. College scholarships, grants, loans, discounts for families, state grants, payment plans; PELL, SEOG, NDSL, FISL, CWS. Scholarship application deadline March 15.

Admissions High school graduation with 16½ units required. GED accepted. Interview recommended. SAT or ACT required; SAT preferred. $15 application fee. Rolling admissions. $100 deposit due on acceptance of admissions offer. *Early Admission* Program. Admission deferral possible. Transfers accepted. Credit possible for CEEB AP and CLEP exams.
Student Life Student government. Newspaper, literary magazine, yearbook. Music and drama groups. Black Student Union. Honorary and professional groups. 2 fraternities and 2 sororities. Single students live at home or on campus. Single-sex dorms. No married-student housing. 30% of students live on campus. 3 intercollegiate sports for men, 3 for women; intramurals. NAIA. Student body composition: 15% Black, 84% White, 1% Other. 13% from out of state.

[J1] MIDLANDS TECHNICAL COLLEGE
Columbia 29250

[1] MORRIS COLLEGE
Sumter 29150, (803) 775-9371
Admissions & Records Officer: Queen W. Spann

- **Undergraduates: 243m, 415w**
- **Tuition (1982/83): $2,348**
- **Room & Board: $1,573; Fees: $54**
- **Degrees offered: BA, BSEd, BFA**
- **Student-faculty ratio: 16 to 1**

A private college affiliated with the Baptist Church, established in 1908. 44-acre small-city campus, 45 miles from Columbia. Served by bus; airport in Columbia.
Academic Character SACS accreditation. Semester system, 2 5-week summer terms. Majors offered in biology, business administration, elementary education, English, fine arts, history, liberal studies, liberal/technical studies, mathematics, physics, political science, religious education, secondary education, and social studies. Distributives and 2 semesters of religion required. Independent study. Honors program. Cooperative work/study, internships. Preprofessional programs in allied health and law. Cross-registration with USC Sumter. Elementary and secondary education certification. TV studio. 94,842-volume library with microform resources.
Financial CEEB CSS. College scholarships, ministerial scholarships, state grants; PELL, SEOG, NDSL, GSL, CWS. Application deadline March 16.
Admissions High school graduation with 18 units required. GED accepted. Interview recommended. SAT or ACT recommended. $10 application fee. Rolling admissions. *Concurrent Enrollment* Program. Transfers accepted. Credit possible for CEEB CLEP exams. Upward Bound program for disadvantaged.
Student Life Student government. Newspaper, yearbook. Music and drama groups. Baptist Student Union. Literary society. Academic, honorary, professional, and special interest groups. 4 fraternities and 4 sororities without houses. 5% of men and 9% of women join. Students must live at home or on campus. Single-sex dorms. 75% of students live on campus. Liquor prohibited. Honor code. Dress code. Smoking in designated areas only. Class, chapel, and convocation attendance mandatory. 3 intercollegiate sports for men, 3 for women; intramurals. AIAW, NAIA, SEAC. Student body composition: 99% Black, 1% Hispanic. 5% from out of state.

[1] NEWBERRY COLLEGE
Newberry 29108, (803) 276-6974
Dean of Admissions: Ray Sharpe

- **Undergraduates: 422m, 298w**
- **Tuition (1982/83): $4,050**
- **Room & Board: $1,900; Fees: $15**
- **Degrees offered: BA, BS, BMus, BMus Ed**
- **Mean SAT 428v, 442m**
- **Student-faculty ratio: 15 to 1**

A private college affiliated with the Lutheran Church, established in 1856. 60-acre small-town campus, 40 miles from Columbia. Served by bus; airport and rail station in Columbia.
Academic Character SACS and professional accreditation. Semester system, 2 5-week summer terms. 37 majors offered in the areas of business administration, computer science, education, fine arts, foreign languages, liberal arts, medical technology, physical education, religion, science, and social sciences. 2 semesters of religion required. Independent study. Honors program. Preprofessional programs in dentistry, law, medicine, nursing, optometry, osteopathy, pharmacy. 3-2 programs in engineering with Clemson; in environmental management and forestry with Duke; in business, computer science, engineering, and physics with Georgia State. Study abroad. Elementary and secondary education certification. 63,000-volume library.
Financial CEEB CSS and ACT FAS. College scholarships, grants, loans, state grants; PELL, SEOG, NDSL, GSL, CWS.
Admissions High school graduation with 18 units required. GED accepted. Interview recommended. Portfolio required for art students. SAT required; ACT may be substituted. $15 application fee. Rolling admissions. $100 deposit due on acceptance of admissions offer. *Early Admission* and *Concurrent Enrollment* programs. Transfers accepted. Credit possible for CEEB AP, CLEP, and college exams.
Student Life Student government. Newspaper, literary magazine, yearbook. Music and drama groups. Academic, religious, service, and special interest groups. 4 fraternities, 2 with houses; 3 sororities, all with houses. Students live with family or on campus. 80% of students live on campus. Liquor prohibited. 75% class attendance required. 2 semesters of phys ed required. 4 intercollegiate sports for men, 4 for women; several intramurals. AIAW, NAIA, SAC. Student body composition: 1% Asian, 10% Black, 1% Hispanic, 88% White. 25% from out of state.

[J1] NORTH GREENVILLE COLLEGE
Tigerville 29688, (803) 895-1410
Director of Admissions: E. Mayson Easterling, III

- **Undergraduates: 316m, 193w; 580 total (including part-time)**
- **Tuition (1982/83): $2,200**
- **Room & Board: $1,500-$1,650**
- **Degrees offered: AA, AS, AM, AAGS**
- **Student-faculty ratio: 13 to 1**

A private college controlled by the South Carolina Baptist Convention, established in 1892. Suburban campus. Served by air, rail, and bus.
Academic Character SACS accreditation. Semester system, 2 4-week summer terms. 2-year transfer programs offered in Bible & religion, business & commerce, English, fine arts, modern foreign languages, natural science & mathematics, social sciences, and health, physical education, & recreation. Distributives and 6 hours of Bible required. Honors program. Cooperative work/study. Preprofessional programs in dentistry, engineering, forestry, law, medicine, nursing, pharmacy, theology. 44,500-volume library.
Financial College scholarships, grants, loans, employment.
Admissions High school graduation required. GED accepted. SAT or ACT useful. $17 application fee. Rolling admissions. $100 deposit due on acceptance of admissions offer. *Early Admission* Program. Transfers accepted. Credit possible for CEEB AP and CLEP exams.
Student Life Student government. Newspaper, literary magazine, yearbook. Music and drama groups. Afro-American Club. Baptist Student Union. Academic, honorary, professional, religious, and special interest groups. Single-sex dorms. Married-student housing. Liquor, dancing, drugs, gambling, firearms, hazing prohibited. Class and chapel attendance expected. 2 hours of phys ed required. 3 intercollegiate sports for men, 2 for women; intramurals. NJCAA.

[J1] ORANGEBURG-CALHOUN TECHNICAL COLLEGE
Orangeburg 29115

[J1] PIEDMONT TECHNICAL COLLEGE
Greenwood 29646

[1] PRESBYTERIAN COLLEGE
Clinton 29325, (803) 833-2820
Director of Admissions & Records: William K. Jackson

- **Undergraduates: 516m, 430w**
- **Tuition (1982/83): $3,905**
- **Room & Board: $2,025; Fees: $320**
- **Degrees offered: BA, BS**
- **Mean SAT 450v, 500m**
- **Student-faculty ratio: 16 to 1**

A private college controlled by the Presbyterian Church, established in 1880, became coed in 1965. 175-acre small-town campus. Served by air.
Academic Character SACS accreditation. Semester system, 2 5-week summer terms. Majors offered in biology, business, chemistry, economics, education, English, fine arts, history, mathematics, modern languages, music, political studies, psychology, religion/philosophy, and sociology. Distributives and 2 semesters of religion required. Independent study. Limited pass/fail, internships. Preprofessional programs in allied health, dentistry, engineering, law, medicine, pharmacy, and theology. 3-2 engineering programs with Auburn and Clemson. 3-2 forestry program with Duke. 3-1 programs in cytotechnology and medical technology. Washington Semester. Marine biology at Gulf Coast Research Station. Study abroad. Elementary, secondary, and special education certification. ROTC. Computer center. Language lab. 129,000-volume library.
Financial CEEB CSS. College scholarships, grants, loans, church-vocation grants, discount for Presbyterian ministers' children, music scholarships, state grants, payment plans; PELL, SEOG, NDSL, FISL, CWS. Application deadlines October 31 (scholarships), April 15 (loans).
Admissions High school graduation with 15 units recommended. Interview recommended. SAT or ACT required. $15 application fee. Rolling admissions. $100 room deposit due on acceptance of admissions offer. *Early Decision* Program. Transfers accepted. Credit possible for CEEB AP and CLEP exams.
Student Life Student Council. Newspaper, literary magazine, yearbook. Music and drama groups. Academic, honorary, political, religious, service, and special interest groups. 6 fraternities with houses; one sorority. Seniors may live off campus. 4 dorms for men, 3 for women. 90% of students live on campus. Honor system. Firearms, gambling, hazing prohibited. 75% class attendance required. One year of phys ed required. 6 intercollegiate sports for men, 3 for women; many intramurals. AIAW, NAIA. Student body composition: 4% Black, 94% White, 2% Other. 49% from out of state.

[1] SOUTH CAROLINA, MEDICAL UNIVERSITY OF
171 Ashley Avenue, Charleston 29403, (803) 792-2300

- **Enrollment: 1,247m, 1,050w; 2,560 total (including part-time)**
- **Tuition (1982/83): $1,062-$1,806 (in-state), $1,738-$2,864 (out-of-state)**
- **Typical Expenses: $4,000**
- **Degrees offered: BSPharm, BSN, BSAllied Health Sciences**

A public university of medicine and allied health professions, chartered in 1824. Urban campus. Air, bus, and rail service.
Academic Character SACS and professional accreditation. Undergraduate programs in pharmacy, nursing, cytotechnology, dental hygiene, extracorporeal circulation, medical records administration, medical technology, occupational therapy, physical therapy, radiologic technology,

respiratory therapy. Certificates in dental assisting, dental lab technology, histotechnology, medical lab technique, opthalmic technology, radiologic technology, respiratory therapy, cytotechnology, histologic technology, physicians' assistant, practical nursing. Divisions include graduate studies in basic medical sciences and allied health sciences; Medicine, Dentistry, Pharmacy, Nursing. PhD, MD, DMD, MD-PhD, MS, PharmD granted. 147,000-volume library.
Financial Some in-state scholarships, student loans.
Student Life Dorms for men and women. 7 national and several local fraternities.

[1] SOUTH CAROLINA, UNIVERSITY OF
Columbia 29208, (803) 777-7700
Director of Admissions: John Bolin

- **Undergraduates: 7,586m, 6,934w; 25,834 total (including graduates)**
- **Tuition (1982/83): $1,180 (in-state), $2,460 (out-of-state)**
- **Room & Board: $1,590**
- **Degrees offered: BA, BS, BFA, BMus, BMus Ed, BMedia Arts, BAEd, BAInter Studies, BAJour, BSBA, BSChem Eng, BSHealth Ed, BSInter Studies, BSMT, BSN, BSPharm, ASEd, ASTech, ASN**
- **Mean SAT 463v, 491m**
- **Student-faculty ratio: 17 to 1**

A public university established in 1801. 262-acre urban campus. Served by air and rail.
Academic Character SACS and professional accreditation. Semester system, 2 5-week summer terms. 8 majors offered in Business Administration, 1 in Criminal Justice, 5 in Education, 4 in Engineering, 2 in Health, 21 in Humanities & Social Science, 3 in Journalism, 1 in Nursing, 1 in Pharmacy, and 7 in Science & Mathematics. Self-designed majors in College of General Studies. Minors offered in some fields and in 4 others. Many foreign language courses. Distributive requirements in some disciplines. Graduates and professional degrees granted. Honors College, honors programs. Phi Beta Kappa. Independent study. Limited pass/fail, internships. 3-1 medical technology program. Exchange programs with over 50 state-supported institutions. International Student Exchange. Exchange programs with Warwick and Kent in England. Elementary and secondary education certification. ROTC, AFROTC, NROTC. Computer facilities. Language labs. Museums. 3,681,701-volume library with microform resources.
Financial CEEB CSS and ACT FAS. University scholarships, grants, loans; PELL, SEOG, NDSL, FISL, NSL, CWS. Priority application deadline February 15.
Admissions High school graduation with college prep program recommended. GED accepted. SAT or ACT required. $25 application fee. Rolling admissions. $115 room deposit due on acceptance of admissions offer. *Early Admission* and *Concurrent Enrollment* programs. Transfers accepted. Credit possible for CEEB AP, CLEP, and university exams. Opportunity Scholars Program for disadvantaged students.
Student Life Student government. Newspaper, literary magazine, yearbook, radio station. Music and drama groups. Debate. Academic, honorary, professional, religious, service, and special interest groups. 20 fraternities and 14 sororities. Freshmen must live on campus. Coed and single-sex dorms. Honors houses. Married-student housing. 30% of all students live on campus. Liquor limited to living quarters and other designated areas. Drugs, firearms, gambling prohibited. Limited class cuts. 9 intercollegiate sports for men, 6 for women; many intramurals. AIAW, NCAA. Student body composition: 0.8% Asian, 13% Black, 0.5% Hispanic, 0.1% Native American, 83% White, 2.6% Other. 18% from out of state.

■[1] SOUTH CAROLINA, UNIVERSITY OF, AT AIKEN
171 University Parkway, Aiken 29801

■[J1] SOUTH CAROLINA, UNIVERSITY OF, AT BEAUFORT
PO Box 1007, Beaufort 29902

■[1] SOUTH CAROLINA, UNIVERSITY OF, COASTAL CAROLINA COLLEGE
Conway 29526

■[J1] SOUTH CAROLINA, UNIVERSITY OF, AT LANCASTER
Lancaster 29720

■[J1] SOUTH CAROLINA, UNIVERSITY OF, SALKEHATCHIE REGIONAL CAMPUS
Allendale 29810

■[1] SOUTH CAROLINA, UNIVERSITY OF, SPARTANBURG
Spartanburg 29303

■[J1] SOUTH CAROLINA, UNIVERSITY OF, SUMTER CAMPUS
Sumter 29150

■[J1] SOUTH CAROLINA, UNIVERSITY OF, UNION REGIONAL CAMPUS
Union 29379

[1] SOUTH CAROLINA STATE COLLEGE
Orangeburg 29117, (803) 531-1073
Director of Admissions: Dorothy L. Brown

- **Undergraduates: 1,434m, 1,759w; 4,073 total (including graduates)**
- **Tuition & Fees (1982/83): $750 (in-state), $1,380 (out-of-state)**
- **Room & Board: $1,476**
- **Degrees offered: BA, BS, BSArt Ed, BSElem Ed, BSEng Tech, BSHPE, BSMus Ed**
- **Mean SAT 300v, 340m**
- **Student-faculty ratio: 16 to 1**

A public college established in 1896. 147-acre small-city campus, 40 miles from Columbia. Served by air and rail in Columbia.
Academic Character SACS and professional accreditation. Semester system, summer term. 47 majors offered by the schools of Arts & Sciences, Education, Home Economics, and Industrial Education & Engineering Technology. Minors in most major fields and in 4 others. Distributives, sophomore comprehensive exam required. Graduate degrees granted. Cooperative work/study, limited pass/fail, internships. Preprofessional programs in agriculture, dentistry, law, medicine, optometry, veterinary medicine. 2-2 nursing programs with Clemson. Elementary and secondary education certification. ROTC, AFROTC. Computer center. Language lab. 217,000-volume library.
Financial Guaranteed tuition. CEEB CSS. College scholarships, grants, loans, payment plans; PELL, SEOG, NDSL, GSL, CWS, college employment program. Application deadline June 1.
Admissions High school graduation with 16 units required. SAT or ACT required. $10 ($15 for out-of-state) application fee. Rolling admissions. $55 deposit due on acceptance of admissions offer. *Early Admission* and *Early Decision* programs. Transfers accepted. Credit possible for CEEB AP exams. Special Service Program for disadvantaged.
Student Life Student government. Newspaper, yearbook. Music groups. Academic, honorary, religious, service, and special interest groups. Fraternities and sororities. Single students must live at home or on campus. Single-sex dorms. Married-student housing. 90% of students live on campus. Freshmen may not have cars on campus. 4 semesters of phys ed required. 8 intercollegiate sports for men, 4 for women; many intramurals. AIAW, NCAA, M-EAC. Student body composition: 93.2% Black, 5.3% White, 1.5% Other. 8% from out of state.

[2 & J2] SOUTHERN METHODIST COLLEGE
760 Broughton Street, SW, Orangeburg 29115

- **Undergraduates: 36m, 30w**
- **Tuition (1980/81): $1,200**
- **Room & Board: $1,700; Fees: $200**
- **Degrees offered: BA, AA, AS**

A private, coed college operated by the Southern Methodist Church, founded in 1956.
Academic Character 4-year programs offered in Bible, Christian education, Christian Ministries, missions, English, history, and social studies. AA in liberal arts, AS in office administration and business administration. 2-year transfer programs offered in general education. One-year business certificate program. Remedial mathematics and English programs.
Admissions High school graduation with 16 units required. Enrollment open to students of all faiths. Rolling admissions. No application deadline.
Student Life Dormitories for men and women. Dining facilities.

[J1] SPARTANBURG METHODIST COLLEGE
Spartanburg 29302, (803) 576-3911
Dean of Admissions & Registrar: A.G. Carter

- **Enrollment: 1,000 men & women**
- **Expenses (1981/82): $3,795-$3,880**
- **Degree offered: AA**
- **Student-faculty ratio: 13 to 1**

A private college controlled by the United Methodist Church, established in 1911. 100-acre urban campus. Served by air, rail, and bus.
Academic Character SACS accreditation. Semester system. 2-year programs offered in liberal arts, early childhood education, supervisory management, criminal justice, business education, interpreting arts for communication with deaf, computer science, and retail merchandising. Distributive requirements. Independent study. Preprofessional programs in dentistry, law, medicine, nursing. 1-3 and 2-3 engineering programs with Clemson.
Financial CEEB CSS and ACT FAS. College scholarships, loans, ministerial scholarships, state grants; PELL, SEOG, NDSL, CWS.
Admissions High school graduation required. GED accepted. SAT required. Rolling admissions. $100 ($50 for commuters) deposit required on acceptance of admissions offer. Transfers accepted. Credit possible for CEEB AP, CLEP, and college proficiency exams.
Student Life Student government. Newspaper, literary magazine, yearbook. Music groups. College Christian Movement. Honorary, service, and special interest groups. Single-sex dorms. Class attendance expected. 2 hours of phys ed required. 5 intercollegiate sports for men, 4 for women; intramurals. WCJCAA.

[J1] SPARTANBURG TECHNICAL COLLEGE
PO Drawer 4386, Spartanburg 29303

[J1] SUMTER AREA TECHNICAL COLLEGE
Sumter 29150

[J1] TRI-COUNTY TECHNICAL COLLEGE
Pendleton 29670

[J1] TRIDENT TECHNICAL COLLEGE
PO Box 10367, North Charleston 29411

[1] VOORHEES COLLEGE
Denmark 29042, (803) 793-3351
Director of Admissions: Iris D. Bomar

- **Undergraduates: 226m, 398w**
- **Tuition (1982/83): $2,156**
- **Room & Board: $1,862; Fees: $173**
- **Degrees offered: BA, BS, AA**
- **Student-faculty ratio: 12 to 1**

A private college affiliated with the Protestant Episcopal Church, established in 1897. 350-acre small-town campus, 50 miles from Columbia. Served by rail and bus; airport in Columbia.

Academic Character SACS accreditation. Semester system, one 6-week summer term. Majors offered in accounting, biology, business administration, business education, elementary education, English, history, mathematics, office administration, social studies, and sociology. Minors required for BS and offered in 5 disciplines. 2-year programs in criminal justice and secretarial science. Courses include Afro-American literature. Distributives and 2 semesters of theology required. Independent study. Credit by exam. ROTC at SC State College. Family Life Institute. Learning Resources Center. 90,000-volume library.

Financial CEEB CSS and ACT FAS. College scholarships, loans, state grants, payment plan; PELL. SEOG, FISL, GSL, NDSL, CWS. Member United Negro College Fund. Application deadline May 1.

Admissions High school graduation with 18 units required. GED accepted. Interview recommended. SAT or ACT required. $10 application fee. Rolling admissions. $25 room deposit due on acceptance of admissions offer. Transfers accepted. Credit possible for CEEB AP, CLEP, and college challenge exams.

Student Life Student government. Newspaper, yearbook. Music and drama groups. NAACP. Academic, honorary, and religious groups. 7 fraternities and 6 sororities without houses. 77% of men and 10% of women join. 95% of students live on campus. 4 semesters of phys ed and 1 semester of health education required. 4 intercollegiate sports for men, 3 for women; intramurals. SAC. Student body composition: 98% Black, 1% Hispanic, 1% White. 23% from out of state.

[J1] WILLIAMSBURG TECHNICAL VOCATIONAL AND ADULT EDUCATION CENTER
601 Lane Road, Kingstree 29556

[1] WINTHROP COLLEGE
Rock Hill 29733, (803) 323-2211
Director of Admissions: James McCammon

- **Enrollment: 1,064m, 2,552w**
- **Tuition (1982/83): $1,012 (in-state), $1,800 (out-of-state)**
- **Room & Board: $1,396**
- **Degrees offered: BA, BS, BMus, BMus Ed, BSW, BVisual Arts**
- **Student-faculty ratio: 14 to 1**

A public college established in 1886, became coed in 1974. 85-acre small-city campus, 20 miles from Charlotte. Served by bus; airport in Charlotte.

Academic Character SACS and professional accreditation. Semester system, 10-week summer term. 39 majors offered by the College of Arts & Sciences, and by the schools of Business Administration, Consumer Science & Allied Professions, Education, and Music. Minor required for a BA. Minors offered in some major fields and 16 others areas. Distributive requirements. Graduate degrees granted. Independent study. Honors programs. Cooperative work/study, limited pass/fail, internships. Preprofessional programs in dentistry, law, medicine, veterinary medicine. 3-1 medical technology program. Charlotte Area Educational Consortium. Study abroad. Elementary, secondary, and special education certification. ROTC at Davidson. Human Development Center. 293,119-volume library with microform resources.

Financial CEEB CSS. College scholarships, grants, loans, PELL, SEOG, NDSL, FISL, CWS. Application deadline February 1.

Admissions High school graduation required. GED accepted. Interview recommended. SAT or ACT required. $15 application fee. Rolling admissions. $100 room deposit due on acceptance of admissions offer. *Early Admission* and *Concurrent Enrollment* programs. Transfers accepted. Credit possible for CEEB AP and CLEP exams.

Student Life Student government. Newspaper, literary magazine, yearbook. Music and drama groups. Model United Nations. Academic, honorary religiou, and special interest groups. 6 fraternities, 1 with housing; 7 sororitie ithout houses. 13% of men and 10% of women join. Coed and single-se dorms Married-student housing. 58% of students live on campus. 75% class attendance required. 4 intercollegiate sports for men, 4 for women; intramurals. AIAW, NAIA. Student body composition: 13% Black, 84% White, 3% Other. 16% from out of state.

[1] WOFFORD COLLEGE
Spartanburg 29301, (803) 585-4821
Director of Admissions: Charles H. Gray

- **Undergraduates: 778m, 296w**
- **Tuition (1982/83): $4,125**
- **Room & Board: $2,300; Fees: $170**
- **Degrees offered: BA, BS**
- **Mean SAT 490v, 500m**
- **Student-faculty ratio: 16 to 1**

A private college affiliated with the United Methodist Church, established in 1854, became coed in 1971. 90-acre urban campus. Served by air, rail, and bus.

Academic Character SACS accreditation. Semester system, 2 5-week summer terms. Majors offered in accounting, biology, chemistry, economics, English, foreign languages, government, history, humanities, intercultural studies, mathematics, philosophy, physics, psychology, religion, and sociology. Self-designed and interdepartmental majors. Distributives and 3 hours of religion required. Independent study. Honors program. Phi Beta Kappa. Cooperative work/study, limited pass/fail, internships. Preprofessional programs in dentistry, law, medicine, ministry, veterinary medicine. 3-2 liberal arts and engineering program with Columbia U and Georgia Tech. Cooperative nursing program with Emory. Cross-registration with Converse offers 11 additional majors. Study abroad. Secondary education certification. ROTC. Language lab. Planetarium. 189,428-volume library with microform resources.

Financial CEEB CSS. College scholarships, grants, loans, ministerial scholarships, state grants, payment plan; PELL, SEOG, NDSL, GSL, CWS. Application deadline March 1.

Admissions High school graduation with 16 units recommended. GED accepted. Interview recommended. SAT or ACT required. $15 application fee. Rolling admissions. $100 ($50 for commuters) deposit due on acceptance of admissions offer. *Early Admission* and *Concurrent Enrollment* programs. Admission deferral possible. Transfers accepted. Credit possible for CEEB AP, CLEP, and college proficiency exams.

Student Life Student Union. Newspaper, literary magazine, yearbook. Music and drama groups. Afro-American Association. Association of Women. Honorary, professional, religious, and special interest groups. 10 fraternities and sororities without houses. 40% of students join. Single students live at home or on campus. Coed and single-sex dorms. No married-student housing. 77% of students live on campus. Class attendance expected. 2 hours of sophomore phys ed required. 9 intercollegiate sports; many club and intramural sports. AIAW, NAIA. Student body composition: 0.8% Asian, 8% Black, 0.5% Hispanic, 90.7% White. 27% from out of state.

[J1] YORK TECHNICAL COLLEGE
Rock Hill 29730

SOUTH DAKOTA *(SD)*

[1] AUGUSTANA COLLEGE
Sioux Falls 57197, (800) 952-3527 or (800) 843-3370
Director of Admissions: Dean A. Schueler

- **Undergraduates: 882m, 1,359w; 2,637 total (including graduates)**
- **Tuition (1982/83): $4,680**
- **Room & Board: $1,755**
- **Degrees offered: BA, AA**
- **Mean ACT 23.3**
- **Student-faculty ratio: 15 to 1**

A private college affiliated with the American Lutheran Church, established in 1860. 100-acre campus in southeastern South Dakota, 15 miles from Minnesota and Iowa. Airport, bus station.

Academic Character NCACS and professional accreditation. 4-1-4 system, May/June miniterm, 8-week summer term. BA offered in accounting, art, biology, business administration, business education, chemistry, comparative literature, computer science, criminal justice, economics, education, engineering physics, English, French, geography, German, government/international affairs, Greek, health/hospital services administration, history, journalism, liberal arts, math, music, nursing, philosophy, physical education, physics, planning, psychology, religion, social studies teaching, social work & community development, sociology, Spanish, theology, and speech, drama, & communications. Self-designed majors. 3-1 major in medical technology. AA offered in aviation, computer science, criminal justice, liberal studies, mortuary science, professional pilot, secretarial science. Distributives and 2 religion courses required. MAT granted. Honors program. Independent study. Pass/fail, cooperative work/study, credit by exam, internships. Several preprofessional programs. 2-2, 3-2, 4-2 engineering programs. Cross-registration with Sioux Falls College, North American Baptist Seminary. YMCA directors program. Living-learning semester in Minneapolis area; several other urban studies programs. Study abroad. Elementary, secondary, and special education certification. 225,000-volume library with microform resources.

Financial ACT FAS. College scholarships, grants, loans, payment plan; PELL, SEOG, NSS, NDSL, GSL, NSL, CWS. Priority application deadline February 15.

Admissions High school graduation with a college prep program required. GED accepted. Interview recommended. ACT or SAT recommended. ACH recommended for placement. $15 application fee. Rolling admissions. Application deadlines September 1 (February 1 for nursing). $100 enrollment and $30 housing deposits required on acceptance of offer of admission. Admission deferral possible. Transfers accepted. Credit possible for summer school credits, CEEB AP and CLEP exams.

Student Life Student government. Newspaper, literary magazine, yearbook. Radio station. Music, drama, and debate clubs. Volunteer groups. Native American Council. Circle K. Honorary, professional, religious, and special interest groups. 6 fraternities and 6 sororities without houses. 23% of men, 21% of women join. 1st- and 2nd-year students from out of town may live off campus only with Dean's permission. Coed, single-sex, special interest, and married-student housing. 60% of students live on campus. Liquor and gambling prohibited. Class attendance required in lower division courses. 2 phys ed credits required. 10 intercollegiate sports for men, 6 for women; intramurals. NCAA, NCIAC. Student body composition: 0.2% Asian, 0.4% Black, 0.7% Native American, 98% White, 0.7% Other. 45% from out of state.

[1] BLACK HILLS STATE COLLEGE

Spearfish 57783, (605) 642-6111
Director of Admissions: Gene Bauer

- **Enrollment: 921m, 1,159w**
- **Tuition (1982/83): $817 (in-state), $1,692 (out-of-state)**
- **Room & Board: $1,425; Fees: $255**
- **Degrees offered: BA, BS, AA**
- **Mean ACT 19.4**
- **Student-faculty ratio: 20 to 1**

A public college established in 1883. 123-acre campus 45 miles from Rapid City. Bus station in Spearfish.

Academic Character NCACS and professional accreditation. Semester system, 2 5-week summer terms. BA, BS offered in accounting, art, biology, business administration, business education, chemistry, communications, criminal justice, elementary education, English, history, industrial arts, mass communications, math, music, office administration, outdoor education, physical education, physical science, physical therapy, political science, social science, sociology, special education, speech, travel industries management. AA offered in accounting, commercial art, computer applications programming, drafting technology, general office secretary, general studies, graphics, legal office secretary, library assistant, medical office secretary, radio & TV operations, travel industries. Certificate in general office secretary possible. Composite majors. Minors. Distributive requirements. MSEd granted. Credit by exam. Independent study, internships. Preprofessional programs in biomedical sciences, agriculture, computer science, forestry, law, wildlife management, and others. Center of Indian Studies. Early childhood, elementary, secondary, and special education certification. ROTC. Art galleries. 170,000-volume library.

Financial ACT FAS. College scholarships and loans, PELL, SEOG, NDSL, FISL, CWS. Application deadline April 1.

Admissions High school graduation or GED required. Rank must be in upper 66% of class. ACT or SAT required. Junior college has open admissions. $15 application fee. Rolling admissions; application deadline 2 weeks before orientation day. $100 room reservation deposit required. Informal early decision, *Early Entrance* programs. Admission deferral possible. Transfers accepted. Credit possible for CEEB AP, CLEP, and college placement exams.

Student Life Student government. Newspaper, magazine, yearbook. Radio station. Music, debate, and drama groups. Native American group. Political and religious groups. Several special interest groups. 2 fraternities (one with house) and 2 sororities without houses. 9% of men, 6% of women join. Single-sex and coed dorms. No married-student housing. 31% of students live on campus. 4 hours of phys ed required. 5 intercollegiate sports for men, 4 for women; intramurals. NAIA, South Dakota Intercollegiate Conference. Student body composition: 1% Black, 6% Native American, 92% White, 1% Other. 10% from out of state.

[1] DAKOTA STATE COLLEGE

Madison 57042, (605) 256-3551
Director of Admissions: Kathy Schneider

- **Undergraduates: 435m, 578w; 1,151 total (including part-time)**
- **Tuition (1982/83): $816 (in-state), $1,692 (out-of-state)**
- **Room & Board: $1,480; Fees: $220**
- **Degrees offered: BS, BSEd, AA**
- **Mean ACT 17**
- **Student-faculty ratio: 17 to 1**

A public college established in 1881. 25-acre urban campus 4 blocks north of the business district of Madison. Bus station nearby.

Academic Character NCACS and professional accreditation. Semester system, 2 4-week summer terms. Bachelor's programs offered in art, biology, business administration, chemistry, English, history, industrial arts, medical record administration, music, physical education, physical education/math, secretarial/office administration, social science, speech & drama. Associate's offered in accounting, agribusiness, data processing, early childhood education, health claims technician, materials management, medical records technician, real estate, respiratory therapy, retail & small business management, secretarial science, social service assistant, travel specialist. Minor required for bachelor's degree; offered in most of the above and in criminal justice, French, health, political science, psychology, sociology, Spanish. Distributive requirements. Independent study, honors program. Internships, cooperative work/study. ROTC. Elementary and secondary education certification.

Financial ACT FAS. College scholarships, state grants; PELL, SEOG, GSL, NDSL, PLUS, CWS.

Admissions High school graduation in top 66% of class (top 50% for out-of-state applicants) required. GED accepted. ACT or SAT required. $15 application fee. Rolling admissions. Informal early decision program. Transfers accepted. Credit possible for CEEB CLEP and college challenge exams.

Student Life Student government. Yearbook. Music, drama, and debate groups. Campus religious groups. Academic and special interest groups. Single students under 21 must live on campus or at home. One coed and 3 single-sex dorms. 50% of students live on campus. Regular class attendance expected. 4 hours of phys ed required. 7 intercollegiate sports for men, 7 for women. NAIA, South Dakota Intercollegiate Conference. Student body composition: 2% Asian, 1% Black, 1% Native American, 96% White. 8% from out of state.

[1] DAKOTA WESLEYAN UNIVERSITY

Mitchell 57301, (605) 996-6511
Associate Director of Admissions: Stephen W. Andresen

- **Enrollment: 190m, 280w**
- **Tuition (1982/83): $3,065**
- **Room & Board: $1,743-$2,088; Fees: $85**
- **Degrees offered: BA, BMEd, AA**
- **Mean ACT 18.7**
- **Student-faculty ratio: 12 to 1**

A private institution affiliated with the United Methodist Church, started in 1885. 8-building campus in the small city of Mitchell.

Academic Character NCACS accreditation. 4-1-4 system, 2 4-week summer terms. Bachelor's degrees offered in American Indian studies, art, athletic training, biology, business administration, chemistry, communication/theatre, community recreation, economics, education, English, foreign languages, library science, math, music, philosophy, nursing, medical technology, physics, political science, history, psychology, sociology, social work, radiologic technology, religion. AA in accounting, computer science, criminal justice, management, monetary & bank management, office management. Minor required. Distributives and one unit in philosophical/theological concept required. Independent study. Directed study. Dual enrollment possible. Credit/no credit option. Travel, exchange, and student-proposed courses possible during Interim. Adult education program. 75,000-volume library.

Financial ACT FAS. University scholarships and grants, United Methodist loans, state grants; PELL, SEOG, NDSL, GSL, CWS, campus part-time work, tuition equalization grant. Application deadline January 1.

Admissions High school graduation in upper ½ of class, ACT or SAT, and evidence of good moral character and future promise required. GED accepted. $10 application fee. Rolling admissions; application deadline January 1. Transfers accepted. Credit possible for CEEB CLEP exams, examinations, or life experience.

Student Life Student government. Newspaper, yearbook, literary magazine. Music, debate and drama groups. Several student-initiated and special interest groups. Single students under 23 must live on campus or at home. Single-sex dorms. Boisterous and disorderly conduct, use of profane language, gambling, abusive use of liquor, and use, consumption, possession or sale of illegal drugs prohibited. ½ unit of phys ed required. 6 intercollegiate sports for men, 6 for women. NAIA, South Dakota Intercollegiate Conference, South Dakota Intercollegiate Athletics for Women.

[J2] FREEMAN JUNIOR COLLEGE

Freeman 57029

[1] HURON COLLEGE

Huron 57350, (605) 352-8721
Admissions Counselor: Donald Rose

- **Enrollment: 250m, 150w**
- **Tuition (1982/83): $3,270**
- **Room & Board: $2,128; Fees: $215**
- **Degrees offered: BA, AA, AAS**
- **Mean ACT 14**

A private college affiliated with the United Presbyterian Church, founded in 1883. Campus is 80 miles northwest of Sioux Falls.

Academic Character NCACS accreditation. 4-1-4 system. Area Majors (2 concentrations or 1 concentration and 2 minors) offered in business, education, music, public service, and preprofessional areas. Self-designed majors. Distributives and 3 semester hours of theology required. MEd granted. Concentrations offered include accounting, agribusiness, art, biology, business administration, chemistry, composition, criminal justice, economics, history, languages, literature, math, music, nursing, philosophy, physical science, physics, political science, psychology, recreation, secretarial science, social science, sociology, speech-communication, theatre, theology, and health, physical education, & recreation. MEd granted in cooperation with Northern State College. Independent and directed studies. Internships. Special topics courses. Elementary, secondary, and special education certification. 48,000-volume library.

Financial Guaranteed tuition. Scholarships, grants-in-aid, work opportunities.

Admissions Rolling admissions. Students are admitted in September and in January.

Student Life Dormitory facilities for men and women on campus. Intercollegiate athletics for men in football, baseball, basketball, wrestling, track; women's intercollegiate athletics in volleyball, basketball, and track. Intramural programs. Student body composition: 10% minority.

[1] MOUNT MARTY COLLEGE

1100 West 5th Street, Yankton 57078

Toll-free: (800) 752-3615 (in-state), (800) 843-3724 (out-of-state)
Director of Admissions: Tom Streveler

- **Undergraduates: 134m, 419w**
- **Tuition (1982/83): $3,900**
- **Room & Board: $1,760**
- **Degrees offered: BA, BS**
- **Student-faculty ratio: 11 to 1**

A private college controlled by the Sisters of St. Benedict, established in 1936, became coed in 1969. Small-city campus.
Academic Character NCACS and professional accreditation. 4-1-4 system, 2 4-week summer terms. Majors offered in accounting, anesthesia, biology, business, chemistry, communication, community journalism, English, elementary education, home economics, mathematics, medical technology, music, nursing, religious education, respiratory therapy, social science, social work, and health, physical education, & recreation. Minors offered in most major fields and in 7 other areas. Self-designed majors. Distributives and 10 hours of religion/philosophy required. Cooperative work/study, pass/fail, internships. Preprofessional programs in dentistry, engineering, law, medicine, optometry, theology, veterinary medicine. 3-1 medical technology program with Sacred Heart Hospital. Cooperative home economics program with SDSU. Cross-registration with 9 area schools. Elementary and secondary education certification. Art gallery. Sacred Music Resource Center. 71,000-volume library with microform resources.
Financial CEEB CSS and ACT FAS. College scholarships, grants, loans; PELL, SEOG, NDSL, FISL, NSL, CWS, college employment. Scholarship application deadline March 1.
Admissions High school graduation required. GED accepted. SAT or ACT required. $10 application fee. Rolling admissions. $50 room deposit due on acceptance of admissions offer. Transfers accepted. Credit possible for CEEB CLEP, departmental challenge exams, and experience.
Student Life Student government. Newspaper, literary magazine, radio station. Music and drama groups. Student Ambassadors. Athletic, academic, honorary, recreational, religious, and special interest groups. Single students live at home or on campus. Single-sex dorms. Intercollegiate basketball for men; volleyball, softball, basketball for women. AIAW, NAIA, 10-KOTA.

[2 & J2] NATIONAL COLLEGE

321 Kansas City Street, Rapid City 57709
Toll-free: (800) 742-8942 (in-state), (800) 843-8892 (out-of-state)
Director of Admissions: Earle G. Sutton

- **Undergraduates: 438m, 632w**
- **Tuition (1982/83): $3,675**
- **Room & Board: $2,469; Fees: $300**
- **Degree offered: BS, AA, AS**
- **Student-faculty ratio: 26 to 1**

A private college established in 1941. 7½-acre urban campus. Airport and bus station nearby.
Academic Character AICS and professional accreditation; NCACS accreditation candidate. Trimester system, 11-week summer term. Majors offered in accounting, business administration, computer data processing, health services administration, and travel & tourism management. Minors offered. Associate degrees offered in the above and in administrative assistant, animal health technology, electronics technology, fashion studies, general studies, livestock production, medical assisting, secretarial science, geophysical surveying. Distributive requirements. Independent study. Credit by exam. Externships, internships. ROTC. 25,000-volume library.
Financial CEEB CSS and ACT FAS. College scholarships, grants, loans, state grants, payment plans; PELL, SEOG, NDSL, FISL, GSL, CWS. Scholarship application deadline April 1.
Admissions High school graduation with 16 units recommended. GED accepted. Interview recommended. ACT required. $25 application fee. Rolling admissions. $70 room deposit due on acceptance of admissions offer. Admission deferral possible. Transfers accepted. Credit possible for CEEB AP, CLEP, college challenge exams, and experiential learning.
Student Life Student government. Newspaper, yearbook. Choir. Rodeo club. Native American organization. Athletic, academic, religious, service, and special interest groups. 2 fraternities, 1 with house; 3 sororities, 1 with house. Students live at home or at school. Coed dorms. Married-student housing. 25% of students live on campus. Liquor prohibited. 2 intercollegiate sports for men, 3 for women; intramurals. NIRA, NLCAA. Student body composition: 0.5% Asian, 5% Black, 5.5% Hispanic, 5.5% Native American, 83.5% White. 40% from out of state.

[G1] NORTH AMERICAN BAPTIST SEMINARY

1321 West 22nd Street, Sioux Falls 57105

[1] NORTHERN STATE COLLEGE

Aberdeen 57401, (605) 622-2544
Director of Admissions & Records: Dr. Richard W. Van Beek

- **Undergraduates: 924m, 1,170w; 2,716 total (including graduates)**
- **Tuition (1982/83): $817 (in-state), $1,692 (out-of-state)**
- **Room & Board: $1,449-$1,263; Fees: $138**
- **Degrees offered: BA, BS, BMus Ed, BSEd, AA**
- **Mean ACT 18**
- **Student-faculty ratio: 22 to 1**

A public college established in 1901. 35-acre small-city campus. Served by air and bus.
Academic Character NCACS and professional accreditation. Semester system, 2 4-week summer terms. 39 majors offered by the divisions of Arts & Sciences, Business & Industry, and Education. Minors offered in most major fields and in 13 other areas. Distributive requirements. Graduate degrees granted. Independent study. Internships, cooperative work study. Preprofessional programs in architecture, engineering, journalism, mortuary science, optometry. 2-2 engineering programs with SD School of Mines and SD State U. 3-1 medical technology program. Cooperative programs with UMinn at Duluth. Study abroad. Elementary, secondary, and special education certification. ROTC. Computer center. Fine arts center. 210,000-volume library with microform resources.
Financial ACT FAS. College scholarships, grants, loans; PELL, SEOG, NDSL, GSL, PLUS, CWS. Priority application deadline March 1.
Admissions High school graduation with 16 units recommended. GED accepted. Interview recommended. ACT required. $15 application fee. Rolling admissions. $50 room deposit due on acceptance of admissions offer. *Early Admission* and *Concurrent Enrollment* programs. Admission deferral possible. Transfers accepted. Credit possible for CEEB AP, CLEP, and departmental exams. Summer enrollment on probation possible.
Student Life Student Association. Newspaper, literary magazine, yearbook. Music and drama groups. Debate. Native American Club. Honorary, political, professional, and religious groups. Students under 21 live at home or in dorms. Coed and single-sex dorms. No married-student housing. 33% of students live on campus. Liquor prohibited. 4 semesters of phys ed required. 9 intercollegiate sports for men, 6 for women; many intramurals. AIAW, NAIA, NCAA, NIC. Student body composition: 0.1% Asian, 0.1% Black, 0.1% Hispanic, 3% Native American, 96% White, 0.7% Other. 5% from out of state.

[J2] OGLALA SIOUX COMMUNITY COLLEGE

Pine Ridge 57770

[J1] PRESENTATION COLLEGE

Aberdeen 57401

[J2] SINTE GLESKA COMMUNITY COLLEGE

Rosebud 57570

[1] SIOUX FALLS COLLEGE

Sioux Falls 57105, (605) 336-2850
Director of Admissions: Earl L. Craven

- **Undergraduates: 336m, 575w**
- **Tuition (1982/83): $3,600**
- **Est. Room & Board: $1,690-$1,840; Fees: $340**
- **Degrees offered: BA, BS, AA**
- **Mean ACT 19**
- **Student-faculty ratio: 21 to 1**

A private college affiliated with the American Baptist Convention, established in 1883. Urban campus.
Academic Character NCACS and professional accreditation. 4-1-4 system, 3- and 2 4-week summer terms. 26 majors offered in the areas of art, biology, business, chemistry, criminal justice, education, engineering, English, history, mathematics, media, medical technology, music, psychology, religion, social science, social work, and speech. Distributives and one course in religion required. MAEd granted. Independent study. Internships. Preprofessional programs in dentistry, law, medicine, mortuary science, veterinary medicine. Cooperative nursing and medical technology programs with Mounds Midway. Cross-registration with 11 area schools. 3-2 engineering program with SD State U. Elementary, secondary, and special education certification. Center for Women. Fine arts center. 75,000-volume library.
Financial CEEB CSS. College scholarships, grants, payment plan; PELL, SEOG, NDSL, FISL, GSL, CWS, college employment program. Recommended application deadline April 1.
Admissions High school graduation in upper half of class required. GED accepted. ACT required. $10 application fee. Rolling admissions. $40 room deposit due on acceptance of admissions offer. *Early Admission* Program. Transfers accepted. Credit possible for CEEB CLEP exams.
Student Life Student government. Newspaper, yearbook, radio and TV stations. Music and drama groups. Honorary, professional, religious, and special interest groups. Single students under 22 live at home or on campus. Single-sex dorms. Married-student housing. 4 phys ed courses required. 7 intercollegiate sports for men, 7 for women; intramurals. AIAW, NAIA, SDIC.

[1] SOUTH DAKOTA, UNIVERSITY OF

Vermillion 57069, (605) 677-5434
Director of Admissions: Gary Gullickson

- **Undergraduates: 2,368m, 2,426w; 6,220 total (including graduates)**
- **Tuition (1982/83): $854 (in-state), $1,884 (out-of-state)**
- **Room & Board: $1,420-$1,500; Fees: $262**
- **Degrees offered: BA, BS, BFA, BLS, AADH, AN**
- **Mean ACT 21**
- **Student-faculty ratio: 18 to 1**

A public university established in 1862. 216-acre small-town campus, 35 miles northwest of Sioux City. Served by bus.
Academic Character NCACS and professional accreditation. Semester system, 8-week summer term. 29 majors offered by the College of Arts & Sciences, 5 by the College of Fine Arts, 4 by the Division of Allied Health, 4 by the School of Business, 9 by the School of Education, 2 by the School of Medicine, and 1 by the School of Nursing. Self-designed majors. Distributive requirements. Graduate and professional degrees granted. Independent study. Honors program. Phi Beta Kappa. Pass/fail, internships. Preprofessional programs in dentistry, law, medicine, mortuary science, optometry, osteopathy, pharmacy, physical therapy, veterinary medicine. 3-1 medical technology program. 2- and 4-year dental hygiene programs. Exchange program with Westfield State College (Mass). Member of University of Mid-America Consortium. Elementary, secondary, and special education certification. ROTC. Business Research Bureau. Child Study Center. Institute of Indian Studies. Museum. Natural sciences field station. History of musical instruments center. 425,000-volume library with microform resources.

Financial CEEB CSS and ACT FAS. University scholarships, loans; PELL, SEOG, NDSL, GSL, CWS. Recommended application deadline March 1.
Admissions High school graduation with 16 units required. ACT required. $15 application fee. Rolling admissions. $35 room deposit due on acceptance of admissions offer. *Early Decision* and *Concurrent Enrollment* programs. Transfers accepted. Credit possible for CEEB CLEP and university placement exams. Upward Bound Program.
Student Life Student government. Newspaper, humor magazine, yearbook, radio and television stations. Music and drama groups. Debate. Athletic, academic, honorary, political, professional, religious, service, and social groups. 9 fraternities and 5 sororities, all with houses. 30% of students join. Freshmen and sophomores under 21 must live at home or on campus. Coed and single-sex dorms. Married-student housing. 38% of students live on campus. 8 intercollegiate sports for men, 7 for women; intramurals. AIAW, NCAA, NCIAC. Student body composition: 1% Black, 3% Native American, 95% White, 1% Other. 21% from out of state.

■[1] SOUTH DAKOTA, UNIVERSITY OF, AT SPRINGFIELD
Springfield 57062, (605) 369-2289
Director of Admissions: Tim White

- **Undergraduates: 543m, 221w**
- **Tuition (1982/83): $809 (in-state), $1,676 (out-of-state)**
- **Room & Board: $1,320; Fees: $125**
- **Degrees offered: BSEd, BSTech, AS**
- **Mean ACT 16.3**
- **Student-faculty ratio: 12 to 1**

A public university established in 1881. 57-acre small-town campus, 96 miles west of Sioux City.
Academic Character NCACS accreditation. Semester system, 2 4-week summer terms. Majors offered in construction & industrial technology, electronics engineering technology, industrial arts, mechanical technology, vocational-technical teacher education. 2-year programs in 8 additional areas. Distributive requirements. Independent study. Cooperative work/study, pass/fail, internships. Numerous preprofessional programs including business administration, business teacher education, dentistry, engineering, medicine, veterinary medicine. Secondary education certification. ROTC. 90,000-volume library.
Financial CEEB CSS and ACT FAS. University scholarships, grants, loans, payment plans; PELL, SEOG, NDSL, FISL, CWS. Priority application deadline April 1.
Admissions High school graduation with 16 units required. ACT required. $15 application fee. Rolling admissions. *Early Admission* Program. Admission deferral possible. Transfers accepted. Credit possible for CEEB AP and CLEP exams.
Student Life Student Senate. Newspaper, yearbook, radio station. Music and drama groups. Debate. Rodeo Club. Athletic, academic, honorary, religious, service, and special interest groups. Single students under 21 live at home or on campus. Single-sex dorms. Married-student housing. 60% of students live on campus. 3.2 beer allowed in dorms. 6 intercollegiate sports for men, 4 for women; intramurals. Student body composition: 1% Asian, 1% Black, 2% Native American, 95% White, 1% Other. 16% from out of state.

[1] SOUTH DAKOTA SCHOOL OF MINES AND TECHNOLOGY
Rapid City 57701, (605) 394-2411, (800) 742-8606 (in-state only)
Registrar & Director of Admissions: Robert H. Moore

- **Undergraduates: 1,500m, 387w; 2,725 total (including graduates)**
- **Tuition (1982/83): $925 (in-state), $2,000 (out-of-state)**
- **Room & Board: $1,599-$1,749**
- **Degree offered: BS**
- **Mean ACT 24**
- **Student-faculty ratio: 19 to 1**

A public college established in 1885. Suburban campus.
Academic Character NCACS and professional accreditation. Semester system. Majors offered in chemical engineering, chemistry, civil engineering, computer science, electrical engineering, geological engineering, geology, mathematics, mechanical engineering, metallurgical engineering, mining engineering, and physics. Minors offered. Distributive requirements; comprehensive exam required in some areas. MS, PhD granted. Limited pass/fail. Cross-registration with Black Hills State. ROTC. Many research institutes. Computer center. Museum. 190,000-volume library with microform resources.
Financial ACT FAS. College scholarships. PELL, SEOG, NDSL, FISL, GSL, CWS. Application deadlines February 15 (scholarships), May 1 (other aid).
Admissions High school graduation in upper 66% of class required. ACT required. $15 application fee. Rolling admissions. $50 room deposit due on acceptance of admissions offer. Transfers accepted. Credit possible for CEEB AP, CLEP, and challenge exams. Probational admission possible.
Student Life Student Association. Music and drama groups. Honorary, political, professional, religious, social, and special interest groups. 4 fraternities with houses. Single students under 21 must live on campus. Coed and single-sex dorms. Drugs prohibited. 3.2 beer permitted in rooms. 6 intercollegiate sports for men, 2 for women; many intramurals. NAIA, SDIC. Student body composition: 0.1% Asian, 0.7% Black, 0.3% Hispanic, 0.1% Native American, 91.4% White.

[1] SOUTH DAKOTA STATE UNIVERSITY
Brookings 57007, (605) 688-4121
Director of Admissions: Vincent O. Heer

- **Enrollment: 3,900m, 3,267w (including graduates)**
- **Tuition (1982/83): $854 (in-state), $1,884 (out-of-state)**
- **Room & Board: $1,500; Est. Fees: $190**
- **Degrees offered: BA, BS, BSN, BSPharm, AA**
- **Mean ACT 21**
- **Student-faculty ratio: 22 to 1**

A public university established in 1881. 1,500-acre small-city campus, 60 miles from Sioux Falls. Served by air, rail, and bus.
Academic Character NCACS and professional accreditation. Semester system, 4- and 8-week summer terms. 28 majors offered by the College of Agriculture, 35 by the College of Arts & Sciences, 8 by the College of Engineering, 8 by the College of Home Economics, and 1 each by the Colleges of Nursing and Pharmacy. Minors offered in 8 additional areas. Distributive requirements. Graduate degrees granted. Independent study. Honors program. Limited pass/fail, internships, credit by exam. Preprofessional programs in dentistry, law, medicine, mortuary science, optometry. Cooperative home economics program with Merrill-Palmer. Study abroad. Secondary education certification. ROTC, AFROTC. Language lab. 300,000-volume library with microform resources.
Financial ACT FAS. University scholarships, grants, loans; PELL, SEOG, NDSL, NSL, HPL, CWS. Application deadlines January 15 (scholarships), March 1 (loans).
Admissions High school graduation with 16 units required. ACT required. $15 application fee. Rolling admissions. Transfers accepted. Credit possible for CEEB CLEP exams.
Student Life Students Association. Newspaper, yearbook. Music groups. Debate. Athletic, academic, honorary, political, religious, service, and special interest groups. 5 fraternities, 3 with houses; 3 sororities without houses. 5% of students join. Single students under 21 must live at home or on campus. Coed and single-sex dorms. Special interest housing. Married-student facilities. 45% of students live on campus. 2 semesters of phys ed required. 11 intercollegiate sports for men, 11 for women; many intramurals. AIAW, NCAA, NCC. Student body composition: 0.4% Asian, 0.4% Black, 0.1% Hispanic, 0.5% Native American, 96.7% White. 10% from out of state.

[1] YANKTON COLLEGE
Yankton 57078, (605) 665-3661
Director of Admissions: David A. Cookson

- **Undergraduates: 148m, 96w**
- **Tuition, Room, Board, & Fees (1982/83): $6,040**
- **Degrees offered: BA, BMus, BSMed Tech**
- **Mean ACT 18; mean SAT 360v, 420m**
- **Student-faculty ratio: 10 to 1**

A private college affiliated with the Congregational Church, established in 1881. Small-city campus, 65 miles northwest of Sioux City.
Academic Character NCACS accreditation. 4-1-4 system, summer term. Majors offered in art, business, biology, chemistry, criminal justice, elementary education, English, history, human services, music, physical education, political science, psychology, recreation, sociology, speech, and theatre. Minors offered. Self-designed majors. Distributive requirements. Independent study and tutorials. Internships, credit by exam. Preprofessional programs in arts management, law, legal assistance, medicine, medical technology, piano pedagogy, seminary, and social science teaching. Elementary and secondary education certification. ROTC at USD. Art center. Observatory. 60,000-volume library.
Financial CEEB CSS and ACT FAS. College scholarships, grants, state aid; PELL, SEOG, NDSL, GSL, PLUS, CWS. Priority application deadline January 1.
Admissions High school graduation with 15 units recommended. Audition required for music majors. SAT or ACT required. $10 application fee. Rolling admissions. $50 deposit due on acceptance of admissions offer. *Early Admission* and *Early Decision* programs. Admission deferral possible. Transfers accepted. Credit possible for CEEB AP and CLEP exams.
Student Life Student Association. Academic, honorary, musical, and special interest groups. Single students must live at home or on campus. Coed and single-sex dorms. Class attendance expected. 6 intercollegiate sports for men, 5 for women; intramurals. NAIA, SDIC. Student body composition: 35% minority.

TENNESSEE (TN)

[P] AMERICAN BAPTIST COLLEGE OF AMERICAN BAPTIST THEOLOGICAL SEMINARY
1800 White's Creek Pike, Nashville 37207

[J1] AQUINAS JUNIOR COLLEGE
4210 Harding Road, Nashville 37205

[1] AUSTIN PEAY STATE UNIVERSITY
Clarksville 37040, (615) 648-7011
Dean of Admissions and Records: Glenn S. Gentry

- **Undergraduates: 2,483m, 2,438w**
- **Tuition (1982/83): $720 (in-state), $2,478 (out-of-state)**
- **Room & Board: $1,898-2,030; Fees: $69**
- **Degrees offered: BA, BS, BFA, BSEd, BSN, AS**
- **Mean ACT 18 composite**
- **Student-faculty ratio: 21 to 1**

A public university established in 1927. 100-acre campus located in small city of Clarksville, 47 miles from Nashville. Served by air and rail.

Academic Character SACS and professional accreditation. Trimester system, 8-week summer term. Majors offered in agriculture, art (6 areas), biology, business (6 areas), chemistry, earth science, economics, education, English, environmental science, French, geography, geology, helath/physical education, history, industrial technology, mathematics, music, music education, nursing, philosophy, physical education, physics, political science, psychology, social welfare, sociology, speech/theatre, and urban affairs & regional development. Graduate and professional degrees granted. Pass/fail for juniors and seniors. Preprofessional programs in dentistry, engineering, law, medical technology, medicine, demonstration farm. 188,215-volume library with microform resources.

Financial ACT FAS (for Federal programs). University scholarships and loans; PELL, SEOG, NSS, NDSL, NSL, Tuition Plan, CWS, university work program. Priority application deadline March 1.

Admissions High school graduation with 16 units required. ACT required. $5 application fee; $25 room deposit (for boarders) required with application. Rolling admissions; suggest applying soon after February 1. *Early Admission* Program. Transfers accepted. Credit possible for CEEB AP and CLEP exams.

Student Life Student government. Newspaper, anthology, yearbook. Music and drama groups. International Relations Club. Academic, professional, honorary, religious, and special interest groups. 7 fraternities and 4 sororities. Married-student housing. 32% of students live on campus. Liquor, drugs, gambling, hazing prohibited on campus. Class attendance required. 3 terms of phys ed required. 7 intercollegiate sports for men, 5 for women; intramurals. AIAW, NCAA, Ohio Valley Conference. Student body composition: 1% Asian, 19% Black, 1.6% Hispanic, 0.2% Native American, 78.1% White. 12% from out of state.

[1] BELMONT COLLEGE

1800 Belmont Blvd., Nashville 37203, (615) 383-7001
Director of Admissions and Registrar: Ronald E. Underwood

- **Undergraduates: 940m, 987w**
- **Tuition (1982/83): $2,500**
- **Room & Board: $1,840-1,940**
- **Degrees offered: BA, BS, BMus, BBA, ASN, AA**
- **Mean ACT 18.8 composite**
- **Student-faculty ratio: 17 to 1**

A private college affiliated with the Tennessee Baptist Convention, established in 1951. 30-acre campus located in Nashville. Served by air, rail, and bus.

Academic Character SACS accreditation. Semester system, 2 5-week summer terms. 43 majors offered in the areas of behavioral sciences, biology, business administration, chemistry & physics, education, health & physical education, history & political science, mathematics, music, nursing, religion & philosophy, and literature, language & communication arts. Minor required for most majors. Minors offered in most major fields and 11 additional areas. 2 semesters of religion required. English comprehensive exam required by junior year. Independent study. Pass/fail, internships, cooperative work/study. Preprofessional programs in dentistry, law, medicine, optometry, pharmacy, theology. 3-1 medical technology program. 3-2 engineering programs with Auburn, U of TN at Knoxville, Georgia Tech; several other cooperative programs with Georgia Tech. Study abroad. Elementary, secondary, and special education certification. ROTC, NROTC at Vanderbilt, AFROTC at TN State. Language lab. 93,712-volume library.

Financial CEEB CSS. College scholarships, grants, loans; PELL, SEOG, NDSL, GSL, Education Funds, College Aid Plan, CWS, college work program. Application deadline March 15.

Admissions High school graduation with 15 units required. GED accepted. Interview required for nursing majors, audition for music majors. ACT or SAT required; ACT preferred. $25 application fee (for boarders), $15 (day students). Rolling admissions; suggest applying in January-February. *Early Decision* and *Early Admission* programs. Transfers accepted. Credit possible for CEEB AP and CLEP exams.

Student Life Student government. Newspaper, magazine, yearbook. Music, debate, and drama groups. Academic, honorary, religious, and special interest groups. 2 women's societies. Freshmen and sophomores must live on campus. No coed dorms. Married-student housing. International housing. 30% of students live on campus. Liquor, gambling, hazing, drugs prohibited. Dress code. Attendance in class and at twice-weekly convocations required. 4 phys ed courses required. 5 intercollegiate sports; intramurals. Volunteer State Athletic Conference. Student body composition: 5.1% Black, 90.4% White. 33% from out of state.

[1] BETHEL COLLEGE

McKenzie 38201, (901) 352-5321
Assistant Director of Admissions: Delores Mann

- **Enrollment: 183m, 180w; 424 total (including part-time)**
- **Tuition (1982/83): $1,980**
- **Room & Board: $1,500**
- **Degrees offered: BA, BS**
- **Student-faculty ratio: 15 to 1**

A private college affiliated with the Cumberland Presbyterian Church, established in 1842. Campus located near Kentucky Lake, in small town of McKenzie, midway between Memphis and Nashville.

Academic Character SACS accreditation. Trimester system, 3 3-week summer terms. Majors offered in accounting, biology, business administration, English, music, religion, applied mathematics, elementary education, general business, lay ministries, music education, science, secondary education, social sciences, and health, physical education & recreation. Self-designed majors. Minors offered in most major fields and in 9 additional areas. Distributive requirements. 6 hours of religion required. Independent study. Honors program. Preprofessional programs in engineering, medical technology, nursing, pharmacy, optometry, physical therapy, dentistry, medicine, cytotechnology, dental hygiene, radiologic technology, medical record administration. Elementary and secondary education certification. 66,000-volume library.

Financial CEEB CSS and ACT FAS. College scholarships and grants, athletic and music scholarships, state grants; PELL, SEOG, NDSL, FISL, CWS.

Admissions High school graduation required. ACT or SAT required. $10 application fee. Rolling admissions. *Early Admission* Program. Transfers accepted. Admission deferral possible. Credit possible for CEEB AP and CLEP exams.

Student Life Student government. Newspaper, yearbook. Drama group. Academic, religious, and special interest groups. 6 fraternities and 3 sororities. Students must live at home or on campus. No coed dorms. 3 hours of phys ed required. 4 intercollegiate sports for men, 2 for women; intramurals. Volunteer State Athletic Conference, NAIA. 16% minority students.

[1] BRYAN COLLEGE

Dayton 37321, (615) 775-2041

- **Enrollment: 258m, 309w; 628 total (including part-time)**
- **Tuition (1982/83): $2,750**
- **Total estimated expenses: $5,250 (does not include books)**
- **Degrees offered: BA, BS**

A private coeducational college organized in 1930. Campus in a rural environment northeast of Chattanooga.

Academic Character SACS accreditation. Semester system. Degrees offered in liberal arts, teacher education, Bible, and business. Remedial mathematics and English programs. 65,000-volume library.

Financial College grants and loans; PELL, SEOG, NDSL, CWS. Two-thirds of students work to earn part of their expenses.

Admissions Rolling admissions. *Early Admission* Program. Transfers accepted. Advanced placement possible.

Student Life Dormitories on campus for men and women. Intercollegiate sports offered in basketball, soccer, tennis, and baseball for men, basketball, volleyball, softball, and tennis for women; intramurals.

[1] CARSON-NEWMAN COLLEGE

Jefferson City 37760, (615) 475-9061
Director of Admissions: Jack Shannon

- **Undergraduates: 810m, 832w**
- **Tuition (1982/83): $3,000 (in-state), $3,100 (out-of-state)**
- **Room & Board: $1,700**
- **Degrees offered: BA, BS, BMus, BSN**
- **Student-faculty ratio: 16 to 1**

A private college affiliated with the Tennessee Baptist Convention, established in 1851. Rural campus located in small town of Jefferson City, 30 miles from Knoxville. Served by bus; airport in Knoxville.

Academic Character SACS and professional accreditation. Semester system, 3-week miniterm in May, 3 3-week summer terms. 42 majors offered in the areas of humanities, social sciences, natural sciences & mathematics, fine arts, applied arts & sciences, business & economics, and nursing. Self-designed majors. Distributive requirements. 2 religion courses required. Independent and accelerated study. Honors program. Pass/fail, internships. Credit by exam and for experience. Preprofessional programs in law, medicine. 3-2 programs in engineering with Georgia Tech, U of Tenn; in forestry with Duke. 3-1 medical technology program. Study abroad. Elementary, secondary, and special education certification. ROTC. Language lab, media center, Home Management House. 150,000-volume library.

Financial College scholarships, grants, and loans; PELL, SEOG, NDSL, FISL, Tuition Plan, deferred payment, CWS. Preferred application deadline for scholarships soon after January 1.

Admissions High school graduation with 16 units required. ACT required. $15 application fee. Rolling admissions; suggest applying early in 12th year. $50 deposit required on acceptance of offer of admission. *Early Decision, Early Admission, ACT-Application* programs. Transfers accepted. Credit possible for CEEB AP and CLEP exams.

Student Life Student government. Newspaper, yearbook. Music, film, debate groups. Black Students Cultural Society. Honorary, academic, professional, religious, and special interest groups. Seniors and students over 21 may live off campus. Married-student housing. 85% of students live on campus. Liquor, hazing, drugs, fireworks, firearms prohibited on campus. Attendance in class and at weekly chapel required. 8 intercollegiate sports for men, 3 for women; intramurals. AIAW, NCAA, Volunteer State Athletic Conference. Student body composition: 5% Black, 94% White, 1% Other. 50% from out of state.

[J1] CHATTANOOGA STATE TECHNICAL COMMUNITY COLLEGE

4501 Amnicola Highway, Chattanooga 37406

[1] CHRISTIAN BROTHERS COLLEGE

650 East Parkway South, Memphis 38104, (901) 278-0100
Director of Admissions: Dayna Street

- **Undergraduates: 729m, 436w**
- **Tuition (1982/83): $3,390**
- **Room & Board: $2,246-$2,886; Fees: $70**
- **Degrees offered: BA, BS, AS**
- **Mean ACT 18 composite**
- **Student-faculty ratio: 15 to 1**

A private college controlled by the Christian Brothers of the Roman Catholic Church, established in 1871, became coed in 1970. 57-acre urban campus in Memphis. Served by air, rail, and bus.
Academic Character SACS accreditation. Semester system, 2 5-week summer terms. Majors offered in biology, business administration (4 areas), chemical engineering, chemistry, civil engineering, electrical engineering, English, history, human development & learning, humanities (4 areas), mathematics, mechanical engineering, medical technology, natural science, and physics. Additional engineering options. Internships. Preprofessional programs in dentistry, law, medicine, nursing, veterinary medicine. Nursing program through St. Joseph Hospital. Cross-registration with LeMoyne-Owen, Memphis Academy of Arts, Memphis Theological Seminary. Montessori workshop in Memphis. Elementary and secondary education certification; kindergarten and special education certification through other Memphis schools. AFROTC nearby. 84,000-volume library.
Financial CEEB CSS and ACT FAS. College scholarships, grants, loans; PELL, SEOG, NDSL, deferred payment, CWS.
Admissions High school graduation with 16 units required. ACT required. $25 application fee. Rolling admissions; suggest applying by August 1. $50 tuition deposit and $25 room deposit (for boarders) required on acceptance of offer of admission. *Early Decision, Early Admission, Concurrent Enrollment* programs. Transfers accepted. Credit possible for CEEB AP and CLEP exams; college has own advanced placement program.
Student Life Student government. Newspaper, magazine, yearbook. Music and drama groups. Academic, religious, and special interest groups. 4 fraternities without houses. Freshmen must live at home or on campus. No coed dorms. 25% of students live on campus. Liquor prohibited, except in dorms and at social functions. Limited class absences allowed. 2 hours of phys ed required. 5 intercollegiate sports for men, 3 for women; intramurals. Student body composition: 0.8% Asian, 10.7% Black, 0.3% Hispanic, 0.1% Native American, 82.9% White. 21% from out of state.

[J1] CLEVELAND STATE COMMUNITY COLLEGE
Cleveland 37311

[J1] COLUMBIA STATE COMMUNITY COLLEGE
Columbia 38401

[J1] CUMBERLAND COLLEGE OF TENNESSEE
Lebanon 37087, (615) 444-2562

- **Enrollment: 158m, 128w; 425 total (including part-time)**
- **Tuition (1981/82): $1,800**
- **Room & Board: $1,350; Typical Expenses: $3,190**
- **Degrees offered: AA, AS, AM**
- **Student-faculty ratio: 15 to 1**

A private coeducational junior college controlled by self-perpetuating board of trustees with independent endowment. Established in 1842. Campus in a small town east of Nashville.
Academic Character SACS accreditation. 4-1-4 system. Majors offered in most liberal arts areas. Curriculum is individual-oriented. 28,500-volume library.
Financial Academic and athletic scholarships are available. Over 70% of students are receiving financial assistance of some kind.
Admissions High school transcripts required. ACT or SAT required. Applicants are admitted in September, January, and June.
Student Life Dormitories for men and women are maintained on campus.

[1] DAVID LIPSCOMB COLLEGE
Nashville 37203, (615) 385-3855, (800) 251-2054 (toll free)
Director of Admissions: Steve Davidson

- **Undergraduates: 1,060m, 1,184w**
- **Tuition (1982/83): $2,448**
- **Room & Board: $1,860; Fees: $150**
- **Degrees offered: BA, BS**
- **Student-faculty ratio: 20 to 1**

A private college affiliated with the Church of Christ, establihsed in 1891. 65-acre campus in Nashville. Served by air, rail, and bus.
Academic Character SACS and professional accreditation. Trimester system, 9-week summer term. 40 majors offered by the departments of art, Bible, biology, business administration, chemistry, education, English, health & physical education, history & political science, home economics, mathematics, modern languages, music, physics & engineering science, psychology, sociology & social work, and speech communication. Distributive requirements. Senior exams. Credit by exam. Preprofessional programs in agriculture, architecture, dentistry, engineering, law, medical technology, medicine, nursing, pharmacy, veterinary medicine. 3-1 medical technology program. 3-2 engineering programs with Georgia Tech, U. Tenn, Auburn, and Vanderbilt. Elementary and secondary education certification. AFROTC, NROTC, ROTC nearby. 138,874-volume library.
Financial CEEB CSS. College scholarships, grants, loans, state grants; PELL, SEOG, NDSL, Tuition Plan, installment plan, CWS. Loan application deadline June 1.
Admissions High school graduation with 15 units required. ACT required. $25 application fee. Rolling admissions; suggest applying in fall. $10 room deposit (for boarders) required on acceptance of offer of admission. *Early Admission* program. Transfers accepted. Credit possible for CEEB AP and CLEP exams.
Student Life Student government. Newspaper, yearbook. Music, debate, oratory, speaking groups. Academic, honorary, religious, service, and special interest groups. 10 fraternities and 11 sororities. 20% of men and 20% of women join. Students must live at home or on campus. No coed dorms. Married-student housing. 70% of students live on campus. Liquor, tobacco prohibited on campus. Attendance at daily chapel and Bible classes required. 3 hours of phys ed required. 6 intercollegiate sports; intramurals. NAIA. Student body composition: 0.6% Asian, 2.8% Black, 0.4% Hispanic, 96.1% White, 0.1% Other. 49% from out of state.

[J1] DYERSBURG STATE COMMUNITY COLLEGE
Dyersburg 38024

[1 and J1] EAST TENNESSEE STATE UNIVERSITY
Johnson City 37614, (615) 929-4213
Dean of Admissions: James W. Loyd

- **Undergraduates: 3,506m, 4,418w; 9,472 total (including graduates)**
- **Tuition (1982/83): $780 (in-state), $1,758 (out-of-state)**
- **Room & Board: $1,600; Fees: $12**
- **Degrees offered: BA, BS, BBA, BFA, BMus Ed, BSEnv Health, BSMT, BSN, BSW, AS**
- **Student-faculty ratio: 23 to 1**

A public university established in 1909. 366-acre urban campus in Johnson City, 20 miles from Bristol. Served by air, bus, and rail.
Academic Character SACS and professional accreditation. Semester system, 2 5-week summer terms. 53 majors offered by the School of Applied Science and Technology, the College of Arts and Sciences, the College of Business, the College of Education, the School of Nursing, and the School of Public and Allied Health. Minor required. Distributive requirements. Graduate and professional degrees granted. Honors program. Cooperative work/study. Preprofessional programs in architecture, dentistry, engineering, medicine, and veterinary medicine. 3-1 programs in medical technology, dentistry, engineering, forestry, medicine. 2-2 and 3-2 programs in engineering. Elementary, secondary, and special education certification. ROTC. Museum. 575,490-volume library with microform resources.
Financial CEEB CSS and ACT FAS. University scholarships, grants, loans; PELL, SEOG, NSS, NDSL, FISL, NSL, CWS. Priority scholarship application deadline April 15.
Admissions High school graduation required. GED accepted. ACT required; SAT accepted. $5 application fee. Rolling admissions; application deadline 2 weeks before registration. *Early Admission* Program. Transfers accepted. Credit possible for CEEB AP, CLEP, and ACT PEP exams; university has own advanced placement program.
Student Life Student government. Newspaper, yearbook, radio station. Music, debate, and drama groups. United Black Students. Academic, political, honorary, religious, service, and special interest organizations. 12 fraternities, 10 with houses, and 7 sororities, none with houses. No coed dorms. Married-student housing. 27% of students live on campus. Liquor, hazing prohibited on campus. 1 year of phys ed required (ROTC, band may be substituted). 10 intercollegiate sports for men, 6 for women; intramurals. AIAW, NCAA, Southern Conference. Student body composition: 0.4% Asian, 3.2% Black, 1.4% Hispanic, 0.4% Native American, 95% White, 0.6% Other. 12% from out of state.

[P] EMMANUEL SCHOOL OF RELIGION
Route 6, Johnson City 37601

[1] FISK UNIVERSITY
17th Avenue, North, Nashville 37203, (615) 329-8500
Director of Admissions: Aline Rivers

- **Undergraduates: 285m, 601w**
- **Tuition (1982/83): $2,275**
- **Room & Board: $2,085; Fees: $350**
- **Degrees offered: BA, BS, BMus**
- **Student-faculty ratio: 13 to 1**

A private university established in 1866. 40-acre urban campus overlooking Nashville. Served by air, bus and rail.
Academic Character SACS and professional accreditation. Semester system. Majors offered in art, biology, chemistry, dramatics & speech, economics, English, French, health care administration & planning, history, management, mathematics, music, music education, physics, political science, psychology, religious & philosophical studies, sociology, and Spanish. Self-designed majors. Distributive requirements. MA granted. Independent study. Honors program. Phi Beta Kappa. Cooperative work/study, pass/fail, internships. Credit by exam. Preprofessional programs in dentistry, law, medicine, mass communication media, theological studies. 5-year MBA program and dual-degree programs in science and engineering with Vanderbilt. 2-2 medical technology, nursing programs. Several exchange programs. Study abroad. ROTC, NROTC at Vanderbilt; AFROTC at Tenn. State. Computer center, language lab. 188,400-volume library with microform resources.
Financial CEEB CSS. University scholarships, grants, loans; PELL, SEOG, NDSL, GSL, CWS. Member United Negro College Fund. Application deadline April 1.
Admissions High school graduation with 15 units required. Health examination required. SAT or ACT recommended. $10 application fee. Rolling admissions; application deadline June 15. *Early Admission* Program. Transfers accepted. Credit possible for CEEB AP exams.

Student Life Student government. Newspaper, magazine, yearbook, radio station. Music, drama, dance groups. Foreign, international student organizations. Academic, religious, and special interest groups. 5 fraternities and 4 sororities. 29% of students join. Students must live at home or on campus. No coed dorms. No married-student housing. 85% of students live on campus. 7 intercollegiate sports for men, 5 for women; intramurals. AIAW, NCAA, SIAC. Student body composition: 99% Black, 1% White. 88% from out of state.

[P] FREE WILL BAPTIST BIBLE COLLEGE
West End Avenue, Nashville 37205

[1 and J1] FREED-HARDEMAN COLLEGE
Henderson 38340, (901) 989-4611
Director of Admissions: Billy R. Smith

- **Undergraduates: 548m, 614w; 1,240 total (including graduates)**
- **Tuition (1982/83): $2,700**
- **Room & Board: $1,690-$1,930**
- **Degrees offered: BA, BS, BBA, AA**
- **Student-faculty ratio: 15 to 1**

A private college affiliated with the Church of Christ, established in 1869. 85-acre campus in small town of Henderson, 17 miles from Jackson. Bus nearby; airport in Jackson.
Academic Character SACS accreditation. Semester system, 2 5-week summer terms. Majors offered in accounting, agribusiness, art, Bible, biology, business, chemistry, communication, computer science, elementary/early childhood education, English, health/physical education, history, home economics, home & family services, instrumental music, management, marketing, mathematics, medical technology, music, office administration, physical education, psychology, school music, secondary education, social work, and speech; several are teaching majors. Self-designed majors. Distributives and 1 Bible class per semester required. Independent study. Honors program. Phi Beta Kappa. Cooperative work/study, internships, field study. Preprofessional programs in law, dentistry, medicine. Cross-registration with Union U and Lambuth College. Elementary, secondary, and special education certification. Child Development Laboratory. 100,000-volume library with microform resources.
Financial ACT FAS. College scholarships, grants, loans, state grants; PELL, SEOG, NDSL, FISL, Tuition Plan, CWS, college work program. Priority application deadline for loans May 15.
Admissions High school graduation required. GED accepted. ACT required. $15 application fee. Rolling admissions; suggest applying by May 1. *Early Admission, Concurrent Enrollment* programs. Transfers accepted. Admission deferral possible. Credit possible for CEEB AP, CLEP, and ACT PEP exams; college has own advanced placement program.
Student Life Student government. Newspaper, magazine, yearbook, radio station. Music, drama, debate groups. Art guild. International club. Professional, religious, service, and special interest groups. 8 coed social clubs. Students must live at home or on campus. No coed dorms. Married-student housing. 85% of students live on campus. Liquor, tobacco, dancing, gambling, firearms, fireworks prohibited on campus. Attendance in class and at chapel required. 2 semesters of phys ed required. 6 intercollegiate sports for men, 3 for women; intramurals. Volunteer State Athletic Conference. Student body composition: 5% Black, 94% White, 1% Other. 61% from out of state.

[G1] HARDING GRADUATE SCHOOL OF RELIGION
1000 Cherry Road, Memphis 38117

[J1] HIWASSEE COLLEGE
Madisonville 37354, (615) 422-3283
Director of Admissions & Financial Aid: James R. Hemphill

- **Enrollment: 255m, 252w; 759 total (including part-time)**
- **Estimated Fees & Expenses: $3,585**
- **Degree offered: AA**
- **Mean ACT 15 composite**
- **Student-faculty ratio: 15 to 1**

A private 2-year college controlled by the United Methodist Church, established in 1849. 600-acre rural campus 2 miles north of Madisonville, 45 miles from Knoxville.
Academic Character SACS accreditation. Trimester system, 2 5-week summer terms. 2-year transfer programs offered in aerospace administration, aerospace technology, agriculture, business administration, business education, communications, elementary education, equitation, forestry, home economics, human services, industrial education, industrial technology, liberal arts, medical technology, music, and physical education. 19 2-year and 13 one-year technology programs. Distributives and 3 credit hours in religion required. Internships. Preprofessional programs in cytotechnology, dentistry, dental hygiene, engineering, medicine, ministry, nursing, optometry, pharmacy, physical therapy, secondary education. 40,000-volume library.
Financial CEEB CSS. College and state scholarships and loans; PELL, SEOG, NDSL, GSL, CWS; college has own work program.
Admissions High school graduation required. GED accepted. ACT or SAT required. Rolling admissions. *Early Admission* Program. Credit possible for CLEP exams.
Student Life Student government. Newspaper, magazine, yearbook. Music and drama groups. International Students. Religious, honorary, service, and special interest organizations. Students must live at home or on campus. Attendance required at chapel and convocations. 6 credit hours of phys ed required. 2 intercollegiate sports. NJCAC. Student body composition: 10% minority.

[J1] JACKSON STATE COMMUNITY COLLEGE
PO Box 2467, Jackson 38301

[J1] JOHN A. GUPTON COLLEGE
Nashville 37203

[1] JOHNSON BIBLE COLLEGE
Knoxville 37920

[1] KING COLLEGE
Bristol 37620, (615) 968-1187

- **Enrollment: 158m, 131w; 332 total (including part-time)**
- **Tuition (1981/82): $2,850**
- **Typical Expenses: $4,595**
- **Degrees offered: BA, BSE, BS**
- **Mean SAT 480v, 520m**

A private coeducational college organized in 1867, and affiliated with the Presbyterian Church. Campus in a small city in the northeast part of the state.
Academic Character SACS accreditation. 4-1-4 system, 5-week summer term. Majors offered in most liberal arts and sciences areas. Accelerated study can lead to degree in two years and eight months.
Financial College offers 24 scholarships of $1,500 or over, 41 scholarships of $750. Loan fund of $40,905; most loans average $593.
Admissions High school transcripts required. SAT required. Freshmen are admitted in September, February, and June.
Student Life Dormitories for men and women are maintained on campus. Dining hall. Intercollegiate athletics (no football).

[1] KNOXVILLE COLLEGE
Knoxville 37921, (615) 546-0751
Director of Admissions and Financial Aid: Joel Harrel

- **Undergraduates: 324m, 171w**
- **Tuition (1982/83): $2,670**
- **Room & Board: $1,845; Fees: $134**
- **Degrees offered: BA, BS**
- **Student-faculty ratio: 20 to 1**

A private college affiliated with the United Presbyterian Church USA, organized in 1867. 39-acre urban campus in northeast Knoxville. Served by air, bus, and rail.
Academic Character SACS accreditation. Trimester system. Majors offered in accounting, biology, business, chemistry, commercial music, communications, early childhood education, elementary education, health/physical education, mathematics/physics, music education, political science, psychology, recreation leadership, religion/philosophy, secondary education, and sociology. Religion courses and comprehensive exams (for seniors) required. Honors program. Preprofessional programs in law, medicine, nursing, social work. Cooperative programs with U of Tennessee in economics, engineering, food and lodging administration, and philosophy. Teacher training. ROTC. Language lab. 80,000-volume library.
Financial CEEB CSS and ACT FAS. College scholarships, grants, loans; PELL, SEOG, NDSL, GSL, deferred payment, CWS. United Negro College Fund.
Admissions High school graduation with 15 units required. SAT or ACT required. $10 application fee. Rolling admissions; suggest applying during 1st semester of senior year. $50 deposit required on acceptance of offer of admission. *Early Decision* Program. Transfers accepted.
Student Life Student government. Yearbook. Music and drama groups. Honorary, academic, and special interest groups. 4 fraternities and 4 sororities without houses. 16% of men and 18% of women join. Students must live at home or on campus. No married-student housing. 84% of students live on campus. Liquor prohibited in dorms. Class attendance required for freshmen. 4 hours of health and phys ed required. 4 intercollegiate sports; intramurals. NCAA, SIAC. Student body composition: 95.1% Black, 4.9% Other. 78% from out of state.

[1] LAMBUTH COLLEGE
Jackson 38301, (901) 427-6743
Director of Admissions: David Ogden

- **Undergraduates: 270m, 468w**
- **Tuition (1982/83): $3,100**
- **Room & Board: $1,650; Fees: $170**
- **Degrees offered: BA, BS, BBA, BMus**
- **Mean ACT 19 composite**
- **Student-faculty ratio: 13 to 1**

A private college affiliated with the United Methodist Church, established in 1843. 50-acre urban campus located in city of Jackson, 75 miles from Memphis. Served by air and bus.
Academic Character SACS accreditation. Semester system, 2 5-week summer terms. 38 majors offered in the areas of art, English, speech & drama, foreign languages, music, religion & philosophy, business administration & economics, education, history & political sceince, psychology, biology, chemistry & physical science, health & physical education, mathematics, physics & computer science, and sociology, social work & family development. Self-designed majors. Distributives and 1 religion course required. Independent study. Honors program. Cooperative work/study, pass/fail, internships. Preprofessional programs in architecture, dentistry, engineering, law, medical technology, medicine, ministry, nursing, pharmacy, physical therapy, religious education, social service, veterinary medicine. 3-2

engineering programs with Memphis State and other schools. Elementary, secondary, kindergarten, and special education certification. Library science certification. Biological field station, business center, interior design laboratory. 110,000-volume library.
Financial CEEB CSS and ACT FAS. College scholarships, grants, loans, ministerial and Methodist grants; PELL, SEOG, NDSL, Tuition Plan, Insured Tuition Payment Plan, CWS, college work program. Priority application deadline April 15.
Admissions High school graduation with 16 units required. GED accepted. SAT or ACT required before registration. $10 application fee. Rolling admissions; suggest applying before August 15. $25 tuition deposit and $25 room deposit (for boarders) required on acceptance of offer of admission. *Early Admission, Early Decision* programs. Transfers accepted. Credit possible for CEEB AP and CLEP exams; college has own advanced placement program.
Student Life Student government. Newspaper, magazine, yearbook. Music, drama groups. Black Student Union. Academic, religious, honorary, professional, and special interest organizations. 3 fraternities with houses and 4 sororities without houses. 40% of men and 40% of women join. Students must live with relatives or on campus. No coed dorms. No married-student housing. 50% of students live on campus. Liquor, drugs, narcotics, weapons prohibited. 2 phys ed courses, including swimming, required. 3 intercollegiate sports for men, 3 for women; intramurals. Volunteer State Athletic Conference. Student body composition: 15% minority. 12% from out of state.

[1] LANE COLLEGE
Jackson 38301, (901) 424-4600
Director of Admissions: Ella R. Maddox

- **Undergraduates: 363m, 362w**
- **Tuition (1982/83): $2,100**
- **Room & Board: $1,460; Fees: $164**
- **Degrees offered: BA, BS**
- **Mean ACT 11.5 composite**
- **Student-faculty ratio: 12 to 1**

A private college affiliated with the Methodist Episcopal Church, established in 1882. 15-acre campus in small city of Jackson, northeast of Memphis. Served by air and bus.
Academic Character SACS accreditation. Semester system. Majors offered in biology, business, chemistry, communications education, computer science, secretarial science, elementary education, English, history, mathematics, music, physical education & health, religion, and sociology. Minor required. Minors offered in most major fields. Distributives and senior exams required. Negro Heritage Room, Haitian art collection. 81,000-volume library.
Financial CEEB CSS and ACT FAS. College scholarships and loans, state grants; PELL, SEOG, GSL, NDSL, CWS. Member United Negro College Fund. Application deadline May 1.
Admissions High school graduation with 15 units required. GED accepted. SAT or ACT required. Rolling admissions. $50 tuition deposit and $25 room deposit (for boarders) required on acceptance of offer of admission. Transfers accepted. Upward Bound Program.
Student Life Student government. Newspaper, yearbook. Music groups. Honorary, academic, and special interest groups. 5 fraternities and 4 sororities. No coed dorms. Over 50% of students live on campus. Liquor prohibited on campus. Dress code. 4 intercollegiate sports for men, 1 for women; intramurals. NCAA, SIAC. Student body composition: 100% Black. Few students from out of state.

[1] LEMOYNE-OWEN COLLEGE
807 Walker Avenue, Memphis 38126, (901) 774-9090
Director of Admissions: Carolyn B. Bishop

- **Undergraduates: 345m, 687w**
- **Tuition (1982/83): $3,700**
- **Degrees offered: BA, BS, BBA**
- **Mean ACT 10.2 composite**
- **Student-faculty ratio: 16 to 1**

A private college affiliated with United Church of Christ and Missionary Baptist Church, established in 1862. Urban campus in Memphis. Air, bus, and rail nearby.
Academic Character SACS accreditation. Trimester system. Majors offered in accounting, art, biology, business administration, chemistry, economics, education, English, health & physical education, history, mathematics, natural science, philosophy, political science, social work, and sociology. Distributive requirements. Independent and accelerated study. Honors program. Cooperative work/study. Internships. Dual-degree program in English. Member Greater Memphis Consortium. Exchange program. Study abroad. Elementary and special education certification. ROTC, AFROTC at Memphis State. Computer center, language lab, museum/gallery. 87,323-volume library.
Financial CEEB CSS. College scholarships, grants, and loans; SEOG, CWS. Application deadlines July 15 (scholarships), September 30 (loans).
Admissions High school graduation with 16 units required. GED accepted. SAT or ACT required. Rolling admissions; suggest applying by January. *Early Admission, Early Decision* programs. Transfers accepted. Credit possible for CEEB AP and CLEP exams. Special Services Program.
Student Life Newspaper, yearbook. Choir, drama group. Academic and special interest organizations. No college housing. Liquor prohibited on campus. Attendance required at weekly chapel. 2 semesters of phys ed required. 4 intercollegiate sports for men, 1 for women. Student body composition: 2% Asian, 98% Black. 6% from out of state.

[1 & J1] LEE COLLEGE
Cleveland 37311, (615) 472-2111
Director of Admissions: Stanley Butler

- **Undergraduates: 590m, 599w**
- **Tuition (1982/83): $2,200**
- **Room & Board: $1,630**
- **Degrees offered: BA, BS, BMus Ed**
- **Student-faculty ratio: 15 to 1**

A private college affiliated with the Church of God, established in 1918. 33-acre campus in Cleveland, 30 miles from Chattanooga. Served by bus; airport and rail in Chattanooga.
Academic Character SACS accreditation. Semester system, 2 5-week summer terms. Majors offered in accounting, biological science, business, chemistry, communications, English, French, history, mathematics, music, music education, natural science, psychology, social science, sociology, Spanish, elementary education, health & physical education, secondary education, and Biblical, Christian, and missionary education. Distributive requirements. Religion required each semester. Independent study. Honors program. Internships. Preprofessional programs in dentistry, medicine, nursing, pharmacy. Study abroad. Elementary, secondary, and special education certification. 92,000-volume library.
Financial CEEB CSS and ACT FAS. College scholarships, grants, and loans, state scholarships and grants; PELL, SEOG, GSL, NDSL, FISL, Tuition Plan, deferred payment, CWS.
Admissions High school graduation required. GED accepted. SAT or ACT required; SAT preferred. $20 application fee. Rolling admissions; suggest applying early in 12th year. $20 tuition deposit and $35 room deposit (for boarders) required on acceptance of offer of admission. *Early Admission, Early Decision, Concurrent Enrollment* programs. Transfers accepted. Credit possible for CEEB AP and CLEP exams.
Student Life Student government. Magazine, yearbook. Music, drama groups. Academic, religious, service, and special interest groups. Freshmen must live at home or on campus. Married-student housing. 55% of students live on campus. Liquor, smoking prohibited on campus. Attendance required at weekly chapel and convocations. 2 semesters of phys ed required. 4 intercollegiate sports for men; intramurals for men and women. NAIA. Student body composition: 0.8% Asian, 6.1% Black, 3% Hispanic, 1.4% Native American, 88.3% White. 75% from out of state.

[1] LINCOLN MEMORIAL UNIVERSITY
Harrogate 37752, (615) 869-3611
Director of Admissions: Conrad Daniels

- **Undergraduates: 472m, 884w**
- **Tuition (1982/83): $2,250**
- **Room & Board: $1,775**
- **Degrees offered: AB, BS, BAS**
- **Mean ACT 17.3 composite**
- **Student-faculty ratio: 20 to 1**

A private university established in 1897. 1,000-acre semi-rural campus in village of Harrogate, 50 miles from Knoxville. Served by bus. Airport in Knoxville.
Academic Character SACS accreditation. Trimester system, 3 3-week summer terms. 2 majors offered by the Division of Basic Studies, 3 by the Division of Behavioral Science, 7 by the Division of Business Administration, 6 by the Division of Career Development, 4 by the Division of Education, 2 by the Division of Fine Arts, 3 by the Division of Humanities, 3 by the Division of Science, and 1 by the Division of Nursing. Self-designed majors. Distributive requirements. Minors offered in all major fields. Independent study. Honors program. Pass/fail, internships. Preprofessional programs in agriculture, forestry, nursing, optometry, pharmacy, veterinary science. 3-2 forestry program with Duke. Other 3-2 programs in law, medicine, dentistry, medical technology. 3-1 programs in dentistry, law, medical technology, medicine. Elementary, secondary and special education certification. ROTC. Home study program. Abraham Lincoln collection. 70,000-volume library.
Financial ACT FAS. University scholarships, grants, loans; PELL, SEOG, CWS. Scholarship application deadline August 15.
Admissions Open admissions; high school graduation recommended. GED accepted. ACT or SAT recommended. $10 application fee. Rolling admissions; suggest applying during 1st half of year. $50 deposit required on acceptance of offer admission. *Early Decision, Early Admission* programs. Transfers accepted. Credit possible for CEEB AP and CLEP exams.
Student Life Student government. Yearbook. Choir, drama group. Academic, service, honorary, and special interest groups. 4 fraternities and 3 sororities. 20% of men and 22% of women join. Coed and single-sex dorms. Married-student housing. 40% of students live on campus. Liquor use restricted on campus. Class attendance required. 6 quarter hours of phys ed required. 5 intercollegiate sports for men, 3 for women; intramurals. Volunteer State Athletic Conference. Student body composition: 6.4% Asian, 5% Black, 0.5% Hispanic, 0.1% Native American, 87% White. 48% from out of state.

[J1] MARTIN COLLEGE
Pulaski 38478, (615) 363-7456
Director of Admissions: Larry Layne

- **Undergraduates: 140m, 100w**
- **Tuition (1982/83): $1,900**
- **Room & Board: $1,700**
- **Degree offered: AA**
- **Student-faculty ratio: 10 to 1**

A private junior college affiliated with the United Methodist Church, established in 1870. Campus located in city of Pulaski, between Nashville and Birmingham, Alabama. Served by bus.

Academic Character SACS accreditation. Semester system, 2 4-week summer terms. 2-year programs offered in art, English, foreign language, music theory & literature, applied music, religion & philosophy, biology, chemistry & physics, engineering graphics, mathematics, physical education, driver education, health, general business, secretarial science, history & political science, psychology, and sociology. Self-designed programs. Preprofessional programs in cytotechnology, dental hygiene, dentistry, engineering, forestry, law, medicine, ministry, nursing, pharmacy, and others. Study abroad possible. 25,000-volume library with microform resources.
Financial ACT FAS. College scholarships, state grants, Methodist loans, PELL, SEOG, NDSL, GSL, CWS. Priority application deadline May 1.
Admissions High school graduation with 12 units required. GED accepted. ACT or SAT required. $10 application fee. Rolling admissions; application deadline August 1. $25 room deposit (for boarders) required on acceptance of offer of admission. *Early Admission* Program. Transfers accepted. Credit possible for CEEB AP and CLEP exams.
Student Life Student government. Newspaper, yearbook. Music and drama groups. Black Student Union. Honorary, religious, and special interest groups. Single students must live at home or on campus. No coed dorms. Attendance at bimonthly assemblies required. 2 hours of phys ed required. 5 intercollegiate sports; intramurals. NJCAA.

[1] MARYVILLE COLLEGE
Maryville 37801, (615) 982-6412
Director of Admissions: Larry M. West

- **Undergraduates: 328m, 322w**
- **Tuition (1982/83): $3,920**
- **Room & Board: $1,995; Fees: $80**
- **Degrees offered: BA, BMus**
- **Mean SAT 475v, 495m**
- **Student-faculty ratio: 13 to 1**

A private college affiliated with the United Presbyterian Church, established in 1819. 350-acre campus in Maryville, 16 miles from Knoxville. Served by bus. Airport 4 miles away.
Academic Character SACS and professional accreditation. 10-3-10-10 system, 6-week summer term. Majors offered in art, biology, business administration, chemistry, economics, elementary education, English, history, interdisciplinary majors, interpreter training for deaf, mathematics, medical technology, music, physical education, physics, political science, psychology, recreation, religion, Spanish. Self-designed majors. Distributives and 1 religion course required. Senior comprehensive exams. Independent study. Honors program. Pass/fail, internships. Field work. Preprofessional programs in engineering, law, medicine. Cooperative program with 12 area schools. 3-2 engineering programs with Georgia Tech, U of Tenn. Study abroad. Washington semester. Elementary and secondary education certification. ROTC at U of Tenn-Knoxville. Environmental Education Center in Great Smoky Mountains, Washington Center for Learning Alternatives. Language lab, art gallery. 115,000-volume library.
Financial CEEB CSS. College scholarships, grants, loans; PELL, SEOG, NDSL, GSL, Insured Tuition Plan, Tuition Plan, Education Funds, CWS.
Admissions High school graduation with 15 units required. Interview encouraged. SAT or ACT required. $10 application fee. Rolling admissions; suggest applying in fall. $100 deposit required on acceptance of offer of admission. *Early Admission* Program. Transfers accepted. Admission deferral possible. Credit possible for CEEB AP and CLEP exams.
Student Life Student government. Newspaper, yearbook. Music, debate, drama groups. Academic, religious, service, and special interest groups. 2 societies for men, 2 for women, 1 for married students; all have rooms. Single students must live with relatives or on campus. Coed and single-sex dorms. No married-student housing. 90% of students live on campus. Freshmen may not have cars on campus. 6 intercollegiate sports for men, 5 for women; intramurals. Student body composition: 4.3% Black, 93.4% White, 2.3% Other. 65% from out of state.

[G1] MEHARRY MEDICAL COLLEGE
Nashville 37208

[J1] MEMPHIS, STATE TECHNICAL INSTITUTE AT
5983 Macon Cove, Memphis 38134

[1] MEMPHIS ACADEMY OF ARTS
Memphis 38112

[1] MEMPHIS STATE UNIVERSITY
Memphis 38152, (901) 454-2000
Dean of Admissions: John Y. Eubank, Jr.

- **Undergraduates: 5,315m, 5,316w; 20,183 total (including graduates)**
- **Tuition (1982/83): $834 (in-state), $2,592 (out-of-state)**
- **Room & Board: $1,718-$2,004**
- **Degrees offered: BA, BS, BBA, BFA, BMus, BMus Ed, BSEd, BSN, BLS, BPS**
- **Mean ACT 19 composite**
- **Student-faculty ratio: 17 to 1**

A public university established in 1912. 200-acre urban campus 7 miles from downtown Memphis. Served by air, bus, and rail.
Academic Character SACS and professional accreditation. Semester system, 1 19-week, 2 6-week summer terms. 33 majors offered by the College of Arts & Sciences, 10 by the College of Business Administration, 13 by the College of Communication & Fine Arts, 28 by the College of Education, and 15 by the College of Engineering. Self-designed majors. Graduate and professional degrees granted. Independent study. Honors program. Pass/fail for upperclassmen. Internships. Credit by exam. Preprofessional programs in law, medicine. 3-1 programs in medical technology, medical record library science; others possible. 5-year masters program in engineering. Nursing program for RNs. Urban & regional studies program in community. Study abroad. Elementary, secondary, and special education certification. ROTC, AFROTC. 625-acre farm. 850,000-volume library with microform resources.
Financial ACT FAS. University scholarships, grants, loans; PELL, SEOG, NSS, NDSL, NSL, College Aid Plan, Education Funds, CWS. Recommended application deadline April 1.
Admissions High school graduation required. GED accepted. ACT required. $5 application fee. Rolling admissions; suggest applying in 2nd half of 12th year. *Concurrent Enrollment* Program. Transfers accepted. Credit possible for CEEB AP exams; university has own advanced placement program.
Student Life Student government. Newspaper, magazine, yearbook, TV station. Music, drama groups. Religious, academic, service, and special interest organizations. 18 fraternities, most with houses, and 11 sororities with suites. No coed dorms. Housing for married and foreign students. 12% of students live on campus. 4 semesters of phys ed required. 7 intercollegiate sports for men, 7 for women; intramurals. Student body composition: 1% Asian, 17.5% Black, 0.2% Hispanic, 0.1% Native American, 81% White, 0.2% Other. 7% from out of state.

[P] MEMPHIS THEOLOGICAL SEMINARY
168 East Parkway South, Memphis 38104

[1] MIDDLE TENNESSEE STATE UNIVERSITY
Murfreesboro 37132, (615) 898-5555
Director of Admissions: W. Wes Williams

- **Undergraduates: 4,062m, 4,179w**
- **Tuition (1982/83): $760 (in-state), $2,518 (out-of-state)**
- **Room & Board: $1,462; Fees: $20**
- **Degrees offered: BA, BS, BBA, BFA, BMus, BSW, BUniv Stu, AA**
- **Mean ACT 18.6 composite**
- **Student-faculty ratio: 21 to 1**

A public university established in 1911, became coed in 1950. 500-acre campus located in small city of Murfreesboro, 32 miles from Nashville. Served by bus; airport in Nashville.
Academic Character SACS and professional accreditation. Semester system, several summer terms. 47 majors offered by the School of Basic & Applied Science, 23 by the School of Business, 33 by the School of Education, and 33 by the School of Liberal Arts. Minor required. Minors offered in 10 areas. Distributive requirements. Graduate and professional degrees granted. Independent study. Honors program. Pass/fail, internships. Preprofessional programs in veterinary science, architecture, engineering, forestry, dentistry, dental hygiene, medicine, medical record administration, nursing, occupational therapy, pharmacy, physical therapy, radiologic technology. Archaeology-religious studies program in Middle East. Elementary and special education certification. ROTC. Language labs, 4 educational labs. 607,000-volume library with microform resources.
Financial CEEB CSS and ACT FAS. University scholarships, grants, loans; PELL, SEOG, NSS, NDSL, NSL, CWS, university work program. Application deadline May 15.
Admissions High school graduation required. GED accepted. ACT or SAT required for students under 21. $5 application fee. Rolling admissions; suggest applying by December 31. $30 housing deposit (for boarders) recommended with application. *Early Admission, Concurrent Enrollment* programs. Transfers accepted. Admission deferral possible. Credit possible for CEEB AP and CLEP exams, and for ACT PEP; university has own advanced placement program.
Student Life Student association. Newspaper, magazine, yearbook, radio station. Music, debate, drama groups. 130 honorary, professional, religious, and special interest organizations. 14 fraternities, 10 with houses, and 7 sororities without houses. 12% of men and 8% of women join. No coed dorms. Married-student housing. 32% of students live on campus. Liquor prohibited on campus. 4 semesters of phys ed required. 8 intercollegiate sports for men, 4 for women; intramurals. AIAW, NCAA, Ohio Valley Conference. Student body composition: 9% Black, 90% White, 1% Other. 6% from out of state.

[P] MID-SOUTH BIBLE COLLEGE
2485 Union Avenue, Memphis 38112

[1] MILLIGAN COLLEGE
Milligan College 37682, (615) 929-0116
Registrar and Director of Admissions: Phyllis D. Fontaine

- **Undergraduates: 301m, 352w**
- **Tuition (1982/83): $3,150**
- **Room & Board: $2,200**
- **Degrees offered: BA, BS**
- **Student-faculty ratio: 14 to 1**

A private college, affiliated with the Christian Church, established in 1881. 135-acre suburban campus 3 miles from Johnson City. Bus and rail in Johnson City.
Academic Character SACS and professional accreditation. Semester system, 2 4½-week summer terms. Majors offered in accounting, Bible, biology, business administration, chemistry, Christian education, elementary education, English, health & physical education, history, human relations (5 areas), humanities, mathematics, missions, music, and secretarial science. Minor required. Distributives and 3 semesters of Bible required. Independent

study. Internships. 3-2 engineering program with Tri-State College, Georgia Tech. Cooperative program with Mid-American College of Funeral Services. Home economics education, nursing programs with East Tennessee State. Dual degree programs with 5 Bible colleges. 3-1 programs in medical technology, law, medicine. Study abroad. Early childhood, elementary, secondary, and special education certification. ROTC at East Tennessee State. 110,000-volume library.
Financial CEEB CSS. College scholarships, grants, loans, state grants, vocational rehabilitation grants, ministerial loans; PELL, GSL, NDSL, FISL, Tuition Plan, deferred payment, CWS, college has own work program. Application deadline April 1.
Admissions High school graduation with 16 units required. ACT or SAT required. $10 application fee. Rolling admissions. $50 tuition deposit and $50 room deposit (for boarders) required on acceptance of offer of admission. *Early Admission* Program. Transfers accepted. Admission deferral possible. Credit possible for CEEB AP and CLEP exams.
Student Life Student government. Newspaper, magazine, yearbook, music, drama groups. International students group. Academic, honorary, professional, religious, service, and special interest groups. Single students must live at home or on campus. No coed dorms. Married-student housing. 83% of students live on campus. Liquor, drugs, social dancing prohibited; smoking restricted. Attendance in class and at twice-weekly convocations required. 2 hours of activity courses required. 7 intercollegiate sports; intramurals. AIAW, NAIA, TIAC, VSAC. Student body composition: 3% Black, 97% White. 72% from out of state.

[J1] MORRISTOWN COLLEGE
417 North James Street, Morristown 37814, (615) 586-5262

- **Enrollment: 66m, 38w**
- **Degrees offered: AA, AS, AAS**

A private coeducational junior college related to the United Methodist Church.
Academic Character SACS accreditation. Semester system. Majors offered in most liberal arts areas. Remedial mathematics and English programs.
Admissions High school graduation required. *Early Admission, Early Decision* programs.
Student Life Dormitories and dining hall for men and women.

[J1] MOTLOW STATE COMMUNITY COLLEGE
Tullahoma 37388

[J1] NASHVILLE STATE TECHNICAL INSTITUTE
Nashville 37209

[P] NASHVILLE YMCA NIGHT LAW SCHOOL
1000 Church Street, Nashville 37203

[J2] O'MORE SCHOOL OF DESIGN
Franklin 37064

[J1] ROANE STATE COMMUNITY COLLEGE
Harriman 37748

[G1] SCARRITT COLLEGE
1008 19th Avenue South, Nashville 37203

[J1] SHELBY STATE COMMUNITY COLLEGE
Memphis 38104

[1] SOUTH, UNIVERSITY OF THE
Sewanee 37375, (615) 598-5931
Director of Admissions: Albert S. Gooch, Jr.

- **Undergraduates: 600m, 400w**
- **Tuition (1982/83): $6,440**
- **Room & Board: $1,630; Fees: $80**
- **Degrees offered: AB, BS**
- **Mean SAT 550v, 600m**
- **Student-faculty ratio: 9 to 1**

A private university controlled by the Episcopal Church, established in 1858, became coed in 1969. 10,000-acre campus including rural village of Sewanee, 50 miles from Chattanooga. Served by air and bus.
Academic Character SACS accreditation. Semester system, 6-week summer term. Majors offered in American studies, Asian studies, biology, chemistry, comparative literature, economics, English, fine arts, French, German, Greek, history, Latin, mathematics, Medieval studies, music, natural resources, philosophy, physics, political science, psychology, religion, Russian, Russian/Soviet studies, and Spanish. Distributives and 2 religion/philosophy courses required. MDiv, DMin granted. Independent study. Phi Beta Kappa. Pass/fail. Preprofessional programs in dentistry, law, medicine, veterinary medicine. 3-2 programs in engineering with Columbia, Duke, Georgia Tech, Rensselaer, Vanderbilt, Washington U. 3-2 forestry program with Duke. Oak Ridge Semester. Study abroad. Secondary education certification. Language labs. 8,500-acre university forest. 435,000-volume library.
Financial CEEB CSS. University scholarships, grants, loans; PELL, SEOG, NDSL, Tuition Plan, CWS. Application deadline March 1.
Admissions High school graduation with 15 units required. Interview encouraged. SAT required. $15 application fee. Application deadline March 1. $150 deposit required on acceptance of offer of admission. *Early Decision, Early Admission* programs. Transfers accepted. Admission deferral possible. Credit possible for CEEB AP exams.
Student Life Student government. Newspaper, magazine, yearbook, radio station. Music, drama, literary groups. Fire department. Honorary, outing, service, and special interest groups. 11 fraternities with houses and 5 sororities. 65% of men and 35% of women join. Students must live at home or on campus. Married-student housing. 95% of students live on campus. Dress code. 2 semesters of phys ed required. 10 intercollegiate sports for men, 8 for women; intramurals. Student body composition: 1% Black, 99% White. 80% from out of state.

[1] SOUTHERN COLLEGE OF OPTOMETRY
1245 Madison Avenue, Memphis 38104

[1] SOUTHERN COLLEGE
Formerly Southern Missionary College
Collegedale 37315, (615) 396-2111
Director of Admissions: Ron Barrow

- **Undergraduates: 642m, 756w; 1,801 total (including graduates)**
- **Tuition (1982/83): $4,160**
- **Room & Board: $2,050**
- **Degrees offered: BA, BS, BMus**
- **Mean ACT 15 composite**
- **Student-faculty ratio: 16 to 1**

A private college controlled by the Seventh-Day Adventist Church (Mormons), established in 1892. 1,000-acre rural campus in Collegedale, 18 miles from Chattanooga. Served by bus.
Academic Character SACS and professional accreditation. Semester system, 4 4-week summer terms. Majors offered in art, biology, chemistry, communication, English, French, German, history, international studies, mathematics, music, music education, phyics, psychology, religion, Spanish, theology, accounting, behavioral science, business administration, business education, computer science, elementary education, health science, home economics, industrial education, long-term health care, management, medical science, medical technology, nursing, and health, physical education & recreation. Minor required. Minors offered in some major fields and in 11 additional areas. Distributives and 12 semester hours of Biblical studies/religion required. Independent study. Internships. Honors program. Preprofessional programs in engineering, health professions, law. 2-2 and 3-2 programs in health professions with Loma Linda U, in engineering with Walla Walla College, in pharmacy with U of Tenn. Adventist Colleges Abroad. Elementary and secondary education certification. Computer center, secondary laboratory school. Civil War collection. 194,797-volume library.
Financial CEEB CSS and ACT FAS. College scholarships, grants, loans, state grants, family rebates; PELL, SEOG, NSS, GSL, NDSL, FISL, Tuition Plan, deferred payment, CWS; college has own work program. Priority application deadline for scholarships and grants April 1.
Admissions High school graduation with 9 units required. GED accepted. ACT required. $15 application fee. Rolling admissions; suggest applying before 2nd half of 12th year. $75 room deposit (for boarders) required by July 1. *Early Admission* Program. Transfers accepted. Admission deferral possible. Credit possible for CEEB AP and CLEP exams; college has own advanced placement program.
Student Life Student government. Newspaper, yearbook, radio station. Religious, academic, social, literary, and special interest groups. Students must live at home or on campus. No coed dorms. Married-student housing. 64% of students live on campus. Liquor, tobacco, theatre attendance, card playing, dancing prohibited. Attendance in class and at convocations, church services, and religious emphasis weeks required. 6 semester hours of phys ed required. No intercollegiate sports. Intramurals. Student body composition: 2% Asian, 6% Black, 4% Hispanic, 88% White. 60% from 8-state Southern Union Conference of Seventh-Day Adventists.

[1] SOUTHWESTERN AT MEMPHIS
2000 North Parkway, Memphis 38112, (901) 274-1800
Director of Admissions: Mary Jo Miller

- **Undergraduates: 540m, 505w**
- **Tuition (1982/83): $5,200**
- **Room & Board: $2,575**
- **Degrees offered: AB, BS, BMus**
- **Mean ACT 26 composite; mean SAT 544v, 584m**
- **Student-faculty ratio: 12 to 1**

A private college affiliated with the Presbyterian Church, established in 1848. 100-acre urban campus in residential section of Memphis. Served by air, bus, and rail.
Academic Character SACS and professional accreditation. Trimester system. Majors offered in anthropology/sociology, art (4 areas), biology, business administration, chemistry, classics, communication, arts, economics, English, foreign languages, French, German, history, international studies, mathematics, music, (7 areas), philosophy, physics, political science, psychology, religion, religion & culture, Spanish, chemical biology, economics/mathematics, and psychobiology. Self-designed majors. Distributives and senior comprehensive exams required. Honors program. Phi Beta Kappa. Pass/fail, internships, field studies. Preprofessional programs in business administration, dentistry, foreign service, international business, law, library science, medical technology, medicine, ministry, pharmacy. 3-2 engineering program with U Tennessee, Vanderbilt, Washington U. Member Southern College University Union; Memphis Consortium. Study abroad.

Elementary, secondary, and special education certification. AFROTC at Memphis State. Art gallery. 182,000-volume library.
Financial CEEB CSS. College scholarships, grants, loans, ministerial grants; PELL, SEOG, NDSL, FISL, Education Funds, CWS. Scholarship application deadline February 1.
Admissions High school graduation with 16 units required. Interview encouraged. SAT or ACT required. $15 application fee. Preferred application deadline February 15. $100 tuition deposit and $100 room deposit (for boarders) required on acceptance of offer of admission. *Early Admission, Early Decision, Concurrent Enrollment* programs. Transfers accepted. Admission deferral possible. Credit possible for CEEB AP exams.
Student Life Student government. Newspaper, magazine, yearbook, journal, radio station. Music, drama groups. Black Student Union. Religious, service, academic, honorary, and special interest organizations. 6 fraternities and 4 sororities without houses. 47% of men and 57% of women join. Students must live at home or on campus. No coed dorms. Language houses. No married-student housing. 84% of students live on campus. Attendance in class may be required. Intercollegiate and intramural sports for men and women. AIAW, NCAA, College Athletic Conference. Student body composition: 2% Black, 98% White.

[J1] STATE TECHNICAL INSTITUTE AT KNOXVILLE
3435 Division Street, Knoxville 37919

[1] TENNESSEE, UNIVERSITY OF
Knoxville 37996, (615) 974-2591
Dean of Admissions and Records: John J. McDow

- **Undergraduates: 11,828m, 10,090w; 28,601 total (including graduates)**
- **Tuition (1982/83): $729 (in-state), $1,761 (out-of-state)**
- **Room & Board: $1,995; Fees: $138**
- **Degrees offered: BA, BS, BFA, BMus, BArch**
- **Mean ACT 21 composite**
- **Student-faculty ratio: 18 to 1**

A public university established in 1794. Urban campus in Knoxville. Served by air and bus.
Academic Character SACS and professional accreditation. Trimester system, 1 10-week, 2 5-week summer terms. 11 majors offered by the College of Agriculture, 14 by the College of Business Administration, 3 by the College of Communications, 16 by the College of Education, 10 by the College of Engineering, 7 by the College of Home Economics, 39 by the College of Liberal Arts, 1 by the College of Nursing, and 1 by the School of Architecture. Self-designed majors. Minors offered. Graduate and professional degrees granted. Independent study. Honors program. Phi Beta Kappa. Cooperative work/study in some colleges. Pass/fail. Credit by exam. Preprofessional programs in several fields. 3-1 programs in dentistry, medicine, pharmacy. Member National, International Student Exchange programs. Elementary, secondary, and special education certification. ROTC, AFROTC. Research organizations, computer center. 1,587,009-volume library with microform resources.
Financial CEEB CSS. University scholarships, grants, loans; PELL, SEOG, NSS, NDSL, FISL, NSL, deferred payment, CWS, university has own work program. Priority application deadline for scholarships March 1.
Admissions High school graduation with 16 units required. GED accepted. ACT required. $10 application fee. Rolling admissions; suggest filing in 11th year or early 12th. $25 room deposit (for boarders) required on acceptance of offer of admission. *Early Admission* Program. Transfers accepted. Admission deferral possible. Credit possible for CEEB AP and CLEP exams.
Student Life Student government. Newspaper, magazine, yearbook, radio station. Music, debate, drama groups. Over 300 academic, honorary, political, professional, religious, and special interest groups. 27 fraternities, 24 with houses, and 20 sororities without houses. 14% of men and 15% of women join. Single freshmen must live with relatives or on campus. Liquor prohibited on campus. 9 intercollegiate sports for men, 6 for women; intramurals. AIAW, NCAC, Southeastern Conference, Tennessee Collegiate Women's Sports Federation. Student body composition: 0.4% Asian, 5.3% Black, 0.3% Hispanic, 0.2% Native American, 90.2% White, 3.6% Other. 14% from out of state.

■[1] TENNESSEE, UNIVERSITY OF, AT CHATTANOOGA
Chattanooga 37401, (615) 755-4157
Dean of Admissions: Ray P. Fox

- **Undergraduates: 3,606m, 3,933w**
- **Tuition (1982/83): $786 (in-state), $2,544 (out-of-state)**
- **Room: $750-$1,120**
- **Degrees offered: BA, BS, BFA, BMus, BSEngr, BSN**
- **Student-faculty ratio: 18 to 1**

A public university established in 1886. 74-acre urban campus in Chattanooga. Served by air and bus.
Academic Character SACS and professional accreditation. Semester system, 3 5-week summer terms. 70 majors offered by the College of Arts & Sciences, the School of Business Administration, the School of Education, the School of Engineering, the School of Human Services, and the School of Nursing. Distributive requirements. Masters degrees granted. Independent study. Honors program. Cooperative work/study. Preprofessional programs in dental hygiene, dentistry, forestry, medicine, nursing, pharmacy, physical therapy. 3-1 and 3-2 programs in engineering with Georgia Tech and Knoxville campus. Elementary and secondary education certification. ROTC. Observatory, computer center. 600,000-volume library with microform resources.
Financial CEEB CSS. University scholarships, grants, loans; PELL, SEOG, NSS, NDSL, GSL, NSL, CWS. Priority application deadline for scholarships March 1.
Admissions High school graduation with 16 units required. GED accepted. SAT or ACT required; ACT preferred. $10 application fee. Rolling admissions; suggest applying by January 1. *Early Decision, Early Admission* programs. Transfers accepted. Credit possible for CEEB AP and CLEP exams.
Student Life Student government. Newspaper, magazine, yearbook. Music, drama groups. International Relations club. Religious, academic, honorary, service, and special interest organizations. 6 fraternities with residential houses and 7 sororities with nonresidential houses. 25% of men and 30% of women join. Students must live at home or on campus. No married-student housing. 10% of students live on campus. Liquor prohibited in dorms. 2 semesters of phys ed required. 9 intercollegiate sports for men, 3 for women; intramurals. Student body composition: 0.6% Asian, 11.4% Black, 0.6% Hispanic, 0.2% Native American, 86.5% White. 10% from out of state.

■[1] TENNESSEE, UNIVERSITY OF, AT MARTIN
University Street, Martin 38328, (901) 587-7000
Director of Admissions: Paul Kelley

- **Undergraduates: 2,029m, 1,994w**
- **Tuition (1982/83): $840 (in-state), $2,600 (out-of-state)**
- **Room: $840**
- **Degrees offered: BA, BS, AA**
- **Student-faculty ratio: 18 to 1**

A public university established in 1900. 600-acre campus in small town of Martin, 125 miles from Memphis. Served by air and bus.
Academic Character SACS and professional accreditation. Trimester system, 2 5-week summer terms. 8 majors offered by the School of Agriculture, 29 by the School of Arts & Sciences, 12 by the School of Business Administration, 5 by the School of Education, 15 by the School of Engineering & Engineering Technology, and 9 by the School of Home Economics. Self-designed majors. Distributive requirements. MS, MBA, MAcc granted. Independent study. Honors program. Cooperative work/study, internships. Preprofessional programs in several fields. 2-year transfer programs in aerospace, chemical, civil, electrical, industrial, mechanical, metallurgical, and nuclear engineering and in engineering mechanics, physics, and science. Study abroad in Japan. Elementary, secondary, and special education certification. ROTC. 150,000-volume library with microform resources.
Financial ACT FAS. University scholarships and loans, state grants; PELL, SEOG, NSS, NDSL, GSL, NSL, CWS. Application deadline March 1.
Admissions High school graduation with 16 units required. ACT required. $10 application fee. Rolling admissions. $50 room deposit (for boarders) required on acceptance of offer of admission. *Early Admission, Early Decision* programs. Transfers accepted. Admission deferral possible. Credit possible for CEEB AP and CLEP exams.
Student Life Student government. Newspaper, magazine, yearbook, radio station. Music, drama groups. Black Student Association. National Organization of Women. Academic, political, honorary, religious, service, and special interest groups. 8 fraternities with houses and 7 sororities without houses. 7% of men and 7% of women join. Single freshmen and sophomores under 25 must live on campus. Married-student housing. 65% of students live on campus. Liquor prohibited on campus. 6 quarters of phys ed or ROTC required. 4 intercollegiate sports for men, 3 for women; intramurals. AIAW, NAIA, NCAA, Gulf-South Athletic Conference. Student body composition: 0.5% Asian, 16% Black, 0.2% Hispanic, 0.1% Native American, 80.3% White. 8% from out of state.

■[1 & G1] TENNESSEE, UNIVERSITY OF, CENTER FOR THE HEALTH SCIENCES
62 South Dunlap, Memphis 38163

■[G2] TENNESSEE, UNIVERSITY OF, SPACE INSTITUTE
Tullahoma 37388

[1] TENNESSEE STATE UNIVERSITY
Nashville 37203, (615) 320-3131
Dean of Admissions: J. Grey Hall

- **Undergraduates: 2,385m, 2,475w**
- **Tuition (1982/83): $720 (in-state), $1,758 (out-of-state)**
- **Room & Board: $1,826; Fees: $72**
- **Degrees offered: BA, BS, BSN, ADN**
- **Student-faculty ratio: 19 to 1**

A public university established in 1912. 450-acre campus in north Nashville; downtown campus for evening classes. Served by air, bus, and rail.
Academic Character SACS and professional accreditation. Semester system, 2 6-week summer terms. 9 majors offered by the School of Agriculture & Home Economics, 4 by the School of Allied Health Professions, 19 by the School of Arts & Sciences, 3 by the School of Business, 6 by the School of Education, 8 by the School of Engineering & Technology, and 1 by the School of Nursing. Distributives and senior project required. Graduate and professional degrees granted. Independent study. Honors program. Cooperative work/study in School of Engineering. Preprofessional programs in dentistry, medicine, physical therapy, social work, veterinary science. 3-1 medical technology program. Natural Science at Gull Coast Lab. Elementary and secondary education certification. AFROTC. 250,000-volume library.
Financial CEEB CSS. University scholarships, grants, loans, state grants; PELL, SEOG, NDSL, GSL, CWS. Application deadline July 15.
Admissions High school graduation with 16 units required. GED accepted. ACT required. Rolling admissions; suggest applying in January or February. $10 room deposit (for boarders) required on acceptance of offer of admission. Transfers accepted. Admission deferral possible. Advanced placement possible.

Student Life Student government. Newspaper, yearbook. Music, drama, debate groups. Academic, honorary, religious, service, and special interest groups. 4 fraternities and 4 sororities. No coed dorms. 50% of students live on campus. Class attendance required. 2 semesters of phys ed required. Intercollegiate and intramural sports. AIAW, NCAA. Student body composition: 0.7% Asian, 91.7% Black, 0.1% Native American, 3.1% White. 25% from out of state.

[1] TENNESSEE TECHNOLOGICAL UNIVERSITY

Cookeville 38501, (615) 528-3317
Dean of Admissions: Hoyle Lawson

- **Undergraduates: 3,735m, 2,562w; 7,927 total (including graduates)**
- **Tuition (1982/83): $771 (in-state), $1,758 (out-of-state)**
- **Room & Board: $1,557**
- **Degrees offered: BA, BS, BSN**
- **Mean ACT 20 composite**
- **Student-faculty ratio: 15 to 1**

A public university established in 1915. 235-acre campus in small town of Cookeville, 80 miles from Nashville. Served by bus.
Academic Character SACS and professional accreditation. Trimester system, 2 5-week summer terms. 16 majors offered by the College of Agriculture & Home Economics, 19 by the College of Arts & Sciences, 6 by the College of Business Administration, 14 by the College of Education, 7 by the College of Engineering, and 1 by the School of Nursing. Distributive requirements. Honors program. Cooperative work/study, internships, pass/fail. Preprofessional programs in dental hygiene, dentistry, forestry, medical records administration, medical technology, medicine, nursing, optometry, pharmacy, physical therapy, veterinary medicine, other allied health fields. Elementary, secondary, and special education certification. ROTC. Computer center, language lab. 550-acre biological research station. 300-acre lab farm. 500,000-volume library.
Financial CEEB CSS and ACT FAS. University scholarships, grants, loans, state academic work scholarships; PELL, SEOG, NDSL, GSL, deferred payment, CWS. Scholarship application deadline April 15.
Admissions High school graduation required. GED accepted. Interview encouraged. ACT required. $5 application fee. Rolling admissions; suggest applying early in 12th year. $25 room deposit (for boarders) required on acceptance of offer of admission. *Early Admission, Concurrent Enrollment* programs. Transfers accepted. Admission deferral possible. Credit possible for CEEB AP, CLEP, and ACT exams; university has own advanced placement program.
Student Life Newspaper, magazine, agricultural journal, radio station. Music, debate, drama, speaking groups. Black Student Organization. Academic, honorary, religious, service, and special interest groups. 13 fraternities and 5 sororities. 65% of men and 6% of women join. Students must live at home or on campus. No coed dorms. Married-student housing. 50% of students live on campus. 6 terms of phys ed, ROTC, or marching band required. 9 intercollegiate sports for men; 3 for women; intramurals. AIAW, NCAA, Ohio Valley Conference. Student body composition: 2.2% Asian, 2.4% Black, 1.1% Hispanic, 0.2% Native American, 94.1% White. 10% from out of state.

[2] TENNESSEE TEMPLE UNIVERSITY

1815 Union Avenue, Chattanooga 37404, (615) 698-6021
Admissions & Assistant Registrar: E.C. Haskell, Jr.

- **Enrollment: 3,378 men and women**
- **Tuition (1982/83): $1,910**
- **Room & Board: $1,980; Fees: $80**
- **Degrees offered: BA, BS, BRE**
- **Mean ACT 16 composite**

A private university affiliated with the Baptist Church, established in 1946. Urban campus in Chattanooga.
Academic Character Semester system, 2 5-week summer terms. Majors offered in Bible, Christian education, missions, pastoral studies, art, broadcasting, business administration, education, English, history, mathematics, missionary health, music, psychology, pulpit communications, and speech communications. Interdisciplinary majors. Minors offered in some major fields and in 10 additional areas. Studies for the Deaf. Distributives, 30 hours of Bible, and Christian service program required. Students must sign a Confession of Faith. Graduate degrees granted. Independent study. Preprofessional seminary studies program. 100,469-volume library with microform resources.
Financial Tuition rates guaranteed for all four years. University scholarships and loans, athletic scholarships, PELL, SEOG, NDSL, GSL, Insured Tuition Payment Plan, CWS; university has own work program.
Admissions High school graduation with 15 units required. GED accepted. ACT or SAT required. $15 application fee. Application deadline August 1. *Early Admission* Program. Transfers accepted. Advanced placement possible.
Student Life Radio station. Single students must live on campus. No coed dorms. Attendance at church services required. 4 intercollegiate sports for men, 3 for women; intramurals. NCCAA, TISA.

[1] TENNESSEE WESLEYAN COLLEGE

Athens 37303, (615) 745-5872
Director of Admissions and Financial Aid: Damon Mitchell

- **Enrollment: 210m, 170w; 467 total (including part-time)**
- **Tuition (1982/83): $2,640**
- **Room & Board: $2,175**
- **Degrees offered: BA, BS, BMus Ed, BApp Sc**
- **Mean ACT 17 composite**
- **Student-faculty ratio: 15 to 1**

A private college affiliated with the United Methodist Church, established in 1857. Small-town campus halfway between Knoxville and Chattanooga.
Academic Character SACS accreditation. Trimester system, 1 9-week and 3 3-week summer terms. 34 majors offered in the areas of business, aviation, behavioral science, sciences, education, church vocations, music, communications, criminal justice, English, health, history, mathematics, psychology, religion & philosophy, and speech & theater. Self-designed majors. Distributives and 6 hours of Biblical and religious studies required. Internships in some programs. Preprofessional programs in dental hygiene, dentistry, engineering, forestry, law, medicine, nursing, optometry, optometric technician, pharmacy, physical therapy. 3-2 engineering and medical technology programs. Elementary, secondary, and special education certification. 58,000-volume library.
Financial CEEB CSS and ACT FAS. College scholarships, grants, and loans; church grants, family grants, state grants, Methodist scholarships, grants and loans; PELL, SEOG, NDSL, GSL, CWS; college has own work program.
Admissions High school graduation with C average required. GED accepted. Interview encouraged. ACT or SAT recommended. $25 application fee. Rolling admissions. Transfers accepted. Credit possible for CEEB AP and CLEP exams.
Student Life Student government. Newspaper, magazine, yearbook. Music and drama groups. Honorary, service, religious, and special interest groups. 2 fraternities and 2 sororities. Students must live at home or on campus. No coed dorms. Liquor, gambling prohibited on campus. 3 phys ed courses required. 5 intercollegiate sports; intramurals. NAIA, AIAW.

[J2] TOMLINSON COLLEGE

PO Box 3030, Cleveland 37311

[1] TREVECCA NAZARENE COLLEGE

Nashville 37203, (615) 248-1200
Director of Admissions: Howard T. Wall

- **Undergraduates: 472m, 489w**
- **Tuition (1982/83): $2,550**
- **Room & Board: $1,860; Fees: $210**
- **Degrees offered: BA, BS**
- **Student-faculty ratio: 15 to 1**

A private college affiliated with the Church of Nazarene, established in 1901. 80-acre campus in Nashville. Served by air, bus, and rail.
Academic Character SACS and professional accreditation. Trimester system, 6-week summer term. 37 majors offered in the areas of business, social sciences, communications, science, education, arts, history, mathematics, physical education, health science, religion, and ministries. Minors offered in 11 additional areas. Distributives and 12 hours of religion required. Independent study. Honors program. Internships. Preprofessional programs in dentistry, engineering, law, medicine, nursing, pharmacy, seminary. Elementary, secondary, and special education certification. NROTC, ROTC at Vanderbilt, AFROTC at Tennessee State. 161,006-volume library.
Financial CEEB CSS and ACT FAS. College scholarships, grants, loans; PELL, SEOG, GSL, FISL, NDSL, Tuition Plan, Education Funds, deferred payment, CWS. Priority application deadline for scholarships April 15.
Admissions High school graduation required. GED accepted. ACT required. $15 application fee. Rolling admissions; suggest applying between January and August. $20 room deposit (for boarders) required on acceptance of offer of admission. *Early Admission* Program. Transfers accepted. Credit possible for CEEB AP and CLEP exams. Academic Enrichment Program.
Student Life Student government. Newspaper, yearbook, radio station. Music, debate groups. Afro-American Society. Academic, religious, service, and special interest organizations. Single students must live at home or on campus. No coed dorms. Married-student housing. 85% of students live on campus. Liquor, tobacco, narcotics, fireworks, weapons prohibited. Dress code. Marriage regulations. Parental permission required to leave Nashville. Attendance at chapel 3 times weekly required. 3 hours of phys ed required. 5 intercollegiate sports for men, 2 for women; intramurals. AIAW, NAIA, Nazarene Intercollegiate Athletic Association, Volunteer State Athletic Conference. 60% of students from out of state.

[1] TUSCULUM COLLEGE

Greeneville 37743, (615) 639-2931;(800) 251-0256 (toll-free)
Director of Admissions and Financial Aid: Estel C. Hurley

- **Enrollment: 140m, 146w; 308 total (including part-time)**
- **Tuition (1982/83): $3,000**
- **Room & Board: $2,030; Fees: $100**
- **Degrees offered: BA, BS**
- **Mean ACT 18 composite; mean SAT 800**
- **Student-faculty ratio: 13 to 1**

A private college affiliated with the United Presbyterian Church, established in 1794. 140-acre campus 5 miles from small city of Greeneville, near the Great Smoky Mountains National Park. Served by bus; airport 40 miles away in Tri-Cities.
Academic Character SACS accreditation. Semester system, 2 4-week summer terms. Majors offered in creative arts, English, biology, business administration, physical education, psychology, social services, elementary education, and special education. Self-designed majors. Distributives and 3 hours of religious studies required. Independent study. Cooperative work/study, internships, pass/fail. Credit for experience. Preprofessional programs in medical technology, dentistry, law, medicine, nursing, pharmacy, veterinary medicine. Study abroad in Denmark. Elementary, secondary, special, and physical education certification. 65,000-volume library with microform resources.

Financial CEEB CSS. College scholarships, state grants; PELL, SEOG, NDSL, GSL, CWS: college has own work program. Application deadline June 15.
Admissions High school graduation required. Interview encouraged. SAT or ACT required. $10 application fee. Rolling admissions; recommended application deadline April 1. $100 deposit required on acceptance of offer of admission. *Early Admission, Early Decision* programs. Transfers accepted. Admission deferral possible. Credit possible for CLEP exams; college has own advanced placement program.
Student Life Student government. Newspaper, yearbook, radio station. Honorary, professional, service, and special interest groups. Students must live at home or on campus. No coed dorms. 1 semester hour of phys ed required. 3 intercollegiate sports for men, 2 for women; club sports. NAIA, VSAC, TISA. Student body composition: 15% minority.

[1] UNION UNIVERSITY
Jackson 38301, (901) 668-1818
Director of Student Enlistment: Carroll W. Griffin

- **Undergraduates: 523m, 859w**
- **Tuition (1982/83): $2,270**
- **Room & Board: $1,480**
- **Degrees offered: BA, BS, BMus, BSN, AS, ASN**
- **Mean ACT 19.2 composite**
- **Student-faculty ratio: 17 to 1**

A private university affiliated with Tennessee Baptist Convention, established in 1825. 150-acre campus in small city of Jackson, 75 miles northeast of Memphis. Air and bus service.
Academic Character SACS and professional accreditation. Semester system, 2 4-week summer terms. Majors offered in accounting, art, business administration, computer science, economics-finance, elementary education, English, English/journalism, French, history, management & marketing, mathematics, music literature, office administration, psychology, religion, social science, social work, sociology, Spanish, biology, chemical physics, chemistry, medical technology, physical education/health, music (8 areas), and nursing (for RNs). Minors offered in 7 areas. 2 courses in religion required. Independent and accelerated study. Honors program. Cooperative work/study. Preprofessional programs in dentistry, law, medicine, pharmacy. CPA program. Elementary and secondary education certification; mental retardation endorsement. ROTC through U of Tenn, Martin. Language lab, computer center. 70,760-volume library.
Financial CEEB CSS. Scholarships, loans; PELL, SEOG, NDSL, deferred payment, CWS. Application deadline May 15.
Admissions High school graduation with 16 units required. GED accepted. Interview encouraged. ACT required; SAT accepted. $10 application fee. Rolling admissions; suggest applying in 1st semester. $10 deposit required on acceptance of offer of admission. *Early Decision, Early Admission, Concurrent Enrollment* programs. Transfers accepted. Admission deferral possible. Credit possible for CEEB AP and CLEP exams.
Student Life Student government. Newspaper, magazine, yearbook. Music, debate, drama, speaking groups. Academic, religious, and special interest organizations. 3 fraternities and 2 sororities. Student suites. Married-student housing. 65% of students live on campus. Attendance at 21 of 36 convocations required. 2 courses in phys ed required. 4 intercollegiate sports for men, 3 for women. NAIA, NCAA. Student body composition: 6.2% Black, 92.7% White. 15% from out of state.

[1] VANDERBILT UNIVERSITY
Nashville 37212, (615) 322-2561
Director of Undergraduate Admissions: Kathlynn Ciompi

- **Undergraduates: 2,644m, 2,763w; 8,911 total (including graduates)**
- **Tuition (1982/83): $6,100**
- **Room & Board: $2,925; Fees: $400**
- **Degrees offered: BA, BS, BSN, BEng**
- **Mean SAT 568v, 611m**
- **Student-faculty ratio: 9 to 1**

A private university established in 1873. 320-acre campus in University Center section of Nashville. Served by air and bus.
Academic Character SACS and professional accreditation. Semester system, 11-week summer term. 36 majors offered by the College of Arts & Sciences, 7 by the School of Engineering, 1 by the School of Nursing, and 5 by the George Peabody College for Teachers. Special majors. Students at College of Arts & Sciences may take courses at schools of Divinity, Engineering, Law, Medicine, Nursing. Distributive requirements. Graduate and professional degrees granted. Independent study for seniors. Honors program. Phi Beta Kappa. Limited pass/fail. Preprofessional programs in health professions, law, social work, speech and hearing. 5-year BA/MBA program. 3-2 engineering programs with several schools. Consortium with 7 Southern Colleges. Oak Ridge Semester. University has off-campus centers in Europe and Ghana. Experiment in International Living. Elementary, secondary, and special education certification. NROTC, ROTC; AFROTC at Tennessee State. Language lab, observatory. 1,400,000-volume library.
Financial CEEB CSS. Scholarships, grants, loans; PELL, SEOG, NDSL, CWS. Preferred application deadline February 15.
Admissions High school graduation with 15 units required. Interview encouraged. SAT required; ACT accepted. English comp ACH required. $15 application fee. Application deadline February 15. $100 deposit required on acceptance of offer of admission. *Early Decision, Early Admission* programs. Transfers accepted. Admission deferral possible. Credit possible for CEEB AP exams.
Student Life Student association. Newspaper, magazine, yearbook, radio station. Music, debate, drama groups. Religious, academic, honorary, service, literary, and special interest groups. 15 fraternities and 10 sororities; all have houses. 45% of men and 40% of women join. Freshmen must live on campus. Married-student, special interest housing. 85% of students live on campus. 13 intercollegiate sports for men, 6 for women; intramurals. SEC. Student body composition: 4% Black, 94% White, 2% Other. 80% from out of state.

[J1] VOLUNTEER STATE COMMUNITY COLLEGE
Nashville Pike, Gallatin 37066

[J1] WALTERS STATE COMMUNITY COLLEGE
Morristown 37814

TEXAS (TX)

[1] ABILENE CHRISTIAN UNIVERSITY
Abilene 79699, (915) 677-1911
Director of Admissions: Clinton E. Howeth

- **Undergraduates: 1,758m, 1,741w; 4,546 total (including graduates)**
- **Tuition (1982/83): $2,370**
- **Room & Board: $1,800; Fees: $225**
- **Degrees offered: BA, BS, BSEd, BSHome Ec, BSMusEd, BBA, BFA, BSN**
- **Mean ACT I9.7 composite**
- **Student-faculty ratio: 25 to 1**

A private university affiliated with the Church of Christ, established in 1906. 102-acre suburban campus. Served by air, rail, and bus.
Academic Character SACS and professional accreditation. Semester system, 2 5½-week summer terms. 67 majors offered by the colleges of Liberal & Fine Arts, Natural & Applied Sciences, Professional studies, and Business Administration. Self-designed majors. Distributives and 15 credits in Bible required; NTECE required of education seniors. Graduate degrees granted. Limited pass/fail, credit by exam. Preprofessional programs in dentistry, engineering, law, medical technology, medicine, optometry, veterinary medicine. Cooperative programs in criminal justice and geology with Hardin-Simmons. Elementary, secondary, and special education certification. ROTC at Hardin-Simmons. 576,246-volume library with microform resources.
Financial CEEB CSS. University scholarships, grants, loans, state grants, payment plan, PELL, SEOG, NDSL, FISL, CWS. Application deadline April 15.
Admissions High school graduation with 15 units required. ACT required. $10 application fee; $50 room deposit due with application. Rolling admissions. *Early Admission* Program. Admission deferral possible. Transfers accepted. Credit possible for CEEB AP and CLEP exams. Special admissions programs.
Student Life Student government. Newspaper, literary magazine, yearbook, radio and TV stations. Music groups. Debates and public speaking. Academic, honorary, religious, service, and special interest groups. 7 social clubs for men and 6 for women, none with houses. 19% of men and 20% of women join. Freshmen must live on campus. No coed dorms. Married student housing nearby. 55% of students live on campus. Liquor, drugs, gambling, hazing, profanity, vulgarity, smoking prohibited. Daily chapel attendance required. Sunday church services and Bible class encouraged. 4 hours of phys ed required. 5 intercollegiate sports for men, 5 for women; many intramurals. AIAW, NAIA, NCAA, LSC. Student body composition: 1% Asian, 3% Black, 2% Hispanic, 94% White. 35% from out of state.

[1] ABILENE CHRISTIAN UNIVERSITY
Garland 75041

[J1] ALVIN COMMUNITY COLLEGE
Alvin 77511

[J1] AMARILLO COLLEGE
Amarillo 79178

[1] AMERICAN TECHNOLOGICAL UNIVERSITY
Killeen 76540

[J1] ANGELINA COLLEGE
PO Box 1768, Lufkin 75901

[1] ANGELO STATE UNIVERSITY
2601 West Avenue North, San Angelo 76909, (915) 942-2041
Admissions Officer: Steven G. Gamble

- **Undergraduates: 2,084m, 2,167w; 5,834 total (including graduates)**
- **Tuition (1982/83): $412 (in-state), $1,492 (out-of-state)**

- **Room & Board: $2,600**
- **Degrees offered: BA, BS, BBA, BMusEd, BSN, AN**
- **Student-faculty ratio: 25 to 1**

A public univeristy established in 1928. 287-acre suburban campus, 200 miles from Austin. Served by air and bus.
Academic Character SACS accreditation. Semester system, 2 5-week summer terms. 36 majors offered by the colleges of Liberal & Fine Arts, Professional Studies, and Sciences. Special majors. Distributive requirements. Graduate degrees granted. Independent study.Preprofessional programs in dentistry, engineering, law, medicine, pharmacy, veterinary medicine. Study abroad. Elementary, secondary, special, and bilingual education certification. ROTC. Fisher Lake Research Center. 408,000-volume library with microform resources.
Financial ACT FAS. University scholarships, loans, payment plan, PELL, SEOG, NDSL, GSL, CWS. Recommended application deadline April 15.
Admissions High school graduatation required. GED accepted. ACT or SAT required. Rolling admissions; suggest applying in fall. $60 room deposit due on acceptance of admissions offer. *Early Admission* and *Concurrent Enrollment* programs. Transfers accepted. Credit possible for CEEB CLEP, SAT, and ACT exams.
Student Life Student government. Newspaper, literary magazine, yearbook. Music and drama groups. Afro-American Association. Chicano Student Organization. Academic, honorary, religious, service, and special interest groups. 4 fraternities, 2 with houses, and 2 sororities without houses. 4% of men and 1% of women join. Single undergraduates live on campus. 25% of students live on campus. Liquor, gambling, narcotics, hazing prohibited. Attendance in class required. 2 semesters of phys ed required. 6 intercollegiate sports for men, 6 for women; intramurals. AIAW, NCAA, LSC. Student body composition: 4.1% Black, 9.5% Hispanic, 84.9% White, 1.5% Other. 4% from out of state.

[P] ARLINGTON BAPTIST COLLEGE
3001 West Division, Arlington 76012

[1] AUSTIN COLLEGE
Sherman 75090, (214) 892-9101
Director of Admissions: Charles Wharton

- **Enrollment: 655m, 531w**
- **Tuition (1982/83): $4,600**
- **Room & Board: $2,200; Fees:$35**
- **Degrees offered: BA**
- **Mean SAT 490v, 520m**
- **Student-faculty ratio: 11 to 1**

A private college affiliated with the Presbyterian Church, established in 1849. 65-acre suburban campus, 60 miles north of Dallas. Served by air and bus.
Academic Character SACS accreditation. 4-1-4 system, 7- and 4-week summer terms. Majors offered in art, biology, business, chemistry, classics, communication, computer science, economics, education, English, foreign languages, history, mathematics, music, philosophy, physical education, physics, political science, psychology, religion, sociology, and in American, Asian, Latin American, and Western Europe studies. Self-designed and special majors. Distributive requirements. MA granted. Independent study. Honors program. Pass/fail. Teaching/learning participation. Internships. Preprofessional programs in dentistry, engineering, law, medicine, ministry, scientific research, teaching. 3-2 engineering programs with NY Polytechnic, SMU, Texas A&M, U Texas at Austin, Washington U. Member consortium with TAGER. Exchange program with American U. Study in Europe, Latin America, Asia. Washington Semester. Austin College in Mexico. Elementary and secondary education certification. Computer center. Language lab. 180,000-volume library.
Financial CEEB CSS. College scholarships, loans, state grants and loans, payment plans, PELL, SEOG, NDSL, CWS. Application deadine June 1; FAF deadline May 1.
Admissions High school graduation with 15 units required. Interview recommended. SAT or ACT required. $20 application fee. Rolling admissions; suggest applying at end of 11th year. $200 deposit due on acceptance of admissions offer. *Early Decision* and *Early Admission* programs. Admission deferral possible. Transfers accepted. Credit possible for CEEB AP, CLEP, and language ACH exams.
Student Life Student government. Newspaper, literary magazine, yearbook. Music groups. Essence of Ebony. Tutorial program. Academic, honorary, political, professional, and service groups. 8 fraternities and 5 sororities, none with houses. 24% of men and 32% of women join. Single students live at home or at school. Coed and single-sex dorms. Language houses. Married-student housing. 90% of students live on campus. Cars must be registered. Community Membership Principle. General Behavior Principle. Honor system. Attendance at convocations with faculty mentor required.. 1 term phys ed required. 8 intercollegiate sports for men, 6 for women; intramurals. AIAW, NAIA, TIAA. Student body composition: 3% Asian, 5% Black, 4% Hispanic, 1% Native American, 86% White, 1% Other. 10% from out of state.

[J1] AUSTIN COMMUNITY COLLEGE DISTRICT
PO Box 2285, Austin 78768

[G1] AUSTIN PRESBYTERIAN THEOLOGICAL SEMINARY
Austin 78705

[J2] BAUDER FASHION COLLEGE
508 South Center Street, Arlington 76010

[1] BAYLOR UNIVERSITY
Waco 76706, (817) 755-1011
Director of Admissions: Herman D. Thomas

- **Undergraduates: 4,015m, 4,714w; 10,412 total (including graduates)**
- **Tuition (1982/83): $2,700**
- **Room & Board: $2,251; Fees: $144**
- **Degrees offered: BA, BS, BAcc, BBA, BFA, BMus, BMus Ed, BSN, BSEd, BSCrimJus, BSHomeEc, BSEng**
- **Student-faculty ratio: 21 to 1**

A private university controlled by the Baptist General Convention of Texas, established in 1845. 350-acre suburban campus. Served by air and bus.
Academic Character SACS and professional accreditation. Semester system, 2 6-week summer terms. 44 majors offered by the College of Arts & Sciences, 18 by the School of Business, 7 by the School of Education, 13 by the School of Music, and 1 by the School of Nursing. Self-designed majors. Distributives, 6 hours of religion, and 2 semesters of University Forum required. Graduate degrees granted. Independent study. Honors program. Phi Beta Kappa. Pass/fail, internships. Credit by exam. 3-2 engineering programs with Case, Texas A&M, Texas Tech, Columbia, Washington U, U Texas. 3-1 forestry program with Duke, 3-1 medical technology program. Cooperative preprofessional programs in accounting, dental hygiene, law, medicine, nursing, pharmacy, physical therapy, with several colleges. Study abroad. Early childhood, elementary, secondary, and special education certification; bilingual, counseling, learning resource specialist preparation. AFROTC. 961,567-volume library with microform resources.
Financial CEEB CSS. University scholarships, grants, loans, music scholarships, payment plans, PELL, SEOG, GSL, NDSL, FISL, CWS. Scholarship application deadline March 1.
Admissions High school graduation with 16 units required. Interview encouraged. SAT or ACT required. $30 application fee. Rolling admissions; suggest applying 1 year before desired enrollment. $100 deposit due on acceptance of admissions offer. *Early Admission* Program. Admission deferral possible. Transfers accepted. Credit possible for CEEB AP and CLEP exams.
Student Life Newspaper, yearbook. Music and fine arts groups. Theatre. Numerous special interest groups. Fraternities and sororities. Single-sex dorms. Married-student apartments. 40% of students live on campus. Academic honor code. Liquor prohibited. 75% class attendance required. Freshmen may not use cars on campus. 4 semesters of phys ed required. Many intercollegiate and intramural sports. NCAA, SAC. Student body composition: 1% Asian, 1.5% Black, 2% Hispanic, 0.3% Native American, 95.2% White. 22% from out of state.

■[G1] BAYLOR COLLEGE OF DENTISTRY
3302 Gaston Avenue, Dallas 75246

■[G1] BAYLOR COLLEGE OF MEDICINE
Houston 77030

[J1] BEE COUNTY COLLEGE
3800 Charco Road, Beeville 78102, (512) 358-3130
Registrar: Anne Nicholson

- **Undergraduates: 1,925**
- **Tuition (1981/83): $4 per semester hour (in-state), $40 (out-of-state)**
- **Room & Board: $1,786**
- **Degrees offered: AA, AS, AAP**
- **Mean ACT 16 composite**
- **Student-faculty ratio: 21 to 1**

A public college established in 1965. Small-city campus.
Academic Character SACS accreditation. Semester system, 2 6-week summer terms. 2-year programs offered in dental hygiene, distribution & marketing, fine arts, health/physical education/recreation, health services, industrial arts, language, office occupations, social sciences, technology, and science, mathematics, & agriculture. Distributive requirements. Preprofessional programs in dentistry, law, medicine, optometry, pharmacy, physical therapy, registered nursing. Center for Independent Study. 33,000-volume library with microform resources.
Financial CEEB CSS. College scholarships, state grants and loans, PELL, SEOG, NDSL, GSL, CWS. Application deadline July 1.
Admissions High school graduation required. GED accepted. ACT recommended. Rolling admissions. Transfers accepted. Credit possible for CEEB CLEP exams; college has own advanced placement program. Upward Bound Program. **Student Life** Student government. Newspaper, magazine. Music groups. Baptist Student Union. Newman Club. Rodeo Club. Honorary, professional, and special interest groups. Married-student housing. 2 intercollegiate sports; intramurals. TJCAC, NJCAA. 43% minority students.

[1] BISHOP COLLEGE
3837 Simpson-Stuart Road, Dallas 75241, (214) 372-8000
Director of Admissions: Fred Warbington, Jr.

- **Undergraduates: 586m, 273w**
- **Tuition (1982/83): $2,500**
- **Room & Board: $1,850**
- **Degrees offered: BA, BS, BSW, BSEd, AA**
- **Student-faculty ratio: 14 to 1**

A private college controlled by the American Baptist Churches, established in 1881. 360-acre suburban campus, 8 miles from downtown Dallas. Served by air, rail, and bus.
Academic Character SACS and professional accreditation. Semester system, 9-week summer term. 26 majors offered by the divisions of Business, Education, Humanities, Natural & Mathematical Sciences, Religion & Philosophy, and Social Sciences. Distributives and senior comprehensive

exam required. Independent study. Honors program. Cooperative work/study, internships, credit by exam. Preprofessional programs in dentistry, engineering, medical technology, nursing, nutrition, pharmacy, physical therapy, physician's assistant, rehabilitation. 3-2 engineering program with Southern Methodist, U Rochester. Many cooperative education programs with other colleges. Study abroad. Elementary and secondary education certificaion. ROTC. Observatory. Ministers Institute. Sabine Farms Community Center. 166,000-volume library.
Financial CEEB CSS. College scholarships, grants, loans, music and athletic grants, state grants and loans, payment plan, PELL, SEOG, GSL, NDSL, CWS.
Admissions High school graduation with 15 units recommended. GED accepted. SAT required. $10 application fee. Rolling admissions. $50 room deposit due on acceptance of admissions offer. *Early Admission* and *Concurrent Enrollment* programs. Transfers accepted. Credit possible for CEEB AP and CLEP exams; college has own advanced placement program.
Student Life Student government. Newspaper, yearbook. Music groups. Religious Emphasis Week. Minister's Lyceum. Academic, honorary, religious, and special interest groups. 4 fraternities and 5 sororities. Single-sex dorms. Married-student apartments. Attendance required in class and at 2 convocations per week. 4 intercollegiate sports; intramurals. NAIA.

[J1] BLINN COLLEGE
902 College Avenue, Brenham 77833, (713) 836-9311
- **Enrollment: 2,792**
- **Degree offered: AA**
- **Mean ACT 16.3**

A public junior college.
Academic Character SACS accreditation. Semester system, 2 6-week summer terms. 2-year programs offered in agriculture, business, liberal arts, and professional areas.
Admissions Freshmen enter either semester. Advanced placement program.
Student Life Single-sex dorms. Dining hall. Student body composition: 13% minority.

[J1] BRAZOSPORT COLLEGE
500 College Drive, Lake Jackson 77566

[1] BROOKHAVEN COLLEGE
Farmers Branch 75234

[1] CEDAR VALLEY COLLEGE
3030 North Dallas Avenue, Lancaster 75134

[J1] CENTRAL TEXAS COLLEGE
US Highway 190, West, Killeen 76541, (817) 526-1211
- **Undergraduates: 1,044m, 777w; 5,291 total (including part-time)**
- **Tuition & Fees (1980/81): $220 (in-state), $560 (out-of-state)**
- **Room & Board: $1,766**
- **Degrees offered: AA, AS, AAS, AGen Ed**
- **Mean ACT 17**

A public junior college.
Academic Character SACS and professional accreditation. Semester system. Courses offered include art, air conditioning & refrigeration, auto body repair, automotive service, business administration, business management, career pilot, child development, communications, cosmetology, computer maintenance, computer science, criminal justice, diesel mechanics, drafting & design, engineering, electronics, farm & ranch agriculture, finance & banking, fire protection, food service, hotel/motel management, maintenance technology, mathematics, mid-management, music, offset printing, photography, physical edcuation, real estate, science, secretarial programs, social science, telecommunications, vocational nursing, welding.
Financial Aid available including PELL, SEOG, NSS, FISL, NDSL, NSL, CWS.
Admissions ACT preferred. $10 application fee. Rolling admissions. $40 room reservation deposit required. *Early Admission* and *Early Decision* programs. Advanced placement program.
Student Life Student body composition: 15% minority.

[J1] CISCO JUNIOR COLLEGE
Route 3, Cisco 76437, (817) 442-2567
Registrar: Olin O. Odom, III
- **Enrollment: 706m, 227w**
- **Tuition (1982/83): $250 (in-state), $400 (out-of-state)**
- **Room & Board: $1,350**
- **Degrees offered: AA, AS**
- **Student-faculty ratio: 15 to 1**

A public college established in 1909. 92-acre rural campus with branches in Clyde and Abilene. Served by bus.
Academic Character SACS accreditation. Semester system, 2 5½-week summer terms. 2-year programs offered in arts & sciences, mathematics & natural sciences, art, engineering, law enforcement, agriculture. Courses in auto mechanics, banking, building trades, child care, cosmetology, data processing, drafting, electronics, fire protection, human services, maintenance mechanics, mid-management, nursing, office occupations, plumbing, real estate, and welding. Distributive requirements for transfer programs.
Financial ACT FAS. College scholarships, grants, state grants, PELL, SEOG, GSL, CWS.
Admissions High school graduation required. GED accepted. ACT or SAT recommended. Rolling admissions. $20 room deposit due on acceptance of admissions offer. *Early Admissions* Program. Transfers accepted. Credit possible for CEEB AP and CLEP exams.
Student Life Student government. Newspaper and yearbook. Music groups. Ranch Day. Honorary, social, and special interest groups. Single-sex dorms. Class attendance required. 4 intercollegiate sports; intramurals. NTJCAC, NJCAA.

[J1] CLARENDON COLLEGE
PO Box 968, Clarendon 79226, (806) 874-3571
Registrar: Leonard D. Selvidge
- **Enrollment: 1,000 men & women**
- **Tuition (1982/83): $25 per semester hour (in-district), $15 (in-state), $30 (out-of-state)**
- **Room & Board: $1,300-$1,450**
- **Degrees offered: AA, AS, AAS**
- **Student-faculty ratio: 33 to 1**

A public college established in 1898. Branch campus in Pampa.
Academic Character SACS accreditation. Semester system, 2 5½-week summer terms. 2-year programs offered in agriculture, business, secretarial science, art, music, speech, biology, chemistry, home economics, education, English, mathematics, and general studies. Distributive requirements. Preprofessional programs in law, nursing, optometry, pharmacy. 20,000-volume library.
Financial ACT FAS. State grants, PELL, SEOG, NDSL, GSL, CETA, CWS. Priority application deadline August 15.
Admissions High school graduation with 15 units required. GED accepted. Rolling admissions. $25 room deposit due on acceptance of admissions offer. *Concurrent Enrollment* Program. Transfers accepted. Credit possible for CEEB CLEP exams.
Student Life Student government. Yearbook. Music and drama groups. Rodeo Club. Collegiate 4-H. Academic, professional, and special interest groups. Single students under 21 must live at home or on campus. Single-sex dorms. 2 hours of phys ed required.

[1] CONCORDIA LUTHERAN COLLEGE
3400 Interstate 35 North, Austin 78705, (512) 452-7661
Registrar/Admissions Officer: Varnes Stringer
- **Enrollment: 485 men & women**
- **Tuition (1982/83): $1,100**
- **Room & Board: $1,008; Fees: $33**
- **Degrees offered: BA, AA**
- **Mean ACT 17.5**
- **Student-faculty ratio: 19 to 1**

A private college controlled by the Lutheran Church-Missouri Synod, established in 1926, became coed in 1955. 20-acre suburban campus. Served by air and bus.
Academic Character SACS accreditation. Semester system. Majors offered in communications, elementary education, general studies, Mexican-American Studies, and management & administration. Distributives and 9 hours of theology required. Pass/fail. Joint programs with area schools. ROTC at U Texas.
Financial ACT FAS. College scholarships and grants, church career stipends, state grants, payment plans; PELL, SEOG, SSIG, NDSL, CWS.
Admissions High school graduation with college prep program recommended. GED accepted. ACT or SAT required. $25 application fee. Rolling admissions. $100 room deposit due on acceptance of admissions offer. $100 refundable deposit required of church-work majors. Transfers accepted. Credit possible for ACT PEP and CEEB CLEP exams.
Student Life Student government. Music, drama, media groups. Honorary, service, and special interest groups. Single students live at home or on campus. Liquor, drugs, firearms, fireworks prohibited. Daily chapel attendance encouraged. 3 hours of phys ed required. 4 intercollegiate sports for men, 3 for women. AIAW, NLCAA.

[J1] COOKE COUNTY COLLEGE
PO Box 815, Gainesville 76240, (817) 688-7731
Director of Admissions & Registrar: Don R. Stafford
- **Enrollment: 264m, 319w; 1,549 total (including part-time)**
- **Tuition (1982/83): $40 per semester hour (in-county), $45 (in-state), $63 (out-of-state)**
- **Estimated Room & Board: $2,000**
- **Degrees offered: AA, AS, AAS**

A public college established in 1924. 132-acre campus.
Academic Character SACS and professional accreditation. Semester system, 2 5-week summer terms. 2-year programs offered by the divisions of Agriculture, Communications & Fine Arts, Allied Health, Business, Industrial & Technical Education, Social Science, Math & Science, Physical Education & Intercollegiate Athletics, and Paramedicine. Distributive requirements. Preprofessional programs in dentistry, engineering, law, medicine, pharmacy, and veterinary medicine. Experimental farm. 35,000-volume library.
Financial ACT FAS. College scholarships, state grants; PELL, SEOG, SSIG, CWS. Application deadline July 1.
Admissions High school graduation required. GED accepted. ACT or SAT required. Rolling admissions. *Early Admission* and *Concurrent Enrollment* programs. Transfers accepted. Credit possible for ACT and CEEB CLEP exams.

Student Life Magazine. Music groups. Circle K. Honorary, professional, religious, and special interest groups. Residential apartments and dormitory facilities available. Intercollegiate basketball and tennis for men and women; intramurals. NJCAA, NTJCAC.

[1] CORPUS CHRISTI STATE UNIVERSITY
6300 Ocean Drive, Corpus Christi 78412
Formerly Texas A&I University at Corpus Christi. Upper level, junior, senior, and graduate courses. SACS accreditation.

[P] CRISWELL BIBLE COLLEGE
525 North Ervay, Dallas 75201

[1] CULLEN COLLEGE OF ENGINEERING
Houston 77004

[1] DALLAS, UNIVERSITY OF
Irving 75061, (214) 579-5119
Director of Admissions: Daniel J. Davis

- **Undergraduates: 561m, 515w; 2,815 total (including graduates)**
- **Tuition (1982/83): $3,300**
- **Room & Board: $2,100-$2,700; Fees: $400**
- **Degrees offered: BA, BSBio Chem**
- **Mean ACT 26; mean SAT 1175**
- **Student-faculty ratio: 15 to 1**

A private university controlled by the Roman Catholic Church, established in 1955. 1,000-acre suburban campus, northwest of Dallas. Served by air, rail, and bus.
Academic Character SACS accreditation. Semester system, 2 5-week summer terms. Majors offered in art, biochemistry, biology, chemistry, classics, drama, economics, education, English, foreign languages, history, mathematics, philosophy, physics, politics, psychology, and theology. Self-designed majors. Distributives, 6 credits in theology, and comprehensive exams required. Graduate degrees granted. Limited pass/fail, credit for activities. Preprofessional programs in architecture, business management, dentistry, engineering, law, medicine. 3-2 engineering program. 3-1 medical technology and physical therapy programs. 5-year MBA program. Sophomore year in Rome. Elementary and secondary education certification. ROTC at U Texas, Arlington; AFROTC at North Texas. Art center. Theater. Language lab. 218,800-volume library with microform resources.
Financial CEEB CSS and ACT FAS. University scholarships, grants, loans, state scholarships, family discounts, payment plans; PELL, SEOG, NCSP, NDSL, GSL, CWS. Application deadline April 1.
Admissions High school graduation with 16 units required. Interview recommended. SAT or ACT required. $15 application fee. Rolling admissions; suggest applying by January 1. $100 deposit due on acceptance of admissions offer. *Early Admission* and *Early Decision* programs. Admission deferral possible. Transfers accepted. Credit possible for CEEB AP and CLEP exams.
Student Life Student government. Literary journal, yearbook. Music, film, and drama groups. Spring Olympics. Academic, social, and special interest groups. Single students live at home or on campus. Single-sex dorms. No married-student housing. 70% of students live on campus. Class attendance expected. 5 intercollegiate sports for men, 4 for women; several intramurals. AIAW, NAIA. Student body composition: 1.7% Asian, 1.6% Black, 5.3% Hispanic, 0.3% Native American, 86.2% White, 4.9% Other. 53% from out of state.

[1] DALLAS BAPTIST COLLEGE
7777 West Kiest, Dallas 75211, (214) 331-8311
Director of Admissions: John Stephens, Jr.

- **Enrollment: 724m, 613w**
- **Tuition (1982/83): $2,840**
- **Room & Board: $2,100; Fees: $150**
- **Degrees offered: BA, BS, BBA, BCareer Arts, BMus**
- **Student-faculty ratio: 24 to 1**

A private college controlled by the Baptist General Convention of Texas, established in 1965. 200-acre suburban campus, 13 miles from downtown Dallas. Served by air, rail, and bus.
Academic Character SACS and professional accreditation. 4-1-4 system, 2 5½-week summer terms. 33 majors offered by the schools of Arts & Sciences, Management & Free Enterprise, Education & Learning Resources, Nursing & Health Sciences, and Christian Faith & Learning. Special majors. Minor in art. Distributives and 12 hours of religion required. Independent study. Internships. Preprofessional programs in dentistry, law, medicine, theology. Study abroad. Elementary and secondary education certification. ROTC. Language lab. 135,552-volume library.
Financial CEEB CSS. College scholarships, grants, loans, state grants, discount for ministers' children, academic scholarships; PELL, SEOG, GSL, NDSL, NSL, CWS. Scholarship application deadline April 1.
Admissions High school graduation with 16 units required. GED accepted. Interview recommended. ACT required; SAT accepted. $25 application fee. Rolling admissions. $50 room deposit required on acceptance of admissions offer. *Concurrent Enrollment* Program. Transfers accepted. Credit possible for CEEB AP and CLEP exams; college has own advanced placement program.
Student Life Student government. Newspaper, literary magazine, yearbook. Music and drama groups. Debate. Baptist Student Union. Academic, athletic, service, and special interest groups. Single-sex dorms. No married-student housing. 20% of students live on campus. Liquor prohibited. Dress code. Class attendance required. Freshmen must attend weekly chapel and special programs. 2 hours of phys ed required. 2 intercollegiate sports for men, 1 for women; intramurals. AIAW, NAIA. Student body composition: 0.4% Asian, 17% Black, 4% Hispanic, 0.6% Native American, 71% White, 7% Other. 15% from out of state.

[P] DALLAS BIBLE COLLEGE
8733 La Prada Drive, Dallas 75228

[2] DALLAS CHRISTIAN COLLEGE
2700 Christian Parkway, Dallas 75234, (214) 241-3371

- **Undergraduates: 64m, 48w; 149 total (including part-time)**
- **Tuition (1982/83): $46 per semester hour**
- **Room & Board: $1,380; Fees: $60-$100**
- **Degrees offered: BA, AA**

A private Christian college emphasizing education for church vocations. Founded in 1950. Suburban campus located 15 minutes from downtown Dallas.
Academic Character AABC accreditation. Semester system. Baccalaureate and associate degrees offered in Bible, secretarial science, professional ministry, Christian education, and music. Remedial English program. 40,000-volume library.
Financial Guaranteed tuition. Scholarships available.
Admissions Open admissions. High school graduation required. ACT and recommendations required.
Student Life Dormitories and cafeteria available. Intercollegiate basketball and baseball.

DALLAS COUNTY COMMUNITY COLLEGE DISTRICT
Dallas — See El Centro College

■[J1] EASTFIELD COLLEGE
Mesquite 75150

■[J1] NORTH LAKE COLLEGE
5001 North MacArthur Blvd., Irving 75062

[P] DALLAS INSTITUTE OF MORTUARY SCIENCE
3906 Worth, Dallas 75246

[G1] DALLAS THEOLOGICAL SEMINARY
3909 Swiss Avenue, Dallas 75204

[J1] DEL MAR COLLEGE
101 Baldwin, Corpus Christi 78404

[2] DEVRY INSTITUTE OF TECHNOLOGY
4250 Beltline Road, Irving 75062

[1] EAST TEXAS BAPTIST COLLEGE
Marshall 75670, (214) 935-7963
Director of Admissions: Paul L. Saylors

- **Undergraduates: 466m, 470w**
- **Tuition (1982/83): $2,040**
- **Room & Board: $2,556; Fees: $270**
- **Degrees offered: BA, BS, BAS, BMus, BSEd, AA, ABA, AS**
- **Student-faculty ratio: 19 to 1**

A private college controlled by the Baptist General Convention of Texas, established in 1912. 160-acre small-city campus, 150 miles east of Dallas. Served by rail and bus.
Academic Character SACS accreditation. Semester system, 2 4-week summer terms. Majors offered in behavioral science, biology, business, chemistry, education, English, history, mathematics, music, physical education, religion, sociology, Spanish, and speech. Minors in most major fields and in 8 others. Distributives, 3 hours of religion, and GRE required. Independent study. Honors program. Preprofessional programs in dentistry, engineering, law, medicine, nursing, pharmacy, theology, veterinary medicine. 3-1 medical technology program. Elementary and secondary education certification. 98,000-volume library.
Financial CEEB CSS and ACT FAS. College scholarships, grants, loans, ministerial grants, state grants, payment plan; PELL, SEOG, NDSL, FISL, CWS. Scholarship application deadline July 1.
Admissions High school graduation with 16 units required. GED accepted. Interview recommended. ACT required. $15 application fee. Rolling admissions; suggest applying in February. $15 room deposit due on acceptance of admissions offer. *Early Admission* Program. Transfers

accepted. Credit possible for CEEB AP and CLEP exams; college has own advanced placement program. Conditional admission possible.
Student Life Student government. Newspaper, yearbook. Music and drama groups. Christian Maturity Council. Baptist Student Union. Athletic, academic, honorary, religious, service, and special interest groups. Students under 21 live at home or on campus. Single-sex dorms. Married-student housing. 65% of students live on campus. Liquor, hazing, gambling prohibited. Dress code. Dean must be notified of marriage intentions. Twice-weekly chapel attendance required. 4 hours of phys ed required. 3 intercollegiate sports for men, 3 for women; intramurals. NAIA, BSC. Student body composition: 4% Black, 1% Hispanic, 1% Native American, 94% White. 14% from out of state.

[1] EAST TEXAS STATE UNIVERSITY

Commerce 74528, (214) 886-5000
Director of Admissions: Phil Ebensberger

- **Undergraduates: 2,482m, 2,437w; 7,767 total (including graduates)**
- **Tuition (1982/83): $240 (in-state), $2,400 (out-of-state)**
- **Room & Board: $3,142; Fees: $330**
- **Degrees offered: BA, BS, BBA, BFA, BGS, BSW, BMus, BMus Ed, BACrim Jus, BSCrim Jus**
- **Mean ACT 18; mean SAT 800**
- **Student-faculty ratio: 15 to 1**

A public university established in 1889. 140-acre campus in a small city 60 miles from Dallas. Served by bus.
Academic Character SACS and professional accreditation. Semester system, 2 6-week summer terms. 11 majors offered by the College of Business & Technology, 8 by the College of Education, 45 by the College of Arts & Sciences. Self-designed majors. Major/minor, broad-field major, or 2 majors required. Distributive requirements. Graduate degrees granted. Independent study. Honors program. Phi Beta Kappa, pass/fail, cooperative work/study, internships. Preprofessional programs in dentistry, law, medicine, optometry, osteopathy, pharmacy, physician's assistant, theology, veterinary medicine. Elementary, secondary, and special education certification. AFROTC. Performing Arts Center. 500,000-volume library with microform resources.
Financial ACT FAS. University scholarships, grants, loans, Hinson-Hazlewood loans; PELL, SEOG, NDSL, FISL, CWS. Application deadline August 1.
Admissions Applicants with ACT 18 or above admitted. GED accepted. ACT required; SAT accepted. Rolling admissions. $50 room deposit required on acceptance of admissions offer. *Concurrent Enrollment* Program. Transfers accepted. Credit possible for CEEB AP and CLEP exams; university has own placement program.
Student Life Student government. Newspaper, literary magazine, yearbook, radio station. Music and drama groups. Debate. Afro-American Student Society. Athletic, academic, honorary, political, religious, service, and special interest groups. 12 fraternities and 7 sororities, all with houses. 11% of men and 12% of women join. Juniors and seniors may live off campus. Coed and single-sex dorms. Married-student housing. 32% of students live on campus. Class attendance required. 4 semesters of phys ed required. 5 intercollegiate sports; intramurals. NAIA, LSC. Student body composition: 0.4% Asian, 11.1% Black, 2.4% Hispanic, 0.9% Native American, 80.6% White, 4.6% Other. 4% from out of state.

[1] EAST TEXAS STATE UNIVERSITY AT TEXARKANA

PO Box 5518, Texarkana 75501

[J1] EL CENTRO COLLEGE

Main and Lamar, Dallas 75202

[J1] EL PASO COMMUNITY COLLEGE

PO Box 20500, El Paso 79998

[P] EPISCOPAL THEOLOGICAL SEMINARY OF THE SOUTHWEST

PO Box 2247, Austin 78768

[J1] FRANK PHILLIPS COLLEGE

PO Box 5118, Borger 79007, (806) 274-5311
Registrar: Maxine Brown

- **Enrollment: 900 men & women**
- **Tuition (1982/83): $108 (in-district), $140 (in-state), $220 (out-of-state)**
- **Room & Board: $1,980; Fees: $16**
- **Degrees offered: AA, AAS**
- **Student-faculty ratio: 20 to 1**

A public college established in 1948. 61-acre small-city campus.
Academic Character SACS accreditation. Semester system, 2 4½-week summer terms. 2-year programs offered in liberal arts, professional, and vocational areas. 2-year transfer programs. Flexible Entry courses. Vocational nursing and career pilot programs. 28,000-volume library with microform resources.
Financial College scholarships, loans, state aid; PELL, SEOG, CWS. Application deadline July 1.
Admissions High school graduation required. GED accepted. Rolling admissions. $50 room deposit due on acceptance of admissions offer. *Early Admission* Program. Credit possible for CEEB AP and CLEP exams.
Student Life Student government. Baptist Student Union. Circle K. Rodeo Club. Honorary, professional, and special interest groups. Single-sex dorms. Dining hall. Class attendance required. 3 intercollegiate sports; intramurals.

[J1] GALVESTON COLLEGE

4015 Avenue Q, Galveston 77550

[J1] GRAYSON COUNTY JUNIOR COLLEGE

Denison 75020

[1] GULF COAST BIBLE COLLEGE

PO Box 7889, Houston 77270, (713) 862-3800

- **Undergraduates: 142m, 84w; 298 total (including part-time)**
- **Tuition (1982/83): $2,380**
- **Room & Board: $1,470-$1,688**
- **Degrees offered: BA, BS**

A private college affiliated with the Church of God.
Academic Character SACS and AABC accreditation. Semester system. Major curricular divisions in practical ministries, Bible & theology, general studies, and professional ministries. Majors in pastoral ministry, music, and elementary education. Major in nursing in cooperation with Houston Baptist U.
Financial Scholarships, loans, government grants, PELL, SEOG, work-study program.
Admissions Rolling admissions. *Early Admission* and *Early Decision* programs. Admission deferral possible. Advanced placement program.
Student Life Single students must live on campus. Married students must find own housing with help from the college.

[1] HARDIN-SIMMONS UNIVERSITY

Abilene 79698, (915) 677-7281
Director of Admissions: Edgar M. Jackson

- **Undergraduates: 632m, 689w; 2,049 total (including graduates)**
- **Tuition (1982/83): $2,760**
- **Room & Board: $1,630-$1,850**
- **Degrees offered: BA, BS, BBS, BEd, BFA, BMus, BBA, BSN**
- **Student-faculty ratio: 19 to 1**

A private university affiliated with the Southern Baptist Convention, established in 1891. 40-acre urban campus, 150 miles west of Forth Worth. Served by air and bus.
Academic Character SACS and professional accreditation. Semester system, 2 5½-week summer terms. 22 majors offered in the liberal arts, 8 in sciences, 9 in behavioral sciences, 26 in education, 8 in music, 5 in business, and 1 in nursing. Minor required. Distributives and 6 hours of Bible required. MA, MEd, MMus granted. Independent study. Preprofessional programs in engineering, law, medicine, nursing, pharmacy, theology, social work. Cooperative programs in agriculture, French, and German with Abilene Christian and McMurry. Study abroad. Elementary, secondary, and special education certification. ROTC. Language lab. 299,443-volume library.
Financial CEEB CSS and ACT FAS (preferred). University scholarships, grants, loans, scholarships for ministerial students and ministers' families, payment plans; PELL, SEOG, NSS, NDSL, GSL, CWS.
Admissions High school graduation with 16 units required. GED accepted. Interview recommended. SAT or ACT required. $25 application fee; $50 room deposit due with admission application. Rolling admissions; suggest applying in early spring. *Early Admission, Early Decision, Concurrent Enrollment* programs. Admission deferral possible. Transfers accepted. Credit possible for CEEB AP, CLEP, and university exams. Opportunity Admission program.
Student Life Student government. Newspaper, literary magazine, yearbook. Music and drama groups. Academic, honorary, religious, social, and special interest groups. Single students must live at home or on campus. Dorms for men and women. Married-student housing. 44% of students live on campus. Twice-weekly chapel attendance required of freshmen and sophomores. 4 semesters of phys ed required. 5 intercollegiate sports for men, 3 for women; many intramurals. NIRA Rodeo. Student body composition: 0.4% Asian, 2.6% Black, 3.5% Hispanic, 0.1% Native American, 89.3% White, 4.1% Other. 13% from out of state.

[J1] HENDERSON COUNTY JUNIOR COLLEGE

Athens 75751

[J1] HILL JUNIOR COLLEGE

Hillsboro 76645

[1] HOUSTON, UNIVERSITY OF

Houston 77004, (713) 749-2236
Director of Admissions: Lee Elliott Brown

- **Undergraduates: 8,906m, 7,052w; 30,692 total (including graduates)**
- **Tuition (1982/83): $420 (in-state), $1,500 (out-of-state)**
- **Room & Board: $2,400-$2,800; Fees: $75**
- **Degrees offered: BA, BS, BBA, BFA, BMus, BAcc, BArch**
- **Mean SAT 999**
- **Student-faculty ratio: 20 to 1**

A public university established in 1927. 384-acre suburban campus, 3 miles from downtown Houston. Served by air, rail, and bus.
Academic Character SACS and professional accreditation. Semester system, 12-week summer term. One major offered by the College of Architecture, 9 by the College of Business Administration, 6 by the College of Education, 5 by the College of Engineering, 1 by the College of Hotel & Restaurant Management, 16 by the College of Humanities & Fine Arts, 8 by the College of Natural Sciences & Mathematics, 1 by the College of Optometry, 1 by the College of Pharmacy, 11 by the College of Social Science, and 8 by the College of Technology. Graduate and professional degrees granted. Honors

program. Preprofessional programs in dentistry, medical technology, medicine, physical therapy. Cooperative African studies program with Rice, Saint Thomas, and Texas Southern. Elementary and secondary education certification. ROTC; NROTC at Rice. Language lab. 1,000,000-volume library with microform resources.
Financial ACT FAS. University scholarships, grants, loans, PELL, NDSL, GSL, FISL, CWS. File FFS by March 1.
Admissions High school graduation with 16 units required. SAT or ACT required; 3 ACH recommended. Rolling admissions; suggest applying by April 15. *Early Admission* and *Early Decision* programs. Transfers accepted. Credit possible for CEEB AP and CLEP exams.
Student Life Student government. Newspaper, literary magazine, yearbook, TV station. Music and drama groups. Debate. Academic, honorary, and religious groups. 14 fraternities, 10 with houses; 10 sororities, 3 with houses. 4% of men and 3% of women join. 8% of students live on campus. Class attendance required. 2 hours of phys ed required. 8 intercollegiate sports for men, 3 for women; intramurals. AIAW, NCAA, SC. Student body composition: 1.3% Asian, 10.3% Black, 7% Hispanic, 0.4% Native American, 76.4% White. 13% from out of state.

■[1] HOUSTON, UNIVERSITY OF, AT CLEAR LAKE CITY
Houston 77058

■[1] HOUSTON, UNIVERSITY OF, DOWNTOWN COLLEGE
Houston 77002

■[1] HOUSTON, UNIVERSITY OF, AT VICTORIA
2302C Red River, Victoria 77901

[1] HOUSTON BAPTIST UNIVERSITY
7502 Fondren Road, Houston 77074, (713) 774-7661
Director of Admissions: Brenda C. Davis

- **Undergraduates: 889m, 1,330w**
- **Tuition (1982/83): $2,400**
- **Room & Board: $1,410; Fees: $48**
- **Degrees offered: BA, BS, BMus, BMus Ed, BSN**
- **Mean SAT 480v, 510m**
- **Student-faculty ratio: 18 to 1**

A private university controlled by the Baptist General Convention of Texas, established in 1960. 158-acre urban campus. Served by air, rail, and bus.
Academic Character SACS and professional accreditation. Quarter system, 2 6-week summer terms. 36 majors offered by the colleges of Business & Economics, Education & Behavioral Studies, Fine Arts, Humanities, and Science & Health Professions. Two majors required. Distributives and 3 Christianity courses required. Graduate degrees granted. Independent study. Limited pass/fail, church internships. Preprofessional programs in dentistry, law, medicine. Transfer programs in nutrition, optometry, pharmacy, physician's assistant, physical therapy, veterinary medicine. 3-1 medical technology program. 3-1 nuclear medicine technology program with Baylor. Study abroad. Elementary, secondary, and special education certification. ROTC, NROTC. Language lab. Research center. 150,000-volume library.
Financial CEEB CSS. University scholarships, grants, loans, tuition discount for ministerial students; PELL, SEOG, NSS, NDSL, FISL, CWS. Application deadline May 1.
Admissions High school graduation required. GED accepted. Interview recommended. SAT or ACT required. $15 application fee. Rolling admissins; suggest applying in fall. $25 tuition and $25 room (for boarders) deposits due on acceptance of admissions offer. *Early Admission* and *Credit-in-Escrow* programs. Transfers accepted. Credit possible for CEEB AP and CLEP exams; university has own placement program. Conditional admission possible.
Student Life Student government. Newspaper, literary magazine, yearbook. Music and drama groups. Debate. Chess club. El Circulo Hispanico. Academic, honorary, professional, and special interest groups. 4 fraternities and 2 sororities without houses. 20% of men and 11% of women join. Single students must live at home, on campus, or in university-approved housing. Single-sex dorms. Married-student housing. 14% of students live on campus. Liquor prohibited. Dress and hair codes. Attendance at 66% of classes required. Convocation attendance mandatory. 2 hours of phys ed required. 5 intercollegiate sports; intramurals. NCAA. Student body composition: 4% Asian, 4% Black, 6% Hispanic, 80% White, 6% Other. 3% from out of state.

[J1] HOUSTON COMMUNITY COLLEGE
22 Waugh Drive, Houston 77007

[J1] HOWARD COUNTY JUNIOR COLLEGE
Big Spring 79720

[1] HOWARD PAYNE UNIVERSITY
Brownwood 76810, (915) 646-2502
Director of Admissions: W. Bennett Ragsdale

- **Undergraduates: 568m, 604w**
- **Tuition (1982/83): $2,100**
- **Room & Board: $1,820; Fees: $220**
- **Degrees offered: BA, BS, BBA, BFA, BGS, BMus Ed**
- **Mean ACT 16**
- **Student-faculty ratio: 14 to 1**

A private university controlled by the Southern Baptist Church, established in 1889. 30-acre small-city campus, 165 miles from Dallas. Served by air and bus.
Academic Character SACS accreditation. Semester system, 5-week and 6-week summer terms. 39 majors offered in the areas of fine arts, humanities, science & mathematics, business administration, religion & philosophy, education, music, and social sciences. Academy of Freedom for superior students. Distributives and 2 semesters of religion required. Independent study. Honors program. Limited pass/fail. Preprofessional programs in dentistry, dental hygiene, medicine, medical technology, nursing, physical therapy, veterinary medicine. Elementary, secondary, and special education certification. ROTC. 119,504-volume library.
Financial ACT FAS. University scholarships, grants, loans, ministerial scholarships, grants, state grants and loans; PELL, SEOG, NDSL, FISL, CWS. Application deadline June 1.
Admissions High school graduation with 15 units recommended. GED accepted. SAT or ACT required. $15 application fee. Rolling admissions; suggest applying by May 1. $25 room deposit due on acceptance of admissions offer. *Early Admission* Program. Transfers accepted. Credit possible for CEEB CLEP exams; university has own placement program.
Student Life Student government. Newspaper, literary magazine, yearbook. Music groups. Academic, religious, and special interest groups. 8 fraternities and 9 sororities, without houses. 29% of men and 40% of women join. Single students must live at home or on campus. Single-sex dorms. Married-student housing. 54% of students live on campus. Liquor prohibited on campus. Twice-weekly chapel attendance required. 4 semesters of phys ed required. 5 intercollegiate sports for men, 2 for women; intramurals. LSC. Student body composition: 0.7% Asian, 7.8% Black, 0.5% Foreign, 6.1% Hispanic, 0.5% Native American, 84.4% White. 12% from out of state.

[1] HUSTON-TILLOTSON COLLEGE
Austin 78702, (512) 476-7421
Admissions Counselor: Paul K. Kimbrough, B.A.

- **Undergraduates: 383m, 272w**
- **Tuition (1982/83): $2,244**
- **Room & Board: $2,018; Fees: $442**
- **Degrees offered: BA, BS**
- **Student-faculty ratio: 12 to 1**

A private college controlled by the United Church of Christ and the United Methodist Church, established in 1934. Urban campus. Served by air and bus.
Academic Character SACS accreditation. Semester system, 5-week summer term. Majors offered in accounting, business, chemistry, economics, English, government, history, hotel & restaurant management, industrial relations & personnel management, marketing, mathematics, music, philosophy & religion, physical education, physics, sociology, and teacher education. Minors offered in most major fields. Distributive requirements. Cooperative work/study. Exchange program with Hamline U. Elementary and secondary education certification. ROTC. 61,913-volume library.
Financial CEEB CSS and ACT FAS. College scholarships, grants, loans, state grants, discounts for ministers' children, payment plans; PELL, SEOG, NDSL, CWS. Scholarship application deadline March 15.
Admissions High school graduation with 15 units required. GED accepted. Interview recommended. SAT or ACT required. $10 application fee. Rolling admissions. Transfers accepted. College has own advanced placement program.
Student Life Student government. Newspaper, yearbook. Academic, honorary, professional, and special interest groups. 4 fraternities and 4 sororities. Students live at home or on campus. Single-sex dorms. Liquor, drugs, firearms prohibited. Class attendance expected. Weekly chapel attendance required. 4 hours of phys ed required. 4 intercollegiate sports for men, 2 for women; intramurals. AIAW, NAIA, BSC. Student body composition: 0.3% Asian, 68.5% Black, 3.5% Hispanic, 1% White, 26.7% Other.

[1] INCARNATE WORD COLLEGE
4301 Broadway, San Antonio 78209, (512) 828-1261
Director of Enrollment: Judith Watson

- **Undergraduates: 182m, 629w; 1,357 total (including graduates)**
- **Tuition (1982/83): $3,136; $3,392 (for nursing)**
- **Room & Board: $1,828; Fees: $100**
- **Degrees offered: BA, BS, BMus, BBA, BSN**
- **Mean SAT 810**
- **Student-faculty ratio: 12 to 1**

A private college controlled by the Sisters of Charity of the Incarnate Word, established in 1881, became coed in 1970. 200-acre suburban campus, 10 minutes from downtown San Antonio. Served by air, rail, and bus.
Academic Character SACS and professional accreditation. Semester system, 2 5-week summer terms. 39 majors offered by the divisions of Humanities & Fine Arts, Natural Science, Nursing, Teacher Education & Home Economics, and Social Sciences, Business Administration, & Multidisciplinary Studies. Minors offered in most major fields and required in some. Distributives and 9 hours of religion or philosophy required; sophomore comprehensive exams. Graduate degrees granted. Independent study. Honors program. Limited pass/fail, cooperative work/study, internships, credit by exam. Preprofessional programs in law and medicine. 3-1 medical technology program. Exchange programs with Oblate College, Our Lady of the Lake, and St. Mary's. Summer study abroad. Elementary, secondary, and special education certification. ROTC at Trinity. Language lab. 141,000-volume library with microform resources.
Financial ACT FAS. College scholarships, grants, loans, state grants; PELL, SEOG, NSL, NDSL, FISL, CWS. Scholarship Priority application deadline for scholarships March 1.
Admissions High school graduation with 16 units required. GED accepted. Interview recommended. ACT or SAT required. $15 application fee. Rolling admissions. *Early Decision* and *Early Admission* programs. Transfers accepted. Credit possible for CEEB AP and CLEP exams.
Student Life Student government. Newspaper, literary magazine. Music and drama groups. Black Student Union. Academic and special interest groups. 2 fraternities and 3 sororities without houses. Freshmen live at home or on

campus. Single-sex dorms. No married-student housing. 21% of students live on campus. Class attendance expected. 2 hours of phys ed required. 2 intercollegiate sports for men, 4 for women; intramurals. Student body composition: 1% Asian, 12% Black, 32% Hispanic, 1% Native American, 49% White, 5% Other. 10% from out of state.

[J1] JACKSONVILLE COLLEGE

PO Box 1747, Jacksonville 75766, (214) 586-2518

- **Undergraduates: 102m, 75w; 271 total (including part-time)**
- **Tuition (1982/83): $50 per semester hour**
- **Room & Board: $180 per month**
- **Degrees offered: AA, AS**

A private college owned and operated by the Baptist Missionary Association of Texas.
Academic Character SACS accreditation. Semester system. Programs offered in the liberal arts. Junior college diploma granted. Remedial English program.
Financial Scholarships available.
Admissions High school graduation required. Admission by entrance exam and individual approval possible for students over 21 and for veterans. *Early Admission* Program.
Student Life Dormitories for men and women. Dining halls.

[1] JARVIS CHRISTIAN COLLEGE

Hawkins 75765, (214) 769-2174
Director of Recruitment & Admissions: Mack D. Johnson

- **Enrollment: 308m, 298w**
- **Est. Tuition (1982/83): $2,250**
- **Room & Board: $1,629; Fees: $358**
- **Degrees offered: BA, BS, BBA, BSEd**
- **Student-faculty ratio: 13 to 1**

A private college controlled by the Christian Church (Disciples of Christ), established in 1912. 340-acre rural campus, 100 miles southeast of Dallas. Airport in Tyler, 20 miles south, or in Longview, 25 miles east.
Academic Character SACS and professional accreditation. Semester system. 16 majors offered by the divisions of Education, Humanities, Science & Mathematics, and Social Science & Business. Self-designed majors. Minors required for BA and BS, offered in most major fields and in 7 others. Distributives, 6 hours of religion, and GRE required. Honors program. Cooperative work/study, internships, credit by exam. Affiliated with Texas Christian U and member of 5-college consortium. UNCF-premedical summer program at Fisk and biomedical program at Meharry. Brookhaven semester. Elementary, secondary, and special education certification. Language and reading labs. TV studio. Library.
Financial ACT FAS. College scholarships, grants, loans, state grants & loans; PELL, SEOG, NDSL, FISL, CWS. Application deadline in early January.
Admissions High school graduation with 16 units required. GED accepted. ACT required. $5 application fee. Rolling admissions. *Early Admission* Program. Transfers accepted. Credit possible for CEEB CLEP exams. Advanced Summer Enrichment Program for entering freshmen. Special admission for promising students.
Student Life Student government. Newspaper, yearbook. United Christian Fellowship. Bible school. Academic, honorary, and special interest groups. 8 fraternities and sororities, 4 social clubs. Permission required to live off campus. Single-sex dorms. Class attendance expected. 4 hours of phys ed required. 3 intercollegiate sports. NAIA. Student body composition: 0.6% Asian, 97.5% Black, 0.6% Hispanic, 0.2% White, 1.1% Other.

[J1] KILGORE COLLEGE

1110 Broadway, Kilgore 75662, (214) 984-8531

- **Undergraduates: 1,104m, 1,104w; 4,180 total (including part-time)**
- **Degrees offered: Associate**

A public, district-controlled junior college.
Academic Character SACS and professional accreditation. Semester system, 2 summer terms totaling 12 weeks. Transfer programs offered in the liberal arts. Preprofessional and vocational-technical programs offered.
Admissions High school graduation or equivalent required.
Student Life Dormitory for men, dormitory for women. Dining hall.

[1] LAMAR UNIVERSITY

Beaumont 77710, (713) 838-8345
Dean of Admissions & Registrar: Elmer G. Rode, Jr.

- **Undergraduates: 4,510m, 4,450w; 14,633 total (including graduates)**
- **Tuition (1982/83): $460 (in-state), $1,540 (out-of-state)**
- **Room & Board: $1,796-$1,894**
- **Degrees offered: BA, BS, BBA, BFA, BGS, BMus, BSW**
- **Mean ACT 18; mean SAT 861**
- **Student-faculty ratio: 22 to 1**

A public university established in 1923. 250-acre suburban campus, 90 miles from Houston. Served by bus; airport 10 miles away.
Academic Character SACS and professional accreditation. Semester system, 2 6-week summer terms. 61 majors offered by the colleges of Business, Education, Engineering, Fine & Applied Arts, Health & Behavioral Sciences, Liberal Arts, and Sciences. Self-designed majors. Minors offered. Distributive requirements. Graduate degrees granted. Honors program. Phi Beta Kappa. Cooperative work/study, internships, pass/fail, credit by exam. Preprofessional programs in allied health fields. 3-1 programs in dentistry, medical technology, medicine. Study abroad. Elementary, secondary, and special education certification. ROTC. Computer center. Museum. Brown Center. 689,000-volume library.
Financial CEEB CSS. University scholarships, grants, loans, state grants and loans; PELL, SEOG, NDSL, FISL, CWS. Application deadlines March 1 (scholarships), April 1 (loans).
Admissions High school graduation with 10 units recommended. SAT, ACT, or TSWE required. Rolling admissions; suggest applying by February 1. $50 room deposit due on acceptance of admissions offer. *Concurrent Enrollment* Program. Transfers accepted. Credit possible for CEEB AP, CLEP, and university exams.
Student Life Student government. Newspaper, magazines. Honorary, professional, religious, service, and special interest groups. 14 fraternities, 3 with houses; 9 sororities, 6 with houses. 4% of men and 3% of women join. Coed and single-sex dorms. Married-student housing. 20% of students live on campus. 4 semesters of phys ed required. 8 intercollegiate sports; club and intramural sports. NCAA, SC. Student body composition: 0.2% Asian, 20% Black, 6% Hispanic, 1% Native American, 70% White, 2.8% Other. 11% from out of state.

[J1] LAREDO JUNIOR COLLEGE

Laredo 78040

[1] LAREDO STATE UNIVERSITY

Laredo 78040

[J1] LEE COLLEGE

Baytown 77520

[1] LETOURNEAU CHRISTIAN COLLEGE

Longview 75607, (214) 753-0231
Director of Admissions: Linda H. Fitzhugh

- **Undergraduates: 899m, 138w**
- **Tuition (1982/83): $3,480**
- **Room & Board: $1,980; Fees: $56**
- **Degrees offered: BA, BS, AS**
- **Student-faculty ratio: 13 to 1**

A private college established in 1946, became coed in 1961. 162-acre urban campus, 130 miles from Dallas. Served by air, rail, and bus.
Academic Character SACS and professional accreditation. Semester system, 6-week summer term. 30 majors offered in the areas of liberal arts & sciences, business, physical education, religion, engineering, and technology. Minors offered in many major fields and in 8 other areas. 4 semesters of Bible required. Independent study. Credit by exam. Flight training. Study abroad. Secondary education certification. Computer center. 120,000-volume library.
Financial CEEB CSS. College scholarships, grants, loans, payment plans; PELL, SEOG, NDSL, GSL, CWS. Scholarship application deadline April 1.
Admissions High school graduation with 16 units required. ACT required; SAT accepted. $20 application fee. Rolling admissions; suggest applying by January 1. $50 deposit due on acceptance of admissions offer. Admission deferral possible. Transfers accepted. Credit possible for CEEB AP and CLEP exams. Giant Step summer program for underprepared students.
Student Life Student government. Newspaper, yearbook, radio station. Music groups. Academic, honorary, religious, and special interest groups. Students must live at home or on campus. Single-sex dorms. Married-student housing. 83% of students live on campus. Liquor and tobacco forbidden on and off campus. Dress and hair code. Class attendance required. Chapel attendance (Tuesday—Friday), 2 convocations per year required. Sunday services of student's choice required. 4 semesters of phys ed required. 6 intercollegiate sports; intramurals. NAIA. Student body composition: 0.6% Asian, 0.9% Black, 0.2% Hispanic, 0.1% Native American, 93.6% White. 80% from out of state.

[J1] LON MORRIS COLLEGE

Jacksonville 75766, (214) 586-2471

- **Undergraduates: 155m, 124w; 317 total (including part-time)**
- **Degrees offered: Associate**
- **Mean ACT 17.8**

A private junior college related to the United Methodist Church.
Academic Character SACS accreditation. Semester system. 2-year programs offered in the liberal arts. Remedial mathematics and English programs.
Financial Federal and state aid available.
Admissions High school transcript required. ACT or SAT required. Rolling admissions. *Early Admission* and *Early Decision* programs.
Student Life Modern dormitories for men and women. Student body composition: 17% minority.

[1] LUBBOCK CHRISTIAN COLLEGE

5601 West 19th Street, Lubbock 79407, (806) 792-3221
Director of Admissions: John King

- **Undergraduates: 575m, 519w**
- **Tuition (1982/83): $2,650**
- **Room & Board: $1,800; Fees: $250**
- **Degrees offered: BA, BS, BSEd**
- **Mean ACT 16.9**
- **Student-faculty ratio: 14 to 1**

A private college affiliated with the Church of Christ, established in 1957. 40-acre urban campus. Served by air, rail, and bus.

Academic Character SACS accreditation. Semester system, 3 4-week summer terms. Majors offered in accounting, agriculture, art, Bible, biology, business, chemistry, education, English, general studies, history, home economics, mathematics, music, physical education, psychology, sociology, Spanish, and speech. Distributives and 14 hours of Bible required. Independent study. Internships. Preprofessional programs in dentistry, engineering, law, medical fields, nursing, veterinary medicine. Cross-registration with South Plains, Texas Tech. Elementary, secondary, and special education certification. ROTC, AFROTC at Texas Tech. Water-research lab. 2 farms. 70,000-volume library.
Financial CEEB CSS and ACT FAS. College scholarships, grants, loans, state grants; PELL, SEOG, NDSL, FISL, CWS, college work program. Application deadline June 1.
Admissions High school graduation required. GED accepted. ACT required. $10 application fee. Rolling admissions; suggest applying by March. $50 deposit due on acceptance of admissions offer. *Early Admission* and *Concurrent Enrollment* programs. Transfers accepted. Credit possible for CEEB AP, CLEP, and ACT PEP exams; college has own advanced placement program.
Student Life Student government. Newspaper, yearbook, radio station. Music and drama groups. Debate. Rodeo Day. Los Conquistadors. Academic, honorary, professional, and special interest groups. 5 fraternities and 5 sororities. 50% of students join. Students under 21 live at home or on campus. Single-sex dorms. Married-student housing. 80% of students live on campus. Liquor and tobacco prohibited. Dress code. Limited class absences. Daily chapel mandatory. 4 hours of phys ed required. 6 intercollegiate sports for men, 3 for women; intramurals. NAIA, TIAA. Student body composition: 4% Black, 4% Hispanic, 1% Native American, 87% White, 4% Other. 31% from out of state.

[J1] MAINLAND, COLLEGE OF THE
8001 Palmer Highway, Texas City 77590

[1] MARY HARDIN-BAYLOR, UNIVERSITY OF
Belton 76513, (817) 939-5811
Director of Admissions: Bill Elliot

- **Undergraduates: 428m, 649w**
- **Tuition (1982/83): $2,250**
- **Room & Board: $1,650-$2,010**
- **Degrees offered: BA, BS, BGT, BBA, BFA, BGS, BMus, BMus Ed, BSEd, BSN**
- **Student-faculty ratio: 18 to 1**

A private university controlled by the Baptist General Convention of Texas, established in 1845. 100-acre small-city campus in central Texas. Served by air, rail, and bus.
Academic Character SACS and professional accreditation. Semester system, 2 5-week summer terms. 35 majors offered by the schools of Arts & Sciences, Business, Creative Arts, Nursing, and Education. Minor required. Minors offered in most major fields and in 3 other areas. Distributives and 6 hours of religion required. Independent study. Honors program. Credit by exam. Preprofessional programs in medicine, pharmacy, theology. Elementary and secondary education certification. AFROTC. Language lab. 105,000-volume library.
Financial ACT FAS. University scholarships, grants, loans, state grants, payment plans; PELL, SEOG, NDSL, NSL, CWS. Application deadline April 1.
Admissions High school graduation with 15 units required. Interview recommended. ACT required. $25 application fee. Rolling admissions; application deadline August 1. $60 room deposit due on acceptance of admissions offer. *Early Decision* and *Early Admission* programs. Admission deferral possible. Transfers accepted. Credit possible for CEEB AP, CLEP, and university proficiency exams. Probationary admission possible.
Student Life Student government. Newspaper, magazine, yearbook. Music and drama groups. Debate. Academic, honorary, social, and special interest groups. Single students must live at home or on campus. 34% of students live on campus. Weekly chapel required. 2 phys ed courses required. 5 intercollegiate sports for men, 3 for women; intramurals. Student body composition: 8% Black, 8% Hispanic, 2% Native American, 79% White, 3% Other. 19% from out of state.

[J1] McCLENNAN COMMUNITY COLLEGE
Waco 76708

[1] McMURRAY COLLEGE
14th and Sayles Blvd., Abilene 79697, (915) 692-4130
Director of Admissions: Doug Wofford

- **Undergraduates: 839m, 709w**
- **Tuition (1982/83): $2,460**
- **Room & Board: $1,740; Fees: $290**
- **Degrees offered: BA, BS, BBA, BMus, BMus Ed, BFA, BSN**
- **Mean ACT 19**
- **Student-faculty ratio: 15 to 1**

A private college controlled by the United Methodist Church, established in 1923. 52-acre suburban campus, 150 miles from Dallas. Served by air and bus.
Academic Character SACS and professional accreditation. Semester system, 2 5-week summer terms. 46 majors offered in the areas of fine arts, liberal arts & sciences, business, education, music, nursing, physical education, religion, and social sciences. Minors offered in most major fields. Courses in Greek and special education. Distributives and 6 hours of religion & philosophy required. Preprofessional programs in dentistry, engineering, law, medicine, physical therapy, veterinary medicine. 3-1 medical technology program. Foreign language programs in cooperation with Abilene Christian and Hardin-Simmons. 2-2 nursing program with Abilene School of Nursing. Elementary, bilingual, secondary, and special education certification. ROTC at Hardin-Simmons. Computer facilities. Language lab. Fine arts center. 145,000-volume library.
Financial CEEB CSS and ACT FAS. College scholarships, grants, loans, tuition reduction for ministers and families, ministerial scholarships, payment plans; PELL, SEOG, NDSL, FISL, CWS. Application deadlines March 1 (scholarships), June 1 (loans).
Admissions High school graduation with 16 units recommended. GED accepted. ACT or SAT required; ACT preferred. $15 application fee. Rolling admissions; suggest applying in January. $100 tuition deposit and $50 room deposit required on acceptance of offer of admission. *Early Admission* and *Concurrent Enrollment* programs. Admission deferral possible. Transfers accepted. Credit possible for CEEB AP and CLEP exams. College has own advanced placement program.
Student Life Student government. Newspaper, literary magazine, yearbook. Music, speech, and drama groups. Debate. Latin-American Club. Academic, honorary, religious, service, and special interest groups. 7 social clubs for men and 6 for women, all without houses. Single students live at home or on campus. Dorms for men and women. Married-student housing. 40% of students live on campus. Liquor, drugs, cheating, and hazing prohibited. Class attendance expected. Attendance at 4 fine arts programs required each semester. 4 semesters of phys ed required. 5 intercollegiate sports for men, 5 for women; intramurals. AIAW, NAIA, TIAA. Student body composition: 0.5% Asian, 9.1% Black, 5.4% Hispanic, 0.5% Native American, 83% White. 15% from out of state.

[J1] MIDLAND COLLEGE
3600 North Garfield, Midland 79701

[1] MIDWESTERN STATE UNIVERSITY
3400 Taft Blvd., Wichita Falls 76308, (817) 692-6611
Director of Admissions: Donita Shaddock

- **Undergraduates: 1,177m, 1,229w; 4,526 total (including graduates)**
- **Tuition (1982/83): $435 (in-state), $1,515 (out-of-state)**
- **Room & Board: $1,449; Fees: $40**
- **Degrees offered: BA, BS, BMus, BMus Ed, BBA, BSEd, BSMed Tech, BFA, BAAS, AA, AAS**
- **Student-faculty ratio: 20 to 1**

A public university established in 1922. 165-acre suburban campus, 150 miles from Fort Worth. Served by air and bus.
Academic Character SACS and professional accreditation. Semester system, 2 5-week summer terms. 8 majors offered by the School of Business Administration & Economics, 7 by the School of Education, 22 by the School of Humanities & Social Science, and 10 by the School of Science & Mathematics. Minor required in most programs. Minors offered in most major fields and in 4 other areas. Distributive requirements. Graduate degrees granted. Honors program. Limited pass/fail, credit by exam. Preprofessional programs in dentistry, engineering, law, medicine, nursing, optometry, osteopathy, pharmacy, veterinary medicine. 3-1 medical technology program with Wichita General Hospital. Cooperative programs in religion with area churches. Elementary, secondary, and special education certification. ROTC. Language lab. 350,620-volume library with microform resources.
Financial ACT FAS. University scholarships, grants, loans; art, debate, journalism, and music awards; state loans; PELL, SEOG, NSS, NDSL, FISL, CWS. Application deadlines April 1 (scholarships), July 1 (loans).
Admissions High school graduation required. GED accepted. ACT or SAT required for applicants under 21. Rolling admissions; suggest applying by June 15. $40 room deposit required on acceptance of admissions offer. *Early Decision* and *Concurrent Enrollment* programs. Transfers accepted. Credit possible for CEEB AP and CLEP exams; university has own advanced placement program. Advised Admission Program.
Student Life Student government. Newspaper, literary magazine, yearbook. Music and drama groups. Debate. Athletic, academic, honorary, religious, service, and special interest groups. 5 fraternities with houses, 5 sororities with chapter rooms. 9% of men and 10% of women join. Students with less than 60 credit hours must live at home or on campus. Single-sex dorms. No married-student housing. 20% of students live on campus. Gambling and hazing prohibited. Class attendance expected. 4 semesters of phys ed required. 4 intercollegiate sports for men, 3 for women; club sports. AIAW, NAIA. Student body composition: 10% minority. 10% from out of state.

[J1] MOUNTAIN VIEW COLLEGE
Dallas 75202

[J1] NAVARRO COLLEGE
PO Box 1170, Corsioana 75110, (214) 874-6501

- **Enrollment: 2,000 men & women**
- **Tuition (1982/83): $240 (in-state), $1,290 (out-of-state)**
- **Room & Board: $1,950**
- **Degrees offered: AA, AS, AAS, AGE**
- **Mean ACT 17**
- **Student-faculty ratio: 35 to 1**

A public college established in 1946. 100-acre rural campus.
Academic Character SACS accreditation. Semester system, 2 5-week summer terms. 2-year programs offered in business, humanities, health occupations, physical education, social & behavioral science, technical education, and science, mathematics, & media instruction. Distributive requirements. Cooperative work/study. Preprofessional programs in dentistry, engineering, law, medicine, nursing, pharmacy, and veterinary medicine. 200-acre farm. TV studio. 30,000-volume library.

Financial College scholarships, loans, grants, work program.
Admissions High school graduation with 16 units required. GED accepted. Rolling admissions. $50 room deposit due on acceptance of admissions offer. *Early Admission* Program. Transfers accepted. Credit possible for ACT PEP, CEEB CLEP, and college challenge exams. Developmental Studies Program.
Student Life Professional, religious, social, service, and special interest groups. Single-sex dorms. Married-student apartments. Class attendance expected. Phys ed required. Intercollegiate and intramural sports. Student body composition: 21% minority.

[J1] NORTH HARRIS COUNTY JUNIOR COLLEGE
2700 W.W. Thorne Drive, Houston 77073

[1] NORTH TEXAS STATE UNIVERSITY
PO Box 13797, Denton 76203, (817) 788-2681

- **Undergraduates: 8,472m, 9,015w; 17,487 total (including graduates)**
- **Tuition (1982/83): $1,100 (in-state), $3,600 (out-of-state)**
- **Room & Board: $2,453**
- **Degrees offered: BA, BS, BFA, BBA, BMus, BAAS, BSB, BSC, BSCS, BSE, BSMT, BSM, BSP, BSW, BSEd, BSHE, BSIA, BSPE**
- **Mean ACT 19; mean SAT 898**
- **Student-faculty ratio: 17 to 1**

A public university established in 1890. 380-acre urban campus, 39 miles from Dallas. Served by bus; airport and rail station in Dallas.
Academic Character SACS and professional accreditation. Semester system, 2 6-week summer terms. 24 majors offered by the College of Arts & Sciences, 13 by the College of Business Administration, 3 by the School of Community Service, 8 by the College of Education, 7 by the School of Home Economics, and 9 by the School of Music. Special majors. Minor required. Distributive requirements. Graduate degrees granted. Independent study. Honors program. Limited pass/fail, credit by exam. Preprofessional programs in allied health, architecture, dentistry, engineering, medicine, theology. 3-1 medical technology program. Elementary, secondary, and special education certification. AFROTC. Language lab. 1,350,000-volume library with microform resources.
Financial CEEB CSS and ACT FAS. University scholarships, grants, loans, payment plans; PELL, SEOG, NDSL, FISL, CWS. Application deadlines March 1 (scholarships), June 1 (loans).
Admissions High school graduation with 16 units recommended. SAT or ACT required. Rolling admissions. $75 room deposit due on acceptance of admissions offer. *Early Decision* and *Early Admission* programs. Transfers accepted. Credit possible for CEEB AP and CLEP exams; university has own advanced placement program.
Student Life Student government. Newspaper, yearbook. Music, drama, and radio-TV groups. Debate. Athletic, academic, honorary, political, religious, service, and special interest groups. 15 fraternities, 14 with houses; 9 sororities, most with houses. Students with over 30 credit hours may live off campus. Coed and single-sex dorms. Some married-student housing. 19% of students live on campus. Drugs and hazing prohibited. Class attendance expected. 4 semesters of phys ed required for freshmen and sophomores. 7 intercollegiate sports for men, 4 for women; intramurals. AIAW, NCAA. Student body composition: 9% Black, 3% Hispanic, 0.1% Native American, 87.9% White. 16% from out of state.

[J1] NORTHWOOD OF TEXAS (NORTHWOOD INSTITUTE)
Cedar Hill 75104, (214) 291-1541

- **Undergraduates: 1,153m, 486w; 1,653 total (including part-time)**
- **Tuition & Fees (1980/81): $850**
- **Room & Board: $1,450**
- **Degree offered: AB**
- **Mean ACT over 13**

A private junior college of business management. Campus located 16 miles from Dallas.
Academic Character NCACS accreditation. Quarter and module system. Programs offered include advertising, hotel & restaurant management, retailing & marketing, fashion, merchandising, business management, executive secretarial, and automotive marketing. Library.
Financial Aid available includes scholarships, athletic scholarships, loans, work-grant programs, part-time off-campus employment.
Admissions ACT required. $15 application fee. Rolling admissions.
Student Life Dormitories and dining hall. Athletics include basketball, soccer, tennis, golf, and baseball

[1] OBLATE SCHOOL OF THEOLOGY
San Antonio 78216

[J1] ODESSA COLLEGE
201 West University, Odessa 79760, (915) 337-5381

- **Undergraduates: 1,146, 1,241; 3,893 total (including part-time)**
- **Tuition (1980/81): $108 (in-district), $130 (in-state), $260 (out-of-state)**
- **Degrees offered: AA, AS, AAS**

A public, district-controlled junior college.
Academic Character SACS and professional accreditation. Semester system, 2 6-week summer terms, 10-day mid-winter term. University transfer courses offered in most preprofessional fields. 2-year courses in automotive mechanics, electrical technology, electronics technology, electronic data processing, heating & air conditioning, inhalation therapy, machine shop, medical technology, mid-management, nursing, police science, radiologic technology, and welding. Certificates of completion granted. Day and evening programs.
Admissions High school graduation required. Non-graduates 19 or older showing evidence of ability to profit from instruction are admitted.
Student Life Limited dormitory space. Dining facilities available. Strong athletics programs in golf, gymnastics, tennis, track, and basketball.

[1] OUR LADY OF THE LAKE UNIVERSITY OF SAN ANTONIO
411 Southwest 24th Street, San Antonio 78285, (512) 434-6711
Director of Admissions: Loretta Schlegel

- **Undergraduates: 414m, 910w**
- **Tuition (1982/83): $2,940**
- **Room & Board: $738-$1,240; Fees: $114**
- **Degrees offered: BA, BS, BAS, BSW**
- **Mean SAT 400v, 350m**
- **Student-faculty ratio: 20 to 1**

A private university controlled by the Congregation of the Sisters of Divine Providence, established in 1911, became coed in 1968. 75-acre urban campus. Served by air, rail, and bus.
Academic Character SACS and professional accreditation. 4-4-1 system, 2 5-week summer terms. 35 majors offered by the colleges of Arts & Sciences, Business & Public Administration, the schools of Education & Clinical Studies, and Social Service. Minors offered. Distributive requirements. Masters degrees granted. Independent study. Limited pass/fail, internships. Preprofessional programs in law, medical technology, medicine, nursing, social work. Cross-registration with Incarnate Word. Study abroad. Elementary, secondary, special, and bilingual education certification. ROTC at St. Mary's. Language lab. 300,000-volume library.
Financial CEEB CSS. University scholarships, grants, loans; PELL, SEOG, NDSL, FISL, CWS. Application deadlines March 1 (scholarships), August 1 (loans).
Admissions High school graduation with 16 units required. GED accepted. SAT or ACT required. $15 application fee. Rolling admissions; suggest applying at end of 11th year. *Early Decision, Early Admission, Concurrent Enrollment* programs. Transfers accepted. Credit possible for CEEB AP and CLEP exams; university has own advanced placement program. Conditional Admission and Summer Challenge programs.
Student Life Student government. Music, film, and drama groups. Academic, honorary, professional, and religious groups. Single-sex dorms. Cafeteria. 15% of students live on campus. Intercollegiate basketball; intramurals. NAIA, AIAW. Student body composition: 9% Black, 53% Hispanic, 34% White, 4% Other. 10% from out of state.

[1] PAN AMERICAN UNIVERSITY
Edinburg 78539, (512) 381-2011
Registrar & Director of Admissions: David Zuniga

- **Enrollment: 3,779m, 5,264w**
- **Tuition (1982/83): $880 (in-state), $4,200 (out-of-state)**
- **Room & Board: $1,755**
- **Degrees offered: BA, BS, BBA, BCJ, BFA, BSW, BSCJ, AAS**
- **Student-faculty ratio: 21 to 1**

A public university established in 1927. 200-acre small-town campus, 15 miles north of Reynosa, Mexico. Rail and bus stations nearby.
Academic Character SACS accreditation. Semester system, 2 6-week summer terms. 8 majors offered by the School of Business Administration, 5 by the School of Education, 1 by the Division of Health Related Professions, 7 by the School of Humanities, 4 by the School of Science & Mathematics, and 9 by the School of Social Sciences. Minors offered in all major fields and in 9 other areas. Distributive requirements. Masters degrees granted. Independent study. Honors program. Cooperative work/study, pass/fail. Preprofessional programs in dentistry, engineering, law, medicine, pharmacy. Elementary and secondary education certification. ROTC. Marine biology lab on Padre Island. Planetarium. Recording and TV studios. 218,394-volume library with microform resources.
Financial University scholarships, grants, loans, Biomedical Sciences Program, College Assistance Migrant Program; PELL, SEOG, NSS, FISL, GSL, NDSL, CWS. Fall application deadline June 1.
Admissions High school graduation with 11 units required. GED accepted. ACT required; SAT accepted. Rolling admissions; application deadline August 2. $20 room deposit due with dormitory application. Transfers accepted. Credit possible for CEEB AP, CLEP, and ACT exams; university has own advanced placement program.
Student Life Student government. Newspaper, yearbook. Music, dance, and drama groups. Debate. Chicano Awareness Organization. Academic, religious, social, service, and special interest groups. 5 fraternities and 2 sororities. Limited housing. Single-sex dorms. Class attendance expected. 4 hours of phys ed required. 5 intercollegiate sports for men, 4 for women; intramurals. NCAA, AIAW. Student body composition: 1% Asian, 1% Black, 71% Hispanic, 1% Native American, 26% White. 1% from out of state.

[J1] PANOLA JUNIOR COLLEGE
Carthage 75633

[J1] PARIS JUNIOR COLLEGE
Paris 75460, (214) 785-7661

- **Undergraduates: 554m, 507w; 2,043 total (including part-time)**
- **District Tuition (1980/81): $4 per hour**
- **In-state Tuition: $4 per hour plus $40 per year**
- **Out-of-state Tuition: $500 per year**
- **Degrees offered: Associate**
- **Mean ACT 16.9**

A public, district-controlled junior college.
Academic Character SACS and professional accreditation. Semester system, 2 6-week summer terms. Comprehensive general academic and applied science programs offered.
Student Life Dormitory facilities for men and women.

[1] PAUL QUINN COLLEGE
1020 Elm Street, Waco 76704, (817) 753-6415

- **Undergraduates: 240m, 235w; 502 total (including part-time**
- **Tuition, Room, Board, & Fees (1980/81): $3,465**
- **Degrees offered: BA, BS**
- **Mean ACT 12**
- **Student-faculty ratio: 13 to 1**

A private college affiliated with the African Methodist Episcopal Church, established in 1872.
Academic Character SACS and professional (social work) accreditation. Semester system, 6-week summer term. Majors offered leading to the degrees of Bachelor of Arts and Bachelor of Science. 80,000-volume library.
Financial Student financial aid available.
Admissions ACT required. Freshmen admitted any term.

[1 & G1] PRAIRIE VIEW AGRICULTURAL AND MECHANICAL UNIVERSITY
Prairie View 77445, (713) 857-3311
Director of Admissions: George H. Stafford

- **Undergraduates: 1,824m, 2,424w; 5,520 total (including graduates)**
- **Tuition (1982/83): $150 (in-state), $1,500 (out-of-state)**
- **Room & Board: $1,600; Fees: $300**
- **Degrees offered: BA, BS, BFA, BMus, BBA, BSN, AA**
- **Mean ACT 16**
- **Student-faculty ratio: 16 to 1**

A public university established in 1876. Campus 46 miles from Houston. Served by bus.
Academic Character SACS and professional accreditation. Semester system, 2 6-week summer terms. 6 majors offered by the College of Agriculture, 21 by the College of Arts & Sciences, 5 by the College of Business, 4 by the College of Engineering, 4 by the College of Home Economics, 6 by the College of Industrial Education & Technology, 1 by the College of Nursing, and several in the College of Education. Minor required. Distributive requirements. Graduate degrees granted. Preprofessional programs in dentistry, medicine, veterinary medicine. Elementary, secondary, and special education certification. ROTC, NROTC (required). 245,000-volume library with microform resources.
Financial CEEB CSS. University scholarships, grants, loans, band scholarships, state loans; PELL, SEOG, NSS, NDSL, NSL, university work program.
Admissions High school graduation with 15 units required. ACT required. Rolling admissions. *Early Admission* Program. Admission deferral possible. Transfers accepted. Credit possible for CEEB AP and CLEP exams.
Student Life Academic, honorary, religious, social, and special interest groups. 4 fraternities and 4 sororities. Students live at home, on campus, or in approved housing. Juniors and seniors may have cars. Hazing prohibited. Class attendance expected. 4 hours of phys ed required. 6 intercollegiate sports for men, 3 for women; intramurals. SAC. Student body composition: 3.6% Asian, 95.8% Black, 0.3% Hispanic, 0.3% Native American.

[J1] RANGER JUNIOR COLLEGE
Ranger 76470, (817) 647-3234

- **Undergraduates: 335m, 90w; 558 total (including part-time)**
- **Degrees offered: AA, AS**

A public, district-controlled junior college.
Academic Character SACS accreditation. Semester system. Transfer programs offered in the liberal arts. Vocational-technical and preprofessional programs also offered.
Admissions High school graduation required. Students admitted in September and January.
Student Life Dormitories and dining hall for men and women.

[1] RICE UNIVERSITY
6100 South Main, Houston 77251, (713) 527-4036
Director of Admissions: Ron W. Moss

- **Undergraduates: 1,549m, 899w; 3,476 total (including graduates)**
- **Tuition (1983/84): $3,700**
- **Room & Board: $3,300; Fees: $200**
- **Degrees offered: BA, BS, BFA, BArch, BMus**
- **Mean SAT 660**
- **Student-faculty ratio: 9 to 1**

A private university established in 1912. 300-acre urban campus. Served by air, rail, and bus.
Academic Character SACS and professional accreditation. Semester system, limited summer term. 39 majors offered in the areas of architecture, art, computer science, engineering, humanities, physical education, mathematics, music, science, and social sciences. Self-designed and special majors. Distributive requirements. Graduate degrees granted. Independent study. Phi Beta Kappa. Pass/fail, internships. Preprofessional programs in dentistry, law, medicine. 5-year programs in accounting, architecture, engineering. Exchange program with Trinity College, Cambridge. Swarthmore semester. Secondary education certification. ROTC, NROTC. Language labs. 1,100,000-volume library with microform resources.
Financial CEEB CSS. University scholarships, grants, loans, state grants, payment plans; PELL, SEOG, NDSL, FISL, part-time employment. FAF deadline February 1.
Admissions High school graduation with 16 units required. Interview required. Audition required for music majors. Architecture applicants should submit portfolio. SAT and 3 ACH required. Application deadline February 1. $100 tuition and $50 room deposits due on acceptance of admissions offer. *Early Decision, Early Admission, Concurrent Enrollment* programs. Admission deferral possible. Transfers accepted. Credit possible for CEEB AP exams.
Student Life Eight residential colleges, each with its own programs and student government. Student Senate. Newspaper, magazine, yearbook, radio station. Music and drama groups. Debate. Black Students Union. Mexican American Students. Chinese Students Association. Academic, honorary, professional, religious, special interest groups. Limited housing for upperclassmen. Coed and single-sex dorms. No married-student housing. 60% of students live on campus. Phys ed required of freshmen. 11 intercollegiate sports for men, 5 for women; several intramural and club sports. AIAW, SAC. Student body composition: 1.2% Asian, 4% Black, 3% Hispanic, 0.2% Native American, 90.8% White, 0.8% Other. 40% from out of state.

[J1] RICHLAND COLLEGE
12800 Abrams Road, Dallas 75231

[1] SAINT EDWARD'S UNIVERSITY
3001 South Congress Avenue, Austin 78704, (512) 444-2621
Director of Admissions & Records: John Lucas

- **Undergraduates: 1,380m, 970w; 2,500 total (including graduates)**
- **Tuition (1982/83): $3,450**
- **Room & Board: $2,340-$3,250; Fees: $224**
- **Degrees offered: BA, BS, BAAS, BLA, BBA**
- **Mean ACT 17; mean SAT 850**
- **Student-faculty ratio: 23 to 1**

A private university controlled by the Roman Catholic Church, established in 1885, became coed in 1966. 180-acre suburban campus. Served by air, rail, and bus.
Academic Character SACS accreditation. Semester system, 3-week and 2 6-week summer terms. 27 majors offered in the areas of behavioral & social sciences, business administration, humanities, teaching & learning, and physical & biological sciences. Distributives and 7 courses in religion required. Graduate degrees granted. Independent study. Honors program. Pass/fail, internships, credit by exam. Preprofessional programs in dentistry, engineering, law, medical technology, medicine, nursing, optometry, pharmacy. Study abroad. Elementary, secondary, and bilingual education certification; special education with U Texas, Austin. ROTC, AFROTC, NROTC at U Texas. Computer center. Learning Resource Center. Language lab. Theatre. 125,000-volume library.
Financial CEEB CSS. University scholarships, grants, loans, academic scholarships; PELL, SEOG, NDSL, GSL, CWS. Scholarship application deadline April 1.
Admissions High school graduation in upper 66% of class required. GED accepted. SAT or ACT required. $20 application fee. Rolling admissions; suggest applying in November. $50 room deposit due prior to entrance. Admission deferral possible. Transfers accepted. Credit possible for CEEB AP, CLEP, and university exams. College Assistant Migrant Program.
Student Life Student government. Newspaper, literary magazine, yearbook. Project Aware Volunteer Program. Academic and special interest groups. Single freshmen under 21 live at home or on campus. Dorms for men and women. No married-student housing. 25% of students live on campus. Liquor prohibited. 4 intercollegiate sports for men, 3 for women; intramurals. AIAW, NAIA, BSC. Student body composition: 1% Asian, 6% Black, 22% Hispanic, 1% Native American, 58% White, 12% Other. 20% from out of state.

[1] SAINT MARY'S UNIVERSITY
1 Camino Santa Maria, San Antonio 78284, (512) 436-3126
Director of Admissions: Fernando A. Yarrito

- **Undergraduates: 1,007m, 972w; 3,333 total (including graduates)**
- **Tuition (1982/83): $3,520**
- **Room & Board: $2,050; Fees: $110**
- **Degrees offered: BA, BS, BAS, BBA**
- **Mean ACT 21; mean SAT 469v, 491m**
- **Student-faculty ratio: 18 to 1**

A private university controlled by the Society of Mary, established in 1852, became coed in 1963. 135-acre suburban campus. Served by air, rail, and bus.
Academic Character SACS accreditation. Semester system, 2 6-week summer terms. 39 majors offered in the areas of arts & sciences, education, engineering, and business & administration. Minors offered in most major fields and in 6 other areas. Courses in Greek and Latin. Distributives and 6 hours of theology required. Graduate degrees granted. Independent study. Cooperative work/study, pass/fail, internships. Preprofessional programs in dentistry, law, medical technology, medicine, pharmacy, veterinary medicine. Exchange with Incarnate Word and Our Lady of the Lake. Elementary and secondary, education certification. ROTC. Language lab. 176,000-volume library.
Financial CEEB CSS. University scholarships, grants, loans, state grants and loans; PELL, SEOG, NDSL, GSL, CWS, university work program. Scholarship application deadline March 31.
Admissions High school graduation with 16 units required. GED accepted. Interview recommended. ACT or SAT required. $15 application fee. Rolling admissions; suggest applying in fall. $50 tuition and $100 room deposits due

on acceptance of admissions offer. *Early Decision* and *Early Admission* programs. Admissions deferral possible. Transfers accepted. Credit possible for CEEB AP, CLEP, and ACT PEP exams. Special admissions programs for underprepared students.
Student Life Student government. Newspaper, literary magazine, yearbook. Music, dance, and drama groups. Black Student Union. Mexican American Student Organization. Debate. Academic, honorary, political, religious, and special interest groups. 9 fraternities, 1 with housing; 5 sororities without houses. 20% of men and women join. Juniors and seniors may live off campus. Single-sex dorms. 35% of students live on campus. Class attendance required. 2 hours of phys ed required. 5 intercollegiate sports for men, 5 for women; intramurals. NAIA, BSC. Student body composition: 0.6% Asian, 5% Black, 35.7% Hispanic, 0.2% Native American, 52.6% White, 5.9% Other. 22% from out of state.

[J1] ST. PHILIP'S COLLEGE
211 Nevada, San Antonio 78203

[1] SAINT THOMAS, UNIVERSITY OF
3812 Montrose Blvd., Houston 77006, (713) 522-7911
Director of Admissions: George A. Knaggs

- **Undergraduates: 630m, 865w; 1,941 total (including graduates)**
- **Tuition (1982/83): $2,800**
- **Room & Board: $2,650; Fees: $250**
- **Degrees offered: BA, BSN, BBA, BMus**
- **Mean SAT 500**
- **Student-faculty ratio: 16 to 1**

A private university controlled by the Basilian Fathers, established in 1947. 15-acre urban campus. Served by air, rail, and bus.
Academic Character SACS accreditation. Semester system, 6-week summer term. 33 majors offered in the areas of art, business, drama, education, liberal arts, mathematics, music, nursing, religion, science, social sciences, and weather. Distributives and one course in religion required. Graduate degrees granted. Internships. Preprofessional programs in dentistry, engineering, law, medical technology, medicine, nutrition, physical therapy. 3-2 engineering program with Notre Dame. Cooperative program with NASA. Study in Rome, Israel, and the Yucatan. Early childhood, elementary, secondary, bilingual, and special education certification. ROTC, NROTC at Rice. Computer center. Storm research institute. 86,000-volume library.
Financial CEEB CSS. University scholarships, grants, loans, state grants; PELL, SEOG, NSS, NDSL, FISL, CWS. Application deadlines March 1 (scholarships), August 1 (loans).
Admissions High school graduation with 16 units required. GED accepted. Interview recommended. SAT or ACT required. $15 application fee. Rolling admissions; suggest applying by February 15. $150 room deposit due on acceptance of admissions offer. *Early Decision, Early Admission, Concurrent Enrollment* programs. Admission deferral possible. Transfers accepted. Credit possible for CEEB AP and CLEP exams; university has own advanced placement program.
Student Life Student government. Newspaper, literary magazine, yearbook. Music and drama groups. Circle K. Academic, honorary, professional, and special interest groups. 2 sororities without houses. 2% of women join. No married-student housing. 10% of students live on campus. Liquor prohibited. Intercollegiate golf for men; intramurals. Student body composition: 8% Black, 16% Hispanic, 66% White, 10% Other. 5% from out of state.

[1] SAM HOUSTON STATE UNIVERSITY
Huntsville 77341, (713) 294-1111
Director of Admissions: H.A. Bass

- **Undergraduates: 4,949m, 5,341w; 10,290 total (including graduates)**
- **Tuition (1982/83): $120 (in-state), $1,200 (out-of-state)**
- **Room & Board: $2,250; Fees: $340**
- **Degrees offered: BA, BS, BAAS, BAT, BBA, BFA, BMus, BMus Ed**
- **Mean ACT 16.8; mean SAT 393v, 418m**
- **Student-faculty ratio: 17 to 1**

A public university established in 1879. Campus in a small city 70 miles from Houston. Airport in Houston.
Academic Character SACS and professional accreditation. Semester system, 2 6-week summer terms. 27 majors offered by the College of Applied Arts & Sciences, 8 by the College of Business Administration, 6 by the College of Education, 17 by the College of Fine Arts, 13 by the College of the Humanities, 8 by the College of Science, and 3 by the Institute of Contemporary Corrections. Minor required in some fields. Special programs in 7 additional areas. Distributives and GRE required. Honors program. Preprofessional programs in dental hygiene, dentistry, engineering, law, medicine, nursing, pharmacy, physical therapy, seminary, veterinary medicine. 3-2 engineering program with Texas A&M. Elementary and secondary education certification. ROTC. Agricultural and criminal justice centers. 617,000-volume library.
Financial CEEB CSS. University scholarships, grants, loans, state grants, payment plan; PELL, SEOG, NDSL, FISL, USAF, CWS. Application deadline March 1.
Admissions High school graduation with 15 units recommended. SAT or ACT required. Rolling admissions. $30 room deposit due on acceptance of admissions offer. *Early Admission* and *Concurrent Enrollment* programs. Transfers accepted. Credit possible for CEEB AP and CLEP exams.
Student Life Student government. Newspaper, yearbook, radio and TV studios. Music and drama groups. Ethnic, political, religious, service, and special interest groups. Freshmen live at home or on campus. Coed and single-sex dorms. Married-student housing. 40% of students live on campus. 2 semesters of phys ed required. Intramural sports. 2% of students from out of state.

[J1] SAN ANTONIO COLLEGE
San Antonio 78284

[J1] SAN JACINTO COLLEGE
8060 Spencer Highway, Pasadena 77505

■[J1] SAN JACINTO COLLEGE—NORTH CAMPUS
5800 Uvalde, Houston 77049

[J1 & 2] SCHREINER COLLEGE
Kerrville 78028, (512) 896-5411
Director of Admissions: Scott J. Goplin

- **Enrollment: 740 men & women (including part-time)**
- **Tuition (1982/83): $1,056-$1,584**
- **Room & Board: $2,105-$2,198**
- **Degrees offered: BA, AA**
- **Mean ACT 20.4**
- **Student-faculty ratio: 23 to 1**

A private college affiliated with the Presbyterian church in the United States, established in 1923, became coed in 1971. Small-city campus, 60 miles northwest of San Antonio.
Academic Character SACS accreditation. 4-1-4 system, 6-week summer term. 2-year transfer and 4-year courses offered in the liberal arts, business, education, law enforcement, secretarial science, and vocational nursing. Minors offered. Distributive requirements; senior thesis required for BA. Independent study. Field employment. Preprofessional programs in dentistry, engineering, law, medicine, pharmacy. 17,000-volume library.
Financial CEEB CSS and ACT FAS. College scholarships, grants, state grants, payment plans; PELL, SEOG, GSL, CWS, college work program.
Admissions High school graduation with 11 units required. GED accepted. SAT or ACT required. $20 application fee. Rolling admissions. $100 deposit due on acceptance of admissions offer. *Early Admission* and *Concurrent Enrollment* programs. Transfers accepted. Credit possible for CEEB AP and ACT exams. Learning Disabilities Program.
Student Life Student government. Literary Magazine. Circle K. Bible study. Special interest groups. Single students under 25 live on campus or at home. Dormitories and dining hall. Class attendance expected. 4 hours of phys ed required. 3 intercollegiate sports for men, 2 for women; intramurals. Student body composition: 11% minority.

[J1] SOUTH PLAINS COLLEGE
Levelland 79336

[P] SOUTHERN BIBLE COLLEGE
PO Box 9636, 10950 Beaumont Highway, Houston 77213

[1] SOUTHERN METHODIST UNIVERSITY
PO Box 296, Dallas 75275, (214) 692-2058
Director of Admissions: Scott F. Healy

- **Undergraduates: 2,754m, 2,750w; 9,200 total (including graduates)**
- **Tuition (1982/83): $5,000**
- **Room & Board: $3,060; Fees: $325**
- **Degrees offered: BA, BS, BBA, BFA, BMus, BSCE, BSEE, BSME**
- **Mean SAT 1,050**
- **Student-faculty ratio: 14 to 1**

A private university affiliated with the United Methodist Church, established in 1911. 164-acre suburban campus, 5 miles from downtown Dallas. Served by air, rail, and bus.
Academic Character SACS and professional accreditation. Semester system, 2 5-week summer terms, January and May inter-terms. 60 majors offered by the schools of Arts, Business Administration, Dedman College (humanities & sciences), and Engineering & Applied Science. Self-designed majors. Minors in many major fields and in 7 others. Distributive requirements. Graduate degrees granted. Independent study. Honors program. Phi Beta Kappa. Limited pass/fail, internships. Preprofessional programs in dentistry, law, medicine. Cooperative program in engineering. Study abroad. Elementary and secondary education certification. AFROTC at North Texas. Computer center. Herbarium. Electron microscopy lab. Seismological observatory. Museums. 1,800,000-volume library with microform resources.
Financial CEEB CSS. University scholarships, grants, loans, ministerial scholarships, scholarships for Methodist ministers' children, federal and state grants and loans, payment plan, student employment. Priority application deadline for scholarships March 1.
Admissions High school graduation with 13 units required. Interview recommended; urged for broadcast/film and journalism majors. Audition required for dance, music, and theatre applicants. SAT or ACT required. $20 application fee. Rolling admissions; application deadline April 1. $200 deposit due on acceptance of admissions offer. Admission deferral possible. Transfers accepted. Credit possible for CEEB AP and CLEP exams.
Student Life Student government. Newspaper, literary magazine, yearbook, radio station. Music, dance, and drama groups. Debate. Athletic, academic, honorary, professional, religious, service, and special interest groups. 15 fraternities and 12 sororities, all with houses. 50% of men and women join. Freshmen live at home or on campus. Coed and single-sex dorms. Co-op dorms. Married-student housing. 51% of students live on campus. 2 hours of phys ed required. 7 intercollegiate sports for men, 4 for women; many

intramurals. AIAW, NCAA, SC. Student body composition: 3% Black, 2% Hispanic, 90% White, 5% Other. 55% from out of state.

[J1] SOUTHWEST TEXAS JUNIOR COLLEGE

Garnerfield Road, Uvalde 78801, (512) 278-4401

- **Undergraduates: 455m, 414w; 2,027 total (including part-time)**
- **Tuition (1980/81): $135 (in-district), $170 (in-state), $311 (out-of-state)**
- **Room & Board: $736; Fees: $50**
- **Degree offered: AA**

A public junior college with a separate adult evening program.
Academic Character SACS accreditation. Semester system. Transfer programs offered for most bachelor degree programs. Terminal majors offered in career pilot technology, secretarial training, data processing, auto mechanics, licensed vocational nursing, agriculture, air conditioning & refrigeration, diesel mechanics, law enforcement.
Admissions High school graduation with 15 units required. Students admitted in September and January.
Student Life Dormitories for men and women.

[1] SOUTHWEST TEXAS STATE UNIVERSITY

San Marcos 78666, (512) 245-2364
Director of Admissions: Debra Evans

- **Undergraduates: 6,706m, 7,092w; 15,288 total (including graduates)**
- **Tuition (1982/83): $120 (in-state), $600 (out-of-state)**
- **Room & Board: $1,926; Fees: $324**
- **Degrees offered: BA, BS, BAAS, BMus, BSin 13 areas, BBA, BFA, BSW, BAIS, BMus Ed, AA, AS, AAS**
- **Student-faculty ratio: 26 to 1**

A public university established in 1899. 180-acre small-city campus, 50 miles from San Antonio. Served by rail and bus; limited air service.
Academic Character SACS and professional accreditation. Semester system, 2 summer terms. 50 majors offered by the schools of Applied Arts, Business, Creative Arts, Education, Health Professions, Liberal Arts, and Science. Minors in all major fields. Distributive requirements. Graduate degrees granted. Independent study. Honors program. Internships. Preprofessional programs in allied health, dentistry, engineering, law, medicine, nursing, pharmacy, veterinary medicine. Study abroad. Elementary, secondary, and special education certification. AFROTC. 717,085-volume library.
Financial ACT FAS. University scholarships, grants, loans, state loans; PELL, SEOG, NDSL, FISL, CWS, university work program. Application deadlines March 15 (scholarships), May 1 (loans).
Admissions High school graduation required. Audition and exams required for music students. ACT or SAT required. Rolling admissions. $50 room deposit due on acceptance of admissions offer. *Early Admission* and *Concurrent Enrollment* programs. Admission deferral possible. Transfers accepted. Credit possible for CEEB CLEP and university proficiency exams.
Student Life Student government. Newspaper, yearbook. Music and drama groups. Honorary and religious groups. 13 fraternities and 9 sororities, 12 with houses. 7% of men and 8% of women join. Single students with less than 60 credit hours live at home or on campus. Coed and single-sex dorms. Special interest housing, co-op dorms. Married-student housing. 32% of students live on campus. Gambling and hazing prohibited. Class attendance required. 4 semesters of phys ed required. 8 intercollegiate sports for men, 5 for women; many intramurals. AIAW, NCAA, LSAC. Student body composition: 0.2% Asian, 3.9% Black, 10.1% Hispanic, 0.3% Native American, 82.1% White, 3.4% Other. 3% from out of state.

[1] SOUTHWESTERN ADVENTIST COLLEGE

Keene 76059, (817) 645-3921
Director of Admissions & Records: Dallas Kindopp

- **Undergraduates: 351m, 393w**
- **Tuition (1982/83): $4,448**
- **Room & Board: $2,260; Fees: $31**
- **Degrees offered: BA, BS, BBA, BMus, AS**
- **Student-faculty ratio: 12 to 1**

A private college controlled by the Seventh-day Adventist Church, established in 1894. 140-acre suburban campus, 25 miles from Fort Worth. Served by rail and bus.
Academic Character SACS and professional accreditation. Semester system, 2 4-week summer terms. 30 majors offered in the areas of business, dietetics, education, home economics, humanities, industrial technology, mathematics, medical technology, music, nursing, physical education, religion, and social sciences. Minors in most major fields and in 9 other areas. Distributives and 12 credits in theology required. Independent study. Several preprofessional programs. Study abroad. Elementary and secondary education certification. 80,000-volume library.
Financial CEEB CSS. College scholarships, grants, loans, state grants; PELL, SEOG, NSS, NDSL, FISL, GSL, CWS. Application deadline August 1.
Admissions High school graduation with 16 units required. ACT required. Rolling admissions; suggest applying between April and July. $30 room deposit due on acceptance of admissions offer. *Early Admission* Program. Transfers accepted. Credit possible for CEEB CLEP exams, college has own advanced placement program.
Student Life Student government. Newspaper, yearbook. Music groups. Academic, religious, and social groups. Students live at home or on campus. Single-sex dorms. Married-student housing. 53% of students live on campus. Liquor, tobacco, drugs, dancing, card playing, vulgarity prohibited. Attendance in class and at weekly chapel required. 4 credits of phys ed required. Student body composition: 3% Asian, 8% Black, 13% Hispanic, 1% Native American, 71% White, 4% Other. 46% from out of state.

[1] SOUTHWESTERN BAPTIST THEOLOGICAL SEMINARY

Fort Worth 76122

TX-111

[J1] SOUTHWESTERN CHRISTIAN COLLEGE

PO Box 10, Terrell 75160, (214) 563-3341

- **Undergraduates: 135m, 121w**
- **Tuition, Room & Board (1980/81): $2,020**
- **Degrees offered: AA, AS**

A private junior college afiliated with the Church of Christ.
Academic Character SACS accreditation. Semester system. Liberal arts and preprofessional curricula offered. Terminal program in business education.
Admissions High school graduates admitted.
Student Life Dormitories for men and women. Intercollegiate and intramural basketball and baseball.

[J1 & 2] SOUTHWESTERN ASSEMBLIES OF GOD COLLEGE

Waxahachie 75165, (214) 937-4010
Director of Admissions: Phil E. Shirley

- **Undergraduates: 282m, 253w**
- **Tuition (1982/83): $1,600**
- **Room & Board: $1,890; Fees: $76**
- **Degrees offered: BA, BS, BSac Mus, AA**
- **Student-faculty ratio: 40 to 1**

A private college controlled by the Assemblies of God, established in 1931, became coed in 1944. 70-acre small-city campus near Dallas. Airport, rail and bus stations in Dallas.
Academic Character AABC accreditation and SACS accreditation for junior college. Semester system, 2 6-week summer terms. Majors offered in Christian education, education/psychology, missions, pastoral ministry/evangelism, and sacred music. One course in religion required each semester. Courses offered in 11 additional areas. Independent study. Internships. 80,645-volume library.
Financial College scholarships, grants, loans, church and state grants, payment plan; PELL, SEOG, NDSL, FISL, CWS.
Admissions High school graduation required. ACT required. $25 application fee. Rolling admissions; suggest applying early in 12th year. $20 room deposit due on acceptance of admissions offer. Admission deferral possible. Transfers accepted. Credit possible for CEEB CLEP exams.
Student Life Newspaper, yearbook. Music groups. Academic, honorary, and religious groups. Single students under 25 live at home or on campus. Coed and single-sex dorms. Married-student housing. 95% of students live on campus. Dress code. Class attendance expected. Church attendance required. 2 hours of phys ed required. 5 intercollegiate sports; intramurals. 53% of students from out of state.

[P] SOUTHWESTERN PARALEGAL INSTITUTE

5512 Chaucer Drive, Houston 77005

[1] SOUTHWESTERN UNIVERSITY

Georgetown 78626, (512) 863-6511
Vice President for Admissions & Student Development: William D. Swift

- **Undergraduates: 418m, 497w**
- **Tuition (1982/83): $4,050**
- **Room & Board: $2,355-$2,445**
- **Degrees offered: BA, BS, BApp Sci, BBA, BSEd, BFA, BMus, BSSoc Sci**
- **Student-faculty ratio: 15 to 1**

A private university controlled by the United Methodist Church, established in 1840. 500-acre small-town campus, 26 miles from Austin. Served by air, rail, and bus.
Academic Character SACS and professional accreditation. Semester system, 3-, 6-, and 8-week summer terms. 39 majors offered by the College of Arts & Sciences and the School of Fine Arts. Self-designed majors. Minors offered in some major fields and in 2 other areas. Distributives and one course in religion required. Seniors take comprehensive exams and GRE. Independent study. Honors program. Limited pass/fail, internships. Preprofessional programs in dentistry, law, medicine, theology. Study abroad. Early childhood, elementary, secondary, and special education certification. 132,000-volume library.
Financial CEEB CSS. University scholarships, grants, loans, state grants and loans, PELL, SEOG, GSL, university work program.
Admissions High school graduation with 16 units required. Audition required for fine arts majors. SAT or ACT required. $10 application fee ($125 after May 1, refundable if admission refused). Rolling admissions; suggest applying in fall. $125 deposit due on acceptance of admissions offer. *Early Admission* Program. Transfers accepted. Credit possible for CEEB AP and CLEP exams.
Student Life Student government. Newspaper, magazine, yearbook. Music and drama groups. Black Organization for Social Survival. Society for Hispanic-Oriented Students. Circle K. Academic, honorary, political, professional, religious, and special interest groups. 4 fraternities with houses; 5 sororities without houses. 40% of men and 45% of women join. Freshmen live at home or on campus. Dorms for men and women. No married-student housing. 75% of students live on campus. Hazing and gambling prohibited. 4 activity courses required. 4 intercollegiate sports for men, 3 for women; intramurals. AIAW, BSAC. Student body composition: 0.5% Asian, 2.5% Black, 3% Hispanic, 0.5% Native American, 93.4% White, 0.1% Other. 8% from out of state.

[1] STEPHEN F. AUSTIN STATE UNIVERSITY

Nacogdoches 75962, (713) 569-2504
Director of Admissions: Clyde Iglinsky

- **Enrollment: 4,600m, 5,200w**
- **Tuition (1982/83): $120 (in-state), $1,200 (out-of-state)**
- **Room & Board: $1,956-$2,198; Fees: $300**
- **Degrees offered: BA, BS, BAAS, BBA, BFA, BMus, BSA, BSEd, BSFor, BSHE, BSN, BSRehab, BSW**
- **Student-faculty ratio: 24 to 1**

A public university established in 1923. 400-acre rural campus, 140 miles from Houston. Served by air and bus.

Academic Character SACS and professional accreditation. Semester system, 2 6-week summer terms. 3 majors offered by the School of Applied Arts & Sciences, 9 by the School of Business, 6 by the School of Education, 4 by the School of Fine Arts, 5 by the School of Forestry, 8 by the School of Liberal Arts, and 6 by the School of Science & Mathematics. Self-designed majors. Minor required. Distributive requirements. Graduate degrees granted. Independent study. Honors program. Cooperative work/study, internships. Preprofessional programs in architecture, dentistry, engineering, hospital administration, medical fields, nursing, pharmacy, physical therapy. Elementary and secondary education certification. ROTC. Computer center. Language lab. 2 farms. Experimental forest. 350,000-volume library with microform resources.

Financial CEEB CSS and ACT FAS. University scholarships, grants, loans, PELL, SEOG, NDSL, CWS. Application deadline April 1.

Admissions High school graduation required. SAT or ACT required. Rolling admissions. $50 room deposit required on acceptance of admissions offer. *Early Admission* and *Concurrent Enrollment* programs. Transfers accepted. Credit possible for CEEB AP, CLEP, and ACT PEP exams; university has own advanced placement program.

Student Life Student government. Newspaper, yearbook, radio and TV stations. Music and drama groups. Ethnic, honorary, professional, religious, service, and special interest groups. 12 fraternities with houses, 6 sororities without houses. 6% of students join. Students under 21 live at home or on campus. Coed and single-sex dorms. Co-op dorms. Married-student housing. 45% of students live on campus. Gambling prohibited. Class attendance expected. 4 hours of phys ed required. 9 intercollegiate sports for men, 7 for women; many intramurals. AIAW, NAIA, LSC. Student body composition: 3% Black, 1% Hispanic, 96% White. 2% from out of state.

[1] SUL ROSS STATE UNIVERSITY

Alphine 79830, (915) 837-8011
Registrar & Director of Admissions: Dorothy M. Leavitt

- **Undergraduates: 691m, 527w; 2,048 total (including graduates)**
- **Tuition & Fees (1982/83): $332 (in-state), $742 (out-of-state)**
- **Room & Board: $1,225**
- **Degrees offered: BA, BS, BBA, BFA, BMus**
- **Student-faculty ratio: 16 to 1**

A public university established in 1917. 600-acre rural campus in small town, 140 miles from Odessa. Served by rail and bus.

Academic Character SACS accreditation. Semester system, 2 5-week summer terms. 26 majors offered by the divisions of Business Administration, Fine Arts, Liberal Arts, Range Animal Science, Science, and Teacher Education. Minor required in some fields; offered in most major areas and in 4 others. Distributive requirements. Masters degrees granted. Internships, credit by exam. Cooperative work/study at Fort Davis. Preprofessional programs in allied health, engineering, physical therapy, veterinary medicine, vocational agriculture. Cooperative programs in forestry and range management with Stephen F. Austin; in vocational agriculture education with Texas Tech. Elementry, secondary, and special education certification. Museum. 203,638-volume library with microform resources.

Financial ACT FAS. University scholarships, grants, loans, state grants, payment plan; PELL, SEOG, FISL, NDSL, CWS, university work program. Application deadline June 1.

Admissions High school graduation required. GED accepted. SAT or ACT required. Rolling admissions; suggest applying by June. $25 room deposit due on acceptance of admissions offer. *Early Admission* and *Concurrent Enrollment* programs. Transfers accepted. Credit possible for CEEB SAT, CLEP, and ACT exams; university has own advanced placement program. Conditional admission possible.

Student Life Student government. Newspaper, literary magazine, yearbook. Music and drama groups. Debate. Circle K. Athletic, academic, honorary, recreational, religious, service, and special interest groups. 2 fraternities with houses. Students under 20 must live on campus or at home. Single-sex dorms. Co-op dorms. Married-student housing. 46% of students live on campus. Attendance in class required. 2 semesters of phys ed required. 6 intercollegiate sports for men, 5 for women; intramurals. NAIA, NIRA. Student body composition: 0.2% Asian, 3% Black, 32.4% Hispanic, 0.2% Native American, 61.7% White, 2.5% Other. 8% from out of state.

[1] TARLETON STATE UNIVERSITY

Stephenville 76402, (817) 336-7851
Director of Admissions: Conley Jenkins

- **Undergraduates: 1,477m, 1,092w; 3,700 total (including graduates)**
- **Tuition (1982/83): $441 (in-state), $1,521 (out-of-state)**
- **Room & Board: $1,958**
- **Degrees offered: BA, BS, BBA, BMus Ed, BSW, BAAS**
- **Mean SAT 850**
- **Student-faculty ratio: 11 to 1**

A public university established in 1899, part of the Texas A&M system. 120-acre small-town campus, 65 miles from Fort Worth. Served by rail and bus.

Academic Character SACS accreditation. Semester system, 2 6-week summer terms. 42 majors offered by the schools of Agriculture & Business, Arts & Sciences, and Education & Fine Arts. Minor recommended. Distributive requirements. MA, MS, MBA granted. Pass/fail. Preprofessional programs in dentistry, engineering, medicine, pharmacy, veterinary medicine. Concurrent enrollment at other colleges possible. Elementary and secondary education certification. ROTC. 700-acre farm. 150,000-volume library.

Financial CEEB CSS. University scholarships, grants, loans, state grants and loans, payment plan; PELL, SEOG, NDSL, FISL, CWS. Application deadline June 2.

Admissions High school graduation required. SAT or ACT required. Rolling admissions; application deadline August 15. $50 room deposit due on acceptance of admissions offer. *Early Decision, Early Admission, Concurrent Enrollment* programs. Transfers accepted. Credit possible for CEEB AP, CLEP, and university challenge exams. Advised admission possible for underprepared students.

Student Life Student government. Newspaper, yearbook. Music and drama groups. Academic, honorary, professional, religious, service, and special interest groups. Single freshmen live at home or on campus. 4 semesters of phys ed required. 7 intercollegiate sports; intramurals. Student body composition: 0.3% Asian, 1.4% Black, 1.1% Hispanic, 0.4% Native American, 96.5% White.

[J1] TARRANT COUNTY JUNIOR COLLEGE DISTRICT

1400 The Electric Service Building, Fort Worth 76102

[J1] TEMPLE JUNIOR COLLEGE

Temple 76501

[J1] TEXARKANA COMMUNITY COLLEGE

Texarkana 75501

[1] TEXAS, THE UNIVERSITY OF

Austin 78712, (512) 471-1711
Director of Admissions: Shirley Binder

- **Undergraduates: 20,301m, 17,810w; 48,145 total (including graduates)**
- **Tuition (1982/83): $120 (in-state), $1,200 (out-of-state)**
- **Room & Board: $2,190-$2,910; Fees: $332**
- **Degrees offered: BA, BS, BBA, BArch, BFA, BJour, BMus**
- **Mean SAT 1,080**
- **Student-faculty ratio: 23 to 1**

A public university established in 1881. 445-acre urban campus. Served by air, rail, and bus.

Academic Character SACS and professional accreditation. Semester system, 2 6-week summer terms. 14 majors offered by the College of Business Administration, 8 by the College of Communication, 7 by the College of Education, 10 by the College of Engineering, 13 by the College of Fine Arts, 33 by the College of Liberal Arts, and 22 by the College of Natural Sciences. 5-year programs in pharmacy and architecture. Distributive requirements. Graduate degrees granted. Honors program. Phi Beta Kappa. Cooperative work/study, pass/fail, credit by exam. Preprofessional programs in many areas. Elementary, secondary, and special education certification. ROTC, AFROTC, NROTC. Computer center. Marine science institute. Observatory. Museum. 4,500,000-volume library with microform resources.

Financial CEEB CSS and ACT FAS. University scholarships, grants, loans, state scholarships; PELL, SEOG, NDSL, GSL, NSL, CWS, assistantships. Application deadline March 1.

Admissions High school graduation with 16 units required. Audition required for music majors. SAT required; ACT accepted. Rolling admissions; application deadline June 1. Transfers accepted. Credit possible for CEEB AP, CLEP, and university exams. Provisional admission possible.

Student Life Student government. Newspaper, magazine, yearbook, radio-television guild. Music and drama groups. Many athletic, debate, academic, professional, religious, service, and special interest groups. 33 fraternities and 21 sororities, all with houses. Freshmen encouraged to live on campus. Coed and single-sex dorms. Co-op housing. Special interest houses. Married-student apartments. 12% of students live on campus. Gambling, drinking, immoral conduct, dishonesty, hazing prohibited. 9 intercollegiate sports; intramurals. AIAW, SC. Student body composition: 1.4% Asian, 2.5% Black, 7.8% Hispanic, 0.2% Native American, 83.3% White, 4.8% Other. 14% from out of state.

■[1] TEXAS, UNIVERSITY OF, AT ARLINGTON

Arlington 76019, (817) 273-3401
Director of Admissions: R. Zack Prince

- **Undergraduates: 6,872m, 4,985w; 20,953 total (including graduates)**
- **Tuition (1982/83): $466 (in-state), $1,546 (out-of-state)**
- **Room & Board: $2,026-$2,312**
- **Degrees offered: BA, BS, BFA, BBA, BMus**
- **Student-faculty ratio: 24 to 1**

A public university established in 1959. 339-acre urban campus, 15 miles from Dallas. Served by air and bus.

Academic Character SACS and professional accreditation. Semester system, 2 5-week summer terms. 8 majors offered by the College of Business Administration, 6 by the College of Engineering, 18 by the College of Liberal Arts, 9 by the College of Science, 5 by the College of Architecture & Environmental Design, 1 by the School of Nursing, and 1 by the Institute of Urban Studies. Distributive requirements. Graduate degrees granted. Honors program. Cooperative work/study, pass/fail. Preprofessional programs in dentistry, law, medicine. Elementary, secondary, and special education

certification. ROTC; AFROTC at Texas Christian. Art gallery. 750,000-volume library with microform resources.
Financial CEEB CSS. University scholarships, grants, loans, payment plan; PELL, SEOG, NSS, NDSL, FISL, CWS. Scholarship application deadline March 15.
Admissions High school graduation with 15 units required. SAT required; ACT accepted. Rolling admissions. *Early Admission* and *Concurrent Enrollment* programs. Transfers accepted. Credit possible for CEEB AP, CLEP, and university proficiency exams. Conditional admission possible.
Student Life Student government. Newspaper, literary magazine, yearbook. Music and drama groups. Academic, honorary, political, service, and special interest groups. 15 fraternities with houses; 9 sororities. 5% of men and 6% of women join. Single freshmen and sophomores live at home or on campus. Coed and single-sex dorms. Limited married-student housing. 7% of students live on campus. Liquor prohibited. 4 semesters of phys ed required of students under 21. 12 intercollegiate sports for men, 8 for women; intramurals. AIAW, NAIA, NCAA, SC. Student body composition: 3.7% Asian, 6.8% Black, 6% Foreign, 3.5% Hispanic, 0.5% Native American, 79.5% White. 5% from out of state.

■[1] TEXAS, UNIVERSITY OF, AT DALLAS
PO Box 688, Richardson 75080

■[1] TEXAS, UNIVERSITY OF, AT EL PASO
El Paso 79968, (915) 747-5550
Director of Admissions: William P. Nelsen

- **Enrollment: 7,881m, 7,555w**
- **Tuition (1982/83): $396 (in-state), $1,476 (out-of-state)**
- **Room & Board: $2,005-$3,009**
- **Degrees offered: BA, BS, BBA, BFA, BMus, BSEd, BSN, BSW, BSCS, BSMT, BSEngs**
- **Student-faculty ratio: 22 to 1**

A public university established in 1913. Urban campus. Served by air, rail, and bus.
Academic Character SACS and professional accreditation. Semester system, 2 6-week summer terms. 9 majors offered by the College of Business Administration, 3 by the College of Education, 6 by the School of Engineering, 20 by the School of Liberal Arts, 3 by the College of Nursing & Allied Health, and 6 by the School of Science. Distributive requirements. Graduate degrees granted. Preprofessional programs in law and medicine. Cooperative engineering, math, physics programs with White Sands. Elementary and secondary education certification. ROTC, AFROTC at New Mexico State. Computer center. Ethnic Study Center. Museum. Seismic Observatory. Radio stations. Border Studies Institute. 618,489-volume library.
Financial CEEB CSS. University scholarships, grants, loans, state grants and loans; PELL, SEOG, NSS, NDSL. Priority application deadline for scholarships March 1.
Admissions High school graduation with 11-12 units required. SAT required; ACT accepted. Rolling admissions; suggest applying before August 1. $60 room deposit due on acceptance of admissions offer. *Concurrent Enrollment* Program. Transfers accepted. Credit possible for CEEB AP exams. Provisional admission possible.
Student Life Newspaper, literary magazine, radio station. Music and drama groups. Debate. Cultural, ethnic, honorary, political, professional, religious, service, and special interest groups. 8 social clubs, 3 with houses. Coed and single-sex dorms. Married-student apartments. 5% of students live on campus. Liquor permitted only in dorm rooms. 6 intercollegiate sports for men, 6 for women; many intramurals. NCAA. Student body composition: 0.7% Asian, 1.7% Black, 43% Hispanic, 0.3% Native American, 45.5% White, 8.8% Other. 14% from out of state.

■[1 & G1] TEXAS, UNIVERSITY OF, AT SAN ANTONIO
San Antonio 78285

■[1] TEXAS, UNIVERSITY OF, AT TYLER
PO Box 9030, Tyler 75701

■[1 & G1] TEXAS, UNIVERSITY OF, HEALTH SCIENCE CENTER AT DALLAS
Dallas 75235

■[1] TEXAS, UNIVERSITY OF, HEALTH SCIENCE CENTER AT HOUSTON—DENTAL BRANCH
Houston 77025

■[1 & G1] TEXAS, UNIVERSITY OF, HEALTH SCIENCE CENTER AT SAN ANTONIO
7703 Floyd Curl Drive, San Antonio 78284

■[1] TEXAS, UNIVERSITY OF, MEDICAL BRANCH
Galveston 77550

■[1] TEXAS, UNIVERSITY OF, OF THE PERMIAN BASIN
Odessa 79762, (915) 367-2011
Director, Admissions & Registrar: Robert T. Warmann

- **Enrollment: 1,610 men & women (including graduates)**
- **Tuition (1980/81): $4 per credit hour (in-state), $40 per credit hour (out-of-state)**
- **Room & Board: $2,100**
- **Degrees offered: BA, BS, BBA**

A public upper-level and graduate university established in 1969. 600-acre small-city campus between Fort Worth and El Paso.
Academic Character SACS accreditation. Semester system, 2 6-week summer terms. 2-year upper level majors offered in anthropology, art, business, chemistry, computer science, criminal justice, earth sciences, economics, engineering, history, humanities, life sciences, literature, mass communications, management, mathematics, physical education, psychology, sociology, speech, and Spanish. Distributives and GRE required. MA, MS, MBA granted. Self-paced study. Contract study. Experiential learning. Audio-cassette learning. Preprofessional programs in dentistry, health sciences, law. Computer facilities. 416,000-volume library with microform resources.
Financial ACT FAS. University scholarships, state grants; PELL, SEOG, GSL, CWS.
Admissions 60 hours of college work required. Rolling admissions. *Concurrent Enrollment* program. Credit possible for CEEB CLEP exams.
Student Life Student government. Literary magazine, yearbook. Special interest groups. Limited number of modular home units available. Married-student housing. Intramural sports. Student body composition: 12% minority.

■[1] TEXAS, UNIVERSITY OF, AT AUSTIN, SCHOOL OF NURSING
1700 Red River, Austin 78701

[1] TEXAS A&I UNIVERSITY
Kingsville 78363, (512) 595-2111
Registrar: Gustavo O. De Leon

- **Undergraduates: 2,078m, 1,595w; 5,355 total (including graduates)**
- **Tuition (1982/83): $120 (in-state), $1,200 (out-of-state)**
- **Room & Board: $1,394; Fees: $128**
- **Degrees offered: BA, BS, BBA, BFA, BMus, BSAg, BSHome Ec, BSEd**
- **Mean ACT 15**
- **Student-faculty ratio: 20 to 1**

A public university established in 1925. 1,574-acre small-city campus, 40 miles from Corpus Christi. Served by rail and bus.
Academic Character SACS and professional accreditation. Semester system, 2 5-week summer terms. 5 majors offered by the College of Agriculture, 20 by the College of Arts & Sciences, 13 by the College of Business Administration, 5 by the College of Engineering, and 5 by the College of Teacher Education. Bilingual degree program. Minors offered. Distributives and GRE required. Graduate degrees granted. Preprofessional programs in dentistry, law, medical technology, medicine, pharmacy, veterinary medicine. Elementary and secondary education certification. ROTC. Computer center. Herbarium. Museum. Language lab. 420,279-volume library.
Financial University scholarships, grants, loans; PELL, SEOG, NDSL, FISL, CWS. Application deadline May 15.
Admissions High school graduation with 16 units required. GED accepted. ACT required; SAT accepted. Rolling admissions. Admission deferral possible. Transfers accepted. Credit possible for CEEB AP and CLEP exams.
Student Life Student government. Newspaper, magazine, yearbook. Afro-American Society. Chicano groups. Academic, ethnic, honorary, political, religious, and service groups. 21 fraternities, 2 with houses, and 8 sororities with rooms. 7% of men and 5% of women join. Students under 21 with less than 60 hours live on campus. Coed and single-sex dorms. Married-student apartments. 29% of students live on campus. 4 semesters of phys ed required. Intramural and recreational sports. Student body composition: 1.4% Asian, 5% Black, 50% Hispanic, 0.1% Native American, 34% White, 9.5% Other. 1.5% from out of state.

[1] TEXAS A&M UNIVERSITY
College Station 77843, (713) 845-1031
Director of Admissions: Billy G. Lay

- **Undergraduates: 16,939m, 10,277w; 35,146 total (including graduates)**
- **Tuition (1982/83): $120 (in-state), $1,200 (out-of-state)**
- **Room & Board: $2,990; Fees: $360**
- **Degrees offered: BA, BS, BBA, BEnv Des**
- **Mean SAT 486v, 517m**
- **Student-faculty ratio: 25 to 1**

A public university established in 1876. 5,200-acre small-city campus, 100 miles north of Houston. Served by air and bus.
Academic Character SACS and professional accreditation. Semester system, 2 5½-week summer terms. 20 majors offered by the College of Agriculture, 3 by the College of Architecture & Environmental Design, 4 by the College of Business Administration, 6 by the College of Education, 17 by the College of Engineering, 4 by the College of Geosciences, 11 by the College of Liberal Arts, 1 by College of Medicine, 8 by the College of Science, 2 by the College of Veterinary Medicine, and 7 by the Galveston marine division. GRE required. Honors program. Cooperative work/study, limited pass/fail, internships. Elementary and secondary education certification. RTOC, AFROTC, NROTC. Language Lab. 1,300,000-volume library with microform resources.
Financial CEEB CSS. University scholarships, grants, loans, state grants and loans; PELL, SEOG, NDSL, GSL, CWS. Application deadline April 1.
Admissions High school graduation with 16 units required. SAT and 2 ACH required. Rolling admissions; suggest applying after September 12. *Early Decision* and *Early Admission* programs. Transfers accepted. Credit possible for CEEB AP and university placement exams.
Student Life Student government. Newspaper, literary magazine, yearbook. Music groups. Discussion and Debate Club. Numerous academic, honorary, technical, and special interest groups. Limited housing; students may apply 10 months in advance. Single-sex dorms. Married-student apartments. 33% of students live on campus. Hazing prohibited. 2 years of phys ed required. 10 intercollegiate sports for men, 10 for women; many intramurals. AIAW, NCAA,

SC. Student body composition: 1% Asian, 1% Black, 3% Hispanic, 1% Native American, 94% White. 9% from out of state.

■[1] TEXAS A&M UNIVERSITY AT GALVESTON

PO Box 1675, Galveston 77553, (713) 766-3200

- **Undergraduates: 392m, 112w; 580 total (including part-time)**
- **Estimated Fees & Expenses (1982/83): $4,400 (in-state), $5,400 (out-of-state)**
- **Degree offered: BS**

A public university. Urban campus in Galveston.

Academic Character SACS and professional accreditation. Semester system. Majors offered in marine sciences, marine biology, marine fisheries, maritime administration, maritime systems engineering, marine transportation, and marine engineering. 3 10-week summer training cruises required for merchant marine officer qualification. Summer School at Sea Program.

Financial Financial aid available through Texas A&M. U.S. Maritime Service cadets may qualify for federal subsidy.

Admissions High school graduation with 16 units required. Applicants must be accepted by Texas A&M. SAT and math ACH required. *Early Decision* and *Early Admission* programs. Advanced placement possible.

[P] TEXAS CHIROPRACTIC COLLEGE

5912 Spencer Highway, Pasadena 77505

[1] TEXAS CHRISTIAN UNIVERSITY

2800 University Drive, Fort Worth 76129, (817) 921-7490
Dean of Admissions: Edward G. Boehm, Jr.

- **Undergraduates: 2,423m, 3,213w; 6,558 total (including graduates)**
- **Tuition (1982/83): $4,000**
- **Room & Board: $1,740; Fees: $390**
- **Degrees offered: BA, BS, BBA, BFA, BGS, BMus, BMus Ed, BSEd, BSN**
- **Mean ACT 22; mean SAT 1010**
- **Student-faculty ratio: 15 to 1**

A private university controlled by the Disciples of Christ, established in 1873. 243-acre suburban campus. Served by air, rail, and bus.

Academic Character SACS and professional accreditation. Semester system, 3-week and 2 5-week summer terms. 72 majors offered by the College of Arts & Sciences, the School of Business, the School of Education, the School of Fine Arts, and the College of Nursing. Self-designed and special majors. Minors offered in most major fields and in 3 other areas. Distributives and one religion course required. Graduate degrees granted. Independent study. Honors program. Phi Beta Kappa. Pass/fail, internships. 3-2 engineering program with Washington U. 3-1 medical technology program. 9-month range management program. Washington Semester. Study abroad. Elementary, secondary, and special education certification. ROTC, AFROTC. Computer center. Observatory. Radio and TV studios. 1,000,000-volume library with microform resources.

Financial CEEB CSS. University scholarships, grants, loans, tuition discounts for dependents of ministers and missionaries of the Christian Church, ministerial student grants, state grants and loans, payment plan; PELL, SEOG, NDSL, GSL, CWS. Application deadline June 1.

Admissions High school graduation with 13 units recommended. GED accepted. Interview recommended. Audition required of music majors. SAT or ACT required. $15 application fee. Rolling admissions. $100 room deposit due on acceptance of offer of admission. *Early Admission* Program. Admission deferral possible. Transfers accepted. Credit possible for CEEB AP and CLEP exams; university has own advanced placement program.

Student Life Student government. Newspaper, literary magazine, radio and TV studios. Music and drama groups. Debate. International Student Association. Academic, honorary, political, professional, religious, service, and special interest groups. 10 fraternities and 12 sororities without houses. 30% of men and 38% of women join. Freshmen and sophomores live at home or at school. Single-sex dorms. Special interest housing. 66% of students live on campus. Liquor permitted in dorm rooms only. Gambling and hazing prohibited. Class attendance expected. 1 year of phys ed required. 11 intercollegiate sports for men, 8 for women; several intramurals. AIAW, NCAA, SAC. Student body composition: 5% Black, 92% White, 3% Other. 42% from out of state.

[1] TEXAS COLLEGE

2404 North Grand, Tyler 75701, (214) 593-8311

- **Undergraduates: 252m, 208w**
- **Tuition (1980/81): $800**
- **Room & Board: $384; Fees: $40**
- **Typical Expenses: $1,710**
- **Degrees offered: BA, BS**
- **Student-faculty ratio: 13 to 1**

A private liberal arts and teacher's college founded in 1894, controlled by the Christian Methodist Episcopal Church. Urban campus located southeast of Dallas.

Academic Character SACS accreditation. Semester system, 6-week summer term. Majors offered by the departments of education (including physical education, health, & recreation), home economics, humanities (including fine arts), natural science & mathematics, and social science (including business education). Special emphasis placed on the training of secondary and elementary teachers. Nursery school affords a laboratory for elementary education majors. 40,000-volume library.

Financial Scholarships, student loan fund, job opportunities.

Admissions High school graduation required. Freshmen take entrance exams, including psychological and English placement tests. Students admitted in September and January.

Student Life 4 fraternities and 3 sororities. 2 dorms for men, 3 for women. No married-student housing.

[P] TEXAS COLLEGE OF OSTEOPATHIC MEDICINE

3600 Mattison Avenue, Fort Worth 76107

[1] TEXAS LUTHERAN COLLEGE

Seguin 78155, (512) 379-4161
Director of Admissions: Robert Miller

- **Undergraduates: 480m, 505w**
- **Tuition (1982/83): $2,800**
- **Room & Board: $1,750-$1,945; Est. Fees:$300**
- **Degrees offered: BA, BS, BMus Ed**
- **Mean SAT 473v, 503m**
- **Student-faculty ratio: 15 to 1**

A private college controlled by the American Lutheran Church, established in 1891. 101-acre rural campus, 35 miles from San Antonio. Served by rail and bus; airport in San Antonio.

Academic Character SACS accreditation. 4-1-4 system, summer term. 27 majors offered in the areas of art, business, education, humanities, music, physical education, sciences, social sciences, and theology. Self-designed majors. Distributives and 7 hours of theology required. Independent study. Honors program. Graded pass/fail, internships. Preprofessional programs in dentistry, engineering, law, medicine, nursing, parish work, pharmacy, theology. 3-1 medical technology program. 2-3 pharmacy program with U Texas. 2-2 nursing and physical therapy programs. Washington Semester. Study abroad. Kindergarten, elementary, secondary, and special education certification. AFROTC at Southwest Texas. Mexican-American Studies Center. Language lab. 120,000-volume library.

Financial CEEB CSS. College scholarships, grants, loans, payment plans; PELL, SEOG, NDSL, FISL, CWS.

Admissions High school graduation with 16 units required. Admission by exam. ACT or SAT required. $10 application fee. Rolling admissions; suggest applying by January 1. $75 deposit due on acceptance of admissions offer. *Early Admission* Program. Transfers accepted. Credit possible for CEEB AP, CLEP, and ACH exams.

Student Life Student government. Newspaper, yearbook. Music and drama groups. Debate. Academic, ethnic, honorary, political, religious, service, and special interest groups. 3 fraternities and 3 sororities without houses. 17% of men and 23% of women join. Upperclassmen may live off campus. Coed and single-sex dorms. No married-student housing. 82% of students live on campus. 3 hours of phys ed required. 5 intercollegiate sports for men, 4 for women; intramurals. AIAW, NAIA, BSC. Student body composition: 4.5% Black, 9.5% Hispanic, 1% Native American, 84% White, 1% Other. 20% from out of state.

[1] TEXAS SOUTHERN UNIVERSITY

Houston 77004, (713) 527-7011
Director of Admissions: William A.T. Byrd

- **Enrollment: 3,481m, 2,872w**
- **Tuition (1982/83): $1,814 (in-state), $1,938 (out-of-state)**
- **Room & Board: $1,850**
- **Degrees offered: BA, BS**
- **Student-faculty ratio: 19 to 1**

A public university established in 1947. Urban campus. Served by air, rail, and bus.

Academic Character SACS and professional accreditation. Semester system, 2 5½-week summer terms. 46 majors offered by the College of Arts & Sciences, and the schools of Business, Communications, Education, Pharmacy, Public Affairs, and Technology. Minors offered. Distributive requirements. Graduate degrees granted. 2-year certificate programs in several areas. Honors program. Cooperative work/study, credit by exam. Cooperative engineering programs with Rice. Elementary and secondary education certification. ROTC at Rice and U Houston; AFROTC at Rice. Over 250,000-volume library.

Financial CEEB CSS. University scholarships, grants, loans, state grants and loans; PELL, SEOG, NDSL, GSL, CWS. Application deadline April 1.

Admissions High school graduation with 15 units required. SAT or ACT required. Rolling admissions; suggest applying by spring of 12th year. Deadline in August. $25 room deposit due on acceptance of admissions offer. Transfers accepted. University has own advanced placement program.

Student Life Student government. Newspaper, yearbook, radio station. Music, dance, and drama groups. SOUL. Honorary and professional groups. Several fraternities and sororities. Freshmen and sophomores live at home or on campus. Married-student housing. 2 hours of phys ed required. 7 intercollegiate sports; intramurals. NCAA. Student body composition: 0.6% Asian, 76.4% Black, 1.3% Hispanic, 0.9% White, 20.8% Other.

■[P] THURGOOD MARSHALL SCHOOL OF LAW

Houston 77004

[J1] TEXAS SOUTHMOST COLLEGE

Brownsville 78520

[J1] TEXAS STATE TECHNICAL INSTITUTE—WACO CAMPUS

Waco 76705, (817) 799-3611
Director of Admissions & Records: Albert Jones

- **Enrollment: 3,521m, 675w; 5,000 total (including part-time)**

- **Expenses (1982/83): $2,500**
- **Degrees offered: AS, AAS**

A public institute established in 1969. 2,200-acre urban campus.
Academic Character SACS accreditation. Trimester system, summer term. 2-year technical and semi-professional programs in aviation maintenance, automotive mechanics, commercial art & advertising, construction equipment maintenance, dental assistant, agricultural & industrial equipment mechanics, two-way radio servicing, TV servicing, environmental engineering technician, automotive merchandising specialist, combination welding, and air conditioning & refrigeration, automotive, biomedical equipment, building construction, chemical, civil engineering, computer science, dental lab, electrical power distribution, electronic, floriculture and ornamental horticulture, drafting & design, instrumentation, laser electro-optic, water & wastewater, and welding technologies. Pre-technical studies. Cooperative work/study, credit by exam.
Financial Institute scholarships, PELL, SEOG, NDSL, FISL, CWS.
Admissions High school graduation required. GED accepted. *Early Admission* and *Early Decision* programs.
Student Life Student government. Newspaper, yearbook. Special interest groups. Dormitories for men and women. Married-student housing. Intramural sports.

■[J1] TEXAS STATE TECHNICAL INSTITUTE—MID-CONTINENT CAMPUS
PO Box 11035, Amarillo 79111

■[J1] TEXAS STATE TECHNICAL INSTITUTE—RIO GRANDE CAMPUS
Harlingen 78550

■[J1] TEXAS STATE TECHNICAL INSTITUTE
Route 3, Sweetwater 79556

[1] TEXAS TECH UNIVERSITY
PO Box 4350, Lubbock 79409, (806) 742-1480

- **Undergraduates: 10,691m, 7,906w; 22,968 total (including graduates)**
- **Tuition (1982/83): $394 (in-state), $1,618 (out-of-state)**
- **Room & Board: $1,870-$2,275**
- **Degrees offered: BA, BS, BMus, BMus Ed, BFA, BBA, BArch, BGS, BSEd, BSInter Trade, BSMT, BSPEd, 11 BSEs**
- **Mean ACT 18.9; mean SAT 432v, 479m**
- **Student-faculty ratio: 18 to 1**

A public university established in 1923. 1,839-acre suburban campus, 323 miles from Dallas. Served by air and bus.
Academic Character SACS and professional accreditation. Semester system, 2 6-week summer terms. 15 majors offered by the College of Agricultural Sciences, 41 by the College of Arts & Sciences, 6 by the College of Business Administration, 3 by the College of Education, 11 by the College of Engineering, and 6 by the College of Home Economics. 5-year BArch program. Self-designed majors. Minor required; minors offered in most major fields and 8 other areas. Distributive requirements. Graduate degrees granted. Independent study. Honors program. Limited pass/fail, credit by exam. Preprofessional programs in health careers, law, ministry, veterinary science. Study abroad. Elementary, secondary, and special education certification. ROTC, AFROTC. Computer center. Language lab. Museum. Planetarium. Seismological observatory. Agricultural research center. 1,500,000-volume library with microform resources.
Financial CEEB CSS and ACT FAS. University scholarships, grants, loans, state grants and loans; PELL, SEOG, NDSL, FISL, CWS. Application deadline April 15.
Admissions High school graduation with 15 units required. SAT or ACT required. Rolling admissions; deadline August 15. $140 deposit due on acceptance of admissions offer. *Early Admission* Program. Transfers accepted. Credit possible for CEEB AP and CLEP exams. Provisional admission possible.
Student Life Student government. Newspaper, literary magazine, yearbook, radio and TV stations. Music and drama groups. Debate. Academic, honorary, professional, religious, service, and special interest groups. 13 fraternities and 15 sororities without houses. 10% of students join. Freshmen under 21 must live on campus. Dormitories for men and women. 32% of students live on campus. Class attendance required. 2 semesters of phys ed required. 8 intercollegiate sports for men, 6 for women; many intramurals. AIAW, NCAA, SAC. Student body composition: 1% Asian, 2% Black, 4% Hispanic, 91% White, 2% Other. 5% from out of state.

[1] TEXAS WESLEYAN COLLEGE
3101 East Rosedale, Fort Worth 76105, (817) 534-0251
Dean of Admissions: Larry L. Smith

- **Undergraduates: 424m, 532w; 1,540 total (including graduates)**
- **Tuition (1982/83): $3,000**
- **Room & Board: $2,140**
- **Degrees offered: BA, BS, BBA, BMus**
- **Mean ACT 18**
- **Student-faculty ratio: 12 to 1**

A private college affiliated with the United Methodist Church, established in 1891. 50-acre urban campus. Served by air, rail, and bus.
Academic Character SACS and professional accreditation. Semester system, 2 5-week summer terms. 32 majors offered by the schools of Business, Education, Fine Arts, and Science & Humanities. Self-designed majors. Minors offered in most major fields and in 4 other areas. German courses. Distributives and 6 hours of Bible required. Business majors take senior comprehensive exams; music majors take comp exams in sophomore and senior years. Honors program. Cooperative work/study, limited pass/fail, internships. Preprofessional programs in dentistry, law, medicine, ministry, college teaching. Study abroad. Elementary and secondary education certification; kindergarten, bilingual, and learning disability endorsement possible. Computer center. Television center. Language labs. 137,282-volume library.
Financial CEEB CSS and ACT FAS. College scholarships, grants, loans, ministerial scholarships, state grants and loans; PELL, SEOG, NDSL, FISL, CWS.
Admissions High school graduation with 16 units recommended. ACT or SAT required. $10 application fee. Rolling admissions. $50 deposit due with application for dorm room. *Early Decision, Early Admission, Concurrent Enrollment* programs. Transfers accepted. Credit possible for CEEB AP and CLEP exams.
Student Life Student government. Newspaper, literary magazine, yearbook. Music and drama groups. Academic, cultural, political, professional, service, and special interest groups. 3 fraternities and 3 sororities, some living facilities. 8% of students join. Coed and single-sex dorms. No married-student housing. 21% of students live on campus. Liquor prohibited in dorm rooms. Class attendance required. 4 hours of phys ed required. 4 intercollegiate sports for men, 4 for women; intramurals. NAIA. Student body composition: 11% Black, 4% Hispanic, 80% White, 5% Other. 3% from out of state.

[1] TEXAS WOMAN'S UNIVERSITY
Denton 76204, (817) 566-1451
Director of Admissions & Registrar: J.E. Tompkins, Jr.

- **Undergraduates: 120m, 3,330w; 7,498 total (including graduates)**
- **Tuition (1982/83): $120 (in-state), $1,200 (out-of-state)**
- **Room & Board: $3,406; Fees: $293**
- **Degrees offered: BA, BS, BFA, BSW**
- **Student-faculty ratio: 18 to 1**

A public university established in 1901. 270-acre urban campus, 35 miles from Dallas. Served by bus; airport in Dallas.
Academic Character SACS and professional accreditation. Semester system, 2 6-week summer terms. 8 majors offered by the College of Education, 4 by the College of Health, Physical Education, & Recreation, 21 by the College of Humanities & Fine Arts, 18 by the College of Natural & Social Sciences, 19 by the College of Nutrition, Textiles, & Human Development, 1 by the College of Nursing, 4 by the College of Health Care Services, and 1 each by the Colleges of Library Science, Occupational Therapy, and Physical Therapy. Major/minor required. Minors offered in all major fields and in 3 other areas. Graduate degrees granted. Honors program. Preprofessional programs in dentistry and medicine. Elementary and secondary education certification. ROTC; AFRTOC at North Texas. Language lab. 550,497-volume library.
Financial CEEB CSS and ACT FAS. University scholarships, grants, loans, state aid; PELL, SEOG, NSS, NDSL, FISL, GSL, CWS.
Admissions High school graduation with 15 units required. ACT or SAT required. Rolling admissions. $25 room deposit due on acceptance of admissions offer. *Early Decision, Early Admission, Concurrent Enrollment* programs. Admission deferral possible. Transfers accepted. Credit possible for CEEB AP exams; university has own advanced placement program.
Student Life Campus government. Newspaper, literary magazine, yearbook. Music and drama groups. Academic, honorary, literary, political, religious, and special interest groups. Students under 21 live at home or on campus. 35% of students live on campus. Class attendance required. 4 hours of phys ed required. 8 intercollegiate sports. AIAW, NCAA. Student body composition: 11.2% Black, 6.5% Hispanic, 0.2% Native American, 76.6% White, 5.5% Other. 10% from out of state.

[1] TRINITY UNIVERSITY
715 Stadium Drive, San Antonio 78284, (512) 736-7207
Director of Admissions: Russell Gossage

- **Undergraduates: 1,136m, 1,240w; 3,269 total (including graduates)**
- **Tuition (1982/83): $4,021**
- **Room & Board: $2,125**
- **Degrees offered: BA, BS, BABA, BSBA, BSEng Sci, BMus**
- **Mean SAT 540v, 560m**
- **Student-faculty ratio: 12 to 1**

A private university affiliated with the Presbyterian Church, established in 1869. 107-acre suburban campus, 4 miles north of downtown San Antonio. Served by air, rail, and bus.
Academic Character SACS and professional accreditation. Semester system, 2 5-week summer terms. 39 majors offered in the areas of art, business, education, engineering, environmental studies, foreign languages, physical education, media, music, science, social science, speech, and cultural studies. Self-designed majors. Courses in Sanskrit, Swedish. Distributive requirements. Masters degrees granted. Independent study. Honors program. Phi Beta Kappa. Pass/fail, internships, credit by exam. Preprofessional programs in dentistry, law, medical technology, medicine, ministry. Study abroad. Administration, counseling, teaching the deaf, elementary, and secondary education certification. ROTC. Communications center. Computer center. Theater. 536,000-volume library with microform resources.
Financial CEEB CSS. University scholarships, grants, loans, tuition exchange plan, discount for ministers' children, ministerial scholarships, payment plans; PELL, SEOG, NDSL, FISL, CWS. Scholarship application deadline February 1.
Admissions High school graduation with 16 units required. Interview recommended. SAT or ACT required. Rolling admissions. $400 deposit due on

acceptance of admissions offer. *Early Decision* Program. Admission deferral possible. Credit possible for CEEB AP and CLEP exams.
Student Life Student government. Newspaper, arts review, yearbook, radio station. Music, film, drama groups. Chicano Students Association. Community Service Program. Academic, political, religious, service, and special interest groups. 6 fraternities and 6 sororities without housing. 10% of men and 15% of women join. Single students live at home or on campus. Coed and single-sex dorms. No married-student housing. 58% of students live on campus. 2 semesters of phys ed required. 11 intercollegiate sports for men, 8 for women; many intramurals. AIAW, NCAA, TIAA. Student body composition: 1.5% Asian, 2.5% Black, 14.5% Hispanic, 80% White, 2% Other. 29% from out of state.

[J1] TYLER JUNIOR COLLEGE
PO Box 9020, Tyler 75711

[J1] VERNON REGIONAL JUNIOR COLLEGE
4400 College Drive, Vernon 76384, (817) 552-6291
Registrar: Roy L. Wiederanders

- **Enrollment: 201m, 371w; 1,500 total (including part-time)**
- **Tuition (1982/83): $180 (in-district), $200 (in-state), $1,200 (out-of-state)**
- **Room: $450**
- **Degrees offered: AA, AS, AFA**
- **Student-faculty ratio: 23 to 1**

A public college established in 1970. 11 branch campuses.
Academic Character SACS accreditation. Trimester system, 9-week summer term. 2-year transfer programs offered in art, agriculture, biology, business, chemistry, drama, education, English, engineering, foreign languages, history, mathematics, music, nursing, physical education, political science, psychology, sociology, and speech. Distributive requirements. Certificate programs. Preprofessional programs in dentistry, medical technology, medicine, pharmacy, veterinary medicine. Learning Resource Center.
Financial College scholarships, grants, state aid; PELL, SEOG, NDSL, GSL, CWS. Priority application deadline July 1.
Admissions High school graduation required. GED accepted. ACT required. Rolling admissions. $50 room deposit due on acceptance of admissions offer. Transfers accepted.
Student Life Student government. Drama Club. Circle K. Rodeo Association. Baptist Student Union. Honorary and special interest groups. Apartment-style housing. Cafeteria. 4 hours of phys ed required. Many intramural sports. Student body composition: 10% minority.

[J1] VICTORIA COLLEGE
Victoria 77901

[1] WAYLAND BAPTIST COLLEGE
Plainview 79072, (806) 296-5521
Director of Admissions: Dr. Dan McLallen

- **Undergraduates: 351m, 307w; 1,406 total (including part-time)**
- **Tuition (1982/83): $1,950**
- **Room & Board: $2,045-$2,297; Fees: $120**
- **Degrees offered: BA, BMus, BS, BSOE**
- **Mean ACT 19**
- **Student-faculty ratio: 17 to 1**

A private college controlled by the Baptist General Convention, established in 1908. 80-acre small-city campus, 45 miles from Lubbock. Served by bus.
Academic Character SACS accreditation. 4-1-4 system, 4 3-week summer terms. 34 majors offered in the areas of business, communications, education, law enforcement, liberal arts, music, physical education, religion, science, and social science. Major/minor required. Minors offered in all major fields and in 5 other areas. 2 religion courses and GRE required. Independent study. Honors program. Cooperative work/study. Preprofessional programs in engineering, law, medical technology, medicine, nursing, optometry, pharmacy, theology. Elementary and secondary education certification. Language lab. 75,000-volume library.
Financial CEEB CSS. College scholarships, grants, loans, ministerial scholarships, payment plan; PELL, SEOG, NDSL, CWS. Scholarship application deadline August 1.
Admissions High school graduation with 15 units required. ACT required. $15 application fee. Rolling admissions. $20 room deposit due on acceptance of admissions offer. *Early Admission* Program. Transfers accepted. Credit possible for CEEB AP exams. College has entrance exams for underprepared applicants.
Student Life Student government. Newspaper, literary magazine, yearbook, radio station. Music groups. Departmental, honorary, religious, and special interest groups. Students must have parental and school approval to live off campus. Married-student housing. 60% live on campus. Permission required to use cars on campus. Liquor, drugs, firearms, hazing prohibited. College must be informed of marriage intentions; written parental permission required. Attendance in class and at weekly chapel required. 4 hours of phys ed required. 5 intercollegiate sports for men, 5 for women; intramurals. NAIA. Student body composition: 0.6% Asian, 4.3% Black, 7% Hispanic, 0.9% Native American, 86.7% White. 32% from out of state.

[J1] WEATHERFORD COLLEGE
300 East Park Avenue, Weatherford 76086, (817) 594-5471
Dean of Student Personnel Services: Larry Hunt

- **Enrollment: 372m, 359w; 1,600 total (including part-time)**
- **Tuition (1982/83): $128 (in-state), $400 (out-of-state)**
- **Room & Board: $1,700-$1,800**
- **Degrees offered: AA, AAS**
- **Student-faculty ratio: 35 to 1**

A public college established in 1921. 90-acre suburban campus.
Academic Character SACS accreditation. Semester system, 2 6-week summer terms, 2 mini-semesters. 2-year programs offered in agriculture, art, arts & sciences, biology, business, chemistry, data processing, drama, engineering, farm management, law enforcement, mathematics, music, physical education, physics, teacher education, vocational nursing, and in vocational-technical areas. Distributive requirements. Preprofessional programs in dentistry, medicine, and veterinary medicine. 48,322-volume library with microform resources.
Financial College scholarships, state grants; PELL, SEOG, CWS.
Admissions Admission by high school graduation or GED required. Non-high school graduates may be admitted on an individual basis. ACT or SAT required for placement. Rolling admissions. $50 room deposit required with application. *Early Admission* Program. Credit possible for CEEB AP and CLEP exams.
Student Life Music groups. Art club. Academic, professional, religious, and special interest groups. Coed dorms. Liquor, drugs, hazing, gambling, firearms, immoral conduct forbidden. Class attendance required. 2 hours of phys ed required. 3 intercollegiate sports; intramurals.

[1] WEST TEXAS STATE UNIVERSITY
Canyon 79016, (806) 656-3331
Director of Admissions: Donald Cates

- **Undergraduates: 2,486m, 2,972w; 6,733 total (including graduates)**
- **Tuition (1982/83): $120 (in-state), $1,200 (out-of-state)**
- **Room & Board: $1,980; Fees: $330**
- **Degrees offered: BA, BS, BBA, BMus, BMus Ed, BAAS, BBEd, BFA, BGS, BSMT, BSN**
- **Student-faculty ratio: 19 to 1**

A public university established in 1909. 124-acre small-town campus, 17 miles from Amarillo. Served by rail and bus; airport in Amarillo.
Academic Character SACS and professional accreditation. Semester system, 2 5-week summer terms. 28 majors offered by the College of Arts & Sciences, 6 by the College of Education, 7 by the School of Agriculture, 8 by the School of Business, 11 by the School of Fine Arts, and 1 by the School of Nursing. Distributive requirements. Masters degrees granted. Independent study. Honors program. Credit by exam. Elementary, secondary, and special education certification. ROTC. Computer center. Farm. Museum. 700,000-volume library.
Financial ACT FAS. University scholarships, grants, loans; PELL, SEOG, NSS, GSL, NDSL, CWS.
Admissions High school graduation with 18 units recommended. ACT or SAT required. Rolling admissions. $40 room deposit due on acceptance of admissions offer. *Early Admission* and *Concurrent Enrollment* programs. Transfers accepted. Credit possible for CEEB AP, CLEP, and university challenge exams.
Student Life Student government. Newspaper, yearbook. Music and drama groups. Debate. El Chicano Club. Athletic, academic, honorary, religious, service, and special interest groups. 8 fraternities, 5 with houses; 6 sororities without houses. 8% of men and women join. Freshmen and sophomores under 21 must live at home or on campus. Single-sex dorms. No married-student housing. 32% of students live on campus. Liquor, gambling, hazing prohibited. 2 semesters of phys ed required. 6 intercollegiate sports for men, 6 for women. NCAA, MVC. Student body composition: 0.7% Asian, 3.6% Black, 5.5% Hispanic, 0.2% Native American, 89% White, 0.8% Other. 11% from out of state.

[J1] WESTERN TEXAS COLLEGE
Snyder 79549, (915) 573-8511

- **Enrollment: 481m, 592w**
- **Tuition (1982/83): $144 (in-state), $720 (out-of-state)**
- **Room & Board: $1,500**
- **Degrees offered: AA, AAS, AGE**
- **Mean ACT 17**
- **Student-faculty ratio: 19 to 1**

A public college established in 1971. Small-town campus, 84 miles southeast of Lubbock. Served by rail.
Academic Character SACS accreditation. Semester system, 6- and 9-week summer terms. 2-year programs offered in agriculture, art, archeology, anthropology, astronomy, biology, business, chemistry, drama, economics, engineering, English, French, geography, geology, German, government, physical education, history, home economics, humanities, mass communication, mathematics, music, philosophy, physics, psychology, religion, sociology, Spanish, speech, and in several vocational fields. Distributive requirements. Learning Resource Center.
Financial College scholarships, state grants; PELL, SEOG, GSL, CWS. Application deadline July 1.
Admissions High school graduation or GED required. Non-high school graduates may be admitted on an individual basis. ACT required. Rolling admissions. $50 room deposit due on acceptance of admissions offer. *Early Admission* and *Early Decision* programs. Transfers accepted. Credit possible for CEEB CLEP exams.
Student Life Student government. Newspaper, literary magazine, yearbook. Honorary, professional, religious, and special interest groups. Liquor, drugs, gambling prohibited. Dress code. Class attendance expected. 4 hours of phys ed required. 2 intercollegiate sports for men, 1 for women; intramurals. WJCAC. Student body composition: 17% minority.

[J1] WHARTON COUNTY JUNIOR COLLEGE
911 Boling Highway, Wharton 77488, (713) 532-4560
Director of Admissions: Ernen M. Haby

- **Enrollment: 707m, 726w; 2,009 total (including part-time)**
- **Tuition (1982/83): $4 per hour (in-state), $40 per hour (out-of-state)**
- **Room & Board: $1,380**
- **Degrees offered: AA, AAS**
- **Student-faculty ratio: 20 to 1**

A public college established in 1946. 90-acre small-town campus, 50 miles southwest of Houston.
Academic Character SACS accreditation. Semester system, 2 6-week summer terms. 2-year transfer, preprofessional, and terminal programs offered by the divisions of Agriculture, Industrial & Technical Occupations, Communications & Fine Arts, Health Occupations, Mathematics & Natural Science, Office Occupations, and Social Sciences & Physical Education. Distributive requirements. Learning Center. 51,478-volume library.
Financial ACT FAS. College scholarships, loans, state grants and loans; PELL, SEOG, NDSL, GSL, CWS.
Admissions High school graduation required. GED accepted. ACT or SAT required. Rolling admissions. $20 room deposit due on acceptance of admissions offer. *Early Admission* and *Early Decision* programs. Credit possible for CEEB AP exams.
Student Life Student government. Newspaper, magazine. Music and drama groups. Mexican-American Student Association. Baptist Student Union. Circle K. Academic, honorary, professional, religious, and special interest groups. Dormitory for men and women. Cafeteria. 2 hours of phys ed required. 7 intercollegiate sports. TJCAC, TJCFC, GCIC. Student body composition: 26% minority.

[1] WILEY COLLEGE
Marshall 75670, (214) 938-8341

- **Undergraduates: 261m, 326w**
- **Tuition (1980/81): $63 per semester hour**
- **Room & Board: $1,544; Fees:$280**
- **Degrees offered: BA, BS, BBA, AA**

A coed college related to the United Methodist Church, founded in 1873 by the Freedman's Aid Society. Campus in northeast Texas.
Academic Character SACS accreditation. Semester system. Majors offered leading to the Associate of Arts, Bachelor of Arts, Bachelor of Science, and Bachelor of Business Administration degrees. Remedial mathematics and English programs. 80,000-volume library.
Financial Financial aid available, including some scholarships.
Admissions *Early Admission* Program. Advanced placement program.
Student Life 4 fraternities and 4 sororities, plus 2 service fraternities and 2 service sororities. 1 dorm for men and 2 for women. Student body composition: 90% minority.

UTAH (UT)

[1] BRIGHAM YOUNG UNIVERSITY
Provo 84602, (801) 378-2507
Dean of Admissions and Records: Robert W. Spencer

- **Enrollment: 11,681m, 10,723w**
- **Tuition (1982/83): $1,220 (for Mormons); $1,830 (others)**
- **Room & Board: $1,934**
- **Degrees offered: BA, BS, BFA, BMus, BInd St**
- **Mean ACT 23 composite**
- **Student-faculty ratio: 24 to 1**

A private university controlled by the Church of Jesus Christ of Latter-Day Saints (Mormons), established in 1875. 500-acre campus in small city of Provo, 45 miles from Salt Lake City. Served by air, bus, and rail.
Academic Character NASC and professional accreditation. 4-4-2-2 system. 91 majors offered by the colleges of Biological & Agricultural Sciences, Business, Education, Engineering Sciences and Technology, Fine Arts & Communications, Humanities, Nursing, Physical & Mathematical Sciences, Physical Education, and Family, Home, & Social Sciences, and by the schools of Library & Information Sciences and Management. Distributives and 14 hours of religion (including 4 on Book of Mormon) required. Graduate degrees granted. Independent study. Honors program. Cooperative work/study. Preprofessional programs in architecture, biomedical engineering, chiropractic medicine, dental hygiene, dentistry, forestry, health administration, law, management, medicine, occupational therapy, optometry, pharmacy, physician's assistant, podiatry, public health, veterinary medicine. Home Study Program. Washington Semester. Study in New York City, Detroit. Study abroad. Elementary, secondary, special education and guidance certification. AFROTC, ROTC. Lab nursery school. Mineralogical museum. School farms. Language lab, computer center. 1,250,000-volume library with microform resources.
Financial CEEB CSS and ACT FAS. University scholarships, grants, church loans, athletic scholarships, PELL, GSL, FISL, deferred payment. Application deadline for scholarships April 30.
Admissions High school graduation required. GED accepted. Interview required. ACT required. $15 application fee. Rolling admissions; application deadline April 30. *Early Decision, Early Admission* programs. Transfers accepted. Credit possible for CEEB AP and CLEP exams.
Student Life Student government. Newspaper, magazine, yearbook, radio and TV stations. Music, dance, debate groups. Honorary, service, and special interest groups. Students must live on campus or in approved housing. No coed dorms. Special interest housing. Married-student housing. 24% of students live on campus. Dress code. Abstinence from liquor, coffee, tea, drugs, tobacco required. Class attendance required. 1 hour of physical fitness and 1 of phys ed required. Several intercollegiate and intramural sports for men and women. AIAW, NCAA, Western Athletic Conference. Student body composition: 0.5% Asian, 0.2% Hispanic, 1.4% Native American, 94.2% White, 3.7% Other. 75% from out of state.

[J1] DIXIE COLLEGE
225 South 700 East, St. George 84770

[J1] LATTER-DAY SAINTS BUSINESS COLLEGE
411 East South Temple Street, Salt Lake City 84111

[1] SOUTHERN UTAH STATE COLLEGE
351 West Center, Cedar City 84720, (801) 586-7700
Director of Admissions: Galen Rose

- **Undergraduates: 934m, 921w**
- **Tuition (1982/83): $735 (in-state); $1,971 (out-of-state)**
- **Room & Board: $1,635**
- **Degrees offered: BA, BS**
- **Mean ACT 19 composite**
- **Student-faculty ratio: 15 to 1**

A public college established in 1897. 105-acre rural campus located in Cedar City, 260 miles from Salt Lake City.
Academic Character NASC and professional accreditation. Trimester system, 2 4-week summer terms. Majors offered in accounting, art, biological science, botany, business administration, business education, chemistry, communication, communication/theatre arts, elementary education, English, family life, history, industrial arts, industrial technology, languages, mathematics, music, physical education, physical sciences, political science, psychology, sociology, theatre arts, and zoology. Distributive requirements. Honors program. Cooperative work/study. Preprofessional programs in agriculture, dentistry, engineering, forestry/range/wildlife sciences, law, medicine, pharmacy, veterinary science. Vocational and certificate programs. Off-campus study. Elementary and secondary education certification. Art gallery, TV studio. 1,000-acre farm, 3,700-acre ranch. 130,000-volume library.
Financial CEEB CSS and ACT FAS. College scholarships, PELL, SEOG, GSL, NDSL, CWS. Priority application deadline March 1.
Admissions High school graduation required. ACT recommended. $10 application fee. Rolling admissions. $50 room deposit (for boarders) required on acceptance of offer of admission. *Early Admission, Concurrent Enrollment* programs. Transfers accepted. Credit possible for CEEB AP and CLEP exams.
Student Life Student government. Newspaper, magazine, yearbook, radio station. Music, dance, debate groups. Shakespeare Festival. Political, cultural, academic, religious, and special interest organizations. Fraternities and sororities. Married-student housing. Liquor prohibited on campus. 3 hours of phys ed required. 6 intercollegiate sports for men, 5 for women; intramurals. AIAW, Rocky Mountain Conference. Student body composition: 0.3% Asian, 0.9% Black, 1.3% Hispanic, 2.8% Native American, 93% White.

[J2] STEVENS HENAGER COLLEGE
2644 Washington Blvd., Ogden 84401

[1] UTAH, UNIVERSITY OF
Salt Lake City 84112, (801) 581-7200
Director of Admissions: Robert Finley

- **Undergraduates: 8,635m, 5,909w; 23,373 total (including part-time)**
- **Tuition (1982/83): $960 (in-state); $2,727 (out-of-state)**
- **Room & Board: $2,684-$2,991**
- **Degrees offered: BA, BS, BFA, BMus, BUniversity Studies**
- **Mean ACT 20 composite**
- **Student-faculty ratio: 20 to 1**

A public university established in 1850. 1,500-acre urban campus in Salt Lake City. Served by air, rail, and bus.
Academic Character NASC and professional accreditation. Trimester system, 8-week summer term. 5 majors offered by the College of Business, 3 by the College of Education, 8 by the College of Engineering, 5 by the College of Fine Arts, 5 by the College of Health, Physical Education, & Recreation, 13 by the College of Humanities, 1 by the College of Nursing, 2 by the College of Pharmacy, 4 by the College of Science, 7 by the College of Social and Behavioral Sciences, 1 by the School of Architecture, and 8 by the State College of Mines and Mineral Institutes. Self-designed majors. Distributive requirements. Independent study. Honors program. Phi Beta Kappa. Pass/fail, internships. Preprofessional programs in dentistry, law, medicine. Exchange programs with 35 US universities. Study abroad. Elementary, secondary, and special education certification. AFROTC, NROTC, ROTC. Institute of Government. Genetics lab, environment research lab. 1,900,000-volume library with microform resources.

Financial CEEB CSS. University scholarships, grants, PELL, SEOG, NSS, NDSL, FISL, Education Funds, CWS. Scholarship application deadline February 1.
Admissions High school graduation required with 16 units recommended. Audition required for ballet majors. ACT required; SAT accepted out-of-state. $25 application fee. Rolling admissions. *Early Admission, Concurrent Enrollment* programs. Transfers accepted. Credit possible for CEEB AP and CLEP exams; university has own advanced placement program.
Student Life Student government. Newspaper, magazine, radio and TV stations. Music, debate, dance, drama groups. Academic, honorary, professional, religious, service, and special interest organizations. 11 fraternities and 10 sororities; all have houses. Married-student housing. 10% of students live on campus. Liquor prohibited on campus. 7 intercollegiate sports for men, 7 for women; intramurals. AIAW, Western Athletic Conference. Student body composition: 1.8% Asian, 0.5% Black, 1.7% Hispanic, 0.7% Native American, 92% White, 3% Other. 16% from out of state.

■[1] EASTERN UTAH, COLLEGE OF

Price 84501, (801) 637-2120
Director of Admissions: William Painter

- **Enrollment: 265m, 254w; 1,134 total (including part-time)**
- **Tuition (1982/83): $651 (in-state); $1,689 (out-of-state)**
- **Room & Board: $2,000 (estimate)**
- **Degrees offered: AA, AS, AAS**
- **Student-faculty ratio: 18 to 1**

A public college, part of the Utah State System of Higher Education, established in 1938. Small town campus.
Academic Character NASC accreditation. Trimester system, several summer terms. 2-year programs offered in the areas of art, business, computer science, ecology, education, engineering, geography, humanities, journalism, languages, library science, mathematics, music, physical education, science, social science, and theatre. Distributive requirements. Preprofessional programs in dentistry, engineering, forestry, management, medicine, medical technology, optometry, pharmacy, physical therapy, veterinary science. Certificates of Completion granted. Learning resources center offers remedial assistance to all students. Women's Resource Center. 25,000-volume library.
Financial CEEB CSS. College scholarships, state aid, PELL, NDSL, GSL, CWS.
Admissions Open admission to all students over the age of 18. ACT required. $5 application fee. Rolling admissions. *Early Admission* Program for students under 18 who have high school transcript and permission of high school principal. Transfers accepted.
Student Life Food service on campus. Dormitories and apartments for men and women; married-student housing.

[1] UTAH STATE UNIVERSITY OF AGRICULTURE AND APPLIED SCIENCE

Logan 84322, (801) 750-1000
Assistant Vice-President, Student Affairs: Bill Sampson

- **Undergraduates: 4,942m, 3,800w; 10,290 total (including graduates)**
- **Tuition (1982/83): $684 (in-state); $2,199 (out-of-state)**
- **Room & Board: $2,400-$2,600 (approx.); Fees: $156 (approx.)**
- **Degrees offered: BA, BS, BLA, BMus, BFA**
- **Student-faculty ratio: 20 to 1**

A public university established in 1888. 130-acre campus in small city of Logan, 80 miles from Salt Lake City. Served by air, bus, and rail.
Academic Character NASC accreditation. Trimester system. 9 majors offered by the College of Agriculture, 11 by the College of Business, 17 by the College of Education, 10 by the College of Engineering, 7 by the College of Family Life, 18 by the College of Humanities, Arts & Sciences, 14 by the College of Natural Resources, and 15 by the College of Science. Minor required. Distributive requirements. MA, EdD, PhD granted. Independent study. Honors program. Phi Beta Kappa. Pass/fail. Cooperative work/study, internships in some programs. Preprofessional programs in foreign service, dentistry, law, medicine. Study in Mexico, Europe, Hawaii. Elementary, secondary, and special education certification. AFROTC, ROTC. Agriculture and engineering experiment stations. Water Research Lab. Wildlife and Fishery Research Unit. Computer center. 1,000,000-volume library with microform resources.
Financial CEEB CSS. University scholarships and grants, state grants; PELL, SEOG, NDSL, FISL, deferred payment, CWS. Application deadlines March 15 (scholarships), August 1 (loans).
Admissions High school graduation required. ACT required. $15 application fee. Rolling admissions; suggest applying after 11th year. *Early Decision, Early Admission* programs. Transfers accepted. Credit possible for CEEB AP and CLEP exams. "Special Services" program.
Student Life Student government. Newspaper, magazine, yearbook, radio and TV stations. Music, debate, drama groups. Academic, professional, honorary, religious, and special interest organizations. 6 fraternities and 3 sororities; all have houses. 5% of men and 6% of women join. Freshmen women expected to live on campus. No coed dorms. Special interest housing. Married-student housing. 25% of students live on campus. Liquor prohibited on campus; smoking restricted. 7 intercollegiate sports for men, 5 for women; intramurals. AIAW, NCAA, PCAA. Student body composition: 0.7% Asian, 0.6% Black, 0.8% Hispanic, 0.4% Native American, 86.3% White, 11.2% Other. 29% from out of state.

■[J1] SNOW COLLEGE

Ephraim 84627, (801) 283-4021
Registrar: Ross P. Findlay

- **Undergraduates: 450m, 350w**
- **Tuition (1982/83): $435 (in-state); $1,305 (out-of-state)**
- **Fees: $65**
- **Degrees offered: AA, AS, AAS**
- **Mean ACT 16.7 composite**
- **Student-faculty ratio: 10 to 1**

A public 2-year college established in 1888. Campus located in small town of Ephraim, 110 miles south of Salt Lake City.
Academic Character NASC accreditation. Trimester system, 2 5-week summer terms. 1 major offered by the Division of Physical Education, 7 by the Division of Humanities & Arts, 13 by the Division of Natural Sciences, 12 by the Division of Social Sciences, Education, Business & Family, and 13 by the Division of Technical & Occupational Education. Distributive requirements. Independent study. Cooperative work/study. Study-travel tours. Diploma and certificate programs. 28,000-volume library.
Financial CEEB CSS and ACT FAS. College scholarships, state grants, PELL, SEOG, GSL, FISL, NDSL, CWS. Recommended application deadline February 15.
Admissions High school graduation required. GED accepted. ACT required. Rolling admissions. *Early Admission, Early Decision* programs. Transfers accepted. Admission deferral possible. Credit possible for CEEB AP and CLEP exams.
Student Life Student government. Newspaper, yearbook. Music, drama, speech organizations. Academic, social, and special interest groups. 70% of students live on campus. Liquor prohibited on campus. 3 terms of phys ed required. 7 intercollegiate sports.

[J1] UTAH TECHNICAL COLLEGE AT PROVO

1395 North 150 East, Box 1009, Provo 84601

[J1] UTAH TECHNICAL COLLEGE AT SALT LAKE

Salt Lake 84107

[1] WEBER STATE COLLEGE

Ogden 84408, (801) 626-6000
Director of Admissions: L. Winslow Hurst

- **Undergraduates: 4,214m, 3,704w; 10,107 total (including part-time)**
- **Tuition (1982/83): $762 (in-state); $2,055 (out-of-state)**
- **Room & Board: $1,950**
- **Degrees offered: BA, BS, BGS, AA, AS**
- **Mean ACT 18.5 composite**
- **Student-faculty ratio: 19 to 1**

A public college established in 1889. 375-acre campus in Ogden, 35 miles from Salt Lake City. Served by bus and rail; airport in Salt Lake City.
Academic Character NASC and professional accreditation. Trimester system, 8-week summer term. 9 majors offered by the School of Business and Economics, 1 by the School of Allied Health Sciences, 6 by the School of Education, 14 by the School of Humanities, 8 by the School of Natural Sciences, 7 by the School of Social Sciences, and 5 by the School of Technology. Minors offered in all major fields and in 10 additional areas. Distributive requirements. MEd granted. Honors program. Cooperative work/study, pass/fail. Preprofessional programs in agriculture, dentistry, engineering, forestry, medicine, pharmacy, range management, veterinary medicine, wildlife management. Study abroad in Mexico. One- and two-year certificates granted. Elementary and secondary education certification. ROTC; AFROTC, NROTC at U of Utah. TV studio, computer center, language lab, herbarium, science museum, planetarium. 285,000-volume library.
Financial College scholarships, PELL, SEOG, SSIG, NSS, GSL, NDSL, NSL, deferred payment, CWS. Application deadline February 1.
Admissions High school graduation with 16 units required. GED accepted. ACT required. $15 application fee. Rolling admissions; suggest applying by August 15. $50 deposit required on acceptance of offer of admission. *Early Admission, Early Decision* programs. Transfers accepted. Admission deferral possible. Credit possible for CEEB AP and CLEP exams.
Student Life Student government. Newspaper, magazine, yearbook, radio station. Music, drama groups. Political, religious, ethnic, service, and special interest organizations. 6 fraternities and 4 sororities; none have houses. Coed and single-sex dorms. No married-student housing. 10% of students live on campus. Liquor prohibited on campus. 3 terms of phys ed required. 7 intercollegiate sports for men, 6 for women; intramurals. AIAW, NCAA, Big Sky Conference. Student body composition: 1% Black, 5% Hispanic, 1% Native American, 93% White. 10% from out of state.

[1] WESTMINSTER COLLEGE

1840 South 1300 East, Salt Lake City 84105, (801) 484-7651
Dean of Admissions: Craig A. Green

- **Undergraduates: 564m, 719w**
- **Tuition (1982/83): $3,180**
- **Room & Board: $2,245; Fees: $100**
- **Degrees offered: BA, BS**
- **Student-faculty ratio: 13 to 1**

A private college established in 1875. 27-acre campus in Salt Lake City, 2 miles from center. Served by air, rail, and bus.
Academic Character NASC accreditation. 4-4-1 system, summer term. 36 majors offered by the faculties of Arts & Letters, Business & Professional Studies, Human & Physical Sciences, and Nursing. Distributive requirements. MEd granted. Honors program. Cooperative work/study, pass/fail, internships. Exchange programs with colleges in Michigan, Ohio, New York, Indiana, Iowa, Missouri. Summer travel-study. Elementary and secondary education certification. ROTC, AFROTC, NROTC at U of Utah. 160,000-volume library.

Financial CEEB CSS and ACT FAS. College scholarships and grants, PELL, SEOG, SSIG, NSS, FISL, GSL, NDSL, NSL, installment plans, CWS; college has own work program. Application deadline for scholarships February 1.
Admissions High school graduation required. GED accepted. Interview encouraged. SAT or ACT required. $20 application fee. Rolling admissions; suggest applying by March 15. $100 tuition deposit and $50 room deposit (for boarders) required on acceptance of offer of admission. *Early Admission, Concurrent Enrollment* programs. Transfers accepted. Admission deferral possible. Credit possible for CEEB AP and CLEP exams; college has own advanced placement program.
Student Life Student government. Newspaper, magazine, yearbook. Music, drama groups. Honorary, religious, academic, and special interest organizations. Freshmen must live at home or on campus. No coed dorms or married-student housing. 11% of students live on campus. 2 semesters of phys ed required. Intramural sports. Student body composition: 4% Asian, 2% Black, 5% Hispanic, 1% Native American, 88% White. 30% from out of state.

VERMONT *(VT)*

[1] BENNINGTON COLLEGE
Bennington 05201, (802) 442-5401
Director of Admissions and Financial Aid: John Nissen

- **Undergraduates: 210m, 390w; 630 total (including graduates)**
- **Tuition (1982/83): $9,620**
- **Room & Board: $2,520**
- **Degree offered: BA**
- **Student-faculty ratio: 9 to 1**

A private college established in 1932, became coed 1969. 550-acre campus 4 miles from Bennington, 175 miles north of New York City, 45 miles east of Albany. Air, rail service to Albany; bus to Bennington.
Academic Character NEASC accreditation. Semester system with Non-Resident Term from January to March, summer terms. 8 divisions; 3 disciplines in Black music, 4 in dance, 3 in drama, 3 in literature and languages, 5 in music, 3 in natural sciences and mathematics, 7 in social science, 8 in visual arts. Students encouraged to pursue work in 4 of the divisions during first 2 years. Tentative plan must be submitted by student before end of second year indicating major during final 2 years. Concentration may be divisional or interdisciplinary. Regular faculty-student meetings regarding program of study. Independent study during latter 2 years (confirmation of Plan) results in senior thesis. Internships (job experience) during Non-Resident Term required. Graduate degrees granted. Pass/fail. Visiting students. Study abroad, terms at other institutions. Post-baccalaureate pre-med and allied health sciences program. Computer center. 100,000-volume library with microform resources.
Financial CEEB CSS. College scholarships and funds; PELL, SEOG, FISL, GSL, CWS. Application deadline February 1.
Admissions High school graduation required. Interview required. SAT or ACT recommended. $25 application fee. Application deadline March 1. $250 deposit required on acceptance of admissions offer. *Early Decision, Early Admission* programs. Transfers accepted. Admission deferral possible.
Student Life Student government. News bulletin, college calendar. Music, drama, dance groups. Tutoring program. Political, academic, special interest groups. Coed and single-sex dorms. 15 self-governing student houses. Freshmen must live on campus. 80% of students live on campus. Men's and women's soccer and tennis teams. Intramurals. Student body composition: 1% Asian, 3% Black, 1% Hispanic, 10% Foreign, 85% White. 95% of students from out of state.

[2] BURLINGTON COLLEGE
90 Main Street, Burlington 05401

[1] and J1] CASTLETON STATE COLLEGE
Castleton 05735, (802) 468-5611
Director of Admissions: Gary Fallis

- **Undergraduates: 600m, 700w; 1,896 total (including graduates)**
- **Tuition (1982/83): $1,380 (in-state); $3,360 (out-of-state)**
- **Room & Board: $2,614; Fees: $162**
- **Degrees offered: BA, BS, AS, AGS**
- **Mean SAT 410v, 430m**
- **Student-faculty ratio: 15 to 1**

A public college established in 1867 in Castleton. 130-acre campus in rural environment 12 miles west of Rutland. Air and bus service.
Academic Character Semester system with 2 5-week summer terms; 3-week workshop term. 27 majors in the areas of art, French, history, literature, math, music, natural sciences, psychology, sociology, Spanish, career programs, business administration, communication, computer information systems, education, nursing, criminal justice, secretarial science, school clerk-librarian. Self-designed majors. MEd granted. Distributive requirements. Independent study, honors program. Cooperative work/study, pass/fail. Preprofessional programs in dentistry, law, medicine, veterinary medicine. Elementary, secondary, and special education certification. NERSP (New England Regional Student Program). International Student Program with Georgetown University. Study abroad. Observatory. Language lab. 72,000-volume library.
Financial ACT FAS and CEEB CSS. College scholarships and grants; PELL, SEOG, NSS, NDSL, FISL, HELP, NSL, CWS. Application deadline March 1.
Admissions High school graduation with 16 units required. SAT or ACT required. $25 application fee. Rolling admissions. December 31 deadline for nursing program. $100 deposit required on acceptance of admissions offer. *Early Admission, Concurrent Enrollment* programs. Transfers accepted. Admission deferral possible. Credit possible for CEEB AP and CLEP exams. Challenge exams in nursing program. Development program for underprepared students.
Student Life Student Association. Newspaper, magazine, yearbook, radio station. Music, drama, dance groups. Athletic, academic, religious, service, and special interest clubs. 2 fraternities, 1 with house; 4% of men join. Students must live on campus or at home. 55% of students live on campus. 7 intercollegiate sports for men, 7 for women; intramurals. AIAW, ECAC, NAIA, NCAA, NECAC, NESCAC. Student body composition: 0.3% Asian, 1% Black, 0.5% Hispanic. 98.2% White. 35% of students from out of state.

[J1] CHAMPLAIN COLLEGE
163 South Willard Street, Burlington 05401, (802) 658-0800
Director of Admissions: Verne L. McDonald

- **Enrollment: 321m, 701w; 1,487 total (including part-time)**
- **Tuition (1983/84): $3,950**
- **Room & Board: $2,975**
- **Degree offered: AS**
- **Student-faculty ratio: 12 to 1**

A private 2-year college established in 1878. Campus located in residential section of city of Burlington. Served by air, bus, and rail.
Academic Character NEASC accreditation. Semester system. 2-year programs offered in accounting, business management, general business, hotel-motel-restaurant management, marketing management & retailing, retailing & fashion merchandising, dental assisting, early childhood education, law enforcement, social services, special education, accounting data processing, data processing, word processing/information processing, court reporting, secretarial studies (4 areas), office management, and liberal studies. Certificate programs. Distributive requirements. Independent study. Credit for work experience. Library with microform resources.
Financial ACT FAS. College scholarships and grants, state grants, PELL, SEOG, NDSL, GSL, PLUS, CWS. Priority application deadline May 1.
Admissions High school graduation required. GED accepted. Interview encouraged. $25 application fee. Rolling admissions. $150 tuition deposit and $50 room deposit (for boarders) required on acceptance of offer of admission. *Early Decision* Program. Transfers accepted. Admission deferral possible. Credit possible for CLEP and ACT PEP exams; college has own advanced placement program.
Student Life Student government. Theatre Program. No coed dorms. Dress code. 5 intercollegiate sports; intramurals. NJCAA.

[1] GODDARD COLLEGE
Plainfield 05667, (802) 454-8311
Coordinator of Admissions: Cynthia Drown

- **Enrollment: 54m, 64w; 118 total (including part-time)**
- **Tuition (1982/83): $6,500**
- **Room & Board: $2,200**
- **Degree offered: BA**
- **Student-faculty ratio: 10 to 1**

A private experimental liberal arts college established in 1938. Rural campus at edge of village of Plainfield, 10 miles east of Montpelier.
Academic Character NEASC accreditation. Semester system. No defined curriculum. Opportunities for study in leadership arts, helping arts, expressive arts, environmental arts, backgrounds, and feminist studies. Special programs in cultural ecology and Native American traditions, aquatic biology, visual arts, individual & group behavior (counseling, psychology), teacher's education, theatre, music & dance. All programs self-designed with independent study, group study, practicums, research, studio work, conferences, workshops. MA granted. Field Semester (off-campus study). Off-Campus Term (less intensive program of studies). 8 semesters may be spent in off-campus independent study and work. 80,000-volume library.
Financial Tuition guaranteed for all four years of study. Financial aid available for needy students.
Admissions Noncompetitive admission. Interview suggested. SAT or ACT suggested. $25 application fee. Rolling admissions. *Early Decision* Program. Advanced placement possible.
Student Life Students must live on campus at least part-time. Most residences are coeducational.

[1] GREEN MOUNTAIN COLLEGE
Poultney 05764, (802) 287-9313, (800) 451-6116 (toll-free)
Dean of Admissions: Douglas W. Durkee

- **Enrollment: 113m, 297w; 424 total (including part-time)**
- **Tuition (1982/83): $5,050**
- **Room & Board: $3,150; Fees: $205**
- **Degrees offered: BS, AA, AFA**
- **Student-faculty ratio: 11 to 1**

A private college established in 1834. 155-acre campus in a scenic recreational area of Vermont, 20 miles from Rutland. Served by bus; airport in Rutland; rail 9 miles away in Whitehall, New York.

Academic Character NEASC and professional accreditation. Semester system. Majors offered in behavioral sciences, elementary education, handicapped education, management, business management, accounting, retail management, and recreation & leisure studies. 2-year programs offered in 10 additional areas. Distributive requirements. Independent study. Externships. 100,000-volume library with microform resources.
Financial CEEB CSS and ACT FAS. College grants, PELL, SEOG, NDSL, GSL, CWS. Application deadline April 1.
Admissions High school graduation required. SAT or ACT required. $20 application fee. Rolling admissions. *Early Admission, Early Decision* programs. Transfers accepted. Credit possible for CEEB AP and CLEP exams.
Student Life Student government. Yearbook. Music group. Honorary, academic, service, and special interest organizations. Students must live at home or on campus. 9 intercollegiate sports. NAC.

[1] JOHNSON STATE COLLEGE

Johnson 05656, (802) 635-2356
Director of Admissions: Jim McWilliam

- **Undergraduates: 426, 453w; 1,413 total**
- **Tuition (1982/83): $1,380 (in-state); $3,360 (out-of-state)**
- **Room & Board: $2,614-$2,714; Fees: $200**
- **Degrees offered: BA, BS, BFA, AS**
- **Mean SAT 900**
- **Student-faculty ratio: 12 to 1**

A public college founded in 1828. 500-acre rural campus 30 miles northeast of Burlington. Bus in Johnson; air, bus, and rail in Burlington.
Academic Character NEASC accreditation. Semester system, 6-week summer term. 28 majors offered in the areas of art, biology, business management, ecology, economics, education, environmental studies, fine arts, health education, mathematics, music, politics, pre-allied medical professions, psychology. Associate degrees in accounting, business information systems, business management. Distributive requirements. MA granted. Independent study. Honors/pass/fail grading. NERSP. Elementary, secondary, and special education certification. Computer center. 87,100-volume library with microform resources.
Financial CEEB CSS and ACT FAS. College scholarships state aid; PELL, SEOG, NDSL, GSL, CWS. Application deadline March 1.
Admissions High school graduation with 16 units required. GED accepted. SAT or ACT reccomended. $25 application fee. Preferred application deadline March 30. Rolling admissions. $100 deposit required on acceptance of admissions offer. Transfers accepted. Admission deferral possible. Credit possible for CEEB AP, CLEP, and ACT PEP exams. Project Access and PROVE program for underprepared students.
Student Life Student government. Newspaper, yearbook, radio station. Music, drama groups. Political, service, athletic, academic, religious, and special interest organizations. Single freshmen and sophomores must live on campus, unless living at home. Special interest, coed dorms. Married-student housing. 55% of students live on campus. 7 intercollegiate sports for men, 5 for women; intramural and club sports. ECAC, NCAA, NESCAC, NAIA. Student body composition: 1% Asian, 2% Black, 1% Hispanic, 1% Native American, 95% White. 33% of students from out of state.

[1] LYNDON STATE COLLEGE

Lyndonville 05851, (802) 626-9371
Director of Admissions: Russell S. Powden, Jr.

- **Undergraduates: 550m, 473w**
- **Tuition (1982/83): $1,380 (in-state); $3,360 (out-of-state)**
- **Room & Board: $2,614**
- **Degrees offered: BA, BS, AA, AS**
- **Student-faculty ratio: 17 to 1**

A public college established in 1911. 175-acre campus in Lyndonville, 9 miles north of St. Johnsbury. Bus in Lyndonville.
Academic Character NEASC accreditation. Semester system, 6-week summer term. 32 majors offered in the areas of behavioral sciences, business, communication arts & sciences, elementary education, English, humanities, meteorology, natural sciences, phys ed, recreation & leisure studies, social sciences. Associate degrees in business, secretarial studies, communications, general studies. Distributive requirements. MEd granted. Independent study. Cooperative work/study, pass/fail, internships. Elementary and secondary education certification. Study abroad. Exchange with other schools. NERSP. AFROTC. 65,000-volume library with microform resources.
Financial CEEB CSS and ACT FAS. College grants and scholarships state aid; PELL, SEOG, NDSL, GSL, FISL, CWS. Application deadline April 1.
Admissions High school graduation with 16 units required. Interview recommended. SAT or ACT required. $25 application fee. Preferred application deadline May 1. Rolling admissions. $100 deposit required on acceptance of admissions offer. Transfers accepted. Credit possible for CEEB AP, CLEP exams; college has own placement program.
Student Life Community council. Newspaper, magazine, yearbook, radio station. Music, drama, outing, foreign language clubs. Athletic, academic, religious, and special interest groups. Social fraternities. Single students not living at home must live on campus. Coed and single-sex dorms. No married-student housing. 50% of students live on campus. 8 intercollegiate sports for men and women; intramurals. NAIA, NCAA, Mayflower Conference. Student body composition: 1% Black, 1% Hispanic, 97% White, 1% Other. 42% of students from out of state.

[1] MARLBORO COLLEGE

Marlboro 05344, (802) 257-4333
Director of Admissions: Nancy Leach

- **Undergraduates: 110m, 118w**
- **Tuition (1982/83): $6,680**
- **Room & Board: $2,700; Fees: $226**
- **Degrees offered: BA, BS**
- **Mean SAT 534v, 519m**
- **Student-faculty ratio: 8 to 1**

A private college established in 1946. Rural campus 2 miles from town of Marlboro, 12 miles from Brattleboro.
Academic Character NEASC accreditation. Semester system. Self-designed concentrations in humanities, art, social sciences, and natural sciences. English requirement. Junior and senior years taught in tutorials. Field studies. Cooperative programs with School for International Training and College of the Atlantic. Study abroad in Italy. 47,625-volume libary.
Financial College work program required. CEEB CSS and ACT FAS. College scholarships, grants, and loans, PELL, SEOG, GSL, PLUS, CWS. Priority application deadline March 1.
Admissions High school graduation required with 15 units recommended. Interview required. Portfolio required for studio arts students. SAT or ACT recommended. $20 application fee. Rolling admissions. $200 deposit required on acceptance of offer of admission. *Early Admission, Early Decision* programs. Transfers accepted. Admission deferral possible. Credit possible for CEEB AP and CLEP exams.
Student Life "Town Meeting" form of student government. Theatre Workshop. Outdoors Program. Coed and single-sex dorms. Cottages and cabins. Individual and team sports.

[1] MIDDLEBURY COLLEGE

Middlebury 05753, (802) 388-3711
Director of Admissions: Fred F. Neuberger

- **Undergraduates: 1,015m, 912w; 1,939 total (including graduates)**
- **Tuition, Room & Board (1982/83): $10,800**
- **Degree offered: BA**
- **Mean SAT 590v, 620m**
- **Student-faculty ratio: 13 to 1**

A private college established in 1800. 500-acre campus in the village of Middlebury, 30 miles south of Burlington. Bus in Middlebury, airport in Burlington.
Academic Character NEASC accreditation. 4-1-4 system. Majors offered in American literature, American studies, art, biology, chemistry, classical studies, classics, East Asian studies, economics, English, environmental studies, French, geography, geology, German, history, Italian, literary studies, math, music, northern studies, philosophy, physics, political science, psychology, religion, Russian, sociology/anthropology, Spanish, theater. Joint majors. Programs in writing, computer science, teacher education. Summer Breadloaf School of English, Breadloaf Writer's Conference, and summer foreign language schools are held on campus. Distributive requirements. MA, MS, DML granted. Independent study. Phi Beta Kappa. Honors program. Honors/pass/fail, internships. Preprofessional programs in medicine, dentistry, veterinary medicine. 3-2 engineering programs with Case Western Reserve, Columbia, Georgia Tech, RPI, University of Rochester. 3-2 business programs with Boston U, Columbia, Dartmouth (Amos Tuck School), NYU, Rutgers, U of Chicago, U of Rochester. 3-2 law program with Syracuse. Exchange with Swarthmore. Junior year at Institute for Architecture and Urban Studies in New York. Washington Semester. Mystic Seaport Program .Study abroad. Elementary and secondary education certification. Computer center. Observatory. 450,000-volume library with microform resources.
Financial CEEB CSS. College scholarships, grants, loans, state aid; PELL, SEOG, NDSL, GSL, CWS. Application deadline January 31.
Admissions High school graduation with 16 units recommended. Interview recommended. SAT and 3 ACH required. $30 application fee. Application deadline January 15. $100 deposit required on acceptance of admissions offer. *Early Decision* Program. Some transfers accepted. Admission deferral possible. Credit possible for CEEB AP exams. Minority recruiting program.
Student Life Student government. Newspaper, magazines, yearbook, radio station. Music, visual arts groups. Language, religious, outing, special interest groups. 6 fraternities with houses; 15% of men and some women join. Coed and single-sex dorms; language houses. 98% of students live on campus. 1 year of phys ed required. 11 intercollegiate sports for men, 11 for women; club and intramural sports. AIAW, ECAC, NCAA, NECAC, NESCAC. Student body composition: 1% Asian, 3% Black, 1% Hispanic, 95% White. 95% of students from out of state.

[1] NORWICH UNIVERSITY-VERMONT COLLEGE

Northfield 05663, (802) 485-5011
Dean of Admissions: William S. Neal

- **Undergraduates: 1,300m, 500w**
- **Tuition, Room & Board (1982/83): $8,700**
- **Degrees offered: BA, BS, AA, AS**
- **Mean SAT 413v, 497m**
- **Student-faculty ratio: 14 to 1**

A private 2-campus university, which became coed when Norwich University (all-male military school established 1819) merged with Vermont College (women's college established 1834) in 1972. 1,000-acre Norwich U campus is in Northfield; Vermont College campus is in nearby Montpelier. Air, bus, and rail service.
Academic Character NEASC and professional accreditation. Semester system with 2 5-week summer terms. 34 majors offered in areas of accounting, biology, business administration, chemistry, communications, computer science, criminal justice, earth science, economics, education, engineering, English, government, history, humanities, international studies, math, medical

technology, military studies, modern languages, philosophy, phys ed, physics, recreation, religion. Associate degrees in 10 areas. Minors in some fields. 5-year 2-degree program. Interdisciplinary majors. Distributive requirements, ROTC required for men. Independent study. Honors program. Internships. Marine Corps Commissioning Program. Russian School on campus. Study abroad. 4- and 2-year ROTC, AFROTC programs. Mountain and Cold Weather Training. Computer services. Learning Skills Center. 150,000-volume library with microform resources.
Financial CEEB CSS. University scholarships; PELL, SEOG, NSS, NDSL, FISL, NSL, CWS. Application deadline March 1.
Admissions High school graduation with 18 units required. Interview recommended. SAT or ACT, ACH recommended. $20 application fee. Rolling admissions. $150 deposit required on acceptance of admissions offer. *Early Admission, Early Decision* programs. Transfers accepted. Admission deferral possible. Credit possible for CEEB AP and CLEP exams. University has own placement exams.
Student Life Student government. Newspaper, magazine, yearbook, radio station. Music groups. Parachute club. Mountain Rescue Team. Service, academic, athletic, honorary, religious, and special interest organizations. No coed dorms. No married-student housing. 90% of students live on campus. Freshmen may not have cars. ROTC cadets at Norwich must wear uniforms. 2 semesters of phys ed required. 12 intercollegiate sports for men, 8 for women; intramural and club sports. ECAC, NCAA, NEIAA. Student body composition: 1% Asian, 3% Black, 1% Hispanic, 1% Native American, 92% White, 2% Other. 80% of students from out of state.

[1] SAINT JOSEPH THE PROVIDER, COLLEGE OF
Clement Road, Rutland 05701

[1] SAINT MICHAEL'S COLLEGE
Winooski 05404, (802) 655-2000
Dean of Admissions: Jerry E. Flanagan

- **Undergraduates: 799m, 820w; 2,054 total (including graduates)**
- **Tuition (1982/83): $5,443**
- **Room & Board: $2,345; Fees: $62**
- **Degree offered: BA**
- **Mean SAT 487v, 509m**
- **Student-faculty ratio: 16 to 1**

A private college affiliated with the Roman Catholic Church. Established 1889, college became coed in 1970. 430-acre campus in Winooski, suburb of Burlington, 90 miles from Montreal. Air, bus, and rail service.
Academic Character NEASC accreditation. Semester system, 6-week summer term. Majors offered in art, accounting, American studies, biology, business administration, chemistry, classics, computer science, economics, elementary education, English literature, environmental science, fine arts, French, history, journalism, math, philosophy, physics, political science, psychology, religion, sociology, Spanish. Self-designed majors. Distributives and 2 courses in religion required. Masters degrees granted; certificate programs offered. Independent study, honors program. Credit by exam. Pass/fail, internships. Preprofessional programs in dentistry, law, medicine. 3-2 engineering program with Clarkson. Exchange programs. Study abroad. Elementary and secondary education certification. Computer center. Observatory. North Campus. AFROTC; ROTC at UVM. 130,000-volume library with microform resources.
Financial CEEB CSS and ACT FAS. College scholarships and grants, state aid; PELL, SEOG, NDSL, FISL, HELP, GSL, CWS. Application deadline March 15.
Admissions High school graduation with 16 units required. Interview encouraged. SAT or ACT required. $20 application fee. Rolling admissions. $150 deposit required on acceptance of admissions offer. *Early Admission* Program. Transfers accepted. Admission deferral possible. Credit possible for CEEB AP and CLEP exams.
Student Life Student government. Newspaper, magazine, yearbook, radio station. Music, drama groups. Service, honorary, religious, and special interest groups. Students must live on campus unless living at home. Special interest and single-sex dorms. 85% of students live on campus. Residence halls have visitation restrictions. 11 intercollegiate sports for men, 11 for women; intramurals. 83% of students from out of state.

[1 and G1] SCHOOL FOR INTERNATIONAL TRAINING OF THE EXPERIMENT IN INTERNATIONAL LIVING
Kipling Road, Brattleboro 05301, (802) 257-7751

- **Enrollment: 228m, 293w; 805 total (including part-time)**
- **Tuition (1982/83): $5,500**
- **Room & Board: $2,300 (for 28 on-campus weeks)**
- **Charges for internship travel not included in above.**
- **Degree offered: BA**
- **Student-faculty ratio: 9 to 1**

A private coeducatinal upper-level undergraduate college established in 1964. Campus in rural area about 40 miles from Bennington and close to the New Hampshire border.
Academic Character NEASC accreditation. Academic calendar is based on a modular plan. World Issues Program. Major offered in international studies. 2-year program features major concentrations in ecology, peace studies & conflict resolution, social/economic development, and intercultural communication. Core component of foreign languages and research, project design and evaluation skills. Graduate programs in language teaching and intercultural administration also available. Overseas internships are an integral component of the program, and last from 7 to 12 months. Undergraduate exchange students from other institutions may enter programs for transfer credit; these include independent study projects, contemporary culture seminars, language study, and some specialized study in international commerce in 14 foreign countries. 26,000-volume library.
Financial Financial aid programs are available for all students.
Admissions Only juniors admitted, in September. Rolling admissions. *Early Admission* Program. Transfers accepted.
Student Life Dormitory and cafeteria available. Some married-student housing. Informal athletic programs.

[1] SOUTHERN VERMONT COLLEGE
Monument Road, Bennington 05201, (802) 442-5427

- **Enrollment: 178m, 184w; 508 total (including part-time)**
- **Tuition (1981/82): $2,550**
- **Degrees offered: BA, AA**

A private coeducational college established in 1926. Formerly Saint Joseph College. Campus in the southwestern corner of the state, 40 miles from Bennington.
Academic Character NEASC accreditation. Semester system. Associate degree programs offered in business, criminal justice, environmental studies, general studies, human services, medical assistant, office accounting, secretarial science. Bachelor degree programs in accounting, business management, communications management, criminal justice management, English, environmental management, human services management. Remedial mathematics and English programs.
Financial Financial aid available for all students.
Admissions Open admissions. Applications accepted at any time.
Student Life Housing available on campus for men and women.

[1] TRINITY COLLEGE
Colchester Avenue, Burlington 05401, (802) 658-0337
Director of Admissions: Jessica Brugger Meserve

- **Undergraduates: 156m, 711w; 887 total (including graduates)**
- **Tuition (1982/83): $4,080**
- **Room & Board: $2,490; Fees: $125**
- **Degrees offered: BA, BS, AA, AS**
- **Mean SAT 434v, 436m**
- **Student-faculty ratio: 17 to 1**

A private college conducted by the Sisters of Mary, founded in 1925. 23-acre campus in the small city of Burlington. Air, bus, and rail service.
Academic Character NEASC and professional accreditation. Semester system, 2 summer terms. Majors offered in education(4 areas), educational studies, English, French, history, human services, modern languages, psychology, social science, social work, social work/developmental disabilities, Spanish, special studies(chemistry, math, US/Canadian cultural studies), accounting, biology, business administration, business technology, medical technology, liberal arts, business administration, office administration. Self-designed majors. Distributives and 1 course in religion required. Independent study. Internships, pass/fail, cooperative work/study. 3-1 program in medical technology with approved hospital. Exchange programs. Study abroad. Early childhood, elementary, secondary, and special education certification. Media Resource Center. Language lab. Learning Resource Center. AFROTC at St. Michael's. 85,313-volume library.
Financial CEEB CSS and ACT FAS. College scholarships and loans, state aid; PELL, SEOG, NDSL, GSL, PLUS, CWS. Application deadline March 1.
Admissions High school graduation required. Interview recommended. SAT or ACT required. $20 application fee; rolling admissions. $100 deposit ($50 for commuters) required on acceptance of admissions offer. *Early Admission* Program. Transfers accepted. Credit possible for CEEB AP and CLEP exams.
Student Life Student government. Newspaper, magazine, yearbook. Choir. Academic, professional, drama, special interest groups. Seniors may live off campus. No married-student housing. 20% of women students live on campus. Class attendance expected. 3 intercollegiate sports. Intramurals. NAIA. 18% of students from out of state.

[J1] VERMONT, COMMUNITY COLLEGE OF
Montpelier 05602

[1] VERMONT, UNIVERSITY OF
Burlington 05405, (802) 656-3370
Director of Admissions: Jeff M.S. Kaplan

- **Undergraduates: 3,272m, 4,408w; 8,680 total (including graduates)**
- **Tuition (1982/83): $2,250 (in-state); $5,800 (out-of-state)**
- **Room & Board: $2,612; Fees: $216**
- **Degrees offered: BA, BS, BEng, BMus, BSEd, AS**
- **Mean SAT 517v, 520m**
- **Student-faculty ratio: 16 to 1**

A public university established 1791. 715-acre campus in Burlington, 100 miles south of Montreal. Air, bus, and rail service.
Academic Character NEASC and professional accreditation. Semester system, one 4- to 8-week summer term. 17 majors offered by the College of Agriculture, 29 by the College of Arts and Sciences, 10 by the College of Education and Social Sciences, 7 by College of Engineering and Mathematics, 5 by the School of Business Administration, 4 by the School of Allied Health Sciences, 5 by the School of Natural Resources, 1 by the School of Nursing. Self-designed majors. Associate degrees in some allied health services. Distributive requirements. Graduate and professional degrees granted. Independent study. Honors programs. Phi Beta Kappa. Cooperative work/study, internships, pass/fail. Preprofessional programs in law, veterinary medicine, medicine, dentistry. Member of Vermont Colleges Consortium. NERSP. Exchange programs. Study abroad. Elementary,

secondary, and special education certification. Government Research and World Affairs Centers. Agricultural Experiment Station. Morgan Horse Farm in Weybridge. Living/Learning Center. Language lab. Computer center. 1,000,000-volume library with microform resources.
Financial ACT FAS. University scholarships; PELL, SEOG, NDSL, health professions loans and grants, CWS. Application deadline March 1.
Admissions High school graduation with 16 units required. Interview recommended. SAT required. $25 application fee. Application deadline February 1. $125 deposit required on acceptance of admissions offer. *Early Decision* Program. Transfers accepted. Admission deferral possible. Credit possible for CEEB AP, CLEP, and university placement exams. Minority student program.
Student Life Student government. Newspaper, magazine, yearbook, radio and TV station. Music, drama, debate, dance groups. Gay Union. Outing, athletic, language, honorary, service, special interest organizations. 15 fraternities and 6 sororities; all with houses. 15% of men and 10% of women join. Freshmen must live on campus or at home. Coed and single-sex dorms. Special interest and married-student housing. 55% of students live on campus. 1 year of phys ed required. Class attendance expected. Extensive intercollegiate and intramural programs. AIAW, ECAC, NCAA, NEIAA, EAIAW, NECAC, Yankee Conference, Olde New England Conference. 53% of students from out of state.

[G1] VERMONT LAW SCHOOL
South Royalton 05068

[J1] VERMONT TECHNICAL COLLEGE
Randolph Center 05061, (802) 728-3391
Director of Admissions and Finanical Aid: Nelberta A. Brink

- **Undergraduates: 620m, 112w; 792 total (including part-time)**
- **Tuition (1982/83): $1,700 (in-state); $3,520 (out-of-state)**
- **Room & Board: $2,614; Fees: $214**
- **Degrees offered: AAS, AE**
- **Student-faculty ratio: 13 to 1**

A public 2-year college established in 1957. Rural campus in village of Randolph, 30 miles from Montpelier. Served by bus.
Academic Character NEASC accreditation. Semester system. 2-year programs offered in agribusiness management technology, dairy farm management technology, architectural & building engineering technology, technical office management, veterinary office assistant, civil engineering technology, electrical & electronics engineering technology, mechanical engineering technology, and surveying technology. Distributive requirements. Independent study. Credit by exam. 1-year pre-technology program. 145-acre farm. 45,000-volume library with microform resources.
Financial CEEB CSS and ACT FAS. College scholarships and emergency loans, state grants, PELL, SEOG, NDSL, GSL, CWS. Application deadline March 1.
Admissions High school graduation with 16 units required. SAT or ACT required. $25 application fee. Rolling admissions. $100 deposit required on acceptance of offer of admission. Transfers accepted. Credit possible for CEEB AP exams; college has own advanced placement program.
Student Life Newspaper, yearbook, radio station. Music clubs. Professional, honorary, and special interest groups. Freshmen must live at home or on campus. Freshmen may not have cars on campus. 4 intercollegiate sports for men, 4 for women; intramurals. NJCAA, NNESCC.

VIRGINIA *(VA)*

[J1 & 1] AVERETT COLLEGE
Danville 24541, (804) 793-7811
Director of Admissions: Walter P. Crutchfield

- **Undergraduates: 400m, 600w**
- **Tuition, Room, & Board: $5,450**
- **Degrees offered: BA, BS**
- **Mean SAT 900**
- **Student-faculty ratio: 18 to 1**

A private college affiliated with the Virginia Baptist General Association, established in 1859, became coed in 1968. 25-acre small-city campus, 50 miles from Greensboro. Served by air, rail, and bus.
Academic Character SACS accreditation. 4-1-4-1-1 system, 2 4-week summer terms. 35 majors offered by the divisions of Business Administration, Education, Fine Arts, Humanities, Mathematics & Natural Science, Physical Education, and Social Sciences. Self-designed majors. Distributives and 6 credits of religion required. MEd granted. Independent study. Pass/fail, internships. Preprofessional programs in dentistry, dental hygiene, law, medicine, nursing. Horsemanship semester in England. Exchange physical education program with Anstey College of Physical Education in England. Elementary, secondary, and special education education certification. Reading center. 75,000-volume library with microform resources.
Financial Tuition, room, and board charges are guaranteed for all four years of study. CEEB CSS. College scholarships, grants, loans, discounts for church-vocation students, minister's children, and simultaneously-enrolled siblings, payment plans; PELL, SEOG, NDSL, FISL, CWS. Application deadline April 1.
Admissions High school graduation with 15 units required. Interview recommended. Riding placement test required for equestrian majors. SAT or ACT required; SAT preferred. $15 application fee. Rolling admissions. $50 deposit due on acceptance of offer of admission. *Early Admission* Program. Admission deferral possible. Transfers accepted. Credit possible for CEEB AP and CLEP exams, and for life experience.
Student Life Student government. Newspaper, literary magazine, yearbook. Music, dance, and drama groups. Academic, honorary, religious, service, and special interest groups. 2 fraternities and 1 sorority. Single-sex dorms. 50% of students live on campus. Honor code. Liquor prohibited. 6 intercollegiate sports for men, 7 for women; intramurals. AIAW, NCAA, Dixie Conference, US and Blue Ridge Field Hockey Associations, Intercollegiate Horse Show Association. Student body composition: 16% Black, 83% White, 1% Other. 35% from out of state.

[J1] BLUE RIDGE COMMUNITY COLLEGE
Weyers Cave 24486

[1] BLUEFIELD COLLEGE
Bluefield 24605, (304) 327-7137
Director of Admissions & Financial Aid: Charles R. Addington

- **Enrollment: 198m, 146w; 387 total (including part-time)**
- **Tuition (1983/84): $2,276**
- **Room & Board: $2,200**
- **Degrees offered: BA, BS, AA**
- **Student-faculty ratio: 11 to 1**

A private college affiliated with the Baptist Church, established in 1922. 85-acre small-town campus.
Academic Character SACS accreditation. 4-1-4 system. Majors offered in behavioral science, business, business-computer information, criminal justice, English, fine arts, general science education, history, music, religion & philosophy, and social science. Distributives and 6 hours of religion-philosophy required. Preprofessional programs in agriculture, dentistry, dental hygiene, engineering, forestry, law, medicine, medical technology, nursing, optometry, pharmacy, and physical therapy. 2-2 engineering program with VPI. Summer theatre. 40,000-volume library.
Financial College scholarships, grants, loans, ministerial aid, state aid; PELL, SEOG, GSL, CWS. Application deadline for SEOG and CWS July 1.
Admissions High school graduation with 12 units recommended. GED accepted. SAT or ACT required. $10 application fee. Rolling admissions. $75 deposit due on acceptance of offer of admission. Transfers accepted. Credit possible for CEEB AP, CLEP, and departmental exams.
Student Life Student government. Yearbook. Baptist Student Union. Service, social, and special interest groups. Juniors and seniors may live off campus. Dorms for men and women. Limited married-student housing. Class attendance required. Weekly convocation, Christian Emphasis Week, Missionary Day, and monthly student government meetings mandatory. 4 hours of phys ed required. 3 intercollegiate sports for men, 3 for women; intramural and club sports. NLCAA.

[1] BRIDGEWATER COLLEGE
Bridgewater 22812, (703) 828-2501
Director of Admissions: Linda F. Glover

- **Undergraduates: 469m, 464w**
- **Tuition (1982/83): $4,100**
- **Room & Board: $2,100; Fees: $600**
- **Degrees offered: BA, BS**
- **Student-faculty ratio: 16 to 1**

A private college affiliated with the Church of the Brethren, established in 1880. 35-acre small-town campus in a rural area, 7 miles from Harrisburg.
Academic Character SACS accreditation. 3-3-1-3 system, 8-week summer term. Majors offered in art, biology, business, chemistry, economics, education, English, French, general science, German, health/physical education, history/political science, home economics, international studies, mathematics, music, philosophy/religion, physical science, physics/math, sociology, and Spanish. Distributives, 6 hours of religion & philosophy, and senior comprehensive exam required. Independent study. Honors program. Internships. Preprofessional programs in 16 areas. 5-year dual-degree engineering program with Georgia Tech. 3-2 forestry program with Duke. Study abroad. Elementary and secondary education certification. Computer center. Language lab. Museum. 85,000-volume library with microform resources.
Financial CEEB CSS. College scholarships, grants, loans, minister's children scholarships, payment plan; PELL, SEOG, NDSL, GSL, CWS. Application deadline March 15.
Admissions High school graduation with 16 units required. Interview recommended. SAT required; 2 ACH recommended. $15 application fee. Rolling admissions; suggest applying before March of 12th year. $100 deposit due on acceptance of offer of admission. *Early Admission* Program. Transfers accepted. Credit possible for CEEB AP and CLEP exams.
Student Life Student government. Newspaper, literary magazine, yearbook, radio station. Music, drama, and film groups. Debate. Academic, honorary, political, religious, service, and special interest groups. Students must live at home or on campus. Single-sex dorms. 88% of students live on campus. Honor system. Liquor, drugs, firearms, fireworks, gambling, hazing, profanity prohibited. Smoking restricted. Weekly convocation attendance mandatory. 2

phys ed activities required. 7 intercollegiate sports for men, 5 for women; intramurals. AIAW, NCAA, ODAC. Student body composition: 2.5% Black, 0.2% Hispanic, 0.1% Native American, 96.4% White, 0.8% Other. 24% from out of state.

[J1] CENTRAL VIRGINIA COMMUNITY COLLEGE
PO Box 4098, Wards Road South, Lynchburg 24502

[1] CHRISTOPHER NEWPORT COLLEGE
Newport News 23606

[J1] DABNEY S. LANCASTER COMMUNITY COLLEGE
Route 60 West, Clifton Forge 24422

[J1] DANVILLE COMMUNITY COLLEGE
Danville 24541

[1] EASTERN MENNONITE COLLEGE
Harrisonburg 22801, (703) 433-2771
Director of Admissions: Ross D. Collingwood

- **Undergraduates: 371m, 650w**
- **Tuition (1982/83): $4,137**
- **Room & Board: $1,926**
- **Degrees offered: BA, BS, AA, AAS**
- **Student-faculty ratio: 14 to 1**

A private college affiliated with the Mennonite Church, established in 1917. 117-acre small-town campus, 1 mile from Harrisonburg. Served by bus; airport 15 miles away.
Academic Character SACS and professional accreditation. Semester system, 3 3-week summer terms. 33 majors offered in the areas of agriculture, art, Bible, business administration, camping & youth ministries, community development, computer science, dietetics, education, home economics, liberal arts, mathematics, medical technology, music, nursing, physical education, science, and social sciences. Minors offered. Distributives and 8 hours of religion required. Masters degrees granted. Certificate programs. Independent study. Internships. Preprofessional programs in dentistry, law, medicine, veterinary science. Member Christian College Coalition. Study abroad. Elementary and secondary education certification. Computer center. Language lab. Planetarium. Observatory. 108,973-volume library.
Financial CEEB CSS and ACT FAS. College scholarships, grants, loans; PELL, SEOG, NSS, NDSL, FISL, GSL, PLUS, CWS. Scholarship application deadline March 1.
Admissions High school graduation with 16 units recommended. Interview recommended. SAT or ACT required; ACT preferred. $15 application fee. Rolling admissions. $100 deposit due on acceptance of offer of admission. *Early Admission* Program. Admission deferral possible. Transfers accepted. Credit possible for CEEB AP and CLEP exams.
Student Life Student government. Newspaper, literary magazine, yearbook, radio station. Music and drama groups. Black Student Union. Academic, religious, service, and special interest groups. Single students under 21 must live with families or on campus. Coed and single-sex dorms. Married-student housing. 60% of students live on campus. Liquor, drugs, tobacco, and dancing prohibited. Attendance in lower level courses and at assemblies required. 6 intercollegiate sports for men, 6 for women; intramurals. AIAW, NCAA, NCCAA, VISA, ODAC. Student body composition: 1% Asian, 2% Black, 3% Hispanic, 94% White. 69% from out of state.

[J1] EASTERN SHORE COMMUNITY COLLEGE
PO Box C, Melfa 23410

[P] EASTERN VIRGINIA MEDICAL SCHOOL
PO Box 1980, Norfolk 23501

[1] EMORY & HENRY COLLEGE
Emory 24327, (703) 944-3121
Director of Admissions: Gordon L. Peck

- **Undergraduates: 416m, 384w**
- **Tuition (1982/83): $3,000**
- **Room & Board: $1,893; Fees: $300**
- **Degrees offered: BA, BS**
- **Mean ACT 24; mean SAT 460v, 500m**
- **Student-faculty ratio: 14 to 1**

A private college affiliated with the United Methodist Church, established in 1836. 150-acre rural campus, 25 miles from Bristol. Bus service 10 miles away in Abington.
Academic Character SACS accreditation. Trimester system, 2 5-week summer terms. 27 majors offered in the areas of business, classics, education, engineering, fine arts, geography, languages, liberal arts, mass communications, mathematics, medical technology, physical education, religion, science, and social sciences. Self-designed majors. Distributives, one religion course, URE, and major comprehensives required. Senior projects. Independent study. Honors program. Limited pass/fail, internships. Preprofessional programs in church vocations, dentistry, law, medicine. 3-2 forestry program with Duke. 3-2 engineering programs with Georgia Tech, NCS, Tulane. Asian studies program with Virginia College and U Virginia. Study abroad. Elementary and secondary education certification. Language lab. 148,000-volume library.
Financial CEEB CSS. College scholarships, grants, loans, grants to church vocation students and ministers' children, payment plans; PELL, SEOG, NDSL, CWS, institutional work program. Application deadline April 1.
Admissions High school graduation with 14-20 units recommended. SAT or ACT required; 3 ACH required for early decision applicants. $15 application fee. Rolling admissions. $100 deposit due on acceptance of offer of admission. *Early Decision* and *Early Admission* programs. Transfers accepted. Credit possible for CEEB AP and college placement exams.
Student Life Student government. Newspaper, literary magazine, yearbook, radio station. Music and drama groups. Honorary, professional, religious, and special interest groups. 6 fraternities and 4 sororities. 25% of students join. Students must live on campus or at home. Single-sex dorms. 75% of students live on campus. Liquor, drugs, firearms, gambling, hazing, membership in secret societies prohibited. 7 intercollegiate sports; club and intramural programs. AIAW, NCAA. Student body composition: 0.2% Asian, 2.3% Black, 0.2% Hispanic, 96.7% White, 0.6% Other. 25% from out of state.

[1] FERRUM COLLEGE
Ferrum 24088, (703) 365-2121
Director of Admissions: F. Ross Ferguson

- **Undergraduates: 850m, 600w**
- **Tuition, Room & Board (1982/83): $4,990**
- **Degrees offered: BA, BS, BSW, AA, AS**
- **Mean SAT 400v, 400m**
- **Student-faculty ratio: 18 to 1**

A private college affiliated with the United Methodist Church, established in 1913. 750-acre rural campus, 35 miles from Roanoke. Bus service nearby; airport and rail station in Roanoke.
Academic Character SACS and professional accreditation. Semester system, 3- and 6-week summer terms. 20 majors offered in the areas of educational theatre, environmental studies, leisure services, psychological studies, public affairs & administration, religious studies, small business enterprise, and social work. Freshmen enroll in Junior Division and receive an associate degree after 2 years of study; they then continue at Ferrum or transfer to another senior college. 80% of students are in the Junior Division, which has 28 majors in the areas of agriculture, business, education, engineering, human services, industrial technology, liberal arts, and preprofessional programs. Distributives and 2 courses in religion required. Independent study. Honors program. Cooperative work/study. Internships and senior seminars required. ROTC. Blue Ridge Institute. Computer center. 66,000-volume library.
Financial CEEB CSS. College scholarships, loans, reductions for Methodist ministers' children, payment plan; PELL, SEOG, GSL, CWS. Preferred application deadlines April 15 (scholarships), March 15 (loans).
Admissions High school graduation required. GED accepted. Interview recommended. $15 application fee. Rolling admissions. $100 deposit due on acceptance of offer of admission. Admission deferral possible. Transfers accepted. Credit possible for CEEB AP, CLEP, and college challenge exams. Academic Challenge Program for academically underprepared students.
Student Life Student government. Newspaper, literary magazine, yearbook, radio station. Music and drama groups. Debate. Black Student Union. Academic and professional groups. Students encouraged to live on campus. Dorms and dining halls for men and women. Limited married-student housing. 90% of students live on campus. Honor code. Liquor prohibited. Class attendance required. 2 semesters of phys ed required. 8 intercollegiate sports for men, 5 for women; club and intramural sports. NJCAA, CC. Student body composition: 12% minority. 15% from out of state.

[1] GEORGE MASON UNIVERSITY
4400 University Drive, Fairfax 22030, (703) 323-2102
Director of Admissions: Patricia M. Riordan

- **Undergraduates: 2,825m, 3,424w; 14,263 total (including graduates)**
- **Tuition (1982/83): $1,176 (in-state), $2,232 (out-of-state)**
- **Room & Board: $3,292**
- **Degrees offered: BA, BS, BFA, BMus, BSEd, BSN, BIndiv Studies**
- **Mean SAT 453v, 503m**
- **Student-faculty ratio: 16 to 1**

A public university established in 1956. 571-acre suburban campus, 16 miles from Washington, DC. North Campus in Fairfax and School of Law in Arlington. Air, rail, and bus service nearby.
Academic Character SACS and professional accreditation. Semester system, 3 5-week and one 8-week summer terms. 47 majors offered by the College of Arts & Sciences, the College of Professional Studies, and the School of Business Administration. Self-designed majors. Distributive requirements. Graduate and professional degrees granted. Cooperative work/study, pass/fail, internships. Preprofessional programs in dentistry, law, medicine, veterinary medicine. Study abroad. Early childhood, elementary, secondary, library science, and vocational education certification. ROTC; AFROTC nearby. Computer center. Electron microscope. Writing Research Center. Center for Bilingual/Multicultural Teacher Preparation. Writers' Conference & Literary Festival. 340,000-volume library with microform resources; 125,000-volume law library.
Financial CEEB CSS. University scholarships, grants, loans, state grants and loans; PELL, SEOG, NDSL, GSL, NSL, CWS. Application deadline April 15.
Admissions High school graduation with 15 units required. SAT or ACT required; ACH recommended. $10 application fee. Rolling admissions. *Early Admission* and *Concurrent Enrollment* programs. Transfers accepted. Credit possible for CEEB AP and CLEP exams.
Student Life Student government. Newspaper, literary magazine, yearbook. Music and drama groups. Debate. Over 100 athletic, academic, honorary, political, religious, and special interest groups. Some apartment-style dorms.

Single-sex dorms. 1000 on-campus housing spaces available. No married-student housing. 5% of students live on campus. Honor code. Beer sold in Rathskeller; other liquor prohibited. 12 intercollegiate sports for men, 9 for women; many intramurals. AIAW, ECAC, NCAA, CCC. Student body composition: 3.4% Asian, 2.9% Black, 2% Hispanic, 0.4% Native American, 89.3% White. 9% from out of state.

[J1] GERMANNA COMMUNITY COLLEGE

Locust Grove 22508

[1] HAMPDEN-SYDNEY COLLEGE

Hampden-Sydney 23943, (804) 223-4388
Dean of Admissions: Robert H. Jones

- **Undergraduates: 750m**
- **Tuition (1982/83): $5,875**
- **Room & Board: $1,825**
- **Degrees offered: BA, BS**
- **Mean SAT 502v, 550m**
- **Student-faculty ratio: 12 to 1**

A private men's college affiliated with the Presbyterian Synod of the Virginias, established in 1776. 565-acre rural campus, 65 miles from Richmond. Bus service 6 miles away in Farmville.

Academic Character SACS accreditation. Semester system, spring short term. Majors offered in biochemistry, biology, biophysics, chemical physics, chemistry, classical studies, economics, economics-mathematics, English, French, Greek, history, humanities, interscience, Latin, Latin & Greek, management economics, mathematics, mathematics-computer science, philosophy, physics, political science, psychology, religion, religion-philosophy, and Spanish. Courses in fine arts. Distributive requirements. Independent study. Honors program. Phi Beta Kappa. Preprofessional programs in business, law, medicine, secondary education. Exchange programs in education, sociology, anthropology with Longwood. Junior/senior exchange with 6 area schools. 3-2 engineering program with Georgia Tech and VPI. Applied chemistry program with VPI. Washington Semester. Appalachian Semester. Study abroad. Secondary education certification with Longwood. ROTC at Longwood. Computer center. Language lab. 140,000-volume library.

Financial CEEB CSS. College scholarships, loans, state scholarships; PELL, SEOG, NDSL, GSL, CWS. Application deadline March 1.

Admissions High school graduation with 16 units required. Interview encouraged. SAT required; 2 ACH required. $25 application fee. Rolling admissions. $200 deposit due on acceptance of offer of admission. *Early Decision* and *Early Admission* programs. Admission deferral possible. Transfers accepted. Credit possible for CEEB AP and CLEP exams.

Student Life Student government. Newspaper, literary magazine, yearbook, radio station. Music and drama groups. Debate. Academic, honorary, religious, and special interest groups. 10 fraternities, 9 with houses. 55% of students join. Students must live in dorms, fraternities, or houses approved by Dean. 92% of students live on campus. Honor code. Class attendance expected. Freshmen must attend 3 convocations. 10 intercollegiate sports; many club and intramural programs. NCAA, ODAC. Student body composition: 1% Black, 97% White, 2% Other. 40% from out of state.

[1] HAMPTON INSTITUTE

Hampton 23368, (804) 727-5328
Dean of Admissions: Ollie M. Bowman

- **Enrollment: 1,299m, 1,931w**
- **Tuition (1982/83): $2,985**
- **Room & Board: $1,500**
- **Degrees offered: BA, BS, BArch**
- **Mean ACT 18m, 18e; mean SAT 800 composite**
- **Student-faculty ratio: 14 to 1**

A private institute established in 1868. 210-acre suburban campus on the James and York rivers, 8 miles north of Norfolk and 80 miles east of Richmond. Served by air, rail, and bus.

Academic Character SACS and professional accreditation. Semester system, 6- and 8-week summer terms. 45 majors offered in the areas of arts & humanities, social sciences, business, education, nursing, and pure & applied sciences. Distributive requirements. Masters degrees granted. Independent study. Honors program. Cooperative work/study, pass/fail. Preprofessional programs in dentistry, law, medicine, pharmacy, social work. 3-2 engineering programs with George Washington U and Old Dominion. Elementary and secondary education certification. ROTC, NROTC. Elementary lab school. Museum. Theatre. 258,319-volume library with microform resources.

Financial CEEB CSS. Institute scholarships, grants, loans, Native American grants, payment plan; PELL, SEOG, NSS, NDSL, CWS. Application deadline July 1.

Admissions High school graduation with 16 units required. SAT or ACT required. $10 application fee. Rolling admissions. $50 tuition deposit and $100 room deposit due on acceptance of offer of admission. *Early Decision* and *Early Admission* programs. Admission deferral possible. Transfers accepted. Credit possible for CEEB AP exams.

Student Life Student government. Newspaper, radio and TV stations. Music and drama groups. Debate. Athletic, academic, honorary, religious, service, and special interest groups. 6 social clubs for men, 4 for women. 5 fraternities and 4 sororities without houses. 7% of men and 8% of women join. Single-sex dorms. Some married-student dorm arrangements possible, if space permits. 69% of students live on campus. Freshmen and sophomores may not have cars. Liquor and drugs prohibited. Class attendance required. Students must inform Dean of marriage intentions. 2 semesters of phys ed and 1 semester of health required. 8 intercollegiate sports; intramurals. CIAA, NAIA, NCAA. Student body composition: 0.1% Asian, 96.6% Black, 0.1% Hispanic, 1.8% White, 1.4% Other.

[1] HOLLINS COLLEGE

Hollins College 24020, (703) 362-6000
Director of Admissions: Sandra J. Lovinguth

- **Undergraduates: 824w; 950 total (including graduates)**
- **Tuition (1982/83): $6,100**
- **Room & Board: $2,650; Fees: $150**
- **Degree offered: AB**
- **Mean SAT 1,002**
- **Student-faculty ratio: 10 to 1**

A private women's college with coed graduate programs, established in 1842. 450-acre suburban campus, 6 miles north of downtown Roanoke. Served by air and bus.

Academic Character SACS and professional accreditation. 4-1-4 system. 34 majors offered in the areas of American studies, classical studies, computer science, economics/business, fine arts, liberal arts, modern languages, music, religion, science, social sciences, statistics, and theatre. Self-designed majors. Distributive requirements. MA, MALS granted. 4-week January special project. Independent study. Honors program. Phi Beta Kappa. Limited pass/fail, internships. Preprofessional programs in law and medicine. 3-2 engineering programs with Washington U, VPI. 3-2 nursing program with UVA. 4-2 architecture program with VPI. Cross-registration with 6 area schools. UN Semester. Washington Semester. Study abroad. Elementary and secondary education certification. ROTC at Washington and Lee. Language labs. 205,000-volume library.

Financial CEEB CSS. College scholarships, grants, loans, payment plans; PELL, SEOG, NDSL, FISL, USAF, GSL, CWS, on-campus employment. Application deadline March 1.

Admissions High school graduation with 16 units required. Interview recommended. SAT required. $20 application fee. Rolling admissions. $400 deposit due on acceptance of admissions offer. *Early Decision* and *Early Admission* programs. Admission deferral possible. Transfers accepted. Credit possible for CEEB AP exams.

Student Life Student government. Newspaper, literary magazine, yearbook. Music, dance, drama, and opera groups. Debate. Community Security Council. Athletic, academic, religious, and special interest groups. Women's dorms. French House. 95% of students live on campus. Honor system. Liquor restricted. Class attendance expected. 8 intercollegiate sports; intramurals. Student body composition: 2% Black, 96% White, 2% Other. 63% from out of state.

[J1] J. SARGEANT REYNOLDS COMMUNITY COLLEGE

Richmond 23230

[1] JAMES MADISON UNIVERSITY

Harrisonburg 22807, (703) 433-6147
Director of Admissions: Francis E. Turner

- **Undergraduates: 3,568m, 4,136w; 8,970 total (including graduates)**
- **Tuition (1982/83): $1,506 (in-state), $2,346 (out-of-state)**
- **Room & Board: $2,164**
- **Degrees offered: BA, BS, BBA, BFA, BGS, BMus, BMus Ed, BSN, BSW**
- **Mean SAT 1,047**
- **Student-faculty ratio: 17 to 1**

A public university established in 1908, became coed in 1966. 365-acre small-city campus, 125 miles from Richmond and Washington, DC. Served by bus; airport 20 minutes away.

Academic Character SACS and professional accreditation. Semester system, 3-, 4-, 6-, and 8-week summer terms. 22 majors offered by the College of Letters & Sciences, 11 by the School of Business, 15 by the School of Education & Human Services, 5 by the School of Fine Arts & Communication, and 1 by the School of Nursing. Minors offered in most major fields and in interdisciplinary studies and secondary education. Distributive requirements. Masters degrees granted. Independent study. Honors program. Limited pass/fail, credit by exam, internships. Preprofessional programs in dentistry, law, medicine, theology. 2-year transfer programs in engineering, physical therapy. Cross-registration with 7 area schools. Study abroad. Elementary, secondary, library science, and special education certification. ROTC. Computer center. Child Development Center. Language lab. TV/film center. Farm. 380,000-volume library with microform resources.

Financial CEEB CSS. University scholarships, grants, loans; PELL, SEOG, NDSL, FISL, CWS. Application deadline March 1.

Admissions High school graduation with 16 units required. GED accepted. Audition required for music majors. SAT required; ACT not accepted. $15 application fee. Rolling admissions. $100 room deposit due on acceptance of admissions offer. *Early Decision* and *Concurrent Enrollment* programs. Transfers accepted. Credit possible for CEEB AP and CLEP exams.

Student Life Student government. Newspaper, literary magazine, yearbook, radio station. Music, dance, and drama groups. Debate. Black Student Alliance. Saturday Adoption Program. Academic, honorary, political, religious, and special interest groups. 9 fraternities and 8 sororities. 10% of students join. Freshmen must live at home or on campus. Coed and single-sex dorms. Language and music houses. No married-student housing. 65% of students live on campus. Seniors and commuters may have cars. Honor system. 2 hours of phys ed required. 12 intercollegiate sports for men, 12 for women; intramurals. AIAW, NCAA. Student body composition: 4% Black, 95% White, 1% Other. 20% from out of state.

[J1] JOHN TYLER COMMUNITY COLLEGE
Chester 23831

[1] LIBERTY BAPTIST COLLEGE
3765 Candlers Mountain Road, Lynchburg 24506, (804) 237-5961
Director of Admissions: Thomas M. Diggs

- **Undergraduates: 1,786m, 1,555w**
- **Tuition (1982/83): $2,000**
- **Room & Board: $2,200; Fees: $270**
- **Degree offered: BS**
- **Student-faculty ratio: 19 to 1**

A private college controlled by the Thomas Road Baptist Church, established in 1971. 4,000-acre small-town campus 50 miles from Roanoke and 100 miles from Richmond. Served by air, rail, and bus.
Academic Character SACS accreditation. Semester system, 2 4-week summer terms. 29 majors offered in the areas of business, communications, education, fine arts, natural sciences & mathematics, religion, and social sciences. Minor required for all non-education majors. Minors offered in all major fields and 16 other areas. Self-designed majors. Distributives and 21 hours of religion required. Independent study. Study abroad. Elementary and secondary education certification. Language lab. TV studio. 133,000-volume library with microform resources.
Financial CEEB CSS. College scholarships, grants, loans, pastors' children scholarships; PELL, SEOG, FISL, CWS. Application deadline August 1.
Admissions High school graduation with 16 units required. GED accepted. Admission granted on personal salvation experience with Jesus Christ, secondary school graduation, transcript, and 3 letters of recommendation. SAT or ACT required. $25 application fee. Rolling admissions. $100 deposit due on acceptance of admissions offer. *Early Admission* and *Concurrent Enrollment* programs. Admission deferral possible. Transfers accepted. Credit possible for CEEB AP, CLEP, and ACT PEP exams. Special admission possible.
Student Life Student government. Yearbook, radio and TV stations. Music and drama groups. Young Americans for Freedom. Students must live at home or on campus. Single-sex dorms. 72% of students live on campus. Liquor, drugs, tobacco, dancing, gambling, movies, profanity prohibited. Social functions chaperoned. Honor code. Strict dress code; hair code for men. Class and chapel attendance required. 4 semesters of phys ed required. 7 intercollegiate sports for men, 5 for women; many intramurals. AIAW, NAIA, NCAA. Student body composition: 0.5% Asian, 3% Black, 1% Hispanic, 1% Native American, 94.5% White. 70% from out of state.

[1] LONGWOOD COLLEGE
Farmville 23901, (804) 392-9251
Director of Admissions: Gary C. Groneweg

- **Undergraduates: 700m, 1,700w; 2,589 total (including graduates)**
- **Tuition (1982/83): $850 (in-state), $1,480 (out-of-state)**
- **Room & Board: $2,005; Fees: $715**
- **Degrees offered: BA, BS, BFA, BMus, BMus Ed, BSBA, BSBEd**
- **Mean SAT 440v, 470m**
- **Student-faculty ratio: 17 to 1**

A public college established in 1839, became coed in 1975. 50-acre small-town campus, 60 miles from Richmond. Served by bus; airport in Richmond.
Academic Character SACS and professional accreditation. Semester system, 2 5-week summer terms. 32 majors offered in the areas of art, business, drama, education, home economics, liberal arts, modern languages, music, physical education, science, and social sciences. Distributive requirements. Masters degrees granted. Independent study. Honors program. Pass/fail, internships. Preprofessional programs in 10 areas with Medical College of Virginia and UVA. Medical technology program with Duke. Engineering programs with Old Dominion and Georgia Tech. Cooperative programs in engineering, nursing, physical therapy. Cross-registration with Hampden-Sydney. Study abroad. Elementary and secondary education certification; library science accreditation. ROTC. Language lab. 200,000-volume library.
Financial CEEB CSS. College scholarships, grants, loans, payment plans; PELL, SEOG, NDSL, CWS. Application deadline April 1.
Admissions High school graduation with 9 units required. Campus visit encouraged. SAT or ACT required; ACH required of language students. $15 application fee. Rolling admissions. $90 deposit due on acceptance of admissions offer. *Early Admission* Program. Admission deferral possible. Transfers accepted. Credit possible for CEEB AP, CLEP, and college proficiency exams.
Student Life Student government. Newspaper, literary magazine, yearbook. Music and drama groups. Academic, honorary, political, religious, service, and special interest groups. 6 fraternities and 11 sororities with space in dorms. 27% of women join sororities. Students must live at home or on campus. Coed and single-sex dorms. Over 90% of students live on campus. Honor code. Liquor restricted to dorm rooms. 4 semesters of phys ed required. 12 intercollegiate sports; intramurals. NCAA. Student body composition: 7% Black, 93% White. 9% from out of state.

[J1] LORD FAIRFAX COMMUNITY COLLEGE
PO Box 47, Middletown 22645

[1] LYNCHBURG COLLEGE
Lynchburg 24501, (804) 522-8100, ext. 300
Dean of Admissions: E.R. Chadderton

- **Undergraduates: 741m, 942w; 2,450 total (including graduates)**
- **Tuition (1982/83): $4,900**
- **Room & Board: $2,400**
- **Degrees offered: BA, BS**
- **Mean SAT 950**
- **Student-faculty ratio: 13 to 1**

A private college affiliated with the Christian Church (Disciples of Christ), established in 1903. 214-acre wooded, suburban campus, 100 miles west of Richmond. Served by air, rail, and bus.
Academic Character SACS accreditation. Semester system, 4 3-week summer terms. 42 majors offered in the areas of American studies, art, business, education, health, journalism, liberal arts, mathematics, medical technology, modern languages, music, nuclear medical technology, nursing, physical education, recreation, religion, science, social sciences, and theatre. Joint BA/BS majors in 8 areas. Minor required. Distributive requirements; varied degree requirement options. Masters degrees granted. Independent study. Honors program. Phi Beta Kappa. Limited pass/fail, internships. Preprofessional programs in dentistry, forestry/wildlife management, journalism, law, library science, medicine, ministry, nursing, optometry, pharmacy, physical therapy, social work, veterinary medicine. 3-2 engineering programs with Old Dominion and Georgia Tech. 3-2 MBA program. 3-2 professional programs possible. Cross-registration with Randolph-Macon Women's College, Sweet Briar. Study abroad. Elementary, secondary, and special education certification. ROTC. Computer center. Language labs. 178,000-volume library with microform resources.
Financial Guaranteed tuition and comprehensive fees. CEEB CSS. College scholarships, grants, loans, ministers' dependent grants, church-vocation grants, payment plan; PELL, SEOG, NDSL, CWS, college work programs. Application deadlines March 15 (scholarships), April 1 (loans).
Admissions High school graduation with 15 units required. GED may be accepted. Interview recommended. SAT or ACT required; 3 ACH required. $15 application fee. Rolling admissions. $100 deposit due on acceptance of admissions offer. *Early Admission* and *Early Decision* programs. Admission deferral possible. Transfers accepted. Credit possible for CEEB AP, CLEP, and college proficiency exams.
Student Life Student government. Newspaper, literary magazine, yearbook, radio station. Music and drama groups. Athletic, academic, honorary, religious, service, and special interest groups. Fraternities and sororities. Seniors may live off campus. Single-sex dorms. Apartments. 90% of students live on campus. Dormitory students may not have cars. 10 intercollegiate sports for men, 8 for women; many club and intramural programs. AIAW, NCAA, ODAC, VIC. Student body composition: 2.5% Black, 0.5% Hispanic, 95.1% White, 1.9% Other. 45% from out of state.

[1] MARY BALDWIN COLLEGE
Staunton 24401, (703) 885-0811
Director of Admissions: Clair Carter Bell

- **Undergraduates: 817w**
- **Tuition, Room & Board (1982/83): $7,680**
- **Degree offered: AB**
- **Student-faculty ratio: 12 to 1**

A private women's college affiliated with the Presbyterian Church of the United States, established in 1842. 50-acre small-city campus, 100 miles west of Richmond. Served by air, rail, and bus.
Academic Character SACS accreditation. Semester system, 4-week May term. 25 majors offered in the areas of art, biology, business, chemistry, economics, English, French, history, mass communications, mathematics, medical technology, music, political science, psychology, religion-philosophy, sociology, Spanish, speech, and theatre. Distributives and senior exams or projects required. Independent study. Phi Beta Kappa. Limited pass/fail, externships. Preprofessional programs in Christian ministry, law, medicine, veterinary medicine. Cross-registration with 6 area schools. Summer marine biology program. Study abroad. Elementary, secondary, and special education certification. ROTC at James Madison. Communications lab. 150,000-volume library.
Financial CEEB CSS. College scholarships, grants, loans, state aid, payment plan; PELL, SEOG, NDSL, FISL, GSL, CWS, college work program. Application deadline March 1.
Admissions High school graduation with 16 units required. Interview welcomed. SAT and 3 ACH required. $20 application fee. Rolling admissions. $200 deposit due on acceptance of admissions offer. *Early Decision* and *Early Admission* programs. Admission deferral possible. Transfers accepted. Credit possible for CEEB AP and college proficiency exams.
Student Life Student government. Newspaper, literary magazine, yearbook. Music, dance, and drama groups. Honorary, service, and special interest groups. Students must live with families or on campus. Women's dorms. 90% of students live on campus. Honor system. 7 intercollegiate sports; intramurals, horse shows. NCAA, ODAC. Student body composition: 1% Asian, 2% Black, 0.5% Hispanic, 96.5% White. 60% from out of state.

[1] MARY WASHINGTON COLLEGE
Fredericksburg 22401, (703) 899-4681
Dean of Admissions & Financial Aid: H. Conrad Warlick

- **Undergraduates: 542m, 1,715w; 2,725 total (including graduates)**
- **Tuition (1982/83): $828 (in-state), $1,960 (out-of-state)**
- **Room & Board: $2,336; Fees: $220**
- **Degrees offered: BA, BS, BLS, BSMT**
- **Mean SAT 502v, 512m**
- **Student-faculty ratio: 16 to 1**

A public college established in 1908, became coed in 1970. 275-acre suburban campus, 50 miles from Richmond. Served by rail and bus.
Academic Character SACS and professional accreditation. Semester system, 1 3-week and 2 4-week summer terms. 35 majors offered by the

departments of Anthropology, Geography & Sociology; Art; Biological Sciences; Chemistry & Geology; Classics, Philosophy & Religion; Dramatic Arts & Dance; Economics, Business & Public Affairs; Education; English, Linguistics, & Speech; Health & Physical Education; History & American Studies; Mathematical Sciences & Physics; Modern Foreign Languages; Music; and Psychology. Self-designed majors. Distributive requirements. Masters degrees granted. Independent study. Honors program. Phi Beta Kappa. Limited pass/fail, credit by exam, internships. Preprofessional programs in dentistry, law, medicine, pharmacy, physical therapy, veterinary science. Study abroad. Elementary and secondary education certification. Language labs. Audio-visual center. Computer center. 275,000-volume library with microform resources.
Financial CEEB CSS. College scholarships, grants, loans; PELL, SEOG, NDSL, FISL, CWS. Scholarship application deadline February 1.
Admissions High school graduation with 16 units recommended. Interview recommended. SAT required; 2 ACH recommended. $15 application fee. Suggest applying by March 1; notification by April 1. $100 deposit due on acceptance of admissions offer. *Early Decision, Early Admission, Concurrent Enrollment* programs. Admission deferral possible. Transfers accepted. Credit possible for CEEB AP and CLEP exams.
Student Life Student government. Newspaper, literary magazine, yearbook, radio station. Music and drama groups. Debate. Academic, honorary, political, professional, religious, and special interest groups. Coed and single-sex dorms. Language houses. 85% of students live on campus. Honor system. 2 credits of phys ed or dance required. 7 intercollegiate sports for men, 9 for women; intramurals. AIAW, NCAA. Student body composition: 2% Asian, 2% Black, 1% Hispanic, 95% White. 23% from out of state.

[1] MARYMOUNT COLLEGE OF VIRGINIA
Arlington 22207, (703) 522-5600
Director of Admissions: Kathryn B. del Campo

- **Undergraduates: 5m, 860w; 1,394 total (including graduates)**
- **Tuition (1982/83): $4,200**
- **Room & Board: $2,650**
- **Degrees offered: BA, BBA, BSN, AA, AAS**
- **Student-faculty ratio: 14 to 1**

A private college primarily for women, conducted by the Religious of the Sacred Heart of Mary, established in 1950. 17-acre suburban campus, 5 miles from Washington. Served by air, rail, and bus.
Academic Character SACS and professional accreditation. Semester system, 3 5-week summer terms. 10 majors offered by the Division of Arts & Sciences, 9 by the Division of Business Administration, 9 by the Division of Education & Human Services, and 1 by the Division of Health Services. Minors offered. Distributives and 1 semester of philosophy of religion required. Masters degrees granted. Internships. Cross-registration with 4 area schools. Elementary and secondary education certification. Learning lab. Computer center. A-V Center. 65,000-volume library with microform resources.
Financial CEEB CSS. College scholarships, grants, payment plan; PELL, SEOG, NDSL, FISL, NSL, CWS, college employment. Scholarship application deadline May 1.
Admissions High school graduation with 16 units recommended. GED accepted. Interview recommended. SAT or ACT required. $20 application fee. Rolling admissions; suggest applying by December. $100 deposit due on acceptance of admissions offer. *Early Admission* Program. Admission deferral possible. Transfers accepted. Credit possible for CEEB AP, CLEP, and college proficiency exams.
Student Life Student-faculty councils. Literary magazine, yearbook. Music and drama groups. International Club. Academic, honorary, political, religious, and social groups. Juniors and seniors may live off campus. Single-sex dorms. 50% of students live on campus. Liquor permitted in specific areas. Honor system. 1 semester of phys ed required. 4 intercollegiate sports; intramurals. AIAW. Student body composition: 3% Asian, 7% Black, 4% Hispanic, 78% White, 8% Other. 60% from out of state.

[J1] MOUNTAIN EMPIRE COMMUNITY COLLEGE
Drawer 700, Big Stone Gap 24219

[J1] NEW RIVER COMMUNITY COLLEGE
Drawer 1127, Dublin 24084

[1] NORFOLK STATE UNIVERSITY
Norfolk 23504, (804) 623-8600
Director of Admissions: James Stence Burton

- **Enrollment: 3,189m, 4,066w (including graduates)**
- **Tuition (1982/83): $862 (in-state), $1,542 (out-of-state)**
- **Room & Board: $960**
- **Degrees offered: BA, BS, BMus, BSW**
- **Student-faculty ratio: 22 to 1**

A public university established in 1935. 110-acre urban campus. Served by bus.
Academic Character SACS and professional accreditation. Semester system, 1 summer term. 10 majors offered by the School of Arts & Letters, 5 by the School of Business, 6 by the School of Education, 17 by the School of Health Related Professions & Sciences, 13 by the School of Social Sciences, 2 by the School of Social Work, and 4 by the School of Technology. Interdisciplinary programs. Distributive requirements. Graduate degrees granted. Honors program. Cooperative work/study. 2-2 industrial arts program with Tidewater Community College. Cross-registration with Old Dominion. Elementary and secondary education certification. ROTC. Computer center. Audio labs. Media center. 200,000-volume library with microform resources.
Financial University scholarships, grants, state aid, PELL, NDSL, student employment.
Admissions High school graduation with 16 units required. GED accepted. SAT required. $10 application fee. Rolling admissions. Transfers accepted. Credit possible for CEEB CLEP exams. Conditional admission possible.
Student Life Student government. Newspaper, yearbook. Music and drama groups. Debate. NAACP. Academic and special interest groups. 4 fraternities and 4 sororities. Coed dorms. 15% of students live on campus. Class attendance expected. 5 intercollegiate sports; intramurals. NAIA, AIAW. Student body composition: 89% Black, 7% White, 4% Other. 16% from out of state.

[J1] NORTHERN VIRGINIA COMMUNITY COLLEGE
8333 Little River Turnpike, Annandale 22003

[1] OLD DOMINION UNIVERSITY
Norfolk 23508, (804) 440-3637
Director of Admissions: Michael E. Malone

- **Undergraduates: 5,975m, 5,979w; 16,486 total (including graduates)**
- **Tuition (1982/83): $1,114 (in-state), $2,074 (out-of-state)**
- **Room & Board: $2,428**
- **Degrees offered: BA, BS, BFA, BSMus, BSBA, BSEE, BSHE, BSPE, BSSE, BSSpE, BSET, BSCE, BSEEng, BSMEng, BSCS, BSDH, BSEH, BSMT, BSN, BSPT**
- **Student-faculty ratio: 30 to 1**

A public university established in 1930. 120-acre urban campus. Air, rail, and bus service nearby.
Academic Character SACS and professional accreditation. Semester system, 3 4-week, 2 8-week, and 1 12-week summer terms. 20 majors offered by the School of Arts & Letters, 7 by the School of Business Administration, 23 by the School of Education, 7 by the School of Engineering, 2 by the School of General Studies, and 18 by the School of Sciences & Health Professions. Distributive requirements. Graduate degrees granted. Independent study. Honors program. Cooperative work/study, limited pass/fail. Cross-registration with 20 area schools. Study in England for student teachers. Elementary, secondary, and special education certification. ROTC, NROTC. Computer center. Child Study Center. Urban research center. Planetarium. 1,000,000-volume library with microform resources.
Financial CEEB CSS. University scholarships, grants, loans, state aid, payment plans; PELL, SEOG, NSS, NDSL, FISL, CWS, university work program. Application deadline April 1; FAF deadline 6 weeks earlier.
Admissions High school graduation with 16 units required. GED accepted. SAT required. $20 application fee. Rolling admissions. $300 room deposit due on acceptance of admissions offer. *Early Admission* and *Concurrent Enrollment* programs. Admission deferral possible. Transfers accepted. Credit possible for CEEB AP, CLEP, and university proficiency exams. EOP for disadvantaged students.
Student Life Student government. Newspaper, literary magazine. Music and drama groups. Debate. Honorary, professional, political, religious, service, and special interest groups. 14 fraternities and 8 sororities, all with houses. Single-sex and apartment-style dorms house 1,500 students. 10% of students live on campus. Honor Code. 13 intercollegiate sports; intramurals. AIAW, ECAC, NCAA. Student body composition: 9% Black, 1.5% Hispanic, 0.5% Native American, 87% White, 2% Other. 19% from out of state.

[J1] PATRICK HENRY COMMUNITY COLLEGE
PO Drawer 5311, Martinsville 24112

[J1] PAUL D. CAMP COMMUNITY COLLEGE
PO Box 737, Franklin 23851

[J1] PIEDMONT VIRGINIA COMMUNITY COLLEGE
Charlottesville 22901

[1] PRESBYTERIAN SCHOOL OF EDUCATION
Richmond 23227

[1 & G1] RADFORD UNIVERSITY
Radford 24142, (703) 731-5371
Director of Admissions: J. Andrew Bales

- **Enrollment: 2,000m, 4,200w (including graduates)**
- **Tuition & Fees (1982/83): $1,254 (in-state), $2,004 (out-of-state)**
- **Room & Board: $2,295**
- **Degrees offered: BA, BBA, BFA, BMus, BS**
- **Mean SAT 490v, 470m**
- **Student-faculty ratio: 19 to 1**

A public university established in 1910, became coed in 1972. 75-acre small-city campus, 45 miles southwest of Roanoke. Served by air and bus.
Academic Character SACS and professional accreditation. Trimester system, 2 5-week summer terms. 64 majors offered in the areas of art, business, computer science, criminal justice, education, foreign languages, home economics, journalism, liberal arts, library science, mathematics, medical technology, music, nursing, physical education, recreation, science, social sciences, speech, and theatre. Self-designed majors. Minors offered. Distributive requirements. Masters degrees granted. Independent study. Honors programs. Limited pass/fail, internships. Preprofessional programs in dentistry, law, medicine. Cooperative chemical engineering program with VPI.

Elementary, secondary, and special education certification. ROTC. Fine Arts Center. Language lab. Laboratory nursery school and kindergarten. 200,000-volume library.
Financial CEEB CSS. University scholarships, grants, loans, payment plans; PELL, SEOG, NDSL, CWS. Application deadline April 15.
Admissions High school graduation with 16 units required. HSET accepted. SAT required. Auditions required for music, dance, and theatre students; portfolio required for art majors. $15 application fee. Rolling admissions. $100 room deposit due on acceptance of admissions offer. *Early Admission* and *Concurrent Enrollment* programs. Transfers accepted. Credit possible for CEEB AP, CLEP, and ACH exams.
Student Life Student government. Newspaper, literary magazine, yearbook. Music, dance, and drama groups. Black Culture Club. Orchesis. Academic, honorary, religious, service, and special interest groups. 6 fraternities and 6 sororities. 6% of women join. Single students under 21 must live on campus or with families. Coed and single-sex dorms. Special interest housing. 65% of students live on campus. Honor system. 6 quarter hours of phys ed required. 6 intercollegiate sports for men, 5 for women; intramurals. Student body composition: 0.3% Asian, 3% Black, 0.6% Hispanic, 95.1% White. 7% from out of state.

[1] RANDOLPH-MACON COLLEGE

Ashland 23005, (703) 798-8372
Director of Admissions: Charles F. Nelson, Jr.

- **Undergraduates: 566m, 359w**
- **Tuition (1982/83): $5,000**
- **Room & Board: $2,200**
- **Degrees offered: BA, BS**
- **Mean SAT 991**
- **Student-faculty ratio: 13 to 1**

A private college affiliated with the United Methodist Church, established in 1830, became coed in 1971. 85-acre small-town campus, 15 miles north of Richmond. Served by rail and bus.
Academic Character SACS accreditation. 4-4-1 system. Majors offered in biology, chemistry, classics, computer science, economics, English, French, German, history, mathematics, philosophy, physics, political science, psychology, religion, Romance languages, sociology, and Spanish. Distributive requirements; senior project in some departments. Independent study. Honors program. Phi Beta Kappa. Cooperative work/study in physics. Preprofessional programs in dentistry, law, medicine, ministry. 3-2 engineering programs with Washington U and Columbia U. 5-year forestry program with Duke. Cross-registration with 6 area schools. Study abroad. Secondary education certification. ROTC at U Richmond. Computer center. Language lab. Observatory. 115,000-volume library.
Financial CEEB CSS. College scholarships, grants, loans, discount for Methodist ministers' children, state aid; PELL, SEOG, NDSL, GSL, PLUS, CWS, college student assistant program. Application deadlines March 1 (scholarships), February 15 (other aid).
Admissions High school graduation with 16 units required. SAT or ACT required; 3 ACH recommended. $20 application fee. Rolling admissions. $200 deposit due on acceptance of admissions offer. *Early Decision* and *Early Admission* programs. Admission deferral possible. Transfers accepted. Credit possible for CEEB AP and college proficiency exams.
Student Life Student government. Newspaper, literary magazine, yearbook. Music and drama groups. Debate. Amnesty International. International Relations Club. Honorary, religious, and special interest groups. Fraternities and sorority, some with houses. Students live at home or on campus. Single-sex dorms. Married-student housing. 95% of students live on campus. Honor Code. 2 semesters of phys ed required. 7 intercollegiate sports for men, 5 for women; many intramurals. NCAA, ODAC. Student body composition: 0.5% Asian, 1% Black, 0.5% Hispanic, 0.5% Native American, 97% White, 0.5% Other. 34% from out of state.

[1] RANDOLPH-MACON WOMEN'S COLLEGE

Lynchburg 24508, (804) 846-7392
Director of Admissions: Robert T. Merritt

- **Undergraduates: 720w**
- **Tuition (1982/83): $5,900**
- **Room & Board: $2,600; Fees: $80**
- **Degree offered: AB**
- **Mean SAT 550v, 550m**
- **Student-faculty ratio: 10 to 1**

A private college affiliated with the Methodist Church, established in 1891. 100-acre suburban campus, 50 miles northeast of Roanoke. Served by air, bus, and rail.
Academic Character SACS accreditation. Semester system. 34 majors offered in the areas of American studies, Asian civilization, classics, communication, education, fine arts, international studies, Latin American studies, liberal arts, mathematics, medical technology, religion, Russian studies, science, social sciences, theatre, and urban studies. Distributive requirements. Independent study. Juniors and seniors may read for honors. Phi Beta Kappa. 3-2 engineering programs with Vanderbilt and Duke. 5-year special education program with UVA. Cross-registration with 8 area colleges. UN and Washington semesters. Study in England, Athens, Rome. Near East Archaeological seminar. Language lab. 150,000-volume library with microform resources.
Financial CEEB CSS. College scholarships, grants, ministerial grants, loans; PELL, SEOG, NDSL, GSL, CWS. Scholarship application deadline March 1.
Admissions High school graduation with 16 units recommended. Interview recommended. SAT or ACT, and 3 ACH required. $20 application fee. Rolling admissions. $300 deposit due on acceptance of admissions offer. *Early Decision* and *Early Admission* programs. Admission deferral possible. Transfers accepted. Credit possible for CEEB AP and CLEP exams.
Student Life Student government. Newspaper, literary magazine, yearbook, radio station. Music, dance, and drama groups. Minority Affairs Club. Women's Coalition. Academic, religious, service, and special interest groups. Single students live at home or on campus. 98% of students live on campus. Class attendance expected. 2 years of phys ed required. 6 intercollegiate sports; intramurals. AIAW. Student body composition: 2.6% Black, 0.4% Hispanic, 94.4% White, 2.6% Other. 70% from out of state.

[J1] RAPPAHANNOCK COMMUNITY COLLEGE

Glenns 23149

[1] RICHMOND, UNIVERSITY OF

Richmond 23173, (804) 285-6262
Dean of Admissions: Thomas N. Pollard, Jr.

- **Undergraduates: 1,372m, 1,097w; 4,215 total (including graduates)**
- **Tuition (1982/83): $5,525**
- **Room & Board: $2,050-$2,250**
- **Degrees offered: BA, BS, BSBA, BMus, BAS, AAS**
- **Mean SAT 494v, 552m (men); 513v, 552m (women)**
- **Student-faculty ratio: 13 to 1**

A private university affiliated with the Baptist Church, established in 1830. 350-acre suburban campus. Served by air, rail, and bus.
Academic Character SACS and professional accreditation. Semester system, summer terms. 43 majors offered in the areas of American studies, business, classics, criminal justice, education, humanities, journalism, mathematics, modern languages, music, physical education, religion, Russian studies, science, social science, speech, theatre, urban and women's studies. Distributive requirements. Graduate and professional degrees granted. Independent studies. Honors program. Phi Beta Kappa. Limited pass/fail, internships. Preprofessional programs in dentistry, forestry, law, medicine. Cooperative forestry program with Duke. New York and Washington programs. Study abroad. Early childhood, elementary, and secondary education certification. ROTC. Undergraduate research program. Computer center. Fine arts center. 410,000-volume libraries with microform resources.
Financial CEEB CSS. University scholarships, grants, loans, ministerial scholarships, state aid, payment plan; PELL, SEOG, NDSL, GSL, CWS, university employment. Scholarship application deadline March 15.
Admissions High school graduation with 16 units required. SAT or ACT, and 3 ACH required. $25 application fee. Application deadline February 1. $250 tuition and $250 room deposits due on acceptance of admissions offer. *Early Decision* and *Early Admission* programs. Admission deferral possible. Few transfers accepted. Credit possible for CEEB AP and CLEP exams.
Student Life Student government. Newspaper, literary magazine, yearbook, radio station. Music and drama groups. Debate. Honorary, religious, service, and special interest groups. 11 fraternities with houses. 45% of men join. Single-sex dorms. No married-student housing. 85% of students live on campus. Honor code. Class attendance expected. 4 semesters of phys ed required. 12 intercollegiate sports for men, 9 for women; many intramurals. AIAW, ECAC, NCAA. Student body composition: 0.8% Asian, 6% Black, 0.2% Hispanic, 0.4% Native American, 92.6% White. 70% from out of state.

[1] ROANOKE COLLEGE

Salem 24153, (703) 389-2351
Director of Admissions: William C. Schaaf

- **Undergraduates: 560m, 569w**
- **Tuition (1982/83): $4,750**
- **Room & Board: $2,075**
- **Degrees offered: BA, BS, BBA**
- **Mean SAT 458v, 485m**
- **Student-faculty ratio: 17 to 1**

A private college affiliated with the Lutheran Church in America, established in 1842. 68-acre suburban campus, 7 miles west of Roanoke. Served by air, rail, and bus.
Academic Character SACS accreditation. 4-1-4 system, 2 4-week summer terms. 27 majors offered in the areas of art, business administration, computer science & statistics, criminal justice, elementary education, fine arts, humanities, international relations, mathematics, modern languages, music, medical technology, radiologic technology, religion, science, social science, and urban studies. Distributive requirements. Independent study. Departmental honors courses. Limited pass/fail, internships. Preprofessional programs in dentistry, law, medicine, optometry, pharmacy, theology, and veterinary medicine. Exchange programs with Hollins, Wagner, and Fairleigh-Dickinson. Member Western Region Consortium. Study abroad. Early childhood, elementary, and secondary education certification. Language lab. 130,000-volume library.
Financial CEEB CSS. College scholarships, grants, loans, reductions for ministerial students and ministers' children, state aid; PELL, SEOG, NDSL, GSL, CWS. Application deadline March 1.
Admissions High school graduation with 16 units required. GED accepted. SAT or ACT required; 3 ACH recommended. $15 application fee. Rolling admissions. $200 deposit due on acceptance of admissions offer. *Early Decision* and *Early Admission* programs. Admission deferral possible. Transfers accepted. Credit possible for CEEB AP and college competency exams.
Student Life Student government. Newspaper, literary magazine, yearbook. Music and theatre groups. Debate. Upward Bound tutoring program. Academic, honorary, and religious groups. 3 fraternities with residence accomodations; 3 sororities without houses. 35% of students join. Students live at home or on campus. Single-sex dorms. 83% of students live on campus.

First-semester freshmen may not have cars. Class attendance required. Drugs prohibited. 1 unit of phys ed required. 7 intercollegiate sports for men, 6 for women; many intramurals. AIAW, NCAA, ODAC. Student body composition: 0.3% Asian, 3% Black, 0.2% Hispanic, 96.5% White. 50% from out of state.

[1] SAINT PAUL'S COLLEGE

Lawrenceville 23868, (804) 848-3111
Director of Admissions: Larnell R. Parker

- **Undergraduates: 313m, 332w**
- **Tuition (1982/83): $2,380**
- **Room & Board: $1,800; Fees: $209**
- **Degrees offered: BA, BS, BSEd**
- **Student-faculty ratio: 16 to 1**

A private college affiliated with the Protestant Episcopal Church, established in 1888. 75-acre rural campus, 60 miles south of Richmond. Served by bus.
Academic Character SACS accreditation. Semester system, 6-week summer term. Majors offered in biology, business, elementary education, English, general science, general studies, history, mathematics, political science, social science, and sociology. Minors offered in 9 areas. Distributives and GRE required. Preprofessional programs in health careers and theology. Cooperative work/study. Elementary and secondary education certification. ROTC. Language lab. 50,000-volume library with microform resources.
Financial CEEB CSS. College scholarships, state aid; PELL, SEOG, NDSL, GSL, CWS.
Admissions High school graduation with 14 units recommended. SAT required. $10 application fee. Rolling admissions. $25 deposit due on acceptance of admissions offer. Transfers accepted. Credit possible for college advanced placement exams.
Student Life Newspaper, yearbook. Choral society. NAACP. L'esprit Libere. Athletic, academic, honorary, and special interest groups. 6 fraternities and sororities. Class attendance required. Dean must be notified of marriage intentions. 4 hours of phys ed required. 6 intercollegiate sports; many intramurals. NCAA, CIAA. Student body composition: 99% Black, 1% Other. 29% from out of state.

[1] SHENANDOAH COLLEGE AND CONSERVATORY OF MUSIC

Winchester 22601, (703) 667-8714
Director of Admissions: Dwight D. Moore

- **Undergraduates: 245m, 440w; 911 total (including part-time)**
- **Tuition (1982/83): $3,650**
- **Room & Board: $2,400; Fees: $270**
- **Degrees offered: BA, BS, BMus**
- **Student-faculty ratio: 8 to 1**

A private college affiliated with the United Methodist Church, established in 1875. 45-acre suburban campus, 70 miles east of Washington, DC. Air, rail, and bus service nearby.
Academic Character SACS and professional accreditation. Semester system, 2 4-week summer terms. 29 majors offered in the areas of biology, chemistry, dance, education, English, equestrian studies, history, management, mathematics, music (applied, church, composition, education, therapy), nursing, philosophy-religion, physical education, psychology-education, recreation therapy, respiratory care, and theatre. Self-designed majors. 2 year programs in nursing and respiratory therapy. Distributives and 1 semester of religion required. Independent study. Honors program. Internships. Elementary and secondary education certification. Computer center. 72,500-volume library.
Financial CEEB CSS. College scholarships, grants, loans, talent award, ministerial aid, state aid, payment plan; PELL, SEOG, NDSL, CWS.
Admissions High school graduation with 10 units recommended. GED accepted. Interview recommended. Audition required for dance, music, and theatre students. $20 application fee. Rolling admissions. $100 deposit due on acceptance of admissions offer. *Early Admission, Early Decision, Concurrent Enrollment* programs. Admission deferral possible. Transfers accepted. Credit possible for CEEB AP, CLEP, and ACT PEP exams.
Student Life Student government. Yearbook. 30 musical groups. Students live at home or on campus. Coed and single-sex dorms. No married-stduent housing. 53% of students live on campus. 2 semesters of phys ed required. Intercollegiate basketball for men; several intramurals. Student body composition: 28% minority. 48% from out of state.

[J1] SOUTHERN SEMINARY JUNIOR COLLEGE

Buena Vista 24416, (703) 261-6181

- **Undergraduates: 293w**
- **Tuition (1982/82): $4,000**
- **Room & Board: 2,075**
- **Degrees offered: Associate**
- **Mean SAT 400v, 400m**

A private, non-denominational junior college for women.
Academic Character SACS accreditation. Semester system. Two-year programs offered in liberal arts, art, music, dramatics, interior design, horsemanship, secretarial science, animal science, merchandising, kindergarten training, and physical education. Remedial English program.
Admissions High school graduation with satisfactory averages and personal qualifications required. Rolling admissions. *Early Admission* Program. Admission deferral possible.
Student Life Women's dorms. About 90% of students live on campus.

[J1] SOUTHSIDE VIRGINIA COMMUNITY COLLEGE

Alberta 23821

[J1] SOUTHWEST VIRGINIA COMMUNITY COLLEGE

Richlands 24641

[1] SWEET BRIAR COLLEGE

Sweet Briar 24595, (804) 381-5548
Director of Admissions: Terry Scarborough

- **Undergraduates: 629w**
- **Tuition (1982/83): $6,700**
- **Room & Board: $2,250; Fees: $60**
- **Degree offered: AB**
- **Mean SAT 500v, 500m**
- **Student-faculty ratio: 8 to 1**

A private women's college established in 1901. 3,300-acre rural campus, 12 miles north of Lynchburg. Served by air, rail, and bus.
Academic Character SACS and professional accreditation. 4-1-4 system. 37 majors offered in the areas of American, French, German, and Italian studies, anthropology, classics, dance, economics, English, government, history, international affairs, mathematics, modern languages, music, philosophy, physics, political economy, psychology, religion, sociology, studio art, and theatre. Self-designed majors. Distributive requirements; senior exam, thesis, or project required. Independent study emphasized. Honors program. Phi Beta Kappa. Limited pass/fail, internships. Preprofessional programs in engineering, law, medicine. 3-2 engineering programs with Columbia, Georgia Tech, Washington U. 3-2 business program with UVA. Junior year environmental studies program. Cross-registration with 7 area colleges. Washington Semester. Exchange with St. Andrew's in Scotland. Study in Europe. Elementary and secondary education certification. Fine arts center. Laboratory nursery school. Museum. Computer facilities. 180,000-volume library with microform resources.
Financial CEEB CSS. College scholarships, grants, loans; PELL, SEOG, NDSL, CWS. Scholarship application deadline March 1.
Admissions High school graduation with 16 units required. Interview recommended. SAT and 3 ACH required. $20 application fee. Application deadline March 1. $300 deposit due on acceptance of admissions offer. *Early Decision* and *Early Admission* programs. Admission deferral possible. Transfers accepted. Credit possible for CEEB AP and college placement exams.
Student Life Student government. Newspaper, literary magazine, yearbook, radio station. Music, dance, and drama groups. Academic, political, service, social, and special interest groups. Students live at home or on campus. 8 women's dorms and 2 houses. 99% of students live on campus. Honors system. 2 semesters of phys ed required. 8 intercollegiate sports; intramurals. Student body composition: 3% Asian, 1% Black, 96% White. 80% from out of state.

[J1] THOMAS NELSON COMMUNITY COLLEGE

PO Box 9407, Hampton 23670

[J1] TIDEWATER COMMUNITY COLLEGE

Portsmouth 23703

[G1] UNION THEOLOGICAL SEMINARY IN VIRGINIA

3401 Brook Road, Richmond 23227

[1] VIRGINIA, UNIVERSITY OF

Box 3728, University Station, Charlottesville 22903, (804) 924-7751
Dean of Undergraduate Admissions: Jean L. Rayburn

- **Undergraduates: 5,589m, 5,526w; 16,385 total (including graduates)**
- **Tuition (1982/83): $1,334 (in-state), $3,260 (out-of-state)**
- **Room & Board: $2,300; Fees: $16**
- **Degrees offered: AB, BSArch, BSChem, BArch Hist, BPlan, BSCom, BSEd, BSN, BSEngs**
- **Mean SAT 570v, 600m**
- **Student-faculty ratio: 10 to 1**

A public university established in 1819, became coed in 1970. 2,000-acre small-city campus. Served by air, rail, and bus.
Academic Character SACS and professional accreditation. Semester system, summer terms. 33 majors offered by the College of Arts & Sciences, 3 by the School of Architecture, 5 by the School of Commerce, 5 by the School of Education, 10 by the School of Engineering & Applied Science, and 1 by the School of Nursing. Self-designed majors. Distributive requirements. Graduate and professional degrees granted. Independent study. Honors program. Phi Beta Kappa. Pass/fail, internships. Preprofessional programs in architecture, business, commerce, education, law, medicine, nursing. Study abroad. Elementary, secondary, and special education certification. ROTC, AFROTC, NROTC. Atomic reactor. Biological station. Computer facilities. Farm. Language labs. Political economy center. Observatories. 2,500,000-volume library with microform resources.
Financial CEEB CSS. University scholarships, grants, loans, payment plans; PELL, SEOG, NDSL, CWS. Application deadline March 1.
Admissions High school graduation with 16 units required. SAT and 3 ACH required. $20 application fee. Application deadline February 1. $250 deposit due on acceptance of admissions offer. *Early Decision* Program. Limited number of transfers accepted. Credit possible for CEEB AP exams.
Student Life Student government. Newspapers, magazines, yearbook, 2 radio stations. Music and drama groups. Debate. Political, professional, religious, service, and special interest groups. 33 fraternities with houses, 13 sororities. 38% of men join fraternities. Unless living at home, freshmen live in dorms for 2 semesters. Coed and single-sex dorms. Married-student apartments. 43% of students live on campus. First-semester students may not have cars. Honor system. 13 intercollegiate sports for men, 10 for women;

many intramurals. AIAW, ACC. Student body composition: 10% Black, 88% White, 2% Other. 35% from out of state.

■[1] CLINCH VALLEY COLLEGE

Wise 24293, (703) 328-2431
Director of Admissions: Sandy Birchfield

- **Undergraduates: 337m, 375w; 956 total (including part-time)**
- **Tuition (1982/83): $864 (in-state), $1,368 (out-of-state)**
- **Room & Board: $1,600-$1,650; Fees: $200**
- **Degrees offered: BA, BS**
- **Student-faculty ratio: 16 to 1**

A public college of the University of Virginia, established in 1954. 350-acre rural campus, 50 miles from Bristol. 65 miles to airport; 45 miles to bus terminal.
Academic Character SACS accreditation. Semester system, 2 5-week summer terms. 22 majors offered in the areas of biology, business, chemistry, education, English, environmental science, history, mathematics, medical technology, mining management, modern languages, performing arts, and social science. Minor required in some departments. Minors available in most majors. Self-designed majors. Distributive requirements. Independent study. Cooperative work/study, pass/fail. Member Western Region Consortium. Study abroad. Elementary, secondary, and special education certification. Computer center. Language lab. Weather station. 85,000-volume library with microform resources.
Financial CEEB CSS. College scholarships, grants, loans, state aid; PELL, SEOG, NDSL, FISL, CWS, college work program. Application deadline May 1.
Admissions High school graduation with 20 units required. GED accepted. SAT or ACT required. $15 application fee. Rolling admissions. $50 room deposit due on acceptance of admissions offer. Transfers accepted. Credit possible for CEEB AP and CLEP exams.
Student Life Student government. Newspaper, literary magazine, yearbook. Music and drama groups. Academic, honorary, political, religious, and special interest groups. 2 fraternities with houses and 2 sororities without houses. 5% of students join. Students live at home or on campus. Single-sex dorms. Married-student housing. Language and special interest housing. 33% of students live on campus. Liquor permitted only in private rooms. Honor code. Class attendance required. 2 hours of phys ed required. 4 intercollegiate sports for men, 3 for women; many intramurals. AIAW, NAIAC. Student body composition: 2% Black, 98% White. 11% from out of state.

[1] VIRGINIA COMMONWEALTH UNIVERSITY

Richmond 23284, (804) 257-1222
Director of Admissions: Dr. Jerrie J. Johnson

- **Enrollment: 7,072m, 10,024w; 20,000 total (including graduates)**
- **Tuition (1982/83): $1,060 (in-state), $2,300 (out-of-state)**
- **Room & Board: $2,146-$2,360; Fees: $238-$338**
- **Degrees offered: BA, BS, BFA, BGS, BMus, BMus Ed, BSW, AS**
- **Student-faculty ratio: 15 to 1**

A public university established in 1968. 2 urban campuses of 54 acres. Served by air, rail, and bus.
Academic Character SACS and professional accreditation. Semester system, several summer terms. 68 majors offered by the College of Humanities & Sciences, the School of the Arts, the School of Business, the School of Community & Public Affairs, the School of Education, the School of Mass Communications, and the School of Social Work. Self-designed majors. Minors offered. Distributive requirements. Graduate and professional degrees granted. Independent study. Honors program. Cooperative work/study, internships. Preprofessional programs in dental hygiene, dentistry, engineering, health sciences, law, medicine, veterinary medicine. 2-2 programs in medical record administration, medical technology, nursing, occupational therapy, pharmacy, and physical therapy with Medical College of Virginia. Dual degree engineering programs with Auburn, Old Dominion, George Washington U. Cross-registration with 4 area schools. Elementary, secondary, and special education certification. ROTC at U Richmond. Computer center. Institute of Statistics. 508,696-volume library with microform resources.
Financial CEEB CSS. University scholarships, grants, loans, payment plan; PELL, SEOG, NSS, NDSL, GSL, NSL, CWS. Priority application deadline for scholarships March 1.
Admissions High school graduation with 10 units required. GED accepted. Audition required for dance, music, and theatre majors. SAT required for applicants under 22. $10 application fee. Rolling admissions. $50 room deposit due on acceptance of admissions offer. *Early Admission* and *Early Decision* programs. Transfers accepted. Credit possible for CEEB AP, CLEP, and university advanced placement exams. Special Services Program for disadvantaged students.
Student Life Student government. Newspaper, literary magazine, Black Student newspaper, yearbook, radio station. Music and drama groups. Over 150 academic, honorary, service, and special interest groups. 7 fraternities, 2 with houses; 3 sororities without houses. Coed dorms. Co-op dorms. 19% of students live on campus. Cars discouraged. 7 intercollegiate sports for men, 65 for women; club and intramural programs. AIAW, NCAA, SBC. Student body composition: 17% Black, 81% White, 2% Other. 12% from out of state.

■[1] VIRGINIA, MEDICAL COLLEGE OF, HEALTH SCIENCES DIVISION OF VIRGINIA COMMONWEALTH UNIVERSITY

12th & Broad Streets, Richmond 23298

[J1] VIRGINIA HIGHLANDS COMMUNITY COLLEGE

PO Box 828, Abingdon 24210

[1] VIRGINIA INTERMONT COLLEGE

Bristol 24201, (703) 669-6101
Dean of Admissions & Financial Aid: Thomas M. Hughes

- **Undergraduates: 125m, 496w**
- **Tuition (1982/83): $3,525**
- **Room & Board: $2,200; Fees: $15**
- **Degrees offered: BA, AA**
- **Mean SAT 400v, 425m**
- **Student-faculty ratio: 13 to 1**

A private college affiliated with the Baptist Church, established in 1884, became coed in 1973. 16-acre urban campus. Airport, bus station nearby.
Academic Character SACS and professional accreditation. Semester system. 31 majors offered by the divisions of Applied & Professional Studies, Behavioral & Social Sciences, Humanities, Natural Sciences & Mathematics, Performing Arts, Physical Education, and Visual Arts, including ballet, creative writing, horsemanship, photography. AA in the areas of allied health, applied & fine arts, drama-speech, general studies, liberal arts, preprofessional, general secretarial, medical lab technology. Distributive requirements. Independent study. Internships. Preprofessional programs in cytotechnology, dental hygiene, laboratory technology, medical record administration, nursing, occupational therapy, pharmacy, physical therapy. Cross-registration with King. Elementary and secondary education certification. Computer center. Language lab. Museum. Riding center. 55,979-volume library with microform resources.
Financial CEEB CSS. College scholarships, grants, loans, payment plans; PELL, SEOG, NDSL, GSL, FISL, CWS, college work program.
Admissions High school graduation with 15 units required. GED accepted. Interview recommended. SAT or ACT recommended. $15 application fee. Rolling admissions. $100 deposit due on acceptance of admissions offer. *Early Admission* and *Concurrent Enrollment* programs. Admission deferral possible. Transfers accepted. Credit possible for CEEB AP and CLEP exams.
Student Life Student government. Newspaper, literary magazine, yearbook, radio station. Music and drama groups. Academic, political, religious, service, and special interest groups. Students must live on campus or at home. No married-student housing. Single-sex dorms. 70% of students live on campus. Liquor prohibited. 4 hours of phys ed required. 1 intercollegiate sport for men, 4 for women; intramurals. Student body composition: 1% Asian, 5% Black, 4% Hispanic, 89% White, 1% Other. 59% from out of state.

[1] VIRGINIA MILITARY INSTITUTE

Lexington 24450, (703) 463-6211
Director of Admissions: Col. William J. Buchanan

- **Undergraduates: 1,329m**
- **Tuition (1982/83): $900 (in-state), $2,730 (out-of-state)**
- **Room & Board: $2,935**
- **Uniform Deposit: $1,200 (for first-year cadets)**
- **Degrees offered: BA, BS**
- **Mean SAT 500v, 550m**
- **Student-faculty ratio: 13 to 1**

A public service academy for men, established in 1839. 134-acre small-town campus, 50 miles from Roanoke. Served by bus; airport in Roanoke.
Academic Character SACS and professional accreditation. Semester system, 2 5-week and one 3½-week summer terms. Majors offered in biology, chemistry, civil engineering, economics, electrical engineering, English, history, mathematics, mechanical engineering, modern languages, and physics. Degree program must be selected before entrance; majors may be changed within program. Distributive requirements. Independent study. Honors program. Phi Beta Kappa. Limited pass/fail. Study abroad. ROTC, AFROTC, NROTC, Marine ROTC. If offered, cadets at graduation must accept commission with obligation for active duty. Computer center. Museum. Research library. 268,316-volume library with microform resources.
Financial CEEB CSS. Institute scholarships, grants, loans, state cadetships; PELL, SEOG, NDSL, FISL, some employment for upperclassmen. Application deadline March 1.
Admissions High school graduation with 16 units required. Interview strongly recommended. Applicants must be unmarried males, 16-22 years old. SAT required; 2 ACH recommended. $15 application fee. Rolling admissions. $100 deposit due on acceptance of admissions offer. *Early Decision* Program. Transfers accepted to first semester only. Credit possible for CEEB AP and departmental exams.
Student Life Student government. Newspaper, literary magazine, yearbook. Music and drama groups. Debate. Cadet groups. Academic, honorary, political, professional, scientific, special interest, and technical organizations. All cadets must live on campus. Seniors may have cars. Liquor and drugs prohibited. Class attendance required. Uniforms mandatory. Cadets may not marry. Strict honor code. 4 hours of phys ed required. 12 intercollegiate sports; 100% intramural participation. NCAA, SC. Student body composition: 2% Asian, 4.7% Black, 1% Hispanic, 92% White. 45% from out of state.

[1] VIRGINIA POLYTECHNIC INSTITUTE AND STATE UNIVERSITY

Blacksburg 24061, (703) 961-6267
Director of Admissions: Archie G. Phlegar

- **Undergraduates: 11,070m, 7,144w; 21,584 total (including graduates)**
- **Tuition (1982/83): $1,155 (in-state), $2,400 (out-of-state)**
- **Room & Board: $1,503; Fees: $126**
- **Degrees offered: BA, BS, BArch, BLand Arch**
- **Mean SAT 1,070**
- **Student-faculty ratio: 11 to 1**

A public university established in 1872. 2,300-acre small-city campus, 40 miles west of Roanoke. Served by bus; airport in Roanoke.
Academic Character SACS and professional accreditation. Trimester system, 2 6-week summer terms. 10 major offered by the College of Agriculture & Life Sciences, 3 by the College of Architecture & Urban Studies, 30 by the College of Arts & Sciences, 7 by the College of Business, 14 by the College of Education, 10 by the College of Engineering, and 4 by the College of Human Resources. Minors offered in most major areas. Distributive requirements in some disciplines. Graduate degrees granted. Independent study. Honors program. Phi Beta Kappa. 5-year cooperative work/study in several areas. Limited pass/fail. Preprofessional programs in dentistry, law, medicine, pharmacy, veterinary medicine. Study abroad. Elementary, secondary, and industrial arts education certification. 2- and 4-year ROTC, AFROTC, NROTC; all cadets wear uniforms and live under military discipline. Agricultural Experimental Station. Energy, industrial, water, and environmental research divisions. Computer center. 1,515,169-volume library with microform resources.
Financial CEEB CSS. Institute scholarships, grants, loans, state aid; PELL, SEOG, NDSL, GSL, CWS. Application deadline March 1.
Admissions High school graduation with 18 units required. Audition or portfolio required for art, music, and theatre majors. SAT and 2 ACH required. $10 application fee. Application deadline January 1. $50 room deposit due on acceptance of admissions offer. *Early Decision* and *Early Admission* programs. Transfers accepted. Credit possible for CEEB AP and departmenta exams.
Student Life Student government, including civilian and cadet student Newspaper, literary magazine, yearbook, radio station. Music and drama groups. Debate. Academic, honorary, religious, service, and special interest groups. Single freshmen live at home or on campus. All cadets must live in dorms. Coed and single-sex dorms. 39% of students live on campus. Cars may not be used during class hours. Honor code. 10 intercollegiate sports for men, 5 for women; many intramurals. AIAW, NCAA, MAC. Student body composition: 4% Black, 95% White, 1% Other. 25% from out of state.

[1] VIRGINIA STATE UNIVERSITY

Petersburg 23803, (804) 520-5000
Director of Admissions: Edward L. Smith

- **Undergraduates: 1,972m, 2,592w**
- **Tuition (1982/83): $1,303 (in-state), $2,108 (out-of-state)**
- **Room & Board: $2,180**
- **Degrees offered: BA, BFA, BS, BSN, BMus, BIndiv Studies**
- **Student-faculty ratio: 16 to 1**

A public university established in 1882. Suburban campus, 20 miles south of Richmond. Air, rail, and bus service in Richmond.
Academic Character SACS accreditation. Semester system, 3- and 6-week summer terms. 12 majors offered by the School of Agriculture, 8 by the School of Business Administration, 11 by the School of Education, 8 by the School of Humanities & Social Sciences, and 8 by the School of Natural Sciences. Masters degrees granted. Honors program. Cooperative work/study. Preprofessional nursing program. ROTC. 207,924-volume library.
Financial CEEB CSS and ACT FAS. University scholarships, grants, loans; PELL, SEOG, NDSL, CWS. Application deadline April 15.
Admissions High school graduation with 16 units recommended. SAT required. $10 application fee. Rolling admissions. Transfers accepted. Credit possible for CEEB AP exams.
Student Life Student government. Yearbook. Music, dance, and drama groups. Debate. Academic, religious, service, and special interest groups. 6 fraternities and 6 sororities. 4 dorms for men, 6 for women, student village complex for men and women. 41% of students live on campus. 4 intercollegiate sports for men, 2 for women; intramurals. CIAA, NAIA, NCAA. Student body composition: 0.33% Asian, 90.14% Black, 0.48% Hispanic, 0.03% Native American, 7.62% White, 1.4% Other. 23% from out of state.

[1] VIRGINIA UNION UNIVERSITY

1500 North Lombardy Street, Richmond 23220, (804) 257-5600
Director of Admissions: Janice Darden Bailey

- **Undergraduates: 566m, 623w**
- **Tuition (1982/83): $2,800**
- **Room & Board: $2,000; Fees: $110**
- **Degrees offered: BA, BS**
- **Student-faculty ratio: 15 to 1**

A private university affiliated with the American Baptist Convention, established in 1865. 55-acre urban campus. Served by air, rail, and bus.
Academic Character SACS accreditation. Semester system, 2 6-week summer terms, 2-week early summer mini-term. 25 majors offered by the Schools of Arts & Sciences, Business Administration, and Education & Psychology. Distributives and 1 semester of religion required. English essay and comprehensive exams sometimes required in junior or senior years. MDiv granted. Independent study. Honors program. Cooperative work/study, field experience. Preprofessional programs in chemical research, dentistry, journalism, law, library science, medical technology, medicine, pharmacy, scientific aid, theology. Dual degree engineering programs with Howard and U Michigan. Career Opportunities program. Cross-registration with Concordia (Minnesota) and Fort Lewis (Colorado). Early childhood, elementary, secondary, and special education certification. ROTC at Virginia State College. School of Theology. Educational Resource Center. Learning Resource Center. Language lab. 130,000-volume library with microform resources.
Financial CEEB CSS. University scholarships, state aid; PELL, SEOG, NDSL, CWS. Member of United Negro College Fund. Application deadline June 1.
Admissions High school graduation with 16 units required. GED accepted. SAT required, $10 application fee. Rolling admissions. $50 deposit required on acceptance of offer of admission. *Early Admission* Program. Transfers accepted. Credit possible for CEEB AP exams. Conditional admission possible. Upward Bound program for academically-deficient students.
Student Life Student government. Newspaper, yearbook, radio station. Music and drama groups. Fine Arts festival. Athletic, academic, honorary, and special interest groups. 8 fraternities and 9 sororities without housing. 5% of men and 4% of women join. Students must live at home or on campus. No married-student housing. Single-sex dorms. 56% of students live on campus. Liquor and drugs prohibited. Class attendance required of freshmen. Students must notify university of marriage intentions. 30 events (assemblies, concerts, etc.) must be attended during first 2 years. 1 semester of phys ed required. 6 intercollegiate sports; intramurals. CIAA, NAIA, NCAA. Student body composition: 95.1% Black, 0.1% Hispanic, 0.5% White, 4.3% Other. 43% from out of state.

[1] VIRGINIA WESLEYAN COLLEGE

Virginia Beach 23502, (804) 461-3232
Director of Admissions: Frank S. Badger

- **Undergraduates: 385m, 471w**
- **Tuition (1982/83): $4,100**
- **Room & Board: $2,150**
- **Degree offered: BA**
- **Mean SAT 477v, 515m**
- **Student-faculty ratio: 16 to 1**

A private college affiliated with the United Methodist Church, established in 1961, became coed in 1966. 300-acre suburban campus. Served by air, rail, and bus.
Academic Character SACS accreditation. Semester system, 2-week January term. 27 majors offered in the areas of American studies, art, business, communications, computer science, education, human services, humanities, mathematics, music, recreation, religion, science, social sciences, and theatre. Self-designed majors. Distributive requirements. Independent and individualized study. Pass/fail, internships, field work. Preprofessional programs in allied health, dentistry, law, medicine, nursing, theology. 3-2 forestry program with Duke. Study abroad. Elementary and secondary education certification. Language lab. 68,000-volume library.
Financial CEEB CSS. College scholarships, grants, loans, Methodist loans, payment plan; PELL, SEOG, NDSL, GSL, CWS. Application deadline August 1.
Admissions High school graduation with 16 units required. Interview recommended. SAT required. $10 application fee. Rolling admissions. $350 deposit due on acceptance of admissions offer. *Early Admission* Program. Admission deferral possible. Transfers accepted. Credit possible for CEEB AP and CLEP exams. Conditional admission possible.
Student Life Student government. Newspaper, literary magazine, yearbook, radio station. Music and drama groups. Black Student Union. Circle K. Academic, honorary, professional, religious, and special interest groups. 2 fraternities and 1 sorority without housese. 10% of men and 5% of women join. Students not living at home live on campus. Single-sex dorms. Academic village arrangement: classrooms, offices, residences, and dining halls. No married-student housing. 62% of students live on campus. 6 intercollegiate sports for men, 2 for women; intramurals. AIAW, NCAA, DIAC. Student body composition: 1% Asian, 10% Black, 1% Hispanic, 87% White, 1% Other. 35% from out of state.

[J1] VIRGINIA WESTERN COMMUNITY COLLEGE

3095 Colonial Avenue, Roanoke 24015

[1] WASHINGTON AND LEE UNIVERSITY

Lexington 24450, (703) 463-9111, ext. 203
Director of Admissions: William M. Hartog

- **Undergraduates: 1,311m; 1,689 total (including graduates)**
- **Tuition (1983/84): $5,800**
- **Room & Board: $2,719; Fees: $70**
- **Degrees offered: BA, BS**
- **Mean SAT 560v, 590m**
- **Student-faculty ratio: 11 to 1**

A private men's university with a coed School of Law. Established in 1749. 95-acre small-town campus, 50 miles from Roanoke. Served by bus.
Academic Character SACS and professional accreditation. 12-12-6 system. 41 majors offered in the areas of art, business, classics, drama, East Asian studies, humanities, journalism, languages, mathematics, natural & physical sciences, religion, and social sciences. Courses in 12 additional areas, including Chinese and Japanese. Self-designed majors. African, Latin American, Russian, and urban studies. Distributive requirements. Senior comprehensive exams required in some majors. JD granted. Independent study. Honors programs. Phi Beta Kappa. Limited pass/fail, internships. Preprofessional programs in dentistry, law, medicine, theology, veterinary science. 3-3 law programs. 3-2 engineering programs with Rensselaer, Washington U, Columbia. 3-2 forestry and environmental management programs with Duke. Cross-registration with 6 area schools. Interuniversity Consortium for Political and Social Research. Faculty exchange with Oxford. Exchange programs with Chinese University, Hong Kong, and Rikkyo University, Japan. Extensive study abroad programs. Luce Scholarships for year in East Asia. Secondary education certification. ROTC. Robert E. Lee Research Program. George C. Marshall Research Foundation. Art collection. Computer center. Nuclear science lab. Communications lab. Observatory. TV studio. Language labs. 568,000-volume library with microform resources.

Financial CEEB CSS. University scholarships, grants, loans, payment plans; PELL, SEOG, NDSL, CWS. Application deadlines February 15 (scholarships), February 29 (loans).
Admissions High school graduation with 16 units required. Interview recommended. SAT and 3 ACH required. $20 application fee. Rolling admissions; application deadline February 15. $250 deposit due on acceptance of admissions offer. *Early Decision* Program. Admission deferral possible. Transfers accepted. Credit possible for CEEB AP and university placement exams.
Student Life Student government. Newspaper, literary magazines, yearbook, radio and TV stations. Music and drama groups. Debate. Religious, professional, and special interest groups. 17 fraternities with houses. 60% of men join. Freshmen not living at home live in dorms. Married-student housing. 40% of students live on campus. Liquor permitted in dorm rooms. Class attendance expected. Honor system. 2 years of phys ed required. 13 intercollegiate sports; many intramurals. NCAA, ODAC. Student body composition: 1% Black, 99% White. 75% from out of state.

[1] WILLIAM AND MARY, COLLEGE OF
Williamsburg 23185, (804) 253-4000
Dean of Admissions: G. Gary Ripple

- **Undergraduates: 2,132m, 2,475w; 6,520 total (including graduates)**
- **Tuition (1982/83): $1,574 (in-state), $4,008 (out-of-state)**
- **Room & Board: $2,602-$2,772**
- **Degrees offered: AB, BS, BBA**
- **Median SAT 1,210**
- **Student-faculty ratio: 15 to 1**

A public college established in 1693. 1,200-acre campus, 40 miles west of Norfolk. Served by air, rail, and bus.
Academic Character SACS and professional accreditation. Semester system, 2 5-week summer terms. 36 majors offered in the areas of anthropology, business administration, classics, computer science, education, fine arts, humanities, mathematics, music, physical education, religion, science, social science, and theatre. Self-designed majors. Minors offered. Courses in Chinese, Portuguese. Distributive requirements. Graduate and professional degrees granted. Independent study. Honors programs. Phi Beta Kappa. Limited pass/fail, internships. Preprofessional programs in dentistry, engineering, medical technology, medicine, public health service, veterinary medicine. 3-2 and 4-2 engineering programs with RPI, Washington, Case Western, and Columbia. 3-2 forestry program with Duke. Study in Europe, the Phillipines. Elementary and secondary education certification. ROTC. Marine Science Institute. Learning Resources Center. Language lab. 717,449-volume library with 1,192,760 manuscripts and documents.
Financial CEEB CSS. College scholarships, grants, loans, state aid, payment plans; PELL, SEOG, NDSL, GSL, CWS. Recommended application deadline between January 1 and February 15.
Admissions High school graduation with strong academic program recommended. Campus visit recommended. SAT required; 3 ACH strongly recommended. $20 application fee. Application deadline January 15. $50 room deposit due on acceptance of admissions offer. *Early Decision, Early Admission, Concurrent Enrollment* programs. Admission deferral possible. Transfers accepted. Credit possible for CEEB AP and college challenge exams.
Student Life Student assembly organizations. Newspaper, literary magazine, yearbook, radio station. Music, dance, drama, and film groups. Debate. Women's Forum. Academic, political, recreational, religious, service, and special interest groups. 10 fraternities and 10 sororities, all with houses. 33% of men and 36% of women join. Freshmen not living at home live on campus. Coed and single-sex dorms. Language houses. 80% of students live on campus. Upperclassmen may have cars. Hazing prohibited. Honor system. 2 years of phys ed required. 14 intercollegiate sports for men, 14 for women; many intramurals. AIAW, ECAC, NCAA, VFISW. Student body composition: 93% White, 7% Other. 30% from out of state.

■[J1] RICHARD BLAND COLLEGE
Petersburg 23805

[J1] WYTHEVILLE COMMUNITY COLLEGE
East Main Street, Wytheville 24382

WASHINGTON *(WA)*

[J1] BELLEVUE COMMUNITY COLLEGE
3000 Landerholm Circle SE, Bellevue 98007

[J1] BIG BEND COMMUNITY COLLEGE
28th and Chanute, Moses Lake 98837

[1] CENTRAL WASHINGTON UNIVERSITY
Ellensburg 98926, (509) 963-1111, (800) 572-4119
Dean of Admissions & Records: James G. Pappas

- **Undergraduates: 2,691m, 2,555w; 6,989 total (including graduates)**
- **Tuition (1982/83): $951 (in-state), $3,219 (out-of-state)**
- **Room & Board: $2,200**
- **Degrees offered: BA, BS, BAEd, BMus**
- **Student-faculty ratio: 23 to 1**

A public university established in 1891. 350-acre rural campus in Ellensburg, 100 miles from Seattle. Served by bus and rail; airport 35 miles away in Yakima.
Academic Character NASC and professional accreditation. Trimester system, 2 4½-week summer terms. 74 majors offered by School of Business & Economics, the School of Letters, Arts & Sciences, and the School of Professional Studies. Self-designed majors. Minors offered in some major fields and in 17 additional areas. Distributive requirements. Masters degrees granted. Independent study. Honors program. Phi Beta Kappa. Cooperative work/study, limited pass/fail, internships. Credit by exam. Preprofessional programs in agriculture, architecture, commerical art, dental hygiene, dentistry, engineering, forestry, law, medical technology, medicine, meterology, nursing, occupational therapy, optometry, pharmacy, physical therapy, veterinary medicine. 3-1 medical technology program. 3-2 physics-engineering program. Study abroad. Elementary, secondary, and special education certification. ROTC, AFROTC. Computer center, language lab. Access to environmental learning center, marine lab. 851,839-volume library.
Financial CEEB CSS. University scholarships, grants, loans; PELL, SEOG, NDSL, GSL, CWS. Application deadline March 15.
Admissions High school graduation required. GED accepted. Interview encouraged. Washington Pre-College Test, SAT, or ACT required. Rolling admissions; suggest applying after December 1. $75 deposit required on acceptance of offer of admission. *Concurrent Enrollment* Program. Transfers accepted. Admission deferral possible. Credit possible for CEEB AP exams; university has own advanced placement program.
Student Life Student association. Newspaper, magazine, radio station, TV channel. Music, drama, debate groups. Academic, honorary, religious, service, and special interest organizations. Single freshmen and sophomores under 21 must live on campus. Coed and single-sex dorms. Special interest and married-student housing. 45% of students live on campus. 2 credits in phys ed required. 9 intercollegiate sports for men, 7 for women; intramurals. AIAW, Independent Conference. Student body composition: 1% Asian, 2% Black, 1% Hispanic, 1% Native American, 93% White, 2% Other. 4% from out of state.

[J1] CENTRALIA COLLEGE
Centralia 98531

[1] CITY COLLEGE
Seattle 98104

[J1] CLARK COLLEGE
Vancouver 98663

[J1] COLUMBIA BASIN COLLEGE
2600 Chase, Pasco 99301

[1] CORNISH INSTITUTE
710 East Roy Street, Seattle 98102

[1] EASTERN WASHINGTON UNIVERSITY
Chaney 99004, (509) 359-2397
Director of Admissions: Glenn E. Fehler

- **Undergraduates: 3,146m, 3,194w; 8,555 total (including graduates)**
- **Tuition (1982/83): $942 (in-state), $3,210 (out-of-state)**
- **Room & Board: $2,220**
- **Degrees offered: BA, BS, BAEd, BMus**
- **Student-faculty ratio: 17 to 1**

A public university established in 1882. 335-acre suburban campus in small town of Cheney, 16 miles from Spokane. Air, bus, and rail in Spokane.
Academic Character NASC and professional accreditation. Trimester system, 2-week and 8-week summer terms. 79 majors offered in the areas of business, social sciences, arts, education, natural sciences, health & recreation, computer science, communications, criminal justice, health fields, engineering, humanities, geography, government, home economics, military science, photography, and environmental sciences. Self-designed majors. Minors in area and cultural studies and in 8 additional areas. Distributive requirements. Masters degrees granted. Independent study. Honors programs. Cooperative work/study, pass/fail, internships. Credit by exam. Preprofessional programs in dentistry, medicine, pharmacy, veterinary medicine. Cooperative language programs with Gonzaga, Whitworth. Study abroad. Elementary, secondary, and special education certification. ROTC. Institute for Technical Studies, Human Development Center, ecology lab. Access to marine lab, primate research center. Computer center, lab school. 400,000-volume library with microform resources.
Financial CEEB CSS. University scholarships, grants, loans, state grants, nursing grants, tuition and fee waivers; PELL, SEOG, NDSL, FISL, GSL, NSL, CWS. Application deadlines April 1 (FAF), May 15 (scholarships), July 1 (loans).
Admissions High school graduation required. GED accepted. Washington Pre-College Test required; SAT or ACT accepted from out-of-state students. Rolling admissions; suggest applying after December 1. $50 tuition deposit

and $80 room deposit (for boarders) required on acceptance of offer of admission. *Early Decision, Early Admission, Concurrent Enrollment* programs. Transfers accepted. Admission deferral possible. Credit possible for CEEB AP exams; university has own advanced placement program.
Student Life Student association. Newspaper, magazine. Music, debate, speaking, drama groups. Black, Chinese, Native American, Chicano organizations. Political, academic, honorary, religious, service, and special interest groups. 5 fraternities and 4 sororities. Coed dorms. Married-student housing. 20% of students live on campus. Liquor allowed in dorms for students over 21. 12 intercollegiate sports for men, 8 for women; intramurals. AIAW, NCAA, NCWSA. Student body composition: 1.1% Asian, 1.4% Black, 1.5% Hispanic, 1.1% Native American, 94.9% White. 5% from out of state.

[J1] EDMONDS COMMUNITY COLLEGE
20000 68th Avenue West, Lynnwood 98036

[J1] EVERETT COMMUNITY COLLEGE
801 Wetmore Avenue, Everett 98201

[1] EVERGREEN STATE COLLEGE, THE
Olympia 98505, (206) 866-6000
Director of Admissions: Arnaldo Rodriguez

- **Undergraduates: 1,268m, 1,430w**
- **Tuition (1982/83): $942 (in-state), $3,210 (out-of-state)**
- **Room & Board: $2,100 (average)**
- **Degrees offered: BA, BS**
- **Student-faculty ratio: 20 to 1**

A public college established in 1967. 1,000-acre suburban campus on Puget Sound in Olympia, 60 miles from Seattle. Served by air, bus, and rail.
Academic Character NASC accreditation. Trimester system, 2 5-week summer terms. Interdisciplinary specialty areas offered in environmental studies, European & American studies, expressive arts, human development & health, management & the public interest, marine sciences & crafts, northwest Native American studies, political economy, and scientific knowledge & inquiry. Annual programs, basic programs offered. MPA granted. Coordinated studies (large group), group contracts (small group), and individual study. Cooperative work/study, pass/fail, internships. Consortium with U of Puget Sound. Exchange programs with St. Mary's College, Kobe U (Japan). Study abroad in Greece. Elementary and secondary education certification. Computer center, media center, self-paced learning lab. Sailing ship for marine studies. 185,000-volume library with microform resources.
Financial CEEB CSS. College scholarships, grants, loans, state grants, tuition waivers, emergency loans; PELL, SEOG, NDSL, FISL, CWS. Priority application deadline April 15.
Admissions High school graduation required. GED accepted. SAT or ACT recommended. $15 application fee. Rolling admissions; application deadline September 1. $50 tuition deposit and $60 room deposit (for boarders) required on acceptance of offer of admission. *Early Admission* Program. Transfers accepted. Admission deferral possible. Credit possible for CEEB AP and CLEP exams.
Student Life Student government. Newspaper, magazine, radio station. Third World Coalition. Native American Students Association. Women's Center. Special interest centers. Limited college housing. Coed and co-op dorms. Married-student housing. 37% of students live on campus. 5 intercollegiate sports; intramurals. AIAW, NAIA, Club Northwest, Northwest Collegiate Women's Soccer Association, US Swimming Congress, US Wrestling Federation. Student body composition: 1.4% Asian, 3.3% Black, 1% Hispanic, 1.5% Native American, 92.8% White. 20% from out of state.

[J1] FORT STEILACOOM COMMUNITY COLLEGE
9401 Farwest Drive, SW, Tacoma 98498

[1] GONZAGA UNIVERSITY
East 502 Boone Avenue, Spokane 99258, (509) 328-4220
Director of Admissions: James T. Mansfield

- **Undergraduates: 1,257m, 948w; 3,056 total (including graduates)**
- **Tuition (1982/83): $4,700**
- **Room & Board: $2,420**
- **Degrees offered: BA, BS, BBA, BEd, BSN (for RNs)**
- **Mean SAT 470v, 510m**
- **Student-faculty ratio: 14 to 1**

A private university controlled by the Society of Jesus (Jesuits), established in 1887. 75-acre urban campus in residential section of Spokane, 10 minutes from downtown. Served by air, bus, and rail.
Academic Character NASC and professional accreditation. Semester system, 6-week summer term. 33 majors offered by the College of Arts & Sciences, 10 by the School of Business Administration, 4 by the School of Education, and 6 by the School of Engineering. Minors offered in most major fields. Distributives, senior thesis or exam, and 3 religion courses required. Graduate and professional degrees granted. Independent study. Honors program. Limited pass/fail. Internships. Credit by exam. 5-year BS-MBA program in engineering. 3-1 programs in medicine possible. Study abroad. International Student Exchange. Elementary, secondary, and special education certification. ROTC; AFROTC, NROTC at Washington State. Computer center, TV center, language labs. Film library. 300,000-volume library with microform resources.
Financial CEEB CSS. University scholarships, grants, loans, state grants, family plan; PELL, SEOG, NDSL, FISL, payment plans, CWS. Application deadline March 1; FAF deadline March 15.
Admissions High school graduation with 16 units required. SAT or ACT required; Washington Pre-College Test accepted in-state. $15 application fee. Rolling admissions; application deadline August 15. $50 tuition deposit and $50 room deposit (for boarders) required on acceptance of offer of admission. *Concurrent Enrollment* Program. Transfers accepted. Admission deferral possible. Credit possible for CEEB AP and CLEP exams and ACT PEP. New Start Program.
Student Life Student government. Newspaper, magazine, yearbook. Music, debate, drama groups. Honorary, service, academic, and special interest groups. Seniors may live off campus. Coed and single-sex dorms. 75% of students live on campus. Attendance in class required. 7 intercollegiate sports for men, 4 for women; intramural and club sports. AIAW, NCAA, WCAC. Student body composition: 2% Asian, 1% Black, 1% Hispanic, 1% Native American, 84% White, 11% Other. 76% from out of state.

[J1] GRAYS HARBOR COLLEGE
Aberdeen 98520

[J1] GREEN RIVER COMMUNITY COLLEGE
Auburn 98002

[J1] HIGHLINE COMMUNITY COLLEGE
Midway 98031

[J1] LOWER COLUMBIA COLLEGE
Longview 98632

[P] LUTHERAN BIBLE INSTITUTE
Providence Heights, Issaquah 98027

[J1] NORTH SEATTLE COMMUNITY COLLEGE
9600 College Way North, Seattle 98103

[1] NORTHWEST COLLEGE OF THE ASSEMBLIES OF GOD
PO Box 579, Kirkland 98033

[J1] OLYMPIA TECHNICAL COMMUNITY COLLEGE
2011 Mottman Road, Olympia 98502

[J1] OLYMPIC COLLEGE
16th and Chester, Bremerton 98310

[1] PACIFIC LUTHERAN UNIVERSITY
PO Box 2068, Tacoma 98447, (206) 531-6900
Dean of Admissions and Financial Aid: James Van Beek

- **Undergraduates: 1,183m, 1,506w; 3,653**
- **Tuition (1982/83): $5,280**
- **Room & Board: $2,370**
- **Degrees offered: BA, BS, BAEd, BBA, BFA, BMus, BSN**
- **Mean SAT 1035**
- **Student-faculty ratio: 14 to 1**

A private university affiliated with the American Lutheran Church, established in 1890. 130-acre suburban campus in Parkland, 7 miles from Tacoma center. Served by air, bus, and rail.
Academic Character NASC and professional accreditation. 4-1-4 system, 2 4½-week summer terms. 29 majors offered by the College of Arts & Sciences, 3 by the School of the Arts, 5 by the School of Business Administration, 22 by the School of Education, 1 by the School of Nursing, and 3 by the School of Physical Education. Self-designed majors. Minors in several major fields and in 7 additional areas. Distributives and 8 hours of religious studies required. MA, MBA granted. Independent study. Honors program. Cooperative work/study, limited pass/fail, internships. Credit by exam. Preprofessional programs in allied health, dentistry, engineering, law, medicine, pharmacy, theology. 3-1 medical technology program. 3-2 engineering programs with Columbia, Stanford. 3-1, 3-2 programs in applied math, computer science, software. Study abroad. Elementary, secondary, and special education certification. AFROTC at U of Puget Sound. Language labs. 265,000-volume library with microform resources.
Financial CEEB CSS. University scholarships, grants, loans, ministers' dependent grants; PELL, SEOG, NSS, NDSL, GSL, NSL, monthly payment plan, CWS, state work program. Application deadlines March 1 (scholarships), February 1 (FAF, loans).
Admissions High school graduation required with 15 units recommended. Interview encouraged. Washington Pre-College Test (in-state), SAT, or ACT required. $25 application fee. Rolling admissions after December 1; suggest applying after October 1. $100 deposit required on acceptance of offer of admission. *Early Decision, Early Admission, Concurrent Enrollment* programs. Transfers accepted. Admission deferral possible. Credit possible for CEEB AP and CLEP exams; university has own advanced placement program.
Student Life Student government. Newspaper, yearbook, radio and TV stations. Music, debate, drama groups. Political, service, academic, honorary, religious, and special interest groups. Single underclassmen under 22 must live at home or on campus. Coed and single-sex dorms. Married-student housing. 65% of students live on campus. Liquor, gambling prohibited. Attendance in class required. Freshmen and sophomores must take 4 semesters of phys ed. 12 intercollegiate sports for men, 4 for women;

intramurals. AIAW, PNIAC, WCIC. Student body composition: 2% Asian, 2% Black, 1% Hispanic, 1% Native American, 94% White. 38% from out of state.

[J1] PENINSULA COLLEGE

1502 East Lauridsen Blvd., Port Angeles 98362, (206) 452-9277
Registrar: Frances Prindle

- **Undergraduates: 421m, 403w**
- **Tuition and fees (1982/83): $513 (in-state); $2,031 (out-of-state)**
- **Degrees offered: AA, AAS**
- **Student-faculty ratio: 13 to 1**

A public college established in 1961. Campus located in the foothills of Olympic Mountains, less then 2 miles from Strait of Juan de Fuca.
Academic Character NACS accreditation. Trimester system, 8½-week summer term. Over 45 2-year transfer programs for the AA degree, and 14 programs for the AAS. Certificate programs. Distributive requirements. Independent study. Honors program. Preprofessional programs in architecture & urban planning, business administration, engineering, forestry, secretarial studies. 35,000-volume library.
Financial CEEB CSS. Grants, loans, special programs aid, state grants and loans, work programs.
Admissions High school graduation required. GED accepted. Rolling admissions. Credit possible for CEEB AP and CLEP exams.
Student Life Student government. Newspaper, magazine. Music and drama groups. Special interest groups. 1 dorm. Intramural sports.

[1] UNIVERSITY OF PUGET SOUND

1500 North Warner Street, Tacoma 98416, (206) 756-3211
Director of Admissions: George H. Mills

- **Undergraduates: 1,235m, 1,548w; 3,159 total (including graduates)**
- **Tuition (1982/83): $5,400**
- **Room & Board: $2,580; Fees: $80**
- **Degrees offered: BA, BS, BAcc Sc, BEd, BMus**
- **Mean SAT 491v, 527m**
- **Student-faculty ratio: 14 to 1**

A private university affiliated with the Methodist Church, established in 1888. 72-acre urban campus in residential section of Tacoma, 35 miles from Seattle. Served by bus and rail; air service between Tacoma and Seattle.
Academic Character NASC and professional accreditation. 4-1-4 system, 2 4½-week summer terms. Majors offered in art, Asian studies, biology, business administration, chemistry, communications/theatre arts, comparative literature, comparative sociology, computer science, economics, education, English, foreign language, geology, history, mathematics, music, natural science, occupational therapy, philosophy, physical education, physical therapy, physics, politics/government, psychology, public administration, religion, urban affairs. Self-designed majors. Programs in 3 additional areas. Distributive requirements. Masters degrees granted. Independent study. Honors program. Cooperative work/study, pass/fail, internships. Preprofessional programs in dentistry, law, medicine, veterinary science. 3-2 program in engineering with Columbia, Oregon State, Washington State, and Washington U (in Missouri). Study abroad. Elementary, secondary, and special education certification. AFROTC. Art gallery, natural history museum. 265,000-volume library.
Financial CEEB CSS. University scholarships, grants, loans; PELL, SEOG, NDSL, GSL, FISL, deferred payment, CWS. Preferred application deadline March 1.
Admissions High school graduation with 17 units required. GED accepted. Interview encouraged. Audition required for music majors. SAT, ACT, or WPCT required. $20 application fee. Rolling admissions; suggest applying by March 1. $75 tuition deposit and $100 room deposit required on acceptance of offer of admission. *Early Decision, Early Admission* programs. Transfers accepted. Admission deferral possible. Credit possible for CEEB AP and CLEP exams.
Student Life Student government. Newspaper, magazine, yearbook, radio station. Music, drama, debate groups. Black Student Union, International Club. Academic, honorary, service, and special interest organizations. 6 fraternities and 6 sororities with houses. 25% of men and 25% of women join. Coed and women's dorms. Language houses. Living Learning houses. 42% of students live on campus. 13 intercollegiate sports for men, 13 for women; intramurals. AIAW, NCAA. Student body composition: 4.3% Asian, 2.5% Black, 0.5% Hispanic, 0.7% Native American, 90.8% White, 1.2% Other. 43% from out of state.

[P] PUGET SOUND COLLEGE OF THE BIBLE

PO Box C2006, Edmonds 98020

[1] SAINT MARTIN'S COLLEGE

Lacey 98503, (206) 491-4700

- **Enrollment: 218m, 145w; 488 total (including part-time)**
- **Tuition (1982/83): $4,312**
- **Room & Board: $2,268; Fees: $110**
- **Degrees offered: BA, BS, BSCE, AA**
- **Mean ACT 20; mean SAT 470v, 490m; mean WPCT VC 51, QC 51**
- **Student-faculty ratio: 15 to 1**

A private college affiliated with the Roman Catholic Order of St. Benedict. Campus in suburban Seattle which is served by air, rail, and bus.
Academic Character NACS and professional accreditation. Semester system, summer term. Majors offered in accounting, biology, chemistry, civil engineering, community service, criminal justice, economics, elementary education, English, history, humane studies, marketing, mathematics, political science, psychology, secondary education, sociology, and special education. Interdisciplinary majors offered in fine arts, environmental science, general science & management. Double majors possible. Courses offered in aerospace studies, art, business administration, college survival, drama, music, philosophy, physical education, physical science, physics, recreation, religious studies, and speech. MAT, MEd granted. Special programs. Remedial mathematics and English programs. Over 88,956-volume library.
Financial College scholarships, grants-in-aid, and loans.
Admissions SAT, ACT, or WPCT required. Rolling admissions. Transfers accepted. Admission deferral possible. Credit possible for CEEB CLEP exams; advanced placement possible.
Student Life 2 intercollegiate sports for men and women; intramurals. Student body composition: 18% minority.

[J1] SEATTLE CENTRAL COMMUNITY COLLEGE

1701 Broadway, Seattle 98122

[1] SEATTLE PACIFIC UNIVERSITY

3307 3rd Avenue W, Seattle 98119, (206) 281-2021
Director of Admissions: Marj Goodwin

- **Undergraduates: 884m, 1,236w; 2,851 total (including graduates)**
- **Tuition (1982/83): $4,464**
- **Room & Board: $2,439**
- **Degrees offered: BA, BS**
- **Student-faculty ratio: 18 to 1**

A private university affiliated with the Free Methodist Church, established in 1891. 25-acre urban campus in residential section of Seattle. Served by air, bus, and rail.
Academic Character NASC and professional accreditation. Trimester system, 2 summer terms. 47 majors offered by the Schools of Business & Economics, Education, Fine & Performing Arts, Health Sciences, Humanities, Natural & Mathematical Sciences, Physical Education & Athletics, Religion, and Social & Behavioral Sciences. Self-designed majors. 5 additional fields of specialization offered. Distributives and 10 credits in Biblical literature required. Masters degrees granted. Independent study. Honors program. Cooperative work/study, pass/fail, internships. Preprofessional programs in dentistry, engineering, law, librarianship, medical technology, medicine, social work, justice. 3-1 medical technology program. 3-2 engineering program with Columbia. Member Christian College Consortium. Elementary, secondary, and special education certification. Island campus for marine biology, botany, wilderness field station. Language lab. 107,822-volume library with microform resources.
Financial CEEB CSS. University scholarships, grants, loans, ministerial candidate loans; PELL, SEOG, NSS, NDSL, FISL, NSL, deferred payment, CWS, state work program. Scholarship application deadline March 1.
Admissions WPCT, SAT, or ACT required. $15 application fee. Rolling admissions; suggest applying between September and May. $50 tuition deposit and $25 room deposit (for boarders) required on acceptance of offer of admission. *Early Admission* Program. Transfers accepted. Credit possible for CEEB AP and CLEP exams.
Student Life Student government. Newspaper, yearbook, music, debate, drama groups. Multi-Ethnic Student Association. International Student Association. Academic, religious, and special interest groups. Single students must live at home or on campus. Coed and women's dorms. Limited married-student housing. 55% of students live on campus. Liquor, tobacco, drugs prohibited on campus. Attendance at 3 chapel services per week required. 5 intercollegiate sports for men, 5 for women; intramurals. NCAA, AIAW. Student body composition: 1.2% Asian, 2.1% Black, 1% Hispanic, 1.9% Native American, 93.8% White. 24% from out of state.

[1] SEATTLE UNIVERSITY

Seattle 98122, (206) 626-5720
Director of Admissions: Michael V. Fox

- **Undergraduates: 2,259m, 2,379w**
- **Tuition (1982/83): $4,725**
- **Room & Board: $2,493**
- **Degrees offered: BA, BS, BCrim Jus, BEd, BPA, BCivil Eng, BEng, BEE, BME, BSN**
- **Mean SAT 460v, 510m**
- **Student-faculty ratio: 16 to 1**

A private university controlled by the Society of Jesus (Jesuits), established in 1891. 45-acre urban campus in Seattle. Served by air, rail, steamship.
Academic Character NASC and professional accreditation. Trimester system, 8-week summer term. 22 majors offered by the College of Arts & Sciences, 6 by the School of Business, 5 by the School of Education, 1 by the School of Nursing, and 15 by the School of Science & Engineering. Alcohol studies. Distributives and 10 hours of religion/theology required. Graduate and professional degrees granted. Honors program for freshmen, sophomores. Cooperative work/study, pass/fail, internships. Preprofessional programs in dentistry, law, medicine, veterinary medicine. Study abroad. Elementary, secondary, special and Montessori education certification. ROTC; AFROTC, NROTC at U of Washington. 325,000-volume library.
Financial CEEB CSS and ACT FAS. University scholarships, grants, loans, family discounts, honors grants; PELL, SEOG, NDSL, GSL, deferred payment, CWS, university has own work program. Scholarship application deadline March 1.
Admissions High school graduation with 16 units required. Interview required in some cases. SAT, ACT, or WPCT required. $15 application fee. Rolling admissions beginning December 1; suggest applying before May 1. $100 tuition deposit and $85 housing deposit required on acceptance of offer of admission. *Early Decision, Early Admission* programs. Transfers accepted. Admission deferral possible. Credit possible for CEEB AP and CLEP exams;

university has own advanced placement program.
Student Life Student government. Newspaper, magazine. Music, debate, drama groups. Political, social, honorary, religious, service, outing, and special interest groups. Freshmen under 21 must live at home or on campus. 30% of undergraduates live on campus. Limited class absences allowed. 4 intercollegiate sports for men, 4 for women; intramurals. NAIA. Student body composition: 13% minority. 25% from out of state.

[J1] SHORELINE COMMUNITY COLLEGE
16101 Greenwood Avenue N, Seattle 98133

[J1] SKAGIT VALLEY COLLEGE
2405 College Way, Mt. Vernon 98273

[J1] SOUTH SEATTLE COMMUNITY COLLEGE
6000 16th Avenue SW, Seattle 98106

[J1] SPOKANE COMMUNITY COLLEGE
North 1810 Greene Street, Spokane 99207

[J1] SPOKANE FALLS COMMUNITY COLLEGE
West 3410 Fort George Wright Drive, Spokane 99204

[J1] TACOMA COMMUNITY COLLEGE
5900 South 12th Street, Tacoma 98465

[1] WALLA WALLA COLLEGE
College Place 99324, (509) 527-2811
Director of Admissions and Records: Orpha Osborne

- **Undergraduates: 890m, 751w; 1,959 total (including graduates)**
- **Tuition (1982/83): $5,115**
- **Room & Board: $2,250; Fees: $54**
- **Degrees offered: BA, BS, BMus, BSBA, BSE, BSW**
- **Student-faculty ratio: 12 to 1**

A private college affiliated with the Seventh-Day Adventist Church (Mormons), established in 1892. 77-acre campus in city of College Place in Walla Walla Valley.
Academic Character NASC and professional accreditation. Quarter system. 53 majors offered in the areas of applied arts, health & physical education, history & social studies, humanities, language arts, mathematics & natural science, and religion & theology. Minor required. Minors offered in most major fields and in 5 additional areas. Distributives, and 16 courses in religion/theology required. Senior comprehensive exams. MA, MS, MEd granted. Honors program. Credit by exam. Preprofessional programs in allied health, architecture, dentistry, dietetics, medical technology, medicine, pharmacy, physical therapy, veterinary science. Study abroad. Elementary and secondary education certification. Marine station. Portland campus. 140,000-volume library with microform resources.
Financial CEEB CSS. College scholarships, grants, loans; PELL, SEOG, BIA grants, NDSL, FISL, NSL, Insured Payment Plan, CWS. Priority application deadline April 1.
Admissions High school graduation with 6 units required. GED accepted. ACT required. $15 application fee. Rolling admissions. $50 deposit required on acceptance of offer of admission. Transfers accepted. Credit possible for CEEB AP and CLEP exams.
Student Life Student government. Newspaper, yearbook. International club, Canadian club. Academic groups. Single students must live at home or on campus. No coed dorms. Married-student housing. 75% of students live on campus. Attendance at chapel, evening services, Sabbath school, and 9 yearly assemblies required. 2 courses in health/phys ed required. Intramural sports. Student body composition: 1% Asian, 2% Black, 1% Hispanic, 0.1% Native American, 75% White, 20.9% Other.

[J1] WALLA WALLA COMMUNITY COLLEGE
500 Tausick Way, Walla Walla 99362

[1] WASHINGTON, UNIVERSITY OF
1400 Northeast Campus Way, Seattle 98195, (206) 543-9686
Director of Admissions and Records: Wilbur Washburn

- **LTotal Enrollment: 18,473m, 16,817w**
- **Tuition (1982/83): $1,176 (in-state); $3,255 (out-of-state)**
- **Room & Board: $2,052**
- **Degrees offered: BA, BS, BBA, BFA, BLA, BMus**
- **Mean ACT 25 composite**
- **Student-faculty ratio: 14 to 1**

A public university established in 1861. 680-acre urban campus in residential area of Seattle. Served by air, bus, and rail.
Academic Character NASC and professional accreditation. Trimester system, 2 part summer term of 9 weeks. 4 majors offered by the College of Architecture & Urban Planning, 69 by the College of Arts & Sciences, 7 by the College of Education, 11 by the College of Engineering, 14 by the College of Fisheries, 8 by the Collge of Forest Resources, 4 by the School of Business Administration, 1 by the School of Dentistry, 4 by the School of Medicine, 3 by the School of Nursing, 2 by the School of Pharmacy, 5 by School of Public Health & Community Medicine, and 1 by the School of Social Work. Self-designed majors. Distributive requirements. Graduate and professional degrees granted. Independent study. Honors program. Phi Beta Kappa. Cooperative work/study, pass/fail, internships. Several preprofessional programs. Study abroad. Elementary, secondary, and special education certification. ROTC, AFROTC, NROTC. Center for Tibetan Studies, Asian Arts. Marine science labs. Computer center, language lab, arboretum. 3,877,238-volume library with microform resources.
Financial CEEB CSS. University scholarships, loans; PELL, SEOG, NDSL, FISL, CWS, state work program. Application deadline March 1.
Admissions High school graduation with 16 units required. Audition required for dance, music majors. SAT, ACT, or WPCT required. $15 application fee. Rolling admissions beginning in January; application deadline May 1. $50 deposit required on acceptance of offer of admission. *Early Admission, Early Decision* programs. Transfers accepted. Credit possible for CEEB AP exams. Educational Opportunity Program.
Student Life Student government. Newspaper, magazine, yearbook, radio and TV stations. Music, debate, drama groups. Special interest organizations. 26 fraternities and 19 sororities; all have houses. Coed dorms. Ethnic and religious housing. Limited married-student housing. 12% of students live on campus. Cars on campus discouraged. Several intercollegiate and intramural sports for men and women. AIAW, NCAA, Athletic Association of Western Universities. Student body composition: 16% Asian, 5% Black, 2% Hispanic, 2% Native American, 75% White. 12% of students from out of state.

[1] WASHINGTON STATE UNIVERSITY
Pullman 99164, (509) 335-5586
Director of Admissions: Stan Berry

- **Undergraduates: 7,908m, 6,189w; 17,048 total (including graduates)**
- **Tuition (1982/83): $1,176 (in-state); $3,256 (out-of-state)**
- **Room & Board: $2,176**
- **Degrees offered: BA, BS, BAcc, BArch, BLA, BMus, BPharm, BSAgr**
- **Student-faculty ratio: 17 to 1**

A public university established in 1890. 339-acre campus located in small town of Pullman, 80 miles south of Spokane. Served by plane.
Academic Character NASC and professional accreditation. Semester system, 6- and 8-week summer terms. 17 majors offered by the College of Agriculture, 3 by the College of Business & Economics, 6 by the College of Education, 11 by the College of Engineering, 6 by the College of Home Economics, 1 by the College of Pharmacy, 53 by the College of Sciences & Arts, and 1 by the Center for Nursing. Distributive requirements. Graduate and professional degrees granted. Independent study. Honors program. Phi Beta Kappa. Cooperative work/study, pass/fail, internships. Preprofessional programs in dentistry, law, medicine. Transfer program in veterinary medicine. 3-1 programs possible. Cross-registration with U of Idaho (agriculture), Eastern Washington U and Whitworth (nursing). Study abroad in several countries. Elementary, secondary, and special education certification. AFROTC, ROTC; NROTC at WSU and U Idaho. Audio-visual center, nuclear reactor, observatory, computer center, language lab, electron microscope center. 1,265,979-volume library with microform resources.
Financial CEEB CSS. University scholarships, grants, loans, health profession loans; PELL, SEOG, NSS, NDSL, FISL, CWS. Application deadlines April 1 (scholarships), June 1 (NDSL).
Admissions High school graduation with 16 units required. WPCT and SAT or ACT required. $15 application fee. Rolling admissions; preferred application deadline May 1. $50 deposit required on acceptance of offer of admission. Transfers accepted. Credit possible for CEEB AP and CLEP exams.
Student Life Student government. Newspaper, magazine, yearbook, radio and TV stations. Music, debate, and drama groups. Academic, honorary, religious, service, and special interest groups. 24 fraternities and 15 sororities; all have houses. 28% of men and 20% of women join. Single freshmen must live at home or on campus. Coed and single-sex dorms. Special interest housing. Married-student housing. 70% of students live on campus. Several intercollegiate and intramural sports for men and women. AAWU, AIAW, PCC (PAC-10). Student body composition: 3% Asian, 2% Black, 1% Hispanic, 1% Native American, 93% White. 16% of students from out of state.

[J1] WENATCHEE VALLEY COLLEGE
1300 Fifth Street, Wenatchee 98801, (509) 662-1651

- **Enrollment: 594m, 571w; 2,416 total (including part-time)**
- **Tuition and Fees (1982/83): $17 per credit (in-state); $68 (out-of-state)**
- **Degrees offered: AA, AAA, AGS**

A public 2-year college established in 1939. 56-acre campus in Wenatchee.
Academic Character NASC accreditation. Trimester system, 8-week summer term. 2-year transfer programs in liberal arts offered, and occupational programs in business administration/management, health technology, office administration, ski management/instruction, and technical & industrial studies; others possible. Certificate programs. Course in Salish Indian language. Distributive requirements. Independent study. Cooperative work/study, pass/fail, internships. Credit by exam, credit for experience. Media center. Member of 2-million volume Washington Library Network.
Financial CEEB CSS. College scholarships, state grants, tuition waivers; PELL, SEOG, GSL, CWS. Application deadline May 1.
Admissions High school graduation required. GED accepted. Rolling admissions after December 1; application deadline September 1. *Early Admission* Program. Transfers accepted. Credit possible for CLEP exams.
Student Life Student government. Newspaper. Music group. Professional, honorary, religious, and special interest organizations. No coed dorms or married-student housing. 3 credits in phys ed required. 3 intercollegiate sports. NACC, NWSA.

[1] WESTERN WASHINGTON UNIVERSITY
Bellingham 98225, (206) 676-3000
Director of Admissions: Richard J. Riehl

- **Undergraduates: 4,881m, 5,410w**
- **Tuition (1982/83): $942 (in-state), $3,210 (out-of-state)**
- **Room & Board: $1,990**
- **Degrees offered: BA, BS, BAEd, BFA, BMus**
- **Mean SAT 495v, 508m**
- **Student-faculty ratio: 22 to 1**

A public university established in 1893. 224-acre urban cmpus in small city of Bellingham, 90 miles from Seattle. Served by air, bus, and rail.
Academic Character NASC and professional accreditation. Trimester system, 6- and 9-week summer terms. 65 majors offered by the College of Arts & Sciences, 8 by the College of Business & Economics, 3 by the School of Education, 12 by the College of Fine & Performing Arts, 6 by the Huxley College of Environmental Studies, and Student-faculty designed majors by the Fairhaven College. Minors offered in most major fields and in 5 additional areas. Programs in East Asian studies, museum training. Distributive requirements. Masters degrees granted. Independent study. Honors program. Cooperative work/study, pass/fail, internships. Credit by exam. Preprofessional programs in architecture, dental hygiene, dentistry, engineering, fisheries, forestry, law, medical technology, medicine, occupational therapy, optometry, pharmacy, physical therapy, social work, theology, veterinary medicine. Study abroad. Elementary, secondary, and special education certification. Environmental studies center, marine lab, computer center. 390,000-volume library with microform resources.
Financial CEEB CSS and ACT FAS. University scholarships, grants, loans, state waivers, state grants; PELL, SEOG, NDSL, GSL, CWS, state work program. Priority application deadline April 1.
Admissions High school graduation with 16 units required. GED accepted. WPCT required in-state; SAT or ACT out-of-state. $15 application fee. Rolling admissions; suggest filing after December 1 (before May 1 for boarders). $50 tuition deposit required 1 week before registration; $60 room deposit (for boarders) required on assignment of room. Transfers accepted. Credit possible for CEEB AP and CLEP exams.
Student Life Student government. Newspaper, magazine, radio and TV stations. Music, debate, drama groups. Outdoor program. Black Unified Society, Women's Center. Religious, academic, professional, service, and special interest groups. Limited university housing. Coed and single-sex dorms, apartments. Married-student housing. 35% of students live on campus. 6 intercollegiate sports for men, 6 for women; intramural and club sports. AIAW, NAIA, Evergreen Conference. Student body composition: 1.4% Asian, 0.9% Black, 0.5% Hispanic, 0.8% Native American, 96.4% White. 6% from out of state.

[J1] WHATCOM COMMUNITY COLLEGE
Bellingham 98226

[1] WHITMAN COLLEGE
Walla Walla 99362, (509) 527-5176
Director of Admissions: William D. Tingley

- **Undergraduates: 586m, 619w**
- **Tuition (1982/83): $5,850**
- **Room & Board: $2,470**
- **Degree offered: AB**
- **Mean SAT 550v, 580m**
- **Student-faculty ratio: 13 to 1**

A private college established in 1859. 45-acre campus located in small city of Walla Walla in the southeastern corner of the state, 235 miles from Portland, Oregon. Served by air and bus.
Academic Character NASC and professional accreditation. Semester system. Majors offered in art, biology, chemistry, dramatic arts, economics, English, foreign languages/literatures, geology, history, mathematics/computer science, music, philosophy, physics, political science, psychology, and sociology. Self-designed majors, interdepartmental majors. Minors offered in most major fields. Distributives and comprehensive exams required. Independent study. Honors program. Phi Beta Kappa. Pass/D/Fail. Internships. Credit by exam. Preprofessional programs in business management, dentistry, engineering, journalism, law, medical technology, medicine, ministry, public service, social work, and others. 3-2 programs in engineering with Caltech and Columbia, in forestry with Duke. 3-3 law program with Columbia. Cooperative science program with Battelle Northwest Labs. Washington, urban semesters. Study abroad. Elementary and secondary education certification. Computer center, language labs. 300,000-volume library.
Financial CEEB CSS and ACT FAS. College scholarships, grants, loans, state grants; PELL, SEOG, NDSL, GSL, Education Funds, Insured Tuition Payment Plan, CWS, state work program. FAF deadline February 15.
Admissions High school graduation with 16 units required. Interview encouraged. SAT, ACT, or WPCT required. $20 application fee. Application deadline March 1. $100 deposit required on acceptance of offer of admission. *Early Decision, Early Admission* programs. Transfers accepted. Admission deferral possible. Credit possible for CEEB AP exams.
Student Life Student government. Newspaper, magazine, yearbook, radio station. Music, drama, debate groups. Cultural activities. Honorary, academic, and special interest groups. 5 fraternities with houses and 5 sororities with section of dorms. 50% of students join. Freshmen and sophomores under 21 must live on campus. Coed and single-sex dorms. Foreign language, ethnic, and other special interest houses. No married-student housing. 80% of students live on campus. Liquor and drugs prohibited. 10 intercollegiate sports for men, 9 for women; intramural and club sports. AIAW, NAIA, NCWSA, Northwest Conference. Student body composition: 5% Asian, 2% Black, 1% Hispanic, 1% Native American, 91% White. 50% from out of state.

[1] WHITWORTH COLLEGE
Spokane 99251, (509) 466-1000
Director of Admissions: Shirlene Short

- **Undergraduates: 840m, 1,081w**
- **Tuition (1982/83): $5,120**
- **Room & Board: $2,240; Fees: $115**
- **Degrees offered: BA, BS**
- **Mean ACT 21; SAT 518v, 510**
- **Student-faculty ratio: 16 to 1**

A private college affiliated with the Presbyterian Synod of Alaska-Northwest, established in 1890. 200-acre suburban campus just outside Spokane. Served by air, bus, and rail.
Academic Character NASC accreditation. 4-1-4 system, 1 6-week and 2 3-week summer terms. Majors offered in biology, business management, chemistry/nutrition, communication studies, earth science, education, English, fine arts, history/political studies, mathematics/computer science, modern languages, physical education/recreation, physics, psychology, religion/philosophy, and sociology. Self-designed and interdisciplinary majors. Distributives and 1 course in religion required. MA, MEd, MAT granted. Independent study. 1 term off-campus study required. Honors program. Internships. Preprofessional programs in dentistry, law, librarianship, medical records, medical technology, medicine, ministry, nursing, social welfare, veterinary medicine. Elementary and secondary education certification. ROTC at Gonzaga. Language lab, computer center. 90,000-volume library.
Financial CEEB CSS. College, federal, and state scholarships, ministerial discounts; PELL, SEOG, NDSL, GSL, CWS. Preferred application deadline March 1.
Admissions High school graduation with 16 units required. Interview encouraged. SAT, ACT, or WPCT required. $15 application fee. Rolling admissions beginning December 1; application deadline August 1. $50 deposit required on acceptance of offer of admission. *Early Decision, Early Admission* Programs. Transfers accepted. Admission deferral possible. Credit possible for CEEB AP and CLEP exams.
Student Life Student government. Newspaper, magazine, yearbook. Music, drama groups. Black Student Union. Religious, academic, honorary, service, outing, and special interest groups. Special interest housing. 80% of students live on campus. Liquor, drugs prohibited on campus. 4 courses in phys ed required. 8 intercollegiate sports for men, 6 for women. PNIAC, IVC. Student body composition: 3% Black, 96% White, 1% Other. 45% from out of state.

[P] YAKIMA SCHOOL OF MEDICAL TECHNOLOGY
1114 West Spruce Street, Yakima 98902

[J1] YAKIMA VALLEY COMMUNITY COLLEGE
PO Box 1647, Yakima 98907, (509) 575-2612

- **Enrollment: 920m, 948w; 2,747 total (including part-time)**
- **Resident Fees (1982/83): $157 per term**
- **Degree offered: AAS**

A public, coeducational junior college.
Academic Character NACS and professional accreditation. Trimester system. Offers 13th and 14th grades in agriculture, nursing, secretarial science, business, and auto mechanics. Remedial mathematics and English programs.
Admissions Freshmen students admitted for any term. Rolling admissions.

WEST VIRGINIA (WV)

[1] ALDERSON-BROADDUS COLLEGE
Philippi 26416, (304) 457-1700
Director of Admissions: Wendell Teets

- **Undergraduates: 254m, 493w; 794 total**
- **Tuition (1982/83): $3,810**
- **Room & Board: $1,585; Fees: $160**
- **Degrees offered: BA, BS**
- **Mean ACT 19; mean SAT 400v, 400m**
- **Student-faculty ratio: 14 to 1**

A private college affiliated with the West Virginia and American Baptist Conventions, established in 1871. 110-acre campus in small town of Philippi, 160 miles from Charleston. Served by air, bus, and rail.
Academic Character NSACS and professional accreditation. Trimester system, 10½-week summer term. 9 majors offered in education & special programs, 4 in health science, 7 in humanities, 4 in natural science, and 12 in social sciences. Self-designed liberal arts majors. Minors offered in most major fields and in 3 additional areas. Liberal arts requirements except in education & special programs. 1 religion course required. Independent study. Cooperative work/study, internships, service projects. Preprofessional programs in dentistry, law, medicine, ministry, Christian education. Nursing

and physician's assistant programs. Cross-registration with Davis and Elkins, Salem, West Virginia, Wesleyan. Study abroad, winter term in Austria. Early childhood, elementary, secondary, and special education certification. 88,000-volume library.
Financial CEEB CSS. College scholarships, grants, and loans, Baptist scholarships; PELL, SEOG, NDSL, GSL, CWS.
Admissions High school graduation with 10 units required. Interview encouraged, required for physician's assistant. ACT required. $10 application fee. Rolling admissions; suggest applying at end of 11th year or beginning of 12th. $50 deposit required on acceptance of offer of admission. *Early Decision, Early Admission, Concurrent Enrollment* programs. Admission deferral possible. Transfers accepted. Credit possible for CEEB AP and CLEP exams; college has own advanced placement program. Special admission program.
Student Life Student government. Newspaper, yearbook, radio station. Music, debate, drama groups. Black Student Alliance. Religious, honorary, academic, and special interest organizations. 4 fraternities and 5 sororities. 20% of students join. Students must live at home or on campus. Single-sex dorms. 75% of students live on campus. Freshmen may not have cars on campus. Liquor, drugs prohibited on campus. 4 intercollegiate sports for men, 3 for women; intramurals. NAIA, WVIAC. Student body composition: 4% Black, 93% White, 3% Other. 56% from out of state.

[P] APPALACHIAN BIBLE COLLEGE

Bradley 25818

[J1] BECKLEY COLLEGE

Beckley 25801

[1] BETHANY COLLEGE

Bethany 26032, (304) 829-7000
Director of Admissions: David Wottle

- **Undergraduates: 477m, 371w**
- **Tuition (1982/83): $5,800**
- **Room & Board: $1,995**
- **Degrees offered: BA, BS**
- **Mean SAT 453v, 497m**
- **Student-faculty ratio: 12 to 1**

A private college affiliated with the Christian Church (Disciples of Christ), established in 1840. 300-acre campus in the village of Bethany, 25 minutes from Wheeling. Airport 55 minutes away in Pittsburgh.
Academic Character NCACS and professional accreditation. Modified semester system, 2 5-week summer terms. Majors offered in art, biology, chemistry, communications, computer science, economics-business, elementary education, English, fine arts, foreign languages, health science, history-political science, mathematics, music, philosophy, physical education, physics, psychology, religious studies, secondary education, social work, sociology, and theatre. Distributives, one religion course, 4 practicums, senior project, UGRE required. Independent study. Honors program. Preprofessional programs in dentistry, engineering, law, medicine, ministry, professional chemistry. Cooperative engineering programs with Columbia, Georgia Tech, Case Western, Washington U (MO). Consortium with Heidelberg, Westminster, Hiram, Muskingham. Washington, UN, Merrill-Palmer semesters. Several programs for study abroad. Elementary and secondary education certification. Language lab, media center. 143,000-volume library with microform resources.
Financial CEEB CSS. College scholarships, grants, loans, payment plan; PELL, SEOG, NDSL, CWS. Application deadline March 15.
Admissions High school graduation with 15 units required. Interview encouraged. SAT or ACT required. $15 application fee. Rolling admissions November through May; suggest applying early in fall. $100 deposit required on acceptance of offer of admission. *Early Admission* Program. Admission deferral possible. Transfers accepted. Credit possible for CEEB AP and CLEP exams; college has own advanced placement program. Programs for learning disabled students.
Student Life Student government. Newspaper, magazines, yearbook, radio and cable TV stations. Music, debate, drama groups. International Relations Club. Academic, religious, honorary, and special interest organizations. 7 fraternities with houses and 4 sororities with suites or houses. 56% of men and 58% of women join. Students must live at home or on campus. Single-sex dorms. Married-student housing. 99% of students live on campus. Freshmen may not have cars on campus. 10 intercollegiate sports for men, 6 for women; intramurals. NCAA, AIAW, PAC. Student body composition: 2% Black, 0.5% Hispanic, 0.5% Native American, 97% White. 84% from out of state.

[1] BLUEFIELD STATE COLLEGE

Bluefield 24701, (304) 325-7102

- **Undergraduates: 630m, 536w; 2,340 total (including part-time)**
- **Tuition & Fees (1980/81): $280 (in-state), $750 (out-of-state)**
- **Degrees offered: BA, BS, BSEd, AS**

A public college organized in 1895. Small-city campus located near the Virginia border.
Academic Character NCACS and professional accreditation. Semester system. Programs offered in the liberal arts, engineering technology, and teacher-training areas.
Financial Some part-time jobs available.
Admissions Open admissions. High school graduation or GED required. ACT required for placement. Students admitted for entrance in September and January.
Student Life Many students commute.

[1] CHARLESTON, UNIVERSITY OF

Charleston 25304, (304) 346-9471, ext. 211, 239
Vice-President & Dean of Admissions: E. Norman Jones

- **Undergraduates: 310m, 463w; 2,021 total (including part-time)**
- **Tuition (1982/83): $3,350**
- **Room & Board: $2,400; Fees: $20**
- **Degrees offered: BA, BS, AA, AS**
- **Student-faculty ratio: 16 to 1**

A private university established in 1888. 35-acre urban campus overlooking Kanawha River, 2 miles from downtown Charleston. Served by air, bus, and rail.
Academic Character NCACS and professional accreditation. Semester system, 4 3-week summer terms. Majors offered in accounting, art, biology, chemistry, computer science, elementary education, English, finance, health education, history-area studies, management, marketing, mass communications, mathematics, music, natural science, nursing, physical education, political science, psychology, radiologic administration, radiologic technology, real estate, recreation, religion-philosophy, respiratory therapy, secondary education, small business management, social sciences, sociology, and speech communication. Self-designed majors. Minors in most major fields and in 4 additional areas. Distributives and senior exam required. Independent study. Honors program. Cooperative work/study, pass/fail, internships. 3-1 medical technology program. Study abroad in Rome, Tokyo. Elementary, secondary, and special education certification. ROTC. Computer center, language lab, greenhouse. 91,729-volume library with microform resources.
Financial CEEB CSS. University scholarships, payment plans; PELL, SEOG, NSS, NDSL, GSL, NSL, CWS, university has own work program. Priority application deadline for scholarships March 1.
Admissions High school graduation with 15 units required. ACT or SAT required. $15 application fee. Rolling admissions; application deadline April 15, January 1 for nursing, radiologic technology. $100 deposit required on acceptance of offer of admission. *Early Decision, Early Admission, Credit-in-Escrow* programs. Admission deferral possible. Transfers accepted. Credit possible for CEEB AP and CLEP exams; university has own advanced placement program.
Student Life Student government. Newspaper, magazine, yearbook, radio station. Music, debate, drama groups. Black Student Advisory Committee. Political, academic, honorary, religious, service, and special interest organizations. 4 fraternities and 3 sororities without houses. 30% of men and 20% of women join. Freshmen must live with relatives or on campus. Single-sex dorms. 25% of students live on campus. 1 year of phys ed required. 5 intercollegiate sports for men, 4 for women; intramurals. AIAW, NAIA, NCAA, WVIAC. 30% of students from out of state.

[1] CONCORD COLLEGE

Athens 24712, (304) 384-3115
Director of Admissions: L.D. Dickens

- **Undergraduates: 760m, 967w; 2,362 total (including part-time)**
- **Tuition (1982/83): $574 (in-state), $1,774 (out-of-state)**
- **Room & Board: $2,047; Fees: $20**
- **Degrees offered: BA, BS, BSW**
- **Mean ACT 17**
- **Student-faculty ratio: 20 to 1**

A public college established in 1872. 120-acre small-town campus, 18 miles from Bluefield and 5 miles from Princeton. Airport and bus station nearby.
Academic Character NCACS and professional accreditation. Semester system, 2 5-week summer terms. Majors offered in art, commercial art, English, geography, history, political science, psychology, sociology, biology, business administration (8 areas), chemistry, community development-regional planning, education (6 areas), mathematics, travel industry management, and social work. Minors offered in most major fields and in 4 additional areas including Appalachian studies. Distributive requirements. Independent study. Honors program. Credit by exam. Preprofessional programs in dentistry, law, librarianship, medicine. 3-1 medical technology programs. 2-2 business administration program with Beckley College. Study abroad in England. Elementary, secondary, and special education certification. Center for Economic Action. 172,000-volume library with microform resources.
Financial CEEB CSS and ACT FAS. College scholarships, grants, loans, payment plan; PELL, SEOG, NDSL, FISL, GSL, CWS, state work program. Priority application deadline April 15.
Admissions High school graduation with 17 units required. GED accepted. Interview encouraged. ACT or SAT required. Rolling admissions; suggest applying before June 1. $50 deposit required on acceptance of offer of admission. *Early Admission* and *Concurrent Enrollment* programs. Transfers accepted. Credit possible for CEEB AP and CLEP exams; college has own advanced placement program.
Student Life Student government. Newspaper, magazine, yearbook, radio station. Music, debate, drama groups. Black Student Union. Political, religious, service, academic, honorary, and special interest organizations. 7 fraternities and 4 sororities housed in Towers Complex. Single students must live at home or on campus. Coed and single-sex dorms. Married-student apartments. 60% of students live on campus. Liquor restricted. 2 hours of phys ed required. 6 intercollegiate sports for men, 4 for women; intramurals. AIAW, NAIA, WVIAC. Student body composition: 5% Black, 95% White. 20% from out of state.

[1] DAVIS AND ELKINS COLLEGE

Elkins 26241, (304) 636-1900
Director of Admissions: David H. Wilkey

- **Undergraduates: 532m, 543w**
- **Tuition (1982/83): $4,370**
- **Room & Board: $2,100; Fees: $55**
- **Degrees offered: BA, BS, AA, AS, AAS**
- **Mean SAT 401v, 425m**
- **Student-faculty ratio: 18 to 1**

A private college affiliated with the Presbyterian Church, established in 1904. 170-acre small-city campus located in the foothills of the Allegheny Mountains, 120 miles from Pittsburgh. Airport nearby.

Academic Character NCACS and professional accreditation. 4-1-4 system, 1 8-week and 2 4-week summer terms. 35 majors offered in the areas of business, art, sciences, education, communication, English, foreign language, health, history, mathematics, political & social sciences, religion-philosophy, theatre, and social service. Self-designed majors. Minors offered. Distributives and senior exam required. Independent study. Pass/fail, internships. Preprofessional programs in dentistry, law, medicine, ministry, veterinary science. 3-2 engineering program with WVU. Forestry programs with Duke, SUNY-Syracuse. Washington Semester. Argonne National Laboratory program. Drew fine arts semester. Study abroad in several countries. Early childhood, elementary, and secondary education certification. Language lab, planetarium, observatory. 80,000-volume library.

Financial CEEB CSS. College scholarships, grants, loans, payment plans; PELL, SEOG, NDSL, CWS. Application deadline April 1; FAF deadline March 1.

Admissions High school graduation with 16 units required. GED accepted. Interview encouraged. SAT or ACT required. $15 application fee. Rolling admissions; suggest applying by March. $100 deposit required on acceptance of offer of admission. *Early Admission* and *Early Decision* programs. Admission deferral possible. Transfers accepted. Credit possible for CEEB AP and CLEP exams.

Student Life Student government. Newspaper, magazine, yearbook, radio station. Music, drama groups. Several academic, honorary, religious, service, and special interest organizations. 4 fraternities and 3 sororities. 40% of men and 35% of women join. Students must live with relatives or on campus. Coed and single-sex dorms. 85% of students live on campus. Liquor prohibited on campus. 2 phys ed credits required. 6 intercollegiate sports for men, 4 for women; intramurals. AIAW, NAIA, NCAA, WVIAC. Student body composition: 4.4% Black, 92.5% White, 3.1% Other. 63% from out of state.

[1] FAIRMONT STATE COLLEGE

Fairmont 26554, (304) 367-4141
Director of Admissions: John G. Conaway

- **Undergraduates: 1,603m, 1,687w; 5,244 total (including graduates)**
- **Tuition (1982/83): $690 (in-state), $1,790 (out-of-state)**
- **Room & Board: $2,144; Fees: $250**
- **Degrees offered: BA, BS, BAEd, AA, AS**
- **Mean ACT 16.4**
- **Student-faculty ratio: 24 to 1**

A public college established in 1867. 80-acre suburban campus 75 miles from Pittsburgh. Served by bus; airport and rail station nearby.

Academic Character NCACS and professional accreditation. Semester system, 2 5-week summer terms. Majors offered in allied health administration, art, biology, business administration, chemistry, criminal justice, engineering technology, English, French, graphics-fine arts, health science, history, home economics, interdisciplinary studies, mathematics, occupational health, physical education, political science, psychology, social work, and sociology. Minor required; minors offered in some major fields and in 9 additional areas. Distributive requirements. Independent study. Pass/fail, internships. Preprofessional programs in dentistry, engineering, journalism, law, medical technology, medicine, pharmacy, physical therapy. Elementary, secondary, and special education certification. ROTC, AFROTC at WVU. 170,000-volume library.

Financial CEEB CSS and ACT FAS. College scholarships, grants, and loans, payment plan; PELL, SEOG, NSS, NDSL, FISL, NSL, GSL, CWS. Scholarship application deadline April 15.

Admissions High school graduation required. GED accepted. ACT required. Rolling admissions. $80 housing deposit (for boarders) required with housing application. *Early Admission, Early Decision, Concurrent Enrollment* programs. Admission deferral possible. Transfers accepted. Credit possible for CEEB AP and CLEP exams; college has own advanced placement program.

Student Life Student government. Newspaper, yearbook, radio program. Music, debate groups. Honorary, religious, and special interest organizations. 6 fraternities, 1 with house, and 4 sororities without houses. 10% of men and women join. Single-sex dorms. 8% of students live on campus. Liquor prohibited in dorms. 2 hours of phys ed required. 8 intercollegiate sports for men, 5 for women; intramurals. NAIA, WVIAC. Student body composition: 8% Black, 1% Hispanic, 89% White, 2% Other. 5% from out of state.

[1] GLENVILLE STATE COLLEGE

Glenville 26351, (304) 523-6311
Dean of Records & Admissions: Mack K. Samples

- **Undergraduates: 589m, 670w; 1,998 total (including graduates)**
- **Tuition (1982/83): $564 (in-state), $1,764 (out-of-state)**
- **Room & Board: $2,040**
- **Degrees offered: BA, BS, BAEd, BABA, BSW, AA**
- **Mean ACT 18**
- **Student-faculty ratio: 17 to 1**

A public college established in 1872. Rural campus in small town of Glenville between Charleston and Clarksburg. Served by bus.

Academic Character NCACS and professional accreditation. Semester system. Majors offered in biology, business administration, chemistry, early childhood education, elementary education, English, history, secondary education (12 areas), social studies, social service, and special education. Distributive requirements. Credit/audit. Preprofessional programs in dentistry, engineering, forestry, law, medical technology, medicine, pharmacy, veterinary medicine. Cooperative program with Parkersburg Community College. Elementary, secondary, and special education certification. Computer center. 300,000-volume library with microform resources.

Financial ACT FAS. College scholarships, state grants; PELL, SEOG, NDSL, FISL, CWS, college has own work program.

Admissions High school graduation with 17 units required. GED accepted. ACT required. Rolling admissions. $25 room deposit (for boarders) required with housing application. *Early Admission* Program. Transfers accepted. Credit possible for CEEB CLEP exams and ACT scores.

Student Life Student government. Newspaper, magazine, yearbook. Music and drama groups. Academic, religious, professional, and special interest organizations. Fraternities and sororities. Single freshmen must live at home or on campus. Dorms for men and women. Married-student housing. 3 hours of phys ed required. Intercollegiate and intramural sports for men and women. Student body composition: 0.2% Asian, 3% Black, 0.1% Hispanic, 0.8% Native American, 93.9% White. 10% from out of state.

[1] MARSHALL UNIVERSITY

Huntington 25701, (304) 696-3160
Director of Admissions: James W. Harless

- **Undergraduates: 3,334m, 5,017w; 11,846 total (including graduates)**
- **Tuition (1982/83): $650 (in-state), $1,380 (out-of-state)**
- **Room & Board: $2,200**
- **Degrees offered: BA, BS, BBA, BFA, BSN, BSW, BSChem, BSCytotechnology, BSMT, AS, AAS**
- **Mean ACT 17.9**
- **Student-faculty ratio: 21 to 1**

A public university established in 1837. 45-acre urban campus in small city of Huntington, 50 miles from Charleston. Served by air, bus, and rail.

Academic Character NCACS and professional accreditation. Semester system, 2 5-week summer terms. 68 majors offered by the colleges of Liberal Arts, Business, Education, and Science, and the schools of Medicine and Nursing. Distributive requirements. MA, MS, MBA, MAJ granted. Independent study. Honors program. Phi Beta Kappa. Pass/fail, internships. Preprofessional programs in health fields. 3-1 cytotechnology and medical technology programs. 2-3 engineering programs possible. 3-2 forestry program with Duke. 5-year speech/language pathology program. Member Regional Council for International Education. Elementary, secondary, and special education certification. ROTC. Computer center, language lab, audio-visual center. 372,105-volume library with microform resources.

Financial CEEB CSS. University scholarships; PELL, SEOG, NSS, NDSL, GSL, NSL, CWS. Application deadline March 1; FAF deadline mid-January.

Admissions High school graduation required. GED accepted. Interview required for nursing majors, audition for music majors. ACT required. Rolling admissions; suggest applying in fall. $50 deposit required on acceptance of offer of admission. *Early Admission* Program. Transfers accepted. Credit possible for CEEB AP and CLEP exams; university has own advanced placement program.

Student Life Student government. Newspaper, magazine, yearbook, radio and TV stations. Music, debate, drama groups. Black United Students. Academic, political, honorary, religious, professional, service, and special interest organizations. 10 fraternities, 8 with houses, and 8 sororities, 7 with houses. Freshmen and sophomores must live at home or on campus. Coed and single-sex dorms. Married-student housing. 26% of students live on campus. Liquor restricted. 2 hours of phys ed required for some majors. 11 intercollegiate sports for men, 6 for women; intramurals. AIAW, NCAA, Southern Conference. Student body composition: 0.5% Asian, 4.7% Black, 0.3% Hispanic, 0.8% Native American, 92.9% White. 16% from out of state.

[J1] OHIO VALLEY COLLEGE

Parkersburg 26101, (304) 485-6192
Director of Admissions: Dennis Ward Cox

- **Enrollment: 129m, 133w; 278 total (including part-time)**
- **Tuition (1982/83): $2,176**
- **Room & Board: $2,184; Fees: $186**
- **Degrees offered: BA, BS, AA, AS, ASec Sc**
- **Student-faculty ratio: 9 to 1**

A private college affiliated with the churches of Christ, established in 1956. 133-acre small-city campus in the Ohio Valley. Served by air, bus, and rail.

Academic Character NCACS accreditation. Semester system, 2 5-week summer terms. BA and BS in Bible offered. 2-year programs offered in secretarial science, business administration, accounting, music, communications, mathematics, natural sciences, physical education, and social sciences. Distributives and 12 hours of Bible required. Independent study. Certificate programs. Preprofessional programs in nursing, medicine, dentistry, engineering.

Financial CEEB CSS. College scholarships, state grants, parental loans; PELL, SEOG, NDSL, FISL, GSL, CWS.

Admissions High school graduation with 15 units required. ACT required. Rolling admissions. *Early Admission* Program. Credit possible for CEEB AP and CLEP exams.

Student Life Student government. Newspaper, yearbook. Music and drama groups. Religious, professional, and special interest organizations. Single students must live with relatives or on campus. Liquor, smoking, gambling, hazing prohibited on campus. Class and daily chapel attendance required. 2 hours of phys ed required. Intramural sports.

[J1] PARKERSBURG COMMUNITY COLLEGE
Route 5, Box 167A, Parkersburg 26101

[1] SALEM COLLEGE
Salem 26426, (304) 782-5011
Director of Admissions: Stephen Ornstein

- **Undergraduates: 512m, 497w**
- **Tuition (1982/83): $3,810**
- **Room & Board: $2,114**
- **Degrees offered: BA, BS, BSW, AA, AS**
- **Mean ACT 18; mean SAT 950**
- **Student-faculty ratio: 15 to 1**

A private college established in 1888. 150-acre small-town campus, 12 miles from Clarksburg. Air, bus, and rail in Clarksburg.
Academic Character NCACS accreditation. Semester system, 2 5-week summer terms. 36 majors offered in the areas of business, art, therapy, sciences, communications, aviation, criminal justice, education, engineering, equestrian studies, humanities, medicine, mining technology, physical education, and political & social sciences. Minors offered in most major fields and in arts with handicapped, music, real estate. Distributive requirements. Internships. Clergy Development Program. Career aviation with Aero-Mech, Inc. Mining technology with National Mine Health and Safety Academy. Elementary, secondary, and special education certification. ROTC. Museum of West Virginia culture. 140,000-volume library.
Financial CEEB CSS. College scholarships, grants, and loans, state grants, payment plans; PELL, SEOG, NSS, NDSL, GSL, NSL, CWS, college has own work program. Preferred application deadline April 15; deadline for state grants March 1.
Admissions High school graduation with 16 units required. GED accepted. Campus visit encouraged. ACT or SAT required. $10 application fee. Rolling admissions; suggest applying 1st semester of 12th year. $100 deposit required on acceptance of offer of admission. *Early Decision, Early Admission, Concurrent Enrollment* programs. Admission deferral possible. Transfers accepted. Credit possible for CEEB AP and CLEP exams. Special acceptance and development program.
Student Life Newspaper, yearbook. Music, debate, drama groups. Foster grandparent program. Political, academic, and special interest groups. 6 fraternities and 2 sororities. 35% of men and 20% of women join. Seniors, veterans, and married students may live off campus. Coed and single-sex dorms. No married-student housing. 80% of students live on campus. 7 intercollegiate sports for men, 5 for women; intramurals. MAIAW, NAIA, WVIAC. Student body composition: 9% Black, 1% Hispanic, 90% White. 75% from out of state.

[1] SHEPHERD COLLEGE
Shepherdstown 25443, (304) 876-2511
Director of Admissions: Karl L. Wolf

- **Undergraduates: 1,550m, 1,550w**
- **Tuition (1982/83): $576 (in-state), $1,776 (out-of-state)**
- **Room & Board: $1,720**
- **Degrees offered: BA, BS, BAEd, AA**
- **Mean ACT 24; mean SAT 1100**
- **Student-faculty ratio: 23 to 1**

A public college established in 1871. 156-acre small-town campus, 70 miles from Washington, DC. Airport and rail station nearby.
Academic Character NCACS and professional accreditation. Semester system, 2 5-week summer terms. Majors offered in accounting, art, biology, business administration, business education, chemistry, data processing, early childhood education, economics, elementary education, English, general science, health education, history, home economics, hotel-motel/restaurant management, library science, marketing, mathematics, music, park administration, physical education, political science, psychology, recreation, safety education, secondary education, social welfare, and sociology. Self-designed majors. Minors offered in most major fields. Distributive requirements. Independent study. Pass/fail, internships. Several preprofessional programs. Early childhood, elementary, middle school, and secondary education certification. AFROTC at U of Maryland-College Park. 468,680-volume library.
Financial CEEB CSS. College scholarships, PELL, SEOG, NSS, NDSL, FISL, NSL, CWS. Scholarship application deadline April 1.
Admissions High school graduation with 18 units required. GED accepted. Interview encouraged. ACT required. Rolling admissions; suggest applying by November 15. $50 deposit required on acceptance of offer of admission. *Early Decision, Early Admission, Concurrent Enrollment* programs. Admission deferral possible. Transfers accepted. Credit possible for CEEB AP and CLEP exams.
Student Life Student government. Newspaper, magazine, yearbook. Music, debate, drama groups. 25 student organizations. 7 fraternities, 1 with house, and 6 sororities without houses. 20% of men and women join. Students must live at home or on campus if housing is available. Coed and single-sex dorms. No married-student housing. 40% of students live on campus. 1 absence per semester hour allowed. 2 semester hours of phys ed required. 6 intercollegiate sports for men, 6 for women; intramurals. NAIA, WVIAC, WRA. Student body composition: 1% Asian, 8% Black, 1% Hispanic, 90% White. 50% from out of state.

[J1] SOUTHERN WEST VIRGINIA COMMUNITY COLLEGE
Logan 25601

[1] WEST LIBERTY STATE COLLEGE
West Liberty 26074, (304) 336-8076
Registrar & Director of Admissions: E. Nelson Cain

- **Undergraduates: 993m, 1,086w; 2,671 total (including graduates)**
- **Tuition (1982/83): $604 (in-state), $1,804 (out-of-state)**
- **Room & Board: $1,974; Fees: $50**
- **Degrees offered: AB, BS, BSBA, AS**
- **Student-faculty ratio: 19 to 1**

A public college established in 1837. 290-acre semi-rural campus in West Liberty, 12 miles from Wheeling. Air, bus, and rail service in Wheeling.
Academic Character NCACS and professional accreditation. Semester system, 2 4-week summer terms. 42 majors offered in the areas of education, business & economics, fine arts, health & physical education, health professions, humanities, natural sciences & mathematics, and social sciences. Minor required of liberal arts majors; minors offered in most major fields and in 8 additional areas. Distributive requirements. Honors program. Credit by exam. 3-2 speech pathology-audiology program with WVU. 2-year transfer programs in engineering, optometry, pharmacy. Elementary, secondary, and special education certification. Language lab, computer services, medical technology lab. 192,000-volume library.
Financial Guaranteed tuition. CEEB CSS and ACT FAS. College scholarships and loans, state grants, payment plan; PELL, SEOG, NSS, NDSL, FISL, NSL, CWS. Application deadline March 1.
Admissions High school graduation required. GED accepted. Audition required for music majors. ACT required. Rolling admissions; suggest applying 1st semester of 12th year. $50 deposit required on acceptance of offer of admission. *Early Admission* and *Concurrent Enrollment* programs. Transfers accepted. Credit possible for CEEB AP and CLEP exams.
Student Life Student government. Newspaper. Music, debate, drama groups. Academic and honorary organizations. 5 fraternities, 1 with house, 4 sororities. 21% of men and 13% of women join. Students must live at home or on campus. Dorms for men and women. Married-student housing. 60% of students live on campus. Liquor restricted. 2 semesters of phys ed required. 9 intercollegiate sports for men, 4 for women; intramurals. NAIA, WVC. Student body composition: 20% minority. 35% from out of state.

[G1] WEST VIRGINIA COLLEGE OF GRADUATE STUDIES
Institute 25112

[1] WEST VIRGINIA INSTITUTE OF TECHNOLOGY
Montgomery 25136, (304) 422-3071
Director of Admissions: Robert P. Scholl, Jr.

- **Undergraduates: 1,734m, 692w**
- **Tuition (1982/83): $478 (in-state), $1,478 (out-of-state)**
- **Room & Board: $2,220**
- **Degrees offered: BA, BS, BSE, BSEE, BSCE, BMET, BET, AS**
- **Mean ACT 19.5**
- **Student-faculty ratio: 15 to 1**

A public institute established in 1895. 112-acre small-town campus, 28 miles southeast of Charleston. Served by bus and rail.
Academic Character NCACS and professional accreditation. Semester system, 2 6-week summer terms. 20 majors offered by the School of Human Studies, 10 by the School of Engineering & Physical Sciences, and 2 by the Community & Technical College. Distributive requirements. Cooperative work/study. Elementary and secondary education certification. ROTC. Computer center. 134,000-volume library with microform resources.
Financial ACT FAS. Institute scholarships and loans, state grants, athletic grants, music scholarships, payment plan; PELL, SEOG, NDSL, FISL, GSL, CWS, state work program, institute work program.
Admissions High school graduation required. GED accepted. ACT required. Rolling admissions. *Early Admission* and *Early Decision* programs. Transfers accepted. Credit possible for CEEB AP and CLEP exams; institute has own advanced placement program.
Student Life Student government. Newspaper, magazine, yearbook. Music, drama groups. Black Student Guild. Women's Association. Service and special interest groups. 5 fraternities and 1 sorority. Freshmen and sophomores must live at home or on campus. Dormitories for men and women. 45% of students live on campus. 2 hours of phys ed required. 8 intercollegiate sports for men; intramurals for men and women. NAIA. Student body composition: 5% Black, 1% Hispanic, 94% White. 15% from out of state.

[J1] WEST VIRGINIA NORTHERN COMMUNITY COLLEGE
Wheeling 26003

[P] WEST VIRGINIA SCHOOL OF OSTEOPATHIC MEDICINE
400 North See Street, Lewisburg 24901

[1] WEST VIRGINIA STATE COLLEGE
Institute 25112, (304) 766-3000
Acting Coordinator of Admissions: Michael Lampros

- **Undergraduates: 2,058m, 2,427w**
- **Tuition (1982/83): $600 (in-state), $1,800 (out-of-state)**
- **Room & Board: $2,010; Fees: $15**
- **Degrees offered: BA, BS, AA, AS, AAS**
- **Student-faculty ratio: 20 to 1**

A public college established in 1891. 87-acre suburban campus in Institute, 10 miles west of Charleston. Air, bus, and rail service in Charleston.
Academic Character NCACS and professional accreditation. Semester system, 2 5-week summer terms. Majors offered in art, biology, business

administration, chemistry, communications, criminal justice, economics, education, English, health physics technology, history, industrial technology, mathematics, political science, psychology, recreation service, social work, and sociology. Distributive requirements. Independent study. Elementary and secondary education certification. ROTC. Computer services. 250,000-volume library.

Financial CEEB CSS and ACT FAS. College scholarships and loans, state grants; PELL, SEOG, NDSL, FISL, GSL, CWS, college has own work program. Application deadline May 15.

Admissions High school graduation with 17 units recommended. GED accepted. ACT required; SAT accepted. Rolling admissions; $50 room deposit (for boarders) required on acceptance of offer of admission. *Early Admission* and *Concurrent Enrollment* programs. Admission deferral possible. Transfers accepted. Credit possible for CEEB AP and CLEP exams.

Student Life Student government. Newspaper, magazine, yearbook. Music and drama groups. Academic and honorary organizations. Fraternities and sororities. Married-student and single-parent housing. 10% of students live on campus. Class attendance required for freshmen and sophomores. 6 intercollegiate sports for men, 4 for women; intramurals. NAIA, WVIAC. Student body composition: 1.7% Asian, 22.3% Black, 76% White. 9% from out of state.

[1] WEST VIRGINIA UNIVERSITY

Morgantown 26506, (304) 293-0111
Dean of Admissions & Records: John D. Brisbane

- **Undergraduates: 8,231m, 6,437w; 21,455 total (including graduates)**
- **Tuition & Fees (1982/83): $850 (in-state), $2,400 (out-of-state)**
- **Room & Board: $2,510**
- **Degrees offered: BA, BS, BS in several areas, AA**
- **Mean ACT 22.8**
- **Student-faculty ratio: 14 to 1**

A public university established in 1867. 74-acre main campus and 725-acre Evansdale campus in Morgantown, 72 miles from Pittsburgh. Served by air and bus.

Academic Character NCACS and professional accreditation. Semester system, 2 6-week summer terms. 9 majors offered by the College of Agriculture & Forestry, 19 by the College of Arts & Sciences, 5 by the College of Business & Economics, 4 by the Creative Arts Center, 1 by the School of Dentistry, 6 by the College of Engineering, 4 by the College of Human Resources & Education, 1 each by the schools of Journalism, Nursing, Pharmacy, Social Work, 3 by the College of Mineral & Energy Resources, 2 by the School of Medicine, and 2 by the School of Physical Education. Graduate and professional degrees granted. Honors program. Credit by exam. Elementary and secondary education certification. ROTC, AFROTC. Experimental farms. 961,828-volume library with microform resources.

Financial CEEB CSS. University scholarships and loans, athletic scholarships; PELL, SEOG, NDSL. Application deadlines January 15 (freshman scholarships), April 1 (loans).

Admissions High school graduation with 10 units required. GED accepted. ACT required. Rolling admissions. *Early Decision* and *Early Admission* programs. Admission deferral possible. Transfers accepted. Credit possible for CEEB AP and CLEP exams; university has own advanced placement program.

Student Life Student government. Newspaper, yearbook, TV station. Music, speaking, drama groups. Several honorary, academic, service, and special interest organizations. 20 fraternities and 11 sororities, all with houses. Freshmen must live at home or on campus. 3 dorms for men, 6 for women. Privately-owned dorms also available. Married-student housing. 24% of students live on campus. Liquor prohibited on campus. 1 year of phys ed required. 12 intercollegiate sports for men, 6 for women; intramurals. AIAW. Student body composition: 0.1% Asian, 2% Black, 0.1% Hispanic, 96.4% White, 1.4% Other. 35% from out of state.

■[J1] POTOMAC STATE COLLEGE OF WEST VIRGINIA UNIVERSITY

Keyser 26726, (304) 788-3011
Assistant Dean for Admissions & Records: Hunter J. Conrad

- **Enrollment: 546m, 548w**
- **Tuition, Room & Board (1982/83): $2,472 (in-state), $3,672 (out-of-state)**
- **Degrees offered: AA, AAS**
- **Mean ACT 16.4**
- **Student-faculty ratio: 24 to 1**

A public junior college established in 1901. 16-acre campus in small city of Keyser, 3 hours from Pittsburgh.

Academic Character NCACS accreditation. Semester system, 2 2-week summer terms. 2-year transfer programs offered in agriculture, business, computer science, economics, education, engineering, forestry, journalism, music, physical education, biology, chemistry, English, geology, history, mathematics, modern languages, physics, political science, psychology, and sociology. 8 programs in career fields and technologies. Certificate programs. Distributive requirements. Pass/fail. Preprofessional programs in dentistry, law, medical technology, medicine, pharmacy, physical therapy, social work, veterinary medicine. College farm, greenhouse. 39,000-volume library.

Financial College scholarships, athletic scholarships, state grants; PELL, SEOG, NDSL, CWS. Application deadline March 31.

Admissions High school graduation with 16 units required. GED accepted. ACT required. Rolling admissions. $50 room deposit (for boarders) required on acceptance of offer of admission. *Early Admission* and *Early Decision* programs. Admission deferral possible. Transfers accepted. Credit possible for CEEB AP and CLEP exams.

Student Life Student government. Newspaper. Music and drama groups. Black Unity. Honorary, religious, political, service, and special interest clubs. 1 fraternity. Single students under 22 must live at home or on campus. Dorms for men and women. 2 hours of phys ed required. 2 intercollegiate sports for men, 2 for women; intramurals. NJCAA.

[1] WEST VIRGINIA WESLEYAN COLLEGE

Buckhannon 26201, (304) 473-7011
Director of Admissions: Wenrich H. Green

- **Undergraduates: 714m, 950w**
- **Tuition (1982/83): $3,600**
- **Room & Board: $2,370; Fees: $386**
- **Degrees offered: BA, BS, BMus Ed, AA**
- **Mean ACT 21; mean SAT 450v, 480m**
- **Student-faculty ratio: 14 to 1**

A private college affiliated with the United Methodist Church, established in 1890. 80-acre small-town campus, 25 miles from Clarksburg. Airport and rail station in Clarksburg.

Academic Character NCACS and professional accreditation. 4-1-4 system, 3 4-week and 2 6-week summer terms. 43 majors offered in the areas of arts, sciences, education, religion & philosophy, business & economics, humanities, political science, health, social science, communication, library science, and fashion merchandising. Major/minor or double major required. Distributives and one religion course required. MAT granted. Independent study. Honors program. Cooperative work/study, pass/fail, internships. Credit by exam. Preprofessional programs in business administration, chemistry, church assistance, dentistry, dietetics, law, medical technology, medicine, ministry, occupational therapy, optometry, pharmacy, physical therapy, religious education, social work. 3-2 and 4-1 engineering programs with U of Pennsylvania. 3-2 engineering program with U of Pittsburgh. 3-2½ forestry program with Duke. 4-college consortium. Cross-registration at College of Boca Raton. Merrill-Palmer semester. Study abroad. Early childhood, elementary, secondary, and special education certification. Language lab. 157,500-volume library.

Financial CEEB CSS and ACT FAS. College scholarships, grants, and loans, Methodist scholarships, ministers' dependents aid, payment plans; PELL, SEOG, NDSL, GSL, NSL, CWS. Application deadlines March 1 (scholarships), April 15 (loans).

Admissions High school graduation with 16 units required. Interview encouraged. ACT or SAT required. $25 application fee. Rolling admissions; suggest applying before May 1. $50 deposit required on acceptance of offer of admission. *Early Decision* and *Early Admission* programs. Admission deferral possible. Transfers accepted in January. Credit possible for CEEB AP and CLEP exams.

Student Life Student government. Newspaper, magazine, yearbook, radio station. Music, drama, debate groups. Academic, honorary, political, religious, service, and special interest organizations. 5 fraternities with houses and 4 sororities without houses. 32% of men and 35% of women join. Juniors and seniors may live off campus. Single-sex dorms. 94% of students live on campus. Class attendance required. 4 semester hours of phys ed required. 9 intercollegiate sports for men, 5 for women; intramural and club sports. AIAW, NAIA, NCAA, WVIAC. Student body composition: 2% Black, 98% White. 70% from out of state.

[1] WHEELING COLLEGE

316 Washington Avenue, Wheeling 26003, (304) 243-2000
Director of Admissions: Dan Saraceno

- **Undergraduates: 327m, 400w; 1,100 total (including graduates)**
- **Tuition (1982/83): $4,350**
- **Room & Board: $2,400; Fees: $100**
- **Degrees offered: BA, BS, BSN**
- **Mean ACT 21; mean SAT 920**
- **Student-faculty ratio: 11 to 1**

A private college controlled by the Jesuit Fathers of the Maryland Province, established in 1954. 65-acre suburban campus in residential section of Wheeling, 60 miles from Pittsburgh. Served by bus; airport and rail station in Pittsburgh.

Academic Character NCACS and professional accreditation. Semester system, 2 6-week summer terms. Majors offered in accounting, banking & finance, behavioral analysis for management, biology, business administration, chemistry, criminal justice, English, fine arts, fine arts management, French, general business, general science, history, marketing, mathematics, medical technology, nursing, philosophy, physics, political science, psychology, public administration, public communications, respiratory therapy, sociology, Spanish, and theology. Self-designed majors. Minors in some major fields and in 3 additional areas. Courses in German. Distributives and 8 hours of religion required. MBA granted. Independent study. Honors program. Cooperative work/study, pass/fail, internships. Credit by exam. Preprofessional programs in dentistry, engineering, law, medicine. 2-2 program in mine engineering with WVU. 2-year transfer program in engineering with U of Detroit. 27-college Jesuit College Exchange Program. Study abroad. 121,000-volume library.

Financial CEEB CSS. College scholarships, grants, loans, state grants, payment plans; PELL, SEOG, NSS, NDSL, FISL, NSL, CWS. Scholarship application deadline March 1.

Admissions High school graduation with 15 units required. GED accepted. Interview encouraged. SAT or ACT required; 2 ACH recommended for nursing majors. $15 application fee. Rolling admissions; suggest applying by December. $100 tuition deposit and $100 room deposit (for boarders) required on acceptance of offer of admission. *Early Admission, Early Decision, Concurrent Enrollment* programs. Admission deferral possible. Transfers accepted. Credit possible for CEEB AP and CLEP exams.

Student Life Student government. Newspaper, magazine, yearbook. Music and drama groups. Students for Intercultural Understanding. Academic, honorary, religious, and special interest organizations. Students must live at home or on campus. Coed and single-sex dorms. No married-student housing. 72% of students live on campus. 3 intercollegiate sports for men, 4 for women, 2 coed; intramural and club sports. WVIAC. Student body composition: 3% Black, 0.3% Hispanic, 95% White, 1.7% Other. 40% from out of state.

WISCONSIN (WI)

[1] ALVERNO COLLEGE

3401 South 39 Street, Milwaukee 53215, (414) 647-5400
Director of Admissions: Stephanie Chapko

- **Undergraduates: 1m, 723w; 1,363 total (including graduates)**
- **Tuition (1982/83): $3,850; $4,150 for nursing**
- **Room & Board: $1,700**
- **Degrees offered: BA, BS, BMus, BSEd, BSMed Tech, BSN, AA**
- **Student-faculty ratio: 16 to 1**

A private women's college affiliated with the School Sisters of St. Francis, organized in 1887. 50-acre wooded campus in residential environment 15 minutes from downtown Milwaukee. Served by air, bus, and rail.

Academic Character NCACS and professional accreditation. Semester system, 2 4-week summer terms. Majors offered in art, art therapy, biology, chemistry, communications, education, English, history, management, mathematics, medical technology, music, nuclear medical technology, nursing, psychology, and religious studies. Support areas required; offered in most major fields and in 8 additional areas. Weekend College grants baccalaureate degrees in management, professional communications, and nursing (for RNs), and associate degree in liberal studies. Independent study. No grades; competence to be shown. Internships. Preprofessional programs in dentistry, law, medicine, veterinary medicine. 3-2 program in engineering with Milwaukee School of Engineering. Early childhood, elementary, secondary education certification. Campus elementary school, Child Development Center, Language lab. 192,089-volume library.

Financial CEEB CSS. College scholarships and grants, music scholarships; PELL, SEOG, NSS, NDSL, NSL, deferred payment, CWS; college has own work program. Suggested application deadline for scholarships March 1.

Admissions High school graduation with 10-12 units required. Audition and exam required for music majors and minors. ACT or SAT required. $10 application. Rolling admissions; suggest applying in 1st semester. $50 tuition deposit and $50 room deposit required on acceptance of offer of admission. *Early Decision* Program. Transfers accepted. Admission deferral possible. Credit possible for CLEP exams.

Student Life Student government. Newspaper. Music and drama groups. Research Center on Women. Academic, honorary, and special interest groups. 27% of full-time students live on campus. Individual sports. Student body composition: 4% Black, 1% Hispanic, 93% White, 2% Other.

[1] BELOIT COLLEGE

Beloit 53511, (608) 365-3391
Director of Admissions: John W. Lind

- **Undergraduates: 552m, 457w; 1,055 total (including graduates)**
- **Tuition (1982/83): $6,450**
- **Room & Board: $2,100; Fees: $136**
- **Degrees offered: BA, BS**
- **Mean ACT 25 composite; mean SAT 527v, 544m**
- **Student-faculty ratio: 12 to 1**

A private college established in 1846. 65-acre campus located in small city of Beloit, 50 miles from Madison and 100 miles northwest of Chicago. Served by air and bus.

Academic Character NCACS accreditation. Semester system. Majors offered in anthropology, art, biochemistry, biology, biology-medical technology, business administration, chemistry, classical civilization, classical philology, comparative literature, economics, economics/management, English composition, English literature, French, geology, German, government, history, international relations, mathematics, mathematics/computer science, modern languages, music, performing arts, philosophy, physics, psychology, religious studies, science for elementary teaching, sociology, Spanish, and theatre arts. Self-designed and interdepartmental majors. Distributive requirements. Independent and accelerated study. Honors program. Phi Beta Kappa. Pass/fail, internships. 3-2 programs in social work with U of Chicago, in engineering with Columbia and Georgia Tech, in forestry with Duke. 4-2 engineering program with Duke. 2-2 medical technology, nursing programs with Rush U. Study abroad. Washington, urban, Argonne semesters. Wilderness field program. Elementary and secondary education certification. Computer center, language lab, observatory. Limnology lab, social science lab. 250,000-volume library with microform resources.

Financial CEEB CSS. College scholarships, grants, loans, PELL, SEOG, NDSL, GSL, CWS. Application deadline March 1.

Admissions High school graduation with 16 units required. Interview encouraged. SAT or ACT required. $20 application fee. Rolling admissions in February-March. $100 deposit required on acceptance of offer of admission. *Early Admission* Program. Transfers accepted. Admission deferral possible. Credit possible for CEEB AP and CLEP exams.

Student Life Student government. Newspaper, magazine, yearbook, radio station. Music and drama organizations. Religious, political, and special interest groups. 4 fraternities and 2 sororities; most have houses. Seniors may live off campus. Coed and single-sex dorms. Language, special interest housing. Co-op dorms. 89% of students live on campus. 8 intercollegiate sports for men, 8 for women; intramural and club sports. NCAA, AIAW, MCAC. Student body composition: 1% Asian, 2% Black, 1% Hispanic, 93% White, 3% Other. 82% from out of state.

[J1] BLACKHAWK TECHNICAL INSTITUTE

PO Box 5009; 6004 Prairie Road, CTY TRK G, Janesville 53547

[1] CARDINAL STRITCH COLLEGE

6801 North Yates Road, Milwaukee 53217, (414) 352-5400
Director of Admissions: Patricia B. Ranger

- **Enrollment: 1,200**
- **Tuition (1982/83): $3,600**
- **Room & Board: $1,950-$2,050**
- **Degrees offered: BA, BFA, BS, AA, AAS**
- **Student-faculty ratio: 10 to 1**

A private college controlled by the Sisters of St. Francis of Assisi, established in 1937. 60-acre urban campus in Milwaukee. Served by air and bus.

Academic Character NCACS and professional accreditation. Semester system, 6-week summer term. Majors offered in art, biology, broad field science, business, chemistry, commercial art, communications arts, computer studies, education, English, French, history, language/business, mathematics, music, natural science, psychology, religious studies, social studies, sociology, Spanish, home economics, and professional arts (for RNs). Distributives and 2 courses in religious studies required. MA granted. Independent study. Pass/fail. Preprofessional programs in business, dentistry, gerontology, law, medical technology, medicine, optometry, veterinary medicine, veterinary science. Study abroad. Early childhood, elementary, secondary, and special education certification.

Financial College scholarships and grants, music scholarships, state grants, and loans, family grants; PELL, SEOG, NDSL, CWS.

Admissions High school graduation with 16 units required. GED accepted. Audition required for music majors. SAT or ACT required. $15 application fee. Rolling admissions. *Early Admission, Early Decision* programs. Transfers accepted. Admission deferral possible. Credit possible for CEEB AP and CLEP exams.

Student Life Student government. Music and drama groups. Afro-American organization. Professional, honorary, religious, and special interest groups. Coed dorm. 16% of students live on campus. 2 intercollegiate sports for men and women; intramurals. 10% minority students.

[1] CARROLL COLLEGE

Waukesha 53186, (414) 547-1211
Dean of Admissions: Frank Hetherington

- **Undergraduates: 527m, 548w**
- **Tuition (1982/83): $5,600**
- **Room & Board: $2,080; Fees: $60**
- **Degrees offered: BA, BS, BSMed Tech, BSN**
- **Student-faculty ratio: 14 to 1**

A private college affiliated with the United Presbyterian Church, established in 1846. 36-acre campus in residential section of city of Waukesha, 18 miles from Milwaukee. Served by bus.

Academic Character NCACS accreditation. 4-1-4 system, 2 6-week summer terms. Majors offered in accounting, art, biology, business administration, chemistry, communication, computer science/physics, criminal justice, economics, education, English, French, geography, German, history, international relations, land use planning, mathematics, medical technology, music, nursing, philosophy, physical education, physics, political science, psychology, religion, social work, sociology, Spanish, theatre arts, and theatre education. Self-designed majors. Minors offered in most major fields and in coaching, secondary education. Distributives and 1 religion course required. Independent study. Pass/fail, internships. Preprofessional programs in dentistry, engineering, journalism, law, medicine, nursing, osteopathy, podiatry, theology, and others. 3-2 engineering programs. BSN with Columbia Hospital. Study abroad. Washington, UN semesters. Elementary, secondary, and early childhood education certification. Computer center. 160,000-volume library.

Financial CEEB CSS. College scholarships, grants, loans, state grants, PELL, SEOG, NDSL, FISL, GSL, Education Funds, deferred payment, CWS. Recommended application deadlines March 15 (scholarships), April 1 (loans).

Admissions High school graduation with 15 units required. Interview encouraged. SAT or ACT required. Rolling admissions; suggest applying by March 15. $100 deposit required on acceptance of offer of admission. *Early Admission, Concurrent Enrollment* programs. Transfers accepted. Admission deferral possible. Credit possible for CEEB AP and CLEP exams; college has own advanced placement program.

Student Life Student government. Newspaper, magazine, yearbook, radio station. Music, debate, drama groups. Independent Women's Association. Black Students Organization. Academic, political, honorary, religious, and special interest groups. 5 fraternities with houses and 4 sororities with suites. 50% of men and 30% of women join. Freshmen and sophomores must live at home or on campus. Coed and single-sex dorms. 85% of students live on campus. Drugs prohibited on campus. Attendance at 3 of 6 confrontations and 3 of 5 convocations required. 2 semesters of phys ed and health required. 9 intercollegiate sports for men, 6 for women; intramurals. CCIW, WICWI, NAIA,

NCAA. Student body composition: 1% Asian, 8% Black, 5% Hispanic, 1% Native American, 85% White. 25% from out of state.

[1] CARTHAGE COLLEGE

Kenosha 53140, (414) 551-8531
Director of Admissions and Financial Aid: Kent Duesing

- **Undergraduates: 487m, 489w; 1,373 total (including part-time)**
- **Tuition (1982/83): $4,575**
- **Room & Board: $1,933; Fees: $76**
- **Degree offered: BA**
- **Mean SAT 950**
- **Student-faculty ratio: 13 to 1**

A private college affiliated with the Lutheran Church in America, established in 1847. 85-acre campus in city of Kenosha, 35 miles from Milwaukee. Served by air, bus, and rail.

Academic Character NCACS and professional accreditation. 4-1-4 system, summer terms. 42 majors offered by the divisions of Business & Economics, Teacher Education, Fine Arts, Humanities, Science & Mathematics, and Social Sciences. Self-designed majors. Distributives and 2 courses in religion required. Independent study. Honors program. Pass/fail, internships. Credit by exam. Preprofessional programs in dentistry, engineering, government, law, library science, medical technology, medicine, nursing, social service, theology, others. 3-2 engineering programs with Washington U, Case Western Reserve. 3-1, 4-1 medical technology programs. Study abroad. January studies in Mexico. Milwaukee Urban Semester. Elementary, secondary, and special education certification. Language lab. 208,539-volume library.

Financial CEEB CSS. College scholarships, grants, loans, state grants, Lutheran loans; PELL, SEOG, NDSL, GSL, Tuition Plan, CWS. Application deadlines February 15 (FAF), May 1 (loans).

Admissions High school graduation with 14 units required. GED accepted. ACT or SAT required; ACT preferred. $15 application fee. Rolling admissions; suggest applying early in 12th year. $200 deposit required on acceptance of offer of admission. *Early Admission, Early Decision* programs. Transfers accepted. Admission deferral possible. Credit possible for CEEB AP and CLEP exams.

Student Life Student government. Newspaper, magazine, yearbook. Music, debate, drama groups. Service, honorary, academic, professional, and special interest groups. 5 fraternities and 4 sororities; none have houses. 30% of men and 35% of women join. Single students must live at home or on campus. Coed and single-sex dorms. 93% of students live on campus. Liquor allowed only in dorms. Attendance required at half of chapel services and convocations. 2 phys ed courses required. 9 intercollegiate sports for men, 6 for women; intramurals. NCAA, CCIW, Chicago Metro Conference for Women. Student body composition: 4% Black, 1% Hispanic, 95% White. 55% from out of state.

[J1 and 2] CONCORDIA COLLEGE

3201 West Highland Blvd, Milwaukee 53208, (414) 344-3400

- **Enrollment: 222m, 247w; 589 total (including part-time)**
- **Tuition (1982/83): $3,300**
- **Room & Board: $1,900**
- **Degrees offered: BA, BSN**

A private coeducational college affiliated with the Lutheran-Missouri Synod.

Academic Character NCACS accreditation. 4-1-4 system. Majors offered in pre-seminary education, education, social work, liberal arts, lay ministry, business, radiological technology, court reporting, and legal, medical, parish, and administrative secretarial. Diplomas offered for two- and three-semester secretarial programs and medical assistant program. Remedial mathematics and English programs.

Admissions SAT or ACT required. GED accepted. Rolling admissions. Advanced placement possible.

Student Life Residence and dining hall.

[J1] DISTRICT ONE TECHNICAL INSTITUTE

620 West Clairmont Avenue, Eau Claire 54701

[1] EDGEWOOD COLLEGE

855 Woodrow Street, Madison 53711, (608) 257-4861
Director of Admissions: Sister Barbara Hubeny

- **Enrollment: 86m, 351w; 726 total (including part-time)**
- **Tuition (1982/83): $3,450**
- **Room & Board: $1,790-$1,840**
- **Degrees offered: BA, BS, AA**
- **Mean ACT 18 composite**
- **Student-faculty ratio: 10 to 1**

A private college controlled by the Dominican Sisters. 55-acre wooded campus in Madison. Served by air and bus.

Academic Character NCACS and professional accreditation. 4-1-4 system, summer term. Majors offered in American studies, applied mathematics & business, art, biology, social studies, business, child life, criminal justice, early childhood, elementary education, English, French, history, mathematics, medical technology, natural science & mathematics, nursing, performing arts, psychology, religious studies, social science, and Spanish. Self-designed majors. Minors offered in some major fields and in 8 additional areas. Independent study. Pass/fail. Cooperative program with UW-Madison. Early childhood, secondary, and elementary education certification. Edgewood Grade School and Edgewood High School on campus; offer opportunities to practice teach and observe.

Financial CEEB CSS. College grants, state grants, PELL, SEOG, NSS, NDSL, GSL, CWS.

Admissions High school graduation with 16 units required. GED accepted. Interview encouraged. ACT required. $10 application fee. Rolling admissions. *Early Admission* Program. Transfers accepted. Credit possible for CEEB AP and CLEP and ACT PEP exams; college has own advanced placement program.

Student Life Student government. Newspaper. Choirs. International club. Religious, professional, and special interest groups. Single students under 20 must live at home or on campus. Coed and single-sex dorms. About 50% of students live on campus. 2 intercollegiate sports for men, 1 for women; intramural and club sports.

[J1] FOX VALLEY TECHNICAL INSTITUTE

1825 North Blue Mound Drive, PO Box 2277, Appleton 54913

[J1] GATEWAY TECHNICAL INSTITUTE

3520 30th Avenue, Kenosha 53140

[1] HOLY REDEEMER COLLEGE

Waterford 53185

[1 and J1] LAKELAND COLLEGE

PO Box 359, Sheboygan 53081, (414) 565-1201

- **Enrollment: 272m, 204w; 758 total (including part-time)**
- **Tuition (1982/83): $4,180**
- **Room & Board: $2,190; Fees: $275**
- **Degree offered: BA**
- **Student-faculty ratio: 15 to 1**

A private college affiliated with the United Church of Christ, organized in 1862. Campus in a rural environment about 40 miles north of Milwaukee. Served by air and bus.

Academic Character NCACS accreditation. 4-1-4 system. Majors offered in teaching, medical technology, health care administration, journalism, business administration, music, sociology, English, German, history, biology, chemistry, mathematics, behavioral sciences, philosophy & religion, art, drama, early child care, writing, accounting, computer programming administration, mental health care, and recreational administration. Preprofessional programs. Remedial mathematics and English programs. 60,000-volume library.

Financial Academic scholarships and work opportunities. Loan fund.

Admissions Rolling admissions. *Early Decision, Early Admission* programs. Advanced placement possible.

Student Life Dormitories for men and women; one coed. Dining hall. Intercollegiate and intramural sports for men and women.

[J1] LAKESHORE TECHNICAL INSTITUTE

1290 North Avenue, Cleveland 53015

[1] LAWRENCE UNIVERSITY

Appleton 54912, (414) 735-6500
Director of Admissions: David E. Busse

- **Undergraduates: 535m, 548w**
- **Tuition (1982/83): $6,675**
- **Room & Board: $2,061**
- **Degrees offered: BA, BMus**
- **Mean SAT 529v, 557m**
- **Student-faculty ratio: 11 to 1**

A private university established in 1847. 72-acre campus on Fox River in small city of Appleton, 100 miles from Milwaukee. Served by air and bus.

Academic Character NCACS and professional accreditation. Trimester system. Majors offered in anthropology, art, biology, chemistry, classics, economics, English, French, geology, German, government, history, mathematics, music, philosophy, physics, psychology, religion, Slavic, sociology/anthropology, Spanish, and theatre-drama. Interdisciplinary majors. Distributive requirements. Independent study. Phi Beta Kappa. Pass/fail. Preprofessional programs in dentistry, law, medicine, business. 3-2 programs in engineering with Columbia, Washington U, Rensselaer, others, in health sciences with Rush Medical Center, in social services administration with U of Chicago, in forestry with Duke. 2-2 health science program. Associated Colleges of the Midwest consortium. Study abroad. Washington, Oak Ridge, urban semesters. Marine biology seminar. Elementary and secondary education certification. Wilderness field station. 325-acre estate in Door County. 230,000-volume library with microform resources.

Financial CEEB CSS. University scholarships, grants, loans, state grants; PELL, SEOG, NDSL, GSL, deferred payment, CWS. Suggested scholarship application deadline March 15.

Admissions High school graduation with 16 units recommended. Interview encouraged. Audition required for music majors. SAT or ACT required. $15 application fee. Rolling admissions after mid-January; suggest applying by March 15. *Early Admission* Program. Transfers accepted. Admission deferral possible. Credit possible for CEEB AP exams; university has own advanced placement program.

Student Life Student-faculty government. Newspaper, magazine, radio station. Music, drama groups. Honorary, service, and city-based organizations. 6 fraternities with houses and 4 sororities with rooms. 32% of students join. Students must live at home or on campus. Coed dorms. Some married-student housing. 98% of students live on campus. 3 terms of phys ed required. 11 intercollegiate sports for men, 10 for women; intramural and club sports. Midwest Conference. Student body composition: 1% Asian, 1.5% Black, 0.5% Hispanic, 0.2% Native American, 96% White. 54% from out of state.

■[G1] PAPER CHEMISTRY, INSTITUTE OF
PO Box 1039, Appleton 54912

[J1] MADISON AREA TECHNICAL COLLEGE
211 North Carroll Street, Madison 53703

[P] MADISON BUSINESS COLLEGE
1110 Spring Harbor Drive, Madison 53705

[1] MARIAN COLLEGE OF FOND DU LAC
45 South National, Fond du Lac 54935, (414) 921-3900
Director of Admissions: Jerome Wiedmeyer

- **Enrollment: 62m, 414w; 563 total (including part-time)**
- **Tuition (1982/83): $3,100**
- **Room & Board: $1,650**
- **Degrees offered: BA, BS, BSBA, BSEd, BSN, BSW**
- **Mean ACT 19.4 composite; mean SAT 417v, 471m**
- **Student-faculty ratio: 10 to 1**

A private college controlled by the Sisters of St. Agnes, established in 1936. 50-acre campus located in small city of Fond du Lac, midway between Milwaukee and Green Bay. Served by air and bus.
Academic Character NCACS and professional accreditation. Semester system, 6-week summer term. Majors offered in art/art education, biology, business administration, chemistry, English, environmental science, history, humanistic studies, human relations, math, nursing, medical technology, psychology, social studies, social work, and teacher education. Minor required. Distributives and 12 credit hours in religion/philosophy required. Independent study. Internships. Preprofessional programs in law, medicine, dentistry, pharmacy, physical therapy, veterinary medicine. Elementary, secondary, and early childhood education. ROTC. 70,000-volume library with microform resources.
Financial CEEB CSS. College scholarships, and loans, state grants, BIA grants, PELL, SEOG, NDSL, GSL, CWS. Application deadline April 15.
Admissions High school graduation with 16 units required. Interview encouraged. ACT or SAT required. $10 application fee. Rolling admissions; application deadline August 15. *Early Admission, Early Decision* programs. Transfers accepted. Admission deferral possible. Credit possible for CEEB AP and CLEP exams; college has own advanced placement program.
Student Life Student government. Music groups. Honorary, professional, religious, and special interest groups. Apartments and women's dorms. 47% of students live on campus. 2 intercollegiate sports for men, 6 for women; intramurals. WCIC, WIC-WAC. 13.1% of students from out of state.

[1] MARQUETTE UNIVERSITY
1217 West Wisconsin Avenue, Milwaukee 53233, (414) 224-7302
Director of Admissions: Leo B. Flynn

- **Undergraduates: 4,321m, 3,610w; 11,802 total (including graduates)**
- **Tuition (1982/83): $4,450; $4,870 for engineering majors**
- **Room & Board: $2,835; Fees: $26**
- **Degrees offered: BA, BS in several fields**
- **Mean ACT 23.7 composite, mean SAT 479v, 534m**
- **Student-faculty ratio: 15 to 1**

A private university conducted by the Society of Jesus (Jesuits), established in 1881. 64-acre urban campus in Milwaukee. Served by air and rail.
Academic Character NCACS and professional accreditation. Semester system, 2 6-week summer terms. Majors offered in accounting, anthropology, biology, biomedical engineering, business administration, business economics, chemistry, civil engineering, computer science, dental hygiene, economics, electrical engineering, English, foreign languages & literature, history, journalism, law enforcement, mathematics, mechanical engineering, medical technology, nursing, philosophy, physical therapy, physics, political science, psychology, social studies, social work, sociology, speech, and theology. Self-designed majors. Minors offered in all major fields and in 9 additional areas. Distributives and theology courses required. Graduate and professional degrees granted. Independent study. Honors program. Phi Beta Kappa. Cooperative work/study, internships. Preprofessional programs in dentistry, law, medicine. Study abroad. Elementary and secondary education certification. ROTC, NROTC. Computer center. 700,000-volume library with microform resources.
Financial CEEB CSS. University scholarships, family discounts, state and nursing grants; PELL, SEOG, NSL, NDSL, FISL, HELP, ALAS, deferred payment, CWS. Preferred application deadline (loans) March 1.
Admissions High school graduation with 16 units recommended. Interview encouraged. SAT or ACT required. $15 application fee. Rolling admissions; suggest applying between October 1 and March 15. $50 deposit required on acceptance of offer of admission. Transfers accepted. Credit possible for CEEB AP and CLEP exams. Educational Opportunity Program.
Student Life Student government. Newspaper, magazine, yearbook. Music and drama groups. Over 200 religious, honorary, academic, and special interest groups. 8 fraternities and 5 sororities. Freshmen and sophomores must live on campus. Coed and single-sex dorms. Some married-student housing. 65% of students live on campus. 8 intercollegiate sports for men, 5 for women; intramurals. AIAW, NCA, WWIAC. Student body composition: 2% Asian, 5% Black, 2% Hispanic, 0.4% Native American, 90.6% White. 50% from out of state.

[J1] MID—STATE TECHNICAL INSTITUTE
500 32nd Street North, Wisconsin Rapids 54494

[J1] WILWAUKEE AREA TECHNICAL COLLEGE
Milwaukee 53203

[1] MILWAUKEE SCHOOL OF ENGINEERING
1025 North Milwaukee, Milwaukee 53201
Dean of Admissions: Owen Cherry

- **Undergraduates: 1,381m, 107w**
- **Tuition (1982/83): $4,605**
- **Room & Board: $2,070**
- **Degrees offered: BA, Blnd Mgmt, AAS**
- **Mean ACT 27**
- **Student-faculty ratio: 20 to 1**

A private college established in 1903. 2½-acre urban campus in Milwaukee. Air, bus, and rail nearby.
Academic Character NCACS and professional accreditation. Trimester system, 11-week summer term. Majors offered in architecture, electrical and mechanical engineering, in biomedical, computer science, electrical, and mechanical engineering technology, and in business administration. MS in engineering management granted. 31,500-volume library.
Financial CEEB CSS and ACT FAS. College scholarships, industry scholarships, NDSL, FISL, deferred payment, CWS.
Admissions High school graduation with 15 units required. GED accepted. Interview required. ACT required. $15 application fee. Rolling admissions. $50 deposit required on acceptance of offer of admission. *Concurrent Enrollment* Program. Transfers accepted. Admission deferral possible. Credit possible for CLEP exams; college has own advanced placement program.
Student Life Student government. Newspaper, magazine. Society of Women Engineers. Professional groups. 9 fraternities, 5 with houses. 5% of men join. Co-op dorms. 50% of students live on campus. Attendance in class required. 3 intercollegiate sports for men, 1 for women; intramurals. NAIA, WICAA. 35% of students from out of state.

[2] MILWAUKEE INSTITUTE OF ART AND DESIGN
207 North Milwaukee Street, Milwaukee 53202

[J1] MORAINE PARK TECHNICAL INSTITUTE
235 North National Avenue, Fond du Lac 54935

[1] MOUNT MARY COLLEGE
2900 North Menomonee River Parkway, Milwaukee 53222, (414) 258-4810
Director of Admissions: Mary Jane Reilly

- **Undergraduates: 669w; 1,111 total including graduates**
- **Tuition (1982/83): $3,616**
- **Room & Board: $2,300; Fees: $160**
- **Degrees offered: BA, BS**
- **Student-faculty ratio: 13 to 1**

A private women's college controlled by the School Sisters of Notre Dame, established in 1913. 80-acre suburban, wooded campus in Milwaukee. Served by air, bus, and rail.
Academic Character NCACS and professional accreditation. Semester system, 2 3-week summer terms. 41 majors offered in the areas of arts, sciences, business, home economics, communications, education, language & literature, history, mathematics, health, philosophy, religion, and social sciences. Self-designed majors. Distributives and theology course required. Independent study. Honors program. Pass/fail, internships in some programs. Preprofessional programs in dentistry, law, medicine, veterinary medicine. Study abroad. Elementary, secondary, and early childhood education certification. ROTC at Marquette. Language lab. 103,000-volume library.
Financial CEEB CSS. College scholarships and grants, PELL, SEOG, NDSL, FISL, deferred payment, CWS. Scholarship application deadline March 15.
Admissions High school graduation with 15 units required. Interview encouraged. SAT or ACT required. $10 application fee. Rolling admissions; suggest applying by December. $50 tuition deposit and $50 room deposit (for boarders) required on acceptance of offer of admission. *Early Decision, Early Admission* programs. Transfers accepted. Admission deferral possible. Credit possible for CEEB AP and CLEP exams.
Student Life Student government. Newspaper, magazine. Music groups. Academic, honorary, and service organizations. 1 dorm. 20% of students live on campus. Liquor, drugs prohibited on campus. 1 semester of phys ed and 3 6-week sessions in lifetime sport required. 2 intercollegiate sports; intramurals. Student body composition: 2% Asian, 5% Black, 1% Hispanic, 91% White. 8% from out of state.

[1] MOUNT SENARIO COLLEGE
Ladysmith 54848, (715) 532-5511

- **Enrollment: 188m, 198w; 503 total (including part-time)**
- **Tuition (1982/83): $3,520**
- **Room & Board: $1,930; Typical Expenses: $950**
- **Degrees offered: BA, BS, BFA, AA**
- **Mean ACT 20 composite**
- **Student-faculty ratio: 12 to 1**

A private coeducational college. Campus in small city in west central part of the state, 60 miles north of Eau Claire and 120 miles northeast of St. Paul, Minnesota.
Academic Character NCACS accreditation. 4-1-4 system, 2 4-week summer terms. Majors offered in art, business administration, early childhood education, elementary education, secondary education, elementary physical education, English, history, mathematics, music, political science,

psychology, and sociology. Interdisciplinary and broadfield majors offered in applied behavioral science, art, business, criminal justice/law enforcement, music management, natural science, social science, and technical management. Associate degree programs in medical assistant, medical technician, and veterinary technician in cooperation with Medical Institute of Minnesota in Minneapolis. Dual-degree program in forestry & engineering offered in cooperation with Michigan Tech. Equestrian studies offered in cooperation with Meredith Manor. Elementary and secondary education certification. 43,0000-volume library.
Financial Guaranteed tuition. Academic and music scholarships available. Student aid program of federal, state, and institutional funds administered. 85% of student body benefits from some form of student aid program.
Admissions High school graduation required. Recommendation from high school counselor or last college attended required. SAT or ACT required. Rolling admissions. *Early Admission, Early Decision* programs. Transfers accepted. Admission deferral possible. Advanced placement possible.
Student Life One residence hall. Central dining hall for resident students. Student body composition: 28% minority.

[P] NASHOTAH HOUSE
Nashotah 53058

[J1] NICOLET COLLEGE AND TECHNICAL INSTITUTE
Rhinelander 54501

[J1] NORTH CENTRAL TECHNICAL INSTITUTE
Wausau 54401

[J1] NORTHEAST WISCONSIN TECHNICAL INSTITUTE
2740 West Mason Street, Green Bay 54303

[1] NORTHLAND COLLEGE
Ashland 54806, (715) 682-4531
Director of Admissions: James L. Miller

- **Undergraduates: 359m, 294w**
- **Tuition (1982/83): $4,190**
- **Room & Board: $2,265; Fees: $180**
- **Degrees offered: BA, BS**
- **Mean ACT 21.2 composite; mean SAT 480v, 515m**
- **Student-faculty ratio: 14 to 1**

A private college affiliated with the United Church of Christ, established in 1892. 65-acre campus in Ashland, 65 miles from Duluth, Minnesota. Served by air and bus.
Academic Character NCACS accreditation. 4-4-1 system, 6-week summer term. Majors offered in art, biology, business administration, chemistry, economics, earth science, elementary education, English, environmental studies, finance, history, management, marketing, mathematics, music, outdoor education, physics, psychology, religions, secondary education, and sociology. Self-designed majors. Minors in 5 additional areas. Distributive requirements. Independent study. Honors program. Cooperative work/study, pass/fail, internships. 3-2 programs in engineering, forestry with Michigan Tech, in natural resources with U of Michigan. Member Lake Superior Association of Colleges and Universities. Study abroad. Computer center, language lab. 750,000-volume library.
Financial CEEB CSS and ACT FAS. College scholarships, talent awards, state grants; PELL, SEOG, NDSL, GSL, FISL, CWS.
Admissions High school graduation required with 16 units recommended. GED accepted. Interview encouraged. SAT or ACT required. Rolling admissions; suggest applying by April 15. $100 tuition deposit and $50 room deposit required on acceptance of offer of admission. *Early Decision, Early Admission, Concurrent Enrollment* programs. Transfers accepted. Credit possible for CEEB AP and CLEP exams; college has own advanced placement program.
Student Life Student government. Newspaper, magazine, yearbook. Music, drama groups. Religious, professional, and special interest groups. 3 fraternities and 3 sororities without houses. 15% of men and 20% of women join. Students must live at home or on campus. Coed and single-sex dorms. No married-student housing. 60% of students live on campus. Liquor restricted. 2 semesters of phys ed required. 4 intercollegiate sports for men, 3 for women; intramurals. NAIA, AIAW. Student body composition: 2% Asian, 3% Black, 1% Hispanic, 6% Native American, 88% White. 65% from out of state.

[1] NORTHWESTERN COLLEGE
Watertown 53094, (414) 261-4352
President and Director of Admissions: Carleton Toppe

- **Enrollment: 275m; 277 total (including part-time)**
- **Tuition (1982/83): $1,320**
- **Room & Board: $1,270; Fees: $32**
- **Degree offered: AB**
- **Student-faculty ratio: 11 to 1**

A private men's college controlled by the Wisconsin Evangelical Lutheran Synod, established in 1865. 38-acre campus in small city of Watertown, midway between Milwaukee and Madison. Served by bus; airport in Milwaukee.
Academic Character NCACS and professional accreditation. Semester system. Courses offered in religion, history, English, German, Latin, Greek, Hebrew, mathematics, science, music, psychology, art, sociology, typing, and physical education. Distributives and 20 credits in religion required. Pre-seminary program only for students who wish to enter the ministry of the Wisconsin Evangelical Lutheran Synod. 40,000-volume library.
Financial CEEB CSS and ACT FAS. College scholarships and grants, state grants, Lutheran grants and loans; PELL, GSL, PLUS, college work program. Application deadline May 1.
Admissions High school graduation required. ACT required. Rolling admissions; suggest applying before August 1.
Student Life Magazine, yearbook. Music, speaking, drama groups. Out-of-town students must live on campus. Dormitories. No married-student housing. Church attendance required. Phys ed required for freshmen. 9 intercollegiate sports; intramurals. Twin Rivers Conference, WCIC.

[1] RIPON COLLEGE
Ripon 54971, (414) 748-8102, (800) 558-0248 (from out-of-state)
Dean of Admissions: John Corso

- **Undergraduates: 529m, 402w**
- **Tuition (1982/83): $6,020**
- **Room & Board: $1,845; Fees: $90**
- **Degree offered: AB**
- **Mean SAT 510v, 540m**
- **Student-faculty ratio: 13 to 1**

A private college established in 1851. 250-acre campus in small town of Ripon, 80 miles from Milwaukee. Served by bus; airport 19 miles away in Oshkosh.
Academic Character NCACS accreditation. Semester system. Majors offered in anthropology, art, biology, business, chemistry, chemistry/biology, drama, economics, English, German, history, Latin American studies, mathematics, music, philosophy, physical education, physics, political science, psychobiology, psychology, religion, Romance languages, sociology/anthropology, and speech. Self-designed majors. Distributive requirements. Independent study. Phi Beta Kappa. Pass/fail, internships. 3-1 programs with professional schools. 3-2 engineering programs with Rensselaer, USC, Washington U. 3-2 forestry and environmental science program with Duke. 3-2 social welfare program with U of Chicago. Member Associated Colleges of the Midwest. Study abroad. Washington, urban semesters. Newberry Library seminars. Elementary, secondary and special education certification. ROTC. Computer center, language labs. 118,000-volume library with microform resources.
Financial CEEB CSS. College scholarships, state scholarships, grants, and loans; PELL, SEOG, NDSL, deferred payment, CWS. Scholarship application deadline March 1.
Admissions High school graduation with 15 units required. Interview encouraged. SAT or ACT recommended. $15 application fee. Rolling admissions. $100 deposit required on acceptance of offer of admission. *Early Admission* Program. Transfers accepted. Admission deferral possible. Credit possible for CEEB AP and ACH scores.
Student Life Student government. Newspaper, magazine, yearbook, journal, radio station. Music, debate groups. Theatre. Academic, honorary, professional, religious, service, and special interest groups. 8 fraternities and 3 sororities; none have houses. 30% of men and 20% of women join. Students must live at home or on campus. Coed and single-sex dorms. 95% of students live on campus. 2 semesters of phys ed required. 10 intercollegiate sports for men, 5 for women; intramurals. AIAW, Midwest Conference. Student body composition: 1% Asian, 2% Black, 1% Hispanic, 96% White. 51% of students from out of state.

[P] SACRED HEART SCHOOL OF THEOLOGY
South Lovers Lane Road, Hales Corner 53130

[G1] ST. FRANCIS SEMINARY, SCHOOL OF PASTORAL MINISTRY
3257 South Lake Drive, Milwaukee 53207

[1] SAINT NORBERT COLLEGE
DePere 54115, (414) 337-3005
Dean of Admissions: Matthew G. Flanigan

- **Undergraduates: 811m, 818w**
- **Tuition (1982/83): $4,445**
- **Room & Board: $2,275 (average); Fees: $50**
- **Degrees offered: BA, BS, BBA, BMus**
- **Mean SAT 515v, 520m**
- **Student-faculty ratio: 16 to 1**

A private college controlled by the Order of St. Norbert, established in 1898, became coed in 1955. 25-acre suburban campus in DePere, 5 miles south of Green Bay. Air and bus in Green Bay.
Academic Character NCACS accreditation. Semester system, 3- and 5-week summer terms. Majors offered in accounting, art, biology, business administration, chemistry, classical languages, communication arts, economics, elementary education, English, French, graphic communication, history, humanities & fine arts, international business, mathematics, music, natural science, philosophy, physcis, political science, psychology, religious studies, sociology, and Spanish. Minor in physical education. Honors program. Internships. Preprofessional programs in engineering, dentistry, law, medicine, optometry, veterinary medicine. 3-2 engineering program with Marquette. 3-1 medical technology program. Study abroad in several countries. Elementary and secondary education certification. ROTC. Language lab. 160,000-volume library.
Financial CEEB CSS. College scholarships, grants, loans; PELL, SEOG, NDSL, GSL, Education Funds, CWS. Scholarship application deadline March 1.

Admissions High school graduation required. PSAT, ACT or SAT required. $15 application fee. Rolling admissions. $125 deposit required on acceptance of offer of admissions. Transfers accepted. Credit possible for CEEB AP and CLEP exams.
Student Life Student government. Newspaper, magazine, yearbook. Music and drama groups. Academic, political, honorary, and special interest organizations. 5 fraternities and 3 sororities; none have houses. 10% of men and 10% of women join. Freshmen must live at home or on campus. Coed and single-sex dorms. No married-student housing. 85% of students live on campus. 9 intercollegiate sports for men, 7 for women; intramural and club sports. NCAA, Midwest Conference. Student body composition: 0.5% Black, 0.5% Hispanic, 0.5% Native American, 98.5% White. 47% of students from out of state.

[1] SILVER LAKE COLLEGE OF THE HOLY FAMILY
Manitowoc 54220

[J1] SOUTHWEST WISCONSIN VOCATIONAL TECHNICAL SCHOOL
Fennimore 53809

[1] VITERBO COLLEGE
LaCrosse 54601, (608) 784-0040
Director of Admissions: M. Ray Duvall

- **Undergraduates: 148m, 660w; 1,113 total (including part-time)**
- **Tuition (1982/83): $3,700**
- **Room & Board: $1,818; Fees: $80-$250**
- **Degrees offered: BA, BS, BArt Ed, BLS, BMus, BEd, BSN, AA**
- **Student-faculty ratio: 12 to 1**

A private college controlled by the Franciscan Sisters of Perpetual Adoration, established in 1890, became coed in 1970. Campus in the Mississippi River Valley, 150 miles from Minneapolis. Served by air, bus, and rail.
Academic Character NCACS and professional accreditation. Semester system, 2 3-week summer terms. Majors offered in accounting, art (4 areas), biology, business administration, chemistry, community-medical dietetics, computer systems management, education, English, home economics, home economics in business, liberal studies, medical record administration, music, musical theatre, nursing, professional management, psychology, religious studies, sociology, and theatre arts. Minors in most major areas and in 6 additional areas. 3 additional minors at UW-LaCrosse. Distributives and 6 hours of religious studies required. Independent study. Cooperative work/study, pass/fail, internships. Preprofessional programs in dentistry, law, medicine, optometry, pharmacy, theology, veterinary medicine. 3-1, 4-1 medical technology programs. Cross-registration with UW-LaCrosse. Elementary and secondary education certification. ROTC at LaCrosse. Nursing center. 67,000-volume library.
Financial CEEB CSS and ACT FAS. College scholarships, state grants, family plan; PELL, SEOG, NSS, NDSL, FISL, GSL, NSL, deferred payment, CWS. Priority application deadline March 1.
Admissions High school graduation with 16 units required. GED accepted. Interview encouraged. ACT or SAT required in some cases; ACT preferred. $10 application fee. Rolling admissions; suggest applying in fall. $100 room deposit (for boarders) required on acceptance of offer of admission. *Early Admission, Concurrent Enrollment* programs. Transfers accepted. Credit possible for CEEB AP and CLEP exams.
Student Life Student government. Newspaper, magazine, yearbook. Music groups. International Students. Religious, academic, professional, and special interest organizations. Freshmen must live with relatives or on campus. Apartments and single-sex dorms. No married-student housing. 55% of students live on campus. Liquor prohibited in dorms. 3 intercollegiate sports for men, 3 for women; intramurals. Twin River Conference. Student body composition: 3% Black, 94% White, 3% Other. 20% of students from out of state.

[J1] WAUKESHA COUNTY TECHNICAL INSTITUTE
Pewaukee 53072

[J1] WESTERN WISCONSIN TECHNICAL INSTITUTE
Sixth and Vine Streets, LaCrosse 54601

[G1] WISCONSIN, MEDICAL COLLEGE OF
8701 Watertown Plank Road, Milwaukee 53226

[1] WISCONSIN SYSTEM, THE UNIVERSITY OF
1220 Linden Drive, 1856 Van Hise Hall, Madison 53706, (608) 262-2321

The University of Wisconsin system consists of 15 separate administrative units headed by Chancellors who are responsible to the President of the System; these units include 13 universities, 11 of which offer baccalaureate and masters degrees and 2 major research institutions offering undergraduate through post-graduate programs, 13 2-year centers and a University Extension. A state-supported system, it includes a land-grant university.

■[1] WISCONSIN, UNIVERSITY OF (Eau Claire)
Eau Claire 54701, (715) 836-5415
Director of Admissions: John L. Kearney

- **Undergraduates: 4,120m, 5,302w; 10,963 total (including graduates)**
- **Tuition (1982/83): $836 (in-state); $3,168 (out-of-state)**
- **Room & Board: $897; Fees: $197**
- **Degrees offered: BA, BS, BFA, BBA, BSN, BMus, BMus Ed**
- **Student-faculty ratio: 19 to 1**

A public university established in 1916. Urban campus located in small city of Eau Claire in northwest Wisconsin, 90 miles from Minneapolis.
Academic Character NCACS and professional accreditation. Semester system, 8-week summer term. 48 majors offered by the schools of Arts & Sciences, Business, Education, and Nursing. Minors offered in 14 additional areas. Distributive requirements. Independent study. Honors program. Cooperative work/study, limited pass/fail, internships. Credit by exam. Preprofessional programs in agriculture, architecture, dentistry, engineering, forestry, law, medicine, mortuary science, occupational therapy, optometry, pharmacy, physical therapy, theology, veterinary medicine. Consortium with UW at LaCrosse, River Falls, Stout. Exchange programs with several foreign universities. Elementary, secondary, and special education certification. Field station, computer center, planetarium. 423,000-volume library with microform resources.
Financial CEEB CSS. University scholarships, scholarships in several major fields, state grants, music loans; PELL, SEOG, NDSL, FISL, NSL, deferred payment, CWS. Application deadline March 1.
Admissions High school graduation with 9 units required. GED accepted. SAT or ACT required. $10 application fee. Rolling admissions. $20 tuition deposit and $75 room desosit (for boarders) required on acceptance of offer of admissions. *Early Admission* Program. Transfers accepted. Credit possible for CLEP exams.
Student Life Student government. Newspaper, magazine, yearbook. Music, debate, speaking, drama groups. Chinese, Indian groups. Academic, honorary, political, religious, service, and special interest organizations. 4 fraternities and 3 sororities; all have houses. 4% of men and 2% of women join. No coed dorms. 34% of students live on campus. 2 credits in phys ed required. 10 intercollegiate sports for men, 7 for women; several intramural sports. NAIA, AIAW, WWIAC, Wisconsin State U Conference. Student body composition: 0.8% Asian, 0.6% Black, 0.4% Hispanic, 0.3% Native American, 97% White, 0.9% Other. 11% of students from out of state.

■[1] WISCONSIN, UNIVERSITY OF (Green Bay)
Green Bay 54302, (414) 465-2111
Director of Admissions: Myron Van de Ven

- **Undergraduates: 1,409m, 1,538w; 4,681 total (including graduates)**
- **Tuition (1982/83): $996 (in-state); $3,328 (out-of-state)**
- **Room & Board: $1,965**
- **Degrees offered: BA, BS, BSW, BSN, AA**
- **Student-faculty ratio: 20 to 1**

A public university established in 1968. 700-acre campus in city of Green Bay. Served by air and bus.
Academic Character NCACS and professional accreditation. 4-1-4 system, 8-week summer term. 9 majors offered in humanities and fine arts, 10 in social sciences, 11 in natural sciences and mathematics, 7 in professional studies. 4 interdisciplinary majors. Self-designed majors. MA, MS granted. Independent study. Honors program. Pass/fail, internships. Preprofessional programs in agriculture, architecture, community development, college teaching, dentistry, engineering, journalism, law, medicine, nursing, pharmacy, social work, theology, veterinary medicine, and hydrology. 3-2, 2-2 engineering programs with UW Madison and Milwaukee. Study abroad. National Student Exchange. Elementary and secondary education certification. ROTC. Computer center. 320,000-volume library with microform resources.
Financial CEEB CSS and ACT FAS; CSS preferred. University scholarships, state grants, BIA grants, talent grants; PELL, SEOG, NDSL, GSL, FISL, CWS. Application deadline March 15.
Admissions High school graduation with 16 units required. $10 application fee. Rolling admissions; suggest applying early in 12th year. *Early Admission* Program. Transfers accepted. Admission deferral possible. Credit possible for CEEB AP and CLEP exams. EOP.
Student Life Student government. Newspaper. Music, dance, theatre groups. Black Student Organization, Native American Club, International Students. About 50 political, academic, environmental, service, religious, professional, and special interest clubs. Coed dorms, apartments. 12% of students live on campus. 6 intercollegiate sports for men, 6 for women; intramurals. AIAW, NCAA. Student body composition: 1% Asian, 1% Black, 1% Hispanic, 2% Native American, 95% White. 8% of students from out of state.

■[1] WISCONSIN, UNIVERSITY OF (La Crosse)
1725 State Street, Lacrosse 54601, (608) 785-8067
Director of Admissions: Gale G. Grimslid

- **Undergraduates: 3,845m, 4,716w**
- **Estimated Tuition (1982/83): $1,112 (in-state), $3,700 (out-of-state)**
- **Room & Board: $1,671**
- **Degrees offered: BA, BS**
- **Mean ACT 19.9 composite**
- **Student-faculty ratio: 19 to 1**

A public university established in 1909. 100-acre campus on Minnesota border, 140 miles from Minneapolis. Served by air, bus, and rail.
Academic Character NCACS and professional accreditation. Semester system, 8-week summer term. 2 majors offered by the College of Education, 22 by the College of Arts, Letters, & Sciences, 6 by the School of Business Administration, 5 by the School of Health and Human Services, and 7 by the School of Health, Recreation, & Physical Education. Minors offered in most major fields in Arts, Letters, & Sciences, and in 7 additional areas. Distributive requirements. MS, MBA, ME granted. Independent study. Honors program. Phi Beta Kappa. Cooperative work/study, pass/fail, internships. Preprofessional programs in architecture, chiropractic, dentistry, engineering, law, forestry, medicine, nursing, optometry, occupational

therapy, pharmacy, veterinary medicine, others. Exchange program with North Carolina A&T, North Carolina Central. Study abroad. Elementary, secondary, and special education certification. ROTC. Audio-visual center. 480,000-volume library with microform resources.
Financial CEEB CSS. University scholarships, state grants; PELL, SEOG, NDSL, GSL, CWS. Priority application deadline March 1.
Admissions High school graduation with 9 units required. GED accepted. ACT required. $10 application fee. Rolling admissions; suggest applying after October 1. *Early Admission* Program. Transfers accepted. Credit possible for CEEB AP and CLEP exams; university has own advanced placement program.
Student Life Student government. Newspaper, magazine, yearbook, TV and radio stations. Music, debate, drama groups. Afro-American Association, Women's Liberation. Academic, political, honorary, religious, service, and special interest groups. 6 fraternities, 3 with houses, and 5 sororities, without houses. 10% of men and 8% of women join. Freshmen and sophomores must live at home or on campus. Coed and single-sex dorms. 33% of students live on campus. Class attendance required. 2 semesters of phys ed required. 10 intercollegiate sports for men, 10 for women; intramural and club sports. NCAA, NAIA, Wisconsin State U Conference. Student body composition: 99% White, 1% Other. 17% of students from out of state.

■[1] WISCONSIN, UNIVERSITY OF (Madison)

140 Peterson Building, 750 University Avenue, Madison 54408, (608) 262-3961
Director of Admissions: David E. Vinson

- **Undergraduates: 15,298m, 13,254w; 42,230 total (including graduates)**
- **Tuition (1982/83): $1,122 (in-state); $3,900 (out-of-state)**
- **Room & Board: $2,225**
- **Degrees offered: BA, BS, BBA, BMus, BNS**
- **Mean ACT 23.8; mean SAT 500v, 572m**
- **Student-faculty ratio: 16 to 1**

A public university established in 1848. 906-acre urban campus in Madison. Served by air and bus.
Academic Character NCACS and professional accreditation. Semester system, several summer terms. 30 majors offered by the College of Agricultural and Life Sciences, 9 by the College of Engineering, 69 by the College of Letters and Sciences, 4 by the School of Allied Health Professions, 11 by the School of Business, 9 by the School of Education, 16 by the School of Family Resources/Consumer Sciences, and 1 each by the Schools of Nursing and Pharmacy. Self-designed majors. Distributive requirements. Graduate and professional degrees granted. Independent study. Honors program. Phi Beta Kappa. Cooperative work/study, pass/fail, internships. Preprofessional programs in allied health fields, behavioral disabilities, elementary education, engineering, journalism, landscape architecture, secondary education, veterinary medicine, business, pharmacy. Transfer programs with Schools of Business, Pharmacy, Medicine, Law. Study abroad. Elementary, secondary, and special education certification. ROTC, AFROTC, NROTC. 3,600,000-volume library with microform resources.
Financial University grants, loans, scholarships, state grants and loans, pharmacy and nursing loans; PELL, SEOG, NDSL, GSL, PLUS, CWS. Priority application deadline March 1.
Admissions High school graduation with 16 units required. Audition required for music majors. $10 application fee. Rolling admissions; apply between October 1 and March 1. *Early Admission* Program. Transfers accepted. Credit possible for CEEB AP and CLEP exams; university has own advanced placement program. Academic Advancement Program.
Student Life Student government. Newspaper, journal, radio and TV stations. Music and drama groups. 28 fraternities, 25 with houses, and 9 sororities, 8 with houses. 8% of men and 7% of women join. Limited on-campus housing; preference given to in-state students. Coed and single-sex dorms, language housing. 23% of students live on campus. Several intercollegiate and intramural sports. AIAW, Big Ten, Western Conference. Student body composition: 1.4% Asian, 2% Black, 0.8% Hispanic, 0.2% Native American, 95.6% White. 26% of students from out of state.

■[1] WISCONSIN, UNIVERSITY OF (Milwaukee)

PO Box 413, Milwaukee 53201, (414) 963-4572
Director of Admissions: Frederick Sperry

- **Undergraduates: 7,088m, 6,834w; 26,663 total (including graduates)**
- **Estimated Tuition (1982/83): $1,154 (in-state); $3,932 (out-of-state)**
- **Room & Board: $2,461**
- **Degrees offered: BA, BS, BBA, BFA, BSE, BSApp Sc, BSN**
- **Student-faculty ratio: 15 to 1**

A public university established in 1885. 90-acre urban campus in residential section 2 miles from downtown Milwaukee. Served by air, rail, and bus.
Academic Character NCACS and professional accreditation. Semester system, 9 summer terms of varying lengths. 7 majors offered by the College of Engineering & Applied Science, 39 by the College of Letters & Science, 5 by the School of Allied Health Professions, 1 by the School of Architecture & Urban Planning, 9 by the School of Business Administration, 11 by the School of Education, 9 by the School of Fine Arts, 1 by the School of Nursing, and 2 by the School of Social Welfare. Self-designed majors. Distributive requirements. Graduate and professional degrees granted. Independent study. Honors program. Phi Beta Kappa. Cooperative work/study, pass/fail, internships. Preprofessional programs in dentistry, law, medicine. 5-year program in engineering and applied science. Dual-degree programs in business-engineering, business-applied science. University Extension is located in downtown Milwaukee. Study abroad. Elementary, secondary, and special education certification. ROTC; NROTC nearby. Early Childhood Center, Study Skills Lab, planetarium, computer center. 2,700,000-volume library with microform resources.
Financial University scholarships; PELL, SEOG, NSS, NDSL, FISL, NSL, deferred payment, CWS.
Admissions High school graduation with 16 units required. GED accepted. Audition required for music majors. $10 application fee. Rolling admissions; priority application deadline August 1. *Early Admission, Concurrent Enrollment* programs. Transfers accepted. Admission deferral possible. Credit possible for CEEB AP and CLEP exams; university has own advanced placement program. EOP.
Student Life Student government. Newspapers, radio station. Music, dance, drama, debate groups. Service, academic, honorary, political, professional, religious, and special interest groups. Fraternities and sororities. Coed dorms. Limited married-student housing. 6% of students live on campus. 8 intercollegiate sports for men, 9 for women; intramurals. WWIAC. Student body composition: 1.1% Asian, 6.5% Black, 1.4% Hispanic, 0.7% Native American, 86.7% White, 3.6% Other. 6% of students from out of state.

■[1] WISCONSIN, UNIVERSITY OF (Oshkosh)

Oshkosh 54901, (414) 424-0202
Director of Admissions: Thomas Snider

- **Undergraduates: 3,476m, 3,484w**
- **Tuition (1982/83): $1,027 (WI & MN residents); $3,361 (others)**
- **Room & Board: $1,750-$2,150**
- **Degrees offered: BA, BS, BArt Ed, BBA, BFA, BHum Serv, BMus, BMus Ed, BSArt, BSChem, BSEd, BSMed Tech, BSN**
- **Student-faculty ratio: 17 to 1**

A public university established in 1871. Urban campus in Oshkosh, 70 miles from Milwaukee. Served by air and bus.
Academic Character NCACS and professional accreditation. Semester system, 8-week and 2 4-week summer terms. 7 majors offered by the College of Business Administration, 15 by the College of Education and Human Services, and 46 by the College of Letters and Science. Minors offered in some major fields and in 18 additional areas. Distributive requirements. Graduate and professional degrees granted. Independent study. Honors program. Pass/fail, internships. Preprofessional programs in architecture, dentistry, engineering, forestry, law, medicine, ministry, mortuary science, pharmacy, veterinary medicine. 3-2 engineering program with UW-Madison. 5-year liberal arts/natural resources with UMichigan-Ann Arbor. 3-1 medical technology programs. Study abroad and in Canadian Rockies and Yukon. Early childhood, elementary, secondary, and special education certification. ROTC. Computer center, TV studio. 500,000-volume library with microform resources.
Financial CEEB CSS. University scholarships, state loans, BIA grants; PELL, SEOG, NSS, NDSL, FISL, NSL, CWS. Application deadline March 31.
Admissions High school graduation with 16 units required. GED accepted. SAT or ACT required. Rolling admissions; suggest applying in fall. $25 tuition deposit and $75 room deposit (for boarders) required on acceptance of offer of admission. *Early Admission* Program. Transfers accepted. Credit possible for CEEB AP and CLEP exams; university has own advanced placement program.
Student Life Student government. Newspaper, magazine, radio station. Music, drama, debate, speaking groups. Academic, political, honorary, religious, service, and special interest groups. Freshmen and sophomores must live at home or on campus. Coed and single-sex dorms. International house. No married-student housing. 30% of students live on campus. 2 credits in phys ed required. 10 intercollegiate sports for men, 9 for women; intramural and club sports. AIAW, NAIA, NCAA, WSUAC, WWIAC. Student body composition: 0.2% Asian, 2.4% Black, 0.3% Hispanic, 0.4% Native American, 96.1% White, 0.6% Other. 4% of students from out of state.

■[1] WISCONSIN, UNIVERSITY OF (Platteville)

725 West Main Street, Platteville 53818, (608) 342-1125
Director of Admissions: Ed Deneen

- **Enrollment: 3,360m, 1,585w**
- **Tuition (1982/83): $1,056 (in-state); $3,388 (out-of-state)**
- **Room & Board: $1,690**
- **Degrees offered: BA, BS**
- **Student-faculty ratio: 18 to 1**

A public university established in 1866. 300-acre rural campus in small city of Platteville, 70 miles from Madison. Served by bus.
Academic Character NCACS and professional accreditation. Semester system, 8-week summer term. 60 majors offered by the Colleges of Agriculture, Arts & Sciences, Education, Engineering, and Business, Industry & Communication. Minors offered in most major fields and in 14 additional areas. Masters degrees granted. Independent study. Honors program. Cooperative work/study, limited pass/fail, internships. Preprofessional programs in chiropractic, commerce, dentistry, journalism, law, medicine, nursing, optometry, osteopathy, veterinary medicine. Study abroad. College of Education year in England. ROTC. 285,000-volume library with microform resources.
Financial CEEB CSS. University scholarships, state, talent and BIA grants; PELL, SEOG, NDSL, CWS. Application deadline March 1.
Admissions High school graduation with 16 units required. ACT or SAT recommended. $10 application fee. Rolling admissions; suggest applying by October 1. $75 deposit required on acceptance of offer of admission. Transfers accepted. Credit possible for CEEB AP and CLEP exams.
Student Life Student government. Newspaper, magazine, yearbook, radio and TV stations. Music, debate, drama groups. Academic, political, honorary, special interest groups. 12 fraternities, 8 with housing, and 4 sororities, 3 with housing. 15% of students join. Single students with fewer than 60 credits must live on campus. 50% of students live on campus. Drugs, gambling prohibited. 2 semesters of phys ed required. 10 intercollegiate sports for men, 6 for women; intramurals. WSU Conference. Student body composition: 0.1% Asian, 1.7% Black, 0.2% Hispanic, 0.1% Native American, 96.9% White, 1% Other. 10% of students from out of state.

■[1] WISCONSIN, UNIVERSITY OF (River Falls)

River Falls 54022, (715) 425-3500
Director of Admissions: W.W. Spaulding

- **Enrollment: 2,602m, 2,402w**
- **Tuition (1982/83): $836 (in-state); $3,168 (out-of-state)**
- **Room & Board: $1,896; Fees: $175**
- **Degrees offered: BA, BS, BFA**
- **Mean ACT 21.5 composite**
- **Student-faculty ratio: 20 to 1**

A public university established in 1874. Campus located in small town of River Falls, 28 miles from St. Paul. Air, bus, and rail in Minneapolis-St. Paul.
Academic Character NCACS and professional accreditation. Trimester system, 8-week summer term. 18 majors offered by the College of Agriculture, 26 by the College of Arts & Sciences, and 7 by the College of Education. Self-designed majors. Minors offered in 14 additional areas. Distributive requirements. MA, MS granted. Independent study. Honors program. Pass/fail, internships. Cooperative work/study. Credit by exam. 2- and 3-year transfer programs in architecture, criminal justice, dentistry, engineering, forestry, home economics, law, medical records librarianship, medicine, mortuary science, music therapy, nursing, optometry, pharmacy, police science, veterinary medicine. Consortium with UW Eau Claire, LaCrosse, Stout. Study abroad. Student teaching in Britain, Australia. Soviet seminar. Elementary, secondary, and special education certification. ROTC, AFROTC, NROTC at U of Minnesota-Minneapolis. 206,000-volume library.
Financial CEEB CSS. University scholarships, Indian scholarships, state grants and loans; PELL, SEOG, NDSL, CWS. Application deadlines March 15 (scholarships), September 1 (loans).
Admissions High school graduation with 16 units required. SAT or ACT recommended. $10 application fee. Rolling admissions; suggest applying in fall. $75 deposit required on acceptance of offer of admission. Transfers accepted. Admission deferral possible. Credit possible for CLEP exams; university has own advanced placement program.
Student Life Student government. Newspaper, magazine, yearbook, radio station. Music, drama groups. Black Student Coalition, Indian Youth Council. Academic, political, honorary, religious, service, and special interest organizations. 5 fraternities and 3 sororities. Freshmen and sophomores must live at home or on campus. Coed and single-sex dorms. 40% of students live on campus. Class attendance required. 3 terms of phys ed required. 10 intercollegiate sports for men, 8 for women; intramurals. WSAC, NCAA. Student body composition: 1% Asian, 2% Black, 1% Hispanic, 1% Native American, 95% White. 40% of students from out of state.

■[1] WISCONSIN, UNIVERSITY OF (Stevens Point)

Stevens Point 54481, (715) 346-0123
Director of Admissions: John A. Larsen

- **Undergraduates: 3,756m, 3,663w; 9,045 total (including graduates)**
- **Tuition (1982/83): $1,120 (in-state); $3,450 (out-of-state)**
- **Room & Board: $1,954-$1,980**
- **Degrees offered: BA, BS, BFA, BMus**
- **Student-faculty ratio: 19 to 1**

A public university established in 1894. 300-acre rural campus in small city of Stevens Point, 110 miles from Madison. Served by air, bus, and rail.
Academic Character NCACS and professional accreditation. Semester system, several summer terms. 51 majors offered by the Colleges of Fine Arts, Letters & Science, Natural Resources, and Professional Studies. Self-designed majors. Minors offered in most major fields and in over 30 additional areas. Distributive requirements. MA, MS, MME, MEPD, MAT granted. Independent study. Honors program. Cooperative work/study, pass/fail, internships. Preprofessional programs in dentistry, engineering, law, medicine, mortuary science, nursing, others. Study abroad in several countries. Elementary, secondary, and special education certification. ROTC. 400,000-volume learning resources center library.
Financial CEEB CSS. University scholarships, state grants and loans, BIA grants; PELL, SEOG, NDSL, GSL, PLUS, CWS. Application deadline March 1.
Admissions High school graduation with 16 units required. GED accepted. $10 application fee. Rolling admissions; suggest applying in fall. *Early Admission* Program. Transfers accepted. Admission deferral possible. Credit possible for CEEB AP and CLEP exams; university has own advanced placement program.
Student Life Student government. Newspaper, magazine, yearbook, radio and TV stations. Music, debate, film, drama groups. Black Student Coalition. Political, religious, honorary, academic, service, and special interest groups. 4 fraternities and 2 sororities. Single freshmen and sophomores must live at home or on campus. Coed and single-sex dorms, special interest housing. No married-student housing. Liquor and smoking restricted. 4 semesters of phys ed required. 10 intercollegiate sports for men, 8 for women; intramural and club sports. WSU Conference, NAIA. Student body composition: 1% Asian, 1% Black, 1% Hispanic, 1% Native American, 96% White, 10% of students from out of state.

■[1] WISCONSIN, UNIVERSITY OF (Superior)

Superior 54880, (715) 394-8101
Director of Admissions: Lowell W. Banks

- **Undergraduates: 826m, 689w; 2,171 total (including graduates)**
- **Tuition (1982/83): $1,010 (in-state); $3,342 (out-of-state)**
- **Room & Board: $2,145**
- **Degrees offered: BA, BS, BFA, BMus, AA**
- **Student-faculty ratio: 15 to 1**

A public university established in 1893. 230-acre urban campus in Superior, next to Duluth, Minnesota. Served by bus. Airport in Duluth.
Academic Character NCACS and professional accreditation. Trimester system, 8-week summer term. Majors offered in art, biology, business, chemistry, communicative arts, computer science, education, English, history, international studies, mathematics, medical technology, music, nursing, physical education, physics, political science, psychology, science, and social studies. Self-designed majors. Minors in 12 additional areas. Distributive requirements. Graduate degrees granted. Independent study. Honors program. Phi Beta Kappa. Cooperative work/study, pass/fail, internships. Preprofessional programs in dentistry, engineering, forestry, law, medicine, nursing, pharmacy, physical therapy, veterinary medicine. Engineering and biology courses with Michigan Tech. Consortium with Lake Superior Association of Colleges and Universities. Study abroad. Elementary, secondary, and special education certification. AFROTC. Field stations. 220,000-volume library.
Financial CEEB CSS and ACT FAS. University scholarships, state grants and loans; PELL, SEOG, NDSL, FISL, CWS, student assistantships. Application deadline March 15.
Admissions High school graduation with 16 units required. GED accepted. ACT required for placement. $10 application fee. Rolling admissions. $75 deposit required on acceptance of offer of admission. *Early Admission, Early Decision, Concurrent Enrollment* programs. Transfers accepted. Credit possible for CEEB AP and CLEP exams; university has own advanced placement program.
Student Life Student government. Newspaper, magazine, yearbook, radio and TV stations. Music, debate, drama groups. Black Student Union. Academic, professional, honorary, religious, service, and special interest groups. 7 fraternities and 2 sororities without houses. 12% of students join. Freshmen and sophomores must live at home or on campus. Coed and single-sex dorms. Special interest housing. 35% of students live on campus. Liquor restricted. 2 terms of phys ed required. 11 intercollegiate sports for men, 5 for women; intramurals. NAIA, NCAA, WSU Conference. Student body composition: 1% Asian, 2% Black, 1% Hispanic, 2% Native American, 91% White, 3% Other. 25% of students from out of state.

■[1] WISCONSIN, UNIVERSITY OF (Whitewater)

Whitewater 53190, (414) 472-1234
Director of Admissions: Irv Madsen

- **Undergraduates: 4,539m, 4,455w; 10,321 total (including graduates)**
- **Tuition (1982/83): $996 (in-state); $3,328 (out-of-state)**
- **Room & Board: $1,622**
- **Degrees offered: BA, BS, BBA, BSEd, AA, AS**
- **Student-faculty ratio: 18 to 1**

A public university established in 1868. 380-acre campus located in small city of Whitewater. Served by bus. Airport and rail 15 miles away in Janesville.
Academic Character NCACS and professional accreditation. Semester system, 4- and 8-week summer terms. 7 majors offered by the College of the Arts, 9 by the College of Business and Economics, 4 by the College of Education, and 23 by the College of Letters & Science. Minors offered in most major fields and in 11 additional areas. Courses in homemaking, Portuguese. Distributive requirements. Graduate degrees granted. Independent study. Honors program. Pass/fail, internships. Elementary, secondary, and special education certification. ROTC. 260,000-volume library.
Financial CEEB CSS and ACT FAS. University scholarships, state grants, BIA grants; PELL, SEOG, NDSL, FISL, deferred payment, CWS. Loan application deadline March 1.
Admissions High school graduation with 16 units required. ACT or SAT required. $10 application fee. Rolling admissions; suggest applying after October 1. $75 deposit required on acceptance of offer of admission. *Concurrent Enrollment* Program. Transfers accepted. Credit possible for CEEB AP and CLEP exams; university has own advanced placement program.
Student Life Student government. Newspaper, yearbook, radio station. Music, dance, drama groups. Several academic, religious, professional, political, service, and special interest organizations. 8 fraternities and 6 sororities. Single students under 21 must live on campus. Coed and single-sex dorms; intensive study housing. 50% of students live on campus. 1 semester of phys ed required. 11 intercollegiate sports for men, 8 for women; intramurals. NCAA, WSU Conference. Student body composition: 0.2% Asian, 1.6% Black, 0.6% Hispanic, 0.2% Native American, 96.1% White, 1.3% Other. 6% of students from out of state.

■[J1] WISCONSIN, UNIVERSITY OF, CENTER SYSTEM

UW Center-Baraboo/Sauk County (Baraboo); 249m, 231w
UW Center-Barron County (Rice Lake); 152m, 215w
UW Center-Fond du Lac; 273m, 265w
UW Center-Fox Valley (Menasha); 503m, 614w
UW Center-Manitowoc County (Manitowoc); 200m, 189w
UW Center-Marathon County (Wausau); 529m, 524w
UW Center-Marinette County (Marinette);192m, 246w
UW Center-Marshfield/Wood County (Marshfield); 220m, 488w
UW Center-Richland (Richland Center); 112m, 139w
UW Center-Rock County (Janesville); 401m, 423w
UW Center-Sheboygan; 351m, 340w
UW Center-Washington County (West Bend); 327m, 351w
UW Center-Waukesha County (Waukesha); 940m, 1,137w

- **Tuition (1982/83): $822-$872 (in-state), $3,080-$3,124 (out-of-state)**
- **Approximate Room & Board: $1,200**
- **Degrees offered: AA, AS**

Academic Character All campuses offer degree credit work for full- or part-time students. NCACS accreditation.
Financial Financial aid is available for all students.
Admissions New students admitted in September, mid-year, and in summer.
Student Life Marathon County Campus has dormitory; student apartments

available at the Marshfield/Wood County, Barron County, Marinette County, and Richland Campuses; other campuses have off-campus housing.

■[1] WISCONSIN, UNIVERSITY OF, PARKSIDE CAMPUS

Box 2000, Kenosha 53141, (414) 553-2000
Director of Admissions: John F. Elmore

- **Undergraduates: 1,499m, 1,306w; 5,368 total (including graduates)**
- **Tuition (1982/83): $981 (in-state); $3,313 (out-of-state)**
- **Degrees offered: BA, BS**
- **Student-faculty ratio: 20 to 1**

A public university established in 1965, became coed in 1968. 700-acre rural campus in Kenosha, 5 miles from Racine, 30 miles from Milwaukee. Served by bus.

Academic Character NCACS accreditation. Semester system, 8-week summer term. 4 majors offered by the Division of Behavioral Science, 11 by the Division of Business and Administrative Science, 2 by the Division of Education, 11 by the Division of Engineering Science, 3 by the Division of Fine Arts, 7 by the Division of Humanities, 7 by the Division of Science, and 5 by the Division of Social Science. Distributive requirements. MPA, MBA granted. Independent study. Honors program. Internships. Credit by exam. Preprofessional programs in architecture, conservation, dentistry, forestry, medicine, optometry, veterinary medicine, veterinary science. Nursing program with UW-Milwaukee and St. Luke's Hospital School of Nursing. Elementary and secondary education certification. ROTC at Marquette. Language lab. 310,000-volume library with microform resources.

Financial CEEB CSS. University scholarships, state grants; PELL, SEOG, NDSL, CWS. Application deadline March 15.

Admissions High school graduation with 9 units required. GED accepted. $10 application fee. Rolling admissions; suggest applying before August 1. *Early Admission, Early Decision, Concurrent Enrollment* programs. Transfers accepted. Credit possible for CEEB AP and CLEP exams.

Student Life Student government. Newspaper, magazine. Music, drama groups. Academic, honorary, religious, service, and special interest organizations. 1 fraternity. No on-campus housing except married-student housing. 10 intercollegiate sports for men, 8 for women; several intramural and club sports. AIAW, NAIA, NCAA. Student body composition: 0.5% Asian, 4.4% Black, 1% Hispanic, 0.2% Native American, 92.5% White, 1.4% Other. 3% of students from out of state.

■[1] WISCONSIN-STOUT, UNIVERSITY OF

Menomonie 54751, (715) 232-1231
Director of Admissions: Donald Osegard

- **Undergraduates: 3,442m, 3,145w; 7,596 total (including graduates)**
- **Tuition (1982/83): $1,056 (in-state); $3,388 (out-of-state)**
- **Room & Board: $1,604-$1,954**
- **Degrees offered: BA, BS**
- **Student-faculty ratio: 23 to 1**

A public university established in 1893. 120-acre campus in small city of Menomonie, 70 miles from Minneapolis-St. Paul. Served by bus.

Academic Character NCACS and professional accreditation. Semester system, 8-week summer term. 35 majors offered by the Schools of Education, Home Economics, Industry & Technoolgy, and Liberal Studies. Minors offered in 19 areas. Graduate degrees granted. Independent study. Honors program. Field experience program. Fashion semester in London. Home economics year at Merrill-Palmer Institute. Elementary, secondary, and special education certification. Audio-visual, photography labs. Child and Family Study Centers. 175,000-volume library.

Financial CEEB CSS and ACT FAS. University scholarships, state grants, BIA grants; PELL, SEOG, NDSL, CWS. Priority application deadline February 15.

Admissions High school graduation with 16 units required. SAT or ACT recommended. $10 application fee. Rolling admissions; suggest applying between October 1 and April 1. $75 deposit required on acceptance of offer of admission. *Early Admission, Early Decision* programs. Transfers accepted. Admission deferral possible. Credit possible for CLEP exams; university has own advanced placement program.

Student Life Student government. Newspaper, magazine, yearbook. Music, debate, drama groups. Political, religious, academic, honorary, service, and special interest organizations. 8 fraternities, 4 with houses, and 5 sororities, 2 with houses. 10% of students join. Freshmen and sophomores must live on campus. Coed and single-sex dorms. Married-student housing. 40% of students live on campus. Liquor use restricted. 1 semester of phys ed required. 11 intercollegiate sports for men, 7 for women; intramurals. AIAW, NAIA, NCAA, WSU Conference. Student body composition: 0.3% Asian, 0.9% Black, 0.3% Hispanic, 0.4% Native American, 98.1% White. 33% of students from out of state.

[P] WISCONSIN CONSERVATORY OF MUSIC

1584 North Prospect Avenue, Milwaukee 53202

[J1] WISCONSIN INDIANHEAD VOCATIONAL TECHNICAL AND ADULT EDUCATION DISTRICT

PO Box B, Shell Lake 54871

WYOMING (WY)

[J1] CASPER COLLEGE

Casper 82601, (307) 268-2256

- **Enrollment: 684m, 713w; 3,371 total (including part-time)**
- **Tuition (1981/82): $380 (in-state), $1,280 (out-of-state)**
- **Degrees offered: AA, AS, AB, AAS**
- **Mean ACT 19.3**

A coed, district-controlled junior college.

Academic Character NCACS and professional accreditation. Semester system. University parallel, technical, and subprofessional programs offered. Terminal program students receive certificate of completion. Remedial mathematics and English programs.

Admissions High school graduation and recommendation required. GED accepted. ACT recommended. *Early Admission* Program. Transfers accepted. Advanced placement possible.

Student Life Housing is in local private homes and in on-campus dormitories.

[J1] CENTRAL WYOMING COLLEGE

Riverton 82501, (307) 856-9291 or 332-9100
Toll-free: (800) 442-1228 (in-state)
Director of Admissions & Records: Letah Chilston

- **Enrollment: 212m, 215w; 846 total (including part-time)**
- **Tuition (1982/83): $336**
- **Room & Board: $1,650**
- **Degrees offered: AA, AS, AAA, AAS**
- **Student-faculty ratio: 13 to 1**

A public community college in Riverton on the banks of the Wind River, and near the Wind River Indian Reservation.

Academic Character NCACS accreditation. Semester system, summer term. 9 majors offered by the Division of Humanities, 28 by the Division of Business, Industry, & Human Services, and 12 by the Division of Physical, Life, & Social Sciences. University transfer, career/technical, and occupational certificate/diploma programs. Distributive requirements. Individualized courses. Credit by exam. Cooperative work/study. Preprofessional programs in law, medicine, dentistry, nursing, pharmacy, veterinary science. Center for Lifelong Learning. A-V Center. Over 26,000-volume library. American Indian Collection.

Financial CEEB CSS and ACT FAS. College scholarships; PELL, SEOG, SSIG, BIA/TRIBAL grants, NDSL, GSL, PLUS, ALAS, CWS.

Admissions Open admissions to person 16 years and older. High school graduation or GED required. ACT recommended. Rolling admissions; file application as soon after February 1 as possible. *Early Admission* Program. Admission deferral possible. Transfers accepted.

Student Life Student government. Theatre, music, art, and debate groups. DECA. Science Unlimited. Outing and ski clubs. Christian Club, Indian Club. Livestock judging, rodeo. One dorm. On-campus apartments available to all students. 4 intercollegiate sports for men, 4 for women; intramurals. Wyoming Community College Athletic Conference, NJCAA.

[J1] EASTERN WYOMING COLLEGE

Torrington 82240, (307) 532-7111
Director of Admissions: Billy G. Bates

- **Enrollment: 182m, 246w; 617 total (including part-time)**
- **Tuition (1982/83): $300 (in-state), $500 (out-of-state)**
- **Room & Board: $1,650**
- **Degrees offered: AA, AAS**
- **Mean ACT 18.6**

A public community college established in 1948.

Academic Character NCACS accreditation. Semester system. Career and transfer programs. 38 majors offered in areas of business, agribusiness, agriculture, health & biological sciences, liberal arts, cosmetology, criminal justice, and refrigeration & air conditioning. Certificate programs. Distributive requirements. Independent and individualized study. Community Educational Service Program. Media, learning centers. 20,000-volume library with microform resources.

Financial College scholarships and loans, activity grants, PELL, SEOG, CWS. Application deadline April 1.

Admissions: High school graduation required. GED accepted. ACT recommended. Rolling admissions; recommend applying at least one month before registration. *Concurrent Enrollment* Program. Transfers accepted. Credit possible for CEEB CLEP exams.

Student Life Student government. Newspaper, literary journal. Music and drama groups. Honor society. Cheerleaders. Livestock judging team. Outing, rodeo clubs. Future Farmers of America. Married-student housing. 2 semesters of phys ed required. 2 intercollegiate sports for men, 3 for women. Wyoming Community College Athletic Conference, NJCAA.

[J1] LARAMIE COUNTY COMMUNITY COLLEGE

1400 East College Drive, Cheyenne 82001

[J1] NORTHWEST COMMUNITY COLLEGE

Powell 82435, (307) 754-6200
Admissions Counselor: Nancy Muecke

- **Undergraduates: 368m, 352w; 1,587 total (including part-time)**
- **Tuition & Fees (1982/83): $420, $880 (out-of-state)**
- **Room & Board: $1,700-$2,070**
- **Degrees offered: AA, AS, AAS**
- **Mean ACT 20; mean SAT 400v, 455m**

A public junior college established in 1946. 950-acre campus located in a small agricultural town.

Academic Character NCACS and professional accreditation. Semester system. Terminal and transfer programs offered in the areas of general studies, liberal arts, arts, education, English, foreign language, geography, history, journalism, music, social sciences, social work, speech communication, agriculture, agri-range management, business, computer science, engineering, home economics, industrial arts education, math, medical lab technology, therapy, physical education, range management, sciences, wildlife management, equestrian studies, office administration, photography, printing, welding technology. Distributive requirements vary with programs. Certificates granted. Independent study. Preprofessional programs in law, dentistry, forestry, medicine, nursing, optometry, pharmacy, veterinary medicine. WICHE student exchange program. Evening, adult, and continuing education programs. Day Care Center.Learning Skills Center. 33,000-volume library.

Financial Guaranteed tuition. College scholarships; athletic, special ability, academic, and activity scholarships; PELL, SEOG, NDSL, GSL, CWS.

Admissions High school graduation required. Non-high school graduates with ability are accepted. ACT or SAT and $10 application fee required from out-of-state students. Rolling admissions; application deadline August 15. *Concurrent Enrollment, Early Admission, Early Decision* programs. Admission deferral possible. Transfers accepted. Credit possible for CEEB AP, CLEP, and college exams, and for military service.

Student Life Student government. Newspaper, yearbook. Several music groups. Drama and debate groups. Young Democrats, Young Republicans. Outing and Rodeo clubs. Academic, honorary, professional, religious, and special interest groups. Single freshmen under 21 must live at home or on campus for one semeseter. One men's, one women's, 2 coed dorms. On-campus apartments for married and single students. Cafeteria. 2 phys ed courses required. 5 intercollegiate sports for men, 5 for women; intramural and recreational sports.

[J1] SHERIDAN COLLEGE

Sheridan 82801, (307) 672-3510
Director of Admissions & Registrar: Bruce Gifford

- **Undergraduates: 250m, 246w; 1,057 total (including part-time)**
- **Tuition (1982/83): $408 (in-state), $1,110 (out-of-state)**
- **Room & Board: $1,864**
- **Degrees offered: AA, AS, AAS**

A public junior college founded in 1948. Small-town campus, with branch campus at Gillette. Airport and bus station nearby.

Academic Character NCACS and professional accreditation. Semester system. Transfer programs offered in agriculture, animal science, range management, crop & weed, farm & ranch management, agricultural education, business, fine arts, humanities, English, history, philosophy, journalism, drama, communication, music, industrial design, commercial & photographic art, social science, business, accounting, secretarial science, sociology, elementary & secondary education, anthropology, physical education, recreation leadership, political science, psychology, engineering, criminal justice, mining engineering, natural sciences, biology, botany, chemistry, forestry, wildlife. Preprofessional majors offered in dentistry, medicine, nursing, optometry, economics, marketing, management, architecture, medical technology, chiropractic, pharmacy, veterinary medicine, business education, physical therapy, office administration, distributive education, forestry & wildlife, occupational therapy. 1- and 2-year terminal programs in secretarial science, general education, practical nursing, dental hygiene, mining technology, mine maintenance, fluid power, diesel, welding, electrical maintenance. WICHE student exchange program. Adult education program. Mining, engineering, agricultural labs. Observatory. Learning Skills Center. Coputer center. Over 30,000-volume library with A-V resources.

Financial College scholarships and loans; athletic, music, activity scholarships; PELL, SEOG, NDSL, CWS. Priority application deadline April 1.

Admissions High school graduation required. GED accepted. Non-high school graduates mnay be admitted on approval of registrar. $55 deposit required with housing application. *Early Admission* Program. Transfers accepted. Credit possible for CEEB CLEP and college exams. Special admission possible.

Student Life Student government. Publications. Music and drama groups. Rodeo, Outing, Ski clubs. Academic, special interest, honorary groups. Dorm housing for 160 students. Cafeteria. No married-student housing. 4 intercollegiate sports for men, 5 for women; intramurals.

[J1] WESTERN WYOMING COLLEGE

2500 College Drive, PO Box 428, Rock Springs 82901, (307) 382-2121
Director of Admissions & Records: Jackie Harrell

- **Undergraduates: 126m, 207w; 1,704 total (including part-time)**
- **Tuition (1982/83): $346 (in-state), $396 (out-of-state)**
- **Room & Board: $1,875**
- **Degrees offered: AA, AAS**
- **Mean ACT 18**

A coed, public junior college established in 1959.

Academic Character NCACS and professional accreditation. Semester system. Transfer programs offered in humanities & fine arts, social science & services, math & natural science, business & management, and preprofessional law, forestry, dentistry, wildlife, medicine, engineering, nursing. Terminal programs in secretarial science, data processing, welding, electricity, chemical technology, keypunch, bookkeeping, building trades, mining technology, X-ray technology, radiologist technician, banking, horse management, medical lab technology, nursing. Distributive requirements. Certificates granted. Independent study, cooperative work/study. Remedial math and English programs. Children's Center. Water Quality Lab. Learning Resource Center. 18,000-volume library with A-V resources.

Financial CEEB CSS. College scholarships, grants-in-aid, athletic grants, civic grants; PELL, SEOG, SSIG, NDSL, CWS, college work program. Priority application deadline April 15.

Admissions High school graduation or equivalent required. GED accepted. ACT recommended. Rolling admissions; suggested deadlines April 1 (allied health programs), April 15 (others). *Concurrent Enrollment* possible. Advanced placement program.

Student Life Student government. Newspaper. Outing and Ski clubs. Honorary, academic, religious, and special interest groups. Women's Center. Apartment-style housing for single and married students. Cafeteria. 2 phys ed courses required. 3 intercollegiate sports for men, 3 for women; intramurals. Western Wyoming Community College Athletic Association, NJCAA.

[1] WYOMING, UNIVERSITY OF

Laramie 82070, (307) 766-5160
Director of Admissions & Registrar: Arland L. Grover

- **Undergraduates: 4,326m, 3,452w; 9,635 total (including graduates)**
- **Tuition (1982/83): $616 (in-state), $2,076 (out-of-state)**
- **Room & Board: $4,100**
- **Degrees offered: BA, BS, BFA, BMus**
- **Mean ACT 20.8**
- **Student-faculty ratio: 11 to 1**

A public university established in 1886. 791-acre campus in a small city in the mountains 2 hours from Denver, Colorado. Air, rail, and bus service.

Academic Character NCACS and professional accreditation. Semester system, 8-week summer term, additional short courses, workshops, and institutes. 10 majors offered by the College of Agriculture, 35 by the College of Arts & Sciences, 4 by the College of Commerce & Industry, 14 by the College of Education, 8 by the College of Engineering, and 3 by the College of Health Sciences. Special and double majors. Degree candidates enroll under 1 of 6 programs: traditional major, self-designed major, professional curriculum, preprofessional curriculum, Honors Program, or non-degree. Distributive requirements. Graduate and professional degrees granted. Independent and accelerated study. Honors program. Phi Beta Kappa. Pass/fail. Cooperative work/study, internships. Preprofessional programs in dentistry, forestry, law, library science, medicine, occupational therapy, optometry, pharmacy, and physical therapy. 2-2 forestry program with approved forestry school and 3-1 programs with other professional schools possible. Exchange program with Universities of AK, HI, ID, MT, NM. Study abroad. Elementary, secondary, and special education certification. ROTC, AFROTC. National Park Service Research Center, Water Resources Research Institute. Museums, art gallery. Language lab. 900,000-volume library.

Financial University scholarships and loans; PELL, SEOG, NSS, NDSL, GSL, NSL, CWS. Application deadline for scholarships and NDSL February 15.

Admissions Open admission to all graduates of accredited WY high schools. Out-of-state graduates eligible if GPA is 2.5 or better. ACT required. Rolling admissions. *Early Admission* Program. Transfers accepted. Credit possible for CEEB AP and CLEP exams, and for university placement exams.

Student Life Student government. Newspaper. Several music, drama, and speaking groups. Religious, academic, honorary, and special interest groups. 9 fraternities, 8 with houses, and 6 sororities with houses. 9% of men, 12% of women join. Single freshmen under 19 must live at home, on campus, or in fraternity or sorority. Married-student housing. 35% of students live on campus. Liquor permitted in some dorms and in Union. 2 semesters phys ed required. 10 intercollegiate sports for men, 8 for women; intramurals. AIAW, NCAA, Western Athletic Conference. Student body composition: 1% Black, 1% Hispanic, 1% Native American, 93% White, 4% Other. 32% from out of state.

U.S. DEPENDENCIES

GUAM (GU)

[1 & J1] GUAM, UNIVERSITY OF
Agana 96910
Director of Admissions: Forrest G. Rogers

- **Enrollment: 732m, 907w; 2,660 total (including part-time)**
- **Tuition (1982/83): $606 (Guam residents), $936 (others)**
- **Room & Board: $2,200; Fees: $58**
- **Degrees offered: BA, BS, BBA, BSW, AA**
- **Student-faculty ratio: 18 to 1**

A public university established in 1952. 100-acre campus in overlooking Pago Bay, 5 miles from Agana. Airport nearby.
Academic Character WASC accreditation. Semester system, 6-week summer term. Majors offered in accounting, agriculture, anthropology, art, biology, chemistry, communications, criminal justice, finance & economics, history, literature, management, marketing, math, nursing, political science, psychology, public administration, science, social sciences, social work, sociology, and bilingual-bicultural-elementary, early childhood, elementary, secondary, and special education. AA offered in business, nursing, library science, criminal justice. Minor required in some programs. Distributive requirements. Masters degrees granted. Independent study, pass/fail, internships. Study in Japan. Elementary, secondary, and special education certification. Marine lab. Research Center. Computer center. 300,000-volume library with microform resources.
Financial Scholarships, grants, loans; PELL, SEOG, NSS, NDSL, FISL, NSL, CWS. Application deadline June 15.
Admissions High school graduation with 15 units required. GED accepted. SAT or ACT, and ACH recommended. $10 application fee. Rolling admissions; application deadline August 3. Refundable 33% tuition deposit and $30 room deposit required on acceptance of admissions offer. *Concurrent Enrollment* Program. Admission deferral possible. Transfers accepted. Credit possible for CEEB CLEP, DANTES, and departmental exams.
Student Life Student government. Newspaper, yearbook. NOW. Micronesian, Filipino, Chinese student groups. Special interest, academic, and service clubs. Coed dorms. Married-student housing. 3% of students live on campus. 2 semesters of phys ed required. 3 intercollegiate sports for men, 1 for women. Student body composition: 70% Asian, 1% Black, 1% Hispanic, 2% Native American, 17% White, 9% Other. 33% from outside of Guam.

[J1] GUAM COMMUNITY COLLEGE
Guam Main Facility, PO Box 23069, Mariana Islands 96921

PUERTO RICO (PR)

[2] AMERICAN COLLEGE OF PUERTO RICO
Bayamon 00619

[1] ANTILLIAN COLLEGE
Mayaguez 00709

[1] BAYAMON CENTRAL UNIVERSITY
PO Box 1725, Bayamon 00619

[G1] CARRIBEAN CENTER FOR ADVANCED STUDIES
Box 41246, Minillas Station, Santurce 00907

[1] CARRIBEAN UNIVERSITY COLLEGE
PO Box 493, Bayamon 00619

[G2] CENTRO DE ESTUDIOS AVANZADOS DE PUERTO RICO EL CARIBE
San Juan 00904

[1] COLEGIO UNIVERSITARIO DEL TURABO
Caguas — see Turabo University

[1] COLEGIO UNIVERSITARIO METROPOLITANO
Cupey 00928

[1] CONSERVATORY OF MUSIC OF PUERTO RICO
Hato Rey 00936

[J2] ELECTRONIC DATA PROCESSING COLLEGE OF PUERTO RICO
Munoz Rivera 555, Hato Rey 00919

[G2] EVANGELICAL SEMINARY OF PUERTO RICO
Ponce de Leon Avenue 776, Hato Rey 00918

[1] INTERNATIONAL INSTITUTE OF THE AMERICAS
Hato Rey 00917

[P] PONCE SCHOOL OF MEDICINE
Ponce 00732

[1] PUERTO RICO, CATHOLIC UNIVERSITY OF
Ponce 00732

- **Enrollment: 4,215m, 7,686w**
- **Tuition (1980/81): $15 all sessions**
- **Approximate Room & Board: $400**
- **Degrees offered: BA, BS, BSEd, BAEd, BSN, BSS, BBA, AS**
- **Mean SAT 500**

A private, bilingual, Roman Catholic university founded in 1948. Urban campus.
Academic Character MSACS accreditation. Semester system, 2 4-week summer terms. BA offered with majors in English, Spanish, French, fine arts, history, social sciences, philosophy, political science, and sociology; BS with majors in biology, chemistry, math, and pre-med; BS in Nursing; BBA with majors in accounting, money & banking, general business economics; BSS; BS in secondary education; BA in elementary education; AS in computer programming and digital electronics. Graduate and professional degrees granted. Diploma programs. Remedial math and English programs. 62,500-volume library.
Financial Guaranteed tuition.
Admissions High school graduation with index of 2.0 required. SAT required. Rolling admissions. Freshmen admitted in August and January. *Early Admission* and *Early Decision* programs. Admission deferral possible. Advanced placement program.
Student Life Limited boarding facilities on campus. Intercollegiate baseball, softball, volleyball, track, and tennis; intramurals.

[1] PUERTO RICO, INTER-AMERICAN UNIVERSITY OF
San German 00753

- **Enrollment: 4,647m, 3,790w**
- **Tuition & Fees (1980/81): $800**
- **Maintenace: $700**
- **Typical Expenses: $1,520**
- **Degrees offered: BA, BAEd, BS**
- **Student-faculty ratio: 19 to 1**

A private, inter-denominational, liberal arts university organized in 1912, first degree granted in 1927. Main campuses at San German and San Juan; regional colleges at Aguadilla, Arecibo, Barranquitas, Bayamon, and Ponce.
Academic Character MSACS accreditation. Semester system, 2 4-week summer terms. Programs include Caribbean-Inter-American studies, biology, chemistry, economics & business administration, education, English, geography, history, home economics, hotel management, linguistics & language teaching, math, music, nursing education, philosophy, physics, political science, psychology, religion, secretarial science, sociology & anthropology, Spanish, and health, physical education, & recreation. Masters and law degrees granted. 70,000-volume library with 15,000-volume law library.
Financial Scholarships, loans; honor, talent, international scholarships; PELL, SEOG, NDSL, FISL, CWS.
Admissions SAT required. Freshmen admitted any semester.
Student Life Dormitories for men and women. Dining hall and cafeteria.

[1] PUERTO RICO, UNIVERSITY OF
GPO Box 4984-G, San Juan 00936
Director of Admissions: Carlos D. Rodriguez

- **Enrollment: 17,361m, 24,965w; 51,159 total (including part-time)**
- **Resident Tuition (1982/83): $1,031 (2-year programs), $1,251 (4- & 5-year programs), $2,500 (medicine & odontology)**
- **Degrees offered: Baccalaureate and associate**

A bilingual, public university system consisting of two 4-year University Campuses at Rio Piedras and Mayaguez, one Medical Sciences Campus at Rio Piedras, two 4-year University colleges at Cayey and Humacao, two 4-year Technological University Colleges at Arecibo and Bayamon, and four 2-year regional colleges at Anguadilla, Carolina, Ponce, and Utuado.

Academic Character MSACS accreditation. Baccalaureate degrees offered in agricultural sciences, agronomy, business administration, education, engineering, general studies, horticulture, home economics, humanities, natural sciences, nursing, occupational & physical therapy, social sciences, medical technology, pharmacy, public communication, computer sciences, electronics, secretarial sciences, nuclear medicine & ultrasound, agricultural education, and health education. Associate degrees granted in several fields in technology or arts & sciences at Bayamon and Arecibo Technological University Colleges, and at regional colleges at Aguadilla, Carolina, Ponce, and Utuado. Many graduate and professional degrees granted. 5,152,594-volume library.
Admissions High school graduation required. Spanish ACH or SAT required. Advanced placement program.

■[1] RIO PIEDRAS CAMPUS
Rio Piedras 00931

[J1] PUERTO RICO JUNIOR COLLEGE
GPO Box AE, Rio Piedras 00928

[J2] RAMIREZ COLLEGE OF BUSINESS AND TECHNOLOGY
1913 Avenue Fernandez Juncos, Santurce 00910

[J1] SACRED HEART, UNIVERSITY OF THE
PO Box 12383, Loiza Station, Santurce

- **Enrollment: 6,000 men & women**
- **Tuition (1980/81): $45 per credit**
- **Room & Board: $800**
- **Degrees offered: Associate**

A private, coed college founded in 1880 by the Religious of the Sacred Heart.
Academic Character MSACS accreditation. Semester system, 2 4-week summer terms. Programs offered in nursing, education, accounting, management, secretarial sciences, horticulture, communications, real estate, physical education, tourism & transportation.
Admissions ACH or SAT required for admission.

[J1] SAN JUAN TECHNOLOGICAL COMMUNITY COLLEGE
958 Ponce de Leon Avenue, Santurce 00907

[1] TURABO UNIVERSITY
Box 1091, Caguas 00626
Formerly Colegio Universitario Del Turabo

VIRGIN ISLANDS *(VI)*

[1 & J1] VIRGIN ISLANDS, COLLEGE OF THE
St. Thomas 00801

- **Undergraduates: 191m, 441w; 2,845 total (including graduates & part-time)**
- **Tuition (1982/83): $468 (VI residents), $1,268 (others)**
- **Room & Board: $1,770**
- **Degrees offered: BA, BS, AA**
- **Student-faculty ratio: 18 to 1**

A public liberal arts college established in 1952. Branch campus on St. Croix.
Academic Character MSACS accreditation. Semester system, 6- and 8-week summer terms. Majors offered in business administration, accounting, English, Spanish, humanities, biology, chemistry, marine biology, math, nursing, social science, social welfare services, teacher education (elementary & secondary preparation). AA programs in accounting, business management, executive secretarial administration, science technology, nursing, construction technology, police science, and agriculture. Masters degrees granted. Remedial math and English programs. 50,000-volume library.
Financial Aid available including scholarships, loans, work-study program.
Admissions High school graduation, GED, or equivalent required. SAT or ACT strongly recommended. Rolling admissions; application deadline April 15. *Early Admission* Program. Admission deferral possible. Advanced placement program.
Student Life Living facilities for 300 full-time students. Several intramural sports. Student body composition: 90% minority.

FOREIGN *(Approved by Regional Accrediting Bodies)*

[1] AMERICAN COLLEGE IN PARIS
31 Avenue Bosquet, Paris France 75007

- **Undergraduates: 700 men & women**
- **Tuition (1982/83): $4,200**
- **Typical Expenses: $5,000**
- **Degrees offered: BA, BFA, AA**
- **Student-faculty ratio: 12 to 1**

An independent, coed, non-sectarian college of arts & sciences, founded in 1961.
Academic Character MSACS accreditation. Degrees licensed by the Delaware State Board of Education. Majors offered in art history, computer science, international business administration, European culture studies, French studies, international affairs, international economics, comparative literature. BFA offered in conjunction with The Parsons School of Design of New York. AA degree programs. Independent study. Remedial math and English programs.
Financial Limited financial aid available.
Admissions Rolling admissions; application deadline July 31. *Early Admission* and *Early Decision* programs. Admission deferral possible. Advanced placement program.

[1] AMERICAN COLLEGE OF SWITZERLAND
1854 Leysin, Switzerland

[J1] AMERICAN SAMOA, COMMUNITY COLLEGE OF
Pago Pago, American Samoa 96799

[1] AMERICAN UNIVERSITY
Cairo, Eqypt

[1] AMERICAS, UNIVERSITY OF THE
Puebla, Mexico

[1] DEREE COLLEGE
Athens, Greece

[J1] FRANKLIN COLLEGE SWITZERLAND
New York Office: 866 UN Plaza, Suite 866, New York NY 10017

- **Undergraduates: 61m, 128w**
- **Tuition (1982/83): $6,000**
- **Degree offered: AA**

A private, coed college with an international program. Campus in Lugano.
Academic Character MSACS accreditation. College offers an international program in the liberal arts with offerings focused on the European and Mediterranean context. Instruction is in English. Required period of academic travel followed by a formal paper on a pre-selected topic. IES diploma awarded to those students undertaking sophomore, junior, or senior year of study abroad.
Admissions 60% of student spots reserved for Americans. High school graduation with a college prep program recommended. SAT or ACT and 3 evaluations required. Rolling admissions. *Early Admission* Program. Admission deferral possible. Advanced placement program.
Student Life Limited space available in college-operated apartments with self-service dining facilities. Independent apartment housing arranged through the College. Athletics include soccer, basketball, hockey, skiing, tennis, swimming, horseback riding, volleyball, and judo.

[1] INSTITUTO TECHNOLOGICO
Monterey N.L., Mexico

[J1] COMMUNITY COLLEGE OF MICRONESIA
PO Box 159, Kolonia, Ponape, Eastern Caroline Islands

[J1] MICRONESIAN OCCUPATIONAL COLLEGE
PO Box 9, Koror, Palau, Western Caroline Islands

[J1] PANAMA CANAL COLLEGE
APO Miami, Florida 34002

- **Undergraduates: 436 men & women; 1,636 total (including part-time)**
- **Tuition (1980/81): $480 (US citizens living in Canal Area/Panama who are US government employees, & other US government employees living in Canal Area; $3,007 (others)**
- **Degrees offered: BSMT, AA, AS, AT**
- **Mean SAT 450**

A public junior college operated by the US government.
Academic Character MSACS accreditation. Semester system, 8-week summer term. Transfer prorgams offered in art, liberal arts, business administration, engineering science, secretarial science, learning resources technology. Preprofessional programs in medicine and nursing. Remedial English program.
Admissions Must be bona fide resident of the Republic of Panama. High school graduation, GED, or entrance exam required. *Early Admission* and *Early Decision* programs. Advanced placement program.
Student Life Dormitory accomodates 45 men and 45 women. Student body composition: 68% minority.

[1] RICHMOND COLLEGE, THE AMERICAN INTERNATIONAL COLLEGE OF LONDON

Queens Road, Richmond, Surrey, England TW10 6JP

- **Undergraduates: 207m, 265w**
- **Tuition (1982/83): £3,250**
- **Room & Board: £1,000**
- **Degrees offered: BA, AA**

A private, coed liberal arts college. Two campuses: freshmen and sophomores in suburban Richmond; juniors and seniors in central London.
Academic Character MSACS accreditation. Semester system, summer term. Majors offered in British area studies, business & economics, English literature, art history, interdisciplinary studies, German, French, Italian, and Spanish. One-year computer science certificate course. 2-year pre-engineering program. Independent study. Internships. Freshmen must earn a minimum 2.0 average to continue in good academic standing; 80% of freshmen complete year in good academic standing. Remedial math and English programs.
Financial Aid available in form of partial scholarships based on academic achievement and financial need.
Admissions SAT required of applicants from American schools. Rolling admissions; no deadline. January and May entrance possible. Transfers accepted.
Student Life Residential facilities available at both campuses. Athletics include soccer, tennis, squash, basketball, and table tennis.

SECTION FOUR

SPORTS INDEX

A section containing information on 47 college and university intercollegiate sports for men and women, with information on colleges offering scholarships in the various sports, and listings of 7 special non-sports activities.

KEY TO SYMBOLS USED:

- □ college offers sport for men
- + college offers sport for women
- ■ college offers sport with scholarships for men
- ‡ college offers sport with scholarships for women
- ★ college offers sport with scholarships for men and women

Archery

Badminton

Baseball

■Ferris State MI
□Ferrum VA
□Findlay OH
□Fisk U TN
□Fitchburg State MA
■Flagler FL
■Florida, U. of FL
■Florida A&M U FL
■Florida Atlantic U FL
■Florida Coll FL
□Florida Inst. of Tech FL
■Florida Southern FL
■Florida State U FL
■Fordham U NY
■Fort Hays State U KS
□Framingham State MA
■Francis Marion SC
□Franklin IN
□Franklin & Marshall PA
□Franklin Pierce NH
■Freed-Hardeman IN
■Friends U KS
□Frostburg State MD
■Furman U SC
■Gadsden State Jr AL
□Gallaudet DC
■Gannon U PA
■Gardner-Webb NC
■Geneva PA
□George Fox OR
■George Mason U VA
■George Washington U DC
□George Williams IL
□Georgetown KY
□Georgetown U DC
■Georgia, U. of GA
□Georgia Coll GA
■Georgia Inst. of Tech GA
□Georgia Southern GA
■Georgia Southwestern GA
■Georgia State U GA
+□Gettysburg PA
□Glassboro State NJ
□Glenville State WV
■Golden Valley Lutheran MN
■Gonzaga U WA
□Goshen IN
+Goucher MD
■Grace IN
■Grand Canyon AZ
□Grand Rapids Baptist MI
□Grand Valley State MI
■Grand View IA
□Greenville IL
□Grinnell IA
□Grove City PA
■Guilford NC
□Gustavus Adolphus MN
□Hamilton NY
□Hamline U MN
□Hampden-Sydney VA
■Hannibal-LaGrange MO
□Hanover IN
□Hardin-Simmons U TX
□Harding U AR
■Hartford, U. of CT
□Harvard/Radcliffe MA
□Harvey Mudd CA
□Haverford PA
□Hawaii, U. of HI
□Heidelberg OH
□Henderson State AR
□Hesser NH
□Hesston KS
□High Point NC
■Highland Comm KS
★Hilbert NY
□Hillsdale MI
□Hiram OH
■Hiwassee TN
□Hobart NY
□Hofstra U NY
□Holy Cross MA
□Hope MI

□Houghton NY
■Howard U DC
■Huntingdon AL
■Huron SD
■Husson ME
■Hutchinson Comm KS
★Illinois, U. of (Chicago Circle) IL
■Illinois, U. of (Urbana) IL
□Illinois Benedictine IL
□Illinois Coll IL
■Illinois Inst. of Tech IL
■Illinois State U IL
□Illinois Wesleyan IL
■Independence Comm KS
■Indiana Central U IN
■Indiana State U. (Terre Haute) IN
■Indiana U. (Bloomington) IN
□Indiana U.-Purdue U. (Indianapolis) IN
+□Indiana U. of Pennsylvania IN
■Iona NY
■Iowa, U. of IA
■Iowa State U IA
■Iowa Wesleyan IA
□Ithaca NY
■Jackson State U MS
■Jacksonville State U AL
■Jacksonville U FL
■James Madison U VA
■Jamestown ND
□John Carroll U OH
■Johns Hopkins U MD
□Judson IL
■Judson Baptist OR
□Juniata PA
□Kalamazoo MI
■Kansas, U. of KS
□Kansas Newman KS
■Kansas State U KS
□Kean NJ
□Kearney State NE
□Keene State NH
□Kemper Military MO
■Kent State U OH
■Kentucky, U. of KY
■Kentucky Wesleyan KY
□Kenyon OH
□Keystone Jr PA
■King's NY
□King's PA
□Knox IL
+□Kutztown State PA
□La Salle PA
□Lafayette PA
□Lakeland WI
□Lamar U TX
■Lambuth TN
■Langston U OK
□Lawrence U WI
■Le Moyne NY
□Lehigh U PA
□Lenoir-Rhyne NC
□LeTourneau TX
□Lewis & Clark OR
■Lewis-Clark State ID
□Lewis U IL
■Liberty Baptist VA
■Lincoln IL
□Lincoln Christian IL
□Lincoln Memorial TN
■Lincoln U MO
□Lincoln U PA
□Lindenwood Colleges MO
■Lindsey Wilson KY
★Linfield OR
■Livingston U AL
□Lock Haven State PA
■Longwood VA
□Loras IA
■Louisburg NC
■Louisiana State U. (Baton Rouge) LA
□Louisiana Tech. U LA
■Louisville, U. of KY

□Lowell, U. of MA
■Loyola Marymount U CA
■Lubbock Christian TX
□Luther IA
□Lynchburg VA
□Lyndon State VT
□Macalester MN
□MacMurray IL
□Maine, U. of (Farmington, Presque Isle) ME
■Maine, U. of (Orono) ME
■Malone OH
□Manchester IN
□Manhattan NY
□Manhattanville NY
■Mankato State MN
□Mansfield State PA
■Marian IN
□Marietta OH
■Marion Military AL
■Mars Hill NC
□Mary Hardin-Baylor, U. of TX
□Maryland, U. of MD
+□Marymount Coll. of Kansas KS
□Maryville MO
□Maryville TN
□Massachusetts, U. of MA
□Massachusetts Inst. of Tech MA
□Massachusetts Maritime MA
■Mayville State ND
□McKendree IL
□McNeese State U LA
■Memphis State U TN
■Menlo CA
■Mercyhurst PA
■Mesa CO
□Messiah PA
□Methodist NC
□Miami, U. of FL
■Miami U OH
■Michigan, U. of MI
■Michigan Christian MI
■Michigan State U MI
■Mid-American Nazarene KS
■Middle Tennessee State TN
□Middlebury VT
■Midwestern State U TX
□Miles AL
□Millersville State PA
□Milligan TN
□Millikin U IL
□Millsaps MS
□Milwaukee Sch. of Engr WI
□Minnesota, U. of (Twin Cities) MN
□Mississippi, U. of MS
■Mississippi Coll MS
□Mississippi Delta Jr MS
■Mississippi Valley State U MS
■Missouri, U. of (Columbia) MO
□Missouri, U. of (Rolla) MO
□Missouri Baptist MO
■Missouri Southern State MO
■Missouri Valley MO
■Missouri Western State MO
□Mitchell CT
□Mohawk Valley Comm NY
□Monmouth IL
□Monmouth NJ
■Montevallo, U. of AL
□Montreat-Anderson NC
□Moorhead State U MN
□Moravian PA
■Morehead State U KY
■Morningside IA
□Morristown TN
□Mount Mercy IA
□Mount Senario WI
□Mount St. Mary's MD
□Mount Union OH
□Muhlenberg PA
□Murray State OK
□Murray State U KY
□Muskingum OH
■Navarro TX

□Nazareth MI
■Nebraska, U. of (Lincoln) NE
□Nebraska Wesleyan NE
■Nevada, U. of (Reno) NV
□New England, U. of ME
□New England Coll NH
□New Hampshire, U. of NH
□New Hampshire Coll NH
■New Haven, U. of CT
□New Jersey Inst. of Tech NJ
★New Mexico, U. of NM
■New Mexico State U NM
■New Orleans, U. of LA
□Newberry SC
□Niagara U NY
□Nichols MA
■Nicholls State U LA
□Norfolk State U VA
□North Adams State MA
■North Alabama, U. of AL
■North Carolina, U. of (Chapel Hill, Wilmington) NC
□North Carolina A&T U NC
■North Carolina State U NC
□North Carolina Wesleyan NC
□North Central IL
□North Dakota State U ND
■North Idaho ID
□North Park IL
+□North Texas State TX
■Northeast Louisiana U LA
+□Northeast Mississippi Jr MS
■Northeast Missouri State MO
□Northeastern U MA
□Northeastern Oklahoma State OK
‡Northern Arizona U AZ
■Northern Colorado, U. of CO
□Northern Iowa, U. of IA
□Northern Kentucky U KY
□Northland WI
■Northwest Missouri State MO
■Northwest Nazarene ID
■Northwestern Coll IA
□Northwestern Oklahoma State OK
■Northwestern State U LA
★Northwestern U IL
■Northwood Inst MI
□Norwich U.-Vermont Coll VT
■Notre Dame, U. of IN
■Nyack NY
□Oberlin OH
□Occidental CA
■Ohio Dominican OH
□Ohio Northern U OH
■Ohio State U OH
□Ohio U OH
□Ohio Valley WV
□Ohio Wesleyan OH
■Oklahoma, U.of OK
■Oklahoma Baptist OK
■Oklahoma Christian OK
■Oklahoma State U OK
■Old Dominion U VA
□Olivet MI
■Oral Roberts OK
+□Oregon Inst. of Tech OR
+□Oregon State U OR
□Otero Jr CO
□Otterbein OH
□Ozarks, Sch. of the MO
■Pace U NY
■Pacific, U. of the CA
■Pacific Lutheran U WA
□Pacific U OR
+□Panama Canal Coll Pa
□Parks Coll IL
□Pearl River Jr MS
□Pembroke State NC
□Pennsylvania, U. of PA
■Pennsylvania State U PA
■Pepperdine U CA
□Peru State NE
■Pfeiffer NC

Basketball

★Ashland ... OH
★Assumption ... MA
■Athens State ... AL
+□Atlantic Christian ... MC
★Auburn U ... AL
+□Augsburg ... MN
+□Augustana ... IL
■Augustana ... SD
+□Aurora ... IL
+□Austin ... TX
★Austin Peay ... TN
+□Averett ... VA
★Avila ... MO
★Azusa Pacific ... CA
+□Babson ... MA
★Baker U ... KS
+□Baldwin-Wallace ... OH
★Ball State U ... IN
+□Baptist Christian ... LA
+□Bard ... NY
+Barnard ... NY
+□Barrington ... RI
+□Bartlesville Wesleyan ... OK
+□Barton Comm ... KS
+□Bates ... ME
★Baylor U ... TX
+□Beaver ... PA
+□Becker Jr ... MA
‡Bee Co ... TX
★Belhaven ... MS
★Bellarmine ... KY
★Belmont ... TN
★Belmont Abbey ... NC
+□Beloit ... WI
★Bemidji State ... MN
★Benedictine ... KS
+Bennett ... NC
★Bentley ... MA
+□Berea ... KY
+□Berry ... GA
+□Bethany ... KS
+□Bethany ... WV
□Bethany Bible ... CA
★Bethany Lutheran ... MN
★Bethany Nazarene ... OK
+□Bethel ... IN
+□Bethel ... KS
+□Bethel ... MN
★Bethel ... TN
+□Bethune-Cookman ... FL
★Biola ... CA
■Birmingham Southern ... AL
■Biscayne ... FL
★Bismarck Jr ... ND
★Black Hills ... SD
+□Blackburn ... IL
★Blinn ... TX
+□Bloomfield ... NJ
+■Bloomsburg State ... PA
‡Blue Mountain ... MS
★Bluefield ... VA
+□Bluffton ... OH
+□Boise State ... ID
★Boston Coll ... MA
★Boston U ... MA
+□Bowdoin ... ME
+□Bowie State ... MD
+□Bowling Green State ... OH
■Bradley U ... IL
+□Brandeis ... MA
+□Brandywine ... DE
★Brevard ... NC
★Briar Cliff ... IA
+□Bridgeport, U. of ... CT
+□Bridgewater State ... MA
+■Brigham Young U.-Hawaii ... HI
+□Brown U ... RI
+□Bryan ... TN
★Bryant ... RI
+Bryn Mawr ... PA
★Bucknell U ... PA
+□Buena Vista ... IA
+□Butler U ... IN
★C.W. Post Coll ... NY

★Cabrini ... PA
‡Caldwell ... NJ
★California, U. of (Berkeley, Irvine, Riverside) ... CA
+□California, U. of (Davis, Los Angeles, San Diego, Santa Barbara, Santa Cruz) ... CA
+□California Baptist ... CA
□California Inst. of Tech ... CA
+□California Lutheran ... CA
□California Maritime ... CA
★California State Poly ... CA
■California State (Bakersfield) . CA
+□California State (Chico, Fullerton, Hayward) ... CA
★California State (Fresno) ... CA
+□California State Coll ... PA
+□Calvin ... MI
★Cameron U ... OK
■Campbell U ... NC
★Campbellsville ... KY
★Canisius ... NY
□Capital U ... OH
□Cardinal Newman ... MO
+□Cardinal Stritch ... WI
+□Carleton ... WI
+Carlow ... PA
+□Carnegie-Mellon U ... PA
★Carroll ... MT
+□Carroll ... WI
★Carson-Newman ... TN
‡□Carthage ... WI
+□Case Western Reserve U ... OH
+□Casper ... WY
+□Castleton State ... VT
□Cathedral ... NY
+□Catholic U. of America ... DC
+□Catholic U. of Puerto Rico ... PR
‡Cazenovia ... NY
+Cedar Crest ... PA
★Cedarville ... OH
★Centenary ... LA
+□Central ... IA
+□Central Arkansas, U. of ... AR
★Central Arizona ... AZ
★Central Coll ... KS
★Central Florida, U. of ... FL
+□Central Methodist ... MO
★Central Michigan U ... MI
★Central Missouri ... MO
★Central State U ... OK
+□Central Washington U ... WA
□Central Wesleyan ... SC
+□Central Wyoming ... WY
★Chadron State ... NE
■Chaminade U ... HI
+□Champlain ... VT
★Chapman ... CA
★Charleston, Coll. of ... SC
★Charleston, U. of ... WV
+Chatham ... PA
+□Cheyney State ... PA
+□Chicago, U. of ... IL
★Chowan ... NC
★Christian Brothers ... TN
+□Cincinnati, U. of ... OH
□Citadel, The ... SC
□City U. (Baruch Coll.) ... NY
□City U. (Medgar Evers) ... NY
+□Claremont-McKenna ... CA
+□Clarion State ... PA
+□Clark U ... MA
+Clarke ... IA
+□Clarkson ... NY
+□Clearwater Christian ... FL
★Cleveland State U ... OH
+□Coe ... IA
★Coker ... SC
+□Colby ... ME
+Colby-Sawyer ... NH
+□Colgate U ... NY
+□College Misericordia ... PA
★Colorado, U. of ... CO
+□Colorado Coll ... CO

★Colorado Sch. of Mines ... CO
+□Colorado State U ... CO
■Columbia Christian ... OR
■Columbia Coll ... MO
+Columbia ... SC
■Columbia Jr ... SC
★Concord ... WV
+□Concordia ... IL
★Concordia ... OR
+□Concordia (Moorhead) ... MN
★Concordia (St. Paul) ... MN
★Concordia Teachers ... ME
★Connecticut, U. of ... CT
+□Connecticut Coll ... CT
+Converse ... SC
★Cooke Co ... TX
+□Coppin State ... MD
+□Cornell Coll ... IA
+□Cornell U ... NY
+□Cowley Co. Comm ... KS
★Creighton U ... NE
★Cumberland ... KY
+□Curry ... MA
+□Daemen ... NY
★Dakota State ... SD
+□Dakota Wesleyan U ... SD
+□Dallas Christian ... TX
★Dana ... NE
+□Daniel Webster ... NH
+□Dartmouth ... NH
★David Lipscomb ... TN
+■Davidson ... NC
★Davis & Elkins ... WV
+□Dawson Comm ... MT
★Dayton, U. of ... OH
+□Dean Jr ... MA
+□Defiance ... OH
+□Delaware, U. of ... DE
+□Delaware Valley ... PA
+□Delta State ... MS
+□Denison U ... OH
★Denver, U. of ... CO
+□DePauw U ... IN
+□Detroit, U. of ... MI
+□Dickinson ... PA
★Dickinson State ... ND
★Dillard U ... LA
+□Dixie ... UT
□Dominican ... CA
+□Dordt ... IA
□D-Q U ... CA
+□Dr. Martin Luther ... MN
★Drake U ... IA
+□Drew U ... NJ
★Drexel U ... PA
■Drury ... MO
+□Dubuque, U. of ... IA
★Duke U ... NC
★Duquesne U ... PA
★D'Youville ... NY
+□Earlham ... IN
★East Carolina U ... NC
+□East Central Jr ... MS
★East Central Oklahoma ... OK
+□East Tennessee State U ... TN
★East Texas Baptist ... TX
★Eastern ... PA
★Eastern Arizona ... AZ
□Eastern Christian ... MD
+□Eastern Connecticut State ... CT
★Eastern Illinois U ... IL
+□Eastern Kentucky U ... KY
★Eastern Montana ... MT
★Eastern Nazarene ... MA
★Eastern New Mexico U ... NM
★Eastern Oklahoma State ... OK
+□Eastern Oregon State ... OR
+□Eastern Washington U ... WA
★Eastern Wyoming ... WY
+□Eckerd ... FL
+□Edgewood ... WI
+□Edinboro State ... PA
+□Elizabethtown ... PA
+□Elmhurst ... IL

+□Elmira ... NY
+Elms ... MA
★Elon ... NC
+□Emerson ... MA
★Emmanuel ... GA
+Emmanuel ... MA
+□Emory & Henry ... VA
★Emporia State U ... KS
+Endicott ... MA
★Erskine ... SC
+□Eureka ... IL
★Evangel ... MO
★Evansville, U. of ... IN
■Fairfield U ... CT
★Fairleigh Dickinson U ... NJ
★Fairmont State ... WV
□Fashion Inst. of Tech ... NY
+■Fayetteville State ... NC
★Ferris State ... MI
+□Ferrum ... VA
+□Findlay ... OH
+□Fisk U ... TN
+□Fitchburg State ... MA
★Flagler ... FL
★Florida, U. of ... FL
★Florida A&M U ... FL
■Florida Coll ... FL
□Florida Inst. of Tech ... FL
★Florida Southern ... FL
★Florida State U ... FL
‡Fontbonne ... MO
★Fordham U ... NY
★Fort Hays State U ... KS
★Fort Lewis ... CO
★Fort Scott Comm ... KS
+□Framingham State ... MA
★Francis Marion ... SC
+□Franklin ... IN
+□Franklin& Marshall ... PA
+□Franklin Pierce ... NH
★Freed-Hardeman ... IN
★Freeman Jr ... SD
★Friends U ... KS
+□Frostburg State ... MD
★Furman U ... SC
★Gadsden State Jr ... AL
+□Gallaudet ... DC
★Gannon U ... PA
★Gardner-Webb ... NC
★Geneva ... PA
+□George Fox ... OR
★George Mason ... VA
★George Washington U ... DC
+□George Williams ... IL
★Georgetown ... KY
+■Georgetown U ... DC
★Georgia, U. of ... GA
+□Georgia Coll ... GA
★Georgia Inst. of Tech ... GA
+□Georgia Southern ... GA
★Georgia Southwestern ... GA
★Georgia State U ... GA
‡Georgian Court ... NJ
+□Gettysburg ... PA
★Glenville State ... WV
★Golden Valley Lutheran ... MN
★Gonzaga U ... WA
★Gordon ... MA
+□Goshen ... IN
+Goucher ... MD
★Grace ... IN
■Grand Canyon ... AZ
+□Grand Rapids Baptist ... MI
+□Grand Valley State ... MI
★Grand View ... IA
★Great Falls, Coll. of ... MT
+□Green Mountain ... VT
+□Greensboro ... NC
+□Greenville ... IL
+□Grinnell ... IA
+□Grove City ... PA
★Guilford ... NC
+□Gustavus Adolphus ... MN
+□Gwynedd-Mercy ... PA

★Northern Oklahoma OK
★Northland WI
★Northwest Missouri State MO
★Northwest Nazarene ID
★Northwestern IA
★Northwestern U IL
★Northwestern Oklahoma State OK
★Northwestern State U LA
★Northwood Inst MI
+□Norwich U.-Vermont Coll VT
+□Notre Dame, Coll. of CA
★Notre Dame, U. of IN
+Notre Dame Coll OH
★Nyack NY
+□Oakland U MI
+□Oberlin OH
+□Occidental CA
□Oglethorpe GA
★Ohio Dominican OH
+□Ohio Northern U OH
★Ohio State U OH
+□Ohio U OH
□Ohio Valley WV
+□Ohio Wesleyan OH
★Oklahoma, U. of OK
★Oklahoma Baptist U OK
★Oklahoma Christian OK
★Oklahoma Panhandle OK
★Oklahoma State U OK
★Old Dominion U VA
+□Olivet MI
★Oral Roberts OK
★Oregon, U. of OR
+□Oregon Inst. of Tech OR
+□Oregon State U OR
+□Otero Jr CO
★Ottawa U KS
+□Otterbein OH
★Ozarks, Sch. of the MO
★Pace U NY
★Pacific, U. of the CA
+□Pacific Christian CA
★Pacific Lutheran U WA
+□Pacific U OR
□Palm Beach Atlantic FL
+□Panama Canal Coll Panama
□Parks Coll IL
★Paul Smith's Coll NY
‡Peace NC
+□Pearl River Jr MS
+□Pembroke State U NC
+□Pennsylvania, U. of PA
★Pennsylvania State U PA
★Pepperdine U CA
+□Peru State NE
★Pfeiffer NC
★Philadelphia Coll. of Textiles PA
★Philander Smith AR
+□Pikeville KY
+Pine Manor MA
★Pittsburg State U KS
+■Pittsburgh, U. of (Johnstown) PA
★Pittsburgh, U. of (Pittsburgh) PA
+□Pitzer CA
+□Plymouth State NH
★Point Loma CA
★Point Park PA
+□Pomona CA
★Portland, U. of OR
★Post Coll CT
+□Potomac State WV
★Prairie View A&M TX
+□Pratt Comm KS
+□Pratt Inst NY
★Presbyterian SC
+□Princeton U NJ
+□Principia IL
★Providence Coll RI
★Puerto Rico, U. of PR
★Puget Sound, U. of WA
★Purdue U IN
★Quinnipiac Coll CT
+□Radford U VA
+□Ramapo NJ
★Randolph-Macon VA
+Randolph-Macon Woman's VA
+□Redlands, U. of CA
★Regis CO
+Regis MA
+□Rensselaer Poly. Inst NY
★Rhode Island, U. of RI
+□Rhode Island Coll RI
★Rice U TX
★Richmond, U. of VA
★Rider NJ
+□Rio Grande OH
+□Ripon WI
+Rivier NH
+□Roanoke VA
★Robert Morris PA
+□Rochester, U. of NY
□Rochester Inst. of Tech NY
+□Rockford IL
★Rockhurst MO
■Rockmont CO
★Rocky Mountain MT
+□Roger Williams RI
★Rollins FL
★Rosary IL
+Rosemont PA
+Russell Sage NY
★Rutgers U NJ
★Sacred Heart CT
★Saginaw Valley MI
★Saint Anselm NH
+Saint Benedict, Coll. of MN
■Saint Catharine KY
+Saint Catherine, Coll of MN
★Saint Edward's U TX
★Saint Francis PA
□Saint John's U MN
★Saint Joseph's U PA
★Saint Leo FL
+□Saint Mary's MD
+Saint Mary, Coll. of NE
★Saint Mary of the Plains KS
★Saint Mary's CA
+□Saint Mary's MN
□Saint Meinrad IN
★Saint Michael's VT
+□Saint Norbert WI
+■Saint Paul's MO
+□Saint Rose, Coll. of NY
+□Saint Scholastica, Coll. of MN
+Saint Teresa, Coll. of MN
■Saint Vincent PA
+□Saint Xavier IL
★Salem WV
+□Salem State MA
+□Salisbury State MD
★Sam Houston State TX
■Samford U AL
+□San Diego, U. of CA
★San Diego State U CA
★San Francisco, U. of CA
+□San Jose Bible CA
+□San Jose State U CA
★Santa Clara, U. of CA
★Santa Fe, Coll. of NM
+□Sarah Lawrence NY
★Schreiner TX
+□Scranton, U. of PA
+Scripps CA
+■Seattle Pacific U WA
+□Seattle U WA
★Seton Hall U NJ
+Seton Hill PA
★Seward Co. Comm KS
★Shaw U NC
+□Shenandoah Coll VA
+□Shepherd WV
★Sheridan WY
★Shippensburg State PA
★Shorter GA
★Siena NY
+□Simon's Rock MA
□Simpson CA
+□Simpson IA
+□Sioux Empire IA
★Sioux Falls SD
+□Skidmore NY
★Slippery Rock PA
+Smith MA
+□Snead State Jr AL
+□Snow UT
+□Sonoma State CA
+□South, U. of the TN
★South Alabama, U. of AL
★South Carolina, U. of SC
+□South Carolina State SC
★South Dakota, U. of SD
★South Dakota State U SD
+□South Dakota Sch. of Mines SD
★South Florida, U. of FL
+□South Georgia Coll GA
★Southeast Missouri State MO
★Southeastern Louisiana U LA
★Southeastern Oklahoma State U OK
★Southern Arkansas U AR
★Southern Baptist AR
★Southern California CA
★Southern Colorado, U. of CO
★Southern Idaho, Coll. of ID
★Southern Illinois U IL
+□Southern Maine, U. of ME
□Southern Methodist SC
★Southern Methodist U TX
★Southern Mississippi, U. of MS
+□Southern Oregon State OR
+Southern Seminary VA
■Southern Tech GA
★Southwest Baptist U MO
+□Southwest Mississippi Jr MS
★Southwest Missouri State U MO
★Southwest State U MN
★Southwest Texas State U TX
+□Southwesten at Memphis TN
★Southwestern Coll KS
■Southwestern Jr. Coll TX
★Southwestern Oklahoma State OK
+□Southwestern U TX
★Spring Arbor MI
★Spring Hill AL
+□Springfield MA
+□St. Ambrose IA
+□St. Andrew NC
★St. Bonaventure U NY
★St. Cloud State MN
★St. Francis IN
■St. Francis, Coll. of IL
★St. Gregory's OK
★St. John Fisher NY
★St. John's KS
★St. John's U NY
+St. Joseph CT
★St. Joseph's ME
★St. Joseph's IN
+□St. Lawrence U NY
★St. Martin's WA
+St. Mary's NC
★St. Mary's U TX
+St. Mary's IN
■St. Mary's MI
+□St. Olaf MN
+□St. Thomas, Coll. of MN
+□St. Thomas Aquinas NY
★Stanford U CA
+□State U. of New York (Albany, Binghamton, Coll. at Alfred at Buffalo, Coll. at Buffalo, Cobleskill, Canton, Coll. at Cornell U., Cortland, Delhi, Farmingdale, Fredonia, Geneseo, Morrisville, New Paltz, Oneonta, Oswego, Plattsburgh, Potsdam, at Syracuse, Stony Brook, Coll. of Tech.) NY
□State U. of New York Maritime Coll NY
★Stephen F. Austin State TX
★Sterling KS
★Stetson U FL
□Stevens Inst. of Tech NJ
+□Stockton State NJ
★Stonehill MA
★Sue Bennett KY
+□Sul Ross State U TX
★Suomi MI
+□Susquehanna U PA
+□Swarthmore PA
+Sweet Briar VA
★Syracuse U NY
★Tabor KS
★Talladega AL
‡Tampa, U. of FL
★Tarkio MO
+□Taylor U IN
★Temple U PA
+□Tennessee, U. of (Chattanooga) TN
★Tennessee, U. of (Knoxville, Martin) TN
+□Tennessee State U TN
+□Tennessee Tech. U TN
★Tennessee Temple U TN
★Texas, U. of (Arlington, Austin, El Paso, San Antonio) TX
★Texas A&M U TX
★Texas Christian U TX
★Texas Lutheran TX
+□Texas State Tech TX
+□Texas Wesleyan TX
‡Texas Woman's U TX
+□Thiel PA
+□Thomas ME
★Thomas More KY
■Tiffin U OH
‡Tift GA
+□Toccoa Falls GA
★Toledo, U. of OH
+□Tougaloo MS
★Towson State U MD
+■Transylvania KY
+□Trenton State NJ
■Trevecca Nazarene AL
+□Tri-State U AL
★Trinidad State Jr CO
+□Trinity CT
+□Trinity IL
+Trinity VT
+□Trinity Christian IL
★Troy State U AL
+□Truett McConnell GA
+□Tufts U MA
★Tulane U LA
★Tulsa, U. of OK
+□Tuskegee Inst AL
★Tusculum TN
+□U.S. Air Force Acad CO
+□U.S. Coast Guard Acad CT
+□U.S. International U CA
+□U.S. Merchant Marine Acad NY
★U.S. Military Acad NY
+□U.S. Naval Acad MD
+□Union NY
‡Union KY
★Union U TN
+□United Wesleyan PA
■Unity ME
+□Upper Iowa IA
+□Upsala NJ
★Urbana OH
+□Ursinus PA
+□Utah, U. of UT
■Utah State U UT
★Utica Coll NY
□Valley Forge Military PA
+□Valparaiso U IN
★Vanderbilt U TN
+□Vassar NY
★Vermont, U. of VT

Bowling

Boxing

Canoeing

Crew

Cricket

Cross Country

+□Anderson ... IN
□Angelo State ... TX
★Appalachian State ... NC
+□Aquinas ... MI
★Arizona, U. of ... AZ
+□Arkansas, U. of ... AR
■Arkansas State ... AR
□Arkansas Tech ... AR
★Ashland ... OH
+□Assumption ... MA
★Auburn U ... AL
+□Augsburg ... MN
+□Augustana ... IL
★Augustana ... SD
+□Aurora ... IL
★Austin Peay ... TN
□Averett ... VA
■Azusa Pacific ... CA
+□Babson ... MA
+□Baker U ... KS
+□Baldwin-Wallace ... OH
★Ball State ... IN
+□Bard ... NY
+Barnard ... NY
□Barrington ... RI
+□Bartlesville Wesleyan ... OK
+□Barton Co. Comm ... KS
+□Bates ... ME
★Baylor U ... TX
+□Beaver ... PA
★Bellarmine ... KY
★Belmont ... TN
+□Beloit ... WI
■Bemidji State ... MN
□Bentley ... MA
□Berea ... KY
+□Berry ... GA
+□Bethany ... KS
+□Bethany ... WV
□Bethel ... IN
+□Bethel ... KS
+□Bethel ... MN
■Biola ... CA
★Biscayne ... FL
+□Bismarck Jr ... ND
★Black Hills State ... SD
+□Bloomsburg State ... PA
□Bluffton ... OH
★Boston Coll ... MA
★Boston U ... MA
+□Bowdoin ... ME
+□Bowling Green State ... OH
★Bradley U ... IL
■Brevard ... NC
+□Bridgewater State ... MA
+□Brown U ... RI
+□Bryan ... TN
+□Bryant ... RI
★Bucknell U ... PA
+□Buena Vista ... IA
□Butler U ... IN
■C.W. Post Coll ... NY
■Cabrini ... PA
+■California, U. of (Berkeley, Riverside) ... CA
□California, U. of (Davis) ... CA
★California, U. of (Irvine) ... CA
+□California, U. of (Los Angeles, San Diego, Santa Barbara, Santa Cruz) ... CA
+□California Inst. of Tech ... CA
+□California Lutheran ... CA
+□California Maritime Acad ... CA
★California State (Bakersfield) . CA
+□California State Coll ... PA
+□California State Poly. U ... CA
+California State U. (Chico) ... CA
■California State U. (Fresno) .. CA
+□California State U. (Fullerton, Hayward) ... CA
□Calvin ... MI
+■Canisius ... NY
+□Capital U ... OH
+□Carleton Coll ... MN
□Carnegie-Mellon U ... PA
+□Carroll ... WI
■Carson-Newman ... TN
‡□Carthage ... WI
□Case Western Reserve U ... OH
+□Castleton State ... VT
+□Catholic U. of America ... DC
★Cedarville ... OH
+■Centenary Coll ... LA
■Central Arizona ... AZ
□Central Arkansas, U. of ... AR
□Central Coll ... KS
+□Central Coll ... IA
★Central Florida, U. of ... FL
+□Central Methodist ... MO
★Central Michigan U ... MI
★Central Missouri ... MO
★Central State U ... OK
□Central Washington U ... WA
□Chaminade U ... HI
■Chapman ... CA
□Cheyney State ... PA
□Chicago, U. of ... IL
+□Cincinnati, U. of ... OH
□Citadel, The ... SC
□City Coll ... NY
+□City U. (Medgar Evers) ... NY
+□Claremont-McKenna ... CA
+□Clarion State ... PA
+□Clark U ... MA
+□Clarkson Coll ... NY
★Cleveland State U ... OH
+□Coe ... IA
□Coffeyville Comm ... KS
+□Colby ... ME
+□Colgate U ... NY
□College Misericordia ... PA
★Colorado, U. of ... CO
★Colorado Sch. of Mines ... CO
+□Colorado State U ... CO
+□Columbia Christian ... OR
★Columbia Coll ... MO
□Concordia ... IL
+□Concordia ... MN
+□Concordia Teachers ... NE
+□Connecticut, U. of ... CT
+□Connecticut Coll ... CT
□Cornell Coll ... IA
+□Cornell U ... NY
□Cumberland Coll ... KY
+□D-Q U ... CA
+□Dakota State ... SD
+□Dakota Wesleyan U ... SD
+□Dallas, U. of ... TX
★Dana ... NE
+□Dartmouth ... NH
■David Lipscomb ... TN
+□Davidson ... NC
■Davis & Elkins ... WV
+□Dayton, U. of ... OH
+□Defiance ... OH
+□Delaware, U. of ... DE
+□Delaware Valley ... PA
+□Delta State ... MS
+□Denison U ... OH
□DePauw U ... IN
□Detroit, U. of ... MI
+□Dickinson ... PA
+□Dickinson State ... ND
+□Dordt ... IA
+□Dr. Martin Luther Coll ... MN
★Drake U ... IA
+□Drew U ... NJ
★Drexel U ... PA
□Dubuque, U. of ... IA
■Duke U ... NC
★Duquesne U ... PA
+□Earlham ... IN
★East Carolina U ... NC
+□East Tennessee State U ... TN
+□Eastern ... PA
+□Eastern Connecticut State ... CT
★Eastern Illinois U ... IL
■Eastern Nazarene ... MA
+□Eastern Oregon State ... OR
□Eastern Washington U ... WA
+□Eckerd ... FL
+□Edinboro State ... PA
+□Elizabethtown ... PA
□Elmhurst ... IL
□Elon ... NC
+Emmanuel ... MA
+□Emory U ... GA
★Emporia State U ... KS
★Evansville, U. of ... IN
+□Evergreen State ... WA
□Fairfield U ... CT
★Fairleigh Dickinson U ... NJ
+□Fairmont State ... WV
★Ferris State ... MI
□Ferrum ... VA
□Findlay ... OH
+□Fisk U ... TN
+□Fitchburg State ... MA
■Flagler ... FL
■Florida, U. of ... FL
□Florida Coll ... FL
+□Florida Inst. of Tech ... FL
+□Florida Southern ... FL
★Florida State U ... FL
+□Fordham U ... NY
★Fort Hays State U ... KS
+□Framingham State ... MA
■Francis Marion ... SC
□Franklin ... IN
+□Franklin & Marshall ... PA
□Franklin Pierce ... NH
■Freed-Hardeman ... TN
□Frostburg State ... MD
■Furman U ... SC
□Gallaudet ... DC
★Gannon U ... PA
□Geneva ... PA
□George Fox ... OR
★George Mason U ... VA
+□George Williams ... IL
+□Georgetown U ... DC
□Georgia, U. of ... GA
★Georgia State U ... GA
■Georgia Tech ... GA
+□Gettysburg ... PA
+□Glassboro State ... NJ
+□Glenville State ... WV
★Golden Valley Lutheran ... MN
+□Gonzaga U ... WA
□Gordon ... MA
+□Goshen ... IN
+Goucher ... MD
★Grace ... IN
□Grand Rapids Baptist ... MI
□Grand Valley State ... MI
+□Green Mountain ... VT
□Greensboro ... NC
□Greenville ... IL
+□Grinnell ... IA
+□Grove City ... PA
+□Gustavus Adolphus ... MN
+□Hamilton ... NY
+□Hamline U ... MN
□Hampden-Sydney ... VA
□Hanover ... IN
+□Hanover ... NY
+□Hardin-Simmons U ... TX
+□Harding U ... AR
+□Harvard/Radcliffe ... MA
+□Harvey Mudd ... CA
★Hastings ... NE
+□Haverford ... PA
+Hawaii, U. of ... HI
+□Hendrix ... AR
□High Point ... NC
★Hillsdale ... MI
□Hiram ... OH
□Hobart ... NY
□Holy Cross ... MA
+□Hope ... MI
+□Houghton ... NY
□Howard Payne U ... TX
+□Humboldt State U ... CA
■Hutchinson Comm ... KS
★Idaho, U. of ... ID
+□Idaho State U ... ID
★Illinois, U. of (Chicago Circle) ... IL
■Illinois, U. of (Urbana) ... IL
□Illinois Benedictine ... IL
★Illinois Inst. of Tech ... IL
★Illinois State U ... IL
□Illinois Wesleyan U ... IL
□Indiana Central U ... IN
★Indiana State U. (Terre Haute) IN
★Indiana U. (Bloomington) ... IN
+□Indiana U. of Pennsylvania ... PA
□Iona ... NY
★Iowa, U. of ... IA
★Iowa State U ... IA
‡□Ithaca ... NY
+□Jacksonville State U ... AL
■Jacksonville U ... FL
★James Madison U ... VA
★Jamestown ... ND
□Jersey City State ... NJ
★John Brown U ... AR
□John Carroll U ... OH
+□Johns Hopkins U ... MD
+□Johnson State ... VT
□Judson ... IL
+□Juniata ... PA
+□Kalamazoo ... MI
■Kansas, U. of ... KS
★Kansas State U ... KS
+■Kansas Wesleyan ... KS
+□Kearney State ... NE
+□Keene State ... NH
★Kentucky, U. of ... KY
■Kentucky Wesleyan ... KY
+□Kenyon ... OH
+■King's Coll ... NY
+□King's Coll ... PA
+□Knox ... IL
+□Kutztown State ... PA
+□La Salle ... PA
+□Lafayette ... PA
+□LaGrange ... GA
■Lake Superior State ... MI
+□Lawrence U ... WI
★Le Moyne ... NY
□Lebanon Valley ... PA
□Lehigh U ... PA
+□LeTourneau ... TX
+□Lewis & Clark ... OR
★Liberty Baptist ... VA
□Lincoln Memorial U ... TN
□Lincoln U ... PA
★Lindsey Wilson ... KY
★Linfield ... OR
+□Lock Haven State ... PA
□Long Island U. (Southampton) ... NY
★Loras ... IA
+□Los Angeles Baptist ... CA
★Louisiana State U. and A&M ... LA
□Louisiana Tech. U ... LA
+□Louisville, U. of ... KY
□Lowell, U. of ... MA
□Loyola Coll ... MD
‡□Loyola Marymount U ... CA
★Loyola U. of Chicago ... IL
□Lubbock Christian ... TX
+□Luther ... IA
+□Lynchburg ... VA
□Lyndon State ... VT
+□Macalester ... MN
+□MacMurray ... IL
+□Maharishi International ... IA
+□Maine, U. of (Orono) ... ME
+□Maine, U. of (Presque Isle) ... ME
□Maine Maritime Acad ... ME
+□Malone ... OH
□Manchester ... IN
□Manhattan Coll ... NY

+□Western Oregon ... OR
■Western State ... CO
+□Western Washington U ... WA
+□Westminster ... MO
□Westminster ... PA
¢Wheaton ... IL
□Wheaton ... MA
★White Plains, Coll. of ... NY
+□Whitman ... WA
+□Whittier ... CA
★Whitworth ... WA
+□Wichita State U ... KS
+□Widener U ... PA
+□Wilkes ... PA
+□Willamette U ... OR
□William & Mary, Coll. of ... VA
□William Jewell ... MO
□William Paterson ... NJ
+□William Penn ... IA
+□Williams ... MA
□Wilmington ... OH
★Winona State U ... MN
+□Wisconsin, U. of (Eau Claire, Green Bay, La Crosse, Oshkosh, River Falls, Stevens Point, Superior, Stout) ... WI
★Wisconsin, U. of (Madison) ... WI
‡□Wisconsin, U. of (Milwaukee) . WI
□Wisconsin, U. of (Platteville, Whitewater) ... WI
□Wittenberg U ... OH
+□Wooster Coll. of ... OH
+□Worcester Poly. Inst ... MA
+□Worcester State ... MA
□Wright State U ... OH
+□Wyoming, U. of ... WY
+□Xavier U ... OH
+□Yale U ... CT
★Yankton ... SD
+□York ... NE
+□York Coll ... PA

Cycling

+□Drew U ... NJ
★Drexel U ... PA
□Pomona ... CA
+□Worcester Poly ... MA

Diving

★Alabama, U. of (University) ... AL
+□Alabama A&M U ... AL
+□Alfred U ... NY
+□Allegheny ... PA
★Arizona State ... AZ
+□Arkansas, U. of (Fayetteville) . AR
★Auburn U ... AL
+□Austin ... TX
+□Babson ... MA
+□Ball State ... IN
+Barnard ... NY
+□Bloomsburg State ... PA
‡□Boston Coll ... MA
■Bradley U ... IL
+□Bridgewater State ... MA
+□Brown U ... RI
★Bucknell U ... PA
+□Butler U ... IN
□California, U. of (Davis) ... CA
+□California, U. of (San Diego) . CA
+□California Inst. of Tech ... CA
+California State U. (Fresno) .. CA
+□California State U. (Fullerton) CA
+□Carleton ... MN
+□Carnegie-Mellon U ... PA
+□Carroll ... WI
‡□Carthage ... WI
+Centenary ... NJ
+Central Arkansas, U. of ... AR
‡Central Missouri State U ... MO
+□Cincinnati, U. of ... OH
+□Claremont-McKenna ... CA
+□Clarion State ... PA
★Cleveland State U ... OH
+□Coe ... IA
+□Colgate U ... NY
+□Colorado Coll ... CO
★Connecticut, U. of ... CT
+□Cornell U ... NY
□Denison U ... OH
+□DePauw U ... IN
+□Dickinson ... PA
★Drexel U ... PA
■Drury ... MO
+□Duquesne U ... PA
■East Carolina U ... NC
□Edinboro State ... PA
+□Emory U ... GA
★Evansville, U. of ... IN
■Ferris State ... MI
★Florida, U. of ... FL
+□Fordham U ... NY
★Fort Lewis ... CO
+□Franklin & Marshall ... PA
★Furman U ... SC
★George Washington U ... DC
+□George Williams ... IL
+□Georgetown U ... DC
+□Georgia, U. of ... GA
+□Gettysburg ... PA
+□Glassboro State ... NJ
+Green Mountain ... VT
+□Grinnell ... IA
+□Gustavus Adolphus ... MN
+□Hamilton ... NY
+□Hamline U ... MN
□Harding U ... AR
+□Harvard/Radcliffe ... MA
+□Harvey Mudd ... CA
+□Hawaii, U. of ... HI
‡□Hendrix Coll ... AR
□Hobart ... NY
+Hood Coll ... MD
+□Hope ... MI
★Illinois, U. of (Chicago Circle) ... IL
★Illinois, U. of (Urbana) ... IL
+□Illinois Benedictine ... IL
‡Illinois State U ... IL
★Indiana U. (Bloomington) ... IN
+□Indiana U. of Pennsylvania ... PA
★Iowa, U. of ... IA
★Iowa State U ... IA
‡□Ithaca ... NY
★James Madison U ... VA
+□John Carroll U ... OH
+□Johns Hopkins U ... MD
★Kansas, U. of ... KS
+Kearney State ... NE
+□Keene State ... NH
★Kent State U ... OH
+□Kenyon ... OH
+Keuka ... NY
+□Knox ... IL
+□La Salle ... PA
+□Lafayette ... PA
+□Lake Forest ... IL
+□Lamar U ... TX
+□Lewis & Clark ... OR
★Lincoln Coll ... IL
□Lowell, U. of ... MA
+□Luther ... IA
+□Lycoming ... PA
+□Macalester ... MN
+□MacMurray ... IL
+Mansfield State ... PA
+□Marist ... NY
+□Mary Washington ... VA
+□Miami, U. of ... FL
★Miami U ... OH
★Michigan, U. of ... MI
★Michigan State U ... MI
+Middlebury ... VT
+□Minnesota, U. of (Twin Cities) MN
★Monmouth Coll ... NJ
‡Montana, U. of ... MT
+Mount Holyoke ... MA
+□Mount Union ... OH
+□Nazareth Coll ... NY
★Nebraska, U. of (Lincoln) ... NE
★Nevada, U. of (Las Vegas) ... NV
‡Nevada, U. of (Reno) ... NV
‡Newcomb ... LA
★North Carolina State U ... NC
★Northeast Missouri State ... MO
+□Northeastern U ... MA
‡□Northern Iowa, U. of ... IA
+□Norwich U./Vermont Coll ... VT
+□Notre Dame, U. of ... IN
+□Oberlin ... OH
★Ohio State U ... OH
+□Ohio U ... OH
+□Ohio Wesleyan U ... OH
★Oklahoma, U. of ... OK
★Old Dominion U ... VA
+Oregon State U ... OR
+Ozarks, Sch. of the ... MO
★Pacific Lutheran U ... CA
+□Pennsylvania, U. of ... PA
★Pepperdine U ... CA
★Pfeiffer ... NC
+□Pittsburgh, U. of ... PA
+□Pitzer ... CA
+Pomona ... CA
□Princeton U ... NJ
+□Principia ... IL
★Puget Sound, U. of ... WA
+□Ramapo ... NJ
+□Redlands, U. of ... CA
+Randolph-Macon Woman's ... VA
+Regis ... MA
+□Rhode Island, U. of ... RI
‡□Rice U ... TX
★Rider ... NJ
□Ripon ... WI
+□Rochester, U. of ... NY
+□Rochester Inst. of Tech ... NY
+□Rockford ... IL
+Salem State ... MA
+Salisbury State ... MD
+San Jose State ... CA
+Scripps ... CA
+□Shepherd ... WV
★Shippensburg State ... PA
★Slippery Rock State ... PA
+Smith ... MA
+□South, U. of the ... TN
★Southern Illinois U ... IL
★Southern Methodist U ... TX
+□Southern Oregon State ... OR
+□Springfield ... MA
+St. Benedict, Coll. of ... MN
+St. Catherine, Coll. of ... MN
+■St. Cloud State ... MN
+□St. Lawrence U ... NY
+St. Mary's ... NC
+□St. Michael's ... VT
+□St. Olaf ... MN
+□St. Rose, Coll. of ... NY
+□St. Thomas, Coll. of ... MN
★Stanford U ... CA
+□State U. of New York (Albany, Alfred, Buffalo, Ceramics Coll., at Cornell, Cortland, Farmington, Maritime Coll., Morrisville, Oswego, Stony Brook) ... NY
+State U. of New York (Buffalo, Syracuse) ... NY
□State U. of New York (Fredonia) ... NY
+□Swarthmore ... PA
+Sweet Briar ... VA
★Syracuse U ... NY
★Temple U ... PA
★Tennessee, U. of (Knoxville) .. TN
□Tennessee State U ... TN
★Texas, U. of (Austin) ... TX
★Texas Christian U ... TX
+Texas Woman's U ... TX
+□Trinity Coll ... CT
+□Tufts U ... MA
+□U.S. Air Force Acad ... CO
+□U.S. Coast Guard Acad ... CT
+□U.S. Naval Acad ... MD
+□Ursinus ... PA
+□Utah, U. of ... UT
+□Valparaiso U ... IN
‡□Vanderbilt U ... TN
+□Vassar ... NY
★Villanova U ... PA
‡Virginia, U. of ... VA
□Virginia Military Inst ... VA
□Wabash ... IN
+□Washington & Jefferson ... PA
□Washington & Lee U ... VA
‡Washington State U ... WA
★Wayne State U ... MI
+Wellesley ... MA
+Wells ... NY
+□Wesleyan U ... CT
+□West Chester State ... PA
★Western Illinois U ... IL
+□Western Maryland ... MD
+□Western Michigan U ... MI
■Western State ... CO
+□Whitman ... WA
+□Whittier ... CA
+□Widener U ... PA
+□Willamette U ... OR
+William & Mary, Coll. of ... VA
+□William Jewell ... MO
□William Paterson ... NJ
+William Smith ... NY
‡William Woods ... MO
‡Wisconsin, U. of (Green Bay) . WI
+□Wisconsin, U. of (LaCrosse, Platteville, River Falls, Stevens Point, Whitewater) . WI
+□Wittenberg U ... OH
+□Worcester Poly. Inst ... MA
★Wright State U ... OH
+□Youngstown State U ... OH

Fencing

+Barnard ... NY
+Boston Coll ... MA
+□Brandeis U ... MA
+Caldwell ... NJ
+□California, U. of (Berkeley) ... CA
□California, U. of (Los Angeles) CA
+□California, U. of (San Diego, Santa Cruz) ... CA
+□California Inst. of Tech ... CA
+□California State U. (Fullerton) CA
+□Carnegie-Mellon U ... PA
+□Case Western Reserve U ... OH
□Chicago, U. of ... IL
+□City U. (Bernard Baruch City Coll) ... NY
★Cleveland State U ... OH
+□Colgate U ... NY
+□Cornell U ... NY
+□Detroit, U. of ... MI
+□Dominican ... CA
+□Drew U ... NJ
+□Duke U ... NC
□Fairfield U ... CT
‡Fairleigh Dickinson U ... NJ
+□Fordham U ... NY
+□George Mason ... VA
‡George Washington U ... DC
+Goucher ... MD
+□Grinnell ... IA
+□Harvard/Radcliffe ... MA
+□Haverford ... PA
+□Hofstra U ... NY
+□Holy Cross ... MA
+□Hunter Coll ... NY
★Illinois, U. of (Chicago) ... IL

■Illinois, U. of (Urbana) ... IL
+□Indiana U. of Pennsylvania ... PA
+□Iowa State U ... IA
+James Madison U ... VA
+□Jersey City State ... NJ
+□Johns Hopkins U ... MD
+□Kean Coll ... NJ
+Kemper Military ... MO
+□Lafayette ... PA
+□Lamar U ... TX
+□Lawrence U ... WI
■Linfield ... OR
+□Lynchburg ... VA
+□Macalester ... MN
+Mary Baldwin ... VA
+□Massachusetts Inst. of Tech ... MA
□Miami U ... OH
□Michigan State U ... MI
□New Jersey Inst. of Tech ... NJ
+□New York U ... NY
★North Carolina, U. of (Chapel Hill) ... NC
+□North Carolina State U ... NC
+□Northwestern U ... IL
+□Notre Dame, U. of ... IN
‡□Ohio State U ... OH
+□Pace U. (Pleasantville) ... NY
+□Pennsylvania, U. of ... PA
+□Pennsylvania State U ... PA
+□Pomona ... CA
+□Pratt Inst ... NY
□Princeton U ... NJ
+Randolph-Macon Woman's ... VA
+□Rensselaer Poly. Inst ... NY
+Rhode Island Coll ... RI
+□Ripon ... WI
□Rutgers U ... NJ
+□San Jose State U ... CA
+□Seton Hall U ... NJ
+□St. Gregory's ... OK
+□St. John's ... NM
★St. John's U ... NY
+St. Mary's ... IN
+□Stanford U ... CA
□State U. of New York (Coll. at Cornell) ... NY
+□State U. of New York (Maritime Coll.) ... NY
+□Stevens Inst. of Tech ... NJ
+Sweet Briar ... VA
★Temple U ... PA
+□Texas, U. of (Arlington) ... TX
+□Tri-State ... IN
+□Trinity Coll ... CT
+□U.S. Air Force Acad ... CO
+U.S. Merchant Marine Acad ... NY
+□U.S. Naval Acad ... MD
■Utica Coll ... NY
□Virginia Military Inst ... VA
★Wayne State U ... MI
+Wellesley ... MA
+□West Chester State ... PA
+□Western Connecticut State ... CT
+□White Plains, Coll. of ... NY
+□William & Mary, Coll. of ... VA
+□William Paterson ... NJ
‡□Wisconsin, U. of (Madison) ... WI
+□Wofford ... SC
+□Worcester Poly. Inst ... MA
+□Yale U ... CT
□Yeshiva U ... NY

Field Hockey

‡Adelphi U ... NY
+Adrian ... MI
+Agnes Scott ... GA
+Albion ... WI
+Albright ... PA
+Alma ... MI
‡American U ... DC
+Amherst ... MA
‡Appalachian State ... NC
‡Ashland Coll ... OH
+Assumption ... MA
+Averett ... VA
+Barrington ... RI
+Bates ... ME
+Beaver ... PA
+Becker Jr. Coll ... MA
‡Bemidji State ... MN
□Bentley ... MA
+Berea ... KY
+Bethany ... WV
+Bloomsburg State ... PA
+Boston Coll ... MA
+Boston U ... MA
+Bowdoin ... ME
+Brandywine ... DE
+Bridgeport, U. of ... CT
+Brown ... RI
+Bryn Mawr ... PA
‡Bucknell ... PA
‡C.W. Post ... NY
‡Cabrini ... PA
+California, U. of (Berkeley) ... CA
+□California, U. of (Davis) ... CA
+California State U. (Chico) ... CA
+Calvin ... MI
+Carleton ... MN
+Carnegie-Mellon ... PA
+Catholic U ... DC
+Cedar Crest ... PA
‡Cedarville ... OH
+Centenary ... NJ
‡Central Michigan U ... MI
+Champlain ... VT
+Chatham ... PA
+Chicago, U. of ... IL
+Cincinnati, U. of ... OH
+Clark ... MA
+Colby ... ME
+□Colgate ... NY
+College Misericordia ... PA
+Colorado State ... CO
+Concordia ... IL
+Concordia (Moorhead) ... MN
+Connecticut, U. of ... CT
+Connecticut Coll ... CT
+Cornell ... NY
+Dartmouth ... NH
+Davidson ... NC
‡Davis and Elkins ... WV
+Dayton, U. of ... OH
+Dean Jr ... MA
+Delaware, U. of ... DE
+Delaware Valley ... PA
+Denison ... OH
‡Denver, U. of ... CO
+DePauw ... IN
+Dickinson ... PA
+Drew ... NJ
‡Drexel ... PA
‡Duke ... NC
+Earlham ... IN
‡Eastern ... PA
‡Eastern Illinois ... IL
+Eastern Kentucky ... KY
+Elizabethtown ... PA
+Elms ... MA
+Endicott ... MA
+Fairfield ... CT
+Fitchburg State ... MA
+Framingham State ... MA
+Franklin ... IN
+Franklin and Marshall ... PA
+Franklin Pierce ... NH
+Frostburg State ... MD
+Georgetown U ... DC
+Gettysburg ... PA
+Glassboro State ... NJ
‡Gordon ... MA
+Goshen ... IN
+Goucher ... MD
+Green Mountain ... VT
+Grinnell ... IA
+Gwynedd-Mercy ... PA
+Hamilton ... NY
+Hanover ... IN
+Harcum Jr ... PA
+Harvard/Radcliffe ... MA
+Haverford ... PA
+High Point ... NC
+Hiram ... OH
+Hofstra ... NY
+Hollins ... VA
+Holy Cross ... MA
+Hood ... MD
+Hope ... MI
+Houghton ... NY
+Immaculata ... PA
+Indiana State ... IN
+Indiana U. (Bloomington) ... IN
+Indiana U. of Pa ... PA
‡Iowa, U. of ... IA
‡Iowa Wesleyan ... IA
‡Ithaca ... NY
‡James Madison ... VA
+Johns Hopkins ... MD
+Johnson State ... VT
+Judson ... AL
+Juniata ... PA
+Kalamazoo ... MI
+Kean ... NJ
+Keene ... NH
‡Kent State ... OH
+Kenyon ... OH
+Keystone Jr ... PA
‡King's Coll ... NY
+□Kutztown ... PA
+La Salle ... PA
+Lafayette ... PA
+Lake Erie ... OH
+Lake Forest ... IL
+Lebanon Valley ... PA
+Lehigh ... PA
+Lock Haven State ... PA
‡Longwood ... VA
‡Louisville, U. of ... KY
+Lowell, U. of ... MA
‡Loyola ... MD
+Luther ... IA
+Lynchburg ... VA
+Lyndon State ... VT
+Maine, U. of (Farmington, Presque Isle) ... ME
‡Maine, U. of (Orono) ... ME
+Manhattanville ... NY
+Marietta ... OH
+Mary Washington ... VA
+Maryland, U. of (College Park) MD
‡Marywood ... PA
+Massachusetts, U. of ... MA
+Massachusetts Inst. of Tech ... MA
+Messiah ... PA
‡Miami U ... OH
‡Michigan, U. of ... MI
‡Michigan State ... MI
+Middlebury ... VT
+Minnesota-Twin Cities, U. of ... MN
+Mitchell ... CT
+Mohawk Valley Comm. Coll ... NY
+Monmouth ... NJ
+Moorhead State ... MN
+Moravian ... PA
+Mount Holyoke ... MA
+Mount St. Mary's ... MD
+Mount Vernon ... DC
+Muhlenberg ... PA
+Muskingum ... OH
+New England Coll ... NH
+New Hampshire, U. of ... NH
+New Hamshire Coll ... NH
□Nichols ... MA
+North Adams State ... MA
‡North Carolina, U. of (Chapel Hill) ... NC
‡Northeast Missouri State ... MO
+Northeastern ... MA
‡Northern Illinois ... IL
‡Northern Iowa, U. of ... IA
‡Northern Michigan ... MI
+Northwestern ... IL
+Norwich U./Vermont Coll ... VT
+Notre Dame ... IN
+Oberlin ... OH
‡Ohio State U ... OH
+Ohio U ... OH
+Ohio Wesleyan ... OH
‡Oklahoma, U. of ... OK
‡Old Dominion ... VA
+Olivet ... MI
‡Pacific, U. of the ... CA
+Pennsylvania, U. of ... PA
‡Pennsylvania State U ... PA
‡Pfeiffer ... NC
+Philadelphia Coll. of Textiles and Science ... PA
+Pine Manor ... MA
‡Pittsburgh, U. of (Pittsburgh) . PA
+Plymouth State ... NH
+Princeton ... NJ
+Principia ... IL
‡Providence ... RI
‡Purdue ... IN
+Radford ... VA
+Ramapo ... NJ
‡Randolph-Macon ... VA
+Randolph-Macon Woman's ... VA
+Rensselaer ... NY
‡Rhode Island, U. of ... RI
‡Richmond, U. of ... VA
‡Rider ... NJ
+Rivier ... NH
+Roanoke ... VA
+Rochester, U. of ... NY
+Rosemont ... PA
+Russell Sage ... NY
+Rutgers U ... NJ
+Salem State ... MA
+Salisbury State ... MD
+San Jose State ... CA
+Scranton, U. of ... PA
‡Shippensburg ... PA
+Siena ... NY
+Simmons ... MA
+Skidmore ... NY
‡Slippery Rock ... PA
+Smith ... MA
+South, U. of the ... TN
+South Dakota State ... SD
‡Southern Illinois ... IL
‡Southwest Missouri State ... MO
+Springfield ... MA
+St. Bonaventure ... NY
□St. John Fisher ... NY
‡St. Joseph's ... PA
+St. Lawrence ... NY
+St. Michael's ... VT
‡Stanford ... CA
+State U. of New York (Brockport, Buffalo, Cobleskill, Coll. at Cornell, Cortland, Delhi, Env. Sci. & Forestry, Oneonta, Oswego, Plattsburgh, Potsdam) ... NY
+Susquehanna ... PA
+Swarthmore ... PA
‡Syracuse ... NY
+Taylor ... IN
‡Temple ... PA
‡Towson State ... MD
+Transylvania ... KY
+Trenton State ... NJ
+Trinity ... CT
+Union ... NY
+Ursinus ... PA
+Valparaiso ... IN
+Vassar ... NY
+Vermont, U. of ... VT
‡Villanova ... PA
‡Virginia, U. of ... VA
+Virginia Commonwealth ... VA
+Washington and Jefferson ... PA
‡Washington State ... WA

+Wellesley ... MA
+Wells ... NY
+Wesley ... DE
+Wesleyan ... CT
+West Chester State ... PA
‡West Virginia Wesleyan ... WV
+Western Connecticut State ... CT
‡Western Illinois ... IL
+Western Maryland ... MD
+Western Michigan ... MI
+Western New England ... MA
+Western Washington ... WA
+Westminster ... PA
+Wheaton ... MA
+□Wheelock ... MA
+□Widener ... PA
+Wilkes ... PA
+William and Mary, Coll. of ... VA
+William Paterson ... NJ
+William Smith ... NY
+Williams ... MA
+Wilson ... PA
+Wisconsin, U. of (Green Bay, Oshkosh, River Falls, Stevens Point) ... WI
‡Wisconsin, U. of (Madison) ... WI
+Wittenberg ... OH
+Wooster ... OH
+Worcester Poly. Inst ... MA
+Worcester State ... MA
+Yale ... CT
+York Coll. of Pennsylvania ... PA
+Youngstown State ... OH

Figure Skating

+□Colgate U ... NY
+□Dartmouth ... NH
+□St. Lawrence U ... NY

Football

■Abilene Christian ... TX
□Adams State ... CO
□Adrian ... MI
□Akron, U. of ... OH
■Alabama, U. of (University) ... AL
□Alabama A&M ... AL
□Alabama State U ... AL
□Albion ... MI
□Albright ... PA
□Alfred U ... NY
□Allegheny ... PA
□Alma ... MI
□American International ... MA
□Amherst ... MA
□Anderson ... IN
■Angelo State ... TX
■Appalachian State ... NC
■Arizona, U. of ... AZ
■Arizona State U ... AZ
■Arizona Western ... AZ
□Arkansas, U. of (Fayetteville, Monticello) ... AR
■Arkansas State ... AR
■Arkansas Tech ... AR
■Ashland ... OH
□Assumption ... MA
■Auburn U ... AL
□Augsburg ... MN
□Augustana ... SD
■Augustana ... MS
□Austin ... TX
■Austin Peay ... TN
■Azusa Pacific ... CA
■Baker U ... KS
□Baldwin-Wallace ... OH
■Ball State ... IN
□Baptist Christian ... LA
□Bates ... ME
■Baylor ... TX
□Beloit ... WI
■Bemidji State ... MN
■Benedictine ... KS
□Bentley ... MA
□Bethany ... KS
□Bethany ... WV
□Bethel ... KS
□Bethel ... MN
□Bethune-Cookman ... FL
■Bismarck Jr ... ND
■Black Hills State ... SD
■Blinn ... TX
■Bloomsburg State ... PA
□Bluffton ... OH
□Boise State U ... ID
■Boston Coll ... MA
■Boston U ... MA
□Bowdoin ... ME
□Bowie State ... MD
□Bowling Green State ... OH
□Bridgewater State ... MA
□Brown U ... RI
■Bucknell U ... PA
□Buena Vista ... IA
□Butler U ... IN
■C.W. Post ... NY
□California, U. of (Davis, Los Angeles) ... CA
□California Inst. of Tech ... CA
□California Lutheran ... CA
□California State Coll ... PA
■California State Poly. U ... CA
□California State U. (Bakersfield, Hayward) ... CA
■California State U. (Fresno) ... CA
+□California State U. (Fullerton) CA
■Cameron U ... OK
□Canisius ... NY
□Capital U ... OH
□Carleton ... MN
□Carnegie-Mellon U ... PA
■Carroll ... MT
□Carroll ... WI
■Carson-Newman ... TN
□Carthage ... WI
□Case Western Reserve ... OH
□Cathedral ... NY
□Catholic U. of America ... DC
□Central ... IA
□Central Arkansas, U. of ... AR
■Central Florida, U. of ... FL
□Central Methodist ... MO
■Central Michigan U ... MI
■Central Missouri ... MO
★Central State U ... OK
□Central Washington U ... WA
■Chadron State ... NE
□Cheyney State ... PA
□Chicago, U. of ... IL
■Chowan ... NC
■Cincinnati, U. of ... OH
□Citadel, The ... SC
□Claremont-McKenna ... CA
□Clarion State ... PA
□Coe ... IA
□Coffeyville Comm ... KS
□Colby ... ME
□Colgate U ... NY
■Colorado, U. of ... CO
□Colorado Coll ... CO
■Colorado Sch. of Mines ... CO
+□Colorado State U ... CO
■Concord ... WV
□Concordia ... IL
□Concordia (Moorhead) ... MN
■Concordia (St. Paul) ... MN
■Concordia Teachers ... NE
■Connecticut, U. of ... CT
□Cornell Coll ... IA
□Cornell U ... NY
□Cowley Co. Comm ... KS
□Curry ... MA
■Dakota State ... SD
□Dakota Wesleyan U ... SD
■Dana ... NE
□Dartmouth ... NH
□Davidson ... NC
□Dayton, U. of ... OH
□Dean Jr ... MA
□Defiance ... OH
□Delaware, U. of ... DE
□Delware Valley ... PA
□Delta State U ... MS
□Denison U ... OH
□DePauw U ... IN
□Dickinson ... PA
■Dickinson State ... ND
+□Dixie ... UT
□Dr. Martin Luther ... MN
■Drake U ... IA
□Dubuque, U. of ... IA
■Duke U ... NC
□Duquesne U ... PA
□Earlham ... IN
■East Carolina U ... NC
□East Central Jr ... MS
■East Central Oklahoma ... OK
□East Tennessee State U ... TN
■Eastern Arizona ... AZ
■Eastern Illinois U ... IL
□Eastern Kentucky U ... KY
■Eastern New Mexico U ... NM
□Eastern Oregon State ... OR
□Eastern Washington U ... WA
□Edinboro State ... PA
□Elmhurst ... IL
■Elon ... NC
□Emory & Henry ... VA
■Emporia State U ... KS
□Eureka ... IL
■Evangel ... MO
■Evansville, U. of ... IN
□Fairfield U ... CT
■Fairmont State ... WV
■Fayetteville State U ... NC
□Ferrum ... VA
□Findlay ... OH
□Fisk U ... TN
□Fitchburg State ... MA
■Florida, U. of ... FL
■Florida A&M U ... FL
■Florida State U ... FL
□Fordham U ... NY
■Fort Hays State U ... KS
■Fort Lewis ... CO
■Fort Scott Comm ... KS
□Framingham State ... MA
□Franklin ... IN
□Franklin & Marshall ... PA
■Friends U ... KS
□Frostburg State ... MD
■Furman U ... SC
□Gallaudet ... DC
■Gardner-Webb ... NC
■Geneva ... PA
■Georgetown ... KY
■Georgetown U ... DC
■Georgia, U. of ... GA
■Georgia Inst. of Tech ... GA
□Georgia Southern ... GA
□Gettysburg ... PA
□Glassboro State ... NJ
★Glenville State ... WV
■Golden Valley Lutheran ... MN
□Grand Valley State ... MI
+□Grinnell ... IA
□Grove City ... PA
■Guilford ... NC
□Gustavus Adolphus ... MN
□Hamilton ... NY
□Hamline U ... MN
□Hampden-Sydney ... VA
□Hampton Inst ... VA
□Hanover ... IN
■Harding U ... AR
□Harvard/Radcliffe ... MA
□Harvey Mudd ... CA
■Hastings ... NE
□Hawaii, U. of ... HI
□Heidelberg ... OH
■Henderson State U ... AR
■Highland Comm ... KS
■Hillsdale ... MI
□Hiram ... OH
□Hobart ... NY
□Hofstra U ... NY
■Holy Cross ... MA
□Hope ... MI
■Howard Payne U ... TX
■Howard U ... DC
□Humboldt State U ... CA
■Huron ... SD
■Hutchinson Comm ... KS
■Idaho, U. of ... ID
□Idaho State U ... ID
■Illinois, U. of (Champaign) ... IL
□Illinois Benedictine ... IL
□Illinois Coll ... IL
■Illinois State U ... IL
□Illinois Wesleyan ... IL
■Independent Comm ... KS
■Indiana Central U ... IN
■Indiana State U. (Terre Haute) IN
■Indiana U. (Bloomington) ... IN
■Indiana U. of Pennsylvania ... PA
□Iona ... NY
■Iowa, U. of ... IA
■Iowa State U ... IA
■Iowa Wesleyan ... IA
□Ithaca ... NY
■Jackson State U ... MS
■Jacksonville State U ... AL
■James Madison U ... VA
■Jamestown ... ND
□Jersey City State ... NJ
□John Carroll ... OH
□Johns Hopkins U ... MD
□Juniata ... PA
□Kalamazoo ... MI
■Kansas, U. of ... KS
■Kansas State U ... KS
□Kansas Wesleyan ... KS
□Kean ... NJ
□Kearney State ... NE
■Kent State U ... OH
■Kentucky, U. of ... KY
□Kenyon ... OH
□Knox ... IL
□Kutztown State ... PA
□Lafayette ... PA
□Lake Forest ... IL
□Lakeland ... WI
□Lamar U ... TX
■Langston U ... OK
□Lawrence U ... WI
□Lebanon Valley ... PA
■Lees-McRae ... NC
□Lehigh U ... PA
■Lenoir-Rhyne ... NC
□Lewis & Clark ... OR
■Liberty Baptist ... VA
□Lincoln U ... PA
■Lincoln U ... MO
■Livingston ... AL
■Livingstone ... NC
□Lock Haven State ... PA
□Loras ... IA
■Louisiana State U ... LA
□Louisiana Tech. U ... LA
■Louisville, U. of ... KY
□Lowell, U. of ... MA
□Lubbock Christian ... TX
□Luther ... IA
□Lycoming ... PA
□Macalester ... MN
■Maine, U. of (Orono) ... ME
□Maine Maritime Acad ... ME
□Manchester ... IN
□Manhattan ... NY
■Mankato ... MN
□Mansfield State ... PA
□Marietta ... OH
■Marion Military Inst ... AL

□Marist ... NY
□Maryland, U. of ... MD
□Maryville ... TN
■Massachusetts, U. of ... MA
□Massachusetts Maritime ... MA
■Mayville State ... ND
□McMurry ... TX
□McNeese State U ... LA
□McPherson ... KS
■Memphis State ... TN
■Menlo ... CA
□Mercyhurst ... PA
■Mesa ... CO
□Miami, U. of ... FL
■Miami U ... OH
■Michigan, U. of ... MI
■Michigan State U ... MI
□Michigan Tech. U ... MI
■Mid-American Nazarene ... KS
■Middle Tennessee State U ... TN
□Middlebury ... VT
■Midland Lutheran ... NE
□Miles ... AL
□Millersville State ... PA
□Millikin U ... IL
□Millsaps ... MS
□Minnesota, U. of (Twin Cities) MN
+□Minnesota, U. of, Tech. Coll .. MN
□Mississippi, U. of ... MS
■Mississippi Coll ... MS
■Mississippi Delta Jr ... MS
■Mississippi Valley State U ... MS
■Missouri, U. of (Columbia) ... MO
■Missouri, U. of (Rolla) ... MO
■Missouri Southern State ... MO
■Missouri Valley ... MO
■Missouri Western State ... MO
□Mobile ... AL
□Monmouth ... IL
□Montana, U. of ... MT
■Montana Coll. of Mineral Sci . MT
□Montana State U ... MT
□Moorhead State ... MN
□Moravian ... PA
■Morehead State ... KY
□Morehouse ... GA
■Morgan State U ... MD
■Morningside ... IA
■Mount Senario ... WI
□Mount Union ... OH
□Muhlenberg ... PA
□Murray State U ... KY
□Muskingum ... OH
■Navarro ... TX
■Nebraska, U. of (Lincoln) ... NE
□Nebraska Wesleyan U ... NE
■Nevada, U. of (Las Vegas, Reno) ... NV
□Newberry ... SC
□New Hampshire, U. of ... NH
■New Haven, U. of ... CT
■New Mexico, U. of ... NM
■New MexicoMilitary Inst ... NM
■New Mexico State U ... NM
■Nicholls State U ... LA
□Nichols ... MA
□Norfolk State U ... VA
■North Alabama, U. of ... AL
■North Carolina, U. of (Chapel Hill) ... NC
□North Carolina A&T State U .. NC
□North Carolina Central U ... NC
■North Carolina State U ... NC
□North Central ... IL
■North Dakota State Sch. of Sci ND
■North Dakota State U ... ND
□North Park ... IL
■North Texas State ... TX
■Northeast Louisiana U ... LA
★Northeast Mississippi Jr ... MS
■Northeast Missouri State ... MO
□Northeastern Oklahoma State U ... OK
□Northeastern U ... MA

■Northern Arizona U ... AZ
■Northern Colorado, U. of ... CO
■Northern Illinois U ... IL
■Northern Iowa, U. of ... IA
■Northwest Missouri State ... MO
■Northwestern ... IA
■Northwestern Oklahoma State U ... OK
■Northwestern State U ... LA
□Northwestern U ... IL
■Northwood Inst ... MI
□Norwich U./Vermont Coll ... VT
■Notre Dame, U. of ... IN
□Oberlin ... OH
□Occidental ... CA
□Ohio Northern U ... OH
■Ohio State U ... OH
□Ohio U ... OH
□Ohio Wesleyan U ... OH
■Oklahoma Panhandle State U OK
■Oklahoma State U ... OK
□Olivet ... MI
■Oregon, U. of ... OR
□Oregon Inst. of Tech ... OR
□Oregon State U ... OR
■Ottawa U ... KS
□Otterbein ... OH
□Pace U. (Pleasantville) ... NY
■Pacific, U. of the ... CA
■Pacific Lutheran U ... WA
□Pacific U ... OR
□Panama Canal Coll ... Panama
□Pearl River Jr ... MS
□Pennsylvania, U. of ... PA
■Pennsylvania State U ... PA
□Peru State ... NE
■Pittsburg State ... KS
■Pittsburgh, U. of ... PA
□Pitzer ... CA
□Plymouth State ... NH
□Pomona ... CA
□Potomac State ... WV
■Praire View A&M U ... TX
□Pratt Comm. Jr ... KS
■Presbyterian ... SC
□Princeton U ... NJ
□Principia ... IL
■Puget Sound, U. of ... WA
■Purdue U ... IN
□Ramapo ... NJ
□Randolph-Macon ... VA
□Redlands, U. of ... CA
□Rensselaer Poly. Inst ... NY
■Rhode Island, U. of ... RI
■Rice U ... TX
■Richmond, U. of ... VA
□Ripon ... WI
□Rochester, U. of ... NY
■Rocky Mountain ... MT
□Roger Williams ... RI
■Rutgers U ... NJ
■Saginaw Valley State ... MI
■Saint Mary of the Plains ... KS
□Saint Norbert ... WI
■Salem ... WV
□Salisbury State ... MD
■Sam Houston State ... TX
□San Diego, U. of ... CA
■San Diego State U ... CA
□San Jose State U ... CA
■Santa Clara, U. of ... CA
+□Shepherd ... WV
■Shippensburg State ... PA
□Siena ... NY
□Simpson ... IA
■Sioux Falls ... SD
■Slippery Rock State ... PA
□Snow ... UT
□Sonoma State ... CA
+□South, U. of the ... TN
■South Carolina, U. of ... SC
□South Carolina State ... SC
■South Dakota, U. of ... SD
□South Dakota Sch. of Mines .. SD

■South Dakota State U ... SD
■Southeast Missouri State ... MO
■Southeastern Louisiana ... LA
■Southeastern Oklahoma State OK
■Southern Arkansas U ... AR
■Southern Colorado, U. of ... CO
■Southern Illinois U ... IL
■Southern Methodist U ... TX
■Southern Mississippi, U. of ... MS
□Southern Oregon State ... OR
□Southwest Mississippi Jr ... MS
■Southwest Missouri State ... MO
■Southwest Texas State U ... TX
■Southwest State U ... MN
■Southwestern ... KS
□Southwestern at Memphis ... TN
■Southwestern Oklahoma State U ... OK
□Springfield ... MS
□St. Ambrose ... IA
■St. Cloud State U ... MN
□St. Francis ... PA
□St. John Fisher ... NY
□St. John's U ... MN
■St. John's U ... NY
■St. Joseph's ... IN
□St. Lawrence U ... NY
■St. Mary's ... CA
□St. Olaf ... MN
□St. Thomas, Coll. of ... MN
■Stanford U ... CA
□State U. of New York (Albany, Brockport, Buffalo, Coll. at Buffalo, Coll. of Ceramics, Coll. of Forestry, Cortland, Maritime Coll.) ... NY
+□State U. of New York Coll. at Cornell ... NY
■Stephen F. Austin ... TX
■Sterling ... KS
□Stonehill ... MA
□Sul Ross State U ... TX
□Susquehanna U ... PA
□Swarthmore ... PA
■Syracuse U ... NY
■Tabor ... KS
■Tarkio ... MO
□Taylor U ... IN
■Temple U ... PA
□Tennessee, U. of (Chattanooga) ... TN
■Tennessee, U. of (Knoxville, Martin) ... TN
□Tennessee State U ... TN
□Tennessee Tech. U ... TN
■Texas, U. of (Arlington, Austin, El Paso) ... TX
□Texas A&I U ... TX
■Texas A&M U ... TX
■Texas Christian U ... TX
■Texas Lutheran ... TX
□Thiel ... PA
■Toledo, U. of ... OH
■Towson State U ... MD
□Trenton State ... NJ
□Trinity ... CT
■Troy State U ... AL
□Tufts U ... MA
■Tulane U ... LA
■Tulsa, U. of ... OK
□Tuskegee Inst ... AL
□U.S. Air Force Acad ... CO
□U.S. Coast Guard Acad ... CT
□U.S. Merchant Marine Acad .. NY
■U.S. Military Acad ... NY
□U.S. Naval Acad ... MD
□Union ... NY
□Upper Iowa ... IA
□Upsala ... NJ
□Ursinus ... PA
□Utah, U. of ... UT
■Utah State U ... UT
□Valparaiso U ... IN
■Vanderbilt U ... TN

■Virginia, U. of ... VA
■Virginia Military ... VA
■Virginia Poly. Inst ... VA
□Virginia State ... VA
□Wabash ... IN
□Wagner ... NY
■Wake Forest U ... NC
□Waldorf ... IA
□Wartburg ... IA
□Washburn U ... KS
□Washington, U. of ... WA
□Washington & Jefferson ... PA
□Washington & Lee ... VA
■Washington State U ... WA
□Washington U ... MO
■Wayne State ... MI
■Wayne State ... NE
■Waynesburg ... PA
■Weber State ... UT
□Wesley ... DE
□Wesleyan U ... CT
□West Chester State ... PA
□West Georgia ... GA
□West Liberty State ... WV
■West Texas State U ... TX
■West Virginia Inst. of Tech ... WV
□West Virginia State ... WV
■West Virginia U ... WV
■West Virginia Wesleyan ... WV
■Western Carolina U ... NC
□Western Connecticut State ... CT
■Western Illinois U ... IL
■Western Kentucky ... KY
□Western Maryland ... MD
□Western Michigan U ... MI
□Western Montana ... MT
□Western New England ... MA
■Western New Mexico ... NM
□Western Oregon ... OR
■Western State ... CO
□Western Washington U ... WA
■Westmar ... IA
□Westminster ... PA
■Wharton Co. Jr ... TX
□Wheaton ... IL
□White Plains, Coll. of ... NY
□Whittier ... CA
■Whitworth ... WA
+□Wichita State ... KS
□Widener U ... PA
□Wilkes ... PA
□Willamette U ... OR
□William & Mary, Coll. of ... VA
□William Jewell ... MO
□William Paterson ... NJ
□William Penn ... IA
□Williams Coll ... MA
□Wilmington ... OH
■Winona State ... MN
□Wisconsin, U. of (Eau Claire, La Crosse, Oshkosh, Platteville, River Falls, Stevens Point, Stout, Superior, Whitewater) ... WI
■Wisconsin, U. of (Madison) ... WI
□Wittenberg U ... OH
■Wofford ... SC
□Wooster, Coll. of ... OH
□Worcester Poly. Inst ... MA
□Worthington Comm ... MN
□Wyoming, U. of ... WY
■Yakima Valley Comm ... WA
■Yankton ... SD
□Yale U ... CT
+□York ... NE
■Youngstown State ... OH

Golf

■Abilene Christian ... TX
□Adams State ... CO
□Adrian ... MI

□Akron, U. of ... OH
■Alabama, U. of (Birmingham) . AL
★Alabama, U. of (University) ... AL
+□Alabama A&M U ... AL
□Albion ... MI
□Albright ... PA
□Allegheny ... PA
□Alma ... MI
□American International ... MA
□American U ... DC
+□Amherst ... MA
□Anderson ... IN
■Angelo State ... TX
□Anna Maria ... MA
★Appalachian State ... NC
□Aquinas ... MI
★Arizona State U ... AZ
■Arizona Western ... AZ
□Arkansas, U. of (Monticello) .. AR
■Arkansas State U ... AR
□Arkansas Tech ... AR
□Ashland ... OH
+□Assumption ... MA
□Atlantic Christian ... NC
■Auburn U ... AL
+□Augsburg ... MN
□Augustana ... IL
■Augustana ... SD
+□Aurora ... IL
+□Austin ... TX
★Austin Peay ... TN
□Averett ... VA
□Babson ... MA
■Baker U ... KS
□Baldwin-Wallace ... OH
+□Ball State ... IN
+□Baptist Christian ... LA
+□Barton Co. Comm ... KS
□Bates ... ME
■Baylor ... TX
+□Beaver ... PA
■Bellarmine ... KY
□Belmont Abbey ... NC
+□Beloit ... WI
■Bemidji State U ... MN
□Benedictine ... KS
□Bentley ... MA
□Berea ... KY
+□Bethany ... KS
+□Bethany ... WV
■Bethany Nazarene ... OK
□Bethel ... IN
□Bethel ... MN
■Bethel ... TN
□Bethune-Cookman ... FL
★Biscayne ... FL
★Bismarck Jr ... ND
+□Black Hills State ... SD
□Bloomsburg State ... PA
□Bluefield ... VA
□Bluffton ... OH
+□Boston Coll ... MA
+□Bowdoin ... ME
+□Bowling Green State U ... OH
■Bradley U ... IL
□Brandeis ... MA
□Brandywine ... DE
+□Brevard ... NC
★Briar Cliff ... IA
□Bridgeport, U. of ... CT
□Bridgewater State ... MA
□Brown U ... RI
+□Bryant ... RI
■Bucknell U ... PA
+□Buena Vista ... IA
□Butler U ... IN
□C.W. Post of Long Island U .. NY
+■California, U. of (Berkeley) ... CA
□California, U. of (Davis, Riverside) ... CA
■California, U. of (Irvine) ... CA
+□California, U. of (Los Angeles, San Diego, Santa Barbara) . CA
□California Inst. of Tech ... CA
□California Lutheran ... CA
+□California State Coll ... PA
■California State U. (Fresno) .. CA
+□California State U. (Fullerton) CA
□Calvin ... MI
■Cameron U ... OK
■Campbell U ... NC
■Campbellsville ... KY
+□Canisius ... NY
□Capital U ... OH
□Carleton ... MN
□Carnegie-Mellon U ... PA
□Carroll ... WI
■Carson-Newman ... TN
□Case Western Reserve U ... OH
□Casper ... WY
■Cedarville ... OH
■Centenary ... LA
+□Central ... IA
□Central Arkansas, U. of ... AR
★Central Florida, U. of ... FL
+□Central Methodist ... MO
■Central Michigan U ... MI
■Central Missouri ... MO
★Central State U ... OK
□Central Washington U ... WA
□Central Wesleyan ... SC
+□Central Wyoming ... WY
□Chaminade ... HI
■Charleston, Coll. of ... SC
★Chowan ... NC
★Cincinnati, U. of ... OH
□Citadel, The ... SC
□Claremont-McKenna ... CA
□Clarion State ... PA
□Clark U ... MA
□Clarkson ... NY
■Cleveland State U ... OH
+□Coe ... IA
+□Coffeyville Comm ... KS
□Colby ... ME
□Colgate U ... NY
■Colorado, U. of ... CO
□Colorado Coll ... CO
★Colorado Sch. of Mines ... CO
+□Colorado State U ... CO
□Concord ... WV
+□Concordia (Moorhead) ... MN
+□Concordia (St. Paul) ... MN
+□Concordia Teachers ... NE
□Connecticut, U. of ... CT
+□Cornell Coll ... IA
□Cornell U ... NY
+□Creighton U ... NE
+□Cumberland ... KY
+□Dakota State ... SD
+□Dakota Wesleyan ... SD
□Dallas, U. of ... TX
★Dana ... NE
+□Dartmouth ... NH
■David Lipscomb ... TN
□Davidson ... NC
■Davis & Elkins ... WV
□Dayton, U. of ... OH
□Defiance ... OH
+□Delaware, U. of ... DE
□Delaware Valley ... PA
□Delta State ... MS
□Denison U ... OH
+□DePauw U ... IN
□Detroit, U. of ... MI
□Dickinson ... PA
□Dickinson State ... ND
+□Dixie ... UT
□Dordt ... IA
□Dr. Martin Luther ... MN
+□Drake U ... IA
■Drexel U ... PA
■Drury ... MO
+□Dubuque, U. of ... IA
★Duke U ... NC
■Duquesne U ... PA
+□Earlham ... IN
★East Carolina U ... NC
+□East Central Jr ... MS
■East Central Oklahoma State . OK
□East Tennessee State ... TN
□Eastern Connecticut State ... CT
□Eastern Illinois U ... IL
□Eastern Kentucky U ... KY
+□Eastern Montana ... MT
★Eastern New Mexico U ... NM
□Eastern Washington U ... WA
+□Eckerd ... FL
□Elmhurst ... IL
+□Elmira ... NY
■Elon ... NC
■Emporia State U ... KS
■Erskine ... SC
+□Eureka ... IL
★Evansville, U. of ... IN
□Fairfield U ... CT
□Fairleigh Dickinson U ... NJ
■Fairmont ... WV
□Fayetteville State U ... NC
★Ferris State U ... MI
□Ferrum ... VA
□Findlay ... OH
+□Fisk U ... TN
□Fitchburg ... MA
■Flagler ... FL
★Florida, U. of ... FL
★Florida A&M U ... FL
★Florida Atlantic U ... FL
□Florida Coll ... FL
□Florida Inst. of Tech ... FL
■Florida Southern ... FL
★Florida State U ... FL
+□Fordham U ... NY
□Fort Hays State U ... KS
□Fort Lewis ... CO
+□Franklin ... IN
+□Franklin & Marshall ... PA
□Franklin Pierce ... NH
□Freed-Hardeman ... TN
★Furman U ... SC
□Gallaudet ... DC
■Gannon U ... PA
■Gardner-Webb ... NC
□George Mason U ... VA
■George Washington U ... DC
■Georgetown ... KY
□Georgetown U ... DC
★Georgia, U. of ... GA
■Georgia Inst. of Tech ... GA
□Georgia Southern ... GA
★Georgia State U ... GA
+□Gettysburg ... PA
□Glassboro State ... NJ
★Glenville State ... WV
□Gonzaga U ... WA
□Goshen ... IN
■Grace ... IN
■Grand Canyon ... AZ
■Grand View ... IA
□Greensboro ... NC
□Greenville ... IL
+□Grinnell ... IA
□Grove City ... PA
■Guilford ... NC
+□Gustavus Adolphus ... MN
□Hamilton ... NY
□Hamline U ... MN
□Hampden-Sydney ... VA
+□Hanover ... IN
□Hardin-Simmons U ... TX
□Harding U ... AR
■Hartford, U. of ... CT
+□Harvard/Radcliffe ... MA
□Harvey Mudd ... CA
★Hastings ... NE
+□Hawaii, U. of ... HI
□Henderson State U ... AR
+□Hendrix ... AR
□High Point ... NC
□Hillsdale ... MI
□Hiram ... OH
□Hobart ... NY
□Holy Cross ... MA
+□Hope ... MI
■Howard Payne U ... TX
+■Huntingdon ... AL
★Husson ... ME
■Hutchinson Comm ... KS
■Idaho, U. of ... ID
□Idaho State U ... ID
★Illinois, U. of (Champaign) ... IL
□Illinois Benedictine ... IL
□Illinois Coll ... IL
+■Illinois Inst. of Tech ... IL
★Illinois State U ... IL
□Illinois Wesleyan U ... IL
□Indiana Central U ... IN
★Indiana U. (Bloomington) ... IN
+□Iona ... NY
★Iowa, U. of ... IA
★Iowa State U ... IA
★Iowa Wesleyan ... IA
□Ithaca ... NY
■Jackson State U ... MS
□Jacksonville ... TX
■Jacksonville State U ... AL
■Jacksonville U ... FL
★James Madison U ... VA
■Jamestown ... ND
□John Carroll U ... OH
□Johns Hopkins U ... MD
+□Juniata ... PA
□Kalamazoo ... MI
★Kansas, U. of ... KS
★Kansas State U ... KS
□Kean Coll ... NJ
□Kearney State ... NE
+□Kemper Military ... MO
■Kent State U ... OH
★Kentucky, U. of ... KY
□Kenyon ... OH
□King's ... PA
+□Knox ... IL
□La Salle ... PA
□Lafayette ... PA
□Lamar U ... TX
+□Lawrence Inst. of Tech ... MI
+□Lawrence U ... WI
■Le Moyne ... NY
□Lebanon Valley ... PA
□Lee ... TN
□Lehigh U ... PA
■Lenoir-Rhyne ... NC
□Lewis & Clark ... OR
□Lewis U ... IL
■Limestone ... SC
□Lincoln Memorial ... TN
■Lincoln U ... MO
□Lindenwood Colleges ... MO
★Linfield ... OR
□Livingston ... AL
★Livingstone ... NC
□Lock Haven State ... PA
□Lon Morris ... TX
□Long Island U. (Southampton) ... NY
‡□Longwood ... VA
+□Loras ... IA
■Louisburg ... NC
★Louisiana State U. (Baton Rouge) ... LA
□Louisiana Tech. U ... LA
■Louisville, U. of ... KY
□Lowell, U. of ... MA
□Loyola ... IL
□Loyola ... MD
+□Loyola Marymount U ... CA
□Luther ... IA
+□Lycoming ... PA
□Lynchburg ... VA
□Macalester ... MN
+□MacMurray ... IL
□Maine, U. of (Orono) ... ME
■Malone ... OH
□Manchester ... IN
□Manhattan ... NY

★Mankato State ... MN
‡□Marian ... IN
+□Marian Coll. of Fond du Lac .. WI
□Marietta ... OH
■Marion Military ... AL
■Marquette U ... WI
□Mary-Hardin Baylor, U. of ... TX
+□Mary Washington ... VA
□Maryland, U. of ... MD
+□Marymount ... KS
+□Massachusetts, U. of ... MA
□Massachusetts Inst. of Tech .. MA
+□Massachusetts Maritime ... MA
+□McKendree ... IL
+□McMurry ... TX
□McNeese State U ... LA
□McPherson ... KS
★Memphis State U ... TN
+■Menlo ... CA
+■Mercyhurst ... PA
+Meredith ... NC
□Methodist ... NC
+□Miami, U. of ... FL
+■Miami U ... OH
★Michigan, U. of ... MI
★Michigan State U ... MI
□Middlebury ... VT
■Middle Tennessee State U ... TN
★Midland Lutheran ... NE
□Millersville State ... PA
□Millikin U ... IL
□Milwaukee Sch. of Engr ... WI
+□Minnesota, U. of, Tech. Coll .. WI
□Mississippi, U. of ... MS
■Mississippi Coll ... MS
■Mississippi Delta Jr ... MS
■Mississippi Valley State U ... MS
□Missouri, U. of (Kansas City) . MO
★Missouri, U. of (Rolla) ... MO
★Missouri Valley ... MO
■Missouri Western State ... MO
+□Mohawk Valley Comm ... NY
□Monmouth ... IL
□Monmouth ... NJ
■Montana, U. of ... MT
■Montevallo, U. of ... AL
+□Moorhead State U ... MN
□Moravian ... PA
+■Morehead State U ... KY
+□Morningside ... IA
+Mount Holyoke ... MA
□Mount Marty ... SD
+□Mount Mercy ... IA
+□Mount Union ... OH
□Mt. St. Mary's ... MD
□Muhlenberg ... PA
+Murray State U ... KY
+□Muskingum ... OH
+□Nazareth Coll ... NY
+□Nebraska, U. of (Lincoln) ... NE
+□Nebraska Wesleyan U ... NE
★Nebraska Western ... NE
★Nevada, U. of
(Las Vegas, Reno) ... NV
+□New England ... NH
□New Hampshire, U. of ... NH
★New Mexico, U. of ... NM
■New Mexico Military ... NM
■New Mexico State U ... NM
■New Orleans, U. of ... LA
□New York U ... NY
□Niagara U ... NY
+□Nichols ... MA
■Nicholls State U ... LA
+□North Adams State ... MA
■North Alabama, U. of ... AL
★North Carolina, U. of
(Chapel Hill, Wilmington) .. NC
□North Carolina, U. of
(Greensboro) ... NC
+■North Carolina State U ... NC
□North Carolina Wesleyan ... NC
□North Central ... IL
★North Dakota State Sch ... ND

□North Dakota State U ... ND
□North Park ... IL
■North Texas State ... TX
■Northeast Louisiana U ... LA
★Northeast Missouri State ... MO
■Northeastern Jr ... CO
□Northeastern Oklahoma State OK
□Northeastern U ... MA
★Northern Colorado, U. of ... CO
★Northern Illinois U ... IL
‡□Northern Iowa, U. of ... IA
■Northwest Nazarene ... ID
★Northwestern ... IA
+□Northwestern Oklahoma
State ... OK
■Northwestern State U ... LA
□Northwestern U ... IL
■Northwood Inst ... MI
□Notre Dame, U. of ... IN
□Oakland U ... MI
+□Occidental ... CA
□Ohio Northern U ... OH
★Ohio State U ... OH
□Ohio U ... OH
□Ohio Wesleyan U ... OH
★Oklahoma, U. of ... OK
■Oklahoma Baptist U ... OK
□Oklahoma Christian ... OK
★Oklahoma State U ... OK
■Old Dominion ... VA
□Olivet ... MI
■Oral Roberts U ... OK
■Oregon, U. of ... OR
+□Oregon State U ... OR
□Otterbein ... OH
+□Pace U (Pleasantville) ... NY
■Pacific, U. of the ... CA
■Pacific Lutheran U ... WA
+□Pacific U ... OR
+□Panama Canal ... Panama
□Paul Smith's ... NY
□Pearl River Jr ... MS
□Pembroke State U ... NC
□Pennsylvania, U. of ... PA
+□Pennsylvania State U ... PA
★Pepperdine U ... CA
+□Peru State ... NE
★Pfeiffer ... NC
□Pikeville ... KY
■Pittsburgh, U. of
(Johnstown) ... PA
□Pitzer ... CA
□Plymouth State ... NH
■Point Loma ... CA
□Pomona ... CA
■Portland, U. of ... OR
★Post Coll ... CT
■Prairie View A&M U ... TX
■Presbyterian ... SC
+□Princeton U ... NJ
□Providence ... RI
+□Puget Sound, U. of ... WA
★Purdue U ... IN
+□Quincy ... IL
■Quinnipiac ... CT
□Radford U ... VA
□Ramapo ... NJ
□Randolph-Macon ... VA
□Redlands, U. of ... CA
□Regis ... CO
□Rensselaer Poly. Inst ... NY
■Rhode Island, U. of ... RI
■Rice U ... TX
■Richmond, U. of ... VA
■Rider ... NJ
□Ripon ... WI
□Roanoke ... VA
■Robert Morris ... PA
+□Rochester, U. of ... NY
+□Rockford ... IL
□Roger Williams ... RI
★Rollins ... FL
+□Rutgers U ... NJ
+Rutgers U. (Douglass) ... NJ

□Sacred Heart U ... CT
■Saginaw Valley State ... MI
□Saint Meinrad ... IN
+□Saint Michael's ... VT
+□Saint Norbert ... WI
+□Saint Rose, Coll. of ... NY
□Saint Thomas, U. of ... TX
□Saint Vincent ... PA
□Salem State ... MA
+□Salisbury State ... MD
■Sam Houston State U ... TX
□San Diego, U. of ... CA
★San Diego State U ... CA
+□San Francisco, U. of ... CA
+□San Jose State U ... CA
□Santa Clara, U. of ... CA
■Schreiner ... TX
□Scranton, U. of ... PA
+Scripps ... CA
■Seton Hall U ... NJ
+□Shaw U ... NC
+□Shenandoah Coll ... VA
+□Shepherd ... WV
★Sheridan ... WY
■Shippensburg State ... PA
★Shorter ... GA
□Siena ... NY
+□Simpson ... IA
□Skidmore ... NY
★Slippery Rock State ... PA
□South, U. of the ... TN
■South Alabama, U. of ... AL
★South Carolina, U. of ... SC
□South Carolina State ... SC
+□South Dakota, U. of ... SD
+□South Dakota Sch. of Mines .. SD
+□South Dakota State U ... SD
★South Florida, U. of ... FL
□South Georgia Coll ... GA
■Southeastern Louisiana U ... LA
□Southeastern Oklahoma State OK
□Southern Arkansas U ... AR
■Southern Colorado, U. of ... CO
★Southern Illinois U ... IL
□Southern Maine, U. of ... ME
‡Southern Methodist U ... TX
■Southern Mississippi, U. of ... MS
+Southern Seminary ... VA
□Southwest Mississippi Jr ... MS
★Southwest Missouri State U .. MO
■Southwest Texas State U ... TX
■Southwestern ... KS
□Southwestern at Memphis ... TN
★Southwestern Oklahoma
State U ... OK
□Southwestern U ... TX
★Spring Hill ... AL
+□Springfield ... MA
□St. Ambrose ... IA
□St. Andrews Presbyterian ... NC
□St. Anselm ... NH
□St. Bonaventure U ... NY
+□St. Cloud ... MN
■St. Edward's U ... TX
■St. Francis, Coll. of ... IL
■St. Francis ... IN
+□St. Francis ... PA
+□St. John Fisher ... NY
□St. John's U ... MN
+■St. John's U ... NY
■St. Joseph's ... PA
■St. Leo ... FL
+St. Mary's ... NC
□St. Mary's U ... TX
+□St. Mary's ... CA
□St. Mary's ... MN
+□St. Olaf ... MN
+□St. Paul's ... MO
+□St. Thomas, Coll. of ... MN
★Stanford U ... CA
□State U. of New York (Albany,
Buffalo, Coll. at Buffalo,
Cobleskill, Coll. at Cornell, Delhi,
Farmingdale, Oswego) . NY

+□State U. of New York
(Cortland, New Paltz,
Maritime Coll.) ... NY
★Stephen F. Austin ... TX
‡Stephens ... MO
■Stetson U ... FL
□Stevens Inst. of Tech ... NJ
+□Stonehill ... MA
□Sul Ross State U ... TX
□Susquehanna U ... PA
□Swarthmore ... PA
+Sweet Briar ... VA
□Tabor ... KS
+□Tampa, U. of ... FL
□Taylor U ... IN
■Temple U ... PA
□Tennessee, U. of
(Chattanooga) ... TN
■Tennessee, U. of
(Knoxville, Martin) ... TN
□Tennessee State U ... TN
□Tennessee Tech. U ... TN
□Tennessee Temple U ... TN
■Texas, U. of (Austin,
El Paso) ... TX
+□Texas A&I U ... TX
★Texas A&M U ... TX
+□Texas Christian U ... TX
■Texas Lutheran ... TX
□Texas Wesleyan ... TX
+Texas Woman's U ... TX
+□Thiel ... PA
+□Thomas ... ME
□Thomas More ... KY
■Tiffin U ... OH
■Toledo, U. of ... OH
+□Tougaloo ... MS
□Towson State U ... MD
□Transylvania ... KY
□Trenton State ... NJ
□Trevecca Nazarene ... TN
□Tri-State ... IN
□Trinity ... CT
★Troy State U ... AL
□Tufts U ... MA
□Tulane U ... LA
★Tulsa, U. of ... OK
+□Tusculum ... TN
+□U.S. Air Force Acad ... CO
+□U.S. Coast Guard Acad ... CT
+□U.S. International U ... CA
□U.S. Merchant Marine Acad .. NY
■U.S. Military Acad ... NY
+□U.S. Naval Acad ... MD
□Union ... KY
+□Union ... NY
■Union U ... TN
□Upper Iowa ... IA
+□Upsala ... NJ
+□Urbana ... OH
□Ursinus ... PA
■Utah State U ... UT
■Utica Coll ... NY
□Valparaiso U ... IN
□Vanderbilt U ... TN
□Vermont, U. of ... VT
□Villanova U ... PA
★Vincennes U ... IN
+□Virgin Islands, Coll. of the ... VI
★Virginia, U. of ... VA
□Virginia, U. of (Clinch Valley) . VA
□Virginia Commonwealth U ... VA
□Virginia Military Inst ... VA
■Virginia Poly. Inst ... VA
□Virginia State U ... VA
+□Virginia Wesleyan ... VA
+□Viterbo ... WI
□Wabash ... IN
+□Wagner ... NY
★Wake Forest U ... NC
□Waldorf ... IA
■Walsh ... OH
+□Wartburg ... IA
+□Washburn U. of Topeka ... KS

+□Washington, U. of .... WA
□Washington & Jefferson ...... PA
□Washington & Lee U .... VA
■Washington State U .... WA
+□Washington U .... MO
■Wayne State U .... MI
□Webber .... FL
★Weber State .... UT
□Wesleyan U .... CT
□West Chester State .... PA
□West Georgia .... GA
□West Liberty State .... WV
■West Texas State .... TX
□West Virginia Inst. of Tech ... WV
+□West Virginia State .... WV
★West Virginia Wesleyan ...... WV
■Western Carolina U .... NC
+□Western Connecticut State ... CT
■Western Illinois U IL
★Western Kentucky U .... KY
+□Western Maryland U .... MD
□Western Michigan U .... MI
■Western State .... CO
■Western Texas .... TX
□Western Washington .... WA
+□Westmar .... IA
+□Westminster .... MO
□Westminster .... PA
■Wharton Co. Jr .... TX
□Wheaton IL
+□White Plains, Coll. of .... NY
□Whitman .... WA
+□Whittier .... CA
★Whitworth .... WA
□Widener U .... PA
□Wilkes .... PA
+□Willamette U .... OR
+□William & Mary, Coll. of ...... VA
□William Jewell .... MO
□William Paterson .... NJ
+□William Penn .... IA
□Williams .... MA
□Wilmington .... OH
■Wingate .... NC
★Winona State .... MN
□Wisconsin, U. of (Eau Claire, Green Bay, Milwaukee, Platteville, River Falls, Stevens Point, Stout, Superior) .... WI
+□Wisconsin, U. of (LaCrosse, Oshkosh, Whitewater) ...... WI
‡□Wisconsin, U. of (Madison) ... WI
□Wisconsin Lutheran .... WI
□Wittenberg U .... OH
■Wofford .... SC
□Wooster, Coll. of .... OH
+□Worcester Poly. Inst .... MA
□Worcester State .... MA
□Wright State .... OH
□Wyoming, U. of .... WY
□Xavier U .... OH
+□Yale U .... CT
□York Coll .... PA
■Youngstown State .... OH

Gymnastics

+Adams State .... CO
‡Alabama, U. of (University) ... AL
+□Alabama A&M U .... AL
‡Arizona, U. of .... AZ
★Arizona State U .... AZ
+Augsburg .... MN
‡Ball State .... IN
+□Bay State Jr .... MA
‡Bemidji State .... MN
+□Boise State .... ID
+□Bowie State .... MD
+Bowling Green State .... OH
+Bridgeport, U. of .... CT
+Bridgewater State .... MA
+Brown U .... RI
+Bryn Mawr .... PA
+■California, U. of (Berkeley) .... CA
+□California, U. of (Davis, Los Angeles, San Diego, Santa Barbara) .... CA
+□California State Poly. U ...... CA
+□California State U. (Chico, Fullerton, Hayward) .... CA
‡California State U. (Fresno) .. CA
+Casper .... WY
+□Catholic U. of Puerto Rico ... PR
‡Centenary .... LA
+Central Arkansas, U. of ...... AR
‡Central Michigan U .... MI
‡Central Missouri .... MO
+□City Coll .... NY
+Clarion State .... PA
+□Colgate U .... NY
+Concordia (Moorhead) .... MN
+Concordia (St. Paul) .... MN
+Connecticut, U. of .... CT
+Connecticut Coll .... CT
+Cornell U .... NY
+□Dartmouth .... NH
‡Denver, U. of .... CO
+□Dixie .... UT
‡Duke U .... NC
+East Tennessee State .... TN
★Eastern Montana .... MT
+Eastern Washington .... WA
+Edinboro State .... PA
‡Emporia State .... KS
‡Florida, U. of .... FL
★Fort Hays State .... KS
‡Furman U .... SC
‡□George Washington U .... DC
+Georgetown U .... DC
★Georgia, U. of .... GA
+Georgia Coll .... GA
■Georgia Inst. of Tech .... GA
+□Glassboro State .... NJ
+Gustavus Adolphus .... MN
+Hamline U .... MN
‡Hofstra U .... NY
+Hunter Coll .... NY
‡Idaho, U. of .... ID
★Illinois, U. of IL
‡Illinois State U IL
★Indiana State U. (Terre Haute) .... IN
‡□Indiana U. (Bloomington) .... IN
+Indiana U. of Pennsylvania ... PA
★Iowa, U. of .... IA
★Iowa State U .... IA
‡Ithaca .... NY
★Jacksonville State .... AL
★James Madison U .... VA
+Kean .... NJ
+Keene State .... NH
★Kent State U .... OH
‡Kentucky, U. of .... KY
‡King's Coll .... NY
+Lamar U .... TX
+Lock Haven State .... PA
‡Longwood .... VA
★Louisiana State U .... LA
+□Lowell, U. of .... MA
+Maine, U. of (Farmington, Presque Isle) .... ME
‡Maine, U. of (Orono) .... ME
‡Mankato State .... MN
+□Maryland, U. of .... MD
‡□Massachusetts, U. of .... MA
+□Massachusetts Inst. of Tech .. MA
‡Mayville State .... ND
★Memphis State .... TN
+□Miami U .... OH
★Michigan, U. of .... MI
★Michigan State U .... MI
+□Minnesota, U. of (Twin Cities) .... MN
+□Mississippi Valley State ...... MS
‡Missouri, U. of (Columbia) ... MO
‡Montana, U. of .... MT
+Montana State .... MT
+Moorhead State .... MN
★Nebraska, U. of (Lincoln) .... NE
+New Hampshire, U. of .... NH
□New Jersey Inst. of Tech ..... NJ
★New Mexico, U. of .... NM
‡North Carolina, U. of (Chapel Hill) .... NC
★North Carolina State .... NC
+Northeastern U .... MA
★Northern Colorado, U. of ..... CO
★Northern Illinios U IL
‡Northern Michigan U .... MI
+Northwest Missouri State ..... MO
+Northwestern U IL
+□Notre Dame, U. of .... IN
★Ohio State U .... OH
★Oklahoma, U. of .... OK
‡Oklahoma State U .... OK
‡Oral Roberts U .... OK
+Oregon State U .... OR
+□Panama Canal Coll ..... Panama
+□Pennsylvania, U. of .... PA
★Pennsylvania State U .... PA
‡Pittsburgh, U. of (Johnstown) .... PA
★Pittsburgh, U. of (Pittsburgh) .... PA
+□Prairie View A&M .... TX
+Radford U .... VA
‡Rhode Island, U. of .... RI
+Rhode Island Coll .... RI
+Rutgers U .... NJ
+Salem State .... MA
‡San Diego State .... CA
+□San Jose State .... CA
‡Seattle Pacific .... WA
+Seattle U .... WA
★Slippery Rock State .... PA
+Smith Coll .... MA
★South Dakota State .... SD
‡Southeast Missouri State ..... MO
★Southern Illinois U IL
‡Southwest Texas State .... TX
+□Springfield .... MA
+St. Catherine, Coll. of .... MN
+St. Mary's .... IN
★Stanford U .... CA
+State U. of New York (Albany, Brockport, New Paltz) .... NY
□State U. of New York (Coll. at Syracuse) .... NY
+□State U. of New York (Cortland, Farmingdale, Coll. at Cornell) .... NY
+Swarthmore .... PA
+Sweet Briar .... VA
■Syracuse U .... NY
★Temple U .... PA
+□Texas, U. of (Austin) .... TX
‡Texas, U. of (El Paso) .... TX
+□Texas A&I U .... TX
+Texas Woman's U .... TX
‡□Towson State .... MD
+Trenton State .... NJ
+□U.S. Air Force Acad .... CO
+□U.S. Coast Guard Acad ...... CT
■U.S. Military Acad .... NY
+□U.S. Naval Acad .... MD
+Ursinus .... PA
+□Utah, U. of .... UT
‡Utah State U .... UT
+Valparaiso U .... IN
+□Vermont, U. of .... VT
+□Washburn U. of Topeka ...... KS
+Washington, U. of .... WA
‡Washington State U .... WA
+□West Chester State .... PA
‡West Virginia U .... WV
‡Western Carolina U .... NC
‡Western Illinois U IL
+□Western Michigan U .... MI
‡Western State .... CO
+Wheaton IL
+□William & Mary, Coll of ...... VA
+Wilson .... PA
‡Winona State .... MN
+Wisconsin, U. of (Eau Claire, River Falls, Superior) ...... WI
+□Wisconsin, U. of (La Crosse, Oshkosh, Platteville, Stout, Whitewater) .... WI
★Wisconsin, U. of (Madison) .... WI
‡Wisconsin, U. of (Milwaukee) .... WI
+Yale U .... CT
‡Youngstown State .... OH

Hammer Throw

□Alfred U .... NY
■Azusa Pacific .... CA
□Davidson .... NC
□Delta State .... MS
★Ferris State .... MI
■Furman U .... SC
□Mary Washington .... VA
□Miami U .... OH
□Redlands, U. of .... CA
□Rhode Island, U. of .... RI
□San Jose State .... CA
■Southern Illinois U IL
□State U. of New York (Coll. of Ceramics) .... NY
■Tennessee, U. of (Knoxville) .... TN
□U.S. Coast Guard Acad ...... CT
■Utah State U .... UT
□Wesleyan U .... CT
+□Whittier .... CA
□Wisconsin, U. of (Stout) .... WI

Hand Ball

+□Dixie .... UT
+□Lake Forest IL
□New Jersey Inst. of Tech ..... NJ
+□Texas A&I U .... TX
+□Virgin Islands, Coll. of the VI
+□Waldorf .... IA

Horseback Riding

+□Averett .... VA
+□Beaver .... PA
+□Becker Jr .... MA
+Berry .... GA
+□California Lutheran .... CA
+Cazenovia .... NY
+Centenary .... NJ
+Colby-Sawyer .... NH
+□Delaware Valley .... PA
+□Drew U .... NJ
+□Fairleigh Dickinson U .... NJ
+Ferrum .... VA
+□Findlay .... OH
+□Fordham U .... NY
+Framingham State .... MA
+Goucher .... MD
+Hollins .... VA
+□Jersey City State .... NJ
+□Kenyon .... OH
+La Salle .... PA
+□Longwood .... VA
+Maria Regina .... NY
+Mary Baldwin .... VA
+□Mary Washington .... VA
+□Miami U .... OH
+Mount Holyoke .... MA
+□New England .... NH
+Pace .... NY

+Randolph-Macon .... VA
+Salem .... NC
+Sarah Lawrence .... NY
+□Skidmore.................... NY
+Smith .... MA
+□South, U. of .... TN
+□Southeastern Oklahoma State .... OK
+Southern Seminary Jr........ VA
+□St. Lawrence U .... NY
+St. Mary's .... NC
+□State U. of New York (Canton, Cobleskill, Potsdam, Stony Brook) .... NY
+Sweet Briar.................. VA
□Valley Forge................. PA
+Virginia Intermont .... VA
+White Plains, Coll. of......... NY

Ice Hockey

★Alaska, U. of................ AK
□American International .... MA
□Amherst.................... MA
□Assumption .... MA
□Augsburg .... MN
□Babson Coll .... MA
□Beloit Coll.................. WI
■Bemidji State .... MN
□Bentley .... MA
□Bethel...................... MN
■Boston Coll .... MA
■Boston U.................... MA
□Bowdoin .... ME
□Bowling Green .... OH
□Brandeis U .... MA
+□Brown U .... RI
□California Inst. of Tech....... CA
□Calvin Coll .... MI
□Canisius Coll .... NY
□Carnegie-Mellon .... PA
+■Clarkson Coll................ NY
+□Colby Coll .... ME
+□Colgate U .... NY
□Colorado Coll .... CO
□Concordia Coll. (Moorhead) .... MN
□Connecticut, U. of .... CT
□Connecticut Coll .... CT
+□Cornell U .... NY
□Culinary Inst. of America..... NY
□Curry Coll.................. MA
□Daniel Webster Coll.......... NH
+□Dartmouth Coll .... NH
□Dayton, U. of .... OH
□Delaware, U. of .... DE
□Denison U.................. OH
■Denver, U. of .... CO
□Dordt Coll.................. IA
□Duquesne U .... PA
□Elmira...................... NY
□Emerson .... MA
■Ferris State .... MI
□Fitchburg State .... MA
□Fordham U .... NY
□Framingham State .... MA
□Franklin Pierce .... NH
■Gannon U .... PA
□Gonzaga U .... WA
■Gordon .... MA
□Grinnell .... IA
□Gustavus Adolphus .... MN
+□Hamilton U .... NY
□Hamline.................... MN
+□Harvard/Radcliffe .... MA
□Hobart .... NY
□Holy Cross .... MA
■Illinois, U. of (Chicago Circle) IL
□Iona .... NY
□Iowa State U .... IA
□Keene State .... NH
■Kent State .... OH
□La Salle .... PA
□Lafayette .... PA
□Lake Forest IL
■Lake Superior State .... MI
□Lawrence U .... WI
□Lehigh U .... PA
□Loras .... IA
□Lowell, U. of................ MA
■Maine, U. of (Orono) .... ME
□Manhattan Coll .... NY
■Mankato State .... MN
□Marist...................... NY
□Massachusetts Inst. of Tech .. MA
□Massachusetts Maritime ...... MA
■Miami U.................... OH
■Michigan, U. of .... MI
■Michigan State U .... MI
□Michigan Tech U .... MI
+□Middlebury .... VT
□Minnesota, U. of (Twin Cities) .... MN
□New Church, Acad. of .... PA
□New England, U. of .... ME
□New England Coll .... NH
+□New Hampshire, U. of........ NH
□New Hampshire Coll .... NH
■New Haven, U. of .... CT
□New Jersey Inst. of Tech ..... NJ
□Nichols Coll .... MA
□North Adams State .... MA
■North Dakota State (Bottineau) .... ND
+□Northeastern U .... MA
■Northern Arizona U .... AZ
□Northern Colorado, U. of..... CO
■Northern Michigan U......... MI
‡Northwestern U............. IL
□Norwich U .... VT
■Notre Dame, U. of .... IN
■Ohio State U .... OH
□Pace U.-Pleasantville......... NY
□Plymouth State .... NH
+□Princeton .... NJ
★Providence Coll .... RI
□Quinnipiac Coll.............. CT
+■Rensselaer Polytech .... NY
+□Rhode Island Sch. of Design . RI
□Ripon Coll .... WI
+□Rochester Inst. of Tech ...... NY
□Roger Williams .... RI
□Salem State .... MA
□Siena Coll .... NY
+□Skidmore................... NY
■St. Anselm .... NH
□St. Bonaventure .... NY
■St. Cloud .... MN
□St. John's U .... MN
□St. John's U .... NY
+□St. Lawrence .... NY
□St. Mary's .... MN
□St. Michael's................ VT
□St. Norbert .... WI
□St. Olaf .... MN
□St. Scholastica .... MN
□St. Thomas .... MN
□St. Vincent .... PA
□Stonehill .... MA
□SUNY (Brockport, Buffalo, Canton, Geneseo, Plattsburgh) .... NY
+□SUNY (Cornell, Cortland, Oswego, Potsdam)......... NY
□SUNY Maritime .... NY
□Trinity Coll .... CT
□Trinity Coll IL
□U.S. Air Force Acad.......... CO
□U.S. Coast Guard Acad ...... CT
□U.S. International U.......... CA
□U.S. Merchant Marine Acad .. NY
■U.S. Military Acad .... NY
□U.S. Naval Acad .... MD
□Union .... NY
□Upsala .... NJ
■Vermont, U. of .... VT
□Villanova .... PA
+□Wesleyan U .... CT
□West Chester State .... PA
□Western Michigan U .... MI
□Western New England Coll ... MA
□White Plains, Coll. of......... NY
□William Paterson Coll .... NJ
+□Williams Coll .... MA
□Wisconsin, U. of (Eau Claire, Stevens Point, Stout, Superior) .... WI
■Wisconsin, U. of (Madison) ... WI
+□Wisconsin, U. of (River Falls) .... WI
□Worcester Polytech .... MA
□Worcester State .... MA
+□Yale........................ CT

Javelin Throw

+□Alfred U.................... NY
■Arkansas State U .... AR
■Austin Peay State............ TN
■Azusa Pacific .... CA
□Bloomsburg State .... PA
■California Lutheran .... CA
□Central Missouri U........... MO
□Chicago, U. of IL
+□Clarion State .... PA
□Colorado Coll .... CO
□Cornell U .... NY
□Davidson Coll .... NC
□Delta State .... MS
□Glassboro State .... NJ
+□Grinnell Coll .... IA
□Gustavus Adolphus .... MN
□Hamilton Coll .... NY
□High Point .... NC
+□Humboldt State............. CA
‡Ithaca...................... NY
■Kansas, U. of .... KS
□Knox Coll IL
□La Salle Coll .... PA
+□Lock Haven State .... PA
□Luther Coll .... IA
+□Mary Washington .... VA
■Miami U.................... OH
■Montana, U. of .... MT
+□Montana State U............ MT
■Nevada, U. of............... NV
□Notre Dame, U. of .... IN
■Pacific Lutheran .... WA
★Puerto Rico, U. of (Rio Piedras campus) ...... PR
+□Redlands, U. of .... CA
□Rhode Island, U. of .... RI
■Southern Illinois U........... IL
■Southern Methodist .... TX
■Tennessee, U. of (Knoxville).. TN
□U.S. Coast Guard .... CT
□U.S. Merchant Marine .... NY
■Utah State U .... UT
□West Virginia Wesleyan ...... WV
+□Whitter..................... CA
+□Williams.................... MA
□Wisconsin, U. of (Stout)...... WI
□Worcester Poly. Inst .... MA

Judo

+□Catholic U .... PR
+□Clarion State .... PA
+□Cumberland Coll .... KY
□New Jersey Inst. of Tech ..... NJ
+□New Mexico Military Inst..... NM
+□Panama Canal Coll .... Pa
★Puerto Rico, U. of (Rio Piedras) .... PR
+□Ripon .... WI
+□Southern Idaho, Coll. of...... ID
□U.S. Merchant Marine Acad .. NY
★Western Texas Coll .... TX

Karate

+□California, U. of (San Diego) .... CA
+□Colgate U .... NY
+□Cumberland Coll .... KY
+□D-Q U .... CA
□Fordham U .... NY
□Louisiana Tech .... LA
+□Mississippi Valley State ...... MS
□New Jersey Inst. of Tech ..... NJ
+□New Mexico Military Inst..... NM
+□Panama Canal Coll ...... France
+□Southern Idaho, Coll. of...... ID
□Stevens Inst. of Tech......... NJ
□U.S. Merchant Marine Acad .. NY
+□Villanova U................. PA
+□Worcester Polytech .... MA

Lacrosse

■Adelphi U .... NY
□Alfred U.................... NY
+□Amherst.................... MA
□Ashland .... OH
□Babson .... MA
+□Bates .... ME
□Baylor U .... TX
+□Bethany.................... WV
+□Boston Coll .... MA
+Boston U.................... MA
+□Bowdoin .... ME
□Brandeis U .... MA
+Bridgewater State............ MA
+□Brown U .... RI
+Bryn Mawr .... PA
■C.W. Post Coll............... NY
□California, U. of (Berkeley) .... CA
+□Castleton State .... VT
+Cedar Crest .... PA
+Centenary .... NJ
□City Coll. of New York .... NY
+□Clarkson .... NY
+□Colby .... ME
+Colby-Sawyer .... NH
+□Colgate .... NY
□Colorado Coll .... CO
□Colorado Sch. of Mines ...... CO
□Connecticut, U. of .... CT
+□Connecticut Coll .... CT
+□Cornell U .... NY
□Creighton U .... NE
+□Dartmouth .... NH
□Dean Jr. Coll .... MA
+□Denison U.................. OH
+□Dickinson .... PA
+□Drew U .... NJ
★Drexel U .... PA
■Duke U .... NC
+Earlham .... IN
□Fairfield U.................. CT
□Fairleigh Dickinson .... NJ
□Fordham U .... NY
+□Franklin & Marshall .... PA
+Frostburg State.............. MD
+□Georgetown U .... DC
+□Gettysburg .... PA
+Glassboro State .... NJ
+Goucher .... MD
■Guilford..................... NC
+Gwynedd-Mercy .... PA
+□Hamilton .... NY
□Hamden-Sydney .... VA
+□Harvard/Radcliffe .... MA
+□Haverford .... PA
□Hobart .... NY
■Hofstra U .... NY
+Hollins .... VA
+Hood .... MD
□Hope....................... MI
‡□Ithaca...................... NY
+□John Hopkins U .... MD

□Kean .... NJ
□Keene State .... NH
□Kentucky, U. of .... KY
+□Kenyon .... OH
□Knox IL
□Kutztown State .... PA
+□Lafayette .... PA
+□Lake Forest IL
□Lawrence U .... WI
+□Lebanon Valley .... PA
+□Lehigh U .... PA
+Lock Haven State .... PA
□Long Island U. (Southampton) .... NY
□Lowell, U. of .... MA
★Loyola .... MD
+□Lynchburg .... VA
□Lyndon State .... VT
+□Marietta .... OH
□Marist .... NY
□Maryland U., of .... MD
+□Massachusetts, U. of (Amherst) .... MA
□Massachusetts Inst. Tech .... MA
□Massachusetts Maritime .... MA
□Miami U .... OH
□Michigan State U .... MI
+□Middlebury .... VT
+□Millersville State .... PA
+Mount Holyoke .... MA
+□Mount St. Mary's .... MD
□Mount Union .... OH
+□New Church, Acad. of the .... PA
+□New England Coll .... NH
+□New Hampshire, U. of .... NH
□New Hampshire Coll .... NH
□New Haven, U. of .... CT
□Nichols .... MA
■North Carolina, U. of (Chapel Hill) .... NC
■North Carolina State U .... NC
+Northeastern U .... MA
□Northern Colorado, U. of .... CO
□Norwich U./Vermont Coll .... VT
□Notre Dame, U. of .... IN
+□Oberlin .... OH
□Ohio State U .... OH
+□Ohio Wesleyan .... OH
+□Plymouth State .... NH
+□Pomona .... CA
+□Princeton U .... NJ
+□Providence .... RI
□Radford .... VA
□Ramapo .... NJ
+□Randolph-Macon .... VA
+Randolph-Macon Woman's .... VA
+□Rensselaer Poly. Inst .... NY
+Rhode Island, U. of .... RI
‡Richmond U., of .... VA
□Ripon .... WI
+□Roanoke .... VA
+□Rochester, U. of .... NY
□Rochester Inst. Tech .... NY
+Russell Sage .... NY
+□Rutgers U .... NJ
+Rutgers U. (Douglass) .... NJ
+□Rutgers U. (Cook, Livingston) .... NJ
+□Saint Michael's .... VT
□St. Vincent .... PA
+□Salisbury State .... MD
‡Shippensburg State .... PA
□Siena .... NY
+□Skidmore .... NY
‡Slippery Rock .... PA
+Smith .... MA
□South, U. of the .... TN
+Southern Maine, U. of .... ME
+□Springfield .... MA
+□St. Mary's Coll. of Maryland .... MD
□State U. of New York (Albany, Buffalo, Canton, Cobleskill, Maritime Coll.) .... NY
+□State U. of New York (Cortland, Oneonta, at Cornell) .... NY
□State U. of New York (Coll. of Ceramics, Env. Sci. & Forestry, Geneseo, Oswego, Potsdam) .... NY
□Stevens Inst. of Tech .... NJ
□Stockton State .... NJ
+□Swarthmore .... PA
+Sweet Briar .... VA
■Syracuse U .... NY
‡Temple U .... PA
★Towson State .... MD
+Trenton State .... NJ
+□Trinity .... CT
+□Tufts U .... MA
□U.S. Air Force Acad .... CO
□U.S. Merchant Marine Acad .... NY
□U.S. Military Acad .... NY
□U.S. Naval Acad .... MD
+□Union .... NY
□Upsala .... NJ
+Ursinus .... PA
+□Vermont, U. of .... VT
+□Villanova U .... PA
★Virginia, U. of .... VA
+□Washington .... MD
□Washington & Lee .... VA
+Wellesley .... MA
+Wells .... NY
+□Wesleyan .... CT
+□West Chester State .... PA
+□Western Maryland .... MD
□Western New England .... MA
★Western Texas .... TX
□Western Washington U .... WA
+Wheaton .... MA
□White Plains, Coll. of .... NY
□Whittier .... CA
□Widener U .... PA
□Willamette U .... OR
+□William & Mary, Coll. of .... VA
+William Smith .... NY
+□Williams .... MA
+Wilson .... PA
+□Wittenburg U .... OH
+□Worcester, Coll. of .... OH
□Worcester Poly. Inst .... MA
+□Yale U .... CT

Polo

□Connecticut, U. of .... CT
+□Cornell U .... NY
+□Skidmore .... NY
+□SUNY at Cornell .... NY
□Valley Forge Military Jr. Coll .... PA
+■Virginia, U. of .... VA

Racquetball

+□Bowie State .... MD
+□Bucknell .... PA
+□Dixie Coll .... UT
+□Fordham U .... NY
+□Lake Forest IL
+□Minnesota, U. of (Tech. Coll.) .... MN
+□New Mexico Military Inst .... NM
+Sweet Briar .... VA
+□Texas A&I U .... TX
□U.S. Naval Acad .... MD
+□Waldorf Coll .... IA

Riflery

□Akron, U. of .... OH
+□Alaska, U. of .... AK
★Appalachian State .... NC
+□Arkansas State .... AR
□California, U. of (Los Angeles) .... CA
□Canisius .... NY
□Centenary .... LA
□Citadel, The .... SC
+□Clarion State .... PA
+□Colorado Sch. of Mines .... CO
□Cornell U .... NY
+□Davidson Coll .... NC
□Delta State .... MS
★Duquesne U .... PA
+□East Tennessee State .... TN
+□Eastern Washington U .... WA
+□Edinboro State .... PA
+□Fordham .... NY
□Furman U .... SC
+□Gannon U .... PA
+□Gettysburg Coll .... PA
+□Hardin-Simmons U .... TX
+□Henderson State .... AR
+□Indiana U. of PA .... PA
□Jacksonville State .... AL
+□John Carroll U .... OH
□Kansas, U. of .... KS
+□Kemper Military Sch. and Coll .... MO
+□Kentucky, U. of .... KY
+□King's Coll .... PA
□La Salle .... PA
+□Lake Superior State .... MI
+□Lehigh .... PA
□Livingston U .... AL
+□Maine, U. of (Orono) .... ME
□Marion Military Inst .... AL
□Massachusetts Inst. of Tech .... MA
+□Massachusetts Maritime .... MA
+□McMurry Coll .... TX
+□McNeese State .... LA
+□Miami, U. of .... FL
□Miami U .... OH
□Missouri, U. of (Rolla) .... MO
+□Missouri Southern State .... MO
+□Mount St. Mary's .... MD
+□Murray State .... KY
□Nebraska, U. of (Lincoln) .... NE
□New Jersey Inst. of Tech .... NJ
+□New Mexico Military Inst .... NM
+□Nicholls State .... LA
+□North Alabama, U. of .... AL
★North Georgia Coll .... GA
□Northeast Louisiana U .... LA
□Northeastern U .... MA
+□Norwich U .... VT
+□Ohio State U .... OH
+□Ohio U .... OH
+□Rensselaer Polytech .... NY
★Rider Coll .... NJ
+□Ripon Coll .... WI
□Scranton, U. of .... PA
★St. John's U .... NY
+□St. Norbert .... WI
□South Florida, U. of .... FL
□Stevens Inst. of Tech .... NJ
+□SUNY Maritime .... NY
□SUNY (Morrisville) .... NY
+□Tampa, U. of .... FL
□Tennessee, U. of (Chattanooga) .... TN
+□Tennessee Tech. U .... TN
+□Texas, U. of (Arlington) .... TX
□Texas, U. of (El Paso) .... TX
+□Texas A&I .... TX
+□Texas A&M .... TX
+□Texas Christian .... TX
+□U.S. Air Force Acad .... CO
□U.S. Coast Guard Acad .... CT
□U.S. Merchant Marine Acad .... NY
■U.S. Military Acad .... NY
□U.S. Naval Acad .... MD
■Valley Forge Military Jr. Coll .... PA
□Villanova U .... PA
□Virginia Military Inst .... VA
+□Wake Forest .... NC
+□Washington and Jefferson .... PA
+□Wentworth Inst. of Tech .... MA
+□West Texas State .... TX
★West Virginia U .... WV
+□Western Carolina U .... NC
★Western Kentucky U .... KY
+□Western Maryland Coll .... MD
+□Westminster Coll .... MO
□William and Mary .... VA
+□Wofford Coll .... SC
+□Worcester Poly. Inst .... MA
□Yeshiva U .... NY

Rodeo

+□Arizona, U. of .... AZ
+□Arkansas, U. of (Monticello) .... AR
+□Barton County Comm. Coll .... KS
+□Bismarck Jr .... ND
★Black Hills State .... SD
+□California State (Fresno) .... CA
+□Casper .... WY
+□Central Arkansas, U. of .... AR
★Central Arizona .... AZ
★Chadron State .... NE
+□Dawson Comm .... MT
+■Dickinson State .... ND
+□Eastern Arizona .... AZ
★Eastern New Mexico .... NM
+□Eastern Oklahoma State .... OK
+□Eastern Oregon State .... OR
★Eastern Wyoming .... WY
+□Fort Hays State .... KS
★Fort Scott Comm .... KS
+Henderson State .... AR
★Hutchinson Comm .... KS
+□Idaho State .... ID
+□McNeese State .... LA
★Midwestern State .... TX
+□Minnesota Tech. Coll., U. of .... MN
+□Montana State .... MT
+□Murray State .... KY
+□Navajo Comm .... AZ
+□Nebraska, U. of (Lincoln) .... NE
+□New Mexico Military Inst .... NM
★New Mexico State .... NM
+□Northeastern Jr .... CO
□Northeastern Oklahoma State .... OK
+□Northern Colorado, U.of .... CO
+□Northern Montana .... MT
★Northwestern State .... LA
★Oklahoma Panhandle .... OK
+□Otero Jr .... CO
+□Pearl River Jr .... MS
□Prairie View A&M .... TX
+□Pratt Comm .... KS
★Sam Houston State .... TX
□Snow Coll .... UT
★Southeastern Oklahoma State .... OK
★Southern Arkansas .... AR
★Southern Colorado, U. of .... CO
★Southern Idaho, U. of .... ID
+□Southwest Texas State .... TX
★Southwestern Oklahoma State .... OK
□Stephen F. Austin .... TX
+□Sul Ross State .... TX
★Tennessee, U. of .... TN
+□Texas A&I U .... TX
+□Texas State Tech .... TX
+□Texas Wesleyan .... TX
+□Vernon Regional Jr .... TX
■Weber State .... UT
+□Western Montana .... MT
★Western Texas .... TX
+□Wharton County Jr .... TX

Rugby

Sailing

Scuba

Cross Country Skiing

Snow Skiing

Water Skiing

Softball

+□Arkansas, U. of (Monticello) .. AR
‡Ashland .... OH
+Assumption .... MA
+Atlantic Christian .... NC
‡Auburn U .... AL
+Augsburg .... MN
+Aurora IL
+Averett .... VA
‡Baker U .... KS
+Baldwin-Wallace .... OH
‡Ball State .... IN
+□Baptist Christian .... LA
+Bard .... NY
+Barrington Coll .... RI
+□Barry U .... FL
+Barton County Comm .... KS
+Bates .... ME
‡Baylor U .... TX
+□Beaver Coll .... PA
+Becker Jr. (Leicester, Worcester) .... MA
+Belhaven .... MS
‡Bellarmine .... KY
+Beloit .... WI
+Bemidji State .... MN
‡Benedictine .... KS
+Berea Coll .... KY
+Bethany .... KS
+Bethany .... WV
+Bethel .... IN
+Bethel .... MN
‡Black Hills State .... SD
+Bloomfield Coll .... NJ
+Bloomsburg State .... PA
+Blue Mountain Coll .... MS
+Bowdoin .... ME
+Bowling Green State .... OH
‡Bradley U IL
+Brandeis U .... MA
+Brandywine .... DE
+Brevard .... NC
‡Briar Cliff .... IA
+Bridgeport, U. of .... CT
+Bridgewater State .... MA
+Brown U .... RI
+Bryan Coll .... TN
‡Bryant .... RI
‡Bucknell .... PA
+Buena Vista .... IA
+Butler .... IN
‡C.W. Post .... NY
‡Cabrini .... PA
‡California, U. of (Berkeley) ... CA
+□California, U. of (Davis, Irvine, San Diego, Santa Barbara) . CA
+California, U. of (Riverside) .. CA
+California Lutheran .... CA
+California State .... PA
+California State (Chico) .... CA
‡California State (Fresno) .... CA
+□California State (Fullerton) ... CA
★California State Polytech .... CA
+Calvin .... MI
‡Cameron .... OK
‡Campbell U .... NC
+Campbellsville .... KY
‡Canisius .... NY
+Capital U .... OH
+Carleton .... MN
+Carnegie-Mellon .... PA
‡Carthage .... WI
+Castleton State .... VT
+Catholic U .... DC
‡Cazenovia .... NY
‡Cedarville .... OH
+Central Coll .... IA
‡Central Coll .... KS
+Central Methodist .... MO
‡Central Michigan .... MI
‡Central Missouri .... MO
+Central Wesleyan .... SC
‡Chadron State .... NE
+Champlain .... VT
‡Chapman .... CA
‡Charleston, U. of .... WV
+Chatham .... PA
+Chicago, U. of IL
‡Chowan Coll .... NC
+Cincinnati, U. of .... OH
+□City Coll .... NY
+Clarion State .... PA
+Clark U .... MA
+Coe .... IA
+Colby .... ME
+□Colgate .... NY
+College Misericordia .... PA
+Colorado State U .... CO
□Columbia Christian .... OR
+Concord Coll .... WV
+Concordia IL
+□Concordia .... MN
+Concordia Teachers .... NE
+Connecticut, U. of .... CT
+Cornell .... IA
+Cowley County Comm .... KS
‡Cumberland Coll .... KY
+Curry .... MA
□Daemen Coll .... NY
+Dakota State .... SD
+Dakota Wesleyan .... SD
‡Dana Coll .... NE
‡Davis and Elkins .... WV
+Dayton, U. of .... OH
+Dean Junior .... MA
+Defiance .... OH
+Delaware, U. of .... DE
+Delaware Valley .... PA
+Delta State .... MS
+DePauw U .... IN
+Dickinson .... PA
+□Dixie Coll .... UT
+Dordt Coll .... IA
+Dr. Martin Luther Coll .... MN
+Drake .... IA
‡Drexel .... PA
+Dubuque, U. of .... IA
+Earlham .... IN
‡East Carolina U .... NC
‡Eastern Arizona Coll .... AZ
‡Eastern Coll .... PA
+Eastern Connecticut State .... CT
‡Eastern Illinois U IL
+Eastern Kentucky U .... KY
+Eastern Nazarene Coll .... MA
+Eastern Oregon State .... OR
+Eastern Washington U .... WA
+Eckerd .... FL
+Edgewood Coll .... WI
+Edinboro State .... PA
+□Elizabeth Seton .... NY
+Elizabethtown .... PA
+Elmhurst IL
+Elmira .... NY
‡Elon Coll .... NC
+Emerson .... MA
+Emmanuel Coll .... MA
‡Emporia State .... KS
+Endicott .... MA
‡Erskine .... SC
‡Evansville, U. of .... IN
+Fairleigh Dickinson .... NJ
‡Ferris State .... MI
+Ferrum .... VA
+Findlay .... OH
+Fitchburg State .... MA
‡Flagler Coll .... FL
‡Florida, U. of .... FL
‡Florida Atlantic U .... FL
+Florida Inst. of Tech .... FL
‡Florida Southern .... FL
‡Florida State .... FL
+Fontbonne .... MO
‡Fort Hays State .... KS
+Fort Scott Comm .... KS
+Framingham State .... MA
‡Francis Marion .... SC
+Franklin and Marshall .... PA
+Franklin Coll .... IN
+Franklin Pierce .... NH
+Friends U .... KS
‡Furman .... SC
+Gallaudet .... DC
+Gannon .... PA
+Gardner-Webb .... NC
‡Geneva .... PA
+George Fox .... OR
‡George Mason .... VA
+George Williams IL
‡Georgetown .... KY
+Georgia Coll .... GA
+□Georgia Southern .... GA
+Georgia Southwestern .... GA
‡Georgia State .... GA
‡Georgian Court .... NJ
+Gettysburg .... PA
+Glassboro .... NJ
+Gordon .... MA
+Goucher .... MD
‡Grace .... IN
+Grand Rapids Baptist .... MI
+Grand Valley State .... MI
‡Grand View .... IA
+Green Mountain .... VT
+Greenville Coll IL
+Grinnell .... IA
+Grove City .... PA
‡Guilford .... NC
+Gustavus Adolphus .... MN
+Gwynedd-Mercy .... PA
+Hampton Inst .... VA
+Hanover .... IN
+Harding .... AR
‡Hartford, U. of .... CT
+Harvard/Radcliffe .... MA
+Heidelberg .... OH
+Hesser .... NH
+Hesston .... KS
+High Point Coll .... NC
+Highland Comm .... KS
+Hillsdale .... MI
+Hiram .... OH
+Hiwassee .... TN
‡Hofstra .... NY
+Hope .... MI
+Houghton .... NY
+Humboldt State .... CA
+Hunter .... NY
‡Huron .... SD
‡Husson .... ME
+Illinois Benedictine IL
+Illinois Coll IL
‡Illinois State IL
+Illinois Wesleyan IL
+Incarnate Word .... TX
‡Indiana Central .... IN
+Indiana State (Terre Haute) .. IN
+□Indiana U .... PA
‡Indiana U. (Bloomington, Purdue) .... IN
+Iona .... NY
‡Iowa, U. of .... IA
‡Iowa Wesleyan .... IA
‡Ithaca .... NY
‡Jacksonville U .... FL
‡Jamestown .... ND
+Jersey City State .... NJ
‡John Brown U .... AR
+Johnson State .... VT
+Judson IL
+Juniata .... PA
‡Kansas, U. of .... KS
‡Kansas State .... KS
+Kansas Wesleyan .... KS
+Kean .... NJ
+Kearney State .... NE
+Keene State .... NH
‡Kent State .... OH
+Kentucky, U. of .... KY
‡Kentucky Wesleyan .... KY
+Keystone Jr .... PA
‡King's Coll .... NY
+King's Coll .... PA
+□Knox IL
+□Kutztown State .... PA
+La Grange .... GA
+La Salle .... PA
+Lafayette .... PA
+Lake Erie .... OH
+Lake Forest IL
‡Lake Superior State .... MI
+Lakeland .... WI
‡Lander .... SC
+Lasell Jr .... MA
+Lawrence .... WI
‡Le Moyne .... NY
■Lee .... TN
+Lehigh .... PA
‡Lenoir-Rhyne .... NC
+Lesley Coll .... MA
+Lewis and Clark .... OR
+Lewis U IL
‡Liberty Baptist .... VA
‡Limestone .... SC
‡Lincoln IL
+Lincoln Memorial U .... TN
‡Lincoln U .... MO
+Lindenwood Coll .... MO
+□Livingstone Coll .... NC
‡Livingston U .... AL
+Lock Haven State .... PA
+Long Island U. (Southampton) .... NY
+Longwood Coll .... VA
‡Loras .... IA
‡Louisburg Coll .... NC
‡Louisiana State and A&M Coll .... LA
+Louisiana Tech .... LA
+Loyola Marymount .... CA
+Luther Coll .... IA
+Lyndon State .... VT
+MacMurray Coll IL
+Macalester .... MN
+Malone Coll .... OH
+Manchester .... IN
+Manhattan Coll .... NY
+Manhattanville .... NY
‡Mankato State .... MN
+Mansfield State .... PA
‡Marian Coll .... IN
+Marian Coll .... WI
+Marietta .... OH
+Marist .... NY
‡Marycrest .... IA
+□Marygrove .... MI
+Maryville .... IN
+Maryville .... MO
‡Marywood .... PA
‡Maine, U. of (Orono) .... ME
+Massachusetts, U. of .... MA
+Massachusetts Inst. of Tech .. MA
‡Mayville State .... ND
+McNeese State .... LA
+Mercy Coll .... MI
‡Mercyhurst .... PA
+Meredith Coll .... NC
‡Mesa Coll .... CO
+Messiah Coll .... PA
+Methodist .... NC
+Miami, U. of .... FL
‡Miami U .... OH
‡Michigan, U.of .... MI
‡Michigan Christian .... MI
‡Michigan State .... MI
‡Mid-America Nazarene .... KS
‡Midwestern State .... TX
+Millersville State .... PA
+Milligan .... TN
+Millikin IL
+□Minnesota, U. of (Tech. Coll., Twin Cities) .... MN
+Mississippi Coll .... MS
+Mississippi Delta Jr .... MS
‡Mississippi U. for Women .... MS
+□Mississippi Valley .... MS
‡Missouri, U. of (Columbia) ... MO

Soccer

□Akron, U. of .... OH
■Alabama, U. of (Birmingham, Huntsville) .... AL
□Alabama A&M .... AL
□Albion .... MI
□Albright .... PA
■Alderson-Broaddus .... WV
+□Alfred .... NY
□Allegheny .... PA
+Allen .... SC
□Allentown Coll. of St. Francis. PA
■Alliance .... PA
□Alma .... MI
□American Coll. in Paris ... France
■American U .... DC
+□Amherst .... MA
□Andrew .... GA
□Anna Maria .... MA
□Appalachian State .... NC
□Aquinas .... MI
□Ashland .... OH
□Assumption .... MA
□Atlantic Christian .... NC
□Augsburg .... MN
□Augustana IL
□Aurora IL
□Austin .... TX
□Averett .... VA
■Avila .... MO
■Azusa Pacific .... CA
+□Babson .... MA
□Baldwin-Wallace .... OH
□Bard .... NY
□Barrington .... RI
□Bartlesville Wesleyan .... OK
+□Bates .... ME
+□Baylor .... TX
+□Beaver .... PA
□Becker Jr .... MA
■Belhaven .... MS
■Bellarmine .... KY
■Belmont Abbey .... NC
+□Beloit .... WI
+■Benedictine .... KS
□Bentley .... MA
+□Berea .... KY
□Bernard M. Baruch .... NY
□Berry .... GA
□Bethany .... KS
□Bethany .... WV
■Bethany Lutheran .... MN
■Bethany Nazarene .... OK
□Bethel .... IN
□Bethel .... KS
□Bethel .... MN
■Biola .... CA
■Birmingham-Southern .... AL
■Biscayne .... FL
+□Black Hills State .... SD
□Blackburn IL
□Bloomfield .... NJ
□Bloomburg State .... PA
□Bluffton .... OH
+□Boston Coll .... MA
■Boston U .... MA
+□Bowdoin .... ME
+□Bowling Green .... OH
□Brandeis .... MA
□Brandywine .... DE
■Brevard .... NC
□Briar Cliff .... IA
□Bridgeport, U. of .... CT
□Bridgewater State .... MA
□Brown .... RI
□Bryan .... TN
+□Bryant .... RI
■Bucknell .... PA
□Cabrini .... PA
+□California, U. of (Berkeley, La Jolla, Santa Barbara, Santa Cruz) .... CA
□California, U. of (Davis, Los Angeles) .... CA
■California, U. of (Riverside) .. CA
+□California Inst. of Tech .... CA
+□California Maritime Acad .... CA
■California State Coll. (Bakersfield) .... CA
□California State U. (Chico) ... CA
■California State U. (Fresno) .. CA
□Calvin .... MI
■Campbell .... NC
+□Canisius .... NY
□Capital .... OH
■Cardinal Newman .... MO
+□Cardinal Stritch .... WI
+□Carleton .... MN
□Carnegie-Mellon .... PA
□Carson-Newman .... TN
□Carthage .... WI
□Case Western Reserve .... OH
+□Castleton State .... VT
□Catholic U .... DC
□Catholic U. of Puerto Rico ... PR
‡Cazenovia .... NY
■Cedarville .... OH
■Centenary .... LA
■Central .... KS
★Central Florida .... FL
□Central Methodist .... MO
■Central Michigan .... MI
□Central Wesleyan .... SC
□Champlain .... VT
■Chapman .... CA
■Charleston, Coll. of .... SC
■Charleston, U. of .... WV
□Cheyney State .... PA
+□Chicago, U. of IL
+Cincinnati, U. of .... OH
□Citadel .... SC
□City Coll .... NY
□City U. of New York (Medgar Evers) .... NY
□Claremont-McKenna .... CA
□Clark .... MA
□Clarkson .... NY
□Clearwater Christian .... FL
■Cleveland State .... OH
□Coe .... IA
■Coker .... SC
+□Colby .... ME
+Colby-Sawyer .... NH
+□Colgate .... NY
+□Colorado Coll .... CO
+□Colorado Mountain (Timberline) .... CO
□Concordia .... NE
□Concordia (St. Paul) .... MN
+■Connecticut, U. of .... CT
□Connecticut Coll .... CT
□Cornell Coll .... IA
□Cornell U .... NY
■Creighton .... NE
+□Curry .... MA
+□Daemen .... NY
□Dakota Wesleyan .... SD
+□Dallas, U. of .... TX
□Daniel Webster .... NH
+□Dartmouth .... NH
□Davidson .... NC
■Davis & Elkins .... MS
□Dayton, U. of .... OH
□Dean Jr .... MA
□Delaware, U. of .... DE
□Delaware Valley .... PA
+□Denison .... OH
■Denver, U. of .... CO
□DePauw .... IN
□Dickinson .... PA
□Dordt .... IA
□Drew .... NJ
■Drexel .... PA
■Duke .... NC
□Earlham .... IN
■East Carolina .... NC
■Eastern .... PA
□Eastern Connecticut .... CT
■Eastern Illinois IL
■Eastern Nazarene .... MA
□Eastern Washington .... WA
□Eckerd .... FL
□Edinboro State .... PA
□Elizabethtown .... PA
□Elmira .... NY
■Elon .... NC
□Emerson .... MA
□Emory .... GA
□Erskine .... SC
□Evansville, U. of .... IN
+□Evergreen State .... WA
□Fairfield .... CT
■Fairleigh Dickinson .... NJ
□Fitchburg .... MA
■Flagler .... FL
■Florida Atlantic .... FL
□Florida Inst. of Tech .... FL
□Florida Southern .... FL
■Fontbonne .... MO
□Fordham .... NY
□Fort Scott Comm .... KS
□Framingham State .... MA
■Francis Marion .... SC
+□Franklin & Marshall .... PA
□Franklin Pierce .... NH
□Freeman Jr .... SD
□Frostburg State .... MD
□Furman .... SC
□Gannon .... PA
■Geneva .... PA
■George Mason .... VA
★George Washington U .... DC
□Georgetown .... KY
□Georgetown U .... DC
□Georgia Coll .... GA
□Georgia Southern .... GA
□Georgia Southwestern .... GA
■Georgia State .... GA
□Gettysburg .... PA
□Glassboro State .... NJ
□Golden Valley Lutheran .... MN
■Gonzaga .... WA
■Gordon .... MA
□Goshen .... IN
■Grace .... IN
□Grand Rapids Baptist .... MI
+□Green Mountain .... VT
□Greenville IL
+□Grinnell .... IA
□Grove City .... PA
■Guilford .... NC
+□Gustavus Adolphus .... MN
+□Hamilton .... NY
□Hamline .... MN
□Hampden-Sydney .... VA
□Hardin-Simmons .... TX
■Hartford, U. of .... CT
□Hartwick .... NY
+□Harvard/Radcliffe .... MA
□Harvey Mudd .... CA
□Haverford .... PA
□Heidelberg .... OH
□Hesston .... KS
□High Point .... NC
□Hiram .... OH
□Hobart .... NY
□Hofstra .... NY
+Hollins .... VA
□Holy Cross .... MA
□Hope .... MI
+□Houghton .... NY
■Howard .... DC
□Humboldt .... CA
□Hunter .... NY
■Husson .... ME
■Illinois, U. of (Chicago Circle) IL
■Illinois Inst. of Tech IL
■Illinois State IL
■Indiana Central .... IN
■Indiana Inst. of Tech .... IN
■Indiana U. (Bloomington) .... IN
□Indiana U. of Pennsylvania ... PA
□Iona .... NY
‡□Ithaca .... NY
□Jacksonville State .... AL
■Jacksonville U .... FL
■James Madison .... VA
□Jersey City State .... NJ
■John Brown .... AR
□John Carroll .... OH
□Johns Hopkins .... MD
□Johnson State .... VT
■Judson IL
■Judson Baptist .... OR
□Juniata .... PA
+□Kalamazoo .... MI
□Kean .... NJ
+□Keene State .... NH
□Kemper Military Inst .... MO
□Kentucky, U. of .... KY
■Kentucky Wesleyan .... KY
□Kenyon .... OH
□Keystone Jr .... PA
□King's Coll .... NY
□King's Coll .... PA
+□Knox IL
□Kutztown .... PA
□La Salle .... PA
+□Lafayette .... PA
□LaGrange .... GA
□Lake Forest IL
□Lakeland .... WI
■Lander .... SC
+□Lawrence .... WI
★Le Moyne .... NY
□Lebanon Valley .... PA
□Lehigh .... PA
+Lesley .... MA
□LeTourneau .... TX
□Lewis IL
+□Lewis and Clark .... OR
■Liberty Baptist .... VA
■Lincoln IL
□Lincoln Christian IL
□Lincoln U .... PA
+□Lindenwood .... MO
□Lock Haven State .... PA
■Long Island U. (Southampton) .... NY
■Longwood .... VA
□Los Angeles Baptist .... CA
□Louisiana Tech .... LA
■Louisville, U. of .... KY
□Lowell, U. of .... MA
■Loyola .... MD
□Loyola Marymount .... CA
■Loyola U. of Chicago IL
+□Luther .... IA
□Lynchburg .... VA
+□Lyndon State .... VT
+□Macalester .... MN
□MacMurray IL
□Maharishi .... IA
□Maine, U. of .... ME
■Maine, U. of (Orono) .... ME
□Maine Maritime .... ME
■Malone .... OH
□Manchester .... IN
+□Manhattanville .... NY
□Marietta .... OH
□Marist .... NY
+□Marlboro .... VT
■Marquette .... WI
□Mars Hill .... NC
□Mary Washington .... VA
■Marycrest .... IA
□Maryland, U. of (College Park) .... MD
□Maryville .... IN
+□Maryville .... MO
+□Massachusetts, U. of .... MA
□Massachusetts Inst. of Tech .. MA
+□Massachusetts Maritime .... MA
□McKendree IL
■Menlo .... CA
■Mercyhurst .... PA
□Messiah .... PA

□Methodist ... NC
□Miami, U. of ... FL
+□Miami U ... OH
■Michigan State ... MI
+□Middlebury ... VT
■Midwestern ... TX
□Millersville ... PA
□Milligan ... TN
+Mills ... CA
□Millsaps ... MS
□Mississippi Coll ... MS
□Missouri Baptist ... MO
■Missouri Southern ... MO
□Mitchell ... CT
+□Monmouth ... IL
□Monmouth ... NJ
□Montreat-Anderson ... NC
□Moravian ... PA
+□Morehead ... KY
□Morningside ... IA
+Mount Holyoke ... MA
■Mount Senario ... WI
+Mount St. Joseph ... OH
+□Mount St. Mary ... NY
■Mount St. Mary's ... MD
□Mount Union ... OH
+Mount Vernon ... DC
□Muhlenberg ... PA
□Muskingum ... OH
□Nazareth Coll. of Rochester ... NY
□Nebraska, U. of (Lincoln) ... NE
■Nevada, U. of (Las Vegas) ... NV
□New Church, Acad. of the ... PA
□New England, U. of ... ME
□New England Coll ... NH
□New Hampshire, U. of ... NH
□New Hampshire Coll ... NH
■New Haven, U. of ... CT
□New Jersey Inst. of Tech ... NJ
+■New Mexico Military Inst ... NM
□New Oreleans, U. of ... LA
□New York U ... NY
□Niagara U ... NY
□Nicholls State ... LA
□Nichols ... MA
□North Adams State ... MA
□North Carolina, U. of (Asheville, Greensboro) ... NC
★North Carolina, U. of (Chapel Hill) ... NC
■North Carolina, U. of (Wilmington) ... NC
■North Carolina State ... NC
□North Carolina Wesleyan ... NC
□North Central ... IL
■North Georgia ... GA
□North Park ... IL
■North Texas State ... TX
■Northeast Louisiana ... LA
□Northeast Missouri ... MO
■Northeastern Christian Jr ... PA
□Northeastern Oklahoma State OK
+□Northern Colorado, U. of ... CO
■Northern Illinois U ... IL
□Northern Kentucky U ... KY
□Northland ... WI
□Northwest Missouri State ... MO
■Northwest Nazarene ... ID
□Northwestern ... IL
□Norwich U./Vermont Coll ... VT
□Notre Dame, Coll. of ... CA
□Notre Dame, U. of ... IN
■Nyack ... NY
□Oberlin ... OH
□Occidental ... CA
□Oglethorpe ... GA
□Ohio Northern ... OH
□Ohio State ... OH
□Ohio U ... OH
+□Ohio Wesleyan ... OH
■Old Dominion ... VA
□Olivet ... MI
+□Oregon Inst. of Tech ... OR
□Pace (Pleasantville/Briarcliff) . NY

■Pacific, U. of the ... CA
★Pacific Lutheran ... WA
+□Pacific U ... OR
□Palm Beach Atlantic ... FL
+□Panama Canal Coll ... Panama
□Parks of St. Louis U ... IL
■Paul Smith's ... NY
□Pembroke State ... NC
□Pennsylvania, U. of ... PA
■Pennsylvania State U ... PA
■Pfeiffer ... NC
■Philadelphia Coll. of Textiles & Science ... PA
■Pittsburgh, U. of ... PA
□Pitzer ... CA
+□Plymouth State ... NH
■Point Loma ... CA
+□Pomona ... CA
★Portland, U. of ... OR
■Post ... CT
□Pratt ... NY
+□Princeton ... NJ
+□Principia ... IL
+■Providence ... RI
■Puerto Rico, U. of ... PR
+■Puget Sound, U. of ... WA
+□Quincy ... IL
■Quinnipiac ... CT
+□Radford ... VA
□Ramapo ... NJ
+■Randolph-Macon ... VA
□Redlands, U. of ... CA
■Regis ... CO
□Rensselaer ... NY
■Rhode Island, U. of ... RI
+□Rhode Island Coll ... RI
□Richmond, U. of ... VA
□Richmond Coll. (Amer. International Coll. of London) ... England
■Rider ... NJ
□Rio Grande Comm ... OH
+□Ripon ... WI
□Roanoke ... VA
■Robert Morris ... PA
+□Rochester, U. of ... NY
□Rochester Inst. of Tech ... NY
□Rockford ... IL
+■Rockhurst ... MO
■Rockmont ... CO
+□Roger Williams ... RI
■Rollins ... FL
□Rutgers (Cook, Livingston, Rutgers) ... NJ
■Sacred Heart ... CT
■Salem ... WV
□Salem State ... MA
□Salisbury ... MD
□San Diego, U. of ... CA
■San Diego State ... CA
■San Francisco, U. of ... CA
□San Jose State ... CA
+■Santa Clara, U. of ... CA
□Sangamon State ... IL
□Scranton, U. of ... PA
■Seattle Pacific ... WA
□Seattle U ... WA
□Seton Hall ... NJ
■Shippensburg ... PA
+□Siena ... NY
+□Simon's Rock of Bard ... MA
+□Skidmore ... NY
■Slippery Rock ... PA
+Smith ... MA
+□Sonoma State ... CA
+□South, U. of the ... TN
■South Alabama, U. of ... AL
■South Carolina, U. of ... SC
■South Florida, U. of ... FL
■Southeast Missouri State ... MO
■Southern California Coll ... CA
+■Southern Illinois U. (Edwardsville) ... IL
□Southern Maine, U. of ... ME

□Southern Methodist ... SC
■Southern Methodist U ... TX
+□Southern Vermont ... VT
□Southwestern at Memphis ... TN
■Spring Arbor ... MI
+□Springfield ... MA
□St. Andrews Presbyterian ... NC
□St. Anselm ... NH
+St. Benedict ... MN
★St. Bonaventure ... NY
■St. Francis, Coll. of ... IL
■St. Francis Coll ... IN
★St. John Fisher ... NY
■St. John's ... KS
+□St. John's ... MN
□St. John's ... NM
■St. John's ... NY
□St. Joseph's ... IN
■St. Joseph's ... PA
+□St. Lawrence ... NY
■St. Leo ... FL
+St. Mary's ... NC
★St. Mary's Coll ... CA
+□St. Mary's Coll ... MN
□St. Mary's Coll. of Maryland ... MD
□St. Mary's U ... TX
□St. Meinrad ... IN
+□St. Michael's ... VT
□St. Norbert ... WI
+□St. Olaf ... MN
+□St. Rose, Coll. of ... NY
□St. Scholastica ... MN
□St. Thomas ... MN
□St. Vincent ... PA
+■Stanford ... CA
+□State U. of New York (Albany, Canton, Cortland, Geneseo, Morrisville, Plattsburgh) ... NY
□State U. of New York (Alfred, Binghamton, Brockport, Buffalo, Cobleskill, Coll. at Cornell, Delhi, Farmingdale, Fredonia, Maritime Coll., New Paltz, Oneonta, Oswego, Potsdam, Utica) ... NY
+□State U. of New York Coll. at Buffalo ... NY
+□State U. Coll. of Ceramics at Alfred ... NY
+□Stephen F. Austin ... TX
□Stetson ... FL
□Stevens Inst ... NJ
□Stockton State ... NJ
+□Stonehill ... MA
□Susquehanna ... PA
□Swarthmore ... PA
+Sweet Briar ... VA
■Syracuse ... NY
■Tabor ... KS
■Tampa, U. of ... FL
■Tarkio ... MO
■Temple ... PA
□Tennessee Tech ... TN
■Tennessee Temple ... TN
+□Texas A&M ... TX
□Texas Christian ... TX
+□Thomas ... ME
■Tiffin ... OH
□Toccoa Falls ... GA
+□Tougaloo ... MS
+□Transylvania ... KY
□Trenton State ... NJ
□Tri-State ... IN
□Trinity Christian ... IL
+□Trinity Coll ... CT
□Trinity Coll ... IL
+Trinity Coll ... VT
+□Tufts ... MA
■Tulsa, U. of ... OK
■Tusculum ... TN
□U.S. Air Force Acad ... CO
□U.S. Coast Guard Acad ... CT
□U.S. International U ... CA
□U.S. Merchant Marine Acad ... NY

■U.S. Military Acad ... NY
□U.S. Naval Acad ... MD
■Union Coll ... KY
+□Union Coll ... NY
□United Wesleyan ... PA
■Unity Coll ... ME
□Upsala ... NJ
□Ursinus ... PA
■Valley Forge Military Jr ... PA
□Vanderbilt ... TN
+□Vassar ... NY
+□Vermont, U. of ... VT
+□Villanova ... PA
□Virgin Islands, Coll. of the ... VI
+■Virginia, U. of ... VA
□Virginia Commonwealth ... VA
□Virginia Military Inst ... VA
+□Virginia Wesleyan ... VA
□Viterbo ... WI
□Wabash ... IN
■Wake Forest ... NC
■Walsh ... OH
■Warner Pacific ... OR
+□Warren Wilson ... NC
□Wartburg ... IA
□Washington, U. of ... WA
□Washington and Jefferson ... PA
□Washington and Lee ... VA
□Washington Coll ... MD
□Washington U ... MO
□Weber State ... UT
+Wells ... NY
+□Wesleyan ... CT
□West Chester State ... PA
□West Liberty State ... WV
□West Virginia Institute of Tech ... WV
■West Virginia Wesleyan ... WV
□Western Baptist ... OR
■Western Carolina ... NC
□Western Connecticut State ... CT
■Western Illinois ... IL
□Western Maryland ... MD
□Western Michigan ... MI
□Western New England ... MA
+□Western Oregon State ... OR
□Westminster ... MO
□Wheaton ... IL
+Wheaton ... MA
■Wheeling ... WV
□White Plains, Coll. of ... NY
+□Whitman ... WA
□Whittier ... CA
□Wilkes ... PA
+□Willamette ... OR
□William and Mary ... VA
□William Jewell ... MO
□William Paterson ... NJ
+William Smith ... NY
+□Williams ... MA
+□Wilmington Coll ... OH
■Wingate ... NC
■Winthrop ... SC
■Wisconsin, U. of (Green Bay, Milwaukee) ... WI
□Wisconsin, U. of (Madison, Platteville) ... WI
+□Wisconsin, U. of (Whitewater) ... WI
□Wisconsin Lutheran ... WI
+□Wittenberg ... OH
■Wofford ... SC
□Wooster ... OH
□Worcester Polytechnic Institute ... MA
□Worcester State ... MA
□Wright State ... OH
■Xavier ... OH
+□Yale ... CT
□Yeshiva ... NY
■York ... NE
□York Coll. of Pa ... PA
□Youngstown ... OH

Squash

□American Coll. in Paris ... France
+□Amherst ... MA
+□Babson ... MA
+□Bowdoin ... ME
+Brown U ... RI
+□Bucknell U ... PA
+□Colby ... ME
+□Colgate U ... NY
+□Dartmouth ... NH
+□Fordham U ... NY
+□Franklin & Marshall ... PA
‡George Washington U ... DC
+□Hamilton ... NY
+Harvard/Radcliffe ... MA
□Hobart ... NY
□Lehigh U ... PA
□M.I.T ... MA
+Middlebury ... VT
+□Pennsylvania, U. of ... PA
+□Princeton U ... NJ
□Rochester, U. of ... NY
+St. Lawrence U ... NY
+Smith ... MA
□State U. of New York (Stony Brook) ... NY
□Stevens Inst. of Tech ... NJ
+Sweet Briar ... VA
+□Trinity ... CT
+□Tufts U ... MA
□U.S. Military Acad ... NY
□U.S. Naval Acad ... MD
+□Vassar ... NY
+□Wesleyan U ... CT
+□Williams ... MA
+□Yale U ... CT

Swimming

★Adelphi U ... NY
+Adrian ... MI
□Akron, U. of ... OH
★Alabama, U. of ... AL
+□Alabama A&M ... AL
+□Albion ... MI
+□Alfred ... NY
+□Allegheny ... PA
+□Alma ... MI
★American U ... DC
+□Amherst ... MA
★Arizona, U. of ... AZ
★Arizona State ... AZ
+□Arkansas, U. of (Fayetteville, Monticello) ... AR
+□Arkansas State ... AR
★Ashland ... OH
★Auburn ... AL
+□Augustana ... IL
+□Austin Coll ... TX
+□Babson ... MA
+■Ball State ... IN
+Barnard ... NY
+□Bay State Jr ... MA
+□Baylor ... TX
+□Beloit ... WI
□Bemidji State ... MN
+□Berea ... KY
+□Bethany ... WV
+□Bloomsburg State ... PA
+□Boca Raton, Coll. of ... FL
‡□Boston Coll ... MA
★Boston U ... MA
+□Bowdoin ... ME
+□Bowie State ... MD
+□Bowling Green State ... OH
■Bradley U ... IL
+□Brandeis ... MA
+Brenau ... GA
+□Brevard ... NC
+□Bridgewater State ... MA
+□Brown U ... RI
+Bryn Mawr ... PA
★Bucknell ... PA
+□Buena Vista ... IA
+□Butler U ... IN
★California, U. of (Berkeley, Irvine) ... CA
+□California, U. of (Davis, Los Angeles, Riverside, San Diego, Santa Barbara) ... CA
+□California Inst. of Tech ... CA
+□California State U. (Chico, Fullerton) ... CA
★California State U. (Fresno) .. CA
+□Calvin ... MI
+□Carleton ... MN
+□Carnegie-Mellon ... PA
+□Carroll ... WI
‡□Carthage ... WI
+□Case Western Reserve ... OH
□Cathedral ... NY
+□Catholic U. of Puerto Rico ... PR
+Centenary ... NJ
+Central Arkansas, U. of ... AR
‡Central Missouri ... MO
+□Central Washington U ... WA
★Charleston, Coll. of ... SC
+□Chicago, U. of ... IL
★Cincinnati, U. of ... OH
□Citadel ... SC
+□City U. of New York (Baruch, City Coll) ... NY
+□Claremont-McKenna ... CA
+□Clarion State ... PA
+□Clark U ... MA
★Cleveland State ... OH
+□Coe ... IA
+□Colby Coll ... ME
+□Colgate ... NY
+□Colorado Coll ... CO
★Colorado Sch. of Mines ... CO
+Colorado State U ... CO
+□Concordia Teachers Coll ... NE
+■Connecticut, U. of ... CT
+Connecticut Coll ... CT
+□Cornell ... IA
+□Cornell U ... NY
+□Creighton U ... NE
+□Dartmouth Coll ... NH
+□Delaware, U. of ... DE
+□Denison U ... OH
★Denver, U. of ... CO
+□DePauw ... IN
+□Dickinson ... PA
+□Dixie Coll ... UT
+□Dordt ... IA
★Drexel ... PA
■Drury ... MO
+□Duke ... NC
+□Duquesne ... PA
★East Carolina U ... NC
★Eastern Illinois U ... IL
□Eastern Kentucky U ... KY
+□Eastern Washington U ... WA
□Edinboro State ... PA
+□Elizabethtown Coll ... PA
+□Emory U ... GA
‡Emporia State ... KS
+□Eureka Coll ... IL
+□Evergreen State ... WA
★Evansville, U. of ... IN
+□Fairfield U ... CT
★Fairmont State ... WV
■Ferris State ... MI
★Florida, U. of ... FL
★Florida A&M ... FL
★Florida State ... FL
★Fordham ... NY
‡□Fort Lewis Coll ... CO
+□Franklin and Marshall ... PA
+□Frostburg State ... MD
★Furman U ... SC
+□Gallaudet ... DC
★George Washington U ... DC
+□George Williams ... IL
+□Georgetown U ... DC
★Georgia, U. of ... GA
+□Georgia Southern ... GA
★Georgia State ... GA
■Georgia Tech ... GA
+□Gettysburg Coll ... PA
+□Glassboro ... NJ
+Goucher ... MD
+□Green Mountain Coll ... VT
+□Greensboro ... NC
+□Grinnell ... IA
□Grove City ... PA
+□Gustavus Adolphus ... MN
+□Hamilton Coll ... NY
+□Hamline ... MN
+□Hannibal-LaGrange ... MO
□Harding ... AR
+□Harvard/Radcliffe ... MA
+□Harvey Mudd ... CA
+□Hawaii, U. of ... HI
+□Henderson State ... AR
‡□Hendrix ... AR
+Hillsdale ... MI
+□Hiram ... OH
□Hobart ... NY
+□Holy Cross ... MA
+Hood ... MD
+□Hope ... MI
★Howard ... DC
+Hunter ... NY
★Idaho, U. of ... ID
★Illinois, U. of (Chicago Circle, Urbana-Champaign) IL
+□Illinois Benedictine ... IL
★Illinois Inst. of Tech ... IL
‡Illinois State ... IL
+Immaculata ... PA
★Indiana U. (Bloomington) ... IN
+□Indiana U. of Pennsylvania ... PA
+□Iona ... NY
★Iowa, U. of ... IA
★Iowa State ... IA
★Iowa Wesleyan ... IA
‡□Ithaca Coll ... NY
★James Madison ... VA
+□Jersey City State ... NJ
+□John Carroll ... OH
+□Johns Hopkins U ... MD
+□Kalamazoo Coll ... MI
★Kansas, U. of ... KS
+Kean Coll ... NJ
+Kearney State ... NE
+□Keene State ... NH
+□Kemper Military Sch. and Coll MO
★Kent State ... OH
■Kentucky, U. of ... KY
+□Kenyon Coll ... OH
+Keuka Coll ... NY
+□King's Coll ... PA
+□Knox ... IL
+□Kutztown State ... PA
+□La Salle ... PA
+□Lafayette ... PA
+□Lake Forest ... IL
+□Lamar ... TX
+□Lawrence ... WI
+□Lehigh U ... PA
+□Lewis and Clark ... OR
★Lincoln ... IL
★Linfield ... OR
+□Livingstone Coll ... NC
+Lock Haven State ... PA
+□Loras ... IA
★Louisiana State U. and A&M Coll ... LA
★Louisville, U. of ... KY
+□Lowell, U. of ... MA
+□Loyola ... MD
+Loyola Marymount ... CA
★Loyola U. of Chicago ... IL
+□Luther ... IA
+□Lycoming Coll ... PA
+□Macalester ... MN
+□MacMurray Coll ... IL
★Maine, U. of (Orono) ... ME
□Manhattan Coll ... NY
+Manhattanville ... NY
★Mankato State ... MN
+Mansfield State ... PA
+Maria Regina ... NY
+□Marist ... NY
+Mary Baldwin ... VA
+□Mary Washington ... VA
+□Maryland, U. of (College Park) ... MD
□Maryland, U. of (Eastern Shore) ... MD
+Marymount ... NY
‡Marymount Coll ... VA
+□Massachusetts, U. of (Amherst) ... MA
+□Massachusetts Inst. of Tech .. MA
★Menlo Coll ... CA
★Mercyhurst ... PA
+□Miami, U. of ... FL
★Miami U ... OH
★Michigan, U. of ... MI
★Michigan State ... MI
+□Michigan Tech ... MI
+Middlebury ... VT
+□Milligan ... TN
+□Millikin ... IL
+Mills ... CA
+□Minnesota, U. of (Tech. Coll) ... MN
□Minnesota, U. of (Twin Cities) ... MN
+□Mississippi Valley State ... MS
★Missouri, U. of (Columbia) ... MO
■Missouri, U. of (Rolla) ... MO
+□Monmouth Coll ... IL
★Monmouth Coll ... NJ
‡Montana, U. of ... MT
+□Morehead State ... KY
+Mount Holyoke ... MA
+Mount St. Vincent ... NY
+□Mount Union ... OH
+□Nazareth Coll. of Rochester .. NY
★Nebraska, U. of (Lincoln) ... NE
★Nevada, U. of (Las Vegas) ... NV
‡Nevada, U. of (Reno) ... NV
+□New Hampshire, U. of ... NH
□New Jersey Inst. of Tech ... NJ
★New Mexico, U. of ... NM
★New Mexico State ... NM
+New Rochelle, Coll. of ... NY
+□New York U ... NY
‡Newcomb ... LA
+□Niagara U ... NY
+□North Adams State ... MA
★North Carolina, U. of (Chapel Hill, Wilmington) .. NC
★North Carolina State ... NC
+□North Central ... IL
+□North Dakota State ... ND
+North Park ... IL
★Northeast Louisiana ... LA
‡□Northeast Missouri State ... MO
+□Northeastern U ... MA
★Northern Colorado, U. of ... CO
★Northern Illinois U ... IL
‡□Northern Iowa, U. of ... IA
‡Northern Michigan U ... MI
+□Northwestern U ... IL
+□Norwich U ... VT
+□Notre Dame ... IN
□Oakland U ... MI
+□Oberlin ... OH
+□Occidental ... CA
+□Ohio Northern ... OH
★Ohio State U ... OH
+□Ohio U ... OH
+□Ohio Wesleyan ... OH
★Oklahoma, U. of ... OK
★Old Dominion ... VA
★Oregon, U. of ... OR
+Oregon State ... OR
+Ozarks, Sch. of the ... MO
★Pacific, U. of the ... CA

+□Pacific Christian . . . . CA
+□Pacific Lutheran U . . . . WA
+□Pacific U . . . . OR
+□Panama Canal Coll . . . . . . Panama
+□Pennsylvania, U. of . . . . PA
★Pennsylvania State U . . . . PA
★Pepperdine U . . . . CA
★Pfeiffer . . . . NC
★Pittsburgh, U. of (Pittsburgh) . . . . PA
+□Pitzer . . . . CA
+□Pomona . . . . CA
+□Prairie View A&M U . . . . TX
+□Princeton U . . . . NJ
+□Principia IL
★Puerto Rico, U. of (Rio Piedras) . . . . PR
★Puget Sound, U. of . . . . WA
★Purdue U . . . . IN
+□Ramapo . . . . NJ
+Randolph-Macon Woman's . . . VA
+□Redlands, U. of . . . . CA
+□Regis . . . . CO
+Regis . . . . MA
+□Rensselaer Poly. Inst . . . . NY
★Rhode Island, U. of . . . . RI
‡□Rice U . . . . TX
★Richmond, U. of . . . . VA
+□Rider . . . . NJ
□Ripon . . . . WI
+Roanoke . . . . VA
■Robert Morris . . . . PA
+□Rochester, U. of . . . . NY
+□Rochester Inst. of Tech . . . . . . NY
+□Rockford IL
‡Rosary IL
+Russell Sage . . . . NY
+□Rutgers U . . . . NJ
+Saint Mary-of-the-Woods . . . . . IN
+□Saint Rose, Coll. of . . . . NY
+Saint Teresa, Coll. of . . . . MN
+Salem State . . . . MA
+Salisbury . . . . MD
+San Diego, U. of . . . . CA
★San Diego State U . . . . CA
★San Jose State U . . . . CA
+Scripps . . . . CA
★Seton Hall U . . . . NJ
+□Shepherd . . . . WV
★Shippensburg State . . . . PA
+Skidmore . . . . NY
★Slippery Rock State . . . . PA
+Smith . . . . MA
+□South, U. of the . . . . TN
★South Carolina, U. of . . . . SC
+South Carolina State . . . . SC
+□South Dakota, U. of . . . . SD
★South Dakota State U . . . . SD
★South Florida, U. of . . . . FL
+□Southern Arkansas U . . . . AR
★Southern Illinois U IL
★Southern Methodist U . . . . TX
■Southern Mississippi, U. of . . . MS
+□Southern Oregon State . . . . . . OR
■Southwest Missouri State U . . MO
‡Southwest Texas State U . . . . . TX
+□Springfield . . . . MA
+St. Benedict . . . . MN
★St. Bonaventure . . . . NY
+St. Catherine . . . . MN
★St. Cloud State U . . . . MN
□St. John's U . . . . MN
★St. John's U . . . . NY
+□St. Lawrence U . . . . NY
+St. Mary's . . . . NC
+St. Mary's . . . . IN
+□St. Olaf . . . . MN
+□St. Thomas, Coll. of . . . . MN
★Stanford U . . . . CA
+□State U. of New York (Albany, Alfred, at Alfred U., Binghamton, Buffalo, Coll. at Buffalo, Cobleskill, at Cornell U., at Cortland, Farmingdale, Geneseo, Maritime Coll., Morrisville, New Paltz, Oswego, Plattsburgh, Potsdam, Stony Brook, at Syracuse) . . . . NY
+State U. of New York (Brockport, Oneonta) . . . . . . NY
□State U. of New York (Fredonia) . . . . NY
+□Stephen F. Austin . . . . TX
+Stephens . . . . MO
□Stockton State . . . . NJ
+□Susquehanna U . . . . PA
+□Swarthmore . . . . PA
+Sweet Briar . . . . VA
★Syracuse U . . . . NY
★Tampa, U. of . . . . FL
★Temple U . . . . PA
★Tennessee, U. of (Knoxville) . . . . TN
□Tennessee State U . . . . TN
★Texas, U. of (Austin) . . . . TX
★Texas A&M U . . . . TX
★Texas Christian U . . . . TX
+Texas Woman's U . . . . TX
■Toledo, U. of . . . . OH
+□Tougaloo . . . . MS
★Towson State . . . . MD
+Trenton State . . . . NJ
+□Trinity . . . . CT
+□Tufts U . . . . MA
★Tulane U . . . . LA
+□U.S. Air Force Acad . . . . CO
+□U.S. Coast Guard Acad . . . . . . CT
+□U.S. Merchant Marine Acad . . NY
★U.S. Military Acad . . . . NY
+□U.S. Naval Acad . . . . MD
+□Union . . . . KY
+□Union . . . . NY
+□Ursinus . . . . PA
+□Utah, U. of . . . . UT
★Utica Coll . . . . NY
+□Valparaiso . . . . IN
‡□Vanderbilt U . . . . TN
+□Vassar . . . . NY
+□Vermont, U. of . . . . VT
★Villanova U . . . . PA
★Vincennes U . . . . IN
□Virgin Islands, Coll. of the VI
★Virginia, U. of . . . . VA
+□Virginia Commonwealth U . . . VA
□Virginia Military Inst . . . . VA
★Virginia Poly. Inst . . . . VA
□Wabash . . . . IN
+□Washington, U. of . . . . WA
+□Washington & Jefferson . . . . . . PA
□Washington & Lee . . . . VA
‡Washington State U . . . . WA
+□Washington U . . . . MO
★Wayne State U . . . . MI
+Wellesley . . . . MA
+Wells . . . . NY
+□Wesleyan U . . . . CT
+□West Chester State . . . . PA
+West Texas State U . . . . TX
★West Virginia U . . . . WV
+□Western Carolina U . . . . NC
★Western Illinois U IL
■Western Kentucky U . . . . KY
+□Western Maryland . . . . MD
+□Western Michigan U . . . . MI
★Western State . . . . CO
□Westminster . . . . PA
+□Wheaton IL
+□Whitman . . . . WA
+□Whittier . . . . CA
+□Widener U . . . . PA
+□Wiley . . . . TX
+□Wilkes . . . . PA
+□Willamette U . . . . OR
+□William & Mary, Coll. of . . . . . . VA
+□William Jewell . . . . MO
+□William Paterson . . . . NJ
+William Smith . . . . NY
‡William Woods . . . . MO
+□Williams . . . . MA
+□Wisconsin, U. of (Eau Claire, La Crosse, Oshkosh, Platteville, River Falls, Stevens Point, Stout, Whitewater) . . . . WI
‡Wisconsin, U. of (Green Bay) . WI
★Wisconsin, U. of (Madison) . . . WI
‡□Wisconsin, U. of (Milwaukee) . WI
+□Wittenberg U . . . . OH
+□Wooster, Coll. of . . . . OH
+□Worcester Poly. Inst . . . . MA
★Wright State U . . . . OH
+□Wyoming, U. of . . . . WY
+□Yale . . . . CT
+□York . . . . NE
+□York . . . . PA
★Youngstown State U . . . . OH

Synchronized Swimming

‡Arizona, U. of . . . . AZ
+Bridgewater State . . . . MA
+Bucknell U . . . . PA
+Clarion State . . . . PA
+Cornell Coll . . . . IA
+Cornell U . . . . NY
‡Illinois, U. of (Chicago Circle) IL
+Lynchburg Coll . . . . VA
‡Michigan, U. of . . . . MI
+National Coll. of Education IL
+Northwest Missouri State . . . . . MO
‡Northwestern U IL
‡Ohio State U . . . . OH
+Richmond, U. of . . . . VA
+Smith . . . . MA
+South, U. of the . . . . TN
+St. Mary's . . . . NC
+State U. of New York (Albany, Brockport) . . . . NY
+Villanova U . . . . PA
+Western Michigan U . . . . MI
+Wheaton . . . . MA
+William & Mary, Coll. of . . . . . . VA

Tennis

□Adams State . . . . CO
★Adelphi . . . . NY
+□Adrian . . . . MI
+Agnes Scott . . . . GA
+□Akron, U. of . . . . OH
★Alabama, U. of . . . . AL
+□Alabama A&M . . . . AL
‡Alabama Christian . . . . AL
+□Alabama State . . . . AL
+Albertus Magnus . . . . CT
+□Albion . . . . MI
+□Albright . . . . PA
+Alfred . . . . NY
+□Allegheny . . . . PA
+□Allentown Coll. of St. Francis de Sales . . . . PA
+□Alma . . . . MI
+□Alvernia . . . . PA
+□American Coll. in Paris . . . France
+□American International Coll . . MA
‡□American U . . . . DC
+□Amherst . . . . MA
+□Anderson . . . . IN
+□Anderson . . . . SC
+□Andrew . . . . GA
★Angelo State . . . . TX
+□Anna Maria . . . . MA
★Appalachian State . . . . NC
+□Aquinas . . . . MI
★Arizona, U. of . . . . AZ
★Arizona State . . . . AZ
★Arizona Western . . . . AZ
+□Arkansas, U. of (Monticello) . . . . AR
★Arkansas State . . . . AR
+□Arkansas Tech . . . . AR
★Armstrong State . . . . GA
+□Ashland . . . . OH
+□Assumption . . . . MA
+□Atlantic Christian . . . . NC
★Auburn . . . . AL
+□Augsburg . . . . MN
+□Augustana IL
★Augustana . . . . SD
+□Aurora IL
+□Austin . . . . TX
★Austin Peay . . . . TN
+□Averett . . . . VA
★Avila . . . . MO
■Azusa Pacific . . . . CA
+□Babson . . . . MA
★Baker . . . . KS
+□Baldwin-Wallace . . . . OH
★Ball State . . . . IN
+□Baptist Christian . . . . LA
+□Bard . . . . NY
+Barnard . . . . NY
+□Bates . . . . ME
+□Bay State Jr . . . . MA
+□Baylor . . . . TX
+□Beaver . . . . PA
+□Becker Jr . . . . MA
■Belhaven . . . . MS
+■Bellarmine . . . . KY
★Belmont . . . . TN
□Belmont Abbey . . . . NC
+□Beloit . . . . WI
‡Bemidji State . . . . MN
‡□Benedictine . . . . KS
+□Bentley . . . . MA
+□Berea . . . . KY
+□Bernard M. Baruch . . . . NY
+□Berry . . . . GA
+□Bethany . . . . KS
+□Bethany . . . . WV
+□Bethany Lutheran . . . . MN
+□Bethany Nazarene . . . . OK
□Bethel . . . . IN
+□Bethel . . . . KS
+□Bethel . . . . MN
★Bethel . . . . TN
□Bethune-Cookman . . . . FL
★Biola . . . . CA
★Birmingham-Southern . . . . AL
★Biscayne . . . . FL
+□Black Hills State . . . . SD
+□Blackburn IL
★Blinn . . . . TX
+□Bloomfield . . . . NJ
+□Bloomsburg State . . . . PA
+□Bluffton . . . . OH
+□Boca Raton, Coll. of . . . . FL
+□Boise State . . . . ID
‡□Boston Coll . . . . MA
★Boston U . . . . MA
+□Bowdoin . . . . ME
+□Bowie State . . . . MD
+□Bowling Green . . . . OH
★Bradley U IL
+□Brandeis . . . . MA
+□Brandywine . . . . DE
+Brenau . . . . GA
‡□Brevard . . . . NC
+□Briar Cliff . . . . IA
+□Bridgeport, U. of . . . . CT
+□Bridgewater State . . . . MA
★Brigham Young (Hawaii) . . . . . HI
+□Brown . . . . RI
+□Bryan . . . . TN
+□Bryant . . . . RI
+Bryn Mawr . . . . PA
★Bucknell . . . . PA
+□Buena Vista . . . . IA
+□Butler . . . . IN
★C. W. Post (Long Island U.) . . NY
‡Cabrini . . . . PA

+■California, U. of (Berkeley) ... CA
+□California, U. of (Davis, La Jolla, Los Angeles, Santa Barbara, Santa Cruz) CA
★California, U. of (Irvine, Riverside) ... CA
□California Inst. of Tech ... CA
+□California Lutheran ... CA
+□California State Coll ... CA
★California State Coll ... PA
★California State Poly ... CA
+California State U. (Chico) ... CA
★California State U. (Fresno) ... CA
+□California State U. (Fullerton) CA
+□Calvin ... MI
‡Cameron ... OK
★Campbell ... NC
★Campbellsville ... KY
+□Canisius ... NY
+□Capital ... OH
+□Carleton ... MN
+□Carnegie-Mellon ... PA
+□Carroll ... WI
★Carson-Newman ... TN
‡□Carthage ... WI
+□Case Western Reserve ... OH
+□Casper ... WY
+□Castleton ... VT
□Cathedral ... NY
+□Catholic U ... DC
+□Catholic U. of Puerto Rico ... PR
‡Cazenovia ... NY
‡Cedar Crest ... PA
★Cedarville ... OH
★Centenary ... LA
+Centenary ... NJ
+□Central ... IA
★Central ... KS
+□Central Arkansas ... AR
★Central Florida ... FL
+□Central Methodist ... MO
★Central Michigan ... MI
★Central Missouri ... MO
★Central State ... OK
+□Central Washington ... WA
+□Central Wyoming ... WY
□Chaminade ... HI
■Chapman ... CA
★Charleston, Coll. of ... SC
★Charleston, U. of ... WV
+Chatham ... PA
+□Cheyney State ... PA
+□Chicago, U. of ... IL
★Chowan ... NC
★Christian Brothers ... TN
★Cincinnati, U. of ... OH
□Citadel ... SC
+□City Coll ... NY
+□Claremont-McKenna ... CA
+Clarion State ... PA
+□Clark ... MA
+□Clarkson ... NY
★Cleveland State ... OH
+□Coe ... IA
+□Coffeyville Comm ... KS
★Coker ... SC
+□Colby ... ME
+Colby-Sawyer ... NH
+□Colgate ... NY
□College Misericordia ... PA
★Colorado, U. of ... CO
+□Colorado Coll ... CO
★Colorado Sch. of Mines ... CO
+□Colorado State U ... CO
‡Columbia Coll ... SC
+□Concord ... WV
+□Concordia ... IL
+□Concordia (Moorhead) ... MN
+□Concordia (St. Paul) ... MN
+□Connecticut, U. of ... CT
+□Connecticut Coll ... CT
+Converse ... SC
★Cooke County ... TX
+□Cornell Coll ... IA
+□Cornell U ... NY
□Cowley County Comm ... KS
+□Creighton ... NE
+□Curry ... MA
+□D-Q U ... CA
+□Dakota State ... SD
+□Dakota Wesleyan ... SD
★Dana ... NE
+□Dartmouth ... NH
+□Davidson ... NC
★Davis & Elkins ... WV
+□Dayton, U. of ... OH
+□Dean Jr ... MA
+□Delaware, U. of ... DE
+□Delta State ... MS
+□Denison ... OH
★Denver, U. of ... CO
+□DePauw ... IN
□Detroit, U. of ... MI
+□Dickinson ... PA
+□Dickinson State ... ND
+□Dixie ... UT
+□Dominican ... CA
+□Dordt ... IA
+□Dr. Martin Luther ... MN
+□Drake ... IA
+□Drew ... NJ
★Drexel ... PA
★Drury ... MO
+□Dubuque, U. of ... IA
★Duke ... NC
★Duquesne ... PA
+□Earlham ... IN
★East Carolina ... NC
+□East Central Jr ... MS
■East Central Oklahoma State ... OK
+□East Tennessee State ... TN
★East Texas Baptist ... TX
+□Eastern Coll ... PA
‡□Eastern Illinois ... IL
+□Eastern Kentucky ... KY
+□Eastern Montana ... MT
+□Eastern Nazarene ... MA
+□Eastern Washington ... WA
+□Eckerd ... FL
+□Edinboro State ... PA
+□Elizabethtown ... PA
+□Elmhurst ... IL
★Elon ... NC
+□Emmanuel ... GA
+Emmanuel ... MA
+□Emory U. Coll ... GA
+□Emory & Henry ... VA
★Emporia State ... KS
+Endicott ... MA
★Erskine ... SC
+□Eureka ... IL
★Evangel ... MO
★Evansville, U. of ... IN
+□Evergreen State ... WA
+□Fairfield ... CT
+□Fairleigh Dickinson ... NJ
+□Fairmont ... WV
+□Fashion Inst. of Tech ... NY
★Ferris State ... MI
+□Ferrum ... VA
+□Findlay ... OH
+□Fisk ... TN
+Fitchburg ... MA
★Flagler ... FL
★Florida, U. of ... FL
★Florida A&M ... FL
★Florida Atlantic ... FL
□Florida Inst. of Tech ... FL
★Florida Southern ... FL
★Florida State ... FL
+□Fontbonne ... MO
★Fordham ... NY
+□Fort Hays State ... KS
‡□Fort Lewis ... CO
+□Fort Scott Comm ... KS
+□Framingham State ... MA
★Francis Marion ... SC
+□Franklin ... IN
+□Franklin & Marshall ... PA
+□Franklin Pierce ... NH
★Freed-Hardeman ... TN
+□Frostburg State ... MD
★Furman ... SC
■Gadsden State Jr ... AL
+□Gallaudet ... DC
★Gannon ... PA
★Gardner-Webb ... NC
+George Fox ... OR
★George Mason ... VA
★George Washington U ... DC
★Georgetown ... KY
+□Georgetown U ... DC
★Georgia, U. of ... GA
+□Georgia Coll ... GA
+□Georgia Southern ... GA
+□Georgia Southwestern ... GA
★Georgia State ... GA
■Georgia Tech ... GA
+□Gettysburg ... PA
+□Glassboro ... NJ
+□Gonzaga ... WA
+□Gordon ... MA
+Goucher ... MD
■Grace ... IN
★Grand Canyon ... AZ
□Grand Rapids Baptist ... MI
★Grand View ... IA
+□Green Mountain ... VT
+□Greensboro ... NC
+□Greenville ... IL
+□Grinnell ... IA
+□Grove City ... PA
★Guilford ... NC
+□Gustavus Adolphus ... MN
+□Gwynedd-Mercy ... PA
+□Hamilton ... NY
+□Hamline ... MN
□Hampden-Sydney ... VA
□Hampton Inst ... VA
+□Hannibal-LaGrange ... MO
+□Hanover ... IN
+Harcum Jr ... PA
+□Hardin-Simmons ... TX
□Harding ... AR
★Hartford, U. of ... CT
+□Harvard/Radcliffe ... MA
+□Harvey Mudd ... CA
★Hastings ... NE
+□Haverford ... PA
+□Hawaii, U. of ... HI
+□Heidelberg ... OH
+□Henderson State ... AR
‡□Hendrix ... AR
+□High Point ... NC
‡□Hillsdale ... MI
+□Hiram ... OH
□Hobart ... NY
□Hofstra ... NY
+Hollins ... VA
‡□Holy Cross ... MA
+Hood ... MD
+□Hope ... MI
+□Hunter ... NY
★Huntingdon ... AL
★Hutchinson ... KS
★Idaho, U. of ... ID
+□Idaho State ... ID
★Illinois, U. of ... IL
□Illinois Benedictine ... IL
+□Illinois Coll ... IL
★Illinois Inst. of Tech ... IL
★Illinois State ... IL
+□Illinois Wesleyan ... IL
+□Incarnate Word ... TX
+■Independence Comm ... KS
+□Indiana Central ... IN
+□Indiana State ... IN
★Indiana U. (Bloomington) ... IN
+□Indiana U. (Purdue at Indianapolis) ... IN
+□Indiana U. of Pennsylvania ... PA
+■Iona ... NY
★Iowa, U. of ... IA
★Iowa State ... IA
★Iowa Wesleyan ... IA
‡□Ithaca ... NY
★Jackson State ... MS
★Jacksonville State ... AL
★Jacksonville U ... FL
★James Madison ... VA
★Jamestown ... ND
+□Jersey City State ... NJ
★John Brown ... AR
+□John Carroll ... OH
+□Johns Hopkins ... MD
+□Johnson State ... VT
‡Judson ... AL
+□Judson ... IL
+□Juniata ... PA
+□Kalamazoo ... MI
★Kansas, U. of ... KS
□Kansas Newman ... KS
★Kansas State ... KS
+□Kean ... NJ
+□Kearney ... NE
+□Keene ... NH
+□Kemper Military ... MO
★Kentucky, U. of ... KY
★Kentucky Wesleyan ... KY
+□Kenyon ... OH
★Keuka ... NY
+□Keystone Jr ... PA
★King's ... NY
+□King's ... PA
+□Knox ... IL
+□Kutztown ... PA
+□La Grange ... GA
+□La Salle ... PA
+□Lafayette ... PA
+Lake Erie ... OH
+□Lake Forest ... IL
★Lake Superior State ... MI
+□Lakeland ... WI
+□Lamar ... TX
★Lambuth ... TN
★Lander ... SC
+Lasell Jr ... MA
+□Lawrence ... WI
★Le Moyne ... NY
□Lebanon Valley ... PA
□Lee ... TN
+□Lees-McRae ... NC
+□Lehigh ... PA
‡□Lenoir-Rhyne ... NC
+Lewis ... IL
+□Lewis & Clark ... OR
■Limestone ... SC
★Lincoln ... IL
★Lincoln ... MO
+□Lincoln Memorial ... TN
+□Lindenwood ... MO
★Linfield ... OR
□Livingston ... AL
★Livingstone ... NC
+□Lock Haven State ... PA
+□Long Island U. (Southampton) ... NY
+□Longwood ... VA
+□Loras ... IA
■Louisburg ... NC
□Louisiana Tech ... LA
★Louisville, U. of ... KY
+□Lowell, U. of ... MA
+□Loyola ... MD
‡□Loyola Marymount ... CA
□Loyola U. of Chicago ... IL
+□Luther ... IA
+□Lycoming ... PA
+□Lynchburg ... VA
+□Lyndon State ... VT
+□Macalester ... MN
+□MacMurray ... IL
+□Maharishi ... IA
+□Maine, U. of (Orono) ... ME
★Malone ... OH
+□Manchester ... IN

★Stephen F. Austin .... TX
‡Stephens .... MO
★Sterling .... KS
‡□Stetson .... FL
+□Stevens Inst. of Tech .... NJ
+□Stonehill .... MA
+□Sul Ross .... TX
+□Susquehanna .... PA
+□Swarthmore .... PA
+Sweet Briar .... VA
‡Syracuse .... NY
+□Tabor .... KS
+□Tampa, U. of .... FL
+□Taylor .... IN
★Temple .... PA
+□Tennessee, U. of (Chattanooga) .... TN
★Tennessee, U. of (Knoxville) .. TN
□Tennessee State .... TN
+□Tennessee Tech .... TN
+□Texas, U. of (Arlington) ...... TX
★Texas, U. of (Austin, San Antonio) .... TX
‡Texas, U. of (Permian Basin) . TX
+□Texas A&I .... TX
★Texas A&M .... TX
★Texas Christian .... TX
★Texas Lutheran .... TX
+□Texas Wesleyan .... TX
+Texas Woman's .... TX
+□Thiel .... PA
+□Thomas .... ME
■Thomas More .... KY
‡Tift .... GA
★Toledo, U. of .... OH
+□Tougaloo .... MS
★Towson State .... MD
‡□Transylvania .... KY
+□Trenton State .... NJ
★Trevecca Nazarene .... TN
□Tri-State .... IN
+□Trinity .... CT
+□Trinity IL
+Trinity .... VT
□Truett-McConnell .... GA
+□Tufts .... MA
★Tulane .... LA
★Tulsa, U. of .... OK
+□Tusculum .... TN
+□Tuskegee .... AL
+□U.S. Air Force Acad .... CO
+□U.S. Coast Guard Acad ...... CT
+□U.S. International U .... CA
□U.S. Merchant Marine .... NY
★U.S. Military Acad .... NY
+□U.S. Naval Acad .... MD
+□Union .... KY
+□Union .... NY
★Union .... TN
+□Upper Iowa .... IA
+□Upsala .... NJ
+□Ursinus .... PA
+□Utah, U. of .... UT
■Utah State .... UT
■Utica .... NY
□Valley Forge Military .... PA
+□Valparaiso .... IN
★Vanderbilt .... TN
+□Vassar .... NY
+□Vermont, U. of .... VT
‡□Villanova .... PA
★Vincennes .... IN
+□Virgin Islands, Coll. of the VI
★Virginia, U. of .... VA
+□Virginia, U. of (Clinch Valley) .... VA
+□Virginia Commonwealth ...... VA
+Virginia Intermont .... VA
□Virginia Military Institute ..... VA
★Virginia Poly. Inst .... VA
+□Virginia Wesleyan .... VA
□Voorhees .... SC
□Wabash .... IN
★Wagner .... NY
★Wake Forest .... NC
■Walsh .... OH
+□Wartburg .... IA
+□Washburn .... KS
+□Washington, U. of .... WA
+□Washington and Jefferson .... PA
□Washington & Lee .... VA
+□Washington Coll .... MD
★Washington State .... WA
★Wayne State .... MI
+□Webb Inst .... NY
★Webber .... FL
★Weber State .... UT
+Wellesley .... MA
+Wells .... NY
+Wesleyan .... GA
+□Wesleyan U .... CT
+□West Chester State .... PA
+□West Florida, U. of .... FL
★West Georgia .... GA
+□West Liberty .... WV
★West Texas .... TX
+□West Virginia Inst. of Tech ... WV
+□West Virginia State Coll ...... WV
★West Virginia U .... WV
★West Virginia Wesleyan ...... WV
★Western Carolina U .... NC
+□Western Connecticut .... CT
★Western Illinois IL
★Western Kentucky .... KY
+□Western Maryland .... MD
+□Western Michigan .... MI
□Western New England .... MA
+Western New Mexico .... NM
+□Western Oregon State .... OR
‡Western State .... CO
+□Western Washington .... WA
★Westmar .... IA
□Westminster .... MO
+□Westminster .... PA
★Wharton County Jr .... TX
+□Wheaton IL
+Wheaton .... MA
+□Wheeling .... WV
+□Wheelock .... MA
‡□White Plains, Coll. of .... NY
+□Whitman .... WA
★Whitworth .... WA
+□Wichita State .... KS
+□Widener .... PA
+□Wilkes .... PA
+□Willamette .... OR
+□William & Mary .... VA
+□William Jewell .... MO
+William Paterson .... NJ
+□William Penn .... IA
+William Smith .... NY
‡William Woods .... MO
+□Williams .... MA
+□Wilmington Coll .... OH
+Wilson .... PA
★Wingate .... NC
★Winona State .... MN
★Winthrop .... SC
+□Wisconsin, U. of (Eau Claire, Green Bay, LaCrosse, Oshkosh, River Falls, Stevens Point, Stout, Whitewater .... WI
★Wisconsin, U. of (Madison) ... WI
‡□Wisconsin, U. of (Milwaukee) . WI
□Wisconsin, U. of (Platteville) .. WI
+□Wisconsin Lutheran .... WI
+□Wittenberg .... OH
□Wofford .... SC
+□Wooster, Coll. of .... OH
+□Worcester Poly. Inst .... MA
+□Worcester State .... MA
+□Wright State .... OH
+□Xavier .... OH
★Yakima Valley Comm .... WA
★Yankton .... SD
+□Yale .... CT
□Yeshiva .... NY
+■York .... NE
+□York Coll. of Pa .... PA
★Young Harris .... GA
■Youngstown State .... OH

Track

★Abilene Christian U .... TX
+□Adrian .... MI
★Alabama, U. of .... AL
+□Alabama, A&M U .... AL
+□Alabama State U .... AL
+□Albion .... MI
+□Albright .... PA
+□Alfred U .... NY
+□Allegheny .... PA
+□Allen U .... SC
+□Alma .... MI
★Angelo State U .... TX
★Appalachian State U .... NC
+□Aquinas .... MI
+□Arkansas, U. of .... AR
■Arkansas State U .... AR
★Ashland .... OH
+□Assumption .... MA
★Auburn U .... AL
+□Augsburg .... MN
+□Austin .... TX
★Austin Peay State U .... TN
□Averett .... VA
★Azusa Pacific .... CA
□Baptist Christian .... LA
□Bartlesville Wesleyan .... OK
+□Barton Co. Comm .... KS
+□Bates .... ME
★Baylor U .... TX
+□Beaver .... PA
■Belmont .... TN
+□Beloit .... WI
□Bentley .... MA
+□Berea .... KY
+□Barry .... GA
+□Bethany .... KS
+□Bethany .... WV
+□Bethel .... KS
+□Bethel .... MN
□Bethune Cookman .... FL
+Blackburn IL
□Bloomsburg State .... PA
+□Bluffton .... OH
★Boston Coll .... MA
★Boston U .... MA
+□Bowdoin .... ME
+□Bowie State .... MD
★Bradley U IL
+□Brandeis U .... MA
■Brevard .... NC
□Bridgewater State .... MA
□Brown U .... RI
+□Bryant .... RI
★Bucknell U .... PA
+□Buena Vista .... IA
■C.W. Post .... NY
+□California, U. of (Davis) ...... CA
+■California, U. of (Riverside) .. CA
+□California Inst. of Tech .... CA
+□California Lutheran .... CA
+□California State .... PA
+□Calvin .... MI
■Campbell U .... NC
■Canisius .... NY
□Carnegie-Mellon U .... PA
■Carson-Newman .... TN
+□Case Western Reserve U ..... OH
+□Catholic U. of America .... DC
★Cedarville .... OH
+□Central Arkansas, U. of ...... AR
+□Central Methodist .... MO
★Central Missouri .... MO
★Central State U .... OK
■Chapman .... CA
+□Cheyney State .... PA
+□Chicago, U. of IL
+□City Coll. of City U .... NY
+□Claremont-McKenna .... CA
+□Clarion State .... PA
+□Clark U .... MA
+□Coe .... IA
□Coffeyville Comm .... KS
+□Colby .... ME
+□Colgate U .... NY
+□Colorado Coll .... CO
★Colorado Sch. of Mines ...... CO
+□Colorado State U .... CO
+□Concord .... WV
+□Concordia (Moorhead) .... MN
+□Concordia Teachers .... NE
□Connecticut, U. of .... CT
+□Cornell .... IA
+□Cornell U .... NY
□Cumberland .... KY
+□Dakota Wesleyan U .... SD
★Dana .... NE
+□Dartmouth .... NH
+□Davidson .... NC
□Delta State U .... MS
+□Denison U .... OH
+□DePauw U .... IN
+□Dickinson State .... ND
+□Dixie .... UT
+□Dordt .... IA
+Dr. Martin Luther .... MN
★Drake U .... IA
+□Dubuque, U. of .... IA
■Duke U .... NC
+Earlham .... IN
★East Carolina U .... NC
■East Central Oklahoma State . OK
+□East Tennessee State U ...... TN
+□Eastern Ketucky U .... KY
+□Eastern Montana .... MT
+□Eastern New Mexico U .... NM
+□Eastern Oregon State .... OR
+□Edinboro State .... PA
□Elon .... NC
+□Emory & Henry .... VA
+□Eureka IL
+□Fairmont State .... WV
■Fayetteville State .... NC
★Ferris State .... MI
□Ferrum .... VA
+□Fisk U .... TN
★Florida, U. of .... FL
★Florida A&M U .... FL
★Florida State U .... FL
★Fordham U .... NY
★Fort Hays State .... KS
+■Fort Scott Comm .... KS
□Franklin & Marshall .... PA
■Furman U .... SC
+□George Fox .... OR
★George Mason .... VA
□Georgetown .... KY
★Georgetown U .... DC
★Georgia, U. of .... GA
■Georgia Inst. of Tech .... GA
□Georgia Southwestern .... GA
+□Gettysburg .... PA
+□Glenville State .... WV
★Golden Valley Lutheran ...... MN
+□Goshen .... IN
□Grand Rapids Baptist .... MI
+□Grand Valley State .... MI
+□Grinnell .... IA
□Grove City .... PA
+□Gustavus Adolphus .... MN
+□Hamline U .... MN
+□Hampton Inst .... VA
□Hanover .... IN
□Harding U .... AR
+□Harvard/Radcliffe .... MA
+□Harvey Mudd .... CA
★Hastings .... NE
+□Haverford .... PA
+□Heidelberg .... OH
□Henderson State .... AR
□High Point .... NC

Track and Field

+□Anderson .... IN
★Angelo State U .... TX
+□Aquinas .... MI
★Arizona, U. of .... AZ
★Arizona State U .... AZ
□Arkansas, U. of (Fayetteville, Monticello) .... AR
★Ashland .... OH
+□Assumption .... MA
★Auburn U .... AL
+□Augustana IL
★Augustana .... SD
+□Austin .... TX
★Austin Peay State U .... TN
□Averett .... VA
★Azusa Pacific .... CA
★Baker U .... KS
+□Baldwin-Wallace .... OH
★Ball State U .... IN
+Barnard .... NY
+□Barton County Comm .... KS
□Bates .... ME
★Baylor U .... TX
■Bellarmine .... KY
■Belmont .... TN
★Bemidji State U .... MN
+□Bethany .... KS
+□Bethel .... KS
□Bethune-Cookman .... FL
■Biola U .... CA
★Bismarck Jr .... ND
★Black Hills State .... SD
■Blinn .... TX
+□Bloomsburg State .... PA
+□Bluffton .... OH
+□Boise State U .... ID
★Boston Coll .... MA
★Boston U .... MA
+□Bowie State .... MD
+□Bowling Green State U .... OH
★Bradley U IL
+□Brandeis U .... MA
■Brevard .... NC
+Bridgewater State .... MA
■Bucknell U .... PA
+□Buena Vista .... IA
□Butler U .... IN
★California, U. of (Berkeley, Irvine) .... CA
+□California, U. of (Davis, Los Angeles, Riverside, Santa Barbara) .... CA
+□California Lutheran .... CA
+□California State .... PA
★California State (Bakersfield) . CA
■California State (Fresno) .... CA
★California State Poly. U .... CA
+□California State U. (Chico, Fullerton) .... CA
■Campbell U .... NC
+□Capital U .... OH
+□Carleton .... MN
□Carnegie-Mellon U .... PA
+□Carroll .... WI
‡□Carthage .... WI
+□Catholic U. of Puerto Rico ... PR
■Cedarville .... OH
+□Central .... IA
■Central Arizona .... AZ
★Central Michigan U .... MI
★Central Missouri State U .... MO
+□Central Washington U .... WA
★Chadron State .... NE
□Chaminade U .... HI
+□Cheyney State .... PA
+□Chicago, U. of IL
★Cincinnati, U. of .... OH
+□City U. of New York (Baruch, City Coll., Medgar Evers) ... NY
+□Claremont-McKenna .... CA
+□Clarion State .... PA
★Cleveland State U .... OH
+□Coe .... IA
□Coffeyville .... KS

+□Colby .... ME
+□Colgate U .... NY
+□ Colorado .... CO
★Colorado, U. of (Boulder) .... CO
★Colorado Sch. of Mines .... CO
+□Columbia Christian .... OR
+□Concordia IL
+□Concordia (Moorhead) .... MN
+□Concordia Teachers .... NE
+□Connecticut, U. of .... CT
+□Coppin State .... MD
+□Cornell U .... NY
★Dakota State .... SD
★Dana .... NE
+□Dartmouth .... NH
■David Lipscomb .... TN
+□Davidson .... NC
+□Defiance .... OH
+□Delaware, U. of .... DE
+□Delaware Valley .... PA
□Delta State U .... MS
□Denison U .... OH
+□DePauw U .... IN
□Dickinson .... PA
+□Dickinson State .... ND
+□Dixie .... UT
■Drexel U .... PA
+□Dubuque, U. of .... IA
■Duke U .... NC
□Earlham .... IN
□East Tennessee State U .... TN
★Eastern Illinois U IL
+□Eastern Kentucky U .... KY
+□Eastern Montana .... MT
+□Eastern Washington U .... WA
+□Edinboro State .... PA
□Elmhurst IL
□Elon .... NC
+□Emory U .... GA
★Emporia State .... KS
★Evansville, U. of .... IN
★Fairleigh Dickinson U .... NJ
★Ferris State .... MI
□Ferrum .... VA
+□Findlay .... OH
+□Fitchburg State .... MA
★Florida A&M U .... FL
★Fort Hayes State U .... KS
■Francis Marion .... SC
+□Franklin .... IN
+□Freeman Jr .... SD
+□Frostburg State .... MD
■Furman U .... SC
+□Gallaudet .... DC
□Gardner-Webb .... NC
□Geneva .... PA
★George Mason U .... VA
+□Georgetown U .... DC
★Georgia, U. of .... GA
+□Gettysburg .... PA
+□Glassboro State .... NJ
★Golden Valley .... WA
■Grace .... IN
+□Greenville IL
+□Grinnell .... IA
□Grove City .... PA
+□Gustavus Adolphus .... MN
+□Hamilton .... NY
□Hamline .... MN
□Harvard/Radcliffe .... MA
+□Harvey Mudd .... CA
★Hastings .... NE
□Haverford .... PA
+Hawaii, U. of .... HI
□Henderson State U .... AR
□High Point .... NC
★Highland Comm. Coll .... KS
★Hillsdale .... MI
□Hobart .... NY
‡□Holy Cross .... MA
+□Hope .... MI
+□Houghton .... NY
■Howard Payne U .... TX
+□Humboldt State U .... CA

+□Hunter .... NY
■Hutchinson Comm. Coll .... KS
★Idaho, U. of .... ID
+□Idaho State .... ID
★Illinois, U. of (Chicago) IL
■Illinois, U. of (Urbana) IL
+□Illinois Benedictine IL
★Illinois State U IL
+□Independence Comm. Coll ... KS
+□Indiana, U. of .... PA
+□Indiana Central U .... IN
★Indiana U. (Bloomington) .... IN
■Iona .... NY
★Iowa, U. of .... IA
★Iowa State U .... IA
★Iowa Wesleyan .... IA
‡□Ithaca .... NY
★Jackson State U .... MS
★James Madison U .... VA
★Jamestown .... ND
+□Jersey City State .... NJ
□Johns Hopkins U .... MD
+□Juniata .... PA
★Kansas, U. of .... KS
★Kansas State U .... KS
+□Kansas Wesleyan .... KS
+□Kearney State .... NE
+□Keene State .... NH
+□Kemper Military .... MO
★Kent State U .... OH
★Kentucky, U. of .... KY
+□Kenyon .... OH
+■King's Coll .... NY
+□Knox IL
+□La Salle .... PA
+□Lafayette .... PA
★Langston U .... OK
+□Lawrence U .... WI
□Lebanon Valley .... PA
□Lehigh U .... PA
+□Lewis and Clark .... OR
★Liberty Baptist .... VA
★Lincoln U .... MO
★Linfield .... OR
+□Lock Haven State .... PA
+■Loras .... IA
★Louisiana State U. A&M .... LA
□Louisiana Tech. U .... LA
★Louisville, U. of .... KY
+□Lowell, U. of .... MA
□Lubbock Christian .... TX
+□Luther .... IA
+□Lynchburg .... VA
+□Macalester .... MN
★Maine, U. of (Orono) .... ME
+■Malone .... OH
★Mankato State U .... MN
□Marietta .... OH
+□Marist .... NY
★Marquette U .... WI
‡Mary Coll .... ND
+□Mary Washington .... VA
+□Maryland, U. of (College Park, Eastern Shore) .... MD
+□Massachusetts, U. of (Amherst) .... MA
□Massachusetts Inst. of Tech .. MA
★Maryville State .... ND
+□McMurry .... TX
□McNeese State U .... LA
+□McPherson .... KS
■Memphis State U .... TN
+■Menlo .... CA
+□Messiah .... PA
+□Methodist .... NC
□Miami, U. of .... FL
★Miami U .... OH
★Michigan State U .... MI
★Mid-America Nazarene .... KS
★Middle Tennessee State U .... TN
+□Middlebury .... VT
★Midland Lutheran .... NE
□Miles .... AL
+□Millersville State .... PA

+□Milligan .... TN
+□Minnesota Tech. Coll .... MN
★Mississippi .... MS
□Mississippi Delta Jr .... MS
★Missouri Valley .... MO
+□Monmouth IL
★Montana, U. of .... MT
+□Montana State U .... MT
+Moorhead State U .... MN
□Morehouse .... GA
★Morgan State .... MD
■Morningside .... IA
★Mount Saint Mary's .... MD
+□Mount Union .... OH
□Muhlenberg .... PA
+□Murray State U .... KY
□Muskingum .... OH
★Nebraska, U. of (Lincoln) .... NE
+□Nebraska Wesleyan U .... NE
■Nevada, U. of (Reno) .... NV
■New Haven, U. of .... CT
★New Mexico, U. of .... NM
■New Mexico State U .... NM
□Niagara U .... NY
+□Nichols .... MA
★North Carolina, U. of (Chapel Hill) .... NC
+□North Carolina A&T State .... NC
★North Carolina State U .... NC
+□North Central IL
★North Dakota State Sch. of Science .... ND
+North Dakota State U. (Bottineau) .... ND
+□North State U .... ND
★North Texas State .... TX
■Northeastern Jr .... CO
+□Northeastern U .... MA
★Northern Arizona U .... AZ
★Northern Iowa, U. of .... IA
+□Northern Montana .... MT
★Northern Missouri State U .... MO
★Northwest Nazarene .... ID
★Northwestern .... IA
■Northwestern State U .... LA
★Northwestern U IL
■Northwood Inst .... MI
+□Norwich U./Vermont Coll .... VT
■Notre Dame, U. of .... IN
+□Oberlin .... OH
+□Occidental .... CA
+□Ohio Northern U .... OH
‡Ohio State U .... OH
+□Ohio Wesleyan .... OH
+□Ohio U .... OH
★Oklahoma .... OK
■Oklahoma Christian .... OK
★Oklahoma Panhandle State ... OK
★Oklahoma State U .... OK
★Old Dominion U .... VA
★Oregon, U. of .... OR
□Oregon Inst. of Tech .... OR
+□Oregon State U .... OR
★Ottawa U .... KS
□Otterbein .... OH
+□Ozarks, School of the .... MO
★Pacific Lutheran .... WA
+□Panama Canal .... Panama
□Pembroke State U .... NC
+□Pennsylvania, U. of .... PA
★Pennsylvania State U .... PA
+□Peru State .... NE
■Philadelphia Coll. of Textiles .... PA
■Pittsburg State U .... KS
★Pittsburgh, U. of .... PA
+□Pitzer .... CA
★Point Loma .... CA
+□Pomona .... CA
★Portland, U. of .... OR
+□Prairie View A&M U .... TX
+□Pratt Comm. Coll .... KS
+□Pratt Inst .... NY
+□Princeton U .... NJ

Trap and Skeet

Volleyball

+□Colgate NY
+College Misericordia PA
+Colorado Coll CO
+Colorado State U CO
+Columbia Christian OR
‡Columbia Coll MO
‡Columbia Coll SC
‡Concord WV
+Concordia IL
‡Concordia OR
+Concordia (Moorhead) MN
+Concordia (St. Paul) MN
+Concordia Teacher's NE
+Connecticut, U. of CT
+Connecticut Coll CT
+Cornell Coll IA
+Cornell U NY
+Cowley County Comm KS
+□Center for Creative Studies MI
‡Dakota State SD
+Dakota Wesleyan SD
+Dallas Christian TX
‡Dana NE
+Daniel Webster NH
+Dayton, U. of OH
+Defiance OH
+Delaware Valley PA
+Denison OH
+DePauw IN
+Dickinson PA
‡Dickinson State ND
+□Dixie UT
+□Dominican CA
+Dordt IA
+Dr. Martin Luther MN
‡Drake IA
‡Drexel PA
‡Drury MO
+Dubuque IA
‡Duke NC
‡Duquesne PA
‡D'Youville NY
+□Earlham IN
‡East Carolina NC
+East Tennessee State TN
+Eastern PA
‡Eastern Arizona AZ
+Eastern Christian MD
+Eastern Connecticut CT
‡Eastern Illinois IL
+Eastern Kentucky KY
‡Eastern Nazarene MA
‡Eastern New Mexico U NM
+Eastern Oregon OR
+Eastern Washington WA
‡Eastern Wyoming WY
+Eckerd FL
□Edinboro State PA
+□Elizabeth Seton NY
+Elizabethtown PA
+Elmhurst IL
+Elmira NY
‡Elon NC
+Emory & Henry VA
‡Emporia State KS
+Endicott MA
‡Erskine SC
+Eureka IL
‡Evangel MO
‡Evansville, U. of IN
‡Fairleigh Dickinson NJ
+Fairmont WV
‡Ferris MI
+Ferrum VA
+Findlay OH
+Fisk TN
+Fitchburg MA
‡Flagler FL
‡Florida A&M FL
+Florida Inst. of Tech FL
‡Florida Southern FL
‡Florida State FL
‡Fontbonne MO
+Fordham NY
+Fort Hays State KS
‡Fort Lewis CO
‡Fort Scott Comm KS
+Framingham MA
+Francis Marion SC
+Franklin IN
+Franklin & Marshall PA
+Franklin Pierce NH
+Friends KS
‡Furman SC
+□Gallaudet DC
+Gannon PA
‡Gardner-Webb NC
‡Geneva PA
+George Fox OR
★George Mason VA
‡George Washington U DC
+□George Williams IL
‡Georgetown DC
‡Georgetown KY
+Georgia, U. of GA
‡Georgian Court NJ
+Gettysburg PA
‡Golden Valley Lutheran MN
‡Gonzaga WA
+Gordon MA
+Goucher MD
‡Grace IN
‡Grand Canyon AZ
+Grand Rapids Baptist MI
+Grand Valley MI
‡Grand View IA
+Green Mountain VT
+Greensboro NC
+Greenville IL
+□Grinnell IA
+Grove City PA
‡Guilford NC
+Gustavus Adolphus MN
+Gwynedd-Mercy PA
+Hamline MN
+Hampton Inst VA
+□Hannibal-LaGrange MO
+Hanover IN
+Harcum Jr PA
+Hardin-Simmons TX
‡Hartford, U. of CT
□Harvard/Radcliffe MA
+Harvey Mudd CA
‡Hastings NE
+Haverford PA
+□Hawaii, U. of HI
+Heidelberg OH
+Henderson State AR
+Hendrix AR
+Hesser NH
+Hesston KS
+High Point NC
‡Hilbert NY
‡Hillsdale MI
+Hiram OH
‡Hofstra NY
+Hollins VA
‡Holy Cross MA
+Hood MD
+Hope MI
+Houghton NY
+Howard DC
‡Howard Payne TX
+□Humboldt CA
+Hunter NY
‡Huntingdon AL
‡Huron SD
‡Husson ME
‡Hutchinson Comm KS
‡Idaho, U. of ID
+Idaho State ID
★Illinois, U. of (Chicago Circle) IL
‡Illinois, U. of (Urbana-Champaign) IL
+Illinois Benedictine IL
+Illinois Coll IL
‡Illinois Inst. of Tech IL
‡Illinois State U IL
+Illinois Wesleyan IL
+Immaculata PA
+Incarnate Word TX
‡Independence Comm KS
‡Indiana Central IN
+Indiana State IN
‡Indiana U IN
+Indiana U. of Pa PA
+Iona NY
‡Iowa, U. of IA
‡Iowa State U IA
‡Iowa Wesleyan IA
‡Ithaca NY
‡Jackson State MS
‡Jacksonville State FL
‡Jacksonville U FL
‡James Madison VA
‡Jamestown ND
‡John Brown U AR
+John Carroll OH
‡Judson IL
‡Judson Baptist OR
+Juniata PA
+Kalamazoo MI
‡Kansas, U. of KS
+Kansas Newman KS
‡Kansas State KS
+Kansas Wesleyan KS
+Kean NJ
+Kearney State NE
+Keene State NH
+□Kemper Military MO
‡Kent State OH
‡Kentucky, U. of KY
‡Kentucky Wesleyan KY
+Kenyon OH
+Keuka NY
‡King's NY
+King's PA
+Knox IL
+□Kutztown PA
+La Grange GA
+La Salle PA
+Lafayette PA
+Lake Erie OH
+Lake Forest IL
‡Lake Superior State MI
+Lakeland WI
+Lamar TX
‡Lambuth TN
+Lasell Jr MA
+Lawrence WI
‡Le Moyne NY
+Lees-McRae NC
+Lehigh PA
‡Lenoir-Rhyne NC
+LeTourneau TX
+Lewis IL
+Lewis and Clark OR
‡Lewis-Clark State ID
‡Liberty Baptist VA
‡Limestone SC
‡Lincoln IL
‡Lincoln MO
+Lincoln PA
+Lincoln Christian IL
+Lindenwood MO
‡Linfield OR
‡Livingston AL
+□Livingstone NC
‡Long Island U. (Southampton) NY
+Longwood VA
‡Loras IA
‡Louisiana State A&M LA
‡Louisville, U. of KY
+Lowell, U. of MA
‡Loyola MD
★Loyola Marymount CA
‡Loyola U. of Chicago IL
+□Luther IA
+Lynchburg VA
+Macalester MN
□Maharishi IA
+Maine, U. of (Farmington, Fort Kent, Machias, Orono) ME
‡Malone OH
+Manchester IN
+Manhattanville NY
‡Mankato MN
‡Manor Jr PA
+Mansfield State PA
+Maria Regina NY
‡Marian IN
+Marian Coll. of Fond du Lac WI
+Marietta OH
+Marist NY
‡Marquette WI
‡Mars Hill NC
‡Mary ND
+Mary Baldwin VA
+Mary Hardin-Baylor TX
+Mary Washington VA
‡Marycrest IA
+Marygrove MI
+Maryland, U. of (Eastern Shore) MD
+Marymount NY
‡Marymount Coll. of Va VA
+Maryville IN
+Maryville MO
‡Marywood PA
+Massachusetts, U. of MA
+Massachusetts Inst. of Tech MA
+Massachusetts Maritime MA
‡Mayville State ND
+McMurry TX
+McNeese LA
+McPherson KS
‡Memphis State TN
+□Menlo CA
‡Mercyhurst PA
+Meredith NC
‡Mesa CO
+Messiah PA
+Methodist NC
+Miami, U. of FL
‡□Miami U OH
‡Michigan, U. of MI
‡Michigan Christian MI
+Michigan Tech. U MI
‡Mid-America Nazarene KS
‡Middle Tennessee State TN
‡Midland Lutheran NE
+Midway KY
+Milligan TN
+Millikin IL
+Mills CA
+Milwaukee Sch. of Eng WI
+□Minnesota Tech MN
+Minnesota-Twin Cities, U. of MN
‡Mississippi U. for Women MS
‡Missouri, U. of (Columbia, Kansas City) MO
+Missouri Baptist MO
‡Missouri Southern MO
‡Missouri Valley MO
‡Missouri Western MO
+Mohawk Valley Comm NY
+Monmouth IL
+Monmouth NJ
‡Montana, U. of MT
‡Montana Coll. of Min. Sci MT
+Montana State MT
‡Montevallo, U. of AL
+Montreat-Anderson NC
+Moorhead State MN
+Moravian PA
‡Morehead State KY
‡Morningside IA
+□Mount Aloysius PA
+Mount Holyoke MA
‡Mount Marty SD
‡Mount Mary WI
‡Mount Senario WI
+Mount St. Joseph OH
+Mount St. Mary NY

‡Weber State .... UT
+Wellesley .... MA
+□Wentworth Inst. of Tech .... MA
+Wesleyan .... GA
+West Chester State .... PA
+West Coast Christian .... CA
‡West Georgia Coll .... GA
+West Liberty State .... WV
‡West Texas State .... TX
+West Virginia Inst. of Tech .... WV
+Western Baptist .... OR
‡Western Carolina .... NC
+Western Connecticut State .... CT
‡Western Illinois U IL
+Western Kentucky .... KY
+Western Maryland .... MD
+Western Michigan .... MI
+Western Montana .... MT
+Western New England Coll .... MA
‡Western New Mexico .... NM
+Western Oregon State .... OR
+Western Washington .... WA
‡Western Wyoming .... WY
‡Westmar .... IA
+Westminster .... MO
+Westminster .... PA
‡Wharton County Jr .... TX
+Wheaton IL
+Wheaton .... MA
+White Plains (Pace) .... NY
+Whitman .... WA
+Whittier .... CA
‡Whitworth .... WA
+□Wiley .... TX
+Wilkes .... PA
+Willamette .... OR
+William Jewell .... MO
+William & Mary .... VA
+William Paterson .... NJ
+William Penn .... IA
‡William Woods .... MO
+□Williams .... MA
+Wilmington .... DE
+Wilmington .... OH
+Wilson .... PA
‡Wingate .... NC
‡Winona State .... MN
‡Winthrop .... SC
+Wisconsin, U. of (Eau Claire, LaCrosse, Oshkosh, River Falls, Stevens Point, Stout, Superior, Whitewater) .... WI
‡Wisconsin, U. of (Madison, Milwaukee) .... WI
+Wisconsin Lutheran .... WI
+Wittenberg .... OH
‡Wofford .... SC
+Wooster, Coll. of .... OH
+Worcester Poly. Inst .... MA
+Worcester State .... MA
+Worthington Comm .... MN
‡□Wright State .... OH
+Wyoming, U. of .... WY
‡Xavier U .... OH
‡Yakima Valley .... WA
‡Yankton .... SD
‡□York .... NE
+York .... PA
‡Youngstown State U .... OH

Water Polo

□Brown U .... RI
■Bucknell U .... PA
■California, U. of (Berkeley, Irvine) .... CA
□California, U. of (Riverside) .... CA
+□California, U. of (Santa Barbara) .... CA
+□California Inst. of Tech .... CA
□California Maritime Acad .... CA
□California State U. (Fresno) .... CA
□Cathedral Coll .... NY
□Claremont-McKenna .... CA
□Cornell U .... NY
■Fordham U .... NY
+□Gonzaga U .... WA
□Grinnell .... IA
□Hampden-Sydney .... VA
□Harvard/Radcliffe .... MA
□Harvey Mudd .... CA
□Johns Hopkins U .... ND
■Kentucky, U. of .... KY
□La Salle .... PA
□Loyola Marymount U .... CA
■Loyola U IL
□Menlo .... CA
■Monmouth .... NJ
‡Northwest Nazarene .... IN
□Occidental .... CA
■Pacific, U. of the .... CA
■Pacific Lutheran .... WA
+□Panama Canal .... Panama
■Pepperdine U .... CA
□Pitzer .... CA
+□Pomona .... CA
□Principia IL
■Puerto Rico, U. of (Rio Piedras) .... PR
□Redlands, U. of .... CA
■Rensselaer Poly. Inst .... NY
□Richmond, U. of .... VA
□Ripon .... WI
□Santa Clara, U. of .... CA
■Stanford U .... CA
□Trinity .... CT
□U.S. Air Force Acad .... CO
□Villanova U .... PA
+□Wiley .... TX

Weight Lifting

□Alabama A&M U .... AL
□Baptist Christian .... LA
+□Dixie .... UT
□Fort Scott Comm .... KS
+□Indiana U. (Bloomington) .... IN
+□Lafayette .... PA
+□Livingstone .... NC
□Louisiana Tech. U .... LA
□Marion Military Inst .... AL
+□McNeese State U .... LA
□New Jersey Inst. of Tech .... NJ
+□Northwestern Oklahoma State .... OK
+□Prairie View A&M .... TX
■Puerto Rico, U. of (Rio Piedras) .... PR
□Texas, U. of (Arlington) .... TX
□Texas Christian U .... TX
□Villanova .... PA
□Washington & Lee .... VA
□Whittier .... CA

Wrestling

□Adams State .... CO
□Adrian .... MI
□Albright .... PA
□Allegheny .... PA
□Alma .... MI
‡American U .... DC
□Amherst .... MA
□Anderson .... IN
■Appalachian State U .... AZ
■Arizona State U .... AZ
■Arizona Western .... AZ
■Ashland .... OH
□Augustana IL
■Augustana .... SD
□Baldwin-Wallace .... OH
■Bemidji State U .... MN
■Bethany Lutheran .... MN
□Bethel .... MN
■Biola U .... CA
■Bismarck Jr .... ND
■Black Hills State .... SD
■Bloomsburg State .... PA
□Boston Coll .... MA
■Boston U .... MA
□Bowdoin .... ME
□Bridgewater State .... MA
□Brown U .... RI
■Bucknell U .... PA
□Buena Vista .... IA
■C.W. Post Center of L.I.U .... NY
□California, U. of (Berkeley, Davis, Los Angeles) .... CA
□California Inst. of Tech .... CA
□California State .... PA
■California State (Bakersfield) .... CA
□California State U. (Chico) .... CA
■California State U. (Fresno) .... CA
+□California State U. (Fullerton) .... CA
□Calvin .... MI
■Campbell U .... NC
□Capital U .... OH
□Carleton .... MN
□Carroll .... WI
■Carson-Newman .... TN
□Carthage .... WI
□Case Western Reserve .... OH
□Catholic U. of Puerto Rico .... PR
■Cedarville .... OH
□Central .... IA
■Central Florida, U. of .... FL
■Central Michigan State .... MI
■Central Missouri State U .... MO
■Central State U .... OK
□Central Washington U .... WA
■Chadron State .... NE
□Chicago, U. of IL
■Chowan .... NC
■Cincinnati, U. of .... OH
□Citadel, The .... SC
□City Coll. of The City U. of New York .... NY
□Claremont-McKenna .... CA
□Clarion State .... PA
□Clarkson .... NY
■Cleveland State U .... OH
□Coe .... IA
□Colgate U .... NY
■Colorado Sch. of Mines .... CO
□Colorado State U .... CO
□Concordia IL
□Concordia .... MN
□Cornell .... IA
□Cornell U .... NY
■Dana .... NE
□Davidson .... NC
□Dayton, U. of .... OH
□Defiance .... OH
□Delaware Valley .... PA
■Dickinson State .... ND
+□Dixie .... UT
■Drake U .... IA
■Drexel U .... PA
□Dubuque, U. of .... IA
■Duke U .... NC
□East Tennessee State U .... TN
■Eastern Illinois U IL
□Eastern Washington U .... WA
□Edinboro State .... PA
□Elmhurst IL
■Elon .... NC
□Emerson .... MA
□Fairleigh Dickinson U .... NJ
■Ferris State .... MI
□Findlay .... OH
■Fort Hays State U .... KS
‡□Fort Lewis .... CO
□Fort Scott Comm .... KS
□Franklin & Marshall .... PA
■Furman U .... SC
□Gallaudet .... DC
■George Mason U .... VA
■George Washington U .... DC
■Georgia Tech .... GA
□Gettysburg .... PA
□Glassboro State .... NJ
■Golden Valley Lutheran .... MN
□Grand Rapids Baptist .... MI
□Grand Valley State .... MI
□Grinnell .... IA
□Gustavus Adolphus .... MN
□Hamline .... MN
□Hampden-Sydney .... VA
□Hampton Inst .... VA
□Hanover .... IN
■Hartford, U. of .... CT
□Harvard/Radcliffe .... MA
□Harvey Mudd .... CA
□Haverford .... PA
□Heidelberg .... OH
□Hiram .... OH
■Hofstra U .... NY
□Hope .... MI
□Humboldt State U .... CA
□Hunter .... NY
■Huron .... SD
□Idaho State .... ID
■Illinois, U. of (Urbana-Champaign) IL
□Illinois Coll IL
■Illinois State U IL
■Indiana Central U .... IN
□Indiana U .... PA
■Indiana U. (Bloomington) .... IN
■Iowa, U. of .... IA
■Iowa State U .... IA
□Ithaca .... NY
■Jacksonville State U .... AL
■James Madison U .... VA
□Jamestown .... ND
□John Carroll U .... OH
□Johns Hopkins U .... MD
□Juniata .... PA
□Kalamazoo .... MI
□Kean .... NJ
■Kearney State .... NE
□Keene State .... NH
□Kemper Military .... MO
■Kent State U .... OH
■Kentucky, U. of .... KY
□Keystone Jr .... PA
□King's .... PA
■King's Coll .... NY
□Knox IL
+□Kutztown State .... PA
□La Salle .... PA
□Lafayette .... PA
■Lake Superior State .... MI
□Lawrence U .... WI
□Lebanon Valley .... PA
□Lehigh U .... PA
□LeTourneau .... TX
■Liberty Baptist .... VA
■Lincoln IL
□Lindenwood .... MO
■Linfield .... OR
+■Livingstone .... NC
□Lock Haven State .... PA
□Longwood .... VA
■Loras .... IA
■Louisiana State U. (A&M) .... LA
□Lowell, U. of .... MA
□Loyola .... MD
□Luther .... IA
□Lycoming .... PA
□Lynchburg .... VA
□MacMurray IL
□Maine, U. of (Orono, Presque Isle) .... ME
□Maine Maritime Acad .... ME
■Malone .... OH
□Manhattan .... NY
■Mankato State U .... MN
□Mansfield State .... PA
■Marquette U .... WI
□Maryland, U. of .... MD

□Maryland, U. of (Eastern Shore) MD
□Massachusetts, U. of (Amherst) MA
□Massachusetts Inst. of Tech MA
□Massachusetts Maritime MA
■Mayville State ND
■Mesa CO
□Messiah PA
■Miami U OH
■Michigan, U. of MI
■Michigan State U MI
□Millikan U IL
□Minnesota, U. of (Twin Cities) MN
+□Minnesota, U. of, Tech. Coll MN
■Missouri, U. of (Columbia) MO
□Mohawk Valley NY
□Monmouth IL
■Montana, U. of MT
□Montana State U MT
□Moorhead State U MN
□Moravian PA
■Morgan State U MD
□Mount Union OH
□Muhlenberg PA
□Muskingum OH
■Nebraska, U. of (Lincoln) NE
■Nevada, U. of (Las Vegas) NV
□New Hampshire, U. of NH
□New Jersey Inst. of Tech NJ
■New Mexico, U. of NM
□New York U NY
□Norfolk State U VA
■North Carolina, U. of (Chapel Hill) NC
□North Carolina A&T State U NC
□North Carolina Central U NC
■North Carolina State U NC
□North Central IL
■North Dakota State Sch. of Science ND
□North Dakota State U ND
■North Idaho ID
□North Park IL
□North Texas State TX
■Northern Arizona U AZ
■Northern Colorado, U. of CO
■Northern Illinois U IL
■Northern Iowa, U. of IA
■Northern Michigan U MI
■Northern Missouri State MO
■Northern Montana MT
■Northern Oklahoma OK
■Northwest Nazarene ID
■Northwestern IA
■Northwestern U IL
□Norwich U./Vermont Coll VT
■Notre Dame, U. of IN
□Oakland U MI
□Ohio Northern U OH
■Ohio State U OH
□Ohio Wesleyan U OH
■Oklahoma, U. of OK
■Oklahoma State U OK
★Old Dominion U VA
□Olivet MI
■Oregon, U. of OR
□Oregon Inst. of Tech OR
□Oregon State U OR
■Pacific Lutheran U WA
□Pacific U OR
+□Panama Canal Pa
■Paul Smith's NY
□Pembroke State U NC
□Pennsylvania, U. of PA
■Pennsylvania State U PA
■Pfeiffer NC
■Pittsburgh, U. of PA
■Pittsburgh, U. of (Johnstown) PA
□Pitzer CA
□Plymouth State NH
□Pomona CA
□Princeton U NJ
■Puerto Rico, U. of (Rio Piedras) PR
■Purdue U IN
□Rensselaer Poly. Inst NY
□Rhode Island RI
■Rider NJ
□Ripon WI
□Rutgers U NJ
■Saginaw Valley State MI
□Saint John's U MN
□Salisbury State MD
□San Jose State CA
□Scranton, U. of PA
■Seton Hall U NJ
■Shippensburg State PA
□Simpson IA
□Sioux Empire IA
■Slippery Rock State PA
□Snow UT
□South, U. of the TN
□South Dakota State U SD
■Southern Illinois U IL
□Southern Oregon State OR
■Southeast Missouri State MO
□Southwest State U MN
□Springfield MA
■St. Cloud State U MN
■St. John Fisher NY
□St. Lawrence U NY
□St. Olaf MN
□St. Thomas, Coll. of MN
■Stanford U CA
□State U. of New York (Albany, Alfred, Binghamton, Brockport, Buffalo, Cobleskill, Coll. of Agriculture & Life Science, Cornell, Cortland, Delhi, Coll. of Environmental Science, Syracuse, Farmingdale, Maritime Coll., Morrisville, Oneonta, Oswego, Potsdam) NY
□Stevens Inst. of Tech NJ
□Susquehanna U PA
□Swarthmore PA
■Syracuse U NY
□Taylor U IN
■Temple U PA
■Tennessee, U. of (Knoxville) TN
□Tennessee, U. of (Chattanooga) TN
□Tennessee Tech. U TN
□Thiel PA
■Toledo, U. of OH
■Towson State U MD
□Trenton State NJ
□Trinity CT
□U.S. Air Force Acad CO
□U.S. Coast Guard Acad CT
□U.S. Merchant Marine Acad NY
□U.S. Military Acad NY
□U.S. Naval Acad MD
□Union NY
□Upper Iowa IA
□Upsala NJ
■Urbana OH
□Ursinus PA
■Utah State U UT
□Valparaiso U IN
■Virginia, U. of VA
■Virginia Military Inst VA
■Virginia Poly. Inst VA
□Wabash IN
■Wagner NY
□Waldorf IA
□Warner Pacific OR
□Wartburg IA
□Washington & Jefferson PA
□Washington & Lee U VA
■Washington State U WA
□Washington U MO
■Waynesburg PA
■Weber State UT
□Wesleyan U CT
□West Chester State PA
□West Liberty State WV
■West Virginia U WV
■Western Illinois U IL
□Western Maryland MD
□Western Michigan U MI
□Western Montana MT
□Western New England MA
■Western State CO
□Western Washington U WA
■Westmar IA
□Wheaton IL
□Whittier CA
■Wilkes PA
□Willamette OR
□William Jewell MO
□William & Mary, Coll. of VA
□William Paterson NJ
□William Penn IA
□Williams MA
■Winona State MN
■Wisconsin, U. of (Madison) WI
□Wisconsin, U. of (Eau Claire, LaCrosse, Oshkosh, Platteville, River Falls, Stevens Point, Stout, Superior, Whitewater) WI
□Wittenberg U OH
□Wooster, Coll. of OH
□Worcester Poly. Inst MA
□Worthington MN
■Wright State U OH
□Wyoming, U. of WY
■Yankton SD
□Yale U CT
□Yeshiva U NY
□York PA
■Youngstown State U OH

Non-Sports Activities

Baton Twirling

+□Akron, U. of OH
+Alabama, U. of AL
+□Albright PA
+□Alma MI
+Appalachian State NC
+Arkansas State AR
+Arkansas Tech. U AR
+Baylor U TX
+□Bloomsburg State PA
+Buena Vista IA
+□California, U. of (Los Angeles) CA
+□California State PA
+□Central Arkansas, U. of AR
+Cincinnati, U. of OH
+Clarion State PA
+Coffeyville Comm KS
+Dayton, U. of OH
+□Delta State MS
+Geneva Coll PA
+Georgia, U. of GA
+□Hampton Inst VA
+□Harding U AR
+Heidelberg Coll OH
+□Indiana U. (Bloomington) IN
★Iowa, U. of IA
+□Jersey City State NJ
+□Kansas State U KS
+Lock Haven State PA
‡Louisiana State U. and A&M LA
+Lubbock Christian TX
+Mansfield State PA
+□Maryland, U. of (College Park) MD
+Massachusetts, U. of (Amherst) MA
+McNeese State LA
+Miami U OH
★Mississippi Coll MS
‡Mississippi Valley State MS
‡Missouri Western State MO
□Mount Union OH
+Muhlenberg Coll PA
+□Murray State KY
‡Navarro Coll TX
+Nebraska, U. of (Lincoln) NE
+Nebraska Wesleyan NE
+□Nevada, U. of (Las Vegas) NV
‡New Mexico State NM
+North Carolina State NC
★Northeast Louisiana U LA
+□Northeastern Oklahoma State OK
+□Northern Arizona U AZ
+Northern Iowa, U. of IA
+□Northern Michigan U MI
+Northwest Missouri State MO
★Northwestern State LA
+□Oklahoma, U. of OK
+Pittsburg State KS
+Pittsburgh, U. of (Pittsburgh) PA
+□Purdue U IN
+□Rhode Island, U. of RI
+Sam Houston State TX
+Shepherd WV
+□Shippensburg State PA
+Slippery Rock State PA
‡South Carolina, U. of SC
‡Southeast Missouri State MO
+Southern Methodist U TX
+St. Paul's MO
+Syracuse U NY
+Temple U PA
+Tennessee, U. of (Knoxville, Martin) TN
+□Texas A&I TX
‡Texas Christian TX
+□Toledo, U. of OH
+□Troy State AL
+□West Chester State PA
+□West Liberty State WV
+□West Virginia Inst. of Tech WV
‡Western Carolina U NC
‡Western Kentucky U KY
+□Westminster Coll PA
+Wilkes Coll PA

Cheerleading

+□Adams State CO
+Adrian Coll MI
+□Akron, U. of OH
+□Alabama, U. of AL
+□Alabama State AL
+□Albright Coll PA
+Alfred NY
+□Allegheny PA
+□Allen U SC
+Allentown Coll PA
+Alliance PA
+□Alma Coll MI
+Alvernia PA
+□American International Coll MA
+□Anderson Coll IN
+□Angelo State TX
+□Appalachian State NC
+□Aquinas MI
+□Arizona Western Coll AZ
+□Arkansas State AR
★Arkansas Tech. U AR
+□Ashland OH
+Assumption MA
+□Atlantic Christian NC
+□Augustana IL
+Baptist Christian LA
+Barrington Coll RI

+Barton County Comm .... KS
+□Baylor U .... TX
+□Bellarmine .... KY
+Berry Coll .... GA
+Bethany Bible Coll .... CA
+□Bethany Coll .... KS
+Bethany Coll .... WV
+□Bethany Lutheran .... MN
+□Bethel Coll .... KS
+□Black Hills State .... SD
+□Blinn Coll .... TX
+□Bloomsburg State .... PA
+□Bluefield Coll .... VA
+Bluffton .... OH
+□Bowie State .... MD
□Bradley U IL
+Brandeis U .... MA
+Brandywine .... DE
+Bridgeport, U. of .... CT
+Bridgewater State .... MA
+□Bucknell .... PA
+Buena Vista .... IA
+□Butler U .... IN
+C.W. Post .... NY
+□California, U. of (Berkeley, Los Angeles) .... CA
+□California Inst. of Tech .... CA
+□California State .... PA
+□California State (Bakersfield) .... CA
□Campbell U .... NC
+□Canisius .... NY
+□Capital U .... OH
+□Carnegie-Mellon .... PA
+□Carroll Coll .... MT
+Carroll Coll .... WI
+□Carson-Newman .... TN
+□Carthage Coll .... WI
+Case Western Reserve .... OH
+□Casper .... WY
+Castleton State .... VT
+Catholic U. of America .... DC
+Cedarville .... OH
+□Centenary .... LA
+□Central Arkansas, U. of ...... AR
+□Central Coll .... IA
+□Central Coll .... KS
+Central Methodist .... MO
+□Central Michigan U .... MI
+Central Missouri .... MO
+Champlain .... VT
+□Cheyney State .... PA
+□Chowan .... NC
+□Christian Brothers .... TN
+□Cincinnati, U. of .... OH
+□City U. (Baruch Coll.) .... NY
+Clarion State .... PA
+Clearwater Christian .... FL
+Coffeyville Comm .... KS
+□Colgate .... NY
+□Concordia IL
+□Concordia Teachers Coll ..... NE
+□Connecticut, U. of .... CT
+Cornell .... IA
+□Cornell U .... NY
★Cumberland Coll .... KY
+□Dakota Wesleyan U .... SD
+□Dana .... NE
+David Lipscomb .... TN
+□Davidson Coll .... NC
+□Davis and Elkins .... WV
+□Dayton, U. of .... OH
+Dean Jr .... MA
+□Delaware Valley .... PA
+□Delta State .... MS
+Denison .... OH
+□DePauw .... IN
+Dickinson .... PA
+Dickinson State .... ND
+□Dixie Coll .... UT
+□Drake .... IA
+□Duquesne .... PA
+□East Carolina .... NC
+□East Tennessee State .... TN

+□Eastern Arizona .... AZ
+□Eastern Connecticut State .... CT
+□Eastern Illinois U IL
+□Eastern Kentucky U .... KY
+Eastern Oklahoma State ..... OK
+□Eastern Washington U .... WA
+□Eastern Wyoming Coll .... WY
+□Eckerd Coll .... FL
+□Edinboro State .... PA
+Elmhurst Coll IL
+Elmira .... NY
+□Elon Coll .... NC
+□Emporia State .... KS
+□Erskine .... SC
+□Evangel Coll .... MO
+□Evansville, U. of .... IN
+□Fairmont State .... WV
+□Fayetteville State .... NC
+Findlay Coll .... OH
+□Florida Southern .... FL
+□Florida State .... FL
+□Fort Hays State .... KS
□Fort Lewis Coll .... CO
+□Fort Scott Comm .... KS
+Framingham State .... MA
+Franklin Coll .... IN
+Freeman Jr .... SD
+□Friends U .... KS
+□Furman U .... SC
+Gannon U .... PA
+Gardner-Webb Coll .... NC
+Geneva Coll .... PA
+□George Mason U .... VA
+□Georgia, U. of .... GA
+□Hampton Inst .... VA
+Harding U .... AR
+Hastings Coll .... NE
+Heidelberg Coll .... OH
+Hesser Coll .... NH
+□High Point Coll .... NC
★Highland Comm .... KS
+□Hiram Coll .... OH
+□Hiwassee Coll .... TN
+□Hofstra U .... NY
+□Hope Coll .... MI
+Houghton .... NY
+□Humboldt State .... CA
+□Hutchinson Comm .... KS
+□Idaho, U. of .... ID
+Illinois Benedictine IL
+Illinois Coll IL
+□Illinois Wesleyan IL
+□Incarnate Word .... TX
+□Indiana Central .... IN
+□Indiana State (Terre Haute) .. IN
+□Indiana U. (Bloomington) .... IN
+□Iona Coll .... NY
+□Iowa, U. of .... IA
+□Jersey City State .... NJ
+□John Carroll U .... OH
+Johnson State .... VT
+□Kansas, U. of .... KS
□Kansas Newman .... KS
+□Kansas State U .... KS
+□Kansas Wesleyan .... KS
+Kearney State .... NE
+Keene State .... NH
+□Kent State .... OH
★Kentucky Wesleyan .... KY
+Keystone Jr .... PA
+King's Coll .... PA
+Knox Coll IL
+□La Grange .... GA
+□La Salle .... PA
+□Lafayette Coll .... PA
+□Lake Superior State .... MI
+Lakeland Coll .... WI
+□Lamar .... TX
+Lebanon Valley .... PA
+Lee Coll .... TN
+□Lenoir-Rhyne .... NC
‡Liberty Baptist .... VA
+□Limestone Coll .... SC
+□Lincoln Memorial .... TN

+Lincoln U .... MO
+Lincoln U .... PA
+□Lindenwood Coll .... MO
+□Lindsey Wilson .... KY
+Lock Haven State .... PA
□Lon Morris .... TX
+Long Island U. (Southampton) .... NY
+□Longwood .... VA
+□Loras Coll .... IA
+□Louisburg Coll .... NC
★Louisiana State U. and A&M .... LA
+□Louisiana Tech .... LA
+□Louisville, U. of .... KY
+□Loyola Marymount .... CA
+Lubbock Christian .... TX
+□Luther .... IA
+Lycoming .... PA
+□Lynchburg .... VA
+□Maine, U. of (Orono) .... ME
+Maine, U. of (Presque Isle) ... ME
+Malone Coll .... OH
+□Manchester .... IN
+□Manhattan Coll .... NY
+□Mankato State .... MN
+Mansfield State .... PA
+Marian Coll .... WI
+Marietta Coll .... OH
+Marion Military Inst .... AL
+□Mars Hill Coll .... NC
+□Mary Washington .... VA
+□Maryland, U. of (College Park) .... MD
+Maryland, U. of (Eastern Shore) .... MD
+Maryville Coll .... MO
+□Maryville Coll .... TN
+□Massachusetts, U. of (Amherst) .... MA
+□Massachusetts Inst. of Tech .. MA
+□McMurry Coll .... TX
+□McNeese State .... LA
+□McPherson .... KS
+□Messiah Coll .... PA
+□Methodist Coll .... NC
+□Miami U .... OH
+□Michigan Christian .... MI
★Mid-America Nazarene .... KS
+□Minnesota, U. of (Twin Cities) .... MN
+□Mississippi Coll .... MS
+□Mississippi Valley .... MS
+□Missouri, U. of (Columbia) ... MO
+Missouri Baptist .... MO
★Missouri Western State ...... MO
+Monmouth Coll IL
+Monmouth Coll .... NJ
+□Montana State .... MT
+□Montevallo, U. of .... AL
+□Moravian Coll .... PA
★Morehead State .... KY
+Mount Senario .... WI
+□Mount St. Clare .... IA
□Mount St. Mary's .... MD
□Mount Union .... OH
+Muhlenberg Coll .... PA
+□Murray State .... KY
+□Muskingum Coll .... OH
‡Navarro Coll .... TX
+□Nebraska, U. of (Lincoln) .... NE
+□Nebraska Wesleyan U .... NE
+□Nevada, U. of (Las Vegas) .... NV
+New Hampshire Coll .... NH
+□New Mexico Military Inst ..... NM
★Niagara U .... NY
+North Carolina, U. of (Asheville) .... NC
+□North Carolina A&T .... NC
+□North Carolina Central .... NC
+□North Carolina State .... NC
+□North Central Coll IL
+North Dakota State (Bottineau) .... ND

+□North Dakota State (Fargo) .... ND
+North Park IL
★Northeast Louisiana U .... LA
+□Northeast Mississippi Jr ...... MS
+□Northeast Missouri State ..... MO
+Northeastern Jr. Coll .... CO
+□Northeastern Oklahoma State .... OK
+□Northern Arizona U .... AZ
+□Northern Iowa, U. of .... IA
+□Northern Michigan U .... MI
+□Northland Coll .... WI
★Northwest Missouri State .... MO
+□Northwest Nazarene .... ID
+□Northwestern .... IA
+Northwestern Oklahoma State .... OK
★Northwestern State .... LA
★Northwood Inst .... MI
+□Notre Dame .... IN
+Nyack Coll .... NY
+□Ohio Dominican .... OH
+□Ohio State .... OH
+□Ohio U .... OH
+□Oklahoma, U. of .... OK
+Olivet Coll .... MI
+□Oregon Inst. of Tech .... OR
+Otterbein .... OH
+□Ozarks, Sch. of the .... MO
+□Pacific Lutheran .... WA
+Panama Canal Coll ..... Panama
‡Paul Smith's Coll .... NY
+□Pearl River Jr .... MS
+□Pembroke State .... NC
+□Pennsylvania, U. of .... PA
+□Peru State .... NE
‡Pfeiffer Coll .... NC
+Philadelphia Coll. of Textiles .... PA
+□Pittsburg State .... KS
+Pittsburgh, U. of (Johnstown) .... PA
+□Pittsburgh, U. of (Pittsburgh) .... PA
+Plymouth State .... NH
+□Point Loma .... CA
+Post .... CT
+Prairie View A&M .... TX
+□Pratt Inst .... NY
+□Purdue U .... IN
+□Redlands, U. of .... CA
+□Rhode Island, U. of .... RI
+Rhode Island Coll .... RI
+□Richmond, U. of .... VA
+□Rider Coll .... NJ
+Robert Morris Coll .... PA
+Rochester Inst. of Tech ...... NY
+□Rockford Coll IL
+□Rockhurst Coll .... MO
+□Rockmont Coll .... CO
+□Rosary Coll IL
+□Sacred Heart .... CT
+□Saginaw Valley State .... MI
+□Salem Coll .... WV
□Salisbury State .... MD
+□Sam Houston State .... TX
+□Samford U .... AL
+□San Diego, U. of .... CA
+□San Diego State .... CA
+Scranton, U. of .... PA
+□Seattle Pacific U .... WA
+□Shenandoah Coll. and Cons. of Music .... VA
+□Shippensburg State .... PA
+□Simpson Coll .... CA
+□Simpson Coll .... IA
+□Sioux Falls .... SD
+Slippery Rock State .... PA
+□Snow Coll .... UT
+□South Carolina, U. of .... SC
+South Carolina State .... SC
+□Southern Arkansas U .... AR

Chess Club

Drill Team

Flying Team

Marching Band

+□Atlantic Christian NC
+□Baylor TX
+□Bethany WV
★Blinn TX
+□Bloomsburg PA
+□Bucknell PA
+□Buena Vista IA
+□Butler IN
+□California, U. of (Berkeley, Davis, Los Angeles) CA
+□California State Coll PA
+□Carnegie-Mellon PA
+□Carroll WI
★Carson-Newman TN
+□Case Western OH
+□Central IA
+□Central Arkansas, U. of AR
+□Central Methodist MO
+□Central Michigan MI
+Central Missouri MO
+□Central Washington WA
+□Cheyney State PA
+Cincinnati, U. of OH
+□Clarion State PA
+Coffeyville Comm KS
+□Colgate NY
+□Concordia NE
+□Connecticut, U. of CT
+□Cornell NY
+□Dayton, U. of OH
+□Delaware Valley PA
+□Delta State MS
+□DePauw IN
+□Dixie UT
+□Drake IA
+□East Carolina NC
+□East Tennessee State TN
★Eastern Arizona AZ
+□Eastern Illinois IL
+□Eastern Kentucky KY
+□Eastern Washington WA
+□Edinboro State PA
★Elon NC
★Emporia State KS
★Evansville, U. of IN
+□Fairmont WV
★Fayetteville State NC
★Florida A&M FL
+□Florida State FL
+□Fort Hays State KS
+□Fort Scott Comm KS
+□Franklin & Marshall PA
+□Friends KS
+□Furman SC
+□Gardner-Webb NC
+□Geneva PA
+□Georgia, U. of GA
+□Georgia Southern GA
+□Gettysburg PA
+□Glassboro NJ
+□Glenville State WV
+□Grand Valley State MI
+□Grove City PA
+□Hampton Inst VA
□Hardin-Simmons TX
+□Harding AR
+□Harvard/Radcliffe MA
★Hastings NE
+Heidelberg OH
+□Henderson State AR
+□Humboldt State CA
+□Idaho, U. of ID
+□Illinois Wesleyan IL
+□Indiana State IN
+□Indiana U. (Bloomington) IN
+□Iowa, U. of IA
★Jacksonville State AL
+□John Carroll OH
★Kansas, U. of KS
+□Kansas State KS
+□Kearney NE
+□Kemper Military MO
★Kent State OH
+□Lafayette PA
+□Lamar TX
★Langston OK
★Lenoir-Rhyne NC
★Liberty Baptist VA
+□Lincoln MO
★Livingston AL
+□Lock Haven State PA
★Louisiana State A&M LA
+□Louisiana Tech LA
★Louisville, U. of KY
+□Maine, U. of (Orono) ME
+□Mankato State MN
+□Mansfield State PA
★Marion Military AL
+□Mars Hill NC
+□Maryland, U. of MD
+□Mass., U. of MA
+□Mass. Inst. of Tech MA
+□McMurry TX
+□McNeese LA
+□Miami U OH
+□Minnesota-Twin Cities, U. of MN
★Mississippi Coll MS
★Mississippi Valley State MS
★Missouri, U. of (Columbia) MO
★Missouri Southern MO
★Missouri Western MO
★Montana, U. of MT
■Morgan State MD
□Mount Union OH
+□Muhlenberg PA
+□Murray State KY
+□Muskingum OH
★Navarro TX
+□Nebraska, U. of NE
+□Nebraska Wesleyan NE
★Nevada, U. of NV
+□New Hampshire, U. of NH
+□New Mexico Military NM
★New Mexico State NM
+□Newberry SC
+□Norfolk State VA
+□North Carolina A&T NC
+□North Carolina Central NC
+□North Carolina State NC
+□North Dakota State ND
+□North Dakota State Sch. of Sci ND
★Northeast Louisiana LA
★Northeast Mississippi Jr MS
+□Northeast Missouri State MO
+□Northeastern Oklahoma State OK
★Northern Arizona AZ
+□Northern Iowa IA
+□Northern Michigan MI
★Northwest Missouri State MO
★Northwestern Oklahoma State OK
★Northwestern State LA
+□Norwich U./Vermont Coll VT
+□Notre Dame, U. of IN
+□Ohio State U OH
+□Ohio U OH
★Oklahoma, U. of OK
+□Olivet MI
+□Otterbein OH
+□Pacific, U. of the CA
+□Pearl River Jr MS
+□Pennsylvania, U. of PA
+□Peru State NE
+□Pittsburg State KS
+□Pittsburgh, U. of (Pittsburgh) PA
+□Prairie View A&M TX
+□Purdue IN
★Rhode Island, U. of RI
+□Rice TX
★Rocky Mountain MT
★Saginaw Valley MI
+□Sam Houston State TX
+□San Diego State CA
+□San Jose State CA
+□Shaw NC
+□Shepherd WV
+□Shippensburg PA
+□Slippery Rock PA
+□Snow UT
★South Carolina, U. of SC
+South Carolina State SC
★Southeast Missouri MO
★Southeastern Louisiana LA
★Southeastern Oklahoma OK
+□Southern Arkansas AR
★Southern Methodist TX
+□Southwest Mississippi Jr MS
+□Southwest Texas State TX
★Southwestern Oklahoma State OK
+□St. Joseph's IN
+St. Mary's IN
+St. Paul's MO
+□State U. of New York (Brockport) NY
+□State U. of New York (Cornell) NY
+□State U. of New York at Buffalo NY
+□State U. of New York Maritime NY
★Stephen F. Austin TX
+□Syracuse NY
★Temple PA
★Tennessee, U. of (Knoxville) TN
★Texas, U. of (El Paso) TX
+□Texas A&I TX
★Texas Christian TX
★Texas Lutheran TX
+□Toledo, U. of OH
★Towson State MD
★Troy State AL
★Tulsa, U. of OK
+□Tuskegee AL
+□U.S. Naval Acad MD
+□United Wesleyan PA
★Utah State UT
■Valley Forge Military PA
★Vincennes IN
+□Virgin Islands, Coll. of the VA
+□Virginia, U. of VA
□Virginia Military Inst VA
+□Virginia State VA
+□Washington State WA
+□Wayne State NE
★Weber State UT
+□West Chester State PA
+□West Georgia GA
+□West Liberty State WV
+□West Virginia Inst. of Tech WV
□West Virginia State WV
★Western Carolina NC
+□Western Kentucky KY
+□Western Michigan MI
+□Westminster PA
★Wharton County Jr TX
+□Wichita State KS
+□William & Mary VA
+□William Penn IA
+□Williams MA
+□Wisconsin, U. of (Eau Claire, Green Bay, La Crosse, River Falls, Stevens Point, Whitewater) WI
+□Wyoming, U. of WY
+□Youngstown State OH

Pep Band

+□Adams State Coll CO
★Alabama, U. of AL
+□Alabama A&M AL
+□Alabama State AL
+□Albright Coll PA
+□Allen U SC
+□Alma Coll MI
+□Anderson Coll IN
+□Anderson Coll SC
+□Appalachian State NC
★Arizona Western Coll AZ
+□Arkansas State AR
+□Arkansas Tech AR
+□Ashland OH
+□Augustana IL
+□Barton County Comm KS
+□Bellarmine KY
+□Beloit Coll WI
+□Benedictine KS
+□Bethany KS
+□Bethel KS
★Bismarck Jr ND
+□Black Hills State SD
+□Bluffton OH
■Bradley U IL
+□Brandeis MA
+□Brevard NC
+□Bucknell PA
+□Buena Vista IA
+□California, U. of (Berkeley, Davis) CA
+□California State PA
□Campbell U NC
+□Capital U OH
+□Carnegie-Mellon PA
+□Carroll Coll MT
+□Carson-Newman TN
+□Carthage WI
+□Case Western Reserve OH
+□Casper Coll WY
★Centenary Coll LA
+□Central Arkansas, U. of AR
+□Central Coll IA
+□Central Coll KS
+□Central Michigan U MI
+Central Missouri MO
★Chadron State NE
+□Chowan NC
+Cincinnati, U. of OH
+□Claremont-McKenna CA
+□Clarion State PA
+□Clarkson NY
+Coffeyville Comm KS
+□Concordia Coll IL
+□Concordia Teachers Coll NE
+□Cornell U NY
+□Cumberland Coll KY
+□Dakota Wesleyan SD
+□Dana Coll NE
+□David Lipscomb TN
+□Davidson Coll NC
+□Dayton, U. of OH
+□DePauw IN
+□Dickinson PA
+□Dickinson State ND
+□Drake IA
+□Duquesne PA
+□Eastern Arizona AZ
+□Eastern Connecticut State CT
+□Eastern Illinois U IL
+□Eastern Montana Coll MT
+□Eastern Oklahoma State OK
+□Eastern Oregon State OR
★Eastern Wyoming Coll WY
+□Edinboro State PA
★Elon Coll NC
★Emporia State KS
+□Erskine SC
★Evansville, U. of IN
+□Fairmont State WV
+□Findlay Coll OH
+□Fort Hays State KS
□Fort Lewis CO
+□Fort Scott Comm KS
+□Friends U KS
+□Furman U SC

INDEX